GARNER'S DICTIONARY OF LEGAL USAGE

Books by Bryan A. Garner

Garner's Modern American Usage (3d ed., Oxford 2009)

Garner on Language and Writing (ABA 2009)

Black's Law Dictionary (editor in chief)
Deluxe Unabridged 9th ed. (West 2009)
Unabridged 9th ed. (West 2009)
Abridged 9th ed. (West 2010)
4th Pocket ed. (West 2011)

Making Your Case: The Art of Persuading Judges, with Justice Antonin Scalia (West 2008)

The Elements of Legal Style (2d ed., Oxford 2002)

Legal Writing in Plain English (Chicago 2001)

Garner's Dictionary of Legal Usage (3d ed., Oxford 2011)

The Winning Brief (2d ed., Oxford 2004)

The Winning Oral Argument (2d ed., West 2009)

The Redbook: A Manual on Legal Style (2d ed., West 2006)

Oxford Dictionary of American Usage and Style (Oxford 2000)

Guidelines for Drafting and Editing Court Rules (4th ed., AOUSC 2004)

A Handbook of Basic Law Terms (West 1999)

A Handbook of Business Law Terms (West 1999)

A Handbook of Criminal Law Terms (West 2000)

A Handbook of Family Law Terms (West 2000)

The Rules of Golf in Plain English, with Jeffrey S. Kuhn (2d ed., Chicago 2008)

Securities Disclosure in Plain English (CCH 1999)

A New Miscellany-at-Law, by Sir Robert Megarry (Garner ed., Hart 2005)

The Chicago Manual of Style, ch. 5, "Grammar and Usage" (16th ed., Chicago 2010)

Texas, Our Texas: Remembrances of the University (Garner ed., Eakin 1984)

GARNER'S DICTIONARY OF LEGAL USAGE

THIRD EDITION

Bryan A. Garner

with a foreword by Judge Thomas M. Reavley

OXFORD
UNIVERSITY PRESS

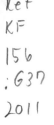

OXFORD
UNIVERSITY PRESS

Oxford University Press, Inc., publishes works that further
Oxford University's objective of excellence
in research, scholarship, and education.

Oxford New York
Auckland Cape Town Dar es Salaam Hong Kong Karachi
Kuala Lumpur Madrid Melbourne Mexico City Nairobi
New Delhi Shanghai Taipei Toronto

With offices in
Argentina Austria Brazil Chile Czech Republic France Greece
Guatemala Hungary Italy Japan Poland Portugal Singapore
South Korea Switzerland Thailand Turkey Ukraine Vietnam

Copyright © 1987, 1995, 2011 by Bryan A. Garner

Published by Oxford University Press, Inc.
198 Madison Avenue, New York, NY 10016
www.oup.com

Oxford is a registered trademark of Oxford University Press

Library of Congress Cataloguing-in-Publication Data

Garner, Bryan A.

Garner's Dictionary of Legal Usage / Bryan A. Garner. — 3d ed.

p. cm.

Rev. ed. of: A dictionary of modern legal usage / Bryan A. Garner. 2d ed. 1995.

Includes bibliographical references and index.

ISBN 978-0-19-538420-8

1. Law—United States—Terminology. 2. Law—United States—Language. 3. Legal composition.
4. English language—Usage—Dictionaries. I. Title. II. Title: Garner's dictionary of legal usage.

KF156.G367 2011

340.03—dc22

2011004242

1 2 3 4 5 6 7 8 9

Printed in the United States of America
on acid-free paper

For my beloved wife,

Karolyne

Garner's Dictionary of Legal Usage

Author
Bryan A. Garner

Associate Editor
Jeff Newman

Associate Editor
Tiger Jackson

Assistant Editor
Shayla R. Edwards

Assistant Editor
Karolyne H.C. Garner

Assistant Editor
Becky R. McDaniel

Assistant Editor
Eliot Turner

Copyeditors
Karen Magnuson
Amy Schneider
Emily Pfaff

Contents

DICTIONARY OF LEGAL USAGE

Foreword

The Honorable Thomas M. Reavley
United States Court of Appeals for the Fifth Circuit

In 1984, a young man named Bryan Garner, the grandson of my erstwhile and esteemed colleague on the Supreme Court of Texas, Justice Meade F. Griffin, joined my Fifth Circuit chambers as one of my law clerks. I knew he had a scholarly bent, but at one point he surprised me with a huge file of index cards that he'd been compiling since his first week of law school—a cache of linguistic jottings that ended up being enshrined in the book you're now reading. An interesting hobby, I thought, until the representative of a Boston publisher sought my help to persuade this 25-year-old Mr. Garner to accept a significant advance payment and allow publication of his book (losing out, I soon discovered, to Oxford University Press). It then dawned on me that I might have a remarkable lexicographer in my office.

The years have verified this and have seen his ongoing achievements. I have watched Bryan closely as he has marched on in a career of prodigious creativity and productivity. He is the acknowledged authority when it comes to legal language and legal rhetoric. Since this book on legal usage first appeared in 1987, he has transformed *Black's Law Dictionary* into the most authoritative law dictionary ever published. He has taken both English usage and (with this book) legal usage to new heights. It is with pride and gratitude that I can herald another contribution by the legal world's most eminent writer and master of language.

Garner's Dictionary of Legal Usage not only defines a wealth of terms and expressions but also offers an abundance of clear, concise directions for their correct and effective use. Although legal terms here receive special attention, the scope of these directions on usage remains as broad as the language itself, whether one's community be that of American English or British English. The dictionary clearly defines many misused or confusing words, legal and nonlegal, and contains much useful information on syntax, pronunciation, and spelling.

Here may be found up-to-date information and practical guidelines on language and style—including discussions of obstacles and pitfalls in communication—all directed toward improved legal writing, whether in judicial opinions, briefs, pleadings, or letters. The entries on generic writing problems, such as SPLIT INFINITIVES, FUSED PARTICIPLES, MISPLACED MODIFIERS, and TITULAR TOMFOOLERY, draw copious examples from legal opinions, briefs, and law-review articles. Garner examines problems peculiar to legal writing, such as BIBLICAL AFFECTATION, LAW REVIEWESE, CITATION OF CASES, and the handling of CASE REFERENCES. These discussions are generally entertaining as well as informative, and many of these topics have never been treated so extensively in a book on legal-writing style.

Lawyers, law students, and general readers interested in clear expression or convincing argument will all find this to be a valuable resource. What is the best noun corresponding to the verb *to recuse*? Do you say you *confected* a pleading? Do you *confront* issues before a judge? Do you *imply* intention from someone's actions, or, as a judge, do you *imply* terms into a contract? Are you fond of using *meaningful* and *hopefully* and *mental attitude*? Are you prone to employ *as to* or to prefer *conclusional* over *conclusory*? Have you *forgone* discovery and stated the *gravamen* of your argument? What do you understand the meaning of *Lochnerize* to be? In the judgment of an appellate court, what are the correct objects of *reverse* and *remand*? Should you have questions or hesitation about the use of these or other expressions in legal writing, the *Dictionary of Legal Usage* offers clear-cut and judicious guidance.

Along with explanations of legal meanings of otherwise ordinary English words, Garner includes law terms that have historically been omitted in the standard unabridged dictionaries, such as *adversarial, conclusory, enjoinable, litigational, pretextual, quashal, recusement,* and *veniremember*. Also recorded are many words having legal meanings that are neglected in the standard dictionaries, such as *duplicitous, imply, judicial, probate, remote,* and *supersede*.

Garner pinpoints differences between any number of near-synonyms: *collateral estoppel* (or *issue preclusion*) and *res judicata; compel* and *impel; concurrent jurisdiction* and *pendent jurisdiction; fictitious, fictive,* and *fictional; incident to* and *incidental to; material* and *relevant; quantum meruit* and *quantum valebant,* and hundreds of similar sets of words. Most of us will find entries that renew explanations of terms and expressions learned in law school and long since forgotten. We may likewise encounter distinctions and nuances that are new to us.

Garner's Dictionary of Legal Usage helps lay to rest some of the linguistic superstitions that many of us grew up with, such as blanket prohibitions against split infinitives, against beginning sentences with *and* or *but,* against using *between* with more than two objects, and so on. Language is rarely if ever governed by absolute proscriptions (see FORBIDDEN WORDS AND PHRASES), and Garner is careful to lead the reader to discriminate and differentiate, rather than to latch on to oversimple formulas that can so easily displace true thought about what constitutes good writing. Surely one of the missions of this book is precisely to foster such thought.

The meaning that language carries, and the spirit it arouses, are the product of words and phrases, *comprehensible* words and phrases. Excess language misdirects. Ambiguous language confuses. Errors in grammar, in diction, in spelling, as well as in fact or logic, distract and destroy confidence. No writer can afford to underestimate the importance of precise, well-placed words. Compiled with the writer's interests in mind, *Garner's Dictionary of Legal Usage* is not only an essential reference but also a lively, personal commentary on legal language as used today.

Preface to the Third Edition

In this new edition, Oxford University Press has given what used to be *A Dictionary of Modern Legal Usage* a new name: *Garner's Dictionary of Legal Usage*. With the name change comes an equally sweeping development of the content.

The idea with this edition was to bring the book into the 21st century with newer (and more) citations—and to replace all the uncited illustrative quotations with citable examples. This undertaking alone involved a monumental effort, and the book has benefited from it both by improved copiousness of illustration and by enhanced accuracy of verbal asssessments.

I have continued to resist the lobbying efforts of certain writers to have citations to their work removed. (Yes, some have actually tried to pressure Oxford University Press with letter-writing campaigns.) Why have I done this? I believe that I should remain dispassionate in citing my evidence. In fact, the indexes at the back of the book have made it easier than ever to know what writers I have cited, and whether those citations are favorable or unfavorable. (They're occasionally neutral.) I persist in believing that the citations confer scholarly value on the work. And let me point out again, as I do on page xiii, that I have cited erroneous usages by my beloved grandfather, my great friend and mentor Charles Alan Wright, and myself. And I have cited my close friend and coauthor, Justice Scalia, unfavorably. As he might well say, "Get over it!" The purpose is never to ridicule, but to educate: I feel an obligation to illustrate points with actual examples, not made-up ones—even though doing so has compounded my own labors.

Dozens of new entries have been added. Two of the most notable appear in the letter I: **indemnify (A)** and INTERPRETATION, MODES OF. For anyone who wonders how serious a revision this work is, reading those entries will give you a good indication.

As with all my other books, I am indebted to many people who have contributed ideas for this one. In addition to those cited on pp. xiv–xv (whose contributions endure), I am grateful to the following scholars and lawyers:

Nancy Burkoff
Christopher Camardello
Shayla R. Edwards
Alexandra B. Garner
Caroline B. Garner
Karolyne H.C. Garner
Ruth Bader Ginsburg
Tiger Jackson
Melissa Lin Jones
Thomas B. Lemann
Morris D. Linton
(the late) Sir Robert Megarry

Brian Melendez
Gary Muldoon
Jeff Newman
Thomas M. Reavley
(the late) William Safire
Antonin Scalia
Ann Taylor Schwing
Eliot Turner
Edward T. Wahl
Peter Walsh
(the late) Charles Alan Wright
Kyu Ho Youm

Dean John Attanasio created the Garner Law Scholars program at the Southern Methodist University School of Law. The GLSers (as they're known) have helped tremendously in researching, cite-checking, and proofreading. Many thanks to Ann R. Chao, Levi Dillon, JoAnn Dodson, Kevin R. Grubbs, Angeline Houghtlin, Timothy Martin, Arrissa K. Meyer, Carrie Nie, Laurie M. Velasco, and Ben A. West.

At Oxford University Press, my editors Casper Grathwohl and Damon Zucca gave invaluable guidance and support as I decided the direction in which to take this third edition. And their colleagues in marketing—Jennifer Quigley, Susan Fensten, and Megan Kennedy—approached the practicalities of publication with enthusiastic verve and savvy insight. At the printing house, Lachina Publishing Services of Cleveland, Ohio, both Jeff Lachina and Jennifer Bonnar ensured a high degree of accuracy and editorial consistency, which are all-too-rare qualities in book publishing today.

My much-trusted colleagues at LawProse, Inc.—Jeff Newman, Tiger Jackson, Shayla R. Edwards, Becky R. McDaniel, and Eliot Turner (see p. vi)—proved enormously helpful in supplying illustrative quotations, double-checking their accuracy, proofreading the text, and supplying the indexes at the back of the book. My undergraduate summer intern, Joshua Fuller, helped track down many original sources.

As always, my copyeditors—first and foremost Karen Magnuson of Portland, Oregon, but also Amy Schneider of Wautoma, Wisconsin, and Emily Pfaff of Carrboro, North Carolina—saved the book from many an editorial glitch. The absence of error, being a negative virtue, is often taken for granted by readers. Yet as I've mentioned, it is a *rara avis* (see LATINISMS) today because of the exigencies of modern book publishing, and I am deeply grateful especially to Karen Magnuson for helping me achieve a high degree of accuracy in all my publications.

This book is dedicated to my wife, Karolyne, whose cheerful enthusiam and contagious smile contributed as much as her thorough knowledge of intellectual-property law. The late William Safire asked me incredulously, after having lunch with the two of us, "Where in the world did you *find* her?" I often ask myself nearly the same question, but it starts with *how*. Anyway, it was at a LawProse seminar—always a good place to be. And I thank my lucky stars.

B.A.G.
Dallas, Texas
January 2011

Preface to the Second Edition

Although there is much new material in this second edition, little need be said by way of introduction. I therefore confine this space to a word about citations and a listing of my literary debts.

Readers familiar with the first edition will note that I have added several thousand new illustrative quotations, with full citations. This represents a significant change in approach.

When writing the first edition, I omitted citations for four reasons. First, I was following the model of H.W. Fowler's *Modern English Usage* (1926), which simply quotes sentences from anonymous sources. (His earlier work, *The King's English* (1906), which he cowrote with his brother, F.G., named sources such as *The Times* but gave no detailed citation.) Second, because the quotations merely reflected what I was reading at the time, they came predominantly from judicial opinions issued by Texas courts and the U.S. Court of Appeals for the Fifth Circuit; having just completed a Fifth Circuit clerkship as I finished the manuscript in 1985, I thought it would not be particularly gracious of me, in a work of this kind, to cite a disproportionately high percentage of Fifth Circuit opinions. Third, since I had begun practicing law in Texas, it seemed imprudent to cite the work of judges before whom I might appear. Finally, the lawyers' briefs from which I drew quotations did not lend themselves to citation.

Although I still quote briefs without citing them, other sources are now fully cited. Why? I now think it helpful to show sources—helpful both legally and lexicographically—so I reject Fowler's approach. Further, the citations in this second edition represent a breadth that was unattainable for the first edition, so I am satisfied that the sources from Texas and surrounding states are only slightly overrepresented, if at all. Finally, I am satisfied that the lexicographic value of citations outweighs the risk of offending someone who has written something that might offend against the language.

I have tried to be dispassionate in my approach to citations. This means, for example, that I have unfavorably cited my own work (see **bequest,** vb.), the work of my grandfather (see ***feoff** (c)), and the work of my mentor, Charles Alan Wright (see **disinterest**). Of course, in Wright's case, there are dozens of other instances in which I quote him favorably.

One more thing about citations. I collected many of them before 1991, when the *Bluebook* began to require first names for authors of books and articles. This caused me no end of needless work, but there were finally a few elusive citations for which neither I nor my research assistants—nor, indeed, my allies in law libraries—could fill in the blanks. In those few instances, I made concessions to the shortness of life and followed the pre-1991 *Bluebook* form.

Readers will find that this edition is much enriched with quotations not only from cases, but also from books and other sources. The shame is that it is not more enriched than it is, for in January 1991 a small lexicographic catastrophe occurred—an event that will no doubt bedevil me for as long as I care about lexicography. That month, I arranged to ship some 40 lawbooks from my office at the University of Texas to the American office of the Oxford Dictionary Department. These books had been thoroughly marked up for excerpting thousands of illustrative quotations, and they represented several years of work. Mysteriously these books—which were to be returned to me for use in preparing this edition—disappeared. They have never been accounted for. And the work that went into marking them can probably never be duplicated.

That loss, though, has been greatly outweighed by the tremendous help I have received from dozens of friends and colleagues. My debts are vast. I must merely list them as an insolvent debtor might do, in schedule form. Some of these friends have simply sent me comments and suggestions without my ever having met them face-to-face. Others

I have known for many years, and I merely prevailed upon them to look over several entries within their areas of expertise; luckily for me, no one ever *seemed* prevailed upon—in fact, quite the opposite. They have all helped in splendid ways:

David Anderson
Michèle M. Asprey
Hans W. Baade
J.H. Baker
Griffin B. Bell
John A. Bell
Vicki V. Bonnington
A.W. Bradley
Jeffrey B. Brawner
John Browning
Robert W. Burchfield
Jenny Burg
Beverly Ray Burlingame
Peter Butt
Thomas Cable
Lauren Chadwick
Neil H. Cogan
Charles Dewey Cole Jr.
Kirsten L. Concha
Edward H. Cooper
Daniel R. Coquillette
Sir Brian Cubbon
Robert O. Dawson
A. Darby Dickerson
Lance E. Dickson
Robert Eagleson
Frank H. Easterbrook
Eric B. Easton
David Elliott
Stephen F. Fink
Betty S. Flowers
Alexandra B. Garner
Caroline B. Garner
Gary T. Garner
(the late) Thomas Gibbs Gee
Lord Goff of Chieveley
Erwin N. Griswold
R.J. Grogan, Jr.
Alan Gunn
(the late) Alan M.F. Gunn
David Gunn
Robert W. Hamilton
Trevor C. Hartley
John L. Hauer
Geoffrey C. Hazard Jr.
Nathan L. Hecht
Dewey R. Hicks Jr.
William B. Hilgers

Nancy Hoagland
William Terrell Hodges
Peter W. Hogg
Steve Holmes
Tony Honoré
Hadley Huchton
Lynn N. Hughes
Laird Hunter
Stanley Johanson
Robert H. Johnston III
Michael E. Keasler
Robert E. Keeton
William Keffer
Elizabeth S. Kerr
Joseph Kimble
N. Stephan Kinsella
Kenneth S. Klein
Karen Larsen
Douglas Laycock
Clyde Leland
Thomas B. Lemann
Sanford Levinson
David J. Luban
Joseph R. Lundy
Peter G. McCabe
Neil MacCormick
Becky R. McDaniel
Thomas O. McGarity
Lord Mackenzie-Stuart
Joseph McKnight
Nanneska N. Magee
Karen Magnuson
John Mann
Thomas Mayo
Sir Robert E. Megarry
Roy M. Mersky
Ernest Metzger
Richard H. Miller
Fred Misko Jr.
B. Prater Monning
James E. Moore
Frederick Moss
Ron Moss
R. Eric Nielsen
John T. Noonan Jr.
James A. Parker
David Peeples
Kenneth L. Penegar

Richard W. Pogue
Rick Prahl
George C. Pratt
Jonathan Pratter
Jack Ratliff
Alan Rau
Hal R. Ray Jr.
Thomas M. Reavley
Charles Rembar
Christopher Ricks
Kenneth F. Ripple
Marlyn Robinson
Kimberly Rogaliner
C. Paul Rogers III
David W. Schultz
Fred Shapiro
David J. Sharpe
Christopher Simoni
A.W.B. Simpson
Katherine Smith
David Simon Sokolow
Bruce S. Sostek
Joseph F. Spaniol
Martin Stanford
Mark E. Steiner
Alicemarie Stotler
Michael Sturley
Pat Sullivan
Barbara M. Tearle
Linda Thomas
Randall M. Tietjen
Michael Tigar
John R. Trimble
John W. Velz
Richard S. Walinski
David M. Walker
Patricia H. Webb
Russell J. Weintraub
Carla Wheeler
Julie J. White
Sir David G.T. Williams
William R. Wilson Jr.
Sir Harry Woolf
Charles Alan Wright
Custis Wright
Suzanne F. Young
Mark G. Yudof

If I've omitted anyone, as I must have, my apologies.

Perhaps my vastest debts are to David M. Walker, of Glasgow, and Beverly Ray Burlingame, of Dallas. These fine scholars read the whole of my first draft and gave detailed comments in the margins. I doubt that there is a page in the book that hasn't been improved by their work.

Law librarians have repeatedly come to my aid. I've received the most help from Roy M. Mersky and his staff at the Tarlton Law Library in Austin. David Gunn in particular has generously run down countless sources for me, with uncommon skill and verve. Likewise, the Southern Methodist University Law Library has been extremely helpful. I cannot overstate how important it was to my research when the director, Gail Daly, gave me two card catalogues for storing lexicographic cards. (That may sound quaint in the age of computers, but index cards remain indispensable to lexicographers everywhere.) Finally, Barbara Tearle and R.G. Logan of the Bodleian Law Library, in Oxford, kindly helped me track down some sources that were otherwise inaccessible. As you might guess, I have never met a law librarian I didn't like.

I'm grateful to Dean Paul Rogers of S.M.U. Law School for allocating research-assistant funds that made it possible for me to have all quotations and citations verified. I don't know another dean who would extend this courtesy to a *former* faculty member, but S.M.U. is a special place.

I've benefited enormously from the teaching I've done in continuing legal education, primarily through LawProse, Inc. From my LawProse colleagues—Betty S. Flowers and John R. Trimble, both English professors at the University of Texas at Austin—I have learned a great deal. Many of the new entries show the influence they have had on me: from Betty I have learned more about the writing process, and from John I have learned more about effective editing. John has also contributed useful terminology, such as "mis-cues," and is largely responsible for my about-face on the subject of contractions.

I've also learned from the thousands of lawyers who have participated in LawProse workshops on legal writing and legal drafting. Through questions and comments, many of these participants have given me a deeper understanding of specific legal-linguistic issues.

The members of the H.W. Fowler Society—a loose organization I founded in order to monitor modern usage—have contributed dozens of examples and ideas for headwords. Most notably, John W. Velz, a great Shakespearean scholar and professor emeritus of English at the University of Texas at Austin, has faithfully sent me hundreds of so-called gleanings. I would not have entries such as the ones on **while away** and *wreckless** if it weren't for him.

This edition owes much to Claude Conyers and Nancy Hoagland of Oxford University Press. Time and again, Claude approved my requests for extraordinary assistance of one kind or another. And Nancy is the author's dream of what a production editor should be: perfectionist and highly proprietary in her approach to the book, but respectful on those rare occasions when I perversely resisted her improvements.

When *DMLU* came out in 1987, my daughter Caroline had just been born some six months earlier. There is a funny photograph of her sitting beside the one-foot-tall pile of manuscript. Now she is eight, and her sister, Alexandra, is three; meanwhile, the manuscript pile has doubled in size. As my girls continue to grow, I'm rather hoping that *DMLU* has reached its full maturity. But I somehow doubt it.

Preface to the First Edition

In 1921, an article in the *American Bar Association Journal* called for a book on "writing legal English."[1] The author of that article, Urban A. Lavery, pointed out that lawyers rarely consult a book on grammar or composition even once to the hundreds of times they consult lawbooks; and yet, as he observed, when convincing argument is to the fore, or clearness of expression is desired, the elements of good writing are often more important than piled-up citations of cases.[2] Since Lavery proclaimed this judgment, many books on "writing legal English" have been published, but none with the broad scope or easy accessibility that might allow readers to resolve at a glance the many grammatical and stylistic questions that arise in legal writing. Filling that gap is the goal of this book.

Anglo-American law has a language of its own, consisting in a vocabulary with an unusually large number of foreign phrases, archaic words and expressions, terms of art, and argot words. Its formal style reflects the dignity and solemnity with which the profession views its mission. These distinctive qualities of legal language—evident alike in the speech and the writing of lawyers—are well enough documented. What has remained uncollected and unscrutinized in any systematic way is the vast body of legal usage.

For a specialist language, the language of law remains remarkably variable, largely because it has been incompletely recorded and mapped. In this respect it is analogous to English before 18th-century grammarians attempted to reduce its variability and make logical its many quiddities. This is not to say, of course, that the language of the law has the malleable capacity of Elizabethan English, which, in the hands of a creative genius like Shakespeare, could be supremely expressive and evocative. Quite the opposite. Stare decisis remains at the core of our system of law—so much so that the continual search for precedents often discourages legal writers from straying beyond precisely how things have been said before. As a result, many locutions have become fossilized in legal language over generations. And the inheritors of that language cannot always distinguish mere form from necessary substance, to the extent that form and substance are ever separable.

Legal traditionalists may be justified in not wanting to throw over too readily what has long served well. Yet tradition alone is not sufficient reason for retaining outmoded forms of language. Modern legal writers must strike a difficult balance in the quest to simplify legal English. They should not cling perversely to archaic language, which becomes less comprehensible year by year, for its own sake. Nor should they seek to jettison every word or phrase that bears the stamp of legal tradition.

As for students of law, they learn the technical language that they will need—the quirks of legal jargon, the peculiar idiomatic expressions, the grammatical idiosyncrasies, the neologisms that cannot be found even in the most current unabridged dictionaries—largely by osmosis. These linguistic matters are, for the most part, seldom discussed by lawyers or law professors; rather, they are part of the spoken and written legal discourse that neophyte lawyers absorb every day and learn to use unconsciously. This casualness in acquiring the language frequently leads to variable and contradictory linguistic habits that need explicating, codifying, and, in some instances, taming.

Granted these basic facts of legal language—the course of its growth, the challenge of its use, the pattern of its acquisition—this book aims at serving three primary functions. First, it helps lawyers chart their way through the bogs of legal language. In the past,

---

1. Lavery, *The Language of the Law*, 7 A.B.A. J. 277 (1921).
2. *Id.* at 280.

anyone wanting such a guide has had to make do with general writing manuals. Though this dictionary lays no claim to comprehensiveness, it offers the legal writer guidance on hundreds of specific points of usage. The advice it gives is generally on the conservative side of usage and grammar, for the simple reason that lawyers generally write in a relatively formal context. Lapses from what has come to be accepted as correct irritate and distract the educated reader, and they make the writing less persuasive. Yet the conservative approach exemplified in these pages aspires to be an *informed* conservatism, one that neither battles hopelessly against linguistic faits accomplis nor remains blind to the inevitable growth and change that occur in language.

Second, the dictionary addresses a great many usage problems that do not ordinarily arise in the writing of persons untrained in the law, and therefore that are not addressed in standard writing guides. Certainly it covers territory common to general guides, as inevitably it must. But one of its chief uses should be in pointing out divergences between legal and lay usage, many of which have previously gone unrecorded. To this end, the dictionary serves lawyers and nonlawyers alike, for it can help both groups bridge the linguistic gulf that separates them, to the degree that is possible. The greater effort here needs to be made by lawyers, who in recent years have become increasingly aware of the importance of using legal language that is simple and direct. Indeed, simplicity and directness, two of the touchstones of good writing, are advocated throughout this dictionary in an effort to tag and to discard legalese and highfalutin jargon.

Third, this work may serve, to some extent, as an instrument of reform. Where lawyers and judges use terms imprecisely or ambiguously (or, indeed, incorrectly), this dictionary often presents standards that will enhance rather than destroy valuable nuances. If ever a prescriptive approach to language is justified, it is in law, where linguistic precision is often of paramount concern, and where ambiguity and vagueness (except when purposeful) are intolerable. Within its compass, the dictionary thus seeks to preserve the rich differentiation in our legal vocabulary, to set out some of the important grammatical usages and traditional idioms, and to oppose slipshod usages that blur well-developed distinctions. Of course, no work of this kind can be a panacea for the problems that occur in legal writing. But such a work can realistically seek to make legal writers sensitive to the aesthetic possibilities of their prose, to goad them into thinking more acutely about what works in a given context, and what does not.

Modern Legal Usage is arranged so that the legal writer, unsure of or puzzled by a particular word or point of grammar, can consult a specific entry addressing the problem at hand. Virtually all the sentences quoted to illustrate legal usage, including linguistic pitfalls, originated in judicial opinions. A few come from statutes, fewer still from lawyers' briefs and other sources. The authors of the quoted specimens generally remain anonymous because ordinarily it's unimportant *who* made a particular mistake. Attention should be focused on the mistake itself, and how to remedy it. Where stare decisis is the ruling principle, citations are necessary; in a dictionary of usage they are not, except of course when documenting usages that are lexicographically noteworthy. Whenever specimens do receive attribution, the importance of that fact lies in documenting the source, not in giving context to the quoted matter; hence subsequent histories of cases cited are not given.

Undertaking to write a dictionary of this kind is a precarious task. For by setting oneself up as an arbiter of usage, one also sets one's prose before the magnifying glasses of readers, who are certain to find blemishes of one sort or another. Such was H.W. Fowler's fate in his *Dictionary of Modern English Usage* (1926), a work that has served me as both exemplar and caution. For whatever may be amiss or at fault in this dictionary, I readily acknowledge full responsibility in advance.

As my manuscript swelled, any number of friends and colleagues looked on with far more than a polite interest. Several have actively contributed to whatever merit the final product has. Randall K. Glover of Austin and Kelly Bowers of Seattle called problematical words to my attention almost daily during the year we worked side by side for Judge Thomas M. Reavley. The judge himself, whose approach to life and law cannot but inspire, gave me advice and encouragement that emboldened me to persevere.

Several fellow lawyers undertook to read large portions of the manuscript and made expert comments throughout. My learned friends Dr. Betty S. Flowers, David Radunsky, Michelle D. Monse, Roy J. Grogan Jr., Hal Roberts Ray Jr., Joe W. Pitts III, Alfredo Estrada, Roger Arnold, Lindsay H. Lew, Kenneth S. Klein, Lisa M. Black, Laura Cale, Sim Israeloff, and Jeffrey B. Brawner have all left the work sharper than they found it. I am indebted also to the late John N. Jackson, whose comments reflected years of thought on the subject of legal-writing style.

The Honorable Robert W. Calvert, formerly Chief Justice of the Supreme Court of Texas, generously read and marked up a prototypical draft of the work; he kept me on the reader's path and gave me a number of useful ideas. I am grateful to Justice Sandra Day O'Connor for corresponding with me on some of the stylistic practices of the United States Supreme Court.

Edmund S.C. Weiner, the accomplished Oxford lexicographer, and Martin S. Stanford, an extremely knowledgeable and thoughtful editor in New York, minutely read the full manuscript and made innumerable improvements. To these two scholars I am especially beholden, as I am to my father, Dr. Gary T. Garner, who spent many hours reading galleys.

Classified Guide to Essay Entries

This guide lists essay entries that may be grouped according to (1) style; (2) grammar and usage; (3) legal lexicology and special conventions; (4) word formation, inflection, spelling, and pronunciation; and (5) punctuation and typography. Essay entries are cross-referenced with words set in small capitals. This guide does not include any entries that are concerned only with the meaning or idiomatic use of title words, or with their spelling, pronunciation, etymology, or inflections.

Style

ABSTRACTITIS

ACRONYMS AND INITIALISMS

ALLITERATION
    A. Pleasant Examples
    B. Unpleasant Examples

AMBIGUITY
    A. Generally
    B. Uncertain Stress Producing Ambiguity
    C. Syntactic Ambiguity
    D. Poor Word Choice Producing Ambiguity

AMERICANISMS AND BRITISHISMS

ANFRACTUOSITY

ANTHROPOMORPHISM

ARCHAISMS

ARGUMENT, MODES OF

BIBLICAL AFFECTATION

BRIEF-WRITING

BURIED VERBS

CASE REFERENCES
    A. Short-Form References
    B. Locatives with
    C. As Attributive Adjectives
    D. Hypallage with
    E. Personification of Cases

CHAMELEON-HUED WORDS

CITATION OF CASES
    A. Beginning Sentences with Citations
    B. Midsentence Citations
    C. Incidental Use of Case Names
    D. Citations in Text

CLICHÉS

COLLOQUIALITY

COMPANY NAMES

CONNOTATION AND DENOTATION

CONTRACTIONS

CUTTING OUT THE CHAFF

DATES
    A. Order
    B. Month and Year
    C. As Adjectives
    D. Written Out
    E. In Contracts

DEFINITIONS
    A. When to Use
    B. Lexical and Stipulative Definitions
    C. Inept Definitional Terms
    D. "Stuffed" Definitions
    E. Placement
    F. Signaling Defined Terms in Text
    G. When to Compose

DOCUMENT DESIGN

DOUBLETS, TRIPLETS, AND SYNONYM-STRINGS

ENUMERATIONS
    A. *First(ly), second(ly), third(ly)*; *one, two, three*
    B. Comma Before the Last Element

ETYMOLOGICAL AWARENESS

EUPHEMISMS

FIRST PERSON
    A. Awkward Avoidance of First Person
    B. The Collegial *we* of Judges
    C. Approaching Autobiography

FLOTSAM PHRASES

FOOTNOTES
    A. Textual Footnotes
    B. For Citations

FORBIDDEN WORDS AND PHRASES
    A. Generally Useless Words and Phrases
    B. Ignorant Malformations

FORMAL WORDS

FORMS OF ADDRESS
    A. Addressing Federal Judges
    B. Addressing State-Court Judges
    C. Four Rules in Using *The Honorable*
    D. *Mr. Justice*; *Mrs. Justice*; *Madam Justice*
    E. Third-Person References
    F. Lawyer-to-Lawyer References
    G. Signing Off
    H. The Lone *sincerely*

FUDGE WORDS

FUSTIAN

GALLICISMS

GOBBLEDYGOOK

HERE- AND THERE- WORDS

ILLOGIC
    A. Illogical Comparison
    B. Danglers and Misplaced Modifiers
    C. Disjointed Appositives
    D. Mistaken Subject of a Prepositional Phrase
    E. Insensitivity to Metaphor

Grammar and Usage

Legal Lexicology and Special Conventions

Word Formation, Inflection, Spelling, and Pronunciation

Punctuation and Typography

Pronunciation Guide

Pronunciations are shown within virgules. Syllables are separated by hyphens in pronunciations, and syllables spoken with the greatest stress are shown in boldface type.

ə	*for all vowel sounds in*	turbid, among, journal, trust, monk
a	*as in*	pact, democrat, drafting
ah	*as in*	alms, father, calm
ahr	*as in*	bargain, argue, pardon
air	*as in*	care, lair, aware
aw	*as in*	law, cause, flaw
ay	*as in*	litigate, delay
b	*as in*	brief, bankruptcy, bench
ch	*as in*	chambers, chance, chief
d	*as in*	deposition, divorce, disclosure
e	*as in*	evidence, appellate, rescue
ee	*as in*	freedom, appeal, pleading
eer	*as in*	peer, gear, weird
f	*as in*	forensic, bailiff, iffy
g	*as in*	guilt, flog, grieve
h	*as in*	hang, holiday, hornbook
hw	*as in*	which, while, whether
i	*as in*	civil, innocent, condition
ɪ	*as in*	trial, right, file
j	*as in*	juror, jail, justice
k	*as in*	clerk, check, county
l	*as in*	law, liberty, legislate
m	*as in*	marshal, matrimony, methods
n	*as in*	none, end, run
ng	*as in*	gang, rank, hung
o	*as in*	modern, confidential, conscience
oh	*as in*	over, parole, quote
ohr	*as in*	lore, floor, bore
oi	*as in*	moist, oyster, toy
oo	*as in*	too, boon, flute
oor	*as in*	poor, boor, tour
or	*as in*	board, court
ow	*as in*	power, our, flower
p	*as in*	primary, plenary, prison
r	*as in*	reporter, reprieve, rules
s	*as in*	sue, swear, sentence
sh	*as in*	shoe, shoulder, push
t	*as in*	term, transact, testify
th	*as in*	thief, theory, ethics
th	*as in*	that, whether, either
uu	*as in*	book, full, woman
v	*as in*	venire, relevant, device
w	*as in*	win, wordy, work
y	*as in*	yes, year, yellow
z	*as in*	zap, dizzy, busy
zh	*as in*	pleasure, vision, leisure

List of Abbreviations

abr. = abridged

adj. = adjective

adv. = adverb

AHD = *The American Heritage Dictionary of the English Language* (4th ed. 2006)

Am. = American

AmE = American English

arch. = archaic

Aus. = Australia; Australian

B9 = *Black's Law Dictionary* (9th ed. 2009)

BrE = British English

c. = century

ca. = (*circa*) around [a given year]

Can. = Canada; Canadian

cap. = capitalized

CDL = *A Dictionary of Law* (Jonathan Law & Elizabeth A. Martin eds., 7th ed. 2009) (in earlier eds., *A Concise Dictionary of Law*)

cf. = (*confer*) compare with

C.J. = Chief Justice

COD = *The Concise Oxford Dictionary of Current English* (8th ed. 1990)

colloq. = colloquial

ed. = edition; editor

e.g. = (*exempli gratia*) for example

Eng. = England; English

esp. = especially

ex. = example

fig. = figuratively

fr. = from (derived from; found in)

Fr. = France; French

G.B. = Great Britain (i.e., England, Scotland, and Wales)

Ger. = German

Gk. = Greek

id. = (*idem*) in the same source

i.e. = (*id est*) that is

J. = Justice; Judge

JJ. = Justices; Judges

J.P. = Justice of the Peace

K.B. = King's Bench

L. = Latin

La. = Louisiana

L.F. = Law French

lit. = literally

L.L. = Law Latin

MEU1 = H.W. Fowler, *A Dictionary of Modern English Usage* (1926)

MEU2 = H.W. Fowler, *A Dictionary of Modern English Usage* (Ernest Gowers ed., 2d ed. 1965)

M.R. = Master of the Rolls

n. = noun

N.B. = (*nota bene*) note well

no. = number

NOAD = *The New Oxford American Dictionary* (2d ed. 2005)

N.Z. = New Zealand

obs. = obsolete

OCL1 = David M. Walker, *The Oxford Companion to Law* (1980)

OCL2 = *The New Oxford Companion to Law* (Peter Cane & Joanne Conaghan eds., 2008)

O.E. = Old English

OED = *The Oxford English Dictionary* (2d ed. 1989) (together with online updates)

O.F. = Old French

orig. = original, originally

Oxford Guide = *The Oxford Guide to English Usage* (1983)

¶ or par. = paragraph

p. = page

P.C. = Privy Council

phr. = phrase

P.J. = Presiding Judge

pl. = plural

pmbl. = preamble

pp. = pages

p. pl. = past participle

prep. = preposition

pron. = pronoun

Q.B. = Queen's Bench

quot. = quotation

q.v.   = (*quod vide*) which see

qq.v. = pl. form of *q.v.*

repr. = reprinted

rev.   = revised by; revision

RH2   = *The Random House Diction-ary of the English Language* (2d ed. 1987)

Scot. = Scotland; Scottish

sing. = singular

SOED   = *The New Shorter Oxford English Dictionary* (4th ed. 1993)

Sp.   = Spain; Spanish

specif. = specifically

s.v.   = (*sub verbo*) under the word

TLS   = *Times Literary Supplement*

U.C.C. = Uniform Commercial Code

U.K.   = United Kingdom (i.e., Great Britain and—since 1922—Northern Ireland)

U.S.   = United States

U.S.C. = United States Code

usu.   = usually

vb.   = verb

W2   = *Webster's New International Dictionary* (2d ed. 1934)

W3   = *Webster's Third New International Dictionary* (1961)

W9   = *Webster's Ninth New Collegiate Dictionary* (9th ed. 1984)

W10   = *Merriam-Webster's Collegiate Dictionary* (10th ed. 1993)

W11   = *Merriam-Webster's Collegiate Dictionary* (11th ed. 2003)

Abbreviations within case names follow established conventions in law.

A

a; an. This entry treats two common problems with the indefinite articles; for advice on using definite and indefinite articles generally, see ARTICLES.

A. Choosing Between *a* and *an*. The indefinite article *a* is used before words beginning with a consonant sound, including *-y-* and *-w-* sounds <a European country> <a one-year limitation>. The other form, *an*, is used before words beginning with a vowel sound <an LL.B. degree> <an SEC subpoena>. Since the sound rather than the letter controls, it's not unusual to find *a* before a vowel or *an* before a consonant. For those who have been wondering, the correct form is *a usufruct* in Louisiana law and *a hypothec* in Scots law.

The distinction between *a* and *an* was not solidified until the 19th century. Up to that time, *an* preceded most words beginning with a vowel, regardless of how the first syllable sounded. The U.S. Constitution reads: "The Congress shall have Power . . . To establish *an uniform* Rule of Naturalization . . . ." U.S. Const. art. I, § 8. But that is no excuse for a modern writer: "Thus retaining *an unique* [read *a unique*] and personal quality style creates nevertheless an essential value in all written expression." Perlie P. Fallon, *The Relation Between Analysis and Style in American Legal Prose*, 28 Neb. L. Rev. 80, 80 (1949).

Writers on usage formerly disputed whether the correct article is *a* or *an* with *historian, historical,* and a few other words. The traditional rule is that if the *-h-* is sounded, *a* is the proper form. If we follow that rule in modern AmE, most people would say *a historian.* Even H.W. Fowler, in the England of 1926, advocated *a* before *historic(al)* and *humble.*

But the theory behind using *an* in such a context is that the *-h-* is very weak when the accent is on the second rather than the first syllable (giving rise, by analogy, to **an habitual offender, *an humanitarian, *an hallucinatory image,* and **an harassed schoolteacher*). So no authority countenances **an history,* though several older ones prefer **an historian* and **an historical.* Justice Benjamin Cardozo wrote: "What we hand down in our judgments is *an hypothesis.* It is no longer a divine command." *Law and Literature,* 52 Harv. L. Rev. 471, 478 (1939). Earlier, Justice Oliver Wendell Holmes had used the same phrase.

Today, however, **an hypothesis* and **an historical* are likely to strike readers and listeners as affectations in need of editing. Anyone who sounds the *-h-* in such words should avoid pretense and use *a.* Hence: *a hypothecation, a hereditament, a hallucinatory image, a harassed schoolteacher.* See **humble.**

B. In the Distributive Sense. *A,* the distributive sense <ten hours a day>, has traditionally been considered preferable to *per,* which originated in commercialese and LEGALESE. It is wrong to consider *a* informal or colloquial in this context. The natural idiom is *sixty hours a week* and *ten dollars a pair,* though it has become common to encounter *sixty hours per week* and *ten dollars per pair.* E.g.:

- "The only high earners (forty dollars *per* [read *an*] hour) were occasional prostitutes." Joel F. Handler, *Women, Families, Work, and Poverty,* 6 UCLA Women's L.J. 375, 398 (1996).
- "Federal land management expenditures, measured in dollars *per* [read *an*] acre, have more than tripled since 1962." Jonathan H. Adler, *Free & Green,* 24 Harv. J.L. & Pub. Pol'y 653, 672 (2001).
- "The workers . . . earned, on average, five dollars *per* [read *an*] hour less than did workers at similar plants around the country." Gerald Torres, *Translation and Stories,* 115 Harv. L. Rev. 1362, 1368 (2002).

Nonetheless, the distributive *per* is at least minimally acceptable, except in the phrase *as per.* (See **as per.**) And in a few contexts, especially when used attributively, *per* is the only idiomatic word. E.g.: "There have also been attempts to reduce the *per-unit* cost through standardization of contracts, notably in the distribution of computer software through 'shrink-wrap licenses.'" Mark A. Lemley, *The Economics of Improvement in Intellectual Property Law,* 75 Tex. L. Rev. 989, 1054 (1997).

A.B. See **able-bodied seaman.**

*abalienate. See **alien,** vb.

abandon = (1) to give up property or some right with the intent of never claiming it again; or (2) in family law, to leave children or a spouse willfully and without an intent to return. In sense 1, a person's losing a billfold (say) and then giving up an unsuccessful search does not mean that the person *abandons* the lost billfold: to *abandon* it, the person would have to take some purposeful action such as throwing it away. For more on this word and its near-synonyms, see **relinquish.**

abandoned property. See **lost property.**

abandonee means, not "one who is abandoned," as the suffix *-ee* might suggest, but "one to whom property rights [in a thing] are relinquished." As in *advancee* (= one to whom money is advanced) and *patentee* (= one to whom a patent has been issued), the suffix *-ee* carries a dative sense. Leff wrote that "there are numerous circumstances in which abandonment of something by one person will have the practical or even legal effect of vesting that thing in a particular other person, who thus may usefully be called an *abandonee.*" Arthur A. Leff, *The Leff Dictionary of Law,* 94 Yale L.J. 1855, 1856 (1985). See -EE (A).

abandum; *abandonum. *Abandum* is the correct spelling of this word, which means "anything

An asterisk (*) precedes words and phrases that are invariably inferior forms.

1

prohibited or ordered to be cast away." *Abandonum* is a historical misspelling.

abate is a FORMAL WORD common in legal contexts, meaning (1) *vb.*, "to nullify; quash; demolish" <to abate a legal action>; (2) *vb.*, "to diminish" <to abate a debt>; or (3) *vb.*, "to remove physically" <to abate a nuisance>; or (4) *vb.*, "to come to an end" <all suits abate upon the death of the plaintiff>. There is, additionally, a technical legal sense that is rarely if ever used today: "to thrust oneself tortiously into real estate after the owner dies and before the legal heir enters" <abatement of freehold>.

Today *abate* is used most often in senses 2 and 3—e.g.:

- (Sense 2) "The rent should *abate* proportionally to the extent the loss of use of the dishwasher and stovetop deprive Boelter of her full normal use of the premises." *Boelter v. Tschantz*, 779 N.W.2d 467, 473–74 (Wis. Ct. App. 2009).
- (Sense 3) "A person who suffers from a nuisance may *abate* it, i.e. remove it, even without giving notice, if he can do so without going on to another's land." William Geldart, *Introduction to English Law* 144 (D.C.M. Yardley ed., 9th ed. 1984).

The adjective is *abatable*—e.g.:

- "Why should a defendant be 'rewarded' with a statute of limitations defense when she causes technically *abatable* harm that is so extensive that the cost of *abating* it exceeds the value of cleanup to plaintiff?" Ronald G. Aronovsky, *Back from the Margins*, 84 Denv. U. L. Rev. 395, 478 (2006). (In that example, it would be preferable to hyphenate *statute-of-limitations defense*, just so, to show the PHRASAL ADJECTIVE.)
- "The court then went on to attack the ostensibly logical premise that an *abatable* nuisance is, by definition, not permanent." Brandon Archer, Note, *Shoo, Odors and Pollutants! Don't Bother Me!*, 59 Baylor L. Rev. 171, 182 (2007).

abator. So spelled.

ABBREVIATIONS. See ACRONYMS AND INITIALISMS & INITIALESE.

*abbuttals. See **abutment**.

abdicate may mean (1) "to disown"; (2) "to discard"; or (3) "to renounce." In legal writing it usually takes on sense 3—e.g.:

- "We did not . . . imply that we had *abdicated* our equitable powers to prevent an unjust forfeiture." *Foundation Dev. Corp. v. Loehmann's, Inc.*, 788 P.2d 1189, 1195 (Ariz. 1990).
- "The majority, as I see it, has *abdicated* its responsibility to enforce federal constitutional norms." *Clemons v. Mississippi*, 494 U.S. 738, 774 (1990) (Blackmun, J., concurring in part & dissenting in part).

abduct; abduce. These words overlap in meaning, but are not interchangeable. Both may mean "to draw away (a limb, etc.) from its natural position" (*OED*). Yet the more common meaning of *abduct* is "to lead away by force." (For a fuller definition, see **abduction**.) Although the *OED* contains a notation that *abduce* is

archaic, *W3* does not label it so; in any event, it is certainly rare.

abductee. See -EE (C).

*abducter. See **abductor** (B).

abduction; kidnapping; *kidnaping; child-stealing. *Abduction* = the act of leading (someone) away by force or fraudulent persuasion. *Black's Law Dictionary* 4 (9th ed. 2009). It constitutes a statutory offense in many states; for example, *abduct* is statutorily defined in one state as "to restrain a person with intent to prevent his liberation by: (A) secreting or holding him in a place where he is not likely to be found; or (B) using or threatening to use deadly force." Tex. Pen. Code Ann. § 20.01 (Vernon 2003).

In England, *abduction* was traditionally given a narrower sense: "the offence of taking an unmarried girl under the age of 16 from the possession of her parents or guardian against their will." *Concise Dictionary of Law* 2 (2d ed. 1990). The *OCL* additionally defines *abduction* in English law as taking "a girl under 18 or a defective woman of any age from the possession of her parent or guardian for the purpose of unlawful sexual intercourse, or a girl under 21 with property or expectations of property from such possession to marry or have unlawful sexual intercourse, or . . . taking away and detaining any woman with the intention that she shall marry or have unlawful sexual intercourse with a person, by force or for the sake of her property or expectations of property."

In current AmE and BrE, *abduction* has virtually no connotations relating to the victim's sex. But in older British legal writing—and at common law—the victim is almost invariably a woman. Abduction of voters, a criminal offense in G.B., is one usage in which the abductee's sex is always irrelevant.

Kidnapping = the act or an instance of stealing, abducting, or carrying away a person by force or fraud, often with a demand for ransom (*W3*). *Kidnapping* (the -*pp*- spelling is preferred) is not restricted in application to children as victims, though the etymology suggests it. *Child-stealing* is the technical statutory term for the abduction of children. See **kidnapping** (B).

abductor. A. Plural Form. *Abductor* forms two plurals: -*tors* and -*tores*. The English plural, *abductors*, is preferable to the Latin plural, *abductores*.

B. And *abducter. This alternative spelling, which is etymologically inferior, is not as widespread as *abductor*.

*aberrance; *aberrancy. See **aberration**.

aberrant, adj.; **aberrational; aberrative.** *Aberrant* = deviating from behavioral or social norms. *Aberrational* = of or relating to an aberration. *Aberrative* = tending toward aberration.

Some writers use *aberrational* when *aberrant*, the more usual word, might work better—e.g.: "Their conduct was so *aberrational* [read *aberrant*], almost unbelievable, that the prosecution and judges found it difficult to sort out the implications of what had transpired." Jay Katz, *Human Sacrifice and Human Experimentation*, 22 Yale J. Int'l L. 401, 411 (1997).

aberration; *aberrance; *aberrancy; aberrant, n. *Aberration* denotes (1) a deviation or departure from what is normal or correct, or (2) a mental derangement. *Aberrance* and *aberrancy* are NEEDLESS VARIANTS.

Although the word *aberration* is not limited to persons, *aberrant* almost always is. As a noun, it means "a deviant; one deviating from established norms."

Aberration and its cognates are occasionally misspelled with -*bb*- and with one -*r*—and these misspellings are what linguists sometimes call autological (that is, they are themselves aberrational). E.g.:

- "Santiago takes issue with canonical Dominican nationalist narratives that repudiate the period of Haitian occupation as an external *abberation* [read *aberration*]." Tayyab Mahmud, *City and Citizenship*, 52 Clev. St. L. Rev. 51, 53 (2005) (paraphrasing Charles R. Venator Santiago).
- "Spotted Bear contends that the 41-month sentence is unreasonable in light of his lack of criminal history [and] the *abberational* [read *aberrational*] nature of the crime." *U.S. v. Spotted Bear*, 207 Fed. Appx. 760, 760 (9th Cir. 2006).
- "Reported data that appeared to be *abberational* [read *aberrational*] (statistically or otherwise) were not included in the calculations." *U.S. v. Valencia*, 34 Media L. Rep. 2494, 2495 (S.D. Tex. 2006).

aberrational; aberrative. See **aberrant.**

abet. See **aid and abet.**

abetment (= the act of abetting) is sometimes erroneously made *abettance* or *abettal*, both NEEDLESS VARIANTS.

abettor. A. And *abetter.* In both BrE and AmE, *abettor* is the more usual spelling; the *OED* states that it "is the constant form of the word as a legal term." *Abettator* is the defunct LAW LATIN term from old English law. See -ER (A) & **perpetrator.** Cf. **bettor.**

　　B. And Its Near-Synonyms: *confederate; conspirator; accomplice; accessory.* See **confederate (A).**

　　C. Compared to *perpetrator; inciter; criminal protector.* See **perpetrator.**

abeyance has a general sense ("a state of suspension, temporary nonexistence, or inactivity" [*OED*]) and a technical legal sense ("expectation or contemplation of law; the position of waiting for or being without a

claimant or owner" [*OED*]). But even in legal contexts, the general lay sense is common—e.g.:

- "Texas would not consider his claim if this action were held in *abeyance.*" *Carter v. Procunier*, 755 F.2d 1126, 1131 (5th Cir. 1985).
- "The statute implicitly recognizes that a child's life cannot be held in *abeyance* while the parent is unable to perform the actions necessary to assume parenting responsibilities." *In re C.L.G.*, 956 A.2d 999, 1005 (Pa. Super. Ct. 2008).

abhorrent, literally "shrinking with horror" (*OED*), in law frequently refers to things in the sense "so far removed from (another thing) as to be repugnant or inconsistent"—e.g.: "The potential for this self-censorship is *abhorrent* to the First Amendment." *Babbitt v. United Farm Workers Nat'l Union*, 442 U.S. 289, 318 (1979) (Brennan, J., concurring in part & dissenting in part).

abide. A. General Senses. *Abide* = (1) to stay <the right of entering and abiding in any state in the Union>; (2) to tolerate, withstand <we won't abide that type of contemptuous behavior>; (3) to obey (construed with *by*) <abide by the law>; (4) to await <our decision must abide the outcome of the general election>; or (5) to perform or execute (in reference to orders or judgments) <as a trial judge, I must abide the judgment of the circuit court>. The last is the strictly legal meaning—e.g.: "Since we do not doubt that the court will promptly proceed to certify . . . and will *abide* our decision before proceeding to trial, we decline to issue a peremptory order at this time." *In re McClelland Eng'rs, Inc.*, 742 F.2d 837, 838 (5th Cir. 1984).

Abide also commonly takes on the sense "to await," as here: "The judgment should be reversed and a new trial granted, with costs to *abide* the event." *Wank v. Ambrosino*, 121 N.E.2d 246, 249 (N.Y. 1954).

Abide by is a PHRASAL VERB meaning "to acquiesce in or conform to"—e.g.:

- "The fact that defense attorneys are, as Bill Stuntz has noted, 'repeat players with whom the government must deal often,' certainly gives the government an added reason to *abide by* its plea agreements." Daniel C. Richman, *Cooperating Clients*, 56 Ohio St. L.J. 69, 93 (1995).
- "Absent evidence to the contrary, we must presume that juries understand and *abide by* a district court's limiting instructions." *U.S. v. Downing*, 297 F.3d 52, 59 (2d Cir. 2002).
- "The Court further added that jurors' emotional involvement and seriousness in considering the gravity of the situation did not mean that the jurors would not follow the court's instructions or *abide by* their oaths." Brooke A. Thompson, *Criminal Law—The Supreme Court Expands the* Witt *Principles to Exclude a Juror Who Would Follow the Law*, 30 UALR L. Rev. 845, 856–57 (2008).

In this sense, omitting the *by* is awkward at best, unidiomatic at worst—e.g.: "A defendant must *abide* [insert *by*] the rules of evidence and procedure." *U.S. v. Bautista*, 145 F.3d 1140, 1151–52 (10th Cir. 1998).

Abiding = lasting, enduring. E.g.:

- "We are left with the *abiding* belief that Hagy's appeal against the city and county was brought frivolously, unreasonably, and without legal or factual foundation." *Hagy v. State*, 51 P.3d 432, 439 (Idaho Ct. App. 2002).
- "The voter's refusal to disaffiliate from the major party may reflect her *abiding* commitment to that party." *Clingman v. Beaver*, 544 U.S. 581, 601 (2005) (per Thomas, J.).

B. Past-Tense and Past-Participial Forms. With the meanings most probably to be found in legal texts ("await" and "execute"), *abided* is the preferred past tense and past participle. In sense 1 ("to stay, dwell"), *abode* is the preferred past tense, and either *abode* or *abided* as the past participle. In other senses, *abided* is the preferred past tense and past participle.

ability; capacity. Whereas *ability* is qualitative, *capacity* is quantitative. *Ability* refers to a person's power of body or mind <a lawyer of great ability>; *capacity*, meaning literally "roomy, spacious," refers figuratively to a person's physical or mental power to receive <her memory has an extraordinary capacity for details>.

For the distinction between *capacity* and *capability*, see **capacity.**

ab initio; in initio. *Ab initio* means "from the beginning" <an act beyond one's legal competence is void *ab initio*>; *in initio* means, as its prefix suggests, "in the beginning." Neither LATINISM seems quite justified in ordinary contexts, although *ab initio*, which in legal writing is used commonly in the phrase *void ab initio*, is common enough not to be particularly objectionable—e.g.:

- "Diversification is generally a response to an unavoidable risk, however, and here the risk can be eliminated *ab initio*." Thomas H. Jackson, *Bankruptcy, Non-Bankruptcy Entitlements, and the Creditors' Bargain*, 91 Yale L.J. 857, 863 (1982).
- "This ignores, *ab initio*, another constant and powerful necessity in human existence: our relationship to one another—the importance to human dignity of community, of collective values, and of 'group rights.'" Peter G. Danchin, *Suspect Symbols*, 33 Yale J. Int'l L. 1, 46 (2008).

Leff noted that the phrase is sometimes used in the sense "thoroughly," roughly equivalent to "from first to last." Arthur A. Leff, *The Leff Dictionary of Law*, 94 Yale L.J. 1855, 1863 (1985). E.g.: "If the defendant is clearly guilty . . . then he will just as clearly be convicted again—with the added benefit that states irritated at holding new trials will have a new (and apparently sorely needed) incentive to comply with the Vienna Convention *ab initio* in future cases." Note, *Too Sovereign but Not Sovereign Enough*, 116 Harv. L. Rev. 2654, 2675–76 (2003).

abjudge; adjudge. These words are antithetical in one sense. *Abjudge* is a rare term (not in most abridged dictionaries) meaning "to take away by judicial decision" (*OED*). *Adjudge*, in contrast, means "to award, grant, or impose judicially" (*id.*). One *abjudges from* and *adjudges to*. For the latter term's other senses, see **adjudge.**

abjudicate is synonymous with *abjudge*. See **abjudge.**

abjure. A. Near-Synonyms Distinguished: *renounce; forswear; swear off; recant; retract.* These verbs share the sense "to disavow a practice, act, statement, or belief that one previously espoused." *Abjure* and *renounce*—the closest synonyms—both connote a solemn and rather public repudiation of an earlier vow, habit, or tenet <abjure using hardball tactics> <the defendant renounced his gang affiliation>. *Forswear*, like its more colloquial sibling *swear off*, suggests a negative oath <it's a sound principle of legal drafting to forswear using the word *shall*>. *Recant* and *retract* emphasize taking back what one has previously said—*recant* implying more of an admission of error, and perhaps a tone of contrition, than *retract* <once the racist implications of his statement were widely recognized, he recanted> <she retracted her earlier statements but refused further comment>.

B. Distinguished from *adjure*. *Abjure* may mean either (1) "to renounce" <Germany abjured the use of force>, or (2) "to avoid" <her evaluation abjured excessive praise>. *Adjure* means "to charge or entreat solemnly; to urge earnestly" <Reagan adjured the Soviets to join him in this noble goal>.

C. Cognate Forms for *abjure* and *adjure*. The noun forms are *abjuration* (or *abjurement*—now defunct) and *adjuration*. The adjectival forms end in *-tory*. The agent nouns are *abjurer* and *adjurer*.

abjurer; *abjuror. The first spelling is preferred. See -ER (A).

able. For the meaning of this word in the phrase *ready, willing, and able*, see **ready, willing, and able.**

able-bodied seaman; able seaman. The former, though much more recent, seems to be the usual term in admiralty law, meaning "a merchant seaman certified for all seaman's duties" (*AHD*). It is abbreviated *A.B.* The phrase *able seaman* is used in the U.S. Shipping Code, 46 U.S.C. § 7307 (2006). It also appears in Herman Melville's *Billy Budd* (1891). To categorize either as a NEEDLESS VARIANT of the other would be difficult and footless. See **seaman** & **mariner.**

aboard. Usually restricted to ships in BrE, this word is used broadly in AmE—e.g.: "Once *aboard* the bus Agent Woodruff announced . . . that he was performing an immigration inspection." *U.S. v. Portillo-Aguirre*, 311 F.3d 647, 650 (5th Cir. 2002).

abode, as past tense of *abide*. See **abide (B).**

abode, place of. This phrase is a pretentious way of referring to someone's home or house. It's also redundant, since *abode* is a place. See REDUNDANCY.

*abolishment; *admonishment. These nouns are inferior to—and much rarer than—the organically derived *abolition* and *admonition*; no longer is there any difference in meaning between the *-ment* and the *-tion* forms. Yet the *-ment* forms, though NEEDLESS VARIANTS, waywardly persist in much legal writing—e.g.:

- "Later cases have heeded this *admonishment* [read *admonition*] and courts have been reluctant to disqualify judges under the due process clause for apparent conflicts of interest." David Scott Coward, Note, *The Adjudicatory Power of the FSLIC over Claims Involving Savings and Loans in FSLIC Receivership*, 88 Colum. L. Rev. 1325, 1358 (1988).
- "With a strong *admonishment* [read *admonition*], the court responded that if a tenure committee was acting in good faith, 'disclosure should not adversely affect the decision-making process.'" James H. Brooks, *Confidentiality of Tenure Review and Discovery of Peer Review Materials*, 1988 BYU L. Rev. 705, 715.
- "Accompanying the then-emergent sentiment favoring the *abolishment* [read *abolition*] of capital punishment came a renewed skepticism regarding conversions accomplished in the shadows of the gallows." Robert N. Strassfeld, *Robert McNamara and the Art and Law of Confession*, 47 Duke L.J. 491, 508 (1997).
- "Epstein then calls not only for the *abolishment* [read *abolition*] of these 'parasitic' rules but also for the enactment of a new rule that will explicitly permit refusal to contract with a person out of discriminatory tastes." Hila Keren, *"We Insist! Freedom Now,"* 11 Mich. J. Race & L. 133, 157 (2005).

abort = (1) (of a pregnancy, project, or mission) to end prematurely; (2) (of a fetus) to cause to be expelled before full development; or (3) (of a pregnant female) to cause to have an abortion. Senses 1 and 2 are more usual than sense 3, which, as an example of HYPALLAGE, strikes many readers as odd. E.g.: "In a case of 1949, the trial judge sentenced a husband who had tried to *abort* his wife and killed her to five years' penal servitude." Glanville Williams, *The Sanctity of Life and the Criminal Law* 155 (1957).

abortee. Logically, one might expect this word to refer to the fetus (one who is aborted)—but by convention, and based on sense 3 of *abort*, the word *abortee* refers to the woman whose miscarriage has been produced. *See* Rollin M. Perkins, *Criminal Law* 100 (1957). Today the word is little used even in legal contexts, perhaps because it seems callous. See -EE.

*aborticide. See **abortion.**

abortifacient; contraceptive. An *abortifacient* is anything intended to produce an abortion. *Contraception* is anything designed to prevent conception. *Abortifacient* should not be used to include *contraceptive*.

abortion; *aborticide; feticide. The word *abortion*, strictly speaking, means no more than "the expulsion of a nonviable fetus" (*W3*). In this sense it is synonymous with *miscarriage*. But today it more commonly applies specifically to an intentionally induced miscarriage—not one that results naturally or accidentally. Though *abortion* was once used interchangeably with *criminal abortion*, that is no longer so with the advent of *legalized abortion*. In the criminal context, then, it is necessary to use the full phrase *criminal abortion* or *crime of abortion*.

*Aborticide = the act of destroying a live fetus. It appears to be a NEEDLESS VARIANT of *abortion*—and a tendentious one. In any event, though, **aborticide* is an ill-formed equivalent of *feticide*. If, as the dictionaries suggest, it is formed on the verb *abort*, then ironically it is what H.W. Fowler called an "abortion," but here is termed a MORPHOLOGICAL DEFORMITY. If it is formed on the noun *abortus* (= an aborted fetus), then it is illogical, for an abortionist does not—except in the grossest imaginable circumstances—"kill" (*-cide*) a fetus that has already been aborted. **Aborticide* is to be avoided in favor of the superior alternative, *feticide* (BrE *fœticide*).

The term *feticide* is often used to denote the killing of a fetus, especially by an assault and battery against the mother.

The current euphemism for *abortion*—a highly charged term since the Supreme Court handed down *Roe v. Wade*, 410 U.S. 113 (1973)—is *pregnancy termination*. See EUPHEMISMS.

ABORTIONS, LINGUISTIC. See MORPHOLOGICAL DEFORMITIES.

abortive; aborted. *Abortive* means "unsuccessful because cut short." It takes on the figurative sense of *aborted* (= cut short), as *an abortive trial*, i.e., one cut short before the verdict by, e.g., settlement of the dispute. (Note that *-ive*, an active suffix, here has a passive sense.) E.g.:

- "Shortly after Oxford's wedding to Anne, he and his guardian quarreled over the latter's role in the prosecution of Oxford's relative the Duke of Norfolk; moreover, Oxford was involved in an *abortive* scheme to rescue the convicted duke from the tower." Peter A. Jaszi, *Brief of Appellant Edward De Vere, Seventeenth Earl of Oxford*, 37 Am. U. L. Rev. 647, 707 (1987).
- "These statutes have been used against government employees who leak classified information to the media, and recently in an *abortive* effort to prosecute private lobbyists who received such leaks." Note, *Media Incentives and National Security Secrets*, 122 Harv. L. Rev. 2228, 2231 (2009).

Abortive is archaic in reference to abortions of fetuses, except in the sense "causing an abortion"; and in that sense, it is a NEEDLESS VARIANT of *abortifacient*. See **abortifacient.**

abound. See **many (B).**

about; approximately. *Approximately* is a FORMAL WORD; *about* is the ordinary, perfectly good equivalent. *About* should not be used, as it often is, with other terms of approximation such as *estimate* or *guess*, because it means "roughly" or "approximately." Hence "roughly about $10,000" is redundant.

above. A. For *above-mentioned*. *Above* is an acceptable ellipsis for *above-mentioned*, and it is much less inelegant—e.g.: "As the *above* arguments indicate, the cornerstone premises in Lessig's overall set of arguments—as well as the overall rhetorical posture of the book—are that amateur-remix-cultural activity is, under current law, criminal activity." Steven A. Hetcher, *Using Social Norms to Regulate Fan Fiction and Remix Culture*, 157 U. Pa. L. Rev. 1869, 1899 (2009).

It was long thought that *above* could not properly act as an adjective. But the word has long been so used in legal writing of the highest quality—e.g.:

- "If the *above* sections were the only law bearing on the matter, [we assume] that they created a civil liability to make reparation to anyone whose rights were infringed." *Slater v. Mexican Nat'l R.R.*, 194 U.S. 120, 126 (1904) (per Holmes, J.).
- "Yet in the middle of the *above* passage from Lord Lindley's opinion there is a sudden and question-begging shift in the use of terms." Wesley Newcomb Hohfeld, *Some Fundamental Legal Conceptions as Applied in Judicial Reasoning*, 23 Yale L.J. 16, 37 (1913).

The *OED* records this use from 1873 and states: "By ellipsis of a pple. as *said, written, mentioned, above* stands attributively, as 'the above explanation.'"

Although some critics have suggested that *above* in this sense should refer only to something mentioned previously on the same page, this restriction is unduly narrow. Still, it's often better to make the reference exact by giving a page or paragraph number, rather than the vague reference made possible by *above*. But idiom will not allow *above* to modify all nouns: **above vehicle* is unidiomatic for *vehicle mentioned above*. Better yet, simply write *the vehicle*, if readers will know from the context which one you're talking about.

A less-than-common and NEEDLESS VARIANT of *above-mentioned* is **before-mentioned*. See **above-mentioned, afore** & **aforesaid**.

B. As an Attributive Noun. This casualism, which has appeared even in Supreme Court opinions, derives from the uses discussed above in (A). E.g.: "Clearly, the *above* is not intended to be an exclusive list of the issues that a Florida attorney may encounter in drafting a trust." Nancy S. Freeman, *Trust Me: Practical Advice for Drafting Florida Trusts*, 83 Fla. B.J. 20, 28 (May 2009).

above-captioned. See **above-mentioned**.

*above-made is an unnecessary compound, and an ugly one—e.g.:

- "Indeed, empirical data tend to support the *above-made* [read *above*] prediction." Jens C. Dammann, *Freedom of Choice in European Corporate Law*, 29 Yale J. Int'l L. 477, 511 (2004).

- "Without a doubt, this is a criticism equally applying to the *above-made* [read *above*] defense proposal." Theresa A. Gabaldon, *Milberg Weiss: Of Studied Indifference and Dying of Shame*, 2 J. Bus. & Tech. L. 207, 241 (2007).

above-mentioned; above-quoted; above-styled; above-captioned. All such compounds should be hyphenated; one sees the tendency nowadays to spell *above-quoted* and *above-mentioned* as single words. Actually, it is best to avoid these compounds altogether by using more specific references; that is, instead of writing the *above-mentioned* court, one should name the court (or, if it has just been named, write *the court, that court*, or some similar identifying phrase). Then again, any of these options may simply be a sign of OVERPARTICULARIZATION, the cure for which would be simply to omit the reference altogether. See **above (A), aforesaid** & **captioned**.

above-referenced. See **reference**, vb.

above-stated. See **above (A)** & **aforesaid**.

above-styled. See **above-mentioned**.

abridgable; abridgeable. *Abridgable* is the preferred spelling in AmE, *abridgeable* in BrE. See MUTE E.

abridge; violate. Constitutional and other rights are often said to be *abridged* or *violated*. But a connotative distinction is possible. *Violate* is the stronger word: when rights are *abridged*, they are merely diminished; when rights are *violated*, they are flouted outright. Following are examples of the milder term:

- "The provision of a new and sanitary building does not [ensure] that it will be operated in a constitutional way . . . and the first amendment can be *abridged* in the cleanest quarters." *Jones v. Diamond*, 636 F.2d 1364, 1375 (5th Cir. 1981).
- "Rather, Coleman asserts, the court first considered the merits of his federal claims and applied the procedural bar only after determining that doing so would not *abridge* one of Coleman's constitutional rights." *Coleman v. Thompson*, 501 U.S. 722, 740–41 (1991) (per O'Connor, J.).
- "Both the trial court and the Court of Appeal held that the potential delay that Jordan's substitution might engender was sufficient to warrant *abridging* Bradley's Sixth Amendment rights." *Bradley v. Henry*, 510 F.3d 1093, 1102 (9th Cir. 2007) (Noonan, J., concurring).

See **adjure** & **violate**.

abridgeable. See **abridgable**.

abridgment; abridgement. Although BrE usually includes the medial *-e-*, AmE omits it. Armed with this knowledge, an American writer should not defend his "misspelling" on grounds of preferring the BrE form. Cf. **acknowledgment** & **judgment**.

abrogate. See **nullify**.

abscond can be both transitive ("to hide away, conceal [something or someone]") and intransitive ("to depart secretly or suddenly; to hide oneself"). The latter is more common today—e.g.: "He sold the cottages, called in the mortgage, and *absconded* with the proceeds." Rupert Cross & J.W. Harris, *Precedent in English Law* 46 (4th ed. 1991).

*__absconder__ (= one who absconds) is illogically formed, and it is rarer than the better-formed *absconder*, the usual agent noun—e.g.:

- "Appellant, age 15, was an *abscondee* [read *absconder*] from a youth development center." *Commonwealth v. Thomas*, 392 A.2d 820, 821 (Pa. Super. Ct. 1978).
- "Evidently, because of loose security safeguards, the *abscondees* [read *absconders*] just walked out of the hotel." *Ledesma-Valdes v. Sava*, 604 F.Supp. 675, 677 (S.D.N.Y. 1985).

See -EE (A). Cf. **escapee.**

abscondence; *abscondment; *abscondsion. The second and third are NEEDLESS VARIANTS rarely found; *abscondence* is the preferred and much more common noun corresponding to the verb *abscond*. E.g.: "Defendant demonstrated a command of the English language not likely to have been acquired during his period of *abscondence*." *People v. Ferrer*, 551 N.Y.S.2d 201, 201–02 (App. Div. 1990). *__Abscondance__* is an infrequent misspelling. See **abscond.**

absconder. See *__abscondee__.

absent (= in the absence of; without) as a preposition typifies LEGALESE. The better choices are *without* and *in the absence of*. E.g.:

- "But virtually no defendants charged with serious crimes will plead guilty *absent* [read *without*] concessions." Nancy Amoury Combs, *Copping a Plea to Genocide*, 151 U. Pa. L. Rev. 1, 22 (2002).
- "The mistrial should be granted without any judicial determination of whether the defendant would be found guilty *absent* [read *in the absence of*] the misconduct." Michael D. Cicchini, *Prosecutorial Misconduct at Trial*, 37 Seton Hall L. Rev. 335, 336 (2007).

For an interesting discussion of how this American LEGALISM has spread into nonlegal contexts, see two pieces by Alan R. Slotkin: *Absent "Without": Adjective, Participle, or Preposition*, 60 Am. Speech 222 (1985); *Prepositional "Absent": An Afterword*, 64 Am. Speech 167 (1989).

absentee, used as an adverb, is a useful linguistic development, especially in the phrase *vote absentee*—e.g.:

- "Our inquiry *as to* [read *into*] why the defendants took . . . Alaniz and her [son and daughter] to vote *absentee* has to begin with whether . . . the request . . . came from Lillian Alaniz herself." *U.S. v. Canales*, 744 F.2d 413, 435 (5th Cir. 1984).
- "Georgia allows any voter to vote *absentee* without having to show identification." Joshua A. Douglas, *Is the Right to Vote Really Fundamental?*, 18 Cornell J.L. & Pub. Pol'y 143, 194 (2008).

It would be cumbersome in that context to have to write, "to vote as an absentee." Although some dictionaries record *absentee* as a noun only, the adverbial usage is increasingly widespread. The word may also function as an adjective <absentee landlord>.

absolute, decree. See **decree absolute.**

absolute, rule. See **decree absolute.**

ABSOLUTE CONSTRUCTIONS. Nominative absolutes, increasingly rare in modern prose, allow writers to vary their syntax while concisely subordinating incidental matter. Such phrases do not bear an ordinary grammatical relation to the rest of the sentence, since the noun or noun phrase does not perform any of the usual functions (subject, object, apposition, etc.) that grammatically attach nouns to other words in the sentence. Yet the whole absolute phrase adverbially modifies some verb. E.g.: "*The court adjourning* [i.e., *When the court adjourned*], we left the courtroom."

This construction often has an antique literary flavor. Few modern writers would use the nominative absolute in the way Herman Melville did: "A drumhead court was summarily convened, *he electing* the individuals composing it." *Billy Budd* 63 (1891). (The pronoun *he* is modified by the participle *electing*; *the individuals composing it* is the object of *electing*. The whole phrase *he electing the individuals composing it* is a nominative absolute, for it has no grammatical function in the statement *A drumhead court was summarily convened.*)

But most modern examples don't strike readers as being so stuffy, as the following examples of the nominative absolute show:

- "It is conceded that the collision was solely the result of Holeman's negligence, *he apparently having been intoxicated* at the time." *Brinkley v. Farmers Elevator Mut. Ins. Co.*, 485 F.2d 1283, 1284 (10th Cir. 1973).
- "*This court having found that* the two types of uses under the trademark maintenance program were not sufficient uses to avoid prima facie proof of abandonment, the district court must specifically address Exxon's intent to resume use of the Humble trademark." *Exxon Corp. v. Humble Exploration Co.*, 695 F.2d 96, 102 (5th Cir. 1982).
- "In *Martin v. Texas, Harlan writing again* for a unanimous Court, the defendant's allegations of discrimination were unsupported by any evidence whatever and were denied." Benno C. Schmidt Jr., *Juries, Jurisdiction, and Race Discrimination*, 61 Tex. L. Rev. 1401, 1471 (1983). (If a pronoun were to be used instead of *Harlan*, the absolute phrase would read "he writing again for the court.")

In the following example, the writer attempted a nominative absolute but incorrectly used the possessive rather than the nominative case: "The trial court concluded [that] Vance was not a good candidate for non-state prison sanction, *his* [read *he*] having 'manipulated the system before.'" *Vance v. State*, 475 So.2d 1362, 1363 (Fla. Dist. Ct. App. 1985).

But blunders with nominative absolutes are nothing new. As commonly printed, the Second Amendment to the United States Constitution contains a mispunctuated absolute construction. The first comma, being quite erroneous, should not appear: "A well-regulated Militia, being necessary to the security of a free state, the right of the people to keep and bear Arms, shall not be infringed." U.S. Const. amend II. If a sentence is to begin that way—*A well-regulated Militia, being necessary to the security of a free state,*—the next word should be *is* or *becomes* or some other verb. The *being*-clause looks to be functioning nonrestrictively in modifying the subject *Militia*, which needs a finite verb in the predicate. Instead, an entirely separate independent clause, with its own subject, appears: *the right of the people to keep and bear Arms shall not be infringed.* So the only way to make sense of the first part of the sentence is as a nominative absolute, the word *being* being a participle that does not relate to the main clause. In short, the Second Amendment ought to have been written in this way: *A well-regulated Militia being necessary to the security of a free state, the right of the people to keep and bear arms shall not be infringed.*

In fact, though, it appears that the constitutional amendment as proposed by Congress in 1789 was correctly punctuated—without a comma after *Militia*—and that later iterations in print, including many in the Supreme Court of the United States, have gotten it wrong. *See* Ross E. Davies, *Which Is the Constitution?*, 11 Green Bag 2d 209 (2008). *See also* William W. Van Alstyne, *A Constitutional Conundrum of Second Amendment Commas*, 10 Green Bag 2d 469 (2007). By any standard, there should be a comma after *State*. A comma after *Arms* is unnecessary and archaic—but passable by 18th-century standards. The comma after *Militia* is incorrect by any standard.

absolute liability. See **strict liability.**

absolve, depending on the context, takes either *of* or *from*. But there is a distinction: one is absolved *of* financial liability, and absolved *from* wrongdoing—assuming that the courts treat one kindly. It's a fine nuance often overlooked. *From* often appears wrongly for *of*—e.g.:

- "If the mother contributed nothing to his support because she was *absolved therefrom* [read, if we must, *absolved thereof*] under that act, no expectation of pecuniary advantage exists." *Gaydos v. Domabyl*, 152 A. 549, 554 (Pa. 1930).
- "In all such cases he would give the court wide discretion as respects costs so that in a proper case an unsuccessful party could be *absolved from* [read *absolved of*] costs or even recover them from the company." William O. Douglas, *Directors Who Do Not Direct*, 47 Harv. L. Rev. 1305, 1326 (1934).

The opposite error (*absolved of* for *absolved from*) sometimes occurs—e.g.:

- "Cnudde . . . considered that Hardgrave's letter completely *absolved her of* [read *absolved her from*] any charges of improper behavior in her teaching methods or in the content of her course." *Kelleher v. Flawn*, 761 F.2d 1079, 1085 (5th Cir. 1985).
- "Instead, they argued, her belief that she was a female classified her as female at the time she signed the license, and

thus *absolved her of* [read *absolved her from*] the charge that she was lying." Robin Conley, *"At the Time She Was a Man,"* 31 Pol. & Legal Anthropology Rev. 28, 32 (2008).

For more senses, see **exculpate** & **release.**

absolvitor. See **assoil.**

abstract, n. American lawyers often use *abstract* as a shortened form of the phrase *abstract of title* (= the history of a particular tract of land, consisting of a written summary of the material parts of every recorded instrument affecting title). An early-20th-century treatise-writer defined the term with florid amplitude:

> An *abstract* may be defined as a condensed history of the title to land, consisting of a synopsis or summary of the material or operative portion of all the various instruments of conveyance which in any manner affect [the] land, or the title thereto, or any estate or interest therein, together with a statement of all liens, charges, or liabilities to which the same may be subject, and of which it is in any way material for purchasers to be apprised. It is usually arranged in chronological order and is intended to show the origin, course, and incidents of the title without the necessity of referring to the original sources of information.
>
> George W. Warvelle, *A Practical Treatise on Abstracts and Examinations of Title to Real Property* § 2, at 2 (3d ed. 1907).

abstract, vb.; **abstractify.** *Abstract* is the CHAMELEON-HUED verb meaning (1) "to separate"; (2) "to summarize" <to abstract a judgment or title>; (3) "to divert"; (4) "to steal"; or (5) "to make (something concrete) abstract."

The *OED* labels sense 4 a EUPHEMISM. In that sense—"to take away secretly, slyly, or dishonestly"—*abstract* is a FORMAL WORD that really beclouds the act it describes. E.g.: "Universal's funds were surreptitiously *abstracted* [read *withdrawn*] and deposited in Richfield's account." *Republic Supply Co. v. Richfield Oil Co.*, 79 F.2d 375, 380 (9th Cir. 1935). A more common word, such as *removed* or *withdrawn*, would undoubtedly be more comprehensible to more readers. The same goes here: "Transfers can range from water right sales, involving the permanent transfer of a water right to temporary water leases where the right to use a certain volume of actual water, or the right to *abstract* [read *remove*] or use water in the future is transferred for a period of time." Oliver M. Brandes & Linda Nowlan, *Wading into Uncertain Waters*, 19 J. Envtl. L. & Prac. 267, 279 (2009).

Abstractify is not listed in the dictionaries, though it has appeared in legal texts. It serves as a pejorative alternative for sense 5 of *abstract*. Perhaps it is a useful invention, for there is no reason for *abstract* to undergo any further degeneration of meaning.

*abstracter. See **abstractor.**

abstractify. See **abstract.**

abstraction means, to nonlawyers, (1) (rarely) "the act of removing"; (2) "an abstract idea";

(3) "abstractedness"; or (4) "a work of abstract art." In law, however, *abstraction* = the act of taking, usu. wrongfully or fraudulently, as in *abstraction of funds.* But in the phrase *abstraction of water* (= the taking of water from a river or other source of supply [*CDL*]), the word connotes no wrongdoing, for in England one may obtain a license. See **abstract,** vb.

ABSTRACTITIS. "How vile a thing . . . is the abstract noun! It wraps a man's thoughts round like cotton wool." Arthur Quiller-Couch, *On the Art of Writing* 109 (1916). *Abstractitis* is Ernest Gowers's term for writing that is so abstract and obtuse (hence abstruse) that the writer does not even know what he or she is trying to say. Far be it from the reader, then, to give such writing a coherent meaning.

One sympathizes with a keen reader like Judge Learned Hand, who wrestled with the Internal Revenue Code: "The words . . . dance before my eyes in a meaningless procession: cross-reference to cross-reference, exception upon exception—couched in abstract terms that offer no handle to seize hold of—leave in my mind only a confused sense of some vitally important, but successfully concealed, purport, which it is my duty to extract, but which is within my power, if at all, only after the most inordinate expenditure of time." Learned Hand, *Thomas Walter Swan*, 57 Yale L.J. 167, 169 (1947).

Perhaps the best antidote to this malady—which in some degree afflicts most sophisticated writers—is an active empathy for one's readers. Rigorous thought about concrete meaning, together with careful revision, can eliminate abstractitis.

Three short examples suffice to illustrate the malady:

- "Win or lose, the County Committee is a focal force of substantiality within the electoral process, whether it be for federal, state or local purposes." *Doherty v. Meisser*, 321 N.Y.S.2d 32, 41 (Sup. Ct. 1971). What is a *focal force of substantiality*?
- "This Note, therefore, structures its analysis around a consideration of definitional methodology and proposes a constitutional definition of religion on the basis of that consideration." Timothy L. Hall, *The Sacred and the Profane*, 61 Tex. L. Rev. 139, 140 (1982). What? The sentence states that the note proposes a definition of religion on the basis of a consideration of methodology, which makes little sense. See OBSCURITY.
- "As used within the context of this book . . . , demonstrative evidence is evidence *which* [read *that*] has, in some form or fashion, been processed." Mark A. Dombroff, *Dombroff on Demonstrative Evidence* 2 (1983). One reads that sentence with mounting expectations of a punch word at the end—yet all we get is the vague word *processed*. What is evidence that has, in some form or fashion, been processed? Been processed by the brain? Unfortunately, even the fuller context of that quotation provides little help.

The first and third examples contain the archetypal abstract words, here termed BURIED VERBS—that is, words ending usually with these suffixes: *-tion, -sion, -ity, -ence, -ance, -ment.* Writers are well advised to take these longish nouns and turn them back into verbs if possible—that is, write *to state*, not *to make a statement*; *to submit*, not *to make a submission*; *to rely on*, not *to evidence a reliance on*; and so on.

The Fowler brothers quote the following sentence—laden with buried verbs—in *The King's English* (1906): "One of the most important reforms mentioned in the rescript is the unification of the organization of judicial institutions and the guarantee for all the tribunals of the independence necessary for securing to all classes of the community equality before the law." Sir Arthur Quiller-Couch's revision eliminates the buried verbs: "One of the most important reforms is that of the courts, which need to be independent within a uniform structure. In this way only can people be assured that all are equal before the law." Arthur Quiller-Couch, *On the Art of Writing* at 109–10.

The late-20th-century vogue in legal theorizing, Critical Legal Studies, was characterized by abstractitis and jargonmongering, the favored words in the field being *purposivist, constitutive, coopting, demobilizing, structuralism, deconstruction, formalism,* and *praxis,* among others. See Louis B. Schwartz, *With Gun and Camera Through Darkest CLS-Land*, 36 Stan. L. Rev. 413, 440 (1984). Some CLS writing reads on this order: "In the reciprocity of roles that are artificial, you think people are more alienated in that bank than I think they are. I think there's more intersubjective zap and unalienated relatedness among tellers." Peter Gabel & Duncan Kennedy, *Roll Over Beethoven*, 36 Stan. L. Rev. 1, 25 (1984). The phrase *intersubjective zap*, by the way, has become a buzz-phrase among CLSers, having now appeared in well over 20 law-review articles. See **Critical Legal Studies.**

By some accounts, abstractitis leads to far worse things. "If concepts are not clear," wrote Confucius, "words do not fit." But he did not stop there: "If words do not fit, the day's work cannot be accomplished, morals and art do not flourish. If morals and art do not flourish, punishments are not just. If punishments are not just, the people do not know where to put hand or foot." Confucius, *Analects* XIII, 3. It is no frivolous assertion to say that, when we descend into abstractitis, more than just our language is afflicted.

Fred Rodell—the Yale law professor, realist, and semanticist who frequently criticized lawyers' language—issued his own inimitable warning about abstractitis: "Dealing in words is a dangerous business, and it cannot be too often stressed that what The Law deals in is words. Dealing in long, vague, fuzzy-meaning words is even more dangerous business, and most of the words The Law deals in are long and vague and fuzzy. Making a habit of applying long, vague, fuzzy, general words to specific things and facts is perhaps the most dangerous of all, and The Law does that, too." Fred Rodell, *Woe Unto You, Lawyers!* 39 (1939).

ABSTRACT NOUNS, PLURALS OF. See PLURALS (B).

abstract of title. See **abstract** & **title.**

abstractor; *abstracter. The *OED* notes that *-or* is "analogically the more regular form"; it is the more usual as well. See -ER (A).

abstruse. See **obtuse.**

abuse, n.; invective; vituperation; obloquy; scurrility; billingsgate; vitriol. All these terms refer to shockingly or inappropriately harsh, coarse language directed at someone. *Abuse*, the broadest, suggests an intemperate person using offensive words <his abuse of his employees was labeled "sailor's talk">—though it can also serve as hyperbole for a reasonable person's moderate displeasure <to me, "litigator" is a term of abuse as compared with "trial lawyer">. *Invective* is highly literate, articulate denunciation that is particularly bitter or intense <"coprophiliac" and "stercoriculous" were put to frequent use in his sesquipedalian invective>. *Vituperation* suggests a verbal onslaught, or a torrent of railing words <he wanted to dissolve the partnership because of what he called his colleague's "penchant for vituperation">. *Obloquy* suggests defamatory language that results in reputational damage <refrain from obloquy, lest you get sued for slander>. *Scurrility* suggests extremely coarse, indecent language <the F-word was a staple of his nonstop scurrility>. *Billingsgate* suggests even more strongly the offensiveness of the language used—although the word is arcane enough to mystify most readers or listeners <he spewed mean, personal billingsgate at the hapless law clerk>. *Vitriol* is scathingly caustic expression; it does not necessarily imply profanity <the debate was filled with vitriol>.

abuse, vb.; misuse; mistreat; ill-treat; maltreat. These verbs share the sense "to deal with in a harmful or wrongful way." *Abuse* is a term of wide application ranging traditionally from the improper use of a device <you're abusing the nib of your pen, and ruining it!> to the seriously wrongful treatment of a person <he physically abused his wife during their short marriage—and she ended up in the emergency room three times>. With *abuse*, the focus is on injurious results. *Misuse*, by contrast, stresses the misapplication of the means, as opposed to the end <they were found to have misused the company car for entirely personal reasons>.

Mistreat, *ill-treat*, and *maltreat* all suggest a moral fault in the agent: deliberateness, wantonness, meanness, or blameworthy ignorance. Most writers on usage have held that there is a distinction between *mistreat* and *maltreat*: "To *mistreat*," write the Evanses, "is to treat badly or wrongly. The word suggests a deviation from some accepted norm of treatment and a deviation always towards the bad. To *maltreat*, to abuse, to handle roughly or cruelly, is to mistreat in a special way. The words are often used interchangeably (Horwill believes that Americans prefer *mistreat* and

English *maltreat*), but *maltreat* is usu. restricted to the rougher forms of mistreating." Bergen Evans & Cornelia Evans, *A Dictionary of Contemporary American Usage* 302 (1957).

abuse of discretion, the phrase denoting a lenient standard of reviewing a lower court's judgment, signifies "no single level of deference or scrutiny." 1 Steven A. Childress & Martha S. Davis, *Standards of Review* § 4.21, at 287 (1986). The "variability [of the phrase] is not hopeless. It just means that generalizations about the standard may not be helpful." *Id.* at 288.

Abuse in this context is not pejorative; the word here is "wholly unrelated to the meaning of the . . . term when used in common parlance." *Beck v. Wings Field, Inc.*, 122 F.2d 114, 116 (3d Cir. 1941). So some writers have proposed substituting *misuse* in place of *abuse. See, e.g., Pearson v. Dennison*, 353 F.2d 24, 28 n.6 (9th Cir. 1965). But the phrase *abuse of discretion* is unlikely to be changed.

abuse of process. See **malicious prosecution.**

abutment; abuttals. An *abutment* is the place at which two or more things touch. *Abuttals*—a term used only in the plural—means "land boundaries." *Abuttals* usually refers to abstract boundaries, and *abutments* usually to physical structures (e.g., the walls of bridges adjoining land). *Abbuttals is a variant spelling to be avoided.

abutter; *abuttor. *Abutter* is the accepted spelling. The word means either (1) "the owner of adjoining land"; or (2) "land that adjoins the land in question." Sense 1 is far more common.

abyss; *abysm. Both nouns signify "a bottomless gulf." *Abyss* is the more current form, and is therefore to be preferred. Though *abysm is obsolescent, the adjective *abysmal* thrives (indeed, in some phrases has become trite) as a figurative term for "immeasurably bad" <abysmal ignorance> <abysmal weather>. *Abyssal* is a technical oceanographic term <the geology of the abyssal deep>.

accede; exceed. *Accede* = (1) "to agree or consent"; (2) "to come into office or a position of stature"; or (3) "to enter a treaty or accord." It is an intransitive verb that takes the preposition *to*. *Exceed*, a transitive verb, means (1) "to surpass"; or (2) "to go beyond the proper limits." The first syllable of *accede* should be pronounced with a short *-a-*, so as to differentiate its sound from *exceed*. For verbs similar in meaning to *accede*, see **assent,** vb.

accent, vb.; accentuate. These synonyms have a latent distinction that might usefully be observed. H.W. Fowler notes that *accent* is more common in literal, and *accentuate* in figurative, senses. Hence one properly *accents* the third syllable of *appellee*, and *accentuates* the weaknesses in an opponent's legal arguments. E.g.:

- "Cyberspace *accentuates* some weaknesses that exist in the shadow of the neoinstitutional endeavor with regard to the nonvirtual world and are brought to light in the virtual world." Niva Elkin-Koren & Eli M. Salzberger, *Law and Economics in Cyberspace*, 19 Int'l Rev. L. & Econ. 553, 579 (1999).

- "People *accentuate* [read *accent*] words and syllables to express shades of emotion and intention." John W. Cooley, *Music, Mediation, and Superstrings*, 2005 J. Disp. Resol. 227, 281.

acceptance; *acceptancy; acceptation; *acception. *Acceptance* corresponds to the active sense of the verb (to accept); *acceptation* corresponds to the passive sense (to be accepted). *Acceptance* = the act of accepting; specif., the final and unqualified expression of assent to the terms of a contractual offer. *Acceptation* = the state of being accepted <widespread acceptation of the doctrine of strict liability in tort was long in coming>. *Acceptancy* is a NEEDLESS VARIANT of *acceptance*, just as *acception* is for *acceptation*.

Following are examples of *acceptation*—the less common word—used correctly:

- "According to the common *acceptation* of the words, ex post facto laws and retrospective laws are synonymous terms." Laura Ricciardi & Michael B.W. Sinclair, *Retroactive Civil Legislation*, 27 U. Toledo L. Rev. 301, 311 (1996).
- "This was truly an undisclosed 'internal sentiment,' so he was held to use the words according to their common *acceptation*." Raoul Berger, *Jack Rakove's Rendition of Original Meaning*, 72 Ind. L.J. 619, 626 (1997).
- "Each land-owner has the entire and unqualified ownership of all water found in his soil, not gathered into natural watercourses, in the common *acceptation* of that term." J. David Aiken, *The Western Common Law of Tributary Groundwater*, 83 Neb. L. Rev. 541, 559 (2004).

acceptance for honor; acceptance supra protest. Both terms mean "a form of acceptance of a bill of exchange to save the good name of the drawer or an endorser" (*CDL*). Both are TERMS OF ART, *acceptance for honor* perhaps being the more generally comprehensible of the two. *Acceptance supra protest* ought to be avoided.

***acceptancy; acceptation.** See **acceptance**.

accepter; acceptor. "The first form is now generally used for one who accepts. The second (earlier) form is the legal term, one who accepts, or undertakes the payment of, a bill of exchange." Margaret Nicholson, *A Dictionary of American-English Usage* 6 (1957). *Acceptor* is also regularly used in law, however, of one who accepts an offer to enter into a contract—e.g.: "From the point of view of the offeror it seems immaterial whether the *acceptor* knew of the offer or not." P.S. Atiyah, *An Introduction to the Law of Contract* 52 (3d ed. 1981).

***acception.** See **acceptance**.

access. A. Generally. As a verb, *access* has its origins in computerese. Like a number of nouns turned into verbs (e.g., *contact*), it now seems increasingly well ensconced in the language. As Ernest Gowers said about *contact*, it is an ancient and valuable right for English-speaking peoples to turn their nouns into verbs when they are so minded. *Gain access to* or some other such equivalent is admittedly ungainly alongside *access*, though the latter still jars sensitive ears—e.g.: "Other electrical units do not *access* the electric energy source through the plug."

B. For *assess*. Sometimes *access* is misused for *assess* (= to evaluate)—e.g.:

- "It still comes down to *accessing* [read *assessing*] the risks against the gains." David Anderson, *On Safari* 16 (2005).
- "Jerome counters the criminalization process by *accessing* [read *assessing*] the situation within the context of his experience [in] law enforcement." Karen S. Glover, *Racial Profiling: Research, Racism, and Resistance* 108 (2009).

***accessary.** See **accessory** (A).

accessible /ak-**ses**-i-bəl/ is sometimes mispronounced as if it were a homophone of *assessable* (= capable of being assessed or evaluated). Worse yet, in a MALAPROPISM, it is sometimes actually confused with *assessable*—e.g.: "This lacuna [i.e., the lack of a study on capital-adequacy rules] may be partly justified by the dearth of an easily *assessable* [read *accessible*] or centralized source for capital-adequacy regulatory data." Bryce Quillin, *International Financial Cooperation* 50 (2008).

accession /ak-**sesh**-ən/ literally means "something added." But it bears several more specific senses in legal contexts: (1) a coming into possession (of an office or right); (2) acquisition of (something connected to one's property) by growth, labor, or the like; and (3) a secondary or subordinate thing that is connected with another thing. Sense 1 is the most common in legal and nonlegal contexts alike <John Roberts's accession to the Chiefship>; senses 2 and 3 are largely peculiar to legal contexts. E.g.:

- (Sense 1) "'*Accession*' [occurs] when the owner of the principal object becomes also owner of its accessory." Thomas E. Holland, *The Elements of Jurisprudence* 218 (13th ed. 1924).
- (Sense 2) "We held that tires and tubes added to a car did not become a part of it by *accession*." *Bank of America v. J. & S. Auto Repairs*, 694 P.2d 246, 251 (Ariz. 1985) (en banc).
- (Sense 3) "It often happened, however, that of the two things united, one was a mere *accession* to the other, a mere secondary or subordinate part." James Hadley, *Introduction to Roman Law* 170 (1881).

accessorial (= [1] of or relating to an accessory; or [2] collateral) appears most commonly in sense 1—e.g.: "We now come to another set of cases in which the English courts have departed from, or at least modified, the derivative theory of *accessorial* liability." Andrew Ashworth, *Principles of Criminal Law* 386 (1991).

Sense 2 has been largely superseded by either *accessory* <accessory promise> or *collateral* <collateral obligation>. See **collateral obligation**.

accessorial obligation. See **collateral obligation.**

accessory, n. **A. And** ***accessary,** n. *Accessory* now predominates in AmE and BrE in meaning both "abettor" and "a thing of lesser importance." Though H.W. Fowler believed a distinction existed between *accessory* and *accessary (the first applying primarily to things, the second to persons), *accessary is now merely a NEEDLESS VARIANT and should be avoided.

B. Pronunciation. Both words discussed in (A) should be pronounced with the first -*c*- as a hard -*k*-sound—hence /ak-**ses**-ə-ree/. A common mispronunciation is /ə-**ses**-ə-ree/.

C. Variable Uses of *accessory* **and** *accomplice.* American writers tend to use *accomplice* to include all principals and accessories before the fact, but to exclude accessories after the fact. Hence the word embraces all perpetrators, abettors, and inciters. *See* Rollin M. Perkins & Ronald N. Boyce, *Criminal Law* 727 (3d ed. 1982).

Other writers use *accomplice* to include all principals and *accessories. Black's,* for example, defines *accomplice* as "a person who is in any way involved with another in the commission of a crime, whether as a principal in the first or second degree or as an *accessory." Black's Law Dictionary* 18 (9th ed. 2009). The *ODL* defines the term as "one who is a party to a crime, either as a principal or as an accessory," and it defines *accessory* as "one who participates in [a crime] but does not bring about the *actus reus* directly." This usage appears to be primarily BrE—e.g.: "We are concerned with the first topic—the parties in different degrees of complicity to a crime, who are termed '*accomplices*.' Accomplices consist of the perpetrator and the accessories." Glanville Williams, *Textbook of Criminal Law* 285 (1978).

Still other writers, however, use *accomplice* and *accessory* as synonyms—e.g.: "A *principal* is a person whose acts fall within the legal definition of the crime, whereas an *accomplice* (sometimes called an '*accessory*' or '*secondary party*') is anyone who aids, abets, counsels, or procures a principal." Andrew Ashworth, *Principles of Criminal Law* 363–64 (1991). See **principal (B)** & *socius criminis.* Cf. *particeps criminis.*

D. And Its Near-Synonyms: *confederate; conspirator; accomplice; abettor.* See **confederate (A).**

accident. A. And *mishap; casualty; incident.* The first three, and sometimes the fourth, denote a chance event that brings injury or loss. *Accident,* the broadest term, refers to an unforeseen event involving an injury or loss that ranges from slight (e.g., spilling a drop from a tepid cup of water) to grave (e.g., running a cruise ship into an iceberg). *Mishap* typically applies to a slight accident, especially one that causes mild annoyance or disappointment. *Casualty* usually implies destruction, especially a serious wounding or loss of life in the military <the troop suffered heavy casualties>. In the context of insurance, *accident* and *casualty* are traditionally distinguished in this way: *accident insurance* covers injuries to oneself by some

lack of care or inattention, or perhaps by some occurrence wholly outside one's control; *casualty insurance* indemnifies the insured for damages resulting from one's liability to someone else for some other injury or loss.

Incident, as it relates to the other three words, is often a EUPHEMISM for *accident* or *near-accident.* But it can refer to something that precipitates a major crisis <caused an international incident>. E.g.: "Available statistics establish that flight engineers have rarely been a contributing cause or factor in commercial aircraft *accidents* or *incidents." Western Air Lines, Inc. v. Criswell,* 472 U.S. 400, 404 (1985) (per Stevens, J.). That use may have been justified for the purposes of one-time DIFFERENTIATION. But literally, the term is simply an abstract word meaning "a discrete occurrence of some importance; a consequential happening." Avoid *incident* in its euphemistic senses, unless you're speaking on behalf of a bureaucracy that has messed up something.

B. And *mistake.* In law, the usual distinction is that an *accident* occurs without the willful purpose of the person who causes it. A *mistake,* by contrast, presupposes the operation of a person's will in producing the event, even though the person has been misled by erroneous impressions.

accidentally. So spelled; *accidently is a solecism. The confusion arises partly from the popular pronunciation and partly from seemingly analogous terms such as *evidently* and *patently.* Cf. **incidentally.**

accident insurance. See **accident (A).**

acclimate; ***acclimatize; acclimation;** ***acclimatization.** *Acclimate* and *acclimation* are the standard terms. *Acclimatize and *acclimatization are NEEDLESS VARIANTS.

accommodable /ə-**kom**-ə-də-bəl/ is so formed—not **accommodatable,* as it is sometimes erroneously written. E.g.: "Equal treatment of inmates is not a legitimate interest when it is accomplished at the expense of denying the exercise of an otherwise *accommodatable* [read *accommodable*] constitutional right." *Goodwin v. Turner,* 908 F.2d 1395, 1405 (8th Cir. 1990) (en banc).

accommodation. So spelled. The word is commonly misspelled with one -*m*-.

accommodatum. See **commodatum.**

accomplice. See **confederate (A).**

***accomptant general.** See **accountant general.**

accord, n. **A. And** *accordance.* To be *in accord* is to be in agreement. E.g.: "This holding was in *accord* with the overwhelming weight of authority in the state courts as reflected in Wigmore's classic treatise on the law of evidence." *U.S. v. Abel,* 469 U.S. 45, 50 (1984) (per Rehnquist, J.).

This phrasing should not be used in place of a more direct statement—e.g.:

- "*We are not in accord with* [read *We reject*] appellant's contention that neither Frank H. McKeyes nor his private bank are in any way bound by the terms of the depositors' five year agreement, which for convenience we refer to as a moratorium." *In re McKeyes's Estate*, 24 N.W.2d 155, 158 (Mich. 1946).
- "Fundamentally, it seems as if *we are not in accord* [read *we disagree*] on the proper application of *Daubert*." Thomas Dillickrath, *A Response to Professor Graham*, 55 U. Miami L. Rev. 1125, 1125 (2001).

To be *in accordance* is to be in conformity or compliance. *In accordance* is sometimes cumbersome, but often useful. E.g.: "Any state-imposed regulations promulgated *in accordance* with this right cannot conflict with the commerce power of the federal government." Andy Taylor, Comment, *Drunk with Power: Does the TABC Know Which Lines to Stay Between?*, 9 Tex. Tech Admin. L.J. 287, 295 (2008). *Out of accordance* = not in conformity.

Accord is misused for *accordance* in the following sentences:

- "Even Justice Scalia is unwilling to say squarely that life sentences for petty offenses are in *accord* [read *accordance*] with the original meaning of the Eighth Amendment." Note, *The Eighth Amendment, Proportionality, and the Changing Meaning of "Punishments*," 122 Harv. L. Rev. 960, 977 (2009).
- "Additionally, this method is in *accord* [read *accordance*] with modern business practices and with sound economic and financial principles." Thierry J. Sénéchal & John Y. Gotanda, *Interest as Damages*, 47 Colum. J. Transnat'l L. 491, 535–36 (2009).

B. And *concord,* n. Both mean "an amicable arrangement between parties, esp. between peoples or nations; compact; treaty." *Accord* is perhaps the less formal word, and the more frequently used today. See **concord (A)** & **treaty.**

accord, vb. **A. And** *afford,* vb. These CHAMELEON-HUED WORDS share the meaning "to furnish or grant," as commonly used in legal texts <accorded (or afforded) all the rights due him under due process>. Yet some DIFFERENTIATION is possible: *accord* has the nuance of granting something because it is suitable or proper <accord litigants a stay of costs pending appeal>. E.g.: "The Court also remarked that unborn children were not *accorded* legal rights in other areas of the law, except upon live birth." Amy Lotierzo, *The Unborn Child, A Forgotten Interest*, 79 Temp. L. Rev. 279, 300 (2006). *Accord* in this sense should usually take a personal object, not an inanimate one; this error most commonly occurs when *accord* is used as a high-sounding substitute for *give*:

- "I cannot subscribe to the Court's sweeping refusal to *accord* [read *give*] the Equal Protection Clause any role in this entire area of the law, and I therefore dissent from both parts of the Court's decision." *Dandridge v. Williams*, 397 U.S. 471, 509 (1970) (Marshall, J., dissenting).
- "We *accord* [read *give*] statutory language its plain, ordinary, and popularly understood meaning, and we *afford*

the language the fullest, rather than narrowest, possible meaning to which it is susceptible." *People v. Kastman*, 779 N.E.2d 333, 339 (Ill. App. Ct. 2002).

The origin of the correct use of *accord* lies in the historical (and still current) sense "to grant (a thing asked) *to* (a person), to give with full consent, to award" (*OED*).

Afford is the more general term, meaning "to furnish (something) as an essential concomitant" <afford to the indigent defendant legal representation>. E.g.:

- "The Sixth Amendment guarantees that a person brought to trial in any federal court must be *afforded* the right to the assistance of counsel before he can be validly convicted." *U.S. v. Burton*, 584 F.2d 485, 488 (D.C. Cir. 1978).
- "If we *afford* relief *to* [this town], will we have to do likewise as each unincorporated village [decides] to incorporate?" *Town of Ball v. Rapides Parish Police Jury*, 746 F.2d 1049, 1062 (5th Cir. 1984).

B. Construing with Prepositions. Intransitively, *accord* takes the preposition *in, to,* or *with,* depending on the context <we accord in our opinions> <we accord to plaintiff his due> <this accords with the prevailing view>.

C. As a Citation Signal. When used as a signal in citations, *accord* ordinarily indicates that the authority cited directly supports the proposition, but in a way slightly different from previously cited authorities. One should include a parenthetical explanation of what that difference is, rather than leaving the reader to search for it. Sometimes it introduces like cases from other jurisdictions. See CITATION OF CASES.

accordance. See **accord (A).**

accord and satisfaction; compromise and settlement. The former appears usually in contractual contexts. Though the two phrases may overlap to some extent, *compromise and settlement* is used in the context of a dispute more probably giving rise to litigation. It applies to all disputes, not just to those arising from contracts. The two substantive words in *compromise and settlement* are broader than those in *accord and satisfaction,* but *compromise* is roughly analogous to *accord,* and *settlement* to *satisfaction.*

An *accord* is an agreement to substitute for an existing debt or obligation some alternative form of discharging that debt; a *satisfaction* is the actual discharge of the debt by the substituted means. Stated otherwise, an *accord* is the agreement to perform (in an alternative way), and the *satisfaction* is the actual performance. Any claim (if disputed, unliquidated, or undisputed and liquidated) may be discharged by an *accord and satisfaction.*

But only a disputed or unliquidated claim may be the basis for a *compromise and settlement.* Though the two words in this phrase have been used with a variety of meanings and even synonymously, at base *compromise* means "an agreement between two or more persons to settle matters in dispute between them";

settlement means "the performance of promises made in a compromise agreement."

according. A. *According to. According to* = (1) depending on; (2) as explained or reported by (a person); or (3) in accordance with. Sense 1: "The Courts exercise what, *according to* our prepossessions, we call a moderating or an obstructive influence." W.W. Buckland, *Some Reflections on Jurisprudence* 43 (1945).

As a form of attribution <according to Corbin, . . .>, *according to* often signals weak writing. A text sprinkled with *according to*'s gives the appearance of having little originality. Avoid the phrase when attributing an idea.

B. *According as.* This phrase means "in a manner corresponding to the way in which; just as." E.g.: "The special law is either favorable or unfavorable *according as* it enlarges or restricts, in opposition to the common rule, the rights of those for whom it is established." Ferdinand Mackeldey, *Roman Law* 164 (1883). (See the quotation from Blackstone under **misdemeanor.**)

C. As a Dangler. For *according* as an acceptable dangling modifier, see DANGLERS (D).

accordingly is a somewhat hifalutin equivalent of *therefore* or *so*, used in stating a conclusion or decision—e.g.:

- "Mother appeals from that juvenile court judgment and argues that the state has not established a 'reasonable likelihood of harm' to the children by a preponderance of the evidence. We agree and, *accordingly*, reverse the judgment finding jurisdiction over the children." *Dep't of Human Servs. v. C.Z.*, 236 P.3d 791, 792 (Or. Ct. App. 2010). (A suggested revision: *We agree and therefore reverse . . . .*)
- "Any argument that rural or wildland character is preserved by the Ordinance is disingenuous because the Ordinance, as indicated by its statement of purpose, is solely focused on the City's community core district—a district that constitutes the urban center of the City. *Accordingly*, we find that the Ordinance was not validly enacted under Idaho Code section 67-6515A." *KGF Dev., LLC v. City of Ketchum*, 236 P.3d 1284, 1289 (Idaho 2010). (A suggested revision: *So we find . . . .*)
- "The Legislature, cross-complainants note, has not expressly declared that 'res judicata or collateral estoppel limits the trial court's power to order relief pursuant to § 17203.' *Accordingly*, they say, no such limitation can be imposed." *In re Fireside Bank Cases*, 115 Cal. Rptr. 3d 80, 86 (Ct. App. 2010). (A suggested revision: *They therefore say that no such . . . .*) On the use of **pursuant to* in the original sentence, see ***pursuant to.

See **according (B).**

according to. See **according (A).**

accost (= to approach and usu. to speak to in an abrupt or challenging manner) has historically had no connotations of physical contact. Hence it would traditionally be considered inappropriate here: "One lady leaving the shop was grabbed by the arm and in a threatening manner told that she had better not go in the place again because it was a 'scab' shop; another lady . . . was likewise *accosted* and told that she ought to be shot for going into that 'scab' shop." *Swing v. American Fed'n*

of Labor, 22 N.E.2d 857, 858 (Ill. 1939). *Accost* is not a strong enough word for that context; *assault* (in the nonlawyer's sense) might have served better.

In the following sentence, the author might not have contemplated physical contact as part of the "initial contact," so the meaning is unclear: "Where the two were strangers and the circumstances of the initial contact were *involuntary—accosted* in parking lots, house break-ins—nearly everyone was certain that a rape had occurred." Susan Estrich, *Real Rape* 13 (1987). Cf. **altercation** & **assault.**

account, n. = (1) a detailed statement of the debits and credits between parties to a contract or to a fiduciary relationship; (2) a statement of monetary transactions; (3) at common law, a legal action used by a lord of a manor to order his bailiff to account for the profits of the manor; or (4) more modernly, a legal action commenced by one who has given another person money to be applied in a particular way, the action being designed to compel the receiver of the money to provide details of the debts owed to the plaintiff. For one variety of sense 4, see **account stated** & **stated.**

accountable takes *for* or *to*, not *from*. E.g.: "Do such rules merely insulate judges from the inconvenience of being held *accountable from* [read *accountable for*] their public actions?" *Grievance Adm'r v. Fieger*, 719 N.W.2d 123, 132 (Mich. 2006). For more on this word and its near-synonyms, see **responsible.**

accountancy. See **generally accepted accounting principles.**

accountant. See **bookkeeper.**

accountant general; *****accomptant general.** The latter spelling—originating in the Renaissance habit of respelling French loanwords on the Latin model—is archaic. Cf. **comptroller.**

accounting. See **generally accepted accounting principles.**

account stated. This phrase bears two distinct meanings: (1) an agreed balance between parties settling an action for debt; (2) a defendant's plea, in response to a bill for an accounting, in which the defendant states that the balance found due on the statement of the account has been discharged and that the defendant holds the plaintiff's release. See **account** & **stated.**

accouter; accouterments; accoutre; accoutrements. As with many other words having this suffix, the *-er* form is AmE, the *-re* BrE.

*****accreditate,** a BACK-FORMATION from *accreditation*, is a NEEDLESS VARIANT of *accredit.*

accrual; *****accruer.** **Accruer*, like **accruement*, is an obsolete form of *accrual*, the general noun corresponding to the verb *accrue*. **Accruer* survives only in the phrase **clause of accruer*. Yet *accrual* has made substantial inroads even into this phrase, so that *accrual* and **accruer* now coexist needlessly. It is time to reject the archaic, and to establish firmly the modern form. Hence we should write *clause of accrual.*

accrue. A. Restriction to Financial Context. At least two critics have recommended that this word be restricted to monetary contexts, quite unaware of its most common meaning in legal contexts. Interest *accrues,* we may be certain, but so do causes of action—at least in jurisdictions in which they do not *arise.* E.g.: "A cause of action *accrues* when the right to sue arises." *Spencer v. Estate of Spencer,* 759 N.W.2d 539, 544 (S.D. 2008). See (B).

But this use should not be extended further to mean "to inure to the benefit of," as here: "The appellate issue turns on whether the tax attributes associated with operations of certain commercial real estate properly *accrued to* [read *inured to the benefit of*] the corporation that held legal title." *Moncrief v. U.S.,* 730 F.2d 276, 277 (5th Cir. 1984).

B. *Accrue* and *arise.* In reference to causes of action, some courts have held that *accrue* and *arise* are synonymous, others that they can be distinguished. *Arise* may refer to the onset of the underlying wrong (e.g., exposure to asbestos), whereas *accrue* may refer to the ripeness of the claim (e.g., contraction of asbestosis or discovery of the disease). We need not set down a rule of usage so much as beware of the ambiguities of these terms in this particular context.

*****accruement.** See **accrual.**

*****accruer.** See **accrual.**

accumulate, accumulative; *cumulate, cumulative.* *Accumulate* is far more common as the verb; **cumulate* is current only in the adjective it yields (*cumulative*). *Accumulate* and **cumulate* both mean "to pile up; collect." **Cumulate,* however, should generally be avoided as a NEEDLESS VARIANT. *Accumulate* has the additional intransitive sense "to increase."

The adjectives demonstrate more palpable DIF-FERENTIATION. In one sense they are synonymous: "increasing by successive addition," in which meaning *cumulative* is the usual and therefore the preferred term. *Cumulative* also means: (1) "relating to interest or a dividend paid to the corpus if not disbursed when due"; or (2) in law, "increasing in force as a result of additional or supporting evidence." In Scots law, *cumulative* is used also to mean "concurrent" <to serve cumulative sentences>.

Accumulative = acquisitive; inclined to amass. It would be salutary to strengthen the distinction and restrict *accumulative* to the sense "acquisitive."

accusation; *accusal.* The first, of course, is current; the second is an obsolete word now classifiable as a NEEDLESS VARIANT. E.g.: "Even families who limit themselves to superficial conversations . . . will recognize the dynamics at work here—the mother-son thing, the mother-daughter thing, the sister-brother thing, the brother-brother thing, the whole stew of tensions and attractions, *accusals* [read *accusations*] and denials." Dan Sullivan, *Total Blame,* L.A. Times, 2 Dec. 1989, at F9. See **charge** (A). Cf. **recusal.**

accusative. See **accusatorial** (B).

accusatorial. A. And *inquisitorial.* *Accusatorial* = (1) of or pertaining to an accuser; or (2) indicating the form of criminal prosecution in which the alleged criminal is publicly accused of the crime and is tried in public by a judge who does not act as the prosecutor <accusatorial procedure>. Sense 2 grew directly out of sense 1, for, in the accusatorial system of criminal trial, the victim (i.e., accuser) made complaint against the offender.

Today, of course, *accusatorial* denotes the common-law system of criminal procedure. It is commonly contrasted with the civil-law term *inquisitorial,* which describes "a system of criminal justice . . . in which the truth is revealed by an inquiry into the facts conducted by the judge" (*CDL*).

Despite its neutral sense in civil law, *inquisitorial* often appears in common-law contexts as a pejorative word—e.g.: "The interrogation described in *Miranda* illustrated the extreme importance that American society placed on criminal prosecution, allowing tricks, cajolery, and even coercion to secure evidence from the suspect[; the] distinction between the *inquisitorial* and the *accusatorial* systems had become blurred." Martin H. Belsky, *Whither Miranda?,* 62 Tex. L. Rev. 1341, 1341 (1984) (book review).

A variant term for *accusatorial procedure* is *adversary procedure,* although the latter term may suggest civil as well as criminal proceedings.

B. And *accusatory; accusative.* *Accusatory* (= accusing; of the nature of an accusation) should not be confused with *accusatorial.* We speak of *accusatory* remarks but *accusatorial* legal systems.

Accusative should be restricted to its grammatical sense relating to the objective case of nouns <him is the accusative case of the third-person masculine singular pronoun>. Yet legal writers often misuse *accusative* for *accusatorial*—e.g.:

- "The feelings, attitudes and relations of the parents of the five-year-old child are strained, *accusative* [read *accusatory*] and acrimonious." *Rodgers v. Hill,* 453 So.2d 1057, 1058 (Ala. Civ. App. 1984).
- "There is no contention herein that the witness was emotional, condemnatory, *accusative* [read *accusatory*] or demanding vindication." *McQueen v. Commonwealth,* 669 S.W.2d 519, 523 (Ky. 1984).

accuse. A. Generally. *Accuse* may be used transitively or, less commonly, intransitively. Here it is intransitive: "It is conceivable that the Court has overstepped its boundaries as the dissenting Justices *accuse.*"

Usually a word for criminal-law contexts, *accuse* has also been used to introduce allegations of noncriminal

---

conduct (as in the preceding quotation). E.g.: "The teams stand *accused*, essentially, of refusing to grant plaintiffs cablecast rights in furtherance of a conspiracy with Cablevision to monopolize cable television trade in Huntington." *Nishimura v. Dolan*, 599 F.Supp. 484, 498 (E.D.N.Y. 1984).

B. And *charge*. See **charge**, vb. (**A**).

accused, n., (= the defendant in a criminal case) was once said to be "more appropriate than either *prisoner* or *defendant*." Archibald Brown, *A New Law Dictionary* 10 (1874). Its superiority to *prisoner*—a word that can prejudice juries (and perhaps even judges)—is unquestionable. But why it should have been considered "more appropriate" than *defendant* is a mystery. Today it is certainly less common in American and British courts than *defendant*, a colorless term: "If you were on trial for a crime, would you rather be called 'the *accused*' or 'the *defendant*'? It seems to me that the latter expression is preferable, as the more neutral." Glanville Williams, *Textbook of Criminal Law* 93 n.3 (1978).

Yet a distinguished criminal-defense lawyer, Bill Wilson of Little Rock, made it a habit in practice (before becoming a federal judge) to use the term *accused*—as if to highlight that the idea that the charges are just "accusations" and to make the government sound more like aggressors. In this view, the term *accuse* has a negative cast to it that reflects worse on the accuser than on the accused.

From a stylistic point of view, *accused* becomes awkward in the possessive case or as a plural: "To determine whether the reference to *the accused's silence* may be cured by an instruction, we consider four factors: (1) the nature of the reference to the *accused's* silence; (2) how it was elicited; (3) whether the district attorney exploited it; and (4) the promptness and adequacy of the cautionary instruction." *Commonwealth v. Robinson*, 550 A.2d 800, 804 (Pa. Super. Ct. 1988). Usually this awkwardness can be remedied by use of the genitive: "the *silence* (or *statement*) of the accused . . ."; or "the *accused person's* silence (or *statement*) . . . ." See POSSESSIVES (F) & PLURALS (D). Cf. **deceased**.

*****accusee** is a NEEDLESS VARIANT of *accused*. E.g.:

- "Later, [Judge Oren R. Lewis] turned to James S. Augus, the senior Justice Department trial lawyer, and accused him of 'shifting the burden of proof from the accuser [the Justice Department] to the *accusee* [read *accused*] . . .'" Robert Meyers, *Courtroom Becomes Classroom*, Wash. Post, 17 March 1979, at C3.
- "This would, of course, suggest Nicholas Daniloff, U.S. News' Moscow correspondent, as the actual *accusee* [read *accused*]." Rance Crain, *Spying Inside the Inside Story*, Advertising Age, 29 Sept. 1986, at 46.

See **accused** & -EE.

accuser; *****accusor.** The *-er* form is standard. See -ER (**A**).

accusing jury. See **grand jury** (**A**).

*****accusor.** See **accuser.**

accustomed. Formerly, the idiom was *accustomed to do*—e.g.: "From the beginning of our legal studies we are *accustomed to think* of law and equity as sharply divided." Carleton K. Allen, *Law in the Making* 413 (7th ed. 1964). But in the mid-20th century, the idiom shifted to *accustomed to doing, accustomed to thinking*, etc. Today the older usage sounds strange to many ears, but some traditionalists stick to it, especially in BrE.

ack-ack. See LAWYERS, DEROGATORY NAMES FOR (**A**).

acknowledge. See **admit** (**A**).

acknowledgment. A. And *acknowledgement*. As with *judgment* and *abridgment*, the spelling without the medial *-e-* is preferable in AmE (but not in BrE).

B. And *verification*. An *acknowledgment* is a formal declaration made in the presence of an authorized officer, such as a notary public, by someone who signs a document and swears to the authenticity of the signature. E.g.: "It is sufficient if the testator states to the witnesses that the signature is his signature. This is known as *acknowledgment* of the signature." Robert Kratovil, *Real Estate Law* 245 (1946).

A *verification*, by contrast, is a formal declaration by which one swears to the truth of the statements in the document. E.g.: "After making demand for judgment for $955, defendants appended a *verification*, notarized and sealed, in which they swore that the facts stated in the [answer were] . . . 'true and correct.'" *Miller v. Master Home Builders, Inc.*, 239 A.2d 696, 697 (Del. Super. Ct. 1968).

a consiliis. See **of counsel.**

*****acquaintanceship** is a NEEDLESS VARIANT of *acquaintance*; it adds nothing to the language except another syllable, which we scarcely need—e.g.:

- "If . . . they do not argue for a startling new interpretation, they may be accused of venturing into an alien field without adequate *acquaintanceship* [read *acquaintance*] with the literature, producing muddled work that merely repeats insights known to every professional." Garrett Epps, *Interpreting the Fourteenth Amendment*, 16 Wm. & Mary Bill Rts. J. 433, 437 (2007).
- "Those doubts arose out of the juror's ongoing *acquaintanceship* [read *acquaintance*] with Mercado, a relationship that the juror failed to disclose until after he had observed Mercado on the witness stand." *State v. Jurado*, 952 A.2d 812, 813 (Conn. App. Ct. 2008).

acquiesce takes *in* or *to*. Some authorities have suggested that *in* is the only proper preposition. Yet the *OED* shows age-old examples with the construction *acquiesce to*, and its labeling that construction obsolete must be deemed a premature judgment, for it is fairly common in legal texts. E.g.: "The defense requested, or at least *acquiesced to*, the inclusion of a voluntary manslaughter instruction in the jury charge." Clara Tuma, *Appeal of Self-Made Error Denied*, Tex. Law., 7 Oct. 1991, at 9. But *acquiesce with* is not in good use. The verb has three distinct syllables: /ak-wee-**es**/. See **assent**, vb.

acquiescence. See **permission.**

acquirer. So spelled—not **acquiror*, as it is sometimes misspelled. E.g.: "The *acquiror* [read *acquirer*] gained a substantial position in the target company's stock." *Gearhart Indus., Inc. v. Smith Int'l, Inc.*, 592 F.Supp. 203, 218 (N.D. Tex. 1984).

acquit. A. Civil and Criminal Contexts. Leff aptly wrote: "One might loosely refer to a party '*acquitted*' in a civil action, though one would ordinarily be tempted to use the terminology only if the cause were quasi-criminal, e.g., an action charging actual fraud, or an intentional physical tort like battery." Arthur A. Leff, *The Leff Dictionary of Law*, 94 Yale L.J. 1855, 1905 (1985). See **exculpate.**
   B. Preposition with. The verb *acquit* takes *of*, not *from*—e.g.: "In the end James was induced to withdraw a letter resigning from the Society, after the Council had passed a resolution *acquitting* him *from* [read *of*] any unfairness." K.M. Elisabeth Murray, *Caught in the Web of Words* 286 (1977).
   C. Past Tense. As a past-tense verb or a past-participial adjective, the form *acquit* is obsolete. It lives only in the LAW FRENCH phrase *autrefois acquit* (= heretofore acquitted). The accepted form today is *acquitted.*

acquittal; acquittance; *acquitment. *Acquittal* is the usual term, meaning both (1) "a release or discharge from debt or other liability"; and (2) "a setting free or deliverance from the charge of an offense by verdict of a jury, sentence of a court, or other legal process" (*W3*). **Acquitment*, a NEEDLESS VARIANT, is obsolete.
   Acquittance is obsolete in all senses except "a written release showing that a debtor has been discharged of an obligation." Perhaps it would be advantageous to allow *acquittance* this commercial meaning, and to leave *acquittal* to the criminal law. E.g.: "There are suggestions in the case that if Mrs. Beer on receipt of the last installment had given Dr. Foakes an '*acquittance*'—that is, an acknowledgment of payment in full—that would have been binding on her." Grant Gilmore, *The Death of Contract* 31 (1974).

acquittal-prone. See **guilt-prone.**

acquittance. See **acquittal.**

*acquittee (= one acquitted of a crime) is an ugly NEOLOGISM; the phrase *acquitted defendant* is ordinarily the better choice. E.g.:

- "The Code also provides that the *acquittee* [read *acquitted defendant*] is entitled to a judicial hearing every six months." *Jones v. U.S.*, 463 U.S. 354, 358 (1983) (per Powell, J.).
- "He is, therefore, not an 'insanity *acquittee*' but a 'criminally insane committee.'" *Glatz v. Kort*, 650 F.Supp. 191, 195 (D. Colo. 1984). [Read *He is therefore not a defendant acquitted by reason of insanity, but one committed to a guardian as criminally insane.*]

See **committee** & -EE. Cf. **convictee.*

ACRONYMS AND INITIALISMS. Seven points merit attention here. First, be aware of the traditional distinction between the two types of abbreviated names. An *acronym* is made from the initial letters or parts of a phrase or compound term. One ordinarily reads or speaks it as a single word, not letter by letter (e.g., *radar* = radio detection and ranging). An *initialism*, by contrast, is made from the initial letters or parts of a phrase or compound term, but is usually pronounced letter by letter, not as a single word (e.g., *r.p.m.* = revolutions per minute).
   Second, the question often arises whether to place periods after each letter in an acronym or initialism. Search for consistency on this point is futile. The trend nowadays is to omit the periods; including them is the more traditional approach. Yet surely if an acronym is spoken as a single word (e.g., ERISA, ERTA), periods are meaningless. If an initialism is made up of lowercase letters, periods are preferable: *rpm* looks odd as compared with *r.p.m.*, and *am* looks like the verb (as opposed to *a.m.*). One method of determining whether to omit or include periods is to follow the form of the organization one names (e.g., IRS, HUD), although inconsistencies are common.
   Third, the best practice is to give the reader some forewarning of uncommon acronyms by spelling out the words and enclosing the acronym in parentheses when the term is first used. A reference to *CARPE Rules* may confuse a reader who does not at first realize that three or four lines above this acronym the writer has referred to a Committee on Academic Rights, Privileges, and Ethics.
   Fourth, capitalization raises various questions. In AmE there is a tendency to print initialisms in all capitals (e.g., FMLA, NJDEP) and acronyms in small capitals (e.g., GAAP, MADD, NASA). Some publications, however, use all capitals for both kinds. But in BrE the tendency is to uppercase only the first letter, as with *Ifor* and *Isa* for *Implementation Force* and *individual savings account*. An influential British commentator once suggested (with little success on his side of the Atlantic) that the lowercasing be avoided: "From the full name to the simplified label three stages can be detected. For instance, the Society [for Checking the Abuse of Public Advertising] . . . becomes first *S.C.A.P.A.*, then *SCAPA*, and finally *Scapa*. In the interests of clarity this last stage might well be discouraged, since thereby the reference is made unnecessarily cryptic." Simeon Potter, *Our Language* 177 (rev. ed. 1966). American writers have generally agreed with this view.
   Fifth, don't use abbreviations that have already been taken. Although it's understandable how a writer in 1959 might have used *PMS* for *primary message systems*, this would be worse than ill-advised today, since *premenstrual syndrome* is more commonly referred to by its initials than by its name. E.g.: "There are ten separate kinds of human activity which I have labeled

Primary Message Systems (PMS). Only the first PMS involves language. All the other *PMS* [read *PMSes*] are nonlinguistic forms of the communication process." Edward T. Hall, *The Silent Language* 45 (1959). The language doesn't easily embrace dual-meaning acronyms. One exception is *IRA*, which has long referred to the Irish Republican Army but in the 1980s came to denote also an individual retirement account. Other examples exist, but all are generally to be avoided. Once everyone thinks of the *FAA* as the Federal Aviation Administration, it's unwise to use that initialism in reference to the Federal Arbitration Act.

Sixth, when an indefinite article is needed before an abbreviation, the choice between *a* and *an* depends simply on how the first syllable is sounded. A vowel sound takes *an*, a consonant sound *a*—hence *an MGM film*, *an SOS*, *a DVD player*, *a UFO*. See **a (A)**.

Seventh, as illustrated under the entry entitled INI-TIALESE, the use in a single text of a number of these abbreviated forms leads to dense and frustrating prose.

act. A. Several Meanings. As jurisprudents have long noted, the term can bear several senses in legal contexts. Sometimes in law as well as in common speech, *act* is "applied to what is purely internal, when an act of the will, or of the conscience, or of the imaginative faculty, is spoken of." Sheldon Amos, *The Science of Law* 100 (6th ed. 1885). Sometimes, too, "the term is limited to the muscular motions of a human being, when these muscular motions are *voluntary*." *Id.* But at other times, *act* "denotes the voluntary muscular motions of a human being attended with some few of their immediate consequences, as in speaking of a good act or a bad act, an act of charity, or an act of violence." *Id.* Finally, it is "used to cover the complex actions of a number of individual persons, and also a long train of complex consequences," as by referring to the "act" of beheading a monarch when it actually covers the actions of the executioners as well as the regicides. *Id.* The authority cited here is admittedly old. But on this point, it's good.

B. And *action*. These are important words in law; yet they are often used indiscriminately. To be sure, the words overlap a great deal, and it is difficult to delineate the distinctions accurately. *Act* is the more concrete <an act of Congress>, *action* the more abstract word <spring into action>. But even *act* is a vague word, "being used in various senses of different degrees of generality. But when it is said that an act is one of the essential conditions of liability, we use the term in the widest sense of which it is capable. We mean by it any event [that] is subject to the control of the human will." M.G. Paulsen & Sanford H. Kadish, *Criminal Law and Its Processes* 212 (1962).

Generally, *act* denotes the thing done, *action* the doing of it. Crabb approaches a workable demarcation:

> When these words are taken in the sense of the thing done, they admit of a . . . distinction. An *act* is the single thing done, or what is done by a single effort, as that is your *act* or his *act*; an *action* may consist of more *acts* than

one, or embrace the causes or the consequences of the action, as a bold *action*, to judge of *actions*, etc.

> Hence it is that the term *act* is more proper than *action* where it is so defined as to imply what is single and simple, as an *act* of authority, an *act* of government, an *act* of folly, and the like; but otherwise the word *action* is to be preferred where the moral conduct or character is in question. We may enumerate particular *acts* of a man's life, as illustrative of certain traits of his character, or certain circumstances of his life; but to speak at large of his *actions* would be to describe his character.

George Crabb, *Crabb's English Synonymes* 24–25 (1917).

As a further gloss, *action* suggests a process—the many discrete events that make up a bit of behavior—whereas *act* is unitary.

C. *Act of omission*. Is it proper to speak of an *act of omission*, or does *act* invariably denote a positive act, i.e., an act of commission? Usage differs: in the phrase *act or omission* (a common phrase in insurance contexts), the word *act* denotes an act of commission, as opposed to a forbearance; but at other times the word appears to include a forbearance as well as an act of commission. So although the phrase *act of omission* may be proper, some readers are likely to sense a MISCUE by wondering whether *of* is a typographical error for *or*.

D. And *enactment*. *Act* has many meanings, but when used as a synonym for *statute*, it is usually clear from the context. Strictly, *enactment* should refer to the passing or enacting of a law (i.e., its enactment), but not to the law once enacted. E.g.:

- "As the state codified the common law of crimes, even if their *enactments* [read *acts*] were silent on the subject, their courts assumed that the omission did not signify disapproval of the principle but merely recognized that intent was so inherent in the idea of the offense that it required no statutory affirmation." *Morissette v. U.S.*, 342 U.S. 246, 252 (1952) (per Jackson, J.).
- "The purpose of an *enactment* [read *act*] is embedded in its words even though it is not always pedantically expressed in words." *U.S. v. Shirey*, 359 U.S. 255, 261 (1959) (per Frankfurter, J.).
- "Nor are legislatures required to provide the correct explanation for the constitutionality of their *enactments* [read *acts*]." Note, *Rationalizing Hard-Look Review After the Fact*, 122 Harv. L. Rev. 1909, 1923–24 (2009).

If the word *act* seemed somehow ambiguous to those writers, they might have used *statute* instead. Finally, **enaction* is a NEEDLESS VARIANT of *enactment*. To sum up, courts pass on the constitutionality of *acts*, not *enactments*; one witnesses the *enactment* of a bill.

In BrE, *Act* (= statute) is usually capitalized so as to prevent MISCUES—e.g.: "When an *Act* was repealed, and the repealing statute itself was subsequently repealed, the first *Act* was revived as from the original time of its commencement." Carleton K. Allen, *Law in the Making* 472 (7th ed. 1964). See **treaty**.

action. A. And *suit*. See **suit (A)**.

B. In Phrases Such as *action in trespass, action in detinue*. Often such phrases are shortened to *trespass, detinue*, etc., and the result is often a MISCUE. In the following sentence, for example, the trespasser and the complainant seem to be transposed: "*Trespass* by Rollin A. Richmond [the plaintiff] against James W. Fiske [the trespasser]." *Richmond v. Fiske*, 35 N.E. 103, 103 (Mass. 1893).

    C. And *act.* See **act (B).**

action; *actio.* In phrases such as *actio(n) ex contractu* and *actio(n) ex delictu, action* is better than *actio.* Better yet is *contract action* or *tort action.*

action, form of. See **form of action.**

actionable has two important senses: (1) "furnishing grounds for a lawsuit"; and (2) "liable to a lawsuit." Sense 1 is the most usual in legal contexts—e.g.:

- "Where words are *actionable per se,* the law presumes malice and conclusively presumes damages without specific proof of injury." *Moore v. Cox,* 341 F.Supp.2d 570, 574 (M.D.N.C. 2004).
- "In that event, plaintiffs would have no *actionable* claim for conversion under Alabama law because defendant's exercise of dominion over their property was not 'wrongful.'" *Murray v. Holiday Isle, LLC,* 620 F.Supp.2d 1302, 1337 (S.D. Ala. 2009).

The word has recently taken on a third sense: "giving rise to an act or action; act-on-able"—e.g.:

- "Many are ambitious visions of a utopian business state—nebulous feel-good credos designed to inspire employees but lacking any *actionable* component." William B. Yanes, *Mission Statements Can Be Inspiring but Impractical,* Investor's Daily, 10 Dec. 1990, at 8.
- "Only [a marketing professional] who understands the real world of lawyering can utilize the data to make recommendations that are precise and *actionable.*" Mercy Jimenez, *The Group,* A.B.A. J., Jan. 1991, at 86.

But most dictionaries do not record any definition consistent with this usage, which is predicated upon a misunderstanding of *action* (= lawsuit) as used in the term (i.e., "giving rise to a lawsuit"). Avoid sense 3.

action at law. See **civil action.**

action for money had and received. See **money had and received, action for.**

action for money paid. See **money had and received, action for.**

action on the case, a LOAN TRANSLATION of the LAW FRENCH *action sur le case,* is the common-law term for a personal tort action. E.g.:

- "This is an *action on the case* by a mother . . . for damages for enticing her minor son, fifteen years of age, to leave the plaintiff's home." *Steward v. Gold Medal Shows,* 14 So.2d 549, 554 (Ala. 1943).
- "The first case is an *action on the case* by Robert Lee Snoddy, suing by next friend, his mother, for personal injuries caused by an automobile truck owned by defendant." *Hightower Box & Tank Co. v. Snoddy,* 50 So.2d 737, 738 (Ala. 1951).

Trespass on the case and *case* alone are variant forms. None of these phrases is used much in modern legal prose, except in historical contexts—e.g.: "The modern torts, for the most part, are the offspring of that prolific '*action on the case*' which began to be developed in the later years of the fourteenth century." C.H.S. Fifoot, *History and Sources of the Common Law* 3 (1949). See **trespass on the case.**

activate. See **actuate.**

ACTIVE VOICE. See PASSIVE VOICE.

act of Congress. See **enactment.**

act of God. See **force majeure.**

act of omission. See **act (C).**

actual. See **constructive (A).**

*actual fact, in. A pomposity for *actually.*

actual fraud. See **fraud (B).**

actuality is frequently a turgid substitute for *reality* or *fact.* E.g.:

- "Here we see the court consciously turning away from the *actualities* [read *realities*] of the business situation, and resorting to the bridge of 'in principle' for the purpose of introducing a theoretical fact situation as the means of reaching what it deemed an obviously just result." George Jarvis Thompson, *The Relation of Common Carrier of Goods and Shipper, and Its Incidents of Liability,* 38 Harv. L. Rev. 28, 42 (1924).
- "From these *actualities* [read *facts*], which are nothing more than the context in which the error arises, a number of factors can be distilled which influence, if not dictate, the conclusion that error is harmless." Dennis J. Sweeney, *An Analysis of Harmless Error in Washington,* 31 Gonz. L. Rev. 277, 286 (1996).
- "Despite its undeniable importance, we do not know much about the *actualities* [read *realities*] of settlement." Kevin M. Clermont, *Litigation Realities Redux,* 84 Notre Dame L. Rev. 1919, 1953 (2009).

*In actuality is virtually always inferior to *actually.*

actuate; activate. The Evanses wrote that *actuate* means "to move (mechanical things) to action" and that *activate* means "to make active." Bergen Evans & Cornelia Evans, *Contemporary American Usage* 10 (1957). The distinction is a fine one not generally followed by dictionaries.

    Typically, *actuate* and **actuation* appear in legal prose as fancy substitutes for *motivate* and *motivation* in a variety of contexts. This usage should generally be avoided on stylistic grounds, but it is not strictly incorrect—e.g.:

- "Many socially desirable behaviors are *actuated* [read *motivated*] by guilt or by the desire to be esteemed by others and by oneself as righteous and generous." Peter H. Schuck, *Affirmative Action: Past, Present, and Future,* 20 Yale L. & Pol'y Rev. 1, 70 (2002).
- "We find that our laws, policies, and institutions appear to be *actuated* [read *motivated*] by the implicitly shared goal of ascending that scale." Robert Hockett, *Human Persons,*

Human Rights, and the Distributive Structure of Global Justice, 40 Colum. Hum. Rts. L. Rev. 343, 409 (2009).

The temptation to use *actuate* rather than *motivate* is much greater where the noun *motive* appears, so that one avoids REDUNDANCY. But a simple rewording usually obviates the need for *actuate*—e.g.:

- "Counsel had the absolute privilege of making such deductions as he saw fit if they were relevant and pertinent to the issues, even though they were false and he *was actuated by improper motives* [read *had improper motives*]." *Irwin v. Ashurst*, 74 P.2d 1127, 1131 (Or. 1938).
- "The showing of invidiousness is made if a defendant demonstrates that *the government's selective prosecution is actuated by constitutionally impermissible motives* [read *the government, in its selective prosecution, was acting on constitutionally impermissible motives*] . . . such as racial or religious discrimination." *U.S. v. Jennings*, 724 F.2d 436, 445 (5th Cir. 1984).
- "Where one exercises a legal right only, *the motive which actuates him is immaterial* [read *one's motivations are immaterial*]." *Maimon v. Sisters of Third Order of St. Francis*, 491 N.E.2d 779, 784 (Ill. App. Ct. 1986).

See **animate.**

actus non facit reum nisi mens sit rea. This MAXIM, phrased in LAW LATIN, is pronounced /**ak**-təs non **fas**-ət **ree**-əm **nis**-ɪ men sit **ree**-ə/. Meaning "an act does not make a person guilty unless his or her mind is guilty," the maxim expresses the criminal-law requirement of mens rea in addition to an *actus reus.* Traceable to the early 12th century, the brocard appears much more commonly in British than in American legal writing—e.g.: "Intent becomes the chief, though not the only, test; and the general rule is formed: *actus non facit reum nisi mens sit rea*, i.e., an act does not make the doer guilty unless his mind is guilty." O. Hood Phillips, *A First Book of English Law* 196 (3d ed. 1955). See **brocard.**

actus reus. See *mens rea* & **overt act.**

A.D. This abbreviation (for *Anno Domini*, not *after death*) is unnecessary after dates in legal documents. In fact, it's absurd to use it with a modern date.

adapt; adopt. These two are occasionally confounded. To *adapt* something is to modify it for one's own purposes; to *adopt* something is to accept it wholesale and use it.

adaptation; adaptive; *adaption; *adaptative. The longer form is preferred in the noun (*adaptation*), the shorter in the adjective (*adaptive*). *Adaption and *adaptative are NEEDLESS VARIANTS.

a dato; a datu. Both LEGALISMS mean "from the date," and both are anachronistic. *A dato* is the better Latin form.

addable. So spelled—not **addible.*

ad damnum [L. "to the damage"] = (1) *adj.*, of, relating to, or constituting the clause stating—in a declaration, writ, or pleading—what damages the plaintiff

demands; (2) *n.*, a prayer for relief that names the amount of damages claimed; or (3) *n.*, the amount of damages that a plaintiff claims in any given case.

Generally, it is possible for legal writers to use clearer phrasing without this LATINISM—e.g.:

- "Thus, even if the statute were retroactively applicable . . . it refers only to the *ad damnum pleading* [read *pleading demanding damages*] and not to the closing argument." *Gumbs v. Pueblo Int'l, Inc.*, 823 F.2d 768, 771 n.1 (3d Cir. 1987).
- "A plaintiff may file a lawsuit *with an ad damnum* [read *claiming damages*] in excess of the amount in the notice of claim." *McFarlane ex rel. McFarlane v. U.S.*, 684 F.Supp. 780, 782 (E.D.N.Y. 1988).
- "Counsel reasoned that each of the original plaintiffs claimed an amount far in excess of $10,000 in the *ad damnum clause of* [read *in the prayer for relief in*] their amended complaint." *Sterling v. Velsicol Chem. Corp.*, 855 F.2d 1188, 1195 (6th Cir. 1988).

added to. See **together with.**

addendum. See **appendix.**

addicted; dependent. Regarding people's reactions to drugs, the distinction between these terms can be an important one. One who is *addicted* to a habit-forming drug has a compulsive physiological need for it. One who is *dependent* on a drug has a strong psychological reliance on it after using it for some time. *Addiction*, then, is primarily physical, whereas *dependency* (also known as *habituation*) is primarily psychological.

*additament is a NEEDLESS VARIANT of *addition*.

additur; increscitur. Neither synonym is as common as the correlative term—*remittitur* (for which see **remitter**)—but *additur* is the more usual of the two, as Traynor explained: "*Additur*, sometimes called *increscitur*, is used . . . to describe an order by which a plaintiff's motion for a new trial on the ground of inadequate damages is denied on the condition that the defendant consent to a specified increase of the award." *Dorsey v. Barba*, 240 P.2d 604, 610 n.1 (Cal. 1952) (en banc) (Traynor, J., concurring in part & dissenting in part).

The term *additur* is an American NEOLOGISM of the early 20th century; it does not occur in English cases, and the first contextual use by an American court suggests its newness: "The order made in this case, might perhaps be termed an '*additur.*'" *Schiedt v. Dimick*, 70 F.2d 558, 563 (1st Cir. 1934). For an interesting but erroneous account of the word—erroneous because it attributes the word first to a *Yale Law Journal* article commenting on the case just cited—see Michael H. Cardozo, *A Word Is Born: "Additur," 1934–*, 2 Scribes J. Legal Writing 143 (1991).

address, vb., = (1) to speak to; (2) to direct (a question, etc.) to (someone); or (3) to call attention to. In sense 3 it is a FORMAL WORD that is sometimes used inappropriately—e.g.: "That portion of the trial court's decree is [not], therefore, assailed by Maria Rosa, as clearly her discontent *addresses* [read *centers on* or *arises out* *of*] the denial of a jury trial on the only factual issues raised having to do with proper division of the estate." *Lopez v. Lopez*, 691 S.W.2d 95, 98 (Tex. App.—San Antonio 1985). That sentence exemplifies HYPALLAGE run amok; generally, *address* should take personal subjects, although by legitimate transference one might say that arguments or pleas *address* certain points. But *discontent* is not a proper subject for the verb.

Here is a correct use of the term: "Plaintiff not only fails to cite a case that contradicts defendant's observation, it fails to *address* this issue at all." *Spacesaver Corp. v. Marvel Group, Inc.*, 621 F.Supp.2d 659, 663 (W.D. Wis. 2009).

Address should be accented on the second syllable both as a verb and as a noun.

addressable is listed in both the *OED* and *W11* as dating from 1953, but much earlier examples exist in law—e.g.: "Inasmuch as counsel themselves say that [the objections] are made not so much to impeach the validity of the act as to show its injustice, a consideration *addressable* to the Legislature, but not to us, no discussion of them is required." *Riley v. Chambers*, 185 P. 855, 859 (Cal. 1919).

addressee. See -EE.

adduce. A. And Its Near-Synonyms: *advance*; *cite*. Each of these verbs relates to bringing forward matter by way of explanation, analysis, illustration, or proof. To *adduce* evidence is to present it as furthering an argument or contention <he adduced sufficient evidence to create a fact issue>. To *advance* a claim, theory, argument, or other contentious point is to put it forward for acceptance or consideration <she advanced a rationale for the ruling>. To *cite* an authority or a passage from an authority is to set it forth in support of an argument <*Miranda* is frequently cited as controlling>. For more on *cite*, see **cite.**

B. And *educe*; *deduce*. All three terms are useful in reference to evidence. To *adduce* is to put forward for consideration something by way of evidence or arguments—e.g.: "In the original panel opinion we held that Rushing's live testimony at trial would have had only cumulative effect on this issue because Wells had access to and did *adduce* testimony concerning the town's supervision and training of Rushing." *Wells v. Rushing*, 760 F.2d 660, 661 (5th Cir. 1985).

To *educe* is to draw out or evoke or elicit—e.g.:

• "We are satisfied that from the evidence thus *educed* [i.e., *developed*, *brought out*] the trial court was justified in finding that the two concerns were practically the same, the latter being merely a continuation of the activities of the former, under the same control and management, but merely under a different name." *Meizlisch v. San Francisco Wool Sorting & Scouring Co.*, 3 P.2d 310, 311 (Cal. 1931).

• "That [divorce] judgment, subsequent to [read *after*] the filing of this suit, was reversed and remanded for retrial by a Texas intermediate court on October 27, 1983, as was *educed* on further showings made in the federal trial court." *Brown v. Hammonds*, 747 F.2d 320, 322 n.3 (5th Cir. 1984).

Here the sense is correct, but the word is matched with the wrong subject: "We need not reach this issue, because *no factual showing was educed* [read either *no showing was made* or *no facts were educed*] by the defendant to negate the allegations of her complaint that the failure to re-employ her resulted from gender-based discrimination." *Simmons v. Lyons*, 746 F.2d 265, 271 (5th Cir. 1984).

To *deduce* is to draw an inference—e.g.:

• "We concluded that the jury reasonably could have *deduced* the distance and inferred that the sale of the narcotics was committed within 1,500 feet of a public elementary school." *State v. Pagan*, 918 A.2d 1036, 1041 (Conn. App. Ct. 2007).

• "The Court found that . . . the facts did not reveal with a sufficient degree of certainty that Van Anraat disposed of information from which he could have *deduced* genocidal intent." Harmen van der Wilt, Comment, *Genocide v. War Crimes in the Van Anraat Appeal*, 6 J. Int'l Crim. Just. 557, 561 (2008).

For the misuse of *deduct* for *deduce*, see **deduce.**

adducible. So spelled—not **adduceable*. Occasionally, *adducible* (or its misspelled variant) is misused for *deducible*—e.g.:

• "Thus, if . . . we determine that the residue of facts is so devoid of evidence of probative value and reasonable inferences *adduceable* [read *deducible*] therefrom, as to preclude guilt beyond a reasonable doubt, we should so declare." *Liston v. State*, 250 N.E.2d 739, 743 (Ind. 1969).

• "On appeal, after . . . presuming the existence of every fact reasonably *adduceable* [read *deducible*] from the evidence, the court must determine whether substantial evidence supports the finding of premeditation and deliberation." *People v. Mitchell*, 183 Cal. Rptr. 166, 171 (Ct. App. 1982).

adduction, n., corresponds to the verb *adduce* but is not nearly as common as that verb. E.g.: "His only reply to Scrope's *adduction* of a named case is, 'Never will you see such an avowry received.'" Carleton K. Allen, *Law in the Making* 194 (7th ed. 1964).

adeem is the verb corresponding to *ademption*. The pair is analogous to *redeem/redemption*.

ademption. A. Two Types. The two types of *ademption* are usefully distinguished. *Ademption by extinction* is the forfeiture of a legacy or bequest by the beneficiary because the property specifically described in the will is not in the estate at the testator's death. *Ademption by satisfaction* occurs when the testator, while alive, gives property to a donee named in the will, with the intention of rendering the testamentary gift inoperative.

B. In the Phrase *work an ademption*. This legal idiom is akin to the lay idiom *work a hardship* (on someone)—e.g.:

- "On appeal, we held that the transfer of the accounts by the guardian did not *work an ademption* because of a statute concerning guardianships of incompetents, the provisions of which precluded ademption of the specific legacies." *In re Estate of Warman*, 682 N.E.2d 557, 561 (Ind. Ct. App. 1997).
- "The extinction of the property bequeathed *works an ademption* regardless of the testator's intent." *In re Estate of Hume*, 984 S.W.2d 602, 605 (Tenn. 1999).

C. And *lapse*. Whereas *lapse* occurs when a beneficiary does not survive to receive property given in a will, *ademption* occurs when the testator otherwise disposes of the property: "Lapse was a matter of no-Henry. *Ademption* is a matter of no-car. To raise the question is usually to answer it. If the testator has no car at his death, what if anything does he want Henry to have? The will should say. If it does not say, the dispute will turn on whether the bequest is specific—in which case it is adeemed by extinction and Henry gets nothing—or general, in which case the executor will have to get a car for Henry." Thomas L. Shaffer, *The Planning and Drafting of Wills and Trusts* 180 (2d ed. 1979).

adequate. A. And *sufficient*. Though originally both words were used in reference to quantity, today there is a trend toward using *adequate* qualitatively, and *sufficient* quantitatively. Hence *adequate* means "suitable to the occasion or circumstances," and *sufficient* means "enough for a particular need or purpose."

In contracts, with respect to *consideration*, a special distinction applies. One rule of consideration is that it need not be *adequate* but it must be *sufficient*. Here, *adequate* consideration means a realistic economic equivalent of the promise it buys, whereas *sufficient* consideration means something having economic value and not stemming from a preexisting legal duty. See **consideration**.

B. *Adequate enough*. This phrase is redundant. Either word alone suffices.

***ad finem; ad fin*.** One would be hard-pressed to justify this Latin phrase (meaning "to the end") in place of the English equivalent. (See LATINISMS.) The phrase is sometimes used in citations in a sense similar to *et seq.*, but the better practice is to cite specific pages, that is, to give an ending as well as a starting point. But if *ad fin.* is to be used, a period should follow the abbreviated form (as just given). See *et seq.*

adherence. A. And *adhesion*. Both words derive from the verb *to adhere*, but *adhesion* is generally literal and *adherence* generally figurative. One should write of *adherence* to tenets or beliefs, and of *adhesion* of bubble gum to the sole of one's shoe. Although the usual word in legal contexts is *adherence* <our adherence to the rule>, even respected writers blunder in their word choice—e.g.: "Can conspirators signify their *adhesion* [read *adherence*] at different times?" Glanville Williams, *Textbook of Criminal Law* 353 (1978).

Yet the standard rules of usage relating to these words find exceptions in the law. One exception to the foregoing advice is the phrase *adhesion contract* or *contract of adhesion*. Said to have been introduced into legal nomenclature by Edwin W. Patterson in *The Delivery of a Life Insurance Policy*, 33 Harv. L. Rev. 198, 222 (1919), the term refers to a standard printed contract prepared by one party, to be signed by the party in a weaker position, usually a consumer, who has little choice about the terms of the contract. The metaphor suggested is that the consumer must *adhere* to the contract as presented, or reject it completely. (Such a contract is also known, more familiarly to nonlawyers, as a *take-it-or-leave-it contract*.) *Adhesion*, then, has a figurative rather than a literal sense in this legal phrase. See **leonine contract**.

Another exception, not so frequently encountered, involves treaties. When a government enters into some but not all of the provisions of a treaty already existing between two other governments, *adhesion* is the term to describe the third government's entrance into the treaty.

B. Preposition *with*. *Adherence*, like *adhesion*, takes the preposition *to*. "This holding mandates close adherence *from* [read *to*] the letter of the law."

adhibit*,** vb., and its noun equivalent ***adhibition are pompous LEGALISMS. To **adhibit* is to apply; an **adhibition* is an application (of something to something else). E.g.:

- "We are importuned by the Dayton Newspapers, Inc., in this original action in this court to *adhibit* [read *apply*] the extraordinary writ of prohibition." *State ex rel. Dayton Newspapers, Inc. v. Phillips*, 351 N.E.2d 127, 139 (Ohio 1976) (Corrigan, J., dissenting).
- "Appellants' *adhibition* [read *application*] of mortality tables and their presentation and argument in the second trial . . . were predicated . . . on the metachronism that Sally was born nineteen years before the accident [that] took her life in 1970." *Hines v. Sweet*, 567 S.W.2d 435, 438 (Mo. Ct. App. 1978).
- "A threshold requirement for the *adhibition* [read *application*] of Title VI to a federal grantee's employment practices appears in § 604." *Guardians Ass'n v. Civil Serv. Comm'n*, 466 F.Supp. 1273, 1281 (S.D.N.Y. 1979).

ad hoc, adv. & adj., is a widespread and useful term meaning "for this specific purpose." Though some witch-hunting Latin-haters have questioned its justification in English (*see, e.g.*, Vigilans [Eric Partridge], *Chamber of Horrors* 26 (1952)), it is firmly established and serves legal language well when used correctly <ad hoc committee>.

By extension—some would say SLIPSHOD EXTENSION—the term has come to mean "without any underlying principle that can be consistently applied"—e.g.: "The majority opinion insufficiently considers the basic and substantive rules of law invoked by plaintiffs' complaint[;] it is an *ad hoc* opinion [that] grants desired relief to needy persons but its effect on established law could be serious." *Davis v. East St. Louis & Interurban Water Co.*, 270 N.E.2d 424, 431 (Ill. App. Ct. 1971). Sometimes the phrase appears to mean "improvised from whatever is at hand" or simply "unsystematic"—e.g.:

- "Lawyers and judges apparently devise [voir dire] questions in a fairly *ad hoc* [read *haphazard* or *unstructured*] way; sometimes prosecutors inadvertently pose questions that work to the advantage of the defense, and vice versa." Eric Schnapper, *Taking* Witherspoon *Seriously*, 62 Tex. L. Rev. 977, 1020 (1984).
- "Although the system has grown in a fairly *ad hoc* [read *unsystematic*] manner, it contains representatives of twenty-one of the twenty-five forest cover types in the United States and covers a broad range of environmental conditions." Holly Doremus, *Data Gaps in Natural-Resource Management*, 83 Ind. L.J. 407, 455 (2008).

Generally speaking, the phrases *on an ad hoc basis* and *in an ad hoc way* are verbose for the adverb *ad hoc*. (See **basis (B).**) Likewise, *ad hoc* should rarely if ever be qualified by *very* or *fairly*. Finally, attempts to condense the phrase into one word have failed and should be forgotten. Cf. **pro hac vice (A).**

ad hominem [L. "to the person"] is shortened from the LATINISM *argumentum ad hominem* (= an argument directed not to the merits of an opponent's argument but to the personality or character of the opponent).

The word is sometimes misspelled **ad hominum*—e.g.:

- "The Petitioners object to the conclusion that it is permissible to challenge an expert witness through an *ad hominum* [read *ad hominem*] argument." *U.S. ex rel. Hamilton v. Ellingsworth*, 692 F.Supp. 356, 369 (D. Del. 1988).
- "The Commonwealth has chosen to couch its appeal in language characterized by an *ad hominum* [read *ad hominem*] attack on the trial judge." *Commonwealth v. Rosario*, 583 A.2d 1229, 1233 (Pa. Super. Ct. 1990) (Cavanaugh, J., dissenting).

ad idem = to the same point or matter; in agreement. E.g.:

- "[The *Talmadge* case], relied on by appellant, turned simply on the fact that the negotiators were never *ad idem* [read *in agreement*] as to price." *Roller v. California Pac. Title Ins. Co.*, 206 P.2d 694, 699 (Cal. Ct. App. 1949).
- "A defense may be asserted when there is a mutual mistake of the parties as to the subject matter, the price, or the terms, going to show the want of a consensus *ad idem*." *MacKay v. McIntosh*, 153 S.E.2d 800, 804 (N.C. 1967).
- "A federal district court cannot, however, declare a treaty signed by the President and ratified by the Senate void on the ground that there was no consensus *ad idem* between the contracting parties." *Elcock v. U.S.*, 80 F.Supp.2d 70, 83 (E.D.N.Y. 2000).

An English equivalent, such as *of the same mind* or *to that effect*, is generally more comprehensible than this Latin phrase, and even more elegant. See FORBIDDEN WORDS. For *consensus ad idem*, see **meeting of the minds.**

adjacent, adj. **A. Preposition with.** *Adjacent* takes the preposition *to*. It was sometimes omitted in pre-20th-century legal writing—e.g.:

- "To son Joseph 400 acres of land *adjacent the land* I live on." Jacob Martin, *Wills of Westchester County, Pennsylvania* 61 (2007) (quoting 1731 will of James Gibbons).
- "Land Sale: September 20, 1808. Joseph Guidry declared that he held title to a tract of land 5 arpents wide in the rear of land owned by Jean Charles Hébert and *adjacent the land* owned by Jacques Faustin." 2 Glenn R. Conrad, *Land Records of the Attakapas District* 64 (1992).
- "It was necessary to grade and gravel portions of the streets *adjacent the property*, and also to reshape the surface of the grounds." 7 California Legislature, *Journal: Appendix Reports* (1893) (report of January 1893).

Today, established idiom demands *adjacent to* in such contexts.

B. And *contiguous*. These words should be distinguished. *Adjacent* = lying near. *Contiguous* = directly abutting or bordering on. See **adjoin.**

adjective law is not a set of rules governing words that modify nouns, but rather the aggregate of rules on procedure. In law as in language, the adjective affects the substantive. E.g.: "The *adjective law* of workmen's compensation, like the substantive, takes its tone from the beneficent and remedial character of the legislation." 3 Arthur Larson, *Workmen's Compensation Law* § 77A.10, at 15-1 (1986).

Adjectival law is a little-used variant—e.g.:

- "A constructive trust frequently is classified as a division of *adjectival* rather than substantive law." 76 Am. Jur. 2d *Trusts* § 222, at 448 (1975).
- "*Adjectival law* relates to the enforcement of rights and duties: in particular, it concerns procedure and evidence." Glanville Williams, *Learning the Law* 19 (11th ed. 1982).

ADJECTIVES. A. Definition. An adjective is a word that modifies a noun. The word is sometimes used sloppily as if it meant "noun"—e.g.: " 'Excellence' is an *adjective* [read *noun*] that describes something which is of the highest quality." *Their Work Stands Out*, Barrister, Summer 1989, at 5.

B. Uncomparable Adjectives. A number of adjectives describe absolute states or conditions and therefore cannot take comparative degrees in *most* or *more*, *less* or *least*, or intensives such as *very* or *quite* or *largely*. The illogic of such combinations is illustrated in this sentence: "Together, the no-fault revolution and courts' reluctance to award permanent alimony are evidence that we have *largely discarded* the assumption that, once married, individuals should be forever tied to one another." Kerry Abrams, *Immigration Law and the Regulation of Marriage*, 91 Minn. L. Rev. 1625, 1699 (2007). The literal meaning of *discard* impinges on the metaphor here: it is hard to imagine a single idea being halfway discarded, though certainly it could be halfway discredited. Deleting *largely* clarifies the meaning.

The best-known uncomparable adjective is *unique* (= being the one and only of a kind). Because something is either unique or not unique, there can be no degrees of uniqueness. Hence **more unique* and **very unique* are incorrect. Yet something may be *almost unique* or not quite unique—if, for example, there were two such things extant. (See **unique**.) Many other words belong to this class, such as *preferable*—e.g.:

- "The *most preferable* [read *preferable*] approach involves a reduction to present value factoring in the contingencies of vesting, maturity, and the pensioner's mortality." *Diffenderfer v. Diffenderfer*, 491 So.2d 265, 269 (Fla. 1986).
- "As the domestic exhaustion of remedies is necessary to any international intervention and is the *most preferable* [read *preferable*] outcome, this possibility was addressed next." Sarah Helena Lord, Comment, *The Nicaraguan Abortion Ban: Killing in Defense of Life*, 87 N.C. L. Rev. 537, 618 (2009).

Following is a short list of uncomparable adjectives:

absolute	inevitable	singular
adequate	infinite	stationary
chief	irrevocable	sufficient
complete	main	unanimous
devoid	manifest	unavoidable
entire	only	unbroken
false	paramount	uniform
fatal	perfect	unique
favorite	perpetual	universal
final	possible	void
ideal	preferable	whole
impossible	principal	

The general prohibition against using these words in comparative senses should be tempered with reason; it has exceptions. For example, Thomas Jefferson used the phrase *more perfect* in the Declaration of Independence, and the phrase then made its way into the U.S. Constitution: "We the People of the United States, in order to form a *more perfect* Union, establish Justice, insure domestic Tranquility, provide for the common defence, promote the general Welfare, and secure the Blessings of Liberty to ourselves and our Posterity, do ordain and establish this Constitution for the United States of America." U.S. Const. pmbl. One writer criticizes this phrase and suggests that it "should read 'to form a *more nearly perfect* Union.'" George J. Miller, *On Legal Style*, 43 Ky. L.J. 235, 246 (1955). Although the Constitution is not without stylistic blemishes, this surely is not one of them, and the suggested edit is pedantic. See **more perfect**.

In short, good writers occasionally depart from the rule, but knowingly and purposefully. Poor writers use uncomparable adjectives indiscriminately, and in the end weaken their writing through hyperbolic qualification. See **weasel words**.

C. Adjectives as Nouns. Words in the English language frequently have the ability to change parts of speech. This tendency is called "functional shift" or "functional variation." So nouns may act as adjectives (*deposition testimony*, *court protocol*) and adjectives as nouns (*corporeals* [BrE] = corporeal things). Legal writers refer to *innocents* (= innocent persons), *immovables*, *movables*, and *necessaries* (= necessary

things). *Indigent* was originally an adjective (15th c.), but it came to be used as a noun (16th c.).

The same process occurred with *hypothetical*, *postmortem*, *principal* (= principal investment), *ignitables*, *potential*, *explosives*, and *recitative*. More modern examples are *finals* (= final examinations) and *classifieds* (= classified advertisements). Similarly, we refer to *the poor*, *the homeless*, *the rich*, *the religious*, and *the destitute*.

Though recent semantic shifts remain unsuitable for formal contexts, we should resist the benighted temptation to condemn all such shifts in parts of speech. Cf. NOUNS AS ADJECTIVES.

D. Adjectives as Verbs. Though noun-to-adjective, adjective-to-noun, and even noun-to-verb transformations are common in English, adjective-to-verb transformations have never been common. They usually have a jargonistic quality (as in the first example below) or a trendy quality (as in the second). Careful writers avoid them or, when quoting someone else, distance themselves by using telltale quotation marks (as Gilmore and Black did):

- "The New York City Fire Commissioner directed that her cargo tanks be '*inerted*' through the introduction of carbon dioxide into the tanks." Grant Gilmore & Charles L. Black Jr., *The Law of Admiralty* 925 (2d ed. 1975).
- "Clinton would be well-advised to *low-key* the task force before it announces anything embarrassing." Joe Klein, *Time to Step Back*, Newsweek, 17 May 1993, at 40.

Cf. NOUNS AS VERBS.

E. Punctuating Coordinate Adjectives. When two adjectives, both modifying the same noun, are related in sense, they should be separated by *and* or by a comma—e.g.: "The purpose of Rule 11 as a whole is to bring home to the individual signer his *personal, nondelegable responsibility*." *Pavelic & LeFlore v. Marvel Ent. Group*, 493 U.S. 120, 126 (1989) (per Scalia, J.).

But when the consecutive adjectives are unrelated, they should have no intervening comma or conjunction—e.g.: "An interesting contrast in judicial philosophy as to the scope of an employee's ethical duty is revealed in a *similar and Texas case* [read *similar Texas case*]." John Schneider & Tom Arnold, *Trade Secrets and the Peripatetic Employee*, 196 PLI/Pat 237, 261 (1985).

Some consecutive adjectives present close questions—e.g.: "The *brief, unsigned Supreme Court opinion* said that the lawyers for Ms. Benten had failed to show a substantial likelihood that the case would be won if it were argued before the United States Court of Appeals for the Second Circuit." Phillip J. Hilts, *Justices Refuse to Order Return of Abortion Pill*, N.Y. Times, 18 July 1992, at 1. Is the fact that the opinion is brief related to the fact that it is unsigned (i.e., per curiam)? If so, the comma is proper; if not, the comma is improper. Because signed opinions tend to be longer than unsigned opinions, the comma is probably justified.

For more on the punctuation of successive adjectives, see PUNCTUATION (D)(1).

F. Proper Names as Adjectives. When a proper name is used attributively as an adjective, the writer should capitalize only that portion used in attribution. In *Southmark Properties v. The Charles House Corp.*, 742 F.2d 862 (5th Cir. 1984), the opinion is scattered with references to "The Charles House property." *The*, however, should be lowercased, for the skeletal phrase is "the property," and only *Charles House* is being used attributively. The definite article, then, derives from the skeletal phrase and not from the name of the party, even though the name of the party is *The Charles House Corporation.*

The practice of using place-names as adjectives is generally to be resisted, although it is increasingly common. Using a city plus the state as an adjective disrupts the flow of the sentence—e.g.: "Farmland's president, Marc Goldman, sent out sleuths who traced the missing containers to an *Elizabeth, N.J., warehouse* he says is filled with discarded bottles of designer water." Edward Felsenthal, *Nobody's Crying Yet, but There Must Be Spilled Milk Somewhere*, Wall St. J., 20 June 1990, at B1. Such constructions contribute to NOUN PLAGUE, lessen readability, and offend sensitive, literate readers.

The disruption is minimal or nonexistent when the city's name occurs without the state—e.g.: "An *Austin jury* returned a verdict in the court of Judge Walter Smith of Waco." *Accountant Found Guilty*, Austin American-Statesman, 21 July 1990, at B6.

G. Pronominal Indefinite Adjectives. Adjectives such as *each*, *any*, *every*, *all*, *no*, and *some* should be used only when they serve some demonstrable purpose. When a subject is plural, such an adjective is usually unnecessary—e.g.: "*All corporate officers* [read *Corporate officers*] must . . . ."

A few conventions with these words are useful in the realm of drafting. First, if a right, privilege, or power is extended, the drafter should use *each* or *a* <each director may>. Second, if a duty is imposed, the drafter should use *each* or *a* <each director must>. And third, if a proscription is set out, the drafter should use *no* <no director may>. See LEGISLATIVE DRAFTING & WORDS OF AUTHORITY.

H. Past-Participial Adjectives. Some past participles work perfectly well as adjectives, and others do not. There can be a *tired* or *irritated* person, but not a *disappeared* person: "In child-support cases for newly born children throughout the state of Maine, the parties are frequently required to notify the mother's *long-disappeared husband* [read *long-gone husband* or *husband, who disappeared long ago,*] of the theoretical interest the presumption of legitimacy assigns him in each case." John Sheldon, *The Good News, and Some Bad News, About the Uniform Parentage Act of 2002*, 18 Me. B.J. 94, 96 n.21 (2003). The reason is that *disappeared* has not been accepted idiomatically as a prepositive adjective, whereas other past participles (such as *tired* and *irritated*) have been. Some legal phrases can be framed either way: hence, *cases decided* and *cases cited*, or *decided cases* and *cited cases*.

I. Phrasal or Compound Adjectives. See PHRASAL ADJECTIVES.

J. Modification of Adjectives Ending in -*ed*. See **very (B).**

K. Adjectives Ending in -*ly*. See ADVERBS (B).

L. Adjectives That Follow the Noun. See POST-POSITIVE ADJECTIVES.

M. Dates as Adjectives. See DATES (C).

adjoin means both "to join" and "to lie adjacent to." In the latter sense, it is transitive and takes a direct object—e.g.: "The park was likened to a garden [that] traditionally (as an appurtenance) *adjoined to* [read *adjoined*] a residence." *Drye v. Eagle Rock Ranch, Inc.*, 364 S.W.2d 196, 206 (Tex. 1963). Etymologically, *adjoining* means "directly abutting; contiguous," as opposed to *adjacent*. See **adjacent.**

adjourn; prorogue; dissolve. All these verbs relate to a public body's deferring or terminating all business. A deliberative body *adjourns* when it suspends business, usually for a brief period but sometimes also indefinitely <adjourn sine die>. E.g.: "But the case was *adjourned* to the court of Exchequer Chamber, where all the judges of England considered difficult cases." Alan Harding, *A Social History of English Law* 105 (1966). The corresponding noun is *adjournment*.

A government, especially in a parliamentary system, *prorogues* the legislature by ending the session, all unenacted business having been quashed. "Magistrates have very wide powers to grant or refuse bail when a person is first brought before them, and the case has to be *adjourned* to a later date." P.S. Atiyah, *Law and Modern Society* 25 (1983). The corresponding noun is *prorogation*.

When a deliberative body is dissolved (or dissolves itself), it no longer exists as previously constituted and cannot take up any further business until a new session with a re-formed membership is duly constituted. See RE- PAIRS. The corresponding noun is *dissolution*.

adjournment; *adjournal. Except in Scotland, *adjournal is a NEEDLESS VARIANT. In Scotland, the *Books of Adjournal* are the records of the Justiciary Court. *Adjournment* = (1) the act of suspending proceedings to another time or place; or (2) an adjourned meeting, i.e., a meeting "scheduled for a particular time (and place if it is not otherwise established) by the assembly's 'adjourning to' or 'adjourning until' that time and place." *Robert's Rules of Order Newly Revised* § 9, at 90 (10th ed. 2000). As *Robert's* points out, because sense 2 is susceptible to confusion with sense 1, the phrase *adjourned meeting* is preferable to *adjournment* in sense 2. Reserve *adjournment* for its ordinary meaning: sense 1.

adjudge; adjudicate. *Adjudge* = (1) to consider judicially; to rule on; (2) to deem or pronounce to be; or (3) to award judicially. *Adjudicate* shares all three meanings of *adjudge* and is more common than *adjudge* in sense 1. In senses 2 and 3, *adjudge* is the more usual term—e.g.:

- (Sense 2) "Nor can [a court of equity] *adjudge* the decree of any other court binding or punish the violation of any decrees but its own." *Day v. Wiswall*, 464 P.2d 626, 630 (Ariz. Ct. App. 1970).
- (Sense 3) "Lucas also filed a bond as required by RCW 7.12.060 in double the amount of his demand, conditioned that he would prosecute his action without delay and pay damages sustained and costs *adjudged* to Stapp if the attachment proved to be wrongfully, oppressively, or maliciously sued out." *Lucas v. Stapp*, 497 P.2d 250, 251 (Wash. Ct. App. 1972).

For examples of *adjudicate* in sense 2, see **adjudicate (B).** For more on these and related verbs, see **judge,** vb.

Adjudge is best used with the object immediately following—e.g.: "The court found him guilty of the charge and *adjudged* him in contempt." *Ex parte Tucker*, 220 S.W. 75, 76 (Tex. 1920). There is a tendency (to be avoided) to insert *as* after *adjudge*, as in the phrase **adjudge as bankrupt* for *adjudge bankrupt.* Cf. **abjudge.**

adjudgment; *adjudgement. See **judgment.**

adjudicataire. See **adjudicator.**

adjudicate. A. Proper Object with. Disputes and controversies are adjudicated, or "settled judicially"; *property* cannot be adjudicated, although conflicting rights in it can be. E.g.:

- "We . . . [reverse the judgment of the Supreme Court of Kansas] insofar as it held that Kansas law was applicable to all of the transactions [that] it sought to *adjudicate.*" *Phillips Petroleum Co. v. Shutts*, 472 U.S. 797, 823 (1985) (per Rehnquist, J.). [A suggested revision: *We . . . reverse the judgment of the Supreme Court of Kansas insofar as it held Kansas law to apply to all the disputed transactions.*]
- "Daughter contends the judgment for quiet title does not comply with the requirements of [the Statute] because it fails to describe with certainty the property *adjudicated* [read *in dispute*]." *Thurmon v. Ludy*, 914 S.W.2d 32, 34 (Mo. Ct. App. 1995).

See **adjudication.** Cf. **litigate.**

B. Meaning "to deem." *Adjudicate* frequently means "to deem or pronounce judicially to be," essentially as an equivalent of sense 2 of *adjudge.* (See **adjudge.**) E.g.:

- "Even assuming that Appellants' claim that PMP is insolvent is correct, PMP has not yet been *adjudicated* a bankrupt, and no execution has been returned unsatisfied because of insolvency or bankruptcy." *Liberty Mut. Ins. Co. v. Treesdale, Inc.*, 419 F.3d 216, 223 (3d Cir. 2005).
- "Minnesota's summary dissolution . . . statute provides that a couple may dissolve their marriage by using a streamlined procedure if . . . no living minor children have been born to or adopted by the parties before or [during] the marriage, unless someone other than the husband has been *adjudicated* the father." Lloyd Cutsumpas & B. Moses Vargas, Comment, *Summary Dissolution: Is Connecticut's Current System as Effective as It Should Be?*, 6 Conn. Pub. Int. L.J. 329, 339 (2007).

- "A few days after the lien was filed, the builder was *adjudicated* a bankrupt." *Redmond v. Kester*, 159 P.3d 1004, 1008 (Kan. 2007).

For more on *adjudicate*, see **adjudge** & **judge,** vb.

adjudicated has come into use as an adjective. So instead of writing, "The ward *was adjudicated* an incompetent," some legists have begun to write, "The ward is *an adjudicated* bankrupt." The adjectival usage purports to give the statement more authority, for it focuses on what the subject *is*, as opposed to what someone *has done to it.*

adjudication; *adjudicature. *Adjudication* = (1) the process of judging; (2) a court's pronouncement of a judgment or decree; or (3) the judgment so given. **Adjudicature* is a NEEDLESS VARIANT. (See **judicature.**) On the plural use of *adjudication*, see PLURALS (B).

Leff wrote that, in modern usage, "*adjudication* can . . . be used as a rough synonym for *litigation*—e.g.: 'the matter is in *adjudication* now.'" Arthur A. Leff, *The Leff Dictionary of Law*, 94 Yale L.J. 1855, 1934 (1985). This SLIPSHOD EXTENSION should be avoided unless, of course, the writer intends to refer to the deliberative process of judges and not to the courtroom proceedings in which lawyers take part. See **adjudicate (A)** & **litigate.**

adjudicative; *adjudicatory; *judicative; judicatory; *judicatorial. As between *adjudicative* and **adjudicatory*, both meaning "having the character or attribute of adjudicating," the former is standard, easier to pronounce, and better sounding. Yet the latter appears with some frequency. So even though we have *adjudicative facts* and *adjudicative hearings*, our legal texts reveal **adjudicatory proceedings* and **adjudicatory action.* There is no need for the two to coexist, for no workable DIFFERENTIATION now appears to be possible. One is best advised to use *adjudicative* in all contexts.

*Judicative is a NEEDLESS VARIANT of *adjudicative.* Likewise, **judicatorial* is a NEEDLESS VARIANT of *judicial.* For *judicatory* (a word with limited currency), see **judicature.** See also **judicative.**

adjudicative facts. See **legislative facts.**

adjudicator; adjudicataire; *judicator. *Adjudicator* = one who adjudicates. If used merely for *judge*, it is a pomposity. But in some contexts it is quite defensible—e.g.: "We find nothing in the history or constitutional treatment of military tribunals which entitles them to rank along with Article III courts as *adjudicators* of the guilt or innocence of people charged with offenses for which they can be deprived of their life, liberty, or property." *U.S. ex rel. Toth v. Quarles*, 350 U.S. 11, 17 (1955) (per Black, J.). *Adjudicataire*, a term from Canadian law, means "a purchaser at a judicial sale" (*W3*). **Judicator* is a NEEDLESS VARIANT of *adjudicator.*

*adjudicature for *adjudication.* See **judicature** & **adjudication.**

adjure (= to charge or entreat solemnly) is some-times misused for two other words, *abhor* and *require*. The first of these is hard to explain but easy to illustrate—e.g.:

- "Although the majority of legal scholars *adjure* strict criminal liability on the grounds that it is indefensible to impose criminal sanctions in the absence of mens rea and that such liability is not an effective deterrent, there are those who make a respectable argument for the rationality of strict criminal liability." *Baker v. State*, 377 So.2d 17, 19–20 (Fla. 1979).
- "Most of us don't dislike lawyers individually; we *adjure* [read *abhor*?] them as a group." *Our Legal System's Put Us in a Box*, Chicago Trib., 23 Aug. 1988, at C19.

This misusage hasn't crept into legal usage to the degree the second error has—that is, *adjure* for *require* or *command*:

- "Arizona law *adjures* [read *requires*] that statutes should be construed to effect their objects." *Knapp v. Cardwell*, 667 F.2d 1253, 1261 (9th Cir. 1982).
- "Assaying the quality of defendant's acts and omissions . . . *adjures* [read *requires*] just such a judgment call." *Swift v. U.S.*, 866 F.2d 507, 511 (1st Cir. 1989).
- "It thus is an aspect of the broader principle that *adjures* [read *requires*] a court to consider the third-party effects of equitable relief and to shape that relief accordingly." *Byron v. Clay*, 867 F.2d 1049, 1051 (7th Cir. 1989) (per Posner, J.).

adjurer; *adjuror. The *-er* spelling is preferred. See -ER (A).

adjuster; *adjustor. *Adjuster* (= one who seeks to determine the amount of loss suffered when an insurance claim is submitted and who attempts to settle the claim) is the preferred spelling. See -ER (A).

adjustment of status. This immigration-law term of art refers to the process of changing or applying to change a lawfully admitted alien's classification from nonimmigrant or temporary resident to permanent resident. Oddly, it is occasionally confused with terms applicable to deporting an alien: "There are a few instances where the BIA [Board of Immigration Appeals] fumbled the language, most notably calling Petitioner's request an '*adjustment of status*' rather than 'withholding of removal.'" *Pathmakanthan v. Holder*, 612 F.3d 618, 625 (7th Cir. 2010). O tempora! O mores! O BIA!

ad litem [L. "for the suit"]. Formerly—and still in English law—a guardian *ad litem* represented only an underage defendant (a next friend or *prochein ami* representing an underage plaintiff). BrE retains this restrictive sense—e.g.: "For purposes of litigation . . . an infant can and must be represented by an adult, who will be called 'the next friend' of an infant plaintiff, the 'guardian *ad litem*' of an infant defendant." William Geldart, *Introduction to English Law* 45 (D.C.M. Yardley ed., 9th ed. 1984). But in modern AmE, underage plaintiffs (as well as defendants) are afforded guardians *ad litem*.

In AmE, the phrase *guardian ad litem* is often short-ened to *ad litem*. E.g.: "As you requested, I called the *ad litem* [i.e., the guardian *ad litem*] today." See **guardian *ad litem***.

adminicular; *adminiculary. *Adminicular* (= corroborative), seen usually in the phrase *adminicular evidence*, is the standard adjectival form of the noun *adminicle*, meaning "supporting or corroborative evidence" (*OED*). **Adminiculary* is a NEEDLESS VARIANT. In Scots law, *adminicle* has the more specific sense "a writing that tends to establish the existence and terms of a lost document."

administer; minister, vb. *Administer* suffices in most legal contexts. It is a transitive verb and, in its most common legal sense, means "to manage and dispose of the estate of a deceased person, either under a will or under letters of administration" (*OED*). E.g.: "The plaintiff administrator was not a trustee of the trust created by her; his duty was to *administer* the property and distribute it to those entitled to receive it." *Geenty v. Phoenix Mut. Life Ins. Co.*, 14 A.2d 720, 723 (Conn. 1940). *Administer* may also mean (1) "to dispense (as justice or as punishment)"; or (2) "to give (an oath)."

The verb *minister*, now exclusively intransitive, shares these last two meanings, albeit only rarely. *Minister* is most commonly used in the sense of attending to others' needs, or, in religious contexts, of administering sacraments. Persons in need are *ministered to*—e.g.: "The victim internally hemorrhaged for ten hours before hospital officials *ministered to* him." *People v. Morse*, 3 Cal. Rptr. 2d 343, 351 (Ct. App. 1992).

*administerial. See **administrative.**

administrable; *administratable; *administerable. The first form is correct; the others are near-abominations, and NEEDLESS VARIANTS to boot. E.g.: "This court did in fact find a more *administratable* [read *administrable*] way to evaluate the property— the trial de novo." *U.S. v. 2,175.86 Acres of Land*, 687 F.Supp. 1079, 1081 (E.D. Tex. 1988).

*administrate is an objectionable BACK-FORMATION from *administration*; it should be avoided as a NEEDLESS VARIANT of *administer*. E.g.: "By the same reasoning, the legislature could delegate the power to promulgate regulations having the force of law to *administrate* [read *administer*] organs of the government." John H. Merryman, *The Civil Law Tradition* 24 (1969).

administrative; *administerial; *administrational. *Administrative* is the general, all-purpose term meaning "of or pertaining to administration or an administration." **Administerial* and **administrational* are NEEDLESS VARIANTS.

administrative-law judge; hearing officer. In U.S. federal law, so-called *hearing officers* had their titles changed in 1978 to *administrative-law judges*. The U.S.

Supreme Court has said that they are "functionally comparable" to U.S. district judges. See **ALJ.**

administrator; executor. Both terms refer to the personal representative who administers the estate of a decedent. An *executor* is named in a will, whereas an *administrator* (usually someone close to the decedent) is court-appointed. There are two kinds of the latter: the first is an *administrator cum testamento annexo* (or *c.t.a.*)—i.e., with the will annexed; the second is an *administrator de bonis non* (or *d.b.n.*), an elliptical phrase for *administrator de bonis non administratis* (= administrator of goods not administered). An *administrator c.t.a.* is appointed if the testator does not name an executor or if the named executor for any reason does not act; an *administrator d.b.n.* is appointed if a prior administrator has begun to act but later dies or is removed.

The phrase *administrator c.t.a.* is often translated *administrator with the will annexed*, a healthy practice that helps minimize the LATINISMS associated with this area of the law.

administratrix. Pl. *administratrixes*, preferably not *administratrices*. But there's less and less justification for this sex-specific term. See SEXISM (C).

admiralty. A. And *maritime law; law of the sea.* *Admiralty* and *maritime* are virtually synonymous in referring to the law of marine commerce and navigation, the transportation at sea of persons and property, and marine affairs in general.

Yet Article III, section 2 of the U.S. Constitution is not redundant in providing, "The judicial power shall extend . . . to all Cases involving admiralty and maritime Jurisdiction." One commentator notes that *admiralty* (dated from ca. 1327 in the *OED*) was the better-known term when the Constitution was drafted, and that *maritime* (*OED*: ca. 1550) was used in conjunction with *admiralty* for two reasons: "(1) to exclude that jurisdiction which the English Admiralty anciently exercised or attempted to exercise over nonmaritime cases arising ashore, and (2) to preclude a resort to those English instances in which common law courts encroached upon the jurisdiction of admiralty." Elijah Jhirad et al., 1 *Benedict on Admiralty* § 101, at 7-3 (7th ed. 1983).

Law of the sea carries a distinct meaning: "the rules governing the relationships between states regarding the use and control of the sea and its resources." Thomas J. Schoenbaum, *Admiralty and Maritime Law* § 2-1, at 20 (1987). So the law of the sea falls within public international law, whereas admiralty or maritime law is a division of private law.

B. *The admiralty.* The phrase *the admiralty* refers to the office of an admiral (fr. Arabic *amir-al-bahr* "chief of the sea") or other person entrusted by the crown with command of the seas and of royal ships. Because the admirals came to have jurisdiction over maritime matters, the phrase by extension came to refer to that jurisdiction. E.g.: "The theory of the case, according to the summary of argument in the Supreme Court

report, was that Chelentis, in a common law action outside *the admiralty*, could recover damages on common law tort principles without regard to the maritime law." Grant Gilmore & Charles L. Black Jr., *The Law of Admiralty* 325 (2d ed. 1975).

admissible; *admissable; *admittable. *Admissible* (the standard word) = (1) allowable; or (2) worthy of admittance (i.e., gaining entry). The other two forms are NEEDLESS VARIANTS to be avoided.

admission. A. And *admittance.* The distinction between these terms is old and useful, but it has a history of being ignored. *Admittance* is purely physical, as in signs that read "No admittance." E.g.:

- "Plaintiff instituted an action . . . to enjoin defendant from refusing her *admittance* to its amusement park because of her race or color, or for any other reason not applicable alike to other citizens." *Fletcher v. Coney Island, Inc.*, 134 N.E.2d 371, 372 (Ohio 1956).
- "A review of the record before us indicates that the occupants of the home were not sufficiently alerted to permit the police to infer that their *admittance* was refused." *State v. Oliver*, 860 N.E.2d 1002, 1004 (Ohio 2007).

Admission is used in figurative and nonphysical senses—e.g.: "The Court held that because the Arizona Supreme Court merely delegated administration of the bar exam grading but retained final authority to grant *admission* to the bar, the conduct was solely that of the court." *Grand River Enters. Six Nations, Ltd. v. Beebe*, 574 F.3d 929, 941 (8th Cir. 2009). *Admission* is also used, however, in physical senses when rights or privileges are attached to gaining entry—e.g.: "The purpose of the labor certification requirement is to prevent the permanent *admission* of aliens to the United States who would compete for jobs that American workers could fill." *Wong v. Napolitano*, 654 F.Supp.2d 1184, 1189 n.3 (D. Or. 2009).

B. And *confession.* In criminal law, a distinction has traditionally existed between these words: an *admission* is a concession that an allegation or factual assertion is true without any acknowledgment of guilt with respect to the criminal charges, whereas a *confession* involves an acknowledgment of guilt as well as of the truth of factual allegations.

C. In Civil Litigation. Although nonlawyers tend to associate *admission* with criminal law (see (B)), it has broad uses in noncriminal evidentiary contexts: "An *admission* is a statement oral or written, suggesting any inference as to any fact in issue or relevant fact, unfavourable to the conclusion contended for by the person by whom or on whose behalf the statement is made." James Fitzjames Stephen, *The Law of Evidence* 23 (1876).

D. Into Evidence. *Evidence*, which may or may not be physical, always requires *admission*—not *admittance*. E.g.:

- "Does due process in a criminal trial require both that the judge find a confession voluntary beyond a reasonable doubt before *admittance* [read *admission*] into evidence and that a jury decide the voluntariness issue anew before using the confession as evidence in reaching its verdict?"

Bruce E. Fein, *Significant Decisions of the Supreme Court* 16 (1972).

- "He was asked to identify the clothes of the victim in order to lay a foundation for their *admittance* [read *admission*] into evidence." *State v. Cox*, 464 So.2d 439, 441 (La. Ct. App. 1985).
- "We review the *admittance* [read *admission*] of evidence under an abuse of discretion standard." *In re Walker*, 515 F.3d 1204, 1213 (11th Cir. 2008). (The phrasing here should be *abuse-of-discretion standard*. See PHRASAL ADJECTIVES.)

admit. A. And Its Near-Synonyms: *acknowledge*; *confess*. These verbs share the sense "to disclose or own up to something reluctantly or despite misgivings." *Admit* emphasizes the reluctance to concede but lessens the suggestion of potential concealment <the mayor admitted that he had been hiring prostitutes for years>. To *acknowledge* in this sense is to make public the truth of something that one might have continued denying or concealing despite rumors or suspicions <he acknowledged his nonmarital child>. *Confess* often applies to what one knows to be illegal, immoral, or otherwise wrong <she confessed her sins>, although it does not always carry such nefarious connotations <I confess that I didn't believe your client could win>.

B. *Admit to. In the sense of disclosing reluctantly, *admit to is generally much inferior to *admit*—e.g.:

- "The United States entered into guilty pleas with individuals who *admitted to* [omit *to*] defrauding the citizens of New Mexico out of millions of dollars." *U.S. v. Vigil*, 476 F.Supp.2d 1231, 1307 (D.N.M. 2007).
- "Suffice it to say [that] Taiwan's government and public do not appear ready to accept cases like that of Sammy 'The Bull' Gravano who, because his testimony was critical in convicting notorious mob boss John Gotti, was sentenced by a U.S. court to only five years in prison after he *admitted to* [omit *to*] killing nineteen people." Margaret K. Lewis, *Taiwan's New Adversarial System and the Overlooked Challenge of Efficiency-Driven Reforms*, 49 Va. J. Int'l L. 651, 673 (2009).

See **confess (to)**.

C. Admit of. *Admit of* = to allow; to be susceptible of—e.g.:

- "Any ambiguity in an insurance contract must be resolved against the insurer and in favor of the insured, and . . . when a policy *admits of* two interpretations the claim for the one sustaining indemnity will be adopted." *Graham v. Equity Nat'l Life Ins. Co.*, 373 So.2d 988, 992 (La. Ct. App. 1979).
- "The easement *admits of* two interpretations." *Meadows Country Club, Inc. v. Unnever*, 702 So.2d 586, 588 (Fla. Dist. Ct. App. 1997).
- "The statement will *admit of* no other possibility but that when Tran shot Bui, he did not have a generalized desire to kill, but the specific desire to kill a rival gang member, as evidenced by the use of the gang moniker." *People v. Tran*, 99 Cal. Rptr. 3d 122, 140 (Ct. App. 2009).

D. Admitted to the bar; called to the bar. The former is the American phrase for qualifying to practice—e.g.: "I was *admitted to the bar* at Chattanooga." William G. McAdoo, *Crowded Years* 40 (1931). The phrase *called to the Bar* is the British phrase for qualifying to practice as a barrister (as distinguished from a solicitor, who is *called to the roll*). *Called to the bar* appears infrequently in AmE. See **called to the bar.** Cf. **barred.**

***admittable.** See **admissable.**

admittance. See **admission (A).**

admitted. See ***self-admitted.**

admonish; monish. See **admonition** & **reprove.**

***admonishment.** See ***abolishment.**

admonition; monition. In general usage, both mean "a warning; caution." *Admonition* is the more common, less technical term <the Supreme Court's admonition that courts ought not to impose constitutional restraints that would inhibit the ability of the political branches to respond to changing world conditions>. *Admonition* has the additional sense "a mild reprimand." See **reprove.**

Monition is the more specialized legal term; it may mean (1) in admiralty and civil-law contexts, "a summons to appear and answer in court as a defendant or to contempt charges"; or (2) in ecclesiastical contexts, "a formal notice from a bishop mandating that an offense within the clergy be corrected." The object of a monition is a *person monished*.

admonitory; *admonitorial; monitory; *monitorial. The *-ory* forms predominate.

adopt. See **adapt.**

adopted. See **adoptive.**

adoption; ratification; novation. In contractual contexts, these three words have deceptively similar meanings. *Adoption* of a contract is accepting it as one's own, or consenting to be bound by it, though it was entered into by someone else acting on one's behalf. A *ratification* is the confirmation of a contract performed or entered into on one's behalf by another who at the time assumed without authority to act as an agent. These two words are near-synonyms. *Novation* has two important meanings: (1) "the substitution of a new contract between parties in place of an existing contract"; and (2) "the substitution of a new party in an existing contract." Sense 1 predominates in American law. See **novation.**

In corporate law, the distinctions have relevance, and are somewhat different, when a promoter enters into a contract that purports to bind a newly formed corporation, or one soon to be formed. If a promoter contracts with a third person when it is understood that the corporation will be formed, the corporation is later properly said to *adopt* the contract. *Ratify*, in contrast, is the proper word when the corporation already existed when the contract was signed. If, after a corporation *adopts* or *ratifies* the contract, the promoter is expressly relieved from liability, the *adoption* or *ratification* becomes a *novation*.

adoptive; adopted. *Adoptive* = (1) related by adoption <an adoptive son>; or (2) tending to adopt <adoptive admissions under Fed. R. Evid. 801(d)(2)(b)>. The phrase **adopted father* is an example of HYPALLAGE, to be avoided in favor of *adoptive father*. The original Latin word, *adoptivus*, applied both to the adopting parent and to the adopted child. But today *adoptive* is almost always used in reference to the adults rather than the children. *Adoptive* is the active form: an adoptive parent is one who has adopted a child. *Adopted* is the passive form: an adopted child is one who has been adopted by a parent.

Here the correct usages are observed:

- "In this special circumstance, where the *adoptive* parents are related to the *adopted* child and to one of the child's natural parents, any perceived inequity of a dual inheritance could be eliminated by limiting the *adopted* child's right to inherit from the *adoptive* kindred in the final adoption decree." *Jenkins v. Jenkins*, 990 So.2d 807, 812 (Miss. Ct. App. 2008).
- "In the years before 1949, children could be adopted by an *adoptive* parent through an application made to the juvenile court or to a board of county commissioners." *In re J.N.H.*, 209 P.3d 1221, 1224 (Colo. Ct. App. 2009).

adpromissor (= surety, bail) has two plural forms in *adpromissors* and **adpromissores*, the latter being unEnglish and therefore inferior. (See PLURALS (A).) The dilemma of choosing between plural forms is easily remedied by writing *sureties*.

ADR. See **alternative dispute resolution**.

*adulter. See **adulterer**.

adulterant; *adulterate. See **adulterous**.

adulteration; adultery. *Adulteration* = (1) the act of debasing, corrupting, or making impure; (2) a corrupted or debased state; or (3) something corrupted or debased. *Adultery* = sexual intercourse engaged in voluntarily by a married person with someone who is not the person's lawful spouse. The Latin verb *adulterare*, from which both English words derive, encompasses all these senses. See **adulterine bastard**.

adulterer; *adulter; adulteress; adultera; adulterator. *Adulterer* is the usual term meaning "one who commits adultery." But the usage issue doesn't stop there because that definition raises the question, Which participant is it, precisely, that commits adultery? The law gives three possible answers:

- Under the canon-law rule, a married participant is an adulterer and an unmarried one is a fornicator. The sex of the participant doesn't matter.
- Under the common-law rule, both participants commit adultery if the married participant is a woman. But if the woman is the unmarried one, both participants are fornicators, not adulterers. This rule is premised on whether

there is a possibility of "adulterating" the blood within a family. (Any offspring from an adulterous union were called *adulterini*.)

- Under modern statutory law, some courts hold that the unmarried participant isn't guilty of adultery (that only the married participant is), but others hold that both participants are adulterers.

The other forms occur much less frequently. **Adulter* is an obsolete variant of *adulterer*; it also had the meaning of *adulterator* (= counterfeiter). *Adulteress* is the feminine form, now disfavored because of the growing awareness of SEXISM—likewise with *adultera*, the term from the civil law. *Adulterator*, as suggested above, derives from the noun *adulteration*, and not from *adultery*.

Today all these terms—and their legal meanings—are somewhat obscure because the legal doctrines themselves have long been somnolent (not to say sleeping around).

adulterine bastard. Leff defined this phrase as "the child of a married woman by a man other than her husband," and commented: "As 'adultery' has come to include sexual relations by a married man with a woman not his wife, whether she is married or not, the term *adulterine bastard* has sometimes come to include a child born to an unmarried woman by a married man. This makes no difference, as no legal consequences presently attach to adulterine bastardy that do not attach to plain old bastardy." Arthur A. Leff, *The Leff Dictionary of Law*, 94 Yale L.J. 1855, 1951 (1985). The form *adulterine bastard* is preferable to *adulterous bastard*, the latter suggesting an unfaithful husband rather than a child produced by adultery.

The very term *bastard* is now being displaced by euphemistic terms in legal contexts. See **bastard, illegitimate child, natural child** & EUPHEMISMS.

adulterous; adulterine; adulterant; *adulterate, adj.; **adulterated.** *Adulterous* and **adulterate* both mean "of, characterized by, or pertaining to adultery," the former term being the more common. E.g.: "We think there was evidence . . . that his conduct and that of the defendant had a legitimate tendency to prove *adulterous* inclination, although insufficient to establish criminal conversation." *Bradstreet v. Wallace*, 150 N.E. 405, 406 n.4 (Mass. 1926). **Adulterate*, adj., more common in Shakespeare's day than in ours, has been relegated to the status of a NEEDLESS VARIANT.

Adulterine = (1) spurious; (2) illegal; or (3) born of adultery <adulterine bastard>. (See **adulterine bastard**.) *Adulterant* = tending to adulterate <adulterant chemicals in the mixture>. *Adulterated* = (1) corrupted or debased <an adulterated culture>; or (2) corrupted by an impure addition <the vintage wine was thoroughly adulterated once the water was added>.

adultery; fornication. *Fornication* often implies that neither party is married, but it may refer to the act of an unmarried person who has sex with a married person. *Adultery* is the proper term when referring to the act of a married person, whether or not the other participant is married. See **adulteration.**

adumbrate (= [1] to foreshadow; or [2] to outline) is a FORMAL WORD that has been called an affectation. But legal writers have considered it serviceable in formal contexts—e.g.:

- "The contours of the action for indemnity among tortfeasors were *adumbrated* by the Louisiana Supreme Court." *Ducre v. Executive Officers of Halter Marine, Inc.*, 752 F.2d 976, 984 (5th Cir. 1985).
- "The majority's holding and reasoning in *Alvarez-Gonzalez II* tended to expand the concept of functional equivalency as *adumbrated* by the Supreme Court fourteen years earlier in *Almeida-Sanchez.*" *U.S. v. Oyarzun*, 760 F.2d 570, 579 (5th Cir. 1985).

advance; advancement. Generally, *advance* refers to steady progress; *advancement* refers to a progression (1) beyond what is normal or ordinary, and (2) involving an outside agent or force. Hence, one might get an occupational *advancement*, but one speaks of the *advance* of civilization. E.g.:

- "It is a compact made between two or more nations, entered into for the common *advancement* [i.e., promotion] of their interests and the interests of civilization." *U.S. v. Samples*, 258 F. 479, 482 (W.D. Mo. 1919).
- "If the State directed seventy percent of the tax credit funds to religious schools and if those schools only admitted students of one religion, then its effect would be the unconstitutional government *advancement* of religion." *Green v. Garriott*, 212 P.3d 96, 116 (Ariz. Ct. App. 2009). (In that sentence, *only* would appear more correctly before *one.*)

In senses suggesting the action of moving up or bringing forth, *advancement* is the proper word—e.g.: "Grunert simultaneously moved for summary judgment and requested a speedy hearing and *advancement* on the court's calendar." *State v. Grunert*, 139 P.3d 1226, 1231 (Alaska 2006).

The distinction gets fuzzier in financial contexts. Although we speak (properly) of *cash advances* and *advances on royalties*, in law *advancement* takes on a sense similar to that which *advance* has in these phrases. Leff defined *advancement* in this sense as "a gift, i.e., an expenditure not legally required, made by a parent to or on behalf of a child, with intention that the value thereof be deducted from the amount that the child would otherwise receive if the parent died intestate." Arthur A. Leff, *The Leff Dictionary of Law*, 94 Yale L.J. 1855, 1952 (1985). E.g.: "The testator, in his lifetime, made gifts which were spoken of as *advancements* to a son named as a beneficiary in the will." *Trustees of Baker Univ. v. Trustees of Endowment*, 564 P.2d 472, 477 (Kan. 1977).

This legal usage is too well entrenched to allow a precisian's attempted "correction" of it: "This use led in turn to the 'hotchpot clause' in deeds and wills, similarly designed to ensure that an *advance* [read *advancement*] inter vivos to one of the class entitled to share in the estate should be brought to account." See **adduce (A).**

advance directive. See **living will.**

*advancee (= [1] one who advances; or [2] one who receives an advance payment) is an unattractive and unnecessary NEOLOGISM. Although the word has been around in law for quite some time, it smacks of newfangled LEGALESE—e.g.:

- "If to the use of the *advancee* [read *recipient*], it may be regarded as a gift or a loan according to circumstances, but if the advance is to be used in the business of the person making it, it could be regarded neither as a gift nor a loan." *Minnesota Mut. Life Ins. Co. v. Fraser*, 222 P. 228, 230 (Wash. 1924).
- "If it can be said to constitute an agreed valuation in any sense, what is valued is the share of the estate [that] the *advancee* [read *designee*?] would receive in the absence of the release." Edward W. Bailey, *Release of the Heir's Expectancy*, 33 Tex. L. Rev. 423, 427 (1955).
- "[Before] 1916, the inheritance or descent article . . . stipulated that the recipient of real property by way of advancement might elect to come into partition with other parceners 'on bringing such advancement, or the value thereof at the time such advancement was received, into hotchpot with the estate descended,' and if he did not, neither the *advancee* [read *recipient*] nor his issue was entitled to claim a share by descent if there was another child unprovided for." *Barron v. Janney*, 170 A.2d 176, 179 (Md. 1961).

See **-EE (A).**

advancement. See **advance.**

advance sheet. See **slip opinion.**

adventitious; adventitial. *Adventitious* means "added extrinsically" or "accidental." It was formerly a legal term meaning "befalling a person by fortune," and was opposed to *profectitious* (= deriving from a parent or ancestor). But these terms are now archaic except in the civil law. *Adventitious* is used today mostly in non-legal senses—e.g.:

- "We believe, given the realities of the administration of justice in the small towns of our Commonwealth and the incidental and *adventitious* nature of the contacts Respondent had with Philip Bartoe, that Respondent's split-second decision was right and in full accord with the instructions of our Supreme Court." *In re McCutcheon*, 846 A.2d 801, 815 (Pa. Ct. Jud. Disc. 2004).
- "Bozzo agreed that opining whether or not *adventitious* agents or extraneous microbial agents are present in oral polio vaccine can result in paralytic polio was not within his expertise." *Strong v. American Cyanamid Co.*, 261 S.W.3d 493, 509 (Mo. Ct. App. 2007).

Adventitial is a medical term that means "of or pertaining to a membrane that covers an organ."

ADVERBS. A. Placement of Adverbs. A fairly well-known manual on legal style long cautioned its readers to avoid splitting verb phrases with adverbs—e.g.: "He *had quickly gone* to the scene of the crime,"

---

recommending instead, "He *quickly had gone* to the scene of the crime." This nonsense apparently derives from a phobia of anything resembling a SPLIT INFINITIVE. Here a phobic writer fell into the awkward phrasing: "The task of questioning veniremen and evaluating their answers is substantially more difficult *than anything that heretofore has been attempted* [read *than anything that has heretofore been attempted* or, better yet, *than anything that has been attempted before*] in the process of jury selection." Eric Schnapper, *Taking* Witherspoon *Seriously*, 62 Tex. L. Rev. 977, 1077 (1984). See HYPERCORRECTION (H) & SUPERSTITIONS (C).

In fact, as all reputable authorities agree, typically the most proper and natural placement of an adverb is after the first auxiliary verb, in the midst of the verb phrase. E.g.: "Under such a scenario, both the Bank and the holder of the McQuinn lien *may still require* the land to secure the liens even after Sellers *have virtually bankrupted* themselves to meet the requirements of the sale contract." *Minor v. Rush*, 216 S.W.3d 210, 215 (Mo. Ct. App. 2007). For a listing of those grammatical authorities from 1782 to the present day, see *Garner's Modern American Usage* 23–24 (3d ed. 2009).

B. Awkward Adverbs. Adjectives ending in *-ly* and *-le* often make slightly cumbersome adverbs, such as *sillily, friendlily, ghastlily, uglily,* and so on. One need not be timid in writing or pronouncing such adverbs when they are called for; but if they seem unnatural, one can easily rephrase the sentence, e.g., *in a silly manner*. Words such as *timely* and *stately*, however, act as both adjectives and adverbs.

In any event, unusual adverbs are to be used sparingly. Some writers display an overfondness for them. One judicial opinion, for example, contains the adverbs *corollarily, consideredly,* and the spurious *widespreadedly. See United Medical Labs. v. Columbia Broadcasting Sys., Inc.,* 404 F.2d 706 (9th Cir. 1968). See **evidentiarily** & *widespreadedly.

C. Adjectives or Adverbs After Linking Verbs. English contains a number of linking verbs (or copulas) apart from *to be*, for example, *appear, become, look, seem, smell, taste*. These verbs connect a descriptive word with the subject; hence the descriptive word following the linking verb describes the subject and not the verb. We say *He turned professional*, not *He turned professionally*.

Legal writers frequently fall into error when they use linking verbs. One must analyze the sentence, rather than memorize a list of common linking verbs, much as this may help. Often an unexpected verb of this kind appears—e.g.: "No other testimonial privilege sweeps so *broadly* [read *sweeps so broad*]." *Trammel v. U.S.*, 445 U.S. 40, 51 (1980) (per Burger, C.J.). The writer is not describing a manner of sweeping, but instead is saying that the privilege *is* broad.

D. Redundantly Formed Adverbs. Some adverbial forms are incorrectly formed by adding *-ly* to words that already function as adverbs. See HYPERCORRECTION (D), **doubtless,** *muchly, overly* & **thus (B).**

E. No Hyphens with Adverbs Ending in *-ly*. See PHRASAL ADJECTIVES (A).

adversary, adj.; **adversarial;** *adversarious;* **adversative; adversive; adverse.** *Adversary*, which can act as both noun and adjective, is the legal term used in phrases such as *an adversary relationship*. E.g.: "The need to develop all relevant facts in the *adversary system* is both fundamental and comprehensive." *U.S. v. Nixon*, 418 U.S. 683, 709 (1974) (per Burger, C.J.). For the term *adversary* and its near-synonyms, see **opponent.**

Until recently, *adversarial* was not listed in most modern dictionaries, though it is fairly common as a near-equivalent of the adjective *adversary*. E.g.:

- "The evolution of this area of the law has been and will remain a product of the interaction of two *adversarial* forces—prosecutors who seek to exclude all scrupled jurors, and defense counsel anxious to retain them." Eric Schnapper, *Taking* Witherspoon *Seriously*, 62 Tex. L. Rev. 977, 1077–78 (1984).
- "Rarely does this type of *adversarial* [read *adversary*] relationship exist between school authorities and pupils." *New Jersey v. T.L.O.*, 469 U.S. 325, 349–50 (1985) (Powell, J., concurring).

In fact, *adversarial* and *adversary* have begun to undergo DIFFERENTIATION: *adversarial* connotes animosity <adversarial conferences>, whereas *adversary* is a neutral, clinical word.

Adversarious (= hostile), though listed in the *OED*, has dropped from the language. *Adversative* is a term of grammar and logic meaning "expressing an antithesis or opposition" <adversative conjunction>. *Adversive* is an anatomical term for "opposite." See **adverse.**

adversary procedure. See **accusatorial (A).**

adversary proceeding = a lawsuit that is ancillary to a main bankruptcy case. E.g.: "The Trust originally disputed the Colleges' request for payment on certain claims and commenced *adversary proceedings* in bankruptcy court." *Claremont McKenna Coll. v. Asbestos Settlement Trust*, 613 F.3d 1318, 1319 (11th Cir. 2010) (per Goldberg, J.).

adverse; averse. Both may take the preposition *to*; *averse* also takes *from*. To be *averse to* something is to have feelings against it <averse to risk>. The term usually describes a person's attitude. To be *adverse to* something—the phrase usually refers to things and not to people—is to be turned in opposition against it <China was adverse to Japan during World War II>.

Adverse is used as an adjective in the phrase *adverse party* (= opposing party) in reference to persons, but seldom elsewhere. In reference to circumstances, *adverse* means "potentially afflictive or calamitous," but most great triumphs come in the face of adverse conditions.

Adverse(ly) to for *against* is a slight pomposity—e.g.:

- "All of these questions were determined *adversely to* [read *against*] the appellants in the lower Court." *Trustee and Bank Both Held Liable to Beneficiaries of Trust*, 63 Banking L.J. 291, 295 (1946). (In that sentence, the second word ought to be deleted. See **of.**)

- "In *Kimberlin I*, the District Court ruled *adversely to* [read *against*] appellants on the clearly established law issue." *Kimberlin v. Quinlan*, 199 F.3d 496, 500 (D.C. Cir. 1999).

adverseness; adversity. For purposes of Article III federal jurisdiction, under the case-or-controversy requirement, should one speak of the need for *adversity* or the need for *adverseness*? The Supreme Court has used both forms—e.g.:

- "Have the appellants alleged such a personal stake in the outcome of the controversy as to assure that concrete *adverseness* which sharpens the presentation of issues upon which the court so largely depends for illumination of difficult constitutional questions?" *Baker v. Carr*, 369 U.S. 186, 204 (1962) (per Brennan, J.).
- "So long as the court does not require such acceptance [of a defendant's tender in settlement of the individual putative class representative's claim], the individual is required to prove his case and the requisite Art. III *adversity* continues." *Deposit Guaranty Nat. Bank v. Roper*, 445 U.S. 326, 341 (1980) (Rehnquist, J., concurring).

The more usual word choice in this context is *adverseness*, which makes sense because *adversity* so often means "misfortune, poverty, and trouble."

The same issue comes up in the field of legal ethics, in the context of the attorney–client privilege. And in that context, the overwhelming favorite is *adversity of interest*, not *adverseness of interest*. But for the reason mentioned above—the promotion of DIFFERENTIATION in meaning, given that *adversity* already has a completely different and well-established meaning—preference should be given to *adverseness*.

adversive. See **adversary.**

advert; avert. To *advert* to something is to refer to it, to bring it up in speech or writing. In AmE, the word is best reserved for formal contexts. In BrE, it appears with some frequency— e.g.: "I must *advert* to the pain suffered and to be suffered by the appellant as a result of the car accident." *Baker v. Willoughby*, [1970] A.C. 467 (H.L.). (See **allude (A).**) The word should not be used in its etymological sense "to turn to," as here: "*Before adverting to* [read *Before turning to*] the factual setting, we briefly outline the legal context in which the issue of fraudulent transfer arises." *U.S. v. Chapman*, 756 F.2d 1237, 1240 (5th Cir. 1985).

To *avert* is to ward off, turn away, or avoid. So a national leader who has failed to *avert* a political scandal might *avert* his or her eyes—e.g.:

- "The abatement rule *averts* the unnecessary and unjustified cost to society of additional criminal litigation, thereby also *averting* a public perception that the judicial process is inefficient." Note, State v. McDonald: *Death of a Criminal Defendant Pending Appeal in Wisconsin*, 1989 Wis. L. Rev. 811, 833.
- "Although we attempt to construe statutes and rules in a way that *averts* needless constitutional tension . . . we cannot create harmony where none exists." *State v. Hansen*, 160 P.3d 166, 168 (Ariz. 2007).

See **avert.**

advertent negligence. See **recklessness.**

advertise. A. And *advertize. The former spelling is standard (AmE, BrE).

B. And *solicit*. To *advertise* is to promote the sale of something by drawing the general public's attention to it. To *solicit* is to seek business from a particular individual or a defined group. The difference is important under the Model Rules of Professional Conduct and state ethics rules. Generally, attorneys may *advertise* their services to the public—with a few restrictions—but may not directly *solicit* clients: "One distinction that makes sense is to view *advertising* as appeals to potential clients generally, as through television or a newspaper advertisement, while *solicitation* focuses on a specific population of potential clients with identified needs. Or we may further refine the distinction by using *solicitation* only where the lawyer's appeal is to a very small group of individuals—say, the dozen injured in a building collapse—rather than to a large group but much smaller than the public generally (the thousands who may have been harmed by a drug's side effects)." Stephen Gillers, *Regulation of the Legal Profession* 403 (2009).

advice. See **advisement.**

*advisatory. See **advisory.**

advise. A. And *counsel*. Both verbs mean "to recommend a course of action." *Advise* often implies professional or technical expertise, but the advice may also be mundane, involving any aspect of human life <they advised us not to take this route to Wrentham!>. *Counsel* suggests a greater degree of accumulated wisdom and deliberative care, and it connotes weightier decisions to be made about matters of greater importance <Tribe counseled the President about Supreme Court nominees>.

B. In Commercialese. In commercial contexts, *advise* takes on a meaning with which nonlawyers are generally unfamiliar. It means "to announce; give formal notice of." E.g.:

- "The former letter of credit *was advised through* Banco di Roma, and the latter letter of credit *was advised through* Monte dei Paschi di Siena." *Lantz Int'l Corp. v. Industria Termotecnica Campana*, 358 F.Supp. 510, 512 n.4 (E.D. Pa. 1973).
- "The confirmed, irrevocable letter of credit *was advised* and made payable *through* Morgan Guaranty Trust Company in New York, with instructions that the credit *be advised* through Fidelity International Bank in New York." *Texas Trading & Milling Corp. v. Federal Republic of Nigeria*, 500 F.Supp. 320, 321 (S.D.N.Y. 1980).

C. For *tell* or *say*. This usage is a pomposity to be avoided—e.g.:

- " 'I had a conversation with Mr. Willard Bunch, who is a member of the Public Defender's Commission, . . . and *I was advised by him* [read *he told me*] that the Public Defender's Commission has zero money, no money at all to comply with any orders such as this Court might enter.' "

Williamson v. Vardeman, 674 F.2d 1211, 1213 (8th Cir. 1982) (quoting the appellant).

- "The court also *advised* [read *told*] the audience of the differences between pleas of not guilty, no contest, and guilty and the possible dispositions for second-degree and first-degree misdemeanors." *Finney v. State*, 9 So.3d 741, 743 (Fla. Dist. Ct. App. 2009).

D. And *instruct*. In traditional BrE, barristers are typically said to *advise* solicitors (or clients through solicitors), whereas solicitors *instruct* barristers. See **attorney (A).**

advisedly means, not "intentionally," but "after careful consideration."

advisement; advice. Judges frequently take matters *under advisement*, meaning that they will consider and deliberate on a particular question before the court. E.g.:

- "The Commission also alleged that Judge Clark failed to report timely or accurately to the Judicial Administrator that fourteen of these nineteen cases had been *taken under advisement*." *In re Clark*, 866 So.2d 782, 783 (La. 2004).
- "[The] court . . . decided to take the matter *under advisement* to determine whether the Court may confirm a plan that provides for bifurcation of a 910-day vehicle claim of a secured creditor who has not objected to the plan." *In re Garner*, 399 B.R. 267, 269 (Bankr. D. Utah 2009).

Advisement is best not used outside the legal idiom for *advice* or *advising* <the advising of entry-level officers>.

adviser; *advisor. The *-er* spelling is sanctioned over the *-or* spelling in the dictionaries. Note, however, that the adjectival form is *advisory*. See **-ER (A).**

advisory; *advisatory. The second is a NEEDLESS VARIANT of *advisory*, which commonly appears in phrases such as *advisory opinion*, *advisory capacity*, and *advisory council*.

advocacy; *advocation. The first is the art or work of an advocate; the second was formerly the term in Scots law for an appellate court's review of lower-court decisions. **Advocation* should not be used, although occasionally it is, where *advocacy* would suffice.

advocate; *advocator. The second is a NEEDLESS VARIANT.

*advocation. See **advocacy.**

advocatory = of or pertaining to an advocate. Hence it corresponds to *advocacy*, not **advocation*. See **advocacy.**

***advocatus diaboli*,** the Latin term for *devil's advocate*, is an example of highfalutin humor and should be used cautiously if at all. Its opposite is *advocatus dei*.

advowson. This archaic legal term, though suggestive of a type of person, refers to a property right in an ecclesiastical office. The right is transferable and inheritable in perpetuity.

AE is a remnant of the Latin digraph, formerly ligatured (æ), appearing in such words as *aegis*

and *praetor*. In most Latinate words in which this digraph once appeared, the initial vowel has been dropped. One sees this tendency still at work in *(a)esthetic*, *(a)eon*, and *(a)ether*. Compare the retention of the digraphs in BrE (e.g., *anaesthetic* and *foetus*) with the shortened forms *anesthetic* and *fetus*, which are prevalent in AmE. See **predial.**

aegis (= auspices; sponsorship) was originally a mythological term meaning "protective shield" or "defensive armor." The word is now used exclusively in figurative senses, usually in the phrase *under the aegis* (not **with the aegis*). One must be careful not to confuse *aegis* with *auspices* (= sponsorship; support). Here the term is used correctly:

- "What has been done regularly under the *aegis* of the law [must] be considered valid." *Dripps v. Dripps*, 366 So.2d 544, 548 (La. 1978).
- "Contracts involving interstate commerce and containing an arbitration provision fall under the *aegis* of federal law." David R. Collins, Comment, *Shrinkwrap, Clickwrap, and Other Software License Agreements*, 111 W. Va. L. Rev. 531, 572 (2009).

Be careful, too, not to confuse *aegis* with leadership in general.

aesthetic; *esthetic. Although some dictionaries have long recorded **esthetic* as the primary form in AmE, the form *aesthetic* remains more common in AmE and BrE alike.

aetiology. See **etiology.**

affect; effect. A. *Affect* for *effect*. In ordinary usage, *affect* is always a verb; it means "to influence; to have an effect on." *Effect*, as suggested by its use in that definition, is primarily a noun meaning "result" or "consequence." To *affect* something is to have an *effect* on it. (See **impact.**) As a verb, *effect* means "to bring about; produce" <they could not effect a coup>.

Affect is often misused for the noun *effect*—e.g.:

- "The laws of New Jersey shall control the *affect* [read *effect*] of the agreement." *Developers Small Bus. Inv. Corp. v. Hoeckle*, 395 F.2d 80, 84 (9th Cir. 1968) (quoting a contract).
- "These side *affects* [read *effects*] can include suicide, drug abuse, homelessness, prostitution, and the risk of HIV/AIDS." Sarah E. Valentine, *Queer Kids: A Comprehensive Annotated Legal Bibliography on Lesbian, Gay, Bisexual, Transgender, and Questioning Youth*, 19 Yale J.L. & Feminism 449, 470 (2008).
- "In his decision, ALJ Stefan addressed plaintiff's claims of pain but noted plaintiff's acknowledgment to her care provider that her medications have helped to relieve her symptoms, and cause her no side *affects* [read *effects*]." *Pardee v. Astrue*, 631 F.Supp.2d 200, 221 (N.D.N.Y. 2009).

Likewise, *effect* is sometimes misused for *affect*. See **effect.**

B. *Effect* for *affect*. *Effect* (= to bring about) is often misused for *affect* (= to influence, have an effect on). The blunder is widespread—e.g.:

- "Opponents say it would *effect* [read *affect*] only a small number of people—in New York an estimated 300 criminals a year—and would have little effect on the causes of crime." Ian Fisher, *Why "3-Strike" Sentencing Is a Solid Hit This Year*, N.Y. Times, 25 Jan. 1994, at A16.

- "It would also *effect* [read *affect*] pensions tied to the rate of inflation and union contracts with automatic adjustments based on inflation." Adam Clymer, *As Parties Skirmish over Budget, Greenspan Offers a Painless Cure*, N.Y. Times, 11 Jan. 1995, at A1.

- "Since counsel's failure to investigate and present mitigating evidence would probably have *effected* [read *affected*] the outcome, defendant was denied a constitutional right." Ellen Marrus, *Effective Assistance of Counsel in the Wonderland of "Kiddie Court,"* 39 Crim. L. Bull. No. 4 (Summer 2003), at 1, 1.

- "Because of the impermanence of economic conditions *effecting* [read *affecting*] decisions 'involving wages, hours or other conditions of employment,' the subject of the initiative petition, collective bargaining and arbitration, was administrative." *In re Initiative Pet. No. 27 of City of Oklahoma City*, 82 P.3d 90, 93 (Okla. 2003).

- "If repatriation is effectively a 'death sentence,' then it would *effect* [read *affect*] a person's interest in his own life, which the Supreme Court has held to be a 'fundamental interest.'" Kit Johnson, *Patients Without Borders: Extralegal Deportation by Hospitals*, 78 U. Cin. L. Rev. 657, 674 (2009).

It could be that the widespread misuse of *impact* is partly an attempt to sidestep the problem of when to use *effect* and when to use *affect*. See **impact**.

affectable. So spelled—not **affectible*.

AFFECTATION, LITERARY. See PURPLE PROSE & LITERARY ALLUSION (B). See also BIBLICAL AFFECTATION.

affected, adj.; **affective; affectional; affectionate.** *Affected*, as an adjective, means "assumed artificially; pretended" <a highly affected accent>; *affective* = emotional <bipolar affective disorder>; *affectional* = pertaining to affection <affectional display>; and *affectionate* = loving, fond <affectionate children>.

Just as *affect* is sometimes misused for *effect*, *affective* is sometimes wrongly placed where *effective* belongs (especially in the mistaken phrase **affective date*)—e.g.:

- "Nor was the formation of new stipulated premium companies prohibited during the several months that elapsed between the adoption of the Code and its *affective* [read *effective*] date." *Drummond Citizens Ins. Co. v. U.S.*, 298 F.Supp. 692, 697 (E.D. Ark. 1969).

- "The new statute has governed property disposition in divorce and annulment actions since its *affective* [read *effective*] date." *Pitsenberger v. Pitsenberger*, 410 A.2d 1052, 1055 (Md. 1980).

We might prefer to call this a typographical error rather than an ignorant bungle. See **affect**.

affection; affectation. The first means "love, fondness"; the second, "pretentious, artificial behavior." In Elizabethan English, these words were used more or less interchangeably, but now each has acquired its own distinct sense—which is good for the language.

Affectation doctrine is sometimes seen for *affects doctrine* in the context of American constitutional law, specifically of the Commerce Clause. E.g.: "For the essence of the *affectation doctrine* [read *"affects" doctrine* or *effects doctrine*] was that the exact location of this line made no difference, if the forbidden effects flowed across it to the injury of interstate commerce." *Mandeville Island Farms, Inc. v. American Crystal Sugar Co.*, 334 U.S. 219, 232 (1948) (per Rutledge, J.). *Affects* is the correct word because the test is whether the activity "affects" commerce. Because the noun corresponding to *affect* (= to influence) is *effect*—not *affectation*—a better phrasing would be *effects doctrine* (i.e., "that has effects"), but it has not gained currency. See **affect** & **effect**.

affectional; affectionate. See **affected**.

affective. See **affected**.

affeer; amerce. Both words mean generally "to fine." Specifically, *affeer* = to fix the amount of (a fine) (*W3*). The variant spellings **affeere* and **affere* should be avoided. *Amerce* = to fine arbitrarily (*OED*), meaning that the amount of the fine is not prescribed by statute, but rather is lodged in the discretion of the court. Etymologically speaking, when being *amerced*, one is "at the mercy" of the court. (For near-synonyms of *affeer* and *amerce*, see **penalize**.)

The noun forms are *affeerment* and *amercement*—**amerciament* having gone the way that all NEEDLESS VARIANTS should. *Amerce* has no agent-noun form. *Affeeror* and **affeerer* are competing forms, the *-or* spelling perhaps the better one because it is more distinctly pronounceable.

affeeror; **affeerer. See **affeer** & **penalize**.

affianced. See **affined**.

affiant /ə-fī-ənt/, a term that began as an Americanism in the mid-19th century, ordinarily means "one who gives an affidavit." More broadly, and less accurately, it refers to any deponent. See **further affiant sayeth naught** & **deponent**.

*afficionado. See **aficionado**.

affidavit [L. "he swore"] is ordinarily a noun referring to a voluntary declaration of facts written down and sworn to by the declarant before an officer authorized to administer oaths. For more, see **evidence (A).**

Occasionally, however, lawyers have used the word as a verb. But a better choice is invariably available—e.g.:

- "This counsel later testified that the reason for filing the Notice of Change of Judge was 'personal to us and the plaintiff, [and that] we *affidavited or noticed* [read *filed an affidavit and notice of*] that change of judge, on Judge Patterson . . . .'" *Hickox v. Superior Court*, 505 P.2d 1086, 1087 (Ariz. Ct. App. 1973) (quoting counsel).

An asterisk (*) precedes words and phrases that are invariably inferior forms.

- "Noteworthily missing from this record, however, is any *affidavited* [read *sworn*] assertion by a representative of the banks." *In re Drexel Burnham Lambert Group Inc.*, 113 B.R. 830, 840 (Bankr. S.D.N.Y. 1990).

The phonetic misspelling **affidavid* is not uncommon. For a redundancy involving this word, see **sworn affidavit.**

affiliation, in BrE, refers to a father's maintenance of illegitimate children. E.g.:

- "The mother has the right to the custody of her illegitimate children, and is bound to maintain them. She may obtain an *affiliation* order against the father from the local police court, either before the child is born or within twelve months after the birth." Anon., *The Home Counsellor* 172 ([London: Odhams Press] ca. 1940–1945).
- "There is the rule [that] requires the testimony of the plaintiff in an action for breach of promise of marriage, and the applicant in an *affiliation* case, to be corroborated by independent evidence." Edward Jenks, *The Book of English Law* 77 (P.B. Fairest ed., 6th ed. 1967).

affined; affianced. *Affined* = closely related; connected. Archaically, *affined* means "obligated." *Affianced* = engaged, betrothed.

affinity. See **kinship.**

affirm. Usually only judgments are *affirmed* by appellate courts; cases are *remanded*; and opinions or decisions are *approved* or *disapproved*. (See JUDGMENTS, APPELLATE-COURT.) The practice of writing "The trial court was *affirmed*" is informally an acceptable ellipsis for "The trial court's judgment was *affirmed*," but such phrasing should not appear in formal legal writing. E.g.: "Had the trial judge followed his initial decision and overruled the motion for new trial without expressing any desire for leniency, *he would be affirmed* [read *his judgment would be affirmed*]." *Equitable Gen. Ins. Co. v. Yates*, 684 S.W.2d 669, 671 (Tex. 1984).

On the use of *affirm* in the sense of taking an oath, see **swear.**

affirmance; affirmation. There is, unfortunately, some overlap of these terms. Yet a useful rule might be formulated: when an appellate court affirms a lower court's judgment, there is an *affirmance*.

In all other contexts, *affirmation* is the preferable term. E.g.: "Finally, we refer to the restatement and *affirmation* of the doctrine in *Hood v. Francis*." *Bank of New York v. Black*, 139 A.2d 393, 397 (N.J. 1958). In the following sentences, *affirmance* is used where *affirmation* would be better:

- "The court held that the instrument was a conveyance and a recognition, acceptance and *affirmance* [read *affirmation*] of the devise, and not a renunciation." *Coomes v. Finegan*, 7 N.W.2d 729, 733 (Iowa 1943).
- "The long established recognition in Massachusetts of the doctrine of independent significance makes unnecessary statutory *affirmance* [read *affirmation*] of its application to pour-over trusts." *Second Bank-State St. Trust Co. v. Pinion*, 170 N.E.2d 350, 354 (Mass. 1960).

The opposite error (*affirmation* for *affirmance*) also occurs, though the appellate idiom has long been established—e.g.:

- "The technical question [was] whether the state appellate court's *affirmation* [read *affirmance*] of the judgment upon the one point of waiver also affirm[ed] all other findings of the state trial court." *Mershon Co. v. Pachmayr*, 220 F.2d 879, 883 (9th Cir. 1955).
- "The Louisiana Supreme Court reversed the appellate court's *affirmation* [read *affirmance*] of summary judgment." *Bradford v. Coody*, 6 So.3d 815, 819 (La. Ct. App. 2008).

Cf. **disaffirmation.**

Quite apart from its ordinary meaning, *affirmation* has a specialized legal sense: "a formal and solemn declaration, having the same weight and invested with the same responsibilities as an oath, by one who conscientiously declines to take an oath" (*OED*). Many American jurisdictions now have statutes permitting *affirmations* under circumstances in which obtaining a notary public's acknowledgment would be inconvenient. The person *affirming* is termed an *affirmant*. See **affirmant & oath.**

affirmant; deponent. One who testifies by deposition and swears to the truth of the testimony is termed a *deponent*. One who, instead of swearing or taking an oath, affirms or solemnly states that the testimony is true, is termed an *affirmant*.

affirmation. See **affirmance.**

affirmative, in the; negative, in the. These phrases have been criticized as jargonistic and pompous. (*See, e.g.,* Quiller-Couch's statement quoted under JARGON (B).) They appear frequently in legal writing and in other types of formal prose. E.g.:

- "The Sixth Circuit, when confronted with the identical question, answered *in the affirmative* and permitted the use of this same deposition." *Dartez v. Fibreboard Corp.*, 765 F.2d 456, 462 (5th Cir. 1985).
- "The sole question raised on this appeal is whether the Texas rule that a defendant prove duress by a preponderance of the evidence violates the due process clause of the fourteenth amendment. Answering *in the negative*, we affirm." *Davis v. McCotter*, 766 F.2d 203, 204 (5th Cir. 1985).

This phrasing is probably better than the closest alternative: "We answer the second certified question 'No.'" *Anthony v. American Gen. Fin. Servs., Inc.*, 697 S.E.2d 166, 175 (Ga. 2010). In the formal context of judicial opinions, *in the affirmative* and *in the negative* should be allowed to exist peacefully. But when these phrases are used of mundane questions in mundane situations, they look foolish.

affirmative action. The phrase is sometimes used generically to denote "a positive step taken," as well as more specifically to denote "an attempt to reverse or mitigate past racial discrimination." *Compare* 15 U.S.C. § 2622(2)(b) (1988) ("the Secretary shall order . . . the person who committed such violation to take *affirmative action* to abate the violation") *with* 29 U.S.C. § 791(b) (1988) ("each department . . .

shall . . . submit . . . an *affirmative action* program for the hiring, placement and advancement of individuals with handicaps").

affirmative pregnant. See **negative pregnant.**

affixture; affixation; *affixion. *Affixture* = the state of being affixed; *affixation* = the act of affixing or the use of an affix. **Affixion = affixation* or *affixture,* but it adds nothing to either; it should be avoided as a NEEDLESS VARIANT.

afflatus; *afflation; *inflatus. For the sense "inspiration" or "supernatural impulse," *afflatus* is the standard term. E.g.:

- "The decisions under the revenue acts have little weight as against legislation under the *afflatus* of the Eighteenth Amendment." *Danovitz v. U.S.,* 281 U.S. 389, 397 (1930) (per Holmes, J.).
- "We are well aware of the fact that counsel cannot be expected to have an *afflatus* through which he conjures up a wonderful story, without the help of his client." *Smith v. Stewart,* 140 F.3d 1263, 1269 (9th Cir. 1998).
- "In this case respondent's divine *afflatus* was the cause of his coming to terms with his conduct and why it was wrong." *Attorney Grievance Comm'n of Maryland v. Weiss,* 886 A.2d 606, 619 (Md. 2005).

*Inflatus and **afflation* are NEEDLESS VARIANTS. The plural of *afflatus* is *afflatuses,* not **afflati.* See PLURALS (A).

afflict. See **inflict.**

affluent /af-loo-ənt/ and *affluence* /af-loo-ənts/ are preferably accented on the first syllable, not the second.

afford. See **accord.**

*affranchise. See **free** & **franchise,** vb.

affray; fray. Both terms, though somewhat quaint, are still used in legal opinions. *Affray* is classically defined as "unpremeditated fighting in a public place that tends to disturb the public peace." E.g.: "To some extent, crimes such as riot, violent disorder, and *affray* appear as inchoate offences of violence or even actual offences of violence." Andrew Ashworth, *Principles of Criminal Law* 35 (1991).

There is some dispute over whether an affray must be in public. From the late 18th century onward, legal writers discussing *affray* said—mistakenly, it seems—that the fighting must occur in public. The germ of the error began with Blackstone's definition of *affray* in 1769 as "the fighting of two or more persons in some public place, to the terror of His Majesty's subjects: for, if the fighting be in private, it is no *affray* but an assault." 4 William Blackstone, *Commentaries on the Laws of England* 145 (1769). In 1822, the first edition of Archbold's *Pleading and Evidence in Criminal Cases* (p. 337) asserted, without support, that the allegation "in a public street or highway" should be charged in the indictment and proved. But the House of Lords has held that Archbold incorrectly grafted this requirement onto the law of affray—that an affray need not be in a public place. *See Button v. Director of Public Prosecutions,* [1966] A.C. 591, 608, 627 (H.L.).

Yet the idea that an *affray* must be public still holds sway in most American jurisdictions. So a leading criminal-law text states: "At common law an *affray* is a mutual fight in a public place to the terror or alarm of the people." Rollin M. Perkins & Ronald N. Boyce, *Criminal Law* 479 (3d ed. 1982).

affreighter. See **charterer.**

affreightment; affretement. Meaning "the hiring of a ship to carry cargo," *affreightment* is standard in common-law countries and in Louisiana (a civil-law jurisdiction). E.g.: "Owners will be more likely to permit their charterers to enter freely into contracts of *affreightment* if the owners know that no 'secret liens' will arise from obscure provisions in subagreements." *Cardinal Shipping Corp. v. M/S Seisho Maru,* 744 F.2d 461, 471 (5th Cir. 1984). *Affretement* is the spelling used in French civil law.

aficionado is often misspelled **afficionado,* as in *Butts v. National Collegiate Athletic Ass'n,* 751 F.2d 609, 613 (3d Cir. 1984).

afore (= before) is a dead ARCHAISM except in the terms **aforesaid,* **aforementioned,* and *aforethought.* Words like **aforedescribed* need not be rescued from oblivion. See **above (A),** **aforesaid* & ***above-mentioned.**

*aforesaid; *aforementioned. These LEGALISMS have little or no justification in modern writing. They often appear in spoofs and complaints—e.g.: "Individual laws . . . may be complicated and forbiddingly so, with the endless paragraphs, their *aforesaids* and *provided howevers.*" Lon L. Fuller, *Anatomy of the Law* 14–15 (1968).

*Aforesaid or **aforementioned* is unnecessary when the reference to what has already been named is clear—e.g.:

- "During her employment she was repeatedly exposed to . . . paint fumes and fiberglass dust in the course of performing her job duties sanding fiberglass fenders. Shortly after leaving Goodyear, appellant filed a claim for workers' compensation benefits, alleging she was unable to work because of bronchitis and injury to her lungs as a result of her exposure to *the aforementioned* [read *these*] fumes and dust particles." *State ex rel. Case v. Industrial Comm'n of Ohio,* 504 N.E.2d 30, 31–32 (Ohio 1986).
- "The complaint alleges that defendants were negligent by . . . failure to advise Plaintiff of the toxic and dangerous characteristics of the chemicals they manufactured and used . . . [and] failing . . . to publish, adopt, and enforce a safety plan concerning exposure to *said aforementioned* [read *these*] dangerous products." *Bingham v. Terminix Int'l Co. LP,* 850 F.Supp. 516, 517 n.2 (S.D. Miss. 1994).

- "For *the aforementioned* [read *these*] reasons, the law's provision for district fiscal officers will probably do little to stem fraud by superintendents." Lydia Segal, *Corruption Moves to the Center*, 36 Harv. J. on Legis. 323, 344 (1999).

See **above-mentioned.**

Worse yet, *aforesaid is a word of imprecision: it sometimes refers to what immediately preceded, to what came just before that, or to everything that has come before. When the reference is intended to be vague, it would be better to use *above-stated* or some other equivalent that is less stilted and legalistic. See FORBIDDEN WORDS (A) & **said** (E).

The word *aforesaid is, of course, a past-participial combination (*afore* + *said*) that is almost always used adjectivally <aforesaid land>. Occasionally, however, it appears as the past participle of a verb: "The association secretly and with intent to deprive appellant of the opportunity of purchasing said property, and with the intent to profit through the information obtained as *aforesaid*, immediately began to negotiate with the owner for the purchase of said property." The literary quality of that sentence speaks for quality of the participial use of *aforesaid. Cf. **said** (A).

aforethought (= thought of in advance) is now used only in the phrase *malice aforethought*. It is essentially synonymous with *premeditated* or *prepense*. See **malice aforethought,** POSTPOSITIVE ADJECTIVES, **prepense** & **willfulness.**

a fortiori /ah-fohr-shee-**ohr**-ee/ is an argumentative term meaning "by even greater force of logic; so much the more." The phrase can be used effectively, but only if you're sure that your readers will get it—e.g.: "If an act is not a civil wrong, it cannot, *a fortiori*, be criminal." Elihu Lauterpacht, *International Law Reports* 387 (1972). (Eng.)

The emphatic form of the term is *a multo fortiori* (= by far the stronger reason).

Legal writers sometimes use *a fortiori* as an adjective, a usage to be resisted—e.g.:

- "We have set forth the other two lines of possible proof only to suggest the *a fortiori* [read *even stronger*] position presented in the instant case." *Hall v. E. I. Du Pont De Nemours & Co.*, 345 F.Supp. 353, 374 (E.D.N.Y. 1972).
- "Clearly, if laws depend so heavily on public acquiescence, the case of conventions is an *a fortiori* [read *even more compelling*] one." P.S. Atiyah, *Law and Modern Society* 59 (1983).
- "The trial court used *Asherman* merely as an *a fortiori* [read *even stronger*] argument rather than suggesting that it was the proper standard." *State v. Hayles*, 727 A.2d 762, 768 n.2 (Conn. App. Ct. 1999).

after-acquired (= obtained after a certain [specified] time) is ordinarily placed before the noun it modifies—e.g.:

- "In Texas, a chattel mortgage upon *after-acquired* personal property is valid where it is clear that the parties contemplated that [the] property would be acquired by the mortgagor and the mortgage sufficiently identifies the property." *Pearson v. Rapstine*, 203 F.2d 313, 314–15 (5th Cir. 1953).

- "Alan Schwartz has argued that a default rule [that] automatically gave a debtor's first major lender a blanket lien to all current and *after-acquired* assets might provide an efficient form of protection against debt dilution." Richard Squire, *The Case for Symmetry in Creditors' Rights*, 118 Yale L.J. 806, 859 (2009).

afterborn, adj., = born after (a certain event, such as the father's death or the birth of a sibling) <an afterborn child>. The word is also used as a noun in pretermitted-child statutes; it means "a child born after the execution of a will" <all afterborns were excluded from the will>. It's a solid word—not hyphenated.

aftereffect. One word.

***after having [+ past participle].** This construction is ordinarily incorrect for *after* [+ present participle]—e.g.:

- "*After having passed* [read *After passing*] a general educational test and given evidence of good character, the candidate must procure himself to be admitted as a student at one of the four Inns of Court above named." Edward Jenks, *The Book of English Law* 66 (P.B. Fairest ed., 6th ed. 1967).
- "The flurry of laches litigation, *after having gone* [read *after going*] on for the better part of ten years, began to subside after the mid-1960's." Grant Gilmore & Charles L. Black Jr., *The Law of Admiralty* 774 (2d ed. 1975).
- "*After having survived* [read *After surviving* or *Having survived*] eight years of attacks during the Reagan administration, the Legal Services Corp. . . . still faces challenges." Nat'l L.J., 14 Oct. 1991, at 1.

afterward; afterword. *Afterward* is an adverb meaning "later" <there was a reception afterward>. *Afterword* is a comment or conclusion that follows the main text in a book <the author's mentor contributed an afterword>.

against. See **contra, versus** & **as against.**

against nature. See EUPHEMISMS & **unnatural.**

against the peace. This phrase was traditionally used in a charging instrument for a misdemeanor, just as *feloniously* was used in a felony indictment. Sometimes the phrase is elaborated to *against the peace of the king* (or *against the king's peace*) or *against the peace and dignity of the state.*

aged ____ years old. A REDUNDANCY. Better phrasings are *age 13*, *13 years old*, and *13 years of age.* The noun is *13-year-old.*

***ageing; aging.** See MUTE E.

agency, as a TERM OF ART, refers to any relationship in which one person (called an *agent*) acts for another (called a *principal*) in commercial or business transactions. Nonlawyers are largely unfamiliar with *agency* used in this way, although they understand the personal noun *agent* as meaning "representative."

Why exactly, you may wonder, is a government agency called an *agency*? The answer has to do with the principal–agent relationship: "Government taxes, spends, builds, paves, educates, punishes, regulates, and so on. Those who actually do this work are the agents of the government, hence the word 'agencies.' In a sense, they are necessary if government is to do anything." John M. Rogers, Michael P. Healy & Ronald J. Krotoszynski Jr., *Administrative Law* 1 (2d ed. 2008).

agenda is (1) the plural form of the Latin noun *agendum*, which means "something to be done" (another, less proper plural of *agendum* being *agendums*); and more commonly, (2) a singular noun meaning "a list of things to be done" or "a program." The plural of *agenda* in sense 2 is *agendas*; decrying *agendas* as a double plural is bootless.

Yet all careful writers should avoid the erroneous form **agendae*, the result of HYPERCORRECTION—e.g.: "Mr. Douglas . . . prepared *agendae* [read *agendas*] for meetings with the trustee and his attorneys." *In re New England Fish Co.*, 33 B.R. 413, 416 (Bankr. W.D. Wash. 1983).

agent; servant. "The words *agent* and *servant* are not synonyms; nevertheless they both relate to voluntary action under employment." *Lemmon v. State*, 3 A.2d 299, 300 (N.J. 1938). An *agent* is a business representative who handles contractual arrangements between the principal and third persons. A *servant*, by contrast, is an employee whose function is to render service, not to create contractual obligations. In the modern legal idiom, *servant* has been almost entirely displaced by *employee*. See **agency** & **employer and employee.**

AGENT NOUNS, FALSE. See -ER (B).

age of capacity; age of consent; age of majority; age of reason. All these terms share the general sense "the age at which a person is legally capable (of doing something)." But over time, each term has assumed a specific sense in a particular context. In the following discussion, the numerical ages listed are established by statute and may vary from jurisdiction to jurisdiction.

Age of capacity, usu. 18, denotes the age when one is legally capable of agreeing to a contract, executing a will, maintaining a lawsuit, and the like.

Age of majority, usu. 18, includes the rights attained at the age of capacity, but is broader because it also includes civil and political rights, esp. the right to vote. See **majority (D).**

Age of consent, usu. 16, denotes the age when one is legally capable of agreeing to marriage (without parental consent) or to sexual intercourse so that, regarding the latter, intercourse with someone under the age of consent is statutory rape. See **statutory rape.**

Age of reason denotes the age when one is able to distinguish right from wrong and is therefore legally capable of committing a crime or tort. It varies from 7 to 14. Seven years is usually the age below which a child is conclusively presumed not to have committed a crime or tort, while 14 years is usually the age below which a rebuttable presumption applies. For related terms, see **child, infant, minority (A)** & **nonage.**

aggrandize; **engrandize; **ingrandize. The last two are NEEDLESS VARIANTS of the first.

aggravate for *annoy* or *irritate*, though documented as existing since the 1600s, has never gained the approval of stylists and should be avoided in formal writing. Strictly speaking, *aggravate* means "to make worse; exacerbate" <writing a second apology might just aggravate the problem>. This meaning obtains in many legal phrases, such as *aggravated assault*. In its proper sense, *aggravate* is opposed to *mitigate* or *extenuate*—e.g.:

- "Here the indignity was of an *aggravated* sort; it occurred at a public place and in the presence of a large number of people." *Anderson v. Pantages Theater Co.*, 194 P. 813, 816 (Wash. 1921).
- "[The state cannot make] the murder of a white victim an *aggravating* circumstance in capital sentencing." *McCleskey v. Kemp*, 753 F.2d 877, 891 (11th Cir. 1985).

Even the brilliant Justice Oliver Wendell Holmes nodded once, misusing *aggravate* for *irritate* in a letter to Sir Frederick Pollock in 1895: "Our two countries *aggravate* [read *irritate* or *annoy*] each other from time to time." 1 *Holmes–Pollock Letters* 66 (1941).

aggravated damages. See **punitive damages.**

aggravated larceny. See **larceny (B).**

aggregable is the preferred form, not **aggregatable*—e.g.: "The Commission notified defendants that their trading activities were *aggregatable* [read *aggregable*]." *Commodity Futures Trading Comm'n v. Hunt*, 591 F.2d 1211, 1227 n.5 (7th Cir. 1979).

aggregate, n.; **aggregation.** Both may mean "a mass of discrete things or individuals taken as a whole," *aggregate* being the more usual term. *Aggregate* /**ag**-rə-gət/ stresses the notion "taken as a whole" (as in the phrase *in the aggregate*), and *aggregation* more "a mass of discrete things." Here the former term is used:

- "[The] price . . . , while of trifling moment to each reader, is sufficient in the *aggregate* to afford compensation for the cost of gathering and distributing [the news]." *International News Serv. v. Associated Press*, 248 U.S. 215, 235 (1918) (per Pitney, J.).
- "It does not, however, deny that in the *aggregate* she was given a disproportionate amount of dangerous and strenuous work." *Davis v. Team Elec. Co.*, 520 F.3d 1080, 1090 (9th Cir. 2008).

In reference to "the act of aggregating," only *aggregation* will suffice—e.g.:

- "There is no allegation that the verdict was determined by *aggregation* and average, by lot, game or chance or other artifice or other improper manner." *Travelers Ins. Co. v. Jackson*, 610 So.2d 680, 681 (Fla. Dist. Ct. App. 1992).
- "Apparently considering multiple takings from the same owner to be the same theft, rather than an *aggregation* of two or more thefts as contemplated by the theft statute, the trial court denied the motion." *Roberts v. People*, 203 P.3d 513, 515–16 (Colo. 2009).

aggregate, vb. **A. Sense.** *Aggregate* /**ag**-rə-gayt/ = to bring together a mass of discrete things or individuals into a whole. The verb is sometimes misused for *total* in reference to sums—e.g.: "Before us [appellant] advances two issues for reversal: that the evidence, properly viewed, revealed a mere failure of communication, not a contempt; and that the fines imposed, *aggregating* [read *totaling*] almost fifteen thousand dollars, were excessive." *In re Reehlman*, 763 F.2d 670, 670 (5th Cir. 1985).

B. *Aggregate together.* This phrase is a REDUN-DANCY—e.g.: "For the purpose of establishing the rate at which capital transfer tax is payable, all property (with certain exceptions) passing on the death is *aggregated together* [read *aggregated*]." William Geldart, *Introduction to English Law* 90 (D.C.M. Yardley ed., 9th ed. 1984).

***aggrievance.** See **grievance.**

***aggrievant.** See **grievant.**

aggrieve (= to bring grief to; to treat unfairly) is now used almost exclusively in legal contexts, and almost always in the form of a past participle. E.g.:

- "An *aggrieved* spouse is not compelled to seek the courts of another state for the protection of her marriage status." *Usen v. Usen*, 13 A.2d 738, 752 (Me. 1940). (Here the term is a past-participial adjective.)
- "The established principle is that suppression of the product of a Fourth Amendment violation can be successfully urged only by those whose rights were violated by the search itself, not by those who are *aggrieved* solely by the introduction of damaging evidence." *Alderman v. U.S.*, 394 U.S. 165, 171–72 (1969) (per White, J.). (Here the term is used as a past participle.)

aggrievement (= an act or instance of causing grief to a person) is illustrated in the *OED* with only one citation, but it appears with some frequency in law—e.g.: "[The exceptions do not] offer reason for *aggrievement*, and signify nothing except general dissatisfaction with the entire report." *Kowalsky v. Am. Employers Ins. Co.*, 90 F.2d 476, 480 (6th Cir. 1937).

The word should not be used as a variant of *grievance*—e.g.: "Another of MacDonald's *aggrievements* [read *grievances*] centers on the deterioration of a bloody footprint, which he was no longer able to distinguish adequately at trial." *U.S. v. MacDonald*, 632 F.2d 258, 270 (4th Cir. 1980).

aging. See MUTE E.

agnate; enate; cognate. In Roman law, an *agnate* is a relative through one's father; an *enate* is a relative through one's mother; and a *cognate* is any relative, through one's father or mother. The corresponding adjectives are *agnatic, enatic,* and *cognatic.* See **kinship** (final ¶).

agnation. See **kinship.**

****a gratia.*** See *ex gratia.*

agréation; agrément. The first is a process, and the second is the usual result of the process. *Agréation* = a diplomatic procedure by which a receiving state makes a prior determination whether a proposed envoy will be acceptable; *agrément* = the approval of a diplomatic representative by the receiving state.

agree. A. Senses with Different Prepositions. To *agree with* is to be in accord with (another) <they agreed with each other>; to *agree to* is to acquiesce in (usu. the performance or specifications of something) <the defendant specifically agreed to those stipulations>. To *agree on* is to come to an agreement (with someone else) about some subject <we agreed on the new branch-office manager>. For more on the sense of *agree* and its near-synonyms, see **assent,** vb.

B. And *concur.* In G.B., appellate judges who join in an opinion are said to *agree*, whereas in the U.S. they *concur*.

C. *Agreed to* and *agreed upon.* These are slightly awkward as PHRASAL ADJECTIVES, but when used before a noun, they should be hyphenated. E.g.:

- "In preparation for trial in November 2002, the trial court issued pretrial and scheduling orders setting cutoff dates and procedures, including procedures for the voluntary and *agreed-upon* exchange of written export reports disclosing all opinions to be expressed at trial." *Rapides Parish Police Jury v. Grant Parish Police Jury*, 924 So.2d 357, 363 (La. Ct. App. 2006).
- "We argue that if the government stopped interfering with people's voluntarily *agreed-to* contracts, a system of de facto privatization could come about." Bryan Caplan & Edward P. Stringham, *Privatizing the Adjudication of Disputes*, 9 Theoretical Inquiries L. 503, 509 (2008).

In a few phrases, *agreed* suffices as an idiomatic ellipsis for *agreed-upon*, as in *agreed verdict* and *agreed judgment.* (See **agreed verdict.**) Generally, though, the entire phrase should appear—e.g.:

- "[As] shown by the charge in the *agreed* [read *agreed-upon*] statement, Jan, at the time of distribution, is the only child of an only child of a child of Hastings." *Maud v. Catherwood*, 155 P.2d 111, 117 (Cal. Ct. App. 1945).
- "Even if the Soviets do use the radar for space tracking, such a reading of the *agreed* [read *agreed-upon*] statement would gut the general prohibition in the ABM Treaty regarding early warning radars." Note, *Legal Models of Arms Control: Past, Present, and Future*, 100 Harv. L. Rev. 1326, 1334 (1987).

A similar ellipsis occurs with *agreed to* and *agreed on*, seemingly on the mistaken notion that one should avoid ending a sentence with a preposition—e.g.:

- "In America there is a famous decision holding that a negotiating party who strings another party along with prolonged negotiations, constantly changing his terms, may be held liable to the other party for actual loss suffered if no contract eventually is *agreed* [read *agreed to*]." P.S. Atiyah, *An Introduction to the Law of Contract* 62 (3d ed. 1981).
- "Mr Dlouhy said the essentials had been *agreed* [read *agreed on*]." Leslie Colitt & John Lloyd, *Comecon Takes First Steps to Dismantle Itself*, Fin. Times, 28 Mar. 1990, at 1.
- "There is the possibility that, due to administrative error, a stem cell may be used for a purpose that was not *agreed*

[read *agreed on*]." Ryan Morgan, *Embryonic Stem Cells and Consent*, 15 Med. L. Rev. 279, 296 (2007).

See PREPOSITIONS (C).

D. Transitive Uses in BrE. BrE often drops the preposition and makes *agree* a transitive verb <they agreed the terms>. To American eyes, the phrasing looks like a typographical error. We can't agree it.

agree and covenant. See **covenant and agree.**

agreed to; agreed upon. See **agreed (c).**

agreed verdict (BrE) = *consent decree* (AmE).

agreement; contract. The first may refer either to an informal arrangement with no consideration (e.g., a "gentlemen's agreement") or to a formal legal arrangement supported by consideration. *Contract* is used only in this second sense. The distinction applies also with the verbs *agree* and *contract*. The intended sense of *agree(ment)* is usually clear from the context.

Although every contract is an agreement, not every agreement is a contract. For example, one may agree to meet a friend at 7:00 p.m. for dinner, and the result is properly called an *agreement*—but not a *contract*, to which a legal obligation attaches. See **bargain.**

agreement, grammatical. See CONCORD (A).

agrees and covenants. See **covenant and agree.**

agrément. See *agréation.*

aid; aide. *Aid* is a noun or verb meaning "help" <aid for tornado victims> <aid a client>. *Aide* is the noun denoting a helper <teacher's aide>.

aid and abet = "to assist the perpetrator of the crime while sharing in the requisite intent." *U.S. v. Martinez*, 555 F.2d 1269, 1271 (5th Cir. 1977). This phrase is a well-known legal DOUBLET that, like most other doublets, has come down to us from the Middle Ages and Renaissance, when embellishing terms with synonyms was common. Singly, *aid* is the more general term, *abet* generally appearing only in contexts involving criminal intent.

Aid and abet is sometimes called a TERM OF ART, but in fact it is, in the words of the chief American and British criminal-law commentators, "unnecessarily verbose" and "antiquated." *See* Rollin M. Perkins & Ronald N. Boyce, *Criminal Law* 724–25 (3d ed. 1982); Glanville Williams, *Textbook of Criminal Law* 288 (1978). It is still used in both AmE and BrE, although in the 1970s England's Law Commission Working Party proposed replacing the phrase with *help*—a proposal that was not accepted. Perkins and Boyce recommend *abet*, which can stand alone unaided.

The agent noun is *aider and abettor*—e.g.:

- "The appellant now makes the further claim that the complaint charged the defendant as an original instigator only, and that he cannot be held liable thereunder as an *aider and abettor*." *Fusario v. Cavallaro*, 142 A. 391, 392 (Conn. 1928).

- "A nonparty need not be formally served with an injunction to trigger *aider and abettor* liability; all that is required is that the *aider and abettor* be given 'fair notice that acting in concert with the named defendants would subject them to contempt proceedings.'" *Select Creations, Inc. v. Paliafito Am., Inc.*, 852 F.Supp. 740, 779 (E.D. Wis. 1994).

See **abettor.**

Sometimes the phrase is made even wordier—e.g.:

- Worst of all: "The prosecutor read that Mr. Wade willfully and knowingly *aided, abetted, encouraged, assisted, advised, and counseled* [read *abetted*] someone who stabbed the victim to death." *In re Wade*, 684 P.2d 731, 733 (Wash. Ct. App. 1984).
- "In other words to be concerned in the commission of a crime it must be shown that the person or persons charged did something knowingly and intentionally in furtherance of a common design or to put it another way that they or he *aided, abetted, and assisted* [read *abetted*] in the perpetration of the offense." *Robertson v. Cain*, 324 F.3d 297, 303 (5th Cir. 2003).

See DOUBLETS, TRIPLETS, AND SYNONYM-STRINGS.

aide. See **aid.**

aide de camp (= military aide) is borrowed from the French and should retain the Gallicized spelling—*aide*—especially considering that *aide* is itself now an English word (meaning "a staff member under one's authority"). In other words, shun *aid-de-camp. The correct plural is *aides-de-camp*. See GALLICISMS.

In BrE, the phrase is often abbreviated *A.D.C.* <he was A.D.C. to General Montgomery in 1943>.

airworthy is used in reference to aircraft and means "fit for flying." The word, surprisingly enough first used in 1829, was analogized from *seaworthy*. See **seaworthy.**

aitiology.* See **etiology.

al barre. See **at bar.**

albeit. This conjunction, though termed "archaic" by Eric Partridge (the British lexicographer), thrives in AmE, both legal and nonlegal. And it still appears in BrE, especially in legal writing. Labeled "literary" in the *COD*, the word *albeit* means "though" and introduces concessive phrases and sometimes subordinate clauses. The even more literary *howbeit*, by contrast, means "nevertheless" and begins principal clauses.

A. Introducing Phrases. The predominant modern use is for *albeit* to introduce concessive phrases:

- "The parties continued to address [the issue], *albeit* in fairly leisurely fashion." *Prudhomme v. Tenneco Oil Co.*, 955 F.2d 390, 395 (5th Cir. 1992).
- "Paralegals perform substantive legal tasks, *albeit* tasks that do not require a license to practice law." *Morris v. Belfor USA Group, Inc.*, 201 P.3d 1253, 1263 (Colo. Ct. App. 2008).
- "The 'handshake' relationship between Tilkin and United was admittedly contractual in nature, *albeit* oral and

terminable at will." *Tilkin & Cagen, Inc. v. United Metal Receptacle Corp.*, 593 F.Supp.2d 996, 998 (N.D. Ill. 2008).

B. Introducing Clauses. *Albeit* may begin a clause, albeit *although* is more common in this context. In fact, *albeit* sounds pretty stuffy in these constructions:

- "Defendants were able in fact to carry out the process successfully in Baltimore and elsewhere, *albeit* they may not have succeeded in treating 'green' or wet concrete surfaces." *Vortex Mfg. Co. v. Ply-Rite Contracting Co.*, 33 F.2d 302, 309 (D. Md. 1929).
- "We think, then, we have for review a decision on a stipulated record, *albeit* the matter was styled as a determination on motions for summary judgment." *Vetter v. Frosch*, 599 F.2d 630, 633 (5th Cir. 1979).
- "There are several devices already in use in various international agreements for doing so, *albeit* they may not be adequate." Edith Brown Weiss, *Climate Change, Intergenerational Equity and International Law*, 9 Vt. J. Envtl. L. 619, 626 (2008).

C. For *even if*. Archaically, *albeit* is sometimes used for *even if* in beginning a clause (a usage to be discouraged)—e.g.: "Separate and distinct false declarations . . . [that] require different factual proof of falsity may properly be charged in separate counts, *albeit* [read *even if*] they are all related and arise out of the same transaction or subject matter." *U.S. v. De La Torre*, 634 F.2d 792, 795 (5th Cir. 1981). The second bulleted quotation under (B) may well fall into this category.

alcoholometer; Alcometer. See **Breathalyzer.**

aleatory; fortuitous; stochastic. These words have similar but distinct meanings. The first two are especially close, meaning "depending wholly on chance." *Aleatory* derives from the Latin word for the game of dice: *alea jacta est* (= the die is cast). *Fortuitous*, meanwhile, carries the suggestion of an accident, usually but not always a happy one. (See **fortuitous.**) As it happens, *aleatory* usually refers to present descriptions or future events that depend on uncertain contingencies—e.g.:

- "The better rule, this court feels, is to respect the *aleatory* nature of the settlement process and to hold both the plaintiff and settling defendant to their gamble." *Doyle v. U.S.*, 441 F.Supp. 701, 711 n.5 (D.S.C. 1977).
- "The 2001 consent judgment in this case is an *aleatory* contract, which simply means it depended upon the uncertain act, i.e., the future purchase of the property by one of the heirs." *Peeler v. Dural*, 958 So.2d 31, 35 (La. Ct. App. 2007).

Fortuitous, meaning "accidental, occurring by chance," typically refers to past events <how fortuitous that the snowstorm shut down the city on the very day my cousin wanted me to stay home from work>. *Stochastic*, the most rarefied of these words, means "random"; it is fairly common in the writing of economic analysts and statisticians. See **fortuitous.** Cf. **adventitious.**

alegal, adj. This late-20th-century NEOLOGISM—lit., "without law"—recognizes the increasingly common view that we should not put every action or event on the plane of legality and illegality. In the view of some scholars, if an action is neither mandated nor prohibited by law, then it should be characterized as *alegal*—e.g.:

- "Think of the many human beings in pre-industrial society related through their dependence on territorial magnates, or guilds, or church organizations. They were not *alegal* institutions." Joseph Vining, *Legal Identity: The Coming of Age of Public Law* 49 (1978).
- "At the free, *alegal* end of the spectrum, realism views judges as charging their own individual courses unencumbered by law in all respects but form." Lewis A. Kornhauser & Lawrence G. Sager, *Unpacking the Court*, 96 Yale L.J. 82, 93 (1986).
- "[Treating] the promises of unmarried cohabitors as contractual words rather than *alegal* words of commitment puts public force behind what is otherwise legally vacuous." Mark Kelman, *A Guide to Critical Legal Studies* 105 (1987).

In using this term, of course, one must respect the boundaries between *alegal* and *illegal*. Otherwise, the same confusion might arise as exists between *amoral* and *immoral*. See **immoral.**

For related terms, see **extralegal** & **nonlegal.**

alias is both adverb (= otherwise [called or named]), as an elliptical form of *alias dictus*, and noun (= an assumed name), today usually the latter. *Alias* refers only to names, and should not be used synonymously with *guise* (= assumed appearance, pretense). See POPULARIZED LEGAL TECHNICALITIES.

alibi. A. As a Noun for *excuse*. The words are not synonymous, although the confusion that has grown out of their meanings is understandable. *Alibi* is a specific legal term referring to the defense of having been at a place other than the scene of a crime. By SLIPSHOD EXTENSION it has come to be used for any excuse or explanation for misconduct, usually one that shifts blame to someone else.

The Evanses wrote of this term:

> Cynicism and the common man's distrust of the law have tinged *alibi* with a suggestion of improbability and even of dishonesty. Purists insist that it should be restricted to its legal meaning, and those who wish to be formally correct will so restrict it. In so doing, however, they will lose the connotation of cunning and dishonesty [that] distinguishes it from *excuse*.
>
> Bergen Evans & Cornelia Evans, *Contemporary American Usage* 24 (1957).

Lawyers perhaps more than others ought to "wish to be formally correct."

B. As an Adverb. In recent years *alibi* has been used as an adverb (meaning "elsewhere" <she proved herself alibi>), but this usage should be eschewed. Although "elsewhere" is the original Latin meaning of *alibi* (originally a locative of L. *alius* "other"), in English it has long served only as a noun, and to hark back to the classical sense is an affectation.

C. As a Verb. Nor should *alibi* be used as a verb, as it is in the following sentences. The first sentence is doubly bad, for the misbegotten verb is based on the misused noun (see (A)):

- "[The defendant,] at the outset of his custodial interrogation, *alibied* [read *provided an alibi, stating*] that he had not been off the naval base after lunch on the 12th." *State v. Franklin*, 241 A.2d 219, 227 (R.I. 1968).
- "Lafon insisted that he and his friends could *alibi* [read *provide alibis for*] one another because they had all attended a party and had not left until 2:00 a.m. the morning of Mergler's disappearance." *Lafon v. Commonwealth*, 438 S.E.2d 279, 282 (Va. Ct. App. 1993).
- "Not only did the plaintiffs not proffer any statistical testimony based on this comparison, they *alibied out of* [read *excused themselves from*] the task (and got the district court to sign a finding) on the grounds that the expense of making such a determination was prohibitive." *Edwards v. City of Houston*, 37 F.3d 1097, 1122 (5th Cir. 1994) (DeMoss, J., dissenting).

The *OED* records this usage from 1909 and labels it colloquial.

alien, vb.; ***aliene; alienate; *abalienate.** When we talk about property changing hands, the best choice of verb is *assign* or *convey* or *transfer* rather than any of these legalistic words. But if some form of *alien* must be used, the most common and therefore the best word in all senses is *alienate*, whether one writes about alienation of property or of affections. Nonlawyers may understand that in certain contexts *alienate* means "to transfer (as property)"; they probably stumble over *alien* as a verb in such a context—much less **abalienate** (a NEEDLESS VARIANT from the civil law). E.g.:

- "The rule of the common law [is that] a man cannot attach to a grant or transfer of property, otherwise absolute, the condition that it shall not be *alienated*, such condition being repugnant to the nature of the estate granted." *Jourolman v. Massengill*, 5 S.W. 719, 725 (Tenn. 1887).
- "Since property owned by tenants by the entireties is not subject to the debts of either spouse, they may *alien* [read *alienate*] it without infringing upon the rights of their individual creditors." *Murphey v. C. I. T. Corp.*, 33 A.2d 16, 18 (Pa. 1943).

**Aliene* is an archaic variant spelling of the verb *alien*.

Alienate frequently takes on the lay sense in legal writing, as in the phrase *alienation of affections*, or as here: "[This] false statement [was] designed to *alienate* supporters of plaintiff and to affiliate them with [the other candidate]." *Shields v. Booles*, 38 S.W.2d 677, 678 (Ky. 1931).

**alienee* (= one to whom ownership of property is transferred) is an unnecessary and obscure equivalent of *grantee*. See the quotation in the following entry.

alienor; *alienist. *Alienor* (= one who transfers property) is equivalent to *grantor*; it should be avoided where *grantor* or *transferor* will serve—e.g.: "Conveying lands by means of a fictitious or collusive suit, commenced by arrangement by the intended *alienee* [read *grantee* or *recipient*] against the *alienor* [read *grantor*]" (quoted in *OED*).

**Alienist*, an obsolescent term for *psychiatrist*, lingers on in law talk—e.g.:

- "Both of the court appointed *alienists* found DePlonty to be mentally ill." *State v. Murphy*, 872 P.2d 480, 483 (Utah Ct. App. 1994).
- "Furthermore, both *alienists* concluded that at the time of the murder Carter could distinguish right from wrong, he understood the nature of his actions, and he was in control of his actions." *Carter v. Galetka*, 44 P.3d 626, 640–41 (Utah 2001).

alimony. See **palimony.**

alio intuitu is not a justified LATINISM, when there are so many more precise alternatives such as *from a different point of view* or *with respect to another case (or condition)*. E.g.: "They were statements made *alio intuitu* [read *under different circumstances*] to other parties, never communicated, so far as appears, to the defendant, or acted upon or intended to be acted upon by him." *Alexander v. Grover*, 77 N.E. 487, 489 (Mass. 1906).

aliquot; aliquant. *Aliquot* = divisible into a larger number or quantity a whole number of times <10 is an aliquot part of 20>. *Aliquant* = not an *aliquot*; that is, not divisible into the larger number or quantity without leaving a remainder <10 is an aliquant part of 21>.

These are technical terms generally best left to technical contexts. *Aliquot* adds nothing to the following sentence: "Compromises are contracts of settlement, and the compromise of one *aliquot* part of a single disputed liability and payment of the balance in full is a settlement of all parts of such single liability." *Nelson-Wiggen Piano Co. v. U.S.*, 84 F.2d 47, 48 (7th Cir. 1936).

One justified technical use of these terms occurs in the field of trusts, where payment of an *aliquot* or *aliquant* part of the consideration for transfer of legal title may determine whether the presumption of a resulting trust will arise. When a payor's contributions for the purchase of property in another's name are *aliquot* parts of the purchase price, some courts presume the contributions to be a gift or loan; when, however, these contributions are *aliquant* parts of the purchase price, the presumption does not arise. See Restatement (Second) of Trusts § 454 cmt. c (1959). This distinction may be obsolescent; the Restatement rejects it in comment b to § 454.

The term *aliquot* is also used in determining whether a gift of property in a will is a specific or a general legacy: "Bequests of all testator's property, an *aliquot* part thereof, or all property except certain things . . . have been held to amount to general legacies." Thomas E. Atkinson, *Handbook of the Law of Wills* 733–34 (2d ed. 1953). See **legacy.**

aliunde (= from another source, from elsewhere) is a LATINISM with little justification in place of an English equivalent. The phrase *evidence aliunde*, for example, means "evidence from outside (an instrument, for example); extrinsic evidence." E.g.: "Thereupon . . .

---

counsel would present their respective reviews of the nature and effect of the state of the record with respect to the existence of *sufficient evidence aliunde* [read *enough other evidence*] to justify admission of the testimony." *U.S. v. Azzarelli Constr. Co.*, 612 F.2d 292, 297 (7th Cir. 1979).

ALJ; A.L.J.; a.l.j. The usual abbreviation for *administrative-law judge* is *ALJ* (without periods)— an abbreviation first used in 1973 and now commonplace. For the first recorded use, see *Hawkins v. Weinberger*, 368 F.Supp. 896, 897 (D. Kan. 1973). The plural is *ALJs*. See **administrative-law judge.** See also ACRONYMS AND INITIALISMS.

The uses of *A.L.J.* in late-19th-century American opinions generally meant either *additional law judge* or *associate law judge.*

all. A. *All (of).* The more formal construction is to omit *of* and write, when possible, "For *all* these reasons, women around the world often find themselves unable to rely on . . . their domestic legal system as a means of legal protection." Martha A. Fineman, *Transcending the Boundaries of Law* 105 (2010).

In two circumstances, though, *all of* is the better choice. The first is when a pronoun follows <all of them>, unless the pronoun is serving as an adjective, either possessive <all my belongings> or demonstrative <all that jazz>. The second is when a possessive noun follows: "*All of* John's property was therefore subject to the IRS lien."

B. With Negatives. *Not all*—as opposed to **all . . . not*—is usually the correct sequence in negative constructions. E.g.:

- "However, *all* American courts *did not* reject it." Roscoe Pound, *The Formative Era of American Law* 89 (1938). A suggested revision: *But not all American courts rejected it.*
- "Students rightfully protest; and while *all of their complaints do not* [read *not all their complaints*] have merit, they too should be heard." William O. Douglas, *Points of Rebellion* 14 (1970).
- "It seems that *all* things were *not* going well in Wheeler's own unit." *Wheeler v. Mental Health & Mental Retardation Auth.*, 752 F.2d 1063, 1065 (5th Cir. 1985). This expanded version of the idiomatic "All is not well" does not work. A suggested revision: *It seems that not all things were going well* or, better, *It seems that all was not well.*

Cf. **every (c).**

C. And *any.* *All* follows a superlative adjective <most of all>; *any* follows a comparative adjective <more than any other>. Constructions such as **more . . . than all* are illogical—e.g.:

- " 'Amoco Ultimate gasoline is superior to all other brands of premium gasoline . . . because it is refined *more than all other* such brands [read *more than any other brand*].' " *Oliveira v. Amoco Oil Co.*, 776 N.E.2d 151, 154 (Ill. 2002) (quoting an advertisement).
- "In the meantime death had silenced the lips of his brother, the one person who *more than all others* [read *more than any other*] was competent to give his version of the matter." *Hudak v. Procek*, 806 A.2d 140, 161 (Del. 2002).

- "Breeding denied Littleton a raise in 2003 because he was still earning *more than all other* West Memphis drivers [read *more than any other West Memphis driver*] except the new lead driver, Cedric Clark, an African-American." *Littleton v. Pilot Travel Ctrs., LLC*, 568 F.3d 641, 646 (8th Cir. 2009).

See OVERSTATEMENT. For *any and all*, see **any and all.**

all and singular is a collective equivalent of *each and every.* It is almost always unnecessary—e.g.: "By separate paragraph [defendant] then *denied that each and every, all and singular, the allegations* [read *denied all the allegations*] contained in plaintiff's original petition." *Dixon v. Mayfield Bldg. Supply Co.*, 543 S.W.2d 5, 7 (Tex. Civ. App.—Fort Worth 1976). See DOUBLETS, TRIPLETS, AND SYNONYM-STRINGS.

all deliberate speed. See **with all deliberate speed.**

allegation; *allegement; **allegatum.** The second and third forms are NEEDLESS VARIANTS.

allegator (= one who alleges) is not often used, even in legal writing, perhaps because of its jocular suggestiveness of *alligator.*

*allegatum. See **allegation.**

allege; contend. To *allege* is formally to state a matter of fact as being true or provable, without yet having proved it. The word once denoted stating under oath, but this meaning no longer applies. To *contend* is to strive against or, in the advocate's sense, means "to state one's position in a polemical way; to submit."

Allege should not be used as a synonym of *assert, maintain, declare,* or *claim. Allege* has peculiarly accusatory connotations. One need not allege only the commission of crimes; but certainly the acts alleged must concern misfeasances or negligence.

allegeable; *allegible. *Allegeable* is the only recognized form of the word.

allegedly does not mean "in an alleged manner," as it would if the adverb had been formed as English adverbs generally are. Follett considered adverbs like this one ugly and unjustified (esp. *reportedly*). See Wilson Follett, *Modern American Usage* 279 (1966). Yet *allegedly* is a convenient space- and time-saver for *it is alleged that* or *according to the allegations.* Though not logically formed, *allegedly* is well established and unobjectionable, if used in moderation. See **reportedly.**

*allegement. See **allegation.**

allegiance. See **fidelity.**

*allegible. See **allegeable.**

***Allen* charge.** See CASE REFERENCES (C) & **dynamite charge.**

aller sans jour. See LOAN TRANSLATIONS.

all fours. See **on all fours.**

allide; collide. The first is used only in a special context in reference to ships in admiralty law. When two ships *allide*, one of them is stationary; ships *collide* when both are moving before impact. *Black's* notes that the distinction is not carefully observed. *Black's Law Dictionary* 88 (9th ed. 2009). See **collision.**

allision. See **collision.**

ALLITERATION. A. Pleasant Examples. "The basic appeal of language," wrote Second Circuit Judge Jerome Frank, "is to the ear." Frank, "The Speech of Judges: A Dissenting Opinion," in *A Man's Reach* 35, 37 (Barbara Frank Kristein ed., 1965). The SOUND OF PROSE is therefore a critical concern. And writers frequently harness sounds for any of several effects. When they repeat sounds, the result is called *alliteration* (which has two subsets: *assonance* for vowels <parody of commonty>, and *consonance* for consonants <the raucous cackles made a cacophony>.

Sometimes alliteration creates a sarcastic tone, as when Vice President Spiro Agnew referred to the *nattering nabobs of negativism*. E.g.:

- "And what is implied by that lovely limpid legalism, 'due process of law'?" Fred Rodell, *Woe Unto You, Lawyers!* 51 (1939).
- "Unblinded by the tweedledum-tweedledee twaddle of much that passes for learned legal argument, . . . he seems essentially a direct, plain-spoken politician." Fred Rodell, *Nine Men* 331 (1955).

At other times it merely creates a memorable phrase—e.g.: "Judges do and must legislate but they can do so only interstitially; they are confined from molar to molecular motions." *Southern Pac. Co. v. Jensen*, 244 U.S. 205, 221 (1917) (Holmes, J., dissenting).

B. Unpleasant Examples. The unconscious or tasteless repetition of sounds, especially excessive sibilance (too many -*s*- sounds, as in the phrase *especially excessive sibilance*), can easily distract readers: "When used by accident it falls on the ear very disagreeably." W. Somerset Maugham, "Lucidity, Simplicity, Euphony," in *The Summing Up* 321, 325 (1938).

Though alliteration is quite common with -*s*- sounds, other unconscious repetitions can occur. In the following sentence (Uniform Probate Code § 2-104), three words in a five-word phrase rhyme: "This section is not to be applied where its application would result in a taking of *intestate estate by the state*." [A possible revision: *This section does not apply when its application would result in the escheat of an intestate estate*.] Although one can avoid the use of *state*, the phrase *intestate estate* is well-nigh unavoidable. (The English Parliament enacted the Intestates' Estate Act, 15 & 16 Geo. VI & 1 Eliz. II, c. 64 (1952).) Sometimes one wishes that we could use the terms *willed* and *unwilled* rather than *testate* and *intestate*—e.g.: "It is familiar law that the will is the source of the beneficiaries' title in the case of *testate estates*, while in *intestate estates* the source of title is the statute." *Greene v. King*, 132 A. 411, 413 (Conn. 1926).

Yet sometimes unpleasant alliteration isn't merely a matter of whether it's conscious or unconscious. That is to say, a writer may use it quite consciously but also quite unpleasantly, through poor literary judgment— e.g.: "The necessarily contextual, contested, and contingent character of substantive liberal principles necessarily prevents them, qua principles, from effectively inhibiting human brutality." Lief H. Carter, *Law and Politics as Play*, 83 Chi.-Kent L. Rev. 1333, 1333 (2008). For a bewilderingly disgusting example involving child abuse, see "Alliteritis" in *Garner on Language and Writing* 512 (2009).

One good way to avoid the infelicity of undue alliteration is to read one's prose aloud when editing. See SOUND OF PROSE, THE.

***all . . . not.** See **all (B).**

allocable is the proper form, not *allocatable*—e.g.: "The division . . . held that the portion of increased tax expense attributable to facilities actually providing intrastate service was properly *allocatable* [read *allocable*] to Narragansett's intrastate operations." *Nepco Mun. Rate Comm. v. FERC*, 668 F.2d 1327, 1346 (D.C. Cir. 1981).

allocatee. See -EE.

allocator; allocatur. *Allocator* = one who allocates. *Allocatur* (lit., "it is allowed") in former practice meant "a certificate duly given at the end of an action, allowing costs" (*OED*).

allocute (= to deliver in court a formal, exhortatory address, i.e., an allocution) is a BACK-FORMATION from the noun *allocution*. (See **allocution.**) Although some years ago the verb might have been viewed as a barbarous MORPHOLOGICAL DEFORMITY, just as *electrocute* once was, we should accept *allocute* as a useful addition to legal language. E.g.: "Although the record does not reveal precisely what his attorney told him concerning the rights he would be relinquishing and the trial judge did not *allocute* the defendant, nothing in the record indicates that the defendant was unaware of the consequences of his waiver." *People v. Butler*, 792 N.Y.S.2d 581, 582 (Ct. App. 2005).

Because *allocution* most properly refers to the court's and not to the criminal defendant's address, it is most properly the court that *allocutes*. But the verb *allocute* has undergone SLIPSHOD EXTENSION analogous to that of *allocution*, so that today the criminal defendants are typically said to be the *allocutors*—e.g.:

- "In light of these differences, courts tend to review the denial of a defendant's right to *allocute* in a more constrained manner than they review the denial of a victim's right to *allocute* under the CVRA." Mary Margaret Giannini, *Equal Rights for Equal Rites?*, 26 Yale L. & Pol'y Rev. 431, 435 (2008).

An asterisk (✱) precedes words and phrases that are invariably inferior forms.

- "Both sides are free to *allocute* as to the amount of the suspended sentence and the period of probation." *State v. Duran*, 967 A.2d 184, 186 (Md. 2009).
- "Lighty attempted to introduce this letter . . . but the district court excluded it, finding that the letter constituted an effort by Lighty to *allocute* to the jury or to present himself as tenderhearted, without subjecting himself to cross-examination." *U.S. v. Lighty*, 616 F.3d 321, 364 (4th Cir. 2010) (per Hamilton, S.J.).

allocution; *allocutus. *Allocution* is inadequately defined by the major dictionaries (usually some variation on "a formal address"). In traditional legal usage, the word refers to a trial judge's asking a criminal defendant to speak in mitigation of the sentence to be imposed. By SLIPSHOD EXTENSION, the word has come to denote the accused person's speech in mitigation of the sentence, rather than the judge's invitation to the accused to speak—e.g.:

- "While failure to afford the defendant his statutory right of *allocution* does not present a federal constitutional issue, that he was not called upon to speak on his own behalf has significance on the issue of whether he intentionally acquiesced in the withdrawal of the promise and surrendered his right to challenge the sentence." *U.S. ex rel. Elksnis v. Gilligan*, 256 F.Supp. 244, 252 (S.D.N.Y. 1966).
- "The record does disclose that appellant was not accorded the right of *allocution*." *Tate v. State*, 524 S.W.2d 624, 626 (Ark. 1975).

*Allocutus is a NEEDLESS VARIANT and an unnecessary LATINISM.

The phrase *victim allocution*—a popular phrase since the 1980s—refers to a crime victim's addressing the court with the objective usually of persuading the sentencer to impose a harsher sentence. Even though this pole-reversal is arguably the result of SLIPSHOD EXTENSION, the phrase is now established in American law—e.g.: "There is no sound reason for limiting *victim allocution* to only victims of violent crimes." *U.S. v. Degenhardt*, 405 F.Supp.2d 1341, 1344 (D. Utah 2005).

allocutory; *allocutive. *Allocutory* is the standard adjective corresponding to the noun *allocution*—e.g.:

- "The right to make *allocutory* and other legal claims should be made effective by a right to counsel at sentencing." Note, *Procedural Due Process at Judicial Sentencing for Felony*, 81 Harv. L. Rev. 821, 833 (1968).
- "*Allocutory* pleas for mercy would have been unavailing and were not allowed." *Harris v. State*, 509 A.2d 120, 125 (Md. Ct. App. 1986).

*Allocutive is a NEEDLESS VARIANT—e.g.: "It was not necessary for counsel to raise the issue of allocution on appeal, Petitioner having made an *allocutive* [read *allocutory*] statement to the court in his direct testimony during his sentencing hearing." *In re Echeverria*, 6 P.3d 573, 582 (Wash. 2000) (en banc).

***allocutus.** See **allocution.**

allodial is the proper adjective, *alodian being an erroneous form.

allodium, allodial; *alodium, *alodial. *Black's Law Dictionary* (9th ed. 2009) and the *OED* list *allodium*

(= land held in fee simple absolute) as standard, *alodium* as a variant; *W3*'s listing is the opposite. Both forms may lay claim to etymological precedent. *Allodium* is the more common and, because unanimity is desirable on this point, should be used to the exclusion of its single-elled counterpart. The plural is generally *allodia*.

The adjective form is *allodial*—e.g.: "There remained scattered tracts of '*allodial*' land (literally, land 'without a lord') which were not incorporated into the system of feudal tenure and whose owners did not even in theory become tenants." Peter Butt, *Land Law* 38 (2d ed. 1988).

all of. See **all (A).**

allograph; autograph. An *allograph* is an agent's writing or signature for the principal. An *autograph*, of course, is one's own signature.

allonge (= a piece of paper attached to a note or other negotiable instrument, usu. to make room for further indorsements) derives from the French verb *allonger* (= to lengthen). Anglo-American lawyers borrowed the word from French law in the mid-19th century. Although *Ballentine's Law Dictionary* (3d ed. 1969) suggests that the word is pronounced /a-lənj/, the better and more common pronunciation is /ə-lonj/.

allow. A. Senses. *Allow* = (1) to give or grant (something) as a right or privilege <she allowed her neighbor an easement>; (2) to approve by not objecting <the court allowed appellee's counsel to reply to the rebuttal>; (3) to make provision for <the rules allow depositions upon written questions>; or (4) in BrE, to sustain (a judgment, claim, or appeal) <the appeal should be allowed>.

B. And *permit*. The words *allow* and *permit* have an important connotative difference. *Allow*, as in sense 2 listed above, suggests merely the absence of opposition, or refraining from a proscription. In contrast, *permit* suggests affirmative sanction or approval.

allowable, though structurally an adjective, often functions as a noun in legal contexts. As a noun it refers to the amount of oil or gas that an operator is allowed to extract from a well or field in one day, under proration orders of a state regulatory commission—e.g.:

- "The Supreme Court of Texas held that Gulf . . . could not be required to go to unnecessary expense to obtain an *allowable* that would permit recovery of its fair share or prevent adverse drainage of oil and gas from the property operated by it." Robert E. Hardwicke & M.K. Woodward, *Fair Share and the Small Tract in Texas*, 41 Tex. L. Rev. 75, 93 (1962).
- "The 1944 BPO, therefore, prescribed a formula to be used in fixing quotas for each well so that each developed lease would be able to currently produce its daily quota, called an *allowable*." *Mobil Exploration & Producing U.S. Inc. v. State Corp. Comm'n*, 908 P.2d 1276, 1283 (Kan. 1995).

See ADJECTIVES (C).

all ready. See already.

all right; *alright. *Alright* for *all right* has never been accepted as standard and probably never will be. Although the phrase is considered unitary, the one-word spelling is simply not all right with traditionalists.

all rise; be upstanding. The first phrase is AmE; the second is BrE. Both commands mean that those present in a courtroom should stand when the judge enters and remain standing until the judge is seated. "You may be seated" follows.

all the; all these. See all (A).

all together. See altogether.

allude. A. And *advert*; *refer*. To *allude* is to refer to (something) indirectly or by suggestion only. To *advert* or *refer* is to bring up directly, *advert* being the more FORMAL WORD. (See advert.) *Allude* is misused for *refer* when the indirect nature of a comment or suggestion is missing—e.g.:

• "Scott made no specific *allusion* [read *reference*] to Defendant Luis L. Gonzalez, who had been arrested by that time." *U.S. v. Gonzalez*, 85 F.Supp.2d 1306, 1309 (S.D. Fla. 1999).
• "There was a passing *allusion* [read *reference*] to a goldfish colored car during petitioner's interrogation at the police station shortly after his arrest—and then nothing more." *Davie v. Mitchell*, 291 F.Supp.2d 573, 594 (N.D. Ohio 2003).

In the following sentences, the writers have created OXYMORONS:

• "There being no words *expressly alluding* [read *referring*] to that contingency, the court is to cure the defect by implication." *Spathariotis v. Estate of Spathas*, 398 P.2d 39, 42 (Colo. 1965).
• "Counsel for the tenant made no *explicit allusion* [read *reference*] to the February 20 letter and no argument based on its existence." *Douglas v. Kriegsfeld Corp.*, 849 A.2d 951, 991 (D.C. 2004) (Schwelb, J., dissenting).

B. And *illude*; *elude*. To *illude* (a rare verb) is to deceive with an illusion. To *elude* (a common verb) is to avoid or escape. Both are sometimes misused for *allude*— e.g.:

• "In fact, appellant conceded in his brief that it was impossible to try him for the murder of Sophie Whalin without *eluding to* [read *alluding to*] the murder of Charles Whalin." *Rodriguez v. State*, 871 S.W.2d 312, 316 (Tex. App.—Amarillo 1994).
• "This report *illudes* [read *alludes? refers?*] to the longevity of the struggle for clean air dating back to 1661 in England." Gordon Morris Bakken, *Reclaim and Pollution Credit Trading*, 33 U. West. L.A. L. Rev. 175, 180 n.24 (2001) (citing an EPA report).

C. For *suggest*. It is erroneous to use *allude* in place of *suggest*. One *alludes to* things, not *alludes that* . . .—e.g.:

• "By citing Perry, Judge Lucero *alludes* [read *suggests*] that the display of monuments in Pioneer Park is its own self-contained property within Pioneer Park." Keenan Lorenz, Summum v. Pleasant Grove City: The Tenth Circuit "Binds the Hands of Local Governments as They Shape the Permanent Character of Their Public Spaces," 85 Denv. U. L. Rev. 631, 645 (2008).
• "Crenshaw *alludes* [read *suggests*] that this omission constitutes evidence that the Board knew that it had failed to comply with the Loan Agreement's requirement." *U.S. ex rel. Crenshaw v. Degayner*, 622 F.Supp.2d 1258, 1277 (M.D. Fla. 2008).

allusion; illusion. The first is an indirect reference <literary allusion>, the second a deception or misapprehension <optical illusion>. For the difference between *illusion* and *delusion*, see illusion. For guidance on allusions, see LITERARY ALLUSION.

allusive; *allusory. *Allusive* is standard.

alluvion; alluvium. In the strictest sense, *alluvion* means "the flow or wash of water against a riverbank," and *alluvium* "a deposit of soil, clay, or the lack of such a deposit caused by an alluvion." But *alluvion* has come to be used for *alluvium*—a regrettable development, for the DIFFERENTIATION is worth preserving. *Alluvio* is the Roman-law equivalent to *alluvion*.

The plural forms of the English terms are *alluvions* and *alluviums* (or, less good, *alluvia*). See PLURALS (A). The adjective for *alluvium* is *alluvial*, the forms *alluvious* and *alluvian* being NEEDLESS VARIANTS. *Alluvion* has no clear-cut adjective other than itself <alluvion waters>.

ally. As a noun, the accent is on the first syllable /al-ɪ/; as a verb, on the second /ə-lɪ/.

almoi(g)n. See frankalmoi(g)n(e).

*alodian. See allodial.

*alodium, *alodial. See allodium.

alongside; *alongside of. The word *alongside*, as a preposition, means "at the side of." Hence, one car is parked *alongside* another, and logs are stacked *alongside* one another. It is unnecessary—and poor style—to write *alongside of*. See of (A).

a lot; *alot. The second construction is always wrong.

already; all ready. *Already* has to do with time <finished already>, and *all ready* with preparation <we are all ready>.

*alright. See all right.

also. See too (A).

altercation. The traditional view is that this word refers to "a noisy brawl or dispute," not rising to the seriousness of physical violence. Traditionally speaking, it's considered a misuse to make it refer to a fight in the physical sense—e.g.: "While serving a term of imprisonment in a North Carolina penitentiary, the respondent Perry became involved in an *altercation* with another inmate; a warrant issued, charging

Perry with the misdemeanor of assault with a deadly weapon." *Blackledge v. Perry*, 417 U.S. 21, 22 (1974) (per Stewart, J.). Leff ill-advisedly wrote that "coming to . . . blows is not totally excluded from the ambit of this term," and used it for a physical affray in his entry on *aggressor.* Arthur A. Leff, *The Leff Dictionary of Law*, 94 Yale L.J. 1855, 2003 (1985). For authority limiting the term to the sense "wordy strife," see the *OED, W2, W3*, and Partridge, *Usage and Abusage* 27 (1973). But in AmE today, the word often denotes some type of scuffling or fighting, especially in police jargon.

alter ego (lit., "other I") = a second self. To nonlawyers, it generally means "a kindred spirit" or "a constant companion." To American lawyers it has a special meaning in the corporate context: "a corporation used by an individual in conducting personal business, the result being that a court may impose liability on the individual by piercing the corporate veil when fraud has been perpetrated on someone dealing with the corporation." *Black's Law Dictionary* 91 (9th ed. 2009). The phrase should not be hyphenated unless it functions as a PHRASAL ADJECTIVE <alter-ego theory>.

alternate; alternative. A. As Nouns. An *alternative* is a choice or option—usually one of two choices, but not necessarily. Some etymological purists argue that the word (fr. L. *alter* "the other of two") should be confined to contexts involving but two choices; Ernest Gowers termed this contention a fetish, and it has little or no support among respected stylistic experts or in actual usage. E.g.:

- "None of the *three alternatives* pretend to show sequence of transactions." *Republic Supply Co. of Cal. v. Richfield Oil Co. of Cal.*, 79 F.2d 375, 379 (9th Cir. 1935).
- "The trial court instructed the jury concerning *three alternatives* under criminal homicide: second-degree murder, manslaughter, and negligent homicide." *State v. Powell*, 872 P.2d 1027, 1031 (Utah 1994).
- "Although the applicable sentencing statute does not provide for enhanced sentencing for repeat offenders, it does mandate that a sentence be selected among *three alternatives*, which do not include probation." *State v. Hamili*, 952 P.2d 390, 395 (Haw. 1998).

Indeed, *alternative* carries with it two nuances absent from the near-synonym *choice*. First, *alternative* may suggest adequacy for some purpose <ample alternative channels>; and second, it may suggest compulsion to choose <the alternatives are liberty and death>.

Alternate, n., means: (1) something that proceeds by turns with another; or (2) one who substitutes for another. Remember that *alternative* is needed far more frequently than *alternate*.

B. As Adjectives. *Alternative* = providing a choice between two or more things; available in place of another. E.g.:

- "Nevertheless, if he has failed to show an unlawful conspiracy and monopoly, he has under his *alternative* demand shown a cause of action to recover damages from either or both of the defendants." *Deon v. Kirby Lumber Co.*, 111 So. 55, 58 (La. 1927).
- "An *alternative* outcome, if rescission is deemed appropriate but the Court questions Plaintiff's ability to tender, would be to grant Plaintiff what she seeks." *Moore v. Wells Fargo Bank, N.A.*, 597 F.Supp.2d 612, 616–17 (E.D. Va. 2009).

Alternate = (1) coming each after one of the other kind, every second one; or (2) substitute.

- (Sense 1) "The earlier cases hold that, where the examined copy is made by one person reading the original and the other holding the copy, it is unnecessary to call both persons as witnesses, and it need not be proved that they *alternately* read and inspected the original and the copy." *Biddy v. State*, 107 S.W. 814, 816–17 (Tex. Crim. App. 1908).
- (Sense 2) "Most States, as well as the Federal jurisdiction, do have statutes providing for *alternate* jurors in criminal cases. In those States where constitutional attacks have been made, the provisions for alternate jurors have been upheld." *People v. Van Camp*, 97 N.W.2d 726, 733 (Mich. 1959).
- (Sense 2) "A similar situation exists relative to . . . naming an attorney to represent the estate, the same attorney who appears here as personal representative, he having been designated as an *alternate* executor." *Phelps v. Goldberg*, 313 A.2d 683, 687 (Md. 1974).

Alternate is sometimes misused for *alternative*—a common mistake, perhaps understandable because of the close sense 2 of *alternate*—e.g.:

- "Nor does it appear likely that further conversations would have convinced counsel to pursue *alternate* [read *alternative*] defenses [i.e., defenses available in place of the primary defense pleaded]." *Mattheson v. King*, 751 F.2d 1432, 1439 (5th Cir. 1985).
- "[T]he introduction of these *alternate* [read *alternative*] theories in public school biology classes would accomplish desirable purposes—and . . . could be accomplished consistently with the Constitution." David Crump, *Natural Selection, Irreducible Complexity, and the Bacterial Flagellum*, 36 Pepp. L. Rev. 1, 3 (2008).
- "These *alternate* [read *alternative*] remedies may incentivize states to act differently and consider that which is 'necessary' in trade interactions to be altogether distinct from that which is 'necessary' in the context of investment relationships." Comment, *The Casualty of Investor Protection in Times of Economic Crisis*, 118 Yale L.J. 1545, 1551 (2009).

Because *alternatives* don't always come in twos, there is no good objection to the phrase *two alternatives* on grounds of REDUNDANCY—e.g.:

- "Where a trust instrument *contains two alternative conditions*, of which the first might be too remote and the second, which actually occurs, is not too remote, the rule is not violated." *Sears v. Coolidge*, 108 N.E.2d 563, 565 (Mass. 1952).
- "A search of the record in this case establishes a likely absence of complete diversity between the parties on *either of two alternative theories*." *Freeman v. Northwest Acceptance Corp.*, 754 F.2d 553, 555 (5th Cir. 1985).

alternative dispute resolution; *alternate dispute resolution. The proper form is *alternative dispute resolution*. The phrase is commonly abbreviated *ADR*. See **alternate (B).**

although . . . yet was formerly a common construction, these two words being considered correlative conjunctions. Today the construction is seen only in the most formal contexts, or in older writings—e.g.: "*Although* [these decisions] do not constitute an unbroken chain, *yet* they are fortified by a wealth of learning, reason, and illustration that render them irresistible as authority." *Smith v. City of Rochester*, 92 N.Y. 463, 481 (1883). In most modern contexts, either conjunction will suffice to give the same meaning as if both were used.

altogether; all together. *Altogether* = completely; wholly <they are altogether frivolous appeals>. *All together* = at one place or at the same time <the defendants were tried all together>.

alumnus. A. Sense. This term is obsolete as a LEGALISM for *foster-child*; today it refers to a former student, esp. a male student, of a particular school, esp. an institution of higher learning. Strictly speaking, one need not be a graduate to be an *alumnus*; one who does not complete a course of study is still an *alumnus*.

The feminine form is *alumna*, and the clipped form (a casualism) is *alum*.

B. The Plural Forms *alumni* and *alumnae*. Most strictly, *alumni* refers to former students who are male, the singular form being *alumnus*. *Alumnae* refers to former students who are female; the singular is *alumna*.

Nowadays, however, *alumni* refers to males and females alike. The same is not true of *alumnae*, which can refer only to women—e.g.: "Throughout its history, the Securities and Exchange Commission has attracted lawyers of the highest quality; among its *alumnae* [read *alumni*], for example, are Mr. Justice William Douglas, Judge Gerhard Gesell, Professor Louis Loss, and Professor Homer Kripke." This statement might come as a surprise to the persons mentioned.

A more common mistake than confusing the gender of these words is confusing their NUMBER, as by using *alumni* or *alumnae* as a singular—e.g.:

- "Welch knew Fenton was an *alumni* [read *alumnus*] of UMR and wondered if Fenton could approach the new dean." *Allison v. Sverdrup & Parcel & Assocs., Inc.*, 738 S.W.2d 440, 446 (Mo. Ct. App. 1987).
- "Nor can it be said that the mere relationship between an *alumnae* [read *alumna*] and her alma mater, even if a close one, automatically imposes a fiduciary duty on the college when accepting a donation." *Abercrombie v. Andrew Coll.*, 438 F.Supp.2d 243, 275 (S.D.N.Y. 2006).

That *alumni* and *alumnae* are plural forms of *alumnus* and *alumna* should be apparent to anyone with even the faintest familiarity with Latin.

a.m., A.M.; p.m., P.M. Although periods are preferred in these abbreviations, it matters not whether capitals or lowercase letters are used—as long as a document is consistent throughout. The lowercase letters are now more common. The phrases for which these abbreviations stand are *ante meridiem* and *post meridiem*, not *meridian*.

But many statutes contain the erroneous forms **post-meridian* and **ante-meridian*, including a Massachusetts statute quoted in *Gallagher v. Crown Kosher Super Mkt. of Mass., Inc.*, 366 U.S. 617, 632 (1961). These misusages are just additional blemishes in books (statute books) that contain one literary blemish after another.

amalgamation. See **merger (A)**.

amatory. See **amorous**.

ambassador; ordinary ambassador; ambassador at large; ambassador extraordinary; legate; nuncio; minister; envoy; internuncio. All these terms designate a diplomatic emissary who serves abroad. The highest-ranking of these emissaries are *ambassadors*, *legates*, and *nuncios*. An *ambassador* is almost invariably a diplomatic agent who resides at a foreign capital <the American ambassador to Nigeria>; an *ambassador at large*, by contrast, has a roving commission and is not assigned to any specific country, and an *ambassador extraordinary* is one employed on particular or unusual occasions. (**Embassador* is a variant spelling.) A *legate* is a papal agent who has the authority to act in the pope's name; a *nuncio* is a papal agent who is not clothed with this authority but serves as an accredited resident ambassador of the Holy See at a foreign seat of government. A *minister* is an agent of the second or third rank. If of the second rank, the ministerial agent may be called an *envoy*—the full title being *envoy extraordinary and minister*. (See POSTPOSITIVE ADJECTIVES.) Although an envoy carries letters of credence to the leader of the state to which accreditation is sought, the envoy is not entitled to the same honors and privileges as an ambassador. An *internuncio* is a papal emissary of the second rank—the ecclesiastical counterpart to an envoy.

ambiance. See **ambience**.

ambidexter denotes a lawyer (esp., in the U.K., a solicitor) who, retained by one party to litigation, abandons that party for the adversary. E.g.: "He is a d—d rascal, and an immoral and base man, and unless ignorance of the law makes a lawyer he is no lawyer—he is an *ambidexter* and a disgrace to his profession." *Goodenow v. Tappan*, 1 Ohio 60, 61 (1823) (quoting a declaration). See LAWYERS, DEROGATORY NAMES FOR (A).

ambience; ambiance. The first form, the English form with the native-sounding pronunciation /am-bee-ənts/, is preferable. The second is a Frenchified affectation that has become a VOGUE WORD. See **ambit**.

ambiguity; vagueness; amphibology; equivocation; tergiversation; double entendre. All these terms refer somehow to a use of language whose meaning is unclear, especially because more than one meaning is possible. An *ambiguity* is susceptible of at least two reasonable interpretations; the term is used most often when a word or phrase, or perhaps a syntactic construction, might be interpreted in either of two quite different senses <the ambiguity of "Please bring me the nails on the counter," when lying on the counter are both nails to be hammered and acrylic nails intended to be affixed to the ends of fingers>. *Ambiguity* tends to result from either slyness or ineptitude (**purposely ambiguous* being simply a blunder, though a common one, for *purposely vague*). *Vagueness*, by contrast, denotes an expression that lacks distinct outlines; the meaning is uncertain because the ambit or scope of the words is fuzzy <the vagueness of a requirement to complete the project "within a reasonable period">. For more on this distinction, see AMBIGUITY (A).

With *amphibology*, we revert again to a duality (or multiplicity) of meanings, this time based on syntax—an *amphibology* being a grammatical construction that might be interpreted in divergent ways because of how the sentence is constructed <"the owner agrees to pay the cost of all construction that is considered reasonable" presents an amphibology: is it the *cost* or the *construction* that must be reasonable?>. (The terms **amphiboly* and **amphibologism* are NEEDLESS VARIANTS.) Most amphibologies result from either carelessness or ineptitude.

When the unclear doubleness of meaning is purposeful, *equivocation* is typically the best word. It usually implies that an expression critical to the thought or the argument switches its sense (this expression being called an *equivoke* /**ek**-wi-vohk/ <the equivocation in labeling illegal aliens "immigrants" and then arguing that "immigrants have been the lifeblood of the U.S. throughout its history" fudges the distinction between legal and illegal alienage>. *Tergiversation*, a bookish synonym of *equivocation*, suggests a greater degree of verbal deceit and intellectual dishonesty. It derives from the Latin word for "to turn (one's) back" and connotes betrayal.

A *double entendre* is an intentional ambiguity typically made for amusement or humor, often with one straightforward, colorless sense and another subtly suggestive, ribald sense. Groucho Marx, like many other comedians, dealt heavily in *double entendres*: "If I told you that you have a beautiful body, would you hold it against me?" Although the idiomatic French phrase is *double entent*, the English GALLICISM (borrowed from French in the 17th century) is spelled *double entendre*, with a halfway anglicized pronunciation /**dəb**-əl on-**ton**-drə/.

AMBIGUITY. A. Generally. Despite what many lawyers seem to believe, ambiguity in the broad sense inheres in all language. Even the most tediously detailed documents that attempt to dispel all uncertainties contain ambiguities; indeed, usually the more voluminous the writing, the more voluminous the ambiguities. (See MYTH OF PRECISION.) Nevertheless, we must strive to rid our writing of ambiguities that might give rise to

misreadings. Drafting especially is a constant battle against ambiguity—a battle that no one can entirely win: "Ambiguity is inherent in any language more complex than grunts, and even a grunt can be ambiguous." Philip Howard, *At the Double, and Be Rather Sharp About It*, The Times (London), 8 Feb. 1991, at 92.

The war against ambiguity should not be waged by overwriting and attempts at hyperprecision through exhaustive specificity. Rather, the legal writer should work on developing a concise, lean, and straightforward writing style, along with a sensitivity to words and their meanings. Once a writer has acquired such a style, ambiguities tend to become more noticeable, and therefore easier to correct. (See PLAIN LANGUAGE (D).) At the same time, an increased linguistic sensitivity allows one to see ambiguities in what might previously have seemed a model of clarity.

What exactly *is* an ambiguity? William Empson, the greatest expounder of ambiguity, has defined it as "any verbal nuance, however slight, which gives room for alternative reactions to the same piece of language." William Empson, *Seven Types of Ambiguity* 19 (1930; Penguin ed. 1977). Courts tend to define ambiguity more narrowly—and one might call this the *legal* sense of the word: "An 'ambiguous' word or phrase is one capable of more than one meaning when viewed objectively by a reasonably intelligent person who has examined the context of the entire integrated agreement and who is cognizant of the customs, practices, usages and terminology as generally understood in the particular trade or business." *Eskimo Pie Corp. v. Whitelawn Dairies, Inc.*, 284 F.Supp. 987, 994 (S.D.N.Y. 1968) (per Mansfield, J.).

Ambiguity should be distinguished from *vagueness*:

> It is unfortunate that many lawyers persist in using the word *ambiguity* to include vagueness. To subsume both concepts under the same name tends to imply that there is no difference between them or that their differences are legally unimportant. Ambiguity is a disease of language, whereas vagueness, which is sometimes a disease, is often a positive benefit. . . . Whereas *ambiguity* in its classical sense refers to equivocation, *vagueness* refers to the degree to which, independently of equivocation, language is uncertain in its respective applications to a number of particulars. Whereas the uncertainty of ambiguity is central, with an 'either-or' challenge, the uncertainty of vagueness lies in marginal questions of degree.
> Reed Dickerson, *The Interpretation of Statutes* 48–49 (1975).

Of course, even highly reputed legal writers confuse the two terms—e.g.:

- "A written constitution must be enormously *ambiguous* [read *vague*] in its general provisions." Edward H. Levi, *An Introduction to Legal Reasoning* 59 (1949).
- "A wise draftsman, when he is dealing with novel issues in course of uncertain development, will deliberately retreat into *ambiguity* [read *vagueness*—there being no such thing as "purposeful ambiguity"]." Grant Gilmore, *The Death of Contract* 76 (1974).

Dickerson, of course, discusses ambiguity from the vantage of the legal drafter rather than that of the poet; for the latter, ambiguity is hardly "a disease of language." As Empson has so well demonstrated, in literature it is often "a positive benefit."

Following are some examples of the more common types of ambiguity in legal writing. Some of these are equivocal only in a technical (or stickler's) sense (i.e., are patent ambiguities); others create real dilemmas in meaning (i.e., are latent ambiguities). Either way, these ambiguities detract from the context in which they appear.

B. Uncertain Stress Producing Ambiguity. "Even if a merchant sells a product, if he is not engaged in . . . selling that particular product in the normal course of business, strict liability may not be imposed." *Lancaster v. W. A. Hartzell & Assocs., Inc.*, 637 P.2d 150, 153 (Or. Ct. App. 1981). Is strict liability prohibited? Or is it a definite possibility? Read the sentence once stressing *may*, the next time stressing *not* in the final clause. Rewording the sentence eliminates the ambiguity. Assuming the writer meant to say that the merchant is immune from liability (and not that he *might* or *may* be immune), he might better have written: *he cannot be held liable* (see **can**) or *he is not subject to liability*. See **may**.

C. Syntactic Ambiguity. The ordering of sentence-parts is basic to clarity. When phrases are arranged with little reflection, ambiguities are certain to arise. Syntactic ambiguities are technically termed *amphibologies*: see the word-entry **ambiguity**.

1. Verbal Correspondence

- "'[T]he parties shall make every reasonable effort to agree upon and have prepared as quickly as possible a contract . . . .'" *Arnold Palmer Golf Co. v. Fuqua Indus., Inc.*, 541 F.2d 584, 588 (6th Cir. 1976) (quoting an agreement). Should the sentence read "to have prepared"? Does *have* correspond syntactically to *shall*, to *make*, or to *agree*? The three possible meanings vary substantially.
- "The artificial entity may sue or be sued as though it were a person, it pays taxes, it may apply for business licenses in its own name, it may have its own bank account, it may have its own seal, and so forth." All the instances of *it* in this sentence have the antecedent *entity*. Yet because of the placement of the first *it*, one is led to believe that the later ones will have a parallel structure ("as though it were a person, as though it pays taxes, as though it may apply."). So the reader is syntactically sidetracked for a moment. See MISCUES.

2. Poorly Placed Modifiers

- "No well shall be drilled within 200 feet of the dwelling or any permanent building of the lessors on the demised premises without *the [lessors' consent]*." *Associated Oil Co. of Wyo. v. Rector*, 50 P.2d 551, 554 (Colo. 1935) (quoting a contract). No well may be drilled without the lessors' consent? (This, obviously, is the intended meaning.) Or is it that the building must be on the land without the lessors' consent?
- "No adjudication was sought or obtained as to whether or not [the law] denied or abridged any right to vote *on account of race or color*." *Whitley v. Johnson*, 260 F.Supp.

630, 631 (S.D. Miss. 1966). The right to vote on account of race or color was abridged? No: the right to vote was abridged on account of race or color.

- "Fear that a jury will wrongly convict an innocent man of rape because it believes a woman who is ambivalent or deceitful after the fact *historically has pervaded the law of rape*." Leslie J. Harris, *New Perspectives on the Law of Rape*, 66 Tex. L. Rev. 905, 905 (1988) (book review). Ambivalent or deceitful historically? No: *historically* is a squinting modifier that should be placed in the midst of the verb phrase: *has historically pervaded*. See ADVERBS (A).
- "The court would be correct in ordering a partial distribution of the amounts of the fund *that has been sought in the motion*." Does the relative pronoun *that* refer to *fund*, *amounts*, or *distribution*? Seemingly the last of these, because the verb (*has*) is singular—and *fund* is not logically the right word. *Amounts* is the right word logically, but it does not fit with *has*.
- "This chilling tale, told in a 13-page report released today by Edward F. Stancik, the Special Commissioner of schools, raised serious questions about the detection and reporting of child abuse *by school officials*." Josh Barbanel, *Girl Writes About Rape by Father but School Ignores Plight*, N.Y. Times, 5 Feb. 1993, at B1. Readers may infer that the story is about *child abuse by school officials*; in fact, however, it is about *detection and reporting by school officials*.
- "Israeli police officers pulled tires away from a burning fire lit in response to the slayings *by Jewish protesters* Tuesday." *2 Israeli Police Gunned Down*, Daily Texan, 31 Mar. 1993, at 3 (adding that "police blamed militant Arabs for the pre-dawn slayings"). Is it *slayings by Jewish protesters* or *fires lit by Jewish protesters*? Though the latter interpretation seems more far-fetched, that is what the writer intended.

NOUN PLAGUE exemplifies one type of poorly placed modifiers. For example, *alimentary canal smuggling* was intended by the U.S. Supreme Court to mean "smuggling contraband goods by concealing them temporarily in one's gut." But the phrase suggests "the smuggling of alimentary canals." E.g.: "A divided panel . . . reversed [defendant's] convictions, holding that her detention violated the Fourth Amendment . . . because the customs inspectors did not have a 'clear indication' of *alimentary canal smuggling* at the time she was detained." *U.S. v. Montoya de Hernandez*, 473 U.S. 531, 533 (1985) (per Rehnquist, J.).

D. Poor Word Choice Producing Ambiguity. "No one has ever told them how to edit syntactic confusion into clear prose." Joseph Williams, *Style: Ten Lessons in Clarity and Grace* 4–5 (1981). To get at the author's true sense, read *transform* for *edit*. Otherwise, *edit . . . into* can read as if it were *insert . . . into*.

These problems are remedied easily enough by thoughtful attention to one's prose, and by editing and revising with the realization that legal writers harm only themselves when they burden readers with these dilemmas in meaning. Drafters who commit these sins do their clients a disservice, unless, of course, the clients enjoy litigation for the sake of litigation. See MISCUES.

---

ambit; ambience. The first means "scope," the second "the immediate environment; atmosphere." Here, *ambit* is correctly used:

- "To the extent any of the challenged testimony falls within the *ambit* of *Crawford*, we conclude that relief is not warranted under any standard of review." *Browning v. State*, 188 P.3d 60, 74 (Nev. 2008).
- "Congress has acted to exclude many discretionary determinations from the *ambit* of judicial review." Shaina N. Elias, Note, *From Bereavement to Banishment*, 77 Geo. Wash. L. Rev. 172, 203 (2008).

These terms are occasionally confused—e.g.:

- "The threshold issue is whether the installation of the first beeper constituted a search within the *ambience* [read *ambit*] of the Fourth Amendment." *U.S. v. Martyniuk*, 395 F.Supp. 42, 44 (D. Or. 1975).
- "Such actions by the Rent Administrator were within the *ambience* [read *ambit*] of authority given to it by D.C. Code 1979 Supp., § 45-1685(a) to carry out the rent stabilization program established under Title II of the Rental Housing Act of 1977." *Granite State Ltd. P'ship v. District of Columbia Rental Accommodations Comm'n*, 422 A.2d 1278, 1281 (D.C. 1980).

See **ambience.**

ambulance-chaser = (1) a lawyer who approaches victims of street accidents in hopes of persuading them to sue for damages; (2) a lawyer's agent who engages in this activity; (3) by extension, one who solicits personal-injury cases for a lawyer, usu. in return for a percentage of the recovery (today an illegal activity in most jurisdictions); or (4) by further extension, one who seeks to profit from the misfortunes of others <that politician is nothing more than a foreign-policy ambulance-chaser>.

According to the 1897 Congressional Record 2961 (24 July), the term originated in New York City, but it had appeared in a Utah newspaper a year earlier (*Ambulance Chasers: Pettifogging Lawyers Who Hunt Up Cases in Which They Can Get Jobs*, Broad Ax (Salt Lake City), 12 Sept. 1896, at 3). The best-known early *ambulance-chaser*—and the reputed coiner of the term—was Abraham Gatner, who in 1907 persuaded a New York law firm to let him sign up accident victims on retainer agreements for the law firm. Actually, though, the term was a misnomer from the beginning: Gatner would not reach the injured person until hours later—and often the next day. *See* Murray T. Bloom, *The Trouble with Lawyers* 118–19 (1970). See LAWYERS, DEROGATORY NAMES FOR (A). Cf. **case-runner.**

ambulatory (lit., "able to walk") has a special sense in the law of wills: "taking effect not from when [the will] was made but from the death of the testator" (*CDL*), or "capable of being revised." A will is *ambulatory* because it is revocable until the testator's death—e.g.:

- "The holding of the chancery court was based on the proposition that a will is *ambulatory*, speaks only at the death of the maker, and the 1955 will having been destroyed in the lifetime of the testatrix, it never had the effect of revoking the 1954 will." *Timberlake v. State-Planters Bank of Commerce & Trusts*, 115 S.E.2d 39, 40 (Va. 1960).

- "For more than a century, we have repeatedly emphasized that because a will is *ambulatory* in nature and because a testator has the right to freely revoke a will until death, an agreement not to revoke a prior will 'demands the most indisputable evidence of . . . agreement.'" *American Comm. for Wiezmann Inst. of Sci. v. Dunn*, 883 N.E.2d 996, 1002 (N.Y. 2008).

ameliorate; *meliorate. *Ameliorate* is the standard term meaning "to make or become better." E.g.:

- "These anomalies, however, appear sufficiently enmeshed in the current tangled web of the jurisprudence on this subject as to be beyond attempted *amelioration* by a panel of this Court." *Findeisen v. North East Indep. Sch. Dist.*, 749 F.2d 234, 241 (5th Cir. 1984) (Garwood, J., concurring).
- "In fact, LG had been prescribed medication since 2004, but even the medication did not *ameliorate* his behavior as shown through his continued fights and multiple suspensions." *Hopgood ex rel. L.G. v. Astrue*, 578 F.3d 696, 703 (7th Cir. 2009).

*Meliorate is a NEEDLESS VARIANT.

It is incorrect to use *ameliorate* as if it meant "to lessen"—e.g.: "The First, Second, and Eleventh Circuits found that any resort to Iranian courts to recover the movant's monetary loss, should the preliminary injunction be denied, would be futile and that the existence of the Iran-United States Claims Tribunal did not '*ameliorate* [read *lessen*] the likelihood of irreparable injury.'" *Enterprise Int'l, Inc. v. Corporacion Estatal Petrolera Ecuatoriana*, 762 F.2d 464, 473 (5th Cir. 1985).

ameliorating waste. See **waste.**

amenability; amenity. These words, of unrelated origin, are occasionally confused. *Amenability* = legal answerability; liability to being brought to judgment <amenability to the jurisdiction of the foreign forum>. For *amenable* and its near-synonyms, see **responsible.**

Amenity = (1) agreeableness; (2) something that is comfortable or convenient; or (3) a convenient social convention. Here the word is almost certainly misused: "Fiat moved to dismiss the action against it for lack of personal jurisdiction, arguing that it was . . . *not susceptible to the amenities of a Massachusetts forum* [read *not amenable to the Massachusetts forum*]." *Boreri v. Fiat S.P.A.*, 763 F.2d 17, 19 (1st Cir. 1985).

amenable takes the preposition *to* <amenable to process>. For more on this word and its near-synonyms, see **responsible.**

amend; emend. Both derive from the Latin verb *emendare* (= to free from fault). *Amend* = (1) to put right, change; or (2) to add to, supplement. This is the general word; the other is more specialized. *Emend* = to correct (as a text).

Amend out has been used to mean "to excise"— e.g.: "This language was *amended out of* the bill by an unanimous vote of the House Judiciary Committee." *State v. Greenough*, 491 P.2d 630, 634 (Or. Ct. App. 1971). (See **a (A).**) *Eliminated from, cut out from,* or *excised from* would have been more felicitous there. See PARTICLES, UNNECESSARY & **out (A).**

The nouns corresponding to *amend* and *emend* are *amendment* and *emendation*.

amendatory; amendable. *Amendatory* = effecting an amendment; *amendable* = capable of being amended.

amended pleading. See **supplemental pleading.**

amendment = (1) a legislative change in a statute or constitution, usu. by adding provisions not in the original; or (2) the correction of an error or the supplying of an omission in process or pleadings. This noun may take either *to* or *of*, usually the former—e.g.: "The continuing episodes of protest and dissent in the United States have their basis in the First *Amendment to* the Constitution, a great safety valve that is lacking in most other nations of the world." William O. Douglas, *Points of Rebellion* 3 (1970). On *amendment* vs. *emendation*, see **amend.**

amends. See **reparation.**

amenity. See **amenability.**

a mensa et thoro (lit., "from board and bed") is a standard phrase in canon law denoting a decree of divorce—now generally outmoded because it does not permit remarriage—that was the forerunner of modern judicial separation. (Such a divorce is distinct from the later divorce *a vinculo matrimonii*, which does allow remarriage.) The LATINISM seems little justified today, but it does indeed occur—e.g.:

- "Mrs. Scheinin filed a complaint for a divorce *a mensa et thoro* . . . on the grounds of desertion and cruelty of treatment and, in addition, alimony, for custody of the children of the marriage, support, and counsel fees." *Ricketts v. Ricketts*, 903 A.2d 857, 868 (Md. 2006).
- "Wife [filed an answer] requesting that she be granted a divorce *a mensa et thoro* on grounds of desertion with leave to merge the divorce into a divorce *a vinculo matrimonii* at the end of the statutory period." *Bryant v. McDougal*, 636 S.E.2d 897, 899 (Va. Ct. App. 2006).

The phrase *divorce from board and bed* is sometimes used instead. But all of them mean "a legal separation." See **divorce.**

amerce. See **affeer** & **penalize.**

amercement; *amerciament; *merciament. *Amercement* [fr. F. *estre B mercie* "to be at [one's] mercy"] = (1) the imposition of a fine; or (2) the fine so imposed. Usually *fining* (sense 1) or *fine* (sense 2) suffices in place of this little-known word. Sometimes, though, an appropriate edit is not at all apparent—e.g.: "It appears that an *amercement* proceeding may properly be initiated by motion in the principal action." *Vitale v. Hotel California, Inc.*, 446 A.2d 880, 882 n.1 (N.J. Super. Ct. 1982).

*Amerciament and *merciament are archaic variants. See **affeer.**

AMERICANISMS AND BRITISHISMS. Throughout this book Americanisms are labeled as "AmE," and Britishisms as "BrE." For guidance on distinctions not covered here, see Norman W. Schur, *English English* (1980); Norman Moss, *British/American Language Dictionary* (1984); and Martin S. Allwood, *American and British* (1964). For differences in editorial style, compare *The Chicago Manual of Style* (16th ed. 2010) with Judith Butcher, *Copy-Editing: The Cambridge Handbook* (4th ed. 2006).

amicable; amiable. The first we borrowed from Latin, the second from French; but the two forms are at base the same word. Yet a useful DIFFERENTIATION has emerged to set these words apart. *Amiable* applies to persons <an amiable judge>, *amicable* to relations between persons <an amicable settlement>.

amicable action. See **friendly suit.**

amicus brief. One *amicus brief*, two *amicus briefs*—not *amici briefs. E.g.: "An aberration of the norm occurred in *Chadha*: both petitioner Chadha and the respondent Justice Department were allowed to reply to the *amici briefs* [read *amicus briefs*]." Barbara H. Craig, *Chadha: The Story of an Epic Constitutional Struggle* 104 (1988). See **amicus curiae.**

amicus curiae; friend of the court. The Latin phrase, being well established, is not likely to be replaced in legal writing by its LOAN TRANSLATION, *friend of the court*. At times lawyers have forgotten the role of the *amicus curiae*—"one who, not as [a party], but just as any stranger might, for the assistance of the court gives information of some matter of law in regard to which the court is doubtful or mistaken, rather than one who gives a highly partisan account of facts." *New England Patriots Football Club v. Univ. of Colorado*, 592 F.2d 1196, 1198 n.3 (1st Cir. 1979) (ellipses omitted).

Amicus curiae practice is less restricted in the U.S. than in England, where "it is customary to invite the Attorney General to attend, either in person or by counsel instructed on his behalf, to represent the public interest, [although] counsel have been permitted to act as *amicus curiae* [read *amici curiae*?] on behalf of professional bodies (e.g., the Law Society)." *Concise Dictionary of Law* 21–22 (2d ed. 1990). In the U.S., virtually anyone with interests affected by the litigation, or indeed with political interest in it, may, when represented by counsel, be approved as an *amicus curiae*.

Amicus is frequently used as an elliptical form of *amicus curiae*. E.g.:

- "An *amicus* argues, and the concurring opinion agrees, that § 1226(e) deprives the federal courts of jurisdiction to grant habeas relief to aliens challenging their detention under § 1226(c)." *Demore v. Kim*, 538 U.S. 510, 516 (2003) (per Rehnquist, C.J.).
- "If any party or *amicus* believes that the revised policies do not conform to this Court's order, then they may file

a statement explaining the basis for that belief." *Plata v. Schwarzenegger*, 556 F.Supp.2d 1087, 1100 (N.D. Cal. 2008).

Amicus also serves as an elliptical adjective—e.g.: "Texas also failed to seek intervention or file an *amicus* brief in a Second Circuit case directly reviewing the contract rate rules." *Texas v. U.S.*, 749 F.2d 1144, 1147 (5th Cir. 1985).

Amicus is sometimes even used as an ellipsis for *amicus brief*: "In its *amicus*, El Salvador explains its interest in securing the ultimate relocation of the pilot station of what it views as its national carrier." *Airline Pilots Ass'n Int'l, AFL-CIO v. TACA Int'l Airlines, S.A.*, 748 F.2d 965, 971 (5th Cir. 1984). This ellipsis is perhaps too elliptical, because *amicus* does not readily suggest itself as a shortened form of *amicus curiae brief* or *amicus brief*, either of which should have appeared in that example. See **amicus brief.**

Although the modern trend is to place the phrase before the noun it modifies, *amicus curiae* is often used as a POSTPOSITIVE ADJECTIVE—e.g.:

- "Where he presents no new questions, a third party can contribute usually most effectively and always most expeditiously by a brief *amicus curiae* and not by intervention." *Crosby Steam Gage & Valve Co. v. Manning, Maxwell & Moore, Inc.*, 51 F.Supp. 972, 973 (D. Mass. 1943).
- "[The] conclusion of the Administrator, as expressed in the brief *amicus curiae*, is that the general tests . . . point to the exclusion of sleeping and eating time of these employees from the work-week and the inclusion of all other on-call time." *Skidmore v. Swift & Co.*, 323 U.S. 134, 139 (1944) (per Jackson, J.).

See POSTPOSITIVE ADJECTIVES. When the phrase appears before the noun, it need not be hyphenated. See PHRASAL ADJECTIVES (B).

Friend of the court, as an equivalent of *amicus curiae*, is primarily journalistic; it appears in many newspapers and journals with a general appeal. E.g.: "In a *friend-of-the-court* brief, the home builders say that permitting lawsuits for damages would show that the Supreme Court recognized 'limits on local regulatory powers that destroy private property rights.'" *Wall St. J.*, 9 Jan. 1985, § 2, at 25. But even this translated phrase must baffle the lay reader not familiar with court practice. The translation is therefore of limited value. See LOAN TRANSLATIONS.

The plural of *amicus curiae* is *amici curiae*. Frequently the singular is wrongly used for the plural:

- "The practice is particularly used in the U.S. Supreme Court, where organizations deeply interested in an area of constitutional law . . . will frequently petition for and be granted permission to participate as *amicus curiae* [read *amici curiae*]." Arthur A. Leff, *The Leff Dictionary of Law*, 94 Yale L.J. 1855, 2012 (1985).
- "The utilities may seek to present their views as *amicus curiae* [read *amici curiae*], and leave to do so is here granted." *Texas v. U.S. Dep't of Energy*, 754 F.2d 550, 553 (5th Cir. 1985).
- "Counsel for respondents, as *amicus curiae* [read *amici curiae*], assert that conclusion as their principal argument before this Court." *U.S. v. Sharpe*, 470 U.S. 675, 683 (1985) (per Burger, C.J.).

The singular is pronounced /ə-**mee**-kəs **kyoor**-ee-ı/ and the plural /ə-**mee**-kee **kyoor**-ee-ı/ or /ə-**mee**-see/. Another acceptable pronunciation of the first word—a common pronunciation in AmE—is /**am**-ə-kəs/.

amid. A. And *among.* *Amid* usually connotes position—e.g.: "*Amid* the public tributes, the one from Felix Frankfurter stood out." Barry Siegel, *Claim of Privilege* 186 (2008). *Among* often connotes a mingling—e.g.: "The will must be made at home or *among* his family or friends." 2 William Blackstone, *Commentaries on the Laws of England* 501 (1766).

B. And *amidst*; *in the midst of*; *mid*; *'mid.* *Amid* and *amidst* are slightly quaint words, especially the latter. Often the word *in* or *among* serves better. (But see **among (B).**) AmE prefers *amid*, BrE *amidst*. *In the midst of* is an informal and wordy equivalent. The preposition *mid* is poetic in all but traditional compounds (e.g., *midnight*, *midstream*) or scientific uses; if the word is appropriate, however, *mid* is better than *'mid*.

amok; **amuck.* The first is standard. Usage authorities once held firmly to the idea that **amuck* is preferable to *amok*—solely on the mistaken notion that **amuck* is older in English and *amok* (though a better transliteration of the Malaysian word) was a late-coming "didacticism." In fact, both forms date from the 17th century. And in any event, *amok* is by far the more common spelling today—e.g.:

- "There are important exceptions—exceptions that ought sufficiently to demonstrate the possibility that the linguistic sense of a profession can run *amok*." Lon L. Fuller, *Legal Fictions* 22 (1967).
- "RICO is a statute run *amok* and no one is beyond its reach." Rick Boucher, *Trying to Fix a Statute Run Amok*, N.Y. Times, 12 Mar. 1989, at 2F.

among. A. And *amongst.* Most forms ending in *-st*, such as *whilst* and *amidst*, are ARCHAISMS. *Amongst* is no exception: in AmE it is pretentious at best. E.g.: "Schools that have offered special composition courses for pre-law students (Illinois, Utah, Wayne State, Loyola of Chicago, *amongst* [read *among*] several others) have generally found them well received and oversubscribed." George D. Gopen, *The State of Legal Writing*, 86 Mich. L. Rev. 333, 355 (1987).

Amongst is more common and more tolerable in BrE, where it doesn't suggest affectation: "The first count of the declaration stated that plaintiff had contracted to perform in the theatre for a certain time, with a condition, *amongst* others, that she would not sing or use her talents elsewhere during the term without plaintiff's consent in writing." *Lumley v. Gye*, [1853] 2 El. & B. 216, 252 (K.B.). But many British stylists fiercely prefer *among* (rightly so, in my view).

Elmer A. Driedger wrote: "To divide *amongst* seems to be a little clearer than to divide *among*; in all other cases *among* is probably to be preferred." *The Composition of Legislation* 78 (1957). His first statement is unfounded: *divide amongst* provides no gain in clarity, and no difference in connotation or denotation.

B. With Mass Nouns. Generally, *among* is used with plural nouns and *amid* with mass nouns. So one is *among* friends but *amid* a crowd. (See **amid**.) *Among* is frequently misused for other prepositions—e.g.:

- "Incompetence in writing English is widespread *among* [read *in*] the legal profession." Robert W. Benson, *The End of Legalese*, 13 N.Y.U. Rev. L. & Soc. Change 519, 570 (1984–1985).
- "*Among* [read *With*] the president's contingent are Mr. Robert Mosbacher, commerce secretary, and around 20 top U.S. executives." Stefan Wagstyl, *Japan Promises to Boost US Imports*, Fin. Times, 8 Jan. 1992, at 1.
- "*Among the evidence* [read *As part of the evidence*] cited in support of these findings, the hearing officer noted that the school psychologist who had administered the plaintiff's . . . triennial evaluation . . . had opined that certain of the plaintiff's low test scores were consistent with persons having these disorders." *Christopher R. v. Commissioner of Mental Retardation*, 893 A.2d 431, 435–36 (Conn. 2006).
- "A thorough search uncovered twenty-four boxes of marijuana interspersed *among a shipment* [read *amid a shipment*] of seafood." *U.S. v. Gordon*, 510 F.3d 811, 813 (8th Cir. 2007).

C. And *between*. See **between (A)**.

amoral. See **immoral**.

***amortise.** See **amortize**.

amortization; *amortizement. The first, pronounced /am-ər-ti-**zay**-shən/, is the regular and preferred form.

amortize; *amortise. The *-ize* form is preferred in both AmE and BrE. The word is pronounced /am-ər-tiz/.

***amortizement.** See **amortization**.

amount; number. *Amount* is used with mass nouns, *number* with count nouns. So we say "an increase in the *amount* of litigation" but "an increase in the *number* of lawsuits."

amount of, an. See SYNESIS.

amphibious, adj., is frequently used in reference to mariners who work both ashore and on ship—e.g.:

- "Our past decisions have enunciated several factors to be evaluated in determining whether an *amphibious* employee becomes the 'borrowed' employee of other than his payroll employer." *Alday v. Patterson Truck Line, Inc.*, 750 F.2d 375, 376 (5th Cir. 1985) (per Tate, J.).
- "Though the Jones Act was intended to be the exclusive remedy for seamen, an *amphibious* worker may recover under state remedies that are credited toward any recovery under the Jones Act or general maritime law." *Rush v. Casino Magic Corp.*, 744 So.2d 761, 765 n.1 (Miss. 1999) (McRae, J., dissenting).

This extended sense of *amphibious* probably had its origin in the phrase of World War II vintage, *amphibious forces*.

amphibology; *amphiboly; *amphibologism. See **ambiguity**.

***amuck.** See **amok**.

an. See **a**.

anachronistic; *anachronous; *anachronic. The last two are NEEDLESS VARIANTS.

anaconda clause. See **Mother Hubbard clause**.

analogous; analogical. These words mean different things. *Analogous* /ə-**nal**-ə-gəs/ = similar in certain respects. The word should be avoided where *similar* suffices, but the two are not perfectly synonymous. *Analogical* /an-ə-**loj**-i-kəl/ = of, by, or expressing an analogy. E.g.: "In Anglo-American law we do not think of *analogical* development of the traditional materials of the legal system as interpretation." Roscoe Pound, *An Introduction to the Philosophy of Law* 106 (1922).

analyse. See **analyze**.

analysis. See ***analyzation** & **in the final analysis**.

analyst; *analyzer; *analyzist. The last two are NEEDLESS VARIANTS.

analytical jurisprudence = a method of legal study that examines law purely in its existing structure (without resort to its history), classifies its terms and concepts, and denies the law any validity unless it derives from or is sanctioned by a determinate sovereign. E.g.: "Austin, the father of English *analytical jurisprudence*, viewed all law as essentially a command of the sovereign power." H.G. Hanbury, *English Courts of Law* 15 (2d ed. 1953).

An adherent to this view of the law is typically referred to as an *analytical jurist*—e.g.: "Early in this century English and American *analytical jurists* produced a good deal of scholarship that resembles the work of legal science in a number of ways, and a revival of analytical jurisprudence is now going on in the common law world." John H. Merryman, *The Civil Law Tradition* 85 (1969). Cf. **sociological jurisprudence**.

***analyzation,** a pseudo-learned variant of *analysis*, has no place in the language—e.g.: "Defense counsel was then provided with ample opportunity to cross-examine to expose any weaknesses in Wagenhofer's credentials or process of *analyzation* [read *analysis*]." *U.S. v. Bartley*, 855 F.2d 547, 552 (8th Cir. 1988). It is what is known as a "nonword." See *Garner's Modern American Usage* (3d ed. 2009) (s.v. *Nonwords*).

analyze; analyse. The first is AmE, the second BrE. *Analyse* does not merit a bracketed *sic* when quoted in an American publication, as here: "The dust jacket tells us: 'In this book, the author brings to bear empirical evidence and legal theory in a critical comparison of English and American discovery, and *analyses* [*sic*] and evaluates the differences between the two systems.'" Kenneth W. Graham Jr., *The Persistence of Progressive Proceduralism*, 61 Tex. L. Rev. 929, 929 (1983) (book review). See *sic* (A).

*analyzer; *analyzist. See **analyst.**

anarchic; *anarchical; *anarchial; anarchist, adj.; ***anarchistic.** The preferred adjectives are *anarchic* (corresponding to *anarchy*) and *anarchist* (corresponding to *anarchism*).

anarchy; anarchism. *Anarchism* is a political theory antithetical to any form of government; *anarchy* is a state or quality of society. Only *anarchy* (= lawlessness, disorder) has pejorative connotations. Sometimes *anarchism* is misused for *anarchy*—e.g.:

- "On July 11, 1988, plaintiffs brought suit, alleging that they had been libeled by Schuster's accusations of dishonesty, character assassination, intimidation and *anarchism* [read *anarchy*]." *Stablein v. Schuster*, 455 N.W.2d 315, 317 (Mich. Ct. App. 1990).
- "Yet if such choices can be 'fundamental' or 'self-defining,' what is to rule out protecting any form of *anarchy* under the banner of liberty, so long as such *anarchism* [read *anarchy*] is 'authentic'?" Michael S. Moore, *Freedom*, 29 Harv. J.L. & Pub. Pol'y 9, 25 (2005). (This is a weird instance of INELEGANT VARIATION.)

ancestor. Only in legal writing does the term *ancestors* include parents as well as grandparents and others more remote. Nonlawyers do not generally think of their fathers and mothers as *ancestors*. See **ascendant** (B).

ancillarity = the quality of being ancillary or of maintaining ancillary jurisdiction (in the U.S., jurisdiction assumed by the federal courts for purposes of convenience to the parties, although the reach of the jurisdiction exercised extends beyond the constitutional or congressional grant). *Ancillarity* is not recorded in any dictionary, but is gaining ground as a legal term—e.g.:

- "Hence it seems quite clear that as concerns venue there are what may be termed 'degrees of *ancillarity*.'" *Lesnik v. Public Indus. Corp.*, 144 F.2d 968, 976 (2d Cir. 1944).
- "Many early decisions seem to go beyond this limited concept of *ancillarity*." *Chicago & N.W. Transp. Co. v. Atchison, Topeka & Santa Fe Ry.*, 367 F.Supp. 801, 805 n.1 (N.D. Ill. 1973).
- "There may be three possible bases for the exercise of federal subject-matter jurisdiction over these third-party claims: admiralty, diversity, or *ancillarity*." *Joiner v. Diamond M Drilling Co.*, 677 F.2d 1035, 1038 (5th Cir. 1982).
- "The concept of *ancillarity* may explain decisions which hold that actions to enforce an alimony or custody decree are outside the diversity jurisdiction if the decree remains subject to modification by the court that entered it." *Lloyd v. Loeffler*, 694 F.2d 489, 492 (7th Cir. 1982).

and. A. Beginning Sentences with. It is a rank superstition that this coordinating conjunction cannot properly begin a sentence. As Wilson Follett and Kingsley Amis pointed out, the same superstition has plagued *but*. But this transitional artifice, though quite

acceptable, should be sparingly used; otherwise, the prose acquires an undesirable staccato effect.

The very best legal writers find occasion to begin sentences with *and*—e.g.:

- "There are certain emergencies of nations in which expedients that in the ordinary state of things ought to be forborne become essential to the public weal. *And* the government, from the possibility of such emergencies, ought ever to have the option of making use of them." *The Federalist* No. 36, at 223 (Alexander Hamilton) (Clinton Rossiter ed., 1961).
- "This period gave rise to what came to be called the law merchant, and saw the hesitant but unmistakable beginnings of the law of intellectual and industrial property. *And* it is to these times that we may trace in recognizable form the patterns of modern shipping and its associated law." Grant Gilmore & Charles L. Black Jr., *The Law of Admiralty* 5 (2d ed. 1975).
- "Acts of Parliament after all are very real laws, as lawyers would unhesitatingly agree. *And* Acts of Parliament have a very tangible 'existence.'" P.S. Atiyah, *Law and Modern Society* 1–2 (1983).
- "Despite errors and failings, Blackstone did manage to put in brief order the rank weeds of English law. But even his picture was partial and defective, like a dictionary that omitted all slang, all dialect, all colloquial and technical words. *And* this imperfect guide was not available to colonials before the 1750s." Lawrence M. Friedman, *A History of American Law* 21 (2d ed. 1985).
- "The judges allowed shifting uses; that is, where a fee was to pass from one person to another upon a contingency. *And* they allowed springing uses." J.H. Baker, *An Introduction to English Legal History* 326 (3d ed. 1990).

See SUPERSTITIONS (D) & **but.**

B. For *or*. Oddly, *and* is frequently misused for *or* where a singular noun, or one of two nouns, is called for. E.g.: "Prisoners' cases are usually heard before federal magistrates *and* district judges." This construction wrongly implies that magistrates and district judges go together—that is, that they hear such cases at the same time. The true sense of the sentence is "magistrates *or* district judges."

Sloppy drafting sometimes leads courts to recognize that *and* in a given context means *or*, much to the chagrin of some judges—e.g.: "We give our language, and our language-dependent legal system, a body blow when we hold that it is reasonable to read 'or' for 'and.'" *MacDonald v. Pan Am. World Airways, Inc.*, 859 F.2d 742, 746 (9th Cir. 1988) (Kozinski, J., dissenting).

For the opposite mistake—*or* for *and*—see the third bulleted quotation under **ancillarity.** For a fuller discussion of the ambiguities caused by these words, see **or** (A).

C. In Enumerations. Legal writers have a tendency, especially in long enumerations, to omit *and* before the final element. To do so in legal writing is often infelicitous: the reader is jarred by the abrupt period ending the sentence and may even wonder whether a part of the enumeration has been inadvertently omitted. One may occasionally omit *and* before the final element in an enumeration with a particular nuance in mind: without *and* the implication is that the series is incomplete—rhetoricians call this construction "asyndeton"; with *and* the implication is that the series is complete. This shade in meaning is increasingly subtle in modern prose. For examples drawn from the writings of Benjamin N. Cardozo, Karl Llewellyn, and Gerald Gunther, see Bryan A. Garner, *The Elements of Legal Style* 160 (2d ed. 2002).

Finally, on the question of punctuating enumerations, the best practice is to place a comma before the *and* introducing the final element. See PUNCTUATION (D)(2).

D. Replaced by *which* in rhetoric. See **which (F)**.

E. Replaced by *if* in rhetoric. See **if (C)**.

*and etc. See **etc.**

and his children; and her children. This phrase ought to be avoided in wills because it gives rise to an interpretive dilemma: is the phrase one of limitation, i.e., does it indicate the size of the estate given? Or is it one of purchase, i.e., does it indicate a gift also to the afterborn children themselves? See **words of purchase.**

and his heirs; and her heirs. These phrases are quintessential pre-20th-century TERMS OF ART—pieces of magical language—formerly necessary to create a fee-simple interest. They are no longer necessary, as it is now possible to say, "I convey to you Blackacre in fee simple," and the words will have that very effect.

*and/or. A. General Recommendation. A legal and business expression dating from the mid-19th century, **and/or* has been vilified for most of its life—and rightly so. The upshot is that "the only safe rule to follow is not to use the expression in any legal writing, document or proceeding, under any circumstances." Dwight G. McCarty, *That Hybrid "and/or,"* 39 Mich. B.J. 9, 17 (1960). Many lawyers would be surprised at how easy and workable this solution is. See **either (D).**

B. A Little History. Lawyers have been among **and/or*'s most ardent haters, though many continue to use it. The term has been referred to as "that befuddling, nameless thing, that Janus-faced verbal monstrosity, neither word nor phrase, the child of a brain of someone too lazy or too dull to express his precise meaning, or too dull to know what he did mean, now commonly used by lawyers in drafting legal documents, through carelessness or ignorance or as a cunning device to conceal rather than express meaning." *Employers' Mut. Liab. Ins. Co. v. Tollefsen*, 263 N.W. 376, 377 (Wis. 1935) (per Fowler, J.). Another court has stated: "To our way of thinking the abominable invention *and/or* is as devoid of meaning as it is incapable of classification by the rules of grammar and syntax." *American Gen. Ins. Co. v. Webster*, 118 S.W.2d 1082, 1084 (Tex. Civ. App.—Beaumont 1938) (per Combs, J.).

These views, in retrospect, are more amusing than insightful. **And/or*, though undeniably clumsy, does have a specific meaning (x **and/or* y = x or y or both). But though the phrase saves a few words, it

"lends itself . . . as much to ambiguity as to brevity . . . . It cannot intelligibly be used to fix the occurrence of past events." *Ex parte Bell*, 122 P.2d 22, 29 (Cal. 1942). **And/or* "commonly mean[s] 'the one or the other or both.'" *Amalgamated Transit Union v. Massachusetts*, 666 F.2d 618, 627 (1st Cir. 1981). This definition suggests the handiest rewording: a good way to avoid the term is to write *unlawful arrest or malicious prosecution, or both,* instead of *unlawful arrest *and/or malicious prosecution.*

Sometimes **and/or* is inappropriate substantively as well as stylistically. Many types of legal documents have been spoiled by the indecisiveness of **and/or*:

- a finding of fact ("associate **and/or* employee");
- a pleading ("officer **and/or* agent");
- an affidavit ("fraud **and/or* other wrongful act");
- a will ("to Ann **and/or* John");
- an indictment ("cards, dice, **and/or* dominoes");
- a judgment (in an action that described the plaintiff by the formula *Jones *and/or Jones, Inc.*).

Courts have not been kind to the word—e.g.: "[T]he highly objectionable phrase *and/or* . . . has no place in pleadings, findings of fact, conclusions of law, judgments or decrees, and least of all in instructions to a jury. Instructions are intended to assist jurors in applying the law to the facts, and trial judges should put them in as simple language as possible, and not confuse them with this linguistic abomination." *State v. Smith*, 184 P.2d 301, 303 (N.M. 1947).

Moreover, the term gives a false sense of precision when used in enumerations: "In an enumeration of duties or powers, either conjunction is generally adequate. If *or* is used, no one would seriously urge that if one enumerated duty or power is performed or exercised, the remainder vanish; and if *and* is used, no one would say that an enumerated duty or power cannot be exercised or performed except simultaneously with all the others." Elmer A. Driedger, *The Composition of Legislation* 79 (1957).

For a superbly edifying essay that supplies still more history, see Sir Robert Megarry, *A New Miscellany-at-Law* 223–32 (Bryan A. Garner ed., 2005).

C. Editing the Hieroglyph. Sometimes **and/or* ought to be replaced by *and* itself—e.g.:

- "There is usually a blackboard, on which issues *and/or* [read *and*] votes may be recorded." Robin T. Lakoff, *Talking Power: The Politics of Language in Our Lives* 122 (1990). (No one would seriously suggest that both issues and votes must be recorded on such a blackboard in a jury room.)
- "Mr Pearce *and/or* [read *and*] his publisher are to be congratulated for working so fast." Joe Rogaly, *Behind the Man from Nowhere*, Fin. Times (Weekend), 27–28 Apr. 1991, at xviii. (If the book has come out promptly, then both the author and the publisher must have worked fast.)

At other times, **and/or* ought to be replaced by *or*—e.g.: "The legal disadvantages of illegitimacy can mostly be avoided by making a will *and/or* [read *or*] adopting the child." Glanville Williams, *The Sanctity of Life and the Criminal Law* 121 (1957). (No one would seriously suggest that one could be put to an election between making a will and adopting a child—i.e., that one could not do both.) For dealing with the construction *either . . . and/or*, see **either (E)**.

D. *Or/and. This reversal of the words is a rare variant of **and/or* with none of the latter's virtues, and all its vices. Rather than hopelessly confuse readers by resorting to its pretended nuance, one should abstain from it completely.

and other good and valuable consideration. See **consideration (D)**.

and which. See **which (C)**.

anecdotal; *anecdotic; *anecdotical. The first is standard; the other forms are NEEDLESS VARIANTS. In reference to evidence, *anecdotal* refers not to anecdotes, but to personal experiences of the witness testifying. Leff trenchantly called *anecdotal evidence* "a term of abuse in assessing a social science argument." Arthur A. Leff, *The Leff Dictionary of Law*, 94 Yale L.J. 1855, 2023 (1985). E.g.: "In probing discriminatory intent, a trial court may examine the history of the employer's practices, *anecdotal* evidence of class members, and the degree of opportunity to treat employees unfairly in the appraisal process." *Lewis v. N.L.R.B.*, 750 F.2d 1266, 1272 (5th Cir. 1985).

The surprisingly common variant **anecdotical* is to be avoided:

- "It is unclear from the plaintiffs' motion what *anecdotical* [read *anecdotal*] and testimonial statements should have been excluded." *In re Richardson-Merrell, Inc. Bendectin Prods. Liab. Litig.*, 624 F.Supp. 1212, 1233 (S.D. Ohio 1985).
- "I have welcomed not only the sustained argument on a theoretical level, but also the *anecdotical* [read *anecdotal*] evidence that has enlivened the study throughout." Hans Ulrich Jessurun d'Oliveira, *Multiple Nationality and International Law*, 101 Am. J. Int'l L. 922, 928 (2007) (book review).

*anent. Theodore M. Bernstein wrote, "Except in legal usage, *anent* [= about] is archaic and semiprecious." Theodore M. Bernstein, *More Language That Needs Watching* 24 (1962). He could have omitted *except in legal usage* and *semi-*.

Another usage critic (following H.W. Fowler) has given somewhat narrower guidelines, for the term is still sometimes used in Scotland: "Apart from its use in Scotch law courts, [*anent*] is archaic." Margaret Nicholson, *A Dictionary of American-English Usage* 25 (1957). Perhaps the best statement is that **anent* "is a pompous word and nearly always entirely useless." Percy Marks, *The Craft of Writing* 47 (1932).

The term was not uncommon through the first half of the 20th century. E.g.: "*Anent* [read *With regard to*] the dismissal, the bank's attorney testified that . . . the memorial company had advertised the property for sale on December 7." *Gandy v. Cameron State Bank*, 2 S.W.2d 971, 973 (Tex. Civ. App.—Austin 1927). Today it occurs only infrequently in legal writing, but examples of it can still be found (especially in the

prose of Judge Bruce Selya of the First Circuit)—e.g.: "The district court denied Fiat's motion to dismiss . . . and ordered the parties to resolve any dispute *anent* [read *about* or *over*] service on that basis." *Boreri v. Fiat S.P.A.*, 763 F.2d 17, 19 (1st Cir. 1985).

ANFRACTUOSITY, or syntactic twisting and turning and winding, has been one of the historical banes of legal prose. It was more common in the late 19th and early 20th centuries than it is today. Let us trace our gradual liberation from anfractuosity, while noting some modern throwbacks. The following is a classic 19th-century example:

> Unless the code, by abolishing the distinction between actions at law and suits in equity, and the forms of such actions and suits, and of pleadings theretofore existing, intended to initiate, and has initiated new principles of law, by which a class of rights and of wrongs, not before the proper subjects of judicial investigation and remedy, can now be judicially investigated and remedied, the facts stated in the plaintiff's complaint in this action, do not constitute a cause of action, and the demurrer of the defendant to that complaint is well taken.
>
> *Cropsey v. Sweeney*, 27 Barb. 310
> (Sup. Ct. N.Y. County, N.Y. 1858).

Here, from 1919, is perhaps the quintessential example of what not to do syntactically:

> Upon the petition of Armour & Co. of New Jersey, Armour & Co. of Texas, a foreign and domestic corporation, respectively, and F.M. Etheridge and J.M. McCormick, of Dallas, Tex., having for its purpose the cancellation of a contract between the city of Dallas, the Texas & Pacific Railway Company, and the Wholesale District Trackage Company, on the ground that it was void, because illegal, and for temporary injunction restraining all parties thereto from performing said contract or any portion thereof pendente lite, and alleging that the petitioners were taxpayers of the city of Dallas, and sued for themselves and all other taxpayers in said city of Dallas, Hon. Horton B. Porter, judge of the Sixty-Sixth district court in Hill county, upon the sworn allegation that the proceeding was a class suit, by fiat indorsed upon the petition in Hillsboro, directed the clerk of the district court of Dallas county to file the petition and docket the cause in the Fourteenth district court in Dallas county, and upon the petitioners entering into a bond in the sum of $10,000, conditioned as required by law, to forthwith issue the temporary injunction.
>
> *City of Dallas v. Armour & Co.*, 216 S.W. 222, 223
> (Tex. Civ. App.—Dallas 1919).

Perish the thought of one idea to a sentence! This phenomenon frequently occurs when one tries to sum up the entire case—the facts and the law—in one sentence. From 1984:

> Here, the hazard—the scaffolding which was unsafe to work on until its guardrail was installed as planned—was a temporary structure, not a part of the ship itself, its gear, or equipment, which was created and used entirely by the independent contractor, who both owned and controlled it.
>
> *Futo v. Lykes Bros. S.S. Co.*, 742 F.2d 209, 221
> (5th Cir. 1984).

And here, from 1985:

> Also of importance, without Ms. Stanlin's testimony that lawn mowers were actually missing from the Four Seasons

store, it is doubtful that the evidence would have proved beyond a reasonable doubt that the delivery by the driver (even if he was Marshall) of two boxes, of unknown content, showed that two lawn mowers, or any, were dropped off at Frederick Street, even though one of the (perhaps previously discarded) boxes indicated that, at least at one time, a lawn mower had been contained within it." *U.S. v. Marshall*, 762 F.2d 419, 422–23 (5th Cir. 1985).

Anfractuosity often leads to grammatical and syntactic blunders. E.g.: "We further hold it was reversible error to deprive the jury of the opportunity to consider the opinions of those who best knew the person whose fate *they* were to determine, and with it, the opportunity to reject, accept, and assign weight to evidence concededly relevant, *which*, as the exclusive arbiters of fact, *was* the jury's sole function." *Cass v. State*, 676 S.W.2d 589, 592 (Tex. Crim. App. 1984). In that sentence, *which* has no clear antecedent, and therefore *was* has no clear subject; *they* refers (loosely) to the jury.

When the syntax becomes so convoluted that it is unwieldy, or when the subject has become so far removed from the verb that readers no longer remember the subject when they reach the verb, it is time to break the sentence up into two or more tractable sentences. As Justice Benjamin Cardozo once wrote, "the sentence may be so overloaded with all its possible qualifications that it will tumble down of its own weight." *Law and Literature* 7 (1930).

Chief Justice William H. Rehnquist offered a solution that would still allow the occasional long sentence: "If a sentence takes up more than six lines of type on an ordinary page, it is probably too long. This rule is truly stark in its simplicity, but every draft I review is subjected to it." *The Supreme Court: How It Was, How It Is* 299 (1987). See SENTENCE LENGTH.

anguishment is a NEEDLESS VARIANT of *anguish*—e.g.: "The trial court award represented special damages for medical, surgical, hospital, and nursing expenses ($1,825.30), property damage ($425.00), . . . and general damages . . . for mental *anguishment* [read *anguish*], humiliation, and embarrassment." *Pierrotti v. Louisiana Dep't of Hwys.*, 146 So.2d 455, 460 (La. Ct. App. 1962).

animadversion was once a legal term meaning "the act of taking judicial cognizance or notice of." Today it means "harsh criticism," as here: "In an Alabama case of 1948, a mother who was convicted of murdering her newly born child received a sentence of twenty years' imprisonment; happily, the conviction was reversed on appeal for lack of evidence, but there was no *animadversion* upon the terrible sentence that the trial court had thought fit to impose." Glanville Williams, *The Sanctity of Life and the Criminal Law* 31 (1957). See **judicial cognizance.**

animate (= to move to action) has been used as a substitute for *actuate*—e.g.:

- "The jury was properly instructed, and it was their peculiar province to determine if the defendant was *animated* by malice. We think there is ample evidence to sustain the verdict." *State v. Acosta*, 242 P. 316, 319 (Nev. 1926).
- "Similarly it was the province of the jury to determine whether Kuk was *animated* by malice, express or implied." *Kuk v. State*, 392 P.2d 630, 632 (Nev. 1964).

Like *motivate*, *animate* is a serviceable replacement for *actuate*, the ready LEGALISM. See *actuate.

animo. See **animus (B).**

animus. A. Generally. *Animus* is a double-edged term. At times it is neutral, meaning "intention; disposition"—particularly the mental element in some conduct. This is the generally accepted legal meaning in legal contexts in G.B. and occasionally in the U.S.—e.g.: "This doctrine was overruled by statute in England, and the jury [is] now permitted to judge of the whole case, and to decide, not merely upon the responsibility of the publication, but upon the *animus* with which it was made." *Harrington v. Butte Miner Co.*, 139 P. 451, 452 (Mont. 1914) (quoting Thomas M. Cooley, *General Principles of Constitutional Law* 281 (1898)).

More often in AmE *animus* denotes ill will, as if it were synonymous with *animosity*—e.g.:

- "Thomas won [the Senate's] approval by 52–48 and said it was 'a time for healing, not a time for anger or for *animus* or animosity.'" Aaron Epstein, *Bush Nominee Carries Closest Vote Since 1888*, Philadelphia Inquirer, 16 Oct. 1991, at 1-A.
- "Plaintiff cannot show pretext because Plaintiff admitted that she failed to timely submit her expense reports and, although she alleges that her supervisor . . . harbored gender *animus* toward her, Human Resources, not [her supervisor], was responsible for the decision to terminate Plaintiff's employment." *Pierri v. Cingular Wireless, LLC*, 397 F.Supp.2d 1364, 1369 (N.D. Ga. 2005).
- "Given the evidence of gender *animus* put forward by Plaintiff, it is conceivable in this case that a jury could find that Plaintiff was intentionally discriminated against on the basis of her sex." *Sturm-Sandstrom v. County of Cook*, 552 F.Supp.2d 945, 951 (D. Minn. 2008).

B. Latinisms. The malevolent sense just mentioned stems perhaps from the several Latin phrases denoting malicious intentions: "Further, the opinion's use of the 'reckless disregard' phrase is followed by the Latin phrase '*animus injuriandi*,' defined as 'The intention to injure, esp. to insult.'" *Mangual v. Rotger-Sabat*, 317 F.3d 45, 66–67 (1st Cir. 2003). Similar phrases are *animus furandi* (= the intention to steal), *animo felonico* (= with felonious intent), and *animus defamandi* (= the intent to defame). These phrases are, happily, obsolescent if not obsolete.

Several neutral *animus* phrases have persisted, especially in the law of wills, yet these LATINISMS generally add nothing to analysis and muddy the waters. We know something is amiss when lawyers begin grammatically misusing Latin terms. For example, *animo revocandi* = with the intent to revoke (a will). In Latin, it is in the ablative case (equivalent to adverbial uses in English), here properly used: "It was generally held in the common-law courts that [upon] the destruction, *animo revocandi*, of a will containing a revocatory clause, a former preserved uncancelled will was thereby revived." *Timberlake v. State-Planters Bank Commerce & Trusts*, 115 S.E.2d 39, 45 (Va. 1960).

But *animo revocandi* is sometimes wrongly used as a noun phrase—e.g.:

- "The admissibility of such evidence for the purpose of establishing the *animo testandi* [read *animus testandi*] when offered for the purpose of supporting the writing as a testamentary disposition, is, in our opinion, the most serious question involved in [this case]." *Noble v. Fickes*, 82 N.E. 950, 953 (Ill. 1907).
- "To effect revocation of a duly executed will, [by] any of the methods prescribed by statute, two things are necessary: (1) The doing of one of the acts specified[;] and (2) accompanied by the intent to revoke—the *animo revocandi* [read *animus revocandi*]." *Thompson v. Royall*, 175 S.E. 748, 749 (Va. 1934).

Just the opposite mistake appears here, the nominative being used where the ablative belongs: "[There can be no conflict] between these ambulatory instruments—these wills—until death, and as the latter were destroyed *animus revocandi* [read *animo revocandi*], they thus never constituted wills under § 64-59, and never revoked the 1938 and 1939 wills." *Timberlake v. State-Planters Bank Commerce & Trusts*, 115 S.E.2d 39, 43 (Va. 1960).

The same sorts of errors occur with other phrases, such as *animus testandi* (= testamentary intent) and *animo testandi* (= with testamentary intent). "The admissibility of such evidence for the purpose of establishing the *animo testandi* [read *animus testandi*] when offered for the purpose of supporting the writing as a testamentary disposition, is, in our opinion, the most serious question involved in this case." We can avoid these embarrassments by sticking to what we all know: English.

Of course, the British seem to know their Latin better, and only rarely misuse *animo* for *animus*, or vice versa. But they are apt to go off the deep end in their proclivity for Latinisms: "The *animus vicino nocendi* may enter into or affect the conception of a personal wrong." *Lonrho Plc. v. Fayed and Others*, [1990] 1 Q.B. 490 (Q.B.D.).

annex, n.; **annexation;** ***annexment;** ***annexion.** *Annex* = something annexed or attached, as an appendix to a brief or a wing of a building. *Annexation* = (1) the act of attaching or incorporating (as territory within a municipality or nation); or (2) the state of having been attached or incorporated. In the parlance of property law, *annexation* refers to the point at which a fixture becomes a part of the realty to which it is attached. *Annexment and *annexion are NEEDLESS VARIANTS of *annexation*. See **appendix.**

annex, vb. See **append,** vb.

annexable. So spelled.

annexation; ***annexment;** ***annexion.** See **annex.**

annihilate is rather too strong a term for *nullify* in legal contexts—e.g.: "Counsel renew their contention that . . . the lapse of 20 years absolutely extinguished and utterly *annihilated* [read *nullified*] the judgment." *Odell v. Green*, 122 N.E. 791, 791 (Ind. Ct. App. 1919). Cf. **nullify.**

annotation; note; lawnote; casenote. An *annotation* is a note that explains or criticizes (usu. a case), esp. to give, in condensed form, some indication of the law as deduced from cases and statutes, as well as to point out where similar cases can be found. In law, *annotations* appear in the *Lawyers' Edition of the United States Reports* and in *American Law Reports* (ALR). *Annotations* usually follow the text of a reported case.

A *note* or *lawnote* is a scholarly legal essay shorter than an article and restricted in scope, usually written by a student for publication in a law review. In this sense *note* and *lawnote* are synonymous, the latter being slightly more specific. A *casenote* is so restricted in scope that it deals only with a single case; *lawnotes*, in contrast, tend to treat many cases in a general area of the law.

announce; ***annunciate; enunciate;** ***enounce.** *Announce*, the best known of these terms, may mean (1) "to proclaim"; (2) "to give notice of"; or (3) "to serve as announcer of." *Annunciate is a NEEDLESS VARIANT, except in religious contexts. *Enunciate* = (1) to formulate systematically; (2) to announce, proclaim; or (3) to articulate clearly. *Enounce is a NEEDLESS VARIANT in sense 1 of *enunciate*.

In reference to judicial opinions, *announce* means "to write for the majority." E.g.: "Mr. Justice Douglas *announced* the judgment of the Court and delivered the following opinion, in which the Chief Justice, Mr. Justice Black and Mr. Justice Reed concur." *Screws v. U.S.*, 325 U.S. 91, 92 (1945).

annoy. See **aggravate.**

annuitant; pensioner. *Annuitant* = a beneficiary of an annuity. E.g.: "A contract to buy an annuity was void where, at the time of the contract, the *annuitant* had died, so that the annuity no longer existed." G.H. Treitel, *The Law of Contract* 249 (8th ed. 1991).

Pensioner = a person receiving a pension. For some purposes the terms are interchangeable. Yet *annuitant* has less disparaging connotations, perhaps because the person it denotes has usually established the annuity, whereas a *pensioner* is generally the beneficiary of a pension provided by a third party, such as the government or an employer. *Pensioner* sometimes suggests one who lives off a very limited fixed income.

annul. See **nullify.**

annulment. So spelled—not *annullment (a common misspelling). See **divorce (A).**

***annunciate.** See **announce.**

answer, n. To nonlawyers, this word denotes a reply to a question or a solution to a problem. In U.S. law, it usually refers to the first pleading of a defendant addressing the merits of the case. In G.B., however, *answer* = (1) a reply to an interrogatory; or (2) a response to a divorce petition. See COMMON-LAW PLEADINGS.

answer, vb.; **respond; reply; replication; rejoin; retort.** In law, some of these terms have specific senses. An *answer* is the defendant's pleading filed in response to a plaintiff's complaint. A *reply* or *replication* may then follow from the plaintiff, and then a *rejoinder* from the defendant in response to the *reply* or *replication*. See COMMON-LAW PLEADINGS.

In motion practice, as opposed to pleading, names are even simpler: a motion is followed by the nonmovant's *response*, and then the movant's *reply*.

In the English language generally, the vocabulary of making statements that are prompted by others' earlier statements is full of nuances. *Answer*, of course, is the most general word. You *answer* a person or a statement when you pay due attention and say or do what you think next appropriate to the situation. You *respond* to a person or stimulus that elicits some kind of statement in return. Because *respond* is somewhat more formal, it is the term used for churchgoers' answers to questions in a catechism or supplications in a litany. You *reply* when you answer directly to a question, charge, argument, or salute (or to the person posing the question, making the charge, etc.). Hence, strictly speaking, you can *answer* a letter merely by acknowledging receipt, but you *reply* only when you address its contents more directly. In traditional usage, you *rejoin* only when answering a *reply*. Today the word is often used indiscriminately with *answer* and *reply*, as if to vary the word choice, but you can also be said (in careful usage) to *rejoin* to an unvoiced question or to someone's objection. You *retort* to sharp words when you verbally retaliate, counterattack, or make a resentful reply.

answerable. See **responsible.**

antagonist. See **opponent.**

ANTE-, ANTI-. The prefix *ante-* means "before," and *anti-* "against." Hence *antecedent* (= something that goes before) and *antipathy* (= feelings against; dislike). In but one word, *anticipate* (= to consider or use before the due or natural time), *ante-* has been changed to *anti-*. In compound words, the prefix *anti-* may cause ambiguities. See **antimarital-facts privilege.**

ante; supra; ubi supra; infra; post. Literally *ante* means "before," and *supra* "above." Some literalists therefore use *supra* for something higher up on the same page and *ante* for something further afield, with corresponding conventions for *infra* and *post*. That practice now has few adherents, at least in the U.S.

Both *ante* and *supra* are today used to refer to a preceding part of the text—however far afield—as in "*supra* at 11." *Ubi supra* was formerly used where *supra* now appears. It means "where above," and really has no place in modern legal writing.

Because *supra* is the more usual term, and because it is desirable that we achieve uniformity on this point, the recommendation here is to use *supra* for general purposes, not *ante*. An additional advantage of *supra* is that it translates directly into English. *See note 5 above* is English; **See note 5 before* is not.

The U.S. Supreme Court is one of few courts that distinguish between the signals *supra* and *ante* in usage; it also makes a distinction between *infra* and *post*. The term *ante* is used to cite a previous opinion published in the same volume of the U.S. Reports, whether or not that opinion is in the same case as that in which the citation appears. For example, *ante* is used in a dissent to cite a page in the majority opinion. *Supra* is used to refer either to earlier pages within the same opinion or to a previously cited authority. The Supreme Court uses *post* correlatively with *ante*, and *infra* with *supra*.

The phrases *ut infra* (= as below) and *ut supra* (= as above) are not current in legal writing, although they were common up to the mid-20th century. See *ex ante* & *infra.*

All these Latin words—*ante, supra, infra, post*—should be used only as signals; they should not replace ordinary English terms in prose. E.g.: "We discuss this argument *infra* [read *below*] and remand for appropriate fact findings." *U.S. v. Cherry*, 759 F.2d 1196, 1210 (5th Cir. 1985). Even in their use as signals, these terms are often vague without some specification of the reference; they are generally best avoided in CITATION OF CASES.

antecedent; prior. Used as adjectives—e.g., to qualify the term *debt*—these words are generally inferior to *earlier* or *preexisting*. Like *previous*, *prior* may occasionally be justified; *antecedent* may on rare occasions be forgivable, but not here:

- "There is no doubt that a bona fide holder of a negotiable instrument, for a valuable consideration, without any notice of facts which impeach its validity, as between the *antecedent parties* [read *previous parties* or *predecessors in interest*], if he takes it under an indorsement made before the same becomes due, holds the title unaffected by these facts, and may recover thereon, although, as between the *antecedent parties* [read *previous parties*], the transaction may be without any legal validity." *Swift v. Tyson*, 41 U.S. 1, 15–16 (1842) (per Story, J.).
- "The allegation of special damages as a matter of aggravation is a substantive allegation of fact, and not an inference of law resulting from facts *antecedently* [read *previously*] stated." *McConnel v. Kibbe*, 33 Ill. 179, 180 (1864).
- "The issue before the Court was whether a discharge of a previous debt was adequate consideration for a bill of exchange, in which case the endorsee would have enjoyed the status of being a holder in due course, notwithstanding

that there were legal impediments to enforcement as between *antecedent parties* [read *previous parties* or *predecessors in interest*] to the note's exchange." Lisa Litwiller, *Re-Examining* Gasperini: *Damages Assessments and Standards of Review*, 28 Ohio N.U. L. Rev. 381, 385 (2002).

The phrase **antecedent to* in place of *before* is a ludicrous pomposity—e.g.:

- "During the course of the trial and *antecedent to* [read *before*] the question complained of it was already established that the claim was filed immediately upon the occasion when he went up to the office of his attorney to see him about the case, so an inquiry as to that occasion was no different than an inquiry as to the time of claim filing." *Texas Employers' Ins. Ass'n v. Hughey*, 266 S.W.2d 456, 458 (Tex. Civ. App.—Fort Worth 1954).
- "*Antecedent to* [read *Before*] a finding of harmless error is a review of the claim of error at issue. The concurring opinion's approach would bar review of the finding of probable cause altogether." *State v. Mitchell*, 512 A.2d 140, 147 n.12 (Conn. 1986).

Cf. **anterior to, *previous to* & **prior to.*

But if the phrase is to be used, it should not lose the particle *to*, as here: "*Antecedent* [insert *to*] this assigned Justice['s (see FUSED PARTICIPLES)] joining the Court, facets of this controversy were here in *In re Powers's Estate*." *In re Estate of Powers*, 134 N.W.2d 148, 155 (Mich. 1965).

antecedents (= background; record) is broader in AmE than in BrE, where it means "an accused or convicted person's background, esp. any previous criminal record or evidence of bad character." In American legal writing, this FORMAL WORD may refer to any witness as well as to an accused—e.g.: "Where the litigation is important the character, reputation and *antecedents* of the main witnesses of the adverse party should be investigated thoroughly." Asher L. Cornelius, *The Cross-Examination of Witnesses* 11 (1929). In such contexts, however, *background* would be a better term.

A 19th-century usage critic stung this word with a venom that has not lost its power: "This use of the word . . . is not defensible . . . [f]or in meaning it is an awkward perversion, and in convenience it has no advantage. . . . [I]t is a needless absurdity. For if, instead of, What do you know of his *antecedents*? it is asked, What do you know of his previous life? or, better, What do you know of his past? there is sense instead of nonsense, and the purpose of the questions is fully conveyed." Richard G. White, *Words and Their Uses, Past and Present* 91–92 (2d ed. 1872). Indeed, *What do you know of his antecedents?* sounds almost as if you're asking about his grammatical prowess.

ANTECEDENTS, AGREEMENT OF NOUNS WITH. See CONCORD (B).

ANTECEDENTS, FALSE. An antecedent is a noun or noun phrase that is referred to by a pronoun. When used correctly and effectively, antecedents are explicitly mentioned, are prominent, and are not far removed from the pronouns that substitute for them.

But a variety of problems can occur, and some of them are here discussed.

A. Ghostly Antecedents. The problem of nonexistent antecedents occurs frequently when a word such as *this* or *it* (see DEICTIC TERMS) is intended to refer, not as it should to a preceding noun, but to the action accomplished in the verb phrase. E.g.:

- "The foregoing sufficiently answers, if any be necessary [read *if any answer be* (or *is*) *necessary*], . . . the suggestion that [the statute] is unconstitutional." *Closson v. Chase*, 149 N.W. 26, 29 (Wis. 1914).
- "To some degree, although not quantified, defendant's sales have declined. Quantification is not required for defendant is not seeking damages therefor [for what?]." *Hart-Carter Co. v. J.P. Burroughs & Son, Inc.*, 605 F.Supp. 1327, 1345 (E.D. Mich. 1985). The writer intended—but failed—to say that plaintiff is not seeking damages for the decline in sales.
- "They are also told that X., a doctor employed by the defendant, will vaccinate anyone who wishes to have this done." Steven Emanuel & Lazar Emanuel, *Emanuel Law Outlines* 59 (2008). What is the noun that acts as antecedent of *this*? We may understand the antecedent *vaccination*, but the sentence itself should supply the antecedent.

A similar problem is raised by using *this* with any one of two or three referents, as here: "Defining racism is a difficult, albeit necessary, task. This is due, in part, to the widespread existence and various expressions of racism, as well as changing understandings of race." Marissa Jackson, *Neo-Colonialism, Same Old Racism*, 11 Berkeley J. Afr.-Am. L. & Pol'y 156, 166 (2009). (What is due to the widespread existence of racism? The task of defining it? The difficulty in defining it? The necessity of defining it? This use of *this* is what English teachers have long called "broad reference.") See ANTICIPATORY REFERENCE (C).

B. False Attraction. In the context of problems with antecedents, false attraction occurs when, instead of referring to the subject, a pronoun such as *this* or *it* refers to a noun appearing between the subject and the pronoun. E.g.: "Harrelson nonetheless contends now that the admission of their testimony was reversible error because *it* had been hypnotically enhanced." *U.S. v. Harrelson*, 754 F.2d 1153, 1180 (5th Cir. 1985). What had been *hypnotically enhanced*? The writer intended to convey that the *testimony*, not its *admission*, had been enhanced by hypnosis. See SUBJECT–VERB AGREEMENT.

C. With Possessives. A noun in the possessive case is not a suitable antecedent for a pronoun because the possessive makes the noun functionally an adjective. The parts of speech of an antecedent and its referent must match—e.g.:

- "Indeed, the Court's reading of the plain language of the Fourth Amendment *is* incapable of explaining even *its* own holding in this case." *Oliver v. U.S.*, 466 U.S. 170, 186 (1984) (Marshall, J., dissenting). What is the subject of *is*, the antecedent of *its*? The intended antecedent is *court*, but the possessive *court's* is merely an adjective modifying *reading*, and is incapable of acting as the antecedent of *it*, or as the subject of *is*. [Read *Indeed, the Court in its reading . . . .*]

- "Would his testimony be the same as *his father's who* [read *that of his father, who*] said the back door was open?" *U.S. v. Pearce*, 912 F.2d 159, 163 (6th Cir. 1990) (quoting appellee's closing argument).

See APPOSITIVES (A), DEICTIC TERMS, POSSESSIVES (H) & **it**.

  D. Remote Antecedents. See MISCUES (C) & REMOTE RELATIVES.

***antecedent to.** See **antecedent**.

antedate; predate. Both words are so commonly used that it would be presumptuous to label either a NEEDLESS VARIANT. One sees a tendency to use *antedate* in reference to documentary materials, and *predate* in reference to physical things and historical facts—e.g.:

- "[The private criminal complaint process's] historical genesis long *predates* our modern system's belief that crime injures society as a whole." *In re Wilson*, 879 A.2d 199, 207 (Pa. Super. Ct. 2005).
- "The SEC has cobbled together a bricolage of agency decisions and statements, all of which *antedate Central Bank*." *SEC v. Tambone*, 597 F.3d 436, 449 (1st Cir. 2010).

The DIFFERENTIATION is worth enhancing.

antemortem; antemortal; premortal; *premortem; premortuary. *Antemortem* corresponds to *postmortem*. (See **postmortem**.) *Premortal* = (1) occurring before the time when human mortality was assumed (i.e., quite ancient); or (2) occurring immediately before death. **Premortem* is a NEEDLESS VARIANT of *antemortem* and *premortal*. *Premortuary* = occurring before the funeral. The distinction between *antemortal* and *premortal* (in sense 2) is that *antemortal* refers to any time before death, whereas *premortal* refers to the time immediately preceding death.

antenuptial. See **prenuptial**.

antepenultimate. See **ultimate**.

***anterior to** for *before* is, like its various bombastic competitors, almost risible. It would be, alas, if some lawyers did not use it with a straight face—e.g.:

- "The contract between this taxpayer and his creditor, which was made *anterior to* [read *before*] the passage of the statute which permitted this sort of a credit upon the taxpayer's income tax, is not attacked in any way as to its bona fides." *Richardson Oils, Inc. v. Thomas*, 61 F.Supp. 414, 415 (N.D. Tex. 1945).
- "The trial tribunal appears to have no system for monitoring filings made *anterior to* [read *before*] the approval order's entry in those cases in which the . . . settlement process remains *sub judice*." *Rowland v. City of Tulsa*, 988 P.2d 1282, 1287 (Okla. 1999).
- "The court instead denied relief on the distinct ground— *anterior to* [read *before*] all of the above, and unknown in nontreaty cases—that the law Hamdan relied upon was not 'judicially enforceable.'" Carlos Manuel Vázquez, *Treaties as Law of the Land: The Supremacy Clause and the Judicial Enforcement of Treaties*, 122 Harv. L. Rev. 599, 603 (2008).

Cf. **antecedent**, ***prior to** & ***previous to**.

ANTHROPOMORPHISM, the attribution of human qualities or characteristics to things, is not uncommon in the language of the law. One common manifestation of this phenomenon occurs in phrases referring to what a statute does or does not *contemplate*—e.g.:

- "The habitual-offender statute *contemplates* an enhanced sentence based on the maximum sentence for an underlying offense. It should not prescribe a particular enhancement for a sentence, which by virtue of plea agreement and adjudication cannot be imposed." *State v. Zachary*, 995 So.2d 631, 633–34 (La. 2008).
- "The statute *contemplates* a cause of action not only for preventing a person from testifying, but also for retaliating against a person for having done so." *Krutchen v. Zayo Bandwidth N.E., LLC*, 591 F.Supp.2d 1002, 1021 (D. Minn. 2008).

Or this, a form of HYPALLAGE: "A *concerned jurisdiction* is one that 'in view either of *its thinking* about the particular substantive issue raised or of its more general legal policies, such as concern for members of the community, can be taken to have *expressed some interest* in regulating an aspect of the multistate transaction in question.'" Arthur Taylor von Mehren & Donald T. Trautman, *The Law of Multistate Problems* 76 (1965).

Occasionally, anthropomorphism reflects poor style, as when a writer refers to the mindfulness of pellucidity: "Notwithstanding the fact that it is centered chiefly in construction, *pellucidity* in legal writing is not *unmindful* of discriminating diction and choice figures of speech." There are no choice figures of speech in that sentence.

ANTI-. See ANTE-.

anticipatable (= that can be expected or anticipated) is listed in the *OED*, with one citation from 1872, but appears in neither *W2* nor *W3*. E.g.: "Stone's statement . . . was elicited to dispel the *anticipatable* suggestion that the government might be using threats of prosecution to induce Schbley to testify favorably." *U.S. v. Fusco*, 748 F.2d 996, 998 (5th Cir. 1984). The quoted sentence illustrates the loose usage of *anticipate* (see **anticipate**); *foreseeable* would have been the better word.

anticipate = (1) to take care of beforehand; to preclude by prior action; forestall; or (2) to expect. Sense 2 has long been considered a SLIPSHOD EXTENSION; it should be avoided in formal legal writing. Lord Evershed, M.R., once addressed this question, saying: "The liking [that] many persons appear to have for the use of words having twice as many syllables as the more natural and proper word to use has, in fairly recent times, undoubtedly led to the use of the word *anticipate* when the correct word is *expect*." *Jarman v. Lambert & Cooke Contractors*, [1951] 2 K.B. 937, 942.

The poor usage is now seemingly ubiquitous—e.g.:

- "Generally the measure of damages for a tort 'is the amount [that] will compensate for all the detriment proximately caused thereby, whether it could have been *anticipated* [read *foreseen*] or not.'" *Valdez v. Taylor Auto. Co.*, 278 P.2d 91, 98 (Cal. Ct. App. 1954).
- "It is clear that the parties and the court still *anticipated* [read *expected*] that further remedial proceedings would take place before the court approved any proposal." *U.S. v. Crucial*, 722 F.2d 1182, 1187 (5th Cir. 1983).
- "Dickirson's conduct in its business operations and the nature of its manufactured products were such that it should have reasonably *anticipated* [read *foreseen*] being haled into court in Louisiana for alleged design or manufacturing defects." *Ruppert v. George Kellett & Sons, Inc.*, 996 So.2d 501, 510 (La. Ct. App. 2008).

The use of *anticipated* in the sense "eagerly awaited" constitutes still further corruption of the word. E.g.: "In the first few weeks of 1994, Britell and her husband eagerly *anticipated* [read *awaited*] the birth of their second child." *Britell v. U.S.*, 150 F.Supp.2d 211, 212 (D. Mass. 2001).

The following sentences illustrate the correct use of the word:

- "Where a debtor brings an equitable petition against his creditor, seeking to compel him to *anticipate* his right of action . . . a judgment sustaining a general demurrer . . . will not operate as a bar to the right of the debtor to set up such defenses in a suit subsequently brought by the creditor on his demand." *Satterfield v. Spier*, 39 S.E. 930, 930 syl. (Ga. 1901). Here *anticipate* = to act prematurely.
- "The plaintiff in the course of the trial may be permitted to amend her petition and show that she did not condone the offense, and we are not authorized beforehand to *anticipate* her rights as a litigant, and by strict construction of her petition deprive her of the benefit of a hearing." *Cope v. Cope*, 77 S.W. 92, 93 (Mo. Ct. App. 1903). Here *anticipate* = to preclude by prior action.

ANTICIPATORY REFERENCE is the vice of referring to something that is yet to be mentioned, but in a grammatical construction that appears to be backward-looking instead of forward-looking. A sentence will be leading up to the all-important predicate but, before reaching it, will refer to something that is contained in the predicate—later in the sentence. Grammatically, the *referent* comes before the *antecedent*. The reader is temporarily mystified. E.g.: "Conflict of laws is the study of whether or not[,] *and if so, in what way*, the answer to a legal question will be affected because the elements of the problem have contacts with more than one jurisdiction." Russell J. Weintraub, *Commentary on the Conflict of Laws* 1 (2d ed. 1980). A suggested revision: *Conflict of laws is the study of whether the answer to a legal problem will be affected because the elements of the problem have contacts with more than one jurisdiction; and if so, how the answer will be affected.*

Only rarely can anticipatory reference be used in a way that does not at least mildly discomfit readers—e.g.: "We think it is clear—*and no party disputes this point*—that the statutory commitment of review of FCC action to the Court of Appeals . . . affords this court jurisdiction over claims of unreasonable Commission delay." *Telecommunications Research & Action Ctr. v. FCC*, 750 F.2d 70, 75 (D.C. Cir. 1984). For an innocuous example with personal pronouns, see the second paragraph in (B) below. The vexatious examples, which are far more common, occur in a variety of forms.

A. As do. This phrasing, when it appears prematurely in a sentence, tends to suggest that the writer feared misusing (or even using) the word *like*—e.g.:

- "Texas, *as do* most jurisdictions, recognizes three general theories of recovery under which a manufacturer of a defective product may be held liable under strict liability principles." *McNeese v. Reading & Bates Drilling Co.*, 749 F.2d 270, 273 (5th Cir. 1985). One must either put *as do most jurisdictions* after the verb, or change the *as do* to *like*.
- "Senators Fisher's and Patterson's statements, *as do* [read *like*] others cited in Warrick's brief, certainly lend themselves to the interpretation that a goal of the legislation was to keep indigents from relocating to Pennsylvania. Another key provision in the statute reinforces this conclusion." *Warrick v. Snider*, 2 F.Supp.2d 720, 724 (W.D. Pa. 1997).

See **like (A)**.

A related error occurs with *have*—e.g.: "The court, *as have* [read *like*] the parties, construes this motion as one for judgment notwithstanding the verdict." Again, the cure is to replace *as have* with the simple preposition that some writers dread—namely, *like*.

B. Pronouns. A pronoun is supposed to have an antecedent—not a consequent. Yet many writers ill-advisedly put their pronouns before their antecedents—e.g.:

- "Assuming *it* applies to claims based on injunctive relief, the *doctrine of res judicata* would not 'bar a suit based on acts of the defendant that have occurred subsequent to the final judgment asserted as a bar.'" *Johnson v. McKaskle*, 727 F.2d 498, 500 (5th Cir. 1984). *It* has no clearly identifiable antecedent: only at the end of the sentence do we realize that *doctrine* is the referent. (On the use of *subsequent to in that sentence, see ***subsequent to**.)
- "After a hearing at which *he* and *his* office manager testified, appellant Reehlman, an orthopedic surgeon, was adjudged in contempt for disobeying a subpoena." *In re Reehlman*, 763 F.2d 670, 670 (5th Cir. 1985).
- "Even if *he* construed the evidence most favorably to the state, a *reasonable juror* should have doubted that the left side of the safe was in the building." *Corbin v. State*, 585 So.2d 713, 717 (Miss. 1991) (Banks, J., concurring). Reverse the positions of *he* and *a reasonable juror*; and consider making the reference nonsexist. See **SEXISM (A)**.

See **ANTECEDENTS, FALSE (A)**.

Occasionally an anticipatory reference by pronoun is acceptable, but only where the "antecedent" follows the reference closely: "Independent[ly] of the scope of *his* response to the auditor's request for information, *the lawyer* . . . may have as part of his professional responsibility . . . ." Robert J. Haft & Michele H. Hudson, *ABA Statement of Policy Regarding Lawyers' Responses to Auditors' Requests for Information*, Liab. Atty. & Acct. for SEC Transact. Appendix 7 (2009).

anticipatory repudiation. See **decline**.

ANTICIPATORY SUBJECTS. See EXPLETIVES.

***anticompete,** like **noncompete,* is a NEEDLESS VARI-ANT of *noncompetition*—e.g.:

- "Berkeley argues that it would be a disservice to the shopping center to allow Drug Fair to obtain the benefit of the *anticompete* [read *noncompetition*] clause." *Berkeley Dev. Co. v. Great Atl. & Pac. Tea Co.,* 518 A.2d 790, 796 (N.J. Super. L. Div. 1986).
- "The court might pay the employer a given sum of money to compensate it for the employee's violation of the *anticompete* [read *noncompetition*] agreement." Edward P. Richards & Katharine C. Rathbun, *Medical Care Law* 13 (1999).

antilapse statute. See **lapse statute**.

antimarital-facts privilege. This is an obtuse name for the evidentiary privilege allowing a spouse not to testify about "marital facts," i.e., intimate facts relating to the marriage. The phrase *antimarital facts* refers to facts whose disclosure tends to harm the marriage. The prefix *anti-* causes the problem, for the privilege is not "antimarital." Yet the disclosure of the facts *is* thought to be "antimarital." The ambiguity caused by the prefix disappears when an alternative name for the privilege is used (e.g., *privilege against adverse spousal testimony, spousal privilege,* or *marital privilege*). The first of these alternative versions is used by the Supreme Court in *Trammel v. U.S.,* 445 U.S. 40, 44 (1980).

antinomy; antimony. These words are not to be confused. *Antinomy* = a contradiction in law or logic; a conflict of authority. *Antimony* = a brittle silvery-white metallic element common in alloys. The first of these, with the root *-nom-* (= law), is the one typically needed in legal contexts—e.g.:

- "The law was taken to be complete and self-sufficient, without *antinomies* and without gaps, wanting only arrangement, logical development of the implications of its several rules and conceptions, and systematic exposition of its several parts." Roscoe Pound, *An Introduction to the Philosophy of Law* 48 (1922).
- "He has even more difficulty in absorbing the notion that *antinomies* among the principles of legal morality may be encountered in the design of legal institutions." Lon L. Fuller, *The Morality of Law* 240 (rev. ed. 1969).

antipathy takes *against, to, toward,* or *for*—e.g.: "In the main, the modern conservative movement's general *antipathy to* government flows from two sentiments: first, it sees government as generally inefficient and often incompetent; second, it sees governmental power and personal freedom as inversely correlated, that is, as a general matter, the more powerful the government, the less free the individual." Carl T. Bogus, *Heller and Insurrectionism,* 59 Syracuse L. Rev. 253, 262 (2008).

The writer of the following sentence haplessly inserted one of the few unidiomatic prepositions: "The court found as a fact that while the defendant had some valid reasons for refusing to renew the plaintiffs' lease, he was also motivated by his *antipathy of* [read *antipathy toward*] the plaintiffs' biracial dating and entertainment practices." *Bills v. Hodges,* 628 F.2d 844, 845 (4th Cir. 1980).

antipiracy (= of or relating to an effort to combat or discourage illegal reproduction, distribution, or use of copyrighted or trademarked products) is so written—solid.

antisuit (= of or relating to a court order prohibiting the filing of another lawsuit against the same party or making the same claim) is a mid-20th-century legal NEOLOGISM that remains unrecorded in most English-language dictionaries. E.g.:

- "Where the two courts involved are a state and a federal court, special attention should be given to such an *antisuit* injunction." *Blanchard v. Commonwealth Oil Co.,* 294 F.2d 834, 839 (5th Cir. 1961).
- "Ordinarily *antisuit* injunctions are not properly invoked to preempt parallel proceedings on the same in personam claim in foreign tribunals." *Laker Airways Ltd. v. Sabena, Belgian World Airlines,* 731 F.2d 909, 915 (D.C. Cir. 1984).

antitrust. So written—without a hyphen.

Anton Piller order. See CASE REFERENCES (C).

a number of people (is) (are). See SYNESIS.

anxious. This word most properly means "uneasy; disquieted; worried." To use the word as a synonym for *eager* is to give in to SLIPSHOD EXTENSION. One unreported opinion contains such a telling misusage that it can't be omitted here (despite the policy in this book of preferring published works): "They weren't nervous; they were just *anxious* [read *eager*] to go fishing." *U.S. v. Metcalf,* 2007 WL 2220424 (E.D. Tenn. 2007).

But where the sense of anticipation is mixed with anxiety, *anxious* is just the word—e.g.:

- "Here the mother's whereabouts were known, she was soon to be released and available for trial, and was *anxious* to retain her children." *In re Welfare of HGB,* 306 N.W.2d 821, 827 (Minn. 1981) (Otis, J., dissenting).
- "The black man feels that he has certain rights and is *anxious* to know what they are and how to procure, protect, and maintain the same." Donald G. Nieman, *From Slaves to Citizens: African-Americans, Rights Consciousness, and Reconstruction,* 17 Cardozo L. Rev. 2115, 2127 (1996) (quoting an 1867 report).

any. A. Singular or Plural. *Any* may be either singular or plural. Here are examples of the (rarer) singular use:

- "Accordingly, we do not reach the question whether *any* of these statements is 'of and concerning' CSI." *Church of Scientology Int'l v. Behar,* 238 F.3d 168, 173 (2d Cir. 2001).
- "We conclude that Weinberger has not demonstrated a prima facie case that *any* of the statements is false or

was made with actual malice and that this factor weighs against the disclosure ordered." *Weinberger v. Maplewood Review*, 648 N.W.2d 249, 256–57 (Minn. Ct. App. 2002).

In those constructions, *any* is really elliptical for *any one*. See **anyone** (A).

B. In Legislation. *Any* is greatly overworked in statutes <if any person shall commit any action upon any other person>. Usually, replacing *any* with the indefinite article *a* or *an* results in heightened readability with no change in meaning.

C. And *all*. See **all** (C).

any and all. The word *all* precisely captures the sense 99 out of 100 times. The one other time, it merely captures the sense. See DOUBLETS, TRIPLETS, AND SYNONYM-STRINGS.

anyhow (= in any way; in any manner) is, in AmE, considered colloquial—almost dialectal—for *anyway* or *nevertheless*. It doesn't fit comfortably in the pages of an august law review—e.g.:

- "To the extent international law does not reflect power politics, realists believe that much of its apparent influence can be explained—or explained away—as nations doing what they would have done *anyhow* [read *anyway*], in the absence of law." Jack Goldsmith & Daryl Levinson, *Law for States: International Law, Constitutional Law, Public Law*, 122 Harv. L. Rev. 1791, 1826 (2009).
- "I do not, without further persuasion, share Mr. Drachsler's view that we should seek declarations of organizational criminality; that technique has had only very limited success in the international trial, and seems to me unnecessary *anyhow* [read *anyway*]." Jonathan A. Bush, *The Prehistory of Corporations and Conspiracy in International Criminal Law*, 109 Colum. L. Rev. 1094, 1250 (2009).

In BrE, however, the word does not seem to strike readers as such a casualism—e.g.: "In many cases it is not for one moment expected that a contracting party will actually perform in person, and when the contracting party is a corporation this would *anyhow* be a physical impossibility." P.S. Atiyah, *An Introduction to the Law of Contract* 283 (3d ed. 1981).

anyone. A. And *any one*. Referring to persons, *anyone* should be spelled as one word. Although once written as two words, the unification of the phrase is complete. *Any one* = any single person or thing (of a number).

Sometimes the phrase is wrongly made one word when, not meaning "anybody," it should be two—e.g.:

- "*Anyone* [read *Any one*] of these facts, standing alone, might amount to no more than suspicion." *U.S. v. Stein*, 53 F.Supp. 911, 913 (W.D.N.Y. 1943).
- "[A question] might arise as to *anyone* [read *any one*] or all of these legitimate 'conceivables.'" *Town of Ball v. Rapides Parish Police Jury*, 746 F.2d 1049, 1062 (5th Cir. 1984).
- "*Anyone* [read *Any one*] of these reasons, alone or in concert with another is sufficient to validate a claim." *Tosco Corp. v. Hodel*, 611 F.Supp. 1130, 1180 (D. Colo. 1985).

B. *Anyone . . . they*. See CONCORD (B) & SEXISM (A).
C. *Anyone else's*. See **else's** & POSSESSIVES (G).

anything; any thing. The distinction is sometimes important in LEGISLATIVE DRAFTING. *Any thing* implies an opposition to *any person*. *Anything* is the far more general word meaning "whatever thing."

anything to the contrary contained herein notwithstanding. See **notwithstanding anything to the contrary contained herein.**

any wise, in. See **wise.**

***apanage.** See **appanage.**

apiece. See **each** (A).

apostasy; *apostacy*. The latter spelling is mistaken, the original Greek word being *apostasia*. E.g.: "Would he then have embraced and defended the *Donovan apostacy* [read *apostasy*] with the same generosity with which he yielded to the *Camara* majority in *Barlow*?" Maurice Kelman, *The Forked Path of Dissent*, 1985 Sup. Ct. Rev. 227, 245.

a posteriori. See **a priori.**

APOSTROPHES. See PUNCTUATION (B).

appall; *appal*. The first is the standard spelling.

appanage; *apanage*. Though in today's French this term is spelled *-p-*, in the French of the 16th century it was spelled *-pp-*. We borrowed the word from the French early in the 17th century, and the *OED* notes that the spellings have been "equally common" in English. The *OED* favors ***apanage*, whereas *W3* favors *appanage*. The latter certainly *appears* more English, and on that basis alone might be deemed preferable.

In its literal and historical sense, *appanage* /**ap**-ə-nij/ means "a grant (as of lands or money) made by a sovereign or a legislative body for the support of dependent members of the royal family" (*W3*). Because Americans are not saddled with such burdens, the term is purely figurative in AmE, meaning "a customary or rightful endowment" (*W3*).

apparatus has the plural forms *apparatuses* and *apparatus*. The first is an English plural and the second the Latin one. When referring to more than one apparatus in Latin, write *apparatus*. But when using English, use *apparatuses*. (It's a fourth-declension noun.) See PLURALS (A).

***Apparati* is a laughable example of HYPERCORRECTION—e.g.:

- "Her testimony indicates that she had definite ideas as to where and how these *apparati* [read *apparatuses*] were to be used." *Clarke v. O'Connor*, 435 F.2d 104, 107 (D.C. Cir. 1970).
- "The court attempted to establish a procedure for determining whether a doctor could disconnect life-sustaining *apparati* [read *apparatuses*] from other patients." Linda F. Gould, *Right to Die Legislation*, 39 Mercer L. Rev. 517, 523 (1988).

apparent is frequently misused in the press, and sometimes in legal writing, in reference to fatal maladies—e.g.:

- "First, there was nothing inherently suspicious in Cascone's *reported death of an apparent heart attack because* [read *reported death—apparently of a heart attack—because*] Cascone had a long history of heart disease, including congestive heart failure, and at the time of admission to the hospital showed heart irregularities." *Cascone v. U.S.*, 370 F.3d 95, 97 (1st Cir. 2004).
- "On September 28, 1986, the decedent *collapsed at home and died of an apparent heart attack* [read *collapsed at home and died, apparently of a heart attack*]." *Kinney v. State*, 941 A.2d 907, 910 (Conn. 2008).

See **evident**. For the sense of *apparent* in *heir apparent*, see **heir (B).**

apparent authority; ostensible authority. Both refer to the authority that an agent appears to have by virtue of the principal's conduct—and that third parties might reasonably assume that the agent actually has. The usual phrase today, in BrE and AmE alike, is *apparent authority.*

appeal, adj. See **appellate** & **appeals,** adj.

appeal, n. **A. Idioms.** In AmE, cases are said to go *on appeal*. In BrE, the idiom *under appeal* is common—e.g.:

- "Their Lordships are of opinion that the decision *under appeal* is not in accordance with that principle." *MacIntosh v. Dun*, [1908] A.C. 390 (P.C.) (appeal taken from Australia).
- "Their Lordships are of opinion that the decision *under appeal* correctly ordered a certificate of succession to be issued giving to the widow of the deceased twelve shares out of twenty-four in the mulk property in Jaffa." *Jaber Elias Ktoia v. Katr Bint Jiryes*, [1941] A.C. 403 (P.C.) (appeal taken from Palestine).

The British phrase *appeal allowed* is equivalent to the American *reversed*. See **appeal allowed, allow** & **on appeal.**

Where American writers would refer to an *appeal from* a judgment, British writers typically refer to an *appeal against* a judgment—e.g.: "Again, in the case of *Harris* in 1952, the speeches were postponed until after the House had intimated that his *appeal against* conviction for larceny would be allowed." H.G. Hanbury, *English Courts of Law* 78–79 (2d ed. 1953).

B. And *certiorari; review.* In referring to consideration by the U.S. Supreme Court of lower-court and state-court judgments, many American lawyers make the mistake of calling the genus by the name of one species; that is, they refer to *appeal* when they mean to include *certiorari* as well. In fact, though, *appeal* is rare in the U.S. Supreme Court. *See* Charles Alan Wright, *The Law of Federal Courts* 775–76 (5th ed. 1994). The more accurate term for the genus—the word that includes *certiorari* as well as *appeal*—is *review*. See **review (A).**

appeal, vb. Depending on the context, *appeal* may be either intransitive or transitive in AmE. Usually one *appeals from* a judgment—e.g.:

- "The defendant *appeals from* a verdict and judgment against him in a slander suit." *Haynes v. Robertson*, 175 S.W. 290, 291 (Mo. Ct. App. 1915).
- "Plaintiff *appealed from* an order sustaining separate demurrers of the defendants on the ground that the complaint does not state a cause of action." *Sorenson v. Chevrolet Motor Co.*, 214 N.W. 754, 754 (Minn. 1927).
- "We find no error in the decrees *appealed from* and they are affirmed." *Home Bldg. Ass'n v. Mackall*, 135 S.E.2d 171, 178 (Va. 1964).

But nearly as often, *appeal* is used transitively in AmE—e.g.:

- "Nolen *appeals* the award of an injunction against him." *Molex, Inc. v. Nolen*, 759 F.2d 474, 475 (5th Cir. 1985).
- "Appellant *appeals* his convictions for possessing a firearm while possessing cocaine . . . and possessing a firearm while a convicted felon." *Fisher v. Commonwealth*, 592 S.E.2d 377, 378 (Va. Ct. App. 2004).

In BrE—in which the transitive use has been obsolete since the late 16th century—one *appeals against* a lower court's decree. E.g.:

- "An erroneous judgment may stand, and acquire an undeserved authority, merely because the losing party does not *appeal against* it." Carleton K. Allen, *Law in the Making* 313 (7th ed. 1964).
- "The architect *appealed against* the master's order to Chapman J. who allowed his appeal and set aside the master's order." *Moon v. Atherton*, [1972] 2 Q.B. 435 (C.A.).

appeal against. See **appeal (A)** & **appeal,** vb.

appeal allowed; appeal dismissed. These British phrases are equivalent to the American phrases *judgment reversed* and *judgment affirmed*. See JUDGMENTS, APPELLATE-COURT.

appeal court. See **appeals,** adj.

***appealer.** See **appellant.**

appeal from. See **appeal (A).**

appeals, adj. In jurisdictions that have a *court of appeals*—as opposed to a *court of appeal*—the alternative wording is *appeals court*, not *appeal court*. E.g.: "A federal *appeals court* in Philadelphia ruled last August that the OMB officials didn't have the authority to do so." Stephen Wermiel, *Supreme Court Will Review OMB's Powers*, Wall St. J., 16 May 1989, at B7. Even so, the term *appellate* is usually more natural-sounding in AmE.

Of course, where, as in California or England, the name of the intermediate appellate court is the *Court of Appeal*, the phrase *appeal court* is entirely proper—e.g.: "Within a week, the High Court decided that Lord Young, the trade secretary, should publish and refer to the Monopolies and Mergers Commission an inspectors' report on the takeover; then a unanimous

---

three-judge *appeal court* decided he need do no such thing." *Curbed in the Courts*, Economist, 28 Jan.–3 Feb. 1989, at 56.

appear. The phrase *it would appear* (it would indeed appear) is invariably inferior to *it appears* or *it seems*. There is no need for the modal verb *would* in this construction, unless a hypothetical subjunctive is intended. Yet legal writers are addicted to this infernal hedging—e.g.:

- "*It would appear* [read *It appears*] to be agnosticism with respect to the existence of tacitly collusive equilibria that are equal to the monopoly level." Alan Devlin, Comment, *A Proposed Solution to the Problem of Parallel Pricing in Oligopolistic Markets*, 59 Stan. L. Rev. 1111, 1118 (2007).
- "*It would appear* [read *It seems*] that the Court's choice to couch its substantive decisions in *BMW* and *Campbell* in procedural terms was the product of a defensive and not particularly convincing effort to ward off comparisons to *Lochner*." Thomas B. Colby, *Clearing the Smoke from Philip Morris v. Williams*, 118 Yale L.J. 392, 404 (2008).
- "*It would appear* [read *It appears*] likely that *Skidmore* review, authorized by *Mead*, may well ensure not a firmer judicial hand, but a situation in which judicial policy preferences play a (still) larger role than they do under *Chevron*." Cass R. Sunstein & Thomas J. Miles, *Depoliticizing Administrative Law*, 58 Duke L.J. 2193, 2221 (2009).

See **would** & SUBJUNCTIVES.

On the difference between *appear* and *make an appearance*, see **appearance, make an.**

appearance, make an; appear, vb. The phrase *make an appearance* contains a BURIED VERB (*appear*), but uncovering the verb may shift the connotation slightly. Many American lawyers believe that a party *makes an appearance* by filing a paper in court or by having a lawyer present, but that to *appear* means to show up personally in court. Some have used this rationale to avoid changing *make an appearance* to *appear* in court rules.

Even so, actual usage supports the idea that *appear* is equivalent to *make an appearance*—e.g.: "In most cases, the husband and wife both desire divorce. If the husband gets his divorce in Nevada and the wife *appears* there—which means that an arrangement is made to have a lawyer in Nevada represent her—there will be no trouble." Max Radin, *The Law and You* 68 (1948).

appellant; appellee. For points of usage, see **plaintiff, defendant.**

appellant; *appealer; *appellor. Perhaps few readers have seen or heard any term other than the first. **Appealer* has not gained currency and should not be introduced as a fancy variant of *appellant*, properly pronounced /ə-**pel**-ənt/.

*Appellor is an archaic term from English law meaning "one who accuses of crime, demands proof of innocence by wager of battle, or informs against an accomplice [by *approvement*]" (*OED*). E.g.: "Appeals of felony continued in use as a means of recovering stolen goods, or of achieving the execution of

an aggressor; but the *appellor* ran the risk of having to fight a battle, or of being severely punished if the appeal failed." J.H. Baker, *An Introduction to English Legal History* 71 (3d ed. 1990).

appellate; appellant, adj.; **appeal,** adj.; **appellative.** *W3* records *appellant* as having been used adjectivally in phrases such as *appellant jurisdiction*, perhaps mainly by nonlawyers. In legal writing, however, the adjective corresponding to the noun *appeal* is invariably *appellate*.

Appellate was defined by Samuel Johnson (1755) as "the person appealed against," the meaning now given to *appellee*. But today the word is used only as an adjective.

In BrE especially, *appeal* itself functions as an adjective in contexts in which Americans would write *appellate*—e.g.: "The judges (at least in England) are not elected by the people, nor are they accountable to anybody (other than *appeal* courts) for their decisions." P.S. Atiyah, *Law and Modern Society* 14 (1983). See **court of appeal(s).**

Appellative, adj., is a specialized grammatical term. *Appellative interrogation* is a variant (and fairly pompous) name for *rhetorical question*. (See RHETORICAL QUESTIONS.) As a noun, *appellative* = term, name. E.g.: "It is a matter of common knowledge, that the *appellative* 'revenue laws' is never applied to the statutes involved in these classes of cases." *U.S. v. Norton*, 91 U.S. 566, 568 (1875) (per Swayne, J.). Occasionally a judge will have some fun with this word—e.g.: "Carrying the adversarial ethic to an extreme, the parties are unable to agree on the spelling of Mr. Ha's first name; the government spells it Solomon while appellant spells it Soloman. We attempt a Solomonic resolution of the *appellative* appellate contretemps, eschewing any textual reference to Ha's given name." *U.S. v. Holmquist*, 36 F.3d 154, 157 n.1 (1st Cir. 1994) (per Selya, J.). See **rhetorical question.**

appellate jurisdiction. See **original jurisdiction.**

appellee is pronounced /ap-ə-**lee**/, not /ə-**pel**-ee/.

*appellor. See **appellant.**

append, vb.; **annex; subjoin; superadd.** These verbs share the sense "to attach or affix to a document, photograph, or the like." To *append* is to add something that is supplemental to but does not become an integral part of the original <three photographs were appended to the report>. To *annex* is to add something in such a way or with such an intention as to have it become an integral part of the original <the store annexed its own addendum of contractual terms that overrode many terms in the mall's printed contract>. *Annex* is more physical in connotation than *attach*, and probably should not be used figuratively—e.g.: "The courts do, nevertheless, at times deny validity to a condition *annexed* [read *attached*] to a testamentary gift where the condition is calculated to influence the future conduct of the beneficiary in manner contrary to the established policy of the State." *In re Liberman*, 18 N.E.2d 658, 660 (N.Y. 1939). *Attach or annex* is an unnecessary DOUBLET: "The affidavits shall be evidenced by a certificate, with official seal affixed, of such officer *attached* or *annexed* [read *annexed*] to such will or testament." Tex. Prob. Code Ann. § 59(a) (Vernon 2003).

To *subjoin* is to add something beneath or below the thing to which it is added, as at the end of a document <the trustees subjoined a telling postscript to the coach's new contract>. *Subjoin* was formerly extremely common in LEGALESE—e.g.: "The majority of the authorities hold the negative view as will appear from the *subjoined* footnote." *First Nat'l Bank of S.C. v. Glens Falls Ins. Co.*, 304 F.2d 866, 870 (4th Cir. 1962). Today the term is rarely used, *subjoined footnote* conveying nothing that *footnote* does not equally clearly convey. Where the word is not, as above, completely superfluous, *join* or *attach* will often suffice in place of this pomposity—e.g.: "We take note of the allegations of criminal activity from police reports that the housing authority *subjoined* [read *attached*] to the termination notice." *Corpus Christi Hous. Auth. v. Lara*, 267 S.W.3d 222, 223 n.2 (Tex. App.—Corpus Christi 2008).

To *superadd* is to add something wholly supererogatory to what is already complete in itself. The word is rare enough that one might well wonder whether it was merely superadded to this entry.

appendix; annex, n.**; addendum; supplement; exhibit.** All these terms refer to supplementary matter that is added to a text, such as a brief, a report, or a book. An *appendix*, or *annex*, is additional material that contributes to the completeness or thoroughness of a relatively full treatment in the main text—as by illustrating or amplifying. An *annex* is typically short and often prepared simultaneously with the main text; an appendix is typically more extensive and often prepared separately later. But an *addendum* or *supplement* suggests that the addition is necessary to complete the treatment or supply deficiencies. An *addendum* is typically briefer and prepared sooner, and a *supplement* is typically more extensive and prepared later. (See **supplemental pleading.**) An *exhibit* is typically a document with a prior independent existence, yet attached to a principal instrument, identified in it, and referred to in it.

appendixes; appendices. Both are correct plural forms for *appendix*, but in AmE *appendixes* is preferable outside scientific contexts (even in reference to books). In BrE, *appendixes* refers to bodily organs and *appendices* refers to back-of-book materials.

appertain; pertain. Some DIFFERENTIATION is possible. Both take the preposition *to*, but *appertain* usually means "to belong to rightfully" <the privileges appertaining to this degree>, whereas *pertain* usually means "to relate to; concern" <the appeal pertains to defendant's Fifth Amendment rights>.

Appertain is a bookish word that typically appears in lofty prose—e.g.:

- "Such suits are in equity being a development of bills *quia timet* or bills of peace remedies, which originated in and *appertained* to the jurisdiction of the court of chancery." *Sanders v. Sanders*, 229 P.2d 164, 166 (Mont. 1951) (Adair, C.J., dissenting).
- "The general principle seems to be that jurisdiction over an inchoate crime *appertains* to the state that would have had jurisdiction had the crime been consummated." Glanville Williams, *Venue and the Ambit of Criminal Law*, (1965) 81 Law Q. Rev. 518, 528.

But sometimes the word appears to have been used merely as a fancy variant of the more usual *pertain*—e.g.: "It would defy common sense to find that class certification is defeated by the possibility of individual questions *appertaining* [read *pertaining*] to one of the elements of one of the case's causes of action." *Lubin v. Sybedon Corp.*, 688 F.Supp. 1425, 1460 (S.D. Cal. 1988).

applicable. A. Pronunciation. For solid authority that the word is preferably pronounced /**ap**-li-kə-bəl/—not /ə-**plik**-ə-bəl/—see Charles Harrington Elster, *The Big Book of Beastly Mispronunciations* 34–35 (2d ed. 2005).

B. Redundancy of. Contracts often require one or more parties to "comply with all applicable laws"—a curious requirement, since they could hardly include *inapplicable* laws in the category. In other words, the word *applicable* in such a provision is a self-evident REDUNDANCY. Hence the following edit is desirable: "Regional centers are required to monitor the SB 962 homes to ensure that they comply with all *applicable laws* [read *laws*] and regulations." *In re Michael K.*, 111 Cal. Rptr. 3d 187, 191 (Ct. App. 2010).

applicant; applicator; *applier. An *applicant* is "one who applies for something (as a position in a firm)." (See **candidate.**) *Applicator* = (1) a device for applying a substance or device (such as a tampon); or (2) one who applies a substance. *Applier is a NEEDLESS VARIANT of *applicator*.

When *applicant* is used merely for *movant* (as in American federal courts), the latter term is preferable. (See **application.**) In G.B., one who seeks a writ of habeas corpus or judicial review by means of mandamus, prohibition, or certiorari is termed an *applicant*.

application. A. And *motion*. In some jurisdictions, this term is merely a variant name for *motion*. Where that is so, *motion* is the better term.

B. And *interpretation*. See **interpretation.**

apply. See **follow** & **run** (C).

applyable. See **applicable** (A).

---

appoint. See **designate.**

appointor, despite its odd appearance, is the accepted spelling of the legal correlative of *appointee*. Avoid **appointer*.

apposite. See **apt.**

APPOSITIVES point out the same persons or things by different names, usually in the form of explanatory phrases that narrow in on the precise meaning of a prior more general phrase. So in the sentence "My brother Brad is a musician," *Brad* is the appositive of *brother*. Usually, in phrases less succinct than *my brother Brad* (in which *Brad* is restrictive), the appositive is set off by commas or parentheses: "Plaintiff's decedent, John Doe, was killed in a plane accident," or, "The appellee in this case (XYZ, Inc.) has counterclaimed against the appellant." In these hypothetical sentences, *John Doe* is an appositive of *decedent*, and *XYZ, Inc.* is an appositive of *appellee*. Two problems crop up with appositives.

A. With Possessives. An appositive should match its antecedent syntactically. Here is the correct use of an appositive with a possessive antecedent: "A cannot confer on C *his*, *A's*, right to possess and deal with the chattel for a partnership purpose." (But the appositive is unnecessary. See MYTH OF PRECISION.)

Having either an antecedent or an appositive that is possessive (and therefore adjectival) matched up with a nominal mate creates awkwardness, as in the following sentences:

- "In this case, [appellant] challenges the district court's grant of *T.J. & Co.'s (Stevenson) motion* [read *Stevenson's motion*] for summary judgment." *Albertson v. T.J. Stevenson & Co.*, 749 F.2d 223, 226 (5th Cir. 1984).
- "In his petition, Wagner misrepresented to the court that federal jurisdiction became apparent during *plaintiff's, Davis*, [read *plaintiff Davis's*] closing argument."
- "We hold that the Appeals Council had the power to reopen the Administrative Law Judge's *(ALJ)* [read *(ALJ's)*] decision." *Cieutat v. Bowen*, 824 F.2d 348, 350 (5th Cir. 1987).

Here are two other examples of appositives that are needlessly awkward:

- "The scope of your brief should not be affected *by the scope of your opponent, the appellant's brief* [read *by the scope of that of your opponent, the appellant*]." Paxton Blair, *Appellate Briefs and Advocacy*, 18 Fordham L. Rev. 30, 41 (1949).
- "[This case concerns] damage that occurred to *appellee-plaintiffs Donald and Doris Taylor's property* in the summer of 1975." *Taylor v. U.S.*, 590 F.2d 263, 264 (8th Cir. 1979). A suggested revision: *the property of the appellee-plaintiffs, Donald and Doris Taylor, . . .*

See POSSESSIVES (G).

B. Punctuation. This problem has been touched on earlier in this entry. Generally, commas (or, less frequently, parentheses) must frame appositives except when the appositive is restrictive. So a person might write *my brother Blair* to distinguish Blair from another brother (say, Brad). But if one had only one brother, the reference would be to *my brother, Blair*.

One telltale signal that the appositive is restrictive is the definite article *the* preceding the noun (e.g., *the maxim nulla poena sine lege is one generally respected by civilized nations*).

When commas are omitted in nonpossessive phrases, the effect is that of a RUN-ON SENTENCE—e.g.: "Plaintiffs offered the testimony of . . . Jesus Leon an airport mechanic." (A comma should appear after the name *Jesus Leon*.) *Newing v. Cheatham*, 540 P.2d 33, 36 (Cal. 1975).

An emphatic appositive is never set off by commas—e.g.:

- "He *himself* [no comma before or after] testified during his deposition that he could not hear any commands from the police once he was inside the car, and that all he could hear was 'banging on the window.'" *Swann v. City of Richmond*, 498 F.Supp.2d 847, 869 (E.D. Va. 2007).
- "Kilby claims that his counsel spent insufficient time interviewing him, even though he *himself* [no comma before or after] testified to hours of conversations with counsel on the phone." *Kilby v. State*, 657 S.E.2d 567, 569 (Ga. Ct. App. 2008).

appraisal. A. And **appraisement.** *W3* treats these as variants; the *OED* definitions suggest some divergence in meaning. Both may mean "the act of appraising; the setting of a price; valuation." But **appraisement*, when connoting the acts of an official appraiser, is the term usually used in reference to valuation of estates; it appears far more frequently in legal than in nonlegal texts. Yet *appraisal* is steadily taking the field.

The more broadly applicable term *appraisal* is also frequent in legal texts, in figurative as well as literal senses. E.g.:

- "This court's *appraisal* of appellant's claim of prosecutorial vindictiveness must adhere to the principles established by the Supreme Court in *Blackledge v. Perry*." *Miracle v. Estelle*, 592 F.2d 1269, 1272 (5th Cir. 1979).
- "Existing critique has focused on international and domestic definitions of human trafficking and *appraisal* of the statutory language." Jayashri Srikantiah, *Perfect Victims and Real Survivors*, 87 B.U. L. Rev. 157, 158 (2007).

Appraisal commonly appears in the writing of lawyers but is more a part of the everyday language. Ironically, however, H.W. Fowler classified it among those words "that have failed to become really familiar and remained in the stage in which the average man cannot say with confidence off-hand that they exist" (*MEU1* 14). Since he wrote that, however, *appraisal* has become the standard term in BrE as well as in AmE, largely because of the American influence. *Appraisal* is now preferred in all ordinary contexts, not **appraisement*.

As with many other pairs of variant word terms, here the vice of INELEGANT VARIATION may tempt the writer—e.g.:

- "If a duty to obtain a full formal *appraisal* exists, it is founded not on any specific statutory requirement that an appraiser be employed or that an *appraisement* [read *appraisal*] take any particular form, but on the more general duty of prudent management." *Carroll v. Carroll*, 903 P.2d 579, 586 (Alaska 1995).

- "In her Inventory and *Appraisement* [Mrs. Mullins] listed the Retirement as community property." *Mullins v. Mullins*, 202 S.W.3d 869, 877 n.1 (Tex. App.—Dallas 2006).

B. And **appraisal valuation.* Though fairly common in AmE contexts regarding corporate law, family law, and estates, **appraisal valuation* is illogical and redundant. E.g.:

- "Wife argues that since Glor's appraisal included a 'business value' of $50,000, and the trial court used that *appraisal's valuations* [read *appraisal*] as to the real estate and the inventory of the business in its division of marital property, it should have also included the $50,000." *Youngberg v. Youngberg*, 194 S.W.3d 886, 890 (Mo. Ct. App. 2006).
- "Contrary to the defendants' contention, the Supreme Court properly accepted the *appraisal valuation* [read *appraisal*] of the six chairs offered by the plaintiff's expert witness, even though the expert was unable to examine the subject chairs." *Goldstein v. Guida*, 904 N.Y.S.2d 117, 119 (App. Div. 2010).

appraise; apprise. The first means "to valuate," the second "to inform." Often *appraise* gets misused for *apprise*:

- "Consideration of the risks inherent in an enterprise is essential if one wishes to be fully *appraised* [read *apprised*] of the risks that a particular job, within that enterprise, gives rise to." Douglas Brodie, *Enterprise Liability: Justifying Vicarious Liability*, 27 Oxford J. Legal Stud. 493, 498 (2007).
- "By the middle of the twentieth century, the attorney general had . . . sufficient personnel as well as the means necessary to keep *appraised* [read *apprised*] of developments in the field." Sara Sun Beale, *Rethinking the Identity and Role of the U.S. Attorneys*, 6 Ohio St. J. Crim. L. 369, 391 (2009).
- "In fact . . . the U.S. Fish and Wildlife Service and the Louisiana Wildlife and Fisheries Commission were fully *appraised* [read *apprised*] of the status of planning by the Corps." *In re Katrina Canal Breaches Consol. Litig.*, 627 F.Supp.2d 656, 673 (E.D. La. 2009).

A rarer mistake is for *apprise* to be misused for *appraise*—e.g.: "The discussion thus far should indicate the limited value of superficial observation in *apprising* [read *appraising*] the effects of Rumbaugh's mental illness." *Rumbaugh v. Procunier*, 753 F.2d 395, 412 (5th Cir. 1985) (Goldberg, J., dissenting). Here, in a famous case, *apprise* is correctly used: "It does not follow that because an officer may lawfully arrest a person only when he is *apprised* of facts sufficient to warrant a belief that the person has committed or is committing a crime, the officer is equally unjustified, absent that kind of evidence, in making any intrusions short of an arrest." *Terry v. Ohio*, 392 U.S. 1, 26 (1968) (per Warren, C.J.).

*appraisement. See **appraisal.**

appreciate = (1) to fully understand; (2) to increase in value; or (3) to be grateful for. The last meaning began as a SLIPSHOD EXTENSION but is now established.

apprehend; comprehend. *Apprehend* = (1) to seize in the name of the law; to arrest <to apprehend a criminal> (for more, see **arrest**); or (2) to lay hold of with the intellect (*OED*). In sense 2, it should not be used as a supposed FORMAL WORD for *believe*, as here:

- "We *apprehend* [read *believe*] that it is unnecessary at this time to cite authority in support of the right in equity to maintain class suits." *City of Dallas v. Armor & Co.*, 216 S.W. 222, 224 (Tex. Civ. App.—Dallas 1919).
- "We *apprehend* [read *believe*] that the Constitution enjoins upon us the duty, however difficult, of distinguishing between the two." *Harisiades v. Shaughnessy*, 342 U.S. 580, 592 (1952) (per Jackson, J.).

Comprehend = (1) to understand, grasp with the mind; or (2) to include, comprise, contain.

apprehension does not always mean "fear," its common lay meaning <she has apprehensions about proceeding>. It frequently takes on noun senses corresponding to the verb *apprehend*—e.g.:

- "The mere *apprehension* [meaning "perception"] of a plaintiff that something may be wrong is not sufficient to begin the prescription." *In re Medical Review Panel of Lafayette*, 860 So.2d 86, 89 (La. Ct. App. 2003).
- "While [the off-duty deputy sheriff] aided in the *apprehension* [meaning "capture"] of the plaintiff and his companions, he identified himself as a store employee." *Smith v. Detroit Entm't LLC*, 338 F.Supp.2d 775, 790 (E.D. Mich. 2004).

See **apprehend.**

apprise. See **appraise.**

appro is an abbreviated form of *approval*, in phrases such as *goods on appro*. Although this type of commercialese may be appropriate for telegrams, it isn't for legal prose.

approbate and reprobate (= to accept and reject), used in the context that one may not accept the benefits of a legal document while challenging some of its conditions, is an unjustified LATINISM that Leff aptly called "insufferably fancy." Arthur A. Leff, *The Leff Dictionary of Law*, 94 Yale L.J. 1855, 2046 (1985). The simpler words used in the definition are preferable.

approbation; approval; approvement. There is no generally accepted distinction between the first two words, except that the first is more unusual and dignified. Follett suggests that we restrict *approbation* to a favorable response on a particular occasion and use *approval* for a general favorable attitude. Wilson Follett, *Modern American Usage* 72 (1966). E.g.: "Again expressing our *approbation* of this doctrine, we conclude that the proof tendered, as declared in the first exception of the defendant below, should have been admitted." *Van Buren v. Digges*, 52 U.S. 461, 476 (1850) (per Daniel, J.).

Follett's distinction would suggest that *approval* be used here: "[The jury trial] has stood the test of experience better than any other legal institution that ever existed among men, and it has met universal *approbation* [read *approval*] among those who lived under it, and by the greatest thinkers who have investigated it impartially." *Jackson v. General Fin. Corp.*, 253 P.2d 166, 168 (Okla. 1953). See **disapprobation.**

Rarely does *approbate* justifiably supersede *approve*—e.g.: "That must follow [that all arranged or Sikh marriages are void] unless the parties knew each other beforehand or *approbated* [read *approved*] the marriage afterwards." *Singh v. Singh*, [1971] 2 W.L.R. 963 (C.A.). For a legal nuance of the verb *approbate*, see **approbate and reprobate.**

Approvement is an old term with two quite distinct meanings at common law: (1) "the act of avoiding a capital conviction by accusing an accomplice; turning king's evidence" (*Black's Law Dictionary* 118 (9th ed. 2009)); and (2) "the conversion to his own profit, by the lord of the manor, of waste or common land by enclosure and appropriation" (*OED*).

approbatory; *approbative. *Approbatory* is the standard form.

appropriable is the adjective corresponding to *appropriate*, vb.—not **appropriatable*. E.g.: "The Preissers have argued lack of standing on the part of the objectors and have contended that they are entitled to decrees, irrespective of the question of availability of *appropriatable* [read *appropriable*] water." *In re Application for Water Rights of Preisser*, 545 P.2d 711, 712 (Colo. 1976) (en banc).

appropriate, vb.; **expropriate.** To *appropriate* is (1) to give to a particular person or organization for a specific purpose <government-appropriated moneys>; or (2) to take from a particular person or organization for a specific purpose. Sense 1 is the more usual in AmE (and better known to the nonlawyer), perhaps because it is better to give than to receive. Following are examples of sense 2, the lawyer's sense:

- "Under this authorization she withdrew from the bank various sums of money, a considerable amount of which she evidently *appropriated* to her own use without any accounting to him." *In re Arnold's Estate*, 107 P.2d 25, 29 (Cal. 1940).
- "The United States Supreme Court there held that a cooperative association of newspapers [that] gathers and distributes news may enjoin a competing news agency from *appropriating* news taken from bulletins issued by the association and from selling it to competitors of the association." *Columbia Broad. Sys., Inc. v. Melody Recordings, Inc.*, 341 A.2d 348, 379 (N.J. Super. Ct. App. Div. 1975).

Expropriate means (1) "to exercise eminent domain over; to take, by legal action, private land for public use"; or (2) "to transfer title to another's property to oneself." See **misappropriate.**

In sense 2, *appropriate* is distinguished from *expropriate* because a private or semipublic entity does the former, whereas a public governmental entity does the latter. The difference between the terms is carefully observed by the courts. E.g.: "It makes no difference in determining the amount to be awarded that the property was *appropriated* and not formally *expropriated*." *Gray v. State, Through Dep't of Highways*, 202 So.2d 24, 30 (La. 1967).

See **arrogate (A).**

appropriation = (1) the exercise of control over property; (2) the bringing about of a transfer of title or of a nonpossessory interest in the property; (3) a public body's act of voting a sum of money for any of various public purposes; or (4) the sum of money so voted.

In the following passage, a court has overstated the traditional significance of the term (sense 1): "Implicit in the meaning of the word *appropriation*, when it comes to competing and equal possessory interests in property, is that the accused person must have exercised 'unauthorized' control over the property." *Freeman v. State*, 707 S.W.2d 597, 605 (Tex. Crim. App. 1986). See **misappropriate.**

approval. See **approbation.**

approve. A. *Approve (of).* *Approve* may be either transitive or intransitive, but in legal usage is usually the former (i.e., it usually takes no *of*). "Thus in our system evidentiary rulings provide the context in which the judicial process of inclusion and exclusion *approves* some conduct as comporting with constitutional guarantees and disapproves other actions by state agents." *Terry v. Ohio*, 392 U.S. 1, 13 (1968) (per Warren, C.J.).

B. And *endorse.* The two should be distinguished. To *approve*, apart from the legal sense of giving official sanction, is to consider right or to have a favorable attitude toward. The verb conveys an attitude or thought. To *endorse* is to support actively and explicitly. The word connotes action as well as attitude.

C. And *approbate.* See **approbation.**

approvement. See **approbation.**

approvingly cited is awkward for *cited with approval*—e.g.: "Judge Rubin found that neither [of two kinds of contracts] met the *Howey* test for an investment contract . . . , a finding *approvingly cited* [read *cited with approval*] in *Moody v. Bache & Co.*" *LTV Fed. Credit Union v. UMIC Gov't Secs., Inc.*, 704 F.2d 199, 203 (5th Cir. 1983). Other awkward variations have appeared—e.g.: "The quoted language from *Whitner* has been *approvingly used* [omit *approvingly*] in construing other portions of the statute." *Hernandez v. State*, 600 S.W.2d 793, 796 (Tex. Crim. App. 1980) (Dally, J., dissenting). The implication here is that, by *using* a precedent, the user implicitly *approves* that precedent.

approximately is almost never as good as *about*—e.g.:

- "Sara, a first-year student, had had a few drinks before she went out that Saturday evening. She recalls having *approximately* [read *about*] ten shots of vodka before going to a fraternity for a party." Rajib Chanda, *Mediating University Sexual Assault Cases*, 6 Harv. Negot. L. Rev. 265, 265 (2001).

- "Appellant said 'you killed my brother' before firing his black handgun *approximately* [read *some*] five times." *State v. Johnson*, 284 S.W.3d 561, 567 (Mo. 2009).
- "*Approximately* [read *About*] three months after the murder, Pace anonymously provided authorities the name of a possible suspect." *State v. Vick*, 682 S.E.2d 275, 278 (S.C. Ct. App. 2009).

See **about.**

***approximately about** is a REDUNDANCY. See **about.**

á prendre. See **profits á prendre.**

a priori; a posteriori. These terms are best left to philosophical contexts. Very simply, *a priori*, the more common term, means "deductively; reasoning from the general to the particular," and *a posteriori* means "inductively; reasoning from the particular to the general, or from known effects to their inferred causes." Here *a priori* is used correctly, although the writer might better have written *deductive*—e.g.: "*Witherspoon*'s teaching is not limited to that particular inference; it counsels against any *a priori* judicial assumptions about the views of veniremen." Eric Schnapper, *Taking* Witherspoon *Seriously*, 62 Tex. L. Rev. 977, 993 (1984).

A priori becomes vague and confusing when it is used to mean "presumably" or "without detailed consideration," as here: "But we cannot say, *a priori*, without evidence, that there is not a sufficient rational distinction between such restaurants and other commercial establishments to warrant a study." *Schafer v. City of New Orleans*, 743 F.2d 1086, 1090 (5th Cir. 1984). This usage is a SLIPSHOD EXTENSION.

Nonlawyers sometimes misuse *a priori* for *prima facie*—e.g.:

- "In short, there is a reasonably persuasive *a priori* [read *prima facie*] case at least for the proposition that the existence of liberal democracy in two powerful countries makes it very unlikely that they will resort to the threat of force in their mutual relations." Tom Farer, *To Shape the Nation's Foreign Policy*, Diogenes, 22 Sept. 2004, at 71.
- "This creates *an a priori* [read *a prima facie*] case for regulation, and may also explain some of the failures that Brown and Jacobs record." Natalie Gold, *Where Rhetoric Meets Reality*, Times Higher Educ. Supp., 20 Nov. 2008, at 48.

apt; likely; liable; prone. When followed by the preposition *to* and an infinitive, these words all denote a greater or lesser possibility of something's occurring. *Apt* suggests a definite tendency or predisposition as gauged from experience <you're apt to work more efficiently if you cultivate other interests outside work> <litigation is always apt to become personal between litigants>. *Likely* emphasizes future probability and therefore takes on a sense of prediction <most likely to succeed> <the company is not likely to win this case>.

Apt for *likely* is a loose usage. But as H.W. Fowler explains, "in British usage *apt* always implies a general tendency; for a probability arising from particular circumstances, *likely* is the word" (*MEU2* 34). The same distinction applies in the best American usage. In the following sentences, *apt* is correctly used of general or habitual tendencies, rather than a likelihood in a particular instance—e.g.: "Indeed, no private cause of action is *apt* [read *likely*] to be brought unless a plaintiff in the position of Panag or Stephens brings it." *Panag v. Farmers Ins. Co. of Wash.*, 204 P.3d 885, 894 (Wash. 2009).

Sometimes *apt* seems entirely apt—e.g.:

- " 'In certain aspects a young child is more *apt* to err than an older person; he or she is *apt* to be more amenable to any influence or suggestion [that] may be made *to them* [delete *to them*] by older persons, and the sanctity of the oath and solemnity of legal proceedings may affect *them* [read *the child*] less than an adult.' " *State v. Ceballos*, 832 A.2d 14, 53 (Conn. 2003) (quoting the defendant).
- "Courts and administrative agencies are given discretionary power in order to individualize the application of law, make it flexible and adaptable to circumstances. Without it, the law is *apt* to be criticized as harsh, unfeeling and unjust." *U.S. v. Copeland*, 369 F.Supp.2d 275, 305 (E.D.N.Y. 2005).

Liable in this sense suggests an exposure to risk or danger, and it suggests only a possibility, perhaps even a fairly remote one, in a cautionary or admonitory statement <if you don't tidy your desk, you're liable to lose control of confidential documents> <a lawyer who doesn't promptly return phone calls is liable to receive client complaints>. *Liable* best refers to something the occurrence of which risks being permanent or recurrent. E.g.:

- "The parties are competitors in this field; and . . . when the rights or privileges of the one are *liable* to conflict with those of the other, each party is under a duty so to conduct its own business as not unnecessarily or unfairly to injure that of the other." *International News Svc. v. Associated Press*, 248 U.S. 215, 235 (1918) (per Pitney, J.).
- "If the act is one that the party ought, in the exercise of ordinary care, to have *anticipated* [read *foreseen*] was *liable* [read *likely*] to result in injury to others, then he is *liable* for any injury proximately resulting from it." *Cirillo v. City of Milwaukee*, 150 N.W.2d 460, 463 (Wis. 1967). In this sentence, *liable* is ill-advisedly used in two senses. The second instance illustrates the sense "legally responsible" (see below).

The idea of recurrence is far more salient in the second than in the first sentence just quoted.

Prone, like *apt*, suggests a tendency, but it always refers to people (not things), and like *liable* it is used in a negative sense <he is prone to mischief>.

a quo; a qua. *A quo* = from which. A court *a quo* is a court from which a case has been removed or appealed. E.g.: "If the court *a quo* has no jurisdiction, then a court *ad quem* gains none by appeal." Eugene A. Jones, *Manual of Equity Pleading and Practice* 12 n.24 (1916).

A qua was originally a solecism for *a quo*. It has gained some degree of currency in legal prose, although *a quo* remains the preferred term. Because *a quo*, the correct form, has persisted alongside the bastardized version, it is not overreaching to say that we should stick with what is correct. It is the only form given, for example, by Arthur A. Leff in his *Dictionary of Law*, 94 Yale L.J. 1855, 2050 (1985). E.g.:

- "Since no written reasons were handed down by the court *a qua* [read *a quo*], our initial task is to define the theory on which recovery may be awarded." *Swan v. Beaubouef*, 206 So.2d 315, 316–17 (La. Ct. App. 1968).
- "On March 30, 1984 the district court *a qua* [read *a quo*] stayed the scheduled execution, dismissed with prejudice the foregoing enumerated claims 2, 4, and 5 and docketed an evidentiary hearing on claims 1 and 3." *Knighton v. Maggio*, 740 F.2d 1344, 1346 (5th Cir. 1984).
- "The sole question posed on appeal is whether the federal court *a qua* [read *a quo*] had personal jurisdiction over the nonresident [defendant]." *Pedelahore v. Astropark, Inc.*, 745 F.2d 346, 347 (5th Cir. 1984).

Cf. **terminus a quo.**

arbiter. See **arbitrator.**

arbitrable (= subject to or appropriate for arbitration) is the correct form, not **arbitratable*. Hence the corresponding noun is *arbitrability*—e.g.: "The appeals-court panel said, 'Since RICO claims are *arbitratable* [read *arbitrable*], we see no reason here for limiting *arbitratability* [read *arbitrability*].'" Wall St. J., 31 Jan. 1991, at B4.

arbitrage; arbitration. *Arbitrage* = the simultaneous buying and selling of currencies or securities at different values in order to profit by price discrepancies. For the sense of *arbitration*, see **arbitration.**

arbitrageur; **arbitrager*. Though English-language dictionaries generally put their entries under the Frenchified *arbitrageur*, some journalists and courts now seem to prefer the naturalized form, **arbitrager*. Yet the GALLICISM is overwhelmingly predominant in print sources.

arbitral. A. And *arbitrary*. *Arbitral* = relating to arbiters or arbitration; *arbitrary* may usually be equated with "capricious; randomly chosen." (See **arbitrary.**) It also has a more and more disused legal meaning: determinable by the decision of a judge or tribunal rather than defined by statute. This, take note, was the *original* meaning of *arbitrary*. Could it be that its other, more modern meanings have grown out of this first one?

Arbitral may correspond to either *arbitrator* or *arbiter*. In legal language, it is almost invariably the adjectival form of *arbitrator* <arbitral discretion>. It also sometimes corresponds to the noun *arbitration*, as in the phrase *arbitral tribunal*. See *Graphic Commun. Union v. Chicago Tribune Co.*, 779 F.2d 13, 15 (7th Cir. 1985). See **arbitrator.**

B. And **arbitrational*; **arbitrative*. Both **arbitrational* and **arbitrative* are NEEDLESS VARIANTS of *arbitral*. E.g.:

- "The witness privilege applies in any judicial, official, investigatory, legislative, or *arbitrational* [read *arbitral*] proceeding." Phillip J. Kolczynski, *The Criminal Liability of Aviators*, 51 J. Air L. & Com. 1, 42 (1985).
- "[Every Kansas corporation can sue and be sued] in all courts and participate . . . in any judicial, administrative, *arbitrative* [read *arbitral*] or other proceeding, in its corporate name." Kan. Stat. Ann. § 17-6102(2) (2009).

arbitrament; **arbitrement*. The first spelling is standard for this word, meaning (1) "the power to decide for others"; or (2) "a decision or sentence." When first imported into English from French in the late 16th century, the word was spelled with *-e-* in the penultimate syllable. Thereafter the spelling was Latinized to *arbitrament*, which the *OED* notes has been the accepted spelling since about 1830. Following is an illustration of sense 1: "When the acts of the citizen in making such exposure are challenged, as not being within the reason of the rule, the court, as in every other case involving considerations of public policy, must itself determine the question as a matter of law, and not leave it to the *arbitrament* of a jury." *Ball v. Rawles*, 28 P. 937, 938 (Cal. 1892).

In sense 2, the word was once common in arbitration contexts; it referred to the arbitrators' decision or award. This particular use is labeled obsolete in Katharine Seide, *A Dictionary of Arbitration* 24 (1970).

arbitrary; unreasonable. These words are extremely complex in law, their senses not readily encapsulated; but their most elemental senses are worth noting. *Arbitrary* = with no purpose or objective. (See **arbitral (A).**) *Unreasonable* = with a purpose that is excessively imposed.

*arbitratable. See **arbitrable.**

arbitrate = (1) (of one or more parties) to settle by, or submit to, arbitration; or (2) (of an arbitral tribunal) to decide a dispute being arbitrated. Though surprisingly common, references to courts' "arbitrating" disputes reflect poor usage—e.g.: "The plaintiff's lawyers would simply tell the plaintiff what he would net if he instructed them to accept the offer; if the plaintiff thought the lawyers were taking too much, he could ask the court to *arbitrate* [read *decide*] the dispute." *Chesny v. Marek*, 720 F.2d 474, 478 (7th Cir. 1983). For more on *arbitrate* and related verbs, see **judge,** vb.

arbitration. A. And *mediation*. Both terms refer to methods of dispute resolution involving a neutral third party. The results of *arbitration* are binding—that is, the parties to the arbitrator's decision are bound by it. In *mediation*, to the contrary, the mediator merely tries to help two disputing parties reach a mutually agreeable solution, but the parties are not bound by a mediated agreement. See **mediation.**

B. "Trying" an Arbitration. To say that an arbitration is *tried* is to betray an ignorance of idiom, as well as the process involved, by treating it as if it were litigation in a public tribunal. And in any event, *arbitration* refers to a process: a *case* may be tried (or arbitrated), but a so-called litigation cannot be tried.

The standard idiom would be to say that an arbitration is *heard* or *conducted*. But legal writers increasingly get it wrong—e.g.:

- "This would be prejudicial to the Hideca-Nereus arbitration which, it was claimed by Hideca, should logically be *tried* [read *heard*] first." *Compania Espanola de Petroleos, S.A. v. Nereus Shipping, S.A.*, 527 F.2d 966, 971 (2d Cir. 1975).
- "The court vacated the arbitration award since the arbitration had been *tried* [read *conducted*] on a totally different theory than the one on which arbitration had been ordered." *Metropolitan Prop. & Liab. Ins. Co. v. Streets*, 856 F.2d 526, 529 (3d Cir. 1988).

*arbitrational; *arbitrative. See arbitral.

arbitrator; arbiter. An *arbitrator* is a person chosen to settle differences between two parties embroiled in a controversy. *Arbiter*, by contrast, is more general, meaning "anyone with power to decide disputes, as a judge." E.g.: "The courts have not been constituted *arbiters* of the fairness, justice, or wisdom of the terms demanded." *J.H. & S. Theatres v. Fay*, 183 N.E. 509, 510 (N.Y. 1932).

The terms do overlap considerably, and they cause confusion on both sides of the Atlantic. Yet when referring to legal arbitration, one should term the resolver of disputes the *arbitrator*—e.g.:

- "Courts have increasingly encouraged arbitration, for it serves as a less costly and expeditious vehicle for resolving disputes of specialized nature, conducted by an *arbiter* [read *arbitrator*] who possesses expertise in that specialized field." *ALS & Assocs., Inc. v. AGM Marine Constructors, Inc.*, 557 F.Supp.2d 180, 185 (D. Mass. 2008).
- "In the prototypical arbitration, when a dispute within the scope of the agreement arises, the parties have a mutual right to initiate the process, and to participate in the selection of an impartial *arbiter* [read *arbitrator*]." *Fiero v. Financial Indus. Regulatory Auth., Inc.*, 606 F.Supp.2d 500, 512 (S.D.N.Y. 2009).

Scots law presents an exception: one appoints an *arbiter* to hold an arbitration.

Leff rightly rejected a distinction of a different nature: "Sometimes a distinction is sought to be made between an *arbiter*, who decides according to rules, and an *arbitrator*, who is free to settle matters in his own sound discretion. But the distinction doesn't hold; *arbiters* often have huge moments of discretionary power, and more important, most *arbitrators* today proceed according to elaborate rules, both procedural and substantive." Arthur A. Leff, *The Leff Dictionary of Law*, 94 Yale L.J. 1855, 2050 (1985). That distinction, in fact, goes back to Roman law, but it has no validity today.

The phrase is always *final* or *ultimate arbiter*, not *arbitrator*. E.g.:

- "It is also clear from case law that goes back to *Marbury v. Madison* that the role of the judiciary was to be the *final arbitrators* [read *final arbiters*] of the Constitution." Maryanne Pitcher, *"Free as Possible"*: Kromko v. Arizona Board of Regents, 40 Ariz. St. L.J. 1161, 1171 (2008).
- "Thus, the most basic functions of the court as interpreter of the Constitution and the *ultimate arbitrator* [read *ultimate arbiter*] of disputes exist in a tenuous balance meant to empower and simultaneously restrain the courts." *Richmond Med. Ctr. for Women v. Herring*, 570 F.3d 165, 172 (4th Cir. 2009).

*Arbitor is a misspelling—e.g.: "Mr. Hong won a countersuit [over] a promised bonus of $742,201 for 2004. The *arbitors* [read *arbiters*] awarded him that amount, plus interest and legal fees." Katie Kuehner-Hebert, *Former Nara CEO Cleared of Blame in Firm's Troubles*, Am. Banker, 28 Aug. 2007, at 6. See **arbitral**.

*arbitrement. See arbitrament.

ARCHAISMS, outmoded words or expressions that are not yet obsolete, abound in the language of the law. This work attempts to treat them individually under specific entries. A great many are collected under the entries FORBIDDEN WORDS, LAWYERISMS & LATINISMS.

Among the archaisms especially to be avoided are the following:

alack	haply	verily
anent	howbeit	whilom
anon	maugre	withal
belike	methinks	wot
betimes	perchance	wroth
divers	shew (for *show*)	
fain	to wit	

One writer aptly says of a similar list: "These are easily avoided by anyone of the least literary sensibility." Herbert Read, *English Prose Style* 9 (1952). See **nay**.

archetypal; *archetypical; *prototypal; prototypical. Inconsistently enough, the preferred adjectival forms are *archetypal* and *prototypical*.

archetype; prototype. These words are close in meaning, but their DIFFERENTIATION should be encouraged. As commonly used, *archetype* means "a standard or typical example," whereas *prototype* means "the original type that has served as a model for successors." *Prototype* is sometimes misused for *archetype*—e.g.: "A *prototype* [read *archetype*] is a representative instance of the class; it may be an average of particular features or simply what comes to the agent's mind, perhaps as a result of recent or spectacular instances." Mario J. Rizzo & Douglas Glen Whitman, *Little Brother Is Watching You: New Paternalism on the Slippery Slopes*, 51 Ariz. L. Rev. 685, 732 (2009).

archive. See document.

An asterisk (✳) precedes words and phrases that are invariably inferior forms.

-ARCHY. See GOVERNMENTAL FORMS.

Arden, Enoch. See **Enoch Arden law.**

*are comprised in. See **comprise (c).**

ARGOT. See JARGON.

*arguendo. In AmE, **arguendo* is unnecessary in place of *for the sake of argument.* Although brevity would commend it, its obscurity to nonlawyers is a distinct liability. E.g.:

- "Second, assuming, *arguendo* [read *for the sake of argument*], that terrorists are entitled to full due-process protections, this Note asserts that a separate inquiry into personal jurisdiction is unnecessary because a due-process analysis is subsumed into the Anti-Terrorism Act." Ozan O. Varol, Note, *Substantive Due Process, Plenary-Power Doctrine, and Minimum Contacts*, 92 Iowa L. Rev. 297, 297 (2006).
- "Assuming *arguendo* [read *for the sake of argument*] that these allegations were established by a preponderance of the evidence, the Government has demonstrated, at most, that Janko was trusted enough to be inducted into al Qaeda's military training program." *Al Ginco v. Obama*, 626 F.Supp.2d 123, 129 (D.D.C. 2009).

*Arguendo is one of those LATINISMS that neophyte lawyers often adopt as pet words to advertise their lawyerliness.

In BrE, the word means something else entirely: "during the course of argument." E.g.: "'This air is too pure for a slave to breathe in,' was already ancient when Serjeant Davy uttered it *arguendo* in 1772." R.E. Megarry, *A Second Miscellany-at-Law* 198 (1973).

argufy = to dispute, wrangle. Krapp calls this term "illiterate or, in cultivated speech, a humorous and contemptuous form of *argue*." George Philip Krapp, *A Comprehensive Guide to Good English* 50 (1927). Lawyers could use a good sarcastic term for *argue*, and *argufy* fills the bill. Cf. **speechify.**

argument; argumentation. An *argument* is (1) the means or process of proof; esp., a series of statements intended to persuade and assist a decision-maker, particularly through analysis and refutation of evidence; or (2) the act or process of debating. E.g.: "Mother has not identified, either in her Rule 60(b)(6) motion, her brief to the ICA, her application for certiorari, or oral *argument* in this court, what errors occurred in the permanent plan hearing that she would have challenged had Yonemori timely appealed on her behalf." *In re RGB*, 229 P.3d 1066, 1094 (Haw. 2010). (On the misuse of the *either . . . or* construction there, see **either (A).**)

Argumentation is (1) the art of logically setting forth premises and drawing conclusions from them; or (2) a chain of arguments or process of reasoning. Sense 1 is the most defensible use. Hence two experienced writers call the first subdivision of a book on advocacy "General Principles of Argumentation." See Antonin Scalia & Bryan Garner, *Making Your Case: The Art of Persuading Judges* xi (2008). Sense 2 verges on sense 1 of *argument*—e.g.:

- "Everyone demands a rational legal practice and a rationally ordered legal science. And everyone agrees that this goal can only be reached by means of rationally convincing *argumentation.*" Ota Weinberger, *Law, Institution, and Legal Politics* 71 (1991).
- "[T]he dialogue is competitive and partisan (advocacy) *argumentation* is used by both sides [in a lawsuit]. However, the goal of the dialogue as a whole is to resolve a conflict of opinions, or at least to throw light on the issue discussed by considering the strongest arguments on both sides of the issue, and seeing how they fare against each other." Douglas N. Walton, *Legal Argumentation and Evidence* 286 (2002).

Those instances are arguable, but the contexts there seem to suggest a sustained analysis or debate. Where that is not so, it might be said that *argumentation* is less good than *argument*—e.g.:

- "[I]t appears to me that the district attorney proceeded with a fair amount of restraint in his closing *argumentation* [read *arguments*], focusing closely on the statutorily enumerated aggravating circumstances." *Commonwealth v. Marinelli*, 910 A.2d 672, 691 (Pa. 2006) (Saylor, J., concurring).
- "By their failure to present any developed *argumentation* [read *arguments*] with respect to the Hospital's liability, the plaintiffs have waived their claim that the district court erred in granting the Hospital's motion for summary judgment." *Borges ex rel. S.M.B.W. v. Serrano-Isern*, 605 F.3d 1, 6 (1st Cir. 2010).

ARGUMENT, MODES OF. The Romans categorized and gave names to several different modes of argument, all of which (both names and modes) are still used today. Although it might be somewhat precious to use some of the more recondite Latin phrases in ordinary contexts (e.g., *argumentum ad crumenam*), they are at least as useful as most things that appear in legal footnotes. Following are some of these phrases, each of which is preceded by *argumentum*:

ab auctoritate	=	from authority (of a statute or case)
ab impossibili	=	from impossibility
ab inconvenienti	=	from inconvenience
a contrario	=	for contrary treatment
ad baculum	=	dependent on physical force to back it up
ad captandum	=	appealing to the emotions of a crowd
ad crumenam	=	appealing to the purse or self-interest
ad hominem	=	based on disparagement or praise of another in a way that obscures the real issue
ad ignorantiam	=	based on an adversary's ignorance
ad invidium	=	appealing to hatred or prejudice
ad misericordiam	=	appealing to pity
ad populum	=	appealing to the crowd
ad rem	=	on the point at issue (what every good judge likes to hear)
ad verecundiam	=	appealing to one's modesty
a fortiori	=	from the stronger case

a simili = by analogy or similarity; from a like case

ex silentio = out of silence (based on the absence of solid evidence)

argumentation. See **argument.**

argumentative; *argumentive. The longer form is the preferred adjective corresponding to *argumentation*.

arise. See **accrue (B).**

arm's-length; *arms-length. In phrases such as *arm's-length transaction*, the correct form is to make *arm* possessive; the phrase is best hyphenated when it appears before the noun it modifies—e.g.:

- "[Before] 1969, an individual purchasing restricted stock was taxed either when the restrictions lapsed or when the stock was sold in an *arm's length* [read *arm's-length*] transaction." *Alves v. Commissioner*, 734 F.2d 478, 481 (9th Cir. 1984).
- "A duty to disclose does not ordinarily arise when parties are engaged in an *arm's length* [read *arm's-length*] transaction." *Clemons v. Home Savers, LLC*, 530 F.Supp.2d 803, 811 (E.D. Va. 2008).
- "Spousal support agreements are not *arms-length* transactions and often involve radically unequal bargaining power." Gregory Klass, *Intent to Contract*, 95 Va. L. Rev. 1437, 1494 (2009).

See PHRASAL ADJECTIVES (A).

An inferior method of signaling the adjectival quality of the phrase is to place quotation marks around it (by referring, for example, to an *"arm's length"* position). This method, to be avoided, appears repeatedly in Geoffrey Hazard, *Triangular Lawyer Relationships*, 1 Geo. J. Legal Ethics 15, 33–34 (1987).

In the phrase *at arm's length* (= not having a confidential relationship), the second two words are not hyphenated.

arraign. See **charge,** vb. (A).

arraignment; indictment. The meanings of these terms vary, depending on the jurisdiction. An *indictment* is the usual instrument charging a person with a felony. It also refers, loosely, to the act of charging someone with a crime. An *arraignment*, within the federal system of the U.S., is the "reading [of] the indictment or information to the defendant or stating to him the substance of the charge and calling on him to plead thereto." Fed. R. Crim. P. 10. See **indictment.**

array; arrayal; arrayment. The three terms differ. *Array* is the most common, meaning (1) "order or arrangement"; (2) "venire; a panel of potential jurors, or a list of impaneled jurors" <after challenges for cause to the first array of jurors in the box>; (3) "clothing"; (4) "militia"; (5) "a large number" <an array of setbacks>; or (6) "a series of statistics or a group of elements." The specific meaning is usually apparent from the context. (See CHAMELEON-HUED WORDS.) By the definition under sense 2, *array* may refer either to a roster of jurors or to the body of jurors collectively.

Arrayal = the act of arraying or ordering. *Arrayment* shares this meaning, but more commonly means "clothing; attire." *Arrayment* developed into another form that is now more generally used in this archaic and learned sense, *raiment*.

Array as a verb has the special legal senses (1) "to impanel a jury for trial" <the jurors have been arrayed on the panel>; and (2) "to call out the names of the jurors one by one" <the defense lawyers scrutinized the jurors as they were arrayed>.

arrearage. See **debt.**

arrears; arrearages. The most common use of either of the terms is the phrase *in arrears* (= behind in the discharge of a debt or other obligation). Current AmE idiom calls predominantly for *in arrears*, whereas a common BrE and older AmE idiom is *in arrear*. *In arrearages* is obsolete.

Arrearage, a LEGALISM, legitimately remains only in the sense "the condition of being in arrears." In all other meanings, *arrears* serves: (1) "unfinished duties" <arrears of work that have accumulated>; and (2) "unpaid or overdue debts" <the creditor has reached an agreement with the debtor on settling the arrears>. E.g.: "The next day Smith paid his child support *arrears* and so was entitled to release." *Commonwealth v. Smith*, 853 A.2d 1020, 1023 (Pa. Super. Ct. 2004).

Yet legal writers frequently use *arrearage* (not even listed in the *COD*) where *arrears* would be preferable. E.g.: "In *Fanchier v. Gammill*, a Nevada Court had awarded a wife alimony which, because of *arrearages* [read *arrears*], she was forced to reduce to a judgment in Mississippi." *Levine v. Levine*, 209 F.Supp. 564, 567 (D. Del. 1962).

In the singular, *arrearage* is common enough in legal texts to be perhaps forgivable, *arrear* being an unnatural-sounding singular. E.g.: "This order recites findings that Franklin paid $1,131 of the $4,531 arrearage found to exist by the 1982 order, leaving an *arrearage* of $3,400 denominated in the order as 'amended *arrearage*.'" *Ex parte Franklin*, 683 S.W.2d 33, 34 (Tex. App.—Tyler 1984). The *OED* records an incorrect American use of *arrears* as a singular: "They constitute a large *arrears* [read *arrear* or *arrearage*], which should be dealt with speedily."

For more on these words, see **debt.**

arrest; apprehend; detain. These verbs share the sense "to limit someone's freedom by holding in custody, esp. as an early step in a possible criminal prosecution." *Arrest* is the general term for seizing and holding a person in custody by legal authority, especially for purposes of pursuing a criminal charge. To *apprehend* is to seize or arrest in the name of the law. To *detain* connotes holding tentatively in custody for questioning and inspection, especially for law-enforcement purposes.

arrest, citizen's. See **citizen's arrest.**

arrest, private. See **citizen's arrest.**

arrestable. So spelled.

arrestee. See -EE.

arrester; *arrestor. The first is the preferred spelling.

arrest warrant. See **capias.**

arrivee. See -EE.

arriving alien. See **asylee (B).**

arrogate. A. And Its Near-Synonyms: *usurp*; *preempt*; *appropriate*, vb.; *confiscate.* These verbs share the sense "to seize or take away, esp. with only questionable authority to do so." *Arrogate*, commonly a reflexive verb <arrogating authority to oneself>, implies an imperious, presumptuous claim to whatever one takes to the exclusion of others <the chair seemed to arrogate to himself the board's authority in corporate matters, expecting the board to rubber-stamp his high-handed actions>. *Usurp* emphasizes a wrongful encroachment into another's rightful place, especially by force <Richard III usurped the throne from Edward V>. *Preempt* suggests a prospective handling of what one wants by foreclosing others' claims or options in advance. Most traditionally, it evokes the idea of a right of first refusal on property, especially on favorable terms <long before this land skyrocketed in value, he had preempted all other buyers with his options>. *Appropriate*, it is true, can mean "to set apart for a particular use" <the legislature appropriated $5 million to improve state parks>, but more often it suggests a conversion of something to one's own use (legally or illegally—with a strong tinge of the latter) <although he was a bailee, he appropriated the lawn equipment to his own use>. (For more, see **appropriate,** vb.) *Confiscate* suggests a sudden or peremptory seizure, perhaps through rightful authority but always with a sense of unfairness <TSA confiscated my new fingernail clippers>.

B. Not a Reflexive. A transitive verb, *arrogate* should not be used reflexively, as here:

- "It is not for this Court *to arrogate itself to the position* [read *to arrogate to itself the authority*] of an international law-making body and read additional factors for consideration into the Treaty." *Westar Marine Servs. v. Heerema Marine Contractors, S.A.*, 621 F.Supp. 1135, 1144 (N.D. Cal. 1985).
- "The present author declines *to arrogate himself to such aptitude* [read *to attribute to himself such aptitude*]." Edward P. Steegmann, Note, *Of History and Due Process*, 63 Ind. L.J. 369, 381 (1988). (One feels somehow grateful for the declination.)

The following sentence illustrates the correct idiom: "John had allowed sheriffs to *arrogate* to themselves

once more the power of hearing pleas of the Crown." H.G. Hanbury, *English Courts of Law* 51 (2d ed. 1953).

arsenious; *arsenous. The first is standard, the second being a NEEDLESS VARIANT. *Arsenious* /ahr-**sen**-ee-əs/ (= of or pertaining to arsenic) should not be confused as being an adjectival form of *arson*. See **arsonable.**

arson; houseburning. *Arson* = (1) *at common law*, the malicious burning of someone else's dwelling house; or (2) *under any of various statutes*, the malicious burning of someone else's or one's own dwelling house or of anyone's commercial or industrial property.

The word *houseburning* denotes the common-law misdemeanor of intentionally burning one's own house that is within the city limits or that is close enough to other houses that they might be in danger of catching fire. The term applies only when no one else is actually damaged by the fire.

arsonable; arsonous. Both terms are omitted from most English-language dictionaries, including the *OED*, *W2*, *W3*, and *AHD*. But they are serviceable. *Arsonable* = (of property) of such a nature as to give rise to a charge of arson if maliciously burned. E.g.: "It is sometimes said that the explanation of this rule is that a chattel is (with certain exceptions) *non-arsonable* property, while a building is *arsonable*, and it is therefore not possible to transfer the malice between the two legal species of property." Glanville Williams, *Criminal Law* 130 (2d ed. 1961).

Arsonous = of or relating to arson. E.g.:

- "After they poured ten gallons of gasoline about the inside of the home in preparation for their *arsonous* act, an unexpected explosion occurred which trapped Frank Owen in the home and resulted in his death." *Smith v. Moran*, 209 N.E.2d 18, 19 (Ill. App. Ct. 1965).
- "He also identified their masks of sanity, ritualistic behavior, alcohol and drug abuse, cruelty to animals, *arsonous* tendencies, and feelings of inadequacy." Stephen Kern, *A Cultural History of Causality* 186 (2004).
- "The clapboard courthouse with its spire seventy-five feet in the air had disappeared, burned to the ground in 1849 by an *arsonous* defendant under indictment, bent on destroying evidence within its wood walls." Philip McFarland, *Hawthorne in Concord* 141 (2005).

Cf. **arsenious.**

artefact. See **artifact.**

artful interpretation; artful construction. See INTERPRETATION, MODES OF (B).

artful pleading. See **well-pleaded complaint.**

article, vb., means "to bind by articles," and is conjugated *articled*, *articling*. An *articled clerk* (who is said to "take articles"), for instance, was formerly the term for an apprentice bound to serve in a solicitor's office in return for learning the trade. The verb is invariably used in reference to apprenticeships. E.g.: "[Among the necessary qualifications for becoming a solicitor is an apprenticeship] or service under articles of clerkship to a practising solicitor for a period varying from two and a half to five years, according to the previous attainments of the clerk. This service is exclusive; and unlike the Bar student, the *articled clerk* cannot devote any part of his attention to matters other than the study and practice of the law." Edward Jenks, *The Book of English Law* 70 (P.B. Fairest ed., 6th ed. 1967).

ARTICLES. A. Omitted Before Party Denominations. It is a convention in legal writing to omit both definite and indefinite articles before words such as *plaintiff, defendant, petitioner, respondent, appellant,* and *appellee*. It is almost as if these designations in legal writing become names, or proper nouns, that denote the person or persons referred to. The convention is a useful one because cutting even such slight words can lead to leaner, more readable sentences. Perhaps the most important aspect of one's preference, though, is to be consistent within a piece of writing. The convention of omitting articles should not spread beyond these few standard party designations, for beyond these standard party-names the convention may seem unidiomatic. E.g.:

- "*Intervenors'* [read *The intervenors'*] opposition to plaintiff's motion has two bases." *Vulcan Pioneers, Inc. v. New Jersey Dep't of Civil Serv.*, 588 F.Supp. 727, 730 (D.N.J. 1984).
- "If *decedent* [read *the decedent*] has no right to recover damages from Piersiak, then Allstate has no responsibility under its policy." *Willett v. Allstate Ins. Co.*, 359 Fed. Appx. 349, 351 (3d Cir. 2009).

See also the examples under (B) of this entry in which *taxpayer* appears without an article.

To some, the practice of omitting these articles may seem symptomatic of LEGALESE. They are entitled to their point of view. The rest of us can enjoy not having to write, "*The plaintiff*, now *the appellant*, sued *the defendant*, now *the appellee*." John Ritchie et al., *Cases and Materials on Decedents' Estates and Trusts* 8 (1982). (In fairness, though, "*Plaintiff*, now *appellant*, sued *defendant*, now *appellee*" is not much better reading.)

B. Wrongly Omitted. There is a contagious tendency in legal writing to omit articles before nouns, perhaps on the analogy of the special legal convention for party-names (see (A)). E.g.: "*Distinction* [read *A distinction*] must be recognized between the review proceeding here involved and those [that] . . . are allowed only . . . through a 'civil action commenced . . . in the district court.'" *White v. U.S.*, 342 F.2d 481, 484 (8th Cir. 1965). In our quest for concision through CUTTING OUT THE CHAFF, however, our writing should not become so abbreviated that we omit necessary articles; articles are more than mere chaff: they are signposts for the reader, who may become temporarily lost without them. There is a tendency, for example, in tax cases to refer to *taxpayer* without an article, as if it were a proper name. E.g.:

- "Federal law also required that *taxpayer* [read *the taxpayer*] make contributions under the Federal Insurance Contributions Act." *Zwiener v. Commissioner*, 743 F.2d 273, 274–75 (5th Cir. 1984).
- "The government appeals the district court's decision that *taxpayer* [read *the taxpayer*] was entitled to use the percentage-of-completion method of accounting." *Koch Indus., Inc. v. U.S.*, 603 F.3d 816, 818 (10th Cir. 2010).

These usages offend a sensitive ear, whether it is the mind's ear or one's actual ear.

Here are a few similar examples:

- "In approaching *solution* [read *the solution*] to this problem we must look somewhat beyond the immediate consequences of *decision* [read *the decision*] in this case." *McCurdy v. McCurdy*, 372 S.W.2d 381, 383 (Tex. Civ. App.—Waco 1963).
- "We conclude that although the award as remitted by *trial judge* [read *the trial judge*] was generous, it was not so gross as to be contrary to right reason." *Smith v. Shell Oil Co.*, 746 F.2d 1087, 1096 (5th Cir. 1984).
- "On the other hand, a revocable living trust with the settlor as trustee has become a common device for people to manage their own assets during *lifetime* [read *their lifetimes*], avoid having to establish a conservatorship in the event of incapacity, and avoid probate upon death." *Weber v. Langholz*, 46 Cal. Rptr. 2d 677, 680 (Ct. App. 1995).

For exceptions to the general rule, see (A) above.

C. Wrongly Inserted. Writers sometimes unidiomatically insert articles where they have no business appearing; this phenomenon is inexplicable, except insofar as we can identify the writer's failure to distinguish between count nouns and mass nouns. E.g.:

- "Only when the nature of the agency relationship is such that the principal would be subject to *a* vicarious liability [omit *a*] as a defendant to another who may have been injured by the agent's negligence." *Frankle v. Twedt*, 47 N.W.2d 482, 486 (Minn. 1951).
- "The Commission has taken the position that it may by its order allow *an* overproduction [omit *an*] for a period of time to meet the market demand." *Clifton v. Koontz*, 325 S.W.2d 684, 691 (Tex. 1959).

D. Repeated. When two or more nouns are connected by a conjunction, it is usually best to repeat the article before each noun. When the article is not repeated, the sense conveyed is that the nouns are identical or synonymous—e.g.: "The committee elected a secretary and treasurer" (one person); "The committee elected a secretary and a treasurer" (two persons).

The article should not be repeated in a second, parallel adjectival phrase—e.g.: "Appellant testified and the United States admitted that P.A.L. was a validly formed and *an* existing corporation [omit *an*]."

E. Indefinite. See **a.**

articulable, not **articulatable*, is the correct form—e.g.: "The government argues that the stop of the car was either part of an 'extended border search' or a '*Terry* stop' based on *articulatable* [read *articulable*] suspicion." *U.S. v. Weston*, 519 F.Supp. 565, 569 (W.D.N.Y. 1981).

artifice is sometimes misspelled **artiface*, as in "a scheme and *artiface* [read *artifice*] to defraud." *U.S. v. Edwards*, 716 F.2d 822, 823 (11th Cir. 1983).

artificial person. See **juristic person.**

artisan; *artizan. The first spelling is standard.

as. A. Causal Words: *as; because; since; for.* In the causal sense, *as* should generally be avoided, because (not *as*!) it may be misunderstood as having its more usual meaning "while," especially when it is placed anywhere but at the beginning of the sentence. H.W. Fowler states: "To causal or explanatory *as*-clauses, if they are placed before the main sentence . . . there is no objection." E.g.:

- "But *as* the case has been discussed here and below without much regard to the pleadings, we proceed to consider the other grounds upon which it has been thought that a recovery could be maintained." *Robins Dry Dock & Repair Co. v. Flint*, 275 U.S. 303, 308 (1927) (per Holmes, J.).
- "*As* I read the Court's opinion to be entirely consistent with the basic principles [that] I believe control this case, I join in it." *Hunter v. Erickson*, 393 U.S. 385, 396 (1969) (Harlan, J., concurring).

But the reverse order is infelicitous unless the reader necessarily knows what is to be introduced by the *as*-clause: "We do not explore the problem further, *as* [read *because*] the issue of damages was not litigated below." *Tramble v. Converters Ink Co.*, 343 F.Supp. 1350, 1355 (N.D. Ill. 1972).

The causal *as* becomes troublesome even at the beginning of a sentence when a temporal *as* appears in the same sentence—e.g.: "*As* Nelda returned to her occupation *as* soon *as* appellant drove her from Newark to New York, and *as* he knew full well that she would do this, one might suppose that the violation of the Mann Act was clearly established." *U.S. v. Ross*, 257 F.2d 292, 293 (2d Cir. 1958). The first and last occurrences of *as* in that sentence are causal, the second and third temporal; the causal words should be changed to *since* or *because*.

Because of the syntactic restrictions on *as*, we are left with three general-purpose causal conjunctions. *Because* is the strongest and most logically oriented of these. *Since* is less demonstratively causal and frequently has temporal connotations. But using *since* without reference to time is not, despite the popular canard, incorrect. (See SUPERSTITIONS (G).) *For* is the most subjective of the three, and the least used. If *because* points out a direct cause–effect relationship, *for* signals a less direct relationship, adding independent explanation or substantiation. Moreover, *for* is a coordinating conjunction, and not, like *because* and *since*, a subordinating conjunction; hence it can properly begin sentences.

B. In Anticipatory Reference. When coupled with *do*-words, *as* can cause mischief of the kind outlined under ANTICIPATORY REFERENCE (A). E.g.: "Both Maryland and the District of Columbia, *as do* [read *like*] most jurisdictions, require that the offending statement be made with knowledge of its falsity or in reckless disregard of the truth to support a finding of false light invasion of privacy." Russell G. Donaldson, *False Light Invasion of Privacy—Cognizability and Elements*, 57 A.L.R.4th 22 (1987). See **like (c).**

C. And *like.* See **like** & HYPERCORRECTION (E).

as against means either "as compared with" or "with respect to; in regard to"—but always with the implication of adversity or conflict—e.g.:

- "If a stick of timber comes ashore on a man's land, he thereby acquires a 'right of possession' *as against* an actual finder who enters for the purpose of removing it." Oliver Wendell Holmes Jr., *The Common Law* 176 (1881).
- "Confessions, if voluntary, are deemed to be relevant facts *as against* the persons who make them only." *Commissioners of Customs & Excise v. Harz & Power*, [1967] 51 Crim. App. 123, 137 (H.L.).

The phrase is sometimes misused for *against* (a misusage dating back, as you'll see, quite some time)—e.g.:

- "Nothing was required to be proved *as against* [read *against*] him, in order to obtain a judgment against him." *Smith v. Hulett*, 65 Ill. 495, 496–97 (1872).
- "The Town of Newton asserts that it was error for this court to permit experts to testify *as against* [read *against*] these defendants." *Hild v. Bruner*, 496 F.Supp. 93, 98 (D.N.J. 1980).
- "An examination of *Vagts'* [read *Vagts's*] article on Nazism reveals further techniques used by these theorists— including the argument that treaties did not apply in changed circumstances . . . and that constitutional law— national law—prevailed *as against* [read *against*] international law." Pieter H.F. Bekker et al., *Making Transnational Law Work in the Global Economy* 25–26 (2010).

Because *as against* is an idiom with a fairly set meaning in English, it should not be used in unfamiliar ways, such as in an ellipsis of *as being against*—e.g.:

- "Any subrogation, reimbursement, assignment, or setoff provision within an insurance policy is void *as against* [read *as being against*] public policy." Jason E. Pepe, *Kansas's Conflict of Laws Rules for Insurance Contract Cases: It's Time to Change Policies*, 46 U. Kan. L. Rev. 819, 838 (1998).
- "On appeal, Farm Bureau raises one argument for reversal: the trial court erred in finding that the 'eluding lawful apprehension or arrest' exclusion contained in Farm Bureau's automobile policy is void *as against* [read *as being against*] public policy." *Southern Farm Bureau Cas. Ins. Co. v. Easter*, 251 S.W.3d 251, 252 (Ark. 2007).

as amended; as it may be amended from time to time. Often a legal drafter will refer to a statute and add to the reference *as amended* or, in full flower, *as it may be amended from time to time.* The extra wording is not surplusage—it establishes what version of the statute controls.

*as and when. This is a redundant expression; either *as* or *when* will suffice—e.g.: "The bill provides that the balances shall be met by the Exchequer *as and when* [read *as*] they mature for payment." (Eng.—ex. fr. Vere Henry Collins, *Right Word, Wrong Word* 19 (1956).)

The variant **when and as* is equally bad—e.g.:

- "A court of equity acts only *when and as* [read *when* or *as*] conscience commands; and if the conduct of the plaintiff be offensive to the dictates of natural justice, then, whatever may be the rights he possesses, and whatever use he may make of them in a court of law, he will be held remediless in a court of equity." *Deweese v. Reinhard*, 165 U.S. 386, 390 (1897) (per Brewer, J.).

- "A detailed description of the patents in this suit, the accused devices, and the parties' litigation history was included in this court's . . . Memorandum and Opinion; it is repeated here *only when and as* [read *only when*] necessary." *Kothmann Enters., Inc. v. Trinity Indus., Inc.*, 455 F.Supp.2d 608, 613 (S.D. Tex. 2006).

as . . . as. A. And *so . . . as.* In positive statements, the *as . . . as* construction is preferred—e.g.:

- "If the guard had thrown [the packaged explosive] down knowingly and willfully, he would not have threatened the plaintiff's safety, *so far as* [read *as far as*] appearances could warn him." *Palsgraf v. Long Island R.R.*, 162 N.E. 99, 101 (N.Y. 1928) (per Cardozo, C.J.).
- "*So long as* [read *As long as*] the courts fail to come to grips with that fact, so long as [read *as long as*] they persist in assuming that every juror has a precise and firmly held position, the process of jury selection will be unpredictable, arbitrary, and ultimately lawless." Eric Schnapper, *Taking* Witherspoon *Seriously: The Search for Death Qualified Jurors*, 62 Tex. L. Rev. 977, 1077 (1984).
- "*Yet, for so long as* [read *Yet as long as*] the Court fails to clarify the nature of its review and grapple openly with the messy choices inherent in its enterprise, its work will remain vulnerable to attack and suspicion." David D. Meyer, Lochner *Redeemed*, 48 UCLA L. Rev. 1125, 1189 (2001).

Through the mid-20th century it was commonly believed that *so . . . as* is preferable to *as . . . as* in negative statements. And it probably still is—e.g.:

- "It is true, there is no locking by the cam against downward movement, and the curtain can be pulled down without touching the pinch handles though not *so easily as* in the Forsyth device." *Curtain Supply Co. v. New Jersey State Ry. Co.*, 142 F. 750, 752 (3d Cir. 1906).
- "He was able to stop the car, but not *so quickly as* if the brake had been in perfect condition." *Layton v. Union Traction Co.*, 76 A. 18, 18 (Pa. 1910).

But *as . . . as* generally serves equally well in such negative statements. Following is a construction in which *not so . . . as* doesn't read as well as *not as . . . as*: "Back at Bennie's Corners, affairs were not going so happily as they were at McGill University." On first reading this sentence, the reader may be temporarily misled into thinking that *so* means "very," in its colloquial sense, as it would if the sentence ended after *happily.* See **as long as; equally as (B)** & **so as.**

B. Repetition of Verb After. Often, when the second *as* in this construction is far removed from the first *as*, the verb is repeated for clarity—e.g.: "Perhaps no area of corporate law *is as* beset with conflicting judicial opinions, variations among statutes, and confusion and uncertainty concerning the likely outcome of litigation *as is* the duty of loyalty." A.A. Sommer Jr., *The Duty of Loyalty in the ALI's Corporate Governance Project*, 52 Geo. Wash. L. Rev. 719, 719 (1984). Yet this separation of related words cannot be recommended.

as at (= as of) is characteristic chiefly of BrE and of financial contexts in AmE. E.g.:

- "This book reflects the law *as at* August 1986." Stanley Berwin, *The Economist Pocket Lawyer* i (1986).
- "The common law took the coldly logical view that bastardy was judged *as at* the date of birth and was indelible." J.H. Baker, *An Introduction to English Legal History* 558 (3d ed. 1990).

as a whole. See **in whole.**

as between (= in a comparison of [usu. two things]) is much more common in legal than in nonlegal writing. In fact, most general English-language dictionaries neglect the phrase. E.g.:

- "The controversy as to the type of law, whether custom or common law or tradition, on the one hand, or legislation, on the other, the controversy as to the relation of law to morals, the discussion *as between* adjudication and administration, *as between* law and equity, *as between* strict and free procedure, all run back to this problem of stability and change." Roscoe Pound, *The Formative Era of American Law* 18 (1938).
- "A judgment gives rights and obligations to litigants *as between* themselves." 1 Ernest W. Chance, *Principles of Mercantile Law* 10 (Percy W. French ed., 13th ed. 1950).
- "This does not mean that in the English courts of the thirteenth century justice was no more than 'justice *as between* man and man.'" Carleton K. Allen, *Law in the Making* 401 (7th ed. 1964).

See **between (D).**

ascendant. A. Spelling. Both as a noun and as an adjective, the spelling *ascendant* is preferred over **ascendent.*

B. And *ancestor; collateral; descendant.* In the language of decedents' estates, both *ascendant* and *ancestor* mean "a person related to an intestate or to one who claims an intestate share in the descending lineal line (e.g., parents and grandparents)." *Ancestor* is the more universally comprehensible word but has two severe disadvantages: first, it is less likely to be understood as referring to a parent; second, it lacks the *-ant* suffix, which makes *ascendant* parallel with *descendant.* See **ancestor.**

Descendant denotes one who is descended from an ancestor—i.e., offspring in any degree, near or remote. E.g.: "No one will deny that a marriage between an *ascendant* and *descendant* in the same line is properly within the forbidden degrees." Max Radin, *The Law and You* 41 (1948). See **descendant.**

A *collateral* is a relative who traces relationship to the intestate through an ancestor in common, but who is not in the lineal line of ascent or descent.

C. In the ascendant. This phrase is sometimes misconstrued to mean "ascending"; actually, it means "dominating; supreme." The phrase has been handed down to us from medieval astrology.

as concerns. See **as regards.**

ascribe (= to attribute to a specified cause) <I couldn't possibly ascribe these sentiments to my parents> is sometimes misused for *subscribe* in the sense "to think of favorably"—e.g.:

- (Right) "A review of existing authority on the state-action doctrine suggests the necessity of specifying the meaning we *ascribe* to the notion of compulsion by the state." *U.S. v. Southern Motor Carriers Rate Conference, Inc.*, 467 F.Supp. 471, 483 n.8 (N.D. Ga. 1979).
- (Wrong) "We simply cannot *ascribe* [read *subscribe*] to the notion, however, that this court should never attempt to set the record straight where the public's perceptions of the judiciary have been manipulated through unfair, incorrect, and misleading reports and comment." *Whitehead v. Nevada Comm'n on Judicial Discipline*, 893 P.2d 866, 936 (Nev. 1995).

as do. See **as** (B) & ANTICIPATORY REFERENCE (A).

as equally. See **equally as** (B) & (D).

as far as. This phrase must be followed by *is concerned* or *goes*, or else idiom is severely violated—e.g.: " 'My treatment was severe, causing no monetary numbers to be put on it, *as far as* damages [add *are concerned*].' " *Maddaloni Jewelers, Inc. v. Rolex Watch U.S.A., Inc.*, 354 F.Supp.2d 293, 307 (S.D.N.Y. 2004) (quoting deposition testimony).

Idiom aside, however, this construction usually signals VERBOSITY. In the sentence just quoted, for example, the writer might have said: "We expect the damages to be insignificant."

as follows; *as follow. *As follows* is always the correct form, even for a long enumeration.

as from, a formal way of dating the onset of something, is more common in BrE than in AmE. E.g.:

- "Eventually it was decided that *as from* 1979 criminal causes in the House of Lords should be reported under the same title as in the court below." Glanville Williams, *Learning the Law* 17–18 (11th ed. 1982).
- "Most building societies credit accounts with monies paid-in by cheque *as from* the date of deposit." *Council Had No Choice*, Fin. Times, 27 Jan. 1990, at 5. See **monies.**

as if; as though. Attempts to distinguish between these idioms have proved futile. Euphony should govern the choice of phrase.

as, if, and when. This phrase, which commonly appears in real estate contracts, could almost always be made *when* with no loss in meaning. See ***as and when, if and when** & DOUBLETS, TRIPLETS, AND SYNONYM-STRINGS.

as in. See **like** (B).

as is; as was. "He bought the company '*as is*.' " Although a martinet of logic might insist on *as was* in the preceding sentence, that phrase is jarringly unidiomatic. *As is*, in the context of that sentence, is really an elliptical form of *on an "as is" basis*, and is infinitely better than that paraphrase. The purpose of the phrase

as is, of course, is for a seller to disclaim warranties and representations.

as it may be amended from time to time. See **as amended.**

ask; inquire; question; interrogate; query. These verbs share the sense "to make an inquisitive statement calculated to elicit a response." To *ask* is simply to pose a question: it is the generic word. To *inquire* is very much the same, but this word implies either that the person who uses the word is engaging in the verbal inflation known as genteelism <may I inquire into the nature of your call?> or that the situation is truly more formal <when speaking to the ambassador, did you inquire about his daughter?>. To *question* is typically to pose one question after another in a penetrating way <the prosecutor questioned the witness for 45 minutes>. To *interrogate* is to engage in formal or systematic questioning, often relentlessly <detainees are interrogated about terrorist activities>. To *query* is to raise a small point, especially a doubtful one, as in the margin of a manuscript <I queried what I think is a typo>.

as long as; so long as. These phrases are not purely temporal constructions; more often than not, they express a condition rather than a time limit <as long as the transferees abide by these restrictions, they may enjoy possession of the land>. See **as . . . as** (A).

as much as or more. When *than* follows these words, the second *as* must appear <as much as or more than>. A common error is to write *as much or more than*.

In the following sentences, however, *as much or more* (not followed by *than*) is correct:

- "Was she not *as much or more* a victim of the system as the astonishingly bright and collected Gregory?" Neil MacCormick, *With Due Respect*, TLS, 22 Jan. 1993, at 3.
- "There can be *as much or more* justice in directing purely prospective application." *Bugosh v. I.U. North Am., Inc.*, 971 A.2d 1228, 1242 n.25 (Pa. 2009) (Saylor, J., dissenting).

See ILLOGIC (A). Cf. **as of.**

as of. A. Generally. *As of* should be used with caution—if at all. Originally an Americanism, the phrase frequently signifies the effective legal date of a document, as when the document is backdated or when the parties sign at different times. When such a nuance is not intended, *as of* is the wrong phrase. It is often inferior to *on*—e.g.:

- "Mattox alleges that her long-term disability benefits, . . . canceled *as of* [read *on*] September 20, 2003, should be reinstated." *Mattox v. Life Ins. Co. of N. Am.*, 536 F.Supp.2d 1307, 1310 (N.D. Ga. 2008).
- "On June 7, 2008, MCS notified Defendants that it intended to terminate the Supplier Agreements *as of* [read *on*] September 7, 2008." *Medical Card Sys. v. Equipo Pro Convalecencia*, 587 F.Supp.2d 384, 386 (D.P.R. 2008).

Cf. **as at.**

B. Used Unnecessarily. Sometimes the phrase needlessly displaces a more direct word—e.g.:

"Arizona had itself not suffered any direct harm *as of the time that* [read *when*] it moved for leave to file a complaint." *Maryland v. Louisiana*, 451 U.S. 725, 743 (1981) (per White, J.).

C. *As of now.* This phrase, along with *as of* itself, has been criticized as a barbarism. Lord Conesford, a curmudgeonly stickler, wrote that "an illiteracy is introduced when the words *as of* precede not a date, but the adverb *now*. *As of now* is a barbarism which only a love of illiteracy for its own sake can explain. What is generally meant is *at present*." Lord Conesford, "You Americans Are Murdering the Language," in *Advanced Composition* 374, 383 (J.E. Warriner et al. eds., 1968).

But *as of now* does not mean "at present"; rather, it means "up to the present time." Follett also disapproved of the phrase, recommending instead *up to now* or *for the present*, but *as of now* is today unobjectionable in AmE.

Still, like its shorter sibling, it sometimes appears needlessly—e.g.: "Norman Mailer is a practiced writer. I am among those who are not convinced that he knows *what* to write, but it is clear he knows *how* to write. His most recent novel, *as of just now,* [delete *as of just now* and surrounding commas] contains the following sentence." Stephen White, *The Written Word* 81 (1984).

as of course. The phrase *as of course*, as opposed to *as a matter of course*, strikes nonlawyer readers as unidiomatic. But in law the idiom is common—e.g.:

- "It does hold that if such transfers are allowed *as of course,* the same right of transfer must be extended to every other child regardless of the dissimilarities of his circumstances." *Dillard v. School Bd. of Charlottesville, Va.*, 308 F.2d 920, 929 (4th Cir. 1962) (Haynsworth, J., dissenting).
- "A motion is not a 'responsive pleading,' within the meaning of rule 15(a), and thus the right to amend *as of course* is not defeated because the other party has filed a motion attacking the pleading." Charles Alan Wright, *The Law of Federal Courts* 450 (5th ed. 1994).
- "[C]osts other than attorneys' fees shall be allowed *as of course* to the prevailing party." Fed. R. Civ. P. 54(d)(1) (2000).

See **of course.**

as of now. See **as of** (c).

as of right is acceptable legal shorthand for *as a matter of right*; the phrase means "by virtue of a legal entitlement"—e.g.:

- "Writs of error to State courts have never been allowed *as of right.*" *Twitchell v. Commonwealth*, 74 U.S. 321, 324 (1868) (per Chase, C.J.).
- "The action for damages is always available, *as of right,* when a contract has been broken." G.H. Treitel, *The Law of Contract* 824 (8th ed. 1991).

***as of yet.** See ***as yet.**

***as per** is commonly understood to mean "in accordance with" or "in accordance with the terms of." *In re Impel Mfg. Co.*, 108 F.Supp. 469, 473 (E.D. Mich. 1952). But it should be commonly eschewed as an unrefined locution.

Originating in commercialese, ***as per** is almost always redundant for *per*. Yet even *per* is a LATINISM in place of which many everyday equivalents will suffice (e.g., *according to* or *in accordance with*)—e.g.:

- "The sellers agree to sell without any restriction and under all lawful guarantees the totality of the property of the said vessel Astree *as per* [read *in accordance with*] clauses and conditions herein stipulated and agree to deliver said vessel to such company as is designated by purchasers." *Caribbean S.S. Co., S.A. v. La Société Navale Caennaise*, 140 F.Supp. 16, 22 (E.D. Va. 1956) (quoting a contract).
- "The prisoner will be placed in the appropriate housing unit for his or her classification *as per* [read *in accordance with*] section 6.0 of this policy." *Roberts v. Mahoning County*, 495 F.Supp.2d 719, 780 (N.D. Ohio 2007) (quoting from an exhibit).

aspersions, to cast is a prolix CLICHÉ for *to asperse*—but the verb is little known. The MALAPROPISM *to cast dispersions* should be heartily aspersed, as this judge did—e.g.: "Plaintiffs also allege that John Bland assisted the authors in . . . 'publishing a misleading and slanderous Local 260 newsletter . . . designed to *cast dispersion* [sic] [read *cast aspersions*] on constitutional delegates.'" *Kirk v. Transport Workers Union*, 934 F.Supp. 775, 782 (S.D. Tex. 1995) ([sic] in original).

aspirant. See **candidate.**

asport; *asporate. *Asport* (the better form) = to carry away or remove feloniously. E.g.: "The crime of larceny entails not only the act of taking property but also of *asporting* it." *People v. Hammon*, 236 Cal. Rptr. 822, 829 (Ct. App. 1987).

Though usually appearing in the context of larceny—hence of personal property—the verb can refer to the illegal carrying away of persons. E.g.: "Between that act and completion of the kidnapping is the drive into the District to the club where Ms. Allwine allegedly worked, finding her there, luring her outside to the car, and effectively restraining and *asporting* her." *Frye v. State*, 489 A.2d 71, 75 (Md. Ct. Spec. App. 1985).

***Asporate** is a poorly formed BACK-FORMATION and a NEEDLESS VARIANT—e.g.:

- "On this venue issue, the trial court interpreted the stipulation between the parties as sufficient to show the truck was *asportated* [read *asported*] from Day County, South Dakota." *State v. Graycek*, 335 N.W.2d 572, 574 (S.D. 1983).
- "The prosecutor . . . add[ed] the value of the pistol first removed from the display case and secreted in the thief's waistband to the value of the second pistol *asportated* [read *asported*] a few minutes later in the same manner." *Sendejo v. State*, 676 S.W.2d 454, 455 (Tex. App.—Fort Worth 1984).

- "A trial court should give a requested charge on false imprisonment as a lesser included charge to kidnapping when the evidence supports a theory that the victim was falsely imprisoned without having been *asportated* [read *asported*] in the manner alleged by the State." *Brown v. State*, 619 S.E.2d 789, 795–96 (Ga. Ct. App. 2005).

asportable (= capable of being asported) is a lexicographic oversight, omitted from most English-language dictionaries, including the *OED*, *W2*, and *W3*. E.g.: "It was a reasonable inference . . . that once inside the department store warehouse the intruders would have access to a whole range of valuable, readily *asportable* consumer goods." *State v. S.G.*, 438 A.2d 256, 260 (Me. 1981).

asportation is a historical TERM OF ART meaning "the act of carrying off." The word denotes a necessary element of larceny. E.g.: "It seems to be the contention of appellees that the doctrine of wrongful *asportation* means that in order to establish conversion it must clearly appear that the taker converted the property to his own use." *Hicks Rubber Co., Distribs. v. Stacy*, 133 S.W.2d 249, 251 (Tex. Civ. App.—Austin 1939). And the meaning, some courts say, has acquired nuances: "The definition of *asportation* has evolved to the point where it seems that the only type of movement considered insufficient as evidence of *asportation* is movement immediately resulting from a physical struggle." *Garza v. State*, 670 S.E.2d 73, 75 (Ga. 2008).

This old word has also been adapted in modern contexts to mean "the act of driving (a vehicle) away"— e.g.: "Defendant argued [that kidnapping] required a completed carjacking, which in turn required *asportation* of the vehicle." *People v. Navarro*, 151 P.3d 1177, 1179 (Cal. 2007). See **larceny, burglary** & **stole, took, and carried away.**

asporter is the agent noun corresponding to *asport*, vb. E.g.: "The evidence did not identify any particular person as the actual *asporter* of the property from the room in which it was stored." *State v. Hollis*, 113 So. 159, 159 (La. 1927).

as regards; as respects; as concerns. *As regards*, a much-maligned phrase, is sometimes inferior to *regarding* or *concerning*, but it is not a solecism. E.g.:

- "It is true that Lady Dufferin's interest was a protected life interest, but she was left free *as regards* dealing with it in one particular way: surrender in favor of persons entitled in remainder." (Eng.) The phrase was a favorite of the great legal scholar Wesley N. Hohfeld, who used it frequently in his *Fundamental Legal Conceptions* (1919).
- "Even then plaintiff delayed five weeks in commencing alternative service and that service when finally effected was technically improper *as regards* the Newspaper and two of the individual defendants." *Porter v. Beaumont Enter. & Journal*, 743 F.2d 269, 271 (5th Cir. 1984).
- "*As regards* matters of history, this includes not only the history of the particular political community in which the question is being contested, but also the history of the idea of religious freedom itself and its relationship to that community." Peter G. Danchin, *Of Prophets and Proselytes*, 49 Harv. Int'l L.J. 249, 286 (2008).

Though *as regards* is no more objectionable than *with regard to*, the whole lot of such phrases is suspect: "Train your suspicions to bristle up whenever you come upon *as regards*, *with regard to*, *in respect of*, *in connection with*, *according as to whether*, and the like. They are all dodges of jargon, circumlocution for evading this or that simple statement." Arthur Quiller-Couch, *On the Art of Writing* 114 (1916). Cf. **regard (A).**

As respects and *as concerns* are equivalent phrases not commonly found outside legal writing. E.g.:

- "*As respects* the federal courts, it is well settled that where the mandate leaves nothing to the judgment or discretion of the court below, and that court mistakes or misconstrues the decree or judgment of this court and does not give full effect to the mandate, its action may be controlled, either upon a new appeal or writ of error if involving a sufficient amount, or by writ of mandamus to execute the mandate of this court." *In re Blake*, 175 U.S. 114, 117 (1899) (per Fuller, C.J.).
- "Presentment is not included as an additional type of formal accusation, since presentments as a method of instituting prosecutions are obsolete, at least *as concerns* the Federal courts." Fed. R. Crim. P. 7(a), adv. comm. note 4.

ass. See **arse** & **pompous ass.**

assail (= to attack) is usually used figuratively in both legal and nonlegal contexts. Both *attack* and *assail* are used of findings and holdings of lower courts with which an appellant is displeased:

- "The appellants *assail* these findings, conclusions and the judgment on the ground that the property was community and that upon the death of Anderson C. Babb, his five children inherited his one-half interest." *Babb v. McGee*, 507 S.W.2d 821, 822 (Tex. Civ. App.—Dallas 1974).
- "Next, appellants *assail* Meyer's qualifications, claiming that because he is a neurologist, he cannot opine on the care provided by an anesthesiologist." *Gelman v. Cuellar*, 268 S.W.3d 123, 128 (Tex. App.—Corpus Christi 2008).
- "Defendants *assail* this methodology, claiming that Parr mistakenly relied on Secure's company-wide profits." *Finjan, Inc. v. Secure Computing Corp.*, 626 F.3d 1197, 1209 (Fed. Cir. 2010).

assassin; *assassinator. The second is an astonishingly common and durable NEEDLESS VARIANT—e.g.:

- "The circumstances show that the *assassinator* [read *assassin*] used a rifle carrying a 32 ball as a bludgeon, with which the victim was beaten to death." *Norris v. State*, 64 S.W. 1044, 1046 (Tex. Crim. App. 1901).
- "Charles Guiteau, the *assassinator* [read *assassin*] of President Garfield, was executed despite medical testimony of insanity." Edward de Grazia, *Murder, Madness and the Law*, 62 Yale L.J. 679, 680 (1953) (book review).
- "The First Amendment should not to be a shelter for the character *assassinator* [read *assassin*] to further his actions that are heedless and reckless or deliberate." *Bartimo v. Horsemen's Benevolent & Protective Ass'n*, 592 F.Supp. 1526, 1532 (W.D. La. 1984).

For the mystifying, cabalistic mathematical sense of *assassinator*, see *Garner's Modern American Usage* 69 (3d ed. 2009).

assassinate. See **kill (A).**

assault; battery. These terms have distinct meanings in criminal and in tort law. Essentially, an *assault* is the use or threat of force upon another that causes that person to have a well-founded fear of physical injury or offensive touching. A *battery* is the use of force or violence on another (in the criminal sense), or any repugnant intentional contact with another (in the tortious sense). Cf. **accost.**

Shooting a gun just to the side of someone, if that person reasonably fears physical injury, or shooting a blank gun directly at someone would be an *assault.* Hitting someone with a bullet makes the act a *battery,* even if the person never knew of the hit. In the tort sense, an uninvited kiss by a stranger would be considered a *battery.* See **battery.**

Leff noted that the distinction is observed only by lawyers, and even by them not consistently: "In ordinary language, and even to some extent in legal talk, the two are conflated, and one speaks of an *assault* frequently in referring to the whole incident, from the threat through its consummation. Indeed, at least in ordinary understanding, use of the word *assault* most likely requires the actual *battery;* most people would not use 'He got angry and *assaulted* her' to describe an incident in which no physical contact was made." Arthur A. Leff, *The Leff Dictionary of Law,* 94 Yale L.J. 1855, 2069 (1985).

assaultee (= one who is assaulted) is a mid-20th-century legal NEOLOGISM omitted from most English-language dictionaries. E.g.:

- "The appellant denied that he assaulted the *assaultee* for any purpose other than getting her money." *McKee v. State,* 33 So.2d 50, 53 (Fla. 1947) (en banc) (Chapman, J., dissenting).
- "The intent to kill may be established by a number of circumstances, such as, the fact that the weapon is directed at some vital spot on the *assaultee's* body." *Caraker v. State,* 84 So.2d 50, 51 (Fla. 1955).
- "Self-defense is relative. It is available as an exculpation, or an excuse for assault, to an *assaultee,* not an assailant." *State v. Brent,* 347 So.2d 1112, 1116 (La. 1977).

See -EE.

assaulter. So spelled—not **assaultor.*

assaultive is the adjective corresponding to *assault*—e.g.:

- "But the armed robbery also shows a character for violence[; and] it was also allowed to be introduced that he's been convicted of an *assaultive* crime involving a gun." *People v. Koontz,* 46 P.3d 335, 363 (Cal. 2002).
- "We need not dwell on the distinction between *assaultive* and non-*assaultive* crimes, for there is a more fundamental flaw in Leahy's thesis." *U.S. v. Leahy,* 473 F.3d 401, 408 (1st Cir. 2007).

assault with intent to commit rape; assault to rape. Both forms occur in criminal cases, the first being somewhat more common. See **rape (c).**

assay; essay. These words, related etymologically, have distinct meanings. *Assay* = to test; to analyze. E.g.:

- "Tenuous theories of liability are better *assayed* in the light of actual facts than in pleader's supposition." *Adato v. Kagan,* 599 F.2d 1111, 1117 (2d Cir. 1979).
- "In both situations the actual degree of harm must be *assayed* in light of the entire jury charge, the state of the evidence, including the contested issues and weight of probative evidence, the argument of counsel and any other relevant information revealed by the record of the trial as a whole." *Almanza v. State,* 686 S.W.2d 157, 171 (Tex. Crim. App. 1984).

Essay, though sometimes used synonymously as a verb with *assay,* most frequently takes on the meaning "to attempt; to try to accomplish." E.g.:

- "But Summers must establish the converse, and it has not *essayed* to do so either in its counterclaim or in its supporting memorandum." *Intamin, Inc. v. Figley-Wright Contractors, Inc.,* 608 F.Supp. 408, 412 (N.D. Ill. 1985).
- "Because the President has not *essayed* to appoint a successor, Gil has continued to serve in that capacity for upwards of six years." *U.S. v. Torres-Rosa,* 209 F.3d 4, 6 (1st Cir. 2000).

Essay so used is quite formal and somewhat archaic; *attempt* or *try* serves better in ordinary contexts. Cf. **endeavor.**

assembly, unlawful. See **riot.**

assent, vb.; **consent; accede; agree; acquiesce; subscribe.** These verbs share the sense "to express a willingness to go along with someone else's wishes or views." *Assent* involves the intellect and applies to propositions or opinions <I simply assented to her view on churchgoing>. *Consent* involves feelings or the will and connotes complying with a request <that's one reason why she consented to marry me>. Of course, one can *assent* or *consent* against one's better judgment. *Accede* suggests a yielding of one's adherence to contrary views or of one's assent <he finally acceded to the encroachment on his land>. *Agree,* in connection with those other words, often implies a prior clash of opinion followed by discussions or negotiations <after seeming to reach a stalemate, they finally agreed on shared responsibilities>. *Acquiesce* suggests forgoing the desire to oppose and silently allowing something despite misgivings <though they wanted their daughter to attend the University of Texas, they finally acquiesced in her adamant desire to attend West Texas A&M>. *Subscribe,* though literally requiring a signature at the bottom, denotes warm approval and at least passive promotion <we subscribe

to the view that government is inherently less efficient than private sector>. In the literal sense of writing one's name or putting one's mark at the bottom of a document, *subscribe* is now purely a LEGALISM. *Sign* almost always suffices more comprehensibly.

assenter; assentor. For "one who assents," *assenter* is standard. *Assentor* has the specialized legal meaning in England of "one who, in addition to the proposer and seconder of a candidate's nomination in an election, signs the nomination paper of that candidate." It should not be used in other senses.

assert. See **maintain (A).**

assertedly. See **reportedly, allegedly** & **confessedly.**

assertive; assertory. The first is the word for ordinary purposes; the second was at one time used by grammarians in reference to sentences or constructions in the form of affirmations. *Assertory* is used in but one legal phrase, *assertory oath*, which denotes a statement of facts under oath.

assertor, not **asserter*, is the usual agent noun corresponding to the verb *assert*. See -ER (A).

assess. See **access (B).**

assessable. See **accessible.**

assessment. A. And *periodic dues*. An *assessment* is (1) the determination of a rate chargeable or an amount due, usu. for tax or fine purposes; (2) the imposition of a fine or a special tax; (3) a valuation for tax purposes; or (4) an audit. *Periodic dues* are regularly required payments made to an organization by a member. *Assessments* are usually made by public entities, but a private organization may levy charges on its members at irregular times for special purposes.

It is redundant to use *periodic dues* and a specific time reference in the same phrase—e.g.: " 'The Union shall certify to the Medical Center the amount that constitutes *periodic monthly dues* [read *monthly dues*].' " *St. John's Mercy Health Sys. v. N.L.R.B.*, 436 F.3d 843, 845 (8th Cir. 2006) (quoting a contract).

B. For Taxation. See **tax.**

asseverate. See **swear.**

assign, n.; **assignee.** Both words mean "one to whom property rights or powers are transferred by another." *Assignee* is more understandable to nonlawyers, who know *assign* as a verb only. But the SET PHRASE *heirs and assigns* is unlikely to disappear; *assign* as a noun almost always appears, as in the phrase just adduced, in the plural.

assign, vb., is frequently merely an inflated synonym of *give*—e.g.: "But I think the principal reasons *assigned* by Judge Wilson and Judge Peters was that under the Act of Congress it did not appear that a case of this kind was excluded from the Circuit Court." William

R. Casto, *There Were Great Men Before Agamemnon*, 62 Vand. L. Rev. 371, 404 (2009).

The verb is a less inflated LEGALISM when used in the sense "to transfer"—e.g.: "As a means of covering his debts, he *assigned* his rights to future royalty income to his creditors." Peter S. Menell, *Bankruptcy Treatment of Intellectual Property Assets: An Economic Analysis*, 22 Berkeley Tech. L.J. 733, 818 (2007). In fact, *assign* is the preferred term for conveying intellectual-property rights.

assignability. See **negotiability.**

assignee. See **assign,** n.

*assigner. See **assignor.**

assignment; assignation. *Assignment* = (1) the transfer of property, or the property so transferred; (2) the instrument of transfer; or (3) a task or job. See **negotiability.**

Assignation = (1) assignment; (2) tryst; or (3) assign (meaning "one to whom property rights or powers are transferred"). *Assignation* is a NEEDLESS VARIANT in senses 1 and 3, and should be confined to sense 2, in which it is truly useful. In sense 1, however, *assignation* is the usual and proper term in Scots law.

assignment of error = a specification of errors made at trial and contained in an application for writ of error directed to an appellate court. On appeal, one *assigns error* to certain alleged prejudicial mistakes at trial. (See **error (A).**) E.g.: "By proper *assignments of error* and cross-errors, the correctness of each of the trial court's conclusions of law and that part of the temporary injunction undertaking to prescribe a form of permissible picketing is challenged." *Roth v. Local Union No. 1460 of Retail Clerks Union*, 24 N.E.2d 280, 282 (Ind. 1939).

assignor; *assigner. In all legal senses, *assignor* is preferred; it is the correlative of *assignee*. **Assigner* has appeared in nonlegal contexts, and there it should remain. See -ER (A).

*assise. See **assize.**

assist, vb., is usually inferior to *help*.

assistance. The phrases *to provide assistance* and *to be of assistance*—containing the nominalized term *assistance*—are generally much inferior to *help*. See BURIED VERBS.

assize, n., = (1) a session of a court or council; (2) a law enacted by such a body, usu. one setting the measure, weight, or price of a thing; (3) the procedure provided for by such an enactment; (4) the court that hears cases involving that procedure; (5) a jury trial; or (6) the jury's finding in such a trial. In short, this word is, historically speaking, a CHAMELEON-HUED WORD.

In the plural (*assizes*), the term refers to the sessions or sittings of a court, especially of a superior court in

England or Wales, held twice a year, at which cases were tried by a judge and jury. The *assizes* ceased to exist in Great Britain after the Courts Act 1971. **Assise* is a variant spelling generally best avoided.

**associate together* is a REDUNDANCY; **associate together in groups* is even worse—e.g.:

- "Because of the threat of harassment against women who *associate together in groups* [read *associate*], servicewomen cannot even turn to each other for relief and support in the face of this daily challenge." Michelle M. Benecke & Kirstin S. Dodge, *Military Women in Nontraditional Fields: Casualties of the Armed Forces' War on Homosexuals*, 13 Harv. Women's L.J. 215, 241 (1990).
- "The Defendants do not dispute that the First Amendment protects the rights of people to *associate together in groups to further* [read *associate in furtherance of*] lawful interests." *Davis v. Phenix City, Ala.*, 513 F.Supp.2d 1241, 1253 (M.D. Ala. 2007).

associational; associative. The *OED* defines these words as virtual synonyms ("of, pertaining to, or characterized by association"). But it also suggests that *associational* refers to particular associations <his associational loyalties>, whereas *associative* refers to association generally. But *W3* suggests that *associative* is now largely confined to contexts involving psychology and mathematics.

Certainly the usual term in legal contexts is *associational*—e.g.:

- "Any thought that due process puts beyond the reach of the criminal law all individual *associational* relationships, unless accompanied by the commission of specific acts of criminality, is dispelled by familiar concepts of the law of conspiracy and complicity." *Scales v. U.S.*, 367 U.S. 203, 225 (1961) (per Harlan, J.).
- "Further, it is extremely doubtful that the rights to visitation asserted by the Thornes are the sort of *associational* rights protected by the First Amendment." *Thorne v. Jones*, 765 F.2d 1270, 1273 (5th Cir. 1985).

assoil; assoilzie; absolvitor. **Assoil* (= to pardon, release, acquit) is an obsolete ecclesiastical term for the reversal of an excommunication. *Assoilzie*, a Scottish dialectal variant, is still used in civil and criminal Scottish cases in the sense "to free of liability by order of court." The Scottish decree is called *absolvitor*.

ASSONANCE. See ALLITERATION (A).

assume; presume. The connotative distinction between these words is that *presumptions* are more strongly inferential and more probably authoritative than mere *assumptions*, which are usually more hypothetical. E.g.:

- " 'Where any document purporting to be 30 years old is produced from any custody which the judge in the particular case considers proper, it is *presumed* that the signature and every other part of such document which purports to be in the handwriting of any particular person is in that person's handwriting.' " *Nicholson v. Eureka*

Lumber Co., 72 S.E. 86, 87 (N.C. 1911) (quoting *Stephen's Digest of the Law of Evidence*).

- "[Defendants] rely upon the ancient legal *presumption*, often mentioned in our cases, that a woman is [considered] legally capable of bearing children at any age." *In re Lattouf's Will*, 208 A.2d 411, 415 (N.J. Super. Ct. App. Div. 1965).

Presumptions lead to decisions, whereas *assumptions* do not—e.g.: "We *assume*, without deciding, that except for the provisions of section 18 of the Decedent Estate Law the trust would be valid." *Newman v. Dore*, 9 N.E.2d 966, 969 (N.Y. 1937). The phrase *we assume, without deciding*, is a favorite of common-law courts.

Where adverbs are concerned, one should always use the common forms derived from *presume*—that is, *presumably* (= I presume; it is to be presumed) or *presumptively* (= there is a presumption at law that). Sometimes writers seem to try to avoid the simple term in favor of an outlandish one—e.g.:

- "It is important to note that this holding prevents a city or a state from adopting any legislation concerning immigration even if the ordinance has the same objective and end result as the federal statute, which is *assumedly* [read *presumably*] to deter illegal immigration." Susan M. Bartlett, *Grass Roots Immigration Reform*, 69 La. L. Rev. 989, 999 (2009).
- "While Sheridan's plea agreement did apparently state that he would testify truthfully if called by the prosecution—*assumedly* [read *presumably*] in conformity with prior statements Sheridan had made to police and authorities, as a result of which the prosecutor proffered the plea bargain in the first place—such a 'condition' does not represent undue coercion, threat, or intimidation." *Woods v. Adams*, 631 F.Supp.2d 1261, 1279 (C.D. Cal. 2009).

Assumptive is pretentious for either *assumed* <assumptive beliefs> or *assuming* or *presumptuous* <an assumptive character>. For the sense of *presumptive* in *heir presumptive*, see **heir** (B).

assuming. See DANGLERS (D).

assumpsit, a LAW LATIN term, means literally "he undertook" or "he promised"—e.g.: "Of the terms used in connection with the subject of restitution, *assumpsit* is one of the oldest and also perhaps one of the most troublesome." Peter W. Davis, Comment, *Restitution: Concept and Terms*, 19 Hastings L.J. 1167, 1182 (1968). The term originally applied to an action for breach of a simple contract, then was extended (after *Slade's Case* [1602]) to cases in which no independent agreement to pay could be proved, and finally applied to implied contracts and quasi-contracts. This CHAMELEON-HUED WORD is no longer widely used by common-law courts; in England the cause of action was abolished by the Judicature Acts of 1873–1875.

assumption, in lay writing, most commonly means "a supposition"; in legal contexts it frequently takes on the older sense "the action of taking for or upon oneself" (*OED*). E.g.: "It is not clear whether ITT also consented to an *assumption* of indebtedness." *Avondale Shipyards, Inc. v. Tank Barge ETS 2303*, 754 F.2d 1300, 1302 (5th Cir. 1985). See **assume.**

assumption of the risk; contributory negligence.
Originally these two were separate doctrines, but *assumption of the risk* has been, in most jurisdictions, subsumed by the doctrine of *contributory* (or *comparative*) *negligence*. Assumption of the risk = the principle that a party who has taken on the risk of loss, injury, or damage consequently cannot maintain an action against the party having caused the loss. An example of assumed risk is the man who volunteers his profile to a friend who wants to practice sword-throwing.

Perhaps because *assumption of the risk* as applied by the courts came to bar otherwise meritorious claims, legal scholars began to point out that *contributory negligence* could be applied to any case involving *assumption of the risk*. And with the rise of *comparative negligence*, the doctrine of *assumption of the risk* became especially unjust if applied to bar a claim. See *volenti non fit injuria* & **comparative negligence.**

assumptive; presumptive. See **assume.**

assurance; insurance. The nouns follow from the verbs; hence the reader might first consult the next entry. Since *ensurance is no longer with us, *insurance* is the nominal form of both *insure* and *ensure*. Usually, *insurance* refers to indemnification against loss (from the verb *insure*); in BrE, *assurance* is sometimes given this meaning, although Partridge notes its decline; its one surviving use in this sense is in reference to life policies. Generally, however, *assurance* = that which gives confidence. See **insurance (B).**

In AmE, *assurance* chiefly means "pledge" or "guaranty." E.g.:

- "The heirs would have no *assurance* that the question of the personal fault of the executor would be properly tried." *Johnston v. Long*, 181 P.2d 645, 651 (Cal. 1947).
- "Because there was evidence that Burke mismanaged the business, refused to pay the Athenses the lottery ticket money, filed suit against them, and refused to *give further assurances of* [better: *to further ensure*] performance, the Athenses assert that a directed verdict for Burke was inappropriate." *Burke v. Athens*, 703 N.E.2d 804, 807 (Ohio Ct. App. 1997).
- "Opposing counsel could not know that the case would be reassigned without having already received *assurance* from the court that [R]espondent's motion would be granted and that a specific hearing date would be set." *Board of Prof'l Responsibility, Wyo. State Bar v. Davidson*, 205 P.3d 1008, 1012–13 (Wyo. 2009).

Assurance also has the specialized, rather rare legal meaning "the act of transferring real property." *Assure* formerly had the corresponding meaning "to convey by deed."

assure; ensure; insure. A. *Assure for ensure.* One person *assures* (makes promises to, convinces) other persons, and *ensures* (makes certain) that things occur or

that events take place. Any object beginning with *that* should be introduced by the verb *ensure*, if the verb is in the active voice. Here *assure*, which always takes a personal object, is properly used: "Zehmer *assured* him that he had no intention of selling the farm and that the whole matter was a joke." *Lucy v. Zehmer*, 84 S.E.2d 516, 518 (Va. 1954).

Assure is often misused for *ensure*—e.g.:

- "The Court's findings were contained in a letter order to counsel, a procedure admittedly more informal than the usual findings which by structure and precision more likely *assure* [read *ensure*] that all relevant issues are disposed of." *Mladinich v. U.S.*, 371 F.2d 940, 941 (5th Cir. 1967).
- "The State's strong interest in *assuring* [read *ensuring*] the marketability of property within its borders and in providing for peaceful resolution of disputes about the possession of that property would support jurisdiction, as would the likelihood that important records and witnesses will be found in the State." *Shaffer v. Heitner*, 433 U.S. 186, 208 (1977) (per Marshall, J.).
- "Trawick also argues that the assistant district attorney and the police promised him that, in return for his statement, they would *assure* [read *ensure*] that he would be expeditiously tried for capital murder." *Ex parte Trawick*, 698 So.2d 162, 175 (Ala. 1997).

Ensure is properly used in the following sentences:

- "The Court there held that the actual jury verdict *ensured* both that there had been probable cause for the grand jury's charge and that the charge was true beyond a reasonable doubt." *U.S. v. Hooker*, 841 F.2d 1225, 1231 (4th Cir. 1988).
- "The independent and adequate state ground doctrine *ensures* that the States' interest in correcting their own mistakes is respected in all federal habeas cases." *Coleman v. Thompson*, 501 U.S. 722, 732 (1991) (per O'Connor, J.).
- "Because the guilty verdict *ensured* that the jury actually made a factual determination that necessarily embraces an affirmative answer to the anti-parties issue, appellant was not deprived of a fair and impartial trial." *Prystash v. State*, 3 S.W.3d 522, 541 (Tex. Crim. App. 1999) (Keller, J., concurring).

B. *Insure* **and** *ensure.* *Insure* should be restricted to financial contexts involving indemnification; it should refer to what insurance companies do; *ensure* should be used in all other senses of the word. Intransitively, *insure* is commonly followed by the preposition *against* <insure against loss>; it may also be used transitively <insure one's valuables>. Following is a commonplace peccadillo:

- "But care must be taken to *insure* [read *ensure*] that the return of the loser does not become the guideline for judgment." Edward R. Cohen, *The Finders Cases Revisited*, 48 Tex. L. Rev. 1001, 1003 (1970).
- "After a bill is enacted, its sponsors must *insure* [read *ensure*] that the law becomes permanent policy, immune to attack or replacement by future Congresses." Harry A. Chernoff et al., *The Politics of Crime*, 33 Harv. J. on Legis. 527, 571 (1996).

C. Noun Forms. See **assurance.**

assurer; *assuror. The *-er* spelling is preferred. See -ER (A) & **underwriter.**

as the case may be. See **case (A).**

as though. See **as if.**

as to is a vague, all-purpose preposition that should be avoided whenever a more specific preposition will fit the context. *As to* does not clearly establish syntactic or conceptual relationships; it hampers the comprehensibility of texts in which it appears. Were it not a phrase, it might justifiably be classed among FORBIDDEN WORDS. And it seems all but addictive to modern legal writers—e.g.: "The *Gregory* rule discussed in *Holmes* said that evidence offered by a defendant *as to* [read *about*] the commission of the crime by another person is admissible if it raises a reasonable inference or presumption *as to* [read *of*] the defendant's innocence and is limited to facts that are inconsistent with his own guilt, but it is not admissible if it merely casts a bare suspicion upon another or raises a conjectural inference *as to* [read *about*] the commission of the crime by another." *Prible v. State*, 245 S.W.3d 466, 469 (Tex. Crim. App. 2008).

   A. Indefensible Uses. To illustrate the slippery variability of *as to*, a list of problematic usages follows; in each example, another preposition would more directly and forcefully express the thought.
1. For *of*:

- "The jury was also instructed that if it believed appellant was guilty of either murder or voluntary manslaughter, but was unsure *as to* [read *of*] which, it was to find him guilty of the lesser offense." *Ruiz v. State*, 691 S.W.2d 90, 93 (Tex. App.—Austin 1985).
- " 'This presumption remains with him throughout the trial until you've been satisfied by the evidence beyond a reasonable doubt *as to* [read *of*] the guilt of the defendant, and the burden of proving the guilt of the defendant beyond a reasonable doubt is on the State.' " *People v. Alexander*, 908 N.E.2d 173, 176 (Ill. App. Ct. 2009) (quoting the trial court). (It would also be better to write *of the defendant's guilt.* See **of (A).**)

2. For *on*:

- "We find no authority for the contention that the rule *as to* [read *on*] the destruction of contingent remainders should be applied to a case where the estate is vested in quality but contingent in quantity." *Kost v. Foster*, 94 N.E.2d 302, 304–05 (Ill. 1950).
- "The Uniform Commercial Code . . . provides guidelines for the incorporation of additional terms, but it is silent *as to* [read *on*] the reconciliation of different terms." *Southern Idaho Pipe & Steel Co. v. Cal-Cut Pipe & Supply, Inc.*, 567 P.2d 1246, 1253 (Idaho 1977).
- "Under the facts of this case, there are disputed issues of material fact which must be resolved by the jury to establish the circumstances upon which the Court must rule *as to* [read *on*] the existence of probable cause." *Carter v. Baker's Food Rite Store*, 787 S.W.2d 4, 8 (Tenn. Ct. App. 1990).

3. For *with*:

- "In the business of life insurance, the value of a man's life is measured in dollars and cents according to his

expectancy, the soundness of his body, and his ability to pay premiums. The same is true *as to* [read *with*] health and accident insurance." *Webb v. McGowin*, 168 So. 196, 198 (Ala. Civ. App. 1935).

4. For *for*:

- "The rule is the same *as to* [read *for*] specialists." *Fox v. Mason*, 124 S.E. 405, 406 (Va. Ct. App. 1924).

5. For *to*:

- "The *answer as to* [read *answer to*] the question of rights of that sort is very difficult to give." 13 Great Britain, Parliament, House of Commons, *House of Commons Papers* 50 (1878).
- "During the whole of it, Mrs. Spooner manifested perfect composure and appeared to be utterly *indifferent as to* [read *indifferent to*] the result." "The Trial of Bathsheba Spooner, William Brooks, James Buchanan, and Ezra Ross for the Murder of Joshua Spooner, Massachusetts, 1778," in 2 *American State Trials* 175, 191–92 (John Davison Lawson ed., 1914).

6. For *by*:

- " 'The court is shocked *as to* [read *by*] the verdict freeing the defendant.' " *Holland v. Sears*, 348 P.2d 538, 540 (Okla. 1960) (quoting the trial court).
- "The government argues that the record does not indicate that Matt and Hank were surprised *as to* [read *by*] the identity of any of those persons." *U.S. v. Chavez*, 845 F.2d 219, 221 (9th Cir. 1988).

7. For *in* or *into*:

- "If the petition is correct *as to* [read *in*] form, the state court 'shall . . . grant such petition . . . and order the recount.' " *Roudebush v. Hartke*, 405 U.S. 15, 21 (1972) (per Stewart, J.).
- "Mr. Abromats then wrote to Mr. Wood inquiring *as to* [read *into*] what amount the Woods were going to claim for 'restitution' and indicating that he required a release of liability as a condition of payment." *Abromats v. Wood*, 213 P.3d 966, 968 (Wyo. 2009).

8. For *applicable to*:

- "That is so fundamental a doctrine *as to* [read *applicable to*] fiduciaries of all sorts, that it is somewhat surprising to find it questioned." *Marcus v. Otis*, 168 F.2d 649, 654 (2d Cir. 1948).
- "It is settled that the rule *as to* [read *applicable to*] the evidence corresponds with the rule *as to* [read *applicable to*] the pleadings." William Henry Rawle, *A Practical Treatise on the Law of Covenants for Title* 129 (4th ed. 2009).

9. Completely Superfluous:

- "The *question is as to* [read *question is*] the validity of the twenty-eighth clause of the will of Mary C. Durbrow, deceased, a childless widow." *In re Durbrow's Estate*, 157 N.E. 747, 748 (N.Y. 1927).
- "The only *real issue* in the case *is as to* [read *real issue . . . is*] the question of insanity." *Brock v. State*, 69 So.2d 344, 345 (Fla. 1954).
- "Section 5(1) says that an application is to be made to the Court having jurisdiction over the subject matter of the award, but it *does not say as to which* [read *does not say which*] Court will have jurisdiction over the subject matter of the award." 13 J. Shipping, Customs & Transport Laws 84 (1986).

- "There is no indication *as to what happened* [read *what happened*] to the third case (an earlier case) listed on the notice." *Commonwealth v. Foster*, 932 N.E.2d 287, 289 n.1 (Mass. App. Ct. 2010).

See **as to whether** & **question as to whether.**

10. Used Twice in One Sentence, with Differing Meanings:

- "It is the contention of the contestant that the residuary legatees under said will so unduly and improperly influenced the testator to make said will in their favor *as to* [read *with regard to*] the residue of this estate *as to render* [read *that they rendered*] the will of no legal effect." *In re Arnold's Estate*, 107 P.2d 25, 27 (Cal. 1940).
- "Petitioner's right to a salary before it was voted to him was so indefinite *both as to* [read *in both*] amount and obligation, *as to be* [read *that it was*] unenforceable." *Wrightsman v. Commissioner*, 111 F.2d 227, 228 (5th Cir. 1940).
- "At the jury trial the defense moved for a judgment of acquittal *as to* [read *on*] all counts, arguing, *as to* [read *with respect to*] the tax-evasion count, that an affirmative act of concealment had to be found to convict the defendant." *U.S. v. Barrilleaux*, 746 F.2d 254, 255 (5th Cir. 1984).
- "The question *as to* [*superfluous*] whether information *as to* [read *about*] particular processes or other matters was 'confidential' or 'secret' is outside the scope of the annotation." L.S. Tellier, *Implied Obligation of Employee Not to Use Trade Secrets or Confidential Information for His Own Benefit or That of Third Persons After Leaving the Employment*, 165 A.L.R. 1453 (1946).

In the first two of those four examples, the final *as to* is a part of the understood phrase *so . . . as to*. (See **so . . . as to**.) The suggested changes of those phrases to clauses beginning with *that* are for the purpose merely of enhancing clarity; apart from the confusion caused by using *as to* twice in different senses, the phrase *so . . . as to* is used in those sentences in a technically proper way.

B. Defensible Uses. The phrase is most justifiable when introducing the discussion of a matter previously mentioned only cursorily in the text:

- "*As to* whether the object [that] this bill discloses was sought to be attained by the members of the union was a lawful one or a valid justification of the threat to strike, the authorities in this country are clearly in conflict." *Kemp v. Div. No. 241, Amalgamated Ass'n of Street & Electric Ry. Employees of Am.*, 99 N.E. 389, 394 (Ill. 1912).
- "*As to* these nine plaintiffs who failed to apply for reappointment, the ruling in *McBee v. Jim Hogg County . . .* requires rejection of their section 1983 claims." *Simmons v. Lyons*, 746 F.2d 265, 268 (5th Cir. 1984).

In beginning sentences in this way, *as to* is equivalent to the more colloquial *as for*.

The phrase is defensible when used for *about*. Nevertheless, it is stylistically inferior to *about* in most contexts, as in the following sentences:

- "The buyer was silent *as to* [better: *about*] the disclaimer." *Southern Idaho Pipe & Steel Co. v. Cal-Cut Pipe & Supply, Inc.*, 567 P.2d 1246, 1254 (Idaho 1977).
- "Complaints *as to* [better: *about*] procedural irregularities in a condemnation case 'must be preserved at the trial court level by motion, exception, objection, plea in abatement, or some other vehicle.'" *Holloway v. Matagorda County*, 686 S.W.2d 100, 101 (Tex. 1985).

- "Any doubt *as to* [better: *about*] the existence of a material fact is to be resolved against the moving party." *In re Ortiz*, 430 B.R. 523, 527 (Bankr. E.D. Wis. 2010).

The phrase is sometimes a passable shorthand form of "with regard to" or "on the question of," a meaning it properly carries when beginning a sentence. E.g.:

- "The trial court entered judgments of nonsuit *as to* all defendants and plaintiff appealed." *Ybarra v. Spangard*, 154 P.2d 687, 688 (Cal. 1945).
- "California has done what we think should here be done; it has made its solution *as to* life insurance proceeds consonant with its other community property law." *McCurdy v. McCurdy*, 372 S.W.2d 381, 383 (Tex. Civ. App.—Waco 1963).
- "The district court erred in denying the new trial sought *as to* the dismissal." *Morris v. Ocean Sys., Inc.*, 730 F.2d 248, 249 (5th Cir. 1984).
- "But the document is silent *as to* whether that is the only permissible use of the property." *Yates v. Dublin Sir Shop, Inc.*, 579 S.E.2d 796, 798 (Ga. Ct. App. 2003).

as to whether. The Fowlers describe it as "seldom necessary" in *The King's English* 344 (3d ed. 1930). That judgment has withstood the test of time. See **as to (A)(9), (B), question as to whether** & **whether (A).**

as was. See **as is.**

as well. When used at the beginning of a sentence, this phrase is a casualism at best—e.g.: "*As well,* [read *Also,*] people are questioning how well the legal system really does protect people's rights." Alan Reid, *Seeing Law Differently* 4 (1992).

as well as. See **together with** & subject–verb agreement (g).

*****as yet** is invariably inferior to *yet* alone, *so far*, or some other equivalent phrase—e.g.:

- "So far as I have been able to ascertain, no court has *as yet* [read *yet* or delete *as yet*] held that such an injunction is entitled to full faith and credit in the sense that the action toward which the injunction is directed must be abated." *James v. Grand Trunk W. R.R. Co.*, 152 N.E.2d 858, 867 (Ill. 1958) (Schafer, J., dissenting).
- "Plaintiff has *as yet* [read *thus far* or delete *as yet*] had no opportunity to testify as to this matter." *Dean v. Michigan Dep't of Natural Res.*, 247 N.W.2d 876, 878 (Mich. 1976).
- "One must question whether the stipulation automatically extended to the *not-as-yet filed claim* [read *yet-unfiled claim* or *yet-to-be-filed claim*]." *Rice v. Glad Hands, Inc.*, 750 F.2d 434, 438 (5th Cir. 1985). See phrasal adjectives.

Cf. **as of (c).**

asylee. A. Generally. A late-20th-century legal neologism, *asylee* is becoming a standard word in the language of the law for "a refugee applying for asylum." It has not yet made its way into most English-language dictionaries. Like many other personal nouns ending in *-ee*, it is illogically formed. But illogical morphology has not presented an obstacle to many other forms ending in *-ee*—e.g.:

- "This portion of the complaint as amended alleges . . . that plaintiffs as a class are '*asylees*.'" *Fernandez-Roque v. Smith*, 539 F.Supp. 925, 932 (N.D. Ga. 1982).
- "The severity of harm to the erroneously excluded *asylee* outweighs the administrative burden of providing an asylum hearing." *Yiu Sing Chun v. Sava*, 708 F.2d 869, 877 (2d Cir. 1983).

See -EE.

The popular press tends to use the phrase *asylum-seeker* (a phrase best hyphenated)—e.g.:

- "More than 10,440 Haitians are in custody at Guantanamo, and more *asylum-seekers* are on cutters offshore." Barbara Crossette, *U.S. Starts Return of Haiti Refugees After Justices Act*, N.Y. Times, 2 Feb. 1992, at 1.
- "*Asylum seekers* poured into Germany last month at the rate of more than one a minute." Christopher Parkes, *Asylum Seekers Flood Germany*, Fin. Times, 5 Aug. 1992, at 1.

Although the preferred pronunciation is /ə-sɪ-**lee**/, many lawyers in the U.S. Department of Homeland Security say /ə-**sil**-ee/.

B. And *arriving alien*; *refugee.* An *asylee* is someone who has been granted asylum—and asylum can be granted only to a person already on U.S. soil. An *arriving alien* is a person who seeks admission into the U.S. A *refugee* is one who applies for refugee status while outside the U.S.

at is incorrect when used with any locative such as *where*—e.g.: "Where is it at?" A curious example appears in the writing of Llewellyn: "Its central notice-filing provisions make it cheap and easy for the prospective seller to find out just *where* he is *at*." Karl N. Llewellyn, *Why We Need the Uniform Commercial Code*, 10 U. Fla. L. Rev. 367, 379 (1957). U.S. District Judge William Terrell Hodges of Florida reports that, as an editor of the law review in 1957, he tried unsuccessfully to persuade Llewellyn to omit the *at*. See PREPOSITIONS (A).

at all events; in any event. These phrases are perfectly synonymous. The first is more common in BrE, the second in AmE. Yet *at all events* does appear infrequently in American texts as well—e.g.:

- "*At all events*, he made no claim of having had training or experience in the field or practice of osteopathy or direct knowledge of the subject, nor to have learned specifically from any osteopathic sources what constitutes the standard practice of that profession in the treatment of severed tendons." *Pedler v. Emmerson*, 49 N.W.2d 70, 80 (Mich. 1951).
- "*At all events*, the cases generally hold that drunkenness does not negate a depraved heart by blotting out consciousness of risk." Wayne LaFave & Austin Scott, *Criminal Law* 621 (2d ed. 1986).

In legal writing these phrases are preferable to *in any case* when used in the same sense, because *in any case* contains the confusingly ambiguous word *case*, which usually refers to a lawsuit in legal contexts. See **case.**

at arm's length. See **arm's-length.**

at bar; at the bar. The phrase *at bar*, meaning "now before the court," derives from the LAW FRENCH phrase *al barre*. *At the bar*, which appears in early decisions such as *Marbury v. Madison* and *McCulloch v. Maryland*, has gradually been displaced in the U.S. by *at bar* in phrases such as in *the case at bar*. E.g.:

- "Within the meaning of malice as used in these opinions in the case *at bar* there was no necessity of proving spite or ill will toward the plaintiff." *Beekman v. Marsters*, 80 N.E. 817, 819 (Mass. 1907).
- "We think that no more was covered than situations substantially similar to those then *at bar*." *Cheney Bros. v. Doris Silk Corp.*, 35 F.2d 279, 280 (2d Cir. 1929).
- "In the case *at bar* it was reasonably foreseeable that a customer would collide with the post while exiting defendant's store carrying merchandise which could obscure view of the post." *Ward v. K Mart Corp.*, 554 N.E.2d 223, 233 (Ill. 1990).

The British tend to use *at the bar*—e.g.: "Until the present argument *at the bar* it may be doubted whether shipowners or merchants were ever deemed to be bound by law to conform to some imaginary 'normal' standard of freights or prices." *Mogul S.S. Co. v. McGregor*, [1889] 23 Q.B.D. 598, 615 (C.A.).

One writer states that *at bar* is used, especially in law schools, to refer to a case already decided and at the time under discussion by professor and students. Arthur A. Leff, *The Leff Dictionary of Law*, 94 Yale L.J. 1855, 2088 (1985). This usage is probably peculiar to certain law schools; to those unfamiliar with it, it smacks of the judge-manqué. See *sub judice.* Cf. **at trial.**

at bench. See **case at bench.**

at circuit. See **circuit, to ride.**

at common law. See **common law (c).**

at fault; in fault. An American critic once wrote that "hunting dogs [that] lose the scent are said to be *at fault*. Hence the phrase means perplexed, puzzled." He added that *in fault* means "in error, mistaken," with this example: "No certified public accountant should be *in fault*." Clarence Stratton, *Handbook of English* 24, 158 (1940). Today, however, *in fault* is seldom used in that way.

The phrase *at fault* is now standard in the sense "responsible for a wrong committed; blameworthy." E.g.: "But the apportionment of the percentages of fault among the parties found *at fault* cannot be accepted from the first trial." *Nichols v. Westfield Indus., Ltd.*, 380 N.W.2d 392, 403 (Iowa 1985) (Uhlenhopp, J., concurring in part & dissenting in part). The phrase is virtually never used synonymously with *perplexed* or *puzzled*.

at first blush. This phrase, common in legal writing, occurs in BrE as well as in AmE. *At first blush* is a homegrown equivalent of the LATINISM *prima facie*, but the two have distinct uses. Rather than serving as a simple adjective or adverb like *prima facie*, the phrase *at first blush* conveys the sense "upon an initial consideration or cursory examination." *Blush* here carries an otherwise obsolete sense: "a glance, glimpse, blink, or look." E.g.:

- "*At first blush*, a reading of [the rule] would [countenance] joinder of the United States as a defendant along with another defendant in a situation such as is present here." *Baumgold Bros., Inc. v. Allan M. Fox Co.—East*, 336 F.Supp. 175, 177 (N.D. Ohio 1972).
- "*At first blush*, we note that when a defendant files a bar complaint or a civil lawsuit against his attorney, there would seem to be an automatic conflict created." *Grady v. Commonwealth*, 325 S.W.3d 333, 345–46 (Ky. 2010).

At first blush is becoming a grossly overworked CLICHÉ. The variant phrase *on first blush is not idiomatic. See **prima facie.**

at hand; in hand. In AmE, the first has ousted the second in most figurative uses, *in hand* being most frequently literal, as in "I have the contract *in hand*." One still occasionally sees the figurative *in hand*, but this is not the current idiom—e.g.:

- "In their briefs in connection with Smith's motion, counsel on both sides state that they have been unable to find any case dealing with the specific problem *in hand* [read *at hand*]." *Grace v. MacArthur*, 170 F.Supp. 442, 444 (E.D. Ark. 1959).
- "In the case *in hand* [read *at hand*], such standards do not exist, although the Codex, and their committee on food labeling, has begun the process to create norms or international recommendations related to foods obtained by genetic manipulation." Javier Guillem Carrau, *Lack of Sherpas for a GMO Escape Route in the EU*, 10 German L.J. 1169, 1190 (2009).

In BrE, however, *in hand* is frequently used in the metaphorical sense—e.g.: "It has been necessary for the courts to consider what amounts to unreasonable conduct in the context of professional skill and judgement where it is recognised that two equally skilled individuals might have very different opinions about the appropriate way of dealing with an *issue in hand*." *Atwood v. Health Serv. Comm'r*, [2008] WL 4264280 (Q.D.).

at issue. See **issue (A).**

at law. See **under law.**

at present. See ***at the present time.**

attach. See **annex.**

attaché case. See **briefcase.**

***attached hereto,** a REDUNDANCY for *attached*, is a LEGALISM to be avoided.

attachment. In the phrase *writ of attachment*, the word *attachment* can bear either of two meanings: (1) the taking into custody of a person to hold that person as security for the payment of a judgment; or (2) the taking into custody of a person's property to secure a judgment or to be sold in satisfaction of a judgment. E.g.:

- (Sense 1) "[Courts of equity] may order a writ of *attachment* for the arrest and detention of the body of the contumacious party until obedience to the decree has been secured." Eugene A. Jones, *Manual of Equity Pleading and Practice* 139 (1916).
- (Sense 2) "The disputed residence was important because a writ of *attachment*—briefly, an order freezing cash or other assets—cannot be obtained against a person unless the person has a foreign address." Joseph Goulden, *The Million Dollar Lawyers* 52–53 (1978).

See **sequestration.**

attainder; attaint, n. Both nouns derive from the (originally French) verb *attaint* (= to accuse, convict). As legal terms they are primarily of historical interest. *Attainder* usually appears in the phrase *bill of attainder* or *act of attainder*; and means "the act of extinguishing someone's civil rights by sentencing the person to death or declaring the person to be an outlaw, usu. in punishment for treason or a felony."

Attaint was formerly used to mean "the conviction of a jury for giving a false verdict" (*OED*). E.g.: "An action called '*attaint*' could be brought against jurors for giving a false verdict, and if it was successful the verdict would be quashed." J.H. Baker, *An Introduction to English Legal History* 156 (3d ed. 1990).

attaint; taint. These terms were originally unrelated, but the senses of the first came to be heavily tainted by erroneous association with the second. *Attaint* = (1) to subject to attainder; to condemn; (2) to touch or affect; or (3) [obs.] to accuse. *Attaint* is justified today only in sense 1; *taint* is otherwise the better word. E.g.:

- "The effect of common law attainder was twofold: forfeiture to the crown of real and personal property, and 'corruption of blood,' which meant that the *attainted* person could neither inherit from his ancestors nor transmit his wealth or title to his heirs." *In re Extradition of McMullen*, 989 F.2d 603, 604 (2d Cir. 1993).
- "In addition to the death sentence, attainder generally carried with it a 'corruption of blood,' which meant that the *attainted* party's heirs could not inherit his property." *Phillips v. Iowa*, 185 F.Supp.2d 992, 999 (N.D. Iowa 2002).

Taint = (1) to imbue with a noxious quality or principle; (2) to contaminate or corrupt; or (3) to tinge or become tinged. *Taint* is by far the more common word in modern writing:

- "It is urged that if evidence is inadmissible against one defendant or conspirator, because *tainted* by electronic surveillance illegal as to him, it is also inadmissible against his codefendant or coconspirator." *Alderman v. U.S.*, 394 U.S. 165, 171 (1969) (per White, J.).
- "We recognize, however, that, under certain circumstances, an illegal search may be so egregious as to *taint* the discovery of evidence." *Commonwealth v. Rood*, 686 A.2d 442, 450 n.11 (Pa. Commw. Ct. 1996).

Taint is just as frequently used as a noun—e.g.: "It was held that such practices . . . were 'not shown to be such as to constitute an unconscientious or inequitable attitude towards its adversary, so as to fix upon complainant the *taint* of unclean hands.'" *Connecticut Tel. & Elec. Co. v. Automotive Equip. Co.*, 14 F.2d 957, 970 (D.N.J. 1926).

attempt. A. *Criminal attempt*. In criminal law, *attempt* refers to the crime of intending to commit a crime, along with taking a step to carry out the crime. E.g.:

- "Mallory thereupon pleaded guilty to the crime of *attempt* to commit burglary of the second degree and was given a short county jail term." *People v. Eastman*, 154 P.2d 37, 38 (Cal. Ct. App. 1944).
- "In England, indeed, the abortion legislation is worded only in terms of *attempt*, it being immaterial for the purpose of the offence whether the abortion itself is effected or not." Glanville Williams, *The Sanctity of Life and the Criminal Law* 180 (1957).

B. And *endeavor*; *assay*. See **endeavor** & **assay**.

attest; witness, vb.; **vouch for.** These verbs share the sense "to testify to the accuracy or authenticity of something." *Attest* suggests a witness's oral or written testimony, given either under oath (as with a notarized signature) or on one's word of honor <three witnesses attested to the signature on the will>. *Attest* often denotes the authentication of a document <an attested copy of the divorce decree>. *Witness* implies a signed statement, but not necessarily having a notary's seal; for example, contracts are often witnessed by anyone that a party asks to watch the document being signed <the buy-sell agreement was witnessed by a different observer for each signer>.

Vouch for is no longer a legal phrase: it simply suggests informal affirmation by a reliable person <a JAG kindly vouched for me as I was trying to enter the Washington Navy Ship Yard>. That is, in modern lay contexts, *vouch* almost invariably means "to answer *for*, be surety *for*" <she vouched for him> <vouched for his honesty>. Archaically, *vouch* means "to call upon, rely on, or cite as authority; to confirm by evidence or assertion"—e.g.: "Jhering, emphasizing the effect of trade and commerce in liberalizing the strict law, *vouched* the introducing of Greek mercantile custom into the law of the old city of Rome." Roscoe Pound, foreword to James Gordley & Arthur Taylor von Mehren, *An Introduction to the Comparative Study of Private Law* xviii (2006). This sense appears to be an extension of the obsolete legal phrase *to vouch to warrant*, meaning "to cite, call, or summon (a person) into court to give warranty of title" (*OED*).

***attestant.** See **attester**.

attestation clause; testimonium clause. Both appear at the end of a will or some other legal instrument. The *testimonium clause* is signed by the testator, the *attestation clause* by the witnesses to the will or some other legal instrument. A typical *testimonium clause* reads: "This will was signed by me on the 14th day of October, 1985, at Wilmington, Virginia." *Testimonium clauses* have traditionally begun with the phrase *in witness whereof*. See **testimonium clause** & **in witness whereof**.

The *attestation clause* recites the formalities required by the jurisdiction in which the will might be admitted to probate. It raises a presumption that the formalities recited have been performed and so aids the proponent of the will at probate. A typical *attestation clause* reads: "The foregoing instrument, consisting of four typewritten pages, was signed and declared by the testator to be her last will in the presence of us, who, at her request, and in her presence and the presence of one another, have subscribed our names as witnesses."

In Scots law, the *attestation clause* is called a *testing-clause*.

attestative; *attestive; *attestational. *Attestative* is the best adjective corresponding to *attestation*; it means "of or relating to attestation." **Attestational* is a NEEDLESS VARIANT. **Attestive* is a NEEDLESS VARIANT of *attesting*.

attester; *attestor; *attestator; *attestant. *Attester* is standard in legal contexts. The others are NEEDLESS VARIANTS. Although the form *attesting witness* sometimes appears, *attester* is more common in print sources.

***at the present day** is inferior to *today*—e.g.: "Criminal proceedings *at the present day* [read *today*] do not result only in death, imprisonment or fine." O. Hood Phillips, *A First Book of English Law* 192 (3d ed. 1955).

***at the present time; *at this time; *at this point in time; at present.** These are inferior to *now*, *nowadays*, or *today*.

***at the same time, while.** See ***while at the same time**.

***at the time that; *at the time when.** These phrases are invariably verbose for *when*.

at the trial. See **at trial**.

at this time; *at this point in time; *at this moment in time. See **at the present time** & **moment in time**, **at this**.

attorn, vb., is pronounced /ə-**tərn**/. See **attornment**.

attorney. A. And Its Near-Synonyms. Lawyers, like people in other walks of life, have long sought to improve their descriptive titles. Boswell relates: "The Society of Procurators, or Attornies, had obtained a royal charter, in which they had taken care to have their ancient designation *Procurators* changed into that of *Solicitors*, from a notion, as they supposed, that it was more genteel." 4 *Life of Johnson* 128 (1791).

The connotations of *attorney* and its near synonyms have historically been quite different in BrE and AmE. Originally, *attorney* denoted a practitioner in common-law courts, *solicitor* one in equity courts, and *proctor* one in ecclesiastical courts; all instructed barristers to appear and argue. *Attorney*, it seems, soon developed an unpleasant smell about it: one commentator writes that the 18th-century efforts "to deodorize the word *attorney* [were] later abandoned, and in the nineteenth century it was supplanted in England by *solicitor*. There *solicitor* lacks the offensive American connotation, as in 'No peddlers or solicitors.' In England, *attorney*, for a lawyer, survives only as *the attorney* (the attorney general), while in America the chief respectable lawyer-solicitor is the *solicitor-general*." David Mellinkoff, *The Language of the Law* 198 (1963).

The two most common terms in AmE, *lawyer* and *attorney*, are not generally distinguished even by members of the profession. In the U.S., *attorney*, *attorney at law*, and *lawyer* are generally viewed as synonyms. But today there seems to be a notion afoot that *attorney* is a more formal (and less disparaging) term than *lawyer*.

Technically, *lawyer* is the more general term, referring to one who practices law. *Attorney* literally means "one who is designated to transact business for another." An *attorney*, technically and archaically (except in the phrase *attorney in fact* [see (B)]), may or may not be a lawyer. Hence Samuel Johnson's statement that *attorney* "was anciently used for those who did any business for another; now only in law." *A Dictionary of the English Language* (1755) (s.v. *attorney*).

From the fact that an *attorney* is really an agent, Bernstein deduces that "a *lawyer* is an *attorney* only when he has a client. It may be that the desire of *lawyers* to appear to be making a go of their profession has accounted for their leaning toward the designation *attorney*." Theodore M. Bernstein, *The Careful Writer* 60 (1965). Yet this distinction between *lawyer* and *attorney* is rarely, if ever, observed in practice.

In the U.S., those licensed to practice law are admitted to practice as "attorneys and counselors." (The -*l*- spelling of *counselor* is preferred in AmE, the -*ll*- spelling in BrE. See DOUBLING OF FINAL CONSONANTS.) This combination of names is unknown in English law, in which *attorney* = solicitor, and *counsellor* = barrister. Yet "in the United States, the term *attorney* has come to have a generic significance that embraces all branches of legal practice." George W. Warvelle, *Essays in Legal Ethics* 53 (1902).

In G.B., a *solicitor* or *attorney* does all sorts of legal work for clients but generally appears only in inferior courts; a *barrister* is a trial lawyer or litigator.

In AmE, *counsel* and *counselor* are both, in one sense, general terms meaning "one who gives (legal) advice," the latter being the more formal term. *Counsel* may refer to but one lawyer <opposing counsel contends> or, as a plural, to more than one lawyer <opposing counsel contend>. See **counsel (B)** & **postman.**

B. Kinds of Attorneys (*attorney in fact*; *attorney at law*). The first means "one with power of attorney to act for another; legal agent." E.g.: "It is held in *Tynan v. Paschal*, that a letter of a decedent to his *attorney in fact* directing him to destroy his will does not operate ipso facto as an immediate revocation of it." *In re McGill's Will*, 128 N.E. 194, 196 (N.Y. 1920). The second means "a licensed lawyer." The plural forms are *attorneys in fact* and *attorneys at law*. See (D).

C. As a Verb. *Attorney*, like *lawyer*, has come to be used as a verb. E.g.: "Among a number of mock trials that lawyers have liked to write is a *Trial of Sir John Falstaff*, wherein the Fat Knight is permitted to answer for himself concerning the charges against him, and *to attorney* his own case." (Eng.) See **lawyer,** vb.

D. Plural. **Attornies* is an obsolete plural of the word (see the quotation from Boswell under (A)); *attorneys* is now the universally accepted plural. Cf. **monies,** which is inferior to *moneys*.

attorney at law. See **attorney (B).**

attorney–client privilege should contain an en-dash or be hyphenated.

attorneydom. See **lawyerdom.**

attorney general, made plural, forms *attorneys general* in AmE, *attorney-generals* in BrE. See PLURALS (E).

attorney in fact. See **attorney (B).**

attorneying. See **attorney (C)** & **lawyer,** vb.

attorney's fees; attorneys' fees; attorney fees; counsel fees. The first of these now appears to be prevalent. See Attorney's Fee Act, 42 U.S.C. § 1988 (1988). The plural possessive *attorneys' fees* is just as good, and some may even prefer that term in contexts in which there is clearly more than one attorney referred to. *Attorney fees* is inelegant but increasingly common. It might be considered a means to avoid having to get the apostrophe right. (But cf. the phrase *expert-witness fees*.) *Counsel fees* is another, less-than-common variant.

The only form to avoid at all costs is **attorneys fees*, in which the first word is a genitive adjective with the apostrophe wrongly omitted. This form appears in Arthur A. Leff, *The Leff Dictionary of Law*, 94 Yale L.J. 1855, 1969 (1985), under *affirmative relief*. See POSSESSIVES (E).

*attornies. See **attorney (D).**

attornment has two analogous senses, the first relating to personal property and the second relating to land. It may mean either (1) "an act by a bailee in possession of goods on behalf of one person acknowledging that he will hold the goods on behalf of someone else" (*CDL*); or (2) a person's agreement to hold land as the tenant of someone other than the original landlord; a tenant's act of recognizing that rent is to be paid to a different person. Both senses are used in BrE and AmE.

An English court has stated that the *attornment* clause in mortgages "is entirely obsolete and at the present time performs no useful purpose." *Steyning & Littlehampton Bldg. Soc'y v. Wilson*, [1951] Ch. 1018, 1020.

The corresponding verb is *attorn*—e.g.: "A tenant who has received possession from his landlord has no right to *attorn* to a third person without first surrendering possession to his landlord or obtaining his consent to such *attornment*." William B. Cunningham, *A Treatise on the Law of Forcible Entry and Detainer* 39 (2d ed. 1895).

attractive nuisance (= a dangerous condition that may attract children onto a property owner's land, thereby causing a risk to their safety) is a seeming OXYMORON. Statements such as the following illustrate the irony of the phrase: "We have no hesitation in affirming the jury's conclusion that the filthy, polluted, weed-choked, garbage plagued drainage canal located near a school . . . constituted an *attractive nuisance*." *Orange County v. Gipson*, 539 So.2d 526, 529 (Fla. Dist. Ct. App. 1989). See **nuisance**.

at trial; at the trial. The shorter form is the more usual and the more idiomatic in AmE—e.g.: "After suing the bank for negligence, the plaintiff testified *at trial* that the bank maintained the account for a month after she brought the fraud to the bank's attention." *Das v. Bank of Am., N.A.*, 112 Cal. Rptr. 3d 439, 452 (Ct. App. 2010). Cf. **at bar**.

In BrE, however, judges still write *at the trial*—e.g.:

- "As a result of that conversation, the petitioner understood that special measures would be taken *at the trial*." *C. v. Her Majesty's Advocate*, [2010] H.C.J.A.C. 89, ¶ 6.
- "I stress that these matters were evidenced by documentation that was produced *at the trial* and that was put to the Claimant during his cross-examination." *Rashford v. Secretary of State for the Home Dep't*, [2010] E.W.H.C. 2200, ¶ 6 (Q.B.).
- "Her interview was admitted in evidence *at the trial* pursuant to the hearsay provisions of the Criminal Justice Act 2003." *R. v. M. (Keith)*, [2010] E.W.C.A. Crim. 2101, ¶ 5.

Still another vanishing idiom is *on* (or *upon*) *the trial*—e.g.:

- "*On the trial* the plaintiff was nonsuited upon the ground that, if any agreement had been made between the plaintiff and the defendant, it was not in writing, but by parol, and was therefore barred at the time the action was commenced." *Mackroth v. Sladky*, 148 P. 978, 980 (Cal. Ct. App. 1915).
- "As no such evidence was produced *upon the trial*, the judgment in favor of the defendant was right, but should not have been 'upon the merits.'" *Ward v. Schwartz*, 161 N.Y.S. 814, 816 (App. Div. 1916) (Shearn, J., concurring).

Today both phrases would be *at trial* in American legal writing. See **trial, at**.

at variance. See **variance**.

at which time is invariably prolix for *when*.

at will. *Employee at will* is an ellipsis for *employee at* [*the employer's*] *will*. *At will* is slowly changing from its position after the noun into a position before the noun it modifies <an at-will employee>. See POSTPOSITIVE ADJECTIVES. Cf. **tenant at will**.

at your disposal; ***at your disposition.** See **disposal**.

atypical; ***untypical.** The preferred term is *atypical*.

auditor. See **bookkeeper**.

aught (= [1] anything; [2] all) is an ARCHAISM to be avoided. E.g.:

- "*For aught that appears* [read *For all that appears*], the essence of what petitioner seeks either has been revealed to him already through the interrogatories or is readily available to him." *Hickman v. Taylor*, 329 U.S. 495, 509 (1947) (per Murphy, J.).
- "*For aught appearing* [read *For all that appears*], Patel has not sought legal entry." *Patel v. Sumani Corp.*, 660 F.Supp. 1528, 1535 (N.D. Ala. 1987).

Cf. **naught**.

auscultator. See LAWYERS, DEROGATORY NAMES FOR (A).

auspices. *Under the auspices* is frequently misconstrued as meaning "in the form of" or "in accordance with." Actually, it means "with the sponsorship or support of." The term is properly used here: "The contest was determinable under the *auspices* of the newspaper company." *Harrison v. Jones*, 184 S.E. 889, 890 (Ga. Ct. App. 1936).

Here are examples of the all-too-frequent misusage:

- "The judgment debtor subject to the proceedings will be deemed, by virtue of his status, to be on notice of whatever remedies that may be invoked *under the auspices of* [read *under*] the statute against his nonexempt assets." Bradley J.B. Toben & Keith C. Livesay, *Article 3827A and the Maturation of the Creditor's Bill Remedy in Texas*, 37 Baylor L. Rev. 587, 620 (1985).
- "Four members of the Court dissented only to our remand to the Court of Appeals *under the auspices of* [read *under* or *in accordance with*] Tex.R.App.P. 50(d)." *Knox v. State*, 769 S.W.2d 244, 246 n.1 (Tex. Crim. App. 1989).
- "The present asset sale, however, is distinguishable because it occurred *under the auspices of* [read *in accordance with*] the state receivership proceeding and the Rhode Island court's approval of that sale." *John T. Callahan & Sons, Inc. v. Dykeman Elec. Co.*, 266 F.Supp.2d 208, 222 (D. Mass. 2003).

See **aegis**.

authentic; genuine; bona fide; veritable. All these adjectives describe something that is precisely what it is said to be or purports to be. What is *authentic* is real, factual, authoritative, and trustworthy <an authentic signed copy>. What is *genuine* is likewise real and true, often with the suggestion of demonstrated provenance and the thing's continued condition from its original form without tampering or adulteration—and certainly not a replica or a mere credible simulacrum <a genuine Roman coin struck during the reign of Julius Caesar>. *Bona fide*, though often used interchangeably with *genuine* or *authentic*, should come into play only when there is a question of good faith or sincerity <a bona fide sale of the stock>. (See **bona fide (c).**) *Veritable* suggests correspondence with the truth, usually with a sense of solemn utterance <we must acknowledge the great deal that is known about the veritable playwright Shakespeare, his life and that of his family, and the detailed records that have been preserved>.

Loosely, *veritable* appears through WORD-PATRONAGE to assert the aptness of designation that is somehow figurative or hyperbolic <he is a veritable master of the law relating to mechanic's liens> <there is a veritable mountain of briefs in the judge's chambers>.

authenticate; certify; validate; verify; substantiate; corroborate. These verbs share the sense "to attest to the truth, accuracy, validity, or genuineness of (something)." *Authenticate* implies that the thing is presumptively genuine but needs further ascertainment by established procedures sufficiently entitled to credit <the birth certificate was authenticated by an expert at the proceeding>. *Certify* suggests a written statement, usually with a signature or seal <the secretary of state certified the election results>. *Validate* is more usual with a legal paper requiring an official seal or stamp, or an officer's signature, before it can take effect <the court's clerk stamped the summons to validate its return> and with a demonstration through reasoning and a credible marshaling of facts <Shakespeare's authorship has been amply validated>. *Verify* suggests establishing the accuracy of a statement or account by testing it against ascertainable facts and perhaps correcting any mistakes found <police verified the witness's statements with video footage>. It can also imply a notary public's having administered an oath to an affiant as opposed to merely acknowledging the authenticity of the witness's signature. *Substantiate* suggests that someone offers evidence in strong support of a point in question or a claim. *Corroborate* presupposes existing evidence or testimony and implies a buttressing of it by further consistent evidence or testimony.

authentication—so spelled—is occasionally misrendered *authentification*. E.g.: "Neither the statutory authority nor the case law require[s] *authentification* [read *authentication*] of the signatures." *Commonwealth v. Gordon*, 633 A.2d 1199, 1204 (Pa. Super. Ct. 1993).

authentic construction; authentic interpretation. See *authentic interpretation* under INTERPRETATION, MODES OF (B).

author is becoming standard as a verb, though fastidious writers still avoid it. Generally it is a highfalutin substitute for *write*, *compose*, or *create*. E.g.:

- "Courts are given the weighty task of balancing, on the one hand, the policy concerns that favor the constitutionally mandated retention of copyright protection for privately *authored* [read *created*] works and, on the other hand, the policy concerns that would permit stripping the author of a privately created work of copyright protection once that work is enacted into law." *Veeck v. Southern Bldg. Code Congress Int'l Inc.*, 293 F.3d 791, 812 (5th Cir. 2002).
- "Noticeably absent from this statute is any authority that after-the-fact privately *authored* [read *written*] legal treatises are a basis to overturn our existing South Dakota court rules and interpretative case law." *State v. Lassiter*, 692 N.W.2d 171, 183 n.9 (S.D. 2005) (Gilbertson, J., dissenting).

Nor is attribution to a collective body among the legitimate uses of this word—e.g.: "Congress adopted an 'inclusionary approach' when it *authored* [read *crafted* or *framed*] this rule." *U.S. v. Wesevich*, 666 F.2d 984, 988 (5th Cir. 1982). *Coauthor* has been considered more acceptable as a verb, perhaps because *co-write* seems deadpan. See NOUNS AS VERBS.

With reference to *the author* (= I), see FIRST PERSON (A).

*authoress. See SEXISM (C).

authority. See **power (B).**

autograph. See **allograph.**

autopsy; postmortem, n. These equivalents are each current in AmE and BrE. *Autopsy* is slightly more common in AmE, *postmortem* in BrE—e.g.: "[The medical examiner] further testified that an *autopsy* is the examination of a deceased person for the purpose of determining the cause and manner of death." *Bryant v. Commissioner of Correct.*, 964 A.2d 1186, 1210 (Conn. 2009) (Palmer, J., concurring).

autrefois /**oh**-tər-foyz/ is a LAW FRENCH term, meaning "on another occasion, formerly," used in the phrases *autrefois acquit* (= a plea in bar of arraignment that the defendant has been acquitted of the offense by a jury) and *autrefois convict* (= a plea in bar of arraignment that the defendant has been convicted of the offense by a jury). These phrases are much more common in G.B. than in the U.S.

autre vie, pur. See *pur autre vie.*

avail, vb., is most properly a reflexive verb only <he availed himself of the opportunity>—e.g.: "For cases where Congress has delegated an agency lawmaking authority . . . but the agency has not *availed* itself of that mechanism, the Court should avoid unduly broad interpretations of the statute and should explicitly discuss the extent to which its analysis precludes agency rulemaking at some future date." William N. Eskridge Jr. & Lauren E. Baer, *The Continuum of Deference*, 96 Geo. L.J. 1083, 1192 (2008). The verb therefore doesn't work in the PASSIVE VOICE—e.g.:

- "Congress meant . . . that damages from or by floods . . . should not afford any basis of liability against the United

States regardless of *whether the sovereign immunity was availed of or not* [read *whether the government availed itself of sovereign immunity*]." *National Mfg. Co. v. U.S.*, 210 F.2d 263, 271 (8th Cir. 1954).

- "Sovereign immunity could not at that time be *availed of* by them for their participation in such wrongful conduct." *Barrett v. U.S.*, 798 F.2d 565, 574 (2d Cir. 1986). [Read: *They could not then avail themselves of sovereign immunity because they had participated in such wrongful conduct.*]

The verb is best not used as a nonreflexive transitive or intransitive verb. In the following specimen, *help, profit,* or *benefit* should replace *avail*: "Even if appropriate, had he known of the defense of voluntary intoxication, it would not have *availed* [read *helped*] him here." *Mullis v. State*, 769 So.2d 475, 475–76 (Fla. Dist. Ct. App. 2000).

availment (= the act of availing oneself of something) has scant support in the *OED* and is omitted from most other English-language dictionaries, but the word is now widely used in American legal writing. E.g.:

- "The employment of the known pure electron discharge above ionization voltages in tubes of the DeForest type was but the *availment* of those skilled in the art of the store of knowledge that had been accumulated and lay ready at hand." *General Elec. Co. v. De Forest Radio Co.*, 23 F.2d 698, 707 (D. Del. 1928).
- "The conditions necessary for *availment* of this provision are not present in the instant suit." *Henderson v. Prudential Ins. Co.*, 238 F.Supp. 862, 866 (E.D. Mich. 1965).
- "If on remand the plaintiffs amend their pleadings accordingly, they will have established a case on the purposeful *availment* issue sufficient to resist dismissal on the face of the pleadings." *Thompson v. Chrysler Motors Corp.*, 755 F.2d 1162, 1173 (5th Cir. 1985).

avails, n. (= profits or proceeds, esp. from a sale of property), is correctly labeled "archaic" in *W3* and in the *SOED*. Legal writers—fond as they are of ARCHAISMS—still occasionally use it. E.g.: "No particular items are selected as representing the *avails* of the trust fund." George G. Bogert & George T. Bogert, *The Law of Trusts and Trustees* § 923, at 390 (2d ed. 1982). *Avail*, the singular form, is frequently used—e.g.:

- "We know that the admonition to the children would be wholly impotent and of no *avail*." *Shenandoah Valley Nat'l Bank of Winchester v. Taylor*, 63 S.E.2d 786, 791 (Va. 1951).
- "The evidence in this regard, to have *avail*, should be of the most satisfactory kind." *Pernod v. American Nat'l Bank & Trust Co. of Chicago*, 132 N.E.2d 540, 542 (Ill. 1956).

Cf. **availment.**

aver. See **swear.**

average is a word that assumes a broad sample of subjects. The word does not mix well with *each*—e.g.: "The Florida League's annual budget for voter registration activity is approximately $80,000, and *each local chapter's annual budget averages approximately* $5,000 [read *each local chapter has an average annual budget of $5,000*]." *League of Women Voters of Fla. v. Browning*, 575 F.Supp.2d 1298, 1307 (S.D. Fla. 2008). See **each (B).**

averageable. So spelled.

averment; *averral. *Averment* is the preferred noun corresponding to *aver* in both AmE and BrE. E.g.:

- "The pleas-in-law are unknown to English law, and one plea on which the respondents' case depends is the relevancy of the *averments.*" *James Miller & Partners, Ltd. v. Whitworth St. Estates*, [1970] 2 A.C. 583, 600 (H.L.) (appeal taken from Manchester).
- "In reviewing the dismissal of a complaint for failure to state a claim, '[w]e must accept all well pleaded *averments* as true and view them in the light most favorable to the plaintiff.'" *Roe v. Abortion Abolition Soc'y*, 811 F.2d 931, 933 (5th Cir. 1987).

*Averral is a NEEDLESS VARIANT. For *aver*, see **swear.**

averse. See **adverse.**

avert (= to turn away, prevent), when used for *advert*, is a MALAPROPISM if it is not merely a typographical error—e.g.: "The Department's Notice did not refer specifically to 'payday loans,' but it did *avert* [read *advert*] to the need to protect Pennsylvania Residents from 'certain Internet lending practices.'" *Cash Am. Net of Nev., LLC v. Commonwealth*, 978 A.2d 1028, 1040 (Pa. Commw. Ct. 2009).

avertible; *avertable. *Avertible* is preferable.

aviate; avigate. No distinction was originally intended with the introduction of *avigate*, although some DIFFERENTIATION in emphasis has emerged. *Aviate*, a BACK-FORMATION of *aviation* first used in the late 19th century, means "to operate an aircraft."

Avigate, a PORTMANTEAU WORD formed from *aviate* and *navigate*, means "to handle and guide (i.e., navigate) an aircraft in the air"—e.g.: "An occasional statute has made it a misdemeanor to operate a train, navigate a vessel, or *avigate* an airplane, while in an intoxicated condition." Rollin M. Perkins & Ronald N. Boyce, *Criminal Law* 999 (3d ed. 1982). *W3* records *avigation* but not *avigate*; the *OED* neglects both words.

In the American law of easements, the usual phrase is *avigational* or *avigation easement*. E.g.:

- "An *avigation* easement . . . permits free flights over the land in question." *U.S. v. Brondum*, 272 F.2d 642, 645 (5th Cir. 1959).
- "We see no reason why an *avigation* easement may not be acquired by prescription in this state." *Drennen v. County of Ventura*, 112 Cal. Rptr. 907, 909 n.2 (Ct. App. 1974).
- "Overflights of aircraft flying into and out of the airport had occurred with such frequency and intensity as to have ripened into the taking of an *avigational* easement." *Fields v. Sarasota-Manatee Airport Auth.*, 512 So.2d 961, 962 (Fla. Dist. Ct. App. 1987).

See **easement (A).**

---

avocation; vocation. These words are almost opposites, although many writers misuse *avocation* for *vocation*. The first means "hobby," whereas the second means "a calling or profession." Here is the common mistake:

- "If the merchant, the grocer, the butcher, and druggist, and other trades and callings are allowed to open their places of business and carry on their respective *avocations* [read *vocations*] during seven days of the week, upon what principle can it be held that a person who may be engaged in the business of barbering may not do the same thing?" *Eden v. People*, 43 N.E. 1108, 1110 (Ill. 1896).
- "The national army consists of professional soldiers, who are in the continuous service of the government, while the members of the militia are taken from the rank and file of the people, all pursuing their respective *avocations* [read *vocations*] in life." *State v. Johnson*, 202 N.W. 191, 192 (Wis. 1925).

Did the writers of those sentences have in mind golf, gardening, and numismatics?

avoid, void, vb.; **avoidance, voidance.** In legal writing these verb and noun pairs are perfectly synonymous. *Avoid*, in law, often means "to make void or to cancel," although in the language of nonlawyers it invariably means "to refrain from" or "to escape or evade." Here are examples of *avoid* in the old-fashioned legal sense:

- "We are next to consider, how a deed may be *avoided*, or rendered of no effect." 2 William Blackstone, *Commentaries on the Laws of England* 308 (1766).
- "While potentially voidable, the settlement payment in PHP was valid until *avoided*." *In re Enron Corp.*, 323 B.R. 857, 877 (Bankr. S.D.N.Y. 2005).

The legal senses of *avoid* and *avoidance* invariably confuse nonlawyers, who are accustomed to the ordinary meanings of these words. It might therefore be advisable to prefer *void* and *voidance*. E.g.: "Plaintiff further argues that method claims are completely independent from the form of apparatus used; that infringement of a method claim is not *avoided* [read *voided*] by utilizing an apparatus differing from the apparatus illustrated in the patent." *Elgen Mfg. Corp. v. Ventfabrics, Inc.*, 314 F.2d 440, 442 (7th Cir. 1963). The archaic sense of *avoid* is ensconced in a number of statutes—e.g.: "The trustee may *avoid* any transfer of an interest of the debtor in property." 11 U.S.C. § 547(b) (1988).

Here the popular meaning of *avoid* appears in a legal context in such a way that a lawyer might at first wonder whether the legal meaning was intended: "The affidavit constitutes nothing more than a recital of unsupported allegations, conclusory in nature. As such it is insufficient to *avoid* summary judgment." *Broadway v. City of Montgomery*, 530 F.2d 657, 660 (5th. Cir. 1976).

In its lay sense "to evade or escape," *avoid* is sometimes misused for *prevent* or *circumvent*—e.g.:

- "The availability of notice before promulgation and wide public participation in rulemaking *avoids* [read *prevents*] the problem of singling out a single defendant among a group of competitors for initial imposition of a new and inevitably costly legal obligation." *National Petroleum Refiners Ass'n v. F.T.C.*, 482 F.2d 672, 683 (D.C. Cir. 1973).
- "The subsequent determination by the court as to the extent of damages *avoids* [read *circumvents*] the problems of collusion and unfairness to the insurer posed by unreasonable settlements between the insured and the claimant." *Somerset S. Props., Inc. v. American Title Ins. Co.*, 873 F.Supp. 355, 358–59 (S.D. Cal. 1994).

avoidable-consequences doctrine. See **mitigation-of-damages doctrine.**

avoidance. See **avoid** & **confession and avoidance.**

avowal; avowry; *avowtry. The noun corresponding to *avow* in its common meaning ("to declare openly") is *avowal*. Its sibling, *avowry*, serves as the noun form corresponding to the specialized common-law meaning of *avow* ("to acknowledge, in an answer, that one has taken something, and to justify the act"). *Avowry* is the equivalent in actions of replevin to the general common-law doctrine of confession and avoidance. E.g.: "The reply of a plaintiff to an *avowry* by a defendant in a replevin action might take one of several forms." F.A. Enever, *History of the Law of Distress* 199 (1931). **Avowtry* is an obsolete synonym of *adultery*.

avulsion. Lawyers may run across the medical as well as the legal use of this word; hence it may be useful to understand the common thread in meaning. Generally, *avulsion* denotes the action of pulling off, plucking out, or tearing away; forcible separation (*OED*).

In land law, *avulsion* refers to the sudden removal of land, by change in a river's course or by the action of flood, to another person's estate—in which event, contrary to the rule of *alluvion* or gradual accretion of soil, it remains the property of the original owner (*OED*). Medically, however, the term has come to denote "a tearing away of a structure or part accidentally or surgically" (*W3*) <avulsion of the diseased limb>. See **alluvion.**

awake; awaken; awakened; awaked. See **wake.**

award over is verbose for *award*—e.g.:

- "What is at stake, so far as the charity is concerned, is the cost of reasonable protection, the amount of the insurance premium as an added burden on its finances, not the *awarding over* [read *awarding*] in damages of its entire assets." *President & Dirs. of Georgetown Coll. v. Hughes*, 130 F.2d 810, 824 (D.C. Cir. 1942).
- "The appellant asserts in his fifth point of error that the trial court abused its discretion by *awarding over* [read *awarding*] one hundred percent of the existing community assets to the appellee." *Falor v. Falor*, 840 S.W.2d 683, 687 (Tex. App.—San Antonio 1992).

See PARTICLES, UNNECESSARY & **over (A).**

awful originally meant "inspiring or filled with awe." E.g.: "No tribunal can approach such a question without a deep sense of its importance, and of the *awful* responsibility involved in its decision." *McCulloch v. Maryland*, 17 U.S. (4 Wheat.) 316, 400 (1819) (per

Marshall, C.J.). The word's meaning has now degenerated to "horrible, terrible."

Hence some writers have experimented with the spelling *aweful in the traditional sense—e.g.: "There were three Lords Justice, as *aweful* as only Victorian judges, perhaps, can be." Viscount Radcliffe, *Not in Feather Beds* 72 (1968). At least one *thinks* the old meaning was meant there. That's the problem. In any event, any supposed distinction between *awful* and *aweful has not prospered in the language.

awoke. See **wake.**

axiom (= an established principle that is universally accepted within a given framework of reasoning or thinking) should not be used of propositions argued for by advocates. If the issue is the subject of controversy, it is not an *axiom*, unless the question is the applicability of an axiom to a given situation.

B

baby, splitting the. See **splitting the baby.**

baby-snatching. See **kidnapping (B).**

***backadation.** See **backwardation.**

backberend; *backberand; *backverinde; backbearing. This Anglo-Saxon term means "having stolen goods in one's possession when apprehended" and refers to a person carrying off stolen property (lit., "bearing it on one's back"). Now confined to historical contexts, the word is most often spelled *backberend*. The other forms are NEEDLESS VARIANTS.

Some writers prefer *backbearing* (often hyphenated in BrE) because it is the most modern form—e.g.: "The first dealt with the criminal taken in the act, and for him there was short shrift. Many local custumals relate the various deaths assigned to the hand-having and *back-bearing* thief." Theodore F.T. Plucknett, *A Concise History of the Common Law* 427 (5th ed. 1956).

BACK-FORMATIONS are words formed by removing an affix from longer words that are mistakenly assumed to be derivatives. This process occurs most commonly when a *-tion* noun is erroneously shortened to make a verb ending in *-te*—e.g., from *emotion* comes *emote*.

Such back-formations are objectionable when they stand merely as NEEDLESS VARIANTS of already extant verbs:

Back-Formation	Usual Word
*accreditate	accredit
*administrate	administer
*asportate	asport
*cohabitate	cohabit
*delimitate	delimit
*evolute	evolve
*indemnificate	indemnify
*interpretate	interpret
*orientate	orient
*registrate	register
remediate	remedy
*solicitate	solicit
*subornate	suborn

Sculpt, arguably a NEEDLESS VARIANT of *sculpture*, is now actually the more common verb.

Many back-formations never gain real legitimacy, some are aborted early in their existence, and still others are of questionable vigor. *Burgle* (back-formed from *burglar*) continues to have a jocular effect (in AmE), as do *effuse*, *emote*, and *laze*. Three 20th-century back-formed words, *choate*, *liaise*, and *surveil*, have come to be used with some frequency in legal contexts.

Many examples have survived respectably, among them *diagnose*, *donate*, *orate*, *resurrect*, and *spectate*. *Enthuse may one day be among these respectable words, although it has not gained approval since it first appeared in the early 19th century. But many have become accepted as legitimate because they have filled gaps in the language and won acceptance through their usefulness. The best rule of thumb is to avoid newborn back-formations that appear newfangled, but not, like a prig, to eschew common back-formations that are useful. Only philologists today recognize as back-formations *beg* (from *beggar*), *jell* (from *jelly*), *peddle* (from *peddler*), *rove* (from *rover*), and *type* (from *typewriter*).

For specific discussions of legal examples, see **asport, novate, *registrate, remediate, *solicitate, subinfeudate & *subornate.**

backpay is commonly spelled as one word in AmE. The British tend to spell it as two words.

***backverinde.** See **backberend.**

backwardation; *backadation. Leff defined this term (having two forms) as, "in stock market parlance, a fee paid by a seller for the privilege of delaying the delivery of securities past their normal delivery date," and puts his main entry under *backadation. See* Arthur A. Leff, *The Leff Dictionary of Law*, 94 Yale L.J. 1855, 2113 (1985). Most dictionaries, however, spell the term *backwardation.* H.W. Fowler included the term in his "ill-favored list" of HYBRID derivatives (*MEU2* 253), but it has become standard.

bad, in law, may mean "not valid"—e.g.: "As though thumbing their noses at a starving woman while self-righteously wrapping themselves in the flag, the Four Horsemen and Roberts held the law *bad*." Fred Rodell, *Nine Men* 241 (1955). The *OED* attests this legal usage from the late 19th century. See **Four Horsemen.**

bad; badly. See ADVERBS (c).

bade. See **bid.**

bad faith; bad-faith. *Bad faith* is the noun phrase <in bad faith>, *bad-faith* the adjectival phrase <bad-faith promises>. See *mala fide.*

bad law. See **bad.**

bad-man theory. "But if we take the view of our friend, the *bad man*, we shall find that he does not care two straws for the axioms or deductions, but that he does want to know what the Massachusetts or English courts are likely to do in fact. I am much of his mind. The prophecies of what the courts will do in fact, and nothing more pretentious, are what I mean by the law." Oliver Wendell Holmes, "The Path of the Law," in *Collected Legal Papers* 172–73 (1920). This famous passage gave a substantial impetus to the realist movement among legal theorists—that one must study the actual behavior of courts and lawyers as well as, or even instead of, theorizing about ultimate sources of law and deductions from those sources. In fact, Holmes did not hold this iconoclastic view but wished to point to the fact that, for the parties, what matters about law is what happens, what the court decides or orders.

The passage gave rise to what theorists now customarily call the *bad-man theory of law.* Karl Llewellyn took the idea a step beyond Holmes's formulation: "The people who have the doing in charge, whether they be judges or sheriffs or clerks or jailers or lawyers, are officials of the law. *What these officials do about disputes is, to my mind, the law itself.*" Karl N. Llewellyn, *The Bramble Bush* 3 (1930) (emphasis in original).

Later writers repeated the name often enough that it has become a basic idea in modern law, especially as framed originally by Holmes—e.g.: "Holmes returned to this idea (which he sometimes referred to as his '*bad man*' theory *of law*) over and over throughout his career." Grant Gilmore, *The Death of Contract* 126–27 n.124 (1974).

bail is a CHAMELEON-HUED legal term. As a noun, it means (1) "the person who acts as a surety for a debt"; (2) "the security or guaranty agreed upon"; or

(3) "release on surety of a person in custody." In sense 3, modern idiom requires *release on bail*, although formerly *in bail* was not uncommon—e.g.:

- "Upon the commitment of appellant to the Williamsburg county jail he employed counsel for the purpose of obtaining his release *in bail.*" *State v. Cockfield*, 120 S.E. 359, 360 (S.C. 1923).
- "Mr. Bartletta was then taken before the recorder and released *in bail* to await the action of the grand jury." *Bartletta v. McFeeley*, 152 A. 17, 17 (N.J. Ch. 1930).

For more on sense 3, together with related words, see **pledge,** n.

As a verb, *bail* means (1) "to set (a person) free for security on the person's own recognizance for appearance on another day" <the prisoner was not bailed but committed>; (2) "to become a surety for"; (3) "to guarantee"; or (4) to place (personal property) in someone else's charge.

Outside legal contexts, the verb *bail* means (1) "to remove (liquid) from (a vessel), esp. with a small container" <bail water from a canoe>; or (2) (colloquially) to leave hurriedly or clandestinely <bail out of a dull party>.

bailable (= admitting of or entitled to bail), together with its antonym *nonbailable*, may refer either to persons or to offenses. E.g.:

- "Furthermore, the record shows that Dovalina's attempted murder charge was *nonbailable.*" *U.S. v. Dovalina*, 711 F.2d 737, 740 (5th Cir. 1983). (One might as naturally have written that Dovalina himself was not *bailable*, because he had been charged with attempted murder.)
- "Even if Congress is free to define *nonbailable* offenses, certainly the allowable justifications are limited." *U.S. v. Affleck*, 765 F.2d 944, 957 (10th Cir. 1985).
- "The police consider acid bath a *bailable* offense not worthy of prosecution as long as the victim is alive irrespective of the extent of disfigurement or deformity the victim suffers." Itoro Eze-Anaba, *Domestic Violence and Legal Reform in Nigeria: Prospects and Challenges*, 14 Cardozo J.L. & Gender 21, 27 (2007).

bail bond. See **bond.**

bail bondsman. See **bailor.**

bailee; bailie. *Bailee* = one to whom personal property is delivered (or *bailed*) without any change in ownership. E.g.: "At common law a *bailee* (i.e., a person to whom the possession of goods is entrusted by the owner) who acted dishonestly had some immunity, since he was considered to be in lawful possession of the goods." L.B. Curzon, *English Legal History* 244 (2d ed. 1979).

Bailie is a term for a Scottish magistrate; it is also a dialectal variant of *bailiff.* See also **bailor, bailiff** & **bailment.**

bailer. See **bailor.**

bailie. See **bailee.**

bailiery; *bailiary. The first is the preferred form of this word, meaning "the jurisdiction of a bailie."

bailiff, n., = (1) in England, a sheriff's officer employed to serve writs, make arrests, and execute process (see **bumbailiff**); or (2) in the U.S., a court officer who keeps order with the parties, attorneys, and jurors during court proceedings. From the 14th century to the 17th, *bailiff* (like *reeve*) denoted an official on a manor or estate with the power to (1) enforce law and order as representative of the lord or master, (2) collect dues and rents from the tenants, and (3) ensure that everyone on the estate had performed services due. Today, in England, *bailiff* denotes an employee who acts as the overseer or superintendent of an estate as related to the land and its profitable uses—but not of the estate's household or financial workings.

bailiff, vb. Primarily in law-school mock trials and moot court, the age-old noun *bailiff* has come to be used as a verb meaning "to act as bailiff." That being so, the newfangled verb will perforce soon infiltrate the speech of the profession. It is an American casualism that should not appear in serious contexts. See NOUNS AS VERBS.

*bailiffry; *bailivia. See **bailiwick.**

bailiwick; sheriffwick; sheriffdom. *Bailiwick* = the office, jurisdiction, or district of a bailiff. Figuratively, it has become synonymous with *domain. Sheriffwick* = the office, jurisdiction, or district of a sheriff.

Because in one sense *bailiff* and *sheriff* are synonymous, the derivatives in *-wick* (lit., "village") have become synonyms. *Bailiwick* is the more common of the two: "A bailiff was popularly referred to as a 'bailie,' and before long a bailie's wick [i.e., village] was expressed as his '*bailiwick*.' And in time this word came to be used to indicate the special territory over which a peace officer exercises his authority as such." Rollin M. Perkins & Ronald N. Boyce, *Criminal Law* 1096 (3d ed. 1982). **Bailiffry* is a NEEDLESS VARIANT, and **bailivia* is an obsolete variant, of *bailiwick.*

In the sense "the office of the sheriff," *sheriffwick* is less common than *sheriffdom*, which was originally a Scotticism. E.g.: "The history of the *sheriffdom* is one of the most important departments of the constitutional history of England." *Grifenhagen v. Ordway*, 113 N.E. 516, 517 (N.Y. 1916). See **sheriffalty.**

bail jump, n., = the act of defaulting on [i.e., "jumping"] one's bail. Though seemingly slang, state and federal courts in the U.S. regularly use the term—e.g.:

- "The presiding judge made the following statement: . . . 'I intend to hold Mr. Lupo for the Grand Jury on the felony *bail jump* in that the warrant has been outstanding since 1970 . . . .'" *People v. Lupo*, 345 N.Y.S.2d 348, 350 (N.Y. City Crim. Ct. 1973).
- "McLennan timely moved to dismiss the indictment prior to trial arguing that it was fatally defective because it did not specifically allege that Chagra's *bail jump*, to which

McLennan was allegedly an accessory, was willful." *U.S. v. McLennan*, 672 F.2d 239, 242 (1st Cir. 1982). On the use of **prior to* in that sentence, see ***prior to.**
- "The sole issue in this prosecution for *bail jump* is whether the evidence is sufficient to show that the person on trial was the same person who earlier had failed to appear in court." *State v. Huber*, 119 P.3d 388, 388 (Wash. Ct. App. 2005).

Whereas a specific instance is referred to as a *bail jump* (or sometimes *bail-jump*), the crime itself is known as *bail-jumping* (an older phrase)—e.g.: "On February 10, 1938, a short affidavit was filed in the Magistrates' Court charging the defendant with the crime of *bail jumping*." *People v. Davis*, 5 N.Y.S.2d 411, 412 (Gen. Sess. 1938). Often the expression serves as a PHRASAL ADJECTIVE—e.g.: "For trial purposes, the harassment charges were severed from the *bail-jumping* charge." *State v. Council*, 245 P.3d 222, 223 (Wash. 2010). See **jump bail.**

bailment = (1) a delivery of personal property by a person (a *bailor*) to another (a *bailee*) who holds it under an express or implied-in-fact contract; (2) the personal property delivered to a bailee; (3) the action of posting bail for a criminal defendant; or (4) the record of one's posting bail for a criminal defendant. The definitions appear in order of decreasing frequency. Sense 1 is by far the most common—e.g.: "Another kind of situation [that] has traditionally been treated as contractual . . . is the relationship created by what is known as a gratuitous *bailment*, i.e., a transaction in which goods are loaned to, or deposited with, another party without payment." P.S. Atiyah, *An Introduction to the Law of Contract* 120–21 (3d ed. 1981).

There are some important distinctions between *bailment* and *sale*: "In bailment the title to the property does not pass to the bailee, but only the possession; in a sale the title passes to the vendee at once." William F. Elliott, *A Treatise on the Law of Bailments and Carriers* 21–22 (1914). But in practice, the terms may be tricky to distinguish because a *bailment* may include an option to purchase, or may be a bailment for the purpose to sell, or may be a conditional sale. In these cases the question is whether the sender has the right to compel a return of the thing sent (making it a bailment), or the receiver has the option to pay for the thing in money (making it more likely a sale). See *id.* at 22–23. *Bailment* differs from *gift* in that "a gift passes ownership and not possession only." *Id.* at 23.

bailor; bailer; bailee; bail bondsman. *Bailor* and *-er* are not at all clearly distinguished in actual legal usage, although they might easily and usefully be given clear DIFFERENTIATION. *Bailor* and *bailee* (i.e., the persons on the giving and receiving ends of a bailment [sense 1]) are correlative personal nouns—e.g.:

- "A bailment relationship arises when the *bailor* agrees to deliver property into the possession of the *bailee*, under terms that the *bailee* accepts, with an understanding that the property will be 'redelivered to the person who delivered it, or otherwise dealt with according to his directions, or kept until he reclaims it, as the case may be.'" Hilary Jay, Note, *A Picture Imperfect: The Rights of Art Consignor-Collectors When Their Art Dealer Files for Bankruptcy*, 58 Duke L.J. 1859, 1884 (2009).
- "This world of contract was inhabited by people in relational pairs: *bailor* and *bailee*, principal and agent, master and servant, principal and factor, landlord and tenant, vendor and purchaser, husband and wife." Roy Kreitner, *Fault at the Contract–Tort Interface*, 107 Mich. L. Rev. 1533, 1536 (2009).

See **bailee** & **-er (A)**.

Bailer (or *bail bondsman*) should be reserved for the sense "one who attaches bail (the surety in criminal law)." Nevertheless, the spelling *bailor* is often used in that sense, and *bailer* appears occasionally in civil contexts. Given the inevitable objections to *bail bondsman* on grounds of SEXISM, we ought to encourage wider use of *bailer* in this sense.

balance of probability; beyond a reasonable doubt. These phrases express two different burdens of proof. In a civil trial, once both sides have presented evidence, the jury is instructed to find for the party that, on the whole, has the stronger case, i.e., the party whose evidence tips the *balance of probability*—however slight the edge may be. But in a criminal trial, the proof necessary for a conviction must be *beyond a reasonable doubt*, because of the presumption of innocence. See **burden of proof** & **preponderance of the evidence**.

balance-sheet insolvency test. See **insolvency**.

ballot. See **vote**.

banc. See **en banc (A)**.

banish, vb., generally takes the preposition *from* <he was banished from the country>. Krapp cites the use "The king *banishes* you his presence," with two objects, but this use is archaic. George Philip Krapp, *A Comprehensive Guide to Good English* 68 (1927).

banknote is one word in both AmE and BrE.

bankrupt, adj.; *bankrout. *Bankrout* is an obsolete form of the word. In the English Renaissance, scholars respelled French borrowings such as *bankrout* on the Latin model, hence *bankrupt*. Many of these respellings did not survive (e.g., *accompt* for *account*); *bankrupt* is one of the few that did. See **comptroller**.

bankrupt, n. Although in popular speech and writing it is common to refer to a *bankrupt*—a usage dating from at least the early 16th century—most modern bankruptcy statutes use the term *debtor* instead. As one treatise states: "Nobody is a *bankrupt*. There is no such person under the Bankruptcy Code." David G. Epstein et al., *Bankruptcy* 6 (1993).

bankruptcy [fr. L. *bancus* "table" + *ruptus* "broken"] = (1) the fact of being financially unable to pursue one's business and meet one's engagements, esp. of being unable to pay one's debts; (2) the fact of having become the subject of bankruptcy proceedings; or (3) the field of law dealing with those who are unable or unwilling to pay their debts. For more on *bankruptcy* and its near-synonyms, see **insolvency (A)**.

Bankruptcy is often misspelled *bankruptsy*.

Bankruptcy Act; Bankruptcy Code. In the U.S., the phrase *Bankruptcy Act* refers to the Bankruptcy Act of 1898; it governed bankruptcy cases filed before 1 October 1979. The phrase *Bankruptcy Code* refers to the Bankruptcy Reform Act of 1978 (frequently amended since then), which governs all cases filed since 1 October 1979.

bankruptcy law; bankrupt law. The normal idiom today is *bankruptcy law(s)*, although *bankrupt law* was once fairly common—e.g.: "Under the *bankrupt law* [read, in more modern terms, *bankruptcy law*] the defendant had the same right to prove up the note for payment in the bankruptcy proceedings that the plaintiffs had, and . . . they were under no obligation to go into the *bankrupt court* [read, in more modern terms, *bankruptcy court*] and prove the claim for the benefit of the surety." *Levy v. Wagner*, 69 S.W. 112, 114 (Tex. Civ. App.—Houston 1902).

*bankruptee, n., is an unnecessary NEOLOGISM equivalent to the well-established noun *bankrupt* (= one that has declared bankruptcy) or *debtor*. E.g.:

- "A judge sets a payback plan on the unsecured debt [that] he thinks the *bankruptee* [read *bankrupt*] can meet in good faith." Lisa J. McCue, *Bankruptcy Changes Called Possible*, Am. Banker, 29 Jan. 1981, at 3.
- "For legal purposes, the family homestead can include up to 200 acres (100 for a single adult) of real property that aren't located within city, town, or village limits, and/or one acre of land, plus any temporary residence if the *bankruptee* [read *bankrupt*] has not acquired another home." Mike Shropshire, *The Nouveau Broke*, D Mag., Nov. 1986, at 89 (inset).
- "The attorney of a trustee in bankruptcy sent letters to the clients of a purchaser of the *bankruptee's* [read *bankrupt's*] assets informing them that the purchaser did not in fact own the assets he claimed to own." Mark C. Lang, *Can Your Client Be Vicariously Liable for Your Intentional Misconduct?*, 16 Prof. Law. 2, 2 (2005).

See **bankrupt, n.**

bankrupt law. See **bankruptcy law**.

*bankruptsy. See **bankruptcy**.

bar, n. In the U.S., all lawyers are members of a bar, whether they are litigators or office practitioners. In G.B., only barristers (in Eng.) and advocates (in Scot.), as opposed to solicitors, make up the *Bar* (the word is customarily capitalized in BrE). See **called to the bar** & **attorney (A)**.

Unified bar and *integrated bar* are interchangeable terms referring to bar associations in which membership is a statutory requisite for the practice of law in a given geographic area.

For the sense of relating to a defendant's judgment on the merits, see **merger (B).**

bar; debar; disbar. The first two have closely related meanings. *Bar* means "to prevent (often by legal obstacle)"—e.g.:

- "Legislative immunity does not, of course, *bar* all judicial review of legislative acts." *Powell v. McCormack*, 395 U.S. 486, 503 (1969) (per Warren, C.J.).
- "The court concluded that these warranty disclaimers did not necessarily *bar* a breach-of-contract claim . . . ." *Reynolds Metals Co. v. Westinghouse Elec. Corp.*, 758 F.2d 1073, 1077 (5th Cir. 1985).
- "*MDY Industries* does not *bar* a gamer's claim to virtual property by adverse possession." Alisa B. Steinberg, *For Sale—One Level 5 Barbarian for 94,800 Won: The International Effects of Virtual Property and the Legality of Its Ownership*, 37 Ga. J. Int'l & Comp. L. 381, 416 (2009).

Bar serves also as a noun <a bar to all claims> <on-sale bar>. (See **merger (B).**)

Debar, a somewhat archaic FORMAL WORD, means "to preclude from having or doing"—e.g.:

- "It would require very persuasive circumstances enveloping Congressional silence to *debar* this Court from re-examining its own doctrines." *Helvering v. Hallock*, 309 U.S. 106, 119 (1940) (per Frankfurter, J.).
- "[A court of record] has the power to amend its records, correct the mistakes of its clerk or other officers of the court, or to supply defects or omissions in the record, and no lapse of time will *debar* the court of the power to discharge this duty." *State v. Cannon*, 94 S.E.2d 339, 342 (N.C. 1956).
- "Here the application for a stay, unlike a motion to *debar* a court from applying a stay, is a disaffirmation of the proceeding below." Peter Demkovitz, *Kuwait Airways Corporation v. Iraqi Airways Company, the Independent, 27 October 1993 English Court of Appeals (Civil Division)*, 7 N.Y. Int'l L. Rev. 200, 203 (1994).

Disbar means "to expel from the legal profession." The corresponding nouns are *debarment* and *disbarment*.

bar entails. See **entail.**

bargain, n.; agreement; contract. Williston sorted these terms out with admirable clarity: "A *bargain* is an agreement of two or more persons to exchange promises, or to exchange a promise for a performance. So defined, *bargain* is at once narrower than *agreement* in that it is not applicable to all agreements, and broader than *contract*, since it includes a promise given in exchange for an insufficient consideration. It also covers transactions [that] the law refuses to recognize as contracts because of illegality." 1 Samuel Williston & W.H.E. Jaeger, *A Treatise on the Law of Contracts* § 2A, at 7 (3d ed. 1957).

bargain, vb. In law, an otherwise obsolete sense persists: "to agree to buy and sell; to contract for." See **grant, bargain, and sell.**

bargained-for exchange. This phrase is sometimes erroneously rendered *bargain for exchange*. Here variations of it are correctly used:

- "The doing of the act constitutes acceptance, the *bargained-for* consideration, and the offeree's performance." Friedrich Kessler, *Contracts: Cases and Materials* 171 (2d ed. 1964).
- "If the termination of obligations were an immediate *bargained-for* right of consequence, he would presumably have taken advantage of his freedom from testamentary obligation to make a new will." *Luff v. Luff*, 359 F.2d 235, 242 (D.C. Cir. 1966).

The origin of the phrase *bargained-for exchange* may be seen from this sentence: "Consideration is something bargained for and given in exchange."

bargainee (= the purchaser in a bargained-for exchange) is more obscure than *purchaser*, but the word is perhaps a useful correlative of *bargainor*. E.g.: "The Statute itself operated to vest the seisin of the bargainor in the *bargainee*." Cornelius J. Moynihan, *Introduction to the Law of Real Property* 183 (2d ed. 1988). See -EE & **bargainer.**

bargainer; bargainor. Though one might suspect that the two forms are synonymous, they are not. *Bargainer* means "one who bargains." *Bargainor* has a more specific legal meaning: "the seller in a bargained-for exchange." See **bargainee.**

bargee. Though illogically formed with the -*ee* suffix, the established form *bargee* (17th c.) is a variant of *bargeman* (14th c.), without the infelicity of SEXISM. E.g.: "The story of the Elmhurst's *bargee* was that off Bedloe's Island a third tug of the railroad . . . came alongside, struck the barge a heavy blow on her port quarter, nearly capsizing her, driving her forward against the barge ahead, and breaking some planks forward." *Sinram v. Pennsylvania R.R.*, 61 F.2d 767, 768 (2d Cir. 1932) (per L. Hand, J.). See -EE (A).

barrack lawyer. See LAWYERS, DEROGATORY NAMES FOR (B).

barrator. See **champertor.**

barratrous is the adjective corresponding to the noun *barratry*—e.g.:

- "The statute is clear that *barratrous* conduct is to be treated as a criminal offense." *Galinski v. Kessler*, 480 N.E.2d 1176, 1179 (Ill. App. Ct. 1985).
- "They simply state that the Master sailed away with the cargo and conclude that this conduct was *barratrous*." *Tradewinds Marketing, Inc. v. General Accident Ins. Co.*, 665 F.Supp. 104, 105 (D.P.R. 1987).

barratry; simony. Why these terms are sometimes confused is not at all apparent. *Barratry* = (1) in criminal law, vexatious persistence in, or incitement to, litigation; (2) in admiralty, (of a master or crew) fraudulent or grossly negligent conduct that is prejudicial to a shipowner; (3) in older Eng. and Scots law, the act of going abroad to purchase a benefice from Rome; or (4) in Scots law, the accepting of a bribe by a judge. The adjective is *barratrous* and the agent noun *barrator*. See **barratrous.**

Simony = the purchase or sale of an ecclesiastical promotion. The adjective is *simoniac(al)*, the agent noun either *simonist* or *simoniac*.

barred is an informal word meaning "admitted to practice (before the bar); licensed." It's most commonly heard in the eastern United States—e.g.: "Interestingly, even though the DC Bar has already opined that being *barred* in D.C. is a prerequisite to performing contract attorney work in the state, many D.C. agencies still continue to staff projects using non-D.C. *barred* J.D.'s. However, many agencies do express high preference for those with the proper D.C. license and most will refuse to pay the standard contract attorney rate without it." My Attorney Blog, *How Much Do Contract Attorneys Make in Terms of Wage Rate?*, http://www.myattorneyblog.com/ (13 Jan. 2008).

barrister = a specialist consultant and pleader belonging to a class of lawyers that is given predominant (formerly exclusive) rights of audience in superior courts. Ordinarily, the word applies to an English or Northern Irish pleader (the Scottish counterpart being an *advocate*). When used in reference to an American lawyer, the word smacks of highfalutin journalese—e.g.: "The prestige and importance of the federal circuit bench [in the U.S.] attracts high-caliber *barristers* [read *lawyers*]." Donald D. Jackson, *Judges* 312 (1974). See **attorney (A), counsel (A), Queen's Counsel & solicitor.**

barristerial (= of or pertaining to a barrister; lawyerly) is, naturally, more common in BrE than in AmE, but it appears in the latter as well—e.g.:

- "Since the 12(e) motion is prone for implementation of *barristerial* shadow boxing, its exercise should be cast in the mold of strictest necessity." *Lincoln Labs. v. Savage Labs.*, 26 F.R.D. 141, 142 (D. Del. 1960).
- "Having taken this position, plaintiffs, in the exercise of commendable *barristerial* caution, have nevertheless submitted documents indicating that . . . Dr. Newman directed the formation of a university-wide Salary Review Committee." *Chang v. University of Rhode Island*, 554 F.Supp. 1203, 1205 (D.R.I. 1983).

basis. A. For *reason*. *Basis* is sometimes used unidiomatically for *reason*—e.g.: "The court, after a full review of the authorities, concluded that there was now no sound *basis* [read *reason*] why the value of life insurance coverage, as well as the cash surrender value, might not be considered in a property division between parties to a divorce action." *Basis* is properly followed by *for* <the basis for the decision>. *Reason*, by contrast, fits with either *for* <the reason for the decision> or *why* (as in the example quoted above). Writers who use *basis why* are probably driven to it by the SUPERSTITION that *reason why* is an error. See **reason (B) & reason why.**

B. On a . . . basis. This long-winded phrase often ousts a simpler, more legitimate adverb—e.g.:

- "To be of practical value as a guide to legal doctrine, a book must be *updated on a regular basis* [read *regularly updated*]." Kent C. Olson, *Legal Information* 55 (1999).
- "One entrepreneur now offers to prepare a fax letter with your imprint and fax it to your list *on a weekly basis* [read *each week*]." George B. Delta & Jeffrey H. Matsuura, *Law of the Internet* 8-78 (2002).
- "In tort actions, the inquiry into the question of negligence is *determined on a case-by-case basis* [read *determined case by case*]." *Doe v. Hawkins*, 42 So.3d 1000, 1010 n.11 (La. Ct. App. 2010).
- "Respondent represented his client *on a contingent fee basis* [read *for a contingent fee*]." *Att'y Grievance Comm'n of Md. v. Thaxton*, 1 A.3d 470, 478 (Md. 2010).

See FLOTSAM PHRASES.

C. Plural Form. The plural of *basis*, as well as *base*, is *bases*. But the pronunciations differ: for *basis*, the plural is pronounced /**bay**-seez/, for *bases* /**bays**-ez/.

bastard, a term of abuse generally, is still used neutrally in the law, in either of two senses: (1) "a child born out of wedlock"; or (2) "a child born to a married woman whose husband, for some provable reason, could not possibly be the father." Sense 1 has always been more common—e.g.:

- "There was judgment rendered in favor of appellees, recognizing them as the sole heirs of Willie Huey and finding appellants to be illegitimate *bastards*." *Succession of Walker*, 288 So.2d 328, 330 (La. 1974). Note the REDUNDANCY of the phrase *illegitimate bastards*.
- "The treatment of non-marital children in Anglo-American law starts with the common law doctrine of *filius nullius*, which literally means that a '*bastard*' is the child of no one, or more accurately that the child 'is therefore of kin to nobody, and has no ancestor from whom any inheritable blood can be derived.'" June Carbone, *The Legal Definition of Parenthood: Uncertainty at the Core of Family Identity*, 65 La. L. Rev. 1295, 1309 (2005) (quoting Blackstone).

Today, however, the law's technical neutrality is not without comic overtones. See **adulterine bastard, illegitimate child, natural child** & EUPHEMISMS.

bastardy = (1) the condition of a bastard; illegitimate birth; or (2) the begetting of bastards; fornication (*OED*). Today in sense 1, *illegitimacy* is the more usual term, and the preferable one for avoiding unduly derogatory connotations. Sense 2 is not common.

Bates stamp, n.; **Bates-stamp,** vb. The noun is the popular name of a self-advancing stamp machine patented in 1891 by the Bates Manufacturing Company, and also refers to the mark it makes—e.g.: "This reference to an 'EDP' designation is to the *Bates stamp* [that] is on each page." *In re Katrina Canal Breaches Consol. Litig.*, 647 F.Supp.2d 644, 657 n.13 (E.D. La. 2009). The verb (hyphenated) means "to affix a distinguishing mark, usu. a number, to each page of a document so that it can be identified in a sequence." E.g.: "[B]ecause the ROA does not appear to be consecutively *Bates-stamped* throughout, the Court will refer to this Court's docket number, part numbers and page numbers for reference to these documents." *Celaya v. Stewart*, 691 F.Supp.2d 1046, 1077 n.5 (D. Ariz. 2010).

Bates should always be capitalized because it is a proper noun. A few writers err—e.g.:

- "Most documents produced by Defendant during discovery are *bates-stamped* [read *Bates-stamped*] as 'MSJ' followed by successive numbers 1 through 2326." *Colon-Fontanez v. Municipality of San Juan*, 671 F.Supp.2d 300, 307 (D.P.R. 2009).
- "Defendants produced this exhibit without pagination, *bates-stamping* [read *Bates-stamping*], or other indication of page order." *Taylor v. Housing Auth. of New Haven*, 267 F.R.D. 36, 68 n.35 (D. Conn. 2010).

battery. To nonlawyers, *battery* connotes physical violence. The legal meaning, however, is "the intentional or negligent application of physical force to, or the offensive contact with, someone without consent." Hence, offensive contact is enough—for example, an unwelcome kiss or caress. E.g.: "The *battery* here was a technical one, and was accompanied by neither physical injury nor violence. It was a mere touching of the person of the plaintiff, a mere incident of the restraint, the false imprisonment." *Fisher v. Rumler*, 214 N.W. 310, 311 (Mich. 1927). As a tort, *battery* is a civil wrong giving rise to a cause of action for damages; as a crime, it is a social harm punished by the state. See **assault.**

bawdy house; house of ill fame; disorderly house. These phrases are three of the EUPHEMISMS by which lawyers have traditionally referred to a brothel or house of prostitution. The quaint phrase *disorderly house* is the broadest of the three, denoting a house where people carry on activities that constitute a nuisance to the neighborhood; these activities might include gambling and drug-dealing as well as prostitution.

beak is a BrE slang term for a magistrate or justice of the peace. E.g.: "In the cities a lone example was set by Henry Fielding (1707–54), the novelist, sitting at Bow Street as the self-styled 'principal Westminster magistrate,' and his brother and successor, Sir John Fielding, 'the Blink *Beak*.' Unpaid, like other magistrates, they spurned the bribes." Alan Harding, *A Social History of English Law* 270–71 (1966). The *OED* quotes many examples from the 16th to the 19th century, including one from Dickens's *Oliver Twist* (1837–1838), and notes that the precise etymology is unknown.

bears the meaning. See DEFINITIONS (c).

bear the relation. See **relation** (B).

because. See **as** (A).

before; by. Cases come *before* courts and are then *reviewed by* those courts. But some writers mar these idioms—e.g.: "Mrs. Davis ultimately sought review *before* [read *by*] the Supreme Court of Tennessee, which granted certiorari because it considered this issue important in the development of the law regarding new reproductive technologies." Nelle S. Paegel, *Use of Stem Cells in Biotechnological Research*, 22 Whittier L. Rev. 1183, 1208 (2001). For *before* as an indicator of time, see **anterior to, *prior to* & **no later than.**

*before-mentioned. See **above-mentioned** & ***aforesaid.**

beg is occasionally used in dissenting opinions in the phrases *beg to differ* and *beg to advise*. These are ARCHAISMS to be eschewed.

For the phrase *beg the question*, see **begging the question.**

*begat; begot. See BIBLICAL AFFECTATION.

beget today appears almost exclusively in figurative contexts—e.g.:

- "The services and gifts must have been rendered with a frequency that *begets* an anticipation of their continuance." *Gaydos v. Domabyl*, 152 A. 549, 552 (Pa. 1930).
- "Breyer's majority opinion undertakes broad judicial policymaking that *begets* a significant expansion of judicial sentencing authority." Craig Green, *Booker and* Fanfan*: The Untimely Death (and Rebirth?) of the Federal Sentencing Guidelines*, 93 Geo. L.J. 395, 425 (2005).
- "On the other hand, an unlawful detention that *begets* knowledge of an outstanding arrest warrant does not always automatically immunize the fugitive from prosecution for crimes discovered during the warrant arrest." *State v. Martin*, 179 P.3d 457, 462 (Kan. 2008).

In its literal sense, *beget* is an ARCHAISM that still appears from time to time—e.g.: "We are told that humankind is created, male and female, for the exclusive sexual communion and partnership that *begets* children." Joan Lockwood O'Donovan, *Law and Redemption*, 36 Pepp. L. Rev. 573, 579 n.1 (2009). The more usual term today is *to conceive* or *to father*.

begging the question does not mean "evading the issue" or "inviting the obvious questions," as some mistakenly believe. The strict (and traditional) meaning of *beg the question* is "to base a conclusion on an assumption that is as much in need of proof or demonstration as the conclusion itself." The formal name for this logical fallacy is *petitio principii*. Following are two classic examples:

- "Reasonable men are those who think and reason intelligently." *Patterson v. Nutter*, 7 A. 273, 275 (Me. 1886). (This statement begs the question: "What does it mean to think and reason intelligently?")
- "Life begins at conception! [Fn.: 'Conception is defined as the beginning of life.']" *Davis v. Davis*, unreported opinion (Cir. Tenn. Eq. 1989). (The "proof"—or the definition—is circular.)

In the following sentence, the writer mangled the SET PHRASE *to beg the question* and misapprehended its meaning (by using *begs* for *ignores*): "Blaming Congress and the Democrats for 'criminalizing of policy differences with the executive branch' *begs* a much larger *issue* here: Should members of the executive branch be allowed to withhold vital information from those members of Congress charged by law to monitor specific actions of the president?" Letter of John M. Burns, Wall St. J., 16 May 1990, at A17.

begin. See **commence.**

beg to. See **beg.**

behalf. A distinction exists between the phrases *in behalf of* and *on behalf of*. The first means "in the interest or in defense of" <he fought in behalf of a just man's reputation>; the second, *on behalf of*, means "as the agent of, as representative of" <on behalf of the corporation, I would like to thank . . .> <she appeared on behalf of her client>.

Upon behalf of is now considered much inferior to *on behalf of*—e.g.: "The answer and motion to dismiss were filed *upon behalf of* [read *on behalf of*] Nationwide and Cowder by a Charleston law firm." *Brison v. Kaufman*, 584 S.E.2d 480, 484 (W. Va. 2003). See **upon.**

behavior. See PLURALS (B).

be in receipt of. See **receipt of, be in.**

belief. Lawyers frequently speak of a *genuine belief*, a *bona fide belief*, or an *honest belief*. In fact, all such phrases are REDUNDANCIES, since it is quite impossible to believe something ungenuinely, in bad faith, or dishonestly.

belligerence; belligerency. *Belligerence* refers to a person's truculent attitude. *Belligerency* has traditionally, in international law, been the preferred term in referring to the status of a state that is at war—e.g.: "Other states are within their rights in declaring themselves neutral in the struggle, and since there can be no neutrals unless there are two belligerents, such a declaration is equivalent to a recognition of the *belligerency* of both parties." J.L. Brierly, *The Law of Nations* 134 (5th ed. 1955).

belongings. See **possessions.**

below is often used by appellate courts to mean "at the trial-court stage." E.g.: "As the district court noted *below*, however, the Supreme Court recently relied on the presumption in a pharmaceutical failure-to-warn case." *N.Y. SMSA Ltd. P'ship v. Town of Clarkstown*, 612 F.3d 97, 104 (2d Cir. 2010). Some appellate courts—especially American ones—avoid this term because it may seem to slight trial judges. See **inferior (B).**

below-mentioned; under-mentioned. The first is AmE or BrE; the second is BrE only. *Below*, like *above*, is frequently used as an ellipsis for *below-mentioned*. See **above.**

bemean. See **demean.**

bench = (1) the court considered in its official capacity <remarks from the bench>; (2) judges collectively <bench and bar>; or (3) the judges of a particular court <the Queen's Bench>. Cf. **court.**

Renaissance lawbooks, in referring to *the Bench*, invariably meant the Court of Common Pleas, not the King's Bench.

bencher, in England, means generally "one who sits on a bench" (*OED*), but particularly refers to a member of the governing body of one of the Inns of Court. E.g.:

- "There was thus little occasion for controversies as to discipline to be brought before the judges, unless the *benchers* failed in the performance of their duties." *People ex rel. Karlin v. Culkin*, 162 N.E. 487, 490 (N.Y. 1928) (per Cardozo, C.J.).
- "In Pennsylvania, Andrew Hamilton, a barrister and *bencher* of Gray's Inn, came to Philadelphia in 1682." Roscoe Pound, *The Development of Constitutional Guaranties of Liberty* 59 (1957).

Benchers are known formally as *Masters of the Bench*.

Archaically, the term was used more generally in reference to magistrates, judges, assessors, and senators.

bench-made. See **judge-made.**

bench memo (AmE) = (1) a short brief submitted by a lawyer to a trial judge, often at the judge's request; or (2) a legal memorandum prepared by an appellate judge's law clerk to help the judge prepare for and participate in oral argument.

bench trial has become—mostly in southern parts of the U.S.—a common equivalent of *trial to the bench* (= a nonjury trial). See **nonjury.**

bench warrant, n., = process that a court issues for the attachment or arrest of a person who has been held in contempt, has been indicted, or has disobeyed a subpoena.

Some legal writers, especially in Texas, have transformed this noun phrase into a PHRASAL VERB—e.g.:

- "Having been *bench warranted* from the Texas Department of Corrections where he is serving time for two prior convictions, appellant is hardly a fit candidate for probation." *Roberts v. State*, 587 S.W.2d 724, 725 n.1 (Tex. Crim. App. 1979).
- "Appellant sought the continuance so that Mr. Babineaux could either be *bench warranted* back to testify or deposed." *Babineaux v. Babineaux*, 761 S.W.2d 102, 103 (Tex. App.—Beaumont 1988). To make that sentence parallel, *either be* should be *be either*. See PARALLELISM.

If the phrase is to be used as a verb, it should be hyphenated: hence *bench-warranted* would have been the better form in both quotations. See NOUNS AS VERBS.

beneficiary. See *cestui que trust* & **devisee.**

benefit, vb. As a verb, *benefit* typically functions more economically and smoothly in the active voice than in the passive—e.g.:

- "After all, the person might have *been benefited by* [read *benefited from*] having received her 'just' rewards earlier rather than later." Mark Strasser, *Wrongful Life, Wrongful Birth, Wrongful Dead, and the Right to Refuse Treatment*, 64 Mo. L. Rev. 29, 67 (1999).
- "One solution is to establish a program of peer educators or counselors so that Roma children can see Roma role models who have *been benefited by* [read *benefited from*] education." Maria Grahn-Farley, *International Child Rights at Home and Abroad*, 30 Cap. U. L. Rev. 657, 676 (2002).

See BE-VERBS (B).

benefited; benefiting. So spelled, with one *-t-*—not two. See DOUBLING OF FINAL CONSONANTS.

benefitee. Though it has not yet made its way into most general English-language dictionaries, this word has appeared frequently in American legal prose since the 1950s. The earliest known use is a 1958 case styled (in full) *Liberty Mut. Ins. Co., a Corporation, Individually and as Use Benefitee of The Howell Co., v. Hartford Accident & Indem. Co.*, 251 F.2d 761 (1958). Soon it had spread—e.g.: "This provision, without undermining the liberal scope of interrogatory discovery, places the burden of discovery upon its potential *benefitee*." David W. Louisell, *Modern California Discovery* 124–25 (1963).

The spelling **benefittee* is incorrect (cf. **benefited**) because the accent falls not on the penultimate syllable but on the last syllable. But the word is almost certainly unnecessary for *beneficiary*. See -EE.

benefit of clergy = (1) at common law (12th c.–19th c.), the right of a clergyman not to be tried for a felony in the King's Court; or (2) by SLIPSHOD EXTENSION, religious approval as solemnized in a church ritual. By invoking the benefit of clergy—usually by reading the so-called *neck verse*—a defendant could have the case transferred from the King's Court (which imposed the death penalty for a felony) to the Ecclesiastical Court (which dispensed far milder punishments). See **neck verse.**

In sense 2, the phrase is not only a slipshod extension but also a POPULARIZED LEGAL TECHNICALITY, appearing most often in reference to children out of wedlock—e.g.:

- "With her, and *without benefit of clergy*, he had five children, and it was his boast that, as each arrived, he dispatched it promptly to a foundling home." René A. Wormser, *The Story of the Law* 215 (1962).
- "Wakefield's generation, twenty years on, didn't just engage in sex *without benefit of clergy*, they talked about it." Rhoda Koenig, *Talkin' 'Bout Their Generation*, N.Y. Mag., 1 June 1992, at 57.

bequeath. A. And *devise; devolve.* *Bequeath* = (1) to give (an estate or effect) *to* a person by will <she bequeathed the diadem to her daughter>; or (2) to give (a person) an estate or effect by will <she bequeathed

her daughter the diadem>. Lawyers and nonlawyers alike use this term metaphorically: "While its origins are somewhat obscure, we know that the marital privilege is *bequeathed* to us by the long evolution of the common law, not by constitutional adjudication." *Port v. Heard*, 764 F.2d 423, 430 (5th Cir. 1985). See **legate.**

Devise = to give property (usu. real property) by will. As a noun, *devise* refers to the realty so given—the analogue for personal property is *bequest*. The Uniform Probate Code uses only the term *devise* to describe giving property by will whether the property is real or personal; it would be bootless to call this well-ensconced terminological shift incorrect. See **devise** & **give, devise, and bequeath.**

Devolve = to pass on (an estate, right, liability, or office) from one person to another. In the context of estates, *devolve* usually takes the preposition *upon*, and sometimes *to*. See **devolve.**

B. For *give.* Using *bequeath* as a fancy equivalent of *give* or *present* is an ignorant pretension—e.g.: "Apparently Mayor Annette Strauss plans to *bequeath* [read *present*] the gift personally to Her Majesty—something rarely done, according to protocol experts. Usually, a gift is *bequeathed* [read *presented*] to the queen's secretary, who then *bequeaths* [read *gives*] it to the queen." Helen Bryant, *Names & Faces*, Dallas Times Herald, 5 Apr. 1991, at A2.

bequest, n.; ***bequeathal; *bequeathment.** *Bequest* = (1) the act of bequeathing; or (2) personal property (usu. other than money) disposed of in a will. (Cf. **legacy.**) *Bequest* is sometimes confused with *behest* (= command). See **devise.**

*Bequeathal and **bequeathment* are NEEDLESS VARIANTS of sense 1 of *bequest*—e.g.:

- "We agree that [the statute] is not applicable, since the trust was demonstrative and not a *bequeathal* [read *bequest*] of specific property." *Estate of Naulin v. Clancy*, 201 N.W.2d 599, 603 (Wis. 1972).
- "The testator's preference for his relatives, it is claimed, was evident from . . . the *bequeathment* [read *bequest*] in Article VI." *Estate of Fleer v. Elmhurst Coll.*, 315 N.E.2d 260, 261 (Ill. App. Ct. 1974).

bequest, vb., is obsolete in place of *bequeath*. Today it amounts to no more than a silly error that has appeared in a would-be Shakespearean scholar's writing: "And by so felicitously using the words newly *bequested* [read *bequeathed*] to English, [Shakespeare], more than any other writer of the English Renaissance, validated the efforts of earlier and contemporary neologists." Bryan A. Garner, *Shakespeare's Latinate Neologisms*, 15 Shakespeare Stud. 149, 151 (1982).

bereave, vb., yields past-tense forms *bereft* and *bereaved*, and the same forms as past participles. *Bereaved* is used in reference to loss of relatives by death. *Bereft* is used in reference to loss of incorporeal possessions or qualities.

An asterisk (*) precedes words and phrases that are invariably inferior forms.

To be *bereft of* something is not just to lack it but to have had it taken away. Hence the following uses are incorrect:

- "[The Mann Act] was not designed to cover voluntary actions *bereft of* [read *lacking*] sex commercialism." *Cleveland v. U.S.*, 329 F.S. 14, 17 (1946) (per Douglas, J.).
- "Because the certification was *bereft of* [read *without*] any clue as to the district judge's reasoning, we could merely vacate the order and remand for a fuller evaluation." *Spiegel v. Trustees of Tufts Coll.*, 843 F.2d 38, 44 (1st Cir. 1988).

Berne-plus; Berne-minus. *Berne-plus* = of or relating to a copyright-treaty provision that affords greater intellectual-property protection than the minimum required by the Berne Convention, either by granting stronger rights or by extending protection to new forms of subject matter. The term arose during the negotiations over the TRIPs Agreement, reflecting the principle that the treaty should incorporate and build on existing international law. The WIPO treaties are said to be "Berne-plus" treaties because they incorporate Berne protections and add even more protections of their own. *Berne-minus* = of or relating to a copyright-treaty provision that affords less intellectual-property protection than is required by the Berne Convention. The United States' reluctance to expressly protect moral rights of authors and artists has been criticized as a "Berne-minus" attitude.

beside (= [1] alongside; or [2] in comparison with) is surprisingly often misused for *besides* (= [1] other than; except; or [2] in addition)—e.g.:

- "When we speak of a unilateral contract, we mean a promise in exchange for which an act or something *beside* [read *besides*] another promise has been given as consideration." Clarence D. Ashley, *What Is a Promise in Law?*, 16 Harv. L. Rev. 319, 319 (1903).
- "Hill is the only man *beside* [read *besides*] Trevino to win on the Senior Tour this year." Jaime Diaz, *At Tradition, Duel Falls Short of Hope*, N.Y. Times, 31 Mar. 1990, at 30.

best efforts; reasonable efforts; commercially reasonable efforts; good-faith efforts. The orthodox view is that a contractual provision requiring *best efforts* imposes extraordinary duties of assiduity: a very high standard of care, regardless of whether the required efforts might be commercially unreasonable. A provision requiring *reasonable efforts* is generally thought to impose a lesser standard of diligence. The other two phrases—*commercially reasonable efforts* and *good-faith efforts*—are essentially NEEDLESS VARIANTS of *reasonable efforts*. In truth, both *best efforts* and *reasonable efforts* are vague phrases, and purposely so. The application of these requirements to the actual situation gives the decision-maker a good deal of latitude. As noted, the majority view is for courts to consider *best efforts* as imposing a higher standard than *reasonable efforts*. But others treat the two as synonymous. Perhaps the safest course is, when possible, to use a *best-efforts* provision when insisting on an opposite number's performance—and to use a *reasonable-efforts* provision for one's own client's performance. Yet the phrases are fuzzy, the judicial

decisions irreconcilable, and the effects admittedly uncertain. For a useful analysis of these problems, see Kenneth A. Adams, *A Manual of Style for Contract Drafting* 133–47 (2d ed. 2008).

bet > bet > bet. *Bet* (not *betted) is the preferred and the far more frequent form of the past tense and the past participle. E.g.:

- "Thus, if a person *betted* [read *bet*] on Salisbury Plain there would be no place within the Act." Hugh P. Macmillan, *Law and Other Things* 158 (1938).
- "The defendant, Portner, answered that the consideration for his check to Caldwell was small pieces of celluloid called 'checks' representing money *betted* [read *bet*] and lost by him in a game of chance." *Scolaro v. Bellitto*, 184 N.E.2d 604, 606 (Ohio Ct. App. 1962).

betrothal; *betrothment. The second form is a NEEDLESS VARIANT.

bettor is the standard spelling for "one who bets or wagers." *Better* has also been used in this sense, but is liable to confusion with the comparative form of *good*. Cf. **abettor (A)**.

between. A. And *among*. *Between* is commonly said to be proper with only two things, and *among* with more than two. Ernest Gowers quite properly called this a "superstition." Quoting the *OED*: "In all senses *between* has been, from its earliest appearance, extended to more than two. . . . It is still the only word available to express the relation of a thing to many surrounding things severally and individually; *among* expresses a relation to them collectively and vaguely: we should not say *the space lying among the three points* or *a treaty among three Powers*" (*MEU2* 57).

The rule as generally enunciated, then, is simplistic. Although it is an accurate guide for the verb *divide* (*between* with two objects, *among* with more than two), the only ironclad distinction is that stated by the *OED*: *between* expresses one-to-one relations of many things, and *among* expresses collective and undefined relations.

So Article VII of the U.S. Constitution uses *between* seemingly to express reciprocal relations: "The Ratification of the Conventions of nine States, shall be sufficient for the Establishment of this Constitution *between* the States so ratifying the Same."

Yet even the more valid distinction is a relatively new one, not observed by the English courts in 1607: "All the Justices, viz., POPHAM, Chief Justice of England, COKE, Chief Justice of the Common Pleas, FLEMING, Chief Baron, FENNER, SEARL, YELVERTON, WILLIAMS, and TANFIELD, JJ., were assembled at Sergeants-Inn, to consult what prerogative the King had in digging and taking of saltpetre to make gunpowder by the law of the realm; and upon conference *between* them, these points were resolved by them all, una voce." *The Case of the King's Prerogative in Saltpetre*, 12 Co. 12 (1607).

In the same case in which Justice Thurgood Marshall several times wrote: "*among* the defendant, the forum, and the litigation," Justice Brennan, in his concurring and dissenting opinion, writes: "*between* the controversy, the parties, and the forum state." *See Shaffer v. Heitner*, 433 U.S. 186, 225 (1977). The latter phrasing might be said to express a more specific individual relation between the named things, the former phrasing (perhaps consciously) expressing a somewhat vaguer relation.

B. *Between* and Numbers. The word *between* may cause problems when used with numbers, particularly if the numbers at either end of the spectrum are intended to be included. E.g.:

- "It is estimated that *between 1 and 3 percent* of the population has an IQ *between 70 and 75* [read *from 70 to 75*] or lower, which is typically considered the cutoff IQ score for the intellectual function prong of the mental-retardation definition." *Atkins v. Virginia*, 536 U.S. 304, 309 n.5 (2002) (per Stevens, J.). "Between one and three" is precisely two.
- "If an employee had completed *between one and five years* [read *from one to five years*] of service with the company, the paid medical benefits would cease on the last day of the third month after the termination occurred." *Communication Workers of Am., AFL-CIO v. Verizon Commun., Inc.*, 255 F.Supp.2d 479, 482–83 (E.D. Pa. 2003).

When you intend to refer to a range of possibilities from a low point to a high point, *from . . . to*, *between . . . and*, or *to* alone is the correct form, not **between . . . to*.

C. *Between you and me*; **between you and I*. Because the pronouns following *between* are objects of the preposition, the correct phrase is *between you and me*. Yet the phrasing **between you and I* is appallingly common: "a grammatical error of unsurpassable grossness," as one commentator puts it. Interestingly, this mistake is committed almost exclusively by educated speakers trying a little too hard to sound refined but stumbling badly. It's almost surely an ingrained instance of hypercorrection based on childhood admonitions not to use *you and me* (or similar compounds) as the subject of the sentence and, what is far more confusing to most people, as a predicate nominative in sentences such as *it is I*. See PRONOUNS (B) & HYPERCORRECTION (B).

D. *Between*; *as between*. Sometimes *as between* (= comparing; in comparison of) is misused for the straightforward preposition. E.g.: "The issue was moot *as between* [read *between*] these parties." *Irwin R. Evens & Son, Inc. v. Bd. of Indianapolis Airport Auth.*, 584 N.E.2d 576, 582 (Ind. Ct. App. 1992). Cf. **as against.**

E. **Between each* and Other Constructions with Fewer than Two Objects. This phrasing is a peculiar brand of ILLOGIC, as in *between each house* or *between each speech* (instead of, properly, *between every two houses* and *between speeches*). Another manifestation of this error is **between . . . or*, with two prepositional objects, rather than *between . . . and*: the misuse results

from confusion between *either . . . or* and *between . . . and*.

between Scylla and Charybdis. See **Scylla and Charybdis, between.**

be upstanding. See **all rise.**

BE-VERBS. A. Wrongly Omitted in Nonfinite Uses. *Be*-verbs, usually in the infinitive or participial form, are often omitted from sentences in which they would add clarity. One explanation is that they are intended to be "understood." (See UNDERSTOOD WORDS.) But this explanation does not excuse the ambiguity and awkwardness often resulting from such omissions. The bracketed verbs in the sentences following were originally omitted:

- "If I thought those two cases [*to be*] in point I should have to consider them very carefully, but I do not." *Wenmoth v. Wenmoth*, [1885] L.R. 37 (C.D.).
- "The annotation necessarily starts with the assumption that the process or information involved was regarded as [*being*] of a secret or confidential nature." L.S. Tellier, *Implied Obligation of Employee Not to Use Trade Secrets or Confidential Information for His Own Benefit or That of Third Persons After Leaving the Employment*, 165 A.L.R. 1453 (1946).
- "'Interception' [*requires*] the use of any electronic, mechanical, or other device. Specifically designated as not [*being*] such devices are telephone or telegraph equipment . . . ." Frank Miller, *Cases and Materials on Criminal Justice Administration* 369 (1986).

B. Circumlocutions with *Be*-Verbs. Verb phrases containing *be*-verbs are often merely roundabout ways of saying something better said with a simple verb. So *be determinative of* for *determine* is verbose. But *be determinative* is all right where there is no object, as here: "It follows that all such attempts are illusory; and, if serviceable at all, are so only to center attention upon which one of the factors may *be determinative* in any given situation." *Moisan v. Loftus*, 178 F.2d 148, 149 (2d Cir. 1950) (per L. Hand, J.).

The following circumlocutory uses of *be*-verbs are common in legal writing, the simple verb ordinarily being preferred:

be abusive of (*abuse*)
be applicable to (*apply to*)
be amendatory of (*amend*)
be applicable to (*apply to*)
be benefited by (*benefit from*)
be conducive to (*conduce to*)
be decisive of (*decide*)
be derived from (*derive from*)
be desirous of (*desire* or *want*)
be determinative of (*determine*)
be dispositive of (*dispose of*)
be in agreement (*agree*)
be in attendance (*attend*)

be indicative of (*indicate*)
be in dispute (*dispute* or *disagree*)
be in error (*err*)
be in exercise of due care (*exercise due care*)
be in existence (*exist*)
be influential on (*influence*)
be in possession of (*possess*)
be in receipt of (*have received*)
be in violation of (*violate*)
be operative (*operate*)
be persuasive of (*persuade*)
be possessed of (*possess*)
be probative of (*prove*)
be productive of (*produce*)
be promotive of (*promote*)
be supportive of (*support*)
be violative of (*violate*)

Many such wordy constructions are more naturally phrased in the present-tense singular: *is able to* (can), *is authorized to* (may), *is binding upon* (binds), *is empowered to* (may), *is unable to* (cannot).

C. Used Unidiomatically in Place of Action Verbs. Always prefer the specific verb that conveys the idea of the action described over an unspecific *be*-verb: "Some of these rules *are* [read *require*] that a statute shall be so construed as to effect the plain and manifest purpose and intention of the Legislature in enacting it." *Goodpaster v. U.S. Mortg. Bond Co.*, 192 S.W. 35, 37 (Ky. 1917).

beyond a reasonable doubt. See **balance of probability.**

beyond cavil. See **cavil, beyond.**

beyond the pale. See **pale, beyond the.**

beyond the shadow of a doubt. See **shadow of a doubt, beyond the.**

BFP = bona fide purchaser. Though the abbreviation is an initialism and not an acronym, the periods are customarily omitted—e.g.: "Having thus failed to comply with federal law, the Bank is hardly in a position to claim the advantageous status of a *BFP* without notice." *First Nat'l Bank v. Lewco Secs. Corp.*, 860 F.2d 1407, 1414 (7th Cir. 1988).

***biannual.** See **biennial** (A).

BIBLICAL AFFECTATION. In many respects the language of the law resembles the language of the King James Version (1611) or of Shakespeare. It is full of the ARCHAISMS we associate either with the Bible or, less commonly, with Shakespeare. As late as the 1980s, the Supreme Court of Mississippi published a sentence containing *doth*, which many readers have encountered only in traditional versions of the Bible. Likewise, *hath* and *hast* appear occasionally in drafting (of a mediocre kind). Courts still occasionally use the Elizabethan ***burthen**, as a variant of *burden*, though it has not been current for several centuries. And much of the syntax of legal prose is biblical: "A

lawyer may never give unsolicited advice to a layman that he retain a client." See ***burthen, doth** & **that** (C).

Even today one can open up law reports and read of a *bounden duty*, as in the line from the *Book of Common Prayer* ("We beseech thee to accept this our *bounden duty* and service.")—e.g.: "It is enough for this purpose that valiant efforts were made to persuade the district to do voluntarily what the United States Supreme Court and the California Supreme Court had held was its *bounden duty*." *Los Angeles Branch NAACP v. Los Angeles Unified Sch. Dist.*, 750 F.2d 731, 752 (9th Cir. 1984) (Pregerson, J., concurring). The origins of the phrase were legal and not religious, but today "when we say *bounden duty* we do not call in any way to mind the bond [that] tied the feudal underling to his lord or the apprentice to his master." Jocelyn Simon, *English Idioms from the Law* (pt. 1), 76 Law Q. Rev. 283, 285 (1960).

Though traditions die hard, these linguistic anachronisms ought not to be perpetuated. They needlessly widen the rift between what is legal and what is lay and unwholesomely lend the air of priestly sanctity to the legal profession. Even the terms *lay* and *legal* used as opposites, much like *lay* and *ecclesiastical*, conjure up this notion; but they are not easily avoided.

It is worth adding to this discussion that citing the Bible as legal precedent is not an admirable practice. Justice Benjamin Cardozo once wrote, "In days not far remote, judges were not unwilling to embellish their deliverances with quotations from the poets. I shall observe toward such a practice the tone of decent civility that is due those departed." *Law and Literature*, 52 Harv. L. Rev. 471, 484 (1939). Yet, even in as religiously diverse a society as the U.S., the practice of quoting from the Bible has persisted. For example:

> [As] far as money buried or secreted on privately owned realty is concerned, the old distinction between treasure-trove, lost property, and mislaid property seems to be of little value and not worth preserving. The principal point of distinction seems to be the intent of the true owner who necessarily is not known and not available. Therefore the evidence on his intent will usually be scant and uncontroverted. . . . I would guess his motivation often to be that of the one-talent servant in the parable in the 25th Chapter of Matthew: "And I was afraid, and went and hid thy talent in the earth . . . ." We should hold that the owner of the land has possession of all property secreted in, on and under his land and continues to hold possession for the true owner, who, incidentally, may not always be the person doing any burying. Matthew 13:44—"Again, the kingdom of heaven is like unto treasure hid in a field; the which when a man hath found, he hideth, and for joy thereof goeth and selleth all that he hath, and buyeth that field." What reason is there for transferring possession to the individual who happens to dig up the property? Or for guessing about the intent or the memory of the person doing the burying? A simple solution for all of these problems is to maintain the continuity of possession of the landowner until the true owner establishes his title.
>
> *Schley v. Couch*, 284 S.W.2d 333, 339–40 (Tex. 1955) (Wilson, J., concurring).

The thing speaks for itself.

bicentennial; bicentenary. See **centennial.**

bid (= to offer a bid) forms *bid* in the past tense. E.g.:

- "The defendant *bid* for the wrong property at an auction sale." William F. Walsh, *A Treatise on Equity* 479 (1930).
- "The tax is computed on the amount *bid* for the property." Robert Kratovil, *Real Estate Law* 48 (1946).

In the sense of *bid farewell* (= to wish someone well upon parting), the past tense is *bade*, rhyming with *glad*, and the past participle is *bidden*—e.g.:

- "If the servant never reads it, but simply delivers it as he was *bidden*, then he is not liable to any action." William Blake Odgers, *A Digest of the Law of Libel and Slander* 161 (1881).
- "Though she did as she was *bidden* and took hold of the child's hand, she did what she could to prevent the child from being hurt." John H. Wigmore, *The Legal System of Old Japan*, 4 Green Bag 478, 480 (1892).

But which past tense is correct in the phrase *to bid fair* (= to seem likely)—is it *bid fair* or *bade fair*? Writers have used both—e.g.:

- "Judicial decision as an agency of legal growth *bade fair* to become sterile." Roscoe Pound, *The Formative Era of American Law* 70 (1938).
- "Certainly the action of *indebitatis assumpsit bid fair* to overtake, at one time or another, most of the other forms of action." J.H. Baker, *An Introduction to English Legal History* 420 (3d ed. 1990).

The *OED* records only *bade fair*, the better form.

bid, n.; **tender,** n. In AmE, both terms are used, whereas in BrE only the latter would appear, in the sense "a submitted price at which one will perform work or supply goods."

biennial, A. And *biannual; semiannual. *Biennial* means "occurring once every two years." *Semiannual* and *biannual both mean "occurring twice a year." The distinctions become important, for example, when employment contracts provide for "*biannual* meetings of the committee to dispose of accident and bonus questions, and any other grievances." *Smith v. Kerrville Bus Co.*, 748 F.2d 1049, 1052 (5th Cir. 1984). It is imprudent to rely on a word like *biannual for such a contractual provision: stick to *semiannual* and *biennial.*

B. And *triennial*, etc. If we scale the numerical summit, we have *triennial* (3), *quadrennial* (4), *quin-quennial* (5), *sexennial* (6), *septennial* (7), *octennial* (8), *novennial* (9), *decennial* (10), *vicennial* (20), *centennial* (100), and *millennial* (1,000).

bigamy; polygamy; *digamy; deuterogamy. *Bigamy* = going through a marriage ceremony with someone when one is already lawfully married to someone else (*CDL*). It may be committed knowingly or unknowingly; if knowing, *bigamy* is a criminal offense.

*Digamy and *deuterogamy* both mean "a legal second marriage occurring after an annulment or a divorce from or the death of the first spouse." *Deuter-ogamy* is the more common term (to the extent that either might be called common!) and is not, like *digamy, liable to confusion with *bigamy*. Hence *digamy should be considered a NEEDLESS VARIANT.

Polygamy is the generic term for "multiple marriages," and encompasses *bigamy*; it is much used by anthropologists, describing both *polygyny* (the practice of having several wives) and *polyandry* (the practice of having several husbands).

big-gun lawyer. See LAWYERS, DEROGATORY NAMES FOR (A).

bilateral contract; unilateral contract. A *unilateral contract* is one in which a promise is given by one party in exchange for the actual performance by the other party. A *bilateral contract* is one in which each party promises a performance, so that each party is an obligor on his own promise and an obligee on the other's promise.

It is a legal solecism to use *unilateral contract* to mean a promise for which no consideration was requested, or for which no sufficient consideration was given. Instead, the phrase "should be reserved for cases in which a legal obligation has been created, but only one party to the obligation has made a promise." 1 Samuel Williston & W.H.E. Jaeger, *A Treatise on the Law of Contracts* § 13, at 26 (3d ed. 1957). If the transaction does not result in a legal obligation, *unilateral offer* or *unilateral promise* may describe the transaction, but not *unilateral contract. Id.* See **synallagmatic contract.**

bill = (1) a formal written complaint, such as a court paper requesting some specific action for reasons alleged; (2) a pleading or court paper in equity, such as a *bill of certiorari*, a *bill of discovery*, a *bill in interpleader*, a *bill of peace*, or a *bill of review*; (3) a legislative proposal offered for debate before its enactment; (4) loosely, an enacted statute; (5) an invoice; or (6) a bill of exchange, i.e., an unconditional order in writing, addressed by one person to another, signed by the person giving it, requiring the addressee to pay on demand, or at a particular future time, a sum certain in money to or to the order of a specified person or to bearer. With such an array of meanings, *bill* is classifiable as a CHAMELEON-HUED WORD. See **suit.**

billa vera. See **true bill.**

bill in chancery; bill in equity. See **chancery.**

billingsgate. See **abuse,** n.

billion. In the U.S. and France, *billion* means "one thousand millions" (= 1,000,000,000); but in G.B., Canada, and Germany, it means "one million millions" (= 1,000,000,000,000). An American *trillion* equals the British *billion.* In BrE, however, the AmE meaning is gaining ground especially in journalism, technical writing, and government statements about finance. See **trillion.**

bill of exchange. Blackstone defined this phrase as "an open letter of request from one man to another, desiring him to pay a sum (of money) named therein, to a third person on his account." 2 William Blackstone, *Commentaries on the Laws of England* 466 (1766). The modern definition has one additional important aspect—negotiability. So a *bill of exchange* has long been held to be "an open letter of request, addressed by one person to a second, desiring him to pay a sum of money to a third, or to any other, to whom that third person shall order it to be paid; or it may be payable to Bearer." Joseph Story, *Commentaries on the Law of Bills of Exchange* 4 (4th ed. 1860). Cf. **check.**

bill of indictment. See **indictment.**

bill of lading. See **lading, bill of.**

bill of particulars; motion for more definite statement. In 1948, the Federal Rules of Civil Procedure were amended to abolish the *bill of particulars*, which was superseded by the *motion for more definite statement.* The latter allows a party who must respond to a pleading to ask the court to require the other party to refile a vague or ambiguous pleading. In several jurisdictions, though, the *bill of particulars* remains in current practice.

bill of rights = a section or addendum, usu. in a constitution, that defines the situations in which a politically organized society will permit free, spontaneous, and individual activity, and that assures members of the society that government powers will not be used in certain ways. The most famous such document is the *Bill of Rights* (conventionally capitalized) of the U.S. Constitution. But England also had a *Bill of Rights of 1689*, which established that the government could not raise revenue without parliamentary authorization.

Does this phrase *Bill of Rights* refer to the first eight or the first ten amendments to the U.S. Constitution? Scholars don't agree. *See* Akhil Reed Amar, *The Bill of Rights* 183–84 & n. (2000); Geoffrey R. Stone, Richard A. Epstein & Cass R. Sunstein, *The Bill of Rights in the Modern State* 541 (1992). But in common usage, all ten are included.

bind = to impose a legal duty on (a person or institution). So courts are said to be *bound* by precedent, and persons who have signed contracts are said to be contractually *bound.*

binder = (1) in property law, a document in which the seller and the buyer of real property declare their common intention to bring about a transfer of ownership, usu. accompanied by the buyer's initial payment; (2) loosely, the buyer's initial payment in the sale of real property; or (3) *in insurance*, an insurer's memorandum giving the insured temporary coverage while the application for an insurance policy is being processed.

binding precedent. See **precedent (B).**

bite at the apple, one. See **one bite at the apple.**

bite at the cherry, one. See **one bite at the apple.**

biweekly; semiweekly. Strictly speaking, *biweekly* = every two weeks, *semiweekly* = twice a week. But because *biweekly* is so commonly used to mean "twice a week," the term is best avoided as ambiguous.

Blackacre is the proverbial example of real estate in hypothetical property problems. Abutting tracts are usually called *Whiteacre, Brownacre,* or some other colorized denomination. These terms have long been a part of the common-law tradition:

- "Where a devise is of *blackacre* to A and of *whiteacre* to B in tail, and if they both die without issue, then to C in fee, here A and B have cross remainders by implication." 2 William Blackstone, *Commentaries on the Laws of England* 381 (1766).
- "The world of bar law is a peculiar place. Every house has a name, usually *Blackacre* or *Whiteacre*." Stephen Labaton, *At the Bar*, 18 Aug. 1989, at 20.

blackletter law. *Black-letter* is a term that describes Gothic or Old English type in antiquated books <black-letter type>. (The word is usually hyphenated in nonlegal contexts relating to typography—but see the final paragraph.) From 1482 to 1679, the medieval Year Books were printed in so-called *Black Letter editions*, which were printed in a heavy Gothic type (and which contain many errors).

By extension the term came to be applied to legal principles that are fundamental and well settled, or statements of such principles in a quasi-mathematical form, because such principles were traditionally printed in boldface type in lawbooks. Law students frequently distinguish between professors with a predilection for *blackletter law* (what the law is) and those whose interest lies more in public policy (why the law is or what it ought to be). See **Blackstone lawyer** & **hornbook law.**

Formerly hyphenated, legal writers have conveniently merged the phrase into a solid word—e.g.:

- "Robinson correctly stated the general understanding as of 1939 in *blackletter* text." Grant Gilmore & Charles L. Black Jr., *The Law of Admiralty* 342 (2d ed. 1975).
- "The format of *blackletter* rule and explanatory comment, familiar from real Restatements, is well suited to its purpose." Douglas Laycock, *The Death of the Irreparable Injury Rule* 266 (1991).

blackmail referred originally to rent payable in cattle, labor, or coin other than silver (i.e., *white money*). Then it came to denote, especially in Scotland, a kind of protection money: payment that robbers extorted from landowners for exemption from their raids. Today the word applies to any menacing demand made without justification—i.e., to illegal extortion generally.

Since at least the late 19th century, the word has been a verb as well as a noun—e.g.: "Thus often arises secret intimidation, enforced confessions, and *blackmailed* pleas of guilty. These sinister dangers were extinguished from the Common Law of England more than six centuries ago." 1 Winston Churchill, *A History of the English Speaking Peoples* 223 (1956).

Blackstonean. The adjective is preferably so spelled. Some writers ill-advisedly make it *Blackstonian*.

Blackstone lawyer = (1) a lawyer with a broad knowledge of blackletter principles; (2) a self-educated lawyer, esp. in antebellum America, whose legal training consists primarily of reading William Blackstone's *Commentaries on the Laws of England*. Sense 2 usually appears in historical contexts—e.g.: "For every Jefferson devoting five full years to legal training, scores of '*Blackstone lawyers*' entered the profession after a few months of study, self-proclaimed masters of one text." Robert A. Ferguson, *Law and Letters in American Culture* 29 (1984). For an example from the writings of Thomas Jefferson, see LAWYERS, DEROGATORY NAMES FOR (A).

blamable. See **blameworthy (B)**.

***blamableness.** See **blameworthiness**.

blame, vb. In the best usage, one *blames* a person or cause *for* something; one does not, in the traditional idiom, *blame* a thing *on* a person or cause. E.g.:

- "Those cases generally failed because the personal-injury claims attempted to *blame non-specific physical symptoms, such as 'chronic fatigue syndrome,' on a range of building conditions* [read *blame a range of building conditions for non-specific physical symptoms such as 'chronic fatigue syndrome'*]." Kevin R. Sido et al., *Architect and Engineer Liability* 62 (2010).
- "I'm sure Mr. Shaw will find some way to *blame this whole debacle on conservatives* [read *blame conservatives for this whole debacle*]." Letter of Jeff Bishop, Ariz. Atty., Jan. 2011, at 8.

See **censure**.

blameful. See **blameworthy (B)**.

blameworthiness; *blamableness. The second is a NEEDLESS VARIANT—e.g.: "The only rational basis for allowing recovery in tort seems to be *blamableness* [read *blameworthiness*]." C.B. Whittier, *Mistake in the Law of Torts*, 15 Harv. L. Rev. 335, 335 (1902).

blameworthy. A. And *culpable*. Though the two words are etymologically equivalent, in 20th- and 21st-century usage the Anglo-Saxon *blameworthy* has tended to appear in noncriminal contexts, the Latinate *culpable* in criminal contexts. Hence *blameworthy* in civil contexts:

- "The indemnitee's conduct is sufficiently *blameworthy* to preclude indemnity." *Bass v. Phoenix Seadrill/78, Ltd.*, 749 F.2d 1154, 1168 (5th Cir. 1985).
- "That finding does not address whether tenants' conduct was sufficiently *blameworthy* that it is appropriate to deny them fees entirely on the claims on which they prevailed

or whether landlord's conduct was sufficiently reasonable that it is appropriate to reach the same result." *Barbara Parmenter Living Trust v. Lemon*, 194 P.3d 796, 803 (Or. 2008).

- "The Court created a new maritime law rule that punitive damages may not exceed compensatory damages in cases in which the defendant's conduct, while sufficiently *blameworthy* to deserve civil punishment, was not actuated by avarice or the purpose of inflicting injury." David W. Robertson & Michael F. Sturley, *Recent Developments in Admiralty and Maritime Law at the National Level and in the Fifth and Eleventh Circuits*, 33 Tul. Mar. L.J. 381, 389 (2009).

And *culpable* in criminal contexts:

- "The issue before us is whether the defense of mistake of fact is available as a defense to negate the *culpable* mental state of criminal negligence." *Williams v. State*, 680 S.W.2d 570, 579 (Tex. App.—Corpus Christi 1984).
- "It is reasonable to presume that the sentencing judge who revokes probation takes a fresh look at the defendant's *culpability* and circumstances and considers at that point in the proceedings the amount of time the defendant should be required to serve." *Ochoa v. Lennon*, 750 F.2d 1345, 1348 (5th Cir. 1985).
- "The foggy conditions that occasioned the accident itself do little to mitigate the Defendant's *culpability*, as it was the Defendant's subsequent flight from the scene that actually gave rise to the criminal charge now before us." *State v. Davenport*, 967 So.2d 563, 566 (La. Ct. App. 2007).

See **guilty**.

Occasionally, however, *culpability* creeps into civil contexts, as here in the context of punitive damages, a hybrid remedy: "[Exemplary damages] are awarded, however, only in cases of extreme *culpability* and are limited to the plaintiff's demonstrable litigation expenses." *Northwestern Nat'l Cas. Co. v. McNulty*, 307 F.2d 432, 436 (5th Cir. 1962). Nevertheless, the writer of that sentence was describing egregious conduct, and *blameworthiness* today hardly seems appropriate for flagrant conduct.

B. And *blameful*; *blamable*. *Blameworthy* and *blamable* both mean "deserving to be blamed," the second being a NEEDLESS VARIANT. *Blameful* (= imputing blame; blaming) has been mistakenly used for *blameworthy*. We need not use up more words for the meaning replicated by *blameworthy* and *blamable*. Cf. **certworthy** & **enbancworthy**.

blawg. See **blog**.

BLENDS. See PORTMANTEAU WORDS.

bloc; block. Political groups or alignments are *blocs*. *Block* serves in all other senses.

blog; weblog; blawg. A *blog*, an aphaeretic shortening of *weblog*, is a website formatted as a personal journal that is usually open to public viewing and comment. *Weblog* was coined in 1995 and shortened to *blog* in 1999. A blog devoted to commenting on or discussing the law and legal issues is sometimes called by the homophonic pun *blawg*, first used in 2002 by an intellectual-property lawyer, Denise Howell. E.g.:

- "Because his *blog* deals with law-related matters, it fits into the subcategory of *blawgs*." Jason Krause, *For the Tech Savvy, the Buzzword Is Blawg*, 1 No. 39 A.B.A. J. E-Report 4 (11 Oct. 2002).
- "Throughout these lengthy proceedings, the judge has offered nothing at all to justify his actions—not a case, not a statute, not a bankruptcy treatise, not a law-review article, not a student note, not even a *blawg*." *In re Complaint of Judicial Misconduct*, 425 F.3d 1179, 1195 (9th Cir. 2005).
- "The [iPad] app features breaking legal news updated continuously every business day, all of the monthly magazine's in-depth articles, and the latest *blawgs* featured in the [ABA] Journal's directory of more than 2,500 legal *blogs*." Darla W. Jackson, *The Year of the iPad?*, 102 Law Lib. J. 513, 516 (2010).

Blog is also used as a verb meaning "to update, maintain, or contribute to a blog."

blood spatter; blood splatter. Although one is tempted to call the semantic differences a bloody mess, let's be more sanguine. A *spatter* is an accidental sprinkling or slight splash of liquid. A *splatter* is a patch or spot of color splashed onto a surface. The first word connotes small or light drops or a small number of them, while the other suggests heavier or more numerous drops. Most legal (and medical) writers, however, usually ignore these differences. *Blood spatter*, which is preferred in AmE and BrE alike, has been used since the 18th century to indicate the presence of drops of blood at a crime scene. E.g.:

- "There was a *blood spatter* 10 x 4 inches on the headboard, about 6 inches from where the head lay." O.J. Brown, *A Case of Double Homicide*, 140 Boston Med. & Surgical J. 301, 302 (1899).
- "There was *blood spatter* throughout the basement." *State v. Rosales*, 998 A.2d 459, 461 (N.J. 2010).
- "Jessica said defendant came to her apartment after midnight the night of the Cross murder with '*blood spatters*, little specks of blood' on his chest and left arm." *People v. Alexander*, 235 P.3d 873, 895 (Cal. 2010).

At least one writer has asserted an additional reason to prefer *spatter*: "'*Blood spatter*' should not be confused with '*blood splatter*.' *Spatter* means to scatter (a liquid) in drops or small splashes; *splatter* has no forensic meaning." James E. Girard, *Criminalistics: Forensic Science and Crime* 38 (2007).

Blood splatter, rare until the 1990s, is now about half as common as *spatter*, even among experts—e.g.:

- "[A criminalist] explained that blood 'smears' result from contact with a bloody object, in contrast to blood '*splatter*,' which is caused by the deposit of airborne blood droplets." *People v. Lewis*, 210 P.3d 1119, 1132 (Cal. 2009).
- "Baden said the killer should have *blood splatter* on his clothes, while Spitz said the killer could have left the scene clean of blood due to the killer's position during the attacks." John J. Miletich et al., *An Introduction to the Work of a Medical Examiner* 26 (2010).
- "Stone testified there were *blood splatters* on the headboard and computer monitor in Dorff's bedroom, both of which

were approximately two and a half feet from Dorff's head." *Tweed v. State*, 779 N.W.2d 667, 669 (N.D. 2010).

blot on title. See **cloud on title.**

blow hot and cold = to take mutually contradictory positions or put forward contradictory views.

- "The plaintiff is *blowing hot and cold* in this case; if we follow him in this latter position, why then he loses the case on the merits." *Hall v. Keller*, 80 F.Supp. 763, 774 (W.D. La. 1948).
- "Inconsistent allegations can be made in separate claims or defenses under F.R.C.P. 8(e)(2); but no authority is known to the undersigned [that] permits *blowing hot and cold* in the same cause of action, as attempted by the proposed amendment." *Steiner v. Twentieth Century-Fox Film Corp.*, 140 F.Supp. 906, 908 (S.D. Cal. 1953).
- "The theory of attack by prior inconsistent statements is not based on the assumption that the present testimony is false and the former statement is true, but rather upon the notion that talking one way on the stand and another way previously is *blowing hot and cold*, and raises a doubt as to the truthfulness of both statements." Charles T. McCormick et al., *Evidence* § 34, at 74 (3d ed. 1984).
- "The theory of attack by prior inconsistent statements is not based on the assumption that the present testimony is false and the former statement true, but rather upon the notion that talking one way on the stand and another way previously is *blowing hot and cold*." *Hernandez v. State*, 273 S.W.3d 685, 689 (Tex. Crim. App. 2008).

For an amusing example of blowing hot and cold, see **Codd's Puzzle.**

blue book = (1) in G.B., a printed report (as of a Royal Commission) presented to Parliament and traditionally softbound in blue covers; (2) in some American states, a compilation of session laws; (3) a volume formerly published to give parallel citation tables for a volume in the National Reporter System; (4) (cap.) the formal name for the citation guide, formerly called *A Uniform System of Citation* (usu. written *Bluebook*); or (5) a stapled notebook with blue covers and usu. with ruled pages, traditionally used for essay answers in law-school examinations.

For more terms connected with sense 1, see **White Paper.**

blue-pencil test = a judicial standard sometimes applied by a court considering an illegal contractual provision and deciding whether to invalidate the entire contract or only the offending words, the standard consisting in whether it would be possible to sever the offending words simply by running a blue pencil through them, as opposed to changing, adding, or rearranging words. E.g.:

- "Despite such criticisms, numerous jurisdictions have presented meritorious justifications for requiring a strict application of the '*blue pencil*' *test*." *Holloway v. Faw, Casson & Co.*, 552 A.2d 1311, 1325 (Md. Ct. Spec. App. 1989).
- "It used to be thought that promises could be severed merely because the '*blue pencil*' *test* was satisfied; but this view no longer prevails. The test may restrict, but it does not determine, the scope of the doctrine of severance." G.H. Treitel, *The Law of Contract* 449 (8th ed. 1991).

blue-sky laws. In the early 20th century, *blue sky* meant "an unsound investment, esp. in fake securities." Hence laws designed to protect gullible investors in securities have been given the name *blue-sky laws*. The phrase is used in BrE as well as in AmE—in the latter, usually in reference to state laws.

As casual JARGON, *blue-sky* (usu. hyphenated) has been transformed into a verb meaning "to approve (the sale of securities) in accordance with *blue-sky* laws." The form of the verb is almost always past tense or past participle—e.g.: "This solicitation and purchase was unlawful under California law because it had not been *blueskyed*." *Hecht v. Harris, Upham & Co.*, 283 F.Supp. 417, 443 (N.D. Cal. 1968). Less commonly, the past-participial adjective means "having blue-sky laws" <blue-skyed states>. See NOUNS AS VERBS.

blunderbuss (= an obsolete firearm that scatters shot and is intended for close-range shooting) is often used figuratively in legal contexts. E.g.:

- "Since double payments can be prevented by a letter or a telephone call, it is unreasonable to accomplish this objective by the *blunderbuss* method of denying assistance to all indigent newcomers for an entire year." *Shapiro v. Thompson*, 394 U.S. 618, 637 (1969) (per Brennan, J.).
- "This claim—on which every serious constitutional question turns—was pleaded in the following *blunderbuss* fashion in each of the complaints." *Elliott v. Perez*, 751 F.2d 1472, 1475 (5th Cir. 1985).
- "Plaintiffs are still unable to provide a comprehensible statement of facts to support their *blunderbuss* approach to the law . . . ." *Kazenercom TOO v. Turan Petroleum, Inc.*, 590 F.Supp.2d 153, 156 (D.D.C. 2008).
- "This court's inquiry was insufficiently nuanced, for such a *blunderbuss* attack on all process technologies is not needed to serve the asserted special needs of information industries." *Cardiac Pacemakers, Inc. v. St. Jude Med., Inc.*, 576 F.3d 1348, 1374 (Fed. Cir. 2009) (Newman, J., concurring in part & dissenting in part).

The more recent sense of *blunderbuss* (= a blundering person) has nothing to do with this sense. The term is infrequently misspelled **blunderbus*.

Sometimes the equivalent *shotgun* or *scatter-gun* is used: "Appellate counsel must recognize that *scatter-gun* contentions are doomed to failure." *Pruitt v. City of Chicago*, 472 F.3d 925, 930 (7th Cir. 2006).

blush, at first. See **at first blush.**

bodily heirs; heirs of the body; *body heirs. The first and second are the classic formulations of the phrase, both unobjectionable. **Body heirs* is much inferior to *bodily heirs* for two reasons: first, generally we should not use a noun adjectivally when we have a serviceable adjective; and second, **body heirs* is so little used that it grates on the legally trained ear.

body corporate is a variant of *corporation* that emphasizes the entity and the members that make it up rather than the abstract notion (*corporation*); *body corporate* is now used more commonly in BrE than in AmE. E.g.: "A *body corporate* cannot be appointed receiver." J. Charlesworth, *The Principles of Company Law* 175 (4th ed. 1945).

*body heirs. See **bodily heirs** & **heir.**

bogus check. See **check, worthless.**

boilerplate [fr. the newspaper business, in which it originally referred to syndicated material in mat or plate form] = (1) ready-made or all-purpose language that will fit in a variety of documents; or (2) fixed or standardized language that is not subject to modification. Sense 1 expresses the lawyer's usual understanding; sense 2 expresses the nonlawyer's common understanding.

The term first entered American legal usage in the 1950s and is today commonly used either as a noun or as an adjective (in phrases such as *boilerplate clause* and *boilerplate language*). The earliest known legal example appeared in Ohio: "After what appears to be the ordinary '*boilerplate*' reference to payment of debts, taxes and costs of administration, the testatrix in the case at bar gave more than usual attention to arrangements in connection with her last rites." *In re Estate of Carrington*, 136 N.E.2d 182, 185 (Ohio Prob. Ct. 1956).

The word is best spelled as one word in AmE. In BrE, it is commonly hyphenated (*boiler-plate*). For an example of boilerplate language, see **attestation clause.**

bolster = (of a courtroom lawyer) to build up a witness's credibility in anticipation of impeachment—a practice generally disallowed by American evidentiary rules. E.g.:

- "The prosecutor may not, among other things, make explicit personal assurances that a witness is trustworthy or implicitly *bolster* the witness by indicating that information not presented to the jury supports the testimony." *U.S. v. Lewis*, 10 F.3d 1086, 1089 (4th Cir. 1993).
- "Attempts to *bolster* a witness by vouching for his credibility are normally improper and an error." *U.S. v. Baptista-Rodriguez*, 17 F.3d 1354, 1372 (11th Cir. 1994).

bombastic is sometimes misconstrued to mean "strident" or "violent." Properly, *bombastic* (lit., "full of stuffing or padding") means "pompous; highfalutin; overblown." The error seems to be on the rise—e.g.:

- "Books about violence published by ISAI appear with loud covers (usually illustrated with raging flames), have a somewhat *bombastic* [read *terroristic* or *incendiary*] title, and use journalistic language and photos of events to urge readers to enter the atmosphere of the violence." Charles A. Coppel, *Violent Conflicts in Indonesia* 209 (2006).
- "The *bombastic* and combative style of Robert Muldoon was itself alienating, even frightening." David Erdos, *Aversive Constitutionalism in the Westminster World*, 5 Int'l J. Const. L. 343, 364 (2007).

- "Haney's tour-de-force analysis of the *bombastic* reign of crime-oriented media leaves no stone unturned." Emily Hughes, *Introduction to a Frank Conversation*, 58 DePaul L. Rev. 591, 595 (2009).

But the misunderstanding is all too common, perhaps because *bombastic* suggests *bomb*.

bona et catalla is the archaic LATINISM from which, by LOAN TRANSLATION, derives the DOUBLET *goods and chattels*.

bona fide. A. And *good-faith*, adj. *Bona fide,* adj., is understood by educated speakers of English; as a legal term, it is unlikely to give way completely to *good-faith.* Cf. **bona fides.**

B. Adjective or Adverb. *Bona fide* was originally adverbial, meaning "in good faith" <the suit was brought bona fide>. The phrase is still used in this way, most often in BrE—e.g.: "The undertaking was given *bona fide,* i.e., without any knowledge that the claim was not a good one." 1 Ernest W. Chance, *Principles of Mercantile Law* 25 (Percy W. French ed., 13th ed. 1950).

Today it is more commonly used as an adjective <it was a bona fide suit>. None of the forms of this term should be hyphenated or written as one word, as *bona fide* sometimes is when functioning as a PHRASAL ADJECTIVE. The opposite of *bona fide* is *mala fide*; the opposite of *bona fides* is *mala fides.* See **mala fide.**

C. Meaning "sincere, genuine." In legal contexts, the adjective *bona fide* should be avoided in the lay sense arrived at through SLIPSHOD EXTENSION, namely, "genuine; not fake." E.g.:

- "Even within the 50-mile area, containers that go directly to the owner of the cargo or to '*bona fide*' [read *genuine*] warehouses are exempted from the Rules." *N.L.R.B. v. Int'l Longshoremen's Ass'n, AFL-CIO,* 473 U.S. 61, 66 (1985) (per Brennan, J.).
- "The Court found that there was no *bona fide* [read *genuine*] dispute that as guarantor of a promissory note executed by Michael E. Hentges, Inc. . . . , Hentges owed the Bank principal of $29,400.00." *In re Hentges,* 351 B.R. 758, 762 (Bankr. N.D. Okla. 2006).

One court has justifiably criticized the phrase *bona fide doubt* in reference to a judge's doubt, saying that the phrase "appears to be a faulty construction of words . . . . [U]nfortunately, it has reached a level of being standard legal idiom in mental competency cases . . . . For purposes of determining whether an evidentiary hearing should be held, . . . '*bona fide doubt*' is a misnomer. It does not convey the correct sense of the test: the question whether an evidentiary hearing is required does not depend on the sincerity, genuineness, etc. of the judge's doubt—we can assume any judge's doubt has these qualities." *Griffin v. Lockhart,* 935 F.2d 926, 929 n.2 (8th Cir. 1991) (citing *DMLU* and recommending instead *sufficient doubt*). See **authentic.**

bona fide purchaser. See BFP.

bona fides, n.; **good faith;** *bonne foi.* Though the adjective *bona fide* has been fully anglicized, the noun phrase *bona fides* has lost much ground—especially in AmE—to *good faith,* n., which is generally preferable. The pronunciation of *bona fides,* /**boh**-nə **fı**-deez/, unlike that of its adjectival sibling, sounds foreign and bombastic. *Bonne foi,* a Frenchified variant, sounds still more so; fortunately, it is rarely encountered.

Typically, one writes, "He executed the contract in *good faith*," not really thinking of *bona fides* as an alternative wording, although admittedly it is sometimes used: "Their *bona fides* was manifest on the record." *Patterson v. Am. Tobacco Co.,* 634 F.2d 744, 748 (4th Cir. 1980).

As in the example just quoted, the noun phrase *bona fides* is singular: *this bona fides,* not **these bona fides.* But writers sometimes mistakenly make it plural—e.g.:

- "Southwestern asserts that it was denied the opportunity to be present and to present evidence when Lowe's *bona fides were* [read *bona fides was*] examined by the Land Office Manager." *Southwestern Petroleum Corp. v. Udall,* 361 F.2d 650, 657 (10th Cir. 1966).
- "He was neither advised at trial that his *bona fides were* [read *bona fides was*] in issue nor given an opportunity to disprove . . . the inference drawn by the court." *Sledge v. J.P. Stevens & Co.,* 585 F.2d 625, 641 (4th Cir. 1978).

bona vacantia (lit., "vacant goods") is a TERM OF ART meaning "property not disposed of by a decedent's will and to which no relative is entitled upon intestacy." E.g.: "I have not been referred to any case in which the Crown sought to interpose a claim to *bona vacantia* between creditors and former members." *In re Banque des Marchands de Moscou (Koupetschesky),* [1957] 3 W.L.R. 637 (C.D.). The phrase should not be used when *unclaimed property* or *ownerless goods* will suffice. Cf. **escheat.**

bond = (1) a written promise to pay a debt or to do some act (e.g., an appeal bond); (2) an interest-bearing certificate of debt that is issued by a corporation or governmental entity usu. to provide for a particular financial need (e.g., a municipal bond); or (3) an insurance agreement whereby a person or corporation becomes a surety to pay, within defined limits, for a financial loss suffered by a second person under certain circumstances (e.g., a bail bond, delivery bond, indemnity bond, or judicial bond). See **debenture.**

In criminal law, *bail bond* (= security for a released prisoner's return for trial) is archaic in BrE but current in AmE. See **bond out.**

bond out (= to post a bail bond and thereby obtain release from [jail]) is an American casualism. E.g.: "They are hastened through the door in the wall, back to the jail where they are either *bonded out,* released to probation, detained for further proceedings, or transported to the penitentiary." Leland P. Anderson, *A More Excellent Way,* 22 Notre Dame J.L. Ethics & Pub. Pol'y 399, 404 (2008). (On the misuse of *either . . . or* in this sentence, see **either (A).**)

bonne foi. See *bona fides,* n.

book, bring to. See **bring to book.**

bookkeeper; accountant; auditor. These terms all denote one who produces, tallies, or checks finance-related records. A *bookkeeper*, in the regular course of business, keeps routine and accurate records of pecuniary transactions by making entries in the books kept for that purpose. An *accountant* is one who is trained not only in bookkeeping but more extensively in organizing systems of record-keeping, ascertaining and reporting on a business's financial situation, and preparing appropriate tax-related documents—and who is authorized under applicable law to practice public accounting. Interestingly, *accountant* is a POPULARIZED LEGAL TECHNICALITY that originally, in the 15th century, denoted "the defendant in an action of account." (See **account,** n.) By extension, in the 16th century, the word came to mean "one whose occupation is the keeping of accounts." More specifically today, a *certified public accountant* (or C.P.A.) is an accountant who has satisfied the statutory and administrative requirements to be registered or licensed as a public accountant. An *auditor* is a financial examiner who checks and verifies the records of a business or an individual to ensure their accuracy or to assess whether irregularities require some corrective action.

bootstrap; bootstrapping. The original expression was one among several variants of *to pull oneself up by one's bootstraps* (a futile effort)—e.g.:

- "It would be as impossible for the directors, in undertaking to contract with themselves, to accomplish any result as it would be for them to undertake to *lift themselves over a fence by their bootstraps.*" *In re State Exch. Bank*, 159 N.E. 839, 840 (Ohio Ct. App. 1927).
- "That would be equivalent to *pulling one's self out of the mire by his own bootstraps.*" *McCarthy v. State ex rel. Harless*, 101 P.2d 449, 453 (Ariz. 1940).
- "To support the doctrine of precedent by reference to precedent would be to try to *pull itself up by its own bootstraps.*" Glanville Williams, *Learning the Law* 88 (11th ed. 1982).

The idea has now been telescoped into the gerund *bootstrapping*—e.g.:

- "It is only by deciding on appeal and on the merits that the claim of foreclosure is insubstantial that this court can [reach its own conclusion]. . . . This appellate *bootstrapping* is the more improper because the question of the adequacy of the foreclosure is in fact not concluded by this appeal." *Pettit v. Olean Indus., Inc.*, 266 F.2d 833, 839 (2d Cir. 1959) (Lumbard, J., dissenting).
- "This argument, too, does not warm us and indeed strikes us as a *bootstrapping* approach." *Hudson v. John Hancock Mut. Life Ins.*, 314 F.2d 16, 23 (8th Cir. 1963).

The term is now often used, especially in law, in the sense "making a success out of one's meager resources."

booty. See **spoils.**

bordereau (= [1] a note of account or, more commonly, [2] a description of reinsured risks) is the singular, *bordereaux* the plural.

The word has recently come to be used as a verb—e.g.: "American and Southeastern Fire Insurance Co., to which the policy had been *'bordereauxed,'* refused payment." *Merchants Nat'l Bank v. Southeastern Fire Ins. Co.*, 751 F.2d 771, 773 (5th Cir. 1985). The proper verb form, however, would be *bordereau* (singular), not *-reaux*. Hence, in the above quotation the word should be *bordereaued.*

bork, vb., an eponym of Robert Bork, President Reagan's unsuccessful nominee for the U.S. Supreme Court, means (1) "(of the U.S. Senate) to reject (a nominee) for the U.S. Supreme Court because of his or her untraditional political and legal philosophy"; or (2) "(of political and legal activists) to embark on a media campaign against (a Supreme Court nominee) in an effort to persuade the Senate to reject the nominee." Originally, the word was usually capitalized, but no longer. It most often appears in sense 2—e.g.:

- "One of the legacies of the Bork nomination is, I think, a contribution to the political dictionary. I'm referring to the verb, *to bork*, which is what Sen. Edward Kennedy, D-Mass., did to Robert Bork. The passive, to be *borked*, is what happened to Bork. Now, what does it mean to be *borked*? Simply this: Your opponents take a matter involving a law and criticize you in terms of policy outcome. You defend yourself by discussing the issue in legal jargon." Terry Eastland, *Reagan's Legacy at Justice Poses Challenge to New President*, Manhattan Law., 1 Nov. 1988, at 12.
- "After they persuaded Ms. Hill to submit an unsworn statement by fax, members of the Senate trio—probably in cahoots with a team of high-powered Washington lawyers, lobbyists and public relations specialists out to '*bork*' the nominee—caused the sensational Hill statement to be leaked to a couple of reputable reporters." William Safire, *The Plumbers' Return*, 17 Feb. 1992, at A11.

both. A. *Both . . . and.* These correlative conjunctions must frame matching syntactic parts—whether nouns, noun clauses, verbs, adjectives, adverbs, etc. Here *both* impermissibly introduces a prepositional phrase when *and* introduces a *noun*: "The chancellor was warranted, *both in law and fact* [read *both in law and in fact* or *in both law and fact*], in his judgment of liability." *Alvis v. J.B. Colt & Co.*, 143 So. 888, 889 (Miss. 1932).

B. *Both . . . as well as.* This construction is both unidiomatic and verbose—e.g.:

- "Gas is measured at the wellhead, and payment is based on the price of gas at the well *both under the lease here in suit as well as under* [read *both under the lease here . . . and under*] most leases." *Wood v. TXO Prod. Corp.*, 854 P.2d 880, 884 (Okla. 1992). Also, it is not advisable to use *well* first as an oil-and-gas term (a noun) and then as an adverb.
- "Atlas Van Lines adopted a new policy to prohibit any affiliated company from handling interstate hauling *both*

under its own name as well as under [read *under its own name as well as under*] the Atlas name." *SCFC ILC, Inc. v. Visa USA, Inc.,* 36 F.3d 958, 970 (10th Cir. 1994).

- "We have for years granted new trials *both under the rule of Tyus as well as under* [read *both under the rule of Tyus and in*] our *Borden* supervisory role as a protector of the integrity of the judicial process." *Fravel v. Haughey,* 727 So.2d 1033, 1043 (Fla. Dist. Ct. App. 1999).

C. Redundancies with. Several wordings with *both* cause redundancies. One is **both . . . each other*—e.g.:

- "Plaintiffs contend that they have alleged that the Shareholder Defendants acted interchangeably with MERS, so that *both* parties were mutual agents of *each other.*" *Trevino v. Merscorp, Inc.,* 583 F.Supp.2d 521, 528 (D. Del. 2008). *Mutual,* of course, aggravates the problem there. A suggested revision: *Each party was the agent of the other.* Or: *The two parties were mutual agents.*
- "*Both* plaintiffs and defendants asserted claims against *each other* under the parties' contract." *Kirschenman v. Elias,* 193 P.3d 60, 60 (Or. Ct. App. 2008). (Delete *against each other.*)

Another troublesome phrasing is **both alike*—e.g.:

- "They argue that whether the legacies in the will are general or specific, they are *both alike* [read *alike*], and both should be taxed pro rata." *Saxon v. Aycock,* 34 S.E.2d 914, 917 (Ga. Ct. App. 1945).
- "This is a relation that exceeds analogy: it is not just that they are *both alike* [read *alike*] in being simultaneously inside and outside the law." Joseph Jenkins, *Inheritance Law as Constellation in Lieu of Redress: A Detour through Exceptional Terrain,* 24 Cardozo L. Rev. 1043, 1052 (2003).

Yet another is **both concurrently*—e.g.: "Happily now, as we shall see, every judge has both a Common Law and an Equity mind, and applies them *both concurrently* [read *concurrently*]." Edward Jenks, *The Book of English Law* 36 (P.B. Fairest ed., 6th ed. 1967).

D. Both (of) the. Though the idiom is falling into disuse, *both the* (or *both these*) has a fine pedigree and continues in formal English—e.g.:

- "The Commission is to promote *both these* purposes." J.L. Brierly, *The Law of Nations* 82 (5th ed. 1955).
- "The hazard, in *both these* respects, could only be avoided, if at all, by rendering that tribunal more numerous." *The Federalist,* No. 65, at 398 (Alexander Hamilton) (Clinton Rossiter ed., 1961).
- "For *both these* reasons, over reliance on foreign authorities diminished." Grant Gilmore & Charles L. Black Jr., *The Law of Admiralty* 46 (2d ed. 1975).

The alternative phrasing, *both of the* (or *both of these*), is increasingly common in AmE.

E. Both . . . equally as. See **equally as (c).**

bottom, vb., may be used literally: "The well was *bottomed* in sand A." Or it may be used figuratively, as it more frequently is in legal contexts:

- "This contention is unsound, and the argument predicated thereon is *bottomed* wholly upon a false premise." *Ford v. Moody,* 276 S.W. 595, 597 (Ark. 1925).
- "The district court properly dismissed plaintiff's section 1983 claim *bottomed* on her assertion of an illegal arrest." *Simons v. Clemons,* 752 F.2d 1053, 1055 (5th Cir. 1985).

This peculiar legal idiom was originally nonlegal, dating in the *OED* from 1637. From a modern stylistic point of view, *base* might be preferable to *bottom* in figurative senses.

The transference to a noun sense of *bottom* is likely to provoke laughter:

- "Title VI on its own *bottom* [read *foundation*] reaches no further than the Constitution." *Guardians Ass'n v. Civil Serv. Comm'n,* 463 U.S. 582, 589–90 (1983) (per White, J.).
- "The question after *Alden,* then, is whether this power stems from Article I, is inherent in the Fourteenth Amendment, or rests on its own *bottom* [read *basis*]." Lauren E. Rosenblatt, Note, *Removing the Eleventh Amendment Barrier,* 78 Tex. L. Rev. 719, 753 (2000).

bottomry; *bottomage. *Bottomry,* denoting a special type of commercial-insurance contract in admiralty, may be used as both noun and verb. **Bottomage* is a NEEDLESS VARIANT from LAW FRENCH.

bound bailiff. See **bumbailiff.**

*bounden. See BIBLICAL AFFECTATION.

bounty, which is becoming an ARCHAISM, is current in the context of wills and estates, although little used elsewhere. It means "munificence; liberality in giving; gift" (*COD*). E.g.:

- "If the court so holds, it will distribute the testator's *bounty* equally among all persons, belonging to the class designated in the will, wherever the person, who by the will was intrusted with such a power, has failed to execute the power." *Milhollen's Adm'r v. Rice,* 13 W. Va. 510, 544 (1878).
- "But the policy which led to the enactment of such statutes is quite different from that under which such trusts are sustained. The former is protection of the debtor and the latter is consideration for the right of the donor or settlor to dispose of his property and control his *bounty* as he wishes, within the limits allowed by law." *State ex rel. Caldwell v. Nashville Trust Co.,* 190 S.W.2d 785, 790 (Tenn. Ct. App. 1945).
- "Their justification is found in the right of the donor to control his *bounty* and secure its application according to his pleasure." *Hines v. Sands,* 312 S.W.2d 275, 279 (Tex. Civ. App.—Fort Worth 1958).

boutique. Since the mid-1980s, *boutique* has, in AmE, denoted a small law firm specializing in one particular aspect of law practice. E.g.:

- "Davis, Everby & Feinberg is a small, *boutique* law firm specializing in litigation." Mark H. Epstein & Brandon Wisoff, *Winding Up Dissolved Law Partnerships,* 73 Cal. L. Rev. 1597, 1625 (1985).
- "Samuel Sterrett . . . resigned Oct. 31 with partner Michael Durney to launch a tax *boutique.*" Jennifer Frey, *Myerson & Kuhn Loses Cabot and Office in D.C.,* Manhattan Law., 7–13 Nov. 1989, at 4.

The word is preferably pronounced /boo-**teek**/, not /boh-**teek**/.

*bracery. See **embracery.**

BRACKETS. See PUNCTUATION (M).

Bracton. This proper name commonly refers both to the 13th-century judge (Henry of Bracton, who sat on the Court of King's Bench and of Assize in the reign of Henry III) and to the book he is thought to have written (*De Legibus et Consuetudinibus Angliae*, ca. 1250). Some historians doubt that Bracton was the author of *Bracton* (italicized when referring to the book)—e.g.: "The author of *Bracton* appreciated this point." J.H. Baker, *An Introduction to English Legal History* 300 (3d ed. 1990).

Brandeis brief. In *Muller v. Oregon*, 208 U.S. 412 (1908), Louis Brandeis persuaded the Court that minimum-hours legislation for women was reasonable—and not unconstitutional—with an unconventional brief that consisted primarily of statistical, sociological, economic, and physiological information. Such a brief has come to be known, since the 1940s, as a *Brandeis brief*, the main characteristics of which are: (1) reliance on extrarecord facts, especially economic and sociological materials, that can be judicially noticed; and (2) lengthiness. E.g.:

- "The brief submitted on the law was . . . five pages, six pages, and on the facts whatever it was, 150 pages . . . . This kind of brief has ever since then been called 'a *Brandeis brief.*'" Felix Frankfurter, *Felix Frankfurter Reminisces* 97 (Harlan B. Phillips ed., 1960).
- "Plaintiff offered no evidence, nothing even in the way of a *Brandeis brief*, from which we might compare factually the problems private tortfeasors and governmental subdivisions have in dealing with stale claims, investigation of claims, and the budget process." *Miller v. Boone County Hosp.*, 394 N.W.2d 776, 783 (Iowa 1986) (Wolle, J., dissenting).
- "Sampson supports his arguments with *Brandeis-brief* type information from studies about the operation of the FDPA." *U.S. v. Sampson*, 486 F.3d 13, 19 (1st Cir. 2007).

breach, n. A. And Its Near-Synonyms: *infraction*; *violation*; *transgression*; *infringement*; *contravention*. These terms all refer to the breaking of a rule. *Breach* typically implies the nonperformance of a contractual obligation, frequently in the phrase *in breach of* (a provision, a contract, etc.) but sometimes also on its own <were the breaches material?>. *Infraction* is more frequent than *breach* in designating the breaking of an officially promulgated rule, especially of a local authority <a clear infraction of the parking rules>. *Violation* connotes a more serious disregard of the law or a willful indifference to the rights of others <they continued missile testing in violation of international law>. *Transgression* implies an act that exceeds the limits of what is allowed—often seriously but sometimes trivially <this act was a clear transgression of the Warsaw Convention> <these unpaid parking tickets, though claimed as an act of civil disobedience, are no more than transgressions of our traffic laws>. *Infringement*, though sometimes used synonymously with *infraction*, typically implies a figurative trespass into another's rightful domain <patent infringement>.

(See **infringe.**) *Contravention* is a going against the meaning of an authoritative text, as if heedless of its plain requirements <the company acted in direct contravention of the agreed judgment entered just two months before>. See **contravene.**

B. Common Misusage. *Breach* can be a troublesome word. Its most frequent legal use is in the phrase *breach of contract*. The word *breach* always suggests its more common cognate, *break*. One can either *breach* or *break* a contract; and another may refer to one's *breach* or *breaking* of it. That much is simple.

In general usage, *breach* is confused with two other words, *breech*, n. (= [1] buttocks; or [2] the lower or back part of something, as a gun bore), and *broach*, vb. (= [1] to make a hole in to let out liquid; or [2] to bring up for discussion). The confusion of *breach* with *breech* consists in writers' mistakenly using the latter where *breach* belongs <breach of a treaty>. The lapse with *broach* occurs when someone writes of *breaching* (read *broaching*) a topic.

The meanings of *breach* and *broach* become close only in reference to dikes or levees and walls (*breach* = to break open; *broach* = to make a hole in). E.g.: "Less than three months ago—in the immediate aftermath of the *breaching* of the Berlin Wall—the Chancellor's closest aides were predicting that five to eight years might still be needed before unity became a reality." David Marsh, *Kohl Takes the Burden of Unity on His Shoulders*, Fin. Times, 22 Feb. 1990, at 3.

breach, more honored in the. Strictly speaking, this phrase refers to an unjust rule that is better broken than obeyed. Often, though, through SLIPSHOD EXTENSION, writers use the phrase to refer to a just rule that, in practice, is often broken. E.g.:

- "Although the obligation of lawyers to cooperate with one another long has been considered a significant professional obligation, it, too, has been more and *more honored in the breach* [read *more often breached*]." Roger J. Miner, *Lawyers Owe One Another*, Nat'l L.J., 19 Dec. 1988, at 13.
- "It is an American custom (perhaps *more honored in the breach*) as well as a Chinese one to show respect for one's elders." Judith Martin, *Ingenuity Can Overcome This Language Barrier*, Chicago Trib., 8 Oct. 1989, at 6C.
- "The code of professional responsibility requires reporting an unethical colleague—a requirement *more honored in the breach* than observance." Raoul L. Felder, *A Degree Isn't a License to Steal*, Newsday (N.Y.), 19 Mar. 1991, at 98.

*breachee is objectionable as an obtuse word meaning "one whose contract has been breached by the other contracting party." E.g.:

- "The *breachor's* initial failure to comply establishes the inadequacy of the *breachee's* remedy at law." *Stewart v. Stewart*, 300 S.E.2d 263, 266 (N.C. Ct. App. 1983). (On the use of **breachor* in that sentence, see **breacher.**)
- "The breacher will offer the *breachee's* expectancy values plus some portion of the surplus." Michael L. Zigler,

Takings Law and the Contracts Clause, 36 Stan. L. Rev. 1447, 1463 n.83 (1984).

- "In a world of perfect judicial information, we could force the breaching party to internalize the costs of breach through damages so that it would only be profitable to breach when the benefits gained exceed the value of the lost performance to the *breachee*." Nathan B. Oman, *Specific Performance and the Thirteenth Amendment*, 93 Minn. L. Rev. 2020, 2028 (2009).

The word is also an illogically formed word because it means not "one who is breached (by another)," but rather "one whose contract has been breached." *Breachee is not, like *refugee*, an established exception. See -EE.

breacher (= a party in breach) is so spelled—not *breachor. See **contract-breaker.**

breach of trust. See **larceny (A).**

***breachor.** See **breacher.**

break, vb. **A. In Contract Law.** *Break* is frequently a casual equivalent of *breach*, vb.—e.g.:

- "The power but not the right to *break* a contract exists, like the power to commit a crime or tort, but the breach is a wrong in either case." William F. Walsh, *A Treatise on Equity* 301–02 (1930).
- "It is a crime to *break* such a contract, if the probable consequence will be to cause injury or danger or grave inconvenience to the community." William Geldart, *Introduction to English Law* 162 (D.C.M. Yardley ed., 9th ed. 1984).

B. As an Element of the Crime of Burglary. In the law of burglary, the word *break* is used in a peculiar sense. It does not require damage to property, yet it is more than crossing an imaginary line when we speak of "breaking into a house." Entering through an open door or window is not breaking; all that is needed is opening a door or window, even if not locked or latched.

break-in, n. So hyphenated.

breaking and entering. See **housebreaking.**

breast (of the court), in the. See LOAN TRANSLATIONS.

Breathalyzer; Intoxilyzer; Drunkometer; alcohol-ometer; Intoximeter. The first three terms and the last term are trademarked names of devices that measure blood-alcohol content, and all are PORTMANTEAU WORDS. *Breathalyzer* (*breath* + *analyzer*) suffers widespread misusage by writers who fail to capitalize it or who misspell it *breathalizer. It isn't yet generic, but it may be on its way—e.g.:

- "Collateral comments made by a defendant during a discussion with the police about the *breathalyzer* may be admissible in evidence where no evidence is offered that the defendant refused the test." Paul J. Liacos et al., *Handbook of Massachusetts Evidence* 472 (8th ed. 2006). (*Breathalyzer* is in lowercase throughout the book.)
- "Both officers then brought defendant to the 'Alcotest room,' where a *breathalyzer* test could be administered

using an Alcotest 7110 machine to measure defendant's blood-alcohol concentration." *State v. Marquez*, 998 A.2d 421, 424 (N.J. 2010). (Note that *Breathalyzer* is here used generically with the brand name of another machine.)

- "Lacking precise interoceptive access to our blood-alcohol levels, we cannot perceive our exact intoxication levels. Few of us own personal *breathalyzers*." Seana Valentine Shiffrin, *Inducing Moral Deliberation: On the Occasional Virtues of Fog*, 123 Harv. L. Rev. 1214, 1221 (2010).

Breathalyze began to be used as a verb in the 1990s—often with an -IZE suffix—and the misusage is spreading. E.g.:

- "Perhaps schools will start drug testing or *breathalyzing* students who drive to school and park their cars on school property or take the school bus." Jonathan M. Ettman, *Vernonia Case Comment: High School Students Lose Their Rights When They Don Their Uniforms*, 13 N.Y.L. Sch. J. Hum. Rts. 625, 662 (1997).
- "Alcohol is regarded as the most frequent cause of traffic crashes, and the likelihood of being *breathalized* is considered low." Kathryn Stewart, *On DWI Laws in Other Countries* 55 (2000).
- "She asserts that the officers were deliberately indifferent to her need for prompt medical care, delaying procurement of an ambulance until she submitted to a *breathalizer* test and provided them with the name of her companion." *Elliott v. County of Monroe*, 115 Fed. Appx. 497, 499 (2d Cir. 2004).
- "After explaining that the parking lot attendant must have disabled her auto-light feature, she *Breathalyzed*, blew a 0.03% BAC, and was forced to do several field sobriety tests which the officer claimed she failed." Andrew Gore, *Know Your Limit: How Legislatures Have Gone Overboard with Per Se Drunk Driving Laws and How Men Pay the Price*, 16 Wm. & Mary J. Women & L. 423, 439 n.142 (2010).

In BrE the standard word is *breathalyser*, and both *breathalyzer* and *breathaliser* are variant spellings. But however spelled, it is never initially capitalized in BrE.

The other terms are less widespread. *Intoxilyzer* (*intoxication* + *analyzer*) is rarely misused, but here is a curious exception: "The officer smelled an *intoxilyzing* [read *intoxicating*] substance on Mayo's breath and noticed that Mayo appeared disoriented." *Mayo v. State*, 843 So.2d 739, 741 (Miss. Ct. App. 2003). *Intoximeter* (*intoxication* + *meter*) is about one-third as common and occasionally misspelled *intoxometer—e.g.: "The case involved the law relating to drink/drive and the accuracy of *intoxometers*." James Holland & Julian Webb, *Learning Legal Rules* 276 (7th ed. 2010). The *Drunkometer* (*drunk* + *meter*), one of the earliest breath-alcohol detectors, was invented in the 1930s, and was the most widely used device until the *Breathalyzer* was introduced in the 1950s. Since then, *Drunkometer* has been infrequently used, perhaps because of its jocular sound. But more often than not, writers have retained its capital letter. *Alcoholometer* (*alcohol* + *hydrometer*) is extremely rare in legal writing—undoubtedly because it is easily confused with the identically named device that measures liquids that are less dense than water. The newer name *Alcometer* appears only slightly more frequently.

In reference to the test performed rather than to the device performing it, *breath test* is the most succinct phraseology, used often by the U.S. Supreme Court and by British courts as well. *Breathalyzer test*, an inferior variant, is also commonly used—e.g.: "When the second officer arrived and the preliminary *breathalyzer test* was administered, Null registered a 0.19, far above the limit for intoxication." *People v. Null*, 233 P.3d 670, 685 (Colo. 2010).

breath of calumny. See **calumny.**

breech. See **breach.**

brethren. The plural form *brethren* has survived only in religious and legal contexts, and almost always in reference to people who aren't brothers by birth. E.g.:

- "In this case I have the misfortune to differ in opinion from a majority of my *brethren*." *Smith v. Richards*, 38 U.S. (13 Pet.) 26, 43 (1839) (Story, J., dissenting).
- "In *Rookes v. Barnard* Lord Devlin, with the unanimous approval of his *brethren*, had laid down that exemplary damages could only be awarded in three types of circumstances." Michael Zander, *The Law-Making Process* 167 (2d ed. 1985).

Courts have considered the word generic in testamentary contexts (i.e., as referring both to males and to females). But most readers are unlikely to see it as gender-neutral: one commentator writes that this EUPHEMISM "gives a not wholly misleading indication of the frequency with which women are appointed as judges." David Pannick, *Judges* 157 (1987). The word is unlikely to flourish in AmE because of its perceived SEXISM. Nor does *brethren and sistren* seem likely to catch on, *sistren* being the analogous archaic plural of *sister*. That plural, unlike its brother, is now chiefly dialectal. See **brother** & **sistren.**

Brothers is sometimes used where *brethren* would normally appear—e.g.: "While I see more ambiguity than do my dissenting *brothers*, it is of no matter because we do not write on a clean slate." *James v. U.S.*, 760 F.2d 590, 606 (5th Cir. 1985) (Higginbotham, J., dissenting).

breve [fr. *brevis* "short"] is the LAW LATIN equivalent of *writ*. Hence, in older texts, *breve originale* means "original writ" and *breve de recto* means "writ of right." E.g.:

- "A writ (*breve* in Latin, *brief* in French) was a thin strip of parchment containing a letter in the name of the king, usually written in Latin, and sealed with the great seal." J.H. Baker, *An Introduction to English Legal History* 67 (3d ed. 1990).
- "Furthermore, novel disseisin only lies in the Royal courts; there is no form of writ corresponding to the *breve de recto*." A.W.B. Simpson, *An Introduction to the History of the Land Law* 28 (1961).

See **writ of right.** Pl. *brevia*.

briber; bribee; bribe-giver; bribe-taker. A *bribe* is a reward or favor given or promised to a person in a position of trust in order that that person's judgment will be skewed or conduct corrupted in one's favor. The one who gives the bribe is termed the *briber*, the one who receives it the *bribee*. E.g.:

- "Made when the allegedly extorted bribe money was being paid, the tape recording in this case is of the actual voices of the *briber* and the *bribee*." *U.S. v. Sopher*, 362 F.2d 523, 525 (7th Cir. 1966).
- "This section does not reach a simple breach of fiduciary duty; it covers only corrupt breaches that involve a bribe. *Briber* and *bribee* are then equally guilty." Tex. Penal Code § 32.43, *Practice Commentary* at 667 (1974).

Some writers use the terms *bribe-giver* and *bribe-taker*, which are undoubtedly clearer to more readers. E.g.:

- "The usual pleas of the *bribe-giver* or *-taker* is that he only followed the example he saw everywhere about him, that he only did directly and candidly what others were doing indirectly and hypocritically." Lon L. Fuller, *Anatomy of the Law* 49 (1968).
- "The starting point in the law of bribery seems to have been when a judge, for doing his office or acting under color of his office, took a reward or fee from some person who had occasion to come before him—and apparently guilt attached only to the judge himself and not to the *bribe-giver*." Rollin M. Perkins & Ronald N. Boyce, *Criminal Law* 527 (3d ed. 1982).

bribery (= the corrupt payment, receipt, or solicitation of a private favor for official action) generally refers to the bribe-giver's actions as well as to the bribe-taker's. (Some jurisdictions restrict *bribe* to the act of the bribe-giver and refer to the bribe-taker's offense as *receiving a bribe*.) A misdemeanor at common law, the offense has been made a statutory felony in most English-speaking jurisdictions.

In the phrase *commercial bribery*, the term has been extended beyond its traditional reference to the act of a government official. *Commercial bribery* refers to the advantage that one competitor secures over other competitors by surreptitious, corrupt dealing with the agents and employees of prospective buyers. See **extortion.**

bribe-taker. See **briber.**

brief, n. = (1) in AmE, the written arguments of counsel for consultation by the court; (2) in BrE, a document by which a solicitor instructs a barrister with an abstract of the pleadings and facts as the barrister prepares to appear as an advocate in court; (3) in BrE, a barrister's authority to appear; or (4) in AmE and BrE, an abstract of all the documents affecting the title to real property (known also as *abstract of title*). See **abstract of title.**

For the LAW FRENCH *brief* (= writ), see **breve.**

brief, vb., occurs primarily in legal, military, diplomatic, and business contexts. In American legal writing, the term refers to preparing a written brief—e.g.:

- "Both the statutory and constitutional issues have been fully *briefed* and argued here." *Dandridge v. Williams*, 397 U.S. 471, 475 (1970) (per Stewart, J.).
- "The next day, counsel *briefed* Andersen's management team, and a participating manager e-mailed the following update to employees." *Roquet v. Arthur Andersen LLP*, 398 F.3d 585, 587 (7th Cir. 2005).

In British legal writing—as in American business, diplomatic, and military contexts—the term refers to preparing, informing, or authorizing a person. E.g.: "Mr. Makin took the view that in telephone conversations with the court he had been told that the hearing on 19 February would be a 'preliminary' hearing. Mr. Makin protested that he had *briefed* counsel for 12 March and that he was only prepared to deal with 'preliminary' matters." *Langley v. N.W. Water Auth.*, [1991] 1 W.L.R. 697, 708 (C.A.). See also **debrief.**

brief, hold a. See **hold a brief for.**

briefcase gets its name from the legal profession, being originally "a case in which lawyers carry their briefs." *Briefcase* and *attaché (case)* are the only terms current in AmE. In BrE, *brief-bag* (for barristers), *deed-case* or *briefcase* (for solicitors), and *attaché case* are used.

briefing attorney. See **clerk.**

briefly = (1) soon; or (2) not for long. It may cause ambiguities in some contexts <he will deliver his speech briefly>. Cf. **presently.**

BRIEF-WRITING. Except on technical points touched on throughout, brief-writing as a discipline is largely beyond the purview of this book. Still, a few points deserve mention here.

First, a hardly disputable point: American judges find most briefs that they read tough going. As one federal appellate judge chastely puts it: "In my experience it is the rare brief-writer who seizes the opportunity to employ the clarity, simplicity, and directness of expression necessary to endow a brief with maximum persuasive force." Roger J. Miner, *Confronting the Communication Crisis in the Legal Profession*, 34 N.Y.L. Sch. L. Rev. 1, 9 (1989). Other federal appellate judges have called most briefs "execrable" and have estimated the number of "truly helpful" briefs at somewhere between 5% and 10%. Though elected judges are generally more forgiving in their assessment, anyone concerned with the literary aspects of practicing law must be troubled by these evaluations.

Second, even though most briefs fall short of most judges' standards, those standards probably ought to be higher than they are. Consider the standard suggested by Karl Llewellyn in a brilliant lecture just a few days before he died: "You need to interest them [the judges] in that brief. You've got to make them feel that when they come to the brief, 'Oh, baby; is it going to be hot.' And they've got to approach the brief with that favorable atmosphere you need." *A Lecture on Appellate Advocacy*, 29 U. Chi. L. Rev. 627, 639 (1962). In

the hands of the right brief-writer, of course, virtually any brief can be "hot." But few are.

Third, the most important—and frequently the most neglected—aspect of any brief is the statement of the issues. Framing issues well has become an all but lost art among modern lawyers. For an explanation of how to frame issues effectively, see ISSUE-FRAMING.

For helpful discussions of the subject, see especially these books: Bryan A. Garner, *The Winning Brief* (2d ed. 2004); Girvan Peck, *Writing Persuasive Briefs* (1984); and Frederick Bernays Wiener, *Briefing and Arguing Federal Appeals* (2d ed. 1967). For a discussion of the most common sin in briefs, see OVERPARTICULARIZATION.

bright-line rule = a judicial rule of decision that is simple and straightforward and that avoids or ignores the ambiguities or difficulties of the problems at hand. The phrase dates from the mid-20th century. The metaphor of a bright line is somewhat older than the phrase *bright-line rule*—e.g.:

- "The difficult part of this case comes with regard to . . . the activity of the Board of Temperance. . . . A *bright line* between that which brings conviction to one person and its influence on the body politic cannot be drawn." *Girard Trust Co. v. I.R.C.*, 122 F.2d 108, 110 (3d Cir. 1941).
- "The *McCambridge* majority opinion . . . agrees that the *Kirby bright-line-rule* is but a mere formalism." J. Gary Trichter, *Bright-Lining Away the Right to Counsel*, Tex. Law., 6 Nov. 1989, at 26.

Cf. **hard-and-fast rule.**

bring an action against is verbose for *sue*—e.g.: "Hynes' mother *brought an action for damages against the company* [read *sued the company for damages*]." C. Gordon Post, *An Introduction to the Law* 86 (1963).

bring error = to seek an appeal, esp. by writ of error. See **error (A).**

bring in (a verdict). Juries are traditionally said to *bring in* a verdict—that is, to bring it back into the courtroom. E.g.:

- "The Judge's summing-up was brief but thorough, and after a short retirement the jury *brought in* a verdict of guilty." Stanley Jackson, *The Life and Cases of Mr. Justice Humphreys* 175 (1952).
- "The jury *brought in* a $4.9 million verdict for the Coliseum." Douglas Laycock, *The Death of the Irreparable Injury Rule* 115 (1991).

bring to book = to arrest and try (an offender). E.g.:

- "The genuinely unfortunate aspect of today's ruling is not that fewer fugitives will be *brought to book*." *Steagald v. U.S.*, 451 U.S. 204, 231 (1981) (Rehnquist, J., dissenting).
- "Since then, however, both Reagan and Bush have been frustrated in their attempts to *bring terrorists to book* and to end the saga of US hostages in Beirut." Simon O'Dwyer-Russell, *£2.5m Reward to Find Lockerbie Bombers*, Sunday Telegraph, 29 Apr. 1990, at 2.
- "It is not the aim of the EC to *bring governments to book* before the European Court of Justice." *Tories Accused of*

Trying to Subvert Brussels Directive, The Times (London), 2 June 1990, at 3.

BRITISHISMS. See AMERICANISMS AND BRITISHISMS.

broach. See **breach.**

broad. See **wide.**

broad brush is a legal METAPHOR signifying a huge generalization—and the CLICHÉ sweeps so very commonly that good editors tend to sweep it out of the texts that it besmirches—e.g.:

- "Congress is much more comfortable painting with *a broad brush* [read *broad generalities*]—'discrimination is forbidden'—than in filling in the details." Linda Greenhouse, *A Changed Court Revises Rules on Civil Rights*, N.Y. Times, 18 June 1989, at E1.
- "The American dream has traditionally used *a broad brush to paint* [read *invidious* (?) *generalities to portray*] a land of inopportunity and inequity with respect to persons of color in general, and African-Americans in particular." Anthony P. Griffin, *Is the Diminution of Civil Rights the Road to a Color-Blind Society?*, 21 Thurgood Marshall L. Rev. 1, 14 (1996).
- "The *broad-brush* [delete the phrase] caricature Ford paints of antiracist activists, combined with his obtuse and uncharitable portrayal of the Jena Six defendants and new civil-rights organizers, reflects two ironic contradictions to his work in The Race Card." Sumi Cho, *Post-Racialism*, 94 Iowa L. Rev. 1589, 1644 (2009).

broad interpretation. See *liberal interpretation* under INTERPRETATION, MODES OF (B).

*brocage. See **brokerage.**

brocard /**broh**-kard/ = an elementary legal principle or maxim, esp. one deriving from Roman law or ancient custom. The word is omitted from most abridged English-language dictionaries, such as *W11* and *AHD*. E.g.:

- "That important and novel legal questions should not be decided in a vacuum is a *brocard*." *U.S. v. Birrell*, 262 F.Supp. 97, 99 (S.D.N.Y. 1967).
- "The *brocard* that a patent is a legally conferred monopoly ordinarily carries precious little value." Edward H. Cooper, *Attempts and Monopolization*, 72 Mich. L. Rev. 373, 416 (1974).
- "Mindful of these precepts, and of the *brocard* that summary judgments should be granted only sparingly in Title VII cases, . . . we find the district court's summary disposition improvident." *Price v. Southwestern Bell Telephone Co.*, 687 F.2d 74, 78 (5th Cir. 1982).

brokerage; brokage. *Brokerage* = (1) the business or office of a broker <real-estate brokerage is a profession requiring knowledge and experience>; or (2) a broker's fee <the brokerage is materially different from the underwriting commission>.

The archaic *brokage* (or, alternatively, **brocage*) means "the corrupt jobbing of offices; the bribe unlawfully paid for any office" (*OED*). In this sense, *brokage* is the lay equivalent of *simony*. See **barratry.**

Brokage is also an archaic NEEDLESS VARIANT of *brokerage*, but it remains the standard form in a single phrase, *marriage brokage*—e.g.:

- "The law of England will not enforce a contract of 'marriage *brokage*.'" Thomas E. Holland, *The Elements of Jurisprudence* 277 (13th ed. 1924).
- "So, also, marriage-*brokage* contracts have long been held to be void." P.S. Atiyah, *An Introduction to the Law of Contract* 242 (3d ed. 1981).
- "A marriage *brokage* contract is one by which a person promises in return for a money consideration to procure the marriage of another." G.H. Treitel, *The Law of Contract* 390 (8th ed. 1991).

brother. This term is often used, by judges, of a male associate on the bench—e.g.:

- "My *Brother* Harlan, while agreeing with the result reached by the Court, deplores the Court's reasoning as 'another step in the onward march of the long-since discredited "incorporation" doctrine.'" *Pointer v. Texas*, 380 U.S. 400, 410–11 (1965) (Goldberg, J., concurring).
- "In my opinion, our trial *brother* [i.e., the trial court judge] fell into legal error by giving any decisive weight to these factors in his piercing inquiry." *Riggins v. Dixie Shoring Co.*, 592 So.2d 1282, 1284 (La. 1992).

See **brethren.**

A substitute for *brother* in this context, perhaps useful in avoiding SEXISM or in referring to a fellow judge who is a woman, is *colleague*: "I disagree with my *colleagues* because I believe the stipulation signed by the two attorneys was at best ambiguous." *Sea-Land Serv., Inc. v. R.V. D'Alfonso Co.*, 727 F.2d 1, 4 (1st Cir. 1984) (Campbell, J., dissenting).

brush, broad. See **broad brush.**

brutum fulmen (= an empty noise; an empty threat) is no TERM OF ART; it is the worst type of LATINISM in the law, expressing a commonplace notion for which a variety of English phrases suffice. E.g.: "[A court of equity] cannot lawfully enjoin the world at large, no matter how broadly it words its decree. If it assumes to do so, the decree is pro tanto *brutum fulmen* [read *ineffectual*] and the persons enjoined are free to ignore it." *Alemite Mfg. Corp. v. Staff*, 42 F.2d 832, 832 (2d Cir. 1930) (per L. Hand, J.).

budget, vb., forms *budgeted* and *budgeting* in AmE, *budgetted* and *budgetting* in BrE. See DOUBLING OF FINAL CONSONANTS.

budget-making is best hyphenated. See **decision-making.**

buggery is a legal term usually meaning "sodomy," but sometimes also "bestiality." *Bugger* (= sodomite) was originally a respectable legal term, though now it is a dialectal term of playful abuse, not necessarily implying sodomy. As the *SOED* chastely notes, *bugger* is "vulgar exc. in law." Here the original meaning obtains, though with contemptuous overtones: "The middle age of *buggers* is not to be contemplated without horror" (Virginia Woolf).

In BrE, *buggery* is the more usual legal term than *sodomy*. It means "anal intercourse by a man with another man or a woman or bestiality by a man or a woman" (*CDL*). E.g.: "*Buggery*[:] One of the circumstances constituting this offence is where the penis penetrates the anus of a male or female, and the maximum penalty is life imprisonment." Andrew Ashworth, *Principles of Criminal Law* 310 (1991). The active bugger is guilty as the *agent*, whereas the receiving bugger is called (and is guilty as) the *patient*. See EUPHEMISM.

bulk, n., sometimes causes writers to doubt which form of the verb to use, singular or plural—e.g.: "The vast *bulk* of recorded crimes *falls* [read *fall*] into the category of property offences." Andrew Ashworth, *Principles of Criminal Law* 39 (1991). Some writers, finding support in the principle of SYNESIS, would write *fall* in that sentence. And they have the better position: when the phrase *bulk of the* is followed by a plural count noun, the verb should be plural—a form attested from the early 19th century in historical dictionaries. Hence, *the bulk of the people are* is better than *the bulk of the people is* (a dehumanizing formulation).

bumbailiff is a BrE slang term for "a bailiff or sheriff's officer who collects debts." *Bum* (= buttocks) was aptly coupled with *bailiff* in this term—actually a corruption of *bound bailiff*—because of the debt-collectors' habit of catching debtors from behind. This humorous word is now obsolescent. See **bailiwick.**

buncombe; *bunkum. This term (meaning "political talk that is empty or insincere") derives from an early-19th-century speech made by a U.S. Congressman representing Buncombe County, North Carolina. He felt compelled, despite other pressing business, to "make a speech for Buncombe" during a session of Congress. *Buncombe* has remained the standard spelling and is to be preferred in any event because it recalls the interesting origin of the word—e.g.:

- "It is doubtful if any . . . political party ever used so much *buncombe* and so little brains as did the Whigs in the presidential contest of 1840." 1 James K. McGuire & Martin Wilie Littleton, *The Democratic Party of the State of New York* 180 (1905).
- "Or would we dig deeply into our stories of neighborliness and *buncombe* and cobble together something almost great?" Thomas Hine, *Don't Blame Mrs. O'Leary,* N.Y. Times, 15 July 1990, § 7, at 13.

The shortened casualism is spelled *bunk* (= nonsense) <that's all bunk!>. A clipped form of *bunkum*, it dated from the early 20th century. Henry Ford immortalized the word when he said, "History is more or less *bunk*."

burden of proof. A. Senses. This ambiguous term refers to two distinct concepts, as James Bradley Thayer was the first to observe in the late 19th century.

See 1 James B. Thayer, *Evidence* 355–64 (1898). Many judicial decisions that ignore the distinction contain muddled reasoning.

The first concept is known more particularly—and unambiguously—as the *risk of nonpersuasion*, the *burden of persuasion*, and the *persuasion burden*. A party meets this burden by convincing the fact-finder to view the facts in a way that favors that party. Today the phrase *burden of proof* most often bears this meaning.

The second concept is known more particularly—and unambiguously—as the *duty of producing evidence*, the *burden of going forward with evidence*, the *production burden*, or the *burden of evidence*. A party meets this burden by introducing enough evidence to have a given issue considered in the case.

One writer explains what has emerged as the modern scholarly consensus: "It is now commonplace that the term *burden of proof* is used in a double sense," adding: "Much confusion would be eliminated if . . . the ambiguous word *proof* [were] entirely discarded." Roy R. Ray, *Texas Law of Evidence* § 41, at 48 (3d ed. 1980).

B. And *onus of proof.* The phrase *burden of proof* is usual in American legal writing; both phrases are used in British legal writing. E.g.: "The judge next directed the jury as to the *onus of proof* upon the issue of provocation." *R. v. Brown*, [1972] 2 Q.B. 229, 235 (C.A.). See **onus** & LOAN TRANSLATIONS.

burglar. See **thief.**

burglarious = of, relating to, or inclined to burglary. E.g.:

- "The completion of the *burglarious* intent is not essential to guilt." Rollin M. Perkins, *Criminal Law* 169 (1957).
- "Although primarily aimed against the carrying of *burglarious* tools, it applies also to the possession of a large variety of other objects with the requisite intent." Glanville Williams, *Textbook of Criminal Law* 819–20 (1978).

Burglariously (L. *burglariter*) was formerly obligatory in indictments for burglary at common law. The word still occasionally appears in more modern contexts—e.g.: "The state argued . . . that . . . he had *burglariously* and feloniously remained in the women's home." *State v. Thomson*, 861 P.2d 492, 495 (Wash. Ct. App. 1993).

burglarize; burgle. *Burglarize* is an American coinage from the late 19th century meaning "to rob burglariously" (*OED*). It is still largely confined to AmE. *Burgle*, a BACK-FORMATION of comparable vintage, has the same meaning; in AmE, *burgle* is usually facetious or jocular, whereas in BrE it is standard and colorless—e.g.: "If you think it is a good idea that the prime minister's house should be *burgled*, it is just as well not to express the thought to a cracksman." Glanville Williams, *Textbook of Criminal Law* 31 (1978).

In American judicial opinions, *burglarize* appears about 30 times as frequently as *burgle*. E.g.:

- "He readily spoke about burglaries, . . . but attributed them to someone named 'George,' a person of bad influence

who forced Heirens to search out places for him to *burglarize.*" *People v. Heirens,* 122 N.E.2d 231, 234 (Ill. 1954).
- "While he was away both apartments were *burglarized* and damaged." *U.S. v. Doby,* 684 F.Supp. 558, 560 (N.D. Ind. 1988).

See **steal** & **rob.**

burglary. A. And *robbery*; *theft*; *larceny*. The precise definitions of these terms vary from jurisdiction to jurisdiction. But it is universal that *people* are the objects of *robbery*; *places* are the objects of *burglary*; and *things* are the objects of *larceny* and *theft*.

Burglary = (1) (in the classic common-law sense) the act of breaking and entering another's house at night with intent to commit a felony (e.g., murder) or—in jurisdictions with statutes making petit larceny a misdemeanor—possibly petit larceny as well; (2) (in the modern AmE sense) the act of breaking and entering a building with the intent to commit a felony (dropping the requirements that it be [a] a house, and [b] at night); or (3) (in the modern BrE sense) the offense either of entering a building, ship, or inhabited vehicle (e.g., a caravan) as a trespasser with the intention of committing one of four specified crimes in it (*burglary with intent*) or of entering it as a trespasser but later committing one of two specified crimes in it (*burglary without intent*). The specified offenses in G.B. are, for *burglary with intent*: (1) stealing; (2) inflicting grievous bodily harm; (3) causing criminal damage; and (4) rape. And for *burglary without intent*: (1) stealing or attempting to steal; and (2) inflicting or attempting to inflict grievous bodily harm.

Robbery = the felonious taking of personal property by force or threat of force from the immediate presence of the victim. *Theft* is a statutory wrong that is broader than *robbery*, although nonlawyers often consider the words synonymous; *theft* means "the taking of personal property belonging to another without his consent, and with the intent to deprive the owner of its value." *Theft* is also broader than *larceny* (= the felonious stealing of personal property; the fraudulent taking and carrying away [*asportation*] of a thing without claim of right), for it includes the lawful acquisition and later misappropriation of the personalty. In England, the common-law felony of larceny was superseded by the Theft Act of 1968. See **asportation.**

In American legal writing, when *of* follows *burglary*, some infelicity or other is almost certain to follow; *burglary of an automobile* would traditionally have been considered a legal blunder, though several states now have statutes that incorporate this phrase; *burglary of a building* is a REDUNDANCY, unless the reference is to a particular building, as in *burglary of the Stokes Building.*

B. And *housebreaking*. *Housebreaking* is a little-used variant of *burglary* in its modern statutory sense (as opposed to the common-law sense). Though the word suggests that it relates only to dwellings, its meaning is broader: "unlawfully breaking into any building, public or private, at any hour, and committing a felony [inside], or, having committed a felony [inside], breaking out." Edward Jenks, *The Book of English Law* 175 (P.B. Fairest ed., 6th ed. 1967). E.g.: "Petitioner was charged with attempted *housebreaking*, and assault with attempt to rape in violation of articles 80, 130, and 134 of the Uniform Code of Military Justice." *Breaking and entering* is a frequently used DOUBLET in that sense.

In Scotland, there is no crime of burglary—only housebreaking—and in that context *house* refers to any secured building. And whereas a *burglary* traditionally occurred at night, a *housebreaking* might occur at any time of day. In Scots law, either offense has historically been called *housebreaking.*

burgle. See **burglarize.**

BURIED VERBS. Jargonmongers call them "nominalizations," i.e., verbs that have been changed into nouns. Without the jargon, one might say that the verbs have been buried in a longer noun—usually a noun ending in one of the following suffixes: *-tion*, *-sion*, *-ment*, *-ence*, *-ance*, *-ity*. It is hardly an exaggeration—no, one hardly exaggerates—to say that, whenever the verb will work in context, the better choice is to use it instead of a buried verb. Hence:

The Verb Buried	*The Verb Uncovered*
arbitration	arbitrate
compulsion	compel
computerization	computerize
conformity, -ance	conform
contravention	contravene
dependence	depend
enablement	enable
enforcement	enforce
hospitalization	hospitalize
identity	identify
incorporation	incorporate
indemnification	indemnify
knowledge	know
litigation	litigate
maximization	maximize
mediation	mediate
minimization	minimize
obligation	obligate, oblige
opposition	oppose
penalization	penalize
perpetration	perpetrate
perpetuation	perpetuate
reduction	reduce
utilization	utilize, use (vb.)
violation	violate

Naturally, you will sometimes need to refer to arbitration or litigation or mediation as a procedure, and

---

An asterisk (✳) precedes words and phrases that are invariably inferior forms.

when that is so you must say *arbitration* or *litigation* or *mediation*. But if a first draft refers to *the mediation of the claims by the parties*, you might well consider having the second draft refer to *the parties' mediating the claims* or to *the time when the parties will mediate their claims*.

Why uncover buried verbs? Three reasons are detectable to the naked eye: first, you generally eliminate prepositions in the process; second, you often eliminate *be*-verbs by replacing them with so-called "action" verbs; and third, you humanize the text by saying who does what (an idea often obscured by buried verbs). See BE-VERBS.

The fourth reason is not detectable to the naked eye: in fact, it is the sum of the three reasons already mentioned. By uncovering buried verbs, you make your writing much less abstract—it becomes much easier for readers to visualize what you're talking about. (Compare: "After the transformation of nominalizations, the text has fewer abstractions; readers' visualization of the discussion is enhanced.") Writing that is laden with buried verbs tends to numb the mind: "In our day, long English words of Latin origin—sometimes in the form of sociological or pseudo-scientific gobbledygook—often have hypnotic or sleep-inducing effects." *Sperbeck v. A.L. Burbank & Co.*, 190 F.2d 449, 450 n.8 (2d Cir. 1951). See ABSTRACTITIS.

Though long neglected in books about writing, buried verbs ought to be a sworn enemy of every serious writer. In legal writing, they constitute a more serious problem even than PASSIVE VOICE—whether in analytical writing, persuasive writing, or drafting.

*burthen is an ARCHAISM and a NEEDLESS VARIANT of *burden* that Shakespeare used frequently and that persisted in legal writing into the 19th century—e.g.: "That the title of the land, when acquired by the community, was taken in the name of the wife, imposes no additional *burthen* [read *burden*] upon the purchaser of inquiring into the equities of the husband and wife in respect to it." *Cooke v. Bremond*, 27 Tex. 457, 460 (1864). It still occasionally burdens legal writing in old quoted matter, but it otherwise has no place in 21st-century prose.

bus, n. & vb. The plural form of the noun (meaning a large vehicle that holds many passengers) is *buses.* The verb (meaning "to transport by bus") is inflected *bus > bused > bused*; the present participle is *busing.* See **busing.**

bush lawyer is an Australian term meaning "a person pretending to have considerable legal knowledge" (*W3*). This term might deserve universal adoption, for we *need* such a name. See LAWYERS, DEROGATORY NAMES FOR (B).

business; industry; commerce; trade; traffic. In their most general senses, these terms refer collectively to the activities by which people try to earn money. *Business* denotes the combined activities by which people make money through goods and services. *Industry* refers mainly to the activities of those engaged in manufacture and production, the construction of buildings, and ventures involving massive labor and major capital. *Commerce* and *trade* imply activities, large and small, involved in the sale of commodities and the provision of services. *Trade* more than *commerce* suggests exchanges of physical goods—but this is only a vague tendency in the word. *Traffic* refers to activities involving the transportation of goods by land, sea, or air <the coal traffic around the world>—sometimes with an association of illegality <drug traffic>.

busing (= the transportation of public-school students to schools outside their neighborhoods, usu. to achieve a racial balance) is so spelled. *Bussing* (which actually denotes kissing) is a misspelling in this context—e.g.: "The court upheld a court-ordered desegregation plan [that] incorporated mandatory *bussing* [read *busing*] in a 'Southern' school district, which was infected with 'de jure' racial segregation." *Citizens Against Mandatory Bussing v. Brooks*, 492 P.2d 536, 540 (Wash. 1972). (Note that the organization's name contained the misspelling.) As a matter of spelling, the single-*s busing* is quite uncontroversial, even if the reality denoted by the word remains emotionally charged—e.g.: "The measures required by those cases often included race-conscious practices, such as mandatory *busing* and race-based restrictions on voluntary transfers." *Parents Involved in Cmty. Sch. v. Seattle Sch. Dist. No. 1*, 551 U.S. 701, 804 (2007) (Breyer, J., dissenting). See **bus.**

Arthur A. Leff knowingly used *bussing* for *busing* in *The Leff Dictionary of Law*, 94 Yale L.J. 1855, 1967 (1985). In his entry under *busing*, Leff took the position that the word is "also properly spelled *bussing*." Accepting that dictum would destroy the DIFFERENTIATION that has evolved between the forms, and therefore it is to be taken as unsound. *Busing* is preferred even in BrE in nonosculatory senses. *See Oxford Guide* 9.

but. A. Beginning Sentences with. It is a gross canard that beginning a sentence with *but* is stylistically slipshod. In fact, doing so is highly desirable in any number of contexts, and most stylebooks that squarely discuss the question say that *but* is better than *however* at the beginning of a sentence. See Garner, "On Conjunctions as Sentence-Starters," in *Garner on Language and Writing* 63–87 (2009). For combinations with *and* and *but* starting sentences, see **and (A).** See also SUPERSTITIONS.

Good writers frequently begin sentences with *but*, and have always done so—e.g.:

- "*But* let it be admitted, for argument's sake, that mere wantonness and lust of domination would be sufficient to beget that disposition." *The Federalist* No. 17, at 119 (Alexander Hamilton) (Clinton Rossiter ed., 1961).
- "When a vessel at sea begins to founder there comes a time when it must be given up as lost. *But* we do not give

the order to abandon ship as soon as, let us say, a fuel pump begins to function erratically." Lon L. Fuller, *Anatomy of the Law* 21 (1968).

- "It is not beyond the bounds of possibility that such a husband might be convicted either of manslaughter or of abetting suicide. *But* he ought not to be." Glanville Williams, *Textbook of Criminal Law* 531 (1978).
- "The strongest case for imposing legal liability arises where there are both benefit and detrimental reliance. *But* it is not necessary that both detriment and benefit should be present in order that the consideration should be good." P.S. Atiyah, *An Introduction to the Law of Contract* 101 (3d ed. 1981).
- "Despite errors and failings, Blackstone did manage to put in brief order the rank weeds of English law. *But* even his picture was partial and defective, like a dictionary that omitted all slang, all dialect, all colloquial and technical words." Lawrence M. Friedman, *A History of American Law* 21 (2d ed. 1985).

B. More than One in a Sentence. Putting this coordinating conjunction (also called a "coordinator") twice in one sentence invariably makes the sentence unwieldy and less than easily readable—e.g.:

- "If an incompetent has no curator, *but* is interdicted, or committed to or confined in a mental institution, the action shall be brought against him, *but* [read *and*] the court shall appoint an attorney at law to represent him." *Alonzo v. Alonzo*, 634 So.2d 54, 57 (La. Ct. App. 1994).
- "*But* the Court does not agree with the argument if the fee being assessed is a fee that counsel requests, *but* [read *and*] is not one yielded by applying the contingency percentage to the past due benefits." *Black v. Astrue*, 584 F.Supp.2d 1278, 1286 (C.D. Cal. 2008).

See the following subsection.

C. For *and*. This is a common mistake. In the following sentences, the second clause follows naturally from the first—it does not state an exception to or qualification of the first—hence *and* is the appropriate conjunction. E.g.:

- "This action was brought by the administrator of Katherine Veach against the Louisville & Interurban Railway Company, to recover damages for [Miss Veach's] death in the sum of $25,000, *but* [read *and*] a trial resulted in a verdict and judgment in favor of the administrator." *Veach's Adm'r v. Louisville & Interurban Ry.*, 228 S.W. 35, 35 (Ky. 1921).
- "Summary judgment is a potent weapon, *but* [read *and*] courts must be mindful of its aims and targets and beware of overkill in its use." *Findeisen v. North East Indep. Sch. Dist.*, 749 F.2d 234, 239 (5th Cir. 1984).

D. Preposition or Conjunction. The use of *but* in a negative sense after a pronoun ("No one *but she* or *her*") has long caused confusion. If we take *but* to be a preposition (meaning "except"), the objective *her* (or *him*) follows. But if we take *but* as a conjunction, the nominative *she* (or *he*) would be proper.

The correct form depends on the structure of the sentence. If the verb precedes the *but*-phrase, the objective case should be used—e.g.:

- "The Office of the Soveraign (be it a Monarch, or an Assembly) consisteth in the end for which he was trusted with the Soveraign Power, namely the procuration of the safety of the people; to which he is obliged by the Law of Nature, and to render an account thereof to God, the Author of that Law, and to none *but him*." Thomas Hobbes, *Leviathan* *175 (1651).
- "PepsiCo represented to plaintiffs that it would not approve the transfer of the Texarkana franchise to anyone *but them*." *Deligiannis v. PepsiCo, Inc.*, 757 F.Supp. 241, 252 (S.D.N.Y. 1991).

But if the *but*-phrase precedes the verb, the nominative case is proper: "None of the defendants *but he* were convicted." This sentence is considered equivalent to "None of the defendants were convicted, *but he was convicted*." *But* acts as a conjunction when it precedes the verb in a sentence such as this, from Thomas Jefferson: "You, however, can easily correct this bill to the taste of my brother lawyers, by making every other word a 'said' or 'aforesaid,' and saying everything two or three times, so that nobody *but we* of the craft *can understand* the diction, and find out what it means." *Jefferson on Jefferson* 44 (Paul M. Zall ed., 2002).

but for (= if not for; except for) has become a useful LEGALISM, as in the following sentences:

- "I also think that the statute is constitutional, and *but for* the decision of my brethren I should have felt pretty clear about it." *Adair v. U.S.*, 208 U.S. 161, 190 (1908) (Holmes, J., dissenting).
- "It is therefore quite plain that *but for* the constitutional prohibition on the operation of segregated public parks, the City of Macon would continue to own and maintain Baconsfield." *Evans v. Abney*, 396 U.S. 435, 453 (1970) (per Brennan, J.).
- "The evidence also showed that, *but for* the negligence of Lee-Vac, the socket never would have failed." *Cities Serv. Co. v. Lee-Vac, Ltd.*, 761 F.2d 238, 240 (5th Cir. 1985).
- "This was not a mixed-motives case such as *Price Waterhouse*, in which it is necessary to decide whether, *but for* the bad motive, the transaction sought by the plaintiff would have gone through." *Bachman v. St. Monica's Congregation*, 902 F.2d 1259, 1263 (7th Cir. 1990).
- "Wife maintained she did not commit adultery prior to signing the paper, and would not have had sex with anyone *but for* the Agreement." *Eason v. Eason*, 682 S.E.2d 804, 806 (S.C. 2009). On the use of *prior to in that sentence, see ***prior to.**

Judge Frank Easterbrook may be the only judge in history to have begun an opinion with *but*, and he did it by using *but for*. See *U.S. v. Duff*, 76 F.3d 122, 124 (7th Cir. 1996) ("*But for* the holding of *Ray v. United States*, this would be a brief opinion."). But to be fair, several judges had previously begun concurring or dissenting opinions with *but for*. See *Davis v. United Cos. Mortgage & Inv. of Gretna*, 551 F.2d 971, 973 (5th Cir. 1977) (Jones, J., dissenting) ("*But for* our precedents by which I am bound."). Easterbrook is apparently a fan of that practice too. See *U.S. v. Campbell*,

324 F.3d 497, 499 (7th Cir. 2003) (Easterbrook, J., concurring) ("*But for* the law of the case, I would vote to vacate the district court's decision and remand with instructions to dismiss for want of jurisdiction.").

In American legal writing, the phrase is frequently used attributively as an adjective, as in *but-for test* or *but-for relationship*. In such phrases, it is better to hyphenate than to use quotation marks around the phrasal adjective. See PHRASAL ADJECTIVES. For *but-for causation*, see CAUSATION (A).

One should avoid using this phrase in two different senses in close proximity, as here (in the third appearance of the phrase): "There is no pretense that the Coliseum would ever be restored to the position it would have occupied *but for* [i.e., were it not for] the wrong. *But for* [i.e., were it not for] the NFL's antitrust violation, the Coliseum would have had college football plus the Raiders, and it would have had the Raiders immediately instead of later. It is true that these losses were short-term, *but for* [i.e., except that for] that period they were irreplaceable, and therefore irreparable." Douglas Laycock, *The Death of the Irreparable Injury Rule* 114 (1991).

butts and bounds. See **metes and bounds.**

but which. See **which (C).**

buy; purchase. As a verb, *buy* is the ordinary word, *purchase* the more FORMAL WORD. Generally, *buy* is the better stylistic choice. As one commentator says, "Only a very pompous person indeed would say he was going to *purchase* an ice-cream cone or a bar of candy." Robert Hendrickson, *Business Talk* 61 (1984). Traditionally, however, *purchase* has been the proper word for real property. See **descent.**

Purchase may also act as a noun; *buy* is informal and colloquial as a noun <a good buy>. See **purchase.**

buyback, n. One word.

buydown, n. One word.

buyer; purchaser. In most contexts, *buyer* is the better term because it is plainer.

buyout. One word.

by. See **before.**

by and between. Though this is a hallowed expression at the outset of contracts, it is unnecessary: *between* alone suffices. E.g.: "The Federal Circuit held that any disputes *by and between* [read *between*] the parties had to be resolved under mandates of that venue provision." Cecilia H. Gonzalez et al., *The Parallel Universes of the USITC and the District Courts*, 10 Sedona Conf. J. 167, 176 (2009). See DOUBLETS, TRIPLETS, AND SYNONYM-STRINGS.

by and through, typical LEGALESE, can be replaced by either *by* or *through*. E.g.:

• "Plaintiff, *by and through* [read *through*] his attorney Laura Robinson, has provided the Court with a litany of ramblings, pleas, and allegations." *Collins v. Educ. Therapy Ctr.*, 184 F.3d 617, 620 (7th Cir. 1999).

• "Mr. Gilmore, *by and through* [read *through*] his attorneys, then filed a response, challenging his mother's standing." *Comer v. Schriro*, 480 F.3d 960, 978 (9th Cir. 2007).

• "January 13, 2006, C.M., *by and through* [read *through*] his attorney ad litem, filed a motion for declaratory judgment asking the lower court to declare that the appellant was his father." Katie S. Allen, Note, *Daddy Dilemma: Should the Truth Matter?*, 30 UALR L. Rev. 815, 833 (2008).

See DOUBLETS, TRIPLETS, AND SYNONYM-STRINGS.

by and with is a classic legal REDUNDANCY with but one legitimate use: "For appointments to constitutional offices the phrase *by and with the advice of the Senate* is a TERM OF ART and should not be changed." Reed Dickerson, *Legislative Drafting* 75 n.4 (1954). See DOUBLETS, TRIPLETS, AND SYNONYM-STRINGS.

byelaw. See **bylaw.**

by-election; *bye-election. *By-election* is preferred in both AmE and BrE.

by its four corners. See **four corners of the instrument.**

by law. See **under law.**

bylaw; byelaw. Not only the spelling but also the sense differs in AmE from that in BrE. In G.B., *byelaws* are regulations made by a local authority or corporation, such as a town or a railway. In the U.S., *bylaws* are most commonly a corporation's administrative provisions that are either attached to the articles of incorporation or kept privately.

The spelling without the *-e-* is preferred in AmE. Though etymologically inferior, *byelaw* (sometimes hyphenated) is standard in British legal texts. E.g.:

• "The general principle—the result of the cases—is 'that a municipal power of regulation or of making *bye-laws* for good government without express words of prohibition does not authorise the making it unlawful to carry on a lawful trade in a lawful manner.'" *Scott v. Glasgow Corp.*, [1899] 1 F. 51 (H.L.).

• "Clause [four] requires the contractor to comply with Acts of Parliament and *bye-laws*." *James Miller & Partners, Ltd. v. Whitworth St. Estates*, [1970] A.C. 583, 604 (H.L.).

For British publications, however, the house style of Oxford University Press is *by-law*. See **ordinance.**

by reason of is typically wordy for *because of*. Although *not guilty by reason of insanity* is a SET PHRASE, in other phrases, the words *by reason of* can usually be improved—e.g.: "*By reason of* [read *Because of*] the injuries aforesaid, the plaintiff has been put to great expense for care and medical treatment." Max Radin, *The Law and You* 102 (1948) (quoting a pleading).

bystander. See **witness (B).**

by the court; per curiam. *By the court* is merely an English translation of *per curiam* (see LOAN TRANS-LATIONS), a term that appears in opinions not attributed to any one member of the court. Contrary to the notion that some lawyers have, *per curiam* opinions usually deal with routine matters that are seen by the judges as having little precedential value; they often dispose of such cases summarily. *Per curiam* opinions should not be construed as exhibiting greater unanimity among members of the court than a signed opinion without a dissent.

Some courts variously use both *per curiam* and *by the court*, of course without DIFFERENTIATION. (Though the practice is now rare, some courts have used merely *the court* for *per curiam* opinions.) It might be best to stick with a single phrase, lest readers of the opinions come to think there must be a distinction. On the one hand, *per curiam* is unambiguous and can be used attributively (*per curiam opinion*), whereas *by the court* may create ambiguities in speech and in writing. Though it is a LATINISM, *per curiam* is a useful and well-established one: it is not likely to be discarded any time soon. On the other hand, *by the court* is at least a comprehensible phrase to all speakers of English, even if they do not all understand its import. Certainly this is the better phrase for popular journalism.

by the later of [date] and [date]; by the later of [date] or [date]. See **later of [date] or [date].**

by virtue of. See **virtue of, in & by.**

C

cab-rank rule = the rule (in G.B.) that a barrister or advocate, if not already engaged, must accept any case in his or her area of practice, however unpopular or disreputable the cause may be. The rule dates back to the 13th century, when the serjeants-at-law were sworn to represent all comers. The METAPHOR, of course, refers to how cabdrivers must line up to accept each fare in turn, without turning away any potential customer in favor of others. Nowadays, in English law practice, the rule is "more celebrated for the way in which it has been ignored." Robert Rice, *Amendment to Cab-Rank Clause Is Welcomed*, Fin. Times, 14 May 1990, at I-12.

cacozelia. See MINGLE-MANGLE.

caducary; *caduciary; *caducous. Most often rendered *caducary* /**kad**-yoo-kair-ee/, the word means (of a bequest or estate) "subject to, relating to, or by way of escheat, lapse, or forfeiture." Labeled "Old Law" in the *OED*, it has nevertheless persisted from Blackstone's day to 21st-century AmE—usually in the phrase *caducary succession*—especially in New York practice. *See, e.g.*, In re Peer's Estate, 245 N.Y.S. 298, 301 (Sur. Ct. 1930) (noting that the amendments "were apparently intended to waive the rights of the State to claim escheat, or rights of '*caducary* successions,' where there were no blood relatives").

The *SOED* entry appears under *caduciary, which is the "nonetymological form" that, according to the *OED*, received the superfluous *-i-* by confusion with *fiduciary*. Perhaps because of its spurious origins, *caduciary has not appeared in recent American or English caselaw. But Scottish texts predominantly use this spelling. One, for example, posits the question "whether the rights of the Crown in England are to be regarded as *caduciary* or successoral." A.E. Anton, *Private International Law* 679 (2d ed. 1990). Like *caducous, the form *caduciary is—outside Scotland—best considered a NEEDLESS VARIANT.

caduce, vb., = to take by escheat or lapse. Derived as a BACK-FORMATION from *caducary*, this NEOLOGISM has achieved a surprising degree of currency. E.g.:

- "The next day, the Government delivered a formal notice that Gulf Ecuador would be *caduced* unless it delivered all funds owed within 30 days." *Phoenix Can. Oil Co. v. Texaco, Inc.*, 658 F.Supp. 1061, 1076 (D. Del. 1987).
- "As it is clear that the Government of Ecuador would not assume the obligation to pay the royalties, and that the contract provided that the companies would pay royalties only on oil they sold, the Government, in effect, *caduced* the plaintiff's royalty rights." *Norsul Oil & Mining Co. v. Texaco, Inc.*, 703 F.Supp. 1520, 1542 (S.D. Fla. 1988).

See **caducary.**

*caduciary. See **caducary.**

caducity = (1) a lapse of a testamentary gift; or (2) the defined period within which a right or claim must be asserted. The term is current mostly in jurisdictions with strong civil-law ties, such as Louisiana and Puerto Rico. E.g.:

- "[T]he *caducity* or inheritable quality of a donation *mortis causa* can be destroyed or rendered ineffective by revocation by the testator or lapse of the legacy." *In re Succession of Buck*, 834 So.2d 475, 477 (La. Ct. App. 2002).
- "An employee has fifteen days after discharge . . . to request reinstatement, provided this request is not made after the lapse of twelve months from the date of the accident. The twelve months is a term of *caducity*." *Castro-Medina v. Procter & Gamble Com. Co.*, 565 F.Supp.2d 343, 349 n.2 (D.P.R. 2008).

*caducous. See **caducary.**

Cain, mark of. See **scarlet-letter.**

calculated = (1) deliberately taken or made <a calculated risk>; or (2) likely <no prospectus may be calculated to deceive>. Sense 2 represents a debasement in meaning that, particularly in criminal-law contexts,

damages the utility of the word even in sense 1. See
SLIPSHOD EXTENSION.

calculus is best confined to mean "a method of calculation" <we should change the calculus somewhat>
and not "calculation" itself. Often *calculus* should
probably be replaced by *calculation*—e.g.:

- "Professor William Fisher, who attempted to establish a framework for such a *calculus* [read *calculation*],
  expressed serious skepticism about the usefulness of his
  analysis for judges." Gideon Parchomovsky & Kevin A.
  Goldman, *Fair Use Harbors*, 93 Va. L. Rev. 1483, 1531
  (2007).
- "While the balance of scales may indeed tip in Grace's
  favor, such a *calculus* [read *calculation*] is far from certain." *In re W.R. Grace & Co.*, 412 B.R. 657, 665 (D. Del.
  2009).

By extension, *calculus* has come to be used as a
VOGUE WORD meaning "a method of analysis" or even
"analysis"—e.g.:

- "In a case like this, in which Congress has not plainly
  marked our course, we must be circumspect in construing the scope of rights created by a legislative enactment
  which never contemplated such a *calculus* [read *analysis*]
  of interests." *Sony Corp. of Am. v. Universal City Studios,
  Inc.*, 464 U.S. 417, 431 (1984) (per Stevens, J.).
- "There is nothing wrong with this balancing *calculus* [oh
  yes there is: read *analysis*] yielding in some sense a basic
  right to liberty. *Such a calculus* [read *It*] protects acts
  themselves, not just illicitly motivated coercion of acts."
  Michael S. Moore, *Freedom*, 29 Harv. J.L. & Pub. Pol'y 9,
  19 (2005).

calendar. In AmE this word is used for *docket* or
cause-list in both civil and criminal cases, but in BrE
the term refers to criminal cases only. See **docket.**

Lawyers often use the word as a verb <the case was
calendared for May 23, 2011>—a centuries-old and
unexceptionable use. E.g.: "It appears that many of
these motions were never *calendared* for hearing or
ruled upon by the trial court." *Slawek v. Slawek*, 698
S.E.2d 768, 769 (N.C. Ct. App. 2010).

call. See **summon.**

called to the bar = (1) in BrE, admitted to practice as a
barrister or advocate; (2) in AmE, admitted to law practice of any kind. Though primarily a BrE locution—
limited strictly to barristers and advocates—the phrase
has achieved some currency among American lawyers.
E.g.: "When I was first *called to the bar*, I received a
very large certificate bearing the Governor's signature
evidencing my appointment as Attorney at Law and
Solicitor in Chancery." Letter of S.B. Rounds (quoted
in William Safire, *I Stand Corrected* 417 (1984)).

In BrE, to be *called within the bar*, as opposed to
merely *to* the bar, is to be appointed King's or Queen's
Counsel.

The noun phrase is *call to the bar*—e.g.: "Timothy,
my former pupil, being by some two or three years the
senior in *call to the Bar*, is detained more often than
not by the claims of his profession." Sarah Caudwell,
Thus Was Adonis Murdered 10 (1981). Sometimes
the phrase is shortened to *call*: "He almost invariably

became a member of the Serjeants' Inn, and ceremo-
nially departed from his Inn of *call*." R.E. Megarry, *A
Second Miscellany-at-Law* 25–26 (1973). See **admit (c).**

calumniate; *calumnize. See **defame.**

calumny, a somewhat old-fashioned equivalent of
defamation, may refer to either (1) the act of falsely
and maliciously misrepresenting the words or actions
of others so as to injure their reputations, or (2) the
false charges or imputations themselves. Although
this term was used at common law as a technical legal
word, today it is more literary than legal. The phrase
breath of calumny is an old CLICHÉ.

The adjective is *calumnious* (*calumniatory
being a NEEDLESS VARIANT), and the agent noun is
calumniator.

came on for hearing; coming on for hearing. These
phrases begin legalistically worded court orders,
often (as with the second example below) as inverted
constructions—e.g.:

- "This matter *came on for hearing* on July 25, 1994, on the
  motion to dismiss filed by Defendant the Resolution Trust
  Corporation (RTC) and the motion for summary judgment filed by Defendants Glenn and Helen Arbogast (the
  Arbogasts)." *Tackett v. Cal. Indep. Trust Deed*, 859 F.Supp.
  1289, 1290 (C.D. Cal. 1994). A suggested revision: *On July
  25, 1994, the court heard the defendants' motion for summary judgment and motion to dismiss.*
- "*Came on for hearing* the 19th day of July, 1995, the EPA's
  Motion to Dismiss for Lack of Jurisdiction as well as
  motions for summary judgment filed by both parties."
  In re Powerlab, Inc., 184 B.R. 511, 512 (Bankr. N.D. Tex.
  1995). A suggested revision: *On July 19, 1994, the court
  heard the EPA's motion to dismiss and both parties' motions
  for summary judgment.*

camera (lit., "chamber"—i.e., the judge's private room)
is used in the phrase *in camera*. See also **chambers** &
in camera.

can. A. And *may*. The distinction between these
words has been much discussed over the years, beginning with Samuel Johnson's *Dictionary of the English
Language* (1755). Generally, *can* expresses physical or
mental ability <he can lift 500 pounds>; *may* expresses
permission or authorization <the guests may now
enter> and sometimes possibility <the trial may end
on Friday>. Although only an insufferable precisian
would insist on observing the distinction in informal
speech or writing (especially in questions such as "Can
I have until August?"), it's often advisable to distinguish between these words.

But three caveats are necessary. First, educated people typically say *can't I* as opposed to the stilted forms
mayn't I and *may I not*. The same is true of other pronouns <why can't she go?> <can't you wait until Saturday?>. Second, *you can't* and *you cannot* are much
more common denials of permission than *you may
not* <no, you can't play with any more than 14 clubs
in your bag>. Third, because *may* is a more polite way
of asking for permission, a fussy insistence on using it
can give the writing a prissy tone.

B. And *could*. These words express essentially the same idea, but there is a slight difference. In the phrase *We can supply you with 5 tons of caliche*, the meaning is simply that we are able to. But in the phrase *We could supply you with 5 tons of caliche if you'd send us a $5,000 deposit*, the *could* is right because of the condition tacked onto the end; that is, there is some stronger sense of doubt with *could*. (See SUBJUNCTIVES.) And in interrogatives, *could* indicates willingness: *Could you meet me at 7 p.m.?* This asks not just whether you're able, but also whether you're willing.

In still another circumstance—in the subordinate clause of a complex sentence—the choice between *can* and *could* depends on the sequence of tenses, as does the choice between any other present- and past-tense verb. If the verb in the main clause expresses a past event, *could* appears in the subordinate clause <She asked me to go so that I could meet my great-aunt>. But if the verb in the main clause expresses a present or future event, *can* appears in the main clause <She is asking me to go so that I can meet my great-aunt> <She will ask me to go so that I can meet my great-aunt>. See TENSES (A).

cancel. This verb preferably makes *canceled* and *canceling* in AmE, *cancelled* and *cancelling* in BrE. Because the primary accent falls on the first syllable, in AmE the *-l-* should not be doubled in the second syllable. Yet the *-ll-* spelling often crops up in American writing—e.g.: "Today we look only at a claim that the subject oil-and-gas leases should be *cancelled* [read *canceled*] for failure to extend their terms through compliance with their shut-in-royalty clauses." *Levin v. Maw Oil & Gas, LLC*, 234 P.3d 805, 819 (Kan. 2010). Note, however, that in *cancellation* the ells are doubled (*-ll-*). See DOUBLING OF FINAL CONSONANTS.

cancel (out). See PARTICLES, UNNECESSARY.

candidacy; candidature. The first is the regular term in AmE, the second in BrE.

candidate; aspirant; nominee; applicant. These terms all denote someone who is under consideration for an office or position. A *candidate* is typically one who seeks or is put forward for an elective office or for a college degree <candidate for the U.S. Senate> <candidates for the degree of J.D.>. An *aspirant* is one who seeks some honor or higher position, whether through election, nomination, or promotion <a lifelong aspirant to the mayorship>. A *nominee* is one who has been named either to represent a party in a forthcoming election <the Republican nominee> or to fill a post that requires confirmation <a Supreme Court nominee>. (Once the confirmation takes place, a *nominee* becomes an *appointee* <the Federal Trade Commissioner is a presidential *appointee*>.) An *applicant* is one who has formally applied for a position, even if the consideration given to the application may be cursory and dismissive (if, for example, the applicant is clearly underqualified) <he was but one in a huge field of applicants>.

cannon. See **canon.**

cannot be heard to say is a trite LEGALISM that expresses the notion of estoppel. E.g.:

• "Certainly if the conduct is eventually found by the National Labor Relations Board to be protected by the Taft–Hartley Act, the State *cannot be heard to say* that it is enjoining that conduct for reasons other than those having to do with labor relations." *Weber v. Anheuser-Busch, Inc.*, 348 U.S. 468, 480 (1955) (per Frankfurter, J.).
• "All parties were familiar with the custom of the industry regarding liability of pilots and mooring masters and *cannot be heard to say* that they were ignorant of the practice of attributing mooring masters' negligence to the shipowner." *Kane v. Hawaiian Indep. Refinery, Inc.*, 690 F.2d 722, 724 (9th Cir. 1982).
• "McElroy *cannot be heard to say* that he and Gemark had agreed on all the terms of the alleged agreement." *McElroy v. Gemark Alloy Refining Corp.*, 592 F.Supp.2d 508, 519 (S.D.N.Y. 2008).

canon; cannon. *Canon* = (1) a corpus of writings <the Scalia canon>; (2) an accepted notion or principle <canons of descent>; (3) a rule of ecclesiastical law (either of the Roman Catholic canon law or of the Anglican Church) <the church canons will not allow it>; or (4) a cathedral dignitary <the canon gave us a tour of Glasgow Cathedral>.

Cannon = (1) a big gun; or (2) the ear of a bell, by which the bell hangs. *Cannon* incorrectly displaces *canon* surprisingly often—e.g.:

• "The district court focused in part on the sections of the Indiana Code that make bailiffs 'at will' employees and [on] the *Cannons* [read *Canons*] of Professional Ethics." *Meeks v. Grimes*, 779 F.2d 417, 420 n.2 (7th Cir. 1985).
• "He was found to be guilty of violation of the *cannons* [read *canons*] of professional ethics by neglecting a legal matter entrusted to him by a client." *Ky. Bar Ass'n v. Lester*, 781 S.W.2d 517, 517 (Ky. 1989).
• "We therefore look to other *cannons* [read *canons*] of statutory interpretation to ascertain congressional intent." *U.S. v. Maciel-Alcala*, 598 F.3d 1239, 1244 (9th Cir. 2010).

The adjective corresponding to *canon* (senses 2–4) is *canonical*. It is perhaps most common as a secularized synonym of *axiomatic*: "Accountants long have recognized that generally accepted accounting principles are far from being a *canonical* set of rules that will ensure identical accounting treatment of identical transactions in all cases." *Grant Thornton, LLP v. FDIC*, 535 F.Supp.2d 676, 709 (S.D. W. Va. 2007). See **axiom.**

canonist = a specialist in ecclesiastical law, esp. in medieval times. A leading historian noted that the English common law "borrows far the greatest number of its fundamental principles from the jurisprudence of the *Canonists*." Henry S. Maine, *Ancient*

Law 132 (17th ed. 1901). Scholars frequently refer to canonists' opinions in discussing moral questions: "According to many of the early *canonists*, the soul was not infused into the infant's body until some time after conception." Glanville Williams, *The Sanctity of Life and the Criminal Law* 196 (1957). Cf. **civilian.**

canon law; church law. These synonymous phrases refer to the codified law governing a church. Traditionally, the phrases refer specifically to the ecclesiastical law governing the Roman Catholic Church, consisting largely of papal bulls, other official decrees, and writings by personages within the church.

canon-law method. See **civil-law method.**

capability. See **capacity** (A).

capable = (1) able to be affected by; of a nature, or in a condition, to allow or admit of; admitting; susceptible (*OED*); (2) having the needful capacity, power, or fitness for (some specified purpose or activity) (*id.*); or (3) having capacity, ability, or intelligence. Sense 1 is far more common today in legal than in lay writing:

• "'Submission to arbitration' is a phrase *capable of* more than one meaning." *Whitworth St. Ests. (Manchester) Ltd. v. James Miller & Partners Ltd.,* [1970] A.C. 583, 600 (H.L.).
• "Allegations of perjured testimony must be supported by substantial factual assertions *capable of* resolution by an evidentiary hearing." *U.S. v. Fishel,* 747 F.2d 271, 273 (5th Cir. 1984).

Sense 2 appears widely in lay and legal writing but is not used in quite the same way: while nonlawyers usually connect a participial phrase to *capable of*, lawyers frequently follow it with a simple noun. E.g.: "The automobiles are *capable of use* in distant States like Oklahoma." *World-Wide Volkswagen Corp. v. Woodson,* 444 U.S. 286, 298 (1980) (per White, J.). Most modern writers would make it *capable of being used.*

capacitas rationalis is a LATINISM whose perpetration in non-Roman contexts is an impeachable offense, what with English phrases like *rational capacity, rational faculties, reason,* and *rationality* to do the work. In the following title, the phrase might refer to the Roman-law doctrine: "Drug Intoxication and the Principle of *Capacita Rationalis*" (N.L.A. Barlow, 100 Law Q. Rev. 639 (1984)).

capacitate (= to qualify; to make legally competent) is a fancy LEGALISM, in place of which *qualify* or *make competent* is more widely comprehensible.

capacity. A. And *capability*. These words overlap, but there are important nuances. *Capacity* = the power to receive, hold, or contain. Figuratively, it refers to mental faculties in the sense "the power to take in knowledge." In law, it is frequently used in the sense "legal competency or qualification" <capacity to contract>. The legal presumption is that adults have capacity to make a will, to undertake financial and property

transactions, and to make decisions about health and welfare (*OCL2*). But it's a rebuttable presumption.

Capability = (1) power or ability in general, whether physical or mental; or (2) the quality of being susceptible of.

B. And *competency*. While *capacity* refers to legal ability or qualification, *competency* is a closely analogous word used in evidentiary contexts, as in *competency to testify*. See **competence.**

C. And *ability*. See **ability.**

capias (L. "that you take," a general term used of writs of attachment or arrest) is generally the shortened form of *capias ad respondendum*, which is a writ to enforce attendance at court. In AmE, the phrase *arrest warrant* has mostly displaced this use of *capias*.

There are also some less well-known species of *capias*, including:

• *capias ad satisfaciendum*, which was formerly used after judgment to imprison the defendant until the plaintiff's claim was satisfied. This phrase is often abbreviated *ca. sa.*, as here: "Another basis for amercement exists where a writ of *ca. sa.* has issued to the sheriff who makes a return that the defendant cannot be found in the county." *Poultrymen's Serv. Corp. v. Winter,* 244 A.2d 308, 309–10 (N.J. Super. Ct. App. Div. 1968). In England, this writ was available in rare cases until 1981.
• *capias utlagatum*, which commands the arrest of an outlawed person.
• *capias in witheram*, which authorizes the sheriff to seize the cattle or goods of a wrongful distrainor.

The word *capias*—as the shortened and anglicized form of *capias ad respondendum*—is a singular noun with the plural *capiases*. Yet *capias* is occasionally misapprehended as being plural as well as singular. E.g.: "On behalf of himself and others similarly situated, Stephen Crane brought an action . . . [complaining] that Dallas County regularly issued misdemeanor *capias* [read *capiases*] without a finding of probable cause by a neutral and detached magistrate." *Crane v. Texas,* 759 F.2d 412, 413–14 (5th Cir. 1985).

capital, adj. Lawyers use this word in two closely allied senses: (1) "punishable by death" <capital crimes>; and (2) "involving capital punishment" <capital cases>. The first example illustrates sense 1, the second and third sense 2:

• "No person shall be held to answer for a *capital*, or otherwise infamous crime, unless on presentment or indictment of a Grand Jury . . . ." U.S. Const. amend. V.
• "A lawyer whose practice is primarily civil may initially face some trepidation in taking on criminal appellate or postconviction *capital* work." Paul J. Bschorr, *Challenges for the Decade,* 17 Litig. 1, 2 (1991).
• "It is not unusual for some complex cases, such as *capital* cases, to have jury deliberations extend beyond three hours." Jay B. Rosman, *Justice in Transition,* 33 Nova L. Rev. 545, 588 (2009).

The *OED* traces these senses to the late 15th and early 16th centuries and lists a lesser-included sense in Roman law, in which *capital* means "involving the loss of civil rights."

Capital can also refer to the money used by an organization, as distinct from income <capital funding>.

capital, n.; **capitol.** The first is a city, the seat of government; the second is a building in which the state or national legislature meets (fr. L. *capitoleum*, the Roman temple of Jupiter). Until October 1698, when the Virginia governor specified that *Capitol* would be the name of the planned statehouse in a village then known as Middle Plantation, the word *capitol* had been used only as the name of the great Roman temple at Rome. *See* Mitford M. Mathews, *American Words* 62–63 (1959).

Capital, whether as a noun or as an adjective (see the preceding entry), is called on far more frequently than *capitol*.

capitalist; capitalistic. *Capitalist* is the general adjective; *capitalistic*, a favorite of Marxists, is pejorative.

CAPITALIZATION. Conventions of capitalization abound in legal writing; several of the more important ones are here discussed. They vary, to be sure, as practices in capitalizing are governed to some extent by personal taste. Sections (A), (B), and (C) below prescribe what might be called "rules" of capitalization, while sections (D), (E), (F), and (G) explain and describe common practices.

A. All Capitals. Avoid them. They impair readability because the eye cannot easily distinguish among characters that are all of a uniform size. Try reading these passages, which are ordered by increasing readability:

EXCEPT AS MAY BE OTHERWISE SPECIFICALLY PROVIDED IN THIS AGREEMENT, ALL NOTICES SHALL BE IN WRITING AND SHALL BE DEEMED TO BE DELIVERED WHEN DEPOSITED IN THE UNITED STATES MAIL, POSTAGE PREPAID, REGISTERED OR CERTIFIED MAIL, RETURN RECEIPT REQUESTED, ADDRESSED TO THE PARTIES AT THE RESPECTIVE ADDRESSES SET FORTH ON EXHIBIT B OR AT SUCH OTHER ADDRESSES AS EITHER PARTY MAY SPECIFY BY WRITTEN NOTICE.

vs.

Except as May Be Otherwise Specifically Provided in This Agreement, All Notices Shall Be in Writing and Shall Be Deemed to Be Delivered When Deposited in the United States Mail, Postage Prepaid, Registered or Certified Mail, Return Receipt Requested, Addressed to the Parties at the Respective Addresses Set Forth on Exhibit B or at Such Other Addresses as Either Party May Specify by Written Notice.

vs.

Except as may be otherwise specifically provided in this Agreement, all notices shall be in writing and shall be deemed to be delivered when deposited in the United States mail, postage prepaid, registered or certified mail, return receipt requested, addressed to the parties at the

respective addresses set forth on Exhibit B or at such other addresses as either party may specify by written notice.

What an odd phenomenon it is that lawyers—whenever they want to draw special attention to passages, such as main issues in a brief or warnings in drafted documents—make them typographically impenetrable. Using all caps is bad enough; underlining them is even worse. If you must use all caps, make sure that they don't run for more than one line.

Writers should avoid using all caps even for the conventions discussed in sections (D)–(G) below. Large and small caps, as in the titles of essay entries in this book, are preferable to all caps because they provide greater typographic variety and are therefore easier on the eye. See DOCUMENT DESIGN.

B. Up-Style Headings. When capitalizing only the initial letters of words (called *up-style* in headings or titles), follow these conventions:

1. Capitalize the first letter of every important word, such as a noun, pronoun, verb, adjective, and adverb, no matter how short the word. So words such as *pi*, *it*, and *be* should be capitalized in headings that use initial caps.

2. Capitalize the initial letter of the first and last word, no matter what part of speech either may be; also, capitalize the first letter of any word that follows a colon or a dash.

3. Put articles (*the, a, an*), as well as conjunctions (*and, or*) and prepositions having four or fewer letters (*of, by, with*), in lowercase.

C. Rules of Law. Named legal rules are variously written with initial letters either capitalized (as if they were titles) or lowercased. But even when we capitalize, the extent of capitalization is not settled; hence we have *the rule in Shelley's case, the Rule in Shelley's case, the Rule in Shelley's Case*, and *The Rule in Shelley's Case*. The first of these is a mere description; the second is not quite logical, since its last noun (*case*) is presented as a descriptive term while its first noun (*Rule*) is treated as a proper noun; the third is the best form, and the most usual; and the fourth makes *the* a part of the name or title, which makes sense for a book or article bearing that name but not for general references to the rule.

Other rules of law have just as many variations. (See, e.g., **Rule against Perpetuities.**) In questionable instances, the best policy is to determine to what extent general legal usage has sanctioned a certain phrase as being a rule of law, and then to capitalize those words essential to the name of the doctrine or rule. Hence *the doctrine of the Destructibility of Contingent Remainders* but *the Rule in Shelley's Case; Destructibility of Contingent Remainders* frequently appears without *the doctrine* or *the rule*, which is not really a part of the name of the rule, but *Shelley's Case* almost never occurs without *the Rule in* preceding it. Likewise *the Rule Forbidding a Remainder to the Grantor's Heirs* and *the Doctrine of Worthier Title*.

D. Vessel Names. These are now more commonly capitalized than not. But the habit of using all capitals is apparently of fairly recent origin. In a typical 19th-century case, *The Harrisburg*, 119 U.S. 199 (1886), the name of the ship had only the first letter capitalized; yet modern cases often write *THE HARRISBURG* when referring to the ship in that case. The older, more conservative convention might seem preferable, since words in all capitals are often distracting and difficult to read. See (A) in this entry. Cf. INITIALESE.

E. Judges' Names. It has long been a tradition, both in English and in American courts, to spell judges' names in all capitals when the names are referred to in judicial opinions—though not elsewhere. (For an older English example, see the quotation under **between (A).**) The U.S. Supreme Court regularly follows this practice. E.g.: "This view garnered three votes in *Arnett*, but was specifically rejected by the other six Justices. *See* [*Arnett v. Kennedy*, 416 U.S. 134, 166–67 (1974)] (POWELL, J., joined by BLACKMUN, J.); *id.* at 177–78, 185 (WHITE, J.); *id.* at 211 (MAR-SHALL, J., joined by DOUGLAS and BRENNAN, JJ.)." *Cleveland Bd. of Educ. v. Loudermill*, 470 U.S. 532, 540 (1985) (per White, J.).

F. Trademarks. Some legal writers prefer to use all capitals in spelling out trademarks. *See, e.g.*, *Conan Props., Inc. v. Conans Pizza, Inc.*, 752 F.2d 145 (5th Cir. 1985). This convention has the advantage of distinguishing between the mark and the party, as here: "In addition, starting from the time of the changeover to *EXXON* as its primary mark, *Exxon* developed plans for extended use of the *HUMBLE* mark, as reflected in numerous internal memoranda." Again, however, using all capitals can be immensely distracting to readers.

G. Party Names. Some people ill-advisedly use all caps for party names: "It is conventional although not essential to put short forms in quotation marks when they are established: JOHN DOE ('DOE'). The quotation marks are dropped for all subsequent references. It is archaic and uselessly wordy to recite 'JOHN DOE (hereinafter referred to as "DOE").'" Barbara Child, *Drafting Legal Documents* 123 (2d ed. 1992). For an example of how distracting it is to use all capitals for party names, see *Schneider v. Indian River Community College Found., Inc.*, 684 F.Supp. 283 (S.D. Fla. 1987). In pleadings and orders, the practice can be maddening. Renounce it.

H. Titles of Office. See TITULAR TOMFOOLERY.

I. Further Reference. For further guidance, see Bryan A. Garner, *The Redbook: A Manual on Legal Style* 53–68 (2d ed. 2006).

capitalize, in the sense "to provide with capital (i.e., money)" is a late-19th-century American NEOLOGISM that has gained universal acceptance—e.g.: "Plaintiffs *capitalized* the project at $3 million." *Sodima v. Int'l Yogurt Co.*, 662 F.Supp. 839, 842 (D. Or. 1987).

capital punishment, whether one is for or against what it denotes, is a legal EUPHEMISM for state-imposed death. See **death penalty.**

capitol. See **capital.**

capitulatory, not **capitulative*, is the adjective corresponding to *capitulation*—e.g.:

- "A party could prevail in an out-of-court settlement, or a defendant might moot the suit by taking unilateral *capitulatory* action." *Smith v. Thomas*, 725 F.2d 354, 356 (5th Cir. 1984).
- "Weisberg begins with what he calls 'the chastened view'—though it might as readily be seen as accommodational, perhaps even *capitulative* [read *capitulatory*], unless, again, we are to take the resolution it describes as inevitable, remaining only to be acknowledged." Nancy A. Weston, *The Fate, Violence, and Rhetoric of Contemporary Legal Thought*, 22 Law & Soc. Inquiry 733, 750 (1997).

caption. The sense "arrest or seizure by legal process" is the oldest for this word; now archaic, that sense has surfaced in several opinions that are, by the law's standards, within living memory—e.g.:

- "That the debt was attachable in confiscation proceedings was held by this court in *Miller v. The United States*, and it was ruled that attachment or seizure could be made without manual *caption* of the visible evidences of the credit." *Brown v. Kennedy*, 82 U.S. 591, 599 (1872) (per Strong, J.).
- "[Replevin] was so useful that it was extended to nearly all cases of unlawful *caption* and detention of chattels." *Largilliere Co. v. Kunz*, 244 P. 404, 405–06 (Idaho 1925).

The usual sense in modern writing—that of a heading—derives ultimately from that legal sense. *Caption* came to be used in the 17th century as a shortened form of *certificate of caption* or *taking*; such a certificate appeared at the top of a legal process to show where, when, and by what authority it was to be served or executed. Lawyers then pressed *caption* into service in a variety of contexts, such as to describe the heading on an abstract of title (where the land is described).

American journalists in turn extended this LEGAL-ISM further by making it refer, in the mid-19th century, to headings of newspaper articles and the like, where the English would have said *title, head*, or *heading*. (See **head.**) Hence in its most common sense today, *caption* is a POPULARIZED LEGAL TECHNICALITY.

captioned, as a short form of *above-captioned* <the captioned cause>, is, like the longer form, unnecessary JARGON. It is preferable to write *this case, that case, the Smith case*, or the like. See **above-mentioned.**

captive. See **prisoner.**

captor; **capturer*. The first is standard, the latter a NEEDLESS VARIANT.

Cardozo is not only widely mispronounced /kahr-**doh**-zə/ instead of /kahr-**doh**-zoh/; it is misspelled **Cardoza* in more than 50 reported cases, such as *State v. Saia*, 302 So.2d 869, 879 (La. 1974) (Summers, J., dissenting); *Brubaker v. Glenrock Lodge Int'l Order of Odd Fellows*, 526 P.2d 52, 59 (Wyo. 1974).

The corresponding adjective is *Cardozan*—e.g.: "*Cardozan* prose is not of consistent quality, but it should not be judged by its worst examples, as it is by his detractors." Richard A. Posner, *Cardozo: A Study in Reputation* 23 (1990). A variant form is **Cardozoean*—e.g.: "Corbin . . . proposed to the Restaters what might be called a *Cardozoean* [read *Cardozan*] definition of consideration." Grant Gilmore, *The Death of Contract* 63 (1974).

carelessness, in law, can be a misleading word because it suggests that a person's actually caring negates carelessness. In the context of criminal and tort law, though, *carelessness* generally states an objective—not a subjective—standard. So regardless of how careful a bicyclist might *try* to be, consciously assessing the risks, that bicyclist still might not reach the objective standard. In short, even those who care deeply can commit legal *carelessness*. Cf. **recklessness.**

carnal knowledge. This phrase, sometimes shortened to *knowledge*, is an old legal EUPHEMISM for sexual intercourse—dating back at least to the 17th century. The phrase is often paired, in references to rape, with *ravish*, a word that today strikes many readers as romanticizing a horrible criminal act. (See **ravish.**) Generally, the phrase *carnal knowledge* might be advantageously replaced with a more direct phrase such as *sexual intercourse*.

carrier. See **underwriter.**

carrying-away, n. See **asportation.**

carte blanche; **carta blanca*. The French form, *carte blanche* (= free permission), is the usual one in English contexts—e.g.: "[The conspirators] chose to give Hellerman *carte blanche* to conceive, manage, and carry out their fraud." *U.S. v. Aloi*, 511 F.2d 585, 600 (2d Cir. 1975). The phrase is pronounced /kahrt **blahnsh**/. The Italian form (**carta blanca*) is a NEEDLESS VARIANT.

Meaning literally "a white card," *carte blanche* does not take an article—e.g.: "With the constitutional amendment and the decisions by the Texas Supreme Court giving the legislature a *carte blanche* [read *carte blanche*; no article] to amend the wrongful death statute, the only option to rectify the injustice is the one that faced the British Parliament in 1846." Jeff Watters, *Better to Kill than to Maim*, 60 Baylor L. Rev. 749, 770 (2008).

But when the term is used attributively, as an adjective, it may well be preceded by an article (so that *a seizure* becomes *a carte blanche seizure*)—e.g.: "According to the warrant, all data on the computer— every single piece—pertains to the investigation and is subject to *a carte blanche* seizure." *U.S. v. Wecht*, 619 F.Supp.2d 213, 245 (W.D. Pa. 2009).

cartel. See **treaty.**

cartelize = to organize into a cartel. (See -IZE (A).) Yet *cartel* has three quite different meanings: (1) "an agreement between hostile nations" (see **treaty**); (2) "an anticompetitive combination, usu. one that fixes commercial prices or otherwise harms competition";

and (3) "a combination of political groups that work toward common goals." Modern usage favors sense 2.

carved in stone. See **stone, etched in.**

carve out (an exception or the like) is a hackneyed METAPHOR in legal writing—e.g.: "We decline to *carve out an exception* to this principle in criminal negligence cases." *State v. Tranby*, 437 N.W.2d 817, 821 (N.D. 1989). As a noun phrase, it takes a hyphen—e.g.: "Far from being a *carve-out* from the Release . . . , the Stock Option Plan clause is itself an exception from an earlier provision of the agreement." *McKissick v. Yuen*, 618 F.3d 1177, 1187 (10th Cir. 2010). See CLICHÉS.

ca. sa. = *capias ad satisfaciendum*. See **capias.**

case. See **cause (A)** & **suit.**

case, law of the. See **law of the case.**

case, trespass on the. See **trespass on the case.**

case at bar. A. And *case-in-chief*. A *case at bar* is a case that the court is presently considering; it may be an original hearing or an appeal. The *case-in-chief* is the evidence presented at trial by a party to support the claim or defense, from the time when the party calls the first witness until the party rests. The terms are occasionally confused—e.g.: "Given the strength of the State's *case at bar* [read *case-in-chief*], it cannot be said that the decision of the trier of fact would have been different had all of the remarks complained of remained unsaid." *People v. Calahan*, 356 N.E.2d 942, 947 (Ill. App. Ct. 1976).

B. And Similar Phrases. *Case at bar* is the most usual expression in which *at bar* is used, but legal and evidentiary issues may be *at bar*, as well as *cases*—e.g.:

- "The case of *National Union* . . . involved a termination clause similar to the one *at bar*." *Kelly Assocs. v. Aetna Cas. & Sur. Co.*, 681 S.W.2d 593, 595 (Tex. 1984).
- "The majority accurately summarizes the statutes *at bar* but detours from their constraint." *State v. Kintz*, 238 P.3d 470, 483 (Wash. 2010) (Sanders, J., dissenting).

See **at bar** & **instant case.**

case at bench is a variant of *case at bar*, cast from the judge's rather than the advocate's point of view. E.g.: "And in this country, Mr. Justice Story felt so strongly on the point that although the *case at bench* was robbery on the high seas . . . ." Rollin M. Perkins & Ronald N. Boyce, *Criminal Law* 144 (3d ed. 1982). Even so, most judges use *case at bar*, not *case at bench*.

casebook. Preferably one word in both AmE and BrE, though it occasionally appears in the latter as two words or as a hyphenated phrase.

casebook method; hornbook method; lecture method. These are the names of different pedagogical techniques in law. The *casebook method* (known also as the *case method*, *casebook system*, or *case system*) was devised in the 1870s at Harvard Law School by Professor Christopher Columbus Langdell. Instead of learning the law from lectures and textbooks, Langdell's students read law cases and then were questioned about them through the Socratic method: they were led to induce principles of law instead of receiving them as predigested deductions. Langdell's *Selection of Cases on the Law of Contracts* (1871) was the first such book of its kind.

The *hornbook* or *lecture method*, by contrast, involves a straightforward presentation of legal doctrine, sometimes interspersed with questions and problems. This method predominates in certain fields of law, such as procedure and evidence, and in civil-law countries.

Scholars continue to debate the merits of one system over the other. These comments from the literature help define the contours of the terms:

- "Under the *casebook method* the student, when confronted with a decision, is expected to analyze it in terms of a knowledgeable separation of superfluous facts from those issues impregnated with legal significance." Arthur D. Austin, *Is the Casebook Method Obsolete?*, 6 Wm. & Mary L. Rev. 157, 161 (1965).
- "The '*casebook method*' of teaching Law is still the vogue in the law schools . . . . In many ways, the old fashioned *hornbook method* of legal education made more sense. It was more direct and more straightforward and you could learn more principles faster." Fred Rodell, *Woe Unto You, Lawyers!* 140–41 (1939).

case-by-case. When used as a PHRASAL ADJECTIVE before the noun <on a case-by-case basis>, the phrase should be hyphenated—but not when it follows what it modifies <the court will draw those lines case by case>.

The phrase *case-to-case* is a variant of *case-by-case*: "Typically federal courts, either by rule or by *case-to-case* determination, follow the forum state's practice." 10 Charles Alan Wright et al., *Federal Practice and Procedure* § 2671, at 228–29 (1983).

caseflow. This NEOLOGISM, dating from 1957 and denoting the processing of legal matters through the systems of a decision-making body, is commonly written as one word. E.g.: Peter A. Sallman, *Observations on Judicial Participation in Caseflow Management*, 8 Civ. Just. Q. 129 (1989).

case-in-chief. This term is useful legal JARGON. It means "the part of a trial in which a party presents evidence to support the claim or defense" (*Black's Law Dictionary* 244 (9th ed. 2009)). E.g.:

- "In numerous cases this Court has held that mention of the fact of the defendant's silence following arrest by the prosecutor in his *case-in-chief* is a violation of constitutional dimension." *U.S. v. Shaw*, 701 F.2d 367, 381 (5th Cir. 1983).
- "During the prosecutor's opening statement and early in the government's *case-in-chief*, a stream of references to the two boys' murders focused the jury on the issue of whether appellant was a child killer as well as being a

drug dealer and an alleged triggerman." *Johnson v. U.S.*, 683 A.2d 1087, 1119 (D.C. 1996).
- "The husband argued that the trial court had erred in failing to grant his motion for a directed verdict at the conclusion of both parties' *case-in-chief*." Joseph W. McKnight, *Family Law: Husband and Wife*, 62 SMU L. Rev. 1149, 1164 (2009).

The phrase should be hyphenated. See **in chief, tenant-in-chief** & **case at bar** (A).

case in which. See **case where** & CASE REFERENCES (B).

case is sealed, the. See **seal** (C).

caselaw; *case-law; *case law. This term appears in modern texts in three ways: as a single word, as a hyphenated phrase, and as two words. Although all three forms can be found in abundance, the phrase is increasingly written as a single solid word—e.g.: "It appears from the *caselaw* and secondary authorities that regulatory actions are more likely to be deemed 'discretionary functions' than non-regulatory actions are." *Dichter-Mad Family Partners v. U.S.*, 707 F.Supp.2d 1016, 1029 (C.D. Cal. 2010). See **common law** (B)(6), **decisional law** & **jurisprudence** (B). Cf. **code law** & **organic law**.

Caselaw (or *decisional law*) is usually opposed to *statutory law* (or *statute law*). Oddly, *caselaw* is often referred to as the *unwritten law*, though it is certainly written. Cf. **unwritten law**.

case lawyer = a lawyer who has something approaching an encyclopedic knowledge of the caselaw within his or her jurisdiction. E.g.:

- "These were still the days of the *case lawyer*, who knew his reports and found his way about them partly by use and wont . . . partly with the help of the *Digests*." Lord Wright, *The Study of Law*, 54 Law Q. Rev. 185, 185 (1938).
- "Since Cardozo was one of the best *case lawyers* who ever lived, the proof was invariably marshalled with a masterly elegance." Grant Gilmore, *The Ages of American Law* 75 (1977). (See **marshal**, vb.)

Cf. **cause lawyer.**

caseload. Listed as two words in *W3*, this term is usually spelled as one word in American legal writing. E.g.: "Cases are then grouped to mix the *caseload* (some civil, some criminal, some agency-administrative) and to spread the work load." Barbara H. Craig, *Chadha: The Story of an Epic Constitutional Struggle* 174 (1988). Cf. **caselaw.**

case method. See **casebook method.**

casenote. See **annotation.**

case of, in the. See **case** (A).

case of first impression = a legal situation that the courts in a given jurisdiction have never before addressed. E.g.:

- "Let us suppose that this was a *case of first impression*, that is, a situation [that] is before an American court for the first time." C. Gordon Post, *An Introduction to the Law* 81 (1963). In that quotation, the word *American* is superfluous.

- "This is a *case of first impression*; however, three foreign jurisdictions, the Ninth Circuit and the states of Washington and Arizona have already addressed the question." *Express Personnel Servs., Inc. v. Belcher*, 86 S.W.3d 498, 501 (Tenn. 2002).

Cf. the inferior LATINISM *res nova* at **res integra.**

case or controversy. This phrase evokes the rule that federal courts in the U.S. do not decide hypothetical cases, or legal questions presented in a vacuum. Instead, the questions must arise in a genuine *case or controversy*.

Interestingly, the phrase has its origins in poor constitutional drafting—that is, drafting that violates the Golden Rule by engaging in INELEGANT VARIATION. Article III, § 2 of the U.S. Constitution describes nine categories of matters that are within the judicial power of the U.S. The first three categories speak of "all Cases" and the next six refer simply to "Controversies." It is because of this that we join the two and say that a federal court can decide only a *case or controversy*. State courts have no such inherent limitation—indeed, many state courts are free to decide matters that would not be a *case or controversy* as federal courts understand the phrase.

Historical considerations aside, the first word swallows the second in this DOUBLET: "a '*controversy*,' if distinguishable at all from a '*case*,' is distinguishable only in that it is a less comprehensive term, and includes only suits of a civil nature." Charles Alan Wright, *The Law of Federal Courts* 60 (5th ed. 1994). See **justiciability.**

CASE REFERENCES. A. Short-Form References. For shorthand reference to a case already mentioned, the usual practice is to use the first name in the case style, or the more distinctive name if the first is fairly common or is a place-name (e.g., *Board of Education*, a state's name, *United States*, etc.). Hence *Erie R.R. v. Tompkins*, when shortened, is *Erie*, not *Tompkins*; but *Marshall v. Mulrenin* usually becomes *Mulrenin*, and *National Mut. Ins. Co. v. Tidewater Transfer Co.* is shortened to *Tidewater*. Case names are not usually abbreviated when the parties' names are short; e.g., *Roe v. Wade* is seldom shortened to *Roe*.

Avoid using a shortened name attributively when it might seem to ridicule the court. One would not want to write *the Seven Elves court* or *the Wolfish court* when referring to the courts that decided *Seven Elves, Inc. v. Eskenazi*, 635 F.2d 396 (5th Cir. 1981), and *Bell v. Wolfish*, 441 U.S. 520 (1979). One judge, referring to *the Petty court*, felt obliged to write "no pun intended." *Welch v. State Dep't of Highways & Pub. Transp.*, 739 F.2d 1034, 1038 (5th Cir. 1984) (Brown, J., concurring). See (C) below.

B. Locatives with. *In which*, not *where*, is the better way of referring to what the facts were or what the court said in a given case. E.g.: "Our conclusion is supported by the supreme court's decision in *Johnson, where* [read *in which*] the defendant sought DNA testing of a Vitullo rape kit." *People v. Sanchez*, 842 N.E.2d 1246, 1253 (Ill. App. Ct. 2006). See **where (B).**

C. As Attributive Adjectives. Some cases have become so well known to the courts that routinely apply them as precedents that these courts have come to use the shortened case names as adjectives. There is no harm in this habit, although case citations might be helpful to the ordinary reader. Rarely, for example, is *Erie R.R. v. Tompkins* cited with the phrase *Erie-bound*. (See *Erie*-**bound.**) Other adjectivally used case names appear in phrases such as these:

- *Terry stop* or *Terry frisk* (fr. *Terry v. Ohio*, 392 U.S. 1 (1968)). See *Terry* **stop.**
- *Miranda warning* (fr. *Miranda v. Arizona*, 384 U.S. 436 (1966)). See **Mirandize.**
- *Allen charge* (fr. *Allen v. U.S.*, 164 U.S. 492 (1896)). See **dynamite charge.**
- *Anders brief* (fr. *Anders v. California*, 386 U.S. 738 (1967)).
- *Anton Piller order*, the former name in BrE for an order by a court in a civil case allowing a party to inspect and remove a defendant's documents, esp. when the defendant might destroy evidence (fr. *Anton Piller K.G. v. Mfg. Processes Ltd.*, [1976] Ch. 55; [1976] 1 All E.R. 779). It is now called a *search order*. See **Woolf reforms.**
- *Mareva injunction*, referring to an interlocutory injunction to restrain a person from removing assets outside the jurisdiction in an attempt to frustrate litigation in England (fr. *Mareva Compania Naviera S.A. v. Int'l Bulk Carriers*, [1980] 1 All E.R. 213). It is now called a *freezing order*. See **Woolf reforms.**

Citation to the full case is especially important when lesser-known cases are referred to adjectively—a practice to avoid. E.g.: "Langa contends that his counsel failed to move for a mistrial when the government elicited co-conspirator hearsay testimony without first securing a *James* ruling." The adjective *James*, which will draw a blank for most readers, refers to *U.S. v. James*, 590 F.2d 575 (5th Cir.) (en banc), *cert. denied*, 442 U.S. 917 (1979).

The precedent itself is sometimes unimportant to the phrase. That is, the case name has merely been adopted to denote certain types of factual situations, as with *Totten trust* (fr. *In re Totten*, 71 N.E. 748 (N.Y. 1904)) and *Mary Carter agreement* (fr. *Booth v. Mary Carter Paint Co.*, 202 So.2d 8 (Fla. Dist. Ct. App. 1967)). When, as in these phrases, the case name is used not to refer to precedent but to describe certain facts or denote types of transactions, citing the case is virtually always unnecessary. See CITATION OF CASES.

D. Hypallage with. It is unobjectionable to write that a certain case *held* something, rather than to say that the court, in that case, held such and such. This practice is an innocuous form of HYPALLAGE. E.g.:

- "*Miranda held* that 'the prosecution may not use statements, whether exculpatory or inculpatory, stemming from custodial interrogation of the defendant unless it demonstrates the use of procedural safeguards effective to secure the privilege against self-incrimination.'" *Estelle v. Smith*, 451 U.S. 454, 466 (1981) (per Burger, C.J.).
- "*National Carbide held* that the Tax Court had improperly failed to distinguish 'agency' and 'practical identity' when it ruled the subsidiaries were true agents." *Moncrief v. U.S.*, 730 F.2d 276, 281 (5th Cir. 1984).
- "Employing the nomenclature of the subsequent result-within-the-risk language, *Palsgraf held* that the defendant was not liable for the plaintiff's injuries because such injuries were not within the risk created by the defendant's negligence." Peter Zablotsky, *Eliminating Proximate Cause as an Element of the Prima Facie Case for Strict Products Liability*, 45 Cath. U. L. Rev. 31, 42 (1995).
- "*Erie held* that federal courts sitting in diversity cases, when deciding questions of 'substantive' law, are bound by state court decisions as well as state statutes." *Serocki v. Meritcare Health Sys.*, 312 F.Supp.2d 1201, 1205 (D.S.D. 2004).

But there is a fine line between this type of hypallage and the fallacious personification of cases mentioned in (E): cases might *hold* something or other, but they probably do not *cite* or *reason* or *argue*.

E. Personification of Cases. This type of ANTHROPOMORPHISM characterizes hack-writing about judicial opinions—e.g.: "*Lopez-Mendoza*, in declining to apply the exclusionary rule to deportation proceedings, cited approvingly cases finding that the absence of *Miranda* warnings did not render otherwise voluntary statements inadmissible in deportation proceedings." *Ramirez-Osorio v. I.N.S.*, 745 F.2d 937, 944 (5th Cir. 1984). The way to correct the problem, of course, is to write *The court in* INS v. Lopez-Mendoza, *etc.*

case runner, n., = a nonlawyer who ferrets out people with potential legal claims through a network of informants (often emergency medical technicians, law-enforcement officials, and court clerks) in order to sell that information to a lawyer who then solicits the potential client's business. See **barratry.**

case-specific = patterned after or adjusted to the facts of a given case <case-specific instructions>. E.g.: Horace E. Johns, *How the Zauderer Decision Impacted Case-Specific Solicitation in Lawyer Advertising*, 26 Comp. Jurid. Rev. 107 (1989). On the use of *impacted* there, see **impact,** vb.

case stated = (1) historically, a procedure by which the Court of Chancery referred difficult legal questions to a common-law court—abolished in 1852; (2) in G.B., a criminal procedure in which the prosecution and the defendant, usu. in a test case, request that a magistrate's court prepare findings along with its decision, so that the parties may then obtain appellate review of a point of law by a three-judge Divisional Court of the Queen's Bench Division; (3) in G.B., a similar procedure in which the parties obtain review of a decision by a lands tribunal or (until 1979) an arbitrator; (4) in the U.S., a civil procedure in which the parties submit an agreed statement of the facts to a trial court so that they can obtain a decision on a point of law; or (5) the factual statement submitted for review under any of the procedures just described.

Fairly uncommon in the U.S., the procedure has been used most frequently in Massachusetts and Pennsylvania. The usual idiom is *upon a case stated*—e.g.:

- "Upon this bill in equity . . . , the facts were agreed. A Superior Court judge properly treated the matter as presented upon a *case stated*." *Moore v. Zoning Bd. of Apps.*, 276 N.E.2d 712, 714 (Mass. 1971).
- "A judgment based upon a *case stated* is not appealable unless the parties expressly have reserved the right to appeal in the *case-stated* submission." *McSwain v. City of Farrell*, 624 A.2d 256, 257 n.2 (Pa. Commw. Ct. 1993).
- "We further described the proceedings as a 'hybrid' one between an adjudication upon a *case stated* and a non-jury trial on stipulated facts." *Warfield v. Shermer*, 910 A.2d 734, 738 (Pa. Super. Ct. 2006).

As the second quoted example shows, when the phrase appears as a PHRASAL ADJECTIVE, it should be hyphenated <case-stated procedure>.

case *sub judice.* See ***sub judice.***

case system. See **casebook method.**

case where is inferior to *case in which*, but the locution is hardly new: "The books are full of *cases where* [better: *cases in which*] a party has gone into equity only to find that he has mistaken the true theory of his case and must sue at law." William M. Lile et al., *Brief Making and the Use of Law Books* 356 (3d ed. 1914). See **where (B)** & CASE REFERENCES (B). Cf. **example where.**

cash damages. See **damages (A).**

casting vote = the deciding vote cast by the presiding officer of a deliberative body when the votes of those deliberating are equal. The U.S. Constitution gives the vice-president the casting vote in the Senate. *See* U.S. Const. art. I, § 3.

cast in stone. See **stone, etched in.**

castle doctrine; my home is my castle; every man's house is his castle. The first of these is the legal incarnation of the latter two, which are popular bywords in legal contexts. The so-called *castle doctrine* is an exception to the *retreat rule*. Under that rule, even the innocent victim of a murderous assault must retreat safely, if possible, instead of resorting to deadly violence unless the victim is in his or her "*castle*" at the time: "That every man's house is 'his *castle*' is a concept that has been echoed down through the ages and the social interest in the security of his '*castle*' has its origin in antiquity; for just as an animal or a bird resents any intrusion into its place of abode, so no doubt did primitive man." Rollin M. Perkins & Ronald N. Boyce, *Criminal Law* 1133–35 (3d ed. 1982). See **retreat rule.**

As for the longer phrases, using the first person forestalls any objections on grounds of sexism, as one writer did in referring to the Fourth Amendment as "the '*my home is my castle*' Amendment." René A. Wormser, *The Story of the Law* 347 (1962). See MAXIMS & SEXISM (A).

casual. Because it is occasionally mistaken for *causal* (and vice versa), *casual* may at first seem wrong in certain contexts even when it is properly intended: "It was precisely that kind of *casual* evidentiary inference that *Witherspoon* expressly condemned: 'It cannot be assumed that a juror who describes himself as having "conscientious or religious scruples" against the infliction of the death penalty . . . thereby affirms that he could never vote in favor of it.'" Eric Schnapper, *Taking* Witherspoon *Seriously*, 62 Tex. L. Rev. 977, 983 (1984). The meaning apparently intended there is "offhand, cursory." But inferences are often *causal* in nature—hence the reader's initial expectation that *causal* would have been the right word. If the writer had chosen *careless* or *desultory* (or some other word) rather than *casual*, the careful reader's expectations would not be undercut. See SOUND OF PROSE, THE.

casualty. See **accident (A).**

casus belli; casus fœderis. *Casus belli* (= an event that provokes war) is both a legal and a literary word—here the latter: "Sherry vomited in the defendant's taxicab on their way home, and this became the *casus belli* of this litigation." *Noble v. Louisville Taxicab & Transfer Co.*, 255 S.W.2d 493, 494 (Ky. 1952). As a term in international law, it refers to a provocative act that, in the opinion of an offended power, justifies making or declaring war.

A *casus fœderis*, by contrast, is (1) a provocative act by one state toward another, entitling the latter to call upon an ally to fulfill the undertakings of the alliance. *See* Ernest M. Satow, *Guide to Diplomatic Practice* app. 1, at 16 (5th ed. 1979) (noting that the two phrases are sometimes confused). By extension, the term has two other meanings: (2) a treaty clause specifying under what circumstances such a duty is owed by an ally; and (3) any treaty provision specifying a condition precedent that triggers a duty of alliance. *See* Aaron X. Fellmuth & Maurice Horwitz, *Guide to Latin in International Law* 50 (2009).

casus incogitati /**kay**-səs in-koj-i-**tay**-tɪ/ (= circumstances unthought of; circumstances that were not addressed in an instrument) is a little-known LATINISM that denotes an idea for which we have frequent need. But will probably never catch on.

casus male inclusus (L. "case wrongly included") denotes the situation that causes a judge-interpreter to believe that legislation is overbroad and covers a case it shouldn't. Like *casus omissus*, the LATINISM does not have a ready English substitute—nor, however, is the phrase very common in American legal writing. Here is a BrE example: "To extend a statute to a regrettably omitted case looks like legislation, whereas refusing to extend it to a *casus male inclusus* is more like imposing a provisional fetter on legislation." Glanville Williams, *Learning the Law* 110 (11th ed. 1982). See *casus omissus.*

casus omissus = a circumstance omitted or not provided for by a statute, rule, or regulation when, in the eyes of the judge-interpreter, it should have been covered. Since this LATINISM has a specific meaning not readily conveyed by a simpler phrase, it should be considered a useful part of the legal vocabulary. It is common in British legal writing—e.g.: "The appellant however contends that the section does not apply because it provides that the disponer (i.e., the wife) shall 'be liable to be taxed': the wife, it is said, is not a taxable person and so this provision does not operate; there is a *casus omissus*." *Reynolds v. Comm'r of Income Tax*, [1966] 1 A.C. 1, 12 (P.C.) (appeal taken from Trinidad & Tobago).

Though unfamiliar to most American lawyers, the phrase does appear occasionally in American law reports—e.g.:

- "The federal courts have treated this as a *casus omissus*, and have divided on the question whether traditional rules of evidence require the exclusion of hearsay offered on direct examination of an expert as the basis of his opinion." *McMunn v. Tatum*, 379 S.E.2d 908, 912 (Va. 1989).
- "[There] is another proposition that we must consider—the concept of *casus omissus*; simply stated, the Latin phrase means that a legislature simply omitted to consider the matter." *Hitt Constr. v. Pratt*, 672 S.E.2d 904, 908 (Va. Ct. App. 2009).

The plural is *casus omissi.*

catalogue; *catalog. Though librarians have come to use *catalog with regularity, *catalogue* is still the better form. *Cataloging makes about as much sense as *plaging. "If the professionals decline to restore the -*u*- to the inflected forms," wrote Follett, "let them simply double the -*g*-." Wilson Follett, *Modern American Usage* 97 (1966). The U.S. Supreme Court has used the more conservative form: "The cases we have reviewed show . . . the impossibility of resolution by any semantic *cataloguing*." *Baker v. Carr*, 369 U.S. 186, 217 (1962) (per Brennan, J.).

catapult, in keeping with the metaphor, is best a transitive and not an intransitive verb. The correct use of this verb in the active voice demands an agent and an object <the men catapulted stones over the wall>. If an agent is omitted, the verb must appear in the passive voice—e.g.: "Gracia was *catapulted* through the windshield opening onto the pavement in front of the truck and sustained a spinal injury." *Gracia v. Volvo Europa Truck, N.V.*, 112 F.3d 291, 293 (7th Cir. 1997). With such a construction, the means is implied.

Yet a common construction today is "He *catapulted* to fame," which at first struck many ears as illogical because the verb, even in figurative uses, so inevitably called to mind the literal sense that, used intransitively, it seemed illogical. But the idiom seems likely to endure—e.g.:

- "Burke *catapulted* to fame as a political thinker, and conservatism emerged as a highly respected, rediscovered political philosophy." Lynn D. Wardle, *A Response to the "Conservative Case for Same-Sex Marriage,"* 22 BYU J. Pub. L. 441, 447 (2008).
- "These newly 'emancipated' suburban laborer–consumers and suburban women–consumers proved to be a mighty coalition, as in 1928 they *catapulted* their patron saint, Herbert Hoover, to the Presidency of the United States." Kenneth A. Stahl, *The Suburb as a Legal Concept*, 29 Cardozo L. Rev. 1193, 1263 (2008).

See METAPHORS.

catchword (BrE) = *keynote* (AmE). E.g.: "At the head [of a case in the law reports] are what are called *catchwords*, indicating briefly what the case is about." Glanville Williams, *Learning the Law* 38 (11th ed. 1982).

categorically (= without qualification) most often accompanies the verb *deny*—e.g.: "At oral argument, . . . Red Dog's attorney *categorically* denied that he has ever contended that Red Dog is or was incompetent." *Red Dog v. State*, 620 A.2d 848, 852 (Del. 1993). For a MALAPROPISM involving this word, see **uncategorically.*

categorical question. See **leading question.**

causa causans. See CAUSATION (B).

causal; causative. These words have, unfortunately, been muddled by legal writers. The meanings should be kept distinct. *Causal* is the more common word, meaning "of or relating to causes; involving causation; arising from a cause." *Causative* = operating as a cause; effective as a cause. These two words share the sense "expressing or indicating cause," although *causal* is preferred for that sense.

In the following sentences, the words are correctly used:

- "Plaintiff may still recover attorney's fees if he can show both a *causal connection* between the filing of the suit and the defendant's action and that the defendant's conduct was required by law." *Williams v. Leatherbury*, 672 F.2d 549, 551 (5th Cir. 1982). (*Causal connection* and *causal link* are SET PHRASES.)
- "She contended that there had been one critical, *causative event* giving rise to the harm she suffered, namely, the failure to have continued to prosecute the municipal court violations complaint." *Bombace v. City of Newark*, 593 A.2d 335, 339 (N.J. 1991).
- "This allegedly negligent and proximately *causative conduct* removes the deaths from the ambit of the . . . definition of 'accident.'" *Columbia Cas. Co. v. Westfield Ins. Co.*, 617 S.E.2d 797, 801 n.6 (W. Va. 2005).

Yet the term *causal*, the more frequent term in legal discourse, is sometimes misused for *causative*—e.g.:

- "[Appellant's] argument is that appellee was asked to pay only for those damages resulting from its defective product and thus was not charged with any injury attributable

to other *causal* [read *causative*] faults." *Shipp v. Gen. Motors Corp.*, 750 F.2d 418, 426 (5th Cir. 1985).
- "The defendant's conduct . . . was fortuitously joined by the *causal conduct* [read *causative conduct*] of another that was also by itself insufficient to accomplish the harm." David W. Robertson, *The Common Sense of Cause in Fact*, 75 Tex. L. Rev. 1765, 1778 (1997).

Less frequently, and from whatever cause, the opposite mistake occurs—e.g.:

- "Although many modern financial outcomes seem to correlate with legal origin, we know correlation is not causation. For one thing, the *causative links* [read *causal links*] offered thus far in legal origins theory are weak." Mark J. Roe, *Legal Origins, Politics, and Modern Stock Markets*, 120 Harv. L. Rev. 460, 465–66 (2006).
- "Today, the Court adds a *causative element* [read *causal element*] to a patient's burden when a health-care provider negligently fails to diagnose or diagnoses improperly, requiring the patient to demonstrate that he would have followed appropriate medical advice had it been given." *Providence Health Ctr. v. Dowell*, 262 S.W.3d 324, 334 (Tex. 2008).
- "The notice was insufficient as a matter of law. It failed to allege any *causative link* [read *causal link*] between the claimed malpractice and the ultimate injury." *Hardacre v. Saginaw Vascular Servs., P.C.*, 762 N.W.2d 527, 528 (Mich. 2009).

See **casual.**

causal challenge = *challenge for cause*. The two-word phrasing allows legal writers a nice parallel for the other type of challenge, the *peremptory challenge*. E.g.:

- "If the Kennedy affidavit is correct, appellant was prevented from intelligently exercising his peremptory and *causal challenges* because of the juror's intentional nondisclosure." *U.S. v. Colombo*, 869 F.2d 149, 151 (2d Cir. 1989).
- "The peremptory challenge, once a challenge not requiring any explanation as to its exercise, is now a pseudo-*causal challenge* that must be justified in all but the most limited circumstances." Robert W. Best, *Peremptory Challenges in Military Criminal Justice Practice*, 183 Mil. L. Rev. 1, 6 (2005).

The phrase **cause challenge* sometimes appears, but *causal challenge* is preferable because it puts the adjective in the true adjectival form. See **challenge for cause.**

causality. See **causation.**

causa mortis (= in contemplation of one's death) is a LATINISM and TERM OF ART used primarily in the phrase *gift causa mortis* (or the thoroughly Latinate phrase *donatio causa mortis*). E.g.:

- "The power of a donor, in a gift *causa mortis*, to revoke the gift and divest the title of the donee is another clear example of the legal quantities now being considered." Wesley Newcomb Hohfeld, *Some Fundamental Legal Conceptions as Applied in Judicial Reasoning*, 23 Yale L.J. 16, 47 (1913).
- "Defendant's assertion that suicide is not the sort of peril that will sustain a gift *causa mortis* finds some support in precedents from other jurisdictions." *Scherer v. Hyland*, 380 A.2d 698, 702 (N.J. 1977).
- "Seminal cases on the law of gifts *causa mortis* invoke a provision of Justinian, who expresses his own debt to

Homer." John M. DeStefano III, *On Literature as Legal Authority*, 49 Ariz. L. Rev. 521, 523 (2007).

As in all these examples, the phrase is normally a POST-POSITIVE ADJECTIVE. But it can also function adverbially—e.g.: "A gift may also be given *causa mortis* whereby it is made in expectation of the donor's death." *Estate of Tahilan v. Friendly Care Home Health Servs.*, 731 F.Supp.2d 1000, 1010 (D. Haw. 2010). In BrE (as in Latin), the phrase is often written *mortis causa*.

causa proxima. See **proximate cause.**

CAUSATION is one of the subjects that have inspired legal writers to don their philosophers' caps and to work out any number of systems of analysis. The general principles of analysis have proved to be more or less universal in Anglo-American jurisdictions, but the terminology of that analysis does vary—hence the explanations in this entry.

As one writer aptly put it, "There are few words in the English vocabulary that have given rise to more legal problems than the words *cause* and *causing*." Note, 88 Law Q. Rev. 451, 451 (1972). Technically speaking, everything that contributes to a given result is, as a matter of fact, a cause of that result. Consider this illustration:

> In homicide by shooting, for example, while the mind turns first to the man who pulled the trigger, it was obviously impossible for him to have committed that homicide (by shooting) without a loaded weapon. As he did not, in all probability, make the gun himself, it is necessary to consider others, such as those who made and sold the weapon, and even the inventor of that particular kind of firearm. Others perhaps were connected with the result because they made the shell or the bullet or the powder, or assembled the finished cartridge. The mind gets lost in the labyrinth of contributory factors long before the possibilities are exhausted. As only a portion of the factors [that] actually contribute to such a result will receive juridical consideration, it is neither necessary nor useful to exhaust the philosophical possibilities of actual causation.
>
> Rollin M. Perkins & Ronald N. Boyce,
> *Criminal Law* 771–72 (3d ed. 1982).

By contrast, though it would be desirable to exhaust the legal terminology of causation, this entry can do no more than discuss the very most common terms. The terminology illustrates the truth of Glanville Williams's observation: "The lawyer is interested in the causal parentage of events, not in their causal ancestry." Glanville Williams, *Textbook of Criminal Law* 328 (1978).

In the end, legal terminology reflects the fact that courts are concerned with determining "cause" from the standpoint of attaching liability, not of ascertaining physical or medical cause. For example, a lawyer might say that A's death was caused by B's negligent driving while a doctor would say it was caused by shock and loss of blood.

A. Proximate cause; legal cause; direct cause; cause in fact. These four terms are essentially synonymous.

The term *proximate cause* has become an indispensable term in American tort law; it means simply "a cause that directly produces an effect; that which in natural and continuous sequence, unbroken by any new independent cause, produces an event, and without which the injury would not have occurred." (See **but for.**) The following definition—perhaps more direct—signals just how fuzzy the phrase is: "a cause of which the law will take notice." The Latin equivalent is *causa proxima*. See **proximate cause.**

The *CDL* does not include an entry on *proximate cause*, since the term *legal cause* is more usual in BrE. That is likewise the term preferred by the American Law Institute. *See* Restatement (Second) of Torts § 9 (1965). *Direct cause* is now increasingly rare.

B. Immediate cause; effective cause; causa causans. These terms are used to denote the last link in the chain of causation (as, e.g., a *supervening cause*). *Causa causans* is little used except in BrE.

C. Producing cause; procuring cause. These terms are virtually synonymous with *proximate cause* but in some jurisdictions are used in particular contexts such as workers' compensation (*producing cause*) and real-estate brokerage (*procuring cause* [of a sale]). The choice of term is usually statutorily prescribed.

D. Intervening cause; supervening cause. These denote a cause that comes into active operation *after* a defendant's negligence, even if that cause does not break the chain of causation. The point is that *intervening* and *supervening* are used, then, in a purely temporal sense in reference to the chain of causation. *Intervening* is the better choice of term, for *supervening cause* is sometimes confused with *superseding cause*. See (E).

In BrE, the equivalent Latinisms *novus actus interveniens* and *nova causa interveniens* are commonly used. See LATINISMS.

E. Superseding cause; sole cause. These phrases denote an *intervening cause* that breaks the chain of causation. So if X shoots Y, who is then stabilized and recovering nicely but soon dies after poor medical treatment, that medical negligence will be held to be a *superseding cause* (a phrase more common than *sole cause*). The phrase *supervening cause* is also sometimes used in this sense, but it should be avoided because of its use also for *intervening cause*. See (D).

causation; causality. *Causation* = (1) the causing or producing of an effect; or (2) the relation of cause and effect. The classic treatise is H.L.A. Hart & Tony Honoré, *Causation in the Law* (2d ed. 1985). In nonlegal writing, *causality* appears often enough in sense 2 that labeling it a NEEDLESS VARIANT is unrealistic.

Causation should never be used simply for *cause*—e.g.:

- "Under the facts of *Kubrick*, the plaintiff had actual knowledge of his injury and its *causation* [read *cause*]." *Dubose v. Kansas City S. Ry.*, 729 F.2d 1026, 1031 (5th Cir. 1984).

- "The carrier in March 1997 requested of Dr. Najjar a diagnosis of claimant's condition and its *causation* [read *cause*]." *Garner v. Clay County Dist. Sch. Bd.*, 798 So.2d 821, 824 n.4 (Fla. Dist. Ct. App. 2001).
- "The nurse's affidavit in the summary record shows in concrete terms that by training, education, and experience she was familiar with the plaintiff's injury and its *causation* [read *cause*]." *Gaines v. Comanche County Med. Hosp.*, 143 P.3d 203, 212 (Okla. 2006) (Opala, J., dissenting).

causative. See **causal.**

cause. A. And *case.* Both terms are used to describe litigated actions, despite some published nonsense to the contrary: "The legal theory of the party may be a *cause* of action. However, the lawsuit itself is not a '*cause.*'" Irwin Alterman, *Plain and Accurate Style in Court Papers* 172 (1987). *Case* is more commonly used, to be sure, but *cause* (= lawsuit) has long been current in the speech and writing of lawyers. E.g.: "Eventually it was decided that as from 1979 criminal *causes* in the House of Lords should be reported under the same title as in the court below." Glanville Williams, *Learning the Law* 17–18 (11th ed. 1982). Indeed, the word *cause* has extended beyond law into popular writing: "It is not necessary here to plead the *cause* of truffles and sauteed mushrooms." P.J. Wingate, *The Fungus Is Still Among Us*, Wall St. J., 3 Apr. 1989, at A12.

The peaceful coexistence of these terms need not be threatened by branding either one a NEEDLESS VARIANT. When writing or speaking for nonlawyers, however, *case* is the clearer term.

B. And *action.* See **suit.**

C. Appropriate Disposition by Courts. See **suit** (final ¶).

D. *Causation* Misused for. See **causation.**

cause célèbre. Traditionally a prosecution or other legal action marked by public notoriety, this GALLICISM now applies to any personality or event causing widespread controversy or interest. Avoid using it as hyperbole.

cause challenge. See **causal challenge.**

cause in fact. See CAUSATION (A).

cause lawyer = (1) a public-interest lawyer who practices law to promote moral or political commitments; or (2) a lawyer who is so deeply committed to a (usu. social) cause that he or she cannot objectively consider issues relating to that cause. The tendentious sense 2 is not common, but it does occur—e.g.: "'*Cause*' lawyers, they say, often lack an adequate understanding of their adversaries' positions, forcing the parties into rancorous, costly lawsuits when more amicable resolutions might be possible." Edward Felsenthal, *Lawyers Who Switch Sides Draw Ire with Big Checks*, Wall St. J., 19 July 1990, at B1, B5. Cf. **case lawyer.**

cause-list is the BrE term corresponding to *docket* or *calendar* in AmE. See **docket** & **calendar.**

cause of action; right of action; ground of action. These terms "should not be confused . . . . They are not interchangeable." *Swankowski v. Diethelm*, 129 N.E.2d 182, 184 (Ohio Ct. App. 1953). *Cause of action* = (1) a group of operative facts, such as a harmful act, giving rise to one or more rights of action; or (2) a legal claim. Writers on civil procedure prefer that the term be confined to sense 1. The acceptance of sense 2 by some courts actually caused the drafters of the Federal Rules of Civil Procedure to avoid the term altogether and to use *claim* instead. *See* Fleming James, *Civil Procedure* § 2.11, at 87 (1965).

Sometimes *cause of action* is misused for *prima facie case* (an old and well-known error)—e.g.:

- "Because Sheehan has failed to make out *its cause of action* [read *a prima facie case*] for bad faith, it may not recover punitive damages." *Westfield Ins. Co. v. Sheehan Constr. Co.*, 580 F.Supp.2d 701, 719 (S.D. Ind. 2008).
- "Therefore, because the government suffered no loss, the relator failed to make out a *cause of action* [read *prima facie case*] under the FCA." *U.S. ex rel. Bauchwitz v. Holloman*, 671 F.Supp.2d 674, 687 n.40 (E.D. Pa. 2009).

See **prima facie case.**

What is equally bad is using *cause of action* as a synonym for *lawsuit*—e.g.: "The court, in its discretion, may award reasonable attorneys' fees as part of the costs to . . . a prevailing party who is an SEA or LEA against the attorney of a parent who files a complaint or subsequent *cause of action* [read *lawsuit*] that is frivolous." 34 CFR § 300.517(a)(ii) (2010).

Right of action has two senses: (1) "the right to make a legal claim in court"; and (2) "a chose in action." Here sense 1 obtains: "No performance on either side can give the unlawful contract any validity, or be the foundation of any *right of action.*" *St. Charles County v. Joint Bd. or Comm'n*, 184 S.W.3d 161, 166 (Mo. Ct. App. 2006). For *chose in action*, see **chose.**

Ground of action is an infrequent variant of *cause of action*—e.g.:

- "On the trial of the action the first *ground of action* failed entirely, as the evidence showed that the defendant recovered the amount he claimed against the plaintiff in said attachment action." *Collins v. Shannon*, 30 N.W. 730, 731 (Wis. 1886).
- "It is the tortious act or negligence of the wrongdoer, and not the consequence, i.e. death, that is the basis or the *ground of action.*" *Peters v. Sidorov*, 855 A.2d 894, 898 (Pa. Super. Ct. 2004).

cause to be. A cartoon some years ago depicted a lawyer at a cocktail party talking with a friend and saying, "I met Joan in law school, where certain sparks were caused to be made." And certain idioms were caused to be learned as well, alas.

This one—*cause to be*—was born of a fear of not sufficiently expressing the idea that an agent may, as opposed to the principal, carry out an act. E.g.: "The directors must *cause books to be kept.*" J. Charlesworth, *The Principles of Company Law* 247 (4th ed. 1945). If the sentence read, "The directors must *keep books*," the result is not to disallow any delegation of bookkeeping matters. In most contexts, this phrase is noxious. See **effect (A)**.

causing death by reckless or dangerous driving. See **manslaughter (B)**.

caution /**kay**-shən/, in civil (and esp. Scots) law, means "security." *Cautionry* /**kay**-shən-ree/ = a surety obligation. *Cautioner* /**kay**-shən-ər/ = a surety.

cautionary; cautious. *Cautionary* /**kaw**-shən-air-ee/ = encouraging or advising caution <cautionary note> <cautionary tale>. *Cautious* = exercising caution <cautious approach> <cautious driver>.

In Scots law, a *cautionary* /**kay**-shən-air-ee/ obligation is one of suretyship. See **caution**.

C.A.V. See *cur. adv. vult.*

caveat /**ka**-vee-aht/, n., (lit., "let him [or her] beware") means, in nonlegal speech and writing, merely "a warning," from the common phrase *caveat emptor* (= let the buyer beware). E.g.: "The expression *caveat emptor* . . . still applies, and so long as the vendor does not actually mislead the purchaser, the purchaser has only himself to blame if he finds that the house is by no means what he thought it was." Anon., *The Home Counsellor* 207 (n.d. [London: Odhams Press, ca. 1940–1945]).

But in legal prose, *caveat* often signifies a notice, usually in the form of an entry in a register, to the effect that no action of a certain kind—such as the probate of a will—may be taken without first informing the person who gave the notice (known as the *caveator*)—e.g.:

- "Dorsey submitted a July 29, 1999 document purporting to be Kennedy's last will and testament for probate by the Gwinnett County Probate Court, and Kennedy's son and stepson filed *caveats*." *Dorsey v. Kennedy*, 668 S.E.2d 649, 650 (Ga. 2008).
- "The Contestants filed a *caveat* against probate, alleging that their father 'died without leaving a valid will, in that the purported will is the result of undue influence and is not supported by sworn witnesses.'" *Estate of Griffith v. Griffith*, 30 So.3d 1190, 1191 (Miss. 2010).

See **caveator**.

caveat, vb., is an AmE extension of the noun use described in the preceding entry—e.g.:

- "The will was successfully *caveated* by the personal representative's step-daughter." *Banashak v. Wittstadt*, 893 A.2d 1236, 1257 (Md. Ct. Spec. App. 2006).
- "On April 10, 2007, appellants filed a petition to *caveat* the will, asserting undue influence and lack of testamentary capacity." *Spry v. Gooner*, 985 A.2d 606, 607 (Md. Ct. Spec. App. 2010).

The verb is inflected *caveated* /**ka**-vee-ə-təd/, *caveating* /**kav**-ee-ə-ting/.

caveatee. See **caveator**.

caveator; contestant. A *caveator* is not one who warns, but one who has entered a caveat, i.e., one who challenges the validity of a will. The person whose interest is challenged is termed the *caveatee*. E.g.: "The district court did require the defendant–*caveatee* to proceed first in order of proof with evidence of due execution. However, the ultimate burden of persuasion was put on the plaintiff–*caveator*." *Curtis v. Curtis*, 481 F.2d 549, 550 (D.C. Cir. 1973). *Caveatrix* is an obsolete form (see SEXISM (C)). See **caveat**.

Contestant is used in jurisdictions in which the procedure of filing a *caveat* is not used—e.g.:

- "We now return to the statute [that] the *contestant* says was disregarded when George and the Gillises subscribed their signatures to the questioned instrument." *In re Demaris's Estate*, 110 P.2d 571, 579 (Or. 1941).
- "*Contestants* argue that the proponent engaged in the unauthorized practice of law by helping the decedent draft her will." *In re Estate of Brevard*, 213 S.W.3d 298, 303 (Tenn. Ct. App. 2006).

See **contestant**.

cavil, beyond (= beyond even the most trivial objection) is a favorite expression of legal writers, especially judges—e.g.:

- "The fact of damage was established *beyond cavil*, but the dollar amount thereof was not proved with mathematical precision." *Wenzler & Ward Plumbing & Heating Co. v. Sellen*, 330 P.2d 1068, 1069 (Wash. 1958).
- "Specifically, it is *beyond cavil* that all women and sexual minorities occupy a subordinated position in society." Berta Esperanza Hernandez-Truyol, *The Gender Bend*, 83 Ind. L.J. 1283, 1319 (2008).
- "Despite the claims of those attempting to market the neuroimaging of deception, it should be *beyond cavil* at this point in time that neuroimages of deception satisfy neither of these tests." Jane Campbell Moriarty, *Visions of Deception: Neuroimages and the Search for Truth*, 42 Akron L. Rev. 739, 755 (2009).

cease. See **stop**.

cease-and-desist order (= an order from a governmental authority directing a person violating the law to stop doing so) should be so hyphenated. (See PHRASAL ADJECTIVES (A).) Usually used in reference to administrative orders, this DOUBLET (*cease-and-desist order*) performs a useful function. Where the doublet functions as a verb phrase and not as an adjective (*We order you to cease and desist*), of course, the hyphens should not appear. The simpler expression *stop order* is confined to securities law.

The phrase *cease-and-desist letter* refers to an analogous demand letter, having no governmental authority behind it but threatening legal action. E.g.: "Last November, Thoroughbred Racing sent *cease-and-desist letters* to several artists who had depicted Easy Goer, winner of last year's Travers Stakes at Saratoga." David Margolick, *At the Bar*, N.Y. Times, 23 Feb. 1990, at B11. See **desist**.

ceasefire. One word in both AmE and BrE.

cede; secede; concede. The distinctions are as follows. *Cede* = to give up, grant, admit, or surrender <the tribe ceded lands by treaty in 1864>. (See **relinquish**.) *Secede* = to withdraw formally from membership or participation in <the South then tried to secede from the Union>. *Concede* = (1) to admit to be true <conceded the point>; (2) to grant (as a right or a privilege) <the company conceded a yearly transportation allowance of $10,000>; or (3) to admit defeat in (as an election) <the candidate conceded the election>.

ceiling, used in the sense of "maximum," is in itself unobjectionable but can sometimes lead to unfortunate mixed metaphors. E.g.: "The Sixth and Fourteenth Amendments guarantee . . . a jury's finding of any disputed fact essential to *increase* the *ceiling* of a potential sentence." *Shepard v. U.S.*, 544 U.S. 13, 25 (2005) (per Souter, J.). One *raises* a ceiling rather than *increases* it.

An English writer on usage quotes a preposterous example about "a *ceiling* price on carpets." In using words figuratively, one must keep in mind their literal meanings. See METAPHORS. Cf. **catapult.**

celui qui trust. See *cestui que trust.*

censor. See **censure (B).**

censorious (= severely critical) is the adjective corresponding to the verb *censure*, not *censor*. E.g.: "As to the manner in which Messrs. Wigmore and Kocourek have executed their task, it is very easy to be *censorious.*" Morris R. Cohen, *Reason and Law* 197 (1961).

censorship (= governmental suppression of material thought to be unsuitable for distribution or viewing on grounds of morality, religion, politics, or national security), whose mention immediately implicates the First Amendment, is one of those politically charged VOGUE WORDS that people use irresponsibly: "Ever since the controversy over federal funding for exhibitions of Robert Mapplethorpe's brutalizing photographs of sadomasochistic behavior erupted a couple of years ago, little cries of '*censorship*' have filled the air like the buzz of locusts wherever politically correct intellectuals congregate. Moreover, it soon became clear that this chorus was determined to construe '*censorship*' so broadly that anyone denied government largesse could claim to be a victim of oppression." *The PC Line on Censorship*, New Criterion, Dec. 1991, at 2.

censure. A. And Its Near-Synonyms: *condemn*; *denounce.* These verbs share the sense "to express disapproval or an unfavorable opinion," but in varying degrees and with varied nuances. *Censuring* implies authority and competence in the criticizing agent—much more than *blame*—as well as serious disapproval <very few members of Congress have been censured by their colleagues>. *Condemn*, stronger in both unfavorableness and finality, often connotes mercilessness

in the critic or judge <130 Islamic scholars condemned terrorism>. *Denounce* surpasses *condemn* in suggesting a stigmatizing in public <the senator denounced his aide for accepting a bribe>.

B. And *censor*. To *censure* is to criticize severely, to castigate. E.g.: "The district court found this argument to be unpersuasive, concluding that Judge Jenevein was *censured* for both his speech and his actions." *Jenevein v. Willing*, 493 F.3d 551, 557 (5th Cir. 2007).

The noun *censure* means "an official reprimand" or "severe criticism"—e.g.: "This Court has now extended Article 37(a), U.C.M.J., far beyond its plain meaning, to include mere presence in the public courtroom to be the equivalent of a *censure*, reprimand, or admonishment." *U.S. v. Harvey*, 64 M.J. 13, 26–27 (App. Armed Forces 2006).

To *censor*, by contrast, is to scrutinize and revise, to suppress or edit selectively—e.g.:

- "The right of the superintendent in the exercise of a reasonable discretion to *censor* the ordinary mail written by a patient who has been adjudged insane is not challenged." *Hoff v. State*, 18 N.E.2d 671, 672 (N.Y. 1939).
- "The United States Supreme Court held that prison officials may implement policies [that] *censor* inmate correspondence if the regulation furthers a substantial government interest unrelated to the suppression of expression, the censorship is no broader than necessary to protect the interest involved, and the inmate whose mail is *censored* is given notice and an opportunity to be heard." *Bundy v. Beard*, 924 A.2d 723, 726 n.3 (Pa. Commw. Ct. 2007).

As a noun, *censor* denotes one who inspects publications, films, and the like before they are published to ensure that they contain nothing heretical, libelous, or offensive to the government. It would be nice to pronounce this use of the term obsolete, but in some countries the censors remain prominent.

centennial; centenary. In all the anniversary designations (*bi-*, *sesqui-*, etc.), whether used as adjectives or as nouns, the *-ial* forms are preferred in AmE, the *-ary* forms in BrE.

***center around** is poor usage for *center on* or *in*. Something can *center on* (avoid *upon*) or *revolve around* something else, but it cannot *center around, as the center is technically a single point. The error is common—e.g.:

- "Bracton's discussion *centres around* [read *centres on*] the word 'heirs.'" Theodore F.T. Plucknett, *A Concise History of the Common Law* 559 (5th ed. 1956).
- "Almost all of his [i.e., Puccini's] works *center around* [read *center on* or *revolve around*] the heroine." J.M. Balkin, *Turandot's Victory*, 2 Yale J.L. & Humanities 299, 315 (1990).
- "In this case, the only point of dispute *centers around* [read *is*] what accounting methods ought to be used in calculating the profits." *Kraatz v. Heritage Imports*, 71 P.3d 188, 205 (Utah Ct. App. 2003).

Center has been used of late as a transitive verb, perhaps to avoid the prepositional dilemma—e.g.: "Computation of pecuniary damages recoverable for a ship's injury in a maritime collision *centers* [i.e., *is at the center of*] this cause." *Hewlett v. Barge Bertie*, 418 F.2d 654, 656 (4th Cir. 1969). But this peculiar phrasing is unidiomatic.

cert, in AmE, is frequently used as a colloquial shortening of *certiorari*: "As a result of this newfound determination to forge ahead with my '*cert*' memos, I managed to finish several more that afternoon." William H. Rehnquist, *The Supreme Court: How It Was, How It Is* 38 (1987). See **certiorari.**

In nonlegal contexts, of course, *cert* can be a shortened form of *certificate, certainty,* or *certify.* In BrE, it appears frequently in the phrase *dead cert* (a complete certainty): "I found some of my American colleagues surprised that their reports of the visit, on a normal day *dead certs* for the front page, had been pushed aside by news of 'Maggie' and her departure." Christopher Hitchens, *In Each Other's Pockets,* The Independent, 16 Dec. 1990, at 27.

certain can cloy as readily as almost any other LEGALISM. The adjectival *said* surpasses it, but not by much: "[The plaintiff] was lawfully possessed of a *certain* donkey, which said donkey of the plaintiff was then lawfully in a *certain* highway, and the defendant was then possessed of a *certain* waggon and *certain* horses drawing the same." *Davies v. Mann,* (1842) 152 Eng. Rep. 588, 588. The *OED* labels this use of *certain,* as well as the phrase *certain of* <certain of his possessions> "somewhat archaic." The phrase *certain of* is here used: "She brought suit under section 1983 in the United States District Court against Rotramel and the city, alleging that their actions had deprived Tuttle of *certain of* his constitutional rights." *Oklahoma City v. Tuttle,* 471 U.S. 808, 811 (1985) (per Rehnquist, J.).

certainly. See **clearly** & **obviously.**

certainty; certitude. *Certainty* = (1) an undoubted fact; or (2) absolute conviction. Sense 2 is very close to that reserved for *certitude,* which means "the quality of feeling certain or convinced." E.g.: "The only thing that gives us slight pause is the question how much *certitude* the agents must have that the premises they are entering, though not listed on the dealer's license as his place of business, really are such." *U.S. v. Cerri,* 753 F.2d 61, 64 (7th Cir. 1985).

Justice Oliver Wendell Holmes stated, rather memorably, "*Certitude* is not the test of *certainty.* We have been cock-sure of many things that were not so." Oliver W. Holmes, "Natural Law," in *Collected Legal Papers* 311 (1920).

Occasionally, writers misuse *certitude* for sense 1 of *certainty*—e.g.: "History is a matter of probability, not *certitude* [read *certainty*]." C. Gordon Post, *An Introduction to the Law* 130 (1963).

certificate = (1) a document in which a fact is formally attested; (2) a document certifying the status or authorization of the bearer to act in a specified way; or (3) a writing made in one court, by which notice of its proceedings is given to another court, usu. by transcript.

A variation of sense 3 denotes one of the three methods of taking a federal case from the court of appeals to the U.S. Supreme Court:

> The court of appeals may certify at any time any question of law in any civil or criminal case for which instructions are desired. The power is that of the court of appeals, and it has been said to be improper for the parties to move for certification. Certification is limited to questions of law, and the questions must be distinct and definite. The Court will dismiss a *certificate* in which the questions are so broad that in effect they bring up the whole case, although when a case has been certified the Court may itself require that the entire record be sent up for decision of the entire matter in controversy.
>
> Charles Alan Wright,
> *The Law of Federal Courts* 777 (5th ed. 1994).

certificate of title. This AmE phrase denotes one of the four types of evidence of title, the other three being abstract and opinion, title insurance, and a Torrens certificate. The *certificate of title*—issued by a lawyer who has examined the public records—is used extensively in the eastern and southern parts of the U.S.

certification. See **certificate.**

certify. See **authenticate.**

certiorari (L. "to be more fully informed") was historically "an original writ issued out of Chancery or the King's Bench, directed in the King's name, to the judges or officers of inferior courts, commanding them to return the records [to the Chancery or King's Bench] of a cause pending before them, to the end that the party may have the more sure and speedy justice." Forrest G. Ferris & Forrest G. Ferris Jr., *The Law of Extraordinary Remedies* 178 (1926). Today *certiorari* refers to a writ or order by which an appellate court comes to review cases of a certain type. The most troublesome aspect of the word is its pronunciation: /sərsh-ee-ə-**rahr**-ee/ or /sərsh-ee-ə-**rair**-ı/. The full formal phrase today is *writ of certiorari,* but this mouthful typically gets clipped to the monosyllable *cert.* See **appeal (B), prerogative writs** & **review (A).**

certitude. See **certainty.**

certworthy; certworthiness. These AmE legal NEOLOGISMS are used as JARGON by those who practice before, closely follow, or sit on the U.S. Supreme Court. *Certworthy* = (of a case) meriting Supreme Court review by grant of a writ of certiorari. E.g.:

- "Accordingly, while I believe the case is not '*certworthy,*' I would affirm the judgment below." *Tipton v. Socony Mobil Oil Co.,* 375 U.S. 34, 38 (1963) (Harlan, J., dissenting).
- "From these circumstances emerges the '*certworthy*' question whether the Fourth Circuit's *Erie* duty obliged

it to certify the false imprisonment issue to the Florida Supreme Court." Robert L. Stern et al., *Supreme Court Practice* 843 (6th ed. 1986).

- "Scholars and the Court generally deem a case '*certworthy*' when the underlying issue on which the lower courts disagree is, in some abstract sense, sufficiently important." Michael F. Sturley, *Observations on the Supreme Court's Certiorari Jurisdiction in Intercircuit Conflict Cases*, 67 Tex. L. Rev. 1251, 1252 (1989).

For an insightful discussion of the term, see David J. Sharpe, *The Maritime Origin of the Word "Certworthiness"*, 24 J. Mar. L. & Com. 667 (1993). Cf. **enbancworthy**.

cesser is a LEGALISM meaning "the premature termination of some right or interest" (*CDL*). E.g.:

- "One cannot devise his property so that it will not be subject to the debts of the devisee unless the devise contains a condition of *cesser* upon an attempted alienation or the estate created is a mere use at the absolute and uncontrolled discretion of the trustee." *Meade v. Rowe's Ex'r & Tr.*, 182 S.W.2d 30, 33 (Ky. 1944).
- "A *cesser* of the use, coupled with any act clearly indicative of an intention to abandon the right, would have the same effect as an express release of an easement, without any reference whatever to time." *Chevy Chase Land Co. v. U.S.*, 733 A.2d 1055, 1097 (Md. 1999).

The word often appears in the phrase *cesser clause* or *cesser provision*—e.g.: "The *cesser* clause in the charter-party does not relieve the charterer from this liability." *Am. Tobacco Co. v. The Katingo Hadjipatera*, 81 F.Supp. 438, 448 (S.D.N.Y. 1948).

cession; session. *Cession* = a giving up, granting; the act of ceding. E.g.: Michael J. Powell, *Professional Divestiture: The Cession of Responsibility for Lawyer Discipline*, 1986 Am. B. Found. Res. J. 31. It is used often of nations or peoples who *cede* land. *Session* (= a meeting or gathering) is used of deliberative bodies <court is in session>.

cestui /sed-ee/ (= beneficiary) commonly appears as an elliptical form of *cestui que trust*. E.g.:

- "He who is in such a fiduciary position cannot serve himself first and his *cestuis* second." *Pepper v. Litton*, 308 U.S. 295, 311 (1939) (per Douglas, J.).
- "The ALR annotation *cited to* [read *cited*] in *In re Taneja* distinguishes the type of cases it discusses (such as this case) from 'cases involving the release of the deed of trust by the trustee in contravention of the terms of the instrument or without the authority of the *cestui*.'" *In re Maximum Developers Invs., LLC*, 428 B.R. 1, 3 (Bankr. D.D.C. 2010). (For more on the correction of *cited to*, see **cite (B)**.)

As with the full phrase, *beneficiary* is a preferable term.

cestui que trust /sed-ee kee **trəst**/ (originally, in LAW FRENCH, *cestuiá que trust*, lit., "that person for whose benefit" or "he who trusts") is a legal ARCHAISM that persists in AmE (in legal contexts only), but is obsolescent in BrE and unknown in Scotland. The phrase is inferior to the simple word *beneficiary*, which is far more widely understood. E.g.: "It may well be that the relation of trustee and *cestui que trust* [read *beneficiary*] may be so acknowledged to exist and to

continue to exist as to prevent the application of the doctrine [of laches]." *Rouse v. Underwood*, 242 Cal. App. 2d 316, 331 (1966).

Other forms of the phrase, such as *celui qui trust* and *cettui que trust*, have appeared—see Sidney S. Alderman, *The French Language in English and American Law*, 7 La. B.J. 33, 37 (1959) (preferring *celui qui trust*)—but they are fairly obscure. The phonetic form *settiki* is more than just fairly obscure. *See* Theodore F.T. Plucknett, *A Concise History of the Common Law* 576 n.2 (5th ed. 1956).

The plural has been variously formed *cestuis que trust*, *cestuis que trusts*, and **cestuis que trustent*. The last of these has aptly been called "hopelessly wrong." Note, 26 Law Q. Rev. 196, 196 (1910). Another writer has sorrowfully remarked: "From time to time, it must be regretfully admitted, the Law Reports have ascribed this deplorable version to one of His Majesty's judges." R.E. Megarry, *Miscellany-at-Law* 33 (1955). Scott and Fratcher explain the trouble: "It is not uncommon to say *cestuis que usent* or *cestuis que trustent* on the theory that the last word in each case is a verb that requires the ending of the French third person plural. But Professor F.W. Maitland has shown that these words are nouns, not verbs, that the term *cestui que use* is an ellipsis, [and] that the full expression is perhaps *cestui a qui oes la terre est tenue*, or something of that sort. If this is true, it is of course absurd to add the plural verb ending." 1 Austin W. Scott & William F. Fratcher, *The Law of Trusts* § 3.2, at 52–53 (4th ed. 1987). The Latin ending in -*ent*, then, is a "hypercorrect" form. See HYPERCORRECTION (A).

The best plural form, in short, is *cestuis que trust*. On elliptical use of the phrase, see **cestui**.

cestui que use /sed-ee kee **yoos**/ (originally, in LAW FRENCH, *cestuiá que use*, lit., "that person for whose use") refers to the beneficiary of a use. (See **use**, n.) Today the term appears primarily in historical contexts, since uses have been abolished in England. E.g.:

- "The chancellor recognized and enforced the rights of the *cestui que use*, and his interest under the deeds became known as an equitable estate, exactly as the interest of the vendee under an executory contract for sale is now known and for the same reason." *State v. Weide*, 135 N.W. 696, 704 (S.D. 1912).
- "The more common general trust, otherwise known as the use, entailed the transfer of legal title (enfeoffment) to a person who was to hold the property (the feoffee to uses) for the benefit of another (the *cestui que use*)." Avesheh Avini, *The Origins of the Modern English Trust Revisited*, 70 Tul. L. Rev. 1139, 1143 (1996).
- "The 'use' allowed the landowner, known as the feoffor, to transfer the land to a 'feoffee to uses,' who in turn could allow another, the *cestui que use*, the use of the land for his benefit." Joshua S. Miller, Note, *Putting Iraq in Trust*, 27 Suffolk Transnat'l L. Rev. 37, 41 (2003).

But some American jurisdictions retain the term; as with *cestui que trust*, *beneficiary* is a preferable term in modern contexts.

On the plural form **cestuis que usent*, see **cestui que trust**. Oddly, Plucknett more or less acknowledges that *cestuis que use* is the better form, and then seven pages later writes **cestuis que usent*. *See* Theodore F.T. Plucknett, *A Concise History of the Common Law* 576 n.2, 579 [*cestuis que use*], 586 [**cestuis que usent*] (5th ed. 1956). Brian Simpson, another legal historian, calls **cestuis que usent* "an expression calculated to give a grammarian bad dreams." A.W.B. Simpson, *An Introduction to the History of the Land Law* 164 (1961). See HYPERCORRECTION (A).

Still other historians, such as J.H. Baker, prefer the spelling *cestuy que use*, presumably because it was the more frequent spelling among medieval lawyers. *See* J.H. Baker, *An Introduction to English Legal History* 285–86, 329 (3d ed. 1990).

ceteris paribus /**kay**-tər-əs **par**-ə-bəs/ (= other things being equal) is, for the most part, an unnecessary LATINISM, since we have the common English phrase, which is better. E.g.: "The fact is, they don't knowingly take losers. *Ceteris paribus* [read *Other things being equal*], the trial lawyer spends his time on the winners. And if a client has a promising case, the lawyer will stake him to it out of sheer self-interest." John A. Jenkins, *The Litigators* xii (1989). Cf. **mutatis mutandis.**

cettui que trust. See ***cestui que trust.***

chain of title = the recorded history of the title to a piece of realty—including all conveyances and encumbrances—from the time of the earliest records of ownership. The phrase draws on the METAPHOR of links (i.e., successive periods of ownership) forming, through time, a connected chain.

chair; chairman; chairwoman; *chairperson. Sensitivity to SEXISM impels many writers to use *chair* rather than *chairman*, on the theory that doing so avoids gender bias. E.g.:

- "Ingrid was *co-chair* of the Network where she voiced concerns for Native women through activism, literature, and community work." Tonya Gonnella Frischner, *Foreword: Flying Eagle Woman*, 3 N.Y.C. L. Rev. 39, 39 (1998).
- "There have been a number of different studies. One of them is the foundation's culpability study that is being headed up by Larry Steinberg, who is the *chair* of that network." Lisa K. Halushka, *Introduction*, 8 Thomas M. Cooley J. Prac. & Clin. L. 1, 50 (2006).
- "On behalf of the Board, the 2006 contract was signed by Karen Bew, the *vice-chair* of the Board." *Randolph v. City of Brigantine Plan. Bd.*, 963 A.2d 1224, 1227 (N.J. Super. Ct. App. Div. 2009).

Certainly *chair* is better than **chairperson*, an ugly and trendy word.

Many readers and writers continue to believe, however, that there is nothing incongruous in having a female *chairman*, since *-man* has historically been sexually colorless. In the federal judicial opinions issued in 1990, *chairman* outnumbered **chairperson* by more than ten to one.

Even so, the nonsexist forms are quickly gaining ground and are likely to prevail entirely within the next couple of decades. If we are to adopt a substitute wording, we ought to ensure that *chair* (which goes back to the mid-17th c.) and not **chairperson* becomes the standard term: "In so ruling, he ignored the uncontradicted testimony of Ms. Connie Mooney, coordinator and *chairperson* [read *chair*] of the Charleston Woman's Health Group." *Doe v. Charleston Area Med. Ctr., Inc.*, 529 F.2d 638, 645 (4th Cir. 1975). See SEXISM (B).

One caveat: if we adopt a term such as *chair*, it must be used in reference to males and females alike. In recent years there has been a lamentable tendency to have female *chairs* and male *chairmen*. This is no better than having *chairwomen* and *chairmen*; after all, in most circumstances in which people lead committees and the like, the sex of the leader is irrelevant. See SEXISM (B).

challenged. See EUPHEMISMS.

challenge for cause (= a lawyer's striking of a veniremember on grounds of bias) is, in AmE, often collapsed into *cause challenge* or *causal challenge*. Of these two shortened forms, *causal challenge* is preferable: "When the judge has concluded the *cause challenges* [read *causal challenges* or *challenges for cause*], the lawyers have the right to exercise a given number of *peremptory challenges*—dismissals for no stated reason." Robin T. Lakoff, *Talking Power: The Politics of Language in Our Lives* 110 (1990). The shorter form (*causal challenge*) corresponds more neatly than the longer form (*challenge for cause*) to the two-word phrase *peremptory challenge*. See **causal challenge.**

chambers. This word refers to a judge's or magistrate's private office. In BrE, it additionally has the sense "the offices occupied by a barrister or group of barristers" (*CDL*). The word is always plural in form, regardless of the number of rooms denoted. Nonlawyers sometimes wrongly make the word singular, as in *judge's chamber*. See, e.g., Margaret Nicholson, *A Dictionary of American-English Usage* (1957), under **camera.**

The one use in which the singular *chamber* is correct is as an adjective: "During this period, however, other events not formally reflected in the record took place. These include *chambers or status conferences* [read *chamber conferences* or *conferences in chambers*]." *Morris v. Ocean Sys., Inc.*, 730 F.2d 248, 249 (5th Cir. 1984).

CHAMELEON-HUED WORDS. "In any closely reasoned problem, whether legal or nonlegal, chameleon-hued words are a peril both to clear thought and to lucid expression." Wesley N. Hohfeld, *Fundamental Legal Conceptions* 35 (1919). More than one great legal mind has made this observation: "When things are called by the same name it is easy for the mind to slide into an assumption that the verbal identity is accompanied in all its sequence by identity of meaning." *Lowden v. N.W. Nat'l Bank & Trust Co.*, 298 U.S.

160, 165 (1936) (per Cardozo, J.). "A word is not a crystal, transparent and unchanged, it is the skin of a living thought and may vary greatly in color and content according to the circumstances and the time in which it is used." *Towne v. Eisner*, 245 U.S. 418, 425 (1918) (per Holmes, J.).

The English language, and therefore the language of the law, teems with words that have many different—sometimes strikingly different—meanings. There are at least two types of chameleon-hued words. The first type consists in words such as *temporal*, which has several distinct meanings: (1) of or relating to time <temporal relations of events>; (2) secular, not spiritual <temporal pastimes>; (3) chronological <temporal sequence>; and (4) of or relating to the temples on the side of one's skull <temporal lobes>.

Similar words abound in the language, and often they are the most important ones. For example, Frankfurter wrote, "I do not use the term *jurisdiction* because it is a verbal coat of too many colors." *U.S. v. L.A. Tucker Truck Lines, Inc.*, 344 U.S. 33, 39 (1952) (Frankfurter, J., dissenting). An English judge has said much the same thing about *condition* in contractual contexts. *See The Varenna*, [1984] Q.B. 599, 618 (calling it "a chameleon-like word [that] takes on its meanings from its surroundings").

The second type consists essentially in words, usually adjectives, that are empty vessels, to be filled with meaning by the reader. Lawyers delight in such terms as *reasonable*, *substantial*, *meaningful*, and *satisfactory*. These terms are often usefully vague, allowing drafters to provide a standard for performance in unforeseen circumstances. It is worth the warning, however, to note that "a competent draftsman would not deliberately pick a word [that] instead of controlling the context is easily colored by it." *In re Coe's Estate*, 201 A.2d 571, 577 (N.J. 1964).

champertor; maintainer; barrator; embracer. The differences are concisely set forth in the following passage: "If a *maintainer* is one who stirs up vexatious suits to which he is not a party, if a *barrator* is one who makes a profession of doing so, if a *champertor* is one who does so for pecuniary gain[,] and if an *embracer* is one who in the course of such proceedings seeks to influence or intimidate judge or jury, it must be admitted that in the minds of the lay public, the chief *maintainers*, *barrators*, *champertors*, and *embracers* of today are the members of the legal profession." Max Radin, *Maintenance by Champerty*, 24 Cal. L. Rev. 48, 66–67 (1935). The word *champertor* is mislabeled obsolete in the *OED*. See **champerty, barratry** & **embracery.**

champertous. See **champerty (c).**

champerty. A. And *maintenance*. These words denote related but distinct offenses. *Champerty*—a subspecies of *maintenance*—is "an illegal proceeding in which a person (often a lawyer) not naturally concerned in a lawsuit engages to help the plaintiff or defendant to prosecute it, on condition that, if it is successful, that person will receive a share of the property in dispute." *Maintenance* is "the action of wrongfully aiding and abetting litigation; the act of sustaining a suit or litigant by a party who has no interest in the proceedings or who acts from an improper motive."

The element of pecuniary return is absent from the notion of *maintenance*. Pollock noted in the late 19th century that "actions for maintenance are in modern times rare though possible." Frederick B. Pollock, *The Law of Torts* 211 (1887). The same might now be said of *champerty*. Contingent fees, which fit within the traditional definition of *champerty*, are now common in the U.S.; they have been excepted from the prohibition of *champerty* and in most cases are proper under American ethical canons. See **contingent fee.**

Misconduct under either name—*champerty* or *maintenance*—is more likely to surface today as a defense to a civil action rather than as a criminal offense. *See* Rollin M. Perkins & Ronald N. Boyce, *Criminal Law* 585 (3d ed. 1982). For an insightful discussion of the status of *champerty* and *maintenance* in American law, see Susan L. Martin, *Syndicated Lawsuits*, 30 Am. Bus. L.J. 485 (1992).

B. Pronunciation. The *Law Student's Pronouncing Dictionary* (1948) gives the pronunciation of *champerty* as /**sham**-pərty/. In AmE, however, the word usually has a hard -*ch*- sound, not an -*sh*- sound.

C. Adjectival Form. The adjective corresponding to *champerty* is *champertous*. E.g.: "For an agreement to be *champertous*, the financier must have no [proper] interest in the litigation to be financed." *U.S. v. Algernon Blair, Inc.*, 795 F.2d 404, 409 (5th Cir. 1986).

chancellor = (1) in England, the nominal head of the Court of Chancery and of the whole judiciary who is also Speaker of the House of Lords and a member of the Cabinet—properly called the Lord High *Chancellor* of Great Britain; (2) in G.B., the single judge of the consistory court of a diocese; (3) the titular head of a university (the vice *chancellor* being equivalent to a president of an American university); or (4) in the U.S., a judge in equity, or on any court denominated "chancery."

Except in a few jurisdictions, such as Delaware, the title isn't ordinarily as exalted in AmE as it is in BrE. Here are typical AmE uses:

- "Plaintiff finally invokes the rule that findings of the *chancellor* on conflicting evidence will not be disturbed unless clearly and palpably against the weight of the evidence." *Pernod v. American Nat'l Bank & Trust Co.*, 132 N.E.2d 540, 543 (Ill. 1956).
- "Indeed, no such finding was made by the *chancellor* in the modification decree here assaulted." *Schaefer v. Schaefer*, 344 So.2d 902, 902 (Fla. Dist. Ct. App. 1977).
- "Although the *chancellor* may have erred in awarding the property to the appellee as her sole property, his decision was not outside the jurisdiction of the chancery court and could not be collaterally attacked." *Murry v. Mason*, 852 S.W.2d 830, 833 (Ark. Ct. App. 1993).

See **chancery, Keeper of the King's Conscience** & **Lord Chancellor.**

chancellor's foot. John Selden, the 17th-century barrister and scholar, said, "Equity is a roguish thing. For law we have a measure, know what to trust to: equity is according to the conscience of him that is Chancellor, and as that is larger or narrower, so is equity. 'Tis all one as if they should make the standard for the measure, a *Chancellor's foot*. What an uncertain measure would this be! One Chancellor has a long foot, another a short foot, a third an indifferent foot; 'tis the same thing in the Chancellor's conscience." John Selden, *Table Talk* (1689) (as quoted in Thomas E. Holland, *The Elements of Jurisprudence* 74 (13th ed. 1924)).

The phrase has continued to stand for inequitable variability in court rulings. E.g.: "The defense of entrapment enunciated in these opinions was not intended to give the federal judiciary a '*chancellor's foot*' veto over law enforcement practices of which it did not approve." *U.S. v. Russell*, 411 U.S. 423, 435 (1973) (per Rehnquist, J.). American courts, alas, have sometimes got the reference wrong: "Hundreds of years ago, likewise, equity ceased to be the measure of the '*King's foot*.'" *U.S. v. Parkinson*, 240 F.2d 918, 921 (9th Cir. 1956).

chance-medley. One criminal-law text defines this quaint legal phrase as "an ordinary fistfight or other nondeadly encounter," suggesting that it would be a loose usage to speak of a homicide resulting from a *chance-medley*. See Rollin M. Perkins & Ronald N. Boyce, *Criminal Law* 1121 (3d ed. 1982). But ever since it was first used in the 15th century, the phrase has referred primarily to deadly encounters—especially in the longer phrase *manslaughter by chance-medley*. A *chance-medley* was excusable as opposed to justifiable homicide. See J.V. Barry, *The Defence of Provocation*, 4 Res Judicata 129, 129 (1949).

There are two views on the etymology of the phrase. One traces the phrase from the Fr. *chance medlée*, meaning "mixed or mingled chance or casualty." In this view, *medley* is a POSTPOSITIVE ADJECTIVE, *chance* being the noun. As the *OED* notes, however, the phrase has been misused by those who took *medley* to be the noun and *chance* to be an adjective—as if the phrase meant "fortuitous medley." It does not. But in an alternative view, *chance* is in fact an adjective, the original having been *chaude*, indicating hot blood. Those who take this view trace the word from *chaude mêlée* (= a killing in the course of a spontaneous, heated quarrel). In support of this latter view, see J.H. Baker, *An Introduction to English Legal History* 601 & n.40 (3d ed. 1990).

chancery; equity. *Chancery* = (1) the office of the Chancellor; (2) a court of equity; or (3) equity. Sense 1 is most usual in England, primarily as a historical usage: "The *Chancery*, in fact, readily abandoned any legal topic as soon as the common law mended its ways and provided a more adequate treatment."

(Eng.) Sense 3 is today almost purely an American extension <principles of chancery>. In the phrase *in chancery*, the term almost vacillates between senses 2 and 3—e.g.: "Before probating the second will it is not necessary to file a bill in *chancery* under the statute to set aside the probate of the former will." *In re Bentley's Will*, 9 S.E.2d 308, 310 (Va. 1940).

Often the term is used attributively, in an adjectival sense—e.g.:

- "The system of *chancery* jurisprudence has been developed as carefully and as judiciously as any part of the legal system, and the judicial power includes it, and always must include it." *Brown v. Kalamazoo Circuit Judge*, 42 N.W. 827, 831 (Mich. 1889).
- "Two of the cardinal principles of *chancery* jurisprudence are that *equity* will not suffer a wrong to be without a remedy, and *equity* looks to the substance, rather than the form." *Watson v. Wolff-Goldman Realty Co.*, 128 S.W. 581, 583 (Ark. 1910).
- "The general rule in Virginia is that a cestui que trust is not bound by a decree rendered against his trustees in a *chancery* suit to which he is not a party." *Parkerson v. Chapman*, 179 F.2d 208, 214 (4th Cir. 1950).

Since the 19th century in AmE, *chancery* has also been synonymous with *bankruptcy* in some states. Hence Thoreau wrote about *going into chancery*, meaning "going bankrupt," in the middle of that century. Such locutions are no doubt restricted to states in which the state bankruptcy courts are called *chancery* courts. Formerly, American legists used *bill in equity* and *bill in chancery* interchangeably. Today in Delaware, the *Court of Chancery* has jurisdiction over insolvency and receiverships of corporations.

Equity has three basic senses that are relevant in comparison to *chancery*: (1) evenness, fairness, justice; (2) the application to particular circumstances of what seems naturally just and right, as contrasted with the application of a legal rule; and (3) the body of principles and rules developed since medieval times and applied by the Chancellors of England and the Courts of *Chancery*. Sense 1 is the general sense used by nonlawyers and lawyers alike; sense 2 is the commonest meaning in legal contexts; and sense 3, in the narrow definition given, is historical and generally British. Senses 2 and 3 are the senses in which *chancery* is sometimes used for *equity*. See **equity.**

change in control; change of control. In references to corporate governance, these phrases are common—about equally common. To minimize the word *of*—something that lawyers need to learn better—prefer *change in control*. See **of.**

channel; *channelize, vb. Because no real DIFFERENTIATION has developed between these terms, **channelize* ought to be branded a NEEDLESS VARIANT. *Channel*, the usual term, means (1) to form channels in, to groove; (2) to guide; or (3) to act as a medium through whom the dead (or absent) supposedly speak. It makes *channeled* and *channeling* in AmE, *channelled* and *channelling* in BrE. See DOUBLING OF FINAL CONSONANTS.

chapter = (1) in G.B., an act of Parliament, each of which is a numbered chapter of the total legislation of the year; (2) a subdivision of a legislative act, comprising a number of sections; or (3) the dean and clergy of a cathedral.

Chapter 11, in AmE, has become synonymous with corporate reorganization for the purpose of handling debts in a structured way, under the protection of a federal bankruptcy court. The phrase is often used attributively—e.g.: "The purpose of a *Chapter 11 filing* is to give a chief executive an opportunity to reorganize a financially troubled business by putting its creditors on hold. When the money problems have been straightened out and the company restored to health, it emerges from the protection of the bankruptcy courts and picks up where it left off." John Taylor, *Bankruptcy Was a Disappointment*, N.Y. Times, 10 Dec. 1989, § 7, at 11.

A common colloquialism nowadays is *to go Chapter 11*: "Of course, Campeau's badly over-extended retailing Empire would soon *go Chapter 11* anyway, throwing thousands out of work and rippling damage through the U.S. economy." Book Note, American Way, Jan. 1992, at 78 (reviewing John Rothchild, *Going for Broke* (1991)).

character; reputation. These words are frequently used in the law of defamation and of evidence. Very simply, the semantic distinction is that *character* is what one is, whereas *reputation* is what one is thought by others to be.

charge, n. **A. In the Sense "accusation."** To write that someone has been *accused* of a *charge* is a REDUNDANCY. E.g.: "In announcing Mr. X's suspension, the [newspaper] management pointed out that 'Mr. X *had neither been accused nor convicted of any charge* (read *had neither been charged nor convicted*).'" (Ex. fr. Wilson Follett, *Modern American Usage* 47 (1966).) [A better revision: *had been neither accused nor convicted.* See PARALLELISM.] See **accuse.**

B. Active and Passive Use. *In charge of* may be used both actively and passively <livestock were left in charge of the foreman> <the foreman was left in charge of the livestock>. The usual passive wording is *in the charge of*, which prevents any possible ambiguities. And to the modern reader, the phrasing without the definite article elicits a pause—e.g.: "Ordinarily the truck was *in charge of* [read *in the charge of*] an employee by the name of William Frierson who kept it over the week-end and also picked up employees every workday morning at a street corner." *Continental Cas. Co. v. Padgett*, 219 F.2d 133, 134 (4th Cir. 1955). To one not accustomed to *in charge of* in the passive construction, subject and object appear to have been confused. That is, the sentence just quoted seems to say that the truck had control of or authority over the employee.

charge, vb. **A. And Its Near-Synonyms:** *accuse; incriminate; *criminate; indict; impeach; arraign.* These verbs share the sense "to allege wrongdoing by someone." But there are important connotative differences. To *accuse* is to declare someone guilty in an immediate and personal way, with sharp disapproval, while to *charge* is to accuse formally of a serious offense. Hence to *accuse* a tournament golfer of cheating is to allege, with resentment, an offense against the rules of golf and a violation of the spirit of the game; but to *charge* a tournament golfer with cheating is to lodge a formal complaint that might well result in the player's disqualification. (Note that one is *accused of*, but *charged with*, a crime.) To *incriminate* is to implicate in a crime or other serious offense <incriminating evidence>—and the term is often used now as a reflexive present participle <self-incriminating>. (**Criminate* is a NEEDLESS VARIANT.) To *indict* is to charge a person with a crime by formal legal process, especially by a grand-jury presentation. To *arraign* is to bring an accused person into court for the purpose of entering a plea to an indictment. To *impeach* is to charge a serious breach of the public trust by an officeholder who is brought before a constitutionally authorized body that deliberates over whether to remove or otherwise punish the officeholder.

B. That-phrase Objects. It is permissible to write, "He *charged* that the prosecutorial misconduct was of constitutional dimensions," although in BrE *charge* generally takes a simple noun, either a person or a thing. E.g.: "Count one *charged* the defendant that on or about October 27, 1969, being an undischarged bankrupt he had obtained credit to the extent of £451 13s. 9d. from Lloyds Bank Ltd without informing the said bank that he was then an undischarged bankrupt." *Regina v. Hartley*, [1972] 2 Q.B. 1.

Both simple nouns and *that*-phrase objects are common in AmE. Here are examples of the latter type:

- "He stated that he gave a lease of the pastureland on his farm to the complainant, but *charged that* the lease he signed, which covered his home, did not contain the verbal agreement entered into by the parties that the lease would be cancelled when the lessor obtained a purchaser for his farm." *Roberts v. Spence*, 209 So.2d 623, 624 (Miss. 1968).
- "The Government's information *charged that* defendants willfully failed to file income tax returns for 1999, 2000, and 2001." *U.S. v. Hall*, 515 F.3d 186, 189 (3d Cir. 2008).

C. *Charge the jury.* When a trial judge *charges* the jury, or gives the jury its *charge*, the judge tells the jurors what the law is and explains that if they believe one version of the facts, they must render their verdict for the plaintiff—but if they believe the other version of the facts, they must render their verdict for the defendant. E.g.: "We conclude that the court properly marshaled the evidence in *charging the jury*." *State v. Andrews*, 927 A.2d 358, 363 (Conn. App. Ct. 2007).

The noun phrase is *jury charge* (= the judge's instructions).

chargé d'affaires. Pl. *chargés d'affaires.* Pluralizing often begets error—e.g.: "Washington is full of *chargé* *d'affaires* [read *chargés d'affaires*]." Sidney S. Alderman, *The French Language in English and American Law*, 7 La. B.J. 33, 37 (1959).

chargee = (1) the holder of a charge upon property, or of a security over a contract (*OED*); or (2) one charged with a crime. Sense 1, though unrecorded in American dictionaries (apart from *W2*), appears more frequently in AmE than in BrE—e.g.:

- "I prefer to regard the gift over as a charge coupled with an ancillary power of sale. The objections are that it is not formally such, and that it gives the trustee greater rights than a *chargee* would have." *Boal v. Metro. Museum of Art*, 292 F. 303, 305 (S.D.N.Y. 1923) (per L. Hand, J.).
- "The critical distinction between trusts and charges for the purposes of resolution of the issues posed in this case is the absence of any fiduciary element in the *chargee's* duty toward the beneficiary of the charge." *Gadekar v. Phillips*, 375 A.2d 248, 255 (Md. Ct. Spec. App. 1977).

Sense 2, which most dictionaries do not record, appears infrequently. E.g.:

- "An indictment performs the office of advising the *chargee* of the charge." *People v. Addison*, 220 N.E.2d 511, 513 (Ill. App. Ct. 1966).
- "She says that a charge of a crime in the vague language of the questioned statute does not apprise the *chargee* with notice of prohibited conduct." *State v. Grinstead*, 206 S.E.2d 912, 918 (W. Va. 1974).

charge the jury. See **charge (c)**.

Charta, Magna. See **Magna Carta**.

charterer; affreighter. Both mean "a person to whom a vessel is chartered in a charterparty." *Charterer* is more usual. See the quotation under **affreightment**.

charterparty; charter-party; charter party [fr. L. *charta partitia* or *carta partita* "a writing divided"]. American dictionaries mostly spell the phrase as two words; some British sources spell it as one; and some sources use the hyphenated spelling. (*See, e.g.,* 3 James Kent, *Commentaries on American Law* 274 (George F. Comstock ed., 11th ed. 1866).) But the trend in AmE and BrE is to make it one—e.g.:

- "Karen and Omar entered into a *charterparty* agreement dated September 26, 1984 under which Karen would provide Omar with a ship, the Motor Vessel Karen, to transport 23,750 tons of wheat." *Karen Maritime Ltd. v. Omar Int'l Inc.*, 322 F.Supp.2d 224, 225 (E.D.N.Y. 2004).
- "The Northern District of Georgia held that the plaintiff could not assert claims against the defendant under the *charterparty* contract, but then contend that the defendant was not a party to the contract for purposes of enforcing the forum-selection clause." *Ormet Primary Aluminum Corp. v. M/V Fu An Cheng*, 681 F.Supp.2d 737, 740 (E.D. La. 2009).
- "The question is raised in the context of a long-term *charterparty* [that] was terminated as a result of the Owners' acceptance of the Charterers' repudiatory breach of the *charterparty*." *Omak Mar. Ltd. v Mamola Challenger Ship. Co.*, [2010] E.W.H.C. 2026 (Comm.).

Of course, "dictionaries lag behind linguistic realities." *Sec. Ctr., Ltd. v. First Nat'l Sec. Ctrs.*, 750 F.2d 1295, 1298 n.4 (5th Cir. 1985) (per Reavley, J.). No doubt more and more dictionaries will come to record *charterparty* as a single word.

Avoid *charter* as an elliptical form of *charterparty* because *charter* has so many other meanings that using it in this way gives rise to ambiguities. The tendency to use *charter* is understandable if we view *charterparty* as two words; the solution is to spell it as one.

chary (= cautious), a FORMAL WORD close in meaning to *wary*, is a favorite word of some legal writers—e.g.:

- "We have been extremely *chary* about extending the 'commercial speech' doctrine beyond this narrowly circumscribed category of advertising." *Dun & Bradstreet, Inc. v. Greenmoss Builders, Inc.*, 472 U.S. 749, 792 (1985) (Brennan, J., dissenting).
- "In its apparent repudiation of direct physical pressures, and of chemicals as a principal means of psychological coercion, the CIA had fashioned a policy more *chary* of existing legal strictures while maintaining the freedom to apply degrees and methods of coercion as severe as those apparently made available after September 11, 2001." William Ranney Levi, Note, *Interrogation's Law*, 118 Yale L.J. 1434, 1471 (2009).

The word sometimes implies "sparing, ungenerous" <chary of praise>.

chaser. See LAWYERS, DEROGATORY NAMES FOR (A).

chasm is pronounced /**kaz**-əm/.

chaste (= untainted by unlawful sexual intercourse; sexually continent or virtuous) is a word that applies to men and women alike. Unfortunately, however, a bias pervades its usual applications so that it almost always refers to women and girls. E.g.: "One view is that a fallen woman who has fully reformed is *chaste*, while another is that chastity before marriage means physical virginity—a woman can be seduced only once. There is nothing *unchaste* about marital intercourse and hence, under either view, a widow or divorcee may be an unmarried female of previously-*chaste* character." Rollin M. Perkins & Ronald N. Boyce, *Criminal Law* 463–64 (3d ed. 1982).

chattelize (= to treat as a chattel) began as a nonlegal word in the 19th century to describe human degradation, as in the phrase *chattelized humanity*. The word has since migrated into legal contexts, as here:

- "When the intangible is *chattelized* in a document, the analogies to property predominate." Eugene F. Scoles & Peter May, *Conflict of Laws* § 19.27, at 758 (1982).
- "This would plainly be true as to ordinary chattels, and '*chattelized*' property like securities should go by the same rule." *Boston Safe Deposit & Trust Co. v. Paris*, 447 N.E.2d 1268, 1271 n.3 (Mass. App. Ct. 1983).

See **chattels**.

chattel mortgage; conditional sales contract. The distinction between these two concepts is important when a buyer of goods cannot pay the entire purchase price at once. In such cases, the buyer makes a down payment, and the rest of the purchase price is payable in installments. Under a *chattel mortgage*, the seller transfers title to the buyer, who gives the seller a mortgage to secure the unpaid balance. Under a *conditional sales contract*, the buyer takes delivery, but the title remains in the seller until the entire purchase price is paid. The latter method, naturally, is more common in installment sales, which usually involve adhesion contracts. See **mortgage.**

In the context of real property, a *conditional sales contract* is often called a *contract for deed*. See **conditional sales contract.**

chattels is commonly defined as "personal property," but this definition misleads. The proper definition is "any property other than freehold land"; a leasehold interest in land, having characteristics of both real and personal property, is termed a *chattel real*. Meanwhile, tangible goods or intangible rights, as in patents, stocks, or shares, are termed *chattels personal*. It is a distinction still recognized (though in the second example below it's a historian using the terms):

- "*Chattels personal* are, properly and strictly speaking, things movable, such as animals, household stuff, money, jewels, etc." *Woodward v. Laporte*, 41 A. 443, 443 (Vt. 1898).
- "In the law of *chattels personal* before the fifteenth century, the treatment of future interests was similar to that of *chattels real*." John Makdisi, *The Vesting of Executory Interests*, 59 Tul. L. Rev. 366, 376 (1984).
- "A cause of action for inverse condemnation accrues the first time damage occurs to lands or *chattels real* [that] was in fact caused by the improvement." *Connolly v. Dallas County, Iowa*, 465 N.W.2d 875, 878 (Iowa 1991). (Note the REMOTE RELATIVE with the *that*-clause.)

The distinction is best observed fastidiously; nevertheless, this terminology is falling into disuse. *Chattel personal* = chose. See **chose.**

cheat = a common-law misdemeanor involving a swindle perpetrated by means of a false token. This wrong—which thrived from the 17th to the 19th centuries—falls today under the rubric of *false pretenses*. See **false pretenses.**

The origin of the word *cheat* is interesting. It derives from *escheat*. In the Middle Ages, the *escheator* was an officer who assessed the value of an escheat—that is, property reverting to the public treasury upon the death of the king's tenant-in-chief for lack of an heir. So corrupt and greedy were the *escheators*, however, that, by the 15th century, the modern sense of *cheat* and *cheater* had developed. Meanwhile, a century later, thieves began to refer to their stolen goods as *cheat*, as if the goods were *escheated* or confiscated. These two uses of the word coalesced into the modern sense. See **escheat.**

cheatee. See -EE (A).

check = an order for payment of money on demand, drawn on a banker, and expressed as being payable either to bearer or to (the order of) a named person. *Cheque* is the BrE spelling. See **bill of exchange.**

check, worthless; bogus check; cold check; false check; rubber check. What should we call an unaltered check that bears the drawer's genuine signature but is drawn on a bank in which the drawer has either no account or insufficient funds? *Rubber check*, which is slang, derives from the idea that the check "bounces"; the phrase suggests that the drawer's account has insufficient funds but not that the drawer has no account, so it is not as broad as the other phrases. *False check* and *bogus check* inappropriately suggest a forgery, which is a different idea altogether. *Cold check*, like *rubber check*, is slang. *Worthless check* is the least objectionable phrase, though it is slightly misleading because the check may finally have some value; despite that shortcoming, criminal-law scholars commonly use *worthless check* (which is not to say that they ever use worthless checks). *See, e.g.*, Rollin M. Perkins & Ronald N. Boyce, *Criminal Law* 385 (3d ed. 1982).

cherry-picking is AmE legal slang for the modern law firm's practice of luring select lawyers from other firms with special inducements. E.g.:

- "Their lawyers will be easy prey in this age of *cherry-picking* and big-firm branching." Steven Brill, *The End of Partnership?*, Am. Law., Dec. 1989, at 3.
- "It's been an incredible decade marked by law firm collapses, mergers[,] and *cherry-picking*." Rita H. Jensen, *Firms Face the New Decade*, Nat'l L.J., 25 Dec. 1989–1 Jan. 1990, at 1.

The verb *cherry-pick* is a BACK-FORMATION: "Dell downplays the effect his attempts to *cherry-pick* will have on San Francisco's legal market." Audrey Duff, *S.F. v. L.A.: Battling for Talent*, Am. Law., May 1990, at 16.

chicanery; *chicane; chicanerous. In contexts other than those involving horse racing and card games, **chicane* has become an archaic and NEEDLESS VARIANT of *chicanery* (= trickery). As the first example shows, this was not always so—e.g.:

- "To appeal from day to day and from court to court upon a question merely of fact . . . is a perpetual source of obstinate *chicane* [read, today, *chicanery*], delay, and expensive litigation." 3 William Blackstone, *Commentaries on the Laws of England* 392–93 (1772).
- "The lack of business ethics displayed by defendant . . . invites and receives the condemnation of all who love fair play and scorn *chicane* [read *chicanery*] and deceit." *Philadelphia Dairy Prods. v. Quaker City Ice Cream Co.*, 159 A. 3, 6 (Pa. 1932).
- "[It] is not uncommon to speak of one as defrauded of his rights who has been wrongfully deprived of them by other means than *chicane* [read *chicanery*] or trickery." *U.S. v. Skeddle*, 989 F.Supp. 873, 885 (N.D. Ohio 1997).

The corresponding adjective, *chicanerous* (= engaging in or exhibiting chicanery) is a useful NEOLOGISM perhaps invented by Professor Arthur Miller of Harvard, the first known user: "It was believed that a pleading containing inconsistent allegations indicated falsehood on its face and was a sign of a *chicanerous* litigant seeking to subvert the judicial process." 5 Charles Alan Wright & Arthur R. Miller, *Federal Practice and Procedure* § 1283, at 372 (1969) (section acknowledged as Miller's). Other uses swiftly followed—e.g.: "The trial judge grounded his dismissal on a finding that 'the United States Attorney's office actions in juggling this case back and forth . . . is [*sic*] vexatious, oppressive, *chicanerous*.'" *U.S. v. Jefferson*, 257 A.2d 225, 226 (D.C. 1969).

For more on this word, see **deception.**

chide. See **reprove.**

chief judge; presiding judge. On each U.S. Court of Appeals (since 1948), the *chief judge* is the senior active judge among those who (1) are not yet 65 years old, (2) have been circuit judges for at least one year, and (3) have never before served as *chief judge.* 28 U.S.C. § 45(a)(1). The *chief judge* generally hears almost as many cases as other judges, acts as the circuit's administrative head, and schedules all court sittings. Before 1948, the position was called *senior circuit judge.*

A *presiding judge* is the senior active judge on a three-member panel that hears and decides cases. One may be a presiding judge one month and the most junior member on a panel the next month. Unlike *chief judge*, then, *presiding judge* is not a permanent title—it is a situational title.

Chief Justice of the United States. Though usage has varied over time, this is now the generally preferred title—not **Chief Justice of the United States Supreme Court* or **Chief Justice of the Supreme Court of the United States.* But that was not always so, as Charles Warren explained with abundant historical evidence:

The official title of the Chief Justice seems to have varied at different periods of the Court's history. Jay was commissioned under the title of "Chief Justice of the Supreme Court of the United States," as were Rutledge, Ellsworth, Marshall, Taney, Chase and White. Fuller was commissioned as "Chief Justice of the United States." The Constitution mentions the office of Chief Justice only once; in Article One, Section three, relative to impeachments in which it is provided—"When the President of the United States is tried, the Chief Justice shall preside." The Judiciary Act of Sept. 24, 1789, provided that the Supreme Court "shall consist of a chief justice and five associate justices." The Act of July 13, 1866, c. 210, for the first time officially used the term "Chief Justice of the United States" providing that "thereafter the Supreme Court shall consist of a Chief Justice of the United States and six associate justices." The Act of April 10, 1869, c. 22, provided that the Court shall "hereafter consist of the Chief Justice of the United States and eight associate justices." The Revised Statutes, Section 673, and the Act of March 3, 1911, c. 231, codifying the laws relating to the judiciary, Section 215, refer to "a Chief Justice of the United States." On the other hand, the statutes relating to the salaries of the Court, viz.: the Act of March 3, 1873, c. 226, the Act of Feb. 12, 1902, c. 547, and the Act of March 3, 1911, c. 231, Section 218,

all refer to "the Chief Justice of the Supreme Court of the United States." *New England Historical and Genealogical Register* (1895), XLIX, 275.

Charles Warren, *The Supreme Court in United States History* 11–12 n.2 (rev. ed. 1928).

Both popular and legal writers use variations on the title—e.g.:

- "*The Chief Justice of the Supreme Court of the United States*, several years ago, was elucidating in the course of the Court's opinion a little point of law." Fred Rodell, *Woe Unto You, Lawyers!* 119 (1939).
- "The *chief justice of the United States Supreme Court* [capitalize *Chief Justice*], Mr. Rehnquist, has said that no rational person could equate a request for aid of counsel with a guilty mind." J. Gary Trichter, *The Civil Law and DWI*, 50 Tex. B.J. 1093, 1096 (1987).
- "During the hearings on Judge John Roberts' nomination to the position of *Chief Justice of the United States Supreme Court*, Roberts similarly endorsed this entrenched notion of the judge as faceless conduit for the rule of law." Susan Bandes, *We Lost It at the Movies*, 40 Loy. L.A. L. Rev. 621, 622 (2007). (For the preferred possessive form of *Roberts*, see POSSESSIVES (A).)

Chief Justiceship; Chiefship. The first is more common, but the second is admirably succinct: "But both Wilson, who had literally applied for the *Chiefship*, and Rutledge, whose friends had campaigned for him, were named Associate Justices." Fred Rodell, *Nine Men* 47 (1955).

child (of tender age or years); young person; juvenile; minor; pupil. In American law, a *child of tender age* or *years* has generally not reached his or her 14th birthday. In English law, *child* itself usually means one who is not yet 14, though some English lawyers, up to the mid-20th century, used *child* to refer to someone under 21.

In most American states, a *juvenile*—a 20th-century statutory word—is one who has not reached the age of 18. *See* Juvenile Delinquency Act, 18 U.S.C. § 5031 (1988). In England, *juvenile* denotes one who has not reached 17—i.e., either a *child* (as defined above) or a *young person* (meaning someone who has reached 14 but is not yet 17).

While *minor* (like *infant*) covers all these categories in most English-speaking jurisdictions, that is not so in Scotland, where *minor* has a more restrictive sense. In Scots law, *minors* are those 16 to 18 years old. Younger persons are called *pupils*. Scots lawyers typically use the word *nonage* to denote the status of *pupils* and *minors*.

Only lawyers could construct a system in which an *infant* can be older than a *child*. See **age of capacity, infancy, infant, minority** & **nonage.**

child *en ventre sa mere.* See *en ventre sa mere.*

child-kidnap. See **kidnapping (B).**

child-slaying. See **infanticide.**

child-stealing. See **abduction** & **kidnapping (B)**.

child support, n. So written. As a PHRASAL ADJECTIVE it is hyphenated <child-support payments>.

chill (= to inhibit, discourage <to chill a person's rights>) is now a common term in American legal JARGON. The standard phrase is *chilling effect*—e.g.: "The majority held that the waiting-period requirement is unconstitutional because it 'has a *chilling effect* on the right to travel.'" *Shapiro v. Thompson*, 394 U.S. 618, 623 (1969) (per Brennan, J.).

The origin of this usage lies in the word's figurative sense, recorded by both the *OED* and *W3*, "to affect as with cold; to check, depress, or lower (warmth, ardour, etc.); to damp, deject, dispirit" (*OED*). All the examples quoted in the *OED* to illustrate this sense involve the *chilling* of something, usually an emotion, that is figuratively warm (enthusiasm, courage, admiration, zeal, etc.).

American lawyers have extended *chill* by applying it to rights and freedoms, to the exercise of rights and freedoms, and even to the persons exercising them. E.g.:

- "The opinions emphasized that such thoughtlessly broad statutes affected not only the immediate litigants but the atmosphere of freedom generally, because they may '*chill* that free play of the spirit which all teachers ought especially to cultivate and practice.'" Robert G. McCloskey, *The American Supreme Court* 204 (1960).
- "The danger that the mere pendency of the action will *chill* the exercise of First Amendment rights requires more specific allegations than would otherwise be required." *Fran. Realty Interstate Corp. v. San Francisco Local Joint Exec. Bd.*, 542 F.2d 1076, 1083 (9th Cir. 1976).
- "The Court purports to save petitioners the uncertainty of possible enforcement of the injunction, and thereby to prevent any *chill* on their First Amendment rights, by vacating the judgment below." *Tory v. Cochran*, 544 U.S. 734, 740 (2005) (Thomas, J., dissenting).

The basic phrase *chilling effect* is sometimes jargonistically elaborated—e.g.: "The purpose of this limitation is to prevent juries from giving awards greatly in excess of what would be reasonable compensation, and thereby imposing a pecuniary '*chill factor*' on the media." *Levine v. CMP Pubs., Inc.*, 753 F.2d 1341, 1342 (5th Cir. 1985). (See SET PHRASES.) Now used indiscriminately, *chill(ing)* and *chilling effect* have become legal CLICHÉS.

chimera. Pl. *-as.* The form *chimera* is now standard, **chimaera* rarely appearing in AmE. The standard plural is *chimeras.*

Chinese Wall = a screening mechanism that protects client confidences by preventing one or more lawyers within an organization from participating in any matter involving that client. A principal purpose of this mechanism is to allow a lawyer to move to a new law firm without the fear of vicariously disqualifying that firm from representing certain clients. Typically, the procedures used in erecting a *Chinese Wall* include prohibiting the lawyer in question from any contact with the case—no access to files, no share in any fees derived from the case, and sometimes even sequestration from those handling the case. *See* M. Peter Moser, *Chinese Walls*, 3 Geo. J. Legal Ethics 399, 400 (1990).

The METAPHOR derives, of course, from the Great Wall of China—not from any ethnic bias. *See, e.g.,* Elizabeth A. Moulton, *We Are Going to Build a Chinese Wall*, 5 Nevada Law. 28–30 (Sept. 1997). Even so, some lawyers worry that the phrase might be understood in a derogatory sense; those who do tend to use a phrase such as *ethical wall*. *See Peat, Marwick, Mitchell & Co. v. Super. Ct.*, 245 Cal. Rptr. 873, 887 (Ct. App. 1988) (Low, P.J., concurring) (criticizing the term as having "an ethnic focus which many would consider a subtle form of linguistic discrimination" and as being inaccurate and politically offensive). Nonetheless, the term has defenders—e.g.: "We agree with PGE that '*Chinese wall*' is an appropriate term and that it does not have the pejorative connotations that made some expert witnesses uncomfortable in using it. As one of humanity's greatest engineering achievements, the Great Wall of China . . . suggests the kind of solidity and impermeability that a potential conflict-of-interest situation requires; we have previously referred to it as a generic term for that kind of barrier." *Portland Gen. Elec. Co. v. Duncan, Weinberg, Miller & Pembroke, P.C.*, 986 P.2d 35, 37 n.2 (Or. Ct. App. 1999).

In conflict-of-interest cases, the phrase dates from about 1977. But earlier references appear in other legal contexts to evoke the idea of artificial insularity. E.g.:

- "Some of them had said the Corn Products Refining Company had built a *Chinese wall* against competitors and kept them in chains." *U.S. v. Corn Prods. Refining Co.*, 234 F. 964, 980 (S.D.N.Y. 1916) (per L. Hand, J.).
- "But we do not think that the state may erect a *Chinese Wall* around itself by adopting regulations." *Barnwell Bros., Inc. v. S.C. State Highway Dep't*, 17 F.Supp. 803, 815 (E.D.S.C. 1937).

Today, however, the phrase almost invariably concerns legal ethics or complex financial transactions.

The phrase is sometimes written *Chinese wall*—e.g.: "Judge Gorton ordered that the Lichten firm institute a '*Chinese wall*' so that henceforth Attorney Getchell would have no exposure whatever to the instant case." *O'Donnell v. Robert Half Int'l Inc.*, 641 F.Supp.2d 84, 85 (D. Mass. 2009). But today the second word is usually capitalized.

Chip Smith charge. See **dynamite charge**.

chirograph = (1) a written deed, subscribed and witnessed; or (2) such a deed in two parts, written head to head, divided by the word "chirographum" in capitals, and the two parts separated by an indented line through the word "chirographum," each party retaining one part. See **party of the first part**.

chit [fr. Anglo-Indian *chitty* "letter; note certificate" (ca. 1673), borrowed from Hindi *chitthī*] = (1) a signed voucher for money received or owed, usu. for food, drink, etc.; or (2) a slip of paper with writing on it. Both meanings are common:

- (Sense 1) "After each meal the Club member is presented with a *chit* upon which he subscribes his name. All chits signed during a month are consolidated and monthly statements are rendered." *Baltimore Country Club, Inc. v. Comptroller of Treasury*, 321 A.2d 308, 310 (Md. 1974).
- (Sense 2) "She was to make memoranda incident to her acts of prostitution, and . . . [w]ould transcribe thereon the amount of money collected from each customer, the time at which she started and finished each transaction, along with her professional identification as 'Pam.' These *chits* . . . were placed . . . in a bag." *Schweinefuss v. Commonwealth*, 395 S.W.2d 370, 373 (Ky. 1965).

choate. Justice Oliver Wendell Holmes wrote to Sir Frederick Pollock in 1878 that he had read in a legal text from California that "the wife on marriage acquires an *inchoate* right of dower which by the death of her husband becomes *choate*." *Holmes–Pollock Letters* 11 (Mark DeWolfe Howe ed., 2d ed. 1961). *Choate*, a BACK-FORMATION from *inchoate*, is a misbegotten word, for the prefix in *inchoate* is intensive and not negative. (See EN- & NEGATIVES (B).) The word derives from the Latin verb *inchoare* "to hitch with; to begin." Yet, because it was misunderstood as being a negative (meaning "incomplete"), someone invented a positive form for it, namely *choate* (meaning "complete").

Holmes described *choate* as an "amusing slip" linguistically. But Justice Antonin Scalia is not amused by it at all. During oral arguments in *I.R.S. v McDermott* in 1992, Justice Scalia corrected a lawyer who used the word: "There is no such adjective. . . . There is *inchoate*, but the opposite of *inchoate* is not *choate*." But because the Supreme Court had used the term repeatedly in *U.S. v. City of New Britain*, 347 U.S. 81 (1954), when Justice Scalia quoted from the case, he pointedly edited it: "The priority of each statutory lien contested here must depend on the time it attached to the property in question and became [no longer inchoate]"). *I.R.S. v. McDermott*, 507 U.S. 447, 452 (1993). Still, as Ben Zimmer has pointed out, the term has been around for nearly two centuries —e.g.: "Of bequests executory or *inchoate*, as distinguished from bequests *choate* and complete in themselves." *See* Ben Zimmer, *On Language: Choate*, N.Y. Times, 3 Jan. 2010, § 7, at 16 (citing 2 R.S. Donnison Roper, *Treatise on the Law of Legacies* 358 (3d ed. 1829)).

In AmE, the word has become more or less standard in the phrase *choate lien*, corresponding to *inchoate lien*. Justice Minton used the word in *U.S. v. City of New Britain*: "The liens may also be perfected in the sense that there is nothing more to be done to have a *choate lien*—when the identity of the lienor, the property subject to the lien, and the amount of the lien are established." 347 U.S. at 84. The three requirements mentioned in that quotation make up what has come to be known in the U.S. as the *choateness doctrine*, which means that "where a security interest arising under state law . . . comes into conflict with a federal tax lien, the state law security interest 'attaches' only

when it becomes *choate*." *J.D. Ct., Inc. v. U.S.*, 712 F.2d 258, 261 (7th Cir. 1983).

Though etymologically misbegotten, the word is now fairly well ensconced in the legal vocabulary. It has supplied a name for a fairly arcane legal doctrine, which is unlikely to be renamed. *Choate* is recognized in legal literature as "an illegitimate back formation" (William T. Plumb, *Federal Liens and Priorities*, 77 Yale L.J. 228, 230 (1967)), but it is used even by those who deprecate its origins.

Pollock heard of the word from Holmes, but otherwise the term *choate* is virtually unknown in BrE. See **inchoate.**

choice of law; choice of jurisdiction. These terms, used in conflicts of law, are occasionally confused. *Choice of law* = the question of which jurisdiction's law applies. *Choice of jurisdiction* = the choice of the country that should exercise jurisdiction over a case. When either phrase is used attributively as a PHRASAL ADJECTIVE, it should be hyphenated <Delaware's choice-of-law rules>. See **conflict of laws.**

chose, n., is a LAW FRENCH word meaning literally "a thing." In modern legal writing, *chose* = chattel personal. E.g.: "There were four reasons why equity could not simply allow the assignee of a legal *chose* to sue the debtor in the Court of Chancery." G.H. Treitel, *The Law of Contract* 578 (8th ed. 1991).

Traditionally, *choses* are of two kinds. *Choses in possession* are tangible goods capable of being actually possessed and enjoyed (e.g., books and clothes); *choses in action* are rights that can be enforced by legal action (e.g., debts or causes of action in tort). E.g.:

- "If the subject of the gift is a *chose in action*, such as a bond, a note, or stock in a corporation, the delivery of the most effectual means of reducing the *chose* to possession or use, such as delivery of the bond, or the note, or the certificate of stock, if present and capable of delivery, is indispensable to the completion of the gift." *Allen-West Comm'n Co. v. Grumbles*, 129 F. 287, 290 (8th Cir. 1904).
- "*Choses in action* are by definition intangible and are therefore incapable of the physical delivery and possession necessary for the assignment, gift, or pledge of personal property." Amelia H. Boss, *Lease Chattel Paper*, 1983 Duke L.J. 69, 79 (1983).
- "A '*chose in action*' means, literally, a thing in action, and is the right of bringing an action, or a right to recover a debt or money, or a right of proceeding in a court of law to procure the payment of a sum of money, or a right to recover a personal chattel or a sum of money by action, or, as it is defined by statute, a right to recover money or personal property by a judicial proceeding." *Citizens Nat'l Bank v. Dixieland Forest Prods., LLC*, 935 So.2d 1004, 1007 (Miss. 2006).

The phrase *chose in action* is sometimes anglicized *thing in action*. Cf. **chattels.**

chose jugée = a matter already settled, and therefore not open to further consideration. This phrase is an unnecessary French equivalent of *res judicata*. See **res judicata.**

Christian name; christian name. See **surname.**

church law. See **canon law.**

***chuse,** an archaic spelling of *choose*, appears in Article I, § 2 of the U.S. Constitution, and indeed throughout the document. The archaic spelling was commonly used in British opinions of the period—e.g.: "She did not *chuse* to expose herself to contempt again. The action then is to depend entirely on the nerves of the actress; if she *chuses* to appear on the stage again, no action can be maintained." *Ashley v. Harrison*, (1793) Peake 256, 258 (K.B.) (spelling modernized at 170 Eng. Rep. 148, 149).

-CIDE. This suffix denotes either the act of slaying [fr. L. *-cīdium* "cutting, killing"] or one who slays [fr. L. *-cīda* "cutter, killer"]. So *fratricide* is either the killing of one's brother or someone who kills his or her brother. The more common words ending in this suffix are these:

homicide	=	the act of killing a person
	=	the killer of another person
infanticide	=	the act of killing a baby
	=	one who kills a baby
matricide	=	the act of killing one's mother
	=	the killer of one's own mother
parricide	=	the act of killing one's father
	=	the killer of one's own father
patricide		See the entry at **parricide.**
regicide	=	the act of killing the king or queen
	=	the killer of the king or queen
suicide	=	the act of killing oneself
	=	one who kills oneself

Though a few others, such as *fratricide* and *sororicide*, are generally known, we also have many less common words ending in -cide. For example, *famicide* (= the destroyer of someone's reputation) was once used as a synonym for *slanderer*. *Prolicide* (= the act of killing offspring either before or soon after birth) is broad enough to subsume both *feticide* (see **abortion**) and *infanticide*. The coinages with this suffix, naturally, are no more sex-neutral than in any other corner of the language: the *OED* records *uxoricide* (= the slayer of one's wife), but *mariticide* (= the slayer of one's husband) is not recorded: it can only be deduced from the adjective *mariticidal* (= of or relating to one who murders her husband).

Scientists have developed *algicides, fungicides, germicides,* and *insecticides* (known also as *pesticides,* though this word can be used more broadly than *insecticides*).

To disinfect their combs and other utensils, American barbers commonly use a trademarked product ominously called *Barbicide*. Hence this suffix, like -EE, is perhaps losing its literal force.

Naturally, wags have seized on this suffix for jocular purposes to make such words as *suitorcide* (a NONCE

WORD meaning "fatal to suitors") and *prenticecide* (= the killing of an apprentice). Justice Holmes's father, the poet Oliver Wendell Holmes, invented a word that some dictionaries label jocular. But perhaps this word ought to be taken seriously: *verbicide*—"that is," Holmes wrote, "violent treatment of a word with fatal results to its legitimate meaning, which is its life." Both "homicide and *verbicide* . . . are alike forbidden." Oliver Wendell Holmes Sr., *An Autocrat at the Breakfast-Table* 10 (1859). One mission of this dictionary is to prevent verbicide in the legal context.

For entries related to this one, see **murder (A)** & **parricide.**

C.I.F. See **cost, insurance, and freight** & **F.O.B.**

c.i.p. = continuation in part. In American patent practice, a *c.i.p. application* is a patent application filed during the lifetime of an earlier application by the same applicant, repeating a substantial part of the earlier application but adding to or subtracting from it. *See* Louis B. Applebaum et al., *Glossary of United States Patent Practice* 24 (1969).

circuit, to ride; to go on circuit; on circuit; at circuit. These phrases refer to the practice of having itinerant courts, similar in some ways to the *Curia Regis* of early common law. State and federal judges in the U.S. commonly *rode circuit* or *went on circuit* through the beginning of the 20th century. Various idioms have emerged from the practice—e.g.:

- "In contrast to the system in England, where judges *went on circuit*, most courts in the United States came to be permanently and locally fixed." René A. Wormser, *The Story of the Law* 427 (1962).
- "For English judges, [having judgments given in Welsh] can hardly have added to the attractions of *going circuit* in Wales." R.E. Megarry, *A Second Miscellany-at-Law* 169 (1973).
- "While the justices of the Supreme Court were not relieved directly of the burden of *circuit riding*, the pressure of their other duties was such that increasingly the circuit court was held by a single district judge." Charles Alan Wright, *The Law of Federal Courts* 6 (5th ed. 1994).

For an interesting account of an English judge *on circuit*, see Frank Douglas MacKinnon, *On Circuit: 1924–1937* (1941).

Lawyers, too, frequently *rode circuit*: "One of [Abraham Lincoln's] nominees was David Davis, a friend from Lincoln's days as a *circuit-riding* lawyer in Illinois." Donald Dale Jackson, *Judges* 333 (1974).

Circuit Court of Appeals. See **Circuit Judge, U.S.**

Circuit Judge, U.S. This is the proper title for a federal appellate judge who sits on a U.S. Court of Appeals (not *Circuit Court of Appeals*). Journalists often incorrectly give the title as *Judge of the Court of Appeals*.

In England, by contrast, a *circuit judge* sits in a county court and hears civil matters.

circuit split. This phrase is used in American legal writing to say that U.S. Courts of Appeals (or state appellate courts) have arrived at contrary holdings on the same point of law. E.g.:

- "It is the dissent that offers a 'novel interpretation' of § 2513, which if adopted would create a *circuit split.*" *U.S. v. Graham*, 608 F.3d 164, 177 (4th Cir. 2010).
- "In *Woodford v. Ngo* . . . the Supreme Court resolved a *circuit split*, holding that 'the PLRA exhaustion requirement requires proper exhaustion.'" *Drippe v. Tobelinski*, 604 F.3d 778, 781 (3d Cir. 2010).
- "In the 1970s and early 1980s, a *circuit split* arose concerning the application of the Confrontation Clause to coconspirator hearsay." Ben Trachtenberg, *Coconspirators, "Coventurers," and the Exception Swallowing the Hearsay Rule*, 61 Hastings L.J. 581, 643–44 (2010).

The concept is expressed in other ways as well, such as *the circuits are split* (on a question). In the past, the phrase *split between* [or *in*] *the circuits* was common— e.g.: "Recognizing that a *split in the circuits* exists and determining that we are not bound by the dictum of *Evans*, we find that *Bailey* and not *Collins* provides the appropriate analysis which we now follow." *United States v. Barnes*, 761 F.2d 1026, 1032 (5th Cir. 1985). But today, the wordy prepositional phrase is more often collapsed into the attributive construction *circuit split*, which is now the dominant form.

The U.S. Supreme Court or Congress is capable of remedying a *circuit split* by laying down an explicit rule of law that the courts of appeals must afterward follow.

CIRCUMLOCUTION. See BE-VERBS (B) & PERIPHRASIS.

circumspection = cautiousness; watchfulness; prudence <the judge exercised circumspection in disbelieving the interested witnesses>. This word is sometimes misunderstood as meaning "examination." E.g.: "The circumstances surrounding the removal are far from typical and present what the Court ascertains as a novel question, requiring almost a complete *circumspection* [read *examination*] of the removal provisions for its resolution." *Heniford v. Am. Motors Sales Corp.*, 471 F.Supp. 328, 331 (D.S.C. 1979).

circumstances. Some writers prefer *in the circumstances* to *under the circumstances*. But the latter is unobjectionable and much more common. E.g.:

- "*Under these circumstances*, we are of the opinion that the sole purpose for which the trust was created has become impossible of accomplishment and has been terminated." *Evans v. Abney*, 165 S.E.2d 160, 163 (Ga. 1968).
- "Certainly, the slasher pictures and the Dirty Harry-inspired vigilante revenge films showed 'no sympathy whatever for the insanity defense, *under any circumstances.*'" Russell D. Covey, *Criminal Madness: Cultural Iconography and Insanity*, 61 Stan. L. Rev. 1375, 1420 (2009).

H.W. Fowler wrote that the insistence on *in the circumstances* as the only right form is "puerile."

circumstantial evidence; indirect evidence. The first is the more common phrase in both AmE and BrE for evidence from which the fact-finder may infer the existence of a fact in issue, but that does not directly prove the existence of the fact. E.g.: "Susman told the jurors his case was going to involve mainly *circumstantial evidence*, a perfectly acceptable way for him to prove his case." John A. Jenkins, *The Litigators* 279 (1989). See **direct evidence.**

citation = (1) an official summons directing a person to appear before a court; or (2) an oral or written reference to a legal authority, usu. a case or statute. The term is used primarily in American and Scottish courts, as opposed to the English courts.

Perhaps that explains why the English authorities cannot agree about to whom a *citation* in sense 1 must be directed. Several say that it must go to a nonparty. See *OCL1*; W.A. Jowitt, *The Dictionary of English Law* 376 (2d ed. 1959); Roger Bird, *Osborn's Concise Law Dictionary* 73 (7th ed. 1983). Another authority of repute, however, defines the word as "a summons to a party to appear." E.R. Hardy Ivamy, *Mozley & Whiteley's Law Dictionary* 80 (10th ed. 1988). Still others define the word as broadly as it is defined in AmE—so that it may be directed either to parties or to nonparties. See *CDL*; P.H. Collin, *English Law Dictionary* 44 (1986); Gavin McFarlane, *The Layman's Dictionary of English Law* 46 (1984). Because usage varies, the narrower definitions are really too narrow to describe BrE accurately.

CITATION OF CASES. The standard works in the field are *The Bluebook: A Uniform System of Citation* (19th ed. 2010) and *The ALWD Citation Manual* (4th ed. 2010). They both provide reliable guidance on hundreds of tricky citational problems, and the editors have tried to make these books easy to use.

American writers have produced a number of ancillary aids for citing cases. Among the useful ones are these: Mary Miles Prince, *Prince's Bieber Dictionary of Legal Abbreviations* (6th ed. 2009); C.E. Good, *Citing and Typing the Law: A Course on Legal Citation and Style* (4th ed. 1997). For identifying obscure citations, especially in historical materials, Marion D. Powers's *Legal Citation Directory* (1971) is useful.

For British form, nearest counterparts to the *Bluebook* are Derek French, *How to Cite Legal Authorities* (2d ed. 2002); Sweet & Maxwell, *Guide to Law Reports and Statutes* (4th ed. 1962); and Donald Raistrick, *Index to Legal Citations and Abbreviations* (3d ed. 2008). For Canadian legal writers, the *Canadian Guide to Uniform Legal Citation* (5th ed. 2002) and Chin-Shih Tang's *Guide to Legal Citation and Sources of Citation Aid: A Canadian Perspective* (2d ed. 1990) are serviceable guides.

A few points not within the purview of those works merit our attention here, the most important being the last.

A. Beginning Sentences with Citations. It is stylistically poor to begin a sentence with a citation—e.g.:

"26 U.S.C. § 7213 provides that it is unlawful for any officer or employee of the United States to wilfully [*sic*] disclose to any person . . . [tax] returns or return information." *U.S. v. Texas Heart Inst.*, 755 F.2d 469, 479 (5th Cir. 1985). A better method is to state the proposition and to place the citation at the sentence's end. For one thing, it is incorrect to begin a sentence with numbers. *See Chicago Manual of Style* § 9.5 (16th ed. 2010); Garner, *The Redbook: A Manual on Legal Style* § 5.5 (2d ed. 2006).

   B. Midsentence Citations. The legal writer's general preference should be not to cite cases in midsentence, for it is distracting to the reader, especially if a citation is longer than 15 or so characters. Only occasionally does it seem appropriate—e.g.: "Our holding in *Harrington v. Bush*, 553 F.2d 190 (D.C. Cir. 1977), requires us to reject Senator Helms's arguments and to deny him standing." *S. Christian Leadership Conf. v. Kelley*, 747 F.2d 777, 780 (D.C. Cir. 1984).

   Courts formerly tried setting off these midsentence citations in parentheses, but the results are little better than any other midsentence citations, and doing so does not conform to the general rules of legal citation. Here is an egregious example:

> The doctrine of incorporation by reference, even if applicable at all where an intent to incorporate in the usual sense is negatived (*In re Estate of York*, 95 N.H. 435, 437, 65 A.2d 282, 8 A.L.R.2d 611; Lauritzen, *Can a Revocable Trust Be Incorporated by Reference*, 45 U. Ill. L. Rev. 583, 600; Polasky, *"Pourover" Wills and the Statutory Blessing*, 98 Trusts & Estates 949, 954–955; compare *Old Colony Trust Co. v. Cleveland*, 291 Mass. 380, 196 N.E. 920; *Bolles v. Toledo Trust Co.*, 144 Ohio St. 195, 58 N.E.2d 381, 157 A.L.R. 1164; Restatement [2d]: Trusts, § 54, cmts. e–j, l), could not import the nonexistent amendment.
> /*Second Bank-State Street Trust Co. v. Pinion*,/ 170 N.E.2d 350, 352 (Mass. 1960).

   C. Incidental Use of Case Names. See CASE REFERENCES.

   D. Citations in Text. Only the hardiest of stylists will own up to this difficult fact: in many types of legal writing—in briefs and memos, for example—the only sensible place for citations is in footnotes. Putting them in the body clutters the text, slows the reader, and hampers the writer's ability to construct a coherent paragraph. Few writing reforms would benefit the legal world more than adopting the following rules: (1) put all citations in footnotes; and (2) ban footnotes for all purposes other than providing citations. For the Garner–Scalia debate on this point, see *Making Your Case: The Art of Persuading Judges* 132–35 (2008). For the Garner–Posner debate, see *Clearing the Cobwebs from Judicial Opinions* and two related articles, 28 Court Review 4–8, 10, 12 (2001).

citator, n., refers, in LEGALESE, not to a person, but to a book that helps lawyers determine the treatment of cases by courts later considering them—whether on appeal or as precedents. By a system of code signs, citators show whether the later cases overrule, follow, limit, or distinguish a given case. Now that this information has been converted to electronic formats, citators have become outmoded.

cite, n. Using *cite* as a noun—in place of *citation*—is a casualism. Some excellent legal writers have used it in this way—e.g.:

- "The *see's* and *cfs.* far outnumber the points that rest on a simple *cite*." Karl Llewellyn, *The Common Law Tradition: Deciding Appeals* 491 (1960).
- "String *cites* are out of style among academic lawyers; for some legal theorists, reading cases is out of style." Douglas Laycock, *The Death of the Irreparable Injury Rule* viii (1991).

Even so, in certain phrases, such as *cite omitted*, the shorter form looks very lax. *See, e.g., U.S. v. David*, 662 F.Supp. 244, 245 (N.D. Ga. 1987) (twice using *cite omitted*). Cf. **quote.**

cite, vb. **A. General Senses and Use.** *Cite*, vb. = (1) to commend <the mayor cited him for his commendable pro bono work>; (2) to set forth as precedent or as binding law <counsel then cited the appropriate statutory provision>; or (3) to summon before a court of law <he was cited for contempt>. For sense 2, see **adduce (A).** For sense 3, see **summon.**

In sense 2, the object of *cite* should be the precedent or statute cited, not the person to whom it is cited. The loose usage is not uncommon in AmE—e.g.:

- "*We are cited to the case of* [read *We are asked to consider* or *The defense cites*] *Lovelady v. State*." *Smith v. State*, 180 S.W.2d 622, 625 (Tex. Crim. App. 1944).
- "A law dictionary such as this, . . . which *cites the reader to leading treatises* [read *cites leading treatises*] such as Wigmore on *Evidence*, . . . can easily instill the suspicion in a diligent patron of law that he has the makings of an advocate." E.J. Bander, *Dictionary of Selected Legal Terms and Maxims* v (2d ed. 1979).
- "I have to assume that if the attorney can't *cite me to case-law* [read *cite caselaw to me*] supporting their proposition that there is none." Hon. Lori Massey, *A View from the Bench: We Are Lawyers, Right?*, College Bull. (newsletter of the College of the State Bar of Texas), Fall 2006, at 2. (Notice other problems: repeated *that, the attorney . . . their.*)

See OBJECT-SHUFFLING.

   B. And **cite to****.** A related problem is using *cite* as an intransitive rather than as a transitive verb—that is, saying that the writer is *citing to a case* rather than *citing a case*. E.g.:

- "How Do You *Cite To* [read *Cite*] a Law Review or Law Journal?" Heading, Andrea B. Yelin & Hope Viner Samborn, *The Legal Research and Writing Handbook: A Basic Approach for Paralegals* 178 (5th ed. 2008).
- "For example, you may *cite to* [read *cite*] a federal wiretapping statute as follows: 18 USCA § 2511." Cathy Okrent, *Torts and Personal Injury Law* 419 (2009).
- "You should never *cite to* [read *cite*] an encyclopedia. . . . It is appropriate to *cite to* [read *cite*] other types of secondary authority. . . . [Y]ou should not *cite to* [read *cite*] A.L.R. annotations. . . . Finally, you can *cite to* [read *cite*] newspaper articles." Katherine A. Currier & Thomas E. Eimermann, *Introduction to Paralegal Studies* 416 (4th ed. 2009).

This looseness results perhaps from the noun form, *citation to*—e.g.: "These claims, and *citations to* cases that [Defendant] acknowledges have rejected his arguments, are set out verbatim in the Appendix." *State v. Speer*, 212 P.3d 787, 792 n.3 (Ariz. 2009). So it might be termed a kind of syntactic BACK-FORMATION.

In sense 3, some people have recently begun writing that a person is *cited to* court. In this casualism, *cite* is shorthand for "to summon with a citation" and is surely inferior to *summon*. E.g: "By the end of the 2000–2001 school year, nearly 350 parents were *cited* [read *summoned*] to court with failure to send, while more than 1000 CPS students were charged with truancy." Elissa Sonnenberg, *Independence Days*, Cincinnati Mag., Oct. 2001, at 169.

C. And *quote*. Lawyers commonly differentiate between these words. To *cite* an authority is to give its substance and to indicate where it can be found. To *quote* is to repeat someone else's exact words and to enclose them in quotation marks. In legal writing, citations routinely follow quotations.

D. And *site*. Given that *cite* is such a familiar term to lawyers, it's rare to see it displaced by the typo *site*, but this does happen—e.g.: "Petitioners *sited* [read *cited*] *Natural Resources Defense Council v. EPA* as precedent for their contention that costs cannot be the primary consideration of the EPA in effectuating a statute to protect the public health." Matthew D. Tait, *A Remedy Even the Plaintiffs Don't Like*, 16 Mo. Envtl. L. & Pol'y Rev. 552, 558 (2009). *Site*, of course, is properly a noun meaning "a place or location."

citizen. A. And Its Near-Synonyms: *subject*; *national*. These terms all denote a person in relation to the sovereign polity to which he or she belongs. *Citizen* = any native or naturalized person who owes allegiance to a country and is entitled to its protection. It is the normal term for referring to anyone in a republic whose status is not that of an alien. *Subject* is (1) one who by birthright or by naturalization owes allegiance to a personal sovereign, such as a monarch or despot; or (2) one who resides in a territory governed by an invading power. In sense 1, it has long been the traditional term in the British Commonwealth <subjects of the Queen>. In short, a *citizen* is a person from a country in which sovereignty is believed or supposed to belong to the collective body of the people, whereas a *subject* is one who owes allegiance to a sovereign monarch.

National = (1) one who lives in a country other than the one in which he or she has the status of citizen or subject; (2) a fellow citizen abroad <he arranged a party for his fellow American nationals in Salzburg>; (3) one born in the territory of a given government but now residing elsewhere, either as an alien or as a naturalized citizen or subject of that country; or (4) in international law, anyone entitled to the protection of a government, regardless of citizenship status.

B. And *resident*. With U.S. citizens, the terms *citizen* and *resident* are generally viewed as being interchangeable in reference to state residency or citizenship. *See* Charles Alan Wright, *The Law of Federal Courts* 265 (5th ed. 1994) (noting that at least two circuit courts have held otherwise—that the terms are related but "not necessarily one and the same thing").

The words are not interchangeable when other political entities (e.g., cities) are the frame of reference, for *citizen* implies political allegiance and a corresponding protection by the state, whereas *resident* denotes merely that one lives in a certain place. E.g.: "Plaintiff, a *citizen* of the State of Washington, seeks a declaratory judgment pursuant to 28 U.S.C. § 400." *Horne v. Title Ins. & Trust Co.*, 79 F.Supp. 91, 92 (S.D. Cal. 1948). (He is a *citizen* of Washington merely by virtue of being a U.S. citizen and residing in that state; yet he would be able to avail himself of the protections of state law—hence *citizen* is appropriate.) It is possible to be a *citizen* of the United States while being neither a *citizen* nor a *resident* of any particular state.

A corporation is not a *citizen* of any state—though it is treated as if it were for jurisdictional purposes. *See* Charles Alan Wright, *The Law of Federal Courts* 447 (5th ed. 1994).

With foreign citizens, the distinction between *resident* and *citizen* becomes acute, since an alien remains a *citizen* of a foreign country but may be a *resident* of a state. For purposes of American diversity jurisdiction in federal courts, the alien's *citizenship*, rather than *residency*, controls, under the principle first laid down in *Breedlove v. Nicolet*, 32 U.S. (7 Pet.) 413, 431–32 (1833). See **citizenship** & **domicile.**

citizenry; citizens. Both are acceptable plurals of *citizen*, *-s* being the more general. Two aspects of *citizenry* distinguish it: first, it is a COLLECTIVE NOUN (although it frequently takes a plural verb), emphasizing the mass or body of citizens; and second, *citizenry* is, as *W2* notes, frequently used by way of contrast to soldiery, officialdom, or the intelligentsia. Here it is opposed to one part of officialdom (some might say *intelligentsia*): "Not only judges but [also] the *citizenry* at large habitually invoke the Constitution." Raoul Berger, *G. Edward White's Apology for Judicial Activism*, 63 Tex. L. Rev. 367, 378 (1984).

citizen's arrest; private arrest. The first phrase is current in both AmE and BrE. The second is a primarily British variant.

citizenship, diversity of. See **diversity.**

citizenship; domicile; residence. *Citizenship* = formal membership in a political unit, esp. a territorial state, with all the attendant rights and privileges; nationality. In other words, *citizenship* "carries with it the idea of identification with the state and a participation in its functions. As a citizen, one sustains social, political,

---

and moral obligation to the state and possesses social and political rights under the Constitution and laws thereof." *Baker v. Keck*, 13 F.Supp. 486, 487 (E.D. Ill. 1936). See **citizen (A).**

Domicile = residency at a particular place accompanied with positive or presumptive proof that the person intends to remain there for an unlimited time. *Mitchell v. U.S.*, 88 U.S. (21 Wall.) 350, 352 (1874). "For purposes of federal diversity jurisdiction, *citizenship* and *domicile* are synonymous." *Hendry v. Masonite Corp.*, 455 F.2d 955, 955 (5th Cir. 1972).

Residence is, for legal purposes, usable in place of *domicile*, but the term is broader because in one sense it is also a FORMAL WORD for "house; home." See **domicile** & **residence.**

city lawyer. See LAWYERS, DEROGATORY NAMES FOR (A).

city part = (in the language of New York state courts) a trial court created to hear slip-and-fall and other personal-injury claims against the City of New York. The proliferation of such suits prompted the creation of a special division composed of various "parts" to dispose of them. *See* David B. Saxe, *An Afternoon in a City Part*, 17 Litig. 1, 1 (Winter 1991).

civic rights. See **civil rights.**

civil action. In so-called code states, this phrase replaced *action at law* and *suit in equity* upon the merger of law and equity in American courts. *See* 1 G.W. Field, *Field's Lawyers' Briefs* 1 (1884). Rule 2 of the Federal Rules of Civil Procedure (1938) established the *civil action* as the "one form of action" in federal courts in the U.S. See **civil suit.**

Civil Code. See **Napoleonic Code.**

civil death, a LOAN TRANSLATION of *mors civilis*, was formerly opposed to *natural death*. At common law, a person who (1) was banished or outlawed, (2) was attainted of felony, or (3) had entered a monastery was said to have suffered a *civil death*: "In one large department of law the fiction [of civil death] is elegantly maintained. A monk or nun cannot acquire or have any proprietary rights. When a man becomes 'professed in religion,' his heir at once inherits from him any land that he has, and, if he has made a will, it takes effect at once as though he were naturally dead." 1 Frederick B. Pollock & F.W. Maitland, *History of English Law* 434 (2d ed. 1899).

Now obsolete in England, this FICTION is still applied in some American states in reference to prisoners. One commentator argues convincingly that the fiction is unnecessary and confusing in the modern world:

> For the sake of preserving the fiction of *civil death*, which satisfied the logic and rules of an earlier day, words are robbed of all ordinary meaning, yet nothing of technical sharpness results. As it is now, the rules that govern the civil rights of prisoners must still be spelled out in statute and case law. In the confusion over the metaphysics of

civil death even earnest men find themselves wandering. Much simpler to drop the whole *civil death* business.
> David Mellinkoff, *The Language of the Law* 328 (1963).

The antonym, *natural life*, is a legal ARCHAISM that lives with us still, although its usefulness too is largely gone. See **natural life.**

civil disobedience (= the principled refusal to obey laws, esp. as part of a political protest aimed at changing the law) originated in Henry David Thoreau's retitled essay of that name (1866), in which he wrote: "Under a government which imprisons any unjustly, the true place for a just man is also a prison." The idea behind *civil disobedience* was refined by Gandhi and Martin Luther King Jr. The latter wrote: "I submit that an individual who breaks a law that conscience tells him is unjust, and who willingly accepts the penalty of imprisonment in order to arouse the conscience of the community over its injustice, has in reality the highest respect for the law." Martin Luther King Jr., *Why We Can't Wait* 86 (1964).

civilian, n., = a lawyer in a civil-law, as opposed to common-law, jurisdiction. As an adjective, *civilian* means "civil-law." In the sentences that follow, the first and third exemplify the noun, the second the adjective:

- "*Jura realia* and *personalia* are expressions occasionally used by modern *civilians* as adjectival forms for *jura in rem* and *in personam*, but only as confined to Property Law." Wesley Newcomb Hohfeld, *Fundamental Legal Conceptions as Applied in Judicial Reasoning*, 26 Yale L.J. 710, 738 (1917).
- "Albert Tate Jr., a *civilian* scholar, then an intermediate appellate court judge, later a justice of the Louisiana Supreme Court and now a member of this court, expressed the view that the 1912 Legislature amended article 467, vastly expanding the items specifically covered." *Equibank v. U.S. I.R.S.*, 749 F.2d 1176, 1179 (5th Cir. 1985).
- "We now know a great deal more about classical Roman understandings of rights (*iura*) . . . and related concepts, as well as their elaboration by medieval and early modern *civilians*." John Witte Jr., *Prophets, Priests, and Kings*, 57 Emory L.J. 1527, 1528 (2008).

Even in legal writing, of course, *civilian* (n. & adj.) appears also in its nonlegal sense ("[of or relating to] a nonmilitary person")—e.g.:

- "A *civilian* trial, in other words, is held in an atmosphere conducive to the protection of individual rights, while a military trial is marked by the age-old manifest destiny of retributive justice." *O'Callahan v. Parker*, 395 U.S. 258, 266 (1969) (per Douglas, J.).
- "At the close of evidence, the military judge discussed proposed instructions with counsel and specifically asked *civilian* defense counsel whether he was requesting instructions on any affirmative defense." *U.S. v. Eslinger*, 69 M.J. 522, 524 (Army Crim. App. 2010).

civil law. A. As Noun. The term *civil law* is ambiguous; legal writers should be careful to specify which meaning they attribute to the term. *Civil law* = (1) (to a common-law practitioner) private law, as opposed to criminal law, administrative law, military law, or ecclesiastical law <civil litigation>; (2) (to a legal historian) the civil law of Rome; (3) (to a comparative-law specialist within the common-law system) the civil-law tradition in civil-code countries; the entire legal system in nations falling within the civil-law tradition; (4) (to a civil-law practitioner) the fundamental content of the legal system (as opposed to public and commercial law)—of persons, of things, of obligations; and (5) (to an ethicist) the law imposed by the state; temporal as opposed to moral law.

Sense 5 is perhaps the rarest one—hence most in need of illustration: "A favorite theory with many of the philosophers is that ethics is an exposition of the moral law as distinguished from the *civil law*; the former being imposed by the conscience, the latter by the power of the state." George W. Warvelle, *Essays in Legal Ethics* 4 (1902).

B. Form of Adjective. Like its sibling *common law*, this term should be hyphenated when it is used as a PHRASAL ADJECTIVE <civil-law jurisdiction>, and written as two words when used as a noun <the civil law of Louisiana>. See **common law** & PHRASAL ADJECTIVES (A).

civil-law method; canon-law method. These refer to methods of determining degrees of blood relationship. Under the *civil-law method*, commonly used in the U.S., you ascertain how closely related a person is to a decedent by counting up or back from the decedent to the nearest ancestor who is common to both the decedent and the relative in question. Then you count down from the ancestor to the relative in question, counting one degree for each generation.

Under the *canon-law method*, you count similarly in each line, and the longer line to the common ancestor determines the degree.

civil lawyer (= civilian, as defined previously) is the usual form, not *civil-law lawyer*—e.g.: "Common lawyers tend to be much less rigorous about such matters than *civil lawyers*." John H. Merryman, *The Civil Law Tradition* 26 (1969). See **civilian.** But cf. **common-law lawyer.**

civil liberties. See **civil rights.**

*****civil offense.** This phrase is a misnomer, *offense* properly referring to a criminal act. The better phrase is *civil wrong*. See **offense.** Cf. **criminal offense.**

civil partnership. See **civil union.**

civil remedy. See **remedy.**

civil rights; civil liberties; civic rights. *Civil rights*, an Americanism, refers generally to the individual rights guaranteed by the Bill of Rights and by the Thirteenth, Fourteenth, Fifteenth, and Nineteenth Amendments, as well as by legislation such as the Voting Rights Act. These rights include especially the right to vote; freedom from involuntary servitude; the enjoyment of life, liberty, and property; privacy; due process; and equal protection of the law. Some of these rights, such as the right to vote, are restricted to citizens; others, such as the rights of due process and equal protection, apply equally to anyone within a jurisdiction.

Some writers distinguish *civil rights* from *political rights*, contending that the latter phrase embraces participation "in the management of government through such practices as voting." Jack Plano & Milton Greenberg, *The American Political Dictionary* 266 (8th ed. 1989). By this definition, then, the right to vote is not a *civil right*. But this discrepancy merely shows that the phrase *civil rights* is fuzzy at the edges.

The phrase *civil liberties* is more widely used than *civil rights*—that is, not just in AmE—to refer generally to the liberties guaranteed to all persons by law or custom against undue governmental interference. *Civil rights* is also sometimes used in this broader sense: "The subject was '*civil rights*,' that is, the liberties of man as man and not primarily as an economic animal." Robert G. McCloskey, *The American Supreme Court* 170 (1960).

Civic rights, a much less common phrase, sounds less weighty than the other two phrases. It often seems to verge on being a NEEDLESS VARIANT of *civil rights*—e.g.: "Lincoln, unwilling to alienate a public opinion that everywhere in the North was implacably, savagely opposed to giving slaves movement or *civic rights*, was, on one occasion in the debates, not above snarling 'nigger.'" Alfred Kazin, *A Forever Amazing Writer*, N.Y. Times, 10 Dec. 1989, § 7 (Book Rev.), at 3.

civil suit. Does this phrase exclude all cases involving the government? Rodell suggests so: "Thus the two sides in what The Law would call a '*civil suit*'—an ordinary case not involving the government—might be required to pick their own expert or experts to settle their dispute for them." Fred Rodell, *Woe Unto You, Lawyers!* 175 (1939). That parenthetical definition is puzzlingly wrong: government lawyers frequently refer to their involvement in *civil suits* or *civil actions*—indeed, the Federal Rules of Civil Procedure provide expressly for *civil actions* in which the government is a party.

civil union; civil partnership. Both terms mean a marriage-like relationship that may be registered with and recognized by civil authorities as meriting some or all of the legal benefits of marriage. *Civil union* is preferred in American law. *Civil partnership* is preferred in British law. In American law, only individual states may authorize civil unions—and dissolutions. Because most states and the federal government do not recognize civil unions as binding, couples who register as partners in a civil union have fewer rights than couples who marry, and the rights granted vary from jurisdiction to jurisdiction. Civil unions are not limited to same-sex couples, which presents an unusual problem. If an opposite-sex couple forms a civil union, they must dissolve the union before contracting marriage with other people in a state that recognizes civil unions. But it's unclear whether the partners are free to marry others without a dissolution in states that do not recognize civil unions. In British law, the Civil Partnership Act 2004 extended marriage-like rights, duties, and protections to same-sex couples who register as civil partners. Partnerships end upon annulment, death, or dissolution.

civil wrong is broader than *tort* or *delict*, embracing also breaches of contract and of trust, breaches of statutory duty, and defects in performing public duties. See **civil offense* & **offense.**

claim. A. Transitive Verb. *Claim* = (1) to take or demand as one's right; or (2) to assert emphatically (something of questionable or questioned credibility). Sense 1 of *claim* often appears without an explicit object (i.e., with the object as an UNDERSTOOD WORD). E.g.: "Plaintiffs are sisters of Mrs. Girard and *claim* as her heirs." *Moss v. Axford*, 224 N.W. 425, 426 (Mich. 1929). That is, they *claim* Mrs. Girard's estate as her heirs.

Sense 2, primarily an Americanism, is subject to SLIPSHOD EXTENSION when writers use *claim* to mean merely "to say." It is groundless, though, to insist that this verb can properly mean only "to lay claim to" or "to demand as one's due," and not "to assert; to allege." *Claim* has long been used in the latter as well as in the former sense. E.g.:

- "Appellants *claimed* that the City did not install the temporary traffic signal within a reasonable time after deciding that a temporary signal was needed." *Sipes v. City of Grapevine*, 146 S.W.3d 273, 280 (Tex. App.—Fort Worth 2004).
- "It was a 'strange coincidence' that a police officer *claimed* to have shot the suspect at the same location around the same time as Celestin was shot." *Celestin v. City of New York*, 581 F.Supp.2d 420, 424 (E.D.N.Y. 2008).

B. Noun. From sense 2 of the verb has grown the noun sense "assertion, contention" <her claim that the immunity applies here>, in addition to the older sense "a right to (something)." To be avoided at all costs is the use of the term in different senses in a single context: "The Government *claims* that Sherlock's *claim* of fifth amendment privilege is moot." *U.S. v. Sherlock*, 756 F.2d 1145, 1146 (5th Cir. 1985). Either substitution eliminates the problem.

claimant. Ordinarily, the word refers to one who asserts a property right or makes a demand, but recently it has been extended to refer also to one who posits a legal claim such as a constitutional privilege, or even one who claims in the sense of "argues." E.g.: "A person whose conduct is clearly within the constitutional scope of a statute may not successfully challenge it for vagueness. . . . The burden is on the *claimant* to show that in its operation the statute is unconstitutional to her in her situation." *Lear v. State*, 753 S.W.2d 737, 740 (Tex. App.—Austin 1988).

claim preclusion; issue preclusion. The first phrase is synonymous with *res judicata* in its strict sense,

without being susceptible to the ambiguities of the LATINISM. The second phrase is synonymous with *collateral estoppel* in its strict sense. Professor Allan Vestal long argued—with considerable success—that courts should use the terms *claim preclusion* and *issue preclusion*; the Restatement (Second) of Judgments follows that usage. "The principal distinction," explains Professor Wright, is that *claim preclusion* "forecloses litigation of matters that have never been litigated. This makes it important to know the dimensions of the 'claim' that is foreclosed by bringing the first action, but unfortunately no precise definition is possible." Charles Alan Wright, *The Law of Federal Courts* 723 (5th ed. 1994). See **collateral estoppel** & **res judicata.**

claim quit. See **quitclaim.**

claim(s) agent; claim(s) adjuster. *Claims* is the standard form. See **adjuster.**

class is not interchangeable with *kind* or *type*. We may have a type or kind of *thing*, but a class of *things*. E.g.:

- "The principle of law which has been attached as the test for decision in this *class of case* [read *type of case* or *class of cases*] is that of whether the language employed by the employer possesses the immediacy and finality of a firing." *Keast v. Commonwealth*, 503 A.2d 507, 509 (Pa. Commw. Ct. 1986).
- "Respondent's acts as set forth in the agreement tendered by the parties falls into this *class of case* [read *type of case* or *class of cases*]." *In re Relphorde*, 644 N.E.2d 874, 875 (Ind. 1994).

class action = a lawsuit instituted by one or more parties on behalf not only of themselves but also of many other parties, when common questions of law and fact are involved. "The *class action* was an invention of equity . . . mothered by the practical necessity of providing a procedural device so that mere numbers would not disable large groups of individuals, united in interest, from enforcing their equitable rights nor grant them immunity from their equitable wrongs." *Montgomery Ward v. Langer*, 168 F.2d 182, 187 (8th Cir. 1948).

The phrase *class-action suit* is wordy for *class action*.

class of, a. See SYNESIS.

clause. In grammar, of course, this word refers to any group of words that contains a subject and a verb. In law, *clause* generally refers vaguely to some unit of a legal instrument or statute—often a paragraph, subdivision, or section. It need not be restricted, in its application, to a single sentence, as some lawyers mistakenly believe.

In G.B., a *clause* in a bill before Parliament becomes a section when the bill is given Royal Assent.

*clause of accruer. See **accrual.**

claw back, vb.; **clawback,** n. As a transitive PHRASAL VERB, *claw back* = (1) to take back money that has already been allocated; or (2) (of a taxing authority) to take back previously granted tax relief. E.g., in sense 1:

"Taxpayers' inability to *claw back* money if property declines in value does not persuade us that there is a problem in the logic of *Pyle*." *Grimes v. I.R.C.*, 851 F.2d 1005, 1009 (7th Cir. 1988).

The noun *clawback* = (1) money taken back; or (2) the loss of previously granted tax relief.

Clawback provision = a penalty in the nature of a tax. E.g.:

- "A blocking statute is a law passed by the foreign government imposing a penalty upon a national for complying with a foreign court's discovery request. France and Britain have passed blocking laws aimed at discovery in American antitrust suits. These statutes are also known by the descriptive moniker: *clawback provisions*." *In re Anschuetz*, 754 F.2d 602, 614 n.29 (5th Cir. 1985).
- "It could make it easier to sue for libel, by granting legal aid for litigants but with stiff *clawback provisions* to discourage frivolous writs." Economist, 28 Jan.–3 Feb. 1989, at 18.

clean hands is a METAPHOR from equity, derived from the maxim *He who comes to equity must come with clean hands*, i.e., must be free from taint of fraud. E.g.:

- "The guiding doctrine in this case is the equitable maxim that 'he who comes into equity must come with *clean hands*.' This maxim is far more than a mere banality." *Precision Instrument Mfg. Co. v. Auto. Maint. Mach. Co.*, 324 U.S. 806, 814 (1945) (per Murphy, J.).
- "The nature of the *unclean-hands* defense in patent and unfair competition litigation and its proper place in the context of the issues presented in such cases has not been clearly established." *Republic Molding Corp. v. B.W. Photo Utils.*, 319 F.2d 347, 349 (9th Cir. 1963).
- "But Phoenix did not make the contributions as required—a delinquency that the trial court termed as 'a classic example of lack of *clean hands*.'" *Kenyon Ltd. P'ship v. 1372 Kenyon St. Nw. Tenants' Ass'n*, 979 A.2d 1176, 1189 (D.C. 2009).

A memorable statement of the principle is: "He that hath committed Iniquity, shall not have equity." Richard Francis, *Maxims of Equity* 5 (1727).

clear, adj. See **evident.**

clear, vb. (= to exonerate), is a casualism common in journalese: "On Monday the jury *cleared* the defendants of charges that they tried to overthrow the Government by force." *U.S. Won't Retry 3 in Bombings*, N.Y. Times, 2 Dec. 1989, at 9.

*clear and convincing clarity. Several state and federal courts have announced **clear and convincing clarity* as the standard for proving actual malice in defamation cases. The phrase is an unfortunate amalgamation of the two phrases *clear and convincing* and *convincing clarity*. See Thomas A. Woxland, *Clear Clarity*, 1 Scribes J. Legal Writing 143–44 (1990). Need it be said that the phrase is a redundant and wordy REDUNDANCY?

clear and convincing evidence. See **preponderance of the evidence.**

clear and present danger. This is the phrase Holmes coined to express his test of whether certain speech is protected by the First Amendment. *See Schenck v. U.S.*, 249 U.S. 47, 52 (1919). Rodell calls this famous formula Holmes's "greatest, and only major, judicial error. The pat phrase was first used in a case where an anti-war extremist, who had urged that young men dodge the draft, was jailed for thus committing a federal crime. . . . Little more than a year later, Holmes himself had cause to regret the '*clear and present danger*' excuse for letting Congress curb freedom of speech, which he had handed his colleagues on the platter of his eloquence." Fred Rodell, *Nine Men* 210 (1955). The Supreme Court later widened the meaning of the phrase, giving, in Rodell's words, its "free-speech-sapping operations the protective cover of the words of Holmes." *Id.*

clear-cut, adj. So hyphenated. E.g.:

- "If treatment decisions in the absence of living wills necessarily require interpreting a patient's prior values, and this process realistically involves some melding of the patient's values with her family's, where is a *clearcut* [read *clear-cut*] line that will prevent nontreatment of persons who are merely inconvenient or 'pleasantly senile'?" Nancy K. Rhoden, *Litigating Life and Death*, 102 Harv. L. Rev. 375, 418–19 (1988).
- "Neither majority nor dissenting opinion came properly to grips with the problem, which was not one of expressing a *clearcut* [read *clear-cut*] 'logical choice' but one of 'balance' between conflicting directives." Walker Gibson, *Literary Minds and Judicial Style*, 6 Scribes J. Legal Writing 115, 132 (1997).

See **doubtless** & **obviously.**

clearly. Exaggerators like this word, along with its cousins (*obviously, undeniably, undoubtedly*, and the like). Often a statement prefaced with one of these words is conclusory, perhaps even exceedingly dubious—e.g.: "It seems to be a familiar joke among some ironic observers that when a judge (some other judge) begins a sentence with a term of utter conviction (*Clearly, Undeniably, It is plain that . . .*), the sentence that follows is likely to be dubious, unreasonable, and fraught with difficulties." Walker Gibson, *Literary Minds and Judicial Style*, 36 N.Y.U. L. Rev. 915, 925 (1961). This skepticism has grown from adverbial abuse. Where the terms are used merely to buttress arguments, they become WEASEL WORDS and actually weaken them. They should be used only where one's bitterest opponent could not object. See **doubtless** & **obviously.**

clearly erroneous. This phrase expresses the standard of review that, in many jurisdictions (such as the U.S. federal courts), an appellate court applies in judging a trial court's treatment of factual issues. A judgment is reversible if it resolves issues in a *clearly erroneous* manner.

clemency; pardon; commutation; reprieve; lenity; leniency; mercy. These terms all denote the reduction

---

An asterisk (∗) precedes words and phrases that are invariably inferior forms.

in the severity of a penalty (usually on grounds of forbearance and compassion) imposed on one who has committed a legal or moral offense. *Clemency* implies an ameliorating forgiveness that lessens the asperities of strict justice or by-the-book punishment. The term evokes particularly the power of the chief executive to pardon or commute a criminal sentence. A *pardon* is a nullification of the remaining penalty due for a violation of the law, with the permission to go scot-free, whether this means an unconditional release from prison, the obliteration of a fine, or an escape from a death sentence. A *commutation* is the executive's replacement of a comparatively severe punishment that has been judicially imposed with one less severe; it is sometimes granted by reason of the wrongdoer's old age or illness, and sometimes because of a disparity between the wrongdoer's sentence and other sentences imposed on similarly culpable people. (See **commute.**) A *reprieve* is a temporary postponement of a penalty, especially a death sentence. *Lenity*, with its more usual lay synonym *leniency* (avoid **lenience*), suggests a relaxation of the enforcement or application of rules. In the phrase *rule of lenity*, it denotes a presumption that an ambiguous penal provision must be interpreted against the enforcing authority and in favor of the person to whom the penalty might apply. *Mercy*, like *leniency*, is a term not confined to law: it suggests a high degree of pitying forbearance that enables one to abstain from judging harshly, from exacting punishment, or from seeking vengeance. In criminal contexts, it often suggests a sentence of life imprisonment as opposed to the death sentence.

*cleptomania. See **kleptomania.**

clergyable; nonclergyable. *Clergyable* = (of an offense) susceptible to benefit of clergy. *Nonclergyable* = (of an offense) punishable without benefit of clergy. E.g.: "Although originally those entitled to benefit of clergy were simply delivered to the bishop for ecclesiastical proceedings, with the possibility of degradation from orders, incarceration, and corporal punishment for those found guilty, during the 15th and 16th centuries the maximum penalty for *clergyable* offenses became branding on the thumb, imprisonment for not more than one year, and forfeiture of goods." *McGautha v. California*, 402 U.S. 183, 197–98 (1971) (per Harlan, J.). See **benefit of clergy** & **neck verse.**

The spelling *clergiable*, though listed as the primary spelling in the *OED* and in most law dictionaries, occurs less frequently than *clergyable* in legal texts.

clerk; law clerk; summer associate; summer clerk; extern; briefing attorney. The rather undignified term *clerk* is used in reference to an American law student who works for a law firm before receiving a law degree and passing the bar exam. In response to the meniality connoted by this term, some lawyers have borrowed *extern* from the medical profession, but its use is not widespread. For *clerks* who work with a firm during the summer months, lawyers have hit upon *summer*

associate or *summer clerk*, which has gained currency throughout the U.S. among firms that recruit heavily.

Law clerk is used both as a synonym of *summer associate* and as a term describing a select graduate who spends a year or two as a judge's apprentice. Unlike law firms' *law clerks*, judges' *law clerks* have usually already passed the bar exam and accepted a permanent position for the following year. Hence, because they are already *lawyers*, the apparent meniality of *law clerk* is especially ironic. Some courts therefore call their clerks *briefing attorneys*, but to one accustomed to the unpretentiousness of *law clerk*, this term seems inflated.

The best advice is to follow the practice of a particular firm or judge: at a firm that hires *law clerks*, they should not call themselves *summer associates* (though the reverse practice is unobjectionable); if a judge hires *law clerks*, they should not parade the name *briefing attorney*. The understated title *law clerk* is to be worn as a badge of honor.

clew. See **clue.**

CLICHÉS. Why is it that, in legal prose, common sense always *dictates* certain actions? That precedents are never to be *lightly overruled*? That to look at something a second time is invariably to *revisit* it? Why are trial judges whom appellate courts agree with always *learned*, but never wise or perspicacious or erudite? Why is any significant evidentiary hearing always termed *full-blown*? Too often in legal writing, parties *strenuously object*; judges write *vigorous dissents*; legal principles are never settled but that they are *well settled*; trial judges always have *sound discretion* rather than mere discretion; exceptions are never created—instead, they are *carved out*; bad statutes are inevitably *constitutionally infirm* rather than invalid or, better yet, unconstitutional; opinions we agree with are invariably *well reasoned*, but almost never cogent or compelling.

Meanwhile, statutory words are *not talismanic*; we don't want to turn rules into *paper tigers* while wending our way through a *statutory mosaic*; as we examine the *parade of horrors* before us, we fear that our opponents have a *private agenda*; going too far, they want to *throw the baby out with the bathwater*. So we respond, naturally: "*If it ain't broke, don't fix it.*"

Clichés should generally be used sparingly in any writing, but especially in legal writing. Yet we are beset with hackneyed phrases inappositely employed in legal briefs and judicial opinions. To begin with, good writers have sensitized themselves to what a cliché is. Acquiring this sensitivity requires some literary taste, but mostly a background that includes wide reading. One need not read very many American judicial opinions to find, e.g., that *We do not write on a clean slate* (or *on a tabula rasa*) is a commonplace often repeated.

General English clichés are also common in legal writing. E.g.:

- "*It all started* on a *fatal day* [read *fateful day*] in December of 1981, when the Equity Shipping Corporation . . .

chartered its vessel to the GHR Energy Corporation." *Coastal (Bermuda) Ltd. v. E.W. Saybolt & Co.*, 761 F.2d 198, 200 (5th Cir. 1985).

- "In the *hallowed days of yore* parties seeking to stay their proceedings in an action at law had to cross the street into a court of equity for an injunction." *Coastal (Bermuda) Ltd. v. E.W. Saybolt & Co.*, 761 F.2d 198, 202 (5th Cir. 1985). (The main clause manages to *sound* like a cliché without actually being one.)
- "*Once upon a time* purists condemned 'ice cream' on the grounds that it isn't cream made of ice, and the logical form should be 'iced cream.'" Eugene Volokh, *Correcting Students' Usage Errors Without Making Errors of Our Own*, 58 J. Legal Educ. 533, 537 (2008). (This example, however, is tongue-in-cheek.)

It would be easy to list hundreds of English-language clichés such as *time is of the essence, crystal clear, proverbial snowball in hell, dire need*, and *flatly refused*; but no purpose would be served. If one finds oneself writing or talking in ready-made phrases, it is time to draw back and frame the thought anew. The occasional cliché may be justifiable, to be sure; it is the habitual use of clichés that is stylistically objectionable. For a fuller discussion, see Eric Partridge, *Dictionary of Clichés* (1963) and James Rogers, *Dictionary of Clichés* (1985).

Finally, if one must use a cliché, do it straightforwardly. Slight variations on clichés are neither clever nor cute. E.g.: "He wore his heresy on his sleeve." (Figuratively, only one's heart (or feelings) can be worn on one's sleeve.) Likewise, one should not change *madding crowd* to **maddening crowd*. See SET PHRASES.

One lawyer has written wittily about the dissolution of his partnership, citing in part "an occupational nervous affliction" that causes lawyers to spout clichés. The culminating altercation, this lawyer recalled, sounded like this:

"You're being arbitrary and capricious!"

"Well, you're being willful and wanton!"

"I'm going to seek affirmative relief."

"Are you suggesting that in futuro we do business separate and apart?"

"I'm telling you that you have been guilty of cruel treatment of me and have inflicted personal indignities upon me, rendering my life burdensome so that it is no longer possible for me to remain your partner!"

"Does this mean that our agreement is null and void?"

"It means that it's of no further force and effect."

"In that event I will no longer be responsible for your debt, default[,] or misdoings," he rejoined. "And I'll want the library for myself, free and clear of any encumbrances."

Edward H. McKinlay, *Legal Cliché Experts*,
49 Fla. B.J. 444 (1975).

client; customer. By definition, a *client* is one who engages the services of a professional, whereas a *customer* gives custom or trade to a business, often on a regular basis. A lawyer or an accountant has *clients*; a grocery store or telephone company has *customers*.

The line of demarcation between these two words has shifted considerably in recent years. By the 1980s, Massachusetts bureaucrats had begun calling welfare recipients their *clients*. See Jon Keller, *Massachusetts's Strange Protest Vote*, Wall St. J., 20 Sept. 1990, at A14. Things had gotten worse by the 1990s. For example, *The Sunday Times* writes of two prostitutes: "Both women took *clients* to their flats." John Davison & Michael Durham, *Prostitutes Go in Fear of London "Ripper,"* Sunday Times, 18 Aug. 1991, at 1-5. See **clientele.**

*clientage. See **clientele.**

cliental = of or relating to a client. The *OED* labels this word "rare," but the Merriam-Webster dictionaries contain no such notation. Still, lawyers have little occasion to use it.

clientele; *clientage; *clientelage; *clientry; clients. *Clients* is the best because it is the least pretentious and most common. *Clientele* has degenerated somewhat in meaning, having been widely used in nonprofessional contexts. E.g.: "The complaint alleges that the plaintiffs are engaged in business as high-grade dressmakers . . . under the name of 'Boue Soeurs,' with the most exclusive *clientele*." *Montegut v. Hickson*, 164 N.Y.S. 858, 860 (App. Div. 1917) (Davis, J., dissenting). Often when *clientele* appears in professional contexts, it is used in reference to the oldest profession. See **client.**

*Clientage, *clientelage, and **clientry* are NEEDLESS VARIANTS of *clientele*.

climactic; *climacteric; climatic. *Climactic* is now established as the adjective of *climax*, though formerly it was thought to be inferior to **climacteric*, which, having lost the battle, is now to be avoided as a NEEDLESS VARIANT. *Climatic* is the adjective corresponding to *climate*; occasionally it becomes a MALAPROPISM for *climactic*.

CLIPPING. See BACK-FORMATIONS.

clog on the equity (of redemption). See **cloud on title.**

closely held corporation; close(d) corporation. These phrases are generally synonymous in denoting a company whose stock is not freely traded and is held by only a few people (often within the same family). *Closely held corporation* is perhaps the phrase that lawyers most commonly use, but *close corporation* is the most common statutory phrase in AmE. In BrE, the term is generally *closed corporation*.

close of the evidence is the legal idiom denoting the end of the presentation of testimony in a trial—e.g.:

- "At the *close of all the evidence* the district court granted an instructed verdict in favor of Westinghouse on nearly all issues." *Reynolds Metals Co. v. Westinghouse Elec. Corp.*, 758 F.2d 1073, 1076 (5th Cir. 1985).

- "At the *close of the evidence*, the trial court submitted Instruction No. 5 . . . to the jury." *State v. D.W.N.*, 290 S.W.3d 814, 817 (Mo. Ct. App. 2009).

close proximity is a common REDUNDANCY.

closing = the completion of a sales contract. On the *closing date*, the seller delivers the deed and the buyer pays the balance of the purchase price.

closing statement; settlement sheet. Both phrases are used in AmE to denote a statement, approved by both buyer and seller, listing all the credits and charges attributable to each one. The credits and charges listed are used to adjust or prorate items in the sales contract and result in a net amount due by the buyer and a different amount due to the seller (other parties, typically, being involved in the transaction).

closure; cloture. The general noun corresponding to the verb *to close* is *closure*. E.g.: "Although *Waller* involved the total *closure* of a trial, the requirement that the trial court make sufficient findings to allow the reviewing court to determine whether . . . a *closure* was justified is equally applicable in the case of a partial *closure*." *U.S. v. Farmer*, 32 F.3d 369, 372 (8th Cir. 1994) (McMillian, J., dissenting).

In AmE, *cloture* is preferred in but one narrow sense: "the procedure of ending debate in a legislative body and calling for an immediate vote." E.g.: "Daschle agreed to schedule a *cloture* vote on repeal of the estate tax, but Republicans fell six votes short (54–44) of the required tally." John D. Graham, *Bush on the Home Front: Domestic Policy Triumphs and Setbacks* 39 (2010). *Closure* is usual in BrE in this parliamentary sense.

clothe. In law, persons are frequently described metaphorically as being *clothed* with certain powers or privileges. E.g.:

- "Mrs. Stordahl, her innocence of wrongdoing established, stands before us *clothed* with the protection equity provides in favor of all bona fide purchasers of interests in property." *Fid. & Deposit Co. v. Stordahl*, 91 N.W.2d 533, 536 (Mich. 1958). (It's mildly risible to imagine Mrs. Stordahl standing before the Michigan Supreme Court innocently *unclothed*.)
- "At the very least, by doing nothing to stop her husband from holding himself out as manager of the center, defendant . . . *clothed* him with apparent authority to do that which managers normally do, including enter into contracts of employment with third persons." *Corman v. Musselman*, 439 N.W.2d 781, 787 (Neb. 1989).
- "Temple's employment by the IRS *clothed* her with the indicia of authority." *U.S. v. Temple*, 447 F.3d 130, 138 (2d Cir. 2006).

If sparingly used, this legal CLICHÉ might be tolerable; but it is sufficient to say merely that a person *has* the powers or privileges in question.

The noun *clothing*, too, was once common as a legal METAPHOR—e.g.: "He is an Emptor Familiæ, and

inherits the legal *clothing* of the person whose place he begins to fill." Henry S. Maine, *Ancient Law* 220 (17th ed. 1901).

cloture. See **closure.**

cloud on title; clog on the equity (of redemption). A *cloud on title* is a defect or potential defect in the owner's title to a piece of land arising, e.g., from a lien, an easement, or a court order. The phrase is generally an American one. E.g.:

- "This mistakenly engrafts upon negotiable instrument law concepts from real property law wherein a defect in the chain of title *casts a cloud* upon subsequent ownership." *Godat v. Mercantile Bank of Nw. County*, 884 S.W.2d 1, 5 n.2 (Mo. Ct. App. 1994).
- "Because the mere presence of the contract on record casts doubt on the owners' otherwise unrestricted right to use and sell the property, we hold the recording of the document *created a cloud on title*, and the trial court erred in refusing a request to order it removed." *Robinson v. Khan*, 948 P.2d 1347, 1347 (Wash. Ct. App. 1998).
- "Either result will facilitate the expeditious and final disposition of assets, and thus enable the debtor (and the debtor's creditors) to achieve a fresh start free of the finality and *clouded-title* concerns Reilly describes." *Schwab v. Reilly*, 130 S.Ct. 2652, 2668 (2010) (per Thomas, J.).

A *clog on the equity* (often written *clog on the equity of redemption*) is any condition or agreement that prevents a mortgagor from getting back the property free from encumbrance upon paying the debt or performing the obligation for which the security was given. The phrase is common in both BrE and AmE. E.g.: "The long-standing common law rule against clauses that '*clog*' a debtor's equity of redemption is for the protection of debtors who are in no position to insist that a creditor omit such clauses from the security agreement at the time it is drafted." *Tropical Jewelers, Inc. v. Nations Bank, N.A.*, 781 So.2d 381, 389 (Fla. Dist. Ct. App. 2000).

The metaphor is an old one in law: Richard W. Turner, in *The Equity of Redemption* 29 (1931), quotes a court that wrote, in 1639: "In some cases . . . the mortgagee will suddenly bestow unnecessary costs upon the mortgaged lands, of purpose to *clogg* the lands, to prevent the mortgager's redemption" (quoting *Bacon v. Bacon*, Tot. 133). See METAPHORS (B).

clue; clew. *Clue* is the only current spelling for the sense "a hint; a bit of evidence." The spelling *clew* survives as a nautical term ("the lower corner of a sail") and as a sewing term ("a ball of thread").

Clue is construed with *to* or *about*, not *as to*.

co-. A. Hyphenation with. Generally, this prefix—which means "together with" or "joint"—does not take a hyphen. Use the hyphen only when (1) the hyphenated form is established (e.g., *co-respondent*, *co-relation*), (2) the unhyphenated form may lead the reader to mistake the syllables (e.g., *co-citation*, *co-heir*), or (3) you believe you're creating a new form (e.g., *co-secretary*).

B. Attaching to Noun Phrase. This creates an awkward construction but is sometimes all but unavoidable, as in *copersonal representative.*

co-appellant; co-appellee. These terms are used to denote the relation of joint parties on appeal. E.g.:

- "The court found that the appellant's attempt to incorporate thirty-six unattached pages of allegations from a *co-appellant's* pleadings failed to give adequate notice as to which allegations were to be adopted." *Bronstein v. Biava,* 838 P.2d 968, 970 (N.M. 1992).
- "Neither the district council *or* [read *nor*] its *co-appellee,* Eastern Petroleum, cite[s] any authority for that position, and we have found none." *Billings v. County Council of Prince George's County,* 989 A.2d 1170, 1177 (Md. Ct. Spec. App. 2010). For more on *or* vs. *nor* in this sentence, see **neither . . . nor (D).**

co-citation is best hyphenated. This word, not uncommon in legal writing, is not listed in the *OED* or in *W3.* E.g.: "A more sophisticated citation-analysis technique, known as 'co-citation analysis,' uses document coupling to measure the number of scholarly documents that have cited any given pair of documents." Yorgo Pasadeos et al., *Influences on the Media Law Literature,* 11 Comm. L. & Pol'y 179, 185 (2006). See CO- (A).

coconspirator. Although hyphenating the word indicates immediately to the reader what the primary word (*conspirator*) is, the one-word spelling is increasingly well established. See CO- (A).

Notably, a *conspirator* is one who plots with another; a "sole conspirator" is impossible. This point has led to some confusion about whether *coconspirator* is redundant. William Safire writes: "To me, a *co-conspirator* is as redundant as a *co-equal.*" *Let's Kill All the Copy Editors,* N.Y. Times (Mag.), 6 Oct. 1991, § 6, at 16.

But like *coequal,* the word *coconspirator* suggests a point of comparison—it is used only where we would otherwise say *fellow conspirator,* as in *his coconspirator* (where we would not, indeed could not, say *his conspirator*).

For analogous examples, see **codefendant, coequal & coplaintiff.** For a similar word with an important difference, see **copartner** (in which *partner* itself suggests the point of comparison, so that *copartner* is unnecessary).

cocounsel. So written—without a hyphen. E.g.: "The fact that *cocounsel* harbored doubts about the chosen strategy is not sufficient to preserve error in the face of the express waiver made by Mr. Standafer on the defendant's behalf." *State v. Spates,* 779 N.W.2d 770, 775 (Iowa 2010). See CO- (A).

C.O.D. = (1) cash on delivery (*COD* & *W3*); (2) collect on delivery (*COD* & *W3*); (3) cash on demand; or (4) costs on delivery (*OED*). Whatever the abbreviation stands for, its effect is the same.

codal (= of or relating to a code), dating from the late 19th century, is an adjective used in some civil-law jurisdictions to refer to the civil code. E.g.:

- "Professor Malone suggested that enterprise liability should be founded directly upon the basic *codal* language, 'Every act whatever of man that causes damage to another obliges him by whose fault it happened to repair it.' La. Civ. Code art. 2315(A) (West Supp. 1985)." *Perkins v. F.I.E. Corp.,* 762 F.2d 1250, 1258 (5th Cir. 1985).
- "Considering the foregoing *codal* articles and jurisprudence, we find that plaintiff did not present sufficient evidence of every element of his case." *Louisiana Weld & Press, LLC v. Loupe Const.,* 31 So.3d 467, 472 (La. Ct. App. 2010).

The word is sometimes (unnecessarily) capitalized: "The *Codal* [read *codal*] provisions taken from the French . . . established the rights of the good faith parties in putative marriages." *Cortes v. Fleming,* 307 So.2d 611, 615 (La. 1973).

The only adjective form of *code* recognized by the dictionaries, however, is *codical* (= pertaining to, or of the nature of, a codex or code). It is not used by civilians in Louisiana.

Codd's Puzzle is the classic parody of inconsistent pleading. Codd, counsel for a defendant charged with stealing a duck, pleaded:

1. that his client had bought the bird;
2. that he had found it;
3. that it had flown into his garden;
4. that its owner had given it to him;
5. that some unknown person or persons had stuffed it into his pocket while he was asleep;
6. that the duck had not existed at any material time; and
7. that his client would if necessary make a full confession.

The lay jury is reported to have acquitted Codd's client. *See* Theo Ruoff, 30 Austral. L.J. 512 (1957).

code; codification. The word *code,* derived from Justinian's *Codex* of A.D. 534 (a collection of legislation), has been applied in several ways in Anglo-American law: (1) to a compilation of existing statutes; (2) to a systematic consolidation of statutory law; (3) to a revision of the whole law, both statutory law and caselaw, reducing its principles to a clear and compact statement. Senses 1 and 2 are better termed *consolidation.*

Citing sense 3 as the primary one, Glanville Williams comments: "For reasons that it would not be flattering to examine in detail, English lawyers have always been hostile (or, at best, indifferent) to this." Glanville Williams, *Learning the Law* 44 (11th ed. 1982).

Specialist lawyers frequently refer elliptically to "the Code" to mean whatever code they deal with most frequently, such as the Civil Code, the Bankruptcy Code, the Uniform Commercial Code, the Family Code, or the Code of Judicial Conduct. Depending on the jurisdiction, these codes may fit any one of the three senses of *code* just enumerated.

Codification, one of Jeremy Bentham's NEOLOGISMS, most properly refers to the process of codifying and not to its result—e.g.: "Although his major aims—codification and complete simplification—have not been achieved, yet to him we owe numerous important legal reforms." Jerome Frank, Introduction to Fred Rodell, *Woe Unto You, Lawyers!* xii (1939). But the word often refers, in a transferred sense, to the finished product—the code itself. See **codify.**

Code Civil. See **Napoleonic Code.**

codefendant. This word, meaning "a joint or fellow defendant," is common; oddly, however, *coplaintiff* is comparatively rare. See CO- (A) & **coplaintiff.**

code law, a more specific term than *statutory law*, is sometimes contrasted, as here, with *caselaw*: "It is written *case-law*, and only different from *code-law* because it is written in a different way." Henry S. Maine, *Ancient Law* 11 (17th ed. 1901). Today, *code law* is preferably two words. Cf. **caselaw.**

Code Napoléon. See **Napoleonic Code.**

code pleading; fact pleading; notice pleading; general pleading. The first two are synonymous phrases referring to the requirement, in some post-common-law pleading, that one allege merely the facts giving rise to the claim, not the conclusions of law necessary to sustain the claim. *See* Charles E. Clark, *Handbook of the Law of Code Pleading* 1–2 (2d ed. 1947). *Code pleading* (as it is usually known) developed originally in New York in the late 1840s, under the influence of David Dudley Field.

The idea of code pleading was to move beyond the formulary technicalities of common-law and equity pleading. The term first appeared in the late 19th century:

- "The only case arising under the modern *code pleadings* and bearing upon this question . . . is *Fosgate v. Herkimer Mfg. & Hydraulic Co.*" *Gibbons v. Martin*, 10 F. Cas. 292, 293 (C.C.D. Or. 1877) (No. 5,381).
- "Under the system of *code pleading*, a technical variance between the allegations and the proof is not deemed material unless the adverse party is prejudiced thereby." *Wilson v. Haley Live-Stock Co.*, 153 U.S. 39, 47 (1894) (per Brown, J.).

In the late 19th and early 20th centuries, code pleading led to gross overpleading. And lawyers came to realize the futility of the endeavor: "'The facts as they actually existed or occurred,' 'the dry, naked, actual facts'—these and these only are to be stated. Can it be done? I think not; it has never been done and never will be done, either by a pleader or by anyone else. Philosophically, logically, it is an impossibility." Walter W. Cook, "The Utility of Jurisprudence in the Solution of Legal Problems," in 5 *Lectures on Legal Topics* 337, 369 (1928).

So, in 1938, the drafters of the Federal Rules of Civil Procedure modified the pleading requirements still further so as to allow *notice pleading* or *general pleading*, which requires merely a "short and plain statement of the claim showing that the pleader is entitled to relief." Fed. R. Civ. P. 8(a). Up to that time, judicial glosses on code pleading had resulted in overpleading that caused "frightful expense, endless delay and an enormous loss of motion." Thomas E. Skinner, *Pre-Trial and Discovery Under the Alabama Rules of Civil Procedure*, 9 Ala. L. Rev. 202, 204 (1957).

code state; noncode state. These terms—current primarily in the early to mid-20th century—distinguished between states that had merged law and equity, and those that had not. E.g.: "In any *code state* in which law and equity have been merged in the same court and in which every action is both legal and equitable in that all rights of the parties, legal and equitable, must be adjudicated therein, the court has full power to give relief . . . [that] the nature of the case calls for, irrespective of whether it would have been classed as a case in equity or a case at law under the old order." William F. Walsh, *A Treatise on Equity* 367 (1930) (referring at pp. 102–03 to "*non-code states* in which equity is still administered as a separate system").

This terminology can be confusing because many readers would think of a *code state* as one having a civil code—i.e., Louisiana.

codex is a NEEDLESS VARIANT of *code*—and a pompous one—unless the writer is referring to one of the ancient European codes (e.g., *Codex Theodosianus* of A.D. 438), a *codex rescriptus* (= a palimpsest, or written-over manuscript), or the like. Pl. *codices*.

codicil; will. *Codicil* = a testamentary supplement that varies or revokes provisions in a will. *Will* = a written or oral expression of one's intention regarding the disposition of one's property at death. See **last will and testament** & **will.**

codification. See **code.**

codifier; codist. Whereas a *codifier* is one who makes a code, a *codist* is one learned in legal codes, esp. in the civil codes of different nations.

codify is best pronounced /kod-i-fɪ/, not /kohd-i-fɪ/. This word, like *codification*, was one of Jeremy Bentham's NEOLOGISMS; it dates from ca. 1800.

codifying statute. See **consolidating statute.**

codist. See **codifier.**

co-employee is a NEEDLESS VARIANT of *coworker*. See CO- (A).

coequal, n. & adj., often means nothing that *equal* does not also mean; it should be rejected in such contexts. E.g.: "All constitutional rights are *coequal* [read *equal*] and must be harmonized with each other and no one such right may be permitted to override or submerge another." 16A C.J.S. *Constitutional Law* § 635 (2009).

The word is useful only in implying the standard of comparison; for example, in a snippet quoted in the *OED*, "the co-eternal and *co-equal* Son," if only *equal* had been used, the reader would wonder, Equal with what? *Co-equal* implies the second and third things with which the Son is said to be equal. This nuance occurs more frequently than one might suspect—e.g.:

- "Rather than creating a set of *coequal* [read *equal*] supreme courts, all competing for business and adopting interpretive fictions to expand their jurisdictions, Article III created a single Supreme Court." James E. Pfander, *Article I Tribunals, Article III Courts, and the Judicial Power of the United States*, 118 Harv. L. Rev. 643, 693 (2004).
- "Church and State were [for most of Western history], quite literally, separate and *coequal* [read *equal*] sovereigns." G. Marcus Cole, *What Is the Government's Role in Promoting Morals? . . . Seriously?*, 31 Harv. J.L. & Pub. Pol'y 77, 80 (2008).

But when that nuance is absent, *equal* suffices. So it is simplistic to say, as William Safire does, that "today's usage frowns on *co-equal* as redundant." *Send in Sovereign for Socialist*, N.Y. Times, 6 Jan. 1991, § 6, at 8, 10. For a mini-tirade on the subject, see Robert C. Cumbow, *The Subverting of the Goeduck*, 14 U. Puget Sound L. Rev. 755 (1991) ("Not only does A equal B, and B equal A, but A and B equal *each other*! Imagine! They're *both* equal *together*!" [etc.]).

On the issue of writing *coequal* as a solid word, see CO- (A). Cf. **coconspirator** & **copartner**.

coercible. So spelled.

coercion, though originally applicable only to physical force, is now commonly used to describe moral and economic pressures. E.g.: "Economic *coercion* can take on many forms and degrees ranging, for example, from discreet impositions in an onerous trade agreement to outright trade embargoes." Noel G. Villaroman, *The Right to Development*, 22 Fla. J. Int'l L. 299, 316 (2010). Such uses are a natural extension of the original sense ("the control by force of a voluntary agent or action").

In criminal law, *coercion* has historically had a more limited sense—*compulsion* being reserved for any action or restraint imposed upon one by another. In this context, *coercion* ordinarily refers specifically to such an action or restraint imposed by a husband on his wife. E.g.: "Under the English 'rule of *coercion*,' the bare command of the husband was a complete defense to the wife, with a few exceptions such as treason or murder." Rollin M. Perkins & Ronald N. Boyce, *Criminal Law* 1062 (3d ed. 1982).

cofelon (= a felon involved in the same crime as another felon) need not be hyphenated. See CO- (A).

cofiduciary = joint fiduciary. The word is best made solid, without a hyphen. See CO- (A).

cognate. See **agnate.**

*cognation. See **kinship.**

cognisance. See **cognizance.**

*cognisant. See **cognizant.**

cognitive; *cognitional. *Cognitive* = of or pertaining to cognition, or to the action or process of knowing. It should be avoided in its use as a jargonistic filler—e.g.: "The totality of the relevant facts supports the finding that the City of Apopka has engaged in a systematic pattern of *cognitive* acts and omissions, selecting and reaffirming a particular course of municipal services expenditures that inescapably evidences discriminatory intent." *Dowdell v. City of Apopka*, 698 F.2d 1181, 1186 (11th Cir. 1983). What the writer might have meant in that sentence is a minor mystery.

Cognitional is a NEEDLESS VARIANT—e.g.:

- "To intend or to have an intention implies that an agent inclines or 'tends' toward some specific object grasped *cognitionally* [read *cognitively*]." Edward C. Lyons, *In Incognito—The Principle of Double Effect in American Constitutional Law*, 57 Fla. L. Rev. 469, 494 (2005).
- "Kant's philosophy saw our perception of the world as dependent on the contingent characteristics of our *cognitional* [read *cognitive*] equipment." Robert P. Burns, *On the Foundations and Nature of Morality*, 31 Harv. J.L. & Pub. Pol'y 7, 10 (2008).

cognitor is an archaic word for *attorney* that derives from Roman law and existed in English only briefly.

cognizable; *cognoscible. *Cognizable* /kog-ni-zə-bəl/ = (1) capable of being known; perceptible; or (2) capable of being, or liable to be, judicially examined or tried; within the jurisdiction of a court of law (*OED*).

Sense 1 is more general—e.g.: "A plea agreement presents both risks and rewards to the defendant and the government; those attendant risks and rewards are *cognizable* at the time the parties enter into the agreement." Kimberly L. Patwardhan, Note, *Fourth Circuit Allows § 3583(c)(2) Sentence Modification*, 43 Suffolk U. L. Rev. 1051, 1057 (2010).

In legal writing, sense 2 is common in the phrase *cognizable claims*—e.g.:

- "Nor do I believe that a criminal suspect who is shot while trying to avoid apprehension has a *cognizable* claim of a deprivation of his Sixth Amendment right to trial by jury." *Tennessee v. Garner*, 471 U.S. 1, 30 (1985) (O'Connor, J., dissenting).
- "The only *cognizable* claims presented were general challenges to the authority of the commissions that would not be affected by the specific proceedings." *Hamdan v. Rumsfeld*, 548 U.S. 557, 677–78 (2006) (Scalia, J., dissenting).

Cognoscible is a NEEDLESS VARIANT that appears in many older texts—e.g. (fr. 17th c.): "No external act can pass upon a man for a crime that is not *cognoscible*." 2 Jeremy Taylor, *Whole Works of the Rt. Rev. Jeremy Taylor* 313 (1835). There is no reason for it today—e.g.: "The quote implies that if the misrepresentations had caused a loss in the plaintiffs' plan accounts, they may have a *cognoscible* [read *cognizable*] claim." Gregory C. Braden et al., *What's New in Employee Benefits*, 39 ALI-ABA 1, 48 (Mar. 2009).

cognizance. A. And *recognizance*. Though superficially similar, these words have unrelated meanings. *Cognizance* = (1) knowledge, esp. as attained by observation or information; or (2) the action of taking judicial notice. Sense 2 is rarer now than it once was. See **judicial notice.**

Recognizance = (1) the bond by which a person engages before a court or magistrate to observe some condition, e.g., to keep the peace, pay a debt, or appear when summoned (*COD*); or (2) the sum pledged as a surety of this bond. See **recognizance.**

B. Pronunciation. Glanville Williams writes of *cognizance*, *recognizance*, and *cognizable*: "we refuse to 'take cognisance of' the intrusive 'g' in speaking, though we do in writing." *Learning the Law* 64 (11th ed. 1982). That may be so in the best speech of English lawyers /**kon**-i-zəns/ (etc.), but not in BrE generally or in AmE—in which the pronunciations are /**kog**-ni-zəns/, /ri-**kog**-ni-zəns/, and /**kog**-ni-zə-bəl/. Cf. **cognoscente.**

cognizant; *cognisant. The -*z*- spelling is preferred in AmE and in BrE.

cognoscente, sing.; **cognoscenti**, pl. This word, almost always used in the plural (-*ti*), is misspelled only a little less frequently than it is used. E.g.:

- "The criminal-defense *cogniscenti* [read *cognoscenti*] will quickly learn that, when this judge's proffer is rejected, the defendant, if convicted, will pay a higher price." *Frank v. Blackburn*, 646 F.2d 873, 901 (5th Cir. 1980) (Rubin, J., dissenting).
- "It is apparent that the *cogniscenti* [read *cognoscenti*] in the jazz tradition bear a striking resemblance to their counterparts [in other fields]." Barbara K. Bucholtz, *On Canonical Transformations and the Coherence of Dichotomies*, 37 U. Rich. L. Rev. 425, 451–52 (2003).
- "These courts have wrestled with the desirability or permissibility, even if not the constitutionality, of various 'no citation' rules, presumably to the sneers or yawns of the *cogniscenti* [read *cognoscenti*], especially those with realist sympathies." Frederick Schauer, *Authority and Authorities*, 94 Va. L. Rev. 1931, 1933 (2008).

Generally, *experts* or *authorities* will suffice, either one being easier to spell—not to mention to pronounce: /kon-yə-**shent**-ee/ or /kog-nə-**shent**-ee/. Writers should be cognizant of the *cogno-* spelling.

*cognoscible. See **cognizable.**

COGSA; C.O.G.S.A.; Cogsa. This acronym, for the Carriage of Goods by Sea Act, is generally rendered *COGSA*, though at least one well-written treatise makes it *Cogsa*. *See* Grant Gilmore & Charles L. Black, *The Law of Admiralty* 93–192 (2d ed. 1975).

cohabit, the verb for *cohabitation*, is analogous to *inhabit*. "To *cohabit* is to dwell together," says one treatise, "so that matrimonial cohabitation is the living together of a man and woman ostensibly as husband and wife." 1 Joel Prentiss Bishop, *Marriage, Divorce, and Separation* § 1669, at 694 (1891).

*Cohabitate is a misbegotten BACK-FORMATION—e.g.:

- "As more couples adopt this lifestyle, our courts will be called upon with increasing frequency to settle disputes over the legal rights of *cohabitating* [read *cohabiting*] couples." Greg Woods, *Loss of Consortium: Extending Recovery to Unmarried Couples in Texas*, 35 Baylor L. Rev. 543, 543 (1983).
- "It was not uncommon for 'respectable' members of the community to turn in their erring brothers and sisters to white legal authorities if they were known to be *cohabitating* [read *cohabiting*] without marrying, maintaining more than one spouse, or violating the obligations of marital monogamy." Katherine M. Franke, *The Domesticated Liberty of* Lawrence v. Texas, 104 Colum. L. Rev. 1399, 1423 (2004).
- "The law, which made New Jersey the fifth state in the country to provide some legal status to *cohabitating* [read *cohabiting*] gay couples, was part of an effort to defuse the Lewis litigation by offering some rights to same-sex families." Andrew Bruck, *Equality in the Garden State*, 2 Harv. L. & Pol'y Rev. 419, 428 (2008).

cohabitant; *cohabitor; *cohabitee. *Cohabitee, though increasingly common (esp. in BrE) for a person living with another as if married, is etymologically the poorest form. (See -EE.) It ought to be avoided—e.g.: "The issue in the case was whether section 1 of the Domestic Violence and Matrimonial Proceedings Act 1976 conferred jurisdiction on a County court judge to order a man who was joint tenant of a council flat to vacate the premises on the application of the female *co-habitee* [read *cohabitant*] who had suffered horrifying violence at his hands." Rupert Cross & J.W. Harris, *Precedent in English Law* 112 (4th ed. 1991).

Cohabitant, derived from the present participle of the Latin verb, is etymologically preferable. (See *OED* 2.) *Cohabitor is a NEEDLESS VARIANT. For still another variant, see **CUPOS.**

*cohabitate. See **cohabit.**

cohabitative; *cohabitive. The general rule is that, in Latinate nouns of this type, the adjectival form derives from the noun form. Hence *cohabitative* is the correct form, following from the noun *cohabitation*.

*cohabitee; *cohabitor. See **cohabitant.**

co-heir (= a joint heir) is generally so hyphenated, though the estimable *Century Dictionary* (1895) makes it *coheir*. (See CO- (A).) E.g.: "A group of persons considered in law as a single unit, might succeed as *co-heirs* to the Inheritance." Henry S. Maine, *Ancient Law* 150 (17th ed. 1901).

cohort; cohorts. AmE legal usage, traditional and formal though it is, has given in to the modern sense (some would say corruption) of this word—e.g.: "Respondent . . . and two *cohorts* were indicted for . . . robbing a savings and loan. . . . The *cohorts* pleaded guilty but respondent went to trial." *U.S. v. Abel*, 469 U.S. 45, 47 (1984) (per Rehnquist, J.).

Traditionally, *cohort* has been a mass noun denoting "a band of warriors." "The extension of *cohort* to nonmilitary uses is natural enough," Follett writes,

> but if the word is to retain its force it should observe two requirements: (1) it should designate members, too numerous to be conveniently counted, of some sort of united group, and (2) it should imply some sort of struggle or contest. *No one of the candidates succeeded in completely marshaling his cohorts before the first ballot / To the legion of the lost ones, to the cohort of the damned*—in such uses the sense of the word is preserved.
>
> Wilson Follett, *Modern American Usage* 99 (1966).

This is a very conservative view of the word, especially given the fact that the sense "colleague, associate, companion" has been by far the most common in the last quarter-century. E.g.: "Senator Biden and his *cohorts* didn't hear, but it appears that thousands of others did." *Mr. Bork's Book*, Wall St. J., 8 Dec. 1989, at A10. Nevertheless, this newer meaning has remained a rather informal one for this respectable word, which in formal writing should retain its older sense.

Follett's sense 1 is common in phrases such as *baby-boom cohort* and *birth cohort*, the latter being defined as a "group, born in the same year, selected for study as the individuals march through time so that researchers can assess the nature and influence of factors affecting their behavior." *See* Dermot Walsh & Adrian Poole, *A Dictionary of Criminology* 22 (1983).

coif. The Order of the *Coif* is an organization of great distinction among those who excel in studying law in American universities. The name comes from the title given to *serjeants-at-law* or *serjeants of the coif*, the barristers of high standing in common-law courts. They took their name, through the linguistic process known as metonymy, from the linen headpieces they wore: "The *coif* (a close-fitting cap of white lawn) [that] the judges wore they wore as serjeants, and neither judge nor serjeant ever doffed his *coif* 'even in the presence of the king, even though he is talking to His Highness.'" Alan Harding, *A Social History of English Law* 174 (1966). See **Order of the Coif.**

Coke, Sir Edward (1552–1634) wrote *The Institutes of the Laws of England* (1628) and compiled 13 volumes of significant cases now referred to as *Coke's Reports*. His name is pronounced as if it were *Cook*, not like the soft drink. See PRONUNCIATION (F). He may be referred to as either *Sir Edward Coke* or (because he was Lord Chief Justice) *Lord Coke. See* F.S. Waddington, Note, *Notes and Queries* (17 Jan. 1885), at 55.

cold blood. The METAPHOR derives from long-outmoded physiological theories about how human blood can boil or become very cold depending on one's passion, physical exertion, or excitement. It signifies what is done "coolly," with time for decision or even reflection.

Though the phrase is part of everyday speech, criminal-law commentators find it useful: "While it is true, to take a test from the homicide cases, that one may incite in the heat of passion what another carries out in *cold blood*, it is also true that one, acting with malicious premeditation, may instigate that which is perpetrated by another at once in the heat of passion." Rollin M. Perkins & Ronald N. Boyce, *Criminal Law* 763 (3d ed. 1982).

cold check. See **check, worthless.**

collaborate. See **corroborate (C).**

collapsible. So spelled.

collate. See **collocate.**

collateral, n., = (1) a person collaterally related to a decedent; or (2) security for a loan. For sense 1, see **ascendant (B)** & **collateral kinship.** For sense 2, see **collateralize** & **pledge.**

collateral estoppel. A. And *issue preclusion*; *res judicata*; *claim preclusion.* The lines of demarcation in meaning are distinct; yet these terms have long caused confusion among judges and advocates. *Collateral estoppel* and *issue preclusion* (= BrE *issue estoppel*) are synonymous; the latter phrase has sprung perhaps from a desire to be more descriptive in naming this legal doctrine. *Collateral estoppel* is the doctrine that prevents the relitigation of an issue that was actually litigated and was a critical and necessary part of the earlier judgment. The judgment on the issues litigated in the first action, then, is binding on the parties in all later litigation in which those issues arise.

Res judicata—also called *claim preclusion*—is the same principle, but broader: when a matter has been finally adjudicated by a court of competent jurisdiction, none of the original parties may reopen or challenge that previous determination. *Res judicata* implies, then, that no further issues exist relating to the dispute, whereas with *collateral estoppel* there may be other adjudicable issues. The best way of remembering these doctrines clearly is to view *collateral estoppel* as a miniature of *res judicata*: the former applies to issues, the latter to entire claims or lawsuits.

One might cite any number of instances in which judges have written *collateral estoppel* when they meant *res judicata* and vice versa. E.g.: "Although the court of appeals in our present case speaks in terms of *res judicata*, . . . the court actually applies principles of *collateral estoppel* in affirming the award of indemnity. . . . *Collateral estoppel* is narrower than *res judicata*. It is frequently [termed] *issue preclusion* because it bars relitigation of any ultimate issue of fact actually litigated and essential to the judgment in a prior suit." *Bonniwell v. Beech Aircraft Corp.*, 663 S.W.2d 816, 818 (Tex. 1984). *See* Fleming James, *Civil*

Procedure 549–50 (1965) (noting that *res judicata* "has been given a good many different meanings" and suggesting, further, that *res judicata* is the genus of which *collateral estoppel* is one species).

B. And *direct estoppel*. The Restatement of Judgments distinguishes between these two phrases in this way: *collateral estoppel* applies to later controversies involving some of the same facts but a different cause of action, whereas *direct estoppel* applies to later controversies involving the same cause of action (where the plaintiff's cause of action is not extinguished by the rules of merger and bar). *See* Restatement of Judgments § 176 (1942). See **merger (B).**

collateralize = (1) to serve as collateral for; or (2) to make (a loan) secure with collateral. This word looks newfangled, and it is, having been recorded only as far back as 1931: "'[H]e found he did not have sufficient paper to *collateralize* the note.'" *Dealer's Fin. Co. v. Coulter*, 3 F.Supp. 114, 115 (W.D. Ark. 1931) (quoting testimony) (antedating *W11*'s earliest citation by ten years).

For real-estate lawyers (conveyancers) and bankers, however, this Americanism is a useful word for summing up what otherwise would take several words. (See **conveyancer.**) Both senses are common—e.g.:

- (Sense 1) "NCFE's obligation to repay them would be *collateralized* by eligible receivables." *U.S. v. Faulkenberry*, 614 F.3d 573, 578 (6th Cir. 2010).
- (Sense 2) "These investments included junk bonds and *collateralized* debt obligations." *Slayton v. American Express Co.*, 604 F.3d 758, 762 (2d Cir. 2010).

collateral kinship. See **kinship.**

collateral obligation; accessorial obligation. Both terms refer to the liability of a person, such as a guarantor, bound on another's debt. *Collateral obligation* has, in modern usage, supplanted *accessorial obligation*. Small wonder.

collateral order = an interlocutory order that is an offshoot from the principal litigation in which it is issued, and that is generally immediately appealable as a "final decision" without regard to whether the principal litigation is final. *See* Charles Alan Wright, *The Law of Federal Courts* 743 (5th ed. 1994).

collateral-order doctrine (= the doctrine, first laid down in *Cohen v. Beneficial Indus. Loan Corp.*, 337 U.S. 541 (1949), that made some collateral orders appealable) is best so hyphenated. See PHRASAL ADJECTIVES (A).

colleague. See **brother.**

collect is a verb sometimes used loosely, especially in the press. As every lawyer knows, being awarded damages is quite a different thing from collecting them: "Under Thursday's ruling, plaintiffs could *collect* [read *seek* or *receive*] damages from local governments only if they proved that discrimination resulted not from the act of an individual but from an official policy." William Choyke, *High Court Backs DISD in*

Rights Suit, Dallas Morning News, 23 June 1989, at 1A. Perhaps most local governments would be good for most judgments, but to use *collect* in this way is sloppy thinking about the law. *Receive*, which sounds closely akin to *collect*, is actually quite different because it connotes a giver (the jury).

The mistake is surprising when it occurs in the prose of model legal writers—e.g.: "If an action *in personam* against the shipowner has been joined to the action *in rem* against the ship, there is no difficulty in *collecting* [read *being awarded*] the deficiency *from* [read *against*] the defendant in the *in personam* action." Grant Gilmore & Charles L. Black Jr., *The Law of Admiralty* 801 (2d ed. 1975).

collectible; *collectable. The *-ible* spelling is preferred.

collective-bargaining agreement. Preferably so hyphenated.

collectively termed. Lawyers frequently use, in definitions, a phrase such as *herein collectively termed* "_____." A question that sometimes arises is whether that last word can be plural, as when the writer enumerates a number of specific railroads and then writes *collectively termed Railroads*. Grammar and common sense alike allow that phrasing. But common sense disallows *herein*. (See **herein.**)

COLLECTIVE NOUNS. Consistency in the use of singular or plural is the main consideration in the skillful handling of collective nouns. A judge who in the beginning of an opinion writes *the jury was* should refer to *jury* as a singular noun throughout. A judge who wishes to emphasize the individual persons more than the body of persons may decide to write *the jury were*.

But switching back and forth between a singular and a plural verb is lamentably common: "Mark Pattison's *Memoirs* is not strictly speaking an autobiography. . . . His *Memoirs* do not so much tell the story of his life. . . . Mark's father, as the *Memoirs* make plain, dominated his son's early years. . . . The *Memoirs* describes clearly . . . ." V.H.H. Green, Introduction, Mark Pattison, *Memoirs of an Oxford Don* 1, 6 (1988).

Apart from the desire for consistency, there is little "right" and "wrong" on this subject: collective nouns take sometimes a singular and sometimes a plural verb. The trend in the U.S. is to regard the collective noun as expressing a unit; hence, the singular is the usual form. When the individuals in the collection or group receive the emphasis, the plural verb is acceptable. E.g.: "The law-of-nature school were not wholly in error." Roscoe Pound, *The Formative Era in American Law* 63 (1938). But generally in AmE writing, collective nouns take singular verbs, as in *the jury finds, the panel is, the faculty demands, the board has decided, the Supreme Court is,* and so on.

Just the opposite habit generally obtains in BrE, where collective nouns tend to take plural verbs. A British text on statute-drafting has even attempted to enshrine this habit, though without giving reasons:

"Though the practice varies, in LEGISLATIVE DRAFT-ING it is advisable to treat collective nouns as plural: that is, such nouns as *authority* or *Board* should be followed by a verb in the plural." Alison Russell, *Legislative Drafting and Forms* 86 (1938). The British tend to write, for example, *the board have*, not *has*—e.g.: "The *board have* considered the report of this further investigation very carefully." *Regina v. Police Compls. Bd. ex parte Madden*, [1983] 1 W.L.R. 447, 450 (Q.B.D.).

BrE has gone so far in some contexts that many Americans would suspect a typographical error: "Oxford were the winners of the 136th University Boat Race, but many will say that Cambridge were the heroes." Richard Burnell, *Oxford Hold Off Brave Light Blues*, Sunday Times, 1 Apr. 1990, at B1.

In the days soon after the American Revolution, not surprisingly, the American practice was closer to the prevailing British practice. E.g.:

- "The House of Representatives shall chuse *their* [modernly, *its*] Speaker and other Officers; and shall have the sole Power of Impeachment." U.S. Const. art. I, § 2.
- "The Senate shall chuse *their* other Officers." U.S. Const. art. I, § 3.

The reversal in practice has become so firmly established in AmE that it is hardly wrong to say that, with certain collective nouns, singular verbs are *preferred*. But one cannot be doctrinaire on this point of usage. The dilemma frequently occurs with nouns such as *majority* and *press* and *faculty*. E.g.:

- "While some plaintiffs have been promoted or otherwise had job changes since November 1985, the majority *remain* [read (in AmE) *remains*] in the same positions and grades they held at that time." *Abundis v. U.S.*, 18 Cl. Ct. 657, 659 (1989). (For examples with *jury*, see the entry under that word.)
- "The First Amendment requires only that the press *have* [read (in AmE) *has*] the same access to a trial as does the public." *Commonwealth v. Upshur*, 882 A.2d 499, 505 (Pa. Super. Ct. 2005).

These are questions more of local idiom than of correct or incorrect grammar. *Majority* can be especially troublesome for those seeking consistency—e.g.: "The majority in *their* [read (in AmE) *its*] footnote 6 *allude* [read *alludes*] to the testimony of [Hinojosa]." *U.S. v. Canales*, 744 F.2d 413, 435 (5th Cir. 1984) (Garza, J., dissenting). This preference for singular verbs with *majority* leads us down unidiomatic paths in sentences such as this, however, in which the noun best takes the plural verb: "The majority of the members of this Court *are* [rather than *is*] satisfied that it was proper to join the two petitions." *Pruchniak v. Sch. Bd. of Elk Point-Jefferson Sch. Dist.*, 691 N.W.2d 298, 300 (S.D. 2004).

On the question whether to use a singular or a plural verb after constructions such as *a number of people* and *a host of problems*, see SYNESIS.

collective work. See **compilation.**

collide. See **allide.**

collision; allision. Both are used, in the U.S. law of admiralty, in reference to vessels that meet each other unexpectedly. In an *allision*, one of the vessels is stationary. In a *collision*, usually both are moving, although *collision* does not necessarily imply force from each of the clashing objects.

Since we have this DIFFERENTIATION in the terminology of admiralty, however, we should observe the distinction, if only in this limited context. E.g.: "The litigation before us arises out of a series of four *collisions* by ships over a two-month period." *Harcon Barge Co. v. D. & G. Boat Rentals, Inc.*, 746 F.2d 278, 283 (5th Cir. 1984).

Here *allision* would have been the better word: "This case arises out of *a collision* [read *an allision*] that allegedly occurred between a tug owned by Dow and a boat docked alongside the plaintiffs' shrimp boat." *Gaspar v. Dowell Div.*, 750 F.2d 460, 461 (5th Cir. 1985). (The docked boat was stationary, presumably.)

But even specialized authorities have used *collision* in this way—e.g.: "The anchored vessel is almost, and usually quite, helpless to avoid *collision*, and moving vessels must keep clear of her." John W. Griffin, *The American Law of Collision* § 145, at 348 (1949). See **allide.**

Although *allision* most commonly applies to two ships, it may also apply to a ship and any stationary object (as a bridge or dock)—e.g.:

- "In the second ruling, the district court addressed liability issues surrounding *allisions* that occurred in the St. Louis harbor when barges from the M/V Anne Holly's tow *allided* with a pier of the Eads Bridge and a moored gambling vessel, the Admiral." *In re American Milling Co.*, 409 F.3d 1005, 1007 (8th Cir. 2005).
- "During Hurricane Katrina, the *MISS TIFF* [read *Miss Tiff*] and the *JACK KING* [read *Jack King*] broke from their moorings on the east branch of the Pascagoula River and *allided* [read *collided*] with a bridge of Interstate 10 approximately 4.7 miles away." *In re Signal Int'l, LLC*, 579 F.3d 478, 484 (5th Cir. 2009). (For more on the preferred form for vessel names, see CAPITALIZATION (D).

collocate; collate. *Collocate* = (1) to arrange in place; to set side by side; or (2) to occur in tandem with something else. *Collate* = (1) to compare minutely and critically; (2) to collect and compare for the purpose of arranging accurately; or (3) to assemble in proper order <he collated the appendixes to the brief>.

Both verbs are useful in legal analysis, *collocate* being perhaps more common, especially in the form of the noun *collocation* (= a distinct arrangement, esp. of words)—e.g.:

- "In considering the general question of property in news matter, it is necessary to recognize its dual character, distinguishing between the substance of the information and the particular form or *collocation* of words in which the writer has communicated it." *Int'l News Serv. v. Associated Press*, 248 U.S. 215, 234 (1918) (per Pitney, J.).
- "If the compilation author clothes facts with an original *collocation* of words, he or she may be able to claim a

copyright in this written expression." *Salestraq Am., LLC v. Zyskowski*, 635 F.Supp.2d 1178, 1182 (D. Nev. 2009).

collogue; colloque. Both are informal words meaning "to confer in private." Krapp labeled *collogue*—the more common word—"colloquial for *talk confidentially.*" George P. Krapp, *A Comprehensive Guide to Good English* 152 (1927). Either would be useful as a verb corresponding to the noun *colloquy*, which is frequently found in legal prose. (See **colloquy.**) Because it is already more common, *collogue* is more likely to gain wide acceptance.

COLLOQUIALITY, within the bounds of modesty and naturalness, is to be encouraged in legal writing as a counterbalance to the frequent use of rigid and pompous formalities. But many people misunderstand the meaning of *colloquiality.* The term is not a label for substandard usages; rather, it means "a conversational style." The writer of this sentence demonstrates an understanding of the term's meaning: "For more than a generation—between 1911 and 1933—securities sales in the United States were regulated nearly exclusively by specialized state statutes known *colloquially* as 'blue sky' laws." Jonathan R. Macey & Geoffrey P. Miller, *Origin of the Blue Sky Laws*, 70 Tex. L. Rev. 347, 348 (1991).

The best legal minds look kindly upon colloquiality: "Although there are no certain guides [in the interpretation of a statute], the *colloquial* meaning of the words [of the statute] is itself one of the best tests of purpose." *Brooklyn Nat'l Corp. v. Commissioner*, 157 F.2d 450, 451 (2d Cir. 1946) (per L. Hand, J.). "The courts will not be astute to discover fine distinctions in words, nor scholastic differentiations in phrases, so long as they are sufficiently in touch with affairs to understand the meaning which the man on the street attributes to ordinary English." *Vitagraph Co. v. Ford*, 241 F. 681, 686 (S.D.N.Y. 1917).

All this is to say that colloquiality is fine in its place. In formal legal writing, occasional colloquialisms may serve to give the prose more variety and texture; they may even be appropriate in judicial opinions in moderation. Still, the colloquial tone should not overshadow the generally serious tone of legal writing, and should never descend into slang.

Good writers would not always agree on where to draw that line. Some judges feel perfectly comfortable using a picturesque verb such as *squirrel away*: "This sufficed, in the absence of any record-backed hint that the prosecution . . . *squirrelled* [read *squirreled*] the new transcript *away.*" *U.S. v. Chaudhry*, 850 F.2d 851, 859 (1st Cir. 1988). Others would disapprove. A stylist like Justice Jackson writes forcefully of *blasting* a party's marriage where nonstylists would probably refer to *terminating the matrimonial relationship. See Rice v. Rice*, 336 U.S. 674, 680 (1949) (Jackson, J., dissenting). Some, like Justice Douglas, would use *pell mell*: "The circuits are in conflict; and the Court goes *pell mell* for an escape for this conglomerate from a real test under existing antitrust law." *Missouri Portland Cement Co.*

v. Cargill, Inc., 418 U.S. 919, 923 (1974) (Douglas, J., dissenting). Others would invariably choose a word like *indiscriminately* instead. Some, like Chief Justice Rehnquist, would use the phrase *Monday-morning quarterbacking. See Vt. Yankee Nuclear Power Corp. v. Natural Res. Def. Council, Inc.*, 435 U.S. 519, 547 (1978). Or *double-whammy. See American Bankers Ass'n v. SEC*, 804 F.2d 739, 749 (D.C. Cir. 1986).

For my part, I side with the colloquialists. In a profession whose writing suffers from verbal arteriosclerosis, some relaxation—and perhaps even some thinning of the blood—is in order. But progress comes slowly. The battle that Oliver Wendell Holmes fought in 1924 is repeated every day in law offices and judicial chambers throughout this country. Remember that Holmes wanted to say, in an opinion, that amplifications in a statute would "stop rat holes" in it. Chief Justice Taft criticized, predictably, and Holmes answered that law reports are dull because we believe "that judicial dignity require[s] solemn fluffy speech, as, when I grew up, everybody wore black frock coats and black cravats." 2 *Holmes–Pollock Letters* 132 (M. Howe ed. 1941). Too many lawyers still write as if they habitually wore black frock coats and black cravats.

colloquy; colloquium. The plural form of *colloquy* (= a formal discussion, as between a judge and counsel) is *colloquies*. Following is a typical use of the word: "The record from the state court contains no *colloquy* between Wiggins and the court with respect to this issue." *Wiggins v. Procunier*, 753 F.2d 1318, 1320 (5th Cir. 1985). (The old word in this sense was *interview*, common in the 19th c.) The verb corresponding to *colloquy* is *collogue.* (See **collogue.**)

Colloquium (= an academic conference or seminar) is frequently misspelled **colloquim. W11* prefers the plural *-quiums*, the (British) *COD -quia*. Many academicians seem to use *colloquia* (and even *auditoria*) merely to avoid possible criticism by colleagues, however unwarranted.

collude; conspire; connive. These verbs are hardly synonymous, but they have in common the idea of cooperating secretly with someone for illicit purposes. To *collude* (lit., "to play together") is to act underhandedly with someone else for purposes of (1) tricking a third party into giving what cannot otherwise be straightforwardly obtained, or (2) somehow upsetting a third party's plans <the largest distributors colluded to fix prices>. To *conspire* (lit., "to breathe together") is to plan and execute in concert with someone else an agreement to commit an unlawful act, with the intent to carry it out, and then to do something in furtherance of that agreement <gang members connived to kidnap the police chief's son>. To *connive* (lit., "to wink together") is to overlook or feign ignorance of what a perpetrator is doing, thereby enabling the perpetrator to commit a wrong that would otherwise be much more difficult to accomplish—e.g.:

- "An instance occurred in England during the last war, when a woman killed her newly born child and her own mother *connived* at the act." Glanville Williams, *The Sanctity of Life and the Criminal Law* 29 (1957).

- "It is often the same citizen who originally supports the passage of such laws who later *connives* at their violation." Lon L. Fuller, *The Anatomy of the Law* 41 (1968).

collusion = (1) an agreement between two or more persons to defraud another; (2) an agreement by which the defendant allows the plaintiff to sue so as to confer jurisdiction on the court; or (3) in divorce proceedings (in the days before no-fault divorces), an agreement between husband and wife for one or the other to commit (or appear to commit) adultery or another marital breach in order to obtain a divorce. In sense 3, *collusion* is (generally) *connivance* for a particular purpose. Joel Prentiss Bishop, 2 *Commentaries on the Law of Marriage and Divorce* 22 (6th ed. 1881). (See **connivance**.) *Collusion* always has the flavor of fraud.

The mistake of misusing *collusion* for *collaboration* is fairly uncommon in law. But H.W. Fowler cites this example: "The two authors, both professors at Innsbruck, appear to be working in *collusion* [read *collaboration*]" (*MEU2* 95).

collusive; *collusory. *Collusive* (= of, relating to, or involving a secret agreement or understanding for illegal or deceitful ends) is preferred; **collusory* is a NEEDLESS VARIANT.

color. In the phrase *under color of state law*, the word *color* = appearance, semblance, guise. The development of this bit of legal JARGON is instructive:

> Sometimes a party put in a plea designed to make what was really a point of fact appear to be a point of law, so as to transfer the decision from the jury to the judge: this was called *colour*. The expression was in due course applied to the title . . . in question. "If the defendant," wrote Blackstone, "in assise or action of trespass, be desirous to refer the validity of his title to the court rather than to the jury, he may state his title specially, and at the same time *give colour* to the plaintiff, bad indeed in point of law, but of which the jury are not competent judges." 3 William Blackstone, *Commentaries on the Laws of England* 309 (emphasis in original).
>
> Jocelyn Simon, *English Idioms from the Law*,
> 76 Law Q. Rev. 429, 440 (1960) (Part 2).

Alongside this sense of an apparent or prima facie title or right there has developed the modern expressions *no color of title*, *no color of right*, and *no color of law*, meaning without any sort of title or right.

colorable is used in law in the sense "having at least a prima facie aspect of justice or validity" (*OED*) <a colorable claim to property>.

The word has been extended to a broader sense, as if it were synonymous with *ostensible* or *apparent*: "Of the documents prepared by the attorneys themselves, none were even colorably prepared in anticipation of this or any other litigation." *U.S. v. Davis*, 636 F.2d 1028, 1040 (5th Cir. 1981). One might be tempted at

first to brand this usage a SLIPSHOD EXTENSION, but it is old—Justice Story used *colorable* in this way in charging a jury in 1814. *See Odiorne v. Winkley*, 18 F. Cas. 581, 582 (C.C.D. Mass. 1814) ("Mere *colorable* alterations of a machine are not enough."). See **color**.

colore officii (= by or under color of office) is a LATINISM without redeeming value. E.g.: "As a general rule, the corporation is not responsible for the unauthorized and unlawful acts of its officers, though done *colore officii*." *Thayer v. City of Boston*, 19 Pick. 511, 511 (Mass. 1837).

The English equivalent serves better, and most readers will not pass it over uncomprehendingly, as they will the Latinism. Further, the English phrase is common—e.g.: "An act is committed *under color of office* if there is a causal connection between the charged conduct and the asserted official authority." *City of Las Cruces v. Baldonado*, 652 F.Supp. 138 (D.N.M. 1986).

color of office. See ***colore officii***.

combination; confederacy; conspiracy. The first two are more neutral than the third: "Appellants announce their willingness to accept this definition [of the boycott], substituting the word 'confederacy' or 'combination' for 'conspiracy.'" *Pierce v. Stablemen's Union, Local No. 8,760*, 103 P. 324, 326 (Cal. 1909).

Combination = the banding together or union of persons for the pursuance of some common goal. The *OED* notes that it was formerly used synonymously with *conspiracy*, but it has appreciated in meaning. E.g.: "A strike is one of the legal means to which parties have a right to resort to enforce a legal *combination*." *Haverhill Strand Theater v. Gillen*, 118 N.E. 671, 673 (Mass. 1918). Today *combination* is often used in antitrust contexts.

Confederacy = a union by league or contract between persons, bodies of men, or states, for mutual support or joint action; a league, alliance, compact (*OED*). The *OED* states that in law this word has traditionally been given a bad sense, as if synonymous with *conspiracy*; no longer is such a meaning predominantly given to the word.

Both *confederacy* and *combination* may refer to an agreement by two or more persons to do an illegal act, but this sense is best reserved for a third word. *Conspiracy* = an agreement between two or more people to behave in a manner that will automatically constitute an offense by at least one of them (e.g., two people agree that one of them will steal while the other waits in a getaway car) (*CDL*).

combine, n., is an American business colloquialism synonymous with *combination*, usually implying fraudulent or anticompetitive ends. Krapp disapproved of this use of the word in 1927, and Bernstein approved of it in 1965, but only as a casualism. So it remains. See **combination.**

come down is the intransitive PHRASAL VERB used of judicial decisions—e.g.:

- "This change in the law has required us to deal with several problems for cases in which sentences were imposed before *Booker* but were on appeal when that decision *came down.*" *U.S. v. Shedrick*, 493 F.3d 292, 302 (3d Cir. 2007).
- "That decision *came down* in mid-January, and although *Herring* produced a five-to-four split in the Court, that division has proved remarkable in terms of our case." *U.S. v. Noster*, 573 F.3d 664, 677 (9th Cir. 2009).

For the transitive counterpart, see **hand down a decision.**

comes now; now comes. Traditionally the standard commencements in pleadings, these phrases are falling into long-overdue disuse. During the late 1980s and early 1990s, judges in four American states (Florida, Louisiana, Michigan, and Texas) were polled on whether they preferred the legalistic opener (*Now comes the plaintiff*, John Jones, by and through his attorneys of record, and would show unto the court the following) as opposed to a plain-language version (*Plaintiff complains of defendant and says*). Not surprisingly, more than 80% of them preferred the shorter, more direct version. Yet many lawyers—most in Texas and probably elsewhere—stick to the tired old wordy forms.

The phrasing *comes now* is an example of archaic INVERSION. *Comes now* is the form for a singular, *come now* for a plural subject. It is not uncommon for modern pleaders to bungle SUBJECT–VERB AGREEMENT with inverted phrases of this kind, as in "*Comes now the plaintiffs*, Russ and Leslie Blanchard" [read *Come now the plaintiffs . . .*]." The wording in a judicial order analogous to this phrase is "*Came on* for consideration the defendant's motion."

Comes now the plaintiff is occasionally mispunctuated—e.g.: "*Comes, now, the plaintiff . . . .*" The first comma in the phrase should follow *plaintiff*, after which the person's name acts as an APPOSITIVE. Placing a comma after the verb betrays the writer's misunderstanding of the inversion of subject and verb. This antiquated wording is sometimes modernized *now comes.*

come to court is the BrE equivalent of *go to trial*—e.g.:

- "Among critics of the existing system is the woman at the centre of last week's trial, an American who waited a year for the case to *come to court.*" *Judges' Old Boy Network Under Fire After Rape Trial*, Sunday Times, 15 Apr. 1990, at A5. (An American journalist writing that sentence would have phrased it *go to trial, reach trial*, or *get to court.*)
- "It took 12 years for the Jack Bernardent case to *come to court.*" Melcher, *Louvre Accused over "Theft" of Tapestries*, The European, 13–15 July 1990, at 2.

See **go to trial.**

comingle. See **commingle.*

coming on for hearing. See **came on for hearing.**

comity = courtesy among political entities (as nations or courts of different jurisdictions), involving esp. mutual recognition of legislative, executive, and judicial acts. The term is often defined as if it were wholly a matter of international law, as here: "*Comity*, in the legal sense, is neither a matter of absolute obligation, on the one hand, nor of mere courtesy and good will, upon the other. But it is the recognition which one nation allows within its territory to the legislative, executive or judicial acts of another nation, having due regard both to international duty and convenience, and to the rights of its own citizens, or of other persons who are under the protection of its laws." *Hilton v. Guyot*, 159 U.S. 113, 163-64 (1895) (per Gray, J.).

But *comity* applies also to political entities within a given country. E.g.:

- "The decision to extradite is a matter of *comity* between sister states." *State v. Robbins*, 590 A.2d 1133, 1138 (N.J. 1991).
- "While our research has not uncovered a reported case involving an attempt by a state or local government to prohibit its employees from contributing to partisan campaigns in other states, we suspect any such attempt would offend the principle of interstate *comity*." *City of Cincinnati v. Ohio Council 8*, 576 N.E.2d 745, 756 (Ohio 1991).

The word is sometimes—especially in BrE—mistaken as meaning "league" or "federation," particularly in the phrase *comity of nations*. For example, Bertrand Russell spoke out in 1915 against World War I and said: "A month ago Europe was a peaceful *comity* of nations . . ." (as quoted in *Differences of Opinion*, Sunday Times, 8 Dec. 1991). Nearly 80 years later the usage persists, but primarily in British writing—e.g.: "What with . . . South Africa's readmission to the *comity* of nations . . . , this is far from fanciful." Ivo Tennant, *Gatting Lobby Holds Out for Change of Heart*, The Times (London), 18 Apr. 1992 (sport section).

commander-in-chief. Pl. *commanders-in-chief.*

COMMAS. See PUNCTUATION (D).

COMMA SPLICES. See RUN-ON SENTENCES.

commemorative; *commemoratory. The usual form is *-tive*; *-tory* is a NEEDLESS VARIANT.

commence; begin; start. Except in describing formal ceremonies or exercises, or legal actions, *commence* is usually unnecessarily stilted for *begin*, with which it is denotatively equivalent. The *OED* notes that "*begin* is preferred in ordinary use; *commence* has more formal associations with law and procedure, combat, divine service, and ceremon[y]." *Commencement* is perhaps justified here: "It is settled that a prevailing party may recover fees for time spent before the formal *commencement* of litigation on such matters as attorney-client interviews." *Webb v. Bd. of Educ. of Dyer County*, 471 U.S. 234, 250 (1985) (Brennan, J., concurring in part & dissenting in part).

But the following examples contain the stilted or wholly unnecessary *commence*:

- "Ilsa then *commenced* [read *began*] living in California with her mother during the school year and spending vacations with her father." *Kulko v. Super. Ct. of Cal.*, 436 U.S. 84, 88 (1978) (per Marshall, J.). (One does not, idiomatically, *commence* to live somewhere.)
- "On the date they *commenced* [read *began*] selling used cars on the premises, Baltimore County zoning regulations permitted such a use." *Antwerpen v. Baltimore County*, 877 A.2d 1166, 1174 (Md. Ct. Spec. App. 2005).
- "This action was *commenced* [read *brought*] by the plaintiffs to recover damages for personal injuries allegedly sustained . . . as the result of a motor vehicle accident that occurred in Queens." *Stancu v. Oh*, 903 N.Y.S.2d 268, 268 (App. Div. 2010).

Commence has long been criticized by stylists when introducing an infinitive. *Begin* is here preferable: "The Mississippi statute *commences* [read *begins*] to run on the date of the wrongful act." *Vidrine v. Enger*, 752 F.2d 107, 108 (5th Cir. 1984).

Definite nuances exist with *start* as opposed to *begin* or *commence*. Usually referring to physical movement, *start* suggests an abruptness not present in *begin* or *commence*; one *starts* to do something or engage in some activity (e.g., to run).

commencement. See **introductory clause.**

commend. See **discommend.**

commensurate; commensurable. In all but mathematical contexts, *commensurable* is a NEEDLESS VARIANT of *commensurate*. *Commensurable* legitimately means "having, or reducible to, a common measure; divisible without remainder by the same quantity" (*OED*). *Commensurate* means: (1) "coextensive"; or (2) "proportionate." Here the rarer term, *commensurable*, is used where its sibling should appear: "The policy initially issued must be read to cover all of the expenses arising from Gina's mental disability, *commensurably* [read *commensurately* (i.e., coextensively)] with coverage for other illnesses, beginning while the policy was in effect, including those incurred during the term of the amendment." *DiPascal v. N.Y. Life Ins. Co.*, 749 F.2d 255, 256–57 (5th Cir. 1985).

commentator; commenter. In law, these ordinary words have special senses. *Commentators* are usually scholars who write within a particular field; *commenters*, in AmE, are those who send comments to an agency about a proposed administrative rule.

commerce. Formerly, *commerce* was usable in all the senses of *intercourse*; hence the phrase *sexual commerce* (= sexual intercourse) in many older legal writings (not necessarily involving prostitution). See **intercourse.** For the general sense of *commerce*, see **business.**

commercial, adj.; **mercantile.** These adjectives both describe whatever involves the money-making aspects of a business enterprise, especially as regards the buying and selling of commodities. *Commercial*, the more common and more general term, refers to anything relating to a transaction or business intended to make a profit <commercial venture> or to the medium by which such a transaction or business is carried on <commercial paper>. *Mercantile* /**mərk**-ən-teel/ overlaps with some meanings of *commercial* <mercantile transactions> but not all (**mercantile paper* is not an accepted or idiomatic phrase). *Mercantile* typically implies the occupation of a merchant, that is, buying and selling—often but not necessarily as a middleman or wholesaler.

commercial bribery. See **bribery.**

commercial domicile. See **domicile (c).**

commercial law = (1) traditionally, the law merchant, i.e., a system of justice that merchants created to govern their affairs separately from the systems of civil, criminal, and ecclesiastical justice; or (2) *in AmE*, the substantive law dealing with the sale and distribution of goods and negotiable instruments and the financing of credit transactions on the security of the goods sold. Sense 2, now the primary sense, has spread beyond AmE: "Today the term '*commercial law*' has assumed a new meaning, a meaning [that] is new at least to Europe, but not so to the United States or to Louisiana. I refer, of course, to the meaning in which the term is used to describe a certain area of expertise in legal practice or learning, or that branch of the law . . . of special interest to business people. It is in this sense that the term is used in the United States in the title of the Uniform Commercial Code." Max Rheinstein, "Problems and Challenges of Contemporary Civil Law of Obligations," in *Essays on the Civil Law of Obligations* 10–11 (Joseph Dainow ed., 1969).

commercially reasonable efforts. See **best efforts.**

commercial paper. See **negotiable instrument.**

commingle; *comingle. *Commingle* (= to mingle together) is now the accepted spelling. **Comingle*, though slightly older, has failed to become standard—e.g.:

- "They had no joint bank accounts, nor did they *comingle* [read *commingle*] any of their accounts." *Wood v. Collins*, 812 P.2d 951, 953 (Alaska Ct. App. 1991).
- "The Court will not allow plaintiff to *comingle* [read *commingle*] its breach of contract claim with a takings claim in this suit as the subject matter of both claims is identical." *Am. Growers Ins. Co. v. Fed. Crop Ins. Corp.*, 210 F.Supp.2d 1088, 1095 (S.D. Iowa 2002).

Mingle has also been used in reference to combining funds—e.g.: "The situation is analogous to one where a wrongdoer *mingles* his own funds with other funds which he has misappropriated." *Marcus v. Otis*, 169 F.2d 148, 150 (2d Cir. 1948). But *commingle*, the more usual term, would ordinarily appear in such a context.

commission. See **commitment.**

commissionee. See -EE.

commissioner; *commissionor. The first spelling is standard.

commissive waste. See **waste.**

*commitee. See **committee.**

commitment; committal; commission. *Commitment* and *commission* are common words that will here be discussed only to the extent that they are confusable with *committal*, which is in all but two specific senses a NEEDLESS VARIANT. In England, a *committal* in civil proceedings is a method of enforcing judgment by obtaining an order that a person be *imprisoned*. E.g.:

- "The mode of enforcing decrees in the time of Henry VI down to the end of the reign of Charles I., where the party was taken, appears to have been by *committal* to the Fleet prison; for the Chancellor could not bind the right, he could only coerce the person." 1 George Spence, *Equitable Jurisprudence* 390 (1846).
- "[The] judge . . . had an inherent jurisdiction to make a *committal* order ex parte [committing a delinquent party to jail]." *Hipgrave v. Hipgrave*, [1962] 2 W.L.R. 1 (P.D.A.D.).
- "It may be that *committal* is the remedy of last resort but . . . the strategy for a case may properly involve the use of imprisonment." *F. v. M.*, [2004] E.W.H.C. 727 (Fam.).

See **committer.**

Committal also has the sense "the action of committing the body to the grave at burial" (*OED*). E.g.: "A decent *committal* of the body to the deep in accordance with the custom in such matters ordinarily discharges the duty which the law imposes." *Brambir v. Cunard White Star Ltd.*, 37 F.Supp. 906, 907 (S.D.N.Y. 1940).

In the sense "the action of committing an insane or mentally retarded person to the charge of another," *commitment* is the usual and the preferred term:

- "The petition was presented to the . . . judge of the Circuit Court of Albemarle County . . . [who] adjudged that Mary's infirmities did not require the *committal* [read *commitment*] of her person to a guardian." *Gilmer v. Brown*, 44 S.E.2d 16, 18 (Va. 1947).
- "The broad rule generally prevails that a valid proceeding to commit a person to an insane asylum or hospital requires, not only adequate notice to the alleged incompetent, but also an opportunity for him to be heard before the order of *commitment* is issued." *In re Sleeper*, 87 A.2d 115, 120 (Me. 1952) (quoting 28 Am. Jur. 676, § 32).

Commitment is also the preferred term in the broad sense of "the action of entrusting, giving in charge": "Few men retain their money in their own custody but commit its care to others, both for the feeling of security that such *committal* [read *commitment*] engenders and the facility with which it may be transferred and paid out by means of checks."

Commission is preferred in the sense "the action of doing or perpetrating (as a crime)." The *OED* records examples of *committal* and even of *commitment* in this sense, but these are anomalous.

committable; *committible. The first is preferred.

committal. See **commitment.**

committee (= a person who is civilly committed, usu. to a psychiatric hospital) is a splendid example of how lawyers take an ordinary English word and give it an alien sense and pronunciation /com-i-**tee**/. The usage invites double takes from both lawyers and nonlawyers: "The civil commitment hearing does not address whether the *committee* has engaged in conduct that constitutes the elements of a crime; rather, that hearing focuses on whether a *committee* is mentally ill or dangerous." *Benham v. Edwards*, 678 F.2d 511, 538 (5th Cir. 1982). *See Hickey v. Morris*, 722 F.2d 543, 547 (9th Cir. 1983) (referring to the "differences between insanity acquittees and civil *committees*"). Of course, those who have had the privilege of serving on more than a few *committees* (in the usual sense) may see this usage as a logical extension of meaning. See ***acquittee.**

Some writers have used the spelling **commitee* to differentiate the legal from the ordinary use of the word. That spelling, however, violates the principles of DOUBLING OF FINAL CONSONANTS and merely suggests that the writer possesses neither an ear for the language nor a computer with a spelling-checker.

Confusingly, *committee* has still another legal sense—especially common in BrE—referring not to the psychiatric patient but to the guardian for the patient. E.g.:

- "In addition to his two brothers, the deceased left three sisters, his next of kin; two of them are lunatics, and Alexander Tweedale the *committee* of their persons and property." *In the Goods of Farquharson Tweedale*, [1874] L.R. 3 P. & D. 204 (P.D.A.D.).
- "The '*committee*' of a person of unsound mind was a single person to whom the care of such person was entrusted by the court, the stress being on the last syllable. *Committees* are no longer appointed." Glanville Williams, *Learning the Law* 64 (11th ed. 1982).

committer; committor. These words constitute one of the few pairs with a clear-cut DIFFERENTIATION arising from these variable suffixes. *Committer* is the general word meaning "one who commits (e.g., a crime)." *Committor* is an uncommon legal term for "a judge who commits an insane or mentally retarded person to the charge of another." See -ER (A).

commodatum; accommodatum. The usual spelling of this term borrowed from Roman law, meaning "a gratuitous loan (of something) for use without compensation," is *commodatum*. It has also been called "a 'loan for use' to distinguish it from a *mutuum*, or a 'loan for consumption.'" Joseph Story, *Commentaries on the Law of Bailments* 194 (Edmond H. Bennett ed., 8th ed. 1870). See **mutuum.**

common. A. And *several*. What is *common* is shared in some way; what is *several* is separate in some way. (See **several.**) But the terms are vague enough that they cause problems when used in several common legal tests: "The distinction between a *common* undivided interest and several and distinct claims is something less than clear. This is to be expected. Except in property law contexts, such terms as *'common'* and *'several'* are poor words for a test of jurisdiction—or anything else—since they 'have little or no clear and ascertainable meaning.'" Charles Alan Wright, *The Law of Federal Courts* 212 (5th ed. 1994) (quoting Benjamin Kaplan, *Continuing Work of the Civil Committee*, 81 Harv. L. Rev. 356, 380 (1967)).

B. And *mutual*. See **mutual.**

commonality; commonness; commonalty; commonage; *commonty. The common character of these words may cause confusion. The ordinary words are *commonality* and *commonness*; although historically the two have overlapped, they are best kept separate, in accordance with the following definitions. *Commonness*, the general noun corresponding to *common*, may mean: (1) "the state or quality of being common" <the commonness today of fax machines>; (2) "the quality of being public or generally used" <the commonness of the thoroughfare>; (3) "the having of run-of-the-mill qualities" <the commonness of his writing>; or (4) "vulgarity" <the commonness of a sot>. *Commonality* = the possession of an attribute in common with another. The term is usual in class-action suits. E.g.: "The district court denied class certification because it found that the petitioner had not satisfied the *commonality* and typicality prerequisites of Federal Rule of Civil Procedure 23 [i.e., the class members' having claims with factual and legal issues in common with one another]." *Shanks v. City of Dallas*, 752 F.2d 1092, 1095 (5th Cir. 1985).

The remaining words are more easily distinguished. *Commonalty* = (1) commoners; the general body of the community (excluding nobility); (2) a municipal corporation (a sense to be avoided with this word, as *corporation* is the ordinary word); or (3) a general group or body. In the following sentence, by contrast, the writer may be using *commonalty* in sense 3—a REDUNDANCY—or may have intended *commonality*: "The Alabama code stood as a statement of the rules of the game that a family of professionals . . . adhered to in recognition of their *commonalty* [read *commonality*?] and because it might, by forcing an affiliation, help keep them out of trouble." Jethro K. Lieberman, *Crisis at the Bar* 56 (1978).

Commonage = (1) the right of pasturing animals on common land; (2) the condition of land held in common; or (3) an estate or property held in common (*OED*). *Commonty, in its existing uses, is a NEEDLESS VARIANT of *commonage*.

commonhold (BrE), referring to condominium ownership, is a new system of tenure in G.B., allowing flats to be sold in freehold. E.g.:

- "*Commonhold*, a new form of flat ownership, has been proposed in a Law Commission report published yesterday. *Commonhold*, another name for the U.S. condominium, would provide an alternative to freehold and leasehold ownership, combining their advantages and removing some of the disadvantages." A.H. Hermann, *Alternative to Leasehold of Flats Proposed*, Fin. Times, 23 July 1987, at I-6.
- "The system of *commonhold*, announced by the Government last month, could deal with many of the problems [that] long leasehold tenants and their landlords are experiencing, says a report published yesterday." *New Lease of Life for Victims of Landlords*, Daily Telegraph, 14 Aug. 1991, at 6.

common intendment. See **intendment.**

common law. A. As Noun—in Broad Contrasts. In modern usage, *common law* is contrasted with a number of other terms. First, in denoting the body of judge-made law based on that developed originally in England, *common law* is contrasted by comparative jurists to *civil law*. Second, "with the development of equity and equitable rights and remedies, *common law* and equitable courts, procedure, rights, remedies, etc., are frequently contrasted, and in this sense *common law* is distinguished from *equity*" (*OCL1*). Third, the term is similarly distinguished from *ecclesiastical law*. Fourth, it is occasionally used to denote the law common to the country as a whole—as distinguished from law that has only local applications. Finally, and perhaps most commonly within Anglo-American jurisdictions, *common law* is contrasted with *statutory law* <statutes in derogation of the common law are to be strictly construed>. See **civil law.**

B. As Noun—Its Specific Senses. The phrase has at least seven senses—and "the precise shade of meaning in which this chameleon phrase is used depends upon the particular context, and upon the contrast that is being made." Glanville Williams, *Learning the Law* 25 n.1 (11th ed. 1982). Among its senses are:

1. in historical England, the "immemorial slow-growing custom declared by juries of free men who gave their verdicts case by case in open court" (1 Winston Churchill, *A History of the English Speaking Peoples* 225 (1956));
2. general law as distinguished from special law such as royal decrees and the local customary law of any district (*see* James Hadley, *Introduction to Roman Law* 43 (1881) (discussing English common law as "common . . . to all parts of the kingdom, in distinction from the local usages"));—in this sense the phrase is analogous to Fr. *droit commun* & Ger. *Gemeinrecht*;
3. in comparative law, a body of law based on the English legal system, as distinct from a civil-law system;
4. "the set of rules that lawyers use to settle any dispute or problem to which no constitution or statute applies" (Fred Rodell, *Woe Unto You, Lawyers!* 20 (1939));
5. the power of judges to create new law under the guise of interpreting it (Glanville Williams, *Learning the Law* 29–30 (11th ed. 1982));

6. modern judge-made law (*see, e.g., Bernard Johnson, Inc. v. Contl. Constructors, Inc.,* 630 S.W.2d 365, 370 n.4 (Tex. App.—Austin 1982) ("The defense of 'privity of contract' having been established by the common law, it obviously may be abolished by statute or by the common law.")); and

7. a widely adopted statute (e.g.: "Carl Zeitz . . . said the judge's ruling appears to be a 'logical extension' of the common laws [dramshop statutes] that hold taverns partly responsible for damages incurred if they serve alcohol to a visibly intoxicated person" (R.B. Smith, *Casinos May Be Held Liable for Drunken Patrons* [sic] *Losses,* Wall St. J., 23 June 1989, at B1)).

Sense 7 is the nonlawyer's unfortunate MISCUE— nothing more. Sense 6 is arguably loose; one book, supporting this sense, states that *common law* is "sometimes referred to as *case law.*" Stephen Foster, *Business Law Terms* 17 (1988). But *common law* really encompasses much more than *caselaw,* which usually refers to a limited number of cases within a field. Still, drawing the line between *caselaw* and *common law*— especially as used in a phrase such as *federal common law*—is a difficult, if not impossible, task. See **caselaw.**

In the U.S.—contrary to popular belief—the common law includes many early English statutes. For example, the crime known as *false pretenses,* unknown to English common law, was made a misdemeanor by an English statute old enough to have been incorporated into the common law of American states. (See **false pretenses.**) Of course, once adopted in the various American states, the common law has grown in a variety of directions, and only rarely does a question of modern American law depend on English common law. As Holmes once acutely observed, "The common law so far as it is enforced in a State, whether called common law or not, is not the common law generally but the law of that State existing by the authority of that State without regard to what it may have been in England or anywhere else." *Black & White Taxicab & Transfer Co. v. Brown & Yellow Taxicab & Transfer Co.,* 276 U.S. 518, 533–34 (1928) (Holmes, J., dissenting). *See generally* Morris L. Cohen, *The Common Law in the American Legal System,* 81 Law Lib. J. 13, 18 (1989).

C. At common law. A LOAN TRANSLATION of the LAW FRENCH *al common ley,* this phrase is the legal idiom used to introduce statements of common-law doctrine—that is, in sense 1 outlined under (B) above. E.g.:

• "*At common law* every person has individually, and the public also has collectively, a right to require that the course of trade should be kept free from unreasonable obstruction." Sir William Erle, *The Law Relating to Trade Unions* 6 (1869).

• "*At common law,* a publisher is subjected to a greater risk of liability than a distributor." Jennifer Benedict, Comment, *Deafening Silence,* 39 Cumb. L. Rev. 475, 478 (2009).

• "*At common law,* kidnapping required proof of both 'an unlawful restraint' and asportation." *Turner v. Commonwealth,* 694 S.E.2d 251, 286 (Va. Ct. App. 2010).

Writers and editors occasionally puzzle over whether to use the present or the past tense after this phrase. In the previous paragraph we see an example of each. The distinction lies here: If the doctrinal statement of immemorial law continues to hold true, the present tense is called for; if the statement is of historical interest and the doctrine long since obsolete, the past tense is appropriate.

Oddly, the preposition *at* is not used in any parallel idiom for civil law.

D. As Adjective. The phrase is hyphenated when it serves as a PHRASAL ADJECTIVE but not when it serves as a noun. Both uses are illustrated in this sentence: "But these are all *common-law* cases, and the *common law* has its peculiar rules in relation to this subject." *The Sea Gull,* 21 F. Cas. 909, 910 (C.C.D. Md. 1865). Cf. **civil law (B).**

common-law cheat. See **cheat.**

common-law lawyer; common lawyer. The better form is *common-law lawyer;* the repetition of *law* is no cause for anxieties about REDUNDANCY—e.g.: "But there the court of appeal, the Privy Council, has been largely composed of *common-law lawyers.*" Oliver Wendell Holmes Jr., *The Common Law* 27–28 (1881). Several learned writers such as John Chipman Gray, Roscoe Pound, and Lawrence Friedman have used *common-law lawyer.*

But many others—mostly British—have used *common lawyer,* as in the title of Frederick H. Lawson's book, *A Common Lawyer Looks at the Civil Law* (1953). Consider:

• "The *common lawyer* is pious and platitudinous about the insularity of English law." Samuel J. Stoljar, *A Common Lawyer's French,* 47 Law Lib. J. 119, 119 (1954).

• "On the whole, the *common lawyers* used the device well, understanding the purpose for which the fiction was created." George W. Paton, *A Textbook of Jurisprudence* 58 (4th ed. 1972).

The *OED,* interestingly, contains examples of the phrase *common lawyer* dating from as early as 1588.

As if to avoid a MISCUE—as by reading *common lawyer* to be analogous to *common strumpet*—at least two eminent writers have taken to hyphenating the phrase:

• "Under either view, the *common-lawyers* seem significantly prominent in the creative days of early equity." Theodore F.T. Plucknett, *A Concise History of the Common Law* 180 n.4 (5th ed. 1956).

• "But the *common-lawyers* . . . were forced into the position of saying that the seisin . . . was in the lord." A.W.B. Simpson, *An Introduction to the History of the Land Law* 150 (1961).

That urge to hyphenate is understandable, but the hyphen belongs in *common-law lawyer* and not in *common lawyer.*

common-law marriage has one meaning in the U.S., another in Scotland, and still another in England. In the U.S., it generally denotes an agreement to marry, followed by cohabitation and a public recognition of the marriage. Common-law marriages are valid in many states, such as Texas, though others have abolished the institution, as New York did in 1932.

In Scotland, the phrase denotes cohabitation for a substantial period with the acquisition of the reputation of being married (an agreement to marry not being necessary).

And in England, *common-law marriage* is now used only of a marriage celebrated according to a common-law form in a place where the local forms of marriage cannot be used (e.g., a desert island), where the local forms are morally unacceptable to the parties (e.g., a Muslim country), or where no cleric is available (*OCL1*). Additionally—and more commonly in BrE—the phrase refers to an illicit union of some duration. As Sir Robert Megarry writes, "The so-called *common-law marriage*, little known in England save as a polite verbal cloak for fornication or adultery of the less ephemeral type, has a respectable ancestry in America." *A Second Miscellany-at-Law* 210 (1973).

In none of these jurisdictions is the phrase to be confused with its near-homophone *common-law mortgage*.

COMMON-LAW PLEADINGS. Until the Judicature Act of 1873, the pleadings allowed in English courts were as follows:

Plaintiff	*statement of claim* or *declaration*
Defendant	*defence* (BrE sp.) or *answer*
Plaintiff	*reply* or *replication*
Defendant	*rejoinder*
Plaintiff	*surrejoinder*
Defendant	*rebutter*
Plaintiff	*surrebutter*

Modern practice has been greatly simplified. In English practice today, the pleadings are generally the plaintiff's *statement of claim*, the defendant's *defence* (BrE sp.), and (sometimes) the plaintiff's *reply*. In American federal practice, the pleadings are generally the plaintiff's *complaint* and the defendant's *answer*, both of which are commonly amended repeatedly. See **pleading (c)**, EQUITY PLEADINGS & WORLD COURT PLEADINGS.

common-law wife is a misnomer of sorts: "No such woman was known to the common law, but [the phrase] means a woman who is living with a man in the same household as if she were his wife. She is to be distinguished from a *mistress*, where the relationship may be casual, impermanent, and secret." *Davis v. Johnson*, [1979] A.C. 264, 270 (per Lord Denning, M.R.). *OCL1* states that "the term *common-law wife* is sometimes applied [no doubt as a EUPHEMISM] to a concubine or mistress where the relationship is of some duration or stability." In AmE, this use of the term is properly considered a corrupt one. See **common-law marriage.**

common lawyer. See **common-law lawyer.**

commonness. See **commonality.**

common pleas, court of. At early common law, common pleas were actions over which the crown did not claim exclusive jurisdiction—as distinguished from *pleas of the crown*. Later, the phrase *common pleas* referred more specifically to civil actions between private citizens.

Through metonymy (as early as the 13th century), *common pleas* came to refer to the court hearing civil actions—a court that lasted in England until 1875, when it was merged into the newly established High Court. Several North American jurisdictions still have courts of common pleas, including the states of Connecticut, Ohio, Pennsylvania, and South Carolina, and the province of Ontario.

common school. See **public school.**

***commonty.** See **commonality.**

commonweal; commonwealth. *Commonweal* = the general welfare or common good. E.g.:

- "The sixteenth-century ideal of the '*commonweal*'—what would now be called 'public policy'—is an originally Roman principle still invoked in the courts." Alan Harding, *A Social History of English Law* 236 (1966).
- "Does the general welfare and common good—the *commonweal*—require that mercy be part of the justice system? I submit that we want a system that allows for both justice and mercy." *State v. Streiff*, 673 N.W.2d 831, 842 (Minn. 2004) (Anderson, J., concurring).

Commonwealth = a nation, state, or other political unit <the British Commonwealth>. For the distinction between this term and *dependency* and *territory*, see **territory.**

commorientes = persons who die at the same time, such as spouses who die in an accident. Although this LATINISM would seem to be useful in the context of simultaneous-death statutes, it is little used in the U.S. outside Louisiana. But it does occasionally surface in general American caselaw:

- "Let me next refer for a moment to the general law governing successions from *commorientes* who perish in a common disaster." *In re Fowles' Will*, 158 N.Y.S. 456, 459 (Sur. Ct. 1916).
- "All of that evidence showed prima facie that husband and wife perished in a common disaster as *commorientes*." *In re Cruson's Estate*, 221 P.2d 892, 900 (Or. 1950).

See **simultaneous death.**

Presumably the term is more common in BrE, for it is included in the compendious *CDL*. And it appears in the work of respected British legists—e.g.: "By reason of the English rule relating to *commorientes* the husband was deemed to have died intestate." R.H. Graveson, *Conflict of Laws* 384 (7th ed. 1974).

In Louisiana usage, *commorientes* has undergone SLIPSHOD EXTENSION to refer not to the persons who die simultaneously, but to the rule of succession regarding such persons. Hence one occasionally sees references to the *doctrine of commorientes*—e.g.:

- "Plaintiff suggests that the *doctrine of commorientes* . . . might have applied but for the assumption by the heirs that the deaths were simultaneous." *Morelock v. Aetna Life Ins. Co.*, 63 So.2d 612, 614 (La. 1953).
- "I do not think it necessary to cope with the difficult problem of whether the doctrine of *commorientes* . . . is applicable to a wrongful death action." *Chateau v. Smith*, 297 So.2d 268, 271 (La. Ct. App. 1974) (Schott, J., concurring).

communication is often used as a count noun in the law of evidence. It refers to any writing or conversation from one person to another or between persons.

Partridge states, in reference to *communicate* and *communication*, that if all you mean by *communicate* is *write* or *tell*, or by *communication* a *note* or a *letter*, then say so. Eric Partridge, *Usage and Abusage* 77 (1973). As a general rule, that advice is well taken; but if the lawyer particularly wishes to emphasize the applicability of a rule of evidence relating to *communications*, use of the longer, broader word is certainly justified.

communicative; *communicatory. The latter is a NEEDLESS VARIANT.

communitize, communitization. A. And *unitize, unitization.* These two sets of terms, from the American law of oil and gas, are sometimes used interchangeably but are usefully distinguished. The following definitions are based on those contained in Howard R. Williams & Charles J. Meyers, *Oil and Gas Terms* 652, 938 (6th ed. 1984). *Unitization* = the joint operation of all or some portion of a producing reservoir. E.g.: "Such leases contain no words of pooling or *unitization*." R.M. Myers, *The Law of Pooling and Unitization* 46 (1957). The verb *unitize* has been traced back to the mid-19th century, though then in a different context.

Communitize and *communitization* are legal NEOLOGISMS dating from the mid-20th century and recorded in no standard nonlegal dictionary. *Communitization* (known also as *pooling*) = the bringing together of small tracts sufficient for the granting of a well permit under applicable rules for the spacing of wells. E.g.:

- "The Carter Oil Company's answer also alleged that there was an agreement between appellees and certain persons to *communitize* a certain other oil lease with that of plaintiff Rhodes." *Rhodes v. Davis*, 28 N.E.2d 113, 115 (Ill. 1940).
- "There was no *communitization* as a matter of law because all of the royalty owners had not executed or ratified the lease." *May v. Cities Serv. Oil Co.*, 444 S.W.2d 822, 827 n.4 (Tex. Civ. App.—Beaumont 1969).

B. And *communize, communization.* Interestingly, the earliest appearance of *communitize* (ca. 1939) was preceded by a variant form—*communize* (= to make classifiable as community property)—which was used during the 1920s through the 1950s. Professor Patrick H. Martin of Louisiana State University, in a letter of September 1989, observed that *communitize* displaced the shorter form because American farmers, especially in Oklahoma, probably did not want their activities in the 1940s through the 1960s being described as "communizing." Imagine the discomfort that the following sentences might have caused during the McCarthy era:

- "It is clear, then, that had the legislature attempted by the Community Property Law to transform property then owned by either spouse from separate into community property, such a provision could not have stood the test of constitutionality. But how is the situation different merely because, instead of a provision of that nature, the act *communizes* the future income from such property?" *Willcox v. Penn Mut. Life Ins. Co.*, 55 A.2d 521, 526 (Pa. 1947).
- "The 1939 Community Property Act, discussed by the administratrix, is only of historical significance, and compliance therewith evidenced an intent by husband and wife to *communize* their property." *Davis's Estate v. Okla. Tax Comm'n*, 246 P.2d 318, 319 (Okla. 1952).

community charge (BrE) = *poll tax* (BrE), i.e., Prime Minister Margaret Thatcher's controversial (and doomed) measure aimed at increasing government revenue. E.g.:

- "The arguments in favour of a *community charge* are as strong as ever. The domestic rate which it replaces was an inequity founded on a fiction." Bruce Anderson, *The Poll Tax Finds a Worthy Champion*, Sunday Telegraph, 21 Jan. 1990, at 19.
- "It must have seemed like a good idea when the Conservative Party proposed it in 1987: a '*community charge*,' the same for every citizen, to cover part of the cost of local government services and replace most real estate taxes. Now, with what has since become known pejoratively as the 'poll tax' and is about to go into effect in England and Wales on April 1, even many of Prime Minister Margaret Thatcher's Conservative Party supporters wish that they had never heard of it." Craig R. Whitney, *Violent Anger Rises in Britain as Date for "Poll Tax" Nears*, N.Y. Times, 10 Mar. 1990, at 2.

community property; separate property. *Community property* = (1) a system of marital-property rights derived from the Spanish law and now existing in eight American states: Arizona, California, Idaho, Louisiana, Nevada, New Mexico, Texas, and Washington; under this system, spouses are co-owners of all real and personal property acquired during the marriage—apart from acquisitions by gift, by will, or by inheritance; or (2) property held under this system.

When used attributively as a PHRASAL ADJECTIVE, the phrase should be so hyphenated: *community-property state*, *community-property rules*, etc. See **ganancial.**

Separate property = property that a married person can sell, give away, or leave to somebody by will without his or her spouse's consent, and that remains that person's undivided property upon divorce. In specific ways, the phrase carries different meanings in community-property jurisdictions and in common-law (or equitable-distribution) jurisdictions. In community-property jurisdictions, separate property refers to a married person's property that is (1) acquired before marriage; (2) acquired during the marriage by gift, by will, or with premarital holdings; or (3) acquired after permanent separation. For the other meanings of *separate property*, see **separate property.**

community service is an increasingly common penal sentence for those whose crimes have injured the community in some way, but who (it is thought) deserve only light punishment. E.g.: "Before his brief declaration, his lawyer, Stephen E. Kaufman, asked Judge Lowe to impose a sentence of *community service*, saying that a jail term would serve no purpose." Stephen Labaton, *GAF Fined; Executive Sentenced*, N.Y. Times, 31 Mar. 1990, at 17.

communization; communize. See **communitize (B).**

commutation. See **clemency.**

commute. A. And *commutate*. *Commutate* is a technical term relating to electricity. *Commute* is the legal term meaning (1) "to exchange (a punishment or penalty) for one of less severity"; or (2) "to change (one kind of payment) into or for another; esp. to substitute a single payment for a number of payments, a fixed payment for an irregular or uncertain one, or a payment in money for one in kind (e.g., a tithe)" (*OED*). Today sense 1 of *commute* is more common <the governor commuted his prison sentence to 60 days of community service>.

B. And *pardon*. To *commute* a punishment or penalty is to reduce it, or to substitute in its place a milder punishment or penalty. To *pardon* one who has been convicted or punished is to excuse that person without exacting any further penalty.

comp is AmE slang for *compensation*—used most often in the phrase *workers' comp*. E.g.: "The House proposal . . . stands a better chance of controlling the *worker comp* drain than the Senate proposal ramrodded by trial lawyer and labor proponents." *Comp Showdown*, Dallas Morning News, 1 Dec. 1989, at 30A.

compact, n. See **treaty.**

compactible; *compactable. The first is preferred.

company; corporation. At common law, the technical legal term for an entity having a legal personality was *corporation*. The word *company* could refer to a partnership or other unincorporated association of persons. In current usage, however, *company* almost always refers to an incorporated company—i.e., a corporation. See **corporation.**

company law is the British equivalent of the American phrase *corporate law*—e.g.:

• "The bill [the 1856 Joint Stock Companies Bill] was passed, and as consolidated in the giant Companies Act of 1862 is the basis of modern *company law*." Alan Harding, *A Social History of English Law* 376 (1966).

• "My Lords, this appeal raises a question of some importance to those concerned with the niceties of *company law*." *Bushell v. Faith*, [1970] A.C. 1099, 1106 (H.L.).

See **corporate law.**

COMPANY NAMES are commonly given abbreviated forms in legal prose. Often writers go to absurd lengths to specify what the short form of the company name is in parentheses—e.g.: *Morgan Data Processing and Filming Co., Inc. (hereinafter "Morgan")*. This habit becomes ridiculous after we have seen three or four parties with distinctive names treated in this way. The better practice in most legal writing is to give the full name when the party is first identified, and then to use the short form thereafter without parenthetical explanation. When companies named, in short form, *Morgan* and *Stevens* and *Broadmoor* and *Datapoint* are involved in litigation or are parties to a contract, nobody will confuse one with another if only these abbreviated names are used. Omitting the cumbersome *hereinafter* phrases also minimizes the somnifacient effects of LEGALESE.

The exception to this advice, of course, occurs when a man named *Morgan* is sued in conjunction with his company *Morgan, Inc.* When names are confusingly similar, it is best to spell out exactly which abbreviation is used with which name, and then to use those forms consistently. This practice does not require *hereinafter*. E.g.: "Plaintiff has sued both John Morgan ('Morgan') and Morgan Inc. ('the Company')."

On the issue of creating acronyms and initialisms from company names—such as "MURB" from Morgan Utility Regulatory Board—see INITIALESE.

comparable; comparative. The first is stressed on the first syllable, the second on the second. *Comparable* = capable of being compared; worthy of comparison <comparable salaries>. *Comparative* = (1) of or pertaining to comparison <a comparative discourse of the laws>; (2) involving comparison <the field of comparative law>; or (3) estimated by comparison <comparative distances>.

Occasionally *comparative* is used where *comparable* is called for: "A new system permits women members of staff to complain if they feel they are being paid less than men of *comparative* [read *comparable*] skill." Simon Hoggart, Observer, 22 Sept. 1991, at 22. Though the *OED* documents this use of *comparative* with four examples ranging from the early 17th to the early 19th century, it labels the usage obsolete.

comparative law. See **jurisprudence (D).**

comparative negligence; contributory negligence. In the U.S., a plaintiff's *contributory negligence* (= his own carelessness for his own safety or interests, which contributes materially to damage suffered by him as a result partly of his own fault and partly of the fault of another person or persons [*CDL*]) has traditionally, in accordance with the common-law rule, acted as a complete bar to recovery. But most states have now adopted statutes providing for *comparative negligence*, which acts to reduce the plaintiff's recovery proportionally to his fault in the damage rather than to bar recovery completely. The terms *contributory negligence* and *comparative negligence* have remained quite distinct.

In G.B., however, the separate term *comparative negligence* is not used. The common-law rule of contributory negligence was altered by the Law Reform (Contributory Negligence) Act of 1945, which provides that "if the plaintiff is partly in fault, his claim is not defeated, but the damages recoverable are to be reduced to such extent as the court or jury thinks just and equitable having regard to the claimant's share in the responsibility for the damage" (*OCL1*). Hence *contributory negligence* in G.B. means roughly what *comparative negligence* means in the U.S.; rather than devising a new term, the English have continued using the old term, but with a new meaning. See **assumption of the risk.**

COMPARATIVES AND SUPERLATIVES. When comparing two items, use a comparative adjective <the greater of the two>; when comparing more than two, use the superlative <the greatest of the three>. The blunder of using the superlative adjective when only two items are compared is quite common—e.g.:

- "In a general way it may be said that there are two classes of these statutes. The *most numerous* [read *more numerous*] class abolishes in terms all distinction between the two crimes and declares that an accessory may be convicted and punished as a principal." *Karakutza v. State*, 156 N.W. 965, 966–67 (Wis. 1916).
- "That is only half the story, and not the *most* [read *more*] important half." Olin Guy Wellborn III, *The Definition of Hearsay in the Federal Rules of Evidence*, 61 Tex. L. Rev. 49, 68 (1982).
- "As stated earlier, claim interpretation is probably *the single most important half* [read *the more important half*] of the two-part infringement analysis." Mark B. Watson, Comment, *Expansion, Compression, and Relief*, 2 Roger Williams U. L. Rev. 91, 108 (1996).

comparator (= something with which something else is compared) "is a new bit of legalese. The word does exist, but is usually used in the scientific context [to denote] an instrument used for making comparisons." *Hein v. Oregon Coll. of Educ.*, 718 F.2d 910, 912–13 n.2 (9th Cir. 1983). But in legal contexts, it frequently appears in discussions of the Equal Pay Act, under which, for example, female plaintiffs contrast their remuneration with that of male *comparators. See id.* at 912. E.g.: "At trial, the EEOC sought to prove that it was entitled to recover the pay of a *comparator* male employed by Smith Pontiac for the period commencing in December 1983." *EEOC v. Mike Smith Pontiac GMC, Inc.*, 896 F.2d 524, 527 (11th Cir. 1990). As the Ninth Circuit observed, "The use of '*comparator*' in the context of the Equal Pay Act has convenience, if not elegance, to commend it." *Hein*, 718 F.2d at 913 n.2.

compare and contrast. See **contrast (B).**

COMPARISONS, FALSE. See ILLOGIC (A).

compel; impel. *Compel* is the stronger word, connoting force or coercion, with little or no volition on the part of the one compelled. *Impel* connotes persuasive urging, with some degree of volition on the part of the one impelled. *Compel* is properly used when the legal process is brought to bear on people's actions—e.g.:

- "He has not yet reached the age of 25 years, and he brings this bill to *compel* the trustees to pay to him the remainder of the trust fund." *Claflin v. Claflin*, 20 N.E. 454, 455 (Mass. 1889).
- "The pleas are no more improperly *compelled* than is the decision by a defendant at the close of the State's evidence at trial that he must take the stand or face certain conviction." *Brady v. U.S.*, 397 U.S. 742, 750 (1970) (per White, J.).

In the following sentences *impel* is properly used, the object (*court*) being an UNDERSTOOD WORD:

- "With these principles in mind, we [the justices of the court of appeals] are *impelled* to agree with the probate court's decision that appellants violated the *in terrorem* clause of decedent's will." *In re Goyette's Estate*, 258 Cal. App. 2d 768, 772 (Ct. App. 1968).
- "Applying these notions to the present case *impels* [the court to] the conclusion that appellant's motion at the close of all the evidence should be read as a motion for a directed verdict." *Elliott v. Group Med. & Surgical Serv.*, 714 F.2d 556, 562 (5th Cir. 1983).

But the courts have been less than punctilious about the distinction between *compel* and *impel*. Sentences like the following are common: "Our analysis *compels* the conclusion that FERC lacks the authority to suspend initial rate filings." *Middle S. Energy, Inc. v. F.E.R.C.*, 747 F.2d 763, 765 (D.C. Cir. 1984). Perhaps this use of *compel* stems from a desire for the court (again, the understood object) to suggest that it simply had no choice in its holding. The device is largely rhetorical and is so clichéd as to be ineffective. Lon Fuller—through the voice of a fictitious judge—subtly mocked the device in a famous article: "For us to assert that the law we uphold and expound *compels* us to a conclusion we are ashamed of . . . seems to me to amount to an admission that the law of this Commonwealth no longer pretends to incorporate justice." *The Case of the Speluncean Explorers*, 62 Harv. L. Rev. 616, 620 (1949). See **impel.**

compellable, primarily a legal term, has traditionally been used in the broad sense "that may be compelled (to do something)." E.g.: "Both Plato and Aristotle approved abortion for this purpose, the latter suggesting that a mother should be *compellable* to commit abortion after she had borne an allotted number of children." Glanville Williams, *The Sanctity of Life and the Criminal Law* 148 (1957).

Today the word is more widely used in the sense "subject to being compelled (to testify)." The term is far more common in BrE than in AmE. E.g.:

- "Not until 1898 were accused persons made competent (but not *compellable*) witnesses at their trial." Theodore F.T. Plucknett, *A Concise History of the Common Law* 437 (5th ed. 1956).
- "It is only within certain limits that husband and wife are competent, and within narrower limits that they are *compellable*, to give evidence against one another, in criminal proceedings." William Geldart, *Introduction to English Law* 49 (D.C.M. Yardley ed., 9th ed. 1984).

compendious means "abridged, succinct," not "voluminous," as several federal judges mistakenly believe—e.g.:

- "We need go no further. Having attentively reviewed the *compendious* record in this long-running suit, we discern no reversible error." *HMG Prop. Investors, Inc. v. Parque Indus. Rio Canas, Inc.*, 847 F.2d 908, 919–20 (1st Cir. 1988) (referring elsewhere to "the hoariness of the controversy and the girth of the record" [at 919]).
- "Of course, Richmond could have built an even more *compendious* record of past discrimination, one including additional stark statistics and additional individual accounts of past discrimination." *City of Richmond v. J.A. Croson Co.*, 488 U.S. 469, 547–48 (1989) (Marshall, J., dissenting).

Perhaps the error stems from the idea that a compendium is, at best, a fairly comprehensive abridgment. But properly speaking, the emphasis falls on *abridgment*, not on *comprehensive*. And some would say that the word does not at all suggest comprehensiveness: "But as a *compendium* of feminist art history . . . and a catalogue—commodious though not, of course, comprehensive—of women artists, this will be an enormously useful work." L. Hughes-Hallet, Book Rev., Sunday Times, 10 June 1990, at 8-10.

compensable. A. And *compensatory*. A nuance exists between these terms. *Compensable damages* = those damages capable of being recovered; damages for which compensation is available. *Compensatory damages* = those damages intended to make the plaintiff whole again; actual damages. *Compensable damages* are hypothetical; *compensatory damages* are those actually awarded or to be awarded to a party.

The form **compensatable* is an error for *compensable*: "[The] loss [is] *compensatable* [read *compensable*] by interest of not more than $405." *Metz v. Tusico, Inc.*, 167 F.Supp. 393, 398 (E.D. Va. 1958).

B. Spelling. *Compensable*—not **compensible*—is the preferred form. The *-ible* spelling is incorrect; the frequency of its use is explained perhaps by a mistaken analogy to *comprehensible*.

*compensatable. See **compensable (A).**

compensate. A. Transitive or Intransitive. *Compensate* may or may not take *for*, and either way means "to make up for, to counterbalance." E.g.: "When it is conceded that mental suffering may be *compensated (for)* in actions of tort, the right of the plaintiff to recover in this case is established." *Mentzer v. W.U. Tel. Co.*,

62 N.W. 1, 5 (Iowa 1895). The modern tendency is to omit *for*, but the sound of a sentence may outweigh the interests of concision.

B. And *recompense*. These verbs are almost precisely synonymous <to recompense the victim for his injuries>, but *recompense* is a FORMAL WORD less commonly used. See **recompense.**

compensation = (1) remuneration; that which is given in recompense; (2) (in AmE) salary or wages; or (3) (in BrE) consideration paid for expropriated land. For an early treatise devoted to compensation in sense 3, see Henry C. Richards & John P.H. Soper, *The Law and Practice of Compensation* (n.d. [1898]); though nearly unknown in AmE, this BrE sense is not confined to lawyers, as witness the lyrics of Jethro Tull's popular song about compulsory purchase, "Farm on the Freeway" ("They say they paid me *compensation* / That's not what I'm chasing, I was a rich man before yesterday.").

In sense 1, the phrase *money compensation* might at first appear to be a REDUNDANCY. But *compensation* can take forms other than money, as John Austin's quotation in the *OED* makes clear by referring to *compensation in money or in kind*. Here Geldart is contrasting *money compensation* with other kinds, such as strict performance in equity: "With few exceptions the only thing that Common Law can do is to give him *money compensation*." William Geldart, *Introduction to English Law* 29 (D.C.M. Yardley ed., 9th ed. 1984). See **pay,** n.

compensatory; *compensative. The second is a NEEDLESS VARIANT. See **compensable (A).** Cf. **recompensive.**

*compensible. See **compensable (B).**

competence; competency. A. Of Persons. Though H.W. Fowler considered *competency* a NEEDLESS VARIANT, these terms have come to exhibit some DIFFERENTIATION, which should be further encouraged. *Competence* usually has the lay sense "a basic or minimal ability to do something." E.g.:

- "It does not follow that *incompetence* of counsel is necessarily established by omission of a claim." *Jones v. Estelle*, 722 F.2d 159, 167 (5th Cir. 1983).
- "An exhaustive study of the deficiencies of applying a mechanism originally developed to decide who owns title to Blackacre . . . is beyond either the demands of this writing or the *competence* and available time of its writer." *State of La. ex rel. Guste v. M/V Testbank*, 752 F.2d 1019, 1032–33 (5th Cir. 1985).

Today *competency* has a specific legal sense: "the ability to understand problems and make decisions; ability to stand trial." A severely mentally retarded person, an incompetent, is said to suffer from legal *incompetency*. *Competency to stand trial* is the usual phrase.

In reference to qualifications in general, as of a witness to a will, *competence* is the usual form—e.g.:

- "The affidavit of Christensen and the combined affidavit of Lott and her father appear to be made on personal knowledge, and both recite facts sufficient to establish the affiants' *competence* to attest to the facts set forth in the affidavits." *Capital Assets Fin. Servs. v. Lindsay*, 956 P.2d 1090, 1094 (Utah Ct. App. 1998).
- "Such facts often go to the legal *competence* [i.e., the qualifications to testify in court] of witnesses or litigants, or the jurisdiction of the court." *People v. Kim*, 202 P.3d 436, 453 (Cal. 2009).

Only when the reference is clearly and solely to mental disability is *competency* the preferred form.

Sometimes *competency* is confused with *competence*—e.g.: "Where the 'station agent' incidentally acts as the telegraph agent in many sparsely settled communities where the business will not permit the employment of a full time telegraph agent, it is apparent that such *competency* [read *competence*] cannot be secured." *Flynn v. Reinke*, 225 N.W. 742, 743 (Wis. 1929).

And vice versa: "[Appellants] contend that their son lacks the mental *competence* [read *competency*] to waive his legal rights, and they maintain that he lacks the competence to decide whether to pursue or waive the benefits of 28 U.S.C. § 2254." *Rumbaugh v. McKaskle*, 730 F.2d 291, 292 (5th Cir. 1984).

Avoid the INELEGANT VARIATION of alternating between the two terms in reference to the same thing, as here: "Enriquez's *competency* challenge is twofold. First, he contends that he was denied due process because the state trial court did not . . . hold a hearing to determine his *competence* [read *competency*] to stand trial. . . . [T]he Supreme Court [has] held that a defendant has a procedural due process right to a *competency* hearing." *Enriquez v. Procunier*, 752 F.2d 111, 113 (5th Cir. 1984).

B. Used of Adjudicative or Rulemaking Bodies. *Competence* is frequently used for qualification or capacity of an official body to act in some way—e.g.:

- "All measures relating to the conduct or to the rights of individuals . . . are within the *competence* of a Legislature with the general powers of legislation conferred by our Constitutions." *Ellingham v. Dye*, 99 N.E. 1, 5 (Ind. 1912).
- "That [12-month] rule recognizes the *competence* of the legislature to choose its words with care." *Va. Dep't of Health v. NRV Real Estate, LLC*, 677 S.E.2d 276, 279 (Va. 2009).
- "With respect to most crimes the credibility of a witness is peculiarly within the *competence* of the jury, whose common experience affords sufficient basis for the assessment of credibility." *State v. Hakala*, 763 N.W.2d 346, 350 (Minn. Ct. App. 2009).

C. Of Evidence. In older legal writing, *competence* referred to the admissibility of evidence. Hence references to the *competence of evidence* were once fairly common. Again, *competency* is a NEEDLESS VARIANT in this context. See **competent** & **incompetence.**

competent is used in archaic senses in the law. Generally the word is used only of persons, whereas in law it is used of courts, of evidence, and of cases. It is even used indefinitely: "In the present case, it was *competent* for the defendants to show that the selling

agent made the alleged representations concerning the horse." *City Nat'l Bank of Columbus v. Jordan*, 117 N.W. 758, 760 (Iowa 1908). This use of the word, in the sense "proper, appropriate," was labeled obsolete by the *OED*. Yet it still appears in legal writing, albeit less and less frequently. E.g.:

- "In the present case it was *competent* for the plaintiff below to show, and he did show, that, as between him and the other signers of the note, he was not a joint maker." *Hecker v. Mahler*, 60 N.E. 555, 556 (Ohio 1901).
- "The general rule is that the recital of a written instrument as to consideration is not conclusive, and it is *competent* to inquire into the consideration and show by parol evidence the nature of the real consideration." *Lakeway Co. v. Leon Howard, Inc.*, 578 S.W.2d 163, 166 (Tex. Civ. App.—Tyler 1979).

More frequently, *competent* = (1) (of a judge or court) having jurisdiction or authority to act <when a court of competent jurisdiction has obtained control of property, that control may not be disturbed by any other court>; (2) (of witnesses) having capacity; qualified to testify in court concerning the material facts <a will is void unless attested by the number of competent witnesses required by statute>; (3) (of a case) within the jurisdiction of the court; or (4) (of evidence) admissible. See **competence** & **incompetent.**

This word is still further complicated in legal contexts by its frequent appearance in its lay sense ("professionally adequate; properly qualified")—e.g.:

- "A jury could conclude that [appellee] had completely failed to fulfill its contractual obligation to provide a *competent* service engineer to supervise installation of the purchased equipment." *Reynolds Metals Co. v. Westinghouse Elec. Corp.*, 758 F.2d 1073, 1077 (5th Cir. 1985).
- "Our review of the sentencing transcript likewise reflects that Keiser's attorney was well prepared and provided *competent* representation at Keiser's sentencing hearing." *U.S. v. Keiser*, 578 F.3d 897, 902 (8th Cir. 2009).

competitive = (1) of, relating to, or based on competition <competitive bidding>; (2) (of business, its products or services, or their pricing) favorable in quality and value when compared with what is otherwise available in the marketplace <our prices are competitive>; (3) constituting or amounting to a competitor <you agree not to work for any competitive business>; or (4) driven by a strong desire to compete and succeed <she is a highly competitive person>. All four senses are standard.

compilation; collective work. *Compilation* = a collection of literary works arranged in an original way; esp., a work formed by collecting and assembling preexisting materials or data that are selected, coordinated, or arranged in such a way that the resulting product constitutes an original work of authorship. *Collective work* = a publication (such as a periodical issue, an anthology, or an encyclopedia) in which several contributions, constituting separate and independent works in their own right, are assembled into a copyrightable whole.

complainant; complainer. *Complainant* is, both in AmE and in BrE (except Scotland), the technical term for one who enters a legal complaint against another. It is traditionally the term used in courts of equity, but by the early 20th century the equity courts had already adopted the term used in courts of law—*plaintiff. See* Walter C. Clephane, *Equity Pleading* vi (1926).

Some writers prefer *complainant* over *prosecutrix* in the context of sexual offenses—e.g.: "In *State v. Connelly*, a turn-of-the-century Minnesota case, the *complainant* was a seventeen-year-old girl who testified that she had been raped by the priest who moved in with his family next door." Susan Estrich, *Real Rape* 44 (1987). See **prosecutrix.**

Complainer is the Scottish equivalent of *complainant.* E.g.: "As soon as he was outside the hotel, the *complainer* was struck on the head and brought to the ground, where he was set upon by a number of individuals." *McInnes v. HM Advocate*, [2010] S.L.T. 266. (Scot.) It is also sometimes used instead of *appellant*— e.g.: "The *complainer* pleaded guilty under a material misapprehension." *Bowes v. McGowan*, [2010] H.C.J.A.C. 55. (Scot.)

In AmE, *complainer* is generally understood as meaning "one who habitually complains." Cf. **pursuer.** See **plaintiff.**

complainee has appeared as a correlative of *complainer*—e.g.: "The action is one seeking to recover concealed assets of the estate of Isabel S. Jones, deceased, which the complainant alleges to be in the possession of *complainee*." *In re Jones's Estate*, 122 N.E.2d 111, 111–12 (Ohio Ct. App. 1952). Perhaps it has something to commend it, but that something is hard to imagine. Proper names would surely be preferable. See -EE & PARTY APPELLATIONS.

complainer. See **complainant.**

complaint, well-pleaded. See **well-pleaded complaint.**

complement. See **compliment.**

compliance. See **suggestibility.**

*complicitous; complicit, adj. Although **complicitous* is the traditional term (dating from the mid-19th century), it appears only rarely in comparison to *complicit*, which is a BACK-FORMATION made on the analogy of *implicit*. Dating from the early 1970s, *complicit* has been an enormously successful NEOLOGISM—e.g.:

- "By validating Florida's rule, today's majority is *complicit* in the Bar's censorship." *Fla. Bar v. Went for It, Inc.*, 515 U.S. 618, 645 (1995) (Kennedy, J., dissenting).
- "Whether Arthur Andersen was altogether misled or, on the other hand, knew the structure of the contract arrangements and was *complicit* to some degree, is not clear at this stage of the case." *Stoneridge Inv. Partners,*

LLC v. Scientific-Atlanta, 552 U.S. 148, 154 (2008) (per Kennedy, J.).

- "Property owners not directly involved or *complicit* in the taking did not have to shoulder the primary burden of rectification." Bernadette Atuahene, *Property Rights & the Demands of Transformation*, 31 Mich. J. Int'l L. 765, 813 n.192 (2010).

Because it is at least as well formed as its alternative and has now established itself as the more common form, *complicit* should be accepted as standard. **Complicitous*, despite its promising beginnings, should now be regarded as a NEEDLESS VARIANT.

complicity, which derives from the idea of being an accomplice, has been extended "to include guilt based upon induced conduct of an *innocent* person." Rollin M. Perkins & Ronald N. Boyce, *Criminal Law* 767 (3d ed. 1982). That broadening of sense is probably a desirable one because the conceptual subtlety involved is unlikely to give rise to a widely adopted verbal subtlety.

compliment; complement. These words are often confounded. The first means "to praise," the second "to supplement appropriately or adequately."

comply takes *with*, not *to*—e.g.:

- "We therefore strike the Amended Answer without prejudice and grant defendant leave to file an answer that *complies* in form *to* [read *with*] the local rules within thirty days." *Linc Fin. Corp. v. Onwuteaka*, 1995 WL 708575, at *2 (N.D. Ill. 1995).
- "Where a defendant *complies to* [read *complies with*] one of the demands for relief in a complaint, does this show that there was indeed a claim stated?" *Osborn v. Painter*, 909 P.2d 960, 962 n.1 (Wyo. 1996).
- "To declare petitioner ineligible for [the residential drug-abuse treatment program] because he *complied to* [read *complied with*] court-ordered release terms is contrary to what Congress intended." *Salvador-Orta v. Daniels*, 531 F.Supp.2d 1249, 1253 (D. Or. 2008).

compose. See **comprise.**

composition means, at common law, (1) the act of adjusting a debt, or avoiding a liability, by compensation agreed to by the parties; or (2) the compensation paid as part of such an agreement. This noun corresponds to the verb *to compound* and often means merely "a compounding." (See **compound,** vb.) E.g.:

- "This being by act of the creditor, since without his participation the *composition* would be ineffective to affect the debt, the surety is discharged." Laurence P. Simpson, *Handbook on the Law of Suretyship* 312 (1950) (corresponding to sense 2 of *compound*).
- "If a slave killed a freeman, he was to be surrendered for one half of the *composition* to the relatives of the slain man, and the master was to pay the other half." Oliver Wendell Holmes Jr., *The Common Law* 17 (1881) (corresponding to sense 3 of *compound*).

Similarly, *compose* is sometimes used as a synonym for *compound* (in the legal sense): "It was . . . an attempt [by the defendant] to *compose* a dispute, . . . to find a mutually satisfactory middle ground between the two divergent conceptions of the original offer to sell." *Frese v. Gaston*, 161 F.2d 890, 891 (D.C. Cir. 1947) (per curiam).

compos mentis. See **non compos mentis.**

compound, vb., has undergone SLIPSHOD EXTENSION from its primarily legal sense. The word has four basic meanings: (1) "to let a fund grow by adding interest earned to the principal, thereby earning more interest"; (2) "to put together, combine, construct, compose" <to compound sand with gravel>; (3) "to settle (any matter) by a money payment, in lieu of other liability" <to compound a debt>; and (4) "to forbear from prosecuting for consideration, or to cause (a prosecutor) so to forbear" <to compound a felony>. For senses 3 and 4—the legal senses—the noun corresponding to this verb is *composition*. (See **composition.**)

Sense 4 has historically been the more common one—e.g.: "Among certain grizzled sea gossips . . . went a rumor perdue that the master-at-arms was a *chevalier* who had volunteered into the king's navy by way of *compounding* for some mysterious swindle whereof he had been arraigned at the King's Bench." Herman Melville, *Billy Budd* 28 (1891).

The word has been sloppily extended because "nonlawyers have misapprehended the meaning of *to compound a felony.* . . . [The word] is now widely abused to mean: to make worse, aggravate, multiply, increase." Philip Howard, *New Words for Old* 19 (1977). Examples of this looseness of diction abound now even in legal writing. E.g.:

- "This deliberate perpetuation of the unconstitutional dual system can only have *compounded* the harm of such a system." *Green v. County Sch. Bd.*, 391 U.S. 430, 438 (1968) (per Brennan, J.).
- "These are largely data drawn at the national level, with a few state overviews added, to show the general picture of diminishing competition for congressional office and the particular effect of redistricting in *compounding* the loss of electoral competition." Samuel Issacharoff & Jonathan Nagler, *Protected from Politics: Diminishing Margins of Electoral Competition in U.S. Congressional Elections*, 68 Ohio St. L.J. 1121, 1122–23 (2007).
- "Respondent led the client in this matter to believe that he was taking care of the situation when in fact he did nothing to remedy his earlier default and only *compounded* the harm to the client." *In re Anderson*, 979 A.2d 1206, 1220 (D.C. 2009).
- "Under this style of reasoning, any further remedy beyond the elimination of formal discrimination runs the risk of *compounding* the loss of personal responsibility that attends normlessness." Joseph E. Kennedy, *The Jena Six, Mass Incarceration, and the Remoralization of Civil Rights*, 44 Harv. Civ. Rights-Civ. Libs. L. Rev. 477, 493 (2009).

It is not quite true, then, at least in the U.S., that "to write 'he *compounded* the offence' (when what is meant is that he did something to aggravate the offence) is to vex every lawyer who reads the sentence,

and to provoke numbers of them to litigious correspondence in defence of their jargon." Philip Howard, *New Words for Old* 20 (1977). Nevertheless, we may justifiably lament the fact that generations of young lawyers will not understand the phrase *to compound a felony* when they see it in the older lawbooks.

Notably, *compound* has also been used in both criminal and civil cases to refer to a settlement (sense 3)—e.g.:

- "The plaintiff had heard from *some one* [read *someone*] not named [that] the defendant had *compounded* the case over a glass of liquor without the accusation being retracted or compensated in any other way." *Johnston v. Lance*, 7 N.C. (Ired.) 448 (1847).
- "[Offenders] usually *pled* [read *pleaded*] guilty or *compounded* the case with the department." Richard Magnus, *The Confluence of Law and Policy in Leveraging Technology*, 12 Wm. & Mary Bill Rts. J. 661, 674 (2004). See **pleaded.**

Whereas *compounding a felony* is a criminal offense, *compounding a civil case* is perfectly proper. In civil contexts, however, *settle* is by far the more common term.

compounder = (1) one who compounds for a liability, debt, or charge; (2) one who compounds a felony or offense; (3) one who pays a lump sum in discharge of a liability requiring recurrent payments; (4) one who, as a stranger to a dispute, tries to help parties settle their differences (an arbitrator with extensive equitable powers was formerly known as an *amicable compounder*); or (5) one who knows of another's crime and agrees, for some reward received or promised, not to inform or prosecute.

compounding a crime = accepting something of value under an unlawful agreement not to prosecute a known criminal offender or to handicap the prosecution. The sense differs from that which many readers would intuitively (and mistakenly) attribute to the phrase (something like *adding to a crime*). See **compound.**

comprehend. In lay contexts, this word means, almost exclusively, "to grasp mentally"; in legal contexts, it frequently means "to include, encompass." E.g.:

- "By confining herself to the use of the generic term, the present testatrix *comprehended* all of the various religious, educational, benevolent, and humanitarian objects that the single word 'charity' connotes." *In re Jordan's Estate*, 197 A. 150, 150–51 (Pa. 1938).
- "No judicial opinion can *comprehend* the protean variety of the street encounter, and we can only judge the facts of the case before us." *Terry v. Ohio*, 392 U.S. 1, 15 (1968) (per Warren, C.J.).
- "The statute thus *comprehends* damages personal to the shipper, such as damages for delay in shipment." *S. Pac. Transp. Co. v. U.S.*, 456 F.Supp. 931, 938 (E.D. Cal. 1978).

See **apprehend.** Cf. **embrace.**

comprise; compose. A. Generally. Correct use of these words is simple, but increasingly rare. The parts *compose* the whole; the whole *comprises* the parts; the whole is *composed* of the parts; the parts are *comprised* in the whole. *Comprise*, the more troublesome word in this pair, means "to contain; to consist of." E.g.:

- "Every act causing an obstruction to another in the exercise of the right *comprised* within this description . . . would, if damage should be caused thereby to the party obstructed, be a violation of this prohibition." *Mogul S.S. Co. v. McGregor*, [1889] L.R. 23 Q.B.D. 598, 607–08 (C.A.).
- "The evidence clearly showed that the committee *comprised* members from inside as well as outside the Bank." *Denton v. First Nat'l Bank of Waco*, 765 F.2d 1295, 1300 (5th Cir. 1985).

A number of mistakes occur with *comprise*:

B. Erroneous Use of **is comprised of.* The phrase **is comprised of* is always wrong and should be replaced by either *is composed of* or *comprises*. E.g.:

- "The law of the professional lawyer *was comprised of* [read *comprised*] rules derived from judges' *dicta*." Alan Harding, *A Social History of English Law* 134 (1966).
- "We also judicially notice that the 123rd Judicial District Court of Shelby County *is comprised of* [read *comprises*] two counties, Panola and Shelby." *Whittington v. State*, 680 S.W.2d 505, 508 (Tex. App.—Tyler 1984).

Sometimes the simplest of verb phrases is what is needed: "In the course of the search, the agents noticed that the ceiling of the barracks was *comprised of* [read *made up of*] removable acoustical tiles." *U.S. v. Cherry*, 759 F.2d 1196, 1199 (5th Cir. 1985). Following is the correct use of *is composed of* where the careless writer would put *is comprised of*: "The biopsy needle *is composed of* a stationary stylet and a retractable cannula that slides over the stylet." *Baran v. Medical Device Techs., Inc.*, 616 F.3d 1309, 1311 (Fed. Cir. 2010) (per Bryson, J.).

C. Comprise for *are comprised in.* E.g.: "Discriminatory tests are impermissible unless shown, by professionally acceptable methods, to be 'predictive of or significantly correlated with important elements of work behavior which *comprise* [read *are comprised in*] or are relevant to the job or jobs for which candidates are being evaluated.'" *Albemarle Paper Co. v. Moody*, 422 U.S. 405, 431 (1975) (per Stewart, J.).

D. Comprise for *constitute.* *Comprise* is more and more commonly used in a sense opposite its true meaning ("to contain, include, embrace"). It should not be used for *compose* or *constitute*. E.g.:

- "To the extent that (pension) rights derive from employment during coverture, they *comprise* [read *constitute*] a community asset subject to division in a dissolution proceeding." *In re Marriage of Brown*, 126 Cal. Rptr. 633, 635 (Ct. App. 1976).
- "The challenges involved are extraordinarily complex; they *comprise* [read *constitute*] a whole other category of issues that require comprehensive regulatory oversight." Jack E. Henningfield & Mitch Zeller, *Could Science-Based Regulation Make Tobacco Products Less Addictive?*, 3 Yale J. Health Pol'y, L. & Ethics 127, 138 (2002).
- "A forced governmental disclosure of ingredients *which comprise* [read *that constitute*] a company's trade secret formula is a facially unconstitutional taking." Delia

Gervin, *You Can Stand Under My Umbrella*, 15 J. Intell. Prop. L. 315, 332 (2008).

E. Comprise for *are.* A related but even odder error is misusing *comprise* for *are*—e.g.: "The appellants *comprise* [read *are*] nine of sixteen defendants convicted in the federal district court . . . on one or more counts of an eleven-count indictment." *U.S. v. Acosta*, 763 F.2d 671, 674 (5th Cir. 1985).

F. Correct use of *comprise.* For a word prone to such a profusion of misuses, it seems only fitting to illustrate its proper use—e.g.:

- "The advisory group, which *comprises* attorneys and representatives of major categories of litigants, will analyze the trends in case filings, the demands on the court's resources, and the principal causes of cost and delay in civil litigation." Theodore R. Tetzlaff, *Federal Courts, Their Rules, and Their Roles*, Litig. 1, 1 (Spring 1992).
- "Together, the first two volumes of 'The Years of Lyndon Johnson' *comprise*, with notes, 1,387 pages." Frank J. Prial, *Author's Kind Word for Johnson*, N.Y. Times, 31 Mar. 1990, at 13.

G. Compose in the sense of *compound.* See **composition**.

compromise = (1) to agree to settle a matter <the parties compromised and dropped their claims against each other>; or (2) to endanger <the disclosure of the information might compromise intelligence sources>. See **accord and satisfaction**.

compromise and settlement. See **accord and satisfaction**.

compromise and settlement agreement. This is the more usual (and the better) wording—not **compromise settlement agreement*.

*compromise settlement agreement. See **compromise and settlement agreement**.

comptroller (= an official in charge of finance, audits, and the like) is pronounced identically with *controller*. To pronounce the *-p-* has traditionally been considered semiliterate. *Comptroller* is used especially of public offices; *controller*, however, means the same thing and is not deceptively spelled. *Comptroller* is more common in AmE than in BrE, where it is archaic.

The strange spelling of *comptroller* originated in the zeal of 15th-century Latinists who sought to respell medieval French loanwords on the "purer" Latin model. Hence *account* became *accompt*, and *count* became *compt*. *Comptroller* is one of the few survivals among such respellings, and it is also one of the bungles perpetrated by those ardent Latinists: the *con-* in *controller* was mistakenly associated with the word *count*, when in fact it is merely the Latin prefix (the true derivation being fr. L. *contrā-rotulātor*). So the respelling should never have been. But we are several centuries too late in correcting it.

compulsive; compulsory. Today, *compulsive* primarily means "of, pertaining to, resulting from, or suggesting psychological obsession." Although it was once commonly used in the sense "mandatory, coercive," that meaning is best denoted today by the word *compulsory*. In short, the two words have undergone DIFFERENTIATION. Therefore, in the following passage, *compulsory* is the better choice—if only to prevent a MISCUE: "Perhaps the most natural usage would take 'damages caused by a public vessel' to mean physical damages arising out of her operation. But there is nothing *compulsive* [read *compulsory*] about such an understanding." Grant Gilmore & Charles L. Black Jr., *The Law of Admiralty* 984 (2d ed. 1974).

compulsory joinder. See **joinder (c).**

compulsory purchase is the BrE term for *expropriation* or the exercise of *eminent domain*. Here the phrase appears in verb form: "Tophams also contended that, since the racecourse would in any event be closed down and left derelict, when it would be *compulsorily purchased* by the local authority for housing purposes, an injunction would be of no benefit to Lord Sefton." *Earl of Sefton v. Tophams, Ltd.*, [1967] 1 A.C. 50, 55 (H.L.). See **compensation, condemn** & **eminent domain.**

compurgator is stuffy for *character witness*, unless (as in the first two examples) the context is historical:

- "The old '*compurgators*' have come to life in our present day 'character witnesses.'" Ephraim Tutt, *Yankee Lawyer* 73 n.* (1943).
- "Although the historical origins of the 'voucher' rule are uncertain, it appears to be a remnant of primitive English trial practice in which 'oath-takers' or '*compurgators*' were called to stand behind a particular party's position in any controversy." *Chambers v. Mississippi*, 410 U.S. 284, 296 (1973) (per Powell, J.).
- "The *Partin* inquiries test the witnesses' capacity and competence; the instant ones place the psychiatrist in the posture of a *compurgator* [read *character witness*]." *U.S. v. Wertis*, 505 F.2d 683, 685 (5th Cir. 1974).
- "All but one witness, including one of appellant's two *compurgators* [read *character witnesses*], testified that appellant could receive a fair trial." *James v. State*, 772 S.W.2d 84, 93 (Tex. Crim. App. 1989) (en banc).

computerize. See -IZE.

comstockery (often capitalized) refers to prudish censorship, or attempted censorship, of supposed immorality in art or literature. In 1873, the American Congress passed the so-called Comstock Law, a federal act to control obscenity, pushed through by one Anthony Comstock (1844–1915), who was a leader of the New York Society for the Suppression of Vice. George Bernard Shaw invented the word *comstockery*, pejorative from the first, when he wrote in the *New York Times* in 1905: "*Comstockery* is the world's standing joke at the expense of the United States."

conceal = (1) to keep from the knowledge of others; refrain from disclosing; or (2) to remove or keep out of sight or notice; to hide. In a statute defining the crime of an accessory after the fact, sense 2 obtains—the word *conceal* implies an act or refusal to act by which the person intends to prevent or hinder a crime's discovery—a mere failure to give information is not enough. *See* Rollin M. Perkins & Ronald N. Boyce, *Criminal Law* 750 (3d ed. 1982).

concede. See **cede.**

concedely. See **confessedly, reportedly** & -EDLY.

***concensus.** See **consensus.**

concept; conception. Both *concept* and *conception* may mean "an abstract idea." *Conception* also means "the act of forming abstract ideas." H.W. Fowler wrote that *conception* is the ordinary term, *concept* the philosophical term. (*MEU1* 88.) Often the latter is used as a high-flown equivalent of a simpler word such as *design, program, thought,* or *idea*. When not used pretentiously for one of those simpler words, *concept* is likely to have negative connotations, as here: "Yet no *concept*, or combination of *concepts*, or rule built out of *concepts*—as all legal rules are built—can of itself provide an automatic solution to the simplest conceivable human problem." Fred Rodell, *Woe Unto You, Lawyers!* 37 (1939).

Wesley Newman Hohfeld used the more appropriate word in titling his *Fundamental Legal Conceptions* (1919). Similarly, the better ordinary use is illustrated here: "That requirement, in safeguarding the liberty of the citizen against deprivation through the action of the State, embodies the fundamental *conceptions* of justice which lie at the base of our civil and political institutions." *Albright v. Oliver*, 510 U.S. 266, 298–99 (1994) (per Stevens, J.).

One prominent legal philosopher has purported to invent a distinction between the terms on another basis: "The contrast between *concept* and *conception* is . . . a contrast between levels of abstraction at which the interpretation of the practice [courtesy] can be studied. At the first level agreement collects around discrete ideas that are uncontroversially employed in all interpretations; at the second the controversy latent in this abstraction is identified and taken up." Ronald Dworkin, *Law's Empire* 71 (1986). Dworkin then immediately adds: "Exposing this structure may help to sharpen argument and will in any case improve the community's understanding of its intellectual environment." *Id.* No, it certainly won't, and neither will reading this passage in its fuller context. The distinction is wholly factitious. Yet others have tried to make it meaningful: "A contrast between levels of abstraction at which the interpretation of the practices can be studied. At the first level agreement collects around discrete ideas [concepts] that are uncontroversially employed in all interpretations; at the second the controversy latent in this abstraction is identified and taken up [to produce conceptions]." Brian Burge-Hendrix, *Epistemic Uncertainty and Legal Theory* 23 (2008) (brackets in original—and citing Dworkin). Epistemic uncertainty indeed!

conceptual; conceptualistic; conceptive; conceptional. These words are very close. *Conceptual* and *conceptional* both mean "of or pertaining to a conception or idea"—*conceptual* being the usual term. *Conceptive* = of or relating to the process of mental conception (i.e., conceiving).

When not being used as a NEEDLESS VARIANT of *conceptual*, the word *conceptional* serves as the adjective corresponding to a different kind of conception (= the fertilization of an egg): "It is not easy to reconcile this attitude with the papal concession of some kinds of *anti-conceptional* measures." Glanville Williams, *The Sanctity of Life and the Criminal Law* 69 (1957).

Conceptualistic = (1) of or relating to the philosophical or psychological doctrine of conceptualism (a nonlegal technical sense); or (2) employing or based on conceptions. In sense 2, *conceptualistic* is more than slightly pejorative: "My initial point is that a substantial degree of conceptualism is inescapable in law, and a substantial degree of *conceptualistic* argument is evident in law." Paul N. Cox, *An Interpretation and (Partial) Defense of Legal Formalism*, 36 Ind. L. Rev. 57, 62 (2003).

concerned with, be. This verb phrase is weak; usually *concern* can be put into the active voice with a gain in directness. E.g.:

- "[The *Green* case] *was concerned with* [read *concerned*] whether a violation [that] continued after a freedom-of-choice plan was initiated required affirmative action." *Geier v. University of Tenn.*, 597 F.2d 1056, 1065 (6th Cir. 1979).
- "This appeal *is primarily concerned with* [read *primarily concerns*] [the plaintiffs'] § 1983 claims." *Forman v. Richmond Police Dep't*, 104 F.3d 950, 954 (7th Cir. 1997).

Cf. **deal with.**

concert = agreement of two or more persons or parties in a plan, design, or enterprise. E.g.: "The Third Circuit reversed, finding direct and circumstantial evidence of *concert* of action tending to show that injurious *concert* also occurred." Steven A. Childress, *A New Era for Summary Judgments*, 116 F.R.D. 183, 185 (1987). This sense thrives in legal language but is all but defunct in lay language, apart from the adjective *concerted*, and the phrase *in concert*. See **concerted.**

In concert = working collectively toward the same end. It does not mean merely "together," though it is sometimes loosely used in that sense—e.g.: "The jury could find that Riley's predisposition, his intoxication, or both factors acting *in concert* [read *together*] proximately caused his injury." *Osborne v. Twin Town Bowl, Inc.*, 749 N.W.2d 367, 380 (Minn. 2008). Here the phrase is correctly used: "Under New Jersey law, a plaintiff asserting a claim for civil conspiracy must demonstrate that a combination of two or more persons acted *in concert* to commit an unlawful act, or to commit a lawful act by unlawful means." *Marshall v. Fenstermacher*, 388 F.Supp.2d 536, 552 (E.D. Pa. 2005). (Note the REDUNDANCY of *a combination . . . acted in concert*: delete *a combination of*.)

concessive; concessionary; *concessional. *Concessive* = of or tending to concession <a concessive stance in negotiating>. *Concessionary* = of or relating to concession or a concession <the concessionary company—i.e., the one with a concession>. *Concessional* is a NEEDLESS VARIANT of either of the previous two; here it appears where *concessive* would serve better: "Generous *concessional* [read *concessive*] treatment of debt-burdened African economies is essential if the continent's development crisis is to end." *Aid and Reform in Nigeria*, Fin. Times, 6 Jan. 1992, at 10.

conciliation. See **mediation (B).**

conciliatory; *conciliative. *Conciliatory* = (1) tending to conciliate; or (2) of or relating to conciliation or mediation. *Conciliative* is a NEEDLESS VARIANT—e.g.:

- "After *conciliative* [read *conciliatory*] efforts failed, plaintiff filed this action." *Barnes v. Lerner Shops of Tex., Inc.*, 323 F.Supp. 617, 619 (S.D. Tex. 1971).
- "Both agencies have incentives to compromise. . . . This *conciliative* [read *conciliatory*] process could be initiated effectively by recognizing areas of common interest." Jerry W. Markham & Rita M. Stephanz, *The Stock Market Crash of 1987*, 76 Geo. L.J. 1993, 2030–31 (1988).

*conciliatrix; *conciliatress.** See SEXISM (C).

concision; conciseness. Drawing a fine distinction, H.W. Fowler wrote that "*concision* means the process of cutting down, and *conciseness* the cut-down state" (*MEU2* 304).

conclude, in law, has these special senses:

1. (of a treaty, convention, or contract) to ratify or formalize. E.g.: "The comparative study of judicial intervention to change or modify a validly *concluded* contract is difficult." Jean-Louis Baudouin, "Theory of Imprevision and Judicial Intervention to Change a Contract," in *Essays on the Civil Law of Obligations* 151 (Joseph Dainow ed. 1969).
2. to bind. E.g.: "The inconsistent statements may be evidentiary as admissions—convincing, persuasive, or of little weight, . . . but in and of themselves, they will not *conclude* a party as a matter of law." *Parkinson v. California Co.*, 233 F.2d 432, 438 (10th Cir. 1956).
3. to estop. This sense is archaic—Lord Coke once wrote that to *conclude* is "to determine, to finish, to shut up, to estoppe, or barre a man to plead or claime any other thing." Sir Edward Coke, *Institutes of the Laws of England* 36b (1628).

conclusion = (1a) the last part or section of a speech or writing, such as the summation to the jury or court; (1b) the final clause or section of a pleading; (1c) the concluding part of a deed or conveyance; (2a) a judgment or statement arrived at by reasoning; (2b) an inferential statement—often an allegation that is insufficiently supported by the underlying facts giving rise to the inference; (3) the concluding, settling, or final arranging (as of a treaty); or (4) an act by which one estops oneself from doing anything inconsistent with it.

*conclusionary; *conclusional. See **conclusive.**

conclusion of fact; conclusion of law. A *conclusion of fact* is an evidentiary inference—a factual deduction drawn from observed or proven facts. A *conclusion of law* is a legal inference—a judicial deduction made upon a showing of certain facts, no further evidence being required.

conclusion to the country. See **pais.**

conclusive; conclusory; *conclusionary; *conclusional. *Conclusive* is the common word, meaning "authoritative; decisive." E.g.:

- "Contemporaneous statements by a sponsor, although far from *conclusive*, are generally entitled to respect." *U.S. v. Meade*, 175 F.3d 215, 219 (1st Cir. 1999).
- "It is not easy to work *backwards* [read *backward*] and *conclusively* infer a malign motive from the acts themselves." *Chamberlin v. Town of Stoughton*, 601 F.3d 25, 31 (1st Cir. 2010).
- "Admissions are rarely *conclusive* of the facts stated." 25 Tex. Jur. 3d, *Criminal Procedure: Trial*, § 1226 (2011).

Most general English dictionaries fail to list *conclusory* as a main entry; the few that do misdefine it. The *OED*, labeling it a variant of *conclusive*, calls it "rare." Yet the word is now quite common in American legal writing—and increasingly in British legal writing—and it does not coincide in meaning with *conclusive*. The DIFFERENTIATION is worth encouraging. *Conclusory* = expressing a factual inference without expressing the fundamental facts on which the inference is based. The word often describes evidence that is not specific enough to be competent to prove what it addresses. For example, the statement "She is an illegal alien" is conclusory, whereas "She told me that she is an illegal alien" is not.

Born in New York, the term has gained widespread currency since it first appeared in the 1920s. E.g.:

- "The motion [is] granted, to the extent of directing the service of an amended complaint, omitting paragraphs 16, 17, and 30, and all *conclusory* matter of the nature pointed out herein." *Ringler v. Jetter*, 201 N.Y.S. 525, 525 (App. Div. 1923).
- "Facts in detail supporting *conclusory* statements herein are available in the record." *People v. Hines*, 29 N.E.2d 483, 487 (N.Y. 1940).
- "So accustomed are we to concentrating on reasons of policy and on the *conclusory* nature of legal categories that we tend to forget how channeled we are by nothing more than a conceptual structure." Joseph Vining, *Legal Identity: The Coming of Age of Public Law* 24 (1978).
- "Ultimately, this [plain-meaning approach to 19th-century boilerplate] produces a largely insensitive and *conclusory* historical inquiry." *Oregon Dep't of Fish & Wildlife v. Klamath Indian Tribe*, 473 U.S. 753, 787 (1985) (Marshall, J., dissenting).

Still, despite its currency—its appearance in tens of thousands of published sources—its absence from dictionaries gives some legal writers pause. The Wyoming Supreme Court in 1987 used the phrase *conclusory affidavits*, and stated in a footnote: "After painstaking deliberation, we have decided that we like the word *conclusory*, and we are distressed by its omission from the English language. We now proclaim that henceforth *conclusory* is appropriately used in the opinions of this court. Furthermore, its usage is welcomed in briefs submitted for this court's review. Webster's, take heed." *Greenwood v. Wierdsma*, 741 P.2d 1079, 1086 n.3 (Wyo. 1987).

Take heed, indeed. Gary W. Saltzgiver, a Michigan lawyer, has sent me a letter from the G.&C. Merriam Company dated 24 November 1976, in which the great dictionary company did not take heed; the letter says that *conclusory* was dropped from Merriam-Webster dictionaries because (1) it is extremely rare, and (2) it is a close synonym of *conclusive*.

Both of those conclusions—or "conclusory statements," we might say—are and were wrong. "A computer search of American judicial opinions, conducted in April 1988, revealed more than 21,000 cases in which *conclusory* appears. It has been used for more than sixty years in state and federal courts, including the United States Supreme Court." Bryan A. Garner, "The Missing Common-Law Words," in *The State of the Language* 235, 239–40 (Sir Christopher Ricks & Leonard Michaels eds., 1990).

Some legal writers, apparently loath to use *conclusory*, have resorted to **conclusional* in the sense previously given:

- "The allegations are vague, *conclusional* [read *conclusory*], or inartistically expressed." *Sanders v. U.S.*, 373 U.S. 1, 22 (1963) (per Brennan, J.).
- "The stricken portions of [the] affidavits contained *conclusional* [read *conclusory*] statements [that] neither the trial court nor this court may consider in passing upon motions for summary judgment." *Public Util. Dist. v. Washington Pub. Power Supply Sys.*, 705 P.2d 1195, 1202 (Wash. 1985) (en banc).
- "While the moving papers contend [that] the employment of new counsel will entail additional expense, the application on this point is *conclusional* [read *conclusory*] and does not establish [that] the hiring would work a substantial hardship." *In re Adler*, 494 N.Y.S.2d 828, 830 (Sur. Ct. 1985).

The *OED* defines **conclusional* as "of or pertaining to the conclusion; final," and calls it not only "rare" but "obsolete" as well. *W3* lists **conclusional*, however, and attributes to it the sense "constituting a conclusion," very nearly the sense here given to *conclusory*. Yet, in American law at least, *conclusory* has become so widespread that **conclusional* should be considered a mere NEEDLESS VARIANT.

Still another such variant is **conclusionary*, which was experimented with for a time and still occasionally appears—but it has lost the battle for supremacy and should be rejected:

- "We are moreover impelled to adhere to the opinion, derived from our experience . . . , that *conclusionary* [read *conclusory*] evidence of this nature is immaterial to the issues." *NLRB v. Donnelly Garment Co.*, 330 U.S. 219, 230 (1947) (per Frankfurter, J.).

- "The defendant's second numbered contention makes a broad *conclusionary* [read *conclusory*] statement." *U.S. v. Boykin*, 275 F.Supp. 16, 17 (M.D. Pa. 1967).
- "Frequently information is sought by way of discovery . . . [that] is susceptible of objective ascertainment and *conclusionary* [read *conclusory*] summarization without its usefulness being impaired." 2 R.M. Milgrim, *Milgrim on Trade Secrets* § 7.06[1], at 7-95 (1988).

Occasionally, *conclusionary is used as a synonym for *concluding* or *final*, as in this vague passage, which ends with a confused parenthetical: "The decision or disposition is the *conclusionary* [read *final*] action of a competent tribunal (the verdict)." John Murray, *The Media Law Dictionary* 29 (1978).

conclusive evidence; conclusive proof. These synonymous phrases have two very different senses. On the one hand, most writers use either phrase to refer to evidence so strong as to overbear any other evidence to the contrary—i.e., evidence that must, as a matter of law, be taken to establish some fact in issue and that cannot be disputed. An example is a certificate of corporation offered as evidence of a company's incorporation. E.g.: "I have no doubt that the words 'conclusive evidence' mean what they say; that they are to be a bar to any evidence being tendered to show that the statements in the minutes are not correct." *Kerr v. John Mottram Ltd.*, [1940] Ch. 657, 660.

On the other hand, some writers mean something less by these phrases: evidence that, though not irrebuttable, so preponderates as to oblige a jury to come to a certain conclusion. E.g.: "The term 'conclusive proof' requires a claimant to sustain his burden merely by proof [that] is clear and convincing." *Bun v. Central Pa. Quarry, Stripping & Constr. Co.*, 169 A.2d 804, 807 (Pa. Super. Ct. 1961). See **preponderance of the evidence.**

conclusory. See **conclusive.**

concomitant. See **incident (B).**

concord. A. And *concordat*. *Concord* is the FORMAL WORD generally meaning "an amicable arrangement between parties, esp. between peoples or nations; compact; treaty." In law the word has sometimes been used as a NEEDLESS VARIANT of *accord* or *compromise* in the senses outlined under **accord and satisfaction.**

The word *concord* also has two archaic legal senses: (1) an in-court agreement in which a deforciant acknowledges that the lands in question belong to the complainant; and (2) an agreement to compromise and settle a case in trespass. See **deforciant.**

Concordat = an agreement between church and state. E.g.: "For decades, under a system affirmed by a 1929 *Concordat* between the Government and the Vatican, Italy's 40,000 priests have been paid in large part out of state funds." Clyde Haberman, *Church Shares Pie with Caesar: How Big a Piece?*, N.Y. Times, 8 Dec.

1989, at 4. Usually, as in the preceding quotation, *concordats* involve agreements with the Catholic Church; one authority defines them as "agreements between the Roman Pontiff and the civil ruler concerning matters of mutual interest to both high contracting parties." Matthew Ramstein, *Manual of Canon Law* 42 (1948). For this and other related terms, see **treaty.**

The word has been the subject of SLIPSHOD EXTENSION, perhaps as writers have been seduced by inflated diction—that is, the possibility of calling a contract between important entities a *concordat*. E.g.: "The case is far stronger for the reason that the purposes for which Temple is operated pursuant to the *concordat* between the University and the Commonwealth, which matured in the legislation of 1965, are public purposes." *Schier v. Temple Univ.*, 576 F.Supp. 1569, 1577 (E.D. Pa. 1984). (On the use of *pursuant to in that sentence, see ***pursuant to.**)

The word *concordat* has also been used as a variant of *concord*, but is to be avoided in that sense as a NEEDLESS VARIANT.

B. And *accord*, n. See **accord (B).**

CONCORD = grammatical agreement of one word with another to which it relates. *Concord* embraces number, person, case, and gender. It applies most often to (1) a subject and its verb; (2) a noun and its pronoun; (3) a noun and its appositive; and (4) a relative and its antecedent. Errors in *concord* are not at all uncommon.

A. Subject–Verb Disagreement. Errors in SUBJECT–VERB AGREEMENT are, unfortunately, legion in legal writing—e.g.:

- "Contracts for the sale of land have been enforced specifically in equity since the fifteenth century because damages *is* [read *are*] not an adequate substitute for the specific land to which the plaintiff is entitled under his contract." William F. Walsh, *A Treatise on Equity* 300 (1930).
- "The largest group of such cases *arise* [read *arises*] on motions for temporary restraining orders or preliminary injunctions." Douglas Laycock, *The Death of the Irreparable Injury Rule* 5 (1991).
- "As usual there *seems* [read *seem*] to be a million things happening around the Texas Law Center." Karen Johnson, *What's Happening at the Texas Law Center?*, Tex. B.J., May 1992, at 514. See SYNESIS.
- "Nothing in either the text of AEDPA or the decisions of the Supreme Court categorically *rule out* [read *rules out*] the availability of habeas relief under the rule set out in *Lowenfield*." *Hooks v. Workman*, 606 F.3d 715, 733 (10th Cir. 2010).

Are these merely symptoms of the decay of 20th- and 21st-century English? Consider: "The adequate narration may take up a term less brief, especially if explanation or comment here and there *seem* [read *seems*] requisite to the better understanding of such incidents." Herman Melville, *Billy Budd* 73 (1891; repr. Signet ed. 1979).

Quoting Melville is not to excuse lapses of this kind: every generation might be more vigilant than it is about its subjects and verbs. But we should not think of these problems as having been unthinkable two or three generations ago.

B. Noun–Pronoun Disagreement. Depending on how you look at it, this is either one of the most frequent blunders in modern writing or a godsend that allows us to avoid SEXISM. Where disagreement can be avoided, I recommend avoiding it; where it cannot be avoided, I recommend resorting to it cautiously because some readers (especially speakers of AmE) may doubt your literacy. E.g.:

- "The *prosecution* contends that *it* has a right pursuant to [Federal Rule of Evidence] 607 to impeach its own witnesses. . . . In addition, *they assert* [read *it asserts*] that a prior inconsistent statement of the witness may be admitted to attack his credibility." *U.S. v. Hogan*, 763 F.2d 697, 701–02 (5th Cir. 1985). (Or use *prosecutors . . . they*.)
- "Yet one can only teach a person something if that person can comprehend and use what is being taught *to them* [delete *to them*]." J.M. Balkin, *Turandot's Victory*, 2 Yale J.L. & Humanities 299, 302 (1990).
- "The Court finds that *the party* has waived *their* [read *its*] right to assert that the stay should be imposed." *In re CFS-Related Sec. Fraud Litig.*, 213 F.R.D. 435, 446 (N.D. Okla. 2003).
- "Each *party* shall bear *their* [read *its*] own costs on appeal." *Committee Concerning Cmty. Improvement v. City of Modesto*, 583 F.3d 690, 716 (9th Cir. 2009).

See **each** (A) & **every** (A).

In BrE—to a surprising degree, and even when the purpose cannot be to avoid sexist usage—this type of disagreement in number is common. For example, Glanville Williams here makes a *firm* become *they*, not *it*: "An all-round practice gives better training than a specialised one—but it may be well worth taking articles in a specialised *firm* if you are assured that *they are* [read *it is*] looking out for a bright young man/woman like you to be a partner." *Learning the Law* 209 (11th ed. 1982).

Even more startling examples abound in BrE—e.g.:

- "It would indeed be rather surprising if it were the same crime to strike a blow at *a person* and then to lock *them* up and keep *them* in custody for six months." K.A. Aickin, *Kidnapping at Common Law*, 1 Res Judicata 130, 130 (1935–1938).
- "Neither father nor mother can deprive *themselves* of *their* rights, except in the case of a separation agreement between husband and wife." William Geldart, *Introduction to English Law* 46 (D.C.M. Yardley ed., 9th ed. 1984).
- "*Anyone* can set *themselves* up as an acupuncturist." Sarah Lonsdale, *Sharp Practice Pricks Reputation of Acupuncture*, Observer Sunday, 15 Dec. 1991, at 4.
- "A starting point could be to give more support to the company *secretary. They are*, or should be, privy to the confidential deliberations and secrets of the board and the company." Ronald Severn, *Protecting the Secretary Bird*, Fin. Times, 6 Jan. 1992, at 8.

And most startling of all: "Under new rules to be announced tomorrow, it will be illegal for *anyone* to donate an organ to *their wife* [read *his wife* or *a spouse*]." Ballantyne, *Transplant Jury to Vet Live Donors*, Sunday Times, 25 Mar. 1990, at A3.

As this seeming sloppiness mounts—and bids fair to invade edited American English—the complaints mount as well. For example: "Columnist James Brady . . . noted on Page 38 that Richard F. Shepard was grammatically incorrect when he wrote, 'Nobody remembers a journalist for their writing.' Perhaps it was Mr. Shepard who wrote the headline for the AT&T ad that appeared on page 37 of the same issue: 'This florist wilted because of *their* 800 service.'" Letter of Jerry Galvin, Advertising Age, 4 Nov. 1991, at 26.

Why is this usage becoming so common? It is the most likely solution to the problems brought on by sexist language—the generic masculine pronoun. Advertisements now say, "*Every student* can own *their* own computer," so as to avoid saying *his computer*—a phrasing that would likely alienate some consumers. The *Macmillan Dictionary of Business and Management* (1988) defines *cognitive dissonance* as "a concept in psychology [that] describes the condition in which *a person's* attitudes conflict with *their* behavior" (p. 38). And the President of the United States, in his 1991 State of the Union address, said: "If *anyone* tells you that America's best days are behind her, then *they're* looking the wrong way." And one of the best-edited American papers allows this: "If the newspaper can't fire him for an ethical breach surely *they* [read *it*?] can fire him for being stupid." Michael Gartner, *U.S. Law Says We Have to Kill Saddam Hussein the Hard Way*, Wall St. J., 31 Jan. 1991, at A15.

C. One Result Wrongly Attributed to Two or More Subjects. Another common mistake—in AmE and BrE alike—is to attribute one result to two separate subjects, when logically a separate result necessarily occurred with each subject. E.g.:

- "Barry Kendall Hogan and Mark Bradford Hogan appeal their *conviction* [read *convictions*] of importing marijuana and conspiracy to import and possession with the intent to distribute the drug." *U.S. v. Hogan*, 763 F.2d 697, 699 (5th Cir. 1985).
- "In school, seats are not assigned, yet students tend to sit in the same seats or nearly the same each time, and sometimes feel vaguely resentful if someone else gets there first and takes 'their' *seat* [read *seats*]." Robin T. Lakoff, *Talking Power* 121 (1990).
- "Undocumented creditors who fail to prove *their claim* [read *their claims*] at the meeting on the 6th February, or such later date as is provided in the Scheme of Arrangement." Notice to Creditors (from Bank of Credit & Commerce (Botswana) Limited), Fin. Times, 6 Jan. 1992, at 10.

The following sentence presents a close call: "The government argues that the *stop of appellees' cars* need be justified only by reasonable suspicion." Or should it be *stops of appellees' cars*? Not if government officers stopped several cars with one action.

concordat. See **concord** (A) & **treaty**.

concubine = (1) a woman who cohabits with a man without being his wife; or (2) a mistress or prostitute. Sense 2 is a loose usage—an example of SLIPSHOD EXTENSION.

concur, to a nonlawyer, means "to agree." To American judges it has two senses: (1) "to join in a judicial decision, adopting the reasoning and result as one's own"; and (2) "to join in a judicial decision while not agreeing with the grounds expressed in the majority opinion supporting the decision." *Concur* takes *in* <concur in the opinion> or *with* <I concur with you>. See **agree (B).**

Sense 2 is really a form of *to concur specially* (= to write specially), that is, to express one's concurrence in a separate opinion. E.g.:

- "Two of the judges *specially concur* upon the ground that the starting of the car . . . was not improper." *Ranous v. Seattle Elec. Co.*, 92 P. 382, 384 (Wash. 1907).
- "Lenroot, Associate Judge, *specially concurs*." *In re Schnell*, 46 F.2d 203, 211 (C.C.P.A. 1931).

concurrence; concurrency. *Concurrence* = (1) accordance, agreement, assent; (2) a vote cast by a judge in favor of the judgment reached, often on grounds differing from those expressed in the majority opinion explaining the judgment; or (3) a separate written opinion explaining such a vote. Sense 1 is the general one, not peculiarly legal—e.g.: "All true legal rights are concurrent in equity, wherever such *concurrence* is material." William F. Walsh, *A Treatise on Equity* 94 (1930). Senses 2 and 3 are omitted from most general English-language dictionaries. But they are common in law—e.g.:

- (Sense 2) "Another variant is the *concurrence* dictated by a desire to produce a badly needed majority opinion instead of a plurality opinion." Bernard E. Witkin, *Appellate Court Opinions* 224 (1977).
- (Sense 3) "There remain, however, two other types of opinion, the *concurrence* and the dissent, which any Justice is free to use at any time he desires." John P. Frank, *Marble Palace* 123 (1958).

Concurrency = (of a criminal sentence) the quality or fact of being concurrent in duration. E.g.:

- "It is settled in this state that where no words of *concurrency* of sentences appear in the judgment entry, the sentences are deemed to be consecutive." *Lee v. State*, 349 So.2d 138, 140 (Ala. Crim. App. 1977).
- "He would then be returned to serve his California sentences, less time gained by *concurrency*." *In re Cain*, 52 Cal. Rptr. 860, 861–62 (Ct. App. 1966).

concurrent; consecutive; cumulative. See **concurrent sentences.**

concurrent interests; co-ownership; estates in community; interests in community. Each of these phrases may be used for the four types of *co-ownership* recognized by Anglo-American law: joint tenancy, tenancy in common, coparcenary, and tenancy by the entireties. See **coparcenary, joint tenancy** (distinguishing that term from *tenancy in common*) & **tenancy by the entireties.**

concurrent jurisdiction; pendent jurisdiction. These terms may confuse even experienced lawyers. *Concurrent jurisdiction* = overlapping jurisdiction; jurisdiction exercised by more than one court at the same time over the same subject matter and within the same territory, the litigant having the initial discretion of choosing the court that will adjudicate the matter. E.g.: "Exceptional but important cases exist . . . [that] raise questions of conflict of laws, particularly in respect of the *concurrent jurisdiction* of two countries with regard to the same crime." R.H. Graveson, *Conflict of Laws* 5 (7th ed. 1974).

That much is well known about *concurrent jurisdiction*. But American caselaw has given the phrase an additional sense, having to do with physical boundaries—especially rivers and other bodies of water. E.g.:

- "It has been decided in many jurisdictions . . . that '*concurrent jurisdiction* on the river' extends only to the water and floatable objects therein, not to bridges, dams, or any other objects of a permanent nature." *Roberts v. Fullerton*, 93 N.W. 1111, 1112 (Wis. 1903).
- "The right to exercise *concurrent jurisdiction* over rivers forming state boundaries will be found discussed by Mr. Rorer in his work on Interstate Law." *State v. Nielsen*, 95 P. 720, 721 (Or. 1908).

Pendent jurisdiction = (in U.S.) exercise by federal courts of jurisdiction over matters falling under the purview of state law, on grounds that the state-law claims are so intertwined with the federal claims that they are best adjudicated in tandem. See **jurisdiction.**

concurrent negligence is an infrequent synonym of *contributory negligence*. For more on that term, see **comparative negligence.**

concurrent resolution = a legislative resolution that does not require the executive's signature and that does not ordinarily have the force of law, such as a measure to regulate Congress's internal affairs. E.g.: "The Act was adopted as a temporary wartime measure, and provides . . . for its termination on June 30, 1943, unless sooner terminated by Presidential proclamation or *concurrent resolution* of Congress." *Yakus v. U.S.*, 321 U.S. 414, 419–20 (1944) (per Stone, J.). The phrase applies to many state legislatures as well—e.g.: "In March, 1873, the General Assembly of Missouri adopted a *concurrent resolution* reciting that grave doubts had arisen as to the constitutionality of the act of March 31st, 1868, just quoted." *Woodson v. Murdock*, 89 U.S. 351, 357 syl. (1874).

concurrent sentences; consecutive sentences; cumulative sentences. These phrases are used in reference to more than one penal sentence assessed against a person. *Concurrent sentences* run simultaneously—i.e., the time served in prison is credited against two or more sentences. *Consecutive sentences* (known also as *cumulative sentences*) run one after the other—i.e., the prisoner begins serving the second sentence only after completely serving the first. E.g.: "Legal usage shows that the phrase [*cumulative sentences*] denotes consecutive sentences, whether imposed under counts of the same indictment or under different indictments, as distinguished from concurrent sentences." *Brosius v. Botkin*, 114 F.2d 22, 23 n.2 (D.C. Cir. 1940). (For the sense of *cumulative* in corporate contexts, see the entry under that word.)

concurring opinion = *concurrence* (sense 3). See **concurrence.**

condemn; contemn. To *condemn*, in one sense, is to render judgment against a person or thing <the court condemned the prisoner to life in prison>. E.g.: "A criminal could not be *condemned* in his absence." Alan Harding, *A Social History of English Law* 121 (1966).

The word has mostly passed from legal usage into general usage in figurative senses <his looks condemn him>. E.g.: "We would have serious doubts about this case if the encouragement of guilty pleas by offers of leniency substantially increased the likelihood that defendants, advised by competent counsel, would falsely *condemn* themselves." *Tollett v. Henderson*, 411 U.S. 258, 263 (1973) (per Rehnquist, J.). For more on this sense, see **censure (A).**

In AmE, *condemn* has the additional legal sense "to pronounce judicially (land, etc.) as converted or convertible to public use, subject to reasonable compensation." E.g.:

- "To *condemn* land is to set it apart or expropriate it for public use." *Wulzen v. Board of Sup'rs of San Francisco*, 35 P. 353, 356 (Cal. 1894).
- "A leasehold interest, of course, is a property interest and consequently may not be *condemned* for a public use without just compensation." *In re Commonwealth*, 447 A.2d 342, 344 (Pa. Commw. Ct. 1982).

To *contemn* is to view with contempt, to disregard; esp., to treat (as a law or court order) with contemptuous disregard. By far the rarer word, *contemn* is occasionally used in the context of a legal sanction of *contempt*. (See **contempt.**) More commonly, however, *contemn* is a literary word. In legal contexts, the related agent noun *contemnor* is common. See **contemn** & **contempt.**

condemnation. See **compulsory purchase** & **eminent domain.**

condemnation money is not a familiar term to most modern lawyers, who would probably suppose it to mean "damages paid by an expropriator of land to the landowner for taking the property." In fact, at least one court has used the term in this way: "The heart of the controversy in this litigation is what disposition should be made of the *condemnation moneys* paid into the District Court by the United States as estimated just compensation for the taking of the Hotel Buckminster, the property of the debtor." *John Hancock Mut. Life Ins. Co. v. Casey*, 141 F.2d 104, 107 (1st Cir. 1944).

But the phrase traditionally refers to something quite different: "damages that a losing party in a lawsuit is condemned to pay." E.g.:

- "The appellant will pay all *condemnation money* and costs [that] may be found against him." *Maloney v. Johnson-McLean*, 100 N.W. 423, 424 (Neb. 1904).
- "Since there was no judgment for plaintiff there was no '*condemnation money*.'" *Allen v. Hartford Accident & Indem. Co.*, 123 P.2d 252, 253 (Okla. 1942).

condemned, n., becomes awkward when used in the possessive—e.g.: "I also believe that a ruling on a *condemned's* competency to waive federal collateral relief should not be cloaked by the hands-off deference of Fed. R. Civ. P. 52(a)." The periphrastic possessive (*of the condemned*) is to be preferred where it is possible. See PLURALS (D) & POSSESSIVES (F). Cf. **accused, deceased** & **insured.**

condemnee, omitted from most English dictionaries, is an American legal NEOLOGISM meaning "one whose property is expropriated for public use or damaged by a public-works project." It dates from the late 19th century—e.g.:

- "Cases between a railroad company and a grantor or *condemnee* fall in the same class." *Illinois Cent. R.R. v. Anderson*, 73 Ill. App. 621, 627 (1898).
- "The *condemnee* whose lands were flooded by the works was permitted to abandon in the appellate court the charge of negligence." *State v. Dart*, 202 P. 237, 239 (Ariz. 1921).
- "A tenant, therefore, is a *condemnee* . . . when its leasehold interest is taken, injured, or destroyed." *In re Commonwealth*, 447 A.2d 342, 344 (Pa. Commw. Ct. 1982).

See -EE.

condemner; condemnor. The *-er* spelling is preferred in the general sense of "one that disapproves." But in the U.S., *-or* predominates in the sense "a public or semipublic entity that expropriates private property for public use." E.g.: "The *condemnor* (i.e., the party condemning) need not wait for possession until the trial has been held." Robert Kratovil, *Real Estate Law* 321 (1946). See -ER (A).

condign = well-deserved. Today the word is generally restricted to forms of punishment, not of praise. To write of *condign awards* or *laurels* is to betray a deafness to modern idiom.

condition. A. And *covenant*. The distinction between these terms is especially important in the law of leases. A broken *condition*, which is a fundamental term of a lease, can be enforced by voiding the contract; a broken *covenant*, by contrast, merely entitles the wronged party to sue for relief, but the wronged party must continue to perform under the contract. See **covenant** & **warranty (B).**

Oliver Wendell Holmes Jr. (as he was before becoming a judge) defined *condition* as "an event, the happening of which authorizes the person in whose favor the condition is reserved to treat the contract as if it had not been made—to avoid it, as is commonly said—that is, to insist on both parties being restored to the position in which they stood before the contract was made." Holmes, *The Common Law* 249 (1881).

B. And *limitation*. A *limitation* specifies the time when an interest (such as a remainder) vests—and how long it will last—whereas a *condition* cuts short the precedent estate and allows an entry for condition broken. *See* A.W.B. Simpson, *An Introduction to the History of the Land Law* 199 n.2 (1961). A *condition* benefits only the grantor, whereas a *limitation* may benefit a stranger. See **remainder.**

conditional limitation is an ambiguous term in American property law, carrying either of two very different senses: (1) an executory interest such as an executory devise, springing use, or shifting use; or (2) a special limitation, i.e., conveyancing language that creates a determinable estate. *See* Cornelius J. Moynihan, *Introduction to the Law of Real Property* 190 (2d ed. 1988). See **condition (B), special limitation** & **springing use.**

conditional revocation. See **dependent relative revocation.**

conditional sales contract = (1) a contract for the sale of goods under which the buyer makes periodic payments and the seller retains title or a security interest in the goods; or (2) a contract for the sale of goods under which the seller has an option to buy back upon a certain condition or event. Sense 1 is the ordinary sense. But some argue that sense 1 is not a true *conditional sale* and that the term should be confined to sense 2. J.P. Adoue, *Remedy of the Seller for Breach of Conditional Sale in Texas*, 4 Tex. L. Rev. 294, 294 (1926). The more usual terms for sense 1 are *retail installment contract* and *retail installment contract and security agreement.*

For the difference between a *conditional sales contract* and a *chattel mortgage*, see **chattel mortgage.**

conditioned that for *on condition that* is a loose usage that almost invariably leads to a MISPLACED MODIFIER (i.e., *conditioned*)—e.g.:

- "Petitioner presents herewith a bond with good and sufficient surety, *conditioned that* [read *on condition that*] your petitioner will pay all costs and disbursements incurred by reason of the removal proceedings should it be determined that said case is not removable or has been improperly removed to this Court." *Fakouri v. Pizza Hut of Am., Inc.*, 824 F.2d 470, 471 (6th Cir. 1987). (Note the LEGALESE in *said case*, etc. See **said.**)
- "The petitioner . . . shall file its bond in the amount of $5,000 with security approved by this Court, naming the Commonwealth as obligee, *conditioned that* [read *on condition that*] if the injunction is dissolved . . . the petitioner shall pay to any person injured all damages sustained by reason of granting the injunction." *Physicians Ins. Co. v. Callahan*, 648 A.2d 608, 619 (Pa. Commw. Ct. 1994).

The phrase is analogous to *provided that.* See **provided that.**

condition of repair is wordy for *condition*. E.g.: "So, in this case, defendant owed no duty to plaintiff as his guest to keep the car tire in such a *condition of repair* [read *condition*] as to prevent a blowout or to replace the worn tire by another." *Wakefield v. Singletary*, 80 N.W.2d 84, 86 (S.D. 1956).

condition precedent; condition subsequent. A *condition precedent* is something that must occur before something else can occur. "The creditor's nonperformance of a *condition precedent* to the principal's duty discharges the surety." Laurence P. Simpson, *Handbook on the Law of Suretyship* 292 (1950).

A *condition subsequent* is something that, if it occurs, will bring something else to an end. See **special limitation, subsequent** & POSTPOSITIVE ADJECTIVES.

condominium. Pl. *-iums*. A judge who used the correct plural once needlessly apologized: "To the purist who winces when Latin is misused, the plural of *condominium* is *condominia*." *Hornstein v. Barry*, 560 A.2d 530, 533 n.4 (D.C. 1989). But a stylist winces at *condominia*. See PLURALS (A).

For the international-law sense of the word, see **confederation.**

condonation; condonement; *condonance. *Condonation* traditionally denotes the complete forgiveness and erasing of a conjugal offense (even to the extent of surrendering all claim for damages against the adulterer) by engaging in sexual intercourse with an adulterous spouse, followed by cohabitation. E.g.: "On any view, if the wife be right in her evidence, the intercourse which she had with her husband in the van in February 1966, amounted to *condonation* of the cruelty which she alleged." *McKenzie v. McKenzie*, [1971] P. 33 (C.A.). To a nonlawyer, the quoted sentence sounds bizarre, as if one *condones* cruelty by later giving in to sexual advances.

The original sense of the word was much broader: "the pardoning of a fault or misdeed, esp. when the pardon is merely implicit, as when a person who has been wronged acts toward the offender as if the offense is forgotten" (*OED*). E.g.: "Every denunciation of existing law tends in some measure to increase the probability that there will be violation of it. *Condonation* of a breach enhances the probability." *Whitney v. California*, 274 U.S. 357, 376 (1927) (Brandeis, J., concurring). Today, in both AmE and BrE, the word is fairly rare—smacking of sesquipedality—and in law is usually confined to discussions of matrimonial offenses.

*Condonance is a NEEDLESS VARIANT. *Condonement* is a technical term in certain card games.

condone; excuse; pardon; forgive. These verbs all share the sense "to refrain from exacting punishment for (a wrong) or from (a wrongdoer)." To *condone* suggests such a friendly bias as to allow someone to see no wrong at all where many if not most would consider a

---

wrong by someone else to have taken place <he condoned her kleptomania>. To *excuse* (opposed to *accuse*) is to overlook without blame <the mutual mistake excuses both parties from performing>. To *pardon* (the antonym of *punish*) is to free someone from the penalty normally due for an offense or from an offender <the governor pardoned Foray soon after the verdict>. To *forgive* (the antonym of *condemn*) is to relinquish any claim to redress while also dispelling any further desire for vengeance and obliterating any lingering sense of grievance <forgive a debt> <forgive an assailant>. In polite nonlegal usage, *excuse, pardon,* and *forgive* all convey the hope that a potential annoyance has caused no real bother. For another related word, see **remit.**

conduce to is often a better and shorter way of saying *be conducive to* — e.g.:

- "The people have an original right to establish, for their future government, such principles as, in their opinion, shall most *conduce to* their own happiness." *Marbury v. Madison,* 5 U.S. 137, 176 (1803) (per Marshall, C.J.).
- "Nothing *conduces to* brevity like a caving in of the knees." Justice Oliver Wendell Holmes, as quoted in Catherine Drinker Bowen, *Yankee from Olympus* 324 (1944) (explaining Holmes's habit of writing opinions while standing).
- "*Panetti* creates the conditions for state and federal courts at all levels to implement certain retributivist ideals that would *conduce to* a fair, accurate, modest, and humane set of principles for reviewing the constitutionality of punishment." Dan Markel, *Executing Retributivism:* Panetti *and the Future of the Eighth Amendment,* 103 Nw. U. L. Rev. 1163, 1166–67 (2009).

See BE-VERBS (B).

When the result is undesirable, *lead* or *contribute* is a better word choice.

confect = to prepare (something), usu. from varied materials. It is a FORMAL WORD, seemingly unbefitting a mundane context in which it means merely "to draft." But Louisiana jurists have long used the word in this sense—e.g.:

- "The record indicates that the Nestlé corporation's third-party claims administrator transferred the file to another office and that this transfer contributed to miscommunications between the attorney's office and the claims office and contributed to some delay in *confecting* [read *processing*] the settlement check." *Bazile v. Nestle USA, Inc.,* 939 So.2d 644, 646 (La. Ct. App. 2006).
- "Here is a very Louisiana story. It's just that most of it took place in Washington, D.C. In September 2005, the body count from hurricanes Katrina and Rita not yet in, the cream of Louisiana's lobbyists began *confecting* [read *drawing up*] an astonishing piece of legislation." Oliver Houck, *Can We Save New Orleans?,* 19 Tul. Envtl. L.J. 1, 5 (2006).
- "The clear and unambiguous language of the Amendment reflects the obvious intent of the parties in *confecting* [read *drafting*] the agreement." *Regional Urology, LLC v. Price,* 966 So.2d 1087, 1092 (La. Ct. App. 2007).

confederacy. See **combination.**

confederate. A. And Its Near-Synonyms in Criminal Law: *conspirator; accessory; abettor; accomplice.* Lawyers use each of these terms to denote one who shares complicity in a criminal or injurious act. *Confederate* is the general term referring to anyone who, in conjunction with someone else, intentionally contributes to the perpetration of an unlawful act, whether criminal or civil. A *conspirator* is one of two or more people who agree to commit an unlawful act, who intend to achieve that objective, and who act in furtherance of the agreement. An *accessory* is a person who aids or contributes in the commission or concealment of a crime. An *abettor* is one who by moral or physical force contributes to the commission of a crime—especially by encouraging others to commit it. An *accomplice* is anyone who participates in the commission of a crime in any culpable way, whether as principal, abettor, or accessory. Although the popular mind distinguishes between *principals* and *accomplices,* the law does not. See **accessory (c).**

B. More on *confederate* **vs.** *conspirator.* Whereas *conspirator* (= one engaged in a conspiracy) always carries negative connotations, *confederate* may be connotatively neutral. Its primary sense is "a person or state in league with another or others for mutual support or joint action; an ally" (*OED*). (See **confederation.**) But *confederate* also—primarily in legal contexts—has what the *OED* calls a "bad sense": "a person in league with another or others for an unlawful or evil purpose; an accomplice."

Sometimes the words are used interchangeably, as here, in an example of INELEGANT VARIATION: "A *conspirator* who had entered a plea of guilty and appeared as a witness against his two *confederates,* was convicted although a nolle prosequi was entered as to the others after two trials failed to reach a verdict." Rollin M. Perkins & Ronald N. Boyce, *Criminal Law* 694 n.94 (3d ed. 1982) (using *confederate* for *coconspirator*).

confederation; federation; condominium; consociation; confiliation. These terms denote various constitutional arrangements for the distribution of political power within the borders of a nation-state. Each one denotes a different allocation or division of governmental functions between a central national government and regional governments or groups.

A *confederation* is a league or union of states, groups, or peoples—each of which retains its sovereignty. The states may delegate some rights and powers to a central authority, but they do not delegate supremacy over their internal affairs, and they retain the right to withdraw from the confederation.

A *federation* is a similarly arranged system with a strong central authority and no true regional sovereignties. In the United States, we speak of the *Sovereign States,* and they do retain extensive rights and powers of their own. But they are always subject to the U.S. Constitution (the fundamental law of the land) and to the powers it gives to the national government.

The distinction between these two words is crucial but subtle. William Safire observes that, in 1789, the United States changed, in Northerners' minds, from a *confederation* to a *federation.* But to Southerners, the nation retained the characteristics of a *confederation*. Later, of course, in 1860, Southerners thought that the union could be dissolved. When the Southern states seceded, they chose the word *confederation* to describe their own grouping—although they did not put a right to secede in their own constitution, an ambiguity noted in the North. *See* William Safire, *Confederacy Rises Again*, N.Y. Times, 29 Sept. 1991, § 6, at 18.

A *condominium* is a joint sovereignty or joint rule by two or more states over a single territorial entity (e.g., the Anglo-Egyptian government of the Sudan, 1899–1955, or the New Hebrides, an Anglo-French colony until 1980).

A *consociation* is a political regime for power-sharing among competing groups within a given geographic area; it involves a coalition of political leaders from all segments of a pluralistic society. (The term *consociation* was coined by Arend Lijphart, the political scientist. See his two books, *Power-Sharing in South Africa* (1985) and *Democracy in Plural Societies* (1977).)

A *confiliation* preserves group rights within a non-federal centralized state, members of each separate ethnic, religious, or linguistic group being afforded autonomy wherever they may be located within the state. For example, their laws of inheritance and marriage, as well as their school systems, are preserved against the operation of majority rule. *See* Albert P. Blaustein & Jay A. Sigler, "Confederation, Condominium, Consociation, Confiliation," in 3 *The Guide to American Law* 138–40 (1983) (these two authors having coined the term *confiliation*).

confer. In Latin, *confer* meant "to compare," whence the present meaning of the abbreviated form of *compare*, namely *cf.* The unabbreviated form *confer* no longer has this meaning; today it means (intransitively) "to come together to take counsel and exchange views" or (transitively) "to bestow, usu. from a position of authority." In this latter sense, one *confers* something *on*, not *in*, another—e.g.:

- "We cannot accept the proposition that appellant's acquiescence in Ilsa's desire to live with her mother *conferred* jurisdiction *in* [read *on*] the California courts in this action." *Kulko v. Superior Ct. of Cal.*, 436 U.S. 84, 94 (1978) (per Marshall, J.).
- "Caselaw *conferred* jurisdiction *in* [read *on*] the Board over these claims." *Lancaster Nursing Ctr. v. Department of Pub. Welfare*, 916 A.2d 707, 711 (Pa. Commw. Ct. 2006). See **convey (B).**

conferee; *conferencee. *Conferee* = (1) a member of or participant in a conference; or (2) one on whom something is conferred. Although this word has the look of a NEOLOGISM, it predates the Declaration of Independence.

- (Sense 1) "We specifically referred to the statements of Senator Orrin Hatch, a *conferee* on the originating act."

In re Goody's Family Clothing, 610 F.3d 812, 817 (3d Cir. 2010).
- (Sense 2) "Under Utah law, unjust enrichment occurs when . . . the *conferee* accepts or retains the benefit under circumstances that make it inequitable." *Nilson v. JPMorgan Chase Bank*, 690 F.Supp.2d 1231, 1251 (D. Utah 2009).

Sense 1 is now the preferred form, leaving *conferencee a needless NEOLOGISM that does further violence both to -EE and to *conference*. It's an ugly bit of conference-goers' jargon. E.g.:

- "Magnan obviously provided McClaskey and the rest of the *conferencees* [read *conference-goers*] with champagne service." Richard Rambeck, *Larry Magnan: Staying at the Westin*, Seattle Bus., July 1989, at 1–8.
- *Conferencees* [read *Conferees*] *Strive to Define Goals of Professionalism*, Dallas Bar Ass'n Headnotes, 15 Aug. 1991, at 4.

As the interpolations just above illustrate, either *conference-goer* or *conferee*, an Americanism dating from the late 18th century, suffices in place of *conferencee.

*conferencee. See **conferee.**

conferment; conferral. Dictionaries suggest that *conferral* is a NEEDLESS VARIANT and that it ought to be treated as such. But caselaw suggests otherwise: in denoting the act of conferring, *conferral* appears in hundreds of federal cases—more than 20 times as often as *conferment*—and in hundreds of state cases—almost six times as often. Judicial usage, then, inclines dramatically toward *conferral*. E.g.: "A distinct feature of our Nation's system of governance has been the *conferral* of political power upon public and municipal corporations for the management of matters of local concern." *Owen v. City of Independence*, 445 U.S. 622, 638 (1980) (per Brennan, J.).

Conferment, on the other hand, appears almost twice as frequently in the popular press as *conferral*. E.g.: "Over the years, Congress has tried to use the denial of MFN—or what might more accurately be called the *conferment* of LFN (least-favored-nation)—status as a stick to make countries behave." Strobe Talbott, *America Abroad*, Time, 3 Aug. 1992, at 53. And respected legal commentators use it—e.g.: "The Acts prohibit the *conferment* on English courts of appellate jurisdiction over Scottish courts." P.S. Atiyah, *Law and Modern Society* 60 (1983).

The question is a straightforward one: are we to model the noun after *referral* or *deferment*? Most linguistic questions like this one were settled hundreds of years ago, but *confer* is one of those verbs for which English speakers have less frequently needed a corresponding noun. Having both forms is wasteful and mildly confusing.

So the question ought to be settled—indeed, it is more important to settle the question than to settle it "correctly." I vote for the traditional form, here used by the U.S. Supreme Court: "The plaintiff here would force the Congress to choose between unconditional *conferment* of United States citizenship at birth and *deferment* of citizenship until a condition precedent is fulfilled." *Rogers v. Bellei*, 401 U.S. 815, 835 (1971) (per Blackmun, J.).

conferrable; *conferable. This word is spelled *-rr-* and is stressed on the second syllable.

conferral. See **conferment.**

confess; confess to. Generally, confessors *confess* crimes, guilt, weaknesses, faults, and the like. Less traditionally—though at least since the 18th century—people have *confessed to* these things. Euphony should govern the phrasing. In the following three examples, *confess to* sounds better than *confess* alone would have:

- "Did ever anybody seriously *confess to* envy?" Herman Melville, *Billy Budd* 39 (1891; repr. Signet ed. 1979).
- "I *confess to* never having attended a tractor pull." William Safire, *Virile Women Target Tobacco Men*, N.Y. Times, 11 Mar. 1990, § 6, at 18.
- "But worse, he was convicted even after the lead witness against him, Ivan F. Boesky, *confessed to* keeping millions of dollars in ill-gotten profits." *Adding Insult to Injury*, N.Y. Times, 15 July 1990, at 2F.

Cf. **admit (A)** & **(B).**

confessed. See ***self-confessed.**

confessedly = (1) by general admission or acknowledgment; or (2) by personal confession (*OED*). Follett too narrowly ruled that "the test of legitimacy for an adverb made from an adjective is that it fit the formula *in* [x] manner" (*Modern American Usage* 279 [1966]), a formula that *confessedly* does not fit. Follett's primary objection was to *reportedly*, the earliest recorded use of which was 1901. But *confessedly* has been used since at least 1640, and undeniably (or perhaps *confessedly*) is useful, especially in legal writing. Still, adverbs ending in -EDLY can be easily overworked. See **reportedly.**

Following are two typical—and unobjectionable—uses of *confessedly*:

- "So far as equitable rules differ from those of the law, they are *confessedly* more just and righteous, and their disappearance would be a long step backward in the progress of civilization." 1 John Norton Pomeroy, *A Treatise on Equity Jurisprudence* xxv (Spencer W. Symons ed., 5th ed. 1941).
- "No poll, no majority vote of the affected, no rule of expediency, and certainly no *confessedly* subjective or idiosyncratic view justifies a judicial determination." Charles D. Breitel, *The Lawmakers*, 65 Colum. L. Rev. 749, 772 (1965).

See **allegedly, reportedly** & -EDLY.

confession. See **admission (B).**

confession and avoidance = a pleading admitting the facts stated by the plaintiff but alleging other facts that destroy their legal effect, in whole or in part. Glanville Williams calls this the *retort courteous* and gives this example: "True, I negligently ran you down, but you were guilty of contributory negligence." *Learning the Law* 21 (11th ed. 1982).

confidant; confidante, n. The forms *confidant* and *confidante* have an interesting history. Until 1700 or so, the English word was *confident* (= a trusty friend or adherent), the correct French forms being *confident* and *confidente*. But early in the 18th century, English writers began substituting an *-a-* for the *-e-* in the final syllable, perhaps because of the French nasal pronunciation of *-ent* and *-ente*.

Today the forms *confidant* and *confidante* predominate in both AmE and BrE, though *confidante* is falling into disuse because of what is increasingly thought to be a needless distinction between males and females. Despite the poor etymology, one can be confident in using *confidant* for either sex, as it is predominantly used in American caselaw. E.g.: "She testified . . . that she was a *confidant* of his." *Spears v. State*, 568 S.W.2d 492, 497 (Ark. 1978). See SEXISM (C).

confide in; confide to. The first phrase (= to trust or have faith in) is more common in general usage <to confide in one's friends>. *Confide to* (= to entrust [an object of care or a task], to communicate [something] in confidence) still commonly appears in legal prose. E.g.:

- "The duty of deciding that question has been *confided* by the Legislature *to* the city council or such other governing board as may be charged with the duty of initiating and performing all street improvement work." *Hannon v. Madden*, 5 P.2d 4, 7 (Cal. 1931).
- "We further held that control of county property is generally *confided to* the Board of Commissioners." *Board of Comm'rs of Crawford County v. Riddle*, 493 N.E.2d 461, 462 (Ind. 1986).
- "Our law *confides to* the jury the difficult task of deciding among often conflicting inferences *which* [read *that*] logically and reasonably may flow from the same basic fact." *State v. Salamon*, 949 A.2d 1092, 1144 (Conn. 2008). (For the useful distinction between *which* and *that*, see **that & which.**)

confidence = (1) assured expectation; firm trust; (2) the entrusting of private matters; or (3) (under the Model Rules of Professional Conduct) information protected by the attorney–client privilege under local law.

Sense 2 has limited currency in general usage, as in the phrase *to take another into one's confidence* (i.e., to tell another private matters in trust). It is more generally used in law, as in this sentence from the Statute of Frauds, 29 Chas. II, c. 3 (1677), which illustrates a use of the word not uncommon today in legal prose: "And . . . from and after the said four and twentieth day of June all declarations or creations of trusts or *confidences* of any lands, tenements, or hereditaments shall be manifested and proved by some writing signed by the party."

Sense 3 is almost unknown to nonlawyers, apart from the legally sophisticated. Even so, it occasionally appears in the press: "If Parliament does not legislate, judges will keep expanding the law of '*confidence*' to stop embarrassing facts being disclosed." Economist, 28 Jan.–3 Feb. 1989, at 18.

confident, n. See **confidant.**

confide to. See **confide in.**

configuration. See **constellation.**

confiliation. See **confederation.**

confinee. See **prisoner.**

confines. Modern usage mandates the plural when referring to boundaries or limits—e.g.:

- "Justice Stone raised the query why statutes should not operate beyond the *confine* [read *confines*] of their literal language to become a basis for new precedents." Charles E. Clark, *The Future of the Common Law*, 47 Yale L.J. 309, 309–10 (1937) (book review).
- "Section 6 of the Second Restatement directs that within the *confine* [read *confines*] of constitutional restrictions, a court will follow a statutory directive of its own state on choice of law." *Marascalco v. International Computerized Orthokeratology Soc'y, Inc.*, 181 F.R.D. 331, 338 (N.D. Miss. 1998).
- "In imperial China, speech as personal conduct and social activity was to be exercised within the strict *confine* [read *confines*] of Confucianism." Kam C. Wong, *Law of Assembly in the People's Republic of China*, 12 Wash. & Lee J. Civ. Rts. & Soc. Just. 155, 159 (2006).

confirm. See **ratify.**

confirmatory; *confirmative. The second is a NEEDLESS VARIANT. In the law of evidence, *confirmatory* is sometimes used as an equivalent of *corroborative*. See **corroborative.**

confirmer; confirmor. The general word for "one who confirms" is *confirmer.* The obsolescent legal term (meaning "one who confirms a voidable estate; the grantor in a deed of confirmation") is spelled *-or.* See -ER (A).

confiscable; *confiscatable. The second is a malformed NEEDLESS VARIANT. E.g.: "Money is defined as *confiscatable* [read *confiscable*] contraband in the Inmate Handbook." *Lowery v. Cuyler*, 521 F.Supp. 430, 431 (E.D. Pa. 1981).

confiscate. See **arrogate** (A).

confiscatory /kən-**fis**-kə-tor-ee/, the adjective corresponding to the verb *confiscate*, means either (1) "of or relating to confiscation"; or (2) "tending to confiscate" (*OED*). E.g.: "The rate of return prescribed by [the commission] . . . would have to be clearly *confiscatory* or outside the purview of the statute to permit judicial interference with the determination." *Safe Harbor Water Power Corp. v. Federal Power Comm'n*, 179 F.2d 179, 201 (3d Cir. 1950). Colloquially, it has been used in the sense "robbing under legal authority" <confiscatory landlords> (*OED*).

conflict, n. (= a lawyer's duty to a client whose interests prevent the lawyer from representing another client), is a slightly transmuted shortening of the phrase *conflict of interest*. See **conflict of interest.**

conflicted, adj., (= affected by conflicting emotions, allegiances, duties, or the like) is psychological cant contributed to the English language by the 1980s. E.g.:

- "William Beard, . . . an adviser to the board of the Other Bar, admits he feels *conflicted* about not reporting illegal drug use by an attorney." Caroline V. Clarke, *Management*, Am. Law., Mar. 1990, at 45.
- "Look who's '*conflicted*' now: the psychiatrists." Pamela Sebastian, *Psychiatrists Hold Mass Meeting as Oedipus Wrecks Mother's Day*, Wall St. J., 11 May 1990, at B1.
- "Much as seems to be the case in the Soviet Union now, the mid-1920's was a period of true flux, of mixed emotions, *conflicted* loyalties, wild uncertainties." Frank Rich, *Life in Moscow After the Revolution*, N.Y. Times, 11 May 1990, at B3.

conflict of interest. Today the phrase "ranges from being a euphemism for the result of outright bribery to describing a situation in which one subject to a duty takes a position inconsistent with that duty." John T. Noonan Jr., *Bribes* 446 (1984).

conflict of laws. The noted commentator Joseph H. Beale noted that "definitions of the subject [*conflict of laws*] are almost as numerous as the authors who have written upon it." 1 Joseph H. Beale, *A Treatise on the Conflict of Laws* 2 (1935). He describes three classes: (1) "definitions that emphasize the solution of the conflict of two laws"; (2) "definitions that emphasize the difference in nationality of the subject of the rights involved"; and (3) "definitions that emphasize the limitation of legislative jurisdiction." *Id.* at 2–3.

Later scholars seem to have avoided the definitional pitfalls. R.H. Graveson, for example, defined *conflict of laws*, sometimes more narrowly referred to as *private international law*, as the "branch of law [that] deals with cases in which some relevant fact has a connection with another system of law on either territorial or personal grounds, and may, on that account, raise a question as to the application of one's own or the appropriate alternative (usually foreign) law to the determination of the issue, or as to the exercise of jurisdiction by one's own or foreign courts." R.H. Graveson, *Conflict of Laws* 3 (7th ed. 1974).

Choice of law, a subset of conflict of laws, concerns the necessity that courts choose between differing substantive laws of interested states. *See* Robert A. Leflar,

The Nature of Conflicts Law, 81 Colum. L. Rev. 1080 (1981). See **choice of law.**

conflict out, vb., = (1) (of a lawyer) to be disqualified by virtue of a conflict between clients' interests; or (2) to disqualify (a lawyer) by virtue of a conflict among clients' interests. E.g.: "His usual outside counsel . . . was *conflicted out*." William Horne, *Inside Moves*, Am. Law., Mar. 1990, at 37. See PHRASAL VERBS.

conflicts (referring to the law of choice of law) is often used as a shortened form of *conflict of laws*. E.g.:

- "It has been specifically held that whether an administrator retains 'in-house doctors' to review claims is irrelevant in the *conflicts* analysis." *Cummins v. Unumprovident Ins. Co.*, 630 F.Supp.2d 687, 701 (M.D. La. 2007).
- "*Conflicts* analysis in corporate law is far more streamlined or even simplistic than the *conflicts of laws* regime applicable to most other areas of law." Faith Stevelman, *Regulatory Competition, Choice of Forum, and Delaware's Stake in Corporate Law*, 34 Del. J. Corp. L. 57, 81 (2009).

conflictual (= of, relating to, or characterized by conflict) is documented in the *OED* from 1961. E.g.: "As to the *conflictual* state of Alabama law arising out of *Lee v. State*, *Brasher v. State*, and *Durham v. State*, I consider that *Brasher* is the paramount authority on the narrow point therein decided." *Kilpatrick v. State*, 285 So.2d 516, 524–25 (Ala. Crim. App. 1973) (Cates, P.J., concurring).

A California court has ill-advisedly flagged with a "[*sic*]" a psychiatrist's use of the word. *See Shapira v. Superior Ct.*, 224 Cal. App. 3d 1249, 1252 (1990): "The diagnosis of organic encephalopathy is . . . inherently *conflictual* [*sic*] with numerous other aspects of this patient's situation."

Scholars writing in the field of conflict of laws have adopted the word in a more limited sense— e.g.: "The *conflictual* aspects of flight obviously arise only in those situations in which some relevant fact has a geographical connection with a foreign country." R.H. Graveson, *Conflict of Laws* 585 (7th ed. 1974).

confluence; *conflux. The second is a NEEDLESS VARIANT.

conform takes the preposition *to* or *with*. H.W. Fowler objected to *conform with*, but most authorities find it quite acceptable. E.g.: "Libya said the investigations *conformed with* international law and did not violate its sovereignty." Paul Lewis, *Libya Offers Some Cooperation in Plane Bombings*, N.Y. Times, 15 Feb. 1992, at A5.

conformable; conformably. These terms are today used almost exclusively in legal contexts. *Conformable* = according in form or character to. E.g.: "The Court of Appeal altered its own order as not being *conformable* to the order pronounced." *In re Swire*, [1885] L.R. 30 Ch.D. 239, 241 (C.A.).

Conformably to = in conformity with; in a manner conformable to. E.g.:

- "If both the law and the constitution apply to a particular case, so that the court must either decide that case *conformably* to the law, disregarding the constitution; or *conformably* to the constitution, disregarding the law; the court must determine which of these conflicting rules governs the case." *Marbury v. Madison*, 5 U.S. (1 Cranch) 137, 178 (1803) (per Marshall, C.J.).
- "*Conformably* to what has been said above, we are of opinion that testatrix . . . did not contemplate or intend that the words 'contracts or debts' should apply to and include those natural obligations and duties [that] a husband . . . owes to his wife." *In re Moorehead's Estate*, 137 A. 802, 807 (Pa. 1927).

The rarer phrase *conformably with* = in accordance with.

conformity; *conformance. *Conformity* is the standard term, **conformance* being a NEEDLESS VARIANT that is not uncommon in legal prose. E.g.:

- "Since it was a destination contract, and the package was not properly delivered in *conformance* [read *conformity*] with the contract, risk remained on the seller." Patricia A. Tauchert, *A Survey of Part 5 of Revised Article 2*, 54 SMU L. Rev. 971, 991 (2001).
- "Although the evidence apparently indicated that the stairs had not been constructed in *conformance* [read *conformity*] with applicable OSHA regulations, the record also supported the conclusion that the plaintiff was aware that the steps had been constructed of two-by-four boards and that the stairs lacked handrails." Deron R. Hicks, *Torts*, 57 Mercer L. Rev. 363, 368 (2005).

Like its corresponding verb, *conformity* takes either *to* or *with*:

- "*Conformity to* state procedure in actions at law . . . was reaffirmed in a permanent statute adopted in 1792." Charles Alan Wright, *The Law of Federal Courts* 424 (5th ed. 1994).
- "The judge's discretion is not unbridled but is . . . to be exercised in *conformity with* the standards governing the judicial office." *Id.* at 629.

confront for *present* is now almost a VOGUE WORD among American judges. It is essentially hyperbolic, suggesting that the court comes "face-to-face with" the issues it decides. E.g.:

- "When *confronted* [read *presented*] with a statute [that] is plain and unambiguous on its face, we ordinarily do not look to legislative history as a guide to its meaning." *Tennessee Valley Auth. v. Hill*, 437 U.S. 153, 184 n.29 (1978) (per Burger, C.J.).
- "The court here *confronts* [read *addresses* or *decides*] issues no less difficult than those discussed in the court's recent opinion concerning the layoffs of firefighters." *Vulcan Pioneers, Inc. v. New Jersey Dep't of Civil Serv.*, 588 F.Supp. 727, 728 (D.N.J. 1984).
- "This case *confronts us with the question of whether* [read *presents the question whether*] a nonresident plaintiff asserting a cause of action based on a tort [that] occurred outside of the [s]tate . . . is exempt from the qualification requirements." *Manookian v. A.H. Robins Co.*, 755 F.2d 1125, 1125 (5th Cir. 1985).

The first of those examples of *confront* is especially inappropriate because the word connotes grappling or resistance, and an unambiguous statute gives no trouble to the interpreter.

confute. See **disprove.**

congeries is a singular noun. *Congery and *congerie are false singular nouns back-formed on the mistaken assumption that *congeries* (Fr. "a collection, aggregation") is the plural of such a noun. All forms but *congeries*, sing. & pl., should be avoided. E.g.: "The analytic bent of most of those now so engaged leads them to reduce 'person' to a *congerie* [read *congeries*] of 'rights.'" John T. Noonan Jr., *Persons and Masks of the Law* xi–xii (1976). See BACK-FORMATIONS.

The word is pronounced /**kon**-jə-reez/ in AmE, and /kən-**jeer**-eez/ or /kən-**jeer**-y-eez/ in BrE.

Congress does not require an article, except in references to a specific session <the 104th Congress>. Although some congressional insiders use *the Congress, this phrasing is a quirk to be avoided. E.g.: "The *Congress* [read *Congress*] has said that interest 'shall be calculated from the date of the entry of the judgment.'" *Affiliated Capital Corp. v. City of Houston*, 793 F.2d 706, 713 (5th Cir. 1986) (Higginbotham, J., concurring).

The possessive form is *Congress's.* See POSSESS-IVES (A).

congressional, like *constitutional*, should be written with the lowercase *c-*, even though the noun corresponding to the adjective is capitalized. See **constitutional.**

*Congressperson is unnecessary for *representative*, *congressional representative*, *Congressman*, or *Congresswoman*. See SEXISM (B).

conjugal. See **matrimonial.**

conjurator.* See **conjurer.

conjure. In the sense "to supplicate, beseech," this verb is accented on the second syllable /kən-**joor**/; in the sense "to play the sorcerer," the first syllable is stressed /**kon**-jər/.

conjurer; **conjuror**; ****conjurator.*** *Conjurator is an obsolete LEGALISM meaning "one joined with others by an oath; a coconspirator." *Conjurer* is the preferred spelling for the word meaning "a magician; juggler."

connectible; **connectable.*** The first is preferred.

connection; **connexion**; **connexity.** The spelling *-tion* is preferred in AmE; *-xion* is an almost obsolete spelling formerly preferred in BrE. The word means

basically (1) "the act of connecting" <the connection of these loose ends>; (2) "the state of being connected" <the connection of these events>; or (3) "a connecting part" <the bridge's connection with the land>.

Lawyers use *connexity* in a distinct way, synonymously with *connectedness* (= the quality of being connected). E.g.: "With [the] similarity of service comes the potential for the public's mistaken assumption of *connexity* between the providers of related services." *Sun Banks of Fla., Inc. v. Sun Fed. Savs. & Loan Ass'n*, 651 F.2d 311, 318 (5th Cir. 1981).

At times, though, it acts as a NEEDLESS VARIANT of *connection*: "As with the antitrust claims, RICO must relate to interstate commerce. But the *connexity* [read *connection*] required is minimal." *Cowan v. Corley*, 814 F.2d 223, 227 (5th Cir. 1987). Cf. **nexus.**

connection with, in. See **in connection with.**

connect together is a common REDUNDANCY. If the intended sense is "to connect with one another," *interconnect* is the appropriate word—e.g.:

- "The parties agree that the second of those two articles (the German II) discloses two monostable multivibrators *connected together* [read *interconnected*] by a delay circuit." *Cleeton v. Hewlett-Packard Co.*, 343 F.Supp. 1215, 1226 (D. Md. 1972).
- "This statute explicitly provides that whoever *connects together* [read *interconnects*] different parts of two notes so as to produce one 'instrument,' with intent to defraud, is guilty of forgery." *State v. Scoby*, 810 P.2d 1358, 1360 (Wash. 1991).
- "Two or more offenses may be joined in a single complaint, indictment, or information if they are based on the same act or transaction, or on two or more acts or transactions *connected together* [read *interconnected*], or constitute parts of a common scheme or plan." *State v. Cook*, 171 P.3d 1282, 1288 (Idaho Ct. App. 2007).

See **together.**

connexity; **connexion.*** See **connection.**

connivance [fr. L. *connīvēre* to blink, wink at] is not, as popularly supposed, conspiracy to act together for an illegal end—although it is a form of collusion. *Connivance* is the act of passively allowing another to act illegally or immorally, especially when one has a duty to stop or report the action. It is silence and neglect when one should be vocal and monitory.

In England, *connivance* is usually confined to marital settings; the *CDL* defines it as "behaviour of a person designed to cause his or her spouse to commit a matrimonial offence." Cf. *Stroud's Judicial Dictionary* (4th ed.) ("the willing consent to a conjugal offence [in the sense of being an accessory before the fact], or a culpable acquiescence in a course of conduct reasonably likely to lead to the offence being committed").

connive. See **collude.**

*connotate. See **connote.**

connotation does not mean "ramification" or "suggestion," as in these two statements by President Carter:

- "The political *connotations* [of the release of the American hostages in Iran] do not concern me."
- "Secretary of State Vance did not want any action with any *connotation* of military action."

In the second sentence, the word is used in the sense of "suggestion," which is close to a correct usage. But words connote; actions do not.

Connotations are the emotive nuances of words, including tone, flavor, and associational senses. Here the term is correctly used:

- "If . . . the title of this article suggests a merely philosophical inquiry as to the nature of law and legal relations—a discussion regarded more or less as an end in itself—the writer may be pardoned for repudiating such a *connotation* in advance." Wesley Newcomb Hohfeld, *Some Fundamental Legal Conceptions as Applied in Judicial Reasoning,* 23 Yale L.J. 16, 20 (1913).
- "Some authorities do suggest that 'issue,' unlike 'children,' has a biological *connotation*." *In re Coe's Estate,* 201 A.2d 571, 576 (N.J. 1964).

Sometimes *connotation* has been confused with *denotation* (= the literal meaning of a term). E.g.: "'Contest of a will' is a term of art, the *connotation* of which is made clear in the context of the appropriate Probate Code sections." *In re Goyette's Estate,* 258 Cal. App. 2d 768, 774 (1968). See the two entries following.

CONNOTATION AND DENOTATION. Those sensitive to language understand not just the dictionary definitions of words and sentences (*denotation*), but the undercurrent of suggestions and implications that inheres in all language (*connotation*). This sensitivity is no less important to the judge interpreting a statute than it is to the literary critic. In a will, for example, connotations may be the real clues to the testator's intent where the literal meanings of words provide no clues.

But connotative sensitivity is also what informs great writing. When complimenting Lord Esher's style, Justice Benjamin Cardozo appreciated the effect of connotation: "What a cobweb of fine-spun casuistry is dissipated in a breath by the simple statement of Lord Esher in *Ex parte Simonds*, that the court will not suffer its own officer 'to do a shabby thing.' If the word *shabby* had been left out, and *unworthy* or *dishonorable* substituted, I suppose the sense would have been much the same. But what a drop in emotional value would have followed. As it is, we feel the tingle of the hot blood of resentment mounting to our cheeks." *Law and Literature,* 52 Harv. L. Rev. 471, 480 (1939).

connote; denote. *Connote* = to imply in addition to the literal meaning; *denote* = to convey the literal meaning; to indicate. *Denote* is rarely if ever misused; *connote*, however, is becoming rarer by the day in its traditional senses, here illustrated: "Even intangible or incorporeal property traditionally *connotes* ownership, possession, and use, with all the rights and privileges normally associated therewith." *Kline v. Kline,* 581 A.2d 1300, 1307 (Md. Ct. Spec. App. 1990).

How is *connote* misused? It is frequently confused with *denote*, just as *literally* is often misused for *figuratively*. E.g.:

- "'Cannot' *connotes* [read *denotes*], not unwillingness, but inability." *Di Bennedetto v. Di Rocco,* 93 A.2d 474, 475 (Pa. 1953).
- "What is at stake for an accused facing death or imprisonment demands the utmost solicitude of which courts are capable in canvassing the matter with the accused to make sure he has a full understanding of what the plea *connotes* [read *means*] and of its consequence." *Boykin v. Alabama,* 395 U.S. 238, 243–44 (1969) (per Douglas, J.).

Further, only words or other symbols can *connote*, not acts. *Connote* isn't a general-purpose equivalent of *suggest* or *associate*—e.g.: "The mere act of sending a child to California to live with her mother . . . *connotes* [read *suggests*] no intent to obtain nor expectancy of receiving a corresponding benefit in that State." *Kulko v. Superior Ct.,* 436 U.S. 84, 101 (1978) (per Marshall, J.). Nor do readers connote—e.g.: "In using the word 'individual' in paragraph (A)(10), we *connote* [read *understand*] a natural person as distinguished from an organization or other artificial person, including an estate." *R.J.R. Nabisco Holdings Corp. v. Dunn,* 657 N.E.2d 1220, 1223 (Ind. 1995). See **connotation.**

In the following sentence, *connote* is used in the sense "to suggest; to lead to the conclusion of." With this example one can see just how mushy this word has become: "If such testimony must necessarily *connote* [read *lead to the conclusion of*] adultery on her part, then it cannot be said that the common law has otherwise closed its eyes to this fact of life." *Davis v. Davis,* 507 S.W.2d 841, 847 (Tex. Civ. App.—Houston [14th Dist.] 1974).

*Connotate is a NEEDLESS VARIANT of *connote*.

connubial. See **matrimonial.**

consanguineous; consanguine; *consanguineal; consanguinean. The preferred legal adjective corresponding to *consanguinity* is *consanguineous* (= descended from the same parent or ancestor). E.g.: "English judges . . . interpreted it as a general prohibition against the succession of the half-blood, and extended it to *consanguineous* brothers, that is to sons of the same father by different wives." Henry S. Maine, *Ancient Law* 125–26 (17th ed. 1901). *Consanguineous* is opposed to *affinal*. See **affinity.**

Consanguine and *consanguineal have been taken up by anthropologists and linguists. *Consanguine* = based on an extended group of blood relations esp. of unilinear descent and constituting the functional familial unit in a society (*W3*). *Consanguineal, which shares this sense, is a NEEDLESS VARIANT of *consanguine*.

Consanguinean is the Roman law term meaning "having the same father." It is opposed to *uterine* (= having the same mother).

consanguinity. See **kinship.**

conscience, vb., has not been recorded in most dictionaries, but legal writers occasionally use it as if it were equivalent to *contemplate*:

- "The Fourteenth Amendment does not *conscience* [read *contemplate*] discretion in such matters." *Workman v. Cardwell,* 338 F.Supp. 893, 901 (N.D. Ohio 1972).
- "The courts of Illinois will not *conscience* [read *allow*] this circumvention of the debtor's right of redemption." *In re Farnik,* 17 B.R. 856, 857 (Bankr. N.D. Ill. 1982).

The only related use recorded in the *OED* is *conscienced* (= having a conscience) <a loose-conscienced person>. For another use of *conscience*, see **Keeper of the King's Conscience.**

conscience, shock the. See **shock the conscience.**

conscionable is not a mere NEEDLESS VARIANT of *conscientious* in its sense of "being guided by one's conscience," though some dictionaries suggest it. As a positive correlative of *unconscionable*, it means "conforming with good conscience; just and reasonable" and refers to things as opposed to persons <a conscionable bargain>. E.g.: "Implied warranties may be limited in duration . . . if such limitation is *conscionable*." 15 U.S.C. § 2308(b) (1988). See **unconscionable.**

consecutive sentences. See **concurrent sentences.**

consensual; *consentaneous; *consentient. *Consensual,* the most common of these terms, means "having or expressing or made with consent." *Consentaneous* and *consentient* are both used in that sense, as well as two others: (1) "unanimous"; or (2) "agreeing." When used for *consensual,* either of the other two words is a NEEDLESS VARIANT; when used in the other two senses, each is easily simplified—as the defining words above suggest.

consensus = a widely held opinion or generally accepted view. Hence two common phrases, *consensus of opinion* and *general consensus,* are prolix. E.g.:

- "Indeed, the *general consensus* [omit *general*] in the courts appears to be that the scientific validity of voice stress tests is even less established than that of polygraph testing." *Dixon v. Conway,* 613 F.Supp.2d 330, 379 (W.D.N.Y. 2009).
- "The *consensus of opinion* [read *consensus*] suggests [that] this decision is wrong and that there may be situations where joint authors will hold title as joint tenants." Clive Thorne, "Copyright," in *Architect's Legal Handbook* 341, 344 (Anthony Speaight ed., 9th ed. 2010).

Sometimes we're accosted by a double REDUNDANCY—e.g.:

- "It was pointed out that there was no *general consensus of opinion* [read *consensus*] that to drink whisky is wrong, or that to be a nurse is discreditable." *Peck v. Tribune Co.,* 214 U.S. 185, 189 (1909) (per Holmes, J.).
- "Sertorius had put the matter before his senate and the *general consensus of opinion* [read *consensus*] was that the loss of territory not under his control was a small price to pay for aid." Nic Fields, *Warlord of Republican Rome: Caesar Against Pompey* 83 (2010).

Because *consensus* refers to the collective unanimous opinion of several people, a consensus of two is impossible: "Unless this is done the two minds may be apart, and there is not that *consensus* [read *agreement*] [that] is necessary according to the English law—I say nothing about the laws of other countries—to make a contract." *Carlill v. Carbolic Smoke Ball Co.,* [1893] 1 Q.B. 256, 269 (C.A.).

Consensus is unrelated to *census*; confusion between the two causes some writers to lapse into the misspelling *concensus*—a form that has appeared several hundred times in American law reports.

consensus *ad idem*. See *ad idem* & **meeting of the minds.**

consent for *concede* is an odd MALAPROPISM—e.g.: "'Yes,' Harry said, *consenting* [read *conceding*] defeat for the moment." Chad Forsythe, *The Eyes of Saul* 176 (2002). For more on *consent,* see **assent,** vb.

***consentaneous.** See **consensual.**

consent decree (AmE) = *agreed verdict* (BrE).

***consentient.** See **consensual.**

**consequent. A. And *consequential. Consequent* = following as a direct result <consequent injuries>. *Consequential,* a rarer and usually legal term, means "following as an indirect or secondary result" <consequential damages>. In its other proper sense, *consequential* may serve as an opposite of *inconsequential,* and hence mean "important," and occasionally "self-important." In the following sentence it means "important; of consequence," a sense prematurely labeled obsolete by the *OED*: "A few months' further delay, pending determination on the governing issue in the District of Columbia litigation, cannot be seriously *consequential*." *Omega Importing Corp. v. Petri-Kine Camera Co.,* 451 F.2d 1190, 1195 (2d Cir. 1971).

In all other senses, *consequent* is the correct term where the choice is between the shorter and longer forms. E.g.:

- "The evidence tended to show that the plaintiff was very much excited, and that the happening of the accident and the *consequent* injury to the casket and the body occasioned her serious mental pain and suffering." *Nichols v. Central Vt. Ry. Co.,* 109 A. 905, 906 (Vt. 1919).
- "The registrar transferred the application to the Divorce Registry so that it might be heard in London; *consequent*

upon that direction, the application came before Mr. Registrar Kenworthy." *O'Brien v. O'Brien and Smith*, [1971] 3 W.L.R. 816 (P.D.A.D.).

B. And *subsequent*. Frequently, *consequent* is misused for *subsequent* (= later), perhaps partly because of the logical fallacy *post hoc, ergo propter hoc* (= after this, therefore because of this), which snares persons who equate sequence with causation, thinking that if one event occurred after another, the second event must have been caused by the first. See **subsequently (B).**

consequentialism. See INTERPRETATION, MODES OF (A).

consequentials, n., = consequential damages. E.g.: "Had the parties excluded *consequentials* by contract, the court would have had to identify the value differential component of the buyer's total loss." 1 James J. White & Robert S. Summers, *Uniform Commercial Code* § 10-4 (5th ed. 2009). (See **differential.**) This legal colloquialism should be discouraged in formal legal writing. Cf. **exemplaries** & **incidentals.**

consequently. See **consequent (A)** & **subsequently (B).**

conservancy. The preferred spelling of this essentially BrE word is *conservancy* (= a commission or court having jurisdiction over a port or river, to regulate the fisheries, navigation, etc. [*OED*]). In all other senses, *conservancy* is a NEEDLESS VARIANT of *conservation*.

conservation. See **conservancy.**

conservational; conservative; conservatory. These words are to be distinguished. *Conservational* = of or pertaining to conservation. *Conservative* = characterized by a tendency to preserve or keep intact or unchanged; believing in the maintenance of existing political and social institutions. *Conservatory* = preservative.

conservator; curator. Both are general as well as specific legal terms. *Conservator* is often used in the sense "a court-appointed guardian of an incompetent" <the conservator shall have the charge of the incapable person>. Primarily a civil-law term (used, e.g., in Scotland), *curator* has an identical meaning; this term has been adopted in a number of common-law jurisdictions, however, as in several American states.

conservatory, adj. See **conservational.**

consider (as) (to be). When followed by a noun, a noun phrase, or an adjective, *consider as* is never justified stylistically; many authorities consider it an error. E.g.:

• "Furthermore, the grand jury is *considered as* [read *considered*] unnecessary, particularly in England, where the preliminary examination is considered sufficient." C. Gordon Post, *An Introduction to the Law* 110 (1963).

• "Such conduct has long been *considered as solicitation* [read *considered solicitation*]." *In re Koffler*, 420 N.Y.S.2d 560, 573 (App. Div. 1979).

But *consider* may properly be followed by the infinitive *to be*, especially if the noun phrase after *consider* is at all long—e.g.: "We acknowledge that two courts *considered* public transportation advertising policies that gave their systems discretion to reject 'controversial' advertisements *to be unconstitutional*." *Ridley v. Massachusetts Bay Transp. Auth.*, 390 F.3d 65, 96 (1st Cir. 2004).

The collocation of *consider* and *as* is acceptable when the phrase is followed by a participial phrase: "He is not *considered as* abandoning his objection because he does not submit to further proceedings without contestation." *Lamarche v. Lussier*, 844 N.E.2d 1115, 1119 (Mass. App. Ct. 2006).

consideration. A. Legal Sense. The law uses *consideration* in a technical sense generally unknown to non-lawyers: "the act, forbearance, or promise by which one party to a contract buys the promise of the other." Generally, a contractual promise is not binding unless it is supported by consideration (or made in a deed). This proposition has, since the 19th century, been known as the *doctrine of consideration*.

This word is one of the lawyer's basic TERMS OF ART, but even lawyers sometimes misconceive the word: "One must be careful not to think of '*consideration*' as if it was synonymous with 'recompense'; rather the word [at common law] connoted some *sound reason* for the conveyance, and the payment of money by the feoffee was only one possible reason." A.W.B. Simpson, *An Introduction to the History of the Land Law* 167 (1961).

B. As a Count Noun. In law, by virtue of the technical meaning explained under (A), *consideration* may be a count noun, whereas in general English usage it is not so used. E.g.: "A basic principle of contract law is that one *consideration* will support multiple promises by the other contracting party." *Fortner v. Fannin Bank in Windom*, 634 S.W.2d 74, 77 (Tex. App.—Austin 1982). Nevertheless, the phrase *other valuable consideration* is used rather than *other valuable considerations*.

C. Idiomatic Constructions. Legal idiom requires *in consideration of* but *as consideration for*, in the sense of the word given under (A).

D. *Valuable consideration* and *good consideration*. The first phrase refers to an act, forbearance, or promise having some economic value; the second refers to natural love or affection, or moral duty. To create an enforceable contract, *valuable consideration* is required. *Good consideration* is no good.

Still, deeds customarily recite a consideration of $1 or $10, plus *other good and valuable consideration* so as to obscure the true price. The DOUBLET is unnecessary, however, as *other valuable consideration* suffices.

Moreover, the full phrase *other good and valuable consideration* is often false, as when all the legal consideration for the contract given is mentioned explicitly. The phrase should be avoided unless it serves a real function, that is, unless the rest of the items of consideration are too numerous and individually trifling to merit specific inclusion or unless the parties to the contract do not wish to recite the true price in a publicly recorded document. The drafter of a contract should have some purpose in mind in using this phrase.

E. *Nominal consideration* and *inadequate consideration*. See **nominal consideration.**

F. *In consideration of the mutual covenants . . . .* See **in consideration of the mutual covenants herein contained.**

G. *In consideration of the premises.* See **in consideration of the premises.**

H. *Past consideration.* This phrase, meaning "an act done or a promise given by a promisee before the making of a promise sought to be enforced," is an OXY-MORON of sorts. For *past consideration* is no consideration, since it has not been given in exchange for the promise sought to be enforced.

consignatary; consignatory. For this civil-law term equivalent to *consignee, Black's Law Dictionary* (9th ed. 2009) gives *consignatory*, and *W3* and *OED* give *consignatary*. The *OED* lists *consignatory* only as a variant of *cosignatory* (= a joint signatory). Historical civilian usage seems to recommend *consignatary*.

consignation. See **consignment.**

consignee (= one to whom goods are consigned) is pronounced /kon-si-**nee**/ or /kon-si-**nee**/. Cf. **commercial paper** & **consignor.** See **negotiable instrument.**

consigner. See **consignor.**

consignment; consignation. These words denote quite different things, though the root concept is the same. *Consignment* is the more usual term in common-law jurisdictions, meaning "the act of delivering goods to a carrier to be transmitted to a designated agent." *Consignation*, primarily a term from Scots and French law, means "the act of formally paying over money, as into a bank, or to a person legally appointed to receive it, often because it is the subject of a dispute."

consignor; consigner. *Consignor* is the technical correlative of *consignee.* A *consignor* dispatches goods to another in *consignment.* In Scots law, a *consigner* is one who makes a *consignation* of money in dispute. The two words are often pronounced differently: *consignor* /kon-si-**nohr**/ or /kən-si-nohr/; *consigner* /kən-si-nər/. See **consignee.**

*****consistence** is a NEEDLESS VARIANT for *consistency.* E.g.: "[Two judges] voted to affirm the rule on institutional considerations, feeling that judicial *consistence* [read *consistency*] on these attachments was more important than the correctness of the attachment pro-cedure itself." *Podolsky v. Devinney*, 281 F.Supp. 488, 492 n.7 (S.D.N.Y. 1968).

consistent with. A. Wrongly Made Adverbial. A common illiteracy in American law is to use this phrase adverbially rather than adjectivally—e.g.: "Medical facilities will be equipped *consistent* [read *consistently*] *with* the standards, and all new health care facility construction will be *consistent with* the standards." *Ruiz v. Estelle*, 679 F.2d 1115, 1167 (5th Cir. 1982). For adverbial uses, *consistently with* (= in a manner consistent with) is the correct phrase.

B. And *not inconsistent with.* When the U.S. Supreme Court reverses and remands a judgment of a federal court of appeals, it directs that the further proceedings be *consistent with* the Court's opinion. But when it reverses and remands a state-court judgment, it directs that the further proceedings be *not inconsistent with* the Court's opinion.

Why the difference? Because *consistent with* shows that the Court retains plenary power over the lower federal court. *Not inconsistent with*, by contrast, shows that the state court is much more independent to fashion its holdings on substantive law.

consist in; consist of. American writers too often ignore the distinction. *Consist of* is used in reference to materials; it precedes the physical elements that compose a tangible thing—cement, for example, *consists of* alumina, lime, silica, iron oxide, and magnesia. *Consist in* (= has as its essence) precedes abstract elements or qualities, or intangible things; e.g., a good moral character *consists in* integrity, decency, fairness, and compassion.

Consist of is often wrongly used for *consist in*—e.g.:

- "The tort of assault *consists of* [read *consists in*] an act intended to cause either harmful or offensive contact with another person or apprehension of such contact, and that creates in that other person's mind a reasonable apprehension of an imminent battery." *Koffman v. Garnett*, 574 S.E.2d 258, 261 (Va. 2003).
- "Conversion *consists of* [read *consists in*] an act in derogation of plaintiff's possessory rights." *Glod v. Baker*, 998 So.2d 308, 317 (La. Ct. App. 2008).
- "The court there noted that, under *King*, a court first must determine whether a defendant's conduct *consists of* [read *consists in*] one act or several acts." *People v. Artis*, 902 N.E.2d 677, 683 (Ill. 2009).

The opposite mistake—using *consist in* for *consist of*—is rare but does occur: "Typically [the bill of complaint in equity] *consisted in* [read *consisted of*] three parts: the narrative, the charging, and the interrogative parts." Fleming James, *Civil Procedure* § 2.4, at 64 (1965).

consociation. See **confederation.**

consolidating statute; codifying statute. A *consolidating statute* collects the legislative provisions on a particular topic and embodies them in a single statute, often with minor amendments and drafting improvements. A *codifying statute*, by contrast, purports to be exhaustive in restating the whole of the law on a particular topic, including prior caselaw as well as legislative provisions. Courts generally presume that a *consolidating statute* leaves prior caselaw intact, whereas a *codifying statute* generally supersedes prior caselaw.

consolidation. See **code, joinder** (B) & **merger** (A).

consols (= [BrE] funded government securities with no maturity date) is invariably in the plural form, because it originated as an abbreviation for *consolidated annuities*. E.g.:

- "In March 1832 the defendant, . . . on the request of Mr. Cuming, consented to act as a trustee . . . and the £5000 *consols* were transferred into their joint names, but no declaration of trust was ever executed." *Clark v. Browne*, [1854] 65 E.R. 510, 512.
- "The testator subsequently acquired the reversionary interest, and an arrangement was carried out under which the *consols* were transferred to him, and he conveyed to the trustees." *In re Campbell*, [1893] 2 Ch. 206, 207.

See **consul.**

consortium; society. In the phrases *loss of consortium* and *loss of society*, the two words are synonymous in the context of husband and wife. *Society*, however, is a broader term, describing other than marital relationships, such as father–child and brother–sister. So generally only a spouse may sue for *loss of consortium* (L. "partnership"—related to *consort*), whereas any close relation may sue for *loss of society*. Both terms refer to the nonpecuniary interests a person may have in the company, cooperation, affection, and aid of another. See **society.**

In England, where only a husband could sue for loss of consortium, the cause of action was abolished as a cause of action by the Administration of Justice Act of 1982. *Consortium* is pronounced /kon-**sor**-shi-əm/ or, more usually, in BrE, /kon-**sor**-di-əm/. The plural is *-tia*.

conspectus; prospectus. These terms are not synonymous. A *conspectus* is a comprehensive survey, summary, or synopsis. A *prospectus* is a document describing the chief features of something that is forthcoming. The plurals are *conspectuses* and *prospectuses*.

conspiracy. See **combination.**

*conspirative; *conspirational. See **conspiratorial.**

conspirator (= one engaged in a conspiracy) finds a NEEDLESS VARIANT in **conspiratorialist*—e.g.: "He ordered Christic and its chief *conspiratorialist* [read *conspirator*], Daniel Sheehan, to pay $1 million toward the defendants' legal bills." L. Gordon Crovitz, *Lawyers Make Frivolous Arguments at Their Own Risk*, Wall St. J., 20 June 1990, at A17. Cf. **confederate** (A).

conspiratorial; *conspirative; *conspiratory; *conspirational. The first is standard; the others are NEEDLESS VARIANTS.

conspire. See **collude.**

*conspire together is a common REDUNDANCY:

- "It maintains that since the 1950's the defendants have *conspired together* [read *conspired*] to conceal and misrepresent the health risks of smoking and the addictive nature of nicotine." *In re Tobacco/Governmental Health Care Costs Litig.*, 83 F.Supp.2d 125, 127 (D.D.C. 1999).
- "This time the particulars allege that he, together with [Wheeler], had *conspired together* [read *conspired*] with persons unknown to supply ecstasy, a controlled drug of class A." *R. v. Lucas*, [2005] EWCA Crim. 2715.
- "It appears that a circle of the colony's most prominent merchants *conspired together* [read *conspired*] to depress the value of bids so as to enable one another to purchase confiscated goods at below-market prices for subsequent resale." Tara Helfman, *The Court of Vice Admiralty at Sierra Leone and the Abolition of the West African Slave Trade*, 115 Yale L.J. 1122, 1144 (2006).

See **together.**

constellation, like *configuration*, is often used figuratively to describe a specific group of facts, as in a case—e.g.:

- "The rationale for this rule, of course, is that each party moving for summary judgment may do so on different legal theories dependent on different *constellations* of material facts." *Bricklayers, Masons & Plasterers Int'l Union of Am., Local Union Number 15 v. Stuart Plastering Co.*, 512 F.2d 1017, 1023 (5th Cir. 1975).
- "The real social impact of workplace behavior often depends on a *constellation* of surrounding circumstances, expectations, and relationships." *Oncale v. Sundowner Offshore Servs.*, 523 U.S. 75, 81–82 (1998) (per Scalia, J.).
- "The *constellation* of uncertainties woven into the very fabric of the modern human condition erodes the social capacity for trust." Rebecca M. Bratspies, *Themed Issue: Perspectives on the New Regulatory Era*, 51 Ariz. L. Rev. 575, 581 (2009).

constitute is often an overblown substitute for *make*. And it is an ARCHAISM to give *constitute*, like *make*, a direct object followed by an objective complement. E.g.:

- "I deem it unnecessary to consider *whether or not* [read *whether*] such an interest would *constitute* [read *make*] her a legal representative of J. P. Robertson after his death, as I do not believe she ever acquired such an interest." *Fort Worth & R.G. Ry. Co. v. Robertson*, 121 S.W. 202, 204 (Tex. Civ. App. 1909) (Dunklin, J., dissenting). For more on *whether or not*, see **whether** (C).
- "No particular words, technical or otherwise, or form of expression in an instrument are necessary to *constitute* [read *make*] it a lease." *F. H. Stoltze Land Co. v. Westberg*, 206 P. 407, 408 (Mont. 1922).

To use *constitute* in the sense "to make up; to compose" is more in accord with modern usage. E.g.: "There was ample personal property for the payment of her debts, and there is no rule to which our attention has been directed, disqualifying him to act as executor by reason of his interest in the property *constituting* the estate." *Lynch v. Jones*, 247 S.W. 123, 126–27 (Mo. 1922). See **comprise (D).**

constitution. The sense referring to a text that sets forth fundamental principles was not usual until the time of the American and French Revolutions. Only since the American declaration in 1787—"We the people of the United States . . . do ordain and establish this *Constitution* for the United States of America"—did the practice of having a written document containing the principles of governmental organization become established. At the same time, *constitution* took on what is now its most common meaning. *See* Kenneth C. Wheare, *Modern Constitutions* 3 (2d ed. 1966).

Originally, the Latin word *consitutiones* referred to the lawmaking utterances of the Roman emperors, especially as collected and abridged in the Theodosian and earlier codes. In the United Kingdom, the word is used in reference to "the collection of rules prescribing the powers of the principal political institutions—Parliament, the government, and the courts—and the rights and liberties of individuals, whether or not they are incorporated in a single document (or in a limited collection of texts)." *English Public Law* 3 (David Feldman ed., 2004). Although British lawyers and politicians frequently refer to the U.K.'s constitution, this looser nontextual sense is said, by the noted contributors to the magnum opus *English Public Law*, to make sense only "in so far as this broader meaning of the term is acceptable." *Id.* at 4.

When referring to the U.S. Constitution, writers customarily capitalize the word *Constitution* whether or not the word appears with the qualifying placename (*U.S.*).

constitutional should not generally be capitalized, though *Constitution* (in reference to the U.S. Constitution or any particular constitution) should be. Cf. **congressional** & **federal.**

The adjective has two meanings: (1) "of or relating to the Constitution" <constitutional rights>; and (2) "proper under the Constitution" <constitutional actions>. Hence sense 1: "The 'sword-wielder' exception to the State's home venue privilege exists where an unlawful invasion of a *constitutional* right is directly threatened in the county where the suit is instituted." *Stovall v. Cooper*, 860 So.2d 5, 8 n.2 (Fla. Dist. Ct. App. 2003). And sense 2: "The Wisconsin statute, which is similar to the Norris–LaGuardia Act, has also been held *constitutional.*" *Swing v. American Fed'n of Labor*, 22 N.E.2d 857, 860 (Ill. 1939) (Farthing, J., dissenting). The opposite of *constitutional* in sense 1 is *nonconstitutional*, and in sense 2 *unconstitutional*. See **nonconstitutional.**

constitutionalism = (1) a constitutional system of government; or (2) adherence to constitutional principles. Sense 2 is now more common—e.g.: "Whatever one may think of Robert Bork's brand of *constitutionalism*,

his willingness to defend that vision openly and forthrightly was admirable." Stephen Macedo, *Stricter Senate Review*, N.Y. Times, 23 Oct. 1991, at A11.

constitutionalist; *constitutionist. The standard form of the term is *constitutionalist* (= [1] one who studies or writes on the Constitution; or [2] a supporter of constitutional principles).

constitutionality (= the quality or state of being constitutional) was originally an Americanism (dating from 1801 in the *OED*), but it is now common in BrE as well.

constitutionalize = (1) to provide with a constitution <to constitutionalize the new government>; (2) to make constitutional; to bring into line with the Constitution <plans to constitutionalize the currently segregated school district>; or (3) to import the Constitution into <the dissenter accused the majority of unnecessarily constitutionalizing its decision>. Senses 2 and 3 are relatively new and are unrecorded in the *OED* and *W3*. Here is an example of sense 3: "*New York Times v. Sullivan* was the first major step in what proved to be a seemingly irreversible process of *constitutionalizing* the entire law of libel and slander." *Dun & Bradstreet, Inc. v. Greenmoss Builders, Inc.*, 472 U.S. 749, 766 (1985) (White, J., concurring).

The (ungainly) noun is *constitutionalization*—e.g.: "I want to . . . discuss the *constitutionalization* of common law since 1937." Erwin Chemerinsky, *The Constitution and the Common Law*, 73 Judicature 149, 150 (1989).

constitutional law = body of law spawned by *Marbury v. Madison*, which declared the judiciary's power to construe the Constitution. Rodell explained it as "the cumulative efforts of the Supreme Court to explain, justify, or excuse the restrictions it lays down." Fred Rodell, *Woe Unto You, Lawyers!* 48 (1939). An infrequent synonym is *fundamental law*.

constitutionally has at least four senses in legal contexts: (1) "in a constitutional manner; in a way that comports with the Constitution" <constitutionally assembled> <constitutionally enacted>; (2) "under the provisions of the Constitution" <constitutionally deficient> <constitutionally impermissible>; (3) "so as to bear on the Constitution" <constitutionally speaking>; and (4) "by the Constitution" <constitutionally prohibited>. Sense 1 is the only legal sense given by the *OED* and *W3*.

*constitutionist. See **constitutionalist.**

constrain = (1) to force; or (2) to confine forcibly. Sense 1 is the more common of the two. It is a favorite word of dissenting judges:

- "As I believe it is jurisprudentially unsound to turn the resolution of this case on an issue which has been expressly waived by the Commonwealth, I am *constrained* to dissent." *Commonwealth v. Ruey*, 892 A.2d 802, 819 (Pa. 2006) (Cappy, J., dissenting).

- "With respect, I am *constrained* to dissent from the majority's approach and I would dismiss this appeal for lack of jurisdiction." *U.S. v. Cooper*, 437 F.3d 324, 341 (3d Cir. 2006) (Aldisert, J., dissenting).
- "I am *constrained* to dissent from the majority opinion's disposition reversing the district court's respective dismissals of the appellants' . . . petitions and remanding for further proceedings." *Etape v. Chertoff*, 497 F.3d 379, 396 (4th Cir. 2007) (Hamilton, J., dissenting).

Sense 2 is primarily literary.

construct for *construe* occurs frequently when non-lawyers write about legal subjects—e.g.: "In his historical interpretation of the Supreme Court's role in *constructing* [read *construing*] the United States Constitution, the late Robert G. McCloskey divided constitutional law into three periods." Barbara H. Craig, *Chadha: The Story of an Epic Constitutional Struggle* vii–viii (1988). See **construction.**

construction is the noun form of both *construct* and *construe*, in law usually the latter. A nonlawyer might think that *construction of statutes* is the business of legislatures, since they *construct* (i.e., build) statutes; but *construction* in that phrase means "the process of construing," which is the business of the courts. See **interpretation.**

The phrase *construction of law* means something slightly different—the "construing" of a statute to cover what it does not explicitly mention.

constructional. See **constructive (B).**

construction lien. See **mechanic's lien.**

construction of law. See **construction.**

construction ut res magis valeat quam pereat. See *interpretation ut res magis valeat quam pereat* under INTERPRETATION, MODES OF (B).

constructive. A. And *actual*. These words are opposed in a variety of legal phrases, for example, *constructive* as against *actual fraud, constructive* as against *actual possession.* When *actual* is used in such a phrase, the extrinsic facts merit the legal conclusion that, e.g., fraud or possession exists. When *constructive* is used, the extrinsic facts do not fall within the strict definition of, say, fraud or possession, but the court finds (or is requested to find), usually on equitable grounds, that the legal conclusion of fraud or possession should apply. Lon Fuller considered the adjective *constructive* a "badge of shame," saying that expressions such as those just mentioned "stand out like ugly scars in the language of the law, the linguistic wounds of discarded make-believes." Lon L. Fuller, *Legal Fictions* 22–23 (1967).

B. And *constructional*. These terms are not to be confused. *Constructive* is given a meaning in law that is unknown elsewhere; it "denotes that an act, statement, or other fact has an effect in law though it may not have had that effect in fact" (*OCL1*). So we have

the phrases *constructive fraud* and *constructive trust* and other phrases describing legal FICTIONS.

Constructional = of or pertaining to the act or process of construing. E.g.:

- "When the taker of a prior interest is one of several heirs of the designated ancestor at the ancestor's death, no *constructional* tendency is sufficiently definite to be capable of statement." *In re Latimer's Will*, 63 N.W.2d 65, 70 (Wis. 1954) (quoting the Restatement of Property).
- "The *constructional* problem is complicated by a so-called rule of repugnancy." Cornelius J. Moynihan, *Introduction to the Law of Real Property* 31 (2d ed. 1988).

constructive fraud; legal fraud. The first is the more common phrase denoting forms of unintentional deception or misrepresentation that are held to be fraudulent. It is also clearer: *legal fraud* might suggest to the unwary that the fraud is, e.g., presumed or sanctioned by law, rather than that it is considered in law to be fraud. See **constructive (A).** For the difference between *fraud in law* and *legal fraud*, see **fraud (C).**

constructive knowledge. See **knowledge.**

constructive manslaughter. See **manslaughter (A).**

constructive seisin. See **seisin (A).**

constructive service. See **substituted service.**

constructive trust. A. Synonyms. The phrase *constructive trust* (= a trust that the law creates against one who has obtained property by wrongdoing) has various equivalents—*trust de son tort, trust ex maleficio, involuntary trust, trust ex delicto*—none of which is as common. Though the other phrases may have some advantages over the confusing phrase *constructive trustee* (see (B)), that term is so common that the others merit being labeled NEEDLESS VARIANTS. See **trust (D).**

B. And *express trust*. Properly speaking, *constructive trust* and *express trust* are not really antonyms because they exist on different verbal planes. As the Restatement of Restitution explains: "The term *constructive trust* is not altogether a felicitous one. It might be thought to suggest the idea that it is a fiduciary relation similar to an *express trust*, whereas it is in fact something quite different . . . . A *constructive trust* does not, like an *express trust*, arise because of a manifestation of an intention to create it, but it is imposed as a remedy to prevent unjust enrichment. A *constructive trust*, unlike an *express trust*, is not a fiduciary relation, although the circumstances [that] give rise to a constructive trust may or may not involve a fiduciary relation." Section 160, cmt. a at 641 (1937).

C. And *resulting trust*. The phrase *constructive trust* is likewise distinguishable from a *resulting trust* (= a trust imposed by law when someone transfers property under circumstances suggesting that he or she did not intend the transferee to have the beneficial interest in the property). A *resulting trust*, then, arises because of the transferor's intention, while the law imposes a *constructive trust* to prevent the wrongful holder of property from being unjustly enriched. The *resulting trustee* is a genuine trustee—in a fiduciary relation to the beneficiary—while the *constructive trustee* has no such fiduciary relation.

construe (= to explain or interpret for legal purposes) applies happily to statutes, rules, and the like—but not to doctrines, as here: "Because it impedes full and free discovery of the truth, the attorney–client privilege is strictly *construed* [read *applied*]." *Weil v. Investment/ Indicators Research & Mgmt., Inc.,* 647 F.2d 18, 24 (9th Cir. 1981).

For another mistaken usage, see **construct.**

construe, strictly. See **strict construction.**

consul; counsel; council. *Consul* = a governmental representative living in a foreign country to oversee commercial matters. *Counsel* = a legal adviser or legal advisers. (See **counsel** & **attorney (A).**) *Council* = a body of representatives. See **council.**

consulate; consulship. *Consulate* = the office, term of office, jurisdiction, or residence of a consul. *Consulship* = the office or term of office of a consul. *Consulate* is the more common and (therefore) the broader term. *Consulship* may be useful in conveying precisely one's meaning.

consult takes the prepositions *with* (documents or other persons), *on* or *upon*, or *about* (a matter). The verb may be used transitively <to consult the will itself> as well as intransitively, in combination with any of the prepositions previously named.

consultation. The English writer Philip Howard has stated that *consultation*

> can mean a conference at which the parties, for example, lawyers or doctors, *consult* or deliberate. Modern legal usage confines this sense to meetings with more than one counsel present. You can have a *consultation* with your doctor on your own. But you must be able to afford the fees of at least two lawyers simultaneously before you can properly describe your meeting with them as a *consultation.*
>
> Philip Howard, *Weasel Words* 57 (1979).

OCL1 defines *consultation* as "a meeting of two or more counsel and the solicitor instructing them for discussion and advice."

No such restrictive meaning is given the term in AmE. If you consult with your lawyer on a certain matter, then that act is *consultation.*

consultative; *consultive; *consultatory; *consultory. The two forms ending in *-ory* are NEEDLESS VARIANTS. Both *consultative* and **consultive* are old, the first recorded from 1583, the second from 1616. Because the adjectival form of Latinate words in *-tion* follows from the noun form, *consultative* is the preferable form—e.g.:

- "[Defendants] have argued that since the Commissioner has only a *consultive* [read *consultative*] role and the I.N.S. may ignore his recommendations, this litigation does not affect him." *Royalton Coll., Inc. v. Clark,* 295 F.Supp. 365, 372 n.4 (D. Vt. 1969).
- "After applying for disability benefits, Denton was directed to see Dr. Jerry Boyd for a *consultive* [read *consultative*] psychological evaluation in July 2005." *Denton v. Astrue,* 596 F.3d 419, 422 (7th Cir. 2010).

See **consultation.**

consume is OFFICIALESE for *eat* or *drink*— e.g.:

- "Other than the facts that she ate pizza for dinner, *consumed* [read *drank*] at least one alcoholic beverage, had an argument with her husband . . . , and . . . left her home upset, Mrs. Sullivan was essentially unable to recall any of the events that took place on the night in question." *In re Sullivan,* 337 B.R. 210, 213 (Bankr. W.D. Mo. 2005).
- "Allen asserted that after *consuming* [read *eating*] the sandwich, her husband developed a salmonella infection and subsequently died as a result of eating the sandwich." *Lakeland Reg'l Med. Ctr., Inc. v. Allen,* 944 So.2d 541, 542 (Fla. Dist. Ct. App. 2006). (The INELEGANT VARIATION could have been avoided by recasting the sentence: *Allen asserted that as a result of eating the sandwich, her husband died of a salmonella infection.*)
- "She emitted a strong odor of alcohol and she admitted *to having consumed* [read *drinking*] alcohol that evening." *State v. Kelley,* 986 A.2d 620, 623 (N.H. 2009). (On the use of **admit to* in this sentence, see **admit.**)

consummate has two pronunciations as an adjective (either /kən-**səm**-it/ or /**kon**-sə-mət/), and still another as a verb /**kon**-sə-mayt/. For its sense, see **inchoate.**

contemn = to treat (as laws or court orders) with contemptuous disregard. E.g.: "We find that jurisdiction exists based on both the inherent power of a court to reach those who knowingly *contemn* its orders and the minimum contacts analysis set out below." *Waffenschmidt v. MacKay,* 763 F.2d 711, 721 (5th Cir. 1985). The *OED* notes that this word is "chiefly a literary word," but it is used just as frequently in legal as in literary contexts. See **condemn.**

contemnee. See **contemner.**

contemner; *contemnor. Most dictionaries list *contemner* (= one who behaves contemptuously or is in contempt) as the standard spelling, and it appears twice as often in print as **contemnor.* The supposed correlative *contemnee* (= one who is treated contemptuously) is exceedingly rare, so there seems little call for the *-or* spelling.

contemplative is accented on the second syllable /kən-**tem**-plə-tiv/.

contemporaneous construction; contemporaneous interpretation. See *contemporaneous interpretation* under INTERPRETATION, MODES OF (B).

contemporary; contemporaneous. Both refer to coinciding periods of time. *Contemporaneous* usually refers to either actions or things, *contemporary* to persons. *Contemporary* has the additional informal meaning "current"—e.g.: "To sound even more *contemporary*, he might have used the euphemism 'pacified,' instead of 'conquered.'" John Phelps Warnock & Harold C. Warnock, *Effective Writing: A Handbook with Stories for Lawyers* 141 (2003). But this sense should be avoided in contexts referring to past times, as here: "Whether Shaw was in fact racist or not is less important than the way in which extracts from Shaw's letters have been edited and packaged, and how this process of shaping could be read as a manifestation of a much more *contemporary* [read *modern*] cultural and political logic." Trevor B. McCrisken & Andrew Pepper, *American History and Contemporary Hollywood Film* 70 (2005). When no other time frame is mentioned, then we may infer "contemporary with us" to denote current rather than historical contexts. **Cotemporaneous* is a NEEDLESS VARIANT of *contemporaneous*; likewise, **cotemporary* is a NEEDLESS VARIANT of *contemporary*.

Here *contemporary* is misused for *contemporaneous*, unless the writer meant to personify the statute mentioned (an unlikely intention): "As the Court acknowledges, [the statute] must be examined in light of 'its *contemporary* [read *contemporaneous*] legal context.'" *Mountain States Tel. & Tel. Co. v. Pueblo of Santa Ana*, 472 U.S. 237, 257 (1985) (Brennan, J., dissenting).

Contemporaneous does not precisely mean "simultaneous"; rather, it means "belonging to the same time or period; occurring at about the same time." Hence the following sentences are correct, although *simultaneous* does not properly fit in each slot filled by *contemporaneous*:

- "Courts regard with particular respect the *contemporaneous* construction of a statute by those initially charged with its enforcement." *Middle S. Energy, Inc. v. F.E.R.C.*, 747 F.2d 763, 769 (D.C. Cir. 1984).
- "An *inter vivos* transfer is to be 'treated as an advancement against the heir's share of the estate only if declared in a *contemporaneous* writing by the decedent or acknowledged in writing by the heir to be an advancement.'" *In re Estate of Soule*, 540 N.W.2d 118, 123 (Neb. 1995) (quoting a Nebraska statute).
- "If the government wishes to rely on any statement of [redacted] it must provide any evidence that he was physically or psychologically coerced prior to or *contemporaneous* with the time that he gave the statement that the government relies on." *Bin Attash v. Obama*, 628 F.Supp.2d 24, 35 (D.D.C. 2009). On the use of **prior to* in that sentence, see **prior to.

For a strange misusage of *contemporaneous*, see *living constitutionalism* under INTERPRETATION, MODES OF (B).

contempt; contemptibility; contemptuousness. These words are quite distinct. *Contempt* = (1) (generally) the act or state of despising; the condition of being despised; or (2) (in law) an action that interferes with the administration of justice. *Contemptibility* = the quality or fact of being worthy of scorn.

Contemptuousness = the quality of being scornful or disdainful. See **contumacity.

contemptible. See **contemptuous** (A).

contempt of court = action that interferes with the administration of justice by the various courts of law. There are several different types. *Direct contempt* is that which occurs in open court (e.g., foul language spoken to a judge). For example, in the 19th century, a drunken lawyer in Tombstone, Arizona, Allen English, upon being fined $25 for *contempt of court*, said to the judge, "Your honor, $25 wouldn't pay for half the *contempt* I have for this court." That statement was a *direct contempt*. By contrast, *constructive contempt* (sometimes called *indirect* or *consequential contempt*) results from actions outside court, such as failing to comply with orders.

Another dichotomy is that between *civil* and *criminal contempt*; the first consists in failing to do something ordered by the court for another litigant's benefit, whereas the second consists in acts that obstruct justice.

contemptuous. A. And *contemptible*. The first means "expressing contempt," the second "worthy of contempt or scorn." Both terms are disparaging, *contemptible* being the stronger of the two. See **contempt**.

B. And *contumacious*. See **contumacious**.

contemptuousness. See **contempt**.

contend. See **allege** & **contest**, vb.

content; contents. When referring to written matter or oral presentation, *content* = the ideas or thoughts contained in the words as opposed to the method of presentation. Follett disapproved the modern tendency to use *content* as well as *contents* for "what is contained," but the usage is old and is now common. E.g.:

- "Since Justice Black did not define the *content* and scope of this exception, that critical task has fallen to the lower courts." Milton Handler & Richard A. De Sovo, *The Noerr Doctrine and Its Sham Exception*, 6 Cardozo L. Rev. 1, 1 (1984).
- "Beyond that, the Court essentially leaves it to the discretion of the individual Member State to determine the *content* and scope of each exception." Sean Pager, *Strictness v. Discretion: The European Court of Justice's Variable Vision of Gender Equality*, 51 Am. J. Comp. L. 553, 563 (2003).

Contents refers to material and nonmaterial ingredients alike—e.g.:

- "The bottles were securely and completely wrapped in paper and tied with a string so that the *contents* of the package could not be seen or observed." *Goodman v. Lane*, 48 F.2d 32, 32–33 (8th Cir. 1931).
- "Buder subsequently executed a codicil to his will in which he bequeathed fifty thousand dollars to each of his grandchildren, made several minor changes not relevant here, and otherwise ratified the *contents* of his will." *Buder v. U.S.*, 7 F.3d 1382, 1384 (8th Cir. 1993).
- "Michael alleges that the trial court improperly admitted into evidence the *contents* of the decedent's previous Will

executed in 2001." *Hamilton v. Hamilton*, 858 N.E.2d 1032, 1038 (Ind. Ct. App. 2006).

Still, *content* is now more common for the nonmaterial things contained in something (as in documents).

The word *contents* should never refer to human beings, as the callous sentence that follows demonstrates: "The impact and disintegration of the aircraft extended over several seconds *before the aircraft and its human contents came to rest* [read *before the aircraft and those aboard came to rest*]." *Pregeant v. Pan Am. World Airways, Inc.*, 762 F.2d 1245, 1250 (5th Cir. 1985).

conterminous. See **coterminous.**

contest, n.; contestation; litiscontestation. These terms are to be differentiated. *Contest* = (1) debate; controversy; dispute <without contest> <will contest>; or (2) a friendly competition. *Contestation* = (1) disputation or controversy, as between parties at law; verbal contention; keen argument (*OED*); (2) the contesting or disputing (of a point or claim) <assertions not open to contestation>; or (3) an assertion contended for <the appellant's contestation is untenable>. *Litiscontestation*, a legal term used primarily in Scots and civil law, means (1) "the formal entry of a suit in a court of law" (*OED*); or (2) "a legal process by which controverted issues are established and a joinder of issues arrived at" (*W3*).

contestant; *contestor. *Contestant* = (1) one who contests a will (*caveator* being a synonym); or (2) a participant in a sporting event. The word has been common only since the mid-19th century. **Contestor* is a NEEDLESS VARIANT for sense 1—e.g.: "Appellant argues that the will *contestors* [read *contestants*] failed to introduce evidence to establish they were interested parties." *Keener v. Archibald*, 533 N.E.2d 1268, 1269 (Ind. Ct. App. 1989). See **caveator** & **contestee.**

contestation. See **contest.**

contested election, in AmE, means either (1) "an election the validity of whose results has been challenged," or (2) "a political race with more than one candidate." Sense 2 is the sole meaning in BrE. See **candidacy.**

contestee is a 19th-century Americanism listed in the *OED* as meaning "a candidate for election who is in the position of having his seat contested by another"— a sense recorded from 1870. Even earlier, though, lawyers had begun to use *contestee* in a sense corresponding to *contestant* or **contestor*, as here:

- "The witness . . . proceeded to state what he had heard the *contestee*, Anthony Banning Jr., say a few days after his father's death, in respect to his father's will." *Banning v. Banning*, 12 Ohio St. 437, 444 (1861).
- "The secretary of the interior found from the evidence that the *contestee* was not a *bona fide* homestead claimant." *Carr v. Fife*, 44 F. 713, 713 syl. 3 (C.C.D. Wash. 1891).

Today the word appears fairly frequently in American legal writing, usually paired against *contestant*—e.g.: "The *contestants* sought to raise various alleged violations of the Kentucky Corrupt Practices Act, the legality of support alleged to have been given the *contestees* by the school superintendent." *Stearns v. Davis*, 707 S.W.2d 787, 787–88 (Ky. Ct. App. 1985). See **contestant** & -EE.

*contestor. See **contestant.**

contiguous means, not merely "close to" or "near," but "abutting." It is commonly misused in the phrase *the forty-eight contiguous states*, which is illogical: only a few states can be *contiguous* to one another. *Contiguous to* for *next to* is sometimes a pomposity. (See **adjacent.** Cf. **adjoin.**) This adjective should always be construed with *to*. E.g.:

- "Its properties are not 'surrounded by' the corporate boundaries of the city because its properties are *contiguous* [read *adjacent*] on one side *to* Nike headquarters, which is not within the corporate boundaries of the city." *Costco Wholesale Corp. v. City of Beaverton*, 136 P.3d 1219, 1225 (Or. Ct. App. 2006).
- "The Nebraska property consists of a house and 12 acres and a separate but *contiguous* parcel of 38 acres." *Mortgage Express, Inc. v. Tudor Ins. Co.*, 771 N.W.2d 137, 142 (Neb. 2009).
- "Though under the 1999 amendment the urban homestead property must be *contiguous*, that requirement is not applicable to the rural homestead." Joseph W. McKnight, *Family: Husband and Wife*, 62 SMU L. Rev. 1149, 1172 (2009).

contingency; *contingence. **Contingence* is a NEEDLESS VARIANT. *Contingency* is sometimes used elliptically for *contingent fee*, as here: "Loftin, . . . who was working on a 40 percent *contingency*, played the role of the homespun Fort Worth boy: His shirttail hanging out, he sniffled from a head cold." Dana Rubin, *Courting Costs*, Texas Monthly, May 1992, at 52, 58. See **contingent fee.**

contingent. See **vested (A).**

contingent fee; contingency fee. The first is the preferred term. It denotes an agreement that no fee will be charged for the lawyer's services unless the lawsuit is successful or is settled out of court. Usually, a *contingent fee* calls for larger compensation to be paid than the lawyer would normally charge, often a percentage of the money recovered or the money saved, to compensate for the risk involved. See **champerty (A)** & **no-win–no-fee system.**

contingent-fee lawyer is a journalistic variation of *plaintiff's lawyer*—and a more specific one, since the two phrases are not always interchangeable. Note that *contingent-fee* is hyphenated when preceding *lawyer* as a PHRASAL ADJECTIVE: "There was nothing new about *contingent-fee lawyers'* moving in when they smelled the kill, but here was an instance when the public at large might benefit from the economic self-aggrandizement of the trial lawyers." John A. Jenkins, *The Litigators* 120 (1989).

contingent remainder; contingent interest. Each phrase is used on both sides of the Atlantic, but the first is more common in both AmE and BrE.

The phrase *contingent remainder* has led to confusion between the interest subject to a condition precedent and a vested defeasible interest subject to a condition subsequent. Unlike a *vested remainder*, a *contingent remainder* is not an estate at all—it is a limitation whereby an estate will vest in interest when a contingent event happens, and then vest in possession when a prior estate ends.

To remedy this confusion, the Restatement of Property discarded the term and substituted in its place a more descriptive phrase *remainder subject to a condition precedent*. Even so, courts continue to use the older term. See **remainder** & **vested remainder.**

continual; continuous. *Continual* = frequently recurring; intermittent. *Continuous* = occurring without interruption; unceasing <the continuous hum of the generator>. The two words are frequently confused, *continuous* typically horning in where *continual* belongs—e.g.:

- "Luckily Mandy liked dogs, for the C.J., in spite of his intelligence, loyalty, and other endearing qualities, involved us in *continuous* [read *continual*] excitement." Ephraim Tutt, *Yankee Lawyer* 197 (1943).
- "Bar associations have *continuously* [read *continually*] tried to define the professional responsibilities of attorneys inside and outside the courtroom." Norman Dorsen & Leon Friedman, *Disorder in the Court* 136 (1973).
- "Minutes after the arrest, Wayne Forrest, a Deputy Attorney General helping prosecute the case, told the presiding judge, Charles R. DiGisi, that the sheriff's office had been engaged in a '*continuous* [read *continual*] course of misconduct' in the Spath case." Robert Hanley, *Courthouse Arrest Roils Trial of Officer in Teaneck Killing*, N.Y. Times, 18 Jan. 1992, at A9.

continuance; continuation; continuity. *Continuance* has virtually opposite senses in lay and legal usage. Generally, it means (1) "keeping up, going on with, maintaining, or prolonging"; or (2) "duration; time of continuing." E.g.:

- "As to each of the four succeeding purchases, conditions precedent were annexed to the right to exercise the option in respect thereto, i.e., the deposit by plaintiff of $1 for each share subject to purchase during the ensuing period and (critical to this action) his *continuance* in defendant's employ." *Lutzker v. Walter E. Heller & Co.*, 172 F.Supp. 77, 82 (S.D.N.Y. 1959).
- "This is so even though the capacity to bear children or the fulfilment of that capacity has not been made a condition of the creation or *continuance* of a valid marriage." Geoffrey Lindell, *Constitutional Issues Regarding Same-Sex Marriage*, 30 Sydney L. Rev. 27, 28 (2008).

But in American law, it means "postponement; the adjournment or deferring of a trial or other proceeding until a future date" <motion for continuance>. E.g.: "In order for us to find that a refusal to grant a *continuance* was an abuse of discretion, the movant must show the denial was prejudicial." *State v. Smith*, 292 S.W.3d 595, 600 (Mo. Ct. App. 2009). See **continue.**

Continuation = continued maintenance; carrying on or resumption of (an action, etc.); that by which a thing is continued (*COD*). E.g.:

- "The privilege extends only to information acquired during the *continuation* of the relation of physician and patient, and does not preclude a physician from testifying as to information respecting a patient which he acquired either before the relation began or after its termination." *State v. Moore*, 204 N.W. 341, 343 (N.D. 1924) (Christianson, J., dissenting) (quoting a state statute).
- "*Continuation* of the use of the property as a municipal park or for another municipal purpose carries out a larger share of Bacon's purpose than the complete destruction of such use by the decree we today affirm." *Evans v. Abney*, 396 U.S. 435, 449 (1970) (Douglas, J., dissenting).
- "The question whether a corporation is *a continuation* of a predecessor has been one of some ferment in the past decade." *Mozingo v. Correct Mfg. Corp.*, 752 F.2d 168, 174 (5th Cir. 1985).

Continuity = connectedness; unbrokenness; uninterruptedness <the continuity of the litigation process was broken up by a number of continuances>.

continuation in part. See **c.i.p.**

continue; stay, vb. "We are accustomed to *continue* an action in the sense of plodding on. But it was possible in Scotland and was once possible in England (and still is in legal language) to *continue* in the sense of knocking off or adjourning." Ivor Brown, *I Give You My Word* 112 (1964). It is this transitive use of *continue* (= to postpone) in legal contexts that yields the legal use of *continuance.*

Only in legal parlance is *stay* current as a transitive verb. Stronger than *continue*, *stay* means "to stop, arrest, delay, prevent (an action or proceeding)" <to stay the proceedings>. E.g.: "All proceedings shall be *stayed* while the Eleventh Circuit considers the appeal." *Deen v. Egleston*, 601 F.Supp.2d 1331, 1347 (S.D. Ga. 2009). See **continuance** & **stay.**

continue liable is an old legal idiom—shorthand for *continue to be liable*. E.g.:

- "There are a number of Tennessee cases [holding] that the father *continues liable* for the support of his minor children even though there has been a divorce and award of custody to the mother." *Livingston v. Livingston*, 429 S.W.2d 452, 458 (Tenn. Ct. App. 1967).
- "[The] policy . . . must be regarded as subsisting in contemplation of law, and the insurer *continues liable* to a third-party claimant until relieved from its obligation." *State Ins. Fund v. Brooks*, 755 P.2d 653, 656 (Okla. 1988).

continuity. See **continuance.**

continuous. See **continual.**

continuum. Pl. *continuums* or **continua*. Avoid the foreign plural. See PLURALS (A).

contorts, n., (= the overlapping domain of contract law and tort law; a specific wrong that falls within that domain) is Professor Grant Gilmore's NEOLOGISM—a PORTMANTEAU WORD (*contract + tort*) dating from the 1970s:

- "I have occasionally suggested to my students that a desirable reform in legal education could be to merge the first-year courses in Contracts and Torts into a single course [that] we would call *Contorts*." Grant Gilmore, *The Death of Contract* 90 (1974).
- "Interestingly, Dean Prosser seems also to recognize this peculiar possibility and to identify it as an issue existing on the fringes of contract and tort law, the so-called 'contort' of recent renown." *Schlange-Schoeningen v. Parrish*, 767 F.2d 788, 793 n.3 (11th Cir. 1985).

contours is such a popular METAPHOR that it has become a VOGUE WORD among lawyers and judges. E.g.: "Because the nature of the newly created right to some extent guides my analysis, I begin by outlining the *contours* of the hearing to which the majority concludes the defendant is entitled." *State v. Fernando A.*, 981 A.2d 427, 450 (Conn. 2009).

contra, n., adj., adv. & prep., is a LEGALISM for *against*, *contrary*, etc. Except as a signal in citations, it should be avoided in favor of its more common equivalents—e.g.:

- "Even if the language of *Alpo Petfoods* and *Wagner Seed* were holdings rather than dicta, we still would be left with the troubling fact that two unreversed decisions of the Higher Authority are *contra* [read *to the contrary*]." *Gersman v. Group Health Ass'n*, 975 F.2d 886, 897 (D.C. Cir. 1992).
- "We respond now to the separate opinion of our able colleague. Judge Johnson's reliance upon *U.S. v. Horsley* as somehow *contra* [read *contrary*] authority plainly reveals a basic misunderstanding of what is meant by what Judge Johnson calls 'unsupported intuition' and 'specific articulable factors.'" *U.S. v. Bentley-Smith*, 2 F.3d 1368, 1379 (5th Cir. 1993).
- "Although there is *contra* [read *contrary*] authority, as a matter of fairness most courts have imposed a special scienter or *mens rea* requirement in CSAEA cases." Paul Anacker & Edward Imwinkelried, *Controlled Substance Analogue Enforcement Act Criminal Defense*, 37 Sw. U. L. Rev. 267, 277 (2008).

contracept, vb., is a BACK-FORMATION that is not yet in most dictionaries. It is a jargonistic word popular among social workers. But lawyers use it as well—e.g.: "Particularly for girls who are just becoming sexually active, the failure to *contracept* [read *use contraception*] is the norm." Michelle Oberman, *Mothers Who Kill*, 8 DePaul J. Health Care L. 3, 68 (2004).

contraceptionist. See **contraceptor.**

contraceptive. See **abortifacient.**

contraceptivism. In the days when contraceptives were illegal, this term referred to unlawful trafficking in contraceptives. *See* Rollin M. Perkins, *Criminal Law* 108 (1957).

contraceptor; contraceptionist. What is the agent noun corresponding to *contraception*? William Safire prefers *contraceptionist*. *See On Language*, N.Y. Times, 30 Dec. 1990, § 6, at 6. But *contraceptor* is five times as common, and usage suggests a worthwhile distinction: a *contraceptor* is one who uses contraception, while a *contraceptionist* is one who advocates its use.

contract, n. & vb. **A. Noun Senses.** The word has many more senses than most dictionaries—even the *OED* and *W3*—acknowledge. In tackling the problem of defining this word, Patrick Atiyah acutely observes: "A definition of a contract presupposes that the law recognizes a single concept of contract. In fact it is doubtful if this is really the case. Certainly there is one very central and powerful concept in the middle of contract law. . . . But contractual obligations arise in such a very wide variety of circumstances, and are based on such a wide variety of grounds, that there is little relationship between cases on the outer extremities of contract law." P.S. Atiyah, *An Introduction to the Law of Contract* 30 (3d ed. 1981). Following are the six primary senses, with subsenses noted:

1. An agreement between two or more parties to do or not to do a thing or set of things; a compact—e.g.: "A *contract* in the popular sense of the word is an agreement between two or more parties." Lawrence Friedman, *Contract Law in America* 15 (1965).

2. **a.** An agreement between two or more parties creating obligations that are enforceable or otherwise recognizable at law—e.g.: "A *contract* is valid if valid under the law of the settled place of business or residence of the party wishing to enforce the contract." Russell Weintraub, *A Defense of Interest Analysis in the Conflict of Laws* [*etc.*], 46 Ohio St. L.J. 493, 498 (1985). **b.** A writing executed by the parties to evidence the terms of such an agreement—e.g.: "The execution of the *contracts* was not a condition of employment." *J.I. Case Co. v. NLRB*, 321 U.S. 332, 333 (1944) (per Jackson, J.). **c.** Arising out of or operating under such an agreement <contract rights> <contract work>. **d.** The legal relation resulting from such an agreement—e.g.: "The *contract* is a subsisting relation, of value to the plaintiff, and presumably to continue in effect." *Landess v. Borden, Inc.*, 667 F.2d 628, 631 (7th Cir. 1981) (quoting William Prosser, *Torts* 726 (2d ed. 1955)). **e.** The task or assignment for which such an agreement has been entered into—e.g.: "The six *contracts* of the defendants, were assigned to, and completed in the name of the New Jersey Wood Paving Company." *American Nicholson Pavement Co. v. City of Elizabeth*, 1 F. Cas. 691, 699 (C.C.N.J. 1874) (No. 309). **f.** In futures markets, the smallest amount of a given commodity that can be exchanged by agreement of traders, i.e., the standard unit of sale—e.g.: "The normal trading unit is one

contract consisting of 5000 bushels." *Cargill, Inc. v. Hardin*, 452 F.2d 1154, 1156 (8th Cir. 1971).

3. More broadly, any legal duty or set of duties not imposed by the law of tort; esp., a duty created by a decree or declaration of a court in the phrase *contract of record*—e.g.: "An obligation of record, as a judgment, recognizance, or the like, is included within the term '*contract*.' A bequest falls under the term '*contract*,' and when the will is admitted to probate it is to be regarded as a *contract of record*." *Quinn v. Shields*, 17 N.W. 437, 442 (Iowa 1883). See **contract of record**. Cf. **quasi-contract**.

4. a. A promise or set of promises, by a party to a transaction, enforceable or otherwise recognizable at law—e.g.: "The defendant agreed to let rooms to the plaintiff; and then, finding that the rooms were to be used for the delivery of blasphemous lectures, declined to carry out his *contract*." William R. Anson, *Some Notes on Terminology in Contract*, 7 Law Q. Rev. 337, 339 (1891). **b.** A writing that expresses such a promise—e.g.: "Whether a number of promises constitute one *contract* (and are non-separable) or more than one is to be determined by inquiring 'whether the parties assented to all the promises as a single whole, so that there would have been no bargain whatever, if any promise or set of promises were struck out.'" *U.S. v. Bethlehem Steel Corp.*, 315 U.S. 289, 298 (1942) (per Black, J.) (quoting *Williston on Contracts*).

5. The division or body of law dealing with contracts. *Often cap.* E.g.: "A general theory of *contract* asserts that there is at least a substantial body of rules which applies to all contracts in common." G.H. Treitel, *An Outline of the Law of Contract* 2 (5th ed. 1979).

6. The terms of a contract, or any particular term—e.g.:

- "It does not appear whether there was any express *contract* as to when the money was payable." *Civil Serv. Coop. Soc'y v. General Steam Navigation Co.*, 2 K.B. 756, 762 n.1 (1903).
- "A similar usage allows *contract* to be applied to . . . the terms or a particular term of a *contract*." R.M. Jackson, *The Scope of the Term "Contract"*, 53 Law Q. Rev. 525, 536 (1937).

B. General Slipperiness. "One moment the word [*contract*] may be *the agreement* of the parties; and then, with a rapid and unexpected shift, the writer or speaker may use the term to indicate the *contractual obligation* created by law as a result of the agreement." Wesley N. Hohfeld, *Fundamental Legal Conceptions* 31 (1919). Legal writers should be sensitive to any such semantic change within a given context.

C. And *promise*. The distinction between these words (despite sense 4 above) has long been urged, and perhaps ought to be observed for conceptual clarity. An influential English writer felt the slippage even in 1845, the words *in strictness* signaling a losing battle: "There is in strictness a distinction between a *promise* and a *contract*; for the latter involves the idea of mutuality, which the former does not." 2 Henry J.

Stephen, *New Commentaries on the Laws of England* 59 (1886). See **promise**, vb.

D. And *covenant*. *Contract* is the general term. *Covenant* now applies to (1) an agreement under seal; (2) an undertaking contained in a deed or implied by law in a deed, as in the phrase *covenant running with the land*; or (3) any specific contractual promise.

E. And *agreement, bargain*. See **agreement** & **bargain**.

F. Contract, vb.; *enter into a contract with*. The tighter wording, *to contract*, is almost always preferable to the longer, *to enter into a contract with*.

G. Formal contract; informal contract. See **formal contract** & **informal contract**.

H. *Verbal contract*. See *verbal contract*.

I. Illegal contract. See **illegal contract**.

J. Pronunciation. As a noun, *contract* is accented on the first syllable /**kon**-trakt/; as a verb, on the second /kən-**trakt**/. Cf. **contrast** & **compact**.

contract breach is inferior to *breach of contract*—e.g.:

- "The instances where tortious conduct merits a punitive award for *contract breach* [read *breach of contract*] are thus narrowly construed." Jonathan S. Solorzano, *An Uncertain Penalty*, 15 Law & Bus. Rev. Am. 779, 782 (2009).
- "Violations of valid conditions are remedied by either a claim for patent infringement or a claim for *contract breach* [read *breach of contract*]." Shubha Ghosh, *Carte Blanche, Quanta, and Competition Policy*, 34 J. Corp. L. 1209, 1223 (2009).

contract-breaker = breacher. E.g.:

- "The wicked *contract-breaker* should pay no more in damage than the innocent and the pure in heart." Grant Gilmore, *The Death of Contract* 14–15 (1974).
- "The option theory of contract also implies that liability for the breach of a contract is strict, that is, that the victim of the breach need not prove fault by the *contract breaker* [read *contract-breaker*] (another reason why specific performance can't be the standard remedy for breach)." Richard A. Posner, *Let Us Never Blame a Contract Breaker*, 107 Mich. L. Rev. 1349, 1351 (2009).

See **breacher**.

contractee (= a person with whom a contract is made) is attested in but one source (dated 1875) in the *OED*; it does not appear in *W3* and is labeled *rare* in *Black's Law Dictionary* (9th ed. 2009). The word was infrequently used in the 19th century—as early as 1815—but fell into disuse in the 20th century, probably for two reasons. First, its meaning duplicates that of *contractor*, so that using the two as correlatives makes little sense. Second, the terminology *offeror* and *offeree* more sharply defines the relationships to be denoted.

Still, a few notable writers have fallen for this word—e.g.: "If a man is induced to contract with another by a fraudulent representation of the latter that he is a great-grandson of Thomas Jefferson, I do not suppose that the contract would be voidable unless the *contractee* [read *contractor* or maybe *offeror*] knew that, for special reasons, his lie would tend to bring the contract about." Oliver Wendell Holmes Jr., *The Common Law* 255 (1881). See -EE.

contract for deed. See **chattel mortgage.**

contract for sale; contract of sale; contract to sell; executory sale. A. Senses. These various phrases have traditionally been used in the law of sales. The newest of them is *contract for sale*, used in the Uniform Commercial Code to include both "a present sale of goods and a contract to sell goods at a future time." U.C.C. § 2-106(1). In G.B., *contract of sale* bears this meaning in the Sale of Goods Act 1893.

The other phrases are narrower because they relate to a future transfer. *Contract to sell* denotes "a contract whereby the seller agrees to transfer the property in goods to the buyer for a consideration called the price." 1 Samuel Williston, *The Law Governing Sales of Goods* § 1, at 2 (1948). Williston notes that this idea is also "not very happily called an *executory sale*." *Id.* at 3. The problem with *executory sale* is that it suggests that a sale has occurred when in fact it has yet to occur.

B. Criticism of *contract for sale* and *contract of sale*. The broadest of these phrases (*contract for sale* and *contract of sale*) have come under criticism because they include two types of transfers: present sales and future sales. Williston complained—unavailingly, in retrospect—that "it is unfortunate . . . to use the same term for two transactions, differing so vitally in their legal effect." 1 Samuel Williston, *The Law Governing Sales of Goods* § 1, at 4 (1948). His recommendation was that "the unambiguous terms, '*contract to sell*' and '*sale*' should be used . . . to express the respective meanings." *Id.*

The consensus of modern scholarly opinion resists this criticism: "The distinction between exchanges that involve promises and those that involve only present transfers is not as sharp as might at first appear, since the law often attaches implied obligations of a promissory character to exchanges involving only present transfers (e.g., the seller usually makes implied warranties in the case of a present sale of goods). The Uniform Commercial Code avoids the distinction [by using the phrase] *contract for sale*." E. Allan Farnsworth, *Contracts* § 1.1, at 4 n.6 (1982).

contract implied in law. See **implied contract** & **quasi-contract.**

CONTRACTIONS. Legal writers have a morbid fear of contractions. Maybe that's because contractions tend to counteract stuffiness—and legal writers everywhere tend to think they should sound stuffy. That's a major psychological cause of poor writing. In fact, though, the more conversational your style is, the more readable it becomes. This is not to say that you should become loose and slangy in your writing, but that you should try to be relaxed and natural. Contractions contribute a lot to this effect. Here's the test. If you would say it as a contraction, write it that way. If you wouldn't, then don't.

Some excellent legal writers use contractions to good effect, especially when driving home a powerful point in the modern idiom. E.g.:

- "What our forefathers said, they said. What they *didn't* say, they meant to leave to us." Charles P. Curtis Jr., *Lions Under the Throne* 7–8 (1947).
- "Of course the bailee would have the action against the thief, if he could be found. But probably that *wasn't* worth very much." Edward Jenks, *The Book of English Law* 272 (P.B. Fairest ed., 6th ed. 1967).
- "You *won't* drive the nail properly if you *don't* hold it straight and so also you *won't* achieve an effective system of law unless you give some heed to what I have called principles of legality." Lon L. Fuller, *The Morality of Law* 200 (rev. ed. 1969).
- "Each of these three solutions is old-fashioned. But many lawyers use them and many lawyers who *don't* use them *don't* understand why they *don't*." Thomas L. Shaffer, *The Planning and Drafting of Wills and Trusts* 202 (2d ed. 1979).
- "This may seem rather curious today: why should a person be unwilling to answer questions properly put to him by duly authorized courts or officials? And if he is unwilling, *isn't* it likely that this is because he has something to hide?" P.S. Atiyah, *Law and Modern Society* 45 (1983).
- "Of course, we do have our property taxes and our inheritance taxes. If we *don't* pay them, we can lose our land." Thomas F. Bergin & Paul G. Haskell, *Preface to Estates in Land and Future Interests* 18 (2d ed. 1984).
- "The only thing left to do is for the jury to engage in a densely textured judgment upon the defendant's conduct—either it was deviant or it *wasn't*." Bruce A. Ackerman, *Reconstructing American Law* 28 (1984).
- "Yet *mightn't* the very Framers who believed the practice to be constitutional in their day nonetheless have been surprised by a suggestion that clergy disqualification therefore could *never* be declared unconstitutional?" Laurence H. Tribe & Michael C. Dorf, *On Reading the Constitution* 12 (1991).
- "You may think *you've* already learned how to discern 'the law,' at least if *you've* completed a semester or so of law school." Linda D. Jellum & David Charles Hricik, *Modern Statutory Interpretation* xxvii (2d ed. 2009).

Using contractions at every turn, of course, can make the writing seem breezy; for most of us, though, that risk is nil: a gentle breeze might refresh our readers. See **cannot** & SUPERSTITIONS (J).

contract of lease. The courts sometimes use this phrase rather than *lease* alone, as if ignoring the fact that a lease is primarily a contract—not a conveyance. "[If] used at all," states one commentator, the phrase *contract of lease* "should be applied merely to the aggregate of the covenants into which the parties may have entered in connection with the making of the conveyance by way of lease." 1 Herbert T. Tiffany, *The Law of Real Property* § 74, at 111 (Basil Jones ed., 3d ed. 1939).

contract of record. This phrase, ironically, denotes "no contract at all, and has nothing whatever to do with the law of contracts." P.S. Atiyah, *An Introduction to the Law of Contract* 31 (3d ed. 1981). A *contract of record* is an obligation imposed by a judgment or recognizance of a court of record; the phrase came about merely because such a judgment or recognizance was enforceable in common-law procedure by the same type of action as was used for contractual cases. For other phrases using *contract* but not truly involving a contract, see **unenforceable contract** & **void contract.**

contract of sale. See **contract for sale.**

contractor. See **independent contractor** & **contractee.**

contract quasi. See **implied contract** & **quasi-contract.**

contracts—like its singular—denotes an entire legal field, as do other plurals such as torts and conflicts. E.g.: "The field of Law known as *Contracts* is one of the most settled, most venerable, and least politically complicated fields of Law." Fred Rodell, *Woe Unto You, Lawyers!* 28 (1939). Cf. sense 5 listed at **contract.**

contract to sell. See **contract for sale.**

contractual is sometimes erroneously written (or pronounced) **contractural*, with an intrusive -*r*-. The *OED* illustrates the blunder with quotations from such reputable publications as *The New York Times* and *The Washington Post.*

  Alas, the word has invaded even higher ground: "There is no essential difference between *contractural* [read *contractual*] and statutory limitations." *Kornberg v. Carnival Cruise Lines, Inc.*, 741 F.2d 1332, 1337 (11th Cir. 1984). The U.S. Supreme Court has *sic*'d this solecism on more than one occasion. See *O'Connor v. Ortega*, 480 U.S. 709, 728 (1987) (quoting a deposition); *Shaffer v. Heitner*, 433 U.S. 186, 191 (1977) (quoting a party's affidavit).

contract under seal. See **seal (B).**

*contractural. See **contractual.**

contradictory; *contradictive; *contradictional; contradictious. *Contradictory* = opposite; contrary. *Contradictious* = inclined to contradict or quarrel; the word is applied to persons. **Contradictive* and **contradictional* are NEEDLESS VARIANTS of *contradictory.*

contradistinction; contrast. These words may be distinguished, if not contradistinguished. *Contradistinction* = distinction by opposition; *contrast* = dissimilarity (but not necessarily opposition). E.g.:

- "These differences in phraseology . . . must not be too literally *contradistinguished* [i.e., be too literally made to seem opposites]." *Brush v. Commissioner*, 300 U.S. 352, 362 (1937) (per Sutherland, J.).
- "The word 'children' in its primary and natural sense is always a word of purchase and not of limitation. . . . It is employed in *contradistinction* to the term 'issue.'" *In re Parant's Will*, 240 N.Y.S.2d 558, 561–62 (Sur. Ct. 1963).

- "The Seventh Amendment preserves the right to a jury trial in 'suits [that] the common law recognized among its old and settled proceedings, and in suits in which legal rights were to be ascertained and determined, in *contradistinction* to those where equitable rights alone were recognized, and equitable remedies were administered.'" *U.S. v. Philip Morris, Inc.*, 273 F.Supp.2d 3, 5 (D.D.C. 2002).

  Contradistinction should not be used where *contrast* suffices. E.g.: "Federal law, *in contradistinction* [read *in contrast*] to other jurisdictions, expressly provides in federal criminal cases that the issue of the defendant's bearing some or all of the cost of incarceration is to be considered at the time of sentencing." *State v. Strickland*, 33 Conn. L. Rptr. 638 (Super. Ct. 2002).

contra proferentem. **A. Sense.** This TERM OF ART names the doctrine that, in interpreting documents, ambiguities are to be construed unfavorably to the drafter. E.g.: "Faced with this ambiguity, the district court adopted the state law rule of contract interpretation *contra proferentem* in fashioning the federal common law." *Phillips v. Lincoln Nat'l Life Ins. Co.*, 978 F.2d 302, 306 (7th Cir. 1992).

  The Latin is literally "against him who offers." A 19th-century authority noted quite rightly that this rule of construction, which normally applies to contracts, "is applicable in pleading, but is not applicable to wills, nor to statutes, verdicts, judgments, etc., which are not words of parties." Henry C. Adams, *A Juridical Glossary* 585 (1886).

  B. Spelled *contra proferentes*. The phrase is sometimes rendered in the plural, *contra proferentes*, an alternative Latin form that is no longer much used—e.g.:

- "The fact that the company appears and interposes a claim to the steamer does not change the legal nature of the proceeding from one in rem to one in personam, so as to bring it within the terms of the special contract on the back of the bill of lading, which are to be *contra proferentes*." *Pacific Coast S.S. Co. v. Bancroft-Whitney Co.*, 94 F. 180, 186 (9th Cir. 1899).
- "I cannot adopt the suggestion that there is in this policy any ambiguous language to be construed *contra proferentes*." *Re Stooley Hill Rubber & Chem. Co. v. Royal Ins. Co.*, [1920] 1 K.B. 257, 274.

contrary. A. *Contrary to* or *contrary from*. *Contrary* takes the preposition *to*. The phrase *contrary from* is no longer standard.

  B. *On the contrary; to the contrary*. *On the contrary* marks a contrast with a statement or an entire argument just mentioned <The respondent argues that we must dismiss the petition. On the contrary, we consider it well taken>. *To the contrary* marks a contrast with a specific noun or noun phrase just mentioned <Reynolds sought relief; Griffin, to the contrary, decided not to litigate>.

  C. And *contradistinction*. See **contradistinction.**

contrast. A. Prepositions with. One *contrasts* something *with* something else, not *to*; but it is permissible to write either *in contrast to* or *in contrast with*.

B. *Compare and contrast.* This is an English teacher's REDUNDANCY.

C. Pronunciation. As a noun, *contrast* is accented on the first syllable /**kon**-trast/; as a verb, on the second /kən-**trast**/.

contrato leonino. See **leonine contract.**

contravene. A. And *controvert.* These words, occasionally confused, should be distinguished. *Contravene* = (1) (of persons) to transgress, infringe (as a law); to defy; or (2) (of things) to be contrary to, come in conflict with. E.g.:

- "The court ruled that the statutory provision was a penalty and that allowing a wrongdoer to insure himself against it would *contravene* public policy." *Northwestern Nat'l Cas. Co. v. McNulty*, 307 F.2d 432, 437 (5th Cir. 1962).
- "It is argued that the regulation, in limiting the amount of money any single household may receive, *contravenes* a basic purpose of the federal law." *Dandridge v. Williams*, 397 U.S. 471, 477 (1970) (per Stewart, J.).

See **violate.** For more on *contravention*, see **breach (A).**

Controvert = to dispute or contest; to debate; to contend against or oppose in argument. E.g.:

- "The appellant's counsel does not very seriously *controvert* the correctness of the answer finding the minor guilty of contributory negligence." *Callies v. Reliance Laundry Co.*, 206 N.W. 198, 199 (Wis. 1925).
- "Under the pleadings, when the issues were joined in fraud, undue influence, failure of consideration, and mistake, the court had jurisdiction to hear and determine the *controverted* facts." *Mabry v. Scott*, 124 P.2d 659, 665 (Cal. Dist. Ct. App. 1942).

For more on *controvert*, see **disprove.**

B. And **controvene.* The form **controvene* is a misrendering caused by confusion between the two words discussed in (A). E.g.: "The State's use of a jailhouse informant to elicit inculpatory information from Wilson *controvened* [read *contravened*] his right to counsel." *Wilson v. Henderson*, 742 F.2d 741, 748 (2d Cir. 1984). The same problem occurs in the noun form—e.g.: "In fact, the Appellees argue that Appellant acted in direct *controvention* [read *contravention*] of their interests." *Winfree v. Philadelphia Elec. Co.*, 554 A.2d 485, 488 (Pa. 1989).

C. And **contravent.* The form **contravent* is a misbegotten BACK-FORMATION innovated by writers who, reaching for the verb corresponding to *contravention*, forgot that *contravene* is the correct form. E.g.: "Decision appears to *contravent* [read *contravene*] clear legislative intent of IEEPA." Jules Lobel, *Emergency Power and the Decline of Liberalism*, 98 Yale L.J. 1385, 1417 n.175 (1989).

*contravent. See **contravene (C).**

contravention. See **breach (A).**

*contravert. See **controvert & contravene (A).**

*contributary. See **contributory, n.**

contribute for *attribute* is nothing less than a MALAPROPISM. But it is surprisingly common in AmE—e.g.:

- "The State simply contends that, from a review of the record, it appears that much of the delay can be *contributed* [read *attributed*] to [Appellant's] trying to obtain counsel, failing to obtain counsel, and trying to dismiss counsel." *Guice v. State*, 952 So.2d 187, 190 (Miss. Ct. App. 2006).
- "The lack of funding necessary to maintain road maintenance can be *contributed* [read *attributed*] to the gasoline tax losing its purchasing power." Nicholas J. Farber, Note, *Avoiding the Pitfalls of Public Private Partnerships*, 35 Transp. L.J. 25, 28 (2008). On the use of *tax* as opposed to *tax's*, see FUSED PARTICIPLES.

contribution; indemnity. These words frequently appear in tandem in the legal phrase *contribution and indemnity*, but many users of the phrase forget the individual significations of the words. *Contribution* is (1) the right to demand that another who is jointly responsible for injury to another contribute to the one required to compensate the victim; or (2) the actual payment by a joint tortfeasor of his share of what is due. It may entail an equal sharing of the loss, but in some jurisdictions entails a payment proportional to one's fault. *Indemnity* is (1) a duty to make good any loss, damage, or liability that another has incurred; or (2) the right of an injured person to claim reimbursement for his loss. Whereas *contribution* involves a partial shifting of the economic loss, *indemnity* involves a complete shifting of the economic loss. See **indemnity.**

Rather than using the phrase *contribution and indemnity* imprecisely and indiscriminately, the party seeking recompense should decide whether he or she is entitled only to one or the other, and then use that term only.

For *contribution's* meaning in equity, see **subrogation (C).**

contributory, adj.; **contributive; contributorial; contributional; *contributary.** Each of these word forms has a different meaning. *Contributory* = (1) making contribution; that contributes to a common fund; or (2) bearing a share toward a purpose or result <contributory negligence>. *Contributive* = having the power of contributing; conducive <exercise is contributive to health>. *Contributorial* = of or relating to a contributor. *Contributional* = of or relating to contribution or to a contribution. **Contributary* is a NEEDLESS VARIANT of *contributory*.

contributory, n.; ***contributary,** n. In the sense "one who, or that which, contributes," *contributory* is now standard—e.g.:

- "The company cannot put the beneficiary on the list of *contributories*." J. Charlesworth, *The Principles of Company Law* 70 (4th ed. 1945).
- "The question was whether a person who was a member of the provisional committee on the formation of a joint

stock company, and had accepted shares in the company, thereby became liable as a *contributory* when the second company failed." R.E. Megarry, *A Second Miscellany-at-Law* 143 (1973).

As with its adjectival use, **contributary* is a NEEDLESS VARIANT.

contributory negligence. See **comparative negligence** & **assumption of the risk.**

control, n. See **power (B).**

controller. See **comptroller.**

*controvene. See **contravene (B)** & **controvert.**

controversion, a fairly uncommon word, is the noun corresponding to *controvert*—e.g.:
- "The fact that Austin's workers' compensation carrier filed a statement of *controversion* is also irrelevant." *Archem Co. v. Austin Indus., Inc.*, 804 S.W.2d 268, 270 (Tex. App.— Houston [1st Dist.] 1991).
- "The record establishes, without *controversion*, that the defendant was twice advised of his constitutional rights." *People v. Kelland*, 567 N.Y.S.2d 810, 812 (App. Div. 1991).

controversy. A. Misspelling. *Controversy* appears surprisingly often in the mangled form **controversary*— e.g.: "We feel that this long-standing *controversary* [read *controversy*] can be significantly reduced and perhaps eliminated." *Evans v. Yankeetown Dock Corp.*, 491 N.E.2d 969, 974 (Ind. 1986).
   B. *Case or controversy.* See **case or controversy.**

controvert. So spelled—not **contravert*, a misspelling that litters more than 150 pages of American caselaw: "To adopt this analysis would be to directly *contravert* [read *controvert*] an express holding of the Court of Appeals." *Harper v. Harper*, 472 A.2d 1018, 1021 (Md. Ct. App. 1984). See **contravene (A)** & **(C).**

controvertible. So spelled.

contumacious; contemptuous. Both terms mean roughly "scornful," but the first is more frequently used as a legal term meaning "willfully disobedient of a court order." E.g.:
- "Finding that the record does not support a finding of *contumacious* conduct or a clear record of unexplained delay, we reverse the dismissal." *Morris v. Ocean Sys., Inc.*, 730 F.2d 248, 249 (5th Cir. 1984).
- "It is well settled in this Circuit that costs, including reasonable attorneys' fees, may be awarded to the party who prosecutes a contempt motion as an appropriate compensatory sanction for *contumacious* behavior." *New York State Nat'l Org. for Women v. Terry*, 952 F.Supp. 1033, 1043 (S.D.N.Y. 1997).

Sometimes in legal writing, *contumacious* bears its lay sense ("recalcitrant"), in which it is chiefly a literary word—e.g.:
- "We should not encourage litigants to act *contumaciously* out of fear that otherwise their constitutional rights will evaporate, nor should we penalize them for dignified rather than vociferous protests of what they consider to

be unwarranted treatment." *U.S. v. Burton*, 584 F.2d 485, 511 (D.C. Cir. 1978).
- "Despite respondent's adamant—even *contumacious*— refusal to cooperate with Hotchkiss or to take the stand as Hotchkiss advised, . . . Hotchkiss succeeded in getting a 'hung jury' on the two most serious charges at the first trial." *Morris v. Slappy*, 461 U.S. 1, 12 (1983) (per Burger, C.J.).

Contemptuous is the more usual term among nonlawyers as the adjective for *contempt*, but it is also used in legal contexts, which usually favor *contumacious*:
- "The [NLRB] petitioned this Court for an adjudication of civil contempt against the Company for violating an . . . order of this Court. . . . The Company's allegedly *contemptuous* conduct consists [in] . . . maintaining an *overly-broad* [read *overbroad*] rule prohibiting employee solicitation and distribution of materials, including union campaign materials." *N.L.R.B. v. Trailways, Inc.*, 729 F.2d 1013, 1016 (5th Cir. 1984).
- "Ordinarily purpose or intent is irrelevant in determining whether an offensive act is *contemptuous*; the nature of the act itself is determinative." *Ex parte Krupps*, 712 S.W.2d 144, 154 (Tex. Crim. App. 1986) (Clinton, J., dissenting).

See **contemptuous (A).**

contumacy; *contumacity; contumaciousness; contumely. **Contumacity* is a long NEEDLESS VARIANT for *contumacy* (= willful contempt of court). *Contumacy*, then, is a particular kind of *contempt of court*. (See **contempt of court.**) E.g.:
- "It cannot be disputed that he has power to issue a citation as he has done in the present case and the [statute] directs that the Judge who issued out the citation shall signify in cases of *contumacy*." *In re Baines*, [1840] 41 E.R. 400 (Ch.).
- "If the accused repents of his *contumacy*, he then has the right to plead to the indictment as if he had not been contumacious." F.P. Ramsay, *An Exposition of the Form of Government and the Rules of Discipline of the Presbyterian Church in the United States* 208 (1898).

The adjectival form is *contumacious.* See **contumacious.**

Contumaciousness should be reserved for the sense "the quality of being contumacious," and should not be used as a longer variant of the preferred noun: "While we do not wish to understate the significance of this omission, we find it to be 'more a matter of negligence than purposeful delay or *contumaciousness* [read *contumacy*].'" *Morris v. Ocean Sys., Inc.*, 730 F.2d 248, 253 (5th Cir. 1984).

Contumely, easily confused with *contumacy*, is a literary word meaning "rude and haughty language." Hence Shakespeare wrote, in *Hamlet*, of "the proud man's *contumely*" (Hamlet 3.1.70).

conundrum. Pl. *conundrums*—not **conundra.* E.g.:
- "In order to avoid *conundra* [read *conundrums*] of this sort it is necessary to abandon the simple dichotomy of 'proprietary' and 'possessory.'" A.W.B. Simpson, *An Introduction to the History of the Land Law* 35 (1961).
- "Not surprisingly, the drafting of the earliest statutes gave rise to a host of judicial *conundrums*." Alan Harding, *A Social History of English Law* 230 (1966).

See **PLURALS (A).**

*conusance—in the *OED*'s words, "an early form of *cognizance*, retained to recent times in legal use"—is a NEEDLESS VARIANT.

convene. See summon.

convener; *convenor. The first is the preferred form. See -ER (A).

convention. See treaty.

*conventional person. See juristic person.

conventional subrogation. See subrogation (B).

conversation, criminal. See criminal conversation & EUPHEMISMS.

conversationalist; *conversationist. The standard term is *conversationalist*. Older authorities preferred *conversationist*, but the word is today no better than a NEEDLESS VARIANT.

conversion means, in tort law, "the wrongful disposition of another's tangible property (other than land) as if it were one's own." It does not include mere acts of damage or even a taking that does not equate with denying the owner's right of property—but it does include acts such as taking possession, refusing to give up the goods on demand, giving them to a third person, or destroying them. This legal sense is virtually unknown to nonlawyers. The adjectival form of the word is *conversionary*.

convey. A. And *conveyance*, vb. *Conveyance*, hypothetically "to accomplish the conveyance of," does not exist except as implied in the form of the agent noun *conveyancer* and the gerund *conveyancing*. This verb denotes what the lawyer does. *Convey* denotes what the seller does (usu. through a lawyer). See conveyancing & conveyor (B).

In the phrase *convey away*, *away* is unnecessary. See PARTICLES, UNNECESSARY.

B. For *confer*. This is an inexplicable lapse. E.g.:

- "Appellee's and appellant's respective citizenships of France and Georgia therefore *conveyed* [read *conferred*] diversity jurisdiction." *Jagiella v. Jagiella*, 647 F.2d 561, 563 (5th Cir. 1981).
- "Although [Defendant's] juvenile adjudication took place in district court under *conveyed* [read *conferred*] jurisdiction, the issue still rests upon the nature of juvenile adjudication in family court." *State v. Riviera*, 993 P.2d 580, 586 n.5 (Haw. Ct. App. 1999).

See confer.

conveyance, n. A. Legal Senses. In law, the noun *conveyance* refers not only to the actual transfer of an interest in land, but also to the document (usually a deed) by which the transfer occurs.

B. For *car* or *automobile*. *Conveyance* is sometimes used as a FORMAL WORD for *car*. It should be avoided when possible. E.g.: "The negligence of a driver of a private *conveyance* [read *car*] was not imputed to the guest." The only context in which it might be justified is that in which the writer intends to be so broad as to cover any vehicle, vessel, or aircraft.

C. And *conveyal*. *Conveyance* is the better noun corresponding to the verb *to convey*; *conveyal* is a NEEDLESS VARIANT.

conveyance, vb. See convey (A).

conveyancer. See conveyor (B).

conveyancing, a term more common in BrE than in AmE, is often understood in a sense analogous to that of *conveyance* (= the document by which land is purchased). E.g.: "It is absolutely essential to understand the two systems of *conveyancing* property in existence, as this will determine . . . the way you go about the process and final registration." Frances James, *Straightforward Guide to Buying and Selling Your Own Home* 82 (2009). Actually, however, it can have a wider import; *conveyancing* comprises the drafting and completion of all kinds of legal instruments, not just those having to do with the transfer of land. E.g.: "A distinction should not be drawn between a gift of the purchase price of the former matrimonial home and a gift of the heritable property itself simply because of the *conveyancing* techniques employed." *Latter v. Latter*, [1990] S.L.T. 805 (Court of Session).

Still, in modern usage, *conveyancing* more and more commonly takes on a more restricted sense: "The law of *conveyancing* is essentially the law relating to the creation and transfer of estates and interests in land." I.R. Storey, *Conveyancing* 3 (2d ed. 1987).

convey and quitclaim. See words of conveyance.

convey and warrant. See words of conveyance.

conveyee (= one to whom property is conveyed) is a legal NEOLOGISM not recorded in dictionaries. E.g.:

- "Since seisin passed to the feoffee at the time of feoffment, or not at all, there could be no springing freehold estate to arise in the *conveyee* out of the estate of the conveyor at a future time." Cornelius J. Moynihan, *Introduction to the Law of Real Property* 163–64 (2d ed. 1988).
- "Sometimes the conveyor produced a knife, which he used to dig a clod of earth from the land or to cut a twig from a tree on the land, and the clod or twig was then handed to the *conveyee* together with the knife." Peter Butt, *Land Law* 455 (2d ed. 1988).

See -EE.

conveyor. A. And *conveyer*. In legal contexts, *conveyor* predominates. Outside law, *conveyer* is the general spelling for "one that conveys." In mechanical uses, however, as in *conveyor belt*, the *-or* spelling is standard.

B. And *conveyancer*. These two terms are distinct. A *conveyor* is the person who transfers or delivers title to another. E.g.:

- "[The] conveyance shall be given effect according to the intention of the *conveyor*." Stanley M. Johanson, *Reversions, Remainders, and the Doctrine of Worthier Title*, 45 Tex. L. Rev. 1, 27 (1966).
- "When the conveyance affects only a part of the *conveyor's* land and, prior to the conveyance, there has been a quasi-easement as between parts of the *conveyor's* land, the prior use of the parcel can help determine the scope of the easement." *R.C.R., Inc. v. Deline*, 190 P.3d 140, 155 (Wyo. 2008). On the use of *prior to* in that sentence, see *prior to.

See -ER (A) & convey.

A *conveyor* must usually have a *conveyancer*, that is, a lawyer specializing in real-estate transactions. E.g.: "The practice of *conveyancers*—lawyers whose business it is to draw up conveyances, wills, and other legal documents—is sometimes valuable evidence of what the law is." William Geldart, *Introduction to English Law* 15 (D.C.M. Yardley ed., 9th ed. 1984). See the English law journal entitled *The Conveyancer*. See also **conveyancing**.

convict, n. See **prisoner**.

convict, vb. In the legal idiom, one is convicted *of* crimes, but *on* counts, or *for* the act of committing a crime. See **conviction**.

convictability, a late-20th-century American NEOLOGISM, refers to the likelihood that a prosecution will result in conviction. Lawyers refer to the *convictability* of cases as well as defendants—e.g.: "The reform effort did not lead more women to report rapes, nor did it change the way prosecutors assessed the '*convictability*' of cases." Susan Estrich, *Real Rape* 88 (1987).

convictable; *convictible. The first is preferred.

convicted. A. Meaning. A person pleads guilty to a felony and receives probation. Has that person been *convicted*? The question matters because, in some states, being *convicted* means that you lose your voting rights. A California court has held that a man who had pleaded guilty, served 90 days in jail, and then withdrawn his guilty plea—whereupon the case was dismissed—had not been *convicted*. See *Truchon v. Toomey*, 254 P.2d 638, 644 (Cal. Ct. App. 1953).

B. Prepositions with. A person is *convicted of* a crime or *convicted for* the act of committing a crime, but is not *convicted in* a crime: "A Palestinian suspected in the bombing of Pan Am Flight 103 was *convicted* today along with three co-defendants *in* [read *for*] a series of attacks in northern Europe four years ago." *Pan Am Bombing Suspect Convicted in Other Attacks*, N.Y. Times, 22 Dec. 1989, at A3.

*convictee. Omitted from most dictionaries, *convictee* is a legal NEOLOGISM and, what is worse, a NEEDLESS VARIANT of the noun *convict*. E.g.:
- "[The] view that inmate violence is to be expected in a maximum security prison that houses violent *convictees* [read *convicts*] has little if any relevance to the instant case." *Madison County Jail Inmates v. Thompson*, 773 F.2d

834, 849 (7th Cir. 1985) (Flaum, J., concurring in part & dissenting in part).
- "We respectfully suggest that the legislature give consideration to amending the probation statute to eliminate optional rejection of probation by a *convictee* [read *convict*]." *State v. Migliorino*, 442 N.W.2d 36, 48 (Wis. 1989).

Cf. **acquittee**. See -EE.

*convictible. See **convictable**.

conviction, it may surprise some readers to know, is used in reference to misdemeanors as well as to felonies. See **convict**, vb.

conviction-prone. See **guilt-prone**.

convince; persuade. Generally, the word *convince* is properly followed by an *of*-phrase or a *that*-clause <he convinced the jury of his client's innocence> <he convinced the jury that his client was innocent>. *Persuade* is usually followed by an infinitive. It is a fall from stylistic grace to write "He *convinced* [read *persuaded*] her to transfer title to him the day before he filed for divorce." *Ware v. Ware*, 161 P.3d 1188, 1196 (Alaska 2007). See **persuade**.

convoke. See **summon**.

co-opt = (1) to recruit (someone) as a member; (2) to assimilate; absorb; to make use of; or (3) to gain the allegiance of (an opponent or potential opponent). The preferred noun form is *co-optation*, not *co-option*; the preferred adjectival form is *co-optative*, not *co-optive. See CO- (A).

coownership (= title giving two or more persons concurrent possession and enjoyment of property) is now written solid. (See CO- (A).) Traditionally, *coownership* has taken three forms: coparcenary, tenancy in common, and joint tenancy. The first of these is now a defunct tenancy. On the others, see **joint tenancy.**

coparcenary, though looking like an adjective, is usually a noun, meaning "an estate in land descended from an ancestor to two or more persons who possess equal title to it"—as when a tenant in tail died intestate and left two female heirs. (See **tail**.) The *OED* notes that a rarer form, ending -*ery*, is "more etymological"; it is also more recognizable as a noun. But this form, like two others—*coparceny and *parcenary—is now classifiable only as a NEEDLESS VARIANT.

The estate was abolished in England in 1925. In the U.S., *coparcenary* came into use in the mid-19th century, mostly in the Northeast and the Midwest. E.g.: "It is contended, that the distinction is merely technical, and does not affect the enjoyment of the estate, whether held in *coparcenary* or in common, as in Maryland there is very little, if any difference." *Gilpin v. Hollingsworth*, 3 Md. 190, 196 (1852). Surprisingly, the estate remains current in some jurisdictions, such as Ohio, which declares by statute: "When a person dies intestate having title or right to any personal property, or to any real estate or inheritance, in this state, the personal property shall be distributed, and the real estate or inheritance shall descend and pass in *parcenary."* Ohio Rev. Code Ann. § 2105.06 (1988).

coparcener. A. And **parcener.* Dating from the 13th century, **parcener* has become a NEEDLESS VARIANT of *coparcener,* which did not appear until the 15th century. The prefix *co-* emphasizes the jointness in the term's meaning "a joint heir." See CO- (A). Cf. **copartner.*

B. And **copartner.* According to one etymological theory, *coparcener* and **copartner* were originally the same word, *partner* having been a corrupt spelling of—a scribal error for—**parcener* in the 13th century. But that is unlikely, since many 14th-century manuscripts spelled the word **parsener,* thus belying the idea that medieval scribes merely confused the *-c-* for a *-t-,* without any sense-association. In any event, DIFFERENTIATION between the words is so complete that few would now associate the two words. See the following entry.

*copartner need not exist alongside *partner.* The joint relationship (i.e., that the existence of one partner implies the existence of one or more other partners) is clear to all native speakers of English. (That jointness is not clear in *parcener*—see **coparcener.**) Because **copartner* adds nothing to the language of the law, it should be avoided. E.g.: "The same form of relief was given at law in cases of contribution between cosureties and *copartners* [read *partners*]." William F. Walsh, *A Treatise on Equity* 90 (1930). See NEEDLESS VARIANTS.

*copartnership is a NEEDLESS VARIANT of *partnership*— e.g.: "Although, in a strict sense, not a *copartnership* [read *partnership*], a joint venture generally is governed by rules and principles applicable to partnership relationships." *Austin P. Keller Constr. Co. v. Commercial Union Ins. Co.,* 379 N.W.2d 533, 535 (Minn. 1986).

copending is an adjective used to describe two or more applications that are simultaneously on file and active in the Patent Office. *See* Louis B. Applebaum et al., *Glossary of United States Patent Practice* 26 (1969). E.g.: "Peerless' argument that the application recited the existence of the *copending* application is misplaced." *Gardco Mfg., Inc. v. Herst Lighting Co.,* 820 F.2d 1209, 1215 (Fed. Cir. 1987).

coplaintiff, though infrequent, is not the NONCE WORD that the *OED* suggests it is. E.g.: "[The stockholder's] application was one for intervention as *coplaintiff." Auerbach v. Bennett,* 393 N.E.2d 994, 999 (N.Y. 1979). The word should not be hyphenated after the first syllable—e.g.: "Daughter to Sir Edward Poole and afterwards wife to and *co-plaintiff* [read *coplaintiff*] with Sir Ralph Dutton." C.H.S. Fifoot, *History and Sources of the Common Law* 425 n.9 (1949). See CO- (A). For the corresponding term, see **codefendant.**

COPULAS, ADVERBS OR ADJECTIVES AFTER. See ADVERBS (C).

copulate. See **fornicate.**

copy, vb., in the sense "to send a copy to" <he copied me with the letter>, is a voguish casualism to be avoided. It is fast becoming standard American lawyer's JARGON. E.g.: "It is therefore legitimate to *copy* [read *send a copy to*] the recipient's boss." Mark H. McCormack, *What They Don't Teach You at Harvard Business School* 138 (1984).

copyeditor. One word.

copyleft is a NEOLOGISM jocularly formed as a counteragent to *copyright.* The brainchild of Richard Stallman, a computer hacker, *copyleft* is a form of copyright that obliges software users to distribute source code for no more than the cost of reproducing it. E.g.: "Stallman's main worry was that some company would take the operating system he wrote, make some changes, and then say that their 'improved' programs were separate inventions and proprietary. To prevent that, he invented a new kind of licensing agreement, the 'Copyleft,' which lets people do anything they want with the software except restrict others' right to copy it." Simson L. Garfinkel, *Programs to the People: Computer Whiz Richard Stallman Is Determined to Make Software Free,* Tech. Rev., Feb.–Mar. 1991, at 52.

copyright, adj.; **copyrighted.** For the sense "secured or protected by copyright," *copyrighted* is the better and by far the more usual form. As an adjective, the form *copyright* is uncommon enough that it does not sufficiently announce what part of speech it is playing—e.g.: "Thanks and appreciation for the use of *copyright* [read *copyrighted*] material." Jefferson D. Bates, *Writing with Precision* xviii (rev. ed. 1985).

copyright, n. See **intellectual property.**

copyright, vb. This verb has existed since the early 19th century. Hence the adjective *copyrightable.* For a mistaken form, see **copywrite.*

copyright troll. See **troll.**

*copywrite is a not infrequent mistake for *copyright,* vb. E.g.: "Ownership of a copyright is something distinct from ownership of a physical object in which the *copywritten* [read *copyrighted*] work is embodied." *Nika Corp. v. City of Kansas City,* 582 F.Supp. 343, 367 (W.D. Mo. 1984).

coram (lit., "in the presence of") begins many of the LATINISMS known to the law. *Coram nobis* (= before us; the court of King's Bench, originally) was the name of a writ of error directed to a court for review of its own judgments and predicated on alleged errors of fact. E.g.: "This is an appeal from a judgment denying this appellant's petition for writ of error *coram nobis." Holman v. State,* 462 So.2d 1035, 1036 (Ala. Crim. App. 1984). *Coram vobis* (= before you) gave its name to the writ of error by an appellate court to a trial court for correction of the latter's error of fact. These phrases are obsolescent if not obsolete in most jurisdictions.

Two other phrases in which *coram* appears are *coram judice* (= in the presence of a judge) and *coram populo* (= in public). Both are unjustifiable LATINISMS. See *coram non judice.*

coram non judice = (1) outside the presence of a judge; or (2) before a judge but not the proper one, or one who cannot take legal cognizance of the matter. This is the one LATINISM beginning with *coram* that is still fairly frequently used. E.g.:

- "The subject-matter is not before it; the proceeding is *coram non judice* and void." *Ex parte Bradley*, 74 U.S. 364, 377 (1868) (per Nelson, J.).
- "This court has often held that where there is a petition or pleading commencing a proceeding in a court of limited jurisdiction seeking a statutory right, such petition or pleading must aver every jurisdictional fact which must exist in order for the court to proceed and, failing to do so, the entire proceeding is *coram non judice* and void." *Jefferson County v. Berkshire Dev. Corp.*, 168 So.2d 13, 16 (Ala. 1964).
- "In view of our holding that the trial court lacked jurisdiction, however, the proceeding is *coram non judice* and it is unnecessary for us to reach such issues." *Boyd v. Boyd*, 653 S.W.2d 732, 737 (Tenn. Ct. App. 1983).

See LATINISMS & *coram.*

core. See **corps.**

corespondent; correspondent. There is an important difference between these terms. In jurisdictions in which appellees are called *respondents*, *corespondent* = co-appellee. But this word has a more specific legal meaning; in divorce suits, when adultery was commonly a ground for divorce, the *corespondent* was the man charged with the adultery and sued together with the wife, or *respondent*. E.g.:

- "A few days later the husband filed a petition for divorce on the ground of the wife's adultery and sought an order for costs against the *corespondent*." *Carter v. Carter*, [1964] P. 1, 2.
- "[The judge] was not satisfied that the wife's adultery had not started earlier than she had said and, because he thought that the wife had not told him the full truth about her association with the *corespondent*, refused to exercise the court's discretion in her favour." *Goldsmith v. Goldsmith*, [1965] P. 188 (C.A.).
- "The husband knew that the wife had committed adultery with the *corespondent* in 1956, but had continued to live with her outwardly as man and wife: the wife did not tell him, and he did not know, that she had also committed adultery with the *corespondent* in 1954." *Inglis v. Inglis*, [1968] P. 639.

A *correspondent*, of course, is a letter-writer, an on-location news-gatherer, or a business representative.

*corollarily, having appeared in fewer than two dozen reported American decisions, may (one hopes) never live more than a shadow of an existence. The *OED* notes that the adjectival use of *corollary* is "rare." The corresponding adverb is not mentioned, but here it is:

- "*Corollarily* [read *As a corollary*], it would follow that such an extent of actual application may occur as to provide substantial probativeness of the reasonableness of the understanding and belief engaged in." *United Med. Labs., Inc. v. Columbia Broad. Sys., Inc.*, 404 F.2d 706, 708 (9th Cir. 1968).
- "Tenneco *corollarily* [read *also*] contends that the trial court erred when it struck affidavits filed by it opposing the motion for summary judgment." *Hanover Petroleum Corp. v. Tenneco, Inc.*, 521 So.2d 1234, 1236 (La. Ct. App. 1988).

See SENTENCE ADVERBS.

corollary; correlation. A *corollary* is an ancillary rule or principle <the assumption-of-the-risk defense is a corollary of the "clean-hands" doctrine in equity>. A *correlation* is a relationship that tends to suggest causality <the correlation between nutrition and success in primary school has long been accepted>.

coroner; *coronator. The second is a NEEDLESS VARIANT.

corpora. See **corpus.**

corporal; corporeal. These terms have undergone DIFFERENTIATION. *Corporal* = of or affecting the body <corporal punishment>. The meaning is unclear here: "He participated in four *corporal* lineups." *Rudolph v. Blackburn*, 750 F.2d 302, 304 (5th Cir. 1984).

Corporeal = having a physical material body; substantial <corporeal beings, as opposed to spiritual ones>. E.g.: "Louisiana law is clear that a domestic animal is considered *corporeal* movable property." *Smith v. University Animal Clinic, Inc.*, 30 So.3d 1154, 1156 (La. Ct. App. 2010).

In the following sentence, *corporeal* is used for *corporal*: "There is no question that a physical beating by one who has no privilege of inflicting such *corporeal* [read *corporal*] punishment intrudes on the victim's liberty interests." *Dwares v. New York*, 985 F.2d 94, 98 (2d Cir. 1993). The *OED* calls this usage obsolete, but it persisted in odd places—e.g.: "it involves idea [*sic*] of punishment, *corporeal* [read *corporal*] or pecuniary." *Black's Law Dictionary* 1133 (6th ed. 1990). It was dropped from the seventh edition (1999). See **corporeal.**

corporate law; corporation law; company law. The usual term in AmE for the law of corporations is *corporate law*. The equivalent in BrE is *company law*. *Corporation law* is a variant phrase occasionally used. See **company law** & **corporate lawyer.**

corporate lawyer; corporation lawyer. There is a subtle distinction. A *corporate lawyer* is either (1) an office practitioner specializing in corporate law, or (2) in-house counsel to a corporation. The phrase is colorless. *Corporation lawyer*, by contrast, is usually connotatively charged, referring to a lawyer, usu. a litigator, who represents major corporations and who makes a name as a "mouthpiece" for profitable ventures that may harm the environment, society, or individuals. In other words, those who use the phrase are not, generally speaking, well disposed to the person referred to—e.g.: "No more than any other President did Lincoln look to merit alone; indeed, his first appointment was one of the worst ever made to the Court, for Noah Swayne of Ohio—named as a barefaced sop to certain business interests who were supporting the war for less than idealistic reasons—was a *corporation lawyer*, as successful as he was callously unethical, who was not to change his spots or his spottiness throughout his long judicial career." Fred Rodell, *Nine Men* 137 (1955). See **corporate law.**

corporateness now has only the sense "the quality of being a body corporate [i.e., a corporation]." E.g.:

- "Equally as well settled as is the principle that plain fraud is not a necessary prerequisite for piercing the corporate veil is the rule that the mere fact that all or almost all of the corporate stock is owned by one individual or a few individuals, will not afford sufficient grounds for disregarding *corporateness*." *DeWitt Truck Brokers, Inc. v. Ray Flemming Fruit Co.*, 540 F.2d 681, 685 (4th Cir. 1976).
- "The alter ego doctrine is equitable in nature, with the test of its application being whether recognition of *corporateness* would produce unjust consequences." *In re Global Waste Co.*, 207 B.R. 542, 547 (Bankr. N.D. Ohio 1997).
- "Because we respect the separate legal status of a corporation and its shareholders, we are equally reluctant to disregard *corporateness* to create liability as we are to disregard *corporateness* to remove liability." *Cambio Health Solutions, LLC v. Reardon*, 213 S.W.3d 785, 790–91 (Tenn. 2006).

Formerly it meant "corpulence" and "bodiliness" as well.

corporation, in the U.S., refers to "an entity (usu. a business) with authority under law to act as a single person, with rights to issue stock and exist indefinitely." In England, *corporation* (or *body corporate*) is defined more broadly as "an entity that has legal personality, i.e., that is capable of enjoying and being subject to legal rights and duties" (*CDL*). Often, in G.B., where *company* is the more usual term, *corporation* is used elliptically to mean a *municipal corporation* (= the authorities of a municipality that carry on civic business). See **company, corporation sole** & **juristic person.** See also **firm** & **body corporate.**

corporation aggregate. See **corporation sole.**

***corporational** is a NEEDLESS VARIANT of *corporate*. E.g.: "A judgment adverse to the plaintiffs on count 2, involving charges that excessive compensation had been paid to the individual defendant as a *corporational* [read *corporate*] officer, was affirmed." *Saigh v. Bush*, 403 S.W.2d 559, 561 (Mo. 1966).

corporation law. See **corporate law.**

corporation lawyer. See **corporate lawyer.**

corporation sole; corporation aggregate. A *corporation sole* is "an individual, being a member of a series of individuals, who is invested by a fiction with the qualities of a [c]orporation." Henry S. Maine, *Ancient Law* 155 (17th ed. 1901). By "a series of individuals," Maine meant that a continuous legal personality is attributed to successive holders of certain monarchical or ecclesiastical positions, such as kings, bishops, rectors, vicars, and the like.

A *corporation aggregate* is merely the full name for what we generally know as a *corporation*; the full phrase generally appears only when a writer contrasts it with a *corporation sole*.

corporatization. See -IZE.

corporeal; incorporeal. The early common law adopted the Roman distinction between *corporeal* (= tangible) and *incorporeal* (= intangible) property, reasoning that land—a material "thing"—has physical substance, whereas a right of way—which is not material—does not. Peter Butt comments that "modern jurisprudence, more familiar with the nature of rights, regards this distinction as unsatisfactory, for *incorporeal* 'things' are simply rights. A right of way, for example, is simply a right over land, and becomes a 'thing' only by a more or less convenient figure of speech. But the medieval lawyers of England preferred to deal with 'things' and so accepted the Roman classification." Peter Butt, *Land Law* 302 (2d ed. 1988). See **corporal** & **hereditament(s).**

corporeal hereditaments = land and fixtures. The defining words are preferable to this highfalutin LEGALISM, the precise meaning of which is unclear even to some seasoned lawyers. See **hereditament(s).**

corps; core. A *corps* is a group (esp. a military unit) working together or doing like tasks <Army Corps of Engineers> <signal corps>. Avoid the misspellings *core* (= the center) and (worse) *corpse* (= a dead body).

corpus; principal; res; trust property; trust estate; subject matter of the trust. These are the various terms used in reference to the property held by a trustee. *Principal*, *trust property*, and *subject matter of the trust* are perhaps most comprehensible to nonlawyers and might be preferred on that account. But the five terms are widely used in legal writing, and it is unlikely that any of them will disappear completely in the next few decades. See **principal.**

Still, the more widely accessible terms may be on the rise. The influential Restatement of Trusts uses *trust property* in preference to *res* because the drafters "felt it unnecessary to drag in a Latin word when English words are available and quite sufficient." 1 A.W. Scott & W.F. Fratcher, *The Law of Trusts* § 3.1, at 52 (4th ed. 1987). See **res.**

Corpus is the Latin word meaning "body." It usually denotes an abstract collection or body <a substantial corpus of legal commentary in this field>. In the following sentences, *corpus* is used in its most usual legal context, involving trusts:

- "These powers include the power to alter or amend the trust instrument or withhold trust assets from beneficiaries, a power to reacquire trust assets at less than fair market value, a power to invade trust *corpus* to support the dependents of the grantor, . . . and the power to pay the trust corpus to the grantor and withhold distributions to beneficiaries." Hudson A. Mead, *A Primer in the Grantor Trust Rules*, 69 Mich. B.J. 1152, 1155 (1990).
- "She authorized the trustees to make direct payments of her trust income and *corpus* to provide for her maintenance, support, and comfort, consistent with the standard of living she previously enjoyed." *In re Chandler*, 767 A.2d 1036, 1041 (N.J. Super. Ct. App. Div. 2001).
- "Upon his death, a landowner directed that his lot be sold and the proceeds added to the *corpus* of a trust for the benefit of all the trust's beneficiaries." *McNabb v. Barrett*, 257 S.W.3d 166, 172 (Mo. Ct. App. 2008).

The plural form is *corpora*. E.g.: "The *corpora* of the trusts were [held] not . . . taxable to the settlor's estate." *State St. Trust Co. v. U.S.*, 263 F.2d 635, 637 (1st Cir. 1959).

Occasionally it is misrendered *corpuses*—e.g.:

- "Different aspects of an article may be protected by different *corpuses* [read *corpora*] of law." David Bender, *Protection of Computer Programs*, 47 U. Pitt. L. Rev. 907, 914–15 (1986).
- "She will have at least $1,500,000 in assets left after the property distribution orders, and current assets and trust *corpuses* [read *corpora*]." *Weinstein v. Weinstein*, 561 A.2d 443, 450 n.4 (Conn. App. Ct. 1989).

The plural is *corpora* even in the phrase *habeas corpus*. See PLURALS (A) & **habeas corpus.**

corpus delicti—meaning "the body of a crime" and emphatically not "dead body"—is generally outmoded as a variant of *actus reus*. The general sense of *corpus delicti* is "the nature of the transgression." E.g.: "The confession in evidence was an extrajudicial confession—voluntary and without pressure, after caution and after the *corpus delicti* had been established." *McDaniel v. Commonwealth*, 32 S.E.2d 667, 670 (Va. 1945).

In cases of felonious homicide, the *corpus delicti* is usually evidence of a death and of a criminal agency as its cause. Thus, *corpus delicti* "has traditionally been established by proof of the dead body and evidence of an unnatural cause of death." *State v. Allen*, 197 N.W.2d 874, 876 (Mich. Ct. App. 1972). But the dead body is not necessary to establish a *corpus delicti*. "Despite clarification of the early confusion about the meaning of the Latin idiom . . . as used in homicide cases, there remains, among many laymen at least, some lingering misunderstanding that the *corpus delicti* in such cases refers to the body of the deceased. It does not, of course, and refers instead to the body (*corpus*) of the wrong (*delicti*), 'the loss sustained.'" *People v. Williams*, 373 N.W.2d 567, 571 (Mich. 1985). See **overt act.**

The phrase is sometimes misspelled **corpus delecti*, a sort of macabre etymological double entendre. See **delecti.*

corpus juris (= the body of law; the law as the sum of laws) is a generic term derived ultimately from the *Corpus Juris Civilis*, the original name of Justinian's code (A.D. 534). E.g.: "The maritime law is not a *corpus juris*—it is a very limited body of customs and ordinances of the sea." *Southern Pac. Co. v. Jensen*, 244 U.S. 205, 220 (1917) (Holmes, J., dissenting).

The term remains well known to American lawyers because of the treatise entitled *Corpus Juris Secundum*; in general contexts, however, it is best to write *body of law*. See LATINISMS.

correctable; *correctible. The first is preferred.

correctional; corrective. *Correctional* = of or pertaining to correction, usu. penal correction <correctional institution>. E.g.: "[He demonstrated] by his plea that he is ready and willing to admit his crime and to enter the *correctional* system in a frame of mind that affords hope for success in rehabilitation." *Brady v. U.S.*, 397 U.S. 742, 753 (1970) (per White, J.). *Corrective* = tending to correct <corrective measures>.

correctitude; correctness. *Correctitude* is a PORTMANTEAU WORD or blend of *correct* and *rectitude*. Referring to what is proper in conduct or behavior, it has moralistic overtones—e.g.:

- "The local political allies of the west tend to be unrepresentative, dissolute, or repressive rulers. . . . Against them Islam seems to provide certainty of belief and *correctitude* of behaviour." Godfrey Jansen, *The Soldiers of Allah*, Economist, 27 Jan. 1979, at 45.
- "Judicial independence is a fragile concept. It is popular at the highest level of abstraction, but it regularly loses support in the face of rulings or statements that clash with various notions of *correctitude*." Steven Lubet, *Judicial Independence and Independent Judges*, 25 Hofstra L. Rev. 745, 749 (1997).

Correctness serves as the noun of *correct*, adj., in all its other senses—e.g.: "The *correctness* of that decision is maintained, upon an able and elaborate discussion of reasons and authorities, in *Langdell on Contracts*." *Lewis v. Browning*, 130 Mass. 173, 175 (1880).

correlation. See **corollary.**

correspondent. See **corespondent.**

corroborate. A. Senses and Uses. *Corroborate* = (1) to support (a statement, argument, etc.) with evidence that is consistent; to confirm; or (2) to confirm formally (a law, etc.). Sense 1 is more common: "The evidence of an accomplice must be *corroborated*." Glanville Williams, *The Sanctity of Life and the Criminal Law* 157 (1957). See **authenticate.**

In either sense, this verb should be transitive <the last witness corroborated the testimony of other witnesses>. **Corroborate with* is inferior to *corroborate*.

Hence one writes, "The circumstances *corroborate* his presence in the city when the crime was committed," not, "The circumstances *corroborate* with his presence in the city when the crime was committed."

B. Pronunciation. In confirmation hearings for judicial appointees, U.S. senators have a bad habit of pronouncing this as if it were spelled *cooberate*, doubtless by confusion with *cooperate*. In October 1991, during Justice Clarence Thomas's confirmation hearings, Senator Joe Biden and other members of the Senate Judiciary Committee consistently pronounced this word as if it were *cooberate*—in other words, *cooperate* with a *-b-* instead of a *-p-*. The correct pronunciation is /kə-**rob**-ə-rayt/.

C. And *collaborate*. The word *corroborate* is occasionally used where *collaborate* (= to work jointly with [another] in producing) belongs, as here: "The defendants *corroborated* [read *collaborated*] to create a cover-up after the murder." *Commonwealth v. James*, 678 N.E.2d 1170, 1179 (Mass. 1997).

corroboration = (1) the confirmation of (a statement) by additional evidence; or (2) the formal confirmation of (a law, etc.). Sense 1 is much more common—e.g.: "Because the testimony of a settlor seeking to revoke a trust is likely to be unreliable, and because solemn written instruments are not to be lightly overturned, strong corroboration of the settlor's testimony is required in order to warrant the granting of relief." *Pernod v. American Nat'l Bank & Trust Co.*, 132 N.E.2d 540, 542 (Ill. 1956).

corroborative; *corroboratory*. The first is standard, *-tory* being a NEEDLESS VARIANT. See **confirmatory.**

corrodible; *corrosible*. The first is preferable because with it the underlying verb, *corrode*, is more readily apparent.

corrupter; *corruptor*. The *-er* spelling is preferred. See -ER (A).

corruptible. So spelled.

cost, insurance, and freight is commonly abbreviated *C.I.F.* For the distinction between it and *F.O.B.*, see **F.O.B.**

***costomal.** See **custumal.**

costs, in the sense of "charges, expenses," is obsolete except in law—the specific definition of the word being either (1) the charges or fees "taxed" by the court, such as filing fees, jury fees, courthouse fees, and reporter fees; or (2) the expenses of litigation, prosecution, or other legal transaction, esp. those allowed in favor of one party against the other. In England—under the *English Rule*—sense 2 applies: *costs* include not only court charges but also a litigant's

attorney's fees. American lawyers sometimes call these *litigation costs*, as opposed to *court costs* (or *costs of court*), which is a more explicit way of using *costs* in sense 1. See **English Rule.**

costs and expenses. This phrase is analogous to **liens and encumbrances*—or, for that matter, **men and human beings*. That is, the phrases consist of a species-word followed by a genus-word. *Expense* is the broader term, referring to "an expenditure of money, time, labor, or resources to accomplish a result" (*Black's Law Dictionary* 658 [9th ed. 2009]). *Costs*, in legal contexts, are usually "the charges or fees taxed by the court, such as filing fees, jury fees, courthouse fees, and reporter fees" (*id.* at 398), although they can also be "the expenses of litigation, prosecution, or other legal transaction, esp. those allowed in favor of one party against the other" (*id.*). So literally, *costs and expenses* is an illogical phrasing. To cure the problem, try *costs and other expenses*. See **liens and encumbrances.**

cosurety. So spelled—without a hyphen. See CO- (A).

cotenancy; cotenant. The words are so spelled—without a hyphen. (See CO- (A).) The most common types of *cotenancies* are *joint tenancy, tenancy by the entireties*, and *tenancy in common*. See **joint tenancy & tenancy by the entireties.**

coterminous; *coterminant*; *coterminate*; *coterminal*; conterminous. *Conterminous* is the oldest and the basic term meaning "having or enclosed within a common boundary." *Coterminous*, an altered form of the original term, shares the meaning of *conterminous* but also means "coextensive in extent or duration." For the sake of DIFFERENTIATION, *coterminous* should be confined to this figurative or metaphorical sense, and *conterminous* reserved for physical and tangible senses. E.g.:

- "It cannot be seriously argued as a general matter that the constitutional limits of congressional power are *coterminous* with the extent of its exercise in the late 18th and early 19th centuries." *O'Callahan v. Parker*, 395 U.S. 258, 280 (1969) (Harlan, J., dissenting).
- "Indeed, the international meaning and extent of access to counsel for persons accused of terrorism is not necessarily *conterminous* [read *coterminous*] with that found in American domestic criminal courts." Charles J. Dunlap Jr. & Linell A. Letendre, *Military Lawyering and Professional Independence in the War on Terror*, 61 Stan. L. Rev. 417, 427 (2008).
- "All attempts to punish profanity as a spiritual crime—that is to say, all attempts to punish that strain of profanity that is *conterminous* [read *coterminous*] with blasphemy—ought now be regarded as blocked by settled understandings of the Religion Clauses." Rodney A. Smolla, *Words "Which by Their Very Utterance Inflict Injury,"* 36 Pepp. L. Rev. 317, 326 (2009).

Coterminant, *coterminate*, and *coterminal* are NEEDLESS VARIANTS.

*cotortfeasor is inferior to *co-tortfeasor*, because the length of the word deceives the eye; in addition, *cotort* (suggesting *cohort*) wrongly seems at first to be the primary word rather than *tortfeasor*. See CO- (A).

couch fee (= sexual favors taken by a lawyer instead of a monetary fee) is a flippant term to denote a serious ethical breach. E.g.: "I had heard sotto voce comments about '*couch fees*' from other lawyers (and not all of them divorce specialists, either), but this Chicagoan was the first to boast about taking sex from a client in lieu of money." Joseph Goulden, *The Million Dollar Lawyers* 31 (1978).

could. See **can** (B) & ***should/could.**

couldn't care less. This is the correct phrasing—not **could care less* (which implies that you do care). E.g.: "While many artists *could* [read *couldn't*] care less about matters of state, others find it a moral imperative to use the power of their craft in protest." J. Harvie Wilkinson III, *Subjective Art, Subjective Law*, 85 Notre Dame L. Rev. 1663, 1684 (2010).

council; counsel. *Council* (= a deliberative assembly) is primarily a noun. *Counsel* (= to advise) is primarily a verb, but in legal writing it is commonly used as a noun in the sense "a legal adviser or legal advisers." Occasionally *council* is misused for *counsel*—e.g.: "It should be noted that claims made against former Mercury General *Council* [read *Counsel*] Susan Skaer, now Tanner, were recently dismissed." Stephanie L. Soondar & Allen Major, *Litigation and Recoupment of Executive Compensation*, 6 Hastings Bus. L.J. 397, 433 n.316 (2010). (Duly noted.) See **advise** (A), **counsel, n.** & **consul.**

councillor; counselor. The first is a member of a council, the second one who gives advice (usu. legal advice). See **attorney** (A).

councilmanic is an unfortunate adjectival form of *councilman*, which itself is objectionable to writers who try to avoid SEXISM. The nonsexist *council member* can substitute for *councilman*—in which case the manic adjective need not intrude.

counsel, n. A. Scope of Term. In BrE, *counsel* is used only of barristers (litigators), whereas in AmE it is frequently used of office practitioners (e.g., *general counsel*) as well as of litigators. See **attorney** (A), **consul, council** & **of counsel.**

B. Number. *Counsel* may be either singular or plural; in practice it is usually plural. But examples of the singular use are common enough:

- "There is no excuse for a *counsel* who has obtained a thorough understanding of the case at bar . . . presenting to the court a statement [that] has no definite plan, which mingles material and immaterial facts, and which is verbose and discursive." William M. Lile et al., *Brief Making and the Use of Law Books* 370 (3d ed. 1914).

- "*Counsel* arguing a case is permitted to assert that a precedent has had unhappy consequences." Michael Zander, *The Law-Making Process* 239 (2d ed. 1985).

More typically, *counsel* is used as a plural. In 1819, for example, the court reporter in *McCulloch v. Maryland* wrote: "The Court dispensed with its general rule, permitting only *two counsel* to argue for each party."

Counsels is sometimes mistakenly used as a plural of *counsel*—especially when nonlawyers are writing about the law:

- "This might seem a strange approach for *counsels* [read *counsel*] responsible for representing not just Valeo and Henshaw but the interests of their employers, the U.S. House and Senate as well." Barbara H. Craig, *Chadha: The Story of an Epic Constitutional Struggle* 73 (1988).

- "Four lawyers were named Nov. 25 to serve as legal *counsels* [read *counsel*] for the transition." *Clinton's Justice Review Team Named*, Nat'l L.J., 7 Dec. 1992, at 2.

C. For *of counsel.* See **of counsel.**

counsel, vb. See **advise** (A).

counsel fees. See **attorney's fees.**

counselless. So spelled in both AmE and BrE. In the wake of *Gideon v. Wainwright*, 372 U.S. 335 (1963) (holding that an indigent criminal defendant must be provided counsel even in a noncapital case), the word is often used in a phrase illustrating HYPALLAGE: *counselless convictions*. See, e.g., *U.S. v. Coyer*, 732 F.2d 196, 200–01 (D.C. Cir. 1984) ("the sentencing court had relied upon *counselless convictions* rendered nugatory by *Gideon v. Wainwright*"). It is not the *convictions* that are counselless, of course, but the *convicts.*

counselor; counsellor; counseling; counselling; counselable; counsellable. The preferred spellings are *counselor, counseling,* and *counselable* in AmE, and *counsellor, counselling,* and *counsellable* in BrE. See DOUBLING OF FINAL CONSONANTS & **attorney** (A) & **councillor.**

count, n. In addition to its use in criminal indictments and informations—in which it means "a part that details or charges a distinct grievance or offense"—this word is used in patent practice to mean "a claim made by the parties to an interference." *See* Louis B. Applebaum et al., *Glossary of United States Patent Practice* 28 (1969). See also **interference.**

countenance, give . . . to is usually an unnecessary PERIPHRASIS for *countenance*, vb. E.g.: "Courts have indeed used language that seems *to give countenance to* [read *to countenance*] the notion that, if a plot is worked out, it cannot be copyrighted." *Sheldon v. Metro-Goldwyn Pictures Corp.*, 81 F.2d 49, 53–54 (2d Cir. 1936).

COUNTER- (= done, directed, or acting against, in opposition to, as a rejoinder or reply to another thing of the same kind already made or in existence [*OED*]) is a common prefix in law because of our adversary system. About half the modern examples in the *OED* are unhyphenated; the better practice nowadays is not to hyphenate such a prefix. Among the law words, both nouns and verbs, beginning with this prefix are these:

counteraccusation	counternotice
counteraffidavit	counteroffer
counteraffirmation	counterperformance
counterappeal	counterpetition
countercondemnation	counterplea
counterdeclaration	counterpromise
counterestoppel	counterproof
counterexplanation	countersign
counterfactual	counterstatement
countergift	countersue
counterinterpretation	countersuggestion
counterlaw	countertitle
counterlegislation	countervindication

Sometimes the prefix is doubled up—e.g.: "And if, by any chance, the boss had come back at Tony with 'How about fifty-five?,' *that* would have been a *counter-counter-offer* involving an Implied, etc." Fred Rodell, *Woe Unto You, Lawyers!* 30 (1939).

counterclaim is one word, unhyphenated. See COUNTER-. For the meaning of *counterclaim*, see **cross-claim.**

counterfactual, n., is, like its better-known synonym *hypothetical*, an attributive noun. E.g.:

- "The 'but for' standard requires the factfinder to address a *counterfactual*: whether a prosecutor would have struck the challenged Afro-American jurors if his decisions had not been clouded by impermissible racial considerations." *Wilkerson v. Texas*, 493 U.S. 924, 926 (1989) (Marshall, J., dissenting).
- "The last *counterfactual* is the easiest." *Shelton v. Office of Workers' Comp. Programs*, 899 F.2d 690, 692 (7th Cir. 1990).

The word sometimes remains an adjective—e.g.: "This type of statement is a *counterfactual* conditional statement, i.e., it is conditional in form and runs counter to fact." *Maddocks v. Bennett*, 456 P.2d 453, 460 n.11 (Alaska 1969).

Whether as a noun or as an adjective, though, *counterfactual* is unusual enough to be slightly pompous in place of *hypothetical*. See COUNTER-.

counterfeit. See **imposture.**

counterfeiting; forgery. These words overlap to some degree. To *counterfeit* (lit., "to imitate") means to unlawfully make false money that passes for the genuine. Before the advent of paper money, the distinction between *counterfeiting* and *forgery* was clear because it referred only to the making of false metallic coins. To *forge* (lit., to falsify or fabricate) is to fraudulently make or alter a document in a way that harms

another's rights. In reference to paper money, then, the two words are virtually interchangeable. See **forgery.** For more on the noun *counterfeit* and its near-synonyms, see **imposture.**

countermand, n. & vb. This word is most commonly a verb meaning (1) "to annul (an earlier command or action) by a contrary command" <the partner countermanded the previous assignment>; or (2) "to recall by a contrary order" <countermanding that shipment>. Sense 1 is most usual—e.g.:

- "The day before the Indianapolis hearing, the judge called Mr. Atanga and, *countermanding* his earlier entry, ordered Mr. Atanga to be in Lafayette the next day." *In re Atanga*, 636 N.E.2d 1253, 1258 (Ind. 1994) (Sullivan, J., dissenting).
- "In fact, Brown's employees testified that they had the authority to *countermand* Fontenot's orders to perform personal work if Freeman was needed at the store." *Hebert v. Cigna*, 637 So.2d 1221, 1225 (La. Ct. App. 1994).
- "In May 1989, Brownlow *countermanded* an order for a piece of equipment that Jones had placed with a dealer on behalf of the Corporation." *Cecil Sand & Gravel, Inc. v. Jones*, 644 A.2d 529, 532 (Md. Ct. App. 1994).
- "The order must be signed by a party, received by the financial institution prior to death, and not *countermanded* by other written order of the same party prior to death." *Jordan v. Burgbacher*, 883 P.2d 458, 463 (Ariz. Ct. App. 1994) (synopsizing a statute). On the use of **prior to* in that sentence, see ***prior to.**

But sense 2 also occurs in legal contexts—e.g.: "The court distinguished *Chan Siew Lai* on the basis that when a bank issues a cashier's check the check becomes the primary obligation of the bank and the purchaser has no authority to *countermand* a cashier's check because of fraud allegedly practiced on the purchaser by the payee." *Godat v. Mercantile Bank of N.W. County*, 884 S.W.2d 1, 4 (Mo. Ct. App. 1994) (en banc).

As a noun, *countermand* refers to either (1) a contrary command or order that revokes or annuls an earlier one; or (2) an action that nullifies something previously executed. Sense 2 is the more specific legal one, but sense 1 predominates in both legal and nonlegal contexts—e.g.: "So far as the record shows, there was no *countermand* of the direction in the telegram and no effort on the part of Dyches or his attorney to have the appeal brought before the appellate court." *Dyches v. Ellis*, 199 S.W.2d 694, 697 (Tex. Civ. App.—Austin 1947).

*Countermandment, labeled "obsolete" in the *OED*, really ought to be so. But because it still lives, it could be more aptly described as a NEEDLESS VARIANT—e.g.: "The Bank contends, however, that in some circumstances a cashier's check should be subject to *countermandment* [read *countermand*], like a certified check, where the issuance is a result of error or fraud and the rights of no other party have intervened." *Foreman v. Martin*, 286 N.E.2d 80, 82 (Ill. App. Ct. 1972).

counteroffer; cross-offer. In the law of contract, a *counteroffer* is an offeree's new offer that varies the terms of the original offer and that therefore constitutes a rejection of the original offer. (See COUNTER-.) A *cross-offer*, by contrast, is an offer made to another in ignorance that the offeree has made the same offer.

counterproof, n. The *OED* prematurely calls this word, meaning "evidence in opposition to other evidence," obsolete. American lawyers continue to find it useful—e.g.:

- "A fair rule either would afford this chance or would restrict the prosecution's *counterproof* in the same way his own is limited." *Michelson v. U.S.*, 335 U.S. 469, 493 (1948) (Rutledge, J., dissenting).
- "If the proof and *counterproof* on the issue depend upon the credibility factors or inferences to be drawn from conflicting evidence, the question is one of fact for the jury." *U.S. v. Martinez*, 429 F.2d 971, 976 (9th Cir. 1970).

See COUNTER-.

countersignature = a second signature attesting to the authenticity of the instrument on which it appears. The *OED* traces this word back to 1842, but in fact it appeared some 35 years earlier in AmE: "The act, as to the *countersignature* by the secretary and recording the same, is directory." *Philips v. Erwin*, 19 F. Cas. 500, 500 (C.C.D. Tenn. 1807) (No. 11,093). *Countersign* is the verb. See COUNTER-.

countersue is a nontechnical way of saying *counterclaim*, vb. E.g.: "Mr. Aboud *countersued*, claiming he had losses of $200,000 because casino employees had given him free drinks." R.B. Smith, *Casinos May Be Held Liable for Drunken Patrons* [sic] *Losses*, Wall St. J., 23 June 1989, at B1. See COUNTER-.

countervail = to counterbalance; to compensate for. This word is probably used 100 times in legal writing for every time it appears in nonlegal writing. E.g.: "The interests of nonminorities in not taking another test do not sufficiently *countervail* these needs."

The word most often appears as a participial adjective. E.g.:

- "Vidrine filed no *countervailing* affidavits." *Vidrine v. Enger*, 752 F.2d 107, 110 (5th Cir. 1984).
- "The *countervailing* accounts of what was testified to in the interview are not nearly as strong in the trial as stated in the EEOC letter." *Coleman v. Home Depot, Inc.*, 306 F.3d 1333, 1340 (3d Cir. 2002).
- "When, as here, no qualifying factor is established, we have no choice but to defer to the legislature even though there may be *countervailing* policy considerations." *Corwell v. Corwell*, 179 P.3d 821, 824 (Utah Ct. App. 2008).

There is nothing inherently wrong with the word, but *countervailing considerations* is on the verge of becoming a legal CLICHÉ.

countervailing equity. See **equity.**

countez was, at common law, the LAW FRENCH term that the court crier used in numbering the jury, but it was soon corrupted into *count these*, as Blackstone explained: "Of this ignorance [of Law Latin and Law French] we may see daily instances in the abuse of two legal terms of ancient French; one, the prologue to all proclamations, '*oyez*, or hear ye,' which is generally pronounced most unmeaningly, 'O yes'; the other, a more pardonable mistake, *viz.* when the jury are all sworn, the officer bids the crier number them, for which the word in law-french is '*countez*'; but we hear it pronounced in very good English, 'count these.'" 4 William Blackstone, *Commentaries on the Laws of England* 334 n. (1769). See *oyez.*

countless applies only to count nouns. E.g.: "She knew my father and I were sick of moving their *countless* baggage, but in public she still believed in maintaining family solidarity." Maxim D. Shrayer, *Homage to Isaac Babel*, Sw. Rev., 1 Jan. 2003, at 144. One may have *countless bags* but not *countless baggage.*

country. In the 12th through the 14th centuries, a jury was a body of neighborhood witnesses summoned to decide by their sworn verdict a dispute between litigants. The controverted facts were said to be tried by the *country* (L. *patria*, Fr. *pays*), which came to be the equivalent in law to "jury." To this day—though somewhat archaically—a litigant demanding a jury sometimes *puts himself (or herself) upon the country* (L. *ponit se super patriam*). So it was in medieval times: "The normal administration of justice was restored in 1218, and the justices found the gaols full of criminals whom they could not try—unless they allowed the accused to '*put themselves upon their country*' (a jury of neighbours), on the general question of guilt or innocence; and that was the solution adopted." Alan Harding, *A Social History of English Law* 61 (1966).

country lawyer (= a rural lawyer, usu. a general practitioner, who knows the ways of the people). Unlike *city lawyer*, the term *country lawyer* carries a connotation that is sometimes neutral, sometimes positive, sometimes negative. E.g.:

- (Neutral) "The testator was a *country lawyer* who had acquired a large estate, both real and personal." *McClellan v. MacKenzie*, 126 F. 701, 702 (6th Cir. 1903).
- (Positive) "The Judge having been a *country lawyer* himself took a fatherly interest in my career." Ephraim Tutt, *Yankee Lawyer* 52 (1943).
- (Negative) "The rule of reason . . . should now allow one to put an antitrust theory of liability or justification into terms that a *country lawyer* can understand." Lawrence A. Sullivan, *The Viability of the Current Law on Horizontal Restraints*, 75 Cal. L. Rev. 835, 847 (1987).

Cf. **city lawyer.**

county, n., in 20th-century American lawyers' slang, is a shortening of *county detective*. E.g.: "Directly opposite on the same corridor was a large room given over to process servers known as '*county detectives*' or '*counties*.'" Ephraim Tutt, *Yankee Lawyer* 87 (1943).

coup de grace. This GALLICISM is sometimes mispronounced /koo də **grah**/, as if the last word were spelled *gras* (as in *pâté de foie gras*). The correct pronunciation is /koo də **grahs**/.

coup d'état; rebellion; revolution; revolt; insurrection; insurgency; putsch. All denote an uprising against those in authority, usually accompanied by violence. The GALLICISM *coup d'état* (koo day-**tah**—often shortened to *coup*) is a sudden and decisive stroke by which those in power are overthrown. The term keeps its diacritical mark but is typically not italicized; the preferred plural form is the anglicized *coups d'états*, not the French *coups d'état*. (The best practice may simply be to shorten the plural form to *coups*, so that the awkwardness of the plural form doesn't arise.) A *rebellion* is usually open and organized resistance to governmental power. The term is typically applied after the fact to a failed attempt or to an uprising that was part of a larger revolution <the Whiskey Rebellion>. A *revolution* is a successful rebellion that has overthrown an old government <the American Revolution>. A *revolt* is usually an armed uprising that does not last long, because it is either soon quelled or immediately successful. An *insurrection* is similar to a *revolt*, often involving a seditious seizure of power for control by one's own party—but often with less truculence than a *revolt* and with greater willingness to compromise with the reigning authority. An *insurgency* is typically a prolonged, guerrilla-type uprising that today often involves frequent terrorist attacks <the Afghan insurgency>. A *putsch* (/puuch/—the term was borrowed from Swiss-German into English) is a small popular uprising, usually short-term; the word is mostly confined to European uprisings <the Munich beer-hall putsch of 1923>. Cf. **sedition.**

COUPLED SYNONYMS. See DOUBLETS, TRIPLETS, AND SYNONYM STRINGS.

coupled with. A. Number. This phrase, like *together with*, results in a singular and not a plural verb when it couples two singular nouns—e.g.: "The absence of crude petroleum and iron ore, *coupled with* limited indigenous supplies of coal and natural gas, *ensures* [not *ensure*] that Japanese industry must import to survive." Roger Buckley, *Japan Today* 67 (2d ed. 1990). See **together with.**

    B. *Coupled with an interest.* This phrase typically appears in a power of attorney to make it irrevocable for as long as the interest remains in effect—so that, for example, the power may survive the principal's death or incompetence. The phrase is not one to be copied by rote from one document to another: its implications need to be closely considered.

    And because the legal implications are not widely known today even to lawyers—apart from those who have made powers of attorney their special interest—a more explicitly worded statement is desirable. Here's what one commentator shrewdly suggests by way of a plain-language statement: "[The principal] acknowledges that this power of attorney is *coupled with an* *interest*, in that the agent has an interest in [refer to whatever is the subject of the power]. As a result, in addition to any other consequences under the law, this power is irrevocable and will survive [the principal's] death or incompetence." Kenneth A. Adams, *A Manual of Style for Contract Drafting* 239 (2d ed. 2008).

couple (of) dozen, hundred, etc. It is slipshod to omit the *of* in such a construction as this: "Is a used toilet seat worth $1 million? Or even a *couple* [read *couple of*] hundred thousand dollars?" Lindsey Gruson, *Is It Art or Just a Toilet Seat? Bidders Will Have to Decide*, N.Y. Times, 15 Jan. 1992, at B1.

coupon is preferably pronounced /**koo**-pon/, not /**kyu**-/.

course, as (a matter) of. See **as of course** & **of course.**

court. A. Metonymy. *Court* is frequently used as a metonymic substitute for *judge*. E.g.:

- "The *court himself*, possessed of a countenance and bearing elsewhere commanding, appeared little more than a pygmy here, in spite of *his* elevation on the bench." (Ex. fr. H.W. Horwill, *Modern American Usage* 88 (1935).)
- "Further, the *circuit court stated that he* would instruct Holman to answer the question and informed Holman that if he did not answer, the court would hold him in contempt." *Holman v. State*, 269 S.W.2d 815, 824 (Ark. 2007).
- "A federal prisoner proceeding pro se appeals the *district court's* refusal to recuse *herself.*" *U.S. v. Patterson*, 292 Fed. Appx. 835, 836 (11th Cir. 2008).
- "The *trial court stated that he* would give the defendant until first thing in the morning to indicate how the defendant wished the *court* to address these observations, and that the *trial court* would ask for responses from counsel at that time." *State v. Campbell*, 983 So.2d 810, 833 (La. 2008).

This usage has sometimes bemused nonlawyers: "In the sometimes-strange jargon of jurists, the words *court* and *judge* were often synonymous." John A. Jenkins, *The Litigators* 155 (1989).

    B. As a Collective Noun. Today *court* is used in AmE as a COLLECTIVE NOUN taking a singular verb. In BrE, the plural verb usually appears with this noun when more than one judge sits on the court: "The *court* of appeal *have* concurred." *Notes*, 14 Law Q. Rev. 336 (1898). Long ago, this construction was common even in the U.S.: "The *Court were* unanimously of opinion, that writs of error to remove causes to this court from inferior courts, can regularly issue only from the clerk's office of this court." *West v. Barnes*, 2 U.S. 401, 401 (1791) (mem.).

court, go to; come to court. The first is the usual AmE phrase, the second the usual BrE phrase. See **come to court.**

court, open. See **open court.**

court costs. See **costs.**

court crier. See **crier.**

courthouse. One word.

court judgment. See **judgment (D).**

court-made is frequently used as an equivalent of *judge-made*—e.g.: "Although it is commonly said that when the United States sues, it comes into court on an equality with private litigants, in fact it enjoys a number of advantages, both statutory and *court-made*." Charles Alan Wright, *The Law of Federal Courts* 127 (5th ed. 1994). See **judge-made.**

court-martial is hyphenated both as noun and as verb. The *OED* lists the verb as colloquial, an observation now antiquated. As to spelling, in AmE, the final *-l* is not doubled in *court-martialed* and *court-martialing*, although in BrE it is. See DOUBLING OF FINAL CONSONANTS. The plural of the noun is *courts-martial*.

In older texts, the term is sometimes rendered *martial court*—e.g.: "A *martial court* must needs in the present case confine its attention to the blow's consequence." Herman Melville, *Billy Budd* 66 (1891; repr. Signet ed. 1979). See POSTPOSITIVE ADJECTIVES.

court of appeal(s). Both forms appear, but *appeals* is more common in AmE, whereas *appeal* is the only form in BrE. The correct form is the statutorily prescribed or the customary form of a given jurisdiction. Following is an example of the less usual American form: "In 93 Cal. App. 2d 43, the *Court of Appeal* affirmed the judgment."

For the proper possessive form with *court of appeals*, see POSSESSIVES (G).

Court of Customs and Patent Appeals. This American court, created in 1909, no longer exists, having been merged in 1982 into the Court of Appeals for the Federal Circuit.

court of first instance = (1) a court in which any proceedings are initiated; or (2) the trial court as opposed to an appellate court. The *CDL* marks sense 2 as a loose usage, but the great historian Theodore F.T. Plucknett appears to have used it in this sense: "There was thus one court of appeal and one *court of first instance*." *A Concise History of the Common Law* 211 (5th ed. 1956). See **first instance.**

Court of International Trade. Originally this court, created in 1909, was known as the Board of General Appraisers, then as the Customs Court, and since 1980 as the Court of International Trade. It hears cases involving customs and duties.

court of justice is a solemn and slightly antique equivalent of *court of law*. E.g.: "Men go from a *court of justice*, after witnessing a severe contest, and in reporting their opinion of the arguments, they will say that one of the advocates had no fault that they can precisely define, and yet there was a prevailing heaviness or a want of impressiveness." Edward T. Channing, "Judicial Eloquence," in *Lectures Read to the Seniors in Harvard College* 98, 103 (1856).

court of law, formerly used in contrast with *court of equity*, is now a formal phrase for *court*, which suffices in ordinary legal contexts. E.g.:

- "Where a contract for the sale of real estate is fair, reasonable, and certain in all of the terms, it is as much the duty of a court of equity to decree specific performance as it is for a *court of law* to award damages for breach of contract." *Boyd v. Mercantile Safe Deposit & Trust Co.*, 344 A.2d 148, 152 (Md. Ct. Spec. App. 1975).
- "Fraud in the inducement of a contract is also ground for an action for damages in a *court of law*." *George Robbrecht Seafood, Inc. v. Maitland Bros. Co.*, 255 S.E.2d 682, 683 (Va. 1979).
- "Appellate courts are *courts of law* and not courts of fact. We cannot judge the credibility and strength of witnesses because trial courts have this responsibility. . . . An 'issue not raised in the circuit court may not be presented for the first time on appeal.'" *Jenkins v. Jenkins*, 325 S.W.3d 924, 928 (Ky. Ct. App. 2010).

Today *court of law* often merely emphasizes the dignity of the judicial institution referred to; but in a few jurisdictions, and certainly in historical contexts, it may usefully distinguish a lawcourt from a court of equity or from some other type of court. See **lawcourt.** Cf. **court of justice.**

Court-packing plan. TI thihis phrase refers to President Franklin D. Roosevelt's plan, presented to Congress on February 5, 1937, to appoint six new justices to the U.S. Supreme Court. It would have enabled him to appoint a new judge to supplement any judge who, upon reaching 70, did not retire. With more than six sitting judges over that age, the plan would have ensured that Roosevelt could win judicial approval of the New Deal program. "The bitter fight that led to the defeat of this '*court-packing*' plan," writes the leading scholar on federal courts, "has given the notion of a nine-man Court such sanctity that it is unlikely that the size will again be changed." Charles Alan Wright, *The Law of Federal Courts* 14 (5th ed. 1994).

court papers = all papers that a party files with the court, including pleadings. Technically, *pleadings* has a restricted sense—referring to complaints, answers, counterclaims, cross-claims, and the like, but not to motions, notices, petitions for leave, and other court papers. American lawyers frequently use *pleadings* loosely as if it were synonymous with *court papers* (known also as *suit papers*)—e.g.: "That record . . . is made up of all the '*suit papers*,' the *pleadings* in the case." John Kaplan & Jon R. Waltz, *Cases and Materials on Evidence* 1 (5th ed. 1984). See **pleadings (B).**

The phrase *court papers* is often shortened to *papers*—e.g.: "The *papers* filed today by the prosecuting team . . . were in response to the motion of Mr. Barry's lawyers." B. Drummond Ayres, *Capital Mayor Used Drugs Many Times, Court Is Told*, N.Y. Times, 21 Apr. 1990, at 8.

court reporter. Before 1900, this phrase usually denoted a set of books, as in *Superior Court Reporter*. By the late 19th century, however, it had taken on a new sense: "one, usu. a stenographer, who records and transcribes court proceedings, depositions, and the like." E.g.:

- "The appellant or plaintiff in error . . . may have the testimony taken in the case transcribed and certified by a *court reporter.*" *Apache County v. Barth*, 177 U.S. 538, 540 (1900) (per Peckham, J., quoting an act passed in 1897 in the territory of Arizona).
- "The transcripts of the Crawford County proceedings cannot be filed by the Supreme Court Clerk because the *court reporter* who transcribed them . . . is not properly certified as a *court reporter.*" *Pullan v. Fulbright*, 685 S.W.2d 151, 153 (Ark. 1985).

For more on the term *reporter*, see **report (A).**

In journalism, the phrase *court reporter* commonly refers to a journalist whose beat is a royal court—e.g.: "The book by Mr Whitaker, the *Daily Mirror*'s *court reporter*, is the most gripping. Charles, he reveals, slept with his mistress, Camilla, two nights before he married Di." *Westenders*, Economist, 19 June 1993, at 94.

courtroom. So spelled—without a space or a hyphen.

Court Street lawyer = a disreputable, wheeling-and-dealing New York lawyer practicing in Brooklyn near Court Street, where many state and federal courts are located. E.g.:

- "Newfield countered the report by writing that the author of the report was a '*Court Street*' *lawyer* 'with ties to the Brooklyn clubhouses' and had interviewed only the plaintiff in preparing the report." *Rinaldi v. Holt, Rinehart & Winston, Inc.*, 366 N.E.2d 1299, 1304 (N.Y. 1977).
- "If Mr. Halpern was not a Wall Street lawyer, nor was he a *Court Street lawyer*, at least not as that term is usually used—a synonym for ambulance chaser, fast talker, exploiter of the miserable." David Margolick, *At the Bar*, N.Y. Times, 9 Feb. 1990, at B11.

See LAWYERS, DEROGATORY NAMES FOR (A).

court suit (BrE) = lawsuit. E.g.: "The legal challenges, involving more than 40 *court suits*, are still far from over." *Towering Troubles*, Economist, 30 Sept.–6 Oct. 1989, at 26.

covenant, n., = (1) a promise made in a deed; or (2) an obligation burdening or favoring a landowner. Sense 1 is the strict one, sense 2 being less fastidious but probably more common. For example, in referring to the various covenants that are implied by law into a lease in the absence of an agreement—such as the *covenant for quiet enjoyment* and the *covenant against encumbrances*—the word *covenant* is synonymous with *term*.

Commentators frequently remark how much *covenant* has slipped from its traditional moorings—e.g.: "In equity, . . . an equitable right *in rem* arises in favor of the covenantee, his heirs and assigns, when the parties intended that the restriction should bind the estate of the covenantor or promisor for the benefit of the land of the covenantee or promisee. The use of

the term '*covenant*' in these cases is hardly justified, because the promise may be without seal or by parol." William F. Walsh, *A Treatise on Equity* 456 (1930). See **condition (A), restrictive covenant, term** & **warranty (A), (B).** Cf. **covenant running with the land.**

covenant, vb. To *covenant* is to enter into a covenant or formal agreement or to agree or subscribe to by solemn promise. E.g.:

- "If a third party has *covenanted* to transfer property to a trust, it is the trustee's duty to take reasonable steps to enforce such a covenant." *Fortune v. First Union Nat'l Bank*, 371 S.E.2d 483, 489 (N.C. 1988) (Meyer, J., dissenting).
- "The landlord's duty arises if he expressly *covenants* to repair at the inception of the lease." *Childress v. Bowser*, 526 N.E.2d 1209, 1211 (Ind. Ct. App. 1988).
- "The farmer expressly *covenants* not to supply seed to any other person, not to save any crop produced from the seed for planting, and not to allow others to use the seed for research." A. Bryan Endres, *State-Authorized Seed Saving*, 9 Drake J. Agric. L. 323, 337 (2004).

Nonlawyers are unaccustomed to the legal uses of the word; ordinarily, in modern contexts, the better practice is to write *agree*. For more on this verb and its near-synonyms, see **promise,** vb. See also **contract (D).**

covenant and agree is a needless doublet common in drafting. *Agree* suffices in virtually every context in which the phrase appears. See DOUBLETS, TRIPLETS, AND SYNONYM-STRINGS.

covenantee = the person to whom a promise by covenant is made. E.g.:

- "And the use thus raised would be executed by the Statute of Uses, thereby transferring the legal estate to the *covenantee.*" Cornelius J. Moynihan, *Introduction to the Law of Real Property* 186 (2d ed. 1988).
- "A restraint is only valid if it goes no further than is reasonably necessary for the protection of the *covenantee*'s interest." G.H. Treitel, *The Law of Contract* 406 (8th ed. 1991). (On the position of *only* in this sentence, see **only.**)

See -EE.

covenant not to compete. See **noncompetition covenant.**

covenant of seisin; covenant of good right to convey. These phrases are synonymous. In a deed, either phrase assures the grantee that the grantor is, at the time of the conveyance, the lawful owner with power to convey the land.

covenantor; covenanter. This agent noun, meaning "the person who makes a promise by covenant," is preferably spelled *-or*. See -ER (A).

covenant running with the land = a covenant that binds subsequent owners. It is also termed a *real covenant*. See **run (B).**

coverages. This plural of what has traditionally been a mass noun is now common—e.g.:

- "In land-based financing, liability insurance merely ensures that a borrower's balance sheet will not be devastated by an accident, whereas, in marine insurance, the liability *coverages* insure that the senior tort, salvage, and general average liens that exist, or that may arise after closing, will not affect the security of the mortgage." Bruce A. King, *Ships as Property: Maritime Transactions in State and Federal Law*, 79 Tul. L. Rev. 1259, 1280 (2005).
- "Failure to provide this information shall constitute a material misrepresentation, which shall result in all insurance *coverages* being void." *Lenhart v. Federated Nat'l Ins. Co.*, 950 So.2d 454, 456 (Fla. Dist. Ct. App. 2007) (quoting an insurance policy).

See PLURALS (B).

covert; overt. *Covert* is best pronounced like *covered*, except with a *-t-* at the end /kəv-ərt/. Still, /koh-vərt/, nearly rhyming with *overt* (but for the accented syllable), is the more common pronunciation in AmE nowadays. See **discovert.**

coverture = the condition or position of a woman during her married life, when she is by law under the authority and protection of her husband (*OED*). The word reeks of SEXISM, although it is unobjectionable in historical contexts—e.g.: "*Coverture* does not protect a married woman from the act of murder, unless it appears that she was under her husband's influence, and acted under the same." *State v. Harris*, 26 So. 64, 65 (La. 1899).

Traditionally used only in reference to wives, this word has recently been applied to husbands as well: "A further question is presented when we consider assets that have come into the ownership of a spouse, or of both spouses jointly, during *coverture*." *Painter v. Painter*, 320 A.2d 484, 493 (N.J. 1974).

Usually, in contemporary contexts, some phrase such as *during marriage* will suffice in place of the legalistic *during coverture*—e.g.:

- "A conveyance or devise to husband and wife, *during coverture* [read *during marriage*], must have the same effect with us as at common law." *Walthall v. Goree*, 36 Ala. 728, 733 (1860).
- "Retirement funds of either spouse, to the extent they are acquired *during coverture* [read *during marriage*], are subject to division as jointly acquired property." *Hodge v. Hodge*, 197 P.3d 511, 514 n.8 (Okla. Civ. App. 2008).

coworker. So spelled—without a hyphen. See CO- (A) & **co-employee.**

cozen is a literary and archaic word meaning "to cheat." E.g.: "The only reason to use the 365/360 method is that it allows banks to *cozen* their borrowers and charge higher-than-agreed-upon amounts of interest." Allan W. Vestal, *No Longer Bending to the Purposes of the Money Lenders: Prohibiting the "Bank Method" of Interest Calculation*, 70 N.C. L. Rev. 243, 248 (1991). The word has never been used as a specific legal term, but there is certainly no reason to avoid it in legal writing.

-CRACY. See GOVERNMENTAL FORMS.

cramdown, a late-20th-century term now common in bankruptcy law, refers to a reorganization plan that creditors are required to accept as long as the plan attains minimum standards established by the Bankruptcy Code. E.g.: "Section 1129(b)(1) of the bankruptcy code [11 U.S.C.] provides that a debtor may 'cram down' its plan over the objection of a creditor 'if the plan does not discriminate unfairly, and is fair and equitable with respect to each class . . . .'" *In re D&F Constr., Inc.*, 865 F.2d 673, 675 (5th Cir. 1989).

creator is a somewhat exalted name for one who establishes a trust—e.g.:

- "The *creator* of a trust may reserve to himself any use of power, beneficial or in trust, which he might lawfully grant to another." *Cleveland Trust Co. v. White*, 16 N.E.2d 588, 597 (Ohio Ct. App. 1937).
- "After assessing federal income taxes, penalties, and interest against the *creators* of the trust . . . the IRS filed transferee tax liens against the trust." Michael Hatfield, *Fifth Circuit Survey: Taxation*, 39 Tex. Tech L. Rev. 1035, 1066 (2007).

See **settlor.**

creature. Legal idiom has developed a peculiar kind of taxonomy, in which legal doctrines or principles are described as *creatures.* E.g.:

- "Adoption is solely a *creature of statute*; it did not exist at common law." *In re P.B. for Adoption of L.C.*, 920 A.2d 155, 156 (N.J. Super. Ct. Law Div. 2006).
- "Equitable subrogation is a *creature of equity*, the object of which is to do substantial justice independent of form or contract relation between the parties." *Countrywide Home Loans, Inc. v. Schmidt*, 742 N.W.2d 901, 902 (Wis. Ct. App. 2007).
- "The rule against perpetuities was a *creature of common law* when these cases were decided, not statute." *Power Gas Mktg. & Transmission, Inc. v. Cabot Oil & Gas Corp.*, 948 A.2d 807, 811 n.3 (Pa. Super. Ct. 2008).
- "In conclusion, New Mexico use immunity law, unlike its federal counterpart, is a *creature of the courts*, and therefore amenable to judicial change." *State v. Belanger*, 210 P.3d 783, 792 (N.M. 2009).

The *OED* quotes the following English example from 1855: "The railway and the rights of the railway are the *creatures of* the Act of Parliament." A useful phrase, *creature of* should not be so overworked as to become another tiresome legal CLICHÉ.

*credal. See **creedal.**

credible; credulous; creditable. *Credible* = believable; *credulous* = gullible, tending to believe; and *creditable* = worthy of credit, laudable. See **incredible.**

credit (= to give credence to) for *believe*, now almost peculiar to legal writing, is an acceptable though slightly pretentious legal idiom:

- "It may be that the court below did not consider such evidence substantial or did not *credit* its validity, but we are unable to determine from a silent record the thought processes of the court below." *Velasquez v. City of Abilene*, 725 F.2d 1017, 1021 (5th Cir. 1984).
- "The jury's deadlock in the present case renders more troubling its split verdict . . . because the split verdict

suggests that the jury had doubts concerning the victim's credibility as a general matter, as it failed to *credit* her testimony about the defendant's earlier attempts to molest her." *State v. Angel T.*, 973 A.2d 1207, 1228 (Conn. 2009).

- "The jury had the option to disbelieve both defendants' proffered defenses and to *credit* the testimony of the eyewitness instead." *Commonwealth v. Vallejo*, 914 N.E.2d 22, 34 (Mass. 2009).

creditable; credulous. See **credible.**

credulity (= gullibility) should not be confused with *credibility* (= believability), as it is in the phrase *it strains credulity*—e.g.:

- "It strains *credulity* [read *credibility*] to argue that Congress simply assumed that one view rather than the other would govern." *Smith v. Wade*, 461 U.S. 30, 93 (1983) (O'Connor, J., dissenting).
- "It simply strains *credulity* [read *credibility*] for the Court to assert that 'propaganda' is a neutral classification." *Meese v. Keene*, 481 U.S. 465, 490 (1987) (Blackmun, J., dissenting).

creedal; *credal. The preferred spelling is *creedal*; the spelling **credal* is a nonstandard variant.

crier (= a court officer who calls the court to order) has the variant spelling *cryer*, which is to be eschewed. Today the bailiff usually acts as *crier*; hence *bailiff* has almost supplanted the term *crier*, which sometimes appears in the phrase *court crier*: "Adam Johnson testified that he was a deputy marshal, and was *court crier* on April 17, 1902, and was in court when the order was made for the open venire." *Richards v. U.S.*, 126 F. 105, 107 (9th Cir. 1903). See **hear ye,** *oyez* & *countez.*

crim. con. See **criminal conversation.**

crime. Blackstone defined a *crime* as "an act committed or omitted in violation of a public law either forbidding or commanding it." 4 William Blackstone, *Commentaries on the Laws of England* 15 (1769). But this definition has long been faulted: "It is not the act omitted [that] constitutes a *crime*, but the omission to act. [And] many acts [that] are not *crimes* are prohibited by public laws." T.W. Hughes, *A Treatise on Criminal Law and Procedure* 5 (1919). The modern definition is any social harm that the law defines and makes punishable. *Black's Law Dictionary* 427 (9th ed. 2009) defines the term as follows: "An act that the law makes punishable; the breach of a legal duty treated as the subject-matter of a criminal proceeding."

Broadly speaking, this term is to be distinguished from *civil wrong* or *tort*. An important point for the novice is to avoid trying to distinguish the two on the basis of the act giving rise to the *crime* or civil wrong, because the same act may be both a *crime* and a civil wrong. For example, a murder may be both criminal and tortious—including such torts as assault, battery, and wrongful death. The act may give rise both to a criminal prosecution (seeking punishment) and to a civil suit for damages (seeking redress).

Interestingly, this distinction is a modern one. In the early days of the common law, criminal law was also the law of torts, so that, as Plucknett put it, "the modern distinction between *crime* and tort is . . . one of those classifications [that] it is futile to press upon mediaeval law." Theodore F.T. Plucknett, *A Concise History of the Common Law* 422 (5th ed. 1956). See **criminal offense.**

crime, infamous. See **infamous crime.**

crime against nature. See EUPHEMISMS.

crimen falsi (lit., "the crime of falsifying") has gradually grown from describing crimes such as perjury and forgery to include any crime involving dishonesty, fraud, or corruption. It is a handy phrase—not a pointless LATINISM—because a paraphrase uses up many more words and is more cumbersome to repeat again and again. E.g.: "This case presents the question whether a district court has the discretion . . . to prohibit the impeachment of a witness with a conviction for a crime involving dishonesty or false statement (a *crimen falsi*)." *U.S. v. Toney*, 615 F.2d 277, 278 (5th Cir. 1980).

The plural form is *crimina falsi*, which is the form that should have appeared here: "The House Committee on the Judiciary amended the bill to permit admission only of prior convictions of *crimen falsi* [read *crimina falsi*]." James McMahon, Note, *Prior Convictions Offered for Impeachment in Civil Trials*, 54 Fordham L. Rev. 1063, 1071 (1986).

The phrase is commonly written with the words reversed (*falsi crimen*). Either version is good Latin—and *falsi crimen* better approximates English word order—but *crimen falsi* is slightly more common.

crime of passion. See *crime passionnel.*

crime passionnel; crime passionel. The English phrase *crime of passion* is perfectly serviceable. But if the GALLICISM must appear, the better form is with two ens (*-nn-*) in the second word.

criminal = (1) of or relating to crime <criminal justice>; or (2) constituting a crime <criminal activities>. The adjective is analogous, then, to *grammatical*, which of course is proper in the phrase *grammatical error* (*grammatical* here meaning not "complying with grammar" but "relating to grammar"). It is quite proper—and hardly risible—to speak of a *criminal judge*, a *criminal lawyer*, or the *criminal bar*, just as it is to speak of the *criminal law.*

criminal abortion. See **abortion.**

criminal action—as opposed to *criminal prosecution*—is, strictly speaking, considered a solecism in BrE, in which *action* is reserved for civil lawsuits. *See* Glanville Williams, *Learning the Law* 4 (11th ed.

1982) ("'[*c*]*riminal action*' . . . is a misnomer"). In AmE, though, the phrase is quite common and quite unobjectionable.

criminal attempt. See **attempt (A).**

criminal conversation = (1) unlawful sexual intercourse with a married person; or (2) a tort action based on such unlawful intercourse. The idea of using *conversation* in this way is not merely modern euphemizing. In the Renaissance, *conversation* fairly routinely referred to sexual intercourse or intimacy. In modern law, then, this phrase—commonly abbreviated *crim. con.*—is an ARCHAISM more than a EUPHEMISM.

At common law, the tort action could be maintained by a husband but not by a wife. In the several American jurisdictions in which it remains a cause of action today, that double standard has been erased, so that wives as well as husbands may sue. *Criminal conversation* was abolished in England in 1857.

To the extent that it can be differentiated from *alienation of affections*, the distinction is this: *criminal conversation* might result, for example, from a one-time act of adultery that does not affect the wayward spouse's affections, whereas an *alienation of affections* occurs when the wayward spouse's emotions are affected in such a way as to deprive the other of consortium.

criminal intent is used in a variety of ways: (1) to refer to the intent to do wrong; (2) to refer to the intent to break a specific law; (3) to serve as the equivalent of *mens rea*, being the mental element requisite for guilt of the offense charged; or (4) to serve as a synonym for criminal negligence. Surveying the semantic confusion, Rollin Perkins has suggested a tidy distinction: "Some other term such as *mens rea* or guilty mind should be employed for more general purposes, and '*criminal intent*' be restricted to those situations in which there is (1) an intent to do the *actus reus*, and (2) no circumstance of exculpation." Rollin M. Perkins & Ronald N. Boyce, *Criminal Law* 834 (3d ed. 1982). See **actus reus** & **mens rea.**

criminality = the quality or fact of being criminal. E.g.: "But the use, until 1963, of the M'Naghten Rules to excuse insane cruelty and refuse divorce on that ground shows that unfortunate hints of *criminality* still attach to a divorce suit (there is generally too much talk of the 'innocent' and the 'guilty' party)." Alan Harding, *A Social History of English Law* 403 (1966). This term has the NEEDLESS VARIANTS *criminalness* and *criminalty*, neither of which should appear in modern legal writing.

criminalize, an Americanism coined in the 1950s, means "to make illegal; to outlaw." E.g.:

- "Relying on . . . Iowa Code § 721.2 . . . , which *criminalizes* subornation of perjury, the Iowa court concluded that . . . Robinson's actions . . . were required." *Nix v. Whiteside,* 475 U.S. 157, 162 (1986) (per Burger, C.J.).

- "Many experts believe that restricting abortion would prove about as successful as Prohibition, when a small but vocal minority managed to *criminalize* liquor." *The Battle over Abortion,* Newsweek, 1 May 1989, at 30. See -IZE.

criminal law, a phrase that often includes the entirety of what we know as the administration of criminal justice, can encompass several legal fields: substantive criminal law, criminal procedure, law enforcement, and penology. Generally, however, a lawyer who speaks of *criminal law* means the substantive criminal law. See **civil law (A).**

criminally = (1) in a criminal manner <he acted criminally>; or (2) under criminal law <criminally liable>. Sense 2 is largely confined to lawyers' writing—e.g.: "The wrongdoer may be prosecuted *criminally*." J.N. Pomeroy, *Equity Jurisprudence* § 1051, at 114–15 (Symons ed., 5th ed. 1941).

criminal mischief. See **malicious mischief.**

criminal negligence. See **negligence (A).**

***criminalness.** See **criminality.**

criminal offense; crime. In distinguishing between these expressions, the U.S. Supreme Court has suggested that the first is broader because it includes petty offenses: "When the change [in Article III of the Constitution] was made from '*criminal offenses*' to '*crimes,*' and made in the light of the popular understanding of the meaning of the word '*crimes,*' . . . it is obvious that the intent was to exclude from the constitutional requirement of a jury the trial of petty *criminal offenses*." *Schick v. U.S.,* 195 U.S. 65, 70 (1904) (per Brewer, J.). Whether this distinction would hold today is doubtful—*criminal offense* seeming to be nothing more than a verbose synonym of *crime.*

criminal protector. See **perpetrator.**

***criminate.** See **incriminate** & **charge,** vb. **(A).**

***criminative; *criminatory.** These are NEEDLESS VARIANTS of *incriminatory.* See **incriminatory** & **criminate.**

criminous = (1) of the nature of a crime; (2) accusing of a crime; or (3) (of a person) guilty of a crime. Although the historical term *criminous clerks* is quite proper in reference to those who at common law availed themselves of the *benefit of clergy*, the word *criminous* is a pompous ARCHAISM when used as a NEEDLESS VARIANT of *criminal*—e.g.:

- "Mr. Fischl's intentions were quite sufficient, in our view, to make his conduct *criminous* [read *criminal*]." *U.S. v. Fischl,* 797 F.2d 306, 311 (6th Cir. 1986).

- "This belief goes beyond the assumption that many suspects are *criminous* [read *criminal*] by nature or profession." Marc Miller, *Pretrial Detention and Punishment,* 75 Minn. L. Rev. 335, 375 (1990).

See **benefit of clergy.**

cripple. See **maim.**

crit. See **Critical Legal Studies (B).**

criterion. A singular noun. Pl. *criteria.* Writers often want to make *criteria* a singular—e.g.:

- "We conclude here, as we did in *Hall,* that the technical classification or denomination of the pleading should not be the determining *criteria* [read *criterion*]." *Saucer v. State,* 779 So.2d 261, 263 (Fla. 2001).
- "It is necessary to highlight a determining *criteria* [read *criterion*]—if not a prerequisite—for effective integration of human rights in peacekeeping operations." Katarina Mansson, *The Forgotten Agenda: Human Rights Protection and Promotion in Cold War Peacekeeping,* 10 J. Conflict & Sec. L. 379, 382 (2005).
- "Reasonable investors would have considered the devaluation of this goodwill an important *criteria* [read *criterion*]." *In re BellSouth Corp. Secs. Litig.,* 355 F.Supp.2d 1350, 1369 (N.D. Ga. 2005).

Cf. **phenomenon.**

Criterion has even been mistaken as a plural, perhaps because *criteria* is so frequently misused as a singular—e.g.: "Plaintiff maintains that these *criterion* [read *criteria*] were purposefully ignored and that Plaintiff, who was 'an ideal candidate for an administrative position,' was disadvantaged by this." *Rios v. Rumsfeld,* 323 F.Supp.2d 267, 276 (D.P.R. 2004). See PLURALS (A).

Critical Legal Studies. A. Generally. *Critical Legal Studies* is a vaguely defined movement involving lawyer-intellectuals—mostly with leftist leanings—who have tried to posit a new method of discussing law by borrowing from deconstructionist philosophy and Marxist rhetoric, among other disparate sources. Adherents generally call themselves *crits, critters,* or *CLSers.* For the most part, their writings are characterized by a newfangled vocabulary and ABSTRACTITIS. See Mark Kelman, *A Guide to Critical Legal Studies* (1987); Roberto Unger, *The Critical Legal Studies Movement* (1983); Louis B. Schwartz, *With Gun and Camera Through Darkest CLS-Land,* 36 Stan. L. Rev. 413 (1984).

B. And *crit; critter.* These are slang words referring to an adherent of Critical Legal Studies. E.g.:

- "Harvard may no longer be 'the Beirut of legal education,' as one *Crit* denied tenure charged, but it's still full of land mines." Ken Emerson, *When Legal Titans Clash,* N.Y. Times, 22 Apr. 1990, § 6, at 26, 28.
- "This is a piece about the *crits* for people who do not like them." John D. Ayer, *Not So Fast on the Crits,* 1 Scribes J. Legal Writing 45 (1990).

critter. See **Critical Legal Studies (B).**

cross, in lawyers' verbal shorthand, refers to *cross-examination.* E.g.: "There's no way you can do a first-rate *cross* if you don't speak the other guy's language." Joseph Goulden, *The Million Dollar Lawyers* 287 (1978) (quoting an anonymous N.Y. lawyer). See **cross-examination.** Cf. **direct.**

cross-claim; counterclaim. In most American jurisdictions, *counterclaim* refers to a claim by a defendant against the plaintiff used as an offset against the original claim; and a *cross-claim* is a claim by one coparty against another, as by one defendant against a codefendant. Each word has been used for the other, but this DIFFERENTIATION should be encouraged and fastidiously followed in practice. *See* Fed. R. Civ. P. 13. *Cross-claim* is now often spelled in the U.S. as one unhyphenated word. See **counterclaim.**

In BrE, *counterclaim* is defined as "a claim brought by a defendant [in a civil proceeding] in response to the claimant's claim, which is included in the same proceedings as the claimant's claim. A *counterclaim* asserts an independent cause of action but is not also a defense to the claim made in the action by the plaintiff" (*ODL*). *Cross-action* is frequently used in BrE for *cross-claim.* These terms are somewhat less restricted in BrE than in AmE, for *cross-claim* may refer to either (1) an action brought by the defendant against the plaintiff, or (2) an action brought by a defendant against a codefendant in the same suit.

***cross-complain,** vb., is a NEEDLESS VARIANT of *cross-claim*—e.g.: "Yassin sued for money he claimed was owed him, and the Solises *cross-complained* [read *cross-claimed*] . . . for breach of contract in connection with the work performed." *Yassin v. Solis,* 108 Cal. Rptr. 3d 854, 856 (Ct. App. 2010).

The same is true of the corresponding nouns—e.g.: "The circuit court held that the statute prohibited enforcement of the indemnification provision and entered an order striking the second count of the *cross-complaint* [read *cross-claim*] and dismissing it with prejudice." *Davis v. Commonwealth Edison Co.,* 336 N.E.2d 881, 883 (Ill. 1975).

cross-examination is hyphenated; *direct examination* is not.

cross-national should always be hyphenated, just as *cross-cultural* should be. Many social scientists drop the hyphens to form single words. Cf. **transnational.**

cross-offer. See **counteroffer.**

cross-question = a question on cross-examination. The hyphen is important because the best *cross-questions* are not cross questions. E.g.: "Certainly it would ordinarily be unfair for a trial court to require an offer of proof during cross-examination. [But] enough must be done to show that the sustaining of an objection to a *cross-question* was error. The *cross-question* must on its face be proper." John Kaplan & Jon R. Waltz, *Cases and Materials on Evidence* 52 (5th ed. 1984).

cruel and unusual punishment. The Eighth Amendment states: "Excessive bail shall not be required, nor excessive fines imposed, nor *cruel and unusual punishments* inflicted." The U.S. Supreme Court has construed the phrase *cruel and unusual punishment* to include not just barbarities such as torture but also punishment that is excessive for the crime committed. *See Coker v. Georgia*, 433 U.S. 584, 598 (1977) (per White, J.) (stating that a death sentence was a disproportionate punishment for rape because "rape . . . in terms of moral depravity and of the injury to the person and to the public . . . does not compare with murder, which does involve the unjustified taking of human life").

But the meaning is still fluid: "*Cruel and unusual punishment* is generally treated as a phrase, a three-word term of art; there appears to be little attempt to examine separately the meaning of either of the two principal words. This is just as well, for major conceptual difficulties might arise if the term 'unusual' were interpreted to have independent definitional significance. For example, if all prison guards routinely beat inmates for the sheer sadistic pleasure of the experience, it could hardly be said that such beatings were unusual. Yet surely courts would agree that the practice violates the Eighth Amendment." 1 Michael B. Mushlin, *Rights of Prisoners* 90 n.1 (2009).

crystallize. See DOUBLING OF FINAL CONSONANTS.

c.t.a. See **administrator.**

cubiclize. See -IZE.

culpa is a civil-law term meaning "actionable negligence." The English words *fault* and *negligence* are far preferable in English contexts. Pl. *-ae.*

culpability. See **guilt.**

culpable; *inculpable; *culpatory; *culpose. *Culpable* (= guilty; blameworthy) is the ordinary word. (See **blameworthy (A).**) **Inculpable* is a troublesome word to be avoided, for it may be interpreted as meaning either "able to be inculpated [i.e., guilty]," or "not culpable [i.e., innocent]." The latter sense has historically been ascribed to the word.

*Culpatory and **culpose* are rare terms, the first meaning "expressing blame," the second "characterized by criminal negligence." Neither has anything to recommend it; one who uses either term in discussing Anglo-American law, or **inculpable* for that matter, is *culpable* of a stylistic infelicity.

culprit has one of the most interesting of all legal etymologies. "According to the legal tradition, found in print shortly after 1700," explains the *OED*, "*culprit* was not originally a word, but a fortuitous or ignorant running together of two words (the fusion being made possible by the abbreviated writing of legal records), viz. Anglo-Fr. *culpable* or L. *culpabilis* 'guilty', abbreviated *cul.,* and *prit* or *prist* = OF. *prest* 'ready'. It is supposed that when the prisoner had pleaded 'Not guilty', the Clerk of the Crown replied with '*Culpable: prest d'averrer nostre bille*,' i.e., 'Guilty: [and I am] ready to aver our indictment'; that this reply was noted on the roll in the form *cul. prist*, etc.; and that, at a later time, after the disuse of Law French, this

formula was mistaken for an appellation addressed to the accused." In short, *culprit* is quintessentially a POPULARIZED LEGAL TECHNICALITY.

Nevertheless, the word still appears in legal contexts to denote a wrongdoer—e.g.: "Some Forces exclude the question of punishment altogether, the Chief Constable refraining from prosecution if the *culprit* has parents or friends or even the Salvation Army to go to and is willing to be looked after; on the other hand there will be prosecution if the *culprit* declares that he is going to do it again." Glanville Williams, *The Sanctity of Life and the Criminal Law* 278–79 (1957).

cultivable; *cultivatable. The shorter form is preferred. E.g.: "The remaining 200 acres is *cultivatable* [read *cultivable*] land." *Sell v. Cohen*, 293 F.Supp. 684, 685 (E.D. Ky. 1968).

*cumbrance is a NEEDLESS VARIANT of *encumbrance.* See **encumbrance.**

cum testamento annexo. See **administrator.**

*cumulate. See **accumulate.**

cumulative, in its general lay sense, means "composed of successively added parts; acquiring or increasing in force or cogency in successive additions" <cumulative effect or argument>. The term has various specific legal senses. The most complex of these, used now chiefly in the corporate field, relates to a system of voting developed originally in 19th-century British school-board elections. *Cumulative voting* = a system of voting, still in use, by which each voter has a number of votes equal to the number of representatives (usu. corporate officers) to be elected, and may either concentrate all his or her votes on one person or distribute them among the candidates.

Cumulative is used of evidence in the sense "tending to prove the same point that other evidence has already been offered to prove." In the context of wills, *cumulative* is sometimes used of legacies in the sense "given by the same testator to the same legatee."

In criminal law *cumulative sentences* are the same as *consecutive sentences.* See **concurrent sentences.**

cupboardman. See LAWYERS, DEROGATORY NAMES FOR (A).

CUPOS is an ACRONYM meaning "a cohabiting unmarried person of the opposite sex"—e.g.:

- "We note the acronym POSSLQ, used in the 1980 census, meaning 'Persons of Opposite Sex Sharing Living Quarters,' which has been criticized because literally it included married couples and communal livers, neither of which is a meretricious relationship. *CUPOS* has been suggested, originating from 'Cohabiting Unmarried Persons of Opposite Sex'. We prefer the latter term." *In re Eggers*, 638 P.2d 1267, 1270 n.2 (Wash. Ct. App. 1982).
- "Her reason for leaving home is that she prefers her own life style of living with this young boy as a *CUPOS* (cohabiting unmarried person of opposite sex)." *Jackman v. State Dep't of Soc. & Health Servs.*, 643 P.2d 889, 890 (Wash. Ct. App. 1982).

See **cohabitant**. See also NEOLOGISMS.

curable. In general English usage this word is used only of diseases; in legal usage, it is used in reference to any defects or deficiencies. Here *curable* = remediable; correctable:

- "The prejudice was of *curable* type and was removed by the instruction of the court." *Liberty Ins. Co. v. Rawls*, 358 S.W.2d 920, 932 (Tex. Civ. App.—Fort Worth 1962).
- "We are confident that such deficiencies in the affidavits are readily *curable*." *Greenwood Utils. Comm'n v. Mississippi Power Co.*, 751 F.2d 1484, 1496 (5th Cir. 1985).
- "We held that a pro se litigant's failure to hand-sign a timely filed notice of appeal is a nonjurisdictional, and therefore *curable*, defect." *Scarborough v. Principi*, 541 U.S. 401, 411–12 (2004) (per Ginsburg, J.).

See **cure**.

cur. adv. vult is the abbreviation of *Curia advisari vult* (= the court wishes to consider the matter). It appears at the end of the written arguments reproduced in British law reports to indicate that the judgment of the court was delivered (as Americans might always expect) on a date later than the hearing, rather than extemporaneously at the conclusion of the hearing, as is common in England. Such a "reserved" judgment carries additional weight as an authority.

An alternative abbreviation is *C.A.V.* or (less commonly) *c.a.v.* And an alternative (and now defunct) spelling is *curia advisare vult*—given by several old law dictionaries such as John Bouvier, *Bouvier's Law Dictionary* (Francis Rawles ed., 3d ed. 1914), and Thomas Tayler, *The Law Glossary* (1877).

curative; *curatory; curatorial. For the meaning "of, relating to, or tending to promote the cure of diseases," *curative* is preferred. *Curative* is also used in the legal sense "corrective" <curative instructions to the jury>. (See **cure** & **curable**.) **Curatory* is a NEEDLESS VARIANT. *Curatorial* = of or relating to a curator <Johnson's curatorial duties at the museum>.

curator. See **conservator**.

*curatory; curatorial. See **curative**.

cure = to correct. In general usage, *cure* is used only in reference to diseases, literal or metaphorical; but in law it is used, as legal JARGON, in reference to any defect or deficiency. So *incurable error* means "error at trial that cannot be corrected by the judge." E.g.:

- "Moreover, even if the agency acts on the administrative reconsideration motion before argument is heard on the judicial review petition, the agency action does not *cure* the jurisdictional defect." *City of New Orleans v. SEC*, 137 F.3d 638, 639 (D.C. Cir. 1998).
- "To *cure* the defect, the challenging party must file a new notice of appeal or petition for review from the now-final agency order." *Melcher v. FCC*, 134 F.3d 1143, 1163 (D.C. Cir. 1998).

- "Aponte suggests that reopening the removal proceedings to allow for briefing is the only way to *cure* the alleged constitutional defect and to ensure a full and fair proceeding before the BIA." *Aponte v. Holder*, 610 F.3d 1, 4 (1st Cir. 2010).

See **curable**.

curfew began as an Anglo-Saxon custom and only in the 1800s came to refer to an official order or regulation to keep off the streets at certain hours. In the 14th century, *corfu* referred to the ringing of a bell every evening at a fixed hour as a signal to cover the fires [O.F. *couvre feu* "cover the fire"]. Even after the ritual of putting out the fires discontinued, the bell-ringing continued as a signal to clear the streets after dark.

***curia advisari vult*.** See ***cur. adv. vult*.**

Curia Regis. See **King's Court**.

currently. See **presently**.

curriculum. Pl. *-a* or *-ums*. The Latin plural is slightly more common, but the Englished version may be gaining ground. E.g.: "Universities multiplied rapidly, first in Italy and then elsewhere, many of them starting as law schools and later broadening their *curriculums*." René A. Wormser, *The Story of the Law* 195 (1962). See PLURALS (A).

curtesy; dower. These medieval common-law terms, which are defunct in England (the rights they represent having been abolished in 1925), live on in several American jurisdictions. The words denote correlative rights. At common law, *curtesy* = the right of a husband, on his wife's death, to a life estate in the land that his deceased wife owned during their marriage. The husband has this right only if a child was born alive to the couple. The word began as a variant spelling of *courtesy* (tenancy by the courtesy of England). Several jurisdictions that retain the terms have abolished the requirement of a child born alive and have reduced the amount from all land to half the land. *Dower* = the right of a wife, on her husband's death, to a life estate in a third of the land that he owned, of which, with few exceptions, she cannot be deprived by any alienation made by him. "The provision for a surviving spouse to receive an elective share replaces the common-law rule that a widow was entitled to *dower*, which was a life estate in a fraction of her husband's lands, and that a widower was entitled to a similar right of *curtesy*." *Russell v. Russell*, 758 So.2d 533, 538 (Ala. 1999). See **dower**.

Inchoate dower and *curtesy initiate* are the terms denoting the spouse's interest in the other spouse's estate while both are living and after the birth of issue capable of inheriting—e.g.:

- "Perhaps the strongest reason for refusing to deduct the value of *inchoate dower* or *curtesy initiate* is that such a deduction would furnish a means for partial evasion of the estate tax, the provisions of which expressly cover marital interests." Note, *Inchoate Dower Held Not Deductible in Computing Value of Husband's Gift of Land to Wife,* 54 Harv. L. Rev. 519, 520 (1941).

- "English dower [was] an ancient inter vivos legal property right in the nature of an inter vivos protective cloud on land title . . . [that] was known as *inchoate dower.*" Charles E. Rounds Jr., *The Common Law Is Not Just About Contracts: How Legal Education Has Been Short-Changing Feminism,* 43 U. Rich. L. Rev. 1185, 1208 (2009).
- "Another reason for the disappearance of dower was its impact on the transferability of real estate when *inchoate dower* attached. Dower thus made it difficult to sell real estate to a bona fide purchaser without both spouses' consent." Colby T. Roe, Comment, *Arkansas Marriage: A Partnership Between a Husband and Wife, or a Safety Net for Support?,* 61 Ark. L. Rev. 735, 740 (2009).

See **initiate tenant by curtesy.**

curtilage (= the land around a house and within an enclosure) is sometimes misspelled **curtilege,* perhaps on the mistaken analogy of *privilege* and *sortilege.*

The term is used in the U.S. and in England but not in Scotland. For police searches under the Fourth Amendment, the *curtilage* is the area within which police may not, in most cases, search without a warrant: "Courts have extended Fourth Amendment protection to the *curtilage*; and they have defined the *curtilage,* as did the common law, by reference to the factors that determine whether an individual reasonably may expect that an area immediately adjacent to the home will remain private." *Oliver v. U.S.,* 466 U.S. 170, 180 (1984) (per Powell, J.). Cf. **messuage.**

custodial interrogation = police questioning begun after a person has been taken into custody or had his or her freedom otherwise curtailed. *See Miranda v. Arizona,* 384 U.S. 436, 444 (1966) (per Warren, C.J.) ("[b]y *custodial interrogation,* we mean questioning initiated by law enforcement officers after a person has been taken into custody or otherwise deprived of his freedom of action in any significant way").

custodian. In law, this word means "guardian" or "protector." It is used euphemistically in lay contexts to mean "janitor."

custody; possession. Whereas one may have *custody* of both persons and things, one may have *possession* of things only. But a further distinction is possible in criminal law: "The distinction between *possession* and *custody* . . . was gradually developed in a long line of decided cases . . . . In general it is important to distinguish between servants and others, because usually a servant who has control of a chattel belonging to his master has *custody* only (and not *possession*), whereas the actual control of a chattel by one not a servant is usually *possession.*" Rollin M. Perkins, *Criminal Law* 196 (1957). See **possession (c).**

custom. See **precedent (e).**

customary law = practices and beliefs that are so vital and intrinsic a part of a social and economic system

that they are treated as if they were laws. *Customary law* is handed down for many generations as unwritten law, though it is usually collected finally in a written code. See **unwritten law.**

customer. See **client.**

customs. See **tax.**

Customs Court. See **Court of International Trade.**

custumal; *costomal. The first is the usual spelling for "a written collection of a city's customs."

cut against; cut in favor of. These CLICHÉS are favorites of the legal profession. Use them sparingly—or perhaps just cut them. E.g.:

- "Although we do not find Murdock particularly relevant here, it *cuts,* if at all, *against* RSR's position." *RSR Corp. v. Brock,* 764 F.2d 355, 368 (5th Cir. 1985).
- "In any event, we find that the first factor *cuts in favor* of the mother and against the father." *In re Marriage of Haslett,* 629 N.E.2d 182, 188 (Ill. App. Ct. 1994).
- "While I cannot pretend that this case drew a crowd to the court room, that the very issues discussed in my opinions were testified to and argued about in a public court room *cuts in favor* of disclosure of my opinions discussing the same issues." *Fudali v. Pivotal Corp.,* 623 F.Supp.2d 25, 28 (D.D.C. 2009).

cut-and-dried case is a CLICHÉ that, when used, needs to be so hyphenated. E.g.: "Take one of the coldest, *cut-and-dried cases* imaginable, a sane man deliberately kills another man in the sight of several reliable witnesses." Fred Rodell, *Woe Unto You, Lawyers!* 105 (1939).

cut in favor of. See **cut against.**

cutting edge is a legal CLICHÉ and a VOGUE WORD—e.g.:

- "By and large, however, the gains made in the safe and efficient administration of our prisons may be attributed to the anonymous professionals who daily toil at the *cutting edge* of our efforts to improve, while at the same time securing our penal institutions." *Abdul Wali v. Coughlin,* 754 F.2d 1015, 1018 (2d Cir. 1985). On the use of **while at the same time* in that sentence, see *****while at the same time.**
- "Norms can also be understood as institutions for social control. The study of these informal mechanisms has recently emerged on the *cutting edge* of legal theory." Geoffrey P. Miller, *The Legal Function of Ritual,* 80 Chi.–Kent L. Rev. 1181, 1186 (2005).

In the cant of our day, every law review seeks to be *on the cutting edge* of the law.

When used as a PHRASAL ADJECTIVE, of course, the phrase is hyphenated—e.g.: "On the other hand, however, the overarching purpose of the LatCrit enterprise—that of creating a coherent, *cutting-edge* body of legal theory and scholarship—has not been nearly as successful." Keith Aoki & Kevin R. Johnson, *An Assessment of LatCrit Theory Ten Years After,* 83 Ind. L.J. 1151, 1181 (2008).

CUTTING OUT THE CHAFF refers to eliminating excess words. It is not an easy task; indeed, verbosity and obscurity are usually the result of facile and slap-dash writing. Judges occasionally confess as much about their own writing. For example: "This opinion is too long. I apologize for its length but I simply didn't have time to write a shorter one." *U.S. v. Price*, 448 F.Supp. 503, 503 (D. Colo. 1978) (echoing Blaise Pascal: "I would have written a shorter letter, but I did not have the time").

Many recurrent phrases are mere deadwood. For example, *Speaking for myself, I think . . .* , aside from being redundant, adds nothing to the sentence when we know who is speaking and have intelligence enough to deduce that the speaker is stating an opinion. Some courts have written (unreasonably) of *reasonable-minded defendants*, as if there might be *reasonable-footed* or *reasonable-chested* defendants; reason is only in the mind.

The following are wordy sentences with more-concise alternatives supplied:

- "*It was a package of small size* [read *It was a small package*]." *Palsgraf v. Long Island R.R.*, 162 N.E. 99, 99 (N.Y. 1928).
- "*In a large part* [*in large part* is idiomatic], it was our anticipation of this type of claim *which* [read *that*] cautioned us for so long against abrogation of the immunity rule." *Holodook v. Spencer*, 324 N.E.2d 338, 344 (N.Y. 1974). [Better: *Our foresight of such claims long cautioned us against abrogating the immunity rule.*]
- "A will is ambulatory in character and subject to change at any time." John Ritchie et al., *Cases and Materials on Decedents' Estates and Trusts* 1017 (1982). [A suggested revision: *A will is ambulatory* or *A will is always subject to change (while the testator lives).*]
- "Discretion is crucial here, for the goal is *that of* [delete *that of*] crafting representative institutions, with everything that such a difficult task entails." Luis Fuentes-Rohwer, *Back to the Beginning: An Essay on the Court, the Law of Democracy, and Trust*, 43 Wake Forest L. Rev. 1045, 1056 (2008).

The unfortunate legal predilection for nouns over verbs, for gerunds over verbal participles, is the cause of much deadweight. E.g.: "The giving of a warning to the person when released of the penalties imposed by this section shall not be a prerequisite to the application of the section." *Sanders v. U.S.*, 809 A.2d 584, 600 n.20 (D.C. 2002) (quoting D.C. Code § 23-1328(b)). [A suggested revision: *When a person is released from prison, this section will apply even if the person did not receive a warning.*] See BURIED VERBS, FLOTSAM PHRASES, REDUNDANCY (A), SUPERFLUITIES & VERBOSITY.

CYBER- is added to words in the growing field of *cyberlaw* (= the area of law dealing with the Internet). One author noted the proliferation of what he calls "this whole *cyber* thing. Look under *C* and you'll find definitions for *cybertorts*, *cyberfraud*, and *cyberattacks* (intriguingly, these are torts, frauds, and attacks committed via computer). You'll see *cybercriminals* in current dictionaries and, much to one's relief, *cybercops* to hunt them down." Adam Freedman, *The Party of the First Part* 220 (2007). Also listed are such terms as *cybersquatting* (= the act of reserving a domain name identical or similar to a company's trademark), *cyberstalking*, *cyberterrorism*, and *cybertheft* (stalking, terrorizing, and stealing via computer). Some sources use the prefix *e-*, as in *e-jurisdiction*, but *cyber-* is more common.

cy pres, cy-pres. A. Generally. This LAW FRENCH term, denoting the doctrine that written instruments should be construed as near to the parties' intention as possible, is predominantly spelled as two words. The British hyphenate the phrase and use an accent grave thus: *cy-près*. Meaning "as near as" and pronounced /SI-**pray**/, *cy pres* (originally *sì près*, *ici-près*, or *aussi-près*) is used in the context of charitable gifts.

This phrase carries different senses modernly and at common law.

> At common law . . . , the Crown exercised its prerogative power to apply funds given for a charitable, but illegal, purpose to some valid charitable purpose without regard for the settlor's intention. Property otherwise given for a particular charitable purpose [that] became incapable of fulfillment was directed by the chancellor under the doctrine of *cy pres* to another charitable purpose [that] fell within the general charitable intention of the settlor.
> The prerogative power, of course, does not exist in this country. The *cy pres* doctrine applied in the United States is a rule of judicial construction designed to approximate as closely as possible the desires of the settlor.
> *La Fond v. City of Detroit*, 98 N.W.2d 530, 534 n.1 (Mich. 1959).

Today, however, the sense is the same in G.B. as in the U.S., the court being bound by this doctrine to make a scheme for the funds to be applied to a charitable purpose as close as possible to the original one.

The state of Georgia has a statute with the following explanation: "When a valid charitable bequest is incapable for some reason of execution in the exact manner provided by the testator, donor, or founder, a court of equity will carry it into effect in such a way as will [as] nearly as possible effectuate his intention." Ga. Code Ann. § 108-202 (1959).

B. As Verb. In rare instances, *cy pres* has been used as a verb meaning "to restructure a gift so that it may reflect as nearly as possible the donor's original gift"—e.g.:

- "[I]t would be the duty of the chancellor to sequester the remainder of the gift and abate its payment or delivery to the hospital, awaiting the correction of abuses, or *to cy pres* the gift." *Hite v. Queen's Hosp.*, 36 Haw. 250, 265 (Haw. Terr. 1942).

- "Rather than permit the funds to accumulate without benefiting the public, the attorney general can bring citations or request the trustees to make application *to cy pres* the funds." Lois G. Forer, *Forgotten Funds: Suggesting Disclosure Laws for Charitable Funds*, 105 U. Pa. L. Rev. 1044, 1059–60 (1957).

This verb use cannot be recommended. But if you're nevertheless curious, it should be inflected *cy-presing* /sɪ **pray**-ing/ and *cy-presed* /sɪ **prayd**/.

D

damage, adj., corresponds to *damages*, n.; that is, *damage claim = claim for damages*. This use of *damage*, dating from the late 19th century, is omitted from most general English-language dictionaries but is common in law. E.g.:

- "If a *damage claim* is within the scope of the arbitration, the arbitrators at common law . . . may depart from the rules of law." Charles T. McCormick, *Handbook on the Law of Damages* § 4, at 19–20 (1935).
- "Nader's *damage action* for fraudulent misrepresentation had exposed the industry's deliberate practice of overbooking to maximize profits." Barbara H. Craig, Chadha: *The Story of an Epic Constitutional Struggle* 62 (1988).
- "Undercapitalization does not simply mean that a company might not have ready cash on hand in whatever amount a plaintiff thinks is necessary to satisfy that plaintiff's *damage claim.*" *Iridex Corp. v. Synergetics USA, Inc.*, 474 F.Supp.2d 1105, 1110 (E.D. Mo. 2007).

But sometimes—especially in BrE—the plural form *damages* is used adjectivally. E.g.:

- "The *Sun* paid £1m in an out-of-court *damages settlement* to the singer Elton John." The Independent, 13 Dec. 1988, at 4.
- "A permanent injunction . . . can translate into more real financial benefit than a *damages judgment* [read, in AmE, *damage judgment*]." Michael Tigar, 17 Litig. 49, 49 (Winter 1991) (book review).

damage, n.; **damages. A.** *Damage* **and** *damages.* "The word *damage*, meaning 'Loss, injury, or deterioration,' is 'to be distinguished from its plural—*damages*—which means a compensation in money for a loss or *damage.*'" *American Stevedores, Inc. v. Porello*, 330 U.S. 446, 450 n.6 (1947) (per Reed, J.) (quoting *Black's*). In the following examples, the two terms are correctly used:

- "After actual *damage* is shown it is unnecessary to show its money extent to sustain a judgment for exemplary *damages.*" *McConathy v. Deck*, 83 P. 135, 135 (Colo. 1905).
- "It is for the factfinder to assess the exact nature of the injury or *damage* sustained by the plaintiff, and to compensate the plaintiff with *damages* for that injury or *damage.*" *Boswell v. Liberty Nat'l Life Ins. Co.*, 643 So.2d 580, 584 (Ala. 1994) (quoting the first ed. of *DMLU*).

But often the words are misused—e.g.:

- "In Massachusetts exemplary damages are not recoverable in an action for libel. . . . Only actual *damage* [read *damages*] may be recovered." *Webb v. Call Publ'g Co.*, 180 N.W. 263, 265 (Wis. 1920).
- "Where the chattel is unique, . . . money *damage* [read *damages*] will be inadequate." William F. Walsh, *A Treatise on Equity* 307 (1930).

- "In order to convict a person of class B arson, the State must prove that the fire caused at least $5,000 in *damages* [read *damage*]." *Capes v. State*, 615 N.E.2d 450, 451 (Ind. Ct. App. 1993).
- "Plaintiff alleges Defendant negligently installed a range cordset which caused a fire resulting in $87,650.42 in *damages* [read *damage*]." *Windham v. Circuit City Stores, Inc.*, 420 F.Supp.2d 1206, 1208 (D. Kan. 2006).

See **money damages.**

In the following sentence, two senses are incorrectly conflated; one recovers *damages* but suffers *damage*: "Ferranti International Signal plans imminent legal action to recover as much as possible of the *damages* it has suffered as a result of an alleged £215m fraud." Hugo Dixon & Charles Leadbeater, *Ferranti Plans Legal Action*, Fin. Times, 18–19 Nov. 1989, at 1. This error bears the technical name ZEUGMA.

An English writer assesses this linguistic situation pessimistically: "It is a melancholy example of the poverty of the language of English Law that it can find no better word than '*damages*' for the compensation [that] it awards in civil cases." Edward Jenks, *The Book of English Law* 207 (P.B. Fairest ed., 6th ed. 1967). But in the upshot, he is correct: "The confusion between '*damage*,' i.e., the loss [that] is the cause of the award of '*damages*,' and '*damages*' themselves, is an endless source of perplexity to students of . . . law. But it would be hopeless now to try to alter the practice." *Id.*

B. *Damage* **and** *injury.* See **injury (B).**

C. *Damages* **in the Context of Restitution.** A leading English authority on the law of contract holds that "a claim for restitution may not, strictly speaking, be one for '*damages*'; its purpose is not to compensate the plaintiff for a loss, but to deprive the defendant of a benefit." G.H. Treitel, *The Law of Contract* 832 (8th ed. 1991). Although this limit on the use of the word *damages* might promote analytical rigor, American lawyers routinely refer to any money acquired by way of judgment—in any type of action—as *damages*.

D. Other Terms with *damages*. For the distinction between *general damages* and *special damages*, see **general damages.** For other types, see **hedonic damages, liquidated damages** & **punitive damages,** as well as **consequentials** & **incidentals.**

damage feasant. See **feasant.**

damages, punitive (or exemplary). See **punitive damages, punitives, punies** & **exemplaries.**

Dame Grand Cross (or Dame Commander) of the Order of the British Empire (O.B.E.). Men who are appointed to the High Court and higher courts are invariably knighted, whereas women are made Dames Commander of the Order of the British Empire. Abbreviation: D.B.E. The mode of salutation is *my lady*. See **my lord.**

damnatory. Though this word might appear to be related to *damnum* and *damnify*, the relation is etymological only. This is not a legal term per se, but a general word equivalent to *condemnatory*, which is more comprehensible. E.g.:

- "[If the] person sued, is proved to have allowed his view to be distorted by malice, it is quite immaterial that somebody else might without malice have written an equally *damnatory* criticism." *Thomas v. Bradbury, Agnew & Co., Ltd.*, [1906] 2 K.B. 627, 638 (C.A.).
- "It is the manufacturers' and merchants' insurance and, when properly employed, is no more *damnatory* than is insurance of property or life." *Whorley v. Patton-Kjose Co.*, 5 P.2d 210, 214 (Mont. 1931).
- "Conceivably, evidence of implied acquiescence in a *damnatory* statement could be the only evidence fixing fault on one accused of civil wrongdoing; certainly the courts can deny such a person an affirmative charge with a better conscience if such evidence is grounded upon a proper predicate." *Robinson v. Morrison*, 133 So.2d 230, 234 (Ala. 1961).

damnify (= to inflict injury upon) is generally an unnecessary LEGALISM for *injure*. The *OED* notes that this word was common in the 17th century but is now rare. One might excuse the word's use in the second example below, but not in the first:

- "I am satisfied that the injured person is *damnified* by having cut short the period during which he had a normal expectation of enjoying life." *Rose v. Ford*, [1937] A.C. 826, 834 (H.L.) (per Atkin, J.). (The writer did not want to repeat *injure*—this use smacks of INELEGANT VARIATION.)
- "It is a claim founded on a special law of Congress waiving the legal immunity of the defendant and creating what was *damnum absque injuria* into a cause to be *damnified*." *F. Mansfield & Sons Co. v. U.S.*, 94 Ct.Cl. 397 (1941).

See **damnum.**

The antonym is much better known: *indemnify*. Though it has the same etymology as *damnify* with a negative prefix (*in-* "not" + *damnum* "loss; damage"), the vowel shifts to *-e-* in the negative form. See **indemnify.**

damnosa haereditas; *damnosa hereditas. Generally, this phrase for "an inheritance more onerous (e.g., because burdened with debts) than profitable" is spelled *haereditas*. Originally a Roman-law term, *damnosa haereditas* has been extended by modern legal writers to refer to anything one acquires that turns out to be disadvantageous.

damnous = of, relating to, or causing a *damnum*. Usually, the term means "causing loss or damage."

The word is obsolescent legal JARGON, not a TERM OF ART—e.g.:

- "The words of the Railways Clauses Act, 'injuriously affected,' do not mean wrongfully in the sense of unlawfully, but '*damnously*,' that is injuriously, affected in the ordinary sense of that word." *Ricket v. Metropolitan Ry.*, [1867] LR 2 HL 175 (HL).
- "I think that there is no doubt that the appellants were *damnously* affected by the works of the railway." *Fleming v. Newport Ry.*, [1883] LR 8 App. Cas. 265 (HL).

See **damnum** & **damnum absque injuria.**

damnum = damage suffered. E.g.: "The loss, *damnum*, is capable of being estimated in terms of money." *Chant v. Read*, [1939] 2 KB 346, 362. This term is hardly justified in any context not involving the doctrine of *damnum absque injuria*. In the sentence quoted it adds nothing. See **damnum absque injuria** & **damnum infectum.**

damnum absque injuria; damnum sine injuria. These synonymous LATINISMS may both be translated *damage without wrongful act*. They denote damage for which there is no legal remedy. A 19th-century commentator stated that *damnum sine injuria*, "standing alone as a sort of compound noun, seems hardly good Latin. English lawyers, however, have so used it since the fifteenth century at the latest." Note, 2 Law Q. Rev. 117, 117 (1886).

Still used with some frequency in British legal writing, the phrases are less common in American legal prose. E.g.:

- "The majority of the court were in favor of arresting judgment . . . on the ground that the plaintiff's privilege of voting was not a matter of property or profit, so that hindrance was merely *damnum sine injuria*." *Watkins v. Secretary of State for the Home Dep't*, [2006] UKHL 17.
- "To my mind, Lord Diplock can hardly have referred to a possible *damnum absque injuria* if he had thought that a substantial claim in fact lay." *SmithKline Beecham Plc. v. Apotex Europe Ltd.*, [2007] Ch 71 (per Jacob, L.J.).
- "Mere annoyance or inconvenience will not support an action for a nuisance because the damages therefrom are deemed *damnum absque injuria* in recognition of the fact [that] life is not perfect." *Bonewitz v. Parker*, 912 N.E.2d 378, 381 (Ind. Ct. App. 2009).

Cf. **injuria absque damno.**

damnum infectum = loss not yet suffered but only apprehended. This LATINISM is more a hindrance than an aid to analysis, for most readers must look it up.

damnum sine injuria. See **damnum absque injuria.**

D & O insurance. See **directors' and officers' insurance.**

DANGLERS are ordinarily unattached participles, either present participles (ending in *-ing*) or past participles (ending usu. in *-ed*), that do not relate syntactically to the nouns they are supposed to modify.

In effect, the participle tries to sever its relationship with its noun or pronoun. Gerunds may also dangle precariously (see (c)). Usually, recasting the sentence will remedy the incoherence, AMBIGUITY, or ILLOGIC.

Danglers are of two types, the majority being unacceptable and a few being acceptable because of long-standing usage. In the normal word order, a participial phrase beginning a sentence (*Running by the lake,*) should be followed directly by the noun acting as subject in the main clause (*I saw the two defendants*). When that word order is changed, as by changing the verb in the main clause to the passive voice, the sentence becomes illogical or misleading: *Running by the lake, the two defendants were seen.* It was not the two defendants who were running, but the witness. This is the unacceptable type of dangling modifier.

Examples of acceptable danglers are easy to come by. We all know that there is nothing wrong with *Considering the current atmosphere in the legislature, it is unlikely that the legislation will pass.* Several other examples are discussed in (D) below.

A. Danglers Ending in *-ing.* In the sentences that follow, mispositioned words have caused grammatical blunders. Perhaps the most common legal sentence containing a dangling participle is this: "Finding no error, the judgment of the district court is affirmed." *See, e.g., In re Gerhardt,* 348 F.3d 89, 93 (5th Cir. 2003). Literally, this sentence says that the judgment found no error; the proper subject, namely, *the court,* remains unmentioned. [A possible revision: *Finding no error, we affirm the judgment of the district court.*] This is the type of problematic dangler cited at the outset: an active participle is followed by a main clause in the passive voice.

The classic example occurs when the wrong noun begins the main clause, that is, a noun other than the one expected by the reader who has digested the introductory participial phrase. E.g.:

- "*Accepting* for present purposes the showing so made, *the facts* of the claim [*were*] as follows." *Martinez v. U.S.,* 728 F.2d 694, 695 (5th Cir. 1984). [A possible revision: *We accept for present purposes the showing made and find the facts to be as follows.* (It is not the facts that *accept*: it is the writer who *accepts* (and *finds*). The error seems to have resulted from the writer's fear of FIRST PERSON.)]
- "*Viewing the record* [read *If we view the record*] in the light most favorable to the non-movant, Ms. Smith's claim for retaliation under Title VII is subject to determination by a jury." *Smith v. TJX Co.,* 609 F.Supp.2d 771, 782 (N.D. Ind. 2009).

The error occurs also when the main clause begins with an EXPLETIVE (e.g., *it* or *there*) after an introductory participial phrase:

- "*Applying* those principles to the facts in the case at bar, *it* is clear that plaintiff cannot recover." *Bailey v. West,* 249 A.2d 414, 418 (R.I. 1969). [A possible revision: *If we apply these principles to the case at bar, it becomes clear that . . . .*]
- "*Turning* to England, *it* ought to be noted first that that country, though late in doing so, participated fully in the

medieval development sketched above." Grant Gilmore & Charles L. Black Jr., *The Law of Admiralty* 8 (2d ed. 1975). [A possible revision: *Though England was late to do so, it participated fully in the medieval development sketched above.*]

- "*Looking* at the passage as a whole, *it* is by no means clear that Lord Atkin meant to confine manslaughter to cases of recklessness in the subjective sense." J.H. Baker, *An Introduction to English Legal History* 226 (3d ed. 1990). [A possible revision: *The passage as a whole does not make clear whether Lord Atkin meant . . . .*]
- "*In considering* whether a product presents an open-and-obvious risk, *it* is necessary to determine whether the particular hazard giving rise to the subject injury was obvious or commonly known." *Lykins v. Fun Spot Trampolines,* 874 N.E.2d 811, 816 (Ohio Ct. App. 2007). [A possible revision: *In considering whether conduct is intentional, the court must determine whether . . . .*]
- "*Applying* these principles to the facts of this case, *it* is clear that appellant entered into a valid and enforceable contract with the Commonwealth." *Carroll v. Commonwealth,* 682 S.E.2d 92, 106 (Va. Ct. App. 2009). [A possible revision: *If we apply these principles to the case at bar, it becomes clear that . . . .*]

Midsentence danglers are just as bad but are harder for the untrained eye to spot. E.g.: "It is the purpose of this note to re-examine the existing law, *placing emphasis upon* [read *to emphasize*] the interests to be protected, and to draw some conclusions as to its adequacy in protecting them." (This is poor writing because it could be included as boilerplate in almost any lawnote imaginable; the writer should craft the language specifically for the case at hand, generalizing, to be sure, but not making it so general that it is well-nigh universal. Further, the writer should have been aware of the natural triad lurking in the sentence, i.e., the infinitive phrases: *to re-examine; to place* [*to emphasize*]; *to draw.*)

B. Past-Participial Danglers. These are especially common when the main clause begins with a possessive—e.g.: "Born on March 12, 1944, in Dalton, Georgia, Larry Lee Simms's qualifications . . . ." Barbara H. Craig, *Chadha: The Story of an Epic Constitutional Struggle* 79 (1988). (Simms's qualifications were not born on March 12—he was.) [A possible revision: *Born on March 12, 1944, in Dalton, Georgia, Larry Lee Simms had qualifications that . . . .*]

But the problem also sometimes appears when a run-of-the-mill noun begins the main clause—e.g.: "*Applied* to the situation at bar, *the likelihood* that a barge will break from her fasts, and the damage she will do, vary with the place and time." *U.S. v. Carroll Towing Co.,* 159 F.2d 169, 173 (2d Cir. 1947) (per L. Hand, J.). [A possible revision: *When those principles are applied to the situation at bar . . . .*]

C. Dangling Gerunds. These are close allies to dangling participles, but here the participle acts as a noun rather than as an adjective:

- "*In handling* this problem *the satellite concept* of illicit commodities developed." Edward H. Levi, *An Introduction to Legal Reasoning* 62 (1949). [A possible revision: *In handling this problem, the courts developed the satellite* concept of illicit commodities. Or: *In the handling of this problem was developed the concept of illicit commodities.*]

- "*In considering* whether conduct is intentional, *it* is unnecessary to ascertain whether the party knew of the rule of law." Glanville Williams, *Criminal Law* 44 (2d ed. 1961). [A possible revision: *In considering whether conduct is intentional, the court need not ascertain whether the party knew of the rule of law.*]
- "*In construing* a criminal statute, *the prisoner* must be given the benefit of the doubt." Edward Jenks, *The Book of English Law* 40 (P.B. Fairest ed., 6th ed. 1967). [A possible revision: *In construing a criminal statute, the court must give the prisoner the benefit of the doubt.*]
- "*In gauging* the force of this argument *it* should be recalled that in many contexts punishments and reward will appear as opposite sides of the same coin." Lon L. Fuller, *Anatomy of the Law* 51 (1968). [A possible revision: *In gauging the force of this argument, one should recall that . . . .*]
- "*In discussing* the definition of contract given in the American Restatement *it* was pointed out that . . . ." P.S. Atiyah, *An Introduction to the Law of Contract* 42 (3d ed. 1981). [A possible revision: *In discussing . . . , one commentator pointed out . . . .*]

D. Acceptable Danglers or Disguised Conjunctions. Any number of present participles have been used as conjunctions or prepositions for so long that they have lost the participial duty to modify specific nouns. In effect, the clauses they introduce are adverbial; they stand apart from and comment on the content of the sentence. Among the commonest of these are *according, assuming, barring, concerning, considering, judging, owing, regarding, respecting, speaking, taking* (usually *account of, into account*). E.g.:

- "*Speaking* geographically, the Atlantic seaboard with a few gaps allows these unions, which become more and more wicked as we cross the Appalachians." Max Radin, *The Law and You* 42 (1948).
- "*Assuming* its maritime nature, almost any type of service claim will today be held within the Lien Act." Grant Gilmore & Charles L. Black Jr., *The Law of Admiralty* 659 (2d ed. 1975).

E. Ending Sentences with. Traditionally, grammarians frowned on *all* danglers, but during the 20th century they generally loosened the strictures for participial constructions at the end of a sentence. Early-20th-century grammarians might have disapproved the following sentences, but they have long been considered acceptable <Robert stepped to the door, seeking his companion> <Tom's arm hung useless, broken by the blow>.

Usually, as in the first of the two examples just noted, the end-of-the-sentence dangler is introduced by a so-called coordinating participle: *seeking* is equivalent to *and sought*. Similarly:

- "Émilie wrote to the false friend, *imploring*: so did the easy-going Marquis, and the fat lady watered *her* letter with her tears." Evelyn Beatrice Hall, *The Life of Voltaire* 121 (1910). (*Imploring = and implored.*)

- "She predeceased him *leaving* a husband and two children." Anthony R. Mellows, *The Law of Succession* 515 (3d ed. 1977). (*Leaving = and left.*)
- "[Students] turned Broad Street into a daytime restaurant destination, *sending* area tax receipts up by 8 percent that year." *Patton Place*, Atlantic, Feb. 2008, at 99. (*Sending = and sent.*)

A few editors would consider each of those participles misattached, but in fact they are acceptable as coordinating participles. As for the few who object, one wonders what they would do with the following sentence: "The boy ran out of the house *crying*."

daresay. So spelled, generally, as one word.

DASHES. See PUNCTUATION (E).

data, technically the plural of *datum*, has, since the 1940s, been increasingly often thought of as a mass noun taking a singular verb. But in formal contexts it is preferably treated as a plural—e.g.: "If new *data do* not fit, either the system must be modified to accommodate *them*, or *they* must be modified to fit the system." John H. Merryman, *The Civil Law Tradition* 67 (1969).

But many writers lapse—e.g.:

- "No finger was lifted to ascertain whether some of the *data was* [read *data were*] available." *Boreri v. Fiat S.P.A.*, 763 F.2d 17, 23 (1st Cir. 1985).
- "It was equally apparent that the *data* gathered on Law and Psychology *was* [read *data . . . were*] not amenable to such categorization." Elizabeth V. Gemmette, *Law and Literature*, 23 Val. U.L. Rev. 267, 268 (1989).
- "Currently there *is no data available* [read *are no data available*] that *measures* [read *measure*] the qualitative differences in how defendants of different races are treated at the various stages of the criminal justice system." Lola Velázquez-Aduilú, *Not Poor Enough*, 2006 Wis. L. Rev. 193, 209 (2006).
- "Although *data raises* [read *data raise*] doubt as to the validity of these perceptions, state legislatures responded by introducing accountability and punishment into juvenile court legislation." Kristin Henning, *What's Wrong with Victims' Rights in Juvenile Court?*, 97 Cal. L. Rev. 1107, 1113 (2009).

The *Oxford Guide* allows the singular use of *data* in computing and allied disciplines; whether lawyers own computers or not, they should use *data* as a plural.

In one particular context, though, *data* is invariably treated as a plural: when it begins a clause and is not preceded by the definite article. E.g.: "*Data* over the last two years *suggest* that the rate at which gay men get AIDS has finally begun to flatten out." Lawrence K. Altman, *Who's Stricken and How*, N.Y. Times, 5 Feb. 1989, at 1.

Datum, the "true" singular, is still used when a single piece of information is referred to—e.g.:

- "The latter statement merely states that a certain *datum* has not been located in records regularly made and preserved." *U.S. v. Yakobov*, 712 F.2d 20, 26 (2d Cir. 1983).
- "This was not a case [in which] some 'presumptively prejudicial' *datum*, like an attempted bribe, had come to light." *Neron v. Tierney*, 841 F.2d 1197, 1203 (1st Cir. 1988).
- "The purpose behind a motion to intervene is a relevant *datum* in the timeliness analysis." *R & G Mortg. Corp. v. Federal Home Loan Mortg. Corp.*, 584 F.3d 1, 12 (1st Cir. 2009).

Because *data* is a count noun, *many data* is correct—e.g.:

- "Numerous expert and representative interests are consulted, and *many data* assembled, often over a long period." Carleton K. Allen, *Law in the Making* 433 (7th ed. 1964).
- "But *much* [read *many*] of the *data* in present personnel files *is* [read *are*] highly subjective." William O. Douglas, *Points of Rebellion* 21 (1970). (In that book, Justice Douglas twice used *data* as a plural on page 19.)

As a historian of the English language once put it, "A student with one year of Latin [knows] that *data* and *phenomena* are plural." Albert C. Baugh, *The Gift of Style*, 34 Pa. B. Ass'n Q. 101, 105–06 (1962).

database. One word.

DATES. A. Order. One may unimpeachably write either *August 8, 2010* or *8 Aug. 2010*. The latter—the BrE method which is also used in the American military—is often better in prose, for it takes no comma.

Of the American method—*May 26, 2010*—the first editor of the *OED* said: "This is not logical: 19 May 1862 is. *Begin* at day, *ascend* to month, *ascend* to year; not *begin* at month, *descend* to day, then *ascend* to year." Sir James A.H. Murray, as quoted in *Hart's Rules for Compositors and Readers at the OUP* 18 n.1 (39th ed. 1983).

B. Month and Year. *February 2011* is better than *February of 2011*. There is no need for a comma between the month and the year.

C. As Adjectives. Modern writers have taken to making adjectives out of dates, just as they have out of PLACE-NAMES. E.g.: "The June 2005 divorce decree . . . awarded him legal and primary physical custody of the children." *Saravia v. Mendoza*, 695 S.E.2d 47, 49 (Ga. Ct. App. 2010). Today this usage occurs even in formal legal prose. The more traditional rendering of the sentence just quoted would be, "The divorce decree of June 2005 awarded him legal and primary custody of the child." Although occasionally using dates adjectivally is a space-saver, the device should not be overworked: it can give prose a breezy, journalistic look.

The usage is particularly clumsy when the day as well as the month is given—e.g.: "The court notes that . . . in *Alpex Computer Corp. v. Nintendo Co.*, the district court reconsidered its July 18, 1991 preclusion order." *Walsh v. First UNUM Life Ins. Co.*, 982 F.Supp. 929, 931 n.1 (W.D.N.Y. 1997). Stylists who use this phrasing typically omit the comma after the year—and

rightly so: in the midst of an adjective phrase (i.e., the date), it impedes the flow of the writing too much.

D. Written Out. Although the validity of a legal document almost never depends on its being dated, lawyers often go to extreme lengths to express the date in words; *1 January 1988* becomes *the first day of January, One thousand nine hundred and eighty-eight.* A waste.

E. In Contracts. To avoid litigation on the question whether *until December 31, 1986* includes all of that day, the drafter should state the matter of inclusion explicitly <this option expires at noon, Pacific Standard Time, on 17 June 2011>.

For another common problem relating to dates in contracts, see **later of [date] or [date].**

datum. See **data.**

Daubert. Francophones and GALLICISM-lovers be warned: *Daubert* is pronounced /**daw**-bərt/, not /doh-**bayr**/. The confusion over how to pronounce *Daubert* began (and apparently should have ended) in the Supreme Court when the Chief Justice said /**daw**-bərt/ in oral argument. The Dauberts' lawyer then chose to mispronounce his clients' name repeatedly rather than correct the Chief Justice. Michael H. Gottesman, *Admissibility of Expert Testimony After* Daubert, 43 Emory L.J. 867, 867 (1994). And so the /**daw**-bərt/ pronunciation was established ex cathedra by a Chief Justice who went uncorrected.

day. Three legal conventions relate to this word. First, when given as the period of a notice, and prescribed as a necessary interval between two acts or events, *day* excludes the day of the notice and the act to be performed. Hence the full number of days prescribed intervenes, unless the law provides otherwise.

Second, when used as a period of time, *day* means the period of 24 hours, beginning at the stroke of midnight.

Third, when used in contrast to *night*, the word ordinarily denotes the period beginning at half an hour before sunrise and ending half an hour after sunset.

day in court is a LOAN TRANSLATION of the LAW FRENCH *jour en banc*, which, by the 17th century, had been translated (partly) to *jour in court*. Whereas the plaintiff ordinarily wants a day in court, the defendant ordinarily wants—in legal parlance—to "go hence without day." (See **go hence without day** & ***sine die.***) E.g.:

- "The principal [suggestion] is that the plaintiff was not made a party to the proceeding, and has not had his *day in court*, in opposition to the final decision [that] ordered the sale." *Howard v. Ry.*, 101 U.S. 837, 847 (1879) (per Clifford, J.).
- "If a party fails to ask for and to secure all relief, both legal and equitable, to which he is entitled in the action, he cannot, after final disposition of the case, bring another action on the same facts for further relief. He has had his

day in court." William F. Walsh, *A Treatise on Equity* 38 (1930).

- "To say Henley has had his *day in court* is an understatement; the circuit court, Wisconsin Court of Appeals, this court, and the U.S. District Court all reviewed the claim that Henley was entitled to a new trial." *State v. Henley*, 787 N.W.2d 350, 369 (Wis. 2010).

Cf. **one bite at the apple.**

d.b.n. See **administrator.**

deadbeat (= a person who evades debts), a 19th-century coinage, is a favorite word of American lawyers trying to collect on judgments. Some use it tendentiously for any judgment debtor, and often the epithet is apt. Even courts use the word in published opinions—e.g.: "The Court's decision is indefensible. It permits a *deadbeat* husband to use the Bankruptcy Code's grace for honest debtors as a slick scheme for euchring his former wife out of her 'sole and separate property' in one-half of the benefits he receives under a pension plan." *Bush v. Taylor*, 893 F.2d 962, 967 (8th Cir. 1990) (Bowman, J., dissenting).

dead capital. See **mortgage.**

deadhand. See **mortmain.**

dead investment. See **mortgage.**

deadline is one word; formerly it was hyphenated.

deadlocked jury. See **hung jury.**

deadly; deathly. The first means "able to cause death." (See **lethal.**) The second means "like death." The CLICHÉ is properly rendered *deathly dull*, not *deadly dull*.

dead man's statute; dead-man statute. The usual form is the possessive *dead man's statute*. When the phrase first appeared, in the late 19th century, it referred to a statutory requirement that all claims against a decedent must be brought within a fixed time (such as two and a half years) from the date when the executor is officially qualified. By the early 20th century, however, the phrase had taken on its modern sense: "a law that makes a decedent's declarations inadmissible as evidence in certain circumstances, as when the witness seeks to support a claim against the estate." E.g.: "That statute, known as the '*dead man's statute*,' provides that an action involving a claim on a succession or the decedent's heir or legatee must be brought within one year of the death of the decedent, or parol evidence is not admissible." *In re Succession of Greer*, 987 So.2d 305, 309 (La. Ct. App. 2008).

Of course, the phrase *dead man* has yielded a variety of terms in the English language, including plant names such as *dead man's fingers* (a type of orchid) and *dead man's hand* (variously an orchid, a fern, or a type of seaweed), as well as *dead man's switch* or *handle* (an automatic shutoff device installed on machinery to protect an operator who releases the controls).

Still, since the early 1980s, some writers have rejected *dead man's statute* on grounds of SEXISM, preferring instead *dead person's statute*: "She argued the '*dead person's statute*' bars Mr. Crowley's testimony because that testimony would be unfair to her." *Ellis v. William Penn Life Ins. Co.*, 873 P.2d 1185, 1187 (Wash. 1994) (en banc). *See Viscito v. Fred S. Carbon Co.*, 636 So.2d 194, 195 n.1 (Fla. Dist. Ct. App. 1994) (exhorting the legislature to amend the statute by changing *man* to *person*). The use of *person* in this context is certainly less vivid than *man*, but the phrase *dead person's statute* may soon seem as natural as *reasonable person* (in place of *reasonable man*). See SEXISM (B) & **reasonable person.**

dead pledge. See **mortgage.**

deal with; deal in. People in business *deal in* what they buy and sell <she deals in stocks and bonds>, but they *deal with* problems or other people <the job entails dealing with demanding clients>. *Deal* should not be used transitively where *deal in* is intended. Although one *deals* cards, one *deals in* oil and other commodities.

But in one context *deal* is transitive, in a phrase originating in the language of the underworld. We say that a person *deals drugs*, not *deals in drugs— e.g.: "The principal witness for the Government was [S.], an undercover detective who had been assigned to investigate allegations that [C.] was *dealing drugs*." Olin Guy Wellborn III, *The Definition of Hearsay in the Federal Rules of Evidence*, 61 Tex. L. Rev. 49, 89 (1982).

Deal with is a vague PHRASAL VERB for which there is almost always a better, more specific substitute—e.g.:

- "Whichever approach is ultimately adopted by the Commission, new commentary will *deal with* [read *discuss*] a lawyer's duty to raise non-frivolous challenges to disclosure requirements external to the rules." Margaret Colgate Love, *Update on Ethics 2000 Project and Summary of Recommendations to Date*, 11 No. 2 Prof. Law. 2, 4 (2000).
- "This article will *deal with* [read *discuss*] eight types of [Alternative Worker Organizations]; however, this list should not be considered complete because the groups will change over time." Alan Hyde, *New Institutions for Worker Representation in the United States*, 50 N.Y.L. Sch. L. Rev. 385, 386 (2006).

Cf. **concerned with, be.** But where *deal with* is roughly equivalent to *handle*, it is unobjectionable: "The Court held that state courts dividing community property in divorce proceedings could not *deal with* nondisability military retirement benefits." John B. McKnight, *Closing the McCarty–USFSPA Window*, 63 Tex. L. Rev. 497, 497 (1984).

death; demise; decease, n.; **surcease.** *Death* is the common word, the other three being FORMAL WORDS (in order of increasing formality) that act almost as EUPHEMISMS. There is nothing wrong with the word *death*, although it has inherently unpleasant connotations. But that is the nature of the subject, and writing *decease* or *surcease* in legal contexts is only a little less ridiculous than writing *going to meet his Maker*. See **demise, deceased** & **surcease.**

death case (sometimes *death action*), as used by the federal courts, commonly means "a criminal case in which the death sentence has been imposed." In criminal cases, then, the phrase has nothing to do with *wrongful death*—e.g.:

- "The measure of an individual's competency under *Rees* to waive federal habeas review in a *death case* is informed by considerations very different from those underlying the standard for competency to stand trial." *Rumbaugh v. Procunier*, 753 F.2d 395, 412 (5th Cir. 1985).
- "In a *death case*, the Constitution requires sentencing juries to consider all mitigating evidence." *Brown v. Payton*, 544 U.S. 133, 148 (2005) (Breyer, J., concurring).

But in tort contexts, lawyers frequently say and write *death case* as a shorthand form of *wrongful-death case*. E.g.: "In *death cases*, the law should allow juries to award money as compensation only for what can reasonably be compensated for by money." Randal R. Craft Jr., *Put Limits on Death Compensation*, N.Y. Times, 8 Oct. 1989, at 2F.

deathly. See **deadly.**

death penalty; death sentence. A phrase dating from the late 19th century, *death penalty* is a plain-speaking alternative to the EUPHEMISM *capital punishment*. *Death sentence*—as opposed to *death penalty*—usually refers to a particular convict's punishment. "The prisoner was convicted, but the *death sentence* (still the penalty for treason) was commuted, and he was released later." William Geldart, *Introduction to English Law* 153 (D.C.M. Yardley ed., 9th ed. 1984). See **capital punishment.**

death-qualified jurors are jurors who cannot be disqualified for serving on a jury under the test set forth in *Witherspoon v. Illinois*, 391 U.S. 510 (1968); in other words, *death-qualified jurors* have been selected because they have no absolute ideological bias against the death penalty. A *death-qualified jury*, then, is held fit to decide cases involving the death penalty. E.g.: "*Death-qualified jurors* may be 'perceptually ready' to view evidence as incriminating and view the prosecution's witnesses in a more positive light than *non-death-qualified jurors*." Christopher Letkewicz, *Stacking the Deck in Favor of Death*, 2 DePaul J. Soc. Just. 217, 247 (2009).

death row is an Americanism dating from the early 1940s (though *W11* dates it only from 1950). E.g.: "A. I was put in *death row*. That's in a line of cells running crossways, east and west, on the *death row*. Q. How far was that, approximately, from the electric chair?" *Daugherty v. State*, 17 So.2d 290, 294 (Fla. 1944) (en banc) (Chapman, J., dissenting) (quoting testimony). Though the phrases in that quotation are *in death row* and *on the death row*, the usual phrase today is *on death row*.

To most speakers of AmE, the term still refers concretely to the area of a prison where those who have been sentenced to death are confined. But there is a tendency to use the term more abstractly in reference to anyone who has been sentenced to death—regardless of the location in a prison.

death sentence. See **death penalty.**

death statute; survival statute. In the context of wrongful-death cases, these phrases must be distinguished. A *death statute* protects the interests of the decedent's family and other dependents, who may recover in damages what they would have received from the decedent if the death had not occurred. A *survival statute*, by contrast, protects the decedent's own interest: the estate recovers for the decedent's pain and suffering before death, medical expenses, lost wages, and (sometimes, oddly) funeral expenses.

The ideas represented by these phrases are a popular subject of law reform: "Historically *death statutes* came first in most jurisdictions and were later supplemented by *survival statutes*. The end result of this secular legislative process will no doubt be that both interests will be protected in all jurisdictions; while the process continues each state must be looked on as a law to itself." Grant Gilmore & Charles L. Black Jr., *The Law of Admiralty* 360 (2d ed. 1975).

debar. See **bar.**

*debark. See **disembark.**

debarkation; *debarcation. The first is the preferred spelling.

debate, vb. & n. In BrE, the verb *debate* equates to AmE *argue*, and the noun *debate* to AmE *argument*. So British lawyers typically use *debate* when American lawyers would write *oral argument* or *argue*. E.g.:

- "Since the matter has been *debated*, it may be desirable for me to say . . . that the test . . . of 'practicability' is that of workability." *In re Tacon Pub. Trustee v. Tacon*, [1954] 2 W.L.R. 66 (C.A.).
- "I would refer first to contracts for the sale of goods which were touched on in the course of the *debate*." *White & Carter (Councils), Ltd. v. McGregor*, [1962] A.C. 413, 437 (H.L.).

See **oral argument.**

de bene esse /də **ben**-ay es-ay/ (lit., "of well-being") denotes the best course of action possible under the circumstances or in anticipation of the future. Though this LAW LATIN phrase is of unknown origin and does not appear in Classical Latin, it serves as useful JARGON in the age-old phrase *deposition de bene esse* (sometimes written *de bene esse deposition*). Such a deposition is taken when the witness will likely be unable to attend a scheduled court hearing. Unlike most depositions, a *deposition de bene esse* is not a so-called discovery deposition but a deposition to preserve testimony.

Formerly, the phrase *appearance de bene esse* was used as a variant of *special appearance*. Today, this substitution is not recommended. One court has even ridiculed it: "[The defendant] is no longer required at the door of the federal courthouse to intone that ancient abracadabra of the law, *de bene esse*, in order by its magic power to enable himself to remain outside even while he steps within." *Orange Theatre Corp. v. Rayherstz Amusement Corp.*, 139 F.2d 871, 874 (3d Cir. 1944). Cf. **esse** & *in esse*.

During the 20th century, the phrase took on another sense in American and British legal writing, namely, "for what it is worth." This use seems pretentious.

debenture; bond. *Debenture* = (1) a writing that acknowledges a debt; (2) a bond secured by nothing more than the credit and financial reputation of the issuer, as opposed to a lien on property; or (3) a customhouse certificate providing for a refund of money paid on duties for imported goods when the importer reexports the goods rather than selling them in the country in which they were imported.

In BrE, *debenture* denotes any security issued by a company other than its shares, including what in AmE are commonly called *bonds*. In AmE, *debenture* generally denotes an instrument secured by a floating charge junior to other charges secured by fixed mortgages; more specifically, it means a series of securities secured by a group of securities held in trust for the benefit of the *debenture* holders. Sometimes a *debenture* is no more than a corporation's unsecured promissory note bearing a fixed rate of interest.

debility; debilitation. *Debility* = weakness; feebleness. *Debilitation* = the act of making weak or feeble; enfeeblement.

debit; debitum. See **debt.**

de bonis asportatis. See **trespass.**

de bonis non. See **administrator.**

debrief, used chiefly in military or espionage operations, means (1) "to interrogate (e.g., a spy) to obtain valuable information"; (2) "to instruct (someone) not to reveal any classified information after that person leaves a sensitive position"; or (3) "(colloquially) to obtain information from (a person) on the completion of a mission or after a journey" (*OED*). Here sense 1 applies: "Driver asserts that the government knew from its '*debriefing*' of the coconspirators pursuant to their plea agreements which of the hundreds of calls were made by Benton to other drug sources." *U.S. v. Driver*, 798 F.2d 248, 251 (7th Cir. 1986).

Some law firms apparently fancy themselves involved in the espionage business. One, in its firm résumé, states: "Feedback is an important part of a summer associate's experience at the firm; in addition to regular informal contact, we have periodic *debriefings* for each summer associate throughout the summer, and one at the conclusion of the summer associate's stay." Even in a figurative sense, this use of *debrief* fails, for the associate no doubt is primarily the recipient, not the source, of the transfer of information; hence, *brief* (= to give important information to) is the correct verb.

debt; indebtedness; debit; debitum; arrear; arrearage. All these terms denote something, usually a monetary sum, that is owed to another. *Debt* usually connotes a definite, readily computable amount owed in return for goods or services, or perhaps real estate.

Indebtedness, though often a puffed-up equivalent of *debt*, is justifiable when it refers to (1) an aggregation of debts owed either to various creditors or to one creditor <the debtor's total indebtedness to 12 creditors> or (2) the state of being indebted <his indebtedness is ongoing>.

- (Sense 1) "Heller elected to declare the entire *indebtedness* due and payable according to the acceleration clauses contained in the notes." *Terrell v. Walter E. Heller & Co.*, 439 P.2d 989, 990 (Colo. 1968).
- (Sense 2) "For purposes of 12 U.S.C. § 82, a national bank's *indebtedness* or liability does not include Federal Funds Purchased . . . [or] obligations to repurchase securities sold." 12 C.F.R. § 7.7518 (1981).

True, *indebtedness* often seems to verge on being a NEEDLESS VARIANT of *debt*. Admittedly, though, in some contexts one can hardly discern what is being referred to: the state of being indebted, an aggregation of debts, or a single debt. See **indebtedness.** Cf. **indebtment.*

Debit is an accounting or bookkeeping term for any item listing on the debt side (the left side) of an account, as opposed to a right-side credit. *Debitum*, an ARCHAISM and a NEEDLESS VARIANT of *debt*, is still sometimes used by Scottish lawyers in traditional phrases such as *debitum fundi* (= a debt of the estate).

Arrear (more commonly in the plural form *arrears*) implies that part of the debt remains unpaid, but not all. *Arrearage*, though used as a needless legalistic synonym of *arrear*, does bear an additional and useful sense: an unpaid dividend that is from a past period and that is due to a holder of preferred stock. See **arrears.**

debut. This word, when used as a verb, is disapproved by 97 percent of the usage panel for the *AHD*, for what that is worth. The forms *debuted* and *debuting* are certainly ugly to the philologist. The *OED*, surprisingly, records examples as far back as 1830. For the moment, however, the verb *debut* has taken on the character of a VOGUE WORD and should be avoided on that account.

decarceration, a word included in none of the major English-language dictionaries, refers to the state-sponsored shutting down of all substandard asylums, prisons, and reformatories, so that those

---

who would ordinarily occupy such institutions are either discharged or denied admission. E.g.: "Those who espoused rehabilitation as the primary purpose of imprisonment included both those who enthusiastically approved of imprisonment and those who favored *decarceration.*" Franklin E. Zimring & Gordon Hawkins, *Dangerousness and Criminal Justice*, 85 Mich. L. Rev. 481, 485 (1986).

decease, n. See **death.**

decease, vb. = to die. "Mr. Leung was not a beneficiary when he *deceased.*" *Leung v. Skidmore, Owings & Merrill LLP*, 213 F.Supp.2d 1097, 1106 (N.D. Cal. 2002). This verbal use of *decease* is even more pompous than the noun use. The straightforward *die* is almost always better. Cf. **death.**

deceased, n.; **decedent.** When these terms are used in the possessive case, no one would argue that *deceased's* is less euphonious than *decedent's.* Yet the term *deceased's* appears frequently in legal prose, especially in BrE, in which *decedent* is obsolete. The awkwardness of *-ed's* can be overcome either by resort to *decedent's* or by writing *of the deceased* (which is, unfortunately, not possible in all contexts). See PLURALS (D) & POSSESSIVES (F). Cf. **accused** & **insured.**

We may find no solace in our unhappy dilemma between these words, for even *decedent* sounds legalistic. Yet it is common in American legal writing—e.g.:

- "Appellant was under no duty to speak or inquire concerning detail of *decedent's* wealth." *In re Borton's Estate*, 393 P.2d 808, 813 (Wyo. 1964).
- "Not only was it inconsistent with [Defendant's] expression of regret for the mother's pain, proving that a *decedent* has asked for what he got is a defense better reserved for the defense of prosecutions such as murder and manslaughter." *Mickens v. Taylor*, 240 F.3d 348, 362 (4th Cir. 2001).
- "Those weather conditions caused the *decedent* to slip and fall between moving railroad cars." *McDonald v. Northeast Ill. Reg'l*, 249 F.Supp.2d 1051, 1056 (N.D. Ill. 2003).

It may be necessary to use *deceased* or *decedent* in a case that involves many parties with the same name, such as a probate dispute or even a wrongful-death action. When that is not the case, the better practice is to use the decedent's name.

deceit = (1) the act of giving a false impression; or (2) a tort arising from a false statement of fact made knowingly or recklessly with the intent that another person should act on it, with the result that the person who acts on it suffers damage. Within this broad definition, *deceit* is capable of sharing in the first four senses of *fraud.* (See **fraud.**)

deceitful. See **dishonest.**

deceive; defraud. To *deceive* is to induce someone to believe in a falsehood. The deceiver may know the statement to be false or may make it recklessly. To *defraud* is to cause injury or loss by deceit. *Defrauding*

leads a person to take action, whereas *deceiving* merely leads a person into a state of mind. But see sense 2 of **deceit.**

deception; fraud; subterfuge; chicanery; double-dealing; self-dealing. All refer to a purposeful misdirection for selfish ends, usually involving ill motives. *Deception* involves an artifice that can but need not involve culpability <his deception swindled the homeowners out of $10,000> <professional illusionists are masters of deception>. *Fraud* always connotes blameworthiness and typically criminality. It usually suggests the perversion of the truth in an attempt to persuade someone to transfer a valuable possession or right. Yet the term is broad enough to encompass any violation of a duty if the violation involves misrepresentation or concealment. (For much more detail, see **fraud.**) *Subterfuge* /səb-tər-fyooj/ is more specifically the evasion by which another is duped, typically as a way of avoiding a duty, a difficulty, or even mere criticism. *Chicanery* connotes petty tricks or sophistry used to gain some advantage, especially in legal proceedings. (See **chicanery.**) *Double-dealing* suggests duplicity of character and two-faced behavior, with strong implications of an ongoing pretense that disguises one's true thoughts, feelings, and motivations. *Self-dealing* suggests participation in a transaction that benefits oneself at the expense of another who is owed a fiduciary duty.

deceptive; *deceptious. The second is a NEEDLESS VARIANT.

decide on is often prolix for *decide*—e.g.:

- "At oral argument, counsel for the United States maintained that it would be up to the prosecutor, when a jury is deadlocked, to request a new panel or to allow the judge to *decide on* [omit *on*] the sentence." *Jones v. U.S.*, 527 U.S. 373, 418 n.21 (1999) (Ginsburg, J., dissenting).
- "The jury's task is particularly awkward when the holdout opposes liability and the jury must *decide on* [omit *on*] damages." Shari Seidman Diamond et al., *Revisiting the Unanimity Requirement*, 100 Nw. U.L. Rev. 201, 205 (2006).
- "The jury must *decide on* [omit *on*] each element . . . beyond a reasonable doubt." Derrick Augustus Carter, *To Catch the Lion, Tether the Goat*, 42 Akron L. Rev. 135, 164 (2009).

See PARTICLES, UNNECESSARY.

decimate. Originally this word meant "to kill one in every ten," but this etymological sense, because it's so uncommon, has been abandoned except in historical contexts. Now *decimate* generally means "to cause great loss of life; to destroy a large part of." Preferably, the word should not be used of a complete obliteration or defeat. Nor should it be used lightly of just any defeat.

decision; opinion; judgment. Technically, in the U.S., judges are said to write *opinions* to justify their *decisions* or *judgments*; they do not write *decisions* or *judgments*. E.g.:

- "The court orally granted the motion and subsequently wrote *a decision* [read *an opinion*] explaining its reasoning." *Isom v. Town of Warren, R.I.,* 360 F.3d 7, 9 (1st Cir. 2004).
- "Chief Justice Taft . . . wrote *a decision* [read *an opinion*] that flatly prohibited congressional encroachments on presidential power." Jonathan T. Molot, *Principled Minimalism,* 90 Va. L. Rev. 1753, 1816–17 (2004).
- "In . . . *Addison v. Holly Hill Fruit Products,* Justice Frankfurter wrote *a decision* [read *an opinion*] approving retroactive rulemaking to fill a gap created by the partial judicial invalidation of an agency exemption from wage and hour legislation." Ann Woolhandler, *Public Rights, Private Rights, and Statutory Retroactivity,* 94 Geo. L.J. 1015, 1053 (2006).

See JUDGMENTS, APPELLATE-COURT & **opinion.** Cf. **speech.**

decisional. See **decisive.**

decisional law; *decision law. The preferred form of this American equivalent of *caselaw* is *decisional law.* E.g.:

- "A good summary of what may be regarded as a consensus view of the *decision law* [read *decisional law*] is the statement quoted earlier in this opinion taken from *Couch on Insurance.*" *Amos v. Allstate Ins. Co.,* 184 P.3d 28, 35 (Alaska 2008).
- "Legislation and *decisional law* promoting gender equality has fostered greater social equality." John G. Culhane, *Marriage Equality?,* 1 Drexel L. Rev. 485, 502 (2009).
- "The addition of the word 'Acts' where it was previously absent signaled that Congress intended to extend the effect of faith and credit where it was previously lacking, and to bring state statutory law up to par with state *decisional law.*" Shawn Gebhardt, Comment, *Full Faith and Credit for Status Records,* 97 Cal. L. Rev. 1419, 1438 (2009).

See **caselaw** & **jurisprudence (B).** See also **decisive.** Cf. **organic law.**

decision-making, n., is a generic term for *deciding* and, though useful in some contexts, is much overworked in current legal writing. The word smacks of sociological cant, and is often merely a grandiloquent way of saying *deciding*: after all, when one makes decisions, one decides.

It is now frequently spelled as one word, even by the U.S. Supreme Court. And the word is so spelled in Paul Brest's book *Processes of Constitutional Decisionmaking* (1975). One sees the same one-wordism tendency at work in the term *budget-making.* These compounds are too bulky to look like anything but jargonistic English; a simple hyphen does a lot. See **budget-making.**

decisive; decisional. *Decisive,* frequently used in the sense "determinative" in legal writing, refers to things as opposed to persons. In lay contexts, of course, *decisive* almost always refers to persons and means "resolute." Following are examples of the legal usage:

- "Defendant points out that he retained his privilege against self-incrimination on the drug charge until sentencing, but that fact is not *decisive*; the police had little interest in gathering additional evidence of the drug charge." *U.S. v. Green,* 592 A.2d 985, 990 (D.C. 1991).
- "This Court's contemplation of paternity matters has generated several *decisive* principles in this significant area of the law." *Marriage/Children of Betty L.W. v. William E.W.,* 569 S.E.2d 77, 81 (W. Va. 2002).
- "But what is unusual about this case, and *decisive* against the *Brady* claim, is that [the] evidence was self-validating, which makes his motivation to fabricate irrelevant." *Mataya v. Kingston,* 371 F.3d 353, 357 (7th Cir. 2004).

Decisional = of, or of the nature of, deciding or a decision. The *OED* notes that *decisional* is "rare." It may have been rare in the 19th century, but today it is common in American legal writing. E.g.:

- "The comments were not related to the *decisional* process as the most recent occurred at least four months before Ramlet's termination, and both were made to employees not involved in the *decisional* process." *Ramlet v. E.F. Johnson Co.,* 507 F.3d 1149, 1153 (8th Cir. 2007).
- "Looking to federal law of due process and the right of cross examination and confrontation as announced by the Supreme Court, I am persuaded that the relevant law is clear, and dictates the conclusion that the state court's *decisional* process was contrary to this clearly established law." *Hall v. Quarterman,* 534 F.3d 365, 381 (5th Cir. 2008) (Higginbotham, J., concurring in part & dissenting in part).
- "Oral argument will not aid the court's *decisional* process, and its denial will not result in prejudice to any party." *Protect Lake Pleasant, LLC v. McDonald,* 609 F.Supp.2d 895, 898 n.4 (D. Ariz. 2009).

See **decisional law.**

declaim; disclaim. The first is what lawyers do in court, the second what manufacturers do in warranties. To *declaim* is to speak formally in public (whence the adjective *declamatory*); this word is frequently misused for *disclaim,* meaning "to make a disclaimer, disavow, repudiate."

declamatory. See **declarative.**

declarant, especially in the context of hearsay evidence, has long been the law's agent noun corresponding to the verb *to state* or *to say.* A *declarant* does not "state vehemently," as the association with *declare* might suggest. E.g.: "Alaska Rule of Evidence 803(3) carves out an exception to the hearsay rule when a statement is not offered to prove the truth of the matter asserted but is offered to prove the *declarant's* state of mind." *State v. McDonald,* 872 P.2d 627, 642 (Alaska Ct. App. 1994).

declaration = (1) at common law, the pleading by which a plaintiff formally presents a claim for relief in a civil action; (2) in the law of evidence, an unsworn statement made by someone having knowledge of facts relating to an event in dispute; (3) in a few American jurisdictions (such as California), a formal written statement resembling an affidavit and attesting, under penalty of perjury, to facts known by the declarant; (4) a U.S. Customs form on which anyone entering the U.S. must record the value of the goods and cash that he or she is bringing into the country; or (5) a document that governs legal rights to certain types of realty, such as a condominium or a residential subdivision.

Sense 3 remains unrecorded in most legal and nonlegal dictionaries. For more on that sense, see **evidence (A)**. For more on sense 1, see COMMON-LAW PLEADINGS, **statement of claim** & **treaty**.

declaration of trust; trust deed; trust agreement. These terms are variously used to name the instrument creating a trust.

declarative; declaratory; declamatory. In grammar we have *declarative* sentences, but in law we have *declaratory* judgments, statutes, and acts. Both words mean "having the function of declaring, setting forth, or explaining"; their DIFFERENTIATION lies in established uses, not in meaning. For virtually all legal contexts, *declaratory* is the word. E.g.: "In the seventeenth and eighteenth centuries, Roman law was taken to be *declaratory* of the law of nature." Arthur T. von Mehren, *The Civil Law System* vii (1957).

Declamatory, which is sometimes confused with *declaratory*, means "haranguing; of or pertaining to declaiming oratorically."

declarative construction; declarative interpretation. See *declarative interpretation* under INTERPRETATION, MODES OF (B).

declarator is not an agent noun, but an old-fashioned equivalent of *declaratory-judgment action* (= a lawsuit in which a legal right or status is declared without the plaintiff's seeking further relief). The form *declarator* remains common in Scots law. See -ER (B).

declaratory. See **declarative.**

declaratory-judgment action. Because the first two words form a PHRASAL ADJECTIVE, they are so hyphenated.

declaratory precedent. See **precedent (C).**

declare. In the context of Anglo-American caselaw, this verb often fosters the legal FICTION "that courts do not 'make' law but only 'discover' or 'declare' it." Lon L. Fuller, *Legal Fictions* 88 (1967). As Fuller suggests, *discover* is equally misleading when used in reference to a court's pronouncements on the law.

declination; *declinature; *declension. All three words are used in denoting the act of courteously refusing, but *declination* now far outstrips the other two in frequency of use. In referring to the act of declining, *declinature and *declension ought to be considered NEEDLESS VARIANTS of *declination*.

decline. A. And Its Near-Synonyms: *refuse; reject; repudiate.* These verbs share the sense "to say no," and they are arranged here from least vehement to most. *Decline,* being the most courteous and neutral, appears commonly in the context of offers, invitations, generosity, and favors. *Refuse* is more decisively negative, sometimes downright discourteous—and it often suggests not agreeing to something that a requester might have expected assent to <despite admitting fault, Marken refused to pay for the damage>. *Reject,* etymologically a "throwing away," is so strong that it suggests wanting nothing to do with a proposal and perhaps even the proposer <our client rejected the settlement offer outright>. In contract law, this is the verb ordinarily used to describe what an offeree does in turning down an offer, or a buyer in refusing tendered goods. *Repudiate,* etymologically a "casting off," connotes an outright disowning with a sense of derision or scorn <Thomas Paine's *Common Sense* repudiated monarchy>, although this connotation is absent in the law of contracts. *Anticipatory repudiation,* as a TERM OF ART, does not require derision or scorn, but only a clear indication that a party to a contract intends not to perform the contract in the future. That doctrine is invoked when the phrase *anticipatorily repudiate* appears—e.g.: "When one party *anticipatorily repudiates* an agreement, the repudiation discharges any remaining duties of performance the other party to the agreement might have." *In re Arlington Hospitality, Inc.,* 368 B.R. 702, 718 (Bankr. N.D. Ill. 2007). See **repudiation.**

B. Noun Forms. *Decline* has two distinct senses that yield distinct noun forms. *Declination* derives from *decline* in the sense "to refuse," and *decline,* n., derives from *decline* in the sense "to go downhill." See **declination.**

deconstruction (= a method of reading by which one finds the subtext beneath the text and inverts their relative importance) for *destruction* is an odd error that might be considered a telling slip of the tongue— e.g.: "Fire is an extremely fast and effective means of *deconstruction.* All urban fires are in some sense manmade." Thomas Hine, *Don't Blame Mrs. O'Leary,* N.Y. Times, 15 July 1990, § 7, at 13.

decorous is pronounced with the primary accent on the first syllable: /**dek**-ə-rəs/.

decree, vb. = (1) to command by decree; or (2) to award judicially; to assign authoritatively. Here sense 2, undifferentiated in most dictionaries, applies because it is construed with a direct object and a *to-* phrase: "But the Probate Court did not *decree* the estate to the widow, and then make her a constructive trustee of such estate for the benefit of the parents." *In re Mahoney's Estate,* 220 A.2d 475, 478–79 (Vt. 1966).

decree; judgment. Traditionally, judicial decisions are termed *decrees* in courts of equity, admiralty, divorce, and probate; they are termed *judgments* in courts of law. E.g.:

- "In the divorce *decree*, the district court denied Wife's request for fees, ordering each party to pay their own attorney fees; costs of the action were taxed to the filing fee." *Singhal v. Singhal*, 208 P.3d 808 (Kan. Ct. App. 2009).
- "In the second above-quoted paragraph in the divorce *decree*, the trial court acknowledges the child support obligation under the temporary orders providing for payments beginning on July 1, 2006." *In re R.F.G.*, 282 S.W.3d 722, 726 (Tex. App.—Dallas 2009).

Nevertheless, in modern usage *decree* is broad enough to refer to any court order, whether or not the relief granted or denied is equitable in nature. E.g.: "The [Supreme] Court's *decrees* are backed only by its own prestige and ultimately by the willingness of the President to help enforce them." Robert G. McCloskey, *The American Supreme Court* 57 (1960). See **judgment (c)**.

decree absolute; decree nisi. These phrases, more usual in G.B. than in the U.S., are very similar. *Decree nisi* = a conditional court decree that will become absolute unless the adversely affected party shows the court, within a specified time, why it should be set aside. In England, a *decree nisi* ordinarily relates to divorce, annulling a marriage, or decreeing that a missing spouse is presumed dead. E.g.:

- "After the hearing of a suit in which a husband petitioned for divorce and the wife respondent cross-prayed for a decree of restitution of conjugal rights, Sachs J. granted the husband a *decree nisi* and made no order as to costs save that the wife's costs should be taxed under the Legal Aid and Advice Act." *Paice v. Paice*, [1957] 1 W.L.R. 1011 (P).
- "That case was similar to the instant one in that a child had been born to the wife petitioner between petition and the *decree nisi* and that the court was not informed of its birth and in consequence did not consider its welfare." *F. v. F.*, [1971] P. 1, 10.

Decree absolute = a ripened decree nisi, that is, one whose time limit has passed, so that the court's decree has become unconditional. In England, a *decree absolute* is ordinarily a decree of divorce, nullity, or presumption of death that ends a legal marriage and enables the parties to remarry. The (conditional) *decree nisi* becomes a (final) *decree absolute* after a time (usually six weeks) if there is no contrary reason.

Rule absolute and *rule nisi* are often used as equivalents of *decree absolute* and *decree nisi*. See **nisi**.

decretal /di-**kree**-təl/ = of or relating to a decree. E.g.:

- "In the bill it is complained that Colorado . . . has refused to permit Wyoming to install measuring devices at the places of diversion . . . , and there is prayer for a *decretal* order permitting such installation." *Wyoming v. Colorado*, 298 U.S. 573, 585 (1936) (per Van Devanter, J.).
- "Judgment of the County Court . . . [is] modified on the law and the facts by inserting after the words 'costs of this action' in the fourth *decretal* paragraph the following words." *Nassau County v. Hardie*, 268 A.D. 1067, 1067 (N.Y. App. Div. 1945).

- "We did not, in our *decretal* statement, 'remand' this case for a particular, prescribed purpose." *U.S. v. Owen*, 553 F.3d 161, 163 n.2 (2d Cir. 2009).

*Decretorial, **decretory*, and **decretive* are NEEDLESS VARIANTS.

Decretal may also be a noun—e.g.: "The precedents [of] compulsion to accomplish governmental *decretals* are found rather in the Court of the Star Chamber, of unhappy memory." *U.S. v. Parkinson*, 240 F.2d 918, 921–22 (9th Cir. 1956). *Decrees* would actually be the better word in that sentence, for *decretals* specifically are "letters containing a papal ruling, particularly one relating to matters of canonical discipline, and most precisely a papal rescript in response to an appeal" (*OCL1*).

decriminalize (= to reclassify [an activity] so that it is no longer considered a crime) is a NEOLOGISM dating only from 1969. Today it is commonplace—e.g.: "As a legislator in Arizona, O'Connor once voted to *decriminalize* abortion." *All Eyes on Justice O'Connor*, Newsweek, 1 May 1989, at 34.

de cursu. See **of course**.

dedicatory; *dedicative; *dedicatorial. The first form is preferred; the other two are NEEDLESS VARIANTS.

deduce; deduct. The first means "to draw a conclusion or inference"; the second means "to subtract." *Deduct* is sometimes misused for *deduce*—e.g.:

- "Under some circumstances good cause for the production of a document may be *deducted* [read *deduced*] from the motion and the circumstances themselves." *Tibbs v. Housing Auth. of New Orleans*, 204 So.2d 70, 72 (La. Ct. App. 1967).
- "Any jury could have reasonably *deducted* [read *deduced*] from this evidence that the codefendant did not serve his full sentence on the prior conviction." *Grigsby v. State*, 833 S.W.2d 573, 575 (Tex. App.—Dallas 1992).
- "We are concerned with what can be *deducted* [read *deduced*] from the evidence." *Morrow v. Fisher*, 51 S.W.3d 468, 473 (Mo. Ct. App. 2001).

See **adduce (b)** & **deducible**.

deducible; deductible. The first means "inferable." E.g.:

- "Nor would the document reveal . . . any information about the nature, scope, or course of the government's investigation or its reliance upon certain evidence not otherwise known or *deducible* by them." *Linsteadt v. I.R.S.*, 729 F.2d 998, 1005 (5th Cir. 1984) (Tate, J., dissenting in part).
- "When the propriety of removal is challenged before the Eleventh Circuit, a case will be remanded unless the jurisdictional amount is clearly stated on the face of the removing documents or readily *deducible* from them." Nicole Ochi, *Are Consumer Class and Mass Actions Dead?*, 41 Loy. L.A. L. Rev. 965, 1004 (2008).

• "A demurrer admits every well-pleaded material fact set forth in the complaint as well as all inferences reasonably *deducible*." *Chester Cmty. Charter Sch. v. Commonwealth Dep't of Educ.*, 996 A.2d 68, 74 (Pa. Commw. Ct. 2010).

Deductible, a favorite word during the tax season, means "capable of being (usu. lawfully) subtracted." It is sometimes misspelled **deductable*. See **deduce.**

deduct. See **deduce.**

deductible. See **deducible.**

deed. A. As Noun Referring to an Instrument. At common law, *deed* referred to any written instrument that was signed, sealed, and delivered. In BrE, this broad sense still applies. In AmE, however, the narrower sense of a writing by which land is conveyed is almost uniformly applicable. See **signed, sealed, and delivered.** For the difference between a *warranty deed* and a *quitclaim deed*, see **grant, bargain, and sell.**

B. As Verb. *Deed*, vb., is an Americanism dating from the early 19th century. Now commonplace in AmE, this verb seems never to be used in BrE, in which solicitors are said to *convey* or *transfer by deed.* The verb *deed* is considerably more economical—e.g.:

• "On December 23, 1952, he *deeded* to Geneva that half of the homestead upon which the improvements had been made." *Green v. Green*, 113 F.Supp. 697, 697 (D. Alaska 1953).
• "[Several factors] sufficiently explain the decedent's motives in *deeding* the property back to her grantor." *Daniels v. Cummins*, 321 N.Y.S.2d 1009, 1013 (Sup. Ct. 1971).

deedcase. See **briefcase.**

deed indented. See **indenture.**

deed of trust; trust deed. The classical form of this term is *deed of trust*, meaning "a deed conveying property in trust, and usu. evidencing a mortgage." But either form suffices, and the second has the advantage of using one-third fewer words. See **of (A).**

deed poll. See **indenture.**

deem = to treat [a thing] as being something that it is not, or as possessing certain qualities that it does not possess. It is a FORMAL WORD often used in legislation to create legal FICTIONS; that is, a statute may provide that something is or is not to be *deemed* something else, or, with a significant difference, that this something is to be *deemed* not something else.

But in general usage, *deem* is archaic for *consider, think, judge,* or *esteem*—e.g.:

• "This merely asserts that the statute may be violated with impunity if only the railroad finds its provisions onerous, or *deems it expedient* [read *thinks it best*] to do so." *Spokane & Inland Empire R.R. v. U.S.*, 241 U.S. 344, 351 (1916) (per White, C.J.).
• "For the present, we *deem it expedient* [read *think it best*] not to attempt to spell out any precise constitutional tests." *Reynolds v. Sims*, 377 U.S. 533, 578 (1964) (per Warren, C.J.).
• "Questions regarding the way Yudof handles the preliminary stages of the lawsuit should therefore not be *deemed*

as [read *considered* or *seen as*] irrelevant in determining his fitness for office." *New President Must Not Let Discrimination Hurt UT*, Daily Texan, 5 Oct. 1992, at 4.
• "The agency *deemed* [read *considered*] it 'irrelevant' because it had not been printed in the two-page, self-made application that Mr. Kirkendall submitted in response to the announcement that invited him to use any written form he wished." *Kirkendall v. Department of Army*, 573 F.3d 1318, 1324 (Fed. Cir. 2009).

deemster. See **dempster.**

de-equitize, vb., is a NEOLOGISM that first appeared in business contexts in the sense "to reduce equity in favor of corporate debt." The corresponding noun form, *de-equitization*, is more common—e.g.:

• "The equity basis supporting business debt seems to be, on the surface, shrinking. . . . The '*de-equitization*' has more than been offset by the large amount of profits that American corporations have been reinvesting." Murray L. Weidenbaum & Kenneth W. Chilton, *Public Policy Toward Corporate Takeovers* 70–71 (1988).
• "At a time when the manufacturing side of many enterprises no longer pulls its own weight, [the C.F.O.] is expected to make money as well as to raise it. What's more, he is essential to the new wave of '*de-equitization*,' the massive re-funding of the nation's private sector with debt rather than the sale of stock." L.J. Davis, *Trailblazers of the New Finance*, N.Y. Times, 4 Dec. 1988, § 6, at 16.

De-equitize has been adopted by legal writers in the sense "to be deprived of an interest in a law firm's profits." It appeared in print only a few times in the 1990s but has since become a VOGUE WORD—e.g.:

• "A growing number of firms are backing up their demands on partners by firing or '*de-equitizing*' those who are consistently unproductive." Susan G. Manch et al., *Maximizing Law Firm Profitability* § 52.04, at 52-6 (1991).
• "So partners worry about having their prerogatives or shares reduced or even being '*de-equitized*' or 'departnerized' or 'pushed off the iceberg' altogether." Marc Galanter & Thomas Palay, *Tournament of Lawyers* 67–68 (1994). See **departner.**
• "Although they are still called 'partners,' their partnership agreements reduce most of them to the de facto status of employees by denying them any claim on the firm's profits and subjecting them to being fired or '*de-equitized*' (demoted by being expelled as equity partners) as if they were employees at will." Richard Posner, *How Judges Think* 167 (2008).
• "The *de-equitization* of a partner as allowed by a partnership agreement may be the functional equivalent of an expulsion and may be treated as such even if that result was not the intention of the partners voting to *de-equitize* their colleague." Robert W. Hillman et al., Revised Uniform Partnership Act § 601, cmt. 4(a) (2010).

de facto. A. And *de jure*. The use of either phrase implies the question whether something exists merely in fact (*de facto*) or by right or according to law (*de jure*).

De facto /di **fak**-toh/ sometimes signals that there is some formal defect that makes the thing described voidable, as in the phrases *de facto contract* and *de facto marriage*. At other times it denotes pure illegitimacy, as in *de facto government* (i.e., one that has displaced the rightful legal government).

De jure /di **joor**-ay/ may be opposed not only to *de facto*, but also to *de gratia* (= by grace or favor), in opposition to which *de jure* means "as a matter of right."

Both phrases were traditionally POSTPOSITIVE ADJECTIVES, but they now commonly precede the nouns they modify <de facto segregation> <de jure corporation>.

B. And *in fact.* Although the terms convey the same notion, their uses are well distinguished. *De facto* is used prepositively, whereas *in fact* is used after the noun it modifies <de facto segregation, attorney in fact>.

C. Two Words, Not One. Some writers have tried to solidify the phrase, but it remains two words—e.g.: "The uniform equality of all as subjects of the state was, for Kant, consistent with *defacto* [read *de facto*] inequalities of a physical, mental, or material nature." Cornelius F. Murphy, *Jurisprudence and the Social Contract*, 33 Am. J. Juris. 207, 218 (1988).

de facto segregation. See **segregation, de facto.**

defalcate. A. And *peculate*; *embezzle.* These three words are broadly synonymous, all three meaning "to misappropriate money in one's charge." *Defalcate* and *peculate*, the latter being slightly more common and referring to public moneys, are FORMAL WORDS that are neutral in color. *Embezzle* is the popular word that is more highly charged with negative CONNOTATIONS. See **defalcation, defalcator, embezzle** & **peculation.**

B. Pronunciation. Several pronunciation guides suggest that it is acceptable to stress this word on the first syllable: /**def**-al-kayt/ or /**def**-əl-kayt/. *See, e.g.,* John B. Opdycke, *Don't Say It: A Cyclopedia of English Use and Abuse* 236 (1939). Others suggest that the corresponding noun may be pronounced /def-al-**kay**-shən/. *See, e.g.,* William H. Phyfe, *20,000 Words Often Mispronounced* 244 (1937).

But these pronunciations have a problem. Anyone who hears them is likely to think of *defecate* and *defecation.* Therefore, if one must utter these words at all, the safest course is to use the following pronunciations, which the better pronunciation guides accept as standard: *defalcate* /dee-**fal**-kayt/ or /di-**fal**-kayt/; *defalcation* /dee-fal-**kay**-shən/.

defalcation may refer either to the act of embezzling or to the money embezzled. E.g.:

- "Who would venture to expose a swindler or a black-mailer, or to give in detail the facts of a bank failure or other corporate *defalcation* [i.e., embezzlement], if every word and sentence must be uttered with judicial calmness and impartiality as between the swindler and his victims, and every fact and every inference be justified by unobjectionable legal evidence?" *Atkinson v. Detroit Free Press Co.*, 9 N.W. 501, 524 (Mich. 1881).
- "Evidence was adduced tending to show that the '*defalcation* [i.e., the money embezzled] was wasted on horse

racing and other forms of gambling.'" *Fidelity & Deposit Co. v. Stordahl*, 91 N.W.2d 533, 535 (Mich. 1958).

- "Having concluded that the debtor was not a fiduciary of Sattler, the court need not reach the question of whether a *defalcation* [i.e., embezzlement] occurred." *In re Shallow*, 393 B.R. 277, 288 (Bankr. D. Conn. 2008).

See **defalcate** & **peculation.**

By SLIPSHOD EXTENSION, some writers have misused *defalcation* in nonbankruptcy contexts when referring merely to a nonfraudulent default or to any failure to meet a duty. E.g.:

- "If the plaintiff asked for contribution for the defendant co-guarantors' proportionate shares of the entire debt (as in this case), he would be going beyond the proper function of contribution to seek advancement rather than reimbursement. This would compel the defendant co-guarantors to assume such risks as the insolvency or *defalcation* [read *default*] of the plaintiff during the period between their payment to him and his payment in discharge of the debt." *Gardner v. Bean*, 677 P.2d 1116, 1119 (Utah 1984).
- "Due to this paralegal's misconduct and failure to fulfill his professional duties, the opposition papers were never filed or served on defendants. This court, under similar circumstances, has previously held that the *defalcations* [read *misconduct* or *negligence*] of a law-firm employee [that] result in a default may constitute excusable law-office failure." *Goldman v. Cotter*, 781 N.Y.S.2d 28, 31 (App. Div. 2004).

To be a *defalcation*, a deficiency must involve some degree of wrongdoing—and the wrongdoing must involve money.

For the pronunciation of *defalcation*, see **defalcate (B).**

defalcator is the agent noun corresponding to *defalcate*—e.g.: "One will not on this basis soothsay that . . . if the *defalcator* be only 'agent' for A but happens to be 'trustee' for B, there will be a difference in result." Karl Llewellyn, *The Common Law Tradition: Deciding Appeals* 442 (1960). See **defalcate.**

defamacast (= a defamatory broadcast) is a PORTMANTEAU WORD and a recent NEOLOGISM that has enjoyed a limited success within law—e.g.:

- "Judge Homer C. Eberhardt of the Georgia Court of Appeals coined a new word, now in general use, which is quite descriptive of being defamed by television, to wit '*defamacast*.'" *Montgomery v. Pacific & S. Co.*, 206 S.E.2d 631, 634 (Ga. Ct. App. 1974).
- "Since a '*defamacast*' . . . is not considered 'slander,' the usual rules of respondeat superior are applicable, as with libel." *Williamson v. Lucas*, 304 S.E.2d 412, 415 (Ga. Ct. App. 1983).
- "Under this '*defamacast*' statute, when a slanderous statement is uttered in or as a part of a visual or sound broadcast, the complaining party shall be allowed only such actual, consequential, or punitive damages as have been alleged and proved." *Riddle v. Golden Isles Broad., LLC*, 666 S.E.2d 75, 78 (Ga. Ct. App. 2008).

The leading American book on tort law suggests that *defamacast*, a "barbarism," was born of a desire to avoid calling defamation by radio or television either *slander* or *libel*. *See* William L. Prosser & W. Page Keeton, *Prosser & Keeton on Torts* § 112, at 787 (5th ed. 1984).

defamation; libel; slander. These three terms are distinguished in English and American law. *Defamation* = an attack upon the reputation of another. It encompasses both *libel* (in permanent form, esp. writing) and *slander* (in transitory form, esp. spoken words). See **libel.**

In Scots law, however, *libel* and *slander* are equivalent to (and therefore interchangeable with) *defamation*.

defamatory; *defamative. *Defamatory* is the usual word; **defamative* is a NEEDLESS VARIANT.

defame; malign; traduce; calumniate; *calumnize. These near-synonyms all mean to speak badly of someone for harmful reasons, often with little regard for the truth. To *defame* is to speak or write in such a way as to give rise to liability for libel or slander. Specifically, *defame* means "to make a false statement about someone to a third person in such a way as to harm the reputation of the person spoken of." See **defamation** & **libel.**

The other terms are less legal and more literary. Both *malign* and *traduce* suggest malevolence, violent bigotry, and passionate prejudice. To *malign* someone or some group is normally to make the object a victim of lies, whether those lies are deliberate or not <the maligning of racial minorities>. To *traduce* is normally to direct aspersions at an individual, often with the suggestion of the resulting damage to the object's reputation <once the newspapers traduced him with false allegations of that scandalous act, it became hard for him to find work in Hollywood>. To *calumniate* is likewise to vilify in such a way as to do serious harm to the object's good name. E.g.: "In each of these submissions defense counsel has elected to *calumniate* opposing counsel in abusive terms e.g., 'vindictive,' 'personal animus toward the defendant' calculated to impugn Ms. Hayes's professional integrity." *U.S. v. Moskovits,* 784 F.Supp. 193, 197 n.3 (E.D. Pa. 1992). **Calumnize* is a NEEDLESS VARIANT that appears sometimes as a bombastic flourish—e.g.: "The second string to the defendant's bench trial bow *calumnizes* [read *criticizes*?] the granting of the motion." *Moores v. Greenberg,* 834 F.2d 1105, 1109 (1st Cir. 1987). (See PURPLE PROSE.) Both *traduce* and *calumniate* sound worse because most readers and listeners, not having copious vocabularies, won't immediately know their meaning—except to intuit that what they denote sounds seriously bad.

default, n. & vb. A *default* is a failure to act when an action is required, esp. the failure to pay a debt—either interest or principal—as it becomes due.

As a verb, *default* may be either transitive or intransitive. Usually it is the latter <she defaulted on the loan>, but the transitive uses are not unusual in legal writing <she defaulted the loan>—e.g.:

- "Further, if the mortgage is later *defaulted* [many would write *defaulted on*], the mortgagee may find that he is not insured if he cannot deliver clear title to the FHA." Robert Kratovil, *Real Estate Law* 191 (1946).
- "The Government advocates untenably that plaintiff should have accepted this offer in order not to *default* the contract, regardless of disproportionate cost." *Aerodex, Inc. v. U.S.,* 417 F.2d 1361, 1364 n.3 (Ct. Cl. 1969).

The agent noun is *defaulter*.

default judgment; judgment by default. The second is somewhat wordy.

defeasance = (1) the rendering null and void (of a previous condition); (2) a condition upon the performance of which a deed or other instrument is defeated or made void, or a contractual provision containing such a condition.

Sense 1 is more usual—e.g.: "The will provision that the interest was to be divided among 'them' every year . . . necessitates the construction that testatrix intended the gift of income also to be subject to *defeasance* by not surviving until the respective dates of distribution." *In re Walker's Trust,* 116 N.W.2d 106, 111 (Wis. 1962).

But sense 2 is not uncommon—e.g.: "The *defeasance* clause the 2009 Noteholders point to . . . is a provision in the Original Indenture." *In re Solutia Inc.,* 379 B.R. 473, 488 (Bankr. S.D.N.Y. 2007).

defeasible. The antonym to this word (*indefeasible*) is known to learned nonlawyers, but *defeasible* itself is almost exclusively a legal term, meaning "capable of being made void." E.g.: "The law enforced the mortgage deed literally as a *defeasible* conveyance to the mortgagee." William F. Walsh, *A Treatise on Equity* 88 (1930). For the phrase *fee simple defeasible*, see **fee simple (F).** For more on *indefeasible* as opposed to *inalienable*, see **indefeasible.**

defective; defectible; deficient. The primary difference to be noted is between the words *defective* (= faulty; imperfect; subnormal) and *deficient* (= insufficient; lacking in quantity). *Defectible*, the least common of the three terms, means "likely to fail or become defective."

The same basic distinction holds for the nouns *defect* and *deficiency*. But *deficiency* is sometimes misused for *defect*—e.g.:

- "The court instead instructed the jury . . . that a product may be defective and unreasonably dangerous because of *design deficiencies* [read *design defects*], and inadequacies in warning and/or instructions for the use and handling of the product." *Bemis Co. v. Rubush,* 401 N.E.2d 48, 58 (Ind. Ct. App. 1980).
- "Plaintiffs assert that these alleged *design deficiencies* [read *design defects*] led to Eveready's sinking." *Northern Ins. Co. v. Point Judith Marina, LLC,* 579 F.3d 61, 64 (1st Cir. 2009).

Blunders of that kind may often result from ill-considered attempts at INELEGANT VARIATION.

Defectible, the least common of the three head-words, means "likely to fail or become defective."

defence. See **defense.**

defend. See **maintain (A).**

defendant. A. Pronunciation. *Defendant* is sometimes pronounced, esp. it seems by law-school professors, with a strong accent on the last syllable, rhyming with *ant*. Presumably, this pronunciation helps legal neophytes remember how to spell the word. Apart from this pedagogically affected pronunciation, the correct way to pronounce the word is /di-**fen**-dənt/.

B. As a Postpositive Adjective. The adjective *defendant* is commonly placed after the noun it modifies when that noun is *party*. E.g.: "The plaintiff, who himself chose both the forum and the *parties defendant*, will not be heard to complain about the sufficiency of the relief obtainable against them." *Provident Tradesmens Bank & Trust v. Patterson*, 390 U.S. 102, 111 (1968) (per Harlan, J.). Some writers use this construction with other nouns, the result being an example of ARCHAISM: "Chief Judge William H. Becker . . . dryly noted that auto companies *defendant* in such situations 'have been unusually evasive and loath to make discovery.'" Joseph Goulden, *The Million Dollar Lawyers* 287 (1978). See POSTPOSITIVE ADJECTIVES.

C. And *prisoner*. In criminal-law contexts, *defendant* is regarded as less prejudicial—and therefore as generally more appropriate—than either *the accused* or *the prisoner*. But *accused* is said to be the norm in Scots law. *See* John A. Beaton, *Scots Law Terms and Expressions* 30 (1982). See **accused** & **prisoner.**

defendant in error = respondent, appellee. See **error (A)** & **plaintiff in error.**

defendant in person. See **pro se.**

defender is used in Scotland for *defendant*, as the name of the party opposite a *pursuer* in civil actions. Cf. **pursuer.**

Elsewhere, the word takes on other senses. Sometimes it appears in reference to one who uses self-defense—e.g.: "Such a *defender*, not being entirely free from fault, must not resort to deadly force if there is any other reasonable method of saving himself." Rollin M. Perkins & Ronald N. Boyce, *Criminal Law* 1121 (3d ed. 1982). At other times it refers to defense counsel in a criminal case—e.g.: "In many other respects the basic duties of professionalism of prosecutor and *defender* are the same." David Mellinkoff, *Lawyers and the System of Justice* 543 (1976). In still other contexts, it refers more broadly to anyone who defends an ideal: "Any such power as that of authorizing the federal judiciary to entertain suits by individuals against the states had been expressly disclaimed, and even resented, by the great *defenders* of the Constitution while it was on its trial before the American people." *Hans v. Louisiana*, 134 U.S. 1, 12 (1890) (per Bradley, J.).

defense; defence. A. Spelling. *Defence* is the BrE, *defense* the AmE spelling. Yet the British spelling was used by American courts through the early 20th century; Judge Learned Hand, for example, used the *-ce* spelling in *Denholm Shipping Co. v. W.E. Hedger Co.*, 47 F.2d 213, 214 (2d Cir. 1931). Today, however, the British spelling is best avoided in the U.S., lest one's writing seem affected.

B. In Criminal Law. Some writers worry that this word can lead to misunderstandings because it is used in different ways. Ordinarily, a *defense* is something that the defendant has the burden of proving. But that is not true of the doctrines of justifiable force, alibi, mistake, and self-defense: "If there is evidence, usually raised by the defendant, that the conduct may have been justifiable, the prosecution bears the burden of proving beyond reasonable doubt that the conduct was *not* justifiable or lawful. Thus, justifiable force is a *defence*, in the sense that it may lead to an acquittal, but the defendant does not have to establish its elements—the prosecution has to negative them." Andrew Ashworth, *Principles of Criminal Law* 110–11 (1991).

Glanville Williams, though, considers these worries pedantic: "A '*defence*' is any matter that the defendant will in practice raise, whether he is legally obliged to do so or not. If the word were confined to matter the burden of proof of which rests on the defendant, there would be virtually no '*defences*' at common law." *Textbook of Criminal Law* 114 n.3 (1978).

C. In Common-Law Pleading. See COMMON-LAW PLEADINGS.

defer; defer to. *Defer*, meaning "to postpone," yields the nouns *deferment* and its NEEDLESS VARIANT *deferral*. *Defer to*, meaning "to give way to," yields the noun *deference.* See **deferment.**

deferment; deferral. *Deferment* is preferable to *deferral* as the noun corresponding to the verb to *defer*—e.g.: "[The company] asserts that the court's ruling . . . mandates *deferral* of the issue of damages." *Cordis Corp. v. Boston Scientific Corp.*, 431 F.Supp.2d 442, 448 (D. Del. 2006). See **defer.**

deferrable; *deferable. The preferred form is *deferrable.* See DOUBLING OF FINAL CONSONANTS.

deferral. See **defer** & **deferment.**

deficiency; deficient. See **defective.**

definite; definitive. These words are increasingly confused. *Definite* = fixed, exact, explicit <the indemnity was expressed in definite words>. *Definitive* = authoritative; conclusive; exhaustive; providing a final solution <the Supreme Court has not given a definitive ruling>.

Although each word is sometimes misused for the other, the more common error is to use *definitive* when *definite* is called for—e.g.:

- "The state board would not have been able to provide the plaintiff the relief sought, namely, interpreting the collective bargaining agreement in the absence of any *definitive* [read *definite*] language." *Santana v. City of Hartford*, 894 A.2d 307, 320 (Conn. App. Ct. 2006).
- "As a member of this panel suggested at oral argument, the agreement should have included more *definitive* [read *definite*] language." *City of Hollywood v. Benoit ex rel. Benoit*, 1 So.3d 1142, 1145 n.4 (Fla. Dist. Ct. App. 2009).

DEFINITIONS. The best advice is to be a minimalist, for "a definition . . . often creates more problems than it solves." *Brutus v. Cozens*, [1972] 3 W.L.R. 521, 525 (per Lord Reid). Yet legal writers—especially drafters of documents—use definitions abundantly, so some guidance is in order.

A. When to Use. The best legal writers and drafters use definitions only when they are necessary—i.e., where there is a gain in clarity and precision. Poor writers and drafters frequently define terms that they either never use again or use perhaps once or twice after the definition. See PLAIN LANGUAGE (D).

If a commonsense shortened name presents itself, use that shortened form. For example, if there is a law firm called Brown, Underwood, Smith, Tennison & Osgood, call it *the Brown firm* or *Brown, Underwood*. But don't invent the acronym *BUSTO* for this purpose. That approach will mire your writing in INITIALESE.

B. Lexical and Stipulative Definitions. Lexical definitions are like dictionary definitions; they purport to give the entire meaning of a word ("'Litigation' means . . ."). Stipulative definitions, by contrast, rely on the ordinary meaning of the word and merely expand a word's meaning ("'Litigation' includes mediation") or contract a word's meaning ("'Litigation' does not include prefiling investigations"). As an English writer put it in the context of statutes, "when an interpretation clause states that a word or phrase 'means . . . ,' any other meaning is excluded, whereas the word 'includes' indicates an extension of the ordinary meaning [that] continues to apply in appropriate cases." Rupert Cross, *Statutory Interpretation* 103 (1976).

When using stipulative definitions—which can be extremely helpful to the drafter—one must be careful not to use counterintuitive definitions, as by saying that the word *dog* is deemed to include all horses. Reed Dickerson made this point authoritatively: "it is important for the legal draftsman not to define a word in a sense significantly different from the way it is normally understood by the persons to whom it is primarily addressed. This is a fundamental principle of communication, and it is one of the shames of the legal profession that draftsmen so flagrantly violate it." *Fundamentals of Legal Drafting* § 7.3, at 144 (2d ed. 1986).

The reason for this admonition, of course, is plain: "whenever we define a word . . . in a manner that departs from current customary usage, we sooner or later unwittingly fall back on the common use and thus confuse the meanings of our terms." Morris R. Cohen, *Reason and Law* 77 (1961). This confusion may occur either in the writer or in the reader. Either way, the result can be dangerous.

Still, some specialists engage in this type of overstipulation. For example, the Longshoremen's and Harbor Workers' Compensation Act defines *vessel* not only as any vessel "upon which or in connection with which" an injury or death may have occurred, but also as "said vessel's owner, owner pro hac vice, agent, operator, charter [*sic*], or a bareboat charterer, master, officer, or crew member." 33 U.S.C. § 902(21) (1988).

C. Inept Definitional Terms. The best practice is to use *means* for a complete definition, *includes* for a stipulated expansion in meaning, and *does not include* for a stipulated contraction of meaning.

Yet many drafters fall into unfortunate forms, such as the following:

1. *Bears the meaning.* Use the tighter *means* instead.

2. *Means and includes.* Use *means* if that is what you mean. The expressions *means and includes* "should not be used because complete and incomplete meaning cannot be stipulated at one and the same time." G.C. Thornton, *Legislative Drafting* 166 (2d ed. 1979).

3. *Includes only.* Use *means* instead.

4. *Shall mean.* "Do not say that the defined words 'shall mean' something or other, as though you were ordering them to do so, or as though you were directing the definitions to go into effect at some later time." Barbara Child, *Drafting Legal Documents* 116 n. (2d ed. 1992). Also to be avoided are the wordy phrases *shall have the meaning* and *shall mean and refer to*.

5. *Is where; is when.* Reword the definition entirely. These phrases are inappropriate ways to introduce definitions. See **is when.**

D. "Stuffed" Definitions. Readers are entitled to assume that definitions—and definitional sections of documents—contain nothing more than definitions. Yet many contractual definitions, such as those in badly drafted insurance policies, contain substantive provisions. Such definitions are called "stuffed" definitions.

E. Placement. When more than a few definitions appear, the drafter is faced with choosing an appropriate place for them within the document. Some drafters place them in a schedule at the end; others collect them at the beginning; still others define them as they appear; and some use a combination of these methods.

It is impossible to frame an absolute recommendation, but a caution is in order against one common practice: putting page after page of definitions at the beginning of a document. If you need more than, say, ten definitions, a schedule at the end is probably a better solution than using the opening pages in this way.

F. Signaling Defined Terms in Text. Drafters' habits vary. The most common way to tell the reader that a term is defined is by using initial capitals—a practice that is not so bad if you keep definitions to a minimum. Others have experimented with boldfacing or italicizing defined terms whenever they appear in text, but this practice can lead to unsightly text. Still others don't signal in any way that a particular word is a defined term, but most legal readers find this practice unacceptable. Drafters who typeset their materials sometimes use running footers to tell the readers which words on a given page are defined in the schedule at the end—a time-consuming and costly practice.

G. When to Compose. There are two advantages to defining terms late in the drafting process. First, you'll be less likely to have a defined term with more than one meaning, because you'll be familiar with the entire document. Second, you won't define terms that aren't used much—or never appear at all.

definitive. See **definite.**

deforce = (1) to keep (lands) from the true owner by means of force; (2) to oust another from possession by force; or (3) to detain (a creditor's money) unjustly and forcibly. Here, the writer apparently mistook *deforce* as a correlative of *enforce*: "An attorney has a lien for his fees which attaches when the suit is filed and service had. . . . If settlement thereof be made without his knowledge . . . his lien is not affected and he may maintain an action to enforce it against him who '*deforced*' the lien." *Downs v. Hodge*, 413 S.W.2d 519, 523 (Mo. Ct. App. 1967).

deforciant; deforcer. In all but Scots law, *deforcer* is a NEEDLESS VARIANT of *deforciant* (= one who deforces). That is unfortunate, since *deforcer* might be more readily understood to anyone who began to learn what the verb *deforce* means. See **deforce.**

defraud. See **deceive.**

defraudation; *defraudment. Lawyers seldom have occasion to use a noun formed from the verb *defraud*, perhaps because the noun *fraud* itself usually suffices. When they find the occasion, however, the word is *defraudation*—e.g.:

- "Benefits obtained by a contracting party subsequent to his *defraudation* are not admissible on the issue of damages." *Philip Chang & Sons Assocs. v. La Casa Novato*, 222 Cal. Rptr. 800, 803 (Ct. App. 1986). On the use of *subsequent to in that sentence, see ***subsequent to.**
- "It was a matter of legal interpretation whether Dauphin County had jurisdiction to try a case involving *defraudation* of a Commonwealth agency." *Commonwealth v. Keenan*, 530 A.2d 90, 94 (Pa. Super. Ct. 1987).
- "The district court concluded that Mr. Bradshaw's *defraudation* of his fourteen victims was part of a single 'scheme or artifice.'" *State v. Bradshaw*, 152 P.3d 288, 289 (Utah 2006).

*Defraudment is a NEEDLESS VARIANT.

***defraudulent** is a NEEDLESS VARIANT of *fraudulent.*

degenerative; *degeneratory. The second is a NEEDLESS VARIANT.

degradation (= a lowering in dignity, character, or quality) is a MALAPROPISM when used for *derogation* (= an abrogation or violation)—e.g.:

- "Immunity from suit is in *degradation* [read *derogation*] of this common-law principle and must therefore be strictly construed." *Bush v. Bush*, 231 A.2d 245, 249 (N.J. Super. Ct. Law Div. 1967).
- "The court concluded . . . that the rebate and veto provisions of the settlement agreement . . . deprived [the third parties], in *degradation* [read *derogation*] of the strong policy favoring settlements, of a chance themselves to compromise Bass' claims against them." *Bass v. Phoenix Seadrill/78, Ltd.*, 749 F.2d 1154, 1158 (5th Cir. 1985).

But the words *degradation* and *derogation* do share one sense: "detraction from the honor or reputation of; lowering or lessening in value or estimation" (*OED*). See **derogation of, in.**

de gratia. See **de facto (A).**

degree is the word used in law for various classifications and specifications, as for steps in *consanguinity* and grades based on the seriousness of crimes. Today most American jurisdictions differentiate first-degree from second-degree murder on the basis of the gravity of the offense (gauged, e.g., by premeditation and purpose), whereas at common law first- and second-degree felons were principals and accessories, respectively. See **consanguinity** & **murder (A).**

dehors is a pompous little LAW FRENCH word (meaning "outside of; beyond the scope of") that should generally be avoided. The plethora of examples, selected from writings of the 1980s and 1990s, indicates the prevalence of this nasty-sounding term /di-**hohr**/. It serves absolutely no purpose but to sound legalistic—e.g.:

- "For present purposes, . . . statutory words [that] are 'ambiguous' are not 'unequivocal,' and judicial ingenuity to resolve the ambiguity, *dehors* [read *outside* or *beyond*] the statute, is inappropriately exercised." *U.S. v. John C. Grimberg Co.*, 702 F.2d 1362, 1378 (Fed. Cir. 1983) (Nichols, J., concurring).
- "This document, assuming it exists, is *dehors* [read *outside*] the record and the Gordons' reliance on such information is improper." *Gordon v. Wisconsin Health Org. Ins. Corp.*, 510 N.W.2d 832, 834 n.2 (Wis. Ct. App. 1993).
- "Because the record of the underlying proceedings in the Court of Claims is *dehors* [read *outside*] the record on appeal, we cannot consider its contents in making our decision." *Lake v. State*, 928 N.E.2d 1251, 1254 (Ill. App. Ct. 2010).
- "Evidence *dehors* [read *outside*] the record shows that it was Jackson who confessed to Loza that she committed the murders." *Loza v. Mitchell*, 705 F.Supp.2d 773, 892 (S.D. Ohio 2010).

The term was formerly spelled as two words—e.g.:

- "These bills are open to the same defenses as other bills; . . . by answer if the objection is for matter *de hors* the record." Eugene A. Jones, *Manual of Equity Pleading and Practice* 64 (1916).
- "A misdescription cannot be rectified by affidavit or evidence *de hors* (from outside the document)." 2 Ernest W. Chance, *Principles of Mercantile Law* 40 (Percy W. French ed., 10th ed. 1951).

DEICTIC TERMS (e.g.: *this, that, it, the*) are "pointing words," that is, words that try to point directly at an antecedent. Etymologically, *deictic* means "capable of proof," and conjures up the notion of pointing to conclusive evidence.

A pointing word such as *this* or *these* should always have an identifiable referent. But in the sentence that follows—an all-too-typical example—the word *these* does not point to one: "Officials at checkpoints that are judicially deemed the functional equivalent of a border have been granted increasingly intrusive power in connection with the search of vehicles at these checkpoints, without any requirement of probable cause or reasonable suspicion. *These* include the power to stop and question occupants about aliens and to search in automobile cavities that could conceal aliens." *U.S. v. Oyarzun*, 760 F.2d 570, 577 (5th Cir. 1985) (Hill, J., concurring). We can deduce, of course, that the writer meant *powers*, though the singular noun *power* is used in the first sentence.

Some writers believe that, in the rule stated at the outset of the preceding paragraph, the phrase "an identifiable referent" means a specific noun. They say that you should never use *this* or *these* without a noun following it. But most grammarians take a more relaxed position: "The antecedent of *this* and *that* may be any single noun . . . . *This* and *that* may also refer to a phrase, clause, or sentence, or even to an implied thought. Reference of this kind must, however, be immediately clear and apparent; otherwise the thought will be obscure." James G. Fernald, *English Grammar Simplified* 40 (Cedric Gale ed., rev. ed. 1979). Fernald is not alone: "*This*, like *that*, is regularly used to refer to the idea of a preceding clause or sentence: 'He had always had his own way at home, and this made him a poor roommate.'/ 'The company train their salesmen in their own school. This [More formally: This practice] assures them a group of men with the same sales methods.'" Porter G. Perrin, *Writer's Guide and Index to English* 794 (rev. ed. 1950) (bracketed language in original). Perrin's notation in his second example accurately describes the difference between *this* and *this practice*: it is a question of formality, not of correctness.

Actually, the grammarians' rule against vague reference is just that: a rule that forbids ambiguities of the kind listed here: "The most important activity is the editing of a college newspaper. *This* has grown with the college." (Ex. drawn fr. Richard Summers & David L. Patrick, *College Composition* 129 (1946).) What has grown with the college? Editing? The newspaper? The

importance of editing the college newspaper? You simply cannot tell what the writer intended—if indeed the writer knew.

All one needs in good writing, then, is a sensitivity to antecedents, whether explicit or implicit. Good writers routinely use pointing words to refer to something that, although clear, is less specific than a particular noun—e.g.:

- "In civilized society men must be able to assume that they may control, for purposes beneficial to themselves, what they have discovered and appropriated to their own use, what they have created by their own labor, and what they have acquired under the existing social and economic order. *This* is a jural postulate of civilized society as we know it." Roscoe Pound, *An Introduction to the Philosophy of Law* 193 (1922).
- "Courts of Quarter Sessions also have the power to make an order that barristers shall have exclusive audience; *this* is usually done in those Sessions where a sufficient number of barristers practice regularly." Pendleton Howard, *Criminal Justice in England* 364 (1931).
- "The inference is that if a given law aims at the common good, it is law, but if it does not achieve its aim there is no moral obligation to obey it. If, however, it does not even aim at the common good, it is not law at all; it is not even legally binding. No lawyer would accept *this*." W.W. Buckland, *Some Reflections on Jurisprudence* 12 (1945).
- "It is said that one cannot delve into the mind but must judge a man on his outward acts. *This* is a half-truth." Glanville Williams, *Criminal Law* 91 (2d ed. 1961).
- "If the trial were nothing but the battle [that] in some respects it resembles, each party would want to leave his opponent guessing about the shape of his array. To some extent *this* is permitted, but not to the point where the opponent would be taken by surprise." Patrick Devlin, *The Judge* 56 (1979).
- "The rule is simply that courts do not use the contempt power to coerce the payment of money. *This* is an important rule for choosing among remedies, but it has nothing to do with irreparable injury." Douglas Laycock, *The Death of the Irreparable Injury Rule* 17 (1991).
- "Normally, the corporation is accountable for a person only if he was an officer, director, or managing agent at the time the deposition was taken. *This* is to protect the party from the admissions of disgruntled former officers or agents." Charles Alan Wright, *The Law of Federal Courts* 612 (5th ed. 1994).

The test for knowing when the word *this* is acceptable in such a context is this: ask yourself, This what? If an answer immediately comes to mind, the word *this* is probably fine. If none comes immediately to mind, you may need to add a noun.

But a word of warning: in each of the examples in the bulleted list above, a noun would have marred the style. One way to spoil such sentences is to insert, after *this*, an abstract noun or noun phrase such as *fact, idea, practice,* or *state of affairs.*

For a related problem with the relative pronoun *which*, also a deictic term, see REMOTE RELATIVES.

de jure has three senses: (1) "of right; lawful"; (2) "as a matter of right"; and (3) "by law." In sense 1 it is contrasted with *de facto* (= in fact, but usu. unlawfully so) <de facto as opposed to de jure segregation>. In sense 2, it is contrasted with *de gratia* (= as a favor gratuitously bestowed). And in sense 3 it is opposed to *de aequitate* (= by equity).

Sense 1 is most usual—e.g.: "That issue will have to be determined in light of the facts that the United States recognizes the West German Government as the *de jure* government over the territory it controls but does not recognize the East German Government." *Omega Importing Corp. v. Petri-Kine Camera Co.*, 451 F.2d 1190, 1191 (2d Cir. 1971). See **de facto (A)**.

de jure segregation. See **segregation, de facto.**

*delapidation. See **dilapidation.**

del credere **agent** (= an agent who guarantees the solvency of the third party with whom the agent makes a contract for the principal) is one of the few Italianisms to have earned a place in Anglo-American law. *Del credere* (It. "of belief or trust") began as an Italian mercantile phrase that English writers borrowed in the 18th century.

delecti* for *delicti* is a misuse that occurs in several LATINISMS, such as *corpus delicti* and *lex loci delicti*. For an example of the latter, see the following sentence: "Most of the numerous inadequacies inherent in *lex loci delecti* [read *lex loci delicti*] also exist in the other traditional *lex loci* rules." *Duncan v. Cessna Aircraft Co.*, 665 S.W.2d 414, 421 (Tex. 1984). See ***corpus delicti*** & ***lex loci delicti.***

delegable is the word, not **delegatable*. Many writers mistakenly use the latter form—e.g.: "He . . . had a wide range of responsibilities not *delegatable* [read *delegable*] to his subordinates." *Holt v. Gamewell Corp.*, 797 F.2d 36, 38 (1st Cir. 1986).

delegate. See **relegate.**

delegatee (= one to whom a debtor's matter is delegated) is not, despite its appearances to the contrary, a NEEDLESS VARIANT of *delegate* (= one who represents or acts for another or a group of others). See -EE.

delegatus non potest delegare. See MAXIMS.

deliberate; deliberative. These words have clear DIFFERENTIATION. *Deliberate* = (1) intentional; fully considered; or (2) unimpulsive; slow in deciding. *Deliberative* = of, or appointed for the purpose of, deliberation or debate (*COD*).

Deliberative is misused for *deliberate* in both sense 1 and sense 2. Here is an example of the former: "A loaded firearm must be considered dangerous. It is an instrument of death. . . . Yet, only *deliberative* [read *deliberate*] action will cause discharge. When properly handled, the gun can be safely used." *Taylor v. Gerry's Ridgewood, Inc.*, 490 N.E.2d 987, 991 (Ill. App. Ct. 1986).

deliberate speed. See **with all deliberate speed.**

deliberative. See **deliberate.**

delict; delictum; *deliction. The preferred term is *tort*. *Delict* (= an offense against the law) is the more common of the two variants here to be discussed, but both are inferior in Anglo-American contexts to the usual word (*tort*). E.g.:

- "Thus recovery of a sum of money by way of penalty for a *delict* [read *tort*] is the historical starting point of liability." Roscoe Pound, *An Introduction to the Philosophy of Law* 149 (1922).
- "The simple fact that one *delict* [read *tort*] has already occurred is in no way indicative of the likely merits of subsequent claims." *Procup v. Strickland*, 792 F.2d 1069, 1081 (11th Cir. 1986) (Johnson, J., dissenting).
- Because there was no specific contractual obligation between the parties and the cause of action does not fit the definition of a *delict* [read *tort*], Richard does not have another remedy at law." *Richard v. Wal-Mart Stores, Inc.*, 559 F.3d 341, 346 (5th Cir. 2009).

Delictum is a Latinate variant used primarily in discussions of Roman law—e.g.:

- "There was another class of obligations, to be looked at presently, which had their origin in a *delictum* (a delict or delinquency), a wrong, unlawful act done by one party to the other." James Hadley, *Introduction to Roman Law* 237 (1881).
- "Bateman Eichler contends that the respondents' *delictum* [read *delict* or *tort*] was substantially par to that of Lazzaro and Neadeau for two reasons." *Bateman Eichler, Hill Richards Inc. v. Berner*, 472 U.S. 299, 312 (1985) (per Brennan, J.).

Additionally, **deliction*, a NEEDLESS VARIANT of *delict*, is not recorded in the dictionaries—e.g.:

- "[The] common-law status of the plaintiff's case is accentuated by the statutory element of *deliction* [read *delict*]." *Schnackenberg v. Delaware, Lackawanna & W. R.R.*, 98 A. 266, 266 (N.J. 1916).
- "The individuals whose alleged *deliction* [read *delict*] caused the death were not sued." *Garber v. Prudential Ins. Co.*, 22 Cal. Rptr. 123, 131 (Ct. App. 1962) (Files, J., dissenting).
- "A suit for damages instituted as a result of a proprietor's violation of the obligation . . . is not a tort action in the sense that *deliction* [read *delict*] in its usual connotation is a necessary element." *Hero Lands Co. v. Texaco, Inc.*, 310 So.2d 93, 97 (La. 1975).

*delictal; *delictive. See **delictual.**

delicti. See ***delecti.**

delictu* for *delicto*, a mistake unknown in English law, has occurred in many dozens of American cases. See ***ex delicto, in flagrante delicto*** & ***in pari delicto.***

delictual; *delictal; *delictive. The preferred form is *delictual*, assuming this word is to be used advisedly in place of its near-equivalent, *tortious*. In civil-law contexts, of course, it is the normal word—e.g.:

- "I would like to raise the question whether we are justified to speak of a general law of obligations including the categories of contractual, *delictual*, quasi-contractual, and quasi-*delictual* obligations, or should we, perhaps, approach each category of obligations separately?" A.N. Yiannopoulos, "Comments and Questions," in *Essays on the Civil Law of Obligations* 45 (Joseph Dainow ed. 1969).
- "The Louisiana Supreme Court held that Article 2971 limited only the innkeeper's contractual, not his *delictual*, responsibility." *Laubie v. Sonesta Int'l Hotel Corp.*, 752 F.2d 165, 167 (5th Cir. 1985).

Delictual may be more useful than its sibling *delict*, for it signifies "of or relating to a tort," whereas *tortious* signifies either "relating to a tort" or "constituting a tort" <tortious conduct>. See **tortious (A).**

*Delictal, recorded in the *OED* as appearing in only one source (in 1913), is a NEEDLESS VARIANT of *delictual*. E.g.:

- "An obscure text suggests that where the *delictal* [read *delictual*] action aimed merely at compensation . . . , they were quite distinct." W.W. Buckland, *A Text-Book of Roman Law* 711 (1921).
- "Much has been and still is being written relative to the distinctions between *delictal* [read *delictual*] liability and contract liability." *Martin v. Martin*, 250 So.2d 491, 493 (La. Ct. App. 1971).
- "We think the rules heretofore set out relating to the right to legal subrogation in conventional debts apply also to *delictal* [read *delictual*] obligations." *A.O. Smith-Inland, Inc. v. Union Carbide Corp.*, 547 F.Supp. 344, 347 (M.D. La. 1982).

Still another NEEDLESS VARIANT is **delictive*—e.g.: "Fault (culpa) involves *delictive* [read *delictual*] conduct of an affirmative or voluntary nature." *Colmenares Vivas v. San Alliance Ins. Co.*, 807 F.2d 1102, 1109 (1st Cir. 1986).

delictum. See **delict.**

delimit; *delimitate. *Delimit*, the preferred form, is not merely a fancy variation of *limit* (= to restrict the bounds of), as many seem to believe. E.g.:

- "The manufacturer may possibly *delimit* [read *limit*] the scope of his potential liability by use of a disclaimer in compliance with [the statute]." *Morrow v. New Moon Homes, Inc.*, 548 P.2d 279, 291 (Alaska 1976).
- "Although the Strasbourg Court emphasizes its own jurisdiction as guardian of the Convention, it also seeks to *delimit* [read *limit*] its jurisdiction vis-a-vis national authorities so as not to replace them." Stefan Sottiaux & Gerhard van der Schyff, *Methods of International Human Rights Adjudication: Towards a More Structured Decision-Making Process for the European Court of Human Rights*, 31 Hastings Int'l & Comp. L. Rev. 115, 134 (2008).

Properly, *delimit* means "to define; delineate," as here: "If the challenged conduct of respondents constitutes state action as *delimited* by our prior decisions, then that conduct was also action under color of state law and will support a suit under § 1983." *Lugar v. Edmondson Oil Co.*, 457 U.S. 922, 935 (1982) (per White, J.).

delinquent, in AmE, can apply to either things or people <delinquent taxes> <juvenile delinquents>. In BrE, it applies only to people.

deliverance, when used for *opinion*, is somewhat grandiose; it is an extension of the Scots law sense "a judicial or administrative order." E.g.:

- "In days not far remote, judges were not unwilling to embellish their *deliverances* with quotations from the poets." Benjamin N. Cardozo, *Law and Literature*, 52 Harv. L. Rev. 471, 484 (1939).
- "Fully aware of Mississippi's imprimatur on § 6 we might—by piecing together some of our own *deliverances* and the District Court opinions dutifully following them—come up with a fair prediction of what Mississippi would hold in this case, but we do not think this a wise course." *Boardman v. United Servs. Auto. Ass'n*, 742 F.2d 847, 851 (5th Cir. 1984).

See **delivery (A)** & **opinion.**

delivery. A. And *deliverance*. *Delivery* is the more usual word to describe a transfer or conveyance (of something), an utterance <a stammering delivery of the speech>, or giving birth. In the law relating to deeds, *delivery* "does not mean transfer of possession, but conduct indicating that the person who has executed the deed intends to be bound by it." G.H. Treitel, *The Law of Contract* 145 (8th ed. 1991). Hence "it is perfectly possible for the grantor to 'deliver' the deed and yet keep possession of it." *Id.* Such a delivery is termed *constructive delivery*.

Deliverance is a legal and religious term usually meaning "rescue, release," although at one time it overlapped with *delivery* in almost every sense. In law, *deliverance* can mean (1) "a jury's verdict"; (2) "in an action of replevin, the delivery of goods unlawfully taken"; or (3) "a judicial opinion or a judgment that a judge delivers." See **deliverance.**

B. And *livery*. The word *livery* has a number of obsolete and archaic senses, but in law has been used in the sense "the legal delivery of property into a person's possession," as in the phrases *livery of seisin* and *to take (or have) livery of*. The student can better understand *livery* by reading it mentally as "delivery." See **livery of seisin.**

C. Cant Uses. It has become voguish in some circles to use *delivery of* where *providing* or *provision for* would normally appear, especially in reference to services. Like any other trendy expression, it ought to be avoided—e.g.:

- "*The delivery of* [read *The provision of*] healthcare services promised by defendants depends on reimbursement adequate to cover the costs of *delivering* [read *providing*] such healthcare." *Rosenberg v. BlueCross BlueShield of Tenn., Inc.*, 219 S.W.3d 892, 897 (Tenn. Ct. App. 2006).
- "[The procedure] addresses the *delivery of* [read *provision of*] dental services to inmates confined within all of the detention facilities of the Metro-Dade Department of Corrections and Rehabilitation." *Dante v. Ryan*, 979 So.2d 1122, 1123 n.2 (Fla. Dist. Ct. App. 2008).

See VOGUE WORDS.

delivery of seisin. See **livery of seisin.**

delusion. See **hallucination** & **illusion.**

delusional; delusive; *delusory; deluded. *Delusional* = of the nature of a delusion. E.g.: "All three experts unanimously concluded that Corcoran's decision to welcome and hasten his own death is based on his *delusional* perception of reality and has no basis in rational thought whatsoever." *Corcoran v. State*, 820 N.E.2d 655, 669 (Ind. 2005). *Delusive* = (1) tending to delude, deceptive; or (2) delusional. Usually sense 1 applies. **Delusory* is a NEEDLESS VARIANT. *Deluded* = deceived; fooled.

demagoguery; *demagogy. *Demagoguery* (= the practices of a political agitator who appeals to mob instincts) is the usual word, **demagogy* being a NEEDLESS VARIANT.

demandant. Formerly, in real actions (i.e., lawsuits over land), the plaintiff was called the *demandant* and the defendant the *tenant.* See **real action.**

demean; bemean. Formerly, authorities on usage disapproved of *demean* in the sense "to lower, degrade," holding that instead it should properly be used reflexively in the sense "to conduct (oneself)." For example, an early usage critic wrote that "*demean* signifies 'to behave' and does not mean *debase* or *degrade*." Frank H. Vizetelly, *A Desk-Book of Errors in English* 62 (1909). The meaning "to behave," now somewhat archaic, is used infrequently in legal contexts—e.g.: "The oath of office now generally administered in all of the states as well as in the federal courts . . . requires [the lawyer] to uphold the law; to *demean* himself, as an officer of the court, uprightly . . . ." *See* former Fed. R. App. P. 46(a) ("I . . . do solemnly swear . . . that I will *demean* myself as an attorney and counselor of this court . . . .") (before I rewrote the rules in 1997).

Yet the more common lay sense is now widespread even in legal prose, and has been with us since at least 1601. E.g.:

- "Nowhere in the common-law world—indeed in any modern society—is a woman regarded as chattel or *demeaned* by denial of a separate legal identity and the dignity associated with recognition as a whole human being." *Trammel v. U.S.*, 445 U.S. 40, 52 (1980) (per Burger, C.J.).
- "This illogical result *demeans* the values protected by the Confrontation Clause." *Richardson v. Marsh*, 481 U.S. 200, 212 (1987) (Stevens, J., dissenting).

Meanwhile, the word *bemean*, with which *demean* was confused in arriving at its popular meaning (= to debase), has become virtually obsolete.

dementia. See **insanity (A).**

demesne (= at common law, a lord's land held as his absolute property and not as feudal property through a superior) is pronounced either /di-**meen**/ or /di-**mayn**/. Today, unless the word appears in a historical context, it is ordinarily figurative—e.g.:

- "Collins, without authorization from the directors, ruled the corporation as a personal *demesne* for the benefit of

himself and his son." *Jackson v. Nicolai-Neppach Co.*, 348 P.2d 9, 20 (Or. 1959).
- "The trial court acted well within its judicial *demesne* in entering summary judgment." *John Miskoff Found., Inc. v. Johnson*, 588 So.2d 675, 675 (Fla. Dist. Ct. App. 1991).

de minimis. A. The Maxim. *De minimis* is a shortened form of the Latin maxim *de minimis non curat lex* (= the law does not concern itself with trifles). E.g.: "Perhaps this is still true today, but if so this area of procedure has become so shrunken as to fall within the maxim *de minimis*." Charles Alan Wright, *The Law of Federal Courts* 291 (5th ed. 1994). Though most legal writers find it legitimate and useful, in practice there is something to Ephraim Tutt's quip that "no one knows exactly what it means." *Yankee Lawyer* 356 (1943).

De minimis non curat lex is a sentence in itself. When invoking the maxim by declaring something to be a mere trifle, one writes that it is *de minimis*. The entire maxim should not be inserted when only the "trifling" portion is called for: "The testimony [regarding] the landscaping in the common areas was unsatisfactory, but this amenity is considered to be *de minimis non curat lex*." *Republic of Tex. Sav. Ass'n v. Island Recreational Dev.*, 680 S.W.2d 588, 592 (Tex. App.—Beaumont 1984). That sentence is grammatically nonsensical. If an entire maxim is used, it should fit into the sentence syntactically. But here we have, in translation, "this amenity is considered to be [*the law does not concern itself with trifles*]." The writer should have ended the sentence with *de minimis*. See MAXIMS.

Perhaps the most memorable use of the phrase is the clever pun created by the late Yale law professor Fred Rodell, who wrote this scandalously funny limerick:

> There was a young fellow named Rex,
> With a very small organ of sex.
> When arraigned for exposure
> He maintained with composure
> "De minimis non curat lex!"

> Fred Rodell, *Rodell Revisited: Selected Writings of Fred Rodell* 259 (Loren Ghiglione, Janet Rodell & Mike Rodell eds., 1994).

B. The Phrase. Lawyers often use the phrase not as a shortened version of the maxim, but in the sense "so insignificant that a court may overlook (it or them) in deciding the issue or case." E.g.:

- "Winter maintains that his unauthorized sales of non-Carvel products were *de minimis* and cannot possibly be deemed to have a sufficient effect on interstate commerce." *Franchised Stores of N.Y., Inc. v. Winter*, 394 F.2d 664, 670 (2d Cir. 1968).
- "The dictum that plaintiff's injury must pass some threshold of seriousness, more than *de minimis*, makes no sense at all." Douglas Laycock, *The Death of the Irreparable Injury Rule* 74 (1991).

The phrase sometimes appears, as in the following sentences, to act merely as a fancy substitute for *minimal*:

- "To require TWA to bear more than a *de minimis* [read *minimal*] cost in order to give Hardison Saturdays off is an undue hardship." *Trans World Airlines, Inc. v. Hardison*, 432 U.S. 63, 84 (1977) (per White, J.).
- "Worsham Sprinkler Co. does not have a family of common marks and spends *de minimis* [read *minimal*] amounts on advertising." *Worsham Sprinkler Co. v. Wes Worsham Fire Prot., LLC*, 419 F.Supp.2d 861, 879 (E.D. Va. 2006).
- "If only *de minimis* [read *minimal*] amounts of nowhere income could be created, rather than the broad swath cut by P.L. 86-272, then the substantive consequences of the throwback rule would be greatly reduced." John A. Swain, *Reforming the State Corporate Income Tax*, 83 Tul. L. Rev. 285, 355–56 (2008).

Sometimes the phrase is used as an attributive noun (meaning "something that is *de minimis*"): "CPI may be barred from asserting its trademark rights nationwide because of its failure to challenge what it may have considered a *de minimis*." *Conan Props. v. Conans Pizza*, 752 F.2d 145, 153 (5th Cir. 1985).

demise, vb. & n. The meanings of the verb *demise* are (1) "to convey by will or lease"; (2) "to pass by descent or bequest"; and (3) "to die."

The corresponding definitions of *demise* as a noun are (1) "the conveyance of an estate by will or lease, or the lease itself"; (2) "the passing of property by descent or bequest"; and (3) "death."

The popular sense of *demise*, of course, is as a noun: "death." Because most nonlawyers understand the word in this sense, the legal senses are likely to bewilder them. The popular meaning is an extension of the legal meanings, for historically the transference of property usually resulted from a sovereign's death. Hence the change of focus from conveyance to death. Sometimes even in legal contexts *demise* carries its noun lay meaning—e.g.:

- "The *demise* of strictly territorial notions of jurisdiction has also carried away the view that the Constitution's protections are strictly territorial." Eugene Kontorovich, *The Constitutionality of International Courts*, 158 U. Pa. L. Rev. 39, 108 (2009).
- "The impact of the different levels of government on free speech cases has gone unnoticed since the mid-century *demise* of Justice Harlan's proposal for First Amendment tailoring." Adam Winkler, *Free Speech Federalism*, 108 Mich. L. Rev. 153, 187 (2009).

See **death.**

Sense 1 of the verb and noun is illustrated in the following sentences. Because even sense 1 contains two quite distinct meanings, a more specific word might be better:

- "If land is *demised* [read *leased*] for the term of one hundred years or more, the term shall, so long as fifty years thereof remain unexpired, be regarded as an estate in fee simple." *Baldwin v. Eidman*, 202 F. 968, 976 (S.D.N.Y. 1913) (quoting a Massachusetts statute).

- "The point in that case was whether one Willmot, agent of the landlord, Smallwood, had notice of a *subdemise* [read *sublease*] by way of mortgage on account of which an alleged forfeiture arose." *Traders Safety Bldg. Corp. v. Shirk*, 237 Ill. App. 1, 13 (1925).

The adjective is *demisable*: "Because this tenure derived its whole force from custom, the lands must have been *demisable* [read *conveyable*] by copy of court roll from time immemorial." W.A. Jowitt, *The Dictionary of English Law* 491 (1959) (s.v. *copyhold*).

democracy. This term, meaning literally "government by the people," is often employed loosely, often tendentiously, often vaguely, and sometimes disingenuously (as when the post–World War II Soviet Union was referred to as a "democracy"). Originally a Greek term, *democracy* was understood by the Greeks in a very different sense from how we understand it today: Greek democracy was an institution limited to male clan members, who were citizens, while a huge population of slaves and other subordinated classes were disenfranchised. The same, of course, might be said of the U.S. before the abolition of slavery and before women gained the right to vote. Notions of democracy change with changing notions of who "the people" are. Throughout history, the term has gradually become more and more inclusive.

demonstrable /di-**mon**-strə-bəl/ is the word, not **demonstratable*, a NEEDLESS VARIANT. E.g.: "Such an inference clearly cannot be supported absent a *demonstratable* [read *demonstrable*] nexus between the defendant and the act sought to be introduced against him." *State v. English*, 383 S.E.2d 436, 438 (N.C. Ct. App. 1989).

demonstrative legacy. See **legacy.**

dempster; deemster. These are variant forms of the same word, which for most purposes has only historical significance. Both mean basically "a judge." *Dempster* was formerly used in Scotland, and *deemster* is still used on the Isle of Man. The *OED* notes that *deemster* "has been used in the general sense as a historical archaism by some modern writers"; the temptation to do so should be resisted.

demur, n. See **demurrer.**

demur, vb.; **demure.** *Demur* = to file a demurrer, which effectively admits the truth of a fact stated but denies that the complainant is legally entitled to relief. E.g.: "The city and the individual defendants *demurred* to each count." *Gillan v. City of San Marino*, 55 Cal. Rptr. 3d 158, 165 (Ct. App. 2007).

Demure is the adjective meaning (1) "sober, grave, serious"; or (2) "coy in an affected way."

demurrable = that may be demurred to. Lawyers have traditionally spoken of *demurrable allegations*, *demurrable indictments*, and the like—e.g.: "There is authority for the position that the indictment must be specific in charging the burglarious intent, and is *demurrable* if it merely alleges an intent to commit 'a felony.'" Rollin M. Perkins & Ronald N. Boyce, *Criminal Law* 266 (3d ed. 1982).

demurrer; *demurral; demur, n.; **demurrage.** A *demurrer* was a common-law pleading that stated that even if the other party's allegations were proved, the other party would not be entitled to succeed, and therefore that the demurring party was entitled in law to succeed on the facts alleged and admitted by the other. E.g.: "The Court of Claims was right in sustaining the *demurrer.*" *Interocean Oil Co. v. U.S.*, 270 U.S. 65, 69 (1926) (per Taft, C.J.). Today, *demurrers* are obsolete in England (since 1883) and in most if not all American jurisdictions. But they are still used in states such as California, Connecticut, Nebraska, Oregon, and Pennsylvania, among others. See -ER (B).

Idiomatically speaking, *demurrers* were said to be *interposed*:

- "The circuit court of Cook county sustained a *demurrer interposed* by appellants to a bill for injunction filed by appellees, and entered a decree dismissing the bill for want of equity." *Kemp v. Div. No. 241, Amalgamated Ass'n of St. & Elec. Ry. Employees of Am.*, 99 N.E. 389, 390 (Ill. 1912).
- "A motion in arrest of judgment or habeas corpus are the only remedies available when no *demurrer* to the indictment is *interposed* before judgment is entered on the verdict." *Jackson v. State*, 644 S.E.2d 491, 496 (Ga. Ct. App. 2007).

Demur, n., is the archaic nonlegal word for "the act of demurring; an objection raised or exception taken to a proposed course of action" (*OED*). The word is now chiefly literary. *Demurral is a NEEDLESS VARIANT of *demur.*

Demurrage is a maritime-law word meaning "a [liquidated] penalty imposed on a charterer of a vessel, or in some instances the consignee of the vessel's goods, for delays in loading or unloading the ship's cargo." *Trans-Asiatic Oil, Ltd. v. Apex Oil Co.*, 804 F.2d 773, 774 n.1 (1st Cir. 1986). It is usually used in the plural: *demurrages.*

denial of justice, an important phrase in international law, has been the object of SLIPSHOD EXTENSION: "The term . . . is sometimes loosely used to denote *any* international delinquency towards an alien for which a state is liable to make reparation. In this sense it is an unnecessary and confusing term. Its more proper sense is an injury involving the responsibility of the state committed by a court of justice." J.L. Brierly, *The Law of Nations* 226–27 (5th ed. 1955).

denization; *denizenation (= the action of making a person a denizen, i.e., a resident alien), a legal term dating from 1601, is sometimes incorrectly rendered *denizenation—e.g.: "During the first three decades of Oklahoma *denizenation* [read *denization*], bar

admission policies in the state remained fairly liberal, thus permitting talented young African Americans to realistically aspire to securing bar membership." R.O. Joe Cassity Jr., *African-American Attorneys on the Oklahoma Frontier*, 27 Okla. City. U. L. Rev. 245, 254 (2002).

denominate. See **denote.**

denote (= to mean; stand for) for *denominate* (= to give a name to; call) is a fairly common error—e.g.:

- "The issue may reasonably be *denoted as* [read *denominated* or, better, *called*] one of procedure." *Arrowsmith v. United Press Int'l*, 320 F.2d 219, 230 (2d Cir. 1963).
- "During what Dr. Huntington *denoted as* [read *denominated*] the 'third wave of democratization' that spread all over Eastern and Central Europe, Macedonia underwent a painful transition." Saso Georgievski, *Separation of Powers in the Republic of Macedonia*, 47 Duq. L. Rev. 921, 921–22 (2009).
- "No one advocates abolishing the crime of murder because it is subject to exceptions; these limits help the criminal law to carry out its underlying policy aims by confining convictions for murder to cases that should be *denoted as* [read *called*] murder." David Crump, *Reconsidering the Felony Murder Rule in Light of Modern Criticisms*, 32 Harv. J.L. & Pub. Pol'y 1155, 1164 (2009).

See **connote.**

denounce; renounce. To *denounce* is to condemn <the scandal caused some longtime supporters to denounce the governor>. To *renounce* is to repudiate <the compromise fell apart when key backers renounced it> or to give up <some protesters renounced their citizenship>. See **censure (A).**

*denouncement. See **denunciation.**

de novo, adv. & adj. This LATINISM, usually an adjective <de novo review>, as an adverb means "anew." E.g.: "We review a summary judgment *de novo.*" *TC Dallas #1, LP v. Republic Underwriters Ins. Co.*, 316 S.W.3d 832, 836 (Tex. App.—Dallas 2010).

denunciation; *denouncement. The second is a NEEDLESS VARIANT.

deny (= to declare untrue; repudiate; to refuse to recognize or acknowledge) is sometimes misused for *refuse* or *deprive.*

   A. For *refuse*. These words are synonymous in certain constructions <he was denied (or refused) this>. But in modern usage *refuse* properly precedes an infinitive, whereas with *deny* this construction is an ARCHAISM: "The Court acknowledged the reprehensibility of such police deception, but *denied* [read *refused*] to [overturn the conviction] on constitutional grounds." *People v. Wright*, 490 N.W.2d 351, 354 (Mich. 1992).

   B. For *deprive*. "[The plaintiff] never really tried to enter into a contract and thus could not have been *denied of* [read *denied* or *deprived of*] his rights to contract or purchase personal property." *Bagley v. Ameritech Corp.*, 220 F.3d 518, 519 (7th Cir. 2000).

depart from, in the context of discussing precedents, is sometimes a EUPHEMISM for *overturn* or *overrule*. When a court says that it *departs from* a precedent, it in effect overturns the precedent, usually without expressly so stating. The expression is more appropriate in referring to mere persuasive authority, as opposed to what would ordinarily be considered binding authority.

departner, n., is extremely rare and appears to be a PORTMANTEAU WORD for either *departnered partner* (see **departner,** vb.) or (less disparagingly) *departing partner*—e.g.: "Under the firm's partnership agreement, when four or more partners leave within a six-month period, the *departners* are obligated to pay a share of the firm's operating expenses, the counterclaims allege." Mark Hansen, *Failed Mergers Lead to Suits*, 79 A.B.A. J. 36, 36 (Feb. 1993).

departner, vb., is a NEOLOGISM meaning (1) "to demote or remove a partner"; (2) "to reduce the equity value of (a partner)"; or (3) "to demote (a partner) from the status of equity partner to nonequity partner." E.g.:

- (Sense 1) "The legal profession continues to grow, albeit more slowly. But all the growth is of older lawyers. This increases pressure on firms to thin their upper ranks to make room for ambitious younger people by mandating earlier retirement, or *departnering* those whose performance lags behind ever-rising standards." Marc Galanter, *Did You Hear the One About . . .* , Tex. Law., 6 Feb. 2006, at 34.
- (Sense 1) "As many as 60 Goldman [Sachs] executives could be stripped of their partnerships this year to make way for new blood, people with firsthand knowledge of the process say. Inside the firm, the process is known as '*de-partnering*.'" Susan Craig, *At Goldman, Partners Are Made, and Unmade*, N.Y. Times, 13 Sept. 2010, at A1.
- (Sense 2) "Plaintiff Walter Demaree worked for Babcock & Brown for nearly seventeen years, during which time he invested heavily in the company. According to Mr. Demaree, Babcock & Brown '*departnered*' him in October 2003, and reduced his percentage of company holdings." *Demaree v. Babcock & Brown Holdings, Inc.*, 2007 WL 2463299, at *1 (W.D. Wash. 2007).

Cf. **de-equitize.**

dépeçage, n. /dep-ə-**sahj**/, is a mid-20th-century borrowing from French law. It derives from the French verb *dépecer* (= to cut up; to dismember), and it means "choice of law issue by issue; the practice of applying rules of different jurisdictions to different issues in a legal dispute"—e.g.:

- "For a long time, courts and writers agreed that a choice-of-law involved a choice of a 'governing' legal system rather than of an individual rule. Much of this ideology remains intact in the language of the courts. But it is increasingly recognized that it is always a rule rather than a legal system to which we are referred . . . . [T]he implementation of this finding has been called *dépeçage*

or *scission*." Albert Ehrenzweig, *Conflicts in a Nutshell* 219 (2d ed. 1970).
- "*Dépeçage* occurs where the rules of one legal system are applied to regulate certain issues arising from a given transaction or occurrence, while those of another system regulate the other issues. The technique permits a more nuanced handling of certain multistate situations and thus forwards the policy of aptness." Arthur T. von Mehren, *Special Substantive Rules for Multi-State Problems*, 88 Harv. L. Rev. 347, 356 n.24 (1974).

dependence; dependency. These variants have undergone DIFFERENTIATION. *Dependence* is the general word meaning (1) "the quality or state of being dependent"; or (2) "reliance." *Dependency* is a geopolitical term meaning "a territory under the jurisdiction of, but not formally annexed by, a nation." (See **territory.**) These words are commonly misspelled *dependance* and *dependancy* (common only in BrE).

For *dependency* in the context of drug use, see **addiction.**

dependent, adj. See **addicted** & **parasitic.**

dependent, n.; **dependant,** n. The older spelling is *-ant*. The *OED* notes: "from the 18th c. often (like the adj.) spelt *dependent*, after L.; but the spelling *-ant* still predominates in the [noun]." *W11* countenances *-ent* over *-ant*. The *COD* continues the Oxonian preference for *-ant*, noting that *-ent* is chiefly American. Certainly the British DIFFERENTIATION in spelling between the adjective (*dependent*) and the noun (*dependant*) is a useful one; but American writers cannot be faulted for using the *-ent* spelling for the noun.

dependent relative revocation. "The doctrine of *dependent relative revocation* is basically an application of the rule that a testator's intention governs; it is not a doctrine defeating that intent." *Linkins v. Protestant Episcopal Cathedral Found. of D.C.*, 187 F.2d 357, 360 (D.C. Cir. 1950). This phrase, common in the American and British law of wills, confuses all but specialists in wills and estates. It has nothing to do with revoking one's dependent relatives; rather, it means that "if a testator revokes [a] will in the mistaken belief that a particular result will ensue, or that a particular set of facts exists when it does not, then the revoked will may still hold good" (*ODL*). The law regards as mutually dependent the acts of destroying one will and of substituting another in its place, when both acts are parts of one plan. The two acts are therefore "related," or *relative*.

We might wish for a less monstrous phrase, such as *conditional revocation*: "The name of this doctrine [*dependent relative revocation*] seems to me to be somewhat overloaded with unnecessary polysyllables. The resounding adjectives add very little, it seems to me, to any clear idea of what is meant. The whole matter can be quite simply expressed by the word 'conditional.'" *In re Hope Brown*, [1942] P. 136, 138 (per Langton, J.).

*depone. See **depose.**

*deponee. See deponent.

deponent (= one who testifies by deposition or affidavit) is sometimes incorrectly rendered *deponee, *deposee, and even *deposer—e.g.:

- "The *deponee* [read *deponent*] hereby designates Mr. Boykin and Mr. Niblack, mentioned above, to act in my behalf with power of attorney." *Watkins v. Boykin*, 536 S.W.2d 400, 402 (Tex. Civ. App.—El Paso 1976).
- "The Superior Court's decision was silent as to plaintiff's questions to both *deposees* [read *deponents*]." *Matheson v. Bangor Publ'g Co.*, 414 A.2d 1203, 1205 (Me. 1980).
- "If there is compelling evidence that a deposition will be a substantial threat to the *deponee's* [read *deponent's*] life, a Court may in its discretion appropriately grant a protective order." *In re Tutu Water Wells Contamination CERCLA Litig.*, 189 F.R.D. 153, 155 (D.V.I. 1999).
- "We note that the record and appellant's brief do not . . . identify what O'Keefe and the *deposer* [read *deponent*] are speaking about in O'Keefe's deposition testimony." *Atanus v. American Airlines, Inc.*, 932 N.E.2d 1044, 1047 n.1 (Ill. App. Ct. 2010).

The *OED* records *deposer as "one who deposes or makes a statement on oath; a deponent," but the sole example is from 1581. *W2* defines it as "a witness; a deponent," and *W3* as "one who deposes; esp: one that testifies." But it might well be misunderstood as denoting the one conducting the deposition rather than the one testifying. Avoid it. See **affiant** & **affirmant**.

deportation; deportment. Both derive ultimately from L. *deportare* (= to carry off; to convey away), but to say that these words have undergone DIFFERENTIATION is a great understatement. *Deportation* = the act of removing (a person) to another country; the expulsion of an alien from a country. (See **removal**.) *Deportment* = the bearing, demeanor, or manners of a person.

deportation proceedings. See **removal proceedings.**

deportment. See **deportation.**

depose; *depone. In legal contexts, to *depose* (vb.) is (1) to bear witness or testify; or (2) to take a deposition of someone. *Depose* also has the historical meaning "to dethrone or kill (a king)." **Depone*, a relatively rare word meaning "to testify," ought to be considered a NEEDLESS VARIANT.

Krapp recorded *depose* as being used in legal contexts for "to state"—e.g.: "The witness *deposes* that he has seen . . . ." George P. Krapp, *A Comprehensive Guide to Good English* 188 (1927). Actually, today that sense survives in AmE only in the doublet *deposes and states* or *deposes and says*, a common phrase in affidavits. (See DOUBLETS, TRIPLETS, AND SYNONYM-STRINGS.) But in BrE it has more currency—e.g.: "The manufacturer's secretary was called and *deposed* that in the previous six years the manufacturer had treated by a similar process 4,737,600 of these garments." *Grant v.*

Australian Knitting Mills Ltd., [1936] A.C. 85, 95 (per Lord Wright).

But the more common use today is the transitive one—e.g.: "The defendant's attorney then *deposed* the plaintiff." As that example illustrates, American lawyers today almost invariably say that the lawyer deposes the witness, not that the deponent deposes. In the following sentence, then, a lawyer would have put the verb to PASSIVE VOICE: "If [the witness] has not *deposed* [read *been deposed*], the other lawyer won't be able to emphasize his pain and suffering by reading the questions and answers to the jury." Joseph C. Goulden, *The Million Dollar Lawyers* 107 (1978). For the misuse of *deposition* as a verb in this sense, see **deposition (c).**

For lawyers, the nonlegal sense ("to dethrone") occasionally causes MISCUES—e.g.: "President George Bush . . . again urged that President Saddam Hussein be *deposed*, saying 'It's only terror that's keeping him in power.'" *Marines Replace Iraqis in North*, Int'l Herald Tribune, 27–28 Apr. 1991, at 1. That is so especially in contexts involving trial preparation—e.g.: "The judge in the drug and racketeering trial of Gen. Manuel Antonio Noriega privately questioned an important prosecution witness this afternoon to determine whether the witness lied when he testified against the *deposed* Panamanian leader last fall." Larry Rohter, *Judge Examines Truthfulness of Noriega Witness*, N.Y. Times, 26 Mar. 1992, at A8.

***deposee; *deposer.** See **deponent.**

deposeth. See -ETH.

depositary; depository; *depositee. Most authorities on usage have agreed through the years that *depositary* is the better term in reference to persons with whom one leaves valuables or money for safekeeping, and that *depository* is preferred in reference to places. But the Uniform Commercial Code contains the term *depositary bank*, and this phrase has therefore become common. E.g.: "Under the new regulation, liability for unauthorized remotely created checks has been shifted from the payor banks to the *depositary banks* (where the checks were deposited)." *U.S. v. Payment Processing Ctr., LLC*, 461 F.Supp.2d 319, 322 n.2 (E.D. Pa. 2006). Following is an example of the traditional use of *depositary*: "The *depositary* in escrow . . . has the absolute duty to carry out the terms of the agreement." *In re Missionary Baptist Found.*, 792 F.2d 502, 504 (5th Cir. 1986).

Depository has continued to be used in reference to places. E.g.: "The landfill served as a *depository* for residential refuse, ash, slag, construction debris, and sewage sludge from a now demolished wastewater-treatment plant operated on a portion of the Inland Site for approximately 60 years." *Lighthouse Pointe Prop. Assocs. LLC v. New York*, 924 N.E.2d 801, 806 (N.Y. 2010).

Depositee is a NEEDLESS VARIANT of *depositary*—e.g.: "A *depositee* [read *depositary*] who made away with the thing was liable *ex deposito*." W.W. Buckland, *A Text-Book of Roman Law* 709 (1921).

deposition. A. As a Noun. In its legal senses, *deposition* is the noun corresponding to *depose*. In civil law the word *deposition* meant "the testimony of a witness. In very old English practice, simply the written testimony of a witness." Edward P. Weeks, *A Treatise on the Law of Depositions* 3 (1880). Today it refers to (1) a witness's out-of-court testimony that is recorded by a court reporter and reduced to writing for later use in court; (2) the session at which such out-of-court testimony is recorded; or (3) in ecclesiastical law, a penalty by which a member of the clergy may be divested of a patronage or other dignity. *Deposition* also serves as the noun for *deposit*—e.g.: "In the event solid waste could not be disposed of through recycling or *deposition* in the landfill, the contractor would be responsible for identifying potential contaminated items." *RISC Mgmt. J.V. v. U.S.*, 69 Fed. Cl. 624, 628 (2006). For more on *deposition* and related words, see **evidence (A)**.

B. *Oral deposition.* This phrase is not a REDUNDANCY because, under most court rules, it is possible to take a *deposition upon written interrogatories* (sometimes called a *deposition on written questions*).

C. As a Verb. *Deposition* serves as the noun for both *depose* and *deposit* <the landfill was unsuitable for hazardous-waste *deposition*>. *Deposition* should not be used as a verb in place of *depose*—e.g.:

- "Need for such documents to impeach *depositioned* [read *deposed*] testimony should be even rarer." *The Jencks Legislation: Problems in Prospect*, 67 Yale L.J. 674, 692 (1958).
- "At that time the arguments reflect he had not *depositioned* [read *deposed*] any of the persons whose written statements were sought with the exception of McMahon." *Rhiner v. City of Clive*, 373 N.W.2d 466, 477–78 (Iowa 1985).

See **depose**.

depository. See **depositary**.

deprecate; depreciate. The first has increasingly encroached on the figurative senses of the second, whereas the second has retreated into financial contexts. Traditionally, *deprecate* means "to disapprove regretfully." E.g.: "One of the earliest and most uncompromising advocates of unlimited sovereignty, Bodin, *deprecated* any attempt to make laws unrepealable." Carleton K. Allen, *Law in the Making* 469 (7th ed. 1964). (For more, see **disapprove (A)**.) And traditionally, *depreciate* means (1) [transitive] to belittle or disparage (something or someone); or (2) [intransitive] to lose value or utility.

Given those traditional senses, the idiom *self-deprecating* is, literally speaking, an unlikely description except perhaps for those suffering from extreme neuroses. *Self-depreciating* (with *depreciate* in its transitive sense) makes more sense, and in fact that is the original phrase—e.g.: "But in him modesty is not an expression of shyness or *self-depreciation* or self-distrust." Felix Frankfurter, "Calvert Magruder," in *Of Law and Life and Other Things* 136, 138 (Philip B. Kurland ed., 1967).

But today *self-deprecating* is 50 times as common in published sources, so it can hardly be called substandard. Still, the traditional phrase does continue to appear.

deprive. See **deny (B)**.

depute, vb.; deputize. To *depute* is to delegate <these responsibilities she deputed to her attorney-in-fact>, and to *deputize* is to make someone else one's deputy or to act as deputy <the sheriff then deputized four people who had offered to help in the search>.

deraign, vb., a legal ARCHAISM still often referred to, means "to settle (a dispute or claim) by combat or wager." A right-minded folk etymologist might conclude that the word was arrived at by metathesis of *derange*.

dereliction = abandonment, esp. through neglect or moral wrong, as in *dereliction of duty*. E.g.:

- "By hypothesis he has committed the gravest *dereliction* possible—a complete repudiation of the trust he expressly assumed." *Marcus v. Otis*, 168 F.2d 649, 657 (2d Cir. 1948).
- "Let's be clear that there are many circumstances—accounting for the overwhelming majority of citations to foreign law—when a judge, sworn to uphold the Constitution, would be in *dereliction* of duty if he or she did not cite foreign legal sources." Stephen Yeazell, *When and How U.S. Courts Should Cite Foreign Law*, 26 Const. Comment. 59, 61 (2009).

The *OED* notes that in legal prose *dereliction* is still used in the neutral sense of physical abandonment; if this sense persists at all in current legal usage, it is obsolescent.

derivative = a contract giving rise to rights and obligations with respect to an underlying asset or other factor, such as debt securities, equity securities, currencies, interest rates, or commodities. *See* John-Peter Castagnino, *Derivatives: The Key Principles* 1 (2009). Cf. **underlying**.

derivative action = a suit by a beneficiary of a fiduciary to enforce a right running to the fiduciary as such. *Goldstein v. Groesbeck*, 142 F.2d 422, 425 (2d Cir. 1944). Synonymous phrases include *derivative suit* and (somewhat more narrowly) *shareholder derivative suit*.

derogate is regularly used in two quite distinct senses in legal prose: (1) transitively, it means "to disparage" <we do not derogate these values, however, if we are unable to find them to be protected by the Constitution>; and (2) intransitively, it is used with the prep. *from* and means "to detract" <the court's position derogates from the highly sensitive discretion that is inherent in the parole function>.

derogation of, in. This phrase is used 99 times in legal contexts for every one use in nonlegal contexts. It means "in abrogation or repeal of (a law, contract, or right)." Hence the maxim: *Statutes in derogation of the common law are to be strictly construed*. In a sense, that maxim is senseless, for, as Grant Gilmore once quipped, "what statute is not?" *The Ages of American Law* 62 (1977). E.g.: "If obtaining Martinez's statement is to be treated as a stand-alone violation of the privilege subject to compensation, why should the same not be true . . . whenever the government so much as threatens a penalty *in derogation of* the right to immunity, or whenever the police fail to honor *Miranda*?" *Chavez v. Martinez*, 538 U.S. 760, 778–79 (2003) (per Souter, J.).

Derogation from is another idiom, meaning "prejudice, destruction (of a right or grant)." E.g.:

- "A grantor cannot be permitted to *derogate from* his absolute grant unless in case of strict necessity." *Adams v. Marshall*, 138 Mass. 228, 236 (1884).
- "Opinion may be expressed through 'rhetorical hyperbole' and 'vigorous epithets,' even in the most pejorative terms, but when the criticism takes the form of accusations of criminal or unethical conduct, or *derogation* [*from*] professional integrity in terms subject to factual verification, the borderline between fact and opinion has been crossed." *Trump v. Chicago Tribune Co.*, 616 F.Supp. 1434, 1435 (S.D.N.Y. 1985).
- "Nothing in this statute, however, implies any *derogation from* the well-established principles embodied in the common-law doctrine of incompatibility." *City of Wildwood v. DeMarzo*, 988 A.2d 1218, 1224 (N.J. Super. Ct. 2010).

See **degradation.**

descend, vb.; **distribute.** In the legal idiom relating to intestacy, real property is said upon death to *descend* (= to pass) to the heirs. E.g.: "If it is a remainder in fee simple it will *descend* on the death of the remainderman intestate to his heirs." Cornelius J. Moynihan, *Introduction to the Law of Real Property* 139 (2d ed. 1988). Personal property, by contrast, is *distributed* to the intestate's next of kin. Hence the phrase *statute of descent and distribution* contains no REDUNDANCY. See **descent (B).** For more on *heirs*, *next of kin*, and *distributees*, see **heir (C).**

descendant. In proper usage, only a decedent is said to have *descendants*—a live parent does not. See **ascendant.**

descender. See -ER (B).

descendible, not **descendable*, is the preferred form.

descent. A. And *purchase*. These words are distinguished in the law of property. *Descent* refers to the acquisition of property by act of law (as by inheritance), whereas *purchase* is acquisition of property by the act of oneself or another (as by will or gift). In legal contexts, then, *purchase* is much broader than the general lay sense of "buying." E.g.: "These incidents did not accrue if the property was acquired through *purchase*, and, in order to obviate this means of curtailing the payment of incidents, title by *descent* was declared to be more worthy than title by *purchase*." *In re Burchell's Estate*, 87 N.E.2d 293, 296 (N.Y. 1949). See **buy, purchase** & **words of purchase.**

B. And *distribution*; *inheritance*. At common law, intestate real property passes by *descent* and intestate personal property passes by *distribution*. Both *heirs* (who take by descent) and *distributees* (who take by distribution) may properly be said to *inherit* or *take by inheritance*. In the U.S., the Uniform Probate Code has simplified the historical terminology, supplanting all these specific terms with the general phrase *intestate succession*. See **descend** & **succession.**

desegregation; integration. No distinction between a legal requirement of *integration* and a legal requirement of *desegregation* is ordinarily observed in legal usage, but the distinction may be important in understanding the constitutional law of race and the schools. Certainly it would be useful, in reference to schools in the U.S., if we distinguished between court-ordered *desegregation* (= the abrogation of policies that segregate races into different institutions and facilities) and court-ordered *integration* (= the incorporation of different races into existing institutions for the purpose of achieving a racial balance).

deserts. See **just deserts.**

*deshabille. See **dishabille.**

designate; name; nominate; elect; appoint. These verbs share the sense "to put forward for an office, position, or honor." *Designate* suggests selection by the person or committee with the power of choosing the incumbent for post. *Name* is synonymous, though it emphasizes the announcement more than the selection. *Nominate*, though etymologically identical with *name*, does not suggest a final choice, but instead a choice that is contingent on others' approval or rejection. *Elect* suggests a final selection with no further approval required. (For the legalistic uses of this word, see **elect.**) *Appoint* implies selection that may be subject to others' approval but will not require a general vote of the electorate.

*designatee. See **designee.**

designedly, in criminal law, is sometimes used synonymously with—but is not as good as—*intentionally*.

designee; *designatee. *Designee* (= a person designated), a word dating from 1925 and commonly used by lawyers, is sometimes displaced by **designatee*, a NEEDLESS VARIANT. E.g.:

- "The commissioner, or a competent *designatee* [read *designee*], is required to inspect and approve all construction work." *Ross v. Consumers Power Co.*, 363 N.W.2d 641, 669 (Mich. 1984).

- "A casino licensee may utilize a dealing shoe or other device designed to reshuffle the cards automatically, provided that the CCC or its authorized *designatee* [read *designee*] has approved such shoe or device." *Doug Grant, Inc. v. Greate Bay Casino Corp.*, 232 F.3d 173, 182 (3d Cir. 2000).

See -EE.

desirable; desirous. *Desirable* is used in reference to things (or people to whom one is attracted), *desirous* in reference to one's emotions. What is *desirable* is attractive and worth seeking; the word applies to anything that arouses a desire. *Desirous* = impelled by desire.

The phrase *be desirous of* is usually a circumlocution for the verb *desire* or *want*. E.g.:

- "Ms. Dorsey offers the information that she and Mr. Blood were raising a four-year-old child as their own, and Mr. Blood *was desirous of assuring* [read *wanted to ensure*] their support." *Dorsey v. Office of Pers. Mgmt.*, 587 F.3d 1111, 1118 (Fed. Cir. 2009).
- "Sadler *was desirous of fixing* [read *wanted to fix*] the time of contamination within the period of Auto-Owners policy coverage." *Sadler v. Auto-Owners Ins. Co.*, 904 N.E.2d 665, 671 (Ind. Ct. App. 2009).
- "The sentencing transcript reveals that the district court *was desirous of doing* [read *wanted to do*] what was 'just' in this case." *U.S. v. Autery*, 555 F.3d 864, 875 (9th Cir. 2009).

See BE-VERBS (B).

Because of the connotations of *desire* still felt in the word *desirous*, it's undoubtedly insensitive to write of a woman who is "desirous" of procuring an abortion—e.g.: "I use the term 'traditional' abortion here to refer to a situation where a woman is *desirous* of terminating her entire pregnancy." Judith F. Daar, *Selective Reduction of Multiple Pregnancy*, 25 U.C. Davis L. Rev. 773, 783 n.44 (1992). [A possible revision: *I use the term 'traditional' abortion here to refer to a situation in which a woman wants to terminate her pregnancy*.]

desist. See **stop.**

de son tort, JARGON from LAW FRENCH (lit., "by his own wrongdoing"), means "wrongful." It is typically used in the two phrases *executor de son tort* (= wrongful executor) and *trustee de son tort* (= wrongful trustee). The phrase denotes the breach of a fiduciary duty.

An *executor de son tort* is a person who, without legal authority, takes it on himself to act as executor or administrator as by acting or dealing with any of the decedent's property, apart from acts necessitated by humanity or necessity (*OCL1*). Usually an *executor de son tort* acts to the detriment of beneficiaries or creditors of the estate.

A *trustee de son tort* acts similarly in respect of a living person's property. E.g.: "Plaintiff contended and the trial court found that when the First Trust was consolidated with the Union Trust Company, the office of trustee, under the terms of the will, thereby automatically became vacant and that the successor, from that time on, acted as *trustee de son tort*." *De*

Korwin v. First Nat'l Bank of Chicago, 179 F.2d 347, 351 (7th Cir. 1949). See *ex maleficio.*

despite. See **regardless (B).**

despite what. See **unlike (A).**

destructible; *destroyable. The second is a NEEDLESS VARIANT. *Destructible*, as well as its corresponding noun *destructibility*, is frequently used in the law:

- "There is ample justification . . . for a search of the arrestee's person and the area 'within his immediate control'—construing that phrase to mean the area from within which he might gain possession of a weapon or *destructible* evidence." *Chimel v. California*, 395 U.S. 752, 763 (1969) (per Stewart, J.).
- "The *destructibility* of contingent remainders posed a threat to the stability of English family settlements of land and the conveyancing bar set to work to circumvent the *destructibility* rule." Cornelius J. Moynihan, *Introduction to the Law of Real Property* 137 (2d ed. 1988).
- "The crux of Shakir's appeal is that because he was already handcuffed at the time Detective Smith searched his bag, he had no access to any weapon or *destructible* evidence that might have been in the bag." *U.S. v. Shakir*, 616 F.3d 315, 317 (3d Cir. 2010).

desuetude /de-swə-tyood/ (= disuse) has, in law, become the name of a doctrine whereby if a statute is left unenforced long enough, it will no longer be regarded by the courts as having any legal effect even though not repealed. It has a limited application in American law, and little if any application in English law: "English law, unlike Roman and Scots law, has never admitted that an Act of Parliament may be repealed or cease to have effect by obsolescence." O. Hood Phillips, *A First Book of English Law* 105 (3d ed. 1955). E.g.: "There is no doctrine of *desuetude* in English law, so a statute never ceases to be in force merely because it is obsolete." Rupert Cross, *Statutory Interpretation* 3 (1976).

detain. See **arrest.**

*detainal. See **detention.**

detainee (= a person held in custody) is a 20th-century NEOLOGISM that has proved useful in legal contexts. E.g.:

- "If an arrest is made without a warrant, however, then regardless of whether the arresting officer believes that probable cause exists, the *detainee* must be promptly brought before a magistrate for a probable cause determination." *U.S. v. Garza*, 754 F.2d 1202, 1211 (5th Cir. 1985).
- "Alexander Hamilton likewise explained that by providing the *detainee* a judicial forum to challenge detention, the writ preserves limited government." *Boumediene v. Bush*, 553 U.S. 723, 744 (2008) (per Kennedy, J.).

See -EE.

detainer. See **detention** & -ER (B).

detention; *detainment; *detainal; detainer. *Detention* = holding in custody; confinement; compulsory delay. **Detainment* and **detainal* are NEEDLESS

VARIANTS. *Detainer* is a specialized legal term meaning (1) "the action of detaining, withholding, or keeping in one's possession"; (2) "the confinement of a person in custody"; or (3) "a writ authorizing prison officials to continue holding a prisoner in custody." See -ER (B).

determent. See **deterrent.**

determinable = (1) liable to be cut short; or (2) capable of being ascertained. Sense 1 is common in the law <determinable fee>, but it generally ought to be avoided in deference to the more universally understandable *terminable*. In a few SET PHRASES, it should be allowed to remain <a possibility of reverter is the future interest left in one who creates a fee simple conditional or a fee simple determinable>. (See **fee simple (F).**) But in other contexts, it ought to be simplified, for it is merely an unnecessary LEGALISM—e.g.:

- "The employment, other than that of the settlor himself, was to be at such weekly wage as the trustee and the society agreed upon and was to be *determinable* [read *terminable*] by a week's notice from the trustee or the society." *Brunker v. Perpetual Tr. Co.* (1937) 59 C.L.R. 140. (Austl.).
- "The parties have stipulated that these deeds conveyed a *fee simple determinable* to the railroad, with the grantors retaining a reversionary interest." *Troha v. U.S.*, 692 F.Supp.2d 550, 563 (W.D. Pa. 2010).

The following sentences illustrate sense 2:

- "This court affirmed the dismissal of the federal claims, but held that the validity of the state-law claims was a matter of state law best *determinable* by the state courts." *Hardy v. University Interscholastic League*, 759 F.2d 1233, 1235 (5th Cir. 1985).
- "The federal definition of developmental disability for purposes of SSI benefits differs from the state definition because it includes a medically *determinable* physical impairment resulting in severe functional limitations and expected to end in death or last at least one year." *Campbell v. State, Dep't of Soc. & Health Servs.*, 83 P.3d 999, 1008 (Wash. 2004).

determinacy, the correct form, is sometimes incorrectly rendered *determinancy*—e.g.:

- "Viewed in this way, *Festo* is a culmination of at least five years of decisions that have placed greater and greater emphasis on certainty and *determinancy* [read *determinacy*] in patent interpretation." *Cases and Recent Developments*, 10 Fed. Cir. B.J. 397, 420 (2000).
- "Additionally, the assessment of skill, with all its apparent *determinancy* [read *determinacy*], is rife with possibilities for manipulation." Michael H. Davis, *Patent Politics*, 56 S.C. L. Rev. 337, 362 (2004).

determinant. See **determiner.**

determinate, adj., = having defined limits; definite; conclusive. *Determinate sentencing* came in response to the phrase *indeterminate sentencing*, which denotes a practice that was common in the U.S. up until the early 1970s (no specific time being set for prison sentences, e.g.: "10 to 20 years"). E.g.:

- "The remedial, coercive nature of the sanction here imposed is manifest. It is remedial and coercive, not punitive, because it is not a *determinate* sentence designed to punish disobedience to a Court order which cannot be redressed." *Delaware State Bar Ass'n v. Alexander*, 386 A.2d 652, 665 (Del. 1978).
- "In a world of mandatory minimums and *determinate* sentences, . . . prosecutors hold a tremendous amount of power." J. McGregor Smyth Jr., *From Arrest to Reintegration*, 24 Crim. Just. 42, 47 (Fall 2009).

The adverb *determinately* is sometimes confused with *determinedly* (= with determination).

determination of whether. The preposition *of* is unnecessary. See **whether.**

determine. A. Archaic Sense. Used without a direct object, *determine* in legal prose is an ARCHAISM in the sense "to terminate; bring or come to an end." E.g.:

- "He had a *determinable* estate; it was never *determined*; he died owning it, and now after the *determination* of the trust it is part of his intestate estate, and to be distributed as such." *State Bank & Trust Co. v. Nolan*, 130 A. 483, 490 (Conn. 1925). (On the use of *determinable* in that sentence, see **determinable.**)
- "If no issue of her body then survive, then all of the principal of said estate then remaining shall be divided among my heirs-at-law in proportion to their heirship and upon the principal of the said fund being distributed in accordance with the direction of this clause, then said trust shall cease and *determine*." *Stempel v. Middletown Trust Co.*, 7 Conn. Supp. 205 (Super. Ct. 1939) (quoting a will).

Nonlawyers are likely to be confused by this legalistic usage; hence a simpler wording might often be called for—e.g.: "The trust will *terminate* [or *end*]."

On the use of the verbose phrase *cease and determine*, see DOUBLETS, TRIPLETS, AND SYNONYM-STRINGS.

B. *Determine* **(***whether***) (***if***).** *Determine if is now regarded as inferior to *determine whether* in formal writing. The latter phrase is five times more common in American judicial opinions.

determiner; determinant. Both mean "that which determines." But there is a latent DIFFERENTIATION: a *determiner* is normally a person who decides, while a *determinant* is a deciding factor—e.g.:

- "Relatively little is known about the *determinants* of U.S. district court judges' publication decisions. [But] evidence suggests that a judge may be more likely to publish a decision if it is 'complex.'" Christopher A. Whytock, *Myth of Mess?*, 84 N.Y.U. L. Rev. 719, 782 (2009).
- "Judge Woodcock also told [the jurors] . . . that they were the sole triers of fact and *determiners* of witness credibility." *U.S. v. Kinsella*, 622 F.3d 75, 81 (1st Cir. 2010).

determine whether. See **determine (B).**

deterrent, n.; **deterrence; determent.** A *deterrent* is that which deters, that is, inhibits or discourages. *Deterrence* is preventing by fear. *Determent* is the act or fact of deterring.

detinet. See **detinuit.**

detinue; replevin; trover. *Detinue* and *replevin* are common-law remedies for the specific recovery of personal property. *Detinue* developed from the writ of debt to provide for the return of wrongfully detained goods (even if not wrongfully taken). The losing defendant had the option, at common law, of returning the property or paying the plaintiff an amount equal to its value, as determined at trial. *Detinue* still exists in many American jurisdictions but was statutorily abolished in England in 1977 (and replaced by the tort of *wrongful interference with goods*).

Replevin originated as an action to test the legality of another's seizure of goods (*distraint*). In England, it has been restricted to this particular situation, whereas in the U.S. *replevin* has become an available remedy for any case of wrongful taking of chattels. See **distraint.**

Trover is a common-law remedy for compensatory damages for conversion of personal property. See **conversion.**

detinuit; detinet. These common-law actions have deceptively similar names. *Detinuit* (lit., "he has detained") = an action of replevin in which the plaintiff already possesses the goods sued upon. *Detinet* (lit., "he detains") = an action alleging simply that the defendant is wrongfully withholding money or chattels.

detrimental reliance = reliance (usu. on another's promise or representation) that turns out to be disadvantageous or to cause a loss. Though it is now a fundamental term in contract law, it did not begin appearing in legal discourse until the mid-20th century. Today, of course, it is commonplace—e.g.:

- "For *detrimental reliance* seems to be the key to promissory estoppel, and it is also, of course, one of the twin legs of the doctrine of consideration." P.S. Atiyah, *An Introduction to the Law of Contract* 125 (3d ed. 1981).
- "*Detrimental reliance* by the promisee can therefore give rise to a proprietary estoppel even though no benefit is conferred on the promisor." G.H. Treitel, *The Law of Contract* 126 (8th ed. 1991).
- "Even if the Government cannot show *detrimental reliance* on our earlier cases, our reexamination of well-settled precedent could nevertheless prove harmful." *John R. Sand & Gravel Co. v. U.S.*, 552 U.S. 130, 139 (2008) (per Breyer, J.).

deuterogamy. See **bigamy.**

devastavit; devisavit. These terms are easily confusable; they call for explanation in modern contexts. *Devastavit* (L. "he has wasted") = the failure of a personal representative to administer a decedent's estate promptly and properly. E.g.:

- "The courts found that he had committed constructive fraud when he participated in the *devastavit*, or wasting,

of a testator's estate." *In re Johnson*, 691 F.2d 249, 256 (6th Cir. 1982).
- "This court has held that an executor who actively contributes to a *devastavit* will be held responsible regardless of his intent." *Johnson v. First Nat'l Bank of Rome, Ga.*, 319 S.E.2d 440, 442 (Ga. 1984).
- "If, however, the administrator did not seek court approval, he could be liable for *devastavit* if he did not act in good faith, with ordinary prudence, and with due regard for the estate's interests." *Kelly v. R.S. Jones & Assocs., Inc.*, 406 S.E.2d 34, 37 (Va. 1991).

See **waste.**

Devisavit is invariably used in the phrase *devisavit vel non* (L. "he devises or not"), which in former practice was an issue sent from an equity or probate court to a court of law to determine the validity of a purported will. E.g.:

- "While the question of '*devisavit vel non*' ('will or no will') is the primary issue in a will contest, and under [the Statute] either party to a will contest has an automatic right to a jury trial, where no genuine issues of material fact have been presented in the pleading stage a motion for summary judgment is properly granted." *In re Launius*, 507 So.2d 27, 29 (Miss. 1987).
- "Summary judgment on the issue of *devisavit vel non* was appropriate despite evidence of undue influence and lack of capacity." *In re Will of Jones*, 669 S.E.2d 572, 573 (N.C. 2008).

See **vel non.**

deviance; *deviancy;** **deviation.** The general term for "an act or instance of deviating" is *deviation* <a ship's deviation from its voyage route> <deviation from orthodox religion>. E.g.: "At a minimum, a military commission can be 'regularly constituted' only if some practical need explains *deviations* from court-martial practice." *Hamdan v. Rumsfeld*, 548 U.S. 557, 632–33 (2006) (per Stevens, J.).

Deviation is more neutral in connotation than *deviance*, which means "the quality or state of deviating from established norms, esp. in social customs." *Deviancy* is a NEEDLESS VARIANT.

deviant; deviate. A. As Adjectives. *Deviant* is normal. The first edition of the *OED* (1928) labeled both of these adjectives "obsolete" and "rare." The *OED Supp.* (1972) deleted the tag on *deviant* and cited many examples in the sense "deviating from normal social standards or behavior." The word is common in legal writing—e.g.: "The government failed to present the expert testimony necessary to establish that the photographs would appeal to the prurient interest of a clearly defined *deviant* group." *U.S. v. Petrov*, 747 F.2d 824, 830 (2d Cir. 1984).

W3 records *deviate* as an adjective, and it is, unfortunately, common in American legal prose—e.g.: "The hospital and morgue staff all testified that no *deviate* sexual intercourse was performed on the complainant while she was under their care and control." *O'Neill v. State*, 681 S.W.2d 663, 667 (Tex. App.—Houston [1st Dist.] 1984). Even so, *deviate* (adj.) is a NEEDLESS VARIANT of *deviant*, the preferred adjective.

Deviant is often used in figurative senses—e.g.: "*Deviant* rulings by circuit courts of appeals, particularly in apparent dictum, cannot generally provide the 'justified reliance' necessary to warrant withholding retroactive application of a decision construing a statute as Congress intended it." *U.S. v. Donnelly's Estate*, 397 U.S. 286, 295 (1970) (per Marshall, J.).

B. As Nouns. Both *deviate* and *deviant* are used as (generally pejorative) nouns meaning "a person who or thing that deviates, esp. from normal social standards or behavior; specif., a sexual pervert." *Deviant* should be preferred since the use derives from the adjectival function. A few writers use **deviationist*, but that word is uncommon enough to be labeled a NEEDLESS VARIANT.

deviation. See **deviance.**

devil, in BrE usage, has an interesting sense: "a junior legal counsel working for a principal" (*SOED*). E.g.: "The term '*devil*' is a regular and serious name [in England] for a young barrister who, in wig and gown, serves without compensation and without fame, often for from five to seven years, supplying a junior with ammunition." Henry S. Drinker, *Legal Ethics* 18 (1953).

The term is also used as a verb, usually in the phrase *to devil for* (*a principal*). E.g.:

- "He *devilled* for his uncle, was made counsel to the Commissioners of Customs in 1840, and soon got a good practice on circuit and at Westminster." 16 William Holdsworth, *A History of English Law* 155 (1966).
- "Judges and advocates who were trained in those days . . . had to spend four years gaining an honours degree, followed by two years unpaid work apprenticed to a solicitor and '*devilling*' for an advocate." Robert Porter, *Fraud Case Fuels Rumour in Gay Scandal*, Sunday Telegraph, 21 Jan. 1990, at 2.

See LAWYERS, DEROGATORY NAMES FOR (A).

devisability; divisibility. The first means specifically "the capability of being given in a will"; the second means more generally "the capability of being divided."

devisavit. See **devastavit.**

devise, n.; bequest; legacy. These words denote types of clauses in wills, each having acquired through DIFFERENTIATION a more or less generally accepted sense among lawyers. A *devise* traditionally disposes of real property (only in legal usage is this word a noun). In the U.S. this tradition has been changed by statutes (see the next entry), but the traditional wording is strongly rooted, and most legal writers confine *devise* to contexts involving real property:

- "A specific *devise* of homestead property is preferred, but the general language of a residuary clause is a sufficiently precise indicator of testamentary intent." *McKean v. Warburton*, 919 So.2d 341, 345 (Fla. 2005).

- "In regard to realty, a *devise* of land cannot be adeemed under the common law except by conveyance of the same land." *In re Estate of Frank*, 189 P.3d 834, 839 (Wash. Ct. App. 2008).

A *bequest* disposes of personal property other than money, although the modern tendency is to include testamentary gifts of money as well as gifts of other personalty—e.g.: "She died in 1925, leaving a will in which she 'asked' her husband 'after his death' to *bequeath* the paintings to the Gallery." *Republic of Austria v. Altmann*, 541 U.S. 677, 681–82 (2004) (per Stevens, J.).

Legacy is the more proper term for a clause disposing of money. Each of the terms may refer not only to the clause in the will, but to the gift itself. See **bequest & will.**

devise, vb.; bequeath. In the traditional legal idiom, one *bequeaths* personal property and *devises* real property. E.g.:

- "In his will, Kenneth purported to *devise* his land and his shares in the Long Company to his four children." *Plains Commerce Bank v. Long Family Land & Cattle Co.*, 440 F.Supp.2d 1070, 1073 (D.S.D. 2006).
- "For estate-planning purposes: the Flecks could *devise* the land to their heirs without the heirs' having to assume responsibility for the operations of the business." *Jarl Invs., LP v. Fleck*, 937 A.2d 1113, 1116 n.1 (Pa. Super. Ct. 2007).

But the restriction to real property has not always obtained: the *OED* quotes an Englishman who in 1347 *devised* his gold ring to a lady companion. Similar usages appeared up to the 18th century.

Under both the Restatement of Property and the Uniform Probate Code (in the U.S.), neither of which distinguishes in terminology between real and personal property, to dispose of any property by will is to *devise* it, the recipients being *devisees* even if the subject of the disposition is personal property. In England, however, *devise* is said to refer properly only to dispositions of real property (*OCL1 & CDL*).

It should not escape our attention that the simple verb *give* almost always suffices as well as, and with less confusion than, *bequeath* or *devise*. See **give, devise, and bequeath.**

The general nonlegal sense of *devise* (= to plan or invent) is also used in legal contexts:

- "The Rule [in Shelley's Case] was *devised* in feudal times to insure feudal landlords the receipt of their rents from their feoffs." *Sybert v. Sybert*, 254 S.W.2d 999, 1001 (Tex. 1953).
- "Administrative rules and regulations which exceed the scope of the statutory enactment they were *devised* to implement are invalid and must be struck down." *Haole v. State*, 140 P.3d 377, 385 (Haw. 2006).
- "The statutes in both cases were *devised* to exempt ongoing periodic wage payments and had only limited relevance in bankruptcy." *In re Sparks*, 410 B.R. 602, 605 (Bankr. S.D. Ohio 2009).

See **bequeath.**

devisee; legatee; heir. These words have traditionally been distinguished, although in practice *devisee* and *legatee* are often used interchangeably. A *devisee* is the recipient of a *devise*. (See **devise**.) *Devisee of land* might once have been considered redundant, but arguably is not redundant in light of the extended meaning in modern legal usage. And the phrasing dates back at least to the 19th century—e.g.: "We are of opinion that this case falls within the general rule, and that the property in question passes to the residuary *devisees*." *Bigelow v. Gillott*, 123 Mass. 102, 107 (1877).

A *legatee* is one who receives a legacy. It is sometimes opposed to *devisee*. E.g.:

- "Traywick was neither a *legatee* or *devisee* under the will . . . and had no right to propound the will for probate." *Sowell v. Sowell's Adm'r*, 41 Ala. 359 (1867).
- "To be an intestate heir is to enjoy an unearned, unchosen status; although the testator can choose a different *devisee* or *legatee*, that position may be similarly unearned or unchosen, from the beneficiary's point of view." Diane J. Klein, *"Go West, Disappointed Heir,"* 13 Lewis & Clark L. Rev. 209, 212 (2009).

An *heir* takes by inheritance (or *descent*) rather than through a will or gift (by purchase); so *heir* is not properly used of a *devisee* or *legatee*. See **descent**.

deviser; devisor; divisor. A *deviser* is one who invents or contrives. A *devisor* is one who disposes of property by will (usu. real property)—e.g.: "The early law of Maryland . . . required that wills devising real property be in writing, signed by the party or someone in his presence and by his express direction, and be attested and subscribed in the presence of the *devisor* by three or four credible witnesses." *Wright v. Nugent*, 328 A.2d 362, 368 (Md. Ct. Spec. App. 1974). *Divisor* is a mathematical term referring to the number by which another number is divided.

For the distinction between *devisor* and *testator*, see **testator (B)**.

devoir /di-**vwahr**/ is a far-fetched, fanciful term when used in place of *duty*, *responsibility*, or *burden*. E.g.:

- "The ALJ's findings were reasonable, responsive to the proof (or the lack thereof) as adduced at the hearing, and consistent with the allocation of the *devoir* [read *burden*] of persuasion." *Migneault v. Heckler*, 632 F.Supp. 153, 159 (D.R.I. 1985).
- "The objectors . . . must carry the *devoir* [read *burden*] of persuasion." *F.T.C. v. Standard Fin. Mgmt. Corp.*, 830 F.2d 404, 411 (1st Cir. 1987).
- "Following a hearing, an immigration judge . . . ruled from the bench . . . that DHS had carried the *devoir* [read *burden*] of persuasion and established that the petitioner was removable." *Peralta v. Holder*, 567 F.3d 31, 32–33 (1st Cir. 2009).

Those examples are all drawn from the sesquipedalian opinions of Judge Bruce Selya of the First Circuit. For more on his penchant to use oddly arcane vocabulary, see Garner, "Smelling of the Inkhorn," in *Garner on Language and Writing* 519 (2009).

devolution; *devolvement. The second is a NEEDLESS VARIANT. *Devolution* means (1) "the passing of the power or authority of one person or body to another" (*OED*); or (2) "the causing of anything to descend or fall upon (anyone)" (*id.*). E.g.:

- (Sense 1) "The circumstance that the settlor specifically reserved a power to appoint a taker means, if it means anything, that she wanted to affirm and emphasize that she desired to retain control of her property up to the time of her death and to direct its *devolution* thereafter." *In re Burchell's Estate*, 87 N.E.2d 293, 298 (N.Y. 1949) (Fuld, J., dissenting).
- (Sense 1) "The reasoning for so deciding is that *devolution* of the property of a decedent is controlled entirely by the statutes of descent and distribution." *In re Mahoney's Estate*, 220 A.2d 475, 477 (Vt. 1966).
- (Sense 2) "The boundary between these two constitutional clauses is blurred by *devolution* of federal policy-making authority to states." *American Greyhound Racing, Inc. v. Hull*, 146 F.Supp.2d 1012, 1080 (D. Ariz. 2001).
- (Sense 2) "Constitutions exist in America to arrest the *devolution* of power over certain key features of life." *Sogg v. White*, 860 N.E.2d 163, 176 (Ohio Ct. Com. Pl. 2006).

devolutive; *devolutionary. The first is the preferred adjective corresponding to the noun *devolution*—e.g.:

- "The Viators took a *devolutive* appeal from the judgments against them in the trial court." *Ragland v. Viator*, 426 So.2d 231, 233 (La. Ct. App. 1983).
- "On June 4, 2005, Entergy took a *devolutive* appeal from that judgment, which is still pending." *Joseph v. Entergy*, 972 So.2d 1230, 1233 (La. Ct. App. 2007).
- "Recent *devolutionary* [read *devolutive*] changes in all major public benefit programs have also expanded states' ability to compete meaningfully with one another." David A. Super, *Privatization, Policy Paralysis, and the Poor*, 96 Cal. L. Rev. 393, 446 (2008).

Devolutionary is a NEEDLESS VARIANT.

Louisiana law allows two types of appeals, *devolutive* and *suspensive*. A *suspensive* appeal suspends the effect of the execution of an appealable order or judgment (La. Code Civ. P. arts. 2087, 2123 (2009)). Accordingly, a *suspensive* appeal requires a security bond for the judgment and court costs, while a *devolutive* appeal requires security for court costs alone (*id.* art. 2124).

devolve = (1) [transitive] to pass on (duties, rights, or powers) to another; or (2) [intransitive] to pass to another by transmission or succession. In sense 2, the verb takes the preposition *on*, *upon*, or *to*. E.g.:

- "The responsibility for prosecuting criminal cases at the trial level *devolves upon* [or *on* or *to*] the state's attorney by reason of his constitutional mandate as implemented by statute." *Sinclair v. State*, 340 A.2d 359, 364 (Md. Ct. Spec. App. 1975).
- "The majority's summary adoption of a code of procedure for video surveillance and its unskeptical deference to the rationale of other circuits is, I respectfully suggest, not consistent with the responsibility that *devolves upon* [or *on* or *to*] us as a court established under Article III of the Constitution." *U.S. v. Koyomejian*, 970 F.2d 536, 551 (9th Cir. 1992) (Kozinski, J., concurring).

- "This peculiar relationship requires that a certain responsibility *devolves upon* [or *on* or *to*] States to ensure the prosperity of its air transport industry and to prevent the industry from collapsing." Ruwantissa Abeyratne, *Investing in Air Transport—A Prudent Move?*, 34 Transp. L.J. 327, 349 (2007).

See **bequeath (A).**

*devolvement. See **devolution.**

devotee. See -EE.

devotion. See **fidelity.**

diagnose. See BACK-FORMATIONS.

diagnosis; prognosis. Courts recognize the important distinction between these words. A *diagnosis* is an analysis of one's present bodily condition with reference to disease or disorder. A *prognosis* is the projected future course of a present disease or disorder. E.g.:

- "As to the *diagnoses* and *prognoses* of the physicians, they are not so clear and consistent as to validate removing the issue of arbitrary and capricious denial of the maintenance and cure from the jury." *Tullos v. Resource Drilling, Inc.*, 750 F.2d 380, 388 (5th Cir. 1985).
- "These records contain charts, test results, *diagnoses*, and *prognoses* of several physicians at the Veterans Administration—including the physicians whom Mr. Peed himself referred to as his primary treating physicians." *Peed v. Sullivan*, 778 F.Supp. 1241, 1243 (E.D.N.Y. 1991).
- "Legislation proposed in several states . . . would authorize physician-assisted suicide but require two qualified physicians to confirm the patient's *diagnosis, prognosis*, and competence." *Washington v. Glucksberg*, 521 U.S. 702, 785 (1997) (Souter, J., concurring).
- "Modern society's current stage of evolution necessitates the recognition that medical science has the means to accurately *diagnose* the PVS patient and deliver a *prognosis* with medical certainty." Justin A. Gonzalez, *Modern Medicine, Murder, and the Mind*, 30 J. Legal Med. 529, 541 (2009).

See **prognosis.**

diagonal. See PUNCTUATION (N).

dialogue; dialog; duologue. *Dialogue* = (1) a conversation between two or more persons; or (2) the exchange of ideas. *Dialog* is a variant spelling predominant in computing contexts. (Cf. **catalogue.**) *Duologue*, a rather uncommon term, means "a conversation between two persons only."

dicta. See **dictum.**

*dictatrix. See SEXISM (C).

diction = (1) enunciation; distinctness of pronunciation; or (2) word choice. Often sense 2 is overlooked. This book addresses in large measure problems of legal diction.

dictum. A. Full Phrase. *Dictum* is a shortened form of *obiter dictum* (= a nonbinding, incidental opinion on a point of law given by a judge in the course of a written opinion delivered in support of a judgment). The full phrase still occasionally appears: "Even if that determination were technically *obiter dictum*, it was not a stray remark on an issue not presented to it." *Dodson v. University of Ark. for Med. Scis.*, 601 F.3d 750, 755 (8th Cir. 2010). Judge Posner has aptly defined *dictum* as "a statement in a judicial opinion that could have been deleted without seriously impairing the analytical foundations of the holding—that, being peripheral, may not have received the full and careful consideration of the court that uttered it." *Sarnoff v. American Home Prods. Corp.*, 798 F.2d 1075, 1084 (7th Cir. 1986).

British legal texts use *dictum* as well as *obiter* as the shortened form of *obiter dictum*. E.g.:

- "The view of Lord Tenterden C.J. in *Collier v. Hicks*, although *obiter*, has always been accepted as authoritative on this aspect of the law." *McKenzie v. McKenzie*, [1971] P.33, 34 (C.A.).
- "In considering the *dicta* cited to us from the cases to which we were referred[,] we bore in mind the importance . . . of interpreting judicial pronouncements in the context of the questions which the court had to decide." *Ball (Inspector of Taxes) v. National & Grindlay's Bank Ltd.*, [1973] Ch. 127, 133–34 (C.A.).

See **obiter dictum.**

B. Types Other than *obiter dictum*. *Obiter dictum* is not the only type of dictum. *Black's* notes also *simplex dictum* (= *ipse dixit*) and *gratis dictum* (= a statement made by a party, but not obligatorily) (*Black's Law Dictionary* 519 [9th ed. 2009]). One can safely assert that *dictum* as used in modern legal writing almost never stands for either of these highly specialized terms. See *ipse dixit*.

Still another type—an important one—is *judicial dictum*, which refers to an opinion by a court on a question that is directly involved, briefed, and argued by counsel, and even passed on by the court, but that is not essential to the decision. *See Cerro Metal Prods. v. Marshall*, 620 F.2d 964, 978 n.39 (3d Cir. 1980). So *judicial dictum* differs from *obiter dictum* because it results from considered controversy, whereas *obiter dictum* is more in the nature of a peripheral, off-the-cuff judicial remark. See Peter J. Bonani, Note, *Judicial Dictum Versus Obiter Dictum*, 16 Temple U.L.Q. 427, 431 (1942). And *judicial dictum* carries more weight: "*Judicial dictum* has been held binding precedent even by modern day 'liberal courts.' *Obiter dicta* [read *Obiter dictum*] on the other hand . . . is not binding authority though it may be persuasive." *Wolf v. Meister-Neiberg, Inc.*, 551 N.E.2d 353, 355 (Ill. App. Ct. 1990).

C. Number. *Dictum* is the singular form of *dicta*, which in law are "remarks made in a judicial opinion that are not binding law." The plural form *dicta* is frequently misused as a singular noun—e.g.:

- "This was *dicta* [read *dictum*]." William F. Walsh, *A Treatise on Equity* 446 n.78 (1930).
- "Such a statement is *dicta* [read *dictum*], and . . . a federal court is bound to follow state court *dicta*." *In re Stutterheim*, 109 B.R. 1006, 1009 (Bankr. D. Kan. 1988).

Able writers generally have no difficulty getting the number correct—e.g.:

- "Pioneer contends that the Constitution of the United States compels us to follow here the *dictum* in the College of California case; it is settled, however, that judicial decisions may be overruled and *dicta* disapproved without violating either the due process clause or the contract clause of the Constitution." *In re Los Angeles County Pioneer Soc'y*, 257 P.2d 1, 9 (Cal. 1953) (per Traynor, J.)
- "The numerous *dicta* in this case *were* repeated some years later and gained force in the repetition." Theodore F.T. Plucknett, *A Concise History of the Common Law* 467 (5th ed. 1956).
- "Fully considered *dicta* in the House of Lords *are* usually treated as more weighty than the *ratio* of a judge at first instance in the High Court." P.S. Atiyah, *Law and Modern Society* 135 (1983).
- "Later *dicta*, as well as a decision at first instance, *support* Romer L.J.'s view." G.H. Treitel, *The Law of Contract* 893 (8th ed. 1991).

D. Articles with. In the legal idiom, *dictum* generally does not take an article unless the article is acting as a DEICTIC TERM. E.g.:

- "The *dictum* in the principal case that the interest in the community royalty of the owner of a tract surrendered by the community lessee is a right in gross is supportable since . . . there is no longer any reversionary interest to which it could be appurtenant." Charles C. Loveless Jr., *Oil and Gas—Community Lease*, 25 Tex. L. Rev. 315, 316–17 (1947).
- "Thus, the *dicta* in the present case is based on the *dictum* in the pre-OEC *Chandler* case." *State ex rel. Juvenile Dep't of Tillamook County v. Beasley*, 840 P.2d 78, 86 (Or. 1992).

Usually, however, the article is unnecessary:

- "The reservation was not an attempt to reserve title to minerals in place, and the decision of the court that such minerals can be owned, or are owned, by the land owner, is *a pure dictum* [omit *a*]." D. Edward Greer, *The Ownership of Petroleum Oil and Natural Gas in Place*, 1 Tex. L. Rev. 162, 172 (1923).
- "The court's cursory treatment of *Hibbs* may well be attributable to the fact that assertion quoted above is pure *dictum* [because] the court then dismissed the lawsuit for failure to state a claim upon which relief can be granted." *University of Tex. at El Paso v. Herrera*, 281 S.W.3d 575, 591 (Tex. App.—El Paso 2008) (Carr, J., dissenting).

In short, the word is sometimes a count noun but is usually not.

E. Lay Sense. In general nonlegal contexts, *dictum* often means (1) "a statement of opinion or belief held to be authoritative because of the dignity of the person making it"; or (2) "a familiar rule." In these lay senses, *dictum* takes an article or another determiner. E.g., in sense 2:

- "It is *a* familiar *dictum* in anatomy that the veins in the great cavities of the body have no valves." Charles A. Todd, *How the Iliac Arteries Act as Valves upon the Venous Flow into the Inferior Vena Cava*, 7 JAMA 600–01 (1886).
- "'Do no harm.' While *that* familiar *dictum* was never part of the Hippocratic oath, it has long been considered one of the precepts of medicine." Elaine Schmidt, *Healing Healthcare*, iSixSigma, Jan.–Feb. 2008, at 1.

dictum page. See **pinpoint citation**.

dietitian; *dietician. The first spelling is preferred.

die without issue. This phrase is ambiguous: does it mean to die without ever having had issue, or to die without having surviving issue? Further, of course, the word *issue* is itself the source of much AMBIGUITY. See **issue (E)**.

differ. See **differ from**.

difference. See **differential (A)**.

different from; different than. Prefer *different from*. The word *than* implies a comparison, i.e., a matter of degree; but *differences* are ordinarily qualitative, not quantitative, and the adjective *different* is not strictly comparative. E.g.: "Minors are treated differently *than* [read *from*] adults in [the criminal justice system]." *People v. Christopherson*, 879 N.E.2d 1035, 1041 (Ill. App. Ct. 2007).

Still, it is indisputable that *different than* is sometimes idiomatic, and even useful since *different from* often cannot be substituted for it—e.g.: "No federal purpose would be impeded by requiring *different* federal venue provisions for diversity actions *than* for federal-question actions." Stanley E. Cox, *Jurisdiction, Venue, and Aggregation of Contacts*, 42 Ark. L. Rev. 211, 283 n.235 (1989). Also, *different than* may sometimes usefully begin clauses, where attempting to use *different from* would be so awkward as to require another construction: "The record also establishes that Wakefield is a *different* person mentally and emotionally *than* he was before his loss of hearing." *Wakefield v. U.S.*, 765 F.2d 55, 57 (5th Cir. 1985).

When *from* nicely fills the slot of *than*, that idiom is to be preferred—e.g.:

- "The fact that the injury occurred in a *different* manner *than* [read *from*] that which might have been expected does not prevent the chauffeur's negligence from being in law the cause of the injury." *Palsgraf v. Long Island R.R.*, 162 N.E. 99, 104 (N.Y. 1928) (Andrews, J., dissenting).
- "If he were to survive a motion to dismiss for failure to state a claim, plaintiff would be seeking adjudication of defendants' alleged wrongdoing that is of a *different* nature *than* [read *from*] that in *Ramirez I*." *Ramirez v. Brooklyn AIDS Task Force*, 175 F.R.D. 423, 429 (E.D.N.Y. 1997).
- "In general, the scholarship notes that voluntary desegregation can pose stigmatic harms, although the voluntary desegregation that the scholarship addresses is of a *different* nature *than* [read *from*] what is implemented today." Derek W. Black, *In Defense of Voluntary Desegregation*, 44 Wake Forest L. Rev. 107, 133 (2009).

The *Oxford Guide* (p. 102) notes that when the adverb *differently* is used, *than* is "especially common . . . and has been employed by good writers since the 17th century" <he did the job differently than she did>. But when *from* is an idiomatic possibility without major surgery on the sentence, it's the preferred word—e.g.:

- "Minors are treated *differently than* [read *differently from*] adults in a variety of ways." Jeffrey M. Banks, *In re Stanford*, 48 S.D. L. Rev. 327, 353 (2003).
- "The Court has suggested, to the contrary, that immigration law operates no *differently than* [read *differently from*] any other power of Congress, and that over no other area is the legislative power more 'complete' than immigration." Adam B. Cox & Cristina M. Rodriguez, *The President and Immigration Law*, 119 Yale L.J. 458, 461 (2009).

Different to is a common British construction, unobjectionable when used by British writers—e.g.: "The agreement was therefore *different* in kind *to* that originally contemplated." *Graves v. Graves*, [2008] L. & T.R. 15 (C.A.).

Writers occasionally use *different* superfluously with *other than*: "The right of the district court to require the commissioners' court, by mandamus, to place a *different* [delete] valuation on the property of the railway company *other than* the value theretofore placed on said property by the commissioners' court is discussed in the case of *Dillon v. Bare*." *State v. Chicago, Rock Island & Gulf Ry.*, 263 S.W. 249, 250 (Tex. 1924).

differentia (= a distinguishing mark or characteristic) is a technical biological term that was long ago appropriated by legal writers, although often it is used merely to mean "a distinction." The term is more common in BrE than in AmE. E.g.:

- "The only *differentia* that can exist must arise, if at all, out of the fact that the acts done are the joint acts of several capitalists, and not of one capitalist only." *Mogul S.S. Co., Ltd. v. McGregor Gow & Co.*, [1889] L.R. 23 Q.B.D. 598, 617 (C.A.).
- "The question in every case is whether the tribunal in question has similar attributes to a court of justice or acts in a manner similar to that in which such courts act. This of necessity was a *differentia* which is not capable of very precise limitation." *Trapp v. Mackie*, [1978] S.C. 283.

The plural is *differentiae.* Cf. **distinguish.**

differential. A. For *difference*. Traditionally, the noun *differential* had only specialized mathematical, mechanical, and biological senses. As a popularized technicality, it was extended to mean "a difference in wage or salary"—e.g.: "Payment [may be] made pursuant to . . . a *differential* based on any other factor other [*sic*] than sex." Equal Pay Act, 29 U.S.C. § 206(d)(1) (1988) (emphasis added).

But the intrusion of this word into the domain of *difference* should stop there. The following use of *differential* was ill-advised: "Most of the foreign news reaches this country . . . at the City of New York, and because of this, and of time *differentials* [read *differences*] due to the earth's rotation, the distribution of news matter throughout the country is principally from east to west." *International News Serv. v. Associated Press*, 248 U.S. 215, 238 (1918) (per Pitney, J.).

B. As Adjective. *Differential*, adj., = (1) of, exhibiting, or depending on a difference; or (2) constituting a specific difference. The adjective is not nearly as often misused as the noun (see (A) above):

- "Under equal protection doctrine, *differential* treatment of parties is constitutional only if adequately related to a sufficient governmental interest." *Tele-Communications of Key West, Inc. v. U.S.*, 757 F.2d 1330, 1340 (D.C. Cir. 1985).
- "The *differential* recognition of the importance of place (to human and non-human systems) is stark and suggests that there is a kind of human frontier—largely unexplored territory—when it comes to place in our thinking about managing marine ecosystems." Seth Macinko, *Fishing Communities as Special Places*, 13 Ocean & Coastal L.J. 71, 72 (2007).

DIFFERENTIATION is the linguistic process by which similar words, usually those having a common etymology, gradually diverge in meaning, each taking on a distinct sense. An appreciation of this linguistic virtue is essential to the true stylist. Meanwhile, that appreciation can lead to a continual disenchantment with the forces that are exerted on language.

Richard Grant White, a 19th-century usage critic, extolled the virtue of *differentiation* while condemning the vice of SLIPSHOD EXTENSION: "The desynonymizing tendency of language enriches it by producing words adapted to the expression of various delicate shades of meaning. But the promiscuous use of two words each of which has a meaning peculiar to itself, by confounding distinctions impoverishes language, and deprives it at once of range and of power." Richard G. White, *Words and Their Uses, Past and Present* 161 (2d ed. 1872).

Legal scholars, too, have warned of what happens when writers lose any sense of differentiation: "If two words have each a precise sense the one including the other, as sanctions are a class of motives, to confuse them is to impoverish the language." W.W. Buckland, *Some Reflections on Jurisprudence* 89 (1945).

different than; differently than. See **different from.**

differ from; differ with. To *differ from* is to be unlike, whereas to *differ with* is to express a divergent opinion—e.g.:

- *Differ from*: "With respect to legacies out of personal estate, the civil law, which in this respect has been adopted by courts of equity, *differs* in some respects *from* the common law in its treatment of conditions precedent." 2 Charles Sweet, *Jarmin on Wills* 15 (6th ed. 1910).
- *Differ with*: "Justice Scalia *differs with* our assessment as to the likelihood that Pap's may resume its nude dancing operation." *City of Erie v. Pap's A.M.*, 529 U.S. 277, 287–88 (2000) (per O'Connor, J.).

difficult of, an archaic construction, is still common in legal prose. E.g.:

- "It had also previously indicated that neither country should take any action, and should ensure that no action was taken, which might aggravate or extend the existing dispute or render it more *difficult of solution.*" Matthew Lippman, *The Convention on the Prevention and Punishment of the Crime of Genocide,* 15 Ariz. J. Int'l & Comp. L. 415, 500 (1998).
- "It must be conceded that a DNA database may be, indeed, already has demonstrated that it may be[,] a valuable tool for solving crimes that otherwise would be *difficult of solution* or would not be solved and could be a boon to those falsely accused, by exonerating them, as it has been to some already." *State v. Raines,* 857 A.2d 19, 64 (Md. 2004).

Formerly this phrasing was seen in literary as well as in legal writing. See **of (c).**

*****digamy.** See **bigamy.**

digital is commonly used as the adjective corresponding to *finger* —e.g.:

- "William Caldwell [argues] . . . that . . . officials subjected him to a *digital* rectal search that violated his fourth, fifth, and eighth amendment rights." *U.S. v. Caldwell,* 750 F.2d 341, 342 (5th Cir. 1984).
- "The issue of *digital* rape was raised at trial." *State v. Roden,* 380 N.W.2d 669, 670 (S.D. 1986).

dignitas is a preposterous LATINISM in place of the ordinary word *dignity*—e.g.: "Indeed, since it was never confirmed, it never possessed the *dignitas* [read *dignity*] of a judgment or order." *Rothman v. RE/MAX of N.Y., Inc.,* 703 N.Y.S.2d 666, 669 (Sup. Ct. 1999).

dignity exists in law in a sense obsolete in nonlegal contexts. It is used to mean "rank; magnitude," esp. in the phrase *of constitutional dignity.* E.g.:

- "A statute and a constitution, [although] of unequal *dignity,* are both 'laws,' and each rest upon the will of the people." *State v. Brantley,* 74 So. 662, 666 (Miss. 1917).
- "The constitutional requirement of substantial equality and fair process can only be attained where counsel acts in the role of an active advocate in behalf of his client, as opposed to that of amicus curiae; the no-merit letter and the procedure it triggers do not reach that *dignity.*" *Anders v. California,* 386 U.S. 738, 744 (1967) (per Clark, J.).
- "As one moves away from the paradigmatic case, the sense of a wrong of constitutional *dignity,* and of a need for a federal remedy, attenuates." *Lauth v. McCollum,* 424 F.3d 631, 633 (7th Cir. 2005).

*****dijudicate.** See **judge,** vb.

dilapidation. So spelled; ***delapidation* is a common misspelling.

dilatory (= tending to cause delay) is commonly used by lawyers <dilatory pleas or exceptions>, but is little known to nonlawyers.

dilemma = a choice between two unpleasant or difficult alternatives. This word should not be used by SLIPSHOD EXTENSION for *plight* or *predicament.* Originally a Greek word meaning "two horns," the word often appears in the CLICHÉ *horns of a dilemma,* but at least the cliché shows ETYMOLOGICAL AWARENESS— e.g.: "I think that Judge Hand would agree that often— though not always—both branches of the antinomy can be served and the *horns of the dilemma* avoided by eschewing a woodenly logical reading of the written law." Archibald Cox, *The Role of the Supreme Court: Judicial Activism or Self-Restraint?,* 47 Md. L. Rev. 118, 124 (1987). Cf. **Hobson's choice.**

The adjective is *dilemmatic.*

dilutee = an unskilled worker added to a staff of skilled workers. See -EE.

diminished, n., in BrE, means "a criminal defense— recognized at common law in Scotland from 1867 and introduced into English law in 1957—that allows one who is on the borderline of insanity to receive a comparatively light sentence." The word is short for *diminished responsibility*—e.g.: "The defence of '*diminished*' (as it is sometimes abbreviated in informal speech) has the superficial attraction of offering an escape from the mad–bad dichotomy." Glanville Williams, *Textbook of Criminal Law* 624 (1978).

diminution; *diminishment. The second is a NEEDLESS VARIANT. "Another consequence of the slide of our adversary system into the police inquisition has been the *diminishment* [read *diminution*] of defence activity." Patrick Devlin, *The Judge* 74 (1979). *Diminution* /dim-i-**nyoo**-shən/ or /**noo**-shən/ is often mispronounced /dim-yoo-**nish**-ən/, by metathesis, and sometimes is erroneously spelled **dimunition.*

diminutive, meaning "small," is not pronounced /di-**min**-ə-tiv/, but rather /di-**min**-yə-tiv/, with a liquid -*u*-.

*****dimunition.** See **diminution.**

diplomat; *diplomatist. The second is a NEEDLESS VARIANT sometimes (but less and less often) used in BrE.

direct is often used as an ellipsis for *direct examination*—e.g.: "His testimony on *direct* did not relate to any inculpatory or exculpatory comments by Mr. P." *U.S. v. Chanya,* 723 F.2d 374, 376 (5th Cir. 1984). Cf. **cross** & **redirect.**

direct cause. See CAUSATION (A).

directed verdict; instructed verdict. The phrases are synonymous. The Federal Rules of Civil Procedure use *directed verdict.* Both phrases exemplify HYPALLAGE, since the jury, and not the verdict, is what is directed or instructed. See **no case.**

direct estoppel. See **collateral estoppel (B).**

direct evidence; original evidence. Both of these phrases are used as antonyms of *hearsay evidence* and *circumstantial evidence* (or *indirect evidence*). *Direct evidence* is more common. As an opposite of *hearsay,* it means "a witness's statement that he or she perceived a fact in issue by one of the five senses or that he or she was in a particular physical or mental state." As an antonym of *circumstantial evidence*, the phrase *direct evidence* means "evidence that proves a fact without any inference or presumption."

It would be helpful by way of DIFFERENTIATION to use *original evidence* as an antonym of *hearsay evidence*, and *direct evidence* as an antonym of *circumstantial evidence*.

direct examination; examination-in-chief. The second is a variant, chiefly BrE, of the first. Though *cross-examination* is so hyphenated, *direct examination*, by convention, is not. See **direct** & **cross-examination.**

direction. See **jury instruction.**

directional. See **directory.**

directorial, not **directoral*, is the adjective corresponding to *director*—e.g.: "The rule's detractors recognize that it is not a complete bar to judicial review of *directoral* [read *directorial*] decision-making." Julia V. Parry, *Special Litigation Committees and the Business Judgment Rule*, 14 Conn. L. Rev. 193, 198 (1981).

directors' and officers' insurance. So written, with the possessives. The phrase is often, in speech and writing, shortened to *D & O insurance*.

directory; imperative. These words are distinguished for purposes of statutory interpretation: "Mandatory provisions [in a statute] have . . . frequently been classified as either *imperative* (when failure to comply renders all subsequent proceedings void) or *directory* (when the subsequent proceedings are valid, though the persons failing to carry out the action enjoined [i.e., mandated] by Parliament may sometimes be punishable)." *F. v. F.*, [1971] P. 1, 11. E.g.: "It has been held that a violation is a substantial and not a mere technical error, inasmuch as such a statute is *imperative* and not *directory*." 16 *Ruling Case Law* 250 (William M. McKinney & Burdett A. Rich eds., 1917).

In the U.S., frequently, the distinction is rather different: *directory* is opposed to *mandatory* and is only a little stronger than *precatory*—e.g.:

- "Statutes [that] regulate and prescribe the time in which public officers shall perform specified duties are generally regarded as *directory* [only]." *Federal Crude Oil Co. v. Yount-Lee Oil Co.*, 52 S.W.2d 56, 61 (Tex. 1932).
- "The written-reasons requirement is a *directory* provision, and therefore, a zoning application is not automatically approved when a government agency fails to state in writing the reasons supporting its denial within the 60-day period." *Johnson v. Cook County*, 786 N.W.2d 291, 296 (Minn. 2010).

In the following sentence, *directional* (= of or relating to, or indicating, spatial direction) is wrongly used for *directory*: "The sentence is a *directional* [read *directory*] provision indicating when and how she is to receive the payments." *Coker v. Coker*, 650 S.W.2d 391, 395 (Tex. 1983) (Spears, J., dissenting).

****directress; **directrix.** See SEXISM (C).

dirt lawyer is a jocular, self-effacing dysphemism in AmE for a real-estate lawyer.

disability. A. And *liability*; *inability*. These words, which overlap only slightly but are sometimes confounded, are best sharply distinguished. *Disability* = (1) the lack of ability to perform some function; or (2) incapacity in the eyes of the law. *Liability* = (1) probability; (2) a pecuniary obligation; (3) a drawback; or (4) a duty or burden <liability for military service>. *Inability* = the lack of power or means.

B. And *disablement*. *Disablement* = (1) the action of crippling or incapacitating; or (2) the imposition of a legal disability. Here sense 1 applies: "Feinberg's harm principle allows a person to consent to all kinds of gross harms. A person might consent to death, permanent *disablement* of a severe kind such as blinding, and so forth." Dennis J. Baker, *The Moral Limits of Consent as a Defense in the Criminal Law*, 12 New Crim. L. Rev. 93, 104 (2009).

disable. See **disenable.*

disabling statute (= a statute that curbs or limits certain rights) is an antonym of *enabling statute* only in the older sense of the latter phrase—i.e., a statute that grants certain rights. See **enabling statute.**

disadvantage, vb., appears regularly in legal writing, but generally only the past-participial form *disadvantaged* appears in lay writing, usually functioning as an adjective <disadvantaged student>. Following are examples of typical legal usage:

- "The State may no more *disadvantage* any particular group by making it more difficult to enact legislation in its behalf than it may dilute any person's vote." *Hunter v. Erickson*, 393 U.S. 385, 393 (1969) (per White, J.).
- "Tomas maintains the statute *disadvantages* or discriminates against one class of individuals because of their physical condition." *Tomas v. Conco Food Distribs.*, 702 So.2d 944, 947 (La. Ct. App. 1997).
- "Defendant contends that the new statute *disadvantages* him by eliminating the thirty-year parole disqualifier." *State v. Fortin*, 969 A.2d 1133, 1139 (N.J. 2009).

disaffirmation; disaffirmance. For the word meaning "repudiation," the distinction drawn at *affirmance* would recommend the form *disaffirmation*. The *COD* recommends *-tion*, but *W11* records only *-ance*, a common form in AmE. Try as we might for consistency, we are unlikely to achieve it here: *disaffirmation* is better, but *disaffirmance* cannot be strongly criticized. E.g.:

- "The defense of fraud at law was ineffective in cases where there was nothing to return unless a rescission or *disaffirmance* of the contract was established." William F. Walsh, *A Treatise on Equity* 497–98 (1930).
- "A guarantor for a minor remains bound although the minor principal may be discharged by *disaffirmance*." *Gervis v. Knapp*, 43 N.Y.S.2d 849, 850 (Sup. Ct. 1943).

- "Although the remedy under the Warranty Act is not the remedy of equitable rescission, it is based on a *disaffirmance* of the contract, while the U.C.C. remedy for breach of warranty is based on affirmance of the contract." *Genetti v. Caterpillar, Inc.*, 621 N.W.2d 529, 547 (Neb. 2001).

See **affirmance**.

disappoint (of) (in). *Disappoint* is used in legal contexts in a sense rare in lay contexts, namely, "to deprive; to frustrate one's expectations." E.g.:

- "The courts will not *disappoint* the interests of those for whose benefit he is called upon to exercise [the power]." *Daniel v. Brown*, 159 S.E. 209, 211 (Va. 1931).
- "A court of equity will then sequester the benefits intended for the electing beneficiary, in order to secure compensation to those persons whom his election *disappoints*." 2 John Norton Pomeroy, *A Treatise on Equity Jurisprudence* § 517, at 462 (Spencer W. Symons ed., 5th ed. 1941).

Usually the term *disappointed* refers to heirs who take neither an intestate share of an estate nor a share by will. E.g.:

- "The testator could not have intended the objects of the power to be *disappointed* of his bounty, by the neglect of the donee to exercise such power in their favour." 1 Thomas Jarman, *A Treatise on Wills* 651 (Charles Sweet ed., 6th ed. 1910).
- "He is known in the law as a *disappointed* legatee, and the doctrine of acceleration of remainders should not be adopted at the expense of *disappointed* legatees." *Sellick v. Sellick*, 173 N.W. 609, 609 (Mich. 1919).

To be *disappointed in* a thing, as opposed to *of* it, is to have received or attained it but to consider it as not measuring up to one's expectations.

Often *disappointed* is used as a past-participial adjective: "An NHS patient has no such choice: nor did a *disappointed* legatee suing a solicitor for negligence in respect of the preparation of a will." John Murphy, *Street on Torts* 179 (12th ed. 2007).

disapprobation, an especially FORMAL WORD meaning "disapproval," is perhaps allowable in weighty contexts—e.g.:

- "On the opening of the cause, Lord Kenyon expressed his *disapprobation* of the action, but . . . his Lordship permitted the cause to proceed." *Ashley v. Harrison*, [1793] 170 E.R. 148.
- "Inquisitorial process occasionally was invoked in other contexts, but generally only as a loose form of *disapprobation*." David Alan Sklansky, *Anti-Inquisitorialism*, 122 Harv. L. Rev. 1634, 1673 (2009).

But in ordinary prose, this noun—like so many other BURIED VERBS ending in *-tion*—leads to top-heaviness. And when denoting the disapproving feelings of ordinary people, it seems especially out of place—e.g.: "Employees, because of their economic dependence upon the Company, may feel the need to sign the petition in order to curry favor with or avoid *disapprobation* [read *disapproval*] by Company officials." *Texaco, Inc. v. N.L.R.B.*, 722 F.2d 1226, 1233 (5th Cir. 1984). See **approbation**.

disapprove. A. And *deprecate*. Both verbs mean "to regard with disfavor" or "to express a negative sentiment about something by objecting to it, usu. on grounds of rules or mores." *Disapprove* connotes displeasure based on principled grounds (ethical, moral, legal, social, etc.) and an unwillingness to accede or acquiesce <the administration disapproves of "wilding" and of "blacking out" as harmful to the student body as a whole>. *Deprecate*, except in the phrase *self-deprecating* (see **deprecate**), connotes regret or apology in the objection <Justice Brown has long deprecated his colleagues' tendency to use legislative history in statutory construction>.

B. Transitive and Intransitive Uses. *Disapprove*, like *approve*, may be transitive (without *of*) <the council disapproved the plans> as well as intransitive (with *of*) <many readers disapproved of the editorial>. The transitive uses appear far more often in legal than in nonlegal writing—e.g.:

- "While we *disapprove* the result of the district court's decision in the instant case, we approve its legal reasoning." *In re Forfeiture of $104,591 in U.S. Currency*, 589 So.2d 283, 285 (Fla. 1991).
- "Congress not only retained the legislative veto but expanded it to allow either house to *disapprove* any portion of a rule the body concluded was a 'single separate rule of law.'" Barbara H. Craig, *Chadha: The Story of an Epic Constitutional Struggle* 69 (1988).
- "We *disapprove* the dicta expressed in that opinion." *State v. Wagner*, 863 So.2d 1224, 1225 (Fla. 2004).

See **approve**.

disassemble. See **dissemble**.

*disassociate; dissociate. Though common, **disassociate* is inferior to *dissociate*, of which it is a NEEDLESS VARIANT. E.g.: "This gives the law a twist [that] *disassociates* [read *dissociates*] it from morality and, I think, to some extent from sound sense." Patrick Devlin, *The Enforcement of Morals* 24 (1968). Eleven years after writing that sentence, Lord Devlin did better: "In the course of their work judges quite often *dissociate* themselves from the law." Patrick Devlin, *The Judge* 4 (1979). See **dissociate**.

disastrous is so spelled—not **disasterous*, a fairly common misspelling.

disbar. See **bar**.

disbarment; disbarring. Both mean "the action of expelling a lawyer from the bar." *Disbarment* is the more common noun in AmE. E.g.:

- "The natural effect of an unreversed *disbarment* order by a state court is to destroy the fair, private, and professional character of the attorney, which is essential for membership in the federal bar." *In re Bennethum*, 196 F.Supp. 541, 542 (D. Del. 1961).
- "But it would stretch fairness to impose a prison term when the usual penalty, according to experts in legal ethics, is *disbarment*." Dorothy J. Samuels, *Behind Mel Miller's Downfall*, N.Y. Times, 21 Dec. 1991, at 14.

- "Clawson did not disclose his convictions or *disbarment*, and he continued to practice law in Arkansas for several years, during which time he represented Wooten." *Wooten v. Norris*, 578 F.3d 767, 771 (8th Cir. 2009).

In BrE, the gerund in *-ing* is common: "By his [defense] the defendant claimed that the benchers in *disbarring* and disbenching him had been activated by malice, and what they had done was without legal effect." *R. v. Visitors to the Inns of Court ex parte Calder*, [1994] Q.B. 1, 45 (C.A.). See **bar.**

disbelief; unbelief; nonbelief; misbelief. *Disbelief* is the mental rejection of something after considering its plausibility; it results from active, conscious decision. *Unbelief* is the mere absence of belief, esp. in religious matters. *Nonbelief* might be a NEEDLESS VARIANT of *unbelief* were it not so very common as to be uncancelable. Besides, it conveniently lacks the connotations of agnosticism—e.g.:

- "*Nonbelief* of the prosecutor in the guilt of the person charged with crime is [evidence] of want of probable cause for the prosecution." *Dunlap v. Chesapeake & Ohio Ry.*, 148 S.E. 105, 107 (W. Va. 1929).
- "The plaintiff opposed the cross motion, contending that its proof raised, at the least, a triable issue of fact as to whether any delay in notification was excusable based upon a reasonable *nonbelief* of any liability on its part." *Surgical Sock Shop II, Inc. v. U.S. Underwriters Ins. Co.*, 854 N.Y.S.2d 214, 215 (App. Div. 2008).

When religion is the subject, *unbelief* is probably the desired word, though here *disbelief* might have been even better to create a longer spectrum: "American society is characterized by a rich diversity spanning the whole spectrum of belief and *nonbelief* [read *unbelief* or maybe *disbelief*]." Steven D. Smith, *Our Agnostic Constitution*, 83 N.Y.U. L. Rev. 120, 162 (2008).

A *misbelief* is an erroneous or false belief.

The preferred agent nouns—just for skeptical readers—are *disbelievers*, *unbelievers*, and *misbelievers*.

disburse; disperse. *Disburse* is chiefly used in reference to distribution of money <the directors disbursed dividends to the stockholders>. *Disperse* is used in reference to scattering of things, such as crowds or diseases.

discharge = (1) to pay a debt or satisfy some other obligation <Jones discharged all the debts>; (2) to release (a bankrupt) from monetary obligations, upon adjudication of bankruptcy <Jones was discharged from those debts>; (3) to dismiss (a case) <case discharged>; (4) to cancel the original provisional force of an injunction or other court order <the T.R.O. was then discharged>; (5) to free (a prisoner) from confinement <the offender was granted a conditional discharge>; (6) to relieve (a jury) of further responsibilities in considering a case <at 6:00 p.m. that Friday, the jury was discharged>; or (7) to fire (an

employee) <employers may hire and discharge when they please>. In sum, *discharge* is a CHAMELEON-HUED WORD.

disciplinary; *disciplinatory. *Disciplinary* = (1) related to discipline <disciplinary rules>; or (2) carrying out punishment <disciplinary measures>. **Disciplinatory* is a NEEDLESS VARIANT.

disclaim. See **declaim.**

disclaimer. See -ER (B).

disclose; expose. There are important differences. *Disclose* = to reveal (any factual matter). *Expose* = (1) to lay bare or unmask (something bad); or (2) to place in a perilous condition.

disclosee (= one to whom information is disclosed) is a NEOLOGISM unrecorded in most English-language dictionaries—e.g.: "Being duly sworn [*disclosee*] pursuant to interposition states . . . ." 2 Roger M. Milgrim, *Milgrim on Trade Secrets* § 7.06[1], at 7-105 (1988) (bracketed interpolation in original). See -EE.

disclosural, a newly formed adjective corresponding to the noun *disclosure*, is a potentially useful NEOLOGISM—e.g.: Bridget Mast, *Disclosural Privacy in Florida*, 22 Stetson L. Rev. 283 (1992).

discomfit, vb.; **discomfiture,** n. *Discomfit* (= to frustrate, disconcert) is best used only as a verb. The preferred noun is *discomfiture*. Ill-trained writers use phrases such as *much to his discomfit*, in which either *discomfort* or *discomfiture* is intended.

*Discomforture is incorrect for either *discomfort* or *discomfiture*—e.g.: "How does a court determine whether a defendant is in fact maintaining a nuisance on his property to the *discomforture* [read *discomfort* or, more likely, *discomfiture*] of his neighbors?" C. Gordon Post, *An Introduction to the Law* 105 (1963).

discomfort. See **discomfit.**

discommend is the opposite of *recommend*, not of *commend*.

disconcertion; *disconcertment. The preferred noun corresponding to the verb *to disconcert* is the rather unusual *disconcertion* /dis-kən-**sərsh**-ən/. **Disconcertment* is a NEEDLESS VARIANT.

discontinuation; discontinuance; discontinuity. See **continuance.**

discontinue. See **stop.**

discover, vb., is generally obsolete in the sense "to uncover, reveal," except in legal JARGON—e.g.: "This rule does not protect a defendant from *discovering* facts indicating moral turpitude on his part unless they amount to a punishable offense." Eugene A. Jones,

Manual of Equity Pleading and Practice 23 (1916). The verb now generally means "to find; to detect." See **discovery.**

For the use in which judges are said to "discover" the common law, see **declare.**

discoverable, in American law, means "subject to pretrial discovery" <discoverable documents of the corporation>. This sense goes beyond the general meaning of "ascertainable."

discovert is not an opposite of *covert* as ordinarily used—*overt* is. *Discovert* means "unmarried, whether widowed, divorced, or never having married," or, more technically, "not subject to the disabilities of coverture." Acceptable in historical contexts, the word is now obsolete because there are no "disabilities of coverture" (i.e., legal disabilities resulting from a woman's being married). See **covert.**

discovery, as a term of legal JARGON, means "disclosure by a party to an action, at the other party's instance, of facts or documents relevant to the lawsuit." E.g.: "The English invented *discovery* while casting about for a substitute for torture for parties unwilling to reveal facts at issue in a lawsuit. Their idea was a good one; but the way it is carried out causes the litigants less torment only in the sense that their agony is mental, not physical." William B. Spawn (ABA president), in a speech before the North Carolina State Bar in 1977 (as quoted in Joseph C. Goulden, *The Million Dollar Lawyers* 286 n. (1978)). See **discover.**

discovery abuse is a broad term that covers many disparate things: "Thus it is useful to subdivide 'abuse' into 'misuse' and 'overuse.' What is referred to as 'misuse' would include not only direct violation of the rules, as by failing to respond to a discovery request within the stated time limit, but also more subtle attempts to harass or obstruct an opponent as by giving obviously inadequate answers or by requesting information that clearly is outside the scope of discovery." Charles Alan Wright, *The Law of Federal Courts* 580 (5th ed. 1994).

"Discovery overuse," by contrast, refers to "asking for more discovery than is necessary or appropriate to the particular case." *Id.* And the term *overuse* "can be subdivided into problems of 'depth' and of 'breadth,' with 'depth' referring to discovery that may be relevant but is simply excessive and 'breadth' referring to discovery requests that go into matters too far removed from the case." *Id.*

discrete; discreet. *Discrete* = "separate; distinct." *Discreet* = "cautious; judicious." *Discreet* is most commonly used in reference to speaking or writing. The usual error is to misuse *discreet*, the more common term in nonlegal language, for *discrete*—e.g.: "Although Texas has moved away from a system of submitting *discreet* [read *discrete*] fact questions on each element of a claim or defense, Texas still employs broad form issues in virtually every case and does not allow the jury to be informed of the effect of its answers." Frank Cicero Jr. & Roger L. Taylor, *Verdict Strategy*, 17 Litig. 41, 42 (Summer 1991).

But the opposite blunder is common—e.g.:

- "Mr. Bradshaw said almost everything the group did locally was *discrete* [read *discreet*]." Peter Applebome, *Bloody Sunday's Roots in Deep Religious Soil*, N.Y. Times, 2 Mar. 1993, at A8.
- "Some city attorneys *discretely* [read *discreetly*] 'pocket' information developed during the lawsuit that might reflect poorly on their client." Joanna C. Schwartz, *Myths and Mechanics of Deterrence*, 57 UCLA L. Rev. 1023, 1065 (2009).
- "According to Tichinin, if the investigation uncovered evidence of an affair, he intended to *discretely* [read *discreetly*] tell the Council." *Tichinin v. City of Morgan Hill*, 99 Cal. Rptr. 3d 661, 668 (Ct. App. 2009).

Discrete is sometimes used meaninglessly—e.g.: "The prosecution apparently made the strikes simply in an effort to procure, from among those summonsed and not disqualified, a jury [that], under the *discrete* [read *peculiar?*] facts of this particular case, would least likely be partial to Leslie." *U.S. v. Leslie*, 759 F.2d 381, 383 (5th Cir. 1985).

discretion is traditionally a mass noun, not a count noun. So references to "the exercise of a sound discretion" and to a court's having "*a* large discretion" are unidiomatic. *See* 6 James W. Moore et al., *Moore's Federal Practice* § 54.70[5], at 54-344, 54-348 (2d ed. 1988) (using the phrases quoted).

***discriminant.** See **discriminatory.**

discriminate, vb., cannot properly be used transitively, as here: "Blacks are *discriminated* [read *discriminated against*] in that city." The same problem crops up in the past-participial adjective—e.g.: "The Secretary's action bars a private suit by the *discriminated employee* [read *employee who has been discriminated against*]." *Marshall v. Sun Oil Co.*, 605 F.2d 1331, 1339 n.8 (5th Cir. 1979).

discriminated, adj. See **discriminate.**

discriminatee = a person unlawfully discriminated against. Few dictionaries record this term, but it is increasingly common in American legal writing. E.g.:

- "It appears advisable to make disposition of that portion of the Board's order which directs the company and the Unions 'jointly and severally to make the *discriminatees* whole for any loss of pay they may have suffered by reason of the discrimination against them.'" *Progressive Mine Workers v. N.L.R.B.*, 187 F.2d 298, 306 (7th Cir. 1951).
- "In the instant case, back seniority . . . is just as necessary to make *discriminatees* 'whole' under Title VI." *Guardians Ass'n v. Civil Serv. Comm'n*, 466 F.Supp. 1273, 1287 (S.D.N.Y. 1979).
- "The NLRB routinely awards backpay to restore *discriminatees* to the economic position they would have enjoyed absent the unfair labor practice." *Warehouse & Office*

Workers' Union v. N.L.R.B., 795 F.2d 705, 718 (9th Cir. 1986).

See -EE.

discriminating. See **discriminatory.**

discrimination has not traditionally been considered a count noun. Hence one should not write *discriminations* for *discriminatory practices* or *instances of discrimination*. See PLURALS (B).

discriminatory; *discriminative; discriminating; *discriminant. Of these, only *discriminative* is ambiguous, it being a NEEDLESS VARIANT of both *discriminatory* (= applying discrimination in treatment, esp. on racial or ethnic grounds) and *discriminating* (= keen; discerning; judicious). *Discriminant* is a NEEDLESS VARIANT of *discriminating*.

Because *discriminatory* has extremely negative connotations, and *discriminating* quite positive connotations, the noun *discrimination* suffers from a split personality, sometimes brought to the surface in judicial writing: "The majority's fallacy lies in using the word *discrimination* as a synonym for *discrimination on the basis of race*. Such usage may suffice in common parlance, but for purposes of analyzing the proof in a § 1981 suit it is, if I may not be misunderstood in so expressing it, too *undiscriminating.*" *Carter v. Duncan-Huggins, Ltd.*, 727 F.2d 1225, 1247 (D.C. Cir. 1984) (Scalia, J., dissenting).

disease of the mind. See **insanity (A).**

disembark is generally considered preferable to *debark* or *disbark*.

disenable is a NEEDLESS VARIANT of *disable*. See **disabling statute.**

disenact, which the *OED* notes as being "rare," is an unnecessary word, since we have *repeal, revoke, set aside, abolish*, and various other more specific words.

disenfranchise; disfranchise. Though *disfranchise* has long been favored in editorial offices, *disenfranchise* is more than 20 times as common and has established itself as the standard term meaning "to deprive of the right to exercise a franchise or privilege, esp. to vote." Some writers, especially of BrE, continue to use the shorter term—e.g.: "A path-breaking extension of effective legal personhood into the ranks of hitherto *disfranchised* minors?" Neil MacCormick, *With Due Respect*, TLS, 22 Jan. 1993, at 3. But *disenfranchise*, with its negative prefix followed by its superfluous intensive prefix, has now taken the field in AmE—e.g.:

- "In *Toney*, the registrar of the same parish misapplied Louisiana election statutes in purging voter lists, resulting in the *disenfranchisement* of many more blacks than whites." *Welch v. McKenzie*, 765 F.2d 1311, 1315 (5th Cir. 1985).
- "The steamroller of *disfranchisement* [read *disenfranchisement*] had recently moved across the South." Martha R.

Mahoney, *What's Left of Solidarity? Reflections on Law, Race, and Labor History*, 57 Buff. L. Rev. 1515, 1577 (2009).

- "In many ways, the recount process being supervised by the Florida Supreme Court represented the last best chance to reduce and judicially remedy some of the inequalities and inaccuracies and *disenfranchisements* that had tainted the initial counting process." Akhil Reed Amar, *Bush, Gore, Florida, and the Constitution*, 61 Fla. L. Rev. 945, 961 (2009).

disentail = to bar the entail (on an estate) and convert (the estate) into a fee simple. See **entail.**

disentitle traditionally takes the preposition *to*, not *from*. E.g.:

- "Although we are not told whether he actually had a gun, he threatened to kill a person and that was enough to *disentitle him to* a sentencing discount under the guideline." *U.S. v. Anderson*, 547 F.3d 831, 832 (7th Cir. 2008).
- "Alabama law has long recognized that the mere fact that a worker resumes work following a work-related accident does not necessarily *disentitle the worker to compensation.*" *Waters Bros. Contractors, Inc. v. Wimberley*, 20 So.3d 125, 135 (Ala. Civ. App. 2009).
- "The Court determines that Huhtamaki's volte face *disentitles it from* [read *disentitles it to*] heightened deference." *Huhtamaki Co. Mfg. v. CKF, Inc.*, 648 F.Supp.2d 167, 173 (D. Me. 2009).
- "Brown's lack of a property interest *disentitles him from invoking* [read *disentitles him to invoke*] the Fourteenth Amendment and hence compels rejection of his Section 1983 claim." *Brown v. City of Ecorse*, 322 Fed. Appx. 443, 446 (6th Cir. 2009).

disfranchise. See **disenfranchise.**

dishabille /dis-ə-**beel**/. So spelled—not *deshabille.*

*disherison; *disinherison.* *Disherison* (= [1] the act of disinheriting; or [2] the state of being disinherited) was labeled obsolete as recently as 1990 in *Black's Law Dictionary* (6th ed.), but it still enjoys limited currency. It ought to be treated as a NEEDLESS VARIANT of *disinheritance*, which is a simpler word that far more readers and listeners will understand—e.g.:

- "Posthumous avarice leading to *disherison* [read *disinheritance*] is bad. Living greediness is bad too." *Gertman v. Burdick*, 123 F.2d 924, 933 (D.C. Cir. 1941).
- "*Disherison* [read *Disinheritance*] of a child invites contest of the will. When a child is *disinherited* a trial judge is likely to submit the will to a jury on an issue of mental capacity, fraud, or undue influence." John Ritchie et al., *Decedents' Estates and Trusts* 142 (1971).

Disinherison, a term generally used in civil law, is likewise a NEEDLESS VARIANT in common-law contexts—e.g.: "The power of *disinherison* [read *disinheritance*] he [Bracton] explains here in the same way as in the case of the fee simple." A.W.B. Simpson, *An Introduction to the History of the Land Law* 62 (1961).

*disherit; *disheritance; *disheritor.** These are NEEDLESS VARIANTS of *disinherit, disinheritance*, and *disinheritor*. E.g.:

- "She was the sister who had been *disherited* [read *disinherited*] by her mother." *Stonesifer v. Swanson*, 146 F.2d 671, 673 (7th Cir. 1945).
- "There is also an almost equally strong presumption against virtual *disheritance* [read *disinheritance*] of testatrix'[s] sole distributee." *In re Vetroock's Will*, 230 N.Y.S.2d 485, 500 (Sur. Ct. 1962).

*disheritor; disinheritor. See ***disherit.**

dishonest; deceitful; lying; untruthful; mendacious. All these adjectives describe someone whose words or actions lack integrity and candor, and therefore credibility. *Dishonest* is broad, implying perhaps an instance or the habit of skewing the truth <a dishonest assertion>, but it may also imply an instance or the habit of stealing or cheating <a dishonest merchant>. *Deceitful* typically suggests a positive intent to mislead, especially by misrepresenting the true character either of oneself or of what is being sold or negotiated, by indulging in falsehoods, by defrauding, or by double-dealing <a deceitful negotiator>. *Lying*, the most brutal and frequent of these adjectives, connotes a habit of stating falsehoods as opposed to a single instance <a lying scoundrel>, although this connotation is absent when the word is used not as an adjective but as a participial verb (that is, "You're lying!" could refer to only one instance, as opposed to a habit). *Untruthful* is a less inflammatory adjective, implying that someone's statements don't square with reality—and the term applies most often not to people but to their assertions <an untruthful report> <an untruthful financial statement>. *Mendacious*, a literary term, is essentially a heightened equivalent of *lying* <a mendacious villain>. See **mendacity.**

disincentive; nonincentive. The first provides an incentive not to do something; the second is no incentive at all.

disinformation; misinformation. These words are not synonyms. *Disinformation* = false information deliberately created and spread <Soviet disinformation of the 1960s>. *Misinformation* = incorrect information.

*disinherison. See ***disherison.**

disinherit. See ***disherit.**

disinheritance. See ***disherison** & ***disherit.**

disintegrative; *disintegratory. The second is a NEEDLESS VARIANT.

disinterest; disinterested; uninterest; uninterested. *Disinterest* is impartiality or freedom from bias or chance of financial benefit—e.g.: "An inherent qualification for a quasi-judicial decision-maker is *disinterest* in the result." *Central Life Ins. Co. v. Aetna Cas. & Sur. Co.*, 466 N.W.2d 257, 261 (Iowa 1991). Hence, *disinterested* means "impartial." For more on this word and its near-synonyms, see **fair (A).**

Uninterest (recorded fr. 1952) means "lack of concern or attention" and *uninterested* "having no concern or care (about something)." E.g.: "If Orenstein believed that Erb knew or would surely find out about paragraph 34, it was not dishonest or opportunistic to fail to flag that paragraph, . . . especially given the *uninterest* . . . that Erb fairly radiated." *Market Street Assocs. Ltd. v. Frey*, 941 F.2d 588, 598 (7th Cir. 1991).

Traditionally, though, the DIFFERENTIATION between these words was not as marked as it might have been: *disinterest* has, in addition to its primary meaning of impartiality, denoted "lack of concern or attention" (i.e., as a synonym of *uninterest*). Given the overlapping nouns, writers have found it difficult to keep the past-participial adjectives entirely separate, and many have given up the fight to preserve the distinction between them.

Nevertheless, the distinction is still best recognized and followed, especially in the law, where the sense of *interest* that gives rise to *disinterested* (as in "interested party") still commonly appears. Because it is a virtue for judges to remain *disinterested*, we had better not forget what that word means—e.g.:

- "Any other rule would make important questions of the title to real estate largely dependent upon the uncertain recollection and testimony of *interested* witnesses." *McBride v. Freeman*, 215 P. 678, 682 (Cal. 1923).
- "In each case 'due process of law' requires an evaluation based on a *disinterested* inquiry pursued in the spirit of science." *Rochin v. California*, 342 U.S. 165, 172 (1952) (per Frankfurter, J.).
- "Ryan obtained credible information from other sources including two *disinterested* witnesses that confirmed Alisha Barbera's claim." *Guntlow v. Barbera*, 907 N.Y.S.2d 86, 96 (App. Div. 2010).

Yet *disinterested* is frequently misused for *uninterested*—e.g.:

- "Many people are *disinterested* [read *uninterested*] in politics and do not vote." Charles Alan Wright et al., *Federal Practice and Procedure* § 3611, at 511 (1984).
- "Today's youth are too self-absorbed and hedonistic, . . . they are separated from the rest of society by an adolescent counterculture, and, more so than in the past, . . . they are *disinterested* [read *uninterested*] in politics and in taking responsibility for society." Sean T. Bradley, *Community Service and Social Responsibility in Youth, James Youniss and Miranda Yates*, 30 Urb. Law. 1114, 1115 (1998) (book review).

disinvestment; divestment. Defined as "consumption of capital," in *W9*, *disinvestment* has come to mean "the withdrawal of investment, esp. for political reasons" (as acknowledged in *W10*, though that nuance was dropped in *W11*). E.g.:

- "About half of the 200 American companies in Kenya have *disinvested* and unemployment is growing." Andrew Hogg, *Frightened Moi Vows He Will Cull Democratic "Rats,"* Sunday Times, 8 July 1990, at 1-20.
- "The dissent's regime would render the permitting process a useless exercise. It would cripple economic expansion in Michigan and probably lead to *disinvestment*." *Preserve the Dunes, Inc. v. Department of Envtl. Quality*, 684 N.W.2d 847, 855 (Mich. 2004).
- "As municipal services could be obtained through contract or through state or regional authorities, the suburbs

could go it alone. Meanwhile, deindustrialization was leading to rapid *disinvestment* in old-line cities." Richard C. Schragger, *Mobile Capital, Local Economic Regulation, and the Democratic City*, 123 Harv. L. Rev. 482, 503 (2009).

Divestment is also used in this sense. See **divesture.*

disjoinder (= the undoing of the joinder of [parties, actions, etc.]) is a useful NEOLOGISM omitted from most legal and nonlegal dictionaries. E.g.:

- "The question of *disjoinder* is not embraced in the present procedure." *People v. Nickel*, 69 N.Y.S.2d 791, 794 (King's County Ct. 1947).
- "Authority for this *disjoinder* of the 'force, violence, or fear' and the 'color of official right' phrases of § 1951(b)(2) was said to be found in [several cases cited]." *U.S. v. Cerilli*, 603 F.2d 415, 428 (3d Cir. 1979) (Aldisert, J., dissenting).

See **joinder.** Cf. **misjoinder.**

dismissal; *dismission. The much older word **dismission* (1547) has given way almost completely to the upstart *dismissal* (1806), considered a mere variant less than a century ago. Today, **dismission* is the NEEDLESS VARIANT.

dismissible. So spelled.

*dismission. See **dismissal.**

disorderly conduct is a vague term embracing an array of petty violations of public decency and order—from the paid-for conduct at a disorderly house (a EUPHEMISM for *brothel*) to fomenting political division—e.g.: "If opposition to the national government should arise from the *disorderly conduct* of refractory or seditious individuals; it could be overcome by the same means which are daily employed against the same evil under the same governments." *The Federalist* No. 16, at 117 (Alexander Hamilton) (Clinton Rossiter ed., 1961).

The Constitution contains a variant phrase, *disorderly behavior*: "Each House may determine the Rules of its Proceedings, punish its Members for *disorderly Behavior*, and with the Concurrence of two thirds, expel a Member." U.S. Const. art. I, § 5.

disorderly house. See **bawdy house.**

disorganized; unorganized. The first means "in confusion or disarray; broken up"; the second means "not having been organized" merely in the negative, but not in the pejorative, sense.

disorient; *disorientate. The longer form is a NEEDLESS VARIANT of the shorter—e.g.: "But people elect not to answer questions for many reasons, starting with the possibility that they are *disorientated* [read *disoriented*] by the experience of being arrested and accused of a serious crime of which they are innocent, and simply do not know how to respond." David

Rose, *To Be Silent Will Imply Guilt*, Observer Sunday, 15 Dec. 1991, at 16. See **orient.**

disparaging (= slighting; insulting) for *disconcerting* or *discouraging* is a MALAPROPISM. E.g.: "The progress of the institutions designed to deal with the environmental issues under NAFTA has been *disparaging* [read *discouraging*]." Bradly Mall, Comment, *The Effect of NAFTA's Environmental Provisions on Mexican and Chilean Policy*, 32 Int'l Law. 153, 172 (1998). See MALAPROPISMS.

dispassionate. See **fair (A).**

dispatent. King's Counsel or Queen's Counsel are appointed to that rank by a so-called *patent*. To be stripped of that rank is, in BrE, to be *dispatented*—e.g.: "He practised for a while in London, but in 1929 he had himself disbarred in England and Ireland, and *dispatented*." R.E. Megarry, *Miscellany-at-Law* 14 (1955). In a footnote, Megarry adds: "The term 'desilked' has mercifully yet to be used." *Id.* See **silk.**

dispel. So spelled—not **dispell.*

disperse. See **disburse.**

dispone is a term from Scots law meaning "to convey formally or in legal form." From the verb are derived the terms *disponer* (= grantor), *disponee* (= grantee), and *disponible* (= capable of being assigned). E.g.:

- "It is implicit in the Ordinance that the husband and no one else can dispose of the wife's income; the husband therefore is the only possible *disponer*." *Reynolds v. Income Tax Comm'r*, [1967] 1 A.C. 1, 7 (P.C.) (appeal taken from Trinidad and Tobago).
- "In order to divest a *disponer* of property in Scots law it was necessary that the disposition granted be recorded in the Register of Sasines or that the interest of the *disponee* be registered in the Land Register as was appropriate." *Sharp v. Thomson*, 1994 S.C. 503 (Outer House).
- "I was referred to the first paragraph of the trust deed which states that the pursuer assigns, *dispones*, conveys and makes over to Maureen Hyslop Roxburgh." *Nicol v. Nine Regions Ltd.*, 2008 S.L.T. 123 (Sh. Ct.).

disposal; disposition. Both nouns answer to the verb *dispose*, but in different ways. *Disposal* implies getting rid of something, as by discarding, destroying, or (possibly) selling or giving away <waste disposal> <asset disposal>. *Disposition*, by contrast, suggests an orderly, well-arranged conclusion or distribution <the final disposition of the estate>.

In the SET PHRASE *at your disposal*, the suggestion is that persons or things are placed under your control for use as you see fit. Although **at your disposition* is also a possible phrasing in English, it is unusual enough that even the best-read readers are likely to wonder whether it might be an unidiomatic blunder. So keep only the former phrasing at your disposal.

---

dispositive; *dispository. In BrE and AmE alike, *dispositive* may mean "conclusive, determinative." In this sense, the word is extremely useful to lawyers— e.g.: "We find the evidence as to the geographic scope of the writ at common law informative but . . . not *dispositive*." *Boumediene v. Bush*, 553 U.S. 723, 748 (2008) (per Kennedy, J.). *Dispository is a NEEDLESS VARIANT—e.g.: "This negative type of evidence is not *dispository* [read *dispositive*] of the guilt issue." *Riley v. Sigler*, 437 F.2d 258, 260 (8th Cir. 1971).

In AmE and Scots law, *dispositive* is the usual word used in reference to testamentary plans, *dispository again being a NEEDLESS VARIANT—e.g.: "The relevant *dispository* [read *dispositive*] provisions of the decedent's will gave two million dollars in real estate, securities or other property to the Hofheinz Family Trust No. 2." *Hofheinz v. U.S.*, 511 F.2d 661, 662 (5th Cir. 1975). In BrE, neither word is used in this way.

disproof; *disproval. The latter is a NEEDLESS VARIANT.

disproportionate; disproportional. See **proportionate.**

disprove; refute; confute; rebut; controvert. These verbs share the sense "to show or try to show by argument that a statement, proposition, or claim is fake or erroneous." *Disprove* emphasizes success in demonstrating the inaccuracy, fallaciousness, and general invalidity of what is being assailed. *Refute* equally stresses the success of the attack and the means of overcoming the opposing argument, usually through a methodical marshaling of evidence and a rigorously analytical and ultimately unanswerable argument. (For more, see **refute.**) *Confute*, a much less common term, is essentially synonymous but perhaps more strongly suggests that the opposing view has been thoroughly vanquished and the opponents reduced to a humble silence.

To *rebut* is to attempt to *refute*, and it suggests the same systematic approach to reasoning. Yet *rebut* doesn't suggest the full achievement of one's end. Hence, while the jury is deliberating, you might say that your colleague *rebutted* the other side's points effectively; only after winning the jury's verdict can you convincingly say that your colleague *refuted* those points. (On the misuse *refute* for *rebut*, see **refute.**) *Rebut* is sometimes wrongly written **rebutt.*

Controvert is a much weaker word, suggesting merely that one contends against an opponent, perhaps in a preliminary attempt at refutation, and perhaps also with some degree of evidence in support of the denial or contradiction. For more on *controvert*, see **contravene (A).**

dispunishable (= not punishable) was a common legal term through the mid-19th century. Today, however, it is uncommon enough that most readers would consider it needlessly obscure.

dispute; disputation. These words should be differentiated. *Dispute* = controversy <goods in dispute>, whereas *disputation* = formal argument or debate.

disqualified; unqualified. These words have quite different senses. *Unqualified* = not meeting the requirements. *Disqualified* = disabled; debarred. An *unqualified* judge should not be a judge. A *disqualified* judge must withdraw from hearing a case when one of the parties is, for example, a close relative.

disqualify. See **recuse.**

disquiet is used in law in the sense of disturbing a person's possession of property, esp. in the civil law of Louisiana—e.g.:

- "The codal article relates to the suspension of the payment of the purchase price when the purchaser is *disquieted* in his possession until the seller restores him to quiet possession." *Lear v. Great Nat'l Dev. Co.*, 41 So.2d 668, 669 (La. 1949).
- "Consideration must also be given to previous jurisprudence because . . . at the time this present litigation was instituted and because of the continuing nature of the disturbances alleged to have *disquieted* plaintiffs' possession, plaintiffs still had a right of action . . . to be maintained and if necessary *quieted* in their possession of the subject property even as to the mineral lease and the right-of-way deed." *Chauvin v. Kirchhoff*, 194 So.2d 805, 813 (La. Ct. App. 1967).

See **quiet.**

disrobe, which ordinarily means "to undress," should not be used in the sense "to remove a judge from the bench"—unless jocularity is clearly intended. In the following example, one cannot say with confidence that humor is intended: "But as of July 1968, no attorneys have been disbarred, no judges *disrobed* and none of the 'excessive' fees dislodged." Murray T. Bloom, *The Trouble with Lawyers* 323 (1970).

dissatisfied; unsatisfied. Some DIFFERENTIATION exists between these words. To be *unsatisfied* is to be less than completely satisfied, whereas to be *dissatisfied* is to be positively bothered by the lack of satisfaction. In law, when one is in arrears, one's debts remain *unsatisfied.*

disseise; *disseize. *Disseise* is the preferred form of this legal word, meaning "to wrongfully deprive (a person) of the freehold possession of real property; to dispossess wrongfully." The act of deprivation is *disseisin.* See **seise.**

disseisor; disseisee. These are the correlative terms for the parties involved in disseisin (= dispossession of a person of estates). E.g.:

- "The dispossessed owner of land, as we have seen, could always recover possession by an action. Though deprived of the res, he still had a right in rem. The *disseisor* acquired only a defeasible estate. . . . The *disseisee* of goods, as well as the *disseisee* of land, has a right in rem." J.B. Ames, *The Disseisin of Chattels*, 3 Harv. L. Rev. 23, 29–30 (1889).
- "In *Ebenhoh*, we held that the *disseizors* [read *disseisors*] were 'entitled to the disputed tract' based on our de novo application of the elements of adverse possession." *Gabler v. Fedoruk*, 756 N.W.2d 725, 731 (Minn. Ct. App. 2008).
- "The rights of adverse possession will soon flow to those who just recently began as unlawful occupiers of the

American tradition. Granted, these *disseisors'* occupation of our tradition has not always been obvious; indeed, secrecy has abounded." Timothy K. Kuhner, *The Corruption of Civilizations*, 13 Roger Williams U.L. Rev. 349, 362 (2008).

See **seisin.**

*disseize. See **disseise.**

dissemble; disassemble. The first means "to present a false appearance," the second "to take apart."

dissent, n.; dissension; *dissention. *Dissent* refers to a difference of opinion, whether among judges or others. *A dissent*, as opposed to *dissent* as an uncountable noun, refers to a dissenting judicial opinion—e.g.:

- "Justices Frankfurter and Roberts concurred in this *dissent*." Samuel Bader, *Coerced Confessions and the Due Process Clause*, 15 Brook. L. Rev. 51, 62 (1948).
- "The *dissent* regards the interest in maintaining our nation's adherence to long-standing principles of international law as not compelling." *Finzer v. Barry*, 798 F.2d 1450, 1464 (D.C. Cir. 1986).

Dissension (the *-sion* spelling is preferred) refers to contentious wrangling or partisan rancor—e.g.:

- "During this period, influenced by *dissension* and disagreement in the state courts, members of Congress repeatedly proposed legislation that would have clarified the effect of sister-state judgments." Stephen E. Sachs, *Full Faith and Credit in the Early Congress*, 95 Va. L. Rev. 1201, 1208 (2009).
- "The adoption of provisions recognizing participatory rights has caused much *dissension* amongst jurists." Miriam Cohen, *Victims' Participation Rights within the International Criminal Court*, 37 Denv. J. Int'l L. & Pol'y 351, 352 (2009).

*Dissention is a mistaken form of *dissension*—e.g.: "A sudden *dissention* [read *dissension*] among those who have gathered lawfully may proceed to violence without amounting to more than an affray." Rollin M. Perkins & Ronald N. Boyce, *Criminal Law* 484 (3d ed. 1982).

dissent, vb., takes *from* or *against*, not *to* or *with*. E.g.:

- "Scalia . . . dissented *with* [read *from*] the court when it ruled that judges must instruct the jury to consider evidence favorable to the defendant when deciding whether to impose the death sentence." Kobayashi, *Mercy Is Not Always Dispensed Justly, Scalia Says*, Honolulu Advertiser, 8 Aug. 1989, at A-3.
- "I *dissent to* [read *from*] the majority opinion's determination that the plaintiff's claims were barred by res judicata." *Beahm v. 7–Eleven, Inc.*, 672 S.E.2d 598, 605 (W. Va. 2008) (Starcher, J., dissenting).
- "The majority's approach in this case infringes upon a defendant's right to be represented by counsel at every 'critical stage' of the trial and undermines the attorney-client privilege and defendants' Fifth Amendment rights. For the foregoing reasons, I *dissent to* [read *from*] this part of the majority's opinion." *State v. Mundon*, 219 P.3d 1126, 1170 (Haw. 2009) (Acoba, J., dissenting).

The preposition *against* is idiomatic but relatively uncommon. E.g.: "But three of Taney's Democratic colleagues violently dissented *against* their Chief's apparently aberrational veto of a state law in order to protect vested rights of a non-agrarian kind." Fred Rodell, *Nine Men* 126 (1955).

dissenter; dissentient, n. *Dissenter* is the standard term in AmE for "one who withholds assent, or does not approve or agree"; *dissentient* is the more usual form in BrE, because the term *dissenter* (usually with an initial cap) has a special religious and social meaning in British history ("i.e., one who dissents or refuses to conform—specif., from the 17th c. on—to the tenets and practices of the Church of England"). E.g.:

- "Lewis J., one of the former *dissentients*, had become C.J." R.E. Megarry, *A Second Miscellany-at-Law* 140 (1973).
- "The real difference between the majority and the *dissentients* in *Maunsell v. Olins* was over the question whether there was an ambiguity." Rupert Cross, *Statutory Interpretation* 145 (1976).

dissenting; dissentient, adj.; **dissentious.** *Dissentient* is sometimes used in BrE where *dissenting* would ordinarily appear in AmE. E.g.:

- "The agent was appointed to execute an instrument of transfer on a *dissentient* shareholder's behalf." Henry Burton Buckley, *The Law and Practice Under the Companies Acts* 320 (3d ed. 1879).
- "Lord Justice Brett, however, delivered a *dissentient* judgment, laying down the general principle." Judah Philip Benjamin, *The Law of Sale of Personal Property* 539 (2d ed. 1888).

The word is not unknown in American legal writing: "Without retracting or in any way departing from our former *dissentient* views, I concur in the action taken by the majority on the instant appeal." *In re King's Estate*, 66 A.2d 68, 72 (Pa. 1949) (Jones, J., concurring). One ambiguity that may be caused by use of *dissentient* is that readers might interpret it as a derogatory word opposite to *sentient*; the true opposite of *sentient* (= feeling), however, is *insentient*. *Dissentious* = given to dissension; quarrelsome.

*dissention. See **dissent, n.**

dissimilar takes the preposition *to* rather than *from*—e.g.:

- "The facts in that case are wholly *dissimilar from* [read *dissimilar to*] the facts in the case before us." *Old Dominion Tel. Co. v. Powers*, 37 So. 195, 197 (Ala. 1904).
- "The goals of a strategic doctrine are not *dissimilar from* [read *dissimilar to*] many of the goals of law." Ganesh Sitaraman, *Counterinsurgency, the War on Terror, and the Laws of War*, 95 Va. L. Rev. 1745, 1836 (2009).

Here the preferable phrasing is illustrated: "Although the listed plans are *dissimilar to* each other in some respects, their common feature is that they provide income that substitutes for wages earned as salary or hourly compensation." *Rousey v. Jacoway*, 544 U.S. 320, 321 syl. (2005). Cf. **disentitle.**

*dissiminate is a fairly common misspelling of *disseminate.*

dissociate; *disassociate. *Dissociate* is the preferred term; **disassociate* is a NEEDLESS VARIANT. *Dissociate* takes the preposition *from.* E.g.:

- "Austin . . . answers that this is to *dissociate* sanction *from* command altogether, confusing sanction and motive." W.W. Buckland, *Some Reflections on Jurisprudence* 89 (1945).
- "*Disassociated with* [read *Dissociated from*] the subject thereof, whatever it may be, a title or name composed of ordinary words, cannot acquire the status of [legally recognized] property[, as] all who speak or write have an inherent right to use any and all words in the English language." *Ball v. United Artists Corp.*, 214 N.Y.S.2d 219, 224 (App. Div. 1961).

See ***disassociate.**

dissolution. See **adjourn, divorce (B)** & **marriage dissolution.**

dissolve. See **adjourn.**

distill; distil. *Distill* is preferred in AmE, *distil* in BrE.

distinct; distinctive. The first means "well defined, discernibly separate" <distinct speech> (see **evident**), and the second means "serving to distinguish, set off by appearance" <a distinctive red bow tie>. *Distinct* speech is well enunciated, whereas *distinctive* speech is idiosyncratically accented, different from that of surrounding speakers. *Distinctive* is sometimes misused for *distinguished* (= notable; famous).

distinguish can be used either transitively, in the sense "to note a difference" <that fact distinguished the first case from the second>, or intransitively, in the sense "to make a distinction" <the court distinguished between premeditated and spontaneous acts>.

In legal contexts, the transitive use appears frequently in the phrase *to distinguish a case*, meaning to provide reasons for deciding a case under consideration differently from a similar case cited as a possible precedent. E.g.: "An apparent precedent may be evaded by '*distinguishing*' the facts, which are never identical in any two cases. Distinguishing may either be genuine or strained." O. Hood Phillips, *A First Book of English Law* 124 (3d ed. 1955). Cf. **differentia.**

distrain, vb., = (1) to seize goods by a legal remedy known as "distress," which entitles a rightful possessor to recover personal property wrongfully taken; or (2) to force (a person, often a tenant), by the seizure and detention of personal property, to perform some duty (such as paying overdue rent). Today sense 2 is the more common one—e.g.:

- "In most states the landlord has the right . . . to seize and sell certain of the tenant's personal property in order to satisfy unpaid rent. This right exists either by virtue of the landlord's right to *distrain* for rent due or by virtue of the landlord's lien." Robert Kratovil, *Real Estate Law* 306 (1946).
- "Three days later he seized the furniture because he had heard that the plaintiff's landlord intended to *distrain* it for arrears of rent." G.H. Treitel, *The Law of Contract* 106 (8th ed. 1991).

See **distraint.**

distrainor; *distrainer. The *OED* states that *-or* is "a more technical form than *distrainer*, and correlative to *distrainee*." Of course, *distrain* itself is a technical word; it may as well have a technical Latinate agent-noun suffix (*-or*). See -ER (A).

distraint; distress. In legal contexts, both mean either "the seizure of goods as security for the performance of a duty" or "the legal remedy authorizing such a seizure." *Distraint* would seem to be the better term, for it looks like the verb from which it derives (Fr. *distraindre*, fr. L. *distringere*) and does not, like *distress*, have an ordinary English meaning. But *distress* is the prevalent term for this sense. See **distrain.**

Though not widely accepted, a possible DIFFERENTIATION appears in one historian's use of *distress* for the legal remedy and *distraint* for the exercise of that remedy: "In practice the remedy of *distress* might not be so effective, for the tenants of the land might be poor men, unable to perform the service, and *distraint* to compel them to do so would be a waste of effort." A.W.B. Simpson, *An Introduction to the History of the Land Law* 50 (1961).

distribute. See **descend.**

distributee. See **heir (C).**

distribution. See **descent (B).**

distrust, vb.; **mistrust,** vb. Both mean "to lack trust or confidence in someone or something." But *distrust* conveys stronger connotations of certainty that something is amiss, even to the point of dread <I distrust him; he is treacherous>. *Mistrust* suggests distinct suspicion and fear, but with something less than certainty <a mistrust of airplane travel>.

dive > dived > dived. So inflected. Avoid **dove.*

divergence; *divergency. The form **divergency* is a NEEDLESS VARIANT of *divergence.*

divers; diverse. These words have distinct meanings. Very simply, *divers* implies severalty, and *diverse* implies difference. *Divers* (= various; sundry) remains a part of AmE only as a curiosity. Formerly it meant not only "various," but "several" as well: "The rent was behind for *divers* years." *Sir Anthony Sturlyn v. Albany*, Cro. Eliz. 67, 78 Eng. Repr. 327 (Q.B. 1587). Today it is an ARCHAISM, and its only accepted meaning is "various," as in Frankfurter's phrase "*divers* judicially inappropriate and elusive determinants." *Baker v. Carr*, 369 U.S. 186, 268 (1962) (Frankfurter, J., dissenting). Other modern examples follow:

- "The appellant used three different substances: cocaine, lysergic acid diethylamide, and methylenedioxymethamphetamine (ecstasy), all on *divers* occasions." *U.S. v. Farano*, 60 M.J. 932, 932–33 (N.M. Ct. Crim. App. 2005).
- "The criminal harassment indictment alleged conduct occurring on *divers* dates from January 5, 2004, through July 10, 2004." *Commonwealth v. Kulesa*, 917 N.E.2d 762, 766 (Mass. 2009).
- "Congress may act in *divers* ways to ensure [n.b., not *insure*] the proper discharge of the government's custodial duty." *U.S. v. Volungus*, 595 F.3d 1, 8 (1st Cir. 2010).

Diverse means "markedly different; unlike." It takes the preposition *from*. E.g.: "Only one member of the plaintiff class named or unnamed must be *diverse from* any one defendant." *Lowery v. Alabama Power Co.*, 483 F.3d 1184, 1193 n.24 (11th Cir. 2007).

Frequently it is used in AmE, without a preposition, to denote a difference in citizenship that gives rise to federal jurisdiction: "The parties are of *diverse* citizenship, and the stakes exceed $75,000, so 28 U.S.C. § 1332 permits the suit to be filed in federal court." *Deng v. Sears, Roebuck & Co.*, 552 F.3d 574, 576 (7th Cir. 2009). See **diversity.**

diversity. As a noun in American legal writing, *diversity* often appears as a shorthand form of the phrase *diversity of citizenship*—e.g.: "Gearench . . . had no burden to prove *diversity* between the original parties or between it and its third-party defendants." *Molett v. Penrod Drilling Co.*, 872 F.2d 1221, 1228 (5th Cir. 1989).

As an adjective in American legal writing, *diversity* is frequently used as a shortened form of the PHRASAL ADJECTIVE *diversity-jurisdiction*—e.g.: "In *diversity* cases, the forum state's choice-of-law rules determine the applicable substantive law." *Rowell v. Franconia Minerals Corp.*, 582 F.Supp.2d 1031, 1038 (N.D. Ill. 2008).

divestiture; *divesture; divestment. The standard noun corresponding to the verb *to divest* is *divestiture*. E.g.: "It is agreed that the history and language of the laws for control of monopolization properly permit the application by the courts of orders requiring *divestiture* of properties of an existing monopolist in order to prevent the continuance of the evil." *U.S. v. Parkinson*, 240 F.2d 918, 919 (9th Cir. 1956). **Divesture* is a NEEDLESS VARIANT.

The other variant, *divestment*, not at all uncommon, might also seem to be a needless variant; yet it appears in a number of SET PHRASES in property law, such as *vested interest subject to divestment*. E.g.:

- "The registration of stock ownership upon the books of the corporation in appropriate statutory language is sufficient to vest legal title, subject to *divestment* if the circumstances surrounding the transaction warrant it." *Frey v. Wubbena*, 185 N.E.2d 850, 854–55 (Ill. 1962).

- "Whether we characterize David's interest as a contingent interest, as a vested interest subject to *divestment*, or as a contingent fee subject to defeasance, it is the quality of his present right in the share which determines whether David's judgment creditors may reach it." *In re Estate of Lane*, 535 N.E.2d 186, 187 (Ind. Ct. App. 1989).

See **disinvestment.**

*dividable. See **divisible.**

dividend; interest. In corporate law, these terms signal an important distinction. *Interest* (= a charge one pays for getting a loan or upon issuing bonds, usu. measured as a percentage of principal) is payable out of the company's assets generally. But a *dividend* (= a share of profits distributed to a shareholder) is a voluntary distribution by the company and does not become a liability until after the company has declared it. Dividends can be declared only out of the assets legally available—especially the company's retained earnings or profits, but not its general assets.

divide up. See PARTICLES, UNNECESSARY.

divisibility. See **devisability.**

divisible; *dividable. The second is a NEEDLESS VARIANT.

divisional court. For an explanation of the divisional courts of the (English) High Court, see **high court.**

divisor. See **deviser.**

divorce. A. And *annulment*. A *divorce* recognizes the existence of a valid marriage, whereas an *annulment* treats the marriage as if it had never existed. Even so, in most jurisdictions the "nonexistence" of the marriage is not considered absolute: any children conceived before an annulment are traditionally considered legitimate.

B. And *dissolution of marriage*. In the 1970s, the word *divorce* was struck from many statutes and replaced by the EUPHEMISM *dissolution of marriage* or *marriage dissolution*. See **marriage dissolution.**

C. Idiom. One gets a divorce from a *spouse*, not from a *marriage*—e.g.: "Another suit . . . commenced . . . by the defendant for a *divorce from a marriage with the plaintiff* [read *divorce from the plaintiff*] . . . was . . . removed to this court." *Sharon v. Hill*, 26 F. 337, 338 (C.C.D. Cal. 1885).

D. *No-fault divorce*. See **no-fault divorce.**

E. *Divorce a mensa et thoro*. See **a mensa et thoro.**

divorcé; divorcée. See **fiancé.**

*divorcement is now obsolete for *divorce* in the sense "the dissolution of the marriage tie," although it persisted in this sense through the early 20th century—e.g.: "In the event of the death or *divorcement* of the wife before the decease of the husband, he shall have the right to designate another beneficiary." Mo. Rev. Stat. § 7895 (1906). David O. Selznick directed Katharine Hepburn in the 1932 film *A Bill of Divorcement*.

Divorcement survives in the general figurative sense "the severance or complete separation of any close relation" <the divorcement of church and state in the U.S.>.

divulgence; *divulgation; *divulgement. Even though the latter two date from the early 17th century, *divulgence*, which dates from the mid-19th century, is now the preferred noun corresponding to the verb *to divulge*.

do. See ANTICIPATORY REFERENCE (A) & **as (B).**

doable. See **practicable (A).**

dock, in British legal writing, means "the enclosure in a criminal court in which the prisoner is placed during trial"—e.g.:

- "Before he died, the little doctor at least had the comfort of knowing that Ethel Le Neve had left the dock a free woman." Stanley Jackson, *The Life and Cases of Mr. Justice Humphreys* 85 (n.d. [1951]).
- "Even where the old rule that a man is to be presumed innocent till proved guilty has not been abrogated by statutes placing on the defence the burden of proving innocence, it may be subtly undermined by the terms used to refer to the man in the *dock*—not 'Mr Smith,' but 'Smith' or 'the accused.'" Alan Harding, *A Social History of English Law* 419 (1966).

See **dock brief.**
American writers sometimes mangle the SET PHRASE *in the dock*—in the following example with a MALAPROPISM: "For the judiciary, then, to say to the sovereign that only judges know what the law is, is one thing. . . . For the judiciary to say this to a man *in the docket* [read *in the dock*] or to a woman sued in tort is quite another." Mary J. Morrison, *Excursions into the Nature of Legal Language*, 37 Clev. St. L. Rev. 271, 285–86 (1989).

dock brief; docker. A *dock brief*, in former English practice, was a brief handed in court directly to a barrister selected from among those present by an indigent criminal defendant in the dock (instead of through the agency of a solicitor), the effect of which was that the barrister then represented the defendant, who was known as a *docker*. See **dock** & **soup.**

docket, in AmE, means "a schedule of cases pending." In BrE, it means "a register of judgments issued by the court."

Docket may be used as a verb in both BrE and AmE—e.g.:

- "The case was *docketed* and tried according to the usual course and practice of the court." *Meece v. Commercial Credit Co.*, 159 S.E. 17, 19 (N.C. 1931).

- "Thereafter he has either 60 or 90 days in which to *docket* the case with the Supreme Court." Charles Alan Wright, *The Law of Federal Courts* 580 (5th ed. 1994).
- "The case was *docketed* in this Court on August 17, 2007, and submitted for decision on the briefs on October 8, 2007." *Miller v. State*, 658 S.E.2d 765, 766 n.1 (Ga. 2008).

See **calendar** & **cause-list.**

dockominium, a PORTMANTEAU WORD made from combining *boat dock* with *condominium*, refers to an idea originated in the early 1980s of selling boat slips, as opposed to renting them. E.g.:

- "Such projects, known informally as '*dockominiums*,' have become very popular in many waterfront communities throughout the metropolitan area, and the developers of many projects are finding more than they expected are being lived in year-round." Anthony DePalma, *Styling Vacation Homes for All Seasons*, N.Y. Times, 6 May 1984, § 8, at 1.
- "The recreational boating system may well be headed toward a system of individual ownership of slip spaces. Just as rental apartments can be converted for sale as condominiums, rental slip spaces can be converted for sale as *dockominiums*." Mark Cheung, *Dockominiums*, 16 B.C. Envtl. Aff. L. Rev. 821, 821 (1989).

doctrinal; doctrinaire; *doctrinary. The first is the neutral term, meaning "of or relating to a doctrine." E.g.: "Indeed, the *doctrinal* commentary upon [*Taddeo*] thus far has been unanimously favorable." *Grubbs v. Houston First Am. Sav. Ass'n*, 730 F.2d 236, 242 (5th Cir. 1984). *Doctrinaire* = dogmatic; slavishly, impractically adhering to dogma. *Doctrinary* is a NEEDLESS VARIANT of *doctrinaire*.

Doctrinaire is sometimes misspelled *doctrinnaire*, on the apparent analogy of *questionnaire*—e.g.: "The Black–Douglas position was too *doctrinnaire* [read *doctrinaire*]." Maurice Kelman, *The Forked Path of Dissent*, 1985 Sup. Ct. Rev. 227, 257.

doctrinal construction; doctrinal interpretation. See *doctrinal interpretation* under INTERPRETATION, MODES OF (B).

***doctrinary.** See **doctrinal.**

doctrine of equivalents (= a judicially created theory for finding patent infringement when the accused process or product falls outside the literal scope of the patent claims, whereby an allegedly infringing process or product might be found to contain an element equivalent to each claimed element of the patented invention) is sometimes mistakenly written *doctrine of equivalence*—e.g.:

- "If the court finds no literal infringement of the element because the accused device has no equivalent structure, then the opportunity of the patentee to show that the device nevertheless infringes under the *doctrine of equivalence* [read *doctrine of equivalents*] has been characterized as taking "two bites at the apple." Robert C. Kahrl, *Patent Claim Construction* § 9.06, at 9-40.1 (2001).
- "The *doctrine of equivalence* [read *doctrine of equivalents*] plays an important role in deciding infringement cases." C.B. Raju & N.S. Sreenivasulu, *Biotechnology and Patent Law* 174 (2008).

doctrine of merger. See **merger** (D).

document; record; archive; muniment; instrument. All these terms refer to a writing, especially one preserved or serving as evidence of something. A *document* is essentially anything written, printed, or extant in a computer. At its broadest, the term denotes any tangible thing on which words, symbols, or marks are recorded. Fed. R. Civ. P. 34(a)(2). *Documents* are divided into two classes: "*Public* or *official documents* include all writing or records made by public officers in any of the three departments of government, setting forth facts [that] such officers are required, in the performance of their duties of their office, to record. All other writings are *private documents*." William Payson Richardson, *The Law of Evidence* 455 (3d ed. 1928). A *record* is a document that has been prepared so that precise knowledge of occurrences will be preserved <the phone company's records show that a call was made at 10:37 A.M.>. An *archive* is a collection or accumulation of documents intended for long-term preservation, especially for the use of scholars and historians <search the archive for the trial notes>. The plural form *archives*, essentially synonymous but perhaps suggesting a miscellany, is more common. (*Archives* can also suggest a place where the collection is kept, as opposed to the collection itself.) A *muniment* is a quite specific kind of document: typically a title deed or charter that is kept and is usable as evidence of ownership. Today this word is most commonly used in the phrase *muniment of title*— e.g.: "A trust may not, under those circumstances, be ingrafted upon a deed absolute in its terms, because if that were the rule deeds would no longer be valuable as *muniments of title*." *Silvers v. Howard*, 190 P. 1, 4 (Kan. 1920). Otherwise, a *muniment* tends to be a public document dealing with national, ecclesiastical, or manorial rights and privileges. An *instrument* is any document with a specifically legal purpose, usually prepared by a lawyer. See **instrument.**

documentary, adj.; *documental. The second is a NEEDLESS VARIANT.

DOCUMENT DESIGN. Traditionally, lawyers have been relatively unconcerned with the look of their documents—even lawyers who consider themselves stylists. This failing (and it is a serious one) had no horrible consequences in the days of typewriters, when the primary design choices were the width of the margins and the amount of underlining and capital lettering.

With the advent of word processing, document design has become much more important as writers are presented with all kinds of new printing options. Failing to use these options knowledgeably will put you at a disadvantage because readers have become accustomed to well-designed documents. In short,

you need to know something about typography and design.

In this space, of course, it is impossible to offer even the simplest primer on the subject. But a dozen rules merit your notice:

1. Understand that the most important decisions you'll make are the font, the type size, the line spacing, the line length, and justification. The basic look and feel of your document will be determined largely by these five factors. For most word-processed documents, you're well advised to use 13-point Garamond, with 1.2-inch margins, and a ragged-right margin. Readability specialists have long insisted that unjustified right margins are more readable than justified ones. In letters, contracts, briefs, and the like, an unjustified right margin avoids all sorts of awkward spacing problems. Leave the fully justified typesetting to publishers.

2. Use a good serifed font, not a sans-serif (except as display type). For text, a readable typeface probably means a serifed typeface, such as the one used throughout this text, as opposed to a sans-serif (/san[z]-**ser**-if/) typeface made up of only straight lines. A serif is a short stroke that projects from the ends of the main strokes that make up a character.

This is a serifed typeface: Century.

This is a sans-serif typeface: Helvetica.

Although sans-serif typefaces often work well in headings and the like, they can be difficult to read in text. Among the better serifed typefaces are Bookman, Caslon, Garamond, Palatino, and Times New Roman. The one typeface to avoid at all costs still predominated in American legal writing in the mid-1990s: Courier. It's an eyesore.

3. Choose a type size of 10–14 points. Most professionally typeset documents use 10- to 12-point type. Federal appellate briefs are required to be 14 points. (Fed. R. App. P. 32.) For letters and most law-office documents, a 13-point setting is a good default.

4. Unless you're producing manuscript for hand-editing, prefer single-spacing over double-spacing. Virtually all professionally printed pages are single-spaced, not double-spaced—books, magazines, newspapers, and so on. Law-office documents were traditionally double-spaced in part because they were typewritten, and a mistake toward the bottom of the page might result in double the retyping for single-spaced text. Also, consider that double-spacing makes for lots of meaningless white space (between every two lines), while single-spacing makes the white space (between paragraphs) meaningful.

5. Ensure that your lines average 45–90 characters, not more or less than that. Ideally, a line of type should accommodate 45 to 90 characters, but the "fine print" that characterizes so many legal documents often spans 150 characters to the line. In text of that kind, the reader's eye tends to get lost in mid-line or in moving from the end of one line to the beginning of the next. One way to improve a document with a large block of text—and, typically, small margins on each side—is to use a double-column format. That design can be extremely helpful, for example, in consumer contracts such as residential leases.

6. Use "smart" quotes and apostrophes, not "straight" ones. You have the technology. Avoid the ugliness of straight hash marks for quotations and apostrophes.

7. Put only one forward space between sentences. This point surprises many people, but the publishing standard (as opposed to the old high-school typewriting-class standard) has always been one forward space after a period or colon. With a proportional typeface, as opposed to monospaced Courier, adding two spaces between sentences disrupts the balance of white space, creating "rivers" within a paragraph.

8. Never underline. Generally, italicizing is preferable to underlining, which was traditionally nothing more than a (poor) substitute for italics. The effect of underlining is to take up white space between lines and therefore to make the lines harder for readers to discern. It also tends to obscure the type's descenders (the parts of g, j, p, q, and y that fall below the baseline), thereby impairing readability.

9. Use boldface only in headings, never in the body. Pockmarking the page with boldfaced words in text is highly distracting and amateurish.

10. Never use all-caps text except for a title or heading of less than one full line. Lawyers grossly overuse all-caps—and initial caps, too, for that matter. A sentence-style heading (such as a point heading in a brief) should appear as a boldface sentence with ordinary capitalization—e.g.:

DO THIS:

1. **Helmsley's claim is barred by limitations because she waited more than three years after discovering her illness to file suit.**

NOT:

1. **HELMSLEY'S CLAIM IS BARRED BY LIMITATIONS BECAUSE SHE WAITED MORE THAN THREE YEARS AFTER DISCOVERING HER ILLNESS TO FILE SUIT.**

AND NOT:

1. **Helmsley's Claim Is Barred by Limitations Because She Waited More than Three Years After Discovering Her Illness to File Suit.**

11. Use white space intelligently. Ample white space makes a page more inviting. The primary ways to create white space on the page are to use generous margins (for letters and briefs, for example, margins greater than one inch), to use headings and subheadings, and to enumerate items in separate paragraphs, subparagraphs, or bulleted lists.

Headings and subheadings are especially helpful in making a document easy to follow. Not only do they serve as navigational aids for your readers, they also

help you as a writer organize your thoughts more logically. See PLAIN LANGUAGE (D).

Enumerating and subenumerating can also be helpful in adding white space. Using a tabulated list allows you not only to display the points better, but also to improve the sentence structure. Ensure that the list falls at the end of the sentence—not at the beginning or in the middle. See ENUMERATIONS & PLAIN LANGUAGE (D).

When you don't mean to imply that one thing in a list is any more important than another—that is, when you're not signaling that there is a rank order—and there is little likelihood that the list will need to be cited, you might use bullet dots. They draw the eye immediately to the salient points and thereby enhance readability. Examples appear throughout this book.

There is a notable difference, however, between how the bullets appear in this book and how they ought to appear in most documents. Although here the bullets fall at the left margin, they should generally be indented farther than a paragraph indent. They are not indented here because a double-column format does not readily lend itself to indentation.

Usually, when you indent an item to be listed—whether it's a bulleted item or an entire paragraph—ensure that the second line of the item does not begin at the left margin. Use hanging indents, with the second line of text beginning just below the first one, as here:

- The managing general partner must send notice to the bankrupt partner before the 180th day after receiving notice of the event that causes the bankruptcy.
- The bankrupt partner and the managing partner must agree on a fair market value for the sale of the interest.

All these devices make the white space on your page meaningful.

12. Rid your text of numerical pollution by footnoting citations. Traditionally, in the days of typewriters, documents couldn't readily be prepared with footnoted citations. Those days are long past. Yet textual citations needlessly overwhelm many a legal paragraph. It's easy to subordinate them while explaining in the text, in your own words, what your authority is: what court said it, and when, for important citations. The rest should be relegated to the foot of the page—with no sentences at all in the footnotes. That way, they're just references. The profession is slow to make this reform, but more and more writers are making the shift year by year. See CITATION OF CASES (D).

For the best extended treatment of document design in law, see Matthew Butterick, *Typography for Lawyers* (2010). It's a superb little book.

Doe, John; Richard Roe. The fictitious names *John Doe* and *Richard Roe* regularly appeared in actions of ejectment at common law (see **ejectment**). *Doe* was the nominal plaintiff, who, by a FICTION, was said to have entered land under a valid lease; *Roe* was said to have ejected *Doe*, and the lawsuit took the title *Doe v. Roe*. These fictional allegations disappeared upon the enactment of the Common Law Procedure Act of

1852. Meanwhile, though, *John Doe*—which began as a LEGALISM—had become a POPULARIZED LEGAL TECHNICALITY.

Beyond actions of ejectment, and especially in the U.S., *John Doe, Jane Doe, Richard Roe, Jane Roe,* and *Peter Poe* have come to identify a party to a lawsuit whose true name is either unknown or purposely shielded.

DOG FRENCH. See LAW FRENCH.

DOG LATIN. See LAW LATIN.

dogma. Pl. *dogmas,* **dogmata.* The English plural is preferred—e.g.: "A number of scholastic and, as it seems to me, unprofitable *dogmas* have grown up [that] tend to obscure the real function of precedent in our legal reasoning." Carleton K. Allen, *Law in the Making* 268 (7th ed. 1964).

dolus (= fraud, deceit, or intentional aggression) is a civil-law term that appears frequently in discussions of general legal principles. E.g.:

- "The typical delict required *dolus*—intentional aggression upon the personality or the substance of another." Roscoe Pound, *An Introduction to the Philosophy of Law* 155–56 (1922).
- "Liability for damage caused by intention (*dolus*) or negligence (*culpa*) was a general principle in Roman law, as it is in Scots law, Roman-Dutch law and French law." O. Hood Phillips, *A First Book of English Law* 226 (3d ed. 1955).

Domesday Book; Doomsday Book. The first is the accepted spelling in modern texts of the name for the great census or survey of England's landholdings, buildings, people, and livestock that was ordered by William the Conqueror and completed (except for several districts in the North) in 1086.

domesticate; ***domesticize.** See **domiciliate.**

domicile; ***domicil. A. Spelling.** *Domicile* is spelled both with and without the final *-e,* but the better and more common spelling is with it.

B. And *residence.* The two words are often "confused as synonymous." *In re Lemen,* 208 F. 80, 82 (N.D. Ohio 1912). They are not: "*Residence* comprehends no more than a fixed abode where one actually lives for the time being. It is distinguished from *domicile* in that *domicile* is the place where a person intends eventually to return and remain." *Catalanotto v. Palazzolo,* 259 N.Y.S.2d 473, 475 (Sup. Ct. 1965).

More specifically, *domicile* means "the place with which a person has a settled connection for certain legal purposes, either because his home is there, or because that place is assigned to him by the law." Restatement of Conflict of Laws § 9, at 17 (1934).

In England, *domicile* means "the country that a person treats as a permanent home and to which he or she has the closest legal attachment." See **citizenship.**

C. *Domicile of origin; domicile of choice; commercial domicile.* *Domicile of origin* = the domicile that is imposed by operation of law on every person at birth. *Domicile of choice* = a domicile chosen by a person having full age and capacity.

Commercial domicile, known also as *quasi-domicile,* "is in no sense true domicile. It is a legal concept used merely as a test of enemy character in time of war. It attaches to any person or firm voluntarily resident or carrying on business in enemy territory or even in enemy-occupied territory. . . . It has chiefly been used to determine the liability of property to seizure, and in a number of cases property itself has been said to possess a commercial domicile." R.H. Graveson, *Conflict of Laws* 221 (7th ed. 1974).

domiciliary is both adjective ("of or pertaining to domicile") and noun ("one belonging to a domicile").

domiciliate; domesticate; ***domesticize.** *Domiciliate* = to establish a domicile or home. *Domesticate* = (1) to tame; or (2) to make a member of the household. Sense 1 here applies: "Before the jury retired, Colonial intimated that it intended to request the court to take judicial notice of the *domesticated* Oregon judgment." *Colonial Leasing Co. v. Logistics Control Group Int'l,* 762 F.2d 454, 457 (5th Cir. 1985). *Domesticize is a NEEDLESS VARIANT of *domesticate.*

dominance; domination. *Dominance* = the fact or position of being dominant. *Domination* = the act of dominating; the exercise of ruling power.

dominant; servient. These terms are usually used in reference to *estates* or *tenements* in the law of easements. A *dominant* estate has the benefit of a servitude or easement over the *servient* estate.

domination. See **dominance.**

dominion. See **power (B).**

dominium is the Roman-law term for absolute ownership. In some contexts it can be "particularly confusing, since in medieval times it is also the word for lordship." J.H. Baker, *An Introduction to English Legal History* 255 (3d ed. 1990).

donate, a BACK-FORMATION from *donation,* was formerly considered a vulgar equivalent of *give.* Today, however, it is a more FORMAL WORD than *give* that is frequently used of charitable bequests.

donatio mortis causa is an unjustified LATINISM for the slightly less Latinate *gift causa mortis.* Pl. *donationes mortis causa.* See *causa mortis.*

donative; donatory. As an adjective, the second is a NEEDLESS VARIANT—e.g.: "This evidence is far short of the clear and convincing proof necessary to rebut the presumption of *donative* intent." *Armstrong v. Daniel,*

232 N.E.2d 218, 221 (Ill. App. Ct. 1967). For the noun sense of *donatory*, see **donee.**

donator. See **donor.**

donatory. See **donative** & **donee.**

donee; donatory, n. *Donee* (= one to whom something is given) is the usual term. E.g.: "Where the inconsistency lies in a gift of the same thing to two persons both *donees* will take some interest in that thing." Anthony R. Mellows, *The Law of Succession* 161 (3d ed. 1977). *Donatory* is a little-used equivalent. See **donor** & -EE.

donor; donator. The second is a problematic word, meaning either (1) "donor" or (2) "donee." It should be avoided in favor of *donor* or *donee.* See **settlor.**

Doomsday Book. See **Domesday Book.**

doomster; doomsman. These are both variants of *deemster* or *dempster.* See **dempster.**

dotal, adj., = (1) at common law, relating to a dower; or (2) in civil law, relating to a dowry. See **dower.**

doth for *does*, though archaic and obsolete, still occasionally appears in judicial pronouncements, such as this, by the Mississippi Supreme Court in 1981: "This Court having sufficiently examined and considered the same and being of the opinion that the same should be denied *doth* order that said motion be and the same is hereby denied." Order quoted in *Jones v. Thigpen*, 741 F.2d 805, 809 (5th Cir. 1984). Methinks, forsooth, that we should throw over this term, as well as the rest of the LEGALESE verily immortalized in that sentence.

The word is also used in orders of the English courts. E.g.: "This court *doth* declare that there was a valid and binding contract." *In re Edwards*, [1958] Ch. 168, 170 (C.A.). See -ETH.

double-dealing. See **deception.**

double entendre originally referred to any verbal expression giving rise to more than one meaning. Now, however, it also connotes that one of those meanings is indecent or risqué. See **ambiguity.**

double jeopardy; former jeopardy. These terms are not precisely the same. *Double jeopardy* is the fact of being prosecuted twice for substantially the same offense. A plea of *former jeopardy* informs the court that one has previously been prosecuted for the same offense. E.g.:

- "Conditioning an appeal of one offense on a coerced surrender of a valid plea of *former jeopardy* on another offense exacts a forfeiture in plain conflict with the constitutional bar against *double jeopardy*." *Green v. U.S.*, 355 U.S. 184, 193–94 (1957) (per Black, J.).
- "The *former-jeopardy* principle is a fundamental feature of our legal system, originating in the common law and later

incorporated into our constitutions." *State v. Brunson*, 393 S.E.2d 860, 864 (N.C. 1990).

- "The first part of each count informed defendant of the nature and character of the criminal offenses with sufficient particularity to enable him to make his defense and, if necessary, to assert *former jeopardy* should he be indicted for the same conduct in the future." *State v. Coven*, 839 P.2d 261, 263–64 (Or. Ct. App. 1992).

DOUBLE NEGATIVES. See NEGATIVES (B).

DOUBLETS, TRIPLETS, AND SYNONYM-STRINGS. Amplification by synonym has long been a part of the English language, and especially a part of the language of the law. In the English Renaissance, this habit was a common figure of speech called *synonymia*. It is often supposed that the purpose of these paired or strung-along synonyms was etymological, that is, that writers in the Middle Ages and Renaissance would pair a French or Latinate term with an Anglo-Saxon approximation as a gloss on the foreign word. So we have, as survivals in legal language, *acknowledge and confess* (Old English and Old French), *act and deed* (Latin and Old English), and *goods and chattels* (Old English and Old French).

The philologist George Philip Krapp argued against this explanation. He saw the purpose of this mannerism as "rhetorical or oratorical rather than etymological." George P. Krapp, *Modern English: Its Growth and Present Use* 251 (1909). He pointed out that such doubling occurred abundantly in Old English, when no substantial foreign element existed in the language, and that it often occurs in later writings without regard for etymology. Although Krapp was undoubtedly correct to emphasize the rhetorical importance of doubling, he was wrong to assume that the figure did not take on a utilitarian significance as well in Middle and early Modern English. The purpose of doubling was dual: to give rhetorical weight and balance to the phrase, and to maximize the understanding of readers or listeners.

Still another explanation has emerged for the particular fondness that lawyers have for this stylistic quirk. It is a cynical one: "This multiplication of useless expressions probably owed its origin to the want of knowledge of the true meaning and due application of each word, and a consequent apprehension, that if one word alone were used, a wrong one might be adopted and the right one omitted; and to this something must be added for carelessness and the general disposition of the profession to seek safety in verbosity rather than in discrimination of language." 1 Charles Davidson, *Precedents and Forms in Conveyancing* 67 (3d ed. 1860).

The phrases most obviously inspired by rhetorical concerns are alliterative. Rhetoricians call them reduplicative phrases—e.g.: *aid and abet*; *have and hold*; *part and parcel*; *trials and tribulations*; *rest, residue, and remainder*; *laid and levied*; and *mind and memory*. Many others, in addition to conveying no nuance in meaning, have no aesthetically redeeming qualities, but even informed opinions on a point of this kind are likely to diverge. Following are two lists, the first containing common doublets in legal writing, the second containing some of the common triplets. Any number of variations, as by inversion (or, with triplets, by reordering), are possible.

Doublets

able and willing
act and deed
agree and covenant
agreed and declared
aid and abet
aid and comfort
all and every
all and singular
all and sundry
amount or quantum
annoy or molest
annulled and set aside (see **annul**)
answerable and accountable
any and all
appropriate and proper
attached and annexed
authorize and direct
authorize and empower
betting or wagering
bills and notes
bind and obligate
by and between
by and through
by and under
by and with
canceled and set aside
cease and come to an end
cease and determine (see **determine (A)**)
chargeable and accountable
claim and demand
covenant and agree
custom and usage
deed and assurance
deem and consider
definite and certain
demises and leases
deposes and says
desire and require
do and perform
dominion and authority
due and owing
due and payable (see **due**)
each and all
each and every
ends and objects
escape and evade
exact and specific
execute and perform
false and untrue
final and conclusive

finish and complete
fit and proper
for and in behalf of
force and effect
fraud and deceit
free and clear
from and after
full and complete
full faith and credit
furnish and supply
good and effectual
goods and chattels
have and hold
indemnify and hold harmless
keep and maintain
kind and character
kind and nature
known and described as
laid and levied
leave and license
legal and valid
liens and encumbrances
made and signed
maintenance and upkeep
make and enter into (a contract)
make and execute
means and includes
messuage and dwelling-house
mind and memory
name and style
new and novel
nominate and appoint
null and of no effect
null and void
object and purpose
order and direct
other and further (relief)
over and above
pains and penalties
pardon and forgive
part and parcel
peace and quiet
perform and discharge
power and authority
premeditation and malice aforethought
release and discharge
repair and make good
restrain and enjoin
reverts to and falls back upon
save and except
seised and possessed (of)
sell and assign
separate and apart
separate and distinct
set aside and vacate
settle and compromise
shall and will

An asterisk (✳) precedes words and phrases that are invariably inferior forms.

shun and avoid
similar and like
sole and exclusive
son and heir
successors and assigns
supersede and displace
surmise and conjecture
terms and conditions
then and in that event
title and interest
total and entire
touch and concern
true and correct
truth and veracity
type and kind
uncontroverted and uncontradicted
understood and agreed
unless and until
uphold and support
used and applied
various and sundry
will and testament

Triplets and Longer Strings

amend, vary, or modify
build, erect, or construct
business, enterprise, or undertaking
cancel, annul, and set aside
changes, variations, and modifications
costs, charges, and expenses
do, execute, and perform
form, manner, and method
general, vague, and indefinite
give, devise, and bequeath
goods, chattels, and effects
grant, bargain, sell, and convey
grants, demises, and lets
hold, possess, and enjoy
initiate, institute, and commence
lands, tenements, and hereditaments
legal, valid, and binding
liberties, rights, and privileges
loans, borrowings, and advances
make, publish, and declare
name, constitute, and appoint
ordered, adjudged, and decreed
pay, satisfy, and discharge
place, install, or affix
possession, custody, and control
promise, agree, and covenant
ready, willing, and able
reconstitution, reorganization, or reconstruction
remise, release, and forever discharge
remise, release, and forever quitclaim
repair, uphold, and maintain
rest, residue, and remainder
right, title, and interest
sell, call in, and convert
signed, sealed, and delivered
situate, lying, and being in

suit, claim, or demand
terminate, cancel, and revoke
terms, stipulations, and conditions
vague, nonspecific, and indefinite
way, shape, or form

One commentator recommends avoiding virtually all coupled synonyms. *See* David Mellinkoff, *Legal Writing: Sense and Nonsense* 189–90 (1982); *The Language of the Law* 349–62 (1963). At least one writer has taken issue with this recommendation on grounds that doublets are a prosodic feature of English and many other languages. He argues: "Since coupled synonyms are by definition redundant, they do not increase the density of ideas contained within a sentence; therefore, they rarely endanger its clarity. Since coupled synonyms add beauty to writing without sacrificing clarity, I see nothing sinful in their moderate use." Robert P. Charrow, 30 UCLA L. Rev. 1094, 1102 (1983) (book review).

The primary problem with such arguments, on either side of the issue, is that they fail to identify the types of writing in which doublets may appear or should not appear. In DRAFTING documents to be interpreted, for example, you must consider the legal effects of this stylistic mannerism. *Stroud's Judicial Dictionary* (4th ed. 1971), under *contiguous* states that *contiguous* is "as nearly as possible" synonymous with *adjoining*, but points to a case in which the phrase *adjoining or contiguous* was read by the court as if it were *adjoining or near to*, "so as to give *contiguous* a cognate, but not identical, meaning with *adjoining*." If the drafter of that phrase meant *contiguous* when writing *contiguous*, then coupling it with *adjoining* caused trouble. (Cf. **adjacent** & **contiguous**.) The problem stems, of course, from the fundamental canon of construing legal documents that states that every word is to be given meaning and nothing is to be read as mere surplusage. In drafting, then, doublets may be given unforeseen meanings by clever interpreters. This danger, however, is more likely to appear with less common doublets and triplets: no judge would interpret *rest, residue, and remainder* as referring to three discrete things.

A second context to be considered is ritual language, as in *the truth, the whole truth, and nothing but the truth*, a resounding phrase that conveys the gravity and majesty of the oath being taken. *Last will and testament* may also properly be placed under the heading of ritual language, which is always directed to a lay rather than to a legal audience, the purpose being as much emotive as it is informational. See **last will and testament.**

A third context in which doubling occurs is that of legal commentary and judicial opinions. Here the coupling of synonyms can rarely be said to "add beauty," as the writer quoted above suggested; rather, it is almost always a blemish. For in this context, legal style most nearly approximates literary style, and amplification by synonym has been out of rhetorical fashion for hundreds of years. Although one might well title a client's will *Last Will and Testament*, if one were to write an opinion construing that document, it would be better to begin, "In this appeal we are called upon to construe the disposition of realty in *John Doe's will*" rather than *John Doe's last will and testament*.

Yet one might well write *vague and indefinite* in patent practice, in which that doublet is generally considered a TERM OF ART describing a patent application that lacks particularity and distinctness. *See* Louis B. Applebaum et al., *Glossary of United States Patent Practice* 126 (1969). The inclusion of both words is widely thought to add a nuance. That is the test in ordinary legal prose: Is a shade of meaning supplied by the second or third synonym, or is it just so much deadwood?

DOUBLING OF FINAL CONSONANTS. Unaccented syllables in inflected words are sometimes spelled differently in AmE and in BrE. Americans generally do not double a final -*l*- before the inflectional suffix, whereas the British generally do. Hence:

AmE	BrE
canceled, canceling	cancelled, cancelling
dueled, dueling	duelled, duelling
funneled, funneling	funnelled, funnelling
initialed, initialing	initialled, initialling
labeled, labeling	labelled, labelling
marshaled, marshaling	marshalled, marshalling
parceled, parceling	parcelled, parcelling
signaled, signaling	signalled, signalling
totaled, totaling	totalled, totalling
traveled, traveling	travelled, travelling
unraveled, unraveling	unravelled, unravelling

The split between AmE and BrE is seen also in words like *jewel(l)er*, *pupil(l)age*, and *travel(l)er*, the British preferring two -*l*-s rather than the one used by Americans. But there are exceptions: British writers use the forms *paralleled* and *paralleling*—just as Americans do—presumably to avoid the ungainly appearance of four -*l*-s in quick succession.

The British always double the final consonant after a full vowel in words such as *kidnapped, -ing* and *worshipped, -ing*. In AmE, *kidnapping* is preferred over **kidnaping* (see **kidnapping (A)**) as an exceptional form (*cf. formatted, formatting*), though *worshiped, -ing* follows the general American rule. *Programmed* and *programming* are the preferred spellings on both sides of the Atlantic, the single -*m*- spellings being secondary variants in AmE; for the probable reason underlying this American inconsistency, see **programmer.**

Writers and editors should make themselves aware of these minor transatlantic differences in spelling and avoid inserting *sic* when quoting a foreign text. (See **sic.**)

Apart from words ending in -*l*- and exceptions noted (*kidnapping, programming*, and *worship(p)ed*), all English-speaking countries follow the same rules on doubling. When a suffix beginning with a vowel is added, the final consonant of the word is repeated only if (1) the vowel sound preceding the consonant is represented by a single letter (hence *bed, bedding* but *head, heading*); or (2) the final syllable bears the main stress (hence *oc-'cur, oc-'curred* but *'of-fer, 'of-fered*).

Among the more commonly misspelled words not already mentioned are these: *biased, busing* (see **bus**), *combated, focused, benefited,* and *transferred.*

doubt. A. *Doubt that; doubt whether.* The first is used primarily in negative sentences and in questions—e.g.: "We do not *doubt that* the $125 per hour rate approved in the circuit court's order is fair and reasonable." *Justice Admin. Comm'n v. Lenamon*, 19 So.3d 1158, 1161 n.3 (Fla. Dist. Ct. App. 2009). *Doubt whether* is used in affirmative statements—e.g.: "Even if the testimony were to be believed, we *doubt whether* Ramey's conduct could be considered so outrageous and so offensive as to bar prosecution of the appellant." *Dravo v. State*, 420 A.2d 1012, 1017 (Md. Ct. Spec. App. 1980).

B. Followed by a Negative. *Doubt* can be a confusing word when followed by a negative—e.g.: "I *doubt* whether the court *will not* take the further step, when necessary." *Tyler v. Judges of the Court of Registration*, 55 N.E. 812, 814 (Mass. 1900). This sentence seems to state merely that the writer thinks the court *will* take the further step referred to.

C. And **misdoubt.* See *****misdoubt.**

doubtful torts; doubtful wrongs. These phrases express a useful nuance in the law of torts. *Doubtful torts* are injuries that are no doubt unlawful wrongs of some sort, but of which we cannot say with certainty that they are torts. *Doubtful wrongs*, by contrast, are injuries that, if they are unlawful, are torts, but are probably not unlawful. *See* T.E. Lewis, *Winfield on Tort* (6th ed. 1954).

doubtless; **doubtlessly.* **Doubtlessly* is incorrect for *doubtless* (a mild expression of certainty), *no doubt* (a stronger expression of certainty), or *undoubtedly* (the strongest of these three expressions of certainty). The word *doubtless* is itself an adverb <the Framers doubtless feared the executive's assertion of an independent military authority unchecked by the people>; therefore, **doubtlessly* is unnecessary. E.g.:

- "Had Zellars been driving in the wrong lane he would *doubtlessly* [read *doubtless*] have had a little more time and a better chance to avoid striking the child." *Nett v. Zellars*, 353 S.W.2d 379, 381 (Ky. 1962).
- "Prejudice *doubtlessly* [read *doubtless*] ensued in this case because credibility was pivotal and the convictions probably would have affected the jury's assessment of T.B.'s

credibility." *Merriweather v. State*, 294 S.W.3d 52, 57 (Mo. 2009).

See ADVERBS (D), **clearly,** HYPERCORRECTION (D) & **obviously.**

doubt of is unidiomatic for *doubt about.* E.g.:

- "The language of the statute leaves no *doubt of* [read *doubt about*] the intent of the General Assembly to eliminate the possibility of armed assaults upon cab drivers by passengers bent upon robbing the drivers." *Meyerson v. Carter*, 316 N.E.2d 240, 243 (Ill. App. Ct. 1974). On the other usage question raised by that example—that of a statute having intent—see HYPALLAGE.
- "A statute does not abrogate or alter the common law unless it is so clearly expressed as to leave no *doubt of* [read *doubt about*] the legislature's intent." *Houle v. School Dist. of Ashland*, 671 N.W.2d 395, 399 (Wis. Ct. App. 2003).
- "Defendant contends . . . the State failed to prove him guilty beyond a reasonable *doubt of* [read *doubt about*] possession of a controlled substance with intent to deliver." *People v. Bailey*, 872 N.E.2d 420, 438 (Ill. App. Ct. 2007).

doubt that; doubt whether. See **doubt** (A).

dove. See **dive.**

dowable = (of a widow) entitled to dower. (See **dower.**) E.g.:

- "The plaintiff inherited the land from his father, who had originally obtained the land through conveyance from the widow's husband; and the plaintiff had agreed to recognize the widow's dower rights, but felt that the pasture area was not *dowable.*" Nancy Isenberg, *Laissez-Unfaire*, 37 Tulsa L. Rev. 929, 938 (2002).
- "He recognized that uncultivated lands were *dowable* (and not exempt from dower) and he incorporated the disputed land within the domesticated landscape of the homestead." *Id.*
- "In holding that Moore's wife was not *dowable*, the Supreme Court of Virginia stated that 'the two instruments were parts of one and the same transaction, and that the seizin of Moore was that instantaneous seizing . . . where the land was merely in transit, and never vested in the husband.'" Abraham M. Ashton, *"Yes, West Virginia, There Is a Special Priority for the Purchase Money Mortgage,"* 107 W. Va. L. Rev. 525, 535 (2005).

dowager; *doweress.* *Dowager* (= a landowner's widow who possesses her dower interest in her deceased husband's land) is now slightly derogatory in nonlegal usage, in the sense "an elderly woman with social standing."

**Doweress*, according to the *OED*, has long been considered a NEEDLESS VARIANT. Nevertheless, it has occurred in good legal writing: "And consequently, a *doweress* [read *dowager*] could not demand dower unless she handed over her late husband's charters." Theodore F.T. Plucknett, *A Concise History of the Common Law* 365 (5th ed. 1956).

dower; dowry. These waning terms are related etymologically (fr. L. *dot-, dos* "gift, marriage portion"), but they are best kept distinct in modern usage. *Dower* = the widow's legal share during her lifetime of the real estate owned by her deceased husband. At common law dower was only a life estate, but in many American jurisdictions dower (or the elective share) has been expanded into a fee—e.g.: "That the widow has *dower* in a defeasible fee though her husband's estate be determined by an executory limitation is asserted in 2 Minor's Institutes (4th Ed.) Ch. VIII, p. 155." *Snidow v. Snidow*, 63 S.E.2d 620, 622 (Va. 1951). See **curtesy.**

Dowry is occasionally used as a synonym of *dower*, but doing so muddles the DIFFERENTIATION between the words. In the best usage, *dowry* means "the money, goods, or real estate that a woman brings to her husband in marriage."

doweress. See **dowager.**

down payment. Two words.

downplay, vb., is not the best usage, *play down* being preferred. E.g.: "Each side also tends to discuss only that role occupied by Wynn favorable to its position and *downplays* [read *plays down*] the other." *Mills Land & Water Co. v. Golden West Ref. Co.*, 230 Cal. Rptr. 461, 466 (Ct. App. 1986). Both expressions are colloquial.

dowry. See **dower.**

draconian; *draconic.* *Draconian* (the usual form) is derived from the name *Draco*, a Greek legislator of the 7th century B.C. who drafted a code of severe laws that included the death penalty for anyone caught stealing a cabbage. Today, *draconian* (sometimes but not usually capitalized) refers to any cruel or excessively severe rule or punishment, not necessarily just legislation.

Sometimes the word is the victim of SLIPSHOD EXTENSION, when applied to any rule or policy that is viewed as harsh though not cruel—e.g.: "Phil Seelig, president of the Correction Officers Benevolent Association, said his organization would appeal the decision to the State Court of Appeals on the ground that random drug testing was unnecessarily *draconian* [read *harsh* or *burdensome*] and violated constitutional protection against unlawful searches." *Court Upholds Drug Testing of Correction Officers*, N.Y. Times, 13 Oct. 1989, at 10.

**Draconic* is a NEEDLESS VARIANT—e.g.: "A general 'control' of the Common Law over statute . . . does not amount to a right to resist even the most *Draconic* [read *Draconian*] statute." Carleton K. Allen, *Law in the Making* 456 (7th ed. 1964).

For a judicial analogue, see **rhadamanthine.**

draft. See **note.**

draft; draught. See **drafter.**

drafter; draftsman; draughtsman; *draftsperson.* *Drafter* is a neutral, nonsexist equivalent preferred by those wary of terms ending in *-man.* *Draftsperson* is a wholly unnecessary NEOLOGISM. See SEXISM (B).

Draughtsman is the older BrE spelling of *draftsman.* E.g.:

- "On the admitted facts the employers did not intend to cease to carry on the business for the purposes of which the employee was employed and its requirements for *draughtsmen* had not diminished." *U.K. Atomic Energy Auth. v. Claydon*, [1974] I.C.R. 128, 131.
- "That type of provision would have been a simple one for the parliamentary *draughtsmen* to insert and for parliament to enact had the restriction been intended." *Clarke v. Clarke*, [2006] Fam. L.R. 90.

In American writing, that spelling smacks of pedantry—e.g.: "He [Samuel Tutt] was thoroughly read in the law, an expert pleader and *draughtsman* [read *draftsman* or, if the book were being written today, *drafter*], reveled in technicalities and, in preparing a case for trial, left no point uncovered." Ephraim Tutt, *Yankee Lawyer* 313 (1943).

Drafting. See LEGISLATIVE DRAFTING.

draftsman. See **drafter.**

draftsmanship; draughtsmanship. The only non-sexist equivalent of these terms is *drafting*, which (unfortunately) refers not only to the art but also to the product.

It is a mistake for American writers to use *draughtsmanship*, the BrE spelling, which appears in Kenneth H. York & John A. Bauman, *Remedies* 182 (1973).

*draftsperson. See **drafter.**

drag > dragged > dragged. *Drug* for *dragged* is a nonstandard dialectal form long common in Southern AmE and seemingly spreading geographically—e.g.:

- "She *drug* [read *dragged*] him out by the ear, pulled him out, beat him up." *Guillory v. Godfrey*, 286 P.2d 474, 477 (Cal. Ct. App. 1955).
- "After the truck turned over, he *drug* [read *dragged*] it a car's length before it stopped." *Keeney v. Odom*, 534 S.W.2d 409, 411 (Tex. Civ. App.—Beaumont 1976).
- "Mr. Call unraveled an approximately 50-pound, two-inch, 40-foot-long hose and *drug* [read *dragged*] it around the front of the truck." *Call v. American Int'l Group, Inc.*, 621 F.Supp.2d 352, 354 (S.D. W. Va. 2008).

dragnet clause. See **Mother Hubbard clause.**

dramshop = a business selling alcoholic drinks; a bar. Of 18th-century origin, the term appears today only in the phrases *dramshop suits*, *dramshop claims*, and *dramshop statutes*. *Dramshop claims* involve allegations that liquor establishments serving underage or obviously intoxicated patrons should be held liable for consequent drunk-driving accidents.

draughtsman. See **drafter.**

draughtsmanship. See **draftsmanship.**

draw. Only in the legal idiom does *draw* retain the sense "to frame (a writing or document) in due form" (*OED*), as a synonym of *draft* <to draw a will>. E.g.:

- "While the petition has been *drawn*, with obvious meticulous care, to avoid the semblance of seeking mandatory relief, in essence and effect it presents no other objective." *American Nat'l Bank v. Sheppard*, 175 S.W.2d 626, 628 (Tex. Civ. App.—Austin 1943).
- "It takes time and knowledge to *draw* a statute carefully." Robert G. McCloskey, *The American Supreme Court* 203 (1960).

More casually—and in nonlegal as well as legal writing—*draw* is coupled with the particle *up*, for a PHRASAL VERB. E.g.: "Of all the many business contracts and legal agreements of every sort that are *drawn up* and signed every day, only a very small fraction are eventually carried to court." Fred Rodell, *Woe Unto You, Lawyers!* 115 (1939).

drawee = payor <drawee bank>. Because lawyers understand *drawee* and *payor* to be synonymous, the coupling of the two in the phrase *drawee/payor* makes little sense—e.g.: "A payee or other true owner of an instrument that is cashed under a forged endorsement may sue directly the *drawee/payor* [read either *drawee* or *payor*] bank." *Lincoln Nat'l Bank & Trust Co. v. Bank of Commerce*, 764 F.2d 392, 397 (5th Cir. 1985).

drink > drank > drunk. So inflected. Avoid *drank* as a past participle—e.g.: "When business people have 'lawyered up' with top-shelf attorneys from prestigious law firms . . . and have *drank* [read *drunk*] their own 'Kool-Aid,' their legal correctness is cemented in their own *mind* [read *minds*]." David C. Albalah & Jesse D. Steele, *For Business Dispute Solutions, Process Matters*, 11 Cardozo J. Conflict Res. 385, 401 (2010).

drink-driving. See **drunk driving.**

droitural; *droiturel. *Droitural* [fr. F. *droit* "a legal right"]—the more common spelling of this uncommon word—means "relating to an ownership right in property, as distinguished from mere possession." E.g.:

- "The law may . . . bar the owner from asserting his rights by a *droitural* action and thus leave these rights suspended in a state of unenforceability." Marian P. Opala, *Praescriptio Temporis and Its Relation to Prescriptive Easements in the Anglo-American Law*, 7 Tulsa L.J. 107, 107 (1971).
- "As a result of these changes, the assize became a '*droitural*' action—that is, it tried right rather than recent possession—and by 1400 the writs of right and entry had been largely driven out of use." J.H. Baker, *An Introduction to English Legal History* 270 (3d ed. 1990).

F.W. Maitland's habitual spelling, **droiturel*, is a variant that is all but obsolete.

drug. See **drag > dragged > dragged.**

drumhead court. The original phrase, *drumhead court-martial*, was an early-19th-century term denoting a military tribunal held around an upturned drum to deal summarily with offenses during military operations. The phrase quickly took on figurative senses,

---

first in reference to any summary court-martial—e.g.: "In the face of the enemy, it is permitted to try an alleged spy summarily before a *drumhead court-martial*, and execute him if found guilty." *Filbin Corp. v. U.S.*, 266 F. 911, 917 (E.D.S.C. 1920).

The phrase was later extended to refer to any tribunal with loose procedures that result in questionable justice. In this extended sense, the phrase is sometimes *drumhead court*, sometimes *drumhead court-martial*—e.g.:

- "It is the protection from arbitrary punishments through the right to a judicial trial with all these safeguards which over the years has distinguished America from lands where *drumhead courts* and other similar 'tribunals' deprive the weak and the unorthodox of life, liberty and property without due process of law." *Barenblatt v. U.S.*, 360 U.S. 109, 162 (1959) (Black, J., dissenting).
- "One of the attorneys in *United States v. Hoffa* was convicted of contempt for saying that the court was conducting a '*drum head court martial*' [read '*drumhead court-martial*'] and 'a star chamber proceeding.'" Norman Dorsen & Leon Friedman, *Disorder in the Court* 150 (1973).

drunk; drunken. Traditionally, *drunk* has been an adjective appearing in the predicate <they were drunk>, whereas *drunken* has preceded the noun <a drunken sailor> <drunken revelry>. Today, the words mostly bear distinct senses. *Drunk* = intoxicated, inebriated. *Drunken* = given to drink; morbidly alcoholic.

We do, however, have the idiom *drunken driving*, defined by the *CDL* as "driving while affected by alcohol." *Drunken* here means "exhibiting or evidencing intoxication." E.g.: "England in the mid-1980s still regulates licensing hours (though not perhaps for much longer) and the age at which people can lawfully buy alcohol, while *drunken driving* is a criminal offence." Simon Lee, *Law and Morals* 1–2 (1986). Because *drunken* implies a habitual state, the phrase *drunk driving* is preferable. See **drunk driving.**

drunk driving (AmE) = *drink-driving* (BrE). The American form—*drunk driving*—exemplifies HYPALLAGE because it is the driver, not the driving, that is drunk. On the less acceptable form—*drunken driving*—see **drunk.**

To American eyes, though, the BrE form looks extremely odd—e.g.:

- "A *drink-driving* offender will probably be charged with one of the specialised offences . . . rather than with careless driving, since the penalty for the former is higher (and can be imprisonment)." Glanville Williams, *Textbook of Criminal Law* 271 (1978).
- "In the West Midlands, 30 officers have been convicted of *drink-driving* in the last two years." Mazher Mahmood, *Drink-Driving Immunity—The Police Force "Perk"*, Sunday Times, 11 Dec. 1988, at A3.

drunken. See **drunk.**

Drunkometer. See **Breathalyzer.**

dualism. See **monism.**

dubious distinction has the dubious distinction of being one of our most overworked CLICHÉS.

dubitante = doubting. The term is used in law reports of a judge who is doubtful about a legal proposition but is loath to declare it wrong—e.g.: "Mr. Justice Rutledge acquiesces in the Court's opinion and judgment *dubitante* on the question of equal protection of the laws."

This term is sometimes used after a judge's name, as an analogue to *concurring* or *dissenting*. It signals that the judge had grave doubts about the soundness of the majority opinion, but not so grave as to spark a dissent. E.g.: "The Court decided to do so, Baggallay L.J. *dubitante* but not *dissentiente* [i.e., doubting but not dissenting]." Carleton K. Allen, *Law in the Making* 493 (7th ed. 1964). See OPINIONS, JUDICIAL (C).

duces tecum. See **subpoena** (C).

due. Traditionally, this word has contained an ambiguity, since it could mean either (1) "payable; owing; constituting a debt"; or (2) "immediately enforceable." Sense 1 relates to the fact of indebtedness, sense 2 to the time of payment. Today, sense 2 is almost invariably the applicable one, as illustrated in an early-20th-century edition of Bouvier: "[*Due*] differs from *owing* in this, that sometimes what is owing is not due: a note payable thirty days after date is owing immediately after it is delivered to the payee, but it is not *due* until the thirty days have elapsed." 1 John Bouvier, *Bouvier's Law Dictionary* 946 (Francis Rawle ed., 3d ed. 1914).

Because a debt cannot be *due* without also being *payable*, the doublet *due and payable* is unnecessary in place of *due*. See DOUBLETS, TRIPLETS, AND SYNONYM-STRINGS.

due and payable. See **due.**

due process of law. When applied to judicial proceedings, this phrase—often shortened to *due process*—traditionally "mean[s] a course of legal proceedings according to those rules and principles which have been established in our system of jurisprudence for the protection and enforcement of private rights." *Pennoyer v. Neff*, 95 U.S. 714, 733 (1877) (per Field, J.).

By the late 19th century, the U.S. Supreme Court had built general substantive principles around the phrase, which scholars came to call *substantive due process*. Rather than forbidding only unfair procedures, the Due Process Clause was held to forbid certain actions no matter how they might be carried out. Substantive due process is today a limited doctrine that, for example, bars most curtailments of free speech (by state governments) and such encroachments into the right of privacy as statutes prohibiting abortions.

Fred Rodell once called the phrase *due process* "that lovely limpid legalism." Fred Rodell, *Woe Unto You, Lawyers!* 51 (1939). It may be lovely, but it is not "limpid" (i.e., clear or transparent). More accurately, Atiyah says: "The fact is that this concept is probably the greatest contribution ever made to modern civilization by lawyers or perhaps any other professional group." P.S. Atiyah, *Law and Modern Society* 42 (1983).

As a PHRASAL ADJECTIVE, it is hyphenated—e.g.:

- "They came close in a couple of cases challenging the *due-process* propriety of laws passed by two Western states." Fred Rodell, *Nine Men* 201 (1955).
- "The early *due-process* legislation was chiefly aimed against irregular or inferior jurisdictions." J.H. Baker, *An Introduction to English Legal History* 538 (3d ed. 1990).

See **law of the land.**

due to is best used to mean "attributable to," and often follows the verb *to be* (sometimes understood in context) <their awards were due to the committee's need for politically expedient recipients>. But the stylist may wish to avoid even correct uses of the phrase, which one writer calls a "graceless phrase, even when used correctly," adding: "Avoid it altogether." Lucile V. Payne, *The Lively Art of Writing* 148 (1965).

The phrase is commonly misused as a conjunctive adverb for *because of, owing to, caused by,* or *on grounds of*—e.g.:

- "Because the state court did not specify whether it denied habeas relief on the merits or *due to* [read *on grounds of*] procedural default, we must interpret the state court's silence." *Stokes v. Procunier,* 744 F.2d 475, 480 (5th Cir. 1984).
- "*Due to* [read *Because of*] the close interrelation between the two rights, and consideration being given to the fact that Wiggins's petition was filed pro se and should therefore be liberally read, we believe that Wiggins's petition fairly raised the issue of his right to counsel." *Wiggins v. Procunier,* 753 F.2d 1318, 1320 (5th Cir. 1985).
- "Religion clauses in state constitutions are generally more detailed and separationist than the Federal Establishment Clause, *due in part to* [read *in part because of*] the widespread enactment of state Blaine amendments prohibiting public funding of religious schools beginning in the 1870s." John Dinan, *Foreword: Court-Constraining Amendments and the State Constitutional Tradition,* 38 Rutgers L.J. 983, 1003 (2007).
- "Gunnar Myrdal understood the 'principle of cumulative causation' as a 'vicious circle' *due to* [read *because of*] the close interrelation of housing, employment, health, civil rights, and political power." John A. Powell, *Structural Racism,* 86 N.C. L. Rev. 791, 797 (2008).

In the following examples, the phrase *due to* is used correctly; but as Payne notes, the sentences might be improved by eliminating it. E.g.:

- "A distinction must be drawn, however, between cases where the difficulties are *due to* uncertainty as to the causation of damage, where questions of remoteness arise, and cases where they *are due to* the fact that the assessment of damages cannot be made with any mathematical accuracy." 11 Hardinge S.G. Halsbury et al., *Halsbury's Laws of England* § 394, at 226 (3d. ed. 1955). [A possible revision: "A distinction must be drawn between cases in which the difficulties *arise from* uncertainty *about what caused* the damage and

those in which difficulties *arise from* the impossibility of assessing damages accurately."]

- "We conclude that . . . the *failure of the government due to* clerical error or oversight . . . does not violate [the statute]." *U.S. v. Walborn,* 730 F.2d 192, 194 (5th Cir. 1984). [A possible revision: *We conclude that the government's failure resulting from clerical error or oversight does not violate the statute.*]

Due followed by an infinitive is not a form of the phrase *due to,* although it looks deceptively similar—e.g.: "The Alabama Supreme Court concluded that since neither the doctrine of mutuality of obligation nor the doctrine of mutuality of remedy supports a refusal to enforce the contract's arbitration clause, the circuit court's denial of the motion to compel arbitration was *due to* be reversed." *Survey of 1996–1997 Developments in Alabama Case Law,* 49 Ala. L. Rev. 323, 337 (1997).

due to the fact that, common in speech, can almost always be boiled down to *because.*

duly authorized. Because *authorize* denotes the giving of actual or official power, *duly* (i.e., "properly") is usually unnecessary. Likewise, *duly* is almost always redundant in phrases such as *duly signed.*

dumb. See **mute.**

dump truck. See LAWYERS, DEROGATORY NAMES FOR (A).

duologue. See **dialogue.**

duplicate, adj.; **duplicative;** *duplicatory; **duplicitous.** Something that is *duplicate* either is made up of two identical parts (such as a business form with a carbon copy) or is an exact copy of something else (such as a photocopy). Something that is *duplicative* either is able to duplicate itself (such as bacteria) or tends to overlap or be redundant with something else (such as a speech or presentation). In its second sense, *duplicative* has pejorative connotations; whereas *duplicate* merely describes, *duplicative* tends to disapprove. *Duplicatory is a NEEDLESS VARIANT. See **multiplicitous (B).**

Courts tend to use the phrase *duplicative litigation.* In fact, it appears almost 20 times as often as *duplicate litigation.* The U.S. Supreme Court favors the former phrase, having enshrined it in one of its tests for having federal courts abstain from hearing cases that could be handled in state courts: "As between federal district courts . . . the general principle is to avoid *duplicative litigation.*" *Colorado River Water Conservation Dist. v. U.S.,* 424 U.S. 800, 817 (1976) (per Brennan, J.).

Duplicitous is a late-19th-century coinage generally understood to mean "deceitful." American and British legal writers have latched onto the word in the sense of doubleness, from the old legal meaning of *duplicity* (= double pleading). A nonlawyer would likely be confused by the following uses of the word:

- "It was further objected that the information was uncertain, *duplicitous*, and made alternative charges and allegations." *State v. Elliott*, 41 Tex. 224, 225 (1874) (per Reeves, J.). (The specimen just quoted antedates the earliest known use [1928] given in *W11*.)
- "The allegation in a single count of a conspiracy to commit several crimes is not *duplicitous*." *Braverman v. U.S.*, 317 U.S. 49, 54 (1942) (per Stone, C.J.).
- "If an offence can be committed intentionally or recklessly, the information or indictment may charge it in those terms. The fact that the mental element is stated in the alternative does not make the charge '*duplicitous*.'" Glanville Williams, *Textbook of Criminal Law* 80 (1978).
- "A *duplicitous* indictment is one charging two separate crimes in the same count." *U.S. v. Ellis*, 595 F.2d 154, 163 (3d Cir. 1979).
- "Acosta argues further that the indictment was *duplicitous* because it joined separate conspiracies into one count." *U.S. v. Acosta*, 763 F.2d 671, 696 (5th Cir. 1985).

Duplicitous should not be extended beyond its sense of doubleness in pleading, indictments, etc., as it is here: "There is a suggestion that some of the work performed by counsel for Baxter was *duplicitous* [read *duplicative*] because of a change in counsel during the preparation stages of the litigation." *Baxter v. Savannah Sugar Ref. Corp.*, 495 F.2d 437, 447 (5th Cir. 1974).

duplicate, n., = (1) a reproduction of an original document having the same substance and often the same validity as the original; or (2) a new original of a document, often made to replace one that is lost or destroyed. Because sense 2 is slightly misleading, the fuller phrase *duplicate original* is more accurate.

duplication. See **duplicity.**

duplicity is frequently used in law as a near-synonym of *duplication*—e.g.:

- "The county prosecutor was even heard boasting to a member of the press that he had a '*duplicity*' of evidence!" Mark McKinnon, "South Toward Home," in *Texas, Our Texas: Remembrances of The University* 145, 146 (Bryan A. Garner ed., 1984).
- "The defendant suggested that the 340 billable hours resulted from a *duplicity* of time spent by the plaintiff's attorney and his five associates." *McClure v. Mexia Indep. Sch. Dist.*, 750 F.2d 396, 403 (5th Cir. 1985).

Those uses of the word are poor. They derive from the true legal meaning "the pleading of two (or more) matters in one plea; double pleading" (*OED*), properly illustrated here: "Pleading had long since ceased to convey any true information, though the rules against '*duplicity*' might require a party to admit all but one of his opponent's falsehoods." Alan Harding, *A Social History of English Law* 332 (1966). The word should not, by SLIPSHOD EXTENSION, be used of other types of doubleness. See **duplicitous.**

The nonlegal sense of *duplicity* (= deceitfulness, double-dealing) is also quite normal in legal contexts—e.g.:

- "An excessive reliance on peer monitoring and informants risks creating a culture of suspicion and *duplicity*." Orly Lobel, *Citizenship, Organization Citizenship, and the Laws of Overlapping Obligations*, 97 Cal. L. Rev. 433, 485 (2009).
- "Indeed, ERA II arguably provided Hatch with an opportunity to lend legitimacy and legal sophistication to an opposition movement often accused of hysteria, *duplicity*, and willful misunderstanding of the law." Serena Mayeri, *A New E.R.A. or a New Era?*, 103 Nw. U. L. Rev. 1223, 1235 (2009).

duress; *duranco*. *Duress* = (1) the infliction of hardship; (2) forcible restraint; illegal imprisonment; or (3) compulsion illegally exercised to force a person to perform some act. *Durance* is an archaic LEGALISM sharing sense 2 of *duress*, for which it is a NEEDLESS VARIANT.

duress of circumstances. See **necessity.**

during such time as is verbose for *while*.

during the course of is almost always verbose for *during*.

dutiable = subject to the levy of a duty, i.e., a tax on goods. E.g.:

- "The dual purpose of the search is to ascertain whether an illegal alien is seeking to cross the border [and] whether contraband or *dutiable* property is being smuggled." *U.S. v. Barbera*, 514 F.2d 294, 296 (2d Cir. 1975).
- "The Federal Circuit also held, as had the CIT, that Ford violated 19 U.S.C. § 1485 because Ford failed to answer Customs' forms fully and failed to promptly disclose information about design changes and their effect on *dutiable* value." Alexandra E.P. Baj, *International Trade Decisions of the Federal Circuit*, 56 Am. U. L. Rev. 1023, 1042 (2007).

duty. See **obligation** & **tax.**

duty, nondelegable. See **nondelegable duty.**

duty-bound. So written. This term from legal JARGON is a PHRASAL ADJECTIVE corresponding to the age-old phrase *bounden duty*.

duty of producing evidence. See **burden of proof (A).**

dwelling-house; dwelling; usual place of abode. Legal writers have traditionally used the quaint terms *dwelling* and *dwelling-house* to denote "a structure in which human beings sleep." These terms named the subject of common-law burglary, which could take place only in a *dwelling-house* and not in a business building. Burglary statutes have, of course, broadened the scope of buildings included within the definition of burglary.

As between *dwelling* and *dwelling-house*, the first is more current in the general language; but the second predominates in legal writing, perhaps because lawyers may fear creating a MISCUE (i.e., if *dwelling* were read as a participial verb and not as a gerund).

The phrase *usual place of abode* often appears in the alternative alongside *dwelling-house* in rules about serving legal papers. The DOUBLET is doubtless justified, since some homeless people cannot be said to live in a *dwelling-house* but can certainly be said to have a *usual place of abode*.

dynamite charge; shotgun instruction; nitroglycerine charge; *Allen* charge; Chip Smith charge. Each of these phrases refers to a supplemental jury instruction given by the court to encourage a deadlocked jury, after prolonged deliberations, to reach a unanimous verdict. The legality of such a jury instruction was upheld in *Allen v. U.S.*, 164 U.S. 492 (1896)—hence the phrase *Allen charge*. See CASE REFERENCES (C).

What is perhaps the most widely used phrase today, *dynamite charge*, originated in the mid-20th century.

It contains a clever pun—as PUNS go in legal terminology—and has appeared in a wide range of legal writings—e.g.: "The jurors were then excused until Monday morning, September 10, 1973. At 11:15 that morning, the judge gave the jury the *Allen* or '*dynamite*' *charge* without any admonition that the majority re-examine its position." *Gray v. Martindale Lumber Co.*, 515 F.2d 1218, 1219–20 (5th Cir. 1975).

Chip Smith charge is the Connecticut version, deriving from *State v. James ("Chip") Smith*, 49 Conn. 376 (1881). E.g.: "It is settled that a '*Chip Smith*' *charge* is an acceptable method of assisting the jury to achieve unanimity." *State v. Wooten*, 631 A.2d 271, 286 (Conn. 1993). The other forms are likewise regional variants; they are exquisite enough that it would be a grave mistake to brand them NEEDLESS VARIANTS.

E

each. A. And Its Near-Synonyms: *apiece*; *severally*; *individually*; *respectively*. These adverbs are all distributive—that is, they refer to every one of the several or many things (or persons) comprised in a group. *Each* and *apiece* (the less formal term) both suggest an equivalence of the items referred to <$5 each> <three books apiece>. *Severally* emphasizes the separateness of each person or thing referred to, implying the same degree for each one <severally responsible> <made bequests to the children severally>. *Individually* stresses the independent treatment of each member of a group <the conspirators were tried individually>. *Respectively* denotes that the persons or things listed match up with items in a previous listing that appears in the same context, each item corresponding to its counterpart in the other list <legacies of $2,000, $3,000, and $4,000 were designated for Michael, Tom, and Lewis, respectively>. Generally speaking, *respectively* is overused—and the best practice is to avoid it altogether. See **respective.**

B. Number. *Each* traditionally takes a singular verb, and the best practice is to write *each . . . is* regardless of whether a plural noun intervenes (*each of the members is*). E.g.:

- "*Each* of the plaintiffs *is* an investor who was persuaded by Coulther to invest in real estate in Costa Rica." *Regions Bank v. Allen*, 33 So.3d 72, 73 (Fla. Dist. Ct. App. 2010).
- "What is notable is that *each* of these doctrines *are extensions* [read *is an extension*] of basic trademark law." Mark A. Lemley & Mark P. McKenna, *Owning Mark(et)s*, 109 Mich. L. Rev. 137, 156 (2010).
- "*Each* of these failures *were* [read *was*] unreasonable under professional norms and independently constitute deficient performance." *Belmontes v. Ayers*, 529 F.3d 834, 859 (9th Cir. 2008).

Pronouns having *each* as an antecedent are traditionally (and most formally) singular.

Sometimes *each* is mistaken as the subject in a sentence in which it acts in apposition, as here:

- "The mortgagor and mortgagee *each has* [read *have*] an insurable interest." Robert Kratovil, *Real Estate Law* 138 (1946).
- "JR's four Tokyo commuter lines *each has* [read *have*] its [read *their*] own color." Peter McGill, *The American Express Pocket Guide to Tokyo* 13 (1988).

See APPOSITIVES (A).

Still another problem occurs with phrases such as *each of us who*. The word *who* is in apposition to *us* and therefore takes a plural verb, but many writers want to make it singular because they mistakenly think that *each* is the subject of the verb—e.g.: "Neither is the practice of law fully intelligible without reference to the inner mind of each of us who *engages* [read *engage*] in law practice." Geoffrey C. Hazard Jr. & Susan P. Koniak, *The Law and Ethics of Lawyering* xxi (1990). For a similar error, see **one of those ——s who (*or* that).**

C. Delimiting the Application of *each*. Especially in contexts in which *all* appears before *each*, it may be important to use defining words after *each*. E.g.: "Suppose a statute required *all directors* to take an oath of secrecy, and imposed a penalty on *each director* in the event of a violation. If half the directors took the oath and half failed, could they all be prosecuted or only those who failed?" Elmer A. Driedger, *The Composition of Legislation* 78 (1957). The remedy lies, of course, in writing that the penalty is imposed on *each director who fails to take the oath*, assuming that is the intended meaning.

each and all. This LEGALISM is no more helpful or necessary than *each and every*. See DOUBLETS, TRIPLETS, AND SYNONYM-STRINGS & **each and every.**

each and every. This trite phrase should generally be eschewed, and especially it should not be plugged in where only one of the adjectives properly modifies what follows. E.g.: "The court has carefully considered *each and every* of the seemingly countless arguments included in both parties' briefs." *Republic of Colombia v. Diageo N. Am. Inc.*, 531 F.Supp.2d 365, 406–07 (E.D.N.Y. 2007). *Each* works fine here, but not *every*, for one cannot say, "The court has considered every of the arguments." One who insists on being bromidic should write: "The court has carefully performed *each and every one* of the seemingly countless arguments." See DOUBLETS, TRIPLETS, AND SYNONYM-STRINGS. Cf. *and/or & if and when.

each other; one another. The traditional view is that the first phrase is used of two persons or entities; the second is best confined to contexts involving more than two. E.g.:

- "Horrible noise on the one hand; money on the other. How do you relate them to *one another* [read *each other*]?" Richard A. Lanham, *Revising Prose* 109 (1979).
- "Dr. Bateman testified this 'well' was the space exactly between two electrode rings where the opposite axial electric fields cancel *one another* [read *each other*] out, resulting in a 'ground plane' of zero AC voltage." *Applera Corp. v. Micromass UK Ltd.*, 204 F.Supp.2d 724, 774 (D. Del. 2002).
- "If the two excess clauses cancel *one another* [read *each other*], as Kentucky law provides, then LMICK's liability rises or falls upon the enforceability of its escape clause." *Great Am. Ins. Co. v. Lawyers Mut. Ins. Co. of Ky.*, 492 F.Supp.2d 709, 713 (W.D. Ky. 2007).

In using these phrases, one must know precisely what is being compared. In the following sentence, *elements constituting the basis of damages* are being compared, although the writer mistook *causes of action* as the units of comparison: "Having examined the jury instructions and the special verdict in this case, we find that the elements constituting the basis of damages of *each* of the two causes of action were not sufficiently distinguished *from one another* [read *from those of the other*] to [ensure] that there was no double compensation." *Braun v. Flynt*, 726 F.2d 245, 251 (5th Cir. 1984). The use of *each* before *one another* is what caused the problem; the writer was guilty of SWAPPING HORSES from *each other* to *one another*.

early on is not the odious locution that some people think. Slightly informal, it is perfectly idiomatic in both AmE and BrE. E.g.: "My pupil master told me *early on* of the client's complaint: 'I want your opinion and not your doubts.'" Lord Denning, *The Discipline of Law* 7 (1979).

earnest (= something given or done beforehand as a pledge or a sign of good faith, esp. a partial payment of the purchase price of goods sold or a delivery of some of the goods themselves, for the purpose of concluding an agreement) generally appears in the phrase *earnest money*. But in Scotland the word is commonly used alone—e.g.: "*Earnest* is to be held merely as evidence of the completion of the bargain. . . . *Earnest* is in no case essential to the completion of the bargain." William Bell, *Dictionary and Digest of the Law of Scotland* (7th ed. 1890) (s.v. *earnest*). For more on *earnest* and related words, see **pledge,** n.

earwitness (= a witness who testifies about something that he or she heard) is formed on the analogy of *eyewitness*. E.g.:

- "The depth of an *earwitness's* familiarity with the voice of the person they claim to have identified can be examined in detail on cross-examination." *U.S. v. Angleton*, 269 F.Supp.2d 868, 875 (S.D. Tex. 2003).
- "Yet while the reliability of eyewitness identification has been a focal point in the news, the scholarly literature, and the courts, the unreliability of *earwitness* identification has gone virtually unnoticed in the caselaw and legal literature." Lawrence M. Solan & Peter M. Tiersma, *Hearing Voices: Speaker Identification in Court*, 54 Hastings L.J. 373, 375 (2003).

Eyewitness and *earwitness* date from the 16th century. For various types of witnesses, see **witness (B).**

easement. A. *Positive* and *Negative Easements*. An easement is a legal or equitable right acquired by the owner of one piece of land to use another's land for a special purpose. *Positive easements* give rights of entry upon another's land, as to cross through to reach one's own land or to discharge water. *Negative easements* consist in the right to prevent the landowner from doing something such as blocking sunlight or erecting buildings that would prevent the use of a runway on nearby land. Cf. **servitude (A).** For *avigational easement*, see **aviate.**

B. Types. An *easement by prescription* arises by adverse use over some specified period, such as 20 years. An *easement in gross* (a rarity) is a personal right benefiting someone who need not—and usually does not—own any land adjoining the servient tenement. An *easement of necessity* arises by reservation (either express or implied) when a landowner sells part of his or her land and leaves no outlet to a highway. An *easement appurtenant* is one created for the benefit of another tract of land.

C. And *right-of-way*. The terms are not synonymous; *right-of-way* (= the right to pass over another's land) is often a type of *positive easement*. But not always: a *right-of-way* may be granted by license (to the person) as well as by easement (inuring to the land)—see (D). See **right-of-way.**

D. And *license*. An easement is a property right; a license is a revocable permission to commit some act that would otherwise be unlawful. An easement is usually created by written instrument; a license is often created orally. An easement is a more or less permanent right; a license is temporary. An easement usually changes ownership as the ownership of the land to which it belongs changes; a license is a purely personal right that cannot be sold. See **license (B).**

E. And *servitude*. See **servitude (A).**

easy judge (= a judge who sentences criminal defendants leniently) is an AmE antonym of *hanging judge*—e.g.:

- "The Court: Has anybody told you that you don't have to worry, that this is an *easy judge*? The Defendant: No, sir." *Stokes v. U.S.*, 366 F.Supp. 879, 881 n.3 (D. Md. 1973) (quoting testimony).
- "The judges develop and decide cases in very different ways. . . . Some have become known as '*easy*' *judges*, others as 'hanging' judges. There *seems* [read *seem*] to be more '*easy*' *judges* than 'hanging' judges, however." *Stieberger v. Heckler*, 615 F.Supp. 1315, 1388 (S.D.N.Y. 1985) (quoting Senator Bellmon).

easy of. See **of** (c).

ecclesiastical law; canon law. Although these generic terms overlap a great deal, *ecclesiastical law* broadly covers all laws relating to a church, whether from state law, divine law, natural law, or societal rules; *canon law* is more restricted, referring only to the body of law constituted by ecclesiastical authority for the organization and governance of a Christian church. See **canon law.**

economic; economical. *Economical* means "thrifty," or, in the current JARGON, "cost-effective." *Economic* should be used for every other meaning possible for the words, almost always in reference to the study of economics. Hence we have *economic studies* and *economic interest* but *economical shopping*. See **uneconomical.**

edict = (1) in Roman law, an intimation by a magistrate (urban or peregrine praetor) stating what actions and defenses would be allowed, and, in the course of time, a settled body of such rules (esp. the Praeterian Edict); (2) a law promulgated by the sovereign and applying either to the entire state or to some of its divisions, but usu. relating to affairs of state; (3) in Scottish ecclesiastical law, an official notice from the pulpit to the congregation; or (4) any formal decree, command, or proclamation. When modern courts refer to their "edicts" (sense 3), they do so usually with a subtle self-mockery, the word *edict* connoting that the issuer is all-powerful.

Though the noun *edict* dates from the 13th century in English, the corresponding adjective, *edictal*, dates only from the early 19th century. It corresponds to sense 1 of *edict*—e.g.: "The *Edictal law* would therefore enforce the dispositions of a Testator, when, instead of being symbolised through the forms of mancipation, they were simply evidenced by the seals of seven witnesses." Henry S. Maine, *Ancient Law* 175 (17th ed. 1901).

EDITORIAL "WE." See FIRST PERSON (B).

-EDLY. Words ending in this way are more pervasive in law than elsewhere. For example, Blackstone wrote that "if one intends to do another a felony, and undesignedly kills a man, this is also murder." 4 William Blackstone, *Commentaries on the Laws of England* *200–01. Lawyers write of *premeditatedly* committed crimes, of *mitigatedly* committed crimes, and of the Warren Court's "*unwarrantedly* sweeping readings of constitutional guarantees . . . ." Jan Deutsch, *Chiarella v. United States: A Study in Legal Style*, 58 Tex. L. Rev. 1291, 1300 (1980).

With words formed in this way, the classic adverbial formula *in a . . . manner* does not work: *allegedly* does not mean "in an alleged manner," *purportedly* does not mean "in a purported manner," and *admittedly* does not mean "in an admitted manner." Rather, the unorthodox formula for these words is *it is . . . -ed that*, i.e., *allegedly* (= it is alleged that) and so on. Instead of bewailing the unorthodoxy of these words in *-edly*, we should welcome the conciseness they promote and continue to use them (if only sparingly). We have many of them, such as *admittedly, allegedly, assertedly, concededly, confessedly, reportedly*, and *supposedly*. See **allegedly, confessedly** & **reportedly.**

Nonetheless, a form ending in *-edly* ought to be avoided if a ready substitute exists: "A bank may indeed be *liable for unauthorizedly revealing* [read *liable for revealing without authorization*] the state of a depositor's accounts to his creditors." *Schuster v. Banco de Iberoamerica, S.A.*, 476 So.2d 253, 255 (Fla. Dist. Ct. App. 1985) (Schwartz, J., dissenting). See **qualifiedly.**

educable. See **educible.**

educe. See **adduce** (B).

educible; educable. The first means "capable of being educed, or drawn out." The second means "capable of being educated."

-EE. A. General Principles. This suffix (fr. French past-participial *-é*) originally denoted "one who is acted upon"; the sense is inherently passive. Hence:

**acquittee*	=	one who is acquitted
arrestee	=	one who is arrested
conscriptee	=	one who is conscripted
detainee	=	one who is detained
educatee	=	one who is educated (by an educator)
ejectee	=	one who is ejected
enrollee	=	one who is enrolled
expellee	=	one who is expelled
inauguree	=	one who is inaugurated
indictee	=	one who is indicted
invitee	=	one who is invited
liberee	=	one who is liberated
permittee	=	one who is permitted
returnee	=	one who is returned
selectee	=	one who is selected
separatee	=	one who is separated
shelteree	=	one who is sheltered
smugglee	=	one who is smuggled
telephonee	=	one who is telephoned

The suffix also has a dative sense, in which it acts as the passive agent noun for the indirect object. This is the sense in which the suffix is most commonly used in peculiarly legal terminology:

abandonee	=	one to whom property rights are relinquished
*advancee	=	one to whom money is advanced
allocatee	=	one to whom something is allocated
allottee	=	one to whom something is allotted
consignee	=	a person to whom something is consigned
covenantee	=	one to whom something is covenanted
deliveree	=	one to whom something is delivered
disclosee	=	one to whom something is disclosed
grantee	=	one to whom property is granted
indorsee	=	one to whom a negotiable instrument is indorsed
lessee	=	one to whom property is leased
patentee	=	one to whom a patent has been issued
pledgee	=	one to whom something is pledged
referee	=	one to whom something is referred
remittee	=	one to whom something is remitted
representee	=	one to whom a representation has been made
seisinee	=	one to whom seisin is transferred
surrenderee	=	one to whom property is surrendered
trustee	=	one to whom something is entrusted
vendee	=	one to whom something is sold
warrantee	=	one to whom a warranty is given

At least two words ending in -*ee* have both a normal passive sense and a dative sense. *Appointee* = (1) one who is appointed; or (2) one to whom an estate is appointed. Sense 2, of course, is primarily legal. And *releasee* = (1) one who has been released; or (2) one to whom an estate is released.

The suffix -*ee*, then, is correlative in sense to -*or*, the active agent-noun suffix: some words ending in -*ee* are formed as passive analogues to -*or* agent nouns, and not from any verb stem. Examples are *indemnitee* (= one who is indemnified; analogue to *indemnitor*) and *preceptee* (= student; analogue to *preceptor*).

These are the traditional uses of the suffix. But there is a tendency today to make -*ee* a general agent-noun suffix without regard to its passive sense or the limitations within which it may take on passive senses. Hence the suffix has been extended to PHRASAL VERBS, even though only the first word in the phrase appears in the -*ee* word. Hence *discriminatee* (= one who is discriminated against), *interferee* (= one who is interfered with), and *tippee* (= one who is tipped off). Then other prepositional phrases have gradually come into the wide embrace of -*ee*: *abortee* (= a woman upon whom an abortion is performed); *confiscatee* (= one from whom goods have been confiscated); **depositee* (= one with whom goods are deposited). Some -*ee* words contain implicit possessives: *amputee* (= one whose limb has been removed); **breachee* (= one whose contract is breached); *condemnee* (= one whose property has been condemned). In still other words, -*ee* does not even have its primary passive sense:

arrivee	=	one who arrives
asylee	=	one who seeks asylum
benefitee	=	one who benefits (or, possibly, "is benefited")
escapee	=	one who escapes
*standee	=	one who stands

Adjudicatee, oddly, has no direct relation to its verb; in civil law, it means "a purchaser at a judicial sale." Finally, the suffix is sometimes used to coin jocular words such as *cheatee* (= one who is cheated).

The upshot of this discussion is that -*ee* has been much abused and that writers must be careful of the forms they use. For active senses we have -*er*, -*or*, and -*ist* at our service; we should be wary of adopting any new active forms in -*ee*, and do our best to see that **standee*, *escapee*, and similar forms wither and die or else remain odd exceptions. Otherwise we risk wasting any sense to be found in this suffix. It was with justifiable concern for the language and for logic that H.W. Fowler noted: "the unskilled workers used to 'dilute' skilled workers in time of war should have been called *diluters* instead of *dilutees*; the skilled were the *dilutees*" (*MEU2* 146). See -ER (A).

B. Word Formation. The principles applying to words ending in -*atable* apply also to agent nouns ending in -*ee* (see *Garner's Modern American Usage* 74 (3d ed. 2009)). So we have *inauguree*, not **inauguratee*; *subrogee*, not **subrogatee* (though the latter is sometimes used mistakenly for the former). See **subrogee.** And some words, such as **probatee* (for *probationer*) and **abscondee*, make no sense at all. See ***probatee.**

C. Stylistic Use of -*ee*/-*or* Correlatives. Stylists know that -*ee* agent nouns are often inferior to more descriptive terms. They sometimes objectify the persons they describe, though the writer may intend no callousness—e.g.: "The government seems to have recognized that in order to assure the safe return of the *abductees* [read *Americans that have been abducted*], they will have to give into the demands of the FARC somehow; hence the offer for leniency." Samantha Kenney, *Regional Shortcomings and Global Solutions*, 14 Conn. Ins. L.J. 557, 577 (2008).

Furthermore, the endings -*or* and -*ee* can be easily transposed by mistake. As a general matter, therefore, good drafters prefer *buyer* and *seller* over *vendee* and *vendor*; *buyer* and *seller* over *bargainee* and *bargainor*; and, in appropriate circumstances, *borrower* and *lender* over *mortgagor* and *mortgagee*. The stakes are often so high that it makes little sense to use forms that increase the possibility of error. See **vendee** & **vendor.**

effect, vb. **A. Generally.** This verb—meaning "to bring about" or "to make happen"—though increasingly rare in English generally, abounds in legal writing. E.g.: "This classification process *effected* by the maximum grant regulation produces a basic denial of equal treatment." *Dandridge v. Williams*, 397 U.S. 471, 518 (1970) (Marshall, J., dissenting).

One writer calls it a "little word whose uses are insufficiently praised." Richard Wincor, *Contracts in Plain English* 33 (1976). True, it can be an effective way of avoiding the awkward contract-drafter's ritual, *remove or cause to be removed* or *produce or cause to be produced*, so as to include agents. (See **cause to be.**) One merely requires the party to *effect removal* or to *effect production*, so that the party may arrange with third parties to do whatever is required. This can undoubtedly aid anyone engaged in drafting.

Often, however, using *effect* as the verb merely spawns wordiness. The verb tends to occur alongside BURIED VERBS, such as *settlement* and *improvement*. E.g.:

- "A system of standardization . . . has, in connection with the service furnished as above, *effected a great reduction in the time lost* [read *reduced the time lost*] by machines in waiting for repair." *U.S. v. United Shoe Mach. Co of N.J.*, 222 F. 349, 371 (D. Mass. 1915).
- "The contract in question was made by defendants . . . *to effect a final settlement of her estate* [read *to settle her estate*]." *D'Avricourt v. Seeger*, 125 So. 735, 736 (La. 1929).
- "The Act, which has been adopted in some other parts of the Commonwealth, has undoubtedly *effected a great improvement in practice* [read *improved practice*]." Marvin Kohl, *Infanticide and the Value of Life* 124 (1978).

B. *Effect* for *affect*. See **affect.**

C. And *effectuate*. Most dictionaries define these words identically, but their DIFFERENTIATION should be encouraged. Although both mean "to accomplish, bring about, or cause to happen," stylists have generally considered *effect* the preferable word, *effectuate* a NEEDLESS VARIANT. No longer need this be so.

The growing distinction—common especially in law—is that *effect* means "to cause to happen, to bring about" <effect a coup>, whereas *effectuate* means "to give effect to, to bring into effect" <effectuate the testator's intentions>. E.g.: "Perhaps nothing more discreditable is involved than an unwillingness to acknowledge in the words of the statute itself the element of discretion that must be exercised in *effectuating* its purposes." Lon L. Fuller, *Anatomy of the Law* 42 (1968).

Of the three confusable terms—*affect*, *effect*, and *effectuate*—the last is the least common. Ordinarily in legal contexts, *effectuate* means "to give effect to" and not "to bring about." So it is *not*, despite what some think, synonymous with *effect*—e.g.:

- "The Board also ordered the following affirmative action which it was found would '*effectuate* [i.e., "give effect to," not "bring about"] the policies' of the Act." *NLRB v. Fansteel Metallurgical Corp.*, 306 U.S. 240, 250 (1939) (per Hughes, C.J.).
- "The rule has been read by courts in a manner that *effectuates* its function of timely notice without creating technical traps for the unwary." *Fluor Eng'rs & Constructors, Inc. v. Southern Pac. Transp. Co.*, 753 F.2d 444, 449 (5th Cir. 1985).

- "To *effectuate* a gift, a donor must deliver property to a donee, or to someone on his or her behalf, with a manifested intent to make a gift of the property." *Banner Life Ins. Co. v. Mark Wallace Dixson Irrevocable Trust*, 206 P.3d 481, 490 (Idaho 2009).

Effect is sometimes misused for *effectuate*—e.g.: "We properly must inquire beyond 'those minimal historic safeguards for securing trial by reason' to ensure that the commands of justice are *effected* [read *effectuated* (i.e., 'given effect')]." *U.S. v. Leslie*, 759 F.2d 366, 375 (5th Cir. 1985). The opposite error occurs here: "In this case, nurses from around the country have earned law degrees to *effectuate* [read *effect*] changes in the health care system." John Katzman, *Heal the System*, Tex. B.J., May 1992, at 474.

In practice, *effectuate* is not trouble-free. Some writers use it fuzzily—e.g.: "If the statutory authority is nothing more than a pretext for *effectuating* personal hostility, an award of monetary damages will be upheld." Mark M. Grossman, *The Question of Arbitrability* 109 (1984). Erroneous forms, too, such as **affectuate*, have popped up (and need to be stamped on)—e.g.:

- "The 'removal period' referred to the statutory 90-day period, beginning when the deportation order became final, within which the Attorney General is required to detain the alien and *affectuate* [read *effectuate*] his removal." *Hersh v. U.S. ex rel. Mukasey*, 553 F.3d 743, 757 n.15 (5th Cir. 2008).
- "Further, it would provide a forum for intergovernmental cooperation while the scope and binding nature would foster a level of regional effectiveness and representation not currently realized by most regional planning bodies, thus avoiding the silence normally accompanying the regional commission's ability to *affectuate* [read *effectuate*] a plan." Andrew P. Gulotta, *Darkness on the Edge of Town*, 28 St. Louis U. Pub. L. Rev. 495, 523 (2009).

See **affect.**

effective; efficacious; efficient; effectual. All these words mean generally "having effect," but they have distinctive applications. *Effective* = (1) having a high degree of effect (used of a thing done or of the doer) <the court's power to fashion an effective equitable remedy>; or (2) coming into effect <effective June 3, 2011>. *Efficacious* = certain to have the desired effect (used of things) <efficacious drugs>. *Efficient* = competent to perform a task; capable of bringing about a desired effect (used of agents or their actions or instruments) <an efficient organization>. *Efficient* increasingly has economic connotations in law that are evident, e.g., in the phrase *cost-efficient*.

Effectual, perhaps the most troublesome of these words in practice, means "achieving the complete effect aimed at." Things, not people, are said to be *effectual*—e.g.:

- "I think that unity of organization is necessary to make the contest of labor *effectual*." *Plant v. Woods*, 57 N.E. 1011, 1016 (Mass. 1900) (Holmes, C.J., dissenting).

- "If that were so, every imperfect security, however invalid as a real right, would be *effectual* as a trust." *Bank of Scotland v. MacLeod (Liquidator)*, [1914] S.C.1 (H.L.).

On the use of *effectually* for *effectively*, see **effectively**.

effective cause. See CAUSATION (B).

effectively; effectually. *Effectively* = (1) in an effective manner; well <to speak effectively>; (2) in effect, actually <the plaintiff is effectively barred from exercising the powers of her office>; or (3) completely or almost completely <the building is now effectively finished>. Sense 2 is common in legal writing—e.g.: "The United States Courts of Appeals are *effectively* [i.e., *in effect*] courts of last resort." Douglas A. Berman & Jeffrey O. Cooper, *In Defense of Less Precedented Opinions*, 60 Ohio St. L.J. 2025, 2029 (1999).

Effectually, by contrast, means "completely achieving the desired result"—e.g.:

- "A defense going far enough to show reasonable and probable cause for making it, would vindicate the good faith of the company as *effectually* [read *effectively*] as would a complete defense to the action." *Travelers' Ins. Co. v. Sheppard*, 12 S.E. 18, 23 (Ga. 1890).
- "We treat the State's motion to stay mandate as *effectually* [read *effectively*] requesting a rehearing and grant the motion." *Johnson v. State*, 792 So.2d 495, 495 n.1 (Fla. Dist. Ct. App. 2001).

See **effectual**.

effects. See **possessions**.

effectually. See **effectively**.

effectuate. See **effect (c)**.

efficacious; efficient. See **effective**.

effluxion of time; efflux of time. Each of these LEGAL-ISMS has traditionally denoted the running of time, especially when that period culminates in the expiration of a lease term or a contractual term, such as an option to purchase, as opposed to some specific action or an event unrelated to a temporal element—e.g.: "The trial court upheld defendants' position that the [provision] was operative only if the contract was terminated prior to the expiration of the five-year term therein provided, and that the restrictive paragraph had no effect if the term ended by *efflux of time*." *Perfection Oil Co. v. Saam*, 264 F.2d 835, 837 (8th Cir. 1959). *Effluxion* has always been more common than the shorter *efflux*, but both are now rare. *Lapse of time* and *passage of time* are much more common—e.g: "There is no indication in the record that [the protection order] was extended, so it has expired by the *lapse of time*." *O'Banion v. Williams*, 175 S.W.3d 673, 675 (Mo. Ct. App. 2005).

The words are pronounced /i-**flək**-shən/ and /i-**fləks**/.

effulge. See BACK-FORMATIONS.

e.g. A. Generally. *E.g.*, the abbreviation for the Latin phrase *exempli gratia* (= for example), introduces representative examples. In AmE, it is preferably followed by a comma (or, depending on the construction, a colon) and is unitalicized. In their fine book on admiralty, Grant Gilmore and Charles L. Black (or their publishers) pedantically put a space between the two letters (*e. g.*), sometimes without a comma following. *See The Law of Admiralty* 10 (2d ed. 1975). In BrE, the periods as well as the comma are sometimes omitted—e.g.: "The problem with seeking a legislative cure for the ethical disease is that most of the perceived outrages are either already illegal (*eg*, Pentagon officials taking bribes) or beyond the reach of the law (politicians' sexual adventures)." *Washington on an Ethics Kick*, Economist, 28 Jan.–3 Feb. 1989, at 19. To American eyes, *eg* looks like *egg* misspelled.

B. With *etc.* Using the abbreviation *etc.* after an enumeration following *e.g.* creates a superfluity, since one expects nothing more than a representative sample of possibilities. But *etc.* might be required after *i.e.* (L. *id est* "that is") to show the incompleteness of the list.

In two editions (5th & 6th), *Black's Law Dictionary* misused *i.e.* for *e.g.* in its entry for *layman*: "One who is not of a particular profession (i.e. non-lawyer)." The abbreviation should be *e.g.*, not *i.e.*, because under the definition a nondoctor as well as a nonlawyer would be a *layman*; the parenthetical *nonlawyer* is intended only to provide an example.

C. Clear Reference. Make it clear what the signal refers to. Consider: "Out-of-pocket losses include medical expenses, lost earnings, and the cost of any labor required to do things that the plaintiff can no longer do himself (*e.g.*, a housekeeper)." But "things the plaintiff can no longer do himself" are not exemplified by *a housekeeper*. (Or does the writer mean *be a housekeeper*?) In any event, wherever readers encounter an *e.g.*, they rightly expect a sampling of appropriate items—not an ambiguous or an all-inclusive listing. In the example given, it might be *e.g.*, *keep house, drive a car, tend the garden*. See **i.e.**

egress; ingress. *Egress* = the right or liberty of going out. *Ingress* = the right or liberty of going in. The correct prepositions are illustrated here: "[The company] breached its duty to furnish Rivers with a safe means of *ingress* to and *egress* from the vessel." *Elevating Boats, Inc. v. Gulf Coast Marine, Inc.*, 766 F.2d 195, 197 (5th Cir. 1985).

The legal phrase *ingress, egress, and regress* = the right to enter, leave, and reenter. Courts and lawyers have sometimes mistaken the import of these terms. For more than a century (1891–1999), *Black's Law Dictionary* (1st–6th eds.) erroneously defined *ingress, egress, and regress* as "the right (as of a lessee) to enter, *go upon* [read *leave*], and *return from* [read *return to*] the lands in question." The same dictionary states that *egress* is "often used interchangeably with the word *access*," apparently confusing *egress* with *ingress*. The error was corrected in the 7th edition (1999).

eight corners. See **four corners of the instrument**.

either. **A. Number of Elements.** Most properly, *either . . . or* can frame only two alternatives, and no more: "[He] testified . . . that in the last few years terrazzo had been used more extensively in entranceways than *either* marble, tile, cement, *or* asphalt [omit *either*]." *Erickson v. Walgreen Drug Co.*, 232 P.2d 210, 211 (Utah 1951).

B. Singular or Plural. When *either* itself is the subject, a singular verb is required—e.g.:

- "Although Michigan conflates the two doctrines, we nevertheless agree that if *either* of these more limited remedies is available, *they* [read *it*] would be the preferred course." *Northland Family Planning Clinic, Inc. v. Cox*, 487 F.3d 323, 335 (6th Cir. 2007).
- "Of course, if either of these findings *are* [read *is*] negative, the regulation is constitutional under the Free Speech Clause." Anna M. Sewell, Note, *Moving Beyond Monkeys*, 114 Penn. St. L. Rev. 1067, 1079 (2010).

Nouns framed by *either . . . or* take a singular verb when they are both singular, or when only the latter is singular. E.g.:

- "There was no evidence that *either* Bundrant *or* Sneed *were accomplices* [read *was an accomplice*] as a matter of law or as a matter of fact and that, of the three, appellant alone was responsible for the burglary of Vick's home." *Cocke v. State*, 201 S.W.3d 744, 749 (Tex. Crim. App. 2006).
- "There was no evidence that *either* Mr. Foy *or* Mr. McDaniel *were* [read *was*] ever personally present or *were* [read *was*] involved in acts in Kansas." *U.S. v. Wesley*, 649 F.Supp.2d 1232, 1237 (D. Kan. 2009).

See CONCORD & SUBJECT–VERB AGREEMENT (E).

C. *Not . . . either.* This phrasing should be a *neither . . . nor* construction. E.g.: "The interests of justice *do not require either a new trial or* [read *require neither a new trial nor*] the entry of a verdict of a lesser degree of guilt." *Commonwealth v. Guy*, 803 N.E.2d 707, 722 (Mass. 2004).

D. *Either or both.* This phrase denotes the meaning generally assigned to *and/or*, but neither phrase finds a place in good legal writing. E.g.:

- "Judicial sanctions in civil contempt proceedings may, in a proper case, be employed *for either or both of two purposes* [read *for either of two purposes*]." *U.S. v. United Mine Workers of Am.*, 330 U.S. 258, 303 (1947) (per Vinson, J.). (If *both* rationales exist, then no one would seriously argue that the sanctions are unavailable.)
- "One must plead *either or both* [delete *or both*] that the state has established a procedure that itself is constitutionally deficient *or that* it has provided no adequate remedy for aberrational departures by its servants from proper procedures [add a comma, and then: *or both*]." *Collins v. King*, 743 F.2d 248, 254 (5th Cir. 1984). For the distinction between *aberrant* and *aberrational*, see **aberrant.**

See *and/or.

E. **Either . . . and/or.* This construction is illogical—e.g.: "Relator responded by producing certain documents, and withholding others *claiming either an attorney-client and/or a work product privilege* [read

claiming the attorney–client privilege or the work-product privilege]." *Federal Deposit Ins. Corp. v. Butler*, 488 So.2d 741, 742 (La. Ct. App. 1986). See ***and/or.**

ejectee. See -EE.

ejectment; ejection; ouster. These terms are deceptively similar but have important differences. *Ejectment* and *ejection* are names of actions at law, whereas *ouster* is a legal wrong. *Ejectment* = (1) ejection of a tenant or occupier from property; or (2) trespass to try title—a legal action in which a person ejected from property seeks to recover possession and damages. This action was abolished in England in 1852 but persists in some American jurisdictions. E.g.: "A legal claim for *ejectment* consists of the following elements: '[p]laintiffs are out of possession; the defendants are in possession, allegedly wrongfully; and the plaintiffs claim damages because of the allegedly wrongful possession.'" *Cayuga Indian Nation of N.Y. v. Pataki*, 413 F.3d 266, 285 (2d Cir. 2005). *Ejection* is the term for a similar action in Scots law.

Ouster is something different: "the act of wrongfully dispossessing someone of any kind of hereditament, such as freehold property" (*CDL*).

ejusdem generis is a canon of construction providing that when general words follow the enumeration of persons or things of a specific meaning, the general words will be construed as applying only to persons or things of the same general class as those enumerated. For example, in the Sunday Observance Act 1677, the language *no tradesman, artificer, workman, labourer or other person whatever* was held not to include a coach proprietor, a farmer, a barber, or a real-estate agent; the general words *or other person whatever* were held confined to persons with similar occupations to those specifically listed—despite the breadth of *whatever*. Similarly, if a lease forbade the tenant to keep *kerosene, camphene, burning fluid, or any other illuminating material*, the general language at the end would not include a light bulb, though it is indisputably an "illuminating material" if the language is taken literally.

The phrase is often used adjectivally—e.g.: "The assembly of machinery is not *ejusdem generis* with 'cleaning, lubricating, and painting.'" Sometimes it functions as an adverb—e.g.: "The general words at the end of the perils clause have been construed *ejusdem generis* with the preceding enumerated perils." Grant Gilmore & Charles L. Black Jr., *The Law of Admiralty* 74 (2d ed. 1975).

The term is pronounced /ee-**joos**-dəm **jen**-ə-ris/, /ee-**yoos**-dəm/, or (BrE) /ee-**jəs**-dəm/, and is occasionally spelled *eiusdem generis* (the classical way, which is Latin but not English).

eke out. Journalists often misuse this PHRASAL VERB by writing, for example, that Smith *eked out* a victory over Jones in the election (as if the phrase meant, in colloquial terms, "squeaked by Jones"). *Eke out* properly means "to supplement, add to, or make go further or last longer." Here the phrase is correctly used:

- "While no particular form for the memorandum is prescribed by statute, it is well settled that the memorandum must be complete in itself, and cannot be *eked out* [i.e., supplemented] by parol evidence." *Gruss v. Cummins*, 329 S.W.2d 496, 501 (Tex. Civ. App.—El Paso 1959).
- "The slender evidence supplied by these ten authors was sought to be *eked out* [i.e., supplemented] by the testimony of five 'professional publishers' and three professional authors." *Exposition Press, Inc. v. F.T.C.*, 295 F.2d 869, 875 (2d Cir. 1961).

One may *eke out* one's income by working nights as well as days. But one does not, properly, *eke out* an existence—e.g.:

- "It is the message that social and economic conditions and opportunities and governmental services are such that many people are unable to support themselves and must rely on the freely given alms of others in order to *eke out an existence* [read *make ends meet*, or some other CLICHÉ] while living on the streets of New York." *Loper v. N.Y. City Police Dep't*, 802 F.Supp. 1029, 1042 (S.D.N.Y. 1992).
- "They are not wealthy and often are just *barely able to eke out an existence* [read *barely able to make ends meet*, or some other CLICHÉ]." *Friends of Vietnam Veterans Mem'l v. Kennedy*, 984 F.Supp. 18, 22 (D.D.C. 1997).

Nor does the phrase mean "to acquire by difficulty or drudgery."

elaborate, vb., is commonly intransitive in nonlegal contexts <to elaborate on a point>, and transitive in legal contexts <to elaborate a point>. E.g.: "Because liability treats the parties as doer and sufferer of the same injustice, tort law *elaborates* legal categories that reflect the singleness of the injustice on both sides and, consequently, the unity of the relationship between plaintiff and defendant." Ernest J. Weinrib, *Correlativity, Personality, and the Emerging Consensus on Corrective Justice*, 2 Theoretical Inquiries L. 107, 116 (2001). Although both *to elaborate* and *to elaborate on* may mean "to work out in detail," the former suggests "to produce by labor," and the latter suggests "to explain at greater length." Awareness of this nuance allows one to choose the apter phrasing.

elect is a LEGALISM meaning "to choose deliberately." A FORMAL WORD generally followed by an infinitive in legal prose, *elect* should not be used where a simple *choose* will suffice. E.g.:

- "None of the defendants *elected* [read *chose*] to file a motion for summary judgment." *Holmes v. Village of Hoffman Estates*, 511 F.3d 673, 678 (7th Cir. 2007).
- "The accused has the means to present a defense through the services of military and civilian defense counsel, or he may *elect* [read *choose*] to represent himself with counsel on stand-by." Morris D. Davis, *In Defense of Guantanamo Bay*, 117 Yale L.J. Pocket Part 21 (2007).
- "The fact that the Petitioner *elected* [read *decided*] to follow his counsel's advices does not exonerate him from any attendant delay attributable to that election." *Kakaygeesick v. Salazar*, 656 F.Supp.2d 964, 987 (D. Minn. 2009).

The changes here suggested are stylistic merely; *elect* cannot be said to be wrong—it is merely symptomatic of LEGALESE.

For more on *elect* and its near-synonyms, see **designate.**

electee (= [1] one chosen or elected; or [2] one to whom the law gives a choice about status) is recorded in the *OED* and supported by a single quotation, from 1593. One might suppose that because *electee* is omitted from most unabridged dictionaries, it was a 16th-century NONCE WORD that is long since defunct. So prudent writers would suppose; yet the word has been successfully revived. E.g., in sense 1: "Petitioners would enjoin the *electees* from acting." *Littig v. Democratic County Comm.*, 38 N.Y.S.2d 214, 216 (Sup. Ct. 1942). Whether this word will gain currency as a correlative of *elector* it is too early to say.

Sense 2 is an illogical use of the -EE suffix, since the *electee* is the person put to the election—the *elector*, in effect: "A section 411 *electee* . . . is qualified to make an election to have his retired pay computed under section 402(d)." *Aflague v. U.S.*, 298 F.2d 446, 449 (Ct. Cl. 1962).

elective. This term is used primarily in relation to political elections. *Elective* = appointed by election; subject to election. In legal writing, however, *elective* is used more broadly of legal choices—e.g.:

- "At the heart of the complaint lies Plaintiff's prayer that the Court . . . hold that the trust failed when Defendant took her *elective* share under the Will." *Hill v. Carman*, 61 F.R.D. 583, 586 (D. Del. 1974).
- "Most states permit a surviving spouse to take an *elective* share of the deceased spouse's estate." *Tensfeldt v. Haberman*, 768 N.W.2d 641, 646 n.7 (Wis. 2009).

elector = (1) esp. in BrE, a legally qualified voter; or (2) in AmE, a member of the electoral college chosen by the states to elect the president and vice president. Sense 1 appears occasionally in AmE, especially in older works—e.g.: "The first view to be taken of this part of the government relates to the qualifications of the *electors* and the elected." *The Federalist* No. 52, at 325 (James Madison) (Clinton Rossiter ed., 1961). Sense 2 is more usual in modern AmE—e.g.: "The President held office for four years and then had to be given—or denied—a second term by *electors* picked by the people." Fred Rodell, *Nine Men* 44 (1955).

electoral (= of or relating to electors), pronounced /ee-**lek**-tər-əl/, is often written and spoken incorrectly as *electorial—e.g.: "The new district would be divided into *electorial* [read *electoral*] subdistricts utilizing the current community college district boundaries." *Liddell v. Board of Educ.*, 733 F.Supp. 1324, 1327 (E.D. Mo. 1990).

eleemosynary /el-ə-**mos**-ə-ner-ee/, related etymologically to the word *alms*, is a FORMAL WORD for *charitable*. It is more common in legal than in nonlegal prose. E.g.:

- "The broad statutory definition of 'charitable organization' includes . . . any benevolent, philanthropic, patriotic, or *eleemosynary* person or one purporting to be such." *Citizens for a Better Env't, Inc. v. Nassau County*, 488 F.2d 1353, 1356 (2d Cir. 1973).
- "Insurance companies are not *eleemosynary* institutions and thus courts cannot require them to provide coverage beyond the scope of the coverage in their contracts unless duly adopted legal requirements compel the companies to provide such coverage." *State Farm Fire & Cas. Co. v. Estate of Mehlman*, 589 F.3d 105, 116 n.11 (3d Cir. 2009).
- "We look to case law to determine if the chancellor acted within his discretion when he determined that the entire 1.8 acres should be used for benevolent, or *eleemosynary*, purposes rather than allowing the land to revert to the Plaintiffs." *Lenoir v. Anderson*, 12 So.3d 589, 593 (Miss. Ct. App. 2009).

ELEGANT VARIATION. See INELEGANT VARIATION.

elemental; elementary. *Elemental* is the more specific term, meaning "of or relating to the elements of something; essential." *Elementary* means "introductory; simple; fundamental."

element of proof. See **proof (C).**

elicit. See **solicit.**

eligible may be equally well construed with either *for* or *to* (an office). *Eligible for* is more common today than *eligible to*, but the latter has unimpeachable credentials—e.g.:

- "No person except a natural born citizen . . . shall be *eligible to* the office of president." U.S. Const. art. II, § 1.
- "No judge of any court . . . shall during the term for which he is elected or appointed, be *eligible to* the legislature." Tex. Const. art. III, § 19.

elisor /ə-**lɪ**-zər/, omitted from *W3* but generally included in unabridged dictionaries, derives from LAW FRENCH and means "a person appointed by a court to return a jury, serve a writ, or perform other duties of the sheriff or a coroner in case of his disqualification" (*W2*). Though comparatively rare, the term is still used in some American jurisdictions. E.g.: "In view of our holding that the *elisor* was an interested person, we do not reach a determination as to the validity of the service of process under Bahamian law." *Wakeman v. Farish*, 356 So.2d 1323, 1325 (Fla. Dist. Ct. App. 1978). The form **eslisor* is a NEEDLESS VARIANT.

ELLIPSES. See QUOTATIONS (E).

eloign; eloin is an archaic legal term meaning "to convey or remove out of the jurisdiction of the court or of the sheriff" (*OED*). Generally the word is spelled *eloign* rather than *eloin*.

elope. The *OED* and many other dictionaries define this term as if it had historically been a "sexist" one in law: "**a.** *Law.* Of a wife: To run away from her husband in the company of a paramour. **b.** In popular language

also (and more frequently) said of a woman running away from home with a lover for the purpose of being married" (*OED*). These definitions suggest that only women can elope, but legal contexts have long made men as well as women elopers—e.g.:

- "If evidence was admitted to show that House had armed himself, and was hunting for Steadman under the impression that the latter had *eloped* with his wife, and was secreting himself in that vicinity, it is difficult to see upon what principle his threats in that connection were excluded." *Alexander v. U.S.*, 138 U.S. 353, 356 (1891) (per Brown, J.).
- "James Campbell had *eloped* with the wife of one Ludlow." *Adger v. Ackerman*, 115 F. 124, 130 (8th Cir. 1902).

else's. Such possessive constructions as *anyone else's* and *everybody else's* are preferred to the obsolete constructions **anyone's else* and **everybody's else*. See POSSESSIVES (G).

elude. See **allude (B).**

elusive; *elusory; *illusive; illusory. *Elusive* (rather than **elusory*) is the usual adjective related to *elude*; *illusory* (rather than **illusive*) is the usual adjective related to *illusion*. Here **illusive* has almost certainly been misused for *elusive*: "The discussion almost inevitably returns to the *illusive* [read *elusive*] subject of what the Supreme Court really held." *B-U Acquisition Group, Inc. v. Utica Mut. Ins. Co.*, 52 B.R. 541, 544 (Bankr. S.D. Ohio 1985). See **illusory.**

EM-, IM-. See EN-.

e-mail. The *e-* is not a prefix but a stand-in for *electronic*. Prefer the hyphenated form here as well as in analogous words such as *e-commerce* and *e-trade*.

emanate = (1) to flow forth, issue, originate from a person or thing as a source; or (2) to proceed from a material source (*OED*). Sense 2 applies to physical senses. E.g.:

- "We also find no evidence that would support a conclusion that the sound *emanating* from a hard-plastic cylindrical container differs when its contents are cocaine and not candy." *Crawford v. State*, 980 So.2d 521, 525 (Fla. Dist. Ct. App. 2007).
- "The officer noticed a 'strong' marijuana odor *emanating* from the car and asked its occupants what they were doing." *State v. Baker*, 221 P.3d 749, 760 (Or. Ct. App. 2009).
- "On September 28, 2007, a Jefferson County Patrol Officer detected strong chemical odors *emanating* from a residence at 3850 Fountain City Road in DeSoto, Missouri." *U.S. v. Turner*, 583 F.3d 1062, 1064 (8th Cir. 2009).

The word is coming to be overworked in sense 1, rising almost to the level of a VOGUE WORD. Its use in the law is old: "In discussing this question, the counsel for the State of Maryland have deemed it of some importance, in the construction of the constitution, to consider that instrument not as *emanating* from the people, but as the act of sovereign and independent

States." *McCulloch v. Maryland*, 17 U.S. (4 Wheat.) 316, 402 (1819) (per Marshall, C.J.).

Judges today seem enamored of the word, which is fast becoming another legal CLICHÉ—e.g.:

- "It appears that the first advancement statute . . . was based on the custom of London and York, and that the custom must have *emanated* from the Roman (or civil) law principle of collatio bonorum[,] requiring a bringing into hotchpot." *Barron v. Janney*, 170 A.2d 176, 179 (Md. 1961). (See **hotchpot**.)
- "At that meeting a proposal authored by Mrs. Shore pursuant to the suggestions *emanating* from a meeting with Central Board officials several days earlier was advanced." *Brody-Jones v. Macchiarola*, 503 F.Supp. 1185, 1220 (E.D.N.Y. 1979). On the use of **pursuant to* in that sentence, see ****pursuant to.**
- "Hypnosis is by its nature a process of suggestion and one of its primary effects is that the hypnotized subject becomes extremely receptive to suggestions that he perceives as *emanating* from the hypnotist." *Alsbach v. Bader*, 700 S.W.2d 823, 829 (Mo. 1985).
- "The final recommendations of the Committee included the following recommendations *emanating* from Dean Feerick's subcommittee, reflecting his commitment to ethical responsibility, academic excellence and public service." James P. White, *John D. Feerick: A Man for All Seasons*, 70 Fordham L. Rev. 2197, 2199 (2002).

emancipate = to set free (as a minor or a slave) from legal, social, or political restraint. In modern legal contexts, one most frequently encounters this term in reference to minors—e.g.: "Plaintiff Adele Gelbman was the passenger in an automobile owned by her and operated by her *unemancipated* 16-year-old son." *Gelbman v. Gelbman*, 245 N.E.2d 192, 192 (N.Y. 1969). See **free.**

emancipation; mancipation. The first means "the act of freeing from slavery," the second "the act of enslaving."

emasculate means literally "to castrate," but has come figuratively to mean "to deprive of strength and vigor, to weaken." The word is a favorite of judges in dissent. E.g.:

- "More important in the long run than this misreading of a federal statute, however, is the Court's *emasculation* of the Equal Protection Clause as a constitutional principle applicable to the area of social-welfare administration." *Dandridge v. Williams*, 397 U.S. 471, 508 (1970) (Marshall, J., dissenting).
- "For the foregoing reasons, I dissent to the majority's *emasculation* of the Mandatory Minimum Sentencing Act." *Commonwealth v. Pittman*, 528 A.2d 138, 146 (Pa. 1987) (Larsen, J., dissenting).
- "I cannot agree with the majority's *emasculation* of the impact rule." *Willis v. Gami Golden Glades, LLC*, 967 So.2d 846, 876 (Fla. 2007) (Cantero, J., dissenting).

Cf. **eviscerate.**

embarrass. Only in legal contexts is this word today used in the sense "to encumber, hamper, impede." E.g.:

- "We think [that] the respective arguments of the parties are considerably *embarrassed* by other factors not touched

upon by the parties." *Carbide Int'l, Ltd. v. State*, 695 S.W.2d 653, 656 (Tex. App.—Austin 1985).
- "In this case, assuming for the purposes of argument that there was a variance, Hickman has not shown he was misled or *embarrassed* in the preparation of his defense." *State v. Hickman*, 191 P.3d 1098, 1102 (Idaho 2008).
- "The *Paredes* court also noted that there are several arguments against a defendant's joinder of offenses, including that the defendant can become *embarrassed* or confounded in presenting separate defenses." *State v. Ridgell*, 199 P.3d 188 (Kan. Ct. App. 2009).

Most nonlawyers would find puzzling these uses of *embarrass*. See EUPHEMISMS.

*****embassador.** See **ambassador.**

embassy; legation. Often assumed to be synonymous, these words should be distinguished. An *embassy* is under an ambassador, and a *legation* is under a minister, envoy, chargé d'affaires, or some other diplomatic agent.

embezzle; misappropriate; steal. *Embezzle* (= to fraudulently convert personal property that one has been entrusted with) is now always used in reference to fiduciaries. *Misappropriate* means "to take for oneself wrongfully" and may or may not be used of a fiduciary. *Steal*, like *misappropriate*, is generally a broader term than *embezzle*; it has the same meaning as *misappropriate*, but much stronger negative connotations. See **defalcate, misappropriate, peculation** & **steal.**

emblements (= [1] crop production, or profits from crops produced by the cultivator's labor; or [2] a common-law doctrine giving the planter of crops ownership rights in those crops after the planter has unexpectedly lost possession of the land before harvest) is a LAW FRENCH term [fr. O.F. *emblaer* "to sow with wheat or oats"] that persists in modern legal writing—but it is surely preferable to its Latin alternative, *fructus industriales*. E.g.: "The duration of a life estate being uncertain, the law encourages the life tenant to cultivate the land by giving him the right to '*emblements*.' This is the right of the legal personal representatives of a deceased life tenant . . . to enter the land after the life estate has come to an end and reap the crops which the life tenant has sown." Peter Butt, *Land Law* 111 (2d ed. 1988). The word is anglicized in pronunciation: /**em**-bli-mənts/.

embrace, in figurative senses, may mean either (1) "to include" or (2) "to adopt." Here sense 1, largely a legal sense, applies:

- "Personal liberty or the right of property *embraces* the right to make contracts for the purchase of the labor of others, and equally the right to make contracts for the sale of one's own labor and the employment of one's individual and industrial resources." *Auburn Draying Co. v. Wardell*, 124 N.E. 97, 99 (N.Y. 1919).
- "The general article . . . was interpreted to *embrace* only crimes the commission of which had some direct impact on military discipline." *O'Callahan v. Parker*, 395 U.S. 258, 271 (1969) (per Douglas, J.).

- "There is no support in the record for the proposition that Bombay's business and goodwill could only be protected by a restrictive covenant *embracing* almost all of the North American continent." *Tandy Brands, Inc. v. Harper*, 760 F.2d 648, 653 (5th Cir. 1985).
- "In *Brown*, we ruled that this right *embraces* the principle that the state cannot prevent parents from choosing for their child a specific educational program but did not include the right to dictate the curriculum at the public school to which parents have chosen to send their children." *Pisacane v. Desjardins*, 115 Fed. Appx. 446, 450 (1st Cir. 2004).
- "We justly celebrate the other rights *embraced* within that Amendment as vital to our democracy as we know it." William V. Luneburg, *The Evolution of Federal Lobbying Regulation*, 41 McGeorge L. Rev. 85, 87 (2009).

Sense 2, used in legal and nonlegal contexts alike, is exemplified in these sentences:

- "While appellants try to argue that dilution cases involve a mixed question of law and fact not governed by the clearly erroneous standard, we cannot *embrace* this argument." *Velasquez v. City of Abilene, Tex.*, 725 F.2d 1017, 1021 (5th Cir. 1984).
- "We have specifically *embraced* the view that the Rehabilitation Act requires affirmative accommodations to ensure that facially neutral rules do not in practice discriminate against individuals with disabilities." *Henrietta D. v. Bloomberg*, 331 F.3d 261, 274-75 (2d Cir. 2003).
- "We agree with Leal that his petition is nonsuccessive, but we cannot *embrace* the full scope of the rule he advocates." *Leal Garcia v. Quarterman*, 573 F.3d 214, 220 (5th Cir. 2009).

embracee. See **embracer.**

embracer; *embraceor. This term, meaning "one guilty of embracery [= the offense of influencing a jury illegally and corruptly]," is best spelled *embracer*, preferred by the *OED* and the *AHD*. W3 and *Webster's New World Dictionary* include their main entries under **embraceor*, with the ill-formed suffix.

Some writers use the NEOLOGISM *embracee* as the correlative of *embracer*—e.g.: "If it takes the form of a bribe and is accepted, both the *embracer* (giver) and *embracee* (taker) are guilty of bribery." Rollin M. Perkins & Ronald N. Boyce, *Criminal Law* 551 (3d ed. 1982).

embracery; *imbracery; *bracery. The first form is standard for this word, which denotes the offense of attempting to corrupt or instruct a jury to reach a particular conclusion by means other than evidence or argument in court, as by bribing or threatening jurors. The popular term for this offense is *jury-tampering*. See **jury-packing.**

*Imbracery and **bracery* are NEEDLESS VARIANTS.

emend. See **amend.**

emigrant; émigré. There is a latent DIFFERENTIA-TION between these words. An *emigrant* is one who leaves a country to settle in another. *Émigré* has the same sense, but applies especially to one in political exile. The first acute accent is often omitted (*emigré*) in AmE.

emigrate. See **immigrate.**

émigré. See **emigrant.**

eminence (= loftiness; prominence) is misused in the following sentence, but whether the desired word is *imminence* (= the quality or state of being ready to take place) or *immanence* (= inherence) is unclear: "The phrase 'imminent danger,' for example, suggested immediacy, inherence, and *eminence* [read *imminence* or *immanence*, either one of which would create a REDUNDANCY]." Edward H. Levi, *An Introduction to Legal Reasoning* 27 (1949).

eminent. See **imminent.**

eminent domain; condemnation; expropriation. The 17th-century civilian Grotius coined the term *eminens dominium*, from which our phrase derives. In BrE, *eminent domain* is primarily a term of international law. In AmE, it refers to the power of federal and local governments to pronounce judicially (land, etc.) as converted to public use. The usual BrE term for this sense is *expropriation*. *Condemnation*, an Americanism, has virtually the same sense: "judicial assignation (of property) to public purposes, subject to reasonable compensation." E.g.: "[The Fifth Amendment's] plain language requires the payment of compensation whenever the government acquires private property for a public purpose, whether the acquisition is the result of a *condemnation* proceeding or a physical appropriation." *Tahoe-Sierra Preservation Council, Inc. v. Tahoe Reg'l Planning Agency*, 535 U.S. 302, 321 (2002) (per Stevens, J.). See **compulsory purchase.**

eminently. See **infinitely.**

emolument. See **pay,** n.

emote. See BACK-FORMATIONS.

empanel; *impanel. *Empanel* (= to swear in [a jury] to try an issue or case) is now the preferred spelling in both AmE and BrE. E.g.: "The trial had already begun; the jury was *empaneled* and opening statements were about to get underway." *Evans v. City of Chicago*, 513 F.3d 735, 751 (7th Cir. 2008). **Impanel* was formerly a common spelling, used, e.g., in *Franklin v. South Carolina*, 218 U.S. 161, 166 (1910).

emphasis added; emphasis supplied. These citation signals are both used to indicate that, in quoting another's words, the writer has italicized some of them. There is no distinction in meaning between the phrases, as some writers occasionally assume. *Emphasis in original* is used to indicate that the italics appear in the original material as here quoted.

An asterisk (✳) precedes words and phrases that are invariably inferior forms.

emphyteusis (= the right of a person who is not the owner of a piece of land to use it as his or her own in perpetuity, subject to forfeiture for nonpayment of a fixed rent) is a civil-law term that appears sometimes in Anglo-American legal writing. E.g.:

- "This is the *Emphyteusis*, upon which the Fief of the middle ages has often been fathered, though without much knowledge of the exact share which it had in bringing feudal ownership into the world." Henry S. Maine, *Ancient Law* 248 (17th ed. 1901).
- "Although the Romans used the term 'dominium,' the holder of land by *emphyteusis* was also treated in many ways as an owner." *Butler v. Baber*, 529 So.2d 374, 381 (La. 1988).

The corresponding adjective is *emphyteutic*.

empiricize, not in the dictionaries, has made an appearance in an American law report: "Just as experienced physicians render diagnoses on the basis of symptoms they sense, but often cannot *empiricize* [= confirm or verify by testing] or articulate, so too, we are told, can those who work among prisoners develop 'senses' concerning the potential for impending disobedience or unrest." *Abdul Wali v. Coughlin*, 754 F.2d 1015, 1018 (2d Cir. 1985).

***empirics** is not in good use for *empiricism*.

***emplead. See **implead.**

employee. A. And *employe*. Although *employé*, the French form, might logically be thought to be better as a generic term, *employée* (which in French denotes the feminine gender) is so widespread (without the accent mark) that it is not likely to be uprooted. *The Wall Street Journal* and a few other publications remain staunch adherents to the form *employe* (minus the acute accent on the final -*e*); but *employee* is standard.

But it did not always have such a stronghold. *Employe* was once common in English. E.g.: "We hardly need repeat the statement . . . that in the Employers' Liability Act Congress used the words '*employé*' and 'employed' in their natural sense, and intended to describe the conventional relation of employer and *employé*." *Hull v. Philadelphia & R.R.*, 252 U.S. 475, 479 (1920) (per Pitney, J.).

B. And *independent contractor*. Both terms refer to a person who works for another, the key distinction being how much control over the work the hirer can assert. An *employee* is subject to a high degree of control in how the work is performed. By contrast, an *independent contractor* is free to choose how to accomplish the work, with little or no supervision or outside control. Although it would seem logical to use *employer* only with its correlative, *employee*, because an employer has the power of control, *independent contractor* is frequently coupled with *employer*—e.g.:

- "As a general rule, an *employer* of an *independent contractor* is not liable for physical harm caused to another by the contractor." *Benson v. Superior Court*, 111 Cal. Rptr. 3d 27, 33 n.5 (Ct. App. 2010).

- "Generally, an *employer* has no duty to ensure that an *independent contractor* performs its work in a safe manner." *Randall Noe Chrysler Dodge, LLP v. Oakley Tire Co.*, 308 S.W.3d 542, 545 (Tex. App.—Dallas 2010).

In these usages, *employer* carries the sense "one who hires another to do work," without a connotation of control. Perhaps the readiest replacement would be *contractee*, but this terms sounds stilted—e.g.: "Examples of relationships that have been recognized in Texas common law as giving rise to a legal duty include . . . that between one supervising or maintaining control over another and the controllee, such as employer/employee, parent/child, and *independent contractor/contractee* under special circumstances." *In re Thrash*, 433 B.R. 585, 597 (Bankr. N.D. Tex. 2010). See **contractee.**

Identifying an independent contractor as an employee is a rare mistake, but it occurs—e.g.: "Finding that the child's injuries were traceable only to the *independent contractor employee's* failure to take routine driving precautions, the court found that because the independent contractor's negligence was unforeseeable, it did not render the *independent contractor's employer*, the municipality, liable." *Nieves-Rosado v. Puerto Rico Hwys. Auth.*, 403 F.Supp.2d 170, 172 (D.P.R. 2005).

The verb *employ* is acceptable for both terms, as it does not necessarily denote control.

employer and employee; master and servant. The first phrase seems to be supplanting the second, which at best sounds antiquarian and, to many, derogatory. Also, *employee* is more transparently distinguishable from *agent* than *servant* is. See **agent.**

empower. See ***impower.

empty-chair defense is an Americanism referring to a common tactic of defendants: when one defendant has settled before trial, the remaining defendant can try to put all fault on the absent one (i.e., the one not occupying a chair at trial).

emulate; immolate. The first is to strive to equal or rival, to copy or imitate with the object of equaling. The second is to kill as a sacrifice.

Emulate is frequently misused, as, e.g., here for *adopt*: "I cannot believe that a company trying to estimate the effect of a marketing tool would *emulate* [read *adopt*] the methods that lawyers use in taking depositions." *Deltak, Inc. v. Advanced Sys., Inc.*, 574 F.Supp. 400, 407 (N.D. Ill. 1983).

EN-; IN-. No consistent rules exist for determining which form of the prefix to use before a given word. In AmE at present, the spellings *entrust, enclose, inquire* (= to ask), and *increase* are standard. The BrE spellings are *entrust, enclose, enquire* (= to ask), and *increase*, but the variants ***intrust** and ***inclose** still appear with some frequency. Especially troublesome to writers are word-pairs with varying prefixes according to inflection: *encrust* but *incrustation*; *engrain* (= to dye in the raw state) but *ingrained* (= deeply rooted).

enabling statute. This phrase was perhaps first used specifically in reference to the act (32 Hen. VIII. c. 28) by which tenants-in-fee and certain others were "enabled" to make leases (*OED*). Now the phrase is used in reference to any statute conferring powers, and in the U.S. usually to a congressional statute conferring powers on executive agencies to carry out various tasks delegated to them. E.g.: "The *enabling* legislation that creates the agency sets out what powers an agency can wield to impact life outside the agency." Lauren Braddy, Note, *Losing the Race Never Run*, 62 Baylor L. Rev. 521, 523 (2010). See **disabling statute** & ***disenable.**

enact. The platitude is that courts adjudicate, rather than legislate. Some judicial decisions seem to belie this principle; still, it is unidiomatic to refer to a court as enacting doctrines: "In addition to the legislative reforms, the Pennsylvania Supreme Court has *enacted* [read *enunciated* or some other word] two new rules regarding the filing of harassing and frivolous lawsuits." Ashley Lynn Griffin, Comment, *The Medical Malpractice Liability Insurance Crisis*, 35 Ohio N.U. L. Rev. 351, 374 (2009).

enacting history. See **legislative history.**

enactment = (1) the action or process of making (a legislative bill) into law <enactment of the bill>; or (2) a statute <a recent enactment>. The word is best not used by legal writers in sense 2, although it has been so used almost from its beginning in the early 19th century. Still, to use *enactment* in sense 2 is to add an unneeded synonym and to muddle a useful distinction. The plural almost always manifests this stylistically poor use: "Congress and the state legislatures are assigned concurrent jurisdiction to prescribe by law the 'Times, Places and Manner' of holding these elections, with *congressional enactments* [read *congressional acts* or *federal statutes*] superseding state laws." Christopher S. Elmendorf, *Refining the Democracy Canon*, 95 Cornell L. Rev. 1051, 1078 (2010). See **act (c).**

Nevertheless, sense 2 is so pervasive that we can do little else but avoid it in our own writing; criticism of its users (as opposed to its use) is unfair, given its pervasiveness. The *OCL1* and *CDL* define *enactment* only in sense 2: "a statute or Act of Parliament, statutory instrument, by-law or other statement of law made by a person or body with legislative powers" (*OCL1*). Likewise, it is used in sense 2 in the Assimilative Crimes Act, 18 U.S.C. § 13 (1982), which states that certain acts or omissions are "not made punishable by any enactment of Congress." Perhaps the use of the term in the last-quoted example arose from the mistaken notion that *act* in *acts and omissions* might

be confused with *act of Congress*. Even were that true, *federal statute* would suffice in place of *act of Congress*.

enate. See **agnate.**

enatic. See **agnate.**

enation. See **kinship.**

en banc; in banc; in banco; in bank. A. Spelling and Pronunciation. *W3* lists only *en banc* (= in full court; F. lit., "on the bench"), the predominant form in English-speaking countries. *In banc* and *in bank* also appear in a few jurisdictions, but these are not widespread. The Arizona courts use *in banc*—as in *Spur Indus., Inc. v. Del E. Webb Dev. Co.*, 494 P.2d 700 (Ariz. 1972) (*in banc*)—and so do the Maryland courts, though the commentators wonder why: "There is no justification for the spelling *in banc* other than the fact that it was used by the drafters of the Maryland Constitution." Paul V. Niemeyer & Linda M. Richards, *Maryland Rules Commentary* 339 (1984).

Unfortunately, the Federal Rules of Appellate Procedure, as well as statutes addressing appellate procedure, used the spelling *in banc* until style revisions of 1994. Judge Jon O. Newman, of the Second Circuit, reluctantly acquiesced to *in banc* in an article discussing *en banc* proceedings: "Grudgingly, I accept the spelling of '*in banc*' adopted by the pertinent statute, 28 U.S.C. § 46(c) (1982), and the federal rule, Fed. R. App. P. 35. Use of the term as it appeared in Old French, '*en banc*,' seems preferable." *In Banc Practice in the Second Circuit*, 50 Brook. L. Rev. 365, 365 n.1 (1984).

The Supreme Court of California, meanwhile, uses *in bank. See, e.g.*, *Kopp v. Fair Political Pracs. Comm'n*, 905 P.2d 1248 (Cal. 1995) (*in bank*). *In banco* is listed in various law dictionaries, but it's rarely if ever used.

En banc being now the usual spelling, the burden falls on English-speaking lawyers to pronounce the word correctly. Certainly the anglicized pronunciation /in **bank**/ is unexceptionable; the French approximation /on **bonk**/ is also common, though some may consider it precious. And reporters are likely to misspell the phrase—e.g.: "'In fact there had been a fair degree of unanimity on this until last September, when the Fifth Circuit sitting *en banque* [read *en banc*] took their renegade path,' said Mr. McDuff." Ronald Smothers, *Challenges to Judicial Elections Revive*, N.Y. Times, 22 June 1991, at 9.

B. Adjective or Adverb. The phrase *en banc* may be either adjectival <en banc proceedings> or adverbial <the court heard the case en banc>. Chief Justice Rehnquist has even used the phrase as a SENTENCE ADVERB: "*En banc*, the Court of Appeals for the Fifth Circuit reversed." *Crawford Fitting Co. v. J.T. Gibbons, Inc.*, 482 U.S. 437, 439 (1987) (per Rehnquist, J.).

enbancworthy (= worthy of being considered en banc) is a term concocted by, and still generally confined to, the judges of the United States Court of Appeals for the Fifth Circuit. As legal JARGON formed on the model of words like *seaworthy* and *airworthy*, it is useful shorthand, though odd-sounding. E.g.:

- "Briefs and oral arguments on rehearing en banc lead the Court to conclude that this case is not *enbancworthy*." *McLaurin v. Columbia Mun. Separate Sch. Dist.*, 486 F.2d 1049, 1050 (5th Cir. 1973).
- "Although standing alone, this problem would hardly be *enbancworthy*, we conclude that action by us is appropriate rather than letting stand the panel's analysis of third-party beneficiary." *Hercules, Inc. v. Stevens Shipping Co.*, 698 F.2d 726, 736 (5th Cir. 1983).
- "The matter at issue is clearly *enbancworthy* because of the far reaching consequences of the panel's holding." *LeClerc v. Webb*, 444 F.3d 428, 430 (5th Cir. 2006) (Stewart, J., dissenting).

Cf. **certworthy.**

The corresponding noun is *enbancworthiness*, and the antonym is *unenbancworthy*—e.g.: "I would agree that this case would be *unenbancworthy* if the panel had avoided the Chambers question on any one of the several grounds suggested." *Maness v. Wainwright*, 528 F.2d 1381, 1382 (5th Cir. 1976) (Goldberg, J., dissenting). Cf. **unenbanc.**

enclose; *inclose. The first spelling is now preferred in all senses. E.g.: "This statute enumerates the following occupational diseases for which recovery is possible: . . . 'carbon monoxide poisoning or chlorine poisoning in any process or occupation involving direct exposure to carbon monoxide or chlorine in buildings, sheds, or *inclosed* [read *enclosed*] places.'" Oliver Pancheri, *Is There Light at the End of the Carpal Tunnel?*, 22 Workers' Comp. L. Rev. 247, 266 (2000) (quoting Idaho statute). See EN-.

*enclosed herewith and ***enclosed herein** are unnecessary for *enclosed*; in both phrases, the first word conveys the idea redundantly expressed by the second. See ***enclosed please find.**

*enclosed please find is archaic deadwood in lawyers' correspondence for *enclosed is* or *I have enclosed*. Whether the phrase was originally commercialese or LEGALESE, it has been cant since its creation.

In referring to a variant form of this phrase—***please find enclosed**—a 19th-century commentator aptly remarked: "A more ridiculous use of words, it seems to me, there could not be." Richard G. White, *Every-Day English* 492 (1880).

enclosure; *inclosure. The first spelling is preferred in all senses. See EN-.

encomium. Pl. *-iums, -ia.* The English plural is preferred—e.g.: "In truth, the book is in no sense a law book, and some of the most enthusiastic *encomiums* of it that I have heard have come from gentlemen who have never opened a law book." Christopher Columbus Langdell, *Dominant Opinions in England During the Nineteenth Century*, 19 Harv. L. Rev. 151, 153 (1906). See PLURALS (A).

*encrease is an obsolete spelling of *increase* used, e.g., in U.S. Const., art. I, § 6. See EN-.

encroach. See **trespass.**

encrust; incrust. See EN-.

encumber. See **incumber.**

encumbrance; *incumbrance; *cumbrance. The preferred spelling of this word, meaning "a claim or liability that is attached to property and that may lessen its value," is *encumbrance* in both AmE and BrE. E.g.: "When title was passed to defendant, it passed free and clear of all *encumbrances* including the covenants to maintain crossings and fencing asserted by plaintiffs." *Koepp v. Holland*, 688 F.Supp.2d 65, 92 (N.D.N.Y. 2010). Yet **incumbrance* is the spelling used in the British Finance Act of 1975. **Cumbrance* is a NEEDLESS VARIANT. See **liens and encumbrances.**

encumbrancer (= a person who holds an encumbrance) is a slightly archaic word that can often be replaced by *lienholder*. (See **lienor.**) A variant spelling to be avoided is **incumbrancer*.

endeavor is a FORMAL WORD for *attempt* or *try*. E.g.: "He then *endeavors* to purchase cocaine from an individual, X." *State v. Davis*, 851 N.E.2d 515, 521 (Ohio Ct. App. 2006).

The same is true of *endeavor* as a noun: "None of these *endeavors* are appropriate for an appellate court reviewing a trial court's custody determination." *In re Marriage of Vandenberg*, 229 P.3d 1187, 1194 (Kan. Ct. App. 2010).

On the difference between the AmE and the BrE spellings, see -OR.

endnote. See **footnote.**

endorse; indorse. The usual spelling in nonlegal contexts is *endorse*. That is the only acceptable spelling of the word when used figuratively to mean "to express approval of." In legal senses relating to negotiable instruments, *indorse* predominates in the U.S., and the word is so spelled throughout the Uniform Commercial Code. This latent DIFFERENTIATION ought to be encouraged. In Great Britain, however, *endorse* is the more frequent spelling, even in the context of commercial paper. See **approve (B).**

*Indorse on the back is a REDUNDANCY; the root *-dors* means "back."

endorsee. See -EE.

endowment has two quite different senses: (1) "the assignment of a wife's dower"; and (2) "the bestowal of money, income, or property to some person or institution."

end product is usually a REDUNDANCY for *product*. Cf. **end result.**

end result is a REDUNDANCY for *result*. Safire calls it "redundant, tautological and unnecessarily repetitive, not to mention prolix and wordy." William Safire, *Peace-ese*, N.Y. Times, 17 Nov. 1991, § 6, at 22. E.g.: "The *end result* [read *result*] of the Supreme Court's labors was that many maritime workers . . . could recover full damages in the unseaworthiness action." Grant Gilmore & Charles L. Black Jr., *The Law of Admiralty* 411 (2d ed. 1975). Cf. **final result** & **ultimate destination.**

ends and objects. See DOUBLETS, TRIPLETS, AND SYNONYM-STRINGS.

enfeoff; *infeoff. See ***feoff.**

enforce; *inforce. A. Spelling. The second spelling is an archaic form whose only vestige appears in *reinforce*. See EN-.

B. "Enforcing" a Contract. Lawyers continually speak of *enforcing* contracts, though this term is not apt unless one is seeking specific performance. Usually, the law merely specifies a remedy for breach of contract—damages—and does not compel performance.

enforceable; *enforcible. *Enforceable* is the preferred, standard spelling in both AmE and BrE. E.g.: "A contract is *enforcible* [read *enforceable*] even though it does not specify the type of deed to be given." Robert Kratovil, *Real Estate Law* 83 (1946).

enfranchise. See **free** & **franchise.**

engage. See **promise,** vb.

English rule, the. American lawyers speak of *the English rule* in many contexts in which English law differs from American law. But throughout the 1980s, the phrase increasingly denoted only one rule: that the losing party in litigation must pay the winner's costs and attorney's fees. E.g.:

- "Most American lawyers abhor *the English rule*. It requires the losing side in a civil suit to pay the winning side's attorneys' costs. This approach would discourage weak or frivolous suits, while encouraging defendants to settle strong suits against them. More generally, it would promote new and less costly ways of resolving conflicts aside from litigation." Robert J. Samuelson, *I Am a Big Lawyer Basher*, Newsweek, 27 Apr. 1992, at 62.
- "I would think real, real seriously about adopting *the English Rule*. You lose, you pay." Michele Galen, *Guilty! Too Many Lawyers and Too Much Litigation*, Business Week, 13 Apr. 1992, at 60, 65 (quoting Scott Turow).

A synonymous phrase—and a sharper one—is *the loser-pays rule.*

engraft; *ingraft. The word is best spelled *engraft*. See EN-.

*engrandize. See **aggrandize.**

engross, *ingross; enroll, *inroll. The preferred spellings are *engross* and *enroll* (AmE), *enrol* (BrE). Both words have to do with the preparation of legal

documents. To *engross* a legal document (as a deed) is to prepare a fair copy ready for execution. To *enroll* it is to enter it into an official record upon execution. See **enrollment.**

enhance. Outside legal contexts, *enhance* means "to make better." In law, it sometimes means "to make harsher" <enhanced sentencing>.

*enjeopard. See **jeopardize.**

enjoin. *Enjoin* has two basic meanings, each the exact opposite of the other. In sense 1, which is positive in intent, *enjoin* means to prescribe, to mandate, or to order that something be done. This sense, used most frequently in BrE (though not wholly unknown in AmE), occurs with either of two prepositions: *upon* or *to*. E.g.:

- "In France and Germany, for example, equity has been a clearly recognized element in the administration of justice, and *enjoined upon* the judge, but assigned to no special jurisdiction." Carleton K. Allen, *Law in the Making* 414 (7th ed. 1964).
- "It is the clause which is common in treaties of reinsurance, providing that the arbitrators are not bound by the strict rules of law but are *enjoined to* decide . . . according to an equitable rather than a strictly legal interpretation of the provisions of the agreement." *Eagle Star Ins. Co., Ltd. v. Yuval Ins. Co.,* [1978] 1 Lloyd's Rep. 357, 361 (C.A.).

In sense 2, which is negative in intent, *enjoin* means to prohibit, to forbid, or to restrain someone by court order from doing a specific act or behaving in a certain way. In this second meaning, the verb takes the preposition *from*—not *to* or *upon*. E.g.:

- "If the Court *enjoined* telephone companies *from* providing service at the filed rate it would then, in effect, be forcing them to break their 'contract' with the FCC and *sua sponte* usurp the authority of the ICC." *Arsberry v. Illinois,* 117 F.Supp.2d 743, 744–45 (N.D. Ill. 2000).
- "The Circuit Court froze Answer Care's assets, *enjoined* the company *from* selling interests in life insurance policies, and appointed Maryland First Financial Corporation to be the receiver for Answer Care." *First Penn-Pac. Life Ins. Co. v. Evans,* 304 F.3d 345, 347 (4th Cir. 2002).

In the sense "to prohibit by injunction," *enjoin* is preferable to the BACK-FORMATION **injunct,* dated in the *OED* from 1872. See **enjoinder** & ***injunction enjoining.**

enjoinable (= capable of being prohibited by injunction), dating from the late 19th century, is contained in no major English dictionary but has proved useful to American judges—e.g.:

- "All such activity would be properly *enjoinable* insofar as it advocated a strike by public employees." *In re Berry,* 436 P.2d 273, 285 (Cal. 1968) (en banc).
- "We find that appellees' use of the house and adjoining premises as a church constitutes a clear and *enjoinable* violation of the restriction in issue here." *Kessler v. Stough,* 361 So.2d 1048, 1050 (Ala. 1978).

- "Justice Black . . . was not convinced that the mining operation would not create an *enjoinable* nuisance." *Kyser v. Township*, 786 N.W.2d 543, 551 (Mich. 2010).

enjoinder; enjoinment; injunction. The words of the Fowler brothers are as apt today as they were at the turn of the 20th century:

> As *rejoin rejoinder*, so *enjoin enjoinder*. The word is not given in the [*OED*], from which it seems likely that Dickens ["Merely nodding his head as an *enjoinder* to be careful."] invented it, consciously or unconsciously. The only objection to such a word is that its having had to wait so long, in spite of its obviousness, before being made is a strong argument against the necessity of it. We may regret that *injunction* holds the field, having a much less English appearance; but it does; and in language the old-established that can still do the work is not to be turned out for the new-fangled that might do it a shade better, but must first get itself known and accepted.
>
> H.W. Fowler & F.G. Fowler, *The King's English* 53 (3d ed. 1931).

The *OED* contains two illustrative examples of *enjoinder*, but *injunction* still generally "holds the field" in both positive and negative senses of *enjoin*.

Yet *enjoinder* has become more common than it was in the Fowlers' day in the sense of "a command, esp. one that prohibits." E.g.: "But the constitutional *enjoinder* against waste does not mean that the riparian owner must . . . clear all water-consuming native growth." *Allen v. California Water & Tel. Co.*, 176 P.2d 8, 18 (Cal. 1946) (en banc). Through SLIPSHOD EXTENSION it has been used as an equivalent of *admonition*, as here: "[Bishop] is also reputed to have written that classical *enjoinder*, 'Hard cases make bad law.'" *Horsley v. State*, 374 So.2d 375, 377 (Ala. 1979) (Beatty, J., dissenting).

Enjoinment, labeled archaic in *W3* and missing from *W2*, is recorded in the *OED* from the 17th century in the sense "the action of enjoining." Today this word might almost be considered common in law; certainly, in denoting the action itself rather than the result of the action (an *injunction*), it is useful. E.g.: "The plaintiffs assert violations of the FLSA related to wage compensation, for which they seek damages and *enjoinment* of future violations." *Bergemann v. Rhode Island*, 676 F.Supp.2d 1, 2 (D.R.I. 2009).

In the following sentence, *enjoinder* is used where *enjoinment* would be more apt: "The trial court's restraint and *enjoinder* [read *enjoinment*] of defendants from interfering in the liquidation is mooted and reversed by virtue of our ruling." *Heard v. Carter*, 285 S.E.2d 246, 249 (Ga. Ct. App. 1981).

See **enjoin.**

enjoy is frequently used in legal writing in the sense "to have, possess." E.g.: "This covenant ensures that the tenant shall *enjoy* the possession of the premises in peace and without disturbance by hostile claimants." The word fails, however, in reference to having or possessing something undesirable, as in "He *enjoys* failing health," labeled a catachrestic use by the *OED*. (That sentence actually looks more jocular than catachrestic.) Occasionally a clever writer recognizes the ironic possibilities of the word: "With a couple of rare exceptions, required by the Constitution, the Justices for the past thirty years have *enjoyed*—and the verb is accurate—the power to refuse to hear any case that anybody, railroaded convict or President of the United States, tries to bring before them." Fred Rodell, *Nine Men* 14 (1955).

enjoyment (= the exercise of a right) occurs now only in legal contexts. E.g.:

- "The right of *enjoyment* implies rights of user, and of acquiring the fruits or increase of the thing, as timber, the young of cattle, or soil added to an estate by alluvion." Thomas E. Holland, *The Elements of Jurisprudence* 210 (13th ed. 1924).
- "A man has no right of light for his windows unless such a right has been acquired by grant or by long *enjoyment*." William Geldart, *Introduction to English Law* 144 (D.C.M. Yardley ed., 9th ed. 1984).
- "Although Eric owned the Manufacturers Life annuity, he had no beneficial interest or right of *enjoyment* in the commuted balance of the annuity, which became payable only after his death." *Boykin v. Law*, 946 So.2d 838, 846 (Ala. 2006).

enlarge has figurative senses (*extend* or *broaden*) in legal writing that it lacks in other contexts. It is used of abstractions like powers and even time. In references to powers, rights, and the like, the METAPHOR conveyed by *enlarge* is entirely natural—e.g.:

- "It was not given a blank legal slate on which to write greatly *enlarged* property rights for patentees." *Rite-Hite Corp. v. Kelley Co.*, 56 F.3d 1538, 1578 (Fed. Cir. 1995).
- "The question is whether the regulation alters or amends the governing statute or case law, or *enlarges* or impairs its scope." *Communities for a Better Env't v. California Res.*, 103 Cal. App. 4th 98, 108 (2002).
- "Although a 'party is entitled to an instruction on any theory of the case reasonably supported by the evidence,' the court does not need to provide additional, more specific instructions 'that do nothing more than reiterate or *enlarge* the instructions in defendant's language' when the court provides the applicable law to the jury." *Ritchie v. Krasner*, 211 P.3d 1272, 1283 (Ariz. Ct. App. 2009).

But in references to time, *extend* is preferable to *enlarge*, which strikes most nonlawyers as unidiomatic—e.g.:

- "The father had filed a modification action previously, and his visitation was *enlarged* [read *extended*]." *Cousens v. Pittman*, 597 S.E.2d 486, 486–87 (Ga. Ct. App. 2004).
- "It would seem that the trial court did not consider that the contractual limitations provisions were saved by the contract language *enlarging the length of* [read *extending*] the limitations period in the event that the preferred provisions were ruled invalid." *St. Paul Travelers v. Millstone*, 987 A.2d 116, 124 (Md. 2010). On the use of **in the event that* in this sentence, see ***in the event that.**

enlargement, in the legal idiom, often means "extension." E.g.: "A significant contributing cause of the failure to file opposition papers . . . was DeMell's failure to file a timely response or a timely motion for an *enlargement* of time." *In re DeMell*, 589 F.3d 569, 571 (2d Cir. 2009). See **enlarge.**

Enoch Arden law. This phrase contains one of the few LITERARY ALLUSIONS that have given names to legal doctrines. "Enoch Arden," a poem by Tennyson, tells the story of a man who, lost at sea for many years, returns home to find his wife married happily to his former rival for her affections; brokenhearted, he resolves that they will not know of his return until after his death. So *Enoch Arden law* = a statute providing for divorce or exempting from liability a person who remarries when his or her spouse has been absent without explanation for a specified number of years, usu. seven. The term first appeared in American caselaw in the 1920s—e.g.: "The '*Enoch Arden law*,' so-called . . . , is an anomaly in the legislative history of the State, and a strict compliance with its terms is required before such extraordinary relief may be granted." *Frankish v. Frankish*, 200 N.Y.S. 667, 668 (App. Div. 1923) (quoting the uncited opinion of *Schubert v. Schubert*).

enormity; enormousness. The historical DIFFEREN-TIATION between these words should not be muddled. *Enormousness* = hugeness, vastness. *Enormity* = outrageousness, ghastliness, hideousness. For example, Alan Dershowitz once said that Noam Chomsky "trivializes the *enormity* of the Chinese massacre [at Tiananmen Square in 1990]." Letter of Alan Dershowitz, *Left's Response to Beijing Massacre*, L.A. Times, 13 July 1989, at 2–6. But President George H.W. Bush was less fastidious: on 10 July 1989, he was buoyed and cheered by what he called "the enormity of this moment," which he said presented a historic challenge to reform the Polish economy.

These writers typify the careful writer's usage:

- "The plaintiff has been beaten, wounded, chained, imprisoned, starved, carried away to a foreign country, and has suffered many '*enormities*.'" Theodore F.T. Plucknett, *A Concise History of the Common Law* 465 (5th ed. 1956).
- "Human beings, in the face of the collective *enormity* of human suffering purport to do what God himself cannot: 'fully resolving every problem.'" William Joseph Wagner, *To the Age of Social Revolution*, 52 Vill. L. Rev. 209, 253 (2008).

But misuse of *enormity* is all too frequent—e.g.:

- "The *enormity* [read *extent*] of the problem was indicated by Congress's findings." *Public Serv. Co. of Ind. v. ICC*, 749 F.2d 753, 756 (D.C. Cir. 1984).
- "Put simply, the *enormity* [read *enormousness*] of the award is matched by the *enormity* [read *enormousness*] of the plaintiff's damages." *Pouliot v. Paul Arpin Van Lines, Inc.*, 235 F.R.D. 537, 551 (D. Conn. 2006). (In this sentence, the writer no doubt intended to refer to the magnitude [*enormousness*] of the award, not its *ghastliness*.)

***enounce.** See **announce**.

enquire. See **inquire**.

enquiry is the regular BrE form for the word equivalent to *question*. By contrast, *inquiry* in BrE means "an official investigation." In AmE, *inquiry* serves in both senses. See EN-. For *inquiry* and its near-synonyms in the sense of "official investigation," see **investigation**.

***en re** is downright wrong for *in re*, but it has occurred in otherwise good prose. See **in re**.

enrichment. See **impoverishment** & **unjust enrichment**.

enroll. See **engross**.

enrollee. See -EE.

enrollment; enrolment (= the official registration of a document) is spelled -*ll*- in AmE and -*l*- in BrE. See **engross**.

en route. Two words. The *en* is best pronounced like "on," an approximation of the French pronunciation; /en/ is acceptable, but /in/ should be avoided.

This term is now voguish in figurative senses—e.g.:

- "In that case . . . it was held, *en route* to a conclusion that such application was not subject to the constitutional objection, that the guarantees of due process and equal protection are not violated if there is a causal connection between the death or injury and the employment." *Chmelik v. Vana*, 201 N.E.2d 434, 437 (Ill. 1964).
- "It is not error in articulating reasons *en route* to a conclusion to indicate that some features of a mark are more distinctive than others." *Sweats Fashions, Inc. v. Pannill Knitting Co.*, 833 F.2d 1560, 1566 (Fed. Cir. 1987).
- "A district court facilitates appellate review by making specific findings *en route* to a fee calculation, and therefore we have reversed when we could not discern whether the district court arrived at its fee award by using the proper factors." *Schlacher v. Law Offices of Phillip J. Rotche & Assocs.*, 574 F.3d 852, 857 (7th Cir. 2009).

***In route** is a solecism—e.g.:

- "The operator instructed Barnes to perform chest compressions while the police were *in route* [read *en route*] to his home." *Barnes v. State*, 768 N.W.2d 359, 360 (Minn. 2009).
- "After the interview and while *in route* [read *en route*] to the Blount County Jail, Officer Webb called Pretrial Services Officer Twilla Tucker, who asked if the defendant wanted an attorney." *U.S. v. Irons*, 646 F.Supp.2d 927, 974 (E.D. Tenn. 2009).
- "Upon reaching the checkpoint, Vargas explained to agents that he was coming from Brownsville, Texas, was *in route* [read *en route*] to Tyler, Texas, and that the trailer was loaded and sealed." *U.S. v. Vargas*, 580 F.3d 274, 277 (5th Cir. 2009).

***ensample** is an ARCHAISM for *example*.

ensue; *insue. The first spelling is standard. E.g.:

- "If the persuasion be used for the indirect purpose of injuring the plaintiff, or of benefiting the defendant at the expense of the plaintiff, it is a malicious act . . . [that is] actionable . . . if injury *ensues* from it." *Bowen v. Hall*, [1880] 50 L.J.Q. B. 305.
- "Sharpe noticed that the first person had gone inside the home. Gunfire *ensued*." *State v. Wilkerson*, 683 S.E.2d 174, 192 (N.C. 2009).

- "Even if we were to presume the trial court erred in admitting the statements from the nurse's notes, no harm *ensued* because the nurse already had testified without objection to these statements." *Wooten v. State*, 267 S.W.3d 289, 309 (Tex. App.—Houston [14th Dist.] 2008).

ensure. See **assure.**

entail, n. & vb. The transitive verb *entail* = (1) (in general usage) to make necessary; to involve; or (2) (in legal usage) to provide that an estate may pass only to the grantee and the heirs of his body, so that none of the heirs can give it away or sell it. Specifically, an *entailed* interest is an equitable interest in land under which ownership is limited to a person and the heirs of his body (either generally or those of a specified class) (*CDL*). E.g.:

- "In *Woolmore v. Burrows*, lands were to be purchased and closely *entailed* to the family estate; and it was decided that every person in esse at the testator's death must have life-estates, and no more." *Knight v. Knight*, [1840] 49 E.R. 58.
- "The creator of the estate has failed to specify successors to take the property in event of expiration of the lineage to which it has been *entailed*." *Gardner v. Grossman*, 57 N.E.2d 440, 442 (Ind. Ct. App. 1944).

See **disentail.**

In addition to sense 2 of the verb, the general nonlegal sense often appears in legal writing—e.g.:

- "The district court's analysis did not *entail* sufficient scrutiny of the particular negligent acts that were found to have been committed." *Pichoff v. Bisso Towboat Co.*, 748 F.2d 300, 303 (5th Cir. 1984).
- "Erroneous removal need not *entail* misconduct." *In re Crescent City Estates, LLC*, 588 F.3d 822, 830 (4th Cir. 2009).
- "While facial challenges, given the breadth of the undertaking, seem to go hand in hand with injunctions, a facial challenge need not *entail* injunctive relief." *Alto Eldorado Partners v. City of Santa Fe*, 644 F.Supp.2d 1313, 1348 (D.N.M. 2009).

There are two noun forms. The noun *entail* (= a fee limited to the grantee's issue or a class of his issue) corresponds only to sense 2 of the verb. E.g.: "Johnson spoke well of *entails*, to preserve lines of men whom mankind are accustomed to reverence." (Eng.) (See **fee tail (A).**) The noun *entailment* corresponds to sense 1 of the verb.

entente. See **treaty.**

enter. A. For *enter into*. Idiomatically speaking, one *enters into a contract* with another; one does not merely **enter a contract*. E.g.:

- "There is no finding that an entirely new oral contract was *entered* [read *entered into*] that could be enforced." *Cate v. Woods*, 299 S.W.3d 149, 154 (Tex. App.—Texarkana 2009).
- "In my view, 'as is' applies to all parties to the contract, and means the property will be conveyed as the title and condition existed at the time the contract was *entered* [read *entered into*], not at the time of closing." *White v. Cooke*, 4 So.3d 330, 335–36 (Miss. 2009) (Dickinson, J., dissenting).

Even so, *to enter into a contract with* is usually prolix for *to contract with*.

B. **Enter in*. The phrase is a REDUNDANCY for *enter*. E.g.:

- "With his presently appealed claims to tens of millions of dollars in punitive damages against defendants enjoying immunity to such claims, to attorneys' fees when he at all times acted *pro se*, and the like, we stand at the gate of the realms of fantasy. We decline to *enter in* [read *enter*]." *Prewitt v. U.S. Postal Serv.*, 754 F.2d 641, 641 (5th Cir. 1985).
- "Appellant . . . appeals an order denying his motion for post-conviction relief, . . . claiming he *entered into* [read *entered*] a plea of *nolo contendere* involuntarily." *Albo v. State*, 808 So.2d 1275, 1275 (Fla. Dist. Ct. App. 2002).
- "He *entered into* [read *entered*] the United States on September 11, 2006, at the Bridge of Americas Port of Entry in El Paso, Texas." *Ruiz v. Campos*, 547 F.Supp.2d 682, 683 (W.D. Tex. 2008).

entering judgment. See **rendition of judgment.**

enter into. See **enter** & **enter in.**

enter into a contract with. See **contract (F).**

entertain = to give judicial consideration to. E.g.:

- "This requirement of a state-law analogue is a jurisdictional prerequisite; if there is no state law under which a private person would be liable, then federal courts do not have subject matter jurisdiction to *entertain* the suit against the Government." *U.S. Aviation Underwriters Inc. v. U.S.*, 530 F.Supp.2d 1315, 1317 (M.D. Ga. 2007).
- "This court lacks jurisdiction to *entertain* plaintiffs' breach-of-contract claim." *Grillasca-Palou v. U.S. Postal Serv.*, 573 F.Supp.2d 493, 495 (D.P.R. 2008).
- "A federal district court has jurisdiction to *entertain* any tort claim brought against the USPS in accordance with the FTCA." *Naskar v. U.S.*, 82 Fed. Cl. 319, 321 (2008).

*enthuse is a widely criticized BACK-FORMATION avoided by writers and speakers who care about their language. E.g.: "When Judge Keller recused himself in the case of *Marshall v. Gates*, Yagman *candidly enthused* [read *stated enthusiastically*] that the result was 'great' for his client." *Standing Comm. on Disc. of U.S. Dist. Ct. for C. Dist. of Cal. v. Yagman*, 856 F.Supp. 1384, 1392 (C.D. Cal. 1994). **Enthused*, adj., is always inferior to *enthusiastic*.

entirety; entireties. See **tenancy by the entireties.**

entitled to, is. See WORDS OF AUTHORITY (G).

entrance; entry. Both *entrance* and *entry* may refer to the act of entering. In reference to structures, *entrance* connotes a single opening, such as a door, whereas *entranceway* and *entry* suggest a longer means of access, as a corridor or vestibule.

entrapment. As several writers on criminal law acknowledge, this term is an inaccurate one—but it is so well established that it is unlikely to be changed. The problem is that *entrap* connotes merely setting a trap, and doing so is not just legal but desirable in bringing to justice those bent on crime, as long as the trap-setter does not instigate the crime. But confusingly, the legal term *entrapment* denotes the investigation of a crime by law-enforcement officers.

entrust, not **intrust*, is now the usual and preferred spelling. **Intrust* is often seen in legal opinions of the late 19th and early 20th centuries. See EN-.

entry. See **entrance.**

entry of judgment. See **rendition of judgment.**

ENUMERATIONS. A. *First(ly), second(ly), third(ly); one, two, three.* The best method of enumerating items is the straightforward *first, second,* and *third.* The forms *firstly, secondly,* and *thirdly* have an unnecessary syllable, and *one, two,* and *three* seem especially informal. E.g.: "This leaves but two possible effects to [the servicemark's] continued use: *One* [read *First*], no one will know what CONAN means. *Two* [read *Second*], those who are familiar with plaintiff's property will continue to associate CONAN with THE BARBARIAN." *Conan Props., Inc. v. Conans Pizza, Inc.,* 752 F.2d 145, 156 (5th Cir. 1985) (Clark, C.J., dissenting). See **firstly.**

B. Comma Before the Last Element. "How to punctuate . . . enumerations," wrote Follett, "is argued with more heat than is called forth by any other rhetorical problem except the split infinitive." Wilson Follett, *Modern American Usage* 397–98 (1966). Fashions in public-school textbooks and journalists' manuals come and go, but only one method is ironclad in avoiding unnecessary ambiguities: inserting a comma before the final member. So *a, b, and c* rather than *a, b and c.* The problems arise with members containing two or more items, as *a and b, c and d, e and f, and g and h.* The last two members are muddled if the comma is omitted. See PUNCTUATION (D)(2).

C. Bullets. See DOCUMENT DESIGN.

D. As a Method for Enhancing Readability. See PLAIN LANGUAGE (D).

enunciate (= to state publicly) is often used in reference to judicial pronouncements, especially where legal doctrines are concerned. E.g.:

- "*Brock,* however, was decided before the requirements of the Double Jeopardy Clause were held to be fully applicable to the states and was based on the standard *enunciated* in *Palko.*" *U.S. v. Stevens,* 177 F.3d 579, 586 n.3 (6th Cir. 1999).
- "The court concluded that the rule *enunciated* in numerous cases regarding the duty of an occupier of property to exercise reasonable care for those invited or lawfully upon the premises should apply." *Elstun v. Spangles, Inc.,* 217 P.3d 450, 453 (Kan. 2009).
- "Others contend that unpublished opinions are justified when no new law is *enunciated* by the case, such that the case will not have unique value as precedent." Erica S. Weisberger, Note, *Unpublished Opinions: A Convenient Means to an Unconstitutional End,* 97 Geo. L.J. 621, 626 (2009).

Strangely, the word is sometimes mispronounced /shee/ in the third syllable—strangely, because this is simply not a word to mispronounce. See **announce.**

*enure. See **inure.**

en ventre sa mere (= *in utero*) is an unnecessary LEGALISM. Instead of *child en ventre sa mere,* write *fetus, unborn child,* or *child in the mother's womb.* E.g.: "A life in being includes a *person en ventre sa mere* [read *child in the mother's womb*] at the time when the will or settlement takes effect." William Geldart, *Introduction to English Law* 41 (D.C.M. Yardley ed., 9th ed. 1984). Cf. **venter.**

enviable; envious. What is *enviable* is worthy of envy or arouses envy. A person who is *envious* suffers from envy. *Envious* usually takes the preposition *of* <she was envious of her sister's success>, but it may take also *against* or *at* <Jane feels envious against Rebecca> <Jane is envious at Rebecca's success> See **jealousy.**

Some writers confuse the two words—e.g.: "Mr. Strauss's financial disclosure statement . . . details what is already widely known: the 72-year-old lawyer is a power broker of abundant wealth and *envious* [read *enviable*] political and corporate connections." Stephen Labaton, *Strauss to Forgo $4 Million in Pay to Take Moscow Post,* N.Y. Times, 13 July 1991, at 3.

envisage; envision. The first has been used since the early 19th century, whereas the second was born in the early 20th century. Today *envision* is more common in AmE, *envisage* being somewhat literary. Both mean "to visualize," but there is perhaps an incipient DIFFERENTIATION under way. As suggested by *W11, envision* means "to picture to oneself," whereas *envisage* means "to view or regard in a certain way." E.g.:

- "We conclude that orders denying appointment of counsel to litigants who [cannot] afford counsel fall into the class of order *envisaged* by *Cohen.*" *Robbins v. Maggio,* 750 F.2d 405, 413 (5th Cir. 1985).
- "Because all of the acts alleged to define the rights of the parties have already occurred, this Court finds that this matter presents an actual controversy, as *envisaged* by Congress and explained by Justice Murphy." *Domino's Pizza LLC v. Deak,* 654 F.Supp.2d 336, 340 (W.D. Pa. 2009).
- "As a magazine publisher, Universal is not one of the archetypal businesses *envisaged* by the FLSA." *Reiseck v. Universal Communs. of Miami, Inc.,* 591 F.3d 101, 106 (2d Cir. 2010).

Envisage seems more appropriate when inanimate objects are the subject; hence *envision,* which denotes a more human process, seems inapposite in this sentence: "The UCC clearly *envisions* [read *envisages*] that a contract came into being under the facts of this case." *Southern Idaho Pipe & Steel Co. v. Cal-Cut Pipe & Supply, Inc.,* 567 P.2d 1246, 1253 (Idaho 1977). Yet it seems quite defensible here: "But there is no doubt that the

Senate *envisioned* no role for the states on Indian lands." *Montana v. Clark*, 749 F.2d 740, 750 (D.C. Cir. 1984).

envoy. See **ambassador.**

envy. See **jealousy** & **enviable.**

eo instante; eo instanti. The dilemma in spelling is best resolved by writing *at the very instant, instantly,* or *immediately.* E.g.:

- "It then decides that title to the legacy passes *eo instanti at* [read *at the moment of*] death." *In re Fenner's Estate,* 3 Pa. D.&C. 3d 421, 423 (Ct. Com. Pl. 1977).
- "If Langdell was right about all useful materials needed for legal education being in the library, then putting lawyering materials in the library *eo instante* [read *immediately*] makes them useful." Louis M. Brown, *Lawyering Decisions: New Materials for Law Libraries to Collect,* 87 Law Lib. J. 7, 21 (1995).
- "Heirs taking under the intestacy statute have no right to renounce an inheritance, which vests in them *eo instanti* [read *instantly*] by operation of law." Adam J. Hirsch, *Revisions in Need of Revising: The Uniform Disclaimer of Property Interests Act,* 29 Fla. St. U. L. Rev. 109, 130 (2001).

epic. See **epochal.**

epilogue. So spelled—not **epilog.* Cf. **prologue.**

epithet; expletive. *Epithet* = (1) an especially apt adjective, whether the quality described is favorable or unfavorable; or (2) an abusive term. Sense 2 is slowly driving out sense 1, a trend to be opposed. *Expletive* = (1) an interjectory word or expression (esp. a profane one); (2) in grammar, a dummy word that fills the syntactic position of another (most commonly *it* or *there*), as in *It is difficult to describe how* . . . or *There are three.* . . . See EXPLETIVES.

epoch = (1) a date of an occurrence that starts things going under new conditions; or (2) "a period of history." Some stylists object to sense 2 as an example of SLIPSHOD EXTENSION, but that extension occurred in the 17th century, and the best writers today use the word in that sense: "Some historians have said that a meaningful history of humankind could be written around *epochs,* with each *epoch* having its own pervasive characteristics, and that the pervasive characteristic of the age in which we live is technological change" (W. Page Keeton).

epochal; **epical.* The first means "marking an epoch, or a new period in chronology." The word should not be used lightly. "The canons trace back to three *epochal* [read *momentous*] Indian law decisions by Chief Justice John Marshall." Charlene Koski, Comment, *The Legacy of* Solem v. Bartlett, 84 Wash. L. Rev. 723, 734 (2009). (John Marshall was Chief Justice through three *epochs*? No, the three decisions marked a change in Indian law; the word choice is a bit hyperbolic.)

*Epical is a NEEDLESS VARIANT of the adjective *epic,* meaning (1) "of or relating to an epic [= a long heroic narrative]"; or (2) "surpassing what is ordinary or usual."

equable. See **equitable.**

equally. This word should not be used with *both,* as it is here: "We want to treat washing machines like automobiles for purposes of a manufacturer liability law because the values and policy goals that determine the choice of a liability rule apply *equally* to *both* [omit *both*] washing machines and automobiles." Marsha Garrison, *Law Making for Baby Making: An Interpretive Approach to the Determination of Legal Parentage,* 113 Harv. L. Rev. 835, 880 (2000). *Both . . . equally* is redundant. See **equally as (c).**

equally as is almost always incorrect. The exceptions are noted under (E).

A. *Equally as . . . as.* This phrasing is incorrect for *as much . . . as* or *as . . . as.* E.g.:

- "The burden of proof (i.e., persuasion) only matters in cases where the factfinder believes it is *equally as* [omit *equally*] possible that the speech is true *as* it is false." Stephanie Leiter, Case Comment, *Philadelphia Newspapers, Inc. v. Hepps,* 18 Rutgers L.J. 687, 702 (1987).
- "As explained above, causation theories that are mere possibilities or, at most, *equally as* [omit *equally*] probable *as* other theories do not justify denying defendant's motion for summary judgment." *Skinner v. Square D Co.,* 516 N.W.2d 475, 484 (Mich. 1994).
- "On the record before us it is at least *equally as* [omit *equally*] probable that, when the FBI investigated TINA97's association with Childress, TINA97's parents or guardian responded appropriately *as* it is probable that the parents or guardian were indifferent." *Attorney Grievance Comm'n of Md. v. Childress,* 770 A.2d 685, 690–91 (Md. 2001).
- "It is *equally as* [omit *equally*] probable that those hired to hand out leaflets do, indeed, embrace the candidate's political views, *as* it is that they do not, resulting, therefore, in an accurate reflection of the candidate support." *State v. Brookins,* 844 A.2d 1162, 1180 (Md. 2004).
- "It is therefore *equally as* possible [omit *equally*] that the attacks came from sport hackers in Guangdong *as* it is that they came from the Chinese government." Susan W. Brenner, *"At Light Speed": Attribution and Response to Cybercrime/Terrorism/Warfare,* 97 J. Crim. L. & Criminology 379, 435 (2007).

B. *As equally as.* This is a variant of the usual blunder illustrated under (A). "To hold otherwise would be to succumb to a nominalism and a rigid trial scenario *as equally* [omit *equally*] at variance *as* ambush with the spirit of our rules." *Quinn v. Southwest Wood Prods., Inc.,* 597 F.2d 1018, 1025 (5th Cir. 1979).

C. *Both . . . equally as.* This is a double REDUNDANCY—e.g.:

- "On the record before us *both are equally as guilty,* and Smith more so, than appellant." *Augustine v. State,* 28 So.2d 243, 247 (Miss. 1946). A suggested revision: *On the record before us, they are just as guilty as appellant, and Smith more so.*
- "An interesting thought is whether a court would hold the joyrider or the operator of the unsecured network

responsible for the damage, because *both are equally as guilty* [read *they are equally guilty*] of the unauthorized access." Taylor E. White, Comment, *Criminal Consequences of Wi-Fi Joyriding*, 62 Ark. L. Rev. 125, 143 n.111 (2009).

See **equally.**

D. Inversion. The phrase is sometimes inverted and rendered *as equally* after NEGATIVES; still it is wrong. E.g.:

- "Although both *Central Steel Drum* and *D.H.M. Industries* involve situations where the actual damages were shown to be less than the liquidated damages, there is no reason that the principles there expressed should *not be as equally* [read *not be equally*] applicable to cases where the actual damages are later shown to exceed the contractual liquidated damages." *Monsen Eng'g Co. v. Tami-Githens, Inc.*, 530 A.2d 313, 318 (N.J. Super. Ct. App. Div. 1987).
- "We fail to see how Richardson is *not as equally* [read *not equally as*] applicable to the present matter as it was to the facts in that case." *City & County of Honolulu v. Sherman*, 129 P.3d 542, 573 (Haw. 2006).

E. Permissible Uses. If the words *equally as* simply appear together, but are really parts of other constructions, all is well—e.g.:

- "If the deceased, in his lifetime, has done anything that would operate as a bar to recovery by him of damages for the personal injury, this will operate *equally as* a bar in an action by his personal representatives for his death." *Brodie v. Washington Water Power Co.*, 159 P. 791, 791 (Wash. 1916) (quoting Tiffany, *Death by Wrongful Act* (1913)).
- "According to the 1996 P & U, 39% of SSS purchasers purchased it primarily to repel insects, 38% purchased it to use *equally as* an insect repellent and a bath oil, and 18% purchased it primarily for use as a bath oil." *Avon Prods., Inc. v. S.C. Johnson & Son, Inc.*, 984 F.Supp. 768, 793 (S.D.N.Y. 1997).

equitable; equable. *Equable* = even; tranquil; level. *Equitable* derives from *equity*, and has associations of justice and fairness, or of that which can be sustained in a court of equity. To nonlawyers it generally means "fair," whereas to lawyers it may mean "fair" but just as often means "in equity" <equitable jurisdiction> <equitable remedies>. For more on *equitable* and its near-synonyms, see **fair (A).**

Even though the administration of law and equity have been merged into unified courts in most American jurisdictions, we continue to speak of *equitable* rights, titles, and remedies, because they had their origins in equity. Such distinctions are useful, and they give parity to legal and equitable rights: after all, "no one suggests that legal rights be called '*equitable*' merely because they have been merged with equity." William F. Walsh, *A Treatise on Equity* 98 (1930). See **equity.**

equitable estoppel. See **estoppel (B).**

equitable waste. See **waste.**

equity is a CHAMELEON-HUED WORD whose senses have never before been adequately broken down. The primary dichotomy is between sense 1, the popular sense, and sense 4, the lawyer's usual sense. When, under sense 4, lawyers contrast *law* with *equity*, they are contrasting the common law with *equity*; the reader or listener must remember that *equity* is law. The word has more than a dozen senses, including subsenses:

1. **a.** In ordinary language, the quality of being equal or fair; fairness, impartiality; evenhanded dealing—e.g.: "In ordinary parlance *equity* is an abstract term, connoting natural justice." Wilbur Larremore, *Continental Regulation of Contempt of Court*, 13 Harv. L. Rev. 615, 621 (1900). **b.** What is fair and right in a given instance; something that is fair and right—e.g.: "The essence of *equity* is the power to do equity. It is a blend of what is fair and what is just." *In re Gloria Mfg. Corp.*, 65 B.R. 341, 347 (E.D. Va. 1985). **c.** Equal or impartial treatment of parties with conflicting claims—e.g.: "[*Equity* de]notes equal and impartial justice as between two persons whose rights or claims are in conflict." *Demers v. Gerety*, 595 P.2d 387, 395–96 (N.M. Ct. App. 1978).

2. The body of principles constituting what is fair and right; natural law—e.g.: "The term *equity* may also be used in a wider sense to cover the whole of the field of natural justice, i.e., good conscience." Cenydd I. Howells, *Equity in a Nutshell* 1 (1966).

3. **a.** The recourse to principles of justice to correct or supplement the law as applied to particular circumstances—e.g.: "The qualities of mercy and practicality have made *equity* the instrument for nice adjustment and reconciliation between the public interest and private needs as well as between competing private claims." *Hecht Co. v. Bowles*, 321 U.S. 321, 329–30 (1944) (per Douglas, J.). **b.** The construing of a law according to its reason and spirit—e.g.: "'*Equitie*' is a construction made by the judges that cases out of the letter of a statute, yet being within the same mischief or cause of the making of the same, shall be within the same remedy that the statute provideth." Coke, *Institutes*, bk. 1, 24b (1628).

4. **a.** The system of law or body of principles originating in the English Court of Chancery and superseding the common and statute law (together called "law" in the narrower sense) when the two conflict—e.g.: "*Equity* [is] in essence, a system of doctrines and procedures which developed side by side with the common law and statute law." L.B. Curzon, *Equity* 4 (1967). **b.** Any system of law or body of principles analogous to Anglo-American equity, such as the praetorian law of the Romans—e.g.: "*Equity* . . . meaning . . . any body of rules existing by the side of the original civil law, founded on distinct principles and claiming incidentally to supersede the civil law in virtue of a superior sanctity inherent in those principles." Henry S. Maine, *Ancient Law* 28 (1870).

An asterisk (✳) precedes words and phrases that are invariably inferior forms.

5. **a.** An equitable right or interest, i.e., one recognizable by a court of *equity*. Often *pl.* E.g.: "Often, however, the term 'balance of *equities*' is used to denote only a balancing of private and public interests." Zygmunt J.B. Plater, *Statutory Violations and Equitable Discretion*, 70 Cal. L. Rev. 524, 535 (1982). **b.** The ownership interest of shareholders in a corporation—e.g.: "She now has *equity* in the professional corporation." **c.** A speculative right or interest in property—e.g.: "Profits realized from the purchase and sale . . . of an *equity* security within a period of less than 6 months are recoverable by the corporation." *Chenery Corp. v. SEC*, 128 F.2d 303, 308 (D.C. Cir. 1942).

6. The right to relief in a court of *equity*, or the reasons for deserving such relief; equitable merit—e.g.: "Where there is equal *equity* in two contending parties, it is always an unpleasant task to decide between them." *Graff v. Smith's Adm'rs*, 1 U.S. 481, 484 (Pa. Ct. Com. Pl. 1789) (per Shippen, J.).

7. A matter that can or must be decided in a court of equity. Usually in the phrase *equity reserved*—e.g.: "Upon the *equity reserved* under and by the said interlocutory order, it is further ordered, decreed and adjudged, that the injunction heretofore granted in this cause be . . . perpetuated." *U.S. v. Nourse*, 31 U.S. 470, 484 syl. (1832).

8. The meaning, intent, or general purpose (of a statute)—e.g.:

- "These cases thus out of the letter, are said to be within the *Equity* of an Act of Parliament." 3 William Blackstone, *Commentaries on the Laws of England* *431 (1765).
- "'[W]ithin the *equity*,' means the same thing as 'within the mischief' of the statute." *Shuttleworth v. Le Fleming*, 19 C.B.N.S. 703 (1865).

Today, this sense is said to "have disappeared as a term of art or as an element of our [modern] jurisprudence." Carleton K. Allen, *Law in the Making* 456 (7th ed. 1964).

9. An equitable remedy—e.g.:

- "Nor is there any *equity* against the Plaintiff in error." *Clarke v. Russel*, 3 U.S. 415, 421 syl. (1799).
- "A remedy in a court of *equity* is frequently called an *equity*." *Harrison v. Craddock*, 178 S.W.2d 296, 301 (Tex. Civ. App.—Galveston 1944).

10. *Civ. law.* Where positive law is absent or ambiguous, the method of deciding cases by natural law or the inferred intent of the legislature—e.g.:

- "*Equity* in the sense that writers in Continental Europe and Latin and Scandinavian countries use it in observing that ideas of equity are the basis of law and are consequently supplementary law." Vilhelm Lundstedt, 25 Tul. L. Rev. 59, 59 (1950).
- "The *equity* of the statute . . . seems to be a continental notion. . . . When the courts spoke of the *equity* of a statute they meant only that adjustment of detail which is necessary when applying a general rule to a specific case." Theodore F.T. Plucknett, *A Concise History of the Common Law* 334–35 (5th ed. 1956).

11. The right to decide matters in equity; equity jurisdiction; equitable power—e.g.: "[*Equity*] describes the power belonging to the judge—a power which must . . . be exercised according to his own standard of right." John N. Pomeroy, *Equity Jurisprudence* § 45, at 46 (1881).

12. **a.** The amount by which the value of a property or an interest in property exceeds secured claims or liens—e.g.: "'[E]*quity*' . . . is the value, above all secured claims against the property, that can be realized from the sale of the property for the benefit of the unsecured creditors." *In re Mellor*, 734 F.2d 1396, 1400 n.2 (9th Cir. 1984). **b.** In accounting, the paid-in capital plus retained earnings.

13. A share in a public company quoted on the stock exchange. E.g.: "On the other hand, investment in shares of public companies quoted on the Stock Exchange ('*equities*') introduced the risk of dependence upon the fortunes of the company selected . . . Investment in *equities* involved risk." William Geldart, *Introduction to English Law* 86 (D.C.M. Yardley ed., 9th ed. 1984).

The term is used in several phrases. A *countervailing equity* is an equitable right or interest that clashes with another. A *latent equity* is an equitable claim that has been concealed from one or more interested parties. (The phrase *secret equity* is synonymous with *latent equity*.) A *natural equity* is that which a conscientious person would consider fair or just in the absence of legal guidance. A *perfect equity* is the interest that a buyer of real estate has after fulfilling all obligations in the purchase, but before receiving the deed. See **chancery.**

equity abhors a forfeiture; the law abhors a forfeiture. The first is the traditional (and correct) maxim. The second has arisen only since the merger of the administration of law and equity—e.g.: "The law abhors forfeiture unless it is plainly intended by the legislature." *E.H. Crump Co. v. Millar*, 391 S.E.2d 775, 778–79 (Ga. Ct. App. 1990).

equity of redemption. See **cloud on title.**

EQUITY PLEADINGS. There were seven distinct forms of pleadings in equity:

- The *bill* (or *information*).
- The *demurrer*.
- The *plea*.
- The *answer*.
- The *cross-bill*.
- The *disclaimer*.
- The *replication*.

See COMMON-LAW PLEADINGS & WORLD COURT PLEADINGS.

equivocation; equivoke. See **ambiguity.**

-ER. A. And -*or*. These agent-noun suffixes can be especially vexatious to the legal writer. The historical tendency in the law has been to make the Latinate *-or* the correlative of *-ee*, hence *indemnitee/indemnitor*, *obligee/obligor*, *transferee/transferor*, *offeree/offeror*, *donee/donor*. Often, however, the choice of suffix seems based on caprice. In the famous contracts case *Household Fire & Carriage Accident Ins. Co. v. Grant*, [1879] 4 Ex.D. 216 (C.A.), Lord Justice Thesiger used the spellings *acceptor* and *offerer*, whereas the modern trend is to write *accepter* and *offeror* in legal contexts. See -EE.

Attempts to confine *-er* to words of Anglo-Saxon origin and *-or* to those of Latin origin are fruitless because so many exceptions exist on both sides of the aisle. Nevertheless, it may fairly be said that Latinate words usually take *-or*, though there are many exceptions—a few of which appear below in the *-er* column:

-er	*-or*
adapter	abductor
conjurer	abettor
corrupter	collector
digester	corrector
dispenser	distributor
eraser	ejector
idolater	impostor
indorser	purveyor
promoter	surveyor

Sometimes there is a distinction in meaning between variant forms of the same word with these two suffixes, as with *bargainer* and *bargainor*, or latent distinctions, as with *bailer* and *bailor*.

B. Suffix *-er* Misleadingly Suggesting Agent Noun in Law Words. In many legal words, the suffix *-er* might seem to signal an agent noun when actually it denotes some nonhuman object or abstract idea. The result, for the less-than-alert legal reader, is a MISCUE. Most such words are LAW FRENCH infinitives that came into use as English nouns invested with technical legal meanings. Among the most common examples are these:

cesser = (1) the neglect to do something; or (2) the premature ending of a term (as of an estate). See **cesser.**

demurrer = a defending party's pleading alleging that, even if the complaining party's allegations are true, there is no reason why the case should proceed further. See **demurrer.**

descender = hereditary succession.

detainer = detention; the action of keeping a person against his or her will, or of keeping property from its owner.

disclaimer = a disavowal or renunciation.

impleader = a procedure by which a litigant brings a new party into the litigation because that party may be liable on a pending claim. See **impleader.**

interpleader = an equitable proceeding in which the court determines which of two or more rival claimants owns property in dispute—the property often being held by a neutral third party called a "stakeholder." See **interpleader.**

nonuser = neglect to use a right. Cf. **user.**

rebutter = in COMMON-LAW PLEADING, the defendant's answer to the plaintiff's surrejoinder. See **rebutter.**

rejoinder = in COMMON-LAW PLEADING, the defendant's answer to the plaintiff's reply or replication. See **rejoinder.**

repleader = a court's allowance of a party to plead anew when the original pleading failed to raise a material issue.

reverter = a reversionary interest that arises when a grant is limited so that it may come to an end. See **reversion.**

surrebutter = in COMMON-LAW PLEADING, the plaintiff's answer to the defendant's rebutter.

surrejoinder = a pleading by which a plaintiff answers to a defendant's rejoinder. See **rejoinder.**

user = the continued use, exercise, or enjoyment of a right. See **user.**

C. And *-re*. Words borrowed from French generally arrived in English with the *-re* spelling. Most such words have gradually made the transition to *-er*. A few words may be spelled only *-re*, such as *acre*, *chancre*, *massacre*, and *mediocre*, because of the preceding *-c-*. Still others—the great majority—have variant spellings, the *-er* ending usually being more common in AmE and the *-re* ending normal in BrE. The following words have variants subject to this distinction: *accouter, -re; caliber, -re; center, -re; goiter, -re; liter, -re; louver, -re; luster, -re; maneuver, -re; meager, -re; meter, -re* (in BrE, *metre* = the measuring device as well as the measure); *miter, -re; niter, -re; reconnoiter, -re; scepter, -re; sepulcher, -re; somber, -re; specter, -re; theater, -re.*

ergo, a slightly archaic equivalent of *therefore*, is occasionally useful for its succinctness. E.g.: "The United States Supreme Court does not recognize the vicarious exclusionary rule; *ergo*, Daan cannot assert the illegality of Bryan's detention and the seizure of the marijuana cigarettes." *People v. Daan*, 161 Cal. App. 3d 22, 28 (1984). But because *ergo* is no longer a part of everyday language, its effective use depends almost entirely on the audience to whom it is directed.

***Erie*-bound** = (of a federal court in the U.S.) required to apply the holding in *Erie R.R. Co. v. Tompkins*, 304 U.S. 64 (1938). This term is frequently used by American federal courts, which must follow the teachings of *Erie v. Tompkins*: where federal laws are not involved, a federal court exercising diversity jurisdiction (and

---

therefore applying state law) must follow the common law of the state in which it sits. *Erie-bound* is fast becoming a CLICHÉ, because the proposition is so well established that ordinarily there need be no invocation of *Erie v. Tompkins* every time a federal court applies state law. Following are two typical examples of use of the phrase:

- "*Erie-bound*, we begin our analysis with the Louisiana Civil Code." *American Int'l. Specialty Lines Ins. Co. v. Canal Indem. Co.*, 352 F.3d 254, 272 (5th Cir. 2003).
- "In the absence of controlling California Supreme Court precedent, the court is *Erie-bound* to apply the law as it believes that court would do under the circumstances." *White v. Starbucks Corp.*, 497 F.Supp.2d 1080, 1088 (N.D. Cal. 2007).

See CASE REFERENCES (C).

The *Erie* case has spawned some less-well-accepted NEOLOGISMS too, including a whimsical NONCE WORD originating in the Second Circuit: "My senior colleague Judge Learned Hand has a way of startling counsel in these '*erieantompkinated*' days by saying, as they approach that inevitable citation: 'I don't suppose a civil appeal can now be argued to us without counsel sooner or later quoting large portions of *Erie Railroad v. Tompkins*.'" Charles E. Clark, *State Law in the Federal Courts: The Brooding Omnipresence of* Erie v. Tompkins, 55 Yale L.J. 267, 269 (1946).

eristic; *eristical. This word, meaning "of or pertaining to controversy or disputation," is best spelled *eristic*.

ermine (the fur of a weasel-like animal) has come to be used figuratively with reference to the ermine in the official robes of judges in England. The word evokes rather grand notions of a judgeship. This use of the word occurs even in the U.S., where ermine is not used in judges' robes. E.g.:

- "The attitude of the judge and the atmosphere of the court room should indeed be such that no matter what charge is lodged against a litigant or what cause he is called on to litigate, he can approach the bar with every assurance that he is in a forum where the judicial *ermine* is everything that it typifies, purity and justice." *State ex rel. Davis v. Parks*, 194 So. 613, 615 (Fla. 1939).
- "When a lawyer dons the *ermine* and mounts the woolsack he assumes a very serious obligation to the people he serves." *Cone v. Cone*, 68 So.2d 886, 887 (Fla. 1953).

Cf. **woolsack.**

err, one of the most commonly mispronounced words in legal contexts, should properly rhyme with *purr*. It is incorrect, from a strict point of view, to mouth it like *air*. See **error (c).**

errant = (1) traveling <knight errant>; (2) fallible, straying from what is proper. Sense 2 overwhelmingly predominates—e.g.:

- "'Invited responses' can be effectively discouraged by prompt action from the bench in the form of corrective instructions to the jury and, when necessary, an admonition to the *errant* advocate." *U.S. v. Young*, 470 U.S. 1, 13 (1985) (per Burger, C.J.).

- "Considering the circumstances, the court finds that for a year, a bond of $400,000 should be made available, against which Defendants may proceed if a jury later determines that the preliminary injunction was *errantly* issued." *Unisource Worldwide, Inc. v. S. Cent. Ala. Supply, LLC*, 199 F.Supp.2d 1194, 1216 (M.D. Ala. 2001).
- "Although the circuit court cited *Holmes*, the court *errantly* decided the case based on its determination that there was a 'per se' conflict—a concept [*that*] *Holmes* itself makes clear has no relevance to this case." *People v. Ortega*, 808 N.E.2d 496, 509 (Ill. 2004).

Errant is properly used of persons or their actions; it is not synonymous with *erroneous*, as some writers apparently think—e.g.:

- "However, merely because of the *errant* [read *erroneous*] application of *Sababu*, we will not equate the lack of a finding of prejudice with the actual absence of prejudice." *U.S. v. Berry*, 64 F.3d 305, 308 (7th Cir. 1995).
- "Highet charged the majority with reaching an *errant* [read *erroneous*] conclusion that Waste Management should be barred from NAFTA arbitration due to its tender of a defective waiver which condoned conduct beyond the intended scope of Article 1121." Jacob S. Lee, Note, *No "Double-Dipping" Allowed*, 69 Fordham L. Rev. 2655, 2677–78 (2001).
- "It appears that the use of the term 'journals' was merely an *errant* [read *erroneous*] pluralization in the notes of the investigating detective." *Taylor v. State*, 982 A.2d 279, 283 n.11 (Del. 2008).

errata. Like *addenda* and *corrigenda*, the plural form *errata* should be used only when one is listing more than one item. If there is only one, the heading should be *erratum*. The English plural *erratums* is not used.

erroneous. See **error (B).**

erroneous mistake is a REDUNDANCY. E.g.: "[T]he Magistrate further found that Plaintiff adequately pled the third element by alleging that it operated under an *erroneous mistake* [read *a mistake*] of fact." *Capital Factors, Inc. v. Heller Fin., Inc.*, 712 F.Supp. 908, 915 (S.D. Fla. 1989).

*erronious is an erroneous spelling of *erroneous*.

error, n. **A. General Senses.** *Error* = (1) a mistake of law in a court's judgment, opinion, or order; (2) an appeal; or (3) *in Scots law*, a mistaken belief by one or both parties about some matter of fact or law material to their bargain—i.e., as an equivalent of the Anglo-American legal term *mistake*. See **mistake (A)** & **mutual mistake.**

To illustrate sense 2, *proceedings in error* are not the same as *erroneous proceedings*, as a nonlawyer might think. In fact, the official name of the highest court in Connecticut is the Supreme Court of Errors. The report in *McCulloch v. Maryland*, 17 U.S. (4 Wheat.) 316, 317 (1819), contains the heading "*Error* to the Court of Appeals of the state of Maryland." This sense developed as an elliptical form of *writ of error*—e.g.: "This motion was granted by the trial court, and the appellant brings *error*." *Austin v. Healthtrust, Inc.*, 951 S.W.2d 78, 78–79 (Tex.

App.—Corpus Christi 1997). See **plaintiff in error & defendant in error**.

B. For *in error* or *erroneous*. This use, though fairly old and increasingly common in AmE, should be avoided, for it wrongly makes *error* adjectival. E.g.:

- "It was *error* [read *erroneous*] to direct a verdict." *Soule v. Bon Ami Co.*, 195 N.Y.S. 574, 577 (Sup. Ct. 1922) (Rich & Kelly, JJ., dissenting).
- "Plaintiff contends that this holding *is error* [read *is in error*]. She asserts that she made out a prima facie case by introducing the note in question." *Thigpen v. Thigpen*, 563 S.W.2d 868, 870 (Tex. Civ. App.—San Antonio 1978).
- "Invited error also occurs when a party independently requests an erroneous instruction and then argues on appeal that the instruction was *error* [read *erroneous*] even though the other party also independently asked for the same instruction." *State v. Lucero*, 220 P.3d 249, 256 (Ariz. Ct. App. 2009).

C. Misused for *err*, vb. This mistake commonly appears in appellate briefs. If we were inclined to be generous to the lawyers who err in this way, we might attribute the mistake to secretaries who misunderstand dictation. Yet the fault cannot rightly be laid on the secretaries. The court in *Stolte v. Mack Fin. Corp.*, 457 S.W.2d 172, 174 (Tex. Civ. App.—Texarkana 1970), subtly highlighted this error in an advocate's brief in three successive points of error. Here is a typical misuse: "Justice Stevens . . . held that the district court *errored* [read *erred*] in granting retroactive relief in *Manhart*." Pamela S. Anderson, *Gender-Based Determination of Retirement Benefits*, 19 Tulsa L.J. 755, 762 (1984). Correctly pronouncing *err* would reduce the frequency of this blunder. (See **err.**)

error, writ of. See **writ of error**.

erstwhile; quondam; sometime; whilom. Each of these terms means "one-time, former, at a former time." By far the most common in AmE and BrE is *erstwhile* (called "literary" in the *OED*). The least common are *quondam* and (even rarer) *whilom*—e.g.: "Gerald Asher, the *whilom* wine merchant and distinguished wine writer, was in town recently to talk about . . . Chardonnay clones." Frank J. Prial, *Wine Talk*, N.Y. Times, 25 Apr. 1990, at C11. The word *sometime*, an invitation to a MISCUE, is often misused as if it meant "occasional, from time to time." See **sometime**.

We need one of these words in English—probably *erstwhile*—because *former* and *one-time* do not always suffice. Our embarrassment of riches, with four synonyms for one sense, is exceeded only by most writers' embarrassment at having to use any one of them in addressing a less-than-learned audience.

escape. A. Legal Senses. In law, the word refers to an unlawful departure from legal custody without the use of force; it does not properly refer to a suspect's avoidance of capture.

In older writings, *escape* was the name of the offense committed by a law-enforcement officer (esp. a jailer) who somehow allowed a suspected criminal to escape, either through inadvertence or because he or she had been bribed. So a jailer convicted of *escape* was one who had been at fault in a prisoner's successful departure from custody. Two modern commentators note that this usage "seems inappropriate." Rollin M. Perkins & Ronald N. Boyce, *Criminal Law* 560 (3d ed. 1982). To be sure, if one asked a group of lawyers (much less nonlawyers) just who had been guilty of escape, almost none today would point to the jailer.

B. *Escape (from)*. As an intransitive verb construed with *from* or *out of*, *escape* means "to gain one's liberty by fleeing, to get free from detention or control" <he escaped from prison>. As a transitive verb taking a direct object, the verb means either (1) "to succeed in avoiding (something unwelcome)" <they escaped suspicion>, or (2) "to elude (observation, search, etc.)" <its significance had previously escaped me>.

escapee (= one who escapes) should more logically be *escaper* or *escapist*. (See -EE (A).) The *OED* suggests that *escapee* is waning in use and that *escapist* is emerging as the standard BrE agent noun. American writers seem to prefer *escaper*. As long as *escapee* is displaced, it might seem to matter little which alternative prevails. But *escaper* might be better for two reasons. First, *escapist* suggests Houdini, i.e., one who makes a living putting on "escapes" from difficult predicaments (also known as an *escapologist*); second, it has irrelevant figurative uses, as in *escapist fiction* (i.e., as the adjective corresponding to *escapism*).

One writer defines *escapee* as "one who has been caught after escaping, or while preparing to escape." Paul Tempest, *Lag's Lexicon* 75 (1950). Perhaps that is how a *lag* (= a convict sentenced to penal servitude) understands the term, but being caught is not really necessary to the definition. Most writers and speakers of English would find nothing wrong with saying, "The *escapees* were never caught"—they would merely find something wrong with the fact of their not being caught.

escape from. See **escape (B)**.

escheat [Law Latin "a falling or happening"] may be both noun and verb. As the former, it means "the lapsing of land to the state (in G.B., to the Crown) upon the death of the intestate owner without heirs." A LAW FRENCH word originally meaning "inheritance," it came to apply at common law to the lord's succession to a tenant's fief when the tenant died seised without heir. From the perceived unfairness of the system—once the lords had begun to abuse it—evolved the aphaeretic form *cheat*. (See **cheat**.)

Escheat is used more commonly as a verb than as a noun in legal writing, as here: "The lands of a person convicted of petty treason . . . or felony *escheated* (i.e. reverted) to his lord." L.B. Curzon, *English Legal History* 233 (2d ed. 1979). But the noun use is hardly uncommon—e.g.: "The court would be less concerned with the influencer's motive in a contest between him and the state claiming an *escheat* than it would be in a contest between him and the donor's surviving spouse." *Escheatment and *escheatage are NEEDLESS VARIANTS.

Originally applied in feudal land law to instances of "failure of title" (when there was no titleholder), *escheat* has been extended—grossly some would say—in AmE. Since World War II, with the enactment of the Uniform Disposition of Unclaimed Property Act in various states—the act itself not using *escheat*—the word is now popularly used by nonlawyers as a verb referring to what happens to abandoned and unclaimed personal property. To the real-property purist, this usage, resulting from both SLIPSHOD EXTENSION and POPULARIZED LEGAL TECHNICALITY, is irksome. Cf. **bona vacantia.**

eschew; eschewal, n. The second syllable of both words is pronounced just as the word *chew* is pronounced, /es-**choo**/. For some reason, many seem to believe that the *esch-* sequence in this term is pronounced *esh-*. It is not. The pronunciation with an *esh-* sound sounds like a sneeze.

escrow [fr. O.F. *escroue* "a roll of writings"] has three noun senses: (1) "a deed delivered but not to become operative until a future date or until some condition has been fulfilled"; (2) "a deposit held in trust or as security" <in escrow>; or (3) "an escrow holder." Sense 1 is the traditional one. Sense 2, labeled "a perversion" in the 4th edition of *Black's Law Dictionary* (1968), was a 19th-century American coinage that is now current in both AmE and BrE. Sense 3, a result of HYPALLAGE, has brevity on its side but little else: it is likely to cause MISCUES.

The verb uses of *escrow*, recorded from 1916, are now common in American legal writing. As a verb, *escrow* means "to put into *escrow* [sense 2]." E.g.:

- "By *escrowing* the funds for the purpose of improving municipal services in the black community, the court took the first step toward ensuring that the unconstitutional disparities would be corrected rather than perpetuated." *Dowdell v. City of Apopka*, 698 F.2d 1181, 1186 (11th Cir. 1983).
- "The cognizant officials of FDIC consented to the sale and to the *escrowing* of proceeds of sale with the rights of all claimants to follow those proceeds." *In re Jeter*, 48 B.R. 404, 409 (Bankr. N.D. Tex. 1985).
- "By *escrowing* the funds the Governor halts the total expenditures of the government as they relate to total revenue, preventing a deficit." *Goldston v. State*, 683 S.E.2d 237, 247 (N.C. Ct. App. 2009).

Today it is common in American real-estate law to speak of *escrowing* all types of documents—that is, holding them with the understanding that they will not be released until some condition is met. This use corresponds to sense 1 of the noun.

escrowee (= the depositary of an escrow) is a curious term, there being no correlative agent noun in *-er* or *-or*. Recorded in *W3* but ignored in the *OED*, the term is not uncommon in modern AmE. E.g.: "The assignment from Avon to the *escrowees* was recorded in the Patent and Trademark Office." *Haymaker Sports, Inc. v. Turian*, 581 F.2d 257, 262 (C.C.P.A. 1978) (Baldwin, J., dissenting). Even so, the phrases *escrow holder* and *escrow agent*—both being precise equivalents—are more widely understandable.

***eslisor.** See **elisor.**

especial; special. Traditionally speaking, *especial* (= distinctive, significant, peculiar) is the opposite of *ordinary*. E.g.:

- "Can it be said that Washington would have subordinated the execution of a public duty to the approval of private individuals who had no *especial* rights in the matter?" *Morris v. U.S.*, 174 U.S. 196, 335 (1899) (White, J., dissenting).
- "As was said in *Sheckell v. Jackson* . . . in reply to a contention that conductors of the public press are entitled to peculiar indulgence and have *especial* rights and privileges, 'the law recognizes no such peculiar rights, privileges, or claims to indulgence.'" *Kimball v. Post Pub. Co.*, 85 N.E. 103, 105 (Mass. 1908).

Special (= specific, particular) is the opposite of *general* <the jury answered special issues>, though increasingly it has ousted *especial* from its rightful territory.

Especial is so rarely used in AmE today—even in learned and legal prose—that some might term it obsolescent. But it does occasionally appear, most often modifying a noun made from an adjective; that is, a writer who might otherwise refer to something that is *especially harsh* would refer to its *especial harshness*, as in this BrE example: "Conduct of the type last named with regard to goods constitutes the tort of conversion, which bears with *especial* harshness on one who has, in all good faith, bought goods from one who had no title to them." William Geldart, *Introduction to English Law* 132 (D.C.M. Yardley ed., 9th ed. 1984).

In the following sentence, *especial* is wrongly used for *special*, used in contrast to *general*: "Positive laws either contain general principles embodied in the rules of law . . . or for *especial* [read *special*] reasons they establish something that differs from those general principles." Wesley N. Hohfeld, *Some Fundamental Legal Conceptions as Applied in Judicial Reasoning*, 23 Yale L.J. 16, 38 (1913) (quoting *Mackelday's Roman Law*).

espousals. See **spousals.**

espouse = (1) to marry or give in marriage; or (2) to adopt or support (as a doctrine or cause). Sense 1, the literal sense, is rarely seen today even in legal writing, but it does occur—e.g.:

- "At this time this person is with him in New Orleans, and the Duke is seeking this divorce to *espouse* her." *Zavaglia v. Notarbartolo*, 69 So. 152, 156 (La. 1915).
- "The next we hear of this marriageable daughter, Stanley, as intermediary, is having his stepson Richmond informed

that the Queen has 'heartily' consented that Richard shall *espouse* her daughter." Stephen Vanderslice, *The Edgeless Sword: Richard III's Desperate End*, 26 Okla. City U. L. Rev. 403, 433 (2001).

Espouse in sense 2 is often misused. In the following sentence, it is used as if it were synonymous with *endorse* (applied to persons as well as things): "In defeating [plaintiff] we do not decry him, nor do we *espouse* [read *endorse*] his adversary." *Fey v. King*, 190 N.W. 519, 523 (Iowa 1922). And here it is incorrectly used for *expound* or *set forth*: "Having *espoused* [read *expounded*] our view of the intent of Congress, we are nonetheless bound by the prior decisions of panels of this circuit." *James v. U.S.*, 740 F.2d 365, 373 (5th Cir. 1984). (The court obviously did not *espouse* a view if it could not follow it.)

Yet the proper use of the word in sense 2 is common—e.g.:

- "This problem might be treated as one covered by the law of negligence. A state not yet ready to *espouse* strict product liability would do just this." John W. Wade, *On the Effect in Product Liability of Knowledge Unavailable Prior to Marketing*, 58 N.Y.U. L. Rev. 734, 759 (1983).
- "Charles II, when he wanted to return to England, was ready to *espouse* this principle in exchange for his throne by declaring 'a liberty to tender consciences, and that no man shall be disquieted or called in question for differences of opinion in matter of religion which do not disturb the peace of the kingdom.'" Steve Bachmann, *Starting Again with the Mayflower . . . England's Civil War and America's Bill of Rights*, 20 Q.L.R. 193, 208 (2000).
- "Since we do not *espouse* [i.e., *adopt*] the *Wagoner* rule, we do not have to resolve this difficulty." *In re Senior Cottages of Am., LLC*, 482 F.3d 997, 1003 n.6 (8th Cir. 2007).

Esq., in AmE, "is often used as a title signifying that the holder is a lawyer." R.D. Rotunda, *Professional Responsibility* 396 (2d ed. 1988). The mild honorific is used nowadays with the names of men and women alike; it is incorrect, however, to use this title with any other title, such as *Mr.* or *Ms.* In BrE, of course, *esquire* is used of any man thought to have the social status of a gentleman. See FORMS OF ADDRESS (F).

One law review has devoted several pages to an article on whether women attorneys should use *esquire*. See Richard B. Eaton, *An Historical View of the Term Esquire as Used by Modern Women Attorneys*, 80 W. Va. L. Rev. 209 (1978). As to the title and purpose of that article, however, it is worth noting that "*Esq.* is . . . not used on oneself, e.g. neither on a card (which bears *Mr.*) nor on a stamped-and-addressed envelope enclosed for a reply (which has merely A-B.X—or A.B.X.—without prefix)." Alan S.C. Ross, "U and Non-U: An Essay in Sociological Linguistics," in *Noblesse Oblige* (Nancy Mitford ed., 1956). But somehow, the idea has gotten out that *Esq.* is something you put after your own name—e.g.: "These [lawyers] assembled here are not ordinary litigators. Instead of appending a mere 'Esq.' after their names, they are 'Factl'—Fellows of the American

College of Trial Lawyers." David Margolick, *At the Bar*, N.Y. Times, 10 Mar. 1989, at 23.

The real question in AmE is not whether women should append *Esq.* to their own names, but whether others should append it to women attorneys' names. The answer: this practice is perfectly acceptable and extremely common. Anyone who is bothered by this practice should pretend that *Esq.*, when used after a woman's name, stands for *esquiress* (recorded in the *OED* from 1596). See SEXISM (C).

-ESS. See SEXISM (C).

essay, vb. See **assay.**

esse (= essence; essential nature) is a pedantic LATINISM. E.g.: "This appeal forces us to acknowledge a lumbering, antediluvian concept that remains embedded in the judicial *esse*." *Coastal (Bermuda) Ltd. v. E.W. Saybolt & Co.*, 761 F.2d 198, 200 (5th Cir. 1985). Cf. *in esse* & *de bene esse.*

essence, time is of the. See **time is of the essence.**

essoign, n. & vb.; **essoin.** *Essoin* /e-**soin**/ is the preferred spelling for both noun and verb; *essoign* is a variant spelling of the noun only. The word (meaning "an excuse for not appearing in court at the appointed time") is used only in BrE. E.g.: "But one cannot wait for ever; that would be unfair to the other party; so a great deal of law is evolved as to the excuses for nonappearance, in technical language the *essoins*, that a man may proffer." F.W. Maitland, *The Forms of Action at Common Law* 20 (1909; A.H. Chaytor & W.J. Whittaker, eds., 1971).

estate = (1) all that a person owns, including both heritable and movable property <she has a modest estate, even if one includes her stock>; (2) the degree, quantity, or nature of a person's rights in land <leasehold estate>; or (3) the land itself <the Biltmore estate>.

estate for years. See **term of years.**

estate planning, though now a commonplace phrase in American law, is an odd EUPHEMISM that may help lawyers avoid confronting their clients too starkly with the dread subject of dying. At least one writer has set his face against the phrase: "An occasional client . . . is probably justified when he calls his personal aggregation of material things an 'estate,' if he wants to call it that. But it is wildly inaccurate to represent that he or anyone else planned it, or that a mere lawyer is going to 'plan' it for him—whatever that means—now that he has it. What is being planned for is death and the fact that one's things go the way of one's mortal coil. 'Estate planning' is an evasive, fawning, pretentious phrase, and I propose to begin by refusing to be associated with it." Thomas L. Shaffer, *The Planning and Drafting of Wills and Trusts* 1 (2d ed. 1979). Shaffer and several other writers use *property settlement* instead of *estate planning*. Shaffer adds: "I regret . . . the connotation the phrase [*property settlement*] has taken from divorce practice." *Id.* at 2 n.1.

estates in community. See **concurrent interests.**

estate tail. See **tail** & **entail.**

*****esthetic.** See **aesthetic.**

estop, vb. **A. Generally.** *Estop* (= to stop, bar, hinder, or preclude) appears most commonly in the passive-voice construction (someone *is estopped* by something)—e.g.: "Petitioner's rule might provide a brighter line for determining whether a patentee *is estopped* under certain circumstances." *Warner-Jenkinson Co. v. Hilton Davis Chem. Co.*, 520 U.S. 17, 32 n.6 (1997) (per Thomas, J.). Yet the active-voice construction (something *estops* someone) does sometimes appear—e.g.: "Determining whether Litton's conduct *estops* it . . . presents a more complicated inquiry." *Litton Sys., Inc. v. Honeywell, Inc.*, 140 F.3d 1449, 1463 (Fed. Cir. 1998). In modern caselaw, the passive construction is about seven times as common as the active. See PASSIVE VOICE.

In the active voice, this verb is sometimes reflexive, in the sense "to be precluded by one's own previous act or declaration from doing or alleging something" (*OED*). E.g.: "By favoring just those two groups and doing so with a virtual quota system for affirmative action in admissions, the law school *estops itself* from proving that its plan to achieve diversity is ingenuous, much less narrowly tailored." *Hopwood v. State of Texas*, 78 F.3d 932, 966 n.24 (5th Cir. 1996) (Wiener, J., concurring).

B. *Estopped to* vs. *estopped from*. Traditionally, it was common to say either that someone is *estopped to do something* or that someone is *estopped from doing something*—that is, either an infinitive or *from* [verb + ing] followed *estopped*. In modern legal usage, *estopped from doing* is more than twice as common—e.g.:

- "The plaintiffs next assert that the bank is, in any event, *estopped from refusing* to loan them the additional $65,000 by its promise to do so." *Whorley v. First Westside Bank*, 485 N.W.2d 578, 582 (Neb. 1992).
- "The district court also found that Logan was *estopped from raising* her breach-of-contract claim." *Logan v. Norwest Bank Minn., N.A.*, 603 N.W.2d 659, 664 (Minn. Ct. App. 1999).
- "The sole issue in this case is whether the Township is equitably *estopped from terminating* Beaver's post-retirement medical benefits." *Middletown Township Policemen's Benevolent Ass'n v. Township of Middletown*, 744 A.2d 649, 651–52 (N.J. 2000).

The less frequent phrasing (*estopped to do*) increasingly sounds a trifle archaic—e.g.: "To the extent that the trial court found that the Village was *estopped to enforce* its ordinances, we find nothing in the record to support a finding of estoppel." *Sandoval County Bd. of Comm'rs v. Ruiz*, 893 P.2d 482, 487 (N.M. Ct. App. 1995). In short, both wordings are fully

acceptable, but the idiomatic trend favors *estopped from* [verb + ing].

estoppel. A. Spelling. The word *estoppel* /es-**top**-əl/ is so spelled. The word is sometimes misspelled **estoppal*, as in Arthur A. Leff, *The Leff Dictionary of Law*, 94 Yale L.J. 1855, 1974, 2104 (1985), under **agency by estoppal* and **authority by estoppal*. For the difference between *estoppel* and *waiver*, see **waiver (c).**

B. Estoppel; estoppel by representation; estoppel in pais; equitable estoppel; promissory estoppel. Most broadly, *estoppel* denotes a bar that precludes a person from denying or contradicting something that he or she has said before or that has been legally established as true. Traditionally, the only real distinction between any of the terms listed above turns on whether the party's statement relates to a present fact or to future conduct.

Estoppel, estoppel by representation, and *estoppel in pais* all relate to a party's saying something about an existing matter of fact. The most usual term today is *estoppel* alone—a shorthand form of *estoppel by representation*.

Promissory estoppel and *equitable estoppel* both relate to a party's saying something about his or her intentions to do something in the future. The phrase *promissory estoppel* has "gradually won out over the term '*equitable estoppel*,' which had been used with some frequency in the earlier cases." Grant Gilmore, *The Death of Contract* 129 n.145 (1974).

Indeed, the term *equitable estoppel* is extraordinarily fuzzy and ought therefore to be avoided. G.H. Treitel criticizes an English decision that "somewhat puzzlingly seems to distinguish between '*promissory*' and '*equitable*' *estoppel*. Terminological difficulty is compounded by the occasional use of the phrase '*equitable estoppel*' to refer to true *estoppel* by representation." *The Law of Contract* 109 (8th ed. 1991). See **promissory estoppel.**

estray is an ARCHAISM used in law for "stray animal"—e.g.:

- "He took the animal up as an *estray*, and proceeded to give the proper *estray* notices under the statute, and in good faith followed all the requirements of the statute relating to *estrays*." *Kinney v. Roe*, 30 N.W. 776, 776 (Iowa 1886).
- "Mr. Maher removed all five animals as *estrays* and completed an *Estray* Livestock Report." *Stanko v. Maher*, 419 F.3d 1107, 1111 (10th Cir. 2005).

See **waifs and estrays.**

estrepement; estrepment. The longer spelling of this word, which means "waste of land caused by a tenant," is more usual—e.g.: "A touchstone . . . is afforded by supposing an attempt at removal by the tenant and a writ of *estrepement* issued or bill in equity filed by the landlord to restrain the removal as the commitment of waste." *In re American Pile Fabrics Co.*, 12 F.Supp. 86, 88 (E.D. Pa. 1935).

et al. is most commonly the abbreviated form of the Latin phrase *et alii* (= and others), though it may also be the masculine singular (*et alius*), the feminine singular (*et alia*), or the feminine plural (*et aliae*). It is used only of persons, whereas *etc.* is used of things. American lawyers commonly write *et al, et. al.*, or *et. al*—all of which are wrong.

The abbreviation does not fit comfortably alongside possessives: "Clifford T. Honicker's chilling account of Louis Slotin's, S. Allan Kline's *et al. encounter* [read *and others' encounters*] with the Nuclear Age is as horrific as it is emblematic." Letter of Glenn Alcalay, N.Y. Times, 10 Dec. 1989, § 6, at 14. Cf. **etc.**

etc. A French proverb states, "God save us from a lawyer's *et cetera*." The point is well taken. More than 400 years ago, John Florio wrote: "The heaviest thing that is, is one *Etcetera*." It is heaviest because it implies a quantity of things too numerous to mention. These are some of the most sensible words ever written on *etc.*:

> Every writer should be on his guard against the excessive use of *etc.* Instead of finishing a thought completely, it is easy to end with an *etc.*, throwing the burden of finishing the thought upon the reader. If the thought is adequately expressed, *etc.* is not needed. If the thought is not adequately expressed, *etc.* will not take the place of that which has not been said. The use of *etc.* tends to become a slovenly habit, the corrective for which is to refrain from using *etc.* except in the *dryest* [read *driest*] and most documentary kind of writing.
>
> George P. Krapp, *A Comprehensive Guide to Good English* 229 (1927).

Lawyers should generally—in pleadings, for example—attempt to be as specific as possible rather than make use of this term. Still, it would be foolish to lay down an absolute proscription against using *etc.*, for often one simply *cannot* practicably list all that should be listed in a given context. Hence, rather than convey to the reader that a list is seemingly complete when it is not, the writer might justifiably use *etc.* (always the abbreviation).

And etc. is an ignorant error, *et* being the Latin *and. Etc.* differs from *et al.* in that it refers to things and not to people. (See **et al.**) The *-t-* in the first syllable of *etc.* should never be pronounced as a *-k-*. On the use of *etc.* with *e.g.* and *i.e.*, see **e.g.**

etched in stone. See **stone, etched in.**

-ETH. At its fringes, legal language retains a few words ending this way—e.g., *deposeth, sayeth*, and *witnesseth*. None is a TERM OF ART. None is even useful. Up to the 17th century, the *-eth* suffix was merely an alternative third-person singular inflection for an English verb; used primarily in southern England, it had, by the end of that century, become obsolete. *She calls* and *he answers* took the place of *she calleth* and *he answereth*.

Perversely, these obsolete forms continue to haunt legal contexts, never with happy results. When using words with this ending, lawyers have long been inconsistent in their approach; for example, a late-19th-century verification stated, "W.J. Bound . . . deposeth and says . . . ." *Dorman v. Crozier*, 14 Kan. 224, 224 (1875) (quoting a verification). Why not *deposeth and sayeth*?

More to the point, modern lawyers commonly mangle tenses when *-eth* crops up, often by thinking that *-eth* signifies a past tense: "E.W. Kelley, being first duly cautioned and sworn, *deposeth* and said that one Paul De Golyer . . . ." *City of Cincinnati v. De Golyer*, 270 N.E.2d 663, 664 (Ohio Ct. App. 1969) (quoting an affidavit). Modern lawyers also misuse *witnesseth* at the outset of a contract as if it were imperative instead of present-tense indicative. The careful legal writer junketh this obsolete dialectal ending. See **doth, saith** & **witnesseth.** See also **further affiant sayeth naught (A).**

ethical; moral. Both adjectives describe a standard of what is right and good, as well as the study and theory of good behavior. *Ethical* implies a relationship to ethics, which is the branch of philosophy dealing with the principles of ideal human conduct and character. But the term also, for lawyers, invokes the various codes of ethics and professional responsibility applicable specifically to the legal profession—and in this sense the word is not so much idealistic as it expresses a minimum standard of conduct that keeps one from transgressing the elaborate set of rules by which each member of the profession must abide. *Moral* is a broader term, implying a basic sense of right and wrong, or good and bad, especially in terms of conduct and conscience. The term evokes notions of prevailing mores, customs, and conventions of a people, often (though not necessarily) with religious overtones.

ethicist; *ethician. *Ethician* is more than two centuries older—dating from the early 17th century—and is therefore given precedence in most English-language dictionaries. Even so, *ethicist* so overwhelmingly predominates in modern usage that *ethician ought to be labeled a NEEDLESS VARIANT. E.g.: "Ethicists and moral theologians offer a variety of explanations for the duty to keep promises." Douglas Laycock, *The Death of the Irreparable Injury Rule* 255 (1991).

ethics; ethos. The distinction escapes many writers, but it is plain. Jeremy Bentham defined *ethics* as "the art of directing men's actions to the production of the greatest possible quantity of happiness, on the part of those whose interest is in view." Bentham, *An Introduction to the Principles of Morals and Legislation* 310 (1823). The singular form *ethic* means "a set of moral principles."

Ethos = the characteristic spirit and beliefs of a community, people, system, or person. Here the nicety keenly appears: "We introduce here no new or radical *ethic* since our *ethos* has never given moral sanction to piracy." *E.I. duPont de Nemours & Co. v. Christopher*, 431 F.2d 1012, 1016–17 (5th Cir. 1970).

---

etiology. Outside the field of medicine (and arguably within it), *etiology* is unnecessary and pompous for *cause*. E.g.:

- "In both cases, we were concerned not with the mere fact that different injuries existed, but with whether those injuries had different *etiologies* [read *causes*]." *In re Van Waters & Rogers, Inc.*, 145 S.W.3d 203, 210 (Tex. 2004).
- "Environmental or public-health injuries, for example, may have complex *etiologies* [read *causes*] that involve the interaction of many discrete risk factors." *Natural Res. Def. Council v. EPA*, 440 F.3d 476, 483 (D.C. Cir. 2006).

Aetiology is the BrE spelling. **Aitiology* is a variant spelling to be avoided.

ETIOLOGY. See CAUSATION.

et seq. When citing a statute, it is better to give the reader an end point as well as a beginning one. Otherwise, the reader is left to conjecture just how many sections are encompassed in 29 U.S.C. § 621 *et seq.* Hence the phrase *et seq.* (short for *et sequentes* = the following ones) should be used sparingly if at all. The problem is exacerbated by the fact that *et seq.* serves also as the abbreviation for the singular *et sequens* (= and the following one), though presumably few users of the phrase know that.

-ETTE. See SEXISM (C).

et ux. See **ux.**

ETYMOLOGICAL AWARENESS is developed only by increased reading and a conscious sensitivity to words and their origins. Ignorance of etymologies can easily lead writers astray, as when a journalist gave the label *holocaust* (Gk. "burnt whole") to a flood. Following are sentences in which writers wandered into etymological bogs:

- "The right to exclude or to expel aliens, or any class of aliens . . . in war or in peace is an inherent and *inalienable* right of every . . . independent nation." *Wong Wing v. U.S.*, 163 U.S. 228, 231 (1896) (per Shiras, J.). Here the root *alien-* causes problems, when we say a country has an *inalienable* right to exclude *aliens*.
- "This is a result [that], if at all possible *consonant* [lit., "sounding together"] with *sound* judicial policy, should be avoided." *Bly v. Rhoads*, 222 S.E.2d 783, 787 (Va. 1976).
- "What we are concerned with here is the automobile and its *peripatetic* [= able to walk up and down, not just *itinerant*] character." *World-Wide Volkswagen Corp. v. Woodson*, 444 U.S. 286, 318 (1980) (Blackmun, J., dissenting). Automobiles can hardly be said to walk.

In the first two specimens, a senseless repetition of the root sense occurs; in the third, the writer has insensitively abstracted and broadened a word still ineluctably tied to its root sense. Cf. VERBAL AWARENESS.

Euclidean; *Euclidian. The *-ean* spelling is standard.

EUPHEMISMS are supposedly soft or unobjectionable terms substituted in place of harsh or objectionable ones. The purpose is to soften; the means is usually indirection. To discerning readers, of course, some euphemisms are objectionable as unnecessarily mealy-mouthed.

We euphemize if we refer to someone not as *drunk*, but as *inebriated* or *intoxicated*; not as a *drug addict*, but (much more vaguely) as *impaired*; not as having *died*, but as having *passed away*; not as *mentally retarded*, but as *exceptional* or *special*.

In some contexts, to be sure, you might prefer a euphemism. If plain talk is going to provoke unnecessary controversy—if talk about *illegitimate children* or *sodomy* will divert attention from your point by offending people—then use an established euphemism.

Indeed, the phrase *illegitimate children* exemplifies the need sometimes to throw over old forms of expression. West Publishing Company's keynote system of indexing legal topics has gone from *Bastards* in the Eighth Decennial Digest (1966–76) to *Illegitimate Children* in the Ninth Decennial Digest (1976–81) to *Children Out-of-Wedlock* in the Federal Digest 3d (1985). Some legal writers use *nonmarital children* to convey the idea. The point, of course, is that we shouldn't scar innocent children with ugly epithets.

Other euphemisms, however, are roundabout and clumsy. Some writers use *rodent operative* or *extermination engineer* in place of *ratcatcher*. We see *pregnancy termination* rather than *abortion*; *sexually ambidextrous* rather than *bisexual*; *armed reconnaissance* rather than *bombing*; *permanent layoff* rather than *firing*. Whatever the unpleasant or socially awkward subject, there are several euphemisms available. In law, *unnatural offense* (or *crime*) *against nature* is not uncommon in place of *homosexuality*. Indeed, Arthur Leff gave *abominable and detestable crime against nature* as a "rather enthusiastic euphemism . . . found in many 19th-century (and some current) statutes, referring to a not fully specified range of sexual crimes." Arthur A. Leff, *The Leff Dictionary of Law*, 94 Yale L.J. 1855, 1866 (1985). The problem that courts encounter—now more than in yesteryear—is deciding what constitutes a *crime against nature* and the like, and whether any criminal statute using such a phrase is so vague as to be unconstitutional. *See* David Abbott, *Crimes Against Language and Nature*, 3 Scribes J. Legal Writing 149 (1992).

Euphemisms are often subtle. Hence *incident* appears in place of *accident* in a U.S. statute limiting total liability to $200 million for a single "nuclear incident," presumably because *incident* sounds vaguer and less alarmist. Today *revenue enhancement* (= tax increase) and *investment* (= increased government spending) are commonly used by American politicians who are reluctant to call things by their more understandable names.

In the mock-heroic style that was popular in the 19th century—and even up to a few decades ago—euphemisms were quite common. In the following sentence, for example, a judge uses an elaborate euphemism for the hymen: "[The statute] further says to the libertine, who would rob a virtuous maiden, under the age of 18 years, of *the priceless and crowning jewel of maidenhood*, that he does so at his peril." *Bishop v. Liston*, 199 N.W. 825, 827 (Neb. 1924).

Some subjects call out for euphemisms or circumlocutions. Explicitness or directness would be undesirable to almost everyone here: "Due process concerns were not offended when a prison inmate was subjected to an attempted *digital* rectal search, based upon a reliable informer's tip." (Advocate's description of *U.S. v. Caldwell*, 750 F.2d 341 (5th Cir. 1984).) Still, the final phrase might advantageously be changed, because *tip* verges on losing its metaphorical quality in that particular context. See **digital.**

In a sense, euphemisms are at war against logical accuracy and clarity. Indeed, they reflect basic human impulses that oppose logical accuracy and clarity: "There are . . . unpleasant truths from which we turn away our minds almost as instinctively as we cover our eyes or turn away our heads from too strong a light or from a horrible sight. And when we cannot but admit such truths, we do not like to speak of them except through euphemisms." Morris R. Cohen, *Reason and Law* 14 (1961). Cohen calls this tendency "a fruitful source of legal fictions." *Id.* See FICTIONS.

EUPHONY. See SOUND OF PROSE, THE.

EUPHUISM. See PURPLE PROSE.

euthanasia; mercy killing. These synonyms are widespread, the first perhaps being more connotatively neutral. *Mercy killing* usually applies to people exclusively, while *euthanasia* applies equally to animals.

euthanize; *euthanatize. *Euthanize* (= to subject to euthanasia) is used most commonly in reference to pets. If we must have such a word, the longer version might seem the better candidate because it is properly formed, strictly speaking, and is older, dating in the *OED* from 1873. But in modern legal writing, *euthanize* predominates to such an extent that it has become the universal standard—e.g.:

- "The Circuit Court of Monongalia County . . . reinstated the magistrate's order to *euthanize* appellant's dog." *State v. Molisee*, 378 S.E.2d 100, 100 (W. Va. 1989) (per curiam).
- "Dr. Ennulat told Ms. Lambiotte that the horse needed to be *euthanized*, and Ms. Lambiotte called her director." *State v. Talley*, 429 S.E.2d 604, 606 (N.C. Ct. App. 1993).

See -IZE (A).

evacuee. See -EE (A).

evanescence is sometimes used incorrectly to mean "departure" or "disappearance." E.g.: "Antonio's untimely *evanescence* [read *departure* or *escape*] was tried in juvenile court as a violation of Welfare and Institutions Code section 871." *In re Antonio F.*, 120 Cal. Rptr. 2d 325, 326 (Ct. App. 2002).

Here the adjective *evanescent* is correctly used in the sense "tending to vanish away":

- "The evidence in *Cupp*, to be sure, was 'highly *evanescent*'; but no less so is any evidence [that] an alerted suspect can dispose of if the police should wait to act until they have obtained a warrant." *Commonwealth v. Skea*, 470 N.E.2d 385, 395 (Mass. App. Ct. 1984).
- "Interests of beneficiaries of private express trusts run the gamut from valuable substantialities to *evanescent* hopes." Jesse Dukeminier, *Perpetuities: The Measuring Lives*, 85 Colum. L. Rev. 1648, 1689 (1985) (quoting R. Powell, *The Law of Real Property*).

evangelical; evangelistic. Today the older term *evangelical* (fr. ca. 1531) is so closely tied with fundamentalist, proselytizing Christians that it should not be applied more generally. *Evangelistic* (fr. ca. 1845), though also redolent with Christian associations, may be used more broadly to mean "militantly zealous."

even date for *the same date* originated in commercialese but has infected lawyers' writing as well. The best practice is to name the date a second time or to write *the same date*. E.g.:

- "For the reasons set forth in the Memorandum of *even date* [read *the same date*], the Court hereby denies Defendant's Motion for Partial Summary Judgment." *EEOC v. Worthington, Moore & Jacobs, Inc.*, 582 F.Supp.2d 731, 738 (D. Md. 2008).
- "The petitioner also attached a copy of the unsigned document, along with a signed trust instrument and warranty deed of *even date* [read *the same date*]." *LaCalle v. Barquin*, 987 So.2d 1245, 1246 (Fla. Dist. Ct. App. 2008).

even if. See **if (c).**

event, in the. The AmE phrase is invariably **in the event that* [+ clause]—an equivalent of *if*. BrE generally favors *in the event of* [+ noun phrase] (usually a BURIED VERB)—a locution that appears also in AmE, sometimes without the *of*. Either phrase is inferior to *if*. See **in the event of** & ***in the event that.**

In BrE, *in the event* also means "in (the) result," a usage likely to result in a MISCUE for American readers—e.g.: "Allowing the appeal, the Court of Appeal stated that although the Swiss were sensitive about their banking secrecy laws by court order from other countries, that by itself would not be a ground for interfering with the order. However, *in the event*, although the documents might prove relevant at a later stage of the proceedings, that was an insufficient ground for upholding the judge's order." *Bank of Crete v. Koskotas*, Fin. Times, 31 May 1991, at 8.

The phrase **in the eventuality* is especially pretentious. E.g.: "The statutes provide that, *in that eventuality* [read *in that event*], the named person shall be deemed to have died immediately after the testator."

*eventuality is a needless pomposity for several everyday words, each of which is more specific: *event, possibility, outcome, contingency, consequences,* or *result.* E.g.: "Bobbitt would be amply protected from this *eventuality* [read *event*]." *Hospital Consultants, Inc. v. Potyka*, 531 S.W.2d 657, 665 (Tex. Civ. App.—San Antonio 1975). See **event, in the.**

eventuate is "an elaborate journalistic word that can usually be replaced by a simpler word to advantage." George P. Krapp, *A Comprehensive Guide to Good English* 231 (1927). E.g.:

- "As a general proposition, one who executes a will believes that the testament covers all contingencies that might *eventuate* [read *occur* or *happen*]." *In re Gautier's Will*, 146 N.E.2d 771, 774 (N.Y. 1957). (Note the INELEGANT VARIATION of *will* and *testament.*)
- "It is quite plain that the Fourth Amendment governs 'seizures' of the person [that] do not *eventuate* [read *result*] in a trip to the station house and prosecution for crime." *Terry v. Ohio*, 392 U.S. 1, 16 (1968) (per Warren, C.J.).
- "[Their] final argument is that their Fifth Amendment rights were not adequately protected by the grant of use immunity by the state court, since it would not protect them from use of their compelled testimony in a federal prosecution, should one *eventuate* [read *ensue* or *occur*]." *Port v. Heard*, 764 F.2d 423, 434–35 (5th Cir. 1985).
- "A term may impose a risk on one of the parties which, if it *eventuates* [read *occurs*], will be to make him poorer." James Gordley, *The Moral Foundations of Private Law*, 47 Am. J. Juris. 1, 18 (2002).
- "A violation of a public duty is a harm in itself; it is not merely the imposition of a risk that might *eventuate* [read *result*] in harm." Guyora Binder, *The Culpability of Felony Murder*, 83 Notre Dame L. Rev. 965, 1019 (2008).
- "Chief among these would be objections about the administrative expense and burden, about the number of false claims of innocence that would be filed, about the impact of reinvestigations on victims and on the public perception, and about other purported harms that might *eventuate* [read *occur*]." Bruce A. Green & Ellen Yaroshefsky, *Prosecutorial Discretion and Post-Conviction Evidence of Innocence*, 6 Ohio St. J. Crim. L. 467, 516 (2009).

every. A. *Every-*: Singular or Plural? Today it is standard BrE to write:

- "Almost *everybody* now seems to be a 'victim' of something—of society or *their* own weaknesses." Susan Crosland, *The Aftershock of Anger*, Sunday Times, 22 Oct. 1989, at B2.
- "The compilation of the *OED* made it possible for *everyone* to have before *them* the historical shape and configuration of the language." Robert W. Burchfield, *Unlocking the English Language* 169 (1989).

But most Americans continue to think of this usage as slipshod, *everybody* requiring a singular; after all, they reason, nobody would say *everybody think* instead of *everybody thinks*. An early usage critic remarked insightfully (while disapproving): "The use of this word is made difficult by the lack of a singular pronoun of dual sex. . . . Nevertheless, this is no warrant for the conjunction of *every* and *them*." Richard G. White, *Every-Day English* 420–21 (1884). Many Americans now take the same stand, thereby making a happy solution elusive. See CONCORD (B) & SEXISM (A).

B. *Each and every.* See **each and every.**

C. *Every . . . not.* This construction often results in an error in logic. Literally, *every one is not* means "none is." But rarely is that what the writer means—e.g.: "*Every important case is not reported* [read *Not every important case is reported*], or at all events not reported in those places where we might reasonably expect to find it." Carleton K. Allen, *Law in the Making* 374 (7th ed. 1964). Cf. **all (B).**

everybody. See **every (A)** & CONCORD (B).

everybody else's. See **else's** & POSSESSIVES (G).

every day, adv.; **everyday,** adj. One tries to accomplish something *every day*; but an *everyday* feat would hardly be worth accomplishing. The two are occasionally confused—e.g.: "But what of the phrase 'per stirpes,' symbolic here of the hundreds of Latin and LAW FRENCH words still used *everyday* [read *every day*] by fully modernized American lawyers whose penchant for foreign languages probably extends no further?" Richard Weisberg, *When Lawyers Write* 99 (1987).

every man's house is his castle. See **castle doctrine.**

every . . . not. See **every (C).**

everyone; everybody. See **every (A),** CONCORD (B) & SEXISM (A).

everyone else's. See **else's** & POSSESSIVES (G).

everyone . . . them. See **every (A),** CONCORD & SEXISM (A).

***everyplace** should be avoided as a vulgarism; *everywhere* is the proper word.

everywhere. See ***everyplace.**

evict. Whether to lawyers or nonlawyers, this word generally means "to expel (a person, esp. a tenant) from land or a building, usu. by legal process." But in law it also means "to recover (property or title to property) *from* a person by legal process."

evidence, n. **A. And Its Near-Synonyms: *testimony; deposition; affidavit; declaration.*** These terms all refer to material presented to a competent legal tribunal to prove or disprove a fact. *Evidence* implies both that the tribunal accepts the material as worthy of consideration and that the party offering the material intends to use it as a means of proof. *Testimony* is the evidence offered by witnesses under oath or on affirmation, typically while on the witness stand in open court. *Deposition*, once interchangeable with *testimony*, now refers typically to out-of-court sworn testimony taken down by a court reporter while the witness is questioned orally by counsel—and it is typically called *deposition testimony*. It is possible, too, to have a deposition by written questions, with written answers. An *affidavit*, by contrast, is a sworn statement obtained and submitted by one side of the dispute without cross-examination. In some jurisdictions, such as California, an affidavit is termed a *declaration*.

B. And *proof.* Strictly speaking, the two words are not synonymous. Unlike *evidence*, the word *proof* should be applied "to the *effect* of the evidence, and not to the *medium* by which truth is established." 1 Simon Greenleaf, *A Treatise on the Law of Evidence* 3 (I.F. Redfield ed., 12th ed. 1866). See **proof.**

C. As a Count Noun. *Evidence* is not generally taken to be a count noun; hence the plural form is unusual at best. E.g.: "Yet in spite of all these *evidences* of judicial humility in these areas, it would be an error to assume that the judiciary had lost self-confidence altogether as a result of its chastening experience in the 1930's." Robert G. McCloskey, *The American Supreme Court* 190 (1960).

D. Other Phrases. See **forensic** (last par.), **give evidence** & **put on.**

evidence, vb.; **evince.** These words, which are lawyers' favorites, are often inferior to *show* or *express* or *indicate*. Properly, to *evidence* something is to be the proof, or to serve as evidence, of its existence or happening or truth. Here it is correctly used:

- "In support of his claim that his oral testimony can be used as proof of a signed writing *evidencing* the contract, Roger cites the comment to UPC § 2-514." *Johnson v. Anderson*, 771 N.W.2d 565, 570 (Neb. 2009).
- "Washington has been unable to point to any specific facts *evidencing* a conspiracy involving the subject Defendants." *Washington v. Florida Dep't of Children & Families*, 595 F.Supp.2d 1291, 1295 (M.D. Fla. 2009).
- "Because the property at issue is real property, an acknowledged writing *evidencing* [wife's] intent to transfer her property to the community was required, and no such writing is in evidence." *In re Estate of Borghi*, 219 P.3d 932, 938 (Wash. 2009).

More often than not, however, it is used loosely for *show, demonstrate,* or *express*:

- "The *Bowers* Court *evidenced* [read *showed* or *expressed*] a subtle devotion to numerical strength in determining the content of fundamental rights." Daniel R. Gordon, *Reconsidering Homosexual Rights in Light of the Reemergence of Southern States' Rights*, 10 Seton Hall L. Rev. 111, 124 (1999).
- "We therefore conclude that the plain language of the statute *evidences* [read *shows*] the intent of the General Assembly to make dissemination of each book or picture or other 'matter' depicting sexual conduct of a child under eighteen years of age a separate and independent crime." *Brown v. State*, 912 N.E.2d 881, 894 (Ind. Ct. App. 2009).
- "The dissent believes that this behavior *evidences* [read *demonstrates*] a mental condition that resembles that of the parents in [other cases]." *In re A.R.D.*, 694 S.E.2d 508, 512 (N.C. Ct. App. 2010).

Evince properly means "to show, exhibit, make manifest," but has been objected to as "a bad word and unnecessary . . . a favourite with callow journalists."

Eric Partridge, *Usage and Abusage* 113 (rev. ed. 1973). It is greatly overworked in legal writing, as the cornucopia of specimens evinces—e.g.:

- "*Raz* holds that each legal system will *evince* laws of at least two types, duty-imposing and power-conferring laws, both of which are norms." James E. Penner, *The Idea of Property in Law* 39 (1997).
- "Although the mother admitted to physically abusing her now adult son on at least one occasion . . . , the record *evinces* that the mother is remorseful and has taken responsibility for these actions." *Ciccone v. Ciccone*, 904 N.Y.S.2d 203, 204–05 (App. Div. 2010).
- "While the contents of the 'Difficult Duty' email are not in dispute, what those contents *evince* is the key question." *Kidwell v. Sybaritic, Inc.*, 784 N.W.2d 220, 240 (Minn. 2010).
- "The authors complain that the family *evinces* 'repronormativity,' meaning that the prevailing legal understanding of the family is still linked to having and raising children." Gerard V. Bradley, *The Role of the Family in Criminal Law*, 33 Harv. J.L. & Pub. Pol'y 1151, 1169 (2010) (reviewing *Privilege or Punish: Criminal Justice and the Challenge of Family Ties*).

*****evidenciary** is wrong for *evidentiary*. See **evidentiary.**

evident; apparent; manifest; patent; distinct; obvious; palpable; plain; clear. These adjectives, all describing what is easily noticed or readily comprehended, overlap to a great degree but are to some extent distinguishable. Although *evident* suggests the presence of visible indications all leading to one conclusion, it can apply to something beyond sensory perception yet elementarily inferable <the defendants' evident relief upon the verdict of acquittal> <an evident breakdown in settlement negotiations>. *Apparent*, a close synonym, is slightly different from *evident* in suggesting not just visible indications but also reasoning, especially through deduction or induction <with experience, it became apparent that contributory negligence was a fundamentally flawed doctrine>. (See **apparent.**) *Manifest* likewise implies outward signs but typically suggests something so openly displayed that its apprehension requires no inference <good conduct is simply good judgment made manifest>. (See **manifest,** adj.) *Patent* (in this sense pronounced /**payt**-ənt/) applies to things that are somewhat more subtle but are, on reflection, undoubtedly existent or true <the patent merits of John Roberts's elevation from a justiceship nomination to that of Chief Justice>. (See **patent,** adj.) *Distinct* suggests a clear delineation that requires no special mental or physical effort to make out, whether by sight <distinct markings>, by hearing <distinct enunciation>, or by intellect <a distinct account in the statement of facts>. (See **distinct.**) *Obvious* implies conspicuousness and therefore ease of discovery <adverse possession must be open and obvious>. *Palpable* suggests what is perceptible through any of the five senses except sight. It especially applies to the sense of touch and, by metaphorical extension, to the intellect as a kind of sixth sense <a palpable sense of doom>. There is nothing wrong with using this word in figurative senses <palpable weaknesses in the argument>, as has been done since at least the 15th century.

Plain and *clear* both apply to something that is instantly understandable and even unmistakable. *Plain* suggests what is common and familiar, as opposed to convoluted and intricate <plain speaking>. *Clear* suggests an absence of anything that muddies or obfuscates <a clear yes–no question>.

evidential. See **evidentiary.**

evidentiarily is the adverb corresponding to *evidentiary,* adj. It is often used—somewhat clumsily—as a SENTENCE ADVERB in the sense "in terms of evidence." E.g.: "It turns out, however, that *evidentiarily* we do not now have such a case before us." *McLaurin v. Columbia Mun. Separate Sch. Dist.,* 486 F.2d 1049, 1050 (5th Cir. 1973) (Coleman, J., concurring). See ADVERBS (B).

evidentiary; evidential. It would be convenient to pronounce *evidential* a NEEDLESS VARIANT and be done with it, but that (older) form seems to predominate in BrE (see *OED* & *COD*). Even so, the *-ary* form—a NEOLOGISM innovated by Jeremy Bentham—also appears in BrE. We might, however, brand *evidential* a NEEDLESS VARIANT in AmE, in which *evidentiary* far outstrips *evidential* in frequency of use. E.g.:

- "If, therefore, the unaltered document is produced for inspection, the facts thus ascertained must, as regards the alleged contractual agreement, be purely *evidential* [read *evidentiary*] in character." Wesley Newcomb Hohfeld, *Some Fundamental Legal Conceptions as Applied in Judicial Reasoning,* 23 Yale L.J. 16, 28 (1913).
- "There is a kind of *evidential* [read *evidentiary*] estoppel." *Holly Hill Citrus Growers' Ass'n v. Holly Hill Fruit Prods., Inc.,* 75 F.2d 13, 17 (5th Cir. 1935).

Still, *evidential* has been useful to some legal theorists, like Hohfeld, in meaning "furnishing evidence" as opposed to "of or relating to evidence" (the sense in which *evidentiary* predominates). If we could enhance this latent DIFFERENTIATION, the language of the law of evidence would be richer for it. Following are two examples from Wesley N. Hohfeld, *Fundamental Legal Conceptions* (1919):

- "An *evidential* fact is one which, on being ascertained, affords some logical basis—not conclusive—for inferring some other fact." Wesley Newcomb Hohfeld, *Some Fundamental Legal Conceptions as Applied in Judicial Reasoning,* 23 Yale L.J. 16, 27 (1913).
- "The facts important in relation to a given jural transaction may be either operative facts or *evidential* facts." *Id.* at 25.

evince. See **evidence,** vb.

eviscerate (= to disembowel) has become a VOGUE WORD among legal writers in its metaphorical applications. Because of its strong meaning, it is not to be used lightly. "To prevent the plain view doctrine from *eviscerating* Fourth Amendment protections, we have imposed a three-prong test that the government must satisfy to justify its application." *Harman v. Pollock,* 586 F.3d 1254, 1264 (10th Cir. 2009).

Here *eviscerate* approaches meaninglessness: "To permit any complainant to restart the limitations period by petitioning for review of a rule . . . would *eviscerate* the congressional concern for finality embodied in time limitations on review." *Montana v. Clark,* 749 F.2d 740, 744 (D.C. Cir. 1984). The META-PHOR of *eviscerating* does not work with a gossamer object like *concern,* even if it is said to be "embodied." Cf. **emasculate.**

evoke (= [1] to call forth; or [2] to bring to mind) is a near-MALAPROPISM when misused for *invoke* (= [1] to call upon; or [2] to cause). E.g.: "[If] Rumbaugh is incompetent to waive his right to federal habeas review, his parents have standing to *evoke* [read *invoke*] a next-friend proceeding." *Rumbaugh v. McKaskle,* 730 F.2d 291, 293 (5th Cir. 1984).

ex-, when meaning "former," should be hyphenated: "A bitter *exemployee* [read *ex-employee*] can do great harm. . . . [W]hen people feel they have been fired 'fairly' . . . they will be reluctant to bad-mouth their *excompany* [read *ex-company*]." Mark H. McCormack, *What They Don't Teach You at Harvard Business School* 199 (1984).

exact from sometimes signals a wordy construction—e.g.: "In the present case, however, *the compelled production of the journal was exacted from defendant's attorneys* [read *the defendant's attorneys were compelled to produce the journal*]." *State v. Barrett,* 401 N.W.2d 184, 191 (Iowa 1987). For the reasons why *production* should be made into the present infinitive of the verb *produce,* see BURIED VERBS.

exalt; exult. To *exalt* is to raise in rank, place in a high position, or extol. To *exult* is to rejoice exceedingly.

Exalt is rather frequently misspelled **exhalt* or **exhault*—e.g.:

- "The serjeant might perform military duties rather less *exhalted* [read *exalted*] than those of a knight." Alan Harding, *A Social History of English Law* 32 (1966).
- "It would be *exhalting* [read *exalting*] form over substance to require the Committee . . . to amend its complaint." *Committee on Professional Ethics & Conduct v. Munger,* 375 N.W.2d 248, 251 (Iowa 1985).

For a similar misspelling, see **exorbitant.**

examination-in-chief. See **direct examination.**

example; exemplar; exemplum; exemplification. *Example* is the general term. *Exemplar* = an ideal or typical example. E.g.:

- "A testator of sound mind may . . . prefer a prodigal son or even an unrepentant sinner to a son who has been an *exemplar* [i.e., an *ideal example*] and pattern of virtue." *In re Liberman,* 18 N.E.2d 658, 660 (N.Y. 1939).
- "The Court of Appeals found critical significance in the fact that the grand jury had summoned approximately

20 witnesses to furnish voice *exemplars* [i.e., typical specimens]." *U.S. v. Dionisio*, 410 U.S. 1, 12 (1973) (per Stewart, J.).

- "The Court's dictum cited the Convention Act as an *exemplar* [i.e., an *ideal example*] of Congress's ability to accord 'domestic effect' to the judgments of similar international tribunals." *Safety Nat'l Cas. Corp. v. Certain Underwriters at Lloyd's, London*, 587 F.3d 714, 736 (5th Cir. 2009).

Exemplum, except in specialized literary senses, is a NEEDLESS VARIANT of *example*. *Exemplification* = (1) (in law) an attested copy of a document <an exemplification is a copy of a record set out either under the Great Seal or under the Seal of the Court>; (2) the act or process of serving as an example <by way of exemplification>; or (3) a case in point.

example in which. See **example where.**

example where is always inferior to *example in which*. See **where (B).** Cf. **case where.**

ex ante; ex post. These LATINISMS, which may act either as adverbs or as adjectives, are likely to confuse most readers. *Ex ante* = based on assumption and prediction; subjective; prospective. *Ex post* = based on knowledge and facts; objective; retrospective. In the following sentences, *prospectively* and *retrospectively* would lead to greater comprehensibility with no loss in the sense:

- "Judges should be aware that their decisions create incentives influencing conduct *ex ante* [read *prospectively*], and that attempts to divide the stakes fairly *ex post* [read *retrospectively*] will alter or reverse the signals that are desirable from *an ex ante* [read *a prospective*] [point of view]." Frank H. Easterbrook, *Method, Result, and Authority: A Reply*, 98 Harv. L. Rev. 622, 622 (1985).
- "Moving from reviewing *ex post* [read *retrospectively*] the conduct's effects and offender's status to determining *ex ante* [read *prospectively*] specific anticompetitive practices that are presumptively illegal is a desirable step." Maurice E. Stucke, *Should the Government Prosecute Monopolies?*, 2009 U. Ill. L. Rev. 497, 542 (2009).

See **ex post facto.**

ex cathedra; ex officio. *Ex cathedra* = (1) (adv.) from the chair or throne; with authority; (2) (adj.) authoritative. Following is a literal adverbial use: "It would, in my judgment, be quite contrary to the concept of a fair trial were this court to have pronounced on them, effectively *ex cathedra* and without reference to the factual context in which they arose." *Coles v. Barracks*, [2007] 1 C.R. 60, 77. Increasingly today, *ex cathedra* has connotations of a peremptory attitude—e.g.: "The Attorney General's letter asserts *ex cathedra* and without citation of a single authority that . . . ." Peter Shane & Harold Bruff, *The Law of Presidential Power* 205 (1988).

Ex officio (= by virtue of one's office) may likewise function either as an adjective <the chair is an ex officio member of all standing committees> or as an adverb <the chair became a member ex officio>. *Ex officiis is a NEEDLESS VARIANT. *Ex officio* should be neither hyphenated nor spelled as one word.

exceed. See **accede.**

except. A. As Verb. *Except* = (1) to exclude, omit <present company excepted>; (2) to object, take exception <I except to that statement>. The latter is the more frequent legal meaning: "After the trial court explained how the State could question Ellis about the other bad acts, trial counsel *excepted* to the ruling, and the trial court granted a continuing objection." *Ellis v. State*, 695 S.E.2d 35, 37 (Ga. 2010).

Sense 2 has given rise to the special legal sense of the word, "to appeal." E.g.: "Defendant timely objected to the testimony, the trial court ruled on the defendant's objection, and defendant *excepted* from the trial court's ruling." *State v. Bass*, 660 S.E.2d 123, 128 (N.C. Ct. App. 2008).

B. As Preposition and Conjunction. When *except* begins a noun phrase rather than a clause (i.e., a phrase with a verb), it is a simple preposition not followed by the relative pronoun *that* <all persons except farmers owning fewer than 500 acres>. But when, as a conjunction, *except* introduces a clause, it should be followed by *that*, which is here incorrectly omitted: "The Court applies joint and several liability for all forfeitable amounts, *except* [read *except that*] Robert McKay shall not be held vicariously liable for the forfeiture of Michael McKay's salary in the amount of $1,492,531." *U.S. v. McKay*, 506 F.Supp.2d 1206, 1215 (S.D. Fla. 2007).

C. As Conjunction. *Except* for *unless* is an ARCHAISM that persists only as a vulgarism. Here is the archaic use: "I devise this land to A and her heirs forever, *except* she should die without heir born of her own body." Will quoted in *Roach v. Martin's Lessee*, 1 Har. 548, 28 Am. Dec. 746 (1835). And here is the modern vulgarism: "Wheat produced on excess acreage may neither be disposed of nor used except upon payment of the penalty, or *except* [read *unless*] it is stored as required by the Act or delivered to the Secretary of Agriculture." *Wickard v. Filburn*, 317 U.S. 111, 119 (1942) (per Jackson, J.). See (E), (G), (H).

D. *Excepting*. This word should not be used as a substitute for *except*, except in the phrase *not excepting*. E.g.:

- "He further provided that the property [should] 'under no circumstances . . . be sold or alienated or . . . at any time . . . devoted to any other purpose or use *excepting so far as herein specifically authorized* [read other purpose or use *than is herein authorized*].'" *Evans v. Abney*, 396 U.S. 435, 448 (1970) (Douglas, J., dissenting).
- "The majority of cases dealing with the problem, *excepting* [read *except*] two, have applied the ruling to the case [that] resulted in the abolishment of the doctrine of sovereign immunity." *Hicks v. State*, 544 P.2d 1153, 1161 (N.M. 1976) (Montoya, J., dissenting).

E. Except as. In drafting, *unless* is preferable to *except as* when referring to a future action—e.g.: "*Except as* [read *Unless*] otherwise stipulated or directed by the court . . . ." Fed. R. Civ. P. 26(a)(2)(B).

Except as may be appropriate when referring to something that an existing rule or statute does—e.g.: "*Except as* otherwise provided in this section . . . ." 11 U.S.C. § 550(a).

F. Except that. This phrase is generally inferior to *but* or some other, more pointed term—e.g.: "The allotments shall be provided in accordance with . . . section 2020(e) of this title (*except that* [read *but*] no household shall begin to receive combined allotments under this section until it has complied with all applicable verification requirements)." 7 U.S.C. § 2026(a)(2).

G. Except when. The word *unless* is usually much preferable—e.g.: "As in the fire cases, strict liability applies *except when* [read *unless*] the destruction of the goods is attributable to acts of God—huge storms and the like—or to violent actions by third persons, to which Holt alluded." Richard A. Epstein, *The Many Faces of Fault in Contract Law: Or How to Do Economics Right, Without Really Trying*, 107 Mich. L. Rev. 1461, 1469 (2009). (Cf. **except as.**) Even with the slightly improved wording, however, this type of wide-open exception makes drafting less easily comprehensible: the reader must research all of federal law to find out whether the exception applies. Such a provision is therefore antithetical to principles of PLAIN LANGUAGE.

H. Except with. This phrase, usually followed by a noun phrase, is ordinarily inferior to *unless* (usually followed by a subject and verb)—e.g.: "*Except with the written consent of the defendant,* [read *Unless the defendant consents in writing,*] the report [must] not be submitted to the court." Fed. R. Crim. App. 32(b)(1).

except as. See **except (E).**

except as otherwise provided. See **notwithstanding anything to the contrary contained herein.**

exceptionable; exceptional. The first is sometimes misused for the second. *Exceptionable* = open to exception; objectionable <she was admonished for her exceptionable behavior>. *Exceptional* = out of the ordinary; uncommon; rare; superior <an exceptional achievement>.

exception proves the rule, the. This phrase is the popular rendering of what was originally a legal maxim, "The exception proves (or confirms) the rule in the cases not excepted" (*exceptio probat regulam in casibus non exceptis*). Originally *exception* in this maxim meant "the action of excepting"—not, as is commonly supposed, "that which is excepted"—so that the true sense of the maxim was that by specifying the cases excepted, one strengthens the hold of the rule over all cases not excepted.

At least two spurious explanations of *the exception proves the rule* exist. One is that because a rule

does not hold in all instances (i.e., has exceptions), the rule must be valid. This misunderstanding of the phrase commonly manifests itself in the discourse of those who wish to argue that every rule must have exceptions. A more sophisticated, but equally false, explanation of the phrase is that *prove* here retains its Elizabethan sense (derived from the Latin) "to test," so that the sense of the phrase is that an exception to a rule "tests" the validity of the rule. This erroneous explanation appears, of all places, in Tom Burnam, *A Dictionary of Misinformation* 79 (1975).

exceptor (= one who excepts or objects) was formerly used in some jurisdictions as an equivalent of *appellant.* E.g.: "*Exceptors* place considerable stress on the case of *Marshall v. Frazier.*" *In re Ree's Estate*, 87 N.E.2d 397, 409 (Ohio Prob. 1947). See **plaintiff** & **except (A).**

except that. See **except (F).**

except when. See **except (G).**

except with. See **except (H).**

excess of, in (= beyond the confines of) is a LEGALISM used in the context of actions ultra vires. The phrase is unobjectionable per se. E.g.:

- "The district court ruled that the regulations had been promulgated *in excess of* the EPA's authority under the Clean Air Act." *U.S. v. Ethyl Corp.*, 761 F.2d 1153, 1154 (5th Cir. 1985).
- "It simply acted *in excess of* the jurisdiction it did have, and we thus conclude that its actions were privileged and that claimants are unable to establish a claim for unlawful imprisonment." *Collins v. State*, 887 N.Y.S.2d 400, 405 (App. Div. 2009).
- "By imposing the remaining challenged fees, the sheriff acted *in excess of* his authority and contrary to the intent of the Legislature." *Souza v. Sheriff of Bristol County*, 918 N.E.2d 823, 832 (Mass. 2010).

See **ultra vires.**

Exchequer is so spelled. Some writers have tried to make it **Exchequor*—e.g.: "This work required a law court in the modern sense made up of a small number of judges of education and ability skilled in the law which sat regularly term after term, generally at Westminster, often at the *Exchequor* [read *Exchequer*]." William F. Walsh, *A Treatise on Equity* 3 (1930).

excise. There are two unrelated verbs *excise*: (1) "to remove"; and (2) "to impose an excise tax on." (See **tax** & **excise tax.**) Here sense 1 applies: "The jury had been selected at the time the sealing order was entered; therefore, *excising* the documents and releasing them to the public, coupled with an admonition to the jury not to listen to news media or discuss the case with others, was an alternative to sealing that should have been considered." *In re Knight Pub. Co.*, 743 F.2d 231, 235 (4th Cir. 1984). To illustrate sense 2, the *OED* quotes Blackstone as follows: "Brandies and other spirits are now *excised* at the distillery." 1 *Commentaries on the Laws of England* 320 (1765). The *OED* labels this sense obsolete, but *W3* and *W11* suggest that it lives on.

***exciseman; excisor.** In view of the modern trend of avoiding needless SEXISM in language, *excisor* is to be preferred.

excise tax has two quite distinct meanings: (1) "a tax imposed on specific commodities that are produced, sold, or transported within a country—for example, liquor and tobacco"; or (2) "a tax imposed on a license to pursue a specified trade or occupation."

excludable; *excludible; *exclusible. The preferred form is *excludable*.

exclusion. See **removal.**

exclusionary = tending to exclude, or characterized by exclusion <exclusionary rule>. This word, recorded first (fr. 1817) in the works of Jeremy Bentham (1748–1832), began as a peculiarly legal word and has remained so.

exclusionary rule. See **no-recourse rule.**

exclusion proceedings. See **removal proceedings.**

exclusive means "with no exceptions" and should be used carefully. An ill-advised use appears in 28 U.S.C. § 1346: "The district courts . . . shall have *exclusive* jurisdiction of civil actions on claims against the United States." This is not so, since circuit courts and the Supreme Court may also properly have jurisdiction on appeal. What was meant is "exclusive *original* jurisdiction." See OVERSTATEMENT.

exclusive federal jurisdiction. See **preemption, federal.**

***ex contractu; ex delicto.** The phrases *in contract* and *in tort* are much preferable to these LATINISMS. E.g.:

- "This court has never held that the bondholder is relieved from proceeding to force the assessing and collecting by reason of any failure or even refusal to assess, reassess, or collect, or that he could have an ordinary action which would lie against a city, either *ex contractu or ex delicto* [read *in contract or in tort*], with the single exception of a suit to recover an assessment against its own property." *Severns Paving Co. v. Oklahoma City*, 13 P.2d 94, 96 (Okla. 1932).
- "[Appellee] maintains that . . . it is entitled to attorney fees and costs incurred in the successful defense against appellant's *ex delicto claim* [read *tort claim*]." *Sullen v. Missouri Pac. R.R.*, 750 F.2d 428, 430 (5th Cir. 1985).
- "On appeal, McGaha contended that the trial court erred in failing 'to discern the distinction between an action *ex contractu* [read *in contract*] and one *ex delicto* [read *in tort*].'" *Cincinnati Ins. Cos. v. Barber Insulation, Inc.*, 946 So.2d 441, 448 (Ala. 2006).
- "The classic distinction between damages *ex contractu* [read *in contract*] and damages *ex delicto* [read *in tort*] is that the former flow from the breach of a special

obligation contractually assumed by the obligor, whereas the latter flow from the violation of a general duty owed to all persons." *Thomas v. State Employees Group Benefits Program*, 934 So.2d 753, 757 (La. Ct. App. 2006).

- "Some breaches of a fiduciary are classified as *ex delicto* [read *tortious*], while others are *ex contractu* [read *contractual*]." *Omega Ctr. for Pain Mgmt., LLC v. Omega Inst.*, 975 So.2d 48, 51 (La. Ct. App. 2007).

See ***delictu.**

ex-convict; *ex-felon. The first is someone who has been released from prison. The second could apply only to one who has been pardoned or cleared—otherwise one remains a felon for life.

exculpate; exonerate; acquit; absolve; vindicate. These verbs share the sense "to free from a charge or blame, esp. as a result of an authoritative finding." To *exculpate* is simply to clear from all blame—traditionally in a matter of no great seriousness, but today increasingly in matters of serious gravity <DNA evidence ultimately exculpated him and saved him from the death sentence>. To *exonerate*, literally speaking, is to free from an onus; the word can be used in civil contexts not involving allegations of wrongdoing <the release exonerated all liens>, but more often today it implies such a thorough contradiction of guilt that all imputations of blame are wiped away <he was exonerated when three witnesses corroborated his alibi>. (See **exonerate.**) To *acquit* is to have a definite finding of "not guilty" by a jury. Suspicion of blameworthiness may indeed linger in a moral sense, but no longer in a legal sense <the jury acquitted the defendant as a result of the bollixed prosecution>. (On the use of this word in a civil context, see **acquit (A).**) To *absolve* suggests a discharge from all obligations and penalties—often in the form of a formal release or an explicit judicial finding. (See **absolve** & **release.**) To *vindicate* is to clear (either a person or the person's actions) from all censure <the defendant's investment strategies were vindicated in the end>. *Vindicate* is alone among these synonyms in possibly referring not just to people but to things as well. For an additional sense of *vindicate*, see **vindicate.**

exculpatee (= one who has been exculpated) is an AmE NEOLOGISM—e.g.: "An exculpatory clause covers the risk of harm sustained by the exculpator that might be caused by the *exculpatee*." *Weaver v. American Oil Co.*, 261 N.E.2d 99, 102 (Ind. Ct. App. 1970). Though rarely heard, the word should—if it must be pronounced at all—be pronounced /ek-skəl-pə-**tee**/. See -EE.

exculpatory; *exculpative. The second is a NEEDLESS VARIANT.

excusal; *excusation. In reference to prospective jurors, the correct phraseology is, e.g., *excusal for* *cause from the venire panel.* **Excusation* is an obsolete word meaning "the action of offering an excuse" (*OED*).

excuse, n.; **justification.** In many areas of the law, these terms are used interchangeably. But they have undergone DIFFERENTIATION in criminal law.

An *excuse* is a defense that arises because the defendant is not blameworthy for having acted in a way that would otherwise be criminal. Traditionally, the following defenses were excuses: duress, entrapment, infancy, insanity, and involuntary intoxication. For another defense, see **alibi (A).**

A *justification*, by contrast, is a defense that arises when the defendant has acted in a way that the criminal law does not seek to prevent. Traditionally, the following defenses were justifications: the defendant's choice of a lesser harm or evil, consent, defense of others, defense of property, self-defense, the use of force to make an arrest, and the use of force by public authority.

excuse, vb. See **condone.**

*ex delictu is a mistaken form of *ex delicto* caused by confusion with the ending of *ex contractu*—e.g.: "An examination of her pleadings only reinforces the *ex delictu* [read *ex delicto*] nature of Ms. Williams' claim." *Page v. U.S. Indus., Inc.,* 556 F.2d 346, 352 (5th Cir. 1977). The reason for the difference is that *delictum* is a second-declension Latin noun whose ablative singular is *delicto,* not *delictu,* whereas *contractus* is a fourth-declension noun whose ablative singular is *contractu.* See **ex contractu.**

execute. A. Senses. *Execute* (= to sign and deliver; to make valid by observing certain required formalities) is lawyers' JARGON used in reference to completing legal documents <she executed her will>. In this sense the word means "to go through the formalities necessary to the validity of (a legal act)—hence, to complete and give validity to (the instrument by which such an act is effected) by performing what the law requires to be done" (adapted fr. *OED*). But the word *sign* is often preferable, especially in communicating with nonlawyers.

Execute also has four more senses in civil-law contexts: (1) "to carry into effect ministerially (a law, a judicial sentence, etc.)"; (2) "to perform or carry out the provisions of a will" (i.e., what the executor does—this use of the term is now somewhat rare—see (C)); (3) "to perform acts of (justice, e.g.) or give effect to a court's judgment"; or (4) "to levy execution (on property of a judgment debtor)" <when the judgment became final, the prevailing plaintiff's attorney had the marshal execute on defendant's nonexempt property>. Sense 4 appears to be peculiar to AmE, and is given in none of the standard unabridged dictionaries. But it falls logically under the second broad sense listed in the *OED*: "to do execution upon." In criminal law, *execute* is "to put to death, esp. by legal sentence." For more on *execute* and related words, see **kill (A).**

B. For *issue.* Though legal instruments and the like are *executed,* writs, warrants, and the like are said to *issue from* (or *be issued by*) courts or other official bodies—e.g.:

- "The bureau [the Federal Bureau of Investigation] said search warrants were *executed* [read *issued*] Thursday on five locations in the Washington area and suburban Atlanta to look for evidence of a wide-ranging criminal conspiracy." Steve McGonigle, *U.S. Treasurer's Home Searched in FBI Influence-Peddling Probe,* Dallas Morning News, 31 Oct. 1992, at 1A.
- "The court *executed* [read *issued*] a Writ of Habeas Corpus Ad Testificandum and had Herrera transported . . . to the Metropolitan Correctional Center in Manhattan for the trial of his action on November 3." *Herrera v. Scully,* 815 F.Supp. 713, 717 (S.D.N.Y. 1993).

See **issue (C).**

C. Used in Reference to Wills. Although the testator *executes* (i.e., performs an action necessary to validate) a will by signing it, the (aptly named) executor is also said to *execute* it when carrying out the will's provisions. This latter use occurs infrequently—e.g.: "Name an executor who is both able and willing to do the job. *Executing* a will can be time-consuming and labor-intensive." G.W. Weinstein, *Planning Your Estate,* Investment Vision, July/Aug. 1990, at 50.

executed contract. See **executory contract.**

*executer. See **executor.**

execution-proof, adj. See **judgment-proof,** adj.

executive agreement. See **treaty.**

executor; *executer. The *-er* spelling is obsolete. An *executor* is (1) "one who does or performs some act"; (2) "one who, appointed in a testator's will, administers the estate"; or (3) in American patent practice, "one who represents a legally incapacitated inventor." In senses 2 and 3, the accent falls (familiarly) on the second syllable /ig-**zek**-yə-tər/; in sense 1, the accent is on the first syllable /**ek**-sə-kyoot-ər/. See **administrator** & **trustee.**

executory; executorial. *Executory* = taking full effect at a future time <an executory judgment> <executory contract>. *Executorial* = of or pertaining to an executor.

executory contract; executed contract. An *executory contract* is one that remains wholly unperformed or for which there remains something still to be done on both sides. An *executed contract* is one that has been entirely performed on one side.

executory limitation. See **special limitation.**

executory sale. See **contract for sale.**

executrix; executress. *Executrix* (pl. *-trices*) is the usual feminine form of *executor,* which may itself serve as a neuter form covering both sexes. Though legal writers have traditionally distinguished between the sexes by suffix, *executor* is now the preferable term for men and women alike. See SEXISM (C).

exegesis; epexegesis; eisegesis. Knowledge of these terms is useful to anyone having to interpret writings. *Exegesis* = explanation or exposition (as of a word or sentence). E.g.: "In interpretation of federal statutes and Congressional intent . . . semantic *exegesis* is not conclusive." *International Union v. Marshall*, 584 F.2d 390, 397 (D.C. Cir. 1978). *Epexegesis* = the addition of a word or words to convey more clearly the meaning implied, or the specific sense intended, in a preceding word or sentence (*OED*). *Eisegesis* = the interpretation of a word or passage by reading into it one's own ideas (*OED*).

exemplar. See **example.**

exemplaries (= exemplary damages) is an attributive noun in AmE—a common part of trial lawyers' JARGON. Cf. **punitives** & **punies.** See **punitive damages.**

exemplary has two almost contradictory connotations: *exemplary damages* make an example out of a wrongdoer, whereas *exemplary behavior* is model behavior. *Exemplary* is sometimes misunderstood as meaning "severe" in phrases such as *exemplary punishment.*

exemplary damages. See **punitive damages.**

exemplification; exemplum. See **example.**

exempli gratia. See **e.g.**

exempt appears commonly in the U.S. as an ellipsis for *tax-exempt.* Usually this usage occurs in contexts in which the reader has already learned that the subject at hand is tax exemptions, and not other types of exemptions. Following is a typical specimen: "An *exempt* organization has the privilege of preferred second- or third-class mailing rates." Craig Weinlein, *Federal Taxation of Not-for-Profit Arts Organizations,* 12 J. Arts Mgmt. & Law 33, 33–34 (Summer 1982).

exemption. See **immunity (A).**

exequatur [fr. L. *exsequor* "let him perform"] = (1) originally, a temporal sovereign's *act* in authorizing a bishop to perform—under authority of the Pope—the clerical and administrative duties of a diocese; later, a sovereign's *right* either to so empower a bishop or to permit the publication of a papal bull; (2) in international law, a receiving state's authorization by which the head of a consular post is admitted to the exercise of his or her functions; or (3) in international law, the executive judgment or order by which a foreign judgment or an arbitral award is made locally enforceable. *See* John P. Grant & J. Craig Barker, *Parry & Grant Encyclopedic Dictionary of International Law* 204 (3d ed. 2009).

exercise for *existence* is a puzzling error. E.g.: "A 'presumption of undue influence' arises from proof of the *exercise* [read *existence*?] of a confidential relation between the testator and such a beneficiary, 'coupled with activity on the part of the latter in the preparation of the will.'" *In re Arnold's Estate*, 107 P.2d 25, 29 (Cal. 1940). (A *confidential relation* is not *exercised.*)

exertive; exertional. *Exertive* = tending to exert or rouse to action (*OED*) <resolve is an exertive emotion>. *Exertional*, though recorded in none of the Oxford or Merriam-Webster dictionaries, has appeared (usually in the negative form) in American law cases in the field of social-security disabilities. *Exertional* = of or pertaining to physical effort. E.g.:

- "He is unable to return to his past relevant work and suffers from a *non-exertional* impairment." *Warmoth v. Bowen*, 798 F.2d 1109, 1110 (7th Cir. 1986).
- "Whenever a *nonexertional* impairment is presented, the Secretary must introduce a vocational expert to testify that jobs in the workplace exist for a person with that particular disability." *Bapp v. Bowen*, 802 F.2d 601, 604 (2d Cir. 1986).

ex facie (= in view of what is apparent, lit., "from the face") is not justified as a legal LATINISM, inasmuch as so many ordinary English words, such as *evidently, apparently,* and *on its face,* suffice in its stead. "*Ex facie* [read *Patently*] those transfers would be the same in form and in effect precisely as the instrument of transfer now before us." *Ridge Nominees, Ltd. v. Inland Revenue Comm'rs,* [1962] Ch. 376, 377–78 (C.A.). Here the phrase is wrongly made adjectival: "The Companies Act, 1948 . . . brought into being that which was *ex facie* [read *evident*] in all its essential characteristics." *Ridge Nominees, Ltd. v. Inland Revenue Comm'rs,* [1962] Ch. 376, 377–78 (C.A.). See **face, on its.**

***ex-felon.** See **ex-convict.**

*ex gratia; *a gratia.* Ex gratia* means "as a favor, not by legal necessity" <*ex gratia* payment>. E.g.: "This punishment is not directly or mainly beneficial to the person injured, though a scheme whereby the State pays compensation *ex gratia* to victims of violence was started in 1964." William Geldart, *Introduction to English Law* 146 (D.C.M. Yardley ed., 9th ed. 1984). **A gratia* is a NEEDLESS VARIANT.

***exhault; *exhalt.** Both are misspellings of *exalt.* See **exalt.**

exhibit. See **appendix.**

***exhorbitant** is a misspelling of *exorbitant.* See **exorbitant.**

ex hypothesi is a needless LATINISM meaning *hypothetically* or *hypothetical.* E.g.: "How can there be a price for what is, *ex hypothesi* [read *hypothetically*], a gratuitous transaction?" P.S. Atiyah, *An Introduction to the Law of Contract* 121 (3d ed. 1981).

exigency; *exigence. The form in *-cy* is standard; the other is a NEEDLESS VARIANT.

exigent; *exigeant. *Exigeant* is a NEEDLESS VARIANT of the standard form, *exigent* (= requiring immediate action).

existing. Legal drafters should use this ambiguous word cautiously. It may mean "existing at the time of the writing" or "existing at some time after the writing," if not specifically put within a time frame.

exit has been an acceptable verb since the early 17th century. Those who object to it on grounds that one does not "entrance" a building have a misplaced prejudice.

exlex; ex lege. Good legal writers have little or no use for these terms. Still, it is well to know their meanings: *exlex* is an adjective meaning "outside the law, without legal authority" <an *exlex* government>, whereas *ex lege* is an adverb meaning "by virtue of law; as a matter of law" <property forfeited *ex lege*>.

ex maleficio = (adv.) by malfeasance; (adj.) tortious. There is no reason why this phrase should not be anglicized. E.g.:

- "[A] fraudulent breach of duty by the [ship's] master, in respect to his owners; or, in other words, a breach of duty in respect to his owners, with a criminal intent, or *ex maleficio* [read *by malfeasance*], is barratry." *Earle v. Rowcroft*, [1806] 8 E. 126, 138 (per Lord Ellenborough).
- "The third-party claim . . . result[ed] from *ex maleficio* [read *false*] deeds fraudulently inducing appellant to issue its bond." *U.S. Fidelity & Guaranty Co. v. Perkins*, 388 F.2d 771, 773 (10th Cir. 1968).
- "A trust imposed *ex-maleficio* [read *because of malfeasance*] . . . springs into existence from the very act of wrongdoing and is applied constructively as a remedy for wrongdoing to prevent unjust enrichment." *Freeman v. Frick*, 207 B.R. 731, 735 (Bankr. N.D. Fla. 1997).

See *de son tort.*

ex necessitate (= of necessity) is a Latinistic pollutant. E.g.:

- "The rule is that executory limitations are void unless they take effect *ex necessitate* [read *of necessity*] and in all possible contingencies within the period of a life or lives in being at the death of the testator and twenty-one years afterwards." *Hall v. Hall*, 123 Mass. 120, 124 (1877).
- "The appeal, however, that we declare the existence of inherent powers *ex necessitate* [read *necessary*] to meet an emergency asks us to do what many think would be wise, although it is something the forefathers omitted." *Youngstown Sheet & Tube Co. v. Sawyer*, 343 U.S. 579, 649–50 (1952) (Jackson, J., concurring).
- "We regard that, however, as nothing more than *an ex necessitate* [read *a necessary*] limitation upon the effect prong in the particular context of annexation to avoid the invalidation of all annexations of areas with a lower proportion of minority voters than the annexing unit." *Reno v. Bossier Parish Sch. Bd.*, 528 U.S. 320, 330–31 (2000) (per Scalia, J.).

See LATINISMS.

ex officio. See **ex cathedra**.

exonerate, in the sense "to free from responsibility," should be used only in reference to people. E.g.: "Contracts to *exonerate* the plaintiff from the payment of debts or demands assumed by the defendant are enforced for a like reason expressed in a different form." William F. Walsh, *A Treatise on Equity* 317 (1930).

Hence the following use, which refers to a rocket booster as opposed to a person, is erroneous: "Held, affirmed for DuPont since there was no evidence that the booster [a component in an explosive device] was responsible for the explosion, and the evidence offered by plaintiff tended to *exonerate* [read *rule out*] the booster." For more, see **exculpate**.

In its sense "to free from encumbrances," of course, *exonerate* is used in reference to burdened property. E.g.:

- "Given the trend in other states to limit the common-law doctrine by requiring specific language indicating an intent to *exonerate* devised property, it would be inappropriate to interpret general language such as 'just debts' as evincing an intent to *exonerate* property passing outside probate." *In re Estate of Vincent*, 98 S.W.3d 146, 149 (Tenn. 2003).
- "In Tennessee, like other jurisdictions, personal property in the form of the residuary estate may be used to *exonerate* devised property passing by will." Thomas E. Clary III, Comment, *Property*—In re Estate of Vincent: *The Tennessee Supreme Court Declines to Extend the Common Law Doctrine of Exoneration to Survivorship Property*, 34 U. Mem. L. Rev. 695, 702 (2004).

Whereas *acquit* takes *of*, *exonerate* takes the preposition *from*: "This . . . required a determination as to whether the wife's legacy . . . was in fact a specific legacy chargeable with the payment of estate obligations or was intended by the testator to be *exonerated from* such obligations." *In re Cannavo's Will*, 300 N.Y.S.2d 731, 733 (Sur. Ct. 1969). See **subrogation (c)**.

ex'or is an archaic abbreviation of *executor*. See **executor**.

exorbitant (lit., "having departed or deviated from one's track [*orbita*] or rut") is sometimes mistakenly spelled *exhorbitant—perhaps because it is confused with *exhort*. E.g.: "Daon's own appraiser agreed that this price was *exhorbitant* [read *exorbitant*]." *Foster v. Daon Corp.*, 713 F.2d 148, 149 (5th Cir. 1983). Cf. the misspellings *exhalt and *exhault: see **exalt**.

exordium. See **introductory clause**.

ex parte; *inter partes*. These correlative terms—legal JARGON, both—are familiar enough to all lawyers to be useful. But they should be simplified for the lay audience.

The first thing to notice about these phrases is that *ex parte* (as presented in the headword) is in roman type, but *inter partes* is italicized. That's because *ex parte* has been naturalized, and *inter partes* hasn't. This is a nettlesome inconsistency. *Ex parte* appears so much more frequently than *inter partes* that it is now, in English-language contexts, treated as an English phrase. But if you were to use both phrases in a given piece of writing, it would make sense to give them parity and italicize both.

An *ex parte* proceeding involves only one party, since the basic meaning of this Latin phrase is "from or on behalf of only one side to a lawsuit." E.g.:

- "Rudolph maintains that the judge was unduly and falsely influenced during an allegedly '*ex parte*' conversation with the prosecution." *Rudolph v. Blackburn*, 750 F.2d 302, 307 (5th Cir. 1984).
- "Because [appellee] declined to participate in this proceeding, the arbitration was conducted *ex parte*." *Fluor Engrs. & Constructors v. Southern Pac. Transp.*, 753 F.2d 444, 450 (5th Cir. 1985).

In an *inter partes* proceeding, more than one party is involved, since *inter partes* means "between (and among) parties; involving all sides to a lawsuit." This term is frequently contrasted with *ex parte*—e.g.:

- "The notice requirement . . . in the context of an *inter partes* judicial proceeding applies with at least equal force in the context of an *ex parte* administrative proceeding." *Bishop v. Commonwealth*, 639 S.E.2d 683, 688 (Va. Ct. App. 2007).
- "In contrast to *ex parte* reexam, a third-party requester participates throughout an *inter partes* case: the requester initiates the proceeding, the patent owner may respond to any office action, and the requester may comment on any response by the owner." *New Medium, LLC v. Barco N.V.*, 582 F.Supp.2d 991, 994 (N.D. Ill. 2008).

This LATINISM—hardly a TERM OF ART—is common in British legal writing—e.g.:

- "My Lords, if this charter is to be read simply as an instrument *inter partes* [read *between parties*], drafted by the contracting parties themselves for the purposes of a particular adventure and expressing the stipulations of their unaided minds, I think that its construction presents no difficulty." *Hansen v. Gabriel Wade & English, Ltd.*, [1924] 19 Ll. L. Rep. 359, 360 (H.L.).
- "There the court was concerned with a statutory provision contained in the Housing Act 1936; here the court is concerned with the construction of an instrument *inter partes* [read *between parties*]." *Compton Group Ltd. v. Estates Gazette Ltd.*, [1978] 36 P. & C.R. 148, 156–57 (C.A.).

In America it is often used in patent- and trademark-related contexts—e.g.:

- "A quarter century later, the federal Trademark Trial and Appeal Board ('Trademark Board') invoked Vaudable's recognition of the famous marks doctrine in several *inter partes* proceedings." *ITC Ltd. v. Punchgini, Inc.*, 482 F.3d 135, 158 (2d Cir. 2007).
- "A request for *inter partes* re-examination of the patents at issue here was pending before the United States Patent Office." *Avery Dennison Corp. v. Alien Tech. Corp.*, 626 F.Supp.2d 693, 700 (N.D. Ohio 2009).

It sometimes appears elsewhere in American legal writing, but it's rarely irreplaceable—e.g.: "Fraud *inter partes* [read *between parties*], without more, should not be a fraud upon the court, but redress should be left to a motion under 60(b)(3) or to the independent action." *Corcoran v. McCarthy*, 778 N.W.2d 141, 147–48 (S.D. 2010).

If the phrase were to be Englished, *interparty*, which already has limited currency, might serve well—but only preceding the noun it modifies.

expatiate; expatriate. *Expatiate* = (1) to wander; or (2) to discourse on (a subject) at length. *Expatriate* = (1) to leave one's home country to live elsewhere; or (2) to banish; exile.

expectancy. A. And *expectant estate*. *Expectancy* = (1) the possibility that an heir apparent or heir presumptive or a presumptive next of kin will acquire property by succession on intestacy; or (2) the possibility that a presumptive legatee or devisee will acquire property by will. *Expectant estate* = a reversion, a remainder either vested or contingent, or an executory interest. *See* Lewis M. Simes & A.F. Smith, *The Law of Future Interests* § 2, at 5–6 (2d ed. 1956).

B. And *expectation*. We have the idioms **life expectancy* and *meet one's expectations*, but aside from distinguishing uses in these phrases, most lawyers would be hard put to set out the distinction. Despite an overlap in actual use, there is a clear-cut DIFFERENTIATION that ought to be observed with care. For *expectancy*, see (A). *Expectation* = the action of mentally looking for someone to come, forecasting something to happen, or anticipating something to be received (*OED*). E.g.:

- "Perhaps the most common recovery sought in contract cases is a reimbursement for damage to what is known as the plaintiff's *expectation* interest." *In re Yeager Co.*, 227 F.Supp. 92, 96 (N.D. Ohio 1963).
- "The statute creates a presumption that parole release will be granted, [which] in turn creates a legitimate *expectation* of release absent the requisite finding that one of the justifications for deferral exists." *Greenholtz v. Inmates of Neb. Penal & Corr. Complex*, 442 U.S. 1, 12 (1979) (per Burger, C.J.).

Here idiom is violated by *life expectation*: "We do not think that earnings for a normal life *expectation* [read *expectancy*] should be considered in formulating the damage awarded." *Rezza v. Cziffer*, 186 So.2d 174, 180 (La. Ct. App. 1966). The opposite error here occurs, *expectancy* for *expectation*: "The court recognized that an injured party cannot recover against a perjuring witness even though perjured testimony interferes with a party's *expectancy* [read *expectation*] in court." Stefan Rubin, *Tort Reform: A Call for Florida to Scale Back Its Independent Tort for the Spoliation of Evidence*, 51 Fla. L. Rev. 345, 350 (1999).

Writers who misguidedly favor INELEGANT VARIATION are especially drawn to these terms. E.g.: "The district court considered the balance due on Todd's repair contract in computing Auto's damages solely in order to ensure that Auto received no more than its expectation. . . . Because the repairers were obligated in solido to *pay this expectancy* [read *pay the amount of this expectation*], the district court correctly subtracted the balance due under the contract from the amount of their total liability." *Todd Shipyards Corp. v. Auto Transp., S.A.*, 763 F.2d 745, 757 (5th Cir. 1985).

expectant heir. See **heir (B).**

expectation. See **expectancy.**

expediency; *expedience. The first is usual; the second is a NEEDLESS VARIANT.

expeditious; expedient; *expediential. *Expeditious* = quickly accomplished; prompt <an expeditious decision>. *Expedient* = (1) desirable; advantageous <a surprisingly expedient device for controlling a difficult problem>; or (2) based on self-interest <a purely expedient decision>. **Expediential* is a NEEDLESS VARIANT.

The word *expedient* was once synonymous with *expeditious*, but this use of the word has long been considered obsolete. Oddly, however, it persists in legal contexts in which *expeditious* would be the better word—e.g.:

- "In addition, the intent of the Declaratory Judgment Act is to promote the simple, *expedient* [read *expeditious*] trial of cases where the . . . questions involved lend themselves readily to trial without the usual formalities to the end that resolution may be speedily achieved." *Gulotta v. Cutshaw*, 258 So.2d 555, 559 (La. Ct. App. 1972).
- "Similarly, a defendant should not be permitted to frustrate the trial court's efforts to conduct an orderly, fair and *expedient* [read *expeditious*] trial, and then benefit from an alleged error by the court which he invited through his own conduct." *People v. Johnson*, 518 N.E.2d 100, 108 (Ill. 1988). (For a discussion of the problem that the word *which* causes in this example, see REMOTE RELATIVES.)
- "[The district court concluded that] there was good cause for terminating him. There is simply too much disparity between TransTexas's payments [to Stanley] and any concessions Stanley may have made for his *expedient* [read *expeditious*] exit from the company." *In re TransTexas Gas Corp.*, 597 F.3d 298, 308 (5th Cir. 2010).

expense, vb., = (in bookkeeping) to charge or record as an expense. E.g.:

- "The Debtors were permitted to *expense* against their monthly income the amount of $1,344.00." *In re Brenneman*, 397 B.R. 866, 872 (Bankr. N.D. Ohio 2008).
- "The records indicate that Richmond Company routinely *expensed* payments on the [credit] card as either fuel or equipment-lease costs, despite the actual itemization reflecting substantial and continuous personal or discrete business uses." *In re Richmond*, 429 B.R. 263, 286 (Bankr. E.D. Ark. 2010).

expiration; expiry. The word *end* is best where it will suffice. *Expiry* is the usual word for "termination" in BrE, whereas in AmE *expiration* is far more common—e.g.:

- "There could be no difficulty here about the date of performance; it was on the *expiry* of the two years." *White & Carter (Councils) Ltd. v. McGregor*, [1962] S.C. 1 (H.L.).
- "The district court denied reinstatement to Marchelos, reasoning that Marchelos had no security interest in his job because he had no reasonable expectation of continued employment beyond the *expiration* of his contract on

August 31, 1979." *Professional Ass'n of Coll. Educators v. El Paso County Cmty. Coll. Dist.*, 730 F.2d 258, 267 (5th Cir. 1984).

expiration; termination. What is it called when a contract comes to an end? If it ends according to the contractual terms, by lapse of time, it's called an *expiration*. If it ends because it's cut short by the occurrence of a condition subsequent or by a party's act, it's definitely called a *termination*.

But is the *expiration* of a contract considered a type of *termination*? That is, can one properly refer to the *termination* of a contract that simply expires through lapse of time? The answer is yes, and it has practical implications for legal drafters. If *expiration* were not simply a species of *termination*, it would be necessary to say things such as this: "Upon the *expiration or termination* of this Agreement, neither party will have any further duty to perform any of its terms." In fact, *termination* alone will do fine in that context. So remember: *expiration* is a subspecies of *termination*.

expire. See **run (A).**

expiry. See **expiration.**

explain. See **explicate.**

explanatorily. See SENTENCE ADVERBS.

EXPLETIVES. In general usage, *expletives* are understood to be curse words or exclamations. This sense was fortified in AmE during the Watergate hearings, when coarse language was omitted from the White House tapes with the phrase *expletive deleted*. In grammar, however, expletives are words that have no special meaning, but stand (usually at the beginning of a clause) for a delayed subject. (See **epithet.**) The two most common expletives are *it* and *there* when beginning clauses or sentences. It is the grammatical sense that applies for the rest of this entry.

A. With Passives. When used after verbs in the passive voice, expletives often give the misimpression that they have antecedents. E.g.:

- "The burial was to take place at Highgate, and *it* was intended to take the body by train from Winooski to Cambridge Junction over the defendant's road, and thence over the connecting road to Highgate." *Nichols v. Central Vt. Ry.*, 109 A. 905, 905–06 (Vt. 1919). (The full passive is *it was intended (by someone) to take the body*; yet, on first reading, *it* appears to refer to *burial*.)
- "Fair warning has now been provided and *it* is expected that the United States Attorney will communicate all of this to the Federal Bureau of Investigation." *U.S. v. Mansker*, 240 F.Supp.2d 902, 911 (N.D. Iowa 2003). (*It* seems at first to refer to *fair warning* when in fact it is merely an expletive.)

See MISCUES.

B. Number. The INVERSION occasioned by expletives sometimes confuses writers about the number of the subject—e.g.:

- "The present order of dismissal does not dispose of all issues because *there remains* [read *remain*] for trial *those issues* raised in Hansen's counterclaim." *Baker v. Hansen*, 679 S.W.2d 480, 481 (Tex. 1984).

- "*There remains* [read *remain*] for trial genuine *issues* of material fact concerning the plaintiff's actual and constructive knowledge." *Paulo v. Cooley, Inc.*, 686 F.Supp. 377, 381 (D.R.I. 1988).

See SUBJECT–VERB AGREEMENT (J).

C. Expletive *it* Alongside Pronoun *it*. Don't use the expletive *it* in the same immediate context as the pronoun *it*—e.g.: "*It* is concluded that *it* [i.e., the road] [became public] between 1975 and 2000." *Hanshaw v. Long Valley Rd. Ass'n*, 116 Cal. App. 4th 471, 476 (2004). [Read *We conclude that the road became public between 1975 and 2000.*] See **it.**

explicate; explain. Though synonymous, these terms are used in different contexts. *Explain* is the ordinary term. *Explicate* (lit., "to open up pleats; to unfold") is more learned and connotes formal, orderly presentation or justification. Oddly, the adjectives *explicable* and *inexplicable* are more frequently used than the verb *to explicate.*

explicit; implicit. *Explicit* = (1) unambiguous <the statute explicitly bars campaigning at the polls>; or (2) graphically lurid <the movie contains explicit sex>. *Implicit* = (1) unstated <long-felt contempt was implicit in her left-handed compliment>; or (2) unqualified <I trust you implicitly>. For more on the loose sense 2 of *implicit*, see **implicit.**

exploitative; *exploitatory; *exploitive. The second and third forms are NEEDLESS VARIANTS.

expose. See **disclose.**

expository; *expositional. The first is standard. The second is a NEEDLESS VARIANT—e.g.: "For *expositional* [read *expository*] ease, I will generally refer only to original *meaning*, with the understanding that my comments also apply to original intent and original understanding." Mitchell N. Berman, *Originalism Is Bunk*, 84 N.Y.U. L. Rev. 1, 22 n.49 (2009).

ex post. See ***ex ante.***

ex post facto is slightly pompous but fairly common when used for *after the fact*. The phrase does have legitimate uses in the sense "retroactive," as in *ex post facto laws*. E.g.: "Application of the newly enacted burden to this defendant thus runs afoul of the *ex post facto* prohibition [i.e., the prohibition against enacting laws that punish retroactively]." *U.S. v. Kowal*, 596 F.Supp. 375, 379 (D. Conn. 1984). An English writer once called this use, which appears in the U.S. Constitution and in Blackstone, "a grotesque misuse of the expression." Note, 34 Law Q. Rev. 8, 9 (1918). His was the grotesque error.

The phrase is often mistakenly shortened. *Ex post* for *ex post facto* is an odd ellipsis without literary legitimacy. "As a rule, therefore, courts will not engage in *ex post inquiries* [read *ex post facto inquiries*] regarding the substantive fairness of contract terms." Maureen B. Callahan, Note, *Post-Employment Restraint Agreements*, 52 U. Chi. L. Rev. 703, 704 (1985). (On the technically correct sense of *ex post*, see **ex ante.**) Yet another strange shortening is *post facto*: "Changes may not be instituted now in the expectation of *post facto* [read *ex post facto*] ratification at some indeterminate future time." *Henderson v. Graddick*, 641 F.Supp. 1192, 1202 (M.D. Ala. 1986). The phrase was formerly spelled *ex postfacto on occasion, but this spelling is archaic. Evident in these elliptical usages is the desire to shorten the three-word phrase, but the desire is simply misplaced here.

Some writers hyphenate the phrase when it functions as a PHRASAL ADJECTIVE <ex-post-facto reasoning>, but the hyphens are unnecessary in this SET PHRASE. See PHRASAL ADJECTIVES (B).

expound; propound. The first means "to explain," the second "to set forth; put forward for consideration." *Expound* is often misused. E.g.:

- "Defendants contend that plaintiffs' First Amendment rights are not abridged by the advertising policy in issue because they are able to utilize the traditional means of *expounding* [read *expressing* or *conveying*] their beliefs through speeches and parades." *Wirta v. Alameda-Contra Costa Transit Dist.*, 434 P.2d 982, 987 (Cal. 1967).
- "To this day, many organized religions *expound* [read *preach* or *express*] traditional views on sex, gender, and sexual orientation that embody and perpetuate conflationary outlooks." Francisco Valdes, *Queers, Sissies, Dykes, and Tomboys: Deconstructing the Conflation of "Sex," "Gender," and "Sexual Orientation" in Euro-American Law and Society*, 83 Cal. L. Rev. 1, 112 n.308 (1995).

Expound is best used transitively: one *expounds* an idea or doctrine; one does not need to *expound on* it—e.g.: "More than traditional in-class exam responses, their papers revealed a desire for catharsis, a chance to *expound on* [omit *on*] many of the frustrations and ironies of the U.S. health care delivery system about which they had learned." Elizabeth Weeks Leonard, *Teaching Health Law*, 37 J.L. Med. & Ethics 139, 144 (2009). Likewise, one *propounds* evidence. See **propound** & **proponent.**

express; expressed. Sometimes within the same writing will be found references to "*express* and implied contracts" and to "*expressed* and implied contracts." The preferred adjective in the sense "specific, definite, clear" is *express*. E.g.: "The decision depends in no way on an agreement, *expressed* [read *express*] or implied." *Pettitt v. Pettitt*, [1970] A.C. 777, 810. See **implied.**

Occasionally, the transitive verb *express* functions as a correlative of *imply*—e.g.: "There are multifarious occasions on which persons who act or speak in the name of a state do acts or make declarations which either express or imply some view on a matter of international law." J.L. Brierly, *The Law of Nations* 61 (5th ed. 1955).

expressible; *expressable. The first is preferred.

expressio unius est exclusio alterius; inclusio unius est exclusio alterius. These interchangeable maxims of interpretation hold that to include or express one thing implies the exclusion of the other, or of the alternative (L. *alterius* meaning "of the other two"). For example, a rule that "each citizen is entitled . . ." implies that noncitizens do not share in the entitlement.

express trust. See **constructive trust (B)**.

expropriate. See **appropriate**.

expropriation. See **eminent domain**.

expunction; *expungement. The second, which is recorded in neither the *OED* nor *W3*, is a NEEDLESS VARIANT that surfaces from time to time—e.g.: "He sought declaratory and injunctive relief, damages, and the *expungement* [read *expunction*] of his prison disciplinary record." *Hewitt v. Helms*, 482 U.S. 755, 764 (1987) (Marshall, J., dissenting).

ex rel., the abbreviation for L. *ex relatione* (= upon the relation or information of), is now used almost exclusively in styles of cases brought by the government on the application of a *relator*, who is a private party that is somehow interested in the matter (as in an action to abate a public nuisance). A typical case style is as follows: *U.S. ex rel. Carter v. Jennings*, 333 F.Supp. 1392 (E.D. Pa. 1971). See **qui tam** & **relater**.

In pre-20th-century lawbooks, *ex rel.* ordinarily denotes that the reporter did not personally witness the proceedings but got an account secondhand.

extemporaneous; extempore, adj.; ***extemporary; *extemporal.** In AmE, the first is the usual form. The others might be considered NEEDLESS VARIANTS, but *extempore* is most common in BrE.

extemporaneously; ex-tempore, adv. In AmE, the second is the Latin-lover's (or Anglophile's) NEEDLESS VARIANT of the first. *Ex-tempore*, like the adjective *extempore*, is the usual form in BrE.

extempore, adj.; ***extemporary.** See **extemporaneous**.

extend. See **enlarge**.

extendable; *extendible; *extensible. The preferred form is *extendable*.

extended opinion = a separate opinion. E.g.:

- "Justice Brennan, joined by Justice Marshall, filed an *extended opinion*, concurring in part and dissenting in part; but that opinion clearly recognized that the Court's opinion left undisturbed a military plaintiff's entitlement to pursue an equitable action to bring constitutional violations to an end." *Wigginton v. Centracchio*, 205 F.3d 504, 513 (1st Cir. 2000).

- "Justice Brennan concurred—but wrote an *extended opinion* analyzing the federal statute at issue from the perspective of the delegation doctrine." Laurence H. Tribe & Patrick O. Gudridge, *The Anti-Emergency Constitution*, 113 Yale L.J. 1801, 1865 (2004).

See **write specially**.

*extendible; *extensible. See **extendable**.

extension; renewal. Both of these words are used in referring to the continuation of a legal contract, such as a lease. But the two have undergone a subtle DIFFERENTIATION with sometimes important ramifications: an *extension* continues the same contract for a specified period, whereas a *renewal* institutes a new contract that replaces the old one. Unfortunately, some courts muddle the two words, using them interchangeably or using both but not defining the difference.

extenuate (= to lessen the seriousness of [a fault or a crime] by partial excuse) should be used only of the fault that is minimized, not of the person. The *OED* cites improper uses (so labeled) such as, "The pursuer's steward . . . *extenuated* himself calmly enough," in which the word is used as if it meant "to extenuate the guilt of; to plead partial excuses for" (*OED*).

extern. See **clerk**.

extinguishment; extinction. Both words are nouns corresponding to the verb *to extinguish*. If there is a DIFFERENTIATION, it is that *extinguishment* refers to the process, and *extinction* to the resultant state. *Extinguishment* means in law "the cessation or cancellation of some right or interest" (*CDL*). E.g.: "Both the Senate bill and House amendments provided for recordation of mining claims and for *extinguishment* of abandoned claims." H.R. Rep. No. 94-1724, at 62 (1976).

extortion; bribery. These terms are sometimes confounded. *Extortion* = (1) the corrupt procurement of something of value by illegal means, such as force or coercion; or (2) the offense committed by a public official who illegally obtains something of value by using his or her office. *Bribery* = the giving or promising of something of value to an officer in return for corrupt behavior. If the briber takes the initiative, it is bribery; if the bribee takes the initiative, it is extortion. See **briber** & **bribery**.

extortionate; *extortionary; *extortive; *extorsive. *Extortionate* (= [1] given to or characterized by extortion; or [2] [of prices] exorbitant) is the standard term, the others being NEEDLESS VARIANTS. E.g.:

- "The vice arises only when he employs *extortive* [read *extortionate*] measures, or when, lacking good faith, he makes improper demands." *State Nat'l Bank v. Farah Mfg. Co.*, 678 S.W.2d 661, 684 (Tex. App.—El Paso 1984).
- "Wright and Armstrong urge, among other things, that the court erred in finding a nexus between the *extortionate* conduct and interstate commerce." *U.S. v. Wright*, 804 F.2d 843, 844 (5th Cir. 1986).

extortioner; *extortionist; *extorter. The first is most usual, the others being NEEDLESS VARIANTS.

*extortive. See extortionate.

EXTRA- (= lying outside the province or scope of) is a prefix that in modern English has formed hundreds of new adjectives, mostly for learned or literary purposes. The prefix has been adopted by many legal writers to form NEOLOGISMS not yet found in unabridged dictionaries. These writers usually do no harm, and in fact occasionally coin useful words. *Extralegal* and *extrajudicial* both date from the early 17th century; *extraconstitutional* dates from the early 19th century. Following are representative examples of 21st-century legal neologisms using this prefix:

- "Our holding in *Bartlett* was based on the plain language of the statute; it did not impose any *extrastatutory* requirements upon municipalities seeking to annex land under the 'forest-preserve exception.'" *Stroick v. Village of W. Dundee*, 744 N.E.2d 1279, 1284 (Ill. App. Ct. 2001).
- "The Court held that *extracontractual* damages to a beneficiary were not among the remedies envisioned by Congress." *BP Corp. N. Am. Inc. Sav. Plan Inv. Oversight Comm. v. Northern Trust*, 692 F.Supp.2d 980, 983 (N.D. Ill. 2010).

extracurial; *extracuriam. The first is the better form because it is a properly formed adjective—e.g.:

- "The decision in *Baker v. Carr* represents a gamble that *extracurial* processes of political adjustment and compromise will produce an issue digestible, as it were, by the Court." Lon L. Fuller, *The Morality of Law* 178 (1964).
- "Much of the *extra-curiam* [read *extracurial*] activity in which the Supreme Court justices have engaged has not been sufficiently consequential to matter." Robert Scigliano, *The Supreme Court and the Presidency* 81 (1971).

extrajudicial. A. And *out-of-court*. These terms are generally equivalent (see (B)). *Out-of-court* is more readily comprehensible to readers and listeners, but it can be awkward. Let euphony govern the word choice—e.g.:

- "The due-process clause should not be treated 'as a uniform command that courts throughout the Nation abandon their age-old practice of seeking information from *out-of-court* sources to guide their judgment toward a more enlightened and just sentence.'" *U.S. v. Adi*, 759 F.2d 404, 411 (5th Cir. 1985).
- "Under the *corpus delicti* rule, a defendant's *extrajudicial* confession was admissible only when there was independent evidence that a death had occurred, and that it resulted from an act of criminal agency." Russell L. Miller, *Wrestling with MRE 304(G): The Struggle to Apply the Corroboration Rule*, 178 Mil. L. Rev. 1, 5–6 (2003).
- "In *Bruton v. United States* the Court reversed the robbery conviction of a defendant who had been implicated in the crime by his codefendant's *extrajudicial* confession." Miguel A. Méndez, *Crawford v. Washington: A Critique*, 57 Stan. L. Rev. 569, 582 (2004).
- "Because professional guidelines focus on lawyers' *extrajudicial* statements regarding matters that are adjudicated

in a court of law, they put the spotlight in the wrong place and on the wrong subjects and are not relevant to corporate practice as it relates to public relations." Michele DeStefano Beardslee, *Advocacy in the Court of Public Opinion*, 22 Geo. J. Legal Ethics 1259, 1260 (2009).

B. Special Sense. Occasionally, this term means "outside the judicial process" as opposed to "out of court"—e.g.: "Saying there had been 'a cascade of *extrajudicial* executions, arbitrary arrests, disappearances and torture,' the [Americas Watch] organization commented that the attitude of the Government of President Alan Garcia 'might best be described as one of resignation.'" Alan Riding, *Human Rights Group Criticizes Peru*, N.Y. Times, 3 Nov. 1988, at 4.

extralegal (= beyond the province of law), dating from the mid-17th century and now in fairly frequent use, is omitted from most legal and nonlegal (extralegal?) dictionaries. E.g.:

- "To a great extent they are *extra-legal*, existing under the sanctions of religion and morality, but not of human law." James Hadley, *Introduction to Roman Law* 248 (1881).
- "They often develop a tendency to pursue their purposes *extra-legally*, or even illegally." J.L. Brierly, *The Law of Nations* 49 (5th ed. 1955).
- "Where law is largely a reflection of *extralegal* morality, what appears in form as retrospective legislation may in substance represent merely the confirmation of views already held." Lon L. Fuller, *The Morality of Law* 92 (1964).

Today the word is written as a solid, without the hyphen. Cf. alegal & nonlegal.

extraordinary writs. See prerogative writs.

extrastatutory. See EXTRA-.

extravagant construction; extravagant interpretation. See *extravagant interpretation* under INTERPRETATION, MODES OF (B).

ex turpi causa non oritur actio. See MAXIMS.

exult. See exalt.

ex vi termini = by the force of the term; by the very meaning of the expression used. This LATINISM has no place in modern legal writing—e.g.:

- "Words that are not actionable *ex vi termini* [read *in themselves*] cannot be made so by an innuendo." *Argabright v. Jones*, 32 S.E. 995, 996 (W. Va. 1899).
- "In the second will there are no words [that] *ex vi termini* [omit *ex vi termini*] import a disposition of real property." *In re Wolfe's Will*, 117 S.E. 804, 806 (N.C. 1923).

*eyeball witness. See eyewitness.

eye of the law. See ANTHROPOMORPHISM.

eyewitness is spelled as one word, not two. Avoid *eyeball witness.* Cf. earwitness. For various types of witnesses, see witness (B).

F

face, on its. In this age-old legal expression, *face* refers to the inscribed side of a document. The full phrase means "in the words of; in the plain sense of" <the document on its face indicates testamentary intent>. The phrase is sometimes used with a possessive noun in place of *its*—e.g.: "The difference between this law and the law in the *McCray* case is that the purpose to control child labor is evident *on the law's face*." Robert G. McCloskey, *The American Supreme Court* 143 (1960). And it is sometimes used figuratively in reference to things other than documents—e.g.: "A libel is harmful *on its face*." *Peck v. Tribune Co.*, 214 U.S. 185, 189 (1909) (per Holmes, J.).

One must be careful of context with this shopworn phrase. When the subject is plural, and the phrase becomes **on their face*, there is a technical failure of CONCORD that can sometimes be risible—e.g.:

- "Most laws, however, discriminate or mete out different treatment *on their face*." Charles H. Clarke, *Equal Protection: Vulnerable Minorities*, 7 Thurgood Marshall L. Rev. 201, 207 (1982). (No one wants to see treatment meted out on anyone's face; though the sentence refers to the face of the statute, nonetheless the imagery suggests something different.)
- "*On their face*, the antitrust-merger guidelines are statements of enforcement policy issued by antitrust-agency leadership." Hillary Greene, *Guideline Institutionalization*, 48 Wm. & Mary L. Rev. 771, 782 (2006).
- "Some of these statutes were held to be unconstitutional *on their face* or as applied." Bradley P. Jacob, *The Defense of Traditional Marriage*, 83 N.D. L. Rev. 1199, 1207 n.46 (2007).
- "Other ERISA rules, which *on their face* seem to prohibit ESOPs, contain exceptions specifically designed to allow them." Sean M. Anderson, *Risky Retirement Business*, 41 Loy. U. Chi. L.J. 1, 14 (2009).

Note that in those last two sentences the plural form **on their faces* would be even worse. See METAPHORS, *ex facie* & **facial**.

face of, in the = in front of; directly opposite; when confronted with. This idiomatic expression has become a part of legal JARGON. E.g.:

- "An act of Congress will also be given effect as domestic law *in the face of* an earlier international agreement of the United States other than a treaty, or a preexisting rule of customary international law." Restatement (Third) of Foreign Relations Law § 115 cmt. a (1987).
- "Energy reliance on coal and oil present[s] an obvious conundrum *in the face of* global warming." Patrick E. Tolan Jr., *Homeland Security Challenges of Global Climate Change*, 54 Loy. L. Rev. 800, 818 (2008).

See **fly in the face of**.

facial = complete; on its face; as a whole. E.g.:

- "The doctrine asserts that the constitutionality of an overbroad law should be judged on its face. The result is that the statute is upheld or invalidated in toto and not as it applies in a particular case. This approach is called '*facial*' review." Peter W. Low et al., *Criminal Law: Cases and Materials* 77 (1982).
- "The cases before us are ones governed by the normal rule that partial, rather than *facial*, invalidation is the required course." *Brockett v. Spokane Arcades, Inc.*, 472 U.S. 491, 504 (1985) (per White, J.).
- "A *facial* challenge may succeed if a legislative scheme is unconstitutional in all or nearly all of its applications." *U.S. v. Booker*, 543 U.S. 220, 274 (2005) (per Stevens, J.).

The adverb *facially* is almost as common as the adjective *facial*. Though it might appear to mean "in a facial manner," *facially* means "on its face"—e.g.:

- "We hold that the plaintiff has standing to challenge the constitutionality of the ordinance, and that the section in its present form is *facially overbroad and unconstitutional* [i.e., *overbroad and unconstitutional on its face*]." *Hill v. City of Houston*, 764 F.2d 1156, 1158 (5th Cir. 1985).
- "The district court was unwarranted in *facially invalidating the statute* [i.e., *invalidating the statute on its face*]." Nathan V. Herron, *Assisted Suicide*, 22 J. Contemp. L. 183, 189 (1996).

facilitate (= to aid; to help) is a FORMAL WORD to be used sparingly, for it often is jargonistic, as is the agent noun *facilitator* (= helper). E.g.: "The commission's improved decision undoubtedly *facilitates* this court's review by clarifying the issues involved." *Public Serv. Co. of Ind. v. ICC*, 749 F.2d 753, 760 (D.C. Cir. 1984). As H.W. Fowler and others have noted, it is better to write that an *action* (e.g., the *court's review*, in the sentence just quoted) is facilitated rather than that the *actor* (e.g., *the court*) is facilitated.

facility. This word is surplusage in phrases such as *jail facility* and *museum facility*.

facsimile transmission. See **fax**.

fact, adj.; **factual.** In phrases such as *fact(ual) question*, the longer form is preferable. Notwithstanding that *fact question* is jarring, it is potentially misleading to the reader. In the following sentence, for instance, the use of *factual* would have circumvented the reader's thinking that *existence of fact* is an unhyphenated PHRASAL ADJECTIVE: "If the proceedings are characterized as a trial on a stipulated record, the existence of *fact questions* [read *factual questions*] will not undermine the result." *John v. Louisiana*, 757 F.2d 698, 703 (5th Cir. 1985). The sentences that follow illustrate the better usage:

- "Petitioners . . . contend that the ICC impermissibly substituted its judgment for the *factual findings* of the state Commission." *Public Serv. Co. of Ind. v. ICC*, 749 F.2d 753, 758 (D.C. Cir. 1984).
- "We are directed by statute and Supreme Court precedent to accord a presumption of correctness to such state court *factual findings*." *Hobbs v. Blackburn*, 752 F.2d 1079, 1082 (5th Cir. 1985).

Notably, *factual* has two meanings: (1) "of or involving facts" <factual issue>; or (2) "true" <a factual depiction>. Here sense 2 is illustrated in a sentence in which *fact* would be not just inferior, but wrong: "Neither of the men testified with sufficient credibility to enable the Court to set out with any confidence a *factual* account of what happened." *U.S. v. Quintana-Ledezma*, 758 F.Supp. 1, 1–2 (D.D.C. 1991). See **fact-finding** & **fact situation.**

Sense 1 of *factual*, the more usual meaning, appears in the following sentences:

- "The rule contemplates that only *factual* questions will be submitted to the jury to which the judge will apply the law, supplementing, if necessary, any *factual* determinations not submitted to the jury." *Sherwood B. Korssjoen, Inc. v. Heiman*, 765 P.2d 301, 304 (Wash. Ct. App. 1988).
- "The state of the *factual* record is not a genuine impediment to analyzing the constitutional question." *Panetti v. Quarterman*, 551 U.S. 930, 981 n.13 (2007) (Thomas, J., dissenting).
- "The weight or credibility of witness testimony is a *factual finding* made by the hearing officer." *K.J.S. v. Department of Children & Family Servs.*, 974 So.2d 1106, 1109 (Fla. Dist. Ct. App. 2007).

fact, n.; **factum.** *Fact* (lit., "a thing done") means "an action performed, an event, an occurrence, or a circumstance." In legal writing, *fact* has the additional particularized sense "an evil deed; a crime." Hence we have the expressions *before the fact, after the fact,* and *confess the fact.*

Factum, the Latinate form of the word, has several meanings: (1) (regarding change in domicile) "a person's physical presence in a new domicile"; (2) "due execution of a will"; (3) "a fact or statement of facts"; and (4) "an act or deed." In senses 3 and 4, the only ones contained in the *OED*, the word has no merit in modern contexts (except in the phrase *fraud in the factum* [senses 2 & 4], for which see **fraud (B)**); few lawyers would understand *factum* when so used. In sense 1, *factum* is perhaps a TERM OF ART; nevertheless, the term calls for elucidation.

Sense 2 occurs frequently in the context of wills, where it is generally no more useful or specific than *execution*: "It might be argued that logically the only question upon the probate was the *factum* [read *execution*] of the instrument." *Eaton v. Brown*, 193 U.S. 411, 413 (1904) (per Holmes, J.). In the SET PHRASE *fraud* or *mistake in the factum*, however, the use of *factum* is well ensconced—e.g.:

- "We are not directly concerned with decedent's lack of testamentary capacity or the due attestation or execution of the will, or such other matters as do not bear upon or tend to prove *fraud in the factum* of the instrument." *In re Cassidy's Estate*, 270 P.2d 1079, 1083 (Ariz. 1954).
- "Another kind of mistake, also traditionally classified as *mistake in the factum*, occurs when the testator errs as to the content of the will." Clark Shores, *Reforming the Doctrine of Reformation*, 26 Gonz. L. Rev. 475, 477 (1990).

- "Since the probate court in such a proceeding merely adjudicates the *factum* [read *execution*] of the will, the superior court on appeal is similarly limited." James C. Rehberg, *Wills, Trusts, and Administration of Estates*, 47 Mercer L. Rev. 387, 396 (1995).

Although *RH2* lists *facta* as the plural of *factum*, the form most common in published sources is *factums*. See PLURALS (A).

*fact, actual. See ***actual fact** & **facts.**

fact-bound. Sometimes written as a single word, it is usually hyphenated as a PHRASAL ADJECTIVE—e.g.:

- "The three [Justices O'Connor, Kennedy, and Souter] tend to be cautious, *fact-bound* judges who decide cases based on their practical effects rather than some lofty, dispassionate doctrine." David A. Kaplan & Bob Cohn, "*Nine Scorpions in a Bottle*," Newsweek, 13 July 1992, at 20.
- "As a general matter, courts should not be in the business of second-guessing *fact-bound* empirical assessments of city planners." *City of Los Angeles v. Alameda Books*, 535 U.S. 425, 451 (2002) (Kennedy, J., concurring).

fact-finder should be hyphenated, not spelled as two words. Likewise, *fact-finding* is best hyphenated. The trend is to make both terms solid, but that trend is at best incipient.

fact-finding = the finding of facts; *factual finding* = a finding of fact. E.g.:

- "We reasoned that defendant was essentially seeking a review of the *fact-finding* process engaged in by the grand jury." *People v. Keizer*, 790 N.E.2d 1149, 1154 (N.Y. 2003).
- "This Memorandum Opinion sets forth the Court's *factual findings* on that issue." *Evans v. Fenty*, 480 F.Supp.2d 280, 281 (D.D.C. 2007).

Fact-finding is often mistakenly used not in reference to the process, but to mean "a finding of fact"—e.g.:

- "The magistrate declined to enter any meaningful *fact-findings* [read *findings of fact*] on the incidents surrounding the workover crew's hotel-room arrangement, which Sylvester contended had precipitated his discharge." *Sylvester v. Callon Energy Servs., Inc.*, 724 F.2d 1210, 1215 (5th Cir. 1984).
- "Constitutional law introduces concerns extraneous to individual *fact-findings* [read *findings of fact*] and adjudications when a societal interest limits the government's exercise of power." David Aaron, *Ethics, Law Enforcement, and Fair Dealing*, 67 Fordham L. Rev. 3005, 3022 (1999).
- "In social-security cases, the question is whether there are a cluster of *fact-findings* [read *factual findings*] by the ALJ that find support in the record and . . . lead to the conclusion that the claimant is not disabled." Morton Denlow, *Substantial Evidence Review in Social-Security Cases as an Issue of Fact*, 2 Fed. Cts. L. Rev. 99, 128 (2007).

See **finding.**

factional; factious; fractious. These words are confusingly similar. *Factional* = of or relating to a faction.

Factious = given to faction; acting for partisan purposes. *Fractious* = refractory, unruly, fretful, peevish.

factitious; fictitious. Both have the basic sense "artificial." *Factitious* = (1) produced artificially by human intervention; not natural; or (2) sham; produced by contrivance. *Fictitious* = imaginary, not real. This second term is often used in reference to testimony, accounts of facts, or stories. See **fictional.**

fact of the matter, the. This phrase is trite FUSTIAN that may serve as a filler in speech, but that generally has no justification in writing. Infrequently it gives the needed rhythm.

factor properly means "an agent or cause that contributes to a particular result." It should not be used, by SLIPSHOD EXTENSION, in the sense "a thing to be considered; event; occurrence." In law *factor* is used also—chiefly in BrE—in the sense "consignee" or "commission agent." E.g.: "Among the more important classes recognised by English law are *'factors,'* who are employed to sell goods for their principal." Thomas E. Holland, *The Elements of Jurisprudence* 303 (13th ed. 1924).

In Scotland, *factor* usually refers to "a manager acting on behalf of an owner of heritable property." Andrew D. Gibb, *Glossary of Scottish Law Terms* 37 (A.G.M. Duncan ed., 2d ed. 1982).

In some American states, meanwhile, *factor* may refer to a garnishee: "In Vermont and Connecticut, he [the garnishee] is also sometimes called *factor,* and the process [of garnishing], *factorizing process.*" Charles D. Drake, *A Treatise on the Law of Suits by Attachment in the United States* § 451, at 386 (7th ed. 1891). This use of *factor* and *factorize* is now infrequent, but it does occur—e.g.: "Debtor became insolvent and plaintiff, a creditor of the debtor, *'factorized'* the $169.88 garnishee owed debtor." *Dick Warner Cargo Handling Corp. v. Aetna Bus. Credit, Inc.,* 538 F.Supp. 1049, 1054 (D. Conn. 1982).

factorize. See **factor** (3d par.).

factotum = a general servant with myriad duties. The correct plural is *-tums,* not *-ta.* E.g.: "The agents suspected that the appellees were driving stolen vehicles, not that they served as *factota* [read *factotums*] of illegal aliens." *U.S. v. Miranda-Perez,* 764 F.2d 285, 289 (5th Cir. 1985). See PLURALS (A).

fact pleading. See **code pleading.**

fact question. See **fact,** adj.

facts cannot literally be false; if something is a fact, then it is by its very nature true. Yet in law one often reads and hears of the "truth" or "falsity" of certain facts. E.g.:

- "Presumably there were good reasons in the interest of justice nearly 100 years ago [that] impelled the court to fetter its own power to get at the *true facts.*" *Re Morris,* [1970] 1 Eng. Rep. 1057, 1063 (Ch.).

- "Such a definition, however, is significantly broader than one including only direct assertions of *untrue facts,* and we find it no more plausible." *Hyman v. Nationwide Mut. Fire Ins. Co.,* 304 F.3d 1179, 1196 (11th Cir. 2002).

- "A concomitant fear of the court when recovery is granted is that the 'innocent' spouse was actually in collusion with the guilty spouse in committing the arson, or at least knew of and consented to the act, but that the *true facts* never came to light." John F. Dobbyn, *Subrogation and the Innocent Spouse Dilemma,* 78 St. John's L. Rev. 1095, 1104 (2004).

In such a context, *facts* is really an elliptical form of *alleged facts.* Hence: "Evidence is relevant if it tends to establish the presence or absence, truth or falsity, of a *fact.*" *Bundick v. Weller,* 705 S.W.2d 777, 780 (Tex. App.—San Antonio 1986). But the best practice is to speak of *false* or *untrue allegations,* not *false* or *untrue facts.* See **true facts.**

facts, judicial. See **judicial notice.**

facts, under the, is an acceptable legal idiom. E.g.:

- "*Under the facts* of the case at bar, we cannot say that the district court erred in allowing the inclusion of this testimony." *Nicholson v. Layton,* 747 F.2d 1225, 1227 (8th Cir. 1984).

- "We ask whether the Kansas uninsured motorist statute mandates coverage *under the facts* presented." *Long v. St. Paul Fire & Marine Ins. Co.,* 589 F.3d 1075, 1079 (10th Cir. 2009).

Cf. **circumstances.**

fact-sensitive; fact-specific. Both are so hyphenated.

fact situation; factual situation. *Fact situation* = a situation with a given set of facts (hypothetical or actual). *Factual situation* = a situation that exists or existed in fact. When coupled with the noun *situation, factual* tends to take on sense 2 listed in the entry under **fact,** adj.

fact-specific. See **fact-sensitive.**

fact that, the. It is imprudent to say, as some have, that this phrase ought never to be used. At times it cannot reasonably be avoided. One writer has suggested that *because* will usually suffice for *the fact that.* See "Vigilans" [Eric Partridge], *Chamber of Horrors* 63 (1952). Yet rarely, if ever, is *because* a good substitute.

Where *the fact that* can be easily avoided, however, it should be. E.g.: "*The fact that* [read *That*] the police officer was engaged in the performance of his duties did not relieve him of the duty of care at intersections." *La Marra v. Adam,* 63 A.2d 497, 502 (Pa. Super. Ct. 1949). See **that (D).**

The common phrase *notwithstanding the fact that* can almost always be replaced by *although* or *even if*—e.g.: "The creditor's release of the principal debtor discharges the surety, *notwithstanding the fact that* [read *even if*] the creditor was induced to execute the release by the principal's fraud." Laurence P. Simpson, *Handbook on the Law of Suretyship* 307 (1950). See **notwithstanding the fact that.**

The pluralized form, as in "*The facts that . . . ,*" is usually unnecessary and awkward for the singular, where the discrete facts discussed are easily considered part of an overall structure or pattern. "*The facts that* [read *The fact that* or *That*] the website gave a direct number to call and that Minnesota residents were on the mailing list were [read *was*] 'more than sufficient evidence that Defendants made a direct marketing campaign to the State of Minnesota.'" Christine E. Mayewski, *The Presence of a Web Site as a Constitutionally Permissible Basis for Personal Jurisdiction*, 73 Ind. L.J. 297, 321 (1997). See FLOTSAM PHRASES.

fact-trier. See **trier of fact.**

factual. See **fact,** adj.

factual finding. See **fact-finding.**

factual situation. See **fact situation.**

factum. See **fact,** n. & *non est factum.*

fail; failure. These are charged words. The late Judge Thomas Gibbs Gee, of the U.S. Court of Appeals for the Fifth Circuit, used to admonish his clerks: "Be gentle with district judges. Never, for example, use *failure* in referring to an action of a district judge." *A Few of Wisdom's Idiosyncrasies and a Few of Ignorance's,* 1 Scribes J. Legal Writing 55, 58 (1990). Likewise, a modern commentator should not say that Justice Benjamin Cardozo, in *Palsgraf*, "failed" to mention the plaintiff's occupation and precise injury; not mentioning these things was no doubt a conscious stylistic choice—not a "failure" at all.

failure. See **insolvency (A).**

fair. A. And Its Near-Synonyms: *just; equitable; impartial; disinterested; dispassionate; objective.* All these adjectives can describe judges who have no personal stake or bias in an outcome and who apply the proper standards without improper influences. *Fair,* the broadest of the lot, suggests the fine judicial quality of being able to consider matters in adjudication without regard for one's own interests, sentiments, or prejudices, often to the point of evenhandedly applying a law that does not square with one's own preferred policy <the judge's decision was unfavorable but fair>. *Just* suggests a nearly perfect alignment with a standard or measure to be followed in arriving at legal decisions; further, it implies what is correct, truthful, and right <the judge handed down a just sentence for the defendant>. *Equitable* suggests a more fluid standard than *just*, evoking the historical courts of equity that would often use discretion to relieve litigants from the harsh strictness of the law courts <an equitable distribution of the testator's estate>. *Impartial* suggests the absence of any attempts to influence the judge, as well as the absence of any preexisting thoughts favoring one side or the other <an impartial magistrate>. *Disinterested* suggests a freedom from any type of bias or other partiality that might arise from having a pecuniary interest in the matter at hand <a disinterested judge has no stake in the litigation>. *Dispassionate* suggests freedom from an inappropriately intense feeling that would mar the judicial temperament; it suggests a cool and calm approach to adjudication <the judge's dispassionate recital of the facts>. *Objective* suggests an ability to give each side its due, patiently, while applying the law as stated, putting aside all matters that are not competent for the judge to consider, and temperately assessing the merits of the case without regard for personal opinions or biases <the judge made an objective ruling>.

B. Misused for *fare. Fair,* properly an adjective, is sometimes misused for the verb *fare* (= [1] to experience good or bad fortune or treatment; or [2] to happen or turn out)—e.g.:

- "From all outward appearances the business was *fairing* [read *faring*] well until Abbott purchased a jet airplane for approximately one million dollars in December of 1974." *Abbott v. Southern Subaru Star, Inc.*, 574 S.W.2d 684, 685 (Ky. Ct. App. 1978).
- "Perhaps Defendants would have *faired* [read *fared*] better by not removing the case to federal court." *Kusper v. Poll Farms, Inc.*, 649 F.Supp.2d 917, 921 (N.D. Ind. 2009).
- "Nonetheless, more and more fathers seem to be *fairing* [read *faring*] well in custody decisions." Gender Fairness Implementation Comm., *Gender Fairness in North Dakota's Courts*, 83 N.D. L. Rev. 309, 338 (2007).

fair comment denotes a defense in libel actions. The substance of it is that the words complained of were honestly made on a matter of public interest. *Fair* does not here mean "balanced; restrained; moderate"; rather, it means "honest; not malicious." The defense is rebutted by proof that the words were uttered maliciously.

fair construction. See *fair interpretation* under INTERPRETATION, MODES OF (B).

fair dealing. See **fair use.**

fair interpretation. See *fair interpretation* under INTERPRETATION, MODES OF (B).

fair play. In legal usage, this phrase, dating from the 18th century at the latest, is the quintessential expression for equitable and impartial treatment. It is often seen in procedural or due-process contexts.

fair use; fair dealing. The defense of *fair use*, in actions for copyright infringement, is also known as *fair dealing* in BrE. The term *fair use* (not *fair usage*) is the one applied in 17 U.S.C. § 107 to describe the kinds of limitations the law places on the exclusive rights of copyright.

fair wear and tear. See **wear and tear.**

fake. See **imposture.**

*falderol. See **folderol.**

fall = to be struck down, often on grounds of unconstitutionality. E.g.:

- "But since the evil aimed at here, child labor, occurs *before* interstate commerce begins, and since the product transported (for example, a can of shrimp) is in itself harmless, the law must *fall*." Robert G. McCloskey, *The American Supreme Court* 145–46 (1960).
- "On the other hand, although initially it was merely the 'hot oil' provisions of the National Recovery Act of 1933 . . . that *fell* as an unconstitutional delegation of legislative power in January 1935, four months later the codes, too, and with them the entire structure of the act, *fell* on similar grounds." Henry J. Abraham, *The Judicial Process* 374 (2d ed. 1968).

fall due is the legal idiom meaning "to become due." It is used in reference to negotiable instruments—e.g.:

- "They collected the notes as they *fell due*." *Cortland Specialty Co. v. Commissioner*, 60 F.2d 937, 938 (2d Cir. 1932).
- "Either party may terminate this agreement at any time by serving written notice on the other party if the other party becomes . . . unable to pay its bills as they *fall due*." Charles Boundy, *Business Contracts Handbook* 61 (2010).

false. A. And *wrong*. Both adjectives describe that which is neither true nor right. *False* suggests deceit in assertions or in thought <false statements> <false notions> and often what is inauthentic or fake <false check>. Only when the context strongly suggests mere error is the connotation of being deceived absent <You say that Shakespeare's first play was produced in 1592? False: it was 1588.>. *Wrong* suggests being askew from the standard of what is true and correct—often with a tinge of moral judgment <painting that vintage car hot pink is plain wrong>. But again, *false* has an overlay of perfidy that is absent from *wrong*: *false advice* is both incorrect and two-faced, while *wrong advice* is simply incorrect.

B. Potential Ambiguity. *False* in a phrase such as *false statement* is potentially ambiguous, since the word may mean either "erroneous, incorrect" or "purposely deceptive."

false allegation. See **facts.**

false arrest. See **false imprisonment.**

false check. See **check, worthless.**

false document. See **forgery.**

false facts. See **facts.**

falsehood. See **lie,** n.

false imprisonment; false arrest. Both are ARCHAISMS, the first being more common and a little less quaint. Both denote the act of detaining a person unlawfully—a common-law misdemeanor and tort.

*false misrepresentation. See **lie.**

false oath. See **perjury.**

false plea; sham plea. Both terms mean "an obviously frivolous or absurd pleading that is made only for purposes of vexation or delay." *Sham plea* (or *pleading*) has been the more common of the two in the U.S.; the *CDL* (British) contains the main entry under *false plea*.

false pretenses, an elliptical form of *obtaining property by false pretenses*, means "knowingly obtaining another's property by means of a misrepresentation of fact with intent to defraud." Though still in use in most American jurisdictions, *false pretences* (as spelled in BrE) has been largely replaced in England by a clearer name: *obtaining by deception*. See **cheat** & **common law (B).**

Some have complained that the phrase *false pretenses* is a REDUNDANCY because *pretense* suggests falsity. That is certainly the connotation today, but formerly *pretense* was a more neutral word denoting "the putting forth of a claim." That it now seems redundant is not a good cause for tampering with the name, unless lawmakers wished to make a wholesale clarification such as *obtaining by deception*.

false representation. See **misrepresentation.**

false swearing. See **perjury.**

falsi crimen. See **crimen falsi.**

family of nations. Writers formerly took a more restrictive view about what this phrase means than most would today: "'The *family of nations*' is an aggregate of States which, as the result of their historical antecedents, have inherited a common civilisation, and are at a similar level of moral and political opinion." Thomas E. Holland, *The Elements of Jurisprudence* 396 (13th ed. 1924). Today, by contrast, virtually any member-state of the United Nations is considered a part of the family of nations. Perhaps the only nations to be excluded are those that regularly engage in state-sponsored terrorism.

fantasy; *phantasy. The first is now the preferred spelling in both AmE and BrE.

fare, n. Because this word, in one of its senses, means "food," the phrase **food fare* is a REDUNDANCY—e.g.:

- "Purchased sandwiches constituted the solid *food fare* [read *food* or *fare*] given the prisoners." *Davis v. North Carolina*, 310 F.2d 904, 910 (4th Cir. 1962).
- "Out-of-town colleagues in town for the American Bar Association annual meeting this month may want to sample Chicago's *food fare* [read *food*, or, perhaps, *cuisine*]." Jerold Jacover, *Lawyers Wax Caloric over Favorite Chicago Restaurants*, Chicago Law., Aug. 1990, at 53.

fare, vb. See **fair (B).**

farmoutee; farmoutor; farm(in)ee; farm(in)or. Readers first encountering these terms may suspect a joke. Who, after all, would use *farmoutor* for someone who farms out work, or *farmoutee* for the person to whom the work is farmed out?

The answer is American oil-and-gas lawyers and businesspeople. The odd thing, though, is that *farmor = farminor = farmoutor*. Usage varies, obviously—but that is so even within a given jurisdiction. Many published sources contain *farmor* and *farmee* as correlatives—e.g.:

- "Generally speaking, a farm-out involves an assignment of, or agreement to assign, leasehold acreage (by the *farmor*) in exchange for an obligation to drill (by the *farmee*)." *Burke v. Blumenthal*, 504 F.Supp. 35, 36 (N.D. Tex. 1980).
- "He claimed that their relationship with Cambridge was transformed from a relationship of lessor-lessee, *farmor-farmee*, to a particular fiduciary relationship because Cambridge had promised in writing to handle future royalty payments with more propriety than it had in the past." *Cambridge Oil Co. v. Huggins*, 765 S.W.2d 540, 542 (Tex. App.—Corpus Christi 1989).

In other sources, the correlative terms are *farmoutor* and *farmoutee*—e.g.:

- "Pan American paid royalties on the same rate to the oil and gas lease royalty owners and transmitted payments at the same rate to its *farmoutees* mentioned in finding No. 13 below, for the period from January 1, 1954, through December 22, 1957." *Waechter v. Amoco Prod. Co.*, 537 P.2d 228, 232 (Kan. 1975) (quoting the trial court).
- "It is first necessary to determine the meaning of the parties in the farmout agreement with respect to 'all costs and expenses incurred in drilling, testing, completing, equipping . . . any test well drilled hereunder . . .' which were the sole responsibility of the *farmoutee*, for which *farmouters* would never be liable, according to the contract." *Continental Oil Co. v. American Quasar Petroleum Co.*, 438 F.Supp. 909, 912 (D. Wyo. 1977).
- "In July 1982, Manges, on behalf of himself, DCRC (Manges) and as agent for the State under the Relinquishment Act, brought suit against Mobil, Exxon, the royalty owners under the lease, and some of the *farmoutees* under the lease." *Scott v. Exxon Corp.*, 763 S.W.2d 764, 765 (Tex. 1988).

Despite the second example above, the spelling *farmoutor* is more common than *-er*—e.g.: "*Farmoutor* should pay rentals and be reimbursed by the farmoutee without liability for improper payment." R.L. Hankinson & R.L. Hankinson Jr., *Landman's Encyclopedia* 188 (2d ed. 1981).

far-reaching is one of our most overburdened adjectival phrases. This otiose METAPHOR should be used cautiously; the phrase should always be hyphenated. E.g.:

- "This question obviously has *far-reaching* significance for judges who have authority over disputed custody arrangements." Harry Brighouse, *How Should Children Be Heard?*, 45 Ariz. L. Rev. 691, 706 (2003).
- "The responsibility of scholars, lawyers, doctors, and judges in the applications of health law is a serious and *far-reaching* matter." David Nachshon, *The Editor's Page*, 25 Med. & L. at i, i (2006).

farther; further. Both are comparative degrees of *far*, but they have undergone DIFFERENTIATION. In the

best usage, the first refers to physical distances, the second to figurative distances. E.g.:

- "The Supreme Court looks no *farther* [read *further*] than whether the distinctions have some 'rational basis.'" *Ball v. Rapides Parish Police Jury*, 746 F.2d 1049, 1058 (5th Cir. 1984).
- "This finding may have stretched the reasonableness inquiry a bit *farther* [read *further*] than the Supreme Court intended." Jeremy J. Jacobs, Bridgers v. Dretke *and More Conflict Surrounding the Requisite Standard for Sufficient* Miranda *Recitations*, 30 Am. J. Trial Advoc. 399, 408 (2006).
- "These sometimes extend no *farther* [read *further*] than to the injury of the private rights of particular classes of citizens, by unjust and partial laws." David Chang, *Structuring Constitutional Doctrine*, 58 Rutgers L. Rev. 777, 792 (2006).

In BrE, *further* is used both physically and figuratively, whereas *farther* is physical only. But there are exceptions, which some would call peccadilloes: "It cannot now be seriously contended that the so-called restrictive force of International Law goes *farther* [read *further*] than this . . . ." Carleton K. Allen, *Law in the Making* 461 (7th ed. 1964) (an English work).

The superlatives—*farthest* and *furthest*—follow the same patterns. E.g.: "With intense questioning, the Justices pushed the lawyers into the *farthest* [read *furthest*] rhetorical corners of their arguments." Linda Greenhouse, *Right-to-Die Case Gets First Hearing in Supreme Court*, N.Y. Times, 7 Dec. 1989, at 1. *Furthermost* is rare for *farthest* (not *furthest*).

F.A.S. See **F.O.B.**

*****fastly** is an obsolete form that now exists only as a nonword, since *fast* serves both as an adverb and as an adjective. Even so, American courts have recently published opinions using the following phrases: **the standard is fastly placed*, **the fastly held rule*, and **fastly becoming so*. In the first two phrases, *firmly*, and in the last, *fast*, would serve better.

fatal. A. In Legal Jargon. In law, this word commonly means "providing grounds for legal invalidity"—e.g.:

- "Mere difficulty in ascertaining the amount of damage is not *fatal*." Charles T. McCormick, *Handbook on the Law of Damages* 101 (West 1935).
- "In general, uncertainty as to the fact of damage is *fatal* to recovery, but not uncertainty as to the amount." Michael D. Brittin, *Constitutional Fair Use*, 20 Wm. & Mary L. Rev. 85, 106 n.120 (1978).
- "Once on inquiry notice, the failure to conduct a diligent investigation is *fatal* to a good-faith defense." Paul Sinclair, *The Sad Tale of Fraudulent Transfers*, 28 Am. Bankr. Inst. J. 16, 79 (2009).

B. And *fateful*. Though both are tied etymologically to the noun *fate*, they have undergone DIFFERENTIATION. *Fatal* means "of or relating to death," while *fateful* means "producing grave consequences." The most common mistake is to use *fatal* when *fateful* would be more appropriate, but sometimes one would be presumptuous to suggest any change, so close is the call: "Like Henry Kissinger and other modern scholars, Mr. Gelb considers the *fatal* turning point not Munich in 1938, but the failure by France and Britain to oppose German reoccupation of the Rhineland in 1936." John Lehman, *The "Heroic" Retreat Was Really a Rout*, Wall St. J., 9 Oct. 1989, at A6.

father-in-law. Pl. *fathers-in-law*.

fault, at; in fault. See **at fault** & **in fault**.

favorite of the law. This phrase, referring to any person or status entitled to extremely generous treatment in legal doctrine, exemplifies the PERSONIFICATION of law in which lawyers habitually engage—e.g.:

- "It has long been said that the surety is a *favorite of the law* and his contract strictissimi-juris." Laurence P. Simpson, *Handbook on the Law of Suretyship* 94 (1950).
- "Homesteads are *favorites of the law* and are liberally construed by Texas courts." *Perry v. Dearing*, 345 F.3d 303, 316 (5th Cir. 2003).

fax. This term is now all but universal, in the face of which *facsimile transmission* became an instant ARCHAISM—and a trifle pompous at that. *Fax* is perfectly appropriate in formal contexts—e.g.: "*Fax* messages seem to occupy an intermediate position." G.H. Treitel, *The Law of Contract* 25 (8th ed. 1991). Pl. *faxes*.

faze. See **phase**.

fealty, a feudal term, formerly meant "the fidelity owed by a feudal tenant or vassal to a lord"—a fidelity implying duties not to do the lord harm or to blacken the lord's reputation, but to facilitate his prosperity. Today it is used figuratively as an ARCHAISM for *fidelity*: "If I begin to quote from the opinions of Mr. Justice Holmes, I hardly know where I shall end, yet *fealty* to a master makes me reluctant to hold back." Benjamin N. Cardozo, *Law and Literature*, 52 Harv. L. Rev. 471, 480 (1939). For more on *fealty* and its near-synonyms, see **fidelity**.

feasance (= the doing or execution of a condition or obligation), though branded "obsolete" in the *OED*, is current in legal usage. Even so, the term is not nearly as common as the negatives *malfeasance* and *misfeasance*. See **malfeasance**.

feasant. Though not listed in the *OED* or in *W3*, this term has been used consistently in American law since the 19th century. The word means merely "doing" and is used primarily in the phrase *damage feasant*, which could almost always be improved by changing the phrase to refer to something "doing" or "causing" damage—e.g.:

- "In *Sackrider v. McDonald*, . . . it was held to be such an abuse of the power of distraining animals *damage feasant* [read *that cause damage*], to impound them before the damages were assessed, as to render the original seizure a trespass." *Webber v. Hartman*, 1 P. 230, 234 (Colo. 1883).

- "It belongs to that small category of personal rights, the assertion of which has always been independent of legal procedure, of which the right to abate a nuisance, under certain circumstances, and the right to distrain cattle *damage feasant* [read *doing damage* or *causing damage*], are examples." *Jones v. Ford*, 254 F. 645, 649 (8th Cir. 1918).
- "When the shipowner's liability presupposes no preceding consensual relation with the injured party, but arises from a base invasion of his interests, it can be safely asserted that the surrender of only the *damage feasant* [read *damage-causing*] vessel is necessary in order to secure limitation." *In re U.S. Dredging Corp.*, 264 F.2d 339, 340 (2d Cir. 1959).

feasible. See **practicable** (A).

feasor. Most commonly appearing in the compounds such as *tortfeasor*, the word *feasor* often appears on its own or in some other combination. Ordinarily it can be simplified—e.g.:

- "The referee in the court below decided the case upon the theory that one joint *feasor* [read *tortfeasor* or *actor*] could not recover from another." *Johnson v. Matson*, 45 F.2d 550, 551 (9th Cir. 1930).
- "On February 17, 1960, counsel for Mahlum having further mulled over the quizzical prospect of paying Carlson, the alleged *non-feasor* [read *nonactor*], the proceeds of the sale of his boat, filed a motion to withhold paying Carlson because the money ought to go to Mahlum when he got his decree." *Mahlum v. Carlson*, 304 F.2d 285, 287 (9th Cir. 1962).
- "Evidence which shows that, following the crime charged, defendant and his *joint crime-feasor* [read *accomplice* or *partner in crime*] possessed weapons with which the crime was committed is relevant." *Ross v. State*, 601 S.W.2d 672, 675 (Mo. Ct. App. 1980).

See **malfeasor, misfeasor** & **tortfeasor**.

federal. This word should be lowercased unless it is part of a title or of an organization's name. See **national**.

federal common law; federal general common law. In *Erie R.R. v. Tompkins*, 304 U.S. 64, 78 (1938), Justice Brandeis declared: "There is no federal general common law." Apart from a so-called *general* common law, however, there is a very substantial *federal common law*, "involving matters in which the federal interest is so strong that the federal courts are free to develop substantive rules to protect that interest." Charles Alan Wright, *The Law of Federal Courts* 292 (5th ed. 1994). The federal common law applies, for example, in disputes between two states.

federal fisc. See **fisc**.

federalism, in AmE, has traditionally referred to the "coordinate relationship and distribution of power between the individual states and the national government." Cathleen C. Herasimchuk, *The New Federalism*, 68 Tex. L. Rev. 1481, 1485 (1990). Cf. **our federalism**.

In U.S. politics, this word is a double-edged sword. It is used by proponents of a strong central government to denote a system in which the national government has broad powers to compel states to conform to policies set by Congress, and by opponents of a strong central government to denote a system in which the states are sovereign entities free to set their own policies subject only to strict construction of the U.S. Constitution. So the word is often employed by political adversaries.

federal jurisdiction, exclusive. See **preemption, federal.**

federally, for *in federal court* or *by federal court(s)*, is unidiomatic among those working with federal courts. E.g.: "The appellant argues that the waiver provision as spelled out *federally* [read *in federal court*] by *Johnson v. Zerbst* and locally by Maryland Rule 719c had not been complied with." *Howell v. State*, 425 A.2d 1361, 1371 (Md. Ct. Spec. App. 1981).

federal preemption. See **preemption, federal.**

federal statute. See **enactment.**

federation. See **confederation.**

fee = an inheritable interest in land, constituting the maximum of legal ownership <fee simple> <fee tail>. Plurals formed from phrases containing this word can be problematic. One textbook, for example, has *fee tails* but *fees simple*. The better practice is to make *fees* plural, whether the phrase is *fees simple absolute*, *fees simple determinable*, or *fees tail*. See POSTPOSITIVE ADJECTIVES.

Fee often acts as an elliptical form of *fee simple absolute*: "Although it is probably good practice to use the word 'absolute' whenever one is referring to an estate in fee simple that is free of special limitation, condition subsequent, or executory limitation, lawyers frequently refer to such an estate as a 'fee simple' or even as a 'fee.' We may find ourselves slipping into that usage as we go along." Thomas F. Bergin & Paul G. Haskell, *Preface to Estates in Land and Future Interests* 24 (2d ed. 1984). See **fee simple.**

For *fee* in the more common sense of remuneration, see **pay,** n.

feebleness literally denotes a debilitated physical state; *feeblemindedness* denotes the mental state. In the following sentence, the two are confused: "The victim was declared 'not competent to testify,' due to her *feebleness* [read *feeblemindedness*], hearing impairment, and the effects of Alzheimer's disease." *McKinney v. State*, 463 S.E.2d 136, 138 (Ga. Ct. App. 1995).

feel. A. For *think***.** *Feel* is a weak and informal substitute for *think, believe, maintain,* or *submit*. E.g.: "In order for this opinion to have any real meaning, we *feel* [read *believe*] the stipulation of facts should be summarized in considerable detail." *Brinkley v. Farmers Elevator Mut. Ins. Co.*, 485 F.2d 1283, 1285 (10th Cir. 1973). When an idea is phrased on an emotional rather than a cognitive level, the resulting sentence seems to minimize the thoughts being reported— e.g.: "She *feels* [read *thinks* or *believes*] that crime prevention must start with helping small children find their way out of poverty and neglect, and that society's resources should go toward better education and housing, not more jails." Bob Cohn & Eleanor Clift, *The Contrary Voice of Janet Reno*, Newsweek, 11 Oct. 1993, at 30.

B. **Feel badly***.** When someone is sick or unhappy, that person feels *bad*—not *badly*. See ADVERBS (C).

C. Feel like. To avoid using *like* as a conjunction, writers usually need to change this phrase to *feel as if*. E.g.: "But on a combined income of $60,000, McDonald and his wife Cindy, who have five children, *feel like* [read *feel as if*] they're just scraping by." Marc Levinson, *Living on the Edge*, Newsweek, 4 Nov. 1991, at 23. See **like (A).**

fee simple. A. Generally. *Fee simple*, the name of the most comprehensive estate in land, "is a term not likely to be found in modern conversation between laymen, who would in all probability find it quite unintelligible. Yet to a layman of the 14th century the term would have been perfectly intelligible, for it refers to the elementary social relationship of feudalism with which he was fully familiar: the words 'fee' and 'feudal' are closely related." Peter Butt, *Land Law* 35 (2d ed. 1988). A *fee simple* was originally an estate that existed only as long as its original owner or any of that owner's heirs were living; since the Middle Ages, the estate has continued indefinitely even when the original owner and all heirs have died.

The phrase *in fee simple* is a LOAN TRANSLATION of the LAW LATIN *in feodo simpliciter*, which appears in the statute *Quia Emptores* (1289).

The common-law fee-simple estates are: (1) fee simple absolute; (2) fee simple conditional; (3) fee simple determinable; and (4) fee simple subject to a condition subsequent. The different estates, which have confusingly similar names—as well as the different names for the same estates—are discussed in the sections that follow. See **fee.**

B. Fee simple with No Other Words. When *fee simple* is used alone, *fee simple absolute* is almost invariably the intended meaning: "Their contention is that the will vested a life estate only in Fred Sybert, while respondent contends that the Rule in Shelley's Case operated to vest a *fee simple* estate in him." *Sybert v. Sybert*, 254 S.W.2d 999, 1000 (Tex. 1953). The plural is *fees simple*. See **fee.**

C. Fee simple absolute; fee simple absolute in possession. Since the Law of Property Act was enacted in 1925, England has had only two legal estates: the *fee simple absolute in possession* and the *term of years absolute*. Hence, "if one retains the old concepts in all strictness the fee simple has been abolished [in England]." A.W.B. Simpson, *An Introduction to the History of the Land Law* 64 n.1 (1961). In AmE, by

---

contrast, *fee simple absolute* is the usual form—not *fee simple absolute in possession.*

In the phrase *fee simple absolute,* the word *absolute* takes on a special meaning: "perpetual."

D. Fee simple conditional. A mostly obsolete estate—lingering only in Iowa, Oregon, and South Carolina—the *fee simple conditional* is an estate restricted to some specified heirs, exclusive of others. This term should not be confused with the similarly named *fee simple subject to a condition subsequent* (see (G)).

E. Fee simple defeasible; qualified fee. These synonyms refer to an estate that ends either because there are no more heirs of the body of the person to whom it is granted, or because a special limitation, condition subsequent, or executory limitation takes effect before the line of heirs runs out. See (F)–(I). See also **defeasible.**

F. Fee simple determinable; fee simple subject to special limitation; fee simple subject to common-law limitation. These synonyms refer to an estate that will automatically end if some specified event ever occurs. If the event is sure to occur (e.g., someone's death), then these terms are inappropriate. The usual phrase is *fee simple determinable.* (See **determinable.**) The future interest retained by the grantor is called a *possibility of reverter.* For more on that phrase, see **reversion.**

G. Fee simple subject to a condition subsequent; fee simple on a condition subsequent; fee simple upon condition; fee simple subject to a power of termination. These terms denote an estate subject to the grantor's power to end the estate if some specified event happens. American lawyers tend to use the phrase *fee simple subject to a condition subsequent,* whereas English lawyers tend to use *fee simple upon condition.* The future interest retained by the grantor is called a *power of termination* or a *right of entry for condition broken.* See **right of entry for condition broken.**

H. Fee simple subject to an executory limitation. This phrase denotes a type of fee simple defeasible (see (E)) subject to divestment in favor of someone other than the grantor if a specified event happens.

I. Fee simple subject to special limitation. See (F).

fee-splitting is, in the view of some lawyers, a EUPHEMISM for a certain type of kickback that lawyers on a contingent fee use to reward other lawyers who send them cases: "One rotten aspect worth mentioning is *fee splitting,* a kind name for kickbacks from personal injury specialists to other lawyers who refer them cases." Letter of John M. Beal, N.Y. Times, 1 Dec. 1989, at 30. In some American states, the practice is considered unethical, but in others it is tolerated.

Even as a noun, the phrase is best hyphenated; but when it functions as a PHRASAL ADJECTIVE, the hyphen is obligatory <fee-splitting arrangements>.

fee tail. A. Generally. A LOAN TRANSLATION of the LAW LATIN *feodum talliatum* (lit., "a cut-down fee"), the phrase *fee tail* means "an estate that is inheritable only by specified descendants of the original grantee."

The TERM OF ART formerly used to create a *fee tail* was the phrase *and the heirs of his* (or *her*) *body.* By special wording, the fee tail might be restricted to male or female descendants: a *tail male* was formerly common, a *tail female* rare. The estate is defunct in most American jurisdictions—the exceptions being Delaware, Maine, Massachusetts, and Rhode Island—and was generally abolished in England in 1925 (though it survives there as an equitable interest). See **entail, fee** & **tail.**

The expressions *estate tail, estate in fee tail, entailed estate, tenancy in tail,* and *entail* (n.) are sometimes used as synonyms.

B. Fee tail general and fee tail special. A *fee tail special* arose if the grant was to a donee and the heirs of his body by a particular spouse. A *fee tail general* arose if no spouse was named.

feign; feint. These words, though they derive from the same French verb (*feindre* "to touch or shape"), have undergone DIFFERENTIATION in English. To *feign* is either to make up or fabricate <she feigned an excuse> or to make a false show of <he feigned illness>. To *feint* is to deliver a pretended blow or attack designed to confuse an opponent momentarily. The word is also, in its older (but still current) sense, used as a noun meaning either a sham or a pretended blow or attack (i.e., the act of *feinting*).

fellow-servant rule (= the common-law doctrine, now generally defunct, holding that an employer could avoid liability to an employee by showing that an injury to the latter was caused by another employee's negligence) should be so hyphenated. See PHRASAL ADJECTIVES.

felo-de-se (lit., "felon with respect to oneself") is a synonym and perhaps a EUPHEMISM for *suicide* (in both senses—i.e., both for the act and for the actor). In modern writing, this GALLICISM seems to appear primarily when the writer wishes to avoid repeating the word *suicide*—e.g.: "English law stigmatised suicide as a felony; the *felo-de-se*'s property was forfeited, leaving his family impoverished." Glanville Williams, *Textbook of Criminal Law* 530 (1978). See **suicide.**

felonious = (1) of, relating to, or involving a felony <felonious intent>; or (2) constituting or having the character of a felony <felonious assault>. In whichever sense, the word is used rarely of persons, almost always of acts. E.g.: "Over the last 25 years five judges . . . have been disciplined for associating with criminals. In most of the cases, the judges performed specific favors for their *felonious friends* [better: *felon-friends*; better still: *felon-fiends*]." Peter Kadzis, *Guilt by Association?,* Nat'l L.J., 22 Apr. 1985, at 1. The *OED* cites but one (19th-century) sentence in which *felonious* is used of a person in the sense of someone who "has committed felony."

felony (originally a LAW FRENCH word meaning "wicked" or "treacherous") was recognized, as early as the 18th century, to be "a term of loose signification even in the common law of England; and of various import in the statute law of that kingdom." *The Federalist* No. 42, at 266 (James Madison) (Clinton Rossiter ed., 1961). Generally, *felony* denotes one of the two classes of crimes at common law, *felonies* being serious crimes and *misdemeanors* being minor crimes. A felony was any offense that involved either the death penalty or a forfeiture of the felon's land and goods.

As that suggests, the difference between a *felony* and a *misdemeanor* is determined solely by the possible punishments: in most American states today, a *felony* is any crime punishable by death or by imprisonment for a year or more, while a *misdemeanor* is any crime with a lesser punishment.

Before the felony–misdemeanor distinction was abolished in England in 1967, it was widely condemned—e.g.: "In form [the criminal law] remains a sprawling and unwieldy mass, and it still contains a number of anachronisms and anomalies—such as the now valueless and inconvenient distinction between felonies and misdemeanours—which hardly a lawyer in the land would be prepared to defend." Carleton K. Allen, *Law in the Making* 353–54 (7th ed. 1964). Odd though it seems, most American lawyers would likely resist any move to abolish the distinction. See **misdemeanor (B).**

felony murder = a death occurring as a result of the commission of a dangerous felony. E.g.: "One day in 1931 while waiting to argue a motion in Part One [a New York court], I was for a time an involuntary spectator at the trial of Eric Martin, a youth, hardly more than a boy, charged with a murder committed during a burglary, that is to say '*felony murder.*'" Ephraim Tutt, *Yankee Lawyer* 324 (1943).

The so-called *felony-murder rule* (so hyphenated) refers to the oft-cited doctrine that any homicide resulting from a felony or attempted felony is murder. The frequent formulation, "Homicide committed while perpetrating or attempting a felony is murder," is too broad because it suggests that mere coincidence is sufficient, as opposed to causation. *See* Rollin M. Perkins, *Criminal Law* 35 (1957). The best formulation today, then, explicitly excepts all felonies that carry no appreciable risk to human safety. Hence, any homicide is considered murder if the death results from a person's committing (or trying to commit) an inherently dangerous felony. Abolished in England in 1957, the *felony-murder rule* remains current in most American jurisdictions.

feme covert; femme covert; femme couvert; femme couverte. Feme covert /fem kəv-ərt/, literally "protected woman" or "sheltered woman," is the traditional term for a married woman. Though it would be spelled differently in modern French, this LAW FRENCH term,

in Anglo-American law, is generally spelled *feme covert* (omitting all the optional letters)—a spelling preferred since Blackstone's time. The plural is *femes covert*. Today, of course, this term (meaning "a married woman") is entirely unnecessary. See **coverture** & LAW FRENCH. For a discussion of other sex-specific forms, see SEXISM (C).

feme sole = (1) an unmarried woman; or (2) a married woman handling the affairs of her separate estate. This LAW FRENCH term is now obsolescent since the distinctions that it denotes are falling into disuse. Following are typical traditional uses:

- "[The house was] to be used and enjoyed by them during their natural lives, subject to their own control and to be managed by them as *femes soles.*" *Smith v. Usher*, 33 S.E. 876, 876 (Ga. 1899).
- "Georgia encouraged the business activity of widows and *femes sole* by abolishing imprisonment for debt for these women in 1847." James W. Ely Jr. & David J. Bodenhamer, *Regionalism and American Legal History*, 39 Vand. L. Rev. 539, 563 (1986).

Historically, *feme* referred primarily to a married woman: hence a *feme sole* was ordinarily a woman who had been divorced or widowed, as opposed to just any unmarried woman. For a discussion of other sex-specific forms, see SEXISM (C).

FEMININE ENDINGS. See SEXISM (C).

FEMININE PRONOUNS USED GENERICALLY. See SEXISM (A).

femme couvert; femme couverte; femme covert. See *feme covert.*

femme sole. See *feme sole.*

fence = (1) a receiver of stolen goods; or (2) a place where stolen goods are sold. Though this use of the word began as underworld slang, it has become standard in criminal law—e.g.:

- "The receivers of stolen goods almost never 'know' that they have been stolen, in the sense that they could testify to it in a courtroom. The business could not be so conducted, for those who sell the goods—the '*fences*'—must keep up a more respectable front than is generally possible for the thieves." *U.S. v. Werner*, 160 F.2d 438, 441 (2d Cir. 1947).
- "There are professional '*fences*' who act as outlets for stolen goods, and goods are sometimes stolen 'to order.'" Andrew Ashworth, *Principles of Criminal Law* 347 (1991).

feodum talliatum. See **fee tail.**

***feoff.** A. And *enfeoff*; ***infeoff.** The usual form of the verb meaning "to put in legal possession (of a freehold interest)" is *enfeoff*. E.g.: "O *enfeoffed* T and his (or her) heirs to the use of A and his (or her) heirs." A. James Casner & W. Barton Leach, *Cases and Text on Property*

320 (1984). The verbs **feoff* and **infeoff* are properly classifiable as NEEDLESS VARIANTS.

B. And *fief.* Both *fief* and **feoff* may be pronounced /feef/ (although the preferred pronunciation of **feoff* is /fef/). Whereas **feoff* is the variant verb, *fief* is a noun denoting a fee, or an estate in land held on condition of homage and service to a superior lord, by whom it is granted and in whom the ownership remains. See **fee.**

C. For *feoffee.* Occasionally, **feoff* is misused for *feoffee*—e.g.: "The Rule [in Shelley's Case] was devised in feudal times to insure feudal landlords the receipt of their rents from their *feoffs* [read *feoffees*], or tenants." *Sybert v. Sybert,* 254 S.W.2d 999, 1001 (Tex. 1953) (Griffin, J., concurring).

D. Pronunciation. The words are pronounced as follows: **feoff* /fef *or* feef/; *enfeoff* /en-**fef** *or* -**feef**/; *fief* /feef/; *feoffee* /fef-**ee** *or* feef-**ee**/.

feoffee /fef-**ee** *or* feef-**ee**/ = the transferee of an estate in fee simple; the person to whom a freehold estate in land is conveyed by feoffment, or a trustee invested with a freehold estate in land. E.g.:

- "Each *feoffee* (recipient of a fief), having received the seisin from his feoffor, would be said to be seised, or possessed of an interest in the land." Thomas F. Bergin & Paul G. Haskell, *Preface to Estates in Land and Future Interests* 11 (2d ed. 1984).
- "The exclusive right they gained was simply to be the first purchaser (or *feoffee*) of Indian land should the tribe agree to sell any of its territory." David Wilkins, *Quit-claiming the Doctrine of Discovery,* 23 Okla. City U. L. Rev. 277, 279 (1998).

See -EE & **feoff* (C).

feoffer. See feoffor.

feoffment /fef-mənt/ (fr. L. *feoffare* "to give one a fief") is an ancient form of conveyance usually involving livery of seisin. (See **livery of seisin.**) At common law, it is the transaction by which a fee is granted. Blackstone defines it as "the gift of any corporeal hereditament to another." 2 William Blackstone, *Commentaries on the Laws of England* 310 (1766). E.g.:

- "New Jersey insists, however, that the feoffor, the Duke of York, was not then the owner of any territory west of the easterly side of the Delaware River, and hence at the time of the *feoffment* had no title to convey." *New Jersey v. Delaware,* 291 U.S. 361, 365 (1934) (per Cardozo, J.).
- "While forfeitures for tortious *feoffment* are now ancient history, premature termination of life estates by merger is not." John V. Orth, *Requiem for the Rule in Shelley's Case,* 67 N.C. L. Rev. 681, 690 (1989).
- "The physical transferring of dollar bills may not be quite as obsolete as the medieval English practice of *feoffment* with livery of seisin, under which land was conveyed with the symbolic handing over of a clod of dirt, but it may be getting there." *U.S. v. Lee,* 232 F.3d 556, 559 (7th Cir. 2000).

feoffor; feoffer. This word, meaning "the transferor of a fee simple," is generally spelled *-or.* E.g.:

- "The *feoffee* (the recipient of a grant of land in fee simple) had positive duties to perform at the direction of the *feoffor* (the transferor of legal title)." Dale A. Oesterle,

Deficiencies of Restitutionary Right to Trace Misappropriated Property in Equity and in UCC § 9-306, 68 Cornell L. Rev. 172, 187 n.29 (1983).

- "Under early common law in England, a result use was held to arise in favor of a person who made a transfer of land by feoffment in fee simple to another, if no consideration was given for the feoffment and no express use was declared by the *feoffor.*" Restatement (Third) of Trusts § 9 (2003).

The *OED* notes that, in old lawbooks (from the 15th to the 17th centuries), *feoffor* was "often misused for *feoffee.*"

ferae naturae (L. "of a wild nature") is the law's rather pretentious way, in referring to animals, of saying "wild." The best modern practice, of course, is simply to use the phrase *wild animals.* See Robert Megarry & H.W.R. Wade, *The Law of Real Property* 65 (5th ed. 1984) (consistently using *wild animals*).

But traditionally, legal writers have not been so straightforward. They formerly used the phrase *ferae naturae* adjectivally, in phrases such as *beasts ferae naturae* or *animals ferae naturae*—e.g.: "Any one who stores up a great bulk of water in a reservoir, or keeps a caravan of beasts *ferae naturae,* is said, by English law, to do so 'at his peril.'" Thomas E. Holland, *The Elements of Jurisprudence* 173 (13th ed. 1924).

By extension, this Latin genitive has come to take on a noun sense in legal writing, so that it means "wild animals" <a caravan of *ferae naturae*>. Though Latin purists would probably consider this use a SLIPSHOD EXTENSION, it is now established in American legal writing. Perhaps the solution is to write *wild animals* instead.

The Latin purists are quite right, however, to lament another development: some writers mistakenly write *fera* rather than *ferae*—e.g.: "Ideas have been compared to *fera naturae* [read *ferae naturae*], property rights . . . which are dependent on possession and are lost by escape of a wild animal and likewise by disclosure of an idea." *Schonwald v. F. Burkart Mfg. Co.,* 202 S.W.2d 7, 12 (Mo. 1947). The best solution is to dispense with the Latin altogether.

Festschrift (= a collection of writings forming a volume presented by the authors as tribute to a [usu. senior] scholar), a German loanword, forms the plurals *Festschriften* and *Festschrifts.* For reasons given at PLURALS (A), the better plural in an English-language context is *Festschrifts.*

feticide. See abortion.

fetus is the clinical term denoting, most broadly, "the product of pregnancy up to the time of birth." Glanville Williams, *Textbook of Criminal Law* 250 (1978). More narrowly, it has been defined as "a viable unborn child." *People v. Smith,* 129 Cal. Rptr. 498, 504 (Ct. App. 1976).

The plural form is *fetuses.* The old BrE spelling—*foetus*—is now disappearing in favor of *fetus.*

A more connotatively charged term, which partisans sometimes find more suitable to their purposes, is *unborn child.*

feu (= a feudal holding) is today obsolete everywhere but in Scotland, where it is used not only as a noun—the counterpart of *fief*—but also as a verb meaning "to give out land upon a feudal arrangement whereby the vassal (buyer) holds land of a superior (the landowner) usually upon the terms that he builds on the land and pays a perpetual rent, or feuduty." Andrew D. Gibb, *Students' Glossary of Scottish Legal Terms* 38 (A.G.M. Duncan ed., 2d ed. 1982). The verb is inflected *feued, feuing*.

feudal; feudatory; *feudatary; *feudatorial. The only important words are *feudal* and *feudatory*, the others being NEEDLESS VARIANTS. *Feudal* = of or relating to a feud or fief. See **fief.**

Feudatory, as an adjective, means "owing feudal allegiance *to*; under the overlordship *of*"; and, as a noun, "one who holds lands by feudal tenure; a feudal vassal." E.g.: "In France, every *feudatory* legislated for his own demesne, but as a necessary result, it followed that an overlord, and even the King, could not legislate for the demesnes of his under-tenants for they were under the jurisdiction of their immediate lord." Theodore F.T. Plucknett, *A Concise History of the Common Law* 317 (5th ed. 1956).

Feudatory sometimes displaces *feudal*—e.g.: "The exclusive right of the first-born to the succession and the rules for entailment of estates were originally promulgated in the 'house laws' of the great *feudatory* [read *feudal*] chiefs, who compelled weak sovereigns to incorporate them in their land grants." Stephen Pfeil, "Law," in 17 *Encyclopedia Americana* 86, 89 (1953).

feudalism. A vague word of modern origin, *feudalism* "was completely unknown in the ages to which we apply it, [being] nothing more than a rough generalisation upon the character of mediaeval society." Theodore F.T. Plucknett, *A Concise History of the Common Law* 507 (5th ed. 1956). Still, the word *feudalism* is "a convenient way of referring to certain fundamental similarities [that], in spite of large local variations, can be discerned in the social development of all the peoples of western Europe from about the ninth to the thirteenth centuries." J.L. Brierly, *The Law of Nations* 2 (5th ed. 1955).

What are those similarities? They involved dependent landholding in return for the rendition of services—typically military service. Society was organized largely through a tenurial system, in which everyone—from king to the lowest landowner—was bound by obligation of service and defense. In the later, more sophisticated forms of feudalism, the rights of defense and service were supplemented by the right of jurisdiction. See **feu.**

feudal system. See **feudalism.**

*feudatary; feudatory; *feudatorial. See **feudal.**

feuduty. See **feu.**

fewer; less. *Fewer* emphasizes number, and *less* emphasizes degree or quantity. **Fewer number* and **fewest number* are illogical tautologies, since *fewer* means "of smaller number." E.g.:

- "If the question before us were what procedure would produce the *fewest number* [read *smallest number*] of death sentences, the power of a trial judge to set aside a jury's verdict might be of substantial importance." *McGautha v. California*, 402 U.S. 183, 305 (1971) (per Brennan, J.). [Or better: *If the question before us were what procedure would produce the fewest death sentences . . . .*]
- "The chosen law will promote the maximum number of interests, while denying the *fewest number* [read *smallest number*]." Marc S. Firestone, *Problems in the Resolution of Disputes Concerning Damage Caused in Outer Space*, 59 Tul. L. Rev. 747, 779 (1985).
- "[These parole officers] are responsible for *a fewer number of* [read *fewer*] parolees so that they can spend more time on 'these special cases that are of high interest to the community and are of a sensitive nature.'" *Flynn v. New York State Div. of Parole*, 620 F.Supp.2d 463, 491 (S.D.N.Y. 2009).

See **less (A).**

*few in number is a common REDUNDANCY.

fiancé; fiancée; divorcé; divorcée. The -*é* forms are masculine, the -*ée* forms feminine.

fiasco (= a complete failure) forms the plural *fiascoes*. See PLURALS (C).

fiat (= a judge's decree) means "let it be done" in Latin. The word in its broad, popular sense has come to connote arbitrariness:

- "A court does not have the power, by judicial *fiat*, to extend its jurisdiction over matters beyond the scope of the authority granted to it by its creators." *Stoll v. Gottlieb*, 305 U.S. 165, 171 (1938) (per Reed, J.).
- "We agree with the Seventh Circuit that a ruling that the marketing of handguns constitutes an ultrahazardous activity would in practice drive manufacturers out of the business and would produce a handgun ban by judicial *fiat*." *Perkins v. F.I.E. Corp.*, 762 F.2d 1250, 1268–69 (5th Cir. 1985).
- "The first [group] claims that the analysis goes too far and invites judges to transform an issue by judicial *fiat*." Camille Gear Rich, *Performing Racial and Ethnic Identity*, 79 N.Y.U. L. Rev. 1134, 1230 (2004).

More technically, *fiat* also denotes in many Anglo-American jurisdictions any one of a number of decrees rendered by a court in pursuance of its jurisdiction. For example, in Texas practice, most motions must contain a *fiat* (to be filled in by the court) fixing the time for a hearing on the motion.

fib. See **lie,** n.

---

fiber is the AmE, *fibre* the BrE spelling. Frequently in asbestosis cases in the U.S., *fibre* appears instead of *fiber*. But the *-er* spelling is preferred in any context in the U.S.

fictional; fictitious; fictive. These forms are distinguishable. *Fictional* = of, pertaining to, or having the characteristics of "an intentional fabrication" of the mind, i.e., of "a convenient assumption that overlooks known facts in order to achieve an immediate goal" (*W3*). This is the adjective to be used of legal FICTIONS. E.g.:

- "There are many instances in which equity has protected purely personal rights, though in some instances the courts have reached that result by finding *fictional* property rights—declaring things property rights that were in truth not of that character." *Fletcher v. Coney Island*, 134 N.E.2d 371, 379 (Ohio 1956).
- "There was no request for attorney's fees by either party. . . . Instead the *fictional* or figurative use of attorney's fees became a collateral issue in a determination of damages." *Kane, Kane & Kritzer, Inc. v. Altagen*, 165 Cal. Rptr. 534, 538 (Ct. App. 1980).

Fictitious = (1) sham; or (2) imaginary. Here sense 1 is illustrated:

- "A Government official [should] be free to make [decisions] without fear or threat of vexatious or *fictitious* suits and alleged personal liability." *Ove Gustavsson Contracting Co. v. Floete*, 299 F.2d 655, 659 (2d Cir. 1962).
- "The name of the payee was *fictitious* so far as the record discloses and that of the drawer a forgery." *State v. Lopez*, 237 P.2d 591, 591 (N.M. 1951).
- "The aspect of the Abscam investigation leading to this bribe began in 1979 when an FBI agent took on the undercover role of one Tony DeVito, president of the *fictitious* Abdul Enterprises." *U.S. v. Kelly*, 748 F.2d 691, 693 (D.C. Cir. 1984).

Sense 2 here obtains:

- "After describing a *fictitious* vehicle on each [certificate], Hill then obtained titles and registrations from the State of Texas." *U.S. v. Davis*, 752 F.2d 963, 967 (5th Cir. 1985).
- "The district court dismissed the claims against the Doe defendants because there were no named parties remaining in the action and because appellants failed to identify the *fictitious* parties by the close of discovery." *Hindes v. FDIC*, 137 F.3d 148, 155 (3d Cir. 1998).

In the following sentences, *fictitious* is used where *fictional* would be better:

- "The decision of Sachs J. in the *Crerar* case will help the probate court to give effect to the wishes of other testators, and to avoid imputing to them a *fictitious* [read *fictional*] knowledge and approval of testamentary documents whose meaning they did not know and would not have approved." *Re Morris*, [1971] P. 62 (quoting *Knowledge and Approval*, 106 L.J. 694 (1956)).
- "Internet Wire, a company offering distribution of company press releases, published this *fictitious* [read *fictional*] press release, and following its publication, the price of Emulex stock plunged." Jennifer O'Hare, *Preemption Under the Securities Litigation Uniform Standards Act*, 56 Ala. L. Rev. 325, 349 (2004).

Fictive = having the capacity of imaginative creation <fictive talent>. Apart from this narrow sense, rarely of use in legal writing, *fictive* is a NEEDLESS VARIANT of both *fictional* and *fictitious*. E.g.: "[T]here has been some *fictive* [read *fictional*] talk to the effect that the reason why a nonresident can be subjected to a state's jurisdiction is that the nonresident has 'impliedly' consented to be sued there." *Olberding v. Illinois Cent. R.R.*, 346 U.S. 338, 341 (1953) (per Frankfurter, J.). (Avoid beginning and ending a sentence with the word *there*.)

FICTIONS. To lawyers, fictions are assumptions that conceal, or presume to conceal, the fact that a rule of law has undergone alteration, its letter remaining unchanged, its operation being modified. *See* Henry S. Maine, *Ancient Law* 21–22 (17th ed. 1901). To nonlawyers, of course, the phrase *legal fiction* means "a surreal untruth."

> In jurisprudence a legal fiction denotes an uncontrovertible averment in an action. In the history of English law legal fictions have had three main functions. The first was to extend the jurisdiction of a court: such was the averment, used to give the Court of Exchequer jurisdiction, that the plaintiff was indebted to the Crown but was the less capable of discharging his debt by reason of the defendant's default to him (which was the true cause of action); or the averment that a contract in fact made abroad was made at the Royal Exchange in Cheapside—a decisive step towards the embodiment into the common law of the whole body of the law merchant. Secondly, legal fictions were designed to avoid cumbersome and archaic forms of action: thus, the fictitious lease, entry and ouster made the action of ejectment applicable to freeholds to the exclusion of the old real actions. Thirdly, fictions were used to extend the scope of a remedy: for example, the allegation that the defendant had found the plaintiff's chattel but refused to deliver it up made the superior remedy in trover not only supersede the action of detinue but also available for most claims in relation to chattels.
> Jocelyn Simon, *English Idioms from the Law*, 76 Law Q. Rev. 283, 304 (1960).

To understand legal fictions we must understand the difference between what is said and what is actually meant: "The best way to talk clearly and precisely and to talk sense is to understand as fully as possible the relation between predication and suggestion, between 'saying' and 'meaning.'" Owen Barfield, "Poetic Diction and Legal Fictions," in *The Importance of Language* 51, 71 (Max Black ed., 1962). A legal fiction is intended not to deceive, but to mask a change in the law; hence it is appropriately termed a "growing pain" in the language of the law. *See* Lon L. Fuller, *Legal Fictions* 21–22 (1967).

Lord Devlin's caution is an apt one: "Legal fictions are dangerous because they have a tendency to spread." Patrick Devlin, *The Judge* 162 (1979).

fictitious; fictive. See **fictional.**

fictitious person. See **juristic person.**

fidelity; allegiance; fealty; loyalty; devotion. These terms all denote an intense personal commitment. *Fidelity* suggests an unswerving observance of duty or faith, especially in matters relating to marriage vows <spousal fidelity>. But *fidelity* can also apply to any type of obligation, whether natural or voluntarily undertaken <a trustee's fidelity>. *Allegiance* suggests adherence to some large cause or to national ties as a matter of principle <a naturalized citizen must swear allegiance>. *Fealty* likewise suggests a supreme duty of faithfulness as a result of a pledge—and the term today appears most often in literary contexts <the interpreter's fealty to the text>. (For more, see **fealty**.) *Loyalty* suggests not only principled commitment but also an emotional, personal attachment to a person or thing <company loyalty>. *Devotion* emphasizes zealous dedication and ardor <the lawyer's devotion to clients' interests>.

fides. See **bona fides** & **mala fide**.

fiduciary; fiducial. *Fiduciary*, as both adjective and noun, is the unvarying legal form of the word <fiduciary relationship> <bound as a fiduciary>. *Fiducial*, used by historians and philosophers in certain contexts, has not found a home in the law.

fief. See **feoff (B).

fiefdom is a NEEDLESS VARIANT of *fief*.

fieri facias (lit., "that you cause to be done") is a LATIN-ISM that has given its name to a writ of execution for the collection of a money judgment; it directs the marshal or sheriff to seize and sell enough of the defendant's property to satisfy the judgment. It is commonly abbreviated *fi. fa.* or *Fi. Fa.* and pronounced /**fi**-fay/, not /**fee**-fah/—e.g.: "*Fi. Fa.* and writs of possession are still in common use, and (retaining their common-law form) have turned out to be the principal survivors of the medieval writ system." J.H. Baker, *An Introduction to English Legal History* 79 (3d ed. 1990).

Fifteen, the. This phrase formerly referred to the old Court of Session, in Scotland. E.g.: "'The Fifteen' decided against the minister and awarded damages against him." Arnold D. McNair, *Dr Johnson and the Law* 54 (1948). Today the Court of Session has 25 (or more) judges.

Fifth Amendment. The idiom is *to take the Fifth Amendment* (= to remain silent in order to avoid incriminating oneself), not *to plead the Fifth Amendment*—e.g.:

- "The possibility that the money possessed by Ms. Perez was generated by another illegal activity, prostitution, was presented when Ms. Perez *pleaded* [read *took*] *the Fifth Amendment* when the state asked her if she earned any of her money from prostitution." *State v. Seventy-Seven Thousand Fourteen & No/100 ($77,014.00) Dollars*, 607 So.2d 576, 585 (La. Ct. App. 1992).
- "They denied beating the defendant, seeing him beaten or that the defendant ever asked for an attorney or *pleaded the Fifth Amendment* [read *invoked the Fifth Amend-*

ment]." *People v. Hendrix*, 620 N.E.2d 1176, 1185 (Ill. App. Ct. 1993).

filch. See **steal** (A).

file is often used as an ellipsis for *file suit*—e.g.: "Prosecutors have broad discretion to decide what charges to *file against* a criminal defendant." *Ex parte Legrand*, 291 S.W.3d 31, 41 (Tex. App.—Houston [14th Dist.] 2009).

filterable; *filtrable. The preferred spelling is *filterable*.

finable. See MUTE E.

final. In reference to judgments, Justice Hugo Black exaggerated only slightly in commenting that "there is no more ambiguous word [than *final*] in all the legal lexicon." *F.T.C. v. Minneapolis-Honeywell Regulator Co.*, 344 U.S. 206, 215 (1952) (Black, J., dissenting). The reason is that the U.S. Supreme Court's holdings on what constitutes a final judgment are inconsistent. But the problem is one of vagueness, properly speaking, not AMBIGUITY, as Black termed it. And though a verbal formula for finality has proved elusive, "in almost all situations it is entirely clear, either from the nature of the order or from a crystallized body of decisions, that a particular order is or is not final." Charles Alan Wright, *Law of Federal Courts* 740 (5th ed. 1994).

final analysis, in the. See **in the final analysis**.

final conclusion; final outcome; final result. These are common REDUNDANCIES, since every *conclusion*, *outcome*, or *result*, as generally understood, is final. E.g.:

- "We do not intimate what the *final result* [better: omit *final*] should be, but as for an alleged violation of the Voting Rights Act . . . we should not write until the court below shows that it considered all of the evidence." *Velasquez v. City of Abilene*, 725 F.2d 1017, 1023 (5th Cir. 1984).
- "In that case, the Washington Supreme Court resolved only a discovery dispute; it did not determine the *final outcome* [omit *final*] of the litigation." *Pierce County v. Guillen*, 537 U.S. 129, 141 (2003) (per Thomas, J.).

Cf. **end result** & **ultimate destination**.

final destination. See **ultimate destination**.

finalize = (1) (transitive) to complete (something); bring (something) to an end; put (something) in final form; or (2) (intransitive) to conclude. Originally an Australianism, *finalize* is a favorite word of jargonmongers. For that reason alone, and also because it is a NEOLOGISM that does not fill a gap in the language, avoid it. E.g.:

- "No decision of this court has squarely held that we have a capricious residual power to '*finalize*' [read *make final* or *bring to an end*] otherwise nonfinal appeals." *Freeman v. Califano*, 574 F.2d 264, 267 (5th Cir. 1978).

- "As a general rule, new constitutional decisions are not applied retroactively to cases that were *finalized* [read *made final*] prior to a new Supreme Court decision." *Goode v. U.S.*, 39 Fed. Appx. 152, 155 (6th Cir. 2002). On the use of **prior to* in that sentence, see **prior to.*
- "The Constitutional Court plays a pivotal role in the process of impeachment through its power to *finalize* the impeachment decision." Jonghyun Park, *The Judicialization of Politics in Korea*, 10 Asian-Pac. L. & Pol'y J. 62, 92 (2008). (Better: . . . *to make the final decision on impeachment.*)

See -IZE.

FINAL PREPOSITION. See PREPOSITIONS (A).

final result. See **final outcome.**

financeable. So spelled.

financer; financier. *Financer* = one who finances a particular undertaking or on a particular occasion. E.g.: "Prior to BAPCPA, vehicle *financers* could be harmed by a debtor who acquired a vehicle in the months leading up to bankruptcy, then filed bankruptcy and crammed the creditor's claim down to the collateral value on the date of filing." *In re Hall*, 400 B.R. 516, 521 (Bankr. S.D. W. Va. 2008). *Financier* = one whose business it is to lend money—e.g.: "As to the fish that filled these eleven invoices, however, the funds necessary to enable these transactions came from an independent *financier*." *Brookridge Funding Corp. v. Aquamarine, Inc.*, 675 F.Supp.2d 227, 235 (D. Mass. 2009).

finders, keepers. See MAXIMS.

finding; holding. A court properly makes *findings of fact* and *holdings* or *conclusions of law*. The writers of the following sentences observed the distinction meticulously:

- "Because we *find* that the jury's *finding* of concurrent fault is amply supported by the evidence, we *hold* that Shell is entitled to full indemnity from PSI." *Smith v. Shell Oil Co.*, 746 F.2d 1087, 1094 (5th Cir. 1984).
- "Therefore, we *hold* that a jury could *find* that Dehart was an actual decisionmaker." *Schafer v. Maryland Dep't of Health & Mental Hygiene*, 359 Fed. Appx. 385, 389 (4th Cir. 2009).

In appellate courts, properly, only *holdings* are affirmed, whereas *factual findings* are disturbed only when clearly erroneous, against the great weight of the evidence, etc., depending on the standard of review. Generally, it is not correct for an appellate court to say that it *affirms* a finding of fact.

Nor should the verb *find* be used when the court rules on a point of law—e.g.:

- "We *find* [read *hold*] that the trial court properly instructed the jury on the Louisiana law of strict liability of the custodian of a defective thing under La. Civil Code art. 2317." *Dobbs v. Gulf Oil Co.*, 759 F.2d 1213, 1215 (5th Cir. 1985).
- "Because we *find* [read *hold*] that the trial court correctly applied the fiduciary exception to the United States' privileged communications, we deny the United States'

petition for a writ of mandamus." *In re U.S.*, 590 F.3d 1305, 1306 (Fed. Cir. 2009).

See JUDGMENTS, APPELLATE-COURT & **fact-finding.**

fine = (1) in common and legal speech, a pecuniary criminal or civil penalty payable to the public treasury; (2) an amicable final agreement or compromise of a fictitious or actual suit to determine the true possessor of land; or (3) historically, a fee paid by a tenant to the landlord at the commencement of the tenancy to reduce the rent payments. In short, in law it's a CHAMELEON-HUED WORD.

For *fine* as a verb meaning "to punish financially," see **penalize.**

finicky is the preferred spelling—not **finnicky. Finical* is a pedantic variant.

finis = end; conclusion. This term should be used just as if one of the defining words were in its place: "But sometimes it denotes the judgment that writes *finis* [read *a finis*] to the entire litigation, after all appellate remedies have been either exhausted or, as here, abandoned." *McDonald v. Schweiker*, 726 F.2d 311, 313 (7th Cir. 1983). Sometimes *finis* is used to signal the end of a book; using it in this way has the sanction of long tradition.

In BrE, the word sometimes denotes a compromise and settlement—e.g.: "The parties then applied to the court to compromise the action; by the terms of the compromise (*finis*) the intending vendor admitted that the land belonged to the intending purchaser because he had given it to him, and the terms of the compromise were recorded in the court records." Peter Butt, *Land Law* 102 (2d ed. 1988).

*finnicky. See **finicky.**

firing the client. When deciding that they will no longer represent a given client, lawyers (like literary agents and accountants) sometimes say that they are "firing" the client—e.g.:

- "In sum, it seems fair to say that the courts look the least favorably on conflicts created by a lawyer filing suit against a current client, and then '*firing*' *the client* who refuses to consent to conflict." Samuel R. Miller et al., *Conflicts of Interest in Corporate Litigation*, Bus. Law., Nov. 1992, at 141, 195.
- "Has the client hired and fired other lawyers? Has another lawyer *fired the client*?" Carole C. Jordan, *Hungry Lawyers Need to Choose Work Carefully*, Nat'l L.J., 12 Apr. 1993, at S16.
- "When one client insisted that he answer his telephone calls, Natsis took an unusual step. 'I *fired the client*,' he says. 'I'm not just a lawyer.'" *Commercial Real Estate Who's Who Towers of Influence: Rising Stars*, L.A. Bus. J., 20 Mar. 1994, § 2, at 11.

This phrasing makes perfect sense when read in light of the relevant *OED* definition of *fire*, which is labeled American slang dating from the late 19th century: "to turn (any one) out of a place; to eject or expel forcibly; to dismiss or discharge peremptorily."

But it is an odd usage, since generally in AmE only the party who hires can be said to *fire*. *W11* perhaps more accurately defines this sense—"to dismiss from a position"—for only the employer can be said to *fire* the employee, not vice versa. One can understand, however, how the usage emerged among lawyers: they retain the upper hand in their client relations if they can be said to *fire* clients, even though they could never go out and "hire" clients.

The age-old struggle to establish just who rejected whom is typified by the following exchange between two friends: "I quit because the boss used repulsive language." "What did he say?" "He said, 'You're fired!'" Anon., as quoted in *The Penguin Dictionary of Modern Humorous Quotations* 258 (Fred Metcalf ed., 1987).

firm. This term is the title under which one or more persons carry on business jointly, or the partnership itself by which they are united for business purposes. A *firm* is not a corporation but an association. Cf. **organization.**

firm offer = one that includes a promise not to revoke it for a specified period.

first and foremost is a CLICHÉ that should not be used merely for *first*. The *OED* describes it as a "strengthened" phrase and dates it from the 16th century.

first blush, at. See **at first blush** & **face, on its.**

first-come-first-served is correct; *first-come-first-serve* is the mistaken rendition that is commonly encountered.

first degree; second degree. See **degree** & **murder (A).**

First Dissenter. See **Great Dissenter.**

first impression, case (or question) of. This phrase is an English equivalent of the LATINISMS *res nova* and *res integra*. E.g.: "King first argues that the district court lacked jurisdiction to revoke his supervised release for violations he committed before the transfer of jurisdiction from the Eastern District of Michigan—a *question of first impression* in our circuit." *U.S. v. King*, 608 F.3d 1122, 1126 (9th Cir. 2010). See **case of first impression** & **res integra.**

first instance. The phrase *in the first instance*, a chameleon-hued and often a FLOTSAM PHRASE, is "now used alternatively to *first*, *at first*, or *in the first place*. It comes from the sense of *instance* as a suit or process in a court of justice. . . . We still speak of a *court of first instance* [i.e., a trial court]." Jocelyn Simon, *English Idioms from the Law*, 76 Law Q. Rev. 429, 433 (1960). E.g.:

- "Another feature of our trial procedure is a consequence of this same defect, namely the want of training of the judges of *first instance* [i.e., trial judges], and is a reproach to our

system." Charles T. McCormick, *Modernizing the Texas Judicial System*, 21 Tex. L. Rev. 673, 688 (1943).
- "At *first instance* Uthwatt, J., thought that the annuitants had a right to the capital sum, the rule being a rule of law." Anthony R. Mellows, *The Law of Succession* 569 (3d ed. 1977).

See CHAMELEON-HUED WORDS & **court of first instance.**

Here the phrase is used for *in the first place*: "The considerations we have discussed support our further determination that these facial attacks should not have been entertained *in the first instance*." Nicholas J. Johnson, *Supply Restrictions at the Margins of* Heller *and the Abortion Analogue*, 60 Hastings L.J. 1285, 1336 (2009). We might classify *in the first instance* as a SET PHRASE, ruling out the variation here in evidence: "The Department has a statutory obligation to give 'the same force and effect' to an out-of-state driving record as though it was entered on the driver's record in Montana in the *original instance* [read *first instance*]." *Chain v. State*, 96 P.3d 1135, 1138 (Mont. 2004). See **instance.**

*firstly, *secondly, *thirdly, etc. are today considered inferior to *first, second, third*, etc. Many stylists prefer using *first* over **firstly* even where the remaining signposts are **secondly* and **thirdly*. See ENUMERATIONS (A).

first option to buy. See **option.**

first part, party of the; first party. See **party of the first part.**

FIRST PERSON. As a general matter, it has been said that "the first person (*I, we, us*) is not usually used in legal writing because in an analysis of fact and law it seems best to have the emphasis on the facts and the law, and not on the analyzer." Norman Brand & John O. White, *Legal Writing: The Strategy of Persuasion* 123 (1976). This statement is true of drafting and of BRIEF-WRITING, but not of other types of legal writing, such as business letters, judicial opinions, and scholarly commentary. It is difficult if not impossible to state a sweeping rule applicable to all legal writing, diverse as it is. Instead, a few specific topics are here addressed in turn.

A. Awkward Avoidance of First Person. Such artifices as *this writer, the present writer*, and other graceless circumlocutions serve no real stylistic purpose and are inferior to the straightforward pronouns *I* and *me*. Late in his career as a legal writer, Jerome Frank confessed that he had long shunned the first-person pronoun, preferring *the writer* to *I* on the assumption that the indirect phrasing signified modesty. With age he became wiser and concluded: "To say *I* removes a false impression of a Jovian aloofness." *Courts on Trial* vii–viii (1950).

Of one common set of self-obscuring devices—*it is suggested that, it is proposed that*, and *it is submitted that*—Fred Rodell observed, "whether the writers really suppose that such constructions clothe them in anonymity so that people cannot guess who is suggesting and who is proposing, I do not know." *Goodbye to Law Reviews—Revisited*, 48 Va. L. Rev. 279, 280 (1962). We do know, however, that these phrases often make sentences read as if they had been "translated from the German by someone with a rather meager knowledge of English." *Id.* See **it is submitted that** & **undersigned**.

None of this should suggest, however, that every personal opinion should include the word *I*. Most opinions are transparently opinions, and they therefore need no direct mention of the writer—e.g.: "Though Holmes is routinely lionized as a great writer, Justice Jackson was the finest writer ever to sit on the high court." No moderately sophisticated reader would assume that this statement is anything more than an opinion. Even so, it is *much* more forceful and convincing when stated without the first person.

B. The Collegial *we* of Judges. The collegial *we* in which judges write their opinions is a useful stylistic device; but it sometimes traverses time with mind-boggling ease: "The court of appeals holding conflicts with *our* holdings in *Hendon v. Pugh*, 46 Tex. 211, 212 (1876) and *Faver v. Robinson*, 46 Tex. 204 (1876). In *Hendon, we* remanded a default judgment." *Uvalde Country Club v. Martin Linen Supply Co.*, 690 S.W.2d 884, 884 (Tex. 1985). It is questionable whether *we* really works when used by a modern court to overleap such a stretch of time; some less strained expression like *this court* might have been better in that sentence.

C. Approaching Autobiography. For a highly autobiographical and first-personish judicial opinion, see *Paine & Williams v. Baldwin Rubber Co.*, 23 F.Supp. 485 (E.D. Mich. 1938) (per Tuttle, J.). This opinion on a patent question is larded with language such as, "I hold that," "I take the case as I would an ordinary patent case," and "It seems to me that . . . ." The capstone, however, is the following passage, which I quote at length to convey the full flavor of the autobiographical style at its most personal and anecdotal:

> My experience began in the country and on the farm. I never laid the carpet directly in contact with the floor. The floor was a pretty rough one. Our loosely compacted base was straw or the old weekly newspapers. The usual thing was to put straw or paper under that carpet to protect it. The purposes were just the same as the purposes that this patent had in mind. It was yielding and would come back with a certain degree of resilience, it made it warmer when the wind got under the house, it protected against the cold, made the temperature more uniform, was nicer to walk over, didn't wear out so quickly. I can't think of any of the things that would be in the Turner patent that were not right in that old carpet with the papers under it, unless it be the fabric, and I say that is not a material part of the claim. That, however, was in a way present. It was not uncommon to cover the floor with straw, place papers over the straw, and then stretch the carpet over the paper. The paper served as a fabric to hold the loose straw in place.

> The carpets of our boyhood were not only flexible but they extended out beyond the margin of the fibrous substance which was underneath the carpet. No one ever carried the straw out to the edge of the carpet. We always kept it back. We didn't want it sticking out with the whiskery effect described. No woman would want straw sticking out around her carpet.
>
> *Id.* at 486–87.

first refusal, right of. See **option**.

fisc [fr. L. *fiscus* "the imperial treasury"] = the public treasury. The *OED* notes that the word is "now rare," but it is not uncommon in American legal writing. E.g.:

- "Any profits obtained, or losses incurred, inure solely to the benefit of the federal *fisc*." *Government Nat'l Mortg. Ass'n v. Terry*, 608 F.2d 614, 619 (5th Cir. 1979).
- "Cases like this . . . cumulatively pose a negligible threat to the *national fisc*." *Swietlik v. U.S.*, 779 F.2d 1306, 1313 (7th Cir. 1985) (Cudahy, J., dissenting).
- "The Legislature has manifested its clear intent to protect the public *fisc* by providing for statutory sovereign immunity and crafting only targeted immunity exceptions relative to Commonwealth agencies." *Piehl v. Philadelphia*, 987 A.2d 146, 157 (Pa. 2009) (Saylor, J., dissenting).

Note well: *public fisc*, unlike *federal fisc*, is a REDUNDANCY.

In Scots law, the word was formerly spelled *fisk*, and it means specifically "the public treasury or 'Crown,' to which estates lapse by escheat" (*OED*).

fishing expedition is a CLICHÉ used to describe (contemptuously) an opponent's attempt, through discovery, to elicit information that might help that opponent. The phrase ought to be given a rest, as the Supreme Court urged long ago: "No longer can the time-honored cry of '*fishing expedition*' serve to preclude a party from inquiring into the facts underlying his opponent's case." *Hickman v. Taylor*, 329 U.S. 495, 507 (1947) (per Murphy, J.).

fisk. See **fisc**.

fit > fitted > fitted; fit > fit > fit. Historically, the verb *fit* became *fitted* in both the past tense and the past participle. Since the mid-20th century, however, AmE has witnessed a shift from *fitted* to *fit*. It began appearing in journalism and even scholarly writing as early as the 1950s. *See* David S. Berkeley, *The Past Tense of "Fit*," 30 Am. Speech 311 (1955). This casualism appears even in what is generally considered well-edited journalism—e.g.:

- "Gordon Getty had never quite *fit* in at his father's oil company." Matt Moffett, Thomas Petzinger Jr. & James B. Stewart, *Courting Disaster*, Wall St. J., 20 Dec. 1985, at 1.
- "Judge Ciparick was overruled by an appeals court, which said that even a lopsided race *fit* the precise wording of the America's Cup deed." L. Gordon Crovitz, *Even Gentlemanly Yachtsmen Go to Court, But Why Let Them?*, Wall St. J., 16 May 1990, at A17.

And it has surfaced in fine scholarly writing—e.g.: "English land tenure, and the English way of life among landed gentry, *fit* [read *fitted*] this social order more than was true in the North." Lawrence M. Friedman, *A History of American Law* 66 (2d ed. 1985).

The traditionally correct past tense still surfaces—especially in BrE—but in AmE it is becoming rarer (and stuffier) year by year—e.g.:

- "We may leave to others the question whether the conception can be *fitted* to our old and modern systems of pleading." W.W. Buckland, *Some Reflections on Jurisprudence* 100 (1945).
- "It is wise before deciding to use it to have regard to the tools with which it can be *fitted* and to the machinery [that] operates it." Patrick Devlin, *The Enforcement of Morals* 20 (1968).
- "Absolute liability also *fitted* into an aspect of the objective theory of contract . . . ." Grant Gilmore, *The Death of Contract* 48 (1974).

Cf. **retrofit.**

fit and proper is a tiresome legalistic doublet with no claim to being either a TERM OF ART or a melodious phrase. One should write either *fit* or *proper*, without yoking them together so predictably. See DOUBLETS, TRIPLETS, AND SYNONYM-STRINGS.

fitted. See **fit.**

fixture = an article that has been attached to land in such a way that, in law, it forms part of the land. The term denotes a special type of property that is a hybrid between real property and personal property: a *fixture*, though considered real property, was once personal property and may be again someday (if removed).

flack. See **flak.**

flagrancy; *flagrance. The second is a NEEDLESS VARIANT.

flagrante delicto. See *in flagrante delicto.*

flair. See **flare.**

flak (= annoying criticism or opposition) is sometimes misspelled *flack*, which is the proper spelling of the term meaning "a press agent." E.g.: "After catching significant *flack* [read *flak*] from customers and the media, Yahoo tried to make peace." Matthew Friedman, *Nine Years and Still Waiting*, 17 Vill. Sports & Ent. L.J. 637, 650 n.73 (2010).

flammable; inflammable. The first is now accepted as standard in BrE and AmE alike. Though examples of its use date back to 1813, in recent years it has become widespread as a substitute for *inflammable*, in which some persons mistook the prefix *in-* to be negative rather than intensive. Traditionally, the forms were *inflammable* and *noninflammable*; today they are *flammable* and *nonflammable*. Purists have lost the fight to retain the older forms. See NEGATIVES (C) & NON-.

flare; flair. *Flare*, n., = a sudden outburst of flame; an unsteady light. *Flair*, n., = (1) outstanding skill or

ability in some field; or (2) originality; stylishness. The most common confusion occurs when *flare* displaces *flair*—e.g.:

- "District Attorney Jerome, who was an intimate friend of Hapgood, turned the actual trial of the case over to Keyran O'Conner, a capable assistant with a *flare* [read *flair*] for picturesque diction." Ephraim Tutt, *Yankee Lawyer* 168 (1943).
- "It is a chance to show we have the imagination and the *flare* [read *flair*] and the vision." Geordie Grieg, *£1 Billion Plan to Restore Britain's Heritage by AD 2000*, Sunday Times, 1 July 1990, at 1-1.

But the reverse mistake also occurs—e.g.: "What can we do with situations in which the constitutional nostrils *flair* [read *flare*]—where there is a sense that there may be something wrong, but one reads through the document and can't quite pin down where that sense comes from?" Laurence H. Tribe & Michael C. Dorf, *On Reading the Constitution* 38 (1991).

Although *flair* is exclusively a noun, *flare* can function as a verb in several senses: (1) to burst into flame; (2) to erupt suddenly; (3) to become suddenly angry; (4) to expand outward in shape; or (5) to signal with a flash of light. Occasionally, *flair* is misused for *flare* in its verb senses, here in sense 2: "The controversy surrounding frozen embryos *flaired* [read *flared*] recently with the death of a wealthy Los Angeles couple and the discovery of two 'orphaned' embryos which the couple had frozen and stored in Australia." Marcia Joy Wurmbrand, Note, *Frozen Embryos: Moral, Social, and Legal Implications*, 59 S. Cal. L. Rev. 1079, 1100 n.18 (1986).

flaunt; flout. Confusion of these terms is so distressingly common that some dictionaries have thrown in the towel and now treat *flaunt* as a synonym of *flout*. But the words are best kept separate. *Flout* means "to contravene or disregard; to treat with contempt." *Flaunt* means "to show off or parade (something) in an ostentatious manner," but is often incorrectly used for *flout*, perhaps because it is misunderstood as a telescoped version of *flout* and *taunt*. E.g.:

- "Despite the fact that both parties *flaunt* [read *flout*] local rules regarding the length of supporting memoranda, neither really addresses the 'successor in interest' notice question in any meaningful way." *Hemstreet v. Banctec, Inc.*, 748 F.Supp. 667, 669 n.2 (N.D. Ill. 1990).
- "CSW *flaunted* [read *flouted*] the rules and failed to properly credit and calculate student refunds." *Jackson v. Culinary Sch. of Wash.*, 788 F.Supp. 1233, 1243 (D.D.C. 1992).

Of course, *flaunt* is most often used correctly—e.g.:

- "Words like 'reasonable,' 'substantial,' and 'satisfactory' *flaunt* their lack of precision." David Mellinkoff, *The Language of the Law* 301 (1963).
- "Reed and Hammonds have been sanctioned on multiple occasions over the past five years, to the point where it almost looks as though they are now *flaunting* their inappropriate conduct." *Janky v. Batistatos*, 259 F.R.D. 373, 382 (N.D. Ind. 2009).

Flout, meanwhile, never seems to cause a problem—e.g.:

- "The offenses did not involve any question of the *flouting* of military authority, the security of a military post, or the integrity of military property." *O'Callahan v. Parker*, 395 U.S. 258, 274 (1969) (per Douglas, J.).
- "To avoid further violence and bloodshed, all state officials, including the governor, must know that they cannot with impunity *flout* federal law." Mitchell F. Crusto, *The Supreme Court's "New" Federalism: An Anti-Rights Agenda?*, 16 Ga. St. U. L. Rev. 517, 558 (2000).

One federal appellate judge who misused *flaunt* for *flout* in a published opinion, only to be *sic*'d and corrected by judges who later quoted him, appealed to *W3* and its editors, who, of course, accept as standard any usage that can be documented with any frequency at all. The judge then attempted to justify his error and pledged to persist in it. *See* William Safire, *I Stand Corrected* 158–59 (1984). Seeking refuge in a nonprescriptive dictionary, however, merely ignores the all-important distinction between formal contexts, on the one hand, in which the strictest standards of usage must apply, and informal contexts, on the other, in which venial faults of grammar or usage may, if we are lucky, go unnoticed (or unmentioned). Judges' written opinions fall into the former category.

For terms similar to *flout* and their usages, see **violate.**

floes (= sheets of ice [fr. Norweg. *flo*, meaning "flat layer"]) should not be confused with *flows*: "Because polar bears are increasingly unable to get to the ice *flows* [read *floes*] on which they used to hunt, they are spending more time in and around Inuit villages, increasing the threat of dangerous interactions with humans." *Panel: Climate Change*, 5 Santa Clara J. Int'l L. 462, 470 (2007) (Wil Burns, moderator).

flood of, a. See SYNESIS.

flotsam; jetsam; lagan. Blackstone called these "the barbarous and uncouth appellations" for goods abandoned at sea. 2 William Blackstone, *Commentaries on the Laws of England* 292–93 (St. George Tucker ed., 1803). *Flotsam* is goods that are cast into the sea and float on the surface of the water. *Jetsam* is goods thrown overboard that sink in the sea and remain under water. *Lagan* /**lag**-ən/ is goods sunk in the sea but attached to a buoy so that they may be found again. **Flotsan* and **ligan* are obsolete spellings of *flotsam* and *lagan*.

These terms have largely outlived their usefulness, except in metaphorical senses. *Flotsam and jetsam* is the CLICHÉ used figuratively to mean "miscellaneous unimportant materials; dispensable articles."

FLOTSAM PHRASES just take up space without adding to the meaning of a sentence. So there is usually no reason, where it is clear whose opinion is being expressed, to write *In my opinion* or *It seems to me that*. Other examples are *hereby, in terms of, on a . . . basis, my sense is that, in the first instance,* and *the fact that*. (Admittedly, some of these phrases may be useful in speech.) A favorite flotsam phrase of lawyers in their pleadings is *at all relevant times*: "*At all relevant times*, he owned shares in the Citi New York Tax Free Reserves Fund." *Halebian v. Berv*, 590 F.3d 195, 199 (2d Cir. 2009). We have enough written words without these mere space-fillers.

flounder; founder. Both verbs signal failure, but the literal senses, and therefore the images conveyed metaphorically, differ. To *flounder* is to struggle and plunge as if in mud. To *founder* is (of a ship) to fill with water and sink, (of a building) to fall down or give way, or (of a horseback rider) to fall to the ground.

flout. See **flaunt** & **violate.**

flowchart, vb. The verbal use of this word is not recorded in the dictionaries, although it was perhaps inevitable, what with the verbal use of *chart*. *W11* records the gerund *flowcharting* but not the verb *to flowchart*, here illustrated: "To the extent that actual, historical vacancies in the employer's workforce can be *flowcharted* with reasonable accuracy, the court should award back pay to the minority employees who . . . would have occupied those vacancies but for discrimination." *U.S. v. U.S. Steel Corp.*, 520 F.2d 1043, 1055 (5th Cir. 1975).

flowed; flown. These words, surprisingly, are frequently confused. *Flowed* is the past tense and past participle of *flow*. *Flown* is the past participle of *fly*. See **overfly.**

flow from. In legal writing, few things *derive from, result from,* or are *caused by* other things; effects always seem to *flow from* causes. This is one of our most overworked legal CLICHÉS. E.g.:

- "Our analysis necessarily *flows from Strickland v. Washington*." *Celestine v. Blackburn*, 750 F.2d 353, 356 (5th Cir. 1984).
- "We also conclude, however, that any fraud by QHL upon McKenzie conferred on Borg-Warner no rights in addition to those *flowing from* its status as a holder of an unperfected security interest." *In re Quality Holstein Leasing*, 752 F.2d 1009, 1015 (5th Cir. 1985).
- "The policy in *Tradesoft* also contained a breach-of-contract exclusion, and the injury there undoubtedly *flowed from* the contractual relationship between the parties." *Houbigant, Inc. v. Fed. Ins. Co.*, 374 F.3d 192, 202–03 (3d Cir. 2004).
- "Substantial rewards often *flow from* unlawful acts, thus providing a powerful incentive which is immediate and certain." Michael Meurer, *Law, Economics, and the Theory of the Firm*, 52 Buff. L. Rev. 727, 746 (2004).

A related locution is *follow from*—e.g.:

- "[The complaint] also states that Swift was substantially certain that Trupiano's injuries would *follow from* its intentional acts." *Trupiano v. Swift & Co.*, 755 F.2d 442, 443 (5th Cir. 1985).
- "From a Kantian perspective, the justification principle *follows from* the notion that people are to be regarded as ends in themselves, not as means to satisfaction of one's own objectives or preferences." Jeffrey R. Seul, *Settling Significant Cases*, 79 Wash. L. Rev. 881, 957 (2004).

flown. See **flowed.**

flycatcher. See LAWYERS, DEROGATORY NAMES FOR (A).

fly in the face of is a legal CLICHÉ. E.g.:

- "In addition to *flying in the face of* the actual language of the [act], the lead opinion's view is contrary to this Court's existing . . . jurisprudence." *Commonwealth v. Santiago,* 855 A.2d 682, 706 (Pa. 2004) (Castille, J., concurring).
- "As the maintenance of two separate actions relating to the same event *flies in the face of* judicial economy, the Court notes that it appears Plaintiff's claims may be pursued in a single action." *Dehaemers v. Wynne,* 522 F.Supp.2d 240, 249 (D.D.C. 2007).

Fly in the teeth of is an inexcusable rendering of the cliché—e.g.: "Neither court is required to accept, as credible, unsupported self-serving testimony that *flies in the teeth of* [read *flies in the face of*] unimpeachable contradictory evidence and universal experience." *New England Merchants Nat'l Bank v. Rosenfield,* 679 F.2d 467, 473 (5th Cir. 1982). Cf. **face of, in the.**

F.O.B.; F.A.S.; C.I.F. These mercantile abbreviations—short for *free on board, free alongside,* and *cost, insurance, and freight*—denote types of contracts for the international sale of goods, and now also sales involving domestic transportation. With an *F.O.B.* contract, the seller's duty is fulfilled by placing the goods aboard the carrier. (Though some writers make the letters lowercase (*f.o.b.*), the capitalized form predominates.) Domestically, the use of *F.O.B.* [*destination*] indicates that freight charges have been paid to transport the goods as far as the named destination, whatever it may be (e.g., seller's plant or buyer's dock).

The term *F.A.S.* is nearly synonymous with *F.O.B.* in the context of contracts of water carriage. The phrasing is commonly *F.A.S. vessel* at a named port. But *F.A.S. vessel* differs from *F.O.B. vessel* in a significant way: "In the former case seller delivers at the wharf but is under no duty to see the loading: a 'received for shipment' bill of lading would be an appropriate document for him to tender. *F.O.B. vessel,* however, requires seller to bear the risk until the loading has been completed; only an 'on board' bill of lading would evidence the completion of his duties." Grant Gilmore & Charles L. Black Jr., *The Law of Admiralty* 106 (2d ed. 1975).

With a *C.I.F.* contract, the seller agrees not only to supply the goods but also to make a contract of carriage with a sea carrier (under which the goods will be delivered at the contract port of destination), to pay the freight, and to insure the goods while they are in transit.

focus, n. Pl. *focuses* or *foci* /**foh**-sɪ/. The plural *foci* may strike readers as pretentious in ordinary prose—e.g.: "The litany of examples reveals a conception of social sharing that differs from the current *foci* [read, perhaps, *focuses*] of the literature along four different dimensions." Yochai Benkler, *Sharing Nicely: On Shareable Goods and the Emergence of Sharing as a Modality of Economic Production,* 114 Yale L.J. 273, 338 (2004).

fogger. See LAWYERS, DEROGATORY NAMES FOR (A).

foia, vb.**; foiable.** In the slang of administrative lawyers, *foiable* documents are subject to disclosure under the Freedom of Information Act (FOIA), and citizens may *foia* (= seek to obtain) them under that Act. Common in oral use, there is little written evidence of these terms. Although the federal statute was passed in 1966, the term *foiable* was not recorded until 2001.

foist (= to falsely present [something] as genuine or superior) takes the preposition *on.* E.g.: "We each have an immunity against others annulling our claims over our property or others *foisting* new claims *upon* [read *on*] us." Leif Wenar, *The Concept of Property and the Takings Clause,* 97 Colum. L. Rev. 1923, 1939 (1997). See **upon.**

When the phrasing is as unidiomatic as **is foisted with,* a different verb is in order—e.g.: "An employer *is foisted with* [read *bears the*] responsibility to a third party if his employee commits a tort in the course of his employment." Stanley Berwin, *Pocket Lawyer* 231 (1986).

*Foist off on is awkward and prolix—e.g.: "In short, the City created a wetlands preserve on Beachwood and then *foisted* the problem *off on* [read *on*] Yamagiwa." *Yamagiwa v. City of Half Moon Bay,* 523 F.Supp.2d 1036, 1101 (N.D. Cal. 2007). The *OED* quotes Charlotte Brontë as having written *foist off on* but labels the phrase "rare."

folderol; *falderol. The first is the preferred spelling for this word, which means either "nonsense" or "a useless trifle."

follow; apply. In the best usage, these terms are distinguishable in describing a court's actions. A court is said to *follow* a precedent when it rules that the precedent bears on and affects the decision on an important point in a pending dispute. Typically, this verb suggests that the court has discretion to choose between two or more lines of authority, or holds the precedent to be persuasive rather than binding. *Apply,* by contrast, usually suggests that a precedent unambiguously binds the decision-maker, so that the decision is more mechanical and less discretionary. Loosely, however, the two verbs are used interchangeably.

follow from. See **flow from.**

following (= after), when used to begin a sentence or clause, often results in a MISPLACED MODIFIER and a MISCUE—e.g.:

- "*Following* [read *After*] a bench trial, the district court voided portions of the plaintiff's settlement agreement." *Bass v. Phoenix Seadrill/78, Ltd.,* 749 F.2d 1154, 1156 (5th Cir. 1985).

- *"Following* [read *After*] a bench trial, the district court found appellant guilty of both counts in March 2003." *State v. Brooks*, 690 N.W.2d 160, 162 (Minn. Ct. App. 2004).

The problem, of course, is that the reader might expect *following* to function as a participle, as here: "*Following* the precedents above, GreenSky's payments and telephone communication alone are insufficient to hale GreenSky into court in North Carolina." *Rossetto USA, Inc. v. GreenSky Fin., LLC*, 662 S.E.2d 909, 916 (N.C. Ct. App. 2008).

foment is incorrect as a noun for *fomentation*—e.g.: "Commanders are not promoted for running a base in a state of debate and *foment* [read *fomentation*]." E. Thomas Moroney, *Military Dissent and the Law of the War: Uneasy Bedfellows*, 58 S. Cal. L. Rev. 871, 889 (1985). It seems likely, however, that the writer confused *ferment* (= agitation) with *foment* (= to incite or rouse).

*****food fare.** See **fare,** n.

fool for a client. From the early 19th century, it has been commonly said: "A man who is his own lawyer has a fool for a client." The earliest recorded variant dates from 1809: "He who is always his own counsellor will often have a fool for his client." *Port Folio* (Philadelphia), Aug. 1809, at 132.

Many occurrences are allusive only. For example, in 1887, when the Alabama Bar Association considered a code of conduct for its members, one suggested provision would have prevented lawyers from conducting their own cases. But that was deleted on constitutional grounds, the proponent of the change saying, "It is one of the American privileges to make a fool of yourself, and it is guaranteed by the Constitution, and I do not see anything wrong with it." Quoted in Walter P. Armstrong Jr., *A Century of Legal Ethics*, 64 A.B.A. J. 1063, 1064 (1978).

Today, the quip is common in AmE and BrE alike—common enough, perhaps, to be a CLICHÉ that fresh writers would prefer to frame anew: "A lawyer never appears to worse advantage than when pleading his own cause." Lon L. Fuller, *The Morality of Law* 188 (1969).

Like many other quotations and SET PHRASES, this one sometimes gets mangled, usually when the writer substitutes *attorney* for *client* as the final word—e.g.:

- "You know, the old expression, someone who represents himself has a *fool for an attorney.*" *U.S. v. Hoffer*, 423 F.Supp. 811, 814 (S.D.N.Y. 1976).
- "The old saying that the person who fights his own case has a *fool for an attorney* may have been invented by lawyers, but there is a lot of truth in it." *Be Careful How You Say "I Quit"*, Sunday Times, 26 Nov. 1989, at E20.
- "Sure, you may be a fool for representing yourself in court but these days—with Yellow-Page lawyers, TV judges, and third-tier law schools that teach Billable Hours 101—you may get a *fool for an attorney*, anyway." Joe Sciacca, *Self-Help Clinic Targets Amateur "Lawyers"*, Boston Herald, 28 Aug. 2000, at 4.

Although, logically speaking, the two formulations add up to the same thing, the original formulation is far wittier because of the ironic turn at the end (shifting from lawyer to client as if they were two persons).

footnote; endnote. Technically, *footnotes* appear at the foot of the page, and *endnotes* at the end of an article or chapter or at the end of a book. But *endnotes* are often called *footnotes*.

FOOTNOTES. A. Textual Footnotes. In modern legal writing, textual footnotes are mostly a scourge. As a writer, you might advantageously learn to detest them.

The thoroughly sensible policy of *The Scribes Journal of Legal Writing*, as stated inside the front cover, merits wide adherence: "We discourage footnotes that contain substantive discussion; footnotes used to cite pertinent materials are fully acceptable."

B. For Citations. In most types of legal writing, footnotes are a splendid place for citations, especially if the citations are followed by brief explanatory parentheticals. See CITATION OF CASES (D).

FOR-; FORE-. These prefixes, it will be observed in many of the entries following, have caused a great deal of confusion. One can usually arrive at the correct prefix for any given word by remembering that *for-* means either "completely" or "against," and that *fore-* means "before." See **forbear** & **forego.**

The two are confused here: "The traditional English approach rests on three doctrines—*unforseen* [read *unforeseen*] mode, mistaken object, and transferred fault." Andrew Ashworth, *Principles of Criminal Law* 174 (1991).

for. See **as** (A).

*****fora.** See **forum.**

for all intents and purposes; to all intents and purposes; *****for all intensive purposes. These synonymous phrases both mean "for practical purposes." They are about equally common—e.g.:

- "On these facts the Seventh Circuit held that the district court erred in referring the case to a magistrate without the consent of the parties because the hearing before the magistrate was, *for all intents and purposes*, a civil trial." *Orpiano v. Johnson*, 687 F.2d 44, 46 (4th Cir. 1982).
- "Here, however, the district court forsook a circumscribed inquiry and, *to all intents and purposes*, fashioned a new and expanded record relative to the petitioner's state court motion for a new trial." *Pike v. Guarino*, 492 F.3d 61, 70 (1st Cir. 2007).

Often this collocation qualifies as a FLOTSAM PHRASE.

Because some people mishear the phrase, the erroneous form *****for all intensive purposes* has arisen—e.g.:

- "It is the Court's opinion that the marriage, *for all intensive purposes* [read *for all intents and purposes*], had ended." *Martin v. Martin*, 820 A.2d 410, 452 (Del. Fam. Ct. 2002).
- "*For all intensive purposes* [read *For all intents and purposes*], the Bareboat Charter Agreement is nothing more than a lease agreement." *Metlife Capital Corp.*

v. Westchester Fire Ins. Co., 224 F.Supp.2d 374, 380 n.5 (D.P.R. 2002).

- "Generally, exhibits attached to a pleading are treated as part of the pleading *for all intensive purposes* [read *for all intents and purposes*]." *Barry Aviation, Inc. v. Land O'Lakes Mun. Airport Comm'n*, 366 F.Supp.2d 792, 796 (W.D. Wis. 2005).

forbade. See **forbid.**

forbear, vb.; **forebear,** n. Though unrelated, these words are confused in every conceivable way. *Forebear*, always a noun, means "ancestor" (usually used in the plural). *Forbear* is the verb meaning "to refrain from objecting to; to tolerate." The verb is inflected *forbear > forbore > forborne*. E.g.: "In general, *forbearing* to bring suit on a potentially stale claim can be consideration to support a contract. More specifically, Unocal actually *forbore* exercising a valid legal option: filing a non-frivolous lawsuit." *Union Oil Co. v. Terrible Herbst, Inc.*, 331 F.3d 735, 742 (9th Cir. 2003).

Forebear, always a noun, means "ancestor" (usually used in the plural). **Forebearer* is an incorrect form of this noun. *Forbear* is occasionally misused for *forebear*:

- "D refused to vacate rooms belonging to the Government which he and his *forbears* [read *forebears*] had occupied for seventy years." Glanville Williams, *Criminal Law* 42 (2d ed. 1961).
- "Our *forbears* [read *forebears*] rejected the closed societies of their birth to come to a land where the boundaries of possible achievement were as expansive as the content of their characters." Anne K. Bingaman, *The Importance of Antitrust in Health Care*, 1995 Utah L. Rev. 373, 374 (1995).

The opposite error, though less common, also occurs (quite ironically, in the second sentence):

- "A promise to *forebear* [read *forbear*], even where a promise is implicit, may be sufficient consideration." L.B. Curzon, *English Legal History* 295 (2d ed. 1979).
- "It is tempting, but I *forebear* [read *forbear*] to comment on Vickers' own English lest someone else go on to find the faults in mine." Letter from H. Young, City Voice [Wellington, N.Z.], 23 Sept. 1993, at 18.

*Forebearance is a nonword, the correct term being *forbearance*—e.g.: "It appears to be settled law that the *forebearance* [read *forbearance*] of some of the salvors to press their claims, whatever the reason for their *forebearance* [read *forbearance*], does not result in a windfall recovery for those who do claim." Grant Gilmore & Charles L. Black Jr., *The Law of Admiralty* 570 (2d ed. 1975).

For the difference between *forbearance* and *omission*, see **omission (B).**

forbid > forbade > forbidden. *Forbid* most traditionally takes the preposition *to* or, less formally, *from*. H.W. Fowler stated that *forbid from doing* is unidiomatic, but it is increasingly common in AmE—e.g.: "[Locke] sharply distinguished the respective spheres

of Church and State and *forbade* each *from meddling* in the other." Clifford Orwin, *Civility*, 60 Am. Scholar 553, 557 (1991).

Even so, *forbid to* remains preferable in formal contexts—e.g.: "Quia Emptores . . . did not *forbid* a tenant in fee simple *to* grant estates smaller than the fee simple absolute." Thomas F. Bergin & Paul G. Haskell, *Preface to Estates in Land and Future Interests* 27 (2d ed. 1984).

The past tense is *forbade* (rhyming with *glad*)—e.g.: "But its governmental superiors *forbade* trash haulers to deal with any other processors." *Department of Revenue v. Davis*, 553 U.S. 328, 346 (2008) (per Souter, J.). *Forbid* is sometimes wrongly used as a past-tense form: "Paul testified she did not think the order *forbid* [read *forbade*] her from trying to make such contacts with her children." *Paul v. Johnson*, 604 So.2d 883, 884 (Fla. Dist. Ct. App. 1992).

Some writers—no doubt those who pronounce *forbade* correctly—mistakenly spell the word **forbad*. E.g.: "Prouty had been found guilty of contempt for violating a decree of divorce against him which *forbad* [read *forbade*] either party to marry again within the time prohibited by the Illinois statute." William F. Walsh, *A Treatise on Equity* 201 (1930). The verb follows its shorter sibling: *bid > bade* /bad/ *> bidden*.

forbidden parts is a EUPHEMISM that is generally too vague to be helpful. But some criminal-law writers have found justifiable uses for the phrase when referring to various jurisdictions in which different bodily parts might be forbidden—e.g.: "The general holding is that the crime [i.e., sodomy] is completed by any penetration into *forbidden parts*." Rollin M. Perkins & Ronald N. Boyce, *Criminal Law* 466–67 (3d ed. 1982).

FORBIDDEN WORDS AND PHRASES. Blanket prohibitions are rarely valid, but they are useful in establishing rules to be flouted only in the rarest instances. It would hardly be an exaggeration to say that no sentence, and no document, would suffer from the absence of the following terms. As one court said, in a different context: "They spell wasted time, trouble for everyone and the delay of justice. Do not use them." *People v. Wright*, 289 N.W.2d 1, 20 (Mich. 1980).

A. Generally Useless Words and Phrases. Each of the following terms is discussed in a separate entry:

   ad idem
   *aforementioned
   *and/or
   *anent
   comes now
   herein
   hereinabove
   hereinafter
   hopefully
   instanter

interface
inter se
*irregardless
know all men by these presents
now comes
ore tenus
parameters
provided that
*pursuant to
quoad
said (for *the*, etc.)
same, n. (for *it*, etc.)
simpliciter
ss.
such (for *the, that*, etc.)
to wit
understood and agreed
vel non
*wheresoever
whosoever
-wise (*taxwise*, etc.)
witnesseth

B. Ignorant Malformations. Some terms have misbegotten by-forms—e.g.:

corpus delecti for *corpus delicti*
idealogy for ideology
miniscule for minuscule

forbore; forborne. See **forbear.**

forceable. See **forcible.**

force and arms, with, is a LOAN TRANSLATION of *vi et armis.* See **trespass** & *vi et armis.*

force and effect is a doublet that has become part of the legal idiom in the phrases *in full force and effect* and *of no force or effect,* neither of which is a TERM OF ART. Either synonym would suffice just as well as the doublet; but the emphasis gained by *force and effect* may justify use of the phrase, more likely in drafting (contracts and statutes) than in judicial opinions. See DOUBLETS, TRIPLETS, AND SYNONYM-STRINGS & OPINIONS, JUDICIAL.

forced portion. See **legitim.**

forceful. See **forcible.**

force majeure; *vis major*; act of God; *damnum fatale.* These phrases, synonymous for all practical purposes, signify "a superior force" (the literal translation of the first two) and denote an event or effect that can be neither anticipated nor controlled. *Force majeure* is the usual form of this LEGALISM; *vis major* is its Latin equivalent. *Act of God* is a common English phrase. These first three phrases are all used in legal writing, the first two appearing almost exclusively there. All have undergone HYPALLAGE, so that the reference is now usually to the destruction caused by forces of nature, rather than to the forces of nature themselves. Also, the phrases refer to an "inevitable" accident— not necessarily just those caused by nature but also

those that occur despite all reasonable precautions. *Damnum fatale* is the Scottish equivalent.

Though *act of God* is the most universal of these terms, it is the least desirable because it so easily misleads:

> As a technical term, *act of God* is untheological and infelicitous. It is an operation of "natural forces" and this is apt to be confusing in that it might imply positive intervention of the Deity. This (at any rate a common understanding) is apparent in exceptionally severe snowfalls, thunderstorms and gales. But a layman would hardly describe the gnawing of a rat as an act of God, and yet the lawyer may, in some circumstances, style it such. The fact is that in law the essence of an act of God is not so much a positive intervention of the Deity as a process of nature not due to the act of man, and it is this negative side [that] needs emphasis.
> T.E. Lewis, *Winfield on Tort* 55–56 (6th ed. 1954).

forcible; forceable; forceful. Oddly, we have *forcible* but *enforceable*. *Forcible,* the usual and preferred term, means "obtaining something by physical strength or a display of violence." E.g.:

- "In an action for *forcible* abduction of children, the father is entitled to damages for the injury done to his feelings." *Stowe v. Heywood,* 7 Allen 118, 123 (Mass. 1863).
- "Piracy, by the law of nations, is any robbery or *forcible* depredation on the high seas without lawful authority." *State v. Hogan,* 58 N.E. 572, 574 (Ohio 1900).

Properly referring only to physical force, *forcible* has frequently been misused for *forceful,* which may be used figuratively as well as literally—e.g.:

- "[T]he Supreme Court of the United States, passing upon the meaning of that provision, has made this *forcible* [read *forceful*] declaration . . . ." *State v. Hester,* 134 S.E. 885, 899 (S.C. 1926).
- "The trial court was also well within its discretion in rejecting the wife's claim that the husband had secret cash stashes as such allegations were unproved; moreover, we are not persuaded by the wife's *forcible* [read *forceful*] argument to the contrary on appeal." *Krystel v. Krystel,* 534 So.2d 914, 914 (Fla. Ct. App. 1988).
- "The active voice is usually more direct and vigorous than the passive. . . . The habitual use of the active voice . . . makes for *forcible* [read *forceful*] writing." William Strunk Jr. & E.B. White, *The Elements of Style* 18 (4th ed. 2000).

The spelling *forceable* at one point seemed entrenched in the phrase *forceable entry and detainer* in Texas, although the Texas Rules have now changed to the spelling *forcible*. *Forceable* frequently appears where *forcible* should—e.g.:

- "The condemned are not [unduly] rushed and are not *forceably* [read *forcibly*] thrust into the chair, except as a last means." Aubrey Holmes, *The Wake of a Lawyer* 54 (1960).
- "The record reflects that defendant physically assaulted a 65-year-old woman at her place of employment, *forceably* [read *forcibly*] taking her money and her vehicle in the process." *People v. Gorrell,* 882 N.Y.S.2d 324, 325 (App. Div. 2009).

Cf. **enforceable.**

forcible detainer; forcible entry; forcible entry and detainer. *Forcible detainer* is the wrongful retention of property by one originally in lawful possession. *Forcible entry* = (1) the act of violently and unlawfully taking possession of land or a tenement against the will of the lawful possessor; or (2) the act of entering land in another's possession by using force against another or by breaking into the premises. *Forcible entry and detainer* is (1) the act of violently taking and keeping possession of lands and tenements without legal authority; or (2) a quick and simple legal proceeding for regaining possession of real property from someone who has wrongfully taken possession, or refused to surrender possession. Of sense 2, a classic authority states that "forcible entry and detainer is essentially an action given to protect actual occupation of real estate against unlawful and forcible invasion, to remove occasion for acts of violence in defending such possession, and to punish a breach of the peace committed in the entry upon or the detainer of real property." William B. Cunningham, *A Treatise on the Law of Forcible Entry and Detainer* 62 (2d ed. 1895). The crucial word is *detainer*, which in law has traditionally denoted "the action of detaining, withholding, or keeping something in one's custody." *Black's Law Dictionary* 513 (9th ed. 2009).

Sometimes the full phrase denoting the lawsuit is shortened to either *forcible entry* (which omits the crucial word and thereby creates an AMBIGUITY) or *forcible detainer*—e.g.:

- "On May 8, 2008, after a hearing, the district court granted Rayls' petition for *forcible entry* [read *forcible entry and detainer*] and directed the clerk to issue a writ of possession requiring Parise to vacate the house." *Rayl v. Parise*, 766 N.W.2d 648, 650 (Iowa Ct. App. 2009).
- "In an action for *forcible detainer* [read *forcible entry and detainer*], Countrywide need only show sufficient evidence of ownership to demonstrate a superior right to immediate possession of the premises." *McGillivray v. Countrywide Home Loans, Inc.*, 360 Fed. Appx. 533, 536 (5th Cir. 2010).

FORE-. See FOR-.

forebear; *forebearance. See **forbear.**

forecast forms the past tense *forecast*, not **forecasted*—e.g.: "It can be shaped to meet real problems that have arisen and not possible problems *forecasted* [read *forecast*]." Patrick Devlin, *The Judge* 182 (1979).

foreclose (a person) *from* (an action) is an archaic construction still used in the law—e.g.: "The State nevertheless maintains that its rule would not *foreclose* prisoners *from* raising *Ford* claims." *Panetti v. Quarterman*, 551 U.S. 930, 943 (2007) (per Kennedy, J.). Today *foreclose* most commonly takes as an object one or more possibilities or choices <his failure of the exam forecloses the possibility of a promotion>. **Forclose* is an erroneous spelling—e.g.:

- "Re-entry will be *forclosed* [read *foreclosed*] because pharmacies will be reluctant to re-stock their shelves with Sandoz's product once consumers begin to identify and

consume other generic products." *Abbott Labs. v. Sandoz, Inc.*, 500 F.Supp.2d 846, 853 (N.D. Ill. 2007).

- "The Court finds that remanding plaintiff's federal claims will not *forclose* [read *foreclose*] defendants' right to federal court adjudication of those claims if defendants make the necessary England reservation on the state court record." *VH Prop. Corp. v. City of Rancho Palos Verdes*, 622 F.Supp.2d 958, 968 (C.D. Cal. 2009).

In the context of a real-estate foreclosure, the idiom requires that you *foreclose* a lien or mortgage (transitive verb) but *foreclose on* a property or on a borrower (intransitive verb)—e.g.:

- "He proposes to *foreclose* the second mortgage." *Swain v. Seamens*, 76 U.S. 254, 273 (1869) (per Clifford, J.).
- "On the following April 10 the Bank instituted an action to *foreclose* its mortgage." Grant Gilmore & Charles L. Black Jr., *The Law of Admiralty* 953 (2d ed. 1975).
- "She was not aware that her marital home had been sold until then; she thought the mortgage company had *foreclosed on* the property." *Arthur v. District of Columbia*, 857 A.2d 473, 482–83 (D.C. 2004).

foregather. See **forgather.**

forego; forgo. The first, as suggested by the prefix, means "to go before." The second is the term meaning "to do without; to pass up voluntarily; waive; renounce." One of the most persistent errors in legal and other writing is the use of *forego* where *forgo* is intended. One court has actually construed *forego* as meaning "voluntarily relinquishing," misspelling the very word it was interpreting. See *O'Neill v. Keegan*, 103 A.2d 909, 911 (Pa. 1954).

Examples of the misuse are legion—e.g.:

- "The public finds it hard to *forego* [read *forgo*] its belief that the law should be so certain that an unequivocal answer could be given in every case." Max Radin, *The Law and You* 13 (1948).
- "The promise of one creditor is regarded as sufficient consideration for the promise of another creditor to *forego* [read *forgo*] part of his claim." James A. MacLachlan, *Handbook of the Law of Bankruptcy* 4 (1956).
- "Must such a one *forego* [read *forgo*] the profit of this transaction at the risk of being held a party to the crime if the surmise proves correct?" Rollin M. Perkins & Ronald N. Boyce, *Criminal Law* 745–46 (3d ed. 1982).

The opposite mistake—misusing *forgo* for *forego*—is less common: "Based on the *forgoing* [read *foregoing*] authorities, we hold that the allegations . . . state a cause of action." *Garrido v. Burger King Corp.*, 558 So.2d 79, 83 (Fla. Dist. Ct. App. 1990).

Forwent and *forewent* are the past-tense forms, and *forgone* and *foregone* the past-participial forms. (See **foregone.**) The past participle *forgone* is more frequent in practice than *forwent*; yet, because legal writing is usually formal in tone, *forwent* is not as uncommon as in general practice. E.g.:

- "He alleged that he *forewent* [read *forwent*] a revocation hearing because of his counsel's ineffectiveness." *Gilbert v. State*, 913 So.2d 84, 86 (Fla. Dist. Ct. App. 2005).

- "Plaintiff's attorneys *forwent* other paying work and paid costs out of pocket, thereby incurring expenses in contesting removal." *Simenz v. Amerihome Mortg. Co.*, 544 F.Supp.2d 743, 746 (E.D. Wis. 2008).

See **foregone.**

foregoing is occasionally mistaken for *following.* "Although the *foregoing quote* [read *following quotation*] is a long one, it succinctly states the entire problem with this regulation: [a long quotation follows, and none precedes this statement]." (Note also the unconscious irony in a *long* quotation that *succinctly* states a proposition!)

foregone is correct in *foregone conclusion* (i.e., a foreordained conclusion), but not when the sense is "passed over" or "done without," as the past participle of *forgo*—e.g.: "He based that part of his holding on the thought that the Aldecoa had '*foregone* [read *forgone*] an opportunity' to engage in the profitable work of property salvage." Grant Gilmore & Charles L. Black Jr., *The Law of Admiralty* 573 (2d ed. 1975). See **forego.**

forehead. The traditional pronunciation of this word rhymes with *horrid.* But in AmE, the word is commonly (and acceptably) pronounced /**for**-hed/.

foreign. In law, this word means "of another jurisdiction," not necessarily "of another country." It is not uncommon for a court in Florida, say, to refer to a judgment of a New Mexico court as a *foreign judgment.* Exceptions occur, however, so one must read carefully. Here *foreign* occurs in the nonlawyer's sense: "The monastery concludes that when the judgment is from a *foreign* country, such a guarantee is not present, and thus New Mexico law should apply to determine if the *foreign* court had personal jurisdiction." *Monks Own, Ltd. v. Monastery of Christ in Desert*, 168 P.3d 121, 125 (N.M. 2007).

forejudge is an archaic equivalent of *prejudge* for which the *OED* includes only one citation more recent than the 18th century, and that from 1860. Perhaps the most notable use of the term was in the Mutiny Act of 1689, 1 Wm. & Mary, ch. 5: "No man may be *forejudged* of Life or Limb, or subjected to any kind of Punishment by Martial Law, or in any other manner than by the Judgment of his Peers, and according to the known and established Laws of this Realm." In modern contexts, however, the word is a fusty ARCHAISM—e.g.: "We do not mean to *forejudge* [read *prejudge*] the substantial and novel question involving disputed evidence of motivation and causation . . . ." *Automatic Radio Mfg. Co. v. Ford Motor Co.*, 390 F.2d 113, 117 (1st Cir. 1968).

foreman; foreperson; presiding juror. The best nonsexist choice is *presiding juror.* Unfortunately, *foreperson* has crept into official court rules. See Fed. R. Crim. P. 6(c). See SEXISM (B).

It is mildly surprising to see *foreman* and *foreperson* used for purposes of INELEGANT VARIATION: "And since the *foreperson* is the single most influential person on a jury, lawyers will do anything to keep good *foreman* material off." Robin T. Lakoff, *Talking Power: The Politics of Language in Our Lives* 114–15 (1990).

forename. See **surname.**

forensic = used in or suitable to courts of law or public debate. E.g.:

- "We need to make explicit the principles that are tacitly presupposed in those everyday patterns of reasoning that are appropriate for deciding issues of fact under the particular constraints that the *forensic* situation imposes." L. Jonathan Cohen, *The Role of Evidential Weight in Criminal Proof*, 66 B.U. L. Rev. 635, 635–36 (1986).
- "The social worker denied having a *forensic* purpose or a law-enforcement purpose in conducting the interviews, but admitted to seeking to determine whether abuse had taken place." *State v. Wyble*, 211 S.W.3d 125, 128 (Mo. Ct. App. 2007).

Other senses have grown out of the primary one. For example, the adjective *forensic* has come to mean "rhetorical" or "argumentative" in certain contexts, the language or manner to which it refers being analogized to courtroom talk. Traditionally *forensics* = the art of argumentative discourse.

Today *forensics*, as a shortening of *forensic ballistics*, is used by police officers to refer to the section of law enforcement dealing with legal evidence relating to firearms. So the phrase *forensic evidence* has cropped up—a phrase understandably deplored by traditionalists but likely to become permanently ensconced in the language. It is especially common in BrE—e.g.:

- "*Forensic evidence* also showed Scottish detectives the bomb was in a brown Samsonite suitcase, similar to one belonging to Khreesat." David Black & Harvey Morris, *Investigators Followed False Trail to Palestinian Cell*, The Independent, 14 Dec. 1990, at 3.
- "Defence lawyers are seeking more details of *forensic evidence* that has lain hidden from them for 16 years." Stewart Tendler, *Six Decide Against Bail Plea*, The Times (London), 19 Dec. 1990, at 3.

foreperson. See **foreman** & SEXISM (B).

foresaid. See **aforesaid.*

*foresake. See **forsake.**

foresee. See FOR- & **anticipate.**

foreseeable is occasionally misspelled **forseeable.* See FOR-.

*foreswear. See **forswear.**

foreword; preface. The word *foreword* denotes a book preface written by someone other than the author. It is often mistaken with its homophone, *forward*—e.g.: "Nathan S. Hefferman, Chief Justice of the Wisconsin Supreme Court, embellishes this concept in his *forward* [read *foreword*] to the book by reducing the title *Modern Appellate Practice* to an acronym." Robert L. Black Jr., Book Rev., 53 U. Cin. L. Rev. 171, 174 (1984).

The word *preface*, by contrast, usually refers to an introductory essay written by the author.

forfeit > forfeited > forfeited. Using *forfeit* as a past participle is an ARCHAISM in AmE and, as the *OED* suggests, in BrE as well—e.g.: "The Cinque Ports alone at this time had a general rule that bailed goods are not *forfeit* [read *forfeited*] by the felony of the bailee." Theodore F.T. Plucknett, *A Concise History of the Common Law* 474 (5th ed. 1956).

The adjectival use—which in some sentences is hardly distinguishable from the past-participial use—is still current in literary BrE. E.g.: "If a man were killed by an animal or thing, it was *forfeit* to the king, who usually sold it and paid the proceeds to the next-of-kin." Glanville Williams, *Textbook of Criminal Law* 29 n.2 (1978).

forfeiture is naturally pronounced /**for**-fi-chər/; pompous speakers are fond of pronouncing the final syllable /tyoor/. See **equity abhors a forfeiture.**

forfend, in all but the literary (and precious) exclamation *Heaven forfend!*, is an ARCHAISM better replaced by *prevent*—e.g.: "To that end it imposes on the homeowner a liability to respond in damages for any injury received because his sidewalks are left in an icy condition—a liability [that] he can, of course, *forfend* [read *prevent*] by scraping the ice off or sprinkling it with sand or ashes." Lon L. Fuller, *Anatomy of the Law* 64 (1968).

forgather; foregather. The first is preferable, so far as either might be said to be "preferable." *Gather* usually suffices.

forgery = (1) a false document, or false part of a document, that someone has tried to make look genuine; or (2) the act of making a false document so that it may be used as if it were genuine. In sense 1, the thing forged must be a document: imitating a sculpture, even with fraudulent intent, is not forgery. And in both senses, the phrase *false document* does not mean a document that tells a lie; it means a document that *is* a lie. See **counterfeiting.**

forgive. See **condone.**

forgo. See **forego.**

form, legal. See **precedent (E).**

formal contract; informal contract. Virtually every legal system has two ways in which promises may become binding as contracts. One is by giving the transaction a certain form in writing (i.e., making a *formal contract*); the other is by complying with the requisites of the transaction in some way other than satisfying requisites of form (i.e., making an *informal contract*). *Formal contracts* were traditionally made under seal; the only test for an *informal contract* is whether it contains the element of "valuable consideration." See **informal contract.**

formalism; formality; formalistic. These words are quite distinct. *Formality* denotes conformity to rules, propriety, or precision of manners. *Formalism*, by contrast, is invariably a pejorative term, meaning "excessive adherence to prescribed forms; use of forms without regard to substantive import." Examples of the rigid, inflexible *formalism* that once characterized English law are legion: "The omission of a single downstroke or contraction sign, or an error of Latin accidence, were fatal mistakes in a writ." J.H. Baker, *An Introduction to English Legal History* 103 (3d ed. 1990).

The corresponding adjective—*formalistic*—is perhaps even more pejorative than *formalism*—e.g.:

- "The distinction between aggravating and mitigating facts has been criticized as *formalistic.*" *McMillan v. Pennsylvania*, 477 U.S. 79, 100 (1986) (Stevens, J., dissenting).
- "The dissenting judge rejected the majority's '*formalistic*, technical and unrealistic application of *Miranda*.'" *Duckworth v. Eagan*, 492 U.S. 195, 200 (1989) (per Rehnquist, C.J.).
- "The Government seizes upon this language as proof positive that the *Eisentrager* Court adopted a *formalistic*, sovereignty-based test for determining the reach of the Suspension Clause." *Boumediene v. Bush*, 553 U.S. 723, 762 (2008) (per Kennedy, J.).

Cf. **legalistic.** See **formulaic.**

FORMAL WORDS are those occupying an elevated level of diction. The English language has several levels of diction, and even synonyms that exist on the different levels: *his honor* is formal, *the judge* is the ordinary phrase, and *the beak* (BrE slang) is vulgar.

The language of the law is perhaps top-heavy with formal words, as the courts are one of the institutions in Western societies that are most fully bedecked with pomp and regalia. Legal language reflects that formality, often quite appropriately. But many lawyers (and especially nonlawyers talking to lawyers, it seems) go overboard, resorting to unnatural pomposities (e.g., *this honorable court* used repeatedly) where ordinary words are called for (e.g., *the court*).

Early in the 19th century, the novelist James Fenimore Cooper worried that "the love of turgid expressions is gaining ground, and ought to be corrected." "On Language," in *The American Democrat* 117 (1838) (repr. in *A Language for Writers* 110, 113 (James R. Gaskin & Jack Suberman eds., 1966)). For stylists, that worry is perpetual, as each generation becomes enamored of its own brands of linguistic inflation: doublespeak, gobbledygook, legaldegook, officialese, and the like. The phrase *formal words* is virtually a EUPHEMISM for those stylistic disturbances. In the left-hand column are some of the chief symptoms:

Formal Word	Ordinary Word
annex	attach
announce	give out
append	attach
approximately	about
assign	give
cease	stop
commence	begin
complete	finish
conceal	hide
deem	consider
demise	death
desist	stop, leave off
detain	hold
determine	end
donate	give
effectuate	carry out
emoluments	pay
employ	use
endeavor	try
evince	show
expedite	hasten
expend	spend
expiration, expiry	end
extend	give
forthwith	immediately, soon
imbibe	drink
inaugurate	begin
indicate	state, show, say
initiate	begin
inquire	ask
institute	begin
interrogate	question
intimate	suggest
necessitate	require
occasion, vb.	cause
peruse	read
portion	part
possess	have
present	give
preserve	keep
prior	earlier
proceed	go (ahead)
purchase	buy
remainder	rest
remove	take away
request	ask
retain	keep
suborn	bribe (a juror or witness)
summon	send for, call
terminate	end
utilize	use

forma pauperis. See **in forma pauperis**.

format, vb., makes *formatted*, *formatting*. See DOUBLING OF FINAL CONSONANTS.

formation. See **formulation**.

formbook. One word.

former and *latter* can apply only to a series of two. The *former* is the first of two, the *latter* the second of two. In contexts in which more than two elements occur, *first* should be used rather than *former*, *last* or *last-mentioned* rather than *latter*. E.g.: "Cities Service sued Lee-Vac and American Hoist. The *latter* [read *last two*] cross-claimed against each other." *Cities Serv. Co. v. Lee-Vac, Ltd.*, 761 F.2d 238, 239 (5th Cir. 1985).

These latter is not an impossibility if the second of the two elements is plural—e.g.: "This cause was brought at the instance of [the] Food and Drug Administration . . . against the individuals named as defendants, praying that *these latter* be restrained from introducing into interstate commerce certain misbranded drugs." *U.S. v. Parkinson*, 240 F.2d 918, 918–19 (9th Cir. 1956).

Former and *latter* can bewilder the reader when the elements referred to are numbers. E.g.: "Thus, in this oath he distinguishes his second invention from the first with the statement that the *latter* contained subject matter not disclosed in the *former*." *Beckman Instruments, Inc. v. Coleman Instruments, Inc.*, 338 F.2d 573, 576 (7th Cir. 1964). The latter here syntactically is "the first," but the context in which this sentence appeared made it clear that the writer meant to say the second invention; that is, he used *latter* in a temporal rather than in a syntactic sense.

May one have a *latter* without a *former*? Strictly speaking, no: even if the word *former* doesn't appear, there should be an idea to which it might attach if it did appear. It was once common to use *latter* without a correlative. E.g.: "In view of what has already been said, very little may suffice concerning a liability as such. The *latter* [i.e., liability], as we have seen, is the correlative of power, and the opposite of immunity (or exemption)." Wesley Newcomb Hohfeld, *Some Fundamental Legal Conceptions as Applied in Judicial Reasoning*, 23 Yale L.J. 16, 53 (1913). Latterly, however, this use of the term is uncommon.

former jeopardy. See **double jeopardy**.

form of action. Although it has virtually no current significance in modern law practice, this phrase is basic to an understanding of Anglo-American legal history. True, the forms of action have been buried, but "they still rule us from their graves." F.W. Maitland, *The Forms of Action at Common Law* 1 (1936).

A *form of action* was a compartment of law and practice associated with a particular writ, each of which had specific forms of process and specific modes of pleading, of trial, of judgment, and of executing the judgment. Some forms of action had exotic names, such as *mort d'ancestor*, *writ of entry in the per and cui*, *writ of besaiel*, and *quare impedit*. In 1830, some 72 forms existed; in 1874, the number had dwindled to 12; and in 1875, they were abolished in England. About the same time, or shortly afterward, they were abolished in most American jurisdictions.

FORMS OF ADDRESS. To avoid professional blunders in correspondence and other writings, the legal writer must know how to refer to judges and other dignitaries. The American rules are much simpler than the British ones. Only a few of the most basic questions are treated here. For a fuller discussion, consult one of the several modern books on forms of address, or a good book of etiquette.

A. Addressing Federal Judges. In addressing judges, err on the side of formality, but not to the point of archaism or pedantry. So in court papers, instead of *To the Honorable Judge of Said Court*, write either *To the Honorable Court* or *To the Honorable Alicemarie H. Stotler, U.S. District Judge*.

In corresponding with the federal judiciary in the U.S., follow these forms:

Chief Justice

Very formal:
    The Chief Justice of the United States
    (address)

    Dear Mr. Chief Justice:

Less formal:
    The Honorable John Roberts
    The Chief Justice of the United States
    (address)

    Dear Chief Justice Roberts:

Associate Justice

    The Honorable Ruth Bader Ginsburg
    The Supreme Court of the United States
    (address)

    Dear Justice Ginsburg:

Other federal judge

    The Honorable William R. Wilson Jr.
    United States District Court, W.D. Arkansas
    (address)

    Dear Judge Wilson:

B. Addressing State-Court Judges. In corresponding with state judges, follow these forms (applicable in most states):

Chief Justice of the highest appellate tribunal

    The Honorable (full name)
    Chief Justice, (name of court)
    (address)

    Dear Chief Justice (surname):

Other state judge

    The Honorable (full name)
    (name of court)
    (address)

    Dear Judge (surname):

C. Four Rules in Using *The Honorable*. First, *Honorable* should be capitalized whenever coupled with a person's name. Second, never write *The Honorable Kagan* or *Hon. Kagan*; *Honorable* always takes a full name:

The Honorable Elena Kagan

Third, abbreviate *Honorable* only in addresses, and omit *The* when abbreviating:

Hon. Elena Kagan

Fourth, when writing a British, Canadian, or Australian correspondent and spelling out the word, use the BrE spelling:

The Right Honourable the Lord Goff of Chieveley

D. *Mr. Justice; Mrs. Justice; Madam Justice*. Many readers, especially in the U.S., find these labels gratuitously sexist. *Justice* alone suffices.

In the U.S. Supreme Court, the *Mr.* disappeared before *Justice* shortly after Justice Sandra Day O'Connor ascended to the bench. See SEXISM.

E. Third-Person References. Whereas British legal writers tend to refer in discourse to *Denning M.R.* and *Woolf J.*—without even a comma after the name—Americans generally refer to *Justice Scalia* (not *Scalia J.*) or *Judge Robert E. Keeton* (on first mention, and later *Judge Keeton*). In third-person contexts, avoid honorifics such as *The Honorable*.

F. Lawyer-to-Lawyer References. The American practice of appending *Esq.* to other lawyers' names is entirely acceptable, but no other titles—not even *Mr.*—may be used in conjunction with it. See **Esq.**

If you prefer not to use *Esq.* (some consider it clubby), a mere *Mr.* or *Ms.* or *Mrs.* (or even *Miss*, if that is the addressee's known preference) will always suffice.

British lawyers often have titles or affiliations that a correspondent is obliged to include after the addressee's name, such as *Q.C.* (Queen's Counsel) and *F.B.A.* (Fellow of the British Academy).

G. Signing Off. When ending a letter, dispense with the archaic flourishes: instead of *I am, my dear sir, Sincerely yours*, write *Sincerely yours*.

In business and personal letters, you may show some individuality in the complimentary close by adopting any of the several standard forms:

Very formal and deferential:
    Respectfully (yours),
    Very respectfully yours,

Less formal, without deference (as in demand letters):
    Very truly yours,
    Yours very truly,
    Yours truly,

General:
    Sincerely yours,
    Yours sincerely,
    Sincerely, (see (H))

Informal:
> With best wishes,
> Best wishes,
> With best regards,
> Best regards,
> Kindest personal regards,
> Best,

Intimate:
> As ever,
> Fondly,
> Yours,
> Yours ever,
> Yours always,

H. The Lone *sincerely*. A foul canard is afoot in the American legal profession: some believe that it is an error to close with *Sincerely, Respectfully, Fondly*, or any other adverb without adding *yours*. Do not believe it: every modern complimentary close contains UNDERSTOOD WORDS. Respected writers from Supreme Court justices to eminent law professors, even great poets, use *Sincerely* without saying whose. *See An Epistolary Essay: The Wright–Garner–Maugans Correspondence on Complimentary Closes*, 2 Scribes J. Legal Writing 83 (1991); *A Sequel to "An Epistolary Essay*," 3 Scribes J. Legal Writing 95 (1992).

formula. Pl. *-as, -ae*. The English plural, ending in *-s*, is preferred in all but scientific writing. Legal writers are somehow fond of the Latinate ending. See PLURALS (A).

formulaic; formulistic; formalistic. *Formulaic* = of, relating to, or constituting a formula. *Formulistic* = fond of formulas. *Formalistic* = adhering unduly to a set way of saying and doing something without regard to its substance or inner meaning.

formulation (= a setting forth systematically) for *formation* (= the act of forming, or the thing formed) is an odd error. In 1993, a newly formed (formulated?) law firm sent out tens of thousands of announcements that read, "X and Y are pleased to announce the *formulation* [*sic*] of their professional corporation for the practice of personal injury law under the name X & Y, P.C."

fornicate; copulate. *Copulate* is a neutral verb referring to the sexual act without regard to legality or the legal status of the parties. *Fornicate* is not neutral: it describes a criminal offense in some American jurisdictions; for example, Virginia Code § 18.2-344 provides that "any person, not being married, who voluntarily shall have sexual intercourse with any other person, shall be guilty of *fornication*, punishable as a Class 4 misdemeanor."

fornication. See **adultery.**

forsake > forsook > forsaken. *Forsake* (= to desert or renounce) is sometimes corrupted into **foresake*.

*forseeable. See **foreseeable.**

for sure is colloquial for *certain* or *certainly*.

forswear; *foreswear. The second does not properly exist. If it did, it might mean "to swear before," since the prefix *fore-* denotes a previous time. *Forswear* is the proper synonym of *renounce* or *abrogate*. See **abjure** (A). Cf. **forego.**

forswearing. See **perjury.**

forte (= a person's strong point) is preferably pronounced with one syllable, like *fort*. But many English-speaking people persist in the two-syllable version, /**for**-tay/, which can hardly be strongly condemned.

for the duration of is verbose for *during*.

for the reason that is prolix for *because*—e.g.: "It is still thought that magistrates are too disinclined to reject police evidence, however implausible, perhaps *for the reason that* [read *because*] they feel the police should always be supported as a matter of principle." P.S. Atiyah, *Law and Modern Society* 26 (1983).

for the sake of (the) argument is a perfectly good phrase that is universally understandable to those who speak English—and therefore much preferable to **arguendo*. Legal stylists frequently use it—e.g.: "But even if, *for the sake of the argument*, we concede the identity of the two Romes, we may go on to observe that the style and trappings of Catholic Rome were quite different from the style and trappings of Imperial Rome." Grant Gilmore, *The Ages of American Law* 68 (1977). The phrase is most commonly rendered without a definite article before *argument*: hence *for the sake of argument*. See ***arguendo.**

forthwith, adv., is a usefully vague term, although it may strike some readers as antiquarian. The writer who intends a precise meaning must be wary: the word has been attributed every shade of meaning from "instantly" to "within 24 hours" to "within a reasonable or convenient time." It is a fuzzy word with no pretense of precision.

Forthwith makes no sense as an adjective, as in the phrase *a forthwith subpoena*.

fortuitous (= occurring by chance) is commonly misused for *fortunate*. Here the correct use of the term is illustrated:

- "Contrary to defendants' argument, the occasional *fortuitous* inclusion of a tenant in the resolution of a claim between the housing authority and the landlord affords no protection to a tenant." *Davis v. Mansfield Metro. Hous. Auth.*, 751 F.2d 180, 185 (6th Cir. 1984).
- "Whether that result would follow it in any other case is entirely *fortuitous*, and it may be that such a result was not intended." *Hofing v. Willis*, 201 N.E.2d 852, 856 (Ill. 1964).
- "Applying tort rules would allow the *fortuitous* location of an accident to determine the situs—and the applicable law—of a contractual controversy." *Grand Isle Shipyard Inc. v. Seacor Marine, LLC*, 589 F.3d 778, 787 (5th Cir. 2009).

See **aleatory.**

In the phrase *fortuitous accident*, the word *fortuitous* is correctly used but it results in a REDUNDANCY: every accident is fortuitous. E.g.:

- "The owners of other non-stationary property such as farm animals or trains [that] may sustain damage in a motor vehicle accident on a public highway are usually not at fault and thus should not be required to maintain their own insurance to cover *fortuitous accidents* [read *accidents*] [that] might occur." *Pioneer State Mut. Ins. Co. v. Allstate Ins. Co.*, 339 N.W.2d 470, 475 (Mich. 1983).
- "The Supreme Court held that *a fortuitous accident* [read *an accident*] in Oklahoma involving a car sold in New York to a local consumer did not provide sufficient contacts between the moving defendants and the forum state." *City of New York v. A-1 Jewelry & Pawn, Inc.*, 247 F.R.D. 296, 334 (E.D.N.Y. 2007).

Fortuity is the seldom-seen noun corresponding to *fortuitous*. E.g.: "The known-loss doctrine is premised on the *fortuity* principle that is inherent in all insurance." *West Bend Mut. Ins. Co. v. U.S. Fid. & Guar. Co.*, 598 F.3d 918, 929 (7th Cir. 2010). *Fortuitousness*, which emphasizes the *quality* as opposed to the *state* of being fortuitous, is also used.

forum. The preferred plural is *forums*—e.g.:

- "Her scepticism is grounded in her suspicion that the legal techniques of interpretation and the *forums* in which interpretation proceeds are biased by the conscious and even more the unconscious mind-sets of bench and bar." Neil MacCormick, *With Due Respect*, TLS, 22 Jan. 1993, at 3.

Avoid the pretentious **fora*—e.g.:

- "Public *fora* [read *forums*] generally are those 'places which by long tradition or by government fiat have been devoted to assembly and debate.'" *ACORN v. City of Phoenix*, 798 F.2d 1260, 1264 (9th Cir. 1986).
- "The government's exclusion of a speaker in traditional or designated public *fora* [read *forums*] is subject to strict scrutiny." *Milwaukee Deputy Sheriffs' Ass'n v. Clarke*, 588 F.3d 523, 530 (7th Cir. 2009).

See PLURALS (A).

forum non conveniens = the doctrine that an inappropriate forum, even though competent under the law, may be divested of jurisdiction if, for the convenience of the litigants and the witnesses, it appears that the action should be instituted in another forum in which the action might originally have been brought. This LATINISM has become a TERM OF ART—e.g.:

- "The common-law *forum non conveniens*, with its stress on contacts and fairness, unhampered by a mythology of power and sovereignty, may yet create a new American law of jurisdiction based on the *forum conveniens*." Albert Ehrenzweig, *Conflict of Laws* 148–49 (1962).
- "A defendant invoking *forum non conveniens* 'bears a heavy burden in opposing the plaintiff's chosen forum.'" *Wilson v. Island Seas Invs., Ltd.*, 590 F.3d 1264, 1269 (11th Cir. 2009).

forum-shopping, n., an Americanism dating from the early 1950s, should be so hyphenated. The phrase refers to the practice of choosing the most favorable jurisdiction or court in which a claim might be heard. Cf. **panel-shopping.**

forwent. See **forego.**

founder. See **flounder.**

fountain of justice is a SET PHRASE, of which **fountainhead of justice* is a mangling: "The king was the *fountainhead* [read *fountain*] of justice." C. Gordon Post, *An Introduction to the Law* 41 (1963).

four, rule of. See **rule of four.**

four corners of the instrument (= the face of a legal document) derives from the age-old view that every deed was supposed to have been written on one skin of parchment having only four corners. The phrase is common in legal JARGON, especially when it is argued that the court should not consider evidence extraneous to the legal document in question. E.g.: "If the *four corners of the deed* provide a coherent expression of the parties' intent, we need search no further, but if an ambiguity or a reasonable doubt appears from a perusal of the particular symbols of expression our horizons must be broadened to encompass the circumstances surrounding the transaction." *Oldfield v. Stoeco Homes, Inc.*, 139 A.2d 291, 297 (N.J. 1958).

Sometimes the phrase is used figuratively of things other than single documents—e.g.: "As a matter of the integrity of the criminal system and its commitment to rule of law, therefore, some level of policing could be required in order to guarantee that the law is meaningful in all *four corners* of the system." Alexandra Natapoff, *Underenforcement*, 75 Fordham L. Rev. 1715, 1770 (2006). (A *system* does not have four corners.)

There is also a doctrine called the *eight-corners rule*—e.g.: "Texas courts follow the '*eight corners*' rule when determining an insurer's duty to defend the insured. Under this rule, a court looks only to the pleadings and the insurance policy to determine whether the duty to defend exists." *Cluett v. Medical Protective Co.*, 829 S.W.2d 822, 829 (Tex. App.—Dallas 1992).

fourfold. See **twofold.**

Four Horsemen. In allusion to the Four Horsemen of the Apocalypse—allegorical figures in the Bible (Rev. 6:1–8)—this phrase formerly referred to four U.S. Supreme Court Justices who consistently opposed New Deal legislation: George Sutherland, Pierce Butler, Willis Van Devanter, and James McReynolds. For an example of a legal writer's use of the phrase, see **bad.**

fours, on all. See **on all fours.**

four unities. In his "Poetics," Aristotle devised "three unities" for dramatic composition, namely, that a play should consist of one main action, should occur at one time (or within 24 hours), and should occur in one place. In allusion to these dramatic principles, real-estate lawyers devised four unities for the creation of a joint tenancy: time, title, interest, and possession. The joint tenants must have the same interest beginning at the same time, deriving from the same title, and consisting of the same undivided possession.

fractious. See **factional.**

framable; *frameable. The *-e-* is best omitted. See MUTE E.

framers in AmE is capitalized only in reference to the drafters of the U.S. Constitution. In all other contexts in which this word refers to legislative drafters, the word is lowercased.

franchise, n., has two quite distinct senses: (1) "the right to vote"; or (2) "the sole right of engaging in a certain business or in a business with a particular trademark in a certain area." Sense 1 is the less common one today, but it remains in use—e.g.: "In earlier times this led to obvious legal changes such as the gradual emancipation of married women, and the spread of the *franchise*." P.S. Atiyah, *Law and Modern Society* 117 (1983).

In English and Scottish legal history, *franchise* also denoted an area enjoying exemption from royal justice. In a franchise, justice was administered by a noble or other person who had a grant of the power to do justice—hence the term *franchise courts.*

franchise, vb.; **enfranchise; *affranchise.** *Franchise* = to grant (to another) the sole right of engaging in a certain business or in a business with a particular trademark in a certain area. (See **franchise,** n.) *Enfranchise* = (1) to set free, release from bondage; (2) to give to a person or class of persons the right to vote; (3) to give to an area or class of persons the right to be represented in an elected body; or (4) to endow with a franchise. For more on senses 1 and 2, along with near-synonyms of *enfranchise,* see **free.** **Affranchise* is a NEEDLESS VARIANT. See **disenfranchise.**

franchiser; franchisor. *Franchiser* is preferred. *W3* contains only the *-er* form; the *OED* lists *-or* as a variant.

frankalmoin; frankalmoign; frankalmoigne; almoign; almoin. This obsolete form of English land tenure—a holding in free alms, in return for prayers—is generally spelled *frankalmoin* in modern texts. *Almoign* and *almoin* are historical variants.

fraud. A. Defining Generally. "Courts refrain from defining fraud," it was once said, "lest they be confronted by their own definition and it be found too broad or too narrow to cover cases that may subsequently arise." Eugene A. Jones, *Manual of Equity Pleading and Practice* 43–44 (1916). *Fraud,* in other words, is a CHAMELEON-HUED WORD. It may mean: (1) a tort consisting in a knowing misrepresentation

made with the intention that the person receiving that misrepresentation should act on it; (2) the misrepresentation resulting in that tort; (3) a tort consisting in a representation made recklessly without any belief in its truth, but made with the intention that the person receiving that misrepresentation should act on it; (4) a misrepresentation made recklessly without any belief in its truth; (5) unconscionable dealing short of actionable deceit at common law; (6) in the context of conspiracy to defraud, a surreptitious taking of property without deception; or (7) in the law of contract, an unconscientious use of the power arising out of the relative positions of the parties and resulting in an unconscionable bargain. Because *fraud* occupies shifting ground, it is best braced with a modifier. See **deception, deceit** & **imposture.**

B. *Fraud in fact; fraud in the factum.* These terms refer to two very different principles. *Fraud in fact* is what is also known as *actual* or *positive fraud,* that is, a concealment or false representation by means of a statement or conduct that causes injury to another. Scienter is usually required. *Fraud in the factum* occurs when a legal instrument (a "factum" at common law) as actually executed differs from the one intended for execution by the person who executes it, or when the instrument may have had no legal existence (as, e.g., because the substance of the document was misrepresented to a blind signatory). See **fact,** n. & **scienter.**

C. *Fraud in law; legal fraud; constructive fraud.* These phrases are deceptively similar. *Fraud in law* is fraud that is presumed under the circumstances, as, for example, when a debtor transfers assets and thereby impairs the efforts of creditors to collect sums due. *Legal fraud* is another term for *constructive fraud* or unintentional deception that causes injury to another. (To complicate matters, it is occasionally also called *fraud in contemplation of law.*) Because *legal fraud* is potentially ambiguous, *constructive fraud* is the better phrase. See **constructive fraud.**

D. And Its Near-Synonyms: *deception; subterfuge; chicanery; double-dealing; self-dealing.* See **deception.**

fraudfeasor (= one who has committed fraud) is a legal NEOLOGISM not listed in most English-language dictionaries or law dictionaries. E.g.:

- "In seeking to choose between a *fraudfeasor* and a negligent party, the Georgia law unfortunately goes with the alleged crook." *Cole v. Cates,* 149 S.E.2d 165, 169 (Hall, J., concurring).
- "Privity is not required between the *fraudfeasor* and the person he is trying to influence to establish a fraud claim." *In re Enron Corp. Sec., Derivative & ERISA Litig.,* 388 F.Supp.2d 780, 784 (S.D. Tex. 2005).

The word should be solid, not hyphenated. E.g.:

- "Failure to correct another's delusion is obviously fraudulent if the circumstances are such that the *fraud-feasor's* [read *fraudfeasor's*] very silence reasonably causes the misapprehension." *Estate of Jones v. Kvamme,* 430 N.W.2d 188, 193 (Minn. Ct. App. 1988).

- "There is no requirement that a *fraud-feasor* [read *fraudfeasor*] must 'sign' or 'certify' a representation, if the speaker intends the hearer to rely on it, and the other necessary elements are satisfied." *Wagner v. Mortgage Info. Servs.*, 261 S.W.3d 625, 641 n.14 (Mo. Ct. App. 2008).

See **feasor.**

*fraudful. See **fraudulent.**

fraud in contemplation of law. See **fraud** (C).

fraud in fact; fraud in the factum. See **fraud** (B).

fraud in law. See **fraud** (C).

fraudulent; *fraudful. The second is a NEEDLESS VARIANT.

fraudulent representation; fraudulent misrepresentation. Although *fraudulent misrepresentation* cannot be called a REDUNDANCY—since not every misrepresentation is fraudulent—it is nevertheless inferior to the *fraudulent representation*. Oliver Wendell Holmes Jr., among others, used *fraudulent representation*. See *The Common Law* 255 (1881).

fray. See **affray.**

free; release; liberate; emancipate; manumit; enfranchise; *affranchise. These verbs share the sense "to set loose without restraint." *Free* is the most general term: it can be used in reference not only to prisoners or slaves but also to anything else that has been confined, encumbered, or trapped <to free a porpoise from the fisherman's net> <she freed her skirt from the car's door>. *Release* more markedly suggests a setting loose or unshackling <release me now> <the bird was released into the wild>. *Liberate*, a more abstract synonym, focuses on the liberty that will result from the setting loose and typically connotes emerging from an unpleasant bondage or constraint <Allied soldiers liberated the inmates of the Nazi work camps>. The word is often used figuratively <if only I could liberate my imagination>. *Emancipate*, in its literal uses, is a legal term meaning "to put an end to one person's legal subjection to another," whether a child who is subject to a parent <the court emancipated 16-year-old Mike after he proved he was mature and self-supporting>, a ward who is subject to a guardian, or a slave who is subject to a slaveholder <Lincoln emancipated the slaves>. (See **emancipate.**) *Manumit* refers more specifically to freeing a person from slavery or putting an end to someone's condition of servitude <in 1838 he manumitted his slaves>. *Enfranchise* goes further by denoting the removal of all legal and political disabilities and the acquisition of full membership in the polity, especially as evidenced by the right to vote. **Affranchise* is a NEEDLESS VARIANT. See **franchise,** vb.

free alongside. See **F.O.B.**

free construction. See *free interpretation* under INTERPRETATION, MODES OF (B).

freedom. See **liberty.**

freedom of contract, a fuzzy phrase often used in 19th-century and early-20th-century judicial opinions, embraced two connected but distinct ideas: "In the first place it indicated that contracts were based on mutual agreement, while in the second place it emphasized that the creation of a contract was the result of a free choice unhampered by external control such as government or legislative interference." P.S. Atiyah, *An Introduction to the Law of Contract* 5 (3d ed. 1981).

free from; free of. Although both are correct, *free from* is preferred by most writers on style. Note the shift in noun forms: *freedom of speech* but *freedom from oppression, pestilence, coercion,* etc.

free gift is a common REDUNDANCY.

freehold has been defined in two quite different ways. Most recently, the *CDL* has defined it as "the most complete form of ownership in land: a legal estate held in fee simple absolute in possession." The *OED* and other modern authorities more accurately define *freehold* as "a tenure by which an estate is held in fee simple, fee-tail, or for term of life." The *CDL*'s definition is unduly restrictive, for a life estate is held in freehold. See **fee, fee simple** & **fee tail.**

freeholder technically means "one who holds an estate in fee simple, an estate in fee tail, or a life estate." In fact, though, most uses of *freeholder* refer to an owner in fee simple absolute. Still, it is incorrect to define *freeholder*, as one book does, as "one who owns land that he or she can transfer without anyone's permission." John W. Reilly, *The Language of Real Estate* 206 (2d ed. 1982). See **freehold, fee simple** & **fee tail.**

free interpretation. See *free interpretation* under INTERPRETATION, MODES OF (B).

free of. See **free from.**

free on board. See **F.O.B.**

free rein. Beware of the common but incorrect rendering *free reign*—e.g.:

- "Considering Mrs. Waldman had *free reign* [read *free rein*] in spending $52,500, we affirm that part of the order allowing the set off for the suit money and costs she claims she is still due." *Waldman v. Waldman*, 612 So.2d 703, 705 (Fla. Dist. Ct. App. 1993).
- "Anderson seemingly had *free reign* [read *free rein*] to provide Bonds whatever muscle creams and supplements he felt appropriate." *U.S. v. Bonds*, 608 F.3d 495, 505 (9th Cir. 2010).

Cf. **rein in.**

---

freezing order. See *Mareva injunction* under CASE REFERENCES (C).

freight = (1) goods transported by water as well as by land (though until recently in BrE it referred only to goods shipped by water); or (2) in a contract for water carriage, the payment made by the sender of goods to the shipowner.

frequently. This adverb can be ambiguous when used with a plural subject and verb. Do individuals do something frequently, or is the characteristic true of a group that may do something only once? Note the MISCUE here: "A study last year by Jack Hadley of the Georgetown University School of Medicine showed that uninsured patients arrived at the hospital sicker than those with health insurance, and *died in the hospital more frequently* [read *more frequently died in the hospital*]." Jane Bryant Quinn, *Woe to the Reformers*, Newsweek, 19 Oct. 1992, at 55. If the phrase *more frequently* is moved after the conjunction *and*, the miscue disappears. See MISPLACED MODIFIERS.

fresh pursuit; hot pursuit. The first is the traditional legal phrase, dating from 1626 in the *OED* and denoting close and continuous chasing of a criminal suspect by police, often across jurisdictional boundaries. The phrase is often used, however, in extended senses: "There is no doubt that during continuance of war a rebel guilty of treason may be slain in actual conflict or *fresh pursuit*." David Lindsay Keir & Frederick Henry Lawson, *Cases in Constitutional Law* 254 (1967).

Hot pursuit, first used in the 1920s, is an equivalent term that is better known among nonlawyers.

friend. Advocates with a sense of tradition and civility typically, during any argument before the bench, refer to an adversary as *my learned friend* or *my friend*—never *my opponent* or *my adversary*. Unfortunately, though, this custom is fading as fast as the bar's other traditions of civility.

friendly suit; amicable action. These synonymous phrases refer to a lawsuit in which all the parties have agreed beforehand to allow a court to resolve the issues involved. *Friendly suit* is more common today—e.g.:

- "The purpose of the correspondence was for Farrell to introduce himself and request Umscheid contact him regarding a settlement of a claim of Umscheid's daughter by a *friendly suit* to be filed in Riley County, Kansas." *In re Farrell*, 21 P.3d 552, 555 (Kan. 2001).
- "Because these proceedings were carried out in 'friendly suit' manner, without the presentation of a countervailing legal position, and without even the objective participation of the Cabinet, the parties lost all benefit of an otherwise adversarial system." *S.J.L.S. v. T.L.S.*, 265 S.W.3d 804, 836 (Ky. Ct. App. 2008).
- "The danger of the *friendly suit* displacing litigation by the real parties in interest is minimized by a liberal practice of allowing intervention or its equivalent—briefs and oral argument by amici curiae." 3 Bernard E. Witkin, *California Procedure* ch. 4, § 27 (5th ed. 2008).

friend of the court. See *amicus curiae*.

frigidity. See **impotence.**

frivolity. See **frivolousness.**

frivolous. Generally speaking, a court filing is frivolous if it has no arguable basis in fact or is unsupported by law, and the attorney or litigant either knew this or failed to reasonably investigate whether any facts existed or might be developed to support the filing. Under Rule 11, courts may sanction an attorney who both knows a filing lacks merit and doesn't make adequate efforts to find any. See *Holgate v. Baldwin*, 425 F.3d 671, 676–77 (9th Cir. 2005). But a filing is not frivolous merely because it is novel or unlikely to succeed.

In immigration law, *frivolous* has a specialized meaning: it describes an asylum application that is deliberately false in any material respect. 8 C.F.R. § 1208.20. If the applicant knows of the falsehood and of the consequences, the application will be denied.

frivolousness; frivolity. In legal writing, both terms refer to an absence of a factual basis or of any legal merit (for a claim, motion, or the like). Although the terms appear with almost equal frequency in the language generally, *frivolousness* is far more common in legal than general writing—e.g.:

- "A finding of factual *frivolousness* is appropriate when the facts alleged rise to the level of the irrational or the wholly incredible, whether or not there are judicially noticeable facts available to contradict them." *Denton v. Hernandez*, 504 U.S. 25, 33 (1992) (per O'Connor, J.).
- "*Frivolousness* is the applicable standard in the *Anders* context because a frivolous appeal 'may be decided without an adversary presentation.'" *U.S. v. 777 Greene Ave.*, 609 F.3d 94, 100 (2d Cir. 2010).

The longer form is preferable, too, because *frivolity* suggests frothy nonseriousness and playfulness—e.g.:

- "Imagination was *frivolity*, and *frivolity* was not on the menu." John D. MacDonald, *Deep Blue Good-By* 274 (1995) (from postscript by Maynard MacDonald).
- "It was one of Craig's pet peeves—along with the superficiality and *frivolity* of New York society." Candace Bushnell, *Trading Up* 255 (2003).
- "It was two days of libertine *frivolity* before the relatively austere season of Lent." JoAnn Ross, *No Safe Place* 42 (2007).

from. See *of* (E).

from hence; from thence. The words *hence* and *thence* (as well as *whence*) are sufficient without the preposition *from* and are therefore preferred singly; yet grammarians have not considered *from hence*, etc., incorrect. *Hence* includes the idea of "from," since it means "from this time; from this place." Boswell, not best known for his achievements in law, used *from thence*: "Mr. Scott of University College, Oxford . . . accompanied [Johnson] *from thence* to Edinburgh." 5 *Life of Johnson* 16 (1791). See **thence** & **whence.**

from henceforth is redundant for *henceforth*, as in: "The will of the giver, according to the form in the deed of gift manifestly expressed, shall be *from henceforth observed* [read *observed henceforth*]." *Raines v. Duskin*, 277 S.E.2d 26, 29 (Ga. 1981) (quoting a statute written in 1285).

from the beginning of time. This phrase, typically found in releases, is essentially an emphatic hyperbole: you're releasing me from all claims you might have had against me from the moment of the Big Bang forward.

from thence. See **from hence.**

from whence. See **from hence, thence** & **whence.**

frontal attack. This late-19th-century expression has become common in legal JARGON to denote a direct attack on a judgment, statute, etc.—e.g.:

- "In fact, when his motion to exclude the informants' out-of-court statements failed, counsel mounted a sustained *frontal attack* on the informants and their statements." *Plascencia v. Alameida*, 467 F.3d 1190, 1198–99 (9th Cir. 2006).
- "He and amicus curiae, an advocacy group for worker rights, mount what is, in essence, a *frontal attack*, on the present statutory and regulatory scheme." *Flick v. PMA Ins. Co.*, 928 A.2d 54, 59 (N.J. Super. Ct. App. Div. 2007).

fructus industriales; fructus naturales. Lawyers might use terms such as *crops* and *perennials*, but instead they have used these LATINISMS. *Fructus industriales* are annual crops produced by labor (e.g., wheat, corn, potatoes, beets); *fructus naturales* are perennial plants (e.g., trees, grasses, perennial bushes). *Fructus naturales* are considered part of the real property, whereas *fructus industriales* usually are not.

fruit; fruits. Idiomatically speaking, one refers to the *fruits of one's labor* and *fruits of a crime*, but to the *fruit of the poisonous tree* (= in a criminal investigation, any tip or lead that results from an illegal search or seizure of evidence)—e.g.: "Not all evidence is the *fruit of the poisonous tree* simply because it would not have come to light 'but for the illegal actions of the police.'" *State v. Hill*, 725 So.2d 1282, 1287 (La. 1998). A leading criminal-law text credits Justice Felix Frankfurter with having coined the phrase in *Nardone v. U.S.*, 308 U.S. 338, 341 (1939). *See* Wayne R. LaFave & Jerold H. Israel, *Criminal Procedure* § 9.3, at 471 (1992).

Often, however, the idiom is paraphrased or foreshortened, and *fruit* is made plural—e.g.:

- "The district court committed no error when it refused to suppress the *fruits* of the recorded conversations." *U.S. v. Chagra*, 754 F.2d 1181, 1183 (5th Cir. 1985).
- "On a motion to suppress the *fruits* of a search in accordance with a warrant, a trial court examines whether the issuing magistrate had a substantial basis for concluding that probable cause existed." *State v. Vanderhors*, 927 So.2d 1011, 1013 (Fla. Dist. Ct. App. 2006).

frustration = the doctrine that, if the entire performance of a contract becomes fundamentally changed without any fault on either side, the contract is considered dissolved. Theoretically—though rarely, it might be said, in pragmatic terms—frustration is imposed automatically by law and does not require either party to do anything. See **impossibility** & **mistake (C).**

FUDGE WORDS are common in mediocre and poor legal writing; they occur seldom in clean, precise prose. The typical phrases are *it would seem to appear that*, *it is suggested that*, and *it is submitted that*. E.g.: "*It would appear to be clear that the Pioneer Society was* [read either *The Pioneer Society was* or *It is clear that the Pioneer Society was*] organized by a group of people who were brought together by their common interest in the history and historical relics of Los Angeles County and the State." *In re L.A. County Pioneer Soc'y*, 257 P.2d 1, 11 (Cal. 1953) (Carter, J., dissenting). Cf. WEASEL WORDS.

fugitive. Only in formal writing does this word mean, in its adjectival sense, "evanescent; fleeting." E.g.:

- "It is no answer to say that complainant spends its money for that which is too *fugitive* or evanescent to be the subject of property." *International News Serv. v. Associated Press*, 248 U.S. 215, 240 (1918) (per Pitney, J.).
- "It is further said that, while that for which the Associated Press spends its money is too *fugitive* to be recognized as property in the common-law courts, the defendant cannot be heard to say so in a court of equity." *Id.* at 262 (Brandeis, J., dissenting).

An even more learned equivalent is *fugacious*—e.g.: "Oil, gas, and other minerals are *fugacious* matter and are subject to capture." *Energy Mgmt. Corp. v. City of Shreveport*, 467 F.3d 471, 476 (5th Cir. 2006) (quoting the district court).

fulfillment; fulfilment. The word is spelled *-ll-* in AmE, *-l-* in BrE.

full age. See **majority (D).**

full-blown is often unnecessary, as in the following example: "The collective knowledge of the investigating officers and agents . . . amounted to probable cause for a *full-blown* arrest of [appellant]." *U.S. v. Webster*, 750 F.2d 307, 319 (5th Cir. 1984). An officer can either arrest or not arrest someone: *full-blown* adds nothing.

The phrase is fast becoming a CLICHÉ in legal writing. E.g.:

- "Short of a *full-blown* commission, a neutral and independent assessment of the legal framework governing the public lands could further illuminate the case for reform." Robert B. Keiter, *Public Lands and Law Reform*, 2005 Utah. L. Rev. 1127, 1224.
- "A canine alert is sufficient to constitute probable cause needed to conduct a *full-blown* search." Eugene D. Bryant, *Snoop Dogs: An Analysis of Narcotics Canine Sniffs of Storage Units Under the Fourth Amendment*, 40 Ga. L. Rev. 1209, 1213 (2006).

---

full-faith-and-credit clause. As a PHRASAL ADJEC-TIVE, *full-faith-and-credit* should be hyphenated.

full-fledged is the phrase, not **fully fledged.*

full force and effect. See **force and effect.**

full power is a common REDUNDANCY. E.g.: "The corporation shall have *full power* to . . . ." The corporation would have just as much power if *full* were deleted.

full-scale, a PHRASAL ADJECTIVE, should be hyphenated—e.g.: "A *full scale* [read *full-scale*] effort to confirm or deny these assertions would require . . . a systematic examination of the cases to see how the treatise has been used." Richard E. Speidel, *On Change and the Law of Contracts*, 71 Fordham L. Rev. 973, 975 (2002).

fully and finally. This DOUBLET is justified in some contexts, as in the phrase *fully and finally discharged*: *fully* refers to the extent of the discharge (as opposed to a partial discharge), and *finally* refers to the time of the discharge (the order is not an interlocutory one). On the other hand, to say that one is *discharged* probably implies that the discharge is both full and final.

*fully fledged. See **full-fledged.**

fulsome (= abundant to excess; offensive to normal tastes or sensibilities) is often incorrectly taken to mean "very full." Here, for example, *fulsome* is used for *fuller*: "For a *more fulsome* [read *fuller*] discussion of this regulatory history, see . . . ." Richard S. Whitt & Stephen J. Schultze, *The New "Emergence Economics" of Innovation and Growth*, 7 J. on Telecomm. & High Tech. L. 217, 255 n.179 (2009).

functus officio is a LATINISM that literally means "having performed his or her office." In practice, the phrase denotes the idea that the specific duties and functions that an officer was legally empowered and charged to perform have now been wholly accomplished, and thus that the officer has no further authority or legal competence based on the original commission.

This term serves the purposes of conciseness but not of lucidity. E.g.:

- "[A trustee's removal may be effected by] his becoming *functus officio*, that is, completing his duties as Trustee, by reason of the estate having been wound up or of some scheme of arrangement having been accepted by his creditors." 2 Ernest W. Chance, *Principles of Mercantile Law* 253 (Percy W. French ed., 10th ed. 1951).
- "It is only when the tribunal is closed, when the jury that decided the case is *functus officio*, and there is no way of getting another one, that the judges are forced themselves to determine what a jury might think." Patrick Devlin, *The Judge* 142 (1979).
- "Pending appeal, the trial judge is *functus officio*, subject to two exceptions and one qualification." *Kirby Bldg. Sys., Inc. v. McNeil*, 393 S.E.2d 827, 831 (N.C. 1990).

Pl. *functi officio.*

fundament = (1) basis; or (2) anus or buttocks. This word can hardly be used without creating a double entendre—e.g.:

- "That policy has remained the *fundament* [read *foundation*] of federal appellate jurisdiction." *Kenyatta v. Moore*, 744 F.2d 1179, 1182 (5th Cir. 1984).
- "It is a closely related *fundament* [read *guide*] of statutory construction that, where Congress codifies prior case law, those prior holdings remain not only good law, but should serve as a valuable touchstone for interpreting the statute." *In re Oot*, 368 B.R. 662, 666 (Bankr. N.D. Ohio 2007).

fundamental law. See **constitutional law.**

fundamental term = a contractual provision that specifies an essential purpose of the contract, so that a breach of that provision through inadequate performance makes the performance not only defective but essentially different from what had been promised. For example, a caterer might have contracted to deliver crepes but instead delivered burritos. The doctrine supplying the innocent party with an excuse if the other party breaches a fundamental term has often been used—since the 1950s—to overcome an exemption clause protecting the culpable party from liability. See **term.**

funds, when used as a count noun, can confuse readers who usually encounter the plural form *funds* as an aggregate <the funds were [= money was] promptly deposited>. The following usage is odd enough to be considered unidiomatic: "*Hundreds of funds* are held for the benefit of students enrolled at the university. *Each of these funds*, which includes funds for endowments, scholarships, and student loans, has a designated fund manager." *Report Accompanies Indictments*, Amarillo Globe-Times, 11 Dec. 1991, at 8C.

funeral; funereal; funerary; *funebrial. *Funeral*, commonly a noun, serves as its own adjective <funeral expenses>. *Funereal*, which is frequently confused with *funeral*, adj., means "solemn, mournful, somber" <funereal dirges>. *Funerary* = of, used for, or connected with burial <funerary pulleys>. **Funebrial* is a NEEDLESS VARIANT of *funereal*. Of *funerary* and **funebrial*, H.W. Fowler wrote that "no one uses [them] if he can help it" (*MEU1* 205).

fungible (= regarded as exchangeable with other property of the same kind) is most commonly an adjective <fungible goods>—as just defined—but it may also serve as a noun <a fungible is any property regarded as exchangeable with other property of the same kind>.

funnily. See ADVERBS (B).

furnish is a useful word in the drafting of contracts because its alternatives—*deliver, give, assign, transmit,* and the like—are often too specific about the means of supplying a thing. *Furnish* can be usefully vague.

further. See **farther.**

further affiant sayeth naught. American lawyers frequently end affidavits with some variation of this sentence: "Further affiant [= the person giving the affidavit] sayeth not." This sentence gives rise to three stylistic dilemmas: first, is it *sayeth* or *saith*; second, is it *not* or *naught*; and third, is the sentence necessary at all?

A. *Sayeth* or *saith*. It is surprising how often American lawyers stop to puzzle over this choice in spelling. (English lawyers use neither spelling because they do not use the phrase.) Both forms are good Elizabethan usage. Among American lawyers who use the phrase, *sayeth* predominates; among American lawyers who rightly pride themselves on their style, the phrase does not appear at all. See -ETH.

B. *Not* or *naught*. The predominant form is **Further affiant sayeth not*. But this is nonsense because it is literally translatable as, "The affiant says not further," or "The affiant does not say further." Does not say what? The form with *naught*, by contrast, makes literal sense: "The affiant says nothing further." E.g.: "Further your affiant sayeth *naught*." *State v. Malkin*, 722 P.2d 943, 944 n.3 (Alaska 1986) (quoting an affidavit).

C. Forbearance. The best choice, stylistically speaking, is to use these phrases not. See **naught.**

FUSED PARTICIPLES. A. The General Rule. H.W. Fowler gave the name "fused participle" to a participle used as a noun (i.e., a gerund) that is preceded by a noun or pronoun not in the possessive case. So *Me going home made her sad* rather than the preferred *My going home made her sad*. The fused participle is said to lack a proper grammatical relationship to the preceding noun or pronoun. No one today doubts that Fowler overstated his case in calling fused participles "grammatically indefensible" and in never admitting an exception. The grammarians Otto Jespersen and George Curme have cited any number of historical examples and have illustrated the absolute necessity of the fused participle in some sentences, barring some recasting of the sentence. E.g.: *The chance of that ever happening is slight*. (One would not want to write, *The chance of that's ever happening is slight*.)

But Fowler had a stylistic if not a grammatical point. Especially in formal prose, the possessive ought to be used whenever it is not unidiomatic or unnatural. In the following sentences, then, possessives would have been better used than the nouns in the objective case:

- "The jury could find that through constant wear the terrazzo slab had over a period of time become smooth, resulting in *it being* [read *its being*] very slippery when wet." *Erickson v. Walgreen Drug Co.*, 232 P.2d 210, 213 (Utah 1951).
- "In the second place, the danger of the *courts reaching* [read *courts' reaching*] an inequitable conclusion by

refusing to modify the results of applying the legal incidents of joint tenancy to the partnership relation is done away with." *In re Ostler's Estate*, 286 P.2d 796, 798 (Utah 1955).
- "He wasn't going to countenance *anybody coming* [read *anybody's coming*] into his house with stolen goods." *Moody v. U.S.*, 377 F.2d 175, 178 (5th Cir. 1967).
- "There is a difference in probability between *one* [read *one's*] intentionally depositing and unintentionally forgetting and the hole-in-the-pocket man." Edward R. Cohen, *The Finders Cases Revisited*, 48 Tex. L. Rev. 1001, 1007 (1970).
- "The district court accepted the prosecutor's representation that it did not believe the additional charge would result in *Krezdorn receiving* [read *Krezdorn's receiving*] a sentence greater than the one initially imposed." *U.S. v. Krezdorn*, 718 F.2d 1360, 1365 (5th Cir. 1983).
- "Defendant claims that that burden shifting . . . will also result in asbestos *manufacturers being* [read *manufacturers' being*] liable for almost any injury caused by a product." *Coffman v. Keene Corp.*, 628 A.2d 710, 721 (N.J. 1993).
- "Some of the 'beauty contests' required by corporate clients or creditors' committees result in *lawyers overstating* [read *lawyers' overstating*] qualifications and experience." Frances Koncilja, *Colorado Bar Association President's Message to Members*, 23 Colo. Law. 2723, 2724 (1994).
- "He says that the medication makes him vulnerable to other *people taking* [read *people's taking*] advantage of him." *In re Williams*, 712 N.E.2d 350, 352 (Ill. App. Ct. 1999).
- "During oral argument in the Appellate Court, members of the court raised a question regarding the propriety of the *trial court granting* [read *trial court's granting*] an oral motion for summary judgment." *Krevis v. City of Bridgeport*, 817 A.2d 628, 631 (Conn. 2003).
- "We see this same pattern for most recurring plaintiffs with each *plaintiff having* [read *plaintiff's having*] a continuing relationship with a particular law firm." Robert B. Thompson & Randall S. Thomas, *The New Look of Shareholder Litigation*, 57 Vand. L. Rev. 133, 189 (2004).
- "This approach would necessarily involve only vague guidelines from the *Court instructing* [read *Court's instructing*] trial courts to consider the nature of the conduct, the wealth of the defendant, and the judge's own sense of proportionality." Jim Gash, *Solving the Multiple Punishments Problem*, 99 Nw. U. L. Rev. 1613, 1634 (2005).
- "The YMCA has not alleged any prejudice that results from the *Court extending* [read *Court's extending*] the limitations period, and the Court does not find any such injury in this case." *Koss v. YMCA*, 504 F.Supp.2d 658, 662 (D. Minn. 2007).
- "There is a difference between a *newspaper publishing* [read *newspaper's publishing*] an investigative report about the questionable loan practices of a bank . . . and a highly regulated Fascination *parlor using* [read *parlor's using*] its public-address system in an attempt to put out of business its competitor's highly regulated Fascination parlor." *Senna v. Florimont*, 958 A.2d 427, 445 (N.J. 2008).
- "We conclude that [the] decision to proceed at trial without *appellant being* [read *appellant's being*] present was not an abuse of discretion." *State v. DeWalt*, 757 N.W.2d 282, 286 (Minn. Ct. App. 2008).

- "Consent to a search by *one having* [read *one's having*] the authority to give such consent constitutes one exception to the warrant requirement." *State v. Williams*, 201 P.3d 371, 377 (Wash. Ct. App. 2009).

But there are many exceptions to this rule of style. The *Oxford Guide* states: "When using most non-personal nouns (e.g. *luggage, meaning, permission*), groups of nouns (e.g. *father and mother, surface area*), non-personal pronouns (e.g. *anything, something*), and groups of pronouns (e.g. *some of them*), there is no choice of construction: the possessive would not sound idiomatic at all." *Oxford Guide* 156 (1983). Examples follow:

- "He must stand on his legal title in an action of ejectment, and he has shown no legal *title passing* to him beyond the description in his deed." *Pereles v. Gross*, 105 N.W. 217, 222 (Wis. 1905).
- "The remainder is subject to being divested on the contingency of *one of the children of Ross Kost dying* before the life tenant and leaving lawful children." *Kost v. Foster*, 94 N.E.2d 302, 305 (Ill. 1950).
- "To the extent that the defendant's argument decreases the possibility of plaintiffs' alleged excessive *speed being* a proximate cause of the collision, it is self-defeating." *Boerner v. Lambert's Estate*, 510 P.2d 1157, 1161 (Wash. Ct. App. 1973).
- "The judgment does not result in the *property being* attached to the locus." Edward R. Cohen, *The Finders Cases Revisited*, 48 Tex. L. Rev. 1001, 1007 (1970).
- "A declaration that coverage exists under the policy subject to proper *facts being shown* at trial is appropriate." *Weiner v. Selective Way Ins. Co.*, 793 A.2d 434, 445 (Del. Super. Ct. 2002).
- "Such positions were normally followed by the local justices, given their convictions about the desirability of local *law becoming* American in form and content whenever possible and as soon as feasible." José Trías Monge, *Legal Methodology in Some Mixed Jurisdictions*, 78 Tul. L. Rev. 333, 336 (2003).
- "Plaintiffs thus seem willing to stake the ripeness of their due-process and equal protection claims on their takings claim *being ripe*." *Alto Eldorado Partners v. City of Santa Fe*, 644 F.Supp.2d 1313, 1349 (D.N.M. 2009).
- "The statute requires us to look at the particular *decision being made* and to ascertain whether that decision is the one Congress has designated to be discretionary." *Mejia Rodriguez v. U.S. Dep't of Homeland Sec.*, 562 F.3d 1137, 1143 (11th Cir. 2009).

B. Unnecessary Participles. Even when there is no choice in the idiom, there is the choice of reconstructing the sentence to avoid the questionable usage. Sometimes it is even possible merely to omit the participle, as here: "To see something *being* [delete *being*] done badly, however, is not to prove that it cannot be done sensibly." Douglas G. Baird, *The Prime Directive*, 75 U. Cin. L. Rev. 921, 930 (2007).

C. No Fused Participle. Adjectival participles sometimes appear on first sight to be fused participles, but they are not. E.g.:

- "This appeal arises from an *order* of the Santa Fe Country District Court *granting* the motion . . . to dismiss on the ground that the action . . . was barred by the doctrine of sovereign immunity." *Hicks v. State*, 544 P.2d 1153, 1153 (N.M. 1976).
- "A landlord is chargeable with knowledge of the situation, actual *knowledge being* unnecessary." Milton R. Friedman, *Friedman on Leases* § 11-14 n.38 (2010).

FUSTIAN (lit., a kind of cotton cloth) has given its name to pompous, empty speech and writing, or highfalutin words for ordinary ideas. The following sentence, for example, might be placed in virtually any judicial opinion on any subject: *The case presents questions of far-reaching importance which demand and have received mature and deliberate consideration by the court.* We could take most of that for granted. See FLOTSAM PHRASES.

futilely, adv., is sometimes misspelled **futiley*—e.g.:

- "The school *futiley* [read *futilely*] offered him assistance to prepare for the Boards, but he rejected any such help." *DeMarco v. University of Health Sciences*, 352 N.E.2d 356, 368 (Ill. App. Ct. 1976) (Burman, J., dissenting).
- "With growing frustration, he scratches *futiley* [read *futilely*] for an unreachable itch somewhere beneath his breastplate." Bruce W. Burton, *Heresy in Antioch*, 35 Gonz. L. Rev. 345, 441 (1999).

future, in (the). See **in future.**

future interest is a phrase that dates from the mid-19th century. *See* 1 Charles Fearne, *Contingent Remainders* 381 (10th ed. 1844). The phrase denotes an interest in property in which the privilege of possession or of enjoyment is future and not present. A noted treatise states that "the interest is an existing interest from the time of its creation, and is looked upon as a part of the total ownership of the land or other thing [that] is its subject matter. In that sense, *future interest* is somewhat misleading, and it is applied only to indicate that the possession or enjoyment of the subject matter is to take place in the future." Lewis M. Simes & Allan F. Smith, *The Law of Future Interests* § 1, at 2–3 (2d ed. 1956).

The future interests commonly recognized are the reversion, the possibility of reverter, the power of termination (known also as the right of entry for condition broken), and the remainder. Some have suggested that this list might be supplemented with the rights of escheat, inchoate dower, and curtesy initiate, but "these interests . . . are not commonly classified as future interests." Cornelius J. Moynihan, *Introduction to the Law of Real Property* 103–04 (2d ed. 1988). See **remainder, reversion** & **right of entry for condition broken.**

G

GAAP. See **generally accepted accounting principles.**

Gaius was a second-century Roman jurist and the author of the *Institutes* (ca. A.D. 1610, a comprehensive treatise on Roman law. As a classical name, *Gaius* preferably makes the possessive form *Gaius',* not *Gaius's:*

- "According to *Gaius's* [read *Gaius'*] way of thinking, crimes can be torts." James Lindgren, *Why the Ancients May Not Have Needed a System of Criminal Law*, 76 B.U. L. Rev. 29, 39 (1996).
- "The modern rationale for assigning blanket liability in *res ipsa* cases frequently echoes *Gaius's* [read *Gaius'*] reasoning that a plaintiff's inability to identify a particular defendant should not be sufficient to defeat an action." G. Gregg Webb, *The Law of Falling Objects*, 59 Stan. L. Rev. 1065, 1080 (2007).
- "The new doctrine formally declared 'nature' the source of the law governing the contested high seas and the newly discovered territories, while substantively it gave legal weight to certain rules and principles contained in *Gaius's* [read *Gaius'*] *Institutes* and Justinian's *Digest*." Lauren Benton & Benjamin Straumann, *Acquiring Empire by Law*, 28 Law & Hist. Rev. 1, 20 (2010).

For more on the possessive form of classical names— and an alternative point of view—see POSSESSIVES (A).

galimony. See *palimony.*

GALLICISMS appear frequently in English prose, and no less frequently in legal than in nonlegal writing. By Gallicisms is not generally meant the LAW FRENCH terminology that is so prevalent in law (e.g., *voir dire, de son tort*), but French terms and phrases of a nonlegal character, such as *blasé, coup de grace, coup d'état, cul-de-sac, joie de vivre, succès d'estime, tête-à-tête,* and *tour de force.* None of these is unduly recherché, to use yet another. But foreignisms of any kind become affectations when used in place of a perfectly good English term, e.g., *peu à peu* for *little by little,* or *en passant* for *in passing,* or *sans* for *without.*

One stylist of high repute cautions sternly against all but thoroughly anglicized Gallicisms: "Of *Gallicisms . . .* it is perhaps not necessary to say much: they are universally recognized as a sign of bad taste, especially if they presuppose the knowledge of a foreign language. A few foreign words, such as *cliché,* have no English equivalent and are in current use; and there may be others [that] are desirable. But except in technical works it will generally be found possible to avoid them." Herbert Read, *English Prose Style* 10 (1952). Cf. LATINISMS.

gaming; gambling. The first is the law's EUPHEMISM for the second—e.g.: "State officialdom, when hoping to sound professional and clinical, uses the term *gaming* as having an ameliorative sense. By contrast, . . . *gambling* has a pejorative connotation." Thomas L. Clark, *Gaming and/or Gambling: You Pays Your Money*, 10 Verbatim 20 (Spring 1984). In traditional legal idiom, a wager or a bet is known as a *gaming contract.* And in the U.K., the Gaming Act 1968 set up the Gaming Board, which regulates gaming.

ganancial (= of, relating to, or consisting of community property) originated as a Spanish-law term, from the Spanish *ganancias* (= earnings, winnings); the Spanish equivalent of *community property* is *gananciales.* The only form of the word to have entered English is the adjective *ganancial,* which unfortunately is omitted from the *OED, RH2, W3,* and most other general English-language dictionaries. E.g.:

- "The husband has the active control and administration of the *ganancial* property during the matrimony." *Stramler v. Coe,* 15 Tex. 211, 215 (1855).
- "Because the legal concept of the community property or *ganancial* system is so foreign to that of the common law, it is frequently very difficult for the judge or lawyer, trained or versed in the common law, to grasp and understand its principles." 1 William Q. de Funiak, *Principles of Community Property* § 3, at 7–8 (1943).
- "The community or '*ganancial*' system was introduced by the Visigothic invaders of the Roman Empire in the early part of the fifth century into what is now Spain and portions of France." *Willcox v. Pennsylvania Mut. Life Ins. Co.,* 55 A.2d 521, 524 (Pa. 1947).

See **community property.**

gantlet; gauntlet. Although *gauntlet* is more common in most senses, *gantlet* is still preferred in one of them. One runs the *gantlet* (= a kind of ordeal or punishment) but throws down the *gauntlet* (= a glove). The trend, however, is to use *gauntlet* for *gantlet.* Like many other trends, it is worth resisting—e.g.:

- "Even if he is initially successful in convincing his client and executing a thoroughly professional draft, it will still have to run the *gauntlet* [read *gantlet*] of many minds." Reed Dickerson, *The Fundamentals of Legal Drafting* § 4.15, at 77 (2d ed. 1986).
- "The Code did not require the taxpayers to run the administrative *gauntlet* [read *gantlet*] in 1985 to obtain a judicial determination of the 1985 value." *Estepp v. Miller,* 731 S.W.2d 677, 682 (Tex. App.—Austin 1987) (Shannon, C.J., concurring).
- "Assume that a bill establishing a federal contract law successfully runs that *gauntlet* [read *gantlet*] and becomes law." Carlos Manuel Vázquez, *The Separation of Powers as a Safeguard of Nationalism,* 83 Notre Dame L. Rev. 1601, 1604–05 (2008).

Gauntlet is correctly used in the following sentences:

- "In substance, the plaintiffs argue, the Department should have ignored the federal administrator's warnings, thrown down the *gauntlet,* litigated the matter and taken its chances on losing federal funds." *Hightower v. Duffy,* 548 N.E.2d 495, 505 (Ill. App. Ct. 1989).
- "At some point, we must throw down the *gauntlet* against the evil of racism." Anthony E. Cook, *The Death of God*

in American Pragmatism and Realism, 82 Geo. L.J. 1431, 1504 (1994).

gaol; gaoler. These are variant BrE spellings of *jail* and *jailer*. The terms are pronounced the same regardless of spelling. See **jail delivery.**

garden-variety, adj. (= of the ordinary or familiar kind), is becoming a garden-variety CLICHÉ in legal prose—e.g.:

- "Only when domestic offenses are treated differently from *garden-variety* [read *typical*] assaults, the argument goes, is the defendant on notice that he may be treated differently in the future as well." *U.S. v. Denis*, 297 F.3d 25, 30 (1st Cir. 2002).
- "This case originated as *a garden-variety* [read *an everyday*], state-law-based contract action." *Vaden v. Discover Bank*, 129 S.Ct. 1262, 1268 (2009) (per Ginsburg, J.).
- "The Supreme Court has previously refused to add narrowing language to a statute (RICO), despite the contention that the statute as written threatened to turn an abundance of *garden-variety* [read *ordinary*] local disputes into violations of federal law." *Wheeler v. Pilgrim's Pride Corp.*, 591 F.3d 355, 384 (5th Cir. 2009).

garnish; garnishee, vb. In AmE, the usual verb form is *garnish* (= to take property, usu. a portion of someone's wages, by legal authority). *Garnishee* is usually reserved for the noun sense ("a person or institution, such as a bank, that is indebted to or is bailee for another whose property has been subjected to garnishment"). The noun corresponding to *garnish* is *garnishment*.

But in BrE, and in a few American jurisdictions, *garnishee* as well as *garnish* is used as a verb—e.g.:

- "A customer's interest in a current account is of a proprietary nature. It is at least a chose in action, for if it were not it could not be *garnisheed* or assigned." *Arab Bank Ltd. v. Barclays Bank*, [1953] 2 Q.B. 527, 538 (C.A.).
- "Asset *garnisheed* Moberly's bank account and collected $11,032.92 from the *garnishee* bank." *Asset Acceptance LLC v. Moberly*, 241 S.W.3d 329, 331 (Ky. 2007).
- "The order by the trial court *garnisheed* whatever debts were due the defendant." *Harrington v. Dyer*, 937 A.2d 77, 81 (Conn. Super. Ct. 2007).

The *OED* gives passing notice to *garnishee* as a verb and its corresponding noun **garnisheement*; the main entries are under *garnish* and *garnishment*.

garnishable (= subject to garnishment), a 20th-century NEOLOGISM omitted from most general English-language dictionaries, is a useful term—e.g.:

- "The Court of Appeals added a qualification to whether a check is a *garnishable* asset." *Water Processing Co. v. Southern Golf Builders, Inc.*, 285 S.E.2d 21, 22 (Ga. 1981).
- "The district court correctly questioned whether such an obligation could be *garnishable* in Texas." *Af-Cap, Inc. v. Republic of Congo*, 462 F.3d 417, 425 (5th Cir. 2006).
- "Even indebtedness that may become due by the lapse of time is *garnishable*, as long as it is due absolutely." *Capital Factors, Inc. v. Alba Rent-A-Car, Inc.*, 965 So.2d 1178, 1182 (Fla. Dist. Ct. App. 2007).

garnishee. See **garnish.**

*garnisheement. See **garnish.**

garnishee order. See **garnishment order.**

garnisher; *garnishor. *Garnisher* is preferred; it is the only spelling listed in *W3* and the prevalent spelling in legal texts—e.g.:

- "The *Garnishors* [read *Garnishers*] are *garnishor* [read *garnisher*]–creditors in Ohio who obtain judgments against debtors when debts are not repaid." *Monroe Retail, Inc. v. RBS Citizens, N.A.*, 589 F.3d 274, 277 (6th Cir. 2009).
- "Edison asserts that the award of attorneys' fees and expenses is not discretionary in this case because the *garnishor* [read *garnisher*] did not obtain a judgment against the garnishee." *Capital One Bank v. Edison Credit Union*, 299 S.W.3d 662, 667 (Mo. Ct. App. 2009).

garnishment. See **sequestration.**

garnishment order (AmE) = *garnishee order* (BrE).

*garnishor. See **garnisher.**

gauntlet. See **gantlet.**

gavel. Though everyone knows what a judge's gavel is, few seem to know the name of the piece of wood that is struck by a gavel. The term is *sound block*.

gazump, (BrE vb.) = (1) [intransitive] to act improperly in the sale of houses, as by raising the price after accepting an offer; (2) [transitive] (of a seller) to treat a buyer of a house unfairly by raising the price after accepting the buyer's offer; or (3) [transitive] (of a competing house buyer) to place a higher bid for a house than the one that the seller has already accepted, thereby encouraging the seller to back out of a contract. This early-20th-century BrE NEOLOGISM, labeled "slang" in the *OED* and in the *COD*, is a word of unknown origin.

The past tense is *gazumped*, not **gazumpted*—e.g.: (sense 3) "During the go-go Thatcher years, it was not uncommon for apartments under contracts 'duly signed by both party's [*sic*] solicitors' to be '*gazumpted*' [read '*gazumped*'] by a higher bidder the day before closing." Paul Schneider, *A Flat in London*, Esquire, Dec. 1991, at 72.

g.b.h.; G.B.H.; GBH. Some English criminal-law writers use this initialism for *grievous bodily harm*—e.g.:

- "Causing grievous bodily harm with intent is an alternative. The abbreviation '*g.b.h.*' is frequently used in conversation, though not in court." Glanville Williams, *Textbook of Criminal Law* 151–52 (1978).
- "The House of Lords has now decided that there can be an 'infliction' of *GBH* without proof of an assault." Andrew Ashworth, *Principles of Criminal Law* 279 (1991).

Though such an initialism may speed communication among specialists, nonspecialists are likely to consider it obscure and off-putting. If it must be used, the best form, for the sake of readability, is *g.b.h.* See ACRONYMS AND INITIALISMS. See also **grievous bodily harm.**

gender has long been used as a grammatical distinction of a word according to the sex assigned to a given noun. It has newly been established in the language of the law in phrases such as *gender-based discrimination*, a usage that some authorities disapprove as jargonistic. Perhaps the main reason for preferring *gender* in such phrases was best summed up in a private conversation with Justice Ruth Bader Ginsburg. In her chambers during June 2009, she told me: "When men see or hear the word *sex*, they think of only one thing."

She played a major role in the semantic shift in which *sex* has narrowed its meaning more often to denote either intercourse <the sex trade> or physical characteristics <sex change>, while *gender* increasingly denotes the social and psychological distinctions between men and women <gender roles>. The expansion of *gender*, which was otherwise a narrow and inflexible word, was arguably much needed in the language because of the distracting duality of *sex*. Here is how Justice Ginsburg tells it: "[F]or me it became altogether clear when my secretary at Columbia said, 'I'm typing these briefs for you and jumping out all over the page is *sex, sex, sex*. Don't you know that for the male audience you are addressing, the first association of the word *sex* is not what you're talking about? So why don't you use a grammar-book term? Use *gender*. It has a neutral sound, and it will ward off distracting associations.' Milicent Tryon was my astute secretary then, and from that day to this I've used *gender*." *Transcript of Interview of U.S. Supreme Court Associate Justice Ruth Bader Ginsburg*, 70 Ohio St. L.J. 805, 817 (2009).

The shift is now irreversible. Many will hail it as progress. Some will decry it as linguistically retrograde. But it is now a linguistic reality.

gendered is a NEOLOGISM meaning "biased in favor of one sex." Built on the newly developed use of *gender*, this adjective dates from the early 1970s. E.g.:

- "In any other employment setting, the use of *gendered* stereotypes suggests sex discrimination." *Weinstock v. Columbia Univ.*, 224 F.3d 33, 58 (2d Cir. 2000).
- "A *gendered* assumption about men played an important role in the legalization of donor insemination." Noa Ben-Asher, *The Curing Law*, 30 Cardozo L. Rev. 1885, 1913 (2009).

See NOUNS AS VERBS.

general. The vogue lately has been to address attorneys general and solicitors general as if they were military officers, that is, simply as *General So-and-So*—e.g.: "May I ask, *General Starr*, in the survey, is this the only statute that has this particular 10-day notice requirement?" Oral Argument of *Michigan v. Lucas*, No. 90-149 (26 Mar. 1991). Despite its prevalence among some of the most esteemed members of the bar and judiciary, it is incorrect. In titles such as *attorney general*, the word *general* is not a noun,

but a POSTPOSITIVE ADJECTIVE—that is, an adjective that follows rather than precedes the noun it modifies, usually for a historical reason: it reflects Romance rather than Germanic (or English) syntax. Postpositive adjectives exist in English largely as a remnant of the Norman French influence during the Middle Ages—an influence most deeply felt in the language of law, politics, religion, and heraldry. *Attorney general* and *solicitor general* are but two examples of this phenomenon. Others include *court-martial* and *notary public*. No one, however, calls a notary public simply "public." And the *general* in *attorney general* is every bit as much adjectival as it is in *general counsel*.

The practice of using *general* as a faux title appears to have been popularized by William Rehnquist, who was otherwise known as a stickler for grammar. He used the term in this way as early as 1980. (Oral Argument of *Fedorenko v. U.S.*, No. 79-5602 (15 Oct. 1980).) Meanwhile, the Chief Justice in that era, Warren Burger, fastidiously addressed the Solicitor General as "Mr. Solicitor General." But from the outset of his chiefship, Chief Justice Rehnquist used *general* as a title, undoubtedly helping to spread the linguistic innovation. (*See* Oral Argument of *Asonia Bd. of Educ. v. Philbrook*, No. 85-495 (14 Oct. 1986).) Lamentably, the practice has continued with Chief Justice Rehnquist's successor and has been adopted by other members of the Court as well. (*See* Oral Argument of *Boumediene v. Bush*, No. 06-1195 (5 Dec. 2007).) Even transcript references to the Solicitor General now simply state "General Clement," "General Kneedler," and "General Kagan." Among the early commentators on this solecism was Michael Herz in *Washington, Patton, Schwarzkopf, and Ashcroft?*, 19 Const. Comment. 663 (2002).

Sticklers will abstain. Others will blithely persist. And the militarization of high legal offices will march forward.

general common law, federal. See **federal common law.**

general consensus. See **consensus.**

general court, in some New England states, refers to the legislature, which historically convened itself as the highest judicial tribunal: "In 1639, Massachusetts Bay had a full system of courts, organized in a way that would not strike a modern lawyer as unduly exotic. The *general court*, acting both as legislature and as the highest court, stood at the crown of the system. As a court, it confined itself mostly to appeals, though its exact jurisdiction was a bit vague." Lawrence M. Friedman, *A History of American Law* 39–40 (2d ed. 1985). See **judicial court.**

general damages; special damages. *General damages* are "those elements of loss or damage [that] need not be claimed or mentioned in the complaint in order to be the subject of proof and recovery at the trial"; and *special damages* are "those which must be specifically claimed and described if recovery for them is to be allowed." Charles T. McCormick, *Handbook on the Law of Damages* § 8, at 32–33 (1935). Another way of expressing the distinction is this: *general damages* are those that the law presumes follow from the type of wrong complained of; *special damages* are those that are alleged to have been sustained in the particular circumstances of the particular wrong, and they must be specifically claimed and proved to have been sustained. The terms, when "used in relation to the problem of pleading, relate to the question, Could the adversary foresee, at the time he reads the complaint, a claim of harm asserted at the trial?" *Id.* n.3. See **damages.**

general intent, in criminal law, is problematic: "Most courts use the term without explanation as though everyone understood it. When an explanation is offered, it is frequently in terms that one suspects the court does not really mean or at least is not willing to generalize across offenses." Peter W. Low et al., *Criminal Law: Cases and Materials* 231–32 (1982). The phrase *general intent* has two senses: (1) negligence involving blameworthy inadvertence; and (2) recklessness involving actual awareness of a risk and the culpable taking of that risk. See **intention (F).**

general intention. See **intention (F).**

general interrogatory. See **special verdict.**

general issue; special issue. At common law, a *general issue* arose in litigation—still arises in some jurisdictions—upon the defendant's filing a general denial, which questioned the truth of every material allegation in the plaintiff's pleading. In a suit based on a contract under seal, the general issue was *non est factum*; in detinue it was *non detinet* ("he does not detain"); in trespass it was "not guilty." See **non est factum.**

A *special issue*, by contrast, arose from pleading by specific as opposed to general allegations. For the most part, *special issues*—long the delight of acutely technical lawyers—have fallen into disuse.

A *general issue* results in *general verdict*—e.g.: "In most federal cases, the traditional *general verdict* is used, by which the jury merely finds for one or the other of the parties." Charles Alan Wright, *The Law of Federal Courts* 674 (5th ed. 1994). See **special verdict.**

generalized (= made general) sometimes wrongly displaces *general*. E.g.: "Notwithstanding . . . the *generalized* [read *general* or *nonspecific*] language of the legislative history, courts and academics have attempted to define swap agreements based on the functioning of markets." *Hutson v. E.I. duPont de Nemours & Co.*, 556 F.3d 247, 259 (4th Cir. 2009). The sentence does not intend to convey that the language was *made general*

(here by the court issuing the injunction), but that it *is general*. Cf. **particularized.**

general jurisprudence. See **jurisprudence (D).**

general legacy. See **legacy.**

generally has three basic meanings: (1) "disregarding insignificant exceptions" <the level of advocacy in this court is generally very high>; (2) "in many ways" <he was the most generally qualified applicant>; or (3) "usually; most of the time" <he generally left the office at five o'clock>. Sense 3 is least good in formal writing, although at times it merges with sense 1.

generally accepted accounting principles; generally accepted accountancy principles. The first is the usual phrase in AmE, the second in BrE. But *accountancy* is used in the U.S. in other phrases and contexts.

The phrases are often abbreviated *GAAP* /gap/— e.g.: "[Financial Accounting Standards Board] standards, also known as *generally accepted accounting principles* ('*GAAP*'), are recognized as authoritative by the Securities and Exchange Commission." *Dreiling v. AOL, Inc.*, 578 F.3d 995, 998 (9th Cir. 2009). Because *GAAP* is an acronym, it should not have periods after each letter. See ACRONYMS AND INITIALISMS.

general pleading. See **code pleading.**

general property; special property. Some legal theorists refer to ownership as *general property* and rightful possession as *special property*. See **possession (B)** & **property (A).**

general verdict. See **special verdict** & **general issue.**

generative; generational. The distinction is clear: *generative* = procreative; *generational* = pertaining to generations. But as useful as the distinction is, writers sometimes miss it. Here the words are used correctly:

- "Certification today covers territory once dominated by a deferral device called 'Pullman abstention,' after the *generative* case, *Railroad Comm'n of Tex. v. Pullman Co.*" *Arizonans for Official English v. Arizona*, 520 U.S. 43, 75–76 (1997) (per Ginsburg, J.).
- "With this rise of aggressive young men generally come *generational* conflict and the erosion of traditional ethical values, norms, and forms of communal construction of justice." Christian Gerlach, *Extremely Violent Societies* 208 (2010).

generic. See **genus (A).**

genericide, a late-20th-century NEOLOGISM in the law of trademarks, means "the loss of a trademark that no longer distinguishes one owner's goods from others' goods." It makes little literal sense, as *-cide* (lit., "killer; slayer" or "killing; slaying") is made to refer merely to the death of a trademark—not its killing. One court calls the term a MALAPROPISM, stating: "It refers to the death of the trademark, not to the death of the generic name for the product. A more accurate term might be *trademarkicide*, or perhaps even *generization*, either of which seems to better capture the idea that the trademark dies by becoming a generic name." *Plasticolor Molded Prods. v. Ford Motor Co.*, 713 F.Supp. 1329, 1344 n.22 (C.D. Cal. 1989). Nevertheless, the word *genericide* is "firmly ensconced in the literature." *Id.* E.g.:

• "In the usual '*genericide*' case a venerable mark has come under attack because, over the course of years, consumers have come to regard it as a name for the genus of a product rather than as a brand name of a particular product from a single source." *G. Heileman Brewing Co. v. Anheuser-Busch, Inc.*, 676 F.Supp. 1436, 1488 (E.D. Wis. 1987).
• "Sometimes *genericide* occurs as a result of the trademark owner's failure to police the mark, resulting in widespread usage by competitors leading to a perception of genericness." 2 J. Thomas McCarthy, *McCarthy on Trademarks and Unfair Competition* § 12:1 (4th ed. 2007).
• "Defendant argues that even if plaintiff ever had any rights to DWG, *genericide* has occurred because plaintiff allegedly chose to let others use DWG without interference." *Autodesk, Inc. v. Dassault Systèmes SolidWorks Corp.*, 685 F.Supp.2d 1001, 1007–08 (N.D. Cal. 2009).

genericness; genericalness; genericism. Although it is odd-looking, *genericness* is now the most widely used noun corresponding to *generic*, adj. It is recorded from 1939 in the *OED* and appears most commonly in reference to trademarks. E.g.:

• "As I view the cases, a defendant alleging invalidity of a trademark for *genericness* must show that to the consuming public as a whole the word has lost all its trademark significance." *Marks v. Polaroid Corp.*, 129 F.Supp. 243, 270 (D. Mass. 1955).
• "The test for *genericness* is whether the public perceives the term primarily as the designation of the article." *Blinded Veterans Ass'n v. Blinded Am. Veterans Found.*, 872 F.2d 1035, 1041 (D.C. Cir. 1989).
• "The Board then reasoned that the addition of the top-level domain extension '.com' did not affect the term's *genericness*." *In re 1800Mattress.com IP, LLC*, 586 F.3d 1359, 1361 (Fed. Cir. 2009).

Despite its specialized currency, *genericness* retains an un-English appearance. Cf. **prolificness.*

Genericalness is listed in the *OED* and *W2*; it does not, like *genericness*, flout principles of English word formation and might be preferred on that ground. It is omitted from *W3*, which labels the adjective *generical* archaic. Nonetheless, it is a rare word—e.g.: "An incontestable mark can be challenged only on the grounds listed in 15 U.S.C. § 1115. *Genericalness* of a mark is one of those grounds." *Park 'N Fly, Inc. v. Dollar Park & Fly, Inc.*, 217 U.S.P.Q. 968, 970 (D. Or. 1982).

Genericism has also appeared—e.g.:

• "There remain two defenses that licensees might make: descriptiveness and *genericism*." James M. Treece, *Licensee Estoppel in Trademark Cases*, 58 Trademark Rep. 728, 738 (1968).

• "We discuss these background trademark principles because they inform our *genericism* analysis of the phrase 'duck tours.'" *Boston Duck Tours, LP v. Super Duck Tours, LLC*, 531 F.3d 1, 11 (1st Cir. 2008).

Labeled rare in the *OED*, *genericism* is perhaps the most realistic alternative to oust *genericness*.

GENITIVES. See POSSESSIVES (G).

genius (= the prevailing character or spirit; characteristic method or procedure) is often used in reference to law. E.g.: "A federal cause of action 'brought at any distance of time' would be 'utterly repugnant to the *genius* of our laws.'" *Wilson v. Garcia*, 471 U.S. 261, 271 (1985) (per Stevens, J.) (quoting *Adams v. Woods*, 6 U.S. 336, 342 (1805) (per Marshall, C.J.)).

The plural *geniuses* is preferred over *genii* except in the sense of demons or spirits—e.g.:

• "That astonishing Chicago—a city where they are always rubbing the lamp, and fetching up the *genii*, and contriving and achieving new impossibilities." Mark Twain, *Life on the Mississippi* 326 (1883; Signet ed. 2001).
• "Recognition and reward for long and laborious effort would have been denied to many inventive *genii* [read *geniuses*] who have contributed so much to almost every phase of human progress." *Nye v. Coe*, 44 F.Supp. 582, 585 (D.D.C. 1942).

See PLURALS (A).

gentlemen's agreement; gentleman's agreement. The first phrase is better, since at least two must agree. One writer defines the phrase as an agreement that "is not an agreement, made between two persons, neither of whom is a gentleman, whereby each expects the other to be strictly bound without himself being bound at all." R.E. Megarry, *A Second Miscellany-at-Law* 326 (1973). A *gentlemen's agreement* differs from a contract because it is unenforceable.

The phrase runs afoul of the drive to eliminate SEX-ISM but is nevertheless widely used. Several alternative phrases are offered in Rosalie Maggio's *Bias-Free Word Finder* (1992)—among them *honorable agreement*, *informal agreement*, and *your word*. But these phrases are patently inadequate. The upshot is that the phrase *gentlemen's agreement* will probably stump many writers who want to be nonsexist.

gentlepersons; gentlepeople. These are occasionally used as neutral terms in salutations, but they have never lost their look of jocularity. *The Second Barnhart Dictionary of New English* (1980) says of *gentleperson*: "often used humorously or ironically." The lawyers who write "Dear Gentlepeople" (they do exist) apparently do so with a straight face, but their readers probably cannot keep one. Better choices are available for salutations: *Ladies and Gentlemen*, for example, or *Dear Counsel* (if all the recipients are lawyers).

genuine. See **authentic.**

An asterisk (✳) precedes words and phrases that are invariably inferior forms.

genus. A. And *species*. Analytical jurists borrowed these terms from logic and biology. A *genus* is a major class or kind of things, which includes several subclasses usually called *species*. The corresponding adjectives are *generic* and *specific*. Hence trademark is a species within the genus of intellectual property; murder is a species of the genus of crime, i.e., it is a particular crime.

B. Plural. The only plural form listed in *W10* was *genera*, but *W11* joined the *OED* and *RH2* in recognizing the variant *genuses*, which has appeared repeatedly in legal writing—e.g.:

- "There are other contentions, or, at least, other species of the above *genuses*." *In re Missouri Pac. R.R.*, 13 F.Supp. 888, 891 (E.D. Mo. 1935).
- "Scholars sought to classify and categorize legal doctrines and cases much as biologists would *genuses* and species." Peter R. Teachout, *Boundaries of Realism*, 67 Va. L. Rev. 815, 825 (1981) (book review).
- "Rather, 'tasty' is 'merely descriptive' and describes a quality found in many *genuses* [read, perhaps, *types*] of salad dressing." *Henri's Food Prods. Co. v. Tasty Snacks, Inc.*, 817 F.2d 1303, 1306 (7th Cir. 1987).

Though purists decry this form, it is undeniably more comprehensible to more people. See PLURALS (A).

gerrymander, an early-19th-century satirical PORTMANTEAU WORD, combines the name of Elbridge Gerry (the governor of Massachusetts) with the ending of *salamander*. When Gerry's party redistricted Massachusetts in 1812 to favor the antifederalists, Essex County was divided in a way that made one voting district look something like a salamander. Hence *gerrymandering* came to refer to the practice of arranging electoral divisions in a way that gives one political party an unfair advantage.

Though the original sense is still the primary one, this word has had its meaning extended. Some legal writers, for example, refer to *jurisdictional gerrymandering*, in which *jurisdiction* may carry either a geographical sense (as in *EEOC v. Int'l Union of Operating Eng'rs*, 553 F.2d 251, 254 n.4 (2d Cir. 1977)) or a sense conveying the idea of legal power (as in Laurence H. Tribe, *Jurisdictional Gerrymandering: Zoning Disfavored Rights Out of the Federal Courts*, 16 Harv. Civ. Rights-Civ. Libs. L. Rev. 129 (1981)).

Those extensions in meaning seem reasonable, but the word has also been subjected to what could only be described as SLIPSHOD EXTENSION: "In the last few years, the 30-second 'attack ad' and the 10-second television news 'sound bite' have become such prominent . . . features of political campaigns that members of Congress have introduced more than two dozen bills in an attempt to *gerrymander* them out of existence." Randall Rothenberg, *Politics on TV: Too Fast, Too Loose?*, N.Y. Times, 15 July 1990, at E1. How the METAPHOR of gerrymandering fits that sentence is anyone's guess.

GERUNDS. The legal writer's prejudice against nouns ending in *-ing* is unfounded. When it comes to CUTTING OUT THE CHAFF, one effective way of reducing

prolixity is to use gerunds directly; so *adjudicating that case was difficult* rather than *the adjudication of that case was difficult*; *presenting the arguments* rather than *the presentation of the arguments*, etc. See BURIED VERBS, FUSED PARTICIPLES (A) & DANGLERS (C).

get. A. Generally. *Get* is good English. Yet many lawyers want to avoid it because they consider it too informal; they prefer *obtain* or *procure*, two FORMAL WORDS. The same tendency is at work here that leads lawyers to shun *before* in favor of **prior to* or **antecedent to*, *later* in favor of **subsequent to*, and the like. Yet confident, relaxed legal writers use the word *get* quite naturally—e.g.:

- "It was until recently a civil offense, called 'alienation of affections,' for which either spouse could *get* damages." Max Radin, *The Law and You* 54 (1948).
- "And if he goes there and *gets* divorced there is no reason why the divorce should not be valid." *Id.* at 65. On other stylistic points in this sentence, see **and (A)** & **reason why (B)**.

See COLLOQUIALITY.

B. Inflections. The past participle *gotten* predominates in AmE, *got* in BrE.

gibe; jibe. *Gibe* is both noun and verb. As a noun, it means "a caustic remark or taunt." E.g.: "The *gibes* hurled at Chancery . . . had led to a determination on the part of some Chancellors that their decisions would be impeccable and would be rooted firmly in precedent." L.B. Curzon, *English Legal History* 129 (2d ed. 1979).

Jibe is generally considered a verb only, meaning "to make things fit, uniform, or consistent." E.g.: "These laws *jibe* well enough with his notions of right and wrong; the trouble is they do not *jibe* with his capacity to act on his own professed convictions." Lon L. Fuller, *Anatomy of the Law* 41 (1968). But Fuller, who was fond of the word, used it also as a noun meaning "agreement; consistency"—e.g.: "What we have here is a lack of *jibe* between words and actions at a level below that of the courts." *Id.* at 24.

gift, it may be surprising to learn, has acted as a verb since the 16th century. E.g.: "All the property was *gifted* property [i.e., it took the form of gifts]." Though this usage is old, it is not now standard. English has the uncanny ability, however, to transform nouns into verbs, and to revive moribund usages. Fifty years ago *contact* was objected to as a verb, though it had been used that way since the early 19th century; few writers now feel uncomfortable using the word as a verb. See NOUNS AS VERBS.

Gift may soon be in the same class—still, cautious writers may prefer to use it only as a noun if the verb causes discomfort, as it well may. E.g.:

- "Traditionally [stock] can be purchased, sold, *gifted*, pledged, bequeathed, and otherwise transferred." Lyman Johnson, *Sovereignty over Corporate Stock*, 16 Del. J. Corp. L. 485, 494 (1991).
- "The Debtor stated that it was liquidated in 1999 and was *gifted* to his sons Matt and Marc, but could not remember

whether the gift-tax return was filed in 2000 or 2001." *In re Jacobs*, 401 B.R. 161, 176 n.19 (Bankr. E.D. Pa. 2009).

One is accustomed to thinking of *gifted children*, but not of *gifted stock*.

gift over. See **over** (A).

gild. See **guild.**

***gipsy.** See **gypsy.**

girl. This word is widely (and understandably) regarded as an affront when used in reference to an adult, just as *boy* would be. But for a female minor, *girl* is the appropriate word; for an odd avoidance of the word in its proper context, see ***minor woman.**

gist /jist/ began as a legal term meaning "the real ground or point (of an action, indictment, etc.)" (*OED*) and has since passed into nonlegal parlance. Today legal writers use it as a nontechnical word, just as it is used by writers at large—e.g.:

- "'The *gist* of the crime lies in the goal ... to obtain money or property under color of official right,' Assistant U.S. Attorney General Christopher Gamiccioni wrote in a legal brief." Joe Ryan, *Ruling Entangles Corruption Sting Cases*, Star-Ledger (Newark, N.J.), 2 June 2010, at 11.
- "[The defendant took a live rocket home and kept it for four years.] The *gist* of his argument is that, because he was a soldier, the rocket was always in the possession and under the control of the United States. This contention fails, and we therefore affirm." *U.S. v. Springer*, 609 F.3d 885, 887 (6th Cir. 2010). See POPULARIZED LEGAL TECHNICALITIES. Cf. **gravamen.**

give. See **bequeath** & **devise.**

give, devise, and bequeath. The leading American scholars on the law of wills and trusts should resolve any doubt: "In drafting wills, 'I give' is an excellent substitute for 'I devise,' 'I bequeath,' and 'I give, devise, and bequeath.' 'I give' will effectively transfer any kind of property, and no fly-specking lawyer can ever fault you for using the wrong verb." Jesse Dukeminier Jr. & Stanley M. Johanson, *Family Wealth Transactions* 11 (1972). They are not alone: "'I give' is better than 'I give, devise, and bequeath.'" Thomas L. Shaffer, *The Planning and Drafting of Wills and Trusts* 170 (2d ed. 1979). See **bequeath, devise** & DOUBLETS, TRIPLETS, AND SYNONYM-STRINGS.

give evidence is more vague and more verbose than *testify*. E.g.:

- "She looked strained and ill, but *gave her evidence* [read *testified* or, perhaps, *gave her testimony*] in a quiet, subdued fashion that was most impressive." Stanley Jackson, *The Life and Cases of Mr. Justice Humphreys* 200 (n.d. [1951]).
- "The prosecutor did not compel Taylor to *give evidence against* [read *testify against*] himself; he was free to remain silent, and did." *U.S. v. Taylor*, 975 F.2d 402, 404 (7th Cir. 1992).

Even if people generally understood *give evidence* as an equivalent of *testify*, the phrase would still be plagued with an AMBIGUITY: *give evidence* sometimes has nothing to do with testimony. E.g.: "The American Bar Association is of the opinion that every candidate for admission to the bar should *give evidence* of graduation from a law school." "Law, American Schools of," in 17 *Encyclopedia Americana* 93, 96 (1953).

give judgment for = to rule in favor of. E.g.:

- "The majority answers yes and on this ground *gives judgment* for the plaintiffs." *Harris v. Zion*, 927 F.2d 1401, 1423 (7th Cir. 1991).
- "The court finds that Paul's patent is valid and that it is being infringed, and *gives judgment for* Paul." Charles Alan Wright, *The Law of Federal Courts* 725 (5th ed. 1994).

give sanction to. See **sanction.**

glance; glimpse. The looker *glances at* something and thereby *gets a glimpse of* it.

Glanvill; Glanvil; Glanville. The purported author of the treatise that was truly the first book on English law (*Tractatus de Legibus et Consuetudinibus Angliae*)—and the justiciar of England from 1180 to 1189—was named Sir Ranulf de Glanvill. Though a few writers spell the name *Glanvil* (and even *Glanville* or *de Glanville*), most modern legal historians make it *Glanvill*.

glimpse. See **glance.**

global (= embracing a number of items or categories) is common in American and British legal writing. E.g.:

- "Ramsey's *global* defense ... was that his wife has set him up out of revenge." *State v. Ramsey*, 124 P.3d 756, 760 (Ariz. Ct. App. 2005).
- "Any such *global* objection to the Commonwealth's expert would have posed a question of admissibility over which the trial court had discretionary control." *Commonwealth v. Puksar*, 951 A.2d 267, 274 (Pa. 2008).

gloss, originally "a word inserted between the lines or in the margin as an explanatory equivalent of a foreign or otherwise difficult word in the text" (*OED*), is used in extended senses in legal contexts—e.g.:

- "Yet the court's elliptical answer neither added [to] nor subtracted any substance from the settled instructions. The answer was sheer tautology, and, at most, a *gloss* on the instructions." *Duda v. Phatty McGees, Inc.*, 758 N.W.2d 754, 762 (S.D. 2008).
- "The State asks us to jump into this morass in order to clarify and put a *gloss* on longstanding principles for evaluating the effectiveness of a defendant's counsel at trial." *State v. Gajewski*, 762 N.W.2d 104, 105 (Wis. 2009).
- "The Police Board's reference to equitable considerations that could toll the statutory period to allow 'actual mediation' reflects a *gloss* on statutory language that the words chosen by Congress do not support." *Blackmon-Malloy v. U.S. Capitol Police Bd.*, 575 F.3d 699, 713 (D.C. Cir. 2009).

As in the second and third examples just quoted, the term often suggests interstitial lawmaking by judges, as opposed to faithful interpretation that refrains from "gap-filling."

In its most extended sense, *gloss* is used as a COL-LECTIVE NOUN equivalent to "pronouncements (usu. by a court); holdings." E.g.: "The act and its judicial *gloss* also provide the manner for distributing the recovery, if any, obtained from a third party [several cases interpreting the act are mentioned]." *Peters v. North River Ins. Co. of Morristown, N.J.*, 764 F.2d 306, 311 (5th Cir. 1985). This sense is analogous to the non-legal sense "a collection of explanations; glossary," and is not really exceptionable.

glossator. The *Glossators* were scholars principally in Bologna who, in the Middle Ages, annotated Justinian's legislation with marginal or interlinear glosses, passage by passage. By convention, the name of this school of annotators is capitalized.

That practice is convenient, for purposes of DIFFER-ENTIATION, because the word *glossator* (always lower-case) also commonly denotes any modern scholar or court who provides glosses—e.g.:

- "Sometimes a *glossator* has relied on supposed purposes of the legislators, or on their debates at the time of enactment, or on their recitals of evils sought to be remedied, or on their putative responses to circumstances strictly contemporary with the enactments." *Richards v. Thurston*, 304 F.Supp. 449, 455 (D. Mass. 1969).
- "Most jurors encounter the arcane language of instructions infrequently—maybe only once in a lifetime—and it is therefore important to give them instructions that do not require scholastic *glossators* to impart meaning." *U.S. v. Ramsey*, 785 F.2d 184, 190 (7th Cir. 1986).

go. See **go to.**

GOBBLEDYGOOK is the obscure language characteristic of jargon-mongering bureaucrats. So *iterative naturalistic inquiry methodology* supposedly refers to a series of interviews. Much legal writing is open to the criticism of being gobbledygook or, more specifically, "legaldegook." One of the purposes of this book is to wage a battle against it. See JARGON, LATINISMS, LEGALESE & OBSCURITY.

"The besetting sin of jurists," writes a well-known Australian authority, "is to conceal threadbare thoughts in elaborate and difficult language. In spite of the difficulties inherent in the subject, the problems of jurisprudence can be expressed in fairly simple language." G.W. Paton, *A Textbook of Jurisprudence* 1–2 (4th ed. 1972).

goes to. See **go to.**

goes without saying, it. Although this phrase is not generally suitable for formal contexts, it may be appropriate in speech or in informal prose. If it goes without saying, then it need not be said.

go hence without day. This phrase, an old standard in defensive pleadings, is routinely used by lawyers who have absolutely no idea what they mean by it. Perhaps they reason just as Chief Justice Fortescue did in the 15th century: "Sir, the law is as I say it is, and so it has been laid down ever since the law began; and we have several set forms which are held as law, and so held and used for good reason, though we cannot at present remember that reason." Y.B. 36 Hen. VI, ff. 25b–26 (1458) (as translated in 3 William S. Holdsworth, *A History of English Law* 626 (3d ed. 1923)).

In fact, the phrase originated in what Sir Matthew Hale, the 17th-century chief justice of the King's Bench, called "the golden age of pleading," before 1500. *See* Margaret Hastings, *The Court of Common Pleas in Fifteenth Century England* 186 (1947). It is but a LOAN TRANSLATION of the LAW FRENCH phrase *aller sans jour* (lit., "to go without day"), used in medieval times. The phrase meant merely that the defendant would like to leave court without any further settings on the court's docket.

At common law, some time after LAW FRENCH fell into disuse, a longer Latin phrase appeared in orders of dismissal: *eat inde sine die*, that is, "that he may go hence without day." The defendant was free to go; he would not have what he did not want—his day in court. This form of order was still used in England until 1733, when use of the English language became compulsory. *See* W.A. Jowitt, *The Dictionary of English Law* 679 (1959). See **sine die** & **day in court.**

Yet the English translation of the phrase, *without day*, cropped up well before 1733. In the 1701 edition of John's Cowel's *Interpreter*, we learn that "to be dismissed without *Day*, is to be finally discharged [by] the Court." Dismissed cases were said to be *put without day.*

American lawyers mindlessly parrot the phrase: in Texas, for example, where most defensive pleadings contain the phrase, not 1 lawyer in 50 can explain what the phrase means. Though *go hence without day* is not current everywhere, it ought to be current nowhere. For a full discussion, see *Garner on Language and Writing* 320–22 (2009).

golden rule. In the realm of morality, everyone knows about the do-unto-others Golden Rule. In law, the phrase *golden rule* takes on other meanings: (1) the interpretive doctrine that words should be given their ordinary sense, as understood in context, unless that would lead to some absurdity or inconsistency with the rest of the instrument; or (2) the principle, in legal drafting, that one should be consistent in terminology by employing one invariable term for one idea; the doctrine that a word or phrase is presumed to bear a consistent meaning throughout a text. For a discussion of the latter principle, see INELEGANT VARIATION.

good, n. See **goods.**

good and valuable consideration. See **consideration (D).**

good behavior is a well-known standard by which judges are considered fit to continue their tenure: "The Judges, both of the supreme and inferior Courts, shall hold their Offices during good Behavior." U.S. Const. art. III, § 1. But the phrase was not original with the constitutional Framers: in 1700, the Act of Settlement provided that judges' commissions would be *quamdiu se bene gesserint*, i.e., "during good behavior." Hence our phrase began as a LOAN TRANSLATION. See *quamdiu se bene gesserint*.

good cause shown is one of the few standard legal expressions that are neither prolix nor inaccessible to nonlawyers. E.g.: "The Oberts argue that the trial court abused its discretion in not granting a new trial for *good cause shown*." *Wagoner v. Obert*, 905 N.E.2d 694, 718 (Ohio Ct. App. 2008). In statutes and rules, the participle *shown* might be considered advisable as placing a burden on the party to demonstrate whatever must be demonstrated. But in advocates' arguments about whether the standard has been met—especially in the argument of the advocate who is doing the showing—the word *shown* is typically inadvisable because it emphasizes the wrong idea: *shown* rather than *good cause*. See SENTENCE ENDINGS. Cf. **show cause** & **probable cause**.

good consideration. See **consideration (D)**.

good faith; good-faith. *Good faith* is the noun phrase <in good faith>, *good-faith* the PHRASAL ADJECTIVE <good-faith efforts>. See **bona fide** & **bona fides**.

good-faith efforts. See **best efforts**.

good law. See **not law**.

good men and true. See **twelve free and lawful men**.

good right to convey. See **covenant of seisin**.

goods has a variety of senses, two of which are here relevant. In the legal sense, *goods* refers to chattels or personalty. In the economic sense, however, it often refers to things that have value, whether tangible or not. For example: "The meaning and value of all *goods* (money, power, love, and so forth) are socially created and vary from one society to the next. Social *goods* do not include privately valued goods, such as sunsets or mountain air." Michael Walzer, *The Limits of "Complex Equality"* 7 (1983).

In the sense "tangible or movable pieces of property," *goods* has traditionally appeared only in the plural form. In recent years, however, *good* has developed the sense "a tangible or movable piece of property other than money." Though still considered unidiomatic by those with sensitive ears (rankled likewise by the shopkeeper's reference to *a pant*), this usage has made such inroads that it is unlikely to be stopped—e.g.: "She claimed that the hospital was the *supplier of a good* [better usage requires *supplier of goods*, even if there is only one kind of goods] subject to Article 2 of the UCC." Arnold J. Goldman & William D. Sigismond, *Business Law* 240 (2006).

goods and chattels. See *bona et catalla* & DOUBLETS, TRIPLETS, AND SYNONYM-STRINGS.

goodwill. Formerly two words, and then for a time hyphenated, the term has now been solidified into one word.

goose case is legal slang for what in legal JARGON is termed *a case on all fours*. E.g.:

- "While there is no '*goose*' *case* in this circuit, Instruction 31 of the Fifth Circuit Pattern Jury Instructions (Criminal Cases) (1979), informs our judgment." *U.S. v. Gaber*, 745 F.2d 952, 954 (5th Cir. 1984).
- "One need not find a '*goose case*' to imbue a warden at a jail with a constitutional duty to protect a prisoner prone to suicide from self-destruction." *Lewis v. Parish of Terrebone*, 894 F.2d 142, 145 (5th Cir. 1990).

For synonyms, see **whitehorse case** & **on all fours**.

got, p.pl. See **get**.

go to, in the sense "to bear on the issue of," is a distinctive legal usage that is current in both AmE and BrE. Oddly, though, it has largely escaped the attention of American and British lexicographers.

Law students frequently say that it puzzles them at first, but soon they begin using it unconsciously. It is commonplace in good legal writing—e.g.:

- "Mistake *going to* the interpretation of the rule of law is not generally a defence." Glanville Williams, *Criminal Law* 183 (2d ed. 1961).
- "Questions of substantive validity *go to* the consistency of the substance of the statute with constitutional provisions." John H. Merryman, *The Civil Law Tradition* 145 (1969).
- "The discretion of the court does not *go* merely *to* terms and conditions, but extends to whether to permit a nonsuit at all." Charles Alan Wright, *The Law of Federal Courts* 696 (5th ed. 1994).

go to court. See **court, go to**.

go to law (= to sue) is an old idiom, and a perfectly good one—e.g.:

- "If . . . a milk company *goes to law* to protest against a state statute setting the price of milk, the past profits—or lack of profits—of the milk distributors, the medical need of milk for slum children, the present financial shape of dairy farmers, the personnel and ability of the government agency doing the price-setting, all may be treated as just as important as the 'due process clause.'" Fred Rodell, *Woe Unto You, Lawyers!* 142 (1939).
- "It may be unreal to suggest that the buyer should resist the demand and *go to law* to enforce his right to the ship without extra payment." P.S. Atiyah, *An Introduction to the Law of Contract* 230 (3d ed. 1981).

go to the jury. See **jury, go to the**.

go to trial (AmE & BrE) = *come to court* (BrE). See **come to court**.

gotten. See **get**.

governance. H.W. Fowler pronounced *governance* an ARCHAISM for which either *government* or *control* would suffice, allowing it only in "rhetorical or solemn contexts" (*MEU1* 220). Yet this noun is standard in law to refer to the running or governing of a corporation—e.g.:

- "When a claim addresses matters of corporate *governance* or other internal affairs of a company, D.C. courts apply the law of the state of incorporation." *City of Harper Woods Employees' Ret. Sys. v. Olver*, 589 F.3d 1292, 1298 (D.C. Cir. 2009).
- "[Defendant] was concerned that large minority stockholders would leverage their voting power so as to unduly interfere in certain areas of corporate *governance.*" *Stilwell v. Office of Thrift Supervision*, 569 F.3d 514, 516 (D.C. Cir. 2009).

Governance does not mean "the quality of a jurisdiction's law that governs in a particular case." E.g.: "While California has a significant interest in the *governance of* [read *having its law govern*] these relationships, Texas has few, if any." *Webb v. Rodgers Mach. Mfg. Co.*, 750 F.2d 368, 374 (5th Cir. 1985).

governmental; government, adj. When we have an adjective (*governmental*) to do the job, one might well wonder why we should resort to a noun (*government*) to do the work of the adjective. Though the trend today is to write *government agency*, some stylists prefer *governmental agency*. Such are the niceties of writing that make the reader's task a little easier. Following are a few examples of the better usage:

- "The city of Akron has not attempted to allocate *governmental* power on the basis of any general principle." *Hunter v. Erickson*, 393 U.S. 385, 395 (1969) (Harlan, J., concurring).
- "Because there's no end to *governmental* mischief, I went snooping around the Census Bureau Web site." Rob Hiaasen, *Spouse Reform Act*, Wash. Post, 1 Aug. 2010, Mag. §, at W22.
- "While many think that the only way to revive the economy . . . is through *governmental* spending, the general feeling is that we can't afford that right now." Mortimer B. Zuckerman, *The Ticking Debt Bomb*, U.S. News & World Rep., 1 Sept. 2010, at 102.

GOVERNMENTAL FORMS. The English language abounds in words to denote almost every conceivable form of government, usually ending in either of the suffixes *-cracy* and *-archy*. Following is a sampling of the hundreds of familiar and arcane terms in the English language, too numerous for inclusion here:

androcracy	=	government by men
autocracy	=	government by a single person
bureaucracy	=	government by administrative bureaus
clerisocracy	=	government by priests or scholars
democracy	=	government by the people
dyarchy	=	government by two rulers
gerontocracy	=	government by the elderly
gynecocracy	=	government by women
hagiocracy	=	government by saints
jurocracy	=	government by the courts
juvenocracy	=	government by youth
kakistocracy	=	government by a country's worst citizens
kleptocracy	=	government by thieves
meritocracy	=	government by those who have the most merit
monocracy	=	government by a single person
ochlocracy	=	government by the mob (also termed *mobocracy*)
oligarchy	=	government by a small group of people
pantisocracy	=	government by all people equally (in a utopia)
plutocracy	=	government by the wealthy
polyarchy	=	government by many persons
stratocracy	=	government by the military
technocracy	=	government by technicians
theocracy	=	government by religious leaders

gownsman (= one who wears a gown as an indication of office or profession) was formerly used in BrE of judges and barristers, but is now more likely to be used in reference to academics. See **silk** & SEXISM (B).

grab law refers not to law but to a kind of lawlessness: it means "aggressive collection practices." The phrase frequently appears in discussions of bankruptcy—e.g.:

- "Such an unfair result is contrary to the policy of the Bankruptcy Act. Its policy is not to subject creditors to the haphazard chance of '*grab law*.' Its chief purpose is to afford all creditors an equal opportunity to realize on their indebtedness." *England v. Sanderson*, 236 F.2d 641, 643–44 (9th Cir. 1956).
- "[The automatic-stay provisions of the Bankruptcy Act were designed for] protection of the estate of the bankrupt against the ravages that would be inflicted on the estate if *grab law* were allowed to govern." Frank R. Kennedy, *The Automatic Stay in Bankruptcy*, 11 U. Mich. J.L. Reform 175, 187 (1978).

Sometimes the phrase is used attributively as a PHRASAL ADJECTIVE and therefore hyphenated—e.g.: "By such *grab-law* tactics Armstrong claims possession of the entire building, which contained the property of six tenants." *In re Process-Manz Press, Inc.*, 369 F.2d 513, 524 (7th Cir. 1966).

GRAMMAR. The very word is considered anathema by many, even those with an advanced education, not so much because it is boring (which it can be) as because it seems intimidating. Often this intimidation causes scoffers to dismiss grammar as an unimportant, trifling pursuit. To be sure, there are more important things in life, but the significance of good grammar should not be underestimated, especially by those engaged in a learned profession.

The courts have frequently addressed the subject with good sense. For example, the Supreme Court of Florida has stated: "The legislature is presumed to know the meaning of words and the rules of grammar, and the only way that a court is advised of what the legislature intends is by giving the generally accepted construction, not only to the phraseology of an act but to the manner in which it is punctuated." *Florida State Racing Comm'n v. Bourquardez*, 42 So.2d 87, 88 (Fla. 1949) (en banc).

Courts give more leeway to nonlawyers but still take a commonsense approach. In examining wills, for example, courts will forgive every error this book is designed to prevent: "When it becomes necessary to do so in order to effectuate the testator's intention as ascertained from the context of the will, the court may disregard clerical mistakes in writing, improper use of capital letters, paragraphing, abbreviation of words, punctuation, misspelling and grammatical inaccuracies, especially where the will is written by a layman who is unlearned, illiterate, or unskilled. In order to ascertain and give effect to the testator's intent, the court may disregard rules of grammar and verbal niceties, but unless a different construction is required, the ordinary rules of punctuation, capitalization, and grammar should be adhered to in construing a will." 95 C.J.S. *Wills* § 612 (1957).

Likewise with contracts: "The use of inapt words or bad English . . . will not affect the validity of the agreement, although it may affect its construction." 17 C.J.S. *Contracts* § 57 (1963). And affidavits: "Where the meaning substantially appears, ordinarily errors or mistakes on the part of the draftsman in the body of [an] affidavit will be overlooked, and mere grammatical errors . . . will not vitiate the effectiveness of the instrument." 2A C.J.S. *Affidavits* § 43 (1972).

The same is true even in pleading: "Bad grammar does not vitiate a declaration, nor do other faults of style have that effect, unless they produce such a degree of obscurity as to give rise to the belief that the tribunal before whom the cause is heard might be misled as to the true issue." 41 Am. Jur. *Pleading* § 28 (1942).

Yet this book seeks to guide legal writers around these pitfalls in the belief that, even if a document's enforceability will not be marred by such lapses, the court's confidence in its reliability may well suffer. But grammar is not to be followed slavishly without regard for what is effective and what is idiomatic. "Wherever by small grammatical negligences the energy of an idea can be condensed, or a word stands for a sentence, I hold grammatical rigor in contempt." Thomas Jefferson, Letter to Madison, 12 Nov. 1801, in 8 *Writings of Thomas Jefferson* 108–09 (1897).

GRAMMATICAL AMBIGUITY. See AMBIGUITY.

grammatical construction; grammatical interpretation. See *grammatical interpretation* under INTERPRETATION, MODES OF (B).

grandfather clause = a clause in the constitutions of some southern American states exempting from suffrage restrictions the descendants of men who voted before the Civil War. The *OED* misleadingly labels this phrase colloquial; it is the only available name for these statutes, and it appears in formal writing. E.g.: "A state law directly denying Negroes the right would be overthrown as a matter of course, and in 1915 the Court had invalidated a so-called '*grandfather clause*' [that] required literacy tests of those who were *not* descendants of those who could vote in 1867." Robert G. McCloskey, *The American Supreme Court* 212 (1960). The phrase has extended senses, too, referring to any statutory or regulatory clause exempting a class of persons or transactions because of circumstances existing before the clause takes effect.

This phrase has given rise to the verb *to grandfather*, meaning "to cover (a person) with the benefits of a grandfather clause." E.g.: "Beginning in 1972, several States passed statutes permitting such acquisitions in limited circumstances or for specialized purposes. For example, Iowa passed a *grandfathering* statute which had the effect of permitting the only out-of-state bank holding company owning an Iowa bank to maintain and expand its in-state banking activities." *North East Bancorp, Inc. v. Federal Reserve Sys.*, 472 U.S. 159, 163 (1985) (per Rehnquist, J.). To be *grandfathered* is to have the advantage of a grandfather clause <get yourself grandfathered by establishing priority in an interest>.

A few writers and speakers—sometimes in jest—have resorted to *grandparent clause* to avoid what might be perceived as SEXISM. But that neutering skews the historical sense and is likely to strike most readers and listeners as silly.

grand jury. A. Generally. In most American states, a prosecutor cannot proceed in a case involving a felony or serious misdemeanor without first coming before a body of (often 23) people who are chosen to sit permanently for at least a month—and sometimes a year—and who, in ex parte proceedings, decide whether an indictment should be issued. This body is known as a *grand jury*. If the grand jury decides that the evidence is strong enough to hold the suspect for trial, it returns a *true bill*, i.e., a bill of indictment, charging the suspect with a specific crime. See **true bill.**

The grand jury was abolished in England—with insignificant exceptions in London and Middlesex—in 1933. Even these exceptions were wiped away by the Criminal Justice Act of 1948.

Historical variants of the phrase *grand jury* include *presenting jury*, *accusing jury*, and *jury of indictment*.

B. And *petit jury*. Whereas a *grand jury* determines whether sufficient evidence exists to accuse a person of a crime and to bring a criminal prosecution, a *petit jury* ultimately determines the guilt or innocence of the accused and may convict only when the government has proved guilt beyond a reasonable doubt. A *petit jury*, then, is what we ordinarily think of as "the jury" in a criminal case. See **petit jury.**

grand larceny. See **larceny (B).**

---

grant = (1) the formal transfer of real property; (2) the document by which such a transfer is effected; or (3) the property transferred. Sense 1 contains a historical AMBIGUITY. Originally, the verb *grant* was used only when the grantor conveyed a nonfreehold interest—that is, carved out a smaller interest—such as an easement or a lease. But today the verb denotes the transferring of the grantor's full interest, as when a fee simple absolute is being conveyed.

grant, bargain, and sell; grant, bargain, sell, and convey. The word *grant* or *convey* alone would seem to suffice, the rest being deadwood. David Mellinkoff sanguinely declared, "*Grant* is sufficient." *Mellinkoff's Dictionary of American Legal Usage* 274 (1992). Yet in some jurisdictions, such as Illinois, *grant, bargain, and sell* is a statutory phrase that creates a warranty deed (creating covenants of title) as opposed to a quitclaim deed (merely conveying whatever interest the landholder possesses)—and *grant* alone will not suffice. See *Wheeler v. Wayne County*, 24 N.E. 625 (Ill. 1890). So do your homework before simplifying *grant, bargain, and sell*. See DOUBLETS, TRIPLETS, AND SYNONYM-STRINGS & **words of conveyance.**

grateful; gratified. Both terms mean "thankful," but *gratified* also means "satisfied" <we gratified our craving for chocolate>.

gratify has long been used in legal writing synonymously with *satisfy* in reference to rules or requirements. Neither the *OED* nor *W3* records this use. E.g.:

- "This averment is in the disjunctive, and does not *gratify* the rule requiring certainty in pleading." *Goldman v. Harford Rd. Bldg. Ass'n*, 133 A. 843, 847 (Md. 1926).
- "The legislative policy to grant the refunds and the statement that its policy should take effect on June first can be *gratified*." *Thomas v. Police Comm'r of Baltimore*, 127 A.2d 625, 628 (Md. 1956).
- "Water and sewerage needs can be *gratified* by the Commission if it deems it expedient and practicable to do so." *City of Bowie v. Wash. Suburban Sanitary Comm'n*, 241 A.2d 396, 400 (Md. 1968).
- "A deliberate act is a free act of the will done in furtherance of a formed design to *gratify* a feeling of revenge." *State v. Jones*, 955 S.W.2d 5, 12 (Mo. Ct. App. 1997).
- "Professor Saul Litvinoff has explained that a contract intended to *gratify* a nonpecuniary interest means a contract made 'to satisfy an interest of a spiritual order.'" *Pinero v. Jackson Hewitt Tax Serv. Inc.*, 594 F.Supp.2d 710, 717 (E.D. La. 2009).

gratis dictum. See **dictum (B).**

gravamen (/grə-**vay**-mən/, preferably not /**grah**-və-mən/) = the point of a complaint or grievance. E.g.:

- "The *gravamen* of plaintiffs' complaint is that defendants engaged in a scheme to defraud them out of their interest in an oil concession." *Kazenercom Too v. Turan Petroleum, Inc.*, 590 F.Supp.2d 153, 159 (D.D.C. 2008).
- "Although Szondy is not claiming statutory aggrievement, the *gravamen* of her claim nevertheless rests on her contention that she is classically aggrieved by Ellis' failure to comply with the notice provisions of [the statute]." *PNC Bank, N.A. v. Kelepecz*, 960 A.2d 563, 571 (Conn. 2008).

- "The general *gravamen* of taxpayers' argument on this issue is its assertion that the trial court made a fundamental error in failing to comprehend the transfer restrictions on the subject properties." *Church St. Assocs. v. County of Clinton*, 959 A.2d 490, 496 (Pa. Commw. Ct. 2008).
- "The *gravamen* of the charge is resisting arrest, not fleeing from a police officer." *State v. Redifer*, 290 S.W.3d 184, 186 (Mo. Ct. App. 2009).

Gravamen is used also of criminal accusations <gravamen of the charge>, but not, properly, of crimes: "*The gravamen of the crime* [read *The gist of the crime*] is that the accused has used a fictitious credit card." See **gist.**

Today, nine out of ten times when this word appears, it is in the phrase *gravamen of the complaint*; since *gravamen* in itself means "the material part of a complaint," the phrase seems redundant. The *OED* quotes no sentences containing *the gravamen of the complaint*, although it quotes several containing *the gravamen of the charge*. Perhaps it is felt in modern prose that the phrase *of the complaint* elucidates the meaning of *gravamen*; if so, the word is recondite on its own and infelicitously redundant in the common phrase.

Gravamen is frequently misused for *crux* or *gist*, both of which are broader—e.g.:

- "The *gravamen* [read *gist*] of the medical opinion in support of petitioners' position is that . . . Rumbaugh is not able to countenance the delay inherent in the continuation of legal proceedings and the possible conversion of his death sentence to life imprisonment." *Rumbaugh on Behalf of Rumbaugh v. McKaskle*, 730 F.2d 291, 292 (5th Cir. 1984).
- "The *gravamen* [read *crux*] of Defendants' arguments is that Dr. Hausman ignored objective evidence of certain banks' willingness to work with Discover on the acquiring side of the business, without the precondition that they work with Discover on the issuing side of the business." *Discover Fin. Servs. v. Visa U.S.A., Inc.*, 582 F.Supp.2d 501, 507 (S.D.N.Y. 2008).
- "The *gravamen* [read *gist*] of the relief sought was the payment of damages, rendering specific performance an inappropriate remedy." *R.P. Brennan Gen. Contractors & Bldg., Inc. v. CPS 1 Realty, LP*, 880 N.Y.S.2d 490, 490 (App. Div. 2009).
- "The act of deliberately leaving custodial restraint constitutes the *gravamen* [read *gist*] of the crime of escape." *State v. Pickel*, 995 A.2d 125, 131 n.10 (Conn. App. Ct. 2010). [A suggested revision: *The essence of the crime of escape is the act of deliberately leaving custodial restraint.*]

*Gravaman is a common misspelling—e.g.: "Fullwood argues that the *gravaman* [read *gravamen*] of the offense of distributing or possessing with intent to distribute in violation of [the Code] is the possession of drugs within one thousand feet of school property." *Fullwood v. Commonwealth*, 676 S.E.2d 348, 351 (Va. Ct. App. 2009).

The plural forms are *gravamens* and *gravamina*, the first being preferred—e.g.: "The *gravamina* [read *gravamens*] of this action are the first four claims." *Mason Tenders Dist. Council Pension Fund v. Messera*, 4 F.Supp.2d 293, 295 (S.D.N.Y. 1998). See PLURALS (A).

graymail originated in the late 1970s as a C.I.A. EUPHEMISM for a certain type of *blackmail*. It refers to the "practice whereby a criminal defendant threatens to reveal classified information during the course of his trial in the hope of forcing the government to drop the criminal charge against him." *U.S. v. Smith*, 780 F.2d 1102, 1105 (4th Cir. 1985). E.g.: "Cases in the context of extraordinary rendition are very likely to present serious questions relating to private diplomatic assurances from foreign countries received by federal officials, and this feature of such claims opens the door to *graymail*." *Arar v. Ashcroft*, 585 F.3d 559, 578 (2d Cir. 2009). The Classified Information Procedure Act (1980), often shortened to the acronym *CIPA*, is informally called the *Graymail Act*. Cf. **greenmail.**

gray mule case. See **whitehorse case.**

Great Britain; United Kingdom. *Great Britain* consists of England, Scotland, and Wales. It differs from *United Kingdom*, which includes Northern Ireland.

Great Charter, the. This phrase is a slightly affected synonym of *Magna Carta*—e.g.: "The ground plan to which the common-law polity has built ever since was given by *the Great Charter*." Roscoe Pound, *The Development of Constitutional Guarantees of Liberty* 18 (1957). See **Magna Carta.**

Great Dissenter; First Dissenter. The *Great Dissenter*—no other judge has even approached his greatness as an author of dissenting opinions—was Justice Oliver Wendell Holmes. The nickname has become standard in American legal parlance—e.g.:

- "Even Justice Holmes, the *Great Dissenter* himself, remarked in his first dissent that dissents are generally 'useless' and 'undesirable.'" William J. Brennan Jr., *In Defense of Dissents*, 37 Hastings L.J. 427, 429 (1986).
- "Anti-formalism in modern habeas interpretation was first heralded by Justice Holmes in his frequently cited dissent in *Frank v. Mangum*. . . . There, the *Great Dissenter* observed . . . ." *Chatman-Bey v. Thornburgh*, 864 F.2d 804, 807 (D.C. Cir. 1988).

In this phrase, the more important word is *great*, not *dissenter*, for Holmes "in fact dissented less often than most of his colleagues." Ruth Bader Ginsburg, *Remarks on Writing Separately*, 65 Wash. L. Rev. 133, 142 (1990).

Interestingly, though, Holmes was not the first to bear this nickname: the phrase was applied originally to the first Justice Harlan. *See* T.J. Knight, *The Dissenting Opinions of Justice Harlan*, 51 Am. L. Rev. 481, 484 (1917). A 1970 Harlan biography by Frank Latham bore the title *The Great Dissenter*.

The so-called *First Dissenter* was Justice William Johnson, who was urged by the president who appointed him, Thomas Jefferson, to write a separate opinion in each case so as to check Chief Justice John Marshall's dominance on the Court. Johnson did so only sporadically, but he disagreed with the majority enough to earn this moniker.

great seal, to take the. This phrase, in BrE, means "to attain the office of Lord Chancellor." E.g.: "The law itself had been changed to permit a Catholic (Lord Rawlinson) *to take the great seal*, but after the fanfare came the silence." *Maths Genius Does His Homework on the Law's Reform*, Sunday Times, 11 Dec. 1988, at A13. The phrase originated in the Lord Chancellor's acting as Keeper of the Great Seal. The Lord Chancellor, who is appointed by being handed the Great Seal, carries it in a bag as the badge of office.

Great Writ has long been used as an exalted synonym for *habeas corpus*—e.g.:

- "There has been a halo about the '*Great Writ*' that no one would wish to dim." *Schneckloth v. Bustamonte*, 412 U.S. 218, 275 (1973) (Powell, J., concurring).
- "The '*Great Writ*,' as it has been called by the Supreme Court from John Marshall's day to this, is available by statute in four different situations." Charles Alan Wright, *The Law of Federal Courts* 351 (5th ed. 1994).
- "President Lincoln's famous suspension of the *Great Writ* has received a significant amount of attention in recent years, meriting a scene to itself within Act I of the American drama." Aaron L. Jackson, *Habeas Corpus in the Global War on Terror*, 65 A.F. L. Rev. 263, 266 (2010).

See **habeas corpus.**

green bag. See LAWYERS, DEROGATORY NAMES FOR (A).

green card. See **visa.**

greenmail, a PORTMANTEAU WORD made from *greenbacks* plus *blackmail*, was coined in the early 1980s. It carries two senses: (1) the act of buying enough stock in a company to threaten a hostile takeover, and of then agreeing to sell the stock back to the corporation at an inflated price; or (2) the money paid for stock in the corporation's buy-back. E.g.:

- "The common law claims and the federal Securities Exchange Act claims arise from the same transaction, i.e., the alleged misrepresentation by the Basses of their motives for acquiring the Texaco stock and the ensuing alleged '*greenmail*' between the Bass defendants and Texaco." *Seagoing Uniform Corp. v. Texaco, Inc.*, 705 F.Supp. 918, 921 (S.D.N.Y. 1989).
- "They are particularly infuriated at a suggestion to offer Goldsmith '*greenmail*,' a controversial American takeover practice whereby a company under siege buys off a predator by giving it a large profit on its shares." Ivan Fallon & Tony Lorenz, *Revealed: Secret Plot to Thwart Goldsmith BAT Bid*, Sunday Times, 26 Nov. 1989, at A1.

The word has also been used as a verb, *to greenmail*, on the analogy of *to blackmail*—e.g.: "A fish company built the billboard in 1971 before the federal government '*greenmailed*' Missouri into regulating billboards." *Icehouse Cold Storage, Inc. v. State Hwys. & Transp. Comm'n*, 23 S.W.3d 651, 652 (Mo. Ct. App. 2000). Cf. **graymail.**

Green Paper. See **White Paper.**

grievable, adj., = of, constituting, or giving rise to a valid grievance. This word is almost certainly an unconscious revival of an old word that the *OED* records as having died off about 1500 (when it meant merely "causing distress"). It suddenly emerged in the mid-20th century—e.g.:

- "While not all '*grievable*' disputes are arbitrable under the contract, this one is." *Engineers Ass'n v. Sperry Gyroscope Co.*, 148 F.Supp. 521, 526 (S.D.N.Y. 1957).
- "The collective-bargaining agreement involved here prohibited without qualification all manner of invidious discrimination and made any claimed violation a *grievable* issue." *Emporium Capwell Co. v. Western Addition Cmty. Org.*, 420 U.S. 50, 66 (1975) (per Marshall, J.).

Its even-more-awkward complement, *non-grievable*, soon followed—e.g.:

- "The Village refused to consider the grievance, declaring it *non-grievable* and stating that Fletcher's only appeal was pursuant to the Fire and Police Commission Act." *Village of Creve Coeur v. Fletcher*, 543 N.E.2d 323, 323 (Ill. App. Ct. 1989).
- "The [plaintiff's] grievance [complaining of his transfer] was returned as '*non-grievable.*'" *Skinner v. Holman*, 672 F.Supp.2d 657, 660 (D. Del. 2009).

For a small essay on the word, see *Garner on Language and Writing* 245 (2009).

grievance; *aggrievance. The second is a NEEDLESS VARIANT.

grievant; grievancer; *aggrievant. The first term is common in AmE in the context of arbitration. *W3* defines *grievant* as "one who submits a grievance for arbitration." E.g.: "[An arbitrator's] job is to define the relief that will compensate the *grievant* if his claim is upheld." *Hotel & Rest. Employees & Bartenders Int'l Union v. Michelson's Food Servs., Inc.*, 545 F.2d 1248, 1254 (9th Cir. 1976).

In practice, *grievant* often refers more narrowly to an employee who registers a complaint with an employer. *See* Katharine Seide, *A Dictionary of Arbitration* 106 (1970). E.g.: "Thomas Rogers and Robert Wilson Jr. (*grievants*), were employed by General Services Administration." *Cornelius v. Nutt*, 472 U.S. 648, 653 (1985) (per Blackmun, J.).

The *OED* lists *grievancer* (= one who occasions a grievance or gives ground for complaint) but not *grievant*, a NEOLOGISM dating back only to 1956: "The *grievant* [was entitled] to have such question submitted to final and binding arbitration." *Wisconsin Motor Corp. v. Wisconsin Employment Relations Bd.*, 79 N.W.2d 119, 122 (Wis. 1956). Thus far, *grievant* has not yet spread beyond American legal writing. It is indisputably a useful term even if one might originally have objected to its formation.

*Aggrievant is a NEEDLESS VARIANT.

grieve, vb., most commonly bears the intransitive sense "to feel grief" <she grieved for many months>, though it may also function transitively <he grieved her death>. It can also, traditionally, be a transitive verb meaning "to cause distress to"—e.g.: "The murders that Gary Tison and Randy Greenawalt committed revolt and *grieve* all who learn of them." *Tison v. Arizona*, 481 U.S. 137, 159 (1987) (Brennan, J., dissenting).

But recently the verb has taken on a new legal meaning: "to bring a grievance for the purpose of protesting." The emergence of this sense is not entirely surprising because it is implied by the words *grievable* and *grievant*. Stylists are not likely to use the verb, but neither are they likely to succeed in expunging it. E.g.:

- "Again, the Union was *grieving* G.E.'s subcontracting." *General Elec. Co. v. N.L.R.B.*, 916 F.2d 1163, 1165 (7th Cir. 1990).
- "Despite their current litigation position that Nemsky's termination could not be *grieved* or arbitrated, it is undisputed that . . . Local 399 and ConocoPhillips had each designated representatives for the purpose of moving forward with arbitration of the grievance." *Nemsky v. ConocoPhillips Co.*, 574 F.3d 859, 866 (7th Cir. 2009).
- "Davis's failure to *grieve* the conditions of his confinement is no bar to his due-process claim because the conditions of his confinement are not the basis on which he alleges he suffered harm." *Davis v. Barrett*, 576 F.3d 129, 133 (2d Cir. 2009).

grievous is frequently misspelled *grievious, just as *mischievous* is frequently misspelled *mischievious. These are grievous and mischievous misspellings (and mispronunciations).

grievous bodily harm, a term commonly used in criminal law and in tort law, is a purposely vague term meaning physical injury that is truly serious. It is purposely vague because, ordinarily, the finder of fact must decide in any given case whether the injury meets this general standard. The term "has no specifically legal meaning." Glanville Williams, *Textbook of Criminal Law* 127–28 (1978). See **g.b.h.**

gross. See **in gross.**

gross negligence. See **negligence (A).**

Grotian is the adjective corresponding to the name *Grotius* (1587–1645), the famous 17th-century Dutch jurist. E.g.: "The doctrines of the *Grotian* school had prevailed." Henry S. Maine, *Ancient Law* 83 (17th ed. 1901).

ground. See **grounds.**

ground of action. See **cause of action.**

grounds. Although one does not count as one ground or two grounds every argument one can muster, it is acceptable to speak of a party's relying on a certain *ground* (= reason). Yet even the writer who has only one reason for a position can take that position *on grounds of* whatever that single reason is.

In the speech and writing of American lawyers, the singular *ground* is loosely equivalent to sense 1 of *ratio decidendi*—that is, the court's basis for a decision. See **ratio decidendi.**

grounds for appeal; grounds of appeal. Either is correct, but *grounds for appeal* is perhaps more common.

groundwater. One word.

group of, a. See SYNESIS.

guarantee. A. And *warranty.* Originally the same word, *warranty* and *guarantee* (or *guaranty*) arrived in the language through different medieval French dialects. Both terms denote undertakings by one party to another to indemnify an assured party against some possible default or defect. But there are important differences.

Guarantee relates to the future, in meaning either (1) the act of giving a security; the undertaking with respect to (a contract, performance of a legal act, etc.) that it will be duly carried out; or (2) something given or existing as security, e.g., to fulfill a future engagement or a condition subsequent.

Warranty relates to the present or past and has somewhat more specific and elaborate senses: (1) a covenant (either express or implied) annexed to a conveyance of realty by which the seller warrants the security of the title conveyed; (2) an assurance, express or implied, given by the seller of goods, that he will be answerable for their possession of some quality attributed to them <the seller hereby disclaims all warranties>; or (3) in an insurance contract, an insured's engagement that certain statements are true or that certain conditions will be fulfilled. See **warranty.**

B. And *guaranty.* The distinction in BrE was formerly that *guarantee* is the verb, *guaranty* the noun. Yet *guarantee* is now commonly used as both noun and verb in both AmE and BrE. Following are examples of the noun use:

- "Negro citizens, North and South, who saw in the Thirteenth Amendment a promise of freedom . . . would be left with [a mere] paper *guarantee* if Congress were powerless to [ensure] that a dollar in the hands of a Negro will purchase the same thing as a dollar in the hands of a white man." *Jones v. Alfred H. Mayer Co.*, 392 U.S. 409, 443 (1968) (per Stewart, J.).
- "[Justice Clark] reasoned that without the exclusionary rule, the fourth amendment *guarantees* would be 'a form of words,' valueless and undeserving of mention in perpetual character of inestimable human liberty." Kimberley D. Reed, *The Exclusionary Rule: Is There Life After Leon?*, 12 Thurgood Marshall L. Rev. 139, 148 (1986).

In practice, *guarantee*, n., is the usual term, seen often, for example, in the context of consumer warranties or other assurances of quality or performance. *Guaranty*, by contrast, is now used primarily in financial and banking contexts in the sense "a promise to answer for the debt of another." *Guaranty* is now rarely

seen in nonlegal writing, whether in BrE or AmE. Some legal writers prefer *guaranty* in all noun senses.

Guaranty was formerly used as a verb but is now obsolete as a variant of *guarantee*, vb. In the following sentence, it appears in its more modern legal use as a noun: "The Westbrooks allege that the bank again required them to sign a personal *guaranty* of the promissory note and another deed of trust securing the *guaranty*." *In re Westbrooks*, 440 B.R. 677, 679 (Bankr. M.D.N.C. 2010).

C. And *guarantor.* Both *guarantee* (fr. 1679) and *guarantor* (fr. 1853) have filled the role of agent noun for the verb *to guarantee*. These words once shared the sense "one who makes a guaranty or gives a security," but today *guarantor* has taken the field, rendering *guarantee* in this sense but a NEEDLESS VARIANT. Oddly, *guarantee* has functioned not only as an equivalent of *guarantor*, but also as a passive correlative of it consistently with other forms in -EE. Thus the *OED* quotes the following specimen of *guarantee* (= a person to whom a guarantee is given): "*Guarantors* are relieved by the *guarantee* being compelled, if one is ready to pay the whole, to sell him the debt of the others." *Gaii Institutionum Juris Civilis Commentarii* 2 (Edward Poste trans., 2d ed. 1875). This use of *guarantee* may have been thought useful in tandem with -*or*. The actual occurrences of it in legal prose are rare.

guarantor. See **guarantee (C)** & **surety.**

guaranty. See **guarantee (B).**

guardhouse lawyer. See LAWYERS, DEROGATORY NAMES FOR (B).

guardian *ad litem*; special guardian. These synonymous phrases denote a court-appointed guardian who acts in litigation on behalf of someone under a disability, such as a minor or an incapacitated adult. E.g.: "The Appellate Division has ruled that no *special guardians*, or *guardians ad litem*, as they've been renamed, are needed in VA estates of less than $2,500." Murray T. Bloom, *The Trouble with Lawyers* 309 (1970). See **ad litem, next friend** & *prochein ami.*

guild, n.; gild, vb. A *guild* is an organization, esp. centered on a trade or craft <Writers Guild>. To *gild* is to coat in gold foil <gild the lily>.

guilt; culpability. *Guilt* is what is determined by a trier of fact. *Culpability* is a matter of fact regardless of whether it ever becomes known. Judge Learned Hand is said to have remarked that anyone can be a killer, but only a jury can make a murderer. See **guilty.**

guilt-prone (opposed to *acquittal-prone*) is coming to be used of juries in the sense "likely to convict (a criminal defendant)." E.g.:

- "[Appellant] contends that the process of excluding from the guilt phase of the trial prospective jurors who are unwilling to consider imposing capital punishment resulted in a jury that was impermissibly *guilt-prone* and unrepresentative of the community." *Mattheson v. King*, 751 F.2d 1432, 1442 (5th Cir. 1985).
- "Young argues in his first proposition [that] the trial judge subtly influenced the voir dire procedure in such a way that the resulting jury panel was *guilt-prone* and death-prone in violation of his Fourteenth Amendment right to due process." *Young v. State*, 992 P.2d 332, 337 (Okla. Crim. App. 1998).
- "Defendant argues that this practice deprived him of a jury made up of a fair and representative cross-section of the community and resulted in the impaneling of a '*guilt-prone*' jury." *State v. Wright*, 584 S.E.2d 109 (N.C. Ct. App. 2003).

A variant is *conviction-prone*—e.g.: "The . . . argument assumes that if the prosecution strikes minority-group members on the basis of their group affiliation, then majority-group members inevitably must be as likely to be as *conviction-prone* as the minority-group members are *acquittal-prone*." *U.S. v. Leslie*, 783 F.2d 541, 560 (5th Cir. 1986). Cf. **death-qualified jurors.**

guilty. Lawyers and nonlawyers alike generally associate this word with criminal contexts. But some highly respected legal writers use it in civil contexts as well—e.g.:

- "The better opinion is that co-tenants in fee are not *guilty* of waste in using and enjoying the property in any way [that] is in accord with the reasonable exercise of prudent

ownership by the average man." William F. Walsh, *A Treatise on Equity* 146 (1930).
- "A person is *guilty* of misrepresentation, though all the facts stated by him are true, if his statement is misleading as a whole because it does not refer to other facts affecting the weight of those stated." G.H. Treitel, *The Law of Contract* 353 (8th ed. 1991).

Sometimes the idea of guilt, when superfluous, can be eliminated through deft editing—e.g.: "The plaintiff was *guilty of contributory negligence* [read *contributorily negligent*] for failing to comply with the planned location of the phone lines." *Ward v. City of Lebanon*, 273 S.W.3d 628, 633 (Tenn. Ct. App. 2008). See **blameworthy** & **liable.**

guilty mind. See *mens rea.*

gunslinger. See LAWYERS, DEROGATORY NAMES FOR (A).

gypsy; *gipsy; Roma; Romani. The first spelling is preferred in AmE, the second in BrE. The term and spelling *gypsy* derive from *Egyptian* because it was believed (erroneously) that the itinerant people had migrated from north Africa. Historically, *gypsy* has a pejorative connotation when applied to people, but is acceptable in phrases such as *gypsy vanner* (a breed of horse) and *gypsy shawl* (a style of garment). *Roma* and *Romani*, the names used by one itinerant tribe, are now the increasingly common terms for most itinerant people.

H

habeas is often used in AmE as an abbreviated form of *habeas corpus*, as in the common phrase *habeas relief*. E.g.:

- "This pro se appeal concerns Timothy Rudolph's second federal *habeas* petition." *Rudolph v. Blackburn*, 750 F.2d 302, 303 (5th Cir. 1984).
- "In 1982, we affirmed the dismissal of a prior petition for federal *habeas* relief." *Daniels v. Blackburn*, 763 F.2d 705, 706 (5th Cir. 1985).
- "Piper's *habeas* argument is directed at invalid waiver of his right to a jury in the death-penalty phase and ineffective assistance of counsel." *Piper v. Weber*, 771 N.W.2d 352, 356 (S.D. 2009).
- "As for petitioner's alleged lack of proficiency with the English language, this court denied a similar argument for equitable tolling in a *habeas* decision issued in 2004." *Oduche v. U.S. Dep't of Homeland Sec.*, 607 F.Supp.2d 676, 682 (D. Del. 2009).

See **habeas corpus.**

habeas corpus, short for *habeas corpus ad subjiciendum et recipiendum* (lit., "that you have the body for submitting and receiving"), is the quintessential justified LATINISM that has taken on a peculiar meaning that no homegrown English term could now supply. (*Have-the-body writ* isn't a serious alternative.)

Though *habeas corpus* has become one of the basic devices to protect civil liberties, it was originally used in *capias* writs not to release people from prison but to secure their presence in custody. In the 16th century, the King's Bench began issuing the writ called *habeas corpus ad subjiciendum*, primarily so that subjects could challenge the constitutionality of imprisonment. In 1679, the writ was legislatively enshrined in the Habeas Corpus Act. Nearly a century later, in the famous *Somersett's Case* (1772), Lord Mansfield held that slavery had no standing in England, so that the writ was sufficient to release a black slave from a ship on the Thames. Today it is considered "perhaps the most important writ known to the constitutional law of England." *Secretary of State for Home Affairs v. O'Brien*, [1923] A.C. 603, 609. See **prerogative writs.**

Today in the United States, *habeas corpus* is employed to bring a person before the court, most frequently to ensure that the person's imprisonment or detention is not illegal. The writ may also be used to obtain judicial review of (1) the regularity of the extradition process, (2) the right to or amount of bail, (3) the jurisdiction of a court that has imposed a criminal sentence, or (4) the constitutionality of a prisoner's conditions of confinement. It is a separate, civil proceeding to enforce the civil right to personal liberty, whether the restraint is under criminal or civil law. It is sometimes referred to in its long form as the *writ of habeas corpus*. At other times it is shortened to *habeas*. Historically, it was often referred to as the *Great Writ*. See **Great Writ** & **prerogative writs.**

When used as a PHRASAL ADJECTIVE, the term need not be hyphenated: "The Senate is scheduled to consider crime legislation, including *habeas-corpus* [read *habeas corpus*] proposals, possibly as soon as next week." Wall St. J., 16 May 1990, at B6. See PHRASAL ADJECTIVES (B).

The plural (rarely used) is *habeas corpora*. See **corpus.**

habendum (L. "to be possessed") denotes the part of a deed that defines the extent of the interest being conveyed and any conditions that attach to that conveyance. The clause beginning "to have and to hold" is the habendum and tenendum combined, though it is traditionally called the *habendum*—e.g.: "The *habendum* clause is as follows: 'To have and to hold, all and singular, the premises above mentioned, unto the said C.M. Dubois, bishop of Galveston.'" *Gabert v. Olcott*, 23 S.W. 985, 986 (Tex. 1893).

The best plural form is not *habenda*, but *habendums*—e.g.: "There were other words in both deeds between the granting clauses and the *habendums* signifying the intention of the grantor." *U.S. v. 31,600 Acres of Land*, 47 F.Supp. 21, 24 (E.D.S.C. 1942).

habitability; *inhabitability. Because of confusion over the prefix *in-*, which is historically intensive and not negative in **inhabitability* (as in *inflammable*), we have startlingly anomalous antonyms: the positive form is *habitability*, the negative form *uninhabitability*. **Inhabitable* is little used today, and it is unfortunately ambiguous now when it *is* used.

habitation is an abstract word best replaced when possible by *house* or *dwelling*.

hack attorney. See LAWYERS, DEROGATORY NAMES FOR (A).

had. See **would have.**

had and received. This DOUBLET has historically been a TERM OF ART in the phrase *money had and received*. In pleading in assumpsit, the plaintiff declares that the defendant *had and received* certain money. In most Anglo-American jurisdictions, the phrase is no longer required in pleadings. See **money had and received, action for.**

had have. This collocation, a so-called double modal, exemplifies dialectal usage—e.g.: "Defense practitioners must determine whether the jurisdiction applies a subjective or objective test with respect to whether the patient would not have consented to the procedure if he or she *had have* [read *had*] been informed of the risk." William G. Cobb, *Defending the Informed Consent Case*, 72 Def. Couns. J. 330, 332 (2005).

had ought, what grammarians call a "double modal," is a substandard usage in place of *ought*—e.g.: "If his services are as valuable as he contended at the trial, he *had ought* [read *ought*] to be able to find substantial employment here or elsewhere." *Roberts v. I-T-E Circuit Breaker Co.*, 316 F.Supp. 133, 134 (D. Minn. 1970). Like most double modals, this one typifies dialectal usage.

haec verba, in. See **in haec verba.**

haeres, the medieval Latin spelling of the Latin word *heres* (= heir), still sometimes appears: "The defendant argued that the Crown was not in possession of the land as it was only *ultima haeres* in real property law." Alastair Davidson, *The Invisible State* 149 (2002). (Aus.) The author erred slightly in his Latin; the correct form is *ultimus*, not *ultima*, before *haeres*.

Hague, The. The definite article in this place-name is invariably capitalized.

***hail into court.** See **hale (B).**

hale. **A. *Hale into court; haul into court.*** These phrases are equally common. In *hale into court*, the verb *hale* means "to compel to go; pull"—e.g.:

- "Taney ordered that the general himself be *haled into court*." Robert G. McCloskey, *The American Supreme Court* 98 (1960).
- "*Hans* was not expressing some narrow objection to the particular federal power by which Louisiana had been *haled into court*, but was rather enunciating a fundamental principle of federalism." *Pennsylvania v. Union Gas Co.*, 491 U.S. 1, 37 (1989) (Scalia, J., concurring in part & dissenting in part).

Haul into court has the advantage of being at once more picturesque because the verb *haul* conjures up a distinct image and is immune from the error discussed in (B)—e.g.:

- "There is even authority that anyone who takes steps deliberately to thwart the enforcement of a judicial decree can be *hauled into court* and dealt with summarily." *U.S. v. Board of Educ.*, 11 F.3d 668, 673 (7th Cir. 1993).
- "Airlines have begun changing their policies even before being *hauled into court*." Reena N. Glazer, Note, *Women's Body Image and the Law*, 43 Duke L.J. 113, 145 (1993).

B. The Solecism *hail into court.* Properly, the verb *hail*—apart from meteorological senses—means (1) "to greet or salute" <they hailed her warmly>; (2) "to praise enthusiastically" <hailed as a great innovator>; or (3) "to call out to" <hail a cab>. Sense 2 is most common in legal writing—e.g.: "Most of the feminist scholars who have treated the battered woman syndrome defense have explicitly endorsed the defense, *hailing* the court's acceptance of the theory as an important first step." Anne M. Coughlin, *Excusing Women*, 82 Cal. L. Rev. 1, 27 (1994).

The blunder *hail into court is surprisingly common—e.g.:

- "When the commission was *hailed* [read *haled*] into court for failing to act, it claimed its process had not yet been appropriately exhausted by the plaintiffs." *Klein v. Sullivan*, 978 F.2d 520, 523 (9th Cir. 1992).
- "The agreement did not designate a specific forum and did not provide any guidance as to where the defendants could be *hailed* [read *haled*] into court." *Preferred Capital, Inc. v. Power Eng'g Group*, 839 N.E.2d 416, 422 (Ohio Ct. App. 2005).
- "When a criminal defendant is initially *hailed* [read *haled*] into court, the status quo is that she cannot alone obviate a jury proceeding while maintaining defenses to the charges." *Commonwealth v. White*, 910 A.2d 648, 664 (Pa. 2006) (Saylor, J., concurring and dissenting).

half (of). The preposition *of* is usually unnecessary—e.g.:

- "The insured may claim for a constructive total where the cost of repair, reconditioning, refloating, or the like would exceed *half* the value." Grant Gilmore & Charles L. Black Jr., *The Law of Admiralty* 84 (2d ed. 1975).
- "*Half* the intentional killings of adult males are in a rage or a quarrel." Glanville Williams, *Textbook of Criminal Law* 477 (1978).
- "The hearing officer ordered ASD to reimburse Parents for *half of* [omit *of*] the cost of this residential program." *Ashland Sch. Dist. v. Parents of Student E.H.*, 587 F.3d 1175, 1180 (9th Cir. 2009).
- "If the hearing officers ruled against the carriers . . . approximately *half of* [omit *of*] the time, how could they be presumed to be biased?" Nancy A. Welsh, *What Is "Important Enough" in a World of Embedded Neutrals?*, 52 Ariz. L. Rev. 395, 464 (2010).

half-yearly. See *biannual.

hallucination; delusion. A *hallucination* results from disturbed perceptions, as when a person "hears voices" or "sees ghosts." A *delusion* is a belief that results from disturbed thinking, as when a person incorrectly imagines that he or she is being persecuted. For the difference between *delusion* and *illusion*, see **illusion**. See also **allusion**.

halve (= to separate into two equal portions) is pronounced like *have*. As with *almond* and *salmon*, the *-l-* is silent. The unfortunate result is that the word is easily misunderstood in speech.

hand down a decision; hand out a decision. The first is the American, the second said to be the traditional British legal idiom, as H.L. Mencken observed in *The American Language* 246 (4th ed. 1960). Following is an example of the American phrase: "It is not extravagant to argue that *Ex parte Young* is one of the three most important decisions the Supreme Court of the United States has ever *handed down*." 17A Charles Alan Wright et al., *Federal Practice & Procedure* § 4231 (3d ed. 2007). The BrE idiom *hand out* is seldom if ever used today.

The traditional idiom has been stretched by journalists, who occasionally use it to refer not to what a judge does, but to what a jury does: "The verdict is noteworthy, lawyers say, because it is believed to be one of the largest sums ever *handed down* in an invasion of privacy case." Paul M. Barrett, *Access to Reagan Videotape Is Limited*, Wall St. J., 16 Feb. 1990, at B6. Cf. **hand up.**

hand up. This idiom traditionally referred to a grand jury's passing a matter on to a criminal court—e.g.:

- "At the time the grand jury reported, five indictments were *handed up*, three of which were sealed and two open." *People v. Bailey*, 149 N.Y.S. 823, 824 (App. Div. 1914).
- "Had these indictments been *handed up* on the 21st, when the district attorney offered to have them prepared, the case . . . would be free from any doubt." *U.S. v. Garsson*, 291 F. 646, 648 (S.D.N.Y. 1923) (per L. Hand, J.).
- "A federal grand jury *handed up* a 28-count indictment against 30 individuals, including the four on appeal in this case, for their participation in the conspiracy." *U.S. v. Rosado-Perez*, 605 F.3d 48, 51–52 (1st Cir. 2010).

Sometimes writers choose the wrong idiom, namely *hand down*—e.g.:

- "The Federal Grand Jury *handed down* [read *handed up*] its indictments on September 15, 1972." Larry A. Van-Meter & Tim McNeese, *United States v. Nixon* 42 (2007).
- "In this case, a Cook County grand jury *handed down* [read *handed up*] indictments against the corporation and five of its corporate officers, charging each with multiple counts of aggravated battery, reckless conduct, and conspiracy." Thomas D. Schneid, *Legal Liability in Safety and Loss Prevention* 135 (2010).

See **hand down a decision.**

hang, vb., = (of a jury) to be unable to reach a verdict. This Americanism dates from the mid-19th century and is still common—e.g.: "Prosecutor Murphy's own rhetoric in the second Hiss trial (after the first jury *hung*) was even more powerful." Daniel Levitt, *Rhetoric in Closing Argument*, 17 Litig. 17, 18 (Winter 1991).

Less commonly, *hang* is used as a transitive verb in the sense "to cause (a jury) to be unable to reach a verdict"—e.g.:

- "One way to *hang* a jury is to have at least one person on it who is likely to raise the hackles of at least one of the others." Robin T. Lakoff, *Talking Power: The Politics of Language in Our Lives* 116 (1990).
- "All that is needed to *hang* a jury is tenacity." Richard H. Menard Jr., *Ten Reasonable Men*, 38 Am. Crim. L. Rev. 179, 196 (2001).

hanged; hung. Coats and pictures are *hung*, and sometimes even juries. But criminals found guilty of capital offenses are *hanged*—at least in some jurisdictions. In perhaps the most disappointing Lerner–Loewe lyric of all time, Henry Higgins (the grammatical shaman of *My Fair Lady*) is made to say that people should be "*hung* / for the cold-blooded murder of the English tongue." The *hung–tongue* rhyme cheapens an otherwise superb scene: a first-rate grammarian like Higgins would never have blundered in such an elementary way. See **hung jury.**

hanging judge (= a judge who is esp. harsh with defendants accused of capital crimes) dates at least from the mid-19th century. Some modern references, though, suggest that the phrase might be older—e.g.: "Too often their attitude appears to be that of the *'hanging judges'* of the seventeenth century." *Ex parte Mouratis*, 21 F.2d 694, 695 (N.D. Cal. 1927). See **maximum [+ name].**

Hansard (= the official reports of the proceedings of the British Parliament) derives from Luke Hansard, printer of the *Journal of the House of Commons* from 1774 to 1828, and his son, Thomas Curson Hansard, printer of the *Parliamentary Debates* during the early 19th century. E.g.: "The debates on all the parliamentary stages are the subject of verbatim reporting in the Official Reports of the Houses of Parliament (known collectively as *Hansard*)." Martin Partington, *Introduction to the English Legal System* 45 (2010–2011).

happily means "fortunately," not "in a happy manner," when used as here:

- "The seventeenth- and eighteenth-century jurists were chiefly teachers and philosophers. *Happily* they had been trained to accept the Roman law as something of paramount authority." Roscoe Pound, *An Introduction to the Philosophy of Law* 43–44 (1922).
- "*Happily*, the Criminal Law Act sweeps aside these anomalies." Glanville Williams, *Textbook of Criminal Law* 349 (1978).

See SENTENCE ADVERBS & **hopefully.**

harass may be pronounced in either of two ways: /**har**-iss/ or /hə-**ras**/. Although the first is often thought to be preferable, the second prevails in AmE (Americans being obtusely impervious to puns). The verb is often misspelled **harrass*—e.g.:

- "Gallups contends that thereafter he was *harrassed* [read *harassed*] by McCrary continually for five days." *Gallups v. Alexander City*, 287 F.Supp.2d 1286, 1292 (M.D. Ala. 2003).
- "Any employee . . . shall be entitled to all relief necessary . . . if that employee . . . is discharged, demoted, suspended, threatened, *harrassed* [read *harassed*], or in any other manner discriminated against in the terms and conditions of employment because of lawful acts done by the employee." 31 U.S.C. § 3730(h) (2010).

harassment. During the Senate's confirmation hearings on the appointment of Justice Clarence Thomas in October 1991, senators divided over whether to say /**hair**-is-mənt/ or /hə-**ras**-mənt/ (and over other issues as well). Because the proceedings were closely watched throughout the U.S., the correct pronunciation became a popular subject of discussion. Although in BrE /**hair**-is-mənt/ predominates—and many Americans (therefore?) consider it preferable—in AmE /hə-**ras**-mənt/ is standard.

hard-and-fast rule. This common CLICHÉ is sometimes useful, in legal prose, but remember to hyphenate it as a PHRASAL ADJECTIVE—e.g.:

- "Few *hard-and-fast rules* are available because whether the model is adequate for a dataset depends on . . . the question being asked, the nature of the lack of fit, and how bad the indicators are." D. James Greiner, *Causal Inference in Civil Rights Litigation*, 122 Harv. L. Rev. 533, 543 (2008).
- "There are no *hard-and-fast* standards as to what facts fulfill the requirements of 'reasonable diligence.'" *Loppnow v. Bielik*, 783 N.W.2d 450, 454 (Wis. Ct. App. 2010).

Cf. the cousin of this phrase, **bright-line rule.**

hard cases make bad law. This catchphrase refers to the danger that a decision operating harshly on the defendant may lead a court to make an unwarranted exception or otherwise alter the law. Glanville Williams wrote wishfully when pronouncing this byword passé: "It used to be said that *hard cases make bad law*—a proposition that our less pedantic age regards as doubtful. What is certain is that cases in which the moral indignation of the judge is aroused frequently make bad law." *The Sanctity of Life and the Criminal Law* 105 (1957). In fact, this CLICHÉ is probably used as frequently today as it ever was—and sometimes unmeaningfully.

hard law. See **soft law.**

hardly. The word may mean "vigorously; harshly" <he was beaten hardly>, but this sense is confusing because the word's primary meaning today is "only just; barely" <the judge said hardly anything>. The difference in placement between *he was beaten hardly* and *he was hardly beaten* is not enough to eliminate doubts about what the writer intends. Still, *hardly* in its primary sense is hardly ever ambiguous—e.g.: "Appellant testified that the police said *hardly* anything during the first interview." *People v. Guillebeau*, 183 Cal. Rptr. 121, 127 (Ct. App. 1982).

hard sell; hard sale. *Hard sell* = pressure tactics used in selling. E.g.:

- "In 1985, David Rainbolt had allegedly 'put the *hard sell*' on Alfred Roberts and represented to him that the dividends on Bancshares' preferred stock were 'guaranteed and no risk.'" *Dotson v. Rainbolt*, 894 P.2d 1109, 1111 (Okla. 1995).
- "After receiving what McGrenera now describes as the '*hard sell*,' Med Resorts and McGrenera entered into a thirty-year contract." *FTC v. Med Resorts Int'l, Inc.*, 199 F.R.D. 601, 604 (N.D. Ill. 2001).

Hard sale = a difficult selling job, usu. on an unlikely buyer—e.g.: "Some solutions for modifying the Joint Plan could be made easily under the framework, while others would be a *hard sale* for some of the federal or state agencies." Zachary L. Lancaster, *Restraining Yellowstone's Roaming Bison*, 20 J. Land Use & Envtl. L. 423, 444 (2005).

An asterisk (*) precedes words and phrases that are invariably inferior forms.

Sometimes the one phrase is misused for the other—e.g.:

- "Plaintiff states . . . that the Apple representative employed '*hard sale* [read *hard-sell*] tactics.'" *Sova v. Apple Vacations*, 984 F.Supp. 1136, 1140 (S.D. Ohio 1997).
- "The fact [that] the chart notes corroborate Dr. Hardwick's testimony as to his habit and routine makes Thomas's challenge to his testimony an especially *hard sell* [read *hard sale*]." *Thomas v. Hardwick*, 231 P.3d 1111, 1117 (Nev. 2010).

hark back is now preferred over **harken back* or **hearken back*—e.g.:

- "We are not *harking back* to Latin bywords without sanction of our highest Court." *In re City of Houston*, 745 F.2d 925, 928 (5th Cir. 1984) (per Reavley, J.).
- "*Harkening back* [read *Harking back*] to their other claims of bias and prejudice, they claim that 'the intent of this punishment is to ruin, rather than correct.'" *Moraski v. Connecticut Bd. of Examiners of Embalmers & Funeral Dirs.*, 967 A.2d 1199, 1216 (Conn. 2009).
- "There is almost a nostalgic quality about it, *harkening back* [read *harking back*] to the days of early America when candidates for office thought it was in bad taste to campaign on their own behalf, instead letting their surrogates do all the dirty work." *Siefert v. Alexander*, 597 F.Supp.2d 860, 888 (W.D. Wis. 2009).

harmless (= not capable of being harmed)—as in the phrase *indemnify and hold harmless*—differs significantly from the lay sense ("not capable of harming"). E.g.: "That subsection authorizes the Secretary of Health and Human Services to *hold harmless* or provide liability insurance for a PHS officer or employee for personal injuries caused by conduct occurring within the scope of his office or employment." *Hui v. Castaneda*, 130 S.Ct. 1845, 1854 (2010) (per Sotomayor, J.) (quoting 42 U.S.C.A. § 233(f)).

The phrase is sometimes written *save harmless*—e.g.: "Amoco would not be fully indemnified and *saved harmless* from any loss." *Patch v. Amoco Oil Co.*, 845 F.2d 571, 572 (5th Cir. 1988). See **indemnify (A).**

hath. See -ETH.

haul. See **hale.**

haul into court. See **hale (A).**

have and hold. See **habendum** & DOUBLETS, TRIPLETS, AND SYNONYM-STRINGS.

havoc, to wreak. Although the phrases *create havoc*, *make havoc*, *play havoc*, and *work havoc* were once common, the usual phrase today is *wreak havoc*. The past tense is *wreaked havoc*, not **wrought havoc* (as many writers mistakenly think)—e.g.: "There are abundant examples of linguistic havoc *wrought* [read *wreaked*] by lawyers and legal scholars as well." Robert C. Cumbow, *The Subverting of the Goeduck: Sex and Gender, Which and That, and Other Adventures in the Language of the Law*, 14 U. Puget Sound L. Rev. 755, 777 (1991).

H.D.C.; H.I.D.C. Both abbreviations denote a "holder in due course," the first being more common. Because they are initialisms and not acronyms, they generally take periods (as opposed to being written *HDC* and *HDIC*), though this battle for reason may already be lost. See ACRONYMS AND INITIALISMS.

Whether one uses *H.D.C.* or *H.I.D.C.*, the indefinite article preceding the initialism should be *an*, not *a*: "In order to be *a HIDC* [read *an H.D.C.*], one must first be a 'holder,' which means that the party must be in possession of the documents of title or an instrument." *In re Singer Prods. Co.*, 102 B.R. 912, 931 (Bankr. E.D.N.Y. 1989).

head has special meanings in legal documents: (1) "a heading in a document (such as a legislative bill, a contract, etc." <the 282-paragraph code was regularly arranged under heads and subheads>; and (2) "in an abstract of title, the description of the land covered by the abstract (sometimes also called the *caption*)" <the head misdefined the realty>. But these uses of *head* may be slowly disappearing; for sense 1, *heading* is now becoming the more usual word, and for sense 2, either *caption* or *property description* is more common. See **subhead.**

heading. See **head,** CAPITALIZATION (B) & DOCUMENT DESIGN.

headlease. In BrE legal writing, this term denotes a primary lease under which subleases are in effect—e.g.: "The former sublease has been destroyed by the forfeiture of the *headlease*, and the court order does not and cannot revive that sublease." Peter Butt, *Land Law* 293 (2d ed. 1988). So *headlessor* is the BrE correlative of *sublessor*, and *headlessee* of *sublessee*. In AmE, the words *lease*, *lessor*, and *lessee* generally refer to the primary lease.

headnote, in AmE and BrE alike, refers to the reporter's summary of a judicial opinion. Usually placed at the beginning of the reported case, the headnote states each rule of law that the case supposedly involves. A synonym of *headnote* is *syllabus*. (See **syllabus.**)

healthcare. Preferably one word. *Healthcare-related issues* is much better than *health-care-related issues*. The one-word version precludes punctuational bungling by writers who don't know how to handle PHRASAL ADJECTIVES.

healthful; healthy. In the best usage, *healthy* means "in good health"; *healthful* means "promoting good health"—e.g.:

- "Prevention efforts also need to address conditions in the economic, social and physical environments that make it difficult for people to make *healthy* [read *healthful*] choices." Edward M. Kennedy, *Health Care as a Basic Human Right*, 22 Harv. Hum. Rts. J. 165, 167 (2009).
- "[Plaintiff] also testified that they do not go out to dinner and the food budget is for *healthy* [read *healthful*], nutritious food." *In re Scott*, 417 B.R. 623, 628 (Bankr. W.D. Wash. 2009).

hearing. For the meaning in Scots law, see **proof (D).**

hearing officer. See **administrative-law judge.**

*hearken back. See hark back.

hearsay evidence; secondhand evidence. The first phrase is the preferred, universally understood term for evidence of the oral statements of someone other than the witness testifying and statements in documents offered to prove the truth of the matter asserted.

Hearsay is sometimes made *heresay*, an error infrequently committed. To do so is heresy. See **direct evidence.**

hear ye, hear ye, hear ye; oyez, oyez, oyez. Both forms of the cry are used today in American courts. The first is archaic English, the second vestigial LAW FRENCH with the same meaning. See **oyez, oyez, oyez** & *countez.*

hedonic damages = damages awarded for the deprivation of the pleasure of being alive. Such damages are not allowed in most jurisdictions. The phrase was innovated in the 1980s—e.g.:

- "An Illinois jury has awarded *hedonic damages.*" Nat'l L.J., Nov. 26, 1984, at 3.
- "The amount of so-called *hedonic damages* was decided following an economist's evaluation of what the youth's enjoyment of life would have been worth had he not been killed." *Court and Government Decisions with Impact on Business, Employees, Consumers,* U.S. News & World Rep., 17 Dec. 1984, at 80.
- "Pushed by a handful of imaginative plaintiff lawyers and expert witnesses-for-hire, *hedonic damages* are sought in personal-injury cases as compensation for the loss of the pleasure of living." Paul M. Barrett, *Accept Hedonic Damages, Study Urges, but Fight for Proper Use,* Wall St. J., 21 Aug. 1989, at 3B.

See **damages.**

hegemony /hi-**jem**-ə-nee/ is a fundamentally political term ("political dominance; the leadership or predominant authority of one state of a confederacy or union over the others") that has been imported into nonpolitical contexts—e.g.:

- "Insured argues that such a provision operates effectively as a forum-selection clause, affording it absolute *hegemony* over the question of the jurisdiction in which any coverage dispute is to be litigated." *Chubb Custom Ins. Co. v. Prudential Ins. Co. of Am.,* 948 A.2d 1285, 1287 (N.J. 2008).
- "Indeed, if the Court were to apply this analytical approach in every case addressing a conflict between a statute and a rule of evidence . . . the legislature, not the judicial department, would possess *hegemony* over all evidentiary rules." *Seisinger v. Siebel,* 203 P.3d 483, 498 (Ariz. 2009) (Eckerstrom, J., concurring in part).
- "The Court's repeated orders . . . ultimately resulted in an effective entrenchment of the Orthodox version of Judaism as far as religious councils were concerned, requiring non-Orthodox representatives to surrender to the Orthodox *hegemony* in their role as council members." Ofrit Liviatan, *Judicial Activism and Religion-Based Tensions in India and Israel,* 26 Ariz. J. Int'l & Comp. L. 583, 609 (2009).

The term verges on being a VOGUE WORD.

height has a distinct -*t*- sound at the end; to pronounce this word as if it were **heighth* is semiliterate.

heightened scrutiny. See **strict scrutiny.**

heinous /**hay**-nəs/—rhyming with "pain us"—is one of the most commonly mispronounced words in legal contexts. It is also frequently misspelled **heinious*—e.g.: "This was a *heinious* [read *heinous*], atrocious, and cruel murder considering the appellant's vicious and pitiless attitude and the brutal manner in which the victim was killed." *Cooks v. State,* 699 P.2d 653, 661 (Okla. Crim. App. 1985).

heir. A. And *heir (at law); (in)heritor.* These terms denote "the person entitled by statute to the land of an intestate." *Heir,* the most common term, is commonly misunderstood: "Laymen—and sometimes first-year law students taking exams—wrongly assume that one who receives real property by will is an heir. Technically, the word 'heir' is reserved for one who receives real property by action of the laws of intestacy, which operate today only in the absence of a valid will." Thomas F. Bergin & Paul G. Haskell, *Preface to Estates in Land and Future Interests* 14 n.32 (2d ed. 1984).

Strictly speaking, *heirs* cannot be determined until the ancestor dies, though we commonly speak of *heirs apparent* and *heirs presumptive* (see (B)). *Heir* ordinarily differs from the term *children,* for a decedent's siblings can be heirs.

Legal heir (= the heir of an intestate by operation of law) is another way of rendering *heir at law*: "There is nothing in the will or in the record that sustains a conclusion that she made the bequest because she wanted to make certain her *legal heirs* would not share in the estate." *La Fond v. City of Detroit,* 98 N.W.2d 530, 532 (Mich. 1959). Still another variant synonymous with *heir at law* is *heir general.* Usually, though, *heir* alone is sufficient.

Inheritor, often used in extended senses <inheritors of the Western tradition>, predominates over *heritor.*

B. Types of Heirs: *expectant heir; prospective heir; heir apparent; heir presumptive.* A living person has no heirs, but various terms have been devised to describe potential heirs. An *expectant heir* is one who has a reversionary or remainder interest in property, or a chance of succeeding to it—e.g.:

- "Before a decedent's death an *expectant heir* has no vested interest in property he may subsequently inherit." *In re Estate of David,* 762 P.2d 745, 746 (Colo. Ct. App. 1988) (Hume, J., dissenting).
- "If Daughter's status as attorney-in-fact were revoked, at that time she would no longer have standing to raise

arguments similar to those included in this appeal, inasmuch as she would only be an *expectant heir* at that time." *In re Guardianship of L.R.*, 908 N.E.2d 360, 365 n.2 (Ind. Ct. App. 2009).

A *prospective heir* is one who may inherit but may be excluded; this term embraces the two other types of heirs, *presumptive* and *apparent*. An *heir presumptive* is a person who will inherit if the potential intestate dies immediately, but who may be excluded if another more closely related heir is born. An *heir apparent* is certain to inherit unless he or she dies first or is excluded by a valid will. Cf. **laughing heir.**

On the placement of the adjectives in these phrases, see POSTPOSITIVE ADJECTIVES. Sometimes the adjectives are used prepositively: "With the exception of the trustee, all of the parties as thus represented—including contingent remaindermen and the *presumptive heirs*—joined in a petition to the court to consider, authorize, and approve the proposed compromise of the litigation." *Mabry v. Scott*, 124 P.2d 659, 662 (Cal. Dist. Ct. App. 1942).

C. *Heir; distributee; next of kin.* Technically, *heir* should refer only to the person entitled to the land of an intestate; either *distributee* or *next of kin* should be used of one entitled to an intestate's personal property. But the technically correct forms are rarely followed even in the ordinary speech of lawyers: "Today the word '*heirs*' usually means those persons designated by the applicable statute to take a decedent's intestate property, real and personal." Jesse Dukeminier & Stanley M. Johanson, *Family Wealth Transactions* 11–12 (1972). See **devisee.**

heirs of the body. See **bodily heirs.**

help; help to. Where the *to* can be idiomatically omitted, it ought to be—e.g.:

- "All this may *help to* [read *help*] explain, though perhaps *not to justify* [read *not justify*], the bias in the legal profession and the courts towards traditional goals and values." P.S. Atiyah, *Law and Modern Society* 87 (1983).
- "Creating a new exception would also *help to shore* [read *help shore*] up the integrity of the special needs doctrine." Ric Simmons, *Searching for Terrorists*, 59 Duke L.J. 843, 908 (2010).

helpmate; *helpmeet. **Helpmeet*, now archaic, was the original form, yet folk etymology changed the spelling to *helpmate*, which is now the prevalent form. Though *helpmate* means "a companion or helper," it is generally restricted in use to one's spouse—e.g.:

- "During the twenty-three years of the marriage, the wife was a mother—seven children—and a *helpmeet* [read *helpmate*] in every sense of the word." *Johnson v. Johnson*, 446 So.2d 622, 625 (Ala. Civ. App. 1983).
- "The permanent loss of sexual relations and his shift from a role as *helpmate* to one as a dependent provides the jury with factually sufficient evidence of a loss of consortium in the future." *Reeder v. Allport*, 218 S.W.3d 817, 821 (Tex. App.—Beaumont 2007).

But it occasionally appears in its broader sense—e.g.:

- "Over time, the gang's targets included Sargent, Sweeney (who survived multiple attempts on his life, but was left paralyzed from the chest down), a rival drug dealer, James Boyden III, and the latter's son and *helpmeet* [read *helpmate*], James Boyden IV." *U.S. v. Houlihan*, 92 F.3d 1271, 1277 (1st Cir. 1996).
- "Schools ideally are *helpmates* to parents in the education of children." *Committee for Educ. Equality v. State*, 294 S.W.3d 477, 512 (Mo. 2009) (Wolff, J., concurring in part).

hence. See **thence.**

henceforth; *henceforward. The second is a NEEDLESS VARIANT. See **from henceforth.**

he or she. The traditional view was that the masculine pronouns are generic, comprehending both male and female. But this view is now widely thought to embody SEXISM. One way to avoid the generic masculine *he*, *his*, and *him* is to use—not at every turn, but sparingly—*he or she*, and *his or her*, and *him or her*. E.g.:

- "Each [juror] indicated that *he or she* could follow the law as directed by the trial court." *Johnson v. State*, 820 So.2d 842, 855 (Ala. Crim. App. 2000).
- "In criminal prosecutions, a juror may be struck for cause if *he or she* has an attorney–client relationship with the prosecutor." *State v. Shimko*, 725 N.W.2d 659 (Iowa Ct. App. 2006).
- "It is true that a person does not have the same expectation of privacy in a hospital room as *he or she* would have at home." *State v. Butler*, 1 So.3d 242, 249 (Fla. Dist. Ct. App. 2008) (Padovano, J., dissenting).

Another way to avoid the problem—not possible in all contexts—is to make the antecedent of the pronoun plural if possible. E.g.: "It is well established that the State cannot exclude jurors from service merely because they have conscientious scruples against the death penalty." *Puckett v. Epps*, 615 F.Supp.2d 494, 507 (S.D. Miss. 2009). The disadvantage of such a wording is that it often too strongly suggests a singleness of mind in the group, as opposed to the uniqueness of an individual mind.

Interestingly, the forms *he or she* and *his or her* have long found acceptance in our typically verbose legal writing. Weseen wrote, "Outside of legal writing, it is not considered good form to use double pronouns, as *he or she*, *his or her*." Maurice H. Weseen, *Crowell's Dictionary of English Grammar* 198 (1928). The phrase is by no means a newfangled concession to feminism. In 1837, the English Wills Act stated: "And be it further enacted, That every Will made by a Man or Woman shall be revoked by *his or her* Marriage (except a Will made in exercise of Appointment . . . .)." 7 Wm. IV & 1 Vict., c. 26 (1837). See SEXISM (A).

hereabouts; *hereabout. This term, meaning "in this vicinity," is preferably spelled with the final *-s*.

hereafter; hereinafter. Perhaps because *hereinafter* sounds especially legalistic, some plain-language advocates have misguidedly recommended *hereafter* in its place. But the two words have distinct meanings;

and in any event, *hereafter* could hardly be cheered as a plain-language triumph over *hereinafter*.

Hereafter = (1) henceforth; or (2) at some future time. The existence of these two meanings may make the word ambiguous, for example in legislation that is said to be *effective hereafter*. A more precise rendering of the intended meaning is *effective with the passage of this Act* or *after the day this Act takes effect*. Sense 1 is the more usual meaning of *hereafter*. A similar AMBIGUITY plagues *heretofore*. See **hitherto.**

Hereinafter = in a part of this document that follows. E.g.: "Motions, in general, shall be submitted and determined upon the motion papers *hereinafter* referred to." *Kasuri v. St. Elizabeth Hosp. Med. Ctr.*, 897 F.2d 845, 855 (6th Cir. 1990) (quoting an Ohio local rule). Often, as in that sentence, the *hereinafter*-phrase ought to be omitted because it does not enhance clarity. Sometimes this compound word may even cloud the thought, as when drafters misuse it for *hereinbefore* and so prompt courts to declare that it really does mean "hereinbefore" in such contexts.

As with *herein*, the legal writer is best advised to make the reference exact, by stating, e.g., *later in this will* or *later in this paragraph* rather than *hereinafter*. Moreover, in introducing abbreviated names, *hereinafter* is redundant: rather than *Mobil Oil Corporation (hereinafter "Mobil")*, one should write *Mobil Oil Corporation ("Mobil")*. See HERE- AND THERE- WORDS & **hereinabove.**

HERE- AND THERE- WORDS. These abound in legal writing (unfortunately, they do *not* occur just here and there), usually thrown in gratuitously to give legal documents that musty legal smell. Following are typical examples:

- "It is not necessary for us to take up each assignment seriatim and reply *thereto*, because from what we have *heretofore* said and what we will *hereinafter* say we have concluded this is a complete answer." *Saunders v. State*, 345 S.W.2d 899, 904–05 (Tenn. 1961).
- "All as fully appears from the affidavit of the publisher *thereof heretofore herein* filed." (From a court paper quoted in *Penn v. Pensacola–Escambia Gov'tal Ctr. Auth.*, 311 So.2d 97, 102 (Fla. 1975).)
- "For value received the undersigned *hereby* assign, transfer, and set over to Union Savings Bank . . . (*herein* called the 'Assignee') Policy No. 8408184 issued by the Ohio Life Insurance Co. (*herein* called the 'Insurer') and any supplementary contracts issued in connection *therewith* (said policy and contracts being *herein* called the 'Policy'), . . . and all claims, options, privileges, rights, title, and interest *therein* and *thereunder* (except as provided in Paragraph C *hereof*)." *Auburn Cordage, Inc. v. Revocable Trust Agreement of Treadwell*, 848 N.E.2d 738, 742 (Ind. Ct. App. 2006) (quoting from a loan and security agreement). (For the *hereby* in this example, see **hereby.**)
- "As used in subsection(a) of this Section, 'improve' means to . . . do landscape work *thereon* or *therefor*, or raise or lower any house *thereon* or remove any house *thereto*, or remove any house or other structure *therefrom*." *Inter-Rail*

Sys., Inc. v. Ravi Corp., 900 N.E.2d 407, 411–12 (Ill. App. Ct. 2008) (quoting from a contract).

These words are generally to be used only as a last resort to avoid awkward phrasing. They certainly shouldn't appear one after another in a stylistically abhorrent passage.

hereby. A. As a Performative Adverb. Although *hereby* is frequently derided as typical LEGALESE, in fact it can serve a useful function as a "performative" adverb. That is, *hereby* denotes that the sentence in which it appears constitutes the legally operative act by which something is done: *I name you as my successor* might be either descriptive of what is done elsewhere or operative in itself. Among the verbs that can usefully be preceded by *hereby* are *assign, disclaim, give, reinstate, reserve, resign, revoke, terminate*, and *withdraw*. For an informed discussion of this issue by a noted plain-language advocate, see Richard C. Wydick, *The Confessions of a Diddle-Diddle Dumb-Head*, 11 Scribes J. Legal Writing 57, 68–74 (2007).

B. As Surplusage. *Hereby* is sometimes a FLOTSAM PHRASE that can be excised with no loss of meaning: *I hereby declare* has no advantages over *I declare*. The verb *declare* simply doesn't need the performative adverb. See HERE- AND THERE- WORDS. Sometimes the word is omitted where you might expect to find it— e.g.: "The writs of scire facias and mandamus are abolished." Fed. R. Civ. P. 81(b). Does that mean that those writs *are hereby* abolished? Or that they *have been* abolished by an authoritative act elsewhere? There is little cause for worry, since Rule 81(b) is itself authoritative and what it says can be taken as true. But one wonders.

hereditable /hə-**red**-i-tə-bəl/ = subject to inheritance—e.g.: "'Children' . . . is not a word of limitation. It does not point to *hereditable* succession." *In re Parant's Will*, 240 N.Y.S.2d 558, 562 (Sur. Ct. 1963).

Apart from its use in the standard phrase *hereditable succession*, *hereditable* is a NEEDLESS VARIANT of *inheritable*—e.g.: "Plaintiff's mother and father then sought genetic counseling at the University of Kansas Medical Center in regard to the risk of birth defects or *hereditable* [read *inheritable*] impairments in future children." *Bruggeman v. Schimke*, 718 P.2d 635, 636–37 (Kan. 1986). See **inheritable.**

hereditament(s). This term, which is best accented on the second rather than the third syllable /hə-**red**-i-tə-mənt/, suggests a relation in meaning to *inheritance*. This is misleading, even though the term did originally mean "things capable of being inherited." Today it means merely "land, real property" and should be avoided as an obscure LEGALISM. It is often redundant—e.g.:

- "In his complaint for divorce he made no reference to either lands or *hereditaments*." *In re Teel's Estate*, 200 P.2d 201, 203 (Cal. Dist. Ct. App. 1948).

• "This court has held that 'a private nuisance is anything done to the hurt, annoyance, or detriment of the lands or *hereditaments* of another, and not amounting to a trespass,' thereby recognizing the obligation to distinguish between the two." *Wilson v. Parent*, 365 P.2d 72, 75 (Or. 1961).

Traditionally, the law distinguished between *corporeal hereditaments* (= tangible items of property, such as land or buildings) and *incorporeal hereditaments* (= intangible rights in land, such as easements). See **corporeal hereditaments** & **lands.**

In England, *hereditament* has the additional sense "a unit of land that has been separately assessed for rating purposes" (*CDL*).

hereditary. See **inheritable.**

heredity for *inheritance* or *inheritability*, though once possible, is today confusingly legalistic. *Heredity* has now been confined largely to biological senses in nonlegal writing. Hence legal writing need not perpetuate an archaic sense of the word—e.g.: "The trial court subsequently determined that the [deed's] reversionary provision lacked words of *heredity* [read *inheritability*] or perpetuity, and it entered judgment for defendant." *Burk v. State*, 607 N.E.2d 911, 912 (Ohio Ct. App. 1992). The nonlegal reader would interpret the quoted sentence as addressing bastardy rather than inheritance.

herein (= in this) is a vague word in legal documents, for the reader can rarely be certain whether it means *in this subsection*, *in this section* (or *paragraph*), *in this document*, or *in this transaction*. A more precise phrase, such as any of the four just listed, is preferable. See HERE- AND THERE- WORDS & **herewith.**

hereinabove is almost always unnecessary for *above*. E.g.:

• "It has also been established *hereinabove* [read *above*] that the directive applies to the processing of the personal data implicated in the online-tracking stage of the fight against P2P copyright infringements." Okechukwu Benjamin Vincents, *When Rights Clash Online*, 16 Int'l J.L. & Info. Tech. 270, 292 (2008).

• "We have concluded as set forth *hereinabove* [read *above*] that Appellants were not entitled to attorneys' fees, but were entitled to prejudgment interest." *Hamilton v. Trans Union Settlement Solutions*, 295 S.W.3d 844, 849 (Ky. Ct. App. 2009).

See **above (B), hereafter** & **hereinbefore.** See also HERE- AND THERE- WORDS.

hereinafter. See **hereafter** & **hereinbefore.**

hereinafter referred to as; hereinafter called. These stilted LEGALISMS are easily avoided. Ordinarily, a parenthetical short form ought to appear without a lead-in—e.g.: "This Daubert-Plus-a-Rigorous-Analysis approach *(hereinafter called 'Daubert Plus' for ease of reference)* [read *('Daubert Plus')*] authorizes the district court to make preliminary factual findings." Heather P. Scribner, *Rigorous Analysis of the Class Certification Expert*, 28 Rev. Litig. 71, 99 (2008).

hereinbefore; hereinafter. In LEGISLATIVE DRAFTING, these words should be avoided, because amendments and repeals may effect a reordering of the statute and make either word inaccurate or misleading. The better practice is to be specific and write *in this act* or *in this section*. See **hereafter** & **hereinabove.** See also HERE- AND THERE- WORDS.

herein fail not (= please adhere closely to your instructions) is legalistic deadwood often found in writs directed to process-servers. E.g.: "In the present case, the subpoena duces tecum commands Lee 'to produce a DNA specimen instanter . . . and *herein fail not* under penalty of law.'" *State v. Lee*, 976 So.2d 109, 124 n.9 (La. 2008). See **herein.**

heres is the Latin equivalent of the singular word *heir*—not of the plural *heirs*. The plural of *heres* is *heredes*.

hereto (= to this) is sometimes misused for *heretofore* (= up to this time)—e.g.: "This fixed rate is reasonable in view of the fact that the Chapter 12 plan process tends to reduce certain risks which FCB has *hereto* [read *heretofore*] been exposed to." *In re Miller*, 98 B.R. 311, 313 (Bankr. N.D. Ohio 1989).

Even when properly used, though, the word is best eliminated—e.g.: "The rights and obligations under this Agreement shall be binding upon . . . the parties *hereto* and their respective successors, heirs, and permitted assigns." *Weinberg v. Dickson-Weinberg*, 220 P.3d 264, 283 (Haw. Ct. App. 2009). A suggested revision: *This Agreement binds the parties as well as their heirs, successors, and assigns.* See HERE- AND THERE- WORDS & **hereafter.**

heretofore. See **hitherto** & **up to now.**

hereunder. This word can almost always be deleted unmisgivingly—e.g.: "That application for an appeal *hereunder* [delete *hereunder*] shall not stay proceedings in the district court unless the district judge or the Court of Appeals or a judge thereof shall so order." 28 U.S.C. § 1292(b). See HERE- AND THERE- WORDS.

herewith. See HERE- AND THERE- WORDS & *enclosed herewith.

heritable. See **inheritable.**

heritor. See **heir (A).**

heritrix; heritress. See SEXISM (C).

hermeneut. See **hermeneutician.**

hermeneutic. See **hermeneutical** & **hermeneutics.**

hermeneutical; hermeneutic, adj. It is tempting to call the latter a NEEDLESS VARIANT, but it is in rather frequent use—often interchanged with *hermeneutical* /hər-mi-**n[y]oo**-ti-kəl/ in single texts for no apparent reason (not even euphony). Stick to *hermeneutical* as the adjective—e.g.: "This little *hermeneutical* fable introduces the three topics of my essay." Steven Mailloux, "Rhetorical Hermeneutics," in *Interpreting Law* *and Literature: A Hermeneutic* [read *Hermeneutical*] *Reader* 345, 345 (Sanford Levinson & Steven Mailloux eds., 1988).

hermeneutician; *hermeneutist; hermeneut. Sound-association is one problem here: *hermeneutician* /hər-mi-n[y]oo-**tish**-ən/ sounds like a cosmetologist of statutes (rhyming, as it does, with *beautician*); *hermeneutist* sounds like a fetishist of unknown propensities; and *hermeneut* sounds like a named salamander. Although the second and third are the more traditional terms for a hermeneutical scholar (both listed, for example, in *W2*), today *hermeneutician* has taken the field in law. E.g.: "Consider the observations of the Italian *hermeneutician* Emilio Betti." Gregory Leyh, Introduction, *Legal Hermeneutics: History, Theory, and Practice* xviii n.5 (Gregory Leyh ed., 1992). But the *hermeneuts* prevail in religious scholarship. A common synonym is *hermeneutical theorist*.

hermeneutics; hermeneutic, n. *Hermeneutics* = the art of interpretation and explanation; specif., the study of deriving meaning from authoritative texts. Although it is fashionable to refer to *a hermeneutic* <a thoroughly Dworkinian hermeneutic>, there is no better reason for this than referring to *a Chomskyan linguistic*. As with other disciplines, such as *economics* and *mathematics*, even the plural form is singular in construction—e.g.: "*Hermeneutics* was governed by a series of regulative maxims to guide and discipline the practical science of interpretation and construction in law and politics." James Farr, "The Americanization of Hermeneutics," in *Legal Hermeneutics: History, Theory, and Practice* 83, 97 (Gregory Leyh ed., 1992).

Although *hermeneutics* has traditionally been the theory underlying a most practical enterprise, in recent years the "discipline" has become increasingly undisciplined. Consider what the hermeneuticians themselves say:

- "The activity of questioning and of adopting a suspicious attitude toward authority is at the heart of hermeneutical discourse. *Hermeneutics* involves confronting the aporias that face us, and it attempts to undermine, at least in partial ways, the calm assurances transmitted by the received views and legal orthodoxies." Gregory Leyh, Introduction to *Legal Hermeneutics: History, Theory, and Practice* xviii (Gregory Leyh ed., 1992).
- "*Hermeneutics* is too much in love with rhetoric, too suspicious of logic. It is, someone like Fiss would add, what people like Unger and especially Goodrich are in favor of, namely, the end of rationality and therefore the legal order as we know it. . . . [H]ermeneutics is either radical or reactionary; it seeks either to undermine the logic of law and legal application or to mystify the law as a body of original meanings and authoritative doctrines handed down from a divine origin through successive generations of priestly interpreters." Gerald L. Bruns, "Law and Language," in *Legal Hermeneutics: History, Theory, and Practice* 23, 26 (Gregory Leyh ed., 1992).

If these things are so, many critical thinkers who are fascinated by the art of interpretation will want little to do with the modern hermeneuticians. Let them be hermeneutically sealed off.

***he/she.** See SEXISM (A) & **he or she.**

hew = (1) to chop, cut; or (2) to adhere or conform (to). Thus sense 1: "A small number of issues may be *hewed* out upfront, particularly with respect to Dolls' numerous (and overlapping) First Amendment Claims." *Dolls, Inc. v. City of Carolville, Iowa*, 425 F.Supp.2d 958, 968 (S.D. Iowa 2006). And sense 2, which is more common in modern legal prose: "This conclusion *hews* to two Supreme Court precedents." *Morris v. Wachovia Sec., Inc.*, 448 F.3d 268, 278 (4th Cir. 2006).

The preferred past participle is *hewn* in BrE and *hewed* in AmE. E.g.:

- (BrE) "No other legal, ethical, or moral schema *has* so consistently *hewn to* [read, in AmE, *hewed to*] the magisterial human experiment of moderation, fairness, efficiency, equality, and justice in social groupings." M. Stuart Madden, *Exploring Tort Law* 48 (2005).
- (AmE) "Other courts *have hewed to* [read, in BrE, *hewn to*] this line." *U.S. v. Troy*, 618 F.3d 27, 32 (1st Cir. 2010) (per Selya, J.).

Heydon's case, rule in. See **mischief rule.**

hiatus. Pl. *hiatuses.* See HYPERCORRECTION (A).

H.I.D.C. See **H.D.C.**

high court; High Court. In AmE, *high court* or *high bench* usually refers to the U.S. Supreme Court—e.g.: "Four protesters, objecting to the Supreme Court's ruling last spring allowing states to further restrict abortions, disrupted the *high court's* session yesterday." *Disorder in the Court*, Wall St. J., 8 Nov. 1989, at B8.

In England and Northern Ireland, by contrast, the *High Court* is a trial and (for some purposes) appellate court having mainly civil jurisdiction and divided into three divisions: the Queen's Bench Division, the Chancery Division, and the Family Division. One judge sits at a trial. Two or three judges usually sit in these divisional courts to review certain proceedings of a lower tribunal or to hear appeals from magistrates' decisions in summary criminal trials. Appeal lies in the Court of Appeal, Civil Division.

In Scotland, the High Court (of Justiciary) is the superior criminal court with trial and appellate jurisdiction.

higher court; upper court. Both phrases are used to denote an appellate court that reviews the judgment of a *lower court. Higher court* is more common in AmE and BrE; *upper court* appears occasionally in BrE. Cf. **inferior (B)** & **lower court.**

---

highest law of the land. See **law of the land.**

high lawyer. See LAWYERS, DEROGATORY NAMES FOR (B).

highly regarded. See **regard (B).**

high seas; open seas. Of these synonyms—meaning "the seas or oceans apart from territorial waters"—the first phrase is now more common.

hijack. Vehicles and planes are *hijacked*, but not people—e.g.:

- "With Davis wielding a .380-caliber gun, the two *hijacked the victim and his car* [read *kidnapped the victim and stole his car*] from the parking lot of a Gwinnett County bowling alley." *Washington v. State*, 581 S.E.2d 518, 521 (Ga. 2003).
- "Defendant contends that the statements the government portrays as admissions are simply responses given by a frightened individual who was '*hijacked* [read *taken*, *seized*, or *arrested*] by armed federal agents.'" *U.S. v. Melendez Santiago*, 544 F.Supp.2d 76, 81 (D.P.R. 2007).

See **skyjack.**

hindering impediment. See **impedient impediment.**

hired gun. See LAWYERS, DEROGATORY NAMES FOR (A).

hire purchase, n., is a late-19th-century BrE NEOLO-GISM equivalent to the AmE phrases *lease-purchase contract* (or *agreement*), *rent-to-own contract* (or *agreement*), and *lease-to-own contract* (or *agreement*). *Hire purchase*, which began as the longer phrase *hire and purchase*, is now usually two words as a noun phrase and hyphenated as a PHRASAL ADJECTIVE <the hire-purchase system>.

It is also sometimes used as a verb phrase (hyphenated): "Where a person examines goods and subsequently makes an offer to buy or *hire-purchase* them, it may be an implied term of the offer that the goods should remain in substantially the same state in which they were when the offer was made." G.H. Treitel, *The Law of Contract* 43–44 (8th ed. 1991).

hire-purchase agreement. See **lease-purchase agreement.**

hirer (BrE) = *lessee* (AmE).

his or her. See **he or she** & SEXISM (A).

historical; historic. *Historical*, meaning "of, relating to, or occurring in history," is needed far more frequently. *Historic* means "historically significant" <the Alamo is a historic building>. Momentous happenings or developments are *historic*; merely documented happenings or developments are *historical*.

In the following sentences, *historic* is correctly used:

- "Chief Justice Cardozo's *historic* and oft-quoted dissent in *Graf v. Hope Bldg. Corp.* has become equity's modern fount in cases [in which] the tyrant demands his dollars and cents on legal time whatever the impact of sickening hardship his victim suffers." *Farr v. Nordman*, 78 N.W.2d 186, 194–95 (Mich. 1956).

- "In *Brown II* the Court referred to its *historic* opinion in *Brown I* as 'declaring the fundamental principle that racial discrimination in public education is unconstitutional.'" *Geier v. University of Tenn.*, 597 F.2d 1056, 1066 (6th Cir. 1979).

Examples of *historic* used incorrectly for *historical* could easily run for several pages, so common is this error—e.g.:

- "The *historic* [read *historical*] option of a maritime suitor pursuing a common-law remedy to select his forum, state or federal, would be taken away by an expanded view of section 1331." *Romero v. International Terminal Operating Co.*, 358 U.S. 354, 371 (1959) (per Frankfurter, J.).
- "Conceivably *historic* [read *historical*] skepticism about the propriety of nonpossessory security in personal property also stems from this mentality." R.E. Speidel et al., *Commercial Law Teaching Materials* 28 (4th ed. 1987).

On the question whether to write *a* or *an historic(al)*, see **a (A).**

historical construction; historical interpretation. See *historical interpretation* under INTERPRETATION, MODES OF (B) & **originalism.**

HISTORICAL PRESENT TENSE IN JUDICIAL OPINIONS. See OPINIONS, JUDICIAL (A).

historico-grammatical construction; historico-grammatical interpretation. See *historico-grammatical interpretation* under INTERPRETATION, MODES OF (B).

hitherto; thitherto. *Hitherto* = up to now, i.e., heretofore. *Thitherto* = up to some specified or implied time in the past, i.e., theretofore. Obviously these ARCHA-ISMS are hardly worth using since the terms just used in defining them—*heretofore* (or *up to now*) and *theretofore*—are perfectly equivalent and much more common. In the following example, a legal writer mistook the import of *hitherto*, which does not properly appear with the past-perfect tense: "The superior court, conceding that it *hitherto* [read *thitherto* or, better, *theretofore*] had refused to enjoin such conduct, recognized 'the growing tendency in courts to grant equitable relief under such circumstances.'" *Colonial Laundries v. Henry*, 138 A. 47, 48 (R.I. 1927). See **up to now.**

hoard, n. or vb.; **horde,** n. A *hoard* is a large collection, esp. of something valuable. To *hoard* is to amass such a collection. A *horde* is a mass of people, esp. and originally a nomadic army.

Hobbesian choice. See **Hobson's choice (C).**

Hobson's choice. A. Generally. This ever-growing CLICHÉ has loosened its etymological tether. Tradition has it that Thomas Hobson (1549–1631), a hostler in Cambridge, England, always gave his customers only one choice among his horses: whichever one was closest to the door. Hence, in literary usage, a *Hobson's choice* came to denote no choice at all—either taking what is offered or taking nothing at all.

BrE writers tend to stick to that sense, as here: "The tribunal . . . concluded that the employees were faced with *Hobson's choice*[,] that they had no real option but to accept the move." *Sheet Metal Components Ltd. v. Plumridge*, [1974] I.C.R. 373, 377 (Nat'l Indus. Relations Ct.).

Though purists resist the change, the prevailing sense in AmE—in legal and nonlegal writing alike—is not that of having no choice at all, but of having two bad choices. E.g.:

- "Ithaca faced a *Hobson's choice* when confronted with Dean's uncompromising and adamant refusal to work on Sunday. Ithaca could either totally capitulate to Dean's demands and require other employees to perform his work or replace Dean with an employee willing to make reciprocal accommodations." *EEOC v. Ithaca Indus., Inc.*, 829 F.2d 519, 521 (4th Cir. 1987).
- "This important public policy will not be advanced by presenting a party with the *Hobson's choice* of either dropping its claim or revealing all confidential communications related to a criminal defense." *Greater Newburyport Clamshell Alliance v. Public Serv. Co.*, 838 F.2d 13, 22 (1st Cir. 1988).

Cf. **dilemma.**

B. Article with. Traditionally—and still in BrE—the phrase takes no article; that is, you are faced not with *a Hobson's choice* but with *Hobson's choice.* In modern AmE, the phrase usually takes either *a* or *the.*

C. "Hobbesian choice." Amazingly, some writers have confused the obscure Thomas Hobson with his famous contemporary, the philosopher Thomas Hobbes (1588–1679). The resulting MALAPROPISM is beautifully grotesque—e.g.:

- "The court need not slap an innocent client with a judgment regardless of the merits, leaving the client with a *Hobbesian choice* [read *Hobson's choice*] of suffering in silence or of making a distasteful claim against his own lawyer." *Fisher v. Crest Corp.*, 735 P.2d 1052, 1058 (Idaho Ct. App. 1987) (Burnett, J., dissenting).
- "Were the law otherwise, the officers' invitation to depart would present the subject of interrogation with a *Hobbesian choice* [read *Hobson's choice*]. To stay could lead to inculpation; to depart surely would." *U.S. v. Sterling*, 909 F.2d 1078, 1082 (7th Cir. 1990).
- "This left Nance the *Hobbesian Choice* [read *Hobson's choice*] of (1) risking a complete loss of federal review of all of his claims or (2) leaving his unexhausted Atkins claim to be raised in a subsequent petition." *Nance v. Norris*, 429 F.3d 809, 810 (8th Cir. 2005) (Melloy, J., dissenting).

hodgepodge. See **hotchpot.**

hoi polloi (= the common people, the masses). Because *hoi* in Greek means "the (plural)," *the hoi polloi* is a technical REDUNDANCY. Nevertheless, *the hoi polloi* overwhelmingly predominates in modern usage.

hold, vb. **A. As Transitive Verb.** When used properly in the legal sense (signifying "to decide," probably from "hold the opinion that"), this verb describes *what* judges do and is therefore transitive. It should not be used intransitively to describe *how* judges do. Here the

intransitive use is wrong: "This Court's task, then, is to decide *how* [read *what*] the Texas state courts would hold when faced with the issue." *Hullum v. Skyhook Corp.*, 753 F.2d 1334, 1337 (5th Cir. 1985). (Courts hold *something*; they do not hold *in a certain manner.* So the noun *what*, not the adverb *how*, is the proper word.) In general English usage, of course, the intransitive use of *hold* is quite acceptable in such clauses as *The argument does not hold.*

B. Hold (to be). *Hold* need not be followed by *to be* or *as*, although *to be* may sometimes add clarity. E.g.:

- "A paper signed by the deceased giving his home to his housekeeper for special favors and services, and ordering his executor after his death to sign a deed and deliver it to her, was *held testamentary* [better: *held to be testamentary*] in character, because what was to be done to make it effective had to be done by the executor." *In re Murphy's Estate*, 75 P.2d 916, 924 (Wash. 1938).
- "It is precisely because we find no ERISA provision at the relevant time mandating participation for all who are eligible that we *hold permissible* [better: *hold to be permissible*] an individual waiver of participation." *Laniok v. Advisory Comm. of Brainerd Mfg. Co. Pension Plan*, 935 F.2d 1360, 1366 (2d Cir. 1991).
- "Under the theory interjected in the case under count VI, MFG was *held to be liable* [read *held liable*] for the breach of plaintiff's employment contract because MFG was the alter ego of Midland Illinois." *Knickman v. Midland Risk Servs.-Ill., Inc.*, 700 N.E.2d 458, 462 (Ill. App. Ct. 1998).

But here the shorter form works better: "The defendant was *held to be liable* [read *held liable*] for breach of contract and conversion." *Held as* <the award was held as permissible> is idiomatically inferior.

C. It was held that. This phrase has traditionally been used in the sense "the law as repeatedly stated by the courts was that"—e.g.: "Previous to the case of *Ackroyd v. Smithson*, *it was held that* an unqualified direction by a testator in his will to sell land, or to buy land with his money, created a complete conversion in equity of the land into money." C.C. Langdell, *Equitable Conversion*, 19 Harv. L. Rev. 1, 1 (1905).

hold a brief for is a lawyers' idiom that has passed into general usage in a broadened sense. Originally, it meant "to be retained as counsel for," but now it generally means merely "to defend or support." E.g.: "In setting forth the claims of the revived natural law of today, I am not *holding a brief for* the old natural law." Roscoe Pound, *The Formative Era of American Law* 29 (1938).

holden is an archaic past participle of *hold*, used as recently as 1850 in *Brown v. Kendall*, 60 Mass. (6 Cush.) 292, 295 (1850): "There certainly are cases in the books, where, the injury being direct and immediate, trespass has been *holden* to lie, though the injury was not intentional." This ARCHAISM has even found its way into 20th-century texts: "The rule has been adopted out of regard to the interests of justice, which

---

cannot be *upholden*." Eugene A. Jones, *Manual of Equity Pleading and Practice* 25 (1916).

holder in due course = a person who in good faith has given value for a negotiable instrument that is complete and regular on its face, is not overdue, and, to the possessor's knowledge, has not been dishonored. See **H.D.C.; H.I.D.C.**

hold harmless. See **indemnify (A).**

holding. As a noun, *holding* involves a determination of a matter of law that is pivotal to a judicial decision. Dicta are not *holdings*:

- "Making a similar observation, the court in *Rosendary Grant* court's *in-dicta holding* [read *dicta*]." Christopher Lilienthal, *New* Grant *Standard May Not Be as Harsh as Feared*, Pa. L. Wkly., 31 Mar. 2003, at 1. (See **dictum.**)
- "See also *Goodtitle v. Kibbe*, . . . (*holding in dicta* that Congress would not have been able 'to grant or confirm a title to land when the sovereignty and dominion over it had become vested in the state.')." *Seneca Nation of Indians v. New York*, 382 F.3d 245, 271 (2d Cir. 2004). Although the opinion may have contained this statement, it is not a statement of law, and it cannot be a holding.

See JUDGMENTS, APPELLATE-COURT & **finding.**

holding over is legal JARGON denoting a tenant's action in continuing to occupy the leased premises after the lease term has expired. E.g.: "The tenant, *holding over* despite efforts to evict him, planted a crop that eventually the landlord harvested."

The tenant is often referred to as a *holdover tenant*—e.g.:

- "In Montana a *holdover tenant* is charged treble rent." Robert Kratovil, *Real Estate Law* 297 (1946).
- "In addition to delineating prohibited conduct, the legislature provided a remedy for landlords with *holdover tenants* and others guilty of forcible entry and detainer and unlawful detainer." *Gorman v. Ratliff*, 712 S.W.2d 888, 890 (Ark. 1986).

holiday (fr. *holy day*) = (AmE) a day on which one is exempt from one's usual work; or (BrE) a vacation. This term has long plagued American courts interpreting time computations in statutes and rules. In 1992, for example, the Supreme Court of Texas decided that *holiday* includes both a day that the commissioners' court in the county where the case is pending has determined to be a holiday, and a day on which the clerk's office for the court in which the case is pending is officially closed. See *In re V.C.*, 829 S.W.2d 772 (Tex. 1992).

Holmesian; *Holmesean. The first is the better and more common spelling.

holograph, n.; ***olograph.** In the law of wills, a *holograph* is a will that is entirely written, dated, and signed in the hand of the testator; in many American states, such a will is valid even if it is not witnessed. E.g.:

- "We address the will, not as a witnessed will, but as a *holograph* since the trial court found it to be a *holograph* and

we deem that issue dispositive here." *In re Estate of Capps*, 154 S.W.3d 242, 246–47 (Tex. App.—Texarkana 2005).
- "We confirmed the will's validity, holding that alterations to a handwritten will that do not affect the substance of the will, and have no impact on the will's testamentary intent, do not invalidate a testator's *holograph*." *Berry v. Trible*, 626 S.E.2d 440, 444–45 (Va. 2006).

The spelling **olograph* is a NEEDLESS VARIANT that has appeared in a few hundred cases—but many hundreds fewer than the etymologically preferable *holograph*. Even so, the spelling **olograph* seems to be prevalent in Louisiana.

The word *holograph* is not to be confused with *hologram* (= a three-dimensional picture).

holographic; holograph, adj. The word *holographic* is the better adjective, not *holograph*—e.g.: "The engrossed copy bearing the *holograph* [read *holographic*] signatures of the makers of the Constitution in the Federal Convention was well known and became famous as a result of its display by the Department of State at the Centennial Exposition at Philadelphia in 1876." Denys P. Myers, *History of the Printed Archetype of the Constitution of the United States of America*, 11 Green Bag 2d 217, 218 (2008).

The form *olographic* is common in Louisiana but not elsewhere.

homage (orig., the ceremony by which the tenant became the lord's "man") is best pronounced /**hom**-ij/. It has been an English word since the 14th century, so it's a silly affectation to use the Frenchified pronunciation /oh-**mahj**/. See **humble.**

home in, not **hone in*, is the correct phrase. In the 19th century, the METAPHOR referred to what homing pigeons do; by the middle of the 20th century, it referred also to what aircraft and missiles do.

And by the 21st century, some writers had begun mistaking the phrase by using the wrong verb, *hone* instead of *home*—e.g.:

- "Roche *hones in* [read *homes in*] on the language in the *Takeda* opinion." *Amgen Inc. v. F. Hoffmann-La Roche, Ltd.*, 580 F.3d 1340, 1355 (Fed. Cir. 2009) (per Schall, J.).
- "Petitioner *hones in* [read *homes in*] on a footnote in *Fox II*." *Heath v. SEC*, 586 F.3d 122, 138 (2d Cir. 2009) (per Straub, J.)
- "This description of the holding in *Wallace hones in* [read *homes in*] on the factual distinction between *Heck* and *Wallace*." *Parish v. City of Elkhart*, 614 F.3d 677, 682 (7th Cir. 2010) (per Flaum, J.).

homeowner. One word.

homered, to be; hometowned, to be. In AmE legal slang, *to be homered* or *to be hometowned* is to be bested in a rural courthouse by a local lawyer, usu. because of a judge's provincial biases. E.g.: "Though city judges are accused of bias as often [as] or more so than country judges, the distressing fact is that outsiders who lose their cases in rural courthouses may charge they've been '*homered*.'" Allen G. Minker, *Justice Out Here*, 17 Litig. 3, 3 (Spring 1991).

Though in both phrases the primary reference is to hometown favoritism, the idiom *to be homered* was no doubt influenced by the baseball term *homer* (= a home run), which is used also as a verb, as in *he homered* (i.e., hit a home run).

homestead, n. In most American states, the land owned and occupied by a husband and wife as their home is known as their *homestead,* as long as the land does not exceed in area or value the limits fixed by law. *Homestead laws* or *homestead rights* exempt a homestead from execution or judicial sale for debt, unless both the husband and the wife have jointly mortgaged the property or otherwise subjected it to creditors' claims.

homestead, vb. The past tense of this verb is *homesteaded*—e.g.: "The Chancellor adjudged the subject property . . . *to be homestead* [read *to be homesteaded* or *to be a homestead*] under Article X of the Constitution." *Kinney v. Mosher,* 100 So.2d 644, 645 (Fla. Dist. Ct. App. 1958). One who homesteads is a *homesteader.* Congress enacted the Homestead Act in 1862.

hometowned, to be. See **homered, to be.**

homicide refers not to a crime (as is commonly thought), but to the lawful or unlawful killing of a person. The word is frequently misspelled *homocide— e.g.: "In *Enmund v. Florida,* the Court dealt with a challenge to a death sentence imposed for aiding and abetting a murder by driving the getaway car for a robbery/homocide [read *homicide*]." Derek S. Bentsen, *Beyond Statutory Elements,* 90 Va. L. Rev. 645, 671 (2004). See **murder (A)** & **-CIDE.** Cf. **suicide (A).**

homogeneous; *homogenous. *Homogeneous* (five syllables) is the usual and the etymologically preferable form. *Homogeneal, **homogenetic,* and *homogenetical are rare forms to be avoided; they have failed to become standard and should be laid to rest.

*hone in. See **home in.**

honesty; integrity; probity; honor. These terms all refer to goodness in character and in action. *Honesty,* denoting uprightness of disposition and conduct, demands a refusal to lie, cheat, or steal under any circumstances. *Integrity* denotes incorruptible morality and insistence on meeting not only one's commitments but also one's high personal standards of conduct. *Probity* is essentially synonymous with *integrity,* though it is more abstract and less well known—and *probity* suggests having proved oneself through tests of virtue. (For misuses of this word, see **probity.**) *Honor* suggests all the above, plus a heightened sense of loyalty to one's family, trade, or profession and adherence to an admirable code of conduct.

In recent years, however, *honor* has undergone a depreciation in meaning—perhaps because of widespread disillusionment and cynicism about leaders but also because of increasing publicity about *honor crimes* (= crimes motivated by the desire to punish someone that the perpetrator believes to have harmed a family's or group's honor). The term "is most often applied to crimes against Muslim women by members of their own families for behavior that leads to perceived social harm, esp. loss of family honor." *Black's Law Dictionary* 428 (9th ed. 2009).

honor. See **honesty.**

Honor, your. See **your Honor.**

Honorable, in AmE, is a title of respect given to judges, members of the U.S. Congress, ambassadors, and the like. It should be used not with a surname only, but with a complete name (e.g., *The Honorable Antonin Scalia*) or with a title of courtesy (e.g., *The Honorable Mr. Scalia*). The abbreviation *Hon.* should be used only in mailing addresses.

In the U.S. Congress, a solecism is televised throughout the land whenever a judge appears to testify. Propped up in front of the judge is a placard that reads, for example, "Hon. Easterbrook" or "Hon. Boudin." Not enough members of Congress, it appears, stop to consult this book.

In the U.K., the title *Honourable* (so spelled) is given to judges of the High Court and equivalents, and to children of viscounts and barons. Members of the Privy Council (which includes ministers of the Crown, Lords Justices of Appeal, and certain others) are styled *Right Honourable.* Judges at circuit courts in England are styled *His Honour Judge So-and-So* and addressed "Your Honour." Cf. **my lord** & **your Honor.**

honorable court, this. Commonly sprinkled throughout briefs, this phrase should be sparingly used, for it tends to nauseate even those judges most susceptible to flattery—e.g.:

- "The petitioner must be granted proper judicial review by *this Honorable Court* regarding these false charges, to clear his record of any wrongdoing for further parole consideration." *Wilwording v. Swenson,* 502 F.2d 844, 847–48 (8th Cir. 1974).
- "The conclusion of the secretary should be upheld upon review by *this Honorable Court.*" *In re Woodrow Wilson Constr. Co.,* 563 So.2d. 385, 390 (La. Ct. App. 1990).
- "The waiver clause states that '. . . if *this Honorable Court* accepts this agreement and sentences him according to its terms and conditions, the defendant waives and surrenders his right to appeal the judgment in the case.'" *U.S. v. Perazza-Mercado,* 553 F.3d 65, 67 n.3 (1st Cir. 2009).

The references should be to *the Court* or *this Court,* apart from the first reference in, for example, the commencement of a pleading. The capitalization of *court* is compliment enough.

honorarium. Pl. *-ia, -iums.* Though *honorariums* has much to commend itself as a homegrown plural—and is the form used by *The New York Times*—*honoraria* generally prevails in AmE and BrE alike. See PLURALS (A).

honoree; honorand. In the early 1950s, these two forms sprang up, both denoting a person who receives an honor. Both words are acceptably formed. The *OED* records only *honorand*, which has probably predominated in BrE. In AmE, however, *honoree* has taken the field—e.g.:

- "We know of no reason . . . why the name of the donor [cannot appear] under the name of the *honoree* thereon." *State ex rel. Singelmann v. Morrison*, 57 So.2d 238, 247 (La. Ct. App. 1952).
- "Neither the hostess nor the *honoree* testified." *State v. Brown*, 160 S.E.2d 508, 511 (N.C. Ct. App. 1968).
- "Of the approximately ninety inquiries from judges to the committee in the past ten years, most have concerned three areas: thirty-five (about 40 percent) have sought guidance on the appropriateness of the inquiring judge's attending events as a guest or an *honoree*." *In re Access to Certain Records of R.I. Advisory Comm. on the Code of Judicial Conduct*, 637 A.2d 1063, 1069 (R.I. 1994) (Lederberg, J., concurring).

See -EE.

hopefully. Use of *hopefully* to mean "it is hoped" (rather than "in a hopeful manner") is widespread, even in legal writing—e.g.:

- "The trial court, *hopefully* imbued with a fair amount of common sense as well as an understanding of the applicable law, views the questioning as a whole." *Wainwright v. Witt*, 469 U.S. 412, 435 (1985) (per Rehnquist, J.).
- "This is a decision which will need to be taken by the parents (*hopefully* without the intervention of the court) in the future." *Evans v. Evans*, [1990] 2 All E.R. 147, 153.

This use of *hopefully* is sometimes defended as being a SENTENCE ADVERB similar to *fortunately* and *certainly* <fortunately, the jury agreed with us [which doesn't mean that the jury agreed in a fortunate manner]>. But the analogy doesn't hold, syntactically, since those adverbs can be rendered into *it is fortunate that* and *it is certain that*—while *it is hopeful that* just doesn't work. Using *hopefully* as a sentence adverb has been condemned for so long that writers employ it at their peril. Its use is a distraction—and careful writers avoid distractions.

horde. See **hoard.**

horizontal restraints; vertical restraints. In the terminology of antitrust law, restraints imposed by agreement between competitors are called *horizontal restraints*; those imposed by agreement between firms at different levels of distribution are called *vertical restraints*. See *Business Elecs. Corp. v. Sharp Elecs. Corp.*, 485 U.S. 717, 730 (1988) (per Scalia, J.).

hornbook law = blackletter law. *Hornbooks* were originally leaves of paper with the alphabet depicted on them; these were covered by a thin plate of translucent horn and mounted on a tablet of wood for use by schoolchildren. By extension, *hornbook* came to be applied to lawbooks containing the rudiments of law. E.g.:

- "It is *hornbook law* that all parties to a contract are necessary in an action challenging its validity or interpretation." *School Dist. of City of Pontiac v. Secretary of U.S. Dep't of Educ.*, 584 F.3d 253, 303 (6th Cir. 2009) (McKeague, J., concurring).
- "It is *hornbook law* that ignorance of the law is generally no defense." *U.S. v. Kilgore*, 591 F.3d 890, 894 (7th Cir. 2010).
- "It is therefore hard to quarrel with the result in *Augusto* under *hornbook law*." Richard A. Epstein, *The Disintegration of Intellectual Property?*, 62 Stan. L. Rev. 455, 504 (2010).

See **blackletter law.**

hornbook method. See **casebook method.**

horse case. See **whitehorse case.**

horse lawyer. See LAWYERS, DEROGATORY NAMES FOR (A).

horseshed, vb., = to prepare (a witness favorable to one's cause, often a client) to testify, esp. with instructions about the proper method of responding to questions while testifying. E.g.:

- "Every trial lawyer knows that the 'preparing' of witnesses may embrace a multitude of other measures, including some ethical lapses believed to be more common than we would wish. The process is labeled archly in lawyer's slang as '*horseshedding*' the witness . . . . [T]he process often extends beyond organizing what the witness knows, and moves in the direction of helping the witness to know new things." Marvin Frankel, *Partisan Justice* 15 (1980).
- "Equally revealing is the slang used to describe the preparation of ordinary witnesses: 'sandpapering' and '*horseshedding*.'" John H. Langbein, *The German Advantage in Civil Procedure*, 52 U. Chi. L. Rev. 823, 835 n.36 (1985).

This old Americanism has evolved since the novelist James Fenimore Cooper used it in a related sense ("to wheedle; to cajole"): "Your regular '*horse shedder*' is employed to frequent taverns where jurors stay, and drop hints before them touching the merits of causes known to be on the calendars." James Fenimore Cooper, *The Redskins* 240 (1846). See **sandpapering.**

host of, a. See SYNESIS.

hotchpot; hotchpotch; hodgepodge. The original form (a LAW FRENCH term referring to a dish mixed by shaking it up), still the preferred legal term, is *hotchpot*. *Hotchpot* was originally the blending of properties to secure equality of division, especially as practiced in cases in which an intestate's property is to be distributed. E.g.: "The advancement being regarded as one in full, the property conveyed could not come into *hotchpot*, and appellees could not share in the distribution of the estate." *Donough v. Garland*, 109 N.E. 1015, 1017 (Ill. 1915). Blackstone called it a "housewifely metaphor" and explained it in Littleton's words: "it seemeth that this word, *hotchpot*, is in English a pudding; for in a pudding is not commonly put one thing alone, but one thing with other things together." 2 William Blackstone, *Commentaries on the Laws of England* 190 (1766) (quoting Co. Litt. 164).

This word was corrupted into *hotchpotch* (used by some courts), then into *hodgepodge*, which is now the usual nonlegal term meaning "an unorganized mixture." E.g.: "Secured creditors are dealt with erratically, tediously, and uncertainly, resulting from a *hodgepodge* of state and federal statutory provisions, bankruptcy and local rules, many conflicting reported cases and varied local customs." *In re Estus*, 695 F.2d 311, 313 n.2 (8th Cir. 1982).

In community-property states in the U.S., the term is also used in reference to the property that falls within the community estate.

hot pursuit. See **fresh pursuit.**

housebreaking. See **burglary (B).**

houseburning. See **arson.**

house counsel; in-house counsel. These variant terms refer to one or more lawyers employed full-time by a company. The shorter phrase, *house counsel*, is stylistically preferable, though both phrases are common.

house of ill fame. See **bawdy house.**

House of Lords. From 1876 until 2009, this phrase contained an ambiguity. In most people's minds, the House of Lords was most commonly known as the upper chamber of the British Parliament. But in 1876, the judicial House of Lords—a subset of the upper chamber—was created. It was a court composed of 11 professionally qualified judges who, together with peers who have had high judicial experience, sat independently of the parliamentary sittings of the House. It usually sat in panels of five, or occasionally seven. In civil matters, it was the court of final appeal for England, Wales, Scotland, and Northern Ireland; in criminal matters, it was the court of final appeal for England, Wales, and Northern Ireland. In 2009 it was superseded by the Supreme Court of the United Kingdom. See **Law Lord** & **Lord of Appeal in Ordinary.**

howbeit. See **albeit.**

however. Most writers have heard that sentences should not begin with this word. But doing so is not a grammatical error; it is merely a stylistic lapse, the word *but* ordinarily being much preferable. E.g.: "*However,* [read *But*] we regard the statutory history of section 702c as being less than univocal on this point, so we cannot assent to appellants' view." For a full discussion of the point, see Bryan A. Garner, "On Conjunctions as Sentence-Starters," in *Garner on Language and Writing* 63 (2009). See also **but (A).**

Yet, used in the sense "in whatever way" or "to whatever extent," *however* is unimpeachable at the beginning of a sentence. E.g.: "*However* extraordinary this new doctrine may appear, it nevertheless has its

advocates." *The Federalist* No. 2, at 37–38 (John Jay) (Clinton Rossiter ed., 1961). See RUN-ON SENTENCES.

howsoever is always inferior to *however*.

hue and cry is an archaic LEGALISM that has passed into the vernacular. At common law it referred either to the public uproar that a citizen was expected to initiate after discovering a crime, or the chase after a felon accompanying such an uproar. The words in this DOUBLET may originally have been distinct, some scholars believing that *hue* may have referred to inarticulate sounds, such as horns or indistinct yells, while *cry* may have referred to distinctly audible words.

Today the phrase simply denotes noisy opposition or controversy—e.g.: "No *hue or cry* was raised until the opposition to the motion to intervene was advanced late in the going." *Maryland-Nat'l Capital Park & Planning Comm'n v. Town of Washington Grove*, 968 A.2d 552, 573 (Md. 2009). See POPULARIZED LEGAL TECHNICALITIES.

humankind; mankind. *Humankind*, a 17th-century creation, is unexceptionable, while *mankind* is, to many people, a sexist word. The prudent writer will therefore resort to *humankind*. E.g.: "Native Americans fulfill this duty through ceremonies and rituals designed to preserve and stabilize the earth and to protect *humankind* from disease and other catastrophes." *Lyng v. Northwest Indian Cemetery Protective Ass'n*, 485 U.S. 439, 460 (1988) (Brennan, J., dissenting). See SEXISM (B).

humble is preferably pronounced with the *-h*-sounded /**hum**-bəl/. (Cf. **homage.**) Inexplicably, the precious pronunciation without sounding the initial *-h*- is common in AmE. One judge went so far as to use *an* before the Humble Oil trademark: "To the contrary, purchasers were informed that the selected shipments would bear the HUMBLE name or be accompanied *by an* HUMBLE *invoice* [read *by a* HUMBLE *invoice*] but were the desired Exxon products." *Exxon Corp. v. Humble Exploration Co.*, 695 F.2d 96, 100 (5th Cir. 1983).

hung. See **hanged.**

hung jury (= a jury whose members cannot arrive at a verdict) does not require apologetic quotation marks, as if signaling that it is slang. It is not; it is a useful legal term (finding a synonymous phrase in *deadlocked jury*). See the quotation in par. 2 under **contumacious.**

hurt (= a legal injury) surprises the nonlegal reader, for whom *hurt* connotes physical or emotional pain only—e.g.:

- "The libelant sustained *hurts* [that] called for 'cure and maintenance.'" *The Quaker City*, 1 F.Supp. 840, 843 (E.D. Pa. 1931).

- "People insist on their legal rights in the context of a relationship in which they have suffered *hurts* and failures of communication." Jonathan M. Hyman & Lela P. Love, *If Portia Were a Mediator*, 9 Clinical L. Rev. 157, 186 (2002).

husband and wife. See **man and wife.**

HYBRIDS, or words made up of morphemes from different languages, have become even more common in the last 75 years than they were in H.W. Fowler's day. Perhaps it is our increasing ignorance of classical tongues, or our disregard for the morphological integrity of the words we coin, that causes the problem. As an American lexicographer once observed, "Not many people care whether a word has Greek and Latin elements mixed in it." Mitford M. Mathews, *American Words* 93 (1959).

Virtually all the hybrids condemned by Fowler (e.g., *amoral, bureaucracy, cablegram, climactic, coastal, coloration, gullible, pacifist, racial, speedometer*) are now passed over without mention even by those who consider themselves purists. Others that Fowler did not mention also fall into this class, such as *antedate, likable, lumpectomy, merriment, postwar, retrofit, riddance, telegenic,* and *transship*. But we also have our own fringe hybrids: *botheration, raticide, monokini,* and *scatteration* (the last being a MORPHOLOGICAL DEFORMITY as well).

In law, one rarely hears complaints about hybrids, though Mario Pei once called *venireman* a product of "the worst kind of hybridization (. . . half Latin, half Anglo-Saxon)." Mario Pei, *Words in Sheep's Clothing* 83 (1969). The nonsexist *veniremember,* of course, solves that problem. See **venireman.**

Other law-related hybrids are widely accepted. *Breathalyzer* (formerly *drunkometer*) has become standard, although in 1965 Gowers wrote that this term was "stillborn, it may be hoped" (*MEU2* 253). (See **Breathalyzer.**) *Creedal* is a near-commonplace. *Quo warranto* is an example dating back to the 13th century. *Automendacity,* a word expressing the idea that a forgery tells not just a lie but a lie about itself—about what the very document is—has proved convenient for writers on criminal law. And Fowler may not be resting in peace. See **creedal** & **quo warranto.**

hygiene used to have something to do with cleanliness and healthfulness, esp. with regard to the body. Then the bureaucrats and psychologists sullied this word with figurative senses, giving us, for example, the phrase *mental hygiene* (*see State of California Dep't of Mental Hygiene v. Bank of Southwest*, 354 S.W.2d 576 (Tex. 1962)). And this: "What she offers in the place of a system of punishment is in fact a system of purely forward-looking *social hygiene* in which our only concern when we have an offender to deal with is with the future and the rational aim of prevention of future crime." H.L.A. Hart, *Crime and the Criminal Law*, 74 Yale L.J. 1325, 1328 (1965) (book review). Careful writers shun this, as they shun all bureaucratic JARGON.

hymeneal. See **matrimonial.**

HYPALLAGE, known also as the transferred epithet, is a figure of speech in which the proper subject is displaced by what would rightfully be the object. Usually hypallage is a mere idiomatic curiosity. It has a distinguished lineage—a famous example being Shakespeare's line from *Julius Caesar*: "This was the most unkindest cut of all." It was not the *cut* that was unkind, but rather the *cutter*. Hence the object has become the subject.

An example from legal language is the phrase "negligent tort." It is the tortfeasor, not the tort, that is negligent. Likewise in these phrases:

abutting owner
angry confirmation fight
arrestable offense
bigamous cohabitation
convictable case
culpable silence
disgruntled complaints
drunk-driving cases
English-speaking countries
extraditable violations
humble opinion
immunized testimony
imprisonable crime
in-custody statements
indictable offense
intestate share
reversible error
uncounseled confession
well-educated home

But this figure of speech can sometimes be used inartfully, or cause problems if the writer is not aware of the true subject—e.g.:

- "The authorities sustain the validity of the direction of the testator, and equity will afford protection to the donor to a charitable corporation in that the attorney general may maintain a suit to *compel the property to be held* for the charitable purpose for which it was given to the corporation." *St. Joseph's Hosp. v. Bennett*, 22 N.E.2d 305, 306–07 (N.Y. 1939). (The *property* is not being *compelled to be held*; someone is *being compelled to hold the property*.)
- "*The arguments* of the parties . . . have *addressed themselves* in considerable part to the propriety of the district court's exercising its equitable jurisdiction to enjoin the strike in question once the findings set forth above have been made." *United Steelworkers of Am. v. U.S.*, 361 U.S. 39, 40–41 (1959) (per curiam). (The *arguments themselves* haven't done the *addressing*; rather, in their arguments, *the parties have addressed themselves*.)
- "The final *subclass* of originalism, what Brest calls 'moderate originalism,' *views* the text of the Constitution as . . . ." Timothy L. Hall, Note, *The Sacred and the Profane: A First Amendment Definition of Religion*, 61 Tex. L. Rev. 139, 152 (1982). (A *subclass* does not *view*.)
- "State *courts* generally *mirrored* this theistic viewpoint." Timothy L. Hall, Note, *The Sacred and the Profane: A First Amendment Definition of Religion*, 61 Tex. L. Rev. 139, 143 (1982). (State *courts* did not *mirror* the point of view discussed; rather, their *decisions* or *opinions* did.)

Hypallage can also lead to faulty METAPHORS: "The defendants in this case . . . have reduced the [husband] to a physical wreck. The *wife . . . is the victim of that wreck.*" *Neuberg v. Bobowicz*, 162 A.2d 662, 670 (Pa. 1960) (Musmanno, J., dissenting). (The writer does not mean to say that the *wife is a victim of her husband,* a paraplegic. Rather, she is a *victim of the defendants' actions.*)

HYPERCORRECTION. Sometimes people strive to abide by the strictest etiquette, but in the process they behave inappropriately. The same human motivations that result in this irony can play havoc with the language: a person will strive for a correct linguistic form but instead fall into error. Linguists call this phenomenon *hypercorrection*—a shortcoming to which legal writers are particularly susceptible.

This foible can have several causes. Often, it results from an attempt to avoid what is incorrectly thought to be a grammatical error. (See SUPERSTITIONS.) At other times, it results when the writer has an incomplete grasp of a foreign language's grammar—but insists on trying to conform to that grammar. And yet again, it sometimes results when the writer allows a misplaced sense of logic to override a well-established idiom. A few of the most common manifestations are enumerated below.

A. False Latin Plurals. One with a smattering of Latin learns that, in that language, most nouns ending in -*us* have a plural ending in -*i*: *genius* forms *genii*, *nimbus* forms *nimbi*, *syllabus* forms *syllabi*, *terminus* forms *termini*, and so on. The trouble is that not all of them do end in -*i*, so traps abound for those who wish to show off their sketchy knowledge of Latin:

Hypercorrect Form	Latin Form	English Form
*apparati	apparatus	apparatuses
*cestuis que trustent	[none]	cestuis que trust
*cestuis que usent	[none]	cestuis que use
*fori	fora	forums
*hiati	hiatus	hiatuses
*ignorami	[vb. in L.]	ignoramuses
*mandami	[vb. in L.]	mandamuses
*mittimi	[vb. in L.]	mittimuses
*nexi	nexus	nexuses
*octopi	octopodes (Gk.)	octopuses
*prospecti	prospectus	prospectuses
*stati	status	statuses

B. *Between you and I. Some users of the English language learn a thing or two about pronoun cases, but little more. They learn, for example, that it is incorrect to say "It is me" or "Me and Jane are going to school now." (See **it is I.**) But this knowledge puts them on tenterhooks: through the logical fallacy known as

"hasty generalization," they come to fear that there is something wrong with the word *me*—that perhaps it's safer to stick with *I*.

They therefore begin to use *I* even when the objective case is called for: "She had the biggest surprise for Blair and *I* [read *me*]." "Please won't you keep this between you and *I* [read *me*]." These are gross linguistic gaffes, but it is perennially surprising how many otherwise educated speakers commit them. See **between (c)** & PRONOUNS (B).

Many writers and speakers try to avoid the problem by resorting to *myself*, but that is hardly an improvement. See **myself.**

C. Number Problems. Sometimes, in the quest for correctness, writers let their sense of grammar override long-established idioms. They may write, for example, "A number of people was there," when the correct form is "A number of people were there." Or they will write, "A handful of problems arises from that approach," instead of "A handful of problems arise from that approach." For more on these correct but "antigrammatical" constructions, see SYNESIS & **number of, a.**

D. Redundantly Formed Adverbs. The forms *doubtless, much,* and *thus* are adverbs, yet some writers overcompensate by adding -*ly* and thereby forming barbarisms: **doubtlessly,* **muchly,* and *thusly—e.g.:

- "The claim was *very muchly* [read *much*] disputed . . . , still there is a Mississippi case holding that it makes no difference whether a claim is liquidated or disputed." *Dix v. Trigger Contractors, Inc.,* 337 So.2d 694, 696 (Miss. 1976).
- "The change in Lewis's representation . . . also *doubtlessly* [read *doubtless*] contributed to counsel's error." *Lewis v. State,* 929 N.E.2d 261, 265 (Ind. Ct. App. 2010).

See ADVERBS (D), **doubtless,** ***illy,** ***muchly** & **thus (B).**

E. *As for like.* When writers fear using *like* as a conjunction, they sometimes fail to use it when it would function appropriately as a preposition or adverb. Hence: "She writes like a lawyer" becomes "She writes as a lawyer." But the latter sentence sounds as if it is explaining the capacity in which she writes. The hypercorrection, then, results in a MISCUE. See **like (A).**

F. *Whom for who.* Perhaps writers should get points for trying, but those who do not know how to use *whom* should abstain in questionable contexts. That is, *against whom, for whom,* and the like may generally be instances in which the writer knows to choose *whom.* But things can get moderately tricky—e.g.: "What someone who intends to mug an approaching stranger *whom* [read *who*] he realizes is grey-haired and sunburnt intends to mug a grey-haired and sunburnt stranger, though it was no part of his aim that the intended victim should be grey-haired and sunburnt." Alan R. White, *Misleading Cases* 60 (1991).

An asterisk (*) precedes words and phrases that are invariably inferior forms.

Although, in that sentence, *whom* may seem to be the object of *realizes*, in fact it is the subject of the verb *is*. See **who** (A) & pronouns (B).

G. Unsplit Infinitives Causing Miscues. Writers who have given in to the most widespread of superstitions—or who believe that most of the readers have done so—avoid all split infinitives. They should at least avoid introducing squinting modifiers into their prose. But many writers do introduce them, and the result is often a miscue or ambiguity—e.g.: "Each is *trying subtly to exert* his or her influence over the other." Mark H. McCormack, *What They Don't Teach You at Harvard Business School* 26 (1984). In that sentence, does *subtly* modify the participle *trying* or the infinitive *to exert*? Because we cannot tell, the sentence needs to be revised in any of the following ways: (1) *Each is subtly trying to exert his or her influence over the other*, (2) *Each is trying to exert his or her influence subtly over the other*, or (3) *Each is trying to subtly exert his or her influence over the other*. See split infinitives (C), superstitions (B) & miscues.

H. Unsplit Verb Phrases. A surprising number of writers believe that it's a mistake to put an adverb in the midst of a verb phrase. The surprise is for them: every language authority who addresses the question holds just the opposite view—that the adverb generally *belongs* in the midst of a verb phrase. (See adverbs (A).) The canard to the contrary frequently causes awkwardness and artificiality—e.g.: "[The majority has] offered up views on an issue that is not currently, but *soon will be* [read *will soon be*], before us." *Cooey v. Strickland*, 588 F.3d 924, 928 (6th Cir. 2009) (Martin, J., dissenting). See superstitions (C).

I. Prepositions Moved from the End of the Sentence. "That is the type of arrant pedantry up with which I shall not put," said Winston Churchill, mocking the pedantry that causes some writers and speakers to avoid ending with a preposition. See prepositions (A) & superstitions (A).

J. Borrowed Articles for Borrowed Nouns. When a naturalized or quasi-naturalized foreignism appears in an English-language context, the surrounding words—with a few exceptions, such as *hoi polloi*—should be English. (See **hoi polloi.**) So one refers to *finding the mot juste*, not *finding le mot juste* (a common error among the would-be literati).

K. Overrefined Pronunciation. Some foreignisms acquire English and American pronunciations. For example, *lingerie* is pronounced in a way that the French would consider utterly barbarous: /lon-zhə-**ray**/, as opposed to /lan-**zhree**/. But for a native speaker of AmE to use the latter pronunciation would be foolish-sounding.

Similarly, American and English printers refer to the more modern typefaces—the ones without small projections coming off the straight lines—as *sans serif* /sanz **ser**-if/, not /sahnz sə-**reef**/. The latter pronunciation may show a familiarity with the French language, but it belies an unfamiliarity both with publishing and with the English language.

Even native-English words can cause problems. The word *often*, for example, preferably has a silent -*t*-, yet some speakers (unnaturally) pronounce it because of the spelling. The next logical step would be to pronounce *administration* /ad-min-i-**stray**-tee-on/, and all other words with the -*tion* suffix similarly. See pronunciation (A).

Hyphens. See punctuation (G) & phrasal adjectives.

hypnotism; hypnosis. These terms are not interchangeable. One might use either term to name the art of mesmerism, but one would never say, "He is under *hypnotism*." *Hypnotism* names only the practice or art; *hypnosis* refers either to the practice or to the state of consciousness itself—e.g.: "One danger of *hypnotism* is the suspect's firm conviction that what he has recalled under *hypnotism* [read *hypnosis*] is accurate." Michael Mello, *Outlaw Executive: "Crazy Joe," The Hypnotized Witness, and the Mirage of Clemency in Florida*, 23 J. Contemp. L. 1, 67 (1997).

The two words are susceptible to inelegant variation, as Chief Justice Rehnquist has demonstrated. See *Rock v. Arkansas*, 483 U.S. 44 (1987) (in which Rehnquist referred to "increased confidence in both true and false memories following *hypnosis*" (at 62) and then to "increased confidence inspired by *hypnotism*" (at 63)).

hypo; hypothet. *Hypothetical* was originally used adjectivally, but has come to be an attributive noun as well. *Hypothet* is an old-fashioned American shortening of *hypothetical* in legal contexts. *Hypo* is now the more widespread legal colloquialism, and it undoubtedly sounds better. E.g.: "In fact, fictional stories ('*hypos*' in the jargon of the law schools) will serve just as well." A.W.B. Simpson, *Trouble with the Case*, TLS, 14–20 Dec. 1990, at 1344.

hypostatize; *hypostasize. The standard form is *hypostatize* (= to make an idea into, or to regard it as, a self-existent substance or person)—e.g.: "It captures and *hypostasizes* [read *hypostatizes*] a moment in the evolution of authorship; and that moment has passed." Carys Craig, *Reconstructing the Author-Self: Some Feminist Lessons for Copyright Law*, 15 Am. U. J. Gender Soc. Pol'y & L. 207, 216 (2007).

hypothecate is not, as some writers believe, a synonym of *hypothesize*. Properly, *hypothecate* is an admiralty and civil-law term meaning "to pledge without delivery of title or possession." *Hypothesize* means "to make a hypothesis," which is a proposition put forward as a basis for argument. President George H.W. Bush, for example, fell into error on 8 August 1990, when, after sending armed forces to Saudi Arabia in the wake of Saddam Hussein's invasion of Kuwait, he said he would not "hypothecate" about this or that scenario. But the confusion is nothing new: "Was the district court, then, bound, in opposition to these facts, to instruct the jury . . . hypothetically . . . ?

[A]ny instruction . . . *hypothecated* [read *hypothesized*] on the absence of such calls, could only tend to confuse or mislead the jury." *Boardman v. Lessees of Reed*, 31 U.S. 328, 344 (1832) (per McLean, J.). **Hypotheticate* is a mistaken form of *hypothecate*.

Hypothecation is best preceded by *a* rather than by *an*—e.g.: "When critical events were unfolding, the Bank and appellants were faced with *an Hypothecation* [read *a Hypothecation*] Agreement that Shearson would not honor." *Richman v. FWB Bank*, 712 A.2d 41, 66 (Md. Ct. Spec. App. 1998). See **a (A).**

hypothetical; *hypothetic, adj. The longer form is now usual—e.g.:

- "With very narrow exceptions not likely to be helpful in our *hypothetic* [read *hypothetical*] and many other cases, they cannot compel the trustee, Cousin Northrop, to ignore dead hand constraints Aunt Essie placed on the use and disposition of the farm when she devised it to him in trust." Rob Atkinson, *The Low Road to Cy Pres Reform*, 58 Case W. Res. L. Rev. 97, 149 (2007).
- "Question 2 of the bankruptcy survey investigates this subject through [a] *hypothetic* [read *hypothetical*] scenario." Ziad Raymond Azar, *Bankruptcy Policy: An Empirical Investigation of 50 Jurisdictions Worldwide*, 82 Am. Bankr. L.J. 407, 426 (2008).

See **hypo.**

I

I; me. See PRONOUNS (B). For the error **between you and I*, see **between (C)** & HYPERCORRECTION (B).

ibid. Short for *ibidem* (= in the same place), this abbreviation is rarely used in legal citations. *Id.*, the abbreviation for *idem* (= the same person or thing), does the same job for a lawyer.

id. See *idem.*

*idealogical. See **ideological.**

idea or concept. Many writers seem unable to say *idea* without adding *or concept*. The habit is a bad one, the two words being virtually interchangeable—e.g.: "They are all appealing to the same fundamental *idea or concept*, though it is extraordinarily difficult to define exactly the nature of that *idea or concept*." Edward Jenks, *The Book of English Law* 2 (P.B. Fairest ed., 6th ed. 1967). In that sentence, *idea* alone would suffice in both places. See **concept.**

idem (= the same), in its abbreviated form *id.*, is used in citations to refer to the cited authority immediately preceding. For example, if footnote 2 reads, "Thomas A. Mauet, *Fundamentals of Trial Techniques* 380 (1980)," footnote 3 might read, "*Id.* at 381."

The full word appears in the LATINISM *idem sonans* (lit., "having the same sound"), which represents a rule of law that a variant spelling of a name in a document will not render the document void if the misspelling is pronounced in the same way as the true spelling (as *Growgan* for *Grogan* on a traffic ticket). E.g.: "Under our random system it sometimes happens that your name is *idem sonans* with mine, and it may be the same even in spelling." Oliver W. Holmes, *The Theory of Legal Interpretation*, 12 Harv. L. Rev. 417, 418 (1899).

identical takes either *with* or *to*. Traditionally, *with* was considered preferable because one has *identity with* something or someone, not *to* it. *Identical to* was

not widely used until the mid-20th century. The *OED*, in fact, quotes illustrative examples only with the phrase *identical with*. Here the older phrasing is used:

- "Under a constitutional provision *identical with* our own, the Missouri courts have held consistently that the question of libel or no libel is for the jury." *Harrington v. Butte Miner Co.*, 139 P. 451, 453 (Mont. 1914).
- "The evidence is that the two prior wills contained residuary devises *identical with* those in the latest will." *Linkins v. Protestant Episcopal Cathedral Found. of D.C.*, 187 F.2d 357, 359 (D.C. Cir. 1951).
- "Criteria for admitting family members are not *identical with* those applied to asylum seekers, economic migrants, and seasonal workers." Liav Orgad & Theodore Ruthizer, *Race, Religion & Nationality in Immigration Selection*, 26 Const. Comment. 237, 246 (2010).

Just as frequently, however, and especially in AmE, *to* appears. It has come to be the predominant nonliterary idiom—e.g.:

- "This parade of difficulties leads to the moral judgment that basic and enhanced chimeras that produce some gametes *identical to* those of humans should not be allowed to breed." Stephen R. Munzer, *Human-Nonhuman Chimeras in Embryonic Stem-Cell Research*, 21 Harv. J.L. & Tech. 123, 144 (2007).
- "Further, the packaging of the counterfeit product can be of deceptively high quality, with the counterfeit product appearing *identical to* the actual medicine." Bryan A. Liang, *Regulating Follow-on Biologics*, 44 Harv. J. on Legis. 363, 383 (2007).

*identificatory; *identificative; *identificational. Try *identifying* instead, or perhaps use *identification* attributively, as the British do <identification parade>. The others are mid-20th-century pomposities.

ideological. So spelled, though many misapprehend its etymology, believing the word is somehow derived from our modern word *idea*, and so misspell it **idealogical*. The blunder has become common enough that it appears in *W3* (cf. ***miniscule**), but inclusion in that dictionary is not a persuasive defense of its use. Like several other, more learned words beginning with *ideo*- (e.g., *ideograph*), *ideology* passed into English through French (F. *idéologie*) and has been spelled *ideo*- in English since the 18th century.

id est. See **i.e.**

idiosyncrasy. So spelled, though often misspelled **idiosyncracy* (as if it denoted a form of government)—e.g.: "Their *idiosyncracies* [read *idiosyncrasies*] are patrician." David Margolick, *Latest Court Candidates Share Similar Histories*, N.Y. Times, 30 May 1993, § 1, at 24.

idyllic (= of, belonging to, or of the nature of an idyll [a short picturesque poem usu. describing rustic life]; full of charm or picturesqueness) is often misused as if it meant *ideal* (= perfect). E.g.: "If unprofessional conduct . . . , deliberately employed as a means of thwarting the prosecution, *was* [read *were*] to be deemed per se ineffective assistance, then the accused would be placed in an *idyllic* [read *ideal*] situation." *Chappee v. Vose*, 843 F.2d 25, 33 (1st Cir. 1988). (On the change of *was* to *were* in that sentence, see SUBJUNCTIVES.)

i.e., the abbreviation for *id est* (L. "that is"), introduces explanatory phrases or clauses. The abbreviation is perfectly appropriate in legal writing. Formerly it was said that, in speaking or reading, the abbreviation should be rendered *id est*. But this is never heard today, whereas the abbreviated letters *i.e.* are frequently heard in lawyers' speech. (See **e.g.**) Generally, a comma follows *i.e.* in AmE (though not in BrE).

if. A. And *whether*. It's good editorial practice to distinguish between these words. *Whether* is generally preferable when you intend to express not a conditional idea, but an alternative or possibility; *if* simply states a condition. Yet *if* is often used when, in formal writing at least, *whether* would be the better word—e.g.: "Based on these observations Agent Fisher inquired *if* [read *whether*] there were any weapons, money, or drugs in the truck." *U.S. v. Martinez*, 356 F.Supp.2d 856, 860 (M.D. Tenn. 2005).

In some contexts, the word choice actually shades the meaning. For example, "Please let me know *if* you need any advice" means to get in touch only if you need advice. "Please let me know *whether* you need any advice" means to advise in any event, whether the answer is yes or no.

B. *If, and only if; if, but only if.* Ordinarily, these phrases add nothing but unnecessary emphasis (and perhaps a rhetorical flourish) to *only if*—e.g.: "Summary judgment is permissible *if and only if* [read *only if*] there is no genuine issue of material fact as to an essential element." *Kinsler v. Berkline, LLC*, 320 S.W.3d 796, 801 (Tenn. 2010).

The variation *if, but only if*, which sometimes occurs in legal writing, is unnecessary and even nonsensical for *only if*. E.g.: "People obey the law *if, but only if*, [read *only if*] they view the law as legitimate." Ann Seidman & Robert B. Seidman, *ILTAM: Drafting Evidence-Based Legislation for Democratic Social Change*, 89 B.U. L. Rev. 435, 472 (2009).

Yet in math and logic, *if and only if* marks a relationship in which if either proposition is true (or false), both are true (or false).

C. For *though, even if,* or *and*. Some writers use *if* in an oddly precious way to mean "though," "though perhaps," "even if," or even "and." Though several dictionaries record this use, it's not recommended because it suggests a kind of prissy affectation—e.g.: "The thrust of this inquiry is to distinguish between the ordinary, *if* [read *and*] occasionally unpleasant, vicissitudes of the workplace and actual harassment." *Noviello v. City of Boston*, 398 F.3d 76, 92 (1st Cir. 2005).

D. And **in the event that*. See **in the event that*.

if, and only if; if, but only if. See **if (B).**

if and when. A. Generally. The single word *if* or *when* typically conveys everything this three-word phrase does. Although the full idiom does emphasize both conditionality and temporality, if a thing is done at a certain time it is ipso facto done. Still, the phrase helpfully sets up two conditions: (1) I won't perform my duty unless you perform yours, and (2) don't expect me to go first. As a popular idiom, *if and when* is not likely to disappear just for the sake of brevity.

H.W. Fowler enumerated a number of suspicions that keen readers are likely to have about users of this phrase: "There is the suspicion that he is a mere parrot, who cannot say part of what he has often heard without saying the rest also; there is the suspicion that he likes verbiage for its own sake; there is the suspicion that he is a timid swordsman who thinks he will be safer with a second sword in his left hand; there is the suspicion that he has merely been too lazy to make up his mind between *if* and *when*" (*MEU1* 254). In short, one is ill advised to use the phrase, which is almost invariably improved when simplified—e.g.:

- "While such an unusual exercise of government power would certainly raise a suspicion that a private purpose was afoot, the hypothetical cases posited by petitioners can be confronted *if and when* [read *if*] they arise." *Kelo v. City of New London*, 545 U.S. 469, 487 (2005) (per Stevens, J.).
- "The judgment further provides that periodic alimony will terminate *if and when* [read *if*] the former wife cohabits with a member of the same or the opposite sex or if the court otherwise orders termination." *J.L.M. v. S.A.K.*, 18 So.3d 384, 387 (Ala. Ct. App. 2008).

An even worse manifestation of the phrase is *if, as, and when*. One of the three words or *whenever* is suitable virtually wherever this phrase appears—e.g:

- "The current summary-judgment motion is denied, but without prejudice to its reassertion *if, as, and when* [read *if*] the Lingafelter judgment becomes final under Illinois law." *Garrett v. Illinois State Toll Hwy. Auth.*, 582 F.Supp.2d 1039, 1040 (N.D. Ill. 2008).
- "Doris and Raoul Hagen's 1976 divorce decree awarded a percentage of Raoul's military retirement pay to Doris to be paid *if, as, and when* [read *as*] he received it." *Hagen v. Hagen*, 282 S.W.3d 899, 900 (Tex. 2009).

- "Appellee was granted a monetary award of $32,900 plus a future sum or sums of money equal to a fractional share of appellant's retirement pension *if, as, and when* [read *whenever*] he receives it." *Heger v. Heger*, 964 A.2d 258, 272 (Md. Ct. Spec. App. 2009).

Cf. **unless and until.**

B. And *when and if.* Perhaps in an attempt to get out of a rhetorical rut, some writers reverse the SET PHRASE and make it *when and if*, with no change in nuance intended. But this inverted construction loses any logical value the original may have had—*when* the thing is done, there is no further question about *if* it will be done. Some other phrasing is usually advisable—e.g.:

- "The possible problems [that] may arise . . . will be addressed *when and if* [read *when*] that issue arises." *In re Grand Jury Matter No. 86-525-5*, 689 F.Supp. 454, 465 (E.D. Pa. 1987).
- "This means that you pay attorneys' fees only *when and if* [read *when*] the attorney recovers money for you." Shae Irving, *Nolo's Encyclopedia of Everyday Law* 347 (7th ed. 2008).

When and if can have a distinct nuance, however, by emphasizing that the event may never happen. Punctuation can help—e.g.: "*When (and if)* the defendant's sanity is restored, the defendant goes to prison to serve any remaining time on the sentence." Paul Bergman & Sara Berman, *The Criminal Law Handbook* 320 (11th ed. 2009).

When *not* is substituted for *and*, the construction emphasizes the inevitability of the event at some point—e.g.: "Most scholars assume it is only a matter of *when—not if—Heller* will be incorporated to the states." Jonathan D. Marshall, *District of Columbia v. Heller*, 59 Syracuse L. Rev. 165, 167 (2008).

if any. Instead of putting *if any* after the noun, try putting *any* before it—e.g.: "The complaint must further show . . . *what voyages or trips, if any* [read *any voyages or trips*] *she* [read *the ship*] has made since the voyage or trip on which the claims sought to be limited arose." Supp. R. Adm. & Mar. Claims F(2).

if, as, and when. See **if and when (A).**

if it ain't broke, don't fix it. This is a favorite CLICHÉ of American lawyers seeking to preserve the status quo—and often merely to entrench mediocrity.

if it be. See SUBJUNCTIVES.

if not is an ambiguous phrase best avoided. It may mean either (1) lit., "(even) if it is (we are, etc.) not; though not" <he was a competent judge, if not a great one>, or (2) "perhaps even" <she was a powerful justice, if not the very most powerful of her generation>. Sense 2 is exemplified in the following sentences:

- "Justices of the peace who handle petty criminal cases and small claims are close to the general public and are an important, *if not* [i.e., *and even an*] essential, element in any state's system of justice." *Brown v. Vance*, 637 F.2d 272, 276 (5th Cir. 1981).
- "While many, *if not most* [read *perhaps even most*], people seek out lawyers for help in matters of personal importance and may, consequently, be vulnerable, the mental health condition of Doe at the time the sexual relationship began is an aggravating circumstance to consider in the imposition of discipline." *Iowa Sup. Ct. Att'y Disc. Bd. v. Marzen*, 779 N.W.2d 757, 769 (Iowa 2010).

Sense 1 is confusing if, as is quite likely, the reader first thinks of the phrase in terms of the more common sense 2: "We are apt *if not* vigilant to overlook the true status of the defendant husband and the defendant wife when they undertook acquisition by the entirety of the home lot." *Cincinnati Women's Servs., Inc. v. Taft*, 466 F.Supp.2d 934, 938 (S.D. Ohio 2005). The sentence means: "We are apt, *if we are not vigilant*, to overlook . . . ." But the reader more familiar with sense 2 will misperceive the sentence as meaning: "We are apt, *and even vigilant*, to overlook . . . ." See AMBIGUITY.

if you will. This phrase typifies the language of those who engage in WORD-PATRONAGE—e.g.: "With regard to a large area of the legal field the experiments of the law, if they can be so called—the engineering appliances, *if you will*—are brought to bear *ex post facto*." Carleton K. Allen, *Law in the Making* 36 (7th ed. 1964). This phrase, meaning in full *if you will allow me to use the phrase*, is almost always (as in the example quoted) best deleted.

ignis fatuus (= will o' the wisp; a delusive hope or desire) forms the plural *ignes fatui*. It is pronounced /**ig**-nis **fach**-ə-wəs/; the plural is /**ig**-neez **fach**-ə-wɪ/.

ignitable. So spelled.

ignominy is accented on the first, not the second, syllable: /**ig**-nə-min-ee/.

ignoramus. Until 1934 in England, if a grand jury considered the evidence of an alleged crime insufficient, it would endorse the bill *ignoramus*, meaning literally "we do not know" or "we know nothing of this." The term was a survival of the medieval practice of having juries act on personal knowledge. Today, the phrases *no bill, no true bill*, and *not a true bill* have replaced *ignoramus.*

By the early 17th century, though, the word *ignoramus* had come to mean, by extension, "an ignorant person." (See POPULARIZED LEGAL TECHNICALITIES.) In 1615, George Ruggle wrote a play called *Ignoramus*, about a lawyer who knew nothing about the law; and this fictional lawyer soon gave his name to all manner of know-nothings, whether lawyers or nonlawyers.

The modern nonlegal meaning appears more frequently in modern legal writing than the historical legal meaning—e.g.:

- "The district court concluded that these witnesses' testimony tended to show that 'even an *ignoramus* in this field would know at least about patrimony laws.'" *U.S. v. Schultz*, 333 F.3d 393, 415 (2d Cir. 2003).
- "This standard, more difficult to satisfy because it depends on the likely reaction of a reasonable consumer rather than an *ignoramus*, appears to have been applied by federal courts ever since." *Aspinall v. Philip Morris Cos.*, 813 N.E.2d 476, 487 (Mass. 2004).

Pl. *ignoramuses*, not **ignorami*. See PLURALS (A).

ignorance. See **mistake** (B).

ignorance of the law is no excuse. See *ignorantia juris.*

ignorant; stupid. Fastidious users of language distinguish between these terms. *Stupid* refers to a lack of innate ability, whereas *ignorant* refers merely to a lack of knowledge on a particular subject. Geniuses are *ignorant* of many facts, but that doesn't make them *stupid*. But *stupid* people can't grasp that they are *ignorant* of even the most basic facts.

ignorantia facti excusat. See MAXIMS.

ignorantia juris is a moderately useful LATINISM denoting the legal doctrine that ignorance of the law is no excuse (rendered in Latin *ignorantia juris neminem excusat* [lit., "ignorance of law excuses no one"]). E.g.:

- "The reliance argument has strong intuitive appeal and further builds on the general criticisms of the *ignorantia juris* principle that it is intolerable to treat individuals as means to an end." Eric W. Treene, Note, *Prayer-Treatment Exemptions to Child Abuse and Neglect Statutes, Manslaughter Prosecutions, and Due Process of Law*, 30 Harv. J. on Legis. 135, 188 (1993).
- "Given the *ignorantia juris* principle, communities rarely feel obliged to announce that the criminal laws in the jurisdiction will be enforced as written." Margaret Raymond, *Penumbral Crimes*, 39 Am. Crim. L. Rev. 1395, 1409 (2002).

See MAXIMS.

Some writers use the phrase *ignorantia legis* rather than *ignorantia juris*. Strictly speaking, *jus* (and its genitive *juris*) means the science of law or the whole body of the law, whereas *lex* (genitive *legis*) means a legislative act or pronouncement, or sometimes the body of enacted law as distinct from principles of common law (or judge-made law). Hence, strictly, *ignorantia juris* means ignorance of the law and *ignorantia legis* ignorance of a specific statute or ordinance. But no such DIFFERENTIATION seems to exist in practice. Ironically, the issue in most cases is ignorance of a specific provision, not of the law in general; but *ignorantia juris* remains the more common form.

ignorantia legis. See *ignorantia juris.*

ignore, when used in reference to a grand jury, means "to sign a bill with *ignoramus*"—e.g.:

- "The grand jury may *ignore* the bill, and decline to find any indictment." *Post v. U.S.*, 161 U.S. 583, 587 (1896) (per Gray, J.).

- "Russo's testimony before the grand jury as to Foster, Baker and Weller, contradicted his testimony before the committing magistrate and in effect made it necessary for the grand jury to *ignore* all three bills." *Commonwealth v. Russo*, 111 A.2d 359, 364 (Pa. Super. Ct. 1955).
- "The grand jury takes it [the case] up anew, and may present or *ignore* the bill, without any reference whatever to the fact that one indictment has been presented and set aside." *State v. Silver*, 398 P.2d 178, 180 (Or. 1965) (en banc).

See **ignoramus.**

ilk correctly means "the same"; hence *of that ilk* means "of that same kind." E.g.:

- "The evidence in this case was of the *ilk* that would tax the patience and wisdom of Solomon." *Mink v. Mink*, 395 S.E.2d 237, 239 (Ga. Ct. App. 1990).
- "While Plaintiff again points to loose similarities of general plot elements, stock characters, and minute, random details of the same *ilk* [read *kind*] discussed above for *Treasure of Khan*, these coincidences between the works are nothing more than that—coincidences of similarities that exist amongst almost any work of this genre." *Doody v. Penguin Group Inc.*, 673 F.Supp.2d 1144, 1161 (D. Haw. 2009).

The word is commonly misapprehended as relating to race or family—it is not that specific. And it commonly carries a pejorative flavor <pimps, thieves, and others of their ilk>.

ill. The comparative form of this adjective is *worse*, the superlative *worst*. The adverb is *ill*—**illy* being an illiterate form. Yet illiteracies have been known to creep into legal writing and even into judicial opinions: see **illy.*

illation (= [1] the act of inferring; or [2] something inferred) is a scholarly term little used today, though a few modern judges are quite fond of it. *Inference* serves better and more understandably—e.g.:

- "The government-knowledge inference generates a strong *illation* [read *inference*] that defendants did not 'knowingly' submit false claims within the meaning of § 3729(a) of the FCA." *U.S. ex rel. Burlbaw v. Orenduff*, 548 F.3d 931, 957 (10th Cir. 2008). [A suggested rewrite: *The government-knowledge inferences strongly suggest that . . . .*]
- "The fact that the southwest corner had been used historically for hotel and function parking since 1945 and was at least partially paved substantially buttresses the *illation* [read *inference*] that the parking was not moved or extended to an area not previously designated for such use at the time it became nonconforming." *Cohen v. Duncan*, 970 A.2d 550, 566 (R.I. 2009). Note the double negatives: see NEGATIVES (A).

illegal; illicit; unlawful. These three terms are fundamentally synonymous. But *illicit* <illicit love affairs> carries moral overtones in addition to the basic sense "not in accordance with or sanctioned by law." See **illicit.**

Illegal is not synonymous with *criminal*, though some writers mistakenly assume that it is. (For an example of this erroneous assumption, see **undocumented alien.**) Anything against the law—even the

Illogic 423

civil law—is, technically speaking, "illegal," but only violations of criminal law are *criminal*. See **illegal contract, nonlegal** & **unlawful**.

illegal alien. See **undocumented alien.**

illegal contract. This phrase is "exceptionally difficult to define." P.S. Atiyah, *An Introduction to the Law of Contract* 38 (3d ed. 1981). The phrase does not denote merely "a contract contrary to the criminal law, although such a contract would indubitably be illegal." *Id.* A contract can be illegal without violating the criminal law because some activities are contrary to the public interest.

illegal entrant. See **undocumented alien.**

illegal entry. This phrase, in some jurisdictions, denotes a lesser-included offense of *burglary*—e.g.: "A murderer, who might get the chair, would be offered a plea to 'manslaughter,' or a burglar, liable for twenty years, one to '*illegal entry*,' depending on how strong the evidence in either case might be." Ephraim Tutt, *Yankee Lawyer* 88 (1943). See **burglary.**

illegible; unreadable. *Illegible* = not plain or clear enough to be read (used of handwriting or defaced printing). *Unreadable* = too dull or obfuscatory to be read (used of bad writing). Impenetrable JARGON is unreadable; only if it is smudged or faint print or incorrigibly bad penmanship is it illegible.

illegitimacy. See **bastardy.**

illegitimate child. Though the phrase is still often used, it is undeniably insensitive. As a far-sighted judge once observed, "There are no *illegitimate children*, only illegitimate parents." *In re Estate of Woodward*, 40 Cal. Rptr. 781, 784 (Dist. Ct. App. 1964). A New York judge contends that "the preferable modern term is *nonmarital child*." Letter of Arthur E. Blyn, *Nonmarital Children*, N.Y. Times, 10 Mar. 1991, at 14. A recent survey found that nearly 40% of contemporary newborns in the U.S. are nonmarital children. See EUPHEMISMS, **bastard** & **natural child.**

illicit (= illegal), when used for *elicit* (= to bring out), is a monumental blunder. One might have thought this error impossible, but it does occur—e.g.:

- "It appears that the purpose in asking the offending questions was to *illicit* [read *elicit*] a response suggesting that Strommen was a person of bad character who had frequent contacts with the police." *State v. Strommen*, 648 N.W.2d 681, 688 (Minn. 2002).
- "We agree with Joseph's assertion that Detective Osmond's statement sought confirmation of Joseph's previous statement and was intended to *illicit* [read *elicit*] a response." *State v. Joseph*, 128 P.3d 795, 809 (Haw. 2006).
- "The power of the voir dire process to *illicit* [read *elicit*] honest answers should not be underestimated, especially when the threat of federal perjury charges looms." *U.S. v. Carona*, 571 F.Supp.2d 1157, 1162 (C.D. Cal. 2008). What does *process* add to that sentence? Nothing: see **process.**

For the proper use of *illicit*, see **illegal.** For the antonym *licit*, see **legal,** adj.

illiterate = (1) unable to read or write; or (2) unlettered. Justice Oliver Wendell Holmes was wont to use this word in sense 2, the heightened sense of the word: "In the case at bar we have an *illiterate* woman writing her own will. Obviously the first sentence, 'I am going on a journey and may not ever return,' expresses the fact that was on her mind as the occasion and inducement for writing it." *Eaton v. Brown*, 193 U.S. 411, 414 (1904) (per Holmes, J.).

ILLOGIC. The writer on language who would dare drag logic into the discussion must do so warily. For centuries, grammarians labored under the mistaken belief that grammar is but applied logic and therefore tried to rid language of everything illogical.

But to paraphrase Justice Oliver Wendell Holmes, the life of the language has not been logic: it has been experience. No serious student believes anymore that grammatical distinctions necessarily reflect logical ones. Our language is full of idioms that defy logic, many of them literary and many colloquial. We should not, for example, fret over the synonymy of *fat chance* and *slim chance*. Applying "linguistic logic" to established ways of saying things is a misconceived effort.

We see that misconceived effort today when armchair grammarians insist that *grammatical error* is an Irish bull; that *I don't think so* is wrong in place of *I think not*; that *the reason why* is wrong (no more so, certainly, than *place where* or *time when*); that *a number of people* must take a singular, not a plural, verb (see SYNESIS); or that, in *Don't spend any more time than you can help*, the final words should be *can't help*. When logic is used for such purposes, it is worse than idle: it is harmful.

That doesn't mean, of course, that logic is of no concern to the writer. For rhetorical purposes, logic is essential. Some readers will look for holes in the wording. In evaluating our own writing, therefore, we should strictly follow idiom and usage, but otherwise apply logic.

The exercise will tighten your prose. Since idiom does not yet prefer *could care less*, much less require it, write *couldn't care less*. (Logically speaking, if you say you *could care less*, then you are admitting that you care to some extent.) No longer might you say, *I was scared literally to death*, because you recognize the literal meaning of *literally* and you are still alive to report how scared you were. Likewise, logic would have you banish such thoughtless words as *preplanned* and use words such as *reiterate* more carefully, so as to distinguish it from *iterate*. See **reiterate.**

An asterisk (✳) precedes words and phrases that are invariably inferior forms.

Logic also rids prose of the various errors in thinking that workaday writers commonly perpetrate. To avoid the ills catalogued below, consider closely how your words and sentences relate to one another.

A. Illogical Comparison. This lapse occurs commonly in locutions like *as large if not larger than*, which, when telescoped, becomes *as large . . . than*; properly, one writes *as large as if not larger than*. Similar problems occur with classes. For example, when members of classes are being compared, a word such as *other* must be used to restrict the class: "Our system of justice is better than any [other] in the world." Our system of justice, after all, is among those in the world.

Another problem of comparison occurs when writers forget the point of reference—e.g.:

- "I cannot ignore our culpability in this situation and, like parricide in the Athenian law, pass it over in silence." *In re Brown*, 454 F.2d 999, 1016 (D.C. Cir. 1971) (Tamm, J., dissenting). *Parricide* didn't pass over anything in silence; rather, the Athenian law passed over *parricide* in silence, the writer means to say. How strange, too, to compare oneself with parricide.

- "Like the young Bentham, an ardent crusader, he [Rodell] *lacks Bentham's patience* [read *lacks patience*]." Jerome Frank, Introduction, *Woe Unto You, Lawyers!* xii (1980 ed). As a comparison of young Jeremy Bentham with old Jeremy Bentham, the sentence does not work, because the source of the comparison is also the source of difference.

- "The Commission is not a judicial body, but a regulatory body, and as such it must have the authority to address each matter before it freely, even if the matter involves issues identical *to a previous case* [read *with those in a previous case*]." *Illinois-American Water Co. v. Illinois Commerce Comm'n*, 751 N.E.2d 48, 52 (Ill. App. Ct. 2001). The sentence compares issues to a case.

- "The issue in this appeal is whether the defendant in an admiralty tort action who settles with the plaintiff without obtaining a release from liability for *other potential defendants* can then be entitled to contribution from them toward the amount it paid to settle its own liability." *Murphy v. Florida Keys Elec. Coop. Ass'n*, 329 F.3d 1311, 1312–13 (11th Cir. 2003). The phrase *other potential defendants* is wrong because any party who has settled is no longer a *potential* defendant.

For related problems, see **as much as or more** & overstatement.

B. Danglers and Misplaced Modifiers. Every dangler or misplaced modifier, to some degree, perverts logic, sometimes humorously. Consider, for example, "I saw the Statue of Liberty flying into Newark." To avoid these disruptions of thought, remember that participles should relate to nouns that are truly capable of performing the action of the participle. Here, for example, note that neither a definition nor a belief construes: "Any definition is likely to distinguish between religion and mere conscientious belief, *construing* the first amendment to govern the former but not the latter." Timothy L. Hall, *The Sacred and the Profane: A First Amendment Definition of Religion*, 61 Tex. L. Rev. 139, 152 (1982). For a fuller discussion of these matters, see DANGLERS & MISPLACED MODIFIERS.

C. Disjointed Appositives. Phrases intended to be in apposition should not be separated. (See APPOSITIVES.) E.g.: "A respected English legal authority on the common law, the view of William Blackstone permeated much of the early thinking on freedom of expression." John Murray, *The Media Law Dictionary* 11 (1978). Blackstone himself, not Blackstone's *view*, is the respected authority.

D. Mistaken Subject of a Prepositional Phrase. This problem crops up usually when a word or phrase intervenes between the noun and the prepositional phrase referring to that noun. Often, as in the first example below, the noun (*vehicle*) functions as an adjective:

- "Defendant Linda G. Okey was the [vehicle] driver in which [read Okey was driving the vehicle in which] the plaintiff's decedent, a minor aged nine, was riding as a passenger." *Tucker v. Okey*, 266 N.E.2d 121, 121 (Ill. App. Ct. 1970).

- "Of the three persons involved, the entire loss fell upon the only one who was himself free from all negligence." William L. Prosser et al., *Torts: Cases & Materials* 662 n.1 (11th ed. 2005). What is the relationship between *the three persons involved*, the *loss* incurred, and the degree of *negligence*? Read *Of the three persons involved, the only one to incur a loss was the one free from all negligence*.

E. Insensitivity to Metaphor. Illogical metaphors abound in American writing. The scholar's *virgin field pregnant with possibilities* is among the more risible examples. Others less humorous are only a little less difficult to spot—e.g.:

- "In my opinion that foundation . . . is not weakened by the fact that it is buttressed by other provisions that are also designed to avoid the insidious evils of government propaganda favoring particular points of view." *F.C.C. v. League of Women Voters*, 468 U.S. 364, 409 (1984) (Rehnquist, J., dissenting). Buttresses serve only to strengthen, not to weaken.

- "This Note examines the doctrine set forth in *Roe v. Wade* and its progeny." Andrea M. Sharrin, Note, *Potential Fathers and Abortion*, 55 Brook. L. Rev. 1359, 1363 (1990). *Roe v. Wade* legalized abortion: don't speak of its progeny!

- "When the district court undertakes to block the untraveled roads by adopting a forward-looking provision, its discretion is necessarily less broad because, without liability findings to mark the way, it is in danger of imposing restrictions that prevent the defendant from forging new routes to serve consumers." *Massachusetts v. Microsoft Corp.*, 373 F.3d 1199, 1224 (D.C. Cir. 2004). What is an *untraveled road*? Travel creates roads; they do not exist in a vacuum.

See METAPHORS (A).

F. Poor Exposition of Sequence. Don't ask your readers to assume what is not logically possible by your very assumptions—e.g.:

- "The obligation of the deceased to transfer certain property, as a minimum, during his life does not negative a desire to leave the other property after death." *Luff v. Luff*, 359 F.2d 235, 243 (D.C. Cir. 1966). A deceased person cannot have obligations of any kind, much less obligations to transfer property during his life. This is an example of the rhetorical figure called "prolepsis."

- "Indeed, the condition of the plane after the crash *eliminates an air collision* [read *was such as to eliminate further speculation about an air collision* or *ruled out an air* collision as the cause of the crash]." *Newing v. Cheatham*, 540 P.2d 33, 40 (Cal. 1975). If *only* we could undo the mishap!

G. Vexatious Little Words with Plain Meanings. Writers often confound their meaning by misusing simple words—e.g.: "To avoid governmental immunity under the public-building exception, the plaintiff must prove that . . . the governmental agency failed to remedy the alleged defective condition *after* [read *in*] a reasonable amount of time." *Renny v. Department of Transp.*, 734 N.W.2d 518, 521–22 (Mich. 2007). If *after* a reasonable amount of time, then the period has become *unreasonable*!

H. Complete Obliviousness in the Task of Writing. We all take leave of our senses, from time to time, especially while composing. We save ourselves, however, by applying our critical faculties while revising. Most of us do, anyway. But some writers don't—e.g.: "The courts are more reluctant in considering extrinsic evidence to construe a will than to construe an inter vivos transfer." [A suggested revision: *Courts are more reluctant to consider extrinsic evidence in construing a will than in construing an inter vivos transfer.*] (The original sentence suggests that courts have a choice of what to construe, as if a judge might say, "Well, here I am considering some extrinsic evidence. Why, I think I'll construe an inter vivos transfer—that would be more fun than a will!")

I. Progression of Tenses. See TENSES.

ill-treat. See **abuse**, vb.

illude. See **allude (B).**

illusion; delusion. These words are used differently despite their similar meanings. An *illusion* exists in one's fancy or imagination. A *delusion* is an idea or thing that deceives or misleads a person about some aspect of the real world. *Delusions* are dangerously wrong apprehensions; *illusions* are also wrong perceptions, but the connotation is far less dire.

For the difference between *illusion* and *allusion*, see **allusion.** For the difference between *delusion* and *hallucination*, see **hallucination.**

illusory; *illusive. The first is preferred; the second is a NEEDLESS VARIANT. See **elusive.**

illustrate, in modern usage, means "to provide a good example of (something); to exemplify." In the following sentence it is used ambiguously: "*Hohfeld's analysis illustrates* [read *In his analysis, Hohfeld examines*] the fallacy of accepting uncritically the 'artificial entity' theory." Robert W. Hamilton, *The Law of Corporations in a Nutshell* 50 (5th ed. 2000). The writer here is not claiming as the sentence seems to do—that Hohfeld's analysis is itself a good example of "the fallacy of accepting uncritically the 'artificial entity' theory." Rather, the sentence is intended to praise Hohfeld's analysis as elucidating the nature of this fallacy.

Illustrate is usually accented on the first syllable: /il-ə-strayt/.

illustrative. A. Pronunciation. Accent the second syllable: /i-ləs-trə-tiv/.

B. And *illustrious*. *Illustrative* means "providing a good illustration or portrayal; representative." *Illustrious* means "distinguished; acclaimed; renowned." Occasionally the words are confounded—e.g.:

- "*Campbell* . . . is *illustrious* [read *illustrative*] of a record where there was evidence that the defendant, if guilty, was guilty of the lesser included offense alone." *Eldred v. State*, 578 S.W.2d 721, 723 (Tex. Crim. App. 1979).
- "Thirteen years after his own law school graduation, he returned to the academy to begin a long and *illustrative* [read *illustrious*] career in law teaching." E. Thomas Sullivan, *A Tribute to Professor Merton C. Bernstien*, 71 Wash. U. L.Q. 1013, 1013 (1993).

*illy. Though once common, **illy* is no longer an acceptable adverb since *ill* itself acts as an adverb. Either *ill* or *poorly* is more serviceable today—e.g.:

- "There are many decisions contrary to this view; but . . . we think they are unsafe, unsound, and *illy adapted* [read *ill-adapted*] to modern conditions." *Tuttle v. Buck*, 119 N.W. 946, 948 (Minn. 1909).
- "Defendant was protesting that it was *illy done* [read *ill-done* or *done poorly*]." *Stevens v. Lakewood Utils. Co.*, 155 N.W. 402, 404 (Mich. 1915).
- "They were either not fully informed or were *illy advised* [read *ill-advised*] as to their rights and duties in the premises." *Park v. Landfried*, 63 S.E.2d 586, 590 (W. Va. 1951).
- "See Trial Transcript at 187 (District Court: 'I have never seen a case so *illy prepared* [read *ill-prepared*].')." *U.S. v. Novak*, 217 F.3d 566, 577 n.27 (8th Cir. 2000).

See **ill** & HYPERCORRECTION (D).

imbibe is a FORMAL WORD meaning "to drink." Unsurprisingly, it occurs more often in legal than in nonlegal contexts—e.g.:

- "Defendants moved for entry of a judgment on the pleadings, arguing that Florida does not have a 'dram shop' act imposing a duty on tavern owners to assure that patrons do not *overimbibe*." *Barnes v. B.K. Credit Servs., Inc.*, 461 So.2d 217, 218 (Fla. Dist. Ct. App. 1984).
- "Generally, courts are reluctant to excuse drivers who refuse chemical testing on the grounds of mental incapacity when those drivers have the capacity to *imbibe* or ingest a chemical substance and choose to drive a car." *Hollis v. State ex rel. Dep't of Pub. Safety*, 183 P.3d 996, 999 (Okla. 2008).

*imbracery. See **embracery.**

immanent. See **imminent.**

immaterial; nonmaterial. Although both may mean "not consisting of a material substance," *immaterial* tends to mean "of no substantial importance; inconsequential." *Nonmaterial*, by contrast, generally means "cultural; aesthetic." *Immaterial* is called for in most legal contexts—e.g.:

- "Most of her objections to Pattie Miller's declaration are erroneously asserted hearsay objections that involve *nonmaterial* [read *immaterial*] facts." *Grant v. Murphy & Miller, Inc.*, 149 F.Supp.2d 957, 974 (N.D. Ill. 2001).
- "If the adverse credibility finding was truly harmless or *nonmaterial* [read *immaterial*] error, it would have been unnecessary to note disagreement with it." *Kumar v. Gonzales*, 439 F.3d 520, 526 (9th Cir. 2006).
- "In this scenario, Democrats would argue that admittedly eligible voters who submitted timely registration forms should not be disenfranchised just because of an innocent, *nonmaterial* [read *immaterial*] error that the state did not give them an opportunity to correct." Edward B. Foley, *The Analysis and Mitigation of Electoral Errors*, 18 Stan. L. & Pol'y Rev. 350, 364 (2007).

immediate cause. See CAUSATION (B).

immemorial. See **time immemorial** & **memory of man runneth not to the contrary.**

immigrant; emigrant. See **emigrant** & **immigrate.**

immigrate; emigrate. *Immigrate* [*im* (into) + *migrate* (to move from one place to another)] = to enter a country with the intention of settling there permanently. *Emigrate* [*e* (from) + *migrate* (to move from one place to another)] = to depart or exit from one country in the hope of settling in another. If you're coming, you're *immigrating*; if you're going, you're *emigrating*. Some countries are plagued by illegal *immigration* (e.g., the United States); others have been plagued by attempts at illegal *emigration* (e.g., the former Soviet Union).

Both verbs are intransitive and hence do not take objects. In the following sentence, *immigrate* is wrongly made transitive—e.g.: "For a lawful permanent resident parent to *immigrate* his child, the parent and child must use a three-step process." *Valenzuela v. Kehl*, 432 F.Supp.2d 192, 196 (N.D. Tex. 2006). [A suggested revision: *When the child of a lawful permanent-resident parent is ready to immigrate, parent and child must follow a three-step process.*]

The agent nouns are *immigrant* and *emigrant* (the GALLICISM *émigré* being a NEEDLESS VARIANT of the latter).

imminent; eminent; immanent. *Imminent* means "certain and very near; impending," as in the legal phrases *imminent bodily harm*, *imminent danger*, and *imminent death*—e.g.:

- "[His conduct] reflects a deliberate action rather than the spontaneous or reflexive conduct [that] occurs at the point when arrest becomes *imminent*." *U.S. v. Bedford*, 446 F.3d 1320, 1326 (10th Cir. 2006).
- "I find convincing Judge Gilman's conclusion that the statute of limitations for bringing a § 1983 method-of-execution challenge starts to run when the prisoner knows or has reason to know of the facts that give rise to the claim and when the prisoner's execution becomes *imminent*." *Getsy v. Strickland*, 577 F.3d 309, 314 (6th Cir. 2009) (Moore, J., concurring).

Imminent does not mean merely "probable," as here incorrectly used:

- "We cannot assume reasonably that the Legislature intended that a statute enacted for the preservation of the life and limb of pedestrians must be observed when observance would subject them to more *imminent* [read *probable*] danger." *Tedla v. Ellman*, 19 N.E.2d 987, 991 (N.Y. 1939).
- "An intoxicated driver presents a *more imminent* [read *greater*] danger than many other crimes—such as concealment of a handgun—and requires less corroboration of an informant's tip." *People v. Ewing*, 880 N.E.2d 587, 597 (Ill. App. Ct. 2007).

Eminent = distinguished, of excellent repute <Judge Friendly of the Second Circuit was long considered an eminent jurist>. The adverb *eminently* is frequently used to mean "very," as in "He is *eminently* deserving of this award," or, "The court's decision was *eminently* fair." See **eminence.**

Immanent, primarily a theological term, means "inherent; pervading the material world" <the immanent goodness of the divine will>.

immolate. See **emulate.**

immoral; unmoral; amoral. These three words have distinct meanings. *Immoral*, the opposite of *moral*, means "evil; depraved." The word is highly judgmental. *Unmoral* means merely "without moral sense; not moral"; it is used, for example, of animals and inanimate objects. *Amoral*, perhaps the most commonly misused of these terms, means "not moral; outside the sphere of morality; being neither moral nor immoral." It is loosely applied to people in the sense "not having morals or scruples"—but this really amounts to a misusage of *immoral*.

immovable, in its fullest sense as a noun in legal parlance, refers to land. But by extension, the word applies also to buildings and other permanent structures as well as trees and servitudes. In law, the word is almost always used in the plural form—e.g.:

- "The appellants argue that the bankruptcy court failed to follow the general conflicts rule of *lex situs*—i.e., that lands and other *immovables* are governed by the law of the state where the property is situated." *In re Morris*, 171 B.R. 999, 1003 (S.D. Ill. 1993).
- "The activity of storing the additives above ground in movable drums and the transporting of the additives in trucks does not relate to the land or other *immovables*." *Bartlett v. Browning-Ferris Indus.*, 683 So.2d 1319, 1322 (La. Ct. App. 1996).
- "Plaintiff contends that sand and gravel are solid minerals and by nature corporeal, and that lesion lies in and only in cases of corporeal *immovables* as distinguished from mineral rights that are classified as incorporeal *immovables* under [the] Civil Code." *Hornsby v. Slade*, 854 So.2d 441, 445 (La. Ct. App. 2003).
- "Archbishop Tsoukalas died . . . and his holographic last will and testament bequeathed the total of his personal property, movables and *immovables*, to the Trust, mistakenly including the Kapandriti lot." *Tsucales v. Holy Xenophone Monastery*, 939 A.2d 1008, 1011 (Pa. Commw. Ct. 2007).

(See ADJECTIVES (C).) Of course, the term *immovable* can also be an adjective <immovable property>.

The spelling *immoveable* is a variant preferred only in Scottish legal writing. See **movable**.

immune can take *to* or *from*, depending on nuance. In the most refined usage, what you're *immune from* can't touch you; what you're *immune to* can touch you, but without effect. E.g.:

- "The fact that Hale viewed husbands as *immune from* rape prosecution is not surprising." Susan Estrich, *Real Rape* 73 (1987).
- "Union wages are more *immune to* the ups and downs of the business cycle than are nonunion wages." Bernt Bratsberg & James F. Ragan Jr., *Changes in the Union Wage Premium by Industry*, 56 Indus. & Lab. Rel. Rev. 65, 70 (2002).
- "The Tribe's sovereignty renders it uniquely *immune to* a private lawsuit without its consent." *Mudarri v. State*, 196 P.3d 153, 163 (Wash. Ct. App. 2008).

immunity. A. And *exemption*. Both denote a freedom from something that is onerous, involves hassle, or otherwise entails unpleasantness. *Immunity* is the broader term, with strong connotations of privilege and freedom from restrictions that apply to most people, *immunity* having been granted only to people who are for some reason viewed with special favor <diplomatic immunity>. Modernly, *immunity* is most often used in the specialized medical sense of the physical power of resisting disease <immunity from diphtheria>. *Exemption* is normally a less sweeping word, referring to some specific release from a legal obligation by which others similarly situated are bound <tax exemption> <exemption from military service>.

B. And *impunity*. While *immunity* is a broad term (see (A)), *impunity* is more specific: it refers merely to a freedom from punishment—e.g.: "If the pendency of an administrative petition conferred *immunity* from both civil forfeiture and criminal liability, a handler could violate the Act with *impunity*." *U.S. v. Riverbend Farms, Inc.*, 847 F.2d 553, 557 (9th Cir. 1988).

immunize = to render immune from or insusceptible to poison or infection (*OED*). By extension it means "to protect (from something bad)." The sense of some contagion or danger is an important element of the word in figurative as well as literal senses—e.g.: "[Justice Brennan] opined that merely because a discrimination fell short of providing an insurmountable barrier did not *immunize* it from the Fourteenth Amendment." *Norton v. Weinberger*, 364 F.Supp. 1117, 1124 (D. Md. 1973). (The Fourteenth Amendment to the U.S. Constitution is generally seen as a good thing, not a bad one. Hence that sentence should have read something like this: *Even if discrimination falls short of an insurmountable barrier, it can still be subject to the Fourteenth Amendment*.)

Through HYPALLAGE, it is often said not that the *witness* is immunized against the effects of his or her testimony, but that the *testimony* is immunized—e.g.: "Yesterday, the high court refused to hear arguments that Mrs. Helmsley is entitled to a pretrial hearing to determine if her indictment is based on *immunized testimony* from an earlier grand jury." Wall St. J., 16 May 1989, at B7. Literally, of course, it was the witness, not the testimony, that was immunized. Notice also that in the sentence quoted, *if* should be *whether*: see **if**.

immure. See **jail,** vb.

impact, n., is not generally understood to be a count noun. But verbal slippage has begun—e.g.: "It is apparent throughout the records that the ICC found Steere's 'melodramatic' list of *adverse impacts upon* [better: *adverse effects on*] the motor-carrier industry unpersuasive." *Steere Tank Lines, Inc. v. ICC*, 724 F.2d 472, 479 (5th Cir. 1984). This use of the noun **impact** is an extension of the verbal use disapproved at **impact,** vb.

impact, vb. *Impact* has traditionally been only a noun. Yet in recent years, it has undergone a semantic shift that has allowed it to function as a verb. Hence: "Five states have adopted plain English laws, but only New Jersey's law severely *impacts upon* [read *affects*] lawyers in their private practice." But uses of that kind become widespread (and also widely condemned by stylists). E.g.:

- "The recently filed pro se application of Charles Rumbaugh dramatically *impacts on* [read *affects*] the issue before us." *Rumbaugh v. McKaskle*, 730 F.2d 291, 293 (5th Cir. 1984).
- "The prior professional activities of a judge are not grounds for disqualification where the record fails to demonstrate the existence of a relationship or interest that clearly and adversely *impacts on* [read *affects*] a party's ability to obtain a fair and impartial trial." *In re Disqualification of Cross*, 657 N.E.2d 1338, 1339 (Ohio 1991).
- "Recognizing students' individual interests as they strive to educate themselves dramatically *impacts on* [read *affects*] how they will respect others' liberty, privacy, and security interests." Roger J.R. Levesque, *Educating American Youth*, 27 J.L. & Educ. 173, 206 (1998).
- "The diversion of funds from legitimate uses in the Medicare program adversely *impacts on* [read *affects*] all Americans." *U.S. v. Gutman*, 95 F.Supp.2d 1337, 1345 (S.D. Fla. 2000).

These uses of the word would be applauded if *impact* were performing any function not as ably performed by *affect* or *influence*. If *affect* as a verb is not sufficiently straightforward in context, then the careful writer might have recourse to *have an impact on*, which, though longer, to many is unquestionably preferable to the jarring impact of *impacts upon*. *Impact* is best reserved as a noun.

Impact has also been used as a transitive verb, but the direct object does not make the verb any more acceptable—e.g.: "Petitioner maintains that the Commission must adhere to the rulemaking requirements of the APA 'when it conclusively affects and substantially *impacts* [better: *redefines*] preexisting rights with a retroactive rule that has the force of law.'" *Middle S. Energy, Inc. v. FERC*, 747 F.2d 763, 772–73 (D.C.

Cir. 1984). Nor should the verb appear as a transitive verb in the passive voice—e.g.: "There was no evidence that, had he joined the medical staff, patient care would then be *impacted* [read *affected*] negatively." *Everhart v. Jefferson Parish Hosp. Dist. No. 2,* 757 F.2d 1567, 1572 (5th Cir. 1985). See NOUNS AS VERBS.

*impanel. See **empanel.**

imparl, vb.; **imparlance,** n. In England, the practice of *imparling* (= obtaining leave of court to adjourn proceedings so that the parties can try to settle the case) was abolished in 1853. Historians occasionally discuss the practice—e.g.: "Instead of putting up a defence Brown asks for 'leave to *imparl*'—that is, he asks the court for an adjournment whilst he talks the matter over with Jones in the hope of reaching a settlement, and he and Jones leave court to have their imparlance." A.W.B. Simpson, *An Introduction to the History of the Land Law* 122 (1961).

The terms *imparl* and its corresponding noun, *imparlance,* now appear more frequently in AmE than in BrE. But even in AmE, the terms are rare enough to be properly classifiable as ARCHAISMS—e.g.:

- "Whereupon Judge Blount held his decision in abeyance for three hours and directed parties and counsel to *imparl* [read *discuss settlement*] during the interim and attempt 'to clear the matter up.'" *Sutton v. Figgatt,* 185 S.E.2d 97, 98 (N.C. 1971).
- "*An imparlance* [read *A settlement conference*] followed and has been held under my supervision, in accordance with the usual regular procedure applicable to pre-trials." *Martinez v. 348 East 104 Street Corp.,* 300 N.Y.S.2d 992, 993 (Sup. Ct. 1969).

impartable; impartible. These are two different words. *Impartable* = capable of being made known or granted (i.e., of being "imparted"). *Impartible* = indivisible. *Impartible* is chiefly legal, used primarily in describing estates <the question is whether the estate is partible or impartible>.

impartial. See **fair (A).**

impassible; impassable. *Impassible* = incapable of feeling or suffering. *Impassable* = not capable of being passed. Cf. **passable.**

impeach = (1) to charge a public official with a crime in office and to constitute a legal tribunal to adjudge whether the official should be removed; esp., in the U.K., to try before the House of Lords at the instance of the House of Commons, and, in the U.S., to try before the Senate at the instance of the House of Representatives <Richard Nixon resigned to avoid being impeached>; (2) to discredit the veracity of (a witness) <counsel thoroughly impeached the witness on cross-examination>; (3) to challenge the authenticity or accuracy of (a document); or (4) in Scotland, to set up the defense, in a criminal case, that another named person committed the crime charged.

In sense 1, *impeach* means, not "to remove from office," but "to bring a charge or accusation against."

Impeachment may, of course, result in removal from office. See **charge,** vb. (A).

In sense 2, there has traditionally been a fine distinction between the *impeaching* of a witness and attacking the witness's credibility: "A witness may be a credible witness generally, but in a particular case be subject to *impeachment* because of prior contradictory statements, bias, motive, interest, corruption, or other matter grown out of the circumstances of the particular case in which he is testifying. In other words, the purpose of an attack upon the credibility of the witness is to show that he is generally unworthy of belief in any cause, whereas the purpose of *impeachment* is to show peculiar circumstances arising in the particular case [that] render his testimony in that case questionable." H. Grady Chandler, *Attacking Credibility of Witnesses by Proof of Charge or Conviction of Crime,* 10 Tex. L. Rev. 257, 257 (1932).

impecunious (= poor; penniless) is sometimes misused as if it meant "hapless," as when someone refers to an *impecunious associate* who is forced by a partner to sign pleadings.

impedient impediment; hindering impediment. *Impedient* = that impedes; obstructive. So *impedient impediment* is the most elementary type of REDUNDANCY. Yet it has acquired a specific legal meaning: "some fact that bars a marriage if known but that does not void the marriage after the ceremony." It is also called *hindering impediment,* which is just as redundant, though less obtrusively.

impediment. See **impedient impediment.**

impel. For the difference between this word and *compel,* see the entry under that word. *Impel to* [+ noun phrase] is a construction not available with *compel.* E.g.: "In the interest of the public good this is a hardness to be endured courageously if not cheerfully by the man whose ideals *impel* him *to* such a course." *Fey v. King,* 190 N.W. 519, 522 (Iowa 1922).

impeller; *impellor. The first spelling is preferred.

imperative. See **directory.**

imperfect, adj. In Roman law and in some modern writings, this word is given a curious sense. An *imperfect* statute is one that prohibits, but does not render void, an objectionable transaction; it provides a penalty for disobedience without depriving a violative transaction of its legal effect.

imperial; imperious. Deriving from the same root (L. *imper-,* "power over a family, region, or state"), these words have been differentiated by their suffixes. *Imperial* = of or belonging to an emperor or empire. *Imperious* = overbearing; supercilious; tyrannical.

Additionally, *imperious* = urgent; absolute; imperative. E.g.:

- "Can we adopt that construction, unless the words *imperiously* require it, which would impute to the framers of that instrument . . . the intention of impeding their exercise by withholding a choice of means?" *McCulloch v. Maryland*, 17 U.S. (4 Wheat.) 316, 408 (1819) (per Marshall, C.J.).

- "Because 'taxes are the life-blood of government, and their prompt and certain availability an *imperious* need,' Congress has created a 'formidable arsenal of collection tools.'" *U.S. v. National Bank of Commerce*, 472 U.S. 713, 734 (1985) (Powell, J., dissenting).

imperium (= supreme authority) forms the plural *imperia*. The word appears frequently in discussions of Roman law, but also in modern contexts—e.g.: "The function was so well performed that not even the monumental indiscretion of the *Dred Scott* decision could quite destroy the judicial *imperium*." Robert G. McCloskey, *The American Supreme Court* 85 (1960).

impermissible. So spelled.

IMPERSONAL "IT." See EXPLETIVES.

impersonation; *personation. The second is a NEEDLESS VARIANT.

impersuadable; *impersuasible. See **persuadable.**

impertinence in nonlegal contexts is taken to mean "presumptuous or forward rudeness of behavior or speech, esp. to a superior; insolence" (*OED*). This sense originated as a colloquialism. In legal contexts, the original sense of the term is retained: "the fact or character of not pertaining to the matter at hand; lack of pertinence; irrelevance." See **impertinent** & **pertinence.**

impertinent does not, in most legal contexts, have its ordinary meaning, "saucy; impudent." Rather, it means "not pertinent or relevant." E.g.: "The court may order stricken from any pleading any insufficient defense or any redundant, immaterial, *impertinent*, or scandalous matter." Fed. R. Civ. P. 12(f). Lawyers should beware in their pleadings of making impertinent statements of either kind. See **impertinence.**

impervious; *imperviable. *Impervious* = not allowing something to pass through; not open to <some people are impervious to reason>. The word should be avoided in the sense "not affected by" <he was impervious to her screams for help> <expert witnesses impervious to harsh cross-examination>. **Imperviable* is a NEEDLESS VARIANT.

impetration, in the sense "the obtaining (of a writ)," is an obsolescent LEGALISM—e.g.:

- "The jury allowed interest only from date of demand, which they fixed as the *impetration* [read *issuance*] of the writ, August 21, 1957, at the figure of $350." *Peyton v. Margiotti*, 156 A.2d 865, 869 (Pa. 1959).
- "Thus, the rule developed that a plaintiff could re-issue the writ (i.e., file the alias) within the statutory period beginning from the *impetration* [read *issuance*] of the unserved writ." *Anderson v. Bernhard Realty Sales Co.*, 329 A.2d 852, 858 (Pa. Super. Ct. 1974).

In its literary sense, *impetration* (= an urgent entreaty) is a FORMAL WORD—e.g.: "Though plaintiff's *impetration* regarding its support of the war effort reflects a commendable attitude, the plaintiff in *Teutsch* was no less well motivated." *Kraemer Mills, Inc. v. U.S.*, 319 F.2d 535, 539 (Ct. Cl. 1963).

impetus. See **impotence.**

impignorate = to mortgage, pledge, or pawn. Any of these more specific, simpler terms should be used rather than this rare, pedantic LATINISM. **Pignorate* is a variant form of the same word.

impinge. See **infringe (B).**

implead; *emplead. The first spelling is standard. See **plead** & EN-.

impleader is recorded in the *OED* only as an agent noun (meaning "one who impleads"), but the word has not been used in that way since the early 18th century. Today it means "a procedure by which a third party is brought into a lawsuit, usu. through a defendant's third-party action." See -ER (B).

implement, vb., is a VOGUE WORD beloved by jargon-mongers, in whose language *policies are implemented.* The phrase *carry out* is usually better, and certainly less vague.

implementer; *implementor. The first spelling is preferred.

implicate = (1) to bring into play; to involve in its nature or meaning, or as a consequence <forcible searching implicates a constitutionally protected interest>; (2) to involve (a person) *in* a charge or crime <each party, striving to implicate the other in this heinous deed>.

implication is the noun corresponding to both *implicate* and *imply.* So it means (1) "the action of implicating, or involving, entangling, or entwining" <Smith's implication of Jones in the crime>; (2) "the action of implying; the fact of being implied or involved" <by necessary implication>; or (3) "that which is implied or involved" <implications of wrongdoing>.

Legal *implication*—an extension of sense 2—occurs when one statement is treated under the law as including another (regardless of what the speaker or writer intended). Contracts, for example, often contain terms implied by law, though the parties never contemplated them.

implication of law. See **imply.**

implicit, meaning "implied," has come to be misused in the sense "complete; unmitigated" <I have implicit trust in her> <I trust her implicitly>. The *OED* labels this usage both erroneous and obsolete; with its resurgence in recent years, one can no longer call it obsolete but can confidently call it erroneous. E.g.:

- "Defendant testified that he was plaintiff's employee and friend and had *implicit* [read *complete* or *unqualified*] trust in and loyalty to plaintiff." *Scafidi v. Johnson*, 409 So.2d 316, 317 (La. Ct. App. 1981).

- "Solicitors take counsel's opinion on difficult questions, and usually rely upon the resulting opinion *implicitly* [read *completely* or *without qualification* or *unquestioningly*]." P.S. Atiyah, *Law and Modern Society* 29 (1983).

See **explicit** & **impliedly**.

implicitly. See **impliedly**.

implied; express. These adjectives are correlative. *Expressed* is sometimes incorrectly contrasted with *implied*. See **express**.

implied contract; quasi-contract. "If a lawyer writes: 'The proper meaning of *implied contract* is contract implied in fact, not *quasi-contract*,' he does not express what is now the invariable usage of lawyers." Glanville Williams, *Language and the Law*, 61 Law Q. Rev. 384, 385 (1945). The terms *implied contract* and *quasi-contract* are now generally considered synonymous in denoting a contract not created by express words but inferred by a court from the conduct of the parties, from some special relationship between them, or because one of them has been unjustly enriched.

Formerly, *implied contract* was limited in use to a contract inferred by the courts by reason of the conduct of the parties or of a special relationship between them (implied in fact), and *quasi-contract* was used of an equitable remedy (also termed *indebitatis assumpsit*) imposed by courts when one party was unjustly enriched to the detriment of the other (implied in law). Some writers—including Scottish lawyers—continue to observe this distinction.

But *implied contract* is a phrase that is best avoided, because it "has given rise to great confusion in the law." 1 Samuel Williston & W.H.E. Jaeger, *A Treatise on the Law of Contracts* § 3, at 9 (3d ed. 1957). The confusion arises precisely because *implied contract* carries the two senses noted above, namely, both *quasi-contract* and *implied-in-fact contract* (= a mutual agreement and intent to promise without any expression in words). See **implied in fact** & **quasi-contract**.

implied in fact; implied in law. The DIFFERENTIATION between these terms is sometimes muddled. *Implied in fact* = inferable from the facts of a case. *Implied in law* = imposed by operation of law, and not because of any inferences that can be drawn about the facts of a case. E.g.:

- "Numerous decisions have held that this waiver of sovereign immunity is limited to express contracts and contracts *implied in fact* and does not extend to contracts *implied in law* or founded upon equitable principles." *Knight Newspapers, Inc. v. U.S.*, 395 F.2d 353, 357 (6th Cir. 1968).
- "Both parties used the phrase 'implied consent' rather loosely to refer to both 'implied in law' and 'implied in fact', so the arguments to the court were sometimes less than precise." *Carrillo v. Houser*, 214 P.3d 444, 449 (Ariz. Ct. App. 2009).

See **implied contract**.

impliedly; implicitly. Though neither form is strictly incorrect, *impliedly* is awkward and characteristic of LEGALESE. H.W. Fowler wrote merely that "*impliedly* is a bad form" (*MEU1* 260). Though almost unknown to nonlawyers, it is a favorite of lawyers. *Impliedly* is old, dating in the *OED* from ca. 1400. Nevertheless, *implicitly* is almost always an improvement—e.g.:

- "By holding that all true speech is privileged, these jurisdictions *impliedly* [read *implicitly*] hold that all media communications are newsworthy and provide true disclosures with greater First Amendment protection than the United States Supreme Court has required to date." Geoff Dendy, *The Newsworthiness Defense to the Public Disclosure Tort*, 85 Ky. L.J. 147, 158 (1997).
- "Many courts *impliedly* [read *implicitly*] hold developers to a higher standard of awareness of restrictions than they do individuals buying property to construct single residences." Laura Pfefferle, *A New Green Government Weapon*, 13 Tul. Envtl. L.J. 471, 492 (2000).
- "If the employee made the promise not to compete shortly after beginning his employment, and the court construed the employer to have *impliedly* [read *implicitly*] promised to retain the employee for some period of time, and the employee then immediately quit the employment, whether the employee's promise should be enforced should depend [on] . . . whether the employee had sufficient information or skills so that the employer could reasonably expect that the (now former) employee would not compete against it." Richard A. Lord, *The At-Will Relationship in the 21st Century*, 58 Baylor L. Rev. 707, 765 (2006).

Used on both sides of the Atlantic, *impliedly* is a graceless LEGALISM with virtually no advantages over *implicitly*, which is much to be preferred. Still, *implied* might be thought to be more concise and direct than *implicit*. Some authorities strain to differentiate the two, but such attempts are futile. See **implicit**.

implied trust. See **trust** (D).

implied warranty of merchantability; implied warranty of fitness for a particular purpose. Legal systems commonly insert a provision into some contracts—particularly those for the sale or supply of consumer goods—warranting that goods supplied under the contract will measure up to a prescribed standard. An *implied warranty of merchantability*, in most jurisdictions, means that the goods (1) pass as described without objection in the trade; (2) are fit for the ordinary uses to which the goods are put; (3) are adequately packaged and labeled; and (4) conform to the factual statements made on the packaging.

An *implied warranty of fitness for a particular purpose* is more specific: if the manufacturer, distributor, or retailer has reason to know a particular use to which the goods are to be put, and the buyer relies on the skill and judgment of the seller in selecting the goods, then the seller implicitly warrants that the goods are fit for that purpose.

imply. A. Uses and Misuses of Legal Senses. Anglo-American judges, who continually evaluate facts, often use the phrase *by implication* (= by what is implied, though not formally expressed, by natural inference), along with its various cognates. Judges (by implication) draw "natural inferences" and thereby decide that something or other was, in the circumstances, "implied." Through the process of HYPALLAGE—a semantic shift by which the attributes of the true subject are transferred to another subject—the word *imply* has come to be used in reference to what the judges do, as opposed to the circumstances. This specialized use of *imply* runs counter to popular lay use and is not adequately treated in English-language dictionaries.

Specifically, the word *imply* often means "(of a court) to impute or impose on equitable or legal grounds." An *implied* contract is not always one implied from the facts of the case, but may be one implied by the court, i.e., imposed by the judge or judges as a result of their inferences.

In using *imply* in this way, courts are said to find a doctrinally posited fact (a condition, restriction, remedy, right of action, or the like) that controls a judicial decision—e.g.:

- "This court cannot, upon some supposed hardship, defeat an estate by *implying* a condition which the grantor has not expressed, nor in the least intimated by the language of his conveyance." *Brown v. State*, 5 Colo. 496, 504 (1881).
- "It would be more literally accurate to acknowledge that . . . the court *implies* the conditions from reasons of equity." *Susswein v. Pennsylvania Steel Co.*, 184 F. 102, 106 (S.D.N.Y. 1910).
- "The difficulty with the arguments seeking to *imply* Mary Silva's survival of Joseph as a condition is that they would result in holding that because it is express that Joseph must survive until the period of distribution to take an inheritable interest, a similar contingency should be *implied* as to Mary." *In re Estate of Ferry*, 361 P.2d 900, 904 (Cal. 1961) (en banc).
- "Judicial willingness to *imply* new remedies in areas governed by federal law has been expressed in a number of ways." *SEC v. Texas Gulf Sulphur Co.*, 312 F.Supp. 77, 91 (S.D.N.Y. 1970).
- "In my view, the Members of Congress merely assumed that the federal courts would follow the ancient maxim '*ubi jus, ibi remedium*' and *imply* a private right of action." *California v. Sierra Club*, 451 U.S. 287, 300 (1981) (Stevens, J., concurring). See MAXIMS.
- "When interpreting the Trust instrument we will not *imply* a condition . . . where none is stated in the language of the five-or-five provision." *In re Estate of Cairns*, 115 Cal. Rptr. 3d 735, 744 (Ct. App. 2010).

When put in the passive voice, *imply* may be especially confusing, because the person who does the implying is left unclear. The user of any unabridged English-language dictionary would either find it hard to divine precisely what *imply* means, or deduce an incorrect meaning: "The remaining provisions of the Insurance Law would lack substance if no private right of action were *implied*." *Corcoran v. Frank B. Hall & Co.*, 545 N.Y.S.2d 278, 284 (App. Div. 1989). In that sentence, the passive voice masks the subject. The writer apparently means to say that a court would

allow such a cause of action: so the court would *imply* a right of action, i.e., impose it on equitable or legal grounds.

This special legal sense is most keenly demonstrated when *imply* is coupled with *impute*, as here: "When deciding the shares, we look to their [the husband's and the wife's] respective contributions and we see what trust is to be *implied* or *imputed* to them." *Cracknell v. Cracknell*, [1971] 3 All E.R. 552, 554.

Often one could actually read *impute* in place of *imply* and have the same sense (read *impute to* for *imply on*): "Under special circumstances the Court may *imply* knowledge *on* the speaker, such as the inventor of a machine, 'who must be fully informed as to [the machine's] good and bad qualities.'" *Brickell v. Collins*, 262 S.E.2d 387, 390 (N.C. Ct. App. 1980).

In some contexts, *imply* seems to take on a slightly different sense, "to read into (a document)," as here: "One has to look merely at what is clearly said. There is no room for any intendment. . . . Nothing is to be read in, nothing is to be *implied*. One can only look fairly at the language used." *Cape Brandy Syndicate v. I.R.C.*, [1921] 1 K.B. 64, 71. But such uses comport with the general sense here outlined, since "reading in" provisions has the same effect as "imputing" them. See **impute**.

The lawyer's *imply* has directly encroached on the word *infer*. Whereas nonlawyers frequently use *infer* for *imply*, lawyers and judges conflate the two in the opposite direction, by using *imply* for *infer*. In analyzing the facts of a case, judges will *imply* one fact from certain others. (*From* is a telling preposition.) Nonlawyers believe they must be *inferring* an additional fact from those already known; if contractual terms are *implied*, they must surely be implied by the words or circumstances of the contract and not by the judges.

Perhaps using this reasoning, some legal writers have recoiled from *imply* and have resorted instead to *infer*. E.g.:

- "Apart from the difficulty of *inferring* a contract where none has been made, no agreement between husband and wife for future separation can be recognized." *Pettitt v. Pettitt*, [1970] A.C. 777, 811 (H.L.).
- "When a party voluntarily accepts a valuable service or benefit, having option to accept or reject it, the Court may *infer* a promise to pay." *Lewis v. Holy Spirit Ass'n*, 589 F.Supp. 10, 13 (D. Mass. 1983).
- "Roger cannot produce a will; therefore, pursuant to the statute, we cannot rely on his oral testimony to *infer* a contract." *Johnson v. Anderson*, 771 N.W.2d 565, 570 (Neb. 2009). On the use of **pursuant to* in that sentence, see ***pursuant to.**

In the following sentence, in which the court writes *implied or inferred from*, the word *implied* adds nothing, unless *by the circumstances* (i.e., *implicit in the circumstances*) is to be understood, and *or* is to be read as *and*: "Rather, the crucial question is when can a waiver of rights be *implied or inferred from* the actions and words of the person interrogated." *McDonald v. Lucas*, 677 F.2d 518, 520 (5th Cir. 1982).

In the following sentences, *infer* might have served better than *imply*. One would be tempted to call these misuses, were some specimens not so ancient—e.g.:

- "There is nothing averred from which the court can *imply* that those conditions were performed." *Cutting v. Myers*, 6 F. Cas. 1081, 1082 (D. Pa. 1818).
- "The requirements of the rule are met if such an intention may be clearly *implied* from the language, the purposes of the agreement, and all the surrounding facts and circumstances." *Salamy v. New York Cent. Sys.*, 146 N.Y.S.2d 814, 817 (App. Div. 1955).

Note that the facts here posited (performance of a condition, intention) are of a lower level of abstraction than those in the examples given at the outset of this entry. Using *imply* with low-level abstractions, as opposed to doctrinally posited facts, is comparatively uncommon in modern legal usage. See **infer.**

Adding still more color to this CHAMELEON-HUED WORD in legal contexts is the ordinary nonlegal sense:

- "There is nothing in the former decision [that] would *imply* that the 'sole discretion' vested in and exercised by the trustees in this case is beyond court review." *In re Ferrall's Estate*, 258 P.2d 1009, 1013 (Cal. 1953) (en banc).
- "We do not mean to *imply* that where joint ownership is set up in conformity with the statutory provisions, a court of equity is thereby foreclosed from looking behind the form of the transaction and determining questions of real and beneficial interest as between the parties." *Frey v. Wubbena*, 185 N.E.2d 850, 855 (Ill. 1962).

It is not wholly surprising that the legal uses of *imply* have not found a place in English-language dictionaries. Common in American and British law alike, the uses here outlined have not yet spread from legal to nonlegal contexts—and may never do so. Moreover, because lexicographic reading programs seldom glean citations from legal texts, lexicographers often overlook linguistic innovation in law. *See* Bryan A. Garner, "The Missing Common-Law Words," in *The State of the Language* 234–45 (Sir Christopher Ricks & Leonard Michaels eds., 1990).

B. The Nonlegal Blunder. Courts are not immune from the general misusage of *infer* for *imply*—e.g.:

- "The courts in both cases *inferred* [read *suggested*] that they would have considered judging the defendants' failure to act under a 'reasonable' time standard, but it was not applicable given the facts." *Snyder v. Nationwide Ins. Co.*, 25 Pa. D.&C. 4th 348, 355 (Pa. Ct. Com. Pl. 1995).
- "At no point in the complaint do plaintiffs allege facts stating or *inferring* [read *implying*] defendants' misrepresentations or omissions caused plaintiffs' loss." *Hardin County Savs. Bank v. City of Brainerd*, 602 F.Supp.2d 1012, 1022 (N.D. Iowa 2008).
- "An adverse determination based on a failure to meet American Community's requirements does not *infer* [read *imply* or *suggest*] that American Community has express discretion to determine when the requirements have been met." *Erker v. American Community Mut. Ins. Co.*, 663 F.Supp.2d 799, 804 (D. Neb. 2009).

See **infer.**

*importunacy. See **importunity.**

importune is a verb meaning "to beg or beseech; entreat." It is also a NEEDLESS VARIANT of the adjective *importunate* (= troublesomely urgent), and an obsolete variant of *inopportune* (= inconvenient; untimely). The intended meaning is often unclear, but perhaps *inappropriate* or *inopportune* would substitute—e.g.:

- "As in *Keser*, and now *Cutbirth*, the trial court, absent exposure to actual evidence, . . . will never have an opportunity to consider whether an innocent man was *importunely* [read *inappropriately*] sentenced." *Cutbirth v. State*, 751 P.2d 1257, 1270 (Wyo. 1988).
- "Although notice and opportunity to defend are not issues here because Jefferson was sued in the initial action, albeit *importunely* [read *inopportunely*?], timeliness is an issue here and notice and opportunity could well be issues in another case." *Reeve v. Union Pac. R.R.*, 790 F.Supp. 1074, 1079 n.4 (D. Kan. 1992).

importunity; *importunacy. **Importunacy* is a NEEDLESS VARIANT of *importunity*, meaning "bothersome pertinacity in soliciting something."

impossibility; frustration. In AmE, writers on the law of contract began using *frustration* instead of *impossibility* shortly after the turn of the 20th century. But as a would-be TERM OF ART, "*frustration* never acquired much precision or clarity of meaning; most of the time it was used as a sort of loose synonym for . . . *impossibility*." Grant Gilmore, *The Death of Contract* 80–81 (1974). Some writers take the view that this change in terminology heralded a change in meaning: that it was "intended to widen the scope of the doctrine of discharge by supervening events." G.H. Treitel, *The Law of Contract* 779–80 (8th ed. 1991). English writers such as Treitel resist the terminological and the corresponding doctrinal change.

Some writers distinguish between *legal impossibility* (e.g., having two spouses simultaneously) and *physical impossibility* (e.g., a person's leaping unaided across the Grand Canyon). See **mistake (B).**

impossible of. See **of (c).**

impost. See **tax.**

impostor; imposter. In most states this word, as it appears in the heading of § 3-405 of the Uniform Commercial Code, is spelled *impostor*. In other states, it is spelled *imposter*. The *-or* spelling is preferred. See -ER (A).

imposture; fraud; fake; sham; counterfeit; simulacrum. These terms all refer to something that is fashioned to resemble something else. *Imposture* denotes not just an object that is false or inauthentic but also an act or practice that is being passed off under an assumed or false character <the claim that the drawings came from Picasso's niece was a huge imposture>. A *fraud* is an imposture that involves an illegal or criminal twisting of the truth <the don't-pay-any-taxes scheme was exposed as a fraud>. (For more of the many senses of this word, see **fraud (A).**) A *fake* is an essentially worthless item that is supposed to be something of some value <the "1803 silver dollar" was an obvious fake>. A *sham* is a close imitation that turns out to be fraudulent <sham affidavit>. (See **sham**.) A *counterfeit* is a close copy of an item, such as legal tender, a stamp, or a bond, especially when the copying depends on tooling or machining <all the $100 bills were counterfeits>. A *simulacrum* /sim-yə-**lak**-rəm/ is a counterfeit that isn't intended to be misrepresented as being real <the wax simulacrum of Princess Diana at Madame Tussaud's seemed stunningly lifelike>. Pl. *simulacrums* or (less good) *simulacra*.

impotence; *impotency. The second is a NEEDLESS VARIANT. *Impotence* in the modern literal sense should be used only in reference to men, a fact not recognized by the writer of this sentence: "Judgments of nullity of marriage may be rendered in all cases, when . . . the parties, or either of them, were at the time of marriage physically and incurably *impotent*." N.J. Stat. Ann. § 2A:34-1(c) (2005). *Black's* notes a rare, archaic use of *impotence* as "a woman's physical inability to engage in sexual intercourse." *Black's Law Dictionary* 825 (9th ed. 2009). But this recondite sense in modern legal writing amounts to an abuse. The corresponding affliction for women, sometimes alleged to be spurious, is *frigidity*. See **potence** & **sterility.**

   Impotence is also used figuratively to mean "powerless"—e.g.: "The gun lobby bemoans the *impotence* of local police forces that cannot protect citizens from violent crime." Andrew D. Herz, *Gun Crazy*, 75 B.U. L. Rev. 57, 95 (1995). This usage often carries a snide connotation.

   Impotence for *impetus* is a MALAPROPISM worthy of Mrs. Malaprop, Mistress Quickly, or Archie Bunker—e.g.: "The main *impotence* [read *impetus*] for recruiting someone who has published is to ensure that he is used to long hours." *Impetus* means "force; impulse."

impoverishment. Only theoretically—not idiomatically—is *impoverishment* an antonym of *enrichment*. Whereas *enrich* means "to make rich *or richer*," *impoverish* means "to make poor; to reduce to indigency." E.g.: "Like many a testator, who, with specific devise and bequest has unwittingly *impoverished* the members of his family after his death, the settlor *impoverished* himself when he conveyed all of his property in trust, and divested himself of the only means of livelihood he had." *Mabry v. Scott*, 124 P.2d 659, 662 (Cal. Ct. App. 1942). Finding a ten-dollar bill *enriches* one to some extent; but for most, losing a ten-dollar bill would not constitute *impoverishment*.

   In the following sentence, *impoverishment* is incorrectly made the correlative of the legal phrase *unjust enrichment*: "Under Louisiana law recovery may be had for unjust enrichment only if the plaintiff proves the amount of his *impoverishment* [read *damages*?]

and that the defendant was enriched to that extent." *McCarty Corp. v. Pullman-Kellogg, Div. of Pullman, Inc.*, 751 F.2d 750, 760 (5th Cir. 1985). See **unjust enrichment.**

*impower is an obsolete spelling of *empower*.

impracticability (= practical impossibility) is sometimes wrongly spelled **impractibility*.

impractical; unpractical. H.W. Fowler had a point in believing that "the constant confusion between *practicable* and *practical* is a special reason for making use of im- and un- to add to the difference in the negatives" (*MEU1* 260), but *unpractical* has not been idiomatically accepted in the U.S. It is not included in some American dictionaries, and even in the (British) *COD* the entry under *impractical* is longer than under *unpractical*. To a few British stalwarts, it may be worth keeping up the fight. For the distinction between *practical* and *practicable*, see **practical.**

imprescriptible; *imprescribable. The first is the preferred form for this word, meaning "not subject to being extinguished by lapse of time under the rules of prescription; that cannot in any circumstances be legally taken away or abandoned" (*OED*). E.g.: "One of the most sacred *imprescriptible* rights of man, is violated." *Slaughter-House Cases*, 83 U.S. (16 Wall.) 36, 110 (1872) (Field, J., dissenting). It is worth warning that "*imprescriptible* is one of the words that are often used without a clear conception of their meaning" (*MEU1* 261). But it may be overstating the case to say that the word is *often* used.

impress, n.; impressment; impression; *impressure. In the legal idiom, constructive trusts are *impressed* by courts upon property obtained by fraud, or the obtaining of which results in unjust enrichment. (See **impress**, vb.) The question remains what to call the act of impressing a constructive trust. The answer is *impressment*—e.g.:

- "The plaintiffs sought compensatory damages, punitive damages, and equitable relief, including the *impressment* of a constructive trust." *Ex parte Wiginton*, 743 So.2d 1071, 1072 (Ala. 1999).
- "When it became apparent to the broker that the purchase-and-sales transaction was . . . contrary to the terms of the brokerage agreement, it sought and obtained a temporary injunction . . . freezing the amount of the commission by the *impressment* of a constructive trust pending further order of the court." *Riverland & Indian Sun L.C. v. L.J. Melody & Co.*, 879 So.2d 1271, 1271 (Fla. Dist. Ct. App. 2004).

   Impress, n., = a characteristic mark or quality. E.g.: "A fixed contract right acquired before marriage was property the 'character of which takes its *impress* from the date of the contract.'" *McCurdy v. McCurdy*, 372 S.W.2d 381, 383 (Tex. Civ. App.—Waco 1963). *Impression* = (1) the impressing (of a mark); (2) the mark impressed; (3) an effect produced on the mind or feelings; (4) a notion (*COD*). *Impressure* is an archaic NEEDLESS VARIANT of *impression*.

impress, vb. This verb is used of a court's imposition of a constructive trust on equitable grounds. For an explanation of characteristic phraseology, see **impress,** n. Following are examples of each of the two legal idioms with this verb:

- "In many cases equity *impresses* a trust upon money or property secured by fraud." William F. Walsh, *A Treatise on Equity* 494 (1930).
- "To determine whether its assets were *impressed* with a trust, Pioneer filed an action for declaratory relief against a member of the society." *In re Los Angeles County Pioneer Soc'y*, 257 P.2d 1, 3 (Cal. 1953).

See OBJECT-SHUFFLING.

impressible; *impressable. The first spelling is preferred.

impression; impressment; *impressure. See **impress,** n.

imprimatur; *imprimatura; *imprimature. The preferred form for ordinary purposes is *imprimatur* (/im-**prim**-ə-tər/ or /im-pri-**mah**-tər/), meaning literally "let it be printed, from the formula used in the Roman Catholic Church by an official licenser, approving a work to be printed." This term (now meaning "commendatory license or sanction") is construed with the preposition *on*—e.g.:

- "Here, the trial judge placed his *imprimatur* on the expert and 'the field of proper police policies and practices' when no foundation for discipline testimony had been laid." Richard F. Suhrheinrich & Molly Carrier Hamilton, *The Sixth Circuit Year in Review*, 25 U. Mem. L. Rev. 365, 455 (1995).
- "While recognizing the frustration of citizens and public officials regarding the lack of enforcement of federal immigration laws, the court reiterates that the 'will of the people' in endorsing the Ordinance does not bestow the *imprimatur* of constitutionality on the Ordinance." *Villas at Parkside Partners v. City of Farmers Branch*, 577 F.Supp.2d 858, 864 (N.D. Tex. 2008).
- "Today the majority blesses with constitutional *imprimatur* a death sentence that could only have been imposed after the jury found that Carlos Caro had previously been convicted of relatively minor, nonviolent drug offenses." *U.S. v. Caro*, 597 F.3d 608, 636 (4th Cir. 2010) (Gregory, J., dissenting).

imprison. See **jail,** vb.

imprisonable crime is a typical example of HYPALLAGE, the perpetrator and not the crime being what is truly imprisonable. Glanville Williams calls *imprisonable* "police jargon, but a convenient word." *Textbook of Criminal Law* 20 n.17 (1978).

improve (= to develop, as land) is a LEGALISM that is generally understandable to most nonlawyers—e.g.:

- "Eighteen thousand dollars of the proceeds of said proposed bond issue is to be used for the purchase of an *improved* parcel of land, now owned by the United States

of America." *State ex rel. Town of S. Charleston v. Partlow*, 55 S.E.2d 401, 402 (W. Va. 1949).
- "[The] supreme court granted the motion, finding that the . . . defendants' remedy for [the] third-party defendants' failure to repay the sum advanced was limited to their retention of the *improved* parcel of land." *Lease Corp. of Am. Inc. v. Resnick*, 732 N.Y.S.2d 266, 268 (App. Div. 2001).

If confusion occurs, it is likely to result from the odd fact that, in lawyers' parlance, an *improvement* to land—say, a ramshackle house—may actually lessen the land's value.

improvident is a FORMAL WORD meaning "heedless; unwary; not circumspect." Judges use the word far more than other writers—e.g.:

- "The chancellor ruled that Gilden's contract was a mere offer until approved by him, and that the trustee acted hastily, with inexperience, and *improvidently*." *Gilden v. Harris*, 78 A.2d 167, 169 (Md. 1951).
- "It is not unreasonable to expect a State's highest legal officer to know the state's law and to bring to this Court's attention the rules of state law that might . . . demonstrate that we granted the writ *improvidently*." *Walpole v. Hill*, 472 U.S. 445, 461 (1985) (Stevens, J., concurring in part & dissenting in part).
- "The dismissal of an appeal as *improvidently* granted has the same effect as if the court had not granted the petition for allowance of appeal in the first place." *Pringle v. Rapaport*, 980 A.2d 159, 175 n.10 (Pa. Super. Ct. 2009).

improviser; *improvisor; improvisator; improvisatore. The usual term for "one who improvises" is *improviser*. The *-or* spelling is not preferred. *Improvisator* is a formal equivalent, and *improvisatore* is an Italianate literary word meaning "one who composes verse or drama extemporaneously."

imprudent; impudent. *Imprudent* = rash; indiscreet. *Impudent* = insolently disrespectful; shamelessly presumptuous.

impugn; oppugn; repugn. *Impugn* = to challenge; to call into question—e.g.:

- "In so finding, the Court in no way *impugns* the integrity of petitioner's counsel." *Baran v. Beaty*, 479 F.Supp.2d 1257, 1275 n.21 (S.D. Ala. 2007).
- "It stands to reason, then, that, amorphous though these notions may be, a judge necessarily *impugns* the integrity and independence of the judiciary when he or she acts out of fear or favor." *Mississippi Comm'n on Judicial Performance v. Osborne*, 16 So.3d 16, 28 (Miss. 2009) (Kitchens, J., dissenting).
- "Where a manifest error of constitutional magnitude exists affecting the truth-seeking function of a criminal prosecution, it is and has been my opinion that such an error *impugns* the integrity of due process and requires redress." *State v. Harris*, 224 P.3d 830, 839–40 (Wash. Ct. App. 2010) (Quinn-Brintnall, J., dissenting).

The noun is *impugnment*.

Impugn does not mean merely "to affect adversely"—e.g.:

- "The agreement's economic realignment of the parties did not *impugn* [read *impair*] the fact-finding process." *Bass v. Phoenix Seaderill/78, Ltd.*, 749 F.2d 1154, 1158 (5th Cir.

1985). In a footnote to this sentence, the court quoted the trial court's conclusion that the agreement "did not *affect* the ability of the court to make accurate findings of fact." *Id.* at 1158 n.6.

- "Where a court finds that the approval process has been *impugned* [read *impaired*], the court may review the transaction and determine whether it satisfies the applicable standard of review." Nadelle Grossman, *Director Compliance with Elusive Fiduciary Duties in a Climate of Corporate Governance Reform*, 12 Fordham J. Corp. & Fin. L. 393, 462 (2007).

See **impugnment.**

Oppugn and *repugn* are less frequently encountered than *impugn. Oppugn* = to controvert or call into question; to fight against. *Repugn* is an ARCHAISM meaning "to offer opposition or strive against; to affect disagreeably or be repugnant to."

impugnment; *impugnation. The second is an obsolete variant. Here is an example of the standard term: "[Appellant] contends that the district judge made many errors in his rulings concerning the conduct of the trial and the admissibility of evidence . . . . The *impugnment* is more than a challenge to specific rulings, however." *Ruiz v. Estelle*, 679 F.2d 1115, 1129 (5th Cir. 1982).

impunity. See **immunity (B).**

impute (= to ascribe; to regard [usu. something undesirable] as being done, caused, or possessed by [*COD*]) takes *to*—e.g.:

- "We are reluctant to *impute* a different meaning *to* the term where it has been used without modification, absent a compelling and certain impetus." *McDonald v. Commissioner*, 764 F.2d 322, 329 (5th Cir. 1985).
- "The Court applied the principles governing civil liability and held that the acts of agents are *imputed to* their employers, who may be penalized when the employees act within the scope of their employment." Daniel L. Cheyette, *Policing the Corporate Citizen*, 25 Alaska L. Rev. 175, 181 (2008).

We see over and over again the growing idiomatic bias in favor of *imputing* undesirable things or qualities—e.g.:

- "If the malice essential to support an action for libel can be found under such circumstances, it must be *imputed*. . . . The law will *impute* malice where a defamatory publication is made without sufficient cause or excuse." *Flynn v. Reinke*, 225 N.W. 742, 743 (Wis. 1929).
- "We ought not *impute* to others instincts contrary to our own." *In re Coe's Estate*, 201 A.2d 571, 575 (N.J. 1964).
- "Lafourche would be negligent only by virtue of an *imputation* of the negligence of another, in this case the negligence of [its employee] Savoie." *Savoie v. Lafourche Boat Rentals, Inc.*, 627 F.2d 722, 723 (5th Cir. 1980).

See **imply (A).**

IN-. See EN- & NEGATIVES (C).

in; into. *In* denotes position, *into* movement or change—e.g.: "But to conclude from this holding that the motorist, who never consented to anything and whose consent is altogether immaterial, has actually agreed to be sued and has thus waived his federal venue rights is surely to move *in* [read *into*] the world of Alice in Wonderland." *Raspante v. Transportation Supply & Mgmt., Inc.*, 214 N.Y.S.2d 583, 590 (Sup. Ct. 1960).

inability. See **disability (A).**

in accord; in accordance. See **accord.**

*in actual fact. See ***actual fact.**

*in actuality. See **actuality.**

inadequate consideration. See **nominal consideration.**

inadmissible; *inadmissable. The first spelling is correct. See **admissible.**

inadvertence; inadvertency. The DIFFERENTIATION between these terms should be encouraged. *Inadvertence* = a fault resulting from not paying attention; a mistake caused by an oversight. E.g.: "We cannot conclude that the district court abused its discretion in taking into account the lulling of Judge Bagley even though there is no suggestion that it was other than the product of oversight or *inadvertence*." *Carbalan v. Vaughn*, 760 F.2d 662, 665 (5th Cir. 1985). *Inadvertency* = the quality or state of being inadvertent <the inadvertency of the act is not disputed>.

*Inadvertancy and **inadvertance* are common misspellings.

inalienable. See **indefeasible.**

in all things. This phrase is LEGALESE commonly found in court papers addressing motions—e.g.: "Having reviewed the record and the applicable law, the Court finds that the bankruptcy judge did not err, and the underlying judgment should be *in all things* affirmed." *Paradise Towing, Inc. v. CIT Group/Sales Fin.*, 368 B.R. 569, 570 (Bankr. W.D. Tex. 2005). Generally it adds nothing.

in any case. See **case (A).**

in any event. See **at all events.**

in any wise. See **wise.**

inapt. Though many English-language dictionaries would suggest that *inapt* is a NEEDLESS VARIANT of *unapt* (and perhaps also of *inept*), it occurs far more frequently in legal writing than *unapt*, which itself ought to be branded as unnecessary.

inasmuch as, *in as much as; insofar as, *in so far as. In modern AmE usage, the standard spelling of each group is *inasmuch as* and *insofar as*, both single words except for the final element. In modern BrE, usage is split: *inasmuch as* is standard and the expression *in so far as* is preferred as four separate words.

However the phrase is spelled, though, *inasmuch as* is almost always inferior to *because* or *since*. See **insofar as.**

inaugural, n.; **inauguration.** The ceremony for a president entering office is an *inauguration*; the speech that the new president makes on this occasion is the *inaugural address*, sometimes shortened to *inaugural*.

inaugurate is a FORMAL WORD, some might say pompous, for *begin* or *start*, being more formal even than *commence*. Sometimes another term, such as *open* or *establish*, is the desired substitute. E.g.: "Thirteen years after *Brown II*, the only step [that] the Tennessee defendants had taken toward dismantling the dual system of public higher education was *inauguration of* [read *setting up* or *starting*] an open-admissions policy." *Geier v. University of Tenn.*, 597 F.2d 1056, 1066 (6th Cir. 1979). Little has changed since Richard Grant White wrote that *inaugurate* "is a word [that] might better be eschewed by all those who do not wish to talk high-flying nonsense." *Words and Their Uses, Past and Present* 128 (2d ed. 1872). See **commence.**

inauguration. See **inaugural.**

in bail. See **bail.**

in banc; in bank; in banco. See **en banc.**

in behalf of; on behalf of. See **behalf.**

in being; *in esse*. John Chipman Gray's classic formulation of the Rule Against Perpetuities reads: "No interest is good unless it must vest, if at all, not later than 21 years after some life *in being* at the creation of the trust." Through this formulation, *in being* has become a TERM OF ART used commonly in discussions of wills and trusts—e.g.:

- "On the date of Mary M. Tilley's death the aforesaid respondents plus six additional great-grandchildren were *in being*." *Industrial Nat'l Bank v. Barrett*, 220 A.2d 517, 520 (R.I. 1966).
- "The record is silent as to which of the grandchildren were *in being* at testator's death." *First-Citizens Bank & Trust Co. v. Barnes*, 210 S.E.2d 519, 521 (N.C. Ct. App. 1975).
- "Decedent's Children and grandchildren were *in being* when the trust was executed." *Estate of Sieber v. Oklahoma Tax Comm'n*, 41 P.3d 1038, 1047 (Okla. Civ. App. 2001).

In esse is a LATINISM equivalent to *in being*. Except as a correlative of *in posse* (= in possibility, but not in actual existence), *in esse* has no justification in place of the Anglo-Saxon phrase: "These words [were] . . . not used in reference to children, who possibly may—but possibly may not—ever be *in esse*, and certainly not to those of whose existence, of course, he would not have any knowledge." *Loockerman v. McBlair*, 6 Gill 177 (Md. 1847). A suggested revision: change *be in esse* to *exist*. See **esse** & ***in esse*.**

in between. Omit *in* when the phrase is followed by one or more objects—e.g.: "On cross-examination, Bishop admitted that Montoya had sat *in between* [omit *in*] him and Garcia, and he could have asked her a question to ask Garcia, but he did not avail himself of this." *Garcia v. State*, 149 S.W.3d 135, 139 (Tex. Crim. App. 2004).

in brief is understood by most readers as meaning "briefly." In American legal writing, however, it sometimes means "in a brief addressed to a court," as here: "[Justice Jackson] meant that an oral argument requires an intense rethinking of your whole case, not in your terms already used *in brief*, but in terms of the questions likely to occur to the judges." George D. Gibson, *Elements of Legal Style*, 22 Bus. Law. 547, 555 (1967).

Inc. Unless otherwise required by syntax, a comma need not follow this abbreviation—e.g.: "Pedernales, *Inc.* was founded in 2011." Increasingly, company names and professional editors are omitting the comma before *Inc.* as well—a good thing, on the whole.

in camera = in the chamber; privately. Though this phrase usually refers to a judge's chambers, it may also refer to a courtroom from which all spectators are excluded. So one cannot be sure where the examination took place in a sentence such as the following: "The appellant contends that the trial judge erred in failing to order the prosecution's files, examined by the judge *in camera*, to be made a part of the record for appellate review, as the appellant requested at the beginning of the trial." *Hamby v. State*, 253 S.E.2d 759, 761 (Ga. 1979). The phrase should not be used in reference to lawyers' offices—e.g.: "Usually, neither side needs to depose its own witnesses because its witnesses' information is generally obtained cooperatively *in camera* [read *in private*]." Peter M. Panken, *The Art of Deposing in Employment Litigation*, 36 Pract. Law. 23, 24 (June 1990).

The phrase may be an adverb that follows the verb it modifies—e.g.: "Judge Leonhard examined *in camera* the State's list of jurors, and to protect the State's work product, he revealed only the criminal histories of the potential jurors." *People v. Hawks*, 899 N.E.2d 632, 633 (Ill. App. Ct. 2008). It may also serve as an adjective that precedes the noun it modifies—e.g. "Defense counsel objected, and much discussion followed, during which defense counsel conceded that he would be bound by the judge's decision following an *in camera* examination of the prosecution's reasons for charge refusal and of materials relating to this *Brady* request." *Rudolph v. Blackburn*, 750 F.2d 302, 304 (5th Cir. 1984). Some writers would hyphenate the phrase in the preceding example. But see PHRASAL ADJECTIVES (B).

The phrase should be used in reference to inspections, but not, through HYPALLAGE, to documents inspected—e.g.: "The plaintiff then filed a motion seeking the 'right to inspection *of the in camera* documents' [read *of the documents that the court had examined in camera*]." *Miles v. M/V Miss. Queen*, 753 F.2d 1349, 1351 (5th Cir. 1985).

In chambers is sometimes used rather than *in camera* in citing an opinion by a single judge. For example, "*Lenhard v. Wolff*, 444 U.S. 1301 (1979) (Rehnquist, J., *in chambers*)." *The Green Bag* has published four volumes of the *In-Chambers Opinions by the Supreme Court of the United States* (2004–2010). Cf. **open court, in.**

incapable is usually applied to persons in modern nonlegal contexts, in the sense "unable; unfit." In law it retains its broader use in reference to things as well as to persons. E.g.: "In certain cases, no doubt, perhaps many cases, a rule [that] a statute attempts to lay down may be *incapable of* practical application till it has been explained by a judge or judges." Edward Jenks, *The Book of English Law* 23 (P.B. Fairest ed., 6th ed. 1967). In such a context, *incapable* means "not allowing or admitting of." See **capable.**

incapacitate; *incapacify; *uncapacitate = to deprive of legal capacity. E.g.: "The central question is . . . whether . . . the events of September 11, 2001 have so *incapacitated* potential jurors . . . that a fair trial [in New York] for Salim would be unlikely." *U.S. v. Salim*, 189 F.Supp.2d 93, 96 (S.D.N.Y. 2002). **Incapacify* and **uncapacitate* are NEEDLESS VARIANTS. See **capacitate.**

incapacitation; incapacity. These words should be distinguished: *incapacitation* = the action of incapacitating or rendering incapable; *incapacity* = lack of ability in some legal respect. See **capacity.**

incarcerate. See **jail,** vb.

in case is generally much inferior to *if.* See **case (A).**

in cases in which is usually verbose for *when, whenever,* or *if.* See **case (A).**

inception; incipiency. Both words mean "beginning; commencement; initiation." The difference is that *inception* refers to the action or process of beginning, whereas *incipiency* refers to the fact or state of having begun. Here the two words show a misguided effort at INELEGANT VARIATION: "The word 'acquired' contemplates the *inception* of title, and as a general rule the character of the title depends upon the existence or nonexistence of the marriage at the time of the *incipiency* [read *inception*] of the right by virtue of which the title is finally extended and perfected." *Fisher v. Fisher*, 383 P.2d 840, 842 (Idaho 1963). *Inception* is far more commonly the appropriate word.

incest, denoting a statutory as opposed to a common-law crime, has been criticized for having an unduly restricted sense. In most English-speaking jurisdictions, a man commits incest by having sexual contact with a female he knows to be his granddaughter, daughter, sister, or mother; a woman commits incest by having sexual contact with her grandfather, father, brother, or son.

incestuous is sometimes mistakenly written **incestious*—e.g.:

- "The *incestious* [read *incestuous*] acts began while the family lived in Texas." *Nance v. Commonwealth*, 237 S.W.2d 537, 537 (Ky. 1951).
- "The problem that may rise in such a definition of *incestious* [read *incestuous*] rape is the categorization of perpetrators." Anjani Kent, *Women and the Law* 288 (2008).

in chambers. See **in camera.**

in chief (= principal, as opposed to collateral or incidental) is legal JARGON denoting the part of a trial, or of a witness's testimony, in which the main body of evidence is presented. E.g.: "While a defendant cannot be compelled to testify, if he elects to do so on his own behalf, he may then be cross-examined as to all matters about which he was examined *in chief*." *Benson v. State*, 602 So.2d 505, 509 (Ala. Crim. App. 1992). Cf. **case-in-chief** & **tenant-in-chief.**

inchoate, pronounced /in-**koh**-ət/ in AmE and /in-koh-ət/ in BrE, means "just begun; not yet fully developed." The prefix is an intensive *in-*, not a negative or privative *in-*. (See **choate.**) The law has found many uses for this word. In criminal law, for example, there are three *inchoate offenses*: attempt, conspiracy, and incitement. The word also appears in other legal contexts—e.g.:

- "We recognize that interpreting the contract to require that the Elders merely be able to furnish water falls short of requiring them to actually furnish water, and that the Bells did not contract only for the Elders' mere, *inchoate* ability to furnish water." *Bell v. Elder*, 782 P.2d 545, 547 (Utah Ct. App. 1989).
- "*Vieux* held first that no vested rights were created because there had not been a congressional or court declaration of abandonment, and second that any *inchoate* rights created by physical abandonment had been extinguished by application of the public highway exception." *Avista Corp. v. Wolfe*, 549 F.3d 1239, 1250 (9th Cir. 2008).
- "Rather than considering whether police knew they lacked probable cause to search the subject apartment, the majority holds that Pollock's *inchoate* suspicion that Harman was 'just somehow intertwined with this' justified what amounts to the warrantless search of a home." *Harman v. Pollock*, 586 F.3d 1254, 1272 (10th Cir. 2009) (Lucero, J., dissenting).
- "In 1920, the state gave notice to all parties interested in the *inchoate* rights of the irrigation company to appear and determine the extent to which those *inchoate* rights

had been realized." *Klamath Irrigation Dist. v. U.S.*, 227 P.3d 1145, 1168 (Or. 2010).

The antonym of *inchoate* is ordinarily either *consummate* <her dower becomes consummate> or *consummated* <they were consummated crimes>. But see **choate.**

The word is sometimes a pomposity that usurps the place of an ordinary word—e.g.: "We find that Apanovitch has simply referred to the suspicions of police officers at an *inchoate stage* [read *early stage*] of the investigation, and we hold that the officers' statements would not have reasonably impeached the testimony of the coroner." *Apanovitch v. Houk*, 466 F.3d 460, 484 (6th Cir. 2006).

See **choate.**

inchoate dower. See **curtesy.**

incidence = occurrence or rate of occurrence <the incidence of syphilis continues to decline>. Using this word as a variant for *instance* (= case or example) is a mistake: "[Hiring] off-duty police officers . . . is the most expensive type of security and in most *incidences* [read *instances*] twice as expensive as the private security that was available in Lawrence at the time." *Weroha v. Craft*, 951 P.2d 1308, 1313 (Kan. Ct. App. 1998). See **incidents** & **instance.**

incident, n. A. And *instance.* An *incident* is an occurrence or happening; an *instance* is an example. See **instance.** Cf. **incidence.**

B. Meaning "a concomitant." This sense, which originated in the feudal law of England, denotes the idea that a thing may be naturally and inseparably connected with something else that is more important. The usage has remained common in legal contexts, especially in the context of either property law or judicial power—e.g.:

- "Courts of justice as an *incident* of their jurisdiction have inherent power to appoint guardians ad litem." *Mabry v. Scott*, 124 P.2d 659, 665 (Cal. Ct. App. 1942).
- "It would appear that section 2035(d) limits the application of the three-year rule to such life-insurance proceeds as would have been includable under section 2042 if a decedent had retained *incidents* of ownership in the life-insurance policy." Keith Buck, Note, *Demise of the Beamed Transfer Theory*, 40 Drake L. Rev. 561, 569 (1991).
- "While Smith characterizes the 'court of competent jurisdiction' question in his case as a factual dispute in his briefing to this court, he has not identified any historical facts regarding any *incident* of jurisdiction that are in dispute." *State v. Smith*, 699 N.W.2d 508, 515 n.10 (Wis. 2005).

For the adjectival use, see **incident to.**

C. And *accident.* See **accident (A)** & EUPHEMISMS.

incidentally; incidently. The first means "loosely; casually" or "by the way," and the second means "so as to be incident; so as to depend on or appertain to something else." The most common mistake with these words is to misuse *incidently* for *incidentally*—e.g.: "Section 474, to the extent it prohibits expression at all, does so only inadvertently and *incidently* [read

incidentally]." *Regan v. Time, Inc.*, 468 U.S. 641, 695 (1984) (Stevens, J., concurring in part & dissenting in part). See **incident to.**

incidentals is elliptical for *incidental damages.* Cf. **consequentials, exemplaries** & **punitives.** See **damages.**

incidently. See **incidentally.**

incidents and *incidence* are homophones that may give listeners trouble. See **incident** & **incidence.**

incident to; incidental to. Though to some extent interchangeable historically, these phrases have undergone a plain DIFFERENTIATION that has gained acceptance among stylists. *Incident to* means "closely related to; naturally appearing with"; *incidental to* means "happening by chance and subordinate to some other thing; peripheral." In the following sentence, *incident to* is properly used: "In an action for fraud, exemplary damages are *incident to* and dependent [on] the recovery of actual damages." *Crawford Chevrolet, Inc. v. Rowland*, 525 S.W.2d 242, 250 (Tex. Civ. App.—Amarillo 1975). Here *incidental to* is correctly used: "He maintains the movement of the victims to the office area was merely *incidental to* his intent to commit aggravated battery or attempted murder." *State v. Turbeville*, 686 P.2d 138, 144 (Kan. 1984).

Incidental is misused for *incident*, a common blunder—e.g.:

- "A half century ago, in that case, we denied damages for wrongful libel of a vessel save when the seizure resulted from bad faith, malice, or gross negligence. *Incidental thereto, on the same grounds we denied* [read *Incident to that denial, we denied on the same grounds*] recovery for attorney's fees incurred in obtaining the release of the vessel seized, without differentiating between attorney's fees and other damages." *Cardinal Shipping Corp. v. M/S Seisho Maru*, 744 F.2d 461, 475 (5th Cir. 1984) (Rubin, J., concurring).
- "A long line of decisions now establishes the government's right to place burdens on citizens when such burdens are *incidental to* [read *incident to*] legitimate regulatory goals, independent of punishment." Daniel L. Feldman & Gerald Benjamin, *Tales from the Sausage Factory* 213 (2010).

Incidental to has even had to be construed as meaning *incident to*, primarily because of slipshod drafting of statutes. *See, e.g., U.S. v. Shursen*, 649 F.2d 1250, 1257 (8th Cir. 1981).

Sometimes courts are inconsistent in their use of these terms in a single opinion: "Closer in point . . . are cases holding that . . . [a club's] outside profits must be . . . strictly *incidental to* [read *incident to*] club activities. . . . Here the rental income was not *incident to* the operation of the club." *U.S. v. Fort Worth Club*, 345 F.2d 52, 57 (5th Cir. 1965). See INELEGANT VARIATION.

Incidental is sometimes wrongly used for *incident*, adj., when the word precedes the noun it modifies—e.g.: "Their primary objective is not to require the defendant to perform a contract, to carry out a trust or to undo the effects of a fraud, but rather to determine the title and *incidental* [read *incident*] right to possession of land." *Connell v. Algonquin Gas Transmission Co.*, 174 F.Supp. 453, 457 (D.R.I. 1959).

incipiency. See **inception.**

incipient; insipient. The first means "beginning; in an initial stage"; the second is an obsolete word meaning "unwise; foolish." Chapter C of J. Gillis Wetler's *Style of Judicial Opinions* (1960) is entitled "Arkansas: American Style, and *Insipient* Transformation." A reading of the first paragraph of that chapter shows that *incipient*, not *insipient*, was the intended word. The misuse, especially for its being in such a prominent place, might be characterized as insipient.

*incitation. See **incitement.**

*incitative; *incitatory. See **inciteful.**

inciteful; *incitive; *incitative; *incitatory. What is the adjective meaning "tending to incite"? Most American dictionaries do not list one, and the *OED* merely records sparse and ancient examples of **incitive*, **incitative*, and **incitatory*—all of which today might be considered NEEDLESS VARIANTS of *inciteful*. This word is a legal NEOLOGISM that first appeared in mid-20th-century AmE. Today it is fairly common—e.g.:

- "Many courts have adopted a rule that 'mere words cannot be sufficient provocation to reduce a murder charge to voluntary manslaughter, no matter how insulting or *inciteful*.'" *State v. Shane*, 590 N.E.2d 272, 277 (Ohio 1992).
- "The statute is the product of a legislative intent to cover intentional *inciteful* acts or conduct aimed at one's opponents as well as one's supporters." *Land v. State*, 426 S.E.2d 370, 373 (Ga. 1993).
- "Livingston's words alone may not have been sufficiently disturbing, *inciteful*, or obscene to qualify as 'behav[ing] in a disorderly manner'; however, the judgment . . . accounted for *both his words and conduct* [read *both his words and his conduct*]." *Livingston v. State*, 995 A.2d 812, 825 (Md. Ct. Spec. App. 2010). (For more on the faulty construction after *both*, see PARALLELISM.)

Unfortunately, the word can be confused with its homophone, *insightful*—e.g.: "*Walker's* significance lies primarily in the circuit court's careful and *inciteful* [read *insightful*] analysis of the training and supervision issues." Martin A. Schwartz, *Section 1983 in the Second Circuit*, 59 Brook. L. Rev. 285, 303 (1993). Where the word isn't clearly a mistake, as in that quotation, the reader (and the listener more so, with no spelling clue) may have to think twice to know whether you are condemning your subject's inflammatory words or praising your subject's enlightening words. So for *inciteful*, consider using an unambiguous alternative such as *antagonistic*, *incendiary*, or *provocative*. See **insightful.**

incitement; *incitation. The second is a NEEDLESS VARIANT.

inciter (= one who incites) is so spelled. See **perpetrator.**

*incitive. See **inciteful.**

inclement. See ***inclimate.**

*inclimate is a spreading MALAPROPISM for *inclement* (= unmerciful; stormy). Because *inclement weather* has become such a common phrase—either a SET PHRASE or a CLICHÉ, depending on whom one asks—many have come to hear the phrase as a redundant comment on the *climate* as well as the *weather*: hence the erroneous **inclimate weather*. E.g.:

- "According to Glascock, the test is used to determine the maximum safe speed at which a vehicle can traverse a curve under the most *inclimate* [read *inclement*] highway conditions, that is, with the highway surface being wet." *Vervik v. State*, 278 So.2d 530, 535 (La. Ct. App. 1973).
- "He also contends that the Secretary's decision to not postpone the February 28th election date due to *inclimate* [read *inclement*] weather was arbitrary and capricious." *Donovan v. Westside Local 174, AFL-CIO*, 783 F.2d 616, 623 (6th Cir. 1986).

*inclose. See **enclose.**

*inclosure is an archaic form of *enclosure*. See **enclosure.**

includable; includible; *inclusible. *Includible* is usual in estate-planning texts, and is a main entry in the *OED*; *includable*, however, is given primary sanction in *W3* and *W11* and is now the more prevalent of the two in more general legal contexts. **Inclusible* is a NEEDLESS VARIANT.

included. See **including.**

includes only. See DEFINITIONS (c).

including is sometimes misused for *namely*. But it should not be used to introduce an exhaustive list, for it implies that the list is only partial. In the words of one federal court, "It is hornbook law that the use of the word *including* indicates that the specified list . . . is illustrative, not exclusive." *Puerto Rico Maritime Shipping Auth. v. ICC*, 645 F.2d 1102, 1112 n.26 (D.C. Cir. 1981). E.g.: "Several business-law courses will be offered next year, *including* [read *namely*] one this summer and four next year."

Included for *including* must be a rare error: "The agreement provides that it 'is an Arizona agreement and that it shall be governed by the laws of the State of Arizona of the United States of America in all matters, *included* [read *including*] but not limited to, validity, obligation, interpretation, construction, performance and termination.'" *Gates Learjet Corp. v. Jensen*, 743 F.2d 1325, 1329 (9th Cir. 1984). See **including but not limited to.**

including but not limited to; *including without limitation; *without limiting the generality of the foregoing. In legal drafting, these cautious phrases are intended to defeat three canons of construction: *expressio unius est exclusio alterius* ("to express one thing is to exclude the other"), *noscitur a sociis* ("it is known by its associates"), and *ejusdem generis* ("of the same class or nature"). See ***expressio unius est exclusio alterius*** & ***ejusdem generis*.**

Even though the word *including* itself means that the list is merely exemplary and not exhaustive, the courts have not invariably so held. So the longer, more explicit variations are necessary in the eyes of many drafters. Of course, the drafters don't help matters when they use these phrases to introduce what looks like a comprehensive list. It's nonsensical to write "all members of Congress, including but not limited to U.S. Senators and members of the House of Representatives." After all, what else could be included by the phrase *members of Congress*?

The most straightforward of these expansive phrases is *including but not limited to*—so written, without commas. (Some drafters ill-advisedly stick a comma after *including* and another after *to*.) The other variants you should abjure. See **abjure.**

inclusible. See **includable.**

inclusio unius est exclusio alterius. See ***expressio unius est exclusio alterius.***

inclusive. This word is often helpful in expressing lengths of time. For example, the phrase *from November 1 to December 15 inclusive* makes clear that both the starting date and the ending date are included; without the word *inclusive*, the meaning is debatable.

incommensurate; incommensurable. See **commensurate.**

incomparable. The primary accent falls on the second syllable—hence /in-**kom**-pə-rə-bəl/, not */in-kəm-**pair**-ə-bəl/. See **comparable.**

incompetence; incompetency. Some lay authorities have stated that *incompetence* is the preferred form, but in legal writing a growing distinction exists between the forms. Reserve *competency* to contexts involving sanity or ability to stand trial or to testify, and use *competence* when referring to less than acceptable levels of ability—e.g.: "The various newspaper stories commenting on both Loehr's alleged *incompetence* [read *incompetency*] and a grand-jury investigation of the District's operations also fall short of *Bollow*." *Loehr v. Ventura County Cmty. Coll. Dist.*, 743 F.2d 1310, 1317 (9th Cir. 1984). These two word-forms are favorites of writers who engage in INELEGANT VARIATION. Be consistent when the sense does not vary. See **competence (A).**

incompetent is the adjective serving both *incompetence* and *incompetency*. Here it is the adjective for *incompetency*: "Their testimony, if accepted, clearly shows that Mary was not totally *incompetent* and at times she was normal and in possession of her mental and physical faculties." *Gilmer v. Brown*, 44 S.E.2d 16, 23 (Va. 1947). And here for *incompetence*: "Appellate lawyers are clearly not *incompetent* when they refuse

to follow a 'kitchen sink' approach to the issues on appeals." *Howard v. Gramley*, 225 F.3d 784, 791 (7th Cir. 2000). See **competent** & **incompetence.**

in concert. See **concert.**

incongruent; incongruous. Both are preferably accented on the second rather than the third syllable (/in-**kong**-groo-ənt/ and /in-**kong**-groo-əs/).

in connection with is invariably a vague, loose connective. Occasionally—very occasionally—it is the only connective that will do: it should always be used as a last resort. E.g.:

- "One of the most difficult problems *in connection with* [read *with*] the duty to take care is the problem of the unforeseeable plaintiff." C. Gordon Post, *An Introduction to the Law* 74 (1963).
- "Status-of-Forces Agreement between the Republic of Cyprus and the United Nations *in connection with* [read *for*] the support, supplementation, and enhancement of the United Nations Interim Force in Lebanon." *United Nations Juridical Yearbook 2008* 30 (2010).
- "The lawyer knew that W.R. Grace appeared to have the law on its side—the Houlihan name was first used and first federally registered *in connection with* [read *for*] Houlihan's Old Place." Stephen Elias & Richard Stim, *Trademark: Legal Care for Your Business & Product Name* 274 (2010).

in consideration of the mutual covenants herein contained. In contract drafting, this hoary phrase supposedly makes clear that the contract cannot fail for lack of consideration. In fact, though, the phrase is deadwood: courts look to the mutual promises to ascertain whether consideration exists, and if one side has promised nothing, vague recitals of consideration will not suffice to save the contract.

in consideration of the premises. Use *therefore* instead.

inconsistency; *inconsistence. Writers on usage formerly tried to distinguish between the forms, reserving *inconsistency* for the sense "the general quality of being inconsistent," and making **inconsistence* mean "an act of an inconsistent nature or an instance of being inconsistent." Today, however, *inconsistency* has ousted *-ce* in all senses. It is high time to brand **inconsistence* as a NEEDLESS VARIANT.

inconsistent pleading. See **Codd's Puzzle.**

in contrast with; in contrast to. These are equally good. See **contrast (A).**

incontrovertible. So spelled.

incorporeal; incorporal. See **corporal** & **corporeal.**

incorporeal hereditament. See **corporeal hereditaments** & **hereditament(s).**

increase; *encrease. See **encrease.**

increasingly less.** See ***increasingly more.

*increasingly more is increasingly—or, rather, more and more—common as a REDUNDANCY. E.g.: "As the business becomes *increasingly more* [read *increasingly* or *more*] competitive, do publishers care which books they publish or what shape the manuscripts are in when they hit the press?" Roger Cohen, *When a Best Seller Is at Stake, Publishers Can Lose Control*, N.Y. Times, 12 May 1991, at 4E.

The phrase **increasingly less* is equally bad: an OXY-MORON. E.g.: "They have *increasingly less* [read *less and less* or *decreasing*] time for thorough first-hand work upon the vast mass of available material." Roscoe Pound, *The Formative Era of American Law* 164 (1938).

incredible; incredulous. *Incredible* = not believable. E.g.:

- "We find *incredible* Wilk's claim that he was unable to present his version of events to the jury, as he testified in his defense for six days." *U.S. v. Wilk*, 572 F.3d 1229, 1234 (11th Cir. 2009).
- "He gave a number of inconsistent, and sometimes inherently *incredible*, statements about the events of that night." *O'Laughlin v. O'Brien*, 577 F.3d 1, 2–3 (1st Cir. 2009).

*Noncredible is a NEEDLESS VARIANT.

Incredulous (= skeptical) is sometimes misused for *incredible*—e.g.:

- "No court is required to believe, or should be bound by improbable, *incredulous* [read *incredible*], or unreasonable evidence supporting a verdict." *Baker Serv. Tools, Inc. v. Buckley*, 500 So.2d 970, 971 (Miss. 1986).
- "As for the record reviews performed by Dr. Korevaar and US Medical Review, both of these reviews are biased to the point of being *incredulous* [read *incredible*]." *Kerper v. Educators Mut. Life Ins. Co.*, 71 Pa. D.&C. 4th 413, 423 (Pa. Ct. Com. Pl. 2004).

See **credible.**

increscitur is a NEEDLESS VARIANT of *additur*—e.g.: F.E. Mathews, *Increscitur* [read *Additur*] *in Personal Injury Cases*, 15 St. Louis L. Rev. 169 (1930). See **additur.**

incriminate; *criminate. *Incriminate* has two important senses: (1) "to charge with a crime" (see **charge, vb. (A)**); and (2) "to indicate involvement in the commission of a crime." The latter sense is more frequent; it applies in the phrase *self-incrimination*—e.g.:

- "When he presents his witnesses, he must reveal their identity and submit them to cross-examination which in itself may prove *incriminating* or which may furnish the State with leads to *incriminating* rebuttal evidence." *Williams v. Florida*, 399 U.S. 78, 83–84 (1970) (per White, J.).
- "Castilho de Oliveira's mother turned over *incriminating* documents and audiotapes to a local prosecutor." *Castilho de Oliveira v. Holder*, 564 F.3d 892, 895 (7th Cir. 2009).

The equivalent verb **criminate* was formerly common in AmE and BrE but seldom appears today—e.g.: "No party or witness shall be required to testify as to any matter which may *criminate* or tend to *criminate*

himself or which shall tend to bring infamy, disgrace, or public contempt upon himself or any member of his family." Ga. Code Ann. § 24-9-27(a) (2010). **Criminate* is now but a NEEDLESS VARIANT of *incriminate*.

incriminatory; *criminatory. The standard is more common, just as *incriminate* is now more common than **criminate*. "He must prove the *criminatory* [read *incriminatory*] character of what it is his privilege to suppress just because it is *criminatory* [read *incriminatory*]." *U.S. v. Weisman*, 111 F.2d 260, 262 (2d Cir. 1940). See **incriminate.**

incrust. See EN-.

inculcatable. So spelled.

inculcate (into) for *indoctrinate*. Although these are both transitive verbs (i.e., they take direct objects), the nature of the objects is different. One *inculcates* values into people; and one *indoctrinates* people with certain values. One does not *inculcate* people, but rather values or beliefs or ideas. The title of a law review article contains this infelicity: Tyll van Geel, *The Search for Constitutional Limits on Governmental Authority to Inculcate Youth*, 62 Tex. L. Rev. 197 (1983). H.W. Fowler noted this aberration and called it "a curious mistake" (*MEU1* 266); no longer is it curious, but it is still a mistake. See OBJECT-SHUFFLING.

*inculpable. See **culpable, inculpatable & nonculpable.**

inculpatable, not **inculpable*, is the correct form of the word meaning "capable of being inculpated." **Inculpable* is, however, a negative form that generally (though ambiguously) means "not culpable; blameless; free from guilt." Use of the term may cause ambiguities. See **culpable & nonculpable.**

inculpate = to accuse or incriminate. Although its antonym (*exculpate*) can be found in nonlegal writing, *inculpate* rarely appears in nonlegal prose. (See **exculpate.**) But it is common in contexts involving criminal law and torts—e.g.:

- "*Bruton* excludes only the statement of a nontestifying codefendant that standing alone directly *inculpates* the defendant." *Daniel v. State*, 677 S.E.2d 120, 123 (Ga. 2009).
- "*Crawford* does not require that a statement *inculpate* a defendant to trigger error under the Confrontation Clause." *U.S. v. Tuyet Thi-Bach Nguyen*, 565 F.3d 668, 674 (9th Cir. 2009).

The adjective is *inculpatory*—e.g.: "Defense counsel heard this testimony of Masorlian, which was exculpatory with respect to her and Brissa and *inculpatory* with respect to petitioner." *U.S. ex rel. Tonaldi v. Elrod*, 782 F.2d 665, 666 (7th Cir. 1986).

incumbent upon or *on* has become a CLICHÉ as a way of expressing a duty or obligation—e.g.:

- "When an individual submits a fee waiver request, it is *incumbent upon* him to clear away any inferences that could cast doubt on his eligibility." *Jarvik v. CIA*, 495 F.Supp.2d 67, 72 (D.D.C. 2007).
- "To the extent Grady did not object at trial to the alleged instances of misconduct, it is *incumbent upon* him to demonstrate plain error." *Grady v. State*, 197 P.3d 722, 733 (Wyo. 2008).

*incumber; encumber. The second is the preferred spelling. See EN-.

*incumbrance. See **encumbrance.**

*incumbrancer. See **encumbrancer.**

incuria. British legal writers use *incuria* (lit., "carelessness") to denote the idea that a case was decided *per incuriam*, that is, in ignorance of the relevant law. E.g.: "Viscount Simon L.C. had erroneously assumed, with the concurrence of the other (including Scottish) peers, that the law of the two countries was the same. *Quaere*, whether this was *incuria*; or is *incuria* unthinkable in the House of Lords?" Carleton K. Allen, *Law in the Making* 257 (7th ed. 1964). See *per incuriam.*

incurrence; *incurment. The second is a NEEDLESS VARIANT of the noun corresponding to the verb *to incur* (= [1] to run into (some undesirable consequence); or [2] to bring upon oneself). E.g.:

- "If it is found, the fault in the *incurrence* of the danger and in remaining in it does not free the defendant from liability." *Clark v. Boston & Maine R.R.*, 182 A. 175, 178 (N.H. 1935).
- "Not only are the tax returns outside of the complaint, the *incurrence* of a liability for taxes is not equivalent to solvency." *In re Die Fliedermaus, LLC*, 323 B.R. 101, 106 (Bankr. S.D.N.Y. 2005).
- "Pivotal to the court's decision . . . was the fact that the trustee did not seek to avoid the *incurrence* of the underlying obligation, instead seeking to avoid the monthly transfer." *In re TSIC, Inc.*, 428 B.R. 103, 115 (Bankr. D. Del. 2010).

Incurrence is sometimes misspelled **incurrance.*

indebitatus assumpsit. See **assumpsit, implied contract** & **quasi-contract.**

indebtedness. See **debt.**

*indebtment, a NEEDLESS VARIANT of *indebtedness* or *debt*, was much more common up to the mid-20th century than it is today. E.g.: "The transfer from Godfrey was a simple collateral security, taken as additional security for the old *indebtment* [read *debt*]." *People's Savs. Bank v. Bates*, 120 U.S. 556, 565 (1887) (per Harlan, J.). A few latter-day examples persist: "The . . . amount due under an absolute *indebtment* [read *debt* or *indebtedness*] may be unascertained or in dispute will not defeat a trustee process." *Loyal Erectors Inc. v. Hamilton & Son, Inc.*, 312 A.2d 748, 752 (Me. 1973). See **indebtedness** & **debt.**

indecency. See **obscenity (B).**

indecent assault is the BrE phrase denoting a statutory crime that includes all forms of sexual assault other than rape, buggery, and attempts to commit either of those crimes. (See **buggery.**) The nearest AmE equivalent is *sexual assault*. See **rape (C).**

indefeasible; inalienable. Both adjectives describe something that belongs to a person without the possibility of divestiture. What is *indefeasible* is not subject to defeasance (= the ending of a status, estate, etc., by conditional limitation). One cannot be deprived of it without agreement or consent <indefeasible title to land>. (**Undefeasible* is a NEEDLESS VARIANT.) What is *inalienable* cannot be transferred to another or otherwise disposed of even with consent <the inalienable rights of life, liberty, and the pursuit of happiness>. Both words strongly suggest what cannot be forfeited, and they are therefore often used without the precise distinction of consensual or nonconsensual transferability.

Inalienable, though not used in the Declaration of Independence, is slightly better formed (with a Latinate prefix as well as suffix)—e.g.:

- "There are many examples of *inalienable* property, including leases that may not be assigned and certain classes of shares in some private companies." Lyria Bennett Moses, *The Applicability of Property Law in New Contexts*, 30 Sydney L. Rev. 639, 652 (2008).
- "An *inalienable* property interest in the body amounts to extending some property principles to the body (the right to exclude, rights of use), but drawing the line at its exchange in contract (the right to include)." Peter Halewood, *On Commodification and Self-Ownership*, 20 Yale J.L. & Humanities 131, 154 (2008).
- "These *inalienable* property rights were argued to derive from a source other than social, political, or legal convention and to fix 'limits on the powers of government.'" Anne Orford, *Jurisdiction Without Territory*, 30 Mich. J. Int'l L. 981, 992 (2009).

Some writers have recently revived **unalienable*, but *inalienable* predominates in modern usage except when quoting the Declaration. See NEGATIVES (B).
   Cf. **feasible.**

INDEFINITE ANTECEDENT. See ANTECEDENTS, FALSE.

indemnifiable; *indemnitable. The first is better.

*indemnificate, a BACK-FORMATION from *indemnification*, is a NEEDLESS VARIANT of *indemnify*. (See **indemnify.**)

indemnification. See **indemnity.**

indemnificatory; *indemnitory. Both mean "of, relating to, or constituting an indemnity." The standard term is *indemnificatory*. The other term, **indemnitory*, is a NEEDLESS VARIANT not recorded in the major unabridged dictionaries, but it occurs occasionally in American legal writing—e.g.:

- "Among these problems are those arising from the possibility of multiple subrogation claims [and from] determining what types or lines of insurance are *indemnitory* [read *indemnificatory*]." *Shelby Mut. Ins. Co. v. Birch*, 196 So.2d 482, 485 (Fla. Dist. Ct. App. 1967) (Andrews, J., dissenting).

- "No decision is necessary at this time on whether the *indemnitory* [read *indemnificatory*] theory should be limited only to owners of premises." *Waller v. J.E. Brenneman Co.*, 307 A.2d 550, 553 (Del. Super. Ct. 1973).

*indemnifier. See **indemnitor.**

indemnify. A. And ***hold harmless; save harmless.*** Are these phrases—*indemnify* and either *hold harmless* or *save harmless*—synonymous? This is a crucial question that has frequently arisen in American litigation, with varying results. The correct answer is most instructive, not just about the phrases at issue but about what happens when lawyers and judges are insufficiently aware of legal terminology and its history. It will be necessary to go into quite some detail in this entry. All the "s.v." references in what follows mean that the dictionaries mentioned are unpaginated, and one must simply look under the term mentioned in its alphabetical place.

First, consider the etymology of *indemnify*. Some authorities suggest that the word derives from *in-* "to take away" + *damnum* "loss." But the better etymology is *indemnis* "harmless" + *-fy* "to make." A steady line of authorities, from the 18th century on, has recorded the meaning of *indemnis* as being translatable as "harmless." Here's how the dictionaries have defined *indemnis*:

- 1735: "without hurt, harm or damage, harmless." Adam Littleton, *Latin Dictionary in Four Parts* (6th ed. 1735) (s.v. *indemnis*).

- 1786: "unhurt, harmless." *Entick's New Latin–English Dictionary* (pt. 2) 221 (William Crackelt ed., rev. ed. 1786).

- 1845: "without hurt, harm, or damage; harmless." Thomas Morrell, *An Abridgment of Ainsworth's Dictionary, English and Latin* (pt. 2) 253 (William Duncan ed., 1845).

- 1891: "without hurt, harm, or damage; harmless." Henry Campbell Black, *A Dictionary of Law* 614 (1891).

- 1893: "without loss, damage or harm; unharmed; one who experiences no loss, or is affected by no loss." J. Kendrick Kinney, *A Law Dictionary and Glossary* 383 (1893).

- 1916: "undamaged." James A. Ballentine, *A Law Dictionary* 234 (1916).

The word *indemnis* is Latin, and the modern verb *indemnify* answers perfectly to the modern French *indemniser*, as the phrase *indemniser d'une perte* is to indemnify someone for a loss. *See* R. Lusum, *French Commercial Terms and Phrases* 90 (1922); *see also* 1 N. Salmon, *Boyer's Royal Dictionary Abridged* (22d ed. 1814) (defining *indemniser* as "to save harmless"); cf. *The Law-French Dictionary* (1701) (defining the LAW FRENCH *indemne* as "saved harmless").

Now let's consider the modern English verb in its own right. The first English-language lexicographer to record a separate entry for *indemnify* was Elisha Coles, who in 1676 defined it as "to save harmless." *An English Dictionary* (1676) (s.v. *indemnify*). Other lexicographers soon followed suit:

- 1707: "to save harmless." *Glossographia Anglicana Nova* (1707) (s.v. *indemnify*).

- 1745: "to save, or bear harmless." Nathan Bailey, *An Universal Etymological English Dictionary* (11th ed. 1745) (s.v. *indemnify*).

- 1755: (1) "to secure against loss or penalty"; (2) "to maintain unhurt." Samuel Johnson, *A Dictionary of the English Language* (1755) (s.v. *indemnify*).

- 1777: "to save, keep, or bear harmless; to secure from charge or danger, etc." Thomas Dyche, *A New General English Dictionary* (16th ed. 1777) (s.v. *indemnify*).

- 1789: "to secure against loss or penalty; to maintain unhurt." Thomas Sheridan, *A Complete Dictionary of the English Language* (2d ed. 1789) (s.v. *indemnify*).

- 1806: "to maintain unhurt, to secure." Noah Webster, *A Compendious Dictionary of the English Language* 156 (1806).

- 1810: "to secure against loss, to maintain unhurt." Thomas Browne, *The Union Dictionary* (1810) (s.v. *indemnify*).

- 1813: "to secure against loss or penalty; to maintain unhurt." *A New Critical Pronouncing Dictionary of the English Language* (1813) (s.v. *indemnify*).

- 1821: "to secure against loss or penalty." Stephen Jones, *A General Pronouncing and Explanatory Dictionary of the English Language* 202 (1821).

- 1828: (1) "to save harmless; to secure against loss, damage, or penalty"; (2) "to make good; to reimburse to one what he has lost." Noah Webster, *An American Dictionary of the English Language* (1828) (s.v. *indemnify*).

- 1845: "to save or free from hurt, injury, or harm; loss, or penalty, or punishment; to save harmless or uninjured." Charles Richardson, *A New Dictionary of the English Language* 417 (2d ed. 1845).

- 1845: "to secure against loss or penalty; to maintain unhurt." John Walker, *Walker's Critical Pronouncing Dictionary and Expositor of the English Language* 287 (John Davis ed., 1845).

- 1850: "to save harmless; to secure against loss, damage or penalty. To make good; to reimburse to one what he has lost." 1 John Boag, *A Popular and Complete English Dictionary* 704 (1850).

- 1861: "to save harmless; to secure against loss, damage, or penalty; to reimburse, to make good." Arnold J. Cooley, *A Dictionary of the English Language* 311 (1861).

- 1867: "to make or save harmless; to secure against loss or damage; to secure from future loss . . . to put one in the situation he was in, before sustaining a loss. In some of the old books, this word is written *indempnify*." 2 Alexander M. Burrill, *A Law*

Dictionary and Glossary 67 (2d ed. 1867) (internal citations omitted).

1879: "to make free of loss. The word is used with two shades of meaning: 1. To make compensation for a loss already sustained; 2. To give assurance or security that one shall have compensation for a loss anticipated. Thus one may speak of indemnifying an owner of land taken for public use, meaning to pay him the value; or of indemnifying the sherrif, meaning to give a bond to reimburse any damages which may be collected from him." Benjamin Vaughan Abbott, *Dictionary of Terms and Phrases Used in American or English Jurisprudence* 596 (1879) (internal citations omitted).

1882: "to indemnify is to make good a loss which one person has suffered in consequence of the act or default of another, and the operation of making good the loss is called indemnification. Thus, if A. fails to pay a debt which he owes to B., and a surety, C., pays it, he is said to indemnify B., and B. is said to obtain indemnification. So, if A. wrongfully causes a loss to B., A. is liable to indemnify B. for the loss which he has sustained." Charles Sweet, *A Dictionary of English Law* 424 (1882).

1890: "to compensate for loss, sustained or anticipated." William C. Anderson, *A Dictionary of Law* 534 (1890).

1891: "to save harmless; to secure against loss or damage; to give security for the reimbursement of a person in case of an anticipated loss falling upon him. Also to make good; to compensate; to make reimbursement to one of a loss already incurred by him." Henry Campbell Black, *A Dictionary of Law* 614 (1891).

1893: "to make or save harmless; to secure against loss or damage; to make good; to reimburse to one what he has lost." J. Kendrick Kinney, *A Law Dictionary and Glossary* 383 (1893).

1914: "to secure or save harmless against loss or damage, of a specified character, which may happen in the future. To compensate or reimburse one for a loss previously incurred. To indemnify is said to be synonymous with 'to save harmless.'" John Bouvier, *Bouvier's Law Dictionary and Concise Encyclopedia* 1532 (Francis Rawle ed., 8th ed. 1914).

1916: "to secure against loss; to compensate for loss." James A. Ballentine, *A Law Dictionary* 234 (1916).

1925: (1) "to protect fully and save harmless"; (2) "to make good"; or (3) "to reimburse another for some loss." James John Lewis, *The Collegiate Law Dictionary* 173 (1925).

1934: (1) "to secure or save harmless against loss or damage, of a specified character, which may happen in the future"; or (2) "to compensate or reimburse for a loss previously incurred. To indemnify is said to be synonymous with 'to save harmless.'" William Edward Baldwin, *Bouvier's Law Dictionary* 535 (Baldwin's Century ed. 1934).

1970: "to save harmless against loss or damage incurred by another; to reimburse another for such loss or damage." Max Radin, *Law Dictionary* 161 (Lawrence G. Greene ed., 2d ed. 1970).

Now an aside. The noun *indemnity* had made its way into English dictionaries long before its verb

sibling, from the early 17th century: John Bullokar defined it as "escaping without damage or hurt." *An English Expositor* (1616) (s.v. *indemnity*). And then Thomas Blount (pronounced /blənt/) recorded it in 1661 and defined it as follows: "eschewing of damage, escaping without hurt, damagelessness." Thomas Blount, *Glossographia* (2d ed. 1661) (s.v. *indemnity*). Interestingly, Blount omitted all reference to *indemnity* and its cognates in his law dictionary nine years later: *see Nomo-Lexicon: A Law-Dictionary* (1670). Then, of course, came Elisha Coles in 1676: "freedom from damage or danger, pardon." Elisha Coles, *An English Dictionary* (4th ed. 1676) (s.v. *indemnity*).

The evidence is overwhelming that *indemnify* and *hold harmless* are perfectly synonymous. The first is Latinate, the second Anglo-Saxon. And it would be possible to multiply 20th- and 21st-century authorities to this effect.

As with many DOUBLETS, TRIPLETS, AND SYNONYM-STRINGS, arguments began to emerge among litigators about whether in fact some distinction did exist between the terms. After all, it had become a commonplace in legal drafting to use the phrase *indemnify and hold harmless* or *indemnify and save harmless*. See, e.g., Hugh M. Spalding, *An Encyclopaedia of Law and Forms* 190 (1879) ("indemnify and save harmless"); Leonard A. Jones, *Legal Forms: Contractual, Business and Conveyancing Forms* 391 (Samuel G. Gifford ed., 7th ed. 1919) ("save, defend, keep harmless, and indemnify"); Clarence F. Birdseye, *Encyclopaedia of General Business and Legal Forms* 1581 (3d ed. 1924) ("protect, indemnify, and keep harmless"); Saul Gordon, *Gordon's Standard Annotated Forms of Agreement* 425 (1932) ("indemnify and hold harmless"). By the mid-20th century, transactional lawyers were accustomed to seeing the phrases constantly, and they seemed rarely to inquire into the precise meanings. By 2010, it was possible for a book on effective contract drafting to include a 23-page discussion of drafting indemnities, with several examples of *indemnify and hold harmless*, without even once raising the issue of the semantic contents of these words. *See* Robert A. Feldman & Raymond T. Nimmer, *Drafting Effective Contracts: A Practitioner's Guide* 5-113 to -136 (2010).

But the courts had already begun invoking the rule about reading nothing in a contract as "mere surplusage." They were charged, as is commonly said, with "giving effect to every word." That's not a bad rule when legal drafters abstain from larding their contracts with surplusage, but it's a horrible rule when they do.

And so, beginning in the late 19th century, there were many ahistorical holdings that *indemnify* isn't at all synonymous with *hold harmless* or *save harmless*. Without so much as a wink at the history of this terminology, courts said such things as this: "There is a distinction between 'indemnify' and 'save harmless,' the latter phrase possessing the more extensive meaning." *Weller v. Eames*, 15 Minn. 461, 467 (1870). And now in many states, courts and commentators have begun to call the *indemnify* language the "indemnity clause" and the *hold harmless* language the "exculpatory clause." *See* Richard J. Lind, *Express Contracts of Indemnity*, 65 J. Kan. B. Ass'n 36, 36 (1996) (distinguishing between exculpatory clauses [*hold harmless*] and indemnity clauses [*indemnify*]); *see also* John Slavich, *Environmental Issues Affecting Emerging Growth Companies*, 31 Bull. Bus. Law Section of the State Bar of Texas 41, 65 (June 1994) (stating that it is "mistaken" to treat *indemnity* and *hold harmless* synonymously).

Take one state as an example: Florida. There the practice just described has emerged in full flower. The *indemnify* language is the "indemnity clause" (covering liabilities to third parties) and the *hold harmless* language is the "exculpatory clause" (releasing first-party liability—that is, so that the *hold harmless* phrase releases a wrongdoing indemnitee where *indemnify* would not have this effect). *See O'Connell v. Walt Disney World Co.*, 413 So.2d 444, 446 (Fla. Dist. Ct. App. 1982); *Van Tuyn v. Zurich Am. Ins. Co.*, 447 So.2d 318, 320 (Fla. Dist. Ct. App. 1984); *Kitchens of the Oceans, Inc. v. McGladney & Pullen, LLP*, 832 So.2d 270, 272 (Fla. Dist. Ct. App. 2002).

And then there's just explicit judicial nonsense, this bit being from California: "Are the words 'indemnify' and 'hold harmless' synonymous? No. One is offensive and the other is defensive—even though *both* contemplate third-liability situations. 'Indemnify' is an offensive right—a sword—allowing an indemnitee to seek indemnification. 'Hold harmless' is defensive: The right not to be bothered by the other party itself seeking indemnification." *Queen Villas Homeowners Ass'n v. TCB Prop. Mgmt.*, 56 Cal. Rptr. 3d 528, 534 (Ct. App. 2007).

True, the majority rule is that *indemnify and hold harmless* is a unitary phrase that means nothing more than *indemnify* alone. *See, e.g., Brentnal v. Holmes*, 1 Root (Conn.) 291, 1 Am. Dec. 44 (1791); *Long v. McAllister-Long*, 221 S.W.3d 1, 10 (Tenn. Ct. App. 2006) (stating that the term *hold harmless* is synonymous with the word *indemnify*, so that a hold-harmless provision in a divorce agreement is nothing more nor less than an indemnity); *Loscher v. Hudson*, 182 P.3d 25, 33 (Kan. Ct. App. 2008) ("'Hold harmless' is synonymous with 'indemnify.'"). Perhaps the best statement on point is that of Vice Chancellor Strine of Delaware, who was presented with an argument to distinguish the terms: "The terms 'indemnify' and 'hold harmless' have a long history of joint use throughout the lexicon of Anglo-American legal practice. The phrase 'indemnify and hold harmless' appears in countless types of contracts in varying contexts. The plain fact is that lawyers have become so accustomed to using the phrase 'indemnify and hold harmless' that it is often almost second nature for the drafter of a contract to include both phrases in referring to a single indemnification right." *Majkowski v.*

American Imaging Mgmt. Servs., LLC, 913 A.2d 572, 588 (Del. Ch. 2006). He added that transactional lawyers everywhere would be surprised to learn that they had unwittingly created additional rights by tacking *and hold harmless* onto *indemnify. Id.*

There has been a welter of needless litigation over the doublet, as litigants have wasted countless dollars fighting over imaginary differences between the words—differences that have no historical justification. And now there is bad law in many states—bad law that is well ensconced. There's an object lesson for all of us: know legal language, its history, and its development; research it when necessary (the literature is startlingly easy to find); and make considered drafting decisions that avoid extra words that don't convey extra meaning—because some court, somewhere, some day, will find extra meaning where there isn't any.

B. Two Senses of *indemnify*. This verb has a double sense, and so does *indemnity*. To *indemnify* may mean either (1) to secure against future losses; or (2) to pay for losses already sustained. It's not a serious AMBIGUITY, typically, because an indemnity covers both situations. The first lexicographer ever to notice this double sense was Noah Webster, who included both definitions in his 1828 *American Dictionary of the English Language.* See his definition under (A) by looking for the year 1828.

C. Intransitive and Transitive Uses of *indemnify*. The verb *indemnify* takes the preposition *from, against,* or *for.* Usually one *indemnifies from* or *against* losses; the *OED* records the transitive sense "to compensate, make up for" <indemnify this defect>, and calls this sense "Obs. rare," but it has been revived: "The agreement did not require Atlas to *indemnify* losses caused by its own negligence." *Sullen v. Missouri Pac. R.R.*, 750 F.2d 428, 433 (5th Cir. 1985). This sense arose apparently through HYPALLAGE, by transference of object from the person compensated to the thing for which that person is compensated.

*indemnitable. See **indemnifiable.**

indemnitee and *indemnitor* are MORPHOLOGICAL DEFORMITIES, since personal suffixes such as *-or* and *-ee* should be applied to verbs, and not to nouns. Yet the words are established beyond question in AmE, where they originated in the 19th century. E.g.:

- "An *indemnitee* owes no obligation whatever to the creditor apart from his promise." Laurence P. Simpson, *Handbook on the Law of Suretyship* 130 (1950).
- "In a contract of indemnity the *indemnitor* agrees to make the *indemnitee* whole for losses incurred when the *indemnitee* is sued." *Sekeres v. Arbaugh*, 508 N.E.2d 941, 946 (Ohio 1987).

See -EE & **indemnitor.**

indemnitor; *indemnifier; *indemnor. The first two words are absolutely synonymous, *indemnitor* being the usual form in American legal writing. E.g.: "That court granted a summary judgment in favor of the *indemnitor*." *Patch v. Amoco Oil Co.*, 845 F.2d 571, 573 (5th Cir. 1988). */Indemnifier* might have been slightly more comprehensible to educated nonlawyers, but it has become a NEEDLESS VARIANT. So has **indemnor*, which appears in some 19th-century lawbooks. See **indemnitee.**

*indemnitory. See **indemnificatory.**

indemnity; indemnification. There is a distinction. *Indemnity* = (1) security or protection against contingent hurt, damage, or loss; or (2) a legal exemption from the penalties or liabilities incurred by any course of action (*OED*). *Indemnification* = the action of compensating for actual loss or damage sustained; the payment made with this object (*OED*).

For more on *indemnity* and related words, see **reparation.** For the distinction between *indemnity* and *contribution*, see **contribution.**

*indemnor. See **indemnitor.**

indenture. This word, essentially a synonym for *contract* or *agreement*, typically appears in the phrases *bond indenture*, the rhyming *debenture indenture*, and *trust indenture*. These all denote agreements of a particular kind. Originally, the document had toothing (hence the root *-dent-*): according to *Black's Law Dictionary* 838 (9th ed. 2009), it traditionally had "the edges serrated, or indented, in a zigzag fashion to reduce the possibility of forgery and to distinguish it from a deed poll [which had straight, smooth sides]."

Historically, any contract requiring counterparts was an *indenture* (or *deed indented*), as opposed to a *deed poll* (requiring only a signature and seal of one party). Here is how an 18th-century lexicographer explained the difference:

> *Indenture* . . . [i]s a writing, containing a conveyance between two or more, indented or cut unevenly, or in and out, on the top or side, answerable to another writing that likewise comprehends the same words. Formerly, when deeds were more concise than at present, it was usual to write both parts on the same piece of parchment, with some word or letters written between them, through which the parchment was cut, either in a straight or indented line, in such a manner as to leave half the word on one part, and half on the other: and this custom is still preserved in making out the indentures of a fine. But at last, indenting only hath come into use, without cutting through any letters at all; and it seems at present to serve for little other purpose, than to give name to the species of the deed.
>
>   3 William Marriot, *A New Law Dictionary* (1798)
>   (s.v. *indenture*).

The same is true today: the word *indenture* serves little purpose other than to intimidate those not intimately familiar with the document so denominated. But it is a stubborn word, and so are its users: so it seems unlikely to budge from its well-ensconced position.

independent. A. Preposition with. *Independent* should take the preposition *of*, not *from*.

B. Adverbial Uses. The proper adverbial phrase is *independently of*—e.g.:

- "Interestingly, defendants do not respond directly to plaintiffs' argument that the earnest money agreement contains contractual obligations *independently of* the disclosure statement." *Archambault v. Ogier*, 95 P.3d 257, 260 (Or. Ct. App. 2004).
- "This court determines this legal question *independently of* the circuit court and court of appeals but benefitting from their analyses." *Loth v. City of Milwaukee*, 758 N.W.2d 766, 768 (Wis. 2008).
- "Plaintiffs are suing for . . . fraud, breach of contract, unjust enrichment, and breach of duty of good faith, claims existing *independent* [read *independently*] of the foregoing statute." *Dierkes v. Blue Cross & Blue Shield of Mo.*, 991 S.W.2d 662, 668 (Mo. 1999).
- "Despite the existence of multiple violations, none occurred *independent* [read *independently*] *of* each other." *North Carolina State Bar v. Sossomon*, 676 S.E.2d 910, 918 (N.C. Ct. App. 2010).

independent contractor. See **employee (B).**

independently of. See **independent (B).**

in derogation of. See **derogation of, in.**

INDETERMINATE SUBJECTS. See EXPLETIVES.

indexes; indices. For ordinary purposes, *indexes* is the preferable plural. E.g.:

- "With all our carefully compiled statute books and elaborate *indexes*, modern legislators often fail to foresee points of rub between their innovations and the body of law against which they are projected." Lon L. Fuller, *Anatomy of the Law* 84 (1968).
- "Case-name and subject *indexes* are maintained on a cumulative basis." Michael Zander, *The Law-Making Process* 211 (2d ed. 1985).

Indices, though less pretentious than **fora* or **dogmata*, is pretentious nevertheless. Some writers prefer it in technical contexts, as in mathematics and the sciences. Though not the best plural for *index*, *indices* is permissible in the sense "indicators"—e.g.: "The existence of one or more of these *indices* does not necessarily preclude a summary determination that certain products or services either are reasonably interchangeable or demonstrate a high cross-elasticity of demand." *C.E. Servs. v. Control Data Corp.*, 759 F.2d 1241, 1246 (5th Cir. 1985). Cf. **appendixes.** See PLURALS (A).

Writers who use the highfalutin form, of course, should spell it correctly. Some misspell it with a mediate *-e-* on the influence of *index*. See, e.g., 10 Cardozo L. Rev., Table of Contents ([Aug.] 1989) ("*indeces*").

*indicant. See **indicative.**

indicate should not appear where *say*, *state*, or *show* will suffice.

indicative; *indicatory; *indicant; indicial. *Indicative* is the usual adjective corresponding to the noun *indication* and meaning "that indicates." *Indicant* and *indicatory* are NEEDLESS VARIANTS except in archaic medical contexts. *Indicial*—the adjective corresponding to both *indicia* and *index*—means (1) "of the nature of an indicia; indicative"; or (2) "of the nature or form of an index." See **indicia.**

indices. See **indexes.**

indicia, the plural of *indicium* (= an indication, sign, token), is treated as a singular noun forming the plurals *indicia* and *indicias*, the former being preferred: "In *Evans v. Newton*, we held that the park had acquired such unalterable *indicia* of a public facility that for the purposes of the Equal Protection Clause it remained 'public' even after the city officials were replaced as trustees by a board of private citizens." *Evans v. Abney*, 396 U.S. 435, 452 (1970) (Brennan, J., dissenting).

The singular *indicium* is still sometimes used—e.g.:

- "Where testimonial statements are at issue, the only *indicium* of reliability sufficient to satisfy constitutional demands is the one the Constitution actually prescribes: confrontation." *Crawford v. Washington*, 541 U.S. 36, 68–69 (2004) (per Scalia, J.).
- "There is no evidence of the appellant's profit margins and, thus, no sound basis for drawing an inference that relative compensation is an *indicium* of control." *U.S. v. Al-Rikabi*, 606 F.3d 11, 16 (1st Cir. 2010).
- "In the absence of either a built-in definition or some reliable *indicium* that the drafters intended a special nuance, accepted canons of construction teach that the word should be given its ordinary meaning." *SEC v. Tambone*, 597 F.3d 436, 442 (1st Cir. 2010).

Compare *data* and *datum*: see **data.** In the civil law, *indicium* is a species of proof similar to common-law circumstantial evidence.

indicial. See **indicative.**

indicium. See **indicia.**

indict; indite. Both words are pronounced /in-**dit**/. *Indict* means "to charge formally with a crime" (see **charge,** vb. (A)); *indite* means "to write, compose, dictate." A literary term, *indite* is rarely used today.

indictable offence. See **summary offence.**

indictable offense. See HYPALLAGE.

indictee (= a person charged with a crime) is not a newfangled passive noun in -*ee*; it has been used in English since the 16th century. See -EE.

***indicter.** See **indictor.**

indictment; information; presentment. In the federal courts of the U.S., a distinction exists between these charging instruments. Any offense punishable by death, or for imprisonment for more than one year

or by hard labor, must be prosecuted by *indictment*; any other offense may be prosecuted by either an *indictment* or an *information*. Fed. R. Crim. P. 7(a). An *information* may be filed without leave of court by a prosecutor, who need not obtain the approval of a grand jury. An *indictment*, by contrast, is issuable only by a grand jury. E.g.: "In some states, while the grand jury still functions, it has lost a great deal of its importance, since the district attorney can begin the case with a simple 'information,' which does as well as the *indictment*." Max Radin, *The Law and You* 110 (1948).

Presentments are not used in American federal procedure; formerly, a *presentment* was "the notice taken, or statement made, by a grand jury of any offense or unlawful state of affairs from their own knowledge or observation, without any bill of indictment laid before them" (*W2*).

Through a historical transference of meaning, *indictment*, which originally referred to the accusation of the grand jury, came to signify in the 16th century the document containing the accusation. (See HYPALLAGE.) In both AmE and BrE, *indictment* may refer to the proceeding or to the charging instrument known more particularly as a *bill of indictment*. See **arraignment.**

To a nonlawyer it may seem strange to see *information* (the charging instrument) used as a count noun: "The court granted the state's motion to join the two *informations* for trial." *State v. Pettigrew*, 3 A.3d 148, 155 (Conn. App. Ct. 2010).

indictor; *indicter. The -*or* spelling is preferred.

indifference; *indifferency. The second is archaic.

indigency; *indigence. *Indigency*, once the less common form, is now four times as common as *indigence* in AmE. *Indigence* ought therefore to be regarded as a NEEDLESS VARIANT.

indirect evidence. See **circumstantial evidence & direct evidence.**

indiscernible; *indiscernable. The first spelling is preferred.

indiscrete; indiscreet. See **discrete.**

indispensable; necessary; proper. Justice Harlan wrote, in *Provident Tradesmens Bank & Trust Co. v. Patterson*, 390 U.S. 102, 118 (1968): "To use the familiar but confusing terminology, the decision to proceed is a decision that the absent person is merely *necessary*, while the decision to dismiss is a decision that he is *indispensable*." With regard to possible parties to a lawsuit, *necessary* refers to those who should be included but need not be, *indispensable* to those without whom the action must be dismissed. In other words, in American legal English *indispensable* means "more necessary than *necessary*." The label *proper* "is used if the party is one who can be joined or not at plaintiff's option." Charles Alan Wright, *The Law of Federal Courts* 495 (5th ed. 1994).

The words *indispensable* and *necessary* are opposed in other legal contexts—e.g.: "This does not mean that the transcript must have been '*indispensable*' to the litigation to satisfy this test; it simply must have been '*necessary*' to counsel's effective performance or the court's handling of the case." 10 Charles Alan Wright et al., *Federal Practice and Procedure* § 2677, at 350–51 (1983).

The two words should not be redundantly coupled when no nuance is intended: "If it becomes *indispensably necessary* [read either *indispensable* or *necessary*] to the case to answer such a question, this Court must meet and decide it." *Baxter v. State*, 224 P.3d 1211, 1222 (Mont. 2009) (Warner, J., concurring). Similarly, the REDUNDANCY *indispensable necessity* occurs at least twice in *The Federalist*.

indisputable should receive its primary accent on the second, not the third, syllable /in-**dis**-pyoot-ə-bəl/. A common and acceptable pronunciation on both sides of the Atlantic is /in-di-**spyoo**-tə-bəl/.

indisputedly, misused for *indisputably* or *undisputedly*, is an odd error—e.g.:

- "Civil commitment *indisputedly* [read *indisputably*] entails a substantial curtailment of liberty." *Project Release v. Prevost*, 551 F.Supp. 1298, 1308 (E.D.N.Y. 1982).
- "She is the mother of three sons, which *indisputedly* [read *indisputably*] makes her the only justice to have experienced pregnancy." *All Eyes on Justice O'Connor*, Newsweek, 1 May 1989, at 34.

indite. See **indict.**

individual was formerly thought to be a newfangled barbarism as a noun substituting for *man*, *woman*, or *person*. Certainly, those more specific terms are generally to be preferred over *individual*, but this word should no longer be stigmatized. Still, *individual* is best confined to contexts in which the writer intends to distinguish the single (noncorporate) person from the group or crowd.

individualize; individuate. Both are commonly used, and they have basically the same sense ("to make individual in character, to give individuality to"); both are also so common that it would be inappropriate to call either a NEEDLESS VARIANT, and subtle writers may in fact intend nuances. *Individualize* is much more common in legal writing—e.g.:

- "This approach injects hypothetical extraneous considerations into the sentencing process and contradicts the judicially approved policy of *individualizing* sentences that are tailored to fit the offender." *U.S. v. Cavazos*, 530 F.2d 4, 6 (5th Cir. 1976).
- "The trial court would be required to evaluate significant quantities of *individualized* extrinsic evidence associated with Humana's affirmative defenses, and the hospitals' response to those defenses would implicate even more

such *individualized* evidence." *Sacred Heart Health Sys. v. Humana Military Healthcare Servs.*, 601 F.3d 1159, 1183 (11th Cir. 2010).

- "The trial court then concluded that generalized, rather than *individualized*, evidence would be sufficient to prove that the permit fees were excessive and that the class members had suffered an ascertainable loss." *Neighborhood Builders, Inc. v. Town of Madison*, 986 A.2d 278, 286 (Conn. 2010).

Indeed, in AmE, *individualize* has become a VOGUE WORD meaning "to humanize; to portray as an individual human being." Hence: "Even if the jury had been presented *individualized* evidence that he was a human being and that he had no extended record of violent crime, we cannot say that counsel was ineffective unless it is shown affirmatively that the death penalty would not have been imposed had the sentencing jury been afforded this testimony." *Milton v. Procunier*, 744 F.2d 1091, 1103 (5th Cir. 1984) (Tate, J., concurring).

Individuate is often used in scientific contexts and in Jungian psychology in highly technical senses, and ought generally to be confined to these uses.

individually. See **each (A).**

individual proprietor. See **sole proprietor.**

individuate. See **individualize.**

indorsation. See **indorsement.**

indorse. See **endorse.**

indorsee. See -EE.

indorsement; *indorsation.* Both terms mean "the act of indorsing"—that is, of placing one's signature on the reverse side of a negotiable instrument, sometimes with an additional notation, to transfer or guarantee the instrument or to acknowledge payment. *Indorsement* is the standard term. *Indorsation*, having always been rare, should be classified as a NEEDLESS VARIANT—e.g.: "The alleged indorsation [read *indorsement*] on the patent from the Grand Council of Rites, signed by Peter Spence, did not purport to give any authority to confer the craft degrees." *Bergera v. U.S.*, 297 F. 102, 107–08 (8th Cir. 1924). See **endorse.**

indorser. So spelled, even though its correlative is -EE. See -ER (A).

indubitably. See **clearly** & **obviously.**

inducement; inductance; induction. *Inducement* ordinarily means "that which influences or persuades." E.g.: "The interests of representative and represented must be so identical that the motive and *inducement* to protect and preserve may be assumed to be the same in each." *Webster v. State Mut. Life Assur. Co. of Worcester, Mass.*, 50 F.Supp. 11, 15 (S.D. Cal. 1943).

In pleading, it has an additional sense in BrE: "Matters of *inducement* are introductory averments stating who the parties are, how connected and other surrounding circumstances leading up to the matter in dispute, but not stating such matter" (quoted in *OED*). Hence: "The first count of the declaration, after the usual *inducement* of the plaintiff's good conduct, stated that, before the [defendant's] speaking and publishing [various] defamatory words . . . the plaintiff was . . . [a] clerk." *Lumby v. Allday*, (1831) 1 Cr. & J. 301, 148 Eng. Rep. 1434 (Ex.).

Induction, in the context of reasoning, means "the establishment of a general proposition from a number of particular instances." *Inductance* is a technical electrical term.

inducing breach of contract. See **tortious interference with contractual relations.**

inductee. See -EE.

induction. See **inducement.**

industrial property. See **intellectual property.**

industry. See **business.**

ineffective; ineffectual; inefficacious; inefficient. See **effective.**

INELEGANT VARIATION. "A draftsman should never be afraid of repeating a word as often as may be necessary in order to avoid ambiguity." Alison Russell, *Legislative Drafting and Forms* 103 (1938). H.W. Fowler referred to as "elegant variation" the ludicrous practice of never using the same word twice in the same sentence. When Fowler named this vice of language in the 1920s, *elegant* was almost a pejorative word, commonly associated with precious overrefinement. Today, however, the word has positive connotations. E.g.: "The opinion is not only accurate as to the state of the law, but is *elegantly* written." *Op. of the Justices to the Senate*, 668 N.E.2d 738, 761 (Mass. 1996).

Lest the reader misapprehend that the subject of this article is a virtue rather than a vice in writing, I have renamed it unambiguously: *in*elegant variation. The rule of thumb with regard to undue repetition is that one should not repeat a word in the same sentence if it can be felicitously avoided. But this is hardly an absolute proscription.

The problem is that if one uses terms that vary slightly in form, the reader is likely to deduce that some DIFFERENTIATION is intended. So one does not write *punitive damages*, *punitory damages, and *punishment damages* all in the same opinion or brief, lest the reader infer that one intends to convey a distinction. Yet one judge did just that in a single dissent. *See Jones v. Fisher*, 166 N.W.2d 175, 224–25 (Wis. 1969) (Hansen, J., dissenting) (using all three forms). Other judges have used alternative forms in a single sentence: "This brings us back to Florida, where the accident occurred, where the action was brought and the damages awarded, and where the *punitory* and deterrent effects of the *punitive* damages awarded in this

case would have their greatest impact." *Northwestern Nat'l Cas. Co. v. McNulty*, 307 F.2d 432, 435 (5th Cir. 1962). See **punitive.**

One frequently encounters writing on criminal law in which *informer* and *informant* are used alternatively, but with no purpose—e.g.: "The second district determined that the possible significance of the *informer's* testimony outweighed any public interest in favor of nondisclosure of an *informant's* identity." *Thomas v. State*, 28 So.3d 240, 244–45 (Fla. Dist. Ct. App. 2010). (See **informant.**) The second use could have been easily avoided by using *him* or *her*. The following example of inelegant variation occurred within the space of two sentences: "The objection is to the breach of the restriction, to the possibility of litigation flowing from that breach, and to the reduced *marketability* of the title with that cloud hanging over it. We believe these factors rendered the title *unmerchantable*." *Johnston v. State Bank*, 195 N.W.2d 126, 129 (Iowa 1972). See **marketable.**

The basic type of variation found objectionable by H.W. Fowler is the simple change from the straightforward term to some slightly more fanciful synonym, as here:

- "Many of the *complainants* in this case were *protestants* [read *likewise complainants*] at the hearing in 1948 when the fuel clause was put in effect." *State ex rel. Utilities Comm'n v. Carolina Power & Light Co.*, 109 S.E.2d 253, 263 (N.C. 1959).
- "A petition may be *attacked* as insufficient to state a cause of action at any stage of the proceedings and may be *assailed* [read *attacked*] on such ground in the appellate court for the first time." *Buda v. Humble*, 517 N.W.2d 622, 624 (Neb. Ct. App. 1994). On the use of *such* in this example, see **such.**
- Plaintiff appears to have abandoned any assertion that . . . the *will* was invalid as to form, arguing only that the trial court erred in failing to annul the *testament* [read *will*] for ingratitude, undue influence, and fraud." *In re Succession of Rachal*, 7 So.3d 132, 133 (La. Ct. App. 2009).

Equally common in modern legal writing is the switch from one form of a word to another. For example, Justice White alternated *contributory neglect* with *contributory negligence* throughout his opinion in *Mosheuvel v. District of Columbia*, 191 U.S. 247, 252 (1903). Similar examples of the distemper are legion:

- "His counsel, with *commendable* candor, includes in his brief a statement to the effect he concedes that. . . . Even in the absence of this *commendatory* [read *commendable*] concession, this court would have no difficulty concluding . . . ." *Redman v. Mutual Benefit Health & Accident Ass'n*, 327 P.2d 854, 860 (Kan. 1958). On the use of *such* in this example, see **such.**
- "The *fictional* John Doe has no constitutional rights to be threatened or violated since there can be no enforcement of a judgment adverse to him. . . . As if confused by too much fiction, in its reasoning the Court returned to the constitutional rights of a *fictional* entity. The defendant John Doe is a *ficticious* [read *fictional*] person created

under the provisions of the statute." Collins Denny, *Uninsured Motorists and the Virginia Court*, 48 Va. L. Rev. 1177, 1186–87 (1962).

- "The only way they would be interested parties as to the *residue* of the decedent's estate would be if the *residuum* [read *residuary*] devise to the trust lapsed such that the *residue* of the estate would then pass to them, in whole or part, as intestate heirs of the decedent." *In re Estate of Corbin*, 66 S.W.3d 84, 90 (Mo. Ct. App. 2001).
- "In this limited situation, however, where the grantor contends that it was not her *intention* [read *intent*] to gift the property by titling it in joint tenancy, summary judgment is inappropriate and the trial court must consider the grantor's rebuttal evidence on the issue of *intent*." *Brousseau v. Brousseau*, 927 A.2d 773, 777 (Vt. 2007).

Certain pairs may lend themselves to this snare: *arbiter* and *arbitrator, adjudicative* and **adjudicatory, investigative* and *investigatory, exigency* and *exigence*. In fact, it sometimes seems that amateurish writers believe that NEEDLESS VARIANTS were made for this specific stylistic purpose.

Particularly confusing are pointless switches from a phrase such as *admiralty law* to *maritime law*—e.g.: "Finally, the court held that traditional concepts of the role of *admiralty law* did not require the finding of a substantial maritime relationship because allowing the parties to pursue state law remedies would not disturb the federal interest of maintaining the uniformity of *maritime law*." Jeanmarie B. Tade, *The Texas and Louisiana Anti-Indemnity Statutes as Applied to Oil and Gas Industry Offshore Contracts*, 24 Hous. L. Rev. 665, 692 (1987).

"The point to be observed," wrote Fowler, "is that, even if the words meant exactly the same, it would be better to keep the first selected on duty than to change guard" (*MEU2* 150).

inept. See **inapt.**

inequity; iniquity. The first means "unfairness"; the second, "evil."

in error. See **error** (B).

in esse; *in posse*. *In esse* = in actual existence; in being. *In posse* = potential; not realized. E.g.:

- "The test for determining whether the insured wage earner contributes to the support of a child *in posse* is whether the wage earner was contributing to the support of the mother at the time of death." *Garcia v. Sullivan*, 883 F.2d 18, 19 n.1 (5th Cir. 1989).
- "The defendant owed no duty of care to a being that was not *in esse* at the time of the negligence." Bonnie Steinbock, *Life Before Birth* 107 (1992).

There is no good reason why the phrases *in being* and *potential* should not be substituted in place of these LATINISMS. See **in being, esse** & *de bene esse*.

in every case. See **case** (A).

in excess of. Wordy for *more than* or *over*. See **excess of, in.**

*inexpense is not, by the normal measures, a legitimate English word; it is listed in no major unabridged dictionary and does not fill a need in the language. E.g.:

- "Even an absentee landlord could *with relative inexpense* [read *rather inexpensively*] employ someone regularly present to remove these hazards." *Liability for Failure to Remove or Render Safe Ice and Snow on Common Passageways and Approaches*, 41 Colum. L. Rev. 349, 352 (1941).
- "The arbitral process, for instance, nearly always exceeds the judicial process in speed, efficiency, and *inexpense* [read *inexpensiveness*]." *Bright v. Norshipco and Norfolk Shipbuilding & Drydock Corp.*, 951 F.Supp. 95, 98 (E.D. Va. 1997).

See NEOLOGISMS & BACK-FORMATIONS.

inexpert, adj.; **nonexpert,** adj. An important distinction exists. *Inexpert* = unskilled <the novice's inexpert cross-examination>. *Nonexpert* = not of or by an expert, but not necessarily unskilled <a rule permitting proof by nonexpert testimony>.

inexplicable (= unexplainable) is accented on the second syllable /in-**ek**-spli-kə-bəl/ or the third /in-ek-**splik**-ə-bəl/.

inexpressible; *inexpressable. The first spelling is correct.

in extenso (= unabridged) is a pompous LEGALISM for the simple English phrase *in full*. E.g.:

- "It is not the duty of this court to sift and glean the record *in extenso* [read *in full*] to find facts which will support an [argument]." *Keplin v. Hardware Mut. Cas. Co.*, 129 N.W.2d 321, 323 (1964).
- "We cited and quoted *in extenso* [read, probably, *extensively*] the Tenth Circuit case of *Thomas v. Hunter*." *Van v. Jones*, 475 F.3d 292, 298 (6th Cir. 2007).

See LATINISMS.

in extremis (= at the point of death; at the last gasp) is better known than most LATINISMS and may be used purposefully as a EUPHEMISM. E.g.: "One may liken the present status of the six debtor entities to a patient *in extremis*, on life support in a hospital." *In re W. Coast Int'l Pain Med., Inc.*, 435 B.R. 569, 578 (Bankr. N.D. Ind. 2010).

in fact. See **de facto** (B).

infamous crime. Originally, an *infamous crime* was one for which part of the penalty was infamy, i.e., being declared ineligible to serve on a jury, hold public office, or testify. These consequences were abolished in the 19th century. In England, the Larceny Act 1861 (repealed) defined *infamous crime* as "the abominable crime of buggery, committed with mankind or with beast." That statutory meaning is long since defunct. More commonly, legal writers equate the phrase with felony.

But it is simplistic to say, as writers occasionally do, that "an 'infamous crime' is a felony." C. Gordon Post, *An Introduction to the Law* 108 (1963). In fact, *infamous crime* is something of a chameleon-hued phrase that takes its meaning from the context. The California Supreme Court has held that, although for some purposes any felony is an infamous crime, in the context of disfranchisement the phrase is limited to crimes involving moral corruption and dishonesty. *See Otsuka v. Hite*, 414 P.2d 412 (Cal. 1966) (en banc).

For purposes of the Fifth Amendment to the U.S. Constitution, which requires an indictment or presentment for "a capital or otherwise infamous crime," the canon of construction termed *ejusdem generis* suggests that we should look to the potential penalty to decide whether a crime is infamous. "The potential penalty is bound to control," says one authority, "because the determination must be made in the early stages of the prosecution." Rollin M. Perkins, *Criminal Law* 19 (1957). (See **ejusdem generis.**) If we translate *capital or otherwise infamous* to "involving capital punishment or similarly grave penalties," it remains problematical to determine what penalty is grave enough to be considered similar to capital punishment.

In sum, *infamous crime* is a vague term in modern usage. See CHAMELEON-HUED WORDS.

infancy = the state or condition of being a minor. E.g.: "At birth a child enters the condition of infancy—a condition [that] ceases at the age of eighteen years, or, rather, at the first moment of the day preceding the eighteenth birthday." William Geldart, *Introduction to English Law* 41 (D.C.M. Yardley ed., 9th ed. 1984). Cf. **nonage.** See **minority (A).**

infant (= a minor) is peculiar to legal language; in nonlegal contexts, *infant* means "a small child; a baby." But in law it is quite possible to write of, say, a *17-year-old infant.* E.g.: "A petition for the expenditure of the funds of an *infant* must comply with the provisions related to *infants*, incompetents, and conservatees." *Collura v. Collura*, 846 N.Y.S.2d 897, 900 (Dist. Ct. 2007). The more usual—and less confusing—term is *minor.* Cf. **infanticide.** See **minority (A)** & **age of capacity.**

infanticide = (1) the killing of a baby, usu. by a parent or with a parent's consent; or (2) a parent who kills a baby, or one who kills a baby with a parent's consent. Sense 2 invariably takes an article <a merciless infanticide>, whereas sense 1 only sometimes takes an article <the infanticide committed by a deranged father> <infanticide committed by a mother with postpartum depression>.

According to one eminent authority, not every killer of a baby has committed infanticide. The killing of another person's child is simple murder or manslaughter. Infanticide, by definition, must be by or on behalf of a parent. *See* Glanville Williams, *The Sanctity of Life and the Criminal Law* 13 (1957).

Despite the legal meaning of *infant* (= a person under the age of majority, usu. 18 years old), the word *infanticide* is restricted to baby-killing. A parent who kills a 17-year-old child would not be called

an "infanticide" (sense 2). (In England, the Infanticide Act applies to the killing of a child up to one year old.) The slightly broader term *child-slaying*, however, might cover situations in which children who are old enough to walk—and up to the age of 18—are killed. By contrast, the most restrictive term is *neonaticide*, which refers to the killing of a newborn. Among the three terms—*infanticide*, *child-slaying*, and *neonaticide*—the first two are the most emotive terms because they are widely known, and the third is a clinical, abstract description that many would read or hear without understanding. See **infant.**

in fault. See **at fault.**

infeasible; *unfeasible.** The first is better.

infect = (1) to taint with crime; or (2) to involve (a ship or cargo) in the seizure to which contraband is liable. This verb is among the more vivid METAPHORS in traditional legal terminology.

infectious is sometimes erroneously rendered **infectuous.* See **contagious.**

infeft is a Scottish variant of *enfeoffed.* See **feoff.*

in feodo simpliciter. See **fee simple (A).**

infeoff. See **feoff.*

infer is generally correctly used in legal writing. Properly, it means "to deduce; to reason from premises to a conclusion." E.g.: "From this difference the court *inferred* that Congress intended subsection (f) to have no deadline." *Lantz v. Commissioner*, 607 F.3d 479, 481 (7th Cir. 2010).

A common mistake among nonlawyers is to use *infer* when *imply* (= to hint at; suggest) is the correct word. Yet this nonlawyer's blunder has occasionally insinuated itself into legal writing. E.g.: "Exclusion from venires focuses on the inherent attributes of the excluded group and *infers* [read *implies*] its inferiority." *U.S. v. Leslie*, 759 F.2d 381, 392 (5th Cir. 1985). See **imply.**

In Scots law, *infer* is used in a special sense: "to involve as a consequence"—e.g.: "In lay usage only a person infers, but in legal usage such and such a course of conduct, for example, infers a penalty." Andrew D. Gibb, *Students' Glossary of Scottish Legal Terms* 45 (A.G.M. Duncan ed., 2d ed. 1982).

inferable. See **inferrable.*

inference. One *draws*, not *makes*, inferences. If one says "to make an inference" (like "to make a deduction"), then many listeners will confuse *inference* with *implication*. The verb *to draw* is therefore clearer. See **infer.**

inferentially. This fancy word often displaces a more common substitute, such as *seemingly* or *we can infer* *that.* The *OED* states that *inferentially* = in an inferential manner, but allows that it is used "sometimes qualifying the whole clause or statement: = as an inference, as may be inferred." This use defies explication but is common in legal writing—e.g.:

- "A jury is entitled to credit the testimony as a factor in the analysis of whether the state has *inferentially* established intent to sell beyond a reasonable doubt." *State v. Wright,* 707 A.2d 295, 299 (Conn. Ct. App. 1998).
- "*Inferentially*, at least, denial of the Rule 2-602(b) request under that circumstance would necessarily amount to an abuse of discretion." *Silbersack v. ACandS, Inc.,* 938 A.2d 855, 861 (Md. 2008).
- "Uncomplicated administrative records in these cases suggest *inferentially*, but unmistakably, that a transfer for fair market value was what each of the appellants intended." *Normand v. Dir. of Office of Medicaid,* 933 N.E.2d 658, 665 (Mass. App. Ct. 2010).

See SENTENCE ADVERBS. Cf. **hopefully** & **thankfully.**

inferior; superior. A. Generally. These comparative adjectives cannot act as adverbs. E.g.: "The statute is unconstitutional not only because it *treats* former mental patients differently from *and inferior to* [read *and as inferior to*] convicts, but also because it presumptively denies former mental patients the opportunity to establish that they no longer present the danger against which the statute was intended to guard." *Galioto v. Department of Treasury,* 602 F.Supp. 682, 690 (D.N.J. 1985).

Only etymologically are these words comparatives; they take *to,* not *than.* They are qualified by *much* or *far,* not by *more,* which is a fairly common error.

B. In Classifying Courts. Traditionally, the hierarchical system of courts within a given jurisdiction is broken down into *inferior courts* and *superior courts.* Many American judges feel uncomfortable with these terms, preferring to speak of *trial courts* and *appellate courts. Inferior* suggests, to many readers and listeners, a lower level of competence.

British legal writers, however, use the classification regularly, not least because many courts have both trial and appellate jurisdiction. In England and Wales, the superior courts include the House of Lords, the Court of Appeal, and the High Court; inferior courts include circuit courts and magistrates' courts.

inferior court. See **inferior (B)** & **higher court.**

*****inferrable; *inferrible.** The preferred form is *inferable*, accented on the second syllable /in-**fər**-ə-bəl/. Seventy-five years ago **inferrible* was considered the best spelling, because of the rule that a consonant should be doubled after a stressed syllable. *Inferable,* which has now ousted the other spelling, is anomalous. See DOUBLING OF FINAL CONSONANTS.

infeudation (= the granting of an estate in fee; enfeoffment) is rarer than both its equivalent, *enfeoffment,* and its derivative, *subinfeudation.* E.g.: "The tenures created during this era of universal *infeudation* were as various as the conditions [that] the tenants made with

their new chiefs or were forced to accept from them." Henry S. Maine, *Ancient Law* 192 (17th ed. 1901). See **subinfeudation.**

in fine is a turgid, legalistic phrase for *in conclusion* or *finally.* E.g.:

- "*In fine* [read *In conclusion,* or *Finally*], the jury would be warranted in finding that the defendants' conduct was a high-handed and unlawful means of collecting a debt." *Ash v. Cohn,* 194 A. 174, 177 (N.J. 1937).
- "*In fine* [read *In conclusion,* or *Finally*], we reject appellants' claim that the district court's treatment of the summaries unduly prejudiced their trial." *U.S. v. Smyth,* 556 F.2d 1179, 1184 (5th Cir. 1977).
- "*In fine* [read *In conclusion,* or *Finally*], we agree with the district court that full restitution would be inappropriate, even though PEU did fail to meet all of its *Hudson* obligations." *Prescott v. County of El Dorado,* 177 F.3d 1102, 1109 (9th Cir. 1999).

infinitely (= endlessly, limitlessly) for *eminently* (= to a high degree) is either gross OVERSTATEMENT or a MALAPROPISM—e.g.:

- "The Court concludes that this distinction is *infinitely* [read *eminently*] reasonable and is a proper approach to maintaining the prison's compelling interest in maintaining security of the institution." *Kelly v. Brewer,* 378 F.Supp. 447, 455 (S.D. Iowa 1974).
- "Greenhouse paints a picture of a jurist who was both confident and *infinitely* [read *eminently*] capable yet highly sensitive to criticism, especially from his fellow jurists." Maxine Goodman, *Becoming Justice Blackmun,* 43 Hous. Lawyer 68, 68 (May–June 2006) (book review).

infirm is frequently used in reference to fatal weaknesses, whether constitutional or statutory. In fact, *constitutionally infirm* might accurately be labeled a legal CLICHÉ. E.g.:

- "The trial court's approach suffers from no *infirmities* warranting reversal." *Folse v. Folse,* 738 So.2d 1040, 1052 (La. 1999).
- "Richards attacks his guilty plea to all counts as constitutionally *infirm* because it resulted from undue coercion by the government." *U.S. v. Kumar,* 617 F.3d 612, 616 (2d Cir. 2010).

See **fatal (A).**

in flagrante delicto (= red-handed; in the act of committing an offense) is a term now more commonly used for polysyllabic humor in nonlegal contexts than as a serious word in law. See LATINISMS.

Some writers mistake the spelling—e.g.:

- "We do not doubt that NASA blushes whenever one of its own is caught *in flagrante delictu* [read *in flagrante delicto* or *red-handed*]." *Norton v. Macy,* 417 F.2d 1161, 1167 (D.C. Cir. 1969).
- "Two wrongs, usually of very unequal weight, should never equal a right to escape when caught *flagrante delictu* [read *in flagrante delicto* or *red-handed*]." *Commonwealth v. Weisenthal,* 535 A.2d 600, 601 (Pa. 1988).

See ITALICS (C).

inflammable. See **flammable.**

*****inflatus.** See **afflatus.**

inflict; afflict. These terms are infrequently confused. *Afflict* takes *with*; *inflict* takes *on*. Living things, especially humans, are *afflicted with* diseases; inanimate objects, especially scourges or punishments, are *inflicted on* people. But misusing *inflict* for *afflict* is increasingly common—e.g.:

- "As the evidence indicates, the severed muscles in the plaintiff's face have *inflicted* [read *afflicted*] him with a tic." *Rogers v. Moody*, 242 A.2d 276, 279 (Pa. 1968).
- "The problems *inflicting* [read *afflicting*] this case and ultimately causing a remand have their genesis in the indictment." *Honc v. State*, 698 S.W.2d 218, 220 (Tex. App.—Corpus Christi 1985).

inflicter; inflictor. The first spelling is better.

influence. The first syllable, not the second, receives the primary accent /**in**-floo-əns/, whether the part of speech is noun or verb.

*****inforce** is an obsolete spelling of *enforce*, except in the prefixed *reinforce*. See EN- & **enforce.**

inform, in the sense "to determine, give form to, permeate," is somewhat archaic, but it is common in scholarly legal writing—e.g.:

- "Our conclusion in this regard is *informed*, in part, by our belief that some measure of deference is owed to CBP due to its considered expertise in carrying out its mission of protecting the border." *Tabbaa v. Chertoff*, 509 F.3d 89, 106 (2d Cir. 2007).
- "Our decision is *informed* in part by the recent opinion of the United States Supreme Court in *Safeco Insurance Co. v. Burr*." *Whitfield v. Radian Guar., Inc.*, 501 F.3d 262, 263 (3d Cir. 2007).
- "The fact that a tortfeasor's payments have never been collateral sources *informs* our analysis of whether a settlement payment made by a tortfeasor's insurer is a collateral source." *Do v. American Family Mut. Ins. Co.*, 779 N.W.2d 853, 862 (Minn. 2010) (Anderson, J., concurring).

informal contract; simple contract; parol contract. These phrases each denote the same idea: a contract that derives its efficacy not from the form of the transaction but from its substance. Williston preferred the term *informal contract* because *simple contract* is misleading. *See* 1 Samuel Williston & W.H.E. Jaeger, *A Treatise on the Law of Contract* § 12, at 22 (3d ed. 1957). The phrase *parol contract* is even more likely to mislead, because, though it suggests an oral contract, it (surprisingly) can be in writing. See **formal contract.**

informant; informer. Both terms are used in reference to those who confidentially supply police with information about crimes. *Informant* is twice as common in American legal contexts, *informer* slightly more common in British ones. The Evanses write that *informant* is neutral, whereas *informer*, which acquired strong connotations of detestation in the 17th and 18th centuries, remains a connotatively charged term. Bergen Evans & Cornelia Evans, *A*

Dictionary of Contemporary American Usage 245 (1957). If that is true in lay contexts, it certainly is not true in legal writing. See INELEGANT VARIATION.

in forma pauperis (= in the form of a poor person; not liable for costs of court) is a TERM OF ART in AmE (but is no longer used in BrE). E.g.:

- "Defendant timely filed a notice of appeal along with a motion to proceed *in forma pauperis*." *State v. Constance*, 248 S.W.3d 696, 697 (Mo. Ct.. App. 2008).
- "The standard for granting a litigant leave to proceed *in forma pauperis* on appeal is more lenient than the standard for granting a COA." Catherine T. Struve, *Power, Protocol, and Practicality*, 84 Notre Dame L. Rev. 2053, 2062 (2009).

Judges frequently use the abbreviation *IFP* <an IFP motion>.

Where less than the entire phrase is used, *pauper* should appear rather than *forma pauperis*. E.g.:

- "Subsequent to the trial court proceedings, plaintiffs filed for *forma pauperis* [read *pauper*] status." *Herbert v. Archdiocese of New Orleans*, 739 So.2d 928, 929 n.1 (5th Cir. 1999). On the use of *subsequent to* in that sentence, see *****subsequent to.**
- "Although the movant neglected to sign the motion itself, he did sign the *forma pauperis* [read *pauper*] affidavit included with the motion." *Penn v. State*, 209 S.W.3d 533, 534 (Mo. Ct. App. 2006).

See **pauper.**

Additionally, in the full phrase one should italicize the *in*, not just *forma pauperis*: "Late in the trial, Wellington, proceeding in *forma pauperis* [read *in forma pauperis*], unsuccessfully submitted an ex parte application." *U.S. v. Nivica*, 887 F.2d 1110, 1117 (1st Cir. 1989). See ITALICS (C).

information. See **indictment** & **knowledge** (A).

information and belief. In traditional pleading, an allegation made only on information—unaccompanied by the pleader's asserting that he or she believes the allegation to be true—is insufficient. It has therefore become standard practice for pleaders to make allegations *on information and belief*.

Among those not used to the practice, it can be confusing. Take a count that reads: "On information and belief, a vice-president of the Bank then recorded the incorrect account number on the deposit slip." Grammatically speaking, *on information and belief* refers to the vice-president's state of mind. Actually, though, the allegation is shorthand for this: *On information and belief, the plaintiff alleges that the vice-president of the Bank then . . . .* The judges and lawyers who read such sentences are never misled because they understand the JARGON, which saves several words. If such a pleading comes before a jury, however, it will likely cause confusion.

informative; *informatory. The second is a NEEDLESS VARIANT, except in bridge, the card game.

informer. See **informant.**

in foro conscientiae (lit., "in the forum of conscience") is used in the sense "privately or morally rather than legally" (*W3*). E.g.:

- "Although the proposal was not accepted by the Borough, its equitable significance *in foro conscientiae* lies in its portrayal of the initial attitude of the complainant toward the project." *Canda Realty v. Borough of Carteret*, 42 A.2d 859, 862 (N.J. Ch. 1945).
- "Since the unextinguished debt remained *in foro conscientiae* as obligatory, it was itself a sufficient consideration for the new promise." *Nyhus v. Travel Mgmt. Corp.*, 466 F.2d 440, 451 (D.C. Cir. 1972).

See LATINISMS.

infra; supra. These ubiquitous signals could advantageously be banished from all legal writing. One writer calls them "disconsolate inadequacies," explaining: "They border on the discourteous unless the point referred to is but a few lines away, and in that event they are not needed." Raymond S. Wilkins, "The Argument of an Appeal," in *Advocacy and the King's English* 277, 281 (George Rossman ed., 1960). See ***ante*** & ***supra.***

infract (= to break in; violate; infringe) is chiefly an Americanism. Even so, it is little used outside legal writing. E.g.:

- "We find that article 6 was *infracted* because no treaty provision justifies the second boarding or the ultimate seizure of the La Rosa." *U.S. v. Postal*, 589 F.2d 862, 872 (5th Cir. 1979).
- "The court's determination that chapter 93A was *infracted* appears sustainable." *Peckham v. Continental Cas. Ins. Co.*, 895 F.2d 830, 842 (1st Cir. 1990).

See **infringe.**

infraction. See **breach (A).**

infrequent; *unfrequent. The second is a NEEDLESS VARIANT.

infringe. A. The Verb Generally. H.W. Fowler held that *infringe* is best used transitively, as here:

- "The court in Laird rejected the claim, ruling that the mere existence of the data gathering system *infringed* no rights since there had been no objective harm or anticipated future harm." *City of Airway Heights v. Dilley*, 724 P.2d 407, 409 (Wash. Ct. App. 1986).
- "Even assuming that the School Board had a racially discriminatory policy or custom as alleged, the enforcement of that policy or custom in this instance was directed at the school and *infringed* no rights of White guaranteed under the Fourteenth Amendment or by contract." *White v. School Bd. of Hillsborough County*, 636 F.Supp.2d 1272, 1277 (M.D. Fla. 2007).

The transitive is especially useful where the passive voice is called for—e.g.: "The defendant has failed to show either that his rights *were infringed* or that there was a procedural irregularity in either 1997 guilty plea." *State v. Otero*, 31 So.3d 1125, 1130 (La. Ct. App. 2010).

Rather than *infringe upon* or *on*, some other verb such as *impinge*, *encroach*, or *trespass* is better when an intransitive verb is desired—e.g.:

- "When a city annexes land within a county's borders, the city *infringes upon* [read *encroaches* or *impinges upon*] a county's governmental function." *Sarpey County v. City of Gretna*, 678 N.W.2d 740, 745–46 (Neb. 2004).
- "It is well established that arbitration is merely a choice of dispute resolution and does not *infringe upon* [read *impinge on*] statutory protections." *Nino v. Jewelry Exch., Inc.*, 609 F.3d 191, 203 (3d Cir. 2010).

See **infract.**

B. And *impinge*. *Impinge* is used intransitively only; it is followed by *on* or *upon* <they impinged on the voter's rights>. *Infringe*, by contrast, may be either transitive or intransitive <to infringe someone's rights> <to infringe on someone's rights>.

Though *impinge* and *infringe* are often used as if they were interchangeable, we might keep in mind the following connotations: *impinge* = (lit.) to strike or dash *upon* something else, whereas *infringe* = to break in (damage, violate, or weaken).

Impinge should not be used without an object to impinge *on*—e.g.:

- "These policies also *impinge* [on what or whom?] when we consider the potential for abuse." *Holodook v. Spencer*, 324 N.E.2d 338, 345 (N.Y. 1974). The writer of that sentence should have supplied the object.
- "Count One also contended that the guidelines' 'definitions for allocating SAF funds to CIOs' are unconstitutionally vague because persons of ordinary intelligence must guess at their meaning, and unlawfully overbroad because they *impinge* [read *impinge on*] constitutionally protected activity." *Rosenberger v. Rector & Visitors of Univ. of Va.*, 18 F.3d 269, 274–75 (4th Cir. 1994).

See **trespass.**

infringement. See **breach (A).**

infringer. So spelled.

in future. This phrase is BrE, perhaps a direct translation of the Latin phrase *in futuro*. AmE uses the definite article: *in the future*. See ***in futuro.***

in futuro is a legalistic LATINISM conveying (or failing to convey) an elementary notion for which the English language has adequate words—e.g.:

- "It is our view that this is not the type of *in futuro* [read *future*] allegation for a warrant that the legislature intended to prohibit by this statute." *Bernie v. State*, 524 So.2d 988, 992 (Fla. 1988).
- "An earlier agreement between plaintiff and the stable contained an exculpatory clause releasing the latter from liability for *in futuro* [read *future*] acts of negligence." *Schmidt v. U.S.*, 912 P.2d 871, 872 (Okla. 1996).
- "Because a permanent injunction acts *in futuro* [read *in the future*] and gives Plaintiff no vested right in the judgment of the trial court, there is no retroactivity bar to applying a new statute after the initial issuance of an injunction." *Landolt v. Glendale Shooting Club, Inc.*, 18 S.W.3d 101, 105 (Mo. Ct. App. 2000).

See **in future** & ***in praesenti.***

ingenious; ingenuous. These words, virtual antonyms, are frequently confused. *Ingenious* means "crafty, skillful, inventive." *Ingenuous* means "artless, innocent, simple."

*ingraft. See **engraft.**

*ingrandize. See **aggrandize.**

ingress. See **egress.**

*ingross. See **engross.**

in gross, when used of servitudes, means "personal as distinguished from appurtenant to land." The phrase may be placed either before or after the noun it modifies—e.g.:

- "A *servitude in gross* threatens the servient owner's autonomy, and thus deserves scrutiny." Gerald Korngold, *Privately Held Conservation Servitudes*, 63 Tex. L. Rev. 433, 464 (1984).
- "This reasoning . . . does not adequately address whether the burden should run if, as in the case of *in gross* conservation *servitudes*, there is never a benefited parcel." *Id.* at 472.

Cf. **run (B).**

*inhabitability. See **habitability.**

in haec verba (= in these words) is the worst sort of puffed-up LATINISM for an ordinary idea—*verbatim* invariably being a good substitute. Often the term is used as an unhyphenated PHRASAL ADJECTIVE. E.g.: "Nevertheless, the use of *in haec verba* pleadings on defamation charges is favored." *Asay v. Hallmark Cards, Inc.*, 594 F.2d 692, 699 (8th Cir. 1979). The sentence would be far more comprehensible without the LATINISM, and with a few more words: *The use of pleadings that give the defamatory words verbatim is favored.* See **verbatim.** Cf. *ipsissima verba.*

in hand. See **at hand.**

inhere. A. Preposition with. *Inhere* takes the preposition *in*; it will not tolerate *within*. "But such was the nature of the federal system; clumsiness and inefficiencies *inhered within* [read *in*] its very structure." Frederick S. Calhoun, *Westering and the Law*, 1 Wyo. L. Rev. 603, 612 n.23 (2001).
B. For *inure.* This MALAPROPISM is a stunning one—e.g.: "The benefit of the enhancement *inhered* [read *inured*] to all users and all listeners, no matter what apparatus was employed for playback purposes." *U.S. v. Chaudhry*, 850 F.2d 851, 855 (1st Cir. 1988). See **inure.**

inherence; inherency. *Inherence* = (1) [generally] the quality of being an essential or innate characteristic; or (2) [in law] the vesting of something by right, grant, or privilege. In general, *inherency* is a NEEDLESS VARIANT. But in intellectual-property law, the *inherency doctrine* is the rule that anticipation of a patent can be inferred despite a missing element in a prior-art reference if the missing element is either necessarily present in or a natural result of the product or process, and a person of ordinary skill in the art would know it.

inherent takes *in*, not *to*—e.g.:

- "These risks are *inherent to* [read *inherent in*] profit-driven private enforcement of an overbroad law like Rule 10b-5." Amanda M. Rose, *Reforming Securities-Litigation Reform*, 108 Colum. L. Rev. 1301, 1363 (2008).
- "I conclude this Part by discussing two limitations on the judicial role *inherent to* [read *inherent in*] the proposed interpretive approach." Goodwin Liu, *Rethinking Constitutional Welfare Rights*, 61 Stan. L. Rev. 203, 228–29 (2008).
- "In lieu of the top-down approach *inherent to* [read *inherent in*] legal scholarship where formal actions by the state determine the extant level of intellectual-property coverage, I adopt the bottom-up approach of the new institutional economics literature." Jonathan M. Barnett, *Property as Process*, 119 Yale L.J. 384, 388 (2009).

The use of *inherent* in the following sentence resulted from ignorance of the word's meaning (as if it were equivalent to *prejudicial* or *inflammatory*): "Nothing in the letters is of such *an inherent* [read *a prejudicial* or *an inflammatory*] nature as to inflame the passions of the jury or invoke its sympathies." *Jackson v. Johns-Manville Sales Corp.*, 750 F.2d 1314, 1319 (5th Cir. 1985). See **inhere.**

inheritability; *inheritableness. *Inheritability* is standard, *inheritableness* being a NEEDLESS VARIANT—e.g.: "The *inheritableness* [read *inheritability*] of a knight's fee was accompanied by the rule of primogeniture." Alan Harding, *A Social History of English Law* 34 (1966).

inheritable; heritable; hereditary. As between the first two, the first is the more common; it means "capable of being inherited"—e.g.:

- "Lands held in feudal knight service immediately after the Conquest were not freely *inheritable.*" Thomas F. Bergin & Paul G. Haskell, *Preface to Estates in Land and Future Interests* 7 (2d ed. 1984).
- "In the twelfth century the term *fee* came to be used to designate an *inheritable* interest in land rather than a mere life interest." Roger A. Cunningham et al., *The Law of Property* 15 n.6 (2d ed. 1993).

Heritable is infrequent enough today to be classed a NEEDLESS VARIANT for most purposes, although it persists in Scotland and in civil-law jurisdictions.

The negative form of the adjective has been rendered both *uninheritable* (*OED*) and *nonheritable* (*W3*). The latter is more common in AmE—e.g.: "It would create an estate in fee simple which . . . would be *nonheritable.*" William F. Fratcher, *Bequests of Orts*, 48 Mo. L. Rev. 476, 478 (1983).

Hereditary has a more restricted sense: "descending by inheritance from generation to generation." E.g.:

---

456 *inheritableness

"From this negative conclusion concerning a claimed constitutional protection, the district court implied a constitutional prohibition against legislative protection of *hereditary* rights to property." *Brady v. City of Dubuque*, 495 N.W.2d 701, 704 (Iowa 1993). See **hereditable** & **heredity**.

***inheritableness.** See **inheritability**.

inheritance. See **descent (B)** & **heredity**.

inheritor; heritor. See **heir (A)**.

inheritrix; inheritress. See SEXISM (C).

inhibitory; *inhibitive. The second is a NEEDLESS VARIANT.

in his own right; in her own right. See **right, in one's own.**

in-house counsel. See **house counsel.**

inimical (= hostile, injurious, adverse), a common word in legal writing, is almost a CLICHÉ in place of *adverse*, especially in collocation with the word *interests*. "The fact of the convictions provided Employer with a reasonable basis to conclude that Claimant had acted in a manner *inimical to* its interests and in a manner that represents a disregard of the standards of behavior that it may expect of an employee." *Smith v. Unemployment Compen. Bd. of Review*, 967 A.2d 1042, 1047 (Pa. Commw. Ct. 2009).

Inimicable for *inimical* is a fairly common error. The *OED* records *inimicable* as a "rare" adjective: it is not rare enough in AmE. E.g.:

- "For anything believed to be *inimicable* [read *inimical*] to his best interests can be thwarted or prevented by simply revoking the trust or amending it in such a way as to conform to his wishes." *Farkas v. Williams*, 125 N.E.2d 600, 607 (Ill. 1955).
- "They argue that Tullos was on board the rig for purposes *inimicable* [read *inimical*] to the legitimate interests of the rig owner and therefore was owed no duty of care by the vessel owner." *Tullos v. Res. Drilling, Inc.*, 750 F.2d 380, 385 (5th Cir. 1985).

in initio. See *ab initio.*

in invitum is unnecessary JARGON meaning "against an unwilling person." E.g.:

- "[A constructive trust is] entirely *in invitum* [read *nonconsensual*] and forced upon the conscience of the trustee for the purpose of working out right and justice or frustrating fraud." *Motley's Adm'rs v. Tabor*, 271 S.W. 1064, 1065 (Ky. 1925).
- "Finally, in *West*, a nonparty was allowed to appeal after having been compelled to participate in the district court proceedings '*in invitum*' [read *unwillingly*]." *In re Grand Jury Proceedings*, 643 F.2d 641, 643 n.2 (9th Cir. 1981).

See LATINISMS.

iniquity. See **inequity**.

in issue. See **issue (A)**.

INITIALESE. Justice Rehnquist (as he then was) once wrote, after stating the facts of a case in which seven different groups of initials were used for identification: "The terminology required to describe the present controversy suggests that the 'alphabet soup' of the New Deal era was, by comparison, a clear broth." *Chrysler Corp. v. Brown*, 441 U.S. 281, 286 n.4 (1979). He was alluding, of course, to one of the most irritating types of pedantry that have gained a foothold in legal writing: the overuse of acronyms and abbreviations. Originally, to be sure, abbreviations were intended to serve the convenience of the reader by shortening names; with their use, cumbersome phrases would not have to be repeated in their entirety. The purported simplifications actually simplified. E.g.: "For the sake of brevity and to avoid confusion, since all persons involved in this litigation, except Mrs. Robinson, have the same surname, we will refer to Mrs. Annie S. Harlan as Annie; to Mrs. Sue Robinson as Sue; to Messrs. Jay W. Harlan and George L. Harlan as Jay and George." *Harlan v. Citizens Nat'l Bank*, 251 S.W.2d 284, 284 (Ky. 1952).

Now, however, many writers seem to have lost sight of this goal: they allow abbreviated names to proliferate in their writing, which quickly becomes a system of hieroglyphs requiring the reader constantly to refer to the original use of the term so that he will understand the significance of the hieroglyphs. It may be thought that this kind of writing is more scholarly than ordinary, straightforward prose. It is not. Rather, it is tiresome and inconsiderate writing; it betrays the writer's thoughtlessness toward the reader and a fascination with the insubstantial trappings of scholarship.

A typical, and by no means exaggerated, example of this vice appeared in *Ryder Energy Distrib. Corp. v. Merrill Lynch Commodities, Inc.*, 748 F.2d 774 (2d Cir. 1984). In this opinion seven hieroglyphs appear, often clumped together. We learn throughout the first few pages of the opinion that REDCO = Ryder Energy Distribution Corporation (why not call it Ryder?); NYME = New York Mercantile Exchange; FCM = futures commission merchant; CFTC = Commodity Futures Trading Commission; EFP = exchange of futures for physical; and TOI = Two Oil, Inc. Braced with this knowledge, if we can hold it, we encounter the following:

> [U]nlike Hutton's, Merrill's duty sprang from two sources. Like Hutton, Merrill had the duty of an FCM representing the buyer—REDCO. In addition, however, Merrill had the duty of an FCM representing the seller—TOI. It was in its capacity as TOI's FCM that Merrill was required, under Form EFP-1, to certify that TOI owned and had possession of enough oil to cover its EFP obligations.

And this:

> The following facts cannot be found in the complaint: REDCO's previous dealings with TOI, REDCO's reasons for conducting an EFP, Merrill's inability to find REDCO an EFP partner, REDCO's introduction of TOI to Merrill, Hutton and NYME's lack of knowledge of TOI's default until June 11, and NYME's instigation of a rules compliance investigation after June 11.

And so it goes throughout the opinion, which would have reached the summit of initialese if only Merrill Lynch Commodities, Inc. had been termed MLCI, and E.F. Hutton & Co. Inc. termed EFHCO.

Almost as bad is *Kierstead v. City of San Antonio*, 643 S.W.2d 118, 120 (Tex. 1982), in which EMT = emergency medical technician, FY = fiscal year, and FPERA = Fire and Police Employee Relations Act: "Both parties presented their interpretations of the application of Art. 1269p, § 6 vis-à-vis the override provision of FPERA, § 20 during the bench trial of the EMTs' claim in November 1979. The trial court awarded the EMTs overtime on the early contracts but denied awards for the FY 1978 and FY 1979 agreements that had specifically mentioned a 56-hour work week obligation for the EMTs." Why not *technician*, a statement that all references to years mean fiscal years, and *the Act*?

The simple solution, of course, is to adopt simplified names for parties and frequently repeated phrases, rather than initials in all capitals that depersonalize and obscure. Instead of referring to "TDMHMR" (Texas Department of Mental Health and Mental Retardation) again and again, one should refer to "the Department" when only one is involved.

In naming something new, one's task is sometimes hopeless: the choice is clear between *ALI–ABA CLE Review* and *American Law Institute–American Bar Association Continuing Legal Education Review*, but one cannot choose either enthusiastically. Both entities must have their due (in part so that they can have their dues), and the acronyms gradually become familiar. But they are not ideal because they are sure to turn off readers initially.

The legal writer should never forget that effective communication takes *two*—the writer and the reader. In the words of Quiller-Couch,

> the obligation of courtesy rests first with the author, who invites the seance, and commonly charges for it. What follows, but that in speaking or writing we have an obligation to put ourselves into the hearer's or reader's place? It is *his* comfort, *his* convenience, we have to consult. To *express* ourselves is a very small part of the business: very small and unimportant as compares with *impressing* ourselves: the aim of the whole process being to persuade.
>
> Arthur Quiller-Couch, *On the Art of Writing* 291–92 (1916).

See ACRONYMS AND INITIALISMS & OBSCURITY (B).

initialing; initialling. *Initialing* is AmE, *initialling* BrE. See DOUBLING OF FINAL CONSONANTS.

initiate is a FORMAL WORD for *begin*, *open*, or *introduce*.

initiate tenant by curtesy; tenant by the curtesy initiate. These phrases are both used, but are falling into disuse. See **curtesy.**

initiative. See **mandate (B).**

initio. See *ab initio.*

*****injoin** is an obsolete spelling of *enjoin*. See EN- & **enjoin.**

injudicious; *****injudicial. The second is a NEEDLESS VARIANT. The antonym of *judicial* is *nonjudicial*. See **judicial.**

*****injunct** (= to enjoin) is a silly and unnecessary BACK-FORMATION—e.g.: "In the sidelines of the jurisprudential inquiries was the strategic importance of the delay caused by the defendant in seeking to *injunct* [read *enjoin*] the prosecution. So long as that civil-law proceeding to *injunct* [read *enjoin*] rolled on, no criminal prosecution could take place." Antoine Masson & Mary J. Shariff, *Legal Strategies* 348 (2009). See **enjoin.**

injunction. *Temporary injunction* (AmE) = *interlocutory injunction* (BrE). *Permanent injunction* (AmE) = *perpetual injunction* (BrE). See **enjoinder.** For the Scots-law equivalent of *injunction*, see **interdict.**

*****injunctional.** See **injunctive.**

*****injunction enjoining** is a common REDUNDANCY—e.g.: "On the basis of these allegations, plaintiff moved for a temporary *injunction enjoining* [better: *injunction prohibiting*] the enforcement of the Michigan injunction." *James v. Grand Trunk W. R.R.*, 152 N.E.2d 858, 860 (Ill. 1958). See **enjoin.**

injunctive; *****injunctional; *****injunctory. *Injunctive* is the standard word—e.g.: "First, a court possesses the independent authority to enforce its own *injunctive* decrees." *SEC v. Homa*, 514 F.3d 661, 673 (7th Cir. 2008). **Injunctional*, a NEEDLESS VARIANT not recorded in the major English-language dictionaries, has now been almost wholly displaced by *injunctive*—e.g.:

- "There is a noticeable absence of judicial attempt so to enumerate the subjects of the remedy or delimit its field as to hamper the power of equity to grant *injunctional* [read *injunctive*] relief." *Funk Jewelry Co. v. State ex rel. La Prade*, 50 P.2d 945, 947 (Ariz. 1935).
- "The *injunctional* [read *injunctive*] prohibition against picketing was supported by evidence of the unlawful purpose." *International Brotherhood of Carpenters & Joiners v. Todd L. Storms Constr. Co.*, 324 P.2d 1002, 1004 (Ariz. 1958).

The other NEEDLESS VARIANT, **injunctory*, is also uncommon—e.g.:

- "She demands *injunctory* [read *injunctive*] relief." *O'Hair v. Paine*, 432 F.2d 66, 67 n.1 (5th Cir. 1970).
- "The issue presented was whether plaintiff had standing . . . to bring this cause of action seeking *injunctory* [read *injunctive*] relief." *Helbig v. Murray*, 558 S.W.2d 772, 774 (Mo. Ct. App. 1977).

injuria. See **injury.**

---

injuria absque damno; injuria sine damno. The English equivalent of each phrase is *injury without damage*, which denotes a legal wrong that causes no actual damage—e.g.:

- "An action cannot be maintained for an *injury without damage. Injuria absque damno* does not constitute a cause of action." *Franks v. North Shore Farms, Inc.*, 253 N.E.2d 45, 49 (Ill. App. Ct. 1969).
- "The issues of sickness and healing, life and death, are too uncertain to be otherwise forecast, but negligence which deprives a man of such probability is more than *injuria sine damno*." *Falcon v. Memorial Hosp.*, 443 N.W.2d 431, 434 (Mich. Ct. App. 1989).

(Cf. **damnum absque injuria**.) In this context, *injuria* and *injury* mean "a legal wrong," not "hurt." See LATINISMS.

injury. A. Generally. Broadly, an *injury* is any harm, damage, wrong, or injustice. In many legal contexts an *injury* is the violation of another's legal right, for which the law provides a remedy. *Injuries* are divided into *real injuries* (such as woundings) and *verbal injuries* (such as slander). They may be criminal wrongs (as with assault) or civil wrongs (as with defamation). Some authorities distinguish *harm* from *injury*, holding that while *harm* denotes any personal loss or detriment, *injury* involves an actionable invasion of a legally protected interest. E.g.:

- "And by *injury* we must understand the infringement of the legal right as distinguished from *damnum* . . . for it is established that the mere fact that the water is in some measure polluted *aliunde*, does not justify further pollution." Edmund W. Garrett, *The Law of Nuisances* 107 (1890). See **damnum**.
- "Although FECA's exclusivity provisions prevent a court from awarding Nichols additional payments for her work-related '*injury*' within the meaning of the act (i.e., her post-traumatic-stress disorder), the provisions do not prevent an award of additional payments for harms that fall outside of FECA's definition of '*injury*.'" *Nichols v. Frank*, 42 F.3d 503, 515 (9th Cir. 1994).

See Restatement (Second) of Torts § 7 cmt. a (1965). *Injuria*, a LATINISM, is ordinarily a NEEDLESS VARIANT in common-law contexts.

B. And *damage*. There is a modern tendency to refer to *damage to property*, but *injury to the person*. It is not an established distinction. Blackstone did not observe it, having titled one section of his great treatise *Injury to Property*, and neither the English nor the American courts have consistently observed it. One could not be faulted for restricting one's usage in this way, but neither could one be faulted for writing *damage to persons* or *injury to property*.

C. And *injuria*. *Injuria*, a LATINISM, is a NEEDLESS VARIANT in common-law contexts. See (A).

Inland Revenue Service. See **Internal Revenue Service.**

in law. See **under law.**

in-law, n., is generally hyphenated or spelled as one word.

in lieu of. A. Generally. The phrase *in lieu of* is now English, and *instead of* will not always suffice in its stead—e.g.:

- "It is to be noted that these homestead provisions first were listed in the Code of 1880 primarily as a protection for the wife *in lieu of* dower which had been abolished by statute." *Grantham v. Ralle*, 158 So.2d 719, 724 (Miss. 1963).
- "Marcontell reached an agreement with Riley, a contractor, permitting him to stay in the house and make repairs *in lieu of* rent." *Van Marcontell v. Jacoby*, 260 S.W.3d 686, 688 (Tex. App.—Dallas 2008).
- "The memorandum stated that *in lieu of* notice of his termination, Elliott would be compensated two weeks' pay." *Cave v. Elliott*, 988 A.2d 1, 4 (Md. Ct. Spec. App. 2010).

B. *In lieu* without *of*. Omitting *of* from the phrase is a sure sign that *instead* would be an improvement over *in lieu*—e.g.:

- "The Court is now empowered to refuse to permit rescission and to award damages *in lieu* [read *instead*]." P.S. Atiyah, *An Introduction to the Law of Contract* 309 (3d ed. 1981).
- "An injunction is sometimes available against a refusal to contract; and it may be that damages can be awarded *in lieu* [read *instead*] even though the refusal gives rise to no cause of action at common law." G.H. Treitel, *The Law of Contract* 925 (8th ed. 1991).

C. For *in view of*. The day after President Clinton announced his healthcare plan in the fall of 1993, a radio host, broadcasting from the lawn of the White House, said to his listeners: "This morning we're going to discuss what state health care means *in lieu of* the President's new federal plan." This mistake—which is spreading—results from a confusion of *in view of* and *in light of*, either of which would have sufficed in that sentence. As it is, *in lieu of* is a MALAPROPISM when used for either of the other phrases.

in light of. See **in lieu of** (C) & **in the light of.**

in limine (= at the threshold or outset; preliminarily) is a LATINISM not likely to be displaced in lawyers' JARGON, especially in the phrase *motion in limine*. But apart from that phrase, *in limine* is easily and advantageously Englished—e.g.:

- "We are faced *in limine* [read *initially*] with a jurisdictional question." *Haynes v. Felder*, 239 F.2d 868, 869 (5th Cir. 1957).
- "If the courts continue to insist on a fiduciary relationship, a restitutionary proprietary claim against a tortfeasor may be defeated *in limine* [read *at the outset*]." Lord Goff of Chieveley & Gareth Jones, *The Law of Restitution* 622 (3d ed. 1986).

in loco parentis (= in the place of a parent) is perhaps a justified LATINISM. Generally, the term applies to guardians and not to trustees, but much depends on context—e.g.:

- "There is some variation in the terminology used to describe a psychological parent-child relationship. Some authorities employ the term 'de facto parent' or '*in loco parentis*' to describe this relationship." *In re Guardianship of Victoria R.*, 201 P.3d 169, 175 n.5 (N.M. Ct. App. 2008).

- "Riley has no standing to sue Alpert for such a claim—it belongs to Alpert's children as his children, not to Riley as holder of the legal interest in trust property held for its beneficial owners. Riley does not stand *in loco parentis* to Alpert's children." *Alpert v. Riley*, 274 S.W.3d 277, 292 (Tex. App.—Houston [1st Dist.] 2008).
- "Public elementary and high school administrators have the unique responsibility to act *in loco parentis.*" *DeJohn v. Temple Univ.*, 537 F.3d 301, 315 (3d Cir. 2008).
- "Foster Parents cannot establish *in loco parentis* status because Father never agreed to the permanent placement of B.R.S. with either CYS or, more importantly, Foster Parents themselves." *In re Adoption of B.R.S.*, 11 A.3d 541, 547 (Pa. Super. 2011).

The *in* is a part of the Latin phrase and should be italicized if the rest of the phrase is in italics. See ITALICS (C).

A clever or not-so-clever law student—it is impossible to know which—once asked whether *in loco parentis* is synonymous with *en ventre sa mère.*

inmate. See **prisoner.**

in memoriam is sometimes misspelled *in memorium—e.g.: "A few days before May 13, 1970, in *memorium* [read *memoriam*] to the dead students at Kent State, white and black students at SFA conducted a large so-called 'candlelight march.'" *McGuire v. Roebuck*, 347 F.Supp. 1111, 1115 (E.D. Tex. 1972).

inner bar = silks (taken collectively). See **silk.** Cf. **outer bar.**

innocence; **innocency.* The second is an obsolete variant.

innocent. See *nocent & **plead innocent.**

innocent until proven guilty. This, the usual rendering of the phrase, is perhaps tendentious because it suggests that guilt will ultimately be proved. Some criminal-law specialists therefore resort to the longer *innocent unless and until proven guilty*, which violates the SET PHRASE but is more legally accurate—e.g.: "The principle that a person should be presumed innocent *unless and until proven guilty* is a fundamental principle of fairness, although its relation to the law of evidence means that it is not always included in discussions of the criminal law." Andrew Ashworth, *Principles of Criminal Law* 74 (1991).

innoculation;* **inocculation.* See **inoculation.

innovative; **innovatory;* **innovational.* The second and third are NEEDLESS VARIANTS of the first:

- "Considerations of this sort did not . . . commend themselves to the judges of 1907 or their immediate successors. It was another unfortunate provision, they doubtless felt, in this *innovatory* [read *innovative*] Act." Patrick Devlin, *The Judge* 113 (1979).
- "Differences in the way firms explore these combinations lead to different *innovational* [read *innovative*] approaches and, ultimately, different degrees of success." Robert P.

Merges, *Commercial Success and Patent Standards*, 76 Cal. L. Rev. 803, 853 (1988).

in no wise. See **nowise.**

Inns of Court. This phrase, a proper noun, refers to four autonomous institutions in which English barristers receive their training: the Honourable Societies of Lincoln's Inn, the Middle Temple, the Inner Temple, and Gray's Inn. These powerful bodies examine candidates for the bar, "call" them to the bar, and award the degree of barrister. Every bar student must join one of them, and every barrister remains a member for life unless he or she resigns or is disbarred. These bodies have been known as *Inns of Court* since the 1420s, though for centuries the phrase denoted primarily the buildings in which the four legal societies were housed.

innuendo. Early in its life as an English word, *innuendo* was a POPULARIZED LEGAL TECHNICALITY. In medieval Latin, *innuendo* (lit., "by nodding; meaning; to wit; that is to say") was used in legal documents to introduce a parenthetical explanation of precisely what a preceding noun or pronoun referred to. Hence Thomas Blount, in his early law dictionary entitled *Glossographia* (1656), wrote that *innuendo* "is a Law term, most used in Declarations and other pleadings . . . to declare and design the person or thing which was named incertain before; as to say, he (*innuendo* the Plaintiff) is a Theef."

By the 17th century, the word had taken on its current meaning, "an oblique remark or indirect suggestion, usu. of a derogatory nature." Because, by its nature, an *innuendo* must be in words, the phrase *verbal innuendo* is a REDUNDANCY—e.g.: "Yes of course sexual harassment by *verbal innuendo* [read *innuendo*] is vulgar." Russell Baker, *Potomac Breakdown*, N.Y. Times, 12 Oct. 1991, at 19. See **verbal.**

Pl. *innuendos.*

innundate.* See **inundate.

inoculation. So spelled. This word is often misspelled *innoculation or **inocculation.*

inoperative is a LEGALISM usually meaning "invalid." E.g.:

- "In the first place, none of the provisions of the contract would be *inoperative*, superfluous, or conflicting if the term 'third party' in the disclaimer is given its broadest interpretation." *Dewakuku v. Martinez*, 271 F.3d 1031, 1042 (Fed. Cir. 2001).
- "If a stipulation of settlement as to such items resulted not from Rule 68 exchanges but from an agreement outside the Rule, then the attorney's-fees provision of Rule 68 likewise would be *inoperative.*" *Nakasone v. Nakasone*, 73 P.3d 715, 720 (Haw. 2003).
- "Dahl maintains that Schweizer's proposed consent to jurisdiction in a Mexican court would be *inoperative* in a Mexican court, as such consents are not recognized under

Mexican law." *Navarrete De Pedrero v. Schweizer Aircraft Corp.*, 635 F.Supp.2d 251, 257 (W.D.N.Y. 2009).

In recent years it has become a VOGUE WORD among government bureaucrats.

In the law of contract, legal writers have given it a special and useful nuance. If a condition precedent fails, it is more precise to say that the contract is *inoperative* rather than *void*—i.e., the validity of the contract itself does not depend on the fulfillment of the condition precedent. *See* P.S. Atiyah, *An Introduction to the Law of Contract* 146–47 (3d ed. 1981).

inopposite is a surprising, and happily infrequent, solecism for *inapposite*.

in order (to) (for) (that). The phrase *in order to* is often wordy for the simple infinitive—e.g.:

- "*In order to* [read *To*] avoid probate and administration, it is often urged that a joint estate in the account has been created." Thomas E. Atkinson, *Handbook of the Law of Wills* 168 (2d ed. 1953).
- "The Supreme Court granted certiorari on a case from the Sixth Circuit *in order to resolve* [read *to resolve*] the conflict among the Circuit Courts of Appeals." *Atlantic Cas. Ins. Co. v. Ramirez*, 651 F.Supp.2d 669, 678 (N.D. Tex. 2009).
- "Despite the upcoming changes, we address the issues raised here *in order to resolve* [read *to resolve*] the conflict between the Courts of Appeal and to give guidance to trial courts as they await the amendment to take effect." *In re Brooks*, 211 P.3d 1023, 1026 n.4 (Wash. 2009).

In order for, which takes a noun, is often wordy for *for*—e.g.:

- "The transformers . . . had been *energized in order for use by Jones* [read *energized for use by Jones*] in the building operations." *Rayner v. R.J. Jones & Sons*, 182 So.2d 353, 358 (La. Ct. App. 1966).
- "Article 4 of the Venezuelan Industrial Property Law requires that trademark licenses must be *recorded . . . in order for use by the licensee* [read *recorded . . . for use by the licensee*] to inure to the benefit of the trademark owner." *Babbit Elecs. v. Dynascan Corp.*, 38 F.3d 1161, 1170 (11th Cir. 1994).

Finally, *in order that*, which needs no reduction, begins a noun phrase expressing purpose—e.g.: "We must vacate the judgment of the district court and remand *in order that* the court may make factual findings under the proper law." *Vanderbilt Univ. v. ICOS Corp.*, 601 F.3d 1297, 1311 (Fed. Cir. 2010) (Dyk, J., concurring in part & dissenting in part). See LEGAL-ISMS AND LAWYERISMS.

in pais (= outside court or legal proceedings) is legal JARGON deriving from LAW FRENCH, meaning literally "in the country (as opposed to in court)." *Matter in pais*, for example, means "a matter of fact that is not in writing." E.g.: "The facts from which equitable estoppels arise are all matters *in pais* as distinguished from records and deeds." 3 John N. Pomeroy & Spencer W. Symons, *Equity Jurisprudence* § 802, at 180 (5th ed. 1941).

Estoppel in pais = an estoppel not arising from a deed or contract, but, for example, from an express statement implied by conduct or negligence. E.g.:

"These articles embody the principal cases of *estoppels in pais*, as distinguished from estoppels by deed or by record." (Eng.) See **estop** & **estoppel (B)**.

in pari delicto is legal JARGON meaning "in equal fault; equally culpable." E.g.:

- "Plaintiffs who are truly *in pari delicto* are those who have themselves violated the law in cooperation with the defendant." *Perma Life Mufflers, Inc. v. International Parts Corp.*, 392 U.S. 134, 153 (1968) (Harlan, J., concurring in part & dissenting in part).
- "The district court dismissed their claim, reasoning that trading on inside information is itself an antifraud violation, and therefore, that the investors were *in pari delicto* with the broker." John H. Walsh, *Can Regulation Protect "Suckers" and "Fools" from Themselves?*, 8 J. Bus. & Sec. L. 188, 229 (2008).

Some writers mistakenly write **delictu*—e.g.: "The court rejected the plaintiff's reliance on Buttrey to defeat the defense of *in pari delictu* [read *in pari delicto*]." *Lank v. New York Stock Exch.*, 405 F.Supp. 1031, 1038 (S.D.N.Y. 1975). Cf. *in flagrante delicto*. See LATINISMS.

in pari materia (= on the same matter or subject) is legal JARGON used in the context of interpreting statutes. The common maxim is that statutes *in pari materia* are to be construed together. Usually the phrase functions as an adjective—e.g.:

- "Sometimes there is, by statute, an appeal from them to the High Court, in which case it may be presumed that the High Court will consider itself bound by its previous decisions *in pari materia*." Carleton K. Allen, *Law in the Making* 237 (7th Cir. 1964).
- "It seems that the present position is that, when an earlier statute is *in pari materia* with a later one, it is simply part of its context to be considered by the judge in deciding whether the meaning of a provision in the later statute is plain." Rupert Cross, *Statutory Interpretation* 128 (1976).

At times the phrase denotes the doctrine and is therefore used as a noun—e.g.: "*In pari materia* finds its greatest force 'when the statutes are enacted by the same legislative body at the [same] time.'" *Mattox v. FTC*, 752 F.2d 116, 122 (5th Cir. 1985).

At other times the phrase is used adverbially—e.g.:

- "The federal estate tax and the federal gift tax . . . are construed *in pari materia*." *Harris v. I.R.C.*, 340 U.S. 106, 107 (1950) (per Douglas, J.).
- "The Maryland constitutional provision is construed *in pari materia* with the Fourth Amendment." *Maryland v. Garrison*, 480 U.S. 79, 83–84 (1987) (per Stevens, J.).

See ITALICS (C) & LATINISMS.

**in pari passu*. See *pari passu*.

in part. See **in whole** & **in pertinent part**.

in pectore. See LOAN TRANSLATIONS.

in personam. A. And *personal*. *In personam* is inferior to *personal* when used in the phrase *in personam jurisdiction* (= jurisdiction over a legal person). In many contexts, however, *personal* cannot substitute for *in personam*:

- "Sovereign immunity extends to *in personam* admiralty claims." *Coastal Holding & Leasing, Inc. v. Maryland Envtl. Servs.*, 420 F.Supp.2d 441, 443 n.8 (D. Md. 2006).
- "*In personam* forfeiture occurs pursuant to [the statute] and is not at issue in this case." *In re Young*, 780 N.W.2d 726, 727 (Iowa 2010). On the use of *pursuant to* in that sentence, see *pursuant to.

A claim *in personam* is one that is vested in a person and that imposes a liability against another person (such as a claim for repayment of a debt).

In personam occurs sometimes after, sometimes before the noun it qualifies. Traditionally it follows—e.g.: "While the vast majority of federal cases are actions *in personam,* there is no constitutional or statutory limitation on the power of a federal court to entertain actions in rem or, under certain circumstances, actions quasi in rem." *In re Joint E. & S. Dist. Asbestos Litig.*, 129 B.R. 710, 798 (Bankr. E.D.N.Y. 1991). Likewise, one refers to a *judgment in personam* (= a judgment rendered against a legal person) and to a *right in personam* (= a right availing against a specific legal person for liability). See POSTPOSITIVE ADJECTIVES.

B. And *in rem*. An action is *in personam* when its purpose is to determine the rights and interests of the parties themselves in the subject matter of the action; an action is *in rem* when the court's judgment determines the title to property and the rights of the parties, not merely among themselves, but also against all persons at any time claiming an interest in the property at issue. *In rem*, then, means "availing against other persons generally and imposing on everyone a legal liability to respect the claimant's right."

Walter Wheeler Cook classified several very different ways in which these phrases are used:

> There seem to be at least four different uses which need to be distinguished: 1. These phrases are used in the classification of the so-called 'primary' rights which legal and equitable actions are supposed to protect and enforce. The classification here is, of course, the well-known one of *rights in rem* and *rights in personam*. 2. The next use has to do with the equally well-known classification of actions as *actions in rem* and *actions in personam*. 3. A third use is in the classification of judgments and decrees as *in rem* or *in personam*. 4. The fourth use refers to the procedure used by a court in the enforcement of its judgment or decree. Here the court is said to *act in rem* or *act in personam*, as the case may be, the usual statement being that the law does the former and equity the latter.
> Walter W. Cook, *The Powers of Courts of Equity,* 15 Colum. L. Rev. 37, 39 (1915).

C. Misspelled *in personum*. This fairly common mistake drew a "[*sic*]" from one court: "On March 31, 1976, attorneys for the other defendant in the case filed an amended motion to dismiss, alleging for the first time as grounds therein that '[t]his court lacks *in personum* [*sic*] jurisdiction over this defendant.'" *Rauch v. Day & Night Mfg. Corp.*, 576 F.2d 697, 699 (6th Cir. 1978).

*in pertinent part; *in relevant part; in part.** The last is best; the second, a variant of the first, is as verbose and jejune as the first. See QUOTATIONS (B).

in point; on point. Both terms, applied to prior judicial decisions, mean "apposite; discussing the precise issue now at hand." *On point* is now the more common phrase, but both are well established in the legal idiom. E.g.:

- "The court referred to the cases cited above but held that they were not *in point* on the question involved under the circumstances there." *O'Keefe v. Wabash R.R.*, 185 F.2d 241, 244 (7th Cir. 1950).
- "We then announced that they were not *in point,* that they were of little help, and that no Iowa decision factually *in point* had been called to our attention." *Martin v. Beatty*, 115 N.W.2d 706, 712 (Iowa 1962).
- "The Licensor-Licensee cases are *on point.* . . . Their holdings do not hinge on findings of bad faith or whether the licensee had prior common law rights in the mark." *Dress for Success Worldwide v. Dress 4 Success*, 589 F.Supp.2d 351, 362 (S.D.N.Y. 2008).
- "Though both cases are *on point,* they were both decided by the court well in advance of its decisions discussing pre-election review of the fundamental and overriding purpose of initiatives." *City of Port Angeles v. Our Water-Our Choice*, 188 P.3d 533, 538 (Wash. Ct. App. 2008).

Case in point is a popular idiom that originated in the law. See **off point** & POPULARIZED LEGAL TECHNICALITIES.

in point of fact is verbose for *in fact* or *actually*—e.g.: "We find no merit in UPMC's claim. *In point of fact* [read *In fact*], it substantially mischaracterizes the record, presenting a tendentious reading of the evidence divorced from what the jury actually considered." *Rettger v. UPMC Shadyside*, 991 A.2d 915, 925 (Pa. Super. Ct. 2010).

in posse. See **in esse.**

in praesenti, which means merely "in the present," is a LATINISM wholly without merit. E.g.:

- "The question here determined is whether there was a valid declaration of trust operating *in praesenti* [omit *in praesenti*] between January 28 and May 3, 1929." *Morsman v. Commissioner*, 90 F.2d 18, 27–28 (8th Cir. 1937).
- "As the District Court erred in dismissing the amended complaint, the case will be remanded for that order to be set aside, after which the appellee should be given an opportunity to plead to an issue, and, if she can, to prove a *gift in praesenti* [read *present gift*]." *Harrington v. Emmerman*, 186 F.2d 757, 762 (D.C. Cir. 1951).
- "Plaintiffs argue that the 1891 Act provides an *in praesenti* [read *current*] grant of a right of way." *Roth v. U.S.*, 326 F.Supp.2d 1163, 1170 (D. Mont. 2003).

See **in futuro.**

in propria persona = pro se. E.g.:

462 *in pursuance of

- "Edward W. Bergquist appeared *in propria persona*." *In re Victoria Co.*, 42 B.R. 533, 534 (Bankr. D. Minn. 1984).
- "He filed a claim of appeal and a brief *in propria persona* in the Court of Appeals." *In re Sanchez*, 375 N.W.2d 353, 355 (Mich. 1985).

See *pro persona* & **pro se.**

***in pursuance of.** See ***pursuant to.**

input, n. & vb. This jargonmonger's word is generally eschewed by careful writers—e.g.:

- "Regardless of their degree of specialization, judges will be heavily dependent on *the inputs* [read *comments* or *information*] they receive from litigants and lawyers when there is little time to dig deeply into a case." Lawrence Baum, *Judicial Specialization and the Adjudication of Immigration Cases*, 59 Duke L.J. 1501, 1544 (2010).
- "This payment compensated for the half hour that it took to *input* the patient data." *U.S. ex rel. Rost v. Pfizer, Inc.*, 736 F.Supp.2d 367, 372 (D. Mass. 2010).

The English have the phrase *input tax*, statutorily defined in the Finance Act of 1977.

inquire; enquire. *Inquire* is a FORMAL WORD for *ask*. In AmE, *in-* is the preferred spelling. See **ask,** EN- & **enquiry.**

inquirer; inquisitor. *Inquirer* is the more general of the two terms, meaning "one who asks questions or investigates." *Inquisitor*, not to be used where *inquirer* is called for, means "one who examines others to obtain information," and carries with it historical connotations of the Spanish Inquisition or trial by inquisition.

inquiry. See **investigation, enquiry** & EN-.

inquisition. See **investigation.**

inquisitive; inquisitorial; *inquisitional. *Inquisitive* = given to inquiry or questioning <a highly inquisitive mind>.

Inquisitorial has quite different connotations: "of the character of an inquisitor; offensively or impertinently inquiring, prying" (*OED*). E.g.:

- "It is simply an empirical predicate of our system of adversary rather than *inquisitorial* justice that cross-examination of a witness who is uncounseled between direct examination and cross-examination is more likely to lead to the discovery of truth than is cross-examination of a witness who is given time to pause and consult with his attorney." *Perry v. Leeke*, 488 U.S. 272, 282 (1989) (per Stevens, J.).
- "Defendant . . . attempts to paint his mother in part as an *inquisitorial* agent of the police, who attempted to solicit a statement where they themselves could not." *State v. Clodfelter*, 691 S.E.2d 22, 30 (N.C. Ct. App. 2010).

To contrast *inquisitorial* with *accusatorial*, see **accusatorial.** For the related noun *inquisition*, see **investigation.**

**Inquisitional* is a NEEDLESS VARIANT of *inquisitorial*—e.g.:

- "A defendant has standing to assert a Fifth Amendment right to due process as a valid objection to the introduction of statements extracted from a nondefendant by

coercion or other *inquisitional tactics* [read *inquisitorial tactics*]." *State v. Samuel*, 623 N.W.2d 565, 570 (Wis. Ct. App. 2000).
- "An underlying principle in the enforcement of our criminal law is that our system is accusatorial, not *inquisitional* [read *inquisitorial*]." *State v. Bilodeau*, 992 A.2d 557, 568 (N.H. 2010).

inquisitor. See **inquirer.**

inquisitorial. See **inquisitive.**

in re; *en re; re. The correct spelling of the two-word version is *in re* (= regarding; in the matter of). Known to nonlawyers as a legalistic term, *in re* was once commonly used at the outset of legal documents, and now is often used before case names (particularly in uncontested proceedings)—e.g., *In re Wolfson's Estate*, which is frequently Englished *In the Matter of Wolfson's Estate*. The *Bluebook* (19th ed.) recommends (p. 90) changing citations that begin *In the Matter of* to *In re*.

Sometimes, in the driest of commercial correspondence, *in re* is shortened to *re*, the ablative inflection of the noun *res*; the ellipsis carries the same meaning as *in re*. Although some authorities object to this use of the term, its conciseness makes it well-nigh irreplaceable. The best practice is to restrict it to use as a signal or introductory title announcing the subject of correspondence, and to avoid using it in sentences as part of one's syntax.

in rebus. See **in rem.**

***in regards to** is semiliterate. The idiomatic phrases are *in regard to*, *in respect to* (or *of*), *with regard to*, and *with respect to*. E.g.:

- "This phone call to Howard on behalf of Servotech was *in regards to* [read *in regard to*] purchasing weapons in the United States for delivery to the Republic of South Africa." *U.S. v. One Boeing 707 Aircraft*, 750 F.2d 1280, 1282 (5th Cir. 1985).
- "Congress amended the statute again in 1996 *in regards to* [read *in regard to*] the electronic creation of child pornography." Cody W. Stafford, *Substantial Effect*, 62 Baylor L. Rev. 290, 292 (2010).
- "A look at the substantive aspects of smart-phone use is important because, even today, the de minimis doctrine is discussed *in regards to* [read *in regard to*] small tasks like turning on lights, starting equipment, and opening the office." Sean McLaughlin, Comment, *Controlling Smart-Phone Abuse*, 58 U. Kan. L. Rev. 737, 761 (2010).

See **as regards.**

in relevant part. See **in pertinent part.**

in rem; *in rebus. The first is accusative singular ("in or against the thing"), the second is ablative plural ("in things"). Both are common parts of lengthier LATINISMS. See **in personam (B).**

in respect of can usually be replaced by a simpler substitute, as the New Zealand Court of Appeal has recognized: "*In respect of* is a phrase used more by lawyers and in official and business documents than in other writing or ordinary speech. Yet it cannot be said to have a precise legal meaning. H.W. Fowler's

Modern English Usage does it justice by recommending that it be used as seldom as possible." *Phonographic Performances (NZ) Ltd v. Lion Breweries Ltd*, [1980] F.S.R. 383.

*inroll. See **engross.**

in route. See **en route.**

insanity. A. And Its Near-Synonyms: *psychosis; lunacy; mania; dementia; mental illness; mental disorder; disease of the mind.* These terms all denote a chronic malfunctioning of mental faculties. *Insanity,* a legal as opposed to a medical term, covers a wide variety of disorders that make the afflicted person incapable of managing personal affairs, performing social duties, or bearing legal responsibility. *Psychosis* is the clinical psychiatric term for mental disease. *Lunacy,* with its sibling *lunatic,* connotes regular or episodic spells of madness and fury, perhaps broken by periods of lucidity; the word retains its strong etymological associations with changes of the moon. *Mania* denotes a spell of frenzied excitement or derangement associated with various mental illnesses. *Dementia* applies to any condition that manifests itself in outward signs of mental deterioration—and it therefore covers a broad field of conditions, including Alzheimer's disease.

The McNaghten rules refer to a "defect of reason, from disease of the mind," a phrase that doctors no longer use. Instead, doctors tend to speak nowadays of *mental illness* or *mental disorder,* the latter being the broader of the two, encompassing any disorder of mind. But neither *mental illness* nor *mental disorder* is precisely synonymous with *disease of the mind,* which includes physically based pathologies such as cerebral arteriosclerosis (diminishing the flow of blood to the brain).

So when it comes to applying the McNaghten rules, and getting expert witnesses to have a common understanding of what they are talking about, "the practical legal position is very confused." Glanville Williams, *Textbook of Criminal Law* 593 (1978). See **McNaghten rules.**

B. Objections to *insanity.* Although this word has a strong hold in criminal law, leading criminal-law writers have tried their best to uproot it. The primary objections are that the word *insanity* (1) is not as clear as *mental disorder,* which more obviously includes disease of the mind, congenital problems, and damage resulting from traumatic injury; (2) suggests misleadingly that it refers to a specific mental condition when in fact it refers to a broad array of conditions; (3) is mere legal JARGON, not a medical term at all. As to the third point, one writer states: "[*Insanity*] is a legal term only, and one that is not used by the psychiatrist; the latter prefers to speak of mental disorder, mental illness, or of psychosis or neurosis." Winfred Overholser, *Psychiatry and the Law,* 38 Mental Hygiene 243, 244 (1954).

in severalty. See **severalty.**

inside of. Omit the *of.* See **of** (C).

insider is sometimes used as a shorthand for *inside trader* or *trader in inside information.* E.g.: Kurt Eichenwald, *Two Firms Are Charged as Insiders,* N.Y. Times, 3 Nov. 1988, at D1.

insider trading; insider dealing; insider tipping. *Insider trading* (= trading by anyone, inside or outside the issuer board, based on any type of material nonpublic information about the issuer of a security or about the market for the security) is the predominant phrase in AmE. E.g.: "Only after being arraigned and fingerprinted did Mr. Wigton learn that he was being charged with *insider trading.*" Steve Swartz & James B. Stewart, *Kidder's Mr. Wigton, Charged as "Insider," Ends His Long Ordeal,* Wall St. J., 21 Aug. 1989, at A10. The phrase *insider dealing* is a primarily BrE variant. The leading text is Marc I. Steinberg & William K.S. Wang, *Insider Trading* (3d ed. 2010).

Insider tipping is the communication by *anyone*—not just a corporate executive or other "insider"—about material nonpublic information relating to a security's issuer or market.

Understandably, the "insider" part of the phrase has been termed a misnomer since *insider trading* and *insider tipping* both refer to activities engaged in by persons who aren't insiders of the corporate issuer. *See id.* at 1 n.5 and accompanying text.

insidious; invidious. A distinction exists between these words. *Insidious* = (of persons and things) lying in wait or seeking to entrap or ensnare; operating subtly or secretly so as not to excite suspicion. E.g.: "The officers of a trust company owe allegiance to the shareholders as well as to the beneficiaries, and the temptation to favor the shareholders may well be more *insidious* than the temptation of an individual trustee to favor himself." *Barker v. First Nat'l Bank,* 20 F.Supp. 185, 189 (N.D. Ala. 1937).

Invidious = offensive; entailing odium or ill will upon the person performing, discharging, or discussing; giving offense to others (*OED*). This term is often used of discrimination, and has been for more than two centuries. E.g.: "He failed to allege motivations of class-based *invidious* discrimination." *Loehr v. Ventura County Cmty. Coll. Dist.,* 743 F.2d 1310, 1320 (9th Cir. 1984). The two words ought not to be used in the same sentence, as here: "Ugly in its practice and *insidious* in its effects, *invidious* racial discrimination deserves protection in no area of society, least of all in the administration of justice in federal courts." *U.S. v. Leslie,* 783 F.2d 541, 574 (5th Cir. 1986) (Williams, J., dissenting). A workable revision might be to drop *insidious* altogether and write "*invidious* in its effects, racial discrimination . . . ."

insightful. This vague one-word CLICHÉ is sometimes misspelled *inciteful*—e.g.: "The most recent and *inciteful* [read *insightful*] opinion, *Liberty Mutual Insurance Co. v. Commercial Union Insurance Co.*, flatly rejected the awareness test and adopted the date of disability as the liability trigger." John Braley, *The Longshore and Harbor Workers' Compensation Act*, 67 Miss. L.J. 759, 792–93 (1998). See **inciteful.**

insignia; *insigne. Today *insignia* (technically plural) is regarded as the singular, *insignias* as its plural. E.g.: "This *insignia* is two feet three inches in length and one foot four inches in height." *Chicago Park Dist. v. Canfield*, 19 N.E.2d 376, 377 (Ill. 1939). Cf. **indicia.**

The Latin singular **insigne* is rarely used, and when it does occasionally appear, it would be better as *insignia*—e.g.: "It was undisputed that he had never made use of the Indian *insigne* [read *insignia*] and had never attempted to imitate or copy the script of printing of the words, White Kitchen, as used by the plaintiff." *Faciane v. Starner*, 230 F.2d 732, 735 (5th Cir. 1956).

insipient. See **incipient.**

insist takes the preposition *on*, not *in*. E.g.: "In a society which *persists and insists in* [read *persists in and insists on*, if the ALLITERATION is really necessary] permitting its citizens to own and possess weapons, it becomes necessary to determine who may and who may not acquire them." *Galioto v. Department of Treasury*, 602 F.Supp. 682, 683 (D.N.J. 1985).

insistence. So spelled—often misspelled **insistance*. See **instance** & ***insistment.**

*insistment, a NEEDLESS VARIANT of *insistence*, appears occasionally in legal writing, though it is not recorded in most English-language dictionaries. E.g.:

- "The *insistment* [read *insistence*] of the plaintiff is twofold." *Jelinek v. Sotak*, 86 A.2d 684, 687 (N.J. 1952).
- "The wife objected, asserting that she would live in one room if need be rather than reside with her mother-in-law, but her spouse remained 'obdurate in his *insistment* [read *insistence*].'" *Koch v. Koch*, 232 A.2d 157, 160 (N.J. Super. Ct. 1967).

in situ (= in its original place; back in place) is a LATINISM used in property law. It is almost always unnecessary.

insofar as (= in such degree as), so spelled in AmE and *in so far as* in BrE, is sometimes misused because its meaning is misunderstood. One does not know exactly what this writer, for instance, had in mind: "*Insofar as important here*, unchallenged instruction No. 5 informed the jury that to convict one of aggravated murder in the first degree the jury must be convinced beyond a reasonable doubt that . . . defendant caused the death . . . in the course of or in furtherance of rape in the first degree or kidnapping in the first degree." *State v. Green*, 616 P.2d 628, 637 (Wash. 1980). A better—and grammatical—way of beginning this sentence would be, *What is important here is that* . . . . See **inasmuch as.**

insoluble; insolvable; *unsolvable. *Insoluble* is used both of substances that will not dissolve in liquids and of problems that cannot be solved—e.g.:

- "The starch, *insoluble* at these conditions, disperses into the bath, while the lactose fully dissolves." *Takeda Pharm. Co. v. Teva Pharm. USA, Inc.*, 668 F.Supp.2d 614, 619 n.12 (D. Del. 2009).
- "I do not . . . consider such problems *insoluble*, since we deal here with purely fungible assets—money." *In re Diet Drugs*, 582 F.3d 524, 557 (3d Cir. 2009) (Ambro, J., dissenting).

Insolvable is used only of problems that cannot be solved; some stylists prefer it to *insoluble*. Judge Henry Friendly, for example, referred to "an essentially insolvable problem." *Schine v. Schine*, 367 F.2d 685, 688 (2d Cir. 1966) (Friendly, J., concurring). Avoid **unsolvable* as a NEEDLESS VARIANT.

insolvency. A. And Its Near-Synonyms: *bankruptcy; receivership; failure; suspension.* These terms, though quite distinct, have in common a suggestion of the inability to meet financial commitments or the state of legally imposed financial oversight. *Insolvency* simply denotes a failure of current resources, so that one is unable to pay debts because of insufficient funds or illiquid assets. *Bankruptcy* is the state of a debtor who has either instituted or been subjected to proceedings under the Bankruptcy Code for liquidation (Chapter 7), for reorganization (Chapter 11), or for restructuring debt (Chapter 13). *Receivership* implies administration of a business or of a person's affairs as a result of litigation, as with the estate of an incompetent, the wholly owned business of a married couple involved in a contentious divorce, or the assets of a corporation undergoing reorganization. Unlike the other terms, *receivership* does not invariably involve insolvency—though insolvency is a frequent concomitant. *Failure*, a popular nonlegal term, denotes the termination of an unprofitable business enterprise. *Suspension*, also a popular nonlegal term, denotes the supposedly temporary cessation of business activities while the principals try to figure out how to make it profitable.

B. More on the Meaning of *insolvency*. *Insolvency* = (1) generally, the inability to pay debts as they mature; (2) under the (U.S.) Bankruptcy Act of 1898, the insufficiency of assets at a fair valuation to pay debts; or (3) under other laws, the insufficiency of assets at a fair salable valuation to pay debts. See James A. MacLachlan, *Handbook of the Law of Bankruptcy* 10–13 (1956). Sense 2, sometimes called the *balance-sheet insolvency test*, is the predominant sense in civil-law jurisdictions. See **bankruptcy.**

insolvent. Nonlawyers are accustomed to using this word as an adjective <an insolvent debtor>, but lawyers sometimes use it attributively as a noun <an insolvent>—e.g.: "An *insolvent* can obey an order not to commit a threatened tort." Douglas Laycock, *The Death of the Irreparable Injury Rule* 76 (1991).

in specie. See **specie.**

inst. = short for *instant*. Wood writes that this was "once a quite respectable legal term, now a piece of commercial jargon for 'the present month' (e.g.: 'We beg to recognise the receipt of your letter of the 25th *inst*.'). Use the name of the month instead." F.T. Wood, *Current English Usage* 123 (1962). The advice is well taken. Cf. **ult.**

installment; instalment. *Instalment* is the BrE spelling, *installment* the spelling preferred in AmE.

instance, vb., = to cite as an instance, to adduce as an example in illustration or proof (*OED*). E.g.:

- "*Benton* does not, however, state that any voluntary dismissal of the first petition makes a subsequent petition second or successive; and the present case may seem one in which the circumstances of the voluntary dismissal make it like the cases *instanced* in *Benton* in which the first petition is to be ignored and the second treated as the first." *Felder v. McVicar*, 113 F.3d 696, 697–98 (7th Cir. 1997).
- "Nor does Bae offer any reason to think that the *instanced* anomalies are somehow ameliorated in cases where the fraudulently obtained item can be replaced cheaply." *U.S. v. Bae*, 250 F.3d 774, 776 (D.C. Cir. 2001).
- "The interactivity among race, culture, gender, and species categories is also a contemporary phenomenon *instanced* through current cultural ideas of certain animals and their appropriate cultural role, function, and space." Maneesha Deckha, *Intersectionality and Posthumanist Visions of Equality*, 23 Wis. J.L. Gender & Soc'y 249, 253 (2008).

instance; instancy. *Instance* "in the sense of urgent solicitation or insistence [always in the phrase *at the instance of*] is a useful word; in any other sense it is useless." Percy Marks, *The Craft of Writing* 53 (1932). Another legitimate meaning of the word is "an illustrative example." Here the word is useless: "It seems plain that *in at least the vast majority of instances* [delete the italicized words] such a purported conveyance of lifetime services would usually (or almost always) be unenforceable and essentially nugatory under applicable state law." *U.S. v. Buttorff*, 761 F.2d 1056, 1061 (5th Cir. 1985).

Following are examples of the use, largely legal, that has substantive value:

- "At the *instance* of their counsel they were given immunity." *State v. Young*, 869 S.W.2d 691, 692 (Ark. 1994).
- "In this lawsuit, Baldwins conceded that Duffield's work was necessary and beneficial to the property but claimed that the work constituted a repair performed at the *instance* of their lessee." *Duffield Constr. v. Baldwin*, 679 N.W.2d 477, 480 (S.D. 2004).
- "The third [ground] is arguably of diminishing significance in view of the fact that states are becoming increasingly susceptible to legal action and accountability at the *instance* of their citizens." Jane Wright, *Retribution but No Recompense*, 30 Oxford J. Legal Stud. 143, 163 (2010).

Instancy, a rare term, means "urgency; pressing nature; imminence" <the instancy of the danger was apparent to all>.

For the misuse of *incidence* for *instance*, see **incidence.**

instance court is an old-fashioned expression for a court of first instance or trial court—e.g.: "The procedure was not as clear either to the *instance courts* or to the Circuit Courts of Appeals as it now seems in the light of the event to the defendants." *Holmberg v. Anchell*, 24 F.Supp. 594, 603 (S.D.N.Y. 1938).

instancy. See **instance.**

instant. See **inst.** & **instant case.**

instantaneously; instantly. "*Instantly* is virtually a synonym of at once, directly, and immediately, though perhaps the strongest of the four. *Instantaneously* is applied to something that takes an inappreciable time to occur, like the taking of an instantaneous photograph, especially to two events that occur so nearly simultaneously that the difference is imperceptible" (*MEU2* 288). E.g.: "He was killed *instantaneously* [read *instantly*] in the collision of that car with the truck driven by the defendant." *Coliseum Motor Co. v. Hester*, 3 P.2d 105, 105 (Wyo. 1931). Cf. **instanter.**

instant case; instant cause; present case; case at bar. These equivalent phrases, though sometimes useful, can often be avoided by *here*, if not used vaguely. Some variation of all these terms may be desirable to avoid verbal tedium, but one should not be so obvious as to lapse into INELEGANT VARIATION.

Instant case is sometimes used where *this case* would be preferable—e.g.:

- "Greenwood then brought *the instant case* [read *this case*] seeking . . . a declaration that the ordinance was valid and constitutional under Missouri law." *City of Greenwood v. Martin Marietta Materials, Inc.*, 299 S.W.3d 606, 614 (Mo. Ct. App. 2009).
- "Plaintiff brought *the instant case* [read *this case*] on May 29, 2008, under the court's diversity jurisdiction, asserting counts for breach of contract, breach of the implied covenant of good faith and fair dealing, promissory estoppel, negligence, and fraud." *Woods v. Era Med LLC*, 677 F.Supp.2d 806, 809 (E.D. Pa. 2010).

Instant (= now under consideration), labeled an ARCHAISM by the *OED*, is alive in the law, and has been extended beyond the basic phrase *instant case*—e.g.:

- "Since the *instant* will has been previously construed as permitting newborn grandnieces and grandnephews to enter the class, the composition of the class has not yet been finally determined." *In re Walker's Trust*, 116 N.W.2d 106, 110 (Wis. 1962).
- "If there were any doubt on this score, defendants have repeatedly represented to this Court, unequivocally and with knowledge that the Court would judicially rely

thereon, that their sole defense to repayment on demand of the *instant* Bonds is their various claims of fraud shortly to be decided at trial." *JPMorgan Chase Bank v. Liberty Mut. Ins. Co.*, 233 F.Supp.2d 550, 553 (S.D.N.Y. 2002).

- "The *instant* paper's central claim concerns the implications of waging a just war on the way it is to be waged, as well as its supposed independence from consequentialist considerations." Ruti Teitel, *The Wages of Just War*, 39 Cornell Int'l L.J. 689, 691 (2006).

- "For purposes of the *instant* settlement agreements, more than sixty-thousand copies of the Notice of Proposed Settlements with PPG and Sherwin-Williams were mailed to potential class members." *In re Auto. Refinishing Paint Antitrust Litig.*, 617 F.Supp.2d 336, 341 (E.D. Pa. 2007).

This bit of legal JARGON ought to be used sparingly if at all. See **case at bar.**

instanter, a silly LATINISM to find in an English-language context, easily makes our list of FORBIDDEN WORDS. Apart from facetiousness, there is no good reason for preferring *instanter* to *instantly* or *at once.* There are several reasons, however, for preferring *instantly.* First, it is universally comprehensible among speakers of English. Second, it conveys the nuances available to either term. Third, it is not, like its cousin the Latinism, pompous (e.g., "Study of, and, if study warrants, changes in land use control cannot be completed *instanter* [read *instantly*].*"). And fourth, it is not susceptible to the AMBIGUITY of *instanter*, which a few courts have held to mean "within 24 hours."

Adding to the utter dispensability of *instanter*, some legal writers have failed to understand that the term is an adverb and have misused it as if it were an adjective: "It [was] . . . an excessive statement made in the heat of closing argument of a hard-fought case, one which was objected to and subjected to [see ALLITERATION] an *instanter* cautionary instruction." *U.S. v. Frascone*, 747 F.2d 953, 958 (5th Cir. 1984). The writer should have used *immediate.*

All that being said, the jocular contexts do exist in which *instanter* is just the word—e.g.: "The worst woman I ever knew . . . had a face [that] for purity and innocence I can only compare with Raphael's 'Madonna,' and some of the best men and women who have crossed my path would have been convicted *instanter* under any laws founded on Cesare Lombroso's theories." F.W. Ashley, *My Sixty Years in the Law* 163 (1936).

instantiate (= to represent by an instance) is a vintage World War II NEOLOGISM of questionable value. E.g.: "The reference to defendant's silence constitutes harmless error; Chapman's fate is to *instantiate* [read *exemplify*] this third rule." *Chapman v. U.S.*, 547 F.2d 1240, 1250 (5th Cir. 1977).

instantly. See **instantaneously.**

in statu quo is a LATINISM properly equivalent to *in statu quo ante* (= in the same condition as previously). Some writers have quite understandably assumed that there was a distinction between *in statu quo* and *in statu quo ante*, and have used the former merely to mean "in the status quo; in the same condition as now exists." In the examples that follow, the phrase is correctly used:

- "In the absence of other rules, the court is to simply leave matters *in statu quo.*" Craig R. Callen, *Cognitive Science and the Sufficiency of "Sufficiency of the Evidence" Tests*, 65 Tul. L. Rev. 1113, 1120–21 (1991).

- "A requirement for rescission based upon unilateral mistake [is that] the other party can be placed *in statu quo.*" *Cameron v. Bogusz*, 711 N.E.2d 1194, 1198 (Ill. App. Ct. 1999).

- "Courts will not reform if the rights of innocent third parties, such as bona fide purchasers or others who have acquired intervening rights who cannot be placed *in 'statu quo,'* are affected." *Chandelle Enters. v. XLNT Dairy Farm, Inc.*, 699 N.W.2d 241, 248 (Wis. Ct. App. 2005).

See ITALICS (C).

But the foregoing discussion is largely beside the point, since the English renditions of the phrase are preferable to the Latinate. One should write *in the status quo* (present condition) or *in the status quo ante* (previous condition). See **status quo.**

instill; instil. The preferred spelling in AmE is *instill.* *Instil* is preferred in BrE. This word takes the preposition *(in)to*, not *with* <he instilled character as well as knowledge into his students>. Use of the latter preposition occurs as a result of confusion of *inspire* with *instill.* See OBJECT-SHUFFLING.

In the following sentence, *instill in* is misused for *confer on*: "Presence within a state, even temporary or transitory presence, is still a common-law basis *instilling competence in* [read *conferring competence on*] the courts of that state to adjudicate claims against a person." *Leab v. Streit*, 584 F.Supp. 748, 755–56 (S.D.N.Y. 1984).

instillation; *instillment. The second is a NEEDLESS VARIANT.

instinct (= imbued, charged, or filled *with*) is a recherché usage that has given the law a memorable idiom:

- "The whole contract is *instinct* with such an obligation." *McCall Co. v. Wright*, 117 N.Y.S. 775, 779 (App. Div. 1909).

- "There are times when reciprocal engagements do not fit each other like the parts of an indented deed, and yet the whole contract . . . may be '*instinct* with an obligation,' imperfectly expressed." *Moran v. Standard Oil Co. of. N.Y.*, 105 N.E. 217, 221 (N.Y. 1914) (per Cardozo, J.).

- "The personal atmosphere of the Court of Appeal today is *instinct* with comity and friendliness." Asquith, L.J., [1950] J.S.P.T.L. 353.

instinctive; *instinctual. The second is a NEEDLESS VARIANT.

institute is a FORMAL WORD for *begin* or *start.* Cf. **commence.** See **begin (B).**

institute proceedings is a highfalutin way of saying *file suit.*

instruct = to give information as a client to (as a solicitor) or as a solicitor to (a counsel); or (2) to authorize (a solicitor or barrister) to act for one. E.g.: "This cause has been carefully *instructed* with evidence by the practisers, who have had the conduct of it." *Evans v. Evans*, [1790] 161 E.R. 466. See **advise (D).**

instructed verdict. See **directed verdict.**

instructions to the jury. See **summing-up.**

instrument = a formal legal document that entails rights, duties, and liabilities, such as a contract, will, note, bill of exchange, money order, share certificate, and the like. E.g.: "Will and Codicil are separate *instruments* in point of execution. One may stand and the other may fall." *In re Estate of Martin*, 771 N.Y.S.2d 292, 294 (Sur. Ct. 2003). Often the word can be supplanted to advantage by *writing* or *document*, terms understandable to nonlawyers.

The word *instrument* strongly suggests a document that is the result of drafting—i.e., a document that sets forth the rights, duties, and liabilities of parties or beneficiaries. To call a piece of written advocacy an *instrument* is to mangle the legal idiom: "No *instrument* [read *document*] of this character [i.e., a brief] is in use in England." William M. Lile et al., *Brief Making and the Use of Law Books* 366 (3d ed. 1914). [Or: *No such document is in use in England.*]

In any event, the phrase *written instrument* and *instrument in writing* are redundancies when a legal instrument is clearly contemplated, since there is no such thing as an *oral instrument*. See **document.** Cf. **statutory instrument.**

insubstantial; *unsubstantial. The second is a NEEDLESS VARIANT.

*insue is an archaic spelling of *ensue*. See **ensue.**

in suit = in dispute, or (engaged) in a lawsuit. E.g.:

- "The district court's function extended . . . to resolution of legal problems incidental to determining the applicability of claimed exemptions to the information *in suit*." *National Org. for Women, Wash., D.C. Ch. v. Social Sec. Admin.*, 736 F.2d 727, 735 (D.C. Cir. 1984).
- "In December 2008, the district court construed certain claims of the patents *in suit*." *Hearing Components, Inc. v. Shure Inc.*, 600 F.3d 1357, 1362 (Fed. Cir. 2010).

The notation in the *OED* that this phrase from legal JARGON is obsolete proved to be premature. Yet the phrase is hardly common.

insurable. So spelled.

insurance. A. Pronunciation. This word is pronounced with the primary accent on the second syllable /in-**shoor**-əns/.

B. Two Species. Insurance is of two kinds. One is insurance against accidents: buildings burning, ships sinking, cars colliding, being injured, and the like.

The other—in BrE frequently called *assurance*—is provision for designated persons on the occurrence of death (*life insurance* [AmE] or *life assurance* [BrE]). See **assurance.**

insurance adjuster (AmE) = *insurance assessor* (BrE).

insurant. See **insured.**

insure. See **assure.**

insured, n., like *deceased* and *accused*, forms an awkward plural and possessive. E.g.: "It is undisputed that the group life-insurance policies fail to define the effective date of an *insured's* retirement benefits under the Social Security Act." *Gravalin v. Reliance Standard Life Ins.*, 592 F.Supp.2d 1184, 1191 (D.N.D. 2009). An equivalent term, *insurant*, solves this infelicity but is little known. See PLURALS (D) & POSSESSIVES (F).

insurer; insuror. The first is standard; avoid the second. See **underwriter.**

insurgence; insurgency. These two words have undergone DIFFERENTIATION. *Insurgence* = a revolt; the action of rising against authority. *Insurgency* = the quality or state of being in revolt; the tendency to rise in revolt (*OED*). See **coup d'état.**

insurrection. See **coup d'état** & **sedition.**

insurrectionary; *insurrectional. The second is a NEEDLESS VARIANT.

in tail. See **tail.**

integrable. So spelled—not **integratable*.

integral; integrant. The second is a NEEDLESS VARIANT as an adjective; but it exists legitimately as a noun (meaning "component"): "A res is a necessary *integrant* of the concept of 'constructive trust.'" *Elliot v. Elliot*, 41 Cal. Rptr. 686, 688 (Dist. Ct. App. 1964).

Integral is often misspelled **intergral*—e.g.:

- "The administering bodies will be an *intergral* [read *integral*] component of the EAI environmental programs." J. Eugene Gibson & William J. Schrenk, *The Enterprise for the Americas Initiative*, 25 Geo. Wash. J. Int'l L. & Econ. 1, 48 (1992).
- "The district court found that the record in this case demonstrated the *intergral* [read *integral*] connection between music therapy and the social and religious beliefs of the Camphill movement." Enid Trucios-Haynes, *Religion and the Immigration and Nationality Act*, 9 Geo. Immigr. L.J. 1, 32 n.168 (1995).

integrant. See **integral.**

integrated bar. This is an odd name for a bar in which membership is compulsory for anyone wishing to practice law. To the nonlawyer, the phrase is likely to give rise to a MISCUE, as one writer recognized with his parenthetical: "Twenty-seven states have *integrated bars*. (Nothing to do with racial relations. All lawyers in these integrated-bar states have to be members of the bar association in order to practice.)" Murray T. Bloom, *The Trouble with Lawyers* 161 (1970). See **bar**, n.

integration. See **desegregation.**

integration clause; merger clause. These synonyms denote a contractual provision stating that the contract represents the parties' complete and final agreement and supersedes all informal understandings and oral agreements relating to the subject matter of the contract.

integrity. See **honesty.**

intellectual property comprises two subdivisions: industrial property and copyright. *Industrial property* includes patents, inventions, trademarks, and industrial designs. *Copyrights* are property rights in literary, musical, artistic, photographic, and film works, as well as in maps and technical drawings. *See* R.P. Benko, *Protecting Intellectual Property Rights* 2–3 (1987).

intelligent. In lay usage this word is usually confined to descriptions of persons; in legal writing it is used just as frequently of acts as it is of persons. An *intelligent* act is one that is carried out comprehendingly. E.g.: "An applicant may attack the voluntary, knowing, and *intelligent* character of a guilty plea entered on the advice of counsel by demonstrating that counsel's representation was below an objective standard of reasonableness." *Dalton v. State*, 654 S.E.2d 870, 874 (S.C. Ct. App. 2007). See HYPALLAGE.

intelligent; intelligible. *Intelligent* means (of persons) "having mental power or grasp." *Intelligible* means (of statements) "understandable."

intend = (1) in ordinary language, to desire that a consequence will follow from one's conduct; or (2) in legal language, to contemplate that consequences of one's act will necessarily or probably follow from the act, whether or not those consequences are desired for their own sake.

intendment = (1) the sense in which the law understands something; or (2) a decision-maker's inference about the true meaning or intention of (a legal instrument). E.g.:

- (Sense 1) "The evidence produced upon the trial, with all its legal *intendments*, . . . failed to fairly tend to prove that the plaintiff's discharge was accomplished by the illegal acts of the defendant." *London Guarantee & Accident Co. v. Horn*, 69 N.E. 526, 533 (Ill. 1903).
- (Sense 2) "*Garza* with its heightened review rubric dispenses entirely with a traditional requirement that all reasonable inferences and *intendments* should be indulged in favor of a jury's verdict." R. Jack Ayres Jr., *Judicial Nullification of the Right to Trial by Jury by "Evolving" Standards of Appellate Review*, 60 Baylor L. Rev. 337, 392 (2008).

Lon Fuller explained the term somewhat differently: "Our institutions and our formalized interactions with one another are accompanied by certain interlocking expectations that may be called *intendments*, even though there is seldom occasion to bring these underlying expectations across the threshold of consciousness. In a very real sense when I cast my vote in an election my conduct is directed and conditioned on the anticipation that my ballot will be counted in favor of the candidate I actually vote for. . . . [T]he institution of elections may be said to contain an intendment that the votes cast will be faithfully tallied." Lon L. Fuller, *The Morality of Law* 217 (rev. ed. 1976).

This specialized legal term should never be used as a fancy variant of *intention* or *intent* (both of which mean "purpose, aim, design, meaning"). (See **intention**.) *Common intendment* = the natural meaning in legal construction. *Intendiment* is an obsolete form of *intendment*.

intense; intensive. The best advice, which is conventional, is to shun *intensive* wherever *intense* will fit the context. *Intensive* is really a philosophical and scientific term best left to philosophers and scientists. We lawyers can make do nicely with *intense*—e.g.:

- "Regulations imposing lesser burdens are subject to less *intensive* [read *intense*] scrutiny, and reasonable, nondiscriminatory restrictions ordinarily will be sustained if they serve important regulatory interests." *Clingman v. Beaver*, 544 U.S. 581, 603 (2005) (O'Connor, J., concurring in part).
- "Given the tangle of inconsistent and incomplete documents introduced into evidence purporting to establish Deutsche Bank as the holder of the Debtor's mortgage, which were submitted during a two-day trial and required *intensive* [read *intense*] scrutiny of hundreds of pages of documents, sanctions may be appropriate." *In re Hayes*, 393 B.R. 259, 269 (Bankr. D. Mass. 2008).

intensely. See **intently.**

intensive. See **intense.**

intention; intent. A. Defining the Terms. "The general legal opinion," writes Glanville Williams, "is that *intention* cannot be satisfactorily defined and does not need a definition, since everyone knows what it means. This is largely true. Trouble has been caused in the past because when judges have offered to give definitions or tests of intention for the benefit of the jury they have used wide language going beyond the ordinary meaning of the word." *Textbook of Criminal Law* 51 (1978). The same must be said of *intent*: "The persistence of the word '*intent*' in complex social problems where conscious intent is either irrelevant or indeterminable probably retards legal process. The cloudy ethical atmosphere that hovers about this term tends to make [analysis] difficult." Edward Stevens Robinson, *Law and the Lawyer* 230 (1935). Still, the two words have subtle connotative differences. See (B).

B. Distinguishing the Terms. If any distinction may be drawn between *intent* and *intention*, it must be connotative: one has evil intent, but good intentions; one has the intent to murder, and the intention to do something either morally neutral or laudable. But this distinction has not been fossilized in the language; often *intent* is used of neutral and even good motives, and arguably one may have bad as well as good *intentions*. Euphony usually governs the choice of word.

The usual phrase is *testamentary intent*, although *testamentary intention* has appeared. Following are sentences in which *intent* appears in reference to gifts or transfers of property:

- "Without a large discretionary power in carrying out the general *intent* of the donor to vary the details of administration, and even the mode of application, many charities would fail by the change of circumstances." *Crow v. Clay County*, 95 S.W. 369, 376 (Mo. 1906).
- "We discovered the *intent* of the grantor from other factors, as shown by the instrument, in order to give full effect to the words of limitation." *In re Burchell's Estate*, 87 N.E.2d 293, 297 (N.Y. 1949).

Intention is also sometimes used either with evil connotations (examples 1 and 2 below) or with neutral connotations (example 3):

- "Mr. Baker admitted that he knowingly submitted the Financial Statement with the *intention* to deceive Plaintiff." *In re Baker*, 419 B.R. 47, 51 (Bankr. E.D. Mo. 2009).
- "The Court finds that while the Board failed to comply with the Sunshine Act its actions were not taken in bad faith nor with an *intention* to deceive the public." *Armstrong v. Mayor & City Council of Baltimore*, 976 A.2d 349, 372 (Md. 2009).
- "Gonzalez's claim that there was no dispute in the present case that Clark had no *intention* of running for the office of mayor is therefore irrelevant." *Gonzalez v. Surgeon*, 937 A.2d 13, 24 n.13 (Conn. 2007).

Intention takes the infinitive form of the verb, not the present participle—e.g.:

- "Ponta Del Gada had opened a restaurant and banquet facility for the general public, and HarMel leased the building with the *intention of running* [read *intention to run*] the operation." *Harvey v. Snow*, 281 F.Supp.2d 376, 378 (D.R.I. 2003).
- "At trial, the government rebutted the 'beard defense' by eliciting testimony from several witnesses about lax enforcement of mafia rules, and about other mob members who had grown facial hair with no *intention of leaving* [read *intention to leave*] the criminal conspiracy." *U.S. v. Carneglia*, 603 F.Supp.2d 488, 494 (E.D.N.Y. 2009).

Intent and *intention* are liable to INELEGANT VARIATION. E.g.:

- "In construing the will, all its provisions should be looked to, for the purpose of ascertaining what the real *intention* [read *intent*, for the sake of consistency] of the testatrix was; and, if this can be ascertained from the language of the instrument, then any particular paragraph of the will which, considered alone, would indicate a contrary *intent*, must yield to the *intention* [read *intent*] manifested by the whole instrument." *McMurray v. Stanley*, 6 S.W. 412, 413 (Tex. 1887).
- "Her *intent* in executing the paper, at least so far as such *intent* is now before us, must be determined by the court as a matter of law.... The [paper writing] does not declare

an *intention* [read *intent*] to revoke the will except through its destruction, either wholly or so far as Hart is concerned by O'Kennedy." *In re McGill's Will*, 128 N.E. 194, 196 (N.Y. 1920).

C. And *motive*. The *motive* is the inducement for doing an act; the *intent* is the resolve to commit an act. Stated differently, *motive* relates to the end; *intent* relates to the means. One court has said of these two words (and two others, *deliberation* and *purpose*): "One reason [that these words] are often confused is that they are used synonymously in ordinary speech." *Snakenberg v. Hartford Cas. Ins. Co.*, 383 S.E.2d 2, 7 n.7 (S.C. Ct. App. 1989). See **motive.**

D. And *purpose*. For the erroneous use of *purpose* for *intention*, see **purpose (B).**

E. *Specific intent* in Criminal Law. *Specific intent* = any intention involved in the definition of a crime. Williams considers the phrase unhelpful: "The adjective 'specific' seems to be somewhat pointless, for the intent is no more specific than any other intent required in criminal law. The most it can mean is that the intent is specifically referred to in the indictment. There is no substantive difference between an intent specifically mentioned and one implied in the name of the crime." Glanville Williams, *Criminal Law* 49 (2d ed. 1961).

But other writers point out that because the test for *specific intent* is subjective rather than objective—and therefore more particularized to a defendant's actual state of mind—it conveys a useful sense: "There is no question . . . that [*specific intent*] refers to a subjective inquiry into the defendant's actual state of mind. For this reason, in a prosecution for a specific-intent crime many courts do not permit an instruction that a person is presumed to intend the natural and probable consequences of his acts. Intent to kill, intent to steal, and intent to rape would all be 'specific intents'. . . . The phrase thus refers to some particular state of mind required by the definition of the offense." Peter W. Low et al., *Criminal Law: Cases and Materials* 230–31 (1982). See **general intent.**

F. *Particular intention; general intention; transferred intention*. These are the three types of criminal intention (or *malice*) from the victim's point of view. *Particular intention* involves a particular victim as its target. *General intention* (sometimes called *general malice*) involves no particular victim (as when someone explodes a bomb to destroy a building), but the intention to harm anyone who ends up being harmed is generally ascribed to the perpetrator. *Transferred intention* (or *transferred malice*) occurs when harm intended for one person befalls another by accident. See **malice.**

intentional. For the distinction between *unintentional* and *involuntary*, see **unintentional.**

intentionalism. See INTERPRETATION, MODES OF (A).

intentional manslaughter. See **manslaughter (A).**

---

intentional murder. See **murder.**

intently; intensely. To act *intently* is to act purposefully (intentionally). To act *intensely* is to act potently or passionately.

intents and purposes, for all. See **for all intents and purposes.**

INTER-; INTRA-. These prefixes have quite different meanings. *Inter-* means "between; among." *Intra-* means "within; in." So *interstate* means "between states" and *intrastate* means "within a state." Lawyers have recently created any number of NEOLOGISMS with these prefixes, primarily with *inter-: interagency, interbranch, intercircuit, intercorporate, intermunicipal,* and the like.

inter alia; inter alios; inter alias. The best course, undoubtedly, is to use *among others,* a phrase that can refer to people or things. The Latin is not so simple. While *inter alia* (= among other things) refers to anything that is not human, *inter alios* (= among other persons) refers to people. The unanglicized form *inter alias* (a rare form in English) means "among other female persons."

Both *inter alia* and *inter alios* are used more in legal writing than elsewhere. *Inter alia* is the much more common phrase—e.g.:

- "The Guidelines required, *inter alia*, maintaining records that show the impact that examinations have on applicants according to race, sex, or ethnic group." *Lopez v. Massachusetts,* 588 F.3d 69, 77 (1st Cir. 2009).
- "The individual stated, *inter alia*, that, at a time when he was approximately 14 years old and working as a male prostitute, he was picked up by Griffith, who allowed him to stay at his residence." *U.S. v. Lecco,* 634 F.Supp.2d 633, 635 (S.D. W. Va. 2009).

Though not common, *inter alios* occurs far more frequently in legal than in nonlegal writing—e.g.: "The Senate Report stated that the residual section was intended to reach, *inter alios,* 'a person who induces another to remain silent or to give misleading information to a Federal law enforcement officer.' " *U.S. v. King,* 762 F.2d 232, 238 (2d Cir. 1985).

The misuse of *inter alia* for *inter alios* is on the rise—e.g.: "The first sentence of the statute specifically lists, *inter alia* [read *inter alios*], judges, probation officers, and mental health professionals for the Nebraska State Patrol as persons entitled to disclosure." *State v. Albers,* 758 N.W.2d 411, 415 (Neb. 2008).

In the following sentence, the phrase is not only wrong but also misplaced: "A contract *between, inter alia, the manufacturer and one of its former employees* [read *between the manufacturer and, inter alios, one of its former employees*], wherein the former employee expressly agreed not to disclose any of the processes and methods of the manufacturer, was an admission of a positive character that such processes and methods were secret." Donald M. Zupanec, *Disclosure of Trade Secret as Abandonment,* 92 A.L.R.3d 138, § 16(b) (Supp. 2010).

interceptor; *intercepter. The first spelling is preferred. See -ER (A).

intercourse. In modern usage, even *lawful intercourse* has sexual overtones that are not to be ignored. The term is best avoided in its traditional sense "mutual dealings and communication." To most modern readers this use of the term is a risible ARCHAISM—e.g.:

- "It would be difficult, if not impractical, to make a fixed classification of rights, or to formulate any general rule to be applied in all cases, because of the great variety of rights which men enjoy in their *intercourse* [read *dealings*] with each other and the infinitely varying circumstances in which they are exercised." *Southern Contracting, Inc. v. H.C. Brown Constr. Co.,* 450 S.E.2d 602, 605 (S.C. Ct. App. 1994).
- "They maintain, with considerable support in the record, that upon their release they ended their *intercourse* [read *contacts*] with Shimek, kept to the straight and narrow, and pursued exemplary lifestyles." *U.S. v. Ahlers,* 305 F.3d 54, 55 (1st Cir. 2002).
- "Some of Walker's school records indicate his ability to maintain appropriate social *intercourse* [read *behavior* or *interaction*]." *Walker v. Kelly,* 593 F.3d 319, 326 (4th Cir. 2010).

Commerce was formerly used in virtually all senses of *intercourse,* including in the phrase *sexual commerce* (= sexual intercourse): "*Sexual commerce or intercourse* and *carnal knowledge* are synonymous terms." 44 Am. Jur. *Rape* § 2 (1942). See **commerce.**

interdict (= to forbid; to restrain) is a FORMAL WORD often occurring in legal writing. E.g.:

- "The defendants argue that . . . all the interests in Bernard's estate will necessarily vest before the expiration of the period *interdicted* by the rule against perpetuities." *Marx v. Rice,* 67 A.2d 918, 920 (N.J. Super. 1949).
- "Both [cases] followed and applied the due-process test set out in *Ferguson* and construed its bias prohibition to *interdict* only actual bias, not the mere appearance of bias." *Levitt v. University of Tex. at El Paso,* 759 F.2d 1224, 1228 (5th Cir. 1985).
- "The right to post a supersedeas bond is a privilege extended to the judgment debtor as a price of *interdicting* the validity of an order to pay money." Elaine A. Carlson, *Reshuffling the Deck: Enforcing and Superseding Civil Judgments on Appeal After House Bill 4,* 46 S. Tex. L. Rev. 1035, 1122 (2005).

The word is pronounced /in-tər-**dikt**/ as a verb, /**in**-tər-dikt/ as a noun.

Interdict is also a civil-law term used as a noun in a sense close to "injunction." E.g.: "On May 27, after a three-day hearing, the court granted a preliminary injunction [that] continued the *interdictions* of the [restraining order]." *Waffenschmidt v. MacKay,* 763 F.2d 711, 714 (5th Cir. 1985). It also serves as a verb: in Scotland, for example, one petitions the court to *interdict* trespass.

interest. For its most general sense, see **right, title, and interest.** For the distinction between *interest* and *dividend* in corporate law, see **dividend.**

interest, legal rate of. The phrase refers to the rate of interest imposed as a matter of law where none is provided for contractually. But it suggests, perhaps misleadingly, a legal ceiling.

interests in community. See **concurrent interests.**

interfere. See **meddle.**

interferee, for *person interfered with*, is legal JARGON without much to be said in its defense—e.g.:

- "The court is not aware of any decisions in which the relationship between the interferer and the *interferee* [read *person interfered with*] was that of co-venturers or prospective co-venturers." *United Euram Corp. v. Occidental Petroleum Corp.*, 474 N.Y.S.2d 372, 375 (Sup. Ct. 1984).
- "Tortious interference with a business relationship . . . has four requirements: . . . (2) knowledge of the relationship or expectancy on the part of the *interferee* [read *party interfered with*] . . . ." *Upjohn Co. v. Riahom Corp.*, 650 F.Supp. 485, 488 n.4 (D. Del. 1986).

See -EE.

interference, in the JARGON of American patent lawyers, has a special legal meaning: an administrative procedure in the U.S. Office of Patent and Trademark to determine (1) who is entitled to the patent when two or more applicants claim the same invention or when an application interferes with an existing patent; or (2) whether a trademark that one applicant seeks to register will cause confusion among consumers with another party's mark. *Black's Law Dictionary* 888 (9th ed. 2009).

interfering with contractual relations. See **tortious interference with contractual relations.**

interim relief. See **interlocutory relief.**

interlocutor = (1) a person who takes part in a dialogue (AmE and BrE); or (2) a judicial pronouncement or court order (Scots law).

interlocutory injunction. See **injunction.**

interlocutory relief; interim relief. *Interlocutory relief* is the phrase used in AmE and BrE to mean "a temporary judicial remedy, such as a preliminary injunction." *Interim relief* is an equivalent term sometimes used in BrE.

intermarriage. One word, but usually a NEEDLESS VARIANT of *marriage*—e.g.: "Some statutes provide that *intermarriage* [read *marriage*] of the parties subsequent to the offense [of seduction] is a bar to prosecution therefor." Rollin M. Perkins & Ronald N. Boyce, *Criminal Law* 464 (3d ed. 1982). On the use of **subsequent to* in that sentence, see *****subsequent to.**

intermarry should not be used for *marry*, which itself necessarily implies mutuality. This old-fashioned LEGALISM suggests to the modern reader a hint that the writer is concerned about miscegenation—e.g.: "Before that time, his daughter, Martha Florence, *had intermarried with* [read *had married*] R.P. Watson, and

five children were born unto them." *Watson v. Wolff-Goldman Realty Co.*, 128 S.W. 581, 581 (Ark. 1910). *Intermarry* should be laid to rest, except when one conveys the nuance of marrying only within a specified group.

intermeddle is always spelled with two *d*'s. One might not have thought **intermedling* to be anything but a typographical error, but it appears that way consistently in a popular primer on torts. For more on this word and its near-synonyms, see **meddle.**

intermeddler, officious. See **officious.**

interment; internment. *Interment* = burial <interment of the remains>. *Internment* = detention, esp. of aliens in wartime <internment of Japanese-Americans during World War II>.

In burial contexts, the word *internment* frequently ousts the proper word—e.g.:

- "The *internment* [read *interment*] or other disposition of the deceased's body is an extremely important emotional catharsis for the family and friends of the deceased." *Shelton v. City of Westminster*, 188 Cal. Rptr. 205, 216 (1982).
- "These cases make clear that the common law rule applies only to individual purchasers of burial spaces for direct *internment* [read *interment*] purposes." *In re Memorial Estates, Inc.*, 90 B.R. 886, 901 (N.D. Ill. 1988).

in terms. See **terms, in.**

in terms of is often nothing more than a FLOTSAM PHRASE—e.g.: "The development in the application of a constitutional provision may be shown *in terms of* [read *through*] the power of the federal government to prohibit commerce." Edward H. Levi, *An Introduction to Legal Reasoning* 62 (1949). See VERBOSITY.

intern. See **jail,** vb.

Internal Revenue Service (U.S.) = Inland Revenue Service (U.K.). Each is referred to informally as *the IRS.*

international. To the international lawyer, the word *international* (= of or relating to the legal relations among states or nations) is an antonym of *municipal* (= of or relating to the internal government of a state or nation). See **municipal.**

International Court of Justice in The Hague. See **World Court.**

international law; *jus gentium;* **law of nations.** These phrases are generally synonymous in meaning "the system of law regulating the interrelationship of sovereign states and their rights and duties vis-à-vis one another." *International law*—the newest of the phrases, a NEOLOGISM dating from 1789 and coined by Jeremy Bentham—is the predominant term nowadays. See *jus gentium.*

But the phrase *international law* also has a broader sense, in which it covers not just the law of nations (as defined above) but also *private international law*, or the conflict of laws. In this broader sense, *international law* is concerned with "the rights of persons within the territory and dominion of one nation, by reason of acts, private or public, done within the dominions of another nation." *Hilton v. Guyot*, 159 U.S. 113, 163 (1895) (per Gray, J.).

internecine /in-tər-**nee**-sin/ (= mutually deadly; destructive of both parties) is often misused in hyperbolic ways—e.g.:

- "The judiciary, in fact and of necessity, has absolutely no interest in *internecine* [read *rancorous*] battles over social etiquette or the unprofessional personality clashes [that] frequently occur among opposing counsel these days." *Amax Coal Co. v. Adams*, 597 N.E.2d 350, 352 (Ind. Ct. App. 1992).
- "A private association of volunteer fire fighters chose to remove four individuals from its membership after *an internecine* [read *a bitter*?] struggle." *Yeager v. City of McGregor*, 980 F.2d 337, 344 (5th Cir. 1993).
- "During the Carter administration, the biggest *internecine* [delete *internecine*] schism within the Democratic Party involved disagreements over health care reform." James F. Blumstein, *Health Care Reform: The Policy Context*, 29 Wake Forest L. Rev. 15, 15 (1994).

internment. See **interment.**

internuncio. See **ambassador.**

interoffice. One word.

inter partes. See **ex parte.**

interpellate. See **interpolate.**

interplead, vb. **A. Who Interpleads.** In an *interpleader*, it is traditionally the adverse parties claiming a right to the property held by the stakeholder that are said to *interplead* their claims. Jowitt, for example, states: "When a person is in possession of property in which he claims no interest, but to which two or more other persons lay claim, and he, not knowing to whom he may safely give it up, is sued by one or both, he can compel them to *interplead*." W.A. Jowitt, *The Dictionary of English Law* 997 (Clifford Walsh ed., 1959).

From the late 19th century, however, it has become common to say that the stakeholder *interpleads* the two contending parties. E.g.:

- "The insurance company *interpleaded* the parties." William F. Walsh, *A Treatise on Equity* 59 (1930).
- "The insurance company, not knowing where the payment should *go as between the three, . . . interpleaded the claimants* [read *go, initiated an interpleader among the three claimants*]." *Metro. Life Ins. Co. v. Baker*, 107 F.Supp. 1, 2 (N.D. Tex. 1952).

See **interpleader (A).**

B. Past Tense and Past Participle. The past-tense and past-participial forms are *interpleaded*, not *interpled*—e.g.:

- "Under the statute it is enough that there 'may' be adverse claims by the *interpled* [read *interpleaded*] parties against the property or fund." *Metro. Prop. & Cas. Ins. Co. v. Shan Trac, Inc.*, 324 F.3d 20, 23 (1st Cir. 2003).
- "For one reason or another, all the *interpled* [read *interpleaded*] parties have fallen by the wayside except Inland and Burek, on the one hand, and the IRS, on the other hand." *Family First Bank v. Kusek*, 657 F.Supp.2d 258, 260 (D. Mass. 2009).

See **plead.**

interpleader. A. General Sense and Uses. *Interpleader* = a suit pleaded between two parties to determine a matter of claim or right to property held by a usu. disinterested third party (called a *stakeholder*) who is in doubt about which claimant should have the property, the purpose of the suit being to determine to which claimant delivery or payment ought to be made. (See **stakeholder.**) Despite its appearance, then, *interpleader* generally denotes a type of lawsuit and not a person; that is, the word is not ordinarily an agent noun. See -ER (B).

The equivalent term in Scots law is *multiplepoinding.*

B. As an Agent Noun. The *OED* lists, as one sense of *interpleader*, "one who interpleads," but notes: "it is doubtful whether the word is more than a dictionary assumption due to a misunderstanding." The sole support for the definition and note is a quotation from Worcester's 1846 dictionary. Today the word is not a "dictionary assumption"; it is a bona fide blunder. E.g.:

- "An interpleader action cannot be maintained if the *interpleader* [read *stakeholder*] asserts any right or interest against interpleaded claimants." *State Comp. Fund v. Superior Court*, 466 P.2d 802, 806 (Ariz. Ct. App. 1970).
- "Affirmed order to allow *interpleaders* [read *interpleading parties*] access to discovery." Stan Soocher, *Court Decisions—U.S. Circuit Courts of Appeals*, Nat'l L.J., 6 Aug. 1990, at 46.

See -ER (B).

interpolate; interpellate. *Interpolate* means "to insert into a text or writing"—e.g.:

- "That is not to say that the specification itself must necessarily describe how to make and use every possible variant of the claimed invention, for the artisan's knowledge of the prior art and routine experimentation can often fill gaps, *interpolate* between embodiments, and perhaps even extrapolate beyond the disclosed embodiments, depending upon the predictability of the art." *AK Steel Corp. v. Sollac & Ugine*, 344 F.3d 1234, 1244 (Fed. Cir. 2003).
- "I prefer to say that literal interpretation of contracts (specifically, a court's refusal to *interpolate* any implied terms—implied conditions, as they are rather confusingly described) creates opportunities for parties to extract surplus that the parties would not have agreed to had they foreseen and made provision against such behavior." Richard A. Posner, *Let Us Never Blame a Contract Breaker*, 107 Mich. L. Rev. 1349, 1360 (2009).

Interpellate, used in legislative reports, means "to question formally; to seek information"—e.g.:

- "Each deputy has the right to *interpellate* the government or its members about matters within their competence."

Constitution of the Czech Republic, art. 53(1), 28 U.S.F. L. Rev. 3, 14 (1993).

- "While the Legislative Yuan is in session, its members shall have the right to *interpellate* the president of the Executive Yuan and the heads of ministries and other organizations under the Executive Yuan." *Additional Articles of the Constitution of the Republic of China*, art. 3(1), 15 Chinese (Taiwan) Y.B. In'tl L. & Affairs 93, 96 (1996–1997).

interpose for *submit* <to interpose a demurrer> is the term traditionally used for pleadings and motions made by the defense. E.g.:

- "In 1993, the Legislature saw fit to codify the *Chalmers* remedy . . . providing that a claimant who timely served and filed a notice of intention but failed to timely *interpose* a claim pursuant to the provisions of § 10 could ask the court for permission to treat the notice of intention as a claim." *Hamilton v. State*, 807 N.Y.S.2d 842, 851 (Ct. Cl. 2005). On the use of **pursuant to* in that sentence, see **pursuant to.*
- "Plaintiffs cannot have been prejudiced by the District's failure to notify them of information to which they could have *interposed* only frivolous substantive objections." *Pachl v. Seagren*, 373 F.Supp.2d 969, 977 (D. Minn. 2005).
- "For the purposes of determining the allowability of a claim, the trustee is given the benefit of any defense available to the debtor of a personal nature which the debtor could have *interposed*, absent bankruptcy in a suit on the claim by the creditor." 4 Lawrence P. King, *Collier on Bankruptcy* ¶ 502.03[2][b] (15th ed. rev. 2005).
- "In all candor, the Court has struggled to understand how defendant's capable attorneys could have *interposed* such an objection in good faith." *Longcrier v. HL-A Co.*, 595 F.Supp.2d 1218, 1247 n.4 (S.D. Ala. 2008).

*interpretate, an obsolete BACK-FORMATION, is a NEEDLESS VARIANT of *interpret*—e.g.:

- "Texas Institute objected to Special Issue 1 . . . in the trial court on the ground that it required the jury [to] *interpretate* [read *interpret*] the contract of the parties." *Texas Instruments, Inc. v. Jordan*, 602 S.W.2d 342, 344 (Tex. Civ. App.—Dallas 1980).
- "Both questions essentially ask us to *interpretate* [read *interpret*] Amendment 425 of the Constitution of Alabama." *Opinion of the Justices No. 327*, 519 So.2d 956, 957 (Ala. 1988).
- "We also apply these rules when *interpretating* [read *interpreting*] administrative rules and regulations." *Qwest Corp. v. State ex rel. Wyo. Dep't of Revenue*, 130 P.3d 507, 511 (Wyo. 2006).
- "The purpose of both the legislative mandate and the rulings in the above-cited cases was to abrogate the prior procedure of our courts in *interpretating* [read *interpreting*] the 'logical' intent of the insured in executing UM coverage (and consequently, determining whether any rejection/selection was knowingly made)." *Wart v. Progressive Sec. Ins. Co.*, 7 So.3d 865, 872 (La. Ct. App. 2009) (Brown, C.J., dissenting).

interpretatio declarativa. See *declarative interpretation* under INTERPRETATION, MODES OF (B).

interpretatio doctrinalis. See *doctrinal interpretation* under INTERPRETATION, MODES OF (B).

interpretatio excedens. See *extravagant interpretation* under INTERPRETATION, MODES OF (B).

interpretatio grammatica. See *grammatical interpretation* under INTERPRETATION, MODES OF (B).

interpretatio historica. See *historical interpretation* under INTERPRETATION, MODES OF (B).

interpretatio historico-grammatica. See *historico-grammatical interpretation* under INTERPRETATION, MODES OF (B).

interpretatio limitata. See *limited interpretation* under INTERPRETATION, MODES OF (B).

interpretatio logica. See *logical interpretation* under INTERPRETATION, MODES OF (B).

interpretation. A. Sense. Generally speaking, *interpretation* is the ascertainment of a text's meaning. It may involve few or many mental processes, depending on the interpreter, but interpretation assuredly takes place whenever a meaning is communicated. An outmoded view is that clear texts are simply discerned and that interpretation takes place "only when there is some ambiguity or doubt arising from other sources." 1 Joseph Story, *Commentaries on the Constitution of the United States* § 401, at 284 (2d ed. 1858). But the more modern view is that "interpretation is a display or an explanation of [an original text's] meaning [and] the retrieval of that meaning, making it plain to those who might be unaware of it." Andrei Marmor, *Law and Interpretation* 155 (1995).

B. And *construction*. There are two schools of thought with regard to how these terms apply to statutes and other types of drafting. One has it that, although "*interpretation* and *construction* are generally regarded as synonymous and used interchangeably, it is not only possible, but desirable as well, to draw a distinction. The word *interpretation* is used with respect to language itself; it is the process of applying the legal standard to expressions found in the agreement in order to determine their meaning. *Construction*, on the other hand, is used to determine, not the sense of the words or symbols, but the legal meaning of the entire contract; the word is rightly used wherever the import of the writing is made to depend upon a special sense imposed by law." 4 Samuel Williston, *Treatise on the Law of Contracts* § 602, at 320 (3d ed. 1961). *See* Frederick Bowers, *Linguistic Aspects of Legislative Expression* 166 (1989) (calling the distinction "in keeping with general hermeneutic terminology"). See **construction.**

The other school of thought—perhaps more consistent with actual usage—utterly rejects Williston's view: "Some authors have attempted to introduce a distinction between *interpretation* and *construction*. Etymologically there is, perhaps, a distinction; but it has not been accepted by the profession. For practical purposes any such distinction may be ignored, in view of the real object of both interpretation and construction, which is merely to ascertain the meaning and will of the lawmaking body, in order that it may be enforced." William M. Lile et al., *Brief Making and the Use of Law Books* 337 (3d ed. 1914).

The supposed dichotomy between these words appears to derive from the theoretical work of Francis Lieber, who in 1839 defined *interpretation* as the discovery and representation of the true meaning of any signs used to convey ideas, and *construction* as the drawing of conclusions about subjects that lie beyond the direct expression of the text but from elements known from and given in the text. Lieber, *Legal and Political Hermeneutics* 1–2, 110–11 n.2 (1839; William G. Hammond ed., 3d ed. 1880). Apart from a few hermeneuticians (see **hermeneutician**), lawyers have never recognized this amorphous distinction. Cf. **construction.**

C. And *application*. When it comes to the use of authoritative texts, these terms denote different mental acts. *Interpretation* = the ascertainment of a text's meaning; specif., the determination of how a text applies to particular facts. *Application* = the process by which, starting with certain facts, one ascertains the legal category under which the facts should be placed, and the rule of law that is to govern them. *See* Francis Lieber, *Legal and Political Hermeneutics* 247 (William G. Hammond ed., 3d ed. 1880).

INTERPRETATION, MODES OF. A. Theories. Interpretation refers to the ascertainment of a text's meaning. Over the millennia, jurists have developed many different theories about how to derive meaning—some of them firmly rooted in the text, and some not. There are four basic theories: *textualism, intentionalism, purposivism,* and *consequentialism.*

Textualism is the doctrine that because words are capable of a relatively objective meaning, the interpreter's role is chiefly or even exclusively to ascertain that meaning from the language in the text. A synonymous phrase is *verbal-meaning theory.*

Intentionalism is a traditional doctrine of interpretation declaring that the judicial interpreter's goal is to discover the legislature's presumed intent. A major critic of this theory was John Chipman Gray, who wrote: "[I]n almost all [cases of statutory interpretation], it is probable, and . . . in most of them it is perfectly evident, that the makers of the statutes had no real intention, one way or another, on the point in question; that if they had, they would have made their meaning clear; and that when the judges are professing to declare what the Legislature meant, they are, in truth, themselves legislating to fill up *casus omissi*." Gray, *The Nature and Sources of the Law* 165 (1916). A synonymous phrase is *legislative-intent theory.*

The other two theories are allied in that they're subjective. *Consequentialism* denotes a doctrine holding that the rightness or wrongness of a judge-interpreter's reading should be assessed according to its consequences. *Purposivism* denotes the interpretive

doctrine that a drafter's "purposes," as divined by an adjudicator, are at least as important as, if not more important than, the words that the drafter has used. Specifically, purposivism advances the idea that a judge-interpreter should seek for an answer to an interpretive problem not in the words of the text but in the general purposes of the text, considering its social, economic, and political context.

B. Specific Interpretive Terminology. The vocabulary of legal interpretation is profuse, and the approaches are manifold. But set out below are the main terms for different styles of interpretation, as settled by legists over the years.

- *artful interpretation*: A type of predestined interpretation involving cunning attempts to show that the text means something that was not, even by the interpreter's own knowledge, the true meaning. (Also termed *artful construction*.)

- *authentic interpretation*: In the civil-law tradition, an interpretation that proceeds from the author or utterer of the text. Though traditionally termed "authentic," this is actually a type of spurious interpretation. "For the civilian, following the Roman texts, the only binding interpretation is 'authentic'—interpretation by the lawmaking organs." 3 Roscoe Pound, *Jurisprudence* 504 (1959). (Also termed *authentic construction.* See *spurious interpretation*.)

- *broad interpretation*: see *liberal interpretation.*

- *contemporaneous interpretation*: **1.** An interpretation given at or near the time when a text was prepared, usu. by one or more persons involved in its preparation. **2.** The doctrine that a legal text should be interpreted in light of the knowledge, needs, and mores existing when the interpretive decision is rendered. (Also termed (in sense 2, when in reference to a constitution) *living constitutionalism, contemporaneous construction.*) Sense 2, invented by Edgar Bodenheimer, is highly unusual because *contemporaneous* is used in a paltering way: typically, *contemporaneous* means "historical" because the relevant time is the drafting, but Bodenheimer makes the relevant time the interpretive event, as if *contemporaneous* were synonymous with *contemporary*. See Bodenheimer, *Jurisprudence: The Philosophy and Method of the Law* 405, 407–08 (rev. ed. 1974). See **contemporary.**

- *declarative interpretation*: An interpretation that settles the meaning of a term that had been vague or ambiguous (as when *game* in reference to animals is settled on which specific animals are and are not covered by the term). (Also termed *interpretatio declarativa; declarative construction.*)

- *doctrinal interpretation*: An interpretation that is based on some doctrine other than fairly deriving the meaning from the text. (Also termed *interpretatio doctrinalis; doctrinal construction.*)

- *extravagant interpretation*: An interpretation that replaces the true meaning of a text with something clearly beyond it. (Also termed *interpretatio excedens; extravagant construction.*)

- *fair interpretation*: An interpretation that a sensible reader, being competent in the language, would give to a drafter's formulation—being careful neither to stretch nor to shrink the words beyond their normal significations. (Also termed *fair construction.*)

- *free interpretation*: An interpretation not based on any specific principle or doctrine other than what the interpreter decides is most desirable. An early statement of this unconstrained approach is as follows: "Nay, whoever hath an absolute authority to *interpret* any written or spoken laws, it is *he* who is truly the Law Giver to all intents and purposes, and not the Person who first wrote or spoke them." Benjamin Hoadly, *Sixteen Sermons* 291 (1754). (Also termed *unrestricted interpretation*; *free construction*.)

- **grammatical interpretation**: An interpretation based on text and context. (Also termed *interpretatio grammatica*; *grammatical construction*.)

- **historical interpretation**: **1.** An interpretation based on original meaning (see **originalism**). **2.** In the civil-law tradition, interpretation derived from regarding the precept as the culmination of a course of historical development disclosing its idea. (Also termed *interpretatio historica*; *historical construction*. See **original intent**.)

- **historico-grammatical interpretation**: An interpretation based on an analysis of history and grammar. (Also termed *interpretatio historico-grammatica*; *historico-grammatical construction*.)

- **interpretation contra legem** /**kon**-trə **leg**-əm/: An interpretation contrary to the words of the text, usu. arrived at for consequentialist (extratextual) reasons.

- **interpretation ut res magis valeat quam pereat**: An interpretation arrived at when alternative readings are possible, one of which (usu. the broader reading) would achieve the manifest purpose of the document and one of which (usu. the narrower reading) would reduce it to futility or absurdity, whereby the judge-interpreter chooses the one that gives effect to the text. (Also termed *construction ut res magis valeat quam pereat*.)

- **liberal interpretation**: A broad interpretation of a text's language, including the use of related writings for deriving meanings, and possibly also a consideration of modern meanings, all with a view to effectuating the "spirit" of the text. (Also termed *loose interpretation*; *broad interpretation*; *liberal construction*; *interpretatio lata*.)

- **limited interpretation**: An interpretation restricted by some principle or doctrine other than a good-faith reading. (Also termed *restricted interpretation*; *interpretatio limitata*; *limited construction*; *restricted construction*.)

- **literal interpretation**: An interpretation based strictly on the exact grammatical sense of unambiguous words. (Also termed *interpretatio verbalis*.)

- **logical interpretation**: An interpretation based on reasoning about the lawmaker's meaning. (Also termed *interpretatio logica*; *logical construction*.)

- **loose interpretation**: see *liberal interpretation*.

- **predestined interpretation**: An interpretation that is consciously or unconsciously influenced by a strong bias that makes the text subservient to the interpreter's preconceived views. (Also termed *interpretatio predestinata*; *predestined construction*.)

- **purposive interpretation**: An interpretation that looks to the "evil" that the statute is trying to correct (i.e., the statute's purpose). (Also termed *teleological interpretation*; *purposive construction*; *teleological construction*.)

- **restricted interpretation**: see *limited interpretation*.

- **spurious interpretation**: An interpretation that makes, unmakes, or remakes meaning rather than discovering it. According to Roscoe Pound, spurious interpretation "puts a meaning into the text as a juggler puts coins, or what not, into a dummy's hair, to be pulled forth presently with an air of discovery." 3 Roscoe Pound, *Jurisprudence* 479–80 (1959). And: "Spurious interpretation as interpretation

is an anachronism in an age of legislation in the maturity of a system of law." *Id.* at 482. "The bad features . . . may be said to be three: (1) that it tends to bring law into disrepute; (2) that it subjects the courts to political pressure; (3) that it invites an arbitrary personal element in judicial administration." *Id.* at 488. (Also termed *spurious construction*.)

- **strict interpretation**: An interpretation according to what the interpreter narrowly believes to have been the specific intentions or understandings of the text's authors or ratifiers, as contrasted with either a fair or a liberal interpretation. (Also termed *strict construction*; *interpretatio stricta*.)

- **systematic interpretation**: In the civil-law tradition, an interpretation derived from analysis of the legal system and fitting the precept into that system. (Also termed *systematic construction*.)

- **teleological interpretation**: see *purposive interpretation*.

- **tortured interpretation**: An interpretation that stretches or shrinks the words beyond the sense that would be given to them by a normal speaker of the language. E.g.: "[T]hey invariably tend to gloss the pitfalls of *interpretatio torta*, that is, of the torture of interpretation and hence of the ultimate incompetence of any and every kind." Miguel Tamen, *Manners of Interpretation* 113 (1993). (Also termed *interpretatio torta*; *tortured construction*.)

- **usual interpretation**: An interpretation on grounds of custom and usage. (Also termed *interpretatio usualis*; *usual construction*.)

- **viperine interpretation**: An interpretation that essentially destroys the text. A few authorities have translated *interpretatio viperina* as simply "a bad interpretation," but this pale rendering has been soundly corrected: "That is a *viperous interpretation* which eats the bowels out of the text. The force of *viperina* is much weakened by the translation 'bad exposition,' given in Branch and Wharton." 2 Alexander Burrill, *A Law Dictionary and Glossary* 595 (2d ed. 1860). (Also termed *viperous interpretation*; *interpretatio viperina*; *viperine construction*.)

interpretation ut res magis valeat quam pereat. See INTERPRETATION, MODES OF (B).

interpretatio predestinata. See *predestined interpretation* under INTERPRETATION, MODES OF (B).

interpretatio torta. See *tortured interpretation* under INTERPRETATION, MODES OF (B).

interpretatio usualis. See *usual interpretation* under INTERPRETATION, MODES OF (B).

interpretatio viperina. See *viperine interpretation* under INTERPRETATION, MODES OF (B).

interpretive; interpretative; *interpretational. Generally, one forms the adjective on the model of the noun form of a word. Hence *prevention* yields *preventive*, not **preventative*. But with *interpretation*, the traditionally correct adjectival form was thought to be *interpretative* (= having the character or function of interpreting; explanatory), which some use consistently—e.g.: "[T]he academicians ask whether state courts shall adopt an *interpretative* or a *noninterpretative* approach to their state constitutions." Shirley S. Abrahamson, *Criminal Law and State Constitutions*, 63 Tex. L. Rev. 1141, 1180 n.157 (1985).

Yet because *interpretive* overtook the longer form during the 20th century, it's now standard. E.g.:

- "My aim is to examine the relative acceptability of *interpretive* [read *interpretative*] and *noninterpretive* [read *noninterpretative*] modes of constitutional adjudication for the generation of Americans who framed the Constitution." Thomas C. Grey, *Origins of the Unwritten Constitution*, 30 Stan. L. Rev. 843, 849 (1978).
- "In light of the continuing debate over *interpretive* [read *interpretative*] versus *noninterpretive* [read *noninterpretative*] modes of constitutional adjudication, the prospect of using established international norms to inform the meaning of constitutional provisions deflects some of the more telling criticisms of *noninterpretive* [read *noninterpretative*] review." Joan F. Hartman, *"Unusual" Punishment*, 52 U. Cin. L. Rev. 655, 691 (1983).
- "[Appellant] filed for rehearing of the new *interpretive* [read *interpretative*] rule under the FPA." *Middle S. Energy, Inc. v. FERC*, 747 F.2d 763, 767 (D.C. Cir. 1984).
- "In light of the *interpretive* [read *interpretative*] methods prescribed by the caselaw, we look to the official comments of the National Conference of Commissioners on Uniform State Laws." *Hennepin County v. Hill*, 777 N.W.2d 252, 256 (Minn. Ct. App. 2010).

*Interpretational is a NEEDLESS VARIANT—e.g.: "The courts do not all follow a single basic *interpretational* [read *interpretive*] technique." James J. White & Robert S. Summers, *Uniform Commercial Code* § 4, at 18 (3d ed. 1988).

interpretivism; noninterpretivism. Among American constitutional lawyers, the terms *interpretivism* and *noninterpretivism* have become standard words for certain doctrines of constitutional interpretation. Although they have been called misleading labels, they are unlikely to disappear. One might have preferred that the words be *interpretationism* and *noninterpretationism*, but the ill-formed versions are probably too well entrenched to be easily uprooted. Cf. **interpretive.**

Interpretivism = the doctrinal view that the only norms in constitutional adjudication are those stated or closely inferable from the text, and that it cannot be left to the judiciary to give moral content from age to age to such concepts as "fundamental liberties," "fair procedure," or "decency." *Noninterpretivism* = the doctrine that the meaning of a legal instrument adopted in the past is subject to historical development and must be ascertained at any given time by recourse to insights and values then and there prevailing; esp., the doctrinal view that constitutional adjudication should not be confined to the text and that courts are justified in resorting instead to modern moral and political ideals that represent the judges' view of sound public policy.

In short, the so-called *interpretivists* "believe that the Court must confine itself to norms clearly stated or implied in the language of the Constitution," while the *noninterpretivists* "believe that the Court may protect norms not mentioned in the Constitution's text or in its preratification history." Erwin Chemerinsky, *The Price of Asking the Wrong Question*, 62 Tex. L. Rev. 1207, 1208–09 (1984). Cf. **strict construction.**

interregnum. Pl. *-nums, -na.* The native English plural (*-ums*) is preferred. See PLURALS (A).

interrogate is a FORMAL WORD for *question*; it suggests formal or rigorous questioning. See **ask.**

interrogatee; *interrogee. *W3* lists **interrogee* (= someone interrogated), not *interrogatee*, but the *OED* lists *interrogatee*, not **interrogee*. Since the agent noun is *interrogator*, it makes more sense to prefer the corresponding passive form, *interrogatee.*

interrogation. See **custodial interrogation** & **interrogatory.**

interrogative; *interrogatory, adj.; ***interrogational.** *Interrogative* (= of, pertaining to, or of the nature of, questioning; having the form or force of a question [*OED*]). The other forms are NEEDLESS VARIANTS.

interrogatory, n.; **interrogation.** *Interrogatory* = a legal questionnaire submitted to an opposing party as part of pretrial discovery. *Interrogation* = (1) the act or process of questioning in depth; or (2) questioning as a form of discourse.

*interrogee. See **interrogatee.**

in terrorem (= as a warning; intimidating) is used in legal JARGON primarily of clauses in wills that threaten to dispossess any beneficiaries who challenge the terms of the will. E.g.:

- "Plaintiffs have also sought *in terrorem* fines. Such fines are imposed prospectively and determine in advance, similarly to liquidated damages provisions, the amount which contemnor must pay to plaintiff upon future violation." *The Enforcement of Resale Price Maintenance*, 69 Yale L.J. 168, 190 (1959).
- "The *in terrorem* clause provides the penalty of forfeiture as against anyone who 'shall contest in any court any of the provisions of this instrument.'" *In re Miller's Estate*, 27 Cal. Rptr. 909, 916 (Dist. Ct. App. 1963).
- "Although it is clear that Rabbi Singer intended to prevent Alexander from contesting the will, these *in terrorem* provisions can reasonably be interpreted to express testator's wish that Alexander not commence court proceedings of any type against the estate plan." *In re Estate of Singer*, 920 N.E.2d 943, 946 (N.Y. 2009).
- "In the case at bar, the Government advances a comparable *in terrorem* argument, contending that Congress must have intended to thwart domestic criminals' ability to make unfettered use of foreign banks for money laundering." *U.S. v. Lloyds TSB Bank PLC*, 639 F.Supp.2d 314, 325 n.7 (S.D.N.Y. 2009).

Justice Frankfurter made literary use of the LATINISM: "There is nothing judicially more unseemly nor more self-defeating than for this Court to make *in terrorem* pronouncements." *Baker v. Carr*, 369 U.S. 186, 270 (1962) (Frankfurter, J., dissenting). See ITALICS (C).

No-contest clause is often used as an anglicized equivalent of *in terrorem clause* in the context of wills—e.g.:

- "While we find that the appellant cannot take under the provisions of the will by virtue of the *no-contest clause*, the testator cannot rewrite sections 41 and 43 of the Probate Code to prevent appellant from exercising her right to take as an heir." *In re Estate of Holtermann*, 23 Cal. Rptr. 685, 692 (Dist. Ct. App. 1962).
- "The question whether a *no-contest clause* in a will has been triggered presents, on appellate review, a mixed question of law and fact." *Keener v. Keener*, 682 S.E.2d 545, 548 (Va. 2009).
- "While *no-contest clauses* in wills and trusts are valid and enforceable in California, it has long been the rule that they must be strictly construed and given no wider scope than is plainly required by their terms." *Bradley v. Gilbert*, 91 Cal. Rptr. 3d 680, 688 (Dist. Ct. App. 2009).

interrupter; *interruptor. The first spelling is preferred. See -ER (A).

inter se (= between or among themselves) is an unjustified LATINISM—e.g.:

- "All of these [books], however divergent *inter se* [delete *inter se*] in their philosophical standpoints or their methods, are essentially and generically of one and the same nature." John Salmond, *Jurisprudence* § 4, at 11 (Glanville L. Williams ed., 10th ed. 1947).
- " 'Consortium' has come to mean the reciprocal rights and duties of both husband and wife *inter se* resulting from the marriage." Janet Boeth Jones, *Necessity of Physical Injury to Support Cause of Action for Loss of Consortium*, 16 A.L.R. 4th 537, 537 n.1 (1982).
- "Based upon the testimony received, the Court issued a finely-detailed order relating to the parties' obligations *inter se* [read *between themselves*] concerning the children, down to the number of times a day telephone calls could be made between the respective residences." *Lo v. Lo*, 878 So.2d 424, 425 (Fla. Dist. Ct. App. 2004).
- "When the GEF first began operations, the World Bank, UNEP, and UNDP agreed *inter se* [read *among themselves*] that it would suffice for the World Bank as Trustee to secure an annual, externally audited financial report from each Implementing Agency and periodic unaudited financial reports to satisfy this responsibility." Sophie Smyth, *A Practical Guide to Creating a Collective Financing Effort to Save the World*, 22 Geo. Int'l Envtl. L. Rev. 29, 61 (2009).

Inter sese is a variant form of the phrase without any difference in meaning—e.g.:

- "Many arrangements for economy of expense and for convenience of administration may be made between carriers without subjecting them to liability as partners or as coadventurers 'either *inter sese* or as to third persons.' " *Berkey v. Third Ave. Ry. Co.*, 155 N.E. 58, 60 (N.Y. 1926) (per Cardozo, J.).
- "The rights of the co-owners *inter sese* are not determined by the . . . Arkansas statutes." *U.S. v. National Bank of Commerce*, 726 F.2d 1292, 1295 (8th Cir. 1984).

interspousal (= between spouses) is a relatively recent legal NEOLOGISM, included in neither the *OED* nor *W3*. It probably originated in and is largely confined to AmE—e.g.:

- "The *interspousal* communication sought to be disclosed appears from the record to have been confidential." *C.M.D. v. J.R.D.*, 710 S.W.2d 474, 478 (Mo. Ct. App. 1986).
- "She argues that the 'something more' test should be applied only to complaints seeking to modify *interspousal* support provisions in independent separation agreements." *Ames v. Perry*, 547 N.E.2d 309, 311 (Mass. 1989). See **spousal.**

interstate; intrastate. These adjectives should not be used adverbially, as here:

- "Since, as we have already said, it is not necessary that the person who uses an interstate facility to further an illegal business know such a facility operates *interstate* [read *in interstate commerce* or *across state lines* or *throughout the states*], it follows that an accomplice, standing in the shoes of such an actor, need not have knowledge of the interstate character of the facility used." *U.S. v. Stern*, 858 F.2d 1241, 1247 (7th Cir. 1988).
- "The Safe Homes for Women Act . . . encompasses much more than the mere concept of 'safe homes'; it also provides law enforcement personnel with the authority to enforce civil protective orders from other states, as well as punish an offender who travels *interstate* [read *across state lines*]." George B. Stevenson, *Federal Antiviolence and Abuse Legislation*, 33 Williamette L. Rev. 847, 872 (1997).
- "A private motor carrier is one [that] transports property when the vehicle travels *interstate* [read *across state lines*], the carrier is the owner, lessee or bailee of the property, and 'the property is being transported for sale, lease, rent, or bailment or to further a commercial enterprise.' " *Syracuse Plastics, Inc. v. Guy M. Turner, Inc.*, 959 F.Supp. 147, 150 (N.D.N.Y. 1997).

See INTER-.

interstitial; *intersticial. The first spelling is preferred.

intervener. See **intervenor.**

*intervenience. See **intervention.**

intervening cause. See CAUSATION (D).

intervenor; intervener. Although most English-language dictionaries prefer *intervener*, the U.S. Supreme Court (predominantly) and the leading American treatise on federal courts (uniformly) prefer *intervenor*. See Charles Alan Wright et al., *Federal Practice and Procedure* § 1902, at 231 n.3 (1986).

BrE writers tend to use *intervener*—e.g.: "We have suggested that an *intervener* should be required to show that there was an emergency and that he did not act officiously but in the defendant's best interests." Robert Goff & Gareth Jones, *The Law of Restitution* 350 (3d ed. 1986).

intervention; *intervenience. The latter is a NEEDLESS VARIANT.

An asterisk (*) precedes words and phrases that are invariably inferior forms.

inter vivos, meaning "between living persons," should be spelled as two words. The phrase may either precede or follow the noun it modifies. Traditionally it functions as an adjective following the noun—e.g.:

- "The rule of law is well settled that in transactions *inter vivos*, where a party stands in confidential relations to another . . . , if the dominant party receives the benefit . . . during the existence of such relation, the party reposing the confidence, on seasonable application to a court of equity, may obtain relief." *McQueen v. Wilson*, 31 So. 94, 95 (Ala. 1901).
- "It is established law that a gift *inter vivos* may be made by the deposit of money in the bank to the credit of another." *First Nat'l Bank of Portland v. Connolly*, 138 P.2d 613, 623 (Or. 1943).
- "The only statutorily permitted restriction on the franchisee's right to transfer *inter vivos* his or her interest in the franchise appears in [the statute]." *Dege v. Milford*, 574 A.2d 288, 291–92 (D.C. 1990).

See POSTPOSITIVE ADJECTIVES.

Often *inter vivos* appears as an adjective preceding the noun—e.g.:

- "Contracts not to revoke a will or devise are enforceable under Alabama law, and *inter vivos* transfers—whether to individuals or trusts—cannot be used to circumvent such contracts." *Self v. Slaughter*, 16 So.3d 781, 788 (Ala. 2008).
- "Gray argued that the resulting *inter vivos* transfer took the house out of the estate and therefore out of the will." *Cragle v. Gray*, 206 P.3d 446, 450 (Alaska 2009).
- "The decedent was one of those persons who, in the end, made disposition of some of his property though *inter vivos* transactions regardless of the consequences to the provisions of his estate plan created years before." *In re Estate of Compton*, 919 N.E.2d 1181, 1184 (Ind. Ct. App. 2010).

Some writers unnecessarily hyphenate this phrasal adjective—e.g.: "In most states these statutes can be evaded by *inter-vivos* [read *inter vivos*] transfers, even deathbed transfers." Thomas L. Shaffer, *The Planning and Drafting of Wills and Trusts* 184 (2d ed. 1979). See PHRASAL ADJECTIVES.

Occasionally the phrase is used adverbially—e.g.: "Moreover it could be argued that the control of an owner, in order to be complete, must include not only the power to give *inter vivos* but also the power to provide for devolution after death as a sort of postponed gift." Roscoe Pound, *An Introduction to the Philosophy of Law* 206 (1922).

inter vivos trust; living trust. These terms denote trusts created by the settlor during his or her lifetime. *Inter vivos*, though a LATINISM, has been so commonly used as a general adjective (see the preceding entry) as to be unobjectionable in legal writing. Even so, *inter vivos trust*, though once more common than *living trust*, seems to be fading.

intestacy. See **testacy.**

intestate (= a person who dies without a will) is an attributive noun, the adjective *intestate* having appeared several centuries before the noun. *Intestate*, n., frequently follows a possessive proper noun,

although literally the usage curiously suggests that the decedent somehow "belonged" to the heir—e.g.:

- "David Kling, the present *plaintiff's intestate*, brought this action in his lifetime, claiming damages for an alleged malicious and willful assault, resulting in severe injuries and a fractured skull, endangering life." *Kling v. Torello*, 87 A. 987, 987 (Conn. 1913).
- "This pond cannot be held to embody perils that were not obvious to *plaintiff's intestate* even though he was a child of seven years and three months of age." *Wood v. Consumers Co.*, 79 N.E.2d 826, 833 (Ill. App. Ct. 1948).
- "*Plaintiff's intestate* had owned four of the wagons, but he was a Cherokee and did not intend to return." Ellen E. Sward, *The Seventh Amendment and the Alchemy of Fact and Law*, 33 Seton Hall L. Rev. 573, 603 (2003).

See **testate.**

Intestate, adj., is usually used in reference to persons, but sometimes, through HYPALLAGE, of property—e.g.: "[The court's] conclusion that under the *Hubinger* case the surplus income is *intestate* is correct." *Stempel v. Middletown Trust Co.*, 15 A.2d 305, 310 (Conn. 1940).

in that is commonly used for *because* or *since* in legal prose, often with considerable awkwardness—e.g.:

- "A pledge differs from a chattel mortgage *in that* [read *because*] in the pledge the general ownership of the goods remains in the pledgor." R.A. Brown, *The Law of Personal Property* 622 (1936).
- "*In that* [read *Because*] we have overruled appellant's fourth ground of error, we also overrule ground of error number five." *Williams v. State*, 680 S.W.2d 570, 577 (Tex. App.—Corpus Christi 1984).

in the absence of is prolix for *without*.

in the affirmative; in the negative. See **affirmative, in the.**

in the case of. See **case (A).**

in the circumstances. See **circumstances.**

in the event of. This phrase, which usually precedes a BURIED VERB, can often be changed to *if*—e.g.: "*In the event of the termination of the Employee's employment* [read *If the Employee's employment terminates*] for any reason, ..." *Amalgamated Butcher Workmen Local Union No. 641 v. Capitol Packing Co.*, 413 F.2d 668, 670 (10th Cir. 1969). See **event, in the & of (A).**

*in the event that is unnecessarily prolix for *if*. And it is poor form in drafting—e.g.:

- "The claimed benefits of a contracting scheme are that when parties can provide for different rules to govern *in the event that* [read *if*] a debtor defaults, those parties can adjust their behavior and prices to create efficiency gains." Elizabeth Warren & Jay Lawrence Westbrook, *Contracting Out of Bankruptcy*, 118 Harv. L. Rev. 1197, 1213 (2005).
- "Now consider a rule that is the opposite of the rule of 'no preliminary injunctions with ex post damages': plaintiff can obtain a preliminary injunction as long as she is willing to assume liability for defendant's costs of complying with the injunction *in the event that* [read *if*] the court, at the conclusion of the case, rules in favor of defendant."

Richard R.W. Brooks & Warren F. Schwartz, *Legal Uncertainty, Economic Efficiency, and the Preliminary Injunction Doctrine*, 58 Stan. L. Rev. 381, 399 (2005).

- "The same should hold true *in the event that* [read *if*] Congress suspends the writ domestically in response to the dangers posed by ongoing military operations on foreign soil." Amanda L. Tyler, *Is Suspension a Political Question?*, 59 Stan. L. Rev. 333, 388 (2006).
- "This conditional amendment will only become effective *in the event that* [read *if*] the U.S. district court issues an order in *Flores* to the effect that the State appropriately addressed the issue of implementing appropriate language-acquisition programs." Eugenia Tunstall, Comment, *The Price of Knowledge*, 39 Ariz. St. L.J. 1325, 1336 n.102 (2007).

See **event, in the.**

*in the eventuality. See ***eventuality.**

in the final analysis; in the last analysis. Both are CLICHÉS—e.g.: "*In the last analysis*, the testator had an absolute right to divert his property from this contestant; he was under no obligation to assign any reason for so doing." *In re Shumway's Will*, 246 N.Y.S. 178, 184–85 (Sur. Ct. 1930). These trite expressions only detract from one's prose. One might better simply state the proposition without the tepid lead-in.

in the first instance. See **first instance.**

in the future. See *in futuro.*

in the interest of is verbose for *for.*

in the last analysis. See **in the final analysis.**

in the light of is inferior to *in light of*, itself a CLICHÉ.

in the midst of. See **amid.**

in the offing. See **offing.**

in the process of. See **process of, in the.**

in the record. See **record (c).**

in the status quo; in the status quo ante. See **in statu quo.**

into. See **in.**

in toto (= completely; entirely; wholly) is a LATINISM expressing such a fundamental notion, and having so many ready English synonyms, that it is seldom if ever justified. E.g.:

- "Neither do all of the plaintiff's policies, taken *in toto* [read *as a whole*], allow, in this Court's opinion, the application of that doctrine to the National YWCA." *National Bd. of YWCA v. YWCA of Charleston, S.C.*, 335 F.Supp. 615, 626 (D.S.C. 1971).
- "That material omission *negates the authorization in toto* [read *completely negates the authorization*]." *Ray v. Young*, 753 F.2d 386, 392 (5th Cir. 1985).

Intoxilyzer; Intoximeter. See **Breathalyzer.**

INTRA-. See **INTER-.**

in transitu is an unjustified LATINISM; the English phrase *in transit* suffices. E.g.:

- "The old equitable right of stoppage *in transitu* [read *in transit*] has been repeatedly held to defeat rights of good-faith purchasers for value." *In re Murdock Mach. & Eng'g Co. of Utah*, 620 F.2d 767, 775 (10th Cir. 1980).
- "Ford also reimburses its dealers for any damage *in transitu* [read *in transit*] and carries insurance to cover the cost of repair." *Ford Motor Co. v. Director of Revenue*, 963 A.2d 115, 118 (Del. 2008).

But many statutes, such as the U.K. Sale of Goods Act, 1979, still bear the phrase.

intrastate. See **interstate.**

*intraversion. See **introversion.**

intra vires (= within the powers [of]) is the antonym of, but is not nearly as familiar as, *ultra vires.* E.g.:

- "Courts interfere seldom to control such discretion *intra vires* the corporation." *United Copper Sec. Co. v. Amalgamated Copper Co.*, 244 U.S. 261, 263–64 (1917) (per Brandeis, J.).
- "What we have said, however, only applies when the tort committed is a wrongful way of doing what the corporation has power to do ('*intra vires* tort,' as it is paradoxically called)." O. Hood Phillips, *A First Book of English Law* 281–82 (3d ed. 1955).
- "The sum it spent on *intra vires* functions would fully absorb the sum paid by the banks together with accrued interest." Aviva Golden, *Digest of Trinity Term* (reporting *In re a Company No. 0013734 of 1991*), Fin. Times, 5 Aug. 1992, at 8.

See LATINISMS. Cf. **ultra vires.**

intrigue, vb., has traditionally meant "to carry on a plot or secret love affair." But today the word most commonly functions as the equivalent of *interest* or *fascinate.* Many editors object to the word when used in this newer sense. E.g.:

- "The question of whether a procedure that affords due process is inherently 'adequate' for the purpose of *Burford* analysis is an *intriguing* [read *interesting* or *fascinating*] one, and may prove critical to deciding certain cases." *Goldstein v. Pataki*, 488 F.Supp.2d 254, 272 (E.D.N.Y. 2007).
- "Although the argument that class proceedings in arbitration are incompatible with the Federal Arbitration Act is an *intriguing* [read *interesting*] one, we are presented with no such argument on this appeal." *In re American Express Merchants' Litig.*, 554 F.3d 300, 310 n.7 (2d Cir. 2009).

But in the end, the traditional use of *intrigue* seems doomed.

introduce in(to) evidence. Although both forms commonly appear, one is demonstrably superior: because the phrase suggests movement (physical or metaphorical), *into* is the better preposition—e.g.:

- "To recover, plaintiff would have had to overcome by no more than a mere preponderance of the evidence the presumption enuring to the government from its *introduction in* [read *introduction into*] evidence of the assessment made." *Kaufman v. Scanlon*, 245 F.Supp. 352, 356 (E.D.N.Y. 1965).

- "The confession was only part of the evidence considered by the jury in determining the guilt or innocence of the defendant; the record reflects that he suffered no prejudice from its *introduction in* [read *introduction into*] evidence." *State v. McCauley*, 272 So.2d 335, 343 (La. 1973).

See **in.**

introductory should never be used in the phrase *be introductory of* (something); instead write *introduce*—e.g.:

- "This, although new as a legislative enactment in this state, *was not introductory of* [read *did not introduce*] a new rule." *Brown v. State*, 113 S.E.2d 618, 619 (Ga. 1960).
- "Although the rule is not of universal application, it is generally true that if an affirmative statute which *is introductory of* [read *introduces*] a new law directs a thing to be done in a certain manner, it may not be done in any other manner, even though there are no negative words." 2 Standard Pennsylvania Practice 2d § 6:52 (2010).

See **be-verbs (b).**

As a noun, *introductory* sometimes serves as a chapter title, but it is inferior to *introduction.*

introductory clause; commencement; exordium. In drafting, these are the three names given to the paragraph, placed at the outset of a contract, that gives introductory material. The best of the three phrases is *introductory clause*, and the worst *exordium*. The phrase *introductory clause* applies aptly even if there is more than one sentence. See **clause.**

Introductory "It" and "There." See expletives, **it** & **there is.**

introversion; *intraversion. The first is the preferred spelling.

intrusion = (1) a person's entering property without permission; (2) a highly offensive invasion of another person's seclusion or private life; or (3) historically, the entry of a stranger, after a particular estate of freehold ends, before a remainder or reversion. *See* 3 William Blackstone, *Commentaries on the Laws of England* 169 (1765). In sense 3 it is distinguished from an *abatement* and *disseisin* as a type of ouster. *Id.*

***intrust** is an obsolete form of *entrust*. See **entrust.**

in trust. See **trust (b).**

inundate. So spelled, though it is often misspelled *inn-*, as here: "Lawyers and judges are among those who are *innundated* [read *inundated*] with these media images." Letter of David A. Sharp, 18 Barrister 6 (Winter 1991–1992).

inure; *enure. The first is the standard spelling in both legal and nonlegal texts. *Inure* = (1) to take effect, come into use; or (2) to make accustomed to something unpleasant; habituate. Sense 1 is the sense that usually appears in legal contexts—e.g.:

- "This stipulation, in our opinion, is also a covenant running with the land, and *inures* to the benefit and advantage of the vendors as against any assignee." *Mesa Mkt. Co. v. Crosby*, 174 F. 96, 102 (8th Cir. 1909).
- "To recover, plaintiff would have had to overcome by no more than a mere preponderance of the evidence the presumption *enuring* [read *inuring*] to the government from its introduction in evidence of the assessment made." *Kaufman v. Scanlon*, 245 F.Supp. 352, 356 (E.D.N.Y. 1965).
- "The damages must *inure* to the exclusive benefit of the surviving spouse and children, if any, or next of kin." 12 Okla. Stat. § 1053 (Supp. 1978).

The noun is *inurement.*

Although in sense 2 persons are *inured* to unpleasant things <many battered women, tragically, become inured to violence>, in sense 1 *inure* is used only of positive effects: *inure to the detriment of* is an idiomatic impossibility. The author of the following sentence lacked idiomatic sensibility: "This Court is satisfied that . . . no prejudice has *inured* [read *resulted*] to the defendants from the manner from which the jury was selected herein." *U.S. v. Levasseur*, 704 F.Supp. 1158, 1165 (D. Mass. 1989). Sense 2 occasionally appears in legal writing: "The steady parade of human savagery [that] is presented to us has an *inuring* effect." *Commonwealth v. Belmonte*, 502 A.2d 1241, 1253 (Pa. Super. Ct. 1985) (Brosky, J., dissenting).

Sometimes *inhere* is misused for *inure*. See **inhere (b).**

in utero. See ***en ventre sa mère.***

invade is the metaphor used in the law of trusts to denote withdrawals from an initial or principal investment. E.g.:

- "Income would have been available to the beneficiaries, and the trustee would have had the power to *invade* the corpus of the trust under certain circumstances." *In re Chambers*, 384 B.R. 460, 463 n.2 (Bankr. E.D. Tex. 2008).
- "The trust gave the trustee the discretion to *invade* the principal or corpus to provide her with a reasonable standard of living." *In re Estate of Gist*, 763 N.W.2d 561, 565 (Iowa 2009).

See **corpus** & **trespass.**

invalidate; *invalid, vb. In the sense "to nullify," the second is a needless variant seen only in legal writing. E.g.: "We turn to the question whether such a meritorious patent is to be *invalided* [read *invalidated*] as held by the court below." *Seiberling v. John E. Thropp's Sons Co.*, 284 F. 746, 756 (3d Cir. 1922). See **nullify (a).**

invective. See **abuse,** n.

inveigh; inveigle. To *inveigh* /in-**vay**/ against something is to rant about or protest it. To *inveigle* /in-**vay**-gəl/ someone to do something is to cajole or coax that person to action.

inventable; *inventible. The first spelling is preferred.

inventory is commonly a verb as well as a noun in legal and business contexts. This use of the word, dating back to the 16th century, is perfectly acceptable—e.g.:

- "The United States Supreme Court and the Georgia Supreme Court have approved of a police procedure [that] *inventories* the contents of a car taken into police custody." *Stoker v. State*, 267 S.E.2d 295, 296 (Ga. Ct. App. 1980).
- "There is evidence that Elsie *inventoried* the materials and kept everything except the stock certificates, which Roger brought to his home." *Estate of Lennon v. Lennon*, 29 P.3d 1258, 1265 (Wash. Ct. App. 2001).
- "In *inventorying* the contents of the vehicle before having it towed, officers found what they believed to be drug paraphernalia with drug residue." *Montgomery v. State*, 904 N.E.2d 374, 376 (Ind. Ct. App. 2009).

invest; vest. These words are synonymous in meaning "to establish (a person) in the possession of any office, position, or property; to endow or furnish (a person or institution) with power, authority, or privilege." *Vest* is more usual in general English usage; the use of *invest* in this sense is chiefly confined to legal writing and evangelical preaching <By the power invested in me by the Holy Spirit, I declare that you shall be instantly healed!>.

Not surprisingly, the legal examples have a different tone from the evangelical ones—e.g.:

- "In a proper legal sense the holder of the legal title is not seized until he is fully *invested* with the possession, actual or constructive." *Seymour, Sabin & Co. v. Carll*, 16 N.W. 495, 495 (Minn. 1883).
- "It was expressly stated that his mere status as a cabinet officer was insufficient to *invest* him with absolute immunity." *Arcoren v. Peters*, 811 F.2d 392, 395 (8th Cir. 1987).
- "Congress has *invested* the court with diversity jurisdiction and unless or 'until Congress decides to alter or eliminate the diversity jurisdiction we are not free to treat the diversity litigant as a second-class litigant.'" *McLaughlin v. Miners & Merchants Bank & Trust Co.*, 758 F.Supp. 375, 381 (W.D. Va. 1991).

See **vest.**

investigable is the proper form—not **investigatable*.

investigation; inquiry; inquisition; probe. These terms all refer to a formal or official examination of some specific occurrence or event in a quest for the truth. *Investigation* implies a systematic tracking down of facts and circumstances, typically from a variety of sources, in hopes of putting together an account that answers, as far as possible, what happened <Watergate investigation>. An *inquiry*—in this sense, as opposed to that of a simple question—often appears in the phrase *official inquiry* and implies something far less extensive and exhaustive than an *investigation*, perhaps as insignificant as making a few phone calls <the inquiry seemed effective, though it took hardly any time>. An *inquisition* is far more ambitious in scope and penetrating in depth; it has frequently been applied to a judicial inquiry in the inquisitorial

system, the purpose being to unearth facts that relate to specific allegations or suspicions. The term is seriously tainted with pejorative connotations from its association with medieval and Reformation efforts by ecclesiastical officials to hunt down heretics by pursuing, persecuting, torturing, and executing victims with relentless fervor <the Spanish Inquisition>. A *probe* (the word dates from 1903 as an Americanism) is essentially a limited investigation with the purpose of detecting criminal activity <Congress's probe into abuses in mortgage lending>.

investigative; investigatory. *W3* calls *investigatory* "chiefly British," but it occurs almost as commonly as *investigative* does in American legal contexts. E.g.:

- "Although Martinez contends that the meaning of 'criminal case' should encompass the entire criminal *investigatory* process, including police interrogations . . . , we disagree." *Chavez v. Martinez*, 538 U.S. 760, 766 (2003) (per Souter, J.).
- "The Confrontation Clause in no way governs police conduct, because it is the trial use of, not the *investigatory* collection of, ex parte testimonial statements [that] offends that provision." *Davis v. Washington*, 547 U.S. 813, 832 n.6 (2006) (per Scalia, J.).
- "An action could still be brought against a prosecutor for conduct taken in an *investigatory* capacity, to which absolute immunity does not extend." *Hartman v. Moore*, 547 U.S. 250, 262 n.8 (2006) (per Souter, J.).

The *COD* lists *investigative* before *-tory*, and it does appear more frequently—e.g.:

- "A second, and related, objection to petitioner's argument is that it assumes that the law of arrest has already worked out the balance between the particular interests involved here—the neutralization of danger to the policeman in the *investigative* circumstance and the sanctity of the individual. But this is not so." *Terry v. Ohio*, 392 U.S. 1, 26 (1968) (per Warren, C.J.).
- "England did not have a professional police force until the 19th century . . . so it is not surprising that other government officers performed the *investigative* functions now associated primarily with the police." *Crawford v. Washington*, 541 U.S. 36, 53 (2004) (per Scalia, J.).
- "We conclude that where a prosecutor submits a motion for a bench warrant to the court applying the law to facts alleged in supporting affidavits signed by witnesses, she is acting not in an *investigative* capacity, but instead as a judicial advocate before the court." *Waggy v. Spokane County Wash.*, 594 F.3d 707, 713 (9th Cir. 2010).

There is certainly no need for the two variants to coexist. We might be well advised to throw over *investigatory* and stick with *investigative*, or to develop some heretofore-unhinted-at DIFFERENTIATION. In any event, the two terms should not be used interchangeably in a single piece of writing, as they are in *Terry v. Ohio*, 392 U.S. 1 (1968). See INELEGANT VARIATION.

invidious. See **insidious.**

in view of. See **in lieu of (c).**

in view of the fact that is a weak equivalent of *because*.

inviolate; inviolable. *Inviolable* suggests that something is incapable of being violated, whereas *inviolate* suggests merely that the thing has not been violated. In practice, however, the words are often used interchangeably. *Inviolate* sometimes appears as a POST-POSITIVE ADJECTIVE. E.g.: "The Court weakens, if indeed it does not in fact submerge, this basic principle by finding, in effect, a grant of substantive legislative power in the constitutional provision for a federal court system, and through it, setting up the Federal Rules as a body of law *inviolate*." *Hanna v. Plumer*, 380 U.S. 460, 475–76 (1965) (Harlan, J., concurring).

in virtue of. See **virtue of, in** & **by**.

invitation to negotiate; invitation to treat. See **offer (B)**.

invite is a verb. Avoid it as a noun displacing *invitation*.

invitee. Although nonlawyers might assume that an *invitee* is someone expressly invited onto property, lawyers use the term to include those who have implied permission to enter the premises, such as postal and delivery workers.

inviter; *invitor. The first is preferred. See **-ER (A)**.

invoke. See **evoke**.

involuntary. An *involuntary* act, as Jeremy Bentham phrased it, is an act "in the performance of which the will has no sort of share: such as the contraction of the heart and arteries." *An Introduction to the Principles of Morals and Legislation* 83–84 n.1 (1823 ed.). For the unusual meaning attributed to the word in the phrase *involuntary manslaughter*, see **manslaughter (A)**. For the distinction between *involuntary* and *unintentional*, see **unintentional**.

involuntary trust. See **constructive trust (A)** & **trust (D)**.

in which. See **where (B)**.

in whole; in part. Wilson Follett wrote that *in whole* is unidiomatic for *as a whole*, the former phrase having been created as a needed parallel of *in part*. He was wrong, unless we want to trace what is idiomatic back before the sixteenth century and ignore steady uses up till the present time. Both *in whole* and *as a whole* are acceptable idioms; indeed, they are not even used in quite the same way. Both mean "as a complete thing," but whereas *as a whole* is the general phrase, *in whole* is always used as a correlative of *in part*. E.g.:

- "Where the compensable injury is caused *in whole or in part* by the act or omission of a third party, the employer shall be subrogated to the right of the employee, his personal representative, his estate or his dependents, against such third party to the extent of the compensation payable under this article by the employer." 77 Penn. Stat. § 671 (2007).

- "Of the 832 petitions disposed during the same period, only thirty-four were granted *in whole or in part*." *McKnight v. Office of Pub. Defender*, 936 A.2d 1036, 1054 n.1 (N.J. Super. Ct. App. Div. 2007).

in witness whereof (= signed), one of the quintessential LEGALISMS, is the phrase that introduces the testimonium clause in a legal document. E.g.: "An appropriate testimonium or concluding clause is '*In witness whereof* I have subscribed my name this —— day of 19—,' although 'Witness my signature this —— day of 19—' will do just as well." Thomas E. Atkinson, *Handbook of the Law of Wills* 820 (2d ed. 1953). See **testimonium clause** & **attestation clause**.

I personally is prolix for a simple *I*. Occasionally it is legitimately used to contrast one's personal opinions with an official stance that one takes for reasons of a position one holds. See FIRST PERSON.

ipse dixit (lit., "he himself said it") = something said but not proved; a dogmatic statement. E.g.: "The realm of procedure is after all the judge's special domain; the construction of statutes is a peculiarly judicial art; and the Court's *ipse dixit* seems more authoritative in these areas than it might if substantive issues of policy were being decided." Robert G. McCloskey, *The American Supreme Court* 204 (1960). Cf. ***probatum***. See **dictum (B)**.

ipsissima verba = the very (same) words. E.g.: "So far as possible, I have tried to preserve the *ipsissima verba* of the original author." P.B. Fairest, Foreword to Edward Jenks, *The Book of English Law* xiv (P.B. Fairest ed., 6th ed. 1967).

Another form of the phrase, *ipsissimis verbis*, means "*in* the very (same) words." In the following example, though, the High Court mangled its Latin with a meaningless phrase, *ipsissima verbis*: "The plaintiffs' affidavit evidence on the inquiry stands uncontradicted . . . and unchallenged. . . . This does not mean that I am obliged to accept it *ipsissima verbis* [read *ipsissima verba*]." *Columbia Pictures Indus. v. Robinson*, [1988] F.S.R. 531, 534 (Ch.) (per Scott, J.).

The phrases are easily simplified—e.g.: "Now Texas has hastened to fall into line, and has enacted this North Dakota resolve *ipsissimis verbis* [read *in the very same words* or *verbatim*]" (ex. fr. G. Krapp, *A Comprehensive Guide to Good English* 334 (1927)). Cf. ***in haec verba***. See **verbatim** & LATINISMS.

ipso facto (= by the fact or act itself; by its very nature) is sometimes replaceable by the phrase *in itself*—e.g.: "Lunacy does not *ipso facto* [read *in itself*] dissolve a partnership unless the articles so provide." 2 Ernest W. Chance, *Principles of Mercantile Law* 9 (Percy W. French ed., 10th ed. 1951). But the LATINISM sometimes seems useful—e.g.: "The court said that the statute was against common right and Magna Carta and *ipso facto* void." Roscoe Pound, *The Development of Constitutional Guarantees of Liberty* 101 (1957). The phrase need not be italicized.

I respectfully submit. It is as easy for an advocate to hedge too much as it is to pound too hard. Some lawyers, arguing a position, use *I respectfully submit* as a verbal tic—even when the statement that follows is quite uncontroversial. The result is an undesirable, namby-pamby tone. See **respectfully.**

ironic; *ironical. Ironic* is standard, **ironical* being a NEEDLESS VARIANT.

IRONY is the use of words whose literal and figurative senses are opposites—that is, it is the difference between what seems to be said and what is meant. The chief weapon of satirists, irony subverts the reader's expectations.

A word of warning: "Most attempts by legal writers to employ irony . . . range from ill-advised to pathetic." Jordan H. Leibman & James P. White, *How the Student-Edited Law Journals Make Their Publication Decisions*, 39 J. Legal Educ. 387, 423 (1989). But the warning should not deter unduly. As the following examples illustrate, irony can be an effective rhetorical tool:

- "The only thing about the appeals [that] we can commend is the hardihood in supposing that they could possibly succeed." *U.S. v. Minneci*, 142 F.2d 428, 429 (2d Cir. 1944) (per L. Hand, J.).
- "Ownership meant no more to [the Shoshone Indians] than to roam the land as a great common, and to possess and enjoy it in the same way that they possessed and enjoyed sunlight and the west wind and the feel of spring in the air. Acquisitiveness, which develops a law of real property, is an accomplishment only of the 'civilized.'" *Northwestern Bands of Shoshone Indians v. U.S.,* 324 U.S. 335, 357 (1945) (Jackson, J., concurring).
- "I cannot say that I know much about the law, having been far more interested in justice." William Temple, the former Archbishop of Canterbury, as quoted in Lord Denning, *The Road to Justice* 1 (1955).
- "We hold that the first amendment does not clothe these plaintiffs with a constitutional right to sunbathe in the nude. . . . They remain able to advocate the benefits of nude sunbathing, albeit while fully dressed." *South Fla. Free Beaches, Inc. v. Miami*, 734 F.2d 608, 610 (11th Cir. 1984) (per Henderson, J.).

One of the most common types of irony is the Swiftian modest proposal, here carried out with some success: "Of course, a simple mechanism for deterring violations such as [police brutality] would be to amend section 1983 to provide that violators will be drawn and quartered. This seems like a very powerful deterrent and might substantially reduce violations of federal rights under color of state law. But aside from problems relating to fairness, this solution also poses problems in the deterrence framework. A powerful deterrent such as drawing and quartering offenders might also deter worthwhile conduct [by the police]. . . . So, the deterrence rationale calls for neither too much nor too little deterrence; we need to find the right amount." *Dobson v. Camden*, 705 F.2d 759, 765 (5th Cir. 1983) (per Goldberg, J.).

irrebuttable; irrefutable. See **rebut.**

irrefragable (= unanswerable; not to be controverted), a useful term in the law, is underused today—so much so that its pronunciation has caused problems even in the Old Country: "In 1955 leading counsel pronounced it [/ir-i-**frag**-ə-bəl/], but Harman J. asserted that it was [/ir-i-**fray**-gə-bəl/]; and so it was for the rest of the case. However, on appeal (on another point) one of the juniors invoked the *Oxford English Dictionary*, and his leader persuaded a reluctant and suspicious Court of Appeal to shift the accent from the third syllable to the second, and pronounce the word [/i-**ref**-rə-gə-bəl/]." R.E. Megarry, *A Second Miscellany-at-Law* 164 (1973). Only Harman J. got it entirely wrong, both of the other pronunciations being acceptable (and the last one given being preferred).

irrefutable. See **rebut.**

irregardless. See **regardless (A).**

irrelevance; *irrelevancy. The first is generally preferred. The only plural form, however, is *irrelevancies*. See **relevance.**

irreparable is pronounced /i-**rep**-ə-rə-bəl/.

irreparable injury is a phrase that "generally produces more dust than light." *Studebaker Corp. v. Gittlin*, 360 F.2d 692, 698 (2d Cir. 1966). Often misunderstood, *irreparable injury* means merely that the injury cannot be remedied through an award of damages. As Douglas Laycock has convincingly shown, "That an injury has little monetary value is often a cause of irreparability, not an antidote." *The Death of the Irreparable Injury Rule* 74 (1991).

irrepleviable; irreplevisable. See **repleviable.**

irrespective of = regardless of. E.g.: "It is true that the author is the owner of the composition as property *irrespective* of its value." William F. Walsh, *A Treatise on Equity* 217 (1930).

Confusion of the words *irrespective* and *regardless* has given rise to the mistaken form **irregardless*. (See **irregardless.*)

irresponsive. See **nonresponsive** & **unresponsive.**

irrevocable; *unrevokable. The first is preferred. It is pronounced /i-**rev**-ə-kə-bəl/.

irritate. See **aggravate.**

IRS. See **Internal Revenue Service.**

is able to is verbose for *can.*

is binding upon is verbose for *binds.*

is comprised of. See **comprise (B).**

-ISE. See **-IZE.**

is entitled to. See WORDS OF AUTHORITY (G).

---

island company. See **offshore company.**

isle (= island) for *aisle* (= a passage for foot traffic) results from mistaking homophones—e.g.: "As she was walking down one of the *isles* [read *aisles*] in the store she slipped on a potato sprout near the potato bin and fell." *Houtchens v. Kyle's Grocery Corp.*, 390 S.W.2d 325, 326 (Tex. Civ. App.—Eastland 1965).

isolable, not **isolatable*, is the correct form. E.g.:

- "We do not believe the events are so easily *isolable*." *U.S. v. Jeffers*, 342 U.S. 48, 52 (1951) (per Clark, J.).
- "The State . . . bas[es] its position on the fact that the petitioner has established no *isolatable* [read *isolable*] prejudice." *Estes v. Texas*, 381 U.S. 532, 542 (1965) (per Clark, J.).

The word is pronounced /ɪ-sə-lə-bəl/.

issuable. In nonlegal contexts this word means "capable of being issued"—and sometimes in legal writing as well. E.g.: "It is fair to say that though the writ of habeas corpus was *issuable* at common law its present form in England has had its origin in the Act of 1679." C. Gordon Post, *An Introduction to the Law* 60 (1963).

But the word carries a special legal sense: "that admits of an issue being taken; in regard to which or during which issue may be joined" (*OED*). E.g.: "No *issuable* fact or condition existed that would authorize the governing board to exercise the discretion confided to it in the passage of that part of the zoning ordinance under attack."

issuance. See **issue (c).**

issue. A. *At issue; in issue. At issue* is the common idiomatic phrase, whereas *in issue* is purely a specialized legal phrase. *At issue* = (1) (of people) in controversy; taking opposite sides of a case or contrary views of a matter; at variance <his views are at issue with mine>; (2) (of matters or questions) in dispute; under discussion; in question <the allegations at issue> (*OED*). The *OED* notes that *in issue* shares sense 2 of *at issue*, but calls it rare.

Having originated in mid-19th-century legal contexts, *in issue* is not at all rare today—e.g.: "In the law of evidence, facts *in issue* are either: (1) facts that, in the pleadings, are affirmed on one side and denied on the other; or (2) in actions without pleadings, all facts from the establishment of which would follow the existence, nonexistence, nature, or extent of any right, liability, disability, or immunity asserted or denied in the case." E.g.:

- "The evidence is directed toward establishing a matter *in issue* other than the defendant's propensity to commit the crime charged." *U.S. v. Zapata*, 871 F.2d 616, 620 (7th Cir. 1989).
- "Where there is a bona fide dispute as to the existence of a contract which covers the dispute *in issue*, a plaintiff is not required to elect his or her remedies, but may proceed on both theories and recover in quantum meruit if he or she fails to establish the right to recover under the disputed contract." *Schwartz v. Pierce*, 870 N.Y.S.2d 161, 166 (App. Div. 2008).

- "The unpublished *Hemminger* opinion discloses too little information to determine whether the sentence there *in issue* was a guidelines-based sentence." *U.S. v. Dews*, 551 F.3d 204, 210 n.10 (4th Cir. 2008).

B. *Issue as to whether; issue of whether.* These phrases are prolix for *issue whether*. Cf. **question (as to) whether.** See **as to (A).**

C. *Issue and issuance. Issuance* was not used until the mid-19th century, up until which time *issue* was the noun corresponding to the verb *to issue*. E.g.: "Under these circumstances, assuming without deciding that they have a proper claim for money damages, the federal Anti-Injunction Act prevents the *issue* of an injunction restraining state proceedings to enforce the state judgment." *Jennings v. Boenning & Co.*, 482 F.2d 1128, 1135 (3d Cir. 1973). A nonlawyer in the U.S. today would think *issuance* to have been an apter term in the sentence quoted.

D. *Join issue.* This phrase may mean: (1) "to submit an issue jointly for decision"; (2) "to accept or adopt a disputed point as the basis of argument in a controversy"; or (3) "to take up the opposite side of a case, or a contrary view *on* a question" (*OED*). The idiom is more common in BrE than in AmE.

The noun phrase is *joinder of issue*. E.g.: "After *joinder of issue*, defendant moved for summary judgment." *Bradley v. Burroughs Wellcome Co.*, 497 N.Y.S.2d 401, 402 (App. Div. 1986).

E. In the Sense of "Offspring" or "Descendants." In the drafting of wills and trusts, the word *issue* invites litigation. English courts—as well as courts in New York and New Jersey—have held that it means all lineal descendants, however remote. Other courts have held that the word refers only to children and not to descendants more remote. And whether it covers adopted children is a question that courts will answer differently. See *In re Upjohn's Will*, 107 N.E.2d 492, 495 (N.Y. 1952). In sum, the word is best avoided altogether.

But if it is not to be avoided, it ought to be used grammatically. The question sometimes arises whether the word should be treated as a singular or as a plural noun. The answer is either—e.g.: "The remaining shares, if any, are combined and then divided in the same manner among the surviving *issue* of the deceased issue [confusing mixed usage of *issue* here] as if the surviving *issue* who *are* [*issue are* works better than *issue is* here] allocated a share had predeceased the decedent, without *issue*." Benjamin C. Wolf, Note, *Resolving the Conflict Between Jewish and Secular Estate Law*, 37 Hofstra L. Rev. 1171, 1178 n.43 (2009). See **die without issue.**

F. *General issue; special issue.* See **general issue.**

issue estoppel. See **issue preclusion** & **collateral estoppel (A).**

ISSUE-FRAMING. A. Generally. There is no more important point in persuasive and analytical writing—and certainly no point that is more commonly bungled—than framing the issue. If you have clearly in mind what question you're addressing, the writing will inevitably be much clearer than it otherwise would be.

That may sound obvious, but in fact very few legal writers frame their issues well. As a result, legal memos and briefs are often diffuse, repetitive, and poorly organized. Sometimes—even to the reader who works hard to find out—memos and briefs do not reveal precisely what question they purport to answer. When confronting such writing, the reader works impatiently to find the point—the gist—the upshot.

Any piece of persuasive or analytical writing must deliver three things: the question, the answer, and the reasons for that answer. The better the writing, the more clearly and quickly those things are delivered. The legal stylist should probably insist that the writing lead the reader to have those things well in mind within 60 seconds of picking up the document, whether it is a brief, an analytical memo, or a judicial opinion.

To do this consistently, open the discussion with a factually specific issue that captures the essence of the problem. The issue should be brief—no more than 75 words—and should be phrased in separate sentences. The format is generally as follows: statement–statement–question. Or, phrased differently: premise–premise–conclusion (followed by a question mark).

Although few legal writers have mastered this technique, it is old. Consider the following issue, framed in 1835:

> A Turk, having three wives, to whom he was lawfully married, according to the laws of his own country, and three sons, one by each wife, comes to Philadelphia with his family, and dies, leaving his three wives and three sons alive, and also real property in this State to a large amount. Will it go to the three children equally, under the intestate law of Pennsylvania? [67 words]
> *Conflict of Laws*, 14 Am. Jurist 275, 275 (1835).

Anyone of moderate legal sophistication can understand that question. And most readers, having seen the question, would probably like to know the answer.

But six American lawyers in ten would probably build up to the question with at least two pages of facts explaining how the Turk came to the U.S., when and where the marriages were solemnized, what the names and birthdates of each of the sons are, and so on. In other words, those six writers would engage in a badly overparticularized statement of facts—a statement that would leave many readers bewildered about the upshot of it all. See OVERPARTICULARIZATION.

Three more of the ten would probably assume that the intended reader knows the facts and therefore dispense with them altogether. The so-called issue in an analytical memo would read something like this: "Is our client entitled to take one-third under Pennsylvania law?" Then the writing would launch into a legal discussion of the intestacy laws. Never mind that the intended reader and the writer do not have an identical understanding of the facts—a point that will likely never emerge if the memo is written in this way. Further, any other reader will remain none the wiser even after reading the entire memo, which as a result can never be useful in future research.

Perhaps the one remaining lawyer of the ten would write an issue more nearly resembling the 1835 version than either the overparticularized or the overvague approach, but perhaps not one in a hundred would frame it with equal brevity and clarity.

B. Deep vs. Surface Issues. A "deep" issue is concrete: it sums up the case in a nutshell—and is therefore difficult to frame but easy to understand. A "surface" issue is abstract: it requires the reader to know everything about the case before it can be truly comprehended—and is therefore easy to frame but hard to understand.

Assume that a defendant is moving for summary judgment. Which of the following statements is more helpful?

1. Can Jones maintain an action for fraud?
2. To maintain a cause of action for fraud under California law, a plaintiff must show that the defendant made a false representation. In his deposition, Jones concedes that neither Continental nor its agents or employees made a false representation. Is Continental entitled to summary judgment on Jones's fraud claim? [49 words]

The longer version asks the reader to do considerably less work. The shorter version sends the reader elsewhere to learn what, precisely, the issue is. Whereas the surface issue says next to nothing about what the court is being asked to decide, the deep issue explains precisely what that something is. To put it differently, the surface issue does not disclose the decisional premises; the deep issue makes them explicit.

The goal is ease of understanding. One way to analyze the difference between a deep issue and a surface issue is to focus on the level of abstraction. Generally speaking, the more abstract an issue is, the more superficial it is: the reader must learn that much more to make any sense of it. The more concrete the issue is, the deeper it is: the reader need hardly exercise the brain to understand.

C. Persuasive vs. Analytical Issues. Unlike the deep-vs.-surface dichotomy, this split is not a matter of good and bad: writing that aims to persuade must have persuasive issues, whereas writing that seeks to analyze in an objective way must have analytical issues. Persuasive issues answer themselves; analytical issues are open-ended.

Karl Llewellyn, one of the great legal thinkers and writers of the 20th century, well understood the importance of a persuasive issue in effective advocacy: "The first art is framing the issue so that if your framing is accepted the case comes out your way. Got that? Second, you have to capture the issue, because your opponent will be framing an issue very differently. . . .

And third, you have to build a technique of phrasing your issue which not only will help you capture the Court but which will stick your capture into the Court's head so that it can't forget it." *A Lecture on Appellate Advocacy*, 29 U. Chi. L. Rev. 627, 630 (1962).

Llewellyn's initial point is the most powerful: the *first* art is framing the issue so that, if your framing is accepted, you win. The persuasive issue, then, can have only one answer. Still, it is far more persuasive than a mere statement of the conclusion. The advocate comes forward simply asking the court to address a straightforward question—e.g.:

- "Texas law provides that a lease predating a lien is not affected in foreclosure. Nelson's lease predates Marshall's lien, on which Marshall judicially foreclosed last month. Was Nelson's lease affected by the foreclosure?" [33 words]
- "Liability-insurance coverage for directors and officers of financial institutions is universally required to recruit well-qualified directors and officers. When the Trew Group acquired First Eastern from the FDIC in 1987, the FDIC agreed to pay the 'reasonable and necessary' operating costs of First Eastern. Is the FDIC obligated to pay the cost of directors' and officers' liability insurance for First Eastern?" [63 words]
- "On dozens of occasions over the course of a decade, United Peoria hired and paid a waste-hauler to haul its hazardous liquid waste to a landfill. In accordance with United Peoria's instructions, the hauler discharged thousands of gallons of United Peoria's waste into the landfill. Were these discharges an 'accident' from United Peoria's point of view?" [57 words]
- "Boskey Insurance issued an excess-insurance policy to BEC for liability exceeding $100,000. BEC represented to Boskey that it had purchased primary coverage for the first $100,000 of liability from Cooper Insurance. If Cooper becomes insolvent, should Boskey be required to step down and provide primary coverage when it never bargained for a role as—or contracted to be—a primary insurer, and when its premium reflected only the risk taken as an excess insurer?" [75 words]

As in the first two examples, an issue often proceeds from the law to the facts. Yet, as in the third and fourth examples, it may nearly as often proceed from the facts to the law. The only key to organizing the statements is to allow the whole to be readily absorbed—and this usually means putting the most easily comprehensible part in the middle of the issue.

These same characteristics hold true with analytical issues, but unlike persuasive ones, they are open-ended. The reader doesn't know the answer upon reading the question, but probably yearns to—e.g.:

- "The Immigration Act § 273 makes it a crime to bring an undocumented alien to the U.S. Meanwhile, the Maritime Act § 2304 makes it a crime for the master of a vessel to fail to rescue persons aboard a vessel in distress. Does a master commit a crime under the Immigration Act when he rescues illegal aliens aboard a ship in distress and brings them to the U.S.? If so, what are his defenses?" [72 words]
- "Mr. and Mrs. Zephyr were killed in the crash of an airplane negligently piloted by Mr. Zephyr. Their daughter, Kate, has sued the estate of her deceased father for the wrongful death of her mother. Does the doctrine of interspousal immunity bar Kate's recovery when there is no marital harmony to preserve?" [52 words]
- "A six-year-old plaintiff rode his bicycle in front of our client's truck before being struck by the truck. Is the six-year-old capable of contributory negligence?" [29 words]
- "In Massachusetts, a dead body is the property of the decedent's family members. As a result, the authority to order an autopsy generally rests with the relatives. In what circumstances is that authority transferred from the family to the medical examiner?" [41 words]

In an analytical memo, such an issue should be followed immediately by a brief answer (with reasons embedded in the answer), so that the question and the answer amount to something resembling an executive summary: the reader understands the gist of the memo merely by reading the first few lines.

D. Readers' Reactions. The purpose of using separate sentences and of limiting the issue to 75 words is to help the reader. A one-sentence issue of 75 or so words is difficult to follow, especially when the interrogative word begins the sentence and the end is merely a succession of *when*-clauses—e.g.:

> Can Barndt Insurance deny insurance coverage on grounds of late notice when Fiver's insurance policy required Fiver to give Barndt notice of a claim "immediately," and when in May 1994, one of Fiver's offices was damaged by smoke from a fire in another tenant's space, and when 10 months later, Fiver gave notice, and when Barndt investigated the claim for 6 months before denying coverage and did not raise a late-notice defense until 18 months after the claim was filed? [81 words]

That is a muddle. Readers forget the question by the time they reach the question mark. Part of the reason is that the time is out of joint: we begin with a present question, then back up to what happened, and then, with the question mark, jump back to the present.

The better strategy is to follow a more or less chronological order, telling a story in miniature. Then, the pointed question—which emerges inevitably from the story—comes at the end:

> Fiver's insurance policy required it to give Barndt Insurance notice of a claim "immediately." In May 1994, one of Fiver's offices was damaged by smoke from a fire in another tenant's space. Ten months later, Fiver gave notice. Barndt investigated the claim for 6 months before denying coverage and did not raise a late-notice claim until 18 months after the claim was filed. Can Barndt now deny coverage because of late notice? [73 words]

Instead of one 81-word-long sentence, we have five sentences with an average length of 15 words. (See SENTENCE LENGTH.) And the information is presented in a way that readers can easily understand.

Because seasoned legal readers are always impatient to reach the issue, the practice of opening a memo, brief, or judicial opinion with the deep issue always satisfies a need that readers feel.

But is the 75-word limit a fair one? Where does it come from? It is the rare case indeed—in fact, I have yet to encounter it—in which issues cannot be framed in 75 words. The 75-word limit is the result of experimentation and informal testing: once an issue goes beyond that length, it is likely to be rambling. You lose the rigor of a concentrated statement. And you probably lose some readers.

It is no accident that the most readable judicial opinions invariably begin with a brief statement of the overarching issue in the case. Among the ablest practitioners of this art was Judge Thomas Gibbs Gee, of the Fifth Circuit, who enshrined it as the first principle in his style sheet for opinions: "Try to state the principal question in the first sentence." *A Few of Wisdom's Idiosyncrasies and a Few of Ignorance's: A Judicial Style Sheet*, 1 Scribes J. Legal Writing 55, 56 (1990).

E. The Importance of It All. These principles of issue-framing may seem elementary at first glance. Yet, judging from most legal writing, they are not at all obvious. And in any event, stylists who cultivate the ability to frame good issues know just how difficult it is: it requires a great deal of mental energy.

It is therefore easy to forgo the effort, and many writers do. Legal writers everywhere seem preoccupied with answers—with conclusions—and rarely with the questions they are answering, or the premises from which their conclusions might follow. As a result, much of the "analysis" and advocacy that goes on is sloppy, or worse.

Even the greatest legal intellects must remain vigilant about these points. One of the most important 20th-century legal philosophers warned about how easy it is to stumble over fundamentals: "One principal source of trouble is obvious: it is always necessary to bear in mind, and fatally easy to forget, the number of different questions about punishment which theories of punishment ambitiously seek to answer." H.L.A. Hart, "Postscript: Responsibility and Retribution," in *Punishment and Responsibility: Essays in the Philosophy of Law* 210, 231 (1968).

issue of whether. See **issue (B).**

issue preclusion (AmE) = *issue estoppel* (BrE). See **collateral estoppel (A)** & **claim preclusion.**

issue sanctions against. See **sanction.**

issue whether. See **issue (B).**

is when; is where. These locutions are improper means of introducing a definition. Instead of writing, "'Livery of seisin' *is where* the grantor delivers possession," one should write, "'Livery of seisin' *is* the grantor's delivery of possession." Examples of ill-phrased definitions abound in legal writing: "*A bill of exchange is when a person takes money* in one country or city upon exchange, and draws a bill whereby he directs another person in another country or city to pay so much to A on order for value received of B and subscribes it." 5 John Comyns & Anthony Hammond, *A Digest of the Laws of England* 131 (1825). The idea of defining is here misplaced. [Read *With a bill*

of exchange, one takes money . . . .] See **where (c)** & **definitions (c).**

it. A. Overuse. This expletive and pronoun often appears too many times in one sentence. Careful writers restrict it (*it*, that is) to one meaning in a given sentence—no more. And still one must be vigilant about whether the antecedent is the closest noun—e.g.:

* "Applying the test of an apportionable or apportioned consideration to the contract in question, *it will be seen* [read *one will see*] at once that *it* [read *such consideration*] is severable." *Gill v. Johnstown Lumber Co.*, 25 A. 120, 120 (Pa. 1892).
* "*It is here that* [read *Here*] the advantage of an absolute sovereign is most apparent, for *it* [read *the sovereign*] makes it possible for immediate effect to be given to the will of the people." H.G. Hanbury, *English Courts of Law* 20 (2d ed. 1953).
* "Within such a unitary jurisdictional framework, the appellate court will, of course, require the trial court to conform to constitutional mandates, but *it* [read *the appellate court*] may likewise require *it* [read *the trial court*] to follow procedures deemed desirable from the viewpoint of sound judicial practice." *Cupp v. Naughten*, 414 U.S. 141, 146 (1973) (per Rehnquist, J.).
* "For *it* is often this sovereign power which gives to the jury *its* place in the constitution. Bereft of *it* [read *the power*], *it* [read *the criminal jury*] will become an expensive and unwieldy fact-finding tribunal which sooner or later will go the way of the civil jury." Patrick Devlin, *The Judge* 145 (1979).

Sometimes a single *it* may be problematic in having no identifiable antecedent: "Paraphrasing the opinion of Judge Vann in *Tabor v. Hoffman*, because an inspection of plaintiff's models may be by fair means, *it* [?] does not justify obtaining the same by unfair means." See ANTECEDENTS, FALSE (A), EXPLETIVES (A) & DANGLERS.

B. Referring to a Person. Although a young baby is often referred to as an *it*, other persons should not be, and especially not judges—e.g.: "In this case an experienced and careful district judge heard and reviewed the quantitative apportionment testimony and exhibits in this case, and *it* [read *he*—i.e., Lucius D. Bunton III] possessed opportunities to assess their convincingness far superior to those of this (appellate) court." *In re Bell Petroleum Servs., Inc.*, 3 F.3d 889, 911 (5th Cir. 1993).

Even in reference to an older child, the word *it* seems inappropriately dehumanizing: "To begin with it was held that a child could not be guilty of crime unless *it* [read *he or she*] had reached the age of twelve." J.W. Cecil Turner, *Kenny's Outlines of Criminal Law* 66 (1952). Perhaps a preferable edit—to avoid *he or she*—would be simply to write *could not be guilty of crime before the age of twelve*. See **he or she.**

ITALICS. A. Generally. H.W. Fowler's shot across the bow is worth heeding: "To those who, however competent on their special subject, have not had enough experience of writing to have learnt [the] rudiments, it comes as natural to italicize every tenth sentence or so as it comes to the letter-writing schoolgirl to underline whatever she enjoys recording" (*MEU1* 304).

How does one avoid overitalicizing? First, if the italicized words appear in quotations, try making the quoted passage shorter. Second, if the italicized words are one's own, try rearranging the sentence so that the italicized words appear at the end. Third, try the deliberate repetition characterizing any one of several rhetorical devices. (*See* Garner, *The Elements of Legal Style* 78–79 (2d ed. 2002).)

Ralph Waldo Emerson overstated the case: "'Tis a good rule of rhetoric [that] Schlegel gives—'In good prose, every word is underscored,' which, I suppose, means, Never italicize." "Lectures and Biographical Sketches," in 10 *Complete Works of Emerson* 169 (1904). By parity of reasoning, of course, one might say we should abolish question marks, exclamation points, and even commas. The point is to italicize only when one *must*.

B. Foreign Phrases. Anglicized terms of foreign origin appear in roman—i.e., nonitalic—type (e.g., bonus). Unnaturalized terms are italicized. Throughout this dictionary, the fuzzy line between naturalized and unnaturalized foreignisms is drawn through the headwords, which appear in either italic or nonitalic boldface type. See GALLICISMS & LATINISMS.

C. Latin Phrases Beginning with *in*. Some writers italicize only *flagrante delicto, forma pauperis, loco parentis, pari materia, statu quo,* and *terrorem.* But the word *in*, which is a part of each of these Latin phrases, ought to be italicized as well.

it being understood. This ABSOLUTE CONSTRUCTION is common in contracts—e.g.:

- "The agreement provided further: 'In addition, we agree to pay to you 2.5% of our net profits derived from exploitation of the Documentary itself in any manner or media. We shall pay you your percentage of net profits *as and when* [read *when*] we receive monies, *it being understood* that there is no guarantee of any profits being generated.'" *Reed v. Freebird Film Prods., Inc.*, 664 F.Supp.2d 840, 842 (N.D. Ohio 2009). For more on the use of *as and when* in this example, see **as and when.*
- "In that Agreement, West Beach and First Financial agreed that the modification executed between CS Assets and West Beach for the Heritage loan 'is subordinate to the mortgage of First Financial . . . for any amount in excess of $2,308,119.00, *it being understood* that additional amounts may accrue pursuant to the original $2,000,000.00 loan.'" *First Fin. Bank v. CS Assets, LLC,* 678 F.Supp.2d 1216, 1223 (S.D. Ala. 2010). On the use of **pursuant to* in that sentence, see **pursuant to.*

itemization is often unnecessary for *list.* See **list.**

iterate. See **reiterate.**

it is I; it is me. In formal English, *it is I* is the preferred expression, *it is me* being passable in the speech of most persons (less commonly in writing).

E.B. White told an amusing story about the fear that so many writers have of making a mistake: "One time

a newspaper sent us to a morgue to get a story on a woman whose body was being held for identification. A man believed to be her husband was brought in. Somebody pulled the sheet back; the man took one agonizing look, and cried, 'My God, it's her!' When we reported this grim incident, the editor diligently changed it to 'My God, it's she!'" E.B. White, "English Usage," in *The Second Tree from the Corner* 150, 150–51 (1954). See PRONOUNS (B).

it is important to note that; it is interesting to note that. These sentence-nonstarters merely gather lint—e.g.:

- "*It is interesting to note that blacks were twice* [read *Interestingly, blacks were twice*] as likely as whites to turn down their first choice." Ian Ayres & Richard Brooks, *Does Affirmative Action Reduce the Number of Black Lawyers?*, 57 Stan. L. Rev. 1807, 1833 (2005).
- "Finally, *it is interesting to note that* [omit the whole phrase] the practice of bundling phones and service has always been less common outside the U.S. and especially uncommon in Europe." Oren Bar-Gill & Rebecca Stone, *Mobile Misperceptions*, 23 Harv. J.L. & Tech. 49, 92–93 (2009).
- "*Anecdotally, it is interesting to note that even those* [read *Anecdotally, even those*] highly critical of what they term the 'politically correct' project of thinking in terms of discrimination may invoke an individual's personal relationships as a sign of their deeper politics of integration." Elizabeth F. Emens, *Intimate Discrimination*, 122 Harv. L. Rev. 1307, 1341 (2009).

Omit them.

it is me. See **it is I.**

it is plain that. See **clearly** & **obviously.**

it is submitted that. This phrase is an especially weak sentence-opener, usually a face-saving mannerism to avoid saying *I think.* Simply omit it and state your point.

its; it's. The possessive form of *it* is *its*; the contraction for *it is* is *it's.* The most common blunder is misusing the contraction *it's* as if it were possessive—e.g.: "In a footnote, the court explains *it's* [read *its*] reference to *Bell Atlantic.*" Alana C. Jochum, Note, *Pleading in Ohio After* Bell Atlantic v. Twombly *and* Ashcroft v. Iqbal, 58 Clev. St. L. Rev. 495, 522 n.208 (2010).

it's me. See **it is I.**

it was held that. See **hold (C).**

it would appear. See **appear.**

iudex. See **judex.**

ius. See ***jus.***

-IZE, -ISE. A. Verbs Ending in *-ize*. Adding the suffix *-ize* to an adjective or noun is one of the most frequently used means of forming new verbs. Many verbs so formed are objectionable. In AmE, *-ize* is more usual than in BrE, in which *-ise* is more common. But even in BrE, *-ize* is preferred to *-ise* in words in which either form of the suffix may appear. The possibility of choice between *-ise* and *-ize* arises only with words ending with the pronunciation *eyes*, not with that of *ice, iss,* or *eez*. For example, in *precise,* the suffix is pronounced *ice,* not *eyes*; in *promise* it is pronounced *iss,* not *eyes*; and in *expertise* it is pronounced *eez*.

Generally, *-ize* verbs are formed on familiar English words or stems—e.g.: *authorize, familiarize, symbolize*; or with a slight alteration to the stem—e.g.: *agonize, dogmatize, sterilize*. A few words have no such immediate stem: *aggrandize* (cf. *aggrandizement*), *appetize* (cf. *appetite*), *baptize* (cf. *baptism*), *catechize* (cf. *catechism*), *recognize* (cf. *recognition*), and *capsize*.

Neologisms in *-ize* generally to be discouraged, for they are invariably ungainly and often superfluous. Thus we have no use for *accessorize, artificialize, cubiclize, fenderize* (= to fix a dented fender), *funeralize, ghettoize, Mirandize, nakedize,* and so on. The law has many of its own curiosities in *-ize* (e.g., *privatize, collateralize, communitize, Lochnerize*), and probably needs no more. Careful writers are wary of new words formed with this suffix.

B. Verbs Ending in *-ise*. Verbs that correspond to nouns having *-is-* as a part of the stem (e.g., in the syllables *-vis-, -cis-, -mis-*), or that are identical with a noun in *-ise,* similarly take *-ise* rather than *-ize* (from which they are precluded). Some of the common verbs in *-ise* are:

advertise
advise
apprise
arise
chastise
circumcise
comprise
compromise
demise
despise
disfranchise
disguise
enfranchise
enterprise
excise
exercise
improvise
incise
merchandise
premise
revise
supervise
surmise
surprise
televise

J

J. is the abbreviation for *Judge* or *Justice.* In American legal writing, one commonly sees references such as *Scalia, J., dissenting.* In British and Canadian legal writing, no comma is used, even in midtext: "The policy reason advanced by La Forest J. seems to me to be quite inadequate to support his rule of irrecoverability. As Wilson J. pointed out, the idea of fiscal disruption hardly seems sufficient to cast the burden of governmental error on the innocent taxpayer." Peter W. Hogg, *Liability of the Crown* 184 (2d ed. 1989). The plural is *JJ.*

jackleg lawyer. See LAWYERS, DEROGATORY NAMES FOR (A).

jactation; jactitation. *Jactation,* lit. "a tossing or swinging of the body to and fro" (*OED*), came figuratively to mean (in both Latin and English) "boasting, bragging, ostentatious display" (*OED*). It is a learned word.

Its sibling *jactitation* derives from the same Latin verb and also has the sense "a boastful declaration"—e.g.: "In the footnoted *jactitation* appended to the byline in the Stanford article, Grantmore bills himself as the 'Henry J. Fletcher Professor of Law and Vance K. Opperman Research Scholar, University of Minnesota Law School.'" Wayne R. LaFave, *Livrebleu 17: Les Conséquences Tragiques Forgées par le Professeur Répugnant Nommé Grantmore,* 2001 U. Ill. L. Rev. 857, 862 (2001).

In law the term applies to boasts of marriage. Specifically, *jactitation of marriage* = a false assertion that one is married to someone to whom one is not in fact married (*CDL*)—e.g.: "In a few cases where women had previously filed suits against their ex-husbands for *jactitation* of marriage, the ex-husband responded by registering a *zina* case against her and her new husband." Julie Dror Chadbourne, *Never Wear Your Shoes After Midnight,* 17 Wis. Int'l L.J. 179, 219 (1999).

But increasingly, *jactitation,* when used at all, appears in its broader sense—e.g.:

- "This is an action in *jactitation* instituted by the eleven named plaintiffs who prayed that defendant be ordered to disclaim title to the property described in plaintiffs' petition." *Holmes v. Wyatt Lumber Co.,* 104 So.2d 293, 293 (La. Ct. App. 1958).
- "This letter, sent to innocent third-party customers of defendant, is clearly a forceful effort to persuade them that they are infringing a valid patent and will face serious consequences unless they divert their trade from plaintiff's product to defendant's. It constitutes (to borrow a term from another field of law) *jactitation* of a patent."

Analytichem Int'l, Inc. v. Har-Len Assocs., 490 F.Supp. 271, 274 (W.D. Pa. 1980).

jail, vb.; **imprison; incarcerate; immure; lock up; intern.** These verbs share the sense "to sequester and confine in a secure place so as to prevent escape." To *jail,* to *imprison* (heightened diction), or to *incarcerate* (popular JARGON) is to *lock up* in prison. *Jail* is the simplest, most direct term, although it may suggest short-term confinement (as with the noun *jail*) <the driver was jailed after refusing a breath test>. *Imprison* implies seizure and confinement of the person, whether or not the lock-up is technically termed a "prison" and whether or not the act is carried out under color of authority <she was falsely imprisoned by her captors>. *Incarcerate,* a term beloved by police and inmates alike, is a kind of genteelism and EUPHEMISM that stylish writers generally prefer to avoid <the suspect was captured, tried, convicted, and incarcerated>. *Immure,* a literary term, suggests a "walling in"—and in a very small space <prisoners were once immured within these inhumane dungeons>. To *intern,* typically during wartime, is to confine within specified boundaries, typically with guards and sentries to prevent escape <during WWI, German Americans were interned in camps>.

jail delivery, in AmE, means "an escape by several prisoners from a jail"; in BrE, the phrase (spelled *gaol delivery*) means "the bringing of prisoners to trial."

jailhouse lawyer. See LAWYERS, DEROGATORY NAMES FOR (B).

Jane Doe; Jane Roe. See **Doe, John.**

JANUS-FACED TERMS. A. The Basic Idea. Janus is an ancient Italian deity, the god of thresholds such as doorways, gates, and even (by figurative extension) the month of January. He is depicted with two faces—one on each side of the head. Hence *Janus-faced terms* are, because of syntactic construction, overburdened in being asked to look backward and forward simultaneously. (Concededly, they sometimes look forward at two different objects, or backward.) As here defined, a word so called upon can properly look one way, but not both.

Commonly known as ZEUGMA, this fault of writing occurs when a verb is incorrectly associated with two subjects or objects, an adjective with two nouns, or a noun with an antecedent and a consequent that are different. Some specimens follow, with short explanations of the problems.

B. Simultaneously Referring to the Case Name and the Named Party. "It is now doubtful whether McCardle (the defendant) would now be sustained," in which the writer means the opinion with the short-title form *McCardle,* though the parenthesis refers to the person. Another such example would be: "Shakespeare's powers were perhaps greatest in *Hamlet,* the most famous of tragedic protagonists," in which the writer is unconsciously referring to the character and the play at the same time. Following is a sentence that

avoids the problem just illustrated: "The *Roskos* court found that the plaintiff, Roskos, was coerced into resignation." *U.S. v. Thompson,* 749 F.2d 189, 194 (5th Cir. 1984).

C. Pronoun Used Also as an Expletive. "As for Mr. Wright's analysis of federal courts, it is always prudent and often a delight to pay attention." In this sentence, *it* first appears to refer to Wright's analysis and then is turned into an introductory filler or expletive. [Read *It is always prudent and often delightful to pay attention to Mr. Wright's analysis of federal courts.*]

D. Two Different Senses of the Same Word. "Why ought Louisiana [the state government] to have power over one who has had an auto accident there [the place]?" The first reference is to a political entity, the second to a geographic area.

E. Word Referred to as a Word, While Purporting to Have Substantive Meaning as Well. "Derived from *Slav,* of which people many were enslaved by the conquering Romans, the word [*slave*] has acquired connotations of servility, timidity, and cowardice" (Bergen Evans). The reference to *Slav* is to the word, not the people; hence the phrase that follows is illogical.

F. Preposition Given Two Meanings. "[The owners will] transact such other business as may properly come before the meeting or any adjournment or postponement thereof." *Kitazato v. Black Diamond Hospitality Invs., LLC,* 655 F.Supp.2d 1139, 1143 (D. Haw. 2009). Here *before* is asked to mean both "in front of" (before the convocation or meeting) and "prior to" (before adjournment). See ZEUGMA AND SYLLEPSIS (A).

JARGON. A. Definition. Jargon refers to the language, spoken and written, that members of any social, occupational, or professional group use to communicate with one another. As used in this book, the term refers to the full range of specialized vocabulary, devised by lawyers to save themselves time and space in communicating with each other, and sometimes even to conceal meaning from those uninitiated into the law.

Jargon covers a broad range of legal vocabulary from the almost slangy (*horse case*) to the almost technically precise (*res ipsa loquitur*). And although an expression that is labeled "jargon" fails to rise to the level of a TERM OF ART, it remains a useful bit of shorthand for presenting ideas that would ordinarily need explaining in other, more circumlocutory terms if persons who lack experience in the law are to understand them.

So a strong in-group property characterizes jargon, which may be acceptable—even desirable—when one lawyer talks with another or addresses a judge. But jargon is unacceptable when the purpose of using it is to demonstrate how much more the speaker or writer knows as a specialist than ordinary listeners or readers do. The intended audience, then, should be the primary concern of a lawyer in deciding which words to use to communicate intelligibly. In a bench trial a lawyer may be justified in referring to the *corpus delicti* (not truly a TERM OF ART), but in a jury trial, a lawyer who uses this term is likely to lead the jury into confusion, puzzlement, and even misjudgment.

As an archetypal example of jargon, the phrase *case on all fours* denotes "a reported case in which the facts and law are so closely similar to the one at hand as to be indistinguishable from it." This phrase, containing only four short words, is much more economical than the definition. But the shorthand phrase, useful as it is to lawyers, remains inscrutable, unless explained, to virtually all nonlawyers. Such jargonistic phrases collectively fall under the rubric of this entry. See **on all fours.**

The following are typical jargonistic words and phrases, all of which are treated in other entries: *adhesion contract* (see **adherence (A)**), *alter ego, Blackacre, case at bar, case-in-chief, clean hands, clog on the equity, cloud on title, conclusory, four corners of the instrument, in personam, instant case, on all fours, piercing the corporate veil, reasonable person, res integra* (or *res nova*), *res ipsa loquitur, sidebar, Whiteacre.* For a related phenomenon, see ABSTRACTITIS. For the opposite tendency, see PLAIN LANGUAGE.

B. Jargonmongering. Some would say that to be a lawyer (or at least a good one) is necessarily to be a jargonmonger, that word-shuffling is the nature of the business. That pessimistic view is not borne out by the evidence of the many successful straight-talking and straight-writing practitioners. If such a jaded view has any validity, the best one can do is to prove its falsity by one's own example.

It is difficult to improve on Sir Arthur Quiller-Couch's seminal analysis of jargon in his book *On the Art of Writing* (1916). He sets out its two primary vices: "The first is that it uses circumlocution rather than short straight speech. It says: '*In the case of* John Jenkins deceased, the coffin' when it means 'John Jenkins's coffin'; and its yea is not yea, neither is its nay nay; but its answer is *in the affirmative* or *in the negative*, as the foolish and superfluous *case* may be. The second vice is that it habitually chooses vague wooly abstract nouns rather than concrete ones" (*id.* at 105). "To write jargon is to be perpetually shuffling around in a fog and cotton-wool of abstract terms" (*id.* at 117). See ABSTRACTITIS.

Nothing nauseates like the real thing: "A supplement to the draft or final EIS on file will be prepared whenever significant impacts resulting from changes in the proposed plan or new significant impact information, criteria or circumstances relevant to environmental considerations impact on the recommended plan or proposed action." 33 C.F.R. § 2502.9(c)(1) (1988). See INITIALESE.

jaywalker (= a pedestrian who crosses a street without heeding traffic regulations) began as an early-20th-century Americanism but is now used also in BrE. In the 1910s, *jay* was a slang term meaning "a stupid, silly person; a simpleton," and at about that time *jaywalker*

and its BACK-FORMATION *jaywalk* came to refer to someone stupid enough to cross streets unsafely. Originally, a *jaywalking* referred only to crossing an intersection diagonally.

J.D.; LL.B. *J.D.* is now the predominantly awarded law degree in the U.S.—*LL.B.* formerly having this distinction. Although it is not actually a doctorate, *J.D.* generally stands for *Juris Doctor* (= doctor of law). In the United States, it is the first professional degree in law at the graduate level, which is then followed by the LL.M. (Master of Laws) and S.J.D. (Doctor of Juridical Science). All American law schools awarded the LL.B. until 1902, when the University of Chicago chose to award the J.D. instead. A few other schools awarded the J.D. as an honor for top graduates and LL.B.s to the rest. But in the 1960s, the J.D. became the standard degree; Yale awarded the last LL.B. in 1971. Some commentators attribute the widespread elevation of the degree to an inflation of academic designation and a desire to distinguish it from undergraduate degrees. *See* Kenneth Kaoma Mwenda, *Comparing American and British Legal Education Systems* 14, 18–20 (2007). In most common-law nations, the LL.B. is an undergraduate degree, although the program of study is almost the same as the J.D. *Id.*

jealousy; envy. The careful writer distinguishes between these terms. *Jealousy* is properly restricted to contexts involving emotional rivalry, whereas *envy* is used more broadly of resentful contemplation of a more fortunate person.

Jeddart justice; Jedburgh justice; *Jedwood justice. The first is now the usual form of this term, meaning "execution first, trial afterwards." The name derives from Jedburgh in Roxburghshire, Scotland, a town near the English border where bands of raiders frequently skirmished on both sides. (*Jeddart* is probably a corrupted form of "Jedworth," the old name of the place.) Apparently of 16th-century origin, *Jeddart justice* "differs from *lynch law* in that it was done by a kind of summary court, not by persons wholly unauthorized" (*OCL1*).

jemmy. See **jimmy.**

jeofails (= mistakes or oversights in pleading), for the most part an obsolete term, is pronounced /jə-**faylz**/. Formerly thought to be the LAW FRENCH form of *j'ai faillé*, meaning "I have made an error," the term is now generally thought to derive from *jocus*, as in *jeopardy* (= *jocus partitus*). *See* John H. Baker & Morris S. Arnold, *Origin of "Jeofail*," 87 Law Q. Rev. 166 (1971).

jeopardize; *jeopard; *enjeopard. H.W. Horwill wrote that in AmE "*jeopard* is preferred to *jeopardize*, the common term in England." *Modern American Usage* 178 (2d ed. 1944). This was not true in 1944, and it is not true today. E.g.: "The appellant has the burden

---

of demonstrating that the error complained of is so clearly prejudicial to substantial rights as to *jeopardize* the fairness and integrity of the trial process." *Flamer v. State*, 953 A.2d 130, 133 (Del. 2008). **Enjeopard* and **jeopard* are NEEDLESS VARIANTS.

jeopardy. See **double jeopardy.**

jet. See LAWYERS, DEROGATORY NAMES FOR (A).

jetsam. See **flotsam.**

jibe. See **gibe.**

Jim Crow law (= a law enacted or purposely interpreted to discriminate against blacks) is an early-19th-century American coinage deriving from *Jim Crow* (1838), a derogatory name for a black man. The institution of American segregation came to be called *Jim Crowism* at about the same time. The earliest known reference in American caselaw to *Jim Crow* as a EUPHEMISM for segregation comes from 1888: "The rear car was set apart by the rules of the company for the accommodation, exclusively, of white people; the other, the front car, was known in Texas as the '*Jim Crow* Car,' and was for the use of colored people, though white people often rode in it." *Houck v. Southern Pac. Ry.*, 38 F. 226, 227 (W.D. Tex. 1888) (per Boarman, J.).

jimmy; jemmy. A burglar's crowbar is spelled *jimmy* in AmE, *jemmy* in BrE.

JJ. (invariably capitalized) is the abbreviation for *judges* or *justices*. Notice that the plural is *JJ.*, not **J.J.*

j.n.o.v. See **judgment** *non obstante veredicto* (D).

jobsite. One word. Cf. **worksite.**

John a Nokes; John a Stiles. These fictitious names of parties in a lawsuit, dating from the 15th and used well into the 19th century, derive from *John atten Oke* (= John who dwells at the oak) and *John atte Stile* (= John who dwells at the stile). They were frequently abbreviated *J.N.* and *J.S. See* Oliver Wendell Holmes Jr., *The Common Law* 25 (1881) (referring to John at Stile).

Occasionally these names are not fictitious. For example, *Stiles v. Blunt*, 912 F.2d 260 (8th Cir. 1990), involves John A. Stiles's candidacy for the Missouri House of Representatives. Cf. **Doe, John.**

John Doe. See **Doe, John.**

join = (1) to unite (several causes of action) in a lawsuit; or (2) to unite (several parties) in a lawsuit.

joinder. A. And *jointure*. These are different words. *Joinder*, the noun corresponding to the verb *to join*, is the usual term in law for the uniting of several causes of action or of parties in a single suit—e.g.:

- "The *joinder* of any person having only a contingent or executory interest in the property proposed to be taken shall not be necessary when the person not joined is virtually represented by any other party or parties defendant." W. Va. Code § 54-2-2 (2008).
- "As this question may very well determine the nondiverse heirs' indispensability here, we are equally ill equipped to rule on the ultimate question of *joinder*." *Jimenez v. Rodriquez-Pagan*, 597 F.3d 18, 27 (1st Cir. 2010).

See **issue** (D) & **join.**

Jointure, a much less common term, means "a widow's freehold life estate in land, made in lieu of dower." E.g.:

- "A *jointure* or any pecuniary provision that is made for the benefit of the intended wife, and in lieu of her dower, shall bar her right to dower provided she assents to the *jointure*." John W. Reilly, *The Language of Real Estate* 261 (2d ed. 1982).
- "It became usual instead to provide in a marriage settlement for some land to be settled on the husband and wife jointly for the life of the survivor, so that a widow would have the land until her death in lieu of a dower. Such a provision was called a '*jointure*.'" J.H. Baker, *An Introduction to English Legal History* 309 (3d ed. 1990).

B. And *consolidation*. Whereas *joinder* has come to be used usually in the sense of uniting parties in a suit, *consolidation* has become in AmE the more usual word for uniting two or more lawsuits into a single suit. See **disjoinder** & **misjoinder.**

C. *Compulsory joinder; permissive joinder*. The Federal Rules of Civil Procedure, which have served as the model for many other sets of court rules, distinguish between *compulsory joinder* and *permissive joinder*. Under Rule 19(a), a party whose presence will not deprive the court of subject-matter jurisdiction must be joined if either of the following is true: (1) in that party's absence, those already involved in the lawsuit cannot receive complete relief; or (2) the absence of such a party, claiming an interest in the subject of the action, might either impair the protection of that interest or leave some party subject to multiple or inconsistent obligations. These provisions equate with *compulsory joinder*, although the word *compulsory* appears nowhere in the rule. Commentators arrived at the name *compulsory joinder* because the rule formerly used the mandatory *shall*. (If a party who falls under this rule cannot be joined for some reason, the court must then decide whether the party is *indispensable* or merely *necessary*. See **indispensable.**)

Permissive joinder, meanwhile, falls under Rule 20, which is given that very heading. Under this rule, persons may be joined as plaintiffs if they assert a right to relief jointly, severally, or in the alternative in respect of the same transaction or occurrence, and if any legal or factual question common to all plaintiffs will arise. Persons may be joined as defendants if any right to relief is asserted against them jointly, severally, or in respect of the same transaction or occurrence, and if any legal or factual question common to all defendants will arise.

D. *Joinder of issue*. See **issue** (D).

join issue. See **issue** (D).

joint adventure. See **joint venture.**

joint and several = together and in separation. When two or more persons bind themselves to do something for another person, their liability on the contract is *joint and several* if both or all first bind themselves by one promise, and then each of them makes a separate promise to the same effect. E.g.:

- "[Appellants] *jointly and severally* covenanted and agreed that they would pay the principal sum of . . . $280,000 on [February 1]." *East River Sav. Bank v. Samuels*, 31 N.E.2d 906, 909 (N.Y. 1940).
- "When a partner dies, his private estate is *jointly and severally* liable . . . for debts and obligations of the firm incurred while he was a partner." 2 Ernest W. Chance, *Principles of Mercantile Law* 14 (Percy W. French ed., 10th ed. 1951).
- "Although Frost's estate is *jointly and severally* liable for the entire judgment, Morrison's estate also argues that it is entitled to a larger judgment." *Capital Investors Co. v. Estate of Morrison*, 800 F.2d 424, 428 (4th Cir. 1986).
- "In the context of a space elevator, any country that 'procured' lift services from the operators of a space elevator could become *jointly and severally* liable for damages." Benjamin Hamilton Jarrell, *International and Domestic Legal Issues Facing Space-Elevator Deployment and Operation*, 7 Loy. L. & Tech. Ann. 71, 95 (2007).

With *joint and several liability*, the liability of two or more obligors may be enforced against them all by a joint action or against any of them by an individual action. *Solidary liability* is used in this sense in Louisiana, Puerto Rico, and civil-law countries. In addition to *joint and several* obligations, Scottish lawyers refer to *conjunct and several* obligations. See **several.**

joint cooperation is a REDUNDANCY.

joint enterprise. Unlike *joint venture*, the phrase *joint enterprise* occurs primarily in criminal law. It is apt when two or more persons set out to commit an offense they have conspired to commit; it should not apply when two or more persons are involved in an unplanned and unforeseen incident that has arisen unexpectedly. See **joint venture.**

jointly and severally. See **joint and several.**

join together is a REDUNDANCY found in the traditional marriage service as a remnant of Elizabethan English. In other contexts, though, it should be recognized as redundant and be trimmed—e.g.:

- "A class action could be desirable here because the legal theories are not necessarily novel, but proving liability in a hurricane could require complex proof, suggesting that it may be beneficial for the Plaintiffs to *join together* [omit *together*] as a class to prosecute their claim." *In re Katrina Canal Breaches Consol. Litig.*, 258 F.R.D. 128, 142 (E.D. La. 2009).
- "Third, and arguably the defining characteristic of most bankruptcy systems, the creditors would *join together* [omit *together*] in a single bankruptcy proceeding, which would gather all the assets and then divide them ratably according to the amount of the creditors' respective debts." Emily Kadens, *The Last Bankrupt Hanged*, 59 Duke L.J. 1229, 1241 (2010).
- "Shareholders can *join together* [omit *together*] and use their collective power to replace the board of a troubled company, but few institutional investors want to take on the challenges of running a public company." Jessica Erickson, *Corporate Governance in the Courtroom*, 51 Wm. & Mary L. Rev. 1749, 1812 (2010).

joint-stock company. So hyphenated. See PHRASAL ADJECTIVES (A).

joint tenancy; tenancy in common. The distinction between these two terms is basic to the law of property. *Joint tenancy* = ownership of property by two or more persons who have identical interests in the whole of the property, with a right of survivorship. *Tenancy in common* = equitable ownership of property by two or more persons in equal or unequal undivided shares, with no right of survivorship. The property for each of these tenancies may be either real (land) or personal (e.g., a bank account), although the *CDL*, which reflects British legal practices, confines its definitions to real property.

jointure. See **joinder (A).**

joint venture; joint adventure. The second, an ARCHAISM, still appears, but *joint venture*—a clearer phrase—ought to displace it. E.g.: "Is friendship a kind of '*joint adventure*' [read '*joint venture*'] such that David's actions could be deemed usurpation of what should have been their joint opportunity?" Ethan J. Lieb, *Friends as Fiduciaries*, 86 Wash. U. L. Rev. 665, 667–68 (2009). Cf. **joint enterprise.**

joint will. See **mutual will.**

joker = an ambiguous clause in a legislative bill inserted to render it inoperative or uncertain in some respect without arousing opposition at time of passage. *See Bennet v. Commercial Advertiser Ass'n*, 129 N.E. 343, 345 (N.Y. 1920). More broadly—and less malignantly—the term may also refer to a rider or amendment that is extraneous to the subject of the bill. E.g.: "Such a holding seems to me to throw both general and special revenue acts wide open as convenient vehicles for the enactment, under the concealment of their titles, of '*joker*' legislation." *Macke v. Commonwealth*, 159 S.E. 148, 151 (Va. 1931) (Epes, J., dissenting).

journal, vb.; **journalize.** Both terms are used in the sense "to record in a journal." *Journalize* is more usual in legal contexts—e.g.:

- "Until the trial court's entry determining the final verdict on a criminal complaint is officially *journalized*, the entry cannot prevent further judgment, since the trial court can always vacate its own judgment and set the case for trial." *Cleveland v. Trzebuckowski*, 709 N.E.2d 1148, 1150–51 (Ohio 1999).

- "It is true that the trial judge issued an oral verdict of guilty on February 23, 2007, but this verdict was not *journalized* until April 9, 2007." *State v. Ludt*, 906 N.E.2d 1182, 1189 (Ohio Ct. App. 2009).

joyrider; joyriding. These early-20th-century American coinages remain colloquialisms—yet criminal-law texts use them because they are the only available terms. *Joyrider* = one who drives someone else's car without permission. The verb, a BACK-FORMATION, is *joyride*.

J.P. = Justice of the Peace. Conventionally, if the abbreviation is used, the plural would be *J.P.'s*, because the abbreviation contains periods—e.g.: "From the *J.P.s* [read *J.P.'s*] odium and contempt spread to the higher justices, usually *J.P.s* [read *J.P.'s*] in their own localities." Alan Harding, *A Social History of English Law* 71 (1966). In the sentence quoted, however, one can understand the author's desire to avoid a MISCUE caused by the apostrophe's seeming to make *J.P.* a possessive. Oddly, however, the same writer used the plural *Q.C.'s* (see *id.* at **junior**).

judex. Reserve this word for historical contexts—e.g.: "English Chancery Courts, heavy borrowers from the civil law, may have derived the system of special masters from the civilian *judex* of the Roman Republic and Early Empire." *U.S. v. Manning*, 215 F.Supp. 272, 292 (W.D. La. 1963). Elsewhere it is just an unnecessary equivalent of *judge*. Pl. *judices*.

judge, vb.; **adjudge; adjudicate; *dijudicate; arbitrate**. These verbs share the sense "to exercise a decision-making power over a dispute or controversy." *Judge* implies critical thinking and impartiality in weighing the evidence, assessing the arguments, and reaching a definitive decision <How did the court judge the merits of the case?>. *Adjudge* stresses the finality of the decision and any award connected with it <$500 was adjudged to the plaintiff>. (See **adjudge**.) *Adjudicate*, which is more formal, stresses the dignity of the proceedings and suggests an imposing hall of justice <the district court must adjudicate the habeas claim>. (See **adjudicate**.) *Dijudicate* (= to decide between; adjudicate) is a rare term without justification in modern writing. *Arbitrate* suggests the binding submission of a disputed matter to an impartial extralegal tribunal constituted for that purpose <the parties agreed to arbitrate their dispute>.

judge; justice. A. An Array of Distinctions. In the U.S., as a general rule, judges sitting on the highest appellate level of a jurisdiction are known as *justices*. Trial judges and appellate judges on intermediate levels are generally called *judges*, not *justices*. (New York, Texas, and a few other jurisdictions depart from these general rules. In New York, *justices* sit on the trial court of general jurisdiction [the Supreme Court, oddly], whereas *judges* sit on the appellate courts. In Texas, *justices* sit on the courts of appeals [between the trial court and the Supreme Court—the latter

being the highest court of civil appeal—which is also composed of *justices*]; *judges* sit on the Texas Court of Criminal Appeals, the highest criminal court, and on trial courts.)

In England and Northern Ireland, similarly, judges of the Supreme Court at trial level are *justices* and at the appellate level *lords justices*. *Judges* sit on circuit courts and *justices* in magistrates' courts.

Horwill wrote that "*judge* carries with it in America by no means such dignified associations as it possesses in Eng. It may mean [in AmE] no more than a *magistrate* of a police court." H.W. Horwill, *Modern American Usage* 180 (2d ed. 1944). *Justice* may also denote, in AmE and BrE alike, a low-ranking judge or inferior magistrate, as in the phrases *justice of the peace* and *police justice*. But when the word refers to the highest American judges—the Justices of the Supreme Court of the United States—the word *Justice* is ordinarily capitalized, even if no particular Justice is named.

Judges often look unkindly on mistakes in their titles, as by inserting "[sic]" after mistakes—e.g.: "By two identical motions filed January 3, 1985 in these related actions, defendant moves for an order 'disqualifying the Honorable Mr. Justice [*sic*] Charles L. Brieant from hearing this matter on the ground that said Honorable Charles L. Brieant was the presiding justice [*sic*] in the trial of *Lamy Optic Industries, Inc. v. Passport International Ltd.*'" *Tenzer v. Lewittinn*, 599 F.Supp. 973, 974 (S.D.N.Y. 1985) (per Brieant, J.). Similarly, Chief Justice Rehnquist, during oral argument, has corrected counsel who have addressed him as "Judge." *See* David Margolick, *At the Bar*, N.Y. Times, 26 Apr. 1991, at B9.

B. In Informal Contexts. In AmE, lawyers conventionally call all but U.S. Supreme Court Justices "judge" in informal settings. *Judge Jefferson* is permissible in talking with the Chief Justice of the Texas Supreme Court, though in referring to him in a conversation with someone else, one would say either *the Chief Justice* or *Chief Justice Jefferson*, or perhaps *Justice Jefferson* (less proper).

In BrE, the conventions are quite different: "Never say 'Justice Smith' or (except for a circuit or county court judge) 'Judge Smith'; these are Americanisms, to be shunned and avoided on this side of the Atlantic." Glanville Williams, *Learning the Law* 64 (11th ed. 1982). Williams is emphatic about this point: do not just shun them—avoid them as well. What are the proper forms? Williams recommends "'Mr. Justice Smith' (or Mrs. Justice Smith, as the case may be) . . . when speaking of him in public." *Id.* He does not mention *Ms. Justice Smith*, the title *Ms.* not having caught on in BrE to the extent it has in AmE.

See **my lord** & FORMS OF ADDRESS (D).

judgeable. So spelled.

judge advocate. Pl. *judge advocates*.

judgeless is a legal NEOLOGISM denoting an unhappy state of affairs—e.g.:

- "To so require would leave a number of rural Texas counties *judgeless* in some criminal cases." *Joshua v. State*, 696 S.W.2d 451, 456 (Tex. App.—Houston [14th Dist.] 1985).
- "Eventually, the jury might be on its own, without even a judge. The last move—from lawless to *judgeless* juries—suggests another process change." Leonard R. Jaffee, *Empathetic Adjustment—An Alternative to Rules, Policies, and Politics*, 58 U. Cin. L. Rev. 1161, 1225 (1990).

judge-made, adj., is used generally as an antonym of *statutory*. E.g.:

- "No system of law—whether it be *judge-made* or legislatively enacted—can be so perfectly drafted as to leave no room for dispute." Lon L. Fuller, *The Morality of Law* 56 (rev. ed. 1969).
- "Such *judge-made* law would be disastrous for press freedom." Economist, 28 Jan.–3 Feb. 1989, at 18.

Since the rise of legal realism in the early 20th century, *judge-made* has been a fairly colorless, connotatively neutral term. *Judge-made* law in the form of "gap-filling" is widely accepted as an inevitable reality. But it once bore strongly disparaging connotations: "Usually the expression [*judge-made*] is employed as a term of disapprobation to characterize a judicial decision or series of decisions, which appears not to be properly or adequately based upon precedent, or which presents some new or unusual conception of legal rights and duties under particular circumstances. Indeed the idea quite generally prevails that such *judge-made* law is not properly law at all, but merely an erroneous interpretation of the law." Alexander Lincoln, *The Relation of Judicial Decisions to the Law*, 21 Harv. L. Rev. 120, 120 (1907).

The exceptions are many, but a latent DIFFERENTIATION appears to be emerging between *judge-made law* and *common law*: though the common law is literally *judge-made* law, modern writers tend to use *judge-made law* in reference to recent developments and *common law* in reference to the remote past.

The phrase *bench-made* is a less frequent variant. *See* Henry J. Abraham, *The Judicial Process* 9 (2d ed. 1968) (*bench-made law*).

judgement. See **judgment.**

judge-shopping = using any of various means to bring a case before a judge who might be more favorably inclined to a litigant than some other judge might be. The phrase is best hyphenated—e.g.:

- "We emphasize that the requirement of showing the unavailability of the trial judge must be strictly met in order to avoid the obvious possibilities of conflict or '*judge shopping*' [read *judge-shopping*] for a favorable ruling." *Shafer v. Northside Inn, Inc.*, 184 N.E.2d 756, 758–59 (Ill. App. Ct. 1962).
- "The chances for *judge-shopping* are significant (although hardly infinite), particularly when dealing with a class with membership in many states." Charles W. Wolfram, *Mass Torts—Messy Ethics*, 80 Cornell L. Rev. 1228, 1232 (1995).
- "Defense attorneys take advantage of the pressures created by a large workload to engage in plea bargaining or '*judge shopping*' [read *judge-shopping*], knowing a court will be more willing to grant continuances if it faces a large backlog." Jeffrey A. Butts, *Delays in Youth Justice* 18 (2010).

judgey (= characteristic of or like a judge) is a NEOLOGISM carrying negative connotations—e.g.: "Edwards is less '*judgey*' than most judges. He is not modest, but neither is he pompous." Donald D. Jackson, *Judges* 324 (1974).

judgitis = the peculiar brand of condescending self-importance to which judges are famously susceptible. Although this derogatory slang word for a judge who suffers from an inflated ego isn't recorded in dictionaries, it's been used for more than 50 years. The *-itis* suffix denotes a kind of inflammation—hence the aptness of the METAPHOR. E.g.:

- "He explained '*judgitis*' was a rare disease, wherein the judge, after taking his position on the bench, tried the case for both sides, and became obsessed with the general power [that] he possessed as a member of the federal judiciary." Welcome D. Pierson, *The Defense Attorney and Basic Defense Tactics* 71 (1956).
- "Judges who believe that the initial letter of their title should be 'G' as in *God* are really not a half-step removed from the deity. They suffer from delusions that are symptomatic of *judgitis*, a horrible disease contracted by ascending to the heights of the bench, characterized by acute astigmatism so they do not recognize former friends." 10 Robert Michael Willes Chitty, *Chitty's Law Journal* 206 (1961).
- "Jack was very attuned to and never succumbed to what he called '*Judgitis*': the judge who can't admit to a mistake; the judge who is sure that politics played a role in everyone else's appointment but not his; and the judge who is offended when old friends call him by his first name." Lewis R. Katz, *Symposium on the Fortieth Anniversary of Mapp v. Ohio*, 52 Case W. Res. L. Rev. 371, 372 (2001).
- "Being fortunate enough to be nominated, confirmed, and appointed to serve on the federal bench often leads to what Judge Ed Devitt called '*judgitis*' or what others refer to as 'forgetting where you came from.'" Robert W. Pratt, *Social Security Judging*, 36 Litig. 3, 63 (Spring 2010).

*****judgmatic.** See **judgmental.**

judgment. A. Spelling. *Judgment* is the preferred form in AmE and seems to be preferred in British legal texts, even as far back as the 19th century. *Judgement* is prevalent in British nonlegal texts, and was thought by H.W. Fowler to be the better form; Glanville Williams states that, in BrE, "*judgement* should really be the preferred spelling." *Learning the Law* 153 (11th ed. 1982). Not in AmE.

B. AmE & BrE Senses. In AmE, a *judgment* is the final decisive act of a court in defining the rights of the parties. It "includes a decree and any order from which an appeal lies." Fed. R. Civ. P. 54(a).

In BrE, *judgment* is commonly used in the sense in which *judicial opinion* is used in AmE: "The facts of this case, which are fully stated in the *judgment* of Lord Hanworth M.R., were briefly as follows." *Payne*

---

v. Cardiff Rural Dist. Council, [1932] 1 K.B. 241, 241. Continental legal systems likewise use *judgment* in this way.

See JUDGMENTS, APPELLATE-COURT, **decision & opinion.**

C. And *decree.* Though *decree* is traditionally the term for a final disposition in equity, the term *judgment* applies, in most American states, to the final disposition made by a court in an equitable as well as in a legal proceeding. *See* Restatement of Judgments, Intro. at 3 (1942). See **decree.**

D. *Court judgment.* This phrase is a REDUNDANCY, though perhaps an understandable one when the likely readers are nonlawyers. For example, the title of the following book might have miscued general readers if the word *court* had been removed: Gini G. Scott et al., *Collect Your Court Judgment* (1991).

E. And *verdict.* See **verdict (D).**

judgment affirmed. See **appeal allowed.**

judgmental; *judgmatic. *Judgmental* = (1) of or relating to judgment; or (2) judging when uncalled for. Sense 2 is now more common <a judgmental critic>, but sense 1 still appears. E.g.: "The evaluation materials provide no guidance on how to apply *judgmental* factors uniformly or how the evaluators are to use outside information." *Carney v. Civil Serv. Comm'n*, 30 P.3d 861, 865 (Colo. Ct. App. 2001). *Judgmatic, called by H.W. Fowler a "facetious formation" because of its irregular formation on the analogy of *dogmatic*, is a NEEDLESS VARIANT of *judicious.* See **judicial.**

judgment as a matter of law. See **judgment** *non obstante veredicto* (A).

judgment-book; judgment-roll. In most jurisdictions, these terms refer synonymously to the book kept by the clerk of court for the entry or recordation of judgments. (See **rendition of judgment.**) But some American jurisdictions call for *entry* of judgments in the *judgment-roll* and mere *recordation* of judgments in the *judgment-book.* The usual term in BrE is *judgment-roll.*

judgment by default. See **default judgment.**

judgment *non obstante veredicto.* **A. And** *judgment notwithstanding the verdict; j.n.o.v.; judgment n.o.v.* In AmE, the tendency is to substitute all these phrases with *judgment as a matter of law.* But of the headwords listed, perhaps the best unabbreviated one is *judgment notwithstanding the verdict.* We must not forget the Latin phrase, however, lest new generations of lawyers come to miss the import of *j.n.o.v.*—an abbreviation that litters many legal texts. See (D).

B. Shortened form of *non obstante veredicto.* The phrase *non obstante veredicto* is sometimes used in the shortened form *non obstante*—e.g.:

- "The jury answered the issues as to bailment and damages for the bailor, but the trial judge entered judgment *non obstante* for the bailee." William M. Cotton, *Presumptions*

and the Burden of Proving a Bailee's Negligence, 31 Tex. L. Rev. 46, 51 (1952).
- "Neither did Airway assert that the trial court erred in overruling its motion for judgment *non obstante* for any of the reasons set forth in its argument." *Airway Ins. Co. v. Hank's Flite Ctr., Inc.*, 534 S.W.2d 878, 882 (Tex. 1976).
- "This appeal . . . requires us to determine whether . . . the trial judge's actions in granting judgment *non obstante* for the defendant, or in the alternative a new trial, were correct." *Eyre v. McDonough Power Equip.*, 755 F.2d 416, 417–18 (5th Cir. 1985).
- "At common law, after trial at *nisi prius*, the cause was heard by the court in bank upon rule for a new trial or motion in arrest or for judgment *non obstante.*" Roscoe Pound, *A Practical Program of Procedural Reform*, 22 Green Bag 438 (1910) (repr. 1 Green Bag 2d 75, 92 (1997)).

C. A Common Misspelling. A surprisingly high percentage of the time, American lawyers mangle the Latin and write *verdicto—e.g.: "If the jury's verdict is clearly arbitrary, the court may enter judgment *non obstante verdicto* [read *veredicto*]." Constance S. Huttner, Note, *Unfit for Jury Determination*, 20 B.C. L. Rev. 511, 534 (1979). All the more reason to stick to *judgment as a matter of law, judgment notwithstanding the verdict*, or *j.n.o.v.*

D. Abbreviation: *j.n.o.v.* *Judgment non obstante veredicto* is usually abbreviated in lowercase. Some courts write *JNOV*, but the capital letters and dropping of periods are distracting. The abbreviation is sometimes shortened to *n.o.v.*: "The appellee . . . may bring his grounds for new trial to the trial judge's attention when defendant first makes *an n.o.v.* [better: *a j.n.o.v.*] motion." *Neely v. Martin K. Eby Constr. Co.*, 386 U.S. 317, 328–29 (1967) (per White, J.).

judgment of his peers. The phrase *judgment of his peers* appears in chapter 39 of Magna Carta. The phrase is "assumed to guarantee trial by jury." C.S. Potts, *Trial by Jury in Disbarment Proceedings*, 11 Tex. L. Rev. 28, 34 (1932). But "modern historical research has definitely determined that trial by jury as we know it, that is, trial before a body of impartial men who hear the evidence and determine defendant's guilt or innocence, did not exist in 1215. . . . What the barons demanded by the '*judgment of peers*' was that the whole case against one of their order should be turned over to them to try; that they should decide what method of proof should be used, whether wager of law, the ordeal, or battle; that they and not the king's judges should act as umpires in applying the selected form of proof; and that they should give the final decision as to the success or failure of the test applied. They did not recognize the king's judges as their 'peers' and still less a jury of freemen of the vicinage." *Id.* at 35. In modern American usage, a defendant's peers are men and women who are of legal age, are citizens of and reside in the locality, understand English, and have never been convicted of a felony.

judgment-proof; execution-proof. Both of these phrases, in reference to a judgment-debtor, mean "having insufficient assets to satisfy a money judgment." Although *judgment-proof* is much more common, *execution-proof* is more accurate: the judgment-creditor may have had little difficulty obtaining the judgment (i.e., winning the lawsuit), but collecting on the judgment through execution may be another matter entirely. So the penniless loser is insulated not from judgment but from execution.

judgment reversed. See **appeal allowed.**

judgment-roll. See **judgment-book.**

JUDGMENTS, APPELLATE-COURT. *Judgment* in this article means the final decree of an appellate court that acts upon a lower-court judgment, whether affirming, reversing, vacating, or whatever. British lawyers ordinarily use *judgment* synonymously with *opinion*, whereas Americans distinguish between the *opinion* (which sets out the reasons for the disposition) and the *judgment* (the pronouncement of the disposition itself). This article, then, reflects primarily American practices.

A cardinal principle of judgment-drafting is that appellate opinions should make explicit how the court is disposing of the judgment or order below. Appellate courts have sometimes left the parties and the trial court uncertain about the status of a case by using vague terms such as *so ordered* and *ordered accordingly*, unaccompanied by a clear statement of the disposition preceding these phrases. This practice is, happily, obsolescent. Of course, if the judgment is particularly complex—as when an appellate court affirms certain parts of the trial court's judgment, vacates another part, and orders the trial court to dismiss what remains as moot—the *so ordered* might be just the phrase for concluding such an admirably precise judgment.

A second important point is that judges should almost make a fetish of the following distinctions: an appeals court affirms, reverses, or modifies *judgments* or *orders*; it agrees with, approves, or disapproves *opinions* or *decisions*; and it remands *cases* (or *causes*) and *actions*. When the lower court lacked jurisdiction, the proper disposition by the appellate court is to *vacate* the judgment of the trial court and *dismiss* the case from the docket of the trial court (or *order* the trial court *to dismiss*). If the trial court had jurisdiction over the case, but entered an order beyond its jurisdiction, the proper disposition is to *vacate* the order and *remand* the case. In each of these circumstances, the appellate court had jurisdiction over the appeal for the limited purpose of making the disposition described. If the appeal raised other issues about the judgment (or order) of the trial court, the proper disposition might add: in other respects the appeal is *dismissed*.

When the appellate court lacks jurisdiction to hear any aspect of the appeal, the proper disposition is usually *appeal dismissed*. Although an appellate court in its opinions may approve or disapprove the trial court's statement or use of legal propositions, the judgment proper operates only on the judgment or order appealed from—that is, appellate courts do not affirm or reverse opinions, only orders or judgments. (The appellate court may, for example, affirm the judgment below but substitute a rationale leading to that judgment.)

The terms *vacate* and *reverse* can be problematic. Practices vary: some courts *reverse* the judgment below when the trial court should have disposed of the case differently, and *vacate* when the trial court may not have been incorrect, but needs to be unconstrained by its former judgment as it carries out the further directions of the appellate court. E.g.: "We *vacate* the judgment of the district court and remand the case for proceedings consistent with this opinion." Still other courts *vacate* only injunctions or administrative orders, or judgments or orders made without jurisdiction, *reversing* all other erroneous dispositions below. Courts ought to encourage consistency among their particular judges in these matters of usage.

With these guidelines in mind, we may usefully consider a number of appellate-court judgments, as well as statements about judgments, that illustrate the pitfalls awaiting the unwary. The first seven examples of poor drafting that follow have been adapted, with some additions, from the excellent discussion of the former Chief Justice of the Supreme Court of Texas, Robert W. Calvert, in his *Appellate Court Judgments*, 6 Tex. Tech L. Rev. 915, 923–24 (1975).

1. *Mistaking the Lower Court for Its Judgment.*

- "To *concur in or affirm* [read *concur in or affirm the order of*] the Interstate Commerce Commission in the current case would be overruling the decision made in the *Houston* case." *Yellow Transit Freight Lines, Inc. v. U.S.*, 221 F.Supp. 465, 468 (N.D. Tex. 1963).
- "The Supreme Court granted certiorari and *affirmed* [read *affirmed the judgment of*] the Fourth Circuit." *P.N. v. Seattle Sch. Dist. No. 1*, 474 F.3d 1165, 1170 (9th Cir. 2007).
- "This Court should *affirm* [read *affirm the judgment of*] the lower court." *Mahaffey v. State*, 316 S.W.3d 633, 643 (Tex. Crim. App. 2010).

The tribunal appealed from is not before the higher court for approval or disapproval, affirmance or reversal; rather, its *judgment* or *order* is.

2. *Mistaking the Case for the Judgment Below.* "The *case* [read *judgment*] is affirmed in part, reversed in part, and remanded with instructions." *Dalton v. Dalton*, 534 S.E.2d 747, 757 (W. Va. 2000). The case or cause remains the same; an appellate-court judgment acts directly upon a previous judgment in the case, but not upon the case itself.

3. *Mistaking the Lower Court's Opinion for Its Judgment.*

- "The *opinion* [read *judgment*] of the trial court is affirmed." *Goetz v. Boyer*, 894 N.E.2d 603, 604 (Ind. Ct. App. 2008).

- "Plaintiffs appealed the *decision* [read *judgment*] of the District Court." *In re Fioravante Settembre*, 425 B.R. 423, 429 (Bankr. W.D. Ky. 2010).
- "The *decision* [read *judgment*] of the trial court is affirmed." *State v. Hernandez*, 690 S.E.2d 582, 663 (S.C. Ct. App. 2010).

The appellate court may agree or disagree with the trial court's opinion or decision; again, however, it affirms or reverses the *judgment*.

4. Mistaking the Appellate Court's Judgment for the Trial Court's. "The *judgment* of the trial court is reversed and rendered." *City of Jackson v. Presley*, 40 So.3d 520, 524 (Miss. 2010). Appellate courts ordinarily have no power or jurisdiction to render a trial court's judgment; yet appellate courts are often authorized to render judgments that should have been rendered by the trial court. [A suggested revision: *The trial court's judgment is reversed; we render judgment for the defendant.*]

5. Purporting to Render a Judgment That the Court Simultaneously Reverses. "We *reverse* and *render* the judgment of the circuit court." *Collins v. Mayor and Council of City of Gautier*, 38 So.3d 677, 680 (Miss. Ct. App. 2010). Similar to #4. [A suggested revision: *The circuit court's judgment is reversed; we render judgment for defendant.*]

6. Mistaking the Judgment for the Case.

- "The amended judgment of the trial court is *affirmed in part, reversed in part, and reversed and remanded in part* [read *affirmed in part, reversed in part, and the case is remanded*]." *Seyler v. Seyler*, 201 S.W.3d 57, 66 (Mo. Ct. App. 2006). (Though it is possible, cases are not ordinarily remanded in part. If the judgment is not stated in sentence form, it is quite proper to write *Affirmed in part, reversed in part, and remanded.*)
- "The judgment of the trial court is reversed *and remanded* [read *and the case is remanded*]." *Franco v. District of Columbia*, 3 A.3d 300, 308 (D.C. 2010). (The judgment of the trial court may be reversed, but only the case may be remanded.)
- "We *vacate and remand* this case to the habeas court." *Johnson v. Roberts*, 694 S.E.2d 661, 664 (Ga. 2010). (Understood, perhaps, are the words *the judgment of the trial court* after the word *vacate*. It is generally best not to rely on UNDERSTOOD WORDS in drafting judgments; yet see the next-to-last paragraph of this article.)

7. Superfluously Granting Judgment After Reversal of a Plaintiff's Judgment. "The judgment of the trial court is reversed *and the judgment is here rendered for the defendants* [omit the italicized words]." *Chemical Express v. City of Roscoe*, 310 S.W.2d 694, 696 (Tex. Civ. App.—Eastland 1958). If the defendant has not filed a counterclaim, the judgment should end after the word *reversed*; the judgment is favorable to the defendant merely in denying the plaintiff recovery.

8. Wrongly Omitting a Remand. "The judgment of the trial Court that the Plaintiff take nothing is reversed and is here rendered that the Plaintiff recover of and from the Defendant." *Blue Bell, Inc. v. Isbell*, 545 S.W.2d 563, 568 (Tex. Civ. App.—El Paso 1976). The judgment is incomplete unless there is only one possible form and measure of relief. If the plaintiff sought damages, the case would have to be remanded to the trial court to determine damages. [Read *We reverse the judgment and remand for a determination of damages.*]

9. Mistaking the Judgment for the Court Below or Its Judgment. "The district court's judgment held plaintiff's patent to be valid in law but not infringed." *Neff Instrument Corp. v. Cohu Electronics, Inc.*, 298 F.2d 82, 85 (9th Cir. 1961).

Finally, it is worth noting that the terms *affirm, reverse, remand,* etc. may have "understood" objects, as here:

- "We *affirm* on all issues with regard to Jack Ballard, but *reverse* insofar as the court held Mary Ballard liable for the 1969 and 1970 deficiencies." *Ballard v. Commissioner*, 740 F.2d 659, 660 (8th Cir. 1984).
- "We *reverse* and *remand* for further proceedings." *Carr v. District of Columbia*, 587 F.3d 401, 402 (D.C. Cir. 2009).
- "We conclude that the reclassification of Appellee's service years was in error and, accordingly, we *reverse*." *Nesselroad v. State Consol. Public Retirement Bd.*, 693 S.E.2d 471, 472 (W. Va. 2010).

These elliptical phrases are unexceptionable.

Lawyers as well as judges must be sensitive to these niceties if they are to draft meaningful prayers in their appellate briefs—and write more precise articles on appellate advocacy: "The appellee's brief should *tell* [read *say*] why *the trial court* [read *the trial court's judgment*] should be affirmed, not why appellant's brief is all wrong." James L. Robertson, *Reality on Appeal*, Litig., Fall 1990, at 3, 6.

*judicable. See **justiciable.**

*judicative; *judicatorial; judicatory. **Judicative* is a NEEDLESS VARIANT of *adjudicative*, while **judicatorial* is a NEEDLESS VARIANT of *judicial*. See **adjudicative** & **judicial.** *Judicatory,* adj., = (1) of or relating to judgment; or (2) by which a judgment may be made; giving a decisive indication; critical. For the noun senses of *judicatory,* see **judicature.**

*judicator. See **adjudicator.**

judicature; judicatory. *Judicature* = (1) a judge's office, function, or authority; (2) a body of judges; or (3) the action of judging or of administering justice through duly constituted courts. It is sometimes used in BrE where *judiciary* usually appears in AmE. (See **judiciary.**) Hence the U.S. statute is the Judiciary Act of 1789, whereas Britain had the Judicature Acts 1873–75 and the Supreme Court of Judicature (Consolidation) Act 1925, now consolidated in the Supreme Court Act 1981. (That Act omits *judicature,* which may be obsolescent in BrE.) *Judicature* is used in a few American names such as the American Judicature Society, which publishes the journal *Judicature,* by its own terms "a forum for fact and opinion relating to all aspects of the administration of justice and its improvement."

But on the whole, *judicature* has generally been far more common in BrE than in AmE. E.g.:

- "It is a basic rule of English *judicature* that our courts do justice in public." *F. v. F.,* [1971] P.D. 1, 14.

- "What in later times were seen as two distinct branches of the constitution—the legislature and the *judicature*—had their origins in a less sophisticated notion of kingship in which legislation and adjudication were not distinguishable." J.H. Baker, *An Introduction to English Legal History* 234 (3d ed. 1990).
- "The Commission observes that in the earlier cases concerning the concept of restriction of competition by object, the Community *judicature* examined cases which related to hardcore restrictions." *Competition Auth. v. Been Indus. Dev. Soc'y Ltd.*, [2009] 4 C.M.L.R. 6.

Judicatory = judiciary; judicature. E.g.: "Confusion . . . would unavoidably result from the contradictory decisions of a number of independent *judicatories*." *The Federalist* No. 22, at 150 (Alexander Hamilton) (Clinton Rossiter ed., 1961). Today, except in specialized senses in Scotland and in the Presbyterian Church, this term should be avoided as a NEEDLESS VARIANT. For its adjectival sense, see ***judicative** & **adjudicative.**

judicial; judicious. *Judicial* = (1) of, relating to, or by the court <judicial officers>; (2) in court <judicial admissions>; (3) legal <the Attorney General took no judicial action>; or (4) of or relating to a judgment <judicial interest at the rate of 4% per annum>. Following are illustrations of the four senses of this complex word.

Sense 1 is the usual sense—e.g.:

- "Other jurisdictions have found a trustee may be *judicially* removed for neglect to perform duties, breach of trust, failure to comply with a court order, and hostility between the trustee and beneficiaries." *Floyd v. Floyd*, 615 S.E.2d 465, 486 (S.C. Ct. App. 2005).
- "[A]ny expansion of the duty of investigation imposed on rental-car agencies is a matter for legislative, not *judicial* action." *Flores v. Enterprise Rent-A-Car Co.*, 116 Cal. Rptr. 3d 71, 81 (Ct. App. 2010).

Sense 2 applies to proceedings—e.g.:

- "An admission in a pleading falls within the scope of a *judicial* confession and is full proof against the party making it." *Erazo v. Morton*, 33 So.3d 952, 954 n.3 (La. Ct. App. 2010).
- "In ruling on a section 2-615 motion, only those facts apparent from the face of the pleadings, matters of which the court can take *judicial* notice, and *judicial* admissions in the record may be considered." *K. Miller Constr. Co., Inc. v. McGinnis*, 938 N.E.2d 471, 477 (Ill. 2010).

With sense 3, the court seems remote from the action—e.g.:

- "[Appellant] then took the witness stand and *judicially* confessed that she committed the offense alleged against her in the indictment." *Gano v. State*, 684 S.W.2d 727, 729 (Tex. App.—Amarillo 1984).
- "Mr. Rogerson . . . was arrested that evening and charged with manslaughter, but in the first week of December last year a grand jury declined to indict him. In the months afterward, . . . Mrs. Wood's husband, Kevin, and other residents who were upset at the lack of *judicial* action have written letters to newspapers and government officials in an attempt to pressure the Attorney General's office to seek an indictment again." Lyn Riddle, *Deer Hunter Is Indicted in Accidental Killing of Woman in Maine*, N.Y. Times, 9 Dec. 1989, at 10.

Sense 4 is one not recorded in most dictionaries, but not uncommon in legal contexts, especially in AmE—e.g.: "Todd's liability for Auto's attorney's fees, therefore, is fundamentally different from, for example, liability for interest on a judgment. . . . Whereas an award of *judicial* interest is collateral to and independent of the action itself, attorney's fees awarded as a result of breach of an implied warranty of workmanlike performance are an integral part of the merits of the case and the scope of relief." *Todd Shipyards Corp. v. Auto Transp., S.A.*, 763 F.2d 745, 756 (5th Cir. 1985). Though hardly unusual, this use of the word is certainly suspect.

Judicious is a much simpler word, meaning "well considered, discreet, wisely circumspect." E.g.:

- "[The] power to interrogate must be *judiciously* exercised, and the examination ought not to be extended beyond that which is reasonably necessary to elicit needed material facts or to clarify testimony." *State v. Hutch*, 861 P.2d 11, 15 (Haw. 1993).
- "Here, the record supports the conclusion that the use of a 15% adjustment was reasonable and a *judicious* application of the Vice Chancellor's valuation expertise." *Montgomery Cellular Holding Co. v. Dobler*, 880 A.2d 206, 224 (Del. 2005).
- "The discretion should be *judiciously* exercised because granting the motion would conflict with one of the underlying purposes of the [Act]." *Larry v. Polk*, 412 F.Supp.2d 542, 545 (M.D.N.C. 2005).
- "Although we disagree with the trial judge's legal conclusions on the difficult and novel issues [that] she faced, we recognize and commend the conscientious and *judicious* manner in which she handled an extraordinarily hard and troubling case." *Boone v. Ballinger*, 228 S.W.3d 1, 14 (Ky. Ct. App. 2007).

*Judgmatic is a NEEDLESS VARIANT of *judicious*. See **judgmental.**

judicial cognizance. See **judicial notice.**

judicial court. In Massachusetts and Maine (and, formerly, New Hampshire), this phrase is not a REDUNDANCY: the legislature was originally called the *general court*, and therefore by distinction *judicial court* emerged in the 17th century and has persisted. See **general court.**

judicial dictum. See **dictum (B).**

judicialize = to treat judicially, arrive at a judgment or decision upon (*OED*). More modernly it has evolved to mean "to take into the province of the courts" and appears usually in a lament—e.g.:

- "A legal process designed to make the law judge-proof has become steadily more *judicialized*, and today the rate of *judicialization* is accelerating throughout the civil law world." J.H. Merryman, *The Civil Law Tradition* 155 (1969).

- "As lawyers we have a natural inclination to '*judicialize*' every function of government." Lon L. Fuller, *The Morality of Law* 176 (rev. ed. 1969).

See -IZE.

The noun *judicialization* (used above in the Merryman quotation) is fairly common—e.g.: "He [Richard A. Epstein] talks, for example, of putting an end to government intervention in the area of labor relations, which he says has led to '*judicialization*' of labor contracts." Deborah Graham, *Conservative Academics: Rising Stars*, Legal Times, 18 Mar. 1985, at 1. Cf. **juridification.**

judicial notice; judicial cognizance. The first phrase (referring to the means by which a court may take as proved certain facts without hearing evidence) is now the more common of the two in both AmE and BrE. A court takes *judicial notice* of a fact for one of two reasons: either it relates to a general legal question (such as statutory construction or constitutionality) that can better be explored by the judge free of evidentiary limitations, or it is so indisputably settled that, although normally within the fact-finder's purview, it can be resolved by the judge without hearing evidence.

The verb phrase is either *notice judicially* or *judicially notice*—e.g.:

- "While there are few absolutes in this area, we can *notice judicially*, if we need, that contemporary wills more often than not use the residuary clause to carry out the most important provisions." *Park Lake Presbyterian Church v. Henry's Estate*, 106 So.2d 215, 222 (Fla. Dist. Ct. App. 1958) (Shannon, J., dissenting).
- "According to professional etiquette, which is *judicially noticed*, a barrister may take instructions only from solicitors and not directly from lay clients." O. Hood Phillips, *A First Book of English Law* 22 (3d ed. 1955).

judicial opinion. See **judgment (B), JUDGMENTS, APPELLATE-COURT & OPINIONS, JUDICIAL.**

judicial review. A. In AmE. *Judicial review* has specialized senses that are not at all apparent in the phrase itself. It means either (1) "the court's power to refuse to enforce an unconstitutional act of either the state or the national government"; or (2) "the court's exercise of that power." E.g.:

- "This right of *judicial review* is indeed the most potent and pregnant fact of Supreme Court power; and its most dramatic and controversial manifestation is in the vetoing by the justices of things done by the other two supposedly equal branches of the national government, the Congress and the President." Fred Rodell, *Nine Men* 36 (1955).
- "Does the Constitution make it clear that the Court has this final authority of '*judicial review*' over national legislative enactments?" Robert G. McCloskey, *The American Supreme Court* 7–8 (1960).

Occasionally—and especially in journalistic writing—*judicial review* is used as a synonym of *appellate review*. But this usage is not strictly proper.

B. In BrE. The BrE uses are quite different because G.B. does not have judicial review in the American sense: courts cannot invalidate primary legislation

(though they review the decisions of lower courts). British writers use *judicial review* to refer to a relatively new procedure in England and Scotland, a procedure that enables a litigant to challenge an administrative action by a public body—and, in England, to secure a declaration; an order for mandamus, certiorari, or prohibition; or an award of damages. E.g.: "The Labour-controlled authority is also among 21 councils contesting a *judicial review* in the High Court next week, in the hope of overturning proposals to cap their poll tax charges." Peter Davenport, *Council Introduces "Austerity Cuts" Because of Poll Tax*, Times (London), 2 June 1990, at 2.

judicial separation. See **separation.**

JUDICIAL WRITING. See OPINIONS, JUDICIAL (B).

judiciary, adj. Ordinarily a noun, *judiciary* is used in *W3* adjectivally in the phrase *with full judiciary authority* (in definition of *en banc*). *W3* records *judiciary* as an adjective equivalent to *judicial*. Today, though, it is rarely so used in legal contexts and should be avoided in that sense as a NEEDLESS VARIANT—e.g.:

- "This procedure agrees with the *judiciary* [read *judicial*] practice in the United States." J.D. Hannan, *The Canon Law of Wills*, Catholic U. Am. Canon Law Studies, No. 86, at 135 (1934).
- "This system of checks and balances was not the result, as in the American Constitution, of a division of power between the legislative, executive, and *judiciary* [read *judicial*] branches of the government." Hans J. Wolff, *Roman Law* 27 (1951).

See ****judicative.**

But in the sense "of or relating to the judiciary," which means something different from *judicial* (= of or relating to a court or courts), the adjective *judiciary* is useful. E.g.: "If the history of the interpretation of *judiciary* legislation teaches anything, it teaches the duty to reject treating such statutes as a wooden set of self-sufficient words." *Romero v. International Terminal Operating Co.*, 358 U.S. 354, 379 (1959) (per Frankfurter, J.). In that sentence, *judicial legislation* would have created a MISCUE, suggesting judicial activism rather than statutes affecting the judiciary. See **judicial.**

judiciary, n. (= the judicial branch of government), is used in both AmE and BrE. (See **judicature.**) E.g.:

- "In *Crouch v. Crouch* . . . [we] gave . . . reasons for the federal *judiciary's* traditional refusal to exercise diversity jurisdiction in domestic-relations cases." *Andrews v. Patterson*, 585 F.Supp. 553, 554 (M.D.N.C. 1984).
- "I believe we should have rights of audience but this is only on condition that we satisfy the *judiciary* and the public that those rights will be exercised completely and fully." Valerie Elliott, *Prosecutors Seek Senior Lawyers*, Sunday Telegraph, 11 Feb. 1990, at 5 (quoting Allan Green, Q.C.).
- "We do not discredit the empirical research cited by Justice Durham in her concurring opinion, which may certainly be useful in the *judiciary's* attempts to improve the

judicial system." *State v. Harmon*, 956 P.2d 262, 273 n.9 (Utah 1998).

- "I suspect that the palpably different volume and content of deference language in school and prison cases may flow from the needs of yet another institution: the *judiciary* itself." Aaron H. Caplan, *Freedom of Speech in School and Prison*, 85 Wash. L. Rev. 71, 92 (2010).

judicious. See **judgmental** & **judicial.**

judiocracy. See **jurocracy.**

jump bail (= to leave [a place] illegally while free on bail) began as slang, but has now become a respectable expression used even by judges in written opinions. E.g.:

- "If the principal *jumps bail* and is not re-arrested, complete and permanent forfeiture of bail seems to be universal." *U.S. v. Ciena*, 195 F.Supp. 511, 511 (S.D.N.Y. 1961).
- "The defendant *jumped bail* before trial." *Supreme Court Ponders Sanction for Violation of Speedy Trial Act*, 56 U.S.L.W. 1176, 1176 (17 May 1988).

See **bail jump.**

jump citation. See **pinpoint citation.**

juncture. The phrase *at this juncture* should be used in reference to a crisis or a critically important time; it is not equivalent merely to "at this time" or "now." When used with these latter meanings, it is a pomposity. Here it is appropriate: "There is no question but that defendant was under arrest and in custody *at this juncture* of the encounter. . . . [T]he defendant (1) had been identified by two people as having robbed them, (2) had been detained, (3) had been searched and (4) was found to have been in possession of a weapon." *People v. Ross*, 748 N.Y.S.2d 845, 847 (N.Y. Sup. 2002). And here it is inappropriate:

- "The controversy *at this juncture merely points up* [read *at this point merely illustrates*] the indefiniteness and uncertainty of the controversial portion of the decree." *Lynch v. Uhlenhopp*, 78 N.W.2d 491, 497 (Iowa 1956).
- "Texas argues . . . that delay of review is not all that it seeks to avoid by petitioning *at this juncture* [read *at this point* or *now*]." *Texas v. U.S. Dep't of Energy*, 764 F.2d 278, 282 (5th Cir. 1985).
- "All that need be said *at this juncture* [read *at this point*] is that under Justice Alito's analysis, Biros fails to present a feasible plan for involving medical professionals of the sort Dr. Heath endorses." *Cooey v. Strickland*, 610 F.Supp.2d 853, 932–33 (S.D. Ohio 2009).

jungle fighter. See LAWYERS, DEROGATORY NAMES FOR (A).

junior (BrE) = a barrister who has not taken silk, regardless of age. E.g.: "To the *juniors*—those who are not Q.C.'s—is reserved the work of drafting pleadings, so that the man who 'takes silk' must start all over again, with as much chance of failing as he ever had." Alan Harding, *A Social History of English Law* 390 (1966). See **silk** & **devil.**

junior party; senior party. In American patent-law practice, *junior party* refers to the applicant involved in an interference who filed later; *senior party* refers to the applicant who filed earlier. See **interference.**

junk bond = a security issued by a company that is too young or has too much debt to earn an investment-grade rating from an agency such as Moody's Investor's Service Inc. or Standard & Poor's Corporation. Such a bond pays a higher return and is considered riskier than an investment-grade bond.

junta; junto. Of Spanish origin, *junta* (= a political or military group in power, esp. after a coup d'état) is pronounced either /**hoon**-tə/ or /**jən**-tə/. It is much more common in AmE than its altered form, *junto* /**jən**-toh/, which has undergone slight DIFFERENTIATION to mean "a self-appointed committee having political aims." Gowers wrote that *junto* "is an erroneous form" (*MEU2* 319), but it appears frequently in BrE where an American would write *junta*—e.g.: "Even so, a compliant civilian government may not be easy for the deeply unpopular *junto* to achieve." *Myanmar: Deja Vu*, Economist, 16 Jan. 1993, at 34 (Am. ed.).

jura. See *jus.*

jural; juristic; *juristical; juridical; *juridic; juratory; juratorial. *Jural* = (1) of or relating to law or its administration; legal; or (2) of or pertaining to rights and obligations <jural relations>. Today, *jural* is more common in sense 2—e.g.:

- "A declaratory-judgment action against an insurer with respect to *jural* relations, either as to present or prospective obligations, is permitted before entry of judgment in the underlying action." *Plaza Restoration, Inc. v. Nationwide Mut. Ins. Co.*, 823 N.Y.S.2d 518, 519 (App. Div. 2006).
- "[T]he party harmed . . . , being under legal disability, is solely reliant upon the court to protect his or her *jural* and other interests." *Malik ex rel. O'Brien v. Malik*, 835 N.Y.S.2d 860, 866 (Sup. Ct. 2007).

In sense 1, *jural* is ordinarily confined to contexts involving legal theory and is often a NEEDLESS VARIANT of simpler terms, such as *legal*—e.g.: "By cutting itself off from the religious root of the historical source of many fundamental *jural* [read *legal*] principles, the liberalist conception deprives itself of the living source of these principles." Alan Cameron, *Foundations of a Liberal Conception of Exploitative Contracts—A Challenge*, 32 Austl. J. Leg. Phil. 127, 139 (2007). But some legal theorists have made a case for it, arguing that, whereas *legal* can be ambiguous in meaning either "pertaining to law" or "conforming to the law," *jural* (in sense 1) unambiguously carries the former meaning. *See, e.g.*, 1 *Dictionary of Philosophy and Psychology* 548 (James Mark Baldwin ed., 1901).

Jural sometimes ill-advisedly displaces the more usual word *justiciable*—e.g.: "If controversies between individuals were decided according to the judge's individual standard of right and wrong, the theory that some questions are not *jural* [read *justiciable*] would not necessarily be recognized." William W. Thayer, *International Arbitration of Justiciable Disputes*, 26 Harv. L. Rev. 416, 416 (1913). The author of that sentence noted the possible synonymy of the terms (*id.* at 416), but this unusual overlapping of senses can't be recommended.

Juristic = (1) of or relating to a jurist, or jurists generally; or (2) of or relating to law or the study of law. Sense 1, though not common, is surely the more useful meaning of this term—e.g.:

- "A few words now as to the authority attached to this *juristic* literature [the Digest]." James Hadley, *Introduction to Roman Law* 65 (1881).
- "The goal of modern Romanistics is to obtain as complete a picture as possible of the evolution of Roman legal institutions and of the forms of *juristic* thinking revealed by them from the earliest stages discernible down to Justinian and beyond." Hans J. Wolff, *Roman Law* 224 (1951).

In sense 2, the word is merely another fuzzy equivalent of *legal*—e.g.: "The transition from unwritten to written code marks a stage in the history of almost every *juristic* [read *legal*] system." Stephen Pfeil, "Law," in 17 *Encyclopedia Americana* 86, 87 (1953). Some might try to justify this use of *juristic* as connoting the idea of law as a science, with its own set of notional constructs, including legal FICTIONS, and its peculiar means of practical deductive reasoning. But this set of connotations is surely lost on most readers. **Juristical*, by the way, is a NEEDLESS VARIANT. See **juristic person.**

Juridical = (1) relating to judicial proceedings or to the law; or (2) of or relating to law. **Juridic* is a NEEDLESS VARIANT. Sense 1 is perhaps justifiable—e.g.: "I cannot believe that the court ever meant . . . to express an inflexible rule or an inexorable *juridical* formula by the use of which we would be able to derive an automatic answer in all cases." *In re Burchell's Estate*, 87 N.E.2d 293, 298 (N.Y. 1949) (Fuld, J., dissenting). But in sense 2, the word is merely a puffed-up equivalent of *legal*—e.g.:

- "Preservation requirements serve overriding *juridical* [read *legal*] interests, including notice, an opportunity to be heard, economy, and efficiency." *Illes v. Jones Transfer Co.*, 539 N.W.2d 382, 390–91 (Mich. Ct. App. 1995).
- "The concept of 'good faith' creates special conduct responsibilities for each case in accordance with the *juridical* [read *legal*] relationship and the end intended by the parties." *Century Packing Corp. v. Giffin Specialty Equip. Co.*, 438 F.Supp.2d 16, 26 (D.P.R. 2006).
- "A citizen of the Russian Federation who has by the day of the appointment attained at least forty years of age, with an irreproachable reputation, who has higher *juridical* [read *legal*] education and an experience in the legal profession of at least fifteen years, who possesses recognised high qualifications in the sphere of law, may be appointed as the Judge of the Constitutional Court of the Russian Federation." Kim Lane Scheppele, *Guardians of the Constitution*, 154 U. Pa. L. Rev. 1757, 1768 n.24 (2006).

Defenders will acknowledge that *juridical* is a highbrow term, but they will argue that it evokes the idea

of law as it appears to the erudite: a hugely elaborate set of principles found in a wide array of sources and requiring some degree of specialized learning, interpretive skill, and logical acumen to put to use. Still, it's hard to make a sound argument that it is superior to *legal*, except to make the user feel somehow more perspicacious. Among the unperspicacious, *juridical* is sometimes mispronounced as if it were spelled **juridicial*, with a soft -*c*-.

Juratory, a rare term today, means "of or pertaining to an oath or oaths; expressed or contained in an oath" (*OED*). *Juratorial*, also rare, means "of or belonging to a jury" (*OED*).

jurat; *jurant. Both mean "one who has taken an oath"; **jurant* is a NEEDLESS VARIANT that is little used. *Jurat* usually refers to a public official as, in Jersey, to a bailiff's assistant. But historically *jurat* could refer to a juror: "The applicant appealed to the Royal Court against the refusal of permission and the appeal was heard by the Bailiff, who had been the Deputy Bailiff when the plan had been adopted, and seven *Jurats*." *Davidson v. Scottish Ministers* (No. 2), [2005] 1 S.C. 7 (H.L.).

Jurat has an additional, and perhaps more common, sense: "a clause placed at the end of an affidavit stating the time, place, and officer before whom the affidavit was made." E.g.: "Camelot objected to the form of the debtors' *jurats* on grounds that a witness must affirm the truth of his or her statements to the best of his or her knowledge, information and belief." *In re Young*, 390 B.R. 480, 491 (Bankr. D. Me. 2008).

jurator = (1) one who swears; or (2) a juror. In sense 2, of course, the word is a NEEDLESS VARIANT. See **juror.**

juratory; juratorial. See **jural.**

jure gentium. See ***jus gentium.***

juridic; juridical. See **jural.**

*juridical person. See **juristic person.**

JURIDICO-, a combining form common in Spanish and French legal writing, has come to be used with some frequency in English as well—e.g.:

- "They were the first to work out methods for the discovery of interpolations in the Digest and to realize that much *juridico*-historical information is found in sources outside of Justinian's *Corpus Iuris*." Hans J. Wolff, *Roman Law* 211 (1951).
- "These relations of production are defined as entailing *juridico*-political (even ideological) conditions as well as economic ones." Catherine Colliot-Thélène, "Afterword" to I. Rubin, *A History of Economic Thought: Part 5* 426–29 (D. Filtzer trans., 1979) (as quoted in Duncan Kennedy, *The Role of Law in Economic Thought*, 34 Am. U. L. Rev. 939, 1000 n.64 (1985)).

The prefix owes its existence to the perceived ineptitude of any derivative from *legal* as the first part of a compound. Writers who use *sociological* and *historico-legal* often feel uncomfortable with the newfangled and ill-formed *lego-*, so they resort instead to *juridico-*.

juridification, a NEOLOGISM dating from the mid-1980s, is a LOAN TRANSLATION of the German word *Verrechtlichung*, which denotes the process of transforming social relations into legal relations—and social conflicts into legal conflicts—primarily through legislation and judicial decisions. Though probably destined never to move beyond the realm of theoretical JARGON, the word usefully describes modern society's increasing reliance on courts to adjudicate questions that were formerly dealt with by other, less formal means (for example, within the family or neighborhood). E.g.:

- "A case exists for lesser *juridification* of labour relations, and for greater reliance on other political and social factors that have generated the transformations the country is now undergoing." Waclaw Szubert, *New Trends in Polish Labour Relations*, 12 Comp. Lab. L.J. 62, 72 (1990).
- "Some observers note the increasing encroachment of law on daily life—the '*juridification*' of the social sphere—with trepidation." Robert Anderson et al., *The Impact of Information Technology on Judicial Administration*, 66 S. Cal. L. Rev. 1761, 1799 (1993).

The verb *juridify,* seemingly a BACK-FORMATION, is somewhat less common—e.g.: "Just as dismissal procedures in Great Britain were increasingly *juridified*, despite the apparent predominance of an entirely different tradition, so attempts to limit the debate on dismissals in the United States to reflections exclusively addressing collective agreements and their implications failed." Spiros Simitis, *Denationalizing Labour Law: The Case Against Age Discrimination*, 15 Comp. Lab. L.J. 321, 324 (1994). Cf. **judicialize.**

jurimetrics, n., = the social science that attempts to "measure" those aspects of justice that are of an empirical nature. The term originated in the early 1960s in Lee Loevinger's article entitled *Jurimetrics: The Methodology of Legal Inquiry*, 28 Law & Contemp. Probs. 5 (1963). E.g.:

- "Those who search for a technological and practical aspect of the law include writers espousing *jurimetrics*." David Forte, *Natural Law and Natural Laws*, 26 U. Bookman 75, 75 (1986).
- "Glendon Schubert, the leader of a school known as Behavioral Jurisprudence and called by some '*Jurimetrics*,' built on the work of Underhill Moore. He sought to develop a systematic, behavioral method for predicting judgments." W.M. Reisman & A.M. Schreiber, *Jurisprudence* 458–59 (1987). Today a journal called *Jurimetrics Journal* publishes papers within the field.

Jurimetrician refers to a lawyer, esp. an academic lawyer, who tries to solve legal problems scientifically.

jurisconsult (= one learned in law, esp. in civil or international law; jurist; a master of jurisprudence [*OED*]) is a well-known word from Roman law but is little used today. Perhaps it merits wider service—e.g.: "The judges [of the International Court of Justice] . . . must be qualified in their own country for the

highest judicial office or be *juris-consults* of recognized capacity in international law." J.L. Brierly, *The Law of Nations* 279 (5th ed. 1955). Despite Brierly's spelling, the term should be solid, not hyphenated.

jurisdiction. A. Senses. In the broad sense of *jurisdiction* as it relates to power, see **power (B).**

B. And *venue*. *Venue* refers to the possible or proper *places* for the trial of a lawsuit, as distinguished from the proper *forums* in which *jurisdiction* (the *power* to hear the case) might be established. *Jurisdiction* over a suit may exist in a particular district, though its venue there would be improper; conversely, the *venue* of a suit may be appropriate in a particular district, though it must be dismissed there for lack of jurisdiction. The most important difference between the two is that a party may consent to be sued in an improper venue, waiving any objection to venue. But a party cannot consent to subject-matter jurisdiction, which the parties cannot confer on a court.

C. Prepositions with. *Jurisdiction* takes either *of* or *over*—e.g.:

- "When the appellate record fails to show that the trial court ruled on the constitutional question, this Court is without *jurisdiction of* an appeal in which this Court's exclusive appellate jurisdiction of constitutional issues is invoked, and the appeal is transferred to the Court of Appeals." *City of Decatur v. DeKalb County*, 668 S.E.2d 247, 250 (Ga. 2008).
- "Because the present cause of action does not arise under federal patent law nor does Metabolite's right to relief necessarily depend on resolution of a substantial question of federal patent law, this court does not have *jurisdiction over* this appeal." *Laboratory Corp. of Am. Holdings v. Metabolite Labs., Inc.*, 599 F.3d 1277, 1279 (Fed. Cir. 2010).

D. *Subject-matter jurisdiction*. See **subject-matter jurisdiction.**

jurisdictional; jurisdictive. *Jurisdictional*, the ordinary word, means "of or relating to jurisdiction"—e.g.:

- "The time limit fixed by Rule 59(e) is *jurisdictional*: it may not be extended by waiver of the parties or by rule of the district court." *Flores v. Procunier*, 745 F.2d 338, 339 (5th Cir. 1984).
- "The only potential way around this *jurisdictional* obstacle would be to measure the seven-day period beginning from the jury's special verdict regarding forfeiture instead of from the jury's guilty verdict." *U.S. v. Hill*, 177 F.3d 1251, 1253 (11th Cir. 1999).

Jurisdictive, a much rarer term, means "having jurisdiction." E.g.: "Turning to the central issue presented in this case, we must decide what court is *jurisdictive* of this suit." *Owner-Operators Indep. Drivers Ass'n v. State*, 541 A.2d 69, 71 (R.I. 1988). The DIFFERENTIATION between the two headwords has only recently emerged, *jurisdictive* being, in its other senses, a NEEDLESS VARIANT of *jurisdictional*. But *jurisdictive* is hardly a useful word: **is jurisdictive of* would be better phrased *has jurisdiction over*.

---

jurisdictionless (= not having jurisdiction) is a late-20th-century NEOLOGISM. E.g.:

- "This after-the-event resuscitation will encourage plaintiffs to try, and District Judges to tolerate, impleaders in the certain knowledge that all will be purified by the Court of Appeals whose wand of dismissal disinfects the infected *jurisdictionless* Court." *Burleson v. Coastal Recreation, Inc.*, 595 F.2d 332, 339 (5th Cir. 1978) (Brown, C.J., dissenting).
- "In a baffling decision, the Court found that deregulation conferred exclusive jurisdiction on the now *jurisdictionless* federal government." Robert C. Fellmeth, *Plunging into Darkness*, 33 Loy. U. Chi. L.J. 823, 827 (2002).
- "The counterargument is that all that is suffered is merely a material loss; what is averted by preventing a *jurisdictionless* court from ruling on a case is an ideological loss." Alex Lees, Note, *The Jurisdictional Label: Use and Misuse*, 58 Stan. L. Rev. 1457, 1491 (2006).

jurisdiction over the subject matter; jurisdiction of the subject matter. See **subject-matter jurisdiction.**

jurisdictive. See **jurisdictional.**

juris doctor. See **J.D.**

juris gentium. See *jus gentium.*

jurisprude, not recorded in the *OED*, is listed in *W3* as a BACK-FORMATION from *jurisprudence* with the meaning "a person who makes ostentatious show of learning in jurisprudence and the philosophy of law or who regards legal doctrine with undue solemnity or veneration." The word was coined with derisive overtones, *prude* being a conscious part of the NEOLOGISM.

The word deserves wider currency, but not without recognition of its pejorative connotations. (For the neutral personal noun corresponding to *jurisprudence*, see **jurisprudent.**) Occasionally, *jurisprude* is misapplied as if it were a neutral noun—e.g.:

- "A judge who focuses upon the natural law intent of the framers might be a clumsy hermeneuticist; he might be a maladroit *jurisprude* . . . , he might make a complete mess of things." Robert H. Bork, *A Time to Speak* 323 (2008).
- "Reaching dramatic levels of criticism of the marital privilege, this florid *jurisprude* claimed: 'It debases and degrades the matrimonial union, converting into a sink of corruption what ought to be a source of purity.'" Ronald L. Goldfarb, *In Confidence: When to Protect Secrecy and When to Require Disclosure* 146 (2009).
- "[Karl] Llewellyn was one of legal theory's most colorful figures: a memorable, if uneven, classroom performer, given to histrionics; a writer with a unique, sometimes bizarre, prose style enlivened and obscured by such terms as 'jurisprude,' 'law-stuff,' . . . and 'skunk-stank.'" Roger K. Newman, *The Yale Biographical Dictionary of American Law* 347 (2009).

jurisprudence. A. Practical and Theoretical Senses. This uncertain term has evolved curiously. The *OED* assigns to it three senses: (1) "knowledge of or skill in law"; (2) "the science that treats of human laws (written or unwritten) in general"; and (3) "a system or body of law." Sense 1, denoting practical skill in the law—the original sense—shifted to create the meanings (2 & 3) that emphasize the body of knowledge

with which skilled practitioners work. For a rather new sense 4, see (B).

Though derivatives of *jurisprudence* exist in a number of Western languages, this shift in meaning from the practical to the theoretical has apparently occurred only in English. Although both senses remain alive, the theoretical one, equivalent now roughly to "philosophy of the law," or "general theory of law," now predominates. The result, one writer has argued, is that "a word of distinguished pedigree and a well-established English meaning not essentially different from that which it bears in other languages has been made to colour like a chameleon and finally emerge as a self-contradictory chimera." A.H. Campbell, *A Note on the Word Jurisprudence*, 58 Law Q. Rev. 334, 339 (1942).

Well, not exactly. We might wish for less confusion, but it looks today as if the theoretical *jurisprudence* (senses 2 & 3) will oust its practical competitor (sense 1), which is labeled archaic by *W3*, and at this point there is little we can do but take note.

But Thomas E. Holland's lament—that many writers use *jurisprudence* as a highfalutin equivalent of *law*—remains a valid caution in many contexts: "The imposing quadrisyllable is constantly introduced into a phrase on grounds of euphony alone. So we have books upon 'Equity Jurisprudence' [as by Story and Pomeroy], which are nothing more nor less than treatises upon the law administered by Courts of Equity. . . . This sacrifice of sense to sound might more readily be pardoned, had it not misled serious and accurate thinkers." Holland, *The Elements of Jurisprudence* 4–5 (13th ed. 1924). In defense of Story and Pomeroy, though, *Equity Law* would certainly have been a confusing (and seemingly oxymoronic) title.

B. For *caselaw.* In AmE *jurisprudence* has been extended further than elsewhere in the English-speaking world, from "body of law" to "caselaw; court decisions." E.g.:

- "The seaman's cause of action against a shipowner for unseaworthiness of the vessel is largely a child of twentieth-century federal *jurisprudence.*" Note, *The Doctrine of Unseaworthiness in the Lower Federal Courts*, 76 Harv. L. Rev. 819, 819 (1963).
- "This holding recognized and applied as part of the general maritime law a principle previously applied by either statute or *jurisprudence* in other contexts." *Roberson v. Rebstock Drilling Co.*, 749 F.2d 1182, 1184 (5th Cir. 1985).

The French term *la jurisprudence* has precisely this sense, as does the German *die Jurisprudenz*. *Caselaw* and *decisional law* are less grandiose terms in English. See **caselaw** & **decisional law.**

C. As a Count Noun. *Jurisprudence* is not properly a count noun—e.g.:

- "Military law, like state law, is *a jurisprudence which exists* [read *a branch of jurisprudence that exists*] separate and apart from the law which governs in our federal judicial establishment." *Burns v. Wilson*, 346 U.S. 137, 140 (1953) (per Vinson, J.).
- "The courts, for many years, refused to acknowledge the existence of 'administrative law' as *a jurisprudence* [read

a branch of jurisprudence]." William H. Chamblee, Comment, *Journey Through the Administrative Process and Judicial Review of Administrative Actions*, 16 St. Mary's L.J. 155, 157 (1984).

D. General, Particular, and Comparative Jurisprudence. The phrase *general jurisprudence* refers to legal theory applied to law and legal systems generally. *Particular jurisprudence* is the scholarly study of the legal system within a particular jurisdiction. *Comparative jurisprudence*, a term in growing use, is preferred by some scholars to *comparative law*.

jurisprudent, n.; **jurisprudential,** adj. *Jurisprudent*, though appearing to be an adjective, is a noun meaning "a jurist, or learned lawyer." E.g.:

- "We have no difficulty with the theoretical concept, expressed in various ways by modern *jurisprudents*, that intentional, willful, or malicious harms of any kind are actionable unless justified." *Trautwein v. Harbourt*, 123 A.2d 30, 40 (N.J. Super. Ct. App. Div. 1956).
- "When there is no rule to follow the court must make one, or, as some *jurisprudents* prefer, 'discover' one." *Britt v. Sears*, 277 N.E.2d 20, 21 (Ind. Ct. App. 1971).

Cf. **jurisprude.**

Jurisprudential = of or relating to jurisprudence. E.g.: "The blending of the civil and criminal paradigms in punitive damages favors the recognition of a 'middleground' *jurisprudential* category with its own set of procedural rules." John G. Cuthane, *Considering Law and Policy Debates: A Public Health Debate* 248 (2010).

jurist. In BrE, this word is reserved for those having made outstanding contributions to legal thought and legal literature—e.g.: "The great German *jurist* Savigny described law as the product of the common consciousness of the people." H.G. Hanbury, *English Courts of Law* 15 (2d ed. 1953). In AmE, it is rather loosely applied to every judge of whatever level, and sometimes even to nonscholarly practitioners who are well respected—e.g.:

- "These topics would lead us into a very enlarged inquiry, incompatible with the object of this summary sketch; but they deserve the attention of all students of the law of prize, and it is to be hoped that some eminent *jurist* will, hereafter, examine them." Joseph Story, *Prize Causes*, 15 U.S. (2 Wheat), App. 1 (1817).
- "I cannot doubt that Livingston will be held the great *jurist* of nineteenth-century America and one to rank with Bentham among English-speaking *jurists*." Roscoe Pound, *The Formative Era of American Law* 167 (1938).

The most common error in AmE is to suppose that *jurist* is merely an equivalent of *judge*—e.g.: "We find no constitutional question concerning the validity of Charles Milton's conviction and sentence of death about which reasonable *jurists* [read *judges*] could differ." *Milton v. McCotter*, 765 F.2d 434, 437 (5th Cir. 1985).

The word has also been appropriated by those who work in legal philosophy—but *jurisprudent* is

the more accurate term in this sense. Sometimes, of course, the senses overlap: "The legal scholar (whom we may, perhaps, here term a *'jurist'* or *'jurisprudent'*) is finally limited only by the communication value of his creations and the usefulness of the resulting concepts." Julius Stone, *Legal System and Lawyers' Reasoning* 205 (1968).

juristic; *juristical. See **jural.**

juristic person; artificial person. These phrases, which are especially common in BrE, are ordinarily defined as "a corporate entity." Holland's definitions are more precise: (1) "a mass of property or a group of human beings that, in the eye of the law, is capable of rights and liabilities"; or (2) "such a mass of property or group of humans to which the law gives a status." *See* Thomas E. Holland, *The Elements of Jurisprudence* 97–98 (13th ed. 1924).

Juristic person is the usual phrase—e.g.:

- "The municipal law of this country, as of other countries, accepts the principle of international law that countries ordinarily accept the existence of *juristic persons* brought into being or recognized as existing in their country of origin." *In re Russian Commercial & Indus. Bank*, [1955] Ch. 148, 157.
- "The phrase includes damages arising from those acts for which a private ship is held legally responsible as a *juristic person* under the customary legal terminology of the admiralty law." Grant Gilmore & Charles L. Black Jr., *The Law of Admiralty* 984 (2d ed. 1975).
- "In other words, do the rights and protections of the CRA extend to *juristic persons* or only to people?" *Safiedine v. City of Ferndale*, 753 N.W.2d 260, 260 (Mich. Ct. App. 2008).

Other names for *juristic person* are **conventional person, fictitious person,* and **juridical person,* all of which should be avoided as NEEDLESS VARIANTS. Cf. **natural person.**

jurocracy (= government by the courts) is recorded in none of the major dictionaries, but it is a useful addition to the language. It appears to have been coined in D.L. Horowitz, *The Jurocracy: Government Lawyers, Agency Programs, and Judicial Decisions* (1977). See GOVERNMENTAL FORMS.

A less-well-formed equivalent is *judiocracy*, coined by a conservative polemicist: "As our judges have become the makers of law, our Congress has become a colony of actors. In an era of judicial restraint, they are going to have to take responsibility for their acts and answer to the electorate. Times change. We move from *judiocracy* [read *jurocracy*] back to old-fashioned democracy." R. Emmett Tyrrell, *Bork, Now More than Ever*, Am. Spectator, Nov. 1987, at 10.

juror; *juryman; *jurywoman; jurator. *Juror* is the modern word. *Juryman and *jurywoman should be avoided on grounds of SEXISM, although they still occasionally appear—e.g.:

An asterisk (❋) precedes words and phrases that are invariably inferior forms.

- "*Jurymen* [read *Jurors'*] affidavits . . . and acknowledgements of judge and both counsel reflect that the jury requested an instruction." *Rissler & McMurry v. Snodgrass*, 854 P.2d 69, 70 (Wyo. 1993).
- "The first method, as described by [Judge Learned] Hand, was to select *jurymen* [read *jurors*] who possessed experiences [that] were especially fitted to the class of facts [that] were before them." *Minner v. American Mortg. & Guar. Co.*, 791 A.2d 826, 834 (Del. Super. Ct. 2000).

Jurator is an obsolete equivalent.

Juror ought to be distinguished from *potential juror* or *veniremember*—e.g.: "When the court was cleared of unchosen *jurors* [read *veniremembers*], the spectators waiting in the corridor were allowed inside." John Bryson, *Evil Angels* 346 (1985). See **venireman.**

jury. Because this word is a COLLECTIVE NOUN in AmE, it usually takes a singular verb. To emphasize the individual members of the jury, we have the word *jurors.* In AmE, *jury* is almost always treated as a singular noun—e.g.:

- "The court is cognizant of the fact that, where a *jury do* [read *jury does*] not decide a case upon prejudice, passion, or mistake, the court has no right to set the verdict aside." *Jeremiah Williams & Co. v. Lamport & Holt*, 224 N.Y.S. 587, 592 (N.Y. City Ct. 1927).
- "A *jury* of twelve *was* chosen." *Thiel v. Southern Pac. Co.*, 328 U.S. 217, 219 (1946) (per Murphy, J.).
- "In all prosecutions of crimes defined by law as felonies, the accused has the right to a jury of 12 members. In all other criminal prosecutions, the legislature may provide for the number of jurors, provided that a *jury have* [read *jury has*] at least six members." *Baker v. State*, 590 N.W.2d 636, 638 (Minn. 1999) (quoting the Minn. statute).

But in BrE, where using plural verbs with collective nouns is common, *jury* usually takes a plural verb— e.g.: "As a result of Shaw's case, virtually any cooperative conduct is criminal if a *jury consider* it ex post facto to have been immoral." H.L.A. Hart, *Law, Liberty, and Morality* 12 (1963). But exceptions do occur in BrE—e.g.: "It is only when this *jury has* determined the facts that the judge is empowered to impose sentence." 1 Winston Churchill, *A History of the English Speaking Peoples* 222 (1956).

Jury is both adjective and noun. Here it acts as an adjective: "Any argument by defense counsel that it took the vote of only one juror to prevent imposition of the death penalty amounted to a request for '*jury* nullification.'" *Hooks v. Workman*, 606 F.3d 715, 734 (10th Cir. 2010) (per Murphy, J.). Of course, legal writers should be aware that, as a general English adjective, *jury* has, in addition to the ordinary legal meaning "of or relating to a jury," the maritime meaning "makeshift" <a jury rig>.

jury, go to the. When a case *goes to the jury*, the jury begins its deliberations—e.g.:

- *Haas Stock-Fraud Trial to* Go to Jury, Headline, Wade Lambert & Paul M. Barrett, Wall St. J., 4 Dec. 1989, at B4.
- "Cynthia Dowaliby was acquitted by the judge before the case *went to the jury*." Janita Poe & Terry Wilson, *Dowaliby*

Case Status Unaltered by Reports, Chicago Trib., 6 Jan. 1993, at 3.

jurybox; *jury-stand. *Jurybox* is the standard term in AmE and BrE alike, though it is often spelled as two words (*jury box*) on both sides of the Atlantic. **Jury-stand* is a NEEDLESS VARIANT.

jury charge. See **charge,** vb. (C).

jury direction. See **jury instruction.**

jury-fixing. See **jury-packing.**

jury instruction (AmE) = *jury direction* (BrE).

jury instructions. See **summing-up.**

juryless (= without a jury) is one of Jeremy Bentham's modest successes as a word-coiner. In the early 19th century, he wrote of "a wicked and *jury-less* Court of Conscience act." Jeremy Bentham, *Scottish Reform Considered* 29 (1808). The word has occurred in many modern contexts—e.g.:

- "The Board differs from a trial judge (in a *juryless* case) who hears and sees the witnesses." *NLRB v. Universal Camera Corp.*, 190 F.2d 429, 432 (2d Cir. 1951) (Frank, J., concurring).
- "The strategy of the English government was to remove litigation to the *juryless* forum of the vice-admiralty courts." Grant Gilmore, *The Ages of American Law* 9 (1977).

jury lottery. Those who are not fond of the jury system use this phrase to describe the unpredictability of juries, especially those that award high amounts of punitive damages. E.g.:

- "But awards far larger than necessary to achieve deterrence are naked and economically counterproductive transfers of wealth through a capricious *jury lottery*." Stuart Taylor Jr., *High Court Should Set Limits in Punitive Damages Sweepstakes*, Manhattan Law., 25 Apr. 1989, at 10.
- "Last week's was a typically absurd case of law by *jury lottery*." L. Gordon Crovitz, *A Legal Rule for the Justices: Never Forget the Consumer*, Wall St. J., 13 Mar. 1991, at A13.

*juryman. See **juror** & SEXISM (B).

jury of indictment. See **grand jury** (A).

jury-packing; jury-tampering; jury-fixing; jury-rigging. *Jury-packing* = contriving to have the jury peopled with those who are predisposed toward one side or the other. *Jury-tampering* = engaging in any activity that might improperly influence one or more jurors. (Another term for *jury-tampering* is *embracery*. See **embracery.**) *Jury-fixing* = corruptly procuring the cooperation of jurors who actually influence the outcome of a trial. *Jury-rigging* = the assembling of a jury in a makeshift manner.

juryroom. One word, increasingly, though the *OED* lists it in hyphenated form and *W3* lists it as two words.

*jury-stand. See **jurybox.**

jury-tampering. See **jury-packing.**

jury trial. Two words, no hyphen.

jury venire. See **venire.**

jury wheel = (traditionally) a contraption, usu. a circular box revolving on a crank, that aids officials in randomly choosing those who will be called in for jury duty. In several jurisdictions today, *jury wheel* has come to apply to the computer methods that have displaced the old-fashioned crank-up devices. E.g.: "Richard J. Masotta, associate director of the Yale University Computer Center, which has a contract with the federal government to compile the master list and the so-called *jury wheel*, also had no answer to the mystery." William Cockerham, *Federal Jury Picks Questioned*, Hartford Courant, 29 July 1992, at A1.

*jurywoman. See **juror** & SEXISM (B).

jus (= law in the most abstract and general sense; a legal right, rule, or principle of law) forms the plural *jura*—e.g.:

- "Other courts have been less precise, creating different categories of real rights: one referring to the *jus in re* where there is evidence of complete and absolute dominion over a thing, and . . . *jus ad rem* (i.e., a right to a thing) when a right is exercisable by one person over the property by virtue of a contract or obligation." *Hawthorne Oil & Gas Corp. v. Continental Oil Co.*, 368 So.2d 726, 730–31 (La. Ct. App. 1979).
- "The rights of use, enjoyment, and disposal are said to be the three elements of property in things. They constituted the *jura in re*." *IP Timberlands Operating Co. v. Denmiss Corp.*, 657 So.2d 282, 294 (La. Ct. App. 1995).

The term is also spelled *ius*. See *jus in rem.*

Inexplicably, one learned writer fell into error by pluralizing the word as if it were a masculine Latin noun rather than a neuter: "The question can be approached from another angle, that of the clarity of the rules about particular aspects of the law, the content of the *iures* [read *iura*], so to speak." E.Z. Tabuteau, *Transfers of Property in Eleventh-Century Norman Law* 225 (1988). For Latinists—and there are still a few in the law—so to speak is an abomination.

jus ad bellum. See *jus in bello.*

jus ad rem. See *jus in rem.*

jus civile; jus gentium. *Jus civile* denoted the legal rules and principles applicable to citizens only—the common law of ancient Rome. *Jus gentium* denoted the legal rules and principles derived from customs of various peoples and nations or from fundamental ideas of right and wrong applicable to foreigners litigating in Rome and later supposed by some to be universal in the human mind. See *jus gentium*, **civil law** (A) & **international law.**

jus cogens = the peremptory norms of international law. E.g.: "Such [peremptory] norms, often referred to as *jus cogens* (or 'compelling law'), enjoy the highest status in international law." *Committee of U.S. Citizens Living in Nicaragua v. Reagan*, 859 F.2d 929, 935 (D.C. Cir. 1988).

jus disponendi (= the right to dispose of property) is an unnecessary LATINISM that masquerades as a TERM OF ART—e.g.:

- "Here, undoubtedly, the devisee is given an estate in fee simple by clear, unambiguous, and explicit words. This carries the *jus disponendi* [read *right of disposition*]." *Farmers Bank of Clinch Valley v. Kinser*, 192 S.E. 745, 746 (Va. 1937).
- "In such case, the founder having the entire *jus disponendi* in disposing [read *right to dispose*] of his own property, sees fit to give to his beneficiary a qualified and limited, instead of an absolute, interest in the income." *Glass v. Carpenter*, 330 S.W.2d 530, 534 (Tex. Civ. App.—San Antonio 1959).

jus gentium; juris gentium; jure gentium. The *jus gentium*, literally, is the law of nations. More specifically, it means either (1) "the body of law governing the status of foreigners in ancient Rome and their relations with foreign citizens" (*jus civile*, by contrast, applying to Roman citizens only); or (2) ever since the time of Grotius (1583–1645), the customary law of nations. See **international law** & **jus civile.**

Juris gentium is the genitive form meaning "of the law of nations"—e.g.: "Tradition . . . was set down as an institution *Juris Gentium*, or rule of the Law common to all Nations." Henry S. Maine, *Ancient Law* 41 (17th ed. 1901). *Jure gentium* is the ablative form meaning "by the law of nations" among other things—e.g.: "Similar instances may be found . . . in common law offences regarded as crimes *jure gentium*, such as piracy on the high seas." R.H. Graveson, *Conflict of Laws* 181 (7th ed. 1974).

jus in bello; jus ad bellum. The first means "the corpus of the laws and customs of war." The second means "the right of making war."

jus in rem; *jus in re; jus ad rem. The distinction is a simple one, although of decreasing importance: "A *jus in [rem]* is a right, or property in a thing, valid as against all mankind. A *jus ad rem* is a valid claim on one or more persons to do something, by force of which a *jus in re* will be acquired." *The Young Mechanic*, 30 F. Cas. 873, 876 (D. Me. 1855). The usual phrase in Anglo-American law is *jus in rem* (lit., "right against a thing"), not **jus in re* (lit., "right in or over a thing"). For the distinction between *in rem* and *in personam*, see **in personam** (B).

jus naturale. See **natural law (A).**

jus non scriptum. See *jus scriptum.*

jus sanguinis = a legal rule whereby a child's citizenship is that of his parents. We have no other name for it.

jus scriptum; jus non scriptum. What is written law (*jus scriptum*), and what is unwritten law (*jus non scriptum*)? In Anglo-Saxon law, *jus scriptum* is exclusively statutory law, together with constitutions, regulations, and treaties; *jus non scriptum* is all law (including caselaw in reported decisions) that has not been officially enacted in some way. But this clear (if strange) distinction does not apply in all legal cultures. In Roman law, the *jus non scriptum* was exclusively customary law; *jus scriptum* was all the rest, whether enacted or unenacted law. And in other legal cultures there are still other nuances. For an insightful discussion, see H.D.H., preface to "The Interpretation of Law by English Medieval Courts," in Theodore F.T. Plucknett, *Statutes and Their Interpretation in the First Half of the Fourteenth Century* v, viii–x (1922). *Jus scriptum* is also known as *lex scripta*; *jus non scriptum* is also known as *lex non scripta.* See **unwritten law.**

just. See **fair (A).**

just deserts (= a reward or punishment that is deserved) is occasionally misrendered **just desserts,* as here:

- "Nor can Horizon avoid its *just desserts* [read *just deserts*] by its pleonastic harping on the fact that its conduct . . . has been impeccable since at least mid-June of 1983." *NLRB v. Horizon Air Servs., Inc.,* 761 F.2d 22, 32 (1st Cir. 1985).
- "When they left, the defendants' own logic suggests that they should have left all their units behind at book immediately and let the new generation of value drivers receive their *just desserts* [read *just deserts*]." *Gelfman v. Weeden Investors, LP,* 859 A.2d 89, 123 (Del. Ch. 2004).
- "Lest the cynical among us suggest that cold logic has robbed the plaintiffs of their *just desserts* [read *just deserts*], we hasten to add that this rule is in no way inequitable." *Negron-Almeda v. Santiago,* 528 F.3d 15, 26 (1st Cir. 2008).

jus tertii (= the right of a third party) generally is not a useful enough LATINISM to justify its presence in legal prose—e.g.:

- "But in the third case, *i.e.,* where the plaintiff was not in possession, the defendant may *set up a jus tertii, i.e.,* [delete the six italicized words immediately preceding] prove that some other person has a better title." O. Hood Phillips, *A First Book of English Law* 230 (3d ed. 1955).
- "Respondents may be correct that petitioner does not possess standing *jus tertii* [read *as a third party*], but this is not the issue." *Phillips Petroleum Co. v. Shutts,* 472 U.S. 797, 805 (1985) (per Rehnquist, J.).
- "In this sense, the threshold for facial challenges is a species of third-party (*jus tertii*) [omit parenthetical phrase] standing, which we have recognized as a prudential doctrine and not one mandated by Article III of the Constitution." *City of Chicago v. Morales,* 527 U.S. 41, 55 n.22 (1999) (per Stevens, J.).

justice. See **judge.**

justice of the peace. See **J.P.**

justiceship; **justicedom; *justicehood.* The first is the usual term; the others are NEEDLESS VARIANTS.

justiciability, in the federal law of the U.S., is a TERM OF ART employed to give expression to the limitation placed upon federal courts by the case-or-controversy doctrine. A matter that is a case or controversy is susceptible of a judicial determination—is justiciable. See **case or controversy** & **justiciable.**

justiciable; **judicable.* The first is preferred in the sense "susceptible of judicial decision; triable" <justiciable cases and controversies>. In the following quotation, however, the word is used nonsensically; Justice Thurgood Marshall, in quoting this sentence, appropriately *sic'd* it: "There has not been enough time in which *justiciably* [*sic*] to decide the case." As quoted in *Dobbert v. Wainwright,* 468 U.S. 1231, 1242 (1984) (Marshall, J., dissenting). **Justiceable* is a fairly common misspelling.

  *Judicable is a NEEDLESS VARIANT—e.g.:

- "Nothing in the present case's complaint rose to the level of a *judicable* [read *justiciable*] constitutional issue." *Mack v. State,* 943 So.2d 73, 76 (Miss. Ct. App. 2006).
- "The ICC will not be a competitor or drain on individual state jurisdiction, but rather a role-model and, more importantly, complementary judicial body for cases which would be otherwise *nonjudicable* [read *nonjusticiable*]." Douglas R. Burgess Jr., *Hostis Humani Generi: Piracy, Terrorism, and a New International Law,* 13 U. Miami Int'l & Comp. L. Rev. 293, 336 (2006).
- "An appellate court must have discretion to control its docket and allot time and attention to those who raise *judicable* [read *justiciable*] issues." *State v. Raiburn,* 171 P.3d 654, 656 (Kan. Ct. App. 2007).

See **jural.**

justicial. The *OED* defines this term as "of or pertaining to justice or its administration"—a use last recorded in 1826. Some noted writers, such as Fred Rodell, have used it as the adjective corresponding to the title *justice,* as in *Supreme Court Justice*—e.g.: "A month after Grant took office, and while the first of the Legal Tender cases was still on its way up to the Court, Congress, perhaps foreseeing trouble, had increased the number of Justices to nine (at which figure, despite Franklin Roosevelt's bid to raise the *Justicial* ante, it has remained ever since)." Fred Rodell, *Nine Men* 158 (1955).

justiciar, n.; **justiciary.** *Justiciar* is obsolete in all but historical senses relating to medieval England and Scotland. *Justiciary* survives in the names *Clerk of Justiciary* and *High Court of Justiciary,* both relating to the supreme criminal courts of Scotland, and as an adjective in related contexts, e.g., *justiciary gowns, justiciary cases,* and *Lords Commissions of Justiciary.*

justification. See **excuse.**

justificatory; *justificative. *Justificatory* is the preferred term, **justificative* a NEEDLESS VARIANT. But *justificatory* itself is often part of a longer phrase that can be tightened—e.g.:

- "So the competence question should be asked and answered, and the court should move on to its substantive economic analysis free of *justificatory excuses* [omit *justificatory*]." Nelson O. Fitts, Note, *A Critique of Noncommercial Justifications for Sherman Act Violations*, 99 Colum. L. Rev. 478, 496 (1999).
- "In other words, if we assume that racial diversity has value, then we have already decided that racial difference can be a consideration that *provides justificatory reasons for* [read *justifies*] certain actions or attitudes." Patrick S. Shin, *Diversity v. Colorblindness*, 2009 BYU L. Rev. 1175, 1210–11.
- "This is accomplished through the drafting of *justificatory reasons* [read *justification*] for judgment." Randal N. M. Graham, *What Judges Want*, 30 Statute L. Rev. 38, 58 (2009).

justify, like *warrant*, generally takes as its object an action or belief, not a person. E.g.: "The instant cases furnish sufficient additional indications of the settlor's intent to *justify* our giving effect to the language of the instrument limiting an estate to the grantor's heirs." *In re Burchell's Estate*, 87 N.E.2d 293, 297 (N.Y. 1949). See **warrant,** vb.

In legal prose, however, this verb frequently takes personal objects. E.g.:

- "I find no such misconduct on the part of the plaintiff that could *justify the defendant* in abandoning her and the six-year-old infant." *Gluckstern v. Gluckstern*, 148 N.Y.S.2d 391, 394 (Sup. Ct. 1955).
- "In evaluating the reasonableness of the officer's conduct the court considered both the circumstances in which the information was given to the officer and the facts that would *justify the officer* in acting on the information without knowing the person's identity or obtaining information for tracing him later." *State v. Fudge*, 42 S.W.3d 226, 231 (Tex. App.—Austin 2001).
- "No Plaintiff has presented any evidence indicating the existence of a relationship with an Agent Defendant that would *justify that Plaintiff* in relaxing his normal vigilance regarding an arms'-length business transaction." *Booker v. American Gen. Life & Accident Ins. Co.*, 257 F.Supp.2d 850, 861 (S.D. Miss. 2003).

This usage is old, and perhaps only today could be considered a LEGALISM: "If, therefore, the process

could be commenced in rem, the authority of *Bynkershoek* would *justify* us . . . ." *Chisholm v. Georgia*, 2 U.S. 419, 425–26 (1793) (per Iredell, J.). Nevertheless, it strikes the modern ear as unidiomatic and illogical.

For more on *justify* and its near-synonyms, see **maintain (A).**

Justinian is a proper noun, the name of the Roman emperor (A.D. 483–565) who was perhaps the greatest legal codifier ever, responsible for promulgating the *Corpus Juris Civilis*.

For the adjective corresponding to his name, some books use *Justinianean* /jəs-tin-ee-**an**-ee-ən/, a clumsy word whose only advantage is that it is distinct from the name itself. Other books use *Justinian* as the adjective as well as the noun (*see, e.g.,* the Hadley quotation under **reception**). The former spelling seems stilted; the latter is quite acceptable.

juvenile. See **child.**

juvenile offender. This phrase, like *juvenile delinquent*, is a technical term deriving from 20th-century legislation. It generally refers to a minor who commits a criminal offense. Just why it offends some—in a juvenile way, one might say—is hard to fathom: "Among all legal expressions that lend themselves to weasely interpretations, there is one that deserves nomination for the Weasel Award. 'Juvenile (or Child) Offender' is a jewel of understatement created by welfare workers and a judiciary subject to political pressures." Mario Pei, *Words in Sheep's Clothing* 87 (1969). What would Mr. Pei have us call such offenders? *Hooligans?*

juxtaposition cannot be a verb; although one may *position* a thing, one may not *juxtaposition* two things. *Juxtapose* is the correct verb form—e.g.:

- "Courts reject efforts of plaintiffs to *juxtaposition* [read *juxtapose*] scenes occurring at different points in two works to show a sequence of events." Nick Gladden, *When California Dreamin' Becomes a Hollywood Nightmare*, 10 J. Intell. Prop. L. 359, 382 (2003).
- "In this Part, we *juxtapose* our evaluation of the practice with five prominent contemporary approaches: originalism, living constitutionalism, minimalism, redemptive constitutionalism, and popular constitutionalism." Nelson Tebbe & Robert L. Tsai, *Constitutional Borrowing*, 108 Mich. L. Rev. 459, 511 (2010).

K

kangaroo court (= a court, often illegitimately held, in which the principles of law and justice are disregarded and perverted) originated in the mid-19th century as American slang but is now an acceptable phrase, if responsibly applied, even in formal writing—e.g.:

- "These arguments contradict basic notions of fairness and, if pushed to their limits, would turn immigration

proceedings into mere *kangaroo courts*." *Khorrami v. Rolince*, 493 F.Supp.2d 1061, 1072–73 (N.D. Ill. 2007).
- "Independent observers called the trial a 'simulated trial,' 'rigged from beginning to end'; 'the whole thing was a cover-up,' and Doe's conviction 'totally incomprehensible factually and legally.' It was a *kangaroo court* to make kangaroos blush." *Doe v. Gonzales*, 484 F.3d 445, 451 (7th Cir. 2007).

An asterisk (*) precedes words and phrases that are invariably inferior forms.

W2 records three particular types of kangaroo courts: (1) "a mock court held by vagabonds or by prisoners in a jail"; (2) "an irregularly conducted minor court in a frontier or unsettled district"; and (3) "formerly, one of a number of courts in Ohio with county-wide jurisdiction, whose judge was paid by fines imposed by him upon conviction of accused persons."

K.B. = King's Bench. See **Queen's Bench.**

K.C. = King's Counsel. See **Queen's Counsel.**

Keeper of the King's Conscience = (historically) the Lord Chancellor, who had the royal power of deciding equitable petitions to the King—a power that gave rise to the system of *equity*. E.g.: "In his character of 'Keeper of the King's Conscience,' [the Chancellor] was held justified in thus exerting the undefined residuary authority which in early times was attributed to an English king." Thomas E. Holland, *The Elements of Jurisprudence* 73 (13th ed. 1924). See **chancellor** & **equity.**

keeper of the peace is a LOAN TRANSLATION of the Latin phrase *custos pacis*, a phrase sometimes Englished as *guardian of the peace*. Our phrase *to keep the peace* derives from the agent-noun phrase.

Keycite, n. & vb. *Keycite* is the trademarked name of the citation-research system introduced by Westlaw in 1997. Users can look up the status of a case, see how often it's been cited and for what points, and do key-number-based research. The noun is always capitalized—e.g.:

- "A *Keycite* search on Westlaw would have revealed to the court that *Hall Motors* had been called into question by *In re Greene.*" *Smith v. Ford Motor Credit Co.*, 301 B.R. 585, 589 (N.D. Ala. 2003).
- "The court took a brief recess to print out the docket entries from the appeal in *United States v. Kennard Gregg*, as well as a Westlaw *KeyCite* showing the denial of the writ of certiorari." *U.S. v. Washington*, 549 F.3d 905, 910 (3d Cir. 2008).

Because the name is a trademark, it isn't proper to use it as a verb. But some writers do so anyway—e.g.:

- "Accordingly, I then *Keycited* decisions on point to learn of subsequent and related decisions." Doug Rendleman, *Irreparability Resurrected?*, 59 Wash. & Lee L. Rev. 1343, 1385 n.203 (2002).
- "A simple Westlaw *keycite* of *Roe* brings up a red flag next to the case name plus notations that *Murphy Bros.* abrogated *Roe* and that several other cases recognize *Roe's* overruling." *Andreshak v. Service Heat Treating, Inc.*, 439 F.Supp.2d 898, 900 n.2 (E.D. Wis. 2006).

Cf. **shepardize.**

keynote. See **catchword.**

key number. This phrase refers to the elaborate indexing system developed by West Publishing Co. for cataloguing the whole of American caselaw with brief (or not-so-brief) headnotes. The phrase is older than many lawyers suspect—e.g.:

- "The section number . . . affixed to the first catchword of the headnote paragraph is a '*key-number*,' unlocking the door to all future and past decisions involving a similar principle." William M. Lile et al., *Brief Making and the Use of Law Books* 41 (3d ed. 1914).
- "The West *Key Number* system gives a crude sense of the numerical dominance of opinions on preliminary relief." Douglas Laycock, *The Death of the Irreparable Injury Rule* 110 (1991).
- "Fortunately or unfortunately, this court's 'opinion' at 179 F.R.D. 328 cannot be located except by serendipity because West Publishing Company does not have a *key number* for 'free legal advice.'" *Bronson & Migliaccio, LLP v. Kinsey*, 228 F.Supp.2d 1315, 1316 (N.D. Ala. 2002).
- "We note that West has a *key number* within Post-Conviction Relief entitled 'Fundamental or Constitutional Error.' This may sometimes confuse prisoners about the need to allege a 'fundamental error' when the prisoner really wishes to make a constitutional claim." *Hughes v. State*, 22 So.3d 132, 137 n.2 (Fla. Dist. Ct. App. 2009).

kidnapping. A. Spelling. The spellings in *-pp-* are, by convention, preferred. But the inferior spelling *kidnaping occasionally appears, as in *People v. Norris*, 706 P.2d 1141 (Cal. 1985) (en banc).

That spelling has its defenders, among them the esteemed Rollin Perkins: "The form with a single 'p' is to be preferred because it is a general rule of spelling that the accent determines whether or not to double the letter when the suffix is to be added to a word ending in a *single consonant* preceded by a *single vowel.* . . . [T]he final consonant is *not* doubled if the word has more than one syllable and the accent is not on the last." Rollin M. Perkins, *Criminal Law* 134 n.1 (1957) (citing the examples of *develop*, *offer*, and *suffer*).

Perkins's final statement, explaining the general rule, is sound. But it overlooks the exceptional nature of *kidnapping*. First, the word is formed on the model of the shorter verb: *nap*, *napping*. Second, up to the 19th century, *kidnap* was generally accented on the second syllable. Third, *kidnapping* is between five and ten times as common as *kidnaping in printed sources. See DOUBLING OF FINAL CONSONANTS.

B. Sense. *Kidnapping* = the act or an instance of taking or carrying away a person without his or her consent, by force or fraud, and without lawful excuse. Glanville Williams addresses the question whether *kidnapping* refers, as its etymology suggests, to the napping of kids:

> Well, apparently not: not in the modern sense. It seems that when the term originated the "kids" who were napped were not the young of the human species but labourers (called "kids") who were recruited by force or guile for agricultural service in the American colonies. And the crime has always been as much concerned with the taking of adults as with the taking of children. Indeed, the original kidnap is the taking of adults: infants were not of much use in the plantations.
>
> Glanville Williams, *Can Babies Be Kidnapped?*
> 1989 Crim. L. Rev. 473, 473.

Williams notes that the generally accepted definition of *kidnap*—given just above—is actually a definition of the term *adult-kidnap*. *Id.* With *child-kidnap* (popularly termed *child-stealing* or *baby-snatching*), the element of force or fraud is often missing, as when someone makes off with a baby-stroller. *Id.* See **abduction.**

kill. A. And Related Verbs: *murder*; *slay*; *assassinate*; *execute.* These verbs share the sense "to take someone's life" or "to deprive of life." *Kill* is so broad that it suggests nothing about the agency, the means of death, or the surrounding circumstances <she killed him> <cigarettes killed him> <he was killed>. *Murder*, in general, denotes the criminal killing of another either in passion or in cold blood, and of course the term carries with it strong tones of moral condemnation. (For nuances, see **murder.**) *Slay*, mostly a literary word, suggests killing by force, especially by striking. *Assassinate* implies the killing of some high personage by treachery, often for political reasons. *Execute* implies either the state's carrying out of the death penalty or the summary action of vigilantes.

B. *Kill . . . dead.* This is a REDUNDANCY popularly promoted (alas) in television commercials touting insecticides that, it is said, will "kill bugs dead."

kind of is a poor substitute for *somewhat*, *rather*, *somehow*, and other adverbs. But it properly functions as a noun, signifying category or class in phrases such as *this kind of writ.* See *****these kind of.**

kindred, n., = relationship by consanguinity. E.g.: "The policy of our laws is that heirs or next of kin, who are in equal degree of *kindred* to the intestate, inherit per capita in equal shares, while those in a more remote degree take per stirpes, or such portion as their immediate ancestor would inherit if living." *Balch v. Stone*, 20 N.E. 322, 324 (Mass. 1889). See **affinity** & **kinship.**

King; Queen. In English legal decisions, if the monarch is a party, he or she is, in civil cases, sometimes called "The King" or "The Queen" in the style of the case. The abbreviated form *R.* (for *Rex* or *Regina*) is also commonly used, especially in criminal cases. Even so, the case name *R. v. Baker* is pronounced "The Queen against Baker." See CASE REFERENCES & **R.**

King's Bench. See **Queen's Bench.**

king's conscience. See **Keeper of the King's Conscience.**

King's Counsel. See **Queen's Counsel.**

King's Court is a LOAN TRANSLATION of the phrase *Curia Regis.* Most historians refer to the *Curia Regis*, but others, such as Plucknett, use *King's Court* as well. *See* Theodore F.T. Plucknett, *A Concise History of the Common Law* 142 (5th ed. 1956).

King's evidence, to turn. See **turn state's evidence.**

king's foot. See **chancellor's foot.**

king's peace. See **against the peace.**

kinship; consanguinity; affinity; *cognation; agnation; enation. All these terms refer to a familial relationship. *Kinship* is the broadest, denoting relationship by either blood or marriage—no matter how remote—and it connotes the closeness of a clan. *Lineal kinship* exists between persons connected in a direct line of descent—such as father and son, grandmother and granddaughter, and the like. *Collateral kinship* exists among those who descend from the same common ancestor but not from one another—such as sister and sister, or cousin and cousin.

Consanguinity denotes relationship by blood. It is a lay as well as a legal term. Here is a classical legal use: "Neither of these two women was related to the testator either by marriage or *consanguinity*, while the contestant was his nephew and his only heir at law." *In re Arnold's Estate*, 107 P.2d 25, 27 (Cal. 1940). Degrees of *consanguinity* are determined differently by the various legal systems of the world. (See **degree.**) Often *consanguinity* is used figuratively—e.g.: "There is apparently no intimate *consanguinity* between the case *sub judice* and the proceeding that pends in an alien jurisdiction." *Coastal (Bermuda) Ltd. v. E.W. Saybolt & Co.*, 761 F.2d 198, 203 (5th Cir. 1985). Yet *relation* might be better than such bombastic uses of *consanguinity.*

Affinity denotes relationship by marriage, and careful legal writers are at some pains to distinguish it from *consanguinity*—e.g.:

- "There is a clear and just moral difference between sexual intercourse of persons related by *consanguinity* (a blood relationship) and that of persons related only by *affinity* (based upon marriage)." *Gish v. State*, 352 S.E.2d 800, 801 (Ga. Ct. App. 1987).
- "While often used together, *consanguinity* and *affinity* are distinct concepts with different definitions[;] we must presume the Texas Legislature was familiar with the definitions and chose to permit petitions filed by individuals related within three degrees of *consanguinity*, but not within three degrees of *affinity*." *In re A.M.S.*, 277 S.W.3d 92, 98 (Tex. App.—Texarkana 2009).

Affinity takes the preposition *between* or *with*, not *to* or *for.*

*****Cognation* is an archaic equivalent of *consanguinity.* *Agnation* denotes relationship through the father's side, and *enation* through the mother's. See **agnate.**

kinsman (= a relative) is less and less used, perhaps because of the desire to avoid sexism. See SEXISM (B).

KITCHEN FRENCH. See LAW FRENCH.

kleptomania; *cleptomania. The first spelling is now standard.

knit has the past-tense forms *knit* and *knitted*, the second being preferred. Cf. **fit.**

*****knitpick.** See **nitpick.**

knock-for-knock agreement (= an arrangement between insurers that each will pay the claim of its insured without claiming against the other party's insurer) should be so hyphenated. See PHRASAL ADJECTIVES.

know all men by these presents (= take notice) is a FLOTSAM PHRASE—as sexist as it is inscrutable to most readers—that needlessly begins many legal documents. Following is a typical beginning of a bond: "*Know all men by these presents* that we, all of the undersigned owners of all of the property described in the surveyor's certificate hereon and shown on this map, have caused the same to be subdivided into lots, blocks, streets and easements and do hereby dedicate the streets and other public areas as indicated hereon for perpetual use of the public." *Oak Lane Homeowners Ass'n v. Griffin*, 219 P.3d 64, 66 (Utah Ct. App. 2009) (quoting boilerplate language from a plat). The phrase originated as a LOAN TRANSLATION of the LATINISM *noverint universi* (= know all persons).

know-how = the information, practical knowledge, techniques, and skill required to achieve some practical end, particularly in industry or technology. *Know-how* is considered incorporeal property, in which rights may be bought and sold. E.g.: "Gates seeks to recover the damages that it allegedly incurred as a result of [Yuasa's] alleged breach of an agreement with [Gates] regarding the nondisclosure of trade-secret technical *know-how.*" *Gates Energy Prods., Inc. v. Yuasa Battery Co.*, 599 F.Supp. 368, 370 (D. Colo. 1983). The phrase is best hyphenated.

knowledge. A. And *personal knowledge; information.* All three terms denote what is or can be known, usually by a person but sometimes also by people generally. *Knowledge* refers to both (1) a fact or body of facts acquired through study, investigation, or observation, often with the implication that it is systematically organized; and (2) an inference or collection of inferences validly drawn from confirmed facts, in such a way that the inference or inferences are considered highly reliable. *Personal knowledge* denotes much more narrowly a fact or cluster of facts acquired by firsthand observation of or participation in events

being inquired into, coupled with a credible degree of recollection.

Information is a broader term, covering the full gamut ranging from all that is meant by *knowledge* to putative facts, unverified and unverifiable facts, and a collection of falsehoods <the information on that website is notoriously unreliable>. The term may refer to one or more facts that are acquired haphazardly <we just happened upon that information> or that are only potentially acquirable <that's the information we need>.

B. And *notice.* As a general matter, *knowledge* requires awareness of a fact or condition, while *notice* requires merely a reason to know of a fact or condition. *Knowledge* is subsumed within *notice* because actual awareness is well above the threshold requirement of a reason to be aware. *See* Restatement (Second) of Agency § 9 (1958). E.g.: "'*Notice*' and '*knowledge*' are not synonyms; when one says of a person that he was 'on notice' of a fact, one may mean just that he should have known, not that he did know." *Shacket v. Philko Aviation, Inc.*, 841 F.2d 166, 170 (7th Cir. 1988). (See **notice.**) The phrase *constructive knowledge* is equivalent to—and inferior to—*notice*.

kudos (fr. Gk. *kydos* "glory") is a singular noun meaning "praise, glory." It is sometimes erroneously thought to be a plural. So *kudo*, a false singular—and therefore *kudoes*, a mistaken plural—has come to plague many texts. E.g.: "I appreciate profoundly the *kudo* [read *kudos*—and read on] for loquacity bestowed upon me by my learned colleague of the majority. . . . I return it to him for placement wherever he is wont to place *kudoes* [read *kudos*]." *Nelson v. Miller*, 480 P.2d 467, 480 (Utah 1971) (Henriod, J., dissenting). Other writers mistakenly use a plural verb with *kudos*, as here:

- "*Kudos are* [read *is*] not awarded for these skills." Gertrude Block, *Effective Legal Writing* 1 (2d ed. 1983).
- "The piece speaks to anyone who cares (or should care) about legal scholarship in the United States. To this extent, and perhaps to this extent only, *kudos are* [read *kudos is*] in order." Ronald J. Krotoszynski Jr., *Legal Scholarship at the Crossroads*, 77 Tex. L. Rev. 321, 331 (1998).

Cf. HYPERCORRECTION (A).

L

label makes *labeled, labeling* (AmE), or *labelled, labelling* (BrE). See DOUBLING OF FINAL CONSONANTS.

laches. A. Sense. *Laches* (LAW FRENCH meaning "remissness, slackness") = unreasonable delay or negligence in pursuing a right or claim, esp. an equitable one, that may disentitle a claimant to relief. The doctrine exemplifies the reserved power of equity to withhold relief otherwise regularly granted when the relief would be unfair or unjust.

The *OED* records a transferred sense—"culpable negligence in general"—which, though appearing in

the work of a famous author, modern lawyers would find difficult to accept. E.g.: "In his heart he felt rather ashamed that his conduct had shown *laches* which others who did not get benefices were free from." George Eliot, *Middlemarch* 375 (1873).

B. Pronunciation. The word is pronounced /**lach**-əz/ (AmE) or /**lay**-chəz/ (BrE).

C. Singular Noun. Though plural in appearance, *laches* is a singular noun that is sometimes incorrectly coupled with a plural verb—e.g.: "*Laches are plead* [read *Laches is pleaded*] as a defense, but the claim here is essentially at law, not in equity." *Levine v,*

Levine, 209 F.Supp. 564, 569 (D. Del. 1962). For more on *plead* (or *pled*) vs. *pleaded*, see **pleaded.**

D. And *limitation*. The guiding principle in distinguishing these two is that "*laches* is not, like *limitation*, a mere matter of time; but principally a question of the inequity of permitting the claim to be enforced." *Galliher v. Cadwell*, 145 U.S. 368, 373 (1892) (per Brewer, J.). An old legal saw states that laches is a penalty for sleeping on one's rights. See **limitations & prescription.**

E. *Run* Idiom Inappropriate. Although we say, idiomatically, that the statute of limitations has *run*, it is not proper to use that verb with *laches*. *Run*, in this context, means "(of a period of time) to come to an end, be complete, expire." Because *laches* does not refer to any specific period of time but is determined after the fact by courts, it cannot be said to have *run*, but merely to *apply* in a given case—e.g.:

- "Because the indemnity action had not yet vested, *laches on the action had not begun to run* [read *the period to which laches might later apply had not begun*]." *Marathon Pipe Line Co. v. Drilling Rig Rowan Odessa*, 761 F.2d 229, 236 (5th Cir. 1985).
- "Only at this point, Grupo Gigante argued, *did the laches clock start to run* [read *did laches apply*] because the 'likelihood of confusion' loomed large." *Tillamook Country Smoker, Inc. v. Tillamook County Creamery Ass'n,* 465 F.3d 1102, 1109 (9th Cir. 2006).

lacuna is a FORMAL WORD for *gap*: "To suggest that a protected person has no such right would posit a *lacuna* between a protected person's rights and an officer's duties." *Town of Castle Rock v. Gonzales*, 545 U.S. 748, 788 n.16 (2005) (Stevens, J., dissenting). The plural *lacunae* is preferable to **lacunas*. See PLURALS (A).

lade (= to load) is an ARCHAISM in all senses, although it frequently appears in shipping contexts. See **laden (A) & lading, bill of.**

laden. A. As a Past Participle Equivalent to *loaded*. To the extent that *laden* lives, it lives primarily as a participial adjective <a laden barge> and not as a past participle. To use *laden* as a part of the verb phrase is to be guilty of ARCHAISM, although it is still used in shipping contexts—e.g.:

- "Mr. Tweedie testified that he paid three claims for cargo that had been *laden* on board but not delivered." *Golcar S.S. v. Tweedie Trading Co.*, 146 F. 563, 566 (S.D.N.Y. 1906).
- "The cart, which had been *laden* with tools and propped up with a little pressure washer to keep it upright, had fallen on top of Cassie." *People v. Beames*, 153 P.3d 955, 962 (Cal. 2007).

See **lade.**

B. For *ridden*. *Ridden* is the more general term, meaning "infested with" or "full of." *Laden* has not shed its strong connotation of "loaded down." Hence a place might be *laden* with things if they had been stacked there; or, more plausibly, a truck or barge might be *laden* with goods. But figuratively, *laden* fails as an effective adjective if the original suggestion of loading is ignored. E.g.: "Hlodan doffed his own life jacket, placed his wallet, wristwatch and other items from his pockets on the deck, and plunged into the *eddy-laden* [read *eddy-ridden*] Mississippi to save Dobbins." *Hlodan v. Ohio Barge Line, Inc.*, 611 F.2d 71, 73 (5th Cir. 1980).

lading, bill of. *Lading* is the Old English equivalent of *loading*. Dating from the 16th century, *bill of lading* = a document acknowledging the shipment of a consignor's goods for carriage by sea (*CDL*). See **laden (A).**

*lady lawyer is an objectionable phrase to a great many lawyers (many but not all of them women). (See SEXISM.) The phrase sometimes merely supplements the already evident bias that some of its users harbor—e.g.: "At the trial, the relator was assigned two attorneys, Mr. Sheridan and Mr. Gellman. A *lady lawyer* [omit *lady*], Katherine Bitses, . . . later became imbued with the cause of Kling after the trial." *U.S. ex rel. Kling v. La Vallee*, 188 F.Supp. 470, 472 (N.D.N.Y. 1960).

laesae majestatis*; **laesae majestas*. See **lese majesty.

lagan. See **flotsam.**

laic; lay. Whereas *laic* means "nonclerical; nonecclesiastical," *lay*, which shares this sense, is broader and encompasses the sense "nonprofessional, not expert, esp. with reference to law and medicine" (*OED*). Lawyers referred to jurors as *lay* ("unlearned; illiterate") in the LAW FRENCH of the Middle Ages. See **laity & layman.**

lain. See **lie & lay.**

*laison. See **liaison.**

laissez-faire; laisser-faire. The first spelling has long been standard. Some British publications, however, continue to use the outmoded spelling *laisser-faire*—e.g.: "Should Hongkong's *laisser-faire* [read *laissez-faire*] government do an about-face to build Hongkong Inc?" *Farewell to Adam Smith*, Economist, 30 Sept.–6 Oct. 1989, at 71.

laity is the noun corresponding to the adjective *lay*. But while *lay* is used about as commonly in legal as in church matters, *laity* appears far more commonly in religious than in legal contexts. Still, the *OED* includes the sense "unprofessional people, as opposed to those who follow some learned profession." E.g.:

- "Fortunately for the bar and for the public, there are no rules of morality for the lawyers [that] do not apply with equal force to the *laity*, and it is well that there should not be." George W. Warvelle, *Essays in Legal Ethics* 32 (2d ed. 1920).
- "For better or worse, the *laity* expects all lawyers to have reasonably informed opinions on certain cases or legal

issues." Sanford Levinson, *For Whom is the* Heller *Decision Important and Why?*, 13 Lewis & Clark L. Rev. 315, 325 (2009).

See **laic** & **layman**.

lame duck (= an officeholder whose powers are greatly reduced because of the impending expiration of his or her term in office, usu. as a result of an electoral defeat or a statutory limitation) was originally an 18th-century British phrase denoting an insolvent businessman. In the early 19th century, the term was extended in BrE to politically bankrupt politicians. By the early 20th century, the modern sense had taken hold in AmE. Today it is common to refer not only to a *lame-duck President* or *lame-duck governor*, but also to a *lame-duck Congress* if the November elections represent significant political changes.

lamentable is preferably accented on the first, not the second, syllable /**lam**-ən-tə-bəl/.

land. When thinking of land, most speakers of English visualize the earth's surface. But in law, the word includes everything above and below the surface—even gases, liquids, and buildings. As a legal concept, then, *land* is an area of three-dimensional space, an inverted pyramid with its tip at the center of the earth and extending outward through the surface of the earth—where natural or imaginary points locate it by reference—and continuing upward to the sky. Land is both immovable and indestructible.

land charge; land law; land tax. Two words in each phrase.

landlocked (= shut in or enclosed by land; almost entirely surrounded by land) is usually used in literal senses in the law. But it has its figurative uses as well: "The Chancellor is no longer fixed to the woolsack. He may stride the quarterdeck of maritime jurisprudence and, in the role of admiralty judge, dispense as would his *landlocked* brother, that which equity and good conscience impel." *Compania Anonima Venezolana de Navegacion v. A.J. Perez Export Co.*, 303 F.2d 692, 699 (5th Cir. 1962).

landlord = (1) at common law, the lord who, under the feudal system, retained the fee of the land; or (2) one who owns or holds real property and lets it out to others.

Some writers have begun to use *landlord* as a verb—e.g.:

- "Learning *landlording* from a book can be difficult." Brian Edwards, *Renting Tips for Landlords*, Chicago Trib., 15 Feb. 1991, at C17.
- Leigh Robinson, *Landlording: A Manual for Scrupulous Landlords* (11th ed. 2010).

The usage seems unlikely to spread, but see NOUNS AS VERBS.

landman. A. Generally. In the law of oil and gas, *landman* refers to a person who, usu. on behalf of an oil company, contracts with landowners for the mineral rights to their land. In this field (as in the oil fields), women as well as men refer to themselves as *landmen*. (A less common variant is *leaseman*.) Many female landmen say they are reluctant to adopt a nonsexist alternative that would apply only to them, because their male counterparts are unlikely to abandon the term. Still, various nonsexist equivalents—such as *exploration manager*, *land manager*, and *land agent*—have achieved limited currency.

A less likely candidate for eventual success is *landwoman*: "Betsy Spomer, a *landwoman* [read *land manager* or *land agent*] for Gulf in Casper, said the company plans to assign a full-time person to resolve differences." *Gulf Temporarily Shelves Little Knife Unit Plan*, Oil & Gas J., 9 Jan. 1984, at 47. See SEXISM (B).

B. Meaning "*terre-tenant.*" *Landman* was formerly used as a LOAN TRANSLATION equivalent to *terre-tenant*. Because this usage is likely to confuse readers, it is best avoided. If an English phrase is needed, *land-tenant* is a better substitute. See **terre-tenant**.

C. And *landsman*. Unlike *landman*, the word *landsman* usually refers to someone who lives and works on land. But it may also refer to an inexperienced sailor—e.g.:

- "The seaman, while on his vessel, is subject to the rigorous discipline of the sea and has little opportunity to appeal to the protection from abuse of power which the law makes readily available to the *landsman*." *Socony-Vacuum Oil Co. v. Smith*, 305 U.S. 424, 430 (1939) (per Stone, J.).
- "This limitation serves much the same purpose for maritime ventures that the corporate fiction serves for the *landsman's* enterprises." *Black Diamond S.S. v. Robert Stewart & Sons*, 336 U.S. 386, 399 (1949) (Jackson, J., dissenting).

See SEXISM (B).

landmark of the law is, as the following quotation suggests, a CLICHÉ to be sparingly bestowed on cases—e.g.:

- "Every decision worthy of preservation as a *landmark of the law* is overwhelmed and buried in a mass of reports." W.T.S. Daniel, *The History and Origin of the Law Reports* 181 (1883).
- "The critical decision is that of Lord Mansfield in *Moses v. MacFerlan* that truly merits the cliché, a *landmark of the law*." Kenneth H. York et al., *Cases and Materials on Remedies* 288 (1992).

See WORD-PATRONAGE.

landowner is written as one word in AmE and BrE. So is *landownership*.

land scrip is an Americanism meaning "a negotiable instrument entitling the holder, usu. an individual or company engaged in public service, to possess specified areas of public land." E.g.:

- "The United States issued *land scrip* to Mann for location on 'unoccupied and unappropriated public lands.'" *Hynes v. Grimes Packing Co.*, 337 U.S. 86, 115 (1949) (per Reed, J.).
- "'Color of title' [includes] a consecutive chain of transfers to the person in possession that . . . is based on a certificate

of headright, land warrant, or *land scrip.*" Tex. Civ. Prac. & Rem. Code § 16.021 (West 1990).

land shark. See LAWYERS, DEROGATORY NAMES FOR (A).

landsman. See **landman (c).**

lands, tenements, and hereditaments. This triplet is the traditional means of referring to real property. Though now frequently used as mere legalistic deadwood, the phrase may be parsed without REDUNDANCY.

Land, of course, denotes the terrestrial earth and what is above and below it, including water. See **land.**

Tenement = anything that might be the subject of common-law tenure. "The word . . . is of a more extensive signification than *land*, which it includes, in addition to most . . . incorporeal things real." 1 Herbert T. Tiffany, *The Law of Real Property* § 10, at 13 (Basil Jones ed., 3d ed. 1939).

Hereditament traditionally includes whatever, upon the owner's death, passes by intestacy. "The term is more extensive in its signification than the word *tenement*, which it generally, though not always, includes, and it may, in England at least, include things of a personal character." *Id.* at 13–14. See **hereditament(s)** & DOUBLETS, TRIPLETS, AND SYNONYM-STRINGS.

land tax. See **land charge.**

land-tenant. See **terre-tenant.**

language in the sense "wording of a document or provision" is peculiar to the law. E.g.: "Where the express *language* of the policy is clear and unambiguous, it will be enforced as written." *Arthur Andersen LLP v. Federal Ins. Co.*, 3 A.3d 1279, 1286 (N.J. Super. Ct. 2010). For an example illustrating the improper pluralizing of this mass noun, see PLURALS (B).

lappage = (1) an overlapping of two claims to land; or (2) the portion of land over which rival claimants have overlapping claims. In AmE, almost every reported example originates in North Carolina—e.g.: "The rules of *lappage* [sense 1] direct that when the title deeds of two rival claimants to land lap upon each other, and neither claimant is in actual possession of any of the land covered by the deeds, the claimant with the better title is deemed in possession of the *lappage* [sense 2]." *Willis v. Mann*, 386 S.E.2d 68, 72 (N.C. Ct. App. 1989).

lapse, vb., = (1) (of an estate or right) to pass away, revert (*to* someone) because conditions have not been fulfilled or because a person entitled to possession has failed in some duty; or (2) (of a devise or grant) to become void. Sense 2 is now much more usual—e.g.: "Suppose a man makes a will leaving all his property to his friend, *A. A* dies before the testator does. The gift to *A* is said to *lapse*. It becomes void, and the

property goes to the testator's heirs." Robert Kratovil, *Real Estate Law* 247 (1946). For the noun sense, see **ademption (c).**

lapse statute; antilapse statute; nonlapse statute. All three phrases denote (in AmE) the same type of statute, the meaning of which is illuminated in the quotations. E.g.:

- "There is no language in the will and it yields no inference . . . contrary to the presumption that the estate should descend and be distributed in accordance with the statute of descent and the *nonlapse statute.*" *Dunlap v. Lynn*, 89 N.W.2d 58, 64 (Neb. 1958).
- "Owners of severed mineral interests challenged the application of a state *lapse statute* that automatically extinguished any mineral interest that had not been used for a period of twenty years." *Op. of the JJ. to the H.R.*, 563 N.E.2d 203, 207 (Mass. 1990).
- "Because he predeceased her, his son, respondent, became the sole beneficiary of her estate by virtue of the *antilapse statute.*" *In re Burns*, 731 N.Y.S.2d 537, 538 (App. Div. 2001).

Today *lapse statute* is the most common phrase, even though it is the least logical (since the effect of the statute is to *prevent* the lapse of testamentary gifts). The most lucid phrase is *antilapse statute.* There are judicial opinions in which both *nonlapse* and *antilapse* appear in reference to the selfsame statute; yet the terms should not be varied in a single writing. See INELEGANT VARIATION.

lapsus linguae; lapsus calami. These LATINISMS are fancy ways of referring to slips of the tongue (*linguae*) or of the pen (*calami*). The phrase *lapsus linguae* is the more common one. For example, in a case in which the trial court incorrectly referred to a witness as "Mrs. Argentine," the appellate court wrote: "This obvious *lapsus linguae* was plainly meant to refer to Mrs. Larsen." *U.S. v. Argentine*, 814 F.2d 783, 787 n.5 (1st Cir. 1987).

As for *lapsus calami* (= a slip of the pen), a good example—though it may have merely been a misprint—occurred in a judicial opinion that looks as if it represents a backslide in First Amendment rights. A judge wrote: "The First Amendment is not a fetish. *Reversed* it must be, but this *reverence* must be tempered with a realistic approach to such problems as that now at bar." *Muir v. Alabama Educ. Television Comm'n*, 656 F.2d 1012, 1015 (5th Cir. 1981). Without *reverence* to prompt the reader to understand that the judge means *Revered* and not *Reversed*, we might be quite confused about his purpose. The errata has been corrected.

larcenable (= subject to larceny) is listed in neither the *OED* nor most other dictionaries, but legal writers occasionally find it useful—e.g.:

- "The common law judges strained the law so as to discover reasons which would place the stealing of certain types of articles outside the scope of larceny, e.g., some domestic animals, growing crops, were held not *larcenable* at common law." L.B. Curzon, *English Legal History* 243–44 (2d ed. 1979).

- "For example, the realty and things which 'savour of the realty' were not *larcenable* at common law." Eli Lederman, *Criminal Liability for Breach of Confidential Commercial Information*, 38 Emory L.J. 921, 941 n.81 (1989).

larcenist; larcener. *Larcenist* (= one who commits larceny) is the ordinary term; *larcener* is a primarily BrE variant. See **thief.**

larcenous = of, relating to, or tainted with larceny; thievish. E.g.:

- "If a check is *larcenously* taken from one's possession, one may sue the thief for common-law conversion." *National Union Fire Ins. Co. v. Bank of Am.*, 240 F.Supp.2d 455, 458 (D. Md. 2003).
- "The defendants claim that . . . they did not have the necessary *larcenous* intent to sustain a judgment against them on a count of statutory theft." *Blackwell v. Mahmood*, 992 A.2d 1219, 1227 (Conn. App. Ct. 2010).

larceny. A. Sense. *Larceny* = the unlawful taking and carrying away of someone else's goods with the intent to appropriate them. With the Theft Act 1968, English law replaced larceny with the statutory crime of theft. Many American states retain the old scheme of *grand larceny* and *petty larceny*, which was first set forth in the Statute of Westminster I, c. 15 (1275). The LAW FRENCH term was *larcyn*, from the LAW LATIN *latrocinium* (fr. *latro* "robber"). See **asportation.**

Classically, *larceny* has differed from *embezzlement* and *breach of trust* in that the latter two involve an employee or bailee already in lawful possession. But modern statutes in many jurisdictions have widened the sense of *larceny* to include common-law embezzlement. *Larceny* also traditionally differs from offenses in which goods are obtained "under false pretenses, cheats, and extortions." Martin L. Newell, *The Law of Defamation, Libel and Slander* 114 (1890). See **embezzle.**

B. Grand and petty larceny; simple and aggravated larceny. Two dichotomies exist in the legal analysis of larceny—at least in the English-speaking jurisdictions that retain *larceny* as a crime. *Petty larceny* (or *petit larceny*) was at common law, and is today in many U.S. states, contrasted with *grand larceny*, the difference lying in the value of the goods stolen. *Simple larceny* is distinguished from *aggravated larceny*, the difference lying in the presence or absence of aggravating circumstances.

C. Spelling: petty larceny or petit larceny. *Petit larceny* is the older spelling of the term (which is still properly pronounced *petty*). The anglicized *petty larceny* is slightly more common, having been adopted for use in Model Penal Code § 223.1(2)(b). The advantage of *petty larceny* is that the correct pronunciation is immediately apparent; the disadvantage is that it suggests a triviality. Merely for the sake of consistency, it would be convenient for writers to follow the Model Penal Code by writing *petty* instead of *petit*. See **petit larceny.**

D. Larceny by trick (and device). The elongation of this phrase—denoting a larceny in which the taker intended to keep the goods even as the rightful possessor, being misled, consensually handed them over—is optional. That being so, the shorter phrase, *larceny by trick*, is recommended.

E. Larceny from the person. This statutory offense is slightly different from *robbery* because it need not involve violence or intimidation—the victim usually being taken unawares. For example, if a thief cuts a necklace and removes it from the owner's neck without her being aware, the thief commits *larceny from the person*. A thief who uses threats or force, on the other hand, commits *robbery*. For more on these distinctions, see **burglary (A).**

largess; largesse. *Largess* (= generous giving; munificence) has long been the standard spelling in English. The GALLICISM was first borrowed into Middle English and was fully anglicized as *largess* by the 16th century. AmE has mostly stuck with that spelling, while BrE has reverted to the Frenchified spelling *largesse*, which now vastly predominates in British contexts. Although the preferred pronunciation is the anglicized /lahr-**jes**/, the word is often pronounced in the French way, that is, /lahr-**zhes**/.

Las Partidas; Las Siete Partidas. These synonymous names (lit., "the seven parts") refer to the Spanish code compiled in 1250 by Alphonso X and based on the civil law, Spanish customary law, and canon law. First enacted in 1348, the code still influences the law of Florida, Louisiana, and Texas. It is referred to as either *Las Partidas* or *Las Siete Partidas*, the latter being slightly more common.

last analysis, in the. See **in the final analysis.**

last but not least is a CLICHÉ to be avoided.

last rites is occasionally misrendered **last rights*—e.g.: "Among these duties are presiding over Sunday and daily masses . . . and delivering *last rights* [read *last rites*]." *Weatherford v. Commercial Union Ins.*, 650 So.2d 763, 769 (La. 1995).

last will and testament is a phrase with ancient resonances. Lord Coke, for example, referred to an *ultima voluntas in scriptis* (= last will in writing). Much ink has been spilled by at least one well-known writer in opposition to this phrase. See David Mellinkoff, *The Language of the Law* 77–79, 331–33 (1963). The argument against it is that coupling *testament* with *will* is redundant, and that *last* is usually inaccurate: "When a testator has been made will-conscious, and likes the habit, *last will* adds spice to a will contest. For example [an actual case]: will No. 1 revoked by will No. 2; a later 'codicil to my last will' held to refer to No. 1, reviving it and revoking No. 2. The testator was talking about his first, not his second, when he said his *last will*" (*id.* at 333).

A curious case, to be sure, and one that might lead some to conclude that *last will and testament* "is redundant, confusing, and usually inaccurate" (*id.*). Yet nonlawyers know the phrase well and understand it as a ceremonious equivalent of *will*. The DOUBLET *will and testament* is no more disturbing than many others that exist undisturbed in our language, and that even enrich it. See DOUBLETS, TRIPLETS, AND SYNONYM-STRINGS, **testament** & **will.**

The only recommendation to be made here is that the phrase be confined to use as a title to the document it refers to, and that general references to the document be couched in the single word *will*. If our goal is to clean up legal writing, there are worthier objects of our reforms than *last will and testament*.

latecoming. Although *latecomer*, the agent noun, dates from the late 19th century and is recorded in most English dictionaries, the adjective *latecoming* is unrecorded in most modern dictionaries. The word— a useful one, surely—appears in several reported American opinions. E.g.:

- "Plaintiffs fear price was the problem here and believe they were simply outbid by a *latecoming* buyer." *Trenta v. Gay*, 468 A.2d 737, 739 (N.J. Super. Ct. Ch. Div. 1983).
- "But the rules vest the trial court, not this court, with the discretionary authority to pass upon *latecoming* motions to amend the pleadings." *Janikowski v. Bendix Corp.*, 823 F.2d 945, 954 (6th Cir. 1987) (Ryan, J., dissenting in part).

latent. See **patent.**

latent ambiguity. See AMBIGUITY.

latent equity. See **equity.**

later. A. Without Temporal Context. *Later* should not be used unless a proper temporal context has first been established—e.g.: "Counsel was Charles Evans Hughes, *later Chief Justice* [read *who was to become Chief Justice*] of the United States." *U.S. v. Guest*, 383 U.S. 745, 767 (1966) (per Stewart, J.). Cf. **then (A).**

B. *Later on.* This collocation is venially verbose for *later*—e.g.: "The District Court emphasized this point again *later on* [read *later*]." *League of United Latin Am. Citizens v. Perry*, 548 U.S. 399, 499 (2006) (Roberts, C.J., concurring in part & dissenting in part).

later of [date] or [date]; later of [date] and [date]. Drafters frequently debate whether the proper conjunction in this phrase is *or* or *and*. The better idiomatic choice is *or*—nine of every ten lawyers believing it is the proper choice.

True, *and* has logic on its side. If we paraphrase by saying *the later of two dates*, it becomes clear that the sense must be plural (conjunctive *and*), not singular (disjunctive *or*). But the wording with *and* sounds as pedantic—and as wrong—as *a number of people was there*. See SYNESIS.

For a brief treatment of this issue, see Richard H. Miller, *A Drafting Dilemma*, 4 Scribes J. Legal Writing 127 (1993).

later on. See **later (B).**

LATINATE PLURALS. See PLURALS (A).

LATINISMS. Can there be any doubt that modern judges and scholars have grown impatient with Anglo-American lawyers' fondness for Latin terminology?

- "On the whole the lesson of this part of our legal history should be that it is dangerous to play with foreign terms unless we know very well what we are about." F.W. Maitland, *The Forms of Action at Common Law* 63 (1909; A.H. Chaytor & W.J. Whittaker eds., 1971).
- "The marvelous capacity of a Latin phrase to serve as a substitute for reasoning, and the confusion of thought inevitably accompanying the use of inaccurate terminology, are nowhere better illustrated than in the decisions dealing with the admissibility of evidence as *res gestae*." Edmund M. Morgan, *A Suggested Classification of Utterances Admissible as Res Gestae*, 31 Yale L.J. 229, 229 (1922).
- "I cannot help deprecating the use of Latin . . . phrases in this way. They only distract the mind from the true problem which is to apply the principles of English law to the realities of the case." *Smith, Hogg & Co. v. Black Sea & Baltic Gen. Ins. Co.*, [1940] A.C. 997, 1003 (per Lord Wright).
- "I think the cases are comparatively few in which much light is obtained by a liberal use of Latin phrases. . . . Nobody can derive any assistance from the phrase *novus actus interveniens* until it is translated into English." *Ingram v. United Auto. Servs., Ltd.*, [1943] 2 All E.R. 71, 73 (per du Parcq, L.J.).
- "Pruitt's letter to the Clerk of the Virginia Supreme Court of Appeals, his correspondence with his attorney, and his petition in the district court spoke of his 'being met with a plea of res judicata' in the state court. It is difficult to follow his line of reasoning or indeed to make any sense out of his prolix and confused arguments. One thing, however, is clear—he, not unlike some lawyers, thought he had discovered magic in a Latin phrase." *Pruitt v. Peyton*, 338 F.2d 859, 861 (4th Cir. 1964).

A century ago, scholars recognized that Latin MAX-IMS had rapidly, for the most part, become obsolete: "The Latin maxims have largely disappeared from arguments and opinions. In their original phraseology they convey no idea that cannot be well expressed in modern English." William C. Anderson, *Law Dictionaries*, 28 Am. L. Rev. 531, 532 (1894). Still, several *Latinisms* have proved themselves useful—often in shortened forms, that is, as phrases and not so much as maxims—such as *de minimis*, *contra proferentem*, *ejusdem generis*, and *noscitur a sociis*.

Despite the overwhelming obsolescence of Latin— more overwhelming in AmE than in BrE—non-lawyers still generally misunderstand the nature of legal language. The linguist Mario Pei, for example, estimated that "half of our specifically legal terminology is Latin." Mario Pei, *Words in Sheep's Clothing* 83 (1969). That statement, of course, is nonsense. Probably more than 90% of our legal terminology is of Latin origin—English words and phrases such as *contract*, *declaratory judgment, issue preclusion, realty, subordinated debt*—but these phrases are English, not Latin.

Nevertheless, legal readers often encounter Latin in modern texts—some of it necessary and some of it not. In legal writing we must distinguish between TERMS OF ART, for which there are no ordinary English equivalents, and those terms that are merely vestigial *Latinisms* with simple English substitutes. The former category comprises useful *Latinisms* such as *prima facie, ex parte, de minimis, habeas corpus, alibi,* and *quorum.* Some words that do have ordinary English equivalents have nevertheless become such standard terms that they are unobjectionable, e.g., *bona fide* (= good faith), *amicus curiae* (= friend of the court), and *versus* (= against). These words have become a part of the English language, or at least necessary parts of the language of the law, and one would be misdirected to rail against them.

The rightful objects of our condemnation are the bombastic, vestigial *Latinisms* that serve no purpose but to give the writer a false sense of erudition. These terms convey no special legal meanings, no delicate nuances apprehended only by lawyers. They are pompous, turgid deadwood. Just as a mathematician would seem ludicrous to write 386/1544 rather than 1/4 merely in an attempt to sound more scholarly, so the lawyer who writes *sub suo periculo* instead of *at his own risk* strikes the reader as a laughable, if vexatious, figure.

Other phrases in this category are illustrated in the following sentences, in which the simple English equivalents are bracketed:

- "But a legacy to one, to be paid when he attains the age of twenty one years, is a vested legacy; an interest which commences *in praesenti* [read *in the present*], although it be *solvendum in futuro* [read *paid in the future*]: and, if the legatee dies before that age, his representatives shall receive it out of the testator's personal estate." 2 William Blackstone, *Commentaries on the Laws of England* 513 (1766).
- "There is a *contradictio in adjecto* [read *contradiction in terms*] when we speak of the general damages appropriate to an indeterminate transaction." *Kerr S.S. Co. v. Radio Corp. of Am.,* 157 N.E. 140, 142 (N.Y. 1927) (per Cardozo, C.J.).
- "Ancillary administration in this state, without assets presently here for administration, would be *mere brutum fulmen* [read *mere empty noise* (lit.), or *ineffective*]." *In re Rogers' Will,* 232 N.Y.S. 609, 613 (App. Div. 1929).
- "A father is directly responsible for the existence of his offspring, and it would accordingly be *contra bonos mores* [read *immoral*] to allow a father to bring children into the world and avoid responsibility for them by himself departing the world." *Lloyd v. Menzies,* 1956 (2) S.A.L.R. 97, 102 (quoting curator *ad litem*'s report).
- "This issue is not before this court for adjudication, although we emphasize, *ex abundanti cautela* [read *out of abundant caution*], that we are not prone to condone the intentional circumvention of the clear legislative purpose of protective statutes." *Ghai v. State,* 465 S.E.2d 498, 500 (Ga. Ct. App. 1995).

Reasonableness dictates that legal writers simplify where possible, allowing the more complicated locutions to stand only if they are legally or linguistically irreducible. Otherwise, our language is easily beclouded (the Latinist would say *obnubilated*) and

becomes, before we know it, a fog of words in which our readers or listeners become hopelessly lost. This is no less true in LEGISLATIVE DRAFTING than in expository writing: "In the selection of words, Latin words and, where possible without a sacrifice of accuracy, technical phraseology should be avoided; the word best adapted to express a thought in ordinary composition will generally be found to be the best that can be used." Henry Thring, *Practical Legislation* 81 (1902).

Words are the primary tools of lawyers. Can we afford, then, to be undiscriminating in our use of those tools? Can we engage in unchecked ABSTRACTITIS with impunity? As Justice Holmes, who was doubtless aware of his oversimplification, wrote toward the end of the 19th century, "We must think things not words, or at least we must constantly translate our words into the facts for which they stand, if we are to keep to the real and the true." Oliver W. Holmes, *Law in Science and Science in Law,* 12 Harv. L. Rev. 443, 460 (1899). Such internal translation is most easily achieved if we use ordinary language when possible. Lawyers must learn the language of the law but wield it carefully, never losing the idiomatic flavor of the vernacular.

Particular *Latinisms*, their utility or their turgidity, are discussed throughout this work under particular entries. For examples of needless Latinity, see **capacitas rationalis** & **res gestae**. See also LAW LATIN, MINGLE-MANGLE & PLAIN LANGUAGE. Cf. GALLICISMS. On questions of pronouncing Latin terms, see PRONUNCIATION (C).

For explanations of *Latinisms*, see *Black's Law Dictionary* (9th ed. 2009); John Trayner, *Latin Phrases and Maxims* (3d ed. 1883); and Aaron X. Fellmeth & Maurice Horwitz, *Guide to Latin in International Law* (2009).

latrine lawyer. See LAWYERS, DEROGATORY NAMES FOR (A).

latter. See **former.**

latterly is an ARCHAISM for *later* or *lately*—e.g.:

- "He noted that the Board, although at one time doubtful of the tour-based feature, had *latterly* [read *later*] abandoned its professed concern over its discriminatory aspects." *National Air Carrier Ass'n v. C. A. B.,* 442 F.2d 862, 873 (D.C. Cir. 1971).
- "He admitted . . . that he had in the past been paid commissions for the sales of houses and that if he had sold any properties *latterly* [read *lately*] he would have been paid commissions." *Rowley v. Commonwealth Unemployment Comp. Bd. of Rev.,* 454 A.2d 217, 218 (Pa. Commw. Ct. 1983).

laudatory; *laudative; laudable. The adjectives *laudatory* and **laudative* both mean "expressing praise." But **laudative* is a NEEDLESS VARIANT, *laudatory* being the common word. *Laudable,* in contrast, means "deserving praise." The distinction is the same as that between *praiseworthy* (= *laudable*) and the active *praiseful* (= *laudatory*).

The misuse of *laudatory* for *laudable* is lamentably common—e.g.:

- "Newton and Einstein both contributed more original labor with more *laudatory* [read *laudable*] results in devising their theories of physical nature than the vast majority of authors protected under copyright law ever could." David Fewer, *Constitutionalizing Copyright*, 55 U. Toronto Fac. L. Rev. 175, 188 (1997).

- "While protecting a juvenile from a criminal record may be *laudatory* [read *laudable*] for purposes of rehabilitation, there is no evidence of legislative intent to protect Moody as an adult from pretrial detention." *Moody v. Campbell*, 713 So.2d 1032, 1034–35 (Fla. Dist. Ct. App. 1998) (Lawrence, J., dissenting).

laughing heir, a LOAN TRANSLATION of the German phrase *der lachende Erbe*, refers to an heir who, being so remotely linked to a deceased relative as to suffer no sense of bereavement, receives a windfall from the estate. E.g.:

- "Rummaging through an old shoe box containing dog-eared letters led to a distant relative living in a trailer park in Terre Haute, Ind. The relative eventually became a '*laughing heir*,' inheriting several hundred thousand dollars." Jay G. Baris, *Personal Finance*, N.Y. Times, 15 Feb. 1987, at C11.

- "Cristina claims that the instant case is a typical '*laughing heirs*' case, and that equity requires that she, an adult child, inherit over more distant relatives." *Amex Assurance Co. v. Caripides*, 179 F.Supp.2d 309, 323 (S.D.N.Y. 2002).

laundry list, in use only since 1958, is the slang phrase American lawyers commonly use to denote a statutory enumeration of items.

law, adj. *Law*, like *legal*, acts as an adjective for *law*, n. No strict DIFFERENTIATION is possible, for we have *law studies* beside *legal studies* and *lawbooks* beside *legal books*; but **legal firm* is an un-English phrase for *law firm*, just as **law doctrine* is not used for *legal doctrine* (yet *common-law doctrine* is universal). The *OED* contains hundreds of examples of the attributive adjective *law*, such as *lawcourt* and *Law Lords*.

Law shares with *legal* the sense "pertaining to the *law* as a body of rules, or as a field of study"—e.g.: "The net amount of back pay they are entitled to receive . . . will depend ultimately upon the decision of fact questions and *law questions* applicable to them alone." *Franklin v. Donoho*, 774 S.W.2d 308, 312 (Tex. App.—Austin 1989). *Legal* has the additional sense "permitted under *law*; not forbidden" <legal acts>, as the antonym of *illegal*.

law, n. This word, by Jerome Frank's sobering assessment, "drips with ambiguity. But it has a traditionally emotive quality which makes it highly serviceable to the legal magicians. There are dozens of discrepant definitions of that word." Jerome Frank, *Courts on Trial* 66 (1950). Those who have tried to define *law* agree only that no definition is fully satisfactory. Still, it is worthwhile to try to sort out the senses.

Roscoe Pound catalogued four meanings for the word *law*. They are:

1. the legal order, that is, the regime that orders human activities and relations through systematic application of the force of politically organized society, or through social pressure, backed by force, in such a society <respect for law>;
2. the aggregate of legislation and accepted legal precepts; the body of authoritative grounds of judicial and administrative action established in an organized society <justice according to law> <systems of law>;
3. the judicial and administrative process, i.e., the process of determining controversies, whether as it actually takes place, or as the public, the jurists, and the practitioners in the courts hold it ought to take place <law is whatever is officially done>;
4. some combination of the previous three definitions <law and morals>.

See Roscoe Pound, *What Constitutes a Good Legal Education*, 7 Am. L. Sch. Rev. 887, 891 (1933).

The word has at least three more senses for lawyers, though:

5. a statute <There should be a law!>;
6. the common law <law but not equity>;
7. the legal profession <one may live greatly in the law as elsewhere>.

The word also has senses in other realms of human activity—senses that lawyers sometimes decry:

8. in science and philosophy, a general formula expressing a de facto uniformity in nature as we find it <law of gravitation>;
9. in science and philosophy, a general formula expressing a necessary property of all conceivable worlds <the law of contradiction, which says that no proposition can at once be both true and false>.

Of the legal senses, (4) and (5) present the most interesting idiomatic distinction. Lawyers distinguish between *a law* (sense 5) and *the law* (sense 4). The former refers to a particular and concrete instance of a legal precept, esp. a piece of legislation. So statutes such as the Sherman Antitrust Act (U.S.) and the Theft Act (Eng.)—or parts of them—can each be called *a law*.

The law, by contrast, is used for something much broader and more general, sometimes together with words describing a recognized branch of legal science, e.g., the law of torts, or with words descriptive of a particular system of law, e.g., the law of the United States.

Most Indo-European languages have different words for the concrete and abstract senses of *law*. For example, in Latin, there is *lex* for the concrete sense, *jus* for the abstract; in Italian, *legge* and *diritto*; in French, *loi* and *droit*; in Spanish, *ley* and *derecho*; in German, *Gesetz* and *Recht*. The English word *right* long ago lost its sense corresponding to the German *Recht*—so English speakers have had to press *law* into double service. See *lex* (A).

An asterisk (✳) precedes words and phrases that are invariably inferior forms.

As a result of our doing so, we have had to confront practical problems that might otherwise have been avoided. In *Swift v. Tyson*, a famous American constitutional-law case, the Supreme Court based its decision in part on the distinction between *law* and *a law* (or *laws*, in the plural): "In the ordinary use of language it will hardly be contended that the decisions of Courts constitute *laws*. They are, at most, only evidence of what the *laws* are; and are not of themselves *laws*." 41 U.S. (16 Pet.) 1, 18 (1842). *Accord* 2 Alexander M. Burrill, *A Law Dictionary and Glossary* 132 (2d ed. 1860) ("*A law* . . . undoubtedly imports an act of the legislature; and the term is quite inapplicable to a decision of a court of justice.").

The decision in *Swift v. Tyson* might have been decided differently, of course, if the statute at issue—the Rules of Decision Act—had declared that state *law*, as opposed to state *laws*, controlled questions of common law as applied by federal courts. So a drafter's lapse—using *laws* where *law* was probably intended—may have resulted in 96 years of bad *law* (not *laws*), until *Swift v. Tyson* was overturned in *Erie R.R. v. Tompkins*, 304 U.S. 64 (1938).

law abhors a forfeiture, the. See **equity abhors a forfeiture.**

law-abiding (= abiding by, maintaining, or submitting to the law) is a PHRASAL ADJECTIVE dating from the early 19th century—e.g.: "Never we trust will the day come when any deadly weapon will be worn or wielded in our peace-loving and *law-abiding* state as an appendage of manly equipment." *State v. Huntly*, 25 N.C. 418, 422 (1843) (per Gaston, J.). See **abide.**

The corresponding noun—an awkward-looking form that does not exactly abide by the laws of English word-formation—is *law-abidingness*. E.g.:

- "*State v. Baird* . . . expressly decides [that] proof of reputation for '*law-abidingness*' has no place in the case." *State v. Shepard*, 67 S.W.2d 91, 94 (Mo. 1933).
- "The defendant's character witnesses . . . testified as to his reputation for honesty and *law-abidingness*." *U.S. v. Londono-Villa*, 898 F.2d 328, 329 (2d Cir. 1990).

law and order. The phrase—originating not in AmE but in 19th-century BrE—is hyphenated only when it functions as an adjective—e.g.: "Had Ervin been extra careful about appearing tough on *law-and-order* issues, he probably never would have done these things." Paul R. Clancy, *Just a Country Lawyer* 202 (1974). As a noun phrase, it should remain unhyphenated: "Then all respect for *law-and-order* [read *law and order*] would vanish." Fred Rodell, *Woe Unto You, Lawyers!* 179 (1939).

lawbook. One word.

lawbreaker; lawbreaking. Each is one word.

law clerk. See **clerk.**

lawcourt is the one-word version of *court of law*. In most modern contexts—wherever the distinction between *courts of equity* and *courts of law* is not

an issue—*lawcourt* is a one-word REDUNDANCY—e.g.: "To do so was its province as fact-finder as well as the *lawcourt* [read *court*]." *City of Saginaw v. Garvey Elevators, Inc.*, 431 S.W.2d 575, 579 (Tex. Civ. App.—Fort Worth 1968).

But in other contexts—especially historical contexts—it provides a concise contrast to *courts of equity*, as here: "In England the *law courts* [read *lawcourts*] at first refused to recognize a decree for money in equity as creating a debt on which an action at law could be maintained." William F. Walsh, *A Treatise on Equity* 67 (1930). See **law,** adj. & **court of law.**

law day. This phrase has undergone a metamorphosis in recent years. Originally, *law day* was the yearly or twice-yearly meeting of one of the early common-law courts. By the 15th century and for a long time after, it came to denote the day appointed for the debtor to discharge a mortgage or else forfeit the property to the mortgagee.

Since 1958, the American Bar Association has sponsored *Law Day* on May 1 of each year—a day in which American schools, public assemblies, and courts draw attention to the importance of law in modern society.

law-driver. See LAWYERS, DEROGATORY NAMES FOR (A).

law factory, a derogatory term for a big law firm, dates from the mid-20th century—e.g.:

- "That is why the center of the nation's law business is in New York City and why the bulk of the nation's influential and profitable law practice is carried on in the Wall Street *law factories*." Fred Rodell, *Woe Unto You, Lawyers!* 155 (1939).
- "Hotchkiss, Levy & Hogan was a typical Wall Street *law factory*, occupying two entire stories in a white-stone office building within spitting distance of J.P. Morgan & Co." Ephraim Tutt, *Yankee Lawyer* 142 (1943).
- "Blood brother to the business trainee off to join Du Pont is the seminary student who will end up in the church hierarchy, . . . the engineering graduate in the huge drafting room at Lockheed, the young apprentice in a Wall Street *law factory*." Roger K. Miller, *Fifty Years of Conforming to the Company*, Wash. Times, 14 May 2006, at B7.

law firm. See **firm.**

LAW FRENCH refers to the Anglo-Norman patois used in legal documents and all judicial proceedings from the 1260s to the reign of Edward III (1327–1377), and used with frequency in legal literature up to the early 18th century. When first introduced into England, this brand of French was the standard language used in Normandy; by the 1300s, through linguistic isolation, it became a corrupted language—by French standards, at any rate. In the 17th century, Sir Edward Coke wrote that *Law French* could not be either "pure or well pronounced," and that one could find within it "a whole army of words, which cannot defend themselves *in bello grammaticali*, in the grammatical war, and yet are most significant, compendious, and effectual to express the true sense of the matter." Edward Coke, *Commentary on Littleton* xxxix–xl (Butler ed., 1832).

English law cases were reported in *Law French* until the end of the 17th century. Even as late as the early 18th century, surprisingly, *Law French* had its apologists: "Really the Law is scarcely expressible properly in English." Roger North, *A Discourse on the Study of the Laws* 13 (ca. 1710). Perhaps the best book written in *Law French* was Sir John Comyn's *Digest of the Laws of England* (1762–1767).

Though *Law French* may be obscure to the English-speaking lawyer, its remnants abound in the language of the law, in common words such as *appeal, arrest, assault, attainder, counsel, defer, defy, demand, demise, disclaimer, escheat, escrow, heir, indictment, interpleader, joinder, laches, larceny, lay, lien, merger, mortgage, negligence, nuisance, ouster, party, process, proof, remainder, reverter, suit, tender, tort, trespass, verdict,* and *voir dire.* There are also remnants somewhat more arcane, such as *cestui que trust* and *en ventre sa mere.*

Law French was always a highly technical language that preserved many old Anglo-Normanisms, but English forms, inflections, word order, and construction finally took it over. A notorious example: in the Salisbury assizes of 1631, a prisoner condemned by the Chief Justice of Common Pleas was said to have "*ject un brickbat a le dit Justice que narrowly mist*"; for that outburst, "*son dexter manus* [was] *ampute*" and the man himself "*immediatment hange in presence de Court.*" One noted writer has referred to Law French as "something very like a Sid Caesar version of a foreign language." Charles Rembar, *The Law of the Land* 178 n.* (1980). Though we have retained much of the vocabulary, Anglo-American lawyers no longer try to communicate with each other in this cabalistic dialect.

For what remains of *Law French,* though, a word about pronunciation is in order. English and, to a lesser extent, American lawyers have generally preserved the medieval pronunciations given to Law French terms—pronunciations that resemble modern English much more than they do modern French. So the "correct" pronunciation of *oyez* is /oh-**yez**/ or /oh-**yes**/, not /oh-**yay**/, and of *autrefois acquit* /oh-tər-foyz/, not /oh-tər-**fwah**/. *See* J.H. Baker, *Manual of Law French* (2d ed. 1990); J.H. Baker, "Law French," in 7 *Guide to American Law* 80–81 (1984). Cf. LAW LATIN. See MINGLE-MANGLE.

lawful. See **legal.**

lawful cause (= good cause; legal justification) is not to be confused with *legal cause* (= proximate cause). See CAUSATION (A).

lawgiver; lawmaker. Both are equivalent to *legislator,* but *lawgiver* suggests one who promulgates an entire code of laws and is therefore more magisterial in tone. E.g.:

- "But Moses was a *lawgiver* as well as a religious leader." *Van Orden v. Perry,* 545 U.S. 677, 690 (2005) (per Rehnquist, C.J.).

- "To the Middle Ages the academic ideal of all Europe as the empire for which Justinian had been the *law-giver* made Roman law a universal law." Roscoe Pound, Foreword to James Gordley & Arthur Taylor von Mehren, *An Introduction to the Comparative Study of Private Law* xvii (2006).

Both *lawgiver* and *lawmaker* are now preferably written as single, unhyphenated words. See **lawmaker.**

law is no respecter of persons, the. See **no respecter of persons, the law is.**

LAW LATIN, formerly sometimes called "dog Latin," is the bastardized or debased Latin formerly used in law and legal documents. For the most part, we have escaped from its clutches. In 1730, Parliament abolished *Law Latin* in legal proceedings, but two years later found it necessary to allow Latin phrases that had previously been in common use, such as *fieri facias, habeas corpus, ne exeat,* and *nisi prius.* As Blackstone would later say, some Latinisms were "not . . . capable of an English dress with any degree of seriousness." 3 William Blackstone, *Commentaries on the Laws of England* 323 (1768).

Brewer's *Dictionary of Phrase and Fable* quotes the following jocular example: "As the law classically expresses it, a kitchen is 'camera necessaria pro usus cookare; cum sauce-pannis, stewpannis, scullero, dressero, coalholo, stovis, smoak-jacko; pro roastandum, boilandum, fryandum, et plum-pudding-mixandum.'" Stevens, *A Law Report* (Daniel v. Dishclout*)* (quoted in Brewer, *Dictionary of Phrase and Fable* (1894), s.v. *Dog-Latin*). *See* John Trayner, *Latin Phrases and Maxims* (4th ed. 1894); E.H. Jackson, *Law Latin* (1897); E. Hilton Jackson, *Latin for Lawyers* (1915); Herbert Broom, *Legal Maxims* (10th ed. 1939). Cf. LAW FRENCH. See MINGLE-MANGLE & LATINISMS.

lawlike (one word meaning "resembling or characteristic of law") is labeled "rare" in the *OED.* The word *is* rare in the law reports, but not in legal commentary—e.g.:

- "Norms are more or less *lawlike* depending upon how formal they are." Larry A. Alexander, *Painting Without the Numbers,* 8 U. Dayton L. Rev. 447, 460 (1983).
- "The essence of a causal generalization is the belief that we attach to the generalization: the belief in its causal or *lawlike* character." Richard W. Wright, *Causation in Tort Law,* 73 Cal. L. Rev. 1735, 1823 (1985).
- "Gordon's basic strategy is to deconstruct the '*lawlike*' qualities of the law by descending into ever finer levels of microstructural analysis." Steve Fuller, *Playing Without a Full Deck,* 97 Yale L.J. 549, 570–71 (1988).

Law Lord. Until 1 October 2009, this title referred to any member of the Appellate Committee of the House of Lords—the Lord Chancellor, the salaried Lords of Appeal in Ordinary, and any peer who held or had held high judicial office. Before the creation of the Supreme Court of the United Kingdom, the Law Lords (usually so capitalized) formed the highest court of appeal in the United Kingdom—roughly equivalent to the Supreme Court of the United States. E.g.:

- "And this was the view of a majority of the *law lords* on that occasion, Lords Brougham and Campbell agreeing with Lord Lyndhurst." *In re Broderick's Will*, 88 U.S. 503, 512 (1874) (per Bradley, J.).
- "The *Law Lords* reached this view by analysing the meaning of the words without regard to their context or legislative intent." Michael Zander, *The Law-Making Process* 95 (2d ed. 1985).

For an excellent account, see *The Judicial House of Lords 1876–2009* (Louis Blom-Cooper et al. eds., 2009). See **House of Lords, Lords** & **Lord of Appeal in Ordinary.**

lawmaker. One word. Although historically this term was thought to be equivalent to *legislator*, the advent of legal realism made it apply just as fully to a judge as to a legislator. So Pound's use of the phrase *legislative lawmaker* is not a careless REDUNDANCY: "But they make the path of the *legislative lawmaker* a rough one." Roscoe Pound, *The Formative Era of American Law* 48 (1938). See **lawgiver.**

lawman = (1) historically, an official whose duty it was to declare the law; (2) a man of law, or lawyer; or (3) a law-enforcement officer. Sense 3 is the only sense recently in general use.

Sense 2 is labeled "obsolete except as a nonce-word" in the *OED*, and it probably *ought* to be obsolete. Yet: "Mispronunciations aside, do the modern *lawmen* [read *lawyers*] who use [legal terms] know something about their origin?" Mario Pei, *Words in Sheep's Clothing* 83 (1969). And in the same year, Glendon Schubert wrote of Justice Robert H. Jackson, "For over forty years, from late adolescence until the very day of his death, his was the life of a *law-man*"—adding "The idiom is that of Karl Llewellyn rather than of Matt Dillon." *Dispassionate Justice* 285 & n.3 (1969). Schubert's use of the term—referring as it does to a particular man—seems more justifiable than Pei's, but either is likely to strike some readers as sexist. See SEXISM (B).

law merchant = a system of customary law that grew up in Europe during the Middle Ages and regulated the dealings of mariners and merchants in all the commercial countries of the world. Many of its principles came to be incorporated into the common law. The plural form is *laws merchant*, the second word (as in the singular) being a POSTPOSITIVE ADJECTIVE. This phrase is a LOAN TRANSLATION of *lex mercatoria*. See **commercial law** & *lex mercatoria.*

lawmonger. See LAWYERS, DEROGATORY NAMES FOR (A).

lawnote. See **annotation.**

law of nations = (1) *jus gentium;* or (2) international law. The phrase *law of nations* began as a LOAN TRANSLATION of *jus gentium* (the common law of peoples) but eventually took on a more restrictive sense, as a synonym of *international law* (= the body of rules and

principles that bind civilized states in their relations with one another). As between these synonyms, "most writers and practitioners have for the past century preferred the term *international law*." John P. Grant & J. Craig Barker, *Parry & Grant Encyclopedic Dictionary of International Law* 336 (3d ed. 2009). A notable exception is J.L. Brierly, *The Law of Nations* (5th ed. 1955). See **jus gentium** & **international law.**

law of nature. See **natural law.**

law of the case = (1) the decision rendered in a former appeal of a case, which by legal doctrine is held to be binding; or (2) the doctrine so holding. So if a case is appealed a second time to a panel of a U.S. Court of Appeals, and a panel with a different makeup from the first panel hears the case the second time, the second panel will generally hold itself bound by the writings of the first panel whether or not its members agree with those earlier writings. This phrase, in Holmes's words, "merely expresses the practice of courts generally to refuse to reopen what has been decided, not a limit to their power." *Messinger v. Anderson*, 225 U.S. 436, 444 (1912) (per Holmes, J.). *Law of the case* is to be distinguished from *res judicata* and *stare decisis*. See **res judicata** & **stare decisis.**

law of the land is a LOAN TRANSLATION of the phrase *lex terrae* (LAW LATIN) or *ley de terre* (LAW FRENCH). First used in Magna Carta (in the phrase *per legem terrae*), the phrase generally means "the law in effect in a country and applicable to all members of the community, whether resulting from the highest court's pronouncements or from legislative enactment." E.g.: "Due process is older than written Constitutions, and the phrase is synonymous with '*law of the land*' as found in Magna Carta." *Horn v. State*, 204 P.3d 777, 783 (Okla. Crim. App. 2009). In AmE, this phrase also sometimes signifies "due process of law."

law of the lex. See **lex (c).**

law of the sea. See **admiralty (A).**

law proper = positive law. Pl. *laws proper*. See **positive law.**

law report. See **report.**

LAW REVIEWESE is the stilted, often jargonistic writing style characteristically found in law reviews. Judge Richard A. Posner, an accomplished stylist who has written in many law reviews, bemoans "the drab, Latinate, plethoric, euphemistic style of law reviews." Posner, *Goodbye to the Bluebook*, 53 U. Chi. L. Rev. 1343, 1349 (1986). Unless the author is a famous one whose prose the editors dare not tamper with, the edited and published writing usually takes on an "official" law-review style that is lacking in personality or individual idiom, overburdened with abstract phraseology, bottom-heavy with footnotes, humorless, and generally unobservant of good grammar and diction. The punctuation is often abysmal. These faults are perhaps ineradicable, at least in the U.S., since law students are called upon to be professional editors when not one in fifty has a background suitable to the task. Nevertheless, the industry and thought that go into publishing a law review are good training, however inconsequential the product often is.

"The ideal law review," writes James C. Raymond in an iconoclastic essay,

> is one that is designed not only to be referred to, but actually (and here comes the revolutionary proposal) to be read. Its articles are selected not on the basis of the number of footnotes they contain, but on the basis of the timeliness of the topic and the soundness of the scholarship. They may have no footnotes or dozens of them—all that are necessary to satisfy the curiosity of intelligent readers who are particularly interested in the topic, but no more.
>
> In the ideal review, articles are also selected, or even solicited, at least partly on the basis of how well their authors can write. Ideal editors are prepared to instruct their assistants and even their contributors on the elements of good writing. They refuse to publish anything that they consider dull, and they have the courage to demand a revision of anything they cannot understand. They know from their own reading that the best legal writers are always more than crabbed logicians of the law. They are capable of clarity without any compromise in precision, and, when the occasion warrants, of eloquence no less memorable than Cicero's.
>
> James C. Raymond, *Editing Law Reviews*, 12 Pepp. L. Rev. 371, 378–79 (1985).

Apart from *The Green Bag*, no such law review yet exists, or is likely to. Still, there is a move afoot to establish faculty-edited law reviews; let us hope that these bring much-needed reform. If they do, then Karl Llewellyn's words would lose their sting: "There is not, as far as I know, in the world an academic faculty which pins its reputation before the public on the work of undergraduate students—there is none, that is, except in the American law reviews." *The Bramble Bush* 107 (1930).

laws. See **law,** n.

law's delay. The possessive is necessary in this phrase, which derives from Shakespeare: "For who would bear . . . the *law's delay* . . . when he might his quietus make with a bare bodkin [i.e., dagger]." *Hamlet* 3.1.69–75. The allusion is sometimes mistakenly rendered in the more emphatic plural, as *the law's delays.*

Law Society = a professional association originally formed in 1825 to prevent abuses among and (later) to regulate solicitors in England and Wales. Separate societies now exist in Australia, Northern Ireland, and Scotland—as well as other jurisdictions in which the dual system of solicitors and barristers exists.

lawsuit. One word, whether in AmE or BrE. See **cause of action, suit** & **suit at law.**

lawyer, n. See **attorney (A)** & *lawyer* under LAWYERS, DEROGATORY NAMES FOR (B).

lawyer, vb.; **lawyering.** The *OED* lists *lawyering* ("colloquial") but not the verb *lawyer*. *W2* contains the verb *lawyer*, defining it as (1) "to conduct a lawsuit against" and (2) "to practice as a lawyer," noting that the term is "rare" in both senses. *W3* omits *lawyer* as a verb and appends the note "often used disparagingly" to *lawyering*.

None of these treatments adequately describes these Americanisms. *Lawyer* is no longer rare as a verb—e.g.: "Of course, ever since lawyers began to *lawyer*, there have been losing counsel aplenty who have so believed in their causes that they have bitterly blamed the court." Karl Llewellyn, *The Common Law Tradition* 3 (1960).

And it has taken on another sense: "to supply with lawyers"—e.g.: "The United States, arguably the most over-*lawyered* country in the world, has approximately 950,000 lawyers admitted to practice, and its law schools are producing around 36,000 new lawyers every year." Ed Weseman, *New Life for Commodity Legal Services*, 26 Of Counsel 10, 12 (2007).

Finally, although *lawyering* may be used disparagingly in some quarters, many lawyers use it as a neutral or even laudatory term to describe what they do—e.g.:

- "If *lawyering* is truly a public profession, it is no more seemly for the members of the bar to live lives of luxury than it was for the clergy of old." Jethro K. Lieberman, *Crisis at the Bar* 227 (1978).
- "This was a prodigious feat of *lawyering* on the part of defense counsel." *People v. Gragg*, 264 Cal. Rptr. 765, 773 (Ct. App. 1989) (referring to defense counsel's obtaining an acquittal for a defendant portrayed as a "brutish" person).
- "The real skill in judging, as it is in *lawyering*, is in being able properly to find and articulate the issues." *Varol v. Blue Cross & Blue Shield*, 708 F.Supp. 826, 827 (E.D. Mich. 1989).

See **attorney (C).**

lawyer-basher, lawyer-bashing. So hyphenated.

lawyerdom (= the world of lawyers) is more than just a NONCE WORD, though most dictionaries do not record it. It first appeared, it seems, in the mid-20th century, and it has been in fairly frequent use ever since—e.g.:

- "[Justice Benjamin Cardozo's] style received wide acclaim in *lawyerdom*." Jerome N. Frank, *Some Reflections on Judge Learned Hand*, 24 U. Chi. L. Rev. 666, 672 (1957).
- "Seliger cannot fairly be placed in a limbo unoccupied by the rest of *lawyerdom*." *Strama v. Peterson*, 561 F.Supp. 997, 999 (N.D. Ill. 1983).
- "Is there any road through the labyrinth of *lawyerdom*?" Glenna Whitley, *Why We Love to Hate Lawyers*, D Mag., May 1991, at 47, 51.

Attorneydom, although considerably older (dating from 1888), is today an occasional variant. E.g.:

- "They were, it seems, not the green cloth bags which afterwards became a synonym for *attorneydom*, but of black buckram." Edmund B.V. Christian, *A Short History of Solicitors* 56 (1896).

- "They also seem less prone to the sort of loophole chicanery and fine-print-chasing endemic to Washington *attorneydom*." Ken Ringle, *The Soviets' Cram Course in Freedom*, Wash. Post, 11 Oct. 1989, at B1.

lawyeress [according to the *OED*] = (1) the wife of a lawyer; or (2) a female lawyer. Neither sense 1, a surprising one, nor sense 2 has much place in modern legal writing. See SEXISM (C) & **lady lawyer.**

lawyering. See **lawyer,** vb.

lawyerish is the disparaging counterpart to *lawyerlike*. E.g.:

- "It is a lengthy, involved, and complicated document 13 typewritten pages in length. . . . Its language is 'lawyerish,' full of technical terms." *Mercantile-Com. Bank & Trust Co. v. Binowitz*, 238 S.W.2d 893, 897 (Mo. Ct. App. 1951).
- "He has nicked his own name down to Dick Thornburgh, from more *lawyerish* Richard L. Thornburgh." J. Randolph Murray, Chicago Trib., 26 Mar. 1989, at 4C.
- "The constitutional amendment . . . is advocated by the people who have lost patience with *lawyerish* logic and want to settle the question once and for all." *The Flag Burners*, Wash. Post, 20 July 1989, at A22.

See **lawyerly.** See also LAWYERS, DEROGATORY NAMES FOR.

lawyerism = (1) a mannerism, esp. of speech or writing, characteristic of lawyers; or (2) the influence, principles, or practices of lawyers. Examples of sense 1 are legion—e.g.: "The use of 'lawyerisms' that becloud clarity of expression is to be avoided." Edward Re, *Brief Writing and Oral Argument* 7 (6th ed. 1987).

Sense 2, however, is less common—e.g.:

- "OAG . . . concluded that control over environmental problems from oil and gas operations on state land lay in not leasing in the first place, the kind of *lawyerism* which drives most clients to ignore the answer they didn't want in the second place." *Michigan Oil Co. v. Natural Res. Comm'n*, 249 N.W.2d 135, 149 n.7 (Mich. Ct. App. 1976).
- "Trial-*lawyerism* 'is the only salient issue of the campaign since there's no judicial record for either candidate,' Ross added." Walter Borges, *In Judge Race, GOP Hits Kidd with TTLA Label*, Tex. Law., 20 Aug. 1990, at 6.

LAWYERISMS. See LEGALISMS AND LAWYERISMS.

lawyerize; lawyerization. Many question the need for such terms, especially since so many NEOLOGISMS formed with the *-ize* suffix are needless and ephemeral. But these words have appeared again and again in legal and nonlegal publications. Sometimes the meaning can be gleaned from the passage—e.g.:

- "We ought to consider the potential impact on the dockets of our busy district courts, and ultimately on our crowded docket, of '*lawyerizing*' prisoner civil litigation." *Merritt v. Faulkner*, 697 F.2d 761, 771 (7th Cir. 1983) (Posner, J., dissenting in part).
- "The *lawyerization* of America has not reached that point." *Sally Beauty Co. v. Nexxus Prods. Co.*, 801 F.2d 1001, 1010 (7th Cir. 1986) (Posner, J., dissenting).

By *lawyerize*, Posner probably means "to put (a thing) under the control of lawyers, the implication being that the adversary system is the only appropriate or effective way to proceed."

In other contexts, the sense is not so easily ascertained—e.g.:

- "Gilmore minimizes the importance of *lawyerizing* and laws through skepticism—how can one make rules in an existence that is fundamentally unknowable and perpetually in flux?" James G. Wilson, *The Morality of Formalism*, 33 UCLA L. Rev. 431, 437 (1985).
- "*Lawyerization* outside urban enclaves has been most dramatic in the state's north-central valley." Gail D. Cox, *100,000 Practitioners*, Nat'l L.J., 21 Nov. 1988, at 1.

In the latter sentence, *lawyerization* seems to mean "populating (an area) with lawyers."

lawyerling. See LAWYERS, DEROGATORY NAMES FOR (A).

lawyerly; lawyerlike. Most American and English dictionaries record *lawyerlike* but not *lawyerly*—this despite the greater currency of the latter word. *Lawyerly* first appeared in Milton's *Eikonoklastes* (1650), but then it fell into a long period of disuse. *See 3 Complete Works of John Milton* 403 (1962) ("the more Lawyerlie mooting on this point"). The first dictionary to record *lawyerly* was, appropriately, written by a lawyer: Noah Webster, *Dictionary of the English Language* (1828). Until recently, however, most other dictionary-makers, being unlawyerly, have ignored the word.

Whether *lawyerly* is a term of praise or of abuse depends on one's general disposition toward lawyers. Sometimes it is used admiringly: "What Marshall did was a stroke of political genius, salted with *lawyerly* adroitness." Fred Rodell, *Nine Men* 87 (1955). Sometimes not—e.g.:

- "But the judges, with *lawyerly* indirection, have not avowed the interest of the judiciary in orderly resort to the courts as a basis for their decision." *Miles v. Illinois Cent. R.R.*, 315 U.S. 698, 706 (1942) (Jackson, J., concurring).
- "With every half line of testimony interrupted by half a page of *lawyerly* harangue, it was exceedingly difficult for the witness to develop his thesis and the search for the truth was well nigh lost in the process." *Watson v. State*, 306 A.2d 599, 608 (Md. Ct. Spec. App. 1973).

Lawyerlike, on the other hand, is almost invariably a term of praise—e.g.:

- "This is not very *lawyerlike*, nor very respectful to the Court." *Rhode Island v. Massachusetts*, 37 U.S. (12 Pet.) 657, 699 (1838) (argument of counsel).
- "Counsel for both sides tried this case on a very high plane and in a very objective, *lawyerlike* fashion." *Reed v. Gulf Oil Corp.*, 217 F.Supp. 370, 373 (D.D.C. 1963).
- "Without exception, despite the emotional overtones of the proceeding, the briefs and oral arguments were temperate, *lawyerlike* and constructive." *South Carolina v. Katzenbach*, 383 U.S. 301, 308 (1966) (per Warren, C.J.).

*lawyerphile. See NONCE WORDS.

LAWYERS, DEROGATORY NAMES FOR. The chief irony of lawyerdom is that poll after poll shows that (1) the public holds lawyers in low esteem, but (2) of all the possible careers that are available, parents would prefer to have their children become lawyers. Whole books could be written about that inconsistency. This is not the place for a discussion of why people disparage lawyers; it is, however, the place to examine the vocabulary with which people do it.

The English language has a formidable stock of disparaging names for lawyers. Of course, every language has its proverbs that reflect poorly in one way or another on lawyers (maybe uncomprehendingly), but probably no other has the range in depreciative vocabulary—from the mild to the harsh. Of course, much depends on who is mouthing the word; some people use *lawyer* itself in derogatory ways—hence the unfortunate tendency for lawyers to call themselves *attorneys* instead of *lawyers*. See **attorney.**

A. Names Actually Given to Lawyers. The following terms have been used at various times and in various places to refer to lawyers in ways that are less than flattering:

- **ack-ack:** (20th–21st-c. AmE criminal cant) a court-appointed lawyer. One writer says that the expression "is both a pun on the World War II antiaircraft gun and also a partial acronym for 'ambulance chaser.'" Joel Homer, *Jargon* 76 (1979).
- **ambidexter:** (16th–19th-c. BrE) an unscrupulous lawyer who takes fees (or sometimes bribes) "with both hands," that is, from both sides of a controversy.
- **ambulance chaser:** (19th–21st c.) a lawyer who solicits business from accident victims at the scene of an accident or shortly thereafter; by extension, an unscrupulous plaintiffs' lawyer—e.g.: "Irresponsible reporters and editors . . . might, for example, describe the lawyer as a 'mob mouthpiece' for representing a client with a serious prior criminal record, or as an '*ambulance chaser*' for representing a claimant in a personal injury action." *Gertz v. Robert Welch, Inc.,* 418 U.S. 323, 355 (1974) (Burger, C.J., dissenting). See **ambulance chaser.**
- **auscultator:** (19th c.) a young German lawyer who has passed his first public exam and is now employed without salary, and without appointment, by the government. *Auscultator* is a fancy equivalent of "listener; one who listens (but doesn't speak)." E.g.: "If he passes, he is sworn in as '*Auscultator*,' and he attaches himself to some inferior court." Walter Copland Perry, *German University Education* 111 (1846).
- **Blackstone lawyer:** (19th–21st-c. AmE) a self-educated antebellum lawyer whose legal training consisted primarily in reading William Blackstone's *Commentaries on the Laws of England.* Thomas Jefferson complained that "a student finds there a smattering of everything, and his indolence easily persuades him that if he understands that book, he is a master of the whole body of law." The "unlettered common people" applied "the appellation of *Blackstone lawyers* to these ephemeral insects of the law." Letter from Thomas Jefferson to Judge John Tyler, 17 June 1812, in 13 *The Writings of Thomas Jefferson* 166–67 (Andrew Lipscomb ed. 1905).
- **chaser:** (20th–21st-c. AmE) an ambulance chaser—e.g.: "Practicing attorneys often tell us [i.e., the disciplinary authorities]: why don't you go get so-and-so, the big guys,

the publicity seekers, the big *chasers*." Murray T. Bloom, *The Trouble with Lawyers* 156 (1970) (quoting Vincent Cullinan, president of the San Francisco Bar, 1967–1968). The term also refers to a "runner" employed by the lawyer for purposes of soliciting business from accident victims.
- **city lawyer:** This term (19th–21st c.) is self-explanatory, except that the people who use the term are usually from rural areas—e.g.: "They talked about the avaricious *city lawyers* who soon would be descending upon the company and demanding private documents." Joseph C. Goulden, *The Million Dollar Lawyers* 283 (1978). See **city lawyer.**
- **country lawyer:** (19th–21st-c. AmE) a rural lawyer. This term can carry positive connotations, but it sometimes suggests modest intellectual abilities—e.g.: "The rule of reason . . . should now allow one to put an antitrust theory of liability or justification into terms that a *country lawyer* can understand." Lawrence A. Sullivan, *The Viability of the Current Law on Horizontal Restraints,* 75 Cal. L. Rev. 835, 847 (1987). See **country lawyer.**
- **Court Street lawyer:** (20th–21st-c. AmE) a (sometimes disreputable) lawyer with a practice—usu. a trial practice—centered in the borough hall area of Brooklyn. E.g.: "Before the Depression, real estate lawyers were typically wheelerdealers, called '*Court Street lawyers*' after the Brooklyn street where many of them set up practice." Rachelle DePalma, *The Role of the Pro in Real Estate Deals,* Crain's N.Y. Bus., 28 Apr. 1986, at 30. Today the term is also used loosely to distinguish lawyers who practice in the outer boroughs (principally Brooklyn) from those, usually white-shoe lawyers, who practice in the federal courts and the state courts of the borough of Manhattan, which is co-extensive with New York County.
- **Cupboardman:** (17th c.) one of an order of disputants at an Inn of Court—so called from their use of a cupboard in one of the halls as a rostrum from which to carry on their disputations. E.g.: "The *Cupboardman* stood at the four corners of the cupboard and each in turn argued the Reader's cases." *Readings and Moots,* 32 Can. L. Times 593, 594 (1912).
- **devil:** (19th–21st c.) a fee-less junior lawyer who works as an apprentice to a senior. E.g.: "The early ambition of the young barrister is to become a '*devil*' to some junior barrister, who always has recourse to such an understudy." Thomas Learning, *A Philadelphia Lawyer in the London Courts* 30 (1911). See **devil.**
- **dump truck:** (20th–21st-c. AmE) an unmotivated criminal-defense lawyer who unskillfully represents indigent defendants through public subsidy. E.g.: "Clients often refer to their public defenders as '*dump trucks*,' a term that apparently derives from the defendant's belief that defenders are not interested in giving a vigorous defense, but rather seek only to 'dump' them as quickly as possible." Suzanne E. Mounts, *Public Defender Programs, Professional Responsibility, and Competent Representation,* 1982 Wis. L. Rev. 473, 474.
- **flycatcher:** (18th–19th c.) one who catches flies. The *OED* cites a 1737 reference to lawyers stating: "Ye scurvy *Flycatchers* ye!"
- **fogger:** (16th–18th c.) a lawyer on the bottom rung of the profession—often preceded by *petty*. See **pettifogger.**
- **green bag:** (17th–19th c.) a lawyer—through the process of metonymy: for their papers, lawyers formerly carried bags made of green canvas or cloth. Although the epithet

is one that many lawyers have borne with pride, there is something at least mildly self-deprecating about equating oneself with a bag.—B.A.G.

- *gunslinger:* (20th–21st-c. AmE) a hired gun—e.g.: "Some lawyers were disturbed when I wrote that lawyers should be 'healers not *gunslingers*' but I have not hesitated to restate it." Warren E. Burger, *Foreward [sic]: American Law Institute Study on Paths to a "Better Way,"* 1989 Duke L.J. 808, 809.

- *hack attorney:* (18th–21st c.) a travesty of a lawyer. E.g.: "They usually end up in what we call the 'bankruptcy mill,' where a *hack attorney* takes their money and provides little or nothing of value." Ralph R. Roberts, Lois Maljak & Paul Doroh, *Foreclosure Self-Defense for Dummies* 120 (2008).

- *hired gun:* (20th–21st-c. AmE) a lawyer who acts like an aggressive gunfighter in the Old West, and who will do anything for a fee—e.g.: "Kevin Mulligan, president of the union, said an agreement was reached in only three months because the '*hired guns*' were not present during negotiations. He said that when the lawyers for both sides were involved in the last contract, the process took 18 months." Carol Stream, *Firefighters Sign 3-Year Contract,* Chicago Trib., 15 May 1992, at 3D.

- *horse lawyer:* (19th–21st-c. AmE) a lawyer of little ability. *See* 3 Richard H. Thornton, *An American Glossary* 196 (Louise Hanley ed., 1962).

- *jackleg lawyer:* (20th–21st-c. AmE) an amateurish and dishonest lawyer—e.g.: "She did have a chat with a couple of lawyers. The lawyers couldn't do a thing. '*Jackleg lawyers,*' she says, and flicks ashes." Wil Haygood, *A Time Revisited,* Boston Globe, 16 Mar. 1989, at 85.

- *jet:* (18th c.) a lawyer, by metonymic reference to the lawyer's black gown.

- *jungle fighter:* (20th–21st-c. AmE) a lawyer who practices in the lower criminal courts—e.g.: "It may well be that the standard of decorum usually prevailing in the sedate precincts of chancery should also be observed by the *jungle-fighters* in the pit of police and criminal courts, but it would be somewhat less than realistic." *Kentucky State Bar Ass'n v. Taylor,* 482 S.W.2d 574, 583 (Ky. 1972).

- *land shark:* (19th–21st c.) a lawyer. E.g.: "'A lawyer!—a *land shark!*—you a lawyer!' were the exclamations of astonishment that burst from every lip." *The Reefer of '76,* in 19 Graham's Lady's & Gentleman's Mag. 104, 104 (1841).

- *latrine lawyer:* (20th–21st-c. AmE) a lawyer who gets business from the rumors spread in the latrine—e.g.: "The *latrine lawyer,* aka s***house lawyer, is usually a rag bag of limited rank and potential, with loads of inaccurate advice, and no lack of believers among those dumb enough to listen." E. Kelly Taylor, *America's Army and the Language of Grunts* 198 (2009) (bowdlerization in original).

- *law-driver:* (17th c.) one who drives or toils at the law; a lawyer who works arduously. E.g.: "Sir, there's an old fellow, a kind of *law-driver,* entreats conference with your worship." Thomas Middleton, *The Phoenix* (1607), in 1 *The Works of Thomas Middleton* 309, 361 (1840).

- *lawmonger:* (17th-c. BrE) a low practitioner of law; a pettifogger—e.g.: "Though this catering *Law-monger* be bold to call it wicked." John Milton, "Colasterion" (1645), in *The Works of John Milton* 233, 259 (Frank A. Patterson et al. eds., 1931).

- *lawyerling:* (19th c.) a new or young lawyer. E.g.: "A wretched English scribe . . . urged on by his paltry, pitiful *lawyerlings,* puts his vile name to his paltry proclamation." Daniel O'Connell, Speech (19 Oct. 1830), 72 *Annual Register* 175, 176 (1831).

- *legal beagle:* (20th–21st c.) a lawyer. Like *legal eagle,* this term is generally found in the speech and writing of non-lawyers, sometimes with positive and sometimes with negative connotations. Sometimes it occurs with dog metaphors—e.g.: "Even if council's *legal beagles* sniff out a loophole to invalidate the petition, the mayor's suggestion to put voter-rejected water metering back on the ballot morally compels the council to repeat the fluoridation vote." Don Martin, *Fluoride Forces Better Brush Up for Battle,* Calgary Herald, 11 Oct. 1991, at B1. See **legal eagle.**

- *legal eagle:* (20th–21st-c. AmE) a lawyer. Like *legal beagle,* this term is almost invariably used by those outside the legal profession, usually with positive connotations. But not always—e.g.: "The *legal eagles* snookered a federal judge into swallowing their sophistry." Samuel Francis, *The Long Count on Executions,* Wash. Times, 1 May 1992, at F3. See **legal eagle.**

- *legalist:* (mid-17th c.) a pedantic, legalistic lawyer—e.g.: "In spite of the severe limitations of world government, global *legalists* believe that international law can solve global problems." Christopher J. Eby, *Global Legalism: The Illusion of Effective International Law,* 38 Denv. J. Int'l L. & Pol'y 687, 689–90 (2010). See **legalist.**

- *leguleian:* (17th–19th-c. BrE) a pettifogger—as the *OED* puts it, "a contemptuous term for a lawyer." E.g.: "You do but that . . . which some silly *Leguleians* now and then do, to argue unawares against their own clients." John Milton, "A Defence of the People of England," in *The Prose Works of John Milton* 1, 179 (J.A. St. John ed., 1910 [Joseph Washington trans., 1692]).

- *lip:* (20th–21st-c. AmE) a criminal lawyer (viewed cynically).

- *long-robe man:* (17th c.) a lawyer (from the long gown). This term is only mildly disparaging if at all. Also termed *man of the long coat.* See **gownsman.**

- *mob mouthpiece:* (20th–21st-c. AmE) a defense lawyer for mobsters—e.g.: "Oscar Goodman has defended a federal judge and the mayor of San Diego, derailed a U.S. attorney general's effort and proudly wears the title '*mob mouthpiece,*' having represented a who's who of alleged crime figures." Robert Macy, *Money's Source "Irrelevant": "Mob Mouthpiece" Fights U.S. Attempt to Seize Fees,* L.A. Times, 6 Apr. 1986, at 2–8.

- *mouthpiece:* (19th–21st-c. AmE & BrE) defense counsel hired to speak at the client's bidding—e.g.: "An attorney is not merely the client's 'alter ego' functioning only as the client's '*mouthpiece.*'" *Morrison v. State,* 373 S.E.2d 506, 509 (Ga. 1988).

- *peat:* (17th c.) a young Scottish lawyer who is considered a particular judge's favorite, esp. through nepotism (*peat* = sweetheart). E.g.: "As Scott tells us in *Redgauntlet,* when a young lawyer was supposed to be under the patronage of a judge, he was termed a *peat,* or pet." *Historical Scottish Proverbs,* 74 Chambers's J. 25, 28 (1897).

- *pettifogger:* (16th–21st-c. BrE & AmE) a petty and disreputable lawyer who niggles over inconsequential details; a "rascally attorney" (*OED*)—e.g.: "Quite the contrary, counsel in that case were not *pettifoggers.*" *Nebeker v. Piper Aircraft Corp.,* 747 P.2d 18, 38 (Idaho 1987). See **pettifogger.**

- *Philadelphia lawyer:* (18th–21st-c. AmE) an ultracompetent lawyer who knows the ins and outs of legal technicalities; also, a shrewdly unscrupulous lawyer. (This term has long been known in AmE and BrE alike. Similar geographic terms are used as regionalisms. For example, *Dallas lawyer* is often snidely used in Fort Worth; *Houston lawyer* is often snidely used in Dallas; and *New York*

lawyer is snidely used by lawyers almost everywhere else.)
See **Philadelphia lawyer.**

- *shady lawyer* (self-explanatory): "A *shady lawyer* named Kantor, who had been assigned as counsel to the defendant, managed by terrifying the mother as to the possible outcome of the case, to extort from her her entire savings amounting to four hundred and thirty-five dollars." Ephraim Tutt, *Yankee Lawyer* 106 (1943).
- *shark*: (19th–21st c.) a lawyer. This nautical reference dates back to at least 1806.
- *ship's lawyer*: (19th–21st-c. AmE) an unskillful lawyer. *See* 3 Richard H. Thornton, *An American Glossary* 348 (Louise Hanley ed. 1962).
- *shyster* = (19th–21st-c. AmE) a professionally unscrupulous lawyer. For the fascinating etymology of this word, see **shyster.** For the distinction between a *pettifogger* and a *shyster*, see **pettifogger.**
- *shyster lawyer* (redundant and self-explanatory): "The *shyster lawyer* assigned by the court wanted to squeeze all the money he could out of the boy's family." Ephraim Tutt, *Yankee Lawyer* 106 (1943). For the etymology, see **shyster.**
- *silk-stocking lawyer*: (19th–21st-c. AmE) a patrician lawyer—e.g.: "'Do you want ivory tower, *silk stocking lawyers* defending these people?' the house speaker shouted at him. Mr. [Gary] Parker replied, 'That's better than no lawyer at all.'" Marianne Lavelle, *Piercing Racism's Heart*, Nat'l L.J., 24 Dec. 1990, at 1.
- *sore-back lawyer*: (20th–21st-c. AmE) a personal-injury lawyer—e.g.: "[My father] really didn't like this bleep I was doing, you know, suing businesses, being a *sore-back lawyer* (legal slang for a personal injury lawyer), and he was oriented the other way." Joe Jamail (as quoted in Steve Coll, *Down Home with Texas' $10.5 Billion Barrister Pennzoil Attorney Joe Jamail*, Wash. Post, 31 July 1986, at B1).
- *stuff gown*: (19th c.) a junior counsel, as opposed to a "silk." Often shortened merely to *stuff.* Cf. **silk.**
- *Tombs lawyer*: (19th–21st-c. AmE) an unscrupulous New York practitioner. Thornton defines the term *Tombs lawyers* as "a class of men in New York, resembling the 'Old Bailey practitioners,' but, if possible, more unscrupulous," with this illustration: "A man as corrupt as sin, as venal as a *Tombs lawyer*." 3 Richard H. Thornton, *An American Glossary* 196 (Louise Hanley ed., 1962).
- *trampler*: (17th c.) a go-between lawyer. E.g.: "He has been a *trampler* of the law, sir; and the devil has a care of his footmen." Thomas Middleton, *A Trick to Catch the Old One* 1.4.38–39 (1608), in *The Chief Elizabethan Dramatists* 690, 693 (William Allan Neilson ed., 1911).
- *underlawyer*: (17th c.) a low-ranking lawyer.
- *waller*: (20th–21st c.) a casually employed legal copyist who lounges against a wall while awaiting employment.
- *white-powder lawyer*: (20th–21st c.) a lawyer who represents cocaine dealers. See **white-powder bar.**
- *white-shoe lawyer* (20th–21st-c. AmE) an establishment lawyer—e.g.: "Lifland rejected Gold's suggestion, appointing *white-shoe lawyer* Leon Silverman of New York's Fried, Frank, Harris, Shriver & Jacobson instead of someone from the ranks of organized labor." Caroline V. Clarke, *Labor's Turn to Take on Manville*, Am. Law., Jan.–Feb. 1991, at 44.

B. Prejudicial Names for Other Forms of Life.
Sometimes, people and things are referred to as lawyers, usually for the purpose of making the reference derogatory—e.g.:

- *barrack lawyer*: (20th–21st-c. BrE criminal cant) a prisoner who thinks he knows all there is to know regarding prison rules. One text defines the phrase as follows: "Generally a solicitor's ex-clerk posing as a lawyer and always ready to give 'expert' advice on 'how to get on special release.'" Paul Tempest, *Lag's Lexicon* 11 (1950).
- *bush lawyer*: (19th–21st-c. Australianism) one who parades a merely fancied knowledge of the law—e.g.: "Well, in the old days in the bush, there were no registered lawyers, so some half-shrewd mug, usually a barber, would set himself up to advise all and sundry. So now anyone who throws around a lot of free advice is called a *bush lawyer.*" Frank Hardy, *Billy Borker Yarns Again* 135 (1967).
- *guardhouse lawyer*: (20th–21st-c. AmE) a jailhouse lawyer. E.g.: "If we are going to administer criminal justice properly to those whose cases call for our attention, if we are going to devote our attention to matters meriting attention and not submerge ourselves in a great bog of rhetorical trivia, mostly dreamed up by *guardhouse lawyers*, we must exercise some degree of rational selection." *Surratt v. U.S.*, 262 F.2d 691, 694 (D.C. Cir. 1958) (Prettyman, C.J., dissenting).
- *high lawyer*: (16th–18th-c. BrE) a mounted highway robber—e.g.: "The legerdemaine [*sic*] of . . . *high Lawyers.*" Robert Greene, *Groats-Worth of Wit* xxix (Dyce ed., 1617). *See* Eric Partridge, *A Dictionary of the Underworld* 331 (1950).
- *jailhouse lawyer*: (20th–21st-c. AmE) an inmate who acquires some legal learning and counsels fellow inmates on drafting complaints and briefs.
- *lake lawyer*: (19th-c. AmE) either of two different fishes, the bow-fin and the burbot—named because of their "ferocious looks and voracious habits." John R. Bartlett, *The Dictionary of Americanisms* 198 (1849).
- *lawyer*: (19th-c. AmE) the black-necked stilt—so named because of its "long bill" (*OED*).
- *lynch lawyer*: (19th-c. AmE) a practitioner of lynch law—e.g.: "In the middle [of the plaza] is planted a tall liberty pole, near which is erected a rude rostrum for *lynch-lawyers* and noisy politicians." Hinton R. Helper, *The Land of Gold* 74 (1855). See **lynch law.**
- *pelican*: (20th–21st-c. AmE) a jailhouse lawyer specializing in appeals. *See* Joel Homer, *Jargon* 78 (1979).
- *sea lawyer*: (19th–21st-c. BrE & AmE) a captious or carping sailor—or, by extension, other person—e.g.: "So long as the teacher acts reasonably the Constitution does not require him to work in an atmosphere of litigious contest with any juvenile *sea-lawyer* who may appear in his class." *Meyers v. Arcata High Sch. Dist.*, 75 Cal. Rptr. 68, 78 (Ct. App. 1969) (Christian, J., dissenting). Originally, in the early 19th century, *sea lawyer* was a name given to the tiger shark.

lawyer's lawyer. This CLICHÉ is among the highest compliments that one lawyer can pay another—e.g.: "Robert Houghwout Jackson was an eloquent spokesman for the pattern of beliefs and feelings characteristic of the political ideology of the American lawyer. More than any other Supreme Court justice of the twentieth century, Jackson was a *lawyer's lawyer.*" Glendon Schubert, *Dispassionate Justice* 1 (1969). For the definitive treatment of all that this phrase embodies, see William H. Harbaugh, *Lawyer's Lawyer: The Life of John W. Davis* (1973). Unfortunately, however, the phrase is coming to be used with little discrimination.

lay, adj. See **laic, laity** & **layman.**

lay; lie. These verbs are commonly misused—even by members of our learned profession. Witness these specimens:

- "He said he played with guns all the time, and that he picked up a pistol *laying* [read *lying*] on the bedside table and began *waiving* [read *waving*] it around." *Still v. State*, 709 S.W.2d 672, 674 (Tex. App.—Tyler 1983).
- "Susman started looking around for a lucrative niche in the Houston legal market, and he thought the big money might *lay* [read *lie*] in plaintiffs' antitrust class action work." John A. Jenkins, *The Litigators* 259–60 (1989).
- "Mr. Armstrong [debating against Alan Dershowitz] was not to be outdone. . . . But Mr. Dershowitz did not *lay* [read *lie*] down." William Glaberson, *Face to Face, 2 Lawyers Feud Away, Slap for Slap*, N.Y. Times, 19 Jan. 1991, at 15.

Very simply, *lie* (= to recline, be situated) is intransitive <he lies on his bed>, whereas *lay* (= to put down, arrange) is transitive only <she laid her hand on his shoulder> <they laid the body in its grave>. The verbs are declined *lie > lay > lain* and *lay > laid > laid*. To use *lay* intransitively to mean "lie," as in **I want to lay down*, is nonstandard, even though (alas) fairly common in speech. See **lie,** vb.

*lay low. See **lie low.**

layman; layperson; lay person; nonlawyer. *Layman* is the most common among these terms and has traditionally been regarded as unexceptionable—in reference to members of both sexes, of course. E.g.: "A *layman* was needed to evaluate the success or failure of my effort to translate rules of law into understandable English prose. Therefore, with infinite patience, my wife read and reread every section of this text." Robert Kratovil, *Real Estate Law* iv (1946). Still, modern writers increasingly avoid *layman* on grounds of SEXISM. For those seeking a nonsexist substitute, *nonlawyer* is the best choice.

W11 records *layperson* from 1972; the one-word form appears to be an Americanism—e.g.: "The average *layperson* would no doubt disagree with A if he said, 'I didn't intend to injure C.'" Here it appears in plural form *lay people*, an alternative to *laypersons*: "If they continue in their druidic isolation, the only course *lay people* might have is what Dick the butcher, in *Henry IV, Part Two*, suggested: 'The first thing we do, let's kill all the lawyers.'" Ronald L. Goldfarb & James C. Raymond, *Clear Understandings: A Guide to Legal Writing* xiii (1982). For the reason to avoid *layperson*, like all other words ending with the *-person* suffix, see SEXISM (B). See also **laity, nonlawyer, people** (A) & BIBLICAL AFFECTATION.

leach, vb.; **leech,** vb. To *leach* is to pass through by percolation, or to separate a solid from a solution by percolation. To *leech* is to apply bloodsuckers to the skin in order to cause bleeding (no longer a favored medical technique); metaphorically, *leeching* occurs when a person acts like a bloodsucker.

Surprisingly often, *leech* is misused for *leach*—e.g.:

- "The advent of agriculture in the Imperial Valley and the Coachella Valley, with its attendant irrigation, *leeching* [read *leaching*], and drainage significantly changed the inflow into the Sea." *U.S. v. Imperial Irrigation Dist.*, 799 F.Supp. 1052, 1058 (S.D. Cal. 1992).
- "Testimony was elicited regarding a condition known as 'new building syndrome,' indicating that new buildings have a greater accumulation of allergens and *leeching* [read *leaching*] of noxious vapors [that] subside with the passage of time." *Champion v. Beale*, 833 S.W.2d 799, 800 (Ky. 1992).
- "Plaintiffs in California, Illinois, and New York are alleging that children whose mothers had implants prior to their conception may have been injured from silicone *leeching* [read *leaching*] through their mothers' bloodstream and breast milk." Todd P. Myers, Casenote, *Ohio Rejects Preconception Cause of Action for DES Grandchildren*, 62 U. Cin. L. Rev. 283, 320 n.267 (1993).

lead > led > led. So inflected. *Lead* is sometimes wrongly used for the past-tense *led*, perhaps on the mistaken analogy of *read/read*, and perhaps also because of confusion with the metal—e.g.: "Claimant has failed to prove that her work injury has *lead* [read *led*] employers to refuse her employment." *Perman v. North Dakota Workers Comp. Bureau*, 458 N.W.2d 484, 486 (N.D. 1990).

leader (at the bar) is a Britishism meaning "the senior barrister for a party in a case." In AmE, *lead counsel* is the usual phrase.

leading case = (1) most strictly, a judicial precedent that first definitely settled an important rule or principle of law and that has since been often and consistently followed; (2) less strictly, an important, often the most important, judicial precedent on a particular legal issue; or (3) loosely, a reported case that determines an issue being litigated; a *ruling case*. (See **ruling case.**) Sense 1 is the classic one, referring to cases such as these:

- *McNaghten's Case*, 8 Eng. Rep. 718, 10 Cl. & Fin. 200 (1843) (first setting forth the grounds of the insanity defense). See **McNaghten.**
- *Palsgraf v. Long Island R.R.*, 162 N.E. 99 (N.Y. 1928) (establishing the doctrine that a defendant's duty in a negligence action is limited to plaintiffs within the zone of apparent danger—to whom damage could be reasonably foreseen).
- *Erie R.R. v. Tompkins*, 304 U.S. 64 (1938) (holding that on questions of state law, a federal court sitting in diversity is bound by the law as declared by the highest state court). See **Erie-bound.**
- *Miranda v. Arizona*, 384 U.S. 436 (1966) (creating the exclusionary rule for evidence obtained improperly from a suspect being interrogated while in police custody). See **Mirandize.**

leading question; categorical question. Nonlawyers frequently misapprehend *leading question* as referring to a question showing hostility or posed just to embarrass or take unfair advantage. Actually, as litigators well know, a *leading question* is one that suggests the answer to the person being interrogated. In Anglo-American law such questions are generally permissible only on cross-examination. *Categorical question*, another name for the same practice, is today little used.

leafleting. This word arises in First Amendment cases, such as *Jews for Jesus, Inc. v. Board of Airport Comm'rs*, 661 F.Supp. 1223, 1224, 1225 (C.D. Cal. 1985), in which the word is spelled *leafletting* on one page and *leafleting* on the next. The better spelling in AmE is *leafleting*; in BrE, *leafletting*. See DOUBLING OF FINAL CONSONANTS.

leap > leaped > leaped. But *leapt* is also an acceptable past-tense and past-participial form. It is unfortunately susceptible to the misspelling **lept*, perhaps on the suggestion of *kept*—e.g.:

- "John J. Sirica *lept* [read *leapt*] to his feet, shouting, 'It ain't fair. It ain't fair!'" *Sirica, 88, Dies; Persistent Judge in Fall of Nixon*, N.Y. Times, 15 Aug. 1992, at 1, 11.
- "McGensey, who by then had reached the top of the wall, *lept* [read *leapt*] down on Rivera." *Gates v. Rivera*, 993 F.2d 697, 698 (9th Cir. 1993).

learned; learnt. As an adjective, *learned* has two syllables, and as a past-tense verb, one. *Learnt* is a BrE variant of the past tense *learned*.

learned counsel; learned friend; learned court. These are tiresome legal CLICHÉS; examples like the following one show just how debased such phrases have become: "*Learned counsel* . . . contend that the delivery of the escrow agreement . . . was in fact a delivery . . . of the oil and gas lease." *Ford v. Moody*, 276 S.W. 595, 597 (Ark. 1925). *Learned friend* is a common variation, as in, "It may be helpful to your Lordship and my *learned friend* if I . . . ," meaning, as David Pannick points out, "it will certainly be helpful to me." Pannick adds that to say "In all fairness to my *learned friend*" means that one is about to "put the legal boot in." David Pannick, *Judges* 153 (1987).

Even *learned court* is likely to sound patronizing, especially when used by an appellate court in reference to a lower court—e.g.: "The *learned court* at special term has found that, [although] the instrument relied upon by the defendant was of a testamentary character, [it] did not comply with the statutory requirements of a will, and [is] therefore void." *Butler v. Sherwood*, 188 N.Y.S. 242, 243 (App. Div. 1921).

learnt. See **learned**.

leasable. So spelled.

lease, n., = (1) a conveyance of real property, usu. in return for rent, made for life, for a fixed period, or at will—but always for less time than the lessor has a right to; (2) both such a conveyance and all other covenants attached to the conveyance; (3) the written instrument in which such a conveyance, together with the covenants, is incorporated; (4) in North America and Australia, a piece of real property that is held on lease; or (5) a temporary conveyance of personal property in return for consideration.

When sense 5 arose in the 19th century, it was considered a loose usage. Today, however, *leases* of cars and office equipment, for example, are common.

lease, vb.; let. *Let* (10th c.) is 300 years older than *lease* (13th c.) in the sense "to grant the temporary possession and use of (land, buildings, rooms, movable property) to another in return for rent or other consideration." But both are well established, and they are equally good. As used by (real) estate agents in BrE, the term "To Let" is more common than the phrase "For Rent," the usual term in AmE.

To say that one *leases* property nowadays does not tell the reader or listener whether one is lessor or lessee. From its first verbal use in the 13th century, *lease* meant "to grant the possession of," but in the mid-19th century it took on the additional sense "to take a lease of; to hold by a lease." This AMBIGUITY has made the preposition used important to clarity: the lessor *leases to* and the lessee *leases from*.

leaseback (= the sale of property on the understanding, or with the express option, that the seller may lease the property immediately upon the sale) dates from the mid-20th century. Though technically a REDUNDANCY, the common phrase *sale and leaseback* helps clarify the meaning.

*leasee. See ***leasor**.

lease for years. See **term of years**.

lease from. See **lease**, vb.

leaseholder (BrE) = *lessee* (AmE). Both terms are used in both speech communities—for example, *leaseholder* is fairly common in American oil-and-gas cases—but *leaseholder* is the more general term in BrE, *lessee* the more general term in AmE.

*lease-lend. See **lend-lease**.

leaseman. See **landman (A)**.

lease-purchase agreement; hire-purchase agreement. The first is standard AmE; the second is the BrE equivalent. The AmE phrase is sometimes written *lease-to-purchase agreement*. See **hire purchase**.

lease to. See **lease**, vb.

*leasor; *leasee. These are blunders for *lessor* and *lessee*. E.g.:

- "The legal status of a third person coming upon a *leasor's* [read *lessor's*] property at the invitation of a *leasee* [read *lessee*] is immaterial." *Flott v. Cates*, 528 N.E.2d 847, 849 (Ind. Ct. App. 1988).

- "The city would require the *leasee* [read *lessee*] to construct at least 55,000 square feet of maintenance hangar space." *Government Actions*, Wash. Post, 12 April 1990, at V5.

See **lessor.**

leave of court = judicial permission to follow a non-routine procedure. In the sense of permission, *leave* had become archaic by the 19th century in every field but law. Rather than just leaving it alone, sometimes lawyers use the word *leave* alone—e.g.: "Your honor, we seek *leave* to amend our complaint under these extraordinary circumstances."

lecture method. See **casebook method.**

led. See **lead.**

leech, vb. See **leach.**

legacy = a gift by will, esp. of personal property and often of money. Several types of legacies are distinguishable. A *specific legacy* or *bequest* is a testamentary gift of property that can be distinguished with reasonable accuracy from the other property forming the testator's estate. A *demonstrative legacy* is paid from a particular source; but if the source is insufficient to satisfy the legacy, then the legacy is paid from the general assets of the estate to the extent that the specific source is lacking. A *general legacy* or *bequest* is a gift of personal property that the testator intends to come from the general assets of the estate.

A *residuary legacy* or *bequest* is a gift of the estate remaining after all claims against the estate have been satisfied, and all specific, demonstrative, and general legacies have been paid out. Cf. **bequest.** See **devise.**

legacy, vb. See **legate.**

legal, adj.; **lawful; licit.** *Legal* is the broadest term, meaning either (1) "of or pertaining to law; falling within the province of law," or (2) "established; permitted, or not forbidden by law." These two senses are used with about equal frequency. See **law,** adj.

Lawful and *licit* share with *legal* sense 2, "according or not contrary to law; permitted by law." *Lawful* is quite common—e.g.: "In March 1977, the company posted a notice on the bulletin board [that] contained a *lawful* statement on the solicitation and distribution of materials." *N.L.R.B. v. Trailways, Inc.*, 729 F.2d 1013, 1018 (5th Cir. 1984). The least frequently used of these terms is *licit* <licit acts> <the licit use of force>, which usually occurs in direct contrast to *illicit.*

Lawful should not be used in sense 1 of *legal*, as it sometimes is—e.g.: "The judgment must be affirmed if it can be sustained on any *lawful* [read *legal*] theory finding support in the pleadings and evidence." *Brazos County Appraisal Dist. v. Sun Operating LP*, 778 S.W.2d 130, 131 (Tex. App.—Texarkana 1989). See **illegal.**

legal, as an attributive noun, means "the legal description of real property" <I have enclosed the legal on the parcel you asked about>. This usage began as surveyors' cant but has gradually infected lawyers' language. See ADJECTIVES (B).

legal assistant. See **paralegal** (B).

legal beagle. See **legal eagle.**

legal cause. See CAUSATION (A).

legal centralism; *legal centrism. The first is the standard phrase to denote a doctrine holding that the legal entities erected by the state occupy the center of legal life and stand in a relation of hierarchic control over other, lesser norms that define appropriate behavior and social relationships, such as the family, the corporation, or business networks. E.g.:

- "This is the defining belief of '*Legal Centralism*,' the almost-universally accepted dogma of legal professionals." David Luban, *Difference Made Legal: The Court and Dr. King*, 87 Mich. L. Rev. 2152, 2184 n.100 (1989).
- "Recently, legal scholars have begun to challenge the fundamental assumption of '*legal centrism*' [read '*legal centralism*'], which emphasizes the importance of the promulgated law as a behavior-guiding force in society." Lynn A. Baker, *Promulgating the Marriage Contract*, 23 U. Mich. J.L. Reform 217, 220 n.20 (1990).

As for the variant form *legocentrism*, see **lego-.**

LEGALDEGOOK = legal gobbledygook; the worst manifestations of LEGALESE. For several years in the early 1990s, the Plain-Language Committee of the State Bar of Texas bestowed its "Legaldegook Awards" to bring attention to what it calls "delightfully atrocious" examples of legal writing. See, e.g., Bryan A. Garner, *The 1993 Legaldegook Awards*, 4 Scribes J. Legal Writing 107 (1993).

The adjective *legaldegooky* originated in the writings of Fred Rodell, who, in his famous essay, wrote: "Else why—once they have won their full professorships, at any rate—do they keep submitting that turgid, *legaldegooky* garbage to law reviews—for free?" *Goodbye to Law Reviews—Revisited*, 48 Va. L. Rev. 279, 288 (1962). See GOBBLEDYGOOK.

legal drafting. See LEGISLATIVE DRAFTING.

legal eagle; legal beagle. Linguists call phrases like these "reduplicative"—other more or less common ones being *fuddy-duddy, hoity-toity, namby-pamby, nolens volens,* and *wishy-washy.* Both *legal beagle* and *legal eagle* are journalists' favorites, and they both seem to be used sometimes with positive connotations, sometimes neutrally, and sometimes with negative connotations. If there is a difference, *legal beagle* seems more frequently to convey the idea (vaguely) of lawyer-as-lapdog—e.g.: "Fuller, meanwhile, has come off to many as the stereotypical high-paid *legal beagle* defending a rich celebrity." Jon Saraceno, *Attorneys Present Dueling Images*, USA Today, 4 Feb. 1992, at 2C.

Legal eagle, an Americanism that is more than twice as common as *legal beagle* in journalistic AmE, provides writers with a little trick for "enlivening" their prose by avoiding the word *lawyer*—e.g.: "Hillary Clinton, feminist, children's rights activist, *legal eagle* and betrayed wife, has won The Family Circle chocolate chip cookie recipe contest." Sandra Gotlieb, *Hillary Bakes Up a Winning Image*, Financial Post, 16 Oct. 1992, at 9. See LAWYERS, DEROGATORY NAMES FOR (A).

LEGALESE. Ironically, many dictionaries label *legalese* a "colloquialism." It denotes what is perhaps the least colloquial of all forms of English writing: the complicated language of legal documents. The *OED* traces *legalese*—the word, not the thing—back to the second decade of the 20th century, with this example: "He signed his name at the foot of a bald formal agreement, written in the most incomprehensible *legalese*." C.J.C. Hyne, *Firemen Hot* 189 (1914).

Though the name for it is fairly new, legalese itself has, throughout the history of Anglo-American law, been a scourge of the profession. Thomas Jefferson railed against statutes "which, from their verbosity, their endless tautologies, their involutions of case within case, and parenthesis within parenthesis, and their multiplied efforts at certainty, by *saids* and *aforesaids*, by *ors* and *ands*, to make them more plain, are really rendered more perplexed and incomprehensible, not only to common readers, but to the lawyers themselves." 1 *The Writings of Thomas Jefferson* 65 (Lipscomb ed., 1903).

The same is true, of course, of all types of legal writing, not just statutes or even just drafting. For a humorous epitome of legalese, the following 19th-century example, describing a collision, is without equal:

> The declaration stated, that the plaintiff theretofore, and at the time of the committing of the grievance thereinafter mentioned, to wit, on, etc., was lawfully possessed of a certain donkey, which said donkey of the plaintiff was then lawfully in a certain highway, and the defendant was then possessed of a certain waggon and certain horses drawing the same, which said waggon and horses of the defendant were then under the care, government, and direction of a certain then servant of the defendant, in and along the said highway; nevertheless the defendant, by his said servant, so carelessly, negligently, unskilfully, and improperly governed and directed his said waggon and horses, that by and through the carelessness, negligence, unskilfulness, and improper conduct of the defendant, by his said servant, the said waggon and horses of the defendant then ran and struck with great violence against the said donkey of the plaintiff, and thereby then wounded, crushed, and killed the same, etc.
>
> *Davies v. Mann*, (1842) 10 M. & W. 546,
> 152 Eng. Rep. 588.

Even in the 20th century, collisions have sounded much the same in legalese—e.g.: "On information and belief, Defendants Newton and Kautz, immediately prior to operating their vehicles on the aforesaid Route 315, had attended a party sponsored by defendant Roach Incorporated on Powell Road in Powell, Ohio; said Defendants left the party at approximately the same time; said Defendants Newton and Kautz were racing their automobiles pursuant to an agreement reached at said party shortly prior to the aforesaid collision." Pleading quoted in *Baird v. Roach, Inc.*, 462 N.E.2d 1229, 1231 (Ohio Ct. App. 1983).

Legalese is often highly compressed—e.g.: "A judgment entered without proper service of the summons is void and subject to attack directly or collaterally." *Hoke v. Motel 6 Jackson*, 131 P.3d 369, 374 (Wyo. 2006). And it flaunts legal ceremony, which arguably has a place in some documents: "In witness, whereof, I have hereunto subscribed my name and affixed my seal the eighteenth of March, in the year of Our Lord, one thousand nine hundred and fifty-five." *Estate of McMillan v. I.R.S.*, 76 T.C. 170, 171 (Tax Ct. 1981) (quoting a will).

We have enough examples, however, of what not to do. The nauseous effect of the passage from *Davies v. Mann*, and other passages throughout this work, should purge readers of any attraction to legalese. See **nauseous**, DOUBLETS, TRIPLETS, AND SYNONYM-STRINGS, LEGALISMS AND LAWYERISMS & PLAIN LANGUAGE.

legal fictions. See FICTIONS.

legal form. See **precedent (E).**

legal fraternity is a traditional phrase that, unfortunately, carries strong associations of maleness—and is therefore unlikely to survive the spreading intolerance toward sexist language. Nonsexist substitutes include *legal community*, *the bar* (in AmE), *bench and bar*, *the legal world*, and the like. On the unflattering side, Fred Rodell referred to the *legal tribe*: "Those amendments begin to look more important than the whole original Constitution; and to any of the *legal tribe*, they are." Fred Rodell, *Woe Unto You, Lawyers!* 56 (1939). See SEXISM.

legal fraud. See **constructive fraud** & **fraud (C).**

legalism; legality. *Legality* = strict adherence to law, prescription, or doctrine; the quality of being legal—e.g.: "A genuine dispute exists as to the *legality* of any ownership claim made by the codepositors." *Legalism* = (1) formalism carried almost to the point of meaninglessness; a disposition to exalt the importance of law or formulated rule in any department of action; or (2) a mode of expression characteristic of lawyers. See **legalist** & **legalistic.** See also *****legalness.**

LEGALISMS AND LAWYERISMS are the circumlocutions, FORMAL WORDS, and ARCHAISMS that characterize lawyers' speech and writing, esp. in drafting. Little can be said by way of advice except that generally lawyers and legislators should try hard to avoid them.

Legalistic	Ordinary
abutting	next to
adequate number of	enough
adjacent to	next to
anterior to	before

Legalistic	*Ordinary*
at the time	when
be able to	can
be authorized	may
be binding upon	bind
be empowered to	may
be unable to	cannot
by means of	by
cause to be done	effect (vb.) *or* have (a thing) done
contiguous to	next to
during such time as	while, during
enter into a contract with	contract with
enter into an agreement with	agree with, contract with
excessive number of	too many
for the duration of	while, during
for the reason that	because
in case	if
in order to	to
in the event that	if
in the interest of	for
it is directed	must
it is the duty	must
it shall be lawful	may
it shall be legal	may
it shall be the duty of	must
it shall not be lawful to	may not, must not
on or about	on, about
or in the alternative	or
per annum	a year, annual
per diem	a day
period of time	period, time
point in time	point, time
*previous to	before
prior to	before
prosecute (a business)	carry on
*pursuant to	under, in accordance with
subsequent to	after
sufficient number of	enough
the reason being that	because
under the provisions of	under
until such time as	until

See LATINISMS & PLAIN LANGUAGE.

legalist = one who adheres to legalistic thinking. E.g.: "Some *legalists* suggest the literal translation of this statute to mean marital assets may be sold only upon entry of a judgment of divorce." *Glatthorn v. Wisniewski*, 566 A.2d 242, 244 (N.J. Super. Ct. Ch. Div. 1989).

legalistic is a rather contemptuous term meaning "formalistic; exalting the importance of formulated rules in any department of action"—e.g.: "In the course of time the inevitable happened, and *legalistic* elaboration of this form of action pursued its stultifying course, so that a mass of complex law grew up around the writ." A.W.B. Simpson, *An Introduction to the History of the Land Law* 29 (1961).

The word has taken on such negative connotations that it has been perverted by at least one writer to mean "without any imaginable legal support"—e.g.: "The Trout of the title is a psychopathic storekeeper who guns down a twelve-year-old girl on the strictly *legalistic* grounds that her foster-brother owes him instalments on a car loan." John Sutherland, *Tangling with the Mob*, TLS, 21 Feb. 1992, at 32. See **legalism**.

legalitarian, adj.; **legalitarianism**, n. The *SOED* records *legalitarianism* as having two senses: (1) "advocacy of conformity with the law"; and (2) "legal egalitarianism." Only sense 2—in which the term is a PORTMANTEAU WORD combining *legal* and *egalitarianism*—is really sensible. E.g.: "Such a result may be acceptable to a *legalitarian*." *Travelers Indem. Co. v. Peacock Constr. Co.*, 423 F.2d 1153, 1160 (5th Cir. 1970) (per Brown, C.J.).

legalize = (1) to make legal; to justify by legal sanction; to authorize; (2) to imbue with the spirit of the law, often making (a thing) legalistic; or (3) to practice as a lawyer. Sense 1 is the common one—e.g.: "[Lithuania's] parliament voted overwhelmingly today to *legalize* rival political parties." Esther B. Fein, *Lithuania Legalizes Rival Parties, Removing Communists' Monopoly*, N.Y. Times, 8 Dec. 1989, at 1.

Sense 2, not so common, still appears—e.g.: "But it is difficult or perhaps impossible for him to avoid a certain distortion of the way in which *legalized* conceptions and legal institutions operate to distribute power in society." A.W.B. Simpson, *Trouble with the Case*, TLS, 14–20 Dec. 1990, at 1344.

Sense 3 is a nonce use illustrated by a single quotation in the *OED*: "Jobson still *legalizes* in Gray's Inn." John R. Leifchild, *Cornwall: Its Mines and Miners* 244 (1855).

legally sometimes functions as a SENTENCE ADVERB in the sense "from a legal point of view." E.g.:

- "*Legally* he knows that of which he has notice." William F. Walsh, *A Treatise on Equity* 509 (1930).
- "*Legally*, however, it seems impossible to differentiate between the sexes, except possibly by confining the theory of maim to the fighting sex." Glanville Williams, *The Sanctity of Life and the Criminal Law* 107 (1957).
- "*Legally*, she contends the trial court erred in focusing only on where as opposed to why she relocated." *McLain v. McLain*, 974 So.2d 726, 735 (La. Ct. App. 2007).

LEGAL MAXIMS. See MAXIMS.

legal memory. See **memory of man runneth not to the contrary** & **time immemorial**.

***legalness** is a NEEDLESS VARIANT of *legality*.

legal portion. See **legitime**.

legal positivism. See **positivism**.

legal rate. See **interest, legal rate of**.

legal science. "The terms *legal science* and *jurisprudence*," writes David M. Walker, "are themselves . . . of very indefinite connotation. The main meanings are probably: all knowledge of and about law; the knowledge of the more theoretical problems of law, as contrasted with knowledge of principles in force; and the systematic analysis and exposition of knowledge of and about law." David M. Walker, *The Scottish Jurists* 6 n.1 (1985).

The term *legal science* is rarely encountered in contemporary writing, perhaps because lawyers know that they are not scientists—perhaps not even to the extent that social scientists might be called "scientists." There are "hard sciences" such as chemistry, physics, biology, and there are "soft sciences" such as sociology, psychology, and political science. Law is a soft science at best; the better view, though, is that it has little enough in common with any science as to make it illegitimate to call it a "science."

legal separation. See **separation**.

legalspeak is another term for *legalese*, with connotations perhaps even more negative. It is formed from the fairly new suffix *-speak*, which came into vogue after George Orwell coined *Newspeak* and *Oldspeak* in his apocalyptic book *1984* (1949). Like its forerunners, *legalspeak* vaguely suggests a conspiracy. E.g.:

* "To use the appropriate *legalspeak*, there was no 'privity'— no direct contact between Becker and Klein." Geoffrey Smith, *Revenge of the Nerds*, Forbes, 22 Oct. 1984, at 102.
* "In China, *legalspeak* makes an unflattering distinction between barristers and lawyers by terming barristers 'big lawyers' and solicitors simply 'lawyers.'" *Point of Order*, Daily Telegraph, 8 Sept. 1990, at 15.
* "Missing from this treatise is the *legalspeak* and stilted language that is characteristic of so many other legal treatises." John J. DiGilio, *Legal Reference Books of 1998*, 91 Law Lib. J. 441, 450 (1999) (reviewing Ralph E. Lerner & Judith Bressler, *Art Law* (1998)).

See LEGALESE & **legaldegook**.

legal subrogation. See **subrogation (B)**.

legal tender = (1) the money—bills or coins— approved by a state; or (2) a tender (of something) that is legally sufficient.

legal title. See **title**.

LEGAL-WRITING STYLE. A sound legal style is not so very different from a sound style in any other realm of writing—except perhaps that it is rarer. As legal writers, we begin with several disadvantages:

* We continually resort to lawbooks that overflow with writing contaminated by stylistic infections— but few readers effectively inoculate themselves.
* Built as it is on precedent, Anglo-American law discourages lawyers from writing differently from their predecessors.
* Our law schools generally shunt legal writing off to the periphery of the curriculum, thereby signaling

in effect that attainments in writing are of minimal importance.

* The modern practice of law does not tolerate the type of revisory process necessary to produce a polished product—the "well-managed" law firm has more work to do than it can complete in a given span of time.
* As a whole, the profession disdains literary accomplishment within law—it believes in a sharp (and illusory) split between style and substance.
* Even those lawyers who care about writing style are often inured to—and therefore help perpetuate— the worst conventions of legal writing.

How often do legal writers overcome these obstacles? Not often.

Why? Perhaps because mistaken notions of "style" mislead so many talented lawyers. They imitate law reviews. (See LAW REVIEWESE.) For continuing-legal-education programs, they try to write "scholarly" papers jam-packed with discursive footnotes. In client letters, they try to sound "professional" but instead come across as pompous. They learn LEGALESE and forget idiomatic English. They become habituated to their *prior to*s, their **pursuant to*s, their *hereinafter*s, their *incident thereto*s, and all their other ballyhoos— and they forget what it is to speak or write directly and simply. They try to be showy instead of being lucid and brief.

Few have written as lucidly and briefly about stylistic excellence in law as Walker Gibson, who delineated the literary contours of legal prose:

> There is no reason why almost any piece of legal writing—and certainly judicial writing—may not move us with its sensitive and wise and gracious handling of language. It is true that the legal writer operates within limiting situations, and he must attend painstakingly to the minutiae of facts that confront him. Yet it is also true that he is engaged in expressing in words the chaos of life, and no poet can say more. Judicial opinions and poetry are obviously not identical forms of expression; yet, in Frost's memorable phrase about poets, the legal writer too is attempting "a momentary stay against confusion." It is hard to think of a finer thing for a man to do.
>
>   A curious humility, or an equally curious arrogance, is apparent in the attitude that legal writers sometimes express toward their performances in language. One hears a lawyer or a judge remark, "Oh, I'm no stylist—I just write down the facts in plain words." This is both humble and arrogant—humble in surrendering elegance to the "creative artists," arrogant in suggesting that only "the facts" really matter. But the situation is surely quite otherwise. The poet or novelist, the historian, the physicist, the appellate judge are all deeply involved in one essential responsibility: the expression of life's complexities in mere man-made words. Wherever he starts, whatever trivial item of human experience he initially confronts, the legal writer can make his stab at eloquence. If Holmes was right, that "a man may live greatly in the law as well as elsewhere," then the consequence is that he must *write*

greatly, for in law as well as in literature there is no other meaning of greatness.
> Walker Gibson, *Literary Minds and Judicial Style*,
> 36 N.Y.U. L. Rev. 915, 930 (1961).

If you care to be a first-rate legal writer, you'll need to read a good deal of superb legal writing—and read attentively. You'll also need to read *about* legal style. Among the works that merit your close study are those listed in the Select Bibliography (pp. 961–62).

*legatary, n. See **legatee.**

legate, n. See **ambassador.**

legate, vb.; **legacy,** vb. Both may mean "to give or leave as a legacy; to bequeath a legacy to." *Legacy* is an ARCHAISM in this verbal sense, and *legate* is rather rare. *Bequeath* is the usual word. See **bequeath.**

legatee; *legatary. *Legatee* = one who is named in a will to take personal property; one who has received a legacy or bequest. In strict common-law terminology, a distinction was drawn between a *legatee* and a *devisee*, the former receiving personal property and the latter real property—e.g.: "A devise or legacy [to a child] shall not lapse [by death], but the property so devised or bequeathed shall vest in the surviving child or other descendant of the *legatee* or devisee, as if such *legatee* or devisee had survived the testator and had died intestate." *In re Maynard's Will*, 307 N.Y.S.2d 503, 503 (Sur. Ct. 1970). But *legatee* is often loosely used for one to whom a devise is given. See **devisee.**

*Legatary, n., is a NEEDLESS VARIANT.

legation. See **embassy.**

*legator, a NEEDLESS VARIANT of *testator*, is used infrequently. It may occasionally mean "one who bequeaths a legacy," as opposed to one who devises real property—but some readers will likely be puzzled. See **devise** & **bequeath.**

legible. See **illegible.**

legislate = (1) [intransitive] to make laws; (2) [transitive] to bring (something) into or out of existence by making laws; to (attempt to) bring about or control by legislation. Sense 1 is the more common one—e.g.: "Montana is free to *legislate* with respect to the liability incurred." *Miller v. Fallon County*, 721 P.2d 342, 347 (Mont. 1986). Sense 2, though, is common enough to be a part of the general language—e.g.: "The critics contend the court far exceeded its authority to interpret the law and instead used *Roe* to *legislate* social policy from the bench." *The Battle over Abortion*, Newsweek, 1 May 1989, at 29.

A BACK-FORMATION from *legislation*, the verb *to legislate* was rarely used before the 19th century. Before that time, laws were said to be not *legislated*, but *enacted* or *ordained*.

legislation = (1) the action of making or giving a positive law in written form, according to some type of formal procedure, by a branch of government constituted to perform this action <legislation is an arduous process>; or (2) what a legislature has enacted; the whole body of enacted laws <the legislation threatens the university's independence>. For a REDUNDANCY involving this term, see **statutory legislation.**

legislative; legislatorial; *legislational. The first corresponds to *legislation*, the second (in good usage) to *legislator*. The third is a NEEDLESS VARIANT of *legislative*. E.g.: Arthur Lenhoff, *Extra-Legislational* [read *Extra-Legislative*] *Process of Law*, 28 Neb. L. Rev. 542 (1949). See **legislatorial.**

LEGISLATIVE DRAFTING. Drafting denotes the specific type of legal writing dealing with legislation, instruments, or other legal documents that are to be construed by others. Statutes, rules, regulations, contracts, and wills are examples. The style is considerably different from that of other legal writing, such as judicial opinions and legal commentary. Many of the worst mannerisms of legalese pervade legal drafting, for the myth of precision has traditionally been one of the drafter's tenets.

A 19th-century English practitioner once delineated the style of good drafting this way:

> [It] is free from all colour, from all emotion, from all rhetoric. It is impersonal, as if the voice, not of any man, but of the law, dealing with the necessary facts. It disdains emphasis and all other artifices. It uses no metaphors or figures of speech. It is always consistent and never contradicts itself. It never hesitates or doubts. It says in the plainest language, with the simplest, fewest, and fittest words, precisely what it means. These are qualities [that] might be used to advantage more frequently than is common in literature, and unfortunately they are not to be found in many legal compositions, but they are essential to good legal composition, and are not essential to literary composition.
> J.G. Mackay, *Introduction to an Essay on the Art of Legal Composition Commonly Called Drafting*, 3 Law Q. Rev. 326, 326 (1887).

Perhaps the most sensible approach to the broad principles of drafting statutes is that of Montesquieu, who discussed the subject in *L'Esprit des Lois*. 39 C. Montesquieu, *L'Esprit des Lois*, ch. 16, 614–17 (Thomas Nugent trans., 1752). I've paraphrased his points:

- The style should be both concise and simple: whatever is grandiose or rhetorical should be omitted as distracting surplusage.
- The words chosen should be, as nearly as possible, absolute—not relative—so as to minimize differences of opinion.
- Statutes should be confined to the real and the actual, avoiding the metaphorical or hypothetical.
- They should not be subtle, but instead comprehensible to the average person.
- They should not confuse the main issue with exceptions, limitations, and modifications, unless such devices are absolutely necessary.
- They should not be argumentative: they should not give detailed reasons for their bases. (This is not to criticize general-purpose clauses, which are quite valuable.)

- They should be maturely considered and practically useful and should not shock the public sense of reason and justice.

Those goals are extraordinarily difficult to attain, and few have succeeded in attaining them. Samuel Williston (1861–1963), the author of many Uniform Acts approved by the Commissioners of Uniform State Laws between 1905 and 1920, was among those few: "Williston was one of the best statutory draftsmen who has ever worked at that mysterious art; he was the most ingenious system-builder in the history of our jurisprudence; he wrote with lucidity and grace." Grant Gilmore, *The Ages of American Law* 134 n.12 (1977).

In fact, complaints about mediocre to horrible statutory drafting have echoed through the decades and centuries—e.g.:

- In 1857, Lord Campbell criticized "an ill-penned enactment, like too many others, putting Judges in the embarrassing situation of being bound to make sense out of nonsense, and to reconcile what is irreconcilable." *Fell v. Burchett*, [1857] 7 E. & B. 537, 539.
- "So unintelligible is the phraseology of some statutes that suggestions have been made that draftsmen, like the Delphic Oracle, sometimes aim deliberately at obscurity, as a disingenuous means of passing a Bill quickly through Parliament." Carleton K. Allen, *Law in the Making* 486 (7th ed. 1964).
- "Parliament has been industrious in multiplying offences, very inartistically drawn, but it is slow to remedy clear absurdities and deficiencies in the law as they come to light." Glanville Williams, *Textbook of Criminal Law* 8 (1978).
- "For over a century and a half, judges have railed against incomprehensible drafting only to be met with the bland reply that the judges are themselves to blame. The existing draftsmen are not only established but entrenched. No other word than pathetic can describe Lord Gardiner's hope in 1971 to 'encourage' them to be simpler." J.A. Clarence Smith, *Legislative Drafting: English and Continental*, 1980 Statute L. Rev. 14, 22.
- "The ultimate style and shape of much legislation is today increasingly unsatisfactory. Many statutes emerge from the parliamentary process obscure, turgid, and quite literally unintelligible without a guide or commentary." P.S. Atiyah, *Law and Modern Society* 127–28 (1983).
- "The Statute Law Society criticized the language of the statutes as: 'legalistic, often obscure and circumlocutious, requiring a certain type of expertise in order to gauge its meaning. Sentences are long and involved, the grammar is obscure, and archaisms, legally meaningless words and phrases, tortuous language, the preference for the double negative over the single positive, abound.'" Michael Zander, *The Law-Making Process* 22 (2d ed. 1985) (quoting the Report of the Renton Committee entitled *Preparation of Legislation*).

Perhaps the current state of affairs results mostly from the fact that "statutory drafting . . . [is] an insufficiently appreciated art." Rupert Cross, *Statutory Interpretation* 12 (1976). That holds as true in the U.S. as it does in Great Britain. Only someone with experience and wisdom recognizes that "there is no more important, exciting, and intellectually rewarding work for a lawyer than that of drafting legislation." Glanville Williams, *Learning the Law* 214 (11th ed. 1982). The accomplished writer who tries legislative drafting will find that it taxes one's literary abilities as much as any other type of writing.

In an important early work on the writing of statutes, George Coode laid down for the first time some important rules of drafting that have formed the basis for modern principles of drafting—and have been routinely ignored in practice. *See* George Coode, *On Legislative Expression* (1842).

The fundamental mode of statutory expression as worked out by Coode is to recite facts concurrent with the statute's operation as if they were present facts, and facts precedent to the statute's operation as if they were past facts.

In elaboration of that deceptively simple statement, what follows is a modernization of Coode's precepts on the use of tenses in statutes, and especially the use of *shall* and *may*. (This adaptation paraphrases Coode as quoted in Elmer A. Driedger's *The Composition of Legislation* 225–28 (1957).)

Coode recognized that much of the trouble in statute-drafting originates in the use of *shall*. Proscriptions that begin "No person *shall* . . ." are inferior to those that begin "No person *may* . . ." because *shall* can be understood in two senses: simple futurity (i.e., *will*) and obligation (i.e., *must*).

The drafter should not attempt to render every action referred to in a statute in a future tense. Some drafters erroneously assume that the words *shall* and *shall not* put the enacting verb into a future tense. Yet in commanding, as in a statute that mandates a certain action, *shall* is modal rather than temporal. Hence it denotes compulsion—the obligation to act—not a prophecy that the person will or will not at some future time perform some act. The commandment "Thou shalt not kill" is not a prediction; it is obligatory in the present tense, continuously through all the time of the law's operation.

Likewise, when the verb *may* is used, the expression is not of a future possibility; instead, it is of permission and authority. The statement "The chair *may canvass* committee members" means that the chair *is authorized to canvass* the committee members.

Yet because the legal action referred to in a statute is sometimes—when *shall* is used—supposed to be in the future tense, drafters often attempt (for the sake of consistency) to express the circumstances that are required to precede the operation of the statute (i.e., all conditions) in the future or future perfect tense. And so in poor drafting language, one frequently finds the following expressions:

- If any person *shall give* [read *gives*] notice, he *may* appeal . . . .
- If the commissioners *shall instruct* [read *instruct*] by an order . . . .

An asterisk (✳) precedes words and phrases that are invariably inferior forms.

- All elections *shall* [read *must*] hereafter, so far as the commissioners *shall direct* [read *direct*] . . . .
- In case any person *shall willfully neglect or disobey* [read *willfully neglects or disobeys*] . . . .
- When such notice *shall have been published* [read *is published*] . . . .
- If any balance *shall have been found* [read *is found*] to be due . . . .

The fear that gives rise to this use of *shall* is that, if the condition for operation of the statute were expressed in the present tense (i.e., when any person is aggrieved), the law would be contemporaneous and would operate *only* on conditions that are met at the moment when the statute is enacted. Likewise, some drafters wrongly assume that if a statute were expressed in the present perfect tense (i.e., when any person has been convicted), the law would be retrospective and would apply *only* to convictions that took place before the act was passed.

These apprehensions are mistaken. An elementary rule of statutory construction is that past tenses never give retrospective effect to a statute unless the intention for retrospectivity is clearly and distinctly framed in words to that effect. Any number of statutes are written in the present or present perfect tense but still are interpreted prospectively only.

If the law is regarded, while it remains in force, as *constantly speaking*, then a simple two-part rule will serve to guide those who draft statutes:

1. Use the *present tense* to express all facts and conditions required to be concurrent with the operation of the legal action—e.g.: "If by reason of the largeness of parishes the inhabitants *cannot* reap the benefits of this Act, two or more overseers *must be chosen*." *Bonan v. Society in Scotland for Propagating Christian Knowledge* (1846) 18 Scot. Jurist 337, 337 (C.S.) (quoting Society's letters-patent). The first clause in this conditional sentence is in the present tense; the main clause that follows contains obligatory language still in the present tense.
2. Use the *present perfect tense* to express all facts and conditions required as precedents to the legal action—e.g.: "When the justices of the peace of any county *assembled* at quarter sessions *have agreed* that the ordinary peace officers *are* not sufficient to preserve the peace, the justices *may* appoint a chief constable." Act for the Establishment of County and District Police Officers 1, 27 Aug. 1839 (in 22 Q. Rev. Juris. at 357 (1839)). The left-branching dependent clauses contain verbs in the past perfect [*assembled, have agreed*] to indicate necessary precedent conditions that now exist [*are*] and thus make legal action possible; the main clause is in the present [permissive] tense to indicate the specific legal action that is open to the justices of the peace.

legislative facts; adjudicative facts. The difference between these phrases is "the cardinal distinction [that], more than any other, governs the use of extra-record facts by courts and agencies." Kenneth C. Davis,

Administrative Law Text § 15.03, at 296 (3d ed. 1972). *Legislative facts*, which are ordinarily general and do not concern the immediate parties, are facts that "help the tribunal to exercise its judgment or discretion in determining what course of action to take"; they come into play "whenever a tribunal engages in the creation of law or of policy." *Id.* They are, for example, the kinds of facts that are used in a Brandeis brief. (See **Brandeis brief.**) *Adjudicative facts* are those found by a court or agency "concerning the immediate parties—who did what, where, when, how, and with what motive or intent." *Id.* In finding adjudicative facts, then, the court or agency performs an adjudicative function.

legislative history; enacting history. The first is the AmE term, and the second BrE, for denoting the background and events leading to the enactment of a statute, including hearings, committee reports, and floor debates.

legislative-intent theory. See INTERPRETATION, MODES OF (A).

legislative veto (AmE) = a practice that, originating in the 1930s and valid until held unconstitutional in 1983, allowed Congress to block a federal executive or agency action within a specified time (usu. 60 or 90 working days) without presidential approval—e.g.: "Short, dark-haired, and tending *toward* stockiness, this pipe-puffing, feisty constitutional expert [Antonin Scalia] had no doubts in his mind about the *legislative veto*'s unconstitutionality, and no hesitancy in speaking his mind to anyone who would listen." Barbara H. Craig, Chadha: *The Story of an Epic Constitutional Struggle* 53 (1988) (which tells the story behind *INS v. Chadha*, 462 U.S. 919 (1983), the case holding the legislative veto unconstitutional).

legislatorial = (1) of or pertaining to a legislator; or (2) of or pertaining to legislation. In sense 2, the word is a NEEDLESS VARIANT of *legislative*. In sense 1, however, the term is useful—e.g.: "An examination of the act impresses that there was *legislatorial* doubt in its enactment." *Hume-Sinclair Coal Mining Co. v. Nee*, 12 F.Supp. 801, 805 (W.D. Mo. 1935). See **legislative.**

legisprudence (= the systematic analysis of statutes as a part of jurisprudence) was coined in 1950 by Julius Cohen in his article *Towards Realism in Legisprudence*, 59 Yale L.J. 886 (1950).

legist = one learned or skilled in the law; a lawyer; a jurist. This word is underused—appearing in only a few modern cases. E.g.:

- "No *legist* meriting deference has noticeably recorded the opinion that a witness could be adjudged in contempt of court for the failure to comply with the terms of a mere summons in such circumstances." *In re Roberts*, 30 A.2d 900, 902 (N.J. Ch. 1943).
- "Certain 'proceedings' were had out of the hearing of the jury panel, in the course of which the Cooperative's *legists* reverted . . . to the above-quoted statement by opposing

counsel." *M & A Elec. Power Coop. v. True*, 480 S.W.2d 310, 313 (Mo. Ct. App. 1972).

legitim. See **legitime.**

legitimacy; legitimation; *legitimization; *legitimatization. *Legitimacy* = the fact of being legitimate. *Legitimation* is the best word for both senses: (1) "the action or process of rendering or authoritatively declaring (a person) legitimate" (*OED*); and (2) "the action of making lawful; authorization" (*id.*)—e.g.: "The initial intrusion may, of course, be *legitimated* not by a warrant but by one of the exceptions to the warrant requirement." *Coolidge v. New Hampshire*, 403 U.S. 443, 471 (1971) (per Stewart, J.). **Legitimization* and **legitimatization* are NEEDLESS VARIANTS.

legitimate, vb. See **legitimize.**

legitimation; *legitimization. See **legitimacy.**

*legitimatize. See **legitimize.**

legitime; legitim. This civil-law term, meaning "the part of a decedent's estate to which his or her issue is entitled as a legal right," is usually spelled *legitime* in Louisiana and *legitim* in Scotland—e.g.:

- "There is no case for imputation of advances where only one of several children claims *legitim*." 4 David M. Walker, *Principles of Scottish Private Law* 127 (3d ed. 1983).
- "A testator may not by testamentary dispositions infringe on the *legitime* of his forced heirs." A.N. Yiannopoulos, *Of Legal Usufruct, the Surviving Spouse, and Article 890 of the Louisiana Civil Code*, 49 La. L. Rev. 803, 803 (1989).

Other terms for *legitime* are *legal portion* and *forced portion*.

legitimize; legitimate, vb.; ***legitimatize.** The first predominates and is now preferred in all senses. It is by far the most common of the three forms. E.g.:

- "Procedural guarantees are hollow unless linked to substantive interests; and no amount of process can *legitimize* some deprivations." *McDonald v. City of Chicago*, 130 S.Ct. 3020, 3090 (2010) (Stevens, J., dissenting).
- "It is not difficult to conclude as Congress did that the 'tain[t]' of such violent activities is so great that working in coordination with or at the command of the PKK and LTTE serves to *legitimize* and further their terrorist means." *Holder v. Humanitarian Law Project*, 130 S.Ct. 2705, 2725 (2010) (per Roberts, C.J.).

Legitimate was previously the preferred verb, and it appears in ancient as well as modern sources—e.g.:

- "This end is undoubtedly better answered by *legitimating* all issue born after wedlock, than by *legitimating* issue of the same parties, even born before wedlock, so as wedlock afterwards ensues." 1 William Blackstone, *Commentaries on the Laws of England* 443 (1765).
- "The courts, increasingly stocked with allies of the president, eventually followed popular opinion, *legitimating* the new constitutional constructions in a series of landmark decisions." Jack M. Balkin, *Commerce*, 109 Mich. L. Rev. 1, 4 (2010).

*Legitimatize is a NEEDLESS VARIANT. See -IZE.

LEGO-, as a prefix meaning "legal," has no etymological warrant. It occurs most frequently (and perhaps occurred originally) in *legocentrism*—a word coined on the analogy of *ethnocentrism*. The following quotation makes its sense apparent: "Lawyers and judges tend to develop a form of tunnel vision which causes them to view the litigation process as if it were the most vital part of our society. We must avoid such '*legocentrism*.'" Gregory Gelfand, *"Taking" Informational Property Through Discovery*, 66 Wash. U. L.Q. 703, 727 (1988). The corresponding adjective, also a NEOLOGISM, is *legocentric*—e.g.: "Gold has a 'legocentric' view of people." J. Alexander Tanford & Sarah Tanford, *Better Trials Through Science*, 66 N.C. L. Rev. 741, 746 (1988). See **legal centralism.**

leguleian. See LAWYERS, DEROGATORY NAMES FOR (A).

lemon law. The word *lemon*, in the sense "something bad or undesirable," originated as an Americanism in the early 20th century. In AmE, the word has increasingly been specialized to refer to cars with persistent problems. Hence, a *lemon law* is a statute designed to protect consumers who buy substandard cars—e.g.: "We noted that under the *Lemon Law* a claimant was required to return the car." *Samuel-Bassett v. Kia Motors Am., Inc.*, 357 F.3d 392, 400 (3d Cir. 2004). Every U.S. state has a lemon law in effect.

BrE was quick to adopt *lemon* but has not narrowed the term, as AmE has. So *lemon law* has a broader sense, referring to faulty consumer goods of any kind—e.g.: "The attempt by Mr Martyn Jones, Labour MP for Clwyd South-West, to introduce a '*lemon law*' to protect consumers buying faulty items has all-party support at Westminster." Julia Langdon, *Consumers' Minister May Try to Squash Lemon Bill*, Sunday Telegraph, 21 Jan. 1990, at 4.

lend. See **loan.**

lend-lease; *lease-lend. Both phrases refer to either (1) "an arrangement made in 1941, under the Lend-Lease Act, whereby sites in British overseas possessions were leased to the United States as bases in exchange for the loan of U.S. destroyers"; or, by extension, (2) "a cooperative arrangement made between friendly entities." The phrase *lend-lease*, which comes directly from the statute, is more common—so it would not be amiss to label **lease-lend* a NEEDLESS VARIANT.

leniency; *lenience. The first form is preferred. See **clemency.**

lenity. See **clemency.**

leonine contract is another term for *adhesion contract*. In Roman law, a *leonina societas* was a partnership in which one party took all the profits and the other all the losses. Cf. the Spanish term *contrato leonino*.

*lept. See **leap.**

lese majesty; *lèse majesty; *leze majesty; *lèse-majesté; *laesae majestas; laesae majestatis. The preferred form of this originally civil-law term—meaning "a crime against the state, esp. against the ruler," or "an attack on a custom or traditional belief"—is the anglicized *lese majesty*. The variant spellings should be avoided. In BrE, the phrase tends to be hyphenated; in AmE it usually is not.

In spelling the full LATINISM naming the crime, however, the phrase is spelled *crimen laesae majestatis*—e.g.: "Counterfeiting has usually been classified as an offense affecting the administration of governmental functions, which unquestionably it is, having been considered *crimen laesae majestatis* and punished as treason at one time in England." Rollin M. Perkins & Ronald N. Boyce, *Criminal Law* 432 (3d ed. 1982). **Laesae majestas* is a hybrid: half LAW LATIN and half LAW FRENCH.

less. A. And *fewer*. *Less* applies to mass nouns <less tonic water, please> or units of measure <less than six ounces of epoxy>. *Fewer* applies to count nouns <fewer than ten guests arrived> or numbers of things <fewer than six limes are left>.

The only exception in using *fewer* occurs when count nouns are so great as to render the idea of individual increments meaningless—e.g.: "A District Court has concurrent jurisdiction under the Tucker Act over suits for *fewer* [read *less*] than $10,000." Here, because the dollars are taken not individually but collectively as an amount, *less* is appropriate. Hence we say *less discovery* but *fewer depositions*; *less testimony* but *fewer witnesses*; *less documentation* but *fewer documents*; *less argumentation* but *fewer arguments*; *less whispering* but *fewer sidebars*; *less ambiguity* but *fewer ambiguities*; *less of a burden* but *fewer burdens*; *less material* but *fewer items*; *less fattening* but *fewer calories*.

Less is used correctly with units of time—e.g.:

- "More than three but *less* than six years after the completion of the cleanup operations, the United States instituted civil actions to recover its cleanup costs." *U.S. v. P/B STCO 213, ON 527 979*, 756 F.2d 364, 366 (5th Cir. 1985).
- "The Supreme Court denied certiorari, and Milton's execution was scheduled again, for June 25, 1985, *fewer* [read *less*] than two hours from this writing." *Milton v. McCotter*, 765 F.2d 434, 436 (5th Cir. 1985).

In the sentence just quoted, *fewer* is used incorrectly not only with a period of time but also with the number *two*, which is illogical. (One hesitates to fault the style of a judge who works under such exigencies.) But if the units of time are countable as whole rather than fractional units, then *fewer* is called for—e.g.: "The time must be not *less* [read *fewer*] than fourteen nor more than twenty-one days after the receipt of the

warrant." H.C. Richards & John P.H. Soper, *The Law and Practice of Compensation* 143 (n.d. [1898]).

Less for *fewer* is an all-too-frequent error—e.g.:

- "Over the years, membership in the organization decreased until in 1941 there were *less* [read *fewer*] than 100 members; at the time of this action there were approximately 58 members still living." *In re Los Angeles County Pioneer Soc'y*, 257 P.2d 1, 11 (Cal. 1953).
- "What the juvenile court system needs is not more but *less* [read *fewer*] of the trappings of legal procedure and judicial formalism." *In re Winship*, 397 U.S. 358, 376 (1970) (Burger, C.J., dissenting).
- "The principal felt that this particular pupil might create *less* [read *fewer*] problems if he remained in the main school building." *Hatton v. Wicks*, 744 F.2d 501, 504 (5th Cir. 1984).

Less power but *fewer powers*: hence the adjective should be *fewer* here: "The establishment of an 'International Competition Policy Office' within the WTO, albeit with *less* [read *fewer*] powers, has also been proposed." Ernst-Ulrich Petersmann, *International Competition Rules for Governments and for Private Businesses*, 72 Chi.-Kent L. Rev. 545, 573 n.14 (1996). See **fewer.**

B. And *lesser*. *Lesser* is an exact synonym of *less*, but is confined to use as an adjective before a noun and following an article <the lesser crime>, thus performing a function no longer idiomatically possible with *less*. Dating from the 13th century, this formal usage allows *lesser* to act as an antonym of *greater*—e.g.: "The *lesser* punishments are just as fit for the *lesser* crimes as the greater for the greater." Oliver Wendell Holmes Jr., *The Common Law* 46 (1881).

Perhaps because of its decreasing use, *lesser* was, especially in the early and mid-20th century, mistakenly supplanted by *less*, which is awkward when used attributively. E.g.:

- "The effect of the creation of a *less* [read *lesser*] estate is to deprive the owner of the fee simple estate of the right of immediate possession." 1 Herbert T. Tiffany, *The Law of Real Property* § 23, at 31 (Basil Jones ed., 3d ed. 1939).
- "Riot, rout, and unlawful assembly are kindred offenses and greater includes the *less* [read *lesser*]." *Commonwealth v. Duitch*, 67 A.2d 821, 822 (Pa. Super. Ct. 1949) (quoting 54 C.J., *Riot*, at 829).

The opposite offense against idiom also occurs: "Even if commercial speech receives *lesser* [read *less*] protection than political speech, it is still treated as speech." Linda L. Berger, *Of Metaphor, Metonymy, and Corporate Money*, 58 Mercer L. Rev. 949, 950 n.3 (2007). The *OED* states that the construction *lesser than* is obsolete.

Should *lesser* (when properly used) seem stilted, one might use *smaller* or, depending on the context, *lower*. Often *smaller* seems more natural. E.g.:

- "*Lease* is conveyance of lands or tenements, usually in consideration of compensation, made for life, for years, or at will, but for *less* [read *a shorter*] time than lessor has in premises, and creates an estate, and is not a mere contract." *Brenner v. Spiegle*, 157 N.E. 491, 492–93 (Ohio 1927).
- "The primary source of income during the marriage was Lance's oil and gas holdings, with a much *lesser* [read

smaller] amount being derived from Rosemarie's interest in the Alliance oil well." *Ruffel v. Ruffel*, 900 A.2d 1178, 1183 (R.I. 2006).

Less is sometimes used in the sense "of lesser seriousness"—e.g.: "He was convicted of three felonies *less* than capital." *Lesser* is commonly used in the phrase from American criminal law, *lesser included offense*: "We also have serious doubts as to whether the offense to which Garrett pleaded guilty in Washington was a '*lesser included offense*' within the [continuing-criminal-enterprise] charge." *Garrett v. U.S.*, 471 U.S. 773, 790 (1985) (per Rehnquist, J.).

lesseeship = the condition or position of a lessee (tenant). E.g.:

- "There must be an ownership or a *lesseeship* in mail stages." *Great Lakes Stages, Inc. v. Laing*, 174 N.E. 784, 786 (Ohio Ct. App. 1930).
- "The defendants argue in the alternative to their theory of *co-lesseeship* that they may assert a violation of their Fourth Amendment rights." *U.S. v. Potter*, 419 F.Supp. 1151, 1154 (N.D. Ill. 1976).

lesser. See **fewer (B)** & **less (B)**.

lesser included offense = a less serious crime than the one charged, but one that an accused necessarily committed in carrying out the more serious crime—e.g.: "Joyriding is a *lesser-included offense* of theft of a motor vehicle." Rollin M. Perkins & Ronald N. Boyce, *Criminal Law* 334 n.97 (3d ed. 1982). As in the preceding quotation, the phrase is often rendered *lesser-included offense*, but it is best not hyphenated because it is not, strictly speaking, a PHRASAL ADJECTIVE.

lessor; lessee. *Landlord* and *tenant* are simpler equivalents that are more comprehensible to most nonlawyers. And they do not run the risk of typographical errors reversing the suffixes.

lest is best followed by a SUBJUNCTIVE. E.g.:

- "[An insanity plea] should be examined with great care *lest* an ingenious counterfeit of the malady *furnish* protection to guilt." *People v. Lawson*, 174 P. 885, 889 (Cal. 1918).
- "Strict scrutiny of the classification which a State makes in a sterilization law is essential, *lest* unwittingly, or otherwise, invidious discriminations *are* [read *be*] made against groups or types of individuals in violation of the constitutional guaranty of just and equal laws." *Skinner v. Oklahoma*, 316 U.S. 535, 541 (1942) (per Douglas, J.).

let (= hindrance or obstacle) is used in the legal doublet *without let or hindrance*. This meaning of *let* is archaic except in law, poetry, and tennis (*let ball* = net ball). The word differs in origin from the verb *let* (= to permit, allow, rent), though both terms appeared in Old English. See DOUBLETS, TRIPLETS, AND SYNONYM-STRINGS.

Nonlawyers have sometimes misunderstood the meaning of *let* in the phrase *without let or hindrance*, as if *let* were an antonym rather than a synonym of

hindrance; e.g., Theodore Dreiser wrote of something descending on somebody "without his let or hindrance," confusing the lay with the legal meaning of *let*.

let, vb. See **lease**.

lethal (= deadly, mortal) is generally used of poisons and medicines in nonlegal usage, but in legal usage still appears in the older sense relating to weapons and wounds as well: "In New York state, the standard for the *lethal* use of force in self-defense has a subjective component in addition to an objective/reasonableness component." Matthew C. Waxman, *The Use of Force Against States That Might Have Weapons of Mass Destruction*, 31 Mich. J. Int'l L. 1, 59 n.270 (2009). Unlike *fatal*, which can be both literal and figurative, *lethal* is ordinarily confined to literal senses. See **fatal**.

letter de cachet. See *lettre de cachet*.

letter of attorney. See **power of attorney**.

letter of the law; *litera legis*. Both denote the strictly literal meaning of the law, rather than the meaning that can be derived from a fair reading of it. Today there is little need for the LATINISM. The phrase *letter of the law* is traditionally opposed to *spirit of the law*—e.g.: "Equity was based upon the idea of natural justice, as opposed to the strict *letter of the law*." 1 Ernest W. Chance, *Principles of Mercantile Law* 2 (Percy W. French ed., 13th ed. 1950). See **spirit**.

letters of credence = the papers appointing a foreign diplomatic agent, who presents them to the head of government to which he or she is accredited—e.g.: "The United States Government is prepared to proceed with the issuance of appropriate *letters of credence* accrediting the United States Ambassador in Belgrade to the new Yugoslav regime." *Artukovic v. Boyle*, 107 F.Supp. 11, 34 n.5 (S.D. Cal. 1952) (quoting an official letter).

letters of marque = licenses to engage in reprisal against citizens or vessels of another nation. E.g.:

- "Formerly it was not uncommon for a state to issue '*letters of marque*' to one of its own subjects, who had met with a denial of justice in another state, authorizing him to redress the wrong for himself by forcible action, such as the seizure of the property of subjects of the delinquent state." J.L. Brierly, *The Law of Nations* 321 (5th ed. 1955).
- "Private maritime wars were legalized by *letters of marque*, allowing a merchant whose ship had been plundered to become a *privateer* and take revenge and compensation from other ships of the offender's nation." Alan Harding, *A Social History of English Law* 306 (1966).

The wordy phrase *letters of marque and reprisal* is traditional and appears, for example, in the U.S. Constitution; nevertheless, it should be avoided.

letters of request. See **letters rogatory**.

---

letters patent. Historically, this phrase, plural in form but singular in sense, denoted an open letter, under governmental seal, granting some right or privilege—e.g.: "In the middle ages all local government was carried on by authority of the king's writs of commission (*letters-patent*)." Alan Harding, *A Social History of English Law* 72 (1966). The phrase was used in opposition to *letters secret* (= governmental documents closed and sealed, and hence not available for general perusal).

In modern law, the phrase *letters patent* has taken on a specialized sense, referring to a governmental grant of the exclusive right to use an invention or design. See **patent.**

letters rogatory; letter(s) of request. Both terms are used in the sense "a request issued to a foreign court requesting a judge to take evidence from a specific person within that court's jurisdiction." *Letters rogatory* has traditionally been the usual term, but it is slowly disappearing: in 1993, the Federal Rules of Civil Procedure were amended to replace the phrase with *letter of request.* Either *letter of request* or *rogatory letter* is used in G.B. Americans use the plural *letters* for the single request, whereas the British use the singular *letter.*

Historically, *letters of request* had a completely different meaning: "a documentary request sent by the judge of one ecclesiastical court to another, esp. to desire that a case may be withdrawn from his own jurisdiction to that of a superior court" (*OED*).

letters secret. See **letters patent.**

letters testamentary = the instrument by which a probate court approves the appointment of an executor under a will and authorizes that executor to administer the estate. In this phrase, *testamentary* acts as a POSTPOSITIVE ADJECTIVE.

lettre de cachet; letter de cachet. The partial anglicization (*-er*) serves no purpose; for this French borrowing, *lettre de cachet* is the preferred spelling. The phrase denotes a warrant issued for the imprisonment of a person without trial. E.g.:

- "The main thrust [of the Fourth Amendment] was directed at the invasion of privacy through general warrants of assistance and *lettres de cachet.*" *Ford v. U.S.*, 352 F.2d 927, 932 (D.C. Cir. 1965).
- "The tendency of Fourth Amendment orthodoxy to focus on citizen autonomy can undoubtedly be attributed to the Framers' fear of arbitrary and unrestrained state incursions on individuals' liberty and property interests. This fear was rooted in early experiences with England's infamous general warrants and writs of assistance and France's *lettres de cachet,* all of which permitted assertions of police power that were unaccountable to magistrate or judge." *Developments in the Law—Race and the Criminal Process,* 101 Harv. L. Rev. 1472, 1500 n.26 (1988).

levee. See **levy.**

leverage, vb. = (1) to provide (a borrower or investor) with credit or funds to improve the ability to speculate and to achieve a high rate of return; or (2) to supplement (available capital) with credit or outside funds. This verb is a mid-20th-century Americanism <a leveraged portfolio is one with a high amount of debt>. The term has definite meaning, but nevertheless may be characterized as a term used primarily by financial jargonmongers. See JARGON (B).

leviable = (1) that may be levied <leviable tax>; or (2) that may be levied upon; capable of being seized in execution <the sheriff found no leviable assets>. Sense 2 is an AmE legalism.

levy; levee. *Levy* is usually a verb meaning (1) "to impose (as a fine or a tax) by legal sanction" <the court levied a fine of $500>; (2) "to conscript for service in the military" <the troops were soon levied>; (3) "to wage (a war)" <the rebels then levied war against the government>; or (4) to take or seize (property) in execution of a judgment—usually with the preposition *on* <the judgment creditor may levy on the debtor's assets>.

Levy may act also as a noun, however, in two senses: (1) "the imposition of a fine or tax, or the fine or tax so imposed"; and (2) "the conscription of men for military service, or the troops so conscripted."

Levee, meanwhile, is the noun meaning "a river embankment; dike; pier." In BrE primarily, it also has the sense "a formal reception." Occasionally *levee* is used as a verb, meaning "to provide with a *levee* (dike)."

lex. **A. Senses.** *Lex* = (1) in Roman law, a legislative bill; (2) a collection of uncodified laws within a jurisdiction; (3) a system or body of laws, written or unwritten, that are peculiar to a jurisdiction or to a field of human activity; or (4) positive law, as opposed to natural law. Some scholars argue that senses 1 and 4 are the correct ones—e.g.: "The positive law formulated and fixed by a legislative body is called *lex, loi, Gesetz*; the general unwritten law is called *ius, droit, Recht.*" 1 Joseph H. Beale, *A Treatise on the Conflict of Laws* 23 (1935).

The plural form of *lex* is *leges.*

B. Anglicizing Phrases Beginning with *lex.* The field known as *conflict of laws* was once rife with phrases—and a few maxims—beginning with the word *lex.* Several of them are discussed in the entries that follow; many are unnecessary LATINISMS that some scholars manage to avoid. For example, Ehrenzweig prefers to anglicize the phrases: "Once both the *place-of-contracting* [i.e., *lex loci contractus*] and the *place-of-performance* [i.e., *lex loci solutionis*] rules had been found unsatisfactory, some courts returned to the law expressly or impliedly intended by the parties, as an alternative or even as an exclusive solution." Albert A. Ehrenzweig, *A Treatise on the Conflict of Laws* 462 (1962). More American scholars than British scholars now make the phrases English; more on both sides of the Atlantic ought to try. See **conflict of laws.**

C. A Redundancy: *law of the lex.* To write *the law of the lex . . . .* is redundant and nonsensical—e.g.: "The

Court of Appeals has differed in determining whether the right to bring an action is of a substantive nature requiring the application of *the law of the lex loci* [read *lex loci*] or a remedy requiring the application of the law of the forum." *Reale v. Herco, Inc.*, as reported in the New York L.J., 13 Sept. 1990, at 21.

lex actus; lex loci actus. The phrase, which means "the law of the place where a document is executed," seems to be a NEEDLESS VARIANT of *lex loci contractus* or *lex loci celebrationis*. The phrase is most often written *lex actus* /leks **ak**-təs/—which is merely a shortened LAW LATIN form of the full phrase *lex loci actus* /leks **loh**-sɪ **ak**-təs/. Graveson has it both ways:

- "The strength of this presumption in favour of the *lex actus* was affirmed by the Court of Appeal in *Jacobs v. Crédit Lyonnais*." R.H. Graveson, *Conflict of Laws* 414 (7th ed. 1974).
- "Capacity is governed by the *lex loci actus*." *Id.* at 402.

lex domicilii /leks dah-mə-**sil**-ee-ɪ/ = (1) the law of the country in which a person is domiciled; or (2) the determination of a person's rights by establishing where, in law, he or she is domiciled—e.g.: "It is . . . in all cases the *lex domicilii* which should determine the right of succession." John Anderson Foote, *Private Int'l Jurisprudence* 253 (Coleman Phillipson ed., 4th ed. 1914).

lex fori /leks **fohr**-ɪ/ = the law of the forum. E.g.:

- "The *lex fori* (the law of the court) governs the procedure and remedies to be applied." René A. Wormser, *The Story of the Law* 493 (1962).
- "The requirement of writing is classified as a rule of evidence and must therefore traditionally be governed by the *lex fori* of any proceedings." R.H. Graveson, *Conflict of Laws* 533 (7th ed. 1974).

Lex fori is sometimes Englished *forum law*: "In conflicts cases concerning the validity of contracts, Professor Ehrenzweig would displace the basic rule pointing to *forum law* [i.e., the law of a particular forum] with the *lex validitatis*."

lex loci /leks **loh**-sɪ/ = (1) the law of the place; local law; or (2) the law of the place where a contract was executed (as a shorthand form of *lex loci contractus*). Sense 2 is increasingly conventional but potentially confusing to nonspecialists because any number of phrases—many more than the six listed here—begin with the words *lex loci*. See **lex loci contractus.**

lex loci actus. See **lex actus.**

lex loci celebrationis /leks **loh**-sɪ sel-ə-bray-shee-**oh**-nəs/ = the law of the place where a legal ceremony, such as a marriage or execution of a contract, was performed—e.g.: "Thus parental consent is classified as a formality, not because it is a formality or bears any resemblance to part of the ceremony of marriage, but because the courts have decided that it should be governed by the *lex loci celebrationis*." R.H. Graveson,

Conflict of Laws 251 (7th ed. 1974). See **lex loci contractus.**

lex loci contractus /leks **loh**-sɪ kən-**trak**-təs/ = the law of the place where the contract was executed—often the proper law by which to decide contractual disputes. E.g.:

- "The *lex loci contractus* (the law of the place where the contract was made) governs the interpretation of a contract." René A. Wormser, *The Story of the Law* 493 (1962).
- "The stipulations were valid by the *lex loci contractus*, but invalid by the law of the forum." Herbert F. Goodrich, *Handbook of the Conflict of Laws* § 110, at 215 (Eugene F. Scoles ed., 4th ed. 1964).

Though it is confusing, given the number of phrases that begin with *lex loci*, this phrase is often shortened just to those two words. See **lex loci.**

Literally, the phrase means "the law of the place of the contract"—as opposed to "where the contract was made"—and this literal meaning can give rise to an AMBIGUITY: "The *lex loci contractus* has always been an ambiguous term, which jurists have interpreted either as the *lex loci celebrationis* or *solutionis*, the law of the place where the contract was entered into, or of that where it was to be performed, according to the tendency of their peculiar views." John Anderson Foote, *Private Int'l Jurisprudence* 337 (Coleman Phillipson ed., 4th ed. 1914). In practice, however, modern courts and scholars invariably use the term to refer to the law of the place where the contract is executed, not performed.

lex loci delicti; *lex loci delictus. **A. Latin vs. English Form.** The best Latin form, *lex loci delicti* (= the law of the place where the tort was committed), is shortened from *lex loci delicti commissi*. The form *delicti* is ten times more common than *delictus* in modern American caselaw. E.g.:

- "A number of American states still follow *lex loci delicti* in their most recent decisions, though the number of such states decreases every year." Robert A. Leflar, *American Conflicts Law* § 132, at 267 (1977).
- "The traditional rule of *lex loci delicti* requires the application of the tort law of the jurisdiction where the injury occurred." *International Paper Co. v. Ouellette*, 479 U.S. 481, 502 n.1 (1987) (per Brennan, J.).

But the best Latin form is the second-best form: Ehrenzweig's anglicized phrase, *place-of-wrong rule* or *place-of-wrong law*, seems the most sensible of the available options.

B. Pronunciation. The phrase *lex loci delicti* is pronounced /leks **loh**-sɪ dee-**lik**-tɪ/. See PRONUNCIATION (C).

C. Mistaken Forms. Perhaps the best argument against the Latin is that English-speaking lawyers—and Americans especially—cannot seem to get the Latin right. The form *lex loci delictus, for example, mangles the Latin on the mistaken analogy of *lex loci contractus*—but the noun *delictus* forms its genitive differently from *contractus*: Being a masculine noun of the fourth declension, *contractus* stays the same in the genitive (*contractus*); *delictus*, meanwhile, is a neuter noun of the second declension, forming *delicti* in the genitive. But legal writers occasionally fall into error—e.g.: "We note that Utah also followed the rule of *lex loci delictus* [read *lex loci delicti*] regarding torts." *Mountain Fuel Supply v. Reliance Ins. Co.*, 933 F.2d 882, 888 (10th Cir. 1991).

The phrase is also sometimes mistakenly rendered *lex loci delecti*—e.g.: "At one time Arkansas courts followed the traditional approach of the First Restatement, termed *lex loci delecti* [read *delicti*] (law of the place of injury)." Carmen L. Arick, Note, *Conflict of Laws—Multistate Torts*, 10 UALR L.J. 511, 516 (1987–1988) (repeatedly using the wrong spelling). Cf. **corpus delicti**. See *delecti.

Another occasional mistake is to write *lex loci delictu*—e.g.: "The cases have read in the forum or *lex loci delictu* [read *lex loci delicti*] limitation provisions." *Amdur v. Lizars*, 39 F.R.D. 29, 36 n.12 (D. Md. 1965).

lex loci rei sitae /leks **loh**-sɪ **ree**-ɪ sɪ-dɪ/ = the law of the place where a thing is situated. This phrase is a NEEDLESS VARIANT of *lex situs*. E.g.: "He is before the Court as a party to the suit not warranting any interference as to the foreign real estate, with the *lex loci rei sitæ* [read *lex situs*]." John Anderson Foote, *Private Int'l Jurisprudence* 208 (Coleman Phillipson ed., 4th ed. 1914). See **lex situs.**

lex loci solutionis /leks **loh**-sɪ sə-loo-shee-**oh**-nəs/ = the law of the place where a contract is performed. E.g.:

- "If a contract made in one country is to be wholly or partly performed in another, it is presumed that the parties intended the mode of performance to be governed by the law of the country of performance (*lex loci solutionis*)." 1 Ernest W. Chance, *Principles of Mercantile Law* 87 (Percy W. French ed., 13th ed. 1950).
- "The courts will give effect to the exchange control regulations of the proper law of the contract and of the *lex loci solutionis*." R.H. Graveson, *Conflict of Laws* 179 (7th ed. 1974).

lex mercatoria; lex mercatorum. The first phrase means "the law merchant"—and the phrase *law merchant*, a TERM OF ART, ought to replace it in modern writing. The second phrase means "the law of merchants," which means something slightly different from *law merchant*. Both phrases ought to be anglicized. See **law merchant.**

lex monetae = the law of the country whose money is at issue. E.g.: "In such cases the meaning of units of that currency, *e.g.* pounds or francs, is determined by reference to the law of the country whose money is in question, sometimes called the *lex monetae*." R.H. Graveson, *Conflict of Laws* 433 (7th ed. 1974).

lex naturae. See **natural law.**

lex non scripta. See **jus scriptum.**

lex patriae. See **personal law.**

lex scripta. See **jus scriptum.**

lex situs /leks **sɪ**-dəs/ = the law of the place where property is located. The phrase is modern LAW LATIN, not classical Latin. E.g.:

- "With regard to contracts concerning land it is governed by the proper law of the contract, usually the law of the country in which the land is situated (*lex situs*)." 1 Ernest W. Chance, *Principles of Mercantile Law* 87 (Percy W. French ed., 13th ed. 1950).
- "The essential validity is governed by the proper law of the transaction, subject in the case of immovables to any overriding provision of the *lex situs*." R.H. Graveson, *Conflict of Laws* 356 (7th ed. 1974).

See *lex loci rei sitae.

lex talionis /leks tal-ee-**oh**-nəs/ = the law of retaliation—the retributive theory of punishment—based on the Mosaic principle of "an eye for an eye, a tooth for a tooth." E.g.:

- "We are content to stand upon ground higher than the common urge of outraged reprisal which revives the *lex talionis*, demanding a life for a life." *Musselwhite v. State*, 60 So.2d 807, 811 (Miss. 1952).
- "The '*lex talionis* of Moses' was literally an 'eye for eye, a leg for a leg.'" *Armstrong v. State*, 444 A.2d 1049, 1052 n.8 (Md. Ct. Spec. App. 1982).

lex terrae. See **law of the land.**

leze majesty. See **lese majesty.**

liability. See **disability (A).**

liability without fault. See **strict liability.**

liable, adj. This term may mean "responsible; subject to liability." In this sense, the word is usually confined to civil contexts in AmE, but in BrE it is used in criminal as well as civil contexts—e.g.:

- "She does not become *liable* merely by assisting her husband to escape punishment for a crime which she knows him to have committed." William Geldart, *Introduction to English Law* 49 (D.C.M. Yardley ed., 9th ed. 1984).
- "Provided the defendant possesses the requisite *mens rea* for the crime charged, he can be held *liable* as a principal." *State v. Spates*, 779 N.W.2d 770, 779 (Iowa 2010).

Liable has three syllables, not two, and is thus pronounced differently from *libel*. See **libel.**

For other uses of *liable*, see **apt** & **responsible.**

liable, continue. See **continue liable.**

liaise, vb., is a BACK-FORMATION from *liaison*, meaning "to establish liaison" or "to act as a liaison officer" <diplomats who liaise with Japanese officials>. First used in the 1920s, this word is still stigmatized as being cant or JARGON. It is pronounced /lee-**ayz**/.

liaison is pronounced either /**lee**-ə-zən/ or /lee-**ay**-zən/, the latter being more common in both AmE and BrE. The nontechnical senses of the word are (1) (n.) "an illicit love affair"; (2) (n.) "communication established for the promotion of mutual understanding;

one who establishes such communication"; and (3) (adj.) "acting as an intermediary" <liaison officer>.

The word is commonly misspelled *laison and especially *liason.

libel; slander. *Libel* is written defamation, *slander* oral defamation. In English, the distinction emerged in the 1600s, before which time both words applied to what was either written or spoken. Perhaps the 17th-century legists were following the distinction observed in Roman law between *famosus libellus* (libel) and *injuria verbalis* (slander). As Gowers points out, the modern distinction is not well fixed in lay minds:

> In popular usage [the terms] are synonymous, meaning a deliberate, untrue, derogatory statement, usually about a person, whether made in writing or orally. In legal usage there are important differences. Each is an untrue and defamatory imputation made by one person about another which, if "published" (i.e. communicated to a third person), can be a ground for a civil action in damages. Such an imputation is a *libel* if made in permanent form (writing, pictures, etc.) or by broadcasting. It is a *slander* if made in fugitive form (e.g. by speaking or gestures). A further distinction is that an action for *slander* cannot ordinarily succeed without proof that actual damage has been caused; in an action for *libel* this is unnecessary. In both cases proof that the allegation was true is a good defence.
>
> *MEU2* 333.

Here *libel* is misused for *slander*: "According to the complaint, the *libel* [read *slander*] was uttered in the presence of only one person." (See **defamation.**) *Verbal slander* is a common REDUNDANCY. See **verbal.** For a mistaken variant of *slander*, see *****slanderize.**

Libel has the additional sense in admiralty "the complaint or initial pleading in an admiralty or ecclesiastical case." The word is used also as a verb in this context—e.g.: "And so, in our own admiralty law, if a ship does you any injury, you '*libel*' or attach, and actually sue, the ship." René A. Wormser, *The Story of the Law* 16 (1962). Hence *libelant*, for which see **libelant.**

libelant; libellant. *Libelant* = an injured sailor. E.g.: "The *libelants* recovered in both Courts below." *Robins Dry Dock & Repair Co. v. Flint*, 275 U.S. 303, 307 (1927) (per Holmes, J.). One *-l-* is preferred in AmE, two in BrE. (See DOUBLING OF FINAL CONSONANTS.) The accent of *libelant* is on the first syllable.

Historically *libelant* has been an admiralty term as just defined, but the word has come to mean additionally "one who publishes a defamatory statement; a libeler." *Libeler* (in BrE *libeller*) is the older and better term for this sense, for it forestalls confusion about what the cause of action is.

libelee, libellee. *Libelee* (= one against whom a libel has been filed) is correlative not with *libeler*, but with *libelant*. The word is spelled *libelee* in AmE, *libellee* in BrE. See -EE.

libeler. See **libelant.**

libelous (= defamatory; constituting libel) is so spelled in AmE; it is *libellous* in BrE. See DOUBLING OF FINAL CONSONANTS.

liberal construction; liberal interpretation. See *liberal interpretation* under INTERPRETATION, MODES OF (B).

liberate. See **free.**

liberty; freedom. These synonyms have connotative distinctions. *Freedom* is the broader, all-encompassing term that carries strong positive connotations. *Liberty*, slightly less emotive, generally suggests the past removal of restraints on specific freedoms.

Pound explained the distinction between Kantian liberty and constitutional liberty as guaranteed in the Bill of Rights:

> Kant's idea of the liberty of each—the free self-assertion of each—limited only by the like liberty of all, was generally accepted. Liberty was a condition in which free exercise of the will was restrained only so far as necessary to secure a harmonious coexistence of the free will of each and the free will of all others. But I am not speaking of the Kantian idea of liberty, in which my generation was brought up. Whatever "liberty" may mean today, the liberty guaranteed by our bill of rights is a reservation to the individual of certain fundamental reasonable expectations involved in life in civilized society and a freedom from arbitrary and unreasonable exercise of the power and authority of those who are designated or chosen in a politically organized society to adjust relations and order conduct, and so are able to apply the force of that society to individuals.
>
> Roscoe Pound, *The Development of Constitutional Guarantees of Liberty* 1 (1957).

license. A. And *licence*. The AmE spelling of the noun and the verb is *license*; that is the BrE spelling of the verb, but *licence* is the BrE spelling of the noun.

B. And *easement*. An *easement* is a right of property; a license is a revocable permission to commit some act that would otherwise be unlawful. An *easement* is usually created by a written document; a *license* is often created orally. An *easement* is more or less permanent; a *license* is temporary. An *easement* cannot be revoked; a *license* is revocable. See **easement.**

licensee = (1) one to whom a license is granted; or (2) one who enters an occupier's property not for business purposes but with the occupier's permission.

licensor; *****licenser. The first spelling is preferred.

licentiate (= one who has obtained a license or authoritative permission to exercise some function) is sometimes used of lawyers—e.g.:

- "Gutterman, a recent *licentiate* in law, had been assisting counsel for Abdell in preparing the case for trial by looking up evidence." *Gutterman v. Commonwealth*, 199 S.E. 508, 509 (Va. 1938).

- "The same caution should be employed in a parallel situation if [the] local custom of a legislative tribunal dictated that its *licentiate* should not obstruct the course of justice in another court." *In re Sawyer*, 260 F.2d 189, 212 (9th Cir. 1958).

licit. See **legal,** adj.

lie, n.; falsehood; untruth; fib; misrepresentation; *suggestio falsi;* **prevarication; terminological inexactitude.** All these terms refer to a statement or assertion that does not square with the truth. *Lie,* a fighting word, carries with it considerable odium because it suggests an outright and purposeful contradiction of the truth. Except in the phrase *white lie* (= an innocuously false statement, usu. made to spare someone's feelings in some benevolent way), *lie* typically bears a strong sense of moral disapproval. Cf. **dishonest.**

Falsehood, a more neutral term, likewise conveys nonconformity with the truth, but less judgmentally so. It is broad enough to encompass a legal FICTION. *Untruth,* too, is milder than *lie*: it does not necessarily connote purposeful untruthfulness. *Fib* is the most euphemistic of all, suggesting a trivially childish lie intended to spare someone (often oneself) from punishment.

Misrepresentation is broad enough to describe a fraudulent as well as a negligent or innocent statement. You may be surprised to learn that, in the law of contracts, the word can also describe a factually accurate statement: "A person is guilty of *misrepresentation* though all the facts stated by him are true, if his statement is misleading as a whole because it does not refer to other facts affecting the weight of those stated." G.H. Treitel, *The Law of Contract* 353 (8th ed. 1991). Typically, though, *misrepresentation* applies to a purposefully misleading statement that conveys a false impression, as by dishonestly touting the advantages of some proposed course of action, by putting actions or events under a false light, or by wrongly suggesting that something to be sold has features or benefits that it does not have.

The phrase **false misrepresentation* is a fairly common REDUNDANCY—e.g.: "MOT alleged (in its complaint) that the Coffeys made several *false misrepresentations* [read *misrepresentations* or *false representations*]." *Moore, Owen, Thomas & Co. v. Coffey,* 992 F.2d 1439, 1445 (6th Cir. 1993).

The final three phrases are variations on the main theme. *Suggestio falsi,* a LATINISM, is an equivalent of *misrepresentation*—literally a "false suggestion" that leads the listener or reader to a seriously incorrect impression, but without a direct lie. (See ***suggestio falsi.***) *Prevarication* is quite similar: an equivocal avoidance of the truth—a paltering. Then, of course, there is Winston Churchill's famous phrase, dating from 1906: *terminological inexactitude.* It is one of the most risible and memorable EUPHEMISMS ever coined.

lie, vb. (= to have foundation in the law; to be legally supportable, sustainable, or proper), is a peculiar legal idiom. E.g.:

- "A writ of certiorari *lies* only to correct errors in law, and not to revise the decision of a question of fact." *New York Cent. R.R. v. Public Serv. Comm'n,* 125 N.E. 176, 177 (Mass. 1919).
- "It is a rule of general application that an action will *lie* for interference with enforceable contractual rights if there be no sufficient justification for the interference." *Conway v. O'Brien,* 169 N.E. 491, 493 (Mass. 1929).
- "The rule is well settled that replevin will not *lie* for money incapable of specific identification." *1967 Senior Class of Pekin High Sch. v. Tharp,* 154 N.W.2d 874, 876 (Iowa 1967).
- "The general rule remains that mandamus will not *lie* to review incidental trial court rulings." Alan Wright et al., *Appellate Practice and Procedure,* 58 SMU L. Rev. 501, 507 (2005).

Lie is used additionally in law in the figurative sense "to reside, exist"—e.g.: "In Massachusetts and New Hampshire, statutes provided for an appeal only if the capturer's vessel had been fitted out by citizens of another state; in all other cases, final appeal *lay* to the state's highest court." Matthew P. Harrington, *The Legacy of the Colonial Vice-Admiralty Courts (Part II),* 27 J. Mar. L. & Com. 323, 343 (1996). Cf. **sound.**

For the difference between *lie* and *lay,* see **lay.**

lie low; lay low. The second phrase is incorrect except as the past tense of the first—e.g.: "Meador told Hunt to *lay low* [read *lie low*] for a while and that they could resume the marijuana business with Dinwiddie in the future." *U.S. v. Dinwiddie,* 618 F.3d 821, 828–29 (8th Cir. 2010). See **lay.**

lien, n., (= a legal right or interest that a creditor has in another's property, lasting usu. until a debt that it secures is satisfied) is pronounced, most properly, /**lee**-ən/ or /lin/; and commonly, but less properly, /leen/. In G.B., it is customary for the lienholder to retain possession of the property on which the lien has been obtained, whereas in the U.S. it is more usual that a lien does not involve retention by the lienholder. In the U.S., when the creditor possesses the collateral, *pledge* is the more usual term. See **pledge** & **liens and encumbrances.*

lien, vb., a 19th-century innovation, is increasingly common, though it is not yet listed in most dictionaries—e.g.: "In addition, the Northcutts allege that the Hancocks wrongfully *liened* the property." *Hancock v. Northcutt,* 808 P.2d 251, 253 (Alaska 1991).

Liened = burdened with a lien. E.g.:

- "The proceeds of the water power are *liened* for the discharge of the canal debt by the act of 1825." *McArthur v. Kelly,* 5 Ohio 139, 151 (1831).
- "Some courts have held *liened* penalty claims allowable." *Simonson v. Granquist,* 369 U.S. 38, 42 (1962) (per Black, J.).

lienable = capable of being subjected to a lien. E.g.: "Certain kinds of labor and materials are not *lienable.*" Robert Kratovil, *Real Estate Law* 203 (1946). This 20th-century Americanism is not listed in the *OED*; it appears in *W3,* but not in its predecessor, *W2.*

liened, adj. See **lien,** vb.

lienee means, in AmE, "one whose property is subject to a lien," but in Australia it is synonymous with *lienholder*. The Australian usage mangles any sense left in the suffix *-ee*. See -EE.

lienholder; *lienor. *Lienholder* is more likely to be understood by nonlawyers—and is more common in published materials. E.g.:

- "The debtor listed the purported *lienholder's* claim as unsecured and the *lienholder* did not object to confirmation of the plan." *In re Simmons*, 765 F.2d 547, 551 (5th Cir. 1985).
- "The debtor must instead disburse these funds in order of priority to *lienors* [read *lienholders*] of record as of the date of bankruptcy filing." *In re Hayes*, 431 B.R. 545, 548 (Bankr. W.D.N.Y. 2010).

*Lienor, an Americanism, is best left unused; it is hardly known in BrE. See **encumbrancer.**

*liens and encumbrances. Though common, this phrase is redundant and illogical because a lien is one type of encumbrance. The better phrasing, then, would be *liens and other encumbrances*, or perhaps just *encumbrances* alone. See DOUBLETS, TRIPLETS, AND SYNONYM-STRINGS. See also **encumbrance.**

lieu of, in. See **in lieu of.**

life-and-death; life-or-death. Though the sense is "relating to a matter of life *or* death," idiom has sanctioned *and* in this PHRASAL ADJECTIVE, not *or*—e.g.:

- "'It's good enough for a *life-and-death* decision,' says one of the judges." James W. McElhaney, *The Law of Experts*, Litig., Summer 1991, at 47, 50.
- "An individual justice has no power to dispose of cases on the merits, but may make a variety of interim orders, sometimes of literally *life-and-death* significance." Charles Alan Wright, *The Law of Federal Courts* 805 (5th ed. 1994).
- "We think the same result should follow when the stakes are not *life and death* but merely 'banishment or exile.'" *Padilla v. Kentucky*, 130 S.Ct. 1473, 1484 n.11 (2010) (per Stevens, J.).

life assurance. See **life insurance.**

life estate = an estate that the grantee holds for life—resulting, for example, from a grant "to X during his life," by will, deed, or trust. Today, most life estates are beneficial interests under trusts, the corpus being personal property, not real property.

life insurance; life assurance. The first is usual in AmE, the second in BrE.

life-or-death. See **life-and-death.**

lifting the corporate veil. See **piercing the corporate veil.**

*ligan. See **flotsam.**

lighted; lit. Both are standard past-tense forms.

light of, in (the). See **in the light of.**

like; as. A. *Like* as a Conjunction. In standard usage, *like* is a preposition that governs nouns and noun phrases, not a conjunction that governs verbs or clauses—e.g.: "In fact, the term 'legal writing' has become synonymous with poor writing: specifically, verbose and inflated prose that reads *like* [read *as if*]—well, *like* [read *as if*] it was written by a lawyer." Steven Stark, Comment, *Why Lawyers Can't Write*, 97 Harv. L. Rev. 1389, 1389 (1984) (though the change does alter the tone). The grammatical function of *like* is adjectival, not adverbial. Hence one does not write, properly, "He argued this case *like* he argued the previous one," but, "He argued this case *as* he argued the previous one." If we change *argue* to *argument*, the word *like* is permissible: "His argument in this case was *like* his argument in the previous one."

This relatively simple precept is generally observed in writing but has been increasingly flouted in American speech. Examples of *like* used conjunctively can be found throughout the Middle English period. Yet the usage has been considered nonstandard at least since the 17th century. For the opposite error (*as* for *like*), see **as (B).**

B. Faulty Comparison: *like in* for *as in*. The phrasing *like in* has never been considered good English, *as in* typically being required—e.g.:

- "This is true even in cases where gains from cooperation have been grossly overstated, *like in* [*as in*] the case of the infamous Cecchini Report of 1988." Petros C. Mavroidis, *The European Union as an International Actor*, 6 Colum. J. Eur. L. 271, 271 n.4 (2000).
- "[The evidence] also does not have strong probative force in showing motive or knowledge *like in* [read *as in*] *Medrano*." *Jackson v. State*, 314 S.W.3d 118, 128 (Tex. App.—Houston [1st Dist.] 2010).

See ILLOGIC (A).

likely has different shades of meaning. Most often it indicates a degree of probability greater than five on a scale of one to ten. The probability is, of course, greater when the word is preceded by a qualifier such as *quite*, *very*, or *extremely*. But it may also refer to a degree of possibility that is less than five on that same scale. See **apt** & **probable.**

limine. See **in limine.**

limitation; repose. A *limitation* period bars a lawsuit if the plaintiff does not sue within a set time from the date when the cause of action accrued. A period of *repose*, meanwhile, bars a lawsuit for a fixed number of years after an action by the defendant (such as manufacturing a product), even if this period ends before the plaintiff suffers any injury. *Beard v. J.I. Case Co.*, 823 F.2d 1095, 1097 n.1 (7th Cir. 1987). Cf. **laches (D).**

For the real-property sense of *limitation*, see **condition (D).**

limitation over. See **over (A).**

---

limitations. When *limitations* is used as an elliptical version of *statute of limitations* or *limitations period*, many writers are unsure whether a singular or plural verb is required. The plural verb is correct. In *statute of limitations*, the verb is controlled by the singular *statute*, not the prepositional phrase. But *limitations* (typically representing *limitations period*) standing alone must be treated as a plural noun and take a plural verb: *limitations are tolled*. E.g.:

- "Does the Court mean to say today that *limitations is tolled* [read *limitations are tolled*] under this Code's section 16.063 if the plaintiff serves the Secretary of State, but not if the plaintiff serves the Transportation Commission Chairman?" *Kerlin v. Sauceda*, 263 S.W.3d 920, 928 (Tex. 2008) (Brister, J., concurring).
- "The Supreme Court held in a misidentification case [that] *limitations are tolled* 'if there are two separate, but related entities that use a similar trade name and the correct entity had notice of the suit and was not misled or disadvantaged by the mistake.'" *State Office of Risk Mgmt. v. Herrera*, 288 S.W.3d 543, 548 (Tex. App.—Amarillo 2009).
- "The majority claims that if a plaintiff is suing on symptoms different from the ones from which he initially suffered, *limitations is tolled* [read *limitations are tolled*]. . . . The majority holds that if a plaintiff has seen a doctor and has been given a clean bill of health, *limitations are tolled* until he is diagnosed." *Pretus v. Diamond Offshore Drilling, Inc.*, 571 F.3d 478, 488–89 (5th Cir. 2009) (Smith, J., dissenting).

limited construction; limited interpretation. See *limited interpretation* under INTERPRETATION, MODES OF (B).

linchpin; *lynchpin. The first spelling is standard.

lineal kinship. See **kinship**.

lines and corners. See **metes and bounds**.

lip. See LAWYERS, DEROGATORY NAMES FOR (A).

liquefy. So spelled. **Liquify* is a common misspelling.

liquidated damages, perhaps originally a EUPHEMISM for *forfeiture* or *penalty*, has, in many jurisdictions, become a TERM OF ART distinguishable from those other terms. *Liquidated damages* applies when the parties to a contract have agreed in advance on the measure of damages to be assessed in the event of default. It should be distinguished from *forfeiture* or *penalty*, which involves a provision imposed as a threat of punishment rather than as a genuine estimate of damages upon default.

Of course, the line between a *penalty* and *liquidated damages* is not always easy to draw. Regardless of what the sum might be called, the courts decide the true nature of the agreed-upon sum. Three conditions commonly lead a court to decide that a sum called "liquidated damages" is really a penalty: (1) if the sum grossly exceeds the probable damages on breach; (2) if the same sum is made payable for any variety of different breaches (some major, some minor); and (3) if a mere delay in payment has been listed among the events of default. See **damages (A)**.

*liquify. See **liquefy**.

lis (= a piece of litigation; a controversy) is brief but, probably to many readers, obscure—e.g.: "The courts are concerned with the practical business of deciding a *lis*." *Attorney-General v. Prince Ernest Augustus of Hanover*, [1957] A.C. 436, 467 (per Lord Normand).

lis pendens; *lis alibi pendens*; *lite pendente*; *pendente lite*. *Lis pendens* (L. "a pending lawsuit"), pronounced /lis **pen**-dənz/, is a useful LATINISM that has given its name to a notice required in some jurisdictions to warn all persons that certain property is the subject matter of litigation, and that any interests acquired during the pendency of the suit must be subject to the outcome of the litigation. Traditionally this notice was called the *notice of lis pendens*, but 20th-century American lawyers shortened the phrase to merely *lis pendens*—e.g.: "The defendant unsuccessfully appealed, claiming insufficient notice of the condemnation proceeding because the *lis pendens* recorded in conjunction with that proceeding failed to describe the subject property adequately." *Caminis v. Troy*, 963 A.2d 701, 708–09 (Conn. App. Ct. 2009).

Lis alibi pendens = a lawsuit pending elsewhere. E.g.: "Where actions *in personam* are started in two courts of concurrent authority of the same country, the plea *lis alibi pendens* is a good defence to the second action." R.H. Graveson, *Conflict of Laws* 144 (7th ed. 1974).

Pendente lite /pen-**den**-tee **li**-tee/, less usually written *lite pendente*, is the same phrase in the present-participial form, meaning "pending the lawsuit; during litigation." In G.B., administrators *pendente lite* are appointed to handle estates in dispute; in the U.S., matters are said to be *pendente lite* when they are contingent on the outcome of litigation.

Sometimes the phrase unnecessarily displaces an English phrase—e.g.: "Respondent is suspended *pendente lite* [read *pending the outcome of this suit*] from the practice of law in this State." *In re Wallingford*, 897 N.E.2d 925, 925 (Ind. 2008). The extra words provide extra comprehensibility.

list. There cannot be a list of one—e.g.: "Appellant is *listed* [read *named*] at the top of the document as 'Guarantor.'" *BankCherokee v. Insignia Dev., LLC*, 779 N.W.2d 896, 900–01 (Minn. Ct. App. 2010).

lit. See **lighted**.

lite pendente. See **lis pendens**.

literal canon; literal rule. These are alternative names for strict constructionism, i.e., the doctrinal view of judicial construction holding that judges should apply the literal words of a statute or document without looking to the purpose behind them. E.g.:

- "Then, should the *literal canon* be dislodged from, or relegated to the position of a presumption in a modern theory of interpretation? . . . [I]t is submitted that the formal approach is within its province most consonant with the

Literary Allusion 547

judicial function." E. Russell Hopkins, *The Literal Canon and the Golden Rule*, 15 Can. B. Rev. 689, 695–96 (1937).

- "The *literal rule* is a rule against using intelligence in understanding language. Anyone who in ordinary life interpreted words literally, being indifferent to what the speaker or writer meant, would be regarded as a pedant, a mischief-maker or an idiot." Glanville Williams, *Learning the Law* 105 (11th ed. 1982).

literal construction. See **original intent** & **strict construction.**

litera legis. See **letter of the law.**

literally = (1) with truth to the letter; or (2) exactly; according to the strict sense of the word or words. The use of this word in the sense "truly, completely," is an example of SLIPSHOD EXTENSION—e.g.: "When there is a subsection of the community listening to her admission of guilt, the wrongdoer has more difficulty avoiding the burden of criminal responsibility, because her fellow citizens, her community, and her peers have *both literally and figuratively* [delete *both literally and figuratively*] become part of the expiation process." Laura I. Appleman, *The Plea Jury*, 85 Ind. L.J. 731, 764 (2010).

When used for *figuratively*, where *figuratively* would not ordinarily be used, *literally* is distorted beyond recognition: "Mr. Gladstone had sat *literally* glued to the Treasury Bench." Because we know it is a META-PHOR, simply say: "Mr. Gladstone had sat glued to the Treasury Bench."

literal rule. See **literal canon.**

literary affectation. See LITERARY ALLUSION (B).

LITERARY ALLUSION, if not too arcane, can add substantially to the subtlety and effectiveness of writing. Allusiveness assumes a common body of literature with which all cultured persons are familiar. The effective writer is wary on the one hand of allusions that are hackneyed, and on the other hand of allusions so learned that they are inaccessible to the average educated reader. It is perhaps easier for judges than for practicing lawyers to use literary allusions, for judges have a guaranteed readership and do not suffer directly if anyone (or everyone) fails to appreciate their allusions. A lawyer submitting a brief to a judge, on the contrary, is likely to be less adventurous in literary flights of fancy. A few specimens follow, with short explanations.

A. Effective Use of Allusion. The following quotations illustrate some of the most common types of allusion used to good effect.

1. *Proverbial.* A good example of effective allusiveness appears in the dissent of Justice Robert W. Hansen of the Wisconsin Supreme Court, in *Jones v. Fisher*, 166 N.W.2d 175 (Wis. 1969). He plays with an old proverb: "The *road* that has brought us to the present state of affairs in regard to punitive damages in Wisconsin courts *is a long one, paved with good intentions.*" *Id.* at 182. Justice Hansen here subtly suggests that this is the road to hell, conjuring up the saying that "the road to hell is paved with good intentions." He might have ruined the effect by quoting the aphorism directly.

2. *Biblical.* "One of the prime concerns addressed in the [Magnuson–Moss Warranty] Act was the warranty wherein the large print *giveth* but the small print *taketh away.*" *Gorman v. Saf-T-Mate, Inc.*, 513 F.Supp. 1028, 1035 (N.D. Ind. 1981). This alludes to Job 1:21: "Naked came I out of my mother's womb, and naked shall I return thither: the Lord gave, and the Lord hath taken away." See BIBLICAL AFFECTATION.

3. *Shakespearean.*

- "La. Rev. Stat. 14:27(a) . . . requires specific intent to commit a crime, and in Stewart's *eyes there is the rub.*" *Stewart v. Blackburn*, 746 F.2d 262, 264 (5th Cir. 1984). This allusion may confuse the reader because of the proximity of *rub* and *eyes.* The phrase *ay, there's the rub* (orig. fr. *Hamlet* 3.1.64) has passed into common parlance.

- "Today, citizen and lawyer alike are faced with a statutory progeny as alarming as the ghostly issue of Banquo were to Macbeth." G.W. Keeton, *The Elementary Principles of Jurisprudence* 88 (2d ed. 1949). (Macbeth, having murdered Banquo, is visited by a crowned apparition of Banquo's son in the presence of the witches [Act 4, scene 1].)

4. *Mythological and Classical.* "This appeal requires this Court to make another trek through that *Serbonian bog* of damages in maritime cases." *Delta S.S. Lines v. Avondale Shipyards, Inc.*, 747 F.2d 995, 997 (5th Cir. 1984). *Serbonian bog* (= a quagmire or predicament from which there is no way of extricating oneself) has become a judges' CLICHÉ, though it may have been fresh when Justice Benjamin Cardozo wrote: "The attempted distinction between accidental results and accidental means will plunge this branch of law into a *Serbonian Bog.*" *Landress v. Phoenix Mut. Life Ins. Co.*, 291 U.S. 491, 499 (1934) (Cardozo, J., dissenting). The Serbonian bog is said to have been between Egypt and Palestine. Milton wrote: "A gulf profound as that *Serbonian Bog,*/ Betwixt Damiata and Mount Casius old,/ Where armies whole have sunk." *Paradise Lost* 2.592.

Here is another typical allusion to ancient history: "Most of the arguments and points made by the en banc opinion have been addressed by our panel opinion, and I will let the matter rest upon what has been said; for me to write more on the subject, which now appears settled by virtue of the majority here and the Second Circuit in *In re Taddeo*, would be largely repetitious and amount to no more than a *Parthian shot.*" *Grubbs v. Houston First Am. Savs. Ass'n*, 730 F.2d 236, 247–48 (5th Cir. 1984) (en banc) (Jolly, J., dissenting). A *Parthian shot* is a parting shot, an allusion to the people of ancient Parthia, noted for their method of fighting on horseback with the bow as their only weapon; after each discharge of an arrow the horse turned as if in flight—hence the modern meaning.

---

5. *Other Literary.* Literary allusions most often arise from classical literature, poetry, or opera—e.g.:

- "There are village tyrants as well as village Hampdens, but none who acts under color of law is beyond reach of the Constitution." *West Virginia State Bd. of Educ. v. Barnette*, 319 U.S. 624, 638 (1943) (per Jackson, J.) (referring to Gray's "Elegy Written in a Country Churchyard").
- "This old but little used section is *a kind of legal Lohengrin*; although it has been with us since the first Judiciary Act, . . . no one seems to know whence it came." *IIT v. Vencap, Ltd.*, 519 F.2d 1001, 1015 (2d Cir. 1975). (Lohengrin, hero of Richard Wagner's opera of the same name and a knight of the Holy Grail, refuses to reveal, even to his wife, the mystery of his origins.)
- "We will not oblige the state to *joust windmills* by requiring that it prove what is not wrong with that which is not there to be seen." *Strahan v. Blackburn*, 750 F.2d 438, 444 (5th Cir. 1985). (In Cervantes' *Don Quixote*, the protagonist Don Quixote tilts at windmills under the delusion that they are giants.)

See Charles Alan Wright, *Literary Allusion in Legal Writing*, 1 Scribes J. Legal Writing 1, 3–4 (1990).

B. Poor Use of Allusion. But *allusion* doesn't always work. Following are some examples with brief explanations of pitfalls.

1. *Hackneyed Allusions.* "What *is and what is not* a sham is the Hamlet-like question that has perplexed the lower courts in the two decades since the Supreme Court, in a 'new and unusual application of the Sherman Act,' enunciated the *Noerr* doctrine." Milton Handler & Richard A. De Sevo, *The* Noerr *Doctrine and Its Sham Exception*, 6 Cardozo L. Rev. 1, 1 (1984). *To be or not to be* (to live or not to live) is rather a different kind of question from what is and is not a sham. Moreover, *To be or not to be* (*Hamlet* 3.1.55) is a greatly overworked phrase.

Hyperbolic allusion, especially if it smacks of BIB-LICAL AFFECTATION, is also ineffective—e.g.: "The words, both singly and conjunctively, have been in common use and generally understood since Moses delivered the commandments and the law to his people, and up to the present time when the words are frequently used decisively to describe a person who is commonly or habitually so intoxicated that his faculties have been impaired, and the words are generally so understood to the extent that they have been practically unquestioned." *People v. Daniel*, 337 P.2d 247, 254 (Cal. Ct. App. 1959) (per Chamberlain, J.). The judge who wrote that, in the process of construing a legal document written in English, merely detracted from his persuasiveness. See OVERSTATEMENT.

2. *Contrived Literariness.* Some judges and advocates, in their quest for originality, go off the deep end. Perhaps the worst manifestation of this phenomenon is what we might term "literary foppery," consisting in the legal writer's going to absurd lengths to display the breadth of his literary knowledge. For example, Laurence Sterne's *Tristram Shandy* is quite irrelevantly dragged into *Farr v. Nordman*, 78 N.W.2d 186, 193 (Mich. 1956) (Black, J., dissenting). Contrived allusions and references invariably detract from the message to be conveyed.

In a striking example of artificially engrafted literariness, an American judge recently peppered one of his opinions with wholly impertinent allusions and references to William Faulkner. The opinion itself discusses the constitutionality under the Fourth Amendment of a lessor's inspection of his land to determine whether the lessee has wrongfully diverted oil production. The first sentence of the statement of facts reads: "The events underlying Auster's claims could have arisen in Yoknapatawpha County, Mississippi, but most of them happened in Calcasieu Parish, Louisiana, where Stream owned the surface and mineral rights in oil-producing property." A footnote, of course, explains that Yoknapatawpha County is the fictional setting of many of Faulkner's novels (and cites works on Faulkner by the renowned critics Cleanth Brooks and Irving Howe). *See Auster Oil & Gas, Inc. v. Stream*, 764 F.2d 381 (5th Cir. 1985). The contrivance has neither purpose nor subtlety.

But worse yet are the headings and subheadings throughout the opinion. We begin with "The Sound and the Fury," which is followed by "Lease in August" (*Light in August*), "The Reivers," "Intruders in the Dust" (*Intruder in the Dust*), "Auster's Gambit" (*Knight's Gambit*), "Go Down, Auster" (*Go Down, Moses*), "Requiem for a Plaintiff" (*Requiem for a Nun*), "Sanctuary," "Microchip! Microchip!" (*Absalom! Absalom!*), "Trooper's Pay" (*Soldiers' Pay*), "As the Wells Lay Pumping" (*As I Lay Dying*), and "The Unvanquished." In short, the references and allusions to Faulkner are entirely factitious. *Id.*

To those with an undiscerning literary sensibility, such contrivances may be appealing. But please see Arnold Bennett, *Literary Taste: How to Cultivate It* (1911).

literatim. See **verbatim.**

litigable; *litigatable. The correct form is *litigable*, not *litigatable—e.g.: "[Courts] have held that this issue is fairly *litigatable* [read *litigable*]." *In re Enron Corp.*, 341 B.R. 141, 169 n.25 (Bankr. S.D.N.Y. 2006).

litigant has denoted "a party to a lawsuit" since the mid-17th century. Originally, in the early 17th century, *litigant* was always an adjective, as in the phrase *party litigant*. Soon, however, the word came to act as a noun, without the necessity of pairing it always with *party*. Rarely nowadays does one encounter the adjectival use of *litigant*; instead, examples like the following abound:

- "It is quite possible that a *litigant* will find that his case will fit some two or three of these pigeon-holes." F.W. Maitland, *The Forms of Action at Common Law* 3 (1909; A.H. Chaytor & W.J. Whittaker eds., 1971).
- "A bait was needed with which to draw *litigants* to the royal courts; the King must offer them better justice than they could have at the hands of their lords." 1 Winston Churchill, *A History of the English Speaking Peoples* 217 (1956).

Cf. **litigator.**

litigate = (1) to be a party to, or carry on, a lawsuit; (2) to make the subject of a lawsuit; to contest at law; or (3) to dispute or contest (a point, etc.). So in sense 1, one *litigates* cases and causes, but in sense 2 one may *litigate* property or consequences, etc.—e.g.: "Qualified immunity is in part an entitlement not to be forced to *litigate* the consequences of official conduct." *Mitchell v. Forsyth*, 472 U.S. 511, 527 (1985) (per White, J.). Cf. **adjudicate (A).**

The phrase *litigate against* (a certain type of opponent) became common in late-20th-century legal writing—e.g.: "New York's highest court ruled that lawyers *litigating against* a corporation can informally interview certain employees without the consent of the corporation's lawyers." Wade Lambert & Edward Felsenthal, *SEC Seeks Injunction on Price Waterhouse*, Wall St. J., 6 July 1990, at B5.

litigated judgment is often a REDUNDANCY—e.g.: "The decision will result in the dismissal of key claims in literally thousands of pending lawsuits—and some *litigated judgments* [read *judgments* or *final judgments*]—and is bound to further depress the number of such suits filed in the future." Rick Schmitt, *California Court Further Restricts Right of Fired Workers to Sue Ex-Employers*, Wall St. J., 26 May 1989, at A3. When used in contrast to *consent judgment*, however, *litigated judgment* makes perfect sense: "The distinction between a consent judgment and a *litigated judgment* has not been widely addressed by Michigan courts." *Trendell v. Solomon*, 443 N.W.2d 509, 510 (Mich. Ct. App. 1989).

litigation, adj.; ***litigational**; ***litigative.** See **litigatory.**

litigation, n. Ordinarily, *litigation* refers to the process of carrying on lawsuits or a specific lawsuit. Hence the plural *litigations* might seem to make little sense. But *litigation* occasionally serves as a synonym for *lawsuit*. Though it may seem unidiomatic to make *litigation* a count noun in this way, the usage is old and is today common. E.g.:

- "The purpose of requiring particularized pleadings is to prevent abusive securities *litigations*." *National Jr. Baseball League v. Pharmanet Dev. Group, Inc.*, 720 F.Supp.2d 517, 527 (D.N.J. 2010).
- "[O]nce one concludes that the challenged *litigations* . . . were not objectively baseless, the matter is closed." *Ginx, Inc. v. Soho Alliance*, 720 F.Supp.2d 342, 364 n.10 (S.D.N.Y. 2010).
- "Patent *litigations* are among the longest, most time-consuming types of civil actions." *Ohio Willow Wood Co. v. Thermo-Ply, Inc.*, 629 F.3d 1374, 1376 (Fed. Cir. 2011).

See PLURALS (B).

litigator. When it originated—in the late 19th century—*litigator* was a NEEDLESS VARIANT of *litigant*, as here: "When a succession is in progress of litigation, the interest of the *litigators* is *deducto aeri aliendo*." *Irwin v. Flynn*, 34 So. 794, 794 syl. 2 (La. 1903). This

sense persisted into the mid-20th century—e.g.: "Government agencies are the heaviest *litigators* in the United States courts." *Lane v. Fitzsimmons Stores, Ltd.*, 62 F.Supp. 89, 91 n.7 (S.D. Cal. 1945). (Cf. **litigant.**) At the same time, the word was coming to refer to a lawyer who specializes in litigation, as an alternative term for *trial lawyer*. See **trial lawyer.**

But now *trial lawyer* and *litigator* have been vaguely differentiated. With the advent, in the U.S., of seemingly endless discovery before trial—which never seems to come—*litigator* has come to connote a lawyer who works in litigation but rarely if ever sets foot in a courtroom. Trial lawyers try cases; litigators, it is sometimes said, merely prepare discovery requests.

litigatory; *litigative; *litigational. There is no single widely accepted neutral adjective corresponding to *litigation* and meaning "of, pertaining to, or involving litigation." *Litigious* is close structurally, but its strong associations with disputatiousness and contentiousness impair its candidacy—in AmE, at any rate. (BrE continues to use *litigious* in neutral contexts.) *Litigable* <litigable claims> and *litigant* <parties litigant> have other specific senses. *Litigation* sometimes functions as an adjective, as in the title of Leon Green's collection of essays *The Litigation Process in Tort Law* (1965). It works in some phrases, such as *litigation battles* or *litigation crisis*, but not in others. See **litigious.**

Litigatory, ***litigational**, and ***litigative** have been pressed into service in the desired neutral sense. *Litigatory* is listed in *W2*, but is omitted from *W3* and has appeared in neither the *OED* nor its *Supplement*. Yet it is no stranger to American legal prose—e.g.:

- "The controlling declaration . . . is that equity can and should intervene whenever it is made to appear that one party, public or private, seeks unjustly to enrich himself at the expense of another on account of his own mistake and the other's want of immediate vigilance—*litigatory* or otherwise." *Spoon-Shacket Co. v. County of Oakland*, 97 N.W.2d 25, 28 (Mich. 1959).
- "Certain Florida cases, though having *litigatory* objectives different from the one at bar, employ the principle." *Brown v. Hutch*, 156 So.2d 683, 686 (Fla. Dist. Ct. App. 1963).
- "Not only do the decided cases lead us to this decision but such ruling accords with modern jurisprudence which seeks to eliminate the hidden *litigatory* pitfall." *Federal Ins. Co. v. Oakwood Steel Co.*, 191 S.E.2d 298, 300 (Ga. Ct. App. 1972).
- "Our affirmance in the present case is predicated upon the purposes and objectives underlying declaratory judgment actions and the *litigatory* posture of the dispute involving the parties herein." *Volkswagenwerk, A.G. v. Watson*, 390 N.E.2d 1082, 1084 (Ind. Ct. App. 1979).
- "Fee awards are intended to attract competent counsel to represent citizens contesting governmental action and to level the *litigatory* playing field." *Bryant v. Commissioner of Soc. Sec.*, 578 F.3d 443, 449 (6th Cir. 2009).

***Litigational**, a NEEDLESS VARIANT of *litigatory*, has been similarly neglected in general English-language dictionaries, though it is not uncommon. E.g.:

- "*Litigational background of both appeals was* [read *In the litigatory background of both appeals was*] a suit instituted by plaintiff." *Morton v. Indemnity Ins. Co.*, 137 So.2d 618, 619 (Fla. Dist. Ct. App. 1962).
- "We now consider briefly a second form of specific jurisdiction . . . relating not only to the plaintiff but also to the taking of evidence and other *litigational* [read *litigatory*] considerations." Arthur Taylor von Mehren & Donald T. Trautman, *Jurisdiction to Adjudicate*, 79 Harv. L. Rev. 1121, 1173 (1966).
- "The *Finney* court recognize[d] that the binding nature of a stipulation of dispositiveness supported the parties in their exercise of *litigational* [read *litigatory*] strategy." *Zeigler v. State*, 471 So.2d 172, 176 (Fla. Dist. Ct. App. 1985).

Litigative is likewise a NEEDLESS VARIANT—e.g.:

- "The transfer of the stock was not actually made until April 1944 because of an unsuccessful *litigative* [read *litigatory*] attempt to prevent the same." *Western Pac. R.R. Corp. v. Western Pac. R.R. Co.*, 85 F.Supp. 868, 870 (N.D. Cal. 1949).
- "For these reasons, I simply cannot accept the shift in the *litigative* [read *litigatory*] burden of proof adopted by the Court." *Columbus Bd. of Educ. v. Penick*, 99 S.Ct. 2982, 2983 (1979) (Stewart, J., dissenting).

litigiosity; litigiousness. If there is a nuance between these words, it is that *litigiosity* denotes the *fact* or *state* of being litigious, whereas *litigiousness* denotes the *quality* of being litigious. The fussiness of this distinction suggests that euphony is a better ground for choice between the two.

In Scots law, however, *litigiosity* has a special sense: "a legal prohibition on a debtor's alienating heritable property to the effect of defeating an action . . . commenced or inchoate" (*OCL1*).

litigious = (1) fond of legal disputes; contentious <our litigious society>; (2) that is the subject of a lawsuit <the litigious property>; or (3) of or pertaining to lawsuits or litigation <dragged into a litigious dispute>. In AmE, the word has been narrowed to sense 1 exclusively. In BrE, however, the word is capable of taking on the neutral senses of (2) and (3)—e.g.:

- "The Statute codified procedure for a new jurisdiction, and may therefore have been more precise than current *litigious* practice." C.H.S. Fifoot, *History and Sources of the Common Law* 27 n.18 (1949).
- "A good deal of *litigious* work is disposed of not in open court but before a judge or master in chambers." Glanville Williams, *Learning the Law* 190 (11th ed. 1982). See **litigatory.**

litigiousness. See **litigiosity.**

litiscontestation, a Scots law term, means "joinder of issue, arising after the defense in a lawsuit has been lodged." The word derives from the Roman term *litis contestatio*, the process by which a legal issue emerges from the opposing statements of the parties, which still occasionally appears in English and American lawbooks: "A discussion of the influence on modern German procedure of the notion involved in the Roman *litis contestatio* (as a pretended contract of submission) will be found in Bullow." Lon L.

Fuller, *Legal Fictions* 89 n.74 (1967). See **contest,** n. & **contestation.**

littoral rights. See **water rights.**

livable; liveable. The spelling *livable* is preferred in AmE, *liveable* in BrE. See MUTE E.

livery. See **delivery (B).**

livery of seisin (= the ceremonial procedure at common law by which a grantor conveyed land to a grantee) is LAW FRENCH (orig. *bail de la seisine*) for *delivery of seisin*. It is sanctioned by centuries of legal usage, and today ordinarily appears only in historical contexts. The ceremony involved going on the land and having the grantor symbolically deliver possession of the land to the grantee by handing over a twig, a clod, or a piece of turf. Alternatively, *livery of seisin* could be accomplished by the grantor's telling the grantee, in view of the land, that possession was given to the grantee, followed by the grantee's entering the land. E.g.:

- "[In] 1540 . . . it was decided that, if a man made a feoffment to perform his will and the will was annexed to the charter of feoffment, and *livery of seisin* was made thereon, he could alter or revoke the will." John Malcolm William Bean, *The Decline of English Feudalism, 1215–1540* 151 n.3 (1968).
- "Land transfers occurred through the ritual of '*livery of seisin*,' or delivery of possession, wherein land changed hands only after the parties traveled to the land being conveyed and the transferor handed the transferee a clump of soil or a tree branch taken from the land." Michelle Andrea Wenzel, *The Model Surface Use and Mineral Development Accommodation Act*, 42 Am. U. L. Rev. 607, 614 (1993).
- "A feoffment, with *livery of seisin*, though once the usual method of conveyance, has long since ceased to be generally employed." Joshua Williams, *Principles of the Law of Real Property* 100 (2006).

The *OED* notes that *livery and seisin* is a common error for *livery of seisin*. See **delivery (B)** & **seisin.**

living constitutionalism. See *contemporaneous interpretation* under INTERPRETATION, MODES OF (B) & **originalism.**

living-tree doctrine is a Canadian doctrine of constitutional interpretation characterizing the constitution as a "living tree" capable of growth and expansion and mandating that it be given a "large and liberal interpretation." This doctrine was first announced in a 1930 decision of the Judicial Committee of the Privy Council. *Edwards v. Canada*, [1930] A.C. 124 (P.C.).

living trust. See *inter vivos* trust.

living will; advance directive. *Living will*, a phrase that dates from the early 1970s, is not a statutory term—in fact, it is really misnamed, because the document to which it refers is not a will at all. It refers to a legal document instructing doctors, relatives, and others when to refrain from using life-support measures to prolong one's life during a catastrophic illness. E.g.:

- "*Living wills* are useful for people who would rather bow out quickly and gracefully than fight for their lives as long as possible." Letter of F. Ackerman, N.Y. Times, 13 Oct. 1989, at 22.
- "Under common law these situations can also be addressed in a *living will*, but the patient would never know it from the materials distributed. . . . There is no reason these *advance directives* should not be physician managed, just as surgical consent forms, anatomical gift forms and do-not-resuscitate orders are." Letter of Alan D. Lieberson, *Law on "Living Wills" Doesn't Go Far Enough*, N.Y. Times, 21 Dec. 1991, at 14.
- "Many states . . . now permit '*living wills*,' . . . and the withdrawal or refusal of life-sustaining medical treatment." *Washington v. Glucksberg*, 521 U.S. 702, 716 (1997) (per Rehnquist, C.J.).

Advance directive refers to a document that is much like a *living will* but broader in scope and more detailed. An advance directive is a durable power of attorney designating a surrogate decision-maker for healthcare matters. An advance directive takes effect upon incompetency—and is "durable" because, unlike most other powers of attorney, it remains in effect during the maker's incompetency—e.g.: "The federal Patient Self-Determination Act now requires hospitals to inform patients of their rights under state law to create '*advance directives*' relating to their medical care and to find out whether patients have such *advance directives*." Thomas Mayo, *Patients' Rights*, Dallas Morning News, 15 Dec. 1991, at 4J.

L.J., an abbreviation for "Lord Justice," is pluralized *LL.J.*

LL.B. See **J.D.**

LL.M. See **J.D.**

loadstar. See **lodestar.**

loadstone; lodestone. This term, meaning "something that strongly attracts," is spelled *loadstone* in BrE and *lodestone* in AmE—e.g.: "The intention of the testator is the guide, or in the phrase of Lord Coke, the *lodestone* of the court." *Jackson v. Phillips*, 96 Mass. 539, 591 (1867). Cf. **lodestar.**

loan; lend. In formal usage, it is best to use *lend* as the verb and *loan* as the noun. But *loan* is considered permissible when used as a verb denoting the lending of money (as distinguished from the lending of articles).

LOAN TRANSLATIONS are English terms arrived at by translating foreign terms into English equivalents. So we arrive at the un-English-sounding *next friend* as a loan translation (or calque) of *prochein ami*. The language of the law has many such terms, usually translated from Latin or French. (See LAW FRENCH & LAW LATIN.) Among the most common loan translations in legal writing are these:

English Term	Foreign Term
action on the case	*action sur le case* (L.F.)
against the form of the statute	*contra formam statuti* (L.)
against the peace	*contra pacem* (L.)
as of right	*de jure* (L.)
a year and a day	*ann et jour* (L.F.)
burden of proof	*onus probandi* (L.)
civil death	*mors civilis* (L.)
damage without injury	*damnum absque injuria* (L.)
dead-hand	*mortmain* (L.F.)
defender of the faith	*fidei defensor* (L.)
friend of the court	*amicus curiae* (L.)
go hence without day	*aller sans jour* (L.F.)
goods and chattels	*bona et catalla* (L.F.)
half-blood	*demy-sangue* (L.F.)
have and hold	*habendum et tenendum* (L.)
	aver et tener (L.F.)
injury without damage	*injuria absque damno* (L.)
in the breast	*in pectore* (L.)
juridification	*Verrechtlichung* (Ger.)
keeper of the peace	*custos pacis* (L.)
King's Court	*Curia Regis* (L.)
know all persons	*noverint universi* (L.)
last will	*ultima voluntas* (L.)
law merchant	*lex mercatoria* (L.)
malice aforethought	*malitia praecogitata* (L.)
mere right	*jus merum* (L.)
	meer dreit (L.F.)
naked contract	*nudum pactum* (L.)
next friend	*prochein ami* (L.F.)
notwithstanding the verdict	*non obstante veredicto* (L.)
on pain of	*sur peine de* (L.F.)
on the high sea	*super altum mare* (L.)
plead not guilty	*plaider de rien culpable* (L.F.)
these presents	*hac praesentes litterae* (L.)
true bill	*billa vera* (L.)
under pain of	*sous pein de* (L.F.)
	sub poena (L.)
unwritten law	*lex non scripta* (L.)
with force and arms	*vi et armis* (L.)

Sometimes the Englished versions require skillful inference to arrive at the meaning—e.g.: "An acceptance, which only remains *in the breast* of the acceptor without being actually and by legal implication communicated to the offerer, is no binding acceptance." *Household Fire & Carriage Accident Ins. Co. v. Grant*, [1878–79] L.R. 4 Ex. D. 216 (C.A.). Others have no literal significance, but have been adopted as legal names (as TERMS OF ART or legal JARGON) for doctrines and causes of action, such as *trespass with force and arms*—e.g.: "Trespass. The declaration stated that defendant . . . *with force and arms* assaulted, debauched, and carnally knew . . . the daughter and servant of the plaintiff." *Margaret Davies v. Williams*, [1847] 116 E.R. 275 (Q.B.).

The tendency toward translating unassimilated foreign terms that are used in law into English is salutary on the whole. *Dead-hand* may never displace *mortmain*, and *friend of the court* may never displace *amicus curiae*, but most of the other foreign-language law terms have fallen into disuse. And most of the loan translations listed above have become familiar. Now there is little call for more loan translations, because legal English increasingly approximates general-purpose English.

loathe; loath; *loth. *Loathe* is the verb meaning "to abhor; detest." *Loath*, with its NEEDLESS VARIANT *loth, is an adjective meaning "reluctant." The verb spelling is frequently used wrongly for the adjective—e.g.:

- "Judges and crown prosecutors were not *loathe* [read *loath*] to intimidate a jury and even to punish the jurymen if they returned a verdict deemed improper by the judge." C. Gordon Post, *An Introduction to the Law* 53 (1963).
- "Yellow has proved itself *loathe* [read *loath*] to loosen its grip on the airport market." *Independent Taxicab Drivers' Employees v. Greater Houston Transp. Co.*, 760 F.2d 607, 609 (5th Cir. 1985).
- "Our courts have generally been *loathe* [read *loath*] to recognize an absolute right to health care." Alison M. Sulentic, *What Catholic School Teaching Says to Catholic Sponsors of School Plans*, 17 J. Contemp. Health L. & Pol'y 1, 3 (2000).

lobby. The legislative senses derive ultimately from the architectural sense of the word. In 19th-century AmE, *lobby* came to denote, through METONYMY, the persons who habitually occupy the lobby in a legislative chamber for the purpose of carrying on business with legislators, esp. influencing their votes. A famous Washington hotel (the Willard) falsely claims that the term was coined in reference to the legislators who once frequented its grand lobby. In fact, though, the legislative sense predates the building of that hotel by nearly a quarter-century. Yet the faux etymology persists.

As a verb, *lobby* has come to mean: (1) to frequent legislative chambers for the purpose of influencing the members' official actions <the group lobbied against the proposed reforms>; or (2) to promote or oppose (a measure) by soliciting legislative votes <the organization lobbied a measure through the House>.

The agent-noun *lobbyist*, meaning "one who lobbies," originated during the American Civil War.

lobbyist; *lobbyer; *lobbier. The second and third forms are NEEDLESS VARIANTS. See **lobby.**

locale; locality. Both terms are frequently used; for the most part they are equivalent, but only *locale* has the sense "the setting or scene of action or of a story."

locate for *set up shop* or *establish residence* is an Americanism that, despite its having been criticized

by several grammarians, has become standard <after several years in the Plaza, the firm located in the Crescent>. *Locate* is transitive in BrE and means "to place" or "to ascertain the whereabouts of." In AmE, the word is used in these senses, but also in the colloquial intransitive sense of "to settle; to begin residing." The sense "to fix or establish in a place" is also distinctively AmE—e.g.: "Subsection (b) of the statute would seem generally to *locate* review of licensing proceedings in the courts of appeals." *Florida Power & Light Co. v. Lorion*, 470 U.S. 729, 736 (1985) (per Brennan, J.). This usage is by no means new—e.g.: "[The 1869 law] is aptly framed to remove from the more densely populated part of the city, the noxious slaughter-houses, and large and offensive collections of animals necessarily incident to [them], and to *locate* them where the convenience, health, and comfort of the people require they shall be located." *The Slaughter-House Cases*, 83 U.S. (16 Wall.) 36, 64 (1872) (per Miller, J.).

LOCATIVES. See CASE REFERENCES (B).

Lochnerize, vb.; **Lochnerization,** n. These terms derive from the case name *Lochner v. New York*, 198 U.S. 45 (1905). *Lochnerize* = to scrutinize and invalidate economic regulations under the guise of enforcing the Due Process Clause. The term carries no small degree of opprobrium: "*Lochnerizing* has become so much an epithet that the very use of the label may obscure attempts at understanding." Laurence Tribe, *American Constitutional Law* 435 (1978). E.g.:

- "Of course we are *Lochnerizing* and intruding into the affairs of a state." *Dunagin v. City of Oxford, Miss.*, 718 F.2d 738, 755 (5th Cir. 1983) (Higginbotham, J., dissenting).
- "Equal protection was so disfavored that, during the heyday of '*Lochnerizing*,' it was called 'the usual last resort of constitutional arguments.'" *Town of Ball v. Rapides Parish Police Jury*, 746 F.2d 1049, 1056 (5th Cir. 1984).
- "Others have decried the purported '*Lochnerization*' of attempts to regulate media as improperly subjecting mere economic regulation to unduly searching constitutional review." Lili Levi, *A "Pay or Play" Experiment to Improve Children's Educational Television*, 62 Fed. Comm. L.J. 275, 299 n.94 (2010).

lockout, n., = (1) an employer's closing of a business or across-the-board dismissal of employees because of disagreement over the terms of employment; or (2) employees' refusal to work because the employer unreasonably refuses to abide by an expired employment contract while a new one is being negotiated.

lock up. See **jail,** vb.

loco parentis. See *in loco parentis.*

locus; situs. Both terms are used in law to mean "a place in which something is situated or is done." *Locus* is the more concrete, specific term: "We hold that at the death of John Girdler's widow . . . his three daughters and granddaughter held undivided equal estates tail in the *locus*." *Hayes v. Hammond*, 143 N.E.2d 693, 698 (Mass. 1957). *Situs*, to the contrary, is more abstract, with a usually broader, territorial sense of "place"—e.g.:

- "Such a decree ought to be entitled to full faith and credit at the *situs* of the land." *Day v. Wiswall*, 464 P.2d 626, 630 (Ariz. Ct. App. 1970).
- "Holding that Mexico rather than Texas was the *situs* of the deposits furthers the general policies of the act of state doctrine." *Callejo v. Bancomer, S.A.*, 764 F.2d 1101, 1125 (5th Cir. 1985).

See **situs.**

locus in quo (= the place where something is alleged to have been done) is common in property law, but is often unnecessary in place of *locus* or *location*. Here it is perhaps justifiable, because its use implicitly incorporates the notion of allegations in a lawsuit: "It is proper to admit photographs of a *locus in quo* even though taken 15½ months after the accident." *Hamilton v. Fean*, 221 A.2d 309, 315 (Pa. 1966).

locus poenitentiae /loh-kəs pen-i-**ten**-shee-ı/ = a point at which it is not too late for a person to change his or her legal position; the possibility of withdrawing from a contemplated course of action, esp. a wrong, before being committed to it. E.g.:

- "He would have us hold that so long as the cause or proceeding in which false testimony is given is not closed there remains a *locus poenitentiae* of which he was entitled to and did avail himself. The implications and results of such a doctrine prove its unsoundness." *U.S. v. Norris*, 300 U.S. 564, 573–74 (1937) (per Roberts, J.).
- "Mrs. Rosenblum enjoyed a *locus poenitentiae*, of which she could take advantage until Jacks or Better somehow changed its position; and she acted promptly in recalling the words of rescission." *Rosenblum v. Jacks or Better of Am. West, Inc.*, 745 S.W.2d 754, 759 (Mo. Ct. App. 1988).

locus sigilli. See **L.S.**

locus standi (= the right to bring an action or to be heard in a given forum) seems to be an unnecessary LATINISM, in view of the more common American legal term *standing*. But *locus standi* is common in BrE—e.g.:

- "First, it may be asked what, if any, *locus standi* the Law Society has in a matter of this kind." *Pearson v. Pearson*, [1971] P. 16.
- "A logically prior question was also raised by the Trustee in these proceedings as to the *locus standi* of Mrs Bayliss to bring an application under Section 303 of the Act if she does not have a contract with the Trustee." *Nicholas Miller (As Trustee in Bankruptcy of Keith Bayliss) v. Donna Jane Bayliss*, [2009] E.W.H.C. 2063 (Ch.).
- "The petitioners' contractual indemnity obligations would not arise unless and until decree was pronounced against their insured in such proceedings, and they were thus too far removed *quoad* both time and status to have any legitimate *locus standi*." *Axa General Ins. Ltd.*, [2010] C.S.O.H. 2.

Formerly it was used in the sense "credentials, established position of high standing." (See **standing.**) The phrase is medieval in origin—it does not appear in classical Roman sources.

lodestar; loadstar. The first spelling is preferred in both AmE and BrE for this term meaning "a guiding star." (The word derives fr. O.E. lād [= way, course] + *star*.) The term has jargonistic uses in setting fees and damages, and these lead to mixed metaphors: "The court increased the adjusted *lodestar* amount by 30 percent to compensate counsel for the delay in receiving payment for the legal services rendered." *Library of Congress v. Shaw*, 478 U.S. 310, 313 (1986) (per Blackmun, J.). (The figurative does not impinge on the literal sense if we write of *raising* a lodestar, but it does so impinge if we write of *increasing* a lodestar.) See METAPHORS (A).

lodestone. See **loadstone.**

LOGIC. See ILLOGIC.

logical construction. See *logical interpretation* under INTERPRETATION, MODES OF (B).

logical fallacy. See **grammatical error.**

logical interpretation. See *logical interpretation* under INTERPRETATION, MODES OF (B).

logomachy /loh-**gom**-ə-kee/ = a contention about words. E.g.:

- "The student of jurisprudence is at times troubled by the thought that he is dealing not with things, but with words, that he is busy with the shape and size of counters in a game of *logomachy*." John C. Gray, *Nature and Sources of the Law* viii (1909).
- "I know for myself that for the past thirty years and more a great part of my daily business has been to give opinions, to argue or to decide as to the meaning of words. These disputes are by no means always barren *logomachies*." Lord Macmillan, *Law and Other Things* 154 (1937).

logorrhea (= diarrhea of the mouth) is an affliction of which lawyers must beware.

long, adv., can stand alone, without *for* preceding it—e.g.: "We have *now for long* [read *now long*] been accustomed, with some archaic survivals, to the doctrine that imposed liability depends in part upon the conscious attitude which a supposititious normal person would take towards the damage resulting from his acts." *Sinram v. Pennsylvania R.R.*, 61 F.2d 767, 770 (2d Cir. 1932) (per L. Hand, J.).

long-arm statute (= a statute providing for the maintenance of jurisdiction over nonresident defendants) derives from the catchphrase *the (long) arm of the law*.

longer than. See **above (A).**

longshoreman. See SEXISM (B).

long-standing, adj. So spelled.

---

looker-on. See **witness (B).**

look over. See **overlook.**

loophole. This term, dating from 1591 (*OED*), originally referred to a narrow vertical opening, widening inward, cut in a wall or door to allow through the passage either cannon fire and other missiles, or light and air. The word *loop* in this compound does not bear its modern sense, but instead derives from the medieval Dutch verb *lupen*, meaning "to lie in wait, watch, or peer."

By the late 1600s, the word had taken on its figurative sense in reference to an ambiguity, omission, or exception in a statute or other legal document. Today this figurative sense prevails—e.g.: "The court was also out to close all *loopholes*, such as the possibility of the brokers and title companies getting legislation giving them the right to do what they had been doing all along." Murray T. Bloom, *The Trouble with Lawyers* 103 (1970).

loose, vb.; **loosen.** Both words mean "to unbind; release." The DIFFERENTIATION between the two is that *loose* generally refers to a complete release <loosing criminals on the community>, *loosen* generally to a partial release <loosening one's belt>. Additionally, *loosen* is figurative more often than *loose*. See **lose.**

loose interpretation. See *liberal interpretation* under INTERPRETATION, MODES OF (B).

loot. See **spoils.**

Lord Chancellor. The plural is sometimes made *Lords Chancellor,* sometimes *Lord Chancellors,* and sometimes *Lords Chancellors.* The prevailing, and the best, form is *Lord Chancellors.* But cf. **lord justice.** See **chancellor** & **Keeper of the King's Conscience.**

Lord Chief Justice; Lord President. Historically, the Lord Chief Justice ranked second to the Lord Chancellor in the English judiciary. After the judiciary was reformed in 2006, the Lord Chief Justice assumed all the judicial functions of the Lord Chancellor, and became the head of the judiciary for England and Wales. The title was also reformed—Lord Chief Justice of England and Wales—for clarification. Northern Ireland and Scotland have their own independent judiciaries, headed by the Lord Chief Justice of Northern Ireland (since 1922) and Lord President of the Court of Session (since 1836).

Lord High Chancellor. See **chancellor.**

lord justice, the title of a judge on the (English) Court of Appeal, is generally pluralized *lords justices.* But *lord justices* might be an improvement. See **Lord Chancellor.**

Lord of Appeal in Ordinary; Lord Ordinary. Terms such as these often baffle those unacquainted with the British legal system. Until 2009, the *Lords of Appeal in Ordinary,* known also as *Law Lords,* sat in the House of Lords as the highest appellate court in the U.K. The

Lords Ordinary sit in Scotland as the trial judges in the Court of Session. See **Law Lord.**

Lord President. See **Lord Chief Justice.**

Lords is sometimes used as an elliptical term for *House of Lords*—e.g.: "Decision-making in the *Lords* does not take place in a vacuum." Alan Paterson, *The Law Lords* 9 (1982). Sometimes the elliptical expression can lead to what seems to be an error in SUBJECT–VERB AGREEMENT. But BrE usage makes *Lords* a singular when the reference is to the House—e.g.: "Oliver Cromwell later explained that the *Lords* was 'very forward to give up the people's rights.'" *Peering Ahead,* Economist, 9–15 June 1990, at 68. See **House of Lords.**

lose; loose. *Lose,* vb., = to suffer the deprivation of; to part with. *Loose* is both adjective and verb, meaning in the latter use "to release; unfasten." Writers sometimes misuse *loose* for *lose*—e.g.:

- "Plaintiff and the other man ran and the police pursued, *loosing* [read *losing*] sight of the two for approximately 30 to 60 seconds." *Stratton v. City of Albany,* 612 N.Y.S.2d 286, 288 (App. Div. 1994).
- "Martini chased defendant, never *loosing* [read *losing*] eye contact with him." *People v. Pulliam,* 626 N.E.2d 356, 357 (Ill. App. Ct. 1994). (In the latter example, notice also the misuse of *eye contact* for *sight.*)

See **loose.**

loser; winner. Courts sometimes use *loser* and *winner* as substitutes for *appellant* and *appellee,* respectively. E.g.: "We may affirm a summary judgment only if the record, read in the light most favorable to the *loser* [i.e., appellant], reveals no genuine issues of material fact and shows the *winners* [i.e., appellees] were entitled to judgment as a matter of law." *Loehr v. Ventura County Cmty. Coll. Dist.,* 743 F.2d 1310, 1313 (9th Cir. 1984).

loser-pays rule. See **English Rule.**

loss-of-bargain damages; lost-expectation damages. These phrases, which should be so hyphenated, both refer to breach-of-contract damages that would place the injured party in the position he or she would have been in had the contract been performed—e.g.: "Another major shift in the law appears to lie in an increased reluctance to award pure '*lost expectation*' *damages,* except perhaps in straightforward commercial cases." P.S. Atiyah, *An Introduction to the Law of Contract* 21–22 (3d ed. 1981).

lost earnings; lost earning capacity. In personal-injury cases, the distinction is an important one. To determine *lost earnings,* the court looks to what a plaintiff actually earned before the injury. To determine *lost earning capacity,* the court looks (more expansively) to the plaintiff"s diminished earning power resulting from the injury.

lost-expectation damages. See **loss-of-bargain damages.**

lost property; mislaid property; abandoned property. At common law, these descriptions governed the disposition of property found by someone other than its original owner. The distinctions are still valid in many English-speaking jurisdictions. Property is said to be *lost* when the owner has involuntarily relinquished possession of it, usually by accident or forgetfulness, and cannot or is highly unlikely to recover it by diligent search. Property is *mislaid* when the owner has intentionally put it in a place and then forgotten it, but may find it by diligent searching. It is *abandoned* if the owner has knowingly forsaken interest in the property.

*****loth.** See **loathe.**

lower court. See **higher court** & **inferior (B).**

loyalty. See **fidelity.**

L.S. (= *locus sigilli*, meaning "place of the seal") is occasionally used on contracts and deeds in place of an actual seal. As contracts under seal have fallen into disuse, so has the need for this abbreviation. See **seal (A), (B).** Cf. **ss.**

lucri causa /loo-kree kaw-zə/ (= for the sake of gain) was once considered a necessary element of larceny: the thief must have been motivated by some purpose of gain or advantage. Today, in jurisdictions that retain larceny as a crime, *lucri causa* is generally considered an inessential element, the intent to deprive the owner of his or her property being sufficient.

lunacy. See **insanity (A).**

lunatic, once a clinical medical description, was formerly used frequently in legal writing—e.g.: "Since the act of 1894 it has not been necessary to issue any process, or have an order of publication, against the *lunatic*." *Rutledge v. Rutledge*, 85 A. 661, 665 (Md. Ct. App. 1912). Today, however, the term is one of opprobrium because of its figurative abuses; it should be used

cautiously if at all. For *lunacy* and its near-synonyms, see **insanity (A).**

luxuriant; luxurious. *Luxuriant*, a favorite word of metaphrasts, means "growing abundantly; lush"—e.g.: "The states have decided that it is better to leave a few of its noxious branches to their *luxuriant* growth, than by pruning them away to injure the vigor of those yielding the proper fruits." James Madison, "Reports on the Virginia Resolutions, 1799–1800," in 4 *Debates of the Several State Conventions on the Adoption of the Federal Constitution* 571 (Jonathan Elliot ed., 2d rev. ed. 1836).

Luxurious = characteristic of luxury. Sometimes the word is confused with *luxuriant*—e.g.: "With his *luxuriously* [read *luxuriantly*] curly white hair, dark bushy eyebrows, olive skin and direct gaze, Judge Botein reminds one lawyer I know of 'an implacable Old Testament Judge.'" Murray T. Bloom, *The Trouble with Lawyers* 168 (1970).

lying. See **dishonest.**

lynch law = the administration of summary punishment, esp. death, for an alleged crime, without legal authority. The phrase connotes mob lawlessness brought about by a perception that justice will be either denied or grossly delayed.

The phrase has an interesting etymology. Originally *Lynch's law*, it took its name from William Lynch (1742–1820) of Virginia, who in 1780 organized his neighbors to maintain order and punish lawlessness in their community. At first the phrase referred to punishments milder than death—whipping, tarring and feathering, burning houses, and the like—but since the late 19th century, the term has been increasingly confined to sentences of death by hanging. The verb *to lynch*, for example, carries that meaning exclusively: "to hang (a person) by lynch law."

lynch lawyer. See LAWYERS, DEROGATORY NAMES FOR (B).

*****lynchpin.** See **linchpin.**

M

MACARONISM. See MINGLE-MANGLE.

Macnaghten; MacNaughton. See **McNaghten.**

maelstrom, originally a Dutch word referring to a grinding or turning stream, is frequently misspelled
*maelstorm—e.g.:

- "Restrictions placed upon human rights have been so recurrent and persistent that labor laws have often been caught up and held lifeless in local *maelstorms* [read *maelstroms*]." David Ziskind, *Labor Laws in the Vortex of Human Rights Protection*, 5 Comp. Lab. L. 131, 137 (1982).

- "The release of the story brought on a *maelstorm* [read *maelstrom*] of criticism in the press." Katherine H. Adams, *Progressive Politics* 142 (1999).

magisterial; magistral. Although *magisterial* carries connotations of nobility, command, and even dictatorialness, it is also the preferred adjective corresponding to the noun *magistrate*—e.g.: "'De novo' means only that the district court shows no deference to *magistral* [read *magisterial*] findings and may conduct rehearings as necessary." Andrew W. Stuart, Note, *I Tell Ya I Don't Get No Respect!*, 23 Law & Pol'y Int'l

Bus. 749, 759 n.40 (1992). *Magistratic* and ***magistratical* are NEEDLESS VARIANTS. *Magistral* = (1) of a master or masters <an absolutely magistral work>; or (2) formulated by a physician <a magistral ointment>.

magistracy; *magistrature; *magistrateship. The first of these is the standard term for the office, district, or power of a magistrate, or body of magistrates. **Magistrature* and **magistrateship* are NEEDLESS VARIANTS.

magistral. See **magisterial.**

magistrate. In both AmE and BrE, *magistrate* is now generally understood as referring to a judicial officer with strictly limited jurisdiction and authority, often on the local level. In G.B., for example, *magistrate* is synonymous with *justice of the peace* and frequently appears in the phrases *police magistrate, metropolitan magistrate, stipendiary magistrate* (now called a *district judge*), and *magistrates' courts*. (See **stipe**.) In Ireland the phrase is *resident magistrate*. The common characteristic is that *magistrate* "generally means a judge of inferior rank." Max Radin, *The Law and You* 110 (1948).

But formerly the word retained a meaning closer to its etymological sense. Derived from L. *magistratus* or *magister* (= master), it once referred to the official first in rank in a branch of government. Hence an emperor, a monarch, or a president might have been termed a *magistrate*. E.g.: "*Edicta*, laws [that] the emperor himself put forth, in his character as highest *magistrate*." James Hadley, *Introduction to Roman Law* 6–7 (1881). So it is that Justice Cardozo referred to Chief Justice Marshall, with the greatest reverence, as the *magistrate* who wrote *Marbury v. Madison*. *See Law and Literature*, 52 Harv. L. Rev. 471, 476 (1939).

But because by the late 20th century the connotations of *magistrate* had fallen so, United States Magistrates—i.e., those at the federal level—lobbied in the late 1980s for a name change. In 1990 they got it, in the Judicial Improvements Act, and they are now called (pleonastically but to them pleasingly) *United States Magistrate Judges*. See **magisterial.**

magistrates' courts. In England—as a result of the Magistrates' Courts Act 1952—this term refers to what were formerly known as *Courts of Summary Jurisdiction*, i.e., the Justices in Petty Sessions and special sessions called Juvenile Courts and Matrimonial Courts.

*magistrateship; *magistrature. See **magistracy.**

Magna Carta; Magna Charta. The usual—and the better—form is *Magna Carta*. *Time* magazine used the secondary spelling and found itself on the defensive: "We were unfairly reproved for our spelling of the document *Magna Charta*. . . . Although many publications use the more familiar *Magna Carta*, most dictionaries prefer the word we used, *charta*, from the Latin word for paper." *Going by the Rules*, Time, 16 Dec. 1991, at 9. Which dictionaries? Not the Oxford dictionaries, the Merriam-Webster dictionaries, or the Random House dictionaries. The *OED* shows that the great document was known exclusively as *Magna Carta* from the 13th to the 17th centuries. And the leading British textbooks, by W.H. McKechnie and J.C. Holt, use *Carta*.

And what about the *Time* editors' argument that *charta* is the Latin word for "paper"? That argument is empty: *charta* and *carta* are variant forms bearing the same meaning in Latin.

Magna Carta does not take a definite article: one says *Magna Carta*, not *the Magna Carta*. E.g.: "Gradually the writ of habeas corpus became the means by which the promise of *Magna Carta* was fulfilled." *Boumediene v. Bush*, 553 U.S. 723, 740 (2008) (per Kennedy, J.).

magnanimous (= big-spirited, high-minded, and generous) has, weirdly, come to be misused as an equivalent of *magnificent*, especially in reference to sums of money. This usage is at best a MALAPROPISM—e.g.:

- "The sum in the general account is not a particularly handsome one in view of the trustees' unpaid obligations, but it is a *magnanimous* [read *magnificent*] amount compared to the balance in the general account on March 19, 1971, which was $11.70." *In re Flying W Airways, Inc.*, 341 F.Supp. 26, 84 (E.D. Pa. 1972).
- "Ex-husband was given 'for spending money' the *magnanimous* [read *magnificent*] amount of $45 per week for working in the grocery store. This does not approach the salary of carryout boys in grocery stores." *Tuttle v. Tuttle*, 399 N.W.2d 876, 879 n.* (S.D. 1986).

*maihem. See **mayhem (C).**

maim; cripple; mutilate; mangle. These verbs share the sense "to commit bodily injury, usu. with malicious intent, so severely as to leave long-lasting physical impairments." *Maim* suggests the loss of a limb or member <he was maimed in the accident and became a double amputee>. (For the noun *maim*, see **mayhem (B)**.) *Cripple* is narrower because it suggests the involvement only of full limbs (not members), and it can refer either to a loss of limb or to a loss of its use—hence an accident could *cripple* someone who retains all four limbs. But the word *cripple* has long been thought to have such a pejorative cast as to be emotionally insensitive. (See EUPHEMISMS.) *Mutilate* suggests physical disfigurement as a result of a violent act, especially the cutting off or removal of a part essential to the whole person <Tyson mutilated his opponent by biting off part of his ear>. *Mangle* does not suggest the loss of a limb, member, or body part, but it does suggest disfiguring injuries from tearing, hacking, or crushing, as well as resultant wounds or cuts of a serious nature <his hand was mangled by the printing press>.

main opinion (AmE) = *majority opinion*. See **majority opinion.**

mainour. This word is a historical curiosity in modern opinions—e.g.: "We are convinced that there was no proof that appellant was 'taken with the *mainour*.'"

King v. State, 645 S.W.2d 782, 785 (Tex. Crim. App. 1981) (explaining, in note 2: "A thief caught with the stolen goods in his possession was said to be taken 'with the *mainour*,' i.e., with the goods in manu, in his hands."). So *with the mainour* is synonymous with *in flagrante delicto*. See **in flagrante delicto.**

mainprise; *mainprize. This word, referring to an old procedure for compelling a sheriff to take sureties for a prisoner's appearance, is generally spelled *mainprise*. The etymological meaning is taking by the hand (fr. Fr. *main* & *pris*).

mainstream, as a verb, is a jargonistic VOGUE WORD to be avoided—e.g.: "I have often tried to wrap my mind around the experience of the *exonerated; reintegrating and mainstreaming* [read *exonerated and reintegrating*] a small population of innocent ex-prisoners who have had the very core *tenant* [read *tenet*] of an American life, their liberty and pursuit of happiness stripped from them." Heather Weigand, *Rebuilding a Life*, 18 B.U. Pub. Int. L.J. 427, 431 (2009). (*Mainstreaming* here adds nothing to *reintegrating*.)

The noun use, of course, is unobjectionable—e.g.: "Precisely because Kehowski's ideas fall outside the *mainstream*, his words sparked intense debate." *Rodriguez v. Maricopa County Cmty. Coll. Dist.*, 605 F.3d 703, 708 (9th Cir. 2010). So is its use as an adjective—e.g.: "[The] 'laboratory of the states' model . . . only works properly when a large number of cases are decided and reported. Otherwise, outliers cannot be separated from *mainstream* decisions." Joshua D.H. Karton & Lorraine de Germiny, *Has the CISG Advisory Council Come of Age?*, 27 Berkeley J. Int'l L. 448, 490 (2009). See NOUNS AS VERBS.

maintain. A. And Its Near-Synonyms: *assert*; *defend*; *vindicate*; *justify*. These verbs share the sense "to support the worthiness of something despite considerable opposition or apathy." *Maintain* suggests strong convictions <Holmes maintained that one could live well in the law> and often defiant perseverance <though mocked by the left and the right alike, Buckley maintained that most drugs should be legalized>. *Assert* suggests an aggressive attempt to persuade <Justice Black asserted that there were simply no exceptions to the First Amendment's freedom of speech>, but it does not always suggest rational argument as opposed to mere bald statement <bizarrely, he asserted a claim under the divine right of kings>. *Defend* suggests attempting to demonstrate the soundness of a position that is being assailed—but it does not express the vehemence of *assert* <the governor defended the mandatory vaccinations>. *Vindicate* in this sense suggests a successful instance of asserting or defending, especially once the passage of time has shown the truth of the matter to be close to what one was asserting or defending. (See **vindicate.**) *Justify* in this sense suggests that the point in dispute has now

become incontestable because of conclusive proof or irrefutable demonstration. For more on the idiomatic use of *justify*, see **justify.**

B. *Maintain a lawsuit*. In this construction, *maintain* is not synonymous with *begin* or *institute*; it embraces the idea of *continuing* or *upholding*. See *Smallwood v. Gallardo*, 275 U.S. 56, 61 (1927) (per Holmes, J.). See **maintenance (B).**

maintainer; *maintainor. The *-er* spelling is preferred in all senses. See **champertor.**

maintenance. A. Legal Senses. *Maintenance* = (1) the care and work put into a building to keep it operating and productive; general repair and upkeep; (2) help in a lawsuit given by a stranger to it who has no lawful cause; meddling in somebody else's litigation; or (3) court-ordered or contractually agreed-upon support for an estranged spouse or for children.

B. For *maintain*. Using *maintenance* as a verb in place of *maintain*, vb. <to maintenance a certain line of inquiry>, is poor. See NOUNS AS VERBS.

C. And *champerty*. See **champerty (A).**

maintenance and cure (= compensation afforded by maritime law to a sailor who gets sick or is injured while working on a vessel) is a TERM OF ART in admiralty contexts—e.g.: "The seaman's right to *maintenance and cure* for illness or injury occurring while he is in the service of the ship is often analogized to workmen's compensation. While the origins of the right are customarily traced back to the mediæval sea codes, it appears to have been first recognized in this country by Justice Story in two cases [that] he decided on circuit." Grant Gilmore & Charles L. Black Jr., *The Law of Admiralty* 281 (2d ed. 1975).

majorat (= [1] the right of primogeniture in Spain, Italy, and other countries; or [2] an estate attached to the right of primogeniture) is pronounced /mə-**zhor**-ə/. In the plural form (*majorats*), the pronunciation remains the same. See **primogeniture.**

majority. A. And *plurality*. These terms are frequently used in reference to judicial opinions, as well as to elections. *Majority* = a group of more than 50 percent (e.g., five of nine judges). *Plurality* = the group with the largest percentage where none of the percentages is 50 percent or more (e.g., four of nine judges, when three have adopted a different position, and two others still another position). See **majority opinion** & **plurality opinion.**

B. Number. *Majority*, like *minority*, is generally used in AmE as a COLLECTIVE NOUN, so that it takes a singular verb. E.g.:

- "The majority *reach* [read *reaches*] their [read *its*] result by drastically misreading the record or ignoring it completely." *People v. Mayoff*, 729 P.2d 166, 179 (Cal. 1986) (Bird, C.J., dissenting).

- "The majority *deem* [read *deems*] it unnecessary to consider Herrera's alternative contentions that Texas has voluntarily waived its sovereign immunity." *University of Tex. at El Paso v. Herrera*, 281 S.W.3d 575, 592 (Tex. App.—El Paso 2008) (Carr, J., dissenting).

But in the phrase *a majority of (people or things)*, the word *majority* is generally treated as a plural in both AmE and BrE—e.g.:

- "The great *majority* of prosecutions *are* in theory private." Patrick Devlin, *The Criminal Prosecution in England* 16 (1960).
- "Of those material exhibits, the *majority are* documents containing Petitioner's statements, and only a *minority* of those statements *are* reliable." *Anam v. Obama*, 696 F.Supp.2d 1, 5 (D.D.C. 2010).

See SYNESIS.

C. References in Dissenting Opinions. In some courts, such as the U.S. Court of Appeals for the First Circuit, it has generally been considered bad form to refer in a dissent to what the "*majority*" says. The thought was that, because the *majority* speaks for the court as a whole, a temperate dissenter should use the term *court* instead of *majority*. See OPINIONS, JUDICIAL.

D. For *full age*. This LEGALISM <age of majority> is common in both AmE and BrE. E.g.: "In the law of contract, persons below the age of *majority* were formerly called infants." G.H. Treitel, *The Law of Contract* 481 (8th ed. 1991). Cf. **minority (A).**

majority opinion (AmE) = the chief opinion of an appellate court when more than one opinion is filed. See **opinion of the court.**

make (= to draw up [a legal document]) is an old legal idiom, dating from the 14th century <they made their wills>. In several phrases, such as *make answer*, it contributes to wordiness—e.g.: "Within twenty days, if the case is to come before the New York Supreme Court, the defendant must *make his answer* [read *answer*] unless he secures an extension of time from the court." C. Gordon Post, *An Introduction to the Law* 134 (1963).

make a mockery of is a CLICHÉ to be avoided.

make an appearance. See **appearance, make an.**

***make and enter into** is a doublet for *make* or *enter into*. See DOUBLETS, TRIPLETS, AND SYNONYM STRINGS. See also **enter.**

make do (= to get by satisfactorily in less-than-ideal conditions; to manage with barely adequate if not inadequate provisions) is so written. **Make due* is a distressingly common blunder—e.g.:

- "Respondent's own testimony showed just the slight difference of $80 per month, despite her claim that the children had to *make due* [read *make do*] with considerably less expensive clothes." *Esposito v. Esposito*, 371 N.W.2d 608, 610 (Minn. Ct. App. 1985).
- "When individuals or organizations satisfice, they *make due* [read *make do*] with means and ends they deem 'good

enough' rather than try in vain to optimize." David M. Frankford, *The Medicare DRGs*, 10 Yale J. Reg. 273, 300 n.87 (1993).

***make efforts** is verbose for *try*—e.g.: "Thus a contract by which a marriage bureau simply undertakes to *make efforts* [read *try*] to find a spouse for a client has been held invalid." G.H. Treitel, *The Law of Contract* 390 (8th ed. 1991).

make good (= to compensate for, restore, or effect) is a legal as well as a lay idiom. Its primary use in law is in the field of contracts—e.g.:

- "Unless the articles so require a company is not legally bound to *make good* losses of fixed capital before distributing current profits." 2 Earnest W. Chance, *Principles of Mercantile Law* 207 (Percy W. French ed., 10th ed. 1951).
- "Fernandez is entitled to indemnification now, whether or not he has already *made good* on his obligations to Goodridge." *Goodridge v. Harvey Group, Inc.*, 778 F.Supp. 115, 133 (S.D.N.Y. 1991).

As in the first example just cited, when this PHRASAL VERB is used transitively (with a direct object), it creates a MISCUE—e.g.: "There is, however, nothing objectionable about a promise to *make good defalcations* for which the promisor is personally responsible." P.S. Atiyah, *An Introduction to the Law of Contract* 231 (3d ed. 1981). The reader may wonder for an instant whether there has been a problem with *bad defalcations*? What is a *good defalcation*, and how does one make it? Of course, the miscue vanishes after a moment's reflection, but the problem with miscues is precisely that they demand a moment's reflection.

The lesson? Prefer *make good on* over *make good*.

make law. When applied to a legislature, this phrase means one thing. When applied to a court, it means quite another: "In applying the expression to the judge, we use it only in a derivative or secondary sense. Otherwise we are in danger of obscuring his essentially interpretative function. In this secondary sense, but only so, the judge does undoubtedly '*make*' law. It is not an original act of creation. Every act of interpretation shapes something new, in a secondary sense." Carleton K. Allen, *Law in the Making* 309 (7th ed. 1964). (For the use of *interpretative* in that quotation, see **interpretive.**)

***make oath and say.** This DOUBLET is an archaic equivalent of *testify*—e.g.: "I, Mark Bishop, *make oath and say* [read *testify*] as follows . . . ." *Watkin Ltd. v. Platt*, 545 So.2d 314, 314 (Fla. Dist. Ct. App. 1989) (quoting an affidavit).

***make provision for** is wordy in place of *provide for*. Further, *provision* is a BURIED VERB.

***make return of** (e.g., a warrant) is wordy for *return*.

make-whole, adj. To be *made whole* is to be returned to the *status quo ante*. The verb phrase *to make whole* has been transformed into the adjectival phrase *make-whole*—e.g.: "Backpay is a *make-whole* remedy intended to restore the employee to the financial situation that would have existed but for the employer's wrongful conduct." *Bonidy v. Vail Valley Ctr. for Aesthetic Dentistry, P.C.,* 232 P.3d 277, 283 (Colo. Ct. App. 2010). See **status quo.**

mala fide; mala fides. Mala fide (= in bad faith) is the adverb or adjective. *Mala fides* /mal-ə **fı**-deez/ (= bad faith) is the noun. Unlike *bona fide,* neither *mala fide* nor *mala fides* is understandable to most nonlawyers, and only infrequently is either phrase encountered in modern legal texts. The best advice is to avoid it and use the well-known Anglo-Saxon equivalent. See **bad faith,** *bona fides* & **good faith.**

The specimens below date from each of the past four centuries:

- "Therefore, we are all of opinion that the defendant ought in justice to refund this money thus *mala fide* recovered." *Moses v. Macpherlan,* [1760] 96 Eng. Rep. 120 (K.B.).
- "If advice given *mala fide,* and loss sustained, entitle me to damages, why, though the advice be given honestly [i.e., *bona fide*], but under wrong information, with a loss sustained, am I not entitled to them [i.e., damages]?" *Lumley v. Gye,* [1853] 2 E. & B. 216 (Q.B.).
- "The petitioner, while not claiming that there was any defense to the note or any irregularity or *mala fides* in the proceeding, alleged that the sale was void as against her." *Scott v. Paisley,* 271 U.S. 632, 634 (1926) (per Sanford, J.).
- "There has been no pleading or proof that the trustees have acted with *mala fides* or a lack of good faith." *Di Portanova v. Monroe,* 229 S.W.3d 324, 331 (Tex. App.— Houston [1st Dist.] 2006).

mala in se; mala prohibita. See *malum in se.*

MALAPROPISMS are incorrectly used words that produce a humorous effect. The term derives from the character Mrs. Malaprop in Sheridan's play *The Rivals;* Mrs. Malaprop loves big words but uses them ignorantly to create hilarious solecisms and occasionally embarrassing double entendres. One of Mrs. Malaprop's famous similes is *as headstrong as an allegory on the banks of the Nile.*

Legal malapropisms are more common than one might expect. One lawyer apparently mistook *meretricious* (= marked by falsity; superficially attractive but fake nevertheless) for *meritorious* with embarrassing consequences: a plaintiff's lawyer, he asked a judge to rule favorably on his client's "meretricious claim." Similarly, Senator Sam Ervin recalled a lawyer who, in arguing that his client had been provoked by name-calling (*epithets*), said: "I hope that in passing sentence on my client upon his conviction for assault and battery, your honor will bear in mind that he was provoked to do so by the *epitaphs* hurled at him by the witness." Quoted in Paul R. Clancy, *Just a Country Lawyer* 121 (1974).

Other illustrations are *nefarious* (= evil) for *multifarious* ("Ties, shirts, shoes, belts, socks, and all the other *nefarious* parts of one's wardrobe") and *voracity* (= greediness with food) for *veracity* ("There would

have been nothing to be gained by trying to impeach the truthfulness or *voracity* of those witnesses."). For still more examples, see **aspersions, avert, categorically, climactic, contribute, degradation, disparaging, dock, evoke, genericide, Hobson's choice (C), illicit, impotence, *inclimate, infinitely, inhere (B), in lieu of (C), magnanimous, meretricious, odious, panacea, petition, prodigious, prospectus (B), querulous, shock the conscience, solace, solicit (A), supersede (D), surcease, underway, *unmercilessly, veracity, waiver (D)** & ***wreckless.**

malefaction. See **malfeasance.**

malefactor /**mal**-ə-fak-tər/ = criminal; felon. Although the term is now primarily literary, the *OED* contains the following quotation of Herbert Spencer from 1862: "By a *malefactor,* we now understand a convicted criminal, which is far from being the acceptation of 'evil-doer'." Herbert Spencer, *First Principles* 438 (1862).

*malefeasance. See **malfeasance.**

malevolent; maleficent. Whereas the first means "wanting evil to befall others," the second means positively "hurtful or criminal to others." Hence *malevolent* has to do with malicious desires, and *maleficent* with malicious actions. See **malice** (final par.).

malfeasance; *malfeazance; *malefeasance; misfeasance; malefaction. Because the words *malfeasance* and *misfeasance* are imprecise in AmE, we begin with the clear-cut BrE distinctions. In BrE, *malfeasance* refers to an unlawful act, whereas *misfeasance* refers to an otherwise lawful act performed in a wrongful manner. **Malefeasance* and **malfeazance* are obsolete spellings of *malfeasance.*

In AmE, *malfeasance* is often confined to the sense "misprision; misconduct or wrongdoing by a public official." *Misfeasance* is a more general word meaning "transgression; trespass."

In AmE, the notion in the word *malfeasance* of public office is sometimes important. But the word is often used of corporate as well as of public officials, and sometimes of other persons—e.g.:

- "Defendants have . . . not cited any persuasive authorities to support their view that Washington, the successor, is tainted in equity by the *malfeasance* of Oaks, its predecessor." *Washington Capitols Basketball Club, Inc. v. Barry,* 304 F.Supp. 1193, 1199 (N.D. Cal. 1969).
- "The contract shall not cover any loss of production . . . due to . . . the neglect or *malfeasance* of the insured." *R & R Farm Enters. v. Federal Crop Ins. Corp.,* 788 F.2d 1148, 1149 n.1 (5th Cir. 1986).

The legislative drafter of the following statutory provision was not unorthodox in using both *malfeasance* and *misfeasance:* "Respondents were classified civil service employees, entitled [under] Ohio Rev. Code Ann. § 124.34 (1984) to retain their positions 'during good behavior and efficient service,' who could not be dismissed 'except for *misfeasance, malfeasance, or nonfeasance* in office.'" *Cleveland Bd. of Educ. v. Loudermill*, 470 U.S. 532, 538–39 (1985) (per White, J.). See **feasance** & **nonfeasance**.

Malefaction (= crime, offense) is a FORMAL WORD that has become an ARCHAISM.

malfeasant, adj., corresponds to the noun *malfeasance*. See **feasant** & **malfeasance**.

malfeasor; malfeasant, n. Although most dictionaries record only *malfeasant* (= a wrongdoer or criminal) as the agent noun, *malfeasor* (a 19th-century coinage) now predominates in American law. To be sure, *malfeasant* does appear as a noun—e.g.:

- "Legislatures . . . have enacted statutes that protect the rights of those who have lawfully assembled from having their assembly disturbed by an unruly contingent of *malfeasants*." *Dempsey v. People*, 117 P.3d 800, 813–14 (Colo. 2005).
- "In the ordinary context, the supervisor is not himself the *malfeasant* who personally acts contrary to instructions . . . , and thus the supervisor's knowledge of an employee's unsafe conduct is imputable to his 'master,' the employer." *W.G. Yates & Sons Constr. Co. v. Occupational Safety & Health Rev. Comm'n*, 459 F.3d 604, 609 n.7 (5th Cir. 2006).

Yet the preferred term today is *malfeasor*, which made its debut in a published judicial opinion in 1854: "It was a serious obstacle to a shipper at Chattanooga to find himself groping in the dark among three distinct carriers, with an inconvenient land porterage interposed, to fix the responsibility for default upon the real *malfeasor*." *Bradford v. South Carolina R.R.*, 7 Rich. 201 (S.C. Ct. App. 1854). *Malfeasor* wasn't recorded in any dictionary, general or legal, until 1999 (*Black's Law Dictionary* 968 (7th ed. 1999)), even though today it is much more common than *malfeasant*—e.g.:

- "[A] *malfeasor* [cannot] be permitted to benefit from his own bad acts." *North Carolina Sch. Bds. Ass'n v. Moore*, 614 S.E.2d 504, 510 (N.C. 2005).
- "The prosecutor may understandably react emotionally to hearing the defense attorneys impugn the testimony of a witness with whom the prosecutor has worked . . . and in so doing threaten the acquittal of a *malfeasor*." *U.S. v. Spinelli*, 551 F.3d 159, 170 n.5 (2d Cir. 2008).
- "Janssen's motion to disqualify counsel is nothing more than 'an attempt by an alleged corporate *malfeasor* to avoid the consequences of its wrongdoing.'" *Commonwealth v. Janssen, Pharmaceutica, Inc.*, 8 A.2d 267, 273 (Pa. 2010) (quoting Commonwealth's brief).

Given that *malfeasant* is also an adjective, *malfeasor* is useful in avoiding ambiguity. See **malfeasant.** Cf. **misfeasor.**

*malfeazance. See **malfeasance.**

MALFORMATIONS. See MORPHOLOGICAL DEFORMITIES.

malice is often ambiguous because it has been diluted in legal writing. Early in the 20th century the dilution was noted and objected to: "When all that is meant by *malice* is an intention to commit an unlawful act

without reference to spite or ill-feeling, it is better to drop the word *malice* and so avoid all misunderstanding." *S. Wales Miners Fed'n v. Glamorgan Coal Co.*, [1905] A.C. 239, 255. But as early as the 19th century, the attenuated legal meaning had taken hold: "*Malice*, in the definition of murder, has not the same meaning as in common speech ['strong ill will'], and . . . has been thought to mean criminal intention." Oliver Wendell Holmes Jr., *The Common Law* 53 (1881).

The legal and nonlegal senses can be pointedly in contrast: "Although when used in its non-legal sense the word clearly denotes an evil or wicked state of mind, at law it does not necessarily have such a connotation; at law it simply means that the actor intentionally did something unlawful. Thus, the legal meaning of '*malice*' is confusing to a non-lawyer because an individual may act with good reason or from humanitarian motives but, as a matter of legal terminology, he has acted with '*malice*' if his act is against the law." Jonathan M. Purver, *The Language of Murder*, 14 UCLA L. Rev. 1306, 1306 (1967). As a noncriminal example, the *malice* requirement in proving libel of a public figure does not involve spite or ill will, only knowing falsity or a reckless disregard for the truth.

Lord Wright suggested that lawyers should use *malevolence* instead of *malice* whenever the idea of ill will is involved. *See Crofter Hand Woven Tweed Co. v. Veitch*, [1942] A.C. 435, 463. Others have suggested avoiding *malice* in the legal sense because "the criminal law ought not to need translation." Glanville Williams, *Criminal Law* 75 (2d ed. 1961). In its place, the phrase *intention or recklessness* could be substituted.

malice aforethought "is a TERM OF ART, if not a term of deception." Glanville Williams, *Textbook of Criminal Law* 208 (1978). In this phrase, in fact, *malice* does not even bear its usual legal meaning. The phrase *malice aforethought* does not "mean a state of the defendant's mind, as is often thought, except in the sense that he knew circumstances which did in fact make his conduct dangerous. It is, in truth, an allegation like that of negligence, which asserts that the party did not come up to the legal standard of action under the circumstances in which he found himself, and also that there was no exceptional fact or excuse present which took the case out of the general rule." Oliver Wendell Holmes Jr., *The Common Law* 62–63 (1881). This phrase, in other words, is neither self-explanatory nor descriptive of a single and invariable frame of mind: it expresses the idea merely that an accused killed the victim intentionally, or under such circumstances that the accused will be treated as severely as if the killing had been intentional. See **malice, aforethought** & **willfulness.**

The word *aforethought*—a 16th-century LOAN TRANSLATION of *prepense* or *praecogitata*—should not obscure the sense, as it is liable to. The word was long ago added to *malice* to indicate a design conceived well before the fatal act, but the cases that arose at common law involved such a variety of killings that the courts placed little emphasis on the idea of a well-laid plan. Today, the only requirement is that the intention not be an *afterthought*. See **prepense.**

One commentator contends that, because "the whole development of the mental requirement of the crime of murder has centered [on] the words *malice aforethought*, it will probably be wise to retain this phrase to express the concept." Rollin M. Perkins, *Criminal Law* 30 (1957). Even so, Perkins suggests *person-endangering state of mind* as a clearer substitute. *Id.* at 38. But even that phrase fails to account for circumstances that justify, excuse, or mitigate.

malicious (= intentional or reckless) bears a legal sense corresponding to the noun *malice*. Glanville Williams recommended substituting the phrase *intentional or reckless* in place of *malicious*. *See Criminal Law* 76 (2d ed. 1961). Likewise, the phrase *intentionally or recklessly* might replace the adverb *maliciously*. See **malice.**

malicious mischief; criminal mischief. The traditional phrase, *malicious mischief*, refers to the common-law misdemeanor of intentionally destroying or damaging another's property. Variant phrases include *malicious mischief and trespass, malicious injury, malicious trespass, malicious damage* (BrE), and *maliciously damaging the property of another*. To avoid the problematic word *malice*, the drafters of the Model Penal Code invented the term *criminal mischief*, a term now used in several American jurisdictions.

malicious prosecution; abuse of process. Charles T. McCormick suggested a demarcation between cases in which "process rightfully issued is wrongfully used, which should be termed *abuse of process*, and cases of malicious procurement of the issuance of process, which should be termed *malicious prosecution*." *Handbook of the Law of Damages* § 109, at 385 (1935). That distinction is as often blurred today as it was in McCormick's time, but it would still promote clear thinking if lawyers observed it.

malign. See **defame.**

malignancy; malignity. *Malignancy* should be confined to denoting any cancerous disease. *Malignity* = wicked or deep-rooted ill will or hatred; malignant feelings or actions.

malodorous. See **odorous.**

malpractice is confined in AmE to negligence or incompetence on the part of a professional (e.g., a lawyer or doctor); in BrE, however, it has this meaning as well as a sense similar to *misfeasance*—e.g.: "The mortgagees are not parties to the *malpractices* of the Waites, and the tenants, who were the victims of those *malpractices*." *Grace Rymer Invs. Ltd. v. Waite*, [1958] Ch. 831. The *OED* records two senses not current in AmE: (1) "illegal action by which a person in a position of trust seeks a personal benefit at the cost of others"; and (2) "a criminal or overtly mischievous action; wrongdoing; misconduct." Cf. **malfeasance.**

maltreat. See **abuse,** vb.

malum in se; malum prohibitum. Pl. *mala in se* and *mala prohibita*. These LATINISMS are frequently used by common-law writers, and knowing the distinction between them helps one understand the relation between morality and law. *Malum in se* = evil in itself; something inherently and universally considered evil. *Malum prohibitum* = wrong merely because it is proscribed; made unlawful by statute. Murder is the usual example of a crime *malum in se*, while running a traffic light is said to be *malum prohibitum*. Still, "a *malum prohibitum* is just as much a crime as a *malum in se*." Oliver Wendell Holmes Jr., *The Common Law* 46 (1881).

The phrases are sometimes used not as nouns, but as POSTPOSITIVE ADJECTIVES—e.g.: "Acts *mala in se* include, in addition to felonies, all breaches of public order, injuries to person and property, outrages upon public decency or good morals, and breaches of official duty, when done wilfully or corruptly. Acts *mala prohibita* include any matter forbidden or commanded by statute, but not otherwise wrong." *Commonwealth v. Adams*, 114 Mass. 323, 324 (1873).

malversation. This arcane term, meaning "official corruption," has on occasion been misrendered *malversion—e.g.:

- "Defalcations under the Act of 1898 were not limited to deliberate *malversions* [read *malversations*]." *In re Johnson*, 691 F.2d 249, 254 (6th Cir. 1982).
- "Although the defendants' expert interpreted the phrase in question to connote more of an 'abuse,' 'misuse,' or '*malversion*' [read '*malversation*'] of Post 12's $7,000, we find . . . that the issue was not whether the term used meant 'embezzlement,' but whether or not it was libelous." *Laniecki v. Polish Army Veterans Ass'n*, 480 A.2d 1101, 1107 (Pa. Super. Ct. 1984).

Cf. **misconduct in office.**

The agent noun, which seems never before to have been recorded in a dictionary, is *malversator*—e.g.: "That case has at times been thought to lay down a different rule, treating the infringer in all cases as a trustee *ex maleficio*, and therefore subject to the severe standard imposed upon *malversators*." *Cincinnati Car Co. v. New York Rapid Transit Corp.*, 66 F.2d 592, 593 (2d Cir. 1933).

The verb form, *malverse, is obsolete.

-MAN; -PERSON. See SEXISM (B).

man. See SEXISM (B).

man and wife. Since the 1960s, this phrase has been steadily decreasing in frequency of use in American judicial opinions. The reason is that it does not accord the female an equal status—i.e., she is referred to only by reference to her marital status. A more balanced phrasing—and one increasingly considered idiomatic—is *husband and wife*. See SEXISM (D).

mancipation. See **emancipation.**

M&A, in late 20th- and 21st-century legal slang, is the abbreviated form of *mergers and acquisitions.*

mandamus, n., was originally a prerogative writ that, up to the 19th century, was used as a writ of restitution for those wrongfully deprived of public offices, as in *Marbury v. Madison*, 5 U.S. 137 (1803). It was instrumental in securing democratic principles in the common law. Since the late 19th century, the writ has grown in use: a superior court issues it to compel a lower court or a government officer to perform mandatory or purely ministerial duties correctly. In England, *mandamus* has, since 1938, been an *order*, as opposed to a writ. See **prerogative writs.**

Pl. *mandamuses.* See HYPERCORRECTION (A).

mandamus, vb., = to order (a lower court or a government official) to perform a specified act. This verb began as a colloquialism in the early 19th century. It is labeled colloquial in *W2* (1934) but has no such notation in *W3* (1961). It has come to appear even in published opinions—e.g.:

- "The prayer was that the county treasurer be *mandamused* to pay . . . the sum of $1,565." *Farson, Son & Co. v. Bird,* 248 U.S. 268, 270 (1919) (per White, J.).
- "Walker urges this Court to issue a Writ of Mandamus to the Court of Appeals ordering that court to *mandamus* Johnson to produce the statement of facts." *Pat Walker & Co. v. Johnson,* 623 S.W.2d 306, 308 (Tex. 1981).

Actually, the use of *mandamus* as a verb is closer to the etymological sense (L. "we charge or command") than the noun use. The brevity of *to mandamus* recommends its more widespread adoption; no valid reasons exist to oppose it.

mandatary. See **mandatory.**

mandate, n. **A. As a CHAMELEON-HUED WORD.** *Mandate* = (1) an order from an appellate court directing a lower court to take a specified action; (2) a judicial command directed to an officer of the court to enforce a court order; (3) in civil law, a written command given by a principal to an agent; (4) in Roman law, a commission by which one person (the mandator) requests someone (the mandatary) to perform some service gratuitously, the commission becoming effective when the mandatary agrees—a synonym in this sense is *mandatum*; (5) in international law, an authority given by the League of Nations to certain governments to take over the administration and development of certain territories (replaced after 1945 by *trusteeship*); or (6) in politics, the electorate's overwhelming show of approval for a given political platform. For more on sense 6, see (B).

B. And Its Near-Synonyms: *initiative*; *referendum*; *plebiscite.* These terms all refer to a means of assessing voters' preferences. *Mandate*, the broadest term, denotes the electorate's strong show of support

for a candidate or a position <in his victory speech, the governor declared a mandate for lowering property taxes>. *Initiative* typically refers to the procedure whereby a clearly defined number of voters may propose a new measure, such as a constitutional amendment, to a legislature or compel a popular vote on the measure <several ballot initiatives succeeded, including the proposal to impose term limits on legislators>. *Referendum*, which is often paired with *initiative* <the state constitution provides specifically for initiative and referendum>, refers to the practice of sending proposed legislative measures to the voters either for approval or objection or for a nonbinding expression of the voting populace's wishes. *Plebiscite* bears two senses: (1) a vote of the people on some measure by a group or body having the right of initiative (idiomatically "having the initiative"), as a binding referendum; or (2) a nation's vote, by the full electorate, on whether the territory in which they live should be constituted under a particular form of government, should merge with either of two nations, or should embark on some other course that would affect the way their government is constituted.

mandate, vb., for *prescribe* is merely verbal sloppiness. "The Federal Rules of Appellate Procedure *mandate* [read *prescribe*] the time for filing a notice of appeal." *In re Cobb*, 750 F.2d 477, 478 (5th Cir. 1985).

mandator. See **mandate,** n. (sense 4).

mandatory; mandatary. H.W. Horwill wrote in the 1930s that *mandatory*—frequently used in AmE— is uncommon in England, and that *obligatory* and *compulsory* are more common. The latter two terms may still be predominant, but *mandatory injunction* is now a common phrase in English law reports. *See, e.g.,* 2 *Jowitt's Dictionary of English Law* 1410 (Daniel Greenberg ed., 3d ed. 2010) (defining it as "an injunction requiring the performance of some act, e.g., the removal of a building or obstruction"). The three words—*mandatory*, *obligatory*, and *compulsory*—are close synonyms. See **directory.**

Mandatary, n. & adj., is a civil-law term appearing (in AmE) mostly in Louisiana. As a noun, it is a close equivalent to what in common-law jurisdictions is called an *agent*, though a mandatary usually (as in Scotland) acts gratuitously—e.g.:

- "As respects liability for misconduct and limitation of action therefor, they are more exactly agents or *mandataries*." *Anderson v. Gailey*, 33 F.2d 589, 592 (N.D. Ga. 1929).
- "The fraud committed by a *mandatary* in exercise of the mandate is regarded as fraud committed by the principal by virtue of the rules governing representation." Saul Litvinoff, *Vices of Consent, Error, Fraud, Duress and an Epilogue on Lesion*, 50 La. L. Rev. 1, 71 (1989).

As an adjective, the word means "of or relating to an agency relationship"—e.g.: "This contract is also a contract of a certain kind; it is a *mandatary* contract, establishing an agency relationship." *Commonwealth Capital Corp. v. Enterprise Fed. Sav. & Loan Ass'n*, 630 F.Supp. 1199, 1201 (E.D. La. 1986).

For the Roman-law sense of *mandatary*, see **mandate,** n. (sense 4).

mandatory injunction; prohibitory injunction. The first requires a positive action; the second requires restraint from action. See **injunction.**

mandatory pro bono. See **pro bono (E).**

mangle. See **maim.**

mania. See **insanity (A).**

manifest, adj., often functions in suspect ways in legal writing: "Someone has observed that whenever a lawyer says that something or other was the manifest intention of a man, '*manifest*' means that the man never really had such an intention." Jerome Frank, *Law and the Modern Mind* 30 (1930). This word is one of those vague terms by which lawyers "create an appearance of continuity, uniformity and definiteness [that does] not in fact exist." *Id.* See **evident,** FICTIONS & **apparent.**

manifesto. Pl. *-os.* See PLURALS (C).

man-killing is still occasionally used in law to refer to a homicidal act, but rarely in nonlegal writing. It is pretty archaic—e.g.:

- "No enlightened jurist now doubts the existence of such a type of moral . . . insanity as homicidal mania or morbid and uncontrollable appetite for *man-killing.*" *Smith v. Commonwealth,* 62 Ky. 224, 231 (Ct. App. 1864).
- "Neither can be used to shoot someone, which is the *man-killing* status intrinsic in a firearm and which is what the Legislature intended to regulate." *People v. Peals,* 720 N.W.2d 196, 210 (Mich. 2006).

See **murder (A)** & SEXISM (B).

mankind. See **humankind** & SEXISM (B).

manner, in a ——. This phrase typifies the style of a writer whose prose reads slowly. *In a professional manner* should be *professionally*; *in a rigid manner* should be *rigidly*; *in a childish manner* should be *childishly.* Good editors do not leave such phrases untouched.

Still, some phrases cannot be made into *-ly* adverbs: *in a Rambo-like manner*; *in a determined manner* (few editors would choose *determinedly*—see -EDLY); *in a catch-as-catch-can manner.* In many such contexts, though, the word *way* would typically be an improvement over *manner.*

manner in which is almost always unnecessarily verbose for *how.*

man-of-law (= a man skilled in law; a lawyer), a word with decidedly positive connotations, is little used today, probably because it is considered sexist. (See SEXISM (B).) Some writers omit the hyphens—e.g.: "Never before had any society taken a professional

man of law—Holmes, about whom I shall have more to say presently—as the embodiment of its dream." Grant Gilmore, *The Ages of American Law* 42 (1977).

man of the long robe. See *long-robe man* under LAWYERS, DEROGATORY NAMES FOR (A).

manpower. See SEXISM (B).

manservant. The plural form of this ARCHAISM, oddly, makes both words in the compound plural: *menservants.*

manslaughter, n. **A.** *Voluntary manslaughter* **and** *involuntary manslaughter.* Because the term *manslaughter* (= unlawful homicide committed without malice aforethought) extends from the verge of murder to the verge of excusable homicide, it became necessary to divide the term into categories. *Voluntary manslaughter* means "an act of murder reduced to manslaughter because of extenuating circumstances such as provocation or diminished responsibility." In some jurisdictions, this crime is known as *intentional manslaughter.*

The other category, by natural contrast, is called *involuntary manslaughter,* but in this phrase the word *involuntary* is used quite unnaturally as a catchall: the phrase means "homicide in which there is no intention to kill or do grievous bodily harm."

In England, *involuntary manslaughter* is subdivided still further into what one commentator calls *straightforward manslaughter* and *constructive manslaughter.* The "straightforward" type "requires the prosecution to prove that the defendant *caused* the death in question by an act or omission, amounting in either case to gross negligence or recklessness (which one is not finally settled) in breach of a duty of care." Glanville Williams, *Textbook of Criminal Law* 224 (1978). *Constructive manslaughter,* in contrast, consists in "a killing in the course of certain kinds of unlawful acts, and then only when the defendant is negligent as to causing bodily injury." *Id.* at 238. See **murder (B).**

B. And *causing death by reckless or dangerous driving.* In 1956, this EUPHEMISM became established in English statutory law "owing to the notorious reluctance of juries to convict of 'motor manslaughter.'" William Geldart, *Introduction to English Law* 158 (D.C.M. Yardley ed., 9th ed. 1984). That's a good lesson in semantics: labels matter.

manslaughter, vb. (= to kill [a person] unlawfully but without malice aforethought), is rightly listed as a colloquialism in the *SOED.* Though hardly common, it has appeared in reported American opinions—e.g.: "In *Burney,* . . . the defendant assaulted victim Williams with a deadly weapon and *manslaughtered* victim Grant during a crowded bar room quarrel culminating in a shooting." *People v. Masters,* 241 Cal. Rptr. 511, 517 (Ct. App. 1988).

manslaughterer (= one who commits manslaughter) is infrequent but arguably useful—e.g.:

- "It was thought that actors whose emotions were stirred by other forms of outrageous conduct . . . also should be punished as *manslaughterers* rather than murderers." *Patterson v. New York*, 432 U.S. 197, 218 (1977) (per Powell, J.).
- "Defendant's planning activity rendered him more culpable than other *manslaughterers*." *People v. Levitt*, 203 Cal. Rptr. 276, 287 (Ct. App. 1984).

mantle; mantel. *Mantle* means, among other things, "a loose robe," and is frequently used by legal writers in figurative senses—e.g.:

- "The Court has decided a series of cases that cloak the States with an increasingly protective *mantle* of 'sovereign immunity' from liability for violating federal laws." *Vermont Agency of Natural Res. v. U.S.*, 529 U.S. 765, 789–90 (2000) (Stevens, J., dissenting).
- "We see no reason to shroud him with a *mantle* of immunity upon the fictitious theory that he was protecting the interests of the corporation." *Industrial Tech. Ventures LP v. Pleasant T. Rowland Revocable Trust*, 688 F.Supp.2d 229, 243 (W.D.N.Y. 2010).

See **clothe.**

Mantel is a different and more common word in everyday speech. It means "a structure of wood or marble above or around a fireplace; a shelf"—e.g.: "Foutch took a gun off the *mantel* and shot Young twice." *People v. Parmly*, 512 N.E.2d 1213, 1215 (Ill. 1987).

In legal writing, the spelling *mantel* is frequently used where *mantle* belongs—e.g.: "For Johnson to now come before this court and attempt to cloak his outrageous conduct in the *mantel* [read *mantle*] of the Article II, Section 16, right of access to the courts is a disgrace to Montana's Constitution." *Emmerson v. Walker*, 236 P.3d 598, 608 (Mont. 2010).

manufacturer. So spelled. Some legal writers mistakenly write **manufacturor*. See -ER (A).

manumit. See **free.**

many. A. And *much*. *Many* is used with count nouns (i.e., those that comprise a number of discrete or separable entities). *Much* is used with mass nouns (i.e., those that refer to amounts as distinguished from numbers). Hence, *many persons* but *much salt*. Here *much* is used incorrectly: "This motion . . . was denied on the ground that the indictment was sufficiently definite in view of the unknown matters involved and the motion called 'for *too much details* [read *too many details*] of evidence.'" *Wong Tai v. U.S.*, 273 U.S. 77, 82 (1927) (per Sanford, J.). Cf. *less* for *fewer*, and note that *less* is the correlative of *much*, whereas *fewer* is the correlative of *many*. See **less (A).**

Sometimes the writer must decide whether a word such as *data* is a count noun (as it traditionally has been) or a mass noun (as it has recently come to be). E.g.: "But *much* [read *many?*] of the data in present personnel files is highly subjective." William O. Douglas, *Points of Rebellion* 21 (1970). Of course, the choice of the singular verb *is* shows that Justice Douglas considered *data* a mass noun—so *much* was the appropriate word.

B. *Many . . . abound*. This phrasing commonly creates a REDUNDANCY—e.g.:

- "Certainly it must be conceded *that many valid reasons abound* [read *that valid reasons abound*] for choosing private over public education." *Cook v. Hudson*, 511 F.2d 744, 752 (5th Cir. 1975) (Clark, J., dissenting).
- "*Many other examples abound* [read *Other examples abound*] in the general statutes of local application passed by the Alabama legislature prior to the adoption of Amendments 375 and 397." *Phalen v. Birmingham Racing Comm'n*, 481 So.2d 1108, 1122 (Ala. 1985). On the use of **prior to* in that sentence, see ****prior to.**

Mareva **injunction.** See CASE REFERENCES (C) & **Woolf reforms.**

margin (= footnotes) occurs today primarily in legal writing, although scholars in all disciplines once commonly used it—e.g.: "The order and decree dismissing the bill is set out in the *margin*." *Goodman v. Lane*, 48 F.2d 32, 33 (8th Cir. 1931). This usage harks back to a bygone era when notes were set out in the outer margins rather than at the foot of the page—though even the foot of the page may rightly be counted as the bottom margin.

mariage de convenance. See **marriage of convenience.**

marijuana; **marihuana*. The first now predominates in judicial opinions and should be preferred. Justice Lewis F. Powell, speaking in 1986 at a luncheon, stated: "The big problem we had in the Court this past Term was how to spell *marijuana*. We were about equally divided between a 'j' and an 'h,' and since I was supposed to be the swing vote on the court, and just to show my impartiality, I added a footnote in a case . . . in which I spelled *marijuana* with a 'j' once and an 'h' in the same sentence." Quoted in *News*, A.B.A. J., 1 Oct. 1986, at 17, 34.

mariner is a serviceable replacement for *seaman*, which not only is considered sexist but also has an awkward homophone. See **able-bodied seaman, seaman** & SEXISM (B).

mariner's will. See **oral will.**

marital. See **matrimonial** & **marriage,** adj.

marital rape was a type of OXYMORON at common law, since a husband was held to be exempt from rape charges if he had nonconsensual sexual intercourse with his wife. The so-called *marital-rape exemption*, though, is gradually disappearing: Anglo-American jurisdictions have generally abolished it. As one writer puts it, abolition "is surely important as a statement of the married woman's autonomy and freedom of choice in sexual matters." Andrew Ashworth, *Principles of Criminal Law* 303 (1991). See **rape (A).**

marital relation is often wordy for *marriage*—e.g.: "A valid divorce terminates the *marital relation* [read *marriage*] and with it the duty of the husband to support his wife and vice versa." Rollin M. Perkins & Ronald N. Boyce, *Criminal Law* 676 (3d ed. 1982). In the plural form, *marital relations* is sometimes used as a EUPHEMISM for sexual relations between husband and wife—e.g.: "In *Pharmacia & Upjohn*, a husband, who became infected with HIV-2 while handling the virus in the course of his employment in a research laboratory, infected his wife after the two engaged in unprotected *marital relations.*" *Gourdine v. Crews*, 955 A.2d 769, 785 (2008).

maritime law. See **admiralty (A).**

marked is pronounced /markt/, as one syllable. The pronunciation /**mar**-kəd/, in two syllables, is an erroneous vestige of the correct adverbial pronunciation /**mar**-kəd-lee/.

marketable. See **salable.**

market overt; open market. The two are mostly distinct. *Market overt* = an open, legally regulated public market where buyers, with some exceptions, acquire good title to products regardless of any defects in the seller's title. *Open market*, though it sometimes shares that sense, generally means "a market with no competitive restrictions on price or availability of products."

Market overt is the less common term—e.g.: "Conceivably the common-law judges might have refused to allow the bailor to recover in detinue against a bona fide purchaser, as they did refuse it against a purchaser in *market overt.*" J.B. Ames, *The History of Trover*, 11 Harv. L. Rev. 374, 379 (1898).

marque, letters of. See **letters of marque.**

***marriable.** See **marriageable.**

marriage, adj. The word *marital* is better than *marriage* in adjectival senses—e.g.: "The Court of Appeals signified in dicta that a classification based on *marriage* [read *marital*] status is permissible." *In re St. Vincent's Serv., Inc.*, 841 N.Y.S.2d 834, 852 (Fam. Ct. 2007). See NOUNS AS ADJECTIVES.

marriage, n. See **common-law marriage.**

marriageable; *marriable. The second is an ARCHAISM to be avoided.

marriage dissolution is a EUPHEMISM for *divorce* or *annulment.* E.g.:

- "The purpose of [The Family Law Act] was to discard the concept of fault in *dissolution of marriage* actions, to minimize the adversary nature of such proceedings, and to eliminate conflicts created only to secure a *divorce.*" *Klemm v. Superior Court*, 142 Cal. Rptr. 509, 513 (Ct. App. 1977). (Note the INELEGANT VARIATION in that sentence [*dissolution of marriage . . . divorce*]. Note also that *dissolution of marriage*, when used adjectivally, needs to

be hyphenated <dissolution-of-marriage actions>. See PHRASAL ADJECTIVES.)

- "A district court, in exercising its broad jurisdiction over *marriage dissolutions*, retains jurisdiction to enforce all terms of approved property-settlement agreements." *Smeal Fire Apparatus Co. v. Kreikemeier*, 782 N.W.2d 848, 863 (Neb. 2010).

That *marriage dissolution* may technically encompass annulments as well as divorces does not redeem it. See **divorce (B).**

marriage of convenience; *mariage de convenance.* The anglicized version is to be preferred over the GALLICISM. But it should be understood rightly: *marriage of convenience* is not "an ill-considered marriage that happens to be convenient to the parties involved," but "a marriage contracted for social or financial advantages rather than out of mutual love."

married. See **wed (B).**

marshal, n., = (1) a law-enforcement officer with duties similar to those of a sheriff; (2) a judicial officer who provides court security, executes process, and performs other tasks for a court; or (3) in England, a recently called barrister who acts as personal officer of and secretary to a High Court judge on circuit. The word is preferably so spelled—not **marshall.**

marshal, as a verb meaning " to arrange in order," in its past-tense and participial forms is frequently misspelled in AmE with a doubled -*l*-. E.g.: "I would reverse based on the preserved errors from the State's initial closing arguments, for much of the same reasons *marshalled* [read *marshaled*] by the Majority opinion in its cumulative effects analysis." *Lawson v. State*, 886 A.2d 876, 900 (Md. 2005). See DOUBLING OF FINAL CONSONANTS.

In BrE, the inflected form is *marshalled*, but the uninflected form is still *marshal*, as in AmE: "If one side can *marshall* [read *marshal*] a precedent that is binding and in point, that will conclude the debate." Michael Zander, *The Law-Making Process* 234 (2d ed. 1985).

martial law; military law. The two are distinct, as a noted commentator suggests: " 'Martial' as opposed to 'military law' is not recognised by the law of England [or of the U.S.]." Thomas E. Holland, *The Elements of Jurisprudence* 377 n.2 (13th ed. 1924). *Martial law* is the body of rules applied on grounds of necessity by a country's rulers when the civil government has failed or looks as if it might fail to function, the armed forces assuming control purportedly until civil processes and courts can be restored to their lawful places. Martial law applies only within a given country—not within occupied enemy territory. *Military law*, on the other hand, refers to the special branch of law that governs military discipline and other rules regarding service in the armed forces. So *martial law* usually applies to civilians as well as soldiers, while *military law* almost never applies to civilians.

Mary Carter agreement, which owes its name to *Booth v. Mary Carter Paint Co.*, 202 So.2d 8 (Fla. Dist. Ct. App. 1967), refers to a contract by which a codefendant settles with the plaintiff and obtains a release, with the further agreement that the codefendant will receive a portion of any amount that the plaintiff may recover from one or more other defendants. In short, the codefendant settles and then joins forces with the plaintiff against the remaining codefendants. See CASE REFERENCES (C).

Some lawyers shorten the phrase to *Mary Carter* <Sinergy then entered into a Mary Carter with the plaintiff>. Much more slangily, lawyers sometimes use the phrase as a verb <Sinergy was Mary Cartered out of the case>.

MASCULINE AND FEMININE PRONOUNS. See SEXISM (A).

mass of, a. See SYNESIS.

mass tort = a large number of tort claims with a common cause—such as a single-accident disaster, a defective product that injures many people, or environmental contamination at a single site—that has injured many victims. This term has, by extension, given rise to some odd JARGON such as *mass litigation* and even *mass defendant*. To avoid giving *mass* these contorted senses, the better practice is to write *mass-tort litigation* and *mass-tort defendant*.

master. A. Meaning "employer." The word *master* was once regularly used to mean "employer" in legal language, and *servant* to mean "employee." But this terminology has long been obsolescent: "Even the legal vocabulary changes; younger lawyers in the spirit of modern labor relations scorn to speak of the law of *master* and servant, under which rubric we used to find the little law that was especially directed to employment." Robert H. Jackson, Foreword to *Jurisprudence in Action* iii (1953). See **employer and employee** & **servant**.

B. Referring to a Parajudicial Officer. During the Middle Ages, the Court of Chancery began appointing officers to assist in various equitable proceedings. These officers were known as *masters*. Though the British Parliament abolished the office in the late 19th century, many American jurisdictions have continued using officers bearing the title *master*, without regard to the equitable or legal nature of the proceedings. Among the functions they may perform are taking testimony, computing interest, valuing annuities, investigating encumbrances on land titles, and the like—virtually always with a written report to the court.

master and servant. See **employer and employee** & **master (A).**

masterful; masterly. *Masterful* describes a powerful, even bullying superior; its antonym is *servile*. *Masterly*

indicates the skill of a master of a profession or trade; its antonym is *unskillful*. A master craftsman is *masterly*; a boorish tyrant is *masterful*. Which is the correct term in the following sentence, from a nonlegal text? "Though Britain's Derek Jacobi looks about as much like Adolf Hitler as Archie Bunker, he evokes the Fuhrer with *masterful* verve." (The actor is *masterly*; Hitler was *masterful*.)

Perhaps one reason the two words are so frequently confounded is that when an adverb for *masterly* is needed, *masterfully* seems more natural than *masterlily*. (See ADVERBS (B).) Indeed, "He writes *masterfully*" strikes one as much less stilted than "He writes *masterlily*." This problem with the adverbial form threatens to destroy a useful distinction between the two adjectival forms. Perhaps *masterlily* would seem less pedantic if we were to use it more often. Barring that, *in a masterly way* is always available.

master of the bench. See **bencher.**

Master of the Rolls = president of the Court of Appeal (Civil Division) in England.

MATCHING PARTS. See PARALLELISM.

material, adj. See **relevant.**

materialman. See **mechanic's lien** & SEXISM (B).

matrimonial; marital; marriage, adj.; **conjugal; connubial; nuptial; hymeneal.** These near-synonyms all mean "of, pertaining to, or characteristic of marriage." *Matrimonial* is the broadest, relating to all aspects of marriage considered as a wedding rite, a legal relation, a spiritual relation, a state of being, or a social institution (hence *matrimonial law* is a comprehensive term). *Marital* is closely synonymous <marital vows> <marital bliss>, but most traditionally (this may surprise you) it describes only the husband and his role in marriage <marital authority>—a connotation that was carried through the 19th century but lingers faintly if at all in modern usage. *Conjugal* connotes reference to married persons and all aspects of consortium, especially sex <conjugal fidelity> <conjugal rights>. (See **consortium.**) *Connubial*, a highbrow word, connotes the state of being married <the couple's connubial experience>. *Nuptial* /nəp-shəl/ refers to the wedding ceremony <Karolyne's nuptial bouquet>. And finally, *hymeneal*, alluding to the Greek god of marriage (Hymen), is a heightened literary word evoking splendor and celebration—rather like the sesquipedalian term *epithalamium* (= a poem written in honor of a bride and bridegroom).

Although *marriage* is sometimes used attributively, in an adjectival sense, the better editorial practice is to reserve *matrimonial* or *marital* for such a use— e.g.: "An aggrieved spouse is not compelled to seek the courts of another state for the protection of her *marriage* [read *marital* or *matrimonial*] status." *Usen v. Usen*, 13 A.2d 738, 751–52 (Me. 1940). See NOUNS AS ADJECTIVES.

matter is sometimes viewed as the lawyer's puffed-up equivalent of *case*. It commonly occurs in contexts such as these:

- "I handled a fascinating *matter* [read *case*] the other day."
- "How many *matters* [read *cases*] are there on the docket?"

And it appears in BrE as well as AmE—e.g.: "It should be noted that section 76(i) extends not only to *matters* arising under the Constitution but also to *matters* involving its interpretation." James Crawford, *Australian Courts of Law* 146 (1982).

Actually, the term derives from the language of equity: "for the Queen's Bench Division we usually talk about 'actions,' denoting the idea of litigants who have a dispute to be determined, whilst in the Chancery Division we are more apt to speak of 'actions and *matters*.' Some of the causes in the Chancery Division are normal litigation between contesting parties, but '*matters*' do not necessarily mean that there is a dispute." R.M. Jackson, *The Machinery of Justice in England* 50–51 (5th ed. 1967).

That quotation suggests a workable distinction for AmE and BrE alike: *case* or *action* refers to a pending lawsuit in which there is a genuine dispute; *matter* refers to any other affair in which a lawyer becomes professionally involved. It therefore makes good sense for law firms to keep records, as they ordinarily do, of "client-matter" numbers. A *matter* might involve legal advice where litigation is never contemplated.

maugre /**maw**-gər/ = despite. Listed as obsolete or archaic in virtually every English-language dictionary, this word is just one more ARCHAISM in which legal inkhornists can indulge. E.g.:

- "*Maugre* this: shall we repudiate such 'excellent method of decision,' as violative of the common law of England in 1791?" *Sunray Oil Corp. v. Allbritton*, 187 F.2d 475, 480–81 (5th Cir. 1951).
- "Complaint is next made that the court erred in permitting the prosecutor to state in his final argument[,] *maugre* timely objection by counsel for the defendant, the following: . . . ." *Shadle v. State*, 194 So.2d 538, 542–43 (Ala. 1967).

maximal. See **maximum**.

MAXIMS. A maxim is a traditional legal principle that has been frozen into a concise expression. There are a few legal and quasi-legal maxims that everyone knows, such as these:

- A man's home is his castle. See **castle doctrine.**
- *Caveat emptor.* See **caveat.**
- Ignorance of the law is no excuse. This phrase is a close LOAN TRANSLATION of *ignorantia juris neminem excusat* (= ignorance of the law excuses nobody). See *ignorantia juris.*
- Possession is nine-tenths of the law. See **possession is nine-tenths of the law.**

Then there are the thousands of maxims dressed up in Latin, few of which most lawyers seem nowadays to know. Among the more common ones are these:

- *Actus non facit reum nisi mens sit rea* (= an act does not make the doer guilty unless his or her mind is guilty). See **actus non facit reum nisi mens sit rea.**
- *Delegatus non potest delegare* (= a person to whom work is delegated cannot himself [or herself] delegate it).
- *De minimis non curat lex* (= the law does not concern itself with trifles). "No one knows exactly what it means." Ephraim Tutt, *Yankee Lawyer* 356 (1943). See *de minimis* (A).
- *Ex turpi causa non oritur actio* (= from an illegal transaction no action arises).
- *Ignorantia facti excusat* (= ignorance of fact excuses, i.e., is a ground for relief).
- *Lex rebrobat moram* (= the law abhors a delay).
- *Nemo commodum capere potest de injuria sua propria* (= no one can benefit from one's own wrong).
- *Nemo debet esse judex in propria cause* (= no one can be a judge in one's own case).
- *Nulla poena sine lege* (= no punishment except in accordance with the law). See **nulla poena sine lege.**
- *Qui facit per alium facit per se* (= he who acts through another acts himself; she who acts through another acts herself).
- *Sic utere tuo, ut alienum non laedas* (= one should use one's own property in a manner that does not injure that of another). See *sic utere.*
- *Transit in rem iudicatam* (= it passes into a matter adjudged, i.e., becomes res judicata).
- *Ubi remedium, ibi ius* (= where there is a remedy, there is a right).
- *Volenti non fit injuria* (= that to which a person consents cannot be considered an injury). See **volenti non fit injuria.**

Though these and other maxims dot the pages of lawbooks—especially older lawbooks—most legal thinkers consider them unnecessary to a mature legal system. Roscoe Pound, for example, suggested that they characterize a legal system still in its formative stages: "A body of primitive law . . . often contains a certain number of sententious legal proverbs, put in striking form so as to stick in the memory but vague in their content." *An Introduction to the Philosophy of Law* 101 (1922). Lon Fuller echoed this view: "Undeveloped systems of law have a decided penchant for such brocards." *Legal Fictions* 34 (1967).

Several writers have suggested that we are better off depositing maxims in the dustbin of history:

- "It seems to me that legal maxims in general are little more than pert headings of chapters. They are rather minims than maxims, for they give not a particularly great but a particularly small amount of information. As often as not, the exceptions and qualifications to them are more important than the so-called rules." 2 James F. Stephen, *History of the Criminal Law of England* 94 n.1 (1883).
- "The fact that the great majority of legal maxims are clothed in the words of a dead language has had, in some

instances, the effect of preventing proper inquiry into their meaning. A phrase couched in Latin seems to some persons invested with 'a kind of mysterious halo.'" Jeremiah Smith, *The Use of Maxims in Jurisprudence*, 9 Harv. L. Rev. 13, 25 (1895).

- "General propositions do not decide concrete cases." *Lochner v. New York*, 198 U.S. 45, 76 (1905) (Holmes, J., dissenting).
- "No one who reflects on the subject can doubt that some useless Latin maxims, and some untrue Latin maxims, have continued current, and that other Latin maxims have been misapplied, when this would not have happened if those maxims had been expressed only in the vernacular." *Sperbeck v. A.L. Burbank & Co.*, 190 F.2d 449, 450 n.8 (2d Cir. 1951).
- "Happily such 'short, dark maxims' are not so common as they once were. When they are used today, it is for the sake of their flavor of antiquity, rather than because of any notion that they are actually explanatory." Lon L. Fuller, *Legal Fictions* 34 (1967).

For the most nearly definitive work on maxims in Anglo-American law, see Herbert Broom, *A Selection of Legal Maxims* (10th ed. 1939). For the most extensive collection of them, authoritatively translated, see *Black's Law Dictionary* 1815–80 (9th ed. 2009). See LATINISMS.

maximum, n. & adj.; **maximal,** adj. More and more frequently, *maximum* (like *minimum*) has come to act as its own adjective—e.g.: "A Hallmark internal memorandum reflects Schoeller's commitment to provide *maximum* quantities to Hallmark through 1990." *Paper Corp. of U.S. v. Schoeller Technical Papers, Inc.*, 773 F.Supp. 632, 634 (S.D.N.Y. 1991).

Maximal usually means "the greatest possible," rather than merely "of, relating to, or constituting a maximum"—e.g.: "It was in the best interests of the children to have *maximal* time with each parent." *Guffin v. Plaisted-Harman*, 232 P.3d 888, 892 (Mont. 2010). See **minimal.**

The plural most commonly listed in dictionaries is *maxima*—e.g.: "To appreciate the truth of this assertion it is only necessary to think of the imposition of prison sentences within the *maxima* allowed by the various statutes." Rupert Cross, *Statutory Interpretation* 41 (1976). But the more down-to-earth choice is *maximums*—e.g.: "A majority of the States pay less than their determined standard of need, and twenty of these States impose *maximums* on family grants of the kind here in issue." *Dandridge v. Williams*, 397 U.S. 471, 481 (1970).

See **minimum** & PLURALS (A).

maximum [+ name] is another way of describing a "hanging judge." The phrase suggests that the judge routinely imposes the maximum possible sentence— e.g.: "But he had been at least as stern in earlier criminal cases, sentencing convicted defendants to long terms, thus earning the nickname '*maximum John*.'" *Sirica, 88, Dies; Persistent Judge in Fall of Nixon*, N.Y. Times, 15 Aug. 1992, at 1, 11. See **hanging judge.**

may = (1) has discretion to; is permitted to <suit may be brought in any district court>; (2) possibly

will <the court may apply this doctrine>; or (3) shall. Sense 3, though a lexical perversion, has come about because "courts have held *may* to be synonymous with *shall* or *must*, usu. in an effort to effectuate legislative intent" (*Black's Law Dictionary* 1068 (9th ed. 2009)), or, as the 6th edition put it, "to the end that justice may not be the slave of grammar."

But no drafter who means *must* should consciously use *may*; the liberties taken by the courts in construing drafters' oversights should not be allowed to change the essential meanings of basic words. See **can (A)** & WORDS OF AUTHORITY (E).

mayhem. A. Several Senses. *Mayhem* = (1) malicious injury to or maiming of a person, originally so as to impair or destroy the victim's capacity for self-defense; (2) violent and damaging action; violent destruction; or (3) rowdy confusion, disruption, chaos. In senses 1 and 2, *mayhem* is a technical term now obsolete in federal law but still found in some state statutes. In sense 3, the term is a POPULARIZED LEGAL TECHNICALITY.

B. And *maim*, n. Though etymologically identical, *mayhem* and *maim* have undergone DIFFERENTIATION: in the best usage, *mayhem* refers to the crime (sense 1) and *maim* to the type of injury required for the crime—e.g.:

- "Specific intent to *maim* may not be inferred solely from evidence that the injury inflicted actually constitutes *mayhem*; instead, there must be other facts and circumstances [supporting] an inference of intent to *maim* rather than to attack indiscriminately." *People v. Ferrell*, 267 Cal. Rptr. 283, 286 (Ct. App. 1990).
- "A prolonged attack is not a necessary legal prerequisite to a finding of *mayhem* where a specific intent to *maim* or disfigure can be inferred from the circumstances of the attack and the severity of the inflicted injuries." *Commonwealth v. Ogden O.*, 864 N.E.2d 13, 16 (Mass. 2007).
- "The prosecutor argued the photographs were relevant to prove defendant's intent to torture and to commit *mayhem*." *People v. D'Arcy*, 226 P.3d 949, 977 (Cal. 2010).

For *maim* as a verb, together with its near-synonyms, see **maim.**

C. And *maihem.** This spelling amounts to nothing more than a NEEDLESS VARIANT.

may it please the court is the standard introductory phrase that lawyers use when speaking to an appellate court. Some people call it LEGALESE, but it is not really in that category. The phrase helps establish a tone of civility and respect in an oral argument.

may not is sometimes the source of AMBIGUITY: it may mean either "is disallowed from" or "might or might not." For example, if an application contained a notice that read, "Applications received after September 30 may not be considered by this office," the question arises whether the office is prohibited from considering it or the decision about considering it depends on how the office exercises its discretion (or whim).

In stating a prohibition, some writers would solve the problem by resorting to *cannot*, but doing so blurs the widely recognized distinction between *can* and *may*. See **can.**

A better way to solve the problem in many contexts is to use the phrase *must not.* So instead of saying that a brief *may not* contain addenda, one might say that a brief *must not* (preferably not *shall not*) contain addenda. (See WORDS OF AUTHORITY (A).) The phrasing with *must* is certainly unambiguous.

In drafted documents, however, the basic phrase at issue—*may not*—is conventionally viewed as unambiguous. Why? Because in legal instruments, one never has occasion to speculate in the sense of "might or might not." So, generally speaking, *may not* does not cause interpretive difficulties in statutes, rules, contracts, bylaws, and the like. But those who want to forestall even a minute possibility of a problem use *must not.* See WORDS OF AUTHORITY (F).

McCulloch v. Maryland. This is the conventional spelling of the groundbreaking case in which the U.S. Supreme Court first used federal constitutional analysis to invalidate a state law. See 17 U.S. (4 Wheat.) 316 (1819). Although the bank cashier involved in that case actually spelled his name *McCulloh* (*see* Charles Alan Wright, *The Law of Federal Courts* 370 n.5 (5th ed. 1994)), the established case name is *McCulloch.*

McKenzie; McKenzie man. In *McKenzie v. McKenzie,* [1970] 3 W.L.R. 472 (C.A.), the Court of Appeal ruled that any litigant is entitled to nonprofessional assistance in court. Hence in BrE, *McKenzie* or *McKenzie man* has come to denote a nonprofessional who attends trial as a party's helper or adviser.

McNaghten; M'Naghten; McNaughton; Macnaghten; MacNaughton; M'Naughten. In 1843, the House of Lords answered a series of questions about what a criminal defendant must show to succeed on the defense of insanity. (*See McNaghten's Case,* [1843] 8 Eng. Rep. 718, 10 Cl. & Fin. 200.) These answers are generally known as the *McNaghten rules* (so spelled). Glanville Williams remarks: "The spelling of the defendant's name in this famous case varies; for simplicity, I have adopted one of the two versions [*McNaghten*] used in the Law Reports, though it is probably [historically] wrong." *Textbook of Criminal Law* 98 n.6 (1978). Historically wrong, perhaps, but so prevalent today that writers everywhere ought to settle on it as the standard spelling.

Justice Felix Frankfurter felt certain that *M'Naghten* was the correct spelling. In 1952, he wrote the editor of *The Times* (London) to reform the spelling used by that newspaper: "It is M'Naghten, not M'Naughten or any of the variants of its misspelling." Felix Frankfurter, "Postscript to M'Naghten's Case," in *Of Law and Life and Other Things That Matter* 1, 1 (Philip B. Kurland ed., 1967). The learned editor of *The Times*— Sir William Haley—produced historical evidence of ten variations, including the prisoner's own version during trial: *M'Naughten.* See *id.*

me; I. See PRONOUNS. For the error **between you and I,* see **between (C).**

mean, adj., = (1) small; (2) obstreperous; or (3) median; average. Readers today often misunderstand sense 1. A *mean-spirited* person is not malevolent or evil; rather, the person has a small spirit, a petty mind.

mean, n.; **median.** Writers should distinguish between these two words. The *mean* is the average. The *median* is the point in a series of numbers above which is half the series and below which is the other half.

meaningful (= full of meaning or expression) has, with some irony, rightly been criticized as a meaningless buzzword, especially when used for *reasonable.* Here its meaning is stretched to the breaking point:

- "[The statute] provide[s] vexatious litigators an opportunity in a *meaningful* [read *reasonable*] time and a *meaningful* [read *reasonable*] manner." *Central Ohio Transit Auth. v. Timson,* 724 N.E.2d 458, 464 (Ohio Ct. App. 1998).
- "Due process requires a *meaningful* hearing at a *meaningful* [read *reasonable*] time before a deprivation of property can occur." *New England Tel. & Tel. Co. v. Conversent Communs. of R.I., LLC,* 178 F.Supp.2d 81, 95 (D.R.I. 2001).

Meaningful has also been used to mean "significant, important," as here: "These guarantees simply provide a mechanism to ensure that a *meaningful* constitutional process occurs." *Burger v. School Bd. of McGuffey,* 923 A.2d 1155, 1163 (Pa. 2007). These uses have made *meaningful* a VOGUE WORD that careful writers avoid.

means and includes. See DEFINITIONS (C).

mean-spirited. See **mean,** adj.

meantime; meanwhile. *In the meantime* is idiomatic; *in the meanwhile* is not. Both *meanwhile* and *meantime* can be used alone <meanwhile, the depositions continued>, though the former more naturally so.

mea sponte. See **sua sponte.**

***meat out.** See **mete out.**

mechanic's lien; mechanic's and materialman's lien. A *mechanic* furnishes labor to the construction of improvements on land; a *materialman* furnishes materials. Because the mechanic and the materialman are usually one and the same, and because the legal distinction between the two is outmoded in most jurisdictions, it has become customary to refer to both in one breath, in the general phrase *mechanic's lien* or *construction lien.*

Such a lien secures payment for labor or materials supplied in improving, repairing, or maintaining real property. In many jurisdictions, the rules for perfecting such a lien are highly technical and rigid.

The word *materialman* is, from the viewpoint of eradicating sexist language, a particularly difficult one to replace. The word *supplier* is a possible candidate, but the word may not need a replacement at all if we merely refer to a *mechanic's lien* or *construction lien*. See SEXISM (B).

meddle; intermeddle; interfere; tamper. These verbs share the sense "to concern oneself with something, esp. someone else's affairs, without necessity or justification." To *meddle* is to interpose oneself in matters that are exclusively other people's concerns <the government should not meddle further with this private contract>. To *intermeddle* is to meddle especially obtrusively and repulsively <being totally unqualified to render medical assistance, and not even having a high-school diploma, he intermeddled when he attempted to perform an emergency tracheotomy on the choking victim—with a No. 2 lead pencil>. To *interfere* is to hamper, frustrate, or meddle in a deleterious way. One interferes *with* someone or something or *in* something by meddling either intentionally or unintentionally <by writing to the court purportedly on behalf of her brother, she was interfering with his legal strategy>. To *tamper* is to make unjustified changes, to pervert by intrusion, or otherwise to try to influence improperly or corruptly <jury tampering>.

media; medium. *Media*, the plural of *medium*, cannot properly be used as a singular. And **medias*, which has recently raised its ugly head, can only be described as illiterate.

Mediums is the correct plural when the sense of *medium* is "a clairvoyant; spiritualist"—e.g.: "A similar state of dissociation seems to account for the manifestations of some 'psychic *mediums*.'" Glanville Williams, *Criminal Law* 37 (2d ed. 1961). Otherwise, the form should be avoided—e.g.:

- "It is true that one of the *mediums* [read *media*] of the lawyer's art is rules, and the lawyer must know rules." James B. White, *The Legal Imagination* xxxv (1973).
- "Reporters for printed *mediums* [read *media*] also focus criticism on television for using all-purpose experts to express an opinion on a wide variety of subjects." Charles Rothfeld, *On Legal Pundits and How They Got That Way*, N.Y. Times, 4 May 1990, at B10.

Media is often used as a shortened form of *communications media*—e.g.: "If one viewpoint monopolizes the *media*, however, the discussion that flows from it will not be full and unrestricted."

median. See **mean.**

*medias. See **media.**

mediate, adj., = occupying a middle position; acting through an intermediate person or thing. It is frequently used in contrast with *immediate*. The Rule in Shelley's Case is often stated thus: "Where the ancestor takes an estate of freehold, and in the same gift or conveyance, an estate is limited either *mediately* or immediately to his heirs, either in fee or in tail, 'the heirs' are words of limitation of the estate, and not words of purchase." *Baker v. Scott*, 62 Ill. 86, 90 (1871).

mediation. A. Generally. *Mediation* "has long been a relatively complex word in English." Raymond Williams, *Keywords: A Vocabulary of Culture and Society* 170 (1976). The most common, but conflicting, senses are the following, for which Williams suggests alternatives (in parentheses): (1) "intermediary action designed to bring about reconciliation or agreement" (*conciliation*); (2) "an activity that indirectly or deviously expresses a relationship between otherwise separated facts, actions, and experiences" (*ideology* or *rationalization*); and (3) "an activity that directly expresses otherwise unexpressed relations" (*form*). Sense 1 is the peculiarly legal one. See **alternative dispute resolution** & **arbitration.**

B. And *conciliation*. The distinction between *mediation* and *conciliation* is widely debated among those interested in alternative dispute resolution, arbitration, and international diplomacy. Some suggest that *conciliation* is "a nonbinding arbitration," whereas *mediation* is merely "assisted negotiation." Others put it nearly the opposite way: *conciliation* involves a third party's trying to bring together disputing parties to help them reconcile their differences, whereas *mediation* goes further by allowing the third party to suggest terms on which the dispute might be resolved. Still others reject these attempts at DIFFERENTIATION and contend that there is no consensus about what the two words mean—that they are generally interchangeable. Though a distinction would be convenient, those who argue that usage indicates a broad synonymy are most accurate.

mediatory; *mediative; mediatorial. The second is a NEEDLESS VARIANT of the first. *Mediatorial*, however, corresponds not to *mediation* but to *mediator*—e.g.: "It is the high province of this Court to interpose its benign and *mediatorial* influence." *Gibbons v. Ogden*, 22 U.S. (9 Wheat.) 1, 184 (1824) (argument of counsel).

medical; medicinal. The first applies to all aspects of a physician's practice, the second only to what is associated with medicines.

medication; medicament. See **medicine.**

medicinal. See **medical.**

medicine; medication; medicament. *Medication* has traditionally meant "the action of treating medically," but through SLIPSHOD EXTENSION it has recently come to mean "a medicinal substance; medicament"—a sense that careful writers avoid. *Medicament* (= a substance taken internally or used externally in curative treatment) and *medicine* (= a substance taken internally in curative treatment) are subsets of the general idea contained in the loose meaning of *medication*.

medicolegal (= involving the application of medical science to law), though perhaps seeming to be a NEOLOGISM, was first used in the early 19th century. It has proved useful enough to be used frequently—e.g.:

- L. Thoinot & A.W. Weysse, *Medico-Legal Moral Offenses* (1911).
- "That these tests are very far from reality cannot, we think, be successfully disputed. Certainly, many competent *medicolegal* writers have so indicated and in our opinion they have proved their case." *U.S. ex rel. Smith v. Baldi*, 192 F.2d 540, 566 (3d Cir. 1951).
- "M-LCS described itself as 'the only full-time consulting firm dedicated to assisting attorneys in all jurisdictions with screening and preparing *medico-legal* cases.'" Joseph Goulden, *The Million Dollar Lawyers* 122 (1978) (quoting advertisement).

The best modern spelling is *medicolegal*—with no hyphen. Cf. **psycholegal.**

medium. See **media.**

meeting of the minds. Grant Gilmore called this phrase "quaintly archaic." *The Death of Contract* 43 (1974). It is not quite a LOAN TRANSLATION, but perhaps a loan paraphrase, of the Roman-law phrase *consensus ad idem.* Justice Oliver Wendell Holmes, Samuel Williston, and others treated *meeting of the minds* with contempt because it denotes a subjective rather than an objective theory of contracts. So it is more than quaintly archaic; as a matter of substantive law, it is long since outmoded. Cf. **mutuality of obligation.**

*meet out. See **mete out.**

*meld together is a common REDUNDANCY.

*meliorate. See **ameliorate.**

member of the bar. While in the U.S. any licensed lawyer is a member of the bar, in G.B. only barristers (and advocates in Scotland) can claim this membership, solicitors being members of the Law Society or the Law Society of Scotland.

member of the legal profession. This phrase is a needless circumlocution for *lawyer.*

memento. So spelled—not **momento.*

memoranda; memorandums. *Memorandum* is always the singular noun. Either *memoranda* or *memorandums* is correct as a plural. No less a writer than Shakespeare used *memorandums* (*Henry IV, Part 1,* 3.3.157–63), but *memoranda* now predominates. See PLURALS (A).

Occasionally the Latinate plural is misused as a singular: "In the discretion of the court [these documents] may be allowed to go to the jury, and be taken out with them when they retire as a *memoranda* [read *memorandum*] of the distances, areas, and quantities

as sworn to by the engineer." John Cassan Waite, *Engineering and Architectural Jurisprudence* 800 (1898).

*memorandize (= to put into a memo), an -IZE NEOLOGISM with little merit, appears to be a NEEDLESS VARIANT of *memorialize.* E.g.: "The two-year leaseback . . . was oral, and is not '*memorandized*' [read *memorialized*] by any writing as required by the statute of frauds." *Truslow v. Woodruff,* 60 Cal. Rptr. 304, 308 n.1 (Ct. App. 1967). See **memorialize.**

memorandums. See **memoranda.**

memorialize (= to preserve the memory of; to supply the memorial of) is a word of great seriousness in lay contexts <to memorialize the plight of European Jews in World War II>. In legal writing, by contrast, it is used in far more mundane contexts—e.g.:

- "This letter *memorialized* the parties' settlement terms." *Wm. Dickson Co. v. Pierce County,* 116 P.3d 409, 411 (Wash. Ct. App. 2005).
- "These promises were reduced to writing, and Grindley and Nahai signed the real estate sales contract *memorializing* the deal." *Golden Atlanta Site Dev., Inc. v. R. Nahai & Sons, Inc.,* 683 S.E.2d 627, 630 (Ga. Ct. App. 2009).

memory, sound mind and. See **mind and memory.**

memory of man runneth not to the contrary. This memorable phrase expresses immemoriality—or the point before which *legal memory* began (fixed as the year 1189), also known as *time immemorial.* By the early 16th century, English courts were coming to use legal memory to restrict the growth of custom, which could be established only if it predated 1189. See **time immemorial.**

The phrase is frequently used in extended senses in American judicial opinions as well as in legal commentary—e.g.: "We are not dealing with a traditional common law crime such as assault and battery, a crime in existence since the *memory of man runneth not to the contrary.*" *Prinz v. Great Bay Casino Corp.,* 705 F.2d 692, 701 (3d Cir. 1983) (A. Leon Higginbotham, J., dissenting).

Though the phrase dates from the 13th century at the latest, some have mistakenly thought it to have less antiquity. The phrase is often attributed to Blackstone, who himself hinted at its antiquity: "Whence it is that in our law the goodness of a custom depends upon it's [sic] having been used time out of mind; or, in the solemnity of our legal phrase, time whereof the *memory of man runneth not to the contrary.*" 1 William Blackstone, *Commentaries on the Laws of England* 67 (1765). The phrase (somewhat mangled) has also been attributed to the King James Version of the Bible (1611): "Myles Ambrose has been around this town . . . since, as the Bible says, the *mind of man runneth not to the contrary.*" *Fourth Annual Judicial Conference of the United States Court of Appeals for*

---

the Federal Circuit, 112 F.R.D. 439, 550 (1987) (David Busby introducing Myles Ambrose).

As in that last example, the phrase is sometimes misrendered *mind of man* (suggesting that no one could *think* otherwise) instead of *memory of man* (suggesting that no one could *remember* otherwise)— e.g.: "We have been operating on this premise for so long that the *mind* [read *memory*] *of a man runneth not to the contrary.*" *Okaw Drainage Dist. v. National Distillers & Chem. Corp.*, 882 F.2d 1241, 1245 (7th Cir. 1989) (quoting Mills, J., the trial judge). Note also that the phrase is *memory of man* (i.e., mankind or humankind), not *memory of a man*, as in the preceding example. See SEXISM (B).

menace. See **threaten.**

mendacious. See **dishonest.**

mendacity; mendicity. The first is deceptiveness, the second beggarliness. A dishonest beggar might be termed a *mendacious mendicant.*

mens rea; actus reus. *Actus reus* = a wrongful act; the element of conduct, as opposed to the mental state, that must be proved to convict a criminal defendant. *Mens rea* = the state of mind that the prosecution, to secure a conviction, must prove that a defendant had when committing a crime. Although these dovetailing TERMS OF ART—both deriving from LAW LATIN— have traditionally been basic to criminal law, one writer cautions against slavish adherence: "This way of dividing up the general elements in crimes is rather 'rough and ready,' and is certainly a better servant than master." Andrew Ashworth, *Principles of Criminal Law* 78 (1991).

Mens rea does not bear a literal meaning (i.e., "bad mind" or "guilty mind"), because one who breaks the law even with the best of motives still commits a crime: "The language is no longer meant to convey the idea of general malevolence characteristic of early common-law usage." Peter W. Low et al., *Criminal Law: Cases and Materials* 627 (1982). The true translation is criminal intention or recklessness. Words typically imposing a *mens rea* requirement include *willfully, maliciously, fraudulently, recklessly, negligently, scienter, corruptly, feloniously,* and *wantonly.* See **mental element.**

Some writers hyphenate the phrase when it appears as a phrasal adjective—e.g.:

- "Such an offense does not have the normal *mens-rea* requirement." Rollin M. Perkins & Ronald N. Boyce, *Criminal Law* 716–17 (3d ed. 1982).
- "It is important to treat common-law *mens-rea* terms, and indeed much of the language of the law, as words that must be translated into ordinary language before one can learn what they mean and how to use them." Peter W. Low et al., *Criminal Law: Cases and Materials* 204–05 (1982).

Although this practice seems laudable within a community that seems impervious to the need for hyphenating phrasal adjectives, it is unnecessary with phrases of foreign origin, such as *mens rea.* See PHRASAL ADJECTIVES (B).

***mental attitude** is a common REDUNDANCY—e.g.: "What distinguishes gross negligence from ordinary negligence, and justifies the imposition of exemplary (punitive) damages, is the *mental attitude* [read *mental state*] of the defendant." *Williams v. McCollister*, 671 F.Supp.2d 884, 889 (S.D. Tex. 2009).

mental disorder. See **insanity** (A).

mental element is a phrase that criminal-law writers often use synonymously with *mens rea.* See **mens rea.**

mental illness. See **insanity** (A).

mentee. See -EE.

mercantile. See **commercial,** adj.

merchantable. See **salable.**

***merciament.** See **amercement.**

mercilessly. See ***unmercilessly.**

mercy. See **clemency.**

mercy killing. See **euthanasia.**

mere right (= a right without possession) is a LOAN TRANSLATION of the LAW LATIN *jus merum*, which appeared in LAW FRENCH as *meer dreit.*

mere scintilla. See **scintilla.**

meretricious (= alluring by false show) has not lost its pejorative etymological connection with the Latin word for "prostitute" (*meretrix*). A *meretricious marriage*, traditionally speaking, is one that involves either two people of the same sex or lack of capacity on the part of one party—e.g.: "The blameless offspring of an acknowledged *meretricious* marriage . . . shall not be bastardized and subjected to the civil consequences which fall upon the fruits of such an unlawful union in England." *Park v. Barron*, 20 Ga. 702, 706 (1856). For a humorous misuse of the word, see MALAPROPISMS.

Today, it would be highly tendentious and objectionable to refer to a legally valid same-sex marriage as a *meretricious marriage.*

mergee is a mid-20th-century NEOLOGISM denoting a participant in a merger. Unlike most nouns formed with the -EE suffix, *mergee* may apply to both the acquired and acquiring corporations, or to the product of the merger. This multiplicity of meaning is most unfortunate—e.g.:

- "It is also contended by appellant that the operating experience of Tennessee Coach Company is an asset within the meaning of T.C.A. 48-519, and *as such* [read *therefore*] was conveyed along with the other assets of said Coach Company to Tennessee Trailways, Inc., the *mergee* [i.e., acquiring] corporation." *Tennessee Trailways, Inc. v. Butler*, 373 S.W.2d 201, 204 (Tenn. 1963).

- "The Commissioner demurred to the bill on the grounds . . . that no statute provided for the transfer of a tax credit earned by a predecessor corporation to a *mergee* [i.e., resulting] corporation." *United Inter-Mountain Tel. Co. v. Moyers*, 426 S.W.2d 177, 178 (Tenn. 1968).
- "This application was apparently precipitated by notification of Texas International Airlines, one of the *mergees* [i.e., acquired corporations] in the Continental/Texas International merger, to the IBT that, on the merger date, all of the employees in the crafts represented by the Teamsters would become subject to Continental's employment policies and its agreement with the union would no longer be effective." *In re Continental Airlines Corp.*, 40 B.R. 299, 301 (Bankr. S.D. Tex. 1984).

Although a few writers have attempted to make a distinction by referring to the acquiring and acquired corporations as the *merger* (or **mergor*) and the *mergee*, the practice hasn't caught on—e.g.:

- "In the event of a true statutory merger, the *mergee* corporation was entitled to the deductions of the other corporation." *E. & J. Gallo Winery v. Commissioner*, 227 F.2d 699, 703 (9th Cir. 1955).
- "Downs continued to solicit each of the *mergees* and made written reports more than five years after the first contact." *Cherry, Bekaert & Holland v. Downs*, 640 F.Supp. 1096, 1099 (W.D.N.C. 1986).

See -EE.

merger. A. And *consolidation; amalgamation*. These terms are distinct in denoting types of corporate restructuring. In a *merger*, one company is absorbed by another, the latter retaining its own name, identity, articles of incorporation, and bylaws, and acquiring all the assets, liabilities, and powers of the absorbed company, which ceases its separate existence. In a *consolidation*, the corporations that are absorbed into a new entity lose their previous identities to form a new corporation.

In English law, the different forms of corporate union are referred to as *amalgamation*. As one writer states in recommending this word, "It is convenient to have some such inclusive term for corporate unions, as they have many elements in common." H.W. Ballantine, *Ballantine on Corporations* § 288, at 680–81 (rev. ed. 1946).

B. And *bar*. In the law of procedure, *merger* describes the effect of a judgment for the plaintiff. Such a judgment extinguishes any claim that was the subject of an earlier lawsuit and merges it into the judgment, so that the plaintiff's rights are confined to enforcing the judgment. *Bar*, on the other hand, describes the effect of a judgment on the merits for a defendant. Such a judgment extinguishes any claim that was the subject of a lawsuit in which judgment was rendered, including parts of that claim that were not raised in the earlier lawsuit.

C. Of Law and Equity. In traditional legal idiom, the joining of the procedural aspects of law and equity is termed "merger"—e.g.: "The history of the *merger* of law and equity, first in New York under the Old Code, and later in twenty-nine other states and territories in which codes similar to the New York Code were adopted, and in England by the Judicature Acts, which took effect in 1875, has been covered in Chapter II." William F. Walsh, *A Treatise on Equity* 96 (1930). Actually, despite Walsh's suggestion that merger did not occur in England until 1875, the fusion of law and equity began in that country with the Common Law Procedure Act 1854.

D. *Doctrine of merger*. This phrase means that something of greater importance subsumes something of lesser importance, but the context determines the precise signification. In the law of contract, for example, *merger* refers to the substitution of a superior form of contract for an inferior form, as when a written contract supersedes all oral agreements and prior understandings. Hence, a *merger clause* (also known as an *integration clause*) states expressly that the contract has this effect.

In criminal law, under the *doctrine of merger*—abolished in some jurisdictions, as in England—a charge of attempt would be defeated if the evidence showed that the defendant had actually committed a felony.

In the property lawyer's vocabulary, the word *merger* denotes the doctrine that, if a greater estate and a lesser estate in the same land become one person's property, the lesser estate is destroyed or "merged" into the greater.

merger clause. See **integration clause** & **merger (D)**.

mergers and acquisitions. See **M&A**.

*merge together is a REDUNDANCY. See **together**.

merit takes the preposition *in* or *to*, not *of*—e.g.: "There is no *merit of* [read *merit to* or *merit in*] the defendant's contention that his age was not proved." *People v. Cavaness*, 171 N.E.2d 56, 59 (Ill. 1961).

meritless. See **unmeritorious**.

meritorious usually refers to parties' claims in AmE, and not to the parties themselves. This restriction does not hold in BrE—e.g.: "There are no doubt a considerable number of cases in which an *unmeritorious* defendant escapes and a *meritorious* plaintiff suffers hardship because of his actions being statute-barred owing to bad advice on the law from his trade union or solicitor." *Central Asbestos Co. v. Dodd*, [1973] A.C. 518, 556 (H.L.).

merits. In legal usage, the *merits* are the elements or grounds of a claim or defense—the substantive consideration to be taken into account in deciding a case, as opposed to extraneous or technical points, esp. of procedure. A judgment is *on the merits* "when it amounts to a declaration of the law as to the respective rights and duties of the parties . . . irrespective of formal, technical, or dilatory objections or contentions." 2 Henry Campbell Black, *The Law of Judgments* 1045 (2d ed. 1902). A judgment on the merits need not be objectively correct: "A judgment may be on the *merits* although an unerring intelligence and infallible sense of moral right might perceive that it worked the wrong; it is not meant that the sentence must be even legally right." *Id.* at 1044.

mesalliance; misalliance. *Mesalliance*, a GALLICISM, means "a marriage with a social inferior; a morganatic marriage." *Misalliance* is best kept distinct in the senses (1) "an improper alliance"; or (2) "a marriage in which the partners are ill-suited for each other." A *mesalliance* /may-zahl-**yahns**/ may be a happy marriage, but a *misalliance* /mis-ə-**li**-əns/ never is.

mesne /meen/ denotes the idea of occupying a middle position. It has two important senses in the law, usually in historical contexts. In feudal contexts, a *mesne lord* is one who holds an estate of a superior lord while being a lord over tenants. The estate of a mesne lord was termed the *mesnalty*. The *OED* notes that *mesne tenant* is "inaccurately used to denote one who holds of a mesne lord."

Mesne may also signify "occurring or performed at a time intermediate between two dates" (*OED*). So *mesne profits* are the profits of an estate received by a tenant in wrongful possession between two dates. E.g.: "The plaintiff relies on legal title to recover possession of the land or of the land and *mesne profits.*" *Foster v. Wilmington Plantation Owners Ass'n*, 696 S.E.2d 85, 88 (Ga. Ct. App. 2010). *Mesne process* = all process issued between the commencement of a lawsuit by the initial writ or pleading and the termination of the suit—e.g.: "The writ upon which the plaintiff was arrested on *mesne process* was of no effect." *Telefsen v. Fee*, 46 N.E. 562, 563 (Mass. 1897).

mesonomic. See **zygnomic.**

messuage /**mes**-wij/ "is usually understood to mean 'a house,' but it includes more than the actual buildings." Henry C. Richards & John P.H. Soper, *The Law and Practice of Compensation* 17 (n.d. [1898]). What else does it include? Generally any garden or orchard associated with the house, and any outbuildings. If the term is used with the degree of particularity specified in its definition, then it may be justified in legal contexts. But often one senses that it's a highfalutin LEGALISM for *house*—e.g.: "Curtilage has been defined as a little garden, yard, field, or piece of void ground, lying near and belonging to the *messuage.*" 7 *The American and English Encyclopedia of Law* 528 (David S. Garland & Lucius P. McGehee eds., 2d ed. 1898). See **curtilage** & **tenement.**

metalaw is a 20th-century NEOLOGISM meaning "a hypothetical legal code based on the principles underlying existing legal codes and designed to provide a framework of agreement between diverse legal systems (orig. conceived as between terrestrial and possible extraterrestrial beings)" (*OED*). The word, then, has a specific sense; it should not be used in vague, half-sensical ways.

METAPHORS. A *metaphor* is a figure of speech in which one thing is called by the name of something else, or is said to be that other thing. Unlike *similes*, which use *like* or *as*, metaphorical comparisons are implicit rather than explicit. (See SIMILES.) Skillful use of metaphor is one of the highest attainments of writing; graceless and even aesthetically offensive use of metaphors is one of the most common scourges of writing, and especially of PURPLE PROSE. Those who use metaphors unrestrainedly and ineffectively almost always fancy themselves supreme stylists; hence the problem of educating readers on the uses and abuses of metaphor is a delicate one, for the worst offenders are likely to consider themselves masterly artists.

A. Mixed and Mangled Metaphors. Lord Keith of Avonholm has shrewdly addressed the use of metaphors in legal writing: "A graphic phrase, or expression, has its uses even in a law report and can give force to a legal principle, but it must be related to the circumstances in which it is used." *White & Carter Councils, Ltd. v. McGregor*, [1962] A.C. 413, 438 (H.L.). The Law Lord displayed a great deal of insight in that passage: the *vehicle* of the metaphor (i.e., the literal sense of the metaphorical language) must be consonant with the *tenor* of the metaphor (i.e., the ultimate, metaphorical sense), which is to say the means must fit the end. In the statement, *That lawyer's brief is a patchwork quilt without discernible design*, the composition of the brief is the tenor, and the quilt is the vehicle.

It is the comparison of the tenor with the vehicle that makes or breaks a metaphor. A writer would be ill advised, for example, to use rustic metaphors in a discussion of the problems of air pollution, which is essentially a problem of the bigger cities and outlying areas. Following are characteristic specimens in which the vehicle of the metaphor is mismatched with the tenor:

- "The rules of offer and acceptance . . . have a *grip on the vision* and indeed on the affections held by no other rules 'of law,' real or pseudo." Karl Llewellyn, *Our Case-Law of Contract*, 48 Yale L.J. 1, 32 (1938). One cannot grip a vision.
- "There are but two *conduits or cables*, the statute of wills, and of descents and distributions by which the Grim Reaper may at the moment of and by the stroke of his scythe flash the transfer and transmission of property and estate to the quick from the dead." *Spinks v. Rice*, 47 S.E.2d 424, 429 (Va. 1948). The Grim Reaper flashes a scythe by means of a conduit or cable?
- "Although Sutter has *clothed* her complaint in the *garb* of a civil-rights action, . . . her claim *boils down* to a demand for custody of the child." *Sutter v. Pitts*, 639 F.2d 842, 844 (1st Cir. 1981). A complaint clothed in a certain garb is boiled down?
- "We need not explore the *full depths* of those issues, however. Our case may be resolved on two *narrower grounds.*" *Cardinal Ship. Corp. v. M/S Seisho Maru*, 744 F.2d 461,

467 (5th Cir. 1984). One might, presumably, avoid full depths by standing on narrow grounds, but not on narrower grounds. Narrower than what?

- "The Court has acquired a *voracious appetite* for judicial activism in its Fourth Amendment jurisprudence, at least when it comes to restricting the constitutional rights of the citizen." *New Jersey v. T.L.O.*, 468 U.S. 1214, 1215 (1984) (Stevens, J., dissenting). Do judges who restrict constitutional rights of citizens feed on judicial activism? The metaphor makes no sense.
- "Equal protection has become a *stout shield* for protecting against the discriminatory *bite* of governmental classification." *Town of Ball v. Rapides Parish Police Jury*, 746 F.2d 1049, 1058 (5th Cir. 1984). What does a stout shield look like? Short and fat? And are shields ordinarily, or ever, used against biting attackers?
- "There is a *long leap*, however, between a public right under the First Amendment to attend trials and a public right under the First Amendment to see a given trial televised. It is a *leap* that is not supported by history." *Westmoreland v. Columbia Broad. Sys., Inc.*, 752 F.2d 16, 23 (2d Cir. 1984). What leaps are supported by history?
- "To assume competency is to let the *enigmas* of psychology *breathe* our miasmic decree." *Rumbaugh v. Procunier*, 753 F.2d 395, 415 (5th Cir. 1985). How do enigmas breathe miasmas?

Yet the greater problem in using metaphors is that one metaphor should not crowd another. The purpose of an image is to fix the idea in the reader's or listener's mind; if disparate images appear in abundance, the audience is left confused or sometimes, at the writer's expense, knee-slapping—e.g.: "*On the one hand*, the contract between the two is a *bipartite umbilical cord fed* by Medicare and Medicaid funds such that Lifetron can be properly termed a recipient of federal financial assistance. . . . *On the other hand*, the *parameters limned* by the Supreme Court . . . *constrain* us to hold that the actions of this private defendant cannot be fairly attributed to the state." *Frazier v. Board of Trustees*, 765 F.2d 1278, 1295 (5th Cir. 1985). This cascade of metaphors bothers the intelligent reader far more than it helps. In fact, the metaphors make no sense: umbilical cords feed, they are not fed; and exactly what shape a bipartite umbilical cord would assume we have no idea, especially if it is (rather grotesquely) resting on a hand.

Badly used metaphors are more forgivable in oratory than in writing, for with the latter the perpetrator can be charged with malice aforethought. Oratorical falls from grace are legion. Some time ago a newspaper article collected some of the oratorical gems of Michigan legislators. E.g.:

- "This bill goes to the very heart of the moral fiber of the human anatomy."
- "From now on, I am watching everything you do with a fine-toothed comb."

The following classic illustration comes from a speech by Boyle Roche in the Irish Parliament, delivered in about 1790: "Mr. Speaker, I smell a rat. I see him floating in the air. But mark me, sir, I will nip him in the bud." (Quoted by Jocelyn Simon, *English Idioms from the Law*, 76 Law Q. Rev. 283, 287 (1960).) Perhaps the supreme example of the comic misuse of metaphor occurred in the speech of a scientist who referred to "a virgin field pregnant with possibilities."

Legal writers must not play fast and loose with their images; they are not, like their speaking counterparts, to be forgiven so easily. To use metaphors badly in prose is amateurish and ultimately embarrassing. Writers should use metaphors sparingly, should wait for the aptest moments, elsewhere using a more straightforward style.

B. Legal Metaphors. The legal idiom abounds in special metaphors not used elsewhere. For example, statutes of limitation are said to *run*, plaintiffs *shoulder* the burden of proof, plaintiffs have *clean* or *unclean hands*, defendants are sometimes *insulated* from liability, agents may be *clothed* with the *mantle* of apparent authority, we have suits to *quiet* title, government action may have a *chilling effect* on First Amendment rights, and we may sue to remove a *cloud* on title. (See CLICHÉS.) These are dormant rather than active metaphors; originally they were creatively expressive, whereas now they are merely expressive. When used with other metaphors, however, they may clash; hence writers must try to be sensitive to the compatibility of dormant with active metaphors.

C. The Overwrought Metaphor. Extended metaphors have been out of fashion for more than a century. The most readers can generally tolerate nowadays is the two-part metaphor—e.g.: "We are faced with the further problem of *fitting the foot* of modern-day use and understanding of gifts of intangible personal property through survivorship arrangements *into the rigid shoe* of common-law principles." *Frey v. Wubbena*, 185 N.E.2d 850, 853 (Ill. 1962). Even that type of sustained metaphor strikes most readers as facile. Here are more examples of metaphorical surfeit:

- "We find no such *hybrid* instrument, with its *dual personality*, self-executing and shifting gears, *chameleon characteristics*, and *Phoenix-like qualities* as yet known to the law." *Spinks v. Rice*, 47 S.E.2d 424, 430 (Va. 1948).
- "At bottom, Chase's action presents the flip side of a familiar aphoristic coin: *if the way to a man's heart lies through his stomach, then so does the way to his bile.* . . . The Constitution requires that correctional facilities meet certain minimum standards of decency, wholesomeness, cleanliness and the like—not that they *cater* to the individual preference of each inmate or that *institutional cuisine be presented and served in a manner which Guide Michelin would applaud.* A jail is, when all is said and done, a penal institution maintained for the purpose of imprisoning those who have committed wrongs against society and thus are receiving their *just desserts*; it is neither a country club, nor a three-star bistro. . . . Chase's complaint is *not judicially digestible* in the form presented." *Chase v. Quick*, 596 F.Supp. 33, 35 (D.R.I. 1984).
- "Notwithstanding Golemis's alarming *diagnosis of the maladies* . . . the ordinance has caused, he has come to the wrong place for an immediate *antidote*. The plaintiff's

present effort to use a federal venue as an *emetic* against the municipal action which (in his view) has tainted the *eupepsia* of his property rights cannot be *swallowed.* . . . [H]e must look to the Rhode Island courts for a *cure.*" *Golemis v. Kirby*, 632 F.Supp. 159, 164–65 (D.R.I. 1985).

- "In the face of this remorseless logic, *Edison lights up* the sky with a barrage of postulates. The asseveration that the disputed phrase must be construed unfavorably to RCI, as the author, has already *blown a fuse* . . . and need not be rehashed. Most of the remaining *surges* are of *low voltage* and do not require discussion." *RCI N.E. Servs. Div. v. Boston Edison Co.*, 822 F.2d 199, 204 (1st Cir. 1987).

mete out, vb. (from an old word for "measure"), is the correct phrase, not *meet out or **meat out.* E.g.:

- "Washington's penalty . . . marks the first time the maximum fine of $10,000 has been *meeted out* [read *meted out*] since O'Brien asked the NBA board of governors to expand his disciplinary powers." Nancy Scannell, *Violence in the NBA: Getting Worse?*, Wash. Post, 16 Dec. 1977, at E1.
- "For Europeans, the death sentences *meeted out* [read *meted out*] to 'rioters' . . . [have] an all too familiar ring." Robert Mauthner, *Salvage from the Wreckage*, Fin. Times, 20 June 1989, at I23.

metes and bounds; butts and bounds; lines and corners. All three phrases are used in deeds and surveys to describe the territorial limits of property, as the surveyor measures distances and angles from designated landmarks and in relation to adjoining properties.

The most familiar phrase is *metes and bounds*, in which *mete* derives from the Latin term *meta* (= a mark or object around which chariots turned in a Roman racecourse). At common law, *mete* denoted a visible object in line with a boundary, such as a stone or tree, showing where a line ended.

The term *butts* "is very obscurely defined in the old books." 1 Alexander M. Burrill, *A Law Dictionary and Glossary* 235 (2d ed. 1859). Today that could be held to include the *OED*, over which Burrill's treatment is an improvement: "In lands of ordinary rectangular shape, *butts* are the lines at the *ends* (Fr. *bouts*), and *bounds* are those on the *sides*, or *sidings*, as they were formerly termed. . . . But in lands of irregular shape, *butts* are the angular points, or corners, where the boundary lines stop and turn in a new direction." *Id.*

A *line* is an imaginary mark that outlines the contours of land, and whose direction and length have been determined by a surveyor. A line is not necessarily straight; it may follow a natural line, such as the bank of a stream. A *corner* marks (1) the beginning or ending point of a line, or (2) the intersection of two or more converging lines. *Lines and corners* are often combined with *metes and bounds* to create a formal property description.

methinks is a creaky ARCHAISM used primarily by the lone judge in dissent—e.g.: "*Methinks* his silence indicates that Baskin had no non-gender-based reason for his action and his superiors well knew it." *Smith v. Texas Dep't of Water Res.*, 818 F.2d 363, 368 (5th Cir. 1987) (Politz, J., dissenting).

Primarily in allusions to *Hamlet* is the word appropriate—e.g.: "*Methinks* my Brothers and Sister protest too much about their general discussion of the writ." *Kuhlmann v. Wilson*, 477 U.S. 436, 463 n.2 (1986) (Brennan, J., dissenting). The Shakespearean line is often misquoted. What Gertrude says of the thespian queen is this: "The lady doth protest too much, *methinks.*" *Hamlet* 3.2.30.

methodology is frequently misused for *method*—so very often, in fact, that it has become hard to object vehemently to the longer word. As most traditionally used, *methodology* means "the science or study of method." But today it's just a more impressive-sounding equivalent to *method* (which stylists continue to prefer)—e.g.:

- "Because this case involves the role of depreciation rates and *methodologies* [read *methods*] in determining the revenue requirements of a regulated utility, we begin by briefly reviewing certain basic principles of regulatory ratemaking." *South Cent. Bell Tel. Co. v. Louisiana Pub. Serv. Comm'n*, 744 F.2d 1107, 1009 (5th Cir. 1984).
- "The recent decision in *Chevron* elaborates on these principles and sets out the appropriate *methodology* [read *method*] for ascertaining whether to afford deference to an agency['s] construction of its governing statute." *Montana v. Clark*, 749 F.2d 740, 745 (D.C. Cir. 1984).

Methodology is correctly used in the following hard-to-locate example: "Writing in a time in which *methodology in the social sciences* [i.e., the study of method in the social sciences] has become the prevailing approach, Professor von Mehren speaks of comparative study of law rather than of comparative law." Roscoe Pound, Foreword in Arthur Taylor von Mehren, *The Civil Law System* vii (1957)

mid; midst. See **amid (B).**

midwife, vb.; **midwive.** The first is the preferred form—e.g.: "This may happen when a writing judge believes with heart and soul that his position is right, but he knows that his majority is shaky; here persuasiveness must *midwive* [read *midwife*] the opinion if it is to come into existence at all." George Rose Smith, *A Primer of Opinion Writing for New Judges*, 21 Ark. L. Rev. 197 (1967).

mien (= demeanor; appearance; bearing) often carries connotations of formidableness <his imposing mien>. The word is pronounced /meen/.

migratory worker. See **undocumented alien.**

milieu is sometimes misspelled **mileau. See, e.g., New Eng. Patriots Football Club, Inc. v. Univ. of Colo.*, 592 F.2d 1196, 1198 (1st Cir. 1979).

The plural *milieus* is preferable to *milieux—e.g.: "But marriages between first cousins are so usual that in many *milieus* they are almost normal." Max Radin, *The Law and You* 42 (1948). See PLURALS (A).

military law. See **martial law.**

military testament. See **oral will.**

militate. See **mitigate.**

millennium [L. *mille* "thousand" + *annus* "year"] forms two plurals: *millennia* and *millenniums*. The preferred plurals are *-ia* in AmE, *-iums* in BrE. But either is acceptable on both sides of the Atlantic. See PLURALS (A).

The word is often deprived of one *-n-* and misspelled **millenium*—e.g.: "Share returns have exceeded eleven percent per year for three decades, even including the declines of the turn of the *millenium* [read *millennium*]." Daniel J.H. Greenwood, *Democracy and Delaware*, 23 Yale L. & Pol'y Rev. 381, 447 (2005). In fact, this misspelling has even found its way into a proper name: the hotel across from the World Trade Center's site in New York City is called *The Millenium*. Perhaps that should be called not a proper name but an improper name.

millionaire is so spelled—not, like *questionnaire*, with *-nn-*. E.g.: "A *millionnaire* [read *millionaire*] with a small pension could qualify for an adjustment under the ordinance." *Halstead v. City of Flint*, 338 N.W.2d 903, 905 (Mich. Ct. App. 1983). For another word susceptible to this problem—*doctrinaire*—see **doctrinal.**

mimic, vb., makes *mimicking* and *mimicked*.

mind and memory is a common DOUBLET <of sound mind and memory> in the context of establishing testamentary capacity. David Mellinkoff called it "a snatch of confusing nonsense. . . . As in England, American lawyers have long recognized that they were using *memory* here in a special way, in the sense of understanding or mind, and that *mind and memory* did no more for testamentary capacity than *mind* alone." David Mellinkoff, *The Language of the Law* 333, 335 (1963).

The snare lies in failing to recognize the phrase as an archaic doublet and in misunderstanding it as setting forth independent criteria for judging testamentary capacity. That is, in this context *mind* historically equated with *memory*. Especially in writing to be read by nonlawyers (as in jury instructions), the second half of this doublet should be avoided. As the law is currently understood, one may be very forgetful and still be "of sound mind and memory." *Sound mind* is sufficient and far less confusing.

In wills, the recitation that the testator is of *sound mind and memory* is falling into disuse for an additional reason: not only does it do no good, it may even raise suspicions about mental capacity. *See* Thomas E. Atkinson, *Handbook of the Law of Wills* 819 (2d ed. 1953). See DOUBLETS, TRIPLETS, AND SYNONYM-STRINGS.

mind of man runneth not to the contrary. See **memory of man runneth not to the contrary.**

MINGLE-MANGLE, known in erudite circles as *macaronism, soraismus,* or *cacozelia,* was a common vice of language in early English opinions. It consists in English larded with Latin or French, as in the following example from *Weaver v. Ward,* decided by the King's Bench in 1616. Try reading this aloud:

> The defendant pleaded . . . that he was . . . a trained soldier in London, of the band of one Andrews captain; and so was plaintiff, and that they were skirmishing with their musquets charged with powder for their exercise in re militari, against another captain and his band; and as they were so skirmishing, the defendant casualiter et per infortunium et contra voluntatem suam, in discharging his piece, did hurt and wound the plaintiff, which is the same, etc. absque hoc, that he was guilty aliter sive alio modo.
>
> Hob. 134, 80 Eng. Rep. 284.

For modern legal readers, mingle-mangle makes for fascinating, if not entirely comprehensible, reading. Following is another Latin-English example, this also from a well-known torts case: "Trespass quare vi & armis clausum fregit & herbam suam pedibus conculcando consumpsit in six acres. The defendant pleads, that he hath an acre lying next the said six acres, and upon it a hedge of thorns, and he cut the thorns, and they ipso invito fell upon the plaintiff's land." *The Case of the Thorns,* 6 Ed. 4, Mich. 7a, pl. 18 (1466) (so summarized in *Bessey v. Olliot & Lambert,* T. Raym. 467 (1681)).

English-French was another mongrel dialect of the law: one early report referred to a prisoner being sentenced who "ject un Brickbat a le dit Justice que narrowly mist & pur ceo immediately fuit Indictment drawn per Noy envers le prisoner & son dexter manus ampute & fix al Gibbet sur que luy mesme immediatement hange in presence de Court." (Quoted fr. Dyer's Reports 188b (1688) in Frederick Pollock, *A First Book of Jurisprudence* 301 (4th ed. 1918).)

The 17th-century English reporters most inclined to engage in mingle-mangle were Rolle and Latch. See LAW LATIN & LAW FRENCH.

minify. See **minimize.**

minim (= something minute) is sometimes used in the context of the maxim *de minimis non curat lex.* E.g.: "The *minim* of the injury here, however, obscures and tempts neglect of the importance of the issue." *Hewlett v. Barge Bertie,* 418 F.2d 654, 656 (4th Cir. 1969). See *de minimis.*

minima. See **minimum.**

minimal; minimum, adj. Both words are used adjectivally, *minimum* as an attributive adjective in phrases such as *minimum wage.* If there is a valid nuance distinguishing these two adjectival forms, it is that *minimal* means "few, little, smallest" <with minimal

disturbance> <minimal support> <minimal objections>, whereas *minimum*, adj., means "consisting in the fewest necessary things, or the least acceptable or lawful amount" <minimum contacts as a basis for jurisdiction> <minimum wage>. E.g.:

- "Many states impose only *minimal* residency requirements on persons petitioning for adoption within their borders." Irving J. Sloan, *The Law of Adoption and Surrogate Parenting* 12 (1988).
- "The purpose of the act is to protect consumers by placing specific *minimum* requirements on the contents of home-improvement contracts." *Benge v. Miller*, 855 N.E.2d 716, 720 (Ind. App. Ct. 2006).

See **maximum** & PLURALS (A).

minimize; minify; *minimalize. *Minimize* and *minify* have distinct meanings, and *minify* is too much neglected. Properly, *minimize* = to keep to a minimum, and *minify* = to belittle, degrade; to represent something as smaller than it really is. **Minimalize* is not a proper word.

minimum, n. The plural given in most dictionaries is *minima*. E.g.: "In so ruling, however, the Court did not dispense with the Sixth Amendment's substantive *minima* of effectiveness." *U.S. v. Owens*, 484 U.S. 554, 568 n.1 (1988) (Brennan, J., dissenting). But surely the better, more natural plural is *minimums*—e.g.: "Was he deprived of a protected property interest and, if so, was the deprivation accomplished without adherence to due-process *minimums?*" *Findeisen v. North East Indep. Sch. Dist.*, 749 F.2d 234, 237 (5th Cir. 1984). See **maximum** & **plurals (A).**

minions of the law is a CLICHÉ referring to police officers or other law-enforcement officers.

*miniscule is one of the commonest misspellings in legal texts, the correct spelling being *minuscule*—e.g.: "There has recently come into the possession of Lincoln's Inn, as the gift of the author's granddaughter, his working copy of the first edition covered and interleaved with *miniscule* [read *minuscule*] writing." P.V. Baker, 103 Law Q. Rev. 650, 651 (1987) (book review). The word derives from the word *minus*, and has nothing to do with the prefix *mini-*. The counterpart—a rarity—is *majuscule* (= [of letters or writing] large or capital).

minister, n. See **ambassador.**

minister, vb. See **administer.**

minor. See **child.**

minority. A. And *infancy; nonage.* These synonyms denote the period during which a person is underage—that is, when a person has not yet reached full age and therefore cannot vote, buy alcoholic beverages, or the like. Notably, a person may be underage for some purposes (such as buying liquor) but not for others (such as voting).

Minority, which is more generally used than either of the others, is the preferable term. It encompasses the full range of persons who fall into underage categories: children, infants, juveniles, young persons, and (in Scotland) pupils. (See **child** & **infant.**) *Minority* is much more common in general usage than its antonym, *majority* (= full age), which is largely confined to legal contexts. See **age of capacity** & **majority (D).**

Infancy is likely to mislead many readers, and *nonage* is obscure to most people of any age. See **infancy, infant** & **nonage.**

B. Singular or Plural? See **majority (B)** & SYNESIS.

*minor woman is an odd combination of EUPHEMISM, MISCUE, and near-OXYMORON that displaces a more natural wording such as *girl, female minor*, or, if the sex of the person is obvious, *minor*. E.g.: "His reference to a 'mature' woman means he does not favor the right of a *minor woman* [read *minor*] to choose to have an abortion without parental or judicial consent." Susan Yoachum, *Wilson Campaign Sticks to Familiar Topics*, S.F. Chronicle, 2 Nov. 1990, at A21.

minuscule. So spelled. See ***miniscule.**

minutia (= a trivial detail; a trifling matter) is the singular of the plural *minutiae* (technically pronounced /mi-**n[y]oo**-shee-ee/, but commonly with a schwa sound in the final syllable). Though much less common than the plural form, *minutia* is hardly unknown. Unfortunately, almost every time it appears it is a misuse for the plural—e.g.: "Once one wades through the unhelpful *minutia* [read *minutiae*], three legal arguments remain." *Lentomyynti Oy v. Medivac, Inc.*, 997 F.2d 364, 370 (7th Cir. 1993).

Then again, the plural form of the noun is sometimes mistakenly coupled with a singular verb—e.g.:

- "We conclude . . . that such *minutiae is* [read *are*] without consequence in determining priority of jurisdiction." *A.E. Staley Mfg. Co. v. Swift & Co.*, 399 N.E.2d 339, 341 (Ill. App. Ct. 1980).
- "We hardly believe such *minutiae is* [read *are*] cause for finding that a wrong principle of law was employed." *Jackson County Bd. of Comm'rs v. State Tax Comm'n*, 343 N.W.2d 255, 260 (Mich. Ct. App. 1983).

Mirandize (= to read an arrestee rights under *Miranda v. Arizona*, 384 U.S. 436 (1966)) was, by the 1980s, common as police-officer slang in the U.S. Today it is a common part of criminal-law parlance—e.g.:

- "First, defendant claims that the trial court erred in ruling inadmissible his exculpatory statements made to the officer after defendant was arrested and *Mirandized.*" *People v. Barrick*, 654 P.2d 1243, 1253 (Cal. 1982) (en banc).
- "So, too, inculpatory words from the suspect, though duly *Mirandized*, might be suppressed as 'fruit' of the unlawful arrest." H. Richard Uviller, *Seizure by Gunshot*, 14 N.Y.U. Rev. L. & Soc. Change 705, 708 (1986).
- "They are read their rights ('*mirandized*') and interrogated." Robin T. Lakoff, *Talking Power: The Politics of Language in Our Lives* 87 (1990).

Surely, though, this -IZE NEOLOGISM is a blemish in place of some acceptable periphrasis, such as *to read* (arrestees) *their Miranda rights*. In the mid-1980s,

23% of the usage panelists for the *Harper Book of Contemporary Usage* (2d ed. 1985) considered the word "a useful addition to the language." A more circumspect 77% disapproved. See -IZE.

misadventure = (1) a mishap or misfortune; or (2) homicide committed accidentally by a person doing a lawful act and having no intention to injure. The word now appears most frequently in the phrases *death by misadventure* and *homicide by misadventure*.

misalliance. See **mesalliance.**

misappropriate; appropriate, vb. *Misappropriate* means "to apply (as another's money) dishonestly to one's own use." E.g.: "Zimmer has failed to prove that Davis has . . . *misappropriated* or threatened to *misappropriate* trade secrets of Zimmer." *Zimmer v. Davis*, 922 N.E.2d 68, 73 (Ind. Ct. App. 2010).

Appropriate has a more neutral, nonaccusatory connotation—e.g.: "Most of those funds are *appropriated* by the General Assembly to the State Department of Education for pass-through to the county boards." *Board of Educ. of Worcester County v. BEKA Indus.*, 989 A.2d 1181, 1206 (Md. Ct. Spec. App. 2010). Still, in meaning "to take from a particular person or organization for a particular purpose," it is tinged with some of the negative connotations made explicit in *misappropriate*—e.g.: "The proper inquiry for a family of marks is to inquire whether the defendant's mark *appropriated* the salient feature of the family of marks." *Lettuce Entertain You Enter. v. Leila Sophia*, 703 F.Supp.2d 777, 785 (N.D. Ill. 2010).

See **appropriate** & **embezzle.**

misbelief. See **disbelief.**

miscarriage. See **abortion.**

miscellaneous must be followed by a plural count noun <miscellaneous charges>; it does not work with an abstract mass noun <miscellaneous legislation>. Though one might refer to *miscellaneous languages* (and thereby include Chinese, English, French, German, and Vietnamese), it makes no sense to write *miscellaneous contract language*, as in Mark M. Grossman, *The Question of Arbitrability* 57 (1984) (section title).

mischief is a slight ARCHAISM as lawyers commonly use it—that is, to denote "a condition in which a person suffers a wrong or is under some hardship, esp. one that a statute seeks to remove or for which equity provides a remedy." E.g.: "It was permissible to consider what the law was before the statute, what '*mischief*' the statute was meant to remedy, and what the statute actually said." Theodore F.T. Plucknett, *A Concise History of the Common Law* 335 (5th ed. 1956).

From this use of *mischief*—common especially in the context of statutory construction—has arisen the phrase *mischief rule*, known also as the *rule in Heydon's case*, ([1584] 3 Co. Rep. 7a). That rule encourages judges construing a statute to consider to what "mischief" the statute was addressed and then to adopt an interpretation that will curtail the mischief and advance the remedy. The *mischief rule* is often contrasted with two other approaches to statutory construction: the *golden rule* and the *plain-meaning rule* (or, as it is termed in BrE, *literal interpretation*). See **golden rule.**

mischievous. So spelled and pronounced—not **mischievious.* Cf. **grievous.**

*misconcept should not displace *misconception*, the ordinary word that is (unlike the shorter form) recognized as a living word in English-language dictionaries—e.g.:

- "The 'impeach' *misconcept* [read *misconception*] was the judge's, not counsel's." *In re Jose S.*, 144 Cal. Rptr. 309, 313 (Ct. App. 1978).
- "Another *misconcept* [read *misconception*] is that it is necessary for the airplane to have a relatively high pitch altitude in order for it to stall." *New Hampshire. Ins. Co. v. U.S.*, 641 F.Supp. 642, 646 (D.P.R. 1986).

misconduct in office; official misconduct. These synonymous phrases refer to the common-law misdemeanor of a public officer's corrupt violation of his or her duties by malfeasance, misfeasance, or nonfeasance. Other synonymous expressions include *misbehavior in office, malconduct in office, malpractice in office, misdemeanor in office, corruption in office*, and *official corruption*. One might justifiably wonder just why there are so many phrases for it. Cf. **malfeasance, malversation** & **nonfeasance.**

misconviction (= the wrongful conviction of an innocent person, usu. as a result of erroneous or fraudulent forensic evidence or mistaken eyewitness identification) is a useful term most fully explained in 2007 by the noted scholar Jane Campbell Moriarty. See her article *"Misconvictions," Science, and the Ministers of Justice*, 86 Neb. L. Rev. 1 (2007). It had been kicking around in the language for many years, sometimes in the sense "a false belief" and sometimes in Moriarty's sense—e.g.: "One of the greatest causes of concern is the extent to which *mis-conviction* is the result of deliberate or negligent behaviour by participants in the criminal justice system." Justina Burnett, *Getting into Law* 105 (2006).

MISCUES. A miscue is an inadvertent misdirection that causes the reader to proceed momentarily with an incorrect assumption about how—in mechanics or in sense—a sentence or passage will end. The misdirection is not serious enough to cause a true AMBIGUITY because, on reflection, the reader can figure out the meaning—e.g.: *The court decided the question did not need to be addressed.* The mere omission of *that* after the verb *decided* induces the reader to believe that *the question* is the direct object—that is, to believe (if only for an immeasurably short moment) that the court decided the question. In fact, of course, the court decided not to decide the question: the writer simply elided the conjunction *that*.

Miscues are of innumerable varieties; the only consistent cure is to develop a keen empathy for the reader. Part of what you must do, then, is to approach even your own text as a stranger might. Further, though, a good edit must involve the kind of skeptical reading in which you imagine how one reader in ten might misread the sentence.

Following are discussions of six of the most common causes of miscues.

A. Unintended Word Association. Sometimes a word appearing late in a passage seems to echo an earlier word to which it really has no relation. In the following example, *barred*, in the final clause, suggests some relation to *disbarred* in the opening sentence: "In 1948 he was found guilty of unprofessional conduct and *disbarred* for three years by a federal judge. The decision was appealed and reversed three years later. In 1958 Fisher, a thin-faced, thinning-haired socialite, was censured by the Illinois Supreme Court for actions against clients—but the Chicago Bar Association had asked that he be *barred* from practice for five years." Murray T. Bloom, *The Trouble with Lawyers* 158 (1970) (quoting an Illinois bar official).

Then again, sometimes the word association is extratextual. In the following examples, the following things occur on first reading: clothes are laid down, litigators try cases, flattery induces a woman to engage in sex, and somebody engages in murder attacks:

- "The Tudor justices enforced laws against Roman Catholic recusants, regulations *laying down the clothes* people might wear and the price they should pay for them." Alan Harding, *A Social History of English Law* 72 (1966). Did 16th-century judges mandate nudity for Roman Catholics?
- "Attorneys from EEOC make particularly interesting speakers as they have been on the front line in trying to settle cases both in and out of court." Bette Ann Stead, *Women in Management* 292 (1978). What litigators do is *try cases*. So when the writer says, *All litigators have had the experience of trying . . .* , the legal reader expects to read about some type of case that litigators try. In this particular sentence, *attempting* would probably be a better choice than *trying*.
- "Flattery induced a woman to submit to intercourse by pretending to perform a surgical operation. He was convicted of rape." Glanville Williams, *Textbook of Criminal Law* 514 (1978). A man named Flattery committed a crime, but his name suggests the wile he might have used in committing it. The miscue might be removed by referring to *Mr. Flattery* instead of *Flattery*.
- "Small-minded, episodic murder attacks the basis of our taken-for-granted values so fundamentally that it generates anxiety." David Canter, *Anxious, Appalled . . . But Still Drawn to Horror*, Sunday Times, 13 Mar. 1994, at 4–6. It looks on first reading as if the noun phrase *murder attacks* is the subject, but *murder* is the subject and *attacks* is the verb.

B. Misplaced Modifiers. When modifying words are separated from the words they modify, readers have a hard time processing the information. Indeed, they are likely to attach the modifying language first to a nearby word or phrase—e.g.:

- "Ms. Connally knew Denotte before she had her surgical procedure on a casual basis." The phrase *on a casual basis*, or perhaps *casually*, belongs after *Denotte*; otherwise, it sounds as if the surgical procedure was a casual one.
- "The right to redeem collateral after default is available to the debtor unless otherwise agreed in writing after default." In that sentence, the reader momentarily believes that the time when default becomes available is important; in fact, though, it is the right that is available. That is, we're not talking about the right to redeem *after default is available*. A suggested revision: *After default, the right to redeem collateral is available to the debtor unless . . . .* Or: *After default, the debtor may redeem collateral unless . . . .*

See MISPLACED MODIFIERS.

C. Remote Antecedents.

- "Until recently, the inns showed themselves particularly ill-equipped to handle the overseas students, including many Africans and such future statesmen as Mr Nehru, who by 1960 made up two thirds of all those called to the English bar." Alan Harding, *A Social History of English Law* 389 (1966). (This sentence involves a REMOTE RELATIVE that makes Mr. Nehru sound like a very big man indeed.)
- "There are various reasons that juries hang, some better than others." Robin T. Lakoff, *Talking Power: The Politics of Language in Our Lives* 126 (1990). (The writer means *some reasons*, not *some juries*, but some readers will not see this immediately.)

See ANTECEDENTS, FALSE (B).

D. Failure to Hyphenate Phrasal Adjectives. The reason for hyphenating phrasal adjectives is precisely to avoid miscues: think of the difference between a *small-claims court* and a *(very) small claims court*. Other, less striking instances abound—e.g.: "The uncontroverted evidence establishes that Super Ships, Inc., never manufactured, sold, or distributed any asbestos containing products to Cereola." Unless the phrase *asbestos-containing products* is hyphenated thus, readers are likely to think at first that the company never manufactured or sold asbestos, as opposed to products containing asbestos. See PHRASAL ADJECTIVES.

E. Misleading Phraseology. In the following example, the phrase *make good*—in the sense "to indemnify"—is paired with *defalcations* (= failures to meet expectations or honor promises) in an odd way. The reader may think at first that the promisor is making defalcations that are good: "There is, however, nothing objectionable about a promise to *make good defalcations* for which the promisor is personally responsible." P.S. Atiyah, *An Introduction to the Law of Contract* 231 (3d ed. 1981).

Sometimes, as in the following example, the confusing syntax results from a preposition (*for*) that appears to have a single-word object (*which*), as opposed to a phrasal object (*which of several payment plans*): "Here there is no problem in using blanks for which of several payment plans the borrower wants to use." Barbara Child, *Drafting Legal Documents* 138 (2d ed. 1992).

Yet again, the first word in a participial phrase (*up the coast of New England*) sometimes seems to be a particle, i.e., a part of a verb (*blew up*): "The storm also blew up the coast of New England." John J. Goldman, *Northeast Slammed by Storm; 7 Killed*, Austin American-Statesman, 12 Dec. 1992, at A1.

F. Ill-Advisedly Deleted *that.* The widespread but largely unfounded prejudice against *that* leads many writers to omit it when it is necessary—e.g.:

- "In *Cox*, the court held a contract indemnifying a casualty company for all liability under the Structural Work Act was void as against public policy." Add *that* after *held*.
- "The court also pointed out an executor cannot appeal for the protection of the interests of a particular devisee or legatee who is able to take an appeal." Add *that* after *pointed out.*
- "In *Pedroza v. Bryant*, the Washington Supreme Court held hospitals [are] subject to the doctrine of corporate negligence." Cherie N. Wyatt, Comment, *Driving on the Center Line*, 46 St. Louis U. L.J. 873, 883–84 (2002). Add *that* after *held.*
- "The Supreme Court held a contract allowing a real-property owner to terminate a listing agreement with a broker before its expiration upon the payment of a specified fee was not a liquidated damages provision." *Morris v. Redwood Empire Bancorp*, 27 Cal. Rptr. 3d 797, 802 (Ct. App. 2005). Add *that* after *held.*

See **that** (A).

G. Omitted Commas. See PUNCTUATION (D) (last par.).

H. Unsplit Infinitives. See HYPERCORRECTION (G).

misdemeanant (= one who has committed a misdemeanor) is the analogue of *felon*. E.g.:

- "It is immaterial, for technical purposes, whether a *misdemeanant* was principal at the fact or before the fact." J.W. Cecil Turner, *Kenny's Outlines of Criminal Law* 89 (16th ed. 1952).
- "Some statutes have provided a penalty for the criminal protector of a *misdemeanant*." Rollin M. Perkins & Ronald N. Boyce, *Criminal Law* 726 n.34 (3d ed. 1982).

Unlike *felon*, however, *misdemeanant* is little known outside the law.

Whether *convicted misdemeanant* is a REDUNDANCY is a close question. Surely most legal readers would not think that it is.

Like *felon*, *misdemeanant* should not refer merely to one suspected or charged, as opposed to one who has been convicted—e.g.: "An officer is not justified in killing a mere *misdemeanant* [read *suspected misdemeanant*] in order to effectuate his arrest, or to prevent his escape after arrest." *Klinkel v. Saddler*, 233 N.W. 538, 541 (Iowa 1930).

The *OED* includes also the lay sense "a person guilty of misconduct," but legal writers should avoid using this technical term in this overbroad sense.

misdemeanor; misdemeanour. A. Spelling. The *-our* is the British spelling, *-or* the American. (See -OR.) The word is archaically spelled *misdemesnors*, as in Blackstone: "Smaller faults, and omissions of less consequence, are comprized under the gentler name of '*misdemesnors*' only." 4 William Blackstone, *Commentaries on the Laws of England* 5 (1769).

B. Modern Uses. Before the distinction between felonies and misdemeanors was abolished by the Criminal Law Act 1967, English lawyers used *misdemeanour* (as they spelled it) to refer to any criminal offense that was neither a felony nor treason. In BrE, the word is primarily of historical interest. But most American jurisdictions retain the felony–misdemeanor distinction. See **felony.**

*****misdoubt,** equivalent to *doubt*, is an unnecessary and confusing ARCHAISM. See **doubt.**

misfeasance. See **malfeasance.**

misfeasor; misfeasant, adj. *Misfeasor* (= one who commits a misfeasance) is the correct agent noun— e.g.: "The establishment of a claim for fraud . . . will in many instances turn on actions taken by the *misfeasor* leading up to the actual transaction." *In re Great Lakes Factors, Inc.*, 331 B.R. 347, 351 (Bankr. N.D. Ohio 2005). *Misfeasant* is the corresponding adjective— e.g.: "National therefore argues that the failure to seek a subordination or discharge might not, in these circumstances, have been a mere negligent mistake but rather, 'reckless, deliberate, unprofessional, incompetent, and possibly *misfeasant*.'" *Wells Fargo Bank v. National Lumber Co.*, 918 N.E.2d 835, 840–41 (Mass. App. Ct. 2009).

As a noun, *misfeasant* sometimes appears where *misfeasor* belongs—e.g.:

- "The *misfeasant* [read *misfeasor*] . . . was the party himself, not any lawyer, so it is not a case of punishing the client for his lawyer's failures, an authorized form of vicarious liability but not one to be imposed lightly." *Lucien v. Breweur*, 9 F.3d 26, 28 (7th Cir. 1993).
- "[T]he conduct involved must be sufficiently egregious to warrant a presumption that the *misfeasant's* [read *misfeasor's*] claims or defenses lack merit." *Cummings v. Cire*, 74 S.W.3d 920, 927 (Tex. App.—Amarillo 2002).
- "The reason for this distinction is that a *misfeasant* [read *misfeasor*] creates a risk of harm; while the *nonfeasant* [read *nonfeasor*], although not creating a risk of harm, merely fails to benefit the injured party by interfering in his or her affairs." *Smit v. Anderson*, 72 P.3d 369, 372 (Colo. Ct. App. 2002).

Cf. **malfeasor,** n.

mishap. See **accident** (A).

misidentification. See **misnomer** (B).

misinformation. See **disinformation.**

An asterisk (✻) precedes words and phrases that are invariably inferior forms.

misjoinder = (1) in civil actions, the improper joinder of parties in an action; or (2) in criminal actions, the improper joinder of distinct offenses in a criminal prosecution. See **joinder.** Cf. **disjoinder.**

mislaid property. See **lost property.**

mislead. See **lead.**

misnomer. A. Legal Sense. *Misnomer* (= the use of a wrong name) in law may mean "a mistake in naming a person or place," whereas in nonlegal contexts it usually refers to a misdescription of a thing—e.g.: "The misnamed corporation under oath timely called attention to the *misnomer*, and the plaintiff amended his petition, procured new citation and service to avoid the *misnomer*." *Consolidated Underwriters v. Adams*, 97 S.W.2d 323, 326 (Tex. Civ. App.—Beaumont 1936).

B. And *misidentification.* A *misnomer*'s effects are relatively minor; a lawsuit is not disrupted by making a correction. But a *misidentification* occurs when the wrong party is brought into a suit. For instance, the party may be correctly named but may happen to have the same name as the person or entity who was actually involved in the transaction. E.g.: "A *misidentification* means the plaintiff has sued the wrong party and limitations is not tolled." *Mantis v. Resz*, 5 S.W.3d 388, 391 n.4 (Tex. App.—Fort Worth 1999). In criminal law, it means that the wrong party is arrested and put on trial.

MISPLACED MODIFIERS. When using participial forms (and especially when beginning a sentence with an -*ing* phrase), one must be sure that the noun introducing the clause that follows is what the participle modifies. Hence the preceding sentence would be incorrect if it read: "When using participial forms . . . , the noun in the main clause must be modified by the participle"—because this construction suggests that a *noun* (as opposed to a writer) can "use" a *participle.* Here is another example: "*After reading* that case, *the initial impulse* of the reader might well be to nominate it for the most arbitrary equal protection decision in recent times." Note the problem that remains here if we change the main clause to "the reader's initial impulse," where *impulse*, not *reader*, is still improperly the subject of the clause. Some of the pitfalls in this area are treated under DANGLERS and MISCUES (B).

The problem often crops up where the writer inserts a passive verb phrase after an introductory participial phrase. E.g.:

- "In determining whether an accident arose out of and in the course of the employment, *each case must be decided* [read *the court must decide each case*] with respect to its own attendant circumstances and not by resort to some formula." *Bell v. Kelso Oil Co.*, 597 S.W.2d 731, 734 (Tenn. 1980).
- "In applying this standard, *the facts and circumstances of each case must be analyzed* [read *the court must analyze the facts and circumstances of each case*] to determine

whether the language used was improper." *Campbell v. State*, 900 S.W.2d 763, 766 (Tex. App.—Waco 1995).

The problem is easily remedied by making certain that an *actor* or *agent* appears in the main clause, and that this actor or agent is the one *doing* something in the participial phrase.

Following is a spate of examples of some misuses to which English sentences are susceptible. Brief comments (in parentheses) are appended before each sentence is recast in an improved form:

- "Awaiting the uncertainties as to quantum of damages, the delay in recovery . . . may increase them." *Bowen v. Morris*, 123 So. 222, 223 (Ala. 1929). (The *delay* awaits *uncertainties*?) [Read *By awaiting (the resolution of all?) uncertainties as to quantum of damages, one may increase, by the delay, the damages incurred.*]
- "Having held that the Commission had the power and authority to pass [the order], and that such action was not arbitrary nor an abuse of discretion, it must follow that this is a suit against the State of Texas, and should be dismissed." *Texas Hwy. Comm'n v. Texas Ass'n of Steel Imps., Inc.*, 372 S.W.2d 525, 535 (Tex. 1963). (What *it* was it that *held*?) [Read *Having held that the commission had the power and authority to pass the order, and that such action was not arbitrary or an abuse of discretion, the court must dismiss this suit against the state of Texas.*]
- "Kast urges that, having found CPL 2.25B to be a procedural rule, we should nevertheless not give effect to the APA's procedural-rules exemption from informal rulemaking requirements because the rule has substantial impact on those regulated." *U.S. Dep't of Labor v. Kast Metals Corp.*, 744 F.2d 1145, 1153 (5th Cir. 1984). (*Having* can here look either way: to *Kast* or to *we*. See JANUS-FACED TERMS (B).) [Read *Kast urges that, even though we have found CPL 2.25B to be a procedural rule, we should not give effect to the APA's procedural-rules exemption to the informal rulemaking requirements.*]
- "Reasoning that 4,000 acres were, as both parties agreed, cleared by July of 1970 as required, and that the lease also required a minimum of 700 acres to be cleared 'each year thereafter,' the contractual obligation mathematically had to be completely performed, and any breach established, by July 1, 1975." *Chapman v. Orange Rice Mill. Co.*, 747 F.2d 981, 983 (5th Cir. 1984). (The *contractual obligation* does not engage in *reasoning*.) [Read *Reasoning that 4,000 acres were, as both parties agreed, cleared by July 1970 as required, and that the lease also required a minimum of 700 acres to be cleared 'each year thereafter,' we have calculated that the contractual obligation had to be completely performed by July 1975.*]
- "Applying the *Baker* rule to this case, plaintiff was arrested on a facially valid warrant and she has therefore alleged no deprivation of a right secured by the Constitution and laws of the United States." *Simons v. Clemons*, 752 F.2d 1053, 1055 (5th Cir. 1985). (The court, not the *plaintiff*, applies *the rule to this case.*) [Read *In applying the Baker rule to this case, we hold that the plaintiff was arrested on a facially valid warrant and therefore had no ground to allege deprivation of a right secured by the Constitution and laws of the United States.*]
- "The record contains ample evidence to support the jury's verdict. Synopsizing, plaintiffs offered evidence which attributed price increases to price-fixing." *In re Corrugated Container Antitrust Litig.*, 756 F.2d 411, 418 (5th Cir. 1985). (The court does the *synopsizing*, not the *plaintiffs*.) Actually, this sentence needs no participle. [Read *The*

record contains ample evidence to support the jury's verdict. In short, the plaintiffs offered evidence that attributed price increases to price-fixing.]

- "No discussion of the subject of reimbursement in Texas can be considered complete without an analysis of the often quoted but incomprehensible case of *Dakan v. Dakan*. Read literally, the Texas Supreme Court addresses only two issues." Michael C. Tighe, Note, *A Chance to Clarify the Confusion Surrounding Reimbursement*, 37 Baylor L. Rev. 255, 261 (1985). (What is read *literally*? *Dakan v. Dakan*, or the Texas Supreme Court?) [Read *Read literally, that Texas Supreme Court case addresses only two issues.*]

- "Treating the papers whereon the appeal was taken as a petition for a writ of common-law certiorari, the petition is hereby denied." *Hedin v. Indian River County*, 610 So.2d 715, 716 (Fla. Dist. Ct. App. 1992). (Is it the *certiorari* that does the *treating*?) [Read *Treating the papers whereon the appeal was taken as a petition for a writ of common-law certiorari, we deny the petition.*]

- "Having determined that none of Mr. Winfield's claims on appeal have merit, the judgment is affirmed." *State v. Winfield*, 5 S.W.3d 505, 517 (Mo. 1999). (The *judgment* has determined that there is no *reversible error*?) [Read *Having determined that none of Mr. Winfield's claims on appeal have merit, we affirm the judgment.*]

misprision. In legal usage, this word usually means "concealment of treason or of felony by one not participating in the treason or felony." The phrase most commonly occurs in the phrases *misprision of felony* and *misprision of treason*. But the word may also refer to seditious conduct itself or to an official's failure to perform duties of public office. More popularly, *misprision* means "misunderstanding, mistake."

Some writers misspell the word **misprison*, perhaps because they mistakenly associate *felony* with *prison* in the phrase *misprision of felony*. E.g.: "A person commits *misprison* [read *misprision*] of felony when he witnesses or has knowledge of a felony being committed or about to be committed, and conceals or fails to give information as to such crime. *Misprison* [read *Misprision*] of felony cannot be committed if the crime is a misdemeanor." Garn H. Webb, *Plain Language Law: Criminal Wrongs (Crimes)* 122 (1981) (consistently so misspelling the word).

misprisor, a NEOLOGISM not to be found in the *OED* or *W3*, is confined to senses derived from the phrase *misprision of felony*—e.g.: "A '*misprisor*' is said to be one who knows of the commission of a felony and does not report it to the proper authorities." Rollin M. Perkins & Ronald N. Boyce, *Criminal Law* 728–29 (3d ed. 1982).

misreliance. Coined in the late 19th century by the scholar John H. Wigmore, *misreliance* denotes a reliance that results from an erroneous belief that a certain fact either exists or will exist (a mistake of fact). *See* Wigmore, *A Summary of Quasi-Contracts*, 25 Am. L. Rev. 695, 696 (1891). E.g.: "One who either knows or believes that he is under no legal obligation to confer a certain benefit upon another and that he

will acquire no right thereby, but nevertheless confers the benefit, cannot justly claim restitution upon the theory of *misreliance*." Frederic Campbell Woodward, *The Law of Quasi Contracts* § 13, at 13 (1913).

misremember means "to remember incorrectly," not "to forget."

misrepresent = (1) to make an untrue statement of fact, usu. with knowledge of its falsity, without belief in its truth, or recklessly; or (2) to conduct malpractice while representing; (of a lawyer) to represent (a client) inadequately. Sense 2 is an odd, unidiomatic use: "Mrs. Johnson has sued Shearman & Sterling, contending she was *misrepresented* by the firm and demanding that it return the nearly $3 million she has already paid." Ronald Sullivan, *Firms Still Jarred by Fallout over Johnson Will*, N.Y. Times, 31 Mar. 1989, at 22.

misrepresentation. See **lie,** n.

misrepresentee is an -EE NEOLOGISM that serves as a correlative to **misrepresentor* (as it is sometimes, alas, spelled)—e.g.: "The *misrepresentee* can, however, still rescind." G.H. Treitel, *The Law of Contract* 321 (8th ed. 1991). Cf. **representee.**

misrepresenter; *misrepresentor. The -*er* spelling is better.

mistake. A. And *error*. These terms both denote something done, left undone, or believed in such a way as to depart from what is proper, accurate, or correct. *Error* suggests deviation from a model or guide <typographical error>, from some kind of standard <grammatical error>, or from an authoritative code <error in admitting the evidence>. *Error* implies a greater degree of blameworthiness than *mistake*, which suggests a faulty idea, a misjudgment, or a misunderstanding <it was a mistake to include that upsetting photograph in the brief>.

B. And *ignorance*. These words, some authorities have said, "do not import the same significance and should not be confounded. Ignorance implies a total want of knowledge in reference to the subject matter. Mistake admits a knowledge, but implies a wrong conclusion." *Hutton v. Edgerton & Richards*, 6 S.C. 485, 489 (1876). But other authorities say that "a mistake, in its legal sense, is 'that result of ignorance of law or of fact which has misled a person to commit that which, if he had not been in error, he would not have done.'" 3 G.W. Field, *Field's Lawyers' Briefs* 109 (1885) (quoting an old equity treatise). The latter authorities, in other words, reject the distinction as being "a refinement too subtle to be applied to the every-day business of life." *Schlesinger v. U.S.*, 1 Cl. Ct. 16, 25 (1863). And they are in the majority.

In fact, *ignorance* is the broader term—it includes *mistake*: "Every mistake involves ignorance but not *vice versa*. Ignorance is lack of true knowledge, either (1) because the mind is a complete blank or (2) because it is filled with untrue (mistaken) knowledge on a particular subject. The first variety, lack of knowledge without mistaken knowledge, may be called simple ignorance. The second variety, lack of true knowledge coupled with mistaken knowledge, is mistake. Ignorance is the genus of which simple ignorance and mistake are the species." Glanville Williams, *Criminal Law* 151–52 (2d ed. 1961).

C. And *frustration*. In the law of contract, *mistake* and *frustration* are "merely different ways of talking about the same thing—that is, the real world has in some way failed to correspond with the imaginary world hypothesized by the parties to the contract." Grant Gilmore, *The Death of Contract* 81 (1974). With either a mistake or frustration, consent may be nullified because of the extreme injustice of holding one of the parties to the contract. See **frustration** & **impossibility**.

D. And *accident*. See **accident (B)**.

E. *Mutual mistake*. See **mutual mistake**.

mistreat. See **abuse**, vb.

mistress. See **common-law wife**.

mistrial has two very distinct senses: (1) "a trial ending without a determination on the merits because of some procedural error or disruption during the proceedings"; or (2) "a trial that ends inconclusively because the jury cannot agree on a verdict." Sense 1 is common to AmE and BrE—e.g.: "When the judge discovered that Brumfield had hired a private detective to spy on the jurors and find out their opinions on smoking, he declared a *mistrial* and shoved Belli's case all the way to the bottom of his docket." Sense 2 occurs primarily in AmE—e.g.: "Bryant explained that the jury in a drug-possession case had been unable to agree, facing a *mistrial*." Donald D. Jackson, *Judges* 92–93 (1974).

mistrust. See **distrust**.

mistry, vb., corresponds only to sense 1 of *mistrial*, but with an even stronger suggestion of fault—e.g.:

- "In the court below, the case was totally misconceived and *mistried*." *Kramer v. Winslow*, 18 A. 923, 927 (Pa. 1890).
- "It is argued . . . that the case was *mistried* for this reason." *Van Riper v. U.S.*, 13 F.2d 961, 963 (2d Cir. 1926) (per L. Hand, J.).
- "The defendant then moved to dismiss the *mistried* RICO count." *U.S. v. Jenkins*, 902 F.2d 459, 462 (6th Cir. 1990).

See **mistrial**.

misusage (= [1] mistreatment; or [2] the incorrect use of language) is increasingly misused for *misuse*, n. (= unauthorized use; misapplication)—e.g.: "There has been no evidence presented as to actual confusion arising from the *misusage* [read *misuse*] of the APOLLO mark." *Apollo Distrib. Co. v. Jerry Kurtz Carpet Co.*, 696 F.Supp. 140, 142 (D.N.J. 1988).

misuse. See **abuse**, vb.

mitigable is the correct form—not **mitigatable*.

mitigate; militate. *Mitigate* = to make less severe or intense; *militate* = to exert a strong influence. Here *mitigate* is correctly used: "In England, the power to *mitigate* the severity of the strict law was originally vested in the king."

*Mitigate against is incorrect for *militate against*; Edmund Wilson called it "William Faulkner's favorite error." *The Bit Between My Teeth* 570 (1965). Faulkner's failings aside, the error is surprisingly common—e.g.:

- "This factor *mitigates* [read *militates*] against immediate review." *Midway Mfg. Co. v. Omni Video Games, Inc.*, 668 F.2d 70, 72 (1st Cir. 1981).
- "Plaintiffs suggest there are two theories [that], if applied to this case, would *mitigate* [read *militate*] against the harsh application of the statute of limitations." *Cramsey v. Knoblock*, 547 N.E.2d 1358, 1364 (Ill. App. Ct. 1989).
- "The current interpretation of AEDPA *militates* against prosecutions of companies for paying ransoms to Somali pirates." Lawrence Rutkowski et al., *Mugged Twice?: Payment of Ransom on the High Seas*, 59 Am. U. L. Rev. 1425, 1441 (2010).

Militate against, of course, is perfectly acceptable: "If the obvious facts *militate against* such an intention as expressed in the document, the court can act upon the real intention as found by the court." (Eng.)

In law, *militate* often takes *for* or *in favor of* as well as *against*. The *OED* calls this use "rare," but today it is common in legal writing—e.g.:

- "There is no testimony or other evidence in the record to indicate whether there was a delay, and if so, whether the delay would *militate for* or *against* a name change." *Scoggins v. Trevino*, 200 S.W.3d 832, 841 (Tex. App.—Corpus Christi 2006).
- "The third factor—legal error—arguably *militates in favor of* issuance of the writ, because the district court may have partly misinterpreted the legal boundaries of the First Amendment privilege we articulated in *Perry I*." *Perry v. Schwarzenegger*, 602 F.3d 976, 981 (9th Cir. 2010).

*Militate toward is unidiomatic—e.g.: "The Government argues that its interest in meeting treaty obligations *militates toward* [read *favors*] a finding that bail is not appropriate for relators post-certification." *Wroclawski v. U.S.*, 634 F.Supp.2d 1003, 1005 (D. Ariz. 2009).

*mitigational. See **mitigatory**.

mitigation-of-damages doctrine, as a PHRASAL ADJECTIVE, should be so hyphenated. A variant name for this doctrine—which requires a plaintiff, after an injury or breach of contract, to use ordinary care to alleviate its effects—is *avoidable-consequences doctrine*.

mitigatory; *mitigative; *mitigational. The first is the preferred form. **Mitigational*, a NEEDLESS VARIANT, sometimes appears where *mitigating* would be the natural word—e.g.: "The issue of ineffective assistance of counsel due to the absence of *mitigational* [read *mitigating*] evidence was first raised by the testimony of several witnesses during the November 16, 1984, evidentiary hearing." *Laws v. State*, 708 S.W.2d 182, 184 (Mo. Ct. App. 1986).

mittimus [L. "we send"] (= a warrant ordering a jailer to detain a person until ordered otherwise) is a Latin verb used in English as a noun. The plural is *mittimuses*—e.g.: "These items are for *mittimuses* issued after the examination is concluded." *U.S. v. Ewing*, 140 U.S. 142, 144 (1891) (per Brown, J.). Through HYPER-CORRECTION, some writers have mistakenly written **mittimi*, which is on the order of **ignorami*—e.g.:

- "In both of these *mittimi* [read *mittimuses*] the crime for which he was convicted was described as forgery." *Green v. State*, 113 F.Supp. 253, 256 (D. Me. 1953).
- "The jail *mittimi* [read *mittimuses*], the accuracy of which *are* [read *is*] not challenged, show that the defendant was represented by counsel and that he exercised his right of allocution." *People v. Montoya*, 640 P.2d 234, 237 (Colo. Ct. App. 1981).

See HYPERCORRECTION (A). Cf. **ignoramus.**

mixed action. See **real action.**

M'Naghten. See **McNaghten.**

mob mouthpiece. See LAWYERS, DEROGATORY NAMES FOR (A).

mobocracy; ochlocracy. *Ochlocracy* is the better word in formal prose for "mob rule," the first term being a MORPHOLOGICAL DEFORMITY. *Ochlocracy* has four centuries of use behind it, *mobocracy* but two. *Mobocracy* also retains a jocular overtone. See GOVERN-MENTAL FORMS.

mockery. See **make a mockery of.**

modality (= a method or procedure) is a pretentious VOGUE WORD: "The mother's expert conceded a lack of awareness of any professional literature documenting the successful use of the *modalities* [read *methods*] he suggested in training the retarded to employ adequate parenting skills." *In re Karen "Y"*, 550 N.Y.S.2d 67, 69 (App. Div. 1989).

MODAL VERBS. See WORDS OF AUTHORITY.

mode; module. There must be something in the root: these words, like *modality*, are inflated VOGUE WORDS.

In proper usage, *mode* means "manner," and *module* means "a unit of size." President George H.W. Bush often entered the "*mode* mode," as when he told a crowd in Los Angeles: "I am not here in the *mode* of politics, I am not here in the *mode* of partisanship, I am not here in the *mode* of blame. I am here to learn from the community." Robert B. Gunnison & Susan Yoachum, *Bush Visits Riot Zone*, San Francisco Chronicle, 8 May 1992, at A1. Such talk proved fruitful for Russell Baker's lively column in *The New York Times*: "President Bush says he is about to enter 'campaign

mode.' Does this mean America will then have president *à la mode*? Absolutely not. Do you think the President is a slice of pie? This is the same answer I had from Mr. Bush's mode handler. . . . The mode Mr. Bush will enter is not a dessert, but a new technological product of the space program. Space-news fans will have noticed that multitudes of modes pour out of NASA press releases." Russell Baker, *In the Mode Mood*, N.Y. Times, 15 Aug. 1992, at 15.

*mode of operandi. See **modus operandi.**

modern-day is invariably inferior to *modern*—e.g.: "Punitive damages . . . are a *modern-day* [read *modern*] analog of 13th century amercements." *Browning-Ferris Indus. of Vt., Inc. v. Kelco Disposal, Inc.*, 492 U.S. 257, 268 (1989) (per Blackmun, J.).

modernly (= in modern times) is accurately described by the *OED* as being "now rare"; more precisely, it might have stated "now rare, except in law." E.g.:

- "*Modernly*, the question of whether the Guarantee Clause is justiciable is less clear." *Wyoming v. U.S. Dep't of Interior*, 360 F.Supp.2d 1214, 1244 (D. Wyo. 2005).
- "*Modernly*, about half of the states do allow duress as a limited defense to murder." Melani Johns, Comment, *Adjusting the Asylum Bar*, 40 Golden Gate U. L. Rev. 235, 251 (2010).

MODIFIERS, MISPLACED. See MISPLACED MODIFIERS.

module. See **mode.**

modus operandi (= a method of operating; a manner of procedure) is often a highfalutin substitute for *method*. Yet it is well established. Pl. *modi operandi*.

The phrase is sometimes misrendered **mode of operandi*. For humorous headnotes using *motor operandi*, see *U.S. v. Aguirre-Valenzuela*, 700 F.2d 161, 161 (Cir. 1983).

moiety. *Moiety*, a legal and literary ARCHAISM, does not, strictly speaking, mean "a small segment or portion," as some writers assume; rather, it means "half." This word should be part of the lawyer's recognition vocabulary, but not of one's working vocabulary, for *half* is the preferable and ordinary word, and the SLIPSHOD EXTENSION of *moiety* makes the word ambiguous. E.g.:

- "The testator devised lands to his wife for life, and at her death one *moiety* [read *half*] to his heirs and the other *moiety* [read *half*] to his wife's heirs, as she might appoint." *Daniel v. Brown*, 159 S.E. 209, 211 (Va. 1931). It might be stylistically preferable merely to say *and the other to his wife's heirs*, thereby halving the number of *halfs*.
- "We believe that in contributing the use of his '*moiety*' [read *half*] in the automobile, he was in fact 'furnishing' the automobile to Clarice, a member of his family." *Marcus v. Everett*, 239 N.W.2d 487, 493 (Neb. 1976).

But is *half* really the right word in the two examples just quoted? The *OED* notes that "loosely," the word *moiety* may denote "one of two (occasionally more) parts (not necessarily equal) into which something is divided." Max Radin's *Law Dictionary* defines the alternative meaning as "a fractional part less than half." Because legal writers use the word in this way almost as often as they do in the sense "half," the word really ought to be avoided altogether.

In American customs law, *moiety* has taken on still another meaning, illustrated in the following examples:

- "Under Customs Law, an informant is paid a '*moiety*' up to, but not exceeding, $50,000. *Moiety* is payment made to an informant who assisted in the seizure and ultimate forfeiture of an object." *U.S. v. Cresta*, 825 F.2d 538, 545 n.3 (1st Cir. 1987).
- "The plaintiff, Mr. Robert Rickard, seeks an award of compensation to informants (otherwise known as *moieties*), pursuant to statutory authority contained in 19 U.S.C. § 1619 (1976)." *Rickard v. U.S.*, 11 Cl. Ct. 874, 875 (1987). On the use of **pursuant to* in that sentence, see ***pursuant to.**

Although a better word might have been found for this type of reward, *moiety* appears to be established JARGON.

momentarily = for a moment. It does not, correctly, mean "in a moment." Cf. **presently.**

*moment in time, at this, is a pomposity for *now*, or sometimes *today* and *nowadays.*

*momento is a misspelling. See **memento.**

monarchical; *monarchial. **Monarchial* is a NEEDLESS VARIANT of *monarchical*, the usual form.

monetary damages. See **money damages.**

monetize; monetarize. The longer form is incorrect for *monetize* (= [1] to put (coins or currency) into circulation as money; [2] to give fixed value as currency; or [3] to purchase debt and thereby free up moneys that would otherwise be used to service that debt). Sense 2: "The benefits flowing from those services are, in theory, as difficult to *monetarize* [read *monetize*] as religious ones." *Hernandez v. Commissioner*, 819 F.2d 1212, 1217 (1st Cir. 1987).

money damages, like *monetary damages*, is a common REDUNDANCY—e.g.: "Where *money damages* [read *damages*] would not afford adequate compensation (as, for example, in the case of a breach of contract to convey land) equity would oblige a defendant to perform specifically his part of the agreement." L.B. Curzon, *English Legal History* 126 (2d ed. 1979). See **damage (A).**

moneyed; *monied. The first is preferred—e.g.: "Commerce might have been used to 'refer to the entire *moneyed* economy . . . .'" Edward H. Levi, *An Introduction to Legal Reasoning* 63 (1949) (quoting the Government's brief in *U.S. v. Darby*, 312 U.S. 100, 103 (1941)). See **monies.**

*moneyed judgment seems like an odd mistake for *money judgment*, a common phrase today. Actually, however, *moneyed judgment* appeared in any number of 19th-century cases. Today it is an ARCHAISM that will strike many readers as an error.

money had and received, action for; money paid, action for. At common law, the *action for money had and received* was one by which the plaintiff could recover money that he or she had paid to the defendant, the money usually being recoverable for either of the following reasons: (1) the money had been paid under mistake or compulsion, or (2) the consideration had wholly failed. The *action for money paid*, by contrast, was one by which the plaintiff could recover money paid not to the defendant, but to a third party in circumstances in which the defendant had benefited.

*monied. See **moneyed.**

*monies is an illogical and misconceived plural. Because it is so common, however, it cannot be labeled a gross error. Still, *moneys* remains the preferred form, used, e.g., in the heading of 18 U.S.C. § 2314 (1988). *Monies* is only as logical as the obsolete plural **attornies*. Cf. **moneyed.**

monish. See **admonition.**

monism; dualism. In international law, *monism* denotes the doctrine that international and domestic law are but two manifestations of the same conception of law. *Dualism*, by contrast, holds that international law and domestic law of the several states are essentially different from each other in three ways: (1) in source; (2) in the relations they regulate; and (3) in substance. *See* 1 Lassa Oppenheim, *International Law* 37 (Hersch Lauterpacht ed., 8th ed. 1955).

monition. See **admonition.**

monitory; *monitorial. See **admonitory.**

monopolization. See **monopoly (C).**

monopoly. A. In Antitrust Law. *Monopoly* is generally understood to mean "control by one supplier or producer over the commercial market within a given region." Nonlawyers often believe that this control must be complete, but the law in various jurisdictions now sets the level of control at a fraction of the overall market. In England, for example, under the Monopolies and Mergers Acts 1948 and 1965, a monopoly existed when the level of control reached one-third of a local or national market. That proportion was lessened by the Fair Trading Act 1973, under which companies can be prevented from controlling more than one-fourth of the supply of a product or service.

In the U.S., under the Sherman Antitrust Act, *monopoly* is an offense that can lead to criminal penalties and divestiture. The offense has two elements: (1) the possession of a "monopoly power" within the relevant market, i.e., the power to fix prices and exclude competitors; and (2) willfully acquiring or maintaining that power "as distinguished from growth or development as a consequence of a superior product, business acumen, or historical accident." *U.S. v. Grinnell Corp.*, 384 U.S. 563, 571 (1966) (per Douglas, J.).

B. In Patent Law. The word can be confusing in patent contexts, in which it bears no connotation of illegality. The solution may be to eliminate its patent-law uses: "Because of its antitrust connotations and association with illegality . . . it often evokes negative reactions inappropriate to a dispassionate analysis of patent law problems." *In re Kaplan*, 789 F.2d 1574, 1578 n.3 (Fed. Cir. 1986). The modern tendency, therefore, is to speak of an *exclusive right* instead of a *monopoly*—that is, the exclusive right to make, use, and sell an invention.

C. And *monopolization*. Properly speaking, *monopoly* refers to the control or advantage itself, or the state of possessing that control or advantage; *monopolization* is the process or act of gaining that control or advantage.

D. And *monopsony*. Whereas *monopoly* (Gk. "sole seller") focuses on the source of goods and services, *monopsony* (Gk. "sole buyer") focuses on their immediate destination: *monopsony* "is the term used to describe a situation in which the relevant market for a factor of production is dominated by a single purchaser." *Permian Basin Area Rate Cases*, 390 U.S. 747, 794 n.64 (1968) (per Harlan, J.). E.g.: "Once El Paso was certified, it held a virtual *monopsony* in the Basin since Southern Union Gas Company, the only other pipeline in the Basin, served only intrastate markets which were already fully utilized." *El Paso Natural Gas Co. v. Sun Oil Co.*, 426 F.Supp. 963, 965 n.5 (W.D. Tex. 1977). The word *monopsony* is far less common than *monopoly*—so much so that a few texts refer erroneously to "monopoly buyers."

monthlong is properly one word in AmE.—e.g.: "After a *monthlong* trial, the jury acquitted the applicant of first-degree murder." *Ferrell v. Wall*, 971 A.2d 615, 617 (R.I. 2009). The same is true of *yearlong*, *weeklong*, and *daylong*.

monument has two legal meanings: (1) "a written document or record" (a sense derived historically from confusion with *muniment*); and (2) in AmE, "any natural or artificial object that is fixed permanently in the soil and referred to in the legal description of land."

moot. A. As Adjective. The *OED* lists only the sense "that can be argued; debatable; not decided, doubtful." Hence a *moot point* was classically seen as one that is arguable. A *moot case* was a hypothetical case proposed for discussion in a "moot" of law students (see (c)). In the U.S., law students practice arguing hypothetical cases before appellate courts in *moot court*.

From that sense of *moot* derived the extended sense "of no practical importance; hypothetical; academic." Hence:

- "There is no other question worthy of notice. We are asked to express an opinion as to the right of the appellants to give bail pending their appeal, but that is now a *moot* point." *Ah How v. U.S.*, 193 U.S. 65, 78 (1904) (per Holmes, J.).
- "There is thus presented the primary question as to whether there is anything for us to decide on this appeal or whether the question has become *moot* because defendant has surrendered possession to plaintiffs." *Price v. Wilson*, 32 A.2d 109, 109 (D.C. Mun. App. 1943).

Today, in AmE, the predominant sense of *moot* is "having no practical significance," in both legal and nonlegal writing. Bernstein and other writers have called this sense of the word incorrect, but it is now a *fait accompli*. To use *moot* in the sense "open to argument" in AmE today is to create an AMBIGUITY, and to confuse most of one's readers. In BrE, the transformation in sense has been slower, and *moot* in its older sense retains vitality. Cf. **mootness.**

B. As Verb. Historically, *moot*, vb., meant "to raise or bring forward (a point or question) for discussion." That sense is still current in BrE, and in older American usage. E.g.:

- "We are now wholly in the realm of politics; not again until the last year was our constitutional question *mooted*." John Gorham Palfrey, *The Growth of the Idea of Annexation*, 13 Harv. L. Rev. 371, 392 (1900).
- "Although the Bar first *mooted* the idea, it was a joint enterprise." *Coming Together*, 130 Solic. J. 289, 289 (1986).

In American legal usage, however, a new sense has taken hold: "to render moot or of no practical significance"—e.g.:

- "These actions presented the *mooted* question [regarding] the coverage of the policy." *Provident Tradesmens Bank & Trust Co. v. Patterson*, 390 U.S. 102, 126 (1968) (per Harlan, J.).
- "The settlement agreement did not *moot* the jurisdictional question." *Giannakos v. M/V Bravo Trader*, 762 F.2d 1295, 1298 (5th Cir. 1985).

C. As Noun. In England, *moot* has the sense "a hypothetical legal problem discussed by students at the Inns of Court for practice" or "the discussion resulting from such a problem." E.g.: "The members of the Inns who had not received their call to the bar took part in these *moots* only in the pleadings, but were trained in the lesser *moots* of the Inns of Courts and Chancery." John Phillip Hill, *Education for the English Bar in the Inns of Court*, 15 Green Bag 114, 120 (1903). This use is unknown in the U.S., although its scent lingers in the phrase *moot court*.

mootness (= the fact or quality of having no practical importance) was an AmE NEOLOGISM when first used in the 1920s—e.g.: "The question of *mootness* is not

---

discussed in the briefs of counsel for the government." *U.S. v. Northern Pac. Ry.*, 18 F.2d 299, 304 (E.D. Wash. 1927). As a noun corresponding to the modern AmE sense of *moot*, the word *mootness* has steadily become more frequent in American legal writing—e.g.:

- "The ruling excepted to, whether on the evidence or on the pleadings, in no wise affects the question of *mootness.*" *Brockett v. Maxwell*, 35 S.E.2d 906, 907 (Ga. 1945). Using *wise* for *way* in this manner is an ARCHAISM. See **nowise** & **wise.**
- "*Mootness* is a question of justiciability. If a case has become moot, . . . then there is no necessity for a judgment." *Ferguson v. Commercial Bank*, 578 So.2d 1234, 1236 (Ala. 1991).
- "The issues in this mortgage foreclosure appeal concern the propriety of the dismissal of the appeal of the named defendant, Joseph Trantino, on the ground of *mootness.*" *Rothstein v. Trantino*, 635 A.2d 813, 813 (Conn. 1994).

Today, the phrase *mootness doctrine* or *mootness rule* denotes the principle that American courts will not decide moot cases—e.g.:

- "The trial court issued another order on December 1 that found the *mootness doctrine* was inapplicable because petitioner was still in custody of the department." *Taylor v. Department of Corrections*, 556 So.2d 494, 494 (Fla. Dist. Ct. App. 1990).
- "There is a strong likelihood that application of the *mootness doctrine* may repeatedly frustrate review." *Peloza v. Freas*, 871 P.2d 687, 688 (Alaska 1994).

See **moot (A).**

mooty, adj., is BrE legal slang meaning "debatable"—e.g.:

- "After discussing a '*mooty*' problem, try to avoid the weak conclusion that 'A is perhaps liable.'" Glanville Williams, *Learning the Law* 124 (11th ed. 1982).
- "'*Mooty*' as the case may be, it is unlikely that there are many *good* points to be made for your side." *Id.* at 164.

moral. See **ethical.**

moral obligation, as used by legal theorists, usually denotes a duty "semi-consciously followed and enforced rather by instinct and habit than by definite sanctions." Henry S. Maine, *Ancient Law* 121 (17th ed. 1901). So a *moral obligation* is not legally enforceable. Further, "its scope has been restricted and the label has become unfashionable." G.H. Treitel, *The Law of Contract* 76 (8th ed. 1991).

moral rights. To most people, this phrase denotes either what is ethically proper or an entitlement under general principles of morality. But the term has a special sense in the field of intellectual property, especially outside the United States. It denotes the right of an author or artist, based on natural-law principles, to guarantee the integrity of a creation despite any transfer of copyright or property-law rights. Moral rights include rights of (1) attribution—that is, the right to be given credit and to claim credit for a work, and to deny credit if the work is changed; (2) integrity—that is, the right to ensure that the work is not changed without the artist's consent; (3) publication—that is,

the right not to reveal a work before its creator is satisfied with it; and (4) retraction—that is, the right to renounce a work and withdraw it from sale or display. Moral rights are recognized by law in much of the world, but very little in the United States.

In other contexts, the phrase bears a more intuitive meaning—namely, circumstances that would cause a reasonable observer to conclude that a sense of right-vs.-wrong militates in favor of a certain outcome even in the absence of a legal ground. E.g.: "[J]ust as erection of medieval cathedrals was sometimes achieved through the impoverishment of parishioners, the majority's protection of the profitability of insurance companies is achieved only at the expense of the legal and *moral rights* of those injured by medical malpractice." *Roberts v. Stevens Clinic Hosp., Inc.*, 345 S.E.2d 791, 813 (W. Va. 1986) (McGraw, J., dissenting).

moral turpitude. A. Generally. *Moral turpitude* = conduct that is fundamentally contrary to justice, honesty, or morality. An act of moral turpitude is often viewed as a violation of prevailing moral standards rather than of a fixed legal standard—not every crime or misdemeanor involves moral turpitude. And because social morals change, nonoriginalists tend to think that the definition does, too. Justice Robert Jackson recognized that treating moral turpitude as a legal standard invites judges to "condemn[] all that we personally disapprove and for no better reason than that we disapprove it." *Jordan v. De George*, 341 U.S. 223, 242 (1951) (Jackson, J., dissenting). In *Posusta v. United States*, Judge Learned Hand wrote: "The test [for crimes involving moral turpitude] is not the personal moral principles of the individual judge or court before whom the application may come; the decision is to be based upon what he or it believes to be the ethical standards current at the time." 285 F.2d 533, 534–35 (2d Cir. 1961). But as a standard, the term *moral turpitude* is less than ideal.

B. In Professional Ethics. Today this term is used mainly in the area of legal ethics; an offense involving *moral turpitude*—such as fraud or breach of trust—traditionally makes a person unfit to practice law.

C. In Military Law. *Moral turpitude* = conduct for which the applicable punishment is a dishonorable discharge or confinement of at least one year.

D. In Defamation. In the common law of libel and slander, the conduct that a person is accused of traditionally had to involve moral turpitude, meaning "an act of baseness, vileness, or depravity in the private and social duties which a man owes to his fellow-men or to society in general, contrary to the accepted and customary rule of right and duty between man and man." Martin L. Newell, *The Law of Defamation, Libel and Slander* 98 (1890).

moratorium. Both *moratoriums* and *moratoria* are fairly common plurals. On the reasons for preferring the native plural *moratoriums*, see PLURALS (A).

more honored in the breach. See **breach, more honored in the.**

more important; more importantly. As an introductory phrase, *more important* has historically been considered an elliptical form of "What is more important," and hence the *-ly* form is thought to be the less desirable. But three points militate against this position. First, if we may begin a sentence, "*Importantly*, jurisdiction in the Supreme Court . . . ," we ought to be able to begin it, "*More importantly*, jurisdiction in the Supreme Court . . . ." See SENTENCE ADVERBS.

Second, the ellipsis does not work with analogous phrases. E.g.: one would not say: "*More notable*, Holmes wrote this opinion . . . ." *More notably* (as opposed to *More notable*) is called for in order that the sentence not sound alien, illogical, and even ungrammatical. The same is true of "*More interestingly*, ..."

And third, if the position of the phrase is changed from the beginning of the sentence in any significant way, the usual ellipsis becomes unidiomatic and *-ly* is quite acceptable. E.g.:

- "But neither, and *more importantly* under the *Bradley* analysis, does the statute or the legislative history direct that the statute be applied prospectively only." *LTV Fed. Credit Union v. UMIC Gov't Secs., Inc.*, 704 F.2d 199, 203 (5th Cir. 1983).
- "Second, and *more importantly*, the evidence did not support the inference that defendant had access to or even knew of the drugs and the scale in the automobile." *Commonwealth v. Thomas*, 752 N.E.2d 835, 840 (Mass. App. Ct. 2001).

The criticism of *more importantly* and *most importantly* has always been rather muted and obscure. Today it has dwindled further, to the point where writers need fear no criticism that can't be dismissed as picayune pedantry.

more interestingly; more interesting. See SENTENCE ADVERBS & **more important.**

more or less (= somewhat) is often used imprecisely in the sense "some degree of," as here: "Keep in mind also that the phraseology used in an instrument quite commonly is not constructed by the grantor himself; the instrument is drafted by someone with *more or less* legal learning." John E. Cribbet et al., *Cases and Materials on Property* 96 (1972). Less legal learning than the grantor possessed?

more perfect. This phrase appears in the preamble to the U.S. Constitution: "We the People of the United States, in Order to form a more perfect Union . . . ." Some critics object that *perfect*, as an absolute quality, should not take a comparative adjective. The answer to those critics is an old one: "It is pedantic to object to the colloquial use of such expressions as 'more universal' [and] 'more perfect.' . . . Of course, superficially viewed, these expressions are incorrect, as there cannot be degrees of universality or of perfection . . . ; yet what is really meant by 'more perfect' for example, is 'more *nearly* perfect.'" Harry T. Peck, "What Is Good

English?" in *What Is Good English? and Other Essays* 3, 16–17 (1899). See ADJECTIVES (B).

***more preferable.** See ADJECTIVES (B) & **preferable.**

more . . . than. A. Parallel Constructions. To create parallel phrasing in the use of this construction, it is often important to repeat the preposition. E.g.: "Most civil audits are *more* favorably settled by an open, honest discussion about what the agent wants *than having* [read *than by having*] the attorney treat the agent as the taxpayer's mortal enemy." Daniel J. Arno, 89 Case & Comment at 53 (Nov.–Dec. 1984). See PARALLELISM & **above (A).**

B. More than one (is) (are). In the phrase *more than one court has held*, the phrase *more than* acts as a compound adverb modifying the adjective *one*. The subject of the clause is the singular noun *court*—hence the singular verb *has*. The same holds true if the singular noun is merely implied, i.e., is an UNDERSTOOD WORD: *more than one has*, not *more than one have*.

For many writers, this principle is counterintuitive because the sense denoted is a plural one. But this is one of the rare instances in English grammar in which the number of the verb is determined not by the meaning of the subject but by its grammatical form. See SYNESIS.

But mistakes are common—e.g.:

- "If one [blood relative] is named, or if *more than* one *are* [read *is*] named, the court, aided by the curator, must make the further finding of whether there are any inheritance rights [that] presently exist." *Massey v. Parker*, 369 So.2d 1310, 1315 (La. 1979).
- "The use of a single culpability score . . . permits the impact of aggravating and mitigating sentencing factors to be considered along the same scale and, where *more than* one *are* [read *is*] present, to offset or accumulate culpability considerations to produce a final sentencing recommendation." Richard S. Gruner, *Towards an Organizational Jurisprudence*, 36 Ariz. L. Rev. 407, 445 (1994). On the use of *towards* in that title as opposed to *toward*, see **toward.**

See SUBJECT–VERB AGREEMENT (K).

C. More . . . than all; more . . . than any. See OVERSTATEMENT.

D. And *over*. See **over (B).**

***more unique.** See ADJECTIVES (B).

more universal. See **more perfect** & ADJECTIVES (B).

moribund (= dying) does not mean "dead." Yet many lawyers misuse the word this way—e.g.:

- "This matrimonial partnership is *completely moribund* [read, perhaps, *dead* or *over*], and cannot be revived." *Wang v. Wang*, 386 N.Y.S.2d 922, 925 (Sup. Ct. 1976).
- "That this rule saves the Clause from being completely *moribund* [read, perhaps, *lifeless*] does not . . . alter the reality that it is insufficient to ensure that federal law is

paramount." *Green v. Mansour*, 474 U.S. 64, 77 (1985) (Brennan, J., dissenting).

MORPHOLOGICAL DEFORMITIES are words derived from other languages, usually Latin or Greek, whose morphemes are so put together as to travesty the lending or borrowing language's principles of word formation. In some philologists' view, one does not combine the inseparable particle *dis-* with nouns to form English verbs (e.g., *dismember*) because it is impermissible by Latin morphology. In Latin, *dis-* was joined only with verbs to form privative verbs (e.g., *disentitle, disregard*).

Any number of examples of ill-formed words made up of classical morphemes exist in modern English: **aborticide, abortuary* (a PORTMANTEAU WORD from *abortion mortuary*), *asylee, Breathalyzer, deflation, drunkometer, homophobe, prosumerism* (a PORTMANTEAU WORD from *pro-consumerism*), *simulcast, slumpflation, stagflation, teletype, urinalysis, workaholic,* and on and on. The importance of knowing something about morphology, or how word elements properly compose whole words, is that we can then create and use NEOLOGISMS that are inoffensive to those who know the English language and other languages. And we can likewise avoid opposition to morphological deformities, which refined writers avoid as much as possible. Cf. HYBRIDS.

mors civilis. See **civil death.**

mortgage, n., = a property owner's promise that, if some obligation is not met, the creditor may take the property to satisfy that obligation. At common law, the word referred only to real property. But in mid-19th-century AmE, the word *mortgage* was extended to apply to personalty as well as realty. Hence, the phrase *chattel mortgage* arose. Still, in actual usage *mortgage* much more frequently applies to real rather than personal property.

The word *mortgage* has two possible etymological meanings. One theory—the better one—holds that the word derives from O.F. *mort gaige* ("dead pledge"), so called because the debt becomes void or "dead" when the mortgagor redeems the pledge. Another theory is that *dead pledge* means the same thing as the current phrases *dead capital* and *dead investment*: while land is in the possession of the lender, it is dead—it gives no return to the owner.

mortgageable. So spelled.

mortgage-holder is less clear than *mortgagee* (= the lending bank) because many readers might take it to mean "mortgagor"—e.g.: "Purchase money *mortgage holders* [read *mortgagees*] may improve their collateral positions by allowing the owner to improve the property at the expense of the mechanics' lienholders." *Shade v. Wheatcraft Indus., Inc.*, 809 P.2d 538, 542 (Kan. 1991).

mortgagor; mortgager; *mortgageor. Sir Edward Coke and William Blackstone used the *-or* spelling;

the lexicographers Samuel Johnson and Noah Webster preferred *-er*, Webster terming *-or* "an orthography that should have no countenance." Noah Webster, *An American Dictionary of the English Language* (1828). The *Law Quarterly Review* and many other British publications use *-er*; the form *-or* predominates in AmE. The **mortgageor* spelling, which appeared in the Year Books, is nowhere used today.

mortis causa. See **causa mortis.**

mortmain (lit., "deadhand") = the condition of lands or tenements held inalienably by an ecclesiastical or other corporation. The term suggests control from the grave, as here in a LOAN TRANSLATION: "The chief purposes of the common-law approach are stated to be a desire to curtail the *deadhand* control of wealth and to facilitate the marketability of property." Lawrence H. Averill Jr. & Ellen B. Brantley, *A Comparison of Arkansas's Current Law Concerning Succession, Wills, and Other Donative Transfers*, 17 UALR L.J. 631, 721 (1995).

The *OED* remarks: "It seems probable that 'dead hand' in English legal use is a metaphorical expression for impersonal ownership, and is unconnected with the older feudal use of *manus mortua* to denote the custom by which serfs (and other classes included under the term *homines manus mortuae*) had no power of testamentary disposition, their possessions, if they died without legitimate offspring, reverting to the lord."

mosaic, vb., is inflected much like *bivouacking* and *mimicking* and *picnicking*—that is, *mosaicking*. Yet intellectual-property writers frequently err—e.g.: "If . . . it is necessary to resort to *mosaicing* [read *mosaicking*], one inevitably runs into difficulty." Jeremy Phillips & Alison Firth, *Introduction to Intellectual Property Law* 55 (4th ed. 2001). *Mosaicking* refers to a method of attacking a patent's validity by combining pieces of prior art in such a way that the obviousness of the invention seems apparent.

most in the sense "quite, very" is an established casualism. Today it is standard English, though less formal than *quite*—e.g.:

- "*Most* [read *Almost*] everybody knows what a statute is, but what is a precedent?" C. Gordon Post, *An Introduction to the Law* 80 (1963).
- "The power of judicial review had a *most* inauspicious beginning." Stephen C. Halpern & Charles M. Lamb, *Supreme Court Activism and Restraint* 156 (1982). The adjective *inauspicious* is actually stronger without a modifier: see WEASEL WORDS.

See **very (A).**

most-favored-nation clause. Commercial lawyers borrowed the diplomatic phrase *most favored nation* (a status that lowers import taxes) and used it to denote a contractual clause ensuring that a given buyer or royalty owner will be treated at least as favorably as any other buyer or royalty owner. The phrase *favored-nation clause* is a variant.

On the same principle, some commercial tenants negotiate a *most-favored-tenant clause*, which ensures that a tenant will be given any negotiating concessions given to other tenants.

most important(ly). See **more important(ly).**

Mother Hubbard clause; anaconda clause; drag-net clause. These synonymous phrases denote a clause stating that a mortgage (more specifically, an *anaconda mortgage*) secures all the debts that the mortgagor may at any time owe to the mortgagee. The METAPHORS underlying the terms are as follows: *Mother Hubbard* suggests that the mortgagor goes to great lengths to satisfy the mortgagee, just as Mother Hubbard (in the popular nursery rhyme) is absurdly solicitous toward her dog. E.g.: "Amerada . . . invokes the 'coverall' (sometimes called the '*Mother Hubbard*') clause in an oil and gas lease from Koch, dated January 19, 1945." *Gardner v. Amerada Petroleum Corp.*, 91 F.Supp. 134, 135 (S.D. Tex. 1950). *Anaconda* suggests that the unsuspecting debtor may get wrapped up in the serpentine clutches of indebtedness. The *dragnet* metaphor suggests a broadly cast net that sweeps in all past and future debts. Today, *Mother Hubbard clause* is the most usual phrase.

motion, n. = an application requesting a court to make a specified order. Though it is properly classifiable as a court paper, a motion is not a pleading. See **court papers, application** & **pleading (B).**

motion, vb., in the sense "to move (as a court)" is labeled obsolete in the *OED*. It ought to be obsolete, but strangely it persists in American legal writing—e.g.:

- "Warrington *motioned* [read *moved*] the court for summary judgment on both the conversion and securities fraud causes of action." *Levitz v. Warrington*, 877 P.2d 1245, 1246 (Utah Ct. App. 1994).
- "On March 24, 1993, Parson *motioned* [read *moved*] the court to increase child support." *Hernandez v. Hernandez*, 640 So.2d 818, 819 (La. Ct. App. 1994).

See **move (that) the court.**

motion for a new trial. See **motion for new trial.**

motion for more definite statement. See **bill of particulars.**

motion for new trial; motion for a new trial. This motion, which dates back to medieval times, is now generally called a *motion for new trial*, without the indefinite article. See ARTICLES (C).

motion in limine should not be hyphenated. See **in limine.**

motivate, -ation. See **actuate.**

motivation. See **motive.**

motive; motivation. *Motive* is, as Wigmore has observed, unfortunately ambiguous: "That which has value to show the doing or not doing of the act is the inward emotion, passion, feeling, of the appropriate sort; but that which shows the probable existence of this emotion is termed—when it is . . . some outer fact—the '*motive*.' For example, the prior prosecution of A by B in a suit at law is said to have been a '*motive*' for A's subsequent burning of B's house. But in strictness the external fact of B's suit cannot be A's '*motive*'; for the motive is a state of mind of A; the external fact does tend to show the excitement of the hostile and vindictive emotion, but it is not identical with that emotion." J.H. Wigmore, *The Science of Judicial Proof* 117 (3d ed. 1937). Cf. **intention (C).**

Motivation, meaning "a mental or an emotional driving force," is often clearer than *motive* would be—e.g.:

- "The legality of a search will not depend on the *motivations* of the police officers involved in the search." *State v. Deneui*, 775 N.W.2d 221, 230 (S.D. 2009).
- "Situations may occur wherein an attorney may use all of his or her peremptory strikes to excuse jurors of only one race without it indicating racial *motivation*." *Dubose v. State*, 22 So.3d 340, 348 (Miss. Ct. App. 2009).
- "Petitioner argues that the letters submitted in postconviction also reveal his true *motivation* for confessing to the murders: to protect Dorothy and their unborn child." *Loza v. Mitchell*, 705 F.Supp.2d 773, 833 (S.D. Ohio 2010).

Cf. **actuate.**

mouthpiece. See LAWYERS, DEROGATORY NAMES FOR (A).

movable, adj. & n., is the preferred spelling in both AmE and BrE. *Moveable*, chiefly a legal variant, should be avoided everywhere but in Scotland, where it is traditional. See **immovable** & **adjectives (C).**

movant; mover. *Movant* (= one who makes a motion to the court) is a late-19th-century Americanism. Among the earliest recorded uses is this one: "The *movants* excepted to the rulings of the court." *Lanning v. Lockett*, 11 F. 814, 814 syl. (C.C.S.D. Ga. 1882).

In the U.S. today, *movant* is far more common than *mover*. It is the form used in most court rules and predominantly in reported cases. E.g.: "On motions for stay pending appeal the *movant* need not always show a probability of success on the merits." *Ruiz v. Estelle*, 650 F.2d 555, 557 (5th Cir. 1981). *Movent is an incorrect variant spelling. (See **applicant.**)

Mover, when used in the sense of *movant*, is a NEEDLESS VARIANT—e.g.: "The court should consider all of the evidence—not just that evidence which supports the *nonmover's* [read *nonmovant's*] case—but in the light and with all reasonable inferences most favorable to the party opposed to the motion." *Michigan Abrasive Co. v. Poole*, 805 F.2d 1001, 1004 (11th Cir.

An asterisk (✳) precedes words and phrases that are invariably inferior forms.

1986). Some people prefer *mover* over *movant* in parliamentary procedure.

move. "We *move the court* to grant a new trial." This construction appears from a logical point of view to be incorrect. Idiom would seem to require: "I *move that the court* grant a new trial." By analogy, one might say: "I hereby *move that we* adjourn," but not "I hereby *move us* to adjourn."

Yet the phrase *moving the court* is of long standing in legal language, including this from the syllabus in *Marbury v. Madison*: "At the last term, . . . William Marbury [et al.] severally *moved the court* for a rule to James Madison." *Marbury v. Madison*, 5 U.S. 137, 137 syl. (1803) (per Marshall, C.J.).

With either of those two constructions, *move* is transitive (*move the court* or *move that the court*), even when the object is understood: *move [the court] for relief* becomes *move for relief*.

moveable. See **movable.**

mover. See **movant.**

much. See **many (A).**

*muchly** has long been considered a substandard form, though several centuries ago it was not so stigmatized. *Much* is the preferred form in all adverbial contexts. Unsurprisingly, the dialectal **muchly* has appeared in reported American opinions—e.g.: "It is clear from the record that the claim was *very muchly* [read *much*] disputed." *Dix v. Trigger Contractors, Inc.*, 337 So.2d 694, 696 (Miss. 1976). See ADVERBS, PROBLEMS WITH (D) & HYPERCORRECTION (D).

mulct. See **penalize.**

multifarious = (1) improperly joining in one pleading distinct matters or claims, and thereby confounding them; (2) improperly joining parties in a lawsuit; or (3) diversified; many and various. Sense 3 is the common, nonlegal sense. In law, sense 1 predominates—e.g.: "The complaint as amended was dismissed . . . on the grounds of *multifarious* pleading and for failure to state a cause of action." *Bates & Rogers Constr. Corp. v. North Shore Sanitary Dist.*, 414 N.E.2d 1274, 1276 (Ill. App. Ct. 1980).

multiparty; multipartite. *Multiparty* is defined by the *OED* as a political term meaning "comprising several parties or members of parties; of an electoral or political system which results in the formation of three or more influential parties." Yet in law, the *party* in this word has come in the U.S. to refer to a party to a lawsuit. E.g.: "When the intervention was allowed, the suit became a *multiparty* action within the meaning of Fed. R. Civ. P. 54(b)." *Borne v. A & P Boat Rentals No. 4, Inc.*, 755 F.2d 1131, 1133 (5th Cir. 1985).

Multipartite (= divided into many parts) is occasionally misused for *multiparty*: "*Multipartite* [read *Multiparty*?] agreements between the debtor and his creditors, or several of them, may bind participating creditors. Non-consenting creditors will not be so

bound." James A. MacLachlan, *Handbook of the Law of Bankruptcy* 4 (1956).

multiplepointing. See **interpleader (A).**

multiplicitous. A. And *multiplicious*. Although both forms (*multiplicitous* and *multiplicious*) have existed in the English language, *W3* states (prematurely) that *multiplicious* is now obsolete. (It is the only form listed in the *OED*.) Certainly it is the rarer term, and it does not immediately reveal its relationship with the noun *multiplicity*. Nonetheless, *multiplicious* appears in the law reports. *See, e.g., U.S. v. Wesley*, 748 F.2d 962, 963 (5th Cir. 1984) ("Wesley argues that his convictions . . . are *multiplicious* and violative of the double jeopardy clause of the fifth amendment."); *U.S. v. Stanfa*, 685 F.2d 85, 88 (3d Cir. 1982) (*multiplicious* used four times in two paragraphs). But this word should not be resurrected: we should avoid multiplicitous forms of this word, and hold steady with *multiplicitous*. (When used—as in the previous sentence—for *multiple*, *multiplicitous* is a pomposity.)

The two forms of the word are susceptible to INELEGANT VARIATION. One judicial writer used both forms in consecutive paragraphs: "Even if a single fact pattern were present, the 'different evidence test' . . . would show that the counts in question were not *multiplicitous*. . . . The chief danger raised by a *multiplicious* [read *multiplicitous*] indictment is the possibility that the defendant will receive more than one sentence for a single offense." *U.S. v. Swaim*, 757 F.2d 1530, 1536–37 (5th Cir. 1985).

B. And *duplicitous*. The distinction is not what one might infer: "An indictment is *multiplicitous* when it charges one offense in several counts. An indictment is *duplicitous* when it charges numerous crimes in a single count." *U.S. v. Jones*, 648 F.Supp. 241, 242 (S.D.N.Y. 1986) (citations omitted). E.g.: "If Lartey has any complaint, it is not that the indictment is *multiplicious* [read *multiplicitous*], but rather that it is *duplicitous*, charging numerous crimes in a single count." *U.S. v. Lartey*, 716 F.2d 955, 968 (2d Cir. 1983). See **duplicitous.**

multiply /muul-tə-plee/ is an adverb as well as a verb /muul-tə-plɪ/—"Bennett's jailmate was a *multiply* convicted felon who admitted on cross-examination that he hoped his testimony against Bennett would earn him a reduced sentence." *U.S. v. Bennett*, 363 F.3d 947, 955 (9th Cir. 2004).

multistate. So spelled, without a hyphen.

multital. See **paucital.**

multitude of, a. See SYNESIS.

mumbo-jumbo. Many critics use this phrase to denote LEGALESE and JARGON—e.g.: "And only the solemn and mystifying *mumbo-jumbo* of legal language keeps the non-lawyers from catching on." Fred Rodell, *Woe Unto You, Lawyers!* 88 (1939).

municipal = (1) of or relating to a town, city, or local governmental unit (as contrasted with *county*, *state*, or *national*); or (2) of or relating to the internal government of a state or nation (as contrasted with *international*). Sense 1 is ordinary. All but international lawyers are likely to find sense 2 odd—e.g.: "It is presumed that *municipal* law is to be interpreted to be in conformity with international law." Michael Zander, *The Law-Making Process* 128 (2d ed. 1985). See **international.**

muniment. See **document.**

murder. A. And *homicide*; *manslaughter*; *man-killing*. *Homicide* is the action of killing another human being; it is the general legal term. *Murder* is the unlawful killing of a human being with malice aforethought. It is the most heinous kind of criminal homicide. At common law, *murder* was not subdivided; but in most American jurisdictions statutes have created *first-degree murder*, *second-degree murder*, and *third-degree murder* (in descending order of reprehensibility). Indeed, *second-degree murder* is the same as common-law *murder*, as defined above. *First-degree murder*, a statutory crime, is the common-law crime of murder with an added element that aggravates the crime (e.g., arson, rape, robbery, burglary, larceny, kidnapping). See **degree.**

Manslaughter, which is a less serious crime than *murder*, is homicide committed without malice aforethought. The Scots-law equivalent is *culpable homicide.*

Man-killing is a nonlegal synonym for *homicide*, used sometimes of nonhuman killers <a man-killing tiger>. But it is a sexist term: see SEXISM (B) & **homicide.** For more on related verbs, see **kill (A).**

B. *Unintentional murder*. This phrase may strike some readers as an OXYMORON, but it is in widespread use—e.g.: "On Tuesday, the [California Supreme Court], in a major break with a 4-year-old precedent, ruled that a killer can be executed for an *unintentional murder*." *Calif. Death Sentence Upheld*, L.A. Times, 15 Oct. 1987, at 1-1. And it is entirely proper to speak of an *unintentional murder*, as when a defendant, for no good reason, shoots a gun into an occupied room and kills somebody inside.

The distinction between *unintentional murder* and *manslaughter*, says one commentator, "has never been drawn with great clarity. What is clear is that murder requires a more culpable level of risk-taking than does manslaughter." Joshua Dressler, *Understanding Criminal Law* 462 (1987). The recklessness involved in unintentional murder is more extreme than that involved in manslaughter.

C. *Murder one*; *murder two*; *murder three*. These are AmE colloquialisms for *first-degree murder*, *second-degree murder*, and *third-degree murder*.

must is used both factually and normatively. The factual use involves a judgment about something that has happened: "She *must* have known that he was there.

Otherwise she never would have begun chanting the message." The normative *must* may be merely a strong *ought* ("You *must* always tell the truth") or an absolute requirement ("To qualify, you *must* be at least 18 years of age").

In drafting, *must* is generally confined to the last of these senses. Many drafters, especially in Australia, Canada, and Great Britain, consider *must* a much better word than *shall* for stating requirements. And the trend seems to be for Americans to adopt this view. See WORDS OF AUTHORITY (A) & (C).

muster. The phrase *to pass muster* began as a military term meaning "to undergo review without censure." Lawyers have picked it up especially in the sense of constitutional review. E.g.:

- "*To pass muster*, these classifications must serve important governmental objectives and be substantially related to achievement of those objectives." *Town of Ball v. Rapides Parish Police Jury*, 746 F.2d 1049, 1059–60 (5th Cir. 1984).
- "The admission of the evidence in this case readily *passes muster*." *Enriquez v. Procunier*, 752 F.2d 111, 115 (5th Cir. 1984).

This SET PHRASE is occasionally mangled: "To *withstand constitutional muster* [read *pass constitutional muster*], a legislative classification must comply with Louisiana's Declaration of the Right to Individual Dignity." *State v. Granger*, 982 So.2d 779, 788 (La. 2008). *Past muster* is an ignorant blunder for *pass muster*: "If either probable cause or exigent circumstances are not established, a warrantless entry will not *past muster* [read *pass muster*]." *Stone v. State*, 279 S.W.3d 688, 692 (Tex. App.—Amarillo 2006).

must needs. See **needs must.**

must not. See WORDS OF AUTHORITY (F).

mutatis mutandis (= the necessary changes having been made; taking into consideration or allowing for the changes that must be made) is a useful LATINISM in learned writing, for the only English equivalents are far wordier. E.g.:

- "How far can the account given above of legal liability responsibility be applied *mutatis mutandis* to moral responsibility?" H.L.A. Hart, "Postscript: Responsibility and Retribution," in *Punishment and Responsibility: Essays in the Philosophy of Law* 210, 225 (1968).
- "The PCF responded by filing near identical pleadings *mutatis mutandis*." *Reed v. St. Charles Gen. Hosp.*, 11 So.3d 1138, 1142 (La. Ct. App. 2009).
- "*Mutatis mutandis*, the task for judges in the search for law and justice in a case of statutory interpretation is ultimately the same." Stephen Wistosky, *How to Interpret Statutes—or Not*, 10 J. App. Prac. & Process 321, 346 (2009).

Cf. *ceteris paribus.*

mute; dumb. In nonlegal contexts, *mute* has come to signify "dumb; destitute of the faculty of speech." But in law, it retains its older use as a synonym of *silent*—e.g.:

"Petitioners' decision to remain *mute* during the deportability phase of the hearing was an appropriate exercise of their Fifth Amendment privilege." *Cabral-Avila v. I.N.S.*, 589 F.2d 957, 959 (9th Cir. 1978). Since *dumb* has also long meant "stupid," avoid it regarding people except in the SET PHRASE *struck dumb*.

MUTE E. In English, an unsounded final *-e-* is ordinarily dropped before the *-ing* and *-ed* inflections, e.g., *create, creating, created; rate, rating, rated; share, sharing, shared*. Exceptions to this rule are verbs with bases ending in *-ee, -ye,* and *-oe*: these do not drop the *-e-* before *-ing*, but they do drop it before *-ed*: *agree, agreeing, agreed; dye, dyeing, dyed; hoe, hoeing, hoed*.

The suffix *-able* often causes doubt when it is appended to a base ending in a mute *-e-*. Generally, the *-e-* is dropped when *-able* is added, but a number of exceptions exist in BrE (e.g., *hireable, liveable, nameable, rateable, ropeable, saleable, sizeable, unshakeable*). But in BrE, forms such as *blamable, exercisable,* and *finable,* which follow the American rule of dropping the *-e-,* are preferred.

The almost universal exception to the AmE rule of dropping the *-e-* before a vowel is that it should be kept if it is needed to indicate the soft sound of a preceding *-g-* or *-c-,* or to distinguish a word from another with a like spelling. E.g., *change, changeable; hinge, hingeing; singe, singeing; trace, traceable*. But even this exception to the rule is not uniform: *lunge* yields *lunging*. Because the given form of a word when inflected is easily forgotten and often the subject of disagreement even among lexicographers, the best course is to keep an up-to-date and reliable dictionary at one's side.

One other difference between AmE and BrE is of interest to legal writers: in AmE, the mute *-e-* is dropped after *-dg-* in words such as *acknowledgment, fledgling,* and *judgment,* whereas the *-e-* is retained in BrE (*acknowledgement, fledgeling,* and *judgement*). British legal writers, however, usually prefer the spelling *judgment*. See **judgment** & **pledgor**.

mutilate. See **maim**.

mutual; common. *Mutual* = reciprocal; directed by each toward the other(s)—e.g.: "This court held that a contract made by *mutual letters* [read *mutual exchange of letters*] was not complete until the letter accepting the offer had been received by the person making the offer." *Lewis v. Browning*, 130 Mass. 173, 175 (1880). *Common* = shared by two or more. *Friend in common* is preferable to *mutual friend,* although the latter has stuck because of Dickens's novel (the title to which, everyone forgets, comes from a sentence mouthed by an illiterate character). See **mutual mistake**.

Like *together, mutual* creates any number of redundant expressions—e.g.: "We have repeatedly held that a party may not assume successive positions in the course of a suit, or series of suits, with reference to the same fact or state of facts, which are inconsistent with each other, or *mutually contradictory* [read *contradictory*]."

Gilmer v. Brown, 44 S.E.2d 16, 19 (Va. 1947). Some of the more common prolixities with this word are *mutual agreement* and *mutual cooperation*. Redundancies are especially common when *mutual* is used in conjunction with *both*; for instance, **mutually binding on both parties,* or: "An invitee enters land with the owner's knowledge and for *the mutual benefit of both* [read *their mutual benefit*]." *Mayer v. Willowbrook Plaza LP*, 278 S.W.3d 901, 909 (Tex. App.—Houston [14th Dist.] 2009). See **together**.

mutuality of obligation (= the fact of both parties to a contract having agreed to be bound in some way) once allowed courts to decide that one party's promise was "illusory" and that the contract therefore failed for lack of consideration. Today, however, "the once powerful slogan of '*mutuality of obligation*' makes its rare appearance . . . as 'the now exploded theory of mutuality of obligation.'" Grant Gilmore, *The Death of Contract* 77 (1974). Cf. **meeting of the minds**.

***mutually agree** is a REDUNDANCY. See **mutual**.

mutually exclusive = each excluding the other. E.g.: "It has always been hard to classify all government activity into three, and only three, neat and *mutually exclusive* categories." Abram Chayes, *The Role of the Judge in Public Law Litigation*, 89 Harv. L. Rev. 1281, 1307 (1976). The phrase must be carefully used.

mutual mistake. Because this phrase, as it is ordinarily employed, involves a misuse of *mutual* for *common,* several writers on the law of contract—such as Cheshire, Fifoot, and Atiyah—have valiantly championed *common mistake* over *mutual mistake*. (See **mutual**.) Alas, the courts have not followed their grammatical lead and continue to refer overwhelmingly to *mutual mistake*.

It would be quite possible—and perhaps desirable—to distinguish between a *common mistake* and a *mutual mistake*. A *common mistake* occurs when both parties make the same mistake: when, for example, parties think that a painting is a genuine Van Gogh but in fact it is a fake. A *mutual mistake* occurs when each party is mistaken about the other's intent: when, for example, I think I am selling you my Honda Accord and you think you are buying my Acura. *Mutual* would be correct because I have mistaken your intent, and you have mistaken mine. But common-law judges typically lump both situations under the name *mutual mistake*.

mutual will; joint will. A *joint will* (sometimes wrongly called a *mutual will*) is one testamentary document executed by two persons. *Mutual wills* are separate documents in which two parties—usu. a husband and wife—establish identical testamentary provisions; such wills may contain or imply a contract not to revoke, so that the death of either party may bind the survivor to make no alteration.

mutuum /**myoo**-choo-əm/ = a transaction (now more usually referred to as a bailment) in which goods are delivered but, instead of being returnable, are replaced by other goods of the same kind. At common law, such a transaction is regarded as a sale or exchange, not as a bailment, because the particular goods are not expected to be returned. A *mutuum* is distinguished from a *deposit* for the same reason and, in the case of a *deposit*, "the property is not . . . transferred or alienated . . . and the depository has the mere possession or custody of the thing." Joseph Story, *Commentaries on the Law of Bailments* 51 (James Schouler ed., 9th ed. 1878). See **commodatum.**

my home is my castle. See **castle doctrine.**

my lady. See **my lord.**

my lord; your lordship. An English judge appointed to the High Court or some even higher court is invariably promoted within society: men are knighted and women are made Dames of the Order of the British Empire. Few become members of the House of Lords, but in court they are all nevertheless addressed *my lord* or *your lordship*, or *my lady* or *your ladyship*.

The *my* and *your* terms are not used interchangeably: *my lord* is used as a vocative in addressing a judge directly ("My lord, this case involves . . ."), whereas *your lordship* appears within a sentence as a polite alternative to *you* ("May it please your lordship, I am counsel for the plaintiff"). Cf. **Honorable** (2d par.).

In Scotland, judges of the Court of Session are, by courtesy, called *Lord X* and addressed in court as *my lord* or *your lordship*, even though they are rarely knighted or raised to the peerage. The origin of this practice was that superior-court judges were originally Lords of the King's Privy Council (i.e., "secret council"), from which the Court of Session evolved.

myriad is more concise as an adjective <myriad drugs> than as a noun <a myriad of drugs>. E.g.: "The Constitution does not empower this Court to second-guess state officials charged with the difficult responsibility of allocating limited public-welfare funds *among the myriad of* [read *among the myriad*] potential recipients." *Dandridge v. Williams*, 397 U.S. 471, 487 (1970) (per Stewart, J.).

myself is best used either reflexively (e.g., "I have decided to recuse *myself*") or intensively (e.g., "I *myself* will sue the corporation on behalf of the class of persons harmed").

But *myself* should not appear as a substitute for *I* or *me*. Using it this way is thought somehow to be modest, as if the reference to oneself were less direct. But it is no less direct, and the writer may unconsciously cause the reader or listener to assume an intended jocularity, or that the writer is somewhat doltish. E.g.:

- "After reconsideration, upon appellees' motion for rehearing, Mr. Justice Brady and *myself* [read *I*] have reached the conclusion that this court has rendered an improper judgment, and that the motion for rehearing should be granted, and the judgment of the trial court affirmed." *Bishop v. Williams*, 223 S.W. 512, 514 (Tex. Civ. App.— Austin 1920). (Is it so difficult to say simply, "We have rendered an improper judgment"?)
- "Those ins and outs are largely a self-learning process, though knowing the experience of someone like *myself* [read *me*] might make the learning shorter, easier, and a lot less painful." Mark H. McCormack, *What They Don't Teach You at Harvard Business School* xii (1984).

See FIRST PERSON.

MYTH OF PRECISION, THE. "Delusive exactness is a source of fallacy throughout the law." *Truax v. Corrigan*, 257 U.S. 312, 342 (1921) (Holmes, J., dissenting). When attacked for their inscrutable use of language, lawyers have traditionally sought refuge in precision, and often silenced their critics by the invocation of precision. Not everyone has been satisfied, however, by the explanation or excuse that legal language, despite its WOOLLINESS and frequent ugliness, is more precise than the general language. In words that still ring true, Jeremy Bentham wrote, in the early 19th century:

> For this redundancy, for the accumulation of excrementitious matter [i.e., legalese] in all its various shapes . . . [and] for all the pestilential effects that cannot be produced by this so enourmous a load of literary garbage,— the plea commonly pleaded . . . is, that it is necessary to *precision*—or, to use the word which on similar occasions they themselves are in the habit of using, certainty.
>
> But a more absolutely sham plea never was countenanced, or so much as pleaded, in either the King's Bench or Common Pleas.
> 3 Jeremy Bentham, *Works* 260 (John Bowring ed., 1843).

A late-19th-century legist wrote, in words less vitriolic but even more telling:

> There is an abundance of affected accuracy in the addition of descriptions to distinguish persons and things needing no distinction, and in the expression of immaterial matters; but real accuracy and precision are attained quite as much by the omission of superfluous phrases, by the avoidance of tautology, by correct references and by a strict adherence to the rules of grammar, as by the use of apt words.
> 1 Charles Davidson, *Precedents and Forms in Conveyancing* 23 (4th ed. 1874).

The truth is that many people, lawyers included, buy into the fallacy that there must be a great deal of precision in LEGALESE. Why else—nonlawyers wonder—would lawyers *talk* so much about precision? Lon Fuller recognized the myth but not the extent of its currency: "For the time being it will be enough to put down one source of obfuscation. This is the notion current among laymen that lawyers, with all their forbidding jargon, have some uncanny ability to convey meaning to one another with great exactitude. Outside the area of a few TERMS OF ART, there is nothing

---

to this belief." *The Anatomy of Law* 26 (1968). What Fuller did not realize is that the myth besots lawyers and nonlawyers alike. What everyone ought to recognize, though, is that, "to fill in the spaces between their 'whereas's' and 'provided however's' lawyers have no resources except those available to any user of language." *Id.*

There is all too little precision in legal language, as many entries in this book should demonstrate. See PLAIN LANGUAGE.

N

naked is often used metaphorically in legal writing in the sense "having nothing that confirms or validates (a thing)." E.g.:

- "The court simply held as a *naked* proposition of law that the contract was illegal and void." *Hubbard v. Mulligan*, 57 P. 738, 741 (Colo. Ct. App. 1899).
- "Plaintiffs argue that, while they do not possess a *naked* ownership interest in the abandoned portion of the road, they possess a lesser, but still protected right in the form of a servitude of use." *Craig v. Grant Parish Police Jury*, 593 F.Supp.2d 901, 906 (W.D. La. 2008).

Naked trespasser describes not one who trespasses unclothed, but a trespasser with absolutely no claim to be present on the land—e.g.: "Had Anderson Strong entered upon this land as a *naked trespasser*, without any property right therein, he would have had no basis for a claim of title until the full period of limitation had run." *Strong v. Garrett*, 224 S.W.2d 471, 474 (Tex. 1949). In trademark law, a *naked license* is a license without provision for the licensor's exercise of quality control. And *naked contract*—a LOAN TRANSLATION of L. *nudum pactum*—denotes a contract not "clothed" with consideration. (See **nudum pactum.**) For the correlative METAPHOR, see **clothe.**

namable. See MUTE E.

name. See **designate.**

namely is generally preferable to the LATINISM *viz.* or to the ARCHAISM *to wit.* But often all three expressions can be avoided—e.g.: "Finally, Part IV turns to the heart of the matter so far as securitization is concerned: *namely,* [omit *namely,*] recharacterization under bankruptcy law." Kenneth C. Kettering, *True Sale of Receivables*, 16 Am. Bankr. Inst. L. Rev. 511, 513 (2008). See **viz.** & **to wit.** See also **including.**

name partner. See **title member.**

Napoleonic Code. American lawyers often refer to the *Napoleonic Code*, or the *Code Napoléon*, as if it were the official name of a single code. Those who do so are wrong on two counts. First, although Napoleon commissioned the codification of French law, his name is only unofficially connected with the product. Second, it is more proper to refer to *Napoleonic codes*, in the plural and with a lowercase *-c-*, as David M. Walker does in the *OCL1*.

The *Napoleonic codes* include the *Code civil* (1804), the *Code de procédure civil* (1806), the *Code de commerce* (1807), the *Code pénal* (1810), and the *Code d'instruction crimenelle* (1811). When American lawyers use the singular phrase, they seem to have in mind the *Code civil* (or *Civil Code*, as rendered in English).

narrative. In Scots law, the *narrative* in a deed is equivalent to the *recitals* in English and American deeds. The *narrative* sets forth the names of the grantor and the grantee, along with the reason for the conveyance.

nation; state. These two words have different meanings. A *nation* is a group of people inhabiting a defined territory, that group being distinct from other groups of people by the fact of its having allegiance to a single government exercising jurisdiction directly over each individual in the group. The *state*, by contrast, is the system of rules—or the machinery—by which jurisdiction is exercised over individuals within the group. It is therefore "illogical and confusing to use the terms '*State*' and '*Nation*' as though they were interchangeable, although this is frequently done. Thus we refer to the 'United *Nations*' although this is in fact an organization of *States*." Edward Jenks, *The Book of English Law* 5 (P.B. Fairest ed., 6th ed. 1967). See **state.**

national. See **citizen (A).**

national; federal. In a nation whose government has a federal system, these two terms might seem interchangeable. But the founders of the United States carefully distinguished them—particularly James Madison, who wrote:

> The Constitution is to be founded on the assent and ratification of the people of America, given by deputies elected for the special purpose; but, on the other [hand], . . . this assent and ratification is to be given by the people, not as individuals composing one entire nation, but as composing the distinct and independent States to which they respectively belong. It is to be the assent and ratification of the several States, derived from the supreme authority in each State—the authority of the people themselves. The act, therefore, establishing the Constitution will not be a *national* but a *federal* act.
> *The Federalist* No. 39, at 243 (James Madison) (Clinton Rossiter ed., 1961).

Thus, as Madison explained, the foundation of the Constitution is *federal*; the operation of governmental powers under the Constitution is *national*; and the method of introducing amendments is *mixed. Id.* at 246.

National Reporter System. See **report (A).**

Native American. See *****native-born citizen.**

*****native-born citizen.** This phrase, though it has been fairly common since the 19th century, reeks of REDUNDANCY—e.g.:

- "The evidence in the record before us is not sufficiently compelling to require that we penalize a naturalized citizen for the expression of silly or even sinister-sounding views [that] *native-born citizens* [read *native citizens*] utter with impunity." *Baumgartner v. U.S.*, 322 U.S. 665, 677 (1944) (per Frankfurter, J.).
- "For the *native-born citizen* [read *native citizen*] it is a right that is truly inalienable." *Kungys v. U.S.*, 485 U.S. 759, 784 (1988) (Stevens, J., concurring).

The modern temptation to brace the adjective *native* may come from two sources. First, in American law, the noun *native* has come to mean either (1) "a person born in the country"; or (2) "a person born outside the country of parents who are (at the time of the birth) citizens of that country and who are not permanently residing elsewhere." Sense 2 represents a slide in meaning, but the judicial writers quoted above could not possibly have wanted to protect against that extended meaning. Second, the phrase *Native American*, meaning *American Indian*, has recently popularized a secondary meaning of *native*, one having to do with heritage and not with birthplace: "one of the original or usual inhabitants of a country, as distinguished from strangers or foreigners; now *esp.* one belonging to a non-European race in a country in which Europeans hold political power" (*OED*).

natural = (1) taking place according to the processes of nature; and (2) taking place according to human experience. In sense 1 everything that occurs is *natural*. In sense 2 "it has the same meaning as 'probable,' 'ordinary,' 'usual,' 'not unlikely,' 'likely,' and several other synonyms." Leon Green, *Are Negligence and "Proximate" Cause Determinable by the Same Test?*, 1 Tex. L. Rev. 243, 245 (1923). In legal contexts, *natural* in sense 2 is a technical term: "Barring divine miracles, which do not loom large on the judicial horizon, everything that happens is *natural*. When the word is used in a more restricted popular sense, a conception of probability is introduced." James Angell McLaughlin, *Proximate Cause*, 39 Harv. L. Rev. 149, 186 (1925). See **unnatural.**

natural child doubles as a term equivalent to *biological child* and as a EUPHEMISM for *bastard, illegitimate child*, or *nonmarital child*. See **bastard** & **illegitimate child.**

natural equity. See **equity.**

naturalist. To most people, Buffon and Darwin were *naturalists*, i.e., 19th-century biologists. But some lawyers use *naturalist* to denote a natural-law adherent—e.g.: "Pufendorf, though differing in his concept of

natural law, was also a '*naturalist*.'" René A. Wormser, *The Story of the Law* 513 (1962). The more usual (and comprehensible) phrase is *natural lawyer*.

natural justice is closely allied with *natural law*. A 19th-century court defined the phrase as "the natural sense of what is right and wrong." *Voinet v. Barrett*, [1885] 55 L.J.Q.B. 39, 41. Although, on its face, the phrase is vague, its application tends to be specific: it usually turns up in discussions about whether a party has been afforded notice and a hearing. However desirable these procedural requirements may be, though, they are anything but "natural." So *natural justice* is really "a serious misnomer," indicating that "lawyers may have underestimated their own contribution to one of the great principles of liberal societies." P.S. Atiyah, *Law and Modern Society* 41 (1983). Cf. **natural law.**

natural law. A. General Sense. Historically a number of senses have been attributed to this term; today the prevailing sense, especially in legal contexts, is "law that determines what is right and wrong and that has power or is valid by nature, inherently, hence everywhere and always." L. Strauss, "Natural Law," in 11 *International Encyclopedia of the Social Sciences* 80, 80 (1968). Because *natural law* and *positive law* are not mutually exclusive, a rule such as "Thou shalt not kill" might be a rule equally in both systems. See **positive law.**

Twentieth-century legal scholars have mostly rejected the notion of *natural law* on positivist grounds, because genuine scientific knowledge cannot validate value judgments, and *natural law* is composed fundamentally of value judgments. Stated differently, the problem with *natural law* is that, if it exists, there is no way to determine whose version of it is correct. The modern user of the term should be aware of the debate surrounding the concept and of the generally low regard in which the concept is now held.

Two synonymous phrases are *law of nature* and *jus naturale*.

B. Incorrect Sense. At least one writer has perversely used the phrase *natural law* as if it referred to the law (or lawlessness) of a state of nature: "Carr relished the good fight, and the opposition's propensity to settle contradicted his own *natural law*." John A. Jenkins, *The Litigators* 350 (1989).

natural lawyer. See **naturalist.**

natural life. The common conveyancing phrase *during his natural life* is better rendered *for life* or *as long as he lives*. See **civil death.**

natural person (= a human being) is unnecessary in place of either *person* or *human being*, except when contrast is made to *juristic person*. Cf. **juristic person.**

natural right, like *natural law* and *natural justice*, is now generally considered a suspect phrase. Property lawyers have traditionally referred to the *natural right* of a landowner to have the land not be deprived of its support from adjacent tracts, to receive water from a stream, and the like. But "it is simpler and more intelligible to talk of the situations in which a landowner can sue in tort without proving the existence of a servitude, than to speak of *natural rights* and attempt to list these." A.W.B. Simpson, *An Introduction to the Land Law* 246 (1961).

naught; nought. These are different spellings of the same word, meaning "nothing." By convention *nought*—especially in BrE—has come to signify the number zero (0). *Naught* is used in all nonmathematical contexts in which "nothing" is meant—e.g.:

- "The decision sets at *naught* the statutory scheme we once described as a 'highly deferential standard for evaluating state-court rulings.'" *Wiggins v. Smith*, 539 U.S. 510, 538 (2003) (Scalia, J., dissenting).
- "Despite Defendants' successful introduction of this evidence in *Herrera Ríos*, their additional efforts appear to have been for *naught*." *Osorio v. Dole Food Co.*, 665 F.Supp.2d 1307, 1344 (S.D. Fla. 2009).

See **further affiant sayeth naught (B).**

nausea, when used for *vomit*, n., is a badly employed EUPHEMISM.

nauseous (= inducing nausea) for *nauseated* is becoming so common that to call it an "error" is to exaggerate. Even so, careful writers follow the traditional distinction in formal writing: what is *nauseous* makes one feel *nauseated*. As of 2011, the U.S. Supreme Court, in its seven uses of either word, has maintained a perfect record—e.g.: "It is made up entirely of repetitive descriptions of physical, sexual conduct, 'clinically' explicit and offensive to the point of being *nauseous*; there is only the most tenuous plot." *Kaplan v. California*, 413 U.S. 115, 116–17 (1973) (per Burger, C.J.).

But lower courts have helped spread the peccadillo—e.g.:

- "After Lesneski moved the van, Fleming said that he felt hot and *nauseous* [read *nauseated*]." *Fleming v. Metrish*, 556 F.3d 520, 523 (6th Cir. 2009).
- "Around 10:00 that morning, Cloaninger began trembling and feeling *nauseous* [read *nauseated*] and flighty." *Cloaninger v. McDevitt*, 555 F.3d 324, 328 (4th Cir. 2009).

nay. Except in the parliamentary procedure of taking votes either *yea* or *nay*—or *aye* and *nay*—the word *nay* smacks of pretentious posturing. E.g.:

- "Moreover, parties must be encouraged, *nay required* [read *even required*], to raise their complaints about the arbitration during the arbitration process itself, when that is possible." *Marino v. Writers Guild of Am., E., Inc.*, 992 F.2d 1480, 1483 (9th Cir. 1993).
- "The district court carefully juxtaposed selections from K-T's Licensed Materials with selections from the MPO program, thereby demonstrating a damning similarity—*nay identity* [read *even identity*]—of organization and language." *Kepner-Tregoe, Inc. v. Leadership Software, Inc.*, 12 F.3d 527, 534 (5th Cir. 1994).

- "I, for one, find it instructive—*nay, daunting* [read *no, daunting* or *even daunting*]—that no Supreme Court case utters so much as a whisper about the doctrine of implied authority that is the centerpiece of the majority's analysis." *Thomas v. INS*, 35 F.3d 1332, 1344 (9th Cir. 1994) (Kozinski, J., dissenting).

See ARCHAISM.

N.B. is the abbreviation for *nota bene* (= note well; take notice).

necessaries; necessities. In legal senses, *necessaries* is the usual term for "things that are indispensable (to life)." E.g.: "Claims for *necessaries* furnished to the beneficiary of a spendthrift or support trust may be enforced against his trust interest." John Ritchie, *Cases & Materials on Decedents' Estates and Trusts* 521 (6th ed. 1982). Though one might suppose that *necessaries* would be the same for everyone, the law does not so hold: "It might be held that ten suits of clothes are *necessaries* for one infant, whereas three suits might not be deemed necessary for another. The whole question turns upon the infant's status in life." 1 Ernest W. Chance, *Principles of Mercantile Law* 44–45 (Percy W. French ed., 13th ed. 1950).

Necessities has the broader sense of "indispensable things," whatever the subject at hand may be.

necessary; necessitous. *Necessary*, the more common word, means "essential." (See **indispensable.**) Almost always used correctly, *necessary* is ill-used when it introduces an infinitive without a BE-VERB preceding it—e.g.: "The only Massachusetts case *necessary to analyze* [read *that it is necessary to analyze* or *that must be analyzed here*] is *Balch v. Stone, supra*, since all other cases from that state followed the *Balch* case without further discussion of the soundness of the rule." *Maud v. Catherwood*, 155 P.2d 111, 118 (Cal. Ct. App. 1945).

Necessitous = placed or living in a condition of necessity or poverty; hard up. E.g.: "It will be found that where a gift results in mere financial enrichment, a trust has been sustained only when the court found and concluded from the entire context of the will that the ultimate intended recipients were poor or in *necessitous* circumstances." *Shenandoah Valley Nat'l Bank of Winchester v. Taylor*, 63 S.E.2d 786, 792 (Va. 1951).

necessitate (= to make necessary) is often inferior to *require*. Yet *require* cannot always substitute for it—e.g.:

- "The ALJ's failure to explain his reason for crediting certain testimony while ignoring more substantial evidence would normally *necessitate* a remand." *Dir., Office of Workers' Comp. Programs, U.S. Dep't of Labor v. Congleton*, 743 F.2d 428, 430 (6th Cir. 1984).
- "Wiggins clearly knew that his insistence on his right to represent himself would, perforce, *necessitate* his giving up his right to counsel." *Wiggins v. Procunier*, 753 F.2d 1318, 1320 (5th Cir. 1985).

necessities. See **necessaries.**

necessitous. See **necessary.**

necessity, in criminal law, denotes a utilitarian idea: that it is sometimes better to break the law than to follow it to the letter. It might lead an appellate court to overturn the murder convictions of four cave explorers who, having gone without food for 21 days and being on the verge of starvation, killed a companion and ate the flesh to survive. Then again, it might not. The doctrine of necessity might lead a court to approve a doctor's decision to perform an illegal, third-trimester abortion in order to save the mother's life. Some writers use *duress of circumstances* as an equivalent phrase.

neck verse. This phrase denotes the first verse of Psalm 51 (*Miserere mei, Deus* "Have mercy on me, O God"), which was traditionally used as a literacy test for an accused to claim *benefit of clergy.* Although judges might choose passages at random, they tended to stick to Psalm 51, with the result that, by the end of the 16th century, half of all convicted felons were able to save their necks by successfully claiming benefit of clergy. See J.H. Baker, *An Introduction to English Legal History* 587 (3d ed. 1990). The reading of the neck verse was abolished in 1707. See **benefit of clergy.**

Needless Variants, two or more forms of the same word without nuance or DIFFERENTIATION, and seemingly without even hope for either, teem in the language of the law. They teem in the English language for that matter, especially in the outer reaches of the language—that is, in technical vocabulary. Unfortunately, the unnecessary coexistence of variant forms, adjectives in *-tive* and *-tory* for example, lead not to precision in technical writing but to uncertainties about authorial intention. (Trusting readers think to themselves, "The writer used *punitive* on the last page but now has pressed into service *punitory—is a distinction intended?")

"It is a source not of strength," wrote H.W. Fowler, "but of weakness, that there should be two names for the same thing [by-forms differing merely in suffix or in some such minor point], because the reasonable assumption is that two words mean two things, and confusion results when they do not" (*MEU1* 373). The confusion is perhaps greatest when writers who are fond of INELEGANT VARIATION discover the boundless mutations of form that exist in law: they will write *res judicata* in one paragraph, *res adjudicata in the next; *a quo* in one sentence, *a qua* in the next; *recusal, recusement,* then *recusation;* and so on.

"On the other hand," we are advised to take note, "it may be much too hastily assumed that two words do mean the same thing; they may, for instance, denote the same object without meaning the same thing if they imply that the aspect from which it is regarded is different, or are appropriate in different mouths, or differ in rhythmic value or in some other matter that may escape a cursory examination" (*MEU1* 373).

Hence the nonlawyer should not jump to assume that *necessaries* is uncalled for in place of *necessities;* that *acquittance* has no place alongside *acquittal;* that *recusancy* is yet another needless variant of the three similar words cited above; that *burglarize* is as good for a British audience as it is for an American one; and so forth. For just such an incorrect assumption, see **wrong.**

Any number of entries throughout this work attempt to ferret out and discriminate between cognate words that have established or emerging distinctions and those that seem, at present, to have neither. To the extent possible, words and phrases rightly classifiable as needless variants ought to be dropped from the language.

need not necessarily is a REDUNDANCY. E.g.:

- "The plaintiff *need not necessarily* [read *need not*] plead a particular fact if that fact is a reasonable inference from facts properly alleged." *Denney v. Drug Enforcement Admin.,* 508 F.Supp.2d 815, 825 (E.D. Cal. 2007).
- "Police officers making arrests *need not necessarily* [read *need not*] believe that the considerations they cite show probable cause." Mathilde Cohen, *Sincerity and Reason-Giving,* 59 DePaul L. Rev. 1091, 1093 (2010).

needs must is an idiomatic phrase deriving from Elizabethan English. Its inverted sibling is *must needs,* which is slightly older. In both phrases, *needs* = necessarily. E.g.: "White is not satisfied, as bolder activists are, to assert that the Justices are not bound by the Constitution; he *needs must* attribute his 'eccentric' views to the Framers." Raoul Berger, *G. Edward White's Apology for Judicial Activism,* 63 Tex. L. Rev. 367, 367–68 (1984).

ne exeat is a LATINISM that has given its name to the writ, no longer widely used, ordering the person to whom it is addressed not to leave the country or the jurisdiction of the court. E.g.: "The purpose of the *ne exeat* bond is to ensure that the orders of the court will not be ignored." *Faris v. Jernigan,* 939 So.2d 835, 840 (Miss. Ct. App. 2006).

The name of the writ derives from the Roman-law writ of *ne exeat republica* (= let him not go out from the republic). See *Foote v. Foote,* 140 A. 312, 313 (N.J. 1928). The medieval writ was *ne exeat regno.*

negate. See **nullify (A).**

negative, vb. This verb—meaning "to deny, nullify, or render ineffective"—was one of the earliest Americanisms, having first appeared in the American colonies in the early 18th century. Today the usage is an ARCHAISM, *negate* having taken over the work formerly handled by the verb *to negative.*

Yet the verb *negative* persists in law, particularly (and oddly) in BrE—e.g.:

- "The jury could not infer any intention to resist or effect their purpose by violence, when the facts plainly *negatived* the intention." Edward Wise, *The Law Relating to Riots and Unlawful Assemblies* 7 (2d ed. 1848).

- "Unless . . . the motive is *negatived*, a wrongful act as against his right . . . is actionable if injury ensue." *Mogul Steamship Co. v. McGregor, Gow & Co.*, [1889] 23 Q.B.D. 598. Modern usage would require the phrasing *if injury ensues*, but this 19th-century British judge was using an archaic SUBJUNCTIVE.
- "The matter of damages is replete with questions of material fact that were not conclusively *negatived* by the customer's evidence before the trial court at the hearing on summary judgment." *Royal Trust Bank of Orlando v. All Fla. Fleets, Inc.*, 431 So.2d 1043, 1045 (Fla. Dist. Ct. App. 1983).

For more immediate comprehensibility to lawyers and nonlawyers alike, *negate* should be adopted as the preferred term.

negative, in the. See **affirmative, in the.**

negative easement. See **easement (A).**

negative pregnant; affirmative pregnant. *Negative pregnant* (= a negative implying or involving an affirmative) is an old POPULARIZED LEGAL TECHNICALITY. The idea usually involves a denial that implies (is pregnant with) its opposite. For example, if a suspected thief is asked, "Did you break into the house at #8 Country Club Drive on Tuesday?" and responds by saying, "No, I didn't do it on Tuesday," the implication is that only the day is wrong. The full phrase is *negative pregnant with an affirmative*.

The *affirmative pregnant* (= a nonresponsive positive statement implying or involving a negative) is not so well known. For example, if a suspected thief is asked, "Did you take the Geochron from the house?" and responds by saying, "I tried to return it the next day!" the implication is that the true answer was "yes."

NEGATIVES. A. Colliding Negatives. Lawyers have become notorious for their proclivity to pile negative upon negative. The result is sentences that most fellow lawyers have a hard time decoding:

- "The order *enjoined* required the five railroad companies to *abstain* from *refusing* to deliver interstate shipments of livestock." (Ex. fr. Frank E. Cooper, *Effective Legal Writing* 29 (1954).)
- "Courts should *not*, by self-imposed impotence, *not* required by the precedents, be less efficacious." *Spathariotis v. Spathas's Estate*, 398 P.2d 39, 42–43 (Colo. 1965).
- "[The trial court] temporarily *enjoined* defendant from *refusing* to supply water service to petitioners' . . . house on account of [their] not having paid a deposit, *without* notice and *without* bond." *Davis v. East St. Louis & Interurban Water Co.*, 270 N.E.2d 424, 425 (Ill. App. Ct. 1971).
- "A plan shall *not* be treated as *not* satisfying the requirements of this section solely because the spouse of the participant is *not* entitled to receive a survivor annuity (whether or *not* an election has been made . . .), *unless* the participant and his spouse have been married throughout the 1-year period ending on the date of such participant's death." Employee Retirement Income Security Act of 1974, Pub. L. No. 93-406, § 205(d), 88 Stat. 829, 863 (1974).

See PLAIN LANGUAGE (D).

B. Not un——; not in——. Double negatives such as *not untimely* are often used quite needlessly in place of a more straightforward wording such as *timely*. Could an action be *not untimely* but somehow not be *timely*?

Sometimes, however, the double-negative form conveys an important nuance. The difference often has to do not with logic but with the burden of proof. For example, many jurisdictions admit customs as law if they are *not unreasonable*. So the party who proves the existence of a custom does not have the further burden of showing that it is *reasonable*. Rather, to defeat the custom, the disputing party must show that it is *unreasonable*. The rule, then, is that customs will be admitted *unless they are unreasonable*, not that they will be admitted *if they are reasonable*.

Such constructions may also have a wider embrace within gray areas. Consider, for example, a set of national rules that allow *local rules not inconsistent with these rules*. Would the same meaning be conveyed by *local rules consistent with these rules*? No: if, for example, the national rules were silent on a question such as the size of paper for filed materials, a local rule specifying such sizes might not be *consistent with* the national rules—but it would certainly be *not inconsistent with* them. *Not inconsistent* prevents clashes; *consistent with* ensures conformity.

Finally, the double-negative form, shorn of any greater context, often connotes something quite different from a positive rendering. E.g.: "The doctrine of equitable conversion is *not unrestricted* in its application." 1 Herbert T. Tiffany, *The Law of Real Property* § 299, at 510 (Basil Jones ed., 3d ed. 1939). The sense is changed by writing, *The doctrine . . . is restricted in its application.*

But when the negatives serve no such identifiable purpose, they ought to be avoided. To say, for example, that a point of law is *not uninteresting* or *not unintelligible* is to engage in a time-wasting rhetorical flourish.

C. Negative Prefixes. The primary negative prefixes in English are *un-*, *in-* (assimilated in many words to *il-*, *im-*, *ir-*), *non-*, and *anti-*. For purposes of simple negation, *in-* is the most particularized of these prefixes, since it generally goes only with certain Latin nouns, and *non-* is the broadest of them, for it may precede virtually any word. As a general rule, it is best to find the most suitable particularized prefix, and if none is really suitable, then to have recourse to *non-*. (*Anti-*, of course, has the special sense "against.") *Un-* usually precedes those Latin verbs ending in the Anglo-Saxon *-ed* (*unexhausted*, *undiluted*, *unsaturated*).

Consistency is often difficult to find with particular roots. For example, *unexhausted remedies* yields *nonexhaustion*, not *unexhaustion*. Likewise, we have *indubitable* but *undoubted*, *irresolute* but *unresolved*, *irrespective* but *unrespected*. From a typographical standpoint, negative prefixes cause trouble with PHRASAL ADJECTIVES, as in *uncross-examined civil deposition*. Roundabout wordings are usually preferable to such telescoping; hence, *a civil deposition in which the witness was not cross-examined*. See NON-.

D. Periphrastic Negatives. Generally, "We dis-agree" is preferable to "We do not agree," unless some emphatic form such as the latter is called for in context to rebut an assertion. Directness is better than indi-rectness; hence *violate* rather than *fail to comply with*; *violate* rather than *do not adhere to*, and the like.

E. *No* and *not*. Lawyers often seem to prefer quaint reversals of modern usage: they say *not* when most native speakers of English would say *no*, and vice versa. This tendency is especially common in the phrase *not more than* (for *no more than*), but it can be seen at work in other phrases as well. The better legal writers stick to the more natural, more modern idiom. E.g.: "Congress has chosen, *wisely or no* [read *wisely or not*], to speak to the precise issue at hand through a Committee Report that was expressly adopted by both Houses." *ACLU v. F.C.C.*, 823 F.2d 1554, 1583 (D.C. Cir. 1987) (Starr, J., dissenting in part). See **not** & ARCHAISMS.

F. Special Problems with *not*. See **not**.

neglect. See **negligence (B)**.

neglectful; *neglective. The second is a NEEDLESS VARIANT that is rare or obsolete.

negligence. A. Senses. In general usage, *negligence* means "carelessness." But in legal usage, *negligence* = (1) the failure to exercise the standard of care that the doer as a reasonable person should have exercised in the circumstances; (2) undue indifference toward the consequences of one's act; or (3) a tort that includes the notions of duty, breach of that duty (unreasonable conduct), and resultant damage.

The term has various gradations: "*Negligence* in law ranges from inadvertence that is hardly more than accidental to sinful disregard of the safety of oth-ers." Patrick Devlin, *The Enforcement of Morals* 36 (1968). *Ordinary* or *simple negligence* is usually suf-ficient to establish liability in a tort action. *Criminal* or *gross negligence* is usually required before the court will impose a penalty. The phrase *gross negligence* has the disadvantage of applying both in civil actions (to increase damages) and in criminal actions (to establish criminal liability); many criminal lawyers therefore prefer *criminal negligence* in criminal-law contexts.

B. And *neglect*. Although in general English usage these terms are not always kept distinct, in law the DIFFERENTIATION is pronounced. *Negligence* stresses a lack of care that gives rise to liability—whether this lack of care manifests itself in the nonperformance of a duty <negligence in failing to pay a bill on time> or the heedless handling of a potentially hazardous task <negligence in operating a forklift>. *Neglect* denotes the act or fact of leaving undone something that ought to have been done <neglect of a duty>. Hence *negligence of a child* refers to the child's carelessness, while *neglect of a child* refers to another's inattention

to or forgetfulness of a child victim—through either negligence or willfulness. Then again, in some con-texts *neglect* may even include inadvertent omission that does not rise to the level of *negligence*. Therefore, *negligent neglect* is not necessarily a REDUNDANCY. Cf. **omission (B)**.

A leading English treatise on criminal law dis-tinguishes *neglect* from *negligence* in the follow-ing way. *Neglect* indicates, as a purely objective fact, that a person has not performed a duty, but it does not indicate the *reason* for the failure. *Negligence*, by contrast, denotes a subjective state of mind and indi-cates a particular reason why the person has failed to perform a duty—namely, because the person has not kept the duty in mind. *See* J.W. Cecil Turner, *Kenny's Outlines of Criminal Law* 108 n.1 (16th ed. 1952). See **negligence (A)**.

C. And *negligency. The word **negligency* is a NEEDLESS VARIANT of *negligence*.

negligent neglect. See **negligence (B)**.

negligible; *negligeable. Avoid the second spelling.

negotiability; assignability. These two terms are related but distinct. The two major ways in which *negotiability* differs from *assignability* are: (1) no notice need be given of the transfer of a *negotiable* instrument; and (2) the transfer of such an instrument is not subject to equitable remedies (i.e., from a claim-ant who might assert a right to or under the instru-ment). See **assignment** & **negotiable instrument**.

negotiable instrument; commercial paper. These terms are not interchangeable. *Commercial paper* is now the more widely used term in the U.S. because of its use in Article 3 of the Uniform Commercial Code. As to the precise distinction, *commercial paper* is the broader term: it may include nonnegotiable as well as negotiable paper, whereas *negotiable instruments* are by definition negotiable ones only.

Generally, a writing is *negotiable* when it is signed by the maker or drawer; contains an unconditional promise or order to pay a sum certain in money, and no other promise, obligation, or power given by the maker or drawer; is payable on demand or at a definite time; and is payable to order or to bearer. The absence of any one of these elements makes commercial paper nonnegotiable.

negotiate = (1) to discuss or conduct a business trans-action, such as a contract or sale; or (2) to transfer (a negotiable instrument, such as a note or bond) in a way that makes the transferee the legal owner of the instrument—e.g. (sense 2): "When a cheque is trans-ferred, whether by delivery or endorsement, it is said to be *negotiated*, and negotiation is a kind of transfer [that] differs in important respects from the ordinary assignment of a contractual right." William Geldart,

Introduction to English Law 124 (D.C.M. Yardley ed., 9th ed. 1984).

neither . . . nor. A. Singular or Plural Verb. When one of the two subjects is singular, and the other is plural, the verb takes its number from the closer subject. So the verb is invariably singular if the second alternative is singular—e.g.: "*Neither the interests of* justice *nor common sense lends* any support to the decision to preserve the single sliver of the Commission's lawmaking power." *Dillon v. U.S.*, 130 S.Ct. 2683, 2705 (2010) (Stevens, J., dissenting). See SUBJECT–VERB AGREEMENT (E).

Moreover, the verb should match the nearest subject in number and person. Sometimes the correct form is admittedly awkward—e.g.: "Neither you nor I *is* [read *am*] likely to change the world." Jefferson D. Bates, *Writing with Precision* 82 (rev. ed. 1988).

B. Number of Elements. These correlative conjunctions should frame only two elements, not more; though it is possible to find modern and historical examples of *neither . . . nor* with more than two members, such constructions are, in Wilson Follett's words, "short of punctilious." E.g.:

- "The old lease *was neither surrendered, abrogated, nor annulled* [read *was not surrendered, abrogated, or annulled*]." *Smith v. Kerr*, 15 N.E. 70, 72 (N.Y. 1888).
- "We believe that the California Supreme Court's application of the minimum-contacts test in this case represents an unwarranted extension of *International Shoe* and would, if sustained, sanction a result that is *neither fair, just, nor reasonable* [read *not fair, just, or reasonable* or *unfair, unjust, and unreasonable*]." *Kulko v. Superior Ct. of Cal.*, 436 U.S. 84, 92 (1978) (per Marshall, J.).
- "Finding the decision by the ICC supported by substantial evidence and *neither arbitrary, capricious nor an abuse of discretion* [read *not arbitrary, capricious, or an abuse of discretion*], we deny the petitions." *Glazer Steel Corp. v. ICC*, 748 F.2d 1006, 1007 (5th Cir. 1984).
- "*Because Rummel neither signed, read, nor heard* [read *Because Rummel did not sign, read, or hear*] the entire document, these notes fail to qualify as a statement under [this] subsection." *U.S. v. Hogan*, 763 F.2d 697, 704 (5th Cir. 1985).

It is permissible, however, to use a second *nor* emphatically in framing three elements: "*Neither* inadvertent failure to provide adequate medical care, *nor* carelessness, *nor* even deliberate failure to conform to the standards suggested by experts is cruel and unusual punishment." *Ruiz v. Estelle*, 679 F.2d 1115, 1149 (5th Cir. 1982). Cf. **either (E).**

C. Parallelism. Not only ought there to be no more than two elements, as explained in (B), but also the elements ought to match each other syntactically. (See PARALLELISM.) E.g.:

- "Ex parte New York No. 1 makes it clear that the State *can neither be proceeded against directly nor impleaded* [read *can be neither proceeded against directly nor impleaded*] in an action brought against the private owners." Grant Gilmore & Charles L. Black Jr., *The Law of Admiralty* 612 (2d ed. 1975).
- "P was held not liable for trespass to the person, the harm being accidental, and due *neither to negligence nor lack of*

caution [read *neither to negligence nor to lack of caution*]." L.B. Curzon, *English Legal History* 256 (2d ed. 1979).

D. *Neither . . . or*. This phraseology is a rank error—e.g.:

- "How is a 'male feminism' possible [that] assumes *neither* a false commonality of male and female experience *or* [read *nor*] a false essentialism?" J.M. Balkin, *Turandot's Victory*, 2 Yale J.L. & Humanities 299, 302 (1990).
- "What if the intervention is *neither* foreseeable *or* [read *nor*] normal, but it leads to the same type of harm?" Steven Emanuel & William Behr, *Torts* 154 (1994).
- "It appears that the admission was *neither* fraudulent *or* [read *nor*] willful and was due to oversight." Charles L. Knapp et al., *Contracts* 92 (2003).

E. Beginning Sentences with. It is permissible, when introducing an additional point of contrast, to begin a sentence with *neither* or (more commonly) *nor*—e.g.: "It is at least problematic whether the now official Catholic view, that a fetus has a full human soul at conception, is consistent with the Thomist tradition. *Nor* was that view thought necessary, in the past, to justify the strongest condemnation of even very early abortion." Ronald Dworkin, *Life's Dominion* 42–43 (1993). See **nor.**

nemine contradicente; nemine dissentiente. Both of these LATINISMS mean "without opposition or dissent." Either phrase may be more accurate than *unanimously* in a given context, for some of those entitled to vote may have abstained. In any event, the definition just given probably serves better than either of the pretentious main entries.

NEOLOGISMS, or invented words, are to be used carefully and self-consciously. Usually they demand an explanation or justification, for the English language is quite well stocked as it is. The most obvious neologisms in -IZE, for example, are to be eschewed. New words must fill demonstrable voids, as *conclusory*, a 20th-century word, does. If a word is invented merely for the sake of novelty, then it is vexatious.

Some writers seem to relish neologisms, as if the new words alone could add freshness to writing. For most readers, they add merely irritation to writing—e.g.:

- "This *would not be contraventive or thwartive of our mandate*." *Buder v. Fiske*, 191 F.2d 321, 324 (8th Cir. 1951). (Why not *would not contravene or thwart our mandate*?)
- Lance S. Hamilton, *Ethnomiseducationalization: A Legal Challenge*, 100 Yale L.J. 1815 (1991). (Since the article is about ideas for which we already have words, why not *ethnocentric education, educational ethnocentrism, ethnocentric miseducation*, or some such phrase?)

Other writers self-consciously state that they have no adequate word. Their efforts are likely to fail (merely because the odds are stacked against neologists), but they have a utilitarian standard in mind—e.g.: "There is no accepted adjective from 'theft,' but the word '*theftous*' will here be used." Glanville Williams, *Textbook of Criminal Law* 645 n.2 (1978).

Legal language has been the source of many neologisms over the past century. In fact, lawyers have probably tended toward the latter of the two opposing disasters that Lon Fuller wrote of: "linguistic stagnation and grotesque fecundity." *Legal Fictions* 22 (1967). So Pollock and Maitland had it, rather uncharacteristically, all wrong: "The licence that the man of science can allow himself of coining new words is one which by the nature of the case is denied to lawyers." 2 Frederick Pollock & F.W. Maitland, *History of English Law* 31 (2d ed. 1905). Rather, "neologisms abound in modern legal writing, though both writer and reader are often unaware that certain commonplace law words have yet to find a home in English dictionaries." Bryan A. Garner, "The Missing Common-Law Words," in *The State of the Language* 235, 237 (Sir Christopher Ricks & Leonard Michaels eds., 1990). See LEGO-.

neonaticide. See **infanticide.**

nephew; niece. Legally speaking, are the children of a spouse's siblings one's *nephews* and *nieces*? No:

- "It is only by courtesy that the children of a husband's or wife's brothers and sisters are called '*nephews*' and '*nieces*.'" *Fedi v. Ryan*, 193 A. 801, 802 (N.J. 1937).
- "It is only 'loosely' that the son of a brother-in-law or sister-in-law is called a *nephew*." *In re Estate of Terney*, 396 P.2d 557, 558 (Or. 1964).

nepotism is best reserved for the sense "bestowal of official favors upon members of one's family," and not attenuated to refer to any friends or political connections. The root sense of *nepot-* in Latin is "nephew; grandson."

NEUTER FORMS. See SEXISM.

new lease on life. See POPULARIZED LEGAL TECHNICALITIES.

news is a singular noun—e.g.: "The *news has* an exchange value to one who can misappropriate it." *International News Serv. v. Associated Press*, 248 U.S. 215, 238 (1918) (per Pitney, J.).

newsagent. One word.

new trial. See **retrial.**

next friend; guardian *ad litem*; *prochein ami*. Technically, an incompetent or minor plaintiff sues by a *next friend*, whereas an incompetent or minor defendant is defended by a *guardian ad litem*; but the duties and powers of the representative are identical regardless of the title. *Dacanay v. Mendoza*, 573 F.2d 1075, 1076 n.1 (9th Cir. 1978).

Nonlawyers occasionally misunderstand *next friend* as if it were literal—e.g.: "We say that a minor brings a suit 'by his *next friend*'; that is, by his nearest friend." Richard Grant White, *Every-Day English* 415 (1880). "Nearest friend" is not a good translation: a *next friend* is usually a parent or general guardian.

The phrase *next friend* is to be preferred to the LAW FRENCH *prochein ami*, of which it is a LOAN TRANSLATION. E.g.:

- "The district court's [order] sought merely to clarify that the amount awarded to the minor children would be paid to their parents as their *next friends*." *Beliz v. W.H. McLeod & Sons Packing Co.*, 765 F.2d 1317, 1326 (5th Cir. 1985).
- "The Supreme Court articulated . . . the standard by which an individual is deemed competent or incompetent to assert his rights for purposes of conferring standing on *next-friend* petitioners." *Franklin v. Francis*, 997 F.Supp. 916, 925 (S.D. Ohio 1998).

See *prochein ami* & **ad litem.**

next of kin. See **heir (C).**

***next preceding** is an awkward phrase, arguably illogical, that commonly appears in drafting. E.g.:

- "In consideration of said sum of $12,500 referred to *in the next preceding paragraph* of this contract, the party of the first part agrees not to . . . ." *Valdosta Drug Co. v. Mashburn Drug Co.*, 188 S.E. 694, 695 (Ga. 1936). The drafting style here is hopelessly archaic and needs to be thoroughly revamped.
- "[Defendants] have willfully abandoned the children for more than four consecutive months *next preceding* [read *before*] the filing of this petition." *In re Stanfill*, 984 S.W.2d 925, 927 (Tenn. Ct. App. 1998).

The best practice in legal drafting is simply to refer to the paragraph by a direct citational reference. For example, a sentence in § 4.4 may refer directly to § 4.3. Whatever practice you adopt, you must be alert not to allow inserted provisions to make either a direct citation to another provision or a reference to the **next preceding* provision inaccurate.

nexus is the law's learned word for *connection* or *multiple connections*. Lawyers have long found it useful—e.g.:

- "The Due Process Clause requires a jurisdictional *nexus* or, as this Court has stated, 'some definite link, some minimum connection, between a state and the person, property or transaction it seeks to tax.'" *MeadWestvaco Corp. ex rel. Mead Corp. v. Illinois Dep't of Rev.*, 553 U.S. 16, 33 (2008) (Thomas, J., concurring).
- "The government has provided adequate evidence of a *nexus* between the firearm and the drug crime." *U.S. v. Norwood*, 603 F.3d 1063, 1072 (9th Cir. 2010).

The acceptable plural forms are *nexuses* (English) and *nexus* (Latin)—e.g.: "When both *nexuses* are established, the litigant will have shown a taxpayer's stake in the outcome." *Flast v. Cohen*, 392 U.S. 83, 103 (1968) (per Warren, C.J.). Some writers have betrayed their ignorance of Latin by writing *nexi*, as if it were a second-declension noun, whereas the word *nexus* is a fourth-declension noun—e.g.:

- "The state's theory would broaden the *Skiriotes* concept of 'citizen' to encompass all American nationals, and hence most if not all of the Bering Sea crabbers, because of their numerous *nexi* [read *nexuses* or *nexus*] with Alaska." *State v. Bundrant*, 546 P.2d 530, 555 (Alaska 1976).

- "The Lees denied that the application and initial premium . . . had been delivered in the District and emphasized the various *nexi* [read *nexuses* or *nexus*] mentioned above with the State of Maryland." *Lee v. Wheeler*, 810 F.2d 303, 304 (D.C. Cir. 1987). (In Latin, *nexi* = persons who have been reduced to quasi-slavery for debt!)

Cf. **apparatus** & **prospectus (A).** See PLURALS (A) & HYPERCORRECTION (A).

nice question = a subtle question. In this phrase, as in other similar ones, *nice* takes on the sense "not obvious or readily apprehended; difficult to decide or settle; demanding close consideration or thought" (*OED*). E.g.:

- "*Nice questions* have arisen as to what constitutes a dedication to the public." William F. Walsh, *A Treatise on Equity* 218 (1930).
- "The cases are divided on this *nice question.*" Charles Alan Wright, *The Law of Federal Courts* 245 (4th ed. 1983).

niece. See **nephew.**

niggardly (= grudging; stingy) derives from an Old Norse word (*hnøggr* "covetous; stingy"); it has nothing to do with the racial slur that is sounded similarly. E.g.: "A tall, heavy-set, good-looking Irishman, he was never *niggardly* about attorney fees." Murray T. Bloom, *The Trouble with Lawyers* 272 (1970). Even so, some speakers and writers have come to shun it just to avoid MISCUES or even serious misunderstandings. For an essay on the subject, see *Garner on Language and Writing* 236–38 (2009).

nihil ad rem (= irrelevant) serves no useful purpose in the language.

nil dicit; nihil dicit [L. "he (or she) says nothing"]. These Latin phrases are used adjectivally to mean "of or relating to a default judgment for the plaintiff entered after the defendant fails to file a timely answer." The form *nil dicit* slightly predominates. A contracted version of *nihil*, the form *nil* appeared even in classical Latin. E.g.: "This is an appeal from the trial court's refusal to grant [First State] a new trial after [Nelson] had been granted a *nil dicit* judgment." *First State Bldg. & Loan Ass'n v. B.L. Nelson & Assocs.*, 735 S.W.2d 287, 288 (Tex. App.—Dallas 1987).

In Texas, a *nil dicit* default judgment is contrasted with a no-answer default judgment: with the latter, the defendant fails both to file an answer and to make an appearance, whereas with a *nil dicit* default judgment, the defendant appears, and may even file preliminary motions, but fails to file an answer.

Some writers hyphenate the expression as a PHRASAL ADJECTIVE <a *nil-dicit* default judgment>. But the norm is to leave Latin phrases unhyphenated, even when they serve as unit modifiers. See PHRASAL ADJECTIVES (B).

NIMBY (= not in my backyard), an acronym dating from the 1980s, refers to the opposition by residents

to a proposal for a new development close to them. *NIMBY lawsuits* are brought by these residents (*NIMBY plaintiffs* or *Nimbies*) to block the development. The term is often used pejoratively to imply that these residents are selfish.

nine (old) men. This phrase, denoting the U.S. Supreme Court, sprang up when, during the early 20th century, the Court blocked progressive legislation largely because of the majority's personal, political, and social views. In 1936, a book appeared in which the phrase was used as the title: Drew Pearson & Robert Allen, *Nine Old Men* (1936). Countless similar uses of the phrase soon began to appear—e.g.:

- "The *nine men* in black robes hold the entire structure of the nation in the hallowed hollows of their hands." Fred Rodell, *Woe Unto You, Lawyers!* 41 (1939). (This use by Fred Rodell anticipates the title of his 1955 book, *Nine Men.*)
- "The '*nine old men*' of the United States Supreme Court are not so infirm that they cannot perform the most surprising handsprings." Ephraim Tutt, *Yankee Lawyer* 444 (1943).
- "After several setbacks Roosevelt vented his frustration with his 'court-packing' plan of 1937, railing at the '*nine old men*' (the youngest was sixty-two, their average age seventy-two) who blocked the path of progress." Donald D. Jackson, *Judges* 338 (1974).
- "[FDR's] success in remaking the Supreme Court of the '*Nine Old Men*' is . . . legend." Harvey G. Hudspeth, "The Roosevelt Court and the Changing Nature of American Liberalism," in 3 *Franklin D. Roosevelt and the Transformation of the Supreme Court* 216 (Stephen K. Shaw et al. eds., 2004).

See **Court-packing plan.**

nisi /**nɪ**-sɪ, **nɪ**-see, **nee**-see, *or* **nis**-ee/ [L. "unless"] = (of a court's ex parte ruling or grant of relief) having validity unless the adversely affected party appears and shows cause why it should be withdrawn. The word is commonly used in the phrase *rule nisi*—e.g.:

- "The motion to appoint counsel was filed and the *rule nisi* issued during pendency of James's notice of appeal." *State v. James*, 438 S.E.2d 399, 400 (Ga. Ct. App. 1993).
- "On October 13, 1992, the mother filed a petition for *rule nisi* requesting that the trial court hold the father in contempt for his failure to pay child support." *Leslie v. Beringer*, 636 So.2d 441, 442 (Ala. Civ. App. 1994).

See **decree absolute.**

nisi prius (lit., "unless before then") refers generally to a civil trial court in which issues are tried before the jury—as opposed to an appellate court. The curious reader may well wonder what the semantic path is from "unless before then" to "trial." The answer lies deep in the recesses of English legal history: the phrase *nisi prius* was a prominent one at the outset of the medieval writ directing the sheriff to summon a jury at Westminster, "unless before" the appointed date the judges of assize arrived in the county where the cause of action arose. If those itinerant justices did arrive, they would try the case locally instead of at Westminster. Because the writ concerned only trial by jury, it became associated with jury trials. In the U.S., the phrase has even been extended to refer to nonjury trials.

A little American law dictionary mangles this etymology, stating: "Literally translated [*nisi prius*] means 'unless the first,' i.e., unless it is the original or first forum it is not a '*nisi prius*' court." Stephen H. Gifis, *Law Dictionary* 320 (3d ed. 1991). The author's mistake lies in trying to find a modern meaning in the phrase *nisi prius*, which even 19th-century law reference works termed "unmeaning in its literal translation." 2 Alexander M. Burrill, *A Law Dictionary and Glossary* 233 (2d ed. 1867).

In England, the *nisi prius* system became defunct in 1971, when it was replaced by the system of Crown Courts. The phrase *nisi prius* is likewise obsolete in most parts of the U.S., but two American jurisdictions—New York and Oklahoma—continue to use the legal ARCHAISM. The phrase is almost always used attributively, that is, modifying a noun that follows—e.g.:

- "Recent jurisprudence, dispositive of all issues raised below, calls for reversal of the *nisi prius* postdecree order." *Evans v. Evans*, 852 P.2d 145, 147–48 (Okla. 1993).
- "The *nisi prius* court's position that any cause of action accrued in 1983 because plaintiff's assignor's right to future payments was rejected, is simply an assertion of an anticipatory breach by defendants." *Vigilant Ins. Co. v. Housing Auth.*, 614 N.Y.S.2d 533, 535 (App. Div. 1994).
- "Here the *nisi prius* judge's signature authenticates the judgment on the face of the memorial." *Aven v. Reeh*, 878 P.2d 1069, 1074 (Okla. 1994).

In most American jurisdictions, the JARGON phrase *nisi prius* would be replaced with *trial court's* in the first example, and with *trial* in the second and third examples.

nitpick is so spelled—not **knitpick*—though pointing this out may seem nitpicky. E.g.: "The *Hovanec* decision upon the facts there presented is hypertechnical, is an indulgence in *knitpicking* [read *nitpicking*], and is an obvious disregard of R.C. 4123.95." *Wires v. Doehler-Jarvis Div. of NL Indus., Inc.*, 345 N.E.2d 629, 632 (Ohio Ct. App. 1974).

nitroglycerine charge. See **dynamite charge.**

no; not. See NEGATIVES (E).

no bill, n. See **ignoramus.**

no-bill, vb. See NOUNS AS VERBS.

nobody. See **no one.**

no case. In English criminal procedure, a submission of *no case* (or *no case to answer*) is the same as the American lawyer's motion for *judgment of acquittal* (in federal practice) or motion for *directed verdict* (abolished by the federal rules but still used in some states). In effect, the defense counsel, at the close of the prosecution's *case-in-chief*, submits to the judge that there is no case that needs answering. British lawyers sometimes use the expression *directed verdict* as well. See **case-in-chief.**

*nocent (= guilty) is obsolete. *Innocent*, the opposite form, is common.

no-compete covenant is an illogical form of *covenant* [or *agreement*] *not to compete* or *noncompetition covenant* [or *agreement*]. It should be avoided in favor of either of these longer phrases. E.g.: "It seems reasonably clear that some allocation of the price to a covenant is necessary if a purchaser wants to deduct any amount for a *no-compete covenant* [read *covenant not to compete*]." See **noncompetition covenant.**

no contest; *nolo contendere*. The English phrase is no doubt preferable merely because it is more comprehensible to more people. Journalists rightly tend to use *no contest* even in jurisdictions in which the plea is called *nolo contendere*. E.g.: "City Manager David Ivory pleaded *no contest* Thursday to two misdemeanor charges of improperly accepting cash from a company that was doing business with the city." Selwyn D. Crawford, *FW Official Pleads No Contest to Getting Cash*, Dallas Morning News, 8 Dec. 1989, at 33A. As a PHRASAL ADJECTIVE, it is hyphenated: *no-contest plea*.

With a plea of *no contest* or *nolo contendere* (lit., "I do not wish to contend"), the defendant does not admit guilt but nevertheless agrees not to offer a defense. The primary legal purpose of such a plea—whichever name is used—is that the defendant retains the right to deny the finding of guilt in any other judicial proceedings.

no doubt. See **doubtless.**

no-fault divorce = divorce on either spouse's unilateral demand, without the necessity of proving elements that the law formerly required, such as adultery or cruelty. During the late 1960s and 1970s, the system of no-fault divorce was adopted throughout the U.S., as well as in England (1969) and Scotland (1977). The phrase is really a misnomer and an OXYMORON, for in divorce there is always enough fault to go around. What the courts and the parties (rightly) wanted to avoid was proving and apportioning fault in routine cases. See **divorce.**

no fewer. See **no less (A).**

no force or effect. See **force and effect.**

noisome is sometimes misconstrued as meaning "noisy; loud; clamorous." In fact, it means "noxious; malodorous." (Cf. **fulsome.**) The word is related etymologically to *annoy*. Justice Benjamin Cardozo, naturally, used it correctly: "If the house is to be cleaned, it is for those who occupy and govern it, rather than for strangers, to do the *noisome* work." *People ex rel. Karlin v. Culkin*, 162 N.E. 487, 493 (N.Y. 1928) (Cardozo, J., concurring).

no later than (= on or before) conveys an important nuance in the language of drafting. It is not equivalent to *before*, which literally does not include the date specified.

Although *within ten days after* might seem stylistically preferable to *no later than ten days after*, the choice is not a stylistic one. The two phrases have different meanings, as the following examples illustrate: (1) a motion for relief filed *within* ten days after entry of judgment; and (2) a motion for relief filed *no later than* ten days after entry of judgment. In the first version, judgment must be entered for the provision to apply; in the second version, no entry of judgment need occur for the provision to apply. If an event triggers the clock, *within* requires one to wait for that triggering event, but *no later than* does not.

nolens volens (= willingly or unwillingly) would be considered a far-fetched LATINISM in most modern legal prose—e.g.: "The contrary view would make the state courts, *nolens volens* [read *willingly or unwillingly*], in effect, inferior federal courts to enforce all federal statutes, whenever Congress so declares." *Walker v. Gilman*, 171 P.2d 797, 816 (Wash. 1946). See **willy-nilly**.

no less. A. And *no fewer*. The phrase *no less*, just like *less*, best refers to amounts or to mass nouns, not countable numbers. (See **less**.) *No fewer* is the better phrase when discussing numbers of things. But some excellent writers have nodded on this point—e.g.:

- "America has already formed treaties with *no less* [read *no fewer*] than six foreign nations." *The Federalist* No. 3, at 42 (John Jay) (Clinton Rossiter ed., 1961).
- "In *no less* [read *no fewer*] than twenty-four states, an acknowledgment by the father, orally or in writing, is sufficient." Max Radin, *The Law and You* 32 (1948).
- "He had appointed *no less* [read *no fewer*] than forty-two new justices of the peace." Fred Rodell, *Nine Men* 86 (1955).
- "The settlor could employ *no less* [read *no fewer*] than three different types of future interest." A.W.B. Simpson, *An Introduction to the History of the Land Law* 217 (1961).
- "Beven identified *no less* [read *no fewer*] than fifty-seven varieties of duty." J.H. Baker, *An Introduction to English Legal History* 476–77 (3d ed. 1990).
- "The point of law involved was one of extreme complexity and it was considered by *no less* [read *no fewer*] than fourteen judges sitting in the Court for Crown Cases Reserved." Rupert Cross & J.W. Harris, *Precedent in English Law* 86 (4th ed. 1991).

B. And *not less*. In drafting, the two phrases are indistinguishable, *no less* being the more natural and therefore the better form. E.g.: "The contract provided that . . . the terminating party had to give notice to the other party '*no less* than 10 days prior to the desired termination date.'" *American Fed'n of State, County &*

Mun. Employees, Local 380 v. Hot Spring County, Ark., 362 F.Supp.2d 1035, 1041 (W.D. Ark. 2004).

In other types of expository writing, however, *no less* connotes surprise: "He weighs *no less* than 300 pounds." That sentence expresses astonishment that he weighs so much. *Not less* is more clinical and dispassionate: "He weighs *not less* than 300 pounds." That sentence states matter-of-factly that he weighs at least that much and maybe more. See NEGATIVES (E).

nolle prosequi; non prosequitur; *nolle prosequitur.
A. As Nouns. The phrase *nolle prosequi* (lit., "not to wish to prosecute") denotes either (1) the legal notice of abandonment of suit; or (2) a docket entry showing that the plaintiff or the prosecution has relinquished the action. *Nolle* is frequently used as a shortened form—e.g.: "We conclude that the nine-month period between the *nolle* and the defendant's rearrest is not properly chargeable as a pretrial delay for purposes of speedy trial analysis." *State v. Gaston*, 503 A.2d 594, 597 (Conn. 1986).

Non prosequitur (lit., "he does not prosecute") is the judgment rendered against a plaintiff who has not pursued the case. *Non pros* is the shortened noun form, here functioning adjectivally: "Appellants contest on appeal the trial court's opening of a *non pros* judgment entered in their favor." *Geyer v. Steinbronn*, 506 A.2d 901, 905 (Pa. Super. Ct. 1986).

*Nolle prosequitur is a hybrid form that is simply meaningless.

B. As Verbs. *Nolle prosequi* is only a noun in England, but has two verb forms in the U.S., *nol-pros* and *nolle pros*. The term means "to abandon a suit or have it dismissed by a *nolle prosequi*." E.g.: "Plaintiff was arrested but never tried, and the charges against him were *nolle prossed*." *Jackson v. Jackson*, 201 S.E.2d 722, 723 (N.C. Ct. App. 1974). The earliest known use occurred in 1878.

Occasionally the phrase *nolle prosequi* is used as a verb in the U.S., although the shorter forms *nolle pros*, *nol-pros*, and *nol-pro* are more usual. E.g.: "Gruskin's decision to permit defendant to admit responsibility for careless driving and to *nolle prosequi* the OUIL [operating a motor vehicle under the influence of intoxicating liquor] charge was an executive function." *People v. Stackpoole*, 375 N.W.2d 419, 424 (Mich. Ct. App. 1985).

Nonpros = to enter a *non prosequitur* against. The past-tense form is *nonprossed*. Blackstone wrote *nonpros'd*. This word dates from about 1755.

nolo (L. "I do not wish") appears frequently as a shortened form of the full phrase, *nolo contendere*—e.g.:

- "The reason the *nolo* plea makes a difference is that it protects defendants in subsequent criminal or civil litigation growing out of the act on which the criminal prosecution is based." Marcia Chambers, *"Nolo" Means You're Guilty Sort Of*, Nat'l L.J., 9 Nov. 1987, at 13.
- "There are provisions for convictions based on *nolo* pleas and for verdicts of conviction that are not yet solidified in a judgment." Paul F. Rothstein, *Needed: A Rewrite*, Crim. Just., Summer 1989, at 20, 21.

nolo contendere (L. "I do not wish to contend") is so spelled. See **no contest.**

nominal = (1) in name only, but not in reality; or (2) of or relating to a noun. Sense 1 is the usual legal sense: a *nominal party* is one who, having some interest in or title to the subject matter of the lawsuit, will not be affected by any judgment—an example being the disinterested stakeholder in a garnishment action. (See **nominal consideration** & **nominal damages.**) Sense 2 is a grammatical one <the adjective *rental* soon came to have nominal uses>.

nominal consideration; inadequate consideration. *Nominal consideration* is only of token value, whereas *inadequate consideration* has substantial value that is patently less than the value of the performance promised or rendered in return. So to buy a $100,000 house, $10 might be termed *nominal consideration* while $30,000 might be termed *inadequate consideration*. The distinction matters in "exceptional cases in which the law treats promises or transfers supported only by *nominal consideration* differently from those supported by substantial or 'valuable' consideration (even though it may be inadequate)." G.H. Treitel, *The Law of Contract* 72 (8th ed. 1991).

nominal damages; substantial damages. *Nominal damages* are "awarded in a trivial amount merely as a recognition of some breach of a duty owed by a defendant to plaintiff and not as a measure of recompense for loss or detriment sustained." *Substantial damages* are "the result of an effort at measured compensation." Charles T. McCormick, *Handbook on the Law of Damages* 85 (1935). *Nominal damages* are symbolic; *substantial damages* are compensatory.

NOMINALIZATIONS. See BURIED VERBS.

nominate. See **designate.**

NOMINATIVE ABSOLUTES. See ABSOLUTE CONSTRUCTIONS.

nominee. See **candidate.**

no more than. See **not more than.**

NON- (= not) is the general-purpose negative prefix that has gained a great deal of ground since the 19th century. *Non-* often contrasts with *in-* or *un-* in expressing a nongradable contrast, rather than the opposite end of a scale, e.g., *nonlegal* as compared to *illegal*, or *nonscientific* as compared to *unscientific*. (See **nonconstitutional.**) Ordinarily, especially in AmE, the prefix is not hyphenated. A number of pitfalls lie in the way of its use, as categorized below. See generally NEGATIVES (B).

A. As a Separable Prefix. Except in a few historical phrases (e.g., the plea of *non assumpsit*), *non-* is properly used only as an inseparable or hyphenated prefix. Some legal writers, though, have tried to make it separable—e.g.:

- "[The Code] seems to reflect a congressional perception that the taxation of the exercise of *non qualified* [read *nonqualified*] stock options should be 'tightened up.'" *McDonald v. Commissioner*, 764 F.2d 322, 333 (5th Cir. 1985).
- "But a trustee also has some *non statutory* [read *nonstatutory*] powers." R.T. Oerton, *Trustees and the Enduring Powers of Attorney Act 1985*, 130 Solic. J. 23, 23 (1986).
- "The mere existence of a written contract governing the same subject matter does not preclude such recovery from *non parties* [read *nonparties*] so long as the other requirements for quasi contracts are met." *Seiden Assocs., Inc. v. ANC Holdings, Inc.*, 754 F.Supp. 37, 40 (S.D.N.Y. 1991).

B. With Nouns and Adjectives. Before adding *non-* to a noun or adjective, determine whether the word being negated has an antonym that would suffice. For example, if *nonpretextual* means merely "valid" or "legitimate," it makes little sense to write: "The State provided a plausible, *nonpretextual* [read *legitimate*], race-neutral justification for dismissing Benitez." *Diomampo v. State*, 185 P.3d 1031, 1039 (Nev. 2008). This infelicity may sometimes derive from tracking statutory language too closely, without searching for the most appropriate word. See SOUND OF PROSE, THE.

Another disadvantage in the use of *non-* is that it is beginning to displace the simplest negative, *not*. For example, "The cases relied upon in the opinion are *non-§ 1983 cases* [read *not § 1983 cases*]." *Grandstaff v. City of Borger*, 779 F.2d 1129, 1133 (5th Cir. 1986) (Hill, J., dissenting). As this example suggests, the use of this prefix to construct phrasal nouns can be especially awkward. "The critical issue before us concerns the order and allocation of proof in a *private, non-class action* [read *private suit, not a class action,*] challenging employment discrimination." *McDonnell Douglas Corp. v. Green*, 411 U.S. 792, 800 (1973) (per Powell, J.).

When adding *non-* to a compound adjective, the meaning can become especially murky: "*non-civil rights suit*"; "*nonper stirpes distribution*." E.g.: "Because the California community-property system already provides protection for a surviving spouse, the policy arguments made in *noncommunity-property states* [read *common-law states*] for allowing spouses to reach Totten trust account funds are of little value." *Estate of Allen*, 16 Cal. Rptr. 2d 352, 357 (Ct. App. 1993). *Noncriminal* can usually be rendered more straightforwardly *civil*; hence *civil trial* rather than *noncriminal trial*, *private school* (in AmE) rather than *nonpublic school*.

But the purpose of some negatives with *non-* is to cover a range of antonyms. For example, *noncivil* might mean more than just "criminal"; it might mean "criminal or administrative." Without an explanation, of course, this type of subtlety will be lost on many readers.

On the whole, *non-* adjectives should be avoided wherever possible, even if the avoidance means using more words. E.g.:

- "We must therefore affirm the District Court's declaratory judgment that the challenged provisions of the Arizona Constitution and statutes, as *applied to exclude nonproperty owners from elections* [read *applied to exclude those who do not own property from elections*] for the approval of the issuance of general obligation bonds, violate the Equal Protection Clause of the United States Constitution." *Phoenix v. Kolodziejski*, 399 U.S. 204, 213 (1970) (per White, J.).
- "In *nonautomobile cases* [read *cases not involving automobile accidents*] there may be a homeowner's policy that triggers the law suit and protects the parent in a direct suit." *Holodook v. Spencer*, 324 N.E.2d 338, 348 (N.Y. 1974).
- "We held unconstitutional a state statute authorizing the use of deadly force against fleeing suspects, not on its face, but only insofar as it authorized the use of lethal force against *unarmed and nondangerous suspects* [read *unarmed suspects who do not appear dangerous*]." *Brockett v. Spokane Arcades, Inc.*, 472 U.S. 491, 502 (1985) (per White, J.). *Unarmed* alone would probably suffice in this sentence.
- "A *nonnegligent plaintiff* [read *plaintiff who is not contributorily negligent*] may recover her total damages regardless of allocated percentages." *Shipp v. General Motors Corp.*, 750 F.2d 418, 425 (5th Cir. 1985).

Using the prefix *non-* with PHRASAL ADJECTIVES produces awkward results, e.g., *nonfact-witness expert, nonincome-producing, noninterest-bearing, nonpar-value, nontaxpaid.* E.g.:

- "It is undisputed that soybean production is *a non-water dependent activity* [read *an activity not dependent on water*]." *Louisiana Wildlife Fed'n, Inc. v. York*, 761 F.2d 1044, 1047 (5th Cir. 1985).
- "In some community-property states, assets [that] you acquire *in a non-community property jurisdiction* [read *while living in a common-law jurisdiction*] are, in effect, converted to community assets for purposes of disposition at death if you reside in the state when you die." Jonathan G. Blattmachr, *The Complete Guide to Wealth Preservation and Estate Planning* 257 (1999).

C. With Verbs. Although we have accepted verbal idioms such as *to nonplus a person* and *to nonsuit a case*, the prefix *non-* should not be used to create new verbs—e.g.: "[The Board] erred by not finding that respondent violated the Texas Term Contract Nonrenewal Act when it *nonrenewed* [read *did not renew*] . . . the petitioner." *Burke v. Central Educ. Agency*, 725 S.W.2d 393, 398 (Tex. App.—Austin 1987) (quoting counsel).

nonact. See **nonfeasance.**

nonage /**non**-ij/ = legal infancy; the condition of being underage. The term is rare today except in legal contexts—e.g.: "Unlike that of, say, a thirteen- or fourteen-year-old child's, this young woman's disability of *nonage* was very near its end." *In re Doe*, 973 So.2d 548, 571 (Fla. Dist. Ct. App. 2008). See **age of capacity** & **minority (A).**

nonbailable. See **bailable.**

nonbelief. See **disbelief.**

NONCE WORDS are terms coined for a particular occasion only. The inventor usually has no hope that the term will become established in the language. Judge Charles E. Clark probably had no hope that his word *erieantompkinated* would catch on. (See **Eriebound.**) The same must have been true of Frank Cooper's *res administrata*. (See **res administrata.**)

But that dictum is not absolute: the person who coined **lawyerphile* as an antonym of *lawyer-basher* surely hoped that the word would suddenly spread throughout the land. It has not. As a failed NEOLOGISM, it became just another forgotten nonce word. See **lawyer-basher.**

nonclergyable. See **clergyable.**

noncode state. See **code state.**

noncompetition covenant. The original phrase was *covenant not to compete* (= a provision in an employment agreement by which the employee agrees not to compete against the employer for some time after the employee leaves the job). In the late 20th century, this four-word phrase was reduced by half to form various phrases, including *noncompetition covenant* or *agreement*, which is preferable to *noncompete covenant* or *no-compete covenant*. The prefix *non-* may be joined to adjectives (as with *nonexistent, nonfatal, nonresponsive*), to nouns (as with *nonoccurrence, nonissue, nonacceptance*), or to present participles (as with *nonpaying, nonsmoking, nonvoting*). It is not at its best, however, when joined to a verb to make an adjective, as in *noncompete*. E.g.: "The plaintiffs rely on four cases [that] they claim support their position that the amounts received pursuant to the *non-compete* [read *noncompetition*] agreements are 'personal service income.'" *Furman v. U.S.*, 602 F.Supp. 444, 451 (D.S.C. 1984). *Noncompete* is not listed in most dictionaries, and we may justifiably hope that it never gains widespread approval. See **NON-, no-compete covenant** & ***anticompete.**

noncompliance. See **breach.**

non compos mentis; compos mentis. These LATINISMS (meaning lit. "not master of one's mind" and "master of one's mind") are now little used. But as long as words such as *insane* and similar words are used figuratively as terms of disparagement, these learned terms may be pressed into service as EUPHEMISMS. *Incompetent*, however, usually serves well in place of *non compos mentis*.

The *OED* contains no examples of *non compos mentis* used as an attributive noun, and it probably should not be so used: "When a minor, lunatic, idiot or *a non-compos mentis* [read *incompetent person*] may be a defendant to a suit and has no guardian . . . , the court shall appoint a guardian *ad litem*." Tex. R. Civ. P. 173 (West 2004). The strange hyphenation in that example suggests that the drafter somehow thought *non-compos* to be a PHRASAL ADJECTIVE and *mentis* a noun related to *men* or *man*. Of course, it really refers to the mind.

Although the plural form is *non compotes mentis*, that form is rarely if ever needed in English. When used as an English adjective, the phrase retains the singular form—e.g.: "It may be said, therefore, that the equitable obligations resting upon . . . committees of persons *non compotes mentis* [read *non compos mentis*] . . . are analogous to those resting upon and given against actual trustees." 4 John N. Pomeroy & Spencer W. Symons, *Treatise on Equity Jurisprudence* § 1088, at 263–64 (5th ed. 1941). See PLURALS (A).

nonconsent. In the context of rape accusations, courts have consistently interpreted this important word as requiring some type of physical resistance. At one time, the burden was rather high: the victim must have exhibited "utmost resistance." Susan Estrich, *Real Rape* 29 (1987). Today, the law having advanced, the meaning is not so rigid.

nonconstitutional; unconstitutional. These terms have distinct meanings. *Nonconstitutional* = of or relating to some legal principle other than a principle found in the U.S. Constitution—e.g.:

- "[*Kent v. Dulles*] did invalidate a burden on the right to travel; however, the restriction was voided on the *nonconstitutional* basis that Congress did not intend to give the Secretary of State power to create the restriction at issue." *Shapiro v. Thompson*, 394 U.S. 618, 649 (1969) (per Warren, C.J.).
- "*Miranda* established a *nonconstitutional* prophylactic rule, the violation of which creates an irrebutable presumption of coercion that is applicable in only a limited number of circumstances." *U.S. v. Cherry*, 759 F.2d 1196, 1209 (5th Cir. 1985).

Unconstitutional (the more familiar word) = in violation of, or not in accordance with, principles found in a constitution, esp. the U.S. Constitution—e.g.: "The three-judge District Court [held] that the Act and regulations in question were *unconstitutional* both under the Equal Protection Clause of the Fourteenth Amendment and under the Constitution of Alaska." *Reetz v. Bozanich*, 397 U.S. 82, 85 (1970) (per Douglas, J.). See **constitutional.**

*****noncredible.** See **incredible.**

nonculpable; *inculpable. Because the second is possibly ambiguous—meaning either "not culpable" or "able to be inculpated"—most criminal-law writers prefer *nonculpable*.

nondelegable duty. In tort law, this phrase does not mean what it literally says: a principal may indeed delegate a *nondelegable duty*, but upon doing so, the principal retains primary (as opposed to vicarious) responsibility if the duty is not properly performed. *See McDermid v. Nash Dredging & Reclamation Co.*, [1987] 3 W.L.R. 212, 215 (per Lord Hailsham). Cf. **duty.**

none. A. Number. *None* = (1) not one; or (2) not any. Hence it may correctly take either a singular or a plural verb—e.g.:

- "*None* of the promises *are* within the statute of frauds." Laurence P. Simpson, *Handbook on the Law of Suretyship* 132 (1950).
- "*None* of these arguments *is* notably strong, let alone conclusive." Andrew Ashworth, *Principles of Criminal Law* 229 (1991).

Generally speaking, *none is* is the more emphatic way of expressing an idea.

B. *Of none effect.* This phrase is an ARCHAISM for *of no effect.*

noneconomic. See **uneconomical.**

*****nonenforceable.** See **unenforceable.**

non est factum (lit., "it is not my deed") is LAW LATIN denoting the plea denying the execution of an instrument sued on—e.g.:

- "The questions in the case arise under the plea of *non est factum*, which puts in issue the execution of the instrument on which the action is brought." *McDonald v. Eggleston*, 26 Vt. 154, 159 (1853).
- "The plaintiff [contended] that the evidence submitted in proof of his plea of *non es factum* demanded a verdict in his favor." *Threlkeld v. Whitehead*, 98 S.E.2d 76, 81 (Ga. Ct. App. 1957).

Pl. *non est factums*. See **fact,** n. & **fraud (B).**

non est inventus. See **not found.**

nonetheless. One word in AmE, three (frequently) in BrE.

nonexpert. See **inexpert.**

nonfeasance; nonact. The two are distinguishable. Whereas *nonact* means merely the failure to act, *nonfeasance* implies the failure to act where a duty to act existed—e.g.: "A compelling showing may include, but is not limited to, adversity of interest, the representative's collusion with an opposing party, or *nonfeasance* by the representative." *State v. Cummings*, 540 S.E.2d 917, 927 (W. Va. 1999). See **feasance.** Cf. **malfeasance.**

*****nonforeseeable** is a NEEDLESS VARIANT of *unforeseeable*.

nonheritable. See **inheritable.**

nonincentive. See **disincentive.**

noninterpretive. See **interpretive.**

noninterpretivism. See **interpretivism.**

nonjudicial. See **injudicious** & **judicial.**

nonjury, adj. Though the phrase *nonjury trial* is current in BrE as well as AmE, the more geographically limited phrase *bench trial* (a condensed version of *trial to the bench*) seems stylistically preferable: the better practice is to name something for what it is rather than for what it is not. Even so, some lawyers and judges, from New York to the State of Washington, find *bench trial* an alien phrase.

Several legal writers, unfortunately, have pressed the adjective *nonjury* into service as an adverb—e.g.: "This case will proceed *nonjury* [read *without a jury*]." *Juckett v. Beecham Home Improve. Prods., Inc.,* 684 F.Supp. 448, 452 (N.D. Tex. 1988).

nonlapse statute. See **lapse statute.**

nonlawyer. It is a curious practice that lawyers (and others who write about law) divide the universe into *lawyers* and *nonlawyers.* But of course they do it of other professions and occupations as well—e.g.: "The Supreme Court later expressly limited the vessel owner's duty to *nonseamen* to situations where the workers were doing 'ship's work.'" *Woessner v. Johns-Manville Sales Corp.,* 757 F.2d 634, 645 (5th Cir. 1985). Although the word *layman* is usually unambiguous, the masculine suffix is a major disadvantage. (See SEXISM (B).) And few would seriously argue that *laypersons* is a palatable alternative. See **layperson.**

nonlegal = (1) not specifically related to law; or (2) not being a lawyer. Sense 1: "Despite what the lawyers say, it *is* possible to talk about legal principles and legal reasoning in everyday *non-legal* language." Fred Rodell, *Woe Unto You, Lawyers!* 12 (1939). Sense 2: "[The] Employment Appeal Tribunal . . . is presided over by a senior judge and behaves very much like an ordinary appeal court, though it also has *non-legal* members." P.S. Atiyah, *Law and Modern Society* 27 (1983). Cf. **alegal** & **extralegal.**

nonlitigious is the antonym of *litigious,* but not in the latter word's prevalent sense today (i.e., "fond of litigation"). Rather, *nonlitigious* corresponds to an older and currently infrequent sense of *litigious* (i.e., "involving litigation"). Hence, *nonlitigious* means not "court-shy" but "not involving litigation"—e.g.: "The legal services considered were 'typical *nonlitigious* matters for which the amount and work requirements would be reasonably foreseeable.'" Murray T. Bloom, *The Trouble with Lawyers* 44 (1970).

nonmarital child. See **bastard, illegitimate child** & **natural child.**

nonmaterial. See **immaterial.**

*****nonmeritorious.** See **unmeritorious.**

nonmovant (= a litigating party other than the one that has filed a motion currently under consideration) is omitted from most English-language dictionaries as well as most law dictionaries. But in American courts, it occurs with great frequency—e.g.:

- "The court should give credence to the evidence favoring the *nonmovant* as well as that 'evidence supporting the moving party that is uncontradicted and unimpeached.'" *Reeves v. Sanderson Plumbing Prods., Inc.,* 530 U.S. 133, 151 (2000) (per O'Connor, J.).
- "The requirement that the *nonmovant* must set forth 'specific facts' means that 'mere denials or conclusory statements are insufficient to survive summary judgment.'" *Enzo Biochem v. Applera Corp.,* 599 F.3d 1325, 1337 (Fed. Cir. 2010).

nonnegotiable. See **negotiable instrument.**

nonobject. See **object.**

*****nonobjectionable** is a NEEDLESS VARIANT of *unobjectionable.*

non obstante veredicto. See **judgment** *non obstante veredicto.*

nonoriginalism; living constitutionalism. These two terms are essentially synonymous, but one noted commentator has suggested a distinction. *Living constitutionalism* denotes the view that, with constitutional provisions concerned centrally with moral values such as liberty and equality, courts should follow evolving or contemporary norms. But *nonoriginalism* need not recognize such an obligation to espouse "enlightened" new interpretations. Mitchell N. Berman, *Originalism Is Bunk,* 84 N.Y.U. L. Rev. 1, 24 n.52 (2009). It seems highly improbable, however, that one who rejects the necessity of following the original meaning of a text would want to replace it with an unenlightened new interpretation. So again, the terms are synonymous. If anything, *living constitutionalism* sounds a little more connotatively palatable than *nonoriginalism,* in the simple sense that it sounds better to be for than against something. Cf. **originalism.**

nonparticipating royalty, used often in oil-and-gas law, is a venial REDUNDANCY: all mineral royalties are nonparticipating.

nonperformance. See **breach.**

nonplussed. The form *-ss-* is preferred.

nonpretextual = not founded on a pretext. E.g.: "[The] reasons to support the termination were . . . found by the jury to be *nonpretextual*." *Wheeler v. Mental Health & Mental Retardation Auth. of Harris County, Tex.,* 752 F.2d 1063, 1071 (5th Cir. 1985). Actually, the jury found that the dismissal was not pretextual—so the finding was a negative one. To say that it "found the dismissal to be nonpretextual" wrongly suggests that the jury answered a question asking whether the dismissal was *nonpretextual*; instead, the jury was asked whether the dismissal was *pretextual,* and it answered "no." See **pretextual** & NON- (B).

nonprobate = other than by will; of or relating to some method of disposition apart from wills—e.g.:

"Termination of joint tenancy and life estate are administrative, *nonprobate* methods to designate the survivor of a property interest." Mark T. Johnson, Comment, *A "Simple" Probate Should Not Be This Complicated*, 2008 Wis. L. Rev. 575, 576 n.1.

nonprofit; not-for-profit. The first is more common, but *not-for-profit* is increasingly used in AmE for greater accuracy: *nonprofit* corporation misleadingly suggests that the corporation makes no profits; but such a corporation actually *does* earn profits and then applies them to charitable purposes. *Not-for-profit* is thought to reveal more accurately that the purpose is not for private gain, though indeed the organization may profit.

Whereas *nonprofit corporation* and *not-for-profit corporation* predominate in AmE, *non-profit-making organization* is the usual BrE phrase.

nonpros. See *nolle prosequi.*

non prosequitur. See *nolle prosequi.*

***nonrebuttable** is a NEEDLESS VARIANT of *irrebuttable*. E.g.: "The fact that two nonresident applicants for a marriage license are of the same sex works an automatic, *nonrebuttable* disqualification of their application to marry in Massachusetts." *Cote-Whitacre v. Department of Pub. Health*, 844 N.E.2d 623, 658 (Mass. 2006) (Marshall, C.J., concurring).

nonrecourse rule. See **no-recourse rule.**

nonrefoulement. See **refoulement.**

nonresponsive, rather than *unresponsive*, is the usual adjective to describe a witness's answer that is somehow off the point—e.g.: "Witnesses are warned to answer questions directly and to the point, and to add nothing superfluous, . . . because extra information may be objected to as '*unresponsive*' [read '*nonresponsive*'] by the cross-examining attorney." Robin T. Lakoff, *Talking Power: The Politics of Language in Our Lives* 90 (1990).

NONRESTRICTIVE CLAUSES. See **that & which.**

non sequitur should be spelled as two words, not hyphenated or spelled as one word. The phrase is frequently misspelled *-tor* or *-tar*.

nonstatutory. This word is sometimes replaceable by *judicial*, *administrative*, or some other descriptive word, as in *judicial policymaking* rather than *nonstatutory policymaking*. If it fits, the more specific word should oust *nonstatutory*.

nonsuit, vb., = (1) of a plaintiff, to seek a voluntary dismissal of (a case or a defendant); or (2) of a court, to dismiss (a case or a defendant) because the plaintiff has failed to make out a legal case or to proffer

sufficient evidence. This verb has been part of lawyers' language since the 16th century. E.g.:

- (Sense 1) "Before trial began, the . . . plaintiffs *nonsuited* all the defendants except [one]." *Quorum Health Res., LLC v. Maverick County Hosp. Dist.*, 308 F.3d 451, 455 (5th Cir. 2002).
- (Sense 2) "The trial court *nonsuited* count II with prejudice." *Carroll v. Curry*, 912 N.E.2d 272, 273 (Ill. App. Ct. 2009).

***nonsuitability.** The preferred antonyms of *suitable* and *suitability* are *unsuitable* and *unsuitableness*. **Nonsuitability*, a NEEDLESS VARIANT of *unsuitableness*, unsuitably suggests a relationship with *nonsuit*. Yet it is perversely used in AmE legal contexts. E.g.: "The Secretary of Agriculture shall, within ten years after September 3, 1964, review, as to its suitability or *nonsuitability* [read *unsuitableness*] . . . for preservation as wilderness, each area." Wilderness Act, 16 U.S.C. § 1132(b) (2011). See **nonsuit.**

***nontaxpaid** is an opaque, ugly word to avoid. E.g.: "Defendant has had a reputation with me for over four years as being a trafficker of *nontaxpaid* distilled spirits." A less concise wording should be used, e.g., *trafficker of distilled spirits upon which no taxes had been paid.*

nontortious. Just as **tortuous* is sometimes misused for *tortious* (see **tortious (B)**), so **nontortuous* has been misused for *nontortious*—e.g.: "Plaintiffs insist that this is not a case involving conflicting claims to the ownership or *nontortuous* [read *nontortious*] use of water." *Friendswood Dev. Co. v. Smith-Southwest Indus., Inc.*, 576 S.W.2d 21, 24 (Tex. 1978).

nontriggerman (= a murder defendant who did not actually kill the decedent and might not have intended to do so) is odd-looking but perhaps necessary—e.g.: "Conservative justices were looking for a case like this one in which to reverse or limit a prior ruling that had prohibited the infliction of the death penalty on a *nontriggerman*—that is, a conspirator who himself had not killed the victim or intended his death." Alan Dershowitz, *Letters to a Young Lawyer* 122 (2009). See SEXISM (B).

nonuser. See **user** & -ER (B).

no one; nobody. These have traditionally been regarded as singular nouns that act as singular antecedents—e.g.: "*No one* should be punished for changing *their* [read *his or her*] religious beliefs." Nicholas Garcés, Comment, *Islam: Till Death Do You Part?*, 16 Sw. J. L. & Trade Am. 229, 230 (2010). See **he or she.**

But the language is changing—BrE more rapidly than AmE—so that *no one . . . they* may soon be regarded as standard. Some consider this change a defilement, others a tremendous advance. However you characterize it, it seems inevitable. See SEXISM (A) & CONCORD (B). Cf. **none.**

***noplace** is a barbarism for *nowhere.*

no pun intended. See WORD-PATRONAGE & PUNS.

no question but that. The *but* in this phrase is unnecessary, the better phrase being *no question that*—e.g.: "There can be *no question but that* [read *no question that*] jurisdiction to review and to affirm or set aside the Secretary's order here involved became fully vested in the court upon the filing of the partnership's petition." *White v. U.S.*, 342 F.2d 481, 482 (8th Cir. 1965).

nor. Where the negative of a clause has already appeared and a disjunctive conjunction is needed, *or* is generally better than *nor.* The initial negative carries through to all the elements in an enumeration. E.g.:

- "When on the witness stand on the trial of this case, however, he could not see the trial judge *nor* [read *or*] an examiner who was within five feet of him *nor* [read *or*] the foreman of the jury six feet away." *Smith v. Sneller*, 26 A.2d 452, 453 (Pa. 1942).
- "The Commonwealth states the plea agreement remained open, a statement which it has not supported by any written communication by it *nor* [read *or*] by any affidavit by the prosecutor." *Boyd v. Waymart*, 579 F.3d 330, 343 (3d Cir. 2009).

See **not** (C) & **neither . . . nor** (D).

no-recourse rule = the traditional common-law rule barring recourse to legislative history as an aid in statutory interpretation. The rule was first announced in the famous copyright case of *Millar v. Taylor*, [1769] 4 Burr. 2303, 98 Eng. Rep. 201 (K.B.). In that case, Justice Willes stated: "The sense and meaning of an Act of Parliament must be collected from what it says when passed into a law; and not from the history of changes it underwent in the house where it took its rise. That history is not known to the other house, or to the Sovereign." 4 Burr. at 2332, 98 Eng. Rep. at 217. Willes therefore interpreted Queen Anne's Copyright Act from its specific language and within its four corners. *Id.* The no-recourse rule was well accepted in 18th-century America. *See* Hans W. Baade, *"Original Intent" in Historical Perspective*, 69 Tex. L. Rev. 1001, 1010–11 (1991). Synonyms are *nonrecourse rule* and (in BrE) *exclusionary rule.*

no respecter of persons, the law is. To many, this English-language legal MAXIM seems to say nearly the opposite of what it actually denotes. The point is not that the law disrespects persons, but that it pays no special regard to one's station in life: speaking ideally (if not idealistically), the law treats a homeless person with the same respect as it would a bishop. E.g.:

- "The law (as we are often told) is *no respecter of persons.* Without being universally true, this is a principle [that] has always applied with special force to the law of homicide. Thus, the villein could not be killed by his lord with impunity. Nor could the slave, even in Anglo-Saxon times, be killed by his master." J.W. Cecil Turner, *Kenny's Outlines of Criminal Law* 104 (16th ed. 1952).

- "The Criminal Court of Appeals in Oklahoma in 1913 spoke in the tradition of this country's dedication to due process and equal protection when it declared that the law is *no respecter of persons.*" *Griffin v. Illinois*, 351 U.S. 12, 19 n.16 (1956) (per Black, J.).
- "The law is *no respecter of persons.* All persons including corporations stand equal before the law and are to be dealt with as equals in a Court of justice." *In re Bendectin Litig.*, 857 F.2d 290, 322 (6th Cir. 1988).

no-right. A *no-right* (= the absence of right against another in some particular respect) is the correlative of a privilege. The term is often discarded as being a purely negative concept—e.g.: "If a *no-right* is something that is not a right, the class of *no-rights* must, it is said, include elephants." John Salmond, *Jurisprudence* 240 n.(u) (Glanville L. Williams ed., 10th ed. 1947). But rightly viewed, negative terms like *no-right* are often useful: "Words like '*no-right*' and 'no duty' may seem uncouth at first sight, but it is surely a clear and useful statement to say that 'right' sometimes means 'no-duty not.'" *Id.*

norm is generally considered a broad term, broader even than "legal rule." A *norm* establishes acceptable and unacceptable standards of behavior; these are addressed to nonlawyers as well as to judges. *Norms* include not only public-policy imperatives (e.g., thou shalt not kill) but also rules for private transactions (e.g., if you offer to make a bargain and the other party accepts, you are contractually bound).

Roscoe Pound explained the so-called *norm* theory of law as viewing law as "a body of *norms* (models or patterns) of conduct or of decisions established or recognized by the state in the administration of justice." *Outlines of Lectures in Jurisprudence* 75 (5th ed. 1943). He conceived of a hierarchy of *norms*, presumably starting with "thou shalt obey the Constitution," and descending through statutes, judicial decisions, regulations, and so on down to commercial customs that a court might recognize.

***normalcy** has traditionally been considered inferior to *normality.* Born in the mid-19th century and later used by President Harding, **normalcy* has never been accepted as standard by the best writing authorities—e.g.:

- Daniel K. Tarullo, *Beyond* Normalcy [read *Normality*] *in the Regulation of International Trade*, 100 Harv. L. Rev. 546, 546 (1987).
- "After [Hurricane] Rita, respondent was absorbed with issues involving the school board and its attempt to return to *normalcy* [read *normal*]." *In re Spruel*, 24 So.3d 198, 200 (La. 2009).

normal wear and tear. See **wear and tear.**

normative (= establishing or conforming to a norm or standard) dates from 1852. The word has grown greatly in popularity since the 1980s—e.g.:

- "A *normative* analysis would require data, not currently available, on the size of the externality created by limited liability and the net effects of regulatory attempts to reduce it." Frank H. Easterbrook & Daniel R. Fischel,

Limited Liability and the Corporation, 52 U. Chi. L. Rev. 89, 114 (1985).

- "If [the description] is meant, however, as a *normative* description of what courts *should* ordinarily do when interpreting [criminal] statutes . . . then I surely do not agree." *Flores-Figueroa v. U.S.*, 129 S.Ct. 1886, 1894 (2009) (Scalia, J., concurring in part).

nostra sponte. See **sua sponte.**

nostrum (= panacea) forms the plural *nostrums*, not *nostra—e.g.: "But advertisements of *nostrums* for restoration of 'lost manhood' have appeared in the daily newspapers for at least fifty years." *U.S. v. Parkinson*, 240 F.2d 918, 921 (9th Cir. 1956). See PLURALS (A).

not. A. Placement of. When used in constructions with *all* and *every*, *not* is usually best placed just before those words. E.g.:

- "Justice Holmes reminded us that *every moral question could not* [read *not every moral question can*] be submitted to the law." Francis R. Kirkham, *Problems of Complex Civil Litigation*, 83 F.R.D. 497, 504 (1979).
- "Under Pennsylvania law, *every contract does not imply* [read *not every contract implies*] a duty of good faith." *Parkway Garage, Inc. v. Philadelphia*, 5 F.3d 685, 701 (3d Cir. 1993).

See **all** (B).

B. *Not . . . nor.* This construction should usually (where short clauses are involved) be *not . . . or*. E.g.: "The verdict exonerating the builder from negligence and finding the lessee culpable is *not inherently inconsistent nor contrary to* [read *not inherently inconsistent with or contrary to*] the instructions." *Erickson v. Walgreen Drug Co.*, 232 P.2d 210, 214 (Utah 1951). See **nor** & NEGATIVES.

C. In Typos. *Not* is a ready source of trouble. Sometimes it becomes *now*, and sometimes it drops completely from the sentence—e.g.: "The Legislature expressly refused to extend the concept of privilege when adopting the discovery procedures. Since privilege is created by statute it *should* [read *should not*] be extended by judicial fiat." John Kaplan & Jon R. Waltz, *Cases and Materials on Evidence* 506 (6th ed. 1988).

Problems of that kind have driven print journalists to "live in perpetual fear of the word *not* either being dropped by a printer or being changed from *not* to *now*. Therefore, wherever possible, they shy away from the word *not*, even at the expense of strict accuracy." Robert Sack, *Hearing Myself Think: Some Thoughts on Legal Prose*, 4 Scribes J. Legal Writing 93, 98 (1993). Notably, it is this very fear that leads newspaper writers to prefer *plead innocent* over the more accurate phrase, *plead not guilty*. See **plead innocent.**

D. And *naught.* See **further affiant sayeth naught** (B).

E. *Not only . . . but also . . . .* See **not only . . . but also.**

notable; noteworthy; noticeable. *Noticeable* = easily seen or noticed (as, e.g., scars); it is generally confined to physical senses. *Notable* (having basically the same meaning) is applied to qualities as well as to material things—e.g.:

- "Today's cases are *notable* for their stark illustration of the inadequacy of the majority's chosen formal analysis." *Zelman v. Simmons-Harris*, 536 U.S. 639, 695 (2002) (Souter, J., dissenting).
- "This last failing is particularly *notable* in view of plaintiff's obligation to plead a set of facts that plausibly give rise to a potential claim." *Lefkowitz v. Bank of N.Y.*, 676 F.Supp.2d 229, 260 (S.D.N.Y. 2009).

Noteworthy, a near-synonym, means "worthy of notice or observation; remarkable." E.g.: "*Noteworthy* to this discussion is that nothing in the rule states that 'fundamental error' is a ground for relief." *Hughes v. State*, 22 So.3d 132, 134 (Fla. Dist. Ct. App 2009).

not all. See **not** (A) & **all** (B).

notarial is the adjectival form of *notary*.

notarize, originally an Americanism dating from the 1930s, is now commonplace in AmE—e.g.: "In order to administer oaths to these workers and to *notarize* their statements for use in civil litigation, petitioner applied in 1978 to become a notary public." *Bernal v. Fainter*, 467 U.S. 216, 218 (1984). In BrE, the word is still, in some quarters, considered something of an atrocity; British lawyers tend to say *notarially validated* instead of *notarized*.

notary; notary public. *Notary* is a common ellipsis of *notary public* in both AmE and BrE. Pl. *notaries public*. In this phrase, *public* is a POSTPOSITIVE ADJECTIVE.

not a true bill. See **ignoramus.**

not . . . because. See **because** (B).

note = lawnote. See **annotation.**

note; draft. A *note* is a simple promise by one party to pay money to another party or to bearer. A *draft* is an order by one person (the drawer) to pay another person (the drawee), demanding that the drawee pay money to a third person (the payee) or to bearer.

not . . . either. See **either** (B).

note up is the approximate British equivalent of the American term *shepardize*. The British call their citators *noter-ups*, or, in some Commonwealth countries, *noter-uppers*. See **shepardize.**

noteworthy. See **notable.**

not-for-profit. See **nonprofit.**

not found is the English-language equivalent of the LAW LATIN *non est inventus*, sometimes abbreviated *n.e.i.* One phrase or the other is commonly used on a sheriff's return of process, saying that the defendant is not to be found in the sheriff's jurisdiction. For obvious reasons, *not found* is preferable.

not guilty. If a jury finds that a criminal defendant is *not guilty*, that finding does not mean (as some mistakenly believe) that the defendant did not commit the act complained of. The defendant may not have had the requisite mental state or may have had some justification or excuse. See **guilty.**

nothing less than. With this phrase, "the risks of ambiguity are very great" (*MEU2* 398). The problem is that the word *less* may function either as an adjective or as an adverb, the resulting senses being contradictory.

When *less* functions as an adjective, the sense of the phrase *nothing less than* is "the same thing as; quite equal to." E.g.: "What the majority has unintentionally accomplished in embracing this case is *nothing less than* the wholesale creation of a World Court." *Alperin v. Vatican Bank*, 410 F.3d 532, 568–69 (9th Cir. 2005).

But even in that sentence, *less* could be read as an adverb, so that the phrase *nothing less than* might mean "any thing other than; something vastly different from." A reader who understands the phrase in that sense is in for a serious MISCUE. And the reader's misunderstanding is entirely understandable, as the following sentence illustrates: "The Hanoverians in Atholl expected *nothing less than* an attack by Lloyd George." 4 Andrew Lang, *A History of Scotland from the Roman Occupation* 504 (1907). Did they expect an attack? Or did they not?

notice, n. A. Senses. *Notice* may refer to two quite different ideas: (1) legal notification required by law or imparted by operation of law as a result of some fact such as the recording of instruments; or (2) information that may be required under a contract. For the distinction between *notice* and *knowledge*, see **knowledge (B).** See also **judicial notice.**

B. Punctuation with. It should be *two weeks' notice*, not *two weeks notice*. The apostrophe is obligatory because there's a genitive within the phrase: *notice of two weeks = two weeks' notice*. It's also permissible to write of *a two-week notice*. But if the *-s* is added, it must have an apostrophe. See POSSESSIVES (C).

C. And *constructive knowledge*. See **knowledge.**

notice, vb. (= to give legal notice to or of), is a LEGALISM that is likely to strike nonlawyers as quite odd—e.g.:

- "Counsel for defendant . . . stated that they did not have [the letter and] had not looked for it, not having been *noticed* to bring it to the trial." *Stewart v. Blackwood Elec. Steel Corp.*, 130 S.E. 447, 448 (W. Va. 1925).
- "Unless you have already done so, *notice* the depositions of all expert witnesses being offered by your opponent."

Mark A. Dombroff, *Litigation: A Trial Preparation Checklist*, 312 PLI/Lit 343, 347 (1986).

- "It was not her duty to *notice* a hearing on the objection, or alternatively, her failure to do so was due to excusable neglect." *In re Nunez*, 196 B.R. 150, 159 (Bankr. App. 9th Cir. 1996).
- "Plaintiff's motion for leave to file a second amended complaint has been *noticed* for a hearing . . . before the U.S. Magistrate Judge." *Hinton v. Trans Union, LLC*, 654 F.Supp.2d 440, 445 n.12 (E.D. Va. 2009).

Notice should be reserved for the giving of legal notice. Avoid using it for providing other types of notice—e.g.:

- "TACA International Airlines, in the midst of collective-bargaining negotiations, *noticed* [read *made known*] its intent to relocate its pilot base." *Airline Pilots Ass'n v. TACA Int'l Airlines*, 748 F.2d 965, 967 (5th Cir. 1984). (To the nonlawyer, this usage confusingly suggests *notice* in the sense "to observe.")
- "It has been *noticed* [read *noted*, i.e., previously in a book] that a record will estop the parties to it and those claiming under them." John Indermaur, *Principles of Common Law* 18 (2009).

notice, judicial. See **judicial notice.**

noticeable. See **notable.**

notice pleading. See **code pleading.**

notice to quit (BrE) = *notice to vacate* (AmE). See **quit.**

notifiable, in BrE phrases such as *notifiable disease* and *notifiable offence*, is built from an old sense of *notify* (not current in AmE): rather than bearing its common meaning ("to give notice of; inform"), *notify* here means "to make known; proclaim; announce." In G.B., some serious diseases (e.g., cholera, diphtheria, scarlet fever, and typhoid) are classed as *notifiable diseases*—that is, they require anyone with knowledge that someone has the disease to contact the authorities. A *notifiable offence* is a serious crime that can be tried in the Crown Court.

notify. See **notifiable.**

not inconsistent with. See **consistent (B)** & NEGATIVES (B).

not law is a phrase that common-law lawyers use when arguing that an old court decision is wrong or obsolete—e.g.: "A decision, to be binding, must not only emanate from high authority, but must be 'good law': if it once earns the reputation of being '*not law*,' it perishes, sometimes by express disapproval, more often by cold disregard. If all else fails, the blame for its defects may be laid at the door of the reporter—sometimes not without cause." Carleton K. Allen, *Law in the Making* 297 (7th ed. 1964).

not less. See **no less (B).**

not more than. The more natural idiom is *no more than*.

not . . . nor. See **not** (B).

not only . . . but also. These correlative conjunctions must frame syntactic parts that match—e.g.:

- "Each of these policies designated *not only* Smith and his wife Sybil as insureds, *but also* a corporate name, Rolling Hills Golf and Racquet Club, Inc." *Smith v. Edward M. Thompson Agency, Inc.*, 430 So.2d 859, 859 (Ala. 1983) (matching parts: noun [*Smith and his wife*], noun [*a corporate name*]).

- "The document that appears in the record of this case contains *not only* Smith's signature *but also* the signature of someone identified as his attorney . . . to sign 'if represented.'" *Smith v. State*, 785 S.W.2d 465, 467 (Ark. 1990) (matching parts: noun [*Smith's signature*], noun [*signature of someone identified*]).

Problems arise when the syntactic parts don't match— e.g.: "That conduct *led not only to revocation of parole but also forfeiture* of street time." *Johnson v. D.C. Det. Ctr.*, 532 F.Supp.2d 4, 6 (D.D.C. 2008) (unmatching parts: prepositional phrase [*led to revocation*], nonsense [*led forfeiture*]). A suggested revision: *led not only to revocation of parole but also to forfeiture of street time.* See PARALLELISM.

One common failing in the *not only* constructions is to omit the *also* after *but*—e.g.:

- "No one has questioned the proposition that the holding covers *not only* such cross-claims *but* [add *also*] impleaders of third parties." Grant Gilmore & Charles L. Black Jr., *The Law of Admiralty* 939 (2d ed. 1975).

- "A publication may be made *not only* intentionally *but* [add *also*] negligently." William Geldart, *Introduction to English Law* 137 (D.C.M. Yardley ed., 9th ed. 1984).

- "The Framers and the citizens of their time intended *not only to protect* the integrity of individual conscience in religious matters, *but* [add *also*] to guard against the civic divisiveness that follows when the government weighs in on one side of religious debate." *McCreary County v. ACLU of Ky.*, 545 U.S. 844, 876 (2005) (per Souter, J.).

See **not** (B).

Another possible construction is *not only . . . but . . . as well.* But a writer who uses this phrasing should not add *also*, which is redundant with *as well*—e.g.:

- "Feminist methods and insights [must] be adopted *not only* by female scholars, *but also* [read *but*] by males *as well*." J.M. Balkin, *Turandot's Victory*, 2 Yale J.L. & Humanities 299, 302 (1990).

- "We cannot quarrel with a conclusion of a school administrator that treating a particular student with such care might be to the advantage *not only* of the pupil *but also* [read *but*] of the other students in the school *as well*." *Hatton v. Wicks*, 744 F.2d 501, 504 (5th Cir. 1984).

- "The finding of nonexistence of a constitutional claim for immunity purposes necessarily decided the whole case *not only* in favor of the officer *but also* in favor of the city *as well* [delete *as well*]." *Brennan v. Township of Northville*, 78 F.2d 1152, 1158 (6th Cir. 1996).

notorious may mean either "famous" or "infamous," though it usually carries strong connotations of unfavorable renown. *Notoriety* is generally more neutral, although it is coming to be tinged with the connotations of its corresponding adjective.

not proven. See **proved.**

no true bill. See **ignoramus.**

not sufficient funds. See **NSF.**

not unreasonable. See NEGATIVES (B).

notwithstanding. A. Grammatical Use. This preposition is an interesting word. In drafting, it commonly means "despite," "in spite of," or "although" and appears in sentences such as this one: "*Notwithstanding* the limitations contained in § 3.5, Mondraff will be offered the first option to quote competitive terms and conditions to Nuboil."

The question that literalist drafters ask is, What doesn't withstand what else? Are the limitations of § 3.5 "not withstanding" (i.e., subordinated to) the present section, or is the present section "not withstanding" (subordinated to) § 3.5? Because the former is the correct reading, some believe that *notwithstanding* should be sent to the end of the phrase in which it appears: *The limitations contained in § 3.5 notwithstanding*, as opposed to *Notwithstanding the limitations contained in § 3.5.*

But that literalist argument is very much in vain, as the *OED* attests with a 14th-century example of *notwithstanding* as a prepositional sentence-starter. This usage has been constant from the 1300s to the present day. In fact, the construction with *notwithstanding* after the noun first appeared more than a century later, and has never been as frequent. The *Century Dictionary* explains: "As the noun usually follows [the word *notwithstanding*], the [word] came to be regarded as a prep. (as also with *during*, ppr.), and is now usually so construed." 3 *The Century Dictionary and Cyclopedia* 4029 (1914). The word does not set up a DANGLER because it does not function as a participle.

B. Followed by *that*. When introducing a verbless phrase, *notwithstanding* need not be followed by *that*. E.g.: "The plurality seems to conclude [that] Article 75 of Protocol I to the Geneva Conventions is binding law *notwithstanding* the earlier decision by our Government not to accede to the Protocol." *Hamdan v. Rumsfeld*, 548 U.S. 557, 654 (2006) (Kennedy, J., concurring in part).

Otherwise, grammar demands that when the term introduces a clause, it should usually be followed by *that*—e.g.:

- "The law is in accord in favoring free competition, since ordinarily it is essential to the general welfare of society, *notwithstanding* [insert *that*] competition is not altruistic but is fundamentally the play of interest against interest." *Goldman v. Harford Road Bldg. Ass'n*, 133 A. 843, 846 (Md. 1926).

- "The instrument is likely to be upheld *notwithstanding* [insert *that*] it includes additionally a reservation of power to amend the trust in whole or in part." *In re Petralia's Estate*, 198 N.E.2d 200, 203 (Ill. App. Ct. 1964).

Even so, the phrase can be boiled down to a simpler wording: see **notwithstanding the fact that.**

C. And *subject to*. The legal drafter often needs these correlative terms, *notwithstanding* to introduce a superordinate provision and *subject to* to introduce a subordinate provision. Hence *Notwithstanding section 7, the maximum expenditure will be $10,000* (suggesting that this ceiling is paramount, even if the calculations under section 7 might seem to lead to a higher number); and *Subject to section 7, the maximum expenditure will be $10,000* (suggesting that this ceiling might be overridden by factors mentioned in section 7). Both phrasings suggest an overlap in coverage; both make explicit the hierarchical effect of the overlap.

notwithstanding anything to the contrary contained herein, an ungainly phrase often placed in complex contracts to introduce the most important provisions, can be fairly said to mean "the true agreement is as follows." It is best used when a lawyer wants one provision in a long, complex contract to override any arguably inconsistent provision.

The better phrasing avoids *herein* by substituting *in this agreement* or *in this contract*. Better yet, the drafter should specify which provision might be read as contradictory. See **herein.**

The statutory equivalent is the phrase *notwithstanding any other provision of law*, as in Fed. R. Evid. 412(a) (1994).

The opposite effect—subordinating the current provision to all others—is achieved by the wording *except as otherwise provided*.

notwithstanding the fact that; notwithstanding that. These legalistic phrases are best replaced by either *although* or *even if*—e.g.: "The freedom that is worth having is freedom to do what you think to be good *notwithstanding that* [read *even if*] others think it to be bad." Patrick Devlin, *The Enforcement of Morals* 108 (1968). See **notwithstanding & fact that, the.**

nought. See **naught.**

NOUN PLAGUE is Wilson Follett's term for the piling up of nouns to modify other nouns. *See* Wilson Follett, *Modern American Usage* 229 (1966). When a sentence has more than three nouns in a row, it generally becomes much less readable. The following sentence is badly constructed because of the noun-upon-noun syndrome, which unfortunately is more common now than in Follett's day: "Consumers complained to their congressman about *the National Highway Traffic Safety Administration's automobile seat belt 'interlock' rule*." One can hardly get to the end of the sentence to find out that we are talking

about a rule. (Actually, many writers today would leave off the possessive after *Administration*.) In the interest of plague control, the following rewrite seems advisable: *the 'interlock' rule applied to automobile seat belts by the National Highway Traffic Safety Administration*.

Readability often drops when three words that are structurally nouns follow in succession, although exceptions such as *fidelity life insurance* certainly exist. But less readable examples such as the following are the rule rather than the exception:

- "Since incentives are inevitably tied to immeasurable subjective evaluations, it is reassuring that the *information generation stimuli* of the adversary model rest in part on other foundations." Edward J. Brunet, *Study in the Allocation of Scarce Judicial Resources*, 12 Ga. L. Rev. 701, 713 (1978).
- "The Court favored governmental concerns rather than *individual right concerns*." Alice Jacobson, Comment, United States v. Montoya de Hernandez, *Swallowing Up Probable Cause*, 17 U. Miami Inter-Am. L. Rev. 609, 617 (1986).

The plague is virtually never endurable when four nouns appear consecutively. E.g.: "The recent decisions in *Primus* and *Ohralik* compel little, if any, change in the current *state attorney solicitation rules*." David. A. Rabin, *Attorney Solicitation*, 12 U. Mich. J.L. Reform 144, 187 (1978). Similarly, what is a *retiree benefit litigation procedure*?

Frequently, noun plague is a cause of AMBIGUITY. E.g.: "My brother Harlan's objections to my *Adamson dissent history*, like that of most of the objectors, relies [*sic*] most heavily on a criticism written by Professor Charles Fairman." *Duncan v. Louisiana*, 391 U.S. 145, 165 (1968) (Black, J., concurring). Here Justice Black means "the history [of the incorporation doctrine] I recited in my dissent in *Adamson*," but the reader could just as easily arrive at "my history of the *Adamson* dissent," or "the history of opinions that dissent from *Adamson*." A couple of prepositions would have remedied the problem.

One aspect of noun plague in legal writing is the traditional (and misguided) preference for nouns over verbs. Jeremy Bentham's so-called substantive-preferring principle was developed as a result of his bias in favor of nouns, which could be modified and multiplied, whereas "a verb slips through your fingers like an eel." 10 Jeremy Bentham, *Works* 569 (John Bowring ed. 1843). So Bentham, like his fellow lawyers, preferred *to give motion to* rather than *to move* and *to give extension to* rather than *to extend*. Even today, lawyers frequently use such circumlocutions.

Another root of the problem is the tendency in modern writing to make adjectives out of nouns and noun phrases, often postponing the true subject until long after the reader has left off hoping for one. E.g.—"This is a breach of contract/Deceptive Trade Practices Act, Tex. Bus. & Comm. Code Ann. (Vernon Supp. 1982–83) (hereinafter referred to as 'the Act') case." *Wolfe Masonry, Inc. v. Stewart*, 664 S.W.2d 102, 102–03 (Tex. App.—Corpus Christi 1983).

Finally, avoid loading a single statement with too many abstract nouns ending in *-tion*. The effect is not a pleasing one—e.g.:

- "The regulation of solicitation involves the *consideration* of whether there are 'ample alternative channels for *communication* of the *information.*'" *In re Koffler*, 420 N.Y.S.2d 560, 573–74 (App. Div. 1979).
- "This case [involves] *protection* against a second *prosecution* for the Washington *importation conviction.*" *Garrett v. U.S.*, 471 U.S. 773, 777 (1985) (per Rehnquist, J.).

See BE-VERBS (B), BURIED VERBS & SOUND OF PROSE (A).

NOUNS AS ADJECTIVES. English has long been noted for its ability to allow words to change parts of speech. The transmutation of nouns into adjectives is one of the most frequently seen shifts of this kind. Usually the change is unobjectionable, as in the first word in each of the following phrases: *law library, state action, telephone wires, home repairs, litigation problems.* Common usages appear in this sentence: "We hold only that the question whether the barge is a *Jones Act vessel* was integral to the *jury question* of *seaman status.*" *Brunet v. Boh Bros. Constr. Co.*, 715 F.2d 196, 199 (5th Cir. 1983).

Occasionally, however, semantic shifts of this kind give rise to ambiguities or play tricks on the reader. For example, it would be unwise for one writing about a statute concerning invalids to call it an *invalid statute.* To make a somewhat different point, the reader's expectations are subverted when a noun is used adjectivally in place of the more usual adjectival form— e.g.: "In 1891 a subdivision of Detroit was planned . . . strictly for *residence* [read *residential*] purposes." *McCurdy v. Standard Realty Corp.*, 175 S.W.2d 28, 31 (Ky. 1943).

Often, of course, the sense conveyed is different when one uses the noun adjectivally as opposed to the adjectival form. For example, *negligence defendant* is something different from *negligent defendant,* the latter being judgmental; *negligence action* means something quite different from *negligent action*; *pornography litigation* seems to mean something different from *pornographic litigation* (which is somehow difficult to visualize).

Finally, relations often become vague when nouns that would normally follow prepositions are adjectives placed before nouns, and the relation-bearing prepositions are omitted. For example, *victim awareness* is a vague phrase; does it mean *on the part of, of, by*? E.g.: "The crime victims' movement led to the passage of several laws enacted to define victims' rights, promote *victim awareness,* and ensure that victims are allowed to exercise these rights in the criminal court process." Kesha Handy, *Federal Crime Victims' Rights*, 46 Hous. Law. 14, 15 (2009). We can deduce that the intended sense is *awareness (on the part of the public) of victims and their rights,* but perhaps we should not ask our

readers to have to make such deductions. The same sort of uncertainty infects *victim restitution* (= full restitution to the victim of a crime).

NOUNS AS VERBS. A type of semantic shift less common than that of noun to adjective is for nouns to act as verbs. Often these usages are considered slangy—e.g.:

- "Form 4 reports will have to be *air-expressed* to the Commission no later than the first business day after a transaction." Committee on Federal Regulation of Securities, *Report of the Task Force on Regulation of Insider Trading Part II*, 42 Bus. Law. 1087, 1102 (1987).
- "Studies have found that a staggeringly high proportion of cases of domestic violence are '*no crimed*' in the London area." Susan S.M. Edwards, *From Victim to Defendant*, 26 Case W. Res. J. Int'l L. 261, 269–70 (1994).
- "'The Firm' . . . for a time even out-*box-officed* 'Jurassic Park.'" Joe Dirck, *Grisham's Latest Loses on Appeal*, Plain Dealer (Cleveland), 22 May 1994, at K1.
- "He'd be as busy *ambassadoring* in Rome as he's been *mayoring* in Boston." David Nyhan, *Bill's Dabble at Diplomacy*, Boston Globe, 2 May 1997, at A23.

Yet nouns used as verbs often make their way into legal parlance and finally into legal print: "A second indictment was presented to the grand jury, and the grand jury *no-billed* the indictment." *D'Ambrosio v. Bagley*, 527 F.3d 489, 499 (6th Cir. 2008). Though writers refer to *fast-tracking* budgets, *tasking* committees, and *mainstreaming* children, English is generally inhospitable to this sort of jargonistic innovation. Legal writers should be wary of adopting usages of this kind.

n.o.v. See **j.n.o.v.**

nova causa interveniens. See CAUSATION (D) & LATINISMS.

novate (= to replace by something new), a 17th-century BACK-FORMATION from *novation*, is labeled "rare" and as peculiar to Roman law in the *OED*. But the word sometimes appears in modern American legal writing—e.g.:

- "He did not *novate* his indebtedness to the Johnstown bank." *Jones v. Costlow*, 36 A.2d 460, 462 (Pa. 1944).
- "The original contract of sale between Rains County and McCallon was *novated* by the commissioners' court." *Simmons v. Ratliff*, 182 S.W.2d 827, 829 (Tex. Civ. App.— Amarillo 1944).
- "There is no 'clear and unequivocal' evidence of . . . Appellants' intention to *novate* the [lease]." *Langhoff Props., LLC v. BP Prods. N. Am. Inc.*, 519 F.3d 256, 263 (5th Cir. 2008).

novation, originally a Roman-law term, denotes the act of substituting for an old contract a new one that either (1) replaces an existing obligation for a new obligation or (2) adds a party who was not a party to the old contract. The word also sometimes refers to the contract that brings about such a substitution. The effect of a novation, unlike that of *subrogation*, is not

---

to transfer liability, but to replace an old liability with a new one. See **adoption** & **subrogation (A)**.

novatory; *novative; *novational. None of these can be said to be common, but *novatory* is used more frequently than the others, which might therefore be labeled NEEDLESS VARIANTS.

novel and concrete. These words appear in virtually all cases involving the misappropriation of commercial ideas. Though they have assumed an "almost talismanic significance," the terms "have nonetheless gained little specific content. Presumably, *novel* means the opposite of *common* or, perhaps, *old*. *Concrete* is probably the antithesis of *abstract*, and also implies that, to be protectable, the ideas must be reduced to tangible form. Beyond this, the decisions offer nothing definitive." Paul Goldstein, *Copyright, Patent, Trademark and Related State Doctrines* 59 (2d ed. 1981).

novelty does not mean "an extreme rarity." Rather, it denotes something both rare *and* new. "Mother-son affairs are so rare as to be regarded as a *novelty*." A. Press et al., *An Epidemic of Incest*, Newsweek, 30 Nov. 1981, at 68. The writer of this sentence could have better written, "Mother-son incest is an extreme rarity." *Oedipus Rex* belies any claim that incest might have to novelty.

noverint universi. See **know all men by these presents.**

novus actus interveniens is the primarily British legal phrase meaning literally "a new intervening act." (See CAUSATION (D) & LATINISMS.) *Novus actus* is sometimes used as an ellipsis for the full phrase—e.g.: "[The option contract] required a *novus actus* on the part of plaintiff." *Bilbo v. Ball*, 188 N.W. 753, 763 (Iowa 1922).

now is sometimes mistakenly used for *present* or *current* as an opposite of *then*, as in *then-owner*. E.g.: "An easement agreement was entered into and recorded, which binds the *now-owners* [read *current owners*] of the two tracts of land." *Sluyter v. Hale Fireworks P'ship*, 262 S.W.3d 154, 159 (Ark. 2007). See **then (A).**

*noways. See **nowise.**

now comes. See **comes now.**

nowhere near is colloquial for *not nearly*.

no-win–no-fee system is a phrase that some journalists use to describe contingent fees. E.g.: "Even the more modest *no-win–no-fee system* would in some cases create a dangerous pressure on lawyers to cheat in order to eat." Stephen Sedley, *Breaking the Law*, London Rev. Books, 18 May 1989, at 3. See **contingent fee.**

nowise (= in no way; not at all) is an adverb that should not be introduced by *in*, although legal writers seem to commit this error more often than not when using the word. *In no way* might even generally be preferable to *nowise*. E.g.: "The statute *in no wise*

[read *nowise* or *in no way*] indicates that the 602(2) definition is only transitory." *ACLU v. F.C.C.*, 823 F.2d 1554, 1568 (D.C. Cir. 1987). Mistaken uses of the word, especially in AmE, are legion.

Formerly spelled as two words, *nowise* should now be consistently treated as a single word. The following examples illustrate the traditionally correct use of the word:

- "The *Allen* disclosure statement is *nowise* comparable in form to the disclosure statement with which this court is concerned." *DeJaynes v. Gen. Fin. Corp. of Ill.*, 442 F.Supp. 377, 382 (S.D. Ill. 1977).
- "The insurer is bound under the contract to pay workers' compensation benefits, not to dispense legal advice, which, indeed, is *nowise* its business." *Costa v. Liberty Mut. Ins. Co.*, 558 N.E.2d 999, 1001 (Mass. App. Ct. 1990).

*Noways, in legal writing at least, is a NEEDLESS VARIANT of *nowise*, although the Evanses state that it is more common in AmE than *nowise*. See Bergen Evans & Cornelia Evans, *A Dictionary of Contemporary American Usage* 326 (1957).

now pending is a common REDUNDANCY, but no less faulty for that—e.g.:

- "Our resolution of the dispute determines the course of proceedings if and when he is rearrested on the *charges now pending* [read *pending charges*]." *U.S. v. Montalvo-Murillo*, 495 U.S. 711, 713 (1990) (per Kennedy, J.).
- "The Security Trust Company, N.A. attacks the validity of the deed of trust in a lawsuit *now pending* [read *pending*] in the United States District Court." *Democratic C. Comm. v. Washington Metro. Area Transit Comm'n*, 21 F.3d 1145, 1147 n.2 (D.C. Cir. 1994).
- "*United States v. Rodriquez, now pending* [read *pending*] before the Court, presents the question 'whether a state drug-trafficking offense . . . qualifies as a predicate offense.'" *Begay v. U.S.*, 553 U.S. 137, 156 n.1 (2008) (Alito, J., dissenting).

noxal (= of or relating to a cause of action against an owner of an animal or slave for damage done by the animal or slave) is, though hardly on every lawyer's lips every day, common enough to merit inclusion in law dictionaries and in English-language dictionaries, from which it is regularly omitted. E.g.: "The 1825 amendment created an exception to the ability of the owner to limit his liability by *noxal* surrender of the animal, a recognized Roman practice that foreshadowed limitation of liability in modern admiralty." William T. Tête, *In Defense of Fault in the Guard Under Article 2317*, 61 Tul. L. Rev. 759, 765 n.37 (1987). The phrase *noxal action* figures importantly in Oliver Wendell Holmes Jr.'s book *The Common Law* (1881).

NSF (= not sufficient funds) acts as an adjective where the full phrase is cumbersome and even ungrammatical <an NSF check>.

nuclear is pronounced /**noo**-klee-ər/, though often it is mispronounced /**noo**-kyə-lər/. Though presidents and other educated persons have had difficulty pronouncing the word correctly, you should if you can.

nudum pactum (= an unenforceable agreement) has taken on different particularized senses within different legal traditions. At common law, of course, a *nudum pactum* was an agreement that failed for lack of consideration. E.g.:

- "An agreement made without consideration is a *nudum pactum*; i.e., it is an agreement [that] is destitute of legal effect." 1 Ernest W. Chance, *Principles of Mercantile Law* 9 (Percy W. French ed., 13th ed. 1950).
- "An agreement [that] did not fall into any of the recognised classes was *nudum pactum*; there was no *causa* and therefore no legal obligation." O. Hood Phillips, *A First Book of English Law* 247 (3d ed. 1955).
- "If the nonbreaching party had entered into a new contract with the breachor, he could still show that the new contract was made without consideration and was thus a '*nudum pactum*.'" *Contempo Design, Inc. v. Chicago & N.E. Ill. Dist. Council of Carpenters*, 226 F.3d 535, 550 (7th Cir. 2000).

In Roman law and civil law, in which consideration is not a necessary element of a contract, the term denoted unenforceability for some other reason, such as lack of a lawful "cause." The anglicized phrase *nude pact* has not been widely used, perhaps because each of those terms carries its own connotative baggage that may cause a MISCUE. See **naked.**

nugatory is not a legal word per se, but it is a learned word favored by lawyers. It means "of no force; useless; invalid." E.g.:

- "Were we to follow the plaintiffs' theory to its logical end, this class action would be governed by a 'crazy quilt' of limitations periods and the federal interest in uniformity would be rendered *nugatory*." *Berger v. AXA Network LLC*, 459 F.3d 804, 814 (7th Cir. 2006).
- "This Court must avoid a construction that would render any part of a statute surplusage or *nugatory*." *Sinicropi v. Mazurek*, 729 N.W.2d 256, 261 (Mich. Ct. App. 2006).

Cf. **otiose.**

nuisance. Etymologically, *nuisance* derives from the Latin *nocere* ("to hurt or harm"), which has also given us the words *annoy*, *noise*, *noisome*, *noxious*, and *obnoxious.*

Some people, realizing that *nuisance* is a recognized legal wrong, therefore assume they might be able to sue people who annoy them. In fact, though, the legal requirement for nuisance is fairly specific: annoyance or disturbance in the enjoyment of property. Unlawful conduct of this kind is commonly put into two classes: (1) the acts of an owner or possessor of land who wrongfully uses that land in a way that unreasonably interferes with the rights of neighboring owners or possessors to enjoy their property; and (2) wrongful interference with easements and other incorporeal rights.

A *public nuisance* (also called a *common nuisance*) interferes with a communal right. Examples include obstructing a highway or allowing trash to accumulate in one's front yard to the annoyance of the neighborhood. A *private nuisance*, on the other hand, is an act that interferes with a person's enjoyment of his or her own land or premises. A common example occurs when someone living in an apartment plays music (or what passes for music) so loudly that the neighboring apartment dweller is unable to read or sleep. See **attractive nuisance.**

null (= void) is perfectly capable of standing alone—e.g.:

- "Even in the compulsory areas, however, the effect of a transfer by unregistered deed is not entirely *null*." Edward Jenks, *The Book of English Law* 298 (P.B. Fairest ed., 6th ed. 1967).
- "The remainder of the judgment is absolutely *null* for failure to properly notify National in the original lawsuit of a claim against it." *Graham v. Payne*, 923 So.2d 866, 869 (La. Ct. App. 2006).

See **null and void.**

nulla bona (= no goods) is a LATINISM that has given its name to the sheriff's return on a writ of execution when he has found no property of the defendant on which to levy. E.g.: "The goods seized were then sold by the sheriff and the proceeds paid to Bird, a return of *nulla bona* being made to the plaintiff's writ." *Bankers Trust Co. v. Galadari*, [1987] 1 Q.B. 222, 227, [1986] 3 All E.R. 794, 798.

null and void. "If the powers of the legislature have not been exercised in conformity with the Constitution, the laws enacted are *null and void*." This doublet is old in the law, is readily understandable to non-lawyers, and is at worst a minor prolixity and a CLICHÉ. Though emphatic, *null and void* is susceptible to the frequent weakness of *void* alone, namely that of being interpreted to mean *voidable*. (See **void.**) But *null and void* is fundamentally innocuous: the fight for PLAIN LANGUAGE has far worse legalistic demons to eliminate. See **null** & DOUBLETS, TRIPLETS, AND SYNONYM-STRINGS.

nulla poena sine lege (= no punishment without a law authorizing it), one of the basic principles of civilized nations, is sometimes shortened to *nulla poena*—e.g.: "The doctrine of *nulla poena* would at first sight seem to require a very rigid criminal law and a severe pruning of the discretion allowed to the court in determining sentence." G.W. Paton, *A Textbook of Jurisprudence* 389 (4th ed. 1972).

A common variation on the phrase is *nullum crimen sine lege* (= no crime without a law authorizing it)—e.g.: "It is usual to begin a discussion of general principles of the criminal law by stating the maxim *nullum crimen sine lege*, sometimes known as the principle of legality." Andrew Ashworth, *Principles of Criminal Law* 59 (1991). See MAXIMS.

nullify. A. And Its Near-Synonyms: *annul*; *negate*; *abrogate*; *invalidate*; *obrogate*. These verbs share the sense "to render something of no account; to deprive of any legal effect." To *nullify* something is to reduce it to nothingness and to deprive it of all efficacy or value <by overriding the President's veto, Congress essentially nullified it>. To *annul* something, especially a law or a legal status, is to neutralize its effect and to erase it, as if it had never existed <the marriage was annulled>. To *negate* something is to destroy its effect <the company's good publicity couldn't negate the bad>. (Cf. **negative,** vb.) To *abrogate* something is to abolish or dispense with it <this law abrogated flood-control immunity>. To *invalidate* something is to negate its force or legality—literally, to deprive it of validity <the Court invalidated corporate spending limits on federal political campaigns>. *Obrogate* is a rare civil-law term meaning "to repeal (a law) by passing a new one."

B. More on *nullify* vs. *annul*. *Nullify* has the broader meaning, and generally carries no necessary implication of legal action—e.g.:

- "The Arizona legislature effectively *nullified* the result in its state by putting prescribing doctors at risk of losing their licenses." Alex Kreit, Comment, *The Future of Medical Marijuana*, 151 U. Pa. L. Rev. 1787, 1796 (2003).
- "The trial court's assertion that juror misconduct *nullified* the verdicts of acquittal is unsupported in Florida law." *Moody v. State*, 931 So.2d 177, 180 (Fla. Dist. Ct. App. 2006).

Cf. **annihilate.**

Annul more strongly suggests abolishing or making nonexistent by legal action <to annul a marriage>. E.g.: "The third paragraph of the answer avers that at the instance of the agents of the appellee the original contract signed by the parties upon which the suit was based was destroyed for the purpose of *annulling* and abrogating it, and the parties all agreeing that this did so *annul* and abrogate it." *Krausgill Piano Co. v. Federal Elec. Co.*, 287 S.W. 962, 962 (Ky. 1926). (See **instance.**)

Annul frequently appears in the verbose phrase *annul and set aside*, in which the last three words are unnecessary. See DOUBLETS, TRIPLETS, AND SYNONYM-STRINGS & **set aside (A).**

nullip, a clipped form of the gynecological term *nullipara* (= a woman who has never borne children), has become common in litigation of mass-tort claims relating to female infertility. The appearance and sound of the word are startling at first, when one considers the context, which seems much more likely to give rise to soft-sounding EUPHEMISMS—e.g.:

- "A prime candidate is the young *nullip* who will settle for nothing less than the most modern, trouble-free method of birth control." *Hawkinson v. A.H. Robins Co.*, 595 F.Supp. 1290, 1305–06 (D. Colo. 1984) (quoting a corporate advertisement).
- "The jury could consider defendant's statement that the Cu-7 was 'excellent for use' with *nullips* as a statement of fact, and not as an opinion." *Kociemba v. G.D. Searle & Co.*, 707 F.Supp. 1517, 1525 (D. Minn. 1989).

nullity = (1) the fact of being legally void <petition for nullity of marriage>; or (2) something that is legally

void <the contract that is now regarded as a nullity>. Sense 2 is now more common—e.g.: "A forged transfer is a *nullity*." J. Charlesworth, *The Principles of Company Law* 89 (4th ed. 1945). But sense 1 also appears from time to time—e.g.: "In questions of *nullity* of marriage, English courts will generally recognise the validity of a foreign decree." R.H. Graveson, *Conflict of Laws* 332 (7th ed. 1974).

nullum crimen sine lege. See **nulla poena sine lege.**

nul tiel is LAW LATIN meaning "no such," and it typically occurs in denials that something exists, as in the names of pleas called *nul tiel record*, *nul tiel corporation*, and *nul tiel debt*—e.g.:

- "Appellant filed an answer containing an allegation that the debt was the debt of another, a plea of '*nul tiel debt*,' and a general denial." *Gregson v. Webb*, 239 S.E.2d 230, 231 (Ga. Ct. App. 1977).
- "The merits would be fully open to examination on a plea of the general issue, which would be nil nebet or non-assumpsit, and not *nul tiel record*." *De la Mata v. American Life Ins. Co.*, 771 F.Supp. 1375, 1381 n.13 (D. Del. 1991).

The phrase is less likely to be replaced than many other JARGON phrases because it is the *name* of a plea, and lawyers are unlikely to adopt a new name such as "the no-such-corporation plea." Even so, many American jurisdictions, including the federal courts, do quite well without the phrase.

NUMBER. See CONCORD, SEXISM (A) & SUBJECT–VERB AGREEMENT.

number of, a. This phrase is generally paired with a plural noun and a plural verb—i.e., *there are a number of reasons* instead of *there is a number of reasons*. The former is correct because of the linguistic principle known as SYNESIS—e.g.:

- "There *is* [read *are*] a number of reasons for this." Patrick Devlin, *The Enforcement of Morals* vii (1968).
- "However, *there is* [read *there are*] a number of exceptions to this rule, whose importance appears to be increasing today." P.S. Atiyah, *An Introduction to the Law of Contract* 260 (3d ed. 1981). (Cf. p. 31: "*There are a number of* different ways of classifying contracts.") On beginning the sentence with *however*, see **however.**
- "The Courts . . . have commented that there *is* [read *are*] *a number of factors* to consider." *Dallas v. State*, 993 A.2d 655, 670 n.4 (Md. 2010) (Bell, J., concurring in part & dissenting in part).

But when *number* is modified with an adjective—that is, when the SET PHRASE that gives rise to the plural locution is changed—the focus shifts to the singular noun *number*, and the verb should become singular. E.g.:

- "There *are* [read *is*] a considerable number of cases in the United States where courts have ordered the employer to pay the bonus notwithstanding language like that just quoted." Lon L. Fuller, *Anatomy of the Law* 128 (1968).
- "*There is a surprising number* of cases in the advance sheets [involving] joint and mutual wills." Thomas L. Shaffer, *The Planning and Drafting of Wills and Trusts* 184 (2d ed. 1979).

- "We take little comfort in his assurances because the predicate of our colleague's optimistic view of future judicial refinement of his new world of secondary liability *is a large number of* expensive and drawn-out pieces of litigation." *Perfect 10, Inc. v. Visa Int'l Serv. Ass'n*, 494 F.3d 788, 798 n.9 (9th Cir. 2007).

See **amount**.

NUMERALS. A. General Guidance in Using. The best practice in legal writing is to spell out all numbers ten and below, and to use numerals for numbers 11 and above. This "rule" has five exceptions:

1. If numbers recur throughout the text or are being used for calculations—that is, if the context is quasi-mathematical—then use numerals.
2. Approximations are usually spelled out <about two hundred years ago>.
3. In units of measure, words substitute for rows of zeros where possible <$3 million, $3 billion>, and digits are used with words of measure <9 inches, 4 millimeters>.
4. Percentages may be spelled out <eight percent> or written as numbers <8 percent or 8%>.
5. Numbers that begin sentences must always be spelled out. (See (c).)

B. Coupling Numerals with Words. In 1992, one lawyer wrote another, saying: "Dear Sally: I really enjoyed seeing you and your two (2) sons in the park last week." All that was missing was the clincher, "Please give my warm wishes to same."

The noxious habit of spelling words out and putting numerals in parentheses decreases the readability of much legal writing, especially drafting. Following is a genuine example from a Canadian court order:

> That of the sum of twelve thousand five hundred dollars ($12,500) payable to the Infant, the sum of twelve thousand dollars ($12,000) be paid to the District Registrar of the Supreme Court of British Columbia, Vancouver, British Columbia, to the credit of the Infant to be held on behalf of the Infant until further order or until she shall attain the age of nineteen (19) years and that the remaining sum of five hundred dollars ($500) together with the sum of one thousand eight hundred and nineteen dollars and ninety-two cents ($1,819.92) be paid to X.Y. Clarke, Solicitor for the Petitioners and the Infant on account of legal fees and disbursements." (Can.)

This belt-and-suspenders practice seems to have originated in a fear of typographical errors: hence, words were used instead of numbers. (And we gained the canon of construction holding that, if ever a discrepancy emerges between spelled-out numbers and numerals, the words control.) But the words did not readily draw the eye to all the important numerical figures, so these were added in parentheses to alert readers. The result is often a bog.

Modern teachers of drafting tend to prefer using the numerals alone. They caution drafters about the urgent necessity of reviewing numerals carefully because, as they note, a misplaced decimal or an added zero (or three) can give rise to malpractice claims. But if clarity and readability are to be primary goals, the belt-and-suspenders approach must be rejected.

If, on the other hand, clarity and readability are not one's primary goal as a drafter—if one is more concerned with unmistakable meaning, however hard a reader might have to work to get at it—then the belt-and-suspenders approach makes perfect sense.

C. Not Beginning Sentences with Numerals. It is stylistically poor to begin a sentence—or, as in the following example, a paragraph—with numerals. E.g.: "1984 saw the publication of three substantial books on the subject." George D. Gopen, *The State of Legal Writing: Res Ipsa Loquitur*, 86 Mich. L. Rev. 333, 364 (1987). Some journals, such as *The New Yorker*, would make that sentence begin, *Nineteen-eighty-four saw the publication . . . .* But most writers and editors would probably simply begin the sentence some other way, as by writing, *In 1984, three substantial books on the subject appeared*. That jibes with the advice of *The Chicago Manual of Style*: "to avoid awkwardness, a sentence can often be recast" rather than begun with a spelled-out year or number. § 9.5 (16th ed. 2010).

D. Round Numbers. Except when writing checks or other negotiable instruments, omit double zeros after a decimal: *$400* is better form than *$400.00*.

E. Decades. As late as the 1970s, editors regularly changed *1970s* to *1970's*. Today, however, the tendency is to omit the apostrophe.

F. Judicial Votes. The preferred method for recording an appellate court's votes in a particular case is to use numerals separated by an en-dash <a 5–4 decision> <voted 6–3 to reverse>. This method, which gives the reader more speed than spelling out the numbers <five-to-four decision>, is standard today—e.g.:

- "The majority was 6–3 and the opinion was by Chief Justice Warren—in itself significant, for the Chief Justice normally reserves for himself those onerous tasks likely to draw the most controversy." Robert A. Liston, *Tides of Justice: The Supreme Court and the Constitution in Our Time* 168 (1966).
- "In the 1974 Term, both Rehnquist and Powell wrote heavily in 6–3 and 5–4 cases, Powell writing in five 5–4 and three 6–3 rulings." Stephen L. Wasby, *The Supreme Court in the Federal Judicial System* 178 (1978).
- "Some would argue that one Justice or two would not make that much difference—and that even the many 5–4 splits would gradually disappear—if the Supreme Court were staffed, as they believe it should be, with men and women who understand that constitutional adjudication is simply the job of correctly reading the Constitution." Laurence H. Tribe, *God Save This Honorable Court* 49 (1985).

For more on the en-dash, see PUNCTUATION (E).

If one prefers to spell out *to* instead of using the en-dash, the phrase must be hyphenated if it functions as a PHRASAL ADJECTIVE—e.g.: "Most of the dissenters in this *5 to 4* [read *5-to-4*] ruling feared that the majority had gone a long way in that direction." Gerald Gunther, *Constitutional Law* 1606 (11th ed. 1985). But if the numbers function adverbially in the sentence, there are no hyphens <voted 5 to 4 to affirm>.

numerous is often merely an inflated equivalent of *many*—e.g.: "*Numerous* [read *Many*] learned and brilliant men have believed in witchcraft." Thomas E. Atkinson, *Handbook of the Law of Wills* 246 (2d ed. 1953).

nuncio. See **ambassador.**

nunc pro tunc (lit., "now for then") is used in reference to an act to show that it has retroactive legal effect—e.g.: "Once the notice of appeal was filed, the trial court lacked jurisdiction to enter the corrected judgment *nunc pro tunc* to the date of the first judgment." *Jesus v. State*, 31 So.3d 309, 310 (Fla. Dist. Ct. App. 2010). The LATINISM is useful legal JARGON, not a TERM OF ART, usually appearing when a court has exercised its "inherent power . . . to make its records speak the truth by correcting the record at a later date to reflect what actually occurred [in earlier court proceedings]." *Ex parte Dickerson*, 702 S.W.2d 657, 658 (Tex. Crim. App. 1986).

nuncupative will. See **oral will.**

nuptial, adj.; **nuptials,** n. Although *nuptial* is in good use as an adjective, the noun *nuptials* (= wedding) is generally a pomposity to be avoided. It should be left to its ineradicable place in newspaper reports of weddings, in which it allows ambitious young journalists to practice INELEGANT VARIATION. The words are pronounced /**nəp**-shəl[z]/—not /**nəp**-shə-wəl[z]/. See **matrimonial.**

nurturance looks like a NEEDLESS VARIANT of *nurture*, but the words have arguably diverged in their connotations. Whereas *nurture* means either "upbringing" or "food," *nurturance*—a 20th-century NEOLOGISM dating from 1938—tends to mean "attentive care; emotional and physical nourishment." If this DIFFERENTIATION persists, then *nurturance* may earn a permanent position in the language. For now, it remains relatively uncommon, and it is hard in any given instance to justify it—e.g.:

- "Albert was also depressed and needed environmental stimulation and *nurturance* [read *nurture*]." *In re Albert B.*, 263 Cal. Rptr. 694, 696 (Ct. App. 1989).
- "[The defendant] is the product of a rather chaotic family life in which his basic needs for structure, discipline, and *nurturance* [read *nurture*] were not met." *Smith v. Mitchell*, 348 F.3d 177, 192 (6th Cir. 2003).
- "The idea that [the defendant] had 'an unusually strong need for what we call *nurturance*' is baffling to the point of being incomprehensible insofar as explaining his alleged brutal murder of a woman." *Thompson v. Bell*, 315 F.3d 566, 605 (6th Cir. 2003) (Moore, J., concurring). Judge Moore seems (quite understandably) to be undercutting a bit of testimonial psychobabble.

O

oasis. Pl. *oases.*

oath. **A. And** *affirmation.* Apart from its nonlegal sense denoting a profane expression, *oath* has two different meanings: (1) a swearing to God that one's statement is true or that one will be bound to a promise; or (2) a statement or promise made when one so swears. An *affirmation* is a similar declaration without the religious invocation. See **affirmant.**
    B. *Under oath* **and** *on oath.* The first is AmE as well as BrE; the second is primarily BrE.

obiit sine prole. See **OSP.**

obiter dictum. **A. Sense.** *Obiter dictum*, in Latin literally "something said in passing," denotes a remark that is made by a judge while delivering judgment but that is unnecessary to the reasoning that has led to that judgment—and is therefore without precedential force. See **dictum (c).**
    B. Plural Form. The plural of *obiter dictum* (= a judge's passing remark) is *obiter dicta*—e.g.: "This passing reference offered no statutory analysis or discussion of the safe harbor itself, and can only be

characterized as *obiter dicta* [read *obiter dictum*]." *In re Cutera Secs. Litig.*, 610 F.3d 1103, 1113 (9th Cir. 2010). A tangential comment is *dictum*; tangential comments are *dicta.* See **ratio decidendi.**
    C. *Obiter* **as a Shortened Form.** *Obiter* is primarily a BrE shortening of the phrase *obiter dictum.* This elliptical form can be confusing when standing for the noun phrase, since *obiter* alone means "by the way"—e.g.: "In *The Christina* three out of five law lords expressed *obiter* doubts about the correctness of the previous English decisions." J.L. Brierly, *The Law of Nations* 193 (5th ed. 1955).
    If the phrase must be shortened, *dictum* is the usual form in AmE and in BrE—e.g.:

- "The Sixth Circuit has similarly viewed the issue, *by obiter* [read *in dictum*], at least." *Sears Roebuck & Co. v. Stockwell*, 143 F.Supp. 928, 932 (D. Minn. 1956).
- "Unless and until the high court directly addresses the constitutionality of factor (i) as delineated by this court, its *obiter characterization* [read *dictum*] remains just that." *People v. Hawthorne*, 841 P.2d 118, 141 n.26 (Cal. 1992).
- "This pronouncement was *obiter* [read *dictum*] because the Court in *Brown* found that the *McClure* test was again not satisfied and therefore the Court was not required to

address the issue of immunity." Adam M. Dodek, *Reconceiving Solicitor Client Privilege*, 35 Queen's L.J. 493, 503 n.35 (2010).

See **dictum (A)**.

D. In Dissenting Judicial Opinions. A British writer states that the phrase *obiter dicta* includes "the content of dissenting judgments made by a particular judge." Stephen Foster, *Business Law Terms* 73 (1988). That statement is itself misplaced *obiter dictum*. As generally used, *obiter dictum* relates to nondispositive remarks in a majority opinion.

object, n. Only in legal writing may persons be *objects*—e.g.:

- "Children or other *objects* born after the period of distribution may of course be included by the effect of express words." Francis Vaughan Hawkins et al., *A Concise Treatise on the Construction of Wills* 73 (1885).
- "Appellee was, as testator's daughter, a natural *object* of her bounty." *Lipscomb v. Young*, 672 S.E.2d 649, 650 (Ga. 2009).

John W. Salmond, the influential legal philosopher, addressed this point head-on: "Certain writers . . . consider that the object of a right means some material thing to which it relates; . . . others admit that a person, as well as a material thing, may be the object of a right." *Salmond on Jurisprudence* 265 (Glanville Williams ed., 11th ed. 1957). So the *subject* of a right is its content (e.g., an entitlement to claim damages), whereas the *object* of a right is the person or thing for whose benefit the right exists.

Moreover, in the legal idiom, some persons may be *objects* while others are *nonobjects*—e.g.:

- "If the donee of a special power makes an appointment to an *object* of the power in consideration of a benefit conferred upon or promised to a *nonobject*, the appointment is ineffective to whatever extent it was motivated by the purpose to benefit the *nonobject*." Restatement of Property § 353 (1940).
- "Plaintiff . . . urges that the power may not be exercised in bad faith or with an intent to benefit a *non-object* [read *nonobject*] of the power, as plaintiff maintains was done here." *Horne v. Title Ins. & Trust Co.*, 79 F.Supp. 91, 94 (S.D. Cal. 1948).

See also **purpose (A)**.

object, vb. **A. And Its Near-Synonyms: *protest*; *remonstrate*.** Each of these verbs relates to opposing something, such as a proposal or a policy, usually by making arguments against it. To *object* is simply to register one's disagreement, usually while stating grounds. To *protest* is to present one's opposition more vehemently, in speech or writing. (See **protest, vb.**) To *remonstrate* is to protest while trying also to convince or persuade <to remonstrate with him about his drunkenness>. The word is preferably pronounced /ri-**mon**-strayt/: it does not, in AmE, rhyme with *demonstrate*.

B. Idiom: *object to ——ing*. The modern idiom uses a present participle, not an infinitive. E.g.: "If a witness *objects to take* [read *objects to taking*] an oath . . . he is to make the promise and declaration as prescribed by the Act of 1869." Edmund Powell et al., *The Principles and Practices of the Law of Evidence* 10 (1869).

objectant; objector. Both words mean "one who contests a will." For purposes of DIFFERENTIATION, *objectant* is perhaps preferable in this sense, since *objector* has other uses in the language of the law, such as "one who objects to the admission of certain evidence at trial," or in the phrase *conscientious objector*.

In the context of wills, then, *objector* might be called a NEEDLESS VARIANT—e.g.:

- "The will made a number of minor bequests to friends, non-profit organizations, and various relatives, including the *objectants*." *In re Will of Falk*, 845 N.Y.S.2d 287, 287 (App. Div. 2007).
- "Wolf's reliance on *Estate of Wheeler*, where our focus was on whether the *objectors* [read *objectants*] to a claim filed against an estate were prevailing parties, is misplaced." *In re Estate of Wolf*, 777 N.W.2d 119, 124 (Wis. Ct. App. 2009).

See **caveator** & **contestant**. Cf. **protestant**.

objectify; objectivize. *Objectify*, dating from the mid-19th century, means either (1) "to make into an object"; or (2) "to render objective." *Objectivize*, dating from the late 19th century, means "to render objective." It would be convenient for the words to undergo further DIFFERENTIATION: *objectify* should be confined to its sense 1, while *objectivize* should preempt *objectify* in the latter's sense 2. See **reify**.

objective. See **fair (A)**.

objector. See **objectant**.

OBJECT-SHUFFLING. This term "describes what unwary writers are apt to do with some of the many verbs that require, besides a direct object, another noun bearing to them a somewhat similar relation, but attached to them by a preposition" (H.W. Fowler, *MEU1* 393)—e.g.:

- "The probability is that the judge himself will *instruct a verdict* of Not Guilty to be returned." P.S. Atiyah, *Law and Modern Society* 21 (1983). The judge will instruct the jury, not the verdict. See HYPALLAGE.
- "Martin does not *cite us* any authority for such a proposition." *Martin v. State*, 176 S.W.3d 887, 906 (Tex. App.—Fort Worth 2005). Martin is not citing the court but a case. A suggested revision: *Martin does not cite any authority for such a proposition.*
- "The majority *substituted the original term 'prior proceeding' with 'prior trial'* [read *substituted 'prior trial' for the original term 'prior proceeding'*]." Jessica Greenwood, Casenote, *Double Jeopardy*, 63 SMU L. Rev. 243, 248

(2010). The other fix would be to change *substituted* to *replaced*.

Unfortunately, there is no simple rule for determining which verbs are reversible and which are not; one must rely on a sensitivity to idiom and a knowledge of what type of subject acts upon what type of object with certain verbs. It is perfectly legitimate, for example, either to *inspire* a person *with* courage or to *inspire* courage *in* a person. *Impress*, likewise, is a reversible word. A court may *impress* a constructive trust *on* property, or *impress* property *with* a constructive trust. Cf. **oust** & **serve**.

But the switch does not work with similar words such as *instill* and *inculcate*. Good teachers *instill* or *inculcate values into* students but cannot properly be said to **instill students with* or **inculcate students with* values. See **inculcate**.

objurgate. See **reprove**.

obligable. So spelled.

obligant. See **obligee** (D).

obligate. See **oblige**.

obligatio. This Roman-law term carries no meaning that is not equally well conveyed by the ordinary English word *obligation*. "Being valid, the state law created an *obligatio*, a personal liability of the owner of the *Hamilton*, to the claimants." *Old Dominion S.S. Co. v. Gilmore*, 207 U.S. 398, 405 (1907) (per Holmes, J.). Rarely did Justice Holmes so indulge himself in such unnecessarily recherché terms.

obligation; duty. Broadly speaking, the words are synonymous in referring to what a person is required to do or refrain from doing—or for the performance or nonperformance of which the person is responsible. But there are connotative nuances. An *obligation* is normally an immediate requirement with a specific reference <his child-support obligations> <Burundi's obligations under the treaty>. A basic word in the civil-law tradition, *obligation* carries a double sense: (1) a duty to act or to refrain from acting; or (2) a mutual legal relationship imposing a complex of rights and duties. Henry Sumner Maine pointed out a "puzzling peculiarity" relating to sense 2—a peculiarity because we are accustomed to acquainting *obligation* with *duty*: "'Obligation' [in Roman law] signified rights as well as duties, the right, for example, to have a debt paid as well as the duty of paying it." Henry S. Maine, *Ancient Law* 270 (17th ed. 1901). In civil law, the term *obligation* embraces contracts, torts, and quasi-contracts.

A *duty* may involve legal compulsion and immediacy, but the word carries an overlay of a moral or ethical imperative <parental duties> <fiduciary duties>. More specifically, *duty* = (1) that which one is required to do or refrain from doing, esp. as occupant of some position, role, or office; or (2) any one of a complex of rights and standards of care imposed by a legal relationship. Sense 2 appears primarily in tort law, in which writers use *duty* only to mean that there could be liability. For *duty* in the tax sense, see **tax**.

obligative. See **obligatory**.

*obligator. See **obligee** (D).

obligatory; obligative. The general term is *obligatory* (= required; mandatory). *Obligative* is a grammatical term in some languages for the mood of a verb expressing obligation or necessity.

oblige; obligate. The differences between these terms lie more in their uses than in their senses. Both words may mean "to bind by law or by moral duty." In legal contexts, the sense of both is usually "to bind by law"—*obligate* occurring more frequently—whereas in lay contexts the sense of moral duty predominates.

Oblige /ə-**blɪj**/ is used in the sense "to bind by legal tie" only in legal writing. E.g.: "The Debtors remained *obliged* to make fifty-one more monthly payments into the distribution fund." *In re Belcher*, 410 B.R. 206, 209 (Bankr. W.D. Va. 2009). *Oblige* has the additional sense "to do a favor for; to bind (someone else) by doing a favor"—a sense not shared by *obligate* <you'll do yourself a favor by obliging him with the title he wants>.

Obliged (= bound by law, duty, or moral tie) often functions adjectivally in a way that *obligated* ordinarily does not—e.g.: "While I agree with the majority's ultimate judgment, I feel *obliged* to write separately to address a troublesome complication in the indictment." *Neal v. State*, 15 So.3d 388, 411 (Miss. 2009) (Kitchens, J., concurring).

Oblige is a casualism in the sense "to comply with a request or desire"—e.g.:

- "The defendants requested that the case be transferred to the superior court, and the magistrate court *obliged*." *Jones v. Equipment King Int'l*, 652 S.E.2d 811, 813 (Ga. Ct. App. 2007).
- "A few days later, the government *obliged* and withdrew the bill, promising the MMA a thorough review of the bill." Martin Lau, *Twenty-five Years of Hudood Ordinances*, 64 Wash. & Lee L. Rev. 1291, 1306 (2007).

obligee; obligor. A. Senses. Several dictionaries, such as *The Random House College Dictionary* (rev. ed. 1995) and *Webster's New World Dictionary* (4th ed. 2007), define *obligee* in its etymological sense, as if it were synonymous with *obligor*. *Random House*, for example, defines *obligee* as "a person who is obligated to another," but that meaning ought to be reserved for *obligor*. An *obligee*, in modern usage, is one to whom an obligation is owed. For an example in which *obligee* and *obligor* are given senses opposite their ordinary current senses, see George J. Bell, *Principles of the Law of Scotland* § 26, at 14 (10th ed. 1899).

B. How to Handle These Terms. The wisest policy is not to handle them at all: where possible, use *creditor* (= obligee) and *debtor* (= obligor) instead. A leading jurist explains why: "Etymologically, '*obligee*' suggests the idea of a person's being obliged, but in current usage this meaning is actually more commonly attached to the term '*obligor*'; but where usage is neither logical nor securely established, one should avoid using potentially misleading expressions." D. Neil MacCormick, "General Legal Concepts," in 11 *The Laws of Scotland: Stair Memorial Encyclopaedia* 1029, at 371 n.3 (1990).

C. Pronunciation. *Obligee* has a soft -*g*- /ob-li-**jee**/, whereas *obligor* has a hard one /ob-li-**gohr**/. *Obligee* is often mispronounced /ob-li-**gee**/, with a hard -*g*-. Cf. **subrogee.**

D. Variations on *obligor*. *Obliger* and **obligator* are NEEDLESS VARIANTS of *obligor*, the usual and therefore the preferable form in legal writing. *Obliger* /ə-**blɪ**-jər/ is the nonlegal form. *Obligant* is also a NEEDLESS VARIANT, except in Scots law, in which it is the predominant form.

oblivious preferably takes the preposition *of* in its strictest sense of "forgetful." (*Oblivion* = forgetfulness or forgottenness, not momentary distraction.) The more popular meaning of *oblivious* today is "unmindful; unaware; unobservant." Today *to* is the more common mate of *oblivious*, though fastidious speakers and writers continue to use *of*.

Oblivious is here used with the correct preposition but in the less traditional sense: "The law does not discriminate between the rescuer *oblivious of* peril and the one who counts the cost." *Wagner v. International Ry.*, 133 N.E. 437, 438 (N.Y. 1921) (per Cardozo, J.).

obloquy. See **abuse,** n.

obnoxious today generally means "offensive; objectionable." But in legal writing, it often carries the sense "contrary"—e.g.:

- "Fully recognizing the general rule of law, that no judgment is to be pronounced against a party without an opportunity of being heard, there is nothing in the record before us which makes the order of the 10th of March, *obnoxious* to this cardinal principle in the administration of justice." *Belt v. Blackburn*, 28 Md. 227, 243 (1868).
- "We do not think the instruction is *obnoxious* to this criticism." *Sollars v. Atchison, Topeka & San Francisco R.R.*, 187 S.W.2d 513, 515 (Mo. Ct. App. 1945).

An even rarer sense of the word, used only in legal and literary contexts, is "exposed to harm or liable to something undesirable." E.g.: "This is a similar case, and it is *obnoxious* to similar criticism" (Eng.) (adapted from *OED* quotation).

*obrogate. See **nullify (A).**

obscenity. A. Sense. The multipronged tests for obscenity have evolved considerably since Justice Potter Stewart remarked, "Perhaps I could never succeed in intelligibly [defining *obscenity*]. But I know it when I see it." *Jacobellis v. Ohio*, 378 U.S. 184, 197 (1964) (Stewart, J., concurring). In 1973, the U.S. Supreme Court spelled out a three-part test: material is obscene if the average person applying contemporary community standards would find that, taken as a whole, the

material appeals to the prurient interest in sex, portrays sexual conduct in a patently offensive way, and lacks serious literary, artistic, political, or scientific value. *Miller v. California*, 413 U.S. 15, 24 (1973).

Because that test involves a variable standard— "contemporary community standards"—the equation varies from locale to locale. In 1983, a judge on the U.S. Court of Appeals for the Second Circuit reluctantly concluded that "the community standards in New York are so low that nothing is obscene." *U.S. v. Various Articles of Obscene Merchandise*, 709 F.2d 132, 138 (2d Cir. 1983) (Meskill, J., concurring).

B. And *indecency*. Neither *obscenity* nor *indecency* named a common-law crime, but each described acts that were considered crimes. The two are sometimes considered interchangeable, although *indecency* is arguably broader because it may encompass anything that is outrageously disgusting.

The High Court of Justiciary, in Scotland, has held that *indecent* and *obscene* are not synonymous. See *McGowan v. Langmuir*, 1931 J.C. 10, 13 (1930). *Indecency* was held to be the milder term: nudity, for example, is indecent but not necessarily obscene. As a matter of degree, therefore, *obscene* is the term to which stronger disapproval attaches.

C. And *obsceneness*. If there is a DIFFERENTIATION between the two, *obscenity* is more of a static fact and *obsceneness* more of a quality. The latter is comparatively rare—e.g.: "The search warrant (1) authorized seizure of all copies of the books in question and (2) was issued without an adversary hearing on the issue of their *obsceneness*." *A Quantity of Copies of Books v. Kansas*, 378 U.S. 205, 215 (1964) (Harlan, J., dissenting).

OBSCURITY, generally speaking, is a serious literary offense. Simple subjects can be made needlessly difficult, and difficult subjects are often made much more difficult than need be.

Obscurity has many possible causes, most of them rooted in imprecise thought or inconsiderateness toward the reader. The root of the problem is invariably psychological: "Most obscurity, I suspect, comes not so much from incompetence as from ambition— the ambition to be admired for depth of sense, or pomp of sound, or wealth of ornament." F.L. Lucas, *Style* 74 (1962). More bluntly still: "The truth is that many writers today of mediocre talent, or no talent at all, cultivate a studied obscurity that only too often deceives the critics, who tend to be afraid that behind the smoke-screen of words they are missing the effectual fire, and so for safety's sake give honour where no honour is due." G.H. Vallins, *The Best English* 106 (1960).

Following is an example of the kind of obscurity typically found in the worst of legal writing: "Upon the other hand, if the defendant in error could not possibly, by the use of reasonable means and due diligence, have procured the information necessary for her to have, in order to make due proof of the death of Archie Hicks, the law did not impose upon her, as a duty, the attempted doing of an impossible thing." *American Nat'l Ins. Co. v. Hicks*, 35 S.W.2d 128, 131 (Tex. Comm'n App. 1931). This obtuseness is due perhaps partly to the metaphysical notion involved, but certainly also to the pompous phraseology. See WOOLLINESS & PLAIN LANGUAGE.

A. Overelaboration. One cannot improve upon what Cardozo wrote about the MYTH OF PRECISION: "There is an accuracy that defeats itself by the overemphasis of details. I often say that one must permit oneself, and that quite advisedly and deliberately, a certain margin of misstatement. . . . [T]he sentence may be so overloaded with all its possible qualifications that it will tumble down of its own weight." *Law and Literature*, 52 Harv. L. Rev. 471, 474 (1939). Edgar Allan Poe put the same point a little differently: "In one case out of a hundred a point is excessively discussed because it is obscure; in the ninety-nine remaining it is obscure because excessively discussed." 2 *The Works of Edgar Allan Poe* 217 (1863). See OVERPARTICULARIZATION.

B. Initialese. Another kind of obscurity results from the overuse of acronyms, with which the reader must repeatedly try to become familiar—e.g.: "The L.C.R.A. has created an EMF policy, which is stricter than the Tex. P.U.C. EMF policy." James H. Stilwell, *Walking the High Wire*, 15 Rev. Litig. 141, 163 (1996). One's writing should be more accessible to readers than that. If it's to contain acronyms, make them few and space them out. See INITIALESE & ACRONYMS AND INITIALISMS.

C. Abstractness. See ABSTRACTITIS.

obsequies; obsequious. These words are unrelated in meaning. *Obsequies*, the noun, is a FORMAL WORD for *funeral*. *Obsequious*, the adjective, means "toadying; bootlickingly attentive."

observance; observation. The DIFFERENTIATION between these two words is complete. *Observance* = the heeding of a rule or tradition; obedience to custom. E.g.: "Probation is conditional liberty dependent upon the *observance* of the terms of probation." *Rivera v. State*, 667 N.E.2d 764, 766 (Ind. Ct. App. 1996). *Observation* = (1) scrutiny; study; or (2) a judgment or inference from what one has seen—e.g.: (Sense 2) "The court hereby makes some additional *observations* regarding the doctrine." *Consejo de Salud Playa Ponce v. Rullan*, 593 F.Supp.2d 386, 389 (D.P.R. 2009).

Observation is frequently misused for *observance*—e.g.:

- "We would be fulfilling our obligation to locate the proper balance between competing demands for effective police protection and strict *observation* [read *observance*] of a suspect's fundamental constitutional rights." *People v. Knapp*, 441 N.E.2d 1057, 1064 (N.Y. 1982) (Jasen, J., dissenting).
- "If the testator's intent can be determined from the will itself, rigid *observation* [read *observance*] of precedent and other rules is not absolute and controlling." *Hudspeth*

v. Hudspeth, 756 S.W.2d 29, 32 (Tex. App.—San Antonio 1988).

Less commonly, *observance* mistakenly displaces *observation*—e.g.: "This proceeding was heard ore tenus by the court, and its questions indicated its keen *observance* [read *observation*] of the demeanor of each and every witness who testified in the case." *Jenkins v. Jenkins*, 232 So.2d 680, 682 (Ala. Civ. App. 1970). (On the use of *ore tenus* in this example, see **ore tenus.**)

observer. See **witness (B).**

obstruction of justice (= interference with the orderly administration of law) is a broad phrase that captures every willful act of corruption, intimidation, or force that tends somehow to impair the machinery of the civil or criminal law. The phrase dates from 1854.

obstructive; *obstructional; *obstructionary. The second and third terms are NEEDLESS VARIANTS.

obtain is a FORMAL WORD for *get*.

obtaining by deception. See **false pretenses.**

obtainment; *obtainance; *obtainal; *obtention. Though all four have appeared in legal writing, *obtainment* is the most natural and the most frequent. The others are NEEDLESS VARIANTS. But the gerund *obtaining* is probably the best choice: *her obtaining a J.D.* is better phrasing than *her obtainment of a J.D.* But perhaps, if she's down-to-earth, she just *got a J.D.*

obtuse; abstruse. *Obtuse* = (1) blunt; dull; or (2) dimwitted. Except in geometry (where an *obtuse* angle is one greater than 90 degrees) and in some sciences, *obtuse* is usually used in the figurative sense 2 <the obtuse sales clerk couldn't figure out my change>. *Abstruse* = arcane; hard to understand <patent terminology can seem abstruse to nonspecialists>. Avoid using *obtuse* when *abstruse* is called for.

obviate. Modern dictionaries that define *obviate* as meaning "to remove" or "to prevent" are unduly restrictive (*see, e.g.,* the NOAD). The *OED* does not even list this sense. Although *obviate* may well carry this meaning, it means more usually "to meet and dispose of or do away with (a thing); to prevent by anticipatory measures" (*OED*). E.g.:

- "Defendant cites the equitable maxim, 'equity acts in personam,' invoked since the days of Coke and Bacon to *obviate* open conflicts between law and equity courts." *James v. Grand Trunk W. R.R.*, 152 N.E.2d 858, 865 (Ill. 1958).
- "The semblance of vindictiveness that arises from the imposition of a harsher sentence the second time around must be *obviated* so that the proceedings do not leave the impression of unfairness to the defendant being sentenced." *U.S. v. Tucker*, 581 F.2d 602, 605 (7th Cir. 1978).
- "Requiring a clear written finding of dependency would *obviate* that problem in most cases." *M.B. v. R.P.*, 3 So.3d 237, 252 (Ala. Civ. App. 2008).

In the sense "to make unnecessary," *obviate* often appears correctly in the phrase *obviate the necessity of* or *need for.* These phrases are not REDUNDANCIES, for the true sense of *obviate the necessity* is "to prevent the necessity (from arising)," hence to make unnecessary. E.g.:

- "My answer to the second question *obviates the necessity* of reaching the first." *Vaughn v. Vermilion Corp.*, 444 U.S. 206, 211 (1979) (Blackmun, J., dissenting).
- "Professor Easterbrook would move us away from this core of first principles toward the periphery populated by managerial techniques—a realm in which the bureaucratic task of punching figures into a supposedly passive and neutral machine *obviates the need* for judges to make and defend hard choices." Laurence H. Tribe, *Constitutional Calculus*, 98 Harv. L. Rev. 592, 621 (1985).

Obviate is sometimes misunderstood as meaning "to make obvious" or "to remedy": "Other courts have extended the duty owed to an invitee by requiring a business premises owner to take reasonable and feasible steps to *obviate* [read *remedy*] dangerous conditions that cannot be encountered with reasonable safety." Jacqueline L. Hourigan, Note, *Negligence*, 73 U. Det. Mercy L. Rev. 613, 621 (1996). Perhaps *remedy* is the word there—but then again, perhaps *make obvious* was the intended sense.

obvious. See **evident.**

obviously, like other dogmatic words (*clearly, undoubtedly, undeniably*), is one that "lawyers tend to use when they are dealing with exceptionally obscure matters." Grant Gilmore, *The Death of Contract* 116 n.63 (1974). See **clearly** & **doubtless.**

*occular. See **ocular.**

occupancy. Most speakers of English, when they hear this word, are likely to think about how full a building is, as in the "occupancy rate" of a hotel. But *occupancy* has a technical legal sense that nonlawyers are likely unaware of: "the taking possession of something having no owner, with a view to acquiring it as property." The term therefore appears often in the context of adverse possession—e.g.:

- "We are of the view that the inquiry must focus on the events that led to defendant's exclusive *occupancy* of the property, which serves as the basis for his adverse possession claim." *Pitson v. Sellers*, 613 N.Y.S.2d 1005, 1006 (Sup. Ct. 1994).
- "Montana law requires *occupancy* and payment of taxes to prove adverse possession." *Lindey's, Inc. v. Goodover*, 872 P.2d 767, 771 (Mont. 1994).

occupant; occupier. These synonyms are both old, and both have historically been used in legal writing to denote "one who takes possession of property." If any distinction in use exists, it is that *occupant* is the usual word in AmE, *occupier* in BrE.

occurrence. So spelled; **occurence* and **occurance* are fairly common misspellings.

ochlocracy. See **mobocracy.**

-OCRACY. See GOVERNMENTAL FORMS.

octopus forms the plural *octopuses,* not **octopi*—e.g.: "This Court does not find the prosecutor's remark that defense counsel were 'trying to cloud the waters' as squid and *octopi* [read *octopuses*] are reputed to do . . . to be anything more than useless bloviation." *Snow v. Reid*, 619 F.Supp. 579, 585 (S.D.N.Y. 1985). See PLURALS (A) & HYPERCORRECTION (A).

ocular is turgid for *visual* or *with one's eyes.* Labeling it a FORMAL WORD is too tepid a description—e.g.: "A trial judge has a perfect right in a proper case such as this to take into consideration his *ocular* [read *visual*] observations made outside the courtroom of the locus in quo." *Russell v. Bartlett*, 139 So.2d 770, 775 (La. Ct. App. 1961). The word is sometimes misspelled **occular.* Cf. **inoculation.**

oculist. See **ophthalmologist.**

*odiferous. See **odorous.**

odious (= hateful) derives from *odium* (= hatred; the reproach that attaches to an act that people despise). E.g.:

- "Discrimination on the basis of race is *odious* and destructive." *Texas v. Johnson*, 491 U.S. 397, 418 (1989) (per Brennan, J.).
- "*Dred Scott* has the *odious* distinction of holding that slaves were still property, subject to return to their owners, even if they managed to find their way to non-slave states." *In re Marriage of Moschetta*, 30 Cal. Rptr. 2d 893, 898 n.14 (Ct. App. 1994).

The old maxim *comparisons are odious* means that it is highly objectionable in everyday life to compare one person (as a child or other family member) with another.

Though *odious* has nothing to do with *odor,* many writers mistakenly believe that it does. The result is nothing short of a MALAPROPISM—e.g.:

- "There is *an odious* [read *an odorous* or *a malodorous*] smell emanating from this case and one wonders for whose benefit the motion to dismiss Vaccaro was filed." *State Farm Mut. Auto. Ins. Co. v. Noble*, 430 S.E.2d 804, 808 (Ga. Ct. App. 1993) (Blackburn, J., dissenting).
- "O'Connell testified that her offices were not provided daily cleaning service, as required under her lease, and that *an odious stench* [read *a stench*] had permeated the hallways as a result of the flooding in the rest-rooms." *Columbus Props., Inc. v. O'Connell*, 644 A.2d 444, 446 (D.C. 1994).

See **odorous.**

odorous; odoriferous; malodorous. *Odorous* = smelly. *Malodorous* = really stinky. *Odoriferous,* a frequently misused term, has historically almost always had positive connotations in the sense "fragrant." It should not be used in reference to foul odors. **Odiferous* is a mistaken shortening of *odoriferous.* See **odious.**

-OES. See PLURALS (C).

of. A. Signaling Verbosity. However innocuous it may appear, the word *of* is, in anything other than small doses, among the surest indications of flabby writing. Some fear that *of*, and the flabbiness it produces, is spreading: "Clearly, *of* is now something more than a mere preposition. It's a virus." *All About Of*, N.Y. Times, 8 March 1992, at 14. The only suitable vaccination is to cultivate a hardy skepticism about its utility in any given context. If it proves itself, fine. Often, though, it will fail to do so.

Some otherwise excellent writers have, on occasion, caught the virus:

- "The second clause *of* the second section *of* the second article empowers the President *of* the United States." *The Federalist* No. 67, at 409 (Alexander Hamilton) (Clinton Rossiter ed., 1961). [A possible revision: *The second clause of Article II, § 1 empowers the President.* (From three *of*s to one.)]
- "On another occasion I have spoken more fully *of* the attempt *of* a leader among American teachers *of* law to give an economic interpretation *of* a well known English case." Roscoe Pound, *The Formative Era of American Law* 88 (1938). [A possible revision: *On another occasion I have discussed how American law teachers have tried to give an economic interpretation of a well-known English case.* (From four *of*s to one.)]
- "Henry II had genius *of* a high order, which never manifested itself more clearly than in his appreciation *of* the inevitability *of* the divergence *of* the paths *of* crime and *of* tort." H.G. Hanbury, *English Courts of Law* 43 (2d ed. 1953). [A possible revision: *Henry II had rare genius, which never manifested itself more clearly than in his appreciation that the paths of crime and of tort would inevitably diverge.* (From six *of*s to two.) The revision also fixes the REMOTE RELATIVE (*which*) and uncovers a BURIED VERB (*divergence*).]
- "To one innocent *of* knowledge *of* the history *of* religions, the preoccupation *of* ecclesiastics, many *of* them celibate, with sexual matters may seem inexplicable." Glanville Williams, *The Sanctity of Life and the Criminal Law* 48 (1957). [A possible revision: *To one who knows nothing about the history of religions, the preoccupation of ecclesiastics—many of them celibate—with sexual matters may seem inexplicable.* (From five *of*s to two.)]
- "In the judicial task *of* supervising the administration *of* estates *of* deceased persons, or *of* controlling the actions *of* trustees, judges are called upon to make simple orders [that] in practice will often be uncontested, and the task is then *of* an administrative character." P.S. Atiyah, *Law and Modern Society* 37 (1983). [A possible revision: *In the judicial task of supervising the administration of decedents' estates, or of controlling trustees' actions, judges are called on to make simple orders that in practice will often be uncontested, and the task is then administrative.* (From six *of*s to three.)]

As the examples illustrate, reducing the *of*s by 50% or so can greatly improve the briskness and readability of the prose.

B. Superfluous in Dates. *December of 2011* should be *December 2011*. See DATES (B).

C. *Difficult of, easy of, impossible of,* etc. This phrasing, illustrated in the examples that follow, is now peculiar to the legal idiom. It is also easily improved—e.g.:

- "The devise is so indefinite and the trust intended to be created so uncertain of its objects and subjects that it is *impossible of execution* [read *impossible to execute*]." *Taylor v. Columbian Univ.*, 226 U.S. 126, 132–33 (1912) (per McKenna, J.).
- "And it is characterized by secrecy, rendering it *difficult of detection* [read *difficult to detect*]." *U.S. v. Rabinowich*, 238 U.S. 78, 88 (1915) (per Pitney, J.).
- "The crucial question, not *easy of answer* [read *easy to answer*], to which the court must direct itself is whether the police conduct revealed in the particular case falls below standards." *Sherman v. U.S.*, 356 U.S. 369, 382 (1958) (Frankfurter, J., concurring).
- "This is not always *a task easy of performance* [read *an easy task to perform*] but the Government is not without adequate—indeed, powerful—means to apprehend and secure the conviction of persons who violate the laws." *U.S. v. Peisner*, 311 F.2d 94, 106 (4th Cir. 1962).
- "We cannot say that this effort was here so *improbable of success* [read *unlikely to succeed*] that all discovery . . . ought to have been denied." *Duke v. University of Tex. at El Paso*, 729 F.2d 994, 996–97 (5th Cir. 1984).

Cf. NOUN PLAGUE. See **difficult of.**

D. *Of a . . . nature.* This phrasing is almost always unnecessary, for the adjective may always be used alone—and with greater force. For example, *act of a tortious nature* reads better as *tortious act.*

E. For *from.* This usage, an ARCHAISM, still appears with some frequency in legal writing—e.g.: "If I order mutton *of* [read *from*] X, and he supplies me with beef, or decomposed mutton, the failure of performance is as complete as if X had supplied nothing." It is commonly seen in the DOUBLET *to recover of and against.* See **purchase (C).**

of a . . . nature. See **of (D).**

of and from. This phrase is a hallmark of—not to say from—musty LEGALESE. The word *from* generally suffices as a replacement—e.g.: "Tenant agrees to indemnify and to hold Landlord harmless *of and from* [read *from*] any such damage, loss, cost or expense." *Nash v. Landmark Storage, LLC*, 283 S.W.3d 605, 607 (Ark. Ct. App. 2008). That sentence could use a thorough overhaul, but the phrase *of and from* is as good a place to start as any. (For *indemnify and hold harmless*, see **indemnify (A).**)

of counsel. This anglicization of the LAW LATIN *a consiliis* is still sometimes applied to "a lawyer employed by a party in a case; esp., one who—although not the principal attorney of record—is employed to assist in the preparation or management of the case or in its presentation on appeal." *Black's Law Dictionary* 401 (9th ed. 2009).

But the term is more commonly used in AmE in reference to a lawyer (usually semiretired) who is affiliated with a private law firm, though not as a member, partner, or associate. The phrase always indicates relationship, and often status as well. The phrase is often shortened to *counsel*. See **counsel.**

The phrase is becoming a title in the minds of American lawyers, many of whom therefore capitalize *Of Counsel* in midsentence. Otherwise, the phrase will create what for many readers is a MISCUE—e.g.: "[The attorney] became '*of counsel*' for the limited purpose of providing transitional services for several selected clients." *Hempstead Video, Inc. v. Village of Valley Stream*, 409 F.3d 127, 136 (2d Cir. 2005). Some writers would delete *of*: *The attorney became counsel for the limited purpose of providing transitional services for several selected clients.*

of course. This phrase, interestingly, seems to have originated as a POPULARIZED LEGAL TECHNICALITY. It appears to have been a LOAN TRANSLATION of the medieval phrase *writ de cursu* (= a writ issued as a matter of course), which in due time became *writ of course*. E.g.:

- "When trespass became a writ *of course*, about 1250, the recovery of unliquidated damages was a well-known practice." William F. Walsh, *A Treatise on Equity* 7 (1930).
- "The barons feared this growth of royal power and it was provided that, henceforth, the Chancellor would seal no writ, which was not an existing writ (known as writ '*of course*'), except with the sanction of the king and council." L.B. Curzon, *English Legal History* 28 (2d ed. 1979).

See **as of course.**

From the sense "as a matter of course," the phrase *of course* took on the sense "naturally; obviously; clearly." Like those defining words, it is sometimes used to fortify lame propositions. It therefore requires careful, responsible use. See **clearly.**

off. See **off of.**

offence. See **offense.**

offender; *offendant, n. The second is a NEEDLESS VARIANT—e.g.: "But once again, many *offendants* [read *offenders*] do well in this category." George D. Gopen, *The State of Legal Writing: Res Ipsa Loquitur*, 86 Mich. L. Rev. 333, 348 (1987).

offense; offence. The first is the AmE spelling, the second the BrE spelling. In BrE and AmE alike, the word is preferably accented on the second syllable /ə-**fents**/. Unfortunately, because American sports-talk puts the accent on the first syllable /**of**-fents/, many American police officers, criminal lawyers, and criminal-court judges have adopted this pronunciation even in the legal sense of the word. The sound of it puts the literate person's teeth on edge.

The word is sometimes used synonymously with *crime*, but at other times it is intended to have a broader meaning. Jeremy Bentham, for example, defined *offense* in two ways: (1) an act that "appear[s] . . . to have a tendency to produce mischief" (Jeremy Bentham, *The Principles of Morals and Legislation* 178 (1823 ed.)); and (2) "an act prohibited, or, (what comes to the same thing) an act of which the contrary is commanded by the law" (*id.* at xix, § 1).

In BrE, and to a lesser extent in AmE, lawyers commonly distinguish *crimes* (at common law) from *offenses* (created by statute). It is common in both speech communities to use *offense* for the less serious infractions and *crime* for the more serious ones. Lawyers would not speak of the "offense" of murder. Nor would they refer to the "crime" of parking a car in the wrong place.

Even so, because *offense* is generally so closely associated with the idea of crime, the phrase *civil offense is needlessly confusing. The phrase *civil wrong* is preferable. See **civil wrong** & **criminal offense.**

offer. A. And *promise*. "There is surely a difference," wrote a 19th-century English scholar, "a profound difference in legal significance, between an *offer* and a *promise*. An *offer* is an expression of willingness to be bound by contract to the person to whom the offer is made, if he accepts the offer unconditionally and within a reasonable time. The offer then becomes a *promise*. A contract is made up of one or more promises and when a contract is made, and not till then, the parties are bound. Therefore an *offer* is revocable, a *promise* is not." William R. Anson, *Some Notes on Terminology in Contract*, 7 Law Q. Rev. 337, 337 (1891). See **promise (A).**

B. *Firm offer*. A *firm offer* contains a promise not to revoke it for a specified period.

C. And *invitation to negotiate*; *invitation to treat*. "The distinction between an *offer* and an *invitation to treat* [or an *invitation to negotiate*] is often hard to draw as it depends on the elusive criterion of intention." G.H. Treitel, *The Law of Contract* 11 (8th ed. 1991). In BrE, the phrase *invitation to treat* denotes an invitation to make an offer, as opposed to an offer in itself; in AmE, the usual term is *invitation to negotiate*. Examples include a menu in a restaurant, wares displayed in a storefront window, and an auctioneer's request for bids. Writers on the law of contract often use roundabout wordings such as *entertainment of bids*, *proposal made to the public*, and *invitation to make an offer*. The last of these has much to be said in its favor because it is immediately comprehensible to a broad spectrum of readers.

D. *Offer* in Criminal Law. Criminal lawyers have given *offer* an odd meaning by making it synonymous with *attempt*. So an *offer to commit battery* is a threat that makes a person reasonably apprehend that he or she is about to be battered—e.g.:

- "That the defendants had in their possession blackjacks does not convert unactionable words into an actionable trespass unless the blackjacks were displayed and produced in such a manner as to amount to an *offer to commit a battery*." *Cucinotti v. Ortmann*, 159 A.2d 216, 219 (Pa. 1960).

- "As an *offer to commit a battery*, an assault is completed when the object of the offer is put in fear of immediate bodily injury." *State v. Tiedman*, 262 N.W.2d 763, 765 (S.D. 1978).

One unfamiliar with this strange phraseology might mistakenly assume that the phrase *offer to commit battery* is contractual in nature and relates to sado-masochism. See **attempt.**

offer of evidence; offer of proof. An *offer of evidence* is the last step in the introduction of evidence. The proponent of tangible evidence (writings, photographs, murder weapons, and the like), after evidence has been marked for identification, allows the judge and opposing counsel the courtesy of examining it before a witness authenticates it. Once the evidence has been authenticated, the proponent says, for example, "Your Honor, we now *offer into evidence* what has been marked Plaintiff's Exhibit No. 5." One "offers" testimonial evidence simply by engaging in direct examination or cross-examination.

An *offer of proof* is a means of preserving the record for appeal. It consists in a lawyer's adducing what that lawyer expects to be able to prove through a witness's testimony. The offer usually occurs outside the jury's presence and only after a judge has sustained an objection to the introduction of the evidence. An offer may be made of tangible evidence, of testimony through questions and answers, or of testimony through the lawyer's own narrative description.

offeror; *offerer. The first is now standard in legal texts, although the second was much used in the 19th century. See -ER (A).

office, vb., has become a commonplace expression among American lawyers in the southwestern U.S., but not among fastidious users of language—e.g.: "There was also a manager of water operations, who supervised the entire water department, but *was not officed* [read *did not have an office*] at the plant." *Bennartz v. City of Columbia*, 300 S.W.3d 251, 254 (Mo. Ct. App. 2009). This is a classic example of the problem discussed under NOUNS AS VERBS.

officer of the court, in the sense "a lawyer," is an Americanism that evokes the close supervision and control that courts exercise over practicing lawyers, the considerable professional duties that lawyers owe to the judicial system, and the privileges that they receive. Although the courtroom lawyer is not an *officer* in the same sense as a bailiff, a marshal, or a police officer, he or she is nevertheless obligated to serve the disciplinary function of controlling the client in court.

The phrase most commonly crops up when one lawyer chides another for an alleged lapse in ethics or etiquette, or when a judge admonishes counsel to keep to a higher standard.

But some judges and legal ethicists object to the term—e.g.:

- "It has been stated many times that lawyers are '*officers of the court*.' One of the most frequently repeated statements to this effect appears in *Ex parte Garland* [71 U.S. 333, 375 (1868)]. The Court pointed out there, however, that an attorney was not an 'officer' within the ordinary meaning of that term. Certainly nothing that was said in *Ex parte Garland* or in any other case decided by this Court places attorneys in the same category as marshals, bailiffs, court clerks, or judges. Unlike these officials, a lawyer is engaged in a private profession, important though it be to our system of justice. In general he makes his own decisions, follows his own best judgment, collects his own fees and runs his own business. The word '*officer*' as it has always been applied to lawyers conveys quite a different meaning from the word '*officer*' as applied to people serving as officers within the conventional meaning of that term." *Cammer v. U.S.*, 350 U.S. 399, 405 (1956) (per Black, J.).

- "By taking the concept of '*officer of the court*' to an extreme, it is quite probable that the society and the judicial system suffer.... [I]t may not only be dangerous but also an indulgence in myth-making, to take the notion that lawyers are literally servile officers of the courts to its logical conclusion." Harry Cohen, *Lawyer Certification, Civility, "Good Moral Character," and Pressures for Conformity*, 25 J. Legal Prof. 101, 113–14 (2001).

The Missouri Supreme Court has pointed out that the concept of an attorney as an *officer of the court* is rooted in English practice. *See Scott v. Roper*, 688 S.W.2d 757, 765–66 (Mo. 1985). But English "attorneys" were not independent practitioners; they were not called to the bar but instead admitted directly by judges, who also regulated them. *Id.* at 766. Their duties were to aid the court directly, sometimes as superior clerks or under-sheriffs. *Id.* And because they were attached to the court, they were granted certain privileges enjoyed by all court staff, including exemption from being sued in other courts or serving in the militia, and given the title of *officer of the court. Id.* These practices did not carry over to American courts, so "we believe that the time has come to abandon invoking the doctrine that lawyers are officers of the court—or, as some courts suggest, public officers—and lay to rest this anachronism from English legal history." *Id.* at 767.

OFFICIALESE = the language of officialdom, characterized by bureaucratic turgidity and insubstantial fustian. The defining characteristic of officialese is the habitual use of inflated language that could be readily translated into simpler terms: "Let us now proceed to perambulate down the corridor to procure our post-prandial libations." As translated: "Let's go down the hall for after-dinner drinks."

Among the linguistically unsophisticated, puffed-up language seems more impressive. Police officers never *get out of their cars*; instead, they *exit their vehicles*. They never *smell* anything; rather, they *detect it by olfaction*. They *proceed* to a *residence* and *observe* the suspect *partaking of food*. Rather than *sending* papers to each other, officials *transmit* them (by hand delivery, not by fax). And among lawyers, rather than *suing*, one *institutes legal proceedings against* or *brings an action against*.

For sound guidance on how to avoid officialese, see Ernest Gowers, *The Complete Plain Words* (Bruce Fisher ed., 2d ed. 1973); and J.R. Masterson & W.B.

Phillips, *Federal Prose: How to Write in and/or for Washington* (1948).

official misconduct. See **misconduct in office.**

officious. In the 18th century, *officious* had positive connotations ("eager to please"). But today it means "sanctimoniously meddlesome; interfering with what is not one's concern, usu. with an air of duty." E.g.: "Some tour managers are *officious*, bad-tempered buggers; others are diplomatic but efficient." Graham Forbes, *Rock and Roll Tourist* 29 (2010). In legal contexts, the word frequently appears in the phrase *officious intermeddler*: "People who fertilize other people's land or play the good Samaritan are '*officious intermeddlers*'—volunteers whom even equity will not aid." Grant Gilmore, *The Death of Contract* 73 (1974).

In the context of diplomacy, the word has a strangely different sense: "having an extraneous relation to official matters or duties; having the character of a friendly communication, or informal action, on the part of a government or its official representatives" (*OED*) <an officious communication>.

But the term is often misused. In the following sentence it is difficult to discern what meaning the writer intended it to have, but it is impossible for a policy to be *officiously applicable*: "It is upon this assumption, that the case will be tried in a convenient forum so that the forum's policies are properly and not *officiously applicable* [read *arbitrarily applied*?] to the case, that Professor Ehrenzweig advances his central suggestion for solution of choice-of-law problems." Russell J. Weintraub, *Commentary on the Conflict of Laws* 9 (1986).

Here the writer apparently mistook its meaning as being "official-looking": "I still lived in the same old dormitory, in a bigger and more *officious* room." Willie Morris, *A Texas Education*, 56 The Alcade 16, 20 (Nov. 1967).

offing. The traditional phrase is *in the offing* (= about to appear). **On the offing* is incorrect and unidiomatic.

off of is nearly always inferior to *off* without the preposition—e.g.: "Mr. Cramer fell or slipped *off of* [read *off*] the ladder and was injured." *Cramer v. Powder River Coal, LLC*, 204 P.3d 974, 980 (Wyo. 2009). The only exception occurs when *off* is part of a PHRASAL VERB, such as *write off*—e.g.:

- "This is a serious difficulty, but it need not lead to the *writing off of* the subjective definition of recklessness." Glanville Williams, *Textbook of Criminal Law* 78 (1978).
- "The subsidiary also boosted its bottom line by maintaining inadequate reserves for bad debts and delaying the *writing off of* uncollectible accounts receivable." *Gebhardt v. ConAgra Foods, Inc.*, 335 F.3d 824, 827 (8th Cir. 2003).

Cf. **outside of.*

off point. Since first used in 1951, this phrase has, in AmE, become the antonym of *on point*—e.g.:

- "The Ohio case is so far *off point* on its facts that one must stretch his imagination to compare that Court's holding and facts to the instant case." *Geurin Contractors, Inc. v. Bituminous Cas. Corp.*, 636 S.W.2d 638, 643 (Ark. Ct. App. 1982).
- "The dissent's cases are *off-point* [read *off point*]." *LeCroy v. Hanlon*, 713 S.W.2d 335, 342 n.10 (Tex. 1986).
- "The plaintiff's argument is *off point*." *U.S. Leasing Corp. v. City of Chicopee*, 521 N.E.2d 741, 744 n.4 (Mass. 1988).

offrecord. See **off-the-record.**

offset, n., is perfectly acceptable in American legal writing. This usage is first recorded in the *OED* as an Americanism from 1769. Nearly 50 years later, John Pickering wrote: "This is much used by lawyers of America instead of the English term *set-off*; and it is also very common, in popular language, in the sense of equivalent. . . . It is not in the dictionaries." J. Pickering, *A Vocabulary* 142 (1816) (emphasis omitted).

Today the word is commonplace, in dictionaries and elsewhere—e.g.:

- "Finally, the Trustee argues that . . . we are, in effect, sanctioning an impermissible *offset* of a fraudulent conveyance against general unsecured claims." *In re United Energy Corp.*, 944 F.2d 589, 597 (9th Cir. 1991).
- "The only statutorily permissible *offset* to an approved progress payment is 'an amount necessary to satisfy any claims, liens or judgments.'" *Christ Gatzonis Elec. Contractor, Inc. v. New York City Sch. Constr. Auth.*, 23 F.3d 636, 641 (2d Cir. 1994).
- "The availability of *offsets* against Social Security benefits is limited." *Lockhart v. U.S.*, 546 U.S. 142, 144 (2005) (per O'Connor, J.).

offset, vb., might be considered inferior to *set off*, although it cannot rightly be condemned as an error. E.g.:

- "The division of property was, or will be, approximately equal and the two amounts would *offset* each other." *Welsh v. Welsh*, 869 S.W.2d 802, 807 (Mo. Ct. App. 1994).
- "The State's asserted interests in modernizing elections and combatting fraud are decidedly modest; at best, they fail to *offset* the clear inference that thousands of Indiana citizens will be discouraged from voting." *Crawford v. Marion County Election Bd.*, 553 U.S. 181, 233 (2008) (Souter, J., dissenting).

What can be condemned as an error—and a gross one—is using **offsetted* as a past tense or past participle. E.g.:

- "NFO then refused to pay Smith, . . . contending that the amount NFO owed Smith was *offsetted* [read *offset*] by the damage caused by Smith's breach of his January 9, 1973 contract." *National Farmers Org. v. Smith*, 526 S.W.2d 759, 763 (Tex. Civ. App.—Corpus Christi 1975).
- "The lower court . . . properly considered . . . the disparity between appellee's earning capacity and appellant's substantial income *offsetted* [read *offset*] by his reasonable expenses and direct support of Eric." *Steenland-Parker v. Parker*, 544 A.2d 1010, 1013 (Pa. Super. Ct. 1988).

See **set-off.**

offshore company; island company. *Offshore company* = a company incorporated or registered outside the jurisdiction where it does its primary business, usu. to obtain some sort of tax or regulatory advantage. In colloquial BrE, the synonym *island company* derives its name from the fact that such companies are often incorporated or registered in the Channel Islands or the Isle of Man. 1 *Jowitt's Dictionary of English Law* 1230 (Daniel Greenberg ed., 3d ed. 2010).

offspring. See **issue (E).**

off-the-record, adj. This is the standard phrase for any comment explicitly not for recordation or attribution. As a PHRASAL ADJECTIVE preceding what it modifies, it should be hyphenated, but not when it follows what it modifies <an off-the-record statement> <a statement off the record>. Some writers have experimented with *offrecord*; that word is not yet standard—e.g.: "The invitation was extended . . . to make some comment on the disclosure. *Offrecord* [read *Off-record*] remarks . . . are not calculated to influence the jury in reaching its verdict." *Walker v. State*, 36 So.2d 117, 119 (Ala. Ct. App. 1948).

of no effect; of none effect. See **none (B).**

of opinion. See **opinion, of (the).**

often, as an adverb, need not be hyphenated in phrases such as the one in the following sentence: "Occurring at the end of eight days of *often-starry* [read *often starry*] and emotional deliberation in State Supreme Court in Manhattan, the verdict ended a highly publicized and sensational murder trial in New York." Ronald Sullivan, *Steinberg Is Guilty of First-Degree Manslaughter*, N.Y. Times, 31 Jan. 1989, at A1.

The word should be pronounced with a silent *-t-*, as with *listen* and *moisten*. It is a badge of linguistic benightedness to sound the *-t-*. For a full essay on the subject, see Charles Harrington Elster, *The Big Book of Beastly Mispronunciations* 354–56 (2d ed. 2005).

***oftentimes** is, in all cases, unnecessary for *often*. E.g.:

- "Evidence of gang affiliation can *oftentimes* [read *often*] be unfairly prejudicial." *U.S. v. Thomas*, 86 F.3d 647, 652 (7th Cir. 1996).
- "Libel lawfare is *oftentimes* [read *often*] used interchangeably with the term libel tourism." R. Ashby Pate, *Blood Libel*, 8 First Amend. L. Rev. 414, 422 (2010).

See REDUNDANCY.

of the essence. In the law of contract, this phrase makes certain stipulations more important than others; any failure to perform such a stipulation justifies a rescission. See **time is of the essence.**

of (the) opinion. See **opinion, of (the).**

olfaction, detect by. This phrase is a laughable pomposity for *smell*. E.g.: "The marijuana was discovered in plain view during the course of a subsequent maritime search of the vessel, and, in any event, the distinctive odor of the contraband weed apparently was ubiquitous and easily *detected by olfaction* on board and well beyond the *Lady Mar.*" *U.S. v. Alvarez-Mena*, 765 F.2d 1259, 1269 (5th Cir. 1985). Here we also have INELEGANT VARIATION (*marijuana . . . the contraband weed*) and misuse of *ubiquitous* (= universal). Cf. **ocular.**

oligopoly; oligopsony. The first denotes control or domination of a market by a few large sellers; the second denotes control or domination of a market by a few large customers. Cf. **monopoly (D).**

***olograph.** See **holograph.**

olographic. See **holographic.**

ombudsman; ombuds; *ombudsperson. *Ombudsman* = (1) an official appointed to receive, investigate, and report on private citizens' complaints about the government; or (2) a similar appointee in a nongovernmental organization. Originally a Swedish word denoting a commissioner, *ombudsman* spread throughout the world during the mid-20th century as governments and other institutions saw the wisdom of having such an official. Though the word entered the English language only as recently as 1959, it caught on remarkably well.

Because of the *-man* suffix, many writers consider it sexist. Some have taken to lopping off the suffix, and though the word *ombuds* looks distinctly un-English and remains unrecorded in most English dictionaries, it is surprisingly common—e.g.: "In Denmark, the Consumers' *Ombuds* has been given statutory responsibility for handling consumer complaints." *Evaluating Electronic Payment Systems in the UK*, Am. Banker, 28 Sept. 1987, at 25.

Several writers have tried *ombudsperson*, but that form should be allowed to wither. (See SEXISM (B).) Others have experimented with *ombuds officer*, which at least satisfies one's desire to have a word that looks as if it denotes a person—e.g.: "Columbia University last week named its first 'ombuds officer' as a reference point on campus for people who have grievances within the university and are looking for options to deal with them." *Campus Life: Columbia*, N.Y. Times, 14 July 1991, § 1, pt. 2, at 31.

Yet the objections to the term seem destined to fail. The U.S. Ombudsman Association is well established, and most of its leaders are content with the name.

omissible; *omittable. The second is incorrect.

omission. A. Generally. Among nonlawyers, this word has a narrower sense than it does among lawyers. To the nonlawyer, an *omission* is either something left out (as of a book or program) or the act of leaving something out. To the lawyer, *omission* serves as a useful antonym of *commission*, ordinarily denoting the failure to do something. E.g.:

- "Nor will the surety be discharged by the creditor's *omission* to inform him." Laurence P. Simpson, *Handbook on the Law of Suretyship* 406 (1950).

- "When we speak of an *omission* we mean something that the accused could have done if he had been minded to do so and had prepared himself in time, or at least something that another in his place could have done." Glanville Williams, *Criminal Law* 4 (2d ed. 1961).

See **omit [+ infinitive]**.

B. And *forbearance*. An *omission* is an unintentional negative act, whereas a *forbearance* is an intentional negative act. Unfortunately, some legal writers use *omission* when they mean *forbearance*—a habit contributing to sloppy analysis.

omit [+ infinitive]. This construction, in which *omit* means "to neglect," appears today primarily in legal prose. E.g.: "A person who wrongfully *omits to perform* a particular act required of him is liable in damages for all of the consequences [that] may ordinarily ensue therefrom." *Valdez v. Taylor Auto. Co.*, 278 P.2d 91, 98 (Cal. Ct. App. 1954). It is a lawyers' expression that is neither JARGON nor LEGALESE, but an obsolescent grammatical construction. See **omission (A)**.

*omittable. See **omissible**.

omnibus, adj. (= relating to many distinct objects at once; comprising a large number of items or particulars), is a LEGALISM most often used in the legislative phrase *omnibus bill*. But *omnibus* also has other uses in legal writing—e.g.: "The appeal brings up for review the denial, after a hearing, of . . . defendant's *omnibus* motion." *People v. Lopez*, 497 N.Y.S.2d 452, 452 (App. Div. 1986). *Omnibus motion* = a motion that makes several requests or asks for multiple forms of relief.

on; upon. These synonyms are used in virtually the same ways. The distinctions are primarily in tone and connotation. *On*, the more usual word, is generally preferable: it is better to write *service on a defendant* than *service upon a defendant*. E.g.:

- "In a hearing *upon* [read *on*] a motion to modify, the burden is *upon* [read *on*] the applicant." *Atkinson v. Atkinson*, 149 P.3d 1055, 1058 (Okla. Civ. App. 2006).
- "This case centers *upon* [read *on*] a parcel of land located adjacent to land owned by the Finkes in the Town of Highland." *Finke v. N. Ind. Pub. Serv. Co.*, 899 N.E.2d 5, 6 (Ind. Ct. App. 2008).
- "The trial court's imposition of a life-without-parole sentence was due in large part to the trial court's dutiful reliance *upon* [read *on*] an order entered by a three-justice panel of this court." *McDowell v. State*, 20 So.3d 1216, 1217 (Miss. 2009).

But *upon* is the better word for introducing the idea of an occurrence or event—e.g.: "*Upon* being served with a request, a party must . . . ."

Avoid altering an idiom in which *on* appears by making it *upon*, as here: "A judgment void *upon its face* [read *on its face*] may be vacated upon proper application regardless of what length of time has intervened since its entry." *Green Ridge Bank v. Edwards*, 372 A.2d 23, 26 n.* (Pa. Super. Ct. 1977). See **face, on its, upon (A)** & SET PHRASES.

on a . . . basis. See **basis (B)**.

on all fours (= squarely on point with regard to both facts and law) is useful legal JARGON that describes a highly pertinent legal precedent. The phrase began as a LOAN TRANSLATION of an old Latin maxim, *Nullum simile est idem nisi quatuor pedibus currit* ("No similar thing is the same, unless it runs on all four feet"). The METAPHOR, as the *OED* explains, is that of a quadruped running evenly—not limping like a lame dog. E.g.:

- "Judges in this way are constantly reasoning not by explicit authority '*on all fours*,' but by analogy." Carleton K. Allen, *Law in the Making* 308 (7th ed. 1964).
- "Once you found cases '*on all fours*' you could sustain a good argument." Frank Maher, *Words, Words, Words*, 14 Melbourne U. L. Rev. 468, 469 (1984).
- "The ranchers' complaint is *on all fours* with the objection of the mushroom growers." *Johanns v. Livestock Mktg. Ass'n*, 544 U.S. 550, 571 (2005) (Souter, J., dissenting). It is odd, though, to say that a complaint is "on all fours" with an objection.

Cf. **whitehorse case**.

Because of the special legal sense, lawyers may create a MISCUE if they suddenly use the phrase in reference to a person on hands and knees: "Coke made an ardent defense of the common-law courts that angered King James so violently that all the judges trembled and Coke himself 'fell flat *on all fours*.' " René A. Wormser, *The Story of the Law* 279 (1962).

on and after (a date) is usually unnecessary for *from* or *since* (a date), unless it is important to convey explicitly the nuance that the date mentioned is included within the scope of applicability. Cf. **on or about**.

on appeal; on the appeal. The first phrase is today considered more idiomatic in AmE—e.g.: "The issue for determination *on the appeal* [read *on appeal*] was the time at which the constitutional right to free primary education ceases." Lee Ann Basser, *Justice for All?*, 8 J. Gender Race & Just. 531, 543 (2005). See **appeal (A)**.

on behalf of. See **behalf**.

on circuit. See **circuit, to ride**.

one. A. The Overdone *one*, n. The impersonal *one* is an uncomfortable word in AmE except when used sparingly (roughly, no more than twice in a sentence—and preferably no more than twice in a paragraph). In droves, it will strike readers as pedantic or schoolmarmish—e.g.: "*One* has an affirmative responsibility toward others when *one* has taken an active part in directing the manner in which these others perform their tasks or when *one* creates or is generally responsible for a dangerous situation that causes harm. . . . *One* is not liable, however, simply because *one* uses the services of an independent contractor. Nor is *one* liable because of the mere fact that the contractor performs his work on *one*'s land or, as in this case, on *one*'s ship." *Futo v. Lykes Bros. S.S. Co.*, 742 F.2d 209, 215 (5th Cir. 1984). Enough said.

B. One . . . he. This expression is inferior to *one . . . one*, partly because of the questionable grammar and partly because of the generic masculine pronoun. (See SEXISM (A).) But the infelicity is common—e.g.:

- "If *one* were thoughtless, *he* [better: *one*] would be apt to say that this is a case in which part of the operative facts creating the original obligation are directly presented to the senses of the tribunal." Clarence Morrow, *Law and Fact*, 55 Harv. L. Rev. 1303, 1328 (1942).
- "A constructive trust, on the other hand, arises when *one* obtains the legal title to property in violation of a duty *he* [better: *one*] owes to another." *Fulp v. Fulp*, 140 S.E.2d 708, 711 (N.C. 1965).

Even worse are constructions on the order of *one . . . such person*—e.g.: "The United States Supreme Court . . . held that *one* may be in custody for habeas corpus purposes despite the fact that *such person* [read *one*] has been released from jail or on personal bond." *Ex parte Williams*, 690 S.W.2d 243, 244 (Tex. 1985). Cf. **one . . . you.**

C. One [+ name]. Using *one* as an adjective before a proper name, as in "*one* Howard James," is a pretentious LEGALISM with a valid pedigree in English, but generally without justification in modern prose. It might even hint at BIBLICAL AFFECTATION, for the *OED* quotes from the Bible: "and of *one* Jesus, which was dead, whom Paul affirmed to be alive." But today, the word *one* looks askance at any name following it.

one and the same is occasionally misrendered *one in the same.

one another. See **each other.**

one bite at the apple; one bite at the cherry. The first is the usual AmE idiom today, the latter the invariably BrE idiom. Each one denotes the idea that a litigant gets but one chance to take advantage of certain opportunities or rights. American courts sometimes use *cherry* in place of *apple*, but the latter fruit vastly predominates. The American version is that rare SET PHRASE that is not so well set, variations on the phrase being more common than the main phrase itself—e.g.:

- "Unless a litigant gets a real *bite at the apple* of discord he should not be foreclosed from another attempt." *Angel v. Bullington*, 330 U.S. 183, 207 (1947) (Rutledge, J., dissenting).
- "Because 'one fair opportunity to litigate an issue is enough,' we generally will not allow a *second bite at a single apple*." *A.J. Canfield Co. v. Vess Beverages, Inc.*, 859 F.2d 36, 37 (7th Cir. 1988) (citation omitted).
- "The interest of finality requires that parties generally get only *one bite at the Rule 59(e) apple* for the purpose of tolling the time for bringing an appeal." *Charles L.M. v. Northeast Indep. Sch. Dist.*, 884 F.2d 869, 871 (5th Cir. 1989).
- "Finality in issue preclusion also serves efficiency by ensuring that parties who have fully and fairly litigated

a particular issue . . . do not receive more than *one bite at the apple*." *Haber v. Biomet, Inc.*, 578 F.3d 553, 557 (7th Cir. 2009).

Some British lawyers insist that their idiom—*one bite at the cherry*—makes more sense because the cherry is a fruit that, by its nature, is eaten in only one bite: it makes little sense to think of multiple bites at a cherry.

But it was not logic that seems to have led American lawyers to speak of apples. Up to the late 1940s, American lawyers, like their British counterparts, regularly said *one bite at the cherry*: dozens of examples appear in the law reports. But by the 1920s on, *cherry* had assumed another sense in AmE, namely "hymen" or "virgin." The *OED* quotes an American book from the 1970s explaining that " '[t]o take or eat a cherry' means to deflower a virgin."

So *one bite at the cherry* may well be the only legal idiom that has changed because its users felt embarrassment over a newfound double entendre.

one . . . he; one . . . his. See **one (B).**

one in [number]; one of every [number]. See SUBJECT–VERB AGREEMENT (M).

*one in the same. See **one and the same.**

one of those ——s who (*or* that). This construction requires a plural, not a singular, verb. Why? Because in this construction, *who* (or *that*) acts as the subject of the upcoming clause, and the relative pronoun takes its number from the plural noun immediately preceding—e.g.: "[It] is one of the few sections of the act that *is* [read *are*] applicable to cases filed after April 20, 2005, but before October 17, 2005." *In re Agnew*, 355 B.R. 276, 280 (Bankr. D. Kan. 2006). The reason for this construction becomes apparent when we reorder the sentence (without changing a word): "Of the few sections of the act that are applicable to cases filed after April 20, 2005, but before October 17, 2005, it is one."

This point of usage trips up even the best writers, so it is common—e.g.:

- "One of the most important and difficult questions *which arises* [read *that arise*] in examining the extent of the parties' duties under a contract is to decide whether the parties are absolutely bound." P.S. Atiyah, *An Introduction to the Law of Contract* 184 (3d ed. 1981).
- "Martin Marietta, however, has not claimed that it was one distributor among many who *was* [read *were*] terminated for failing to price-fix." *O.K. Sand & Gravel, Inc. v. Martin Marietta Corp.*, 819 F.Supp. 771, 797 (S.D. Ind. 1992).

For similar errors, see **crime** (last par.) & **each (A)** (last par.).

one . . . one. See **one (B).**

oneself. One word.

one . . . you. This shift from third person to second is even worse than *one . . . he*. (See **one (B).**) E.g.: "*One* hears—and if *you* are like me, *you* acquiesce in—many complaints about the decline of civility in Western society." Clifford Orwin, *Civility*, 60 Am. Scholar 553, 553 (1991). [One possible revision: *You hear—and if you are like me, you acquiesce in—many . . . .*]

on his own application is LEGALESE for *at his request.*

on information and belief. See **information and belief.**

on its face. See **face, on its.**

onlooker. See **witness (B).**

only is perhaps the most frequently misplaced of all English words. Its best placement is precisely before the words intended to be limited. The more words separating *only* from its correct position, the more awkward the sentence; and such a separation can lead to ambiguities. (Cf. **solely.**) E.g.:

- "These public rights can *only* be destroyed by proper municipal action." *Hwy. Holding Co. v. Yara Eng'g Corp.*, 123 A.2d 511, 515 (N.J. 1956). (Put *only* before *by.*)
- "A *pro se* complaint . . . can *only* be dismissed for failure to state a claim if it appears beyond a doubt that the plaintiff can prove no set of facts in support of his claim which would entitle him to relief." *Estelle v. Gamble*, 429 U.S. 97, 106 (1976) (per Marshall, J.). (Put *only* before *if.*)
- "The state need *only* perform if the defendant has performed his obligations." James Edward Bond, *Plea Bargaining and Guilty Pleas* 240 (1981). (Put *only* before *if.*)
- "*Erie* is *only* applicable where there is no controlling federal statute." Steven Emanuel & Lazar Emanuel, *Civil Procedure* 233 (2008). (Put *only* before *where.*)

on oath. See **oath (A).**

on or about is the lawyer's hedge-phrase for dates, used especially in pleadings—e.g.: "Ortiz alleges that *on or about* June 14, 2008, he was summoned to serve as a juror." *Ortiz-Skerrett v. Rey Enters., Inc.*, 692 F.Supp.2d 201, 202 (D.P. R. 2010). If the date is known with certainty, *on* is preferable. See FUDGE WORDS & **on and after.**

on pain of. See **pain of, on.**

on point. See **in point** & **off point.**

on the appeal. See **on appeal.**

on the contrary. See **contrary (B).**

*****on the offing.** See **offing.**

on the part of. This phrase is usually verbose—e.g.: "The accident was not due to any voluntary action *on the part of the plaintiff* [read *by the plaintiff*]." *Potthast v. Metro-N. R.R. Co.*, 400 F.3d 143, 150 (2d Cir. 2005).

on the record. See **record (C).**

on trust. See **trust (B).**

onus, lit., "a burden" (L.), usually carries the extended meaning "a disagreeable responsibility; obligation." In law, it also acts as an elliptical form of *onus probandi*, meaning *burden of proof.* E.g.:

- "The mode of suing for and recovering penalties and forfeitures does not necessarily include any rules . . . as to the *onus probandi.*" *The Abigail*, 1 F. Cas. 36, 37 (C.C.D. Mass. 1824).
- "The principle governing a movant's burden of proof for postjudgment vacation relief is vastly different from that which applies to the allocation of *onus probandi* and of the pleading burden in prejudgment stages." *Davidson v. Gregory*, 780 P.2d 679, 684 n.19 (Okla. 1989).
- "Upon a death-benefit claimant rests the *onus probandi.*" *American Mgmt. Sys. v. Burns*, 903 P.2d 288, 291 n.12 (Okla. 1995).

Onus of proof is a BrE compromise between *onus probandi* and *burden of proof*—e.g.:

- "The question of *onus of proof* is only a rule for deciding on whom the obligation of going further, if he wishes to win, rests." 1 Thomas Beven, *Negligence in Law* 128 (2d ed. 1895).
- "There is a preliminary question for the judge . . . whether there is any [evidence] upon which a jury can properly proceed to find a verdict for the party producing it upon whom the *onus of proof* is imposed." *Coughran v. Bigelow*, 164 U.S. 301, 307 (1896) (per Shiras, J.).

See **burden of proof (B)** & LOAN TRANSLATIONS.

op. cit. is the abbreviation for *opere citato* (= in the work cited). It was a signal formerly used where today a short-form citation would appear. *Op. cit.* is no longer used in legal citations and is obsolescent in other scholarly writing.

open court, in. This phrase, sometimes contrasted with *closed court* or *in camera*, means "during the public proceedings of a court." E.g.:

- "Only once was Judge Taylor ever seen at a dead standstill *in open court*, and the Cunninghams stopped him." Harper Lee, *To Kill a Mockingbird* 167 (1960).
- "It is difficult to imagine acceptance of a system under which, instead of trial *in open court*, a quiet and secluded inquiry by a committee of social scientists would determine whether an individual should be subjected to compulsory detention." Lon L. Fuller, *Anatomy of the Law* 55 (1968).
- "When a defendant pleads *in open court*, there is less need for counsel to develop the record and refine claims to present to an appellate court." *Halbert v. Michigan*, 545 U.S. 605, 630 (2005) (Thomas, J., dissenting).

Cf. **in camera.**

open-ended; open-endedness. Both are so hyphenated.

open market. See **market overt.**

open seas. See **high seas.**

open the door. This legal CLICHÉ generally denotes one of two ideas: (1) that one party makes it possible (i.e., "opens the door") for the other party to do something tending to be prejudicial; or (2) that a court or policymaker is embarking on a *slippery slope.* (See **slippery slope.**)

An asterisk (✳) precedes words and phrases that are invariably inferior forms.

- (Sense 1) "It would be ironic to hold that when a State embarks on such desirable experimentation it thereby *opens the door* to scrutiny by the federal courts, while States that choose not to adopt such procedural provisions entirely avoid the strictures of the Due Process Clause." *Hewitt v. Helms*, 459 U.S. 460, 471 (1983) (per Rehnquist, J.).
- (Sense 2) "In adopting the rule it does, the Court *opens the door* to countless similarly situated prisoners to withdraw their guilty pleas many years after they were entered." *Henderson v. Morgan*, 426 U.S. 637, 659 (1976) (Rehnquist, J., dissenting).

operable; *operatable; operative; operational. *Operable* is now commonly used in the sense "practicable; capable of being operated." **Operatable* for *operable* is an occasional error—e.g.: "The fact that [the machinery] was not '*operatable*' [read *operable*] after some repairs had been completed did not render it 'unrepairable.'" *Arizona Container Corp. v. Consolidated Freightways*, 522 P.2d 772, 774 (Ariz. Ct. App. 1974).

Operative = (1) having effect; in operation; efficacious <the statute is now operative>; or (2) having principal relevance <*may* is the operative word of the statute>.

Operational = engaged in operation; able to function; used in operation. E.g.: "While a rate of slightly under ten 'violent' incidents per month may seem shocking at first hearing even for a sizable correctional institution, this statistic must be evaluated in light of the fact that no *operational* definition of 'violence' has been tendered." *Wheeler v. Sullivan*, 599 F.Supp. 630, 646 (D. Del. 1984).

ophthalmologist; oculist; optometrist; optician. The first two designate an M.D. whose specialty is the eye, although *ophthalmologist* is now more usual. An *optometrist* (with the degree of O.D.) is licensed to prescribe glasses and contact lenses, as well as some medicines for the eye. An *optician* makes the glasses in accordance with the prescription.

ophthalmology /of-thə[l]-**mol**-ə-jee/ is often mispronounced /op-/ and misspelled **ophthamology* or **opthamology*.

opine today usually connotes the expression of a judgment based on insufficient grounds. Because it suggests the giving of an idle opinion, it cheapens the opinion given. Formerly, however, the word was used in the sense "to express or pronounce a formal or authoritative opinion" (*OED*). The *OED* calls this sense rare; yet, in American law at least, this usage could hardly be accurately described as rare. Examples abound in which the verb is used of courts' pronouncements, without any suggestion of insufficiency of evidence. E.g.:

- "The Court of Appeals *opined* that a taxpayer would not have standing to challenge a President's favorable reference to religion in a State of the Union address." *Hein v. Freedom From Religion Found., Inc.*, 551 U.S. 587, 612 (2007) (per Alito, J.).

- "The Supreme Court *opined* that the intention of a patent monopoly is to reward an inventor for the public disclosure of his invention." Alex Osterlind, *Staking a Claim on the Building Blocks of Life*, 75 Mo. L. Rev. 617, 637 (2010).

Hence the older neutral sense remains alive in law, perhaps because a verb corresponding to *opinion* is badly needed. But the available choice, *opine*, leaves open the potential for many a playful ambiguity.

Sometimes it is unclear whether cheapening is intended—e.g.: "The expert witness will *opine* that these images are real." *U.S. v. Lee*, 64 M.J. 213, 215 (Armed Forces App. 2006). One can hardly be said to *opine* about one's own thoughts: "I merely *opine* that I am hard-pressed to imagine a more appropriate case for [the use of legislative history] than the present one." *Gonzalez v. Southern Pac. Transp. Co.*, 755 F.2d 1179, 1191 (5th Cir. 1985). [Read *I would be hardpressed to imagine* . . . .] See **opinion**, vb.

opinion, n. *Opinion* is the AmE term for a judicial deliverance, i.e., the court's statement explaining its decision, including points of law, statements of fact, *rationes decidendi*, and dicta. The BrE equivalent is *judgment*, but the word *opinion* is also frequently used there. (See **judgment (B).**) In BrE, *opinion* more commonly refers to advice given by counsel on facts set out in a case or in a memorandum submitted to counsel. See **decision** & **deliverance.**

opinion, vb., is a NEEDLESS VARIANT of *opine*—e.g.:

- "Dr. Battalora *opinioned* [read *opined*] that the accident caused only multiple muscle strains." *Bergeron v. Firestone Tire & Rubber Co.*, 482 So.2d 54, 56 (La. Ct. App. 1986).
- "Unless a risk premium is necessary to attract competent counsel, Justice O'Connor *opinioned* [read *opined*] that one should not be granted." *Shakman v. Democratic Org. of Cook County*, 677 F.Supp. 933, 940 (N.D. Ill. 1987).

See **opine.**

opinion, of (the). Modern idiom requires *of the opinion*. To omit the definite article is to use an ARCHAISM peculiar to law—e.g.:

- "We are *of opinion* that the findings of fact as made by the trial court are supported by sufficient competent evidence." *Peoples Ice & Fuel Co. v. Dickey Oil Co.*, 65 P.2d 319, 329 (Kan. 1937).
- "The Court is *of opinion* that the gist of this offense is the attempt to influence the action of the Federal Housing Administration." *U.S. v. Melvin*, 148 F.Supp. 204, 205 (D.C. Cir. 1957).

Today, *of the opinion* seems to outnumber *of opinion* in legal opinions by three or four occurrences to one, in both BrE and AmE—e.g.:

- "We are *of the opinion* that this appeal may be decided at this time, without further briefing or argument." *State v. Vashey*, 912 A.2d 416, 417 (R.I. 2006).
- "The court is *of the opinion* that Ms. White suffered an injury which is chronic and permanent." *White v. Progressive Sec. Ins. Co.*, 6 So.3d 860, 862 (La. Ct. App. 2009).

opinion of the court. This phrase denotes the American-style judicial opinion that, though written usually by a single judge, speaks for the court as a whole. Within the common-law tradition, the alternative is *seriatim opinions*, in which each judge on the bench pronounces an individual opinion. For a brief history of how Chief Justice John Marshall established the opinion of the court in American law, see Bryan A. Garner, "Opinions, Style of," in *The Oxford Companion to the Supreme Court of the United States* 706, 707 (Kermit L. Hall ed., 2d ed. 2005).

opinion rule; rule against opinions. The first is the preferred phrase for the principle that a witness should testify to facts, not opinions, and that a non-expert witness's opinions are often excludable from evidence. *Black's Law Dictionary* 1202–03 (9th ed. 2009). The second is a common variant. This rule of evidence carries different senses in AmE and in BrE, primarily because of the different understandings of the word *opinion*:

> The opinion rule, though it developed from practices and expressions of the English courts, seems to be emphasized more generally and enforced more inflexibly here [in the U.S.] than in the mother country. In the first place a rule against "opinions" may have had a different meaning for the English judge. We are told that in English usage of the 1700s and earlier *opinion* had the primary meaning of "notion" or "persuasion of the mind without proof or certain knowledge." It carried an implication of lack of grounds, which is absent from our present-day term *opinion* in this country. We use the word as denoting a belief, inference, or conclusion, without suggesting it is well- or ill-founded.
>
> Charles T. McCormick, *Handbook of the Law of Evidence* 22 (Edward W. Cleary ed., 2d ed. 1972).

OPINIONS, JUDICIAL. Writing a judicial opinion is a peculiar task—quite different in many ways from writing other types of expository prose. The primary difficulty lies in giving either a "yes" or a "no" answer to what is often an extremely complicated problem. The decision generally must be consistent with previous judicial decisions, while conforming to the judge's notions of what justice dictates. Often, and especially in difficult cases, the doctrine of stare decisis plays tug-of-war with conscientious fairness. The dilemma is especially acute because some of the most intractable problems of society and of individual human lives must be reduced to simple yea-or-nay dichotomies. Not all the uncertainties can be plumbed by the judge writing an opinion; the task is to justify one's determination, crude as the framework may be for minimizing the possibly substantial merits of the losing side.

John Wigmore identified six shortcomings of judicial opinions: (1) undiscriminating citation of authority; (2) unfamiliarity with controlling precedents; (3) mechanical treatment of judicial questions; (4) misconception of the doctrine of precedents; (5) overconsideration of points of law; and (6) certain deficiencies peculiar to one-judge opinions. 1 John Wigmore, *Evidence* § 8, at 615–18 (3d ed. 1940). Electronic research has probably minimized #2, but exacerbated #1. Overcrowded court dockets have minimized #5 but exacerbated #3. Criticisms #4 and #6 remain perennial problems.

There are so many aspects of writing effective judicial opinions that no short treatment could pretend to cover even the primary ones. But a few short observations may be helpful. The reader who needs more detailed guidance may read any number of articles or books on the subject. (See LEGAL-WRITING STYLE.) But all in all, we still must await production of a first-rate treatise on this subject.

A. Tense. It is generally best in judicial opinions to write in the present tense when referring to the parties or facts before the court that have or seem to have continuing validity, from all that appears in the record. So if a judge writes, "The defendants *were* citizens of Clarksville, Tennessee," the reader must wonder whether they have moved or died. What the judge here doubtless meant is that these persons *were* defendants, but now that the trial is over they are no longer. Using the past tense in this way needlessly puzzles the reader, even though the author knows that the past tense is technically correct because the opinion is being written some time after the trial or sitting. Yet in narrating past events, of course, the past tense is normal.

Less troublesome, but also to be avoided, is the mannerism of using the future tense, as in "The judgment *will be* affirmed." Such statements often appear toward the beginning of an opinion, so that at the end, the court may conclude, "The judgment *will be, and hereby is,* affirmed." This messing about with tenses is unnecessary. The writing judge should be direct: "We affirm the judgment below."

B. Judicial Humor. Drollery and judicial opinions almost invariably make an unhappy combination. "The form of opinion which aims at humor from beginning to end is a perilous adventure, which can be justified only by success, and even then is likely to find its critics almost as many as its eulogists." Benjamin N. Cardozo, *Law and Literature*, 52 Harv. L. Rev. 471, 483 (1939). One of those critics of judicial humor was the late Justice George Rose Smith of the Arkansas Supreme Court, who observed, "Judicial humor is neither judicial nor humorous. A lawsuit is a serious matter to those concerned in it. For a judge to take advantage of his criticism-insulated, retaliation-proof position to display his wit is contemptible, like hitting a man when he's down." George R. Smith, *A Primer of Opinion Writing, for Four New Judges*, 21 Ark. L. Rev. 197, 210 (1967). Justice Smith cited an egregious example of attempted stream-of-consciousness humor: *Hampton v. North Carolina Pulp Co.*, 49 F.Supp. 625 (E.D.N.C. 1943); it is one of the worst opinions that have come to my attention. For an example of failed poeticism and wasteful drivel, see *U.S. v. Sproed*, 628 F.Supp. 1234 (D. Or. 1986).

Lest we assume, however, that judicial writing should be cheerless and sober-sided, it is worth noting Cardozo's tempered judgment: "In all this I would not convey the thought that an opinion is the worse for being lightened by a smile. I am merely preaching caution." *Law and Literature*, 52 Harv. L. Rev. 471, 484 (1939).

C. Separate Opinions. Judges, and especially appellate judges in the majority, write not just for themselves but for the entire court. In concurring and dissenting opinions, of course, the writing usually becomes more individualistic:

> If a judge is occasionally possessed of an uncontrollable desire to express his personal views instead of having them continually absorbed in the compromise pronouncements of the court, he may gratify that urge by the writing of concurring or, if so disposed, even dissenting, opinions. But a concurring opinion must justify itself by furnishing a different reason for the court's decision, and even then should not be resorted to unless the writer of the majority opinion refuses to accept and incorporate the suggested additions or amendments. A concurring opinion which merely says the same thing in other language is not only valueless as a contribution to the science of the law but is somewhat a reflection on the colleague to whom was assigned the duty of explaining the views . . . of the court.
> Horace Stern, *The Writing of Judicial Opinions*, 18 Pa. Bar Ass'n Q. 40, 44 (1946).

See *dubitante* & **write specially.**

D. Drafting Mandates. See JUDGMENTS, APPELLATE-COURT.

opponent; adversary; antagonist. All three terms refer to a person against whom one contends or fights, without necessarily suggesting any personal animus against that person. An *opponent* is one on the opposite side of a dispute, argument, political contest, etc. An *adversary* is essentially the same, although the term can suggest a greater degree of hostility. An *antagonist* is one against whom a person is involved in harsh combat and fierce fighting (whether literal or figurative), as if battling a nemesis.

oppress; repress. *Oppress*, which has the more negative connotations of the two, means "to subject (a person or a people) to inhumane or other unfair treatment; to persecute." *Repress*, a closely related word, means either: (1) "to keep under control"; or (2) "to reduce (persons) to a subordinate position."

oppression = (1) in criminal law, any harm, other than extortion, that a public officer corruptly causes to a person; or (2) in the law of contract, coercion to enter into an illegal contract—used as a basis for allowing a person to recover money paid or property transferred under an illegal contract. In sense 2, as G.H. Treitel notes, *oppression* is "used in a somewhat broad sense." *The Law of Contract* 437–38 (8th ed. 1991).

oppugn. See **impugn.**

opt; opt in; opt out (= to choose or decide) is usually followed by *to* or *for*—e.g.:

- "Thiessen *opted to* receive the lump-sum payment." *Nebraska EEOC v. State Employees Ret. Sys.*, 471 N.W.2d 398, 400 (Neb. 1991).
- "By *opting for* a *Pierringer*-type release, Unigard obviously was interested in more protection than the covenant not to sue or the general release would provide." *Unigard Ins. Co. v. Insurance Co. of N. Am.*, 516 N.W.2d 762, 765 (Wis. Ct. App. 1994).

But in the language of class actions, plaintiffs are said to have the choice of *opting in* or *opting out* of the class—e.g.: "Defendants propose that this Court employ an *opt in*, rather than an *opt out*, procedure in this class action." *Andrews Farms v. Calcot, Ltd.*, 258 F.R.D. 640, 656 (E.D. Cal. 2009). In fact, the phrase has been extended to the persons who *opt in* or *out*; in modern American legal JARGON, they are known as *opt-ins* or *opt-outs*.

*****opthamology.** See **ophthalmology.**

optician. See **ophthalmologist.**

optimacy; optimality. *Optimacy* = aristocracy. *Optimality* = idealness.

optimum is generally the noun, *optimal* generally the adjective. Although *optimum* is often used attributively <optimum conditions>, the adjective should be used in adjectival senses where it idiomatically fits <optimal conditions>—e.g.: "He testified [that] Ron's *optimum* [read *optimal*] solution is to find a kidney donor." *Corkern v. Smith*, 960 So.2d 1152, 1159 (La. Ct. App. 2007). Cf. **maximum.**

opt in. See **opt.**

option; right of preemption; first option to buy; right of first refusal. These terms are usefully distinguished in the law of contract. An *option* is an offer that, specifying the amount of consideration, becomes a contract when the offeree (or *optionee*) accepts it. For example, if Beverly has a three-year option to buy Charlie's house for $200,000, she may exercise that option, and make the sales contract binding, at any time within that period.

A *right of preemption* is a potential buyer's contractual right to have the first opportunity to buy, at a specified price, if the seller chooses to sell. For example, if Beverly has a right of preemption on Charlie's house for five years at $200,000, Charlie can keep the house for five years (in which case Beverly's right expires); but if he wishes to sell during those five years, he must offer the house to Beverly for $200,000. Beverly, in turn, can either buy or refuse to buy; if she refuses, Charlie can sell to somebody else. Nonlawyers often call Beverly's right an *option*, but lawyers ought to be more fastidious in their use of language. Of course, the synonymous phrase, *first option to buy*, is perfectly apt and perhaps even more descriptive than *right of preemption*.

A *right of first refusal* is a potential buyer's contractual right to meet the terms of a third party's offer if the seller intends to accept that offer. For example, if three conditions are met—Beverly has a right of first refusal on the purchase of Charlie's house, Ted offers to buy the house for $300,000, and Charlie intends to accept Ted's offer—then Beverly can match Ted's offer and thereby trump it.

option, vb. (= to grant or take an option on), dates from ca. 1926, but remains JARGON—e.g.: "The three acres *optioned* for sale lie largely within the 300 feet immediately east of the John R. Junkin Drive." *Dicks v. City of Natchez*, 319 So.2d 214, 216 (Miss. 1975). It may be useful legal slang, but it is best restricted to speech.

optionee; *optioner. See **optionor.**

option-giver; option-holder. These terms are more comprehensible than *optionor* and *optionee*. E.g.: "In the present context, an option may be defined as a right possessed by one person (the *option-holder*) to insist that another person (the *option-giver*) grant or transfer a specified interest in land." Peter Butt, *Land Law* 171 (2d ed. 1988).

option-holder. See **option-giver.**

optionor; *optioner. The *-or* form is now prevalent. It has the advantage of being more strictly accurate as a correlative of *optionee* (= the grantee in an option contract), although *option-giver* is clearer. See **option-giver.**

optometrist. See **ophthalmologist.**

opt out. See **opt.**

or. A. And *and*. "*Every* use of 'and' or 'or' as a conjunction involves *some* risk of ambiguity." Maurice B. Kirk, *Legal Drafting: The Ambiguity of "And" and "Or"*, 2 Tex. Tech L. Rev. 235, 253 (1971) (emphasis in original). So in the main text of *Words and Phrases* (2010)—including pocket parts—the word *and* takes up 71 pages of digested cases interpreting it in myriad ways, and the word *or* takes up another 68 pages of digested cases interpreting it in an equally broad array of senses. Virtually every book on drafting legal documents contains a section on the potential ambiguity of the two words.

Authorities agree that *and* has a distributive (or several) sense as well as a joint sense, and that *or* has an inclusive sense as well as an exclusive sense. Hence:

- The "several *and*": A and B, jointly or severally.
- The "joint *and*": A and B, jointly but not severally.
- The "inclusive *or*": A or B, or both.
- The "exclusive *or*": A or B, but not both.

See Scott J. Burnham, *The Contract Drafting Guidebook* 163 (1992). "The meaning of *and* is usually *several*. . . . The meaning of *or* is usually inclusive." *Id.* See **and (B).**

B. For *or else*. By itself, *or* should not be asked to do the work of *or else*—e.g.: "Every clause in the contract is 'understood and agreed' *or* [read *or else*] it would not be written into it." Richard Wincor, *Contracts in Plain English* 29 (1976).

C. Beginning Sentences with. Like *and* and *but*, the word *or* is a perfectly appropriate word with which to begin a sentence—e.g.: "Thus a politically organized society may be under a patriarchal king, or, as so frequently in a Greek city-state, a tyrant, a more or less absolute ruler with no title to be king. *Or* it may be under an oligarchy, a caste derived from priestly heads of kin-groups." Roscoe Pound, *The Development of Constitutional Guarantees of Liberty* 4–5 (1957).

D. *Or/and*. See *****and/or.**

-OR, -ER. See -ER (A).

-OR; -OUR. The AmE-vs.-BrE rules are a little complicated. All agent nouns but *saviour* (BrE) take *-or* in both the AmE and BrE (e.g., *actor*, *investor*). The distinction between AmE (*-or*) and BrE (*-our*) usage occurs in abstract nouns. Hence the British write *behaviour, colour, flavour,* and *humour,* whereas Americans write *behavior, color, flavor,* and *humor.* But the following words end in *-or* on both sides of the Atlantic: *error, horror, languor, liquor, pallor, squalor, stupor, terror, torpor,* and *tremor. Glamour* is the primary exception to the rule of *-or* in AmE.

In BrE, nouns ending in *-our* change to *-or* before the suffixes *-ation, -iferous, -ific, -ize,* and *-ous* (e.g., *coloration, honorific*). But *-our* keeps the *-u-* before *-able, -er, -ful, -ism, -ist, -ite,* and *-less* (e.g., *honourable, labourer, colourful*).

oral. See **verbal** & **parol.**

oral argument (AmE & BrE) = *oral debate* (BrE). In AmE, the phrase is ordinarily *in* or *at oral argument*, but *on oral argument* also appears, especially in New York. E.g.: "The disclosure proposed and described by Wallenstein *on oral argument* would go only to particulars as to the results of the committee's investigation and work." *Auerbach v. Bennett*, 393 N.E.2d 994, 1004 (N.Y. 1979). See **debate.**

oral contract; *verbal contract. The first—the correct phrase—outnumbers the second by more than ten to one in American judicial opinions. See **verbal** & **parol (A).**

oral deposition. See **deposition (C).**

oral instrument. See **instrument.**

oral will; nuncupative will; sailor's will; soldier's will. The broadest term is *oral will*, of which there are two types, both obsolescent: *nuncupative wills* and *soldiers' and sailors' wills.*

Nuncupative will is an English adaptation of the LAW LATIN phrase *testamentum nuncupativum* (= an oral will). If *nuncupative wills* are valid in a given jurisdiction, the amount that may be conveyed in them is usually limited by statute. Ordinarily, the will must be made in the testator's last illness, and usually at home unless the testator falls ill elsewhere. Two competent witnesses are usually required.

Soldiers' and sailors' wills derive from ancient military and maritime custom; in England the privilege derives from statute. The soldier must be in military service, or the sailor at sea, and, in some jurisdictions, a single witness must be present. In Great Britain, the phrases *soldier's will*, *mariner's will*, and *military testament* are used.

Nuncupative is often used as broadly as *oral*, that is, to encompass soldiers' and sailors' wills—e.g.:

> A *nuncupative* will is not required to be in writing. It may be made by one who, at the time, is in actual military service in the field or doing duty on shipboard at sea, and in either case in actual contemplation, fear, or peril of death, or by one who, at the time, is in expectation of immediate death from an injury received the same day. It must be proved by two witnesses who were present at the making thereof, one of whom was asked by the testator, at the time, to bear witness that such was his will, or to that effect.
>
> Cal. Prob. Code § 54 (repealed).

Yet the usual practice is to use *nuncupative* only in reference to the second type of will mentioned in the statute just quoted—i.e., an oral will made in contemplation of imminent death from an injury recently incurred—to distinguish it from *soldiers' and sailors' wills. Oral* encompasses every one of these types.

orate. See **perorate** & BACK-FORMATIONS.

ordain and establish. This DOUBLET has a fine pedigree: "We the people of the United States, in order to form a more perfect Union, establish Justice, insure domestic Tranquility, provide for the common defence, promote the general Welfare, and secure the Blessings of Liberty to ourselves and our Posterity, do *ordain and establish* this Constitution for the United States of America." U.S. Const. pmbl. In most modern contexts, *establish* alone suffices, *ordain* being archaic in all but its religious senses. See **legislate.**

ordeal. See POPULARIZED LEGAL TECHNICALITIES.

order = (1) a command or direction; (2) a judge's written direction; or (3) a written instrument (such as a check), made by one person and addressed to another, directing that other to pay money or deliver something to someone named in the instrument. In sense 2, a court's order may be either interlocutory (on some intermediate matter) or, more broadly, final (and therefore dispositive of the entire case).

In sense 2, *order* is distinguished from *judgment* and *decree*: "An *order* is the mandate or determination of the court upon some subsidiary or collateral matter arising in an action, not disposing of the merits, but adjudicating a preliminary point or directing some step in the proceedings." 1 Henry Campbell Black, *The Law of Judgments* 3 (2d ed. 1891). Hence rulings on most motions are *orders*, not *judgments*.

ordered, adjudged, and decreed. In many American jurisdictions, this wordy phrase routinely appears in court orders. The simple word *ordered* is generally much preferable—e.g.: "It is therefore *ordered, adjudged, and decreed* [read *ordered*] that Plaintiffs take nothing by their suit against Defendant Dallas County, Texas." *Posey v. Southwestern Bell Tel. LP*, 430 F.Supp.2d 616, 631 (N.D. Tex. 2006). See DOUBLETS, TRIPLETS, AND SYNONYM-STRINGS.

***orderee** is an unnecessary NEOLOGISM that surely will not survive with the fittest words in the language—e.g.:

- "The formal requirements of Rule 34 are . . . a safeguard by means of which the *orderees* are insured adequate apprisal of the terms of the court's mandate to them." *SEC v. Los Angeles Trust Deed & Mortgage Exch.*, 24 F.R.D. 460, 464 (S.D. Cal. 1959). [A possible revision: *Rule 34 ensures that the ordered parties will be adequately apprised of the court's mandate.*]
- "May [court orders] be ignored or disobeyed without sanction as here, creating a weakening of the court's authority through deliberate superimposition of the *orderee's* own judgment?" *Lamons v. State*, 335 S.E.2d 652, 656 (Ga. Ct. App. 1985) (Beasley, J., dissenting). [A possible revision: *May court orders be ignored and disobeyed with impunity? If so, a person under court order can weaken the court's authority merely by ignoring the order.*]

See -EE (C).

order of licence. See **parole.**

Order of the Coif. This was the name, formerly, of the order of serjeants-at-law, the highest order of counsel at the English Bar. Through the mid-19th century, they had a monopoly over practice in the Court of Common Pleas. But when, by statute, that court was opened to the whole Bar in 1846, the Order began to wither. Nathaniel Lindley was the last serjeant to be appointed (1875) and to die (1921).

In the U.S. today, the origins of this order are not widely known among lawyers. But they all know that one must excel in law school to be elected to the Order of the Coif, an honorary legal fraternity composed of select law students. Students at American law schools who earn a J.D. degree and graduate in the top 10% of their class are eligible for membership. See **coif.**

ordinance; ordnance; ordonnance. *Ordinance* (= a municipal [i.e., city] law) is common in AmE but rare in BrE, where *by-law* serves this purpose. In AmE, *bylaw* is generally used to mean "a corporate rule or regulation not included in the articles of incorporation." See **bylaw.** *Ordnance* = military supplies; cannon; artillery. *Ordonnance* = the ordering of parts in a whole; arrangement.

ordinarily prudent person; ordinary prudent person. With compound modifiers, either two adjectives before a noun or an adverb and an adjective before a noun, one must look closely at the sense to determine whether the first word is properly an adjective or an adverb. One such problematic phrase in law is *ordinar(il)y prudent person*, familiar in discussions of torts. One sees both *ordinary* and *ordinarily* in the cases, but the latter is more logical, because *ordinary* modifies *person*, whereas *ordinarily* modifies the adjective *prudent*.

The intended meaning, of course, is *person of ordinary prudence*. We do not mean *an ordinary person*; we mean *a person who is prudent to an ordinary degree*. One problem is that *ordinarily* in one sense means "often; usually." And if we (incorrectly) give it that sense, we end up with a person who is *ordinarily* (but not always) prudent—i.e., one who sometimes may be given to imprudence. Because of that slight AMBIGUITY, one cannot be dogmatic in preferring *ordinarily prudent person* over *ordinary prudent person*. But it is preferable nevertheless—e.g.: "*Ordinarily prudent persons* . . . would not run at a rate of 20 to 25 miles per hour onto such a crossing." *Veach's Adm'r v. Louisville & Interurban Ry.*, 228 S.W. 35, 36 (Ky. 1921).

On the variant phrase, *ordinarily prudent man*, see SEXISM (B).

Ordinary, Lord of Appeal in. See Lord of Appeal in Ordinary.

ordinary law. In AmE—though not in BrE—this phrase is contrasted with *organic* or *constitutional law. Ordinary law* consists primarily of regular statutes, which may prove unconstitutional; *organic law*, or *constitutional law* (as it is more generally called), is superordinate and relatively fixed in its words, if not in its interpretation. Cf. **organic law.**

ordinary negligence. See negligence (A).

ordinary prudent person. See ordinarily prudent person.

ordinary scrutiny. See strict scrutiny.

ordnance; ordonnance. See ordinance.

or else. See or (B).

ore tenus is an adverbial LATINISM meaning "by word of mouth." Either *oral* or *orally* is preferable to this term, which in most contexts ought to be considered a FORBIDDEN WORD. E.g.:

- "Judge Wyzanski has referred to the 'enormous, nearly cancerous, growth of exhibits, depositions, and *ore tenus* [read *oral*] testimony' in antitrust cases." John R. Allison, *Arbitration Agreements and Antitrust Claims*, 64 N.C. L. Rev. 219, 247 (1986) (quoting *U.S. v. Grinnell Corp.*, 236 F.Supp. 244, 247 (D.R.I. 1964)).
- "Following an *ore tenus* proceeding, the trial court determined that the employee's injury did not 'arise out of and in the course of his employment.'" *Strickland v. Marshall Constr. & Repair, Inc.*, 553 So.2d 591, 592 (Ala. Civ. App. 1988).

The phrase *ore tenus rule* now serves, in AmE, as the name for the presumption that a trial court's findings of fact are correct and should not be disturbed on appeal unless clearly wrong or unjust. The phrase seems to have come about through the realization that live witnesses, testifying orally, may make a very different impression from that which their words on paper make. E.g.: "As the evidence before the trial court was by stipulation of the parties and no testimony was taken orally, the *ore tenus rule* of review is not applicable to this appeal." *Kessler v. Stough*, 361 So.2d 1048, 1049 (Ala. 1978). But the more usual wording is *clearly-erroneous rule*. See **clearly erroneous.**

organic law. In law, the term *organic* is just as chameleon-hued and troublesome as in the general language. (*See Garner's Modern American Usage* 598 (3d ed. 2009).) In a civil-law jurisdiction such as Louisiana, *organic law* refers to decisional law. E.g.:

- "Louisiana *organic law* allows an individual to contract concerning liability for negligence in all cases where such a contract is not contrary to public policy." *Diamond Crystal Salt Co. v. Thielman*, 395 F.2d 62, 63 (5th Cir. 1968).
- "Article XI, section 3 is a 'self-executing' constitutional provision, which was adopted to bypass legislative and executive control and to provide the people of Florida a narrow but direct voice in amending their fundamental *organic law*." *Browning v. Florida Hometown Democracy*, 29 So.3d 1053, 1063 (Fla. 2010).

See **decisional law.**

But the phrase has an entirely different sense in the common-law tradition: *Bouvier's Law Dictionary* defined *organic law* as "the fundamental law or constitution of a state or nation" and used the phrase in that sense. For example, in defining the "United States of America," Bouvier stated: "the republic whose *organic law* is the constitution adopted by the people of the thirteen states which declared their independence of the Government of Great Britain on the fourth day of July, 1776." *BLD* 3370 (8th ed. 1914). The phrase is still used in this sense: "At the time when our *organic laws* were adopted, criminal trials both here and in England had long been presumptively open." *Richmond Newspapers, Inc. v. Virginia*, 448 U.S. 555, 569 (1980) (per Burger, C.J.). Cf. **ordinary law.**

Confusingly, the phrase *organic statute* is used of a legislative act establishing an administrative agency.

organization. Many legal writers use this as a general term that includes companies, partnerships, foundations, nationalized industries, government departments, and the like. Cf. **firm.**

orient; *orientate. The second is a NEEDLESS VARIANT of *orient*, which means "to get one's bearings or sense of direction." The longer variant (a BACK-FORMATION from *orientation*) seems especially common in BrE: "Victor was anxious and depressed, was *well-orientated* [read *well oriented*] but had a poor short-term memory." *Hinton v. Leigh*, [2009] E.W.H.C. 2658 (Ch.), at ¶ 123. Cf. **disorient.**

original evidence. See **direct evidence.**

original instance. See **first instance.**

original intent; original meaning; original understanding. These phrases commonly appear in discussions of constitutional interpretation. *Original intent* (= the subjective intention of the framers or ratifiers of an authoritative text) denotes a legal FICTION, since the idea of a collective but identical intent is something that cannot be said to exist in the preparation or adoption of a text.

Original meaning = the sense conveyed by a text, esp. an important text such as the Constitution, at the time of adoption or as reconstructed by a later court from what an informed, reasonable member of the community would have understood at the time of adoption according to then-prevailing linguistic meanings and interpretive principles. A synonymous phrase is *original public meaning.*

Original understanding = the collective perceptions and beliefs of the informed public at the time of adoption or ratification—esp. but not exclusively of those who participated in ratification. Cf. **strict construction.**

originalism; nonoriginalism; living constitutionalism. *Originalism* = (1) the doctrine that a legal text should be interpreted through the historical ascertainment of the meaning that it had or would have had to a fully informed observer at the time when the text first took effect; esp., the doctrine that those authorized to make a legal instrument effective meant to set forth ascertainable meanings by the language of the instrument and that the interpreter's duty is to understand, as best as can be determined, what the text would have meant to contemporaneous readers; (2) the doctrine that a legal text should be interpreted through the historical ascertainment of the actual or presumed intent of those who prepared it or gave it legal effect. Sense 1 is the preferred use of the term: it is an objective test, not a subjective one. Common synonyms (in both senses) are *historical interpretation* and *interpretivism.* See **interpretivism** & *historical interpretation* under INTERPRETATION, MODES OF (B).

Nonoriginalism = a family of interpretive approaches maintaining that a text need not be interpreted strictly in accordance with its original meaning or the intentions or understandings of its framers or ratifiers. It is essentially synonymous with *living constitutionalism,* but one noted commentator has suggested a distinction. *Living constitutionalism* denotes the view that, with constitutional provisions concerned centrally with moral values such as liberty and equality, courts should follow evolving or contemporary norms. But *nonoriginalism* need not recognize such an obligation to espouse "enlightened" new interpretations. Mitchell N. Berman, *Originalism Is Bunk*, 84 N.Y.U. L. Rev. 1, 24 n.52 (2009). It seems highly improbable, however,

that one who rejects the necessity of following the original meaning of a text would want to replace it with an unenlightened new interpretation. So again, the terms are synonymous. If anything, *living constitutionalism* sounds a little more connotatively palatable than *nonoriginalism* because it typically seems better to be for than against something.

original jurisdiction; primary jurisdiction. The first phrase, meaning "jurisdiction to take cognizance of a case at the outset, to try it, and to decide the issues," is usually contrasted with *appellate jurisdiction.* In the U.S., *primary jurisdiction* is original jurisdiction that lies in an administrative agency.

original meaning. See **original intent.**

original precedent. See **precedent (c).**

original public meaning. See **originalism.**

original understanding. See **original intent.**

orphan. Although in the popular mind *orphan* refers to a child whose mother and father are both dead, courts have sometimes interpreted the word differently. Historically, a child became an orphan when the father died. Depending on the facts at hand, *orphan* may be held to include a child who has lost only one parent. *See In re Byrd's Will*, 308 N.Y.S.2d 97, 102 (Sur. Ct. 1970). Some areas of law, such as immigration, broaden the definition to cover children whose parents are living but unwilling to support them or incapable of supporting them. *See, e.g.*, 8 U.S.C. § 1101(b)(1)(f). But the courts seem uniformly to have included in their definition of *orphan* the idea that the person so described be a minor.

orphanhood; *orphancy; *orphandom. The first is the usual word, the other two being NEEDLESS VARIANTS.

orphan's court. In some American states today— such as Delaware, Maryland, and Pennsylvania—this phrase denotes a probate court. (The orphan's courts originated in England but have long since become defunct there.) Generally speaking, the jurisdiction of an *orphan's court* is not limited to orphans or even to minors—a good reason, perhaps, to jettison the phrase in the few places where it still occurs.

Although the plural possessive form *orphans' court* might have made better sense, the singular possessive *orphan's* has long been standard. The form without an apostrophe is poor—e.g.: "At this point Judge Terzian had to point out rather sadly to Mrs. MacFarlane that even though she was chief judge of the probate court—called *orphans court* [read *orphan's court*] in Maryland—she couldn't do any more." Murray T. Bloom, *The Trouble with Lawyers* 215 (1970).

orse. is the abbreviated form of *otherwise* (sometimes with, sometimes without a period)—e.g.: "The only recorded case we can find in this area is that of *Corbett v. Corbett* (*orse Ashley*) decided by the Honourable Mr.

Justice Ormrod." *City of Columbus v. Zanders*, 266 N.E.2d 602, 606 (Franklin County Mun. Ct., Ohio 1970). The punctuation dilemma can be avoided by abstaining from this arcane abbreviation and simply spelling out the word. See **otherwise.**

or which. See **which (c).**

-os. See PLURALS (c).

OSP; *obiit sine prole.* The Latin phrase means "he died without issue"; the translation suffices if we are to write out a phrase. The abbreviation may sometimes be justified, if the targeted readers are certain to understand its import.

As with many other LATINISMS, American lawyers often get it wrong. For example, the 5th edition of *Black's Law Dictionary* (1979) defines *obit sine prole* ("he dies without issue") in the past tense when in fact it is present tense. The past-tense form is *obiit.*

ostensible authority. See **apparent authority.**

*ostensively for *ostensibly* (= from all that appears) is a solecism. E.g.: "Although deposit insurance coverage is a function that *ostensively* [read *ostensibly*] could be handled by private enterprise, the United States also wanted to and did direct the FDIC to protect the public interest." *Rauscher Pierce Refsnes, Inc. v. FDIC*, 789 F.2d 313, 315 (5th Cir. 1986).

ostrich defense is a colloquialism that disparages a criminal defendant's claim not to have known of the criminal activities of his or her associates. E.g.:

- "Whether or not Ramirez's implicit *ostrich defense* was credible is not for this court to determine." *State v. Amezola*, 741 P.2d 1024, 1033 (Wash. Ct. App. 1987) (Swanson, J., dissenting).
- "Instead, [the appellees] have simply ignored [the estoppel issue] and adopted the *ostrich defense* in addition to their attempted use of the Archimedean Lever." *Capitol Fish Co. v. Tanner*, 384 S.E.2d 394, 396 (Ga. Ct. App. 1989) (Deen, P.J., concurring).

other. See **otherwise (a).**

other good and valuable consideration. See **and other good and valuable consideration** & **consideration (d).**

otherwise. A. And *other*. Most properly, *other* is the adjective, *otherwise* the adverb—e.g.:

- "An interested person may appear before an agency or its responsible employees for the presentation, adjustment, or determination of an issue, request, or controversy in a proceeding, whether interlocutory, summary, *or otherwise* [read *or other* or, better, *of some other kind*], or in connection with an agency function." *Systems Plus, Inc. v. U.S.*, 69 Fed.Cl. 757, 767 (Fed. Cl. 2006).
- "It is undisputed that Mr. Lee never took any step, substantial *or otherwise* [read *or other* or, better, *or not*], to travel to California." *U.S. v. Lee*, 603 F.3d 904, 919 (11th Cir. 2010).

In considering this usage, one commentator wrote that "to pronounce this *otherwise* inadmissible would be to fly in the face of a strongly established usage. But usage, which can allow on sufferance, cannot prevent it from being rejected by more exact writers." Wilson Follett, *Modern American Usage* 242–43 (1966).

B. *Otherwise than*. This phrase is often misused for *other than*. Driedger is wrong to characterize *otherwise than* generally as "useful to specify one predicate modifier and expressly exclude all others." Elmer A. Driedger, *The Composition of Legislation* 86 (1957). Its legitimate uses are few, *other than* being the phrase typically called for—e.g.:

- "An obligation to design something in a certain way is not violated simply because the actual impact of the design turns out *otherwise than* [read *other than*] intended." *Mark H. v. Lemahieu*, 513 F.3d 922, 936 (9th Cir. 2008).
- "The issue of simultaneous death arises when there is insufficient evidence that two individuals died *otherwise than* [read *other than*] simultaneously." Victoria J. Haneman & Jennifer M. Booth, *120 Hours Until the Consistent Treatment of Simultaneous Death*, 34 Nova L. Rev. 449, 449–50 (2010).

But sometimes the force of the phrase is genuinely adverbial, and when that is true *otherwise than* is the correct phrasing—e.g.: "Under Rule 141, the trial court has discretion, for good cause stated on the record, to allocate costs *otherwise than* as provided by law or the Texas Rules of Civil Procedure." *Hatfield v. Solomon*, 316 S.W.3d 50, 67 (Tex. App.—Houston [14th Dist.] 2010).

C. *Other . . . other than*. A fairly common mistake is to repeat *other* in the phrase *other than*, particularly when one or more words intervene—e.g.: "Factors such as these play a role under the Act's four exceptions—the seniority differential under the specific seniority exception, the shift differential under the catch-all exception for differentials 'based on any *other* factor *other than* sex.'" *Corning Glass Works v. Brennan*, 417 U.S. 188, 204 (1974) (per Marshall, J.). Either one of the *others* should be dropped.

D. *Otherwise expressed*. This is cumbersome and jarring for "in other words." E.g.: "As a consequence this court has declared that in such a case the allowable diminution is 'the amount necessary to convert the unsound structure into a sound one,' or *as otherwise expressed* [read *in other words*], 'the cost of repairs necessary to make the thing whole.'" *Connell v. Davis*, 940 So.2d 195, 208 (5th Cir. 2006). See **to put it another way.**

E. As a Conjunction. The slipshod usage of the conjunctive *otherwise* occurs primarily in BrE—e.g.:

- "Nor, indeed, need we wait for it to happen, *otherwise* no law could be passed and no magistrate appointed." George Buchanan, *Law of Kingship* 129 (Roger A. Mason & Martin S. Smith trans., 2006). (A semicolon is needed before *otherwise*.)
- "You have to have several clients, you have to exhibit some choice over when and where you will work, you

have to provide your own tools and equipment *otherwise* there will be a presumption that you are not really self-employed." Len Shackleton & Nigel Meager, *Modernising European Union Labour Law* 11 (2007). (A semicolon is needed before *otherwise*.)

For further elucidation of this common error, see RUN-ON SENTENCES.

otiose /oh-shee-**ohs**/ = unneeded; not useful. The word is used more by lawyers than by other writers. E.g.:

- "It would imply an unworthy conception of the federal judiciary to give weight to the suggestion that acknowledgment of this power will tempt some *otiose* or timid judge to shuffle off responsibility." *Louisiana Power & Light Co. v. City of Thibodaux*, 360 U.S. 25, 29 (1959) (per Frankfurter, J.).
- "Since statutory tolling would apply during that period if the petition was properly filed, equitable tolling during that period on account of egregious misconduct would be *otiose*." *Martin v. Ryan*, 318 Fed. Appx. 457, 459 (9th Cir. 2008).
- "If this analysis is correct, double-patenting attacks are largely *otiose*." Miles Hastie, *Sanofi-Aventis and Double Patenting*, 22 I.P.J. 155, 161 (2010).

Cf. **nugatory.**

ought. A. Infinitive Following. *Ought* should always be followed by an infinitive, whether the phrase is *ought to* or *ought not to*—e.g.:

- "Theaters [that] patronized that union *ought not to be* patronized by the public." *Trade Unions*, 50 Banking L.J. 454, 454–55 (1933).
- "*Ought* it *to be* made punishable when adultery is not?" Patrick Devlin, *The Enforcement of Morals* 1 (1968).
- "When a case as well considered and as recently decided as *Free Speech Coalition* is put aside (after a mere six years) there *ought to be* a very good reason." *U.S. v. Williams*, 553 U.S. 285, 320 (2008) (Souter, J., dissenting).

As a sham badge of scholasticism, American law professors tend to omit the particle *to* when the expression is in the negative or interrogative. But there is no warrant for this usage—e.g.:

- "The question is not: what must we do?; but rather: what *ought we do* [read *ought we to do*]?" Erwin N. Griswold, *Renvoi Revisited*, 51 Harv. L. Rev. 1165, 1184 (1938).
- "This does not mean that we *ought not* [read *ought not to*] listen to what shareholder primacy advocates have to say, only that we *ought not* [read *ought not to*] uncritically accept it as gospel." Leonard I. Rotman, *Debunking the "End of History" Thesis for Corporate Law*, 33 B.C. Int'l & Comp. L. Rev. 219, 270 (2010). (The author's possible argument that including the second *to* would create a SPLIT INFINITIVE is weak. A suggested revision: . . . *we ought not to accept it uncritically as gospel*.)
- "We *ought not* [read *ought not to*] celebrate incrementalism because it will normally be difficult to know whether incremental changes in law, and especially in legislated law, are desirable." Saul Levmore, *Interest Groups and the Problem with Incrementalism*, 158 U. Pa. L. Rev. 815, 827 (2010).

A few legal writers extend this pedant's solecism beyond negatives and interrogatives—e.g.: "Neither need the laws be interpreted so as to protect those who *ought* [read *ought to*] know better from their own indolence." *Hamel v. Prudential Ins. Co.*, 640 F.Supp. 103, 105 (D. Mass. 1986).

B. And *should*. *Ought* should be reserved for expressions of necessity, duty, or obligation; *should*, the slightly weaker word, expresses mere appropriateness, suitability, or fittingness.

-OUR. See -OR.

our federalism is an odd name for a legal doctrine, but in AmE this phrase denotes the controversial doctrine "that federal courts must refrain from hearing constitutional challenges to state action under certain circumstances in which federal action is regarded as an improper intrusion on the right of a state to enforce its laws in its own courts." Charles Alan Wright, *The Law of Federal Courts* 339–40 (5th ed. 1994). The leading case on this point is *Younger v. Harris*, 401 U.S. 37 (1971). Perhaps because of its strange appearance—with the possessive first-person pronoun—the phrase is sometimes written *Our Federalism*, with initial capitals. See **federalism.**

***ourself; *theirself.** **Ourself* is technically ill-formed, since *our* is plural and *self* is singular. But it is established in the editorial or royal style. **Theirself* is indefensible, however.

oust = (1) to eject, dispossess, or disseise (construed with *of*); or (2) to exclude, bar, or take away (construed with *from* or *of*). Hence, idiomatically speaking, one may either *oust a court of jurisdiction* or *oust jurisdiction from a court*. Today the first of those expressions is more common—e.g.: "Parties to a contract cannot *oust* a court *of* jurisdiction by agreement." *Bohl v. Hauke*, 906 N.E.2d 450, 454 (Ohio Ct. App. 2009). But the alternative wording has persisted—e.g.: "The district court clearly has subject-matter jurisdiction over this case, unless the [Act] applies so as to *oust* the court's jurisdiction." *U.K. Ministry of Def. v. Trimble Nav. Ltd.*, 422 F.3d 165, 168 (4th Cir. 2005). See OBJECT-SHUFFLING.

In the language of nonlawyers, *oust* is generally confined to figurative uses. But lawyers continue to use the word in literal, concrete senses—e.g.: "Courts have treated the tenant-shareholder as an owner or landlord, rather than a tenant, for the purpose of permitting him to *oust* a preceding tenant under provisions permitting such action by a landlord." 1 *American Law of Property* § 3.10, at 201 (A.J. Casner ed., 1952).

ouster. See **ejectment.**

out. A. As an Unnecessary Particle in Phrasal Verbs. *Out* commonly appears superfluously in phrases such as **calculate out*, **distribute out*, **segregate out*, and **separate out*. (Colloquially, it occurs in *lose out*, *test out*, and *try out*.) E.g.: "Defendants' motion does not *segregate out* [read *segregate*] Plaintiff's various claims in a coherent manner." *Carey v. Maricopa County*, 602

F.Supp.2d 1132, 1136 (D. Ariz. 2009). See PHRASAL VERBS & PARTICLES, UNNECESSARY.

But sometimes *out* is necessary, as here: "Manufacturers have a duty of due care to *design out* dangers that might arise from a product's foreseeable misuses." Joseph A. Page, *Liability for Unreasonably and Unavoidably Unsafe Products*, 72 Chi.-Kent L. Rev. 87, 88 n.3 (1996). The phrase *design out* (= to rid of [an undesirable characteristic]) is common in patent and products-liability contexts.

B. As a Noun. This usage <counsel was looking for an out> is a casualism.

outcomes, a formerly uncommon plural form, has all the flavor of voguish GOBBLEDYGOOK—e.g.: "By equitable, I mean we have to ask what it will take to create schooling *outcomes* that place black and brown children on equal footing with their white, middle-class peers." Gloria J. Ladson-Billings, *Can We at Least Have* Plessy?, 85 N.C. L. Rev. 1279, 1288 (2007). Cf. PLURALS (B).

outer bar; utter bar. *Outer bar* is the more usual form of this English phrase meaning "junior barristers, collectively, who sit outside the bar of the court, as opposed to Queen's Counsel, who sit within it" (*CDL*). Though an American should perhaps hesitate to tell English lawyers which of the two terms to use, *outer bar* at least makes literal sense to any reader or listener. Cf. **inner bar.**

Utter bar, an older form, is still occasionally used. When students are "called to the Bar," they are called to the *degree of the Utter Bar* and become *Utter Barristers*. But *Utter Barrister* is a rare term; "junior" (as opposed to "silk") is preferred. See **junior** & **silk.**

outlawry = (1) the action of putting a person out of the protection of the law; or, more usually, (2) defiance of the law. It is not synonymous with *proscription*—i.e., as a noun corresponding to the verb *to outlaw*—though here it is erroneously used in that sense: "Wright came to believe that the proponents of the *outlawry* [read *proscription*] of war did not expect immediate effects from the Pact but rather were thinking in terms of generations." Gerhard Von Glahn, *Law Among Nations* 578 (1981). The context makes it clear that renunciation of war is the subject of discussion (hence *the outlawing of war*); *outlawry* does not work, although one might feebly argue that war here is being personified. See ANTHROPOMORPHISM.

out-of-court. See **extrajudicial (A).**

out of time. Generally, this phrase refers to persons and means "having no more time available" <you're out of time>. In law, however, the phrase sometimes refers to things other than persons and means "untimely" <the motion was ruled to be out of time>. E.g.: "The question was whether s. 8(1) of the Foreign Judgements (Reciprocal Enforcement) Act 1933 applied in favour of the defendant to a claim for money due on bills of exchange bought in England against a German company in whose favour a judgment had been given by a German court on an identical claim because, by German, unlike English law, it was *out of time*." Rupert Cross, *Statutory Interpretation* 137 (1976).

*__outside of,__ in the sense "apart from" or "aside from," is always inferior to *outside* alone—e.g.: "History of a system of law is largely a history of borrowings of legal materials from other legal systems and of assimilation of materials from *outside of* [read *outside*] the law." Roscoe Pound, *The Formative Era of American Law* 94 (1938). Cf. **off of.**

over. A. Special Legal Uses. In the law of property, particularly of vested and contingent interests, *over* when used after a noun denoting the interest means that the interest named, whether vested or contingent, is preceded by some other possessory interest. For example, a *limitation over* includes a second estate in the same property to be enjoyed after the first estate granted expires. E.g.: "A conveyance by a grantor with a *limitation over* to his heirs was said to be governed by the doctrine of worthier title, under which a *limitation over* to a grantor's heirs resulted in an automatic reversion in the grantor and nullified the *limitation over*." *In re Burchell's Estate*, 87 N.E.2d 293, 296 (N.Y. 1949).

A *gift over* is one that follows another's life estate or fee simple determinable. E.g.:

- "If the first granddaughter died without issue, her heirs could take nothing because of the express provisions for *gift over* in such case." *Orme v. Northern Trust Co.*, 172 N.E.2d 413, 419 (Ill. App. Ct. 1961).
- "Since the sisters all predeceased George, the defendants assert that the alternative *gifts over* failed." *Hofing v. Willis*, 201 N.E.2d 852, 855 (Ill. 1964).

Remainder over is one type of *gift over*. Although *remainder* itself connotes a preceding estate, the phrase *remainder over* is a common one. E.g.:

- "They alleged that an 1857 will had devised a life estate in the land to Martha A. Sanders, with *remainder over* to her children." *Malone v. Bowdoin*, 369 U.S. 643, 644 n.2 (1962) (per Stewart, J.).
- "He devised the stock to Stephen C.S. as an absolute gift, and there was no *remainder over* if Stephen C.S. failed to pay Blechstein the dividends." *In re Estate of Stephano*, 981 A.2d 138, 141 (Pa. 2009).
- "When the eldest son of the family became of age or married, his father would convey the family lands to himself in trust for life, to his son for life, with *remainder over* to unborn heirs." Calvin H. Johnson, *Taxing the Consumption of Capital Gains*, 28 Va. Tax Rev. 477, 490 (2009).

The plural form is *gifts over, remainders over,* etc.

B. For *more than*. This casual sense of *over* is accepted even in formal writing—e.g.:

- "The auditorium was filled to capacity with *over* eight hundred persons present." *Terminiello v. City of Chicago,* 337 U.S. 1, 2 (1949) (per Douglas, J.).
- "When a prima facie case of trademark abandonment exists because of nonuse of the mark for *over* two consecutive years, the owner of the mark has the burden to demonstrate that circumstances do not justify the inference of intent not to resume use." *Exxon Corp. v. Humble Exploration Co., Inc.,* 695 F.2d 96, 99 (5th Cir. 1983).
- "The Porter and Geoghan cases each reportedly involved *over* 200 victims and gave rise to dozens of lawsuits." Timothy D. Lytton, *Clergy Sexual Abuse Litigation,* 39 Conn. L. Rev. 809, 854 (2007).

Cf. **above (A)** & **more . . . than.**
    C. In *pay over.* See **pay over.**
    D. *Over-* as a Combining Form. See **overly.**
    E. *Over . . . under.* See VERBAL AWARENESS.

overall is invariably a VOGUE WORD, often a lame SENTENCE ADVERB. E.g.:

- "A contextual interpretation furthers Congress' original purpose, is less likely to encourage random punishment, and is consistent with the statute's *overall* history." *U.S. v. Ressam,* 553 U.S. 272, 283 (2008) (Breyer, J., dissenting). (In that sentence, *Congress's* would have been the better possessive form. See **Congress.**)
- "*Overall*, the balance of factors, especially the weight of the avoidance of piecemeal litigation factor, qualifies this case as an exceptional one in which abstention is warranted." *Doré v. Wormley,* 690 F.Supp.2d 176, 193 (S.D.N.Y. 2010).
- "This interpretation, advanced by the Secretary, emphasized the *overall* voluntary nature of NCLB." Andrew G. Caffrey, *No Ambiguity Left Behind,* 18 Wm. & Mary Bill Rts. J. 1129, 1148 (2010).

All three quoted sentences would read better without *overall.*

overarching. The *-ch-* is not pronounced like a *-k-*: /oh-vər-**ahr**-ching/.

overbreadth; vagueness. In American law, these terms are usefully distinguished. The *vagueness* doctrine, based on due process, requires that a penal statute state explicitly and definitely what acts are prohibited, so as to preclude the lack of fair warning and arbitrary enforcement. *Overbreadth*, by contrast, concerns the First Amendment and relates to civil as well as criminal law. A statute is *overbroad* if it seemingly prohibits not only acts that it may legitimately forbid but also acts protected by First Amendment freedoms.

overbroad. See **overbreadth** & **overly.**

overflown is the correct past participle for *overfly* <the jets had overflown Phoenix>, but not for *overflow*, which properly makes *overflowed* <the river had overflowed its banks>. See **overfly.**

overfly (= to fly over in an airplane) is uncommon except in legal usage and pilots' JARGON. Following are examples from legal writing:

- "There was no negligence in not having enough fuel to *overfly* Rome, because that was a scheduled stop." *Sakaria v. Trans World Airlines,* 8 F.3d 164, 168 (4th Cir. 1993).
- "By abrogating the landowner's right to exclude in favor of the public's right to *overfly* land—a necessity of modern aviation—the courts prioritized competing uses." Randall Bezanson & Andrew Finkelman, *Trespassory Art,* 43 U. Mich. J.L. Reform 245, 284 (2010).

See **aviate.**

overlook; oversee. The first is sometimes misused for the second. To *overlook* is to neglect or disregard <they didn't overlook the project's defects>. To *oversee* is to supervise or superintend <a project overseen by four managers>. *Look over* is also differentiated from *overlook*; it means "to examine." See **oversight.**

overly. Although this word is old, dating from about the 12th century, it is best avoided because it has long since fallen into disrepute. (Words sometimes do this.) *Overly* is almost always unnecessary because *over-* may be prefixed at will: *overbroad, overrefined, overoptimistic, overripe,* etc. When it is not unnecessary, it is merely ugly. Some usage authorities consider *overly* semiliterate, although the editors of the Merriam-Webster dictionaries have used it in a number of definitions. Certainly this adverb should be avoided whenever possible. *Over-* as a prefix usually serves well—e.g.: "Disregarding, as we must, the *overelaborate* language of the act and looking to the substance rather than to the form of things, the question presented . . . is, does the act . . . delegate to the industrial commission judicial powers which may be exercised only by a court?" *Town of Holland v. Village of Cedar Grove,* 282 N.W. 111, 117 (Wis. 1938). When *over-* is awkward or ugly-sounding, one might have recourse to *too* or *unduly* <an unduly lax standard>. E.g.:

- "In our own country, the grand jury system has been looked upon as inflexible and *overly* [read *unduly*] formal." C. Gordon Post, *An Introduction to the Law* 109–10 (1963).
- "We are not scientists—not even social scientists—nor were meant to be. Let us not be *overly* [read *unduly*] depressed at that not altogether depressing thought." Grant Gilmore, *The Death of Contract* 4 (1974).

In any event, one should always be consistent within a piece of writing: in one U.S. Supreme Court opinion, we find, in successive paragraphs: "We agreed with the District Court that the statute was not *overly broad* or vague . . . . A declaratory judgment of a lower federal court that a state statute is . . . *overbroad* or vague . . . will likely have a more significant potential for disruption of state enforcement policies." *Steffel v. Thompson,* 415 U.S. 452, 473–74 (1974) (per Brennan, J.). (*Overbroad* is always preferable to *overly broad.*)

Other specimens follow, with suggested improvements:

- "The national public policy reflected both in Title VII of the Civil Rights Act of 1964 and in § 1981 may not be frustrated by the development *of overly technical* [read *of overtechnical* or *unduly technical*] judicial doctrines of standing or election of remedies." *Hackett v. McGuire Bros., Inc.*, 445 F.2d 442, 446–47 (3d Cir. 1971).

- "This interpretative method was deemed *overly* [read *unduly*] speculative and too far removed from the statutory text." *Gabelli Global Multimedia Trust Inc. v. Western Inv. LLC*, 700 F.Supp.2d 748, 760 (D. Md. 2010). (On *interpretative* vs. *interpretive*, see **interpretive.**)
- "Potential litigants may become *overly cautious* [read *too cautious*] in creating materials so as to not risk disclosing sensitive information in future litigation." *In re City of New York*, 607 F.3d 923, 942 (2d Cir. 2010).

See ADVERBS (D).

One last point. *Overly* should never displace a word such as *especially*. What does it mean for a piece of writing to be *overly persuasive*? "Justice Ginsburg's effort to rebut the majority's legislative history was brief and not *overly* [read *especially*] persuasive." James J. Brudney, *The Supreme Court as Interstitial Actor*, 70 Ohio St. L.J. 889, 899 (2009).

OVERPARTICULARIZATION. This word describes, better than any other, the besetting sin of practicing lawyers' prose. One judge, satirizing the overparticularized style, deduces that lawyers work on the following principles (among others): "Every sentence should begin with a date, or at least have a date somewhere in it. No attempt should be made to explain the facts in relative time, such as several months before or several days after. Dates are important, even if they have nothing to do with any issue in the case. . . . Please do not try to limit the factual summary to subjects material to the issues in the case, since the Court's curiosity about irrelevancies is unbounded." Nathan L. Hecht, *Extra-Special Secrets of Appellate Brief Writing*, 3 Scribes J. Legal Writing 27, 29 (1992).

Hence, the wise admonition of Judge Thomas Gibbs Gee, whose formulation gave this sin its name: "No overparticularization, which can throw your reader off by causing him to try to keep track of things that do not matter. For example—do not write 'On April 1, 1990' unless the day is significant. Instead, write 'Last spring.'" *A Few of Wisdom's Idiosyncrasies and a Few of Ignorance's: A Judicial Style Sheet*, 1 Scribes J. Legal Writing 55, 57 (1990).

To illustrate the contrast between an overparticularized style and a more pointed style, consider these alternative versions of the opening paragraph in an appellate brief:

1. This is an appeal by Plaintiff, Trenton Medical Center, under section 19 of the Administrative Procedure and Texas Register Act, Article 6252-13a, V.T.C.S., from an order of the Texas Health Facilities Commission granting a Certificate of Need to Charter Fenton, Inc., a wholly-owned subsidiary of Acland Medical Corporation for Fenton Hospital, Houston, Texas. On December 10, 1984, the Commission accepted and dated the application of Fenton for a Certificate of Need to construct, equip and operate an 80-bed psychiatric and addictive disease facility containing 43,410 square feet to be located in northwest Houston. Fenton originally proposed 60 psychiatric and 20 addictive disease beds but later amended its application to 64 psychiatric and 16 addictive disease beds. Plaintiff filed a Notice of Intent to become a party to the application of Fenton which request was accepted by the Commission on January 11, 1985. Defendants, Post and Hospital Group, also filed and were accepted as parties to the application of Fenton.

2. This case involves contradictory decisions by the Texas Health Facilities Commission concerning three applications to build new 80-bed psychiatric hospitals in Houston.

   The hearing officer who heard all the evidence found a "proven need for two of the three" new hospitals. The Commission voted 3–0 to adopt her report but voted 2–1 to deny as "unnecessary" one of the two hospitals she recommended.

   Neither the Commission majority's stated findings of fact nor substantial record evidence supports this illogical result. The real reason for the majority's action arbitrarily violated the Commission's own rules of procedure. The result, if not rejected, would prevent elderly psychiatric patients in a 21-county area from receiving care that neither the newly approved hospital nor any existing hospital will provide.

The second version contains none of the clutter that plagues the first. Instead of worrying about the number of beds and the number of square feet—not to mention Article 6252-13a—the writer of the second version focuses immediately on the true issues in the case and on the human drama that gave rise to the dispute.

The sad fact is that, although virtually every lawyer and judge who examines the two will pronounce the second version far superior, every one of them hailing from the U.S. will also confess that the first is conventional and the second unusual. See OBSCURITY (A).

overreach = (1) to circumvent, outwit, or get the better of by cunning or artifice; (2) to defeat one's object by going too far; or (3) in BrE, to replace (an interest in land) with a direct right to money. Sense 1 often applies in legal contexts—e.g.: "If, from a consideration of all the facts concerning the situation of the parties . . . at the time the contract was made, and the trial court concludes that the intended wife was not *overreached*, the contract should be sustained." *In re Ward's Estate*, 285 P.2d 1081, 1084 (Kan. 1955).

Most American lawyers would likely be puzzled by sense 3—e.g.: "Any equitable interest . . . may be '*overreached*'; that is, transferred from one form of capital to another as the trustees, having the legal estate, may decide." Alan Harding, *A Social History of English Law* 401 (1966).

overrule; overturn; reverse; set aside; vacate. *Overrule* is often employed in reference to procedural points throughout a trial, as in evidence <"Objection!" "Overruled.">. *Overrule* also denotes what a superior court does to a precedent that it expressly decides should no longer be controlling law, whether that precedent is a lower court's or its own.

Overturn is somewhat broader: it describes any judicial reasoning, including express overruling, by which a court partly or completely abolishes an earlier rule of law. Whereas *overruling* and *overturning* are both ordinarily abrupt, one-time acts, *overturning* may also (in its broadest use) indicate a long-term process by which courts gradually whittle away the authority of a precedent.

Reverse, by contrast, is much narrower than either *overrule* or *overturn*: it describes an appellate court's change to the opposite result from that by the lower court in a particular case.

Set aside and *vacate* are synonymously used to denote an appellate court's wiping clean the judgment slate in a particular case. The effect is to nullify the previous decision, usually of a lower court, but not necessarily to dictate a contrary result in further proceedings. See JUDGMENTS, APPELLATE-COURT & **set aside (B).**

*****overrulement,** an unlikely and unsightly American NEOLOGISM, was coined apparently because of a perceived need for a noun corresponding to the verb *to overrule*. A better phrasing is invariably possible if one merely uncovers the BURIED VERB—e.g.:

- "The statute in such a case expressly allows a discretionary appeal *on the overrulement of a demurrer* [read *when a demurrer is overruled*]." *State ex. rel. Southerland v. Town of Greeneville*, 297 S.W.2d 68, 71 (Tenn. 1956).
- "[*Beecher's*] positions as authority on that question *has* [read *have*] been greatly weakened if not destroyed by *overrulement sub silentio* [read *overruling sub silentio*]." *Bigelow v. Walraven*, 221 N.W.2d 328, 335 (Mich. 1974). (See SUBJECT–VERB AGREEMENT (B).)
- "There are at least two reasons why this Court should reverse the trial court's order for a new trial in this case, even without *overrulement of* [read *overruling*] *Javis*." *Snow v. Freeman*, 315 N.W.2d 125, 126 (Mich. 1982) (Ryan, J., dissenting).

Cf. *****overthrowal.**

oversee. See **overlook.**

oversight = (1) an unintentional error; or (2) intentional and watchful supervision. For sense 2, *oversight* is an unfortunate choice of word: *supervision* is preferable. Indeed, *administrative oversight* sounds less like a responsibility than like a bureaucratic botch. See **overlook.**

OVERSTATEMENT. Such words as *clearly, patently, obviously,* and *indisputably* are generally rightly seen as weakening rather than strengthening the statements they preface. They have been debased. Some scholars have mused that when a writer begins a sentence with one of these words, the statement following it is probably questionable. See **clearly.**

Unconscious overstatement is also a problem in legal discourse. It's never good to overstate one's case, even in minor unconscious ways, since the writing will lose credibility. Good writers remain wary of injudicious exaggeration. Perhaps the most common pitfalls involve comparisons, relative evaluations, and missing qualifications—e.g.:

- "More black students are presently enrolled at the University of Texas Law School *than have attended the school in all its history* [read *than have attended the school in previous years cumulatively,* or *than have, all told, been heretofore admitted,* or *than in all its history up to three years ago*]."
- "The approach used *in the United States* [read *in the U.S. judicial system*] to achieve information input and accurate output is mainly adversarial in nature."
- "In 1971, Congress enacted two important statutes—the Federal Election Campaign Fund Act and the Federal Election Campaign Act—both designed to reduce the corrupting influence of money on the political process." (No doubt the writer intended to say that 1971 saw the enactment of two major statutes designed to reduce financial corruption in campaigns; what the writer has said, however, is that 1971 saw the enactment of two major statutes, which, incidentally, had to do with reducing . . . . The problem is most easily identifiable if one reads the sentence without the names of the statutes set off by long dashes. The root of the problem is *both*, which makes the clause it introduces nonrestrictive rather than restrictive. The unconscious misstatement is eliminated when we omit *both*.)
- "Perhaps Senator Kennedy is at his best with those *who count most in the world*—his family." Though one might get the impression from various catchpenny tabloids that the Kennedy family *does* comprise "those who count most in the world," this is not what the writer intended to convey. [Read *who for him count most in the world* or *who count most in the world to him.*] See ILLOGIC (A).

overt. See **covert.**

overt act is sometimes used in criminal-law contexts, particularly in treason, as an equivalent of *actus reus* or *corpus delicti*. The phrase *overt act*, as opposed to the synonymous phrases, emphasizes the idea that the act is "open," and therefore perceptible to anyone who is there to observe it. But no one need be there to perceive it: "For legal purposes an act done in complete secrecy is an overt act or *actus reus* if later it can be proved against the defendant (as if he confesses to it)." Glanville Williams, *Textbook of Criminal Law* 32 (1978).

Because *overt act* is more widely comprehensible than either of the LATINISMS just mentioned, writers on the criminal law might achieve greater clarity if they uniformly adopted it. See ***actus reus*** & ***corpus delicti.***

overthrow is a synonym of *invalidate*, but it is more picturesque—e.g.: "Tax laws were queried and sometimes *overthrown* on the ground that the state had no 'jurisdiction to tax' the source in question." Robert

G. McCloskey, *The American Supreme Court* 152–53 (1960).

*****overthrowal,** like **overrulement*, is a NEOLOGISM that is neither recorded in most English-language dictionaries nor needed as part of the legal vocabulary. (See **overrulement.*) The noun *overthrow* or the present participle *overthrowing* will serve in virtually any context in which one might be tempted to use **overthrowal*—e.g.:

- "It is entirely clear that what was done herein . . . is not an *overthrowal* [read *overthrow* or *overthrowing*] of the state assessment and levy upon discernible grounds of illegality." *In re Gould Mfg. Co.*, 11 F.Supp. 644, 651 (E.D. Wis. 1935).
- "*Overthrowal of* [read *Overthrowing*] the verdict is unwarrantable." *Sears v. Mid-City Motors, Inc.*, 136 N.W.2d 428, 431 (Neb. 1965).

overturn. See **overrule.**

over . . . under. See VERBAL AWARENESS.

OVERWRITING. See PURPLE PROSE.

owing, adj.; **owed.** Although *owing* in the sense of *owed* is an old and established usage, the more logical course is simply to write *owed* where one means *owed*. The active participle may sometimes cause ambiguities or mislead the reader, if only for a second. E.g.:

- "We must consider whether to recognize a new liability *owing from* [read *owed by*] parents to their children for negligent supervision." *Holodook v. Spencer*, 324 N.E.2d 338, 340 (N.Y. 1974).
- "Such suit was based upon a sworn account alleged to be *owing* [read *owed*] by such defendants as partners." *Kantor v. Herald Pub. Co.*, 645 S.W.2d 625, 626 (Tex. App.—Tyler 1983).
- "Cleland admitted that a child-support arrearage accrued while Jeremy was a minor and was still *owing* [read *owed*] when Jeremy turned 18." *SRS v. Cleland*, 213 P.3d 1091, 1094 (Kan. Ct. App. 2009).

See PASSIVE VOICE (B).

owing to is an acceptable dangling modifier now primarily confined to BrE—e.g.: "No doubt until the time of Lord Nottingham the application of precedents was uncertain, *owing largely to* the scarcity of reliable reports." Carleton K. Allen, *Law in the Making* 380 (7th ed. 1964). See DANGLERS (D). Cf. **due to.**

own, in the sense "to admit," is now chiefly confined, in AmE, to the PHRASAL VERB *own up to*. But Learned Hand and several other accomplished legal writers have showed fondness for the one-word verb—e.g.: "It must be *owned* that the law upon the subject is not free from doubt." *Schmidt v. U.S.*, 177 F.2d 450, 451 (2d Cir. 1949) (per L. Hand, J.).

ownership (= title) implies the right of control over an object, quite apart from any actual or constructive control. The word has both a physical sense (e.g., ownership of a house) and a figurative sense (e.g., ownership of a copyright). See **possession (B).**

The word *ownership* is subject to nearly the same doubleness of meaning as *property*: "While it is usual to speak of *ownership of land*, what one owns is properly not the land, but rather the rights of possession and approximately unlimited use, present or future. In other words, one owns not the land, but rather an estate in the land. This is, in some degree, true of any material thing. One owns not the thing, but the right of possession and enjoyment of the thing." 1 H.T. Tiffany, *The Law of Real Property* § 2, at 4 (Basil Jones ed., 3d ed. 1939). See **property.**

OXYMORONS are immediate contradictions in terms, as in the word *bittersweet*. Any number of relative oxymorons exist in legal parlance, such as *all deliberate speed* (from the U.S. desegregation cases), *attractive nuisance*, *compelled consent*, *equitable servitude* (servitude in equity), *innocent fraud*, *intentional negligence*, *involuntary bailee* (not actually a bailee at all), *ordered liberty*, *substantive due process* (substantive process?), and *premeditative afterthought*. One criminal-law writer tried to invent the phrase *partial absolute liability*, which (understandably) did not take root. See Gerhard O.W. Mueller, *On Common Law Mens Rea*, 42 Minn. L. Rev. 1043, 1068 (1958). Other examples abound—e.g.:

- "As far as beauty contests for business go, this one was *pretty ugly.*" Stephanie Francis Ward, *What You Don't Do May Matter More Than What You Do*, 2 No. 25 A.B.A. J. E-Report 6 (2003).
- "Wearing a button or an arm band is *passive activity* that does not inherently distract students during the curriculum portion of the school day, unlike raising one's fist in the air." *Holloman ex rel. Holloman v. Harland*, 370 F.3d 1252, 1299 (11th Cir. 2004) (Wilson, J., concurring in part & dissenting in part).
- "Conway is a school that you'd want your son or daughter to attend. . . . It's a very positive place to be as opposed to Gateway which is *controlled chaos.*" *Webb-Edwards v. Orange County Sheriff's Office*, 525 F.3d 1013, 1023 (11th Cir. 2008).
- "In some states, prisoners served *increasingly less* time because of a combination of generous good-time and emergency releases." Nora V. Demleitner, *Good Conduct Time*, 61 Fla. L. Rev. 777, 781 (2009).
- "Additional property was also *found missing*, but everything eventually turned up in a janitor's closet." *Marion County Coroner's Office v. EEOC*, 612 F.3d 924, 927 (7th Cir. 2010).
- "The *conspicuous absence* of any mention of the House having a role in the confirmation process could, therefore, be construed as a definite signal that there was no intent for that chamber to participate in the confirmation process." *Fox v. Grayson*, 317 S.W.3d 1, 8 (Ky. 2010).

Cf. **consideration (H), unearned income, contract of record, unenforceable contract, unknown suspect** & **void contract.** See **suicide victim.**

---

oyer and terminer (lit., "to hear and determine") is a phrase still sometimes encountered in modern legal writing. At common law, the commissioners of *oyer and terminer* heard criminal cases. In some American states, the phrase *courts of oyer and terminer* formerly denoted the higher criminal courts. (Delaware, New Jersey, and Pennsylvania had such courts through the mid-20th century.) The pure LAW FRENCH form—*oyer et terminer*—is less frequently seen.

When Lord Eldon was Lord Chancellor, from 1801 to 1827, the Chancery was so hypertechnical and inefficient that it became known as a court of "*oyer sans terminer*." See J.H. Baker, *An Introduction to English Legal History* 130 (3d ed. 1990).

oyez, oyez, oyez. This is the cry heard in court to call the courtroom to order when a session begins. The word *oyez* was the LAW FRENCH equivalent of *hear ye* in the Middle Ages. (See **hear ye.**) The pronunciation was first /oh-**yets**/, later /oh-**yes**/ or /oh-**yez**/. Hence in Anglo-American courts the word has traditionally been pronounced "oh yes" (the pronunciation given in the *OED*). Sometimes today *oyez* is given the Frenchified pronunciation /oh-**yay**/. For Blackstone's view on pronouncing this word, see **countez.**

It was no doubt this triplet incantation to which Clarence Darrow alluded when he wrote, "When court opens, the bailiff intones some voodoo singsong words in an ominous voice that carries fear and respect at the opening of the rite." "Attorney for the Defense," in *Verdicts Out of Court* 313, 314 (1963). The incantation and surrounding pomp typical of many appellate courts is as follows: "At precisely 1:00 p.m. the marshal announced, 'The Honorable, the Chief Justice and the Associate Justices of the Supreme Court of the United States. *Oyez! Oyez! Oyez!* All persons having business before the Honorable, the Supreme Court of the United States, are admonished to draw near and give their attention, for the Court is now sitting. God save the United States and this Honorable Court.'" Barbara H. Craig, *Chadha: The Story of an Epic Constitutional Struggle* 202–03 (1988).

*Oyes, a variant spelling, is not now widely current.

P

pace /**pay**-see/ or /**pah**-chay/ [L. "with peace to"] = with all due respect to. This term is used most often when the writer expresses a contrary position—e.g.: "It is true, *pace* Savigny, that the reason and utility on which such customs rest often arise from purely local conditions." Carleton K. Allen, *Law in the Making* 98 (7th ed. 1964).

pacifist; *pacificist. *Pacifist* is the established form. Etymologists formerly argued that **pacificist* is the better-formed word, but it is almost never seen.

pact; paction. See **treaty.**

paid over. See **pay over.**

pain of, on. The phrase *on pain of death* was once common in law to express a prohibition the violation of which would result in the death penalty. The phrase has passed into lay contexts, in which it is ordinarily facetious. But it remains as a shortened phrase *on pain of* in legal usage. In this phrase, *pain* means "suffering or loss inflicted for a crime or offense; a punishment ranging from death to a small fine." E.g.:

- "'It is forbidden to all others to meddle with the said exorcisms, *on pain of* being punished according to law.'" Alexander Dumas, "Urbain Grandier," in 4 *Celebrated Crimes* 1324–25 (1896).
- "According to the principles of scientific jurisprudence, a rule [that] people are called upon to obey, *on pain of* some disagreeable consequence if they fail, ought first to be clearly and plainly stated." Edward Jenks, *The Book of English Law* 23 (P.B. Fairest ed., 6th ed. 1967).
- "We do not interpret this requirement to be a regimented procedure that must be explicitly performed *on pain of* reversal." *Jones v. State*, 920 So.2d 465, 476 (Miss. 2006).

See LOAN TRANSLATIONS.

pair forms the plural *pairs*. Using *pair* as a plural is incorrect—e.g.: "They found two *pair* [read *pairs*] of glasses on the ground." *People v. Memory*, 105 Cal. Rptr. 3d 353, 362 (Ct. App. 2010). On the question whether a phrase such as *pair of shoes*, as a subject, takes a singular or a plural verb, see SYNESIS.

pais (lit., "country") = the district or vicinage where the accused lives or where a crime was committed. A remnant of LAW FRENCH (fr. *pays*), this word sometimes signifies, in a transferred sense, the jury drawn from the district. Hence a *conclusion to the country* (a LOAN TRANSLATION) is a jury request and a *trial per pais* is a jury trial. See *in pais*.

palate; palette; pallet. The *palate* is the roof of the mouth or the sense of taste. A *palette* is an artist's paint-mixing board. A *pallet* is (1) a short platform for shipping, stacking, or storing goods; or (2) an improvised bed, especially on the floor.

pale, beyond the. This phrase, which has passed into lay parlance in the sense "bizarre; outside the bounds of civilized behavior," derives from the legal sense of *pale* from English history ("a district or territory within determined bounds, or subject to a particular jurisdiction"). In medieval Ireland, the district around Dublin, settled by the English and considered a law-abiding area, was known as the *Pale* or *within the Pale*. The land beyond that area was characterized as wild "bandit country."

In legal writing the phrase is often used figuratively but with ETYMOLOGICAL AWARENESS, as here:

- "The judgment of the Court of Appeals below turned on its determination that an interpretation of Rule 68 to include attorney's fees is *beyond the pale* of the judiciary's rulemaking authority." *Marek v. Chesny*, 473 U.S. 1, 35 (1985) (Brennan, J., dissenting).

- "The action of the Commissioner in reconstituting the Board in order to produce a result more to his liking seems *beyond the pale*." *In re Alappat*, 33 F.3d 1526, 1577–78 (Fed. Cir. 1994) (Plager, J., concurring).
- "While the Court concludes that the FTC's interpretation is clearly beyond the *'Chevron pale,'* this does not end the Court's inquiry, as the interpretation may be entitled to some degree of deference." *New York State Bar Ass'n v. FTC*, 276 F.Supp.2d 110, 139 (D.D.C. 2003) (per Walton, J.).

See POPULARIZED LEGAL TECHNICALITIES.

palette. See **palate.**

palimony (= a court-ordered allowance paid by one member to the other of a couple that, though unmarried, formerly cohabited) is a PORTMANTEAU WORD first recorded in 1979. Though it has become fairly common, it is jocular in most contexts. E.g.: "*Trimmer v. Van Bomel* . . . [was] a '*palimony*' case concerning an alleged oral agreement by which a wealthy widow was to pay her former male companion 'costs and expenses for sumptuous living and maintenance for the remainder of his life.'" *Gregg v. U.S. Indus., Inc.*, 715 F.2d 1522, 1537 (11th Cir. 1983). *Galimony*, a similar form that is even more jocular, has been used in reference to *palimony* between lesbians.

pallet. See **palate.**

palming off; passing off. The two terms are perfectly synonymous ("putting into circulation or dispersing of fraudulently" [*OED*]), both being used with almost equal frequency in AmE and BrE. *Passing off* is more peculiarly legal. E.g.:

- "The court therefore found that the local companies did not necessarily have the intent of *passing off* the advertisements as the work of the Hollywood studios." Nicole Griffin Farrell, Comment & Note, *Frankly, We Do Give a . . . Darn!*, 2003 Utah L. Rev. 1041, 1053–54.
- "Trademark law prevents one company from confusing consumers by *passing off* its goods as those of another company." Lauren Beth Emerson, Note, *Termination of Transfer of Copyright*, 75 Fordham L. Rev. 207, 211 (2006).

Palming off is used additionally in lay senses, and might be called a POPULARIZED LEGAL TECHNICALITY—e.g.: "It can happen that a state falls into the hands of groups that *palm off* injustice as justice, . . . creating a peace that in actuality is dictatorship." Pope Benedict XVI, *A Turning Point for Europe* 53 (2010). See **passing off.**

palpable. See **evident.**

pamphlet. This word is pronounced with the *-ph-* as if it were an *-f-*. A great many people incorrectly say /**pam**-plət/ instead of /**pam**-flət/. Similar mispronunciations occur with *ophthalmology* and *amphitheater.*

panacea (= cure-all; nostrum) is sometimes confused with other words. E.g.: "To allow the State to raise new matters not brought out in the original appeal or on rehearing would *open up a panacea* [read *open a Pandora's box* or, better, *bring a plethora*] of problems by way of precedent." *Laday v. State*, 685 S.W.2d 651, 654 (Tex. Crim. App. 1985). This is a MALAPROPISM.

pandemic = (of a disease) prevalent over the whole of a country or continent, or over the whole world. The word is usually adjectival, but may be used as a noun: "The international community pledged $1.9 billion in international aid to prepare for an avian flu *pandemic*." Elizabeth Weeks, *After the Catastrophe*, 85 N.C. L. Rev. 223, 259 (2006).

panel-shopping, analogous to *forum-shopping*, refers to panels usually consisting of three members of a court. E.g.: "[The 'law of the case doctrine'] discourages *panel shopping* at the circuit level, for in today's climate it is most likely that a different panel will hear subsequent appeals." *Lehrman v. Gulf Oil Corp.*, 500 F.2d 659, 662 (5th Cir. 1974). The hyphenated form is preferable. See **forum-shopping.**

panic, vb., makes *panicked* and *panicking.* Usually intransitive, *panic* has also appeared as a transitive verb, meaning "to affect with panic." E.g.: "Their goal . . . was simply to *panic* us enough to get us spending more and more time and money on ever greater security measures at home and military ventures abroad." Donald MacDonald, Letter to the Editor, N.Y. Times, 24 Jan. 2010, at D9.

paper has a special legal sense in the phrase *commercial paper* (= negotiable documents and bills of exchange). The plural *papers* often refers to pleadings and other court documents <we filed all the necessary papers>. See **negotiable instrument** & **court papers.**

papers. See **court papers.**

paperwork. One word.

paradigm. A. Sense. *Paradigm* = (1) an example, pattern; (2) a pattern of grammatical changes within a language; (3) a theoretical framework; or (4) a prevailing attitude, esp. within education or scholarship.

B. Plural. The preferred plural is *paradigms*, not *paradigmata. See PLURALS (B).

C. For *paragon*. The term *paragon* (= a model of perfection) is sometimes displaced by *paradigm*, especially in the phrase *paragon of virtue*. E.g.:

- "Bradford, previously convicted of rape, burglary and attempted murder, is no *paradigm* [read *paragon*] of virtue." *U.S. v. Bradford*, 78 F.3d 1216, 1224 (7th Cir. 1996).
- "In order to establish a usable legal standard for negligence, courts developed the common-law concept of the reasonable person—that *paradigm* [read *paragon*] of virtue who sets the bar by always exercising reasonable care."

Young v. Gastro-Intestinal Ctr., Inc., 205 S.W.3d 741, 752 (Ark. 2005) (Imber, J., dissenting).

- "If they achieve those objectives, the law is good, the law is just, and their attorneys are *paradigms* [read *paragons*] of virtue." Yitzchok Adlerstein, *Lawyers, Faith, and Peacemaking: Jewish Perspectives on Peace*, 7 Pepp. Disp. Resol. L.J. 177, 183 (2007).

paragraph. In drafting, a *paragraph* is a subdivision usually numbered for reference and sometimes, in citations, indicated by the character ¶. The term can be confusing, however, because a drafted *paragraph* often consists of many individual paragraphs in the conventional sense of the word. At other times, it may consist of a two- or three-word phrase. When using cross-references, then, it is often more helpful to give the full citation—as, for example, by referring to "Rule 4(A)(4)(b)(ii)." That way, the terminology for each subdivision does not impede clarity.

parajudge has been used to refer to U.S. Magistrate Judges, who have some adjudicative power, but not the extent of power vested in Article III judges: "Under the '*para-judge*' rationale, the Magistrates Act comports with Article III [of the U.S. Constitution] because it subjects magistrates' rulings to de novo determination by a federal district judge." *U.S. v. Saunders*, 641 F.2d 659, 663 (9th Cir. 1980). The unhyphenated one-word form is best in AmE.

A minor judicial officer, such as a hearing officer, local magistrate, master, or referee may also be termed a *parajudge*.

paralegal. A. Senses and Usage. *Paralegal* = (1) (adj.) of, relating to, or associated with law in an ancillary way; or (2) (n.) a paralegal aide.

In BrE, the term is sometimes spelled as two words, as it was repeatedly in the following article: "Compare that with the UK's largest single law firm Clifford Chance with 985 fee earners comprising 195 partners, 577 assistant solicitors, 206 articled clerks and 7 *para legals*." Robert Rice, *Profession Still Bashful About the Business of Making Money*, Fin. Times, 9 Apr. 1990, at 12.

B. And *legal assistant*. In sense 2, *paralegal* is rivaled in AmE by the term *legal assistant*. Some prefer calling themselves *paralegals*; others prefer calling themselves *legal assistants*. The two terms are about equally common.

paralegaling is a colloquialism to name what it is that a paralegal (or *legal assistant*) does. The term is similar to *bailiffing* (see **bailiff**). See NOUNS AS VERBS.

One text uses the more formal term *paralegalism* (= the calling of a paralegal)—see William P. Statsky, *Introduction to Paralegalism* (5th ed. 2009).

paralegalism. See **paralegaling**.

PARALEIPSIS is a rhetorical tactic whereby a speaker or writer mentions something in disclaiming any mention of it. For example, a less-than-scrupulous cross-examiner would engage in paraleipsis if he stated, "Mr. Smith, I won't bring up your unsavory past as a drug-dealer, but I would like to ask you some questions about your prior business dealings with the plaintiff." To which the fitting response is "Objection!" preferably after *unsavory*. Among the most common phrases introducing a paraleipsis are *to say nothing of, not to mention*, and *needless to say*.

In the following example of judicial paraleipsis, the judge appears to be suggesting a tactic to one of the parties: "I purposely refrain from commenting on the possibility of any relief against Malcolm Devers' attorney, Dalonas, which may be available to the defendants, or any title company that may have insured a Radnor Heights fee for one of them." *Devers v. Chateau Corp.*, 792 F.2d 1278, 1299 (4th Cir. 1986) (Murnaghan, J., dissenting).

And in the following example, Morris Cohen may have had in mind the difference between *referring* and *alluding*, but the resulting paraleipsis is nevertheless damning: "We need not refer to the Texas governor who pardoned hundreds of criminals for his political advantage." Morris R. Cohen, *Reason and Law* 65 (1961) (referring to that very governor). The unfortunate thing about this passage is that Cohen shifts the reader's negative impression away from the individual perpetrator and onto the state. For a brief account of Governor Pa Ferguson's malfeasances in granting pardons—and his subsequent impeachment—see T.R. Fehrenbach, *Lone Star: A History of Texas and the Texans* 638–39 (1968).

PARALLELISM refers to matching parts, i.e., analogous sentence-parts that must match if the sentence is to make strictly logical sense—and the best grammatical sense. The problem of unparallel sentence-parts usually crops up in the use of correlative conjunctions and in lists:

- "[Its] continuance is contingent upon legally recognized rights of tenure, transfer, and of succession [delete second *of* or insert *of* before *transfer*] in use and occupancy." *In re O'Connor's Estate*, 252 N.W. 826, 827 (Neb. 1934).
- "Marketing quotas *not only embrace* [read *embrace not only*] all that may be sold without penalty *but also* what may be consumed on the premises." *Wickard v. Filburn*, 317 U.S. 111, 119 (1942) (per Jackson, J.).
- "No person in this country who is committed to prison on a charge of crime can be kept long in confinement because he can insist upon either being let out on bail *or else of being* [read *or else being*] brought to speedy trial." Alfred Denning, *Freedom Under the Law* 9 (1949).
- "These [copyright] exceptions were based *not only on* long-time library practice, *but also* [insert *on*] the recognition that libraries provide significant benefit to society and are a public good." Estelle Derclaye, *Copyright and Cultural Heritage* 132 (2011). A better correction would put the preposition *on* before *not only*, so that it connects to its two objects, *practice* and *recognition*.

Failures of parallelism are especially common in cumulative sentences—e.g.: "The defendants *admitted* the publication of the article, *disavowed* any intention to defame and injure the plaintiff in his good name and reputation; [make the semicolon a comma to match the punctuation before *disallowed*, then insert *and*] *denied* that the article was maliciously composed, printed, or published; that the article appeared simply as a news item, [make the comma a semicolon to match the punctuation before *that the article appeared*] and [insert *that the article* to match the other *that*-clauses] was brought in by one of its news gatherers." *Webb v. Call Publ'g Co.*, 180 N.W. 263, 264 (Wis. 1920). This sentence tries to do too much: it has a series of three main verbs, the last of which has a series of three *that*-phrase objects.

Less troubling is a lack of parallelism where two or more sentence-parts are balanced by *and*; but even this should be avoided—e.g.:

- "[The boy's] operation [of the car] was therefore unlawful and *negligence* [read *negligent*] per se." *Cirosky v. Smathers*, 122 S.E. 864, 865 (S.C. 1924).
- "Johann was a tall, thin man, dark-haired, near-sighted, not bad-looking, and *a fop* [read *foppish*]." George Richard Marek, *Beethoven: Biography of a Genius* 131 (1969). Here we have a string of adjectives—all implicitly modifying *man*—but the writer changes the last in the string to a noun phrase.

See PLAIN LANGUAGE (D).

paralyze; paralyse. The first spelling is the only one used in AmE; the second (as well as the first) is used in BrE.

parameters. Technical contexts aside, this jargonistic VOGUE WORD is not used by those with a heightened sensitivity to language. To begin with, only a specialist in mathematics or computing knows precisely what it means: it is a mush word. Second, when it does have a discernible meaning, it is usurping the place of a far simpler and more straightforward term. Though the word does not appear in the best legal writing, it does abound—e.g.:

- "The purpose of pleadings is to put one's opponent on notice as to the *parameters* [read *grounds*] of the forthcoming battle." *Bilano v. Young*, 665 S.W.2d 536, 543 (Tex. App.—Corpus Christi 1983).
- "Although it would have been appropriate to outline the *parameters* [read *elements*] of agency for purposes of the entrapment charge, a reading of the court's instructions . . . satisfies us that the jury was neither misled nor confused." *U.S. v. Frascone*, 747 F.2d 953, 957 (5th Cir. 1984).
- "Other ILO instruments establish affirmative rights related to work, but within broad *parameters* [read *guidelines*] that allow many interpretations." Berta E. Hernández-Truyol & Jane E. Larson, *Sexual Labor and Human Rights*, 37 Colum. Hum. Rts. L. Rev. 391, 417 (2006).
- "Where, however, the officer is not confined to the *parameters* [read *boundaries*?] of a department program, and thus has considerable discretion to choose the places he searches, pretext is irrelevant and the search is governed only by a general assessment of objective reasonableness." Michael R. Dimino Sr., *Police Paternalism*, 66 Wash. & Lee L. Rev. 1485, 1533 (2009).
- "We do not decide the *parameters* [read *limits*] of tribal-court jurisdiction over the same subject matter." *Garcia v. Gutierrez*, 217 P.3d 591, 594 (N.M. 2009).

Rarely is the word used in the singular, but it does occur: "The dismissal in the instant case falls within the *parameter* of the present rule." *Clifford Ragsdale, Inc. v. Morganti, Inc.*, 356 So.2d 1321, 1323 (Fla. Dist. Ct. App. 1978).

Sometimes writers use *perimeter*, whose meaning has influenced the senses of *parameter*, ostensibly to sidestep any criticisms for the use of *parameter*. E.g.:

- "The plurality continued that the immunity extended even to malicious acts that were within the outer *perimeter* of the federal employee's line of duty." *Dretar v. Smith*, 752 F.2d 1015, 1016 (5th Cir. 1985).
- "All that is left for the district court to decide on . . . is whether specific acts and allegations fall within this *perimeter*." *Austin Mun. Secs., Inc. v. National Ass'n of Secs. Dealers, Inc.*, 757 F.2d 676, 694 (5th Cir. 1985).

Although this usage makes literal sense, *limit* or *boundary* or *border* would be a simpler term for the same notion.

*paramouncy. See **paramountcy.**

paramount means "superior to all others" or "most important"—not merely "important."

paramountcy is the noun corresponding to the adjective *paramount*. It is not often seen but is quite proper—e.g.: "One of these principles is undoubtedly the *paramountcy* of EEC law over municipal or national law." P.S. Atiyah, *Law and Modern Society* 62 (1983). **Paramouncy* is a NEEDLESS VARIANT.

A more familiar word, such as *supremacy* or *preeminence*, will almost always be a better choice.

paraphrase is occasionally misrendered *paraphraze*, as in *Eades v. Drake*, 332 S.W.2d 553, 556 (Tex. 1960). See **rephrase.**

parasitic, in reference to damages, does not mean merely "additional." Rather, the term means, in the words of Lord Denning, M.R.,

> that there are some heads of damage which, if they stood alone, would not be recoverable: but, nevertheless, if they can be annexed to some other legitimate claim for damages, may yet be recoverable. They are said to be *parasitic* because, like a parasite, in biology, they cannot exist on their own, but depend on others for their life or nourishment. . . . I do not like the very word *parasite*. A parasite is one who is a useless hanger-on sucking out the substance of others. *Parasitic* is the adjective derived from it. It is a term of abuse. It is an opprobrious epithet. The phrase *parasitic damages* conveys to my mind the idea of damages which ought not in justice to be awarded, but which

somehow or other have been allowed to get through by hanging on to others. If such be the concept underlying the doctrine, then the sooner it is got rid of the better. . . . I hope it will disappear from [the textbooks] after this case.

> *Spartan Steel & Alloys Ltd. v. Martin & Co.,*
> [1973] Q.B. 27, 34–35.

Parasitic should not be used as a fancy variant of *dependent*, as here: "The legal characterization of an individual's mental state under *Rees* is *parasitic* [read *dependent*] on the factual conclusions rendered by those testifying on the issue." *Rumbaugh v. Procunier*, 753 F.2d 395, 413 (5th Cir. 1985). The quotation from Lord Denning makes plain the metaphorical baggage that *parasitic* carries with it; and unless the METAPHOR is perfectly apt, the word should not be used.

parcel, n. (= a tract of land), is now primarily a LEGAL-ISM. E.g.: "Individual households own *parcels* of land, but many elements of value are held in common by a larger group." Lee Anne Fennell, *Homeownership 2.0*, 102 Nw. U. L. Rev. 1047, 1102 (2008).

parcel out is a common PHRASAL VERB in the legal idiom. E.g.: "Oversaturation of the character might cause it to lose value more quickly than if the copyright owner could *parcel out* the character in smaller doses." Thomas F. Cotter, *Memes and Copyright*, 80 Tul. L. Rev. 331, 381 (2005).

*parcenary. See **coparcenary.**

*parcener. See **coparcener (A).**

pardon, n. See **clemency.**

pardon, vb. See **commute (B)** & **condone.**

parens patriae (= the father of a country) refers in Great Britain to the king or queen, particularly as the sovereign (historically speaking) was thought to have a kind of guardianship over the nation and persons in need of care. E.g.: "At common law the king is *parens patriae*, father of his country, which is but the medieval mode of putting what we mean today when we say that the state is the guardian of social interests." Roscoe Pound, *The Spirit of the Common Law* 68 (1921).

In the U.S., *parens patriae* refers to the state as a sovereign—e.g.: "Two interests that traditionally justify intrusive state action are the state's police power and its *parens patriae* interest." Christyne E. Ferris, *The Search for Due Process in Civil Commitment Hearings*, 61 Vand. L. Rev. 959, 966 (2008).

parentelic method; parentelic system. These phrases denote one scheme of computation used to determine the paternal or maternal collaterals entitled to inherit. The name derives from the technical term *parentela* (= a person's issue). E.g.:

• "Under the laws of succession and marriage there are three different methods for determining degrees of relationship. The most common is the civil law method, used in Virginia to determine relationships in succession law.

The second is the *parentelic method*, used in succession law in other states. The third is the canon law method, developed to establish the limits of permissible marriages between relatives." William J. O'Shaughnessy Jr., Note, *Proxy Decisionmaking for the Terminally Ill: The Virginia Approach*, 70 Va. L. Rev. 1269, 1292–93 (1984).

• "This pattern of intestate inheritance resembles the common law's *parentelic system* for the descent of land." Carolyn S. Bratt, *A Primer on Kentucky Intestacy Laws*, 82 Ky. L.J. 29, 49 (1993–1994).

PARENTHESES. A. Syntactic Effect. Words contained within parentheses do not affect the syntax of the rest of the sentence. E.g.: "[We must determine] whether each (or both) appellants are entitled to immunity." *Elliott v. Perez*, 751 F.2d 1472, 1482 (5th Cir. 1985). The writer of that sentence could have avoided this error (*each appellants are*) by reading the sentence without the parenthetical phrase. See PUNCTUATION (H).

B. Overuse of. Virtually any punctuation mark is subject to an annoying overuse, but this is especially true of parentheses—and long dashes—which to be effective must be used sparingly. When they appear at all frequently in writing, they tire the reader's eye, add to the burden of decoding, and cloy the reader's interest. The sentence begins to sag with the qualifications here and there. The following is a two-sentence example from an opinion published in 1985:

> Marshall also relies upon his cross-examination of the government investigator (Ms. Sandlin) and of a government witness (Bitner; the Four Seasons manager and the custodian of its records—although he was not called upon by the government to authenticate the Four Seasons lawnmower records) as showing the unreliability of Ms. Sandlin's opinion that three (or any) lawn mowers were actually missing, as she had testified on the basis of her deductions from the (incomplete) Four Seasons records. . . . However, in the first place, if the testimony of Marshall's witnesses was to be believed (which was for the jury to determine), Marshall could not have been at the Frederick Street residence at the time Lee (thus mistakenly) believed that he saw him there.
>
> *U.S. v. Marshall*, 762 F.2d 419, 422 (5th Cir. 1985).

None of these parenthetical interpolations is syntactically or stylistically justified.

C. With Appositives. See APPOSITIVES (B).

pari delicto, in. See *in pari delicto.*

pari materia, in. See *in pari materia.*

pari passu (= with equal pace; equally; at the same time) is an adverb as well as an adjective. The phrase is frequently used in contracts when several persons are paid at the same level or out of a common fund. E.g.: "Hence when this £25 is withdrawn and mixed with £175 in the second account, the charges extend over the whole resulting £200, but only to the extent of £25, and this is divided up *pari passu* amongst the ten." (Eng.)

The phrase **in pari passu* is wrong, *in* being no part of the phrase. In the following example, the writer appears to have meant *in pari materia*: "The Supreme Court has indicated that fee statutes using the same language are to be interpreted *in pari passu* [read *in pari materia* or *pari passu*]." James Moore et al., *Moore's Federal Practice* ¶ 54.77[.5-3], at 54-499 (1988). See **in pari materia.**

Parliament. The definite article (*the*) is unnecessary before this word when it is used as a proper noun (i.e., in reference to a particular parliament). E.g.: "Most socialist members of *Parliament* voted against the amendment while a significant number of members abstained." Balázs Schanda, *Religious Freedom Issues in Hungary*, 2002 BYU L. Rev. 405, 428. Cf. **Congress.**

parliamentary need not be capitalized except when one is referring to the doings of a particular parliament. Unlike *congressional*, which should not be capitalized, *parliamentary* as a lowercase adjective has other senses, most commonly in denoting procedural rules for governing meetings. So there may be more justification for the uppercase *Parliamentary* than an uppercase *Congressional*.

parliamentary history (BrE) = *legislative history* (AmE). See **legislative history.**

parody; satire. *Parody* = an imitative work that comments, usu. through humor, directly on another person's expression or creative style (as in art or literature) and has both social value and entertainment value. *Satire* = a work that uses irony, wit, or sarcasm to expose, ridicule, or scorn the follies and vices of humanity or organizations. Like a *parody*, a *satire* may use a specific work as a platform, but unlike a *parody*, the work is not the target. The distinction is important under the fair-use exception to copyright law: "*Parody* needs to mimic an original to make its point, and so has some claim to use the creation of its victim's (or collective victims') imagination, whereas *satire* can stand on its own two feet and so requires justification for the very act of borrowing." *Campbell v. Acuff-Rose Music, Inc.*, 510 U.S. 569, 580–81 (1994) (per Souter, J.). Sometimes the terms are confused—e.g.: "It is the rule in this Circuit that though the *satire* [read *parody*] need not be only of the copied work and may . . . also be a *parody* [read *satire*] of modern society, the copied work must be, at least in part, an object of the *parody*, otherwise there would be no need to conjure up the original work." *Rogers v. Koons*, 960 F.2d 301, 310 (2d Cir. 1992).

parol. A. Senses. *Parol* is most commonly used as an adjective equivalent to *oral*—e.g.:

- "No one has claimed in this case that the alleged *parol* promise to settle the underlying lawsuit for a specific range of dollars is consistent with the language of the original contract." *Creamer v. Helferstay*, 448 A.2d 332, 338–39 (Md. 1982).
- "Payless further contends that the 'deed speaks for itself, it is clear and unambiguous and therefore Appellant's *parol*

assertions as to the intent and import of the document are irrelevant and immaterial.'" *Hutchins v. Payless Auto Sales, Inc.*, 38 P.3d 1057, 1062 (Wyo. 2002).

In contract law, however, *parol* includes the written as well as the spoken word. So a *parol contract* is any contract that is not under seal. See **informal contract.**

Parol may also act as a noun meaning "word of mouth." E.g.: "Cruz does not dispute the principle asserted by Davis—that an agreement or stipulation that no party shall be bound by a contract unless all parties sign it—may be proven by *parol*." *Rael v. Davis*, 83 Cal. Rptr. 3d 745, 753 (Ct. App. 2008). *By parol* (= by word of mouth) is the most common construction with the noun *parol*, but *in parol* (= in something said or spoken; in a statement or declaration) is also used—e.g.:

- "To be sufficient under the statute of frauds, a writing must be complete in itself, leaving nothing to rest in *parol*." *Kenby Oil Co. v. Lange*, 42 P.3d 201, 204 (Kan. Ct. App. 2002).
- "Every essential element of the sale must be expressed in writing, and a contract for the sale of land which is partly in writing and partly in *parol* falls within the Statute of Frauds." *Edwards v. Sewell*, 656 S.E.2d 246, 249 (Ga. Ct. App. 2008).

B. Pronunciation. *Parol* is most properly pronounced /**par**-əl/. Yet, in AmE, it is frequently pronounced like *parole*, namely /pə-**rohl**/. That pronunciation is acceptable.

C. Spelled *parole*. This variant spelling is uncommon enough to make it undesirable—e.g.: "Again, at this date the law had barely begun to acquire experience in the handling of *parole evidence* [read *parol evidence*]." Theodore F.T. Plucknett, *A Concise History of the Common Law* 56 (5th ed. 1956). But it is the usual form in Scotland.

parol contract. See **simple contract** & **informal contract.**

parole. A. In Penal Law. *Parole* (= the conditional release of a prisoner from jail before he or she serves the full sentence) has long been the standard term in AmE; it existed in British military terminology in a related sense from the 17th century, and in the 20th century became standard in BrE in the American sense. *Ticket-of-leave* and *order of licence* were earlier BrE variants; *release on licence* is still a common equivalent in British legal contexts.

B. In Immigration Law. Although most lawyers are familiar with its criminal-law sense, *parole* has a unique sense in immigration law: "temporary admission to the United States of an alien for urgent humanitarian reasons or for a significant public benefit, until the conditions supporting admission cease to exist or are found to be inadequate." Aliens who qualify for parole include asylum-seekers and emergency-aid providers.

C. And *parol*. For *parole* as a variant spelling of *parol*, see **parol (c)**.

parolee. See **probationer**.

parol-evidence rule (= the rule that evidence cannot be admitted—or if admitted, cannot be used—if it has the effect of adding to, varying, or contradicting a legal instrument) is commonly thought of as an evidentiary rule, but "it is probably best regarded as a rule of substantive law." P.S. Atiyah, *An Introduction to the Law of Contract* 161–62 (3d ed. 1981). The question of admissibility is really only secondary, the primary question being whether, if admitted, the evidence will have the legal effect of varying the instrument.

parricide; patricide. *Parricide* is the more usual word meaning (1) "the murder of one's own father"; or (2) "one who murders his own father." E.g. (sense 2): "The contention that quadriplegia is 'punishment enough'—like the *parricide*'s claim that he deserves mercy as an orphan—is one addressed to the sentencing court's discretion alone." *U.S. ex rel. Villa v. Fairman*, 810 F.2d 715, 717–18 (7th Cir. 1987).

It is also used in extended senses, such as "the murder of the ruler of a country" and "the murder of a close relative." These are not examples of SLIPSHOD EXTENSION, however, for even the Latin etymon (*parricida*) was used in these senses.

part. See **portion** & **city part**.

part, in. See **in pertinent part**.

partake is construed with either *in* or *of* in the sense "to take part or share in some action or condition; to participate." *In* is the more common preposition in this sense: "Steele knew that Clouthier had recently refused to eat both lunch and dinner, and had refused to *partake* in free time." *Clouthier v. County of Contra Costa*, 591 F.3d 1232, 1246 (9th Cir. 2010).

Of is common when the sense is "to receive, get, or have a share or portion *of*; to have something *of*, possess a certain amount *of*"—e.g.:

- "The inclusion of the Commandments monument in this group has a dual significance, *partaking of* both religion and government, that cannot be said to violate the Establishment Clause." *Van Orden v. Perry*, 545 U.S. 677, 691–92 (2005) (per Rehnquist, J.).
- "The notion of definitional information, however, *partakes of* scope, meaning, and clarity together." Jeffrey A. Lefstin, *The Formal Structure of Patent Law and the Limits of Enablement*, 23 Berkeley Tech. L.J. 1141, 1220 (2008).
- "It is well understood that legal reasoning *partakes of* moral judgment in cases in which judges routinely exercise delegated or common law-making authority." Harry T. Edwards & Michael A. Livermore, *Pitfalls of Empirical Studies That Attempt to Understand the Factors Affecting Appellate Decisionmaking*, 58 Duke L.J. 1895, 1945–46 (2009).

part and parcel is an idiomatic DOUBLET and CLICHÉ that emphasizes the sense of "an essential or integral portion; something essentially belonging to a larger whole." E.g.: "The need to label a person a professional is *part and parcel* of a 'professional malpractice' action." *Racine County v. Oracular Milwaukee, Inc.*, 767 N.W.2d 280, 286 (Wis. Ct. App. 2009). See DOUBLETS, TRIPLETS, AND SYNONYM-STRINGS.

partially; partly. Whenever either word could suffice in a given context, *partly* is the better choice. *Partially* occasionally causes AMBIGUITY because of its other sense "in a manner exhibiting favoritism." *AHD* notes that *partly*, which has wider application, "is the choice when stress is laid on the part (in contrast to the whole), when the reference is to physical things, and when the sense is equivalent to *in part, to some extent*" <partly to blame> <a partly finished building>. "*Partially* is especially applicable to conditions or states in the sense of *to a certain degree*; as the equivalent of *incomplete*, it indirectly stresses the whole" (*AHD*) <partially dependent> <partially contributory>.

*partially undisclosed principal. See **principal (c)**.

partial payment; part payment. Although *part payment* is common in the lawbooks, *partial payment* is more idiomatic today.

partial performance; part performance. Although *part performance*, like *part payment*, can be found throughout many fine books, *partial performance* is the more natural-sounding phrase.

partible; *partitionable. The longer form is a NEEDLESS VARIANT not recorded in the dictionaries. *Partible* = subject to partition; separable <the concurrent estate is partible>.

particeps criminis is an unjustified LATINISM in view of our simpler equivalent *accessory*. E.g.: "Where the conveyance is founded in actual fraud the grantee is regarded as a *particeps criminis* [read *accessory*], and is not entitled to reimbursement, or to have the conveyance stand for any purpose of reimbursement or indemnity, for the consideration paid." *Blount v. Blount*, 95 So.2d 545, 560 (Miss. 1957). The plural form is *participes criminis*.

PARTICIPLES, PROBLEMS WITH. See ADJECTIVES (H), DANGLERS (B), FUSED PARTICIPLES & MISPLACED MODIFIERS.

PARTICLES, UNNECESSARY. Any number of English verbs are regularly given particles in informal or colloquial contexts, and these particles often help to establish the informality or colloquiality of the writing. So a Good Samaritan *helps out* a person rather than merely *helping* that person, litigants *fight out* a dispute rather than merely *fighting* it.

Unnecessary particles seem to find a more hospitable climate in BrE than in AmE—e.g.:

- "By a strange coincidence, on the very same day, so-called animal rights activists *injured up* [read *injured*] a 13-month-old baby in Bristol." Richard Ingrams, *Observer*, 24 June 1990, at 18.
- "Competition in high schools . . . has not *slackened off* [read *slackened*]." Roger Buckley, *Japan Today* 93 (2d ed. 1990).

The following examples are best avoided in legal prose: *award over* (*award*), *continue on* (*continue*), *convey away* (*convey*), and *proceed on* (*proceed*).

Slight DIFFERENTIATION is possible with a number of phrases, such as *die off* (*die*), *face up to* (*face*), *lose out* (*lose*), *meet up with* (*meet*), *pay off* or *pay out* (*pay*) (see **pay** & **pay over**); with these phrases, the particles arguably add a nuance to the verb. One must always be on guard to ask whether the particles in one's writing pull their weight or give, instead, a breezy, slangy quality to the prose.

PARTICLE VERBS. See PHRASAL VERBS.

particular intention. See **intention (F).**

particularized is sometimes misused for *particular*—e.g.: "Under a rules-based system, a predetermined legal result flows from the existence of certain *particularized* [read *particular*] facts." Lance J. Phillips, Note, *The Implications of IFRS on the Functioning of the Securities Antifraud Regime in the United States*, 108 Mich. L. Rev. 603, 616 (2010). The sense there is not "made particular" but "particular"; hence *particularized* is the wrong word for the context. Cf. **generalized.**

particular jurisprudence. See **jurisprudence (D).**

***parties hereto** is, 99 times out of 100, a rank REDUNDANCY. The one other time, either *parties to this case* or *parties to this agreement* would be preferable.

partisan; *partizan. The first is the preferred spelling in both AmE and BrE. Although the term denotes "one who takes part or sides with another," it has connotations of "a blind, prejudiced, unreasoning, or fanatical adherent" (*OED*).

partition. To a nonlawyer this is something that separates, especially one part of a space from another; to a lawyer, *partition* = a division of real property into severalty.

The word is also commonly a verb in legal writing; it means "to divide (land) into severalty" <action for partitioning an inheritance>. E.g.: "Any one of a number of co-owners was entitled to have the property '*partitioned*,' i.e. divided, or at any rate to have the property sold and his share paid out to him." William Geldart, *Introduction to English Law* 78 (D.C.M. Yardley ed., 9th ed. 1984). See **partible.**

Both as a noun and as a verb, the word *petition* is sometimes misused for *partition*, the result being a gross MALAPROPISM—e.g.:

- "Children over approximately age 9 sat in an 11 by 14 enclosure, partially *petitioned* [read *partitioned*] off from the main waiting room." *Doe v. New York City Dep't of Soc. Servs.*, 670 F.Supp. 1145, 1181 (S.D.N.Y. 1987).
- "Structural components include walls, *petitions* [read *partitions*], floors, ceilings, windows, doors, [etc.]." Jacob Mertens, *Mertens Law of Federal Income Taxation* § 45.51, at 120 (1990).

***partitionable.** See **partible.**

***partizan.** See **partisan.**

partly. See **partially.**

partner. See **copartner** & **coparcener (B).**

partnership = (1) a voluntary joining together for business purposes by two or more persons of money, goods, labor, and skill, upon an agreement that the gain or loss will be divided proportionally between them; or (2) the relation that exists between those who carry on a business in common for the purpose of profit.

part payment. See **partial payment.**

part performance. See **partial performance.**

party is a LEGALISM that is unjustified when it merely replaces *person*. If used as an elliptical form of *party to the contract* or *party to the lawsuit*, *party* is quite acceptable as a TERM OF ART—e.g.: "According to the common law, any contract may be terminated by either *party* with due notice." Geoff Davenport et al., 47 *Termination of Employment Digest* 348 (2002). See **party of the first part.**

Fred Rodell's quip is worth remembering: "Only The Law insists on making a '*party*' out of a single person." Fred Rodell, *Woe Unto You, Lawyers!* 28 (1939). See **third party.**

PARTY APPELLATIONS. Generally, in briefs and opinions, it is best to humanize parties by calling them by their names—e.g.: "Jones" and "Smith." Otherwise, the reader is continually forced to rethink who is the petitioner and who the respondent; who the appellant and who the appellee; or, worse yet, who was plaintiff below, now appellee (or is it appellant?). It is easier to remember that Mr. Gulbenkian is the appellant than that the appellant is Gulbenkian, for every case has an appellant, but not every case has a Gulbenkian. *See* Fed. R. App. P. 28(d).

Problems arise, however, with matters of procedure. "Gulbenkian failed to preserve error" is an invidious legal FICTION, since it was Gulbenkian's attorney, not Gulbenkian, who failed to preserve error. Judicial opinions should avoid obscuring the responsibility for procedural mistakes. In such contexts, *appellant*, *appellee*, *plaintiff*, and other such appellations are preferable, for they more nearly connote attorney and client jointly. Even phrasing the statement "Counsel for appellant failed to preserve error" would be appropriate, although from the lawyer's perspective it is a harsher statement. See **plaintiff, defendant.**

party in interest = a natural or juristic person having a legal or economic interest in litigation or arbitration. E.g.: "The trouble, however, with appellants' position in this case is that no stipulation was presented to the court signed by all *parties in interest.*" *In re Dardis's Will*, 115 N.W. 332, 333 (Wis. 1908).

party litigant. See POSTPOSITIVE ADJECTIVES.

party of the first part; party of the second part. These phrases—which have traditionally appeared in many types of instruments—are the worst types of ARCHAISMS. Not only are they cumbersome and verbose, they also invite mistakes. A glance at volume 31 of *Words and Phrases* (1957) hints at the amount of litigation caused by drafters who have inadvertently transposed *first* and *second.*

The best modern practice, in contractual drafting, is to use either real names or functional labels such as *buyer* and *seller; licensor* and *licensee; publisher* and *author;* and the like.

The most that can be said for the old phrases is that they have a mildly interesting history. Parties entering into contracts were once divided into classes, or "parts," according to their property interests in the transaction. Generally, the owner or seller was the *party of the first part* and the buyer was the *party of the second part*—e.g.:

- "Know all men by these presents, that John Doe, of the county of Arapahoe, in the state of Colorado, *party of the first part*, for and in consideration of the sum of $5,000, to him in hand paid by Richard Roe, of the county of Arapahoe and state aforesaid, *party of the second part*, the receipt of which is hereby acknowledged, does hereby grant, bargain and sell unto the said *party of the second part*, his heirs and assigns, the following goods and chattels, viz . . . ." W.S. Walker, *Sayler's American Form Book* 97 (4th ed. 1913) (from a form chattel mortgage).
- "The said *party of the first part*, for and in consideration of the sum of $1,000, in hand paid, at and before the sealing of these presents, the receipt whereof is hereby acknowledged, has granted, bargained, sold, aliened, conveyed and confirmed, and by these presents does grant, bargain, sell, alien, convey and confirm, unto the said *party of the second part*, his heirs and assigns, all [describe property]." W.S. Walker, *Sayler's American Form Book* 132 (4th ed. 1913) (from a form warranty deed to secure a loan).
- "This agreement entered into between _____ *party of the first part*, and _____ *party of the second part*." Samuel G. Kling, *The Legal Encyclopedia for Home and Business* 93 (1957) (simple form contract so punctuated).

These are the once-common uses, but there are two historically unwarranted variations.

First, during the 20th century the historical divisions between buyers and sellers fell apart: contract drafters came to use *party of the first part* for whichever party was named first. Often, that party was the one with the greatest degree of bargaining power—e.g.:

"The *party of the first part* covenants and agrees to drill for the *party of the second part* [i.e., the landowner], its successors or assigns, a well for petroleum or gas. . . . The *party of the second part* covenants and agrees to pay to the *party of the first part*, provided the *party of the first part* shall complete said well in the manner, to the depth, and of the dimensions hereinafter specified, and when the said well shall be so completed, at the rate of [$___]."

Robert T. Donley, *Coal, Oil and Gas in West Virginia and Virginia* 360 (1951) (from a form contract for drilling an oil or gas well).

Second, the idea of a *party of the third part* gradually arose, though this would have traditionally been considered a solecism. In most contracts, there were but two sides (or "parts"), so that in multiparty contracts there would be *parties of the first part* and *parties of the second part*. The idea was that a *third party* was a stranger to the contract. So a turn-of-the-century dictionary described *third parties* as a "term used to include all persons who are not parties to the contract, agreement, or instrument of writing by which their interest in the thing conveyed is sought to be affected." Walter A. Shumaker & George F. Longsdorf, *The Cyclopedic Dictionary of Law* 909 (1901). But by the mid-20th century, drafters were using *party of the third part* to describe not a stranger, but another party to the contract—e.g.:

Whereas the *party of the first part* has made certain discoveries relating to the manufacture of synthetic rubber, apparently of material commercial value, and has associated the *party of the second part* with him to further the marketing thereof, and the *party of the third part* is willing to form and finance a company to manufacture and market the same, if he finds to his satisfaction, after investigation, that said discoveries are valuable commercially . . . . Samuel G. Kling, *The Legal Encyclopedia for Home and Business* 101 (1957) (from a form agreement to organize a corporation).

Any question about whether *party of the third part* is proper usage is best answered by saying that all these ancient expressions are poor usage in modern drafting. See **chirograph, party** & PERSON.

party-opponent is generally hyphenated, as in Fed. R. Evid. 613(b), though there is hardly a good rationale for writing it this way.

pass. A. Judicial Senses. The phrase *pass on* or *pass upon* has a peculiar meaning in legal writing, namely, "to decide." It is used primarily of questions of law—e.g.:

- "When our courts first came to *pass upon* constitutional questions, what they read in Coke's Second Institute . . . appeared but a common-law version of what they read in French and Dutch publicists as to an eternal and immutable natural law . . . ." Roscoe Pound, *The Spirit of the Common Law* 75 (1921).
- "The state courts have power to *pass on* both state and federal questions." Charles Alan Wright, *The Law of Federal Courts* 795 (5th ed. 1994).

Yet the phrase has been used also in reference to juries, which of course decide questions of fact—e.g.:

- "It is not the province of this court to *pass upon* the weight of evidence . . . . We think there was a fair question for the jury, and they must *pass upon* it uninfluenced by any intimation from us." *Heyne v. Blair*, 62 N.Y. 19, 23 (1875).
- "Some [courts] have nearly gone to the extent of holding that where the language is severe, the jury should *pass*

upon the case under proper instructions." *Sylvester v. Armstrong*, 84 P.2d 729, 734 (Wyo. 1938).

B. Testamentary Senses. In the context of wills and estates, *pass* (= to transfer or be transferred) may be either transitive or intransitive. Ordinarily it is intransitive—e.g.:

- "The purpose . . . of the makers [was] that the property of the one first to die *pass* at his or her death as he or she directs by and under that instrument." *Spinks v. Rice*, 47 S.E.2d 424, 427 (Va. 1948).
- "It is elementary that no interest in the decedent's property *passes* by descent or will until the death of the decedent." *Awtry's Estate v. Commissioner*, 221 F.2d 749, 759 (8th Cir. 1955).

But it may also be transitive—e.g.:

- "The judgment of the county court construing the first paragraph of the will to *pass* all personal property possessed by the testator at his death to his widow except as otherwise stipulated in his will is affirmed." *In re Schaech's Will*, 31 N.W.2d 614, 618 (Wis. 1948).
- "In the eyes of state legislatures, estate recovery was a dangerous public relations move which robbed senior citizens of the opportunity to *pass* property to loved ones." Diane Lourdes Dick, *The Impact of Medicaid Estate Recovery on Nontraditional Families*, 15 U. Fla. J.L. & Pub. Pol'y 525, 536 (2004).

passable; passible. *Passable* means "capable of being passed; open"; *passible* means "feeling; susceptible to pain or suffering." Cf. **impassible.**

passed. See **past.**

passerby. Pl. *passersby*.

passim (= here and there) is used in citing an authority in a general way and indicates that the point at hand is treated throughout the work. Specific references are preferred in legal citations; when a general reference is called for, *see generally* is the signal most frequently used. *Passim* is especially useful in the index of authorities contained in the front matter of a brief.

passing off. A. Form. As a noun phrase, *passing off* should be two words. A few writers have hyphenated the phrase—e.g.: Suman Naresh, *Passing-Off, Goodwill, and False Advertising*, 45 Cambridge L.J. 97 (1986)—but this rendering of the phrase is recommended only when it acts as a PHRASAL ADJECTIVE. See **palming off.**

B. And *reverse passing off.* Whereas *passing off* denotes falsely representing one's own product as that of another in an attempt to deceive purchasers, *reverse passing off* denotes falsely representing another's product as one's own in a similar attempt to deceive.

*****passive tense.** See PASSIVE VOICE (I).

PASSIVE VOICE. A. Generally. "Avoid the passive," one often hears; yet many do not really understand what voice is in grammar, let alone what the passive

voice is. "Voice" refers to the relationship between the subject of a clause and its verb: if the verb performs the action of the subject (as in "Jane hit the ball"), the verb is active, whereas if the subject is acted upon (as in "The ball was hit by Jane"), the verb is passive.

True, the two sentences say essentially the same thing, but the emphasis is changed. The passive results in a wordier sentence, disrupts the ordinary sequence of events in the reader's mind, often causes DANGLERS, and often obscures the actor. Consider: "The ball was hit." As in that sentence, passive voice may lead to vagueness, or lend itself to purposeful obfuscation (see (E)). Small wonder that politicians find so many uses for the passive (e.g., "Mistakes were made"—President Reagan's response to intense questioning about the Iran-Contra debacle). See PLAIN LANGUAGE (D).

More to the point, although the passive voice has its occasional legitimate uses—usually, when the actor is either unimportant or unknown—its frequent use makes a piece of writing much less interesting and readable. Avoiding the passive is good general advice; but one should not make a fetish of it. Following are different types of passive voice with their own peculiar problems, along with suggested remedies.

B. The Otiose Passive. This is the type of passive that results from lazy thinking, as in "The ball was hit by Jane." This syntax subverts the English-speaking reader's reasonable expectation of a direct actor–action–consequence sequence, unless a departure from that sequence is somehow an improvement. E.g.:

- "Common trust fund legislation *is addressed to* [read *addresses*] a problem appropriate for state action." *Mullane v. Central Hanover Bank & Trust Co.*, 339 U.S. 306, 307 (1950) (per Jackson, J.).
- "[The fee-simple interest] *could have been conveyed by her* to the defendant." *Caccamo v. Banning*, 75 A.2d 222, 224 (Del. Super. Ct. 1950). A suggested revision: *She could have conveyed the fee-simple interest to the defendant*.
- "*It is insisted by Sue* [read *Sue insists*] that the power of appointment given George in their mother's will was nonexclusive." *Harlan v. Citizens Nat'l Bank of Danville*, 251 S.W.2d 284, 285 (Ky. 1952).
- "After both sides had rested, *a conference was had between the trial judge and counsel* [read *the trial judge and counsel conferred* (or *had a conference*)]." *Valdez v. Taylor Auto. Co.*, 278 P.2d 91, 93 (Cal. Dist. Ct. App. 1955).

C. Confusion of Active and Passive Constructions. Consider the following sentences:

- "Defendant's corn on storage at the debtor's business establishment was removed by the debtor, with no credit being given to the defendant and *was done so without* [read *the debtor did so without*] any approval or authority of the defendant." *Ducker v. Lohrey*, 33 B.R. 973, 975 (Bankr. S.D. Ohio 1983).
- "This 360-page record may be fairly summarized, *as did appellant's counsel* in his argument before this Court, by stating that the State's witnesses recount a brutal, unprovoked attack." *Gregory v. State*, 401 S.W.2d 594, 594 (Tex. Crim. App. 1966).

If the first clause is to be passive in the latter specimen quoted, then the second must also be passive [read *as was done by appellant's counsel*] to make the clauses parallel. But the best version would be to write both clauses in the active voice. The last example above might look like this: *We may fairly summarize this 360-page record, as appellant's counsel did in his argument before this Court, by stating that the State's witnesses recount a brutal, unprovoked attack.*

Here the combination of active and passive constructions leads to problems of syntax and logic: "In his affidavit in opposition to defendants' motion, plaintiff Nishimura acknowledges *that plaintiffs were never interested in, much less sought* [read *that plaintiffs never had an interest in, nor sought*], rights to produce and distribute the teams' games on an exclusive, metropolitan-wide basis." *Nishimura v. Dolan*, 599 F.Supp. 484, 498 (E.D.N.Y. 1984).

D. The Ambiguous Passive. Here an AMBIGUITY is caused by the writer's failure to specify who is acting in each instance: "[To avoid dermatitis], skin contact [with the epoxy] must be minimized, rigorous personal cleanliness encouraged [by the user?], and suitable protective equipment used by the operator." Robert L. Harris & Frank Arthur Patty, *Patty's Industrial Hygiene* 1290 (2000). The operator, hardly the one to *encourage* personal cleanliness, must *practice* it. The manufacturer is encouraging cleanliness.

E. Active Wrongly Used for Passive. With a few verbs, it has become voguish to use the active construction where, according to sense, the passive should appear. "The cases *divide* [read *can be divided*] into two categories, roughly paralleling the sometimes fuzzy distinction between legislative and interpretative rules." *Montana v. Clark*, 749 F.2d 740, 745 (D.C. Cir. 1984). Cf. the colloquial British usage—e.g.: "In his usual merry provocative way he looked me in the eye and said: 'You need your head *examining* [read *examined*].' He was Deputy High Steward of the University, I discovered." James M. Dyce, *Stress: The Dilemma of Success* 81 (1982).

For a discussion of the *amount owing* and *amount owed* as idiomatic alternatives, see **owing.**

F. The Dishonest Passive. Sometimes the passive is used (but not as in this sentence!) in a way that is of questionable honesty. In a negligence case in which plaintiffs—a minor and his mother—have accused the retailer defendant of negligence in selling lighter fluid to the minor, this sentence occurs: "The minor plaintiff attempted to fill said lighter with fluid and *was caused* to set himself on fire." *Van Skike v. Zussman*, 318 N.E.2d 244, 248 (Ill. App. Ct. 1974). *Was caused to* is superfluous and misleading—one immediately wonders, *by whom*?

G. The Double Passive. The problem here is using one passive immediately after another. E.g.:

- "Had an absolute liability theory been intended *to have been injected* into the Act, much more suitable models could have been found." *Dalehite v. U.S.*, 346 U.S. 15, 45 (1953) (per Reed, J.).

- "A specified portion of such shares shall mean such portion of the votes *entitled to be cast* in respect of such shares by virtue of the provisions of such articles of incorporation." Karen Ann Rolcik & Mark Warda, *How to Form a Corporation in Texas* 94 (2004). Votes are not *entitled to be cast*; rather, persons are *entitled to cast* votes.

H.W. Fowler writes that "monstrosities of this kind . . . are as repulsive to the grammarian as to the stylist" (*MEU2* 138).

In legal writing, the problem is especially common where the verb *attempt* appears—e.g.:

- "[Police] have been several times employed when poaching *has been attempted to be prevented*, and satisfactorily." Great Britain, Parliament: House of Commons, *Reports from Commissioners* 293 (1861). [A suggested revision: *The police have been satisfactorily employed several times to prevent poaching.*]

- "Whether [the statute of limitations] may or may not [be pleaded] does not depend upon the conclusive character of the evidence by which the action *is attempted to be supported.*" Joseph Kinnicut Angell & John Wilder May, *A Treatise on the Limitation of Actions at Law and Suits in Equity* 83 n.4 (1869). [A suggested revision: *Whether the statute of limitations may be pleaded does not depend on the conclusive character of the evidence offered to support the action.*]

- "It must be that what *was attempted to be guarded against* was injury in the insured resulting from fire while in a building." *Houlihan v. Preferred Acc. Ins. Co. of N.Y.*, 111 N.Y.S. 1048, 1050 (App. Div. 1908). [A suggested revision: *The purpose must be to protect the insured from injury resulting from a fire while in a building.*]

This construction is likewise common with *seek*—e.g.:

- "*A distinction is sought to be drawn between* [suggested revision: *Plaintiff seeks to distinguish*] the case just cited and the case at bar, on the ground that [the cited] case was one at equity and the case before us is one at law." *Florida State Hosp. for Insane v. Durham Iron Co.*, 17 S.E.2d 842, 846 (Ga. Ct. App. 1941).

- "The issue was not a complete denial of the right of access to deep water, but only a balancing of that right against the public-trust interests existing in the state-owned lands and waters over which *that right was sought to be exercised* [suggested revision: *the property owners sought to exercise that right*]." Joseph J. Kalo, *North Carolina Oceanfront Property and Public Waters & Beaches*, 83 N.C. L. Rev. 1427, 1474 (2005).

Some double passives are defensible—e.g.: "Offerings made in compliance with Regulation D *are not required to be registered* with the Securities and Exchange Commission under the 1933 Securities Act." Stephen P. Jarchow, *Institutional and Pension Fund Real Estate Investment* 240 (1990). As Fowler notes, "In legal or quasi-legal language this construction may sometimes be useful and unexceptionable: *Diplomatic privilege applies only to such things as are done or omitted to be done in the course of a person's official duties. / Motion made: that the words proposed to be left out stand part of the Question*" (*MEU2* 139). But these are of a different kind from *are sought to be included* and *are attempted to be refuted*, which can be easily remedied by recasting. "The rule," states the

Oxford Guide (p. 148), "is that if the subject and the first passive verb can be changed into the active, leaving the passive infinitive intact, the sentence is correctly formed." Here, for example, a recasting of the first passive verb form into the active voice results in a sentence that makes sense:

Passive/Passive: The prisoners were ordered to be shot.

Active/Passive: He ordered the prisoners to be shot.

But in the following example, a recasting of the first passive verb into the active voice does not make sense:

Passive/Passive: The contention has been attempted to be made.

Active/Passive: He attempted the contention to be made (un-English).

Sense can be restored to this sentence by casting both parts in the active voice:

Active/Active: He attempted to make the contention.

H. Special Active Use with *issue*. In contexts discussing mandamus and other writs, *issue* is used actively where most nonlawyers would make it passive—e.g.:

- "At the last term, viz., December term, 1801, William Marbury [et al.] severally moved the court for a rule to James Madison, Secretary of State of the United States, to show cause why a mandamus should not *issue* [a nonlawyer would write *be issued*] commanding him to cause to be delivered [better: *commanding him to deliver*] to them respectively their several commissions as justices of the peace." *Marbury v. Madison*, 5 U.S. (1 Cranch) 137, 137–38 (1803) (per Marshall, C.J.).
- "If the duty imposed by a statutory provision leaves a discretion in whom it is imposed . . . , mandamus will not *issue* to compel performance of that duty in a specific way." Richard Akinnola, *Abiola, Democracy, and Rule of Law* 228 (1997).

See **issue**.

I. *Passive tense. A rudimentary knowledge of grammar precludes such solecisms as **passive tense*. There is no such thing in English: only *past tenses* (denoting time) and the *passive voice* (denoting the relationship between the subject and a transitive verb). But the blunder is a common one—e.g.:

- "His use of the *passive tense* [read *passive voice*] here could obscure one important part of his formulation." Elizabeth Garrett, *Legislating* Chevron, 101 Mich. L. Rev. 2637, 2637–38 (2003).
- "Following these averments are a series of statements about Cooper and Plaintiff, all employing the *passive tense* [read *passive voice*] to state that Cooper 'was observed' in various activities and situations." *Bird v. Bird*, 668 S.E.2d 39, 43 (N.C. Ct. App. 2008).
- "We agree with Dillingham that by writing article 5.14's demand requirement in the *passive tense* [read *passive voice*] (barring suit until 'a written demand is filed'), the Legislature did not require that shareholders send the demand personally, as opposed to having someone do so on their behalf." *In re Schmitz*, 285 S.W.3d 451, 457 (Tex. 2009).

pass muster. See **muster.**

pass on; pass upon. See **pass (A).**

past; passed. *Past* can be a noun <a blast from the past>, a preposition <half past the hour>, an adjective <reminiscing about past adventures>, or an adverb <a past-due notice>, but not a verb. The word occurs in many redundant phrases, such as *past history*, *past track record*, *past record*, and *past experience*. All these are REDUNDANCIES because the noun denotes something that by its very nature is rooted in the past. *Passed* is the past tense and past participle of the verb *pass* in all its senses <she passed the test> <he passed out> <the motorcyclist had passed three cars>.

past consideration. See **consideration (H).**

past experience is a common REDUNDANCY. See **past.**

pastime is sometimes misspelled **pasttime*. The misspelling derives from a misunderstanding of the word's origin, *pass* (vb.) + *time*, not *past* + *time*.

PAST-PARTICIPIAL ADJECTIVES. See ADJECTIVES (H).

patdown, n., (= frisk) is one word.

patent, adj.; **latent,** adj.; **patent,** n. & vb. The first two words are adjective antonyms: what is *patent* /**pay**-t[ə]nt/ is readily apparent or visible; what is *latent* /**lay**-t[ə]nt/ is hidden or undeveloped. The noun *patent* /**pat**-[ə]nt/ denotes a government grant of right, privilege, or authority, especially today the limited-term intellectual-property right granted to an inventor to exclude others from making or trading in his or her invention. The verb means "to obtain a patent." See **evident.**

patentable began as a 19th-century Americanism but is now widely used in BrE as well as AmE.

patent ambiguity. See AMBIGUITY.

patent attorney; patent agent. Three types of people may represent inventors before the U.S. Patent & Trademark Office (P.T.O.): *patent attorneys*, *patent agents*, and inventors themselves. *Patent attorneys* and *patent agents* are registered to practice before the P.T.O. and may perform nonlegal services such as preparing applications, negotiating licenses, and prosecuting patents. But only *patent attorneys* can also give legal advice and opinions and provide other legal services related to patents. Kinney & Lange, P.A., *Intellectual Property Law for Business Lawyers* 13–14 (2009).

patentee; patent-holder; patent-owner. Under the Patent Act (35 U.S.C. § 100(d)), all title-holders of a patent, whether or not they were inventors, are termed *patentees*. Although it might seem helpful to distinguish a *patentee* as a person to whom a patent is issued and either a *patent-owner* or *patent-holder* as the current owner, the Act uses only the umbrella term *patentee* for all title-holders. See -EE.

patent troll. See **troll.**

paterfamilias. In the usual English-language sense ("the male head of the household"), the preferred plural is *paterfamiliases*. In the Roman-law senses ("the head of a Roman household" or "a free Roman citizen"), the plural is *patresfamilias.*

patricide. See **parricide.**

paucital; multital. *Paucital* = in personam; *multital* = in rem. These legal terms were used by Wesley N. Hohfeld and other legal philosophers but are not recorded in most dictionaries. Now generally disused, the terms appeared mostly in early-20th-century academic writing—e.g.:

- "If B owes A a thousand dollars, A has an affirmative right in personam, or *paucital* right, that B shall transfer to A the legal ownership of that amount of money. If, to put a contrasting situation, A already has title to one thousand dollars, his rights against others in relation thereto are *multital* rights, or rights in rem." Wesley Newcomb Hohfeld, *Fundamental Legal Conceptions as Applied in Judicial Reasoning*, 26 Yale L.J. 710, 718–19 (1917).
- "Some of such overspreading classifications consist of the following: relations in personam ('*paucital*' relations), and relations in rem ('*multital*' relations)." *Id.* at 712.

See **in rem** & **in personam.**

paucity means "dearth; fewness" <a paucity of cases deciding this issue>. E.g.: "There was no *paucity* of evidence from which defendant could have been found guilty as charged." *U.S. v. Devine*, 787 F.2d 1086, 1087 (7th Cir. 1986). The word indicates a small quantity, not a complete lack of something, as the following sentences erroneously suggest:

- "Since there is *a complete paucity of* [read *no*] decisional law on the issue involved here, it might be wise, at this juncture, to defer to certain language contained within the preface of the AMA Guides themselves." *Adams v. Industrial Comm'n*, 547 P.2d 1089, 1096 (Ariz. Ct. App. 1976) (Wren, J., dissenting).
- "In the court's view, it was not necessary to reach this issue, which is essentially a matter of affirmative defense, because of the *total paucity* [read *absence*] of evidence probative of the basic elements of the plaintiff's case." *Murphy v. Owens-Corning Fiberglas Corp.*, 447 F.Supp. 557, 572 (D. Kan. 1977).
- "There was *a complete paucity of* [read *no*] proof relating to a proximate cause between Plaintiff's minority age and his injuries." *Tierney v. Black Bros. Co.*, 852 F.Supp. 994, 1001 (M.D. Fla. 1994).

pauper is no longer used in lay contexts except for historical or humorous purposes. But it is still used by straight-faced lawyers and judges of impecunious parties in litigation. E.g.: "The Court recognized [that] the mandatory language of Ind.P.C.R. 1, § 9 requires the public defender to represent a *pauper appellant* from the denial of post-conviction relief and recognizes no exception to the rule." *Majors v. State*, 441 N.E.2d 1375, 1378 (Ind. 1982). See *in forma pauperis.*

pawn. See **pledge.**

pawnor; pawnee. The *pawnor* is the owner of an item of goods who transfers it to another, the *pawnee*, as security for a debt. E.g.: "Chattels could pass on death in other ways than those here described: e.g., on the death of a *pawnor* before redemption, the property passed to the *pawnee*." J.H. Baker, *An Introduction to English Legal History* 435 (3d ed. 1990). Nonlegal writers and dictionaries use the spelling *pawner*.

pay, n.; **compensation; wage; salary; stipend; fee; emolument; remuneration; recompense.** These terms all denote money that is earned for one's labor or services. *Pay* is the most general, usual term <total pay package>. *Compensation* is essentially equivalent, although it can embrace not just pay received in return for services rendered, but also money paid for a loss (as with damages). *Wage* or *wages* applies mainly to compensation paid daily or weekly for labor, especially for blue-collar labor <a mechanic's wage> <the maid's daily wage>. *Salary* normally refers to fixed compensation paid periodically over a longer time for white-collar work. In BrE, the equivalent of *salary* for a teacher, officeholder, or minister is *stipend*, but in AmE *stipend* usually suggests a modest payment made to someone who is appointed to carry out an assignment over a specified period <the semesterly stipend for research assistants>. *Fee* refers to the price asked by and paid to a professional (broadly defined) <lawyer's fee> <Arnold Palmer's appearance fee>. *Emolument* is a high-flown equivalent of *pay*, used especially as a plural in reference to officeholders <the emoluments of office>. *Remuneration* and *recompense* /**rek**-əm-pen[t]s/ are much the same, except that they can more broadly denote compensation anywhere on the pay scale, from the most modest to the greatest <what remuneration do you require?> <what can I give you by way of recompense?>. With *recompense*, there is an additional suggestion of requiting, paying back, or making amends—though the word is not always colored in this way. See **recompense.**

pay, vb.; **pay up.** The second means "to discharge completely (a debt)," while the first may refer to partial or total payments. So because of this slight DIFFERENTIATION, *up* is not a needless particle. Cf. **pay over.** See PARTICLES, UNNECESSARY.

payor. Although the *OED* and *W3* have their main entries under *-er*, the *-or* spelling is more common in American legal writing. E.g.: "If the customer writes the check locally, that is, in the metropolitan area in which the customer's bank is located, the *payor* bank often will receive the check on the very day that the customer writes it." Ronald J. Mann, *Making Sense of Payments Policy in the Information Age*, 93 Geo. L.J. 633, 644 (2005). Ironically, the spellings are *payor* but *taxpayer*. In BrE the spelling *payer* is common.

pay over. Though appearing to be a REDUNDANCY, this common legal idiom is often justifiable. *Over* signifies in this phrase the perfective aspect of the verb (the payment is completed); *pay* alone is imperfective. This is not to say that *pay over* is justified in all the examples quoted below, but it might well be in the first and third:

- "Upon her death, the principal was to be *paid over* by the trustees to such persons as the settlor might appoint by will, or in default of such appointment, to the settlor's heirs at law and next of kin as in intestacy." *In re Burchell's Estate*, 87 N.E.2d 293, 298 (N.Y. 1949) (Fuld, J., dissenting).
- "The fact that the money was *paid over* [read *paid*] to the wife, for her support and the support of her children, certainly does not conflict with the order of the court." *National Auto. & Cas. Ins. Co. v. Queck*, 405 P.2d 905, 912 (Ariz. Ct. App. 1965).
- "The amounts withheld constitute a special fund held in trust for the benefit of the United States and are *paid over* quarterly." *U.S. v. Novelli*, 381 F.Supp.2d 1125, 1132 (C.D. Cal. 2005).
- "Although the companies' tax filings accurately stated its tax liabilities, Easterday, through the corporation, repeatedly failed to *pay over* [read *pay*] to the Internal Revenue Service the full amount of payroll taxes due." *U.S. v. Easterday*, 564 F.3d 1004, 1006 (9th Cir. 2009).

See PARTICLES, UNNECESSARY.

pay up. See **pay.**

peace, against the. See **against the peace.**

peaceable; peaceful. Generally, *peaceful* refers to a state of affairs; *peaceable* refers to the disposition of a person or a nation. The two words overlap some, but a strict DIFFERENTIATION is worth encouraging.

peace of mind; piece of (one's) mind. Whereas *peace of mind* is calm assurance, a *piece of one's mind* is something a person says in a fit of pique. But the two are surprisingly often confused—e.g.:

- "The policyholder should recover for mental distress caused by the insurance company's bad faith conduct because insurance is purchased to provide *piece* [read *peace*] of mind." *D'Ambrosio v. Pennsylvania Nat'l Mut. Cas. Ins. Co.*, 431 A.2d 966, 972 (Pa. 1981).
- "The weaker party does not enter into the contract primarily for profit, but to secure an essential service or product, financial security or *piece* [read *peace*] of mind." Henry H. Perritt Jr., *Implied Covenant: Anachronism or Augur?*, 20 Seton Hall L. Rev. 683, 710–11 (1990).
- "Kansas courts have allowed recovery under nuisance theory to include annoyance, discomfort, inconvenience, endangerment of health, and loss of *piece* [read *peace*] of mind." Charles C. Steincamp, Note, *Toeing the Line*, 32 Washburn L.J. 190, 233 (1993).
- "Restrictions on obnoxious noise and public indecency protect people's sensibilities and *piece* [read *peace*] of mind, not their liberty." Samuel Freeman, *Criminal Liability and the Duty to Aid the Distressed*, 142 U. Pa. L. Rev. 1455, 1487 n.112 (1994).

peak; peek. The distinction is so elementary as not to call for explanation. But mistakes do occur— e.g.: "[The court held] that citizens must be notified of entries and seizures pursuant to 'sneak and *peak* [read *peek*]' warrants which authorize a surreptitious entry for purposes of looking around or taking photographs." Ronald J. Bacigal, *The Right of the People to Be Secure*, 82 Ky. L.J. 145, 186 n.272 (1993–1994).

On the misuse of *peak* for *pique*, see **pique.**

peat. See LAWYERS, DEROGATORY NAMES FOR (A).

peccadillo. Pl. -*oes*. See PLURALS (C).

peccavi (lit., "I have sinned") = an acknowledgment or confession of sin. The word is pronounced /pə-**kah**-vee/.

pectore, in. See LOAN TRANSLATIONS.

peculate. See **defalcate.**

peculation is essentially a fancy equivalent of—perhaps even a polite EUPHEMISM for—*embezzlement*. But the *OED* suggests a narrower meaning for *peculation*: "the appropriation of public money or property by one in an official position." If that were correct, then a public official *peculates* whereas a corporate employee *embezzles*.

Indeed, *peculation* was once used in this narrower sense—e.g.: "The power to control and direct the appropriations, constitutes a most useful and salutary check upon profusion and extravagance, as well as upon corrupt influence and public *peculation*." 2 Joseph Story, *Commentaries on the Constitution of the United States* § 1348, at 222 (5th ed. 1891).

Today, however, the word routinely refers to violations of private trusts—e.g.: "But to analogize petitioners' scheme to a conventional case of *peculation* by an employee, whether public or private, is to disregard the facts of this case." *Parr v. U.S.*, 363 U.S. 370, 398–99 (1960) (Frankfurter, J., dissenting). That being so, there is little to commend the word in comparison with the more usual term *embezzlement*. See **defalcate** & **embezzle.**

peculiar province. See **province, the peculiar.**

pecuniary; pecunious. The suffixes distinguish these words. *Pecuniary* = relating to or consisting of money. *Pecunious* = moneyed; wealthy. (Its opposite is *impecunious*, meaning "destitute.")

The adverb corresponding to *pecuniary* is *pecuniarily*—e.g.: "Under the 'person aggrieved' test, a party must demonstrate that they are directly and adversely *pecuniarily* affected by the order at issue." *In re City of Vallejo*, 408 B.R. 280, 298–99 (Bankr. App. 9th Cir. 2009).

pedal. See **peddle.**

peddle (= to sell) often has a perjorative bent—e.g.: "Pixelon was undercapitalized, *illiquid* [read *was illiquid*], had taken insider loans, was in dispute with several of its key managers, and was desperate for the infusion of capital that would come from the shares that defendants were trying to *peddle*." *Greer v. Advanced Equities*, 683 F.Supp.2d 761, 771 (N.D. Ill. 2010). (For more on why *was* is needed before *illiquid*, see PARALLELISM.)

Peddle is also misused for the verb *pedal*, especially in phrases such as *soft-pedal* (orig., to use the muffling pedal on a piano) and *backpedal* (= orig., to pedal a bicycle backward). E.g.:

- "Can these rules remove any incentives an accounting firm might have to *soft-peddle* [read *soft-pedal*] an audit report in order to keep consulting business? Perhaps not." Amy Shapiro, *Who Pays the Auditor Calls the Tune?*, 35 Seton Hall L. Rev. 1029, 1059 (2005).
- "Once P1 has made her valuation, it is irrevocable; P1 cannot *backpeddle* [read *backpedal*] when she learns what sort of transfer P2 selects." Lee Anne Fennell, *Revealing Options*, 118 Harv. L. Rev. 1399, 1430 (2005).

pederasty. So spelled. Cf. **buggery.**

pediatrician; *pediatrist. The first is the common, preferred term, meaning "a physician who specializes in children's medicine." The second, a NEEDLESS VARIANT, has the liability of causing confusion with *podiatrist* (= a foot doctor).

peek. See **peak.**

pejorative. So spelled, though sometimes mistakenly spelled *perjorative, as in the following examples:

- "The majority resorts to *perjoratives* [read *pejoratives*]." *Compagnie des Bauxites de Guinea v. Insurance Co. of N. Am.*, 651 F.2d 877, 889 (3d Cir. 1981) (Gibbons, J., dissenting).
- "The female-gendered term is slightly *perjorative* [read *pejorative*] of this species of prosecution." Helen Leskovac, *Legal Writing and Plain English*, 38 Syracuse L. Rev. 1193, 1202 (1987).

pelican. See LAWYERS, DEROGATORY NAMES FOR (B).

penal; punitive; penological. *Penal* = of or relating to punishment or retribution. *Punitive* = serving to punish; intended to inflict punishment. *Penological* = of or relating to the study of the philosophy and methods of punishment and treatment of persons found guilty of crime. So the words have distinct senses.

Penological is often used inappropriately for *penal*, perhaps because the usual phrase is *the state's penological interest*, and the state's interest sounds more clinical and dispassionate if *penological* rather than *penal* is used. That is not, however, a justification for misusing the word. E.g.: "The State by this statute, or any other statute fixing a penalty of a fine, has declared its *penological* [read *penal*] interest—deterrence, retribution and rehabilitation—satisfied by a monetary payment, and disclaimed, as serving any *penological* [read *penal*] purpose in such cases, a term in jail." *Williams v. Illinois*, 399 U.S. 235, 264 (1970) (Harlan, J., concurring). See EUPHEMISMS.

penal institution is a EUPHEMISM for *prison*.

penalize; fine; amerce; affeer; mulct; sconce. All these verbs mean "to punish by deprivation." But there are nuances. *Penalize* connotes that there has been a violation of a law or rule intended to maintain discipline or fair treatment for everyone subject to it. It suggests the imposition by duly constituted authorities of a monetary penalty or the forfeiture of an advantage <late taxpayers are penalized at least 5% of the total tax due>. To *fine* is to exact an amount within certain limits prescribed by law.

To *amerce* is to impose a monetary penalty with great discretion on the part of the decision-maker—"arbitrarily," in the *OED*'s words. Etymologically speaking, when being *amerced*, one is "at the mercy" of the court. Today, it is little more than a pretentious LEGALISM—e.g.:

- "To treat that clause as though it were a redundant or an insubstantial part of the agreement is to flout familiar experience of the readiness of juries to *amerce insurance companies* [read *hold insurance companies liable*]." *Watson v. Employers Liab. Assurance Corp.*, 348 U.S. 66, 75–76 (1954) (Frankfurter, J., concurring).
- "When we provided . . . that costs were to be awarded to defendants and intervenors, we did not intend to *amerce the plaintiffs with* [read *hold the plaintiffs liable for*] all of the costs of the litigation since its inception." *Environmental Def. Fund, Inc. v. Froehlke*, 368 F.Supp. 231, 254 (W.D. Mo. 1973).

See **amercement.**

To *affeer* is to fix the precise amount of (a fine). The variant spellings *affeere and *affere should be avoided. The agent noun is *affeeror* or *affeerer, the -*or* spelling perhaps the better one because it is more distinctly pronounceable.

Mulct is similar to *amerce*, except that it often carries overtones of an oppressive exaction made by use of force <the colonists mulcted the indigenous tribes of their gold whenever an uprising seemed imminent>. Pronounced /məlkt/, the word is rarely encountered outside the law, and only infrequently within it—e.g.: "Let them then be *mulcted* to the uttermost in the penalty that Parliament has prescribed." Patrick Devlin, *The Enforcement of Morals* 60 (1968). *Mulct* has the additional sense "to deprive or divest of," and it carries pejorative connotations of mercilessness or deceit. E.g.: "The panel opinion also permits a jury to *mulct* the defendant in a defamation action of more than compensatory damages." *Levine v. CMP Publ'ns, Inc.*, 753 F.2d 1341, 1342 (5th Cir. 1985).

To *sconce* is to impose a petty fine, originally in Oxbridge but now also elsewhere, for a slight breach of rules or etiquette.

pend, vb. (= [of a lawsuit] to be awaiting decision or settlement; to be pending), is a sense unrecorded by the *OED* and *W3*. In this novel AmE legal sense *pend* is really a BACK-FORMATION from the present-participial form *pending* <the case has been pending for three years>. The word dates from the early 20th century—e.g.:

- "The matter is really not procedural or controlled by the rules of court in which the litigation *pends*." *Oklahoma*

Natural Gas Co. v. Oklahoma, 273 U.S. 257, 259–60 (1927) (per Taft, C.J.).

- "While plaintiff's case *pended* [read *was pending*] in the trial court, . . . the defendant had presented itself as contestant of any right of the plaintiff to obtain valid judgment." *Car & Concepts, Inc. v. Funston*, 601 S.W. 2d 801, 803 (Tex. Civ. App.—Ft. Worth 1980).

Pending sounds more natural in most contexts in which *pend* appears.

pendant. See **pendent.**

pendency; *pendence. *Pendency* (= the state or condition of being pending or continuing undecided) is the familiar legal term. E.g.: "Likewise, accrual of interest during *pendency* of an appeal stops if the judgment creditor rejects the judgment debtor's offer to tender payment of the judgment, costs, and interest." *Niemeyer v. Wendy's Int'l, Inc.*, 782 N.E.2d 774, 777–78 (Ill. App. Ct. 2002). **Pendence* is a NEEDLESS VARIANT. E.g.: "I do believe that he has started to mature some during the *pendence* [read *pendency*] of this case and through the course of his trial." *State v. Holloway*, 482 N.W.2d 306, 315 (S.D. 1992).

pendens. See **lis pendens.**

pendent; pendant. The first is an adjective literally meaning "hanging, suspended"; the second is a noun meaning "something suspended, as a chain around one's neck."

Pendent, common in the legal phrase *pendent jurisdiction*, is occasionally misspelled *pendant*. E.g.: "The Court is not inclined to grant injunctive relief on plaintiff's *pendant* [read *pendent*] State anti-dilution claim." *Home Box Office v. Showtime*, 665 F.Supp. 1079, 1087 (S.D.N.Y. 1987).

pendente lite (= while the action is pending) is sometimes misspelled **pendent lite*. See **lis pendens.**

pendent jurisdiction. See **concurrent jurisdiction.**

penetrable is preferable to **penetratable*.

penitentiary (= a reformatory or correctional prison) originally referred to an ecclesiastical office (i.e., a person appointed to deal with penitents). The idea of reform is embedded in the root meaning. Although for some time rehabilitation was not a major objective of American prisons, today it is on the rise.

penological. See **penal.**

pensioner. See **annuitant.**

penultimate. See **ultimate.**

penumbral; *penumbrous. The second is a NEEDLESS VARIANT.

people. A. And *persons*. *People* is general, *persons* specific. One refers to *English-speaking people* (or *peoples*)

but to *the twelve persons on the jury. Persons* should virtually always be used with small, specific numbers.

B. And *state*. A *people* (collectively) consists of a great many persons united by a common language and by similar customs—usually the result of common ancestry, religion, and historical circumstances. A *state* is a great many persons, generally occupying a given territory, among whom the will of the majority—or of an ascertainable class of persons—prevails against anyone who opposes that will. A *state* may coincide exactly with one *people*, as in France, or may embrace several, as in the U.S.

*peoplekind is an unnecessary formation for *mankind* or *humankind*. E.g.: "Their perceptions were not necessarily wrong; but they were a reflection of the 'general consent of mankind,' not *peoplekind* [read *humankind*], much less *womankind*." Cheryl B. Preston, *This Old House: A Blueprint for Constructive Feminism*, 83 Geo. L.J. 2271, 2309 (1995). See **humankind.**

people's court. This phrase originated, oddly enough, as a propagandistic phrase for totalitarian regimes—e.g.: "The custom of prejudging guilt or innocence and of injecting evidence and opinions upon the trial by publicity can easily proceed to such a point that verdicts in highly publicized American cases will no more really represent the jurors' dispassionate personal judgment on the legal evidence than do those of '*People's Courts*' we so criticize abroad." Robert H. Jackson, *The Advocate: Guardian of Our Traditional Liberties*, 36 A.B.A. J. 607, 609 (1950).

In the 1980s, a television show named "The People's Court" (Wapner, J., presiding) became extremely popular. Since that time, the phrase has come to mean a court in which ordinary people can solve their petty and not-so-petty disputes.

PER-. This prefix may mean "through" (*perspicuous, impervious*), or it may act as an intensive (*perfervid, perforce, perchance*).

per. A. In Citations. *Per* is used to indicate the judge who has written a majority opinion. E.g.: *In re City of Houston*, 745 F.2d 925 (5th Cir. 1984) (per Reavley, J.). The *Bluebook* now recommends omitting *per*; it is sometimes useful, however, when a writer cites a case and believes that the authorship of the opinion is in some way noteworthy.

Even so, *per* should be avoided in text when no citation is involved—e.g.: "The dissent, *per* [read *by*] Justice White, objected that the majority's discussion of summary judgment rules is confusing and inconsistent." Steven A. Childress, *A New Era for Summary Judgments*, 116 F.R.D. 183, 187 (1987).

B. For *a*. Ordinarily in distributive senses, *a* or *an* has traditionally been considered preferable to *per* <25 miles an hour>. But *per* may become a necessary substitute for *a* when it is used as part of a PHRASAL ADJECTIVE—e.g.:

- "Entwistle calculated a *per*-winch profit figure of $3.20." *Pierce v. Ramsey Winch Co.*, 753 F.2d 416, 440 (5th Cir. 1985).
- "The defendant contends the award of $150,000.00 *per* parent is excessive, and the plaintiffs contend it is abusively low." *Schexneider v. Louisiana Dep't of Health & Hosps.*, 660 So.2d 508, 510 (La. Ct. App. 1995).

See **a (B).**

peradventure is archaic in what used to be its primary sense, "perhaps." In the hackneyed phrase *beyond peradventure*, it means "doubt." E.g.:

- "The meaning intended for the term in that subdivision is plain *beyond all peradventure*." *In re Gautier's Will*, 146 N.E.2d 771, 773 (N.Y. 1957).
- "It is clear *beyond peradventure* that the income tax on wages is constitutional." *Stelly v. Commissioner*, 761 F.2d 1113, 1115 (5th Cir. 1985).

Beyond peradventure of a doubt* is a REDUNDANCY: "Kentucky law is clear *beyond peradventure of a doubt that* [read *beyond peradventure that*] the only property right existing with regard to the continuance of a public way is that a landowner has a right of reasonable access to the public highway system." *Wessels Constr. & Dev. Co. v. Commonwealth*, 560 F.Supp. 25, 27 (E.D. Ky. 1983). Cf. **cavil, beyond.

per annum is unnecessary for *a year, per year*, or *each year*. Cf. **per diem.**

per anum (= through the anus), a EUPHEMISM appearing in contexts relating to sex crimes, is so spelled—not *per annum* (= per year), as some writers mistakenly render it: "Buggery is copulation *per annum* [read *per anum*] by a man with either another man or with a woman." Rollin M. Perkins & Ronald N. Boyce, *Criminal Law* 465 (3d ed. 1982). A better, more straightforward phrase than *copulation per anum* would be *anal copulation* or *anal sex.*

per capita. A. And *per caput.* The first is the frequently used plural ("by heads"), the second the rare singular ("a head; by the head").
B. And *per stirpes.* Both phrases (meaning, respectively, "by heads" and "by stocks") are commonly used in the context of wills and estates. They denote different methods for calculating what the heirs or next of kin will receive. For example, in an intestate succession *per capita*, all claimants entitled to intestate shares take equally regardless of the share to which an ancestor through whom they claim would have been entitled. In succession *per stirpes*, the shares are determined usually at the first generation of takers: for example, if one family stock has skipped a generation because a child has predeceased the decedent, the grandchildren of the decedent would divide among themselves an amount equal to what their deceased parent would have been entitled to.

Per stirpes (= by family stocks) is sometimes cited as a term of art that cannot be simplified. In fact, though, the phrase is ambiguous in ways explained in the entry TERMS OF ART. Leading writers on wills and estates generally recommend avoiding it. *See, e.g.*, Stanley M. Johanson, *In Defense of Plain Language*, 3 Scribes J. Legal Writing 37, 37–38 (1992).

percent; per-cent; per cent; per cent.; per centum. This sequence illustrates in reverse the evolution of this word, originally a phrase. Today it is best spelled as a single word. The plural of *percent* is *percent*; adding an *-s*, though not uncommon, is substandard.

In most writing, *75%* is easier to read than *75 percent* or (worse yet) *seventy-five percent.*

percentage of, a. One writes, "A high percentage of it *is* there," but "A percentage of them *are* there." Cf. **proportion.** See SYNESIS.

per centum. See **percent.**

perceptible. See **perceptive.**

perceptive (= keenly intuitive) for *perceptible* (= appreciable; recognizable) is an infrequent error—e.g.: "Those professions that have tried that solution have paid handsomely without *perceptive* [read *perceptible*] improvement in their images." Bob Dunn, *Contemplating Our Future*, Tex. B.J., May 1992, at 448.

perchance is an ARCHAISM for *perhaps*—e.g.: "I even went so far as to march down the hall to the Baltimore City Bar Library to ask the librarian whether my predecessor clerk had, *perchance*, left a gun in the library." Peter F. Axelrad et al., *Tributes to Judge Lawrence F. Rodowsky*, 60 Md. L. Rev. 785, 803 (2001).

per contra (= on the other hand; to the contrary; by contrast) may seem to be a useful LATINISM because of its brevity, but the English words are much more widely understood. E.g.: "That doctrine . . . had as its major premise the idea that the shipowner's liability for unseaworthiness is based on negligence. *Per contra* [read *By contrast*], both Mahnich and Sieracki had made clear that negligence had no part in the brave new world of unseaworthiness." Grant Gilmore & Charles L. Black Jr., *The Law of Admiralty* 395 (2d ed. 1975).

per curiam (= by the court) is primarily an adjective <per curiam opinion>, but is sometimes used as an elliptical form of *per curiam opinion*. E.g.: "In the *per curiam* denying rehearing in *Bennett*, the en banc court for this circuit unanimously agreed on the statement of governing criteria by which a municipality's § 1983 liability is to be determined." *Shelton v. City of College Station*, 754 F.2d 1251, 1257 (5th Cir. 1985).

In still other contexts, the phrase is used adverbially—e.g.: "Presumably no one would have quarreled with the *Calbeck* majority if it had . . . reversed the Fifth Circuit *per curiam*." Grant Gilmore & Charles L. Black Jr., *The Law of Admiralty* 422 (2d ed. 1975). See **by the court** & *per incuriam.*

per diem = for or by the day <per diem fee>. Generally, it makes more sense to write *a day* <$50 a day> or *daily* <daily fee>. (See **a (B).**) *Per diem*, a LATINISM, has been defended when it is positioned before the noun it modifies, but *daily* is undoubtedly an improvement. In no legal context, one can safely say, is *per diem* the best available phrase.

perempt, vb., in legal slang, is sometimes used as a BACK-FORMATION from *peremptory challenge*, the sense being "to exercise a peremptory challenge against"—e.g.: "The trial court erred to the prejudice of appellant Joseph in allowing the prosecutor to *perempt* jurors with reservations about the death penalty." *State v. Joseph*, 653 N.E.2d 285, 303 (Ohio 1995). For another sense of the word, see **preempt.**

peremption. See **preemption.**

peremptory, adj., = admitting no contradiction or denial; incontrovertible. "Hence, the trial court erred by failing to give a *peremptory* instruction to the jury on plaintiff's liability to defendants for breach of the contingent-fee agreement, as defendants requested." *Pereira v. Thompson*, 217 P.3d 236, 253 (Or. Ct. App. 2009). *Peremptory* was originally a term from Roman law, meaning "that destroys, puts an end to, or precludes all debate, question, or delay" (*OED*) <peremptory edict>.

Since the early 20th century, *peremptory* has often been used as an elliptical form of *peremptory challenge* or *strike*, which denotes the removal of a veniremember without a showing of cause—e.g.:

- "The trial judge went upon the theory that . . . plaintiff should have exhausted his *peremptories* upon the other two [jurors]." *Martin v. Farmers' Mut. Fire Ins. Co.*, 102 N.W. 656, 658 (Mich. 1905).
- "After all *peremptories* have been taken, or the parties satisfied, the jury shall then be sworn as a body to try the cause." *Avila v. U.S.*, 76 F.2d 39, 41 (9th Cir. 1935).
- " 'You had *peremptories* still left that you could have exercised, had you thought you were not getting a fair jury.' " *People v. Hancock*, 40 N.W.2d 689, 698 (Mich. 1950) (quoting the trial judge).
- "While the fact that the jury included members of a group allegedly discriminated against is not conclusive, it is an indication of good faith in exercising *peremptories*, and an appropriate factor for the trial judge to consider in ruling on a *Wheeler* objection." *People v. Turner*, 878 P.2d 521, 536 (Cal. 1994).

Cf. **causal challenge.**

The word is sometimes mistakenly written *preemptory*, no doubt as a result of the writer's mistakenly associating the word with the verb *preempt*—e.g.:

- "On Friday, Judge John Ouderkirk of State Superior Court dismissed a black woman after a challenge for cause and a black man after a *preemptory* [read *peremptory*] challenge by the prosecutor. In making *pre-emptory* [read *peremptory*] challenges, lawyers do not have to give a reason for wanting a prospective juror dismissed." *Jury Queries Resume in Beating Case*, N.Y. Times, 8 Aug. 1993, at 17.
- "The State may not exercise its *preemptory* [read *peremptory*] challenges for purely racial reasons." *Wilson v. State*, 884 S.W.2d 904, 907 (Tex. App.—San Antonio 1994).

For the correct use of *preemptory*, see **preemptive.**

peremptory challenge. See **peremptory.**

perfect /pər-**fekt**/, vb., = to bring to completion; to complete, finish, consummate; to carry through, accomplish (*OED*). This sense, now mostly legal, usually appears in reference to perfecting appeals and perfecting liens. E.g.: "A cadre of lawyers in Albany specializes in the art of *perfecting* bar appeals." Stephen Labaton, *At the Bar*, N.Y. Times, 18 Aug. 1989, at 20.

perfect equity. See **equity.**

perfectible. So spelled.

perfect-tender rule = the less-than-robust rule that, in contracts between merchants, every aspect of the seller's performance is a condition of the buyer's liability, so that the buyer is privileged to reject the goods if the seller deviates even slightly from the contractual requirements. The phrase should be so hyphenated. See PHRASAL ADJECTIVES.

perimeter. See **parameters.**

per incuriam is not the opposite of *per curiam* (= by the court); rather, it means "through inadvertence; in ignorance of the relevant law." Today it is used more commonly in BrE than in AmE. E.g.:

- "The decision in *Dixon* was justified by a finding that the *Ioannou* judgment was given *per incuriam* (that the court had failed to consider other relevant matters—that is, the true intention behind the legislation)." Charles Barrow et al., *Briefcase on Employment Law* 82 (2000).
- "A decision made *per incuriam* (by carelessness) is made in ignorance of a relevant authority and is not therefore a binding precedent." Paul Chynoweth, *The Party Wall Casebook* 166 n.1 (2003).
- "It was held that these earlier decisions of the Court of Appeal were *per incuriam* since the decisions were based on a clearly discernible error." Andrew Mitchell & Minel Dadhania, *As Level Law* 67 (2003).

periodic dues. See **assessment.**

periodic tenancy; tenancy from month to month; tenancy from year to year. The phrase *periodic tenancy* is the genus of which both *tenancy from month to month* and *tenancy from year to year* are species. A *periodic tenancy* continues for a year—or any fraction of a year—and for successive equivalent periods until terminated by either party with proper notice. This type of tenancy most commonly arises when a lease term ends and is automatically (and repeatedly) renewed another month or year.

Within the Anglo-American classifications of property rights, the *periodic tenancy* has a dual nature:

"Periodic tenancies of all types are now considered to be non-freehold 'estates in land,' although they are also 'chattels real'—i.e., personal rather than real property." Roger A. Cunningham et al., *The Law of Property* 82 (2d ed. 1993). See **chattels** & **estate.**

Though *periodic tenancy* is a general term, it is often used interchangeably with the more specific phrases (*tenancy from month to month* and *tenancy from year to year*); such periods other than months or years are highly unusual. But one commentator praised the vagueness of *periodic tenancy*, noting that it "has the virtue of being so indefinite that it may not be criticized for inaccuracy." Frank Bobbitt, *Tenancy from Year to Year and Related Estates*, 8 Tex. L. Rev. 325, 326 (1930). Still, the more specific phrases are often preferable, when accurately used, because they are more universally comprehensible.

The more specific terms are often written *month-to-month tenancy* and *year-to-year tenancy*, the hyphens being necessary in a PHRASAL ADJECTIVE that precedes the noun.

period of time is usually unnecessary in place of either *period* or *time.*

PERIPHRASIS = a roundabout way of writing or speaking. Many a legal writer uses "jargon to shirk prose, palming off *periphrasis* upon us when with a little trouble he could have gone straight to the point." Arthur Quiller-Couch, *On the Art of Writing* 108 (1916). See JARGON, EUPHEMISMS & REDUNDANCY.

PERIPHRASTIC COMPARATIVES. See COMPARATIVES AND SUPERLATIVES.

***perjorative** is a misspelling of *pejorative.* See **pejorative.**

perjure is now used only as a reflexive verb—e.g.: "The spousal testimonial privilege recognizes that some honorable people might choose to *perjure themselves* rather than incriminate their spouses or go to jail for contempt." David A. Super, *The New Moralizers*, 104 Colum. L. Rev. 2032, 2059 (2004). See **perjury.**

perjured; perjurious; *perjurous; *perjurial. *Perjured* is now the usual adjective corresponding to *perjury*—e.g.: "At sentencing, the district court imposed an obstruction of justice enhancement upon Dr. Kaufman based upon his *perjured* testimony at trial." *U.S. v. Kaufman*, 546 F.3d 1242, 1269 (10th Cir. 2008). The word *perjurious* is somewhat broader because it means "involving perjury" as opposed to the more specific sense of *perjured* (= characterized by perjury). So it is possible to speak of a person's *perjurious* tendencies but not of *perjured* tendencies.

**Perjurous* is an obsolete spelling of *perjurious*, which is analogous in formation to *injurious.* E.g.:

- "The purpose of this *perjurous* [read *perjurious*] declaration was to convince the district court to impose specific performance of an earlier plea offer with an attendant low sentence." *U.S. v. Arakelian*, 218 Fed. Appx. 76, 78 (2d Cir. 2007).

- "Prisock was recalled to the stand and recanted his *perjurous* [read *perjurious*] testimony." *In re Prisock*, 5 So.3d 319, 321 (Miss. 2008).

The form **perjurial*, a NEEDLESS VARIANT, has no warrant: "There is a sea of motions, demands, claims, counterclaims and plenty of innuendoes on each side as to the *perjurial* [read *perjurious*] aptitude of the other." *Rocket Mining Corp. v. Gill*, 417 P.2d 120, 120 (Utah 1966).

perjurer. So spelled—not **perjuror.**

***perjurial; perjurious; *perjurous.** See **perjured.**

perjury; false swearing; forswearing. The popular meaning of the first two terms is the same, namely, "swearing to what the witness knows to be untrue." *Forswearing* is a little-used equivalent of *false swearing*; *forswearing* also means, of course, "repudiating; renouncing." The technical DIFFERENTIATION at common law between *perjury* and *false swearing*, apart from their being separate indictable offenses, is that *perjury* connotes corruption and recalcitrance, whereas *false swearing* (or *false oath*) connotes mere falsehood without these additional moral judgments.

permanence; permanency. Both forms are used frequently. The two share the sense "the quality or state of being permanent." But while *permanence* emphasizes durability <the permanence of the snow>, *permanency* emphasizes duration <the permanency of fees tail>.

permanent injunction. See **injunction.**

permission; acquiescence. *Permission* connotes an authorization to do something, whereas *acquiescence* connotes the passive failure to object to someone's doing something.

permissive; *permissory. The second is a NEEDLESS VARIANT.

permissive joinder. See **joinder (c).**

permissive waste. See **waste.**

permit. See **allow (b).**

permit of = to leave room for <the words permit of more than one interpretation>. This phrase is common in contexts involving the interpretation of drafted documents, or statutes.

permittee. See -EE.

permute; *permutate. *Permute*, vb., is—apart from specialized mathematical uses—merely a fancy equivalent of the verb *to change.* **Permutate* is a NEEDLESS VARIANT.

perorate; orate. *Perorate* means "to conclude a formal address," although it is infrequently misunderstood as meaning "to declaim rhetorically or emotionally." *Orate*, a BACK-FORMATION, was once widely considered objectionable or merely humorous; yet it is losing this stigma.

peroration refers, most strictly, to the concluding part of a speech. And the word ordinarily bears that sense—e.g.:

- "In an eloquent *peroration*, Brennan concluded by observing . . . ." Geoffrey R. Stone, *Justice Brennan and the Freedom of Speech*, 139 U. Pa. L. Rev. 1333, 1352 (1991).
- "At the time, I thought my *peroration* was brilliant. I concluded my argument by rising with oratorical fervor." Stanley Mosk, *Culpability, Restitution, and the Environment*, 21 Ecology L.Q. 551, 554 (1994).

But through SLIPSHOD EXTENSION—primarily because the closing of a speech is typically the most impassioned and rhetorical part—some writers have used the word as if it referred to any rhetorically charged speech or writing. E.g.: "Professor Tribe's *perorations* [read *comments*? *rhetoric*?] about the not-so-absolute absolutes should seem a very sorry affair against at least the science of general relativity." Stanley L. Jaki, *Patterns over Principles: The Pseudoscientific Roots of Law's Debacle*, 38 Am. J. Juris. 135, 144 (1993).

In any event, the word is unacceptably strained when asked to refer to opening remarks—e.g.: "*After opening with a passionate peroration* [read *After opening passionately*], the dissent begins its technical-legal analysis by quoting a New Deal dissent in *United States v Butler*, one of the Old Court's last desperate struggles on behalf of a Madisonian understanding of limited national powers." Bruce Ackerman, *Liberating Abstraction*, 59 U. Chi. L. Rev. 317, 327 (1992). Was Ackerman perhaps straining for an alliteration that led him astray of the sense?

Some writers seem to use the word with little idea of its true meaning. One can only guess at the authors' intentions in the following passages:

- "Harvey cites one judge's *peroration* [read *praise*?] of the merits of the British law of evidence as evidence that the judge was 'certifiable,' and, in the style of Rumpole, alludes to the law in general as a sort of formality." Richard H. Underwood, *Logic and the Common Law Trial*, 18 Am. J. Trial Advoc. 151, 155 n.12 (1994).
- "The *Cooney* court preceded its discussion of interest analysis with a similar *peroration* [read *allusion* or *reference*?] to the fact that the conflict did not involve conduct-regulating rules." Aaron D. Twerski, *A Sheep in Wolf's Clothing*, 59 Brook. L. Rev. 1351, 1361 (1994).

perpetrate. See **perpetuate.**

perpetrator; abettor; inciter; criminal protector. These terms name the four different kinds of criminally culpable parties at common law. *Perpetrator* = one who, with mens rea, has caused a socially harmful occurrence either personally or through some tool or innocent agent (see **mens rea**). *Abettor* = one who is present at the scene of a crime, either actually or constructively, and who, with mens rea, either helps the perpetrator commit the crime or stands by with intent—known to the perpetrator—to help if needed, or otherwise encourages the perpetrator. *Inciter* = one who, with mens rea, helps, commands, or encourages another to commit a crime without being either actually or constructively present when it is carried out. *Criminal protector* = one who is in no way tainted with guilt of a crime when perpetrated but who, with full knowledge of the facts, later conceals the offender or helps prevent detection, arrest, trial, or punishment. See Rollin M. Perkins & Ronald N. Boyce, *Criminal Law* 723–26 (3d ed. 1982).

In the crime of treason, all such parties are principals. In misdemeanors, the first three are principals, and *criminal protectors* are not punishable. In felonies:

- Perpetrators are principals in the first degree.
- Abettors are principals in the second degree.
- Inciters are accessories before the fact.
- Criminal protectors are accessories after the fact.

Cf. **accomplice.** See **principal (B).** See also **confederate.**

perpetuable. So spelled—not *perpetuatable.

perpetual injunction. See **injunction.**

perpetuate (= to make last indefinitely; prolong) and *perpetrate* (= to commit or carry out) are surprisingly often confounded. E.g.:

- "In 1988, Federal District Judge James L. Kinf dismissed the suit as baseless, accused Mr. Shean of knowingly *perpetuating* [read *perpetrating*] a fraud and fined the Christie Institute." Michael Kelly, *Perot Shows Penchant for Seeing Conspiracy*, N.Y. Times, 26 Oct. 1992, at A10.
- "This allowed Ogle to use said document to *perpetuate* [read *perpetrate*] a fraud on a bank lending institution in connection with a $100,000 loan." *Taylor v. Sullivan*, 613 N.Y.S.2d 397, 398 (App. Div. 1994).

The word *perpetuate* is correctly used in the following sentence: "Without an eye to cultural and human progression, putting stock in 'tradition' and precedent could entrench tyranny and *perpetuate* human injustices." Deana Pollard Sacks, *Elements of Liberty*, 61 SMU L. Rev. 1557, 1577–78 (2008).

per procurationem = by proxy. The phrase is abbreviated *per pro.*, *p. proc.*, *p. pro.*, or *p.p.*

perquisite; prerequisite. *Perquisite*, often shortened to *perk*, means "a privilege or benefit given in addition to one's salary or regular wages." *Prerequisite* = a previous condition or requirement.

per quod; **per se.** Literally, *per quod* = whereby. In all tort actions, *per quod* once introduced the allegations giving rise to special damages by a showing of consequences stemming from the defendant's acts. *Per se* violations required no such showing. The phrases survive in defamation cases. *See, e.g., Kurz v. The Evening News Ass'n*, 375 N.W.2d 391, 394 (Mich. Ct. App. 1985). E.g.: "The law has always made a distinction between false imputations that may be actionable in themselves, or *per se*, and those that may be actionable only on allegation and proof of special damage, or *per quod*." *Layne v. Tribune Co.*, 146 So. 234, 238 (Fla. 1933).

Unfortunately, though, the use of *per se* in defamation contexts is ambiguous because it invites confusion with another distinction in the law of defamation: that between words that are facially defamatory ("You're an embezzler") and words that amount to subtle, veiled defamations. Statements of the latter type require some pleading and proof of innuendo or explanation. But this distinction, valuable as it is, has nothing whatever to do with whether special damages must be proved. Even so, some American courts have been misled by the linguistic similarity between *actionable per se* and *defamatory per se*. *See* Charles T. McCormick, *Handbook of the Law of Damages* § 113, at 417–18 (1935).

per se (lit., "through [or *in, by, of*] itself") = (1) standing alone; in itself, or (2) as a matter of law. The phrase is both adverb and adjective. Formerly used almost always after the adjective or noun it modifies, today it is commonly used before—e.g.:

- "Illinois courts have frequently noted that objects that are not *per se* deadly weapons may be used in such a manner as to become deadly weapons." *People v. Kipfer*, 824 N.E.2d 1246, 1259 (Ill. App. Ct. 2005).
- "Plaintiff disagrees, contending that the gunshot wound he suffered in Vietnam resulted in a *per se* disabling seizure disorder and a *per se* disabling organic mental disorder when evaluated under listings 11.02(A) and 12.02(A) and (B), respectively." *Bolden v. Commissioner of Soc. Sec.*, 556 F.Supp.2d 152, 162 (E.D.N.Y. 2007).
- "And while resale-price maintenance is no longer *per se* illegal under federal law, it almost certainly remains so under the law of some states." Henry C. Thumann, *Multijurisdictional Regulation of Monopoly in a Global Market*, 2008 Wis. L. Rev. 261, 267.
- "The Supreme Court's *Philadelphia Bank* decision created a virtual *per se* rule that linked merger legality to the market shares of the merging firms." Herbert Hovenkamp, *United States Competition Policy in Crisis: 1890–1955*, 94 Minn. L. Rev. 311, 355 (2009).

The phrase usually takes no punctuation, even though its English equivalent *in itself* or *of itself* is ordinarily set off by commas. When, however, *per se* is used as a direct functional equivalent of one of these phrases, it should be set off: "That the propriety, *per se*, of searches of law offices is an area of some controversy makes it more, not less, imperative that public officials not disregard the strictures of the fourth amendment." *Klitzman, Klitzman & Gallagher v. Krut*, 591 F.Supp. 258, 265 (D.N.J. 1984).

When used before the noun it modifies, *per se* often means "absolute." E.g.:

- "We are not disposed to fashion a *per se* rule requiring reversal of every conviction following tardy appointment of counsel." *Chambers v. Maroney*, 399 U.S. 42, 54 (1970) (per White, J.).
- "This inquiry calls for line-drawing but no fixed *per se* rule can be expressed or applied in any particular case." *Aguillard v. Edwards*, 765 F.2d 1251, 1255 (5th Cir. 1985).

Per se has become a TERM OF ART in antitrust law, referring to an outright violation of the antitrust statutes. The Supreme Court of the United States has defined *per se* antitrust violations as those "which because of their pernicious effect on competition and lack of any redeeming virtue are conclusively presumed to be unreasonable and therefore illegal without elaborate inquiry as to the precise harm they have caused or the business excuse for their use." *Northern Pac. Ry. v. U.S.*, 356 U.S. 1, 5 (1958) (per Black, J.). *Per se* is not absolute in American antitrust law: there may be behavior that is a *per se* violation of the statute, yet the violator may still raise defenses, such as impossibility because of market conditions.

The phrase has been extended in antitrust contexts well beyond its usual sense, from *per se illegality* to *per se rules* or *analysis* to *per se language*—e.g.: "*Per se* language expresses a mood of undoubted hostility to a practice." 7 Phillip Areeda, *Antitrust Law* § 1510, at 417 (1986). See **per quod**.

persecute. See **prosecute**.

persevere. Because this word is frequently a victim of the intrusive *-r-*, it is often mispronounced (and misspelled) **perservere*.

-PERSON. For a discussion of this suffix, see SEXISM (B).

person. This word illustrates the tendency lawyers have to take an ordinary English word and give it an unnatural meaning: "So far as legal theory is concerned, a person is any being whom the law regards as capable of rights and duties. Any being that is so capable is a person, whether a human being or not, and no being that is not so capable is a person, even though he be a man." J.W. Salmond, *Jurisprudence* 299 (P.J. Fitzgerald ed., 12th ed. 1966). Lon Fuller, among others, has questioned whether *person* is the most desirable word for the concept. *See* Lon L. Fuller, *Legal Fictions* 12–14 (1967). What term might be better? Fuller suggests *legal subject* or *right-and-duty bearing unit*. *Id.* On second thought, perhaps *person* is not quite so bad.

PERSON. It is important in any piece of writing, and especially in drafting, not to confuse one's references to persons, as by switching the voice through which the prose is set down. The writer should not change the person through whom the writing speaks, as by slipping in and out of third person, with first person interspersed.

Following is an example from a will quoted in an opinion: "The said party of the first part . . . does hereby remise, release and forever quitclaim unto the said party of the second part, his heirs and assigns forever, all of the real estate of the said Ella F. Sherwood [the party of the first part], wherever situate, to have and to hold the same unto the party of the second part, his heirs, executors, administrators and assigns forever, and for the same considerations, *I do* hereby sell . . . unto the party of the second part, all personal property." *Butler v. Sherwood*, 188 N.Y.S. 242, 243 (App. Div. 1921).

Here is another specimen, in which *testator* = party of the first part. "This conveyance and transfer are made upon the condition that the party of the second part, *my husband*, survive *me*, and the same is intended to vest and take effect only upon *my decease*, and until said time the same shall be subject to revocation upon the part of the *party of the first part*." *Butler v. Sherwood*, 186 N.Y.S. 712, 712 (Sup. Ct. 1921).

In both of these examples, certainly, use of the first person would be preferable throughout. See FIRST PERSON & **party of the first part.**

persona is singular, not plural—*personae* being the plural. Hence: "*Jowitt's Dictionary of English Law* in two volumes is quite detailed and because of its articles on long forgotten legal *persona* [read *personae* or, better yet, *personages*], incidents and maxims is an amusing read in itself." P.H. Kenny, *Studying Law* 47 (1985). (That sentence really needs a comma after *maxims*— and another after *incidents*. See PUNCTUATION (D).)

persona grata. See **persona non grata.**

personal. See **in personam (A)** & **real.**

personal action. See **real action.**

personal injury. When used as a noun phrase, two words unhyphenated; when used as a PHRASAL ADJECTIVE, hyphenated—e.g.: "But over the past year, *personal-injury attorneys* have been successful in having a number of such laws overturned." *Court in Washington Voids a Law Limiting Some Jury Awards*, Wall St. J., 1 May 1989, at B5.

personal knowledge. See **knowledge (A).**

personal law = the law that governs a given person in family matters, usu. regardless of where the person goes. In common-law systems, *personal law* refers to the law of the individual's domicile. (See *lex domicilii*.) In civil-law systems, it refers to the law of the individual's nationality (and is sometimes called *lex patriae*). E.g.: "Succession to immovables on the basis of the *personal law* of the decedent, as distinct from the law of the situs, has long been the rule in a substantial number of civilian jurisdictions." Alfred Hill, *The Judicial Function in Choice of Law*, 85 Colum. L. Rev. 1585, 1647 (1985). The effect of the differing systems is that, in civilian countries, personal law follows the person, whereas in common-law countries it does not.

Still other, religion-based systems establish a *personal law* for some aspects of life such as marriage, divorce, inheritance, legitimacy, adoption, and many types of capacity—e.g.:

• "While the Hindu Code retains *personal law* for Hindus, that *personal law* has almost entirely eliminated traditional caste distinctions." Jamie Cassels, *Bitter Knowledge, Vibrant Action*, 1991 Wis. L. Rev. 109, 116 n.29 (book review).

• "While article 44 of the constitution envisages the eventual adoption of a uniform civil code, Hindus, Muslims and other religious communities are still subject in many respects to their *personal law*." *Id.* at 111 n.9.

• "All members of a religious community, whether a majority or minority—Jews, Muslims, and members of different Christian communities in Israel; Muslims and Hindus in India—may be subject to a religion-based family law that is applied by religious courts. Like power sharing, a *personal law* can provide an important degree of autonomy and cohesion even for minorities that are territorially dispersed." Henry J. Steiner, *Ideals and Counter-Ideals in the Struggle over Autonomy Regimes for Minorities*, 66 Notre Dame L. Rev. 1539, 1542 (1991).

Though limited in Anglo-American law, the concept still applies to some degree: although American and English courts look chiefly to the law of the person's domicile, a person of full age and capacity may establish a desired personal law merely by choosing a given place—the place where that law is in effect—as a domicile.

personal property; personalty. Broadly defined, *personal property* "includes not only tangible movables, but also such intangible rights as bank deposits, commercial paper, corporate shares, life-insurance policies and the like." Ray Andrews Brown, *The Law of Personal Property* v (2d ed. 1955). For the historical basis for the distinction between *real property* and *personal property*, see **real.**

Personalty, a synonym of *personal property*, is contrasted with *realty*. E.g.: "*Personalty* is transferred, leased, hired, mortgaged, lent in very simple ways. As a rule it can be done by word of mouth. It is very different with *realty*." Max Radin, *The Law and You* 124–25 (1948). The word should not be confused with *personality*.

For the distinction between *realty* and *personalty*, see **realty (B).**

personal representative is a broad term for a person who, upon another's death, collects the decedent's property, pays the debts, and distributes what is left among those entitled under a will or under the rules of succession on intestacy. The two types of personal representatives are *executors* and *administrators*. See **administrator.**

personal service. See **substituted service.**

personalty. See **personal property.**

personam, in. See **in personam.**

persona non grata; persona grata. The established plurals are *personae non gratae* and *personae gratae*. See PLURALS (A).

*personation. See **impersonation.**

personnel may take either a singular or a plural verb, depending on whether it is intended as a COLLECTIVE NOUN.

persons. See **people.**

person . . . them; person . . . they. See CONCORD (B).

perspective. See **prospectus** (B).

perspicuous; perspicacious. *Perspicuous* is to *perspicacious* as *intelligible* is to *intelligent*. *Perspicuous* may be defined etymologically as "see-through-it-ive-ness"; it means "clear; lucid; seen readily," and is applied to thought and expression—e.g.: "Great lawyers distinguish themselves by their *perspicuity* in discerning the rules and applying them, while great judges make their mark by the effectiveness of their decisions and the forcefulness of their expression." John V. Orth, *A Bridge, a Tax Revolt, and the Struggle to Industrialize*, 84 N.C. L. Rev. 1927, 1927 (2006). *Perspicacious* = penetrating in thought; acutely discerning; keen; shrewd <a scholar as perspicacious as Charles Alan Wright>.

per stirpes. See **per capita** (B) & **stirpital.**

*****per stirpital.** See **stirpital.**

persuadable; *persuadible; *persuasible. The preferred form is *persuadable*.

persuade; convince. One *persuades* another *to do* something, but one *convinces* or, archaically, *persuades* another *of* something. Either *persuade* or *convince* may be used with a *that*-phrase object, although *persuade that* occurs seldom outside law. American judges seem addicted to the expression. E.g.:

- "The burden is on the defendant to *persuade* us *that* his sentence is inappropriate." *Laster v. State*, 918 N.E.2d 428, 434 (Ind. Ct. App. 2009).
- "We are not *persuaded that* the evidence against Hawkins related to the carjacking counts was overwhelming." *U.S. v. Hawkins*, 589 F.3d 694, 706 (4th Cir. 2009).

See **convince.**

persuaded that, we are. See **we are persuaded that.**

*****persuadible; *persuasible.** See **persuadable.**

persuasion burden. See **burden of proof** (A).

persuasive burden. See **burden of proof** (A).

persuasive precedent. See **precedent** (B).

pertain. See **appertain.**

pertinence; *pertinency. The first is now the usual and preferred form—e.g.:

- "Curiously, despite its obvious *pertinency* [read *pertinence*], counsel for neither party cited *Graystone* to the district court in this case." *McMullen v. Bay Ship Mgmt.*, 335 F.3d 215, 218 (3d Cir. 2003).
- "The Court reasoned that, because the core of criminality under the statute is the *pertinency* [read *pertinence*] of the questions to the subject under inquiry, . . . the indictment

had to do more than simply repeat the statutory language, it had to descend to particulars." *U.S. v. Russell*, 639 F.Supp.2d 226, 235 (D. Conn. 2007).

See **impertinence.**

pertinent part, in. See **in pertinent part.**

peruse means "to read with great care." It should not be used merely as a fancy substitute for *read*. It is pronounced /pə-**rooz**/, and the noun *perusal* /pə-**rooz**-əl/.

Peter Poe. See **Doe, John.**

petition. For the misuse of this word for a similar-sounding word, see **partition.**

petitioner. See PARTY APPELLATIONS & **plaintiff.**

petitioner, respondent. For points of usage, see **plaintiff, defendant.**

petitio principii. See **begging the question.**

petit jury. A. And *petty jury.* *Petit jury* is now the accepted spelling in AmE; the development is perhaps a favorable one, for nonlawyers are likely to read *petty* in its modern sense even though they are familiar with the phrase. (See **petty offense.**) A *petit jury* (= a trial jury) is contrasted with a *grand jury* (= the jury that decides whether to hand down an indictment or information). E.g.:

- "Using a statutorily specified number of peremptory challenges, parties may exclude qualified prospective jurors from the *petit jury* without assigning any reason for the challenge." Deana Kim El-Mallawany, Comment, Johnson v. California *and the Initial Assessment of* Batson *Claims*, 74 Fordham L. Rev. 3333, 3336 (2006).
- "Courts are hesitant to apply diversity rationales to *petit juries*, and will generally look only at juror representation across a larger community." Justin D. Levinson, *Forgotten Racial Equality*, 57 Duke L.J. 345, 415 (2007).

Cf. **grand jury.**

In BrE, *petty jury* seems to be the predominant spelling—e.g.: "A prisoner who is indicted is tried by a *petty jury*." O. Hood Phillips, *A First Book of English Law* 25 (3d ed. 1955).

B. Pronunciation. *Petit jury* should be pronounced in the same way as *petty jury*. But in some American jurisdictions—such as Texas, alas—the pronunciation /**pet**-it/ has taken hold. See HYPERCORRECTION (K).

petit larceny; petty larceny. See **larceny** (C).

petitory /**pet**-i-tor-ee/ is an adjective used in reference to suits seeking to try title to real property or to a vessel, independently of possession—e.g.:

- "Real actions were brought to recover lands, tenements, or hereditaments. They were of two classes, *petitory* and *possessory*. In *petitory* actions the controversy was concerning the property and right. In *possessory* actions the dispute was in relation only to the possession." Edwin E. Bryant, *The Law of Pleading Under the Codes of Civil Procedure* 4 (1899).

- "The heirs converted the matter into a *petitory* action by claiming ownership of the property." *Reily v. State*, 864 So.2d 223, 225 (La. Ct. App. 2003).

pettifogger. Like *shyster*, the word *pettifogger* is a contemptuous term for *lawyer*. But there is a difference, as explained here, rather magniloquently:

> The *pettifogger*, as a lawyer, is an unlearned, little, mean character, lacking in ability, sound judgment, or good common sense, while the *shyster* may be possessed of much learning, great ability or an abundance of shrewdness and cunning, but he is a trickster and a dishonest schemer; he is a fomenter of litigation, strife, and discord in the community; he is a manufacturer of evidence, a fosterer of perjury and a promoter of bribery; he is a cunning thief, who conceals his perfidy and rascality under the cloak of the law; he cunningly abuses the noble profession to which he has been admitted as a weapon of offense in deeds of unjust oppression, scheming knavery and the procurement of confidence and the repose of trust, which he basely abuses, when there is opportunity to profit by so doing.
>
> R. L. Harmon, addressing Alabama Bar Ass'n in 1897 (quoted in George W. Warvelle, *Essays in Legal Ethics* 69 (1902)).

Modern lawyers and judges use the term *pettifogger* with some frequency—e.g.: "Quite the contrary, counsel in that case were not *pettifoggers*." *Nebeker v. Piper Aircraft Corp.*, 747 P.2d 18, 38 (Idaho 1987). See **shyster** & LAWYERS, DEROGATORY NAMES FOR.

The corresponding abstract noun is *pettifoggery* (= legal chicanery)—e.g.: "The opposition of Goodman and Dorsey to the motion to compel discovery was specious, replete with linguistic legerdemain, half truths, and *pettifoggery*." *In re Marriage of Lemen*, 170 Cal. Rptr. 642, 649 (Ct. App. 1980).

petty jury. See **petit jury.**

petty larceny. See **larceny (C)** & **petit larceny.**

petty offense. In G.B., this phrase (spelled *petty offence* in BrE) has dropped from the criminal law because it was thought to minimize unduly a serious infraction of the law. In the U.S., some have wondered whether a *petty offense* is actually a crime. It is, despite the misleading terminology: a repealed federal statute provided that any misdemeanor "the penalty for which . . . does not exceed imprisonment for a period of six months or a fine of not more than $5,000, or both, is a *petty offense*." 18 U.S.C. § 1(3) (1983). See **petit jury (A).**

***phantasy.** See **fantasy.**

phase for *faze* (= to disconcert) is a disconcertingly common blunder—e.g.: "The fact that the *Ohio* Supreme Court had ignored this slip and treated the tax as what, practically speaking, it was, didn't *phase* [read *faze*] the U.S. Supreme Court." Fred Rodell, *Woe Unto You, Lawyers!* 81 (1939). In Rodell's case, the

mistake was probably an editor's error; on page 134 of the same book appears a correct use: "That will not *faze* the law schools."

The mistake often appears in the negative adjective ***unphased** (for *unfazed*)—e.g.:

- "NYCERS, apparently *unphased* [read *unfazed*] by the absence of any express legislative authority, maintains that it is nevertheless empowered to carve out substantial exclusions from the statutorily constituted membership class." *Doctors Council v. New York City Employees' Ret. Sys.*, 514 N.Y.S.2d 922, 933 (App. Div. 1987).
- "The people who are not dissuaded, however, are strongly attracted to the absence of constraints, and relatively *unphased* [read *unfazed*] by the absence of support." James M. Doyle, *"It's The Third World Down There!,"* 27 Harv. Civ. Rights-Civ. Libs. L. Rev. 71, 105 (1992).
- "*Unphased* [read *Unfazed*] by the absence of those critical terms, the court simply decided to superimpose 18 U.S.C. § 2's broad accomplice liability onto 21 U.S.C. § 848(e)(1)(B)." Brian Serr, *Of Crime and Punishment, Kingpins and Footsoldiers, Life and Death*, 25 Ariz. St. L.J. 895, 910 (1993).

Perhaps this misusage is simply an unfortunate linguistic phase; if not, many will find it hard to remain unfazed.

Ph.D. (= Philosophical Doctor; Doctor of Philosophy) requires the periods.

phenomenon. This is the singular noun, *phenomena* being the plural—e.g.: "The contemporary, fast-paced, and evolving character of these *phenomena* presented challenges." Pablo J. Boczkowski, *News at Work* 10 (2010). But many writers misuse the plural as if it were singular—e.g.: "The Supreme Court recently explained this *phenomena* [read *phenomenon*] in *Powers v. Ohio*." *People v. Boston*, 586 N.E.2d 326, 332 (Ill. App. Ct. 1991) (Johnson, J., dissenting). The singular is also misused as the plural—e.g.: "We don't have a theory that takes into account all these *phenomenon* [read *phenomena*]." Peter Alexander & Rick Halpern, *Racializing Class, Classifying Race* 216 (2000). Cf. **criterion.**

Philadelphia lawyer. In colonial America, Philadelphia was the center of legal, literary, and scientific endeavors. During that period, the phrase *Philadelphia lawyer* took on the meaning "a shrewd and learned lawyer." Why? One explanation is that the phrase resulted from Andrew Hamilton's successful defense of the New York printer John Peter Zenger against libel charges in 1735—a case that helped establish freedom of the press in the U.S. Observers are said to have noted that a *Philadelphia lawyer* got Zenger off. But because the *OED* records no uses of the term until 1788, the origin remains obscure.

Even today, though, the term is used in much the same way as it was in the late 18th century—e.g.: "Employers say the rules are hopelessly complex and costly. 'A *Philadelphia lawyer* can't even figure these out,' says Kenneth Morrissey, FMC Corp. employee benefits manager." *Labor Letter*, Wall St. J., 11 Feb. 1992, at 1A. In other contexts, predictably, the phrase merely denotes a lawyer who hails from Philadelphia. What is difficult to say is what the phrase *connotes* in such a context. See LAWYERS, DEROGATORY NAMES FOR (A).

philosophical; *philosophic. The second is a NEEDLESS VARIANT.

PHRASAL ADJECTIVES. A. General Rule. When a phrase functions as an adjective—an increasingly frequent phenomenon in 21st-century English—the phrase should ordinarily be hyphenated. Seemingly everyone in the literary world knows this except lawyers. For some unfathomable reason—perhaps because they are accustomed to slow, dull, heavy reading—lawyers resist these hyphens.

But professional editors regularly supply them, and rightly so. The primary reason for them is that they prevent MISCUES and make reading easier and faster. Hence:

adverse-possession claim
affirmative-action policy
agency-enabling statute
blank-check authority
breach-of-contract claims
child-support payments
civil-rights case
conditions-of-confinement claim
conspiracy-law dispute
criminal-law setting
death-penalty case
federal-question case
flag-desecration statute
food-stamp-eligibility rule
fundamental-rights cases
good-faith exception
grand-jury probe
hate-crime statutes
home-rule provisions
in-court testimony
late-term abortion
least-restrictive-remedy test
levels-of-generality problem
minimum-wage laws
ordinary-meaning analysis
paid-in capital
personal-injury lawyer
purchase-money mortgage
quality-of-life considerations
real-estate practice
rent-control ordinance
same-sex marriage
show-cause order
social-choice theory
states'-rights argument
stop-and-frisk procedures
subject-matter jurisdiction
textual-integrity canon
third-degree assault
two-party check

verbal-meaning criterion
white-collar crime

When the reader encounters such a phrasal adjective, he or she is not misled into thinking momentarily that the modifying phrase is really a noun itself. (See MISCUES (D).) The following examples demonstrate the hesitation caused by a missing hyphen:

- "Perhaps . . . it would have been possible to harmonize the *presumption of authority provisions* [read *presumption-of-authority provisions*] with the *duty to inquire provision* [read *duty-to-inquire provision*]." Grant Gilmore & Charles L. Black Jr., *The Law of Admiralty* 674 (2d ed. 1975). Elsewhere in their book, Gilmore and Black show better stylistic judgment—see (C).
- "Mackey was questioned by the Court about his five *armed robbery convictions* [read *armed-robbery convictions*] only because he chose to testify and tried to deny his guilt. Thus, there is no merit to the Fifth Amendment *right to remain silent violation claim* [read *right-to-remain-silent-violation claim*]." *U.S. v. Mackey*, 299 F.Supp.2d 636, 642 (E.D. La. 2004).
- "As the legal community and press became more interested in *comparative law firm economics* [read *comparative law-firm economics*], *public service* [read *public-service*] and *pro bono* representation decreased in importance." Paul J. Bschorr, *Challenges for the Decade*, Litig., Summer 1991, at 1, 1. See **pro bono publico.**
- "There is no statute of limitations in the original statute, though courts have implied a *ten year statute of limitations* [read *ten-year statute of limitations*]." Ariel Meyerstein, *The Law and Lawyers as Enemy Combatants*, 18 U. Fla. J.L. & Pub. Pol'y 299, 331 n.158 (2007).
- "Even if the Court would concede that perhaps the requirement of an 'actual tax deficiency' is really a *court made rule* [read *court-made rule*], the question still stands whether a requirement for an actual tax deficiency sans intent . . . is the correct interpretation of the tax-evasion statute." Gurpreet Bal, *Bringing it All Back Home*, 5 Hastings Bus. L.J. 367, 376 (2009).

Hyphenating these phrasal adjectives also minimizes NOUN PLAGUE. For instance, *common law* is the noun phrase and *common-law* the PHRASAL ADJECTIVE; when the phrase has no hyphen, the reader does not expect a noun to follow it.

One sees the pronounced improvement in readability especially when two compound adjectives modify one noun:

- common-law mirror-image rule
- long-latency occupational-disease cases
- 13-year-old court-ordered busing plan

Following are examples in which enlightened legal writers supplied the necessary hyphens:

- "To the *law-of-nature school*, lawmaking was but an absolute development of absolute principles." Roscoe Pound, *An Introduction to the Philosophy of Law* 92 (1922).
- "The main plea was that the entire *separate-but-equal doctrine* be discarded." Fred Rodell, *Nine Men* 323 (1955).
- "*Rank-and-file lawyers* were too untrained for Chitty." Lawrence M. Friedman, *A History of American Law* 146 (2d ed. 1985).
- "The petition . . . argues that the ruling 'took a major step away from settled law' in the First Amendment's *free-exercise-of-religion clause*." Wade Lambert & Wayne E.

Green, *Subway-Begging Ban Is Backed on Appeal*, Wall St. J., 11 May 1990, at B2.

When a compound modifier begins with an adverb that ends in *-ly*, the hyphen is dropped—e.g.:

- "This is the *legally-relevant* [read *legally relevant*] feature." Glanville Williams, *Criminal Law* 20 (2d ed. 1961).
- "With the *hotly-contested* [read *hotly contested*] Second Congressional District primary six days away, supporters of Sen. Bob Smith gathered last night." M.L. Elrick, *Kemp Coy on Plans for 1996*, Concord Monitor (N.H.), 8 Sept. 1994, at B1.

B. Phrasal Adjectives of Foreign Origin. A few phrasal adjectives, such as *bona fide, ex officio, mens rea, pro rata*, and *res ipsa loquitur*—in which the words generally have no English meaning when taken alone—are usually treated as exceptions to the rule of hyphenation.

Still, some writers grant them no exemption from hyphens—e.g.:

- "An entirely different approach to the problem of distinguishing preparation from attempt is suggested by the *res-ipsa-loquitur test*." Peter W. Low et al., *Criminal Law: Cases and Materials* 134 (1982).
- "The origins of the common-law *mens-rea* requirement are obscure." *Id.* at 200.
- "On one view, there is a *prima-facie* duty of care." Rupert Cross & J.W. Harris, *Precedent in English Law* 45 (4th ed. 1991).

Cf. **alter ego.**

C. Snakelike Compounds. Instead of toying with snakelike compounds, writers are usually well advised to rework the sentence—e.g.:

- "Each contract included *a waiver-of-all-rights-to-subrogation clause* [read *a clause waiving all rights to subrogation*]." *Horizon Petroleum Co. v. Barges Dixie 162, 234 & 236*, 753 F.2d 382, 383 (5th Cir. 1985).
- "We found no merit in any other issue raised, *including an ineffective-assistance-of-counsel claim* [read *including a claim of ineffective assistance of counsel*]." *Austin v. McCotter*, 764 F.2d 1142, 1142 (5th Cir. 1985).

Here is a particularly ugly specimen: "We, though, are *law-of-the-case bound* in this matter and thus cannot reconsider this contention." *Todd Shipyards Corp. v. Auto Transp., S.A.*, 763 F.2d 745, 753 (5th Cir. 1985). A suggested revision: *We are bound by the law of the case and thus cannot reconsider this contention.*

Some writers do use them, usually to create a jocular or self-mocking tone—e.g.:

- "For the political law of Holmes's time was, with a few . . . lapses and interludes, merely a more concentrated continuation of the *let-business-alone-and-let-it-run-the-country* jurisprudence that had come to full flower late in the preceding century." Fred Rodell, *Nine Men* 185 (1955).
- "The *no-lien-for-partial-execution-of-affreightment-contracts rule* of the Pacific Export case does have the merit of running both ways, as the so-called 'dead freight' cases show." Grant Gilmore & Charles L. Black Jr., *The Law of Admiralty* 639 (2d ed. 1975).

Sometimes phrasal adjectives incorporate so many disparate elements that, when combined with

the noun that follows, they have an effect similar to NOUN PLAGUE—e.g.: "A *child-sex-abuse defendant's* Sixth Amendment right to confront witnesses against him was violated." *Screening Defendant from Accuser Violates Confrontation Clause*, 57 U.S.L.W. 1001, 1003 (U.S. 5 July 1988).

D. Suspension Hyphens. When two phrasal adjectives have a common element at the end, and this ending portion (usually the last word) appears only with the second phrase, insert a suspension hyphen after the unattached words to show their relationship with the common element. The hyphens become especially important when the phrases are compounded in this way—e.g.:

- "The Government argues that this designation is ineffective because it reflects a *ten-* rather than *two-year* federal sentence." *U.S. v. Naas*, 755 F.2d 1133, 1137 (5th Cir. 1985).
- "A court faced with enforcing a *general-* or *public-interest law*, however, should give vent to its imagination, since such a law is designed—like the antitrust statutes—to vest discretion in the judicial branch." Laurence H. Tribe, *Constitutional Calculus*, 98 Harv. L. Rev. 592, 614 (1985).

Here the hyphens are not supplied, to the reader's puzzlement: "The situs of this case is the small city of Apopka, Florida located *in the fern and foliage growing region* [read *in the fern- and foliage-growing region*] north of Orlando." *Dowdell v. City of Apopka*, 698 F.2d 1181, 1184 (11th Cir. 1983) (per Vance, J.).

For more on the use of hyphens, see PUNCTUATION (G).

E. Amount or Period of Time. With compound adjectives denoting periods of time and amounts, plurals should be dropped in the adjectival phrase—e.g.: "The record is silent as to whether or not Annie Belle was born after a normal *nine months pregnancy* [read *nine-month pregnancy*]." *Lawson v. Baker*, 351 S.W.2d 571, 574 (Tex. Civ. App.—Houston 1961). Likewise, one should write *three-week hiatus, fourteen-hour-a-day schedule*, and *four-year decline.* The exception is with fractions <a two-thirds vote>.

F. Proper Noun. When a name is used attributively as a phrasal adjective, it ordinarily remains unhyphenated. E.g.: "The *Terry Maher strategy* put immediate pressure on rival bookshop chains." Raymond Snoddy, *Book Price War Looms in Britain*, Fin. Times, 28–29 Sept. 1991, at 1.

G. Phrasal Adjectives Following the Noun. When predicative, phrasal adjectives are not usually hyphenated <this rule is well worn> <this is a well-worn rule>. Exceptions include *short-lived*, which is always hyphenated.

H. Phrases with Only One Element Joined. When the first or second element in a phrasal adjective is compound, it too needs to be hyphenated: *post-cold-war norms*, not *post-cold war norms*. Otherwise, as in the example just quoted, *post* appears more closely related to *cold* than *war* does. E.g.: "Palumbo wants a *Domesday book-style appraisal* [read *Domesday-book-style appraisal*] of all cultural buildings with a cash breakdown of the needed repairs." Geordie Grieg, *£1 Billion to Restore Britain's Heritage by AD 2000*, Sunday Times, 1 July 1990, at 1-1.

PHRASAL VERBS are verbs that are made up of more than one word, often a verb and a preposition. When using a phrasal verb, one must be certain to include the entire phrase and not just the primary verb. So statutes are *struck down*, not just *struck*. Likewise, contracts are *entered into*, not just *entered*. *Sue out* means something different from *sue* (see **sue out**). We must respect, then, the latter part of phrasal verbs as much as the earlier. *Prove up, make whole, hold over, hand down* or *out* (an opinion), *make payment for*, and *work out* (a settlement) are a few of the phrasal verbs common in law. Generally, writers should not be timid in using phrasal verbs; they are usually not substandard or even colloquial, unless the particle is unnecessary. (See PARTICLES, UNNECESSARY.) For a full collection of verbs of this kind, see G.W. Davidson, *Chambers Pocket Guide to Phrasal Verbs* (1982).

When one phrasal verb is part of a DOUBLET, an AMBIGUITY may arise if an adverb occurs in the midst of the phrasal verb—e.g.: "In no case shall a corporation purchase or make payment, *directly or indirectly*, for its own shares when there is reasonable ground for believing that the corporation is insolvent." Tex. Bus. Corp. Act art. 2.03(F) (Vernon 1973). Does the phrase *directly or indirectly* apply to *purchase*? If so, read *purchase or make payment for, directly or indirectly*.

In the following specimen, the writer left the phrasal verb incomplete, apparently out of fear of using an unnecessary particle: "*Drawing* [read *Drawing on*] the principle that the acquisition of or attempt to acquire monopoly power is illegal only if not accomplished by legitimate means such as 'product, business acumen, or historic accident,' appellee observes that [appellant's] sole theory of exclusionary conduct . . . is unsupported by the record." *C.E. Servs., Inc. v. Control Data Corp.*, 759 F.2d 1241, 1247 (5th Cir. 1985). Cf. **strike.**

PHRASING refers to syntactic structures, their graceful logic or maladroit clumsiness. The writer should have some sense of how best to order the parts of a sentence, so that it will be logically, and preferably even elegantly, constructed. Many of the specific maladies of construction are discussed throughout this work. Hence this entry can do little more than exemplify some of the general problems and offer remedies—e.g.:

- "The jury made a special finding that the defendant, in firing the bomb, exercised reasonable care." *Scanlon v. Wedger*, 31 N.E. 642, 642 (Mass. 1892). This sounds as if the bomb was fired *in order to pursue such care*! A suggested revision: *The jury made a special finding that the defendant exercised reasonable care in firing the bomb.*
- "The Erie had contended that application of the Pennsylvania rule was required, among other things, by section 34 of the Federal Judiciary Act of September 24, 1789." *Erie R.R. v. Tompkins*, 304 U.S. 64, 71 (1938) (per Brandeis, J.). This phrasing suggests that the Pennsylvania rule was not just required, but mandated, demanded, necessitated ("among other things"). A suggested revision: *The Erie had contended that application of the Pennsylvania rule was required by, among other things, section 34* . . . .

- "The plaintiff having conveyed away by deed purporting to convey a fee simple interest, the lands in question and having had them conveyed back to her, is now . . . seized of a fee simple interest." *Caccamo v. Banning*, 75 A.2d 222, 224 (Del. Super. Ct. 1950). A suggested revision: *Having purported to convey* (less redundant than *having conveyed away*) *a fee simple interest in the lands in question, and having had them conveyed back to her, the plaintiff is now seised* (the better spelling) *of a fee simple interest.*
- "In the case of a vested remainder, there is a person in being ascertained and ready to take who has a present right of future enjoyment." *Oak Park Trust & Savs. Bank v. Baumann*, 438 N.E.2d 1354, 1358 (Ill. App. Ct. 1982). This is downright ungrammatical. A suggested revision: *. . . there is a person in being, ascertained and ready to take, who* . . . .

P.I., in lawyers' slang, refers to "personal-injury law." E.g.: "Tingey finally quit Galane's firm in frustration over his mentor's refusal to take the steady, well-paying personal injury (*PI*) cases that would have amply subsidized Galane's other legal work." John A. Jenkins, *The Litigators* 18 (1989). This initialism is best written with periods after each letter. See ACRONYMS AND INITIALISMS.

picaresque; picturesque. These words are quite different. *Picaresque* = roguish. *Picturesque* = fit to be the subject of a picture; strikingly graphic.

piece of (one's) mind. See **peace of mind.**

piercing the corporate veil; lifting the corporate veil. The first phrase is the AmE phrase, the second the BrE phrase, meaning "the act of disregarding the veil of incorporation that separates the property of a corporation from the property of its security holders."

Sometimes *pierce* is used in extended, elliptical senses, as here: "[Were a corporation to attempt to perpetrate a fraud on the court by] improperly creating or destroying diversity jurisdiction, . . . we would not elevate form over substance but would accomplish whatever *piercing* and adjustments were considered necessary to protect the court's jurisdiction." *Panalpina Welttransport GmBh v. Geosource*, 764 F.2d 352, 355 (5th Cir. 1985). The *piercing* referred to apparently would entail judicial directives or sanctions against corporate officials—in effect, the court would disregard the veil of incorporation.

pilfer. See **steal (A).**

pillage. See **spoils.**

pinpoint citation; jump citation; dictum page. The first is the most usual of these synonymous phrases, which denote the page on which a quotation or relevant passage appears, as opposed to the page on which a case or article begins. For example, in the following citation, the number 595 denotes the pinpoint citation: *Groh v. Brooks*, 421 F.2d 589, 595 (3d Cir. 1970). Sometimes the pinpoint citation coincides with the first page of the case or article cited, as here: *State v. Jones*, 919 N.E.2d 739, 739 (Ohio 2009).

Today, *jump citation* is nearly as common as *pinpoint citation*. But *dictum page* appears to be obsolescent; it was used in the *Bluebook* in the 1950s but has long since been abandoned, perhaps because it misleadingly suggests that the quoted matter is dictum as opposed to the holding of the court. See **dictum.**

pique ([1] to irritate; or [2] to excite or arouse) is sometimes confused with *peak*. The proper phrase is *to pique someone's interest*—e.g.: "This court has held that statements designed to gain the trust and assurance of co-conspirators, to provide incentives for negotiations and to *peak* [read *pique*] interest are also in furtherance of a conspiracy." *U.S. v. Blakeney*, 942 F.2d 1001, 1020–21 (6th Cir. 1991).

For still another misuse, see **peak.**

pitiable; pitiful; piteous; pitiless. *Pitiable* = calling for or arousing pity. E.g.:

- "The vast majority of criminals who come into the dock at Assizes or Sessions are *pitiable* creatures, a nuisance rather than a danger to the state." Patrick Devlin, *The Criminal Prosecution in England* 112 (1960).
- "The fiction always seems *pitiably* obvious and naïve—in retrospect." Lon L. Fuller, *Legal Fictions* 93 (1967).

Pitiful, strictly, means "feeling pity," but in modern speech and writing it is almost always used in the sense "contemptible." The word *piteous* "had become misused as a form of *pitiable* as early as Shakespeare's time: for him hearts could be *piteous* in the active sense and corpses in the passive." Ivor Brown, *I Give You My Word & Say the Word* 235 (1964). Today *piteous* is archaic and poetic—not a word for ordinary uses. *Pitiless* = showing no pity.

PLACE-NAMES AS ADJECTIVES. See ADJECTIVES (F).

place of abode. See **abode, place of.**

place-of-wrong rule; place-of-wrong law. See **lex (loci) delicti (A).**

place under surveillance. See **surveillance, place under.**

place where. This phrase is perfectly idiomatic. There is no good reason to insist on *place that*. Cf. **reason (B).**

plagiarize is often misspelled **plagarize* or **plagerize*.

plain. See **evident.**

plain, it is. See **clearly.**

PLAIN LANGUAGE. A. Generally. Albert Einstein once said that his goal in stating an idea was to make it as simple as possible but no simpler. If lawyers everywhere adopted this goal, the world would probably change in dramatic ways.

But there is little reason for hope when so many legal writers seem to believe that to seem good or competent or smart, their ideas must be stated in the most complex manner possible. Of course, this problem plagues many fields of intellectual endeavor, as the philosopher Bertrand Russell noted:

> I am allowed to use plain English because everybody knows that I could use mathematical logic if I chose. Take the statement: "Some people marry their deceased wives' sisters." I can express this in language [that] only becomes intelligible after years of study, and this gives me freedom. I suggest to young professors that their first work should be written in a jargon only to be understood by the erudite few. With that behind them, they can ever after say what they have to say in a language "understanded of the people." In these days, when our very lives are at the mercy of the professors, I cannot but think that they would deserve our gratitude if they adopted my advice.
>
> Bertrand Russell, "How I Write," in *The Basic Writings of Bertrand Russell* 63, 65 (Robert E. Egner & Lester E. Denonn eds., 1961).

But the professors have not heeded Russell's advice. Since Russell wrote that essay in the mid-1950s, things have gotten much worse in fields such as biology, linguistics, literary criticism, political science, psychology, and sociology. And they have gotten worse in law.

Consider the following statutory provision, a 260-word tangle that is as difficult to fathom as any algebraic theorem:

> 57AF(11) Where, but for this sub-section, this section would, by virtue of the preceding provisions of this section, have in relation to a relevant year of income as if, for the reference in sub-section (3) to $18,000 there were substituted a reference to another amount, being an amount that consists of a number of whole dollars and a number of cents (in this sub-section referred to as the "relevant number of cents")—
>
> (a) in the case where the relevant number of cents is less than 50—the other amount shall be reduced by the relevant number of cents:
>
> (b) in any case—the other amount shall be increased by the amount by which the relevant number of cents is less than $1.
>
> (12) Where, but for sub-section (5), this section would, by virtue of the preceding provisions of this section, have effect in relation to a relevant year of income as if, for the reference in sub-section (3) to $18,000, there were substituted a reference to another amount, being an amount that consists of a number of whole dollars and a number of cents (in this sub-section referred to as the "relevant number of cents") then, for the purposes of the application of paragraph 4(b)—
>
> (a) in a case where the relevant number of cents is less than 50—the other amount shall be reduced by the relevant number of cents; or
>
> (b) in any case—the other amount shall be increased by the amount by which the relevant number of cents is less than $1.
>
> Income Tax Assessment Act [Australia] § 57AF(11), (12) (as quoted in David St. L. Kelly, "Plain English in Legislation," in *Essays on Legislative Drafting* 57, 58 (David St. L. Kelly ed., 1988)).

That is the type of drafting that prompts an oft-repeated criticism: "So unintelligible is the phraseology of some statutes that suggestions have been made that draftsmen, like the Delphic Oracle, sometimes aim deliberately at obscurity." Carleton K. Allen, *Law in the Making* 486 (7th ed. 1964).

With some hard work, the all-but-inscrutable passage above can be transformed into a straightforward version of only 65 words:

> If either of the following amounts is not in whole dollars, the amount must be rounded up or down to the nearest dollar (or rounded up if the amount ends with 50 cents):
>
> (a) the amount of the motor-vehicle-depreciation limit; or
>
> (b) the amount that would have been the motor-vehicle-depreciation limit if the amount had equaled or exceeded $18,000.
>
> Revision based on that of Gavin Peck (quoted in Kelly, *supra*, at 59).

Few would doubt that the original statute is unplain and that the revision is comparatively plain. True, the revision requires the reader to understand what a "motor-vehicle-depreciation limit" is, but some things can be stated only so simply.

When it comes to the legislative jungle of the tax code, as Justice Robert H. Jackson once wrote, "It can never be made simple, but we can try to avoid making it needlessly complex." *Dobson v. Commissioner*, 320 U.S. 489, 495 (1943) (per Jackson, J.).

Still, some might protest that, after all, the law is a learned profession. Some seem to find an insult in the suggestion that lawyers should avoid complex verbiage. They want to express themselves in more sophisticated ways than nonprofessionals do.

Their objection needs a serious answer because it presents the most serious impediment to the plain-language movement. There are essentially four answers.

First, those who write in a difficult, laborious style risk being unclear not only to other readers but also to themselves. When you write obscurely, you're less likely to be thinking clearly. And you're less likely to appreciate the problems that are buried under such involuted prose. For the private practitioner, this could increase the possibility of malpractice.

Second, obscure writing wastes readers' time—a great deal of it, when the sum is totaled. An Australian study conducted in the 1980s found that lawyers and judges take twice as long deciphering legalistically worded statutes as they do plain-language revisions. Law Reform Comm'n of Victoria, *Plain English & the Law* 61–62 (1987).

Third, simplifying is a higher intellectual attainment than complexifying. Writing simply and directly is hard work, but a learned profession ought not to shrink from the challenge. In fact, the hallmark of all the greatest legal stylists is precisely that they take difficult ideas and express them as simply as possible. No nonprofessional could do it, and most lawyers can't do it. Only extraordinary minds are capable of the task.

Still, every lawyer—brilliant or not—can aim at the mark.

Fourth, the very idea of professionalism demands that we not conspire against nonlawyers by adopting a style that makes our writing seem like a suffocating fog. Unless lawyers do the right thing and reform from within, outside forces may well cause a revolution that will marginalize the legal profession. See LEGALESE, LEGALISMS AND LAWYERISMS & OBSCURITY.

B. Definitions. "Plain language," generally speaking, is "the idiomatic and grammatical use of language that most effectively presents ideas to the reader." Garner, *The Elements of Legal Style* 5–13 (2d ed. 2002). Some have tried to reduce "plain language" to a mathematical formula, but any such attempt is doomed to failure. And that is no indictment of the idea: "It is no criticism that Plain English cannot be precisely, mathematically defined. Neither can 'reasonable doubt' or 'good cause.' Like so many legal terms, it is inherently and appropriately vague." Joseph Kimble, *Plain English: A Charter for Clear Writing*, 9 Thomas M. Cooley L. Rev. 1, 14 (1992).

The fundamental principle is that anything translatable into simpler words in the same language is bad style. That may sound like a facile oversimplification that fails when put into practice—but it isn't and it doesn't.

C. An Old Idea. Of course, legal discourse has long been ridiculed for its incomprehensibility. Jonathan Swift skewered LEGALESE when he wrote of a society of lawyers who spoke in "a peculiar cant and jargon of their own, that no other mortal can understand." *Gulliver's Travels* 154 (1726).

What is less well known than the ridicule is that good legal writers have long advocated a plain-language style. In the mid-19th century, for example, the leading authority on LEGISLATIVE DRAFTING said that most legal documents can be written in "the common popular structure of plain English." George Coode, *On Legislative Expression* xxx (1842). A generation later, an English lawyer explained that good drafting "says in the plainest language, with the simplest, fewest, and fittest words, precisely what it means." J.G. Mackay, *Introduction to an Essay on the Art of Legal Composition Commonly Called Drafting*, 3 Law Q. Rev. 326, 326 (1887). Other writers could be cited, decade by decade, up to the present day. In short, there is nothing new about the idea.

D. Plain-Language Principles. "No lawyer can now safely navigate," writes a well-known law professor, "without knowing the problems of legalese and the principles of plain English." Robert W. Benson, *The End of Legalese*, 13 N.Y.U. Rev. Law & Soc. Change 519, 573 (1984–1985). Experienced editors have arrived at these plain-language principles through induction—through carrying out the principles again and again. Once you have revised hundreds of legal documents for the purposes of clarifying and simplifying, you can fairly accurately predict what problems the next document might hold in store.

Of these principles, perhaps the most important is to reject the MYTH OF PRECISION. Traditionally, lawyers have aimed for a type of "precision" that results in cumbersome writing, with many long sentences collapsing under the weight of obscure qualifications. That "precision" is often illusory for two reasons: (1) AMBIGUITY routinely lurks within traditional, legalistic language; and (2) when words proliferate, ambiguities tend to as well.

Of course, where clarity and precision are truly at loggerheads, precision must usually prevail. But the instances of actual conflict are much rarer than lawyers often suppose. Precision is not sacrificed when the drafter uses technical words where necessary and avoids JARGON that serves no substantive purpose. As one commentator puts it, "What is often called 'legal phraseology' is no more than inept writing or the unnecessary use of obscure or entangled phrases." Samuel A. Goldberg, "Hints on Draftsmanship," in *Drafting Contracts and Commercial Instruments* 7, 8 (Research and Documentation Corp. ed., 1971).

As a rule, whether one is drafting legislation, contracts, or other documents, clarity is just as important as precision. In fact, clarity helps ensure precision because the drafter with an obscure style finds it less easy to warrant what the draft itself says.

The main work of the legislative drafter is "to state the law in a form clearer and more convenient than that in which it has hitherto existed, and that is a task for experts." J.L. Brierly, *The Law of Nations* 80 (5th ed. 1955). Of course, some influences leading to complexity cannot be overcome; among these are the difficulty of the subject matter itself and the fact that a final draft may reflect a compromise between different points of view. But with hard work, other obscurantist influences—the ones that are linguistically based—can be overcome: long-windedness, needless jargon, and inconsistent style resulting from collaborative efforts.

The chief guidelines are as follows:

1. Achieve a reasonable average sentence length. Strive for an average sentence length of 20 words—and, in any event, ensure that you are below 30 words. Doing this involves following a maxim that, unfortunately, makes some legal drafters unnecessarily nervous: "If you want to make a statement with a great many qualifications, put some of the qualifications in separate sentences." Bertrand Russell, "How I Write," in *The Basic Writings of Bertrand Russell* 63, 65 (Robert E. Egner & Lester E. Denonn eds., 1961). See SENTENCE LENGTH.

2. Prefer short words to long ones, simple to fancy. Minimize jargon and technical terms so that you achieve a straightforward style that non-lawyers as well as lawyers can understand. This means rejecting LEGALISMS such as *pursuant to* (under, in accordance with), *prior to* (before),

subsequent to (after), *vel non* (or not, or the lack of it).

3. Avoid double and triple negatives. No reader wants to wrestle with a sentence like this one: "The investments need not be revalued at intervals of not more than two years if the trustee and the beneficiaries do not disagree." [Read: *If the trustee and beneficiaries agree, the investments need not be revalued every two years.*] See NEGATIVES (A).

4. Prefer the active voice. *Notice must be given* compares poorly with *The tenant must give notice* because (a) the first version does not spell out who must give notice, and (b) readers take in a sentence more easily if it meets their expectation of a subject–verb–object structure. See PASSIVE VOICE.

5. Keep related words together. In well-constructed sentences, related words go together—especially subject and verb, verb and object. See PHRASING.

6. Break up the text with headings. Headings and subheadings make the structure of a document overt, allowing readers to find their way around the document quickly and easily. See DOCUMENT DESIGN.

7. Use parallel structures for enumerations. See PARALLELISM, ENUMERATIONS & DOCUMENT DESIGN (F), (G).

8. Avoid excessive cross-references. The writer who becomes zealous about cross-referencing usually creates linguistic mazes. The problem is that readers are asked to hold in mind the contents of several different provisions simultaneously. For a choice example, see WOOLLINESS.

9. Avoid overdefining. Although definitions are sometimes helpful, legal drafters grossly overuse them. Whenever you send the reader elsewhere in a legal document to understand what you're saying in a given provision, you impede understanding. And many drafters "pass the buck" in this way repeatedly for a single term, by using cross-references in definitions. See—if you like, but this is not intended as a pass-the-buck cross-reference—DEFINITIONS (A).

10. Use recitals and purpose clauses. In contracts, recitals help the reader understand what the drafter hopes to accomplish; in legislation, purpose clauses serve this function. Except in the simplest drafting projects—such as straightforward buy–sell agreements—you should generally presume that these orienting devices are necessary. And even simple documents should have descriptive titles (not *Agreement*, but *Agreement Restricting Stock Transfers*).

Finally, to gauge how effectively the principles are carried out, plain-language advocates recommend that certain documents be tested on typical readers. For documents that go out by the thousands and hundreds of thousands (like government forms) and for major

---

An asterisk (✳) precedes words and phrases that are invariably inferior forms.

legislation, time spent in testing at the front end can save enormous amounts of time and money in the long run.

E. Efforts to Use Plain Language. Since the 1970s, most American states have passed some type of plain-language legislation, and several federal statutes exist as well. *See* Joseph Kimble, *Plain English: A Charter for Clear Writing*, 9 Thomas M. Cooley L. Rev. 1, 31–35 (1992). Statutes of this type have not caused the problems that skeptics once warned of—unworkable standards, fatal ambiguities, decline in the quality of drafting. In fact, an empirical study would probably confirm precisely the opposite effects.

In addition to plain-language legislation, lawyers in many English-speaking jurisdictions have formed commissions and committees to promote plain language. In the U.S., for example, the State Bar of Michigan formed such a committee in 1979 and the State Bar of Texas in 1990; other state bar associations have begun to follow suit. In Australia, the Centre for Plain Legal Language has done much to promote the movement. In British Columbia, the Plain Language Institute thrived for a time and produced much good literature before being disbanded in 1993 for lack of governmental funding; other Canadian groups soon took up the slack. In England, the Plain English Campaign—a grassroots consumer organization—has met with considerable success. England is also the home of Clarity, an international organization that studies and promotes plain language in law. All these efforts have depended primarily on the determination of specific individuals.

Their opponents—the naysayers—have an increasingly difficult time as more and more excellent work is published in the field of plain language. For example, in 1994 Martin Cutts, an English writing consultant, redesigned and rewrote an act of Parliament: the Timeshare Act 1992. In doing so, he convincingly showed what immense improvements are possible in legislative drafting if only the official drafters approached their task with a greater command of plain-language principles. *See* Martin Cutts, *Lucid Law* (1994). The enduring problem—here as elsewhere—is whether reform can take place while the old guard remains.

In some places, though, official and semi-official bodies are changing standard forms. For example, the English Law Society's 1990 and 1992 editions of the Standard Conditions of Sale use "language that is as direct as the subject-matter allows, sentences that are relatively short and jargon-free, and a layout that is clear." Peter Butt, *Plain Language and Conveyancing*, Conv. & Prop. Law., July–Aug. 1993, at 256, 258. Similarly, in 1992 the Law Society of New South Wales issued a "plainer" form of contract for the sale of land—"plainer" than its predecessor, though not yet quite "plain." *Id.* In the early 1990s, the Real Estate Forms Committee of the State Bar of Texas issued plain-language forms for deeds, deeds of trust, leases, and other forms. These are but a few examples.

For a challenging but partly tongue-in-cheek approach to a legislative mandate for plain language,

see David C. Elliott, *A Model Plain-Language Act*, 3 Scribes J. Legal Writing 51 (1992).

F. The Trouble with the Word *plain*. It is unfortunate that the SET PHRASES *plain language* and *plain English* contain the word *plain*. For that word, to many speakers of English, suggests the idea of "drab and ugly." But plain language is not drab: it is powerful and often beautiful. It is the language of the King James Version of the Bible, and it has a long literary tradition in the so-called Attic style of writing. *See* Garner, *The Elements of Legal Style* 5 (2d ed. 2002).

Despite the unfortunate associations that the word *plain* carries, it has become established and is without a serious competitor. As a result, plain-language advocates must continually explain what they mean by "plain" language—or else critics and doubters will misunderstand it.

G. Prospects. We can point to significant progress in this area, but it remains sporadic. In the end, E.B. White may have been prescient: "I honestly worry about lawyers. They never write plain English themselves, and when you give them a bit of plain English to read, they say, 'Don't worry, it doesn't mean anything.'" E.B. White (as quoted in Thomas L. Shaffer, *The Planning and Drafting of Wills and Trusts* 149 (2d ed. 1979)).

There are those who say that "lawyers spend half their time trying to understand what other lawyers wrote; and the other half of their days writing things that other lawyers spend half their time trying to understand." Samuel A. Goldberg, "Hints on Draftsmanship," in *Drafting Contracts and Commercial Instruments* 7, 10 (Research & Documentation Corp. ed., 1971). That cynical view holds true only when poor writing becomes pervasive; and alas, there is some truth in it today.

Beyond the mere inconveniences of obscurity, however, people actually suffer from it. Not least among the sufferers are judges who must try to make sense out of nonsense. But the vexation that judges feel pales in comparison with the economic and emotional suffering that clients often experience.

It is hardly an overstatement to say that plain-language reform is among the most important issues confronting the legal profession. And until this reform occurs, the profession will continue to have a badly tarnished image—no matter how many other altruistic endeavors it carries out. If we want the respect of the public, we must learn to communicate simply and directly.

H. A Plain-Language Library. Those wishing to consult further sources in the field may find helpful the books listed in the Select Bibliography under "Plain English" (see p. 962).

plainly. See **clearly** & **obviously.**

plaint = a written statement of a cause of action, used to bring suit in a county court in England. Following is a 19th-century example of this term as still used in England: "The defendant refused to deliver them up, and the plaintiff consequently brought a *plaint . . .* to recover the notes." *Bridges v. Hawkesworth*, [1851] 21 L.J.Q.B. 75, 76.

The term is used in AmE only in nonlegal senses— e.g.: "Socrates repeatedly follows an admission that poets can speak truth with the *plaint* that they cannot explain the truth they speak." Kenji Yoshino, *The City and the Poet*, 114 Yale L.J. 1835, 1845 (2005).

plaintiff; complainant; demandant; objectant; exceptor. *Plaintiff* = the party who brings suit in a court of law. This party may have other special names, depending on the jurisdiction and the cause of action asserted. (See, e.g., **pursuer.**) *Complainant* is used in even more general senses of any party who brings a complaint. *Demandant* = one who makes a demand or claim, usu. a creditor.

The remaining terms are quite distinct from the others. *Objectant* = one who objects. *Exceptor* = one who objects or takes exception. See **exceptor** & **objectant.**

plaintiff, defendant; petitioner, respondent; appellant, appellee. A. Capitalizing. The American lawyer's conventions are generally as follows. To refer to a party in the present case, write: "Wisely, *Plaintiff* has chosen . . . ." It is generally better, of course, to use the party's real name. (See PARTY APPELLATIONS.) To refer to a party in some other (usually reported) case, write: "In *Jones v. Smith*, the *plaintiff* . . . ."

B. Articles before. It is often useful in legal writing to omit *the*, *a*, or *an* before *Plaintiff* and other designations of parties in the present dispute, for cutting even such slight words can lead to leaner, more readable sentences.

Still, omission of articles can cause problems where two party denominations are proximate: "[The] motion preserves no error because it refers to only one *plaintiff* and because it fails to specify which *plaintiff defendant* contends failed to prove a prima facie case." *Elliott v. Group Med. & Surgical Serv.*, 714 F.2d 556, 561 (5th Cir. 1983). Inserting *the* between *plaintiff* and *defendant* removes the impediment to reading. See ARTICLES (A).

C. Relative Pronouns with. Though personal relative pronouns (i.e., *who* and *whom*) are normally used with these denominations, when *plaintiff*, etc., is a company, corporation, or entity other than an individual or a set of easily identifiable individuals, then *which* is correct in nonrestrictive clauses. The restrictive relative pronoun *that*, of course, may be used with either persons or companies. See PARTY APPELLATIONS & **that & which.**

plaintiff in error; defendant in error. In some jurisdictions, the first is an equivalent of *appellant* or *petitioner*, the latter an equivalent of *appellee* or *respondent*, when the appeal is by writ of error. E.g.: "After the documents were sent, the *plaintiff in error* filed an assignment of errors, which served the same purpose as a complaint in the trial court, and the *defendant in error* filed a plea in response." Clark A.

Donat, *Every Attorney Deserves a Second Chance*, 62 Ark. L. Rev. 831, 838 (2009). See **error (A).**

plaintiff's lawyer; plaintiffs' lawyer; plaintiff lawyer. For one who regularly represents plaintiffs—in the U.S., usually on contingent fees—the predominant form is *plaintiff's lawyer*. But *plaintiffs' lawyer* might be better for this purpose, since the singular possessive (*plaintiff's lawyer*) is often used in reference merely to one who represents a plaintiff in a particular action.

Plaintiff lawyer misleadingly suggests one who is a party to a lawsuit, as opposed to the one handling the lawsuit. E.g.: "Sanctions were sought in some 700 federal cases and granted in just over half. It's usually the *plaintiff lawyer* [read *plaintiff's lawyer*] who's fined." L. Gordon Crovitz, *Lawyers Make Frivolous Arguments at Their Own Risk*, Wall St. J., 20 June 1990, at A17.

plaintive was for centuries used interchangeably with *plaintiff* in legal prose. But now the sense "being or pertaining to the plaintiff in a suit" (*OED*) is an ARCHAISM, probably obsolete. The sole current meaning of *plaintive* is as an adjective: "sorrowful; mournful."

playwright, n.; playwriting. Sometimes the two are confused. E.g.: "Poets and *playwrites* [read *playwrights*] often use different meter and rhyme schemes when dealing with different characters." Paul T. Wangerin, *Skills Training in "Legal Analysis"*, 40 U. Miami L. Rev. 409, 438 (1986). For a similar error, see *****copywrite.**

plea; pleading, n. A *plea* is now given only in criminal cases, although at common law a defendant's answer to the plaintiff's complaint was termed a *plea*. In U.S. federal courts today, the only criminal pleas are *guilty*, *not guilty*, and *nolo contendere*. A *pleading* is the complaint or answer in a civil case, or the criminal indictment and the answer in a criminal case.

plea bargain, n.; plea-bargain, vb. As a noun, the phrase means "an agreement between the prosecution and the defense in a criminal case to allow the defendant to plead guilty or testify against others in return for a reduced charge or some other prosecutorial concession." The phrase dates only from the 1960s—e.g.: "This is not the usual case of an asserted *plea bargain*." *People v. Bannan*, 110 N.W.2d 673, 675 (Mich. 1961). The noun phrase *plea bargaining* is slightly older, dating from the 1950s.

As an intransitive verb, *plea-bargain* (hyphenated) means "to make a plea bargain."

plead. A. Sense. *Plead* does not ordinarily mean, as some nonlawyers think, "to argue a case in court." Eric Partridge amended his note on *lawyer* in *Usage and Abuse* by quoting a British lawyer who corrected Partridge's "layman's misusages" as follows: "A barrister does not '*plead*' in Court. He argues a case in Court, or—colloquially—*does* a case in Court. Pleadings are the written documents preparatory to a case, e.g., Statement of Claim, Defence in a civil action,

Petition or Answer in divorce." *Usage and Abusage* 379 (1973). See **pleaded.**

B. Loose Usage with Objective Complement. In AmE, criminal lawyers increasingly say that they will *plead a client guilty*—e.g.:

- "I had made a deal with the District Attorney's office to *plead him guilty* for four years in the State penitentiary for all cases." Aubrey Holmes, *The Wake of a Lawyer* 43 (1960).
- "Defendant contends, therefore, that in so doing defense counsel effectively *pleaded defendant guilty* to first-degree murder." *People v. Clark*, 565 N.E.2d 1373, 1380 (Ill. App. Ct. 1991).

Instead of this slipshod use of *plead*, the better phrasing in the sentences above would have been *have my client plead guilty* and *pleaded guilty on defendant's behalf.*

pleaded; *pled; plead. Traditionally speaking, *pleaded* is the best past-tense and past-participial form. Commentators on usage have long said so, pouring drops of vitriol onto *has pled and *has plead*—e.g.:

- "Say, 'He *pleaded* guilty' (not '*pled*' or '*plead*')." Sherwin Cody, *Dictionary of Errors* 118 (1905).
- "Careful speakers use *pleaded.*" Frank H. Vizetelly, *A Desk-Book of Errors in English* 167 (1906).
- "The past tense is *pleaded*. The use of *pled* or *plead* is colloquial." C.O. Sylvester Mawson, *Style-Book for Writers and Editors* 178 (1926).
- "These past tense forms [*plead* and *pled*] are by some authorities condemned as entirely incorrect, and by others classified as colloquial. The correct past tense of *plead* is *pleaded*, as 'He *pleaded* illness as an excuse.'" Maurice H. Weseen, *Crowell's Dictionary of English Grammar and Handbook of American Usage* 470 (1928).
- "The surely correct forms of the verb *to plead* in the past tense and past participle are *pleaded*, *has pleaded*. Colloquially, *plead* and *pled* are used as the past tense." Clarence Stratton, *Handbook of English* 245 (1940).
- "*Pleaded* is the approved past tense of *plead*. тнus: *He pleaded* (not '*pled*' or '*plead*') *not guilty*." Alexander M. Witherspoon, *Common Errors in English and How to Avoid Them* 135 (1943).

The problem with these strong pronouncements, of course, is that *pled and *plead* have gained some standing in AmE, as the Evanses noted in mid-century: "In the United States *pleaded* and *pled* are both acceptable for the past tense and for the participle. In Great Britain only the form *pleaded* is used and *pled* is considered an Americanism." Bergen Evans & Cornelia Evans, *A Dictionary of Contemporary American Usage* 372 (1957). The variant forms might not be the best usage, but neither can they be condemned as horrible.

Nevertheless, *pleaded* is the predominant form in both AmE and BrE—e.g.:

- "Elsewhere, it is generally required that the mitigating circumstances be *pleaded.*" Edwin E. Bryant, *The Law of Pleading Under the Codes of Civil Procedure* 248 (1899).
- "Contentions of law do not have to be *pleaded.*" Patrick Devlin, *The Judge* 56 (1979).
- "No case was to be *pleaded* at Superior Court for less than a three pound fee." Lawrence M. Friedman, *A History of American Law* 100–01 (2d ed. 1985).

- "Harding *pleaded* guilty to a conspiracy charge in the attack on Olympic silver medalist Nancy Kerrigan and resigned from the U.S. Figure Skating Association." Bob Baum, *Harding Pleads Guilty*, San Diego Union-Tribune, 17 Mar. 1994, at A1.

The spelling *plead* as a past tense (for *pled) appeared in the 18th century, apparently on the analogy of *read > read*. (Cf. **lead.**) E.g.: "The parties dispute whether the causes of action apparently *plead* [read *pleaded*] by Plaintiff are cognizable under California and Ohio law." *Cheers Sports Bar & Grill v. DIRECTV, Inc.*, 563 F.Supp.2d 812, 817 (N.D. Ohio 2008). One problem with this form is that many readers will suffer a MISCUE by seeing *plead* at first as a present-tense verb.

The other variant form, *pled, dates from the 16th century. It is nearly obsolete in BrE except as a dialectal word. Nor is it considered quite standard in AmE, although it is a common variant in legal usage—e.g.:

- "In the second count of their petition, they *pled* [read *pleaded*] their title specially." *Jensen v. Wilkinson*, 133 S.W.2d 982, 983 (Tex. Civ. App.—Galveston 1939).
- "Defendant *pled* [read *pleaded*] guilty to the lesser offense." *State v. Carlberg*, 375 N.W.2d 275, 277 (Iowa Ct. App. 1985).

pleader; *pleador. Only the first is correct.

plead guilty to is sometimes misrendered *plead guilty of*, which is really just a confusion of two legal idioms: one pleads *to* a charge but is guilty *of* a crime. E.g.: "Mr. Krikava's wife, Carol, and son, Kevin, pleaded guilty *of* [read *to*] perjury and received only probation, since the guidelines allow leniency for defendants who plead guilty." Dirk Johnson, *A Farmer, 70, Saw No Choice; Nor Did the Sentencing Judge*, N.Y. Times, 20 July 1994, at A1, A9.

pleading. A. Senses. *Pleading* = (1) the art of preparing formal written statements in lawsuits; (2) a document containing the written allegations of fact that each party is required to communicate to the opponent before trial, so that each will know what contentions must be met by the evidence; or (3) oral advocacy of a case in court. Sense 3 is found more frequently in nonlawyers' writing than in lawyers'—unless one goes back to the 14th century, when pleadings were oral.

B. And *court paper*. In sense 2, *pleading* should be distinguished from *court paper*, which is a broader term. Motions, briefs, and affidavits are *court papers*, not *pleadings*. Examples of pleadings are complaints, petitions, counterclaims, and answers. A late-19th-century writer's explanation shows that this usage is time-honored: "*Pleadings* are the formal allegations of the parties of their respective claims and defences." Edwin E. Bryant, *The Law of Pleading Under the Codes of Civil Procedure* 178 (1899).

C. And *prayer*. The *pleading* is the document in which a party in a legal action sets out the cause of action or defense. A *pleading* consists of (1) a commencement; (2) a body (or charging part); (3) a *prayer*, or demand for judgment; (4) a signature; and, when required, (5) a verification. The *prayer*, which usually appears at the end of the pleading, is the request for relief from the court. E.g.: "The court merely held that if there is a requirement that the complainant specifically plead for prejudgment interest, a *prayer* for general relief will not satisfy that requirement if the *pleadings* also contain a specific *prayer* for a different kind of interest." *Consolidated Cigar Co. v. Texas Commerce Bank*, 749 F.2d 1169, 1174–75 (5th Cir. 1985).

A typical *prayer* reads: "Wherefore, defendant prays that plaintiff take nothing in this action (etc.)." A plain-language equivalent might read: "For these reasons, defendant requests that the court enter judgment that the plaintiff take nothing (etc.)." See **prayer.**

D. And *plea.* See **plea.**

E. **Pleadings in Various Forums.** See COMMON-LAW PLEADINGS, EQUITY PLEADINGS & WORLD COURT PLEADINGS.

pleading, inconsistent. See **Codd's Puzzle.**

plead innocent. It used to be that only journalists made the mistake of writing *plead innocent* rather than *plead not guilty*, but now this phrase has made it even into judges' writing: lawyers should avoid the phrase, as there is no such thing as a plea of innocent. Journalists, on the other hand, avoid *not guilty* merely because the word *not* might get accidentally dropped or changed to *now*. See **not (c).**

***pleador.** See **pleader.**

plea in abatement; plea of abatement. In jurisdictions in which the plea is used, *plea in abatement* is the usual form.

***please find enclosed,** like its inverted sibling, **enclosed please find*,** is an old-fashioned, stilted phrase that lawyers are fond of using in letters. Better, more modern substitutes include *I am sending with this letter, I have enclosed, I am enclosing,* and *Enclosed are (or is).* See ***enclosed please find.**

plebiscite. See **mandate (B).**

***pled.** See **pleaded.**

pledge, n.; **earnest; token; pawn; bail; collateral.** These terms all denote something given and to be held as a guarantee of the satisfaction of some agreed-upon condition. *Pledge* refers to anything, including one's word, given to another as security for the payment of a debt or the performance of some other obligation. *Earnest* originally referred to something of value given by a buyer to a seller to make a bargain binding, but today it generally refers to something that serves as a promise of further performance to come—especially part of a price paid in advance as evidence that a bargain has been struck and negotiations ended. (See **earnest.**) *Token* in this sense refers to whatever is given to guarantee the genuineness of a thing or the good faith of a person. *Pawn* refers to an object of some value held for a time and liable to redemption by the owner: the item is typically deposited with a pawnbroker as security for the money loaned on it. *Bail* in this sense refers to a security, such as cash or a bond, for the release of a prisoner who must appear in court at a future time. *Collateral* refers to property that is pledged as security against a debt.

pledge, vb. See **promise,** vb.

pledgeable. So spelled.

pledgee = (1) one with whom a pledge or pawn is deposited; or (2) a person who takes a pledge (esp. an American college student who undertakes to enroll in a fraternity or sorority). Sense 1 makes some sense, but sense 2 is apt to bother careful readers (the college student really being a *pledger,* not a *pledgee*). See -EE (A).

pledger; pledgor. The most logical spelling is *pledger,* not *pledgor* or ***pledgeor.** Even so, *pledgor* is more than 50 times as common as *pledger* in American judicial opinions, largely because it is the regular correlative of *pledgee.* See MUTE E.

plenary is a FORMAL WORD for *full, complete,* or *entire.* E.g.: "By exercising its discretion to deny the motion in such a situation, a district court would permit development of a fuller record and would save time if disposition of the motion would require the same time and effort as a *plenary trial.*" Bradley Scott Shannon, *Should Summary Judgment Be Granted?*, 58 Am. U. L. Rev. 85, 109–10 (2008). Here *full trial* would be better.

plenitude. So spelled. A common misspelling is ***plentitude**—e.g.: "The rule is a salutary one in view of the different jurisdictions of the state courts and of this court. It leaves in both the full *plentitude* [read *plenitude*] of their powers." *Adams v. Russell*, 229 U.S. 353, 361 (1913) (per McKenna, J.).

plentiful; *plenteous. No distinction in meaning being possible, writers should prefer the prevalent modern form, *plentiful.* ***Plenteous** is archaic and poetic—in modern prose, a NEEDLESS VARIANT.

***plentitude.** See **plenitude.**

PLEONASM. See VERBOSITY.

plunder. See **spoils.**

plurality opinion = an appellate opinion without enough judges' votes to constitute a majority, but having received the greatest number of votes of any of the opinions filed. E.g.: "Three justices, in the *plurality opinion* of Justice Rehnquist, took the position that § 16 of the Clayton Act does not meet the second half of the *Mitchum* test." Charles Alan Wright, *The Law of Federal Courts* 302 (5th ed. 1994). The term dates from about 1960, when Justice Whittaker used it in *U.S. v.*

Kaiser, 363 U.S. 299, 328 n.2 (1960) (Whittaker, J., dissenting). See **majority** (A).

PLURALS. A. Borrowed Words. Words transported into the English language from other languages, especially Greek and Latin, present some of the most troublesome aspects of English plurals. At a certain point borrowed words become thoroughly anglicized and take English plurals. But while words of Latin and Greek origin are still new and only questionably naturalized, writers who see the words as primarily foreignisms use the native-language plurals. Then again, with certain words, the foreign plurals become so well established that anglicization never takes place.

So many variations on this theme have occurred that it is impossible to make valid generalizations. *Minimum* makes *minima* but *premium* makes *premiums*; *pudendum* makes *pudenda* but *memorandum* makes either -*dums* or -*da*; *colloquium* generally makes -*quia* in BrE, -*quiums* preferably in AmE. The only reliable guide is a certain knowledge of specific words, or habitual reference to a usage guide.

In words with a choice of endings, one English and the other foreign, we should generally prefer the English plural. It is an affectation for college professors to insist on using *syllabi* rather than *syllabuses*. The fear of being wrong or sounding unacademic even leads some of them to use forms like *auditoria* and *stadia*.

H.W. Fowler called the benighted stab at correctness "out of the frying pan into the fire." Many writers who try to be sophisticated in their use of language are susceptible to writing, e.g., **ignorami* and **octopi*, unaware that neither is a Latin noun that, when inflected as a plural, becomes -*i*. The proper plural of the Greek word *octopus* is *octopodes*; the proper English plural is *octopuses*. *Ignoramus* makes only *ignoramuses*, for in Latin the word is a verb, not a noun. For several similar examples, see HYPERCORRECTION (A).

French words also present problems. *Fait accompli* becomes *faits accomplis* and *force majeure* becomes *forces majeures*. But then we have the LAW FRENCH words such as *feme sole*, which becomes *femes sole*, and *feme covert* (or *femme couverte*), which as a plural becomes *femes covert* (or *femmes couvertes*). The best policy is to make a habit of consulting a good dictionary, and to use it discriminatingly.

B. Mass (Noncount) Nouns. A recent trend in the language is to make plurals for mass nouns—general and abstract nouns that cannot be broken down into discrete units, and that therefore should not have plural forms. One example of this phenomenon is the psychologists' and sociologists' term *behaviors*, as if the ways in which one behaves are readily categorizable and therefore countable. Granted, one can have good or bad behavior, but not, properly, *a* good behavior or *a* bad behavior. Following are examples of other words infected by the contagion.

1. *Coverages.* "The court cited approvingly an earlier holding that an insurance agent's responsibility to advise clients of necessary and available *coverages* is a question of breach rather than duty." Shane Ham, *Assignability of Professional Negligence Claims Against Insurance Agents*, 50 Ariz. L. Rev. 647, 655–56 (2008).

2. *Discriminations.* "Class legislation helped to strike down at least some *discriminations* against minorities, but it also helped strike down laws that came to be associated with majorities." V.F. Nourse & Sarah A. Maguire, *The Lost History of Governance & Equal Protection*, 58 Duke L.J. 955, 996 (2009).

3. *Inactions.* "If I live with a sense of responsibility for the shape of the world, then the avoidable suffering of others must always show itself as one of the consequences of my actions and *inactions*." Louis E. Wolcher, *The End of Technology*, 79 Wash. L. Rev. 331, 384 (2004).

4. *Languages.* "In China's case, when the economic reality demands it in the long run, the provisions might be interpreted and tailored further to differentiate the two types of relationships in enforcement because the statutory *languages* are created to be open-ended." Youngjin Jung & Qian Hao, *The New Economic Constitution in China*, 24 Nw. J. Int'l L. & Bus. 107, 142 (2003).

5. *Litigations* and *attentions.* "Most writers largely ignore the problems of institutional division of labor at work in criminal law and focus their *attentions* almost exclusively on the merits of that conduct and perhaps on the legal role of the actor." Malcolm Thorburn, *Justifications, Powers, and Authority*, 117 Yale L.J. 1070, 1075 (2008).

"A sprawling, hit-or-miss, costly, and confusing series of civil *litigations* across many states is an absurd way to control a vital national and international form of communication." *Ramirez v. Dollar Phone Corp.*, 668 F.Supp.2d 448, 465 (E.D.N.Y. 2009).

6. *Managements.* "Those investment decisions are typically based, in some measure, on descriptions of the financial positions of competing firms provided by the firms' *managements*." David B. Kahn & Gary S. Lawson, *Who's the Boss?*, 53 Emory L.J. 391, 392 (2004).

7. *Outputs.* "One might conclude that there was too much product differentiation and too much of collateral *outputs* such as advertising." Herbert Hovenkamp, *United States Competition Policy in Crisis: 1890–1955*, 94 Minn. L. Rev. 311, 348 (2009).

8. *Participations.* Sometimes this phenomenon occurs through attributive uses, as where *participation* is substituted for *unit of participation*: "In another 27%, the target either has been sold or gone bankrupt, effectively terminating all-equity *participations*." William W. Bratton, *Hedge Funds and Governance Targets*, 95 Geo. L.J. 1375, 1141 (2007). The same principle is at work when *proofs* is substituted for *elements of proofs*.

C. Words Ending in -*o*. Fowler laid down a number of guiding principles for words ending in -*o*: first, monosyllables and words used as freely in the plural as in the singular usually have *-oes* (*embargoes*, *heroes*, *noes*, *potatoes*, *vetoes*); second, alien-looking words, proper names, words that are seldom used as plurals, words in which *-o-* is preceded by a vowel, and shortened words (e.g., *photo*) do not take the *-e-* (*embryos*, *hippos*, *kilos*, *ratios*). Good dictionaries guide users to the preferred spellings.

D. Nouns Formed from Past-Participial Adjectives. These are usually awkward and alien-looking to nonlawyers. But they are commonplace in legal writing—e.g.: "The court reviewed the subject policy and concluded that the members were individual *insureds* covered by the policy." Michael A. Dorelli, *Recent Developments in Indiana Business and Contract Law*, 42 Ind. L. Rev. 847, 875 (2009). See **condemned, deceased** & **insured.** See also POSSESSIVES (F).

E. Compound Nouns. Plurals of compound nouns made up of a noun and a POSTPOSITIVE ADJECTIVE are formed by adding *-s* to the noun: *courts martial, heirs presumptive.* The British and Americans differ on the method of pluralizing *attorney general.* Those words in which the noun is now disguised add *-s* at the end of the word, as with all compounds ending in *-ful*: *lungfuls, spoonfuls, handfuls.*

F. Proper Names. Although few books on grammar mention the point, proper names often cause problems when writers try to make them plural. The rule is simple: most take a simple *-s*, while those ending in *s*, *x*, or *z*, or in a sibilant *ch* or *sh*, take *-es*. Hence:

Singular Form	Plural Form
Adam	Adams
Adams	Adamses
Bush	Bushes
Church	Churches
Cox	Coxes
Flowers	Flowerses
Jones	Joneses
Levy	Levys
Lipschutz	Lipschutzes
Mary	Marys
Rabiej	Rabiejs
Shapiro	Shapiros
Sinz	Sinzes
Thomas	Thomases

Plurals like these are often erroneously formed by calling (say) Mr. and Mrs. Sinz either *the Sinz* or *the Sinz'*. The latter form, with the apostrophe, merely results from confusion with possessives—and even *the Sinz'* is not a good possessive (the correct forms being *Sinz's* in the singular and *Sinzes'* in the plural).

G. Parenthetical Plurals. Competent drafters should avoid creating parenthetical plurals and think of better ways to express a thought. A parenthetical plural is formed when an "(s)" is tacked onto a singular noun. The purpose is to indicate that the statement applies to one or more members of the category. See Amy Einsohn, *The Copyeditor's Handbook* 116 (2d ed. 2005).

But the practice produces serious drafting problems. Does such a noun take a singular or plural verb? If a pronoun refers to the parenthetical plural, should it be singular or plural? And what about nouns that don't take a simple *-s* (e.g., *party*)? Using *(s)* as a shortcut produces ungainly, unsightly sentences—e.g.:

- "Plaintiff says that he had at least one year after disability of the minor *beneficiary(s)* to bring the suit, which would extend *their* right to bring such action beyond the six-year deadline of May 26, 1963." *Hemingway v. Shull*, 286 F.Supp. 243, 245 (D.S.C. 1968). A suggested revision: *one year after disability of a minor beneficiary to bring the suit, which would extend the beneficiary's right . . . .*
- "The state alleged defendant's intent in entering the schools was to commit a felony sexual offense against *a student(s)*." *State v. Schleve*, 775 So.2d 1187, 1193 (La. Ct. App. 2000). The article *a* is necessarily singular. A suggested revision: *one or more students.*
- "[T]he Court shall issue an Order directing specific performance of the Agreement and, if the *Defendant(s) fail(s)* to comply with this Order, the Court shall, if appropriate under applicable legal principles, issue an Order of contempt." *Arevalo v. Colorado Dep't of Human Servs.*, 72 P.3d 436, 438 (Colo. Ct. App. 2003) (quoting a settlement agreement). A suggested revision: *if the defendant fails . . . .*

ply (= layer; fold) forms the plural *plies*. *Plys* is incorrect—e.g.: "These [characteristics] included the tire's size, its maximum inflation pressure, its maximum load, the number of *plys* [read *plies*]." Jerry L. Mashaw & David L. Harfst, *Regulation and Legal Culture: The Case of Motor Vehicle Safety*, 4 Yale J. on Reg. 257, 287 n.70 (1987).

p.m. See **a.m.**

Poe, Peter. See **Doe, John.**

poetic justice, nowadays a CLICHÉ, refers to the system exemplified in older fiction in which villains always receive condign punishments, and heroes their fitting rewards.

point, in. See **in point** & **off point.**

point, off. See **off point.**

point, on. See **in point** & **off point.**

point in time, at this. See **at the present time.**

point of fact. See **in point of fact.**

point of law. This phrase refers to a discrete proposition or issue of law arising from the facts established in a given case. It is often shortened to the one word *point.*

point of view. See **viewpoint.**

point out; point to; point up. *Point out* = (1) to observe; or (2) to call to others' attention. *Point to* = to direct attention to (as an answer or solution). *Point up* = to illustrate. *Point up* is perhaps comparatively more frequent in legal than in nonlegal writing. E.g.: "For

Mr. Lucas, the case *points up* a key pitfall of seeking capital punishment." Dan R. Barber, *Law Could Curb Texas Executions*, Dallas Morning News, 18 Apr. 1993, at 35A.

police, though a COLLECTIVE NOUN, is generally construed as a plural both in AmE and in BrE.

policy; polity. *Policy*, by far the more common of these words, means "a concerted course of action followed to achieve certain ends; a plan." It is more restricted in sense than *polity*, which means (1) "the principle upon which a government is based"; or (2) "the total governmental organization as based on its goals and policies." Sense 2 is more usual—e.g.:

- "But only together did they form the achievement that enabled the peaceful coexistence of persons of different beliefs in one *polity* and the recognition of the diversity as legitimate." Dieter Grimm, *Conflicts Between General Laws and Religious Norms*, 30 Cardozo L. Rev. 2369, 2371–72 (2009).
- "Though they are not elaborated in detail in most formal constitutions, in a very real sense these rules constitute the *polity*." Tom Ginsburg & Zachary Elkins, *Ancillary Powers of Constitutional Courts*, 87 Tex. L. Rev. 1431, 1448 (2009).

policyholder; *policyowner. *Policyholder* is preferably spelled as one word. **Policyowner* is a NEEDLESS VARIANT.

policy-making should be hyphenated. Cf. **decision-making.**

***policyowner.** See **policyholder.**

politic, adj.; **political.** The adverbial forms are *politicly* (= in a politic manner; shrewdly; prudently) and *politically* (= in a political or partisan way or manner).

***politicalize.** See **politick** (2d par.).

political rights. See **civil rights.**

politick, vb.; **politicize.** *Politick*, a BACK-FORMATION from *politics*, at one time was not recognized as an acceptable word. Today it is more common in AmE than in BrE, and means "to engage in partisan political activities."

Politicize has a similar sense "to act the politician," but also the broader sense "to render political" <politicizing judicial races>. **Politicalize* is a NEEDLESS VARIANT.

politics may be either singular or plural. Today it is more commonly singular than plural <politics is dirty business>, although formerly the opposite was true.

polity. See **policy.**

pollicitation is an antique civilian LEGALISM meaning "an offer not yet formally accepted, and therefore usu. revocable." E.g.:

- "By a *promise* we mean accepted offer as opposed to an offer of a promise, or, as Austin called it, a *pollicitation*." William R. Anson, *Principles of the Law of Contract* 6 (Arthur L. Corbin ed., 3d Am. ed. 1919).

- "Conventional obligations were subdivided into promise, *pollicitation* or offer, paction and contract." William W. McBryde, *The Law of Contract in Scotland* 2 (1987).

polygamy; polyandry; polygyny. The first is the broadest term, referring to a person's being simultaneously married to more than one spouse. *Polyandry* is the practice of having more than one husband; *polygyny* is the practice of having more than one wife. See **bigamy.**

pony case. See **whitehorse case.**

Ponzi scheme = a fraudulent investment scheme in which money placed by later investors pays artificially high dividends to the original investors, thereby attracting even larger investments. The scheme takes its name from Charles Ponzi, who in the late 1920s was convicted and punished for fraudulent schemes he conducted in Boston. E.g.:

- "This was a proposal to furnish services on a commercial basis, and since we have always refused to distinguish for First Amendment purposes on the basis of content, it is no different from an advertisement for a bucket shop operation or a *Ponzi scheme* which has its headquarters in New York." *Bigelow v. Virginia*, 421 U.S. 809, 831 (1975) (Rehnquist, J., dissenting).
- "The scheme was kept afloat by paying interest on existing certificates with the proceeds of new certificate sales. . . . It was . . . a massive *Ponzi scheme*." Tim O'Brien, *Some Firms Never Learn*, Am. Law., Oct. 1989, at 63, 64.

pooling; unitization. See **communitize (A).**

POPULARIZED LEGAL TECHNICALITIES. H.W. Fowler observed that when technical terms pass into everyday speech and writing, two things often occur. First, the popular use more often than not misrepresents the original meaning; second, free indulgence in terms of this sort results in a tawdry style. These observations are no less true with legal technicalities than with those of other kinds.

The prime example is *alibi*, which in law refers to the defense in a criminal case of proving that one was elsewhere when the crime was committed. Nonlawyers snatched up the term and, through misunderstanding perhaps coupled with SLIPSHOD EXTENSION, came to use it as a synonym for *excuse*, especially a lame excuse. Today even lawyers misuse the term in this way. See **alibi (A).**

As the *OED* will confirm, any number of common expressions have their origins in law, such as these:

accountant
benefit of clergy
beyond the pale
case in point
culprit
follow suit
forestall
gist
have no right to
hold in contempt
homage

hue and cry
in his (or her) own right
innuendo
in point
moot point
new lease on life
of course
on point
ordeal
palming off
posse
premises (a place)
read the Riot Act
self-defense
sidebar
signed, sealed, and delivered
special pleading
time is of the essence
vested interest
vouch for
wear and tear

For other, mostly historical examples from the legal lexicon, see the discussions under **alias, compound, gist, ignoramus, hue and cry** & **pale, beyond the.**

populous; populace; populist. *Populous* (= thickly populated) is sometimes confused with *populace* (= residents collectively; the population of a designated place) and *populist* (= of or relating to a movement claiming to represent the whole of the people). All the possible errors are startling ones—e.g.:

- *Populace* for *populous*: "Michigan is a state of nearly 10 million people, the eighth most-*populace* [read -*populous*] state in the nation." Ronald G. Ehrenberg, *What's Happening to Public Higher Education?* 159 (2007).
- *Populous* for *populace*: "It has a disgruntled *populous* [read *populace*], a restless *populous* [read *populace*] that might explode anytime." Charles H. Ferguson, *No End in Sight: Iraq's Descent into Chaos* 500 (2008).
- *Populous* for *populist*: "The advent of the Jacksonian era and its emphasis on democratic *populous* [read *populist*] ideals . . . promoted . . . the notion that . . . judges should be popularly elected." Norman Krivosha, *Acquiring Judges by the Merit Selection Method*, 40 Sw. L.J. (Special Issue), May 1986, at 15, 15.

pore (= to read carefully) should not be confused with *pour*, as it frequently is—e.g.:

- "Appellants' representatives spent about two and one-half years *pouring* [read *poring*] over the books and records of the Cincinnati School System in an effort to find something that was wrong." *Deal v. Cincinnati Bd. of Educ.*, 419 F.2d 1387, 1394 (6th Cir. 1969).
- "Ms. Besso . . . now spends her evenings *pouring* [read *poring*] over brochures from Boston, Boulder, Colo., and Nashville." Sara Rimer, *Fleeing Los Angeles: Quake Is the Last Straw*, N.Y. Times, 18 Feb. 1994, at A1, A10.

This error may well occur because *poring* appears less often in print than in speech.

portend (= to foretell or foreshadow) should not be used as a substitute for *mean*. "This development *portends* [read *means*] hope for those seeking new trials in [shaken baby syndrome] cases." Deborah Tuerkheimer, *The Next Innocence Project*, 87 Wash. U. L. Rev. 1, 55 (2009). The word *portend* necessarily has negative connotations.

portentous (=[1] prophetic; [2] wondrous; [3] solemn; or [4] pompous) is so spelled. But the word is sometimes incorrectly written *portentious or *portentuous—e.g.:

- "The court made a significant observation *portentious* [read *portentous*] of things to come." *O'Brien v. Barnes Bldg. Co.*, 380 N.Y.S.2d 405, 420 (Sup. Ct. 1974).
- "Can anyone imagine . . . a responsible government administrator . . . issuing regulations with as *portentuous* [read *portentous*] [an] effect as here on the same factual certainties that EPA had?" *Ethyl Corp. v. EPA*, 541 F.2d 1, 87 n.81 (D.C. Cir. 1976) (en banc) (Wilkey, J., dissenting).

portion; part. There are connotative differences. *Portion* = share (as of an estate or of food). It is an entity cut or as if cut away from the whole <his portion of the contract> <her portion of the grain>. *Part*, in contrast, merely connotes a constituent part of the whole <part of a house, a country, etc.>.

In a common-law "strict settlement," a *portion* is a lump sum paid in trust to a settlor's children and receivable by them once they reach the age of majority or marry.

PORTMANTEAU WORDS. Lewis Carroll improvised this term to denote words formed by combining the first part of one word with the last part of another. (Linguists use the term *blend* to name an example of this phenomenon.) Thus *insinuendo* was arrived at by combining *insinuation* with *innuendo*; *quasar* is from *quasi* and *stellar*; *aerobicise* derives from *aerobic exercise*. Other recent innovations are *avigation*, from *aviation* and *navigation*, *pictionary* for *picture-filled dictionary*, and *videbut* for *video debut*. Most portmanteau words are NONCE WORDS that do not gain currency; others, like *brunch (breakfast + lunch)*, become standard. Among 20th- and 21st-century portmanteau coinages are these:

Breathalyzer (*breath + analyzer*)
brotel (*brothel + hotel*)
defamacast (*defamatory + broadcast*)
galimony (*gal + alimony*)
gazwelcher (*gazump + welcher*)
litigotiation (*litigation + negotiation*)
palimony (*pal + alimony*)

For other examples, see **avigate, contorts, correctitude, departner, dockominium, gerrymander, greenmail, irregardless, legalitarian** & **sexting.**

posit (= [1] to set in place, fix; or [2] to postulate or lay down as the basis for argument) should not be used for *to present*, as here: "The social group *posited* [read *presented*] below may prove effective in utilizing the Department's willingness to recognize domestic violence as a basis for asylum." Marisa Silenzi Cianciarulo & Claudia David, *Pulling the Trigger*, 59 Am. U. L. Rev. 337, 377 (2009).

positive (= having real existence) is a common meaning of the word in law, but little used in nonlegal writing today. E.g.: "[The] wrong was actuated by a *positive* design to injure the third person to whom the duty was due." *Shields v. Booles*, 38 S.W.2d 677, 680 (Ky. 1931).

positive easement. See **easement (A).**

positive fraud. See **fraud (B).**

positive law. This term is sometimes used with little idea of its precise sense. *Positive law*, referring primarily to statutes and regulations, might be defined as "coercively implemented law laid down within a particular political community by political superiors, to govern members of the community, as distinct from moral law or law existing in an ideal community or in some nonpolitical community."

Associated originally with John Austin's jurisprudence, *positive law* is frequently used by common-law writers. E.g.:

- "*Positive law*, the law applied and enforced in the courts, is the means by which the state [secures people in their natural rights] and is morally binding only so far as it conforms to natural law." Roscoe Pound, *The Development of Constitutional Guarantees of Liberty* 74 (1957).
- "Something like efficient breach theory is part of our *positive law* to this limited extent, but we do not need the irreparable injury rule to implement it." Douglas Laycock, *The Death of the Irreparable Injury Rule* 248–49 (1991).

Unfortunately, as several writers have pointed out, Austin used *positive* differently in different phrases. In *positive law*, it means "set by a political superior"; in *positive morality* (also an Austinian phrase), it means "set by human authority." *See* W.W. Buckland, *Some Reflections on Jurisprudence* 84–85 (1945). Hence Buckland's barb: "One may use a term in any sense one will, provided one uses it always in the same sense. Austin makes considerable use of the right, but is not very careful of the proviso." *Id.* Cf. **natural law (A).**

positivism. H.L.A. Hart once bemoaned that issues can be "clouded by the use of grand but vague words like 'Positivism' and 'Natural Law.' Banners have been waved and parties formed in a loud but often confused debate." H.L.A. Hart, *Law, Liberty, and Morality* 2 (1963). The confusion has not abated, and *positivism* has remained vague—if not downright ambiguous. Whereas general philosophers tend to use the word as shorthand for *logical positivism* (a system involving formal verification of empirical questions), legal philosophers use the word to denote the theory of *positive law* (which postulates that legal rules are valid only because they are enacted by an existing political authority). E.g.:

- "In the literature of legal *positivism* it is of course standard practice to examine at length the relations of law and morals." Lon L. Fuller, *The Morality of Law* 204 (rev. ed. 1969).
- "What, then, is law? The basic answer, which is the essence of legislative *positivism*, is that only statutes enacted by the legislative power could be law." John H. Merryman, *The Civil Law Tradition* 24 (1969).

Cf. **natural law (A).** See **positive law.**

posse, in. See *in esse.*

posse comitatus (lit., "the power of the county") = a body of able-bodied citizens called together by the sheriff to suppress riots, pursue felons, or act in military defense of the country. E.g.: "Horizontal and nationwide class divisions had by 1700 made the *posse comitatus* unusable as a police force, since it included the very classes [that] were prone to riot." Alan Harding, *A Social History of English Law* 270 (1966). The American frontier term *posse* originated as a shortened form of this early common-law term.

possess. The passive construction *to be possessed of* is a LEGALISM for the active verb *to possess.* E.g.: "If A *was possessed of land* [read *possessed land*] under a ten-year lease from B, the owner of the fee, B, and not A, was said to be seised." 1 *American Law of Property* 12–13 (A.J. Casner ed., 1952).

possession. A. Senses. Of this CHAMELEON-HUED WORD, a legal philosopher pessimistically states: "The search for [its] 'proper' meaning . . . is likely to be a fruitless one." G.W. Paton, *A Textbook of Jurisprudence* 553 (4th ed. 1972). Generally speaking, it can have one of four senses: (1) "the fact of having or holding property in one's power"; (2) "the right under which one may exercise power over something at pleasure, to the exclusion of all others"; (3) the detention or use of something with the intention to hold it as one's own; or (4) (esp. in plural), "something that a person owns or controls; property."

The classic senses are 1 and 4; sense 2 is commonly considered a corruption (see (B)); and sense 3 is a predictable extension of meaning similar to the extension that *property* has undergone. See **property (A).**

B. And *ownership.* In sense 2, *possession* becomes confused with *ownership*—and legal writers ought to distinguish the two rigorously. Technically, *ownership* is a legal status: the aggregate of rights that give a person the fullest power to enjoy, destroy, or dispose of a thing; one of these rights is to possess the thing. *Possession*, meanwhile, is purely a matter of fact: a thief may acquire possession of a billfold, but the owner retains the rights of ownership. *Ownership* is always rightful, whereas *possession* might not be so. See **ownership.**

C. And *custody.* *Possession* and *custody* are usefully differentiated in criminal law. A person who takes shoes to a shoe-repair shop may leave the shoes for a few days to have new soles put on; in that event, the shoe-repairer takes *possession.* A shoe-repairer who can fix the shoes on the spot, while the customer waits, takes *custody* only.

Why the distinction? At common law, the cobbler with *possession* of shoes would, upon proof of misappropriation, be guilty of embezzlement. But the cobbler with *custody* would, on the same proof, be guilty of the lesser crime of *larceny*. See **custody.**

For more on these words in a different context, see **possession, custody, or control.**

possession, custody, or control. This phrase commonly appears in discovery requests that require another party to produce documents: one party asks another to produce all documents or things in the other's *possession, custody, or control.* The broadest of the three is generally considered *control*, since a person could turn something over to a fiduciary, thereby relinquishing possession and custody, but retaining control. See **possession (c)** & DOUBLETS, TRIPLETS, AND SYNONYM-STRINGS.

possession is nine-tenths of the law. Originally, in the 17th century—and well into the 19th—the catchphrase was *possession is nine parts* (or *points*) *of the law*, there supposedly being ten parts or points of the law. The substance of the idea was that one's having possession threw onto any other claimant the burden of showing an even better claim to possess. Throughout the 20th century and to the present, the phrase has generally been *nine-tenths* (not *nine parts*) in AmE and BrE alike.

It is a popular phrase, not really a legal one, and legal writers often slight the idea behind it when using it. E.g.:

- "This rule partakes of the old adage that so frequently guides laymen in practical action, that *possession is nine tenths of the law.*" *In re Estate of Barassi*, 71 Cal. Rptr. 249, 254 (Ct. App. 1968).
- "Although we are familiar with the maxim, '*possession is nine-tenths of the law*,' we prefer to apply the remaining one-tenth." *U.S. v. One 1985 Cadillac Seville*, 866 F.2d 1142, 1146 (9th Cir. 1989).

See MAXIMS.

possessions; belongings; effects. These terms all refer to everything that one might own that is not considered real property—or, collectively, all the personal property one owns. *Possessions* denotes the aggregate of things owned, regardless of value <once discovered, all his possessions were meticulously catalogued by the auction house>. *Belongings* suggests items more closely associated with the owner or the owner's sentiments, including not only clothes and toiletries but also family albums, valuable keepsakes, and the like <he lost all his treasured belongings in the fire>. *Effects* is a term intermediate between *possessions* and *belongings*, but closer to the former: it refers primarily to items of movable personal property <all her effects were divided among her surviving family members>.

possessive; possessory; *possessorial. The terms *possessive* and *possessory* have undergone DIFFERENTIATION. *Possessive* = (1) exhibiting possession or the desire

to possess; (2) [in grammar] denoting possession. *Possessory* = (1) of or pertaining to a possessor <possessory rights>; (2) arising from possession <possessory interest>; or (3) that is a possessor <possessory conservator>. *Possessorial is a NEEDLESS VARIANT of *possessory*.

On *possessory* as opposed to *petitory actions*, see **petitory.**

POSSESSIVES. A. Singular Possessives. The best practice, advocated by Strunk and White in *The Elements of Style* and by every other authority of superior standing, is to add -*'s* to all singular possessives, hence *witness's*, *Vitex's*, *Jones's*, *Congress's*, *testatrix's*. So misunderstood is the rule that *witness's* actually gets a "[*sic*]" in *Yeager v. Greene*, 502 A.2d 980, 982 (D.C. 1985).

Legal stylists generally follow the rule just stated—e.g.:

- "Harvard and *Holmes's* executors resolved to allow the collection of *Holmes's* papers, which mainly consisted of letters, to be microfilmed and made available generally to scholars." G. Edward White, *The American Judicial Tradition* 557 (2007).
- "[A jury] may believe part of a particular *witness's* testimony, but disbelieve other parts of that *witness's* testimony." *Smith v. State*, 932 A.2d 773, 776 (Md. Ct. Spec. App. 2007).
- "The will did not provide for her husband nor indicate the *testatrix's* intention not to provide for him." *Hall v. Kalfayan*, 118 Cal. Rptr. 3d 629, 634 (Ct. App. 2010).

There are two exceptions to this rule. The first is that biblical and classical names ending in -*s* take only an apostrophe, hence *Aristophanes' plays*, *Grotius' writings*, *Jesus' suffering*, *Moses' discovery*. Some writers ill-advisedly ignore this exception—e.g.: "From its very beginning, the aim of Justinian's legislation was more ambitious than that of *Theodosius's* [read *Theodosius'*] codification had been." Hans J. Wolff, *Roman Law* 170–71 (1951). The *Chicago Manual of Style* abandoned its support of this exception in its 16th edition (2010) at Rule 7.18, even though "when these forms are spoken, the additional *s* is generally not pronounced." Its examples include *the Ganges's source* and *Xerxes's armies*. That advice seems premature. See **Gaius.**

The second exception is for singular names and terms formed from a plural. Thus *Scribes*, the name of the organization devoted to improving legal writing, makes *Scribes'* as a possessive (*Scribes' president*). The same holds true for *General Motors*: "A merger by General Motors will excite great interest in an enforcement agency simply because of *General Motors's* [read *General Motors'*] size." E.W. Kintner, *An Antitrust Primer* 95 (2d ed. 1973).

B. Plural Possessives. To form the plural possessive, an apostrophe is added to the -*s* of the plural, e.g., *bosses'*, *Joneses'*, *octopuses'*, *Sinzes'*. The one exception is for plurals not ending in -*s*, for which -*'s* is added as in the singular possessive: *brethren's*, *children's*, *men's*, *women's*.

The apostrophe is surprisingly often misplaced or omitted—e.g.: "The so-called 'Married *Womens'*

An asterisk (*) precedes words and phrases that are invariably inferior forms.

[read *Women's*] Acts' permit them to sue and be sued as if they were *femes sole*." Eugene A. Jones, *Manual of Equity Pleading and Practice* 32 n.29 (1916).

C. Units of Time or Value and the Genitive Adjective. The idiomatic possessive should be used with periods of time and statements of worth. *Two weeks' notice* needs the apostrophe because it is merely another rendering of *notice of two weeks* (the genitive version). E.g.:

- "The stipulation included a provision requiring *sixty days*['] *notice* before either party moved out of Bannock County if such move would make the parenting plan in the stipulation impractical." *Allbright v. Allbright*, 215 P.3d 472, 473 (Idaho 2009). The correct phraseology is *sixty days' notice*, just as it is *several years' experience* and *two months' time*.
- "The trial court suspended defendant's sentence and placed him on *36 months probation* [read *36 months' probation*], conditional upon defendant serving 90 days in county jail." *People v. Tarris*, 103 Cal. Rptr. 3d 278, 281 (Ct. App. 2009).
- "According to the allegations in the amended complaint, however, *six million dollars worth* [read *six million dollars' worth*] of these warrants were exercised by Perseus-Soros, which had inside information about the upcoming merger with Genzyme." *Vladimir v. Bioenvision Inc.*, 606 F.Supp.2d 473, 489 (S.D.N.Y. 2009).

D. Of Inanimate Things. Possessives of nouns denoting inanimate objects are generally unobjectionable. Indeed, they allow writers to avoid awkward uses of *of*—e.g.: *the book's title*, *the article's main point*, *the system's hub*, *the envelope's contents*, and *the car's price tag*. See **of (A).**

The old line was that it is better to use an "*of* phrase rather than the *'s* to indicate possession when the possessor is an inanimate object. Write *foot of the bed*, not *the bed's foot*." Robert C. Whitford & James R. Foster, *Concise Dictionary of American Grammar and Usage* 96 (1955). The *foot of the bed*, of course, is a SET PHRASE, so the example is not a fair one. Whenever it is not a violation of idiom, the possessive in *'s* is preferable—e.g.: "Rectrix purports to bring this claim under the *First Amendment's guarantee* of free speech." *Rectrix Aerodome Ctrs., Inc. v. Barnstable Mun. Airport Comm'n*, 632 F.Supp.2d 120, 130 (D. Mass. 2009).

But such possessives can be overdone: "§ *922(f)'s* unambiguous language regarding the section's applicability requires us to decline the invitation to extend § *922(f)'s* coverage." *John W. Stone Oil Distrib., Inc. v. M/V Mr. W. Bruce*, 752 F.2d 184, 186–87 (5th Cir. 1985). In fact, it is often best to avoid use of possessives with statutes: "The court, relying on § *1471(a)'s* legislative history [better: *the legislative history of section 1471(a)*], found that 'the regulation . . . was not reasonably adopted.'" *U.S. v. Garner*, 749 F.2d 281, 284 (5th Cir. 1985).

The practice of using possessives with case names becomes preposterous when later courts interpolate full citations, as here: "Consistent with *Milliken* [*v. Bradley*, 433 U.S. 267, 97 S.Ct. 2749, 53 L. Ed. 2d 745 (1977)]*'s* teachings, a remedial order must be carefully tailored to correct the constitutionally infirm condition." *U.S. v. Crucial*, 722 F.2d 1182, 1189 (5th Cir. 1983).

E. Incorrect Omission of Apostrophe. Possessive apostrophes are increasingly omitted nowadays. Avoid this sloppy habit. E.g.: "Brown had hired Jack Rogers, a Lake Charles attorney, to procure *Governor Edwards* [read *Governor Edwards's*] signature." *Brown v. Maggio*, 730 F.2d 293, 294 (5th Cir. 1984). Where two possessives are proximate, writers will often inadvertently omit one: "We have considered the import and admissibility of the Alexanders' expert *witnesses testimony* [read *witnesses' testimony*] touching upon the drilling of additional wells." *Amoco Prod. Co. v. Alexander*, 594 S.W.2d 467, 477 (Tex. Civ. App.—Houston [1st Dist.] 1979). See **attorney's fees.**

F. Past-Participial Adjectives as Attributive Nouns. It can be awkward to use a past-participial adjective attributively <the disadvantaged> <the accused>. With such phrases as *the insured's death* and *the deceased's residence*, it is better to use an *of*-phrase; hence *the death of the insured* and *the residence of the deceased*. (Better yet, one might prefer *decedent* to *deceased*.) See **accused, condemned, insured & deceased.** See also PLURALS (D).

G. Phrasal Possessives. A so-called phrasal possessive is to be avoided when possible, so that one does not end up with sentences like this: "*That strange man who lives down the block's daughter* [read *The daughter of that strange man who lives down the block*] was arrested last week." Genitives with *of* are only slightly longer. More important, however, they are correct—e.g.:

- "DHS submitted evidence that the appellant's parental rights had been terminated to the *child in question's sibling* [read *sibling of the child in question*]." *Carroll v. Arkansas Dep't of Human Servs.*, 148 S.W.3d 780, 784 (Ark. Ct. App. 2004).
- "Both sides of this controversy rely on federal court jurisprudence and both argue that the *other one's* [read *other's*] position is inconsistent with federal arbitration law." *Oklahoma Oncology & Hematology P.C. v. US Oncology, Inc.*, 160 P.3d 936, 944 (Okla. 2007).
- "You didn't hear any proof that it was anything outside the norm of *anybody else's* childhood growing up experiences." *State v. Banks*, 271 S.W.3d 90, 136 (Tenn. 2008).
- "We conclude that we cannot determine, on the basis of the record before this court, whether the panel abused its discretion when it relied on the *plaintiff in error's criminal record* [read *criminal record of the plaintiff in error*]." *State v. Peay*, 959 A.2d 655, 657 (Conn. App. Ct. 2008).
- "The *court below's verdict* [read *verdict of the court below*] holding defendant Christopher Frick personally liable for the apparent damages to plaintiff's property is against the manifest weight of the evidence." *H. Park Partners, LLC v. Frick*, 910 N.E.2d 527, 528 (Ohio Ct. App. 2009).
- "The offeror can either propose a new offer in light of the newly discovered evidence or proceed to trial and present all the evidence in an attempt to be compensated fairly by the *trier of fact's decision* [read *decision of the trier of fact*]." *One Star, Inc. v. Staar Surgical Co.*, 102 Cal. Rptr. 3d 195, 201 (Ct. App. 2009).
- "The Supreme Court granted a petition for certiorari to review the *Court of Appeals'* decision." *State v. Evans*, 688 S.E.2d 583, 585 (S.C. Ct. App. 2009).

With a phrase such as *court of appeals*, the possessive is acceptable and widely used <the court of civil
appeals' opinion uses substantially the same alter-ego
test that is stated in the briefs>. The other established
forms of phrasal possessives are variations on *anybody else's* <the court's ruling disposed of no one else's
claim>. See **else's.**

H. Followed by Relative Pronouns. The relative
pronoun *who* should not follow a possessive noun. E.g.:
"Or there may have been inimical voices raised among
the committee, such as *Palffy's* or Nikolaus *Esterhazy's*,
who just then had had an unpleasant brush with the
composer." George R. Marek, *Beethoven* 382 (1969).
[Read *Or there may have been raised among the committee inimical voices, such as those of Palffy or Nikolaus
Esterhazy, who just then had had an unpleasant brush
with the composer.*] See ANTECEDENTS, FALSE (C).

I. Attributive Possessives. Businesses are often
named with a proper single name in possessive form,
as *McDonald's* or *Sambo's*. Although possessive in
form, these are functionally nouns, as in *Sambo's
brings this action*, etc. How, then, does one make a possessive of the noun *Sambo's*? One court did it this way:
"On February 26, 1973, *Sambo's* Certificate of Authority to do business in this state was forfeited." *Farris v.
Sambo's Restaurants, Inc.*, 498 F.Supp. 143, 147 (N.D.
Tex. 1980). The judge should have written *Sambo's'*,
because *Sambo's certificate* = certificate of Sambo,
whereas *Sambo's' certificate* = certificate of Sambo's,
the latter being the desired sense. Likewise, when
Buddy's Food Store is shortened to *Buddy's*, one writes
of *Buddy's' manager*. But good PHRASING requires *the
manager of Buddy's.*

J. With Appositives. See APPOSITIVES (A).

possessor (= one who possesses) has the special legal
sense "one who takes, occupies, or holds something
without ownership, or as distinguished from the
owner" (*OED*). E.g.:

• "The element of express notice may be satisfied by showing . . . that there were unequivocal acts, open and public,
[that] made the *possessors'* occupation so visible, hostile,
and notorious as to presume notice to the *nonpossessor*."
Williams v. Screven Wood Co., 619 S.E.2d 641, 644 (Ga.
2005).
• "The misappropriation theory only bars trading on confidential information that a defendant uses for his or her
own gain in breach of a fiduciary, contractual, or similar
obligation to the *owner or rightful possessor* of the information." Palmer T. Heenan et al., *Securities Fraud*, 47 Am.
Crim. L. Rev. 1015, 1050 (2010).

possessorial; possessory. See **possessive.**

possibility of reverter. See **reversion.**

possible. See **practicable** (A) & **probable.**

POSSLQ /**pos**-el-kyoo/ is an ACRONYM for "person of
the opposite sex sharing living quarters." It was used
in the 1980 U.S. census in order to count unmarried

couples living in the same household. But because
it literally includes married couples, roommates,
siblings, and others, it's criticized as producing misleading data. *See, e.g.*, Grace Ganz Blumberg, *Legal
Recognition of Same-Sex Conjugal Relationships*, 51
UCLA L. Rev. 1555, 1569 n.70 (2004). Yet demogra-
phers continue to use the acronym, even though in the
1990 census it was replaced with *unmarried partner*.
In the early 1980s, the word tended to be in lowercase
(*posslq*), but in more recent writing it is usually set in
all capitals. Cf. **CUPOS.**

POST-, when used for *since* or *after* to create a SEN-
TENCE ADVERB, is a sloppy way of achieving brevity.
"*Post*-Roe [read *Since* Roe], states have continued
to pass legislation regulating abortion to the extent
allowed by the Supreme Court's decisions." Jeffrey D.
Jackson, *Blackstone's Ninth Amendment*, 62 Okla. L.
Rev. 167, 219 (2010). See PRE-.

post. See **ante.**

postbankruptcy. One word.

post facto. See **ex post facto.**

posthaste is archaic in all but its adverbial sense.

post hoc (L. "after this") is often used in the mistaken
sense "[of or relating to] the fallacy of assuming causality from temporal sequence [i.e., *post hoc, ergo propter hoc*]." Avoid the slipshod habit—e.g.:

• "In applying these criteria, it is important that a district
court resist the understandable temptation to engage in
post hoc [read *after-the-fact*] reasoning by concluding
that, because a plaintiff did not ultimately prevail, his
action must have been unreasonable or without foundation." *Christiansburg Garment Co. v. EEOC*, 434 U.S. 412,
421–22 (1978) (per Stewart, J.).
• "Petitioners observe correctly that if the lawyer's brief for
the ICC had simply announced its clarifying analysis in
the form of allegations or new explanations, such would
constitute pure *post hoc* [read *after-the-fact*] rationalization not entitled to any consideration by this court. The
clarifying opinion of the Commission, however, differs
sharply from *after-the-fact* rationalizations made by attorneys or by courts." *Public Serv. Co. v. ICC*, 749 F.2d 753,
759 (D.C. Cir. 1984).

See *post hoc, ergo propter hoc.*

post hoc, ergo propter hoc [L. "after this, therefore
because of this"] denotes the fallacy of confusing
sequence with consequence. Two common usages,
since for *because* (acceptable) and *consequent* for
subsequent (unacceptable), exemplify the fallacy:
they originated when speakers and writers confused
causality with temporality. The following specimen
demonstrates a canny use of the maxim: "Here, as elsewhere in the law, *propter hoc* must be distinguished
from *post hoc*." *Hennigan v. Ouachita Parish Sch. Bd.*,
749 F.2d 1148, 1152 (5th Cir. 1985) (per Rubin, J.).
See **post hoc.**

postjudgment. One word.

postman. From ca. 1678 until 1875, this word was equivalent to *lawyer*; more particularly, it referred to a barrister in the Court of Exchequer who had precedence in motions except in Crown business. This rank was eliminated by the Judicature Acts, which merged the Exchequer with the Court of Queen's Bench. The *OED* records that "the name was derived from the post, the measure of length in excise cases, beside which he took his stand." Surely this sense of the word was unrelated to another sense recorded by the *OED*: "a hireling writer of libels or scurrilous falsehoods." But see LAWYERS, DEROGATORY NAMES FOR. See also **attorney** (A) & SEXISM (B).

postmortem. See **autopsy**.

postnuptial (= made, occurring, or existing after marriage) refers to the time after the wedding, not after a divorce. E.g.: "The district court found the *postnuptial* reconciliation agreement valid and considered its terms when equitably dividing the couple's property." *In re Marriage of Cooper*, 769 N.W.2d 582, 583 (Iowa 2009).

POSTPOSITIVE ADJECTIVES follow, rather than precede, the nouns they modify, generally because they follow Romance rather than Germanic (or English) syntax. They exist in English largely as a remnant of the Norman French influence during the Middle Ages, and especially in the century following the Norman Conquest. The French influence was most pronounced in the language of law, politics, religion, and heraldry.

In law as in these other fields, French phrases were adopted wholesale—syntax and all—and soon passed into the English language unchanged, though in English, adjectives almost invariably precede the nouns they modify. Following is a list of frequently used law-related phrases with postpositive adjectives:

accounts payable
accounts receivable
act malum in se (see **malum in se**)
ambassador extraordinary (see **ambassador**)
annuity certain
appearance corporal
attorney general (see **general**)
body corporate (see **body corporate**)
body politic
brief amicus curiae (see **amicus brief** & **amicus curiae**)
chattels personal (see **chattels**)
chattels real (see **chattels**)
condition precedent (see **condition precedent**)
condition subsequent (see **condition precedent**)
corporation de facto (see **de facto**)
corporation de jure (see **de facto**)
court martial
date certain
decree absolute (see **decree absolute**)
easement appurtenant (see **easement** (B))
fee simple (see **fee**)

fee simple defeasible (see **fee**)
fee simple determinable (see **fee**)
fee tail (see **fee**)
gap certain
heir apparent (see **heir**)
law merchant (see **law merchant**)
letters patent (see **letters patent**)
letters rogatory (see **letters rogatory**)
letters testamentary (see **letters testamentary**)
notary public (see **notary**)
offense mala prohibita (see **malum in se**)
parties defendant (see **defendant** (B))
parties litigant (see **litigatory**)
postmaster general (see **general**)
president-elect
queen regent (*or* regnant) (see **queen regnant**)
secretary general (see **general**)
sum certain
sum total
surgeon general (see **general**)
twelve men good and true (see **twelve free and lawful men**)

On the troublesome issue of pluralizing the nouns in phrases such as these, see PLURALS (E).

At least two common English nouns, *things* and *matters*, often take postpositive adjectives that are ordinarily prepositive. So we say that someone is interested in *things philosophical*, or *matters philological*. And the adjective *alive* is always postpositive <the cattle were still alive>.

Sometimes a writer will attempt to create a prepositive adjectival phrase where properly the phrase would normally and most idiomatically be postpositive. The result is ungainly indeed: "It would be similar, in other words, to determining whether *complained of conduct* [read *the conduct complained of*] was prejudicial before determining whether or not it was constitutional error." Sam Kamin, *An Article III Defense of Merits-First Decisionmaking in Civil Rights Litigation*, 16 Geo. Mason L. Rev. 53, 93 (2008).

There is, however, a tendency in modern writing to make prepositive adjectival phrases out of what formerly would have been postpositive. So instead of having *payments past due*, we just as often see *past-due payments*: "In billing Burch for *past-due payments* at a rate in excess of the legal rate of interest, the accused's goal was not only to encourage timely payment of his bills, but, if timely payment did not occur, to collect a clearly excessive fee." *In re Conduct of Campbell*, 202 P.3d 871, 687 (Or. 2009).

post-sentencing should be hyphenated for visual reasons. See PUNCTUATION (G).

posttrial. One word.

postverdict. One word.

potence; potency. Oddly, *potency* is more common in the positive, and *impotence* in the negative. See **impotence**.

potentiality is jargonistic when used merely for *potential, n.*

potential juror; prospective juror. These phrases are equally good plain-language translations of *veniremember*—e.g.:

- "Although he did not mention the Federal sentencing, the judge instructed a group of more than 50 *prospective jurors* that a verdict in the Denny case would not be reached." *Jury Queries Resume in Beating Case*, N.Y. Times, 8 Aug. 1993, at 17.
- "The decision by Judge Glenn Berman in New Brunswick forced attorneys to begin qualifying additional candidates for a pool of *potential jurors* to sit on the trial of Nathaniel Harvey, 44." Jim O'Neill, *12 Potential Jurors Get Boot at Murder Trial*, Star-Ledger (Newark, N.J.), 29 Oct. 1994, at 19.

See **venireman.**

pour. See **pore.**

pouree trust. See **pourover.**

pourover, an estate-planning term, refers to testamentary assets that are incorporated into a living trust. E.g.: "Despite . . . a later statute authorizing *pourovers* by will into an *inter vivos* trust . . . doubts were occasionally expressed whether a revocable trust would be upheld if it purported to be effective after the settlor's death." Stanley M. Johanson, *Revocable Trusts and Community Property*, 47 Tex. L. Rev. 537, 541 (1969).

Before it transformed into a noun in the late 1960s, *pourover* was an adjective denoting a statute that allows this type of incorporation of testamentary assets into a living trust—e.g.:

- "Probably the most common motives and purposes of testators in using living trusts and *pour-over wills* are as follows . . . ." Thomas H.B. Whipple, *Principles of Business Writing* 164 (1924).
- "The statute should specifically provide that in the case of a true *pour-over gift* by will, the property should be added to the inter vivos trust and thereafter be administered as part of it, not as a testamentary trust." 10 *Monthly Digest of Tax Articles* 10 (1959).
- "In enacting the first full bodied *pour-over statute* with all privileges and rights in the settlor during life, the legislature specifically reserved to the surviving spouse, the right to elect against the will." *Purcell v. Cleveland Trust Co.*, 200 N.E.2d 602, 606 (Ohio Prob. Ct. 1964).

Both as adjective and as noun, the word is preferably solid (*pourover*), not hyphenated or (heaven forbid) two words.

At least one writer considers *pourover* a misnomer because, he says, "wills and insurance contracts do the pouring; the trust is pouree." Thomas L. Shaffer, *The Planning and Drafting of Wills and Trusts* 207 (2d ed. 1979). He therefore uses the phrase *pouree trust*, but this phrase seems unlikely to catch on. And in any event, *pourover trust* is no less logical than *spillover*

pond, in which the pond does no spilling but instead holds the water that is spilled.

power. A. Senses. For lawyers, the most important senses are these: (1) "the ability to do something, esp. to alter a legal relation by doing or not doing a given act"; (2) "legal authorization"; (3) "a document giving legal authorization"; and (4) "political ascendancy or influence."

When used in sense 2, the word is frequently coupled with *right*. But the coupling is often superfluous, as Jeremy Bentham explained:

> *Powers*, though not a species of *rights* . . . , are yet so far included under rights that wherever the word *power* may be employed, the word *right* may also be employed: The reason is, that wherever you may speak of a person as having a *power*, you may also speak of him as having a *right* to such *power*: but the converse of this proposition does not hold good: there are cases in which, though you may speak of a man as having a *right*, you cannot speak of him as having a *power*, or in any other way make any mention of that word. On various occasions you have a *right*, for instance, to the services of the magistrate: but if you are a private person, you have no *power* over him: all the power is on his side. This being the case, as the word *right* was employed, the word *power* might perhaps, without any deficiency in the sense, have been omitted.
>
> Jeremy Bentham, *An Introduction to the Principles of Morals and Legislation* 224 n.1 (1823).

B. And Its Near-Synonyms: *authority; jurisdiction; control; dominion.* These words are related to one another in denoting the prerogative or capacity to determine, command, rule, or govern. *Power* in this sense refers to the capacity to rule by virtue of rank or office. Although *authority* is often used synonymously with *power*, it most specifically denotes power possessed by one over another—hence one has the *power* (not *authority*) to decide what to do next, but a boss has the *authority* (or, less normally, the *power*) to determine the roles that subordinates will play. *Authority* is more precise than *power* in conveying what is needed to keep people from infringing others' rights. A chief justice exercises administrative *authority* within a court—not, idiomatically, *power*. As plurals, the words both denote those who hold power or authority <the powers that be> <please alert the authorities>. *Jurisdiction* suggests both the legal power and the legal authority to determine, command, rule, or govern to a specified, limited extent (the boundaries usually being either geographic or nonphysical) <the court has jurisdiction over this case>. (See **jurisdiction (A).**) *Control*, as it relates to this cluster of terms, emphasizes the possession and exercise of the authority either to manage and direct or to regulate the allocation or progress of things <client control> <the fire was out of control>.

Dominion connotes supreme sovereignty, literal or figurative <the king and his dominion>, or both control and possession <we must determine who had dominion over the diamond bracelet>. It is a FORMAL WORD—e.g.:

- "Alford argues that the evidence presented as to that count failed to demonstrate that she had any *dominion* or control over any marijuana in the Western District of Texas." *U.S. v. Acosta*, 763 F.2d 671, 682 (5th Cir. 1985).
- "A defendant's control and *dominion* over a vehicle can indicate knowledge." *U.S. v. Parker*, 583 F.3d 1049, 1058 (8th Cir. 2009).
- "Constructive possession results when a person knowingly has the power and intention to exercise *dominion* over an object." *Howard v. State*, 684 S.E.2d 297, 298 (Ga. Ct. App. 2009).

power of attorney; letter of attorney. The first is the usual phrase in both AmE and BrE. *Letter of attorney* is a BrE variant that refers properly to the *document* giving one authority to act on another's behalf, rather than to the *authority* itself. But *power of attorney* is used both for the document and for the authority given by the document. The plural is *powers of attorney*. See PLURALS (E).

power of termination. See **right of entry for condition broken** & **fee simple (G).**

p.p. is an ambiguous abbreviation, since it may be short for *propria persona* (= in one's proper or own person), or *per procurationem* (= by proxy). (The abbreviation for *pages* (*pp.* or *pp*), of course, has no internal period.) For more on *per procurationem*, see *per procurationem.*

practicable. A. And *possible*; *feasible*; *doable*. All mean essentially "capable of happening or of being caused to happen." What is *possible* does or might exist or occur <any possible reason>. What is *practicable* can be readily brought about through available means under current conditions <a completely practicable plan> <not just possible but practicable technologies>, perhaps with a suggestion of doing so at a reasonable cost. What is *feasible* is highly possible and even seems to be practicable, though less definitely so; yet success appears likely if the project, plan, or scheme is to be undertaken, again with the hint of economic reasonableness <purposeful cultural changes are not feasible in such a short period>. What is *doable* is capable of being accomplished or advanced immediately, but with little or no regard for the cost involved.

B. And *practical*. While *practicable* refers invariably to things, *practical* refers either to things or to people, relating to actual human life, people's daily needs, or the conditions for meeting those needs. What is *practical* is unquestionably useful and serviceable in everyday life—and can be produced in an economically efficient way. A *practical* person is one who habitually approaches challenges both realistically and reasonably.

practice; practise. In AmE, *practice* is both the noun and the verb; in BrE, *practice* is the noun, *practise* the verb. Occasionally *practise* is used by American

writers, but *practice*, n. & vb., is the preferred spelling. One well-known exception to the general rule in the U.S. is the lawyers' organization called the Practising Law Institute.

practise. See **practice.**

practiser. See **practicioner.**

practitioner; practiser. The first is the term primarily used in AmE and BrE for "one who exercises a profession or occupation." The second is used almost exclusively in BrE, though not commonly—e.g.:

- "Most treatises seem to have been intended solely for the use of the *practiser*." Joseph Story, *The Law of Bailments*, 7 Am. Jurist & L. Mag. 128, 130 (1832).
- "These lessons lead to a conclusion widely shared by *practisers* in this field." Jean-Pierre Le Gall & Patrick Dibout, *Taxation of Corporate Mergers in the European Community*, 8 Int'l Bus. L.J. 992, 1038 (1990).

The variant *practicer* sometimes occurs in AmE— e.g.: "Technically, [Washington] Irving was a *practicer* of law until after the death of Matilda Hoffman in 1809." 1 Stanley Thomas Williams, *The Life of Washington Irving* 26 (1971). (This usage, *practicer of law*, sounds like the usage of someone unfamiliar with the practice of law.)

praecipe /**pre**-sə-pee/ (lit., "command") denoted, at common law, a writ ordering a defendant to do some act demanded by the plaintiff or demandant, or to explain why (*ostensurus quare*) he or she should not do it. A *praecipe* action aims not at compensation for misconduct but at restoration of a right. For example, *praecipe in capite* was, at common law, the principal writ for the recovery of land in the King's Court. *Praecipe quod reddat* was used (1) to claim chattels or debts that the defendant held unjustly; (2) to make the defendant perform a covenant; or (3) to obtain an accounting of moneys received. *Praecipe quod permittat* was used to order the defendant to allow the plaintiff to have or do something.

A modern example occurs in a court paper filed in the Supreme Court of British Columbia: "*Praecipe*. Required: To search for an Appearance entered on behalf of the Defendant XYZ Corporation. DATED _____. [Signature] Solicitor for the Plaintiff." (Can.)

A Pennsylvania judge writes that "*praecipe* may be correctly used as a verb as well as a noun." T.J. Terputac, *A Handbook of English Usage* 250 (1989). Primarily in Michigan and Pennsylvania, the word is used as a verb in three senses: (1) "to move for entry of judgment"; (2) "of a court, to rule (a case) ready for trial"; or (3) "of a lawyer, to move for a trial setting on the court's docket."

The use as a verb seems to have originated in Michigan, in senses 2 and 3—e.g.:

- (Sense 2) "The defendant Runnells filed a plea September 12, 1924, and the case was *praeciped* on that date as ready for trial." *Robinson v. Sample*, 219 N.W. 661, 661 (Mich. 1928).

- (Sense 3) "During this period of time petitioners could have *praeciped* the cause for trial." *Hailey v. Wolf*, 30 N.W.2d 437, 439 (Mich. 1948).

Later, these senses appeared in Pennsylvania. Sense 2: "A notice of rehearing by the Board . . . [stated] that the case had not been *praeciped* for trial or otherwise disposed." *Cudo v. Hallstead Foundry, Inc.*, 539 A.2d 792, 797 (Pa. 1988) (Flaherty, J., dissenting).

Sense 1, however, is more common today in Pennsylvania—e.g.:

- "On May 23, 1979, Evans, as attorney for Fitelson *praeciped* the arbitration award for judgment, because the time period for entry of an appeal from the arbitration award had passed." *Becker v. Evans*, 496 F.Supp. 20, 20 (M.D. Pa. 1980).
- "When no responsive pleading was received from DPW within thirty days, the claimant *praeciped* for entry of default judgment." *Pennsylvania Inst. Health Servs., Inc. v. Commonwealth*, 647 A.2d 692, 694 n.2 (Pa. Commw. Ct. 1994).
- "The Gas Companies discontinued their other claims and *praeciped* for the entry of judgment." *Kilmer v. Elexco Land Servs.*, 990 A.2d 1147, 1151 (Pa. 2010) (per Baer, J.).

Most American lawyers would doubtless consider these uses of the word obscure, to say the least. In most parts of the U.S., lawyers don't *praecipe* a case for trial; they simply *ask for a trial setting*. Nor do they *praecipe* for entry of judgment; they *move* for entry of judgment.

praedial. See **predial.**

pray, in the legal sense "to request earnestly," is a survival from Elizabethan usage, as in Shakespeare's "a conqueror that will *pray* in aid for kindness, where he for grace is kneeled to." *Antony & Cleopatra*, 5.2.27–28. The religious sense of *pray* grew alongside the broader secular sense, and neither it nor *prayer* should be viewed as symptomatic of BIBLICAL AFFECTATION (see **prayer**). E.g.:

- "[The] complaint additionally *prays* for injunctive relief including back pay as well as an order that Plaintiff receive a name-clearing hearing and that he be reinstated to the position of Dean of the College." *Gies v. Flack*, 495 F.Supp.2d 854, 858 (S.D. Ohio 2007).
- "Defendant objected to a continuance and *prayed* for no restitution because of the failure of evidence." *Cooks v. State*, 23 So.3d 863, 864 (Fla. Dist. Ct. App. 2009).

prayer = (1) a request addressed to the court that appears at the end of a pleading; or (2) in British parliamentary practice, a negative resolution that challenges a statutory instrument. E.g.:

- (Sense 1) "When plaintiffs seek damages, questions about the reliability of the plaintiffs' *prayer* for relief can be resolved by reference to analogous case law involving the $75,000 amount in controversy." Sarah S. Vance, *A Primer on the Class Action Fairness Act of 2005*, 80 Tul. L. Rev. 1617, 1628 (2006).

- (Sense 2) "But even if a group of Members decide to challenge such an instrument (by what is called a '*prayer*')—there is no guarantee that the government will provide time for a debate or the opportunity of a vote." Michael Zander, *The Law-Making Process* 70 (2d ed. 1985).

See **pray** & **pleading** (C).

PRE- [+ noun]. Such a construction may be used adjectivally, as in the following examples:

- "The neutral mechanism, far from being the discriminatory act, is merely the means by which the *pre-act* and *pre-limitations* disparate treatment is carried forward into the actionable time frame." *Sobel v. Yeshiva Univ.*, 839 F.2d 18, 29 (2d Cir. 1988).
- "But the prosperous fur-trading days of Astor and Chouteau were, in a sense, *pre-law*." Robert MacCrate, *The Making of the American Lawyer*, 34 S.D. L. Rev. 227, 227 (1989).

But making the *pre-* phrase into an adverb modifying a verb is a poor substitute for the idiomatic construction: *before* plus the noun. E.g.:

- "Defendant could have responded that he did inform the police and this statement was made *prearrest and pre-Miranda* [read *before they arrested him and read him his rights*]." *People v. Sutton*, 464 N.W.2d 276, 277 n.3 (Mich. 1990).
- "Even *pre-Heller* [read *before Heller*], that strategy would have been bizarre and ineffective." Robert A. Levy, *Second Amendment Redux*, 33 Harv. J.L. & Pub. Pol'y 203, 215 (2010).

See POST-.

preamble (= [1] an introductory statement stating the reasons for and objectives of a document such as a contract, statute, charter, or constitution; or [2] the first words (of a patent claim) that identify a field of art) takes the preposition *to* or, less commonly, *of*. The corresponding adjective is *preambular*.

precatory (= of, relating to, or expressing entreaty or supplication) is a word not much used outside the law. *Precatory words* in a will, or in motions at shareholders' meetings, are words praying or expressing a desire that a thing be done; ordinarily, *precatory* words are not binding. The word is usually opposed to or contrasted with *mandatory*. E.g.:

- "Buchanan thus construed the statutory 'condition' as *precatory* rather than as mandatory." David J. Barron & Martin S. Lederman, *The Commander in Chief at the Lowest Ebb*, 121 Harv. L. Rev. 941, 985 (2008).
- "In most companies in which *precatory* shareholder proposals to dismantle staggered boards were passed, management chose to ignore them." Michal Barzuza, *Delaware's Compensation*, 94 Va. L. Rev. 521, 544 (2008).

precautionary; precautious. These terms have undergone DIFFERENTIATION since they were first used in the 18th century. *Precautionary* = (1) suggesting or advising provident caution; or (2) of, relating to, or of the nature of a precaution. *Precautious* = using precaution; showing caution or care beforehand. See **cautionary.**

precede. A. And *proceed.* These words are sometimes confused even by otherwise literate professionals. Both may mean "to go ahead," but in different senses. *Precede* = to go ahead of; to come before. *Proceed* = to go ahead; to continue. For a common misspelling, see (B).

B. Misspelled **proceed.* This misspelling seems to result from confusion with *proceed*—e.g.: "In Exclusion 10, the general terms *preceed* [read *precede*] the specific terms." *Sommers v. State Farm Fire & Cas. Co.,* 764 So.2d 87, 91 (La. Ct. App. 2000). It occurs in print surprisingly often: *see, e.g., Drennen Land & Timber Co. v. Angell,* 475 So.2d 1166, 1171–72 (Ala. 1985).

C. For *preface.* This seems to be an anomalous error—e.g.: "Here is a good place to retrogress and discuss a short essay that *precedes* [read *prefaces*] the triad of Being-Nothing-Becoming." David Gray Carlson, *Hegel's Theory of Quality,* 22 Cardozo L. Rev. 425, 448 (2001).

precedence. A. And **precedency.* Today *precedence* serves more ably for all purposes and is standard. **Precedency* is a NEEDLESS VARIANT that was used through the beginning of the 19th century.

B. And *precedents.* Pronunciation of these words is traditionally distinguished in AmE. The first is often thought to be best pronounced with the second syllable stressed, i.e., /prə-**seed**-əns/, whereas the second has the primary accent on the first syllable, i.e., /**pres**-ə-dəns/. *Precedence* is nevertheless acceptably pronounced /**pres**-ə-dəns/ in AmE, as it is usually sounded in the common phrase *take precedence over.* In BrE, /**pres**-ə-dəns/ is the only known pronunciation.

*precedency. See **precedence.**

precedent, adj., is inferior to *prior* or *previous,* except when used as a POSTPOSITIVE ADJECTIVE in a phrase such as *condition precedent.* E.g.: "Though the old case law is quite messy on the effect of taking a note for a *precedent* [read *prior*] debt, the case law is quite clear that a person who sells goods or otherwise gives value in an immediate exchange for a bank note has accepted that bank note as a complete discharge of the underlying claim." James Steven Rogers, *Unification of Payments Law and the Problem of Insolvency Risk in Payment Systems,* 83 Chi.-Kent L. Rev. 689, 697 (2008). This adjective is best pronounced /pri-**seed**-ənt/, although /**pres**-ə-dənt/ is acceptable.

The adjective *precedent* (= preceding in time or order) should not be used for *precedential* (= of the nature of, constituting, or relating to a precedent)— e.g.: "Louisiana courts should apply civilian *precedent* [read *precedential*] theory to those areas primarily based on the civil-law and common-law *precedent* [read *precedential*] theory to those areas based on the American common law." Jason Edwin Dunahoe,

Note, *Jurisprudence Disorientee,* 64 La. L. Rev. 679, 698 (2004).

precedent, n. **A. And** *stare decisis.* A *precedent* is a decided case that furnishes a basis for determining an identical or similar case that may arise later, or a similar question of law. *Stare decisis,* by contrast, is the practice of applying precedents to later cases.

B. As a Shortened Form of *binding precedent.* The word *precedent* alone is ambiguous, since it is a CHAMELEON-HUED WORD. That is, we have both *binding precedents* and *persuasive precedents,* and they do not carry the same weight of authority: a *binding precedent* must be followed, whereas a *persuasive precedent* need not be. Usually, a lawyer who uses the word *precedent* means *binding precedent.*

Without the qualifying adjective, however, the term can be very broad indeed: "If the term '*precedent*' is construed sufficiently broadly, there are very few cases in which there is literally none to serve as an analogy, however remote." Rupert Cross & J.W. Harris, *Precedent in English Law* 204 (4th ed. 1991).

C. *Original precedent; declaratory precedent.* Some writers distinguish between judicial deliverances that merely declare existing law (*declaratory precedents*) and those that lay down new law (*original precedents*). In fact, though, the difference is one of degree and not of kind: "If we have a case [that] deals with certain facts by applying an acknowledged rule, we really have an addition to the rule, because we now know that a certain kind of fact falls within it, and in the nature of things we can never have two sets of facts [that] are precisely similar. No precedent is purely '*declaratory*' or purely '*original.*'" William Geldart, *Introduction to English Law* 11 (D.C.M. Yardley ed., 9th ed. 1984).

D. Meaning "a legal form." In England, Australia, and Canada, lawyers use *precedent* to refer to a legal form. American lawyers speak of a *form,* while Scots lawyers speak of a *style.* See **style.**

E. And *custom.* The historian Plucknett, like other writers, has emphasized the distinction between *precedent* and *custom:* one case constitutes a *precedent,* whereas several cases serve as evidence of a *custom.* Theodore F.T. Plucknett, *A Concise History of the Common Law* 347 (5th ed. 1956).

precedential ordinarily means "furnishing a guide or rule for subsequent cases." E.g.: "The likely *precedential* effect of ICTY decisions in ICC proceedings should be a major concern motivating scholars and practitioners to understand obstacles to criminal liability in ICTY cases." Richard P. Barrett & Laura E. Little, *Lessons of Yugoslav Rape Trials,* 88 Minn. L. Rev. 30, 32 (2003). See **precedent,** n.

precedents. See **precedence.**

preceding, when used simply for *before,* is best replaced by that word—e.g.: "Her account of the day's events *preceding* [read *before*] Large's arrest are in essence in agreement with Large's testimony." *Daves v.*

State, 327 S.W.3d 289, 295 (Tex. App.—Eastland 2010). Cf. *next preceding.

*preceed. See precede (B).

precipitancy; *precipitance; precipitation. *Precipitancy* = excessive or unwise haste in action; rashness. **Precipitance* is a NEEDLESS VARIANT. *Precipitation* = (1) haste, hurry; (2) the act of precipitating <the precipitation of the riot is still a mystery>; or (3) something precipitated (as rain or snow).

precipitate, adj.; **precipitous; *precipitant.** These words are quite different, though often confused. *Precipitate* /pri-**sip**-i-tət/ = sudden; hasty; rash; showing violent or uncontrollable speed. The word is applied to actions, movements, or demands. E.g.: "Henry ensured that the only effect of *precipitate* action by a claimant should be the delay of the fulfillment of his claim, and the increase of its cost." H.G. Hanbury, *English Courts of Law* 39 (2d ed. 1953).

Precipitous /pri-**sip**-i-təs/ = like a precipice; steep. It is properly applied to physical things—rarely to actions, except when the METAPHOR of steepness is apt. But *precipitous* is frequently misused for *precipitate*—e.g.:

- "The presence of an equity trustee may comfort shareholders and minimize *precipitous* declines in share price upon bad financial news and may prevent such a decline in the face of enhanced debt or debt reorganization negotiations." Kelli A. Alces, *Strategic Governance*, 50 Ariz. L. Rev. 1053, 1099 (2008).
- "While lenders generally do not accelerate *precipitously* [read *precipitately*], the option to accelerate upon a covenant violation gives the lender significant leverage over management." Frederick Tung, *Leverage in the Board Room*, 57 UCLA L. Rev. 115, 134 (2009).

Precipitant is a NEEDLESS VARIANT of *precipitate*—e.g.: "The facts presented in this case tend to show that Mr. Adam's mental facilities declined rather *precipitantly* [read *precipitately*]." *In re Fletcher*, 345 B.R. 592, 596 (Bankr. N.D. Ohio 2006).

precipitation. See **precipitancy.**

precipitous. See **precipitate.**

precision; precisian; precisionist. *Precision* = accuracy. *Precisian* = a person who adheres to rigidly high standards (often with regard to moral conduct). *Precisionist* = a person who prizes absolute correctness of expression and performance, esp. in language and ritual.

preclusive; *preclusory. The second is a NEEDLESS VARIANT.

precondition is usually unnecessary in place of *condition*—e.g.: "For months the Government tried in vain to persuade him that he and the ANC should abandon some of the cornerstones of their strategy as a *pre-condition* [read *condition*] for future negotiations." Fred Bridgland, *Freedom Brings Mandela His Greatest Challenge*, Sunday Telegraph, 11 Feb. 1990, at 3.

precontractual; precontract, adj. Contract scholars—not contractual scholars—disagree in their practice: Grant Gilmore refers to *precontractual duties*, whereas G.H. Treitel refers to *precontract negotiations*. Gilmore's practice is probably better for two reasons: first, because *precontract* is also a noun meaning "an agreement to marry," it may give rise to ambiguities; and second, it is better to use a genuinely adjectival form when it is available.

predate. See **antedate.**

predatory; predacious; *predaceous; *predative; *predatorial. *Predatory* = preying on other animals. The word is applied figuratively in the phrase from antitrust law, *predatory pricing*. The forms **predaceous*, **predatorial*, and **predative* are NEEDLESS VARIANTS. The spelling *predacious* has undergone DIFFERENTIATION and means "devouring; rapacious."

predecease (= to die before), a Shakespearean coinage, has become a legal genteelism: "She *predeceased* him leaving a husband and two children." Anthony R. Mellows, *The Law of Succession* 515 (3d ed. 1977). And it surely has a place: if one says, *She died before him . . .* , the words *She died* resonate in the mind—the reader wonders how and why. But the legal writer usually wants to focus on something else entirely: "Should she *predecease* her husband, even this incipient right is automatically extinguished." Robert Kratovil, *Real Estate Law* 226 (1946). The writer who used *die before* in that sentence would lose some readers. Lawyers, in short, sometimes need to talk about death without thinking about it.

predecisional (of, relating to, or occurring during the time before a decision) is a mid-20th-century legal NEOLOGISM. E.g.:

- "Occasionally, on particular facts, a *predecisional* release has been criticized for the outside appearances it created." *FTC v. Cinderella Career & Finishing Schs., Inc.*, 404 F.2d 1308, 1323 (D.C. Cir. 1968).
- "Finding that the documents are relevant as well as deliberative and *predecisional*, the court was willing to look at many of the documents in camera to see if they should be released because of governmental misconduct." *Convertino v. U.S. Dep't of Justice*, 674 F.Supp.2d 97, 104 (D.D.C. 2009).

predestined construction; predestined interpretation. See *predestined interpretation* under INTERPRETATION, MODES OF (B).

predial /**pree**-dee-əl/ (= consisting of or pertaining to or attached to the land), the rough equivalent of *real* in the phrase *real property*, is usually so spelled in Louisiana. But it's *praedial* in Scotland.

The usual phrase in law is *predial servitude*, which means, in Scots and civil law, "a servitude affecting land, such as a right of way, of light, of support, and the like." E.g.: "A *predial servitude* is a charge on a servient estate for the benefit of a dominant estate." La. Civ. Code Ann. art. 646 (West 1980). See **servitude (A).**

predicable; predicative; predicatory. *Predicable* = that may be predicated or affirmed. *Predicative* = having the quality of predicating, affirming, or asserting. *Predicatory* = of or pertaining to a preacher.

predicate, vb. (= [1] to affirm a statement or proposition; or [2] to found, base), is usually construed with *on* in modern writing. E.g.: "In *Cuban*, the court reached a middle-ground conclusion, rejecting the SEC's attempt to *predicate* insider trading liability *on* a confidentiality agreement while noting that such liability could be premised on the violation of an agreement not to trade on confidential information." Tyler J. Bexley, *Reining in Maverick Traders*, 88 Tex. L. Rev. 195, 214 (2009).

predicate nominatives. See PRONOUNS (B).

predicative; predicatory. See **predicable.**

predominant; predominate. *Predominant* is the standard adjective; *predominate* /pri-**dom**-i-nət/ is a NEEDLESS VARIANT. In good usage, *predominate* is the verb, *predominant* the adjective. Readers may be confused when *predominate* is used adjectivally—e.g.:

• "The *predominate* [read *predominant*] theoretical justification was that loss of these benefits would incentivize addicts to get clean and turn their lives around." Erin E. Patrick, *Lose Weight or Lose Out*, 58 Emory L.J. 249, 285 (2008).
• "Courts must carefully scrutinize guilt determinations based largely or exclusively on evidence that has been the *predominate* [read *predominant*] cause of wrongful convictions." Cynthia E. Jones, *The Right Remedy for the Wrongly Convicted*, 77 Fordham L. Rev. 2893, 2893 (2009).

Cf. **preponderantly.**

preempt; perempt. These words should be distinguished. *Preempt* (now generally spelled as one word without a hyphen) is a BACK-FORMATION from its noun, *preemption*. To *preempt* is to handle or acquire beforehand to the exclusion of others, or to take precedence over. For more, see **arrogate (A).**

To *perempt*, by contrast, is to quash, do away with, or extinguish. The *OED* and *W3* record *perempt* as an obsolete or archaic term, but it is current at least in Louisiana in intransitive uses—e.g.:

• "The Louisiana Supreme Court has made it clear that a cause of action for legal malpractice can *perempt* and extinguish even if the client never discovers that cause of action." *Atlas Iron & Metal Co. v. Ashy*, 918 So.2d 1205, 1213 (La. Ct. App. 2006).
• "Because La. Rev. Stat. Ann. § 9:5606 *perempts* this claim, the Campbells do not have a viable cause of action against Stone Insurance." *Campbell v. Stone Ins., Inc.*, 509 F.3d 665, 672 (5th Cir. 2007).

preemption, federal; exclusive federal jurisdiction. Though many American legal writers fail to distinguish between these phrases, and use *preemption* for both senses, one jurist insists that, properly speaking, *federal preemption* should be kept distinct from *exclusive federal jurisdiction*: "In the former, federal substantive law supplants state law, but, absent other provisions, both state and federal courts have concurrent jurisdiction of actions arising under that law; in the latter, only the specified federal instrumentalities have jurisdiction of the matter, irrespective of the law to be applied." 1 *Moore's Federal Practice* ¶ 0.160, at 189 (2d ed. 1981).

preemption; peremption. *Preemption*, by far the more common word, means: (1) "the right to buy before others"; (2) "the purchase of something under this right"; (3) "an earlier seizure or appropriation"; (4) "the occupation of (public land) so as to establish a preemptive title"; or (5) in AmE, Congress's legislatively taking over of an entire subject matter so as to make it inherently federal. See **preempt.** For more on sense 5, see **preemption, federal.** For *right of preemption*, see **option.**

Peremption is a rare legal term meaning "the act or process of quashing" (*W3*), "a nonsuit." It is rare everywhere, apparently, but in Louisiana. E.g.:

• "*Peremption* is but a form of prescription, a species thereof, but with the characteristic that it does not admit of interruption or suspension." *Flowers, Inc. v. Rausch*, 364 So.2d 928, 931 (La. 1978).
• "The trial court granted Ms. Juneau's exception of *peremption* because the plaintiffs' objection to candidacy failed to name the Honorable Jay Dardenne, in his official capacity as the Louisiana Secretary of State, as a defendant." *Scaglione v. Juneau*, 41 So.3d 1287, 1288 (La. Ct. App. 2010).

Peremption and its derivatives are used throughout *Equilease Corp. v. M/V Sampson*, 756 F.2d 357 (5th Cir. 1985). *See* N. Stephan Kinsella, *A Civil Law to Common Law Dictionary*, 54 La. L. Rev. 1265, 1285 (1994).

preemptioner; preemptor. These words should be differentiated. A *preemptioner* holds the right to purchase public land by preemption—e.g.: "A *preemptioner* acquires no present right to affect the property, but holds only a general contract right to acquire a later interest should the property owner decide to sell." *Old Nat'l Bank v. Arneson*, 776 P.2d 145, 148 (Wash. Ct. App. 1989).

A *preemptor* actually acquires land by using this right—e.g.: "The *preemptor* . . . is entitled to no lesser means of receiving the offer than is provided to the seller by the third party offeror." *Gyurkey v. Babler*, 651 P.2d 928, 932 (Idaho 1982). Of course, *preemptor* serves also as the general agent noun corresponding to the verb *preempt*.

preemptive; preemptory; peremptive; peremptory. The adjectives most commonly used and distinguished are *preemptive* (= relating to or of the nature of preemption) and *peremptory* (= [1] conclusive;

absolute; or [2] arbitrary; not requiring shown cause). See **peremptory.**

But the two other forms have bona fide existences. *Preemptory* correctly means "of or relating to a preemptor" (but is sometimes misused for *preemptive*). (For the correct use, see **preemptioner;** for the incorrect use, see **preemptory.**) *Peremptive* = of or relating to peremption. E.g.: "Authority exists in Louisiana cases to support the proposition that a prescriptive period defined in a statute conferring a right is actually a *peremptive* period." *Equilease Corp. v. M/V Sampson,* 756 F.2d 357, 360 (5th Cir. 1985). See **preemption.**

Preemptory for *peremptory* is a fairly common mistake. Properly, the former means "of or relating to a preemptor." See **preemptioner.**

Preemptive Phrases. See anticipatory reference.

preemptor. See **preemptioner.**

preemptory. See **preemptive.**

preestablished. So spelled.

preexisting. So spelled.

preface. See **foreword** & **precede (c).**

prefatory; *prefatorial; *prefatial. The last two terms are needless variants of the first.

prefer, which generally means "to like better," survives in a number of older senses in legal writing. For example, the *OED* records the sense "to advance oneself or one's interests," exemplified here: "Since the signing of the 1957 Rome Treaty, event after event has illustrated that the member states *prefer* to feather their own nests." Sam-Sang Jo, *European Myths: Resolving the Crises in the European Community/European Union* 35 (2007). But additionally, *prefer* has the sense "to lay (a matter) before anyone formally for consideration, approval, or sanction; to bring forward (as an indictment)" <to prefer charges>. Hence:

- "The applicant had an opportunity to establish his innocence when the court-martial charge was *preferred* against him by demanding trial by court-martial thereby requiring the prosecution to establish his guilt beyond a reasonable doubt." *Metz v. U.S.,* 61 Fed.Cl. 154, 162 (2004).
- "There is substantial evidence in the record to support the hearing officer's determination that the disciplinary charges were not *preferred* against the petitioner as retaliation for his commencement of a civil action against the Town and members of the police department." *Kaufman v. Wells,* 867 N.Y.S.2d 533, 535 (App. Div. 2008).

preferable /pref-ər-ə-bəl/ is inherently a comparative adjective. So it shouldn't be used with *more*—e.g.: "While immunity is a good solution to the problem of obscenity generally, the problem of defamation can only be solved either through a return to distributor liability (costly to free speech) *or, more preferably* [read *or, preferably*], the weakening of anonymity for defamatory posters." Paul Ehrlich, *Communications Decency Act § 230,* 17 Berkeley Tech. L.J. 401, 408 (2002). See comparatives and superlatives & adjectives (b).

pregnancy termination. See **abortion.**

pregnant, negative. See **negative pregnant.**

prejudge. See **forejudge.**

prejudice, n. & vb. **A. Generally.** *Prejudice* is a legalism for *harm,* n. & vb. In ordinary discourse, it is a lawyer's pomposity—e.g.: "All these types of election advocacy can form the basis for an inference by a sitting judge that a particular ruling may *prejudice* his chances for reelection." Mark Spottswood, *Free Speech and Due Process Problems in the Regulation and Financing of Judicial Election Campaigns,* 101 Nw. U. L. Rev. 331, 360 (2007). Often *prejudice* refers to legal harm—e.g.: "The trial court's error in refusing the separate verdict forms that would have resolved this issue *prejudiced* the defendants." *People v. Moore,* 922 N.E.2d 435, 453 (Ill. App. Ct. 2009).

Sometimes the past participle *prejudiced* almost gives rise to a miscue, as some readers might take it to mean "having a strong bias against (something)"— e.g.: "The Louisiana revocatory action is available to a creditor who is *prejudiced* [i.e., *harmed*] at the time by a fraudulent transfer made by his debtor." Albert Tate Jr., "The Revocatory Action in Louisiana Law," in *Essays on the Civil Law of Obligations* 133, 133 (Joseph Dainow ed., 1969).

B. *With prejudice; without prejudice.* These terms are used in reference to whether a future action is barred. For example, if a court dismisses a lawsuit *with prejudice,* the court has adjudicated the merits of the case, so the dismissal constitutes a bar to future action. A *dismissal without prejudice* is not an adjudication on the merits; hence no right or remedy is foreclosed to the parties.

Increasingly, writers are placing *with(out) prejudice* before the noun *dismissal*—but the resulting phrasal adjective jars the reader familiar with the legal idiom: "Government counsel told the justices that the district judge erred by not performing the balancing test the act mandates for choosing between *with-* and *without-prejudice* dismissal." *Supreme Court Ponders Sanction for Violation of Speedy Trial Act,* 56 U.S.L.W. 1176, 1176 (17 May 1988).

prejudicial. A. And *prejudiced.* *Prejudicial* (= tending to injure; harmful) applies to things and events; *prejudiced* (= harboring prejudices) applies to people. The meaning of a sentence can frequently be made clearer by using *harmful* in place of *prejudicial.*

Occasionally, writers misuse *prejudicial* for *prejudiced*—e.g.: "Indeed the rule shields the deliberations

---

and conclusions of the chosen representatives of the board only if they possess a disinterested independence and do not stand in a dual relation which prevents an *unprejudicial* [read *unprejudiced*] exercise of judgment." *Auerbach v. Bennett*, 393 N.E.2d 994, 1001 (N.Y. 1979).

B. And *pre-judicial.* The hyphen makes an important difference. *Pre-judicial* was used in Roman law in reference to a class of preliminary actions in which questions of right or fact, usually as relating to status, were determined. Today the hyphenated form is often used somewhat differently, in reference to a time before a given person became a judge—e.g.: "Pay less attention to what nominees say in interviews and their confirmation hearings, and pay more attention to where they worked in their *pre-judicial* careers." Michael C. Dorf, *Does Federal Executive Branch Experience Explain Why Some Republican Supreme Court Justices "Evolve" and Others Don't?*, 1 Harv. L. & Pol'y Rev. 457, 459 (2007). See PUNCTUATION (G).

The more usual term is *prejudicial*, discussed in (A). E.g.:

- "The plaintiff objects to the introduction of this testimony, even for the limited purpose of impeaching his credibility, on the ground that the probative value of this old conviction does not substantially outweigh its *prejudicial* effect under the applicable evidentiary rule." Andrew J. Wistrich, Chris Guthrie & Jeffrey J. Rachlinski, *Can Judges Ignore Inadmissible Information?*, 153 U. Pa. L. Rev. 1251, 1306 (2005).
- "The Court also agreed with the defendant that the admission of evidence of the defendant's liability insurance was improper and *prejudicial.*" James E. Wildes, *Tort Developments in 2006*, 81 Conn. B.J. 63, 71 (2007).

preliminary injunction. See **temporary restraining order.**

preliminary to, when used merely as an equivalent of *before*, is a silly pomposity—e.g.: "*Preliminary to* [read *Before*] reaching the award itself, courts have been faced with a number of procedural hurdles that required balancing the interests of parents and districts around the question of notice." Solomon A. Metzger, *Compensatory Education Under the Individuals with Disabilities Education Act*, 23 Cardozo L. Rev. 1839, 1850 (2002). Cf. **preparatory to,** ***prior to*** & **antecedent.**

premeditated (= consciously considered beforehand) appears mostly in criminal-law contexts <premeditated murder>. Because it invariably precedes a bad act of some kind, the word has taken on strongly negative connotations.

premeditatively, adv., is used much more often than the corresponding adjective, *premeditative.* The adverb provides an alternative to the awkward term *premeditatedly*, which is also common. E.g.:

- "Defendant was charged with willfully, deliberately, and *premeditatively* murdering her with malice aforethought." *State v. Hansen*, 225 N.W.2d 343, 345 (Iowa 1975).

- "It is his position that the judges have *premeditatively* used the appointment process to take control of the indigent defender system in Caddo Parish." *Walker v. State*, 917 So.2d 1229, 1234 (La. Ct. App. 2005).
- "It is Carter's position that trial counsel should have emphasized the shorter time span to show the attack occurred in a heat of passion rather than deliberately and *premeditatedly.*" *Carter v. Mitchell*, 443 F.3d 517, 533 (6th Cir. 2006) (per Suhrheinrich, J.).

See -EDLY.

premia. See **premium.**

premise; premiss. Both refer to "a previous statement or proposition from which another is inferred as a conclusion." The first is the AmE, the second the BrE spelling.

premises. A. As a Popularized Legal Technicality. *Premises* (= a house or building) has a curious history in legal usage. Originally, in the sense of things mentioned previously, it denoted the part of a deed that sets forth the names of the grantor and grantee, as well as the things granted and the consideration. Then, through HYPALLAGE in the early 18th century, it was extended to refer to the subject of a conveyance or bequest as specified in the premises of the deed. Finally, it was extended to refer to a house or building along with its grounds. In short, someone who says, "No alcohol is allowed on these premises," is engaging unconsciously in a POPULARIZED LEGAL TECHNICALITY.

The term always takes a plural verb—e.g.: "The *premises* were put under surveillance." And it is improper to shorten *premises*—in the sense of a building together with its grounds—to the singular *premise.* E.g.: "[A no-knock provision allows] law-enforcement officers to enter *a premise* [read *premises*] forcibly, without announcing their presence before entering, under certain circumstances." Ralph De Sola, *Crime Dictionary* 103 (1982).

B. Other Senses in Drafting. The word *premises* is sometimes used in the sense of matters (usually preliminary facts or statements) previously referred to in the same instrument. In practice, this usage is often inarticulate and confusing, since the subject matter constituting the *premises* is rarely specified in the instrument. For example, one who writes *wherefore, premises considered* in the prayer of a court paper would be hard pressed to say what the premises are, other than everything that has gone before.

Occasionally, too, lawyers use *premises* in the logical, syllogistic sense of the grounds or bases for a legal argument or legal reasoning. See ISSUE-FRAMING.

premiss. See **premise.**

premium. Pl. *premiums.* The form ***premia*** is hopelessly pedantic: "Tender offers entail substantial *premia* [read *premiums*] compared with the prices shares carry before the bids—and afterward, should the offers be defeated." *Flamm v. Eberstadt*, 814 F.2d 1169, 1174 (7th Cir. 1987). See PLURALS (A).

premortal; *premortem. See **antemortem.**

premortgage. So spelled, without a hyphen.

premortuary. See **antemortem.**

prenuptial; antenuptial. *Prenuptial* is far more common in AmE today; *antenuptial* is the usual term in BrE. Oddly, *antenuptial* does not appear in many English-language dictionaries. Yet Google Books (as of 18 November 2010) finds 145,000 instances of the term in print, and the word appears quite often in legal writing—e.g.:

- "Under the rules of the English common law, the husband was liable for his wife's *antenuptial* and postnuptial obligations." Isidor Loeb, *The Legal Property Relations of Married Parties* 153 (1900).
- "The husband also sought a division of the parties' property and debts pursuant to an *antenuptial* agreement." *Blasdel v. Blasdel*, 27 So.3d 1288, 1289 (Ala. Civ. App. 2009). On the use of *pursuant to in that sentence, see ***pursuant to.**
- "The marital unity rule extinguishing *antenuptial* actions for tort between spouses was abolished in Tennessee many years after the Court decided *Raines*." *Creech v. Addington*, 281 S.W.3d 363, 376 n.14 (Tenn. 2009).

Cf. **postnuptial.**

The phrase *prenuptial agreement* is commonly shortened to *prenup* (a casualism).

preowned for *used*. See EUPHEMISMS.

preparatory; preparative. As an adjective, *preparative* is a NEEDLESS VARIANT of *preparatory*. It is a legitimate noun, however, meaning "something that prepares the way for something else."

preparatory to, used in the sense "in preparation for," is legalistic—e.g.:

- "The demolition of the two-story building and the four-story building constituted work *preparatory to* [read *in preparation for*] the construction of the building." *Waikiki Resort Hotel, Inc. v. City & County of Honolulu*, 624 P.2d 1353, 1360 (Haw. 1981).
- "On April 6, 1994, defendant mailed proxy materials to its shareholders *preparatory to* [read *in preparation for*] the annual meeting scheduled for May 11, 1994." *Smith v. Orange & Rockland Utils., Inc.*, 617 N.Y.S.2d 278, 279 (Sup. Ct. 1994).
- "This privilege covers communications adjunct or *preparatory to* [read *in preparation for*] legal proceedings such as communications to an attorney." *Long v. Marubeni Am. Corp.*, 406 F.Supp.2d 285, 294 (S.D.N.Y. 2005).

The phrase is likewise pretentious in place of *before*—e.g.: "Upon the appellant's conviction and *preparatory to* [read *before*] sentencing, the trial court ordered a presentence report." *Robinson v.*

Commonwealth, 413 S.E.2d 661, 661 (Va. Ct. App. 1992). Cf. ***preliminary to,** ***prior to** & **antecedent.**

prepense. The phrase *malice prepense* is obsolete for *malice aforethought*. See **aforethought** & **malice aforethought.**

***preplan** is illogical for *plan* because one can plan something beforehand only. E.g.: "Ninety percent of wasting time and standing in line can be eliminated with a little *preplanning* [read *planning*] and some common sense." Mark H. McCormack, *What They Don't Teach You at Harvard Business School* 212 (1984). See ILLOGIC & REDUNDANCY.

preponderance of the evidence; clear and convincing evidence. The first phrase, denoting the greater weight of the evidence, is the "traditional measure of persuasion in civil cases." John W. Strong et al., *McCormick on Evidence* § 340, at 575 (4th ed. 1992). The phrase *clear and convincing evidence*—as well as half a dozen or so variations, such as *clear, convincing, and satisfactory evidence*—denotes a "more exacting measure." *Id.* But this heightened standard, however expressed, remains fuzzy: "It has been persuasively suggested that [the standard] could be more simply and intelligibly translated to the jury if they were instructed that they must be persuaded that the truth of the contention is 'highly probable.'" *Id.* at 575–76. See **burden of proof** & **balance of probability.**

preponderantly; *preponderately. The better form is *preponderantly*, though the NEEDLESS VARIANT *preponderately* is becoming commonplace—e.g.: "For an award of supplemental earnings benefits, the claimant must *preponderately* [read *preponderantly*] prove an inability to earn 90 percent of pre-injury wages." *Britton v. Morton Thiokol, Inc.*, 604 So.2d 130, 134 (La. Ct. App. 1992).

Preponderate should be used only as a verb, not as an adjective—or, by derivation, as an adverb. Cf. **predominate.**

PREPOSITIONS. A. Ending Sentences with. The spurious rule about not ending sentences with prepositions is a remnant of Latin grammar, in which a preposition was the one word that a writer could not end a sentence with. But Latin grammar never should have been thought to straitjacket English grammar. If the SUPERSTITION is a "rule" at all, it is a rule of rhetoric and not of grammar, the idea being to end sentences with strong words that drive the point home. That principle is sound, of course, but not to the extent of meriting lockstep adherence.

Churchill's witticism about this preposterous bugaboo should have laid it to rest. When someone once upbraided him for ending a sentence with a preposition, he rejoined, "That is the type of arrant pedantry up with which I shall not put." Avoiding a preposition at the end of the sentence sometimes leads to just such a preposterous monstrosity.

Perfectly natural-sounding sentences end with prepositions, particularly when a verb compounded with a preposition appears at the end (as in *follow up* or *ask for*). E.g.: "The unlawful act must have some causal connection with the injury complained of." *Larrimore v. American Nat'l Ins. Co.*, 89 P.2d 340, 343 (Okla. 1939). When one decides against such formal (sometimes downright stilted) constructions as *of which*, *on which*, and *for which*—and instead chooses the relative *that*—the preposition is necessarily sent to the end of the sentence: "I must respectfully dissent, for this is a point on which I must insist" becomes far more natural as, "I must respectfully dissent, for this is a point that I must insist on."

Moreover, good writers often end their sentences with prepositions—e.g.:

- "But the admission of consuls into the United States, where no previous treaty has stipulated it, seems to have been nowhere provided for." *The Federalist* No. 42, at 265 (James Madison) (Clinton Rossiter ed., 1961).
- "At first sight it is little to the credit of Montesquieu's and Vico's contemporaries that their work was not followed up." Frederick Pollock, "The History of Comparative Jurisprudence," in *Essays in the Law* 1, 22 (1922).
- "Sound objectives became confused and were even lost sight of." Fleming James, *Civil Procedure* § 2.5, at 66 (1965).
- "There is always some unrepealed junk that nobody will make an effort to get rid of." Patrick Devlin, *The Enforcement of Morals* 126 (1968).
- "The trouble is that Holmes failed to keep in mind his own profound insight into the complex interplay between new materials drawn from life and old materials from the past which have not yet been sloughed off." Grant Gilmore, *The Ages of American Law* 53 (1977).
- "The involuntary bailee can be quickly disposed of. He is one who has been sent goods that he did not ask for." Glanville Williams, *Textbook of Criminal Law* 694 (1978).
- "The result of this was that agreements in restraint of trade were frequently made and frequently abided by." P.S. Atiyah, *An Introduction to the Law of Contract* 248 (3d ed. 1986).
- "Perhaps it is possible for a particular case to be either within or without the judicial power, depending on the court it is in." Charles Alan Wright, *The Law of Federal Courts* 50 (5th ed. 1994).

See HYPERCORRECTION (I) & SUPERSTITIONS (A).

For an interesting—and incorrect—example involving *where it is at*, see **at.**

B. Redundancy of. Writers often repeat prepositions unnecessarily when there are intervening phrases or clauses. E.g.: "Clearly, the grandparents, *with* whom the minor children had lived *with* [delete the first *with*] for over two years, have a statutory priority to adopt the children." *L.R. v. Department of Children & Fams.*, 822 So.2d 527, 531 (Fla. Dist. Ct. App. 2002). Cf. **so as** [+ infinitive].

C. Wrongly Elided. But just as often, necessary prepositions are wrongly omitted, usually because of the proximity of the same preposition performing a different function—e.g.: "An acceptance which requests a change [*of*] or addition to the terms of the offer is not thereby invalidated unless the acceptance is made to depend on an assent to the changed or added terms." Restatement (Second) of Contracts § 61 (1981).

Occasionally prepositions are omitted for fear of ending a sentence with one—e.g.:

- "He participated in this much worse event than any of his prior criminal history *that we are aware* [read *that we are aware of*]." *People v. Smith*, 39 Cal. Rptr. 2d 513, 514 n.2 (Ct. App. 1995). Or, one might say, *of which we are aware.*
- "An owner of land may sell portions of it and make restrictions as to its use for the benefit of himself as well as for the benefit of those *to whom he sells* [*whom he sells to*]." *Gambrell v. Nivens*, 275 S.W.3d 429, 436–37 (Tenn. Ct. App. 2008).

The writers should not have feared writing *aware of* and *sells to*. See (A).

There is at least one other type of problem caused by prepositions wrongly omitted: an AMBIGUITY may result. For example, *Attorney Solicitation* is the title of a law review article; yet from the title, one does not know whether the article refers to the solicitation of, or solicitation by, attorneys. That anyone with legal knowledge would presume the latter does not vindicate the writer's vagueness. See NOUN PLAGUE. See also (E).

D. Correctly Matching with Verbs. A useful rule of thumb—by no means to be taken as an absolute rule—in determining what preposition to use with a given verb is to follow the prefix of that verb. Hence *inhere in*, *comport with* (L. *com-* "with"), *attribute to* (L. *ad-* "to"), and so on. But there are many exceptions. *Impute* takes *on*, *oblivious* takes *of*, and *in respect* can take either *of* or *to*, though *with respect* takes only *to*.

The verbs used in criminal law are sometimes tricky. Following are the correct prepositions for some of the common verbs:

acquitted *of* burglary
acquitted *on* an indictment, count, or charge of burglary
charged *in* (AmE) or *on* (BrE) an indictment or count
charged *with* murder
convicted *of* burglary
convicted *on* an indictment, count, or charge of burglary
indicted *for* embezzlement
indicted *on* a charge of embezzlement
pleaded guilty *to* a charge or count of murder
pleaded guilty *to* murder
sentenced *on* an indictment, count, or charge
tried *on* an indictment, count, or charge

Many other verbs are treated throughout this work. Readers with an interest in a more detailed, comprehensive treatment of this subject may benefit from the following works: Morton Benson et al., *The BBI Combinatory Dictionary of English: A Guide to Word Combinations* (1986); Frederick T. Wood, *English*

Prepositional Idioms (1967); and A.P. Cowie & R. Mackin, *The Oxford Dictionary of Current Idiomatic English* (1975).

E. Repetition of After Conjunctions. Often it is useful in avoiding AMBIGUITY to repeat the preposition governing the noun after *or* or *and*. E.g.: "Is it a question *of* law or *of* fact?"

A statute drafter's failure to repeat such a preposition resulted in litigation that worked its way to the U.S. Supreme Court. The question arose whether an agency could remove a case under the following provision:

> (a) A civil action or criminal prosecution commenced in a State court against any of the following persons may be removed by them to the district court of the United States. . . .
>
>   (1) Any officer of the United States or [of] any agency thereof. . . .

The Supreme Court used grammatical analysis in concluding that the removal by an agency was improper: "We find that . . . the first clause of § 1442(a)(1) grants removal power to only one grammatical subject, '[a]ny officer,' which is then modified by a compound prepositional phrase: 'of the United States or [of] any agency thereof.'" *International Primate Protection League v. Tulane Educ. Fund*, 500 U.S. 72, 79–80 (1991). See (c).

F. Getting It Wrong. Writers often use the incorrect preposition—e.g.:

- "If a spouse must receive an elective-share trust, and subsequently a QTIP interest, there are significant consequences *to* [read *for*] the surviving spouse." Lauren B. Epstein, *The QTIP Trust and the Elective Share Trust*, 53 Fla. L. Rev. 965, 983 n.143 (1999).
- "The debtor's argument that he was a simple, unsophisticated, and inexperienced individual, ignorant *to* [read *of*] the meaning of tenants by the entirety, is belied by his sophistication, experience, conduct, and constant reliance on counsel." *In re Adam*, 406 B.R. 717, 732 (Bankr. E.D. Va. 2009).

See **as to (A).**

prerequisite; requisite. Rarely is *prerequisite* used with the degree of punctilio that Eric Partridge prescribed: "Properly, a *prerequisite* has to be obtained or fulfilled before a *requisite* can be attended to. In short, *prerequisite* is rarely permissible." Vigilans [Eric Partridge], *Chamber of Horrors* 114 (1952). Probably it is more accurate to say that *prerequisite* simply includes a time element, whereas *requisite* does not. See also **perquisite.**

prerogative; *prerogatory. *Prerogative* (= of, relating to, or exercising an exclusive right or privilege) is the standard term. **Prerogatory* is a NEEDLESS VARIANT— e.g.: "At this time, a *prerogatory* [read *prerogative*] writ is not before the court in this case." *Mott v. England*, 604 P.2d 560, 564 (Wyo. 1979).

prerogative writs. During the 16th century, this name was given to administrative writs such as mandamus, certiorari, habeas corpus, and prohibition—each of which was originally in the nature of an administrative order from a superior official commanding a subordinate to do something, give some information, or the like. As a major legal historian notes, however, the name *prerogative writs* "was not altogether apt, because in the early stages of their expansion these writs were mainly used to curb prerogative activity by councillors and conciliar courts." J.H. Baker, *An Introduction to English Legal History* 165–66 (3d ed. 1990).

The phrase *extraordinary writs*, which is perfectly equivalent, is more genuinely descriptive, and therefore preferable.

*prerogatory. See **prerogative.**

prescribe, vb. In lay writing, *prescribe* is transitive only: doctors prescribe drugs and moralists prescribe rules of conduct. Yet some writers blunder.

In the civil-law tradition, as in Louisiana and Scotland, *prescribe* has a special intransitive sense: "[of an action] to suffer prescription; to lapse, to become invalid or void by passage of time; to be no longer capable of prosecution" (*OED*). E.g.:

- "We need not unravel this jurisprudence to determine whether any of his trespass claims for damages for the actual taking of his property have *prescribed* [i.e., *become void by passage of time*]." *Mississippi River Transmission Corp. v. Tabor*, 757 F.2d 662, 671 (5th Cir. 1985).
- "Generally, in workers' compensation cases, all claims for payments *prescribe* [i.e., *cease to be capable of prosecution*] one year after the accident giving rise to the claim occurred." *Ardoin v. Firestone Polymers, LLC*, 30 So.3d 177, 182 (La. Ct. App. 2009).
- "Respondent agreed to represent Mr. Wells, who had a cause of action for battery against Jimmy Pepitone [that] was about to *prescribe* [i.e., *lapse*]." *In re Wells*, 36 So.3d 198, 205 (La. 2010).

Cf. **prescription.**

The civilian sense of *prescribe* has also been employed transitively (and therefore in the PASSIVE VOICE)—a sense not listed in the *OED*: "It was shown that the property involved was the same property as that in a suit brought in the Louisiana court a few years earlier where the same restrictive covenant was held *to have been prescribed* by two years['] continued violation." *Warner v. Walsdorf*, 277 F.2d 679, 680 (5th Cir. 1960). See **proscribe.**

prescription. In law, this term frequently refers to the legal effect that the passage of time has on a person's rights or obligations. That effect may be to establish those rights or obligations (positive prescription), fortify them (another type of positive prescription), or extinguish them (negative prescription). For example, under the (English) Prescription Act 1832, a right to an easement may be established through continual use over 20 years' time. In the U.S., periods for prescription vary from state to state: they are sometimes 10, 15, or 20 years. Cf. **proscription.**

present, adj. Phrases such as *the present testator* and *the present trust* have become common spin-offs of *the present case* and *the present writer.* (See FIRST PERSON (A).) Rarely, however, does this *present* serve any purpose: it hasn't in the past and it won't in the future. See **instant case.**

present, vb. See **confront.**

presentable has nearly opposite senses in nonlegal and legal contexts. Whereas fops go to great lengths to make themselves "presentable," criminals subject to presentment are also said to be "presentable"— e.g.: "The grand jury may indict an accused for any 'indictable or *presentable* offense found to have been committed or to be triable within the county.'" *State v. Spradlin,* 12 S.W.3d 432, 434 n.3 (Tenn. 2000) (quoting a Tennessee statute).

present case. See **instant case.**

presenter; *presentor. The preferred spelling is *-er.* The two legal senses are (1) "a person who makes a presentment"; and (2) "a person who presents a petition, bill, etc. (i.e., makes a presentation)." For more detail on sense 1, see **presentment.**

presentiment. See **presentment.**

presenting jury. See **grand jury (A).**

presently contains an AMBIGUITY. In the days of Shakespeare, it meant "immediately." Soon its meaning evolved into "after a short time" (perhaps because people exaggerated their promptitude); this sense is still current. Then, chiefly in AmE, it took on the additional sense "at present; currently." Some writers deprecate this sense, but the *Oxford Guide* states that it is "widely used and often sounds more natural than *at present.*" It certainly appears in formal legal prose in this sense, especially in AmE. But *now* or *currently* is invariably a better choice—e.g.:

- "Widespread inconsistency in defining male and female *presently* occurs even though some courts have adopted a bright-line rule." Rachel Duffy Lorenz, Comment, *Transgender Immigration,* 53 UCLA L. Rev. 523, 555 (2005).
- "*Presently* pending before the Court is defendant's motion to dismiss the amended complaint for lack of subject matter jurisdiction or, in the alternative, for failure to state a claim upon which relief can be granted." *Marsoun v. U.S.,* 591 F.Supp.2d 41, 42 (D.D.C. 2008).

Cf. **momentarily.**

presentment; presentiment. The first means "the act of presenting or laying before a court or other tribunal a formal statement about a matter to be dealt with legally." (For the special sense of *presentment* in criminal law, see **indictment.**) The second means "a vague mental impression or feeling of a future event."

*presentor. See **presenter.**

presents, know all men by these. See **know all men by these presents.**

present time, at the. This phrase is wordy for *now.*

present writer is today generally considered inferior to *I* or *me.* See **present** & FIRST PERSON (A).

preservation; *preserval. The second is a NEEDLESS VARIANT.

presidence; presidency. The first means "the action or fact of presiding"; the second means "the office or function of president."

president. In corporate law, the term is used differently in AmE and BrE. In AmE, *president* often denotes the chief executive director of a company; but in BrE, it is a title usually given to a nonexecutive former head of a company.

presiding judge. See **chief judge.**

presiding juror. See **foreman** & SEXISM (B).

prestatutory. So spelled. See PUNCTUATION (G).

presumably. See **presumptively.**

presume. See **assume.**

presumption. A. Generally. *Presumption* = (1) a legal inference or assumption that a fact exists, based on the known or proven existence of some other fact or facts; or (2) a judicially applied prediction of factual or legal probability. E.g.:

- "The provision creates a conclusive *presumption* of carrier knowledge that a shipment contains tobacco when it is marked as originating from a Maine-licensed tobacco retailer." *Rowe v. New Hampshire Motor Transp. Ass'n,* 552 U.S. 364, 372 (2008) (per Breyer, J.).
- "Bonney presented very little evidence to rebut the *presumption* of insanity or the evidence that she might be at risk to herself and others if she were to be released." *Bonney v. State,* 673 S.E.2d 102, 105 (Ga. Ct. App. 2009).

In American law, the most basic distinction is between a *presumption of law* and a *presumption of fact.* A *presumption of law* is a rule of law by which the finding of a basic fact gives rise to a presumed fact capable of being rebutted. A *presumption of fact* is simply an argument; it is an inference that may be drawn from the establishment of a basic fact, but need not be drawn as a matter of law—e.g., that the possessor of recently stolen goods is the thief. This distinction is increasingly rejected. See **rebuttable presumption.**

British lawyers distinguish between the following types: (1) presumptions *juris et de jure,* which are irrebuttable; (2) presumptions *juris,* which are rebuttable by evidence; and (3) presumptions of fact, which are merely inferences.

B. *Presumption of innocence; presumption of sanity.* In criminal law, a *presumption* is not an inference drawn from facts but rather an assignment of the burden of proof. A defendant is entitled to a *presumption* *of innocence* and doesn't have to produce any evidence to support it. The prosecution must overcome the presumption by proving guilt beyond a reasonable doubt.

A defendant who asserts insanity as an affirmative defense bears the burden of overcoming the *presumption of sanity* by adducing evidence that he or she was insane when committing the crime.

presumptive; presumptuous. *Presumptive* = (1) giving reasonable grounds for presumption or belief; warranting inferences; or (2) based on presumption or inference. E.g., in sense 2: "The expense of keeping informed from day to day of substitutions among even current income beneficiaries and *presumptive* remaindermen . . . would impose a severe burden on the plan." *Mullane v. Central Hanover Bank & Trust Co.*, 339 U.S. 306, 318 (1950) (per Jackson, J.). (For *heir presumptive*, see **heir (B).**) *Presumptuous* = arrogant, presuming, bold, forward, impudent.

presumptively; presumably. These words are often used synonymously in English prose, but in legal writing are commonly differentiated. *Presumptively* = by legal presumption. E.g.: "The literal words of the statute are *presumptively* conclusive of legislative intent, but that presumption may be defeated by contrary indications of intent also evident on the face of the statute." *Presumably* = as one may presume or reasonably suppose; by presumption or supposition.

*presumptively presumed is redundant for *presumed*—e.g.:

- "It has been noted by more than one court that one who is the founder, chief stockholder, president and member of the board of directors or a corporation should be *presumptively presumed* [read *presumed*] to be a person responsible under § 6672 for the collection and payment of employee withholding taxes." *Kinnie v. U.S.*, 771 F.Supp. 842, 849 (E.D. Mich. 1991).
- "[T]he labeling of the product complies with all federal regulations, and is *presumptively presumed* [read *presumed*] safe to use, and that there is no caveat, warning, or other limitation that is mandatory." Robert L. Stephens Jr., CLE Presentation, *Getting Your Evidence and Expert Testimony Admitted into Court in Montana*, 30906 NBI-CLE 53 (2006).

Perhaps what the authors intended was *conclusively presumed*.

presumptuous. See **presumptive.**

pretence. See **pretense.**

pretense; pretence. The AmE spelling is *-se*, the BrE spelling *-ce*. See **false pretenses.**

pretentious (= making claim to great merit or importance) for *pedantic* (= overrating or parading book-learning or technical knowledge) is an unthinking blunder: "The line between owner and repairman is dull and elusive at best; fortunately, Congress has for future cases ended this sometimes *pretentious* [read *pedantic*] distinction." *Pichoff v. Bisso Towboat Co.*, 748 F.2d 300, 303 (5th Cir. 1984).

pretermit. A. Connotation of Purposefulness. *Pretermit* generally connotes "to overlook or ignore purposely"—e.g.:

- "Our finding [that] the exceptions of lis pendens were properly sustained renders all other issues moot, and therefore, we *pretermit* discussion of these issues." *Calbert v. Batiste*, 31 So.3d 332, 332 n.3 (La. 2010).
- "*Pretermitting* whether trial counsel's performance was deficient due to his failure to obtain an electronic enhancement of the videotape prior to trial, Faulkner has failed to show that he was prejudiced as a result of trial counsel's inaction." *Faulkner v. State*, 697 S.E.2d 914, 916–17 (Ga. Ct. App. 2010).

Yet in the legal phrase *pretermitted child statutes*, the word *pretermitted* means "neglected or overlooked accidentally." E.g.: "*Pretermitted* statutes do not restrict testamentary freedom and therefore should be encouraged." Terry L. Turnipseed, *Why Shouldn't I Be Allowed to Leave My Property to Whomever I Choose?*, 44 Brandeis L.J. 737, 779 (2006). This sense derives from Roman law, which had the special term *preterition* for the omission by a testator to mention in his will one of his children or natural heirs.

B. For *prevent*. *Pretermit* does not properly mean "to prevent, preclude, or obviate"—though legal writers commonly seem to attribute those meanings to the word. E.g.:

- "It is incorrect in reading the 'subject only to' language as *pretermitting* [read *precluding*] a reading of the contract as a whole to flesh out the extent of Global Marine's obligation under § XV(C)." *Weathersby v. Conoco Oil Co.*, 752 F.2d 953, 956 (5th Cir. 1984).
- "This remand *pretermits* [read *obviates*] the necessity of reviewing Blue Cross's denial on the merits." *Lafleur v. Louisiana Health Serv. & Indem. Co.*, 563 F.3d 148, 160 (5th Cir. 2009).
- "When such a prejudicial error of law skews the trial court's finding of a material issue of fact and causes it to *pretermit* [read *preclude*] other issues, the appellate court is required, if it can, to render judgment on the record by applying the correct law and determining the essential material facts de novo." *Key v. Monroe City Sch. Bd.*, 32 So.3d 1144, 1149 (La. Ct. App. 2010).

C. In Immigration Law. Although the *OED* declares *pretermit* in the sense of "to suspend or terminate" rare, it's actually quite common in U.S. immigration courts, especially in the phrase *motion to pretermit* (= an attempt to preemptively terminate an alien's application pending in immigration court)—e.g.:

- "The evidence of Lara-Rivas's use of a false U.S. passport to obtain a California driver's license was properly admitted in support of the government's *motion to pretermit* his adjustment application." *Lara-Rivas v. Mukasey*, 270 Fed. Appx. 526, 526 (9th Cir. 2008).

An asterisk (✳) precedes words and phrases that are invariably inferior forms.

- "At a hearing, the government made an oral *motion to pretermit* Jeronimo's motion for cancellation of removal. The Immigration Judge ('IJ') granted the government's oral motion and denied Jeronimo cancellation of removal." *Jeronimo v. U.S. Attorney Gen.*, 330 Fed. Appx. 821, 822 (11th Cir. 2009).
- "The IJ held, and the BIA affirmed, that Toribio's request for cancellation of removal should be *pretermitted* and further denied on the merits for failure to satisfy this standard." *Toribio-Chavez v. Holder*, 611 F.3d 57, 64 (1st Cir. 2010).

Because *pretermit* has other senses, it is not always clear in immigration contexts what it actually means. And it can cause confusion among generalist judges. Only the most ingenious and astute judge, like Judge Richard A. Posner, is likely to sort out the semantic nuances:

> Because the petitioner was barred from receiving a waiver of inadmissibility, she could not apply for an adjustment of status. But rather than say that, the immigration judge "pretermitted" the application. This word is used by the immigration court and the Board of Immigration Appeals whenever an alien is found ineligible to apply for some form of relief. The common dictionary meanings of "pretermit" are to leave undone, to neglect, to omit, to overlook intentionally, to let pass without mention or notice, to interrupt or terminate, to suspend indefinitely. It might seem that because the petitioner's application for adjustment of status is premature and will remain so until the ten years are up, it is the last meaning of *pretermit*—to suspend indefinitely—that is the one the Board intends. It is the sense in which the word is used in the only regulation of the Board that we've found that uses it.
>
> That would mean that the petitioner's application for adjustment of status would be put in the freezer until she became eligible to apply in ten years. But that is not correct. To obtain legal residence in the United States, she must, when she becomes eligible to apply for permission to reapply for admission, apply for that permission. If permission to enter is granted, she can then reapply for adjustment of status—but not before. To say that her application for adjustment of status has been "pretermitted" is therefore unnecessarily vague; her application has been dismissed. *Gonzalez-Balderas v. Holder*, 597 F.3d 869, 870 (7th Cir. 2010) (per Posner, J.).

pretextual (= constituting a pretext), though not recognized in the *OED*, *W11*, or *W3*, is common in American legal writing. E.g.:

- "Whether the purpose of the statute is to screen the courts against *pretextual* grievances or to protect the respondent . . . , we need not inquire." *Cameron v. Cameron*, 56 S.E.2d 384, 388 (N.C. 1949).
- "There is no evidence to support a contention that the arrest for the traffic violation was *pretextual*." *State v. Moody*, 443 S.W.2d 802, 804 (Mo. 1969).
- "[Audio's] explanation for [Muhammad's] suspension and subsequent discharge is *pretextual*." *Muhammad v. Audio Visual Servs. Group*, 380 Fed. Appx. 864, 869 (11th Cir. 2010).

See **nonpretextual.**

pretrial. One word, unhyphenated. See PUNCTUATION (G).

prevalent is accented on the first, not the second, syllable: /**prev**-ə-lənt/.

prevarication. See **lie,** n.

prevent now ordinarily takes *from*, although archaically it is used with a direct object and a participle. E.g.: "The release or return may not operate to *prevent* future action to collect *from* the same or other property owned by obligor." Tex. Fam. Code. § 157.321 (Vernon 2008). In BrE this usage remains common.

Prevent there causes ugly and ungrammatical constructions—e.g.: "Officer Valdivia's hidden intent *prevented there* from being a completed act of prostitution." *Wooten v. Superior Ct.*, 113 Cal. Rptr. 2d 195, 212 (Ct. App. 2001). A suggested revision: *Officer Valdivia's hidden intent prevented the completion of an act of prostitution.*

See **pretermit (B).**

preventive; *preventative. The correct form is *preventive*— as both noun and adjective—although the corrupt, extrasyllabled form **preventative* is unfortunately common. E.g.:

- "As for . . . misplaced words—possibly the best *preventative* [read *preventive*] is a secretary who majored in English composition." Mortimer Levitan, *Confidential Chat on the Craft of Briefing*, 1957 Wis. L. Rev. 59, 62.
- "It is in no sense a *preventative* [read *preventive*] remedy, but is prospective merely." 52 Am. Jur. 2d *Mandamus* § 9, at 337 (1970).
- "Greater willingness to make doctors liable means that they are forced to practise what is called '*preventative* [read *preventive*] medicine' and order costly, complicated, and often unnecessary tests." Reginald W.M. Dias & Basil S. Markesinis, *Tort Law* 3 (1984).

preverdict. So spelled—without a hyphen. See PUNCTUATION (G).

previous. See **prior.**

previously; before, adv. Although **previous to* is much inferior to *before* as a preposition, just the opposite holds true for the adverbs. *Previously* is better than *before*, at least when the adverb comes before the verb— e.g.: "As *before* [read *previously*] mentioned, residency is a question of physical fact and intention or belief is not a relevant consideration." *Wall Rose Mut. Ins. Co. v. Manross*, 939 A.2d 958, 969 (Pa. Super. Ct. 2007).

*previous to for *before* is unnecessarily highfalutin— e.g.: "At no time *previous to* [read *before*] its brief on the merits before this Court did respondent argue that the question might not be properly presented." *California State Bd. of Equalization v. Sierra Summit, Inc.*, 490 U.S. 844, 846 n.3 (1989) (per Stevens, J.).

One sometimes even finds *previously to*—e.g.:

- "The requisites . . . are to be performed at the time of, and *previously to* [read *before*] entering into the contract." *Levinson v. Boas*, 88 P. 825, 829 (Cal. 1907).

- "Parker testified the jacket had been given to him some time *previously to* [read *before*] December 16 by Weaver." *Weaver v. State*, 481 So.2d 832, 834 (Miss. 1985).
- "Indiana trial courts lack authority to enforce even an agreed-upon division of property insofar as it divides amounts of gross military retirement pay that were, *previously to* [read *before*] the decree, waived." *Bandini v. Bandini*, 935 N.E.2d 253, 262 (Ind. Ct. App. 2010).

See ***prior to.** Cf. **anterior** & **antecedent.**

prevision = foresight. E.g.: "Life will have to be made over, and human nature transformed before *prevision* so extravagant can be accepted as the norm of conduct, the customary standard to which behavior must conform." *Palsgraf v. Long Island Ry.*, 162 N.E. 99, 100 (N.Y. 1928) (per Cardozo, C.J.). The word is not to be confused with the ordinary term, *provision*.

prideful. See **proud.**

prima facie (= at first sight) may function as either an adjective or an adverb, here as an adverb: "Publication of such language *prima facie* constitutes a wrong without any allegation or evidence of damage other than that which is implied or presumed from the fact of publication." Occasionally, the phrase even serves as a SENTENCE ADVERB—e.g.: "*Prima facie*, a crime will be tried in the county in which it was committed." Edward Jenks, *The Book of English Law* 50 (P.B. Fairest ed., 6th ed. 1967).

Adjectival uses are perhaps even more common today—e.g.:

- "Worthy should not have been dismissed from the action unless it was clear that BPS could not establish *prima facie* liability on any of them." *BPS, Inc. v. Worthy*, 608 S.E.2d 155, 160 (S.C. Ct. App. 2005).
- "The required *prima facie showing* is not especially burdensome." *Rodriguez-Quiñones v. Lehigh Safety Shoe Co.*, 736 F.Supp.2d 445, 455 (D.P.R. 2010).

On hyphenating this phrase when it functions as an adjective, see PHRASAL ADJECTIVES (B).

Sometimes the phrase appears to have been misused for *per se*, as here: "In libel, with perhaps some exceptions, defamatory matter is *prima facie libelous* [read *per se libelous*]." *Ransom v. Matson Nav. Co.*, 1 F.Supp. 244, 247 (W.D. Wash. 1932). See **at first blush.**

prima facie case = (1) the establishment of a legally required presumption that may be rebutted; or (2) the plaintiff's burden of producing enough evidence to permit the fact-trier to infer the fact at issue. *Texas Dep't of Cmty. Affairs v. Burdine*, 450 U.S. 248, 254 n.7 (1981) (per Powell, J.). *Black's* defines *prima-facie case* as "a party's production of enough evidence to allow the fact-trier to infer the fact at issue and rule in the party's favor," and as "the establishment of a legally required rebuttable presumption." (*Black's Law Dictionary* 1310 (9th ed. 2009)). E.g.: "Until he has proved that the defendant will in that case profit at

his expense, he has not made out a *prima facie case* to be paid anything, and until he has proved how much that profit will be, his *prima facie case* is not complete." *Gillis v. Cobe*, 59 N.E. 455, 594 (Mass. 1901).

primary, in the JARGON of insurers, is sometimes used as an attributive noun for *primary beneficiary*. Following is an example from a life-insurance policy: "When the insured dies, payment will be made in equal shares to the primary beneficiaries living when payment is made. If a *primary* dies after the first payment is made, that *primary*'s unpaid share will be paid in equal shares to other *primaries* living when payment is made."

primary jurisdiction. See **original jurisdiction.**

primary liability. See **vicarious liability.**

primary responsibility. See **vicarious liability.**

prime (= to take priority over) is a usage unknown to lay writing. E.g.:

- "Travis County's lien *primed* all other liens on such property." *In re First Magnus Fin. Corp.*, 415 B.R. 416, 426 (Bankr. D. Ariz. 2009).
- "In the event of conversion to Chapter 7, the lien would *prime* the rights of the trustee to recover his or her administrative expenses." *In re Successor Borrower Servs., LLC*, 426 B.R. 68, 70 (Bankr. W.D.N.Y. 2010).

primer, in the sense of "an introductory or refresher book," is always pronounced /**prim**-ər/. The undercoat to paint is pronounced /**prɪ**-mər/.

primogenital; *****primogenitary;** *****primogenitive.** For the adjective corresponding to *primogeniture*, the prevailing form—though it may breed MISCUES—is *primogenital*. The other choices are NEEDLESS VARIANTS. See **primogeniture.**

primogeniture; *****primogenitureship;** **primogenitor.** *Primogeniture* means (1) "the fact or condition of being the firstborn of the children of the same parents"; or (2) (at common law) "the right of succession or inheritance belonging to the firstborn, often involving the exclusion of all other children." In many civil-law countries, the equivalent term for sense 2 is *majorat*.

**Primogenitureship* is a NEEDLESS VARIANT of *primogeniture*—e.g.: "Considering that the purpose of introducing the words 'heirs and assigns' into deeds and wills was to prevent the operation of the principle of *primogenitureship* [read *primogeniture*], . . . it becomes readily apparent that the words as used here are meaningless and inaptly used." *Whitehead v. McCoy*, 29 A.2d 729, 731 (N.J. Ch. 1943).

Primogenitor denotes "the first parent; earliest ancestor." (Loosely, it is used for *progenitor* [= forefather, ancestor].) See **progenitor.**

principal, n. **A. And** *principle,* n. In lay usage, it is usually enough to remember that *principal* (= chief; primary; most important) is almost always an adjective, and *principle* (= a truth, law, doctrine, or course of action) is virtually always a noun. Although *principle* is not a verb, we have *principled* as an adjective. (See **principled.**)

In legal language, *principal* is often a noun, an elliptical form of *principal person* or *actor,* primarily in agency law and criminal law. *Principal* also acts as a shortened form of *principal investment* in the context of investments, banking, and trusts. See **corpus** & **res.**

Misusing *principal* for *principle* is fairly common—e.g.: "The *principals* [read *principles*] underlying the anti-trust laws are as old as the early English statutes against combinations in restraint of trade and price-fixing agreements." Stephen Pfeil, "Law," in 17 *Encyclopedia Americana* 86, 92 (1953).

Likewise, the opposite error sometimes occurs—e.g.:

- "My *principle* [read *principal*] disagreement is . . . ." Lloyd L. Weinreb, *Fair's Fair: A Comment on the Fair Use Doctrine,* 103 Harv. L. Rev. 1137, 1140 (1990).
- "[The] portfolio of currently available securities . . . will return *principle* [read *principal*] and interest in future years to replace the lost nominal earnings." George A. Schieren, *On Using Minimum-Cost Portfolios to Determine Present Value,* 4 J. Legal. Econ. 47, 51 (1994).

B. Criminal Law: *principal* **and** *accessory.* At common law, *principal in the first degree* = the perpetrator of a crime; *principal in the second degree* = one who helped at the time of the crime; *accessory before the fact* = one who successfully incited a felony; and *accessory after the fact* = one who, knowing a felony has been committed, tried to help the felon escape punishment.

American and English experts in criminal law have written how advantageous it would be to speak in terms other than *principals* and *accessories* to crimes. In the U.S., for example, it "is much less confusing . . . to speak of a perpetrator of second degree murder, or an abettor of first degree murder, than it is to refer to a *principal* in the first degree to murder in the second degree, or a *principal* in the second degree to murder in the first degree." Rollin M. Perkins & Ronald N. Boyce, *Criminal Law* 735 (3d ed. 1982). The Model Penal Code is not worded in terms of *principals* and *accessories.* For more, see **confederate.**

In Great Britain, the Criminal Law Act 1967 abolished the distinction between felonies and misdemeanors, consequently abolishing accessories and making every participant a principal. The better English authorities recommend *perpetrator* (= the person who in law performs the offense). *See* Glanville Williams, *Textbook of Criminal Law* 285–86 (1978). See **perpetrator.**

C. Agency Law: *undisclosed principal; unidentified principal;* **unnamed principal;* **partially undisclosed principal.* The first two phrases are quite distinct. An *undisclosed principal* is a principal whose existence a third party lacks notice of when an agent interacts with the third party on the principal's behalf. An *unidentified principal* is a principal whose identity (as opposed to existence) a third party lacks notice of when the agent and the third party interact. Among the undesirable synonyms of *unidentified principal* are **unnamed principal* and **partially undisclosed principal.* *See* Restatement (Third) of Agency § 1.04 cmt. b (2006).

D. Meaning "principal investment." See **corpus.**

principled, as often used of decisions and judgments, means "resting on reasons that in their generality and neutrality transcend the immediate result involved." *See* Herbert Wechsler, *Toward Neutral Principles of Constitutional Law,* 73 Harv. L. Rev. 1, 19 (1959). When used of persons, *principled* means "having principles or scruples."

prior; previous. The adjective *prior* or *previous* for *earlier* is within the stylist's license; **prior to* and **previous to* in place of *before* are not. See **antecedent,** **previous to* & **prior to.*

prioritize. Writers with sound stylistic priorities avoid this word. See **-IZE.**

prior restraint = censorship before publication. E.g.: "Unless we assume that the statute is a mere symbolic gesture, we must conclude that it will create a significant *prior restraint* on adult access to protected speech." *U.S. v. American Library Ass'n, Inc.,* 539 U.S. 194, 225 (2003) (Stevens, J., dissenting).

*prior to is a terribly overworked lawyerism. Only in rare contexts is it not much inferior to *before.* Even the U.S. Supreme Court has suggested that the phrase is "clumsy," noting that "legislative drafting books are filled with suggestions that . . . *prior to* be replaced with the word *before.*" *U.S. v. Locke,* 471 U.S. 84, 96 n.11 (1985) (per Marshall, J.). Nevertheless, examples abound in virtually any piece of legal writing:

- "The agency also began using its pattern of violations authority *which* [insert comma before *which*] had lain dormant for many years *prior to* [read *before*] *Sago.*" C. Gregory Ruffennach, *Free Markets, Individual Liberties, and Safe Coal Mines,* 111 W. Va. L. Rev. 75, 102 n.158 (2008). For more on the nonrestrictive *which*-clause in this sentence, see **that & which.**
- "Petitioner requested withdrawal of his motion for voluntary departure *prior to* [read *before*] expiration of his 30-day departure period." *Dada v. Mukasey,* 554 U.S. 1, 22 (2008) (per Kennedy, J.).

As Bernstein has pointed out, you should feel free to use **prior to* instead of *before* only if you are accustomed to using **posterior to* for *after.* Theodore M. Bernstein, *The Careful Writer* 347 (1979). Cf. **antecedent,** **anterior to,* **preliminary to,* **previous to* & **subsequent to.*

prise. See **prize.**

*prisoned is a NEEDLESS VARIANT of *imprisoned.*

prisoner; inmate; confinee; captive; convict. These terms all denote one who is deprived of liberty and held in custody. *Prisoner* can be a general term <are you holding me prisoner?>, but it most commonly denotes someone who is being kept in a prison or penitentiary <the prisoners are allowed one exercise period each day>. *Inmate* and *confinee* bear a similar sense: they typically refer to one who is confined either for a shorter period or in a low-security facility. (*Inmate* can also mean "one who shares a dwelling with others," but this sense is archaic.)

Confinee (= a person held in confinement), though it appears in *RH2*, is missing from most major English dictionaries, such as the *OED* and *W3*. Sometimes it looks suspiciously like a mere EUPHEMISM for *prisoner*—e.g.: "There's also plenty of recreational opportunities and commonly a rather sizable contingent of well-educated and formerly prominent *confinees*." Paul Galloway, *Celebrity Cons Put Prisons on Guard*, Chicago Trib., 29 Oct. 1989, at 1C. At other times, though, it performs the useful function of distinguishing between those confined for criminal offenses and those confined (perhaps temporarily) for other reasons—e.g.: "*Thompson* rejected a claim that Treatment Center patients were entitled to an annual review similar to the one afforded *confinees* under Chapter 123." *Pearson v. Fair*, 935 F.2d 401, 413 (1st Cir. 1991). See NEOLOGISMS.

Captive connotes a seizure by force, as with a prisoner of war or someone held for ransom; it often suggests subjugation or forced labor as much as it does imprisonment. *Convict*, though literally applicable to an accused person who has been found guilty of a crime, applies more often to such a person with a particular set of associations: an imprisoned person serving a long sentence for a serious offense and wearing the distinctive garb of those so situated.

privacy, right of. See **right of privacy.**

private Act. See **public Act.**

private arrest. See **citizen's arrest.**

private bill. See **public Act.**

private international law. See **conflict of laws** & **international law.**

private law. See **public law.**

private prosecutor. See **prosecutor.**

private school. See **public school.**

privilege is a slippery legal word most commonly denoting a person's legal freedom to do or not to do a given act. In the 19th century, it was not clearly distinguished from *right*—e.g.:

- "The word 'right' is defined by lexicographers to denote, among other things, property, interest, power, prerogative, immunity, *privilege* (*Walker's Dict.*, word 'Right')." *People v. Dikeman*, 7 How. Pr. 124, 130 (N.Y. Sup. Ct. 1852).

- "The words 'right' or '*privilege*' have, of course, a variety of meanings, according to the connection or context in which they are used. Their definition, as given by standard lexicographers, include 'that which one has a legal claim to do,' 'legal power,' 'authority,' 'immunity granted by authority,' 'the investiture with special or peculiar rights.'" *U.S. v. Patrick*, 54 F. 338, 348 (M.D. Tenn. 1893).

Wesley Newcomb Hohfeld noted that *privilege* in legal usage includes (1) the "privilege" of a landowner to enter the land (*Some Fundamental Legal Conceptions as Applied in Judicial Reasoning*, 23 Yale L.J. 16, 52–53 (1913)); (2) a homeowner's "privilege" to eject a trespasser (*id.* at 35 n.39); (3) a "privilege" to utter a libel (i.e., a privileged communication) (*id.* at 39–40); (4) a criminal defendant's "privilege" against self-incrimination (*id.*); and (5) a person's "privilege" to enter another's land by license (*id.* at 43–44). He drew distinctions between rights, licenses, and privileges, and defined *privilege* as the opposite of or negation of a *duty* and as the correlative of *no-right* (i.e., the lack of a right). *Id.* at 29, 32. But the unclear usages Hohfeld noted a century ago still persist.

The word is often misspelled **priviledge*. The pages of American law reports are riddled with examples followed by "[*sic*]." It even appears mistakenly in law reviews—e.g.:

- "The court accepted his argument that the disclosure would violate his *priviledge* [read *privilege*] against self-incrimination since he was charged with violating the plaintiff's trademark." Sue Holloway, *"Black Box" Agreements*, 23 Cal. W. Int'l L.J. 199, 211 n.98 (1992).

- "The assignee argued that the *priviledge* [read *privilege*] only encompassed the specific machines manufactured *prior to* [read *before*] the application date." F. Andrew Ubel, *Who's on First?—The Trade Secret Prior User or a Subsequent Patentee*, 76 J. Pat. & Trademark Off. Soc'y 401, 410 (1994). For the use of **prior to* in that sentence, see ***prior to.**

privileges and immunities; privileges or immunities. The first phrasing appears in Article 4, § 2 of the U.S. Constitution; the second appears in the Fourteenth Amendment. The *Privileges and Immunities* Clause is the important one: "The Citizens of each State shall be entitled to all Privileges and Immunities of Citizens in the several States." This seminal clause prohibits a state from favoring its own citizens by discriminating against nonresidents who come into the state. *See Toomer v. Witsell*, 334 U.S. 385, 396 (1948).

The *Privileges or Immunities* Clause, by comparison, is obscure and unimportant: "No State shall make or enforce any law which shall abridge the privileges or immunities of citizens of the United States." Five years after the Fourteenth Amendment was ratified, the Supreme Court read this clause as being limited to privileges of national, as opposed to state, citizenship. *See The Slaughter House Cases*, 83 U.S. (16 Wall.) 36, 55 (1873). And these privileges, while not trivial, are extremely limited; they encompass such liberties as being able to cross state lines freely and being able to vote in national elections.

privity; privy. In a nonlegal literary sense, a *privity* is something kept secret <there were several privities between just them>. To a lawyer, it is a relationship between two parties that is recognized by law, usually a mutual interest in a transaction or thing <in privity of contract>.

Privy likewise has different associations for nonlawyers and lawyers. To nonlawyers it is an adjective meaning "secret; private," or a plural noun (*privies*) meaning "outhouse; toilet." Lawyers mean no harm in calling other people *privies*; a *privy* in law is one who is a partaker or has any part or interest in any action, matter, or thing. E.g.: "[Collateral estoppel] bars the same parties or their *privies* from relitigating in a later proceeding legal or factual issues that were actually raised and necessarily determined in an earlier proceeding." *Mullins v. State*, 294 S.W.3d 529, 534 (Tenn. 2009).

The word is also used adjectivally in this legal sense—e.g.: "The trial court granted Mrs. Bridges' motion for summary judgment, on the theory that the children are not *privies* in law, fact, or estate with appellee." *Richardson v. Bridges*, 389 S.E.2d 215, 216 (Ga. 1990). Still, *privy* is used in its lay senses in legal writing—most commonly "participating in the knowledge of something private"—and the legal reader must be adept at discerning which sense is intended: "Because the parties had stipulated prior to trial that Christen had a prior trafficking conviction in 1995, the jury was not *privy* to this information." *State v. Christen*, 976 A.2d 980, 984 n.5 (Me. 2009).

prize; prise. *Prize* is the spelling for all senses but one: to *prise* is to pry or force open. Yet in AmE *prize* often appears in this sense. The DIFFERENTIATION is worth promoting. For the piratical sense of *prize*, see **spoils.**

pro and con; pro et con. The English rendering—*pro and con*—is preferred. The other is the LATINISM for "for and against."

The plural *pros and cons* is commonly used as a noun phrase—e.g.: "The agency must provide notice to the public by undertaking the required rulemaking process so that the *pros and cons* can be weighed." *California Sch. Bds. Ass'n v. State Bd. of Educ.*, 113 Cal. Rptr. 3d 550, 575 (Ct. App. 2010). Or it may be adverbial: "The issues raised by the pleadings have not been dispelled by the affidavits filed *pro and con* on the motion for summary judgment." *Fleischmann v. Donner*, 300 So.2d 26, 26 (Fla. Dist. Ct. App. 1974). One should not depart from the SET PHRASE: "Now we are obliged to advert to those elements of proof and legal concepts *pro and contra* [read *pro and con*] bearing upon the validity of the instrument in question." *In re Estate of Powers*, 134 N.W.2d 148, 158 (Mich. 1965).

Pro and con has also been used as a verb phrase <to pro-and-con the issue>, and although today this use sounds somewhat odd, it has the sanction of long

standing. The *OED* and *W3* record another use not here recommended: the phrase has been used prepositionally <arguments pro and con the proposal>, but in such a context the native-English *for and against* would be better.

probable; likely; possible. These words—in order of decreasing strength—express gradations of the relative chance that something might happen. With a coin toss, for example, you cannot say that it is *probable* that it will turn up heads, though you might say that it is *likely*. (Of course, it would be equally likely to turn up tails.) The word *likely*, then, as Glanville Williams puts it, is "a strong '*possible*' but a weak '*probable*.'" Glanville Williams, *Criminal Law* 59 (2d ed. 1961). And the word *possible*, of course, embraces a wide gamut: everything from the remotest chance to a 100% certainty.

probable cause. The Fourth Amendment to the U.S. Constitution states that neither arrest warrants nor search warrants may issue without a prior showing of "*probable cause*." The standard probably began as a looser one than *good cause*—looser because more guesswork is involved in deciding whether cause is "probable" (i.e., "provable," from the Latin *probabilis*—not merely "likely") than whether it is "good."

Today, however, *probable cause* is such an important constitutional standard that it is rarely thought of in conjunction with *good cause*. It now has an established place as a TERM OF ART, though its precise contours will probably always remain vague. Cf. **good cause shown.**

probate, n., = the act by which a testamentary document is judicially established as having been a testator's final will. But the word has been extended well beyond that traditional sense. Today it often includes everything that a personal representative does in handling a decedent's estate.

As an adjective, the word takes on still other shades of meaning. *Probate code* = the entire statutory law of decedents' estates, substantive as well as procedural. *Probate law* = the law of succession, including both statutes and caselaw. See ***probatum*** & **proof (B).**

probate, as a transitive verb, is an Americanism. The word means "to admit (a will) to proof" <the will was probated in 1992>. By extension, it is sometimes said that a lawyer *probates an estate*.

During the 20th century, *probate* acquired unrelated senses, as the BACK-FORMATION from *probation*: (1) "to grant probation to (a criminal)"; and (2) "to reduce (a sentence) by means of probation." E.g.:

- (Sense 1) "A suspended sentence shall have the effect of *probating* the defendant." *Wood v. State*, 21 S.E.2d 915, 918 (Ga. Ct. App. 1942).
- (Sense 2) "The conviction['s] . . . validity plays no necessary part in the consideration of whether a *probated* prison term should be continued." *U.S. v. Francischine*, 512 F.2d 827, 828 (5th Cir. 1975).

****probatee** is a NEEDLESS VARIANT of *probationer*—
e.g.: "Oregon's statutes required that a *probatee* [read
probationer] not be required to pay said fees unless he
is or will be able to do so . . . [and] that the *probatee*
[read *probationer*] may petition to have the unpaid
portion 'forgiven.'" *White Eagle v. State*, 280 N.W.2d
659, 661 (S.D. 1979). See *-EE*.

probation = (1) a procedure by which a convicted
offender is released, subject to court-imposed conditions, rather than being sent to prison; or (2) the act
of proving judicially (a will, etc.).

Sense 2, recorded in Scottish law dictionaries but
rarely elsewhere, is attested in the *OED* by two 16th-
century citations and nothing more recent. Although
it is still used in some stock phrases such as *admit to
probation* (Scot.), it is otherwise fairly uncommon. But
it was revived in 20th-century AmE—e.g.:

- "When an estate is in process of *probation*, the authority
  to sue for its assets rests in the administrator or executor."
  Demmer v. Stroude, 40 F.Supp. 795, 796 (N.D. Tex. 1941).
- "The district court . . . remanded the estate to the probate
  court for completion of administration thereof, which in
  effect ordered *probation* of the will without limitation as
  to the property to be administered." *In re Estate of Jones*,
  366 P.2d 792, 793 (Kan. 1961).
- "The caveators further alleged that 'their rights will be
  affected to their prejudice by the *probation* of said instruments as the Last Will and Testament and First Codicil.'"
  In re Will of Ashley, 208 S.E.2d 398, 399 (N.C. Ct. App.
  1974).

probationary; ****probational;** ****probatory.** The second
and third are NEEDLESS VARIANTS. See **probative.**

probationer; parolee. *Probationer* = a person, esp. a
convict, on probation. (See **probation** & ****probatee.**)
Parolee = one released on parole. See **parole.**

probative; ****probatory.** *Probative* = (1) tending or
serving to prove; (2) exploratory; serving to test; or
(3) in Scots law, self-proving <a probative deed>.
In the law of evidence, sense 1 is invariably the one
intended, though it is of more recent origin. E.g.: "Evidence even upwards of nine years old has been found
probative of intent." *U.S. v. Impastato*, 535 F.Supp.2d
732, 736 (E.D. La. 2008). See **probity.**

**Probatory is a NEEDLESS VARIANT of either *probative* (most commonly) or *probationary*.

probativeness. See **probity.**

****probatory.** See **probationary** & **probative.**

probatum /proh-**bay**-təm/ = something proved or
conclusively established. (Cf. *ipse dixit.*) It sometimes
appears in its plural form (*probata*) and is usually
nothing but a highfalutin equivalent of *proof*—e.g.:
"Defendant Griffin contends there is a fatal variance between the *allegata* [read *allegations*] and the
probata [read *proof*], arguing that the State's proof
that he struck Dexter Harper with his feet and fists is

insufficient to support his conviction for aggravated
assault by shooting Dexter Harper with a handgun."
Griffin v. State, 449 S.E.2d 341, 343 (Ga. Ct. App.
1994). See LATINISMS.

probe. See **investigation.**

probity means "honesty; integrity." E.g.: "It is beyond
either human capacity or the demands of justice that
the trial judge decide correctly every issue arising in
the trial. What is required is not a perfect score, but
fairness, *probity*, and the avoidance of substantial prejudice." *Ruiz v. Estelle*, 679 F.2d 1115, 1132 (5th Cir.
1982). For more on this term and its near-synonyms,
see **honesty.**

Unfortunately, *probativeness*, which means "the
quality of tending to prove something," and its adjective, *probative*, are frequently confused with *probity*.
E.g.:

- "The standard for admissibility was one of relevance and
  probity [read *probativeness*] balanced against possible
  prejudicial effects." Shubha Ghosh, *Fragmenting Knowledge, Misconstruing Rule 702*, 1 Chi.-Kent J. Intell. Prop.
  1, 40 (1999).
- "Unexcepted hearsay evidence creates this risk because
  it is frequently *probative* on the issue of the existence of
  a material fact, but its *probity* [read *probativeness*] does
  not make it reliable evidence." Chris Funderburg, *Evidence
  Law at SOAH*, 10 Tex. Tech Admin. L.J. 423, 430 (2009).
- "The Defendants challenge the relevance and *probity* [read
  probativeness] of the prior lawsuits." *Gray v. City of Hammond, Indiana*, 693 F.Supp.2d 823, 833 (N.D. Ind. 2010).

Probity is also occasionally misused for *propriety*—
e.g.: "The ISO standards are not binding on Euclid,
and Euclid contests the *probity* [read *propriety*] of
using these standards." *Bartley v. Euclid, Inc.*, 158 F.3d
261, 279 n.2 (5th Cir. 1998).

problematic; problematical. Both forms appear in
modern writing. Though *problematic* is now more
usual, euphony may sometimes lead a writer to choose
problematical.

problem-solving, a VOGUE WORD among lawyers and
social scientists, is best avoided when possible. E.g.:
"This technique of *problem-solving* [read *solving problems*] lacks rationality." *Oklahoma Bar Ass'n v. Denton*,
598 P.2d 663, 667 (Okla. 1979).

**pro bono publico. A. Historical and Grammatical
Development.** The phrase *pro bono publico* is an old
one in Anglo-American law. Originally, it was not
restricted to a lawyer's duty, but instead referred to
anything done for the public good. The phrase can be
found in Coke's 17th-century commentary on Littleton's *Tenures*: "It appeereth that owners are in that case
bound *pro bono publico* to maintain houses and mills
which are for habitation and use of men." Co. Litt.
200b (1628). As in that example, the early British and
American uses of the phrase were adverbial, and they
related to anything done for the public good—e.g.:

- "In the case of charity, the King, *pro bono publico*, has an original right to superintend the case thereof, so that, abstracted from the statute of Eliz., relating to charitable uses, and antecedent to it, as well as since, it has been every day's practice to file informations in Chancery, in the Attorney-General's name, for the establishment of charities." *Eyre v. Countess of Shaftesbury*, 2 P. Wms. 103, 119, 24 Eng. Rep. 659, 664 (1722). On the use of *antecedent to* in that sentence, see **antecedent.**
- "Indeed, I know of no case, where the doctrine of relation, which is a mere fiction of law, is allowed to prevail, unless it be in furtherance and protection of rights, *pro bono publico*." *In re Richardson*, 20 F. Cas. 699, 702 (D. Mass. 1843).
- "It is sought here to hold a municipal corporation, acting *pro bono publico*, responsible not only for its own neglect to repair, but also for that of its officer in failing to observe the ordinance for the inspection of the bridge." *Weightman v. Corporation of Wash.*, 66 U.S. (1 Black) 39, 44–45 (1861) (per Clifford, J.).

Today, of course, the phrase refers primarily to a lawyer's services performed for the public good (see (B)), but this usage is comparatively recent. Few reported decisions predating the 1970s refer to this lawyerly duty. But there is a late-19th-century reference in an Illinois opinion to a lawyer's acting for a client *pro bono publico*: "McKenzie & Calkins, *pro bono publico*." *Board of Educ. v. Arnold*, 1 N.E. 163, 163 (Ill. 1884).

The adverbial uses have persisted, usually when the full phrase appears, as opposed to the shortened form *pro bono* (see below)—e.g.: "In a time when the need for legal services among the poor is growing and public funding for such services has not kept pace, lawyers' ethical obligation to volunteer their time and skills *pro bono publico* is manifest." *Mallard v. U.S. Dist. Court for S. Dist. of Iowa*, 490 U.S. 296, 310 (1989) (per Brennan, J.).

The adjectival uses, however, are perhaps the most common today—e.g.:

- "Although one proposal requiring mandatory *pro bono publico* work by attorneys was recently voted down by the American Bar Association, the very proposal itself indicates the awareness of the bar of its obligation to protect the right of indigent litigants." *Caruth v. Pinkney*, 683 F.2d 1044, 1049 (7th Cir. 1982).
- "A lawyer should aspire to render at least (50) hours of *pro bono publico* legal services per year." Model Rules of Professional Conduct Rule 6.1 (1994).
- "The Commission sought to accentuate the duties of lawyers that transcended their responsibilities to clients—for example, by . . . requiring lawyers to devote a portion of their time to *pro bono publico* work." Marc Galanter, *Predators and Parasites*, 28 Ga. L. Rev. 633, 642 (1994).

Lawyers have shortened the phrase to *pro bono*. It is typically a phrasal adjective—unhyphenated, of course, as a phrase of foreign origin (see PHRASAL ADJECTIVES (B))—modifying a simple noun or noun phrase—e.g.:

- "It is reasoned that an attorney, as an officer of the court, has the duty to assist the court, without compensation, in the administration of justice and, similarly, that every attorney is deemed to have consented to *pro bono*

appointments by virtue of having accepted his license to practice law." *State v. Oakley*, 227 S.E.2d 314, 318–19 (W. Va. 1976).
- "At the time that the 1853 law was passed, there was no clear conception of '*pro bono* work.' Those who debated the bill appeared to contemplate that one might do some uncompensated service for a constituent, a friend or a relative, but not for a needy stranger." Lisa G. Lerman, *Public Service by Public Servants*, 19 Hofstra L. Rev. 1141, 1176 (1991).
- "Lawyers tend not to find time to fulfill their *pro bono* obligations." Harry T. Edwards, *The Growing Disjunction Between Legal Education and the Legal Profession*, 91 Mich. L. Rev. 34, 68 (1992).
- "*Pro bono* work will, by definition, take some time away from ordinary law practice, but there is no reason to think that it will compromise the 'ethic of excellence' with regard either to free or paying clients." Steven Lubet, *Professionalism Revisited*, 42 Emory L.J. 197, 204 (1993).
- "I have never found a case of a lawyer disbarred for not performing *pro bono* service." Patrick L. Baude, *An Essay on the Regulation of the Legal Profession and the Future of Lawyers' Characters*, 68 Ind. L.J. 647, 658 (1993).
- "A lawyer has an obligation to render public interest and *pro bono* legal service." N.Y. Jud. Law app., Code of Professional Responsibility EC 2–25 (McKinney Supp. 1994).

At times, the phrase *pro bono* is even used as a noun phrase itself, that is, as a short form of *pro bono work* or *pro bono services*, as in the title of the following article: Lewis S. Calderon et al., *Mandatory Pro Bono for Law Students: Another Dimension in Legal Education*, 1 J.L. & Pol'y 95 (1993). E.g.:

- "Those who previously performed voluntary *pro bono* for the poor will suddenly feel cheated out of their voluntary goodwill as the bar or the state coerces them into satisfying a minimum number of hours." B. George Ballman Jr., *Amended Rule 6.1*, 7 Geo. J. Legal Ethics 1139, 1164 (1994).
- "One of the strongest arguments against mandatory *pro bono* for licensed lawyers is the negative effect that such a plan might have on lawyers' intrinsic motivation." Elena Romerdahl, *The Shame of the Legal Profession*, 22 Geo. J. Legal Ethics 1115, 1128 (2009).

B. Arguments over Modern Meaning. For a phrase whose modern content was only fairly recently acquired, *pro bono* has generated many hot debates about meaning. Broadly speaking, there are two camps: those who support a wide definition and those who support a narrow one.

Broadly, *pro bono* legal services include any uncompensated work that a lawyer performs for the public good. Some guides adopt the broad definition. For example, a Georgia guide defines *pro bono service* as "any uncompensated services performed by attorneys for the public good . . . , [including] civic, charitable and public service activities, as well as activities that improve the law, the legal system, and the legal profession." *State Bar of Georgia Handbook* 10 (Supp. 1993). The narrow definition, by contrast, limits the work specifically to services performed for indigents, as opposed to charitable organizations such as symphonies, museums, and the like. E.g.:

- "The purpose of a narrow definition of *pro bono* is to ensure that legal aid is provided to those who need it most—the poor." Kim Schimenti, Comment, *Pro Choice for Lawyers in a Revised Pro Bono System*, 23 Seton Hall L. Rev. 641, 693 n.254 (1993).

- "At Tulane, *pro bono* work is synonymous with poverty law and hence *pro bono* projects may not encompass work for the government such as working for the offices of the Public Defender or the District Attorney." Lewis S. Calderon et al., *Mandatory Pro Bono for Law Students*, 1 J.L. & Pol'y 95, 103–04 (1993).

One reason for preferring the broad over the narrow definition is that specialists—such as those lawyers who work exclusively in corporate mergers and acquisitions—may find it difficult to take up the causes of indigents, especially if that work were to involve court appearances. The literature on pro bono work reflects this very problem: "The focus must be on the definition of '*pro bono* services.' Such a term should be broadly defined to provide ample opportunities for contributions by all types of lawyers engaged in different specialties." "*. . . In the Spirit of Public Service*": *A Blueprint for the Rekindling of Lawyer Professionalism*, 112 F.R.D. 243, 297 (1986). Also, though one can hardly imagine more important work than what is done on behalf of the poor, society inarguably benefits from many other public services that lawyers perform. It is therefore difficult, if not impossible, to justify a dogmatic insistence on the narrow definition on historical grounds or linguistic grounds—indeed, on any grounds other than one's own modern view of sound public policy.

In any event, of course, it is quite misleading to define *pro bono* as meaning merely "unpaid," as here: "He was a strong proponent of requiring lawyers to perform '*pro bono*'—unpaid—services." Glenn H.W. Fowler, *Robert McKay, 70, Legal Scholar and Head of 1971 Attica Panel*, N.Y. Times, 14 July 1990, at 11.

C. Roman or Italic? Most legal writers today treat the phrase *pro bono* as being fully anglicized; therefore, they do not italicize it. (It is italicized in the preceding sentence only because it is a phrase being referred to as a phrase.)

D. Hyphenating the Phrasal Adjective. Some writers hyphenate *pro bono* when it serves as an adjective. Others, however, who see *pro bono* as a SET PHRASE that needs no hyphen, have the better position—e.g.:

- "In Atlanta, for example, five local bar associations have recruited 1,025 attorneys to do *pro-bono* [read *pro bono*] indigent defense as part of the 1,000 Lawyers for Justice, which has taken on 305 cases thus far this year." Peter Applebome, *Indigent Defendants, Overworked Lawyers*, N.Y. Times, 17 May 1992, at 18.
- "The U.S. legal profession, more than any other, has fostered the idea of countervailing legal power, supporting legal services for the poor, [and] imposing a generalized obligation of *pro-bono* [read *pro bono*] service." David M. Trubek et al., *Global Restructuring and the Law*, 44 Case W. Res. L. Rev. 407, 426 (1994).

See PHRASAL ADJECTIVES (B).

E. *Mandatory pro bono*. Some writers have suggested that the phrase *mandatory pro bono* is an OXYMORON—e.g.:

- "Because pro bono publico service historically has referred to charitably donated assistance, the term '*mandatory pro bono*' is itself a problem—a classic oxymoron, not unlike *jumbo shrimp* and *military intelligence*." Esther F. Lardent, *Mandatory Pro Bono in Civil Cases*, 49 Md. L. Rev. 78, 79 (1990).
- "In a sense, the concept of *mandatory pro bono* is an oxymoron, like military music." Roger C. Cramton, *Mandatory Pro Bono*, 19 Hofstra L. Rev. 1113, 1132–33 (1991).

The reason, of course, for seeing the phrase as a contradiction in terms is that, in the modern American lawyer's mind, *pro bono* equates with "voluntary." It has always been hard to compel charity—and impossible to compel charitableness.

proceduralist (= a specialist in legal procedure) is a 20th-century legal NEOLOGISM. E.g.:

- "So wrote one of America's greatest *proceduralists*, Judge Charles E. Clark, in a 1945 dissent." Charles Alan Wright, *The Law of Federal Courts* 678 (4th ed. 1983).
- "There is a widespread belief among *proceduralists*, both judges and scholars, that the pleading rules should be used to control the federal docket, especially expensive, complex, and time-consuming class actions." Roy L. Brooks, *Conley and Twombly: A Critical Race Theory Perspective*, 52 How. L.J. 31, 61 (2008).
- "The complexities of managing and resolving disputes in a federal trial court call upon the judge's skill and expertise as a manager, a *proceduralist*, a realist, and a legalist who must interpret and apply a range of substantive laws." Maureen N. Armour, *Remembering Judge Sanders*, 62 SMU L. Rev. 1547, 1559 (2009).

procedural law; substantive law. Separating these two phrases presents no small conundrum. The problem, as Justice Frankfurter once observed, is that "*substance* and *procedure* are the same keywords to very different problems. Neither *substance* nor *procedure* represents the same invariants. Each implies different variables depending upon the particular problem for which it is used." *Guaranty Trust Co. v. York*, 326 U.S. 99, 108 (1945). The decision whether a particular issue is "substantive" or "procedural" may vary depending on whether the context relates to a court's rulemaking power, to resolving a question concerning conflict of laws, or to applying state or federal law.

Traditionally, *substantive law* (one of Bentham's coinages) denotes the law that lays down people's rights, duties, liberties, and powers. Hence, substantive law addresses such issues as what rights one has against trespassers. By contrast, *procedural law* (also called *adjective law*) consists of the rules by which one establishes one's rights, duties, liberties, and powers—either by litigation or otherwise. How to start an arbitration or a lawsuit and proceed with it—or how to get a clerk to issue a writ—is a matter of procedural law. See **adjective law.**

In some contexts—usually involving the law of a single jurisdiction—the dichotomy seems admirably straightforward. In criminal law and procedure, *substantive law* declares what acts are crimes and imposes penalties, while *procedural law* sets the steps by which a violator is brought to punishment. Similarly, in civil law and procedure, *substantive law* defines the rights and duties of persons, while *procedural law* defines the steps in having a right or duty judicially defined or enforced.

proceed. See **precede** (A).

proceeding; proceedings. In reference to business done by a tribunal of any kind, *the proceeding* and *the proceedings* are interchangeable. And both are so common that it would be impossible to brand either one as inferior. But if several hearings are referred to, *proceedings* is the better choice.

proceeds, n. (= the value of land, goods, or investments when converted into money), takes a plural verb. But some writers want to write *proceeds is* instead of the correct form, *proceeds are*—e.g.: "Appellants raise the legal question of whether the District Court . . . infringed on their rights to seek further relief under Montana law after the $50,000 in insurance *proceeds is* [read *proceeds are*] distributed." *Infinity Ins. Co. v. Dodson*, 14 P.3d 487, 491 (Mont. 2000).

Proceeds in this sense is accented on the first syllable /**proh**-seeds/, not the second. But the verb use <she proceeds slowly> is /prə-**seeds**/.

process has the special legal senses (1) "the proceedings in any action or prosecution" <due process>; and (2) "the summons by which a person is cited to appear in court" <service of process>. Sense 2 is especially baffling to nonlawyers unfamiliar with legal procedures. E.g.: "A person charged with or convicted of a felony and released on bail who, in order to evade the *process* of the court, willfully fails to appear as required, is guilty of a felony." *People v. Walker*, 59 P.3d 150, 158 (Cal. 2002).

In sense 2, *process* may serve either as a count noun (as in the preceding example) or as a mass noun (as in *service of process*).

process of, in the. Often useless verbiage. Cut it.

processual (= of or relating to a legal process) began as a 19th-century term used by legal historians writing about Roman law. In the latter half of the 20th century, though, American legal writers adopted it—e.g.:

- "That court would . . . promptly have reversed and remanded for due hearing and with firm suggestion that the board examine and then conform to the *processual* religion of the act of 1952." *Superx Drugs Corp. v. State Bd. of Pharmacy*, 125 N.W.2d 13, 18 (Mich. 1963).
- "The clear statement and the standardless delegation doctrines are *processual* in nature." Franklin E. Fink, Note, Abourezk v. Reagan: *Curbing Recent Abuses of the Executive Immigration Power*, 21 Cornell Int'l L.J. 147, 178 (1988).

prochein ami (= a "next friend" who represents an underage plaintiff's interests in litigation) is preferably so spelled. E.g.: "Sugimoto also represents Kristy Lacaran-Chong, a minor, as *prochein ami* or next friend." *Wong-Leong v. Hawaiian Indep. Refinery, Inc.*, 879 P.2d 538, 541 n.2 (Haw. 1994). *Prochein amy (used by Blackstone), *prochain ami, and *prochain amy are variant spellings to be avoided. See **next friend** & LOAN TRANSLATIONS.

proconsulate; *proconsulship. The second is a NEEDLESS VARIANT.

procreative; *procreational. The first is standard, *procreational being a NEEDLESS VARIANT.

procuration; procurement; *procurance; procuracy. Traditionally, *procuration* has meant "the act of appointing another as one's attorney-in-fact or agent." By transference the term has referred also to the authority vested in a person so appointed. E.g.: "Any trading done without the express authorization from Poplar Grove, through Carter Wilkinson, was done 'outside the limits of his *procuration*.'" *Poplar Grove Planting & Refining Co. v. Bache Halsey Stuart Inc.*, 465 F.Supp. 585, 592 (M.D. La. 1979).

Finally, *procuration* has been used as the generic noun for *procure*, but this broad sense is best reserved for *procurement*—e.g.:

- "Active *procuration* [read *procurement*] of the execution of the will did not give rise to this presumption even where there was opportunity." *In re Dopkins' Estate*, 212 P.2d 886, 891 (Cal. 1949).
- "If, however, the warrant was issued under authority of state law then every requirement of Rule 41 is not a *sine qua non* to federal court use of the fruits of a search predicated on the warrant, even though federal officials participated in its *procuration* [read *procurement*] or execution." *U.S. v. Sturgeon*, 501 F.2d 1270, 1273 n.5 (8th Cir. 1974).

Procurement has had another, more restricted sense in legal contexts: "persuading or inviting a woman or child to have sexual intercourse." E.g.: "Defendant, Linda Sue Esch, appeals the judgment of conviction entered on a jury verdict finding her guilty of . . . two counts of *procurement* of a child for sexual exploitation." *People v. Esch*, 786 P.2d 462, 464 (Colo. Ct. App. 1989). *Procurance is a NEEDLESS VARIANT.

Procuracy /**prok**-yə-rə-see/ = a letter of agency; the document empowering an attorney-in-fact to act.

procurator. See **attorney** (A).

procure is a FORMAL WORD for *get* (the ordinary word)—even more formal than *obtain*.

procurement. See **procuration.**

procuring breach of contract. See **tortious interference with contractual relations.**

procuring cause. See CAUSATION (C).

prodigality; profligacy. *Prodigality* means "lavishness; extravagance." *Profligacy* means primarily "salaciousness; licentiousness," but it also shares the sense of *prodigality*.

prodigious for *prestigious* is a MALAPROPISM—e.g.: "The American Law Institute is one of the most select and *prodigious* [read *prestigious*] legal organizations in this country."

producible. So spelled; **producable* and **produceable* are infrequent misspellings.

producing cause. See CAUSATION (C).

production burden. See **burden of proof (A).**

productive of, be. See BE-VERBS (B).

products liability; product liability. The general area of law is known as *products liability*. Occasionally one sees the singular form *product liability*, usually in reference to a particular product of a particular manufacturer. When the phrase is used adjectivally, it should be hyphenated <products-liability case>. See PHRASAL ADJECTIVES.

pro et con. See **pro and con.**

profane; profanatory. That which is *profane* is irreverent or blasphemous; that which is *profanatory* tends to make (something) profane.

proferens = the party that proposes or adduces a contract or a condition in a contract. E.g.: "If the clause contains language which expressly exempts the person in whose favour it is made (hereinafter called 'the *proferens*') from the consequence of the negligence of his own servants, effect must be given to that provision." *Smith v. South Wales Switchgear Ltd.*, [1978] 1 All E.R. 18 (H.L.). The plural is *proferentes*. See *contra proferentem* (A).

profert in curia; *profert in curiam. Profert in curia (= to produce a deed in court simultaneously with a related pleading) has always been the preferred form and now is the only accepted form. **Profert in curiam* was always far less common, and by 1950 it had mostly disappeared from legal writing. It should now be treated as a NEEDLESS VARIANT.

profession. This word has been much debased of late, primarily at the hands of egalitarians who call any occupation a profession. In any American city today, a person seeking a job as a barber, manicurist, or manager of a fast-food store turns in the classified advertisements to the section "Professions." A lawyer looking for a change in jobs turns to "Advanced Degree Required," a section of its own rather than a subsection of "Professions."

Traditionally there have been but three professions: theology, law, and medicine. These were known either as *the three professions* or as *the learned professions*. The term was ultimately extended to mean "one's principal vocation," which embraces prostitution as well as medicine. (*The oldest profession* originally had an irony much stronger than it has today.)

The restricted sense of *profession* no doubt strikes many people as snobbish and anachronistic. What about university professors, atomic physicists, and engineers? Perhaps three professions are not enough, but we ought at least to use *some* discrimination, with emphasis on "prolonged specialized training in a body of abstract knowledge." William J. Goode, *Encroachment, Charlatanism, and the Emerging Profession*, 25 Am. Soc. Rev. 902, 903 (1960). Professional training "must lead to some order of mastery of a generalized cultural tradition, and do so in a manner giving prominence to an *intellectual* component." Talcott Parsons, "Professions," 12 *International Encyclopedia of Social Science* 536, 536 (1968).

Notably, the traditional, artificially restricted view of the term has long been considered archaic. Holmes wrote in 1896: "It is not likely . . . that anybody will be prejudiced against business or will take formal views of the dignity of callings such as a hundred years ago put the ministry first, law and medicine next, and below them all other pursuits." Oliver Wendell Holmes, "The Bar as a Profession," in *Collected Legal Papers* 153, 153 (1952).

On the other side of the Atlantic, hardly a generation later, Lord Justice Scrutton wrote that, although *profession* used to be confined to the three learned professions, by 1919 it had a broader meaning: "A '*profession*' in the present use of language involves the idea of an occupation requiring either purely intellectual skill, or of manual skill controlled, as in painting and sculpture, or surgery, by the intellectual skill of the operator, as distinguished from an occupation which is substantially the production or sale or arrangements for the production or sale of commodities." *Commissions v. Maxse*, [1919] 1 K.B. 647, 657 (C.A.).

proffer is chiefly a literary and legal term; it is equivalent to *offer*, and, like that word, may be both noun and verb. So, as a noun:

- "The trial court considered the *proffer* by the defense before excluding the eyewitness expert testimony." *People v. Aguilar*, 918 N.E.2d 1124, 1135 (Ill. App. Ct. 2009).
- "A rational trier of fact could conclude that the facts in her *proffer*, if proven, were sufficient to satisfy the elements of the compulsion defense." *State v. Leprowse*, 221 P.3d 648, 650 (Mont. 2009).

And as a verb:

- "Defendants *proffer* a conflicting version of the facts." *Lopez-Machin v. Indupro*, 668 F.Supp.2d 320, 322 (D.P.R. 2009).

An asterisk (✳) precedes words and phrases that are invariably inferior forms.

- "Counsel's *proffered* reasons for failing to offer Dr. Ofshe's testimony are also problematic." *Lunbery v. Hornbeak*, 605 F.3d 754, 764 (9th Cir. 2010).

It is occasionally misspelled **profer*—e.g.: "But the very point of the article, of course, is based on the *pro-ferred* [read *proffered*] fact that Rehnquist is rapidly becoming the chief declarer of what the Constitution requires." Sanford Levinson, *Law as Literature*, 60 Tex. L. Rev. 373, 398–99 (1982).

profferer. So spelled—not *-or*.

profits. In drafting, this word is often vague, so it is generally best defined. *Gross profits*, for example, is usually different from *gross receipts*, and whatever is to be deducted ought to be mentioned explicitly in the definition. Even more obviously in need of definition is *net receipts*, which patently involves deductions of some kind.

profits à prendre, known also as *right of common*, denotes the right exercised by one person to enter another's land and take away some part of the soil, such as the profits from the soil. As its form suggests, *profits à prendre* is a LAW FRENCH survival; it remains fairly common. E.g.: "The rights Beaubien granted to the settlers were *profits à prendre* or, in more modern parlance, easements appurtenant to the land owned or occupied by the original settlers." *Lobato v. Taylor*, 70 P.3d 1152, 1156 (Colo. 2003).

Profit à prendre has been rendered *profit a' prendre* by some for whom the grave accent apparently was not typographically possible. *See, e.g.*, *McDonald v. Board of Miss. Levee Comm'rs*, 646 F.Supp. 449, 469 (N.D. Miss. 1986). Omitting the accent completely from this phrase is preferable, however, to using an apostrophe in its stead.

profligacy. See **prodigality.**

pro forma (= as a matter of form; for the sake of form) usually has a slightly depreciative tone in modern usage. The term need not be hyphenated as an adjectival phrase. See ADJECTIVES (C).

progenitor. A *progenitor* is one that yields *progeny*—e.g.: "As March 1, 1913, receded in time, the 1913 basis became increasingly moot, and the other initial basis rules, the illegitimate progeny of 1913 basis, became far more important than the *progenitor* rule itself." Calvin H. Johnson, *The Legitimacy of Basis from a Corporation's Own Stock*, 9 Am. J. Tax Pol'y 155, 174 (1991). See **primogenitor.**

progeny. A. Plural in Sense. *Progeny* is usually plural in sense and hence takes a plural verb. E.g.: "The *prog-eny* of *Williamson v. U.S.* indicates [read *indicate*] that *Williamson* requires reversal only when the specific defendant was picked out for the informer's effort by a government agent." Another word is required when the sense is singular, as in the following sentence: "In a *Blanchard progeny* [read *In a case that follows the rule in* Blanchard], *Chavers v. Exxon Corp.*, we quoted from

and explained *Blanchard's* holding." *Sullen v. Missouri Pac. R.R.*, 750 F.2d 428, 431 (5th Cir. 1985).

B. Insensitively Used. In the context of the famous abortion case, *Roe v. Wade*, this METAPHOR shows a lack of VERBAL AWARENESS: "Part I of this Note exam-ines the doctrine set forth in *Roe v. Wade* and its *prog-eny*." Andrea M. Sharrin, Note, *Potential Fathers and Abortion*, 55 Brook. L. Rev. 1359, 1363 (1990).

prognosis; prognostication; prognostic, n. *Prognosis* is ordinarily used in medicine to mean "a forecast of the probable course and termination of an illness." (See **diagnosis.**) *Prognostication* is more general, denoting "a prediction or prophecy" or "a conjecture of some future event formed upon some supposed sign." E.g.:

- "Despite plaintiff's *prognostications*, in the 16 years since *Joseph* was decided, not a single case has relied on it for the concept of immunity." *Pecoraro v. Balkonis*, 891 N.E.2d 484, 493 (Ill. App. Ct. 2008).
- "Because *Grange* provides such precedent in Mississippi, there is no room for *prognostications* as to whether the state high court, as presently constituted, would come to the same conclusion." *Plunkett v. State Farm Mut. Auto. Ins. Co.*, 347 Fed. Appx. 994, 996 (5th Cir. 2009).

Prognostic = an advance indication or omen.

program; programme. *Program* is the AmE, *pro-gramme* the BrE spelling. The ending *-am* is used in BrE, however, in reference to computer programs.

programmatic. So spelled in both BrE and AmE.

programmer; programming. The best spellings are in *-mm-* whether in AmE or in BrE. The double *-m-* in AmE appears to be descended from *programme*, the BrE spelling. A few American dictionaries give prior-ity to *programer* and *programing*, but these forms are rare in practice. See DOUBLING OF FINAL CONSONANTS.

pro hac vice. A. Meaning and Uses. This LATINISM, meaning "for this occasion or particular purpose," is not easily simplified in much legal writing. Often it is used adjectivally—e.g.:

- "In *Shaw*, the trial judge sanctioned an objecting *pro hac vice* attorney who appeared unable to provide reasonable identification of his objector client." Edward Brunet, *Class Action Objectors*, 2003 U. Chi. Legal F. 403, 444.
- "The court imputed to the *pro hac vice* owner the notice and knowledge received by the insurer and the attorneys retained by the insurer." *Pargman v. Vickers*, 96 P.3d 571, 578 (Ariz. Ct. App. 2004).

The phrase is also used adverbially when a lawyer who has not been admitted to practice in a particular juris-diction is admitted for the purpose of conducting a particular case—e.g: "Debtor disputes this and states that he was admitted *pro hac vice* on March 25, 1999." *Ball v. A.O. Smith Corp.*, 321 B.R. 100, 107 (N.D.N.Y. 2005). Cf. **ad hoc.**

B. Pronunciation. The phrase is usually pro-nounced /proh hak **vis**/ or /**vɪ**-see/ or /**vee**-chay/.

C. Incorrect Form. The phrase is sometimes mis-spelled **pro haec vice*—e.g.: "Chappee also argued to the SJC that he was denied effective assistance of counsel because his local lawyer neglected to move Simon's admission *pro haec vice* [read *pro hac vice*]." *Chappee v. Vose*, 843 F.2d 25, 33 n.5 (1st Cir. 1988). The difference between *hac* and *haec* is that *haec* is nominative, while *hac* is ablative (the case governed by *pro*). Cf. **in haec verba.**

prohibit takes the preposition *from.* Formerly, this verb could be construed with *to* <the law prohibits persons to litter>, but this construction is now an ARCHAISM.

prohibition. A. Writ of Prohibition. This writ was a prerogative order issued to prevent either a lower court from exceeding its jurisdiction or a tenant from committing waste. Unlike *certiorari, prohibition* is anticipatory and preventive rather than after-the-fact and remedial. See **prerogative writs.** Cf. **certiorari.**

B. And *proscription. Proscription* implies a written prohibition, whereas *prohibition*, in its everyday sense, connotes nothing about whether it appears in writing. See **proscription.**

prohibitive; prohibitory. These terms have undergone a latent DIFFERENTIATION that needs to be further encouraged. *Prohibitive* may mean generally "having the quality of prohibiting," but more and more in modern prose it has the sense "tending to preclude consumption or purchase because of expense" <the costs are prohibitive>. So the phrase *prohibitively expensive* is a REDUNDANCY—e.g.: "Today, the economics of law practice make it *prohibitively expensive* [read *prohibitive*] to litigate small claims." Roger J. Miner, *Confronting the Communication Crisis in the Legal Profession*, 34 N.Y.L. Sch. L. Rev. 1, 7 (1989).

Frequently used in the phrase *prohibitory injunction*, the word *prohibitory* has carved out a niche in the law in the sense "expressing a prohibition or restraint"—e.g.:

- "This language is intended to protect consumers as well as business competitors; its *prohibitory* reach is not limited to deceptive or fraudulent acts, but extends to any unlawful business conduct." *Morris v. Redwood Empire Bancorp*, 27 Cal. Rptr. 3d 797, 802 (Ct. App. 2005).
- "The difference between a rights-granting statute and a purely *prohibitory* statute is significant in determining the existence vel non of an implied private right of action." *San Juan Cable LLC v. Puerto Rico Tel. Co.*, 612 F.3d 25, 32 (1st Cir. 2010). (See **vel non.**)
- "In their response, Plaintiffs . . . request a *prohibitory* injunction requiring Clear Channel to stop using its signs." *Reudy v. Clear Channel Outdoors, Inc.*, 693 F.Supp.2d 1091, 1111 (N.D. Cal. 2010).

prohibitory injunction. See **mandatory injunction.**

prolificacy; *prolificness. The first is the better-formed and more usual word—e.g.: "Perfection over *prolificacy* is Def Leppard's mode: No whine before its time." Robert J. Hawkins, *Def Leppard Wants to*

Be Perfect, Not Prolific, San Diego Union-Tribune, 17 Sept. 1992, at 12.

The NEEDLESS VARIANT **prolificness* is a poorly formed HYBRID (a Latin base with an Anglo-Saxon suffix)—e.g.:

- "[Judge Richard A. Posner's] *prolificness* [read *prolificacy*] is no surprise to anyone familiar with his academic output: 11 books and more than 100 articles." David Ranii, *The Next Nominee?*, Nat'l L.J., 26 Nov. 1984, at 1.
- "In *Irving*, there would have been no dispute because all Indians would have had equal claims in all land, irrespective of the *prolificness* [read *prolificacy*] of their ancestors." T. Nicolaus Tideman, *Takings, Moral Evolution, and Justice*, 88 Colum. L. Rev. 1714, 1729–30 (1988).

Cf. **genericalness.**

PROLIXITY. See VERBOSITY.

prologue. So spelled—preferably not **prolog.*

promise, n. **A. Moral and Legal Senses.** *Promise* is frequently used in two different senses in law. One is the lay sense, in which *promise* denotes a pledge to which the law attaches no obligation. In the other, the legal sense, *promise* is synonymous with *contract.* One commentator insists on the latter meaning as the only one appropriate to legal contexts: "It is not conceivable . . . that the term *promise* as a legal idea can mean anything except words of promise to which the law annexes an obligation." Clarence D. Ashley, *What Is a Promise in Law?*, 16 Harv. L. Rev. 319, 319 (1903). Because those words frequently remain unheeded, the acute reader must carefully determine what the word means in a given context; the acute writer should take pains to make that meaning clear. For more on this distinction, see the Anson quotation under **pollicitation.** See also **offer** & **contract (C).**

B. Promises and Policies in Drafting. The drafter often has a choice between stating an obligation either as a promise or as a policy. For example, a credit-card agreement might say: "The cardholder must make at least the minimum payment by the fifth day of each month." In signing the agreement, the cardholder makes what is in the nature of a promise.

To phrase the same obligation as a policy, the agreement might say: "The minimum balance is due on the fifth day of each month."

The difference, of course, is that the promissory language puts the obligation more emphatically. The policy language is more polite and slightly more vague. The substantive content is likely the same, but the language of promise is more likely to result in a common understanding of who must do what. See WORDS OF AUTHORITY.

promise, vb.; **covenant; engage; pledge; contract.** These verbs share the sense "to bind oneself to an agreement." To *promise* is to give an assurance, often with little or no expectation of how it is to be performed <he promised that he would deliver his

manuscript by June 30>. To *covenant* is to promise or undertake formally, as in a written contract <the granter covenanted not to encumber the property in any way>. For more on this word, see **covenant, vb.** To *engage* is to enter into a more assuredly binding agreement that is not to be broken <he engaged his favorite line editor, K. Magnuson, who purged the proofs of every last blemish>. *Pledge* implies the voluntary and solemn giving of a promise <he pledged 5% of his royalties to his alma mater>. *Contract* implies entering into a legally binding agreement (typically containing many promises, or covenants) <he contracted with a publisher>; the verb typically precedes either *for* or *to*, but often it needs neither <we have contracted an amicable deal>.

promisee is the preferred spelling, not **promissee.*

promisor; promiser. The usual legal spelling is *-or* (as the correlative to *promisee*), but *-er* is equally good. E.g.: "To allow him to keep such a payment or other consideration would be giving the *promisor* something for nothing." See *-ER* (A).

The spelling **promissor* is an inferior ARCHAISM: "The *promissor* [read *promisor*] denied he had ever made the contract under consideration." *Burford v. Pounders*, 199 S.W.2d 141, 144 (Tex. 1947).

*promissee. See **promisee.**

promissory. So spelled.

promissory estoppel. A. And *quasi-contract.* These phrases are closely related but distinct. *Promissory estoppel* ordinarily refers to the situation in which a plaintiff seeks recovery for loss or damage suffered as a result of relying on the defendant's promises or representations. *Quasi-contract* refers to the situation in which a plaintiff seeks reimbursement for some benefit that he or she has conferred on the defendant. One well-known writer believed that the law might have done well with one or the other but not both: "It would seem, as a matter of jurisprudential economy, that both situations could have been dealt with under either slogan but the legal mind has always preferred multiplication to division." Grant Gilmore, *The Death of Contract* 88–89 (1974). See **quasi-contract.**

B. And *equitable estoppel.* The phrase *equitable estoppel* is an outmoded equivalent of *promissory estoppel.* See **estoppel (B).**

promissory note (= an unconditional promise in writing to pay a person a sum of money) formerly had the synonym *writing obligatory*, but that phrase has long since become an ARCHAISM.

promoter. So spelled—not **promotor.*

promotive = tending to promote. E.g.:

- "He, Baletsa, and others were all working toward making Access a viable business operation. His activities in this regard were essential *promotive* activities." *In re Access Cardiosystems, Inc.*, 340 B.R. 127, 148 (Bankr. D. Mass. 2006) (per Boroff, J.).

- "Decisions from other jurisdictions may have persuasive authority if well reasoned and *promotive* of justice." *Cucos, Inc. v. McDaniel*, 938 So.2d 238, 243 (Miss. 2006).

See BE-VERBS (B).

*promotor. See **promoter.**

promulgate, a word perhaps too well liked by lawyers, means (1) "to make known by public declaration"; or (2) "to disseminate (some creed or belief), or to proclaim (some law, decree, or tidings)" (*OED*). E.g., in sense 2: "It is my desire that any disbursements made under this paragraph shall be made to persons who believe in the fundamental principles of the Christian religion and in the Bible and who are endeavoring to *promulgate* the same." *In re Small's Estate*, 58 N.W.2d 477, 479 (Iowa 1953) (quoting a will).

For the mistaken use of *propagate* for *promulgate*, see **propagate.**

prone. See **apt.**

prong. Courts often use this word to describe one part of a multifaceted—and often formalistic—legal test. The METAPHOR effectively shows that each part of the test must be met for a particular doctrine to apply: just as prongs are necessary to hold a stone in a piece of jewelry, so each element of a test (i.e., each "prong") must be satisfied before the legal doctrine applies. Justice Wiley B. Rutledge was one of the earliest American users of this word in this figurative sense. *See Oklahoma Press Publ'g Co. v. Walling*, 327 U.S. 186, 192 (1946).

Since the mid-20th century, the word has all but become a VOGUE WORD. From 1970 to 1975, it appeared in only 9 opinions of the U.S. Supreme Court; from 1985 to 1990, though, it appeared in some 55. Meanwhile, the other federal courts and state courts have come to use it with great frequency. For a discussion of the opinion-writing style typified by layered sets of "prongs" and "hurdles" and other tests, see Garner, "Opinions, Style of," in *The Oxford Companion to the Supreme Court of the United States* 607, 607–08 (1992).

PRONOUNS. A. Underused in Legal Writing. "It is not simply that referential pronouns are avoided only where their use could raise genuine confusion; [in legal writing] they seem to be eschewed as a species." David Crystal & Derek Davy, *Investigating English Style* 202 (1967). The result is often a sentence that no native speaker of English—other than a lawyer— would ever perpetrate, such as: "Then Tina became very lethargic, at which time Tina was taken to the emergency room."

Why the fear of pronouns? Because lawyers have overlearned the lesson that pronouns sometimes have ambiguous referents. That being so, they (the lawyers, not the referents) swear off using them (the pronouns, not the lawyers) altogether. The result, to paraphrase Fred Rodell, is that many legal sentences read as if they have been translated from the German by someone who barely knows English.

Clunkers can be avoided by judiciously using pronouns and by finding other ways to avoid repeating nouns—e.g.: "After the persons obligated under the loan failed to pay *the loan* [delete the previous two words] as required, the bank foreclosed on the collateral and caused *the collateral* [read *it*] to be sold."

B. Nominative and Objective Case. There are four essential rules concerning personal pronouns. First, if the pronoun is the subject of a clause, it must always be in the nominative case <she is friendly>. Second, if the pronoun is the object of a verb, it must be in the objective case <this is between her and me>. Third, if a pronoun is the object of a preposition, it must always be in the objective case <it was the fault of them, not their children>. If a prepositional phrase contains two or more objects, all the objects are in the objective case <please tell only me and him>. *Like*, a preposition, is followed by the objective case <you're starting to sound like me> <they looked like us>. Fourth, if the pronoun is the subject of an infinitive, it must be in the objective case <she wanted him to sing another song>.

One might think that a work of this kind, catering as it does to members of a learned profession, could pass over the differences between subjects and objects in pronouns. The sentences that follow, however, belie that thought: the first was written by a lawyer, the second by a law professor. The third appears to have been written by a complete idiot:

- "We will need to confer with *whomever* works on this project and then have *he* or *she* draft a motion for summary judgment."
- "Third, the fault is said to lie in part with *we* 'eccentric professors.'"
- "[This] view of the authority of the Bible causes *he or she* [read *him or her*] to quote the Bible to you in a judgmental way." David Cobia, *The Complete Idiot's Guide to Evangelical Christianity* 84 (2007).

In the first example *whoever* should be the subject of *works* in the noun clause, and the pronouns should be *him* and *her* as objects of *have*. In the second, *us* should be the object of the preposition *with*. See **who (A)** & HYPERCORRECTION (F).

Debilitated grammar seems ubiquitous—e.g.:

- "I would hold that Dr. Rowland, when he made his will, intended by these words 'coinciding with' to cover *he* [read *him*] and his wife dying together in just such a calamity as in fact happened." *Re Rowland*, [1963] 1 Ch. 1 (C.A.) (Lord Denning, M.R., dissenting).
- "Are we really that much smarter than *them* [read *they*]?" John B. Mitchell, *Current Theories on Expert and Novice Thinking*, 39 J. Legal Educ. 275, 275 (1989).
- "Winston [Churchill] was crouched like a great bird over the unusually small table, giving tea to his son Randolph, several years younger than *me* [read *I*]." Lord Hailsham, *Sad Memories of Dear Winston*, Sunday Times, 8 July 1990, at 3–16.
- "Rafael Macedo de la Concha, Mexico's attorney general, claims that use of the Verichip by *he* [read *him*] and his subordinates *have* [read *has*] been vital in Mexico's

struggle with drug cartels." Crystal Spivey, *Breathing New Life into HIPAA's UHID*, 9 DePaul J. Health Care L. 1317, 1333 n.100 (2006).

- "[T]he police did not believe that the story presented by *she* [read *her*] and Kennedy was plausible." Jessica Cullivan, Comment, *Why the* Kennedy v. Louisiana *Holding Does Not Afford Missouri a Voice*, 44 New Eng. L. Rev. 453, 460 (2010).

For **between you and I*, see **between (c)** & HYPERCORRECTION (B).

C. Predicate Nominatives. A predicate nominative is a pronoun in the nominative case appearing after a copula (or linking verb), usually a form of the verb *to be*. "It is *I*," one writes, for instance, or, in formal contexts: "It seems to be *she*," "You appeared to be *I*," and so on. When the situation is formal, these constructions are not affectations; they are traditionally considered obligatory. For example, the following error occurred merely because of an imperfect knowledge of grammar, together with aspirations to correctness: "There are no placards on the bench with the justices' names, so you may not know who is *whom* [read *who*]." Barbara Boyer, *Confessions of an Avid Arguer*, 25 Wyo. Law. 23, 26 (Dec. 2002).

Nevertheless, in informal contexts and primarily in speech, it is quite acceptable today to say "It's me." On formal occasions, or if one is particularly fastidious in language, one should feel perfectly comfortable saying "It is I." See **it is I.**

D. Pronouns, Preemptive. See ANTICIPATORY REFERENCE (C).

E. Restrictive and Nonrestrictive Relative Pronouns. See **that & which.**

PRONUNCIATION. A. General Principles. The best course is to follow the pronunciation current among educated speakers in one's region. The Texas pronunciation of *voir dire* /vohr **dir**/ differs markedly from the New York pronunciation /vwah **deer**/, and it would be inappropriate for a Texas lawyer to affect the New York pronunciation. On this point, H.W. Fowler still speaks to us with clarion wisdom: "The ambition to do better than our neighbours is in many departments of life a virtue; in pronunciation it is a vice; there the only right ambition is to do as our neighbours do" (*MEU1* 466). See HYPERCORRECTION (K).

A few words have universally accepted pronunciations and rejected mispronunciations; where prescriptions on pronunciation appear in this book, the preferred pronunciation is generally preferred, regardless of the jurisdiction.

When it comes to words that are seldom pronounced by English-speaking people—as with any learned word, such as those from the law—the advice to conform with our neighbors' pronunciation becomes problematic. For here we find diversity, not uniformity—the result of the infrequency with which the words are pronounced. "Where there is a diversity of opinion and practice among reasonable [and educated] people, there must be also an equally broad charity in judgment. Could anything be more absurd than to stigmatize as incorrect a pronunciation which is actually in general use . . . ?" George P. Krapp, *The Pronunciation of Standard English in America* iv (1919).

B. Commonly Mispronounced Lawyers' Words. Many words that prove troublesome to lawyers are listed throughout this work, with the correct pronunciation noted. Among the most frequently mispronounced words in the law are *err* /ər/, *substantive* /**səb**-stən-tiv/, and (formerly) *cestui* /**set**-ee/. See **pamphlet.**

C. Latin Terms. Pronunciation of Latin terms that survive in the language of the law is always troublesome for lawyers, since so few are trained in Latin and all are compelled to use such terms in the course of practice. The difficulty is—depending on one's point of view—exacerbated or ameliorated by the existence of three distinct methods of Latin pronunciation. As an example, *sub judice* is pronounced in two quite different ways, with minor variations on each (see **sub judice**).

Of the three methods of Latin pronunciation—Anglo-Latin, classical Latin, and Italianate—only one has found a permanent home in law: Anglo-Latin. For those who have studied Latin in high school and college, this legal preference can be bothersome because the resulting pronunciations can sound uncouth—e.g.:

Law-Latin Term	Anglo-Latin Pronunciation	Classical Pronunciation
nisi prius	/nɪ-sɪ **prɪ**-əs/	/nee-see **pree**-əs/
ratio	/**ray**-shee-oh	/**rah**-tee-oh
decidendi	dees-i-**den**-dɪ/	day-see-**den**-dee/
sine die	/**sɪ**-nee **dɪ**-ee/	/**see**-nay **dee**-ay/

Further, several legal LATINISMS are primarily read and not spoken (e.g., *expressio unius est exclusio alterius*). Most of the common Latinisms, such as *de minimis*, *de facto*, and *ipso facto*, have readily apparent pronunciations. One should attempt to cultivate a sensitivity to the way Latin terms are pronounced within the professional community of one's geographic area, and stay within the mainstream in that community. Of course, using dictionaries is always helpful. (See LAW LATIN.) For more on this interesting subject, see H.A. Kelly, *Lawyers' Latin: Loquenda ut Vulgus?*, 38 J. Legal Educ. 195 (1988).

D. Law French. Lawyers generally pronounce Law-French words just as they were pronounced in the Middle Ages. To give them a modern French pronunciation, as by mouthing *oyez* as if it were /oh-**yay**/ instead of /oh-**yes**/ or /oh-**yez**/, is a type of vulgarism.

E. BrE Idiosyncrasies. Glanville Williams notes several instances in which "lawyers still jealously retain the archaic pronunciations of English words." *Learning the Law* 63–64 (11th ed. 1982). Among them are these:

assured, n.	/ə-**shur**-əd/
cognisance (BrE spelling)	No -g- pronounced.
recognisance (BrE spelling)	No -g- pronounced.
record, n.	/ri-**kord**/

F. Some Famous Judges' Names. If there's one term you definitely want to pronounce correctly, it's the name of the judge before whom you're appearing. But *all* proper names are worth getting right, including those belonging to these personages:

> Brougham /broom/ *or* /**broo**-əm/, not /brahm/ *or* /brohm/
> Cardozo /kahr-**doh**-zoh/, not /kahr-**doh**-zə/
> Coke /kuuk/, not /kohk/
> Posner /**pohz**-nər/, not /**pahz**-nər/
> Scalia /skə-**lee**-ə/, not /**skayl**-yə/
> Sotomayor /soh-toh-mɪ-**yohr**/, not /soh-toh-**mair**/
> Taney /**tah**-nee/, not /**tay**-nee/

proof. A. Evidence Carrying Conviction. Whereas *evidence* includes all the means by which any alleged matter of fact can be established or disproved, *proof* is the result of evidence: the evidence may or may not be sufficient to establish the alleged facts—that is, may or may not amount to *proof*. See **evidence (B).**

B. For *probate*. *Proof* has the general legal senses (1) "evidence that determines the judgment of a court"; and, more specifically, (2) "an attested written document that constitutes legal evidence." In practice, sense 2 translates into the idiomatic equivalent of *probate*: "Bearing these opposing considerations in mind, the court is of the opinion that the will should be admitted to *proof*." *Eaton v. Brown*, 193 U.S. 411, 414 (1904) (per Holmes, J.). *Proving a will* = obtaining probate of a will. See **probate, n.**

C. For *element of proof*. Generally, of course, *proof* is a mass noun. But when *proof* is used as an ellipsis for *element of proof* (as a type or a piece of evidence), it often takes the plural form *proofs*—e.g.:

- "Under [FELA] the test of a jury case is simply whether the *proofs* justify with reason the conclusion that employer negligence played any part, even the slightest, in producing the injury or death." *Rogers v. Mississippi Pac. R.R.*, 352 U.S. 500, 506 (1957) (per Brennan, J.).
- "It is also the product of a procedure in which the litigant is assured of an opportunity to present *proofs* and arguments for a decision in his favour." Lon L. Fuller, *Anatomy of the Law* 159 (1968).
- "Rendering the decision in this manner, I believe, would do justice to the parties and allow both sides on remand to present appropriate *proofs* and arguments to the trial court." *Meyers v. Woods*, 871 N.E.2d 160, 178 (Ill. App. Ct. 2007).

See PLURALS (B).

D. Meaning "hearing" in Scots Law. In Scotland, *proof* also means "a hearing at which evidence is heard," as when a judge rules by saying, "I will allow a *proof*."

E. Ambiguity of the Phrase *burden of proof*. See **burden of proof (A).**

F. *Proof beyond a reasonable doubt*. See **balance of probability.**

propaganda, a singular mass noun, makes the plural *propagandas*. It is sometimes mistakenly thought to be a plural in the class of *data* and *strata*.

propagate (= to reproduce or extend) is occasionally confused with *promulgate* (= to proclaim; put [a law] into action)—e.g.:

- "The Department determined that the F.L.S.A. governed the wage claims, but did not then look to the regulations *propagated* [read *promulgated*] under the Act." *Stewart v. Region II Child & Family Servs.*, 788 P.2d 913, 916–17 (Mont. 1990).
- "Commissioner Beman testified that the issuance of the preliminary injunction would have dire consequences for the PGA. He testified that the PGA would not be able to *propagate* [read *promulgate*] any rules for the professional tournaments that it oversees." *Gilder v. PGA Tour, Inc.*, 936 F.2d 417, 421 (9th Cir. 1991).

*propelment. See **propulsion.**

proper. See **indispensable.**

pro per. See **pro persona.**

properly. Placement of this word in relation to a linking verb or copula may affect meaning in significant ways: *be properly* means something different from *properly be.* The latter phrase means that the thing in question (the subject) is proper, or that it is proper for the thing to be done <this question may properly be raised on appeal>, whereas the former means that the thing should be done in a proper way <briefs should be properly submitted>. See BE-VERBS.

pro persona (= for one's own person; on one's own behalf) is a LATINISM used in some jurisdictions as an equivalent of *pro se* and *in propria persona.* E.g.: "Defendant has raised a number of other issues in a *pro persona* brief." *State v. Kreps*, 706 P.2d 1213, 1218 (Ariz. 1985). The phrase is sometimes shortened to *pro per* <a pro per litigant>. See **pro se** & *in propria persona.*

property. A. Legal Meaning. Hohfeld elucidated uses that were conventionally viewed to be correct and incorrect. The traditional legal meaning of the term is "a right over a determinate thing, either a tract of land or a chattel." The transferred sense that nonlawyers commonly attach to the term is "any external thing over which the rights of possession, use, and enjoyment are exercised." *See* Wesley N. Hohfeld, *Fundamental Legal Conceptions* 28–29 (1919). So the correct emphasis was seen as being on the rights over a thing, and not on the thing itself.

Today, however, even in legal writing, *property* generally carries the nontechnical sense Hohfeld disapproved of. Felix Cohen, for example, graphically defined the term as a thing that could be labeled: "That is *property* to which the following label can be attached. To the world: Keep off unless you have my permission, which I may grant or withhold. Signed:

Private citizen. Endorsed: The state." *Dialogue on Private Property*, 9 Rutgers L. Rev. 357, 374 (1954).

B. As a Count Noun. Generally, *property* used as a count noun is realty agents' cant in AmE. E.g.:

- "[The] agency also reserves the 'right to grant access rights, including vehicular access, over and across the Property' to *one adjacent property* [read *one adjacent piece of property*] at no cost to either [the] agency or the grantee." *San Jose Parking, Inc. v. Superior Ct.*, 2 Cal. Rptr. 3d 505, 511 (Ct. App. 2003).
- "The rapid increase in the number of abandoned homes precludes a city from stepping in and taking control of *every property* [read *all the property*]." Creola Johnson, *Fight Blight*, 2008 Utah L. Rev. 1169, 1236.
- "Ramirez indicated to Agent Smith that in the beginning she filled out the purchase contracts with the information she received from Uribe on the persons who wanted to buy *a property* [omit *a*]." *U.S. v. Ramirez*, 574 F.3d 869, 873 (7th Cir. 2009).
- "Large cities . . . now mandate green building standards for commercial *properties* [read *property*]." Katherine A. Trisolini, *All Hands on Deck*, 62 Stan. L. Rev. 669, 706 (2010).

property description. See **head.**

property-settlement. See **estate planning.**

prophesy; prophecy. *Prophesy* is the verb meaning "to predict or foretell," *prophecy* the noun meaning "a prediction or foretelling." Some writers mistake the noun and the verb—e.g.:

- "*Prophesy* [read *Prophecy*] as to whether there will be speedy and widespread adoption can not be safely indulged in at this early time." 1 Samuel Williston, *The Law Governing Sales of Goods* (Joseph J. O'Connell ed., 1948) (1960 Supp. at 3).
- "Plaintiffs thus acknowledge that their *prophecied* [read *prophesied*] losses may readily be compensated by money damages." *Schmidt v. Enertec Corp.*, 598 F.Supp. 1528, 1544 (S.D.N.Y. 1984).

The words are pronounced differently. The last syllable in *prophesy* is pronounced "sigh," whereas the last syllable in *prophecy* is pronounced "see."

prophylactic, n. To an educated nonlawyer, this word is synonymous with *condom.* Doctors use the term for anything that prevents disease. To lawyers, it means "anything that is designed to prevent (something undesirable)." E.g.: "The Court recognized that the predeprivation notice and hearing were necessary *prophylactics* against a wrongful discharge." *Findeisen v. North East Indep. Sch. Dist.*, 749 F.2d 234, 238 (5th Cir. 1984). The example quoted does not demonstrate the keenest linguistic sensitivity: in view of the nonlawyer's understanding, it is perhaps unwise to use *prophylactic* in the same sentence with *discharge.* See VERBAL AWARENESS.

Prophylactic is also frequently an adjective in legal writing <a prophylactic rule>.

proponent; *propounder. Both mean "one seeking to have a will admitted to probate." The usual term is *proponent*, the form **propounder* being a NEEDLESS VARIANT.

proportion, n., should not be used when *part* or *portion* is intended. See **portion.**

One writes, "A high proportion of it *is*," but "A high proportion of them *are*." Cf. **percentage of, a.** See SYNESIS.

proportion, vb.; ***proportionalize; *proportionate,** vb. The second and third are NEEDLESS VARIANTS.

proportionate; proportional; *proportionable. The distinction to be observed is between *proportional* and *proportionate*; admittedly, at times the distinction is foiled by the frequent interchangeability of the terms. Nevertheless, it is possible to formulate the nuance that *proportional* = (1) of or relating to proportion; or (2) in due proportion; whereas *proportionate* = proportioned; adjusted in proportion. As a Latinate perfect passive participle, *proportionate* suggests the conscious proportioning of an agent.

This nice distinction aside, *proportionate* seems to be used more commonly in legal writing than *proportional*. E.g.:

- "In small groups, a *proportionably* [read *proportionately*] higher percentage of the members participate than in large groups." Adam M. Chud & Michael L. Berman, *Six-Member Juries*, 67 Tenn. L. Rev. 743, 758 (2000).
- "The court reasoned there is an implied rule among co-guarantors that each is required to pay his or her *proportionate* share of a debt." John Krahmer, *Commercial Transactions*, 61 SMU L. Rev. 657, 668–69 (2008).
- "Application of comparative negligence holds a criminally negligent defendant responsible for the full amount of the victim's economic losses that resulted from the defendant's *proportionate* fault." *People v. Millard*, 95 Cal. Rptr. 3d 751, 779 (Ct. App. 2009).
- "The League would assert that without the entering-player pool, drafted rookies might consume *disproportionate* salary-cap space because they have significant bargaining power with their drafting clubs." Sean W.L. Alford, Comment, *Dusting Off the AK-47*, 88 N.C. L. Rev. 212, 260 (2009).

Especially is this so in the negative form of the word: "The particular preferred legatees, by an exact effectuation of their gifts, would receive only the *proportionably* [read *proportionately*] reduced amounts." *In re Van Brunt's Estate*, 287 N.Y.S. 269, 274 (Sur. Ct. 1936).

*Proportionable is an ARCHAISM that still sometimes occurs in legal writing—e.g.: "The note for additional interest shall be *proportionably* [read *proportionately*] reduced." Cf. **commensurate.**

propound (= [1] to put forward [a will] as authentic; [2] to put forth for consideration or discussion; or [3] to make a proposal; to propose) is easily used correctly, as the examples following demonstrate. E.g.:

- "To the extent that such a distinction is not made in practice, legislators have strong incentives to *propound* multiple interpretations of the act, hoping that a sympathetic judge will subscribe to their point of view." Daniel B. Rodriguez & Barry R. Weingast, *The Positive Political Theory of Legislative History*, 151 U. Pa. L. Rev. 1417, 1447 (2003).
- "Even the most restrictive theory *propounded* by Judge Bork concludes that the First Amendment safeguards 'explicitly political' speech." Sonja R. West, *The Story of Me*, 84 Wash. U. L. Rev. 905, 957 (2006).
- "A legal fiction is a statement *propounded* with a complete or partial consciousness of its falsity, but accepted because of its utility." Christine Hayes, *Rabbinic Contestations of Authority*, 28 Cardozo L. Rev. 123, 134 (2006).
- "The Federal Circuit's inequitable-conduct jurisprudence might profit from a renewed focus on *propounding* clear standards that can be easily applied by lower courts and the public." Randall R. Rader, *Always at the Margin*, 59 Am. U. L. Rev. 777, 785 (2010).

For the misuse of this verb, see **expound.**

*propounder. See **proponent.**

proprietary; proprietorial; *proprietory. The last is an erroneous form. The adjectival form corresponding to the noun *proprietor* is either *proprietary* or *proprietorial*. *Proprietary* also means "of, relating to, or holding as property."

In the following sentence, *proprietorial* is almost certainly misused for *proprietary*: "The contracts were negotiated not with the band's company, The Beatles, Ltd., which held the rights, but with NEMS, which did not possess any *proprietorial* [read *proprietary*] rights whatsoever, being simply a management organization." Albert Goldman, *The Lives of John Lennon* 335 (1988).

propulsion; *propelment. The first is the usual term, **propelment* a NEEDLESS VARIANT.

propulsive; *propulsory. The second term is a NEEDLESS VARIANT.

pro rata, adv., should be spelled as two words. E.g.: "The Nutt Firm was to provide one million dollars per year in capital contributions, with any further necessary contributions to be paid *pro rata* by the other co-venturers." *Barrett v. Jones, Funderburg, Sessums, Peterson & Lee, LLC*, 27 So.3d 363, 365 (Miss. 2009). *Proportionately* will sometimes serve in place of *pro rata*.

On the question whether to hyphenate *pro rata* when it functions as a phrasal adjective—that is, *pro-rata distribution* as opposed to *pro rata distribution*— see PHRASAL ADJECTIVES (B).

prorate (= to divide or assess proportionately) is an Americanism, although the British have now adopted the noun form *proration*. Instead of the AmE *prorating*, common in the law of oil and gas, the British use *prorationing*.

prorogation. See **adjourn.**

prorogue; prorogate. *Prorogue* = (1) to postpone; (2) to discontinue the meetings of (a legislative assembly, usu. Parliament) for a definite or indefinite time without dissolving it; or (3) to discontinue meeting until the next session. *Prorogate* is a NEEDLESS VARIANT except in Scots and civil law, in which the term means "to extend by consent (the jurisdiction of a judge or court) to a cause in which jurisdiction would otherwise be incompetent." See **adjourn.**

proscribe; prescribe. *Proscribe* means to prohibit, *prescribe* to impose authoritatively. Yet some writers blunder—e.g.: "Doctors will be liable for malpractice if, instead of running necessary tests and *proscribing* [read *prescribing*] medicine, they treat every illness with bloodletting." James Forrest McKell Jr., Note, *Chatter, Clatter, and Blinks*, 2010 Duke L. & Tech. Rev. 10, 11. Here both are correctly used: "Due process of law requires that a penal statute or ordinance state with reasonable clarity the act it *proscribes* and must also *prescribe* fixed standards for adjudging guilt when that person stands accused." *State v. Bloss*, 637 P.2d 1117, 1128 (Haw. 1981). See **prescribe.**

proscription; prescription. Like the corresponding verbs, these nouns are sometimes confused. Sometimes it is difficult to determine whether the use is proper or improper, as here: "The hallmark of IFRS is that the metrics for so many of its provisions are principles-based as contrasted with more specific rules-based *proscriptions* [read *prescriptions*?]." James D. Cox, *Coping in a Global Marketplace*, 95 Va. L. Rev. 941, 958 (2009). If the writer meant to say that the provisions of the statute were principles-based prohibitions, *proscription* was the correct word; but if the writer meant to say that the statute laid down principles-based provisions, *prescription* would have been the correct word.

Even more serious is the MISCUE caused by *medical proscription* in the following example: "Gill . . . alleges only that Rudnickey forced him to paint despite his complaints that paint fumes made him 'dizzy and nauseous.' In the absence of any medical *proscriptions* known to Rudnickey, his decision to ignore Gill's complaints amounted to nothing more than a mere negligent act." *Gill v. Mooney*, 824 F.2d 192, 195 (2d Cir. 1987). See **prohibition (B).**

pro se = on one's own behalf. The phrase is two words, and should not be hyphenated. Functionally, the phrase may be either adjectival or adverbial. Here it is the former: "Petitioner's response did not show cause why this court should not limit his ability to file *pro se* actions and papers in this court." *Franklin v. State*, 25 So.3d 645, 645 (Fla. Dist. Ct. App. 2009). Just as frequently it is adverbial, as here: "Father appeals *pro se* and argues that his incarceration has resulted in a substantial change in his income, and therefore, he is entitled to a reduction of his child-support obligation." *In re Paternity of E.C.*, 896 N.E.2d 923, 924 (Ind. Ct. App. 2008). See *in propria persona* & **pro persona.**

prosecutable. So spelled.

prosecute; persecute. Heaven forbid that one with legal training should confuse these terms. *Prosecute* = to begin a case at law for punishment of a crime or of a legal violation. *Persecute* = to oppress, coerce, or treat unfairly, often out of religious hatred.

Today *prosecute* is largely confined to criminal contexts (= to institute legal proceedings against [a person] for some offense), but the word survives as an ARCHAISM in civil contexts in the sense "to carry out or engage in a legal action; to follow up on a legal claim." E.g.:

- "A statute of Illinois provided that no action should be brought or *prosecuted* in that State for damages occasioned by death occurring in another State in consequence of wrongful conduct." *Kenney v. Supreme Lodge of the World, Loyal Order of Moose*, 252 U.S. 411, 414 (1920) (per Holmes, J.).
- "A lessee, who in good faith is *prosecuting* work for development with reasonable diligence, will be protected against cancellation of his lease." *Little v. Page*, 810 S.W.2d 339, 340 (Ky. 1991).
- "The defendants *prosecuted* an appeal assigning numerous grounds of error, none of which involved the fact that the original complaint was unsigned." *Hoover v. West Virginia Bd. of Medicine*, 602 S.E.2d 466, 471 (W. Va. 2004).
- "Anderson *prosecutes* this appeal, arguing that the trial court erred in failing to grant his motion for a directed verdict and in admitting certain documentary evidence of a Florida conviction." *Anderson v. State*, 874 So.2d 1000, 1002 (Miss. Ct. App. 2004).

When used in reference to something other than law, *prosecute* generally means "to carry on." In this sense, the term is a LEGALISM and an ARCHAISM <he continued to prosecute his business>. E.g.: "All unexpended balances of appropriations prior to May 15, 1928, made for *prosecuting* work of flood control on the Mississippi River, are made available under this title."

prosecution meant originally (fr. 16th c.) "the following up, continuing, or carrying out of any action, scheme, or purpose, with a view to its accomplishment or attainment." Then it came to be associated with criminal law in the 18th century and took on the meaning "a criminal proceeding in which an accused person is tried."

Today, both in AmE and in BrE, it is also used for *prosecutor* or *prosecutors*, the process of HYPALLAGE having done its usual work—e.g.:

- "The trial court prevented the defendant from introducing testimony regarding her reputation in the community for truthfulness after the *prosecution* made an issue of the defendant's character." *People v. Falls*, 902 N.E.2d 120, 121 (Ill. App. Ct. 2008).

- "In this case, the *prosecution* argued that there was no need to perform the type of tests that are seen on certain *CSI* television shows because those tests would not have worked." *Foster v. State*, 961 A.2d 526, 529 (Del. 2008).

In BrE, the word often takes a plural verb: "It is not altogether clear from the authorities what is the degree of risk that the *prosecution have* to prove." Glanville Williams, *Textbook of Criminal Law* 73 (1978).

prosecutional; *prosecutive. See **prosecutorial.**

prosecutor = (1) a legal officer who represents the state in criminal proceedings; or (2) a private person who institutes and carries on a suit—esp. a criminal suit—in court. Sense 2, though increasingly rare, persists primarily in BrE—e.g.:

- "A private *prosecutor* may relieve the local authority of some expense, but here the private prosecutor may receive from the local authority part of the cost he incurs." R.M. Jackson, *The Machinery of Justice in England* 324 (5th ed. 1967).
- "In some types of criminal case the title of the case will not contain *Rex* or *Reg.* before the 'v.,' but will contain the name of a private person. This happens when the case is tried summarily before magistrates (*i.e.* justices of the peace); here the name of the actual *prosecutor* (*e.g.* a policeman) appears instead of the nominal prosecutor, the Queen." Glanville Williams, *Learning the Law* 17 (11th ed. 1982).

See **prosecution.**

prosecutorial; prosecutory; *prosecutive; *prosecutional. The most common term in criminal-law texts is *prosecutorial*; but this variant is not included in *W3*. *Prosecutory* and its NEEDLESS VARIANT **prosecutive*—less common words in legal writing—are defined as "of or pertaining to prosecution." A distinction might obtain if we restricted *prosecutorial* to be the adjective for *prosecutor*, already its primary function. E.g.: "The *prosecutorial* decision not to prosecute has a deterrent effect on police misconduct." *See, e.g.,* Bennett L. Gershman, *Prosecutorial Misconduct* (1985); Joseph F. Lawless, *Prosecutorial Misconduct: Law, Procedure, Forms* (1985).

But sometimes *prosecutorial* appears where *prosecutory* might be more appropriate—e.g.:

- "In *Decker*, we recognized that the grant of immunity is normally a *prosecutorial* [read *prosecutory*] function." *Dependency of Q.L.M. v. State Dep't of Soc. & Health Servs.,* 20 P.3d 465, 471 (Wash. Ct. App. 2001).
- "The purpose of a statute of limitations is to protect a defendant against delay and the use of stale evidence and to provide an incentive for efficient *prosecutorial* [read *prosecutory*] action in criminal cases." *State v. Nielsen*, 44 S.W.3d 496, 499 (Tenn. 2001).
- "Defendant contends that the relative lack of *prosecutorial* [read *prosecutory*] interest in denying immunity renders this case unique; we are unpersuaded." *State v. Belanger,* 170 P.3d 530, 532 (N.M. Ct. App. 2007).

*Prosecutional is but a NEEDLESS VARIANT not countenanced by the dictionaries.

prosecutrix /pro-sə-**kyoo**-triks/, a word traditionally used in reference to a female who brings criminal charges against a sexual assailant, has been objected to on grounds that it is sexist and obscurantist. *See Allen v. State*, 700 S.W.2d 924, 935–36 (Tex. Crim. App. 1985) (Miller, J., concurring). Judge Miller offers *victim* as a clearer, more sympathetic term. But *victim* would surely be prejudicial and ineffective if, for example, it has not been established that a rape actually took place or who the rapist was. (Cf. **complainant.**) Judge Miller observes that "if *prosecutrix* is used to refer to the female victim of a sexual assault, would not the term *prosecutor* be appropriate for a male victim of a sexual assault?" *Id.* at 936 n.2.

Of course, *prosecutor* is not today much used in that sense (but see sense 2 under that headword). And it is that lack of equivalency that lends some credence to the charge that the word evinces a discriminatory bias in the language. (See SEXISM (C).) More likely, however, the language of the law has not needed a word for adult male victims of sex crimes.

One admirable device that judges have begun using when writing about rape cases—a device that doesn't attach an awkward, aggressive-sounding epithet to the victim—is to use a pseudonym, such as *Mary Doe*, when presenting a factual narrative.

proselytize; *proselyte, vb. The first is preferred, the second being a NEEDLESS VARIANT.

prospective heir. See **heir (B).**

prospective juror. See **potential juror.**

prospectus. A. Plural Form. The correct English plural is *prospectuses*—and it is the only form listed in English dictionaries. The Latin plural is *prospectus* (a fourth-declension noun), not **prospecti*, the product of ignorant hypercorrection. E.g.:

- "Bismarck Realty prepared *prospecti* [read *prospectuses*] on the property." *Bismarck Realty Co. v. Folden*, 354 N.W.2d 636, 638 (N.D. 1984).
- "Put and call option trading on an underlying security is directly affected by the *prospecti* [read *prospectuses*], representations and omissions of the issuer of the underlying security." *Tolan v. Computervision Corp.*, 696 F.Supp. 771, 775 (D. Mass. 1988).

Cf. **apparatus.** See HYPERCORRECTION (A).

B. For *perspective*. This is a gross MALAPROPISM—e.g.:

- "While there is a technical difference in wording, we think that the article fairly places in the proper *prospectus* [read *perspective*] the testimony given at the May 30 hearing." *Kinloch v. News & Observer Publ'g Co.*, 314 F.Supp. 602, 605 (D.N.C. 1969).
- "Viewed in its proper *prospectus* [read *perspective*], § 5 of the Fourteenth Amendment appears as a positive grant of legislative power, authorizing Congress to exercise its discretion in fashioning remedies to achieve civil and political equality for all citizens." *Pennsylvania v. Local Union No. 542*, 347 F.Supp. 268, 296 (E.D. Pa. 1972).

Properly, of course, *prospectus* = a printed document describing the chief features of a school, commercial enterprise, forthcoming book, or the like. See **conspectus.**

prostate. See **prostrate.**

prostitution, meaning in one sense "the act of debasing," is connotatively charged with its other sense of harlotry. E.g.: "The *New York World* called it 'a conscious *prostitution* of his court to the services of one side in a vile partisan squabble.'" Charles Lane, *Edward Henry Durell*, 13 Green Bag 2d 153, 162 (2010). Where the tone is intentionally provocative or connotatively charged, it may be the right word. *Prostitution* should not be used, however, wherever *debasement* might adequately be used.

In criminal law, the word was once confined to a female's taking money in exchange for sexual intercourse with a man. Today, however, the law recognizes that males as well as females engage in prostitution.

prostrate, vb. & adj.; **prostate,** n. These are very different words, but they are sometimes confused. In its verb sense, to *prostrate* oneself is to kneel down in humility or adoration. As an adjective, *prostrate* means either "lying face down" or "emotionally overcome." The noun *prostate*, by contrast, refers to the gland found in male mammals, surrounding the urethra at the base of the bladder.

The most common mistake is to say *prostrate gland when one means *prostate gland*—e.g.:

- "He described acid phosphatase as an enzyme from the *prostrate* [read *prostate*] gland of a male person." *State v. Williams*, 196 S.E.2d 248, 249 (N.C. 1973).
- "The *Connell* plaintiff alleged that defendant physician breached a 'continuing duty to disclose material facts' (the physical examination findings, specifically, enlargement of the *prostrate* [read *prostate*] gland) relevant to the decedent's condition (eventually diagnosed as cancer)." Jennifer S.R. Lynn, *Connecticut Medical Malpractice*, 12 Bridgeport L. Rev. 381, 441 (1992).
- "One strain of mice, whose males develop enlarged *prostrate* [read *prostate*] glands, will be used to test potential drug treatments for *prostrate* [read *prostate*] enlargement as well as suspected carcinogens." Michael E. Sellers, Note, *Patenting Nonnaturally Occurring, Man-Made Life*, 47 Ark. L. Rev. 269, 271–72 (1994).

protagonist. Literally, *protagonist* = the chief character in a drama; by extension, it means "a champion of a cause." It should not be used loosely of any upholder or supporter of a cause; it should refer to a prominent and active supporter. E.g.: "Perhaps the *protagonists* [read *supporters*] of today's competing constitutional norms are about to reach out to each other and engage in conversation and compromise." William E. Nelson et al., *The Liberal Tradition of the Supreme Court Clerkship*, 62 Vand. L. Rev. 1749, 1805 (2009).

Protagonist is all too frequently confused with *antagonist*. E.g.:

- "A test formulated in the previous century for a controversy between two friendly states is hardly relevant to contemporary controversies, involving high expectations of violence, between nuclear-armed *protagonists* [read *antagonists*]." Myres McDougal & Florentino Feliciano, *Law and Minimum World Public Order* 230 (1961).
- "During the ensuing imbroglio, Leahy admittedly fired the weapon. The *protagonists'* [read *antagonists'*] versions of what happened differ materially." *U.S. v. Leahy*, 473 F.3d 401, 404 (1st Cir. 2007).

In the following sentence, the writer attempted to use *protagonist* figuratively in its dramatic sense but failed in the METAPHOR because a drama has only one protagonist: "Slugs, larvae, nematodes, and rodents form the supporting cast in this trademark drama; the *protagonists* [read *principal characters*] are the terms *Larvacide* and *larvicide*." *Soweco, Inc. v. Shell Oil Co.*, 617 F.2d 1178, 1181 (5th Cir. 1980).

Perhaps the most objectionable watering-down of the meaning of *protagonist* occurs when it is used as an equivalent of *proponent*—e.g.: "These regional groupings then eventually *metamorphasized* [read *metamorphosed*] into something much more profound . . . than could have been envisioned by the original *protagonists* [read *proponents*] of economic integration." James D. Wilets, *A Unified Theory of International Law, the State, and the Individual*, 31 U. Pa. J. Int'l L. 753, 769 (2010).

pro tanto (= to that extent; as far as it goes) is a defensible LATINISM commonly used in law. No other word quite works without substantial rewording. It may be used adjectivally—e.g.:

- "An innocent change of position disenriching the recipient will provide a *pro tanto* defense." Peter Birks, *Unjust Enrichment and Wrongful Enrichment*, 79 Tex. L. Rev. 1767, 1787 (2001).
- "There is a difference with a Chapter 11 discharge because debts are not discharged *pro tanto* based on the value received as in judicial enforcement outside bankruptcy; they are discharged entirely." Charles W. Mooney Jr., *A Normative Theory of Bankruptcy Law*, 61 Wash. & Lee L. Rev. 931, 1053 (2004).
- "Congressional easing of Article IV's demands is hardly equivalent to a *pro tanto* dissolution of the union." Gillian E. Metzger, *Congress, Article IV, and Interstate Relations*, 120 Harv. L. Rev. 1468, 1503 (2007).
- "The petitioner formulated the argument that the Smith Act's membership clause had been repealed *pro tanto*." David Yerushalmi, *Shari'ah's "Black Box"*, 2008 Utah L. Rev. 1019, 1079.
- "A society without exclusive friendships would be sad; a society with fewer properly raised children is *pro tanto* deprived of the future value of humanity." Roderick M. Hills Jr., *Do Families Need Special Rules of Criminal Law?*, 88 B.U. L. Rev. 1425, 1431 (2008).

protectable; ***protectible.** The first is preferred. Inconsistencies often arise even within one piece of writing. *See, e.g.*, Westlaw headnotes 1 and 5 of *Velo-Bind, Inc. v. Scheck*, 485 F.Supp. 102, 102 (S.D.N.Y. 1979).

protective; ***protectory.** The second is a NEEDLESS VARIANT.

---

pro tem is the abbreviation for *pro tempore* (= for the time being). This fairly common LATINISM is used as a POSTPOSITIVE ADJECTIVE in phrases such as *mayor pro tem.*

protest, n.; protestation. The difference is that *protest*, the ordinary word, usually refers to a formal statement or action of dissent or disapproval, whereas *protestation*, a learned word, generally denotes a solemn affirmation.

protest, vb., is transitive or intransitive in AmE but is solely intransitive in most BrE writing. In G.B., one writes, "They *protested against* discrimination," but not, "They *protested* discrimination." Eric Partridge considered the latter, which is acceptable AmE usage, incorrect and quoted an American writer as an offender against idiom. *See Usage and Abusage* 248 (1973). The phrase *protest against* is common also in AmE. E.g.: "Sixty-five protestors had been arrested for *protesting against* the Vietnam War." Martin H. Belsky, *A Practical and Pragmatic Approach to Freedom of Conscience*, 76 U. Colo. L. Rev. 1057, 1057 (2007). In AmE, however, *against* is regularly omitted. An exception to the general British legal idiom is the phrase *protest a bill of exchange*. For more on *protest* and its near-synonyms, see **object (A).**

protestant /**prot**-ə-stənt/ (= a protesting person) is often used in law to mean "one who protests an administrative decision." E.g.: "Once the petitioner makes out its prima facie case, however, a presumption is created that the new authority will be consistent with the public convenience and necessity and the burden of proof is shifted to the *protestants* to show that it will not." *Steere Tank Lines, Inc. v. ICC*, 724 F.2d 472, 475 (5th Cir. 1984). Cf. **caveator, contestant** & **objectant.**

protestation. See **protest, n.**

prothonotary means generally "the chief clerk of a court of law." The word is pronounced /proh-**thon**-ə-tar-ee/ or /proh-thə-**nod**-ə-ree/.

The spelling with the *-h-* is prevalent in both AmE and BrE (**protonotary* is a variant)—that is, to the extent that any form of this obsolescent word can be called "prevalent" at all. The office was abolished in England in 1837, the last holder surviving until 1874. But the term lingers in some American jurisdictions. E.g.:

- "The trustee may, on the other hand, obtain an adjudication of his management of the trust by filing his account in the office of the *prothonotary* of the court." *Princess Lida v. Thompson*, 305 U.S. 456, 463 (1939) (per Roberts, J.).
- "As in Florida, a private party may obtain a prejudgment writ of replevin through a summary process of ex parte application to a *prothonotary*." *Fuentes v. Shevin*, 407 U.S. 67, 75–76 (1972) (per Stewart, J.).

protocol. See **treaty.**

prototype. See **archetype.**

prototypical. The usual and preferred form is *prototypical*, not **prototypal*. Cf. *****archetypical.**

protuberate is frequently misspelled and mispronounced as if it were **protruberate*, perhaps out of confusion with *protrude*. The adjective, likewise, is *protuberant*, not **protruberant*—e.g.: "Physical examination revealed plaintiff to be a very healthy appearing person with a *protruberant* [read *protuberant* or *protruding*] abdomen." *Coleman v. Califano*, 462 F.Supp. 77, 79–80 (N.D.N.Y. 1978).

proud; prideful. The connotative distinction to bear in mind is that *prideful* suggests excessive pride, haughtiness, and disdain. A favorite word of charismatic and evangelical Christians, *prideful* is also moralistic in tone.

prove; prove up. Generally, it is sufficient to use *prove* transitively, and hence to write, "He attempted to *prove* his title to the land." A common Americanism in law, however, is the phrasal verb *prove up* (= to adduce or complete the proof of right to (something); to show that one has fulfilled the legal conditions). E.g.: "The state failed to *prove up* the elements required for a racketeering offense under Minnesota law." *Fraction v. Minnesota*, 678 F.Supp.2d 908, 913 (D. Minn. 2008). The *OED* indicates that this usage has spread to Canada. See PHRASAL VERBS & PARTICLES, UNNECESSARY.

proved; proven. *Proved* is the universally preferred past participle of *prove*. Often, however, *proven* illadvisedly appears—e.g.:

- "In *Beaumont v. Feld*, a bequest to 'Catharine Earnley' was *proven* [read *proved*] to have been intended for Gertrude Yardley, and was given to the latter." *In re Gibbs' Estate*, 111 N.W.2d 413, 418 (Wis. 1961).
- "Since the serious bodily injury suffered by complainant at the hands of Appellant was *proven* [read *proved*] beyond a reasonable doubt, the error, if any, was harmless." *Mitchell v. State*, 681 S.W.2d 163, 166 (Tex. App.—Houston [14th Dist.] 1984).

In AmE and BrE alike, the past participle *proved* is much more common than *proven*—e.g.: "Our system does not interfere till harm has been done and has been *proved* to have been done with appropriate mens rea." H.L.A. Hart, "Punishment and the Elimination of Responsibility," in *Punishment and Responsibility: Essays in the Philosophy of Law* 158, 182 (1968).

Like *stricken*, however, *proven* is properly used only as an adjective. E.g.:

- "The existence of substantial equity in pledged collateral is usually the main concern, and its *proven* existence is readily accepted as protection of a mortgagee's financial interests while the automatic stay prevents it from foreclosing." *In re Heather Apartments LP*, 366 B.R. 45, 51 (Bankr. D. Minn. 2007).
- "Defendant's attempt to distinguish *Feldman* on the *proven* facts of that case, as compared to the allegations in this case, is wholly unpersuasive." *Friedman v. 24 Hour Fitness USA, Inc.*, 580 F.Supp.2d 985, 992 (C.D. Cal. 2008).

See **stricken.**

Proven has survived as a past participle in legal usage in two phrases: first, in the phrase *innocent until proven guilty*; second, in the verdict *not proven*, a jury answer no longer widely used except in Scots law. As for *not proven*, one writer has defined this verdict as meaning, "Not guilty, but don't do it again." William Roughead, *The Art of Murder* 131 (1943).

provenance; provenience. Both are FORMAL WORDS for *origin* or *source*. *Provenience* is chiefly an Americanism, but *provenance* prevails throughout the English-speaking world—including AmE.

proves the rule, the exception. See **exception proves the rule, the.**

prove too much = to make an overbroad argument; (of an argument) to be overbroad. E.g.:

- "A very common criticism of Vaihinger is to say that he *proves too much*. If everything is a 'fiction,' then the meaning of the word 'fiction' has been lost, and 'as if' has become simply 'is.'" Lon L. Fuller, *Legal Fictions* 123 (1967).
- "The government's argument *proves too much*. If an 'acquisition' as that term is used in the acquisition clause is also required under the notice clause, then the notice alternative would be rendered surplusage." *Cole v. Harris*, 571 F.2d 590, 596 (D.C. Cir. 1977).

prove up. See **prove.**

provided that. A. Provisos Generally. Writers on drafting have long cautioned drafters not to use provisos. In fact, the words *provided that* are a reliable signal that the draft is not going well.

The problem—recognized five centuries ago by Coke—is that the phrase means too many different things: *provided that* may create an exception, a limitation, a condition, or a mere addition. Sometimes the phrase is the functional equivalent of *if*—e.g.: "*Provided that* [read *If*] an order of restitution is within the bounds of the statutory framework, we review the order for an abuse of discretion." *U.S. v. Batson*, 608 F.3d 630, 632–33 (9th Cir. 2010).

The matter contained in the proviso is often preferably integrated into a subordinate clause introduced by *but*—e.g.: "No person who has not attained the age of twelve years shall be competent to testify, *provided that*, if the court finds that any such person understands the nature and obligation of the oath, such person shall be competent to testify." This statute is best rephrased: "Persons who are at least 12 years old are competent to testify, but a person under that age is also competent if the court finds that the person understands the nature and obligation of the oath." (Ex. fr. Irving Younger, *Persuasive Writing* 6, 6–7 (1990).) See **proviso.** For an expanded treatment of why provisos are undesirable and of ways to remove them expertly, see Garner, *Legal Writing in Plain English* 107–12 (2001).

B. And *providing that*. As between *provided that* and *providing that*—assuming one wants to create a proviso despite what is said under (A)—the former is the preferred phrasing.

province, the peculiar, is a legal CLICHÉ throughout common-law countries. E.g.: "It is most important in legislation to avoid intermeddling with *the peculiar province* of Ethics or Divinity." Denis Caulfield Heron, *An Introduction to the History of Jurisprudence* 57 (2009).

provincial, in a country without provinces, has been narrowed primarily to its extended meaning, "parochial, narrow." Yet it still carries its primary sense, "of or relating to a province"—e.g.: "Bidding adieu to his London friends, Barry Sullivan immediately set out on a *provincial* tour extending over four months." Robert M. Sillard, *Barry Sullivan and His Contemporaries* 121 (2008).

proving a will. See **proof (B).**

provision. See **prevision** & **proviso.**

provision of law is usually unnecessary for *law* or *provision*.

provisions, under the. See **under the provisions.**

proviso generally has a narrower sense than *provision* (= a term or subpart in a legal instrument). In drafting, a *proviso* is either a clause that is inserted in a legal or formal document and that makes some condition, stipulation, exception, or limitation, or a clause upon whose observance the operation or validity of the instrument depends—and it is normally introduced by the words *provided that*. E.g.: "The company should answer for all injury resulting, whether to the feelings or the purse, one or both, subject to the *proviso* that the injury must be the natural and direct consequence of the negligent act." *Mentzer v. Western Union Tel. Co.*, 62 N.W. 1, 7 (Iowa 1895). For the reasons to avoid provisos, see **provided that (A).**

The plural is *provisos*, not **provisoes*.

provocation; revenge. In criminal law, killing in *provocation* is one type of killing in *revenge*, but generally *provocation* is considered quite separate. It gives rise to action in the heat of the moment, whereas *revenge* refers to planned, cold-blooded killing.

provocative; *provocatory. The second is a NEEDLESS VARIANT.

prox. See **ult.**

proximate; proximal. Both mean "lying very near or close." Yet *proximal* is primarily a technical, scientific term, whereas *proximate* is the ordinary term with the additional senses (1) "soon forthcoming;

imminent"; (2) "next preceding" <proximate cause>; and (3) "nearly accurate; approximate."

proximate cause, an anglicization of the LATINISM *causa proxima*, is a TERM OF ART having little to do with physical causation, emphasizing instead the continuity of the sequence that produces an event. The meaning is elusive: "a cause of which the law will take notice." The phrase is basic to tort law in AmE and is also used, though much less frequently, in BrE. One commentator rather uncharitably terms *proximate cause* "concise gibberish." David Mellinkoff, *The Language of the Law* 401 (1963). See CAUSATION (A).

Synonymous phrases—now, for the most part, rejects—are *primary cause, efficient cause, efficient proximate cause, efficient adequate cause, legal cause,* and *jural cause.*

proximo. See **ult.**

proxy, in corporate law, has three distinct senses: (1) "a person who is authorized to vote another's shares"; (2) "the grant of authority by which a person is so authorized"; or (3) "the document granting that authority."

prudent; prudential. *Prudent* = exhibiting prudence. *Prudential* = pertaining to, considered from the point of view of, or dictated by prudence. E.g.:

- "One focus of attention is a set of *prudential* guidelines proposed by the American Bar Association to guide the courts' discretionary choices in using this remedy." Ronald M. Levin, *"Vacation" at Sea*, 53 Duke L.J. 291, 297 (2003).
- "The court's rejection of this argument appears to be centered on *prudential* concerns about the appropriate role of the judiciary once the government defines its selected groups." Jenny Rivera, *An Equal Protection Standard for National Origin Subclassifications*, 82 Wash. L. Rev. 897, 940 (2007).

"To call an act *prudent,*" wrote H.W. Fowler, "is normally to commend it; to call it *-ial* is more often than not to disparage it. A prisoner's refusal to go into the witness-box is prudential but not prudent if he refuses for fear of giving himself away but actually creates prejudice against himself, prudent but not prudential if it deprives the prosecution of a necessary link in the evidence but is dictated merely by bravado, and both or neither in conditions as easy to invent" (*MEU1* 473).

prurience; *pruriency. The second is a NEEDLESS VARIANT.

pseudonym = a fictitious name. In law, common pseudonyms for persons involved in suits are *John Doe, Jane Doe,* and *Richard Roe.* Here the word is wrongly used for *euphemism* (= a more or less neutral word or phrase used in place of an expression that is considered disagreeable in some way): "Still others assume that diversity is simply a *pseudonym* [read *euphemism*] for affirmative action." Steven A. Ramirez, *The New Cultural Diversity and Title VII*, 6 Mich. J. Race & L. 127, 143 (2000). See EUPHEMISMS.

PSITTACISM is the parrotlike use of language. If there is a malady endemic in legal writing, it is the habit of mechanically repeating old wads of verbiage that reflect neither true reasoning nor feeling. Many legal opinions and law-review articles teem with ready-made legal phrases strung end on end. Each formula gives itself away with the first word or two, so that the adept reader knows what the psittacistic writer will say before finishing. *In derogation of* is rarely followed by anything other than *the common law*; and so endemic are such phrases as *case of first impression, it is well established that,* and *notwithstanding anything herein to the contrary* that they finally numb the intellect of both reader and writer. For more examples, see CLICHÉS.

George Orwell's thinking was as penetrating here as elsewhere: "Modern writing at its worst does not consist in picking out words for the sake of their meaning and inventing images in order to make the meaning clearer. It consists in gumming together long strips of words [that] have already been set in order by someone else, and making the results presentable by sheer humbug." George Orwell, "Politics and the English Language," in *Shooting an Elephant and Other Essays* 77, 85 (1945).

The best legal writers attempt to formulate their thoughts anew. Their writing is fresh and original. And it is rare.

psychic; *psychal; psychical; psychological. *Psychic* = (1) of or relating to the psyche; (2) spiritual; or (3) paranormal. *Psychical* (= of or relating to the mind) is contrasted with *physical.* *Psychal is a NEEDLESS VARIANT. *Psychological* = (1) of, pertaining to, or of the nature of psychology; dealing with psychology; or (2) of or pertaining to the objects of psychological study; of or pertaining to the mind; mental (*OED*). The *OED* states that sense 2 of *psychological* is a loose usage, but it is now firmly established.

psycholegal (= involving the psychological implications of the legal process) is a late-20th-century NEOLOGISM—e.g.: Wallace D. Loh, *Psycholegal Research: Past and Present*, 79 Mich. L. Rev. 659 (1981); Gary B. Melton & Ralph B. Pliner, "Adolescent Abortion: A *Psycholegal* Analysis," in *Adolescent Abortion, Psychological and Legal Issues* 1 (G.B. Melton ed., 1986); Richard L. Wiener, *A Psycholegal and Empirical Approach to the Medical Standard of Care*, 69 Neb. L. Rev. 112 (1990). Cf. **medicolegal.**

psychological. See **psychic.**

psychosis. See **insanity (A).**

pubes, a term that occasionally arises in criminal cases, refers either to the area surrounding a person's external genitals or to pubic hair. It is sometimes mispronounced /pyoobs/, though properly it has two syllables /**pyoo**-beez/.

public, a COLLECTIVE NOUN, usually takes a singular verb in AmE <public is> and a plural verb in BrE <public are>.

public Act; private Act; public bill; private bill. In British statutory law (or "statute law," as it is known in BrE), a *public Act* is one that a court may take judicial notice of, whereas a *private Act* is one whose terms must be proved in court. But every Act passed since 1850 is considered public in this sense unless the Act expressly provides otherwise (a rarity). (For the reason behind capitalizing *Act*, see **act (c).**)

A *public bill* is one brought by a government minister or by a private member who has won a place on the ballot allowing him or her a chance to bring in the bill. A *private bill* is one promoted by a person or body (such as a local authority) to regulate its own affairs. Public and private bills are subject to different parliamentary procedures.

*publically. See **publicly.**

publication = (1) (in the law of defamation) the communication of defamatory words to someone other than the person defamed; or (2) (in the law of wills) the formal declaration made by a testator at the time of signing the will that it is the testator's will. Following are examples of sense 2, in which the word is a TERM OF ART:

- "There is no point in '*publishing*' the will at the beginning; the witnesses will not be likely to see the *publication* there. It should be at the end of the will. In any case, 'I declare that this is my will' is a *publication*." Thomas L. Shaffer, *The Planning and Drafting of Wills and Trusts* 171 (2d ed. 1979).
- "Substantial compliance relating to the *publication* of a will and attesting by witnesses is all that is required, and no formal request that witnesses sign or express declaration that instrument is testator's will is required." *In re Estate of Speers*, 179 P.3d 1265, 1271 (Okla. 2008).

In sense 1 as in sense 2, the verb corresponding to *publication* is *to publish*. In the law of defamation, to *publish* is to make public. E.g.: "Since truth is commonly a defense to libel charges, such a right will give historians the incentive to *publish* accurate, factually based statements." Hannes Rösler, *Dignitarian Posthumous Personality Rights*, 26 Berkeley J. Int'l L. 153, 190 (2008). Spoken as well as written defamation is said to be *published*.

public bill. See **public Act.**

public fisc. See **fisc.**

publicist (= [1] one who specializes in public or international law; or [2] a commentator on the law of nations) ordinarily means "publicity agent" to nonlawyers. Hence the legal use of the term generally requires explanation if the audience is a broad one.

public law = (1) international law; the law of nations; (2) constitutional law, criminal law, and administrative law taken together; (3) legislation enacted for the benefit of the public as a whole, operating on all people in similar circumstances—as opposed to *private law*; or

(4) published law. Sense 4 is by far the least common— e.g.: "A case decided is called a 'precedent,' and becomes at once *public law*, which, under many circumstances, binds a court to make the same decision in any future case similar to it." William M. Lile et al., *Brief Making and the Use of Law Books* 26 (3d ed. 1914).

publicly, not **publicically*, is the adverb—e.g.: "Clearly, the legislature intended a municipality to be able to condemn *publically* [read *publicly*] held land in some circumstances or it would not have enacted section 11-61-2." *Village of Woodridge v. Board of Educ.*, 933 N.E.2d 392, 409 (Ill. App. Ct. 2010).

public person. To most speakers of English, this phrase suggests a celebrity. But legal theorists use it quite differently: "By a '*Public person*' we mean either the State, or the sovereign part of it, or a body or individual holding delegated authority under it." Thomas E. Holland, *The Elements of Jurisprudence* 127 (13th ed. 1924).

public policy. In the context of policy-making, this phrase connotes the art of ruling wisely <implementing sound public policy>. The phrase refers vaguely to matters regarded by the legislature or by the courts as being of fundamental concern to the state and the whole of society.

In the context of contract law, *public policy* connotes an overriding public interest that may justify a court's decision to declare a contract void. In this context, too, the phrase is vague: "*Public policy* is a variable notion, depending on changing manners, morals and economic conditions. In theory, this flexibility of the doctrine of *public policy* could provide a judge with an excuse for invalidating any contract which he violently disliked." G.H. Treitel, *The Law of Contract* 424 (8th ed. 1991).

Today this term, when used as a noun, is not preceded by an article: "The trial court's ruling was particularly problematic in light *of the public policies* [read *of public policies*] favoring arbitration and the settlement of complex class actions." *In re Cellphone Termination Fee Cases*, 104 Cal. Rptr. 3d 275, 288 (Ct. App. 2009).

public school; common school; private school. In AmE, the first two terms are synonyms for free schools supported by taxes. *Public school* is now preferred. Although *common school* has largely fallen from ordinary discourse, it appears in many state constitutions and judicial opinions—e.g.:

- "The general assembly shall make such provisions, by taxation, or otherwise, as, with the income arising from the school trust fund, will secure a thorough and efficient system of *common schools* throughout the state." Ohio Const., art. VI, § 2 (1851).
- "The legislature shall provide for the maintenance and support of a system of free *common schools*, wherein all the children of this state may be educated." N.Y. Const. art. XI, § 1 (1894).

- "Today's *public school* districts are direct descendants of 19th-century '*common schools*.'" *Baier v. Mayer Unified Sch. Dist.*, 232 P.3d 747, 752 n.10 (Ariz. Ct. App. 2010).

In BrE, the term *common school* is used because a *public school* is often neither free nor open to the general public. It is the equivalent of an American *private school*—e.g.:

- "It was easy to stress the importance to the young boy, with very great potential, of maintaining his expectations, his relationships within and without the school, and his opportunity to develop scholastically and in the round within a prestigious school that opened the prospects of a subsequent admission, either as a scholar or perhaps simply as a fee-payer, to a leading English *public school*." *Re A.*, [2006] E.W.C.A. Civ. 830, ¶ 6.
- "She also wanted to send the children to *public school* at 'vast cost'." *Mack v. Lockwood*, [2009] E.W.H.C. 1524, ¶ 33 (Ch.).
- "[T]he *public schools* and universities . . . are 'economic operators' offering their educational services 'on the market' for educational services, in competition with one another and with state-funded schools." *R. (ex rel Chandler) v. Secretary of State for Children, Schs. & Families*, [2009] E.W.H.C. 219, ¶ 160 (Admin.).

In Scotland, a *public school* is "a school under the management of an education authority." *D. v. Glasgow City Council*, [2007] C.S.I.H. 72, ¶ 19.

publish. See **publication.**

pudendum (= a genital organ) forms the plural *pudenda* (= genitals). See PLURALS (A).

puffing (= the action of praising a thing excessively but in general terms, esp. to advertise it) is perfectly appropriate in formal contexts; it is not a casualism. E.g.:

- "Ours may be, for *puffing* purposes, a 'government of checks and balances,' but there is no check at all on what the Supreme Court does." Fred Rodell, *Nine Men* 4 (1955).
- "General commendations, commonly known as dealer's talk, seller's statements, or *puffing*, do not amount to actionable misrepresentations where the parties deal at arm's length and have equal means of information and are equally well qualified to judge the facts." 41 Tex. Jur. 3d *Fraud & Deceit* § 28 (1985).

While American writers tend to stick to the gerund *puffing*, British writers frequently refer to particular statements as "mere *puffs*."

puisne (= younger or of lower rank), sometimes used in reference to a superior court judge who is less than a chief judge, is pronounced like *puny*. Etymologically, the LAW FRENCH *puisne* is *puis-né* (= later-born). The term has been extended in English legal usage to apply to mortgagees and other incumbrancers; it is also used in England as an attributive adjective in the sense "a puisne judge" <five puisnes upheld the plea>. E.g.:

- "Often the court consisted of the Lord Chief Justice and two *puisne* judges, with a second and third court consisting of three *puisnes*." R.M. Jackson, *The Machinery of Justice in England* 123 (5th ed. 1967).
- "The motions were heard by Lord Chief Justice Mansfield sitting with his *puisnes*, Willes and Ashurst." Patrick Devlin, *The Judge* 122 (1979).

PUNCTUATION. A. Generally. Judges and jurists have written more nonsense about punctuation than about any other facet of the language. The well-known dictum that "punctuation is not a part of the statute" has given rise to even more surreal pronouncements: "Punctuation at any rate is not a part of the English language." *Kansas City Life Ins. Co. v. Wells*, 133 F.2d 224, 227 (8th Cir. 1943). Just as surreally, courts have minimized the effect of punctuation with outré statements: "Punctuation or the absence of punctuation will not of itself create ambiguity." *Anderson & Kerr Drilling Co. v. Bruhlmeyer*, 136 S.W.2d 800, 803 (Tex. 1940).

Can that be so? The resolution of at least two capital cases has rested on no more than how the court interpreted a comma. See *U.S. v. Palmer*, 16 U.S. (3 Wheat.) 610, 636 (1818) (in which Johnson, J., dissenting, stated: "Men's lives may depend upon a comma"); *Rex v. Casement*, [1917] 1 K.B. 98 (1916).

And consider the following statement shorn of the punctuation marks: "Woman—without her, man would be a savage."

The fallacies underlying the statements quoted in the first paragraph are too obvious to require extensive explanation. And occasionally—though not often enough—the courts refute them: "Punctuation is a rational part of English composition, and it is sometimes quite significantly employed. I see no reason for depriving legal documents of such significance as attaches to punctuation in other writings." *Houston v. Burns*, [1918] A.C. 337, 348.

Lawyers and judges have long mistrusted punctuation as a guide to meaning. See Richard C. Wydick, *Should Lawyers Punctuate?*, 1 Scribes J. Legal Writing 7 (1990). Historically speaking, there are three primary reasons for this mistrust: (1) the uncertain state of English punctuation during the 17th and 18th centuries, a formative period for modern law; (2) the fact that printers typically controlled punctuation more than drafters; and (3) the age-old canard that English statutes were traditionally unpunctuated. See *id.* at 16–19. Wydick persuasively concludes that judges "should create a rebuttable presumption that legal documents have been punctuated in accordance with ordinary English usage, and they should use the punctuation, along with all of the other guides to meaning, when they interpret legal documents." See *id.* at 24.

Following, then, are the basic principles for punctuating in accordance with ordinary English usage. These principles are adapted, with elaboration, from the *Oxford Guide* (pp. 193–97). First, though, a warning. Poor punctuation often signals writing problems that go deeper than one might think: "Most errors of punctuation arise from ill-designed, badly shaped sentences, and from the attempt to make them work by means of violent tricks with commas and colons and such like." Hugh Sykes Davies, *Grammar Without Tears* 167 (1951).

B. The Apostrophe [']. This punctuation mark is used in English for either of two purposes: (1) to indicate the possessive case <Lord Mansfield's speech> <Mother Jones's recipe>; and (2) to mark the omission of one or more elements and the contracting of the remaining elements into a meaningful expression <we will = we'll> <department = dep't> <2011 = '11>.

On the misuse of an apostrophe to denote a plural, see PLURALS (F).

C. The Colon [:]. This mark may link two grammatically complete clauses by indicating a step forward from the first to the second: the step may be from an introduction to a main theme, from a cause to an effect, from a general statement to a particular instance, or from a premise to a conclusion. E.g.: "The remedy is simple[:] the United States Supreme Court can eliminate the conflict by simply taking up an appropriate case for review." *Kidwell v. State*, 696 So.2d 399, 405 (Fla. Dist. Ct. App. 1997). The colon is also used, and perhaps more commonly, to introduce a list of items, often after expressions such as "for example"; "namely"; "the following"; "as follows"; and "including." E.g.: "The following Judges were present[:] Judge J. Fritz Thompson, Richard V. Evans, E.M. Creel, Robert J. Wheeler, C.B. Smith, John Denson, J. Edgar Bowron, Gardner Goodwyn (from Bessemer), J.Q. Smith, and Leigh M. Clark." *Hale v. State*, 186 So. 163, 165 (Ala. 1939).

D. The Comma [,]. This is the least emphatic mark of punctuation, and the one used in the greatest variety of circumstances:

1. To separate adjectives that each qualify a noun in the same way <a cautious[,] reserved person>. E.g.:

   - "Is there to be one standard for the old, repulsive laws that preferred whites over blacks, and a *different, more forgiving* standard for new laws that give blacks special benefits in the name of historical redress?" Linda Greenhouse, *Signal on Job Rights*, N.Y. Times, 25 Jan. 1989, at 1.
   - "It almost goes without saying that the job of the president of the L.I.R.R. is not a weekday warrior's position—it is not a *five-days-a-week, 9-to-5* job." Matthew L. Wald, *Senator Assails L.I.R.R. Chief as Out of Touch*, N.Y. Times, 21 Apr. 1994, at B6.

   But when adjectives qualify the noun in different ways, or when one adjective qualifies a noun phrase containing another adjective, no comma is used—e.g.: "a distinguished [no comma] foreign journalist"; "a bright [no comma] red tie." E.g.: "I could quote dozens of similar remarks by *eminent, legal scholars* [read *eminent legal scholars*] and lawyers." Jerome Frank, *Courts on Trial* 61 (1949).

2. To separate items (including the last from the penultimate) in a list of more than two—e.g.: "the defendants, the third-party defendants[,] and the counterdefendants." The question whether to include the serial comma has sparked many arguments in law offices and judges' chambers. It is easily answered in favor of including the final comma, for its omission may cause ambiguities, whereas its inclusion never will—e.g.: "A and B, C and D, E and F[,] and G and H." When the members are

compound, calling for *and* within themselves, clarity demands the final comma. See ENUMERATIONS (B).

3. To separate coordinated main clauses—e.g.: "Cars will turn here[,] and coaches will go straight." There are two exceptions: first, when the main clauses are closely linked (e.g., "Do as I tell you [no comma] and you will not regret it."); and second, when the subject of the second independent clause, being the same as in the first, is not repeated (e.g., "Remedies that prevent harm altogether are often better for plaintiffs [no comma] and are always closer to the ideal of corrective justice." Douglas Laycock, *The Death of the Irreparable Injury Rule* 4 (1991)).

4. To mark the beginning and ending of a parenthetical word or phrase <I am sure[,] however[,] that it will not happen> <Fred[,] who is bald[,] complained of the cold>.

   Some writers mistakenly omit the second comma—e.g.:

   - "Scienter, or knowledge of the falsity of representation[,] is required." William F. Walsh, *A Treatise on Equity* 490 (1930).
   - "Mr. Rifkin's lawyer, John Lawrence[,] insisted that Mr. Rifkin did not know what he was doing and often drove around in a haze after strangling victims." John T. McQuiston, *Rifkin Guilty of Murder as Long Island Jury Rejects Insanity Defense*, N.Y. Times, 10 May 1994, at A16.

   Still others leave out both commas, often creating a MISCUE: "Such warrantor must as a minimum remedy such consumer product within a reasonable time and without charge." 15 U.S.C. § 2304(a)(1) (1988). (A comma is needed after *must* and after *minimum*; otherwise, one reads *as a minimum remedy* as a single phrase.)

   Note that with restrictive clauses—that is, those that are necessary to define the antecedent or to limit it—*no* commas are used. E.g.: "Men [no comma] who are bald [no comma] should wear hats." / "Facts [no comma] not unlike those found in this record [no comma] were considered in that case." See **that & which.**

5. To separate a participial or verbless clause, a salutation, or a vocative—e.g.: "Having had breakfast[,] I went for a walk." / "The sermon *over* [or *being over*], the congregation filed out." / "Fellow lawyers[,] the bar must unite in seeking reform of the system of electing judges." (N.B.: Not "The sermon[,] being over[,] . . ."; and no comma with restrictive expressions like "My friend Judge Smith" or "my son John.")

6. To separate a phrase or subordinate clause from the main clause so as to avoid misunderstanding. E.g.: "In the valley below[,] the villages looked very small." / "In 1982[,] 1918 seemed like the distant past." (N.B.: A comma should not be used to separate a phrasal subject from its predicate, or a verb from an object that is a clause. E.g.: "A car with

such a high-powered *engine, should* [read *engine should*] not fail on that hill." / "They believed, that [read *believed that*] nothing could go wrong.")

7. To distinguish indirect from direct speech. E.g.: "They answered[,] 'Here we are.'"

8. To mark the end of the salutation, e.g., "Dear Mr. Crosthwaite[,]"; "Dear Rebecca[,]", etc. and the complimentary close, e.g., "Very truly yours[,]"; "Yours sincerely[,]"; etc. In formal letters, the salutation is separated from the body by a colon "Dear Sir[:]"; "Dear Madam[:]"; etc.

Writers cause needless confusion or distraction for their readers when they insert commas erroneously:

- *The Archaic Comma Preceding a Verb.* Formerly, it was common for writers to insert a comma in the main clause before the verb, but this practice has been out of fashion since the early 20th century. Today it is considered incorrect. E.g.: "Whether or not a contract has been modified, [omit the comma] is a question of fact for the jury." / "Only if this were true, [omit the comma] could it be said that plaintiffs received their bargained-for equivalent of the $30,000 payments."

  Even those who understand this principle are tempted sometimes to place a comma after a compound subject. That temptation should be resisted— e.g.: "Co-owners who are not joint tenants, tenants by the entireties, or owners of community property, [omit the comma] are tenants in common." Robert Kratovil, *Real Estate Law* 222 (1946).

- *Misplaced Emphasis.* "I, accordingly, [read *accordingly* without the embracing commas] dissent." / "We, therefore, [read *therefore* without the embracing commas] conclude that the ancient doctrine of sovereign immunity has lost its underpinnings." (N.B.: If the emphasis in the preceding sentence is to fall on *We*—as clearly separated from some other group and its thinking—the commas should stand; but if the emphasis is to fall on the *therefore* as a simple consequence of our reasoning from the evidence, then the commas should be omitted. See **therefore (D).**)

- *Compound Sentences.* As explained in #3 in the preceding list, no comma appears before the conjunction in a compound sentence when the second clause has an understood subject—e.g.: "The problem has not yet arisen, [omit comma] and is of little practical importance." P.S. Atiyah, *An Introduction to the Law of Contract* 57 (3d ed. 1981). / "These are cases in which plaintiff seeks some equitable remedy, [omit comma] and is remitted to a legal remedy instead." Douglas Laycock, *The Death of the Irreparable Injury Rule* 100 (1991).

- *Dates.* No comma is needed between the month and year in dates written "December 1984" or "18 December 1984"; a comma is required when the date is written "December 18, 1984." See DATES (B).

- *The Comma Splice.* See RUN-ON SENTENCES.

The omission of commas can often blur the sense of a sentence, as in the following examples:

- "Substantial performance cannot occur where the breach is intentional [insert a comma] as it is the antithesis of material breach."

- "Because, prior to their filing [insert a comma] consignor's claims will be subordinate to those of lien creditors, in practice the consignee's creditors will have effective claims to the consigned goods."

- "Something may be said for it, since it furnishes a simple, if arbitrary [insert comma] test."

E. The Dash [— ; –]. There are two kinds of dashes, which typesetters are able to distinguish by their length. First, the *em-dash*, which is as wide as the square of the type size, is used to mark an interruption in the structure of a sentence. In typewriting, it is commonly represented by two hyphens, often with a space at either end of the pair (--). A pair of em-dashes can be used to enclose a parenthetical remark or to mark the ending and the resumption of a statement by an interlocutor. E.g.:

- "Both attorneys have obviously entered into a secret pact—complete with hats, handshakes, and cryptic words—to draft their pleadings entirely in crayon on the back sides of gravy-stained paper place mats, in the hope that the Court would be so charmed by their child-like efforts that their utter dearth of legal authorities in their briefing would go unnoticed." *Bradshaw v. Unity Marine Corp., Inc.*, 147 F.Supp.2d 668, 670 (S.D. Tex. 2001).

- "The courts were endeavouring to find the compromise— always difficult—between substantial justice and a proper discipline of form." Carleton K. Allen, *Law in the Making* 401 (7th ed. 1964).

The em-dash can also be used to replace the colon.

In legal writing, em-dashes are the second most underused mark of punctuation (*periods* being the most underused). Whether in drafting or in persuasive writing, dashes can often clarify a sentence that is clogged up with commas. Imagine the following sentences if commas replaced the well-chosen em-dashes:

- "He may make no pretension—he generally makes no pretension—to be an expert in any of these fields, but he would be a little ashamed if he was crassly ignorant of them." Max Radin, *The Law and You* 11 (1948).

- "In some jurisdictions, the judge, when using a special verdict, need not—should not—give any charge about the substantive legal rules beyond what is reasonably necessary to enable the jury to answer intelligently the questions put to them." Jerome Frank, *Courts on Trial* 141 (1949).

- "If this be the correct principle—and, so far as we are aware, it has never before been laid down in terms—there seems to be no reason why it should not apply equally to the Divisional Court of the Queen's Bench." Carleton K. Allen, *Law in the Making* 240 (7th ed. 1964).

- "Why should not all people—Blacks as well as Whites—be allowed to appear, by right, before a tribunal that is impartial and not a stooge for the powerful Highway Lobby, to air their complaints and state their views?" William O. Douglas, *Points of Rebellion* 86 (1970).

- "When the plaintiff's attorney files a certificate stating that he or she believes a defendant cannot be personally served, because after diligent inquiry within the state where the complaint is filed the defendant's place of residence cannot be ascertained—or, if ascertained, that it is beyond the territorial limits of personal service as provided in this rule—this defendant must be served by publication in a newspaper published in the county where the property is located." Fed. R. Civ. P. 71A (1992 draft of Style Subcommittee, Standing Committee on Federal Practice and Procedure).

Second, the *en-dash*, which is half as wide as an *em-dash*, is distinct (in print) from the *hyphen*. It is ordinarily equivalent to the word *to*. In typewriting, it is commonly represented by one hyphen, occasionally with a space at either end (-). But the better practice is to use the en-dash <the 1914–1918 war> <Dallas–Toronto–Quebec route> <pages 68–70>.

Sometimes the en-dash suggests tension and carries the sense "versus." For example, in circumstances involving a disjunction, the en-dash is usually preferable to the slash—e.g.: "If we manage to get that far, the absurdity of attempting to preserve the nineteenth-century contract–tort dichotomy [not *contract/tort dichotomy*] will have become apparent." Grant Gilmore, *The Death of Contract* 90 (1974).

F. The Exclamation Mark [!]. This mark is used after an exclamatory word, phrase, or sentence. It usually counts as the concluding full stop, but need not. E.g.: "Hail, Source of Being! Universal Soul!" It may also be used within square brackets, after or in the midst of a quotation, to express the editor's amusement, dissent, or surprise. Rarely is the exclamation mark called for in legal writing.

G. The Hyphen [-]. In all but one context, AmE is much more inhospitable to hyphens than BrE. Words with prefixes are generally made solid: *nonstatutory* (not *non-statutory*), *pretrial* (not *pre-trial*), *posttrial* (not *post-trial*), *preemption* (not *pre-emption*). This no-hyphen style seems aesthetically superior, but reasonable people will differ on such a question. They can agree, however, that the hyphen must appear when an AMBIGUITY, MISCUE, or eyesore results without it—e.g., *pre-judicial* (career), *re-sign* (the petition), *post-sentencing*. See RE- PAIRS.

And what is that one context in which AmE is hospitable to the hyphen? See PHRASAL ADJECTIVES.

H. Parentheses [(...)]. These marks enclose words, phrases, and even whole sentences (but usually not more than a whole paragraph). If what is enclosed is a full sentence, the closing parenthesis includes the end punctuation; if not, the end punctuation is swept outside, as in the previous sentence here. More specifically, parentheses are used as follows:

1. To indicate interpolations and remarks by the writer of the text, e.g., "Mrs. X (*as I will call her*) now spoke."
2. To specify, in one's own running text, an authority, definition, explanation, reference, or translation.
3. To indicate, in the report of a speech, interruptions by the audience.

4. To separate reference letters or figures that do not need a full stop, e.g., (1)(a).

I. The Period or Full Stop [.]. This mark is used in two ways. First, it ends all sentences that are not questions or exclamations. The next word should normally begin with a capital letter.

Second, it indicates abbreviations (see ACRONYMS AND INITIALISMS). If a point marking an abbreviation comes at the end of a sentence, it also serves as the closing full stop. E.g.: "She also kept dogs, cats, birds, etc[.]" But where a closing parenthesis or bracket intervenes, a period is required: "She also kept pets (dogs, cats, birds, etc[.).]" When a sentence concludes with a quotation that ends with a period (i.e., a full stop), question mark, or exclamation mark, no further period is needed. E.g.: "He cried, 'Be off!' [no period] But the child would not move."

J. The Question Mark [?]. A question mark follows every question that expects a separate answer; the next word should begin with a capital letter. "He asked me, 'Why are you here?' A foolish question." (N.B.: A question mark is not used after indirect questions, e.g.: "He asked me why I was there.") A question mark may be placed in brackets after a word, etc., whose accuracy is doubted, e.g., "Sangad Anurugsa[?]"

K. Quotation Marks [" "]. In using quotation marks (or "inverted commas," as the British call them), writers and editors of AmE and BrE have developed conventions that are markedly different.

1. In AmE, double quotation marks are used for a first quotation; single marks for a quotation within a quotation; double again for a further quotation inside that; etc. In BrE, the practice is exactly the reverse at each step.
2. With a closing quotation mark, practices vary. In AmE, it is usual to place a period or comma within the closing quotation mark, whether or not the punctuation so placed is actually a part of the quoted matter. E.g.: "Joan pointedly said, 'We do not intend to see "Les Miserables."'" In BrE, by contrast, the closing quotation mark comes before all punctuation marks, unless these marks form a part of the quotation itself (or what is quoted is *less* than a full sentence in its own right). E.g.: 'Joan pointedly said, "We do not intend to see 'Les Miserables'."' (N.B.: In this specimen, the outermost quotation marks indicate that a printed source is being quoted directly.)

When question and exclamation marks are involved, AmE and BrE practice is the same. E.g.: (AmE) "Did Nelson really say, 'Kiss me, Hardy'?"; (BrE) 'Did Nelson really say, "Kiss me, Hardy"?' But when the question or exclamation mark is an integral part of what is being quoted, it is swept inside all quotation marks (i.e., inverted commas). E.g.: (AmE) "Banging her fist on the table, she exclaimed, 'And that's *that*!'"; (BrE) 'Banging her fist on the table, she exclaimed, "And that's *that!*"' (N.B.: When the ending of an interrogatory or an exclamatory sentence coincides with the ending of another sentence that embraces it, the stronger mark of punctuation is sufficient to terminate *both* sentences; i.e., a period [i.e., a full stop] need not also be included after the question mark or exclamation mark inside the final quotation mark.)

As to quotations that are interrupted to indicate a speaker, AmE and BrE again show different preferences. In AmE, the first comma is swept within the quotation mark. E.g.: "Sally," he said, "is looking radiant today." In BrE, the first comma (usually) remains outside the inverted comma, just as though the attribution could be lifted neatly out of the speaker's actual words. E.g.: 'Sally', he said, 'is looking radiant today'. See QUOTATIONS (B).

3. In nonlegal citations, quotation marks (and roman type) are often used when citing titles of articles in magazines, chapters in books, poems not published separately, and songs. (Titles of books and magazines are usually printed in italics in nonlegal citations.) See CITATION OF CASES.

L. Semicolon [;]. This mark separates those parts of a sentence between which there is a more distinct break than a comma can signal, but that are too closely connected to be made into separate sentences. Typically these will be clauses of similar importance and grammatical construction. E.g.: "To err is human; to forgive, divine." (N.B.: The comma here flags the dropping of a word: *is*.)

M. Square Brackets ([ ]). These enclose comments, corrections, explanations, interpolations, notes, or translations that were not in the original text but have been added by subsequent authors, editors, or others. E.g.: "My right honorable friend [John Smith] is mistaken."

In legal writing, brackets are customarily used for adjustments in quoted matter, such as making lowercase a letter that was uppercase in the source of the quotation ("The court stated that '[a]nother problem in determining the existence of apparent authority relates to the extent of the knowledge of the person invoking the doctrine.'") or signifying an omission of an inflection in a word ("If the trustees 'fail[ ] to reelect or reemploy the superintendent' without giving notice, his contract is automatically reviewable.").

This last use—bracketing empty space—should not supplant the ellipsis, as here: "The *choice of* [ ] *forum* [read *choice of . . . forum*] was made in an arm's-length negotiation." *Snyder v. Smith*, 736 F.2d 409, 419 (7th Cir. 1984) (quoting *The Bremen v. Zapata Off-Shore Co.*, 407 U.S. 1, 12 (1972)).

For further inquiry, the following works are useful: Karen E. Gordon, *The Well-Tempered Sentence: A Punctuation Handbook for the Innocent, the Eager, and the Doomed* (1983); G.V. Carey, *Mind the Stop* (1977 ed.); Harry Shaw, *Punctuate It Right!* (1963); and Eric Partridge, *You Have a Point There: A Guide to Punctuation and Its Allies* (1953; repr. 1978).

N. Virgule [/]. Known popularly as the "slash," arcanely as the "solidus," and somewhere in between as the "diagonal," the virgule is a mark that doesn't appear much in first-rate writing. Some writers use it to mean "per" <50 words/minute>. Others use it to mean "or" <and/or> or "and" <every employee/independent contractor must complete form XJ42A>. Still others use it to indicate a vague disjunction, in which it's not quite an *or* <the novel/novella distinction>. In this last use, the en-dash is usually a better choice. (See (E).) In all these uses, there's almost always a better choice than the virgule. Use it as a last resort.

But the virgule has legitimate uses as well: (1) to separate run-in lines of poetry <To be, or not to be: that is the question: / Whether 'tis nobler in the mind to suffer / The slings and arrows of outrageous fortune>; (2) to show pronunciations (as they're shown throughout this book) <*ribald* is pronounced /**rib**-əld/>; (3) to separate the numerator and the denominator in a fraction <19/20>; (4) in Internet addresses <http://www.oed.com>; and (5) in informal jottings, to separate the elements in a date <11/17/2010>.

punies. American trial lawyers use this shortened word as a slang for *punitive damages*—e.g.:

• "Klausner, who says he has at least six clients with whistleblower actions, says last week's ruling is terrific. 'It's great if you know you can get *punies* from a government agency.'" Henry Gottlieb, *Whistleblower Punitives Allowed in Public Sector*, N.J.L.J., 6 Dec. 1993, at 1 (quoting Stephen Klausner, a lawyer in Somerville, N.J.).

• "A San Francisco County Superior Court jury awarded secretary Rena Weeks $6.9 million in *punies* from Baker & McKenzie—with 1,642 attorneys, the world's largest law firm—and $225,000 from rainmaker Martin Greenstein, whom Ms. Weeks had accused of unwanted sexual attention." Thom Weidlich, *Baker Verdict Not Major Concern*, Nat'l L.J., 19 Sept. 1994, at A6.

Cf. **punitives.**

punishable. When used in reference to a person, *punishable* means "liable to punishment" <she is not legally punishable>. When used in reference to a crime, it means "entailing punishment" <an offense punishable by a $500 fine>. The latter sense—a good illustration of how HYPALLAGE works—is now the more common one.

punitive; *punitory. *Punitive* (= involving or inflicting punishment) is a word much more common in legal than in nonlegal texts. *Punitory is a NEEDLESS VARIANT. These two forms are commonly used by those who practice INELEGANT VARIATION. E.g.: "Considered as strictly *punitory* [read *punitive*], the damages are for the punishment of the private tort, not of the public crime." Thomas B. Colby, *Beyond the Multiple Punishment Problem*, 87 Minn. L. Rev. 583, 621 (2003). Even worse: "The law with respect to *punitive damages* is that in order to justify the *infliction* [read *imposition*?] of *punitory damages* [read *punitive damages*] for the commission of a tort, the act complained of must have been done wantonly or maliciously." *Stenson v. Laclede Gas Co.*, 553 S.W.2d 309, 315 (Mo. Ct. App. 1977).

punitive damages; exemplary damages; vindictive damages; aggravated damages; retributory damages. The first two terms are by far the most common in both AmE and BrE. Each one tells only half the story, for the two-pronged rationale for awarding such damages in civil cases is (1) to punish the defendant, and (2) to make an example of the defendant so as to deter others. *Exemplary damages* appears to be the more usual phrase in BrE (although the *CDL* and the *OCL1* mention only punishment as the basis), whereas in AmE the term *punitive damages* is slightly more frequent. (Colloquially, the phrase is sometimes shortened in AmE to *punitives* and even *punies*.) See **punitives** & **punies**.

The other forms, sometimes used in strings (as in the following example), should be avoided as NEEDLESS VARIANTS. E.g.:

- "The Illinois Breach of Promise Act reflects a compromise position that allows recovery of 'actual' damages suffered by the nonbreaching party, but bars all *punitive, exemplary, vindictive,* or *aggravated damages.*" Michelle Oberman, *Sex, Lies, and the Duty to Disclose,* 47 Ariz. L. Rev. 871, 890 (2005).
- "On appeal, defendants argued that the damages were excessive, and the courts responded that in cases of willful wrong, *punitive damages, vindictive damages,* or *exemplary damages* were permitted." Benjamin C. Zipursky, *A Theory of Punitive Damages,* 84 Tex. L. Rev. 105, 158 (2005).

See **parasitic** & **smart money.**

punitives, a shortened form of *punitive damages,* is a casualism—e.g.:

- "Not only that, Corboy wanted juries to concentrate on the compensatory damages, because that money was *tax-free* to the client (unlike *punitives,* which were taxed just like one huge paycheck)." John A. Jenkins, *The Litigators* 369 (1989).
- "Richard B. Miller led the defense team that saw the jury award Pennzoil more than $7 billion in compensatory damages and another $3 billion in *punitives.*" *Pennzoil v. Texaco,* Litig., Winter 1991, at 14, 14.

Cf. **punies** & **exemplaries.**

*****punitory.** See **punitive.**

Puns. Plays on words—known popularly as puns and professorially as paronomasia—can add zest to writing if artfully used. H.W. Fowler and Bernstein have dispelled the notion that puns are the lowest form of wit. Bad puns, of course, create a bad impression in either speech or writing. But the well-wrought pun often serves to reinforce the point one is making. The good pun gives the sentence added meaning in both (or all) its senses, and it is not too obvious.

Puns seem increasingly popular in American legal prose. Some are good and some are not. The title of a law-review article by Robert P. Mosteller, *Simplifying Subpoena Law: Taking the Fifth Amendment Seriously,* 73 Va. L. Rev. 1 (1987), plays effectively on two English idioms, *to take the Fifth Amendment* and *to take (something) seriously.* Both senses fit the purpose

of the article, hence the aptness of the pun. A more strained but nevertheless clever pun occurred to the federal appellate judge who wrote: "*Ticonic's* cloth cannot be cut to fit Interfirst's *suit.*" *Interfirst Bank v. FDIC,* 777 F.2d 1092, 1097 (5th Cir. 1985) (discussing *Ticonic Nat'l Bank v. Sprague,* 303 U.S. 406 (1938)). Here *suit* carries the double sense, on the one hand, of completing the tailoring METAPHOR (cutting cloth for a suit) and, on the other hand, of denoting the lawsuit at issue. Yet another aesthetically pleasing pun is this subtle one from the pen of Justice Frankfurter: "The liability rests on the inroad [that] the automobile has made on the decision of *Pennoyer v. Neff,* . . . as it has on so many aspects of our social scene." *Olberding v. Illinois Cent. R.R.,* 346 U.S. 338, 341 (1953) (per Frankfurter, J.). Ordinarily, of course, *inroad* is an abstract word, but Justice Frankfurter's placement of *automobile* near it gives the word a new and unexpected concrete sense; again, the pun is felicitous.

Chief Justice William Rehnquist has used puns that would probably delight some readers and perturb others—depending entirely on their views on issues other than linguistic matters. One case, for example, involved several Indiana nightclubs that wanted to feature totally nude dancers. When Indiana officials began enforcing an indecent-exposure statute requiring dancers to wear "pasties" and G-strings, several dancers sued to enjoin enforcement of the statute on First Amendment grounds. Chief Justice Rehnquist's opinion upholding the statute concluded in this way: "It is without cavil that the public indecency statute is '*narrowly tailored*'; Indiana's requirement that the dancers wear at least pasties and a G-string is *modest,* and the *bare* minimum necessary to achieve the state's purpose." *Barnes v. Glen Theatre, Inc.,* 501 U.S. 560, 572 (1991) (per Rehnquist, C.J.).

Probably half the puns one sees in modern legal writing, though, are the empty kind of wordplay in which one of the senses is inapposite or, at worst, gibberish. Some ill-wrought specimens:

- "The bells do not *toll* the limitations statute while one ferrets the facts." *Prather v. Neva Paperbacks, Inc.,* 446 F.2d 338, 341 (5th Cir. 1971). (The pun here is *toll,* which on the obvious level [*bells . . . toll*] means, nonsensically, "to ring"; the legal sense of *toll,* the one that gives meaning to the sentence, is "to abate." The pun in no way contributes to the sense; in fact, it is more likely to confuse than to enlighten.)
- "[An official] cannot hide behind a claim that the particular factual predicate in question has never appeared *in haec verba* in a reported opinion. If the application of settled principles to this factual tableau would inexorably lead to a conclusion of unconstitutionality, a prison official may not take solace in *ostrichism.*" *Little v. Walker,* 552 F.2d 193, 197 (7th Cir. 1977). (*Ostrichism* here apparently means "the practice of hiding one's head in the sand," foreshadowed earlier in the sentence in the phrase *hide behind a claim.* The pun is on *ostracism* [= exclusion from association with another or others], but this near-homophone has nothing to do with the meaning of the sentence. Hence the writer has been at pains to create a

punning NEOLOGISM whose suggestiveness bewilders, rather than charms, the reader.)

As Charles Lamb once observed, "A pun is not bound by the laws which limit nicer wit. It is a pistol let off at the ear; not a feather to tickle the intellect." "Popular Fallacies—. . . That the Worst Puns Are the Best," in *Essays of Elia and Last Essays of Elia* 306, 306–07 (1906). Still, in punning one must not abandon the intellect, for then one becomes a nuisance to the reader. Lamb also cautioned that puns sometimes show "much less wit than rudeness," adding: "We must take in the totality of time, place, and person." *Id.* at 308.

pupil. See child.

pupilage; pupillage. The -*l*- spelling is AmE, the -*ll*- spelling BrE.

pur autre vie—a LAW FRENCH phrase meaning "for another's life"—is pronounced /pər **oh**-tər **vee**/. E.g.: "The grantee of a life tenant generally took an estate *pur autre vie*, measured by the grantor's life, not the grantee's." 1 *American Law of Property* 124 (A.J. Casner ed., 1952). The phrase is sometimes spelled *per autre vie*.

purchasable. See **salable**.

purchase. A. Meaning Generally "to buy." In legal writing, the verb *purchase* commonly appears as an equivalent of *buy*. So used, *purchase* is a FORMAL WORD that most good editors would probably want to change to *buy*.

 B. Special Legal Sense. *Purchase* = to acquire real property other than by descent. So in very technical legal parlance, gifts are *purchased* by those who receive them. The following sentence conveys this special legal sense of the word (here as a noun): "A third party who deals in good faith with a personal representative with respect to a transaction involving a *purchase*, sale, lease or other encumbrance of real property of a business may rely on the notice that the personal representative must file." Gerry W. Beyer, *Wills and Trusts*, 61 SMU L. Rev. 1179, 1190 (2008). This legal technicality appears also in the phrases *words of purchase* and *take by purchase*.

 C. Choice of Preposition. The verb *purchase* may take *from* or *of*, though the latter form is an ARCHAISM. E.g.: "The amount of shares which I have *purchased of* NBTY or any other security has never been enough to affect the market price in any stock." *Davidov v. U.S.*, 415 F.Supp.2d 386, 390 (S.D.N.Y. 2006). See **words of purchase, buy** & **descent (A)**.

purchase money. Two words as a noun phrase <the return of the purchase money>; hyphenated as a PHRASAL ADJECTIVE <purchase-money resulting trust> <purchase-money mortgage>.

purchaser; *purchasor. The first is the only correct spelling. Usually, *purchaser* can advantageously be made *buyer*. See **buyer** & **purchase (A)**.

purloin. See **steal (A)**.

PURPLE PROSE, or ostentatious writing, has a certain fascination for some legal writers, as it does for many an aspiring novelist. Good writing *uses* words; purple prose *parades* them. The danger is that, "unless the pen be guided by the hand of genius, there is apt to result a sacrifice of legal sense to purely artificial verbiage. . . . An ornate, pretentious, grandiose style, replete with superfluous frills and rhetorical extravagances, can act only as an undesirable distraction." Horace Stern, *The Writing of Judicial Opinions*, 18 Pa. B. Ass'n Q. 40, 42 (1947).

Similes are especially likely to turn purple. Whereas METAPHORS are quite acceptable in legal writing, copious SIMILES tend to signal overwriting: "Getting information on the judgment-debtor's assets was like working at a deep archeological dig, or perhaps more akin to ferreting out the proverbial needle in an oversized haystack, all the while knowing that time's winged chariot was right upon one's heels, like a relentless juggernaut."

Rarely can a short sentence turn purple, but this one comes as close as any: "A miniscule [*sic*] error must coalesce with gargantuan guilt, even where the accused displays an imagination of Pantagruelian dimensions." *Chapman v. U.S.*, 547 F.2d 1240, 1250 (5th Cir. 1977).

Purple prose is seductive: it may skew the literary sensibilities especially of those who purport to be stylists, and is most common among those who fancy themselves talented writers. To name three guilty parties, Norman Brand and John O. White, in their otherwise solid book *Legal Writing: The Strategy of Persuasion* 111–12 (1976), offer up as an example of a "well-written decision" the following, by Justice Carlin of New York:

> This case presents the ordinary man—that problem child of the law—in a most bizarre setting. As a lowly chauffeur in defendant's employ he became in a trice the protagonist in a breath-bating drama with a denouement almost tragic. It appears that a man, whose identity it would be indelicate to divulge[,] was feloniously relieved of his portable goods by two nondescript highwaymen in an alley near 26th Street and Third Avenue, Manhattan; they induced him to relinquish his possessions by a strong argument *ad hominem* couched in the convincing cant of the criminal and pressed at the point of a most persuasive pistol. Laden with their loot, but not thereby impeded, they took an abrupt departure and he, shuffling off the coil of that discretion which enmeshed him in the alley, quickly gave chase through 26th Street toward 2d Avenue, whither they were resorting "with expedition swift as thought" for most obvious reasons. Somewhere on that thoroughfare of escape they indulged the stratagem of separation ostensibly to disconcert their pursuer and allay the ardor of his pursuit. He then centered on for capture the man with the pistol whom he saw board the defendant's taxicab, which quickly veered south toward 25th Street on 2d Avenue where he saw the chauffeur jump out while the cab, still in motion, continued toward 24th Street; after the chauffeur relieved himself of the cumbersome burden of his fare the latter also is said to have similarly departed from the cab before it reached 24th Street. . . . The chauffeur—the ordinary man in this case— acted in a split second in a most harrowing experience. To call him negligent would be to brand him coward; the court does not do so in spite of what those swaggering heroes, "whose valor plucks dead lions by the beard," may bluster to the contrary. The court is loathe to see the plaintiffs go without recovery even though their damages were slight, but cannot hold the defendant liable upon the

facts adduced at the trial. Motions, upon which decision was reserved, to dismiss the complaint are granted with exceptions to plaintiffs. Judgment for defendant against plaintiffs dismissing their complaint upon the merits. *Cordas v. Peerless Transp. Co.*, 27 N.Y.S.2d 198, 199, 202 (N.Y. City Ct. 1941).

This very opinion has been justly criticized for its purplishness in Ronald L. Goldfarb & James C. Raymond, *Clear Understandings* 142–43 (1982).

purport, n., = that which is conveyed or expressed, esp. by a formal document. As a noun, this term is now primarily a legal word (the verb *to purport* being common). E.g.:

- "The clear *purport* of Title II is to guarantee that qualified disabled persons enjoy meaningful access to public services, programs, and activities." *Iverson v. City of Boston*, 452 F.3d 94, 99 (1st Cir. 2006).
- "We cannot ignore the plain *purport* of the New York statute at issue here." *Arias v. Figueroa*, 930 A.2d 472, 477 (N.J. Super. Ct. App. 2007).

The verb—meaning "to profess or claim falsely" or "to seem to be"—is much more common—e.g.:

- "Although the trial court *purported* to grant Sewell additional time to file a notice of appeal, no provision of the appellate rules permits trial courts to expand the time limit prescribed by Appellate Rule 9." *Sewell v. State*, 939 N.E.2d 686, 687 (Ind. Ct. App. 2010).
- "The nondelegation doctrine still *purports* to absolutely prohibit the delegation of legislative power." Mark D. Rosen, *From Exclusivity to Concurrence*, 94 Minn. L. Rev. 1051, 1100 (2010).

purported, adj., = reputed; rumored. It does not mean "alleged," as here erroneously used: "We need not address the department's remaining claims concerning *purported* [read *alleged*] violations of sovereign immunity and fundamental fairness." *In re Matthew F.*, 4 A.3d 248, 255 n.13 (Conn. 2010).

purpose, n. **A. And** *object*, n. A British writer suggests that *purpose* is more restricted than *object*. J. Charlesworth, *The Principles of Company Law* 16–17 (4th ed. 1945). That may be because *object* is more of a CHAMELEON-HUED WORD capable of bearing many meanings. But the two words are close synonyms in denoting "something one sets before oneself as a thing to be done; the end one has in view." In fact, the *OED* uses each word in defining the other.
B. And *intention*. Statutory drafters sometimes use *purpose* as if it were synonymous with *intention*. But as Glanville Williams has observed, *purpose* ought not to include recklessness or a mere knowledge of probability, as *intention* generally does. *See Textbook of Criminal Law* 93 (1978). See **intention (B).**

purpose, vb., = to set as a goal for oneself; to intend; to resolve. This FORMAL WORD is little used now in nonlegal contexts. Even in law it has a musty smell—e.g.: "Each order *purposed* to deny the Rule 60(b) motion

that had been filed in that subset of cases." *In re High Voltage Eng'g Corp.*, 544 F.3d 315, 317 (1st Cir. 2008).

purpose approach. See **mischief rule.**

purposeful. See **purposive.**

purposely; purposefully. The first means "on purpose; intentionally"; the second means "with a specific purpose in mind; with the idea of accomplishing a certain result."

Some writers fall into INELEGANT VARIATION with these words—e.g.: "The State did not exceed its authority in defining the crime of murder as *purposely* causing the death of another with prior calculation or design. . . . [T]he jury's verdict reflects that none of her self-defense evidence raised a reasonable doubt about the State's proof that she *purposefully* [read *purposely*] killed with prior calculation and design." *Martin v. Ohio*, 480 U.S. 228, 233 (1987) (per White, J.).

purposive; purposeful. H.W. Fowler and the *OED* editors objected to *purposive* as an ill-formed hybrid. Today, however, it is usefully distinguished in one sense from *purposeful* (= [1] having a purpose; or [2] full of determination). *W11* records under *purposive* the sense "serving or effecting a useful function though not as a result of planning or design."

But in other senses it is a NEEDLESS VARIANT of *purposeful*, as in the following examples:

- "If the person who deprives you of them could show that you would not have used them, you are not entitled to lost income, but you are entitled to have them back, so that their subsequent nonuse is once again an instance of your *purposiveness* [read *purposefulness*] rather than that of your injurer." Arthur Ripstein, *As If It Had Never Happened*, 48 Wm. & Mary L. Rev. 1957, 1967 (2007).
- "Textualists view the *purposive* [read *purposeful*] use of unexpressed legislative intent as illegitimate, but they also view it as dangerous to the separation of powers." Note, *Textualism as Fair Notice*, 123 Harv. L. Rev. 542, 554 (2009).

purposive construction; purposive interpretation. See *purposive interpretation* under INTERPRETATION, MODES OF (B).

purposivism. See INTERPRETATION, MODES OF (A).

pursuance of, in. See **pursuant to.

*pursuant to = (1) in accordance with; (2) under; (3) as authorized by; or (4) in carrying out. Because the phrase means so many things, it is rarely—if ever—useful. Lawyers are nearly the only ones who use the phrase, and they often use it imprecisely. Following are some well-taken edits:

- "The petitioners bring this petition *pursuant to* [read *under*] the provisions of the *Infants Act*, R.S.B.C. 1979, c. 196." (Can.)
- "*Prior to* [read *Before*] the execution of both the aforementioned letters, the County Court of Woodward County issued an order to disburse funds *pursuant to an application authorizing payment* [delete italicized language] of

$33.00 per month." *Western State Hosp. v. Stoner*, 614 P.2d 59, 64 (Okla. 1980). For more on **prior to* in this sentence, see **prior to.

- "[Appellant] is a state prisoner incarcerated in the Louisiana State Penitentiary in Angola, Louisiana, *pursuant to* [read *for*] a 1964 aggravated rape conviction." *Brown v. Maggio*, 730 F.2d 293, 294 (5th Cir. 1984).
- "*Pursuant to* [read *Under*] the mandate of the Supreme Court in *Escondido* ..., the decision of the Federal Energy Regulatory Commission to grant a license in these proceedings is reversed." *Escondido Mut. Water Co. v. FERC*, 743 F.2d 1321, 1321 (9th Cir. 1984).

British legal writers often use **in pursuance of*—e.g.: "An application by a person claiming to be entitled to any money paid into the Bank of England *in pursuance of* [read *under*] section 15 of the Companies Act of 1890, shall be made in such form and manner as the Board of Trade may ... direct." 2 Baron Nathaniel Lindley & Walter Barry Lindley, *A Treatise on the Law of Companies* 1475 (1902). This usage was formerly common in the U.S.

Partridge was wrong to call this phrase "OFFICIALESE for *after.*" *Usage and Abusage* 257 (1973). It may be officialese, but it does not, ordinarily, mean "after." Still, at least one American lawyer has privately admitted making the mistake of treating the phrase as an antonym of **prior to*. See **under.**

pursuer; defender. These are the names equivalent to *plaintiff* and *defendant* in Scots and canon law. E.g.: "The *pursuer's* allegations were that a man came into the branch of the bank at which the *pursuer* was teller, tendered certain silver coins and asked for notes in exchange." Alexander Mackenzie Stuart, *Recent Leading Scots Cases*, 36 Jurid. Rev. 281, 282 (1924). (Scot.)

purview. In the context of LEGISLATIVE DRAFTING, this neglected word denotes the body of a statute following the preamble, traditionally beginning with the language, *Be it enacted that* . . . . It was therefore an easy extension in meaning that gave *purview* its most common sense today (i.e., "scope; area of application")—a sense that borders on CLICHÉ: "The Hughes Court held that the right to dissent, protest, and march for that purpose was within the *purview* of the First Amendment." William O. Douglas, *Points of Rebellion* 5 (1970).

put, n.; call, n. *Put* is often used as a noun in securities law in the sense "an option to sell securities." E.g.:

- "The mirror image of *call* options, *put* options give parties the right to sell their entitlements to others without their consent." Richard R.W. Brooks, *The Efficient Performance Hypothesis*, 116 Yale L.J. 568, 576–77 (2006).
- "Section 20(d) provides that anyone who would violate SEC regulations by insider trading in securities would also be liable for conduct with respect to certain derivatives of those securities, including *puts, calls*, options, and security-based swap agreements." *SEC v. Rorech*, 673 F.Supp.2d 217, 226 (S.D.N.Y. 2009).

In such contexts, *put* is usually contrasted with *call* (= an option to buy securities).

put, vb., often means either (1) "to hypothesize for purposes of illustration" <in the case put>; or (2) "to argue (a case)" <even bishops appeared in court personally to put their cases>.

put another way. See **to put it another way.**

putative = supposed; believed; reputed. E.g.: "New York law required that certain classes of *putative* fathers receive notice of a pending adoption proceeding." Kayla Britton, Note, *You Shall Always Be My Child*, 43 Ind. L. Rev. 499, 505 (2010). *Putative marriage*, a term originally from canon law, denotes a marriage that, though legally invalid, was contracted in good faith by at least one of the parties. E.g.:

- "Given Jiang's questionable asylum claim, which was based on a forced abortion performed on his *putative* wife . . . , Jiang's former attorney reasonably advised Jiang to withdraw his asylum claim in favor of obtaining voluntary departure." *Jiang v. Mukasey*, 522 F.3d 266, 270 (2d Cir. 2008).
- "There may have been no quasi-community property contributions, as the *putative* marriage lasted only 19 months, and during that time, the *putative* spouse was the family's principal breadwinner." *Trustees of IL WU-PMA Pension Plan v. Peters*, 660 F.Supp.2d 1118, 1136 (N.D. Cal. 2009).

put on = (1) to call (a person) as a witness; or (2) to adduce (evidence)—e.g.:

- (Sense 1) "If a man has a record, you just don't *put him on* the stand. *Put on* his wife, his brother, his father and mother, but don't let him take the stand." Aubrey Holmes, *The Wake of a Lawyer* 51 (1960).
- (Sense 2) "'We just *put on* the evidence and went ahead without him,' said Assistant District Attorney Tom D'Amore." Melvin Belli, *Courts Specialize in Drugs*, Dallas Morning News, 1 July 1990, at 33A.

put oneself upon the country (= to demand a jury trial) is an ARCHAISM that still occasionally appears in modern defense pleadings. For an explanation of its common-law origins, see **country.**

put option. See **put.**

putrefy; *putrify. The second is a misspelling.

putsch. See **coup d'état.**

put to one's law. At common law, this phrase meant "to compel a person to undergo a judicial test, such as compurgation, ordeal, or combat." Magna Carta (1215), for example, contains a provision that states: "Let no bailiff be able to *put any one to his law* by his own simple word without credible witnesses." More modernly, the phrase means "to put a person to trial."

pyramiding inferences, rule against. This rule, followed in some jurisdictions, prohibits a fact-finder from piling one inference on another to arrive at a conclusion. But it is a confusing and unhelpful METAPHOR, as Judge John Minor Wisdom has aptly observed: "The so-called *rule against pyramiding inferences*, if there really is such a 'rule' and if it is anything more than an empty pejorative, is simple legalese fustian to cover a clumsy exclusion of evidence having little or no probative value." *NLRB v. Camco, Inc.*, 340 F.2d 803, 811 (5th Cir. 1965). Other leading authorities likewise cast doubt on it: "Whatever the vitality of the supposed *rule against pyramiding inferences*, it ought

not to be taken as forbidding the use of one presumption as the mechanism for establishing the basic fact of another." 21 Charles Alan Wright & Kenneth W. Graham Jr., *Federal Practice and Procedure* § 5125, at 603 (1977). See LEGALESE.

Q

Q.B.D. = Queen's Bench Division. See **Queen's Bench.**

Q.C. = Queen's Counsel. **A. Plural Form.** Though some writers make the plural form *Q.C.s*, the better form is *Q.C.'s*.

B. Punctuation with. When the title appears in midsentence, a comma goes before and after it: "Roman law texts were also cited by Sir Sidney Kentridge, *Q.C.*, counsel for the claimants." Basil Markesinis & Jörg Fedtke, *The Judge as a Comparatist*, 80 Tul. L. Rev. 11, 96 n.279 (2005).

Some writers omit the periods in this abbreviation— e.g.: "If a client wants to employ a Queen's Counsel or senior barrister, he must also employ—at two-thirds the *QC*'s fee—a junior barrister as well." Anthony Sampson, *Anatomy of Britain* 149 (1962). The prevailing style—in BrE and AmE alike—is to include the periods.

Q.E.D. is the abbreviation for *quod erat demonstrandum* (= which was to be proved or demonstrated).

Q.E.F. is the abbreviation for *quod erat faciendum* (= which was to be done).

qq.v. See *quod vide.*

qua (= in the capacity of; as; in the role of) is often misused and is little needed in English. "The real occasion for the use of *qua*," wrote H.W. Fowler, "occurs when a person or thing spoken of can be regarded from more than one point of view or as the holder of various coexistent functions, and a statement about him (or it) is to be limited to him in one of these aspects" (*MEU1* 477). Fowler's example of a justifiable use of the term is this: "*Qua* lover he must be condemned for doing what *qua* citizen he would be condemned for not doing." This proper use of the term is seldom seen today, especially in AmE.

One is hard-pressed to divine any purpose but rhetorical emphasis in the examples following:

• "States retain sovereignty despite the fact that Congress can regulate States *qua* States in certain limited circumstances." *U.S. v. Lara*, 541 U.S. 193, 218 (2004) (Thomas, J., concurring).

• "The critical issue is not whether a particular branch of the federal government is responsible for the delay; it is whether the individual petitioner versus the government *qua* government is responsible." *Singh v. Still*, 470 F.Supp.2d 1064, 1068 (N.D. Cal. 2007).

• "A crime, as opposed to any manner of civil offense, is a direct affront to the sovereign; the sovereign *qua* sovereign is therefore a party to such suits in its role as prosecutor."

La. State Bd. of Nursing v. Gautreaux, 39 So.3d 806, 815 (La. Ct. App. 2010).

Nor do most unemphatic modern uses justify the choice of *qua* over *as*. Indeed, these are the very types of uses that Fowler rightly objected to—e.g.:

• "The right of fair comment, though shared by the public, is the right of every individual who asserts it, and is, *qua* [read *as claimed by*] him, an individual right whatever name it be called by, and comment by him which is coloured by malice cannot from his standpoint be deemed fair." *Thomas v. Bradbury, Agnew & Co., Ltd.*, [1906] 2 K. B. 627, 638.

• "*Qua* [read *To test its claims as a*] patent, we should at least have to decide, as tabula rasa, whether the design or machine was new and required invention." *Cheney Bros. v. Doris Silk Corp.*, 35 F.2d 279, 280 (2d Cir. 1929).

• "Our concern with lawyers' ethics is almost entirely concerned with their behavior *qua* [read *as*] lawyers." John A. Humbach, *A Response to Russell Pearce*, 23 Pace L. Rev. 599, 600 (2003).

quadrennial; *quadriennial. The second is a NEEDLESS VARIANT.

quaere; query. *Quaere* is the Latin word meaning "question." The original form of *query*, *quaere* is now but a NEEDLESS VARIANT in any sense other than a technical one: it is sometimes appended or prefixed to doubtful statements. E.g.: "Whether a plea in abatement is not the proper mode of defense when the facts relied on do not appear of record, *quaere*." *Engelke & Feiner Milling Co. v. Grunthal*, 35 So. 17, 18 (Fla. 1903).

The term is used occasionally in modern writing—e.g.:

• "*Quaere*, whether the bank would have been allowed . . . to plead a Section 7426 counterclaim." *U.S. v. National Bank of Commerce*, 726 F.2d 1292, 1298 (8th Cir. 1984).

• "One can affix one's signature to a document by writing thereon, and one can affix one sheet of paper to another with a staple or sticky tape; but *quaere* as to a paper clip." Arthur A. Leff, *The Leff Dictionary of Law*, 94 Yale L.J. 1855, 1969 (1985).

Using *quaere* for *query* is precious—e.g.: "The decision on . . . defendant's *quaere* [read *query*] will render moot the necessity for a discussion of the Government's remaining contentions." *U.S. v. Certain Parcels of Land*, 67 F.Supp. 780, 789 (S.D. Cal. 1946). The form *quere* is a misspelling.

For *query* as a verb, see **ask.**

quai. See **quay.**

qualified fee = fee simple defeasible. See **fee simple (E)**.

qualifiedly (= in a qualified fashion) is an adverb that often ought to be made back into an adjective—e.g.: "Statements by the employer explaining the plaintiff's discharge *were not qualifiedly privileged* [read *had no qualified privilege*]." Pamela G. Posey, Note, *Employer Defamation*, 30 Wm. & Mary L. Rev. 469, 475 n.37 (1989). Unfortunately, adverbs ending in *-edly* are unqualifiedly fashionable in modern legal writing. See -EDLY.

QUALIFIERS, PREEMPTIVE. See ANTICIPATORY REFERENCE.

qualitative; *qualitive. The longer form is preferred. The adjective corresponds to *quality* in the sense of character or nature, not in the sense of merit or excellence. Cf. **quantitative.**

quamdiu se bene gesserint (= for as long as they behave themselves) is so spelled. This LATINISM, apparently introduced in the Act of Settlement of 1700, has traditionally been used in the appointment of judges for life, but today we use the sensible English-language equivalent: *during good behavior.* See **good behavior.**

quandary—a word of unknown origin—refers to a mental state of perplexity or confusion. E.g.:

- "The juror was left in a *quandary* as to whether to follow that instruction or the immediately preceding one it contradicted." *Francis v. Franklin*, 471 U.S. 307, 324 (1985) (per Brennan, J.).
- "Meanwhile, the trial courts have rendered divergent judicial interpretations of the attorney–client privilege and thereby created a *quandary* for patent agents and their clients." James J. Merek & David A. Guth, *The Attorney–Client Privilege and U.S. Patent Agents*, 76 J. Pat. & Trademark Off. Soc'y 591, 594 (1994).

As a result of SLIPSHOD EXTENSION, however, the word is often misapplied as if it referred to a difficult problem, dilemma, or enigma detached from any state of mind—e.g.:

- "While Exxon's definition accords more readily with everyday notions of 'natural gas,' these notions do not, without more, resolve the definitional *quandary* [read *problem*]." *Exxon Corp. v. Lujan*, 970 F.2d 757, 760 (10th Cir. 1992).
- "The *quandary* [read *difficulty* or *problem*] in this case is that case law has combined and shuffled the definitions of domicile, bona fide residence, legal residence and residence into a mix that resulted in the declaration by the court in *In re Ozias' Estate* . . . that residence and domicile are interchangeable and synonymous." *Genrich v. Williams*, 869 S.W.2d 209, 210 (Mo. Ct. App. 1993).
- "Crucial medical facts . . . would be presented, the shape of the ethical *quandary* [read *problem* or *dilemma*] would be sketched, and the care provider's position clarified." John D. Arras, *Principles and Particularity*, 69 Ind. L.J. 983, 987 (1994).

quanta. See **quantum.**

quantificational. See **quantitative.**

quantify; *quantitate. The second is a NEEDLESS VARIANT newly popular with social scientists, whose choice

of terms has never been a strong recommendation for the use of those terms.

quantitative; *quantitive. The preferred form is *quantitative*, not **quantitive*. Variants such as **quantificational* should be avoided. Cf. **qualitative.**

quantity (usu. "portion; amount") is used by legal theorists in a sense borrowed from logic: "the extent in which a term in a given logical proposition is to be taken" (*W3*). E.g.:

- "While, no doubt, in the great majority of cases no harm results from the use of such expressions, yet these forms of statement seem to represent a blending of nonlegal and legal *quantities* which, in any problem requiring careful reasoning, should preferably be kept distinct." Wesley Newcomb Hohfeld, *Some Fundamental Legal Conceptions as Applied in Judicial Reasoning*, 23 Yale L.J. 16, 49 (1913).
- "If, however, the problem is analyzed, it will be seen that as of primary importance, the grantor has two legal *quantities*: the privilege of entering and the power, by means of such entry, to divest the estate of the grantee." *Id.*

The *OED* notes that *quantity* in the sense "length or duration of time" exists now only in the legal phrase *quantity of estate* <the quantity of estate is 99 years>.

quantum, a favorite word of lawyers and judges, means "amount; share, portion; the required, desired, or allowed amount." Ordinarily in legal writing it appears as an inflated synonym of *amount*—e.g.:

- "Petitioners envision that the *quantum* [read *amount*] of risk necessary to make out an Eighth Amendment claim will vary according to the severity of the pain and the availability of alternatives." *Baze v. Rees*, 553 U.S. 35, 47 (2008) (per Roberts, C.J.).
- "The double jeopardy analysis hinges entirely on the state-law question of what *quantum* [read *amount*] of punishment the state legislature intended." *Jones v. Sussex I State Prison*, 591 F.3d 707, 710 (4th Cir. 2010).
- "A court could . . . provide the same *quantum* [read *amount*] of equitable relief for statutory violations as would the Patent Act if it did not contain a specific recognition of equitable relief." James M. Fischer, *What Hath Ebay v. Mercexchange Wrought?*, 14 Lewis & Clark L. Rev. 555, 575 (2010).

Occasionally the word causes problems in sense. The term should not be used for *thing, character, state,* or the like—e.g.: "The starting point for this reflection is . . . to recognize that freedom and necessity are not separate and distinct *quanta* [read *things*], but are and will forever remain in dialectical relation to one another." Michael Halley, *Thoughts on the Churn Law*, 104 Nw. U. L. Rev. Colloquy 132, 146 (2009). And given the modern, technical sense of the word, the writer should beware of creating a MISCUE by pairing it with *amount*—e.g.: "The consequences of that . . . failure will *amount to* [read *determine*] the *quantum* of the compensation he will have to pay." Kenneth H. York et al., *Cases and Materials on Remedies* 65 (5th ed. 1992). See VERBAL AWARENESS.

The only accepted plural of this word is *quanta*. The erroneous form **quantums* is occasionally seen. E.g.: "This court has stated that dishonesty, fraud, deceit, and misrepresentation are four different violations, that may require different *quantums* [read *quanta*] of proof." *In re Romansky*, 825 A.2d 311, 315 (D.C. 2003). This foreign plural is one of the exceptions to the general rule enunciated in the entry PLURALS (A). Following are examples of the correct plural:

- "There is a large difference between the two things to be proved (guilt and probable cause), as well as between the tribunals which determine them, and therefore a like difference in the *quanta* and modes of proof required to establish them." *Brinegar v. U.S.*, 338 U.S. 160, 173 (1949) (per Rutledge, J.).
- "Absent hard data, I would rather err on the side of receiving little additional benefit from imposing additional *quanta* of liability than err by adhering to *Robins*'s inequitable rule." *Ex rel Guste v. M/V Testbank*, 752 F.2d 1019, 1052 (5th Cir. 1985).

quantum meruit; quantum valebant; quantum valebat. These counts were used at common law by pleaders in suits in assumpsit, and they are still used today. *Quantum meruit* = the reasonable value of services; *quantum valebant* = the reasonable value of goods and materials. *Quantum meruit* means literally "as much as he or she had earned," and shows no signs of waning in legal use. The term, however, "is ambiguous; it may mean (1) that there is a contract 'implied in fact' to pay the reasonable value of the services, or (2) that, to prevent unjust enrichment, the claimant may recover on a quasi-contract (an 'as if' contract) for that reasonable value." *Martin v. Campanaro*, 156 F.2d 127, 130 n.5 (2d Cir. 1946).

The distinction between *quantum meruit* and *quantum valebant* is that *quantum meruit* (often termed *quasi-contract*) is used of an action to recover for services that the plaintiff has performed, and *quantum valebant* is used to recover for the value of goods that the plaintiff has supplied without a price having been set. E.g.: "Although such fees are recoverable in an action based on *quantum meruit* or *valebant*, no attorneys' fees are recoverable if the *quantum meruit* or *valebant* claim is an insignificant part of the relief sought by a party." *Todd Shipyards Corp. v. Jasper Elec. Serv. Co.*, 414 F.2d 8, 18 (5th Cir. 1969). See **quasi-contract.**

Quantum valebant and *quantum valebat* both appear in the cases; and both are correct Latin: *quantum valebant* means "as much as they were worth," whereas *quantum valebat* means "as much as it was worth." Hence the choice is between using the singular or plural Latin construction. As a matter of usage, *valebant* predominates among American legal writers who use the phrase, and *valebat* among British legal writers. (Scots lawyers tend to use *quantum valeat* [= as much as it may be worth].) But the phrases are gradually falling into disuse.

quare clausum fregit (= whereas he or she has broken the close) is often the short form for *trespass quare clausum fregit*, which is the technical term for unlawfully entering land that is visibly enclosed. See **trespass.**

quash = (1) to suppress or subdue; to crush out, beat into pieces; or (2) to annul; to make void (as a writ or indictment); to put an end to (as legal proceedings). Sense 2 is the more frequent legal meaning: "Their petition for writ of certiorari was granted on December 11, 1980, but was subsequently *quashed* for lack of prosecution." *Gonsalves v. Alpine Country Club*, 727 F.2d 27, 28 (1st Cir. 1984).

In AmE, a *motion to quash* is usually a motion to nullify a writ or subpoena. In BrE, by contrast, *quash* has broader uses. For example, an indictment or a conviction may be said to be *quashed*—e.g.:

- "The indictment can and must be *quashed*." Patrick Devlin, *The Criminal Prosecution in England* 102 (1960).
- "The Court of Appeal Criminal Division unanimously *quashed* a conviction where the jury foreman had announced that the conviction was agreed to by ten of the jury but failed to state that two had dissented!" Michael Zander, *The Law-Making Process* 95 (2d ed. 1985).

Though convictions are *quashed* in BrE, lower-court decisions are said to be *reversed*, and jury verdicts are *set aside*. See **set aside (A).**

quashal, the American noun corresponding to the verb *to quash*, is recorded in no major English-language dictionary. Yet it is fairly common in legal writing in the U.S. <quashal of the writ>, and it is useful.

The word first appeared in the late 19th century—e.g.:

- "Yet the judgment might . . . have been put there nunc pro tunc, even during the pending of the motion, with the effect of removing the ground of *quashal*." *Adams v. Higgins*, 1 So. 321, 324 (Fla. 1887).
- "When the appellate proceeding is irregular, . . . the policy of our statutes as to a regular hearing on the merits in due course of procedure is not contravened by a *quashal* or summary disposition." *Holland v. Webster*, 29 So. 625, 630 (Fla. 1901) (Mabry, J., dissenting).
- "It is urged by relator as his grounds for *quashal*, that the opinion of the Court of Appeals is in conflict with [another] case." *Mergenthaler Linotype Co. v. Davis*, 251 U.S. 256, 258 (1920) (per McReynolds, J.).

Since those early uses of the word, of course, it has come to be used occasionally in most American jurisdictions. E.g.: "Like the *quashal* of the subpoena, this injunctive relief was related to the central purpose of a proceeding that is essentially criminal in nature." *Lee v. Johnson*, 799 F.2d 31, 42 (3d Cir. 1986) (Becker, J., dissenting). H.W. Fowler might find fault with its formation in *-al*, but the etymon is appropriately Latin and

---

there appears to be no serviceable alternative. Even if there were, *quashal* has taken hold.

quasi—pronounced /**kwah**-zee/ or /**kway**-zı/— means "as if; seeming or seemingly; in the nature of; nearly." It has been called "senseless jargon" by an 18th-century judge and "that ancient question-beggar" by a 20th-century legal theorist (Lon Fuller). Corbin wrote sensibly (though not quite idiomatically) of *quasi*: "The term *quasi* is introduced as a weasel word that sucks all the meaning *of* [read *from*] the word that follows it; but this is a fact the reader seldom realizes." *Corbin on Contracts* 27 (1st ed. 1952). See WEASEL WORDS.

Maine, by contrast, wrote idiomatically but took a great many words to say merely that *quasi* signals a strained (though not *violently* strained) analogy:

> This word "*quasi*," prefixed to a term of Roman law, implies that the conception to which it serves as an index is connected with the conception [being compared, and that] the comparison is instituted by a strong superficial analogy or resemblance. It does not denote that the two conceptions are the same or that they belong to the same genus. On the contrary, it negatives the notion of an identity between them; but it points out that they are sufficiently similar for one to be classed as the sequel to the other . . . .
> Henry S. Maine, *Ancient Law* 286 (17th ed. 1901).

In legal writing, *quasi* should generally appear as a hyphenated prefix. E.g.:

- "While that concern may result in the creation of '*quasi*-property rights' in communicative symbols, the focus is on the protection of consumers, not the protection of producers as an incentive to product innovation." *Bonito Boats, Inc. v. Thunder Craft Boats, Inc.*, 489 U.S. 141, 157 (1989) (per O'Connor, J.).
- "The remedy of *quasi*-specific performance is not available because it applies only after the testator's death." Jason Thomas King, *Lifetime Remedies for Breach of Contract to Make a Will*, 50 S.C. L. Rev. 965, 971 (1999).
- "The communications are actually *quasi*-privileged because the communications are not considered privileged in limited situations with a court order." Alvin O. Boucher, *Implied Waiver of Physician and Psychotherapist–Patient Privilege*, 83 N.D. L. Rev. 855, 864 n.65 (2007).

The term has been prefixed to any number of adjectives and nouns, such as the following:

quasi-compulsory
quasi-contract
quasi-contractual
quasi-corporation
quasi-criminal
quasi-delict
quasi-domicile
quasi-estoppel
quasi-heir
quasi-judge
quasi-judicial
quasi-larceny
quasi-legal
quasi-legislation
quasi-legislative
quasi-monopoly

quasi-negotiable
quasi-possession
quasi-proprietary
quasi-public
quasi-remainder
quasi-rent
quasi-right
quasi-rule
quasi-theft
quasi-tort
quasi-usufruct

quasi-contract; contract implied in law. The terms are now regarded as synonymous in referring not to a contract at all, but to the FICTION necessary to promote justice by preventing unjust enrichment. *See U.S. v. Neidorf*, 522 F.2d 916, 919 (9th Cir. 1975), *cert. denied*, 423 U.S. 1087 (1976). Some writers express a strong preference for the phrase *quasi-contract*: "What is best called *quasi-contract* our lawyers call *contract implied in law*, though there is no agreement." W.W. Buckland, *Some Reflections on Jurisprudence* 63 (1945). See **implied contract.**

The irony, of course, is that whichever name one chooses, the thing being described is not a contract at all: "*Quasi-contracts* are a heterogeneous collection of cases [that] themselves have little more in common than the fact that one person is held obliged to restore or pay for some benefit received from another in order that a just result should be reached in the circumstances of the case." P.S. Atiyah, *An Introduction to the Law of Contract* 35 (3d ed. 1981). See **promissory estoppel (A), assumpsit, quantum meruit** & **unjust enrichment.**

The phrase *quasi-contract* should be hyphenated.

quasi-domicile. See **domicile (C).**

quasi ex contractu = (1) as if from a contract; or (2) in the nature of quasi-contract. E.g.: "Having been so benefited, the defendant is liable, *quasi ex contractu*, independently of contract or agency." *Hughes v. Monnahan*, 165 N.W.2d 231, 233 (Minn. 1969). See *ex contractu* & **quasi-contract.**

quaternary, adj. & n., is often misspelled **quarternary*. The adjective means "consisting of four parts," the noun "a set of four things."

quay; quai. The first spelling is preferred.

que, in the phrases *cestui que trust* and *cestui que use*, is pronounced /kee/ or /kə/, not /kyoo/.

Queen. See **King** & **R.**

queen regnant; queen regent; queen consort; queen dowager. *Queen regnant* denotes a queen who rules in her own right. *Queen regent* denotes a queen who rules on behalf of another, such as a child king. *Queen consort* denotes the wife of a reigning king. And *queen dowager* denotes the widow of a deceased king. The plural forms are *queens regnant, queens regent,* and *queens consort.*

Queen's Bench. At common law, the *Court of Queen's Bench* was one of three central courts that administered different branches of the law; it issued prerogative writs to inferior courts and public officers, heard trespass cases as well as some personal actions, and had appellate jurisdiction in civil and criminal cases by writ of error. In 1875, when the English court system was reorganized, the *Queen's Bench Division* became one of the five divisions composing the High Court of Justice. Then, in 1880, two other divisions—Common Pleas and Exchequer—were merged into the Queen's Bench Division, which today hears actions founded on contract or tort, applications for judicial review, and some appeals from magistrates' courts. For more on the High Court, see **high court.**

Queen's Counsel. See **Q.C.** & **silk.**

Queen's evidence, to turn. See **turn state's evidence.**

quere; query. See *quaere.*

querist. See **questioner.**

querulous (= apt to complain; whining) is a MALAPROPISM when used for *query-like.* E.g.: "*Querulous of* [read *Skeptical of? Doubtful about?*] the procedure by which the state court rendered its judgment disbarring Liedtke, we simply refused to rely thereon as the basis for removing him from our roll of attorneys." *Liedtke v. State Bar of Tex.,* 18 F.3d 315, 317 n.7 (5th Cir. 1994).

query; question. See **ask.**

question, vb. See **ask.**

*questionary. See **questionnaire.**

question (as to) whether; question (of) whether. The best phrasing is *question whether*—e.g.:

- "If a person is accused of murder the *question whether* he was or was not legally responsible for the death may be intended to raise the *issue whether* the death was too remote a consequence of his acts for them to count as its cause." H.L.A. Hart, "Postscript: Responsibility and Retribution," in *Punishment and Responsibility: Essays in the Philosophy of Law* 210, 220 (1968). On *issue whether,* see **issue (B).**
- "This leaves the *question whether* there are any impersonal or institutional measures available that may serve as a kind of prophylaxis against the introduction of distortions into the law at the level of enforcement." Lon L. Fuller, *Anatomy of the Law* 37 (1968).
- "The real difference between the majority and the dissentients in *Maunsell v. Olins* was over the *question whether* there was an ambiguity." Rupert Cross, *Statutory Interpretation* 145 (1976).

The phrases *question as to whether* and *question of whether* are common prolixities. Examples of *question as to whether* are legion in the prose of lawyers and judges—e.g.:

- "When the suit is brought only against state officials, a *question arises as to whether* [read *question arises whether*] that suit is a suit against the State itself." *Pennhurst State Sch. & Hosp. v. Halderman,* 465 U.S. 89, 101 (1984) (per Powell, J.).
- "As to the data created during the life of RCM Biothane, a *question arises as to whether* [read *question arises whether*] plaintiffs required permission to access that data." *Joseph Oat Holdings, Inc. v. RCM Digesters, Inc.,* 665 F.Supp.2d 448, 458 (D.N.J. 2009).

Even where *question* means "doubt," the preferred form is *question whether*: "[There is] a *question as to whether* [read *question whether*] the defendant could be convicted on a theory of aiding and abetting for statements made after the unsuccessful attempt." *U.S. v. Khalil,* 279 F.3d 358, 369 n.3 (6th Cir. 2002).

The only context in which *question as to whether* might be justified is where an intervening phrase might cause an AMBIGUITY or awkwardness: "The dispute regarding the proper interpretation of section 610 of the CDA is part of a broader *question* of statutory interpretation *as to whether* the term 'person' when used in a statute includes the sovereign and the sovereign's officials acting in their official capacities." Thomas L. McGovern et al., *A Level Playing Field,* 36 Pub. Cont. L.J. 495, 497 (2007).

The other common prolixity is *question of whether*—e.g.:

- "We do not answer *the question of whether* [read *the question whether,* or *whether*] the requested photographs are public records." *DeLong v. Parmelee,* 236 P.3d 936, 954 (Wash. Ct. App. 2010).
- "There are . . . plausible arguments on both sides of the *question of whether* [read *question whether*] a decision by the primary reviewing court in consolidated petitions for review is binding on other courts of appeals." Jeffrey C. Dobbins, *Structure & Precedent,* 108 Mich. L. Rev. 1453, 1457 (2010).

Yet *question of whether* is preferred when one uses the idiom *it is a question of . . .* , as in "a question of ethics" or "a question of materiality"—e.g.: "It is a *question of whether* the court acted without reference to any guiding rules or principles." *Jones v. Jones,* 64 S.W.3d 206, 209 (Tex. App.—El Paso 2001).

question-begging is the adjectival form of the phrase *begging the question.* The phrase is commonly found in the writing of dissenting judges—e.g.:

- "Indeed, Justice Brickley's conclusion that, since there is no evidence that Juillet was a drug dealer, the only reason for his 'delivery of drugs' was Bleser's incessant requests, . . . is classical *question-begging.*" *People v. Juillet,* 475 N.W.2d 786, 817 (Mich. 1991) (Boyle, J., concurring in part & dissenting in part).

- "Until this case I would have agreed with the majority's repeated, but *question-begging* assertion that the contours of the Sixth Amendment Confrontation Clause are identical to those of Missouri's face-to-face guarantee, but only because I had not imagined, and this Court had not faced, a statutory procedure that so clearly abrogates a constitutional guarantee." *State v. Naucke*, 829 S.W.2d 445, 465 (Mo. 1992) (Robertson, C.J., dissenting).

See **begging the question**.

questioner; querist. The first is the ordinary, more natural term.

questionnaire; *questionary. The second word is a NEEDLESS VARIANT.

question (of) whether. See **question (as to) whether**.

quia timet (lit., "because he or she fears") denotes a legal doctrine under which a party seeks equitable relief because of a concern over future probable injury to certain rights or interests. *Quia timet* often forms a PHRASAL ADJECTIVE; when it does, the words should not be hyphenated <quia timet injunction>. See PHRASAL ADJECTIVES (B).

quick originally meant "alive," as in the surviving phrase *the quick and the dead*, used by one judge to turn a nice phrase: "There are but two conduits or cables, the statute of wills, and of descents and distributions by which the Grim Reaper may at the moment of and by the stroke of his scythe flash the transfer and transmission of property and estate to the *quick* from the dead." *Spinks v. Rice*, 47 S.E.2d 424, 429 (Va. 1948).

Up to the 19th century, *quick* was used as an equivalent of *live* or *alive* in general contexts, as in the Apostles' Creed: "From thence he shall come to judge *the quick* and the dead." Here is a specimen from 1865: "The defendant proved that Dygert was arrested January 2, 1862, on a justice's warrant, issued on the complaint of the plaintiff, for procuring an abortion of a *quick* child, on the plaintiff, at Ilion, Herkimer county, July 5, 1861." *Bettinger v. Bridenbecker*, 63 Barb. 395 (N.Y. Sup. Ct. 1865). Today this usage would be an affected ARCHAISM.

The illogical phrase *quick with child*—referring to a pregnant woman—began in the 15th century as an inversion of the strictly logical phrase *with quick child*. The *OED* labels the phrase "rare or obsolete," but naturally legal writers continue to use it: "A woman is '*quick with child*' . . . after she has felt the child alive within her." Rollin M. Perkins, *Criminal Law* 100 (1957).

quid pro quo (= this for that; tit for tat) is a useful LATINISM, for the only English equivalent is *tit for tat*, which is unsuitable in formal contexts. E.g.:

- "The plaintiffs have attempted to formulate the settlement within the traditional framework of a *quid pro quo* offered by the defendants in exchange for releases from further liability." *Dann v. Chrysler Corp.*, 198 A.2d 185, 200 (Del. Ch. 1964).

- "Issue ads like WRTL's are by no means equivalent to contributions, and the *quid pro quo* corruption interest cannot justify regulating them." *Federal Election Comm'n v. Wisconsin Right to Life, Inc.*, 551 U.S. 449, 478–79 (2007) (per Roberts, C.J.).

The word *exchange* does not quite capture the right sense.

Quid pro quo is wrongly used in the following example: "The exclusivity of the statutory compensation remedy against the employer was designed to counterbalance the imposition of absolute liability; there is *no comparable quid pro quo* [read *no comparable balancing*] in the relationship between the employer and third persons." *Federal Marine Terminals, Inc. v. Burnside Ship. Co.*, 394 U.S. 404, 413 (1969) (per Stewart, J.).

The best plural is *quid pro quos; quids pro quos* is a pedantic alternative. *Quids pro quo is incorrect—a good example of HYPERCORRECTION.

quiescence; *quiescency. The *-ce* form is standard, *quiescency being a NEEDLESS VARIANT. *Quiesence is a fairly common misspelling. *See, e.g.*, Alison A. Clarke, Note, *State Legislation Denying Subsistence Benefits to Undocumented Aliens*, 61 Tex. L. Rev. 859, 866 (1983).

quiet, adj. In the so-called *covenant for quiet enjoyment*, the word *quiet* means "free from disturbance" or "peaceful," not merely "free from noise." Plucknett equates *quiet enjoyment* with *seisin*: "If A unjustly and without a judgement disseised B of his free tenement, then it seemed reasonable that B should be restored to the enjoyment of his property upon satisfactory proof, first, that he was in *quiet enjoyment* (that is to say, seised), and secondly, that A had turned him out." Theodore F.T. Plucknett, *A Concise History of the Common Law* 358 (5th ed. 1956). See **seisin.**

quiet, vb.; **quieten.** The preferred verb form is *quiet*, as in the phrase *to quiet title*. E.g.:

- "After the seller sued to *quiet* title, the court held the buyer was entitled to specific performance because the seller had not cancelled the contract." *Queiroz v. Harvey*, 204 P.3d 390, 395 (Ariz. Ct. App. 2008).
- "The City argues that attorney's fees are not available in actions for adverse possession, trespass to try title, or suits to *quiet* title." *City of Dallas v. Turley*, 316 S.W.3d 762, 771 (Tex. App.—Dallas 2010).
- "In 2006, the Toledo Museum of Art brought a claim to *quiet* title to a Paul Gauguin painting." Jessica Grimes, Comment, *Forgotten Prisoners of War*, 15 Roger Williams U. L. Rev. 521, 532 (2010).

Chiefly a Britishism, *quieten* was considered a superfluous word by the great British writer on usage, H.W. Fowler; it is to be avoided.

Adjectivally, the phrase *quiet title* is hyphenated: "In the earlier *quiet-title* case in which the government's conduct was found to be unreasonable, the 'innocent spouse' issue was raised." *Sliwa v. Commissioner*, 839 F.2d 602, 610 (9th Cir. 1988).

quietus /kwɪ-**ee**-təs/ forms the plural *quietuses*.

qui facit per alium facit per se. See MAXIMS.

quiritary; *quiritarian. *Quiritary* (= "in accordance with Roman civil law; legal, as opposed to equitable") is preferably so spelled. The second form is a NEEDLESS VARIANT.

quit = (1) to stop; or (2) to leave. For sense 1, the past tense is *quit* <the defendant then quit making the harassing phone calls>. For sense 2, the past tense is *quitted.* E.g.:

- "If he had, before the expiration of the period limited by the law of Tennessee, *quitted* his residence in Missouri, and joined his family in New York, for the purpose of making the latter state his residence in fact, he would have been entitled to bring his action within the period fixed by the laws of New York." *Penfield v. Chesapeake, O. & S.W. R.R. Co.*, 134 U.S. 351, 361 (1890) (per Harlan, J.).
- "The troopers came back to Braund's property only a few minutes after they *quitted* it." *Braund v. State*, 12 P.3d 187, 196 (Alaska Ct. App. 2000).

See **stop.**

qui tam [L. "who as well"] = an action under a statute that allows a private person to sue for a penalty, part of which the government or some specified public institution will receive. Etymologically speaking, the plaintiff is a suitor "who as well" sues for the state. E.g.:

- "The False Claims Act . . . includes provisions allowing private citizens to bring civil suits on behalf of the government. They're based on a principle called *qui tam.*" Rick Wartzman & Paul M. Barrett, *For Whistle-Blowers, Tune May Change,* Wall St. J., 27 Sept. 1989, at B1.
- "A statutory *qui tam* action is one brought against a public official to recover a penalty (treble damages) for the commission of injurious acts or for a failure to act in obedience to some duty." *State v. Town of Canute*, 858 P.2d 436, 440–41 (Okla. 1993) (Opala, J., dissenting).

Qui tam lawsuits originated in the 13th century—when private persons would seek to protect the king's interest—and were embodied in statutes during the 15th century. In the U.S., *qui tam* lawsuits have "been in existence . . . ever since the foundation of our government." *Marvin v. Trout*, 199 U.S. 212, 225 (1905) (per Peckham, J.). They are usually reported as being in the name of the government *ex rel.* (= on the relation of) the private citizen. See *ex rel.*

quitclaim, vb. & adj. [L.F. "to proclaim free"]. *Quitclaim,* vb., = (1) to renounce or give up (a claim or right); or (2) to convey all of one's interest in (property) to whatever extent one has an interest. These senses are closely related, sense 2 having grown out of sense 1. Today, sense 2 is the more usual one—e.g.:

- "[This] tract of land [was] *quitclaimed* by R.E. Janes to R.E. Janes Gravel Co." *Thompson v. Janes*, 245 S.W.2d 718, 723 (Tex. Civ. App.—Austin 1952).

- "The Objectors fail to recognize that those 200 landowners are not part of this class since USRV *quitclaimed* any interests to those rights-of-way prior to this action, and those landowners may pursue any possible claims independent from this action." *Hefty v. All Other Members of the Certified Settlement Class*, 638 N.E.2d 1284, 1292 (Ind. Ct. App. 1994). On the use of **prior to* in that sentence, see ****prior to.**
- "The record reveals that Raymond *quitclaimed* the property to Esther on September 10, 1990." *Ross v. Ross*, 638 N.E.2d 1301, 1303 (Ind. Ct. App. 1994).
- "Hocherl subsequently *quitclaimed* her interest in the ranch to Pete Stampter." *Sandstrom v. Sandstrom*, 880 P.2d 103, 104 (Wyo. 1994).

Occasionally the verb is used intransitively—e.g.: "The undersigned hereby remises, releases and forever *quitclaims* unto [plaintiff], all right, title and interest of the undersigned in and to the [adjoining] property." *Davis v. Nelson*, 880 S.W.2d 658, 663 (Mo. Ct. App. 1994) (quoting release).

The traditional way of quitclaiming property is to convey all of one's "right, title, and interest." See **right, title, and interest.**

The word *quitclaim*—formerly two words, then hyphenated, and now invariably one word—functions as an adjective as well, usually in the phrase *quitclaim deed* (= a deed that, without warrantees of title, purports to convey only whatever interest the landholder possesses). E.g.:

- "Northrup had previously conveyed all her right, title and interest in The Strip to the Wallaces by virtue of the 1962 *quitclaim deed* referenced above." *Cloer Land Co. v. Wright*, 858 P.2d 110, 112 (Okla. Ct. App. 1993).
- "Two years later, while the parties were still separated but not yet divorced, Mr. Clark prepared, executed and delivered to Mrs. Clark a *quitclaim deed* which said that he was conveying to Mrs. Clark 'all of [his] right, title, and interest' in the house they had purchased." *Clark v. Clark*, 644 A.2d 449, 450 (D.C. 1994).

For the distinction between a *quitclaim deed* and a *warranty deed*, see **grant, bargain, and sell.**

Occasionally, *quitclaim* even functions as a noun, as a shortened form of *quitclaim deed*—e.g.: "Because Campbell's conveyance was only by *quitclaim* and transferred only whatever 'right, title, and interest' he had in 1960, Campbell's heirs have a claim to their proportionate share of the land in question." *Rogers v. Ricane Enters., Inc.*, 884 S.W.2d 763, 769 n.5 (Tex. 1994).

quite = (1) entirely; completely; (2) very; or (3) fairly; moderately. Sense 3 occurs in BrE only, in which the word has undergone pejoration. To say that something is *quite good* is a compliment in AmE but nearly the opposite in BrE: "Some years ago I was hired by an American bank. I received a letter from the head of human resources that started: 'Dear John, I am *quite* pleased that you have decided to join us.' That '*quite*' cast a cloud. Then I discovered that in American English 'quite' does not mean 'fairly' but 'very.'" John Mole, *Body Language of World Business*, Sunday Times, 8 July 1990, at 6-1.

quittance = (1) the discharge from a debt or obligation; or (2) the document serving as evidence of the discharge. For the related word *acquittance*, see **acquittal.**

quitter; quittor. For "one who quits," *quitter* is preferred. *Quittor* = an inflammation of the feet, usu. in horses.

quoad (= as regards; with regard to) is a LATINISM that is easily Englished. E.g.: "The test is whether the compact enhances state power *quoad* [read *regarding*] the national government." *U.S. Steel Corp. v. Multistate Tax Comm'n,* 434 U.S. 452, 473 (1978) (per Powell, J.). The term often appears in the phrase *quoad hoc* (= with regard to this). E.g.: "When [a justice] undertakes the issuing of a warrant of arrest which commands and secures the arrest, and possibly the imprisonment, of the person charged he *quoad hoc* [omit *quoad hoc,* which is superfluous] acts ministerially." *Broom v. Douglass,* 57 So. 860, 866–67 (Ala. 1912).

quo animo (lit., "with what intention or motive"), an arcane LATINISM, is used by some legal writers as an equivalent of *animus.* "The further requirement—the *quo animo*—is that he be shown to have intended to deprive the owner of the object." *Commonwealth v. Garcia,* 707 N.E.2d 378, 380 (Mass. 1999). Those legal writers are, happily, becoming rarer. See **animus.**

The correct use of the phrase is not as a noun, but as an adverb—e.g.: "Indeed, once it is established that a payment has been accepted as rent, which is a question of fact, waiver results as a matter of law, and the question of *quo animo* [i.e., with what intention] the payment was accepted is irrelevant." Peter Butt, *Land Law* 284 (2d ed. 1988). Even this use, though, is questionable in modern writing.

quod erat demonstrandum. See **Q.E.D.**

quod erat faciendum. See **Q.E.F.**

quod vide = which see. The abbreviation *q.v.* (pl. *qq.v.*) often appears in cross-references in reference books.

quondam (= former) is an ARCHAISM. See **erstwhile.**

quorum. Pl. *quorums.* See PLURALS (A).

QUOTATIONS. A. Use of Quoted Material. The deft and incidental use of quotations is a rare art. Legal writers—especially the bad ones—are apt to quote paragraph after paragraph in block quotations (see (B)). Those who do this abrogate their duty, namely, to *write.* Readers tend to skip over single-spaced mountains of prose, knowing how unlikely it is that so much of a previous writer's material pertains directly to the matter at hand. Especially to be avoided is quoting another writer at the end of a paragraph or section, a habit infused with laziness. The skillful quoter

subordinates the quoted material to his or her own prose and uses only the most clearly applicable parts of the previous writing. And even then, one must weave it into one's own narrative or analysis, not allowing the quoted to overpower the quoter.

B. Handling Block Quotations. The best way to handle them, of course, is not to handle them at all: quote smaller chunks. Assuming, though, that this goal is unattainable—as most legal writers seem to think—then the biggest challenge is handling the quotation so that it will actually get read. The secret is in the lead-in.

Before discussing how a good lead-in reads, let us look at how 98% of them read. They are dead:

- The court observed: . . . .
- The court held: . . . .
- The court further held: . . . .
- As stated by the court: . . . .
- Rule 54(d) states: . . . .
- As the court specifically stated: . . . .
- The statute reads in pertinent part: . . . .
- The *Miranda* court stated: . . . .
- According to the 5th Circuit: . . . .
- That opinion enunciated the definition of the term "fixture" as follows: . . . .

Anyone who wants to become a good legal stylist must vow to try *never* to introduce a quotation in this way. Readers are sure to skip the quotation.

The better practice is to state the upshot of the quotation in the lead-in. With this method, the lead-in becomes an assertion, and the quotation becomes the support. The reader feels as if the writer has asserted something concrete and often, out of curiosity, wants to verify that assertion.

Consider, for example, how differently the following passage would read if the colon introducing the quotation followed *observed* instead of *bystanders*:

> As one Texas court has observed, modern legal practice is designed to prevent the vexatious suing of innocent bystanders:
>
>> Our statutes of limitation afford ample time for investigation before the institution of suit. Before and after that point, our rules of practice afford many means of investigating the circumstances of the case and of ascertaining the proper identity of the parties sued. We are unable to find any legal excuse for appellant's having sued the wrong corporation or for his delay in ascertaining this fact.

When the writer gives the upshot in the introductory words, readers are not left hunting for the central idea of the quotation.

This method has the benefit not only of ensuring that the quotation is read, but also of enhancing the writer's credibility. For if the lead-in is pointed as well as accurate, the reader will agree that the quotation supports the writer's assertion.

C. Punctuating the Lead-In. Writers usually have four choices: a colon, a comma, a period (i.e., no lead-in, really—only an independent sentence before the quotation), or no punctuation. A long quotation ordinarily requires a colon. Some writers, though, let the lead-in and the quotation stand as separate sentences, as in the following example:

> As part of the "balancing" of equities, the Act provides that the statutory remedies shall serve as the employee's *exclusive remedy* if that employee sustains an injury compensable under the Act.
>
>> No common law or statutory right to recover damages from the employer, his insurer . . . or the agents or employees of any of them for injury or death sustained by any employee while engaged in the line of his duty as such employee, other than the compensation herein provided, is available to any employee who is covered by the provisions of this Act, to anyone wholly or partially dependent on him . . . or anyone otherwise entitled to recover damages for such injury.
>>
>> Ill. Rev. Stat. ch. 48, ¶ 138.5(a) (1986).

The writer there crafted a good lead-in by summarizing the provision in plain English. Letting the lead-in stand as one sentence, though, can leave the quotation in a sort of syntactic limbo. A colon, by contrast, helps the reader see how the quotation fits into the text: the quotation simply amplifies the lead-in.

When is it best to use no punctuation at all? Only when the introductory language moves seamlessly into the quoted material—e.g.:

> Professor Bobbitt thinks that the view that moral arguments should generally be excluded from constitutional discourse
>
>> justifies, for example, the phenomenon of federal habeas corpus, for which it is otherwise difficult to give good grounds. Habeas corpus severs the constitutional decision from the moral question of guilt or innocence, so that the former can be dispassionately weighed as one suspects it seldom can be in the context of a trial. At the same time federal habeas corpus gives the matter to a group of deciders whose customary business is, by comparison to state courts, largely amoral.

The mere fact that what is being introduced is a block quotation does not mean that some additional punctuation is necessary.

D. American and British Systems. In AmE, quotations that are short enough to be run into the text (usually fewer than 50 words) are set off by pairs of *double* quotation marks (". . ."). In BrE, quoted text that is not long enough to be a block quotation is set off by *single* quotation marks ('. . .'). See PUNCTUATION (K).

E. Ellipses. A good way to trim down a bloated quotation—and therefore to increase the odds of having it read—is to cut irrelevant parts. When you omit one or more words, you show the omission by using ellipsis points (a series of three period-dots) with one space between them:

> The court may require any attorney . . . who vexatiously multiplies the proceedings to personally satisfy the excess costs, expenses, and attorneys' fees reasonably incurred because of that conduct.

Use a fourth period-dot when the omission falls between sentences in the quoted material or when your ellipsis ends a sentence.

The spacing between the last word of the sentence and the first ellipsis point depends on whether the last word before the ellipsis ends a sentence. In the following example, *intent* is the last word of the first sentence, and it therefore ends with a period followed by three ellipsis points:

> A circuit court must initially determine, as a question of law, whether the language of a purported contract is ambiguous as to the parties' intent. . . . If the terms of an alleged contract are ambiguous or capable of more than one interpretation, however, parol evidence is admissible to ascertain the parties' intent.

But if *intent* were not the last word of the first sentence, then the three ellipsis points would come first, and the (typographically identical) period after. The only difference would be the space between *intent* and the first dot:

> A circuit court must initially determine, as a question of law, whether the language of a purported contract is ambiguous as to the parties' intent . . . . If the terms of an alleged contract are ambiguous or capable of more than one interpretation, however, parol evidence is admissible to ascertain the parties' intent.

That distinction—a hairsplitting distinction, in the minds of some—is one that careful legal writers adhere to. In nonlegal writing, though, the convention is to close up the space before the first of four ellipsis points.

Finally, when you omit more than one paragraph in a block quotation, use a whole line for the three ellipsis points (centered), which should have five to seven spaces between them—e.g:

> Everyone is familiar with the general distinction between what people mean to say and what they expect or hope will happen as a result of their having said it. People often say "Don't bother" when they hope the person they are speaking to will ignore what they have said and will indeed bother. The distinction is especially important when people give orders to make requests in language that is normally understood as abstract or in some other way requiring judgment.
>
> .   .   .
>
> The late-eighteenth-century authors of the Eighth Amendment (as we have defined them) declared that "cruel and unusual punishments" are unconstitutional. What did they intend to say?
>
> Ronald Dworkin, *Life's Dominion: An Argument About Abortion, Euthanasia, and Individual Freedom* 134–35 (1993).

---

quote (properly a verb) for *quotation* is a casualism that sometimes appears in formal contexts—e.g.: "This *quote* . . . clearly draws a distinction." *U.S. v. Sells Eng'g, Inc.*, 463 U.S. 418, 463 (1983) (Burger, C.J., dissenting). The problem with *quotation* is that, to the writer who hopes to deliver goods quickly, the three syllables sound and read as if they are taking too much time. The single syllable of *quote*, meanwhile, sounds apt to such a writer. And it sounds more and more natural all the time, as it seems to predominate in spoken English.

The negative form, too, is a casualism—e.g.: "The only other citation provided by plaintiffs in support of their position is a *misquote*." *UAL Corp. v. Mesa Airlines, Inc.*, 88 F.Supp.2d 910, 913 (N.D. Ill. 2000). See **cite (c).**

quo warranto (lit., "by what authority?") is the HYBRID name (L. *quo* + A.S. *warrant*) of the common-law writ enshrined in two statutes enacted in 1289, each known as *Statutum de Quo Warranto*. Through this writ, a relator sought to discover either the extent of royal manors or the warrants by which royal rights and royal estates had passed to corporations or private individuals. Today, the writ is obsolete in England but persists in the U.S., where it is generally used to inquire into the authority by which a public office is held or a franchise is claimed. See **prerogative writs.**

The hybrid nature of this LAW LATIN term is apt to throw the linguist into a fit: "The term . . . is to a linguist a horripilating hybrid, using an English term like 'warrant' with a Latin ablative ending and combining it with a Latin interrogative pronoun." Mario Pei, *Double-Speak in America* 73 (1973).

q.v. See *quod vide.*

R

R., the abbreviation for either *Regina* (= Queen) or *Rex* (King), is often used in G.B. in place of *The Queen* or *The King* in criminal case names.

racial discrimination; race discrimination. The first phrase is slightly better because, other things being equal, the adjective (*racial* or *race*) should have the form as well as the function of an adjective (hence *racial*). But predictably, idiomatic English is not entirely consistent: we speak of *racial equality* but *race relations*. Cf. **sex.**

rack. See **wrack.**

racketeering. The noun *racketeering* refers either to the business of racketeers or to a system of organized crime traditionally involving the extortion of money from business firms by intimidation, violence, or other illegal methods. Oddly, this noun, as well as the verb *racketeer*, is characterized by the *OED* as an Americanism, whereas the adjective *racketeering* is exemplified in that dictionary only by British quotations. If the verb and its derivative forms began as Americanisms, they will inevitably spread to BrE, given the inroads already made.

In 1970, the U.S. Congress passed the Racketeer Influenced and Corrupt Organizations Act (RICO), 18 U.S.C. §§ 1961–68 (1988), which led to a resurgence of the word in AmE. Today *racketeering* often has the broad sense "the practice of engaging in a fraudulent scheme or enterprise."

railroad; railway. As nouns these words are virtually equivalent. Both mean (1) a permanent roadway made of a line of rails to provide a track for locomotives and the cars they draw, or self-propelled vehicles built to run on rails; or (2) a company that owns such a roadway and its assets. In BrE, *railway* is the preferred term. In AmE, a small or local railroad that uses only light equipment, such as commuter trains or streetcars, may also be called *light rail.*

The two words are abbreviated *R.R.* and *Ry. Railroad* is used universally as a verb <passenger railroading>, figuratively as well as literally—e.g.: "By contrast, the perception that legislative proposals are being *railroaded* through Congress produces fractiousness and impedes the dialogue—both between members of Congress themselves and between members of Congress and key constituency groups." Lynn S. Branham, *The Prison Litigation Reform Act's Enigmatic Exhaustion Requirement*, 86 Cornell L. Rev. 483, 539 (2001). This sense is now used in BrE as well as AmE.

rainmaker, in AmE, refers to a lawyer who, generally through wide contacts and high standing within the business community, generates a great deal of business for a law firm. E.g.:

- "It is well known that law firms often have partners who are socially prominent due to their civic, charitable, or political activities. They may do little legal work; their job is to bring in new clients. They are the '*rainmakers*.'" Frederick C. Moss, *The Ethics of Law Practice Marketing*, 61 Notre Dame L. Rev. 601, 670 (1986).
- "A proficient '*rainmaker*,' Manley accounted for substantial annual Finley Kumble billings—in excess of $14 million in 1984." *Manley v. AmBase Corp.*, 337 F.3d 237, 240 (2d Cir. 2003).

raise. A. And *rear*. The old rule, still somewhat observed, is that crops and livestock are *raised* and children are *reared*. But *raised* is now more common and fully standard regarding children, and the only option in the SET PHRASE *born and raised.*

B. "*Raising*" a Use. In the traditional legal idiom, to create a use (in the sense of equitable ownership) was to *raise* a use—e.g.:

- "The rule requiring a consideration to *raise a use*, has become merely nominal." *Jackson ex. dem. Hudson v. Alexander*, 3 Johns. 484, 492 (N.Y. Sup. Ct. 1808).
- "Consideration was essential to *raise a use* under the statute." *Chase Fed. Savs. & Loan Ass'n v. Schreiber*, 479 So.2d 90, 99 (Fla. 1985).
- "At the beginning of the sixteenth century it was settled that *a use could be raised* without a transfer of the seisin by means of a bargain and sale." Cornelius J. Moynihan, *Introduction to the Law of Real Property* 176 (2d ed. 1988).

See **use.**

Rambo. This is the name of the "hero" in David Morrell's novel *First Blood*, which was popularized in the film by that name and in *Rambo: First Blood Part II* and *Rambo III*. The character Rambo is a Vietnam veteran who is madly bent on violent revenge.

By an almost natural extension, the term came in the 1980s to denote ultra-aggressive lawyers, especially litigators. The *SOED* defines *Rambo* (with the initial capital) as "a man given to displays of physical violence or aggression, a macho man." But among American lawyers, the term has lost its sex-specific character, so that it is perfectly natural to speak of a female litigator as being a *Rambo*.

Sometimes, as in the first example quoted below, *Rambo* appears alone, but more often it is used attributively in the phrases *Rambo litigator*, *Rambo lawyer*, and *Rambo tactics*—e.g.:

- "I do not say to trust the untrustworthy or to retreat before *Rambos*." Thomas M. Reavley, *Response to "One Year After Dondi,"* 17 Pepp. L. Rev. 851, 852 (1990).
- "The headlines of the late 1980s and early 1990s gleefully referred to '*Rambo*' lawyers and unethical trial tactics, judges incessantly complained about uncivil behavior in the courts, and certain attorneys even prided themselves as 'warriors' who employ hardball tactics and take no prisoners." Roland Garcia, *Saluting the Architects of Freedom*, 39 Hous. Law. 6, 6 (Feb. 2002).
- "An egregious, and sleazy, example of the *Rambo* tactics Wilde used is . . . depos[ing] one of Kolupar's friends about Kolupar's employment as a topless dancer." *Kolupar v. Wilde Pontiac Cadillac, Inc.*, 668 N.W.2d 799, 808 (Wis. Ct. App. 2003).
- "One practitioner candidly recommends lawyers openly gossip and 'brand' *Rambo lawyers* as a means of discouraging incivility." Melissa S. Hung, *A Non-Trivial Pursuit*, 48 Santa Clara L. Rev. 1127, 1161 n.272 (2008).

Cf. LAWYERS, DEROGATORY NAMES FOR.

rape. A. Defined. Some authorities, especially older ones, define *rape* as "carnal knowledge of a woman forcibly against her will." 4 William Blackstone, *Commentaries on the Laws of England* 210 (1769). But the better view is that force should not be an element of the definition because if it is, then one must resort to a fictional "constructive force," which includes the threat of force. See **constructive.**

A better traditional, common-law definition is as follows: "A man commits rape when he engages in intercourse (in the old statutes, carnal knowledge) with a woman not his wife; by force or threat of force; against her will and without her consent." Susan Estrich, *Real Rape* 8 (1987). Gradually, the definition has been simplified. One criminal-law text defines it simply as "sexual intercourse with a female person without her consent." Rollin M. Perkins & Ronald N. Boyce, *Criminal Law* 197 (3d ed. 1982). See **marital rape.**

This definitional change took place in many American states during the 1970s. The pre-1974 rape statute in Texas defined *rape* as "the carnal knowledge of a woman without her consent and obtained by force, threats or fraud." Tex. Penal Code Ann. § 1183 (Vernon 1961). A 1974 amendment changed the definition so that a person is guilty of rape "if he has sexual intercourse with a female not his wife and without the female's consent." *Id.* § 21.02 (Vernon 1974). For the more modern development, see (C).

B. And *seduction.* Traditionally, the law has distinguished between *rape* and *seduction*. If consent is altogether lacking, the offense is called *rape*. If the consent is unfairly obtained—as through phony tenderness or false promises of an enduring relationship—the act is called *seduction*.

Seduction was a statutory crime against women of any age in 37 American states until the late 20th century. It was variously regarded as a crime involving injury to reputation (*State v. Mallonee*, 69 S.E. 786, 787 (N.C. 1910)) up to a crime of physical violence (*U.S. v. Williams*, 55 F.Supp. 375, 377 (D. Minn. 1944)). A complainant could sue in tort for economic damages and for personal damages, such as mental anguish and loss of reputation. Parents also had standing to sue for the loss of a daughter's services and earnings. Mary Ann Mason, *From Father's Property to Children's Rights* 6 (1996). Now, where the crime still exists, it is limited to the seduction of children under the age of consent.

C. And *sexual assault; indecent assault.* During the 1980s, many American jurisdictions abolished rape as a separate offense and created a new offense called *sexual assault*, defined in Texas as follows: "a person commits an offense if the person intentionally or knowingly caused the penetration of the anus or female sexual organ of another person who is not the spouse of the actor by any means, without that person's consent." Tex. Penal Code Ann. § 22.011(a) (Vernon 1983). The result is that the statute covers not just females, but also males who are homosexually assaulted.

There are several variations. In New Jersey, *simple sexual assault* is defined as an act of sexual penetration committed when the "actor uses physical force or coercion, but the victim does not sustain severe personal injury." N.J. Stat. Ann. § 2C:14-2(c)(1) (West 1982). The Model Penal Code, however, is drafted much more broadly:

> A person who has sexual contact with another not his spouse, or causes such other to have sexual contact with him, is guilty of sexual assault, a misdemeanor, if . . . he

knows that the contact is offensive to the other person . . . . Sexual contact is any touching of the sexual or other intimate parts of the person for the purpose of arousing or gratifying sexual desire.

> Model Penal Code § 213.4 (1980).

One state—Pennsylvania—even uses the term *indecent assault* as opposed to *sexual assault*. Under the Pennsylvania statute, a person who has "indecent contact" with another not his or her spouse is guilty of indecent assault if:

- the other person does not consent;
- the actor knows that the other person has a mental defect that impairs consent;
- the actor knows that the other person is unaware of the act;
- the actor has drugged the person;
- the other person is in custody in a hospital or other institution where the actor has supervisory or disciplinary authority; or
- the actor is more than 18 years old and the other person is under 14.

See 18 Pa. C.S.A. § 3126 (1994). Under that same Pennsylvania statute, *indecent contact* is defined as "any touching of the sexual or other intimate parts of the person for the purpose of arousing or gratifying sexual desire, in either person." *Id.* § 3101.

In G.B., *indecent assault* is the usual term for a lesser offense than rape: touching without consent. It is punishable by up to two years' imprisonment. *See* Tony Honoré, *Sex Law* 65–68 (1978).

rape shield law. See **shield law.**

rare. See **scarce.**

rarefy is often misspelled **rarify*—e.g.:

- "This was high ground indeed; the Supreme Court found the air too *rarified* [read *rarefied*]." Grant Gilmore & Charles L. Black, *The Law of Admiralty* 224 (2d ed. 1975).
- "The *rarified* [read *rarefied*] rules underlying this rigid and time-bound conception of the term 'equity' were hardly at the fingertips of those who enacted § 502(a)(3)." *Great-West Life & Annuity Ins. Co. v. Knudson*, 534 U.S. 204, 224 (2002) (Ginsburg, J., dissenting).

Cf. **stupefy.**

ratable; rateable. In AmE, the spelling *ratable* is preferred, while in BrE *rateable* is more common.

The adverb *ratably* is frequently used in legal writing in the sense "pro rata; proportionately" <they will share ratably in the assets>. E.g.:

- "Co-owners must, as a rule, contribute *ratably* toward payment of taxes, special assessments, mortgages and repairs of the property." Robert Kratovil, *Real Estate Law* 223 (1946).
- "Those [withdrawals] . . . from the deposit accounts were . . . to be borne *rateably*." Lord Goff of Chieveley & Gareth Jones, *The Law of Restitution* 75 (3d ed. 1986).
- "Any expense in the first category cannot be *ratably* apportioned across all classes of income." *Boeing Co. v. U.S.*, 537 U.S. 437, 451 (2003) (per Stevens, J.).

See MUTE E.

rate-making, n. & adj., is best hyphenated.

rather unique. See ADJECTIVES (B).

ratification = (1) in contract law, a person's binding adoption of an act already completed, but either not done in a way that originally produced a legal obligation or done by a stranger having at the time no authority to act as the person's agent; (2) in constitutional law, the process by which an amendment to the constitution is adopted; (3) in domestic law, the process by which a state indicates acceptance of the obligations contained in a treaty; or (4) in international law, the final confirmation by the parties to an international treaty, usu. including the documents reflecting the confirmation. See **adoption.**

ratify; confirm. These verbs share the sense "to approve something tentatively done or prepared so that it has full legal validity." Although the words are often interchangeable, *ratify* connotes a greater degree of approval and is therefore more typically used in reference to a highly significant matter that requires full participation by the ratifying body, as with a constitution, treaty, or corporate action requiring after-the-fact approval. *Confirm* emphasizes the assent of the agent to something's validity, as with an appointment of someone to a post <the President's nominee was confirmed by the Senate>.

ratio /**ray**-shee-oh/ frequently serves as a shorthand form of *ratio decidendi*—e.g.:

- "Fully considered *dicta* in the House of Lords are usually treated as more weighty than the *ratio* of a judge at first instance in the High Court." P.S. Atiyah, *Law and Modern Society* 135 (1983).
- "The *ratio* . . . of a case is its central core of meaning, its sharpest cutting edge." Michael Zander, *The Law-Making Process* 225 (2d ed. 1985).

The plural is *rationes*. See *ratio decidendi*.

ratiocination; rationalization. *Ratiocination* /**ray**-shee-oh-sə-**nay**-shən/ = the process or an act of reasoning—e.g.: "It is not our duty to unravel the *ratiocinations* of the jury's collective logic." *Odom v. U.S.*, 377 F.2d 853, 857 (5th Cir. 1967). *Rationalization* = (1) an act or instance of explaining (away) by bringing into conformity with reason; or (2) (colloq.) the finding of "reasons" for irrational or unworthy behavior. Sense 2 is responsible for the negative connotations of *rationalization* among nonlawyers—e.g.: "Proper legal decisions should never be mere *rationalizations* fronting for political correctness." *Caperton v. A.T. Massey Coal Co.*, 679 S.E.2d 223, 294 (W. Va. 2008) (Benjamin, acting C.J., concurring).

ratiocinative; *ratiocinatory. The second is a NEEDLESS VARIANT.

ratio decidendi /**ray**-shee-oh des-i-**den**-dɪ/ (lit., "the reason for deciding") = (1) the rule of law on which a court says its decision is founded; or (2) the rule of law on which a later court or analyst thinks that a previous court founded its decision. So even though this term is basic to the common-law system of precedents, it is more than a little ambiguous. Still, sense 2 is much less common in practice than sense 1. As the *OCL1* notes, a literal translation of the phrase ("the reason for the decision") is unsatisfactory "because the reason may in fact be something other, such as the judge's dislike of the defendant. Nor is the *ratio* the decision itself, for this binds only the parties [by *res judicata*] whereas the *ratio* is the principle which is of application to subsequent cases and states the law for all parties." See **res judicata.**

Because judicial opinions often contain no clearly ascertainable *ratio decidendi*, finding it often demands insight and independent judgment. But many writers use this term without concerning themselves with the AMBIGUITY or the subtleties—e.g.:

- "Lower courts read the opinions of this Court with a not unnatural alertness to catch intimations beyond the precise *ratio decidendi*." *Johnson v. U.S.*, 333 U.S. 46, 56 (1948) (Frankfurter, J., dissenting in part).
- "The words of an opinion are not scriptural admonitions or statutory mandates; we are bound by the rationale of a decision, its *ratio decidendi*, not its explanatory language." *Daniels v. Morris*, 746 F.2d 271, 275 (5th Cir. 1984).
- "The *ratio decidendi* was the statute's perceived purpose, i.e., 'to achieve equality of employment opportunities.'" *Smith v. City of Jackson*, 544 U.S. 228, 262 (2005) (O'Connor, J., concurring).

The plural form is *rationes decidendi* (**ray**-shee-oh-neez des-i-**den**-dɪ)—e.g.:

- "The substitution of negligent non-military personnel in place of military personnel would have no effect on these *rationes decidendi*." *Sheppard v. U.S.*, 294 F.Supp. 7, 9 (E.D. Pa. 1969).
- "A general rule of interpretation, unlike other common law rules, can never be rendered more specific by the *rationes decidendi* of later cases." Rupert Cross, *Statutory Interpretation* 168 (1976).

See **stare decisis.** Cf. **dictum (A)** & **obiter dictum (B).**

rational. See **reasonable.**

rationale (= a reasoned exposition of principles; an explanation or statement of reasons) is not to be confused with *rationalization* (= the act of explaining away something). See **ratiocination.**

Rationale is three syllables, although H.W. Fowler believed that it should be four syllables based on etymology (*-ale* being two syllables). Today, his preferred pronunciation would be considered terribly pedantic in most company. The final syllable is pronounced like that in *morale* or *chorale*. See **ratio decidendi.**

rationalization. See **ratiocination.**

rationalize for *analogize* or *harmonize* is an unlikely error—e.g.:

- "Appellants have called to our attention the recent Supreme Court case of *Indian Towing Co. v. U.S.*, . . . but it is difficult to *rationalize that case with* [read, depending on the sense, *analogize that case to* or *harmonize that case with*] the one at bar." *Tillman v. U.S.*, 232 F.2d 511, 514 (9th Cir. 1956).
- "In *Smith*, the Eighth Circuit Court of Appeals attempted to *rationalize its cases* [read *harmonize its cases*] holding that, 'even without a pattern, . . . the timing . . . sufficed to establish causal connection.'" *Martinez v. Cole Sewell Corp.*, 233 F.Supp.2d 1097, 1117 (N.D. Iowa 2002).

ration allotment is a REDUNDANCY. E.g.: "The jury was justified in inferring that the applications . . . for *ration allotments* [read *rations*, or, less good, *allotments*] for . . . the W and W Cafeteria, were prepared and filed with the Rationing Board by the appellant." *Franks v. U.S.*, 164 F.2d 795, 796 (8th Cir. 1947). Either word would be sufficient.

ravish (= to rape) is now more literary or archaic than is appropriate for modern legal contexts—e.g.:

- "To *ravish* a woman is to have carnal connection with her forcibly and without her consent." *Niederstadt v. Nixon*, 505 F.3d 832, 837 (8th Cir. 2007).
- "[The] defendant was indicted on the charge that he 'unlawfully, willfully and feloniously did *ravish*, abuse, and carnally know' [the victim] who was at the time physically helpless." *State v. Atkins*, 666 S.E.2d 809, 812 (N.C. Ct. App. 2008).

One problem with *ravish* is that it has romantic connotations: it means not only "to commit rape," but also "to fill with ecstasy or delight." The latter sense renders the word unfit for acting as a technical or legal equivalent of *rape*. The term describing the act should evoke outrage; it should not be a romantic abstraction, as *ravish* is.

-RE; -ER. See **-ER (c).**

re. See **in re** & **res.**

rea. See *reus.*

reaction; effect. Justice Oliver Wendell Holmes once nodded and misused *reaction* (= response) for *effect* (= outcome): "The question then is narrowed to whether the exercise of its otherwise constitutional power by Congress can be pronounced unconstitutional because of its possible *reaction* [read *effect*] upon the conduct of the States in a matter upon which I have admitted that they are free from direct control." *Hammer v. Dagenhart*, 247 U.S. 251, 278 (1918) (Holmes, J., dissenting). The states had a *reaction to* Congress's action; Congress had an *effect on* the states.

reactionary; *reactionist; *reactionarist. The second and third are NEEDLESS VARIANTS.

reading the Riot Act. The English "Riot Act," 1 Geo. I, stat. 2, c. 5 (1714) (repealed 1973), made it a capital offense for 12 or more rioters to assemble for an hour after a magistrate proclaimed that the rioters must disperse. As an astute 19th-century commentator observed, the magistrate's proclamation "is commonly, but very inaccurately, called reading the Riot Act." 1 James F. Stephen, *A History of the Criminal Law of England* 203 n.1 (1883). Why inaccurately? Because the statute itself was not read. Instead, a proclamation was read, calling on rioters to disperse.

By the early 19th century, the phrase *read the riot act* (usually with the last two words in lowercase) had become a catchphrase meaning "to tell someone off"— e.g.: "Spartech's plant manager at the time '*read the riot act*' to Spartech employees, telling them they had to 'get it right.'" *High Concrete Tech., LLC v. Korolath of New Eng., Inc.*, 665 F.Supp.2d 883, 888 (S.D. Ohio 2009). See POPULARIZED LEGAL TECHNICALITIES.

read on. Yes, please do. This phrase is one of the most bizarre bits of legalese in the legal lexicon. In patent practice, a patent claim is said to *read on* a prior-art reference (a previous patent) when it contains all the same features as the predecessor. It describes an infringing product or process. If all the patent claims "read on" an earlier patent, the invention infringes—or if the patent hasn't been issued yet, it won't be.

ready, willing, and able. This phrase traditionally describes a prospective buyer of property who can legally and financially consummate a proposed deal. A less common variant is *ready, able, and willing*. See DOUBLETS, TRIPLETS, AND SYNONYM-STRINGS.

real, when used adverbially in place of *really* or *very*, is bad English—e.g.:

- "Competition in recent years hasn't been *real* [read *very*] friendly." L. Gordon Crovitz, *Even Gentlemanly Yachtsmen Go to Court, but Why Let Them?*, Wall St. J., 16 May 1990, at A17.
- "In the early days (meaning the *real* [read *very*] early days like fifty, sixty, or seventy years ago, or more), membership records were routinely destroyed." Donald S. Gray, *Members Old & New*, 41 Orange County Law. 4, 4 (Aug. 1999).
- "The juvenile's therapist stated that the juvenile passed two social-skills groups and that he 'participates *real* [read *very*] well in group.'" *Commonwealth v. Ronald R.*, 877 N.E.2d 918, 920 (Mass. 2007).

real; personal. The distinction between *real property* (or *realty*) and *personal property* (or *personalty*) is as old as Roman law, but the curious terminology is much more recent. From the early 17th century on, land was commonly called *real property* and chattels were called *personal property* merely because land could be recovered specifically in a real action, but chattels could be made the subject only of a damage action. See **real action.**

real action; personal action; mixed action. The distinctions between these three were fundamental to the common law. *Real actions* involved a *res*, or land, and a plaintiff (or demandant) claiming some interest in the land. *Personal actions* involved debts, personal duties, or damages arising from any cause. *Mixed actions* partook of the nature of the other two, as when the

plaintiff claimed both real property and damages. See **demandant** & **real.**

real contract. This phrase, common among civilians, is rarely used by common-law writers and judges. Still, it describes an obligation enforced at common law from the earliest times: "A *real contract* is an obligation arising from the possession or transfer of a res. The *real contracts* known to the common law were enforced by the actions of account, detinue, and debt." 1 Samuel Williston & Walter H.E. Jaeger, *A Treatise on the Law of Contracts* § 8, at 19 (3d ed. 1957). For the most part, these forms of action fell into disuse with the rise of assumpsit. See **assumpsit.**

real covenant. See **covenant running with the land.**

real estate. A. Quaint Objection to the Phrase. Richard Grant White's (19th-century) view of this phrase— "a pretentious intruder from the technical province of law"—remains surprisingly apt:

> Law makes the distinction of real and personal estate; but a man does not, therefore, talk of drawing some personal estate from the bank, or going to Tiffany's to buy some personal estate for his wife; nor, when he has an interest in the national debt, does he ask how personal estate is selling. He draws money, buys jewels, asks the price of bonds. *Real estate*, as ordinarily used, is a mere big-sounding, vulgar phrase for houses and land, and, so used, is a marked and unjustifiable Americanism. Our papers have columns headed in large letters, "Real Estate Transactions," the heading of which should be Sales of Land.
>
> Richard Grant White, *Words and Their Uses, Past and Present* 150 (2d ed. 1872).

B. And *real property*. Nonlawyers such as realtors have pedantically tried to distinguish these terms: "*Real estate* includes all of the components in the definition of land plus artificial things (placed by humans) permanently attached. . . . The term *real property* includes everything in the definition of *real estate* and also the legal rights, interests, and privileges associated with the ownership of *real estate*." Gerald R. Cortesi, *Mastering Real Estate Principles* 21 (2003). But this supposed distinction is surely mistaken. Statutes and courts usually give both terms the same meaning—e.g.:

- "Wisconsin Stat. § 70.03 defines 'real property,' 'real estate,' and 'land' for the purposes of tax assessment as 'not only the land itself but all buildings and improvements thereon, and all fixtures and rights and privileges appertaining thereto.'" *ABKA Ltd. P'ship v. Bd. of Rev. of Village of Fontana-On-Geneva Lake*, 603 N.W.2d 217, 221 (Wis. 1999).
- "'*Real property*' means land, buildings, fixtures, and all other improvements to land. The terms 'land,' 'real estate,' 'realty,' and 'real property' may be used interchangeably." Fla. Stat. § 192.001(12) (2010).
- "K.S.A. 77-201 Eighth defines the terms 'real property' and 'real estate' to include land and all rights thereto 'and interest therein' for purposes of statutory construction. . . . K.S.A. 79-102 defines the terms 'real property' and 'real estate' as including 'not only the land itself' but 'all buildings, fixtures, improvements, mines, minerals, quarries, mineral springs and wells' and the 'rights and privileges

appertaining thereto.' This simply means that the terms broadly include any rights and privileges that are associated with ownership of any of the listed properties." *In re Lipson*, 238 P.3d 757, 760 (Kan. Ct. App. 2010).

See **property (A)**.

real-estate agent. See **realtor**.

real evidence = the physical evidence (such as clothing or a knife wound) that itself has played a direct part in the incident in question. Historically there is a distinction between *immediate real evidence* and *reported real evidence*. *Immediate real evidence* is evidence that is already before the tribunal. *Reported real evidence* is not present at the tribunal, "but the existence of it is conveyed to [the court] through the medium of witnesses or documents." T.W. Hughes, *An Illustrated Treatise on the Law of Evidence* 165 (1907). Today *real evidence* is generally synonymous with *immediate real evidence*. See **evidence**.

real facts. See **fact** & **actual fact, in**.

real party in interest. So written, though a few judges have ill-advisedly made this noun phrase *real-party-in-interest* or *real party-in-interest*. Only as a PHRASAL ADJECTIVE—as in *real-party-in-interest provision*—does the phrase need hyphens.

real property. For the historical basis for the distinction between *real property* and *personal property*, see **real**. For debunking of the supposed distinction between *real property* and *real estate*, see **real estate (B)**.

realtor (= a real estate agent or broker) has two syllables, not three: /**reel**-tər/. This Americanism is a MORPHOLOGICAL DEFORMITY, since the *-or* suffix in Latin is appended only to verb elements, and *realt-* is not a verb element. But the term is too well established in AmE to quibble with its makeup. The shortness of the word commends it.

Some authorities suggest that it should be capitalized and used only in its proprietary trademark sense, that is, "a member of the National Association of Realtors"; the organization invented and registered the trademark in 1916. Because comparatively few people know about the trademark, in AmE the term is used indiscriminately of real-estate agents generally. In BrE, real-estate agents are known as *estate agents*; *realtor* is virtually unknown there, and *real estate* is only a little better known to British nonlawyers.

realty. A. Sense. The only current sense of this term is the legal one, "real property." Formerly, the term could denote both "royalty" and "a reality." See **real estate**.

B. Precise Difference Between *realty* and *personalty*. Anglo-American courts have disagreed about whether an estate in land less than a freehold is properly considered *realty* or *personalty*. (At common law, a tenant for years was not regarded as having an interest in realty.) Today, courts most often use the terms "*real estate* and *real property* in a broad sense as applicable to any estates in land, whether freehold or less than freehold, as well as to land itself, regarded as the object of rights." 1 Herbert T. Tiffany, *The Law of Real Property* § 3, at 7–8 (Basil Jones ed., 3d ed. 1939). The increasing use of *realty* and its cognates in the broader sense, to include nonfreehold as well as freehold estates, is attributable to "the fact that it corresponds to the ordinary use of the expression . . . among members of the community in general" (*id.* at 8)—otherwise known as SLIPSHOD EXTENSION.

rear. See **raise (A)**.

reason. A. *Reason . . . is because.* This construction is traditionally regarded as grammatically loose, since *reason* implies *because* and vice versa. After the noun *reason* plus a *be*-verb or other linking verb, a noun phrase, predicate adjective, or *that*-clause should appear. Some good writers have perpetrated the error—e.g.:

- "The *reason* that most of us chatter so much *is not because* [read *that*] we suppose ourselves more competent than counsel." Charles E. Wyzanski Jr., "A Trial Judge," in *Whereas—A Judge's Premises* 3, 3 (1965).
- "The *reason* why words are so important *is because* [read *is that*] words are the vehicle of thought." Lord Denning, *The Discipline of Law* 5 (1979). (Better yet, delete *The reason why . . . is*: *Words are important because they are the vehicle of thought.*)
- "The *reason* for this standard *is because* [read *is that*] only the trier of fact can be aware of the variations in character and tone of voice that bear so deeply on the listener's understanding." *Kuebel v. Charvet's Garden Ctr., Inc.*, 30 So.3d 885, 895 (La. Ct. App. 2009).

Variations on the phrase, such as *reason . . . is due to*, are no better—e.g.:

- "The *reason* there is nothing but oral testimony *is due to* [omit *due to*] appellate counsel's failure to obtain a written waiver." *Coddington v. Langley*, 202 F.Supp.2d 687, 698 (E.D. Mich. 2002).
- "Part of the *reason is due to the fact that* [read *reason is that*] existing immigration restrictions are keeping people from receiving higher wages in foreign countries." Andrés Solimano, *International Migration in the Age of Crisis and Globalization* 57 (2010).

Although *reason is because* is bad English, it is not nearly as malodorous as *where . . . at*. See **where (D)**.

B. *Reason why* and *reason that*. Both forms are quite correct. It is an unfortunate SUPERSTITION that *reason why* is objectionable as a REDUNDANCY. True, it is mildly redundant—in the same way as *time when* and *place where*—but it has long been idiomatic, and good writers have long regarded the phrase as unimpeachable English—e.g.:

- "The *reason why* a lawyer does not mention that his client wore a white hat when he made a contract . . . is that he foresees that the public force will act in the same way whatever his client had upon his head." Oliver W. Holmes,

"The Path of the Law" (1897), in *Collected Legal Papers* 167, 168 (1952).

- "There is another *reason why* Austin's 'General Jurisprudence' cannot be called a philosophy." W.W. Buckland, *Some Reflections on Jurisprudence* 42 (1945).
- "There is no *reason why* the divorce should not be valid." Max Radin, *The Law and You* 65 (1948).
- "There are also various *reasons why* certain people may by rule be exempted from the normal workings of the criminal law." Morris R. Cohen, *Reason and Law* 51 (1961).
- "The other *reason why* we tend to relegate the fiction to the past lies in our failure to realize that the law will be faced, in the future, with essentially *new* situations." Lon L. Fuller, *Legal Fictions* 94 (1967).
- "Packer captured the *reason why* the humanitarian focus is erroneous." Peter W. Low et al., *Criminal Law: Cases and Materials* 26 (1982).
- "The *reason why* the other is not liable is that he is an undisclosed principal." G.H. Treitel, *The Law of Contract* 634 (8th ed. 1991).
- "The *reason why* this and other mitigating evidence was unavailable is that respondent's counsel failed to conduct a constitutionally adequate investigation." *Schriro v. Landrigan*, 550 U.S. 465, 482 (2007) (Stevens, J., dissenting).
- "There are numerous *reasons why* this counterintuitive theory is unsound." *Christian Legal Soc'y v. Martinez*, 130 S.Ct. 2971, 2996 (2010) (Stevens, J., concurring).

Moreover, *reason that* is often a poor substitute—as in any of the examples just quoted—just as *time that* and *place that* are poor substitutes when adverbials of time and place are called for. But cf. the indefensible REDUNDANCY in (A).

C. And *basis*. See **basis (A)**.

*reasonability. See **reasonableness**.

reasonable; rational. Generally, *reasonable* means "according to reason," while *rational* means "having reason." Yet *reasonable* is often used in reference to persons in the sense "having the faculty of reason" <reasonable person>. When applied to things, the two words are perhaps more clearly differentiated: "In application to things *reasonable* and *rational* both signify according to *reason*; but the former is used in reference to the business of life, as a *reasonable* proposal, wish, etc.; *rational* to abstract matters, as *rational* motives, grounds, questions, etc." George Crabb, *Crabb's English Synonymes* 589 (John H. Finley ed., 2d ed. 1917).

reasonable doubt, beyond a. See **balance of probability**.

reasonable efforts. See **best efforts**.

reasonable man. See **reasonable person**.

reasonable-minded is prolix for *reasonable*—e.g.:

- "Second, the Court says that the intrusion was not a serious one because a *reasonable-minded* [read *reasonable*] citizen would in fact want to be present at a search of his house unless he was fleeing to avoid arrest." *Michigan v. Summers*, 452 U.S. 692, 711 n.4 (1981) (Stewart, J., dissenting).
- "We will uphold the verdict if there is any interpretation of the evidence that could lead a *reasonable-minded* [read

reasonable] jury to find the defendant guilty beyond a reasonable doubt." *U.S. v. Cole*, 525 F.3d 656, 661 (8th Cir. 2008).

See REDUNDANCY.

reasonableness; *reasonability. The second is a NEEDLESS VARIANT.

reasonable person. Most modern American opinions refer to a *reasonable person* instead of a *reasonable man*, the age-old sexist standard, which Lord Radcliffe called "the anthropomorphic conception of justice." *Davis Contractors Ltd. v. Fareham U.D.C.*, [1956] A.C. 696, 728. (See SEXISM (B).) The reasonable person—a hypothetical legal standard—acts sensibly, takes proper but not excessive precautions, does things without serious delay, and weighs evidence carefully but not overskeptically. The reasonable person, being neither perfect nor indifferent, has been termed "a psychological tour de force." Edward Stevens Robinson, *Law and the Lawyers* 212 (1935).

When the locution functions as a PHRASAL ADJECTIVE, it should be hyphenated—e.g.: "If Parliament had intended to require people to live up to the objective, *reasonable-man standard* it would surely have said so." Glanville Williams, *Criminal Law* 145 (2d ed. 1961).

reasonable wear and tear. See **wear and tear**.

rebellion. See **coup d'état**.

rebound; re-bound. See RE- PAIRS.

rebuke. See **reprove**.

rebus, in. See **in rem**.

rebut. See **disprove**.

rebuttable presumption (= a legal presumption subject to valid rebuttal) becomes illogical when the phrase is turned into an adverb and a verb, so avoid, e.g., **presume rebuttably* and **rebuttably presume* and stick to the standard phrase—e.g.: "We also adopt a *rebuttable presumption* that a release benefits only those specifically designated." *Podraza v. New Century Physicians*, 789 N.W.2d 260, 268 (Neb. 2010).

rebuttal; *surrebuttal. *Rebuttal* (= the act of rebutting) is often used in legal writing, and with good reason: it is much broader than *rebutter*, which is the name of the pleading intended to rebut. See **rebutter**.

*Surrebuttal is not an answer to a rebuttal; it is a NEEDLESS VARIANT of *surrebutter*, a common-law pleading. See COMMON-LAW PLEADINGS.

rebutter = (1) (formerly) a defendant's answer to a plaintiff's surrejoinder; the pleading that followed the rejoinder and surrejoinder, and that might in turn be answered by the surrebutter; or (2) one who rebuts. Sense 1 is the only strictly legal sense of the term. See -ER (B) & COMMON-LAW PLEADINGS.

recant. See **abjure (A)**.

receipt, as a verb, began as an Americanism in the 18th century and has now spread to BrE. It is commercialese, but there is no grammatical problem in writing "The bill must be *receipted*" or "The sale was *receipted*." *Receipt* is ordinarily used in the PASSIVE VOICE—e.g.:

- "The addressee will not be permitted to examine the contents of a COD parcel until it has *been receipted for* and all charges are paid." *United States Postal Guide* 103 (1913).
- "The signature log maintained by The Post Box showed that various packages had been *receipted for* by 'Captain N.'" *U.S. v. Garces*, 32 M.J. 345, 347 (Ct. Military App. 1991).

Still, *to be receipted for* is a graceless phrase—e.g.: "Property so seized shall *be receipted for* by such officer who shall . . . sign the receipt." *Joe Flynn Rare Coins, Inc. v. Stephan*, 526 F.Supp. 1275, 1283 (D. Kan. 1981). [A suggested revision: *The officer must sign and deliver a receipt for the seized property.*] Cf. **receiptor.**

receipt and sufficiency of which are hereby acknowledged. This recital, common in contractual language, is almost always unnecessary and unhelpful. And when *is* appears instead of *are*, it is ungrammatical.

receipt of, be in. This insipid phrase, which usually occurs in letters, is to be avoided as OFFICIALESE or commercialese or LEGALESE.

receiptor (= [1] a person who receipts property attached by a sheriff; or [2] a bailee) is noted as being an Americanism by the *OED*. It dates from the early 19th century. The *-or* spelling is preferred to *-er*. See **receipt.**

receivables (= debts owed to a business and regarded as assets) began in the mid-19th century as an Americanism but is now current in BrE as well. It is the antonym of *payables*. See ADJECTIVES (C).

receive. See **reception.**

receiver is used in both AmE and BrE in the specific legal sense of "a person appointed by a court, or by a corporation or other person, for the protection or collection of property." Usually the *receiver* administers the property of a bankrupt, or property that is the subject of litigation, pending the outcome of a lawsuit.

receivership. See **insolvency (A).**

recense. See **revise.**

recension (= the revision of a text) is not to be confused with *rescission*. (See **rescission.**) E.g.: "The *recension* of statute law is not only destructive but constructive when it takes the form of codifying and consolidating acts." Carleton K. Allen, *Law in the Making* 476 (7th ed. 1964).

reception is the term commonly used to denote the adoption of an existing legal system originally developed elsewhere. E.g.:

- "It is more remarkable that this revived Justinian law should find a similar *reception* in Germany." James Hadley, *Introduction to Roman Law* 38 (1881).
- "Despite the efforts of early law reformers, all of the original states, and most of the later ones, adopted English common law insofar as it was deemed applicable to local conditions. This '*reception*' of the common law, as it came to be called, was accomplished either by express statutory or constitutional provision or by judicial decision." Peter W. Low et al., *Criminal Law: Cases and Materials* 40 (1982).

The corresponding verb, *receive*, is commonly used in an analogous sense—e.g.:

- "According to a theory [that] was popular half a century ago, the Canon Law of the Western Church was, even before the Reformation, not regarded as wholly binding on the ecclesiastical courts in England, but only to the extent to which it was '*received*' or acknowledged by courts in England." Edward Jenks, *The Book of English Law* 30 (P.B. Fairest ed., 6th ed. 1967).
- "To this day, an occasional case still turns on whether some statute or doctrine had been '*received*' as common law in this or that state." Lawrence M. Friedman, *A History of American Law* 111 (2d ed. 1985).

receptioning (= to do the job of a receptionist) is American law-firm cant that illustrates the same tendency in modern usage as *paralegaling* and *bailiffing*. See NOUNS AS VERBS.

recidivate is a formal equivalent of *relapse, backslide, fall back into crime*, or *rape (etc.) again*. As an intransitive verb, it takes no direct object <the possibility that he might recidivate is remote>. Invented in the early 1500s, it fell into disuse toward the end of the following century, but 20th-century legal writers revived it—e.g.:

- "Dr. Bohn would not testify to a reasonable degree of medical or psychological certainty that there was a substantial likelihood Tweedy would *recidivate*." *In re Tweedy*, 488 N.W.2d 528, 532 (Neb. 1992).
- "The trial court . . . should consider . . . the base rate statistics for violent behavior among individuals of this person's background (e.g., data showing the rate at which rapists *recidivate*, the correlation between age and criminal sexual activity, etc.)." *In re Linehan*, 518 N.W.2d 609, 614 (Minn. 1994).
- "The court emphasized Kreitinger's 'serious criminal history of financial frauds' and found that she was 'extremely' likely to '*recidivate*.'" *U.S. v. Kreitinger*, 576 F.3d 500, 504 (8th Cir. 2009).

recidivous; recidivist. The first is the preferred adjective. The second is the noun meaning "one who habitually relapses into crime" (*OED*).

reciprocity; reciprocation. *Reciprocity* = (1) the state of being reciprocal; or (2) the mutual concession of advantages or privileges for purposes of commercial, diplomatic, or other relations. *Reciprocation* = the action of doing something in return. Though *reciprocity* is by far the more common term, some legal writers use *reciprocation* erroneously in its place, especially in sense 2: "Neither statute requires a *reciprocation* [read *reciprocity*] of the regional limitation." *Northeast Bancorp, Inc. v. Federal Reserve Sys.*, 472 U.S. 159, 175 (1985) (per Rehnquist, J.). See **mutual.**

*recision; *recission. See **rescission.**

recital; recitation. These words overlap but are distinguishable. The drafting term is *recital*, referring to the preliminary statement in a deed or contract explaining the background of the transaction and showing the existence of facts, or, in pleading, introducing a positive allegation. E.g.:

- "The *recitals* also lay out the revised per-share price that should have applied . . . to achieve the intended minority interest." *Curia v. Nelson*, 587 F.3d 824, 827 (7th Cir. 2009).
- "It is questionable as to whether this argument is even preserved, because it is developed to some extent in the *recitation* [read *recital*] of facts, but not in the argument section of the brief." *Milanouic v. Holder*, 591 F.3d 566, 570 (7th Cir. 2010). The *as to* in this sentence is superfluous. See **as to.**

More generally, *recital* may mean "a rehearsal, account, or description of some thing, fact, or incident"—e.g.: "The *recitals* in the warrant affidavit [are] strong evidence that Lanpher believed that Schiele had identified one of his attackers." *Morris v. Lanpher*, 563 F.3d 399, 403 (8th Cir. 2009).

Recitation often connotes an oral delivery before an audience, whether in the classroom or on stage. Yet it is more often the general noun meaning "the act of reciting"—e.g.:

- "*West Virginia State Board of Education v. Barnette* . . . struck down compulsory *recital* [read *recitation*] of the secular Pledge of Allegiance as it then existed." Douglas Laycock, *Theology Scholarships, the Pledge of Allegiance, and Religious Liberty*, 118 Harv. L. Rev. 155, 229 (2004).
- "The jury . . . began a *recitation* of its verdicts that started with a response of 'hung' as to the first charge." *Whitfield v. State*, 867 A.2d 168, 175 (Del. 2004).

reckless. See **wanton.** For an interesting error, see ***wreckless.**

recklessness. In legal contexts, this term is used with several gradations of meaning, but the primary emerging sense is that recklessness occurs when the actor does not desire the consequence but foresees the possibility and consciously takes the risk. Another term for *recklessness* is *advertent negligence*. Cf. **carelessness.**

reckon (= to count or compute) is an ARCHAISM. E.g.: "Petitioner *reckons* that of the 76-month sentence for the 1992 convictions, 36 months are attributable to the sentencing enhancement and 40 months are attributable to the substantive offenses." *Saravia-Paguada v. Gonzales*, 488 F.3d 1122, 1126 n.6 (9th Cir. 2007). The word is dialectal in the sense "to suppose, think" <I reckon the judges will affirm>.

reclaim; re-claim. See RE- PAIRS.

recognizance; reconnaissance; *reconnoisance. *Recognizance* = a bond or obligation, made in court, by which a person (called the *recognizor*) promises to perform some act or observe some condition (as to appear when called on, to pay a debt, or to keep the peace). E.g.: "The judge may either set bail, remand the defendant, or release her on her own *recognizance*." Josh Bowers, *Punishing the Innocent*, 156 U. Pa. L. Rev. 1117, 1132 (2008).

In BrE, the *-g-* in *recognisance* (as it is usually spelled in BrE) is silent, reflecting that the current spelling is really only a latter-day Latinization of the spelling of the LAW FRENCH term **conusance*. But in AmE, the *-g-* is regularly sounded.

Reconnaissance = a preliminary survey; a military or intelligence-gathering examination of a region. **Reconnoisance* is an older spelling of *reconnaissance*; it is also a NEEDLESS VARIANT of *recognizance* and of *recognition*. The verb corresponding to *reconnaissance* is *reconnoiter, -re.* See **cognizance (A), reconnoiter** & **-ER (C).**

recollect. A. And *remember*. The distinction is a subtle one worth observing. To *remember* is to recall what is ready at hand in one's memory. To *recollect* is to find something stored further back in the mind.

B. And *re-collect*. See RE- PAIRS.

*recommend against. *Recommend* is a word with positive connotations; in all the examples in the *OED*, it is construed with *to*. The antonym of *recommend* is *discommend*, which should appear in place of **recommend against* in the following sentence: "The faculty members voted sixteen to three to *recommend against* [read *discommend*] promoting Qamhiyah." *Qamhiyah v. Iowa State Univ. of Sci. & Tech.*, 566 F.3d 733, 738 (8th Cir. 2009). See **discommend.**

*recompensable is a NEEDLESS VARIANT of *compensable*—e.g.: "They have failed to establish a valid basis for penalizing Defendants with the denial or reduction of their otherwise *recompensable* [read *compensable*] costs." *In re Williams Secs. Litig. WCG Subclass*, 558 F.3d 1144, 1151 (10th Cir. 2009). See **compensable (A).**

recompense. A. Generally. This word, both a transitive verb ("to repay, compensate") and a noun ("payment in return for something"), is a FORMAL WORD that is equivalent to but more learned than *compensate* or *compensation*. In BrE the noun is sometimes spelled *-ce.*

Recompense is used more frequently as a noun than as a verb—e.g.:

- "For students who are the victims of peer harassment, a variety of means (failing formal resolution) exist to ameliorate the abusive environment or to seek *recompense* for injuries." Gail Sorenson, *Peer Sexual Harassment*, 92 Ed. Law Rep. 1, 16 (1994).
- "I conclude that a 'reasonable fee' means not the reasonableness of the agreed-upon contingent fee, but a reasonable *recompense* for the work actually done." *Gisbrecht v. Barnhart*, 535 U.S. 789, 811 (2002) (Scalia, J., dissenting).

Although *compensate* is a much more common verb than *recompense*, the latter does frequently appear—more commonly in law than elsewhere. E.g.:

- "It is possible to find exceptions, to be sure: a famous author tells a dunce tale at the expense of an industrial worker who loses a finger by accident, is *recompensed*, and decides to lose another." Richard Delgado & Jean Stefancic, *Scorn*, 35 Wm. & Mary L. Rev. 1061, 1092 (1994).
- "The government has never been *recompensed* for the money that George Gilley fraudulently obtained from it." *U.S. v. Goforth*, 465 F.3d 730, 732 (6th Cir. 2006).

See **pay** & **compensate (B)**.

B. And Its Needless Variants. Both as a noun and as a verb, *recompense* has its NEEDLESS VARIANTS. The variant noun is **recompensation*—e.g.:

- "Also, the trial court awarded Travelers $70,330.78 in *recompensation* [read *compensation*]." *Scamardo v. New Orleans Stevedoring Co.*, 595 So.2d 1242, 1245 (La. Ct. App. 1992).
- "To the extent that the participants or beneficiaries would seek *recompensation* [read *recompense* or *compensation*] for medical benefits paid, the Funds assert a subrogation claim in their thirteenth cause of action." *Eastern States Health & Welfare Fund v. Phillip Morris, Inc.*, 729 N.Y.S.2d 240, 244 (Sup. Ct. 2000).

The needless verb is **recompensate*—e.g.: "Dragt undertook to hold the property for development by DeTray and to *recompensate* [read *recompense* or *compensate*] DeTray for his capital contributions." *Dragt v. Dragt/DeTray, LLC*, 161 P.3d 473, 480 (Wash. Ct. App. 2007).

C. And Its Near-Synonyms in the Noun Sense "pay." See **pay,** n.

recompensive (= compensatory) is a rare term whose use in modern prose strikes the reader as a straining for the recherché term.

reconnaissance; *reconnoisance. See **recognizance.**

reconnoiter; reconnoitre. The verb form corresponding to the noun *reconnaissance* is preferably spelled *-er* in AmE and *-re* in BrE. See **recognizance.**

record. A. Usage and Sense. Although *record* frequently refers to an official court report, it also has a much broader meaning: "[a *record*] is a written memorial made by a public officer, authorized by law to perform that function, and intended to serve as evidence of something written, said, or done." George W. Warvelle, *A Practical Treatise on Abstracts and Examinations of Title to Real Property* 68 (3d ed. 1907). So the term includes everything from a legislative act to a transcript of judicial proceedings to an enrolled deed. For more on *record* and its near-synonyms, see **document.**

Record has come to be used adjectivally as shorthand for *in the record*. E.g.: "In the final analysis, then, there is no *record support* for a prima facie case of discrimination against the Hispanic juror." *Gray v. Brady,*

592 F.3d 296, 305 (1st Cir. 2010). It is preferable not to collapse the prepositional phrase into a nominal adjective in this way because some readers will likely have a MISCUE. See NOUN PLAGUE.

B. And *transcript; report of proceedings; statement of facts*. Generally, a *transcript* or *report of proceedings* is an official copy of the recorded proceedings in a trial or hearing. The Texas rules of appellate procedure define two types of record. The *reporter's record* is synonymous with *report of proceedings* or *transcript*. The *clerk's record* contains all documents filed with the clerk of the court. Tex. R. App. P. 34.5, 34.6. See **report of proceedings.**

C. *In the record; on the record*. What is the difference? The distinction proved significant in Supreme Court oral arguments on 9 November 2010: something *on the record* has been transcribed by a court reporter, usually in open court, at the direction of the judge. Something *in the record* has been incorporated in the papers that pertain to a lawsuit, whether transcribed, supplemented by affidavit, or otherwise filed and kept with the documents that are sent to an appellate court for review. Hence *in the record* is the broader term.

D. BrE Pronunciation. In British legal English, the noun *record* "is pronounced like the verb, with the stress on the second syllable." Glanville Williams, *Learning the Law* 63 (11th ed. 1982).

recordation; *recordal. The second is not a proper word, though it has erroneously appeared in such phrases as "*recordal* of a trademark with the Treasury Department." *Recordation* is the word. E.g.: "The supplemental complaint requests that both the Customs Service and Art's Way remove the *recordal* [read *recordation*] of the DION registration to permit unimpeded entry of the machinery into the United States." *B. & R. Choiniere Ltd. v. Art's-Way Mfg. Co.*, 207 U.S.P.Q. (BNA) 969, 971 (N.D.N.Y. 1979).

recorder = (1) in BrE, a practicing barrister who acts as a usu. part-time judge, esp. in a crown court; or (2) in AmE, a person with whom a deed or mortgage to be recorded is deposited.

record reveals that, the. This phrase is responsible for more sprawling sentences than perhaps any other stock phrase in appellate judicial opinions. And it is redundant: any facts being related by an appellate court *must* (with a few exceptions) be revealed in the record.

recount; re-count. See RE- PAIRS.

recourse; resort. *Recourse* = (1) application to a person or entity for help; or (2) the right of a holder of a negotiable instrument to demand payment from the drawer and indorsers when the first liable party fails to pay. The term is used in the idiomatic phrases *have recourse to* and *without recourse*. The latter is the peculiarly legal phrase that, when added to the indorsement of commercial paper, protects the indorser from liability to the indorsee and later holders. *Resort* (= that which one turns to for refuge or aid) is closely related to sense 1 of *recourse*.

recover (= to secure by legal process) takes *from* or *against* in modern usage. The collocation *recover of is an ARCHAISM for *recover from*. E.g.:

- "If the plaintiff can *recover of* [read *recover from*] these defendants upon this cause of action, then a customer of his, who was injured by the delay occasioned by the stopping of his work, could also recover from them." *Lowe's Home Ctr., Inc. v. Gen. Elec. Co.*, 381 F.3d 1091, 1095 (11th Cir. 2004).
- "IDX shall *recover of* [read *recover from*] Leon its costs on appeal." *Leon v. IDX Sys. Corp.*, 464 F.3d 951, 963 (9th Cir. 2006).

Cf. **of (E).**

recoverable = compensable. The term originally meant "capable of being recovered or regained," but was extended in legal usage, because of the nature of damages, to "capable of being legally obtained." E.g.: "The Carmack Amendment has not changed the common-law rule that special damages are usually not *recoverable* in a breach of contract action." *Spray-Tek, Inc. v. Robbins Motor Transp., Inc.*, 426 F.Supp.2d 875, 886 (W.D. Wis. 2006). Strictly speaking, the special damages are not to be *recovered*, for they are being awarded for the first time to the complainant; but this usage is quite permissible in the legal idiom. See **compensable.**

recover back might appear to be a legal REDUNDANCY. E.g.: "If one, by fraud procures a sham bid on his property . . . [the] injured party may *recover back* the sum so lost by him in the sale of his property, or the sum realized by the other, with interest." 12 *American Law Register* 267 (2010).

But in common-law terminology a distinction exists between *to recover* (= to obtain, as in recovering damages) and *to recover back* (= to secure the return of, as in recovering back money paid incorrectly, as by mistake). E.g.: "Once the plaintiff has rescinded, he is entitled to *recover back* what he gave under the contract." *Griggs v. E.I. DuPont de Nemours & Co.*, 385 F.3d 440, 446 (4th Cir. 2004).

***recover of.** See **recover.**

recreate; re-create. The first means either "(of a pastime or relaxation) to refresh or agreeably occupy" or "to amuse oneself, indulge in recreation" (*COD*); the second means "to create anew." The hyphen makes a great difference—e.g.:

- "Allowing these claims to go forward will *re-create* a loophole for abusive securities litigation that Congress intended, through SLUSA, to close." *LaSala v. Bordier et Cie*, 519 F.3d 121, 142 (3d Cir. 2008).
- "While post-enforcement judicial review can mimic these features, it cannot fully *recreate* [read *re-create*] them." David L. Franklin, *Legislative Rules, Nonlegislative*

Rules and the Perils of the Short Cut, 120 Yale L.J. 276, 317 (2010).

See RE- PAIRS.

recreational; ***recreative.** The first is the preferred adjective corresponding to the noun *recreation*. E.g.: "During this additional time the employees variously slept, ate, played cards or engaged in other *recreative* [read *recreational*] activities." *Madera Police Officers' Ass'n v. City of Madera*, 194 Cal. Rptr. 648, 651 (Ct. App. 1983).

recrimination. Today, *recrimination* is used mainly in criminal law in the sense "an accused person's counteraccusation against the accuser." The accusation may be for the same or a different offense—e.g.: "In many simple assault situations, there are bound to be accusations and *recriminations* based either on the immediate circumstances or the parties' long-term relationship." *Holder v. Town of Sandown*, 585 F.3d 500, 506 (1st Cir. 2009).

Historically, in a divorce suit, *recrimination* was a countercharge that the complainant was guilty of an offense constituting a ground for divorce. When both parties to the marriage committed marital misconduct that would be grounds for divorce, neither could obtain a fault divorce. *Recriminations* are now virtually obsolete because of the prevalence of no-fault divorce. See **collusion, connivance** & **condonation.**

recriminatory; ***recriminative.** The second is a NEEDLESS VARIANT.

rectification = a court's equitable correction of a contractual term that is misstated, as where the rent is wrongly recorded in a lease or the area of land is recited incorrectly in a deed. To a degree, this term applies also to statutory construction—e.g.: "It would be a mistake to suppose that the Courts never indulge in milder acts of *rectification*. Something of the sort happens whenever 'and' is read as 'or' or vice versa; but these milder acts of *rectification* are most exceptional." Rupert Cross, *Statutory Interpretation* 25 (1976).

recur; reoccur. To *recur* is to happen over and over, esp. at irregular intervals. To *reoccur* is to happen again.

recurrence; ***recurrency; reoccurrence.** *Recurrence* is the preferred form, *reoccurrence* being a secondary variant meriting only careful avoidance. *Recurrency is a NEEDLESS VARIANT.

recusal; recusation; recusement; recusancy; ***recusance.** The preferred noun form of the verb *recuse* (= to remove [oneself] as a judge considering a case) is *recusal*, though its earliest known use is as recent as 1950: "On the 13th of April, Judge Longshore filed an order of *recusal* accompanied by an order vacating his former order." *Methvin v. Haynes*, 46 So.2d 815, 817 (Ala. 1950).

Recusation and *recusement* (the latter not listed in the *OED*) are now NEEDLESS VARIANTS in common-law contexts. *Recusation* is not uncommon, especially in civil-law writing. *See, e.g., State v. DeMaio*, 58 A. 173 (N.J. 1904); *Stewart v. Reid*, 38 So. 70 (La. 1905). Although *recusation* is understandably common in Louisiana, it persists, oddly, in other jurisdictions. E.g.:

- "Canon 3C(1)(a) is basically a broad standard by which a judge should sua sponte determine the matter of *self-recusation* [read *recusal*]." *State v. Smith*, 242 N.W.2d 320, 323 (Iowa 1976). (See **sua sponte**.)
- "Once a prosecutor recuses himself, the *recusation* [read *recusal*] applies to all aspects of the case." *Daugherty v. State*, 466 N.E.2d 46, 49 (Ind. Ct. App. 1984).
- "The plaintiff asserts the 'essence' of his motion for *recusation* [read *recusal*] is what the trial justice 'himself said and how he has ruled.'" *Barber v. Town of Fairfield*, 486 A.2d 150, 152 (Me. 1985).
- "The trial judge admitted making these remarks upon defendant's motion for . . . continuance and *recusation* [read *recusal*]." *State v. Majors*, 325 S.E.2d 689, 690 (N.C. Ct. App. 1985).
- "Absent proof of personal bias requiring *recusation* [read *recusal*] . . . the principal factors considered by us in determining whether further proceedings should be conducted before a different judge [include] . . . whether reassignment would entail waste." *Armco, Inc. v. United Steelworkers of Am.*, 280 F.3d 669, 683 (6th Cir. 2002).

For an example of INELEGANT VARIATION with *recusal* and *recusation*, see *Reilly v. Southeastern Pa. Transp. Auth.*, 489 A.2d 1291, 1297–98 (Pa. 1985).

Recusement appears far less commonly—e.g.:

- "Plaintiff filed a challenge for Mr. Booker's *recusement* [read *recusal*] upon the ground that he had prejudged the case." *Cobble Close Farm v. Board of Adjustment*, 92 A.2d 4, 10 (N.J. 1952).
- "Following our opinion . . . , the Honorable Paul M. Marko . . . entered an order of *recusement* [read *recusal*] in the fall of 1982." *Irwin v. Irwin*, 455 So.2d 1118, 1119 (Fla. Dist. Ct. App. 1984).

Recusancy is a different word, meaning "obstinate refusal to comply." **Recusance* is a NEEDLESS VARIANT of *recusancy*.

recuse; disqualify. The two words are not quite interchangeable in modern legal usage. *Disqualify* might always be used in place of *recuse*, but the reverse does not hold true. *Disqualify*, the broader term, may be used of witnesses, for example, as well as of judges, whereas *recuse* is applied only to someone who sits in judgment (usually judges or jurors).

Recuse is almost invariably reflexive; that is, judges are said to *recuse themselves. Disqualify* may also be used reflexively <under these circumstances, the judge should disqualify herself from sitting in the case>. Just as commonly, though, lawyers use this verb nonreflexively <his years began to disqualify him from more active work>.

Recuse is by far the more interesting word, primarily because of its inadequate treatment in English-language dictionaries. Both *recuse* and its legal cognates are missing from *AHD* and were not included in Merriam-Webster dictionaries until the publication of *W10* (1993). The word might seem to be moribund in BrE, for the *Chambers 20th Century Dictionary* says: "to reject, object to (e.g. a judge) (arch.)." The sense of objecting to is fairly rare—e.g.: "[One-half of the plantation] with lien privilege to contribute to or *recuse* the contribution of the sum of [$7,347.30]." *Grant v. Buckner*, 172 U.S. 232, 237 (1898) (quoting trial-court decree).

How the word evolved from that sense of objecting, as reflected in the *OED*, to the modern sense is curious indeed. Today, when we say *recuse*, we almost always mean "to remove (oneself) as judge in a legal matter." The one exception appears to be the phrase *motion to recuse*, in which the meaning is "to seek to have (a judge) removed from participating in the adjudication of a legal matter." Hence we encounter specimens such as these:

- "This motion denied, the trustee moved to *recuse* the examiner for bias and prejudice." *N.L.R.B. v. Phelps*, 136 F.2d 562, 565 (5th Cir. 1943).
- "Motion to *recuse* the Chief Justice denied." *Kerpelman v. Attorney Grievance Comm'n*, 450 U.S. 970, 970 (Mem. Op.).
- "Motion to *recuse* Justice Powell denied." *Ernest v. United States Attorney*, 474 U.S. 1016, 1016 (Mem. Op.).

But these are the exceptions in modern usage. Today, 99% of the occurrences of *recuse* are reflexive.

How, then, did we get from (1) "to object to (a judge) as prejudiced" (*OED*) to (2) "to remove (oneself) as an adjudicator"? Surprisingly, the Supreme Court appears to have deprecated the newer meaning just after the turn of the 20th century, by enclosing the word in telltale quotation marks: "The plaintiffs, when the case was called for trial, filed a written motion or petition, challenging the right of the presiding judge to hear the case, and praying that he '*recuse*' himself." *McGuire v. Blount*, 199 U.S. 142, 143 (1905) (per Day, J.).

Yet a reporter of the Court's opinions had used the word in this sense more than a half-century before, in what appears to be the earliest use of the reflexive: "The judge *recused* himself, and the suit, by consent of the parties, was transferred for trial to the District Court." *Fourniquet v. Perkins*, 48 U.S. (7 How.) 160, 165 (1849) (reporter's rendition of appellant's argument).

In the 19th and early 20th centuries, the word was not at all common. In fact, a computer search reveals only 38 cases in which the uninflected verb *recuse* appeared before 1950, and 3,219 cases between 1950 and 1989. The paucity of uses before 1950 may explain the notation in *W2* that *recuse* is "obs. exc. in Civil and Canon Law."

Because *recuse* is virtually always reflexive today, it cannot be used in the PASSIVE VOICE, unlike *disqualify*. To say that a judge is *disqualified* is perfectly idiomatic, but to say one is *recused* is not.

When used reflexively, both verbs sometimes take an understood object. These are nothing more than lawyers' elliptical expressions—e.g.:

- "Had Black *disqualified*, he would have departed from the traditions of 150 years." John P. Frank, *Disqualification of Judges*, 56 Yale L.J. 605, 636 (1947).
- "Relief . . . for failure to *recuse* on the merits." 13A Charles Alan Wright et al., *Federal Practice and Procedure* § 3550, at 627 n.8 (1984).

recusement. See **recusal.**

redact. See **revise.**

redeemable; *redemptible. Eschew the second; it is pedantic, unnecessary, and irredeemable.

redemption, equity of. See **cloud on title.**

redemptive; *redemptory; redemptional. *Redemptive* = tending to redeem; redeeming. **Redemptory* is a NEEDLESS VARIANT. *Redemptional* = of or pertaining to redemption—e.g.: "Having been divested of ownership prior to the sale and having incurred penalties for delinquent non-payments which it has paid, its personal obligation for the *redemptional* penalty became a myth." *Weston Inv. Co. v. State*, 180 P.2d 962, 965 (Cal. Ct. App. 1947).

redhibition. Louisiana is the only American jurisdiction in which this civil-law term is used. It denotes the voidance of a sale as the result of an action brought on account of some defect in something sold, on grounds that the defect renders the thing sold either useless or so imperfect that the buyer would not have purchased it if the buyer had known of the defect. *Redhibitory* is the usual adjectival form.

redintegration. See **reintegration.**

redirect is a common shorthand form of *redirect examination*, which in American usage follows cross-examination. E.g.:

- "Often the attorney, in cross-examination of a witness, produces from him statements that create an impression favorable to his own client. If the impression is misleading, it may lodge in the minds of the jurors and become ineradicable unless corrected; to correct it, the opposing attorney may readdress additional questions to his own witness. This is called the *redirect*." C. Gordon Post, *An Introduction to the Law* 121 (1963).
- "On *redirect*, the Government inquired whether Lowe had any reason to try to protect himself." *U.S. v. Edwards*, 716 F.2d 822, 825 (11th Cir. 1983).
- "Several times, on direct and *redirect*, McLoren was asked, with varying specificity, what had spurred him to be more forthcoming with DDA Semow than when initially questioned by Detectives Tauson and Neumann." *Hein v. Sullivan*, 601 F.3d 897, 910 (9th Cir. 2010).

The equivalent BrE term is *re-examination*. See **re-examination.** Cf. **direct.**

redound, now used most commonly in the CLICHÉ *to redound to the benefit of* (which is verbose for *to benefit*), may also be used in negative senses <to redound against or to the shame of>.

redress. See **reparation.**

redressable; *redressible. The first spelling is standard.

red tape. Lawyers and government officials formerly used red ribbons (called "tapes") to tie together their papers. Gradually during the 19th century, these red ribbons came to symbolize rigid adherence to time-consuming rules and regulations. Writers such as Scott, Longfellow, and Dickens used the term *red tape*, and now it has become universal—but its origins are widely forgotten.

reduce should not be used as a reflexive verb when the subject is inanimate—e.g.:

- "The question *reduces itself* [read *is reducible* or *may be reduced*] to whether a private litigant has standing to instigate such enforcement in that court." *Lang v. French*, 154 F.3d 217, 222 (5th Cir. 1998).
- "This case *reduces itself* [read *is reducible*], therefore, to the proposition that a valid and binding oral contract existed between the parties." *Brooks & Co. Gen. Contractors v. Randy Robinson Contracting, Inc.*, 513 S.E.2d 858, 860 (Va. 1999).

REDUNDANCY. Washington Irving wrote that "redundancy of language is never found with deep reflection. Verbiage may indicate observation, but not thinking. He who thinks much says but little in proportion to his thoughts." Lawyers should think much about those words, and begin to write less. (See CUTTING OUT THE CHAFF.) Following are some of the typical manifestations of redundancy in legal writing.

A. General Redundancy. This linguistic pitfall is best exemplified, rather than discoursed on:

- "The mere fact that the association acquired its knowledge *later in point of time* [omit *in point of time*] gave the appellant no superior legal position over the association." *Goldman v. Harford Rd. Bldg. Ass'n*, 133 A. 843, 846 (Md. 1926).
- "This type of obligation imposes an undue restriction on alienation or an *onerous burden* in perpetuity." *Nicholson v. 300 Broadway Realty Corp.*, 164 N.E.2d 832, 835 (N.Y. 1959). Because *onus* = "burden," *onerous burden* is redundant.
- "These two paragraphs are the *least legible and the most difficult to read* [omit *and the most difficult to read*] in the instrument, but they are most important in the evaluation of the rights of the contesting parties." *Henningson v. Bloomfield Motors, Inc.*, 161 A.2d 69, 73 (N.J. 1960). In context, the sentence related exclusively to *legibility* and had nothing to do with *readability*.
- "At the outset, this court must state that it is not *adverse* [read *averse*,] as a matter of principle, to any *new innovations* [omit *new*] in expediting the just termination of litigation." *Perry v. Mohawk Rubber Co.*, 63 F.R.D. 603, 606 (D.S.C. 1974). On the misuse of *adverse* for *averse*, see **adverse.**
- "A woman with a permanent disability who claims she received a low *test* score for the law school entrance *exam test* because the *test*-givers wouldn't accommodate her has

sued them for emotional distress." Lauren Blau, *LSAT Target of Woman's Suit*, L.A. Daily J., 15 Nov. 1995, at 3. *Test* appears thrice, once in the redundant phrase *exam test*, quadrupling the pleonasm.

- "*Religious hymns* [read *Hymns*] were playing in the background." Jennifer Emily, *Documents: Mom Thanked God After Attack*, Dallas Morning News, 16 Dec. 2004, at B4.

See *while at the same time & oftentimes.

B. Awkward Repetitions. Samuel Johnson once advised his readers to "avoid ponderous ponderosity." The repetition of roots was purposeful, of course. Many legal writers, however, engage in such repetitions with no sense of irony, as in the phrases *build a building, refer to a reference, point out points, an individualistic individual*. As great a writer as he was, Chief Justice Marshall seems not to have had a stylistic design in the following repetition, though he may have been striving for a rhetorical effect: "The question is, *in truth, a question of supremacy* [read *is, in truth, one of supremacy*]." *McCulloch v. Maryland*, 17 U.S. 316, 433 (1819) (per Marshall, C.J.). In the sentences that follow, however, the repetitions are mere thoughtless errors:

- "The plaintiff's *number was number* [read *number was*] 37." *McCallister v. Patton*, 215 S.W.2d 701, 701 (Ark. 1948).
- "Notice was *mailed* [read *sent*] by registered mail." *State v. Rufenacht*, 754 P.2d 339, 340 (Ariz. Ct. App. 1988).
- "*This judicially required warrant requirement* [read *This judicial requirement of a warrant*] has been described as a 'narrow one.'" 1 L. Electronic Surveillance 3:52 (2010).
- "The resolution of the board of directors accepting property for shares must *specify the specific* [omit *specific*] property involved." 25 Mo. Prac. Code, Bus. Orgs. 13.10 (2010).

See *injunction enjoining.

C. Common Redundancies. Many of these are treated in separate entries. It is useful to be aware that phrases such as the following are redundant: *named nominee, adult parent* (but maybe this is no longer redundant), *to plead a plea, *cost-expensive, *active agent, *end result, *erroneous mistake, *integral part, past history* (arguably established), *connect up* or *together, *future forecast, *merge together, *mingle together, join together* (arguably acceptable), *mix together*. For idiomatic redundancies in the form of coupled synonyms, see DOUBLETS, TRIPLETS, AND SYNONYM-STRINGS.

redundancy pay. See **severance pay.**

reek; wreak. These homophones are occasionally confused. *Reek* = to give off an odor or vapor. As a noun, *reek* = an odorous vapor. *Wreak* = to inflict <to wreak havoc>.

reenactment is now written as a solid—without a hyphen after *re*. See PUNCTUATION (G).

reenforce. See **reinforce.**

reenter; reentry. Both terms are best not hyphenated.

reestablish should not be hyphenated.

re-examination, primarily a BrE term, is equivalent to the AmE term *redirect examination*. Following are examples of the noun and verb forms:

- "In *re-examination,* as in examination in chief, leading questions are ordinarily not permitted, unless they concern some matter not in dispute, when they are allowed in order to save time." Pendleton Howard, *Criminal Justice in England* 367 (1931).
- "Witnesses examined in open court must be first examined in chief, then cross-examined, and then *re-examined.*" (Eng.)

See **direct examination & redirect.**

refer. See **allude (A) & revert (A).**

referable; *referrable; *referible. The preferred form is *referable*, which is accented on the first syllable; otherwise, the final -*r* would be doubled. The sense is "capable of being referred to." E.g.: "We think [the district court] was referring to all of the 'other downward departures' sought by Stevens, and not just the one *referable* to the Bible studies, which is the next item that the Court took up." *U.S. v. Stevens*, 223 F.3d 239, 248 (3d Cir. 2000).

Referrable often mistakenly appears; the form is old, but has long been held inferior to *referable*. E.g.: "Mr. Yushuvayev also asserts . . . that 'there is no claim that he committed any overt act *referrable* [read *referable*] to such conspiracy.'" *Yushuvayev v. U.S.*, 532 F.Supp.2d 455, 475 n.23 (E.D.N.Y. 2008). *Referible* is a seldom-seen NEEDLESS VARIANT.

refer back is a common REDUNDANCY, *refer* alone nearly always being sufficient. E.g.:

- "We also will not address Cancel-Alegría's qualified immunity argument, which simply *refers back to* [read *refers to*] her misguided merits argument." *Mercado-Berrios v. Cancel-Alegria*, 611 F.3d 18, 28 n.10 (1st Cir. 2010).
- "The term *refers back to* [read *refers to*] the service discussed within the main body of the statute." *Sakarapanee v. Dep't of Homeland Sec.*, 616 F.3d 595, 599 (6th Cir. 2010).

Cf. **relate back.** See **return back & revert (B).**

Refer back may be justified in those rare instances in which it means "to send back to one who or that which has previously been involved"—e.g.: "This case is *referred back* to Magistrate Judge McCarthy for further proceedings." *U.S. v. Mason*, 660 F.Supp.2d 479, 480 (W.D.N.Y. 2009).

reference, n. See **allude (A) & referral.**

reference, as a verb meaning "to provide with references," is defensible—e.g.:

- "We also find that, like the Harvard plan Justice Powell *referenced* [read *referred to*] in *Bakke*, the Law School's race-conscious admissions program adequately ensures that all factors that may contribute to student body diversity are meaningfully considered alongside race in admissions decisions." *Grutter v. Bollinger*, 539 U.S. 306, 337–38 (2003) (per O'Connor, J.).

- "Appellant's primary argument against this conclusion is that the district court improperly *referenced* the military court's discussion of the underlying facts of his conviction." *U.S. v. Whetzell*, 594 F.3d 624, 626 (8th Cir. 2010).

See NOUNS AS VERBS.

referendum. Pl. *-da, -dums.* The English plural *-dums* seems to be on the rise—e.g.:

- "[The] electorate has occasionally taken matters into its own hands, through ballot initiatives or *referendums*." *Vieth v. Jubelirer*, 541 U.S. 267, 363 (2004) (Breyer, J., dissenting).
- "[They] also supported the Washington constitutional amendment establishing initiatives and *referendums* and sponsored the 1934 blanket primary initiative." *Washington St. Grange v. Washington St. Republican Party*, 552 U.S. 442, 446 n.2 (2008) (per Thomas, J.).

See PLURALS (A) & **mandate** (B).

*referrable. See **referable.**

referral; reference. Both mean "the act of referring." *Reference* is the broader, general term. *Referral*, which began as an Americanism in the early 20th century but now is used commonly in BrE as well, means specifically "the referring to a third party of personal information concerning another" or "the referring of a person to an expert or specialist for advice."

reflection; reflexion. The first spelling is preferred in both AmE and BrE. *Reflexion* was formerly common in British writing. H.W. Fowler recommended *-ction* in all senses (*MEU1* 489).

reform, n.; **reformation.** Both terms denote an amelioration or improvement. But *reform* is more minute and particular, referring to any single attempt to make things better, whether by a measure intended to curb corrupt practices or an amendment to cure a flawed statute. *Reformation*, by contrast, is a more abstract term denoting an entire movement for change, especially when that change is intended for the improvement of morality, religion, or the general polity.

reform, vb.; **re-form.** See RE- PAIRS.

reformation. See **reform,** n.

refoulement /ri-**fowl**-mənt/ is a French term meaning "expulsion or return of a refugee from one state to another where his or her life or liberty would be threatened." It originally appeared as a title for Article 33 of the 1951 Geneva Convention Relating to the Status of Refugees, which reads: "No contracting state shall expel or return ('*refouler*') a refugee in any manner whatsoever to the frontiers of territories where his life or freedom would be threatened." (*See Lin v. Rinaldi*, 361 F.Supp. 177, 183 (D.N.J. 1973).) The title of that article of the Convention, *Refoulement*, is enclosed in quotation marks, no doubt signifying that in 1951 it was taken as a foreign word.

Its earliest known use as an English term, in the negative form, appears in *Chun v. Sava*, 708 F.2d 869, 877 n.25 (2d Cir. 1983): "The United States appears to recognize a liberty interest, the right of *nonrefoulement* for a refugee." *See also Ramirez-Osorio v. I.N.S.*, 745 F.2d 937, 944 (5th Cir. 1984) ("There is a sufficiently secured right of *nonrefoulement . . .* to give rise to a protectible liberty interest"). The word is yet to be recorded in an English dictionary.

refractory; refractive. These terms have undergone DIFFERENTIATION. *Refractory* = stubborn, unmanageable, rebellious. E.g.: "The estate given [to] the *refractory* legatee by the will was held for the purpose of indemnifying the disappointed legatee." *Sellick v. Sellick*, 173 N.W. 609, 611 (Mich. 1919). *Refractive* = that refracts light.

refrain; restrain. Both mean generally "to put restraints upon," but *refrain* is used in reference to oneself in the sense "to abstain" <he refrained from exchanging scurrilities with his accuser>, whereas *restrain* is used of another <the police illegally restrained the complainant from going into the stadium>.

refugee. See **asylee** (B).

refuse. See **deny** (A) & **decline.**

refutation; *refutal. The second is an ill-formed NEEDLESS VARIANT of *refutation*. It is hardly ubiquitous, but it has turned up in some unlikely places—e.g.:

- "An evaluation is not subject to complete objective confirmation or *refutal* [read *refutation*]." *U.S. v. Jones*, 856 F.2d 146, 151 (11th Cir. 1988).
- "[A given book discusses] criticisms of Savigny's ideals and present[s] selected *refutals* [read *refutations*] by Savigny." Stephen A. Siegel, Lochner *Era Jurisprudence and the American Constitutional Tradition*, 70 N.C. L. Rev. 1, 76 n.384 (1991).
- "The railroad's wholesale *refutal* [read *refutation*] thereof notwithstanding, the parties have failed to present any evidence on this factual issue." *McGraw v. Norfolk & W. Ry.*, 500 S.E.2d 300, 309 n.9 (W. Va. 1997).

refutative; *refutatory. The second is a NEEDLESS VARIANT.

refute. See **disprove.**

regard. A. As a Noun in the Phrases *with regard to* and *in regard to*. These two phrases are correct, but the forms **with regards to* and **in regards to* are, to put it charitably, poor usages—e.g.: "*With regards to* [read *With regard to*] the Defendant's second assertion, that the officers exceeded the scope of his consent because he was not 'present' during their search of the room, this argument is unpersuasive as well." *U.S. v. Hicks*, 631 F.Supp.2d 725, 737 (E.D.N.C. 2009). The acceptable forms are best used as introductory phrases. Usually, however, they may advantageously be replaced by some simpler phrase such as *concerning, regarding,* *considering*, or even the simple prepositions *in*, *about*, or *for*.

The plural form, *regards*, is acceptable only in the phrase *as regards*. In other words, *with regards to is bad form—e.g.:

- "He became furious at the mere mention of George F. Will, the columnist who accused him recently of 'judicial exhibitionism' *with regards to* [read *with regard to*] his trade-agreement ruling." Ruth M. Bond, *At Center of Trade-Accord Storm, Judge Bristles but Watches Image*, N.Y. Times, 17 Sept. 1993, at B11.
- "Newton contends he was denied procedural due process both *with regards to* [read *with regard to*] his ATCS certificate and his employment, and that those constitutional violations preclude qualified immunity." *Newton v. Utah Nat'l Guard*, 688 F.Supp.2d 1290, 1305 (D. Utah 2010).

See **as regards**, ***in regards to** & **respect**.

B. As a Verb in the Phrases *highly regarded* and *widely regarded*. The verb *regard* commonly appears in these two combinations. The one phrase, *highly regarded*, is a vague expression of praise; the other, *widely regarded as* ——, usually ends (i.e., the blank is usually filled) with words of praise—though it would certainly be possible to say that someone is *widely regarded as beneath contempt*. It is a mistake, however, to truncate the latter phrase—to say *widely regarded* in place of *highly regarded*—e.g.: "The most *widely regarded* [read *highly regarded*] proposal for tackling tropical deforestation is the Compensated Reductions Plan." Randall S. Abate & Todd A. Wright, *A Green Solution to Climate Change*, 20 Duke Envtl. L. & Pol'y F. 87, 106 (2010).

regardless. A. And *irregardless. *Irregardless, a semiliterate PORTMANTEAU WORD from *irrespective* and *regardless*, should long ago have been stamped out. *Irregardless is common enough in speech in the U.S. that it has found its way into judicial opinions. *See, e.g., State ex rel. Fisher v. McKinney*, 85 N.E.2d 562, 563 (Ohio Ct. App. 1949).

On the second day of the U.S. Supreme Court's 1986–1987 term, Chief Justice Rehnquist upbraided a lawyer who used *irregardless, saying: "I feel bound to inform you there is no word *irregardless* in the English language. The word is *regardless*." Linguistic fastidiousness is no less important in oral than in written argument.

In American legal writing, most of the published examples of *irregardless appear in quoted testimony, in which the word is followed by "[*sic*]" in three of every four instances. Of the handful of published examples that originated in a federal judge's writing—as opposed to originating as oral statements that are later quoted—a third appear in a single Illinois judge's opinions.

Although this widely scorned word seems unlikely to spread and flourish, careful users of language must continually stamp on it when they encounter it.

B. And *despite*. *Regardless* (= without regard to) should not be used for *despite* (= in spite of). E.g.: "The ICJ found that those named individuals were entitled to review and reconsideration of their U.S. state-court convictions and sentences *regardless of* [read *despite*] their failure to comply with generally applicable state rules governing challenges to criminal convictions." *Medellin v. Texas*, 552 U.S. 491, 491 syl. 1 (2008).

C. *Regardless whether. *Regardless* takes the preposition *of*. It is incorrect to write **regardless whether*—e.g.:

- "Our constitutional analysis of donations to and spending by nonconnected nonprofits applies *regardless whether* [read *regardless of whether*] a nonprofit has registered as a political committee with the FEC." *Emily's List v. Federal Election Comm'n*, 581 F.3d 1, 8 n.7 (D.C. Cir. 2009).
- "Aspects of U.S. patent law will be required to prove causation in this case *regardless whether* [read *regardless of whether*] it is adjudicated in the United States or Canada." *Touchcom, Inc. v. Bereskin & Parr*, 574 F.3d 1403, 1418 (Fed. Cir. 2009).

See **whether**.

regards. See **regard (A)** & **as regards**.

regard to, in; with regard to. See ***in regards to** & **regard (A)**.

Regina. See **R.**

register; registrar. Both terms refer to the governmental officer who keeps official records. The *OED* notes that *register* was commonly used in this sense from 1580 to 1800 and that *registrar* is now the usual word. But in AmE *register* retains vitality: various levels of government have *registers of deeds*, *registers of wills*, *registers of copyrights*, *registers of patents*, and the like. As a matter of AmE usage, a *registrar* is usually a school official, whereas a *register* is usually one who records documents for state or local government.

Apart from the agent-noun sense, the general meaning of *register* today is "a book or other record in which entries are made during the course of business." E.g.: "A *register* of the proprietors of patents is kept at the Patent Office, and all assignments, licences, amendments, and revocations must be entered therein." 2 Ernest W. Chance, *Principles of Mercantile Law* 160 (Percy W. French ed., 10th ed. 1951).

***registerable.** See **registrable**.

registrable, not *registerable, is the preferred spelling—e.g.:

- "Since 1925 restrictive covenants have been *registerable* [read *registrable*]." P.S. Atiyah, *An Introduction to the Law of Contract* 284 (3d ed. 1981).
- "Otherwise *registerable* [read *registrable*] marks do not acquire generic character by participating in electronic commerce." *In re Hotels.com*, 573 F.3d 1300, 1304 (Fed. Cir. 2009).

An asterisk (*) precedes words and phrases that are invariably inferior forms.

registrant /**rej**-i-strənt/ does not rhyme, in the final syllable, with *restaurant*—even though this mispronunciation is common with the Securities and Exchange Commission.

registrar. See **register.**

registrate is an ill-conceived BACK-FORMATION from *registration*, the verb *register* being standard—e.g.: "Sgt. L. Gaspard obtained a motor vehicle registration on a dark blue Dodge van . . . *registrated* [read *registered*] to Rex Racheau." *State v. Racheau*, 467 So.2d 544, 546 (La. Ct. App. 1984). It is true, however, that *registrate* is correctly used when denoting the setting of pipe-organ stops.

regress. See **egress.**

regretful; regrettable. Errors made are *regrettable*; the persons who have committed them, assuming a normal level of contrition, are *regretful*. But writers often misuse *regretful* for *regrettable*—e.g:

- "The psychiatrists all agreed that it was not likely that the appellant would have had a lucid moment on the date of this *regretful* [read *regrettable*] incident." *Harris v. State*, 648 S.W.2d 47, 50 (Ark. 1983) (Purtle, J., dissenting).
- "This is the fourth time the Court has sustained the imposition of the death penalty. *Regretfully* [read *Regrettably*], its decision does nothing to clarify the confusion or to harmonize the inconsistencies of the Court's capital-murder jurisprudence." *State v. DiFrisco*, 645 A.2d 734, 773 (N.J. 1994) (Handler, J., dissenting).
- "*Regretfully* [read *Regrettably*], a legislature is seldom called upon to decide between right and wrong." *State v. Gainer*, 447 S.E.2d 887, 897 (W. Va. 1994).

regulable = able to be regulated; susceptible to regulation. **Regulatable* is incorrect, but it does occasionally appear—e.g.: " 'Commercial speech' . . . was *regulatable* [read *regulable*] under the law at that time." *Insurance Adjustment Bureau v. Insurance Comm'r*, 542 A.2d 1317, 1319 n.2 (Pa. 1988).

regulation. See **rule.**

regulatory; *regulative. The two forms of the adjective are both common, but *regulatory* predominates. That form is accented in AmE on the first syllable /**reg**-yə-lə-tohr-ee/, in BrE often on the third /reg-yə-**lay**-tə-ree/. **Regulative* should be considered a NEEDLESS VARIANT.

reign. See **free reign** & **rein in.**

reimbursement. See **subrogation (c).**

reinforce (= to strengthen) is the preferred form, though the base verb is *enforce*, not **inforce*. (Likewise with *reinstate*.) Rather than hyphenate or use a diaeresis and retain the *-e-* in such words (e.g., *re-enforce*, *reënforce*), the *-e-* in each word is changed to *-i-* when the prefix is added. *Re-enforce* (= to enforce again) is sometimes seen in AmE.

rein in, not **reign in*, is the correct form of the phrase meaning "to check; to restrain." The metaphorical image is of the rider pulling on the reins of the horse to slow down (i.e., "hold your horses"). But many writers get it wrong—e.g.:

- "Regulatory schemes are necessary [for] . . . *reigning in* [read *reining in*] unbridled upset of the environment and its ecological systems by miners." *U.S. v. Doremus*, 658 F.Supp. 752, 755 (D. Idaho 1987). Notice the striking insensitivity to METAPHOR in this example: it is impossible to *rein in* (much less *reign in*) an *unbridled* horse—yet the writer has pushed the two images together. See VERBAL AWARENESS.
- "This statement was but an echo [that] *reigned in* [read *reined in*] the defense encampment by which it was environed." *Primeaux v. Leapley*, 502 N.W.2d 265, 275 (S.D. 1993) (Henderson, J., dissenting).
- "Fairchild asserts that she had to *reign in* [read *rein in*] her own speech during the August 16 comment session." *Fairchild v. Liberty Indep. Sch. Dist.*, 597 F.3d 747, 755 (5th Cir. 2010).

Cf. **free rein.**

reintegration; redintegration. *Reintegration* is the usual form of the word in the sense "the act of restoring to a state of wholeness; renewal; reconstruction." *Redintegration* was formerly more common in this sense; it is still used in scientific and other technical contexts.

reiterate; iterate. It is perhaps not too literalistic to use *iterate* in the sense "to repeat," and *reiterate* in the sense "to repeat a second time [i.e., to state a third time]." The distinction is observed only by the most punctilious writers, *reiterate* being the usual term in either sense.

reject. See **decline.**

rejoin. See **answer,** vb.

rejoinder; surrejoinder. A *rejoinder*, in former practice, was the pleading served by a defendant in answer to the plaintiff's reply (the pleading in answer to the defense). A *surrejoinder* was a plaintiff's pleading in reply to a defendant's rejoinder. See -ER (B) & COMMON-LAW PLEADINGS.

*reknowned. See **renowned.**

relate back is not a REDUNDANCY in law; rather, the phrase invokes the doctrine of *relation back*—e.g.:

- "He later sought to amend his petition to add an ineffective-assistance-of-counsel claim, but the court held that the amendment did not *relate back* to the initial pleading." *Sanchez-Llamas v. Oregon*, 548 U.S. 331, 364 n.3 (2006) (Ginsburg, J., concurring).
- "The December Order, making child support retroactive to October 2007, was not a modification of child support, but *related back* to the Decree." *In re Brinley*, 244 P.3d 339, 341 (Mont. 2010).

relater; relator. The first is the preferred spelling in the sense "narrator; one who relates." *Relator* is the legal term meaning "one who applies for a writ of mandamus or quo warranto on grounds that a defendant has breached—or threatens to breach—a public duty." E.g.:

"If the attorney general grants *relator* status, the *relator* generally takes an active part in the proceeding and is responsible for court costs and other expenses of litigation." Terri Lynn Helge, *Policing the Good Guys*, 19 Cornell J.L. & Pub. Pol'y 1, 47 (2009). See *ex rel.*

relate to <a jury can relate to that experience>, when used as in the example just given, is a voguish expression characteristic of popular American cant in the 1970s and 1980s. It is unlikely to lose that stigma.

relation. A. And *relative*. These terms are interchangeable in the sense "a person who is kin," although currently *relative* is much more usual.

B. Legal Sense. Some legal scholars, most notably Professor Leon Green, have used *relation* as "the best term available to express the value of one human being to another. . . . Relations may be classified as family relations, trade relations, professional and political relations, labor relations, and general social relations." Leon Green, *Cases on Injuries to Relations* 1 (1940).

C. And *relationship*. *Relation* is the broader term in this pair, since *relationship* refers either to kinship or to the fact of being related by some specific bond. The phrase *in relationship with* is almost always incorrect for *in relation to*. To be correct, the phrase would almost have to be *in his* (or *her* or *its*) *relationship with*, etc.

relational = of or relating to relations between persons. E.g.: "The court also concluded that the reasons SOSF gave for firing the two—that Griffin had '*relational* difficulties' with other employees and that Yarden's services were no longer needed—were not pretextual." *Griffin v. Sisters of Saint Francis, Inc.*, 489 F.3d 838, 842 (7th Cir. 2007). The term is distinct from the adjective *relative*. See **relation (c).**

relation back, in legal JARGON, refers to the doctrine that an act done at a later time is considered in the eyes of the law to have occurred at an earlier time. E.g.:

- "Courts have generally looked to the *relation-back* doctrine in this circumstance to determine whether the post-statutory amendment relates back to the original filing." Lonny Sheinkopf Hoffman, *In Retrospect: A First Year Review of the Class Action Fairness Act of 2005*, 39 Loy. L.A. L. Rev. 1135, 1140 (2006).
- "Under the '*relation back*' doctrine, added claims or defenses may . . . be treated as if they were part of the original pleadings, so that even the statute of limitations does not act as a complete bar." Michael L. Moffitt, *Customized Litigation*, 75 Geo. Wash. L. Rev. 461, 468 (2007).
- "The *Scarborough* Court explained that the *relation-back* doctrine allowed the amendment because the amendment 'arose out of the conduct, transaction, or occurrence set forth or attempted to be set forth in the initial application.'" *Jackson v. Kotter*, 541 F.3d 688, 695 (7th Cir. 2008).

See **relate back.**

One court has ill-advisedly hyphenated the phrase throughout, both when (as a PHRASAL ADJECTIVE) it needs the hyphen <the relation-back rule> and when (as a noun) it does not <the doctrine of relation back>. *See Lemelson v. Synergistics Research Corp.*, 669 F.Supp. 642, 647–48 (S.D.N.Y. 1987).

relationship. See **relation (c).**

relative, n.; **relation.** See **relation (a).**

relative to; ***relatively to.** *Relative to* is a variant of *in relation to* or *in comparison with*; usually one of these longer phrases adds clarity. Partridge called *relative to* GOBBLEDYGOOK. In no event is *relatively to proper. "*Relatively to* [read *In relation to*] her, his act was not negligent."

The phrase is also an awkward substitute for *concerning* or *regarding*: "The latter part of the paragraph contains language similar to that of paragraph (a) *relative to* [read *concerning*] the discharge of the corporation's liability if an agreement is signed by the parties."

relator. See **relater.**

***relatrix.** See SEXISM (c).

relay; re-lay. See RE- PAIRS.

release. A. Senses. *Release* = (1) liberation from an obligation, duty, or demand; (2) a written discharge, acquittance, or receipt; (3) a written authorization or permission for publication; (4) the act of conveying an estate or right to another, or of legally disposing of it; (5) a deed or document effecting a conveyance; (6) the action of freeing or fact of being freed from restraint or confinement; or (7) a document giving formal discharge from custody. For one sense of the verb *release*, together with near-synonyms, see **free.**

B. And *re-lease*. See RE- PAIRS.

releasee. The *OED* defines the word as "one to whom an estate is released," but the usual sense today—in AmE and BrE alike—is "one who is released," either physically or by contractual discharge. The following examples illustrate these two senses:

- "A hearing shall be held . . . within a reasonable time, unless a hearing is waived by the probationer, parolee or conditional *releasee*." Wyo. Stat. § 7-13-408 (1985) (as quoted in *Pisano v. Shillinger*, 814 P.2d 274, 280 (Wyo. 1991)).
- "When the actions or representations of the *releasee* so impair the mind and judgment of the releasor that he fails to understand the nature or consequence of his release, there has been no meeting of the minds." *Haller v. Borror Corp.*, 552 N.E.2d 207, 210 (Ohio 1990).

The correlative word is usually *releasor* in legal usage, though most dictionaries record only *releaser*. The *-or* form follows the typical preference for such spellings in answer to an *-ee* form. See -EE.

An asterisk (✻) precedes words and phrases that are invariably inferior forms.

*releasement, once a fairly common word, is now merely a NEEDLESS VARIANT of *release*—e.g.: "Their dispute concerning the advisability of the *releasement* [read *release*] in lieu of calling the police continued throughout the remainder of the afternoon." *Chavkin v. Rotter*, 245 N.Y.S.2d 435, 436 (App. Div. 1963). See release (A) & *divorcement.

release on licence. See parole.

releasor; releaser. See releasee.

relegate; delegate. To *relegate* is to consign to an inferior position or to transfer for decision or execution. E.g.: "State courts are more familiar with the issues involved in local land-use and zoning regulations, and . . . this makes it proper to *relegate* federal takings claims to state court." *San Remo Hotel, LP v. City & County of San Francisco*, 545 U.S. 323, 350 (2005) (Rehnquist, C.J., concurring). To *delegate* is to commit (as powers) to an agent or representative.

relevance; relevancy. The first is preferred in both AmE and BrE. *Relevancy* was the predominant form in American and British writings on evidence of the 19th century, but now *relevance* is more common except in Scotland. See irrelevance.

relevant; material. These terms both describe facts that might have some bearing on a point or dispute being considered. A *relevant* fact has a possible traceable connection, especially a conceivable probative connection, to the matter at hand. A *material* fact is one so closely connected to the point under consideration that it is indispensable to a proper assessment.

Relevant is sometimes misused for *applicable* or *appropriate*. E.g.: "We thus recognize the possibility, as we did in *Jenkins*, that the attorney's cost for paralegal services will supply the *relevant* [read *appropriate*] metric for calculating the client's recovery." *Richlin Sec. Serv. Co. v. Chertoff*, 553 U.S. 571, 585 (2008) (per Alito, J.).

Material, the victim of lawyers' SLIPSHOD EXTENSION, is frequently used in the sense "significant"— e.g.: "An immediate appeal would *materially* [i.e., significantly] advance the ultimate termination of the litigation." *In re NSB Film Corp.*, 167 B.R. 176, 180 (Bankr. App. 9th Cir. 1994).

relevant part, in. See in pertinent part.

relic; relict; relique. *Relic* = a surviving trace or memorial; something interesting because of its age. E.g.:

- "Today, decisions such as *Mochan* and *Donoghue* are widely viewed as *relics*." Peter W. Low et al., *Criminal Law* 41 (1982).
- "It is a little ironic and telling that lethal injection, hailed just a few years ago as the humane alternative in light of which every other method of execution was deemed an unconstitutional *relic* of the past, is the subject of today's challenge." *Baze v. Rees*, 553 U.S. 35, 104 (2008) (Thomas, J., concurring).

Relique is an archaic spelling of the word.

Relict = widow; survivor. Because *relict* is used only in legal writing, is unknown to nonlawyers, is sometimes mistaken for *relic*, and invariably means merely "widow" or "widower," we might justifiably seek to conform to general English usage and write *widow(er)*. Some legal writers have resorted to the tautologous DOUBLET *widow and relict*—e.g.: "Your petitioner would respectfully state that she was the late *widow and relict* of J.M. Cunningham, dec'd." *Cunningham v. Dellmon*, 237 S.W. 450, 451 (Ark. 1922). Widows and widowers unfamiliar with the term will not take kindly to being called *relicts*.

relief. See remedy.

relief over. See over (A).

relinquish; surrender; abandon; cede; waive. These verbs share the sense "to give up something." *Relinquish* means precisely that, or sometimes more specifically "to let (something) out of one's control, possession, or ownership." The thing being relinquished can be tangible <the officer relinquished his choke-hold> or intangible <relinquish all tort claims>. To *surrender* is to submit after a struggle, usually from being forced to do so. To *abandon* is to relinquish finally, completely, and purposefully, with no possibility of resumption. (See abandon.) To *cede* is to transfer lands, territories, or geopolitical rights as a result of treaty negotiations or an adverse decision from a tribunal. To *waive* is to intentionally relinquish a known right, not by force or necessity but by choice. The word implies a refusal to insist on the continuation of a right, claim, immunity or on the continued observance of a rule. See waive (A).

relique. See relic.

relitigate. *RH2* aside, *relitigate* (= to litigate again) is not recorded in most English-language dictionaries, but it has been widely used since the mid-19th century and is unquestionably useful. E.g.:

- "He would still be free to *relitigate* the issue whether the driver had had his permission and thus whether the insurance proceeds should not be credited against his personal liability." Charles Alan Wright, *The Law of Federal Courts* 500 (5th ed. 1994).
- "We see no reason why preclusion based on a lesser showing would have been appropriate if the order of the two actions had been switched—that is, if the United States had brought the first suit itself, and then sought to *relitigate* the same claim through the contractor." *Taylor v. Sturgell*, 553 U.S. 880, 906 n.13 (2008) (per Ginsburg, J.).

The corresponding noun, *relitigation*, is equally common.

rem. See in rem & res.

remainder. See rest, residue, and remainder & DOUBLETS, TRIPLETS, AND SYNONYM-STRINGS.

remainder; reversion. These terms are distinguishable on two grounds. First, a *reversion* always arises in the creator of a particular estate or in the creator's heirs; a *remainder* can never arise in the creator of the estate or in the creator's heirs. Second, a *reversion* may arise without any intent, express or implied, that the reversioner take; a *remainder* arises only when the instrument creating the present estate shows an intent that the remainderman take. See **over (A)** & **reversion.**

remainderman (= the person to whom a remainder is devised) was formerly two words but is now regularly spelled as a single word—e.g.:

- "Affirmative waste as a concept stems from an early English common-law concern that the interests in land held by reversioners or *remaindermen* be protected from depredations by life tenants." *McMahon v. Eke-Nweke*, 503 F.Supp.2d 598, 604 (E.D.N.Y. 2007).
- "The children asserted that the decedent's wife had received only a life estate and not a fee simple interest in certain property and that they were the *remaindermen* of that property." *In re Estate of Florence*, 307 S.W.3d 887, 892 (Tex. App.—Fort Worth 2010).

A possible nonsexist equivalent is *remainderer*, but it is extremely rare—e.g.: "In the mean time the *remainderer* would have had a right to anticipate payment." *Mellon's Appeal*, 8 A. 183, 187 (Pa. 1887). See SEXISM (B).

remainder over. See **over (A).**

remainder subject to a condition precedent. See **contingent remainder.**

remand, n.; *remandment. The second is a NEEDLESS VARIANT, as is *remission*. See **remission.**

remand, vb. A. Objects. People as well as cases may be *remanded* (or "sent back"): *remand* = (1) to send (a case) back to the court from which it came for some further action; or (2) to recommit (an accused) to custody after a preliminary examination—e.g.:

- (Sense 1) "We vacate the judgment of the Supreme Court of Virginia and *remand* the case for further proceedings not inconsistent with the opinion in *Melendez-Diaz v. Massachusetts*." *Briscoe v. Virginia*, 130 S.Ct. 1316 (2010) (per curiam).
- (Sense 2) "[The court] revoked his probation and *remanded* him to the custody of the Secretary of Corrections to serve his original sentence." *State v. Baker*, 95 P.3d 135, 136 (Kan. Ct. App. 2004).

B. *Remand back* as a Redundancy. *Remand* alone is preferable to *remand back*—e.g.:

- "[The facts] are sufficiently compelling to support a claim of persecution on account of imputed political opinion and to require a *remand back* [omit *back*] to the BIA for a credibility determination." *Molina-Morales v. I.N.S.*, 237 F.3d 1048, 1052 (9th Cir. 2001) (Fletcher, J., dissenting).
- "If the removing party does not demonstrate fraudulent joinder, the district court must *remand back* [omit *back*] to state court based on the lack of subject-matter jurisdiction." *Saginaw Hous. Comm'n v. Bannum, Inc.*, 576 F.3d 620, 624 (6th Cir. 2009).

See **send back.**

C. Pronunciation. *Remand* is pronounced /rə-**mand**/ both as a noun and as a verb.

*remandment. See **remand,** n.

*remanent. See **remnant.**

remark; re-mark. See RE- PAIRS.

remedial; remediable. *Remedial* (= providing a remedy; corrective; curative) is frequently pejorative in general English-language contexts <remedial learning>. In law, however, it usually acts as the adjective for *legal remedy*: "The statute of limitations is a *remedial* device only and does not affect the substantive rights of the parties." *Manning v. Fort Deposit Bank*, 619 F.Supp. 1327, 1331 (W.D. Tenn. 1985).

Remediable = capable of being remedied. E.g.: "Third, and most important, a holding that Arar, even if all of his allegations are true, has suffered no *remediable* constitutional harm legitimates the Government's actions in a way that a state-secrets dismissal would not." *Arar v. Ashcroft*, 585 F.3d 559, 638 (2d Cir. 2009).

remediate is a BACK-FORMATION from *remediation*— and is generally a NEEDLESS VARIANT of *remedy*. E.g.:

- "[The agency is charged with the] solemn responsibility for *remediating* [read *remedying*] discrimination." *Hinfey v. Matawan Reg'l Bd. of Educ.*, 391 A.2d 899, 907 (N.J. 1978).
- "In some legislative schemes designed to *remediate* [read *remedy*] or prevent harm to certain portions of the public, the doctrine of equitable tolling has been allowed." *Dawe v. Old Ben Coal Co.*, 754 F.2d 225, 228 (7th Cir. 1985).

There is, however, one exception: in environmental law, the word has become an established term of art— e.g.: "The district court entered judgment for RSR, holding that International's Environmental policies obligated it to indemnify RSR for *remediation* costs incurred by the EPA at Harbor Island." *RSR Corp. v. International Ins. Co.*, 612 F.3d 851, 854 (5th Cir. 2010) (per Garwood, J.).

remediless; *remedyless. As *penny* makes *penniless*, so *remedy* makes *remediless* (= without remedy; lacking any remedies)—e.g.:

- "The risk selected by the plaintiffs to pursue their tort claim under a collective liability theory which ultimately failed, thus leaving them *remedyless* [read *remediless*], was willingly assumed." Nina H. Compton & J. Douglas Compton, *DPT Vaccine Manufacturer Liability*, 20 N.M. L. Rev. 531, 549 (1990).
- "There were all sorts of problems with this characterization of marriage, including the fact that husbands would frequently desert their wives, leaving them *remediless* and without any property or other means of support." Margaret F. Brinig & Steven M. Crafton, *Marriage and Opportunism*, 23 J. Legal Stud. 869, 881 (1994).

remedy; relief. *Relief* has historically been more commonly used in the context of courts of equity, and *remedy* in the context of courts of law. And so one generally speaks of *legal remedies* and of *equitable relief. See* C.C. Langdell, *A Brief Survey of Equity Jurisdiction* (pt. 2), 1 Harv. L. Rev. 111, 111 (1887).

*remedyless. See **remediless.**

remember. See **recollect (A).**

remise = to give up, surrender, make over to another, release (any right, property, etc.) (*OED*). Though traditionally used in quitclaim deeds, the term is fast becoming a legal ARCHAISM. Several words—such as those just used in defining *remise*—are more specific and more widely understood.

remise, release, and forever quitclaim. See **words of conveyance.**

remissible. So spelled.

remission. As a noun meaning "the act of remanding," *remission* is a NEEDLESS VARIANT of *remand*, n. Here is an example suggesting the writer's indulgence in INELEGANT VARIATION: "An appellate court 'may *remand* the cause . . . .' The procedure for *remission* [read *remand*] of the cause to the lower court . . . is further regulated and controlled generally by the rules of the appellate courts." 14A Stephen M. Flanagan, *Cyclopedia of Federal Procedure* § 69.01, at 65 (1984). See **remand, remit, remittance** & **renvoi.**

In BrE, *remission* refers not only to the sending back of a case to a lower court, but also to the part of a prison sentence that a convict is allowed not to serve (e.g., *remission* for good conduct in prison).

remit = (1) to pardon; (2) to abate, slacken; mitigate; (3) to refer (a matter for decision) to some authority, send back (a case) to a lower court; (4) to send or put back; or (5) to transmit (as money). Senses 1 and 2 are uncommon today. Sense 4 is frequent in legal writing—e.g.:

- "The breach by the landlord of his covenant does not justify the refusal of the tenant to perform his covenant to pay rent. . . . The tenant is *remitted* to the right to recoup himself in the damages resulting from the landlord's breach of his covenant to repair." *Mitchell v. Weiss*, 26 S.W.2d 699, 700–01 (Tex. Civ. App.—El Paso 1930).
- "In *remitting* [the] members of this class to a solution at the ballot box, rather than dangling the carrot of reform by judicial injunction before them, the district court followed the course of wisdom and practicality." *Hawkins v. Town of Shaw, Miss.*, 461 F.2d 1171, 1185 (5th Cir. 1972) (Roney, J., dissenting).
- "In those few difficult cases, the State should bear the burden of *remitting* the defendant for further psychological observation to ensure that he is competent to defend himself." *Medina v. California*, 505 U.S. 437, 467 (1992) (O'Connor, J., concurring).

Sense 5 is also quite common <upon receiving the demand letter, she promptly remitted the amount due>.

Sense 3, once common in legal prose, still appears, here as a synonym of *remand*—e.g.:

- "We shall conclude that the verdicts were fully supported, but there is a need in the interests of justice to *remit* the case to the trial judge so he may pass anew on the motion in his discretion." *Commonwealth v. Guy G.*, 758 N.E.2d 643, 644 (Mass. App. Ct. 2001).
- "The Supreme Court held preclusion did not bar the plaintiffs' federal claims because a party *remitted* to state court by an abstention order has the right to return to federal court." *DLX, Inc. v. Kentucky*, 381 F.3d 511, 531 (6th Cir. 2004).
- "Defendants' motion . . . poses . . . the issue whether Emigra should be permitted to gain that access by asserting antitrust claims rather than being *remitted* to state court to pursue its trade-secret and unfair-competition claims." *Emigra Group, LLC v. Fragomen, Del Rey, Bernsen & Loewy, LLP*, 612 F.Supp.2d 330, 338 (S.D.N.Y. 2009).

See **remission.**

remittance; *remittal; remission; *remitment. *Remittance* corresponds to sense 5 of *remit*, and means "money sent to a person, or the sending of money to a person." E.g.: "The Greers challenged . . . the amount of those penalties in the Tax Court, arguing that they had made a *remittance* in 1995 that paid their tax liability and thus reduced their penalties." *Greer v. Commissioner*, 557 F.3d 688, 688 (6th Cir. 2009). **Remitment* is a NEEDLESS VARIANT.

Remission is the noun corresponding to senses 1 through 4 of *remit*; it means either "forgiveness" or "diminution of force, effect, degree, or violence." See **remit.** **Remittal* is a NEEDLESS VARIANT.

remitter; *remittor; remittitur. *Remitter* = (1) one who sends a remittance; (2) a principle by which a person having two titles to an estate, and entering on it by the later or more defective of these titles, is held to hold it by the earlier or more valid one; or (3) the act of remitting a case to another court. (See **remit.**) The spelling **remittor* is inferior.

Remittitur = (1) the process by which the court reduces the damages awarded in a jury verdict; or (2) the action of sending the transcript of a case back from an appellate to a trial court, or the notice for doing so. For sense 2, the usual phrase is *remittitur of record.*

remittitur; remittitur of record; *remittor. See **remitter.**

remnant; *remanent. The second is an archaic spelling to be avoided.

remonstrate. The second syllable is accented /ri-**mon**-strayt/ in AmE, the first syllable /**rem**-ən-strayt/ in BrE. For this word and its near-synonyms, see **object (A).**

remote has a special legal meaning in contexts involving the rule against perpetuities: "beyond the 21 years after some life in being by which a devise must vest." E.g.: "The Rule Against Perpetuities invalidates interests that are inalienable because their ownership vests too *remotely*." Heather M. Marshall, Note, *Instead of Asking "When," Ask "How"*, 44 New Eng. L. Rev. 763, 766 (2010). See **in being** & *in esse.*

REMOTE RELATIVES. Surprisingly few grammarians discuss what has become an increasingly common problem: the separation of the relative pronoun (*that, which, who*) from its antecedent. For example, in the sentence "The files sitting in the courtroom that I was talking about yesterday are in disarray," the word *that* strictly modifies *courtroom*, not *files*. But many writers today would intend to have it modify *files*—they would loosely employ a "remote relative."

The best practice is simply to ensure that, whatever the relative pronoun, it immediately follow the noun that it modifies. As the following examples illustrate, lapses involving *which* are extremely common:

- "This work required a law court in the modern sense made up of a small number of judges of education and ability skilled in the law *which* sat regularly term after term, generally at Westminster, often at the Exchequer." William F. Walsh, *A Treatise on Equity* 3 (1930). *Which* modifies *court* (21 words and 7 nouns before). [A possible revision: *This work required a law court in the modern sense: one that was made up of a small number of judges of legal education and ability and that sat regularly term after term, generally at Westminster, often at the Exchequer.*]
- "States, like individuals, often put forward contentions for the purpose of supporting a particular case *which* do not necessarily represent their settled or impartial opinion." J.L. Brierly, *The Law of Nations* 61 (5th ed. 1955). *Which* modifies *contentions* (9 words and 3 nouns before). [A possible revision: *States, like individuals, often put forward contentions that support a particular case but do not necessarily represent their settled opinion.*]
- "If a terrorist places a bomb by the front door of a Cabinet Minister, *which* does damage but fortunately does not kill anybody, could this be an attempt to murder?" Glanville Williams, *Textbook of Criminal Law* 371 (1978). *Which* modifies *bomb* (9 words and 3 nouns before). [A possible revision: *If a terrorist places a bomb by the front door of a Cabinet Minister and that bomb does damage but fortunately does not kill anybody, could this be an attempt to murder?*]
- "The convenience of the litigants is the next quality in the administration of justice *which* I shall consider." Patrick Devlin, *The Judge* 59 (1979). *Which* modifies *quality* (6 words and 3 nouns before). [A possible revision: *The convenience of the litigants is the next quality that I shall consider in the administration of justice.*]
- "There are today a great many other bodies exercising quasi-judicial powers *which* are not regarded strictly speaking as courts, though many of them do perform functions very closely analogous to those of ordinary courts." P.S. Atiyah, *Law and Modern Society* 27 (1983). *Which* modifies *bodies* (4 words and 2 nouns before). [A possible revision: *There are today a great many other bodies exercising quasi-judicial powers; these bodies are not regarded strictly speaking as courts, though many of them do perform functions very closely analogous to those of ordinary courts.*]
- "People may have claims against each other and against the State *which* are of a moral or political character." *Id.* at 112. *Which* modifies *claims* (8 words and 3 nouns before). [A possible revision: *People may have moral and political claims against each other and against the State.*]

- "Legislators are constantly making decisions about law reform *which* depend on moral values." Simon Lee, *Law and Morals* 3 (1986). *Which* modifies *decisions* (4 words and 2 nouns before). [A possible revision: *Legislators are constantly making decisions about law reform, and many of these decisions depend on moral values.*]

But *that* is almost as troublesome, and when used remotely is even more likely to cause confusion—e.g.:

- "The law has a way of looking at family relationships *that* is different, or may be different, from the moral, the social, or the religious way." Max Radin, *The Law and You* 17 (1948). *That* modifies *way* (6 words and 2 nouns before). [A possible revision: *The law has a way of looking at family relationships—a way that is different, or may be different, from the moral, the social, or the religious way.*]
- "All groups seem to develop noticeable characteristics, so that some can recognize sailors, clergymen, actors and other occupational groups *that* are not at all hereditary and hardly attributable to any definite physical cause." Morris R. Cohen, *Reason and Law* 42 (1961). *That* modifies *characteristics* (13 words and 6 nouns before). [A possible revision: *All groups seem to develop noticeable characteristics that are not at all hereditary or attributable to any definite physical cause, but that allow some people to recognize sailors, clergy, actors, and other occupational groups.*]
- "There is another important aspect of the case, and that is whether, in placing so heavy a burden on the jury, it has brought about a shift of responsibility for decisions in the moral field *that* affects the democratic process I have endeavoured to describe." Patrick Devlin, *The Enforcement of Morals* 98 (1968). What affects the democratic process? The *moral field*? The *responsibility* for decisions? The *shift* in that responsibility? The answer seems to be *shift* (9 words and 4 nouns before). [A possible revision: *There is another important aspect of the case, and that is whether the heavy burden placed on the jury has brought about a shift of responsibility for decisions in the moral field—a shift that affects the democratic process I have endeavoured to describe.*]
- "The plain fact is that in most cases where doubt can arise as to whether a particular situation is covered by a statute, no intellectual resources are available to the legislature in deciding the question *that* are not equally available to the judge." Lon L. Fuller, *Anatomy of the Law* 33 (1968). *That* modifies *resources* (10 words and 3 nouns before). [A possible revision: *In most cases in which doubt can arise about whether a particular situation is covered by a statute, the legislature has no intellectual resources that are not equally available to the judge.*]
- "The most important changes in the law of future interests *that* the Statute of Uses wrought may be summarized in one sentence." Thomas F. Bergin & Paul G. Haskell, *Preface to Estates in Land and Future Interests* 113 (2d ed. 1984). *That* modifies *changes* (7 words and 3 nouns before). [A possible revision: *The most important changes that the Statute of Uses wrought in the law of future interests can be summarized in one sentence.*]
- "Lee Feltman, Esq., . . . appeals from an order of the district court, Edelstein, J., *that* adopted the findings and recommendations of Magistrate Gershon." *Sassower v. Sheriff of Westchester County*, 824 F.2d 184, 185 (2d Cir. 1987). Does that sentence refer to *an order that adopted* or *the district court that adopted*? It looks as if the writer

meant to refer to *order* (7 words and 3 nouns before), not *court*. [A possible revision: *Lee Feltman, Esq., . . . appeals from a district-court order that adopted the findings and recommendations of Magistrate Gershon . . . .*]

Even *who* is used remotely, but its meaning is much more frequently clear—e.g.:

- "Gibson was a Democrat of Jackson's type (Jackson wished to put him on the Supreme Court of the United States), the son of a prosperous and successful man of business in a frontier community, who was also a colonel in the Revolutionary army." Roscoe Pound, *The Formative Era of American Law* 85 (1938). *Who* may modify either *son* (13 words and 4 nouns before) or *man* (7 words and 3 nouns before). It seems to modify the more remote of the two—*son*. [A possible revision: *Gibson was a Democrat . . . , the son of a prosperous and successful man of business in a frontier community. Gibson was also a colonel in the Revolutionary army.*]
- "The question whether one of a gang *who* is arrested at the scene of the crime continues to be 'present' there is considered in § 134." Glanville Williams, *Criminal Law* 354 (2d ed. 1961). *Who* modifies *one* (4 words and 2 nouns before.) [A possible revision: *The question whether a gang member who is arrested at the scene of the crime continues to be "present" there is considered in § 134.*]
- "Patricia Buthmann and Tim Tyroler on Tuesday lost their effort to block being evicted from the Casa Carranza apartments . . . because they allowed a woman to stay with them *who* possessed two syringes suspected to be drug paraphernalia." Kris Mayes, *Renters Run Afoul of Eviction Law*, Phoenix Gazette, 29 Sept. 1994, at B1. At first, the relative pronoun *who* may seem to modify *them* as part of an archaic construction; in fact, it modifies *woman* (5 words and 2 nouns before). [A possible revision: *. . . because a woman who stayed with them possessed two syringes thought to be drug paraphernalia.*]

At times, the remote relative may even appear in a phrase such as *in which*—e.g.: "The unexpected announcement renewed speculation about the 74-year-old Pope's broader state of health, particularly because he planned an important speech at the United Nations on the family *in which* he was expected to discuss the Vatican's views of the recent population conference in Cairo." Alan Crowell, *Pope, Citing His Health, Cancels His Planned Trip to New York*, N.Y. Times, 23 Sept. 1994, at A1. *In which* modifies *speech* (8 words and 3 nouns before). [A possible revision: *The unexpected announcement renewed speculation about the 74-year-old Pope's broader state of health, particularly because he planned an important speech at the United Nations on the family. He was expected to discuss the Vatican's views of the recent population conference in Cairo.*]

As in the example just quoted, remote relatives often seem to result from the writer's ill-advised combining of two sentences into one. Among the advantages of avoiding remote relatives—avoiding MISCUES and even AMBIGUITY—is that you also improve your average SENTENCE LENGTH. For more on using *that* and *which* correctly, see **that & which.**

removable. This is the preferred spelling in both AmE and BrE, not **removeable*. See MUTE E.

removal; exclusion; deportation. All these terms are used in highly technical senses in immigration law. *Exclusion* = the denial of an alien's lawful entry into the United States after a hearing to determine admissibility. *Deportation* = the expulsion from the United States of an alien who has violated immigration laws. In 1997, the Illegal Immigration Reform and Immigrant Responsibility Act consolidated these terms into *removal*, which carries both meanings. 8 C.F.R. § 240.

removal proceedings; deportation proceedings; exclusion proceedings. In immigration law, these phrases denote the three types of proceedings before and after the Illegal Immigration Reform and Immigrant Responsibility Act of 1996 (110 Stat. 3009–546). Before April 1997 (the Act's effective date), *deportation proceedings* were initiated against a person already in the U.S. to determine whether the person would be allowed to stay, and *exclusion proceedings* were initiated against a person seeking admission to the U.S. Both actions are now consolidated under the term *removal proceedings*. Because the older terms define different proceedings, they are typically used for proceedings that were pending before April 1997, but not later. *Removal proceedings* is the term used for those. But confusion is understandably common—e.g.:

- "On June 13, 1995, he received notice that *removal proceedings* [read *deportation proceedings*] had been initiated against him for overstaying his visa." *Alrefae v. Chertoff*, 471 F.3d 353, 355 (2d Cir. 2006).
- "The defendant has lost his status as a TPS alien, and a *deportation proceeding* [read *removal proceeding*] is currently pending in the Executive Office of Immigration Review." *U.S. v. Garcia-Ochoa*, 607 F.3d 371, 373 (4th Cir. 2010). (The defendant entered the U.S. in 1998. *Id.*)
- "The government did not base its second *deportation proceedings* [read *removal proceedings*] against Bravo-Pedroza on a new conviction as here." *Poblete Mendoza v. Holder*, 606 F.3d 1137, 1141 (9th Cir. 2010). (The first proceeding began in 2004. *Id.* at 1140.)

Many judicial opinions use at least two of these terms, perhaps because the nature of a *removal proceeding* is less clear than in its predecessor terms. And though the immigration-law orthodoxy is to insist on *removal proceedings*, it seems unfortunate to have an ambiguous genus-term covering two very different species.

remove; removal. In law, these terms have procedural senses that are generally unknown to nonlawyers. *Removal* = the transfer of an action from a court on one jurisdictional level to a court on another level. So in the U.S., some state-court actions may be *removed* to federal court if the proper statutory basis exists. (The correlative term for transferring the action back to state court is *remand*. See **remand.**) In England, *removal* is the transfer of a High Court action from a district registry to London (or vice versa) or of a county-court action to the High Court (or vice versa).

remove; re-move. See RE- PAIRS.

*removeable. See **removable.**

remuneration. So spelled; **renumeration* is an all-too-common misspelling and mispronunciation. See **pay,** n.

renant; *reniant. At early common law, *renant* (the more common spelling) meant "denying." **Reniant* is a variant form.

render = (1) to make, cause to be <render worthless>; or (2) to give <render judgment>. In sense 2, *render* is a FORMAL WORD worthy of describing judicial actions, although generally it appears in this context primarily in AmE: judicial decisions are *rendered*; nonjudicial responses are *given*. "The Court seizes upon the petitioner's seven-word response, 'Uh, yeah, I'd like to do that,' *rendered* [read *uttered*] during a colloquy [that] could not have taken five minutes." *Smith v. Illinois*, 469 U.S. 91, 100 (1984) (Rehnquist, J., dissenting). Such an inarticulate statement from a habeas corpus petitioner should hardly be said to have been *rendered*.

In AmE, the usual expression is that judgment is *rendered*; in BrE it is commonly written that judgment is *given*. E.g.: "Summary judgment was *given* for the claimants." Justine Thornton, *Significant UK Environmental Cases*, 21 J. Envtl. L. 323, 329 (2009).

rendezvous. A. Plural Form. The singular noun *rendezvous* has an identical plural form—i.e., *rendezvous*, not *-vouses*.

B. Verb Inflections. As a verb, *rendezvous* makes *rendezvouses* in the third-person present tense, and *rendezvoused* in the past tense. (In both inflected forms, the root *-s-* is silent.) The present participle is *rendezvousing* /**ron**-day-voo-ing/.

rendition. The prevalent meaning today—"the action of rendering; giving out or forth"—began as an Americanism but has now become universal. BrE retains an older, quasi-legal sense as well: "the surrender of a suspected or convicted person, usu. betw. two Commonwealth countries."

rendition of judgment; entry of judgment. Courts have traditionally distinguished between *rendition of judgment* (= the oral or written ruling containing the judgment entered) and *entry of judgment* (= the formal recordation of a judgment by the court). It has been said that *rendition* is the ultimate judicial act, whereas *entry* is merely ministerial in nature and evidentiary in purpose.

This distinction at one time posed problems in some cases in which no terminal judicial act was required, as with a jury's general verdict. In current American practice (Fed. R. Civ. P. 58), the verdict *rendered* by a jury or the decision *rendered* by the judge is converted into an "inchoate" judgment, effective upon *entry*.

renege; renegue; *renig. The first is the preferred form in AmE, the second the standard spelling in BrE, although the first is making inroads. **Renig* is a variant spelling in AmE—a NEEDLESS VARIANT.

renewal. See **extension.**

renewal of judgment; revival of judgment. "Generally speaking there exists an important distinction between *revival* and *renewal* of judgments. *Revival*, by judicial decree on scire facias, removes dormancy and authorizes belated issuance of a writ of execution. Conversely, *renewal*, by civil action on the judgment, consists [in] a new money judgment endowed with its own actionability, executability, and creation of a lien." Stefan A. Riesenfeld, *Creditors' Remedies and Debtors' Protection* 101 (1979).

*reniant. See **renant.**

*renig. See **renege.**

renounce. See **denounce** & **abjure (A).**

*renouncement. See **renunciation.**

renowned. So spelled; **reknowned* is wrong but fairly common for *renowned*. E.g.: "Byatt is *reknowned* [read *renowned*] for her intelligence." Mira Stout, *What Possessed A.S. Byatt*, N.Y. Times, 26 May 1991, § 6, at 13, 14. The noun form is *renown*; there is no verb, though the past participle *renowned* functions as an adjective.

rent, n.; **rental,** n. Generally, one should not use *rental* where *rent* will suffice. *Rental* denotes the amount paid as rent, the income received from rent, or a record of rental payments received (e.g., the Grossvener Estate rental). *Rental* sometimes encroaches on *rent* itself: "The lessee agrees to pay the agreed-upon *rental*." If the writer had merely meant that the lessee must pay the rent (as opposed to a specific sum due periodically, e.g., monthly), then *rent* would have been the better term.

rent, vb., is ambiguous insofar as it may refer to the action taken by either the lessor or the lessee; the word has had this doubleness of sense from at least the 16th century. Both the lessee and the lessor are *renters*, so to speak, though this term is usually reserved for tenants. Cf. **lease,** vb.

rental, n. See **rent,** n.

rent charge; rentcharge; rent-charge = the right to receive an annual sum from the income of land, usu. in perpetuity, and to retake possession if the payments are in arrears. Hyphenated in the *OED*, this word is now one word in BrE (as in the Rentcharges Act of 1977) and two words in AmE.

*renumeration. See **remuneration.**

renunciation; *renouncement. The second is a NEEDLESS VARIANT.

---

renvoi /ren-**voi**/ (F. "sending back") = the problem arising in private international law when one country's rule on conflict of laws refers a case to the law of a foreign country, and the law of that country refers the case either back to the law of the first country (*remission*) or to the law of a third country (*transmission*) (*CDL*). Within federal systems such as that of the U.S., *renvoi* applies when one state's conflicts rule refers the case to the law of another state. See **remission**.

reoccur. See **recur.**

reoccurrence. See **recurrence.**

reorganization. In bankruptcy, *reorganization* is the financial restructuring of a corporation, esp. in the repayment of debts under a plan created by a trustee and approved by a court. In tax contexts, *reorganization* is the restructuring of a corporation, as by a merger or recapitalization, in order to improve its tax treatment under the Internal Revenue Code.

repairable. See **reparable.**

RE- PAIRS. Many English words (like *repair*) beginning with the prefix *re-* take on different meanings depending on whether the prefix is hyphenated or is closed up. Some of these words, whose two different senses with and without the hyphen should be self-explanatory, are as follows:

re(-)bound	re(-)dress	re(-)prove
re(-)call	re(-)form	re(-)search
re(-)claim	re(-)lay	re(-)sent
re(-)collect	re(-)lease	re(-)sign
re(-)count	re(-)mark	re(-)sound
re(-)cover	re(-)move	re(-)store
re(-)create	re(-)place	re(-)treat

reparable; repairable. Of these two terms, the first term has acquired a broader meaning. Used of damages, losses, or injuries, *reparable* means "capable of being set right again." Used of things, *repairable* means "capable of being repaired." The antonyms of these words are *irreparable* and *unrepairable*.

reparation; redress; amends; restitution; indemnity. These terms all refer to making good on a loss that one has either contributed to or agreed to take responsibility for. *Reparation* (most commonly a plural) originally suggested atonement for an offense, and it still carries this connotation <war reparations> <reparations to Japanese Americans interned during World War II>; normally, *reparations* are payments intended (even if by fiction) to restore things to their previous conditions. *Redress* more strongly implies that a wrong has been done, and it can suggest a getting even <I'll seek my redress in court>. *Amends* suggests a less serious offense and often simply a misunderstanding <let me make amends, please>. *Restitution* suggests a full restoration in value of what someone has been deprived of <the thief was ordered to make full restitution in addition to serving jail time>. *Indemnity* refers

to the contractual reimbursement or compensation for loss, damage, or liability.

reparative; *reparatory. The second is a NEEDLESS VARIANT.

repay. A. Sense. This word means "to pay back"—it should not refer to paying something for the first time, however long the sum has been due. E.g.:
- "Earlier this year, Michael took out a $45,000 loan to *repay* [read *pay*] the back taxes and interest he owed." *For Special Cases, a "Tax Therapist"*, N.Y. Times, 8 Dec. 1989, at 27.
- "Anthony claims that the other sentences are short because tax offenders generally *repay* [read *pay*] what they owe, suffer disproportionately to the loss they cause, and are easy to rehabilitate." *U.S. v. Anthony*, 545 F.3d 60, 68 n.8 (1st Cir. 2008).

B. **Repay back.*** This is a REDUNDANCY.

repealer = (1) one who repeals; or (2) a legislative act abrogating an earlier act. Sense 2, of recent origin, is the more common one—e.g.: "While Congress might simply have struck the 1950 statute, in considering the *repealer* the point was made that the existing statute provided some express procedural protection." *Hamdi v. Rumsfeld*, 542 U.S. 507, 542–43 (2004) (Souter, J., dissenting in part). See -ER (B).

*repeat again; *repeat back. Both are REDUNDANCIES.

repel; repulse. *Repulse* (= to drive or beat back [an assailant]) denotes primarily a physical act of resistance, or a METAPHOR based on such resistance—e.g.: "The attack upon the representatives, indeed, had already been launched, and, after an initial victory, had been *repulsed*." C.H.S. Fifoot, *History and Sources of the Common Law: Tort and Contract* 358 (1949). *Repel*, by contrast, is primarily figurative. Hence *repel* is the verb corresponding most closely in meaning to the adjective *repulsive*, and a person who experiences *repulsion* is *repelled*. In the following sentences, *repel* is acceptably used as a near-synonym of *rebut*:
- "The owner of the servient estate must rebut the presumption of right, by . . . protest and objection under such circumstances as to *repel* the presumption." *Walton v. Knight*, 58 S.E. 1025, 1026 (W. Va. 1907).
- "In such cases the burden of proof rests upon the party claiming the benefit under the transaction to *repel* the presumption thus created by law by showing a severance of the relation." *King v. King*, 4 So.2d 740, 743 (Ala. 1941).
- "The circumstances *repel* any thought of fraud and speak cogently of the integrity of the instrument under review." *In re Demaris's Estate*, 110 P.2d 571, 586 (Or. 1941).

repellent; repulsive. Both mean, literally, "causing to turn away." *Repulsive* is the stronger word; it applies to whatever disgusts or offends in the extreme. **Repellant*, a variant spelling of *repellent*, is to be eschewed. See **repel.**

repetitive; repetitious; *repetitional; *repetitionary. A certain DIFFERENTIATION is emerging between the first two terms. *Repetitive* generally means "repeating;

containing repetition." It is a largely colorless term. *Repetitious*, which has taken on pejorative connotations, means "containing tedious repetitions." E.g.:

- "And even when testimony is limited to relevant areas, they have the further obligation to ensure that the presentation of evidence does not become rambling and *repetitious*." *U.S. v. Smith*, 452 F.3d 323, 332 (4th Cir. 2006).
- "We have constantly preached to attorneys that they should avoid *repetitious* allegations and averments in complaints, warning against the reviled 'shotgun pleadings' style." *Watts v. Florida Int'l Univ.*, 495 F.3d 1289, 1299 (11th Cir. 2007).

Repetitional and *repetitionary* are NEEDLESS VARIANTS of *repetitive*.

rephrase for *paraphrase*. One cannot use these two words interchangeably. One may *paraphrase* either statements or persons, but one may *rephrase* only statements. The writer of this sentence incorrectly used *rephrase* for *paraphrase*: "To *rephrase* [read *paraphrase*] Justice Frankfurter, newspapers are inherently available to all as a mode of expression." Note, *Local Government Equal Time Broadcast Regulation*, 61 Tex. L. Rev. 175, 179–80 (1982).

replace; re-place. Here *replace* is used for *re-place*: "Where land or chattels have been wrongfully taken from a person, he can be *replaced* [read *re-placed*] substantially in the position which he formerly occupied by restoring to him in specie that which was taken from him." Restatement of Torts § 901 cmt. a (1939). See RE- PAIRS. For the difference between *replace* and *substitute*, see **substitute**.

repleader. See -ER (B).

*repleat. See **replete**.

replenish makes the noun *replenishment*, not *repletion* (= a surfeit, plethora).

replete means not "complete," but "abundantly supplied with; full to overflowing." *Repleat* is an infrequent misspelling—e.g.: "Appellants' response . . . is *repleat* [read *replete*] with broad references to factual allegations [that] Appellants indicate that they will prove at a future time." *Proctor v. White*, 155 S.W.3d 438, 443 (Tex. App.—El Paso 2004).

repletion. See **replenish**.

repleviable; *replevisable. Blackstone was ahead of his time in using *repleviable* rather than *replevisable*, which is now rightly considered a NEEDLESS VARIANT. The antonym of *repleviable* is *irrepleviable*. See **replevy**.

replevin; replevy, n. *Replevin* is the name of both a writ and a cause of action. *Replevy*, preferably a verb, is an archaic variant of *replevin* as a noun, although it still appears—e.g.:

- "At issue was a *replevy* [read *replevin*], a PJR dependent on a preexisting interest in the property." Elizabeth A. Alquist, Note, *Balancing the Checklist*, 26 Conn. L. Rev. 721, 740 (1994).
- "In *Bollman*, . . . which concerned *replevy* [read *replevin*] of a piano, the plaintiff argued that 'before an action of *replevin* for personal property can be maintained . . . a demand for possession must be made.'" *Lackawanna Chapter of Ry. & Locomotive Historical Soc'y, Inc. v. St. Louis County*, 606 F.3d 886, 889 (8th Cir. 2010).

See **replevy** & **detinue**.

replevin, vb., is an obsolete variant of the verb *replevy*. (See **replevy**.) When *replevin* is used as a verb in modern American legal writing, it is simply an error—e.g.:

- "The manufacturer wrongfully *replevined* [read *replevied*] a printing press." *Cummins v. Brodie*, 667 S.W.2d 759, 766 (Tenn. Ct. App. 1983).
- "Purchase of *replevined* [read *replevied*] vehicle by judge and cover-up." *Mississippi Judicial Performance Comm'n v. Walker*, 565 So.2d 1117, 1130 (Miss. 1990) (Appendix B).
- "The Tate County Circuit Court ordered that the goods be *replevined* [read *replevied*] from David, in accordance with the terms of the settlement agreement." *Madison v. Madison*, 922 So.2d 832, 833 (Miss. Ct. App. 2006).

*replevisable. See **repleviable**.

replevy, vb., = (1) [transitive] to regain possession of (personal property) under a provisional remedy that allows the plaintiff, upon giving security, to regain the disputed property from the defendant and to hold it until the court decides who owns it; (2) [transitive] to regain possession of (personal property) by a successful action in replevin; or (3) [intransitive] to bring an action for replevin.

Though sense 3 is fairly infrequent, senses 1 and 2 are common. The distinction between them involves merely the stage that the litigation has reached: if the lawsuit is still pending, sense 1 applies—e.g.:

- "The cardinal question in every replevin action is whether the plaintiff was entitled to immediate possession of the property *replevied* at the commencement of the action." *International Harvester Credit Corp. v. Lech*, 438 N.W.2d 474, 477 (Neb. 1989).
- "The mortgagee-finance company *replevied* the automobile from the purchaser, who then settled with the finance company by agreeing to pay the balance due on the mortgage." *People v. Jory*, 505 N.W.2d 228, 233 (Mich. 1993).
- "The failure of the court to order a bond that complies with the replevin statute threatens the security of the person whose property is *replevied*." *Child's Play Ltd. v. A & A, Inc.*, 642 A.2d 170, 172 (Me. 1994).

If, by contrast, the litigation has concluded and the plaintiff has prevailed, sense 2 applies—e.g.: "Lienholder *replevied* the vehicle and recovered attorney fees and costs from the wrecker service." *Sharp v. State*, 877 P.2d 629, 630 (Okla. 1994).

Sometimes one cannot tell, without the fuller context, whether sense 1 or sense 2 applies—e.g:

- "PCA 'picked up and sold' some cattle and defendant Hopkins *replevied* the 88 head and sold them." *Central Prod. Credit Ass'n v. Hopkins*, 810 S.W.2d 108, 110 (Mo. Ct. App. 1991).
- "Homeowners allege that SCOF did not properly credit the individual accounts for items it *replevied* from the corresponding lots." *Dave Kolb Grading, Inc. v. Lieberman Corp.*, 837 S.W.2d 924, 933 (Mo. Ct. App. 1992).

Only personal property can be *replevied*, as the following statement acknowledges: "In any event, someone out there had better tell the creditors who repossessed and hauled away center pivot systems from debt-ridden irrigators that those creditors have *replevied* real estate—quite a legal phenomenon to say the least." *Mapco Ammonia Pipeline, Inc. v. State Bd. of Equalization & Assessment*, 471 N.W.2d 734, 749 (Neb. 1991). See **replevin**. Cf. **detinue**.

*replicatable is incorrect for *replicable*—e.g.: "The feeders' argument assumes . . . the mechanical (and therefore *replicatable* [read *replicable*]) application of such fixed numbers." *In re Beef Indus. Antitrust Litig.*, 542 F.Supp. 1122, 1141 (N.D. Tex. 1982).

replication. See **answer,** vb. & COMMON-LAW PLEADINGS.

reply. See **answer,** vb. & COMMON-LAW PLEADINGS.

report. A. And *reporter.* Traditionally, a law *report* is a written account of a proceeding and judicial decision, and the *reporter* is the person responsible for making and publishing that account. (Cf. **court reporter.**) In AmE, however, *reporter* has been blurred into *report*—primarily because of West Publishing Company's "National Reporter" system (established in 1879), each *Reporter* being a set of books containing judicial opinions from a geographic area within the country. Formerly, fastidious writers tried to distinguish the senses by capitalizing one but not the other, as the following quotation suggests, but this practice is not widely followed. E.g.: "It may not come amiss to remark that the National Reporter System is usually spoken of as the '*Reporters*,' and one of the component parts of that system is in like manner spoken of as a '*Reporter*.' Wherever, in this or the succeeding chapters of this work, the word is used with a capital, it refers to one or more of the parts of the National Reporter System. When the word '*reporter*' is used without capitalization, it refers to the person who reports or edits the cases in any series of reports to which reference is being made." William M. Lile et al., *Brief Making and the Use of Law Books* 37 (3d ed. 1914).

A similar extension of *reporter* occurred in 19th-century Scotland, where the *Scottish Law Reporter* appeared from 1865 to 1925.

B. The Reports. In BrE, "the Reports" are Coke's 13 volumes that began to appear in 1600. Coke tried to present every previous authority bearing on each case he reported, and his work has remained the historian's first entrance into the study of medieval caselaw.

reportedly. "Newspapermen and broadcasters live on a steady diet of this adverb," wrote Wilson Follett. "Yet it is so lacking in the characteristics of a respectable adverb that one would like to see its use confined to cable messages, where it saves money and can await translation into English." *Modern American Usage* 279 (1966). E.g.: "Approximately fifteen minutes later, the officer stopped a red car traveling away from the general area where *the shots reportedly had been fired* [read, according to Follett, *where the shots had been reported*]." *U.S. v. Johnson*, 592 F.3d 442, 451 (3d Cir. 2010).

To be sure, adverbs in *-edly* are often cumbersome and opaque (at first). *Reportedly* is not nearly as common in legal writing as *allegedly, confessedly,* and *assertedly.* All such forms ought to be avoided unless there is virtually no other concise way of saying what needs to be said. If that test is met, as it often is, we should use *reportedly* or any of the other terms without apology. See -EDLY, **allegedly** & **confessedly.**

reporter. See **report** (A).

report of proceedings. This term is used in various American jurisdictions to refer to the verbatim transcript of any on-the-record proceedings before a judge. In Texas, the anomalous phrase *statement of facts* is used in this sense. See **record** (B).

Reports, the. See **report** (B).

repose is not "indefinite dormancy," but rather suggests temporary rest, after which there will again be activity. Hence, in the following pronouncement, the court was not aspersing the doctrine in question as strongly as it might have thought: "As to sovereign immunity, that doctrine, insofar as it has been created by courts, seems headed for a deserved *repose*." *City of Albuquerque v. Garcia*, 508 P.2d 585, 587 (N.M. 1973). This is slovenly writing that makes little sense—why "insofar as it has been created by the courts," which is ambiguous? The judge might better have written, "Sovereign immunity as created by the courts seems to be moribund." This says the same thing in almost half the words. See CUTTING OUT THE CHAFF.

Statute of repose is a curious AmE legal usage for a statute that sets up a legal defense, usu. by the passage of time. It differs from a period of *limitation* because it bars a suit a fixed number of years after the defendant acts in some way (as by manufacturing a product), whereas *limitation* bars an action if the plaintiff does not file suit within a set time from the date when the cause of action accrues. E.g.:

- "Common-law jurisdictions refer to this type of limitation as a *statute of repose*, while states with civil codes use the term peremptive period." *Stanley v. Trinchard*, 579 F.3d 515, 518 n.3 (5th Cir. 2009).
- "The District Court determined that section 4A-505 of the U.C.C. posed a procedural bar—a one-year *statute of repose* on claims that an account was wrongfully debited based on a payment order." *ReAmerica, S.A. v. Wells Fargo Bank Int'l*, 577 F.3d 102, 105 (2d Cir. 2009).

See **limitation.**

repository; *repositary. The first spelling is standard. Cf. **depositary.**

represent; re-present. See RE- PAIRS.

representation; misrepresentation. These two words require care: if by *fraudulent representation* one really means *fraudulent misrepresentation*, then the latter phrase should be used. Cf. **false representation.**

representations and warranties. Although most contracts have a section so designated, there is widespread doubt about the precise difference between a *representation* and a *warranty*. One theory, not far from the truth, is that a *representation* amounts to a statement that the present situation is so-and-so, while a *warranty* is a guarantee that it will be so in the future. In fact, though, there are four salient differences between them: (1) a *warranty* is conclusively presumed to be material (therefore giving rise immediately to a claim for breach), while the burden is on the party claiming breach to show that a *representation* is material; (2) a *warranty* must be strictly complied with in every particular, while substantial truth is the only requirement for a *representation*; (3) a *warranty* is an essential part of a contract, while a *representation* is usually only a collateral inducement; and (4) an express *warranty* must be written on the face of the document, while a *representation* may be written or oral.

Some have asked this: if the *warranty* gives so much more protection than a *representation*, why not simply use *warranty* alone—without *representation*? It's a fair point, perhaps, but here's the reason for sticking to both: some parties to a contract don't want merely a guarantee that so-and-so will be so in the future; they also want an eye-to-eye statement (*representation*) that the thing is so now. If it later turns out not to have been so when the *representation* was made, then the party claiming breach can complain of a lie. (See **lie.**) If only a *warranty* were in place, the breaching party could simply say, "I'll make good on your losses—as I always said I would—but I never told you that such-and-such was the case." Hence *representations and warranties.*

representee (= one to whom a representation has been made), a word that originated in the 17th century and then was disused for nearly two centuries, reemerged in 20th-century discussions of contract law. It has become fairly common as a correlative of *representor*—e.g.:

- "It is presumed that the *representor* in pursuing his own economic interest will necessarily protect the rights of the *representees* who have the same economic interest." *In re Will of Levy*, 496 N.Y.S.2d 911, 912 (Sur. Ct. 1985).
- "Each [doctrine] is based on a representation followed by reliance on the part of the *representee*." G.H. Treitel, *The Law of Contract* 109 (8th ed. 1991).

- "Washington courts have . . . discussed the plaintiff's education . . . and whether oral misrepresentations were 'contradicted' by written documents in the *representee's* possession." *Swartz v. KPMG LLP*, 476 F.3d 756, 762 (9th Cir. 2007).

See -EE. Cf. **misrepresentee.**

repress. See **oppress.**

reprieve. See **clemency.**

reprimand. See **reprove.**

reprise, n.; **reprisal.** *Reprise* = (1) an annual deduction, duty, or payment out of a manor or estate, as an annuity or the like; or (2) (in music) a repetition. *Reprisal* = an act of retaliation, usu. of one nation against another but short of war.

reproach. See **reprove.**

reprobate (= to reject [as an instrument or deed] as not binding on one) is, in Scots law, the antonym of *approbate*. See **approbate.**

reprove; reprimand; admonish; reproach; rebuke; chide; upbraid; objurgate. These verbs share the sense "to criticize with disapproval, usu. in hopes of rectifying a flaw." To *reprove* is to lay fault humanely and with restraint, in the expectation that the person so corrected will improve. To *reprimand* is to reprove severely and formally, and usually both publicly and officially. To *admonish* is to reprove mildly, but with warnings or cautions. To *reproach* is to reprove by expressing dissatisfaction, unhappiness, and perhaps even derision. To *rebuke* is to scold pointedly and sternly. To *chide* or *upbraid* is to rebuke or to take to task over some matter of only moderate or little significance. To *objurgate* is to chide more formally—and with a greater sense of intimidation (partly because the word itself is intimidating).

republish; revive. In the law of wills, there is a distinction between these verbs. *Republishing* involves bringing forward in time a will that has remained continuously valid since its making. *Reviving* a will involves restoring to effectiveness a will or codicil that has been revoked.

repudiate. See **decline.**

repudiation; rescission. *Repudiation* = a contracting party's words or actions that indicate an intention not to perform the contract in the future. *Rescission* = a party's unilateral unmaking of a contract for a legally sufficient reason, such as the other party's material breach.

Though the definitions suggest precise meanings for these terms, they are frequently confused. The main problem is that *repudiation* is a common-law term, whereas *rescission* is an equitable one. Hence, as P.S. Atiyah points out, "most books on the law of Contract discuss the right to repudiate the contract for breach of condition in a section on Remedies, while they treat of the right to rescind a contract in the section on Misrepresentation. Indeed, so different are *repudiation* and *rescission* believed to be, that serious confusion is caused in the law of sale of goods by the fact that the Sale of Goods Act regulates the former but not the latter." P.S. Atiyah, *An Introduction to the Law of Contract* 294 (3d ed. 1981). To compound the trouble, lawyers indiscriminately use *repudiation* for both a rightful and a wrongful termination.

For more on the verb *repudiate* and its near-synonyms, see **decline.**

repudiatory; *repudiative. Despite the *OED*'s suggestion to the contrary, *repudiatory* is the usual term—**repudiative* being a NEEDLESS VARIANT.

repugn. See **impugn.**

repugnant. This word, in law, is frequently used in its oldest sense, "inconsistent with; contrary or contradictory to." Legal writers use the word most commonly when contrasting two things—e.g.:

• "The annexing of such incidents to the contract would be *repugnant* to the express terms [of the contract]." *Nebraska Land & Feeding Co. v. Trauerman*, 98 N.W. 37, 39 (Neb. 1904).
• "The idea of judicial application of constitutional provisions and of judicial refusal to give effect to legislation *repugnant* to the Constitution . . . goes back to refusal of the common-law courts to give effect to acts of Parliament 'impertinent to be observed.'" Roscoe Pound, *The Development of Constitutional Guarantees of Liberty* 96–97 (1957).
• "Because the statute itself is not *repugnant* to the Constitution and can by its terms comport with the Sixth Amendment, the Court does not have the constitutional authority to invalidate it." *U.S. v. Booker*, 543 U.S. 220, 283 (2005) (Stevens, J., dissenting in part).

In nonlegal usage, *repugnant* today denotes "causing distaste or aversion."

repulse. See **repel.**

repulsive. See **repellent.**

reputation. See **character.**

reputational (= of or pertaining to reputation) is not recorded in *W3*, but dates from 1921 in the *OED*. The term is useful to legal writers—e.g.:

• "Nor is any liberty or *reputational* interest implicated." *Findeisen v. North East Indep. Sch. Dist.*, 749 F.2d 234, 240 (5th Cir. 1984) (Garwood, J., concurring).
• "Management may well value more highly the time that would be expended in litigation and any *reputational* effects of a loss, whereas plaintiffs might well assign a high value to the potentially recoverable damages." David M. Phillips, *Principles of Corporate Governance*, 52 Geo. Wash. L. Rev. 653, 686 (1985).

• "The victim . . . would incur not only the costs entailed in mounting a defense, he likely would sustain a *reputational* loss as well, and neither loss would be compensable under federal law." *Hartman v. Moore*, 547 U.S. 250, 267 (2006) (Ginsburg, J., dissenting).

requestee. Though recorded in neither the *OED* nor other major English-language dictionaries, *requestee* has achieved limited currency in law as a correlative of *requester* (or, less good, *-or*). E.g.:

• "The burden as to the first prong would be on the *requestee* as the movant, while the burden as to the second prong is on the requestor." *Cielock v. Munn*, 262 S.E.2d 114, 115 (Ga. 1979).
• "[The Freedom of Information Act] does not require that information must be helpful to the *requestee* before the government must disclose it." *Stolt-Nielsen Transp. Group Ltd. v. U.S.*, 534 F.3d 728, 734 (D.C. Cir. 2008).

See -EE.

requiescat in pace. See **R.I.P.**

require. See **necessitate.**

requisite. See **prerequisite.**

*requisite requirement is a patent REDUNDANCY.

requisition = (1) an authoritative, formal demand; or (2) a governmental seizure of property.

requital; *requitement. The second is a NEEDLESS VARIANT.

res; re; rem. *Res* (= thing), pronounced like *race* in AmE but like *reese* or *rays* in BrE, is used in a number of different ways in legal contexts. Most often it is a synonym of *principal* or *corpus* in reference to funds. E.g.:

• "When Sellers are not suing to enforce the trust obligations or to preserve their shares of the trust *res*, but instead are suing the trustee in tort for damages resulting from a breach of his fiduciary duties, we believe that the statute of limitations must accrue from the time that the trustee openly repudiates those duties." *Weis-Buy Servs., Inc. v. Paglia*, 411 F.3d 415, 423 (3d Cir. 2005).
• "Then, as now, the jurisdiction of courts adjudicating rights in the bankrupt estate included the power to issue compulsory orders to facilitate the administration and distribution of the *res*." *Central Va. Cmty. Coll. v. Katz*, 546 U.S. 356, 362 (2006) (per Stevens, J.).

See **corpus.**

Yet it is often used in its literal sense "thing," in reference to a particular thing, known or unknown. E.g.:

• "In a sense, the married couple once owned the entirety of the marital *res*, over which Jennifer no longer had any claim; but, of course, the married couple no longer existed after the divorce." *In re Bledsoe*, 569 F.3d 1106, 1117 (9th Cir. 2009).
• "After reviewing this precedent, we conclude a state must exert some element of physical control over the *res* to satisfy the possession requirement." *Aqua Log, Inc. v. Georgia*, 594 F.3d 1330, 1335 (11th Cir. 2010).

See **thing.**

In more prudish days, *res* was even used in legal writing as a EUPHEMISM for "sexual organ"—e.g.: "The weight of authority, both English and American, is that although [for rape to be proved] some penetration must be shown beyond a reasonable doubt, it need not be full penetration; nothing more than *res in re* being requisite." 44 Am. Jur. *Rape* § 3, at 903 (1942). In Latin, *rem* is the accusative case of the singular noun, and *re* is the ablative case (as in *In re Snooks*).

Res is the plural as well as the singular form: "German law uses the word 'thing' only for *res* that are corporeal." G.W. Paton, *A Textbook of Jurisprudence* 508 (4th ed. 1972). See *jus in rem* & *in personam* (B).

*res adjudicata. See **res judicata (A)**.

res administrata is a NEOLOGISM meaning "res judicata as applied to administrative decisions." E.g.:

- "Nor is there any agreement as to precisely what degree of similarity should exist between the received conventions of res judicata and what might be called the doctrine of '*res administrata*.'" Frank E. Cooper, *State Administrative Law* 503 (1965).
- "Principles of res judicata—perhaps better dubbed '*res administrata*'—can apply to successive proceedings before a single agency." 18 Charles Alan Wright et al., *Federal Practice and Procedure* § 4475, at 762 (1981).

rescindable; *rescissible. The first form is better because of its more recognizable relation to the verb. It is the only form listed in the *OED*; *W3* contains both. Cf. **rescissory**.

*rescindment is a NEEDLESS VARIANT of *rescission*.

*rescissible. See **rescindable**.

rescission; *recision; *recission; *rescision; *rescindment. In the sense "an act of rescinding, annulling, vacating, or canceling," *rescission* is the standard and the etymologically preferable spelling. **Rescindment* is a NEEDLESS VARIANT of that word.

On the question of spelling, some writers have been misled by their smattering of Latin: perhaps they have realized that **recision* is from the Latin noun *recisio*, meaning "a cutting back, or lopping off." And through the process known as folk etymology, these writers may have wrongly thought **recision* to be the correct form, *rescission* a corruption. Yet *rescission* is the true Latin form (fr. the accusative *rescissionem*) as well as the true English form. *Rescission* is preferable also because of the consistency of spelling between verb and noun (*rescind/rescission*).

Yet the inferior spelling remains annoyingly common—e.g.:

- "We are not called upon to address whether in an action for fraud in the inducement of a contract, Jones must elect between the remedies of damages and *recision* [read *rescission*] of the contract." *DeCoatsworth v. Jones*, 639 A.2d 792, 797 n.3 (Pa. 1994).

- "The letter to petitioner Mobil states that the Government is imposing a lease suspension—rather than a cancellation or *recision* [read *rescission*]." *Mobil Oil Exploration & Producing S.E., Inc. v. U.S.*, 530 U.S. 604, 631 (2000) (Stevens, J., dissenting).
- "[T]he defendant sought only the remedy of specific performance, which we explained imposed a lesser burden than *recision* [read *rescission*] or withdrawal of the plea." *U.S. v. Williams*, 510 F.3d 416, 427 (3d Cir. 2007).

Some courts even mistakenly combine the misspelling **recision* with the correct spelling to arrive at still other, less frequent misspellings: **recission* and **rescision*. The former appears, e.g., in *Malone v. Safety-Guard Mfg. Co.*, 748 F.2d 312, 314 (5th Cir. 1984).

The sound of the *-ss-* in *rescission* is like that in *precision*, not that in *permission*. This is one of very few words in the English language in which the *-ss-* has the sound /zh/ instead of /sh/. Two others are *fission* (in AmE) and *abscission*. Cf. *-mission* (with /sh/) in its many forms.

For the distinction between *rescission* and *repudiation*, see **repudiation**.

rescissory; *rescissionary; *rescissional. *Rescissory* is the standard adjective corresponding to the noun *rescission* and the verb *to rescind*. E.g.: "Through its fraud action, Cinerama seeks . . . an award of *rescissory* damages." *Cede & Co. v. Technicolor, Inc.*, 542 A.2d 1182, 1186 (Del. 1988). **Rescissionary* and **rescissional* are NEEDLESS VARIANTS. Cf. **rescindable**.

research; re-search. See RE- PAIRS.

reserve, vb. In legal drafting, *reserve* is sometimes used when the better word is *except*, as legal commentators have long noted—e.g.: "Grantors before the time of Coke had used the word *reserve* when the plain intent was to take out of the operation of the conveyance some part of the property which would otherwise have fallen within the description used in the conveyance. Here the subject-matter was, of course, proper for an *exception*, and the strictly accurate words would have been, according to Coke, '*exceptis, salvo, praeter*, and the like.'" Harry A. Bigelow & J.W. Madden, *Exception and Reservation of Easements*, 38 Harv. L. Rev. 180, 181 (1924). *Reserve* historically referred to a new thing that was being created, such as rents. *Id.* at 180. See **except**.

res gestae (lit., "things done") has, it seems, irrevocably ensconced itself in the terminology of the law of evidence. But Wigmore considered it "not only entirely useless, but even positively harmful." 6 J.H. Wigmore, *Evidence in Trials at Common Law* § 1767, at 255 (James H. Chadbourn ed., 4th ed. 1976). And recent writers have said that the "ancient phrase can well be jettisoned, with due acknowledgment that it served its era in the evolution of evidence law." Edward W. Cleary, *McCormick on Evidence* § 288, at 836 (3d ed. 1984).

The phrase is generally defined as "the events at issue or others contemporaneous with them." In the law of evidence, *res gestae* may be either a rule of relevance that makes testimony about the events forming part of the *res gestae* admissible, or an exception to the hearsay rule allowing for the admissibility of *res gestae* (e.g., if they accompany or explain a declarant's contemporaneous state of mind or physical sensations). See TERMS OF ART.

Res gesta, the singular form, is also sometimes used, as in R.N. Gooderson, *"Res Gesta" in Criminal Cases* (pt. 2), 1957 Cambridge L.J. 55 (so spelled throughout).

residency. A. And *residence*. Although both are used in the sense "the act or fact of living in a given place for some time," only *residence* is used as a FORMAL WORD—some would say pomposity—for "house" <a three-story residence>.

It would be useful to restrict *residence* to that sense and to use *residency* in the sense "domicile," but there is little consistency in today's usage. Following are some typical uses, with suggested revisions in brackets for the first two specimens:

- "Both those favoring lengthy *residence* [read *residency*] requirements and those opposing all requirements pleaded their cases during the congressional hearings on the Social Security Act." *Shapiro v. Thompson*, 394 U.S. 618, 646 (1969) (Warren, C.J., dissenting).
- "It is not irrational to believe that a United States citizen father who has spent at least five years in *residence* [read *residency*] during his teenage years would have more of a connection with this country to pass on than, say, a father who lived in the United States between the ages of one and ten." *U.S. v. Flores-Villar*, 536 F.3d 990, 998 (9th Cir. 2008).
- "Although the Louisiana state bar may have reciprocity with other states, citizens could leave the country and establish *residency* abroad, and, as the majority states, Louisiana does not have reciprocity with other nations." *LeClerc v. Webb*, 419 F.3d 405, 430 (5th Cir. 2005) (Stewart, J., dissenting in part).

B. And *domicile*. These terms are not synonyms in legal contexts. *Residency* usually just means bodily presence as an inhabitant in a given place; *domicile* usually requires bodily presence plus an intention to make the place one's home. See **citizenship** & **domicile**.

resident. See **citizen (B)**.

residuary; residual; *residuous. In the context of residues of estates and trusts, *residuary* is the preferred adjective. The *residuary* clause in a will "disposes of property of the testator not otherwise disposed of." George E. Gardner, *Handbook of the Law of Wills* 418 (1903). E.g.:

- "His will did not mention the paintings, but it did name a *residuary* legatee, namely, Ferdinand's niece, Maria Altmann, by then an American citizen." *Republic of Austria v. Altmann*, 541 U.S. 677, 705 (2004) (Breyer, J., concurring).
- "Since the beneficiaries named in the *residuary* clause of a New York will inherit everything in the estate that is not subject to a specific bequest, these beneficiaries are

regarded as the 'universal heirs' for purposes of German law." *Nordwind v. Rowland*, 584 F.3d 420, 430 (2d Cir. 2009).

Yet there are many examples of *residual* used in such contexts—e.g.:

- "Therefore, they contend that it is 'equitable' for this Court to 'restore' the money to Robert's *residual* [read *residuary*] estate under theories of unjust enrichment." *Freedman v. Freedman*, 116 F.Supp.2d 379, 380 (E.D.N.Y. 2000).
- "The decedent in his will gave specific instructions as to how the *residual* [read *residuary*] estate was to be administered and how the expenses of his estate were to be handled in the event the residue estate was insufficient." *Lurie v. Comm'r*, 425 F.3d 1021, 1026 (7th Cir. 2005).

Residual and *residuary* are susceptible to INELEGANT VARIATION: "They claim to have an interest in Wilbert's *residuary* [read *residual*] trust as *residual* beneficiaries of the estate." *In re Will of Frye*, 764 N.W.2d 783, 783 n.3 (Iowa Ct. App. 2009).

When one writes of a person's capabilities and functions remaining after an injury, *residual* is the correct term—e.g.: "The ALJ . . . [found] that Purnell retained the *residual* function capacity to perform a limited range of light work activity." *Purnell v. Astrue*, 662 F.Supp.2d 402, 411 (E.D. Pa. 2009).

*Residuous is a NEEDLESS VARIANT of the other two words.

residuary legacy. See **legacy**.

residue; residuum; residual, n.; **residuary,** n. Both *residue* and *residuum* mean "that which remains." *Residue* is the usual and preferred term for contexts involving estates. It means "the part of a decedent's estate remaining after payment of all debts, expenses, statutory claims, taxes, and testamentary gifts . . . have been made" (*Black's Law Dictionary* 629 (9th ed. 2009)). E.g.:

- "Virginia and another child, Charles D. Wilkinson, were to receive the rest and *residue* of Virginia's estate." *Wilkinson v. U.S.*, 440 F.3d 970, 972 (8th Cir. 2006).
- "In his will, Dr. Stern bequeathed the *residue* of his estate, including any interest in the painting, to the Foundation." *Vineberg v. Bissonnette*, 548 F.3d 50, 54 (1st Cir. 2008).

Although Blackstone wrote that "the surplus or *residuum* must be paid to the residuary legatee" (2 William Blackstone, *Commentaries on the Laws of England* 514 (1766)), *residuum* is now to be avoided in such contexts: "In certain cases where the *residuum* was given to named persons in distinct parcels or in unequal shares, this court has held that a lapsed legacy did not go to the residuary legatees." *Tumlin v. Butler*, 448 S.E.2d 198, 199 (Ga. 1994).

Residuum is a technical term used correctly in chemical contexts—e.g.: "Deodorizer distillate is the *residuum* of the soybean oil manufacturing process; it is a chemically undefined solid remaining after deodorized soybean oil is taken from feedstock oil." *Archer Daniels Midland Co. v. U.S.*, 561 F.3d 1308, 1314 (Fed. Cir. 2009). The plural is *residua*.

Residue and *residuum* often tempt those who fancy INELEGANT VARIATION. In the phrase *residue of a residue*, there is nothing wrong with repeating the word *residue*. Varying the form of the word is an affectation—e.g.: "Some courts have held that the gift passes by intestacy on the theory that there can be no *residue of a residuum* [read *residue of a residue*]." John Ritchie et al., *Case and Materials on Decedents' Estates and Trusts* 988 (6th ed. 1982).

Residual, n., = a remainder; an amount still remaining after the main part is subtracted or accounted for (*OED*). E.g.: "If some *residual* still remains, that *residual* amount will revert to the reversion fund discussed above." *Bynum v. District of Columbia,* 412 F.Supp.2d 73, 80 (D.D.C. 2006).

Residuary, when used elliptically as a noun for such full phrases as *residuary estate* (= *residue*), is uncommon and possibly confusing. It should be avoided. E.g.:

- "When a court decision threatened to invalidate those publicity rights, the California legislature intervened by enacting a statute to protect the rights for the *residuary* [read *residual*] beneficiary of her will." Joshua C. Tate, *Immortal Fame,* 44 Ga. L. Rev. 1, 5–6 (2009).
- "The *residuary* [read *residue*] of her estate was to be placed in trust with the income to be distributed to her nephew." *Iowa Superior Court Attorney Disciplinary Bd. v. Wagner,* 768 N.W.2d 279, 282 (Iowa 2009).

The word sometimes even elliptically denotes *residuary beneficiary,* a usage that can cause confusion—e.g.:

- "It was this reversion which passed to the *residuaries* [read *residuary beneficiaries*]." *Reeves v. American Sec. & Trust Co.,* 115 F.2d 145, 148 (D.C. Cir. 1940).
- "[This] conduct denied the nieces their inheritance as *residuaries* [read *residuary beneficiaries*] of the estate." *Krevatas v. Wright,* 518 So.2d 435, 438 (Fla. Dist. Ct. App. 1988).

*residuous. See **residuary.**

residuum. See **residue.**

resign is almost always intransitive in the U.S. <resign from office>, but is often transitive in England <resign the office>.

resign; re-sign. See RE- PAIRS.

res integra; res nova. These terms are moderately common in legal writing. Both mean "an undecided question; a case of first impression"; *res nova* is used primarily in AmE and *res integra* in BrE. Following are examples of the latter:

- "The court added that if it were *res integra* it would hold that calling a man a rogue or a woman a whore in public company is actionable." *Cooper v. Seaverns,* 105 P. 509, 512 (Kan. 1909).
- "James Kent, then a judge in New York's state supreme court, indicated that, were the question one of first impression ('*res integra* to our law'), he would have been inclined to follow . . . the civil law." Robert E. Mensel, *A*

Diddle at Brobdingnag, 38 U. Mem. L. Rev. 97, 110–11 (2007).

American legal writers use *res nova* far more often than *res integra*—e.g.:

- "Requiring the matter to be considered *res nova* by every single trial judge in every single case might seem to some to pose serious administrative difficulties." *Rock v. Arkansas,* 483 U.S. 44, 65 (1987) (Rehnquist, C.J., dissenting).
- "This case does not implicate deference concerns under the Antiterrorism and Effective Death Penalty Act because the issue is *res nova.*" *Richie v. Mullin,* 417 F.3d 1117, 1119 n.1 (10th Cir. 2005).
- "Although this issue of statutory interpretation is *res nova* in this circuit, the Tax Court, the D.C. Circuit, and the Federal Circuit have each resolved it." *Curr-Spec Partners, LP v. Commissioner,* 579 F.3d 391, 393 (5th Cir. 2009).

See **first impression, case of.**

The plural forms are *res integrae* and *res novae.*

res ipsa loquitur (= the thing speaks for itself) is known in G.B. but is far more common in the U.S., where it has become familiar enough that *res ipsa case* and even *resipsy* (also spelled *resipsey*) have become lawyers' elliptical colloquialisms. *Res ipsa loquitur* is one of those LATINISMS that have become so common in lawyers' JARGON, or more specifically as TERMS OF ART, that their usefulness is unquestioned.

The phrase refers to the doctrine allowing that, in some circumstances, the mere fact of an accident's occurrence raises an inference of negligence so as to establish a prima facie case. "The rule bearing this name *warrants* the inference of negligence but does not *compel* such an inference." *Johnson v. U.S.,* 333 U.S. 46, 48 (1948) (per Douglas, J.) (quotation marks and brackets omitted).

Many writers tend toward the elliptical dropping of the final word in the phrase—e.g.:

- "*Res ipsa* belongs to the world of negligence." *Jones v. Williams,* 286 F.3d 1159, 1167 (9th Cir. 2002) (Silverman, J., concurring).
- "Although they deny relying on the doctrine of *res ipsa loquitur* to prove their case, the plaintiff's claim . . . is essentially a *res ipsa* claim." *Borger v. CSX Transp., Inc.,* 571 F.3d 559, 566 (6th Cir. 2009).
- "I therefore respectfully dissent from the majority's invocation of *res ipsa* in a case where it was not warranted." *Gass v. Marriott Hotel Servs., Inc.,* 558 F.3d 419, 435 (6th Cir. 2009) (Boggs, C.J., dissenting).

It may be just as well to leave the last word off, because it is commonly misspelled. American judicial opinions contain examples of **locquitur, *locquitor, *loquiter, *loquitor,* and **loguitur,* among other variations.

The phrase is often used attributively, as in, "She sought to recover on a *res ipsa loquitur* theory." Generally, because it is a foreign phrase, it is not hyphenated when so used. See PHRASAL ADJECTIVES (B).

*resistable. See **resistible.**

resister; resistor. *Resister* is the term meaning "one who resists." *Resistor* is a technical electrical term.

resistible; *resistable. The first spelling is preferred.

resistor. See **resister.**

res judicata. A. And *res adjudicata. The phrase meaning literally "a thing adjudicated" is now universally spelled *res judicata.* The other form, **res adjudicata,* ought to be rejected as a NEEDLESS VARIANT.

But the spelling *adjudicata* was formerly common—e.g.:
- "The jury's verdict of not guilty necessarily confirmed Bruce's title and rendered the issue *res adjudicata.*" Ephraim Tutt, *Yankee Lawyer* 70 (1943).
- "[The] rule . . . involves a departure from the ordinary principles of *res adjudicata.*" Lon L. Fuller, *Legal Fictions* 4 (1967).

Though occasionally in use as late as the 1960s, *adjudicata* is almost never seen in contemporary legal writing.

B. And *collateral estoppel.* See **collateral estoppel (A).**

C. Preposition with. *Res judicata,* which needs no italics, takes *of* or *to.* E.g.:
- "An acquittal on one [indictment] could not be pleaded as *res judicata* of the other." *Dunn v. U.S.,* 284 U.S. 390, 393 (1932) (per Holmes, J.).
- "Certainly the judgments entered are *res judicata* of the tax claims . . . whether or not the basis of the agreements on which they rest reached the merits." *U.S. v. International Bld'g Co.,* 345 U.S. 502, 506 (1953) (per Douglas, J.).
- "Our holding that the Alabama Supreme Court's application of *res judicata* to nonparties violated due process turned on . . . understanding . . . that the first suit was brought in a representative capacity." *Taylor v. Sturgell,* 553 U.S. 880, 897 (2008) (per Ginsburg, J.).

In American legal writing the phrase is frequently used as a kind of predicate adjective, as here: "A judgment is not *res judicata* as to, or legally enforceable against, a nonparty." *Provident Tradesmens Bank & Trust Co. v. Patterson,* 390 U.S. 102, 110 (1968) (per Harlan, J.). See **res administrata** & *chose jugée.*

D. Plural. The plural, rarely used nowadays, is *res judicatae*—e.g.: "In the north . . . the accumulation of *res judicatae* led to the redefinition of custom." Marie Seong-Hak Kim, *Civil Law and Civil War,* 28 Law & Hist. Rev. 791, 794 (2010).

res nova. See **res integra.**

resolvable; *resolvible; resoluble. The first is far more common than the others in meaning "able to be resolved." E.g.: "If this is an accurate picture of how the constitutional system evolves—turning potential dead ends into uncomfortable but *resolvable* conflicts—it suggests how unique were the sectional disputes that led to the Civil War." Sanford Levinson & Jack M. Balkin, *Constitutional Crises,* 157 U. Pa. L. Rev. 707, 748 (2009). *Resoluble* has the liability of meaning also "capable of being dissolved again." The variant spelling **resolvible* is to be avoided.

resort. See **recourse.**

resound; re-sound. See RE- PAIRS.

respect. A. *In respect of* and *with respect to.* These phrases are usually best replaced by simpler expressions, such as single prepositions. See **in respect of, regard** & **as regards.**

B. *With respect, with great respect,* etc. David Pannick sardonically remarks: "The barrister presents his arguments *with respect, with great respect,* or, on difficult occasions, *with the greatest of respect.* The degree of respect voiced is, of course, in inverse proportion to the willingness indicated by the judge to agree with the arguments being advanced." David Pannick, *Judges* 153 (1987).

respecter of persons. See **no respecter of persons, the law is.**

respectfully. The term is greatly overworked in lawyers' writing directed at judges, often with the effect of conveying either sycophancy or sarcasm. E.g.: "Plaintiff '*respectfully* submits that [she] has followed the required court procedures' by making 'multiple efforts to obtain clarification that the case was suspended' such that she 'did not . . . willfully disregard the court set hearing.'" *Peterson v. Archstone,* 677 F.Supp.2d 167, 168 (D.D.C. 2010). See **I respectfully submit** & **respective.**

respective; respectively. Legal writers tend to overuse these pedantic terms. *Respectively* ought to mean "each one in relation to that one's own situation." E.g.: "Appellee's and appellant's *respective* citizenships of France and Georgia therefore supported diversity jurisdiction." *Jagiella v. Jagiella,* 647 F.2d 561, 563 (5th Cir. 1981). It would be more natural, however, to write, "Appellee's citizenship of France and appellant's citizenship of Georgia therefore supported diversity jurisdiction."

Typically, *respectively* is not needed at all—e.g.: "In fact their decisions are much more consistent and ours are much less consistent than they appear *respectively* [delete *respectively*] in theory." Roscoe Pound, *The Formative Era of American Law* 123–24 (1938). The same criticism applies to the adjective *respective*—e.g.: "The order in which contracting parties must perform their *respective* [delete *respective*] obligations depends on the distinction between conditions precedent, concurrent conditions, and independent promises." G.H. Treitel, *The Law of Contract* 662 (8th ed. 1991). As H.W. Fowler wrote, "Delight in these words is a widespread but depraved taste; like soldiers and policemen, they have work to do, but, when the work is not there, the less we see of them the better; of ten sentences in which they occur, nine would be improved by their removal" (*MEU1* 500). For more on *respectively* and other distributive adverbs, see **each (A).**

A well-known formbook contains a petition for recovery of unpaid rent with the closing, just before the line for the lawyer's signature, "Respectively submitted." One might have hoped that everyone would know the difference between *respective* and *respectful*. See **respectfully.**

respond. See **answer,** vb.

respondeat superior [L. "let the principal answer"] is a maxim that embodies the rule of vicarious liability. The phrase is invariably used as a noun—e.g.: "Under the ordinary rules of *respondeat superior,* the ship-owner is responsible for his actions." Grant Gilmore & Charles L. Black Jr., *The Law of Admiralty* 520 (2d ed. 1975). The first word is sometimes misspelled **respondiat.*

respondent is the PARTY APPELLATION generally used opposite *petitioner,* whether the petitioner seeks a writ of error, a writ of mandamus, or some other type of relief. Both *respondent* and *petitioner* are used most often on appeal and not in the trial court. But that has not always been true of *respondent*: in equity cases, formerly, the *orator* was the complainant and the *respondent* was the defendant.

responsibility, when used in the sense "liability to be made to account or pay," is a LEGALISM not generally understood by nonlawyers, although its sense is sometimes deducible. Whereas nonlawyers use this term in moral senses, lawyers give it legal senses—e.g.: "Each defendant's ultimate monetary *responsibility* depends on the number of defendants ultimately held liable." *Schettino v. Roizman Dev., Inc.,* 730 A.2d 797, 801 (N.J. 1999). See **vicarious liability.**

In criminal contexts, *responsibility* refers to either (1) guilt; or (2) mental fitness to answer in court for one's actions.

responsible; liable; answerable; accountable; amenable. All these adjectives can mean "required to make good on a fault or deficiency." You can be *responsible* for fulfilling an obligation, administering an office, or paying to make up for a default <the attorney general is responsible to the citizens for enforcing the state's laws>. You can be *liable* if the law makes you responsible for your own or someone else's default <a guarantor is liable for the borrower's debt>. You are *answerable* if you can be called to account because of a legal violation or the neglect of a duty <the lane-jockey was clearly answerable for the wreck he caused>. You are *accountable* if you have been entrusted with something or you have become bound to be called on to justify your actions in the execution of that trust <officeholders are accountable to the electorate as a whole>. You are *amenable* if you are subject to the control of or to repudiation by a higher authority <even the Secretary of State is amenable to the law of the land> or open to accepting something <the parties were amenable to mediation>.

-RESS. See SEXISM (C).

rest, vb., = (AmE) to voluntarily conclude presenting evidence in a trial <after that testimony, the defense rested>. The idiom that one or the other side to a lawsuit *rests* dates from the late 19th century.

restaters = authors of the Restatements of the American Law Institute. E.g.: "Indeed, this very problem has been addressed by the learned *restaters* in Comment F to § 611, Restatement (Second) of Torts (1977)." *Hinerman v. Daily Gazette Co.,* 423 S.E.2d 560, 578 (W. Va. 1992).

As in the preceding quotation, the word often appears to be limited to the reporters on a particular Restatement, but sometimes the word appears to refer to the entire membership of the Institute, and sometimes with a sneering tone that says more about the writer than about the restaters—e.g.: "Just as legal realism undercut the symmetrical doctrines beloved of the *restaters* of the ALI, so law and economics and CLS, from different ends of the spectrum, have undercut much of the rationality that Hart and Sacks put into training the legal generation who were at law school in the fifties." Robert Stevens, 44 J. Legal Educ. 152, 154 (1994) (reviewing Anthony T. Kronman, *The Lost Lawyer: Failing Ideals of the Legal Profession* (1993)).

restaurateur. So spelled. **Restauranteur* is a common error—e.g.:

- "I would also have doubted seriously the advisability of excluding the ordinary *restauranteur* [read *restaurateur*] as an 'ultimate consumer.'" Ray J. Aiken, *Let's Not Oversimplify Legal Language,* 32 Rocky Mtn. L. Rev. 358, 361 (1960).
- "An example of negligence that does not lead to liability thanks to the fireman's rule would be a homeowner's or *restauranteur's* [read *restaurateur's*] negligent failure to turn off a stove, thereby starting a fire that leads to a responding firefighter being injured." Robert H. Heidt, *When Plaintiffs Are Premium Planners for Their Injuries,* 82 Ind. L.J. 745, 745–46 (2007).

rest in peace. See **R.I.P.**

restitution. According to the leading English authorities, "the law of *restitution* is the law relating to all claims, quasi-contractual or otherwise, [that] are founded upon the principle of unjust enrichment." Robert Goff & Gareth Jones, *The Law of Restitution* 3 (3d ed. 1986). This modern use of the term *restitution,* derived from Roman law, began as an Americanism but is now established in BrE as well.

At common law, *restitution* was ordinarily used to denote the return or restoration of some specific thing or condition. But 20th-century usage has extended the sense of the word to include not only the restoration or giving back of something, but also compensation, reimbursement, indemnification, or reparation for benefits derived from—or loss caused to—another.

For more on this term and its near-synonyms, see **reparation.**

restitutionary; *restitutional; *restitutive; *restitutory. Restitution being a common subject in law, we find any number of examples of *restitutionary* and *restitutional in law reports, although our unabridged dictionaries record only *restitutive and *restitutory. These last two are little known to American and British lawyers.

The standard form is *restitutionary*, and all other forms can properly be regarded as NEEDLESS VARIANTS. E.g.:

- "The earliest proceedings in common-law courts were *restitutionary* in nature." Restatement of Restitution 5 (1937).
- "From the time of Lord Mansfield *restitutionary* remedies were dependent on the dictates of 'natural justice and equity' on which he laid stress." Charles Alan Wright, *Cases on Remedies* 59 (1955).
- "*Restitutionary* remedies are designed to restore to plaintiff all that defendant gained at plaintiff's expense." Douglas Laycock, *Modern American Remedies* 3 (1985).
- "There are three forms of damages typically awarded to compensate for breach of contract: expectation damages, *restitutionary* damages, and reliance damages." *Southern Cal. Fed. Sav. & Loan Ass'n v. U.S.*, 422 F.3d 1319, 1334 (Fed. Cir. 2005).

restive, despite its misleading appearance, does not mean "restful." Formerly it meant "stubborn, refusing to budge," but now it has become synonymous with *restless*, a development that some language critics lament.

restoration; *restoral. The second is a NEEDLESS VARIANT.

restore; re-store. See RE- PAIRS.

restrain. See **refrain.**

rest, residue, and remainder. This collocation is beloved by drafters of wills. Those who strive for simplicity and PLAIN LANGUAGE usually write *all other property* instead. See DOUBLETS, TRIPLETS, AND SYNONYM-STRINGS & **residue.**

restricted construction; restricted interpretation. See *limited interpretation* under INTERPRETATION, MODES OF (B).

RESTRICTIVE AND NONRESTRICTIVE CLAUSES. See **that & which.**

restrictive covenant = a private agreement, usu. in a deed or lease, that restricts the use and occupancy of real property, most commonly by specifying lot size, building lines, architectural styles, and the uses to which the property may be put. Formerly, such covenants were used in the U.S. to racist ends: "Finally, '*restrictive covenants*'—whereby property-owners in 'white sections' of Northern cities contracted never to sell or rent to people 'not of the Caucasian race'— were dealt a long-range death-blow in a set of rulings which said that state courts could not enforce such contracts, even in private lawsuits, without violating the Fourteenth Amendment." Fred Rodell, *Nine Men* 295 (1955). See **covenant.**

resultant, n., for *result* is an ARCHAISM—e.g.:

- "For the legislative purpose is the *resultant* [read *result*] of the pressure of conflicting interests in the legislature." Jerome Frank, *Courts on Trial* 302 (1950).
- "Human preferences do not seem to be the *resultants* [read *result* or *results*] of a few simple causes, but rather of a large scale and measured under experimental conditions." Morris R. Cohen, *Reason and Law* 105 (1961).
- "The rationale for the Second Circuit's extension of the attorney-client privilege to communication to a nonlawyer accountant by the lawyer's client was the *resultant* [read *result*] of two conflicting forces." *Murray v. Board of Educ.*, 199 F.R.D. 154, 156 (S.D.N.Y. 2001).

resulting trust. See **constructive trust** (C).

resurface, vb. Like *surface*, *resurface* can be both intransitive and transitive. *Resurface* = (1) to come to the top again <he resurfaced in the middle of the pond>; or (2) to put a new surface on <the state resurfaced the road>.

retain is a FORMAL WORD for *keep*.

retainage; retainer. *Retainage* (AmE) = a percentage of what a landowner sets aside for a contractor, withholding the sum until the construction has been satisfactorily completed and all mechanics' liens either released or expired. Though the word is fairly common in American property law, it is omitted from every major English-language dictionary and from most law dictionaries.

Retainer = (1) a client's authorization for a lawyer to act in a case; (2) a fee paid to a lawyer to secure legal representation. A *special retainer* results in employment for a specific project. A *general retainer* results in employment for a specific length of time instead of for a specific project.

retaliation; retribution. As a type of punishment, *retaliation* (= the proportioning of punishment to the extent of the resulting harm) has been confused with *retribution* (= the proportioning of punishment to the blameworthiness of the offender). But they are two distinct concepts: "In a given situation, *retaliation* and *retribution* may have diametrically opposed implications for the proper level of punishment, for a person whose conduct is highly reprehensible may fortuitously fail to cause harm, and a person's conduct may accidentally result in great harm though he did nothing wrong." David J. Karp, *Causation in the Model Penal Code*, 78 Colum. L. Rev. 1249, 1257 n.21 (1978).

retaliatory; retaliative. The two forms have undergone DIFFERENTIATION. The former means "of, relating to, or constituting retaliation" <retaliatory eviction>, whereas the latter means "vindictive, tending to retaliation" <a retaliative landlord>.

reticence; *reticency. The second is a NEEDLESS VARIANT.

reticent (= reserved; disinclined to speak freely; taciturn) is frequently misunderstood as being synonymous with *reluctant*. E.g.: "Big companies in the software and information-technology sectors will undoubtedly support the reform, while companies in biotechnology and pharmaceutical sectors will be *reticent* [read *reluctant*] to do so." Jay P. Kesan & Andres A. Gallo, *The Political Economy of the Patent System*, 87 N.C. L. Rev. 1341, 1401 (2009). Occasionally, the line between taciturnity and reluctance is an extremely subtle one—e.g.: "Many cases go unreported because of a *reticence* on the part of the victims to publicly accuse close relatives, much like the silence that often cloaks child abuse." Jon Nordheimer, *A New Abuse of Elderly: Theft by Kin and Friends*, N.Y. Times, 16 Dec. 1991, at A1.

retire. In the legal idiom, a jury is customarily said to *retire* for deliberations—e.g.:

- "After the jury had *retired* to deliberate, the court informed counsel that some communication had been received from the jury." *People v. Allen*, 197 N.W.2d 874, 878 (Mich. Ct. App. 1972).
- "Before the jury *retired*, the district court held a sidebar discussion and invited objections and corrections to its instructions." *Burke v. McDonald*, 572 F.3d 51, 56 (1st Cir. 2009).

The noun *retirement* is much less common in this sense, but it does appear from time to time, especially in BrE: "The Judge's summing-up was brief but thorough, and after a short *retirement* the jury brought in a verdict of guilty." Stanley Jackson, *The Life and Cases of Mr. Justice Humphreys* 175 (n.d. [1951]).

retorsion; *retortion. Both spellings are used in international law in referring to "retaliation in kind for discourteous, unkind, or unfair acts, such as high tariffs or discriminatory duties." The *OED* gives preference to *retortion, but most international-law texts use *retorsion*. See 2 L. Lassa Oppenheim, *International Law* 134 (7th ed. 1952). So *retortion is now best considered a NEEDLESS VARIANT.

retort. See **answer,** vb.

retract. See **revoke** & **abjure (A).**

retractable. So spelled—not *retractible.

*retractible. See **retractable.**

retraction; retractation. In the figurative sense "the act of recanting" or "a statement in recantation," *retraction* is usual in AmE, *retractation* in BrE. In BrE, *retraction* is the noun corresponding to *retract* in literal senses ("to draw back," etc.).

retreat; re-treat. See RE- PAIRS.

retreat rule = the criminal-law doctrine holding that even the innocent victim of a murderous assault must choose a safe retreat, if there is one, instead of resorting to deadly force, unless either of the following circumstances exists: (1) the victim is in his or her

"castle" at the time (see **castle doctrine**); or (2) the assailant is a robber or one whom the victim is trying to arrest—e.g.:

- "The *retreat rule* occasioned strong controversy in the United States, where it was of practical importance because of the prevalence of handguns." Glanville Williams, *Textbook of Criminal Law* 460 (1978).
- "This Court departed from what had been the traditional *retreat rule* and held that a defendant faced with felonious attack on a public street was justified in standing his ground and, if necessary, destroying the person making the felonious act." *People v. Aiken*, 828 N.E.2d 74, 77 (N.Y. 2005).

retrial; new trial. These terms are interchangeable. A *retrial* is defined as "a *new trial* of an action that has already been tried." A *new trial*, as the term is usually used, is a retrial. Sometimes *re-examination* is used for *retrial*. But the only perceptible reason for using the longer word instead of the shorter is that it might be thought a weightier, more euphonious expression: "In this instance exactitude and clearness have been sacrificed to rhetorical effect. *New trial* is the statutory, and therefore the exclusive and appropriate method of re-examining issues of fact." 1 Thomas Carl Spelling, *A Treatise on New Trial and Appellate Practice* 2 (1903).

retribute, vb. (= to pay back; to visit retribution upon), a 17th-century BACK-FORMATION from *retribution*, is labeled "rare" in the *OED*. But modern writers on criminal law are reviving it after centuries of disuse. E.g.:

- "The just deserts principle does not prescribe a scale of penalties . . . beyond suggesting that punishments must be felt to be deserved, that is, felt somehow to *retribute* (pay back) for the moral and material injuries crimes cause." Ernest van den Haag, *Punishment: Desert and Crime Control*, 85 Mich. L. Rev. 1250, 1256 (1987).
- "Robbins had only *retributed* [read *paid back*] the past humiliations of William Jessup and other American sailors." Ruth Wedgwood, *The Revolutionary Martyrdom of Jonathan Robbins*, 100 Yale L.J. 229, 316 (1990).
- "In criminal cases involving racial animus, the prosecutorial veto has a profound impact on the community since the prosecutor neither deters prohibited hate crime conduct nor *retributes* [read *pays back*] the victimization of the targeted group." Tamara F. Lawson, *Whites Only Tree*, 8 U. Md. L.J. of Race, Religion, Gender & Class 123, 131 (2008). Note the unjustifiably unhyphenated phrasal adjectives *hate-crime* and *whites-only*. See PHRASAL ADJECTIVES.

retribution. See **retaliation.**

retributive; retributory; *retributional; *retributionary. *Retributive* = characterized by, or of the nature of, retribution (*OED*). E.g.:

- "The fact that it is natural to hate a criminal does not prove that *retributive* punishment is justified." Glanville Williams, *The Sanctity of Life and the Criminal Law* 60 (1957).

- "Yet it is certainly something [that] should prevent our dismissing all *retributive* theory out of hand." H.L.A. Hart, *Law, Liberty, and Morality* 60 (1963).
- "Current decisions by state legislatures . . . to retain the death penalty as a part of our law . . . rest in part on a faulty assumption about the *retributive* force of the death penalty." *Baze v. Rees*, 553 U.S. 35, 78 (2008) (Stevens, J., concurring).

Retributory = involving, producing, or characterized by retribution or recompense (*OED*). The only sense that *retributory* has that is lacking in *retributive* is that of causing or producing retribution. But euphony often governs the choice of term.

*Retributional and **retributionary* are NEEDLESS VARIANTS not contained in the major English-language dictionaries. But they appear fairly frequently—e.g.:

- "The connection . . . turns upon the conspiracy between the Texas defendants and Moses to subject the plaintiffs to *retributional* [read *retributive*] abuse without regard to constitutional rights." *Williams v. Garcia*, 569 F.Supp. 1452, 1454 (E.D. Mich. 1983).
- "A tort defendant who has used or marketed annoyance-tech devices would likely be viewed by courts as breaching the peace or enabling *retributional* [read *retributive*] behavior against another likely to spur violence, if discovered by the victim." Robert F. Blomquist, *Annoyancetech Vigilante Torts and Policy*, 73 Alb. L. Rev. 55, 69 (2009).
- "The death penalty is typically justified as a means of retribution or deterrence. When *retributionary* [read *retributive*], the severity of the punishment must typically be proportional to the culpability for the crime." Pramila A. Kamath, *Blinded by the Bright-Line*, 77 U. Cin. L. Rev. 321, 323 (2008).

retributory damages. See **punitive damages.**

retroactive; retrospective; retrogressive. In law, the first two terms are used synonymously in reference to statutes that extend in scope or effect to matters that have occurred in the past. E.g.:

- "The court refused to give effect to a *retroactive* statute creating a special tribunal to try certain suits by a bank against its officers." Roscoe Pound, *The Formative Era of American Law* 57 (1938).
- "It is presumed that a statute does not have *retrospective* effect." Michael Zander, *The Law-Making Process* 128 (2d ed. 1985).

The one advantage of *retrospective* is that it corresponds etymologically to its antonym, *prospective*.

Retrogressive = retrograde; tending to go back to an inferior state; returning to a worse condition. E.g.: "The court found that Senate Districts 2, 12, and 26 were *retrogressive* because in each district, a lesser opportunity existed for the black candidate of choice to win election under the new plan than under the benchmark plan." *Georgia v. Ashcroft*, 539 U.S. 461, 474 (2003) (per O'Connor, J.).

retrofit, n. & vb. The noun *retrofit* is a HYBRID meaning "a modification of equipment or a building to include developments not available at the time of original manufacture or construction." The term has been extended to use as a verb in both literal and figurative senses—e.g.:

- "On appeal Ronald has sought to *retrofit* his case by downplaying the degree to which his recovery was based on Bonnette's false statements of love and sexual desire." *Askew v. Askew*, 28 Cal. Rptr. 2d 284, 289–90 (Ct. App. 1994).
- "Plaintiff's position was that the astragal should have been removed by Coke and the door *retrofitted* with some sort of synthetic rubber cushion." *Fontana v. Coca-Cola Enters., Inc.*, 632 So.2d 811, 814 (La. Ct. App. 1994).

As in the immediately preceding example, the past-tense form should be *retrofitted*, not *retrofit*—e.g.:

- "To do so, Westinghouse has invested in a series of advanced technologies [that] are standard to new plant designs and [that] can be *retrofit* [read *retrofitted*] into existing units." *Wholesale Power Contracts*, Pub. Util. Fortnight, 16 Mar. 1989, at 67, 72.
- "Existing cars should be *retrofit* [read *retrofitted*] with meters, for an installation fee." Steven N. Brautigam, Note, *Rethinking the Regulation of Car Horn and Car Alarm Noise*, 19 Colum. J. Envtl. L. 391, 438 (1994).

Cf. **fit.**

return, n., = (1) a court officer's bringing back of an instrument to the court that issued it—as when a sheriff returns a citation; (2) the officer's indorsement on such an instrument, reporting what the officer did or found—as in a return of *nulla bona*; or (3) an income-tax filing. See **make return of** & **nulla bona.**

return back is a fairly common REDUNDANCY. Cf. **refer back** & **revert (B).**

returnee. See -EE.

reurge. Solid—no hyphen.

reus; rea. These are the masculine and feminine forms of the term used in Roman, civil, and canon law to denote "a defendant." The plural forms are *rei* and *reae*. *Reus* is the more commonly encountered form.

reuse. Solid—no hyphen.

revalidate; revive. When used in reference to reestablishing the validity of revoked wills, these words are quite distinct. *Revalidation* consists in repetition of the formalities of execution of the will previously revoked. *Revival* consists in revocation of the superseding or revoking will (i.e., the will that displaced or invalidated the original will).

revenge. See **provocation.**

*revengeful. See **vindictive (A).**

reverence, vb.; **revere.** The first is a FORMAL WORD equivalent to the second. E.g.: "More specifically, how does a desire to end one's life fit into a social context that *reverences* human life?" Melvin I. Urofsky, *Justifying Assisted Suicide*, 14 Notre Dame J.L. Ethics & Pub. Pol'y 893, 916 (2000). See *lapsus linguae.*

reversal; reversion; reverter. The first is the noun corresponding to the verb *to reverse.* The second and third are nouns corresponding to the verb *to revert.* H.W. Fowler quotes the following misuse of *reversion* for *reversal*: "The *reversion* [read *reversal*] of our free-trade policy would, we are convinced, be a great detriment to the working class" (*MEU2* 524). For the distinction between *reversion* and *reverter*, see **reversion.** Cf. **revert.**

reverse, vb.; **overrule.** An appellate court *reverses* a decision when it overturns what a lower court has done in the same case; it *overrules* a decision when, in a later case, it disapproves or disallows its own earlier decision involving a factually similar problem. See JUDGMENTS, APPELLATE-COURT.

reverse discrimination. This term refers to treating minorities preferentially, usu. through affirmative-action programs, in a way that adversely affects members of a majority group. The term first became popular with the U.S. Supreme Court's decision in *Regents of Univ. of Cal. v. Bakke*, 438 U.S. 265 (1978).

But the word is older. The *Second Barnhart Dictionary of New English* (1980) traces it back to 1971, and neither John Algeo's dictionary of neologisms, *Fifty Years Among the New Words* (1991), nor Jonathon Green's *Tuttle Dictionary of New Words Since 1960* (1992) takes it back any further.

In fact, though, the term was coined in the early 1960s, apparently by a state-court judge: "These constitutional guarantees mean that a non-white pupil has just as much right to be educated in a public school as a white pupil, but it also means, and equally so, that a child should not be enrolled or transported to a certain schoolhouse because he is white or non-white. To apply such a test, overtly or covertly, is *reverse discrimination* making racial membership a qualification for such a move, when it really should be irrelevant and immaterial." *Strippoli v. Bickal*, 248 N.Y.S.2d 588, 599 (Sup. Ct. 1964) (per William G. Easton, J.).

The next use in American caselaw—the first federal example—occurred four years later: "The history leads the court to conclude that Congress did not intend to require '*reverse discrimination*'; that is, the act does not require that Negroes be preferred over white employees who possess employment seniority." *Quarles v. Philip Morris, Inc.*, 279 F.Supp. 505, 516 (E.D. Va. 1968).

reverse passing off. See **passing off (B).**

reversible. So spelled.

reversible error has been wrongly criticized on grounds that "*error* cannot be *reversed* per se, although its results can be remedied." William F. Haggerty, *Of Bards, Beguilers, and Barristers*, 66 Mich. B.J. 784, 785 (1987). Yet this is an acceptable example of HYPALLAGE.

reversion; reverter. Both are reversionary interests in property having been conveyed. A *reversion* is an interest in land arising by operation of law whenever the owner of an estate grants to another a particular estate, e.g., a life estate or a term of years, but does not dispose of the owner's entire interest (*OCL1*). A *reverter* is a lesser interest—a possibility that the land might revert—arising when a grant is limited so that it might terminate. A *reversion* occurs automatically upon termination of the prior estate (as when a life tenant dies), whereas a *reverter*—usually termed a *possibility of reverter*—under orthodox theory, does not occur automatically, but is subject to a return to the grantor when a condition is breached (as upon the lapse of a conditional fee).

Reverter and *reversion* are susceptible to INELEGANT VARIATION. Justice Brennan, in his dissent in *Evans v. Abney*, 396 U.S. 435, 450–59 (1970), switches back and forth between the terms in describing the single interest that heirs had in a fee simple subject to condition subsequent. The correct term to describe such an estate is *power of termination* or *right of entry for condition broken*. See **remainder, reversal** & -ER (B).

reversionary; *reversional. The second is a NEEDLESS VARIANT—not common but hardly unknown: "They do afford an inference of an intention to invest full power in his wife to effectuate a complete separation of the 'home place' by conveyance from any *reversional* [read *reversionary*] interest on behalf of his estate." *Geyer v. Bookwalter*, 193 F.Supp. 57, 61–62 (W.D. Mo. 1961).

reversioner = the grantor or heir in reversion; one who possesses the reversion to an estate. E.g.:

- "Affirmative waste as a concept stems from early English common-law concern that the interests in land held by *reversioners* or remaindermen be protected from depredations by life tenants." *McMahon v. Eke-Nweke*, 503 F.Supp.2d 598, 604 (E.D.N.Y. 2007).
- "The defendant, sitting on the land, asserts a claim to only a life estate, and asks the court to allow him to 'pray aid' of the *reversioner*, that is, to allow the party who will claim the land after his death to intervene in the action." Thomas Lund, *Activist Judges of the Early Fourteenth Century*, 2008 Utah L. Rev. 471, 494–95.

See **reversion** & **remainder.**

revert = (1) (of property) to return by reversion; (2) to return to a former state; to go back to (as a former state or condition); or (3) to turn (eyes or steps) back.

A. *Revert* for *refer*. This is a curious mistake: "By *reverting* [read *adverting* or *referring*] to the language of the contestant's petition, we can see that the contestant admits that the document under consideration actually bears the testator's and attesters' signatures." *In re Demaris's Estate*, 110 P.2d 571, 580 (Or. 1941). Even if the writer intended in this sentence to say that we were "going back" to focus on particular words, the use of *revert* was ill-advised, for sense 3 subsumes the connotations of sense 2 of returning to a former state or condition.

B. *_Revert back._ This REDUNDANCY is common in AmE, less so in BrE. E.g.:

- "Many lawyers feel uncomfortable in a mediation and may sometimes *revert back* [read *revert*] to an adversarial mentality." Kevin Tan, *The Singapore Legal System* 435 (1999).
- "An outstanding legal claim that is abandoned by the trustee *reverts back* [read *reverts*] to the original debtor-plaintiff." *Moses v. Howard Univ. Hosp.*, 606 F.3d 789, 795 (D.C. Cir. 2010).

Cf. **return back** & **refer back.**

reverter. See **reversal** & **reversion.**

revest = to vest a second time. E.g.:

- "By breaking bulk, the bailee determines the bailment, and . . . the goods at once *revest* in the possession of the bailor." Oliver Wendell Holmes Jr., *The Common Law* 177 (1881).
- "CAF violated the terms of the donation certificate, which called for title to *revest* in the USAF if the CAF no longer wished to retain the F-82." *Secretary of U.S. Air Force v. Commemorative Air Force*, 585 F.3d 895, 898 (6th Cir. 2009).
- "The bankruptcy court discharged Vickie Lynn Marshall's preexisting debts and caused the property remaining in the bankruptcy estate to be *revested* in her." *In re Marshall*, 600 F.3d 1037, 1045 (9th Cir. 2010).

The corresponding noun is *revestment*—e.g.: "In addition to the State's right of *revestment* under the condition . . . , the reservation reserved to the State the right of entry and use." *Turiano v. State*, 519 N.Y.S.2d 180, 185 (Ct. Cl. 1987).

review, n. **A. And** *appeal; certiorari.* The word *review* denotes a genus, of which *appeal* and *certiorari* are species. In reference, then, to all types of appellate scrutiny—however the cases may have arrived in the appellate court—*review* is the most accurate term. See **appeal (B).**
    B. And *_reviewal._ *_Reviewal_ is a NEEDLESS VARIANT.

*revisal. See **revision.**

revise; redact; recense. The first is the ordinary word that serves in most senses. The second and third terms are used especially of revising texts with close scrutiny. *Redact* = (1) to make a draft of; or (2) to edit. In American legal writing it is often used in the sense "to edit out or mask the privileged, impertinent, or objectionable matter in a document." *Recense* is more of a literary term in modern usage; it relates to scholarly editing of ancient texts and the like.

reviser; revisor. Although both forms appear in modern legal prose, the *-er* form is preferred—e.g.: "Although the Shawnee try to discount this as just a *reviser's* note, this statement was legislatively enacted as part of the public law and is a good indication of Congressional intent, even though it is not an operative part of the statute itself." *Shawnee Tribe v. U.S.*, 423 F.3d 1204, 1215–16 (10th Cir. 2005).

revision; *revisal. The second is a NEEDLESS VARIANT—e.g.: "The legislature provided for new editions periodically, including a *revisal* [read *revision*] in 1837, prepared by a committee of three, including James Iredell, Jr., who followed in his father's footsteps." Laura F. Edwards, *The Forgotten Legal World of Thomas Ruffin*, 87 N.C. L. Rev. 855, 883 (2009).

revisionary; *revisional; *revisory. *Revisionary* = of, pertaining to, or made up of revision <revisionary methods>. *_Revisional_ is a NEEDLESS VARIANT. *Revisory* = having power to revise; engaged in revision <a revisory board>.

revisor. See **reviser.**

revisory. See **revisionary.**

revitalize has become a VOGUE WORD among politicians and businesspeople <to revitalize the inner city>.

revival of judgment. See **renewal of judgment.**

revive. See **revalidate** & **republish.**

reviver; revivor. The two forms mean different things. *Reviver* = one who or that which revives. *Revivor* is a primarily BrE legal term denoting a proceeding for the revival of a suit or action abated by the death of one of the parties, or by some other circumstance (*OED*). E.g.: "Section 60-2404 holds that a dormant judgment may be revived upon certain conditions by the judgment creditor filing a motion for *revivor* within two years of the date at which the judgment becomes dormant." *Vanover v. Cook*, 260 F.3d 1182, 1187 (10th Cir. 2001).

revocability is pronounced /rev-ə-kə-**bil**-i-tee/.

revocable; *revokable. The first form is preferred; the word is pronounced /**rev**-ə-kə-bəl/. *_Revokable_ (as well as *revokeable*) is a NEEDLESS VARIANT. See **irrevocable.**

revocatory; *revocative. The first is preferred, whether in common-law phrases such as *revocatory acts* or *revocatory powers*, or in the civil-law phrase *revocatory action* (*see, e.g.,* Quebec Civ. Code art. 1032).

*revokable. See **revocable.**

revoke; retract. These two words are nearly synonymous. *Revoke* = to annul by taking back; *retract* = to withdraw or disavow. In the idiom of contract law, an offer is *revoked*, while an anticipatory repudiation of a contract is *retracted*.

revolt; revolution. See **coup d'état.**

rewrite is both noun and verb, although *write* itself cannot be a noun. E.g.: "As a result, Justice Adkins's *rewrite* of the *Doran* holding, taken verbatim from the throw away dicta in *Canney*, came home to roost." Peter H. Seed, *Florida's Sunshine Law: The Undecided Legal Issue*, 13 U. Fla. J.L. & Pub. Pol'y 209, 233 (2002).

Rex; Regina. See **R.**

rhadamanthine; *rhadamantin. *Rhadamanthine* /rad-ə-**man**-thən/, an exotic term meaning "of or relating to a rigorous or inflexible judge," is best so spelled. The word is a type of LITERARY ALLUSION (see (D)), Rhadamanthus being, in Greek mythology, Zeus and Europa's son who served as one of the judges in the lower world. E.g.:

- "I do not suggest that every such *rhadamanthine* ruling restricting access to the courts is motivated solely by a desire to reduce judicial workload." Bernard S. Meyer, *Justice, Bureaucracy, Structure, and Simplification*, 42 Md. L. Rev. 659, 685 (1983).
- "In a series of cases . . . , some courts have utilized a *rhadamanthine* construction of the procedural requirements of the Rule." David S. Day, *Discovery Standards for the Testimonial Expert Under Federal Rule of Civil Procedure 26(b)(4)*, 133 F.R.D. 209, 217 (1990).
- "The court believes that entering judgment in favor of AT&T on all claims solely because of preemption would [be] an overly *rhadamanthine* decision." *Rebaudo v. AT&T*, 562 F.Supp.2d 345, 351 (D. Conn. 2008). On the use of *overly* for *unduly*, see **overly.**

See **draconian.**

RHETORICAL QUESTIONS—those posed without the hope or expectation of an answer, often because the answer is obvious—especially when not unusually long, should end with a question mark. E.g.: "Who would deny that the victim of a nuisance may have it abated regardless of the intent of the offending party?" *Jolley v. Powell*, 299 So.2d 647, 648 (Fla. Dist. Ct. App. 1974). Rhetorical questions quickly become tiresome if overused.

***rhodomontade.** See **rodomontade.**

rhyme or reason is a CLICHÉ to be avoided—e.g.: "An agency may not, *without rhyme or reason* [read *without reason*], create conflicting lines of precedent governing materially identical situations." *South Shore Hosp., Inc. v. Thompson*, 308 F.3d 91, 102 (1st Cir. 2002).

Richard Roe; Jane Roe. See **Doe, John.**

RICO (an acronym for the Racketeer Influenced and Corrupt Organizations Act) should be written in all capitals—not written *Rico*, as it predominantly appears in *Chapman & Cole v. Itel Container Int'l B.V.*, 116 F.R.D. 550 (S.D. Tex. 1987) (using both forms).

Some writers, especially journalists, have begun to use the acronym as a verb meaning "to sue under RICO"—e.g.:

- "In my view, reputable businesses would not be *RICOed* if injured plaintiffs had an across-the-board express federal

commercial/consumer fraud damages remedy." Arthur F. Mathews, *Shifting the Burden of Losses in the Securities Markets*, 65 Notre Dame L. Rev. 896, 962 (1990).
- "The plaintiff can't sue under the substantive law—here, the securities law—but hopes to get into court anyway by *RICOing* someone." L. Gordon Crovitz, *While Senate Fiddles, the Supreme Court Has Real Work to Do*, Wall St. J., 9 Oct. 1991, at A15.

So used, the word is a casualism.

rid > rid > rid. The past-tense and past-participial form **ridded* is now obsolete.

ridden. See **laden (B).**

right, adj.**; righteous; rightful.** *Right* = correct, proper, just. *Righteous* = morally upright, virtuous, or law-abiding. This term has strong religious connotations, often of unctuousness. *Rightful* = (1) (of an action) equitable, fair <a rightful dispossession>; (2) (of a person) legitimately entitled to a position <the rightful heir>; or (3) (of an office or piece of property) that one is entitled to <his rightful inheritance>.

These terms are sometimes confused. In the following specimen, *rightfully* is misused for *rightly*: "The jury *rightfully* [read *rightly*] could reason that Marr knew the conditions through which he [had] to fly." *U.S. Fire Ins. Co. v. Marr's Short Stop*, 680 S.W.2d 3, 5 (Tex. 1984). For a similar distinction—that between *purposely* and *purposefully*—see **purposely.**

right, n., is "one of the most ambiguous words in the English language." W.W. Buckland, *Some Reflections on Jurisprudence* 32 (1945). The most widely used definition is "an interest or expectation guaranteed by law." The nature of the guarantee—especially its enforcement—leads to endless gradations in meaning.

right, as of. See **as of right.**

right, in one's own. Originally, this phrase referred to a person's particular title or claim to something. The phrase still sometimes bears this literal sense—e.g.:

- "Mrs. Brayman lacks standing to assert this cause of action in *her own right* or on behalf of her daughter, and the appellees were entitled to summary judgment as a matter of law." *Brayman v. DeLoach*, 439 S.E.2d 709, 711 (Ga. Ct. App. 1993).
- "An association has standing to bring suit on behalf of its members when *its members* [read *they*] would have standing to sue *in their own right.*" *Friends of the Earth, Inc. v. Laidlaw Envtl. Servs. (TOC), Inc.*, 528 U.S. 167, 181 (2000) (per Ginsburg, J.).
- "She had not served long enough to have earned any benefits *in her own right.*" *U.S. v. Moore*, 504 F.3d 1345, 1349 (11th Cir. 2007).

Today, however, the word has an extended sense referring to an individual characteristic or qualification that a person might otherwise be thought to hold in common with someone else—e.g.: "They had inherited considerable property from their father, an unsuccessful Congregational clergyman turned successful lawyer, and their mother, a wealthy woman *in her own right*." Carolyn C. Jones, *Dollars and Selves: Women's Tax Criticism and Resistance in the 1870s*, 1994 U. Ill. L. Rev. 265, 276. That sentence conveys the idea that the mother did not owe her wealth to her successful husband.

But if such a distinction is not intended, the phrase is often merely a superfluity, the victim of SLIPSHOD EXTENSION—e.g.:

- "If Edell's redirect examination was devastating *in its own right* [delete *in its own right*], it also had far exceeded the bounds of permissible questioning." John A. Jenkins, *The Litigators* 207 (1989).
- "At the Rule 29.15 hearing, trial counsel testified that McAffee had a criminal record *in her own right* [delete *in her own right*]." *State v. Harris*, 870 S.W.2d 798, 817 (Mo. 1994).

See SUPERFLUITIES.

right but not obligation. This phrase, common in contracts, makes explicit that a party has the right but not the legal duty to do something. Because the conferment of a right sometimes implies an obligation to exercise that right, the phrase is a useful one.

righteous; rightful. See **right,** adj.

right of action. See **cause of action.**

right of common. See **profits à prendre.**

right of entry; right of reentry. The first is the standard phrase, to which the second adds nothing.

right of entry for condition broken; right of entry for breach of condition; power of termination. All three phrases refer to the rights of the grantor and the grantor's successors after conveyance of a fee simple conditional, which creates a possibility of reverter. Though the most common phrase is *right of entry (for condition broken)*, the word *right* is something of a misnomer: "The *right of entry* is not, strictly speaking, a 'right' in the sense of being a present legally enforceable claim. It is rather a power to terminate the granted estate on breach of the specified condition." Cornelius J. Moynihan, *Introduction to the Law of Real Property* 112 (2d ed. 1988). Hence, the trend is to use *power of termination. See* Restatement of Property § 24, at 60, special note to cmt. b (1936). See **reversion** & **fee simple (G).**

Some authorities use the phrase *right of entry for breach of condition*, but the modern trend is to prefer *power of termination. See* Roger A. Cunningham et al., *The Law of Property* 44–45 (2d ed. 1993).

right of first refusal; right of preemption. See **option.**

right of privacy; right to privacy. Although the phrase commonly appears with either preposition, *right of privacy* predominates.

When functioning as a noun, the phrase remains unhyphenated. But when it is used as a PHRASAL ADJECTIVE, it is preferably hyphenated <right-of-privacy case>.

right of reentry. See **right of entry.**

right of survivorship (= a joint tenant's right to succeed to the whole estate upon the death of the other joint tenant—in the case of only two such tenants, and analogously when more than two are involved) is a LOAN TRANSLATION of the Latin phrase *jus accrescendi*. Deeds often make the right explicit by stating that the grantees are to hold "as joint tenants with the right of survivorship."

right-of-way = (1) a person's legal right, established by usage or by contract, to pass through grounds or property owned by another, or the land so used; (2) in AmE, the right to build and operate a railway line or highway on land belonging to another, or the land so used; or (3) the right to take precedence in traffic. The plural is *rights-of-way. See* **easement (C).**

right reason. An American court writes: "We conclude that, although the award as remitted by the trial judge was generous, it was not so gross as to be contrary to *right reason*." *Smith v. Shell Oil Co.*, 746 F.2d 1087, 1096 (5th Cir. 1984). The *OED* states that the phrase *right reason* is now rare; yet it remains common in much legal writing. It ought to be rare, since *reason* alone suffices in most contexts—or so reason tells us.

As might be expected, the phrase has a history: it is a LOAN TRANSLATION of the Latin phrase *rectam rationem*. Borrowed by St. Thomas Aquinas directly from Aristotle, *right reason* was one method of discovering the essence of natural law. E.g.:

- "Natural law, or *jus naturale*, as defined by Roman philosophers and jurists, is that law which is naturally discerned by *right reason*, as opposed to the law found necessary and made by man for the safe conduct of the state under localized conditions or by agreement for the preservation of international rights." "Law, Natural," in 17 *Encyclopedia Americana* 104, 105 (1953).
- "[The] essence [of natural law] is that there is an abstract justice, either God-given or ascertainable by man's '*right reason*,' and that laws are just or unjust in so far as they conform to or violate the pure, abstract, ultimate rules of conduct." René A. Wormser, *The Story of the Law* 482 (1962).

Whether the phrase *right reason* is outmoded depends largely on one's view of natural law. (See **natural law.**) In any event, though, the phrase hardly belongs in a context in which a court finds an award of damages reasonable, as in the sentence quoted at the outset of this entry.

right, title, and interest. This phrase, one of the classic triplets of the legal idiom, is the traditional language for conveying a quitclaim interest. (See **quitclaim** & DOUBLETS, TRIPLETS, AND SYNONYM-STRINGS.) Technically, only one of the three words is necessary, as the broad meaning of *interest* includes the others: though you can have an *interest* without having *title* and perhaps without a given *right*, you cannot have *title* or a *right* without having an *interest*.

Therefore, the more modern drafting style is to replace the triplet with the broadest of the three words—e.g.: "When a parcel of land is used or purchased in violation of federal narcotics laws, all of the offending owner's *right, title, and interest* [read *interest*] immediately *transfer* [read *transfers*] to the government, regardless of when the forfeiture action is instituted." Damon G. Saltzburg, Note, *Real Property Forfeitures as a Weapon in the Government's War on Drugs*, 72 B.U. L. Rev. 217, 221 (1992).

Still, some traditionalists prefer to keep from varying the age-old idiom, which uses only two additional words. Why, they reason, create a test case with their documents merely to find out whether *interest* is indeed broad enough to encapsulate *right* and *title*?

American lawyers, when given the choice in transactional drafting—the pros and cons on both sides of the argument—split about equally on the two sides.

right to die. As a noun phrase, *right to die* is three words <advocates of the right to die>; but as a PHRASAL ADJECTIVE, it should be hyphenated: "Both sides of a *right-to-die* case received a skeptical hearing today at the Supreme Court." Linda Greenhouse, *Right-to-Die Case Gets First Hearing in Supreme Court*, N.Y. Times, 7 Dec. 1989, at 1.

right-to-lifer (= an opponent of abortion rights) is journalese. And it's generally pejorative—e.g.: "The cast of characters includes . . . Attorney General Dick Thornburgh, a strident *right-to-lifer* who took the questionable step of asking the court to reconsider *Roe*." *The Battle over Abortion*, Newsweek, 1 May 1989, at 28.

right to privacy. See **right of privacy.**

rigorous (= extremely strict, austere) should not be misused for *rigid*, as here: "The objection was primarily that the court did not adequately portray the *rigorous* [read *rigid*], inflexible, absolute character of the duty to supply and keep in order seaworthy appliances [that] the law . . . imposes." *Cox v. Esso Ship. Co.*, 247 F.2d 629, 636 (5th Cir. 1957).

riot; unlawful assembly. An *unlawful assembly* is a meeting of three or more persons who intend either to commit a violent crime or to carry out some act, lawful or unlawful, that will constitute a breach of the peace. A *riot* is an unlawful assembly that has begun to fulfill its common purpose of breaching the peace and terrorizing the public.

Riot Act, reading the. See **reading the Riot Act.**

R.I.P.; *requiescat in pace*; rest in peace. The phrase *requiescat in pace* means "may he (or she) rest in peace." The abbreviated form, though commonly taken to be a shortened form of the English phrase, stands for the Latin phrase.

riparian rights. See **water rights.**

rising of court. This increasingly rare term, generally used as an antonym of *sitting* or *session*, refers to the court's final adjournment of the term. Loosely, however, it is also used in reference to a recess or temporary break in the court's business, as at the end of the day. E.g.: "The court gave judgment to Fail and Otho L. Hays for the amounts due them respectively, and ordered, in default of payment of the judgments within ten days from the *rising of court*, a sale of the mortgaged property." *Hays v. Galion Gas Light & Coal Co.*, 29 Ohio St. 330, 332 (1876).

risk = (1) the hazard of property loss covered by an insurance contract, or the degree of such a hazard; (2) a person or thing that the insurer considers a hazard; or (3) a known danger to which a person assents, thus foreclosing recovery for injuries suffered <assumption of the risk>. For more on sense 3, see **assumption of the risk** & ***volenti non fit injuria.***

risk of nonpersuasion. See **burden of proof (A).**

rob. See **steal.**

robber. See **thief.**

robbery = aggravated larceny, i.e., larceny from the person by violence or intimidation. "The non-lawyer speaks of 'robbing a bank' by driving a tunnel into the strong-room; but this is not legal usage. In law, *robbery* implies force or the threat of it." Glanville Williams, *Textbook of Criminal Law* 791 (1978). See **burglary (A).**

rodomontade; *rhodomontade. Pronounced /rod-ə-mən-**tayd**/, the word, meaning "boastful talk," is preferably spelled *rodomontade*.

Roe, Richard; Jane Roe. See **Doe, John.**

rogatory letter. See **letters rogatory.**

role; roll. These two words are sometimes confused. *Roll* has many senses, including bankroll, but the only sense that seems to cause problems is "a list or register" <the teacher took roll>. *Role*, by contrast, means "a function or part, as in a drama."

The most common error is the use of *roll* where *role* belongs—e.g.:

- "Perhaps it is time once again to call to the prosecutor's attention the particularly sensitive *roll* [read *role*] played by the government attorney." *U.S. v. Anchondo-Sandoval*, 910 F.2d 1234, 1238 (5th Cir. 1990).
- "The court obviously . . . believed [that] the reason given by the State's attorney for striking Venireperson Austin was the real reason, and that race did not play a *roll* [read *role*] in the State's decision." *State v. Davis*, 835 S.W.2d 525, 527 (Mo. Ct. App. 1992). On the use of *Venireperson*

Austin in the preceding example, see TITULAR TOMFOOL-ERY & **venireman**.

But the opposite blunder also occurs—e.g.: "The Departmental Disciplinary Committee now moves for an order . . . accepting respondent's affidavit of resignation from the practice of law and striking his name from the *role* [read *roll*] of attorneys." *In re Percy*, 785 N.Y.S.2d 911, 911 (App. Div. 2004).

Roma. See **gypsy**.

Romani. See **gypsy**.

Romanist = one who is versed in or practices Roman law; a lawyer of the Roman school. The term, generally capitalized, has also been a pejorative epithet for Roman Catholics.

Roman law = (1) the law of the Roman people; or (2) civil law. Max Radin calls sense 2 "improper," saying, "It is extremely important . . . to separate the two terms." Max Radin, *Law Dictionary* 302 (2d ed. 1970). But not all writers do separate them—e.g.: "By civil law—or *Roman law*, or *Roman civil law*—is meant that system of law in operation in the Roman Empire and set forth particularly in the compilations of Roman jurists (Justinian and his successors) and comprising the Institutes, the Codex, the Digest and the Novels collectively called the *Corpus Juris Civilis*." C. Gordon Post, *An Introduction to the Law* 34 (1963). See **civil law**.

routinize is an -IZE NEOLOGISM best avoided as GOB-BLEDYGOOK. E.g.:

- "Administration is a means of *routinizing coercion* [read *making coercion routine*]."
- "Business men . . . want to settle and *routinize* [read *and to make routine*] both practice and expectation." Grant Gilmore & Charles L. Black Jr., *The Law of Admiralty* 15 (2d ed. 1975).
- "[The] court gives the appearance of almost *routinizing contempt* [read *making contempt routine*]." *State v. Steven B.*, 94 P.3d 854, 860 (N.M. Ct. App. 2004).

royalty. See **nonparticipating royalty**.

rubber check. See **check, worthless**.

ruin, n.; **ruination.** The first is the ordinary term; the second is humorous and colloquial. E.g.: "Protecting people from financial *ruination* [read *ruin*] and enabling them to buy vital, but otherwise unaffordable, services generates large benefits." Henry J. Aaron, *Health Care Rationing: Inevitable but Impossible?*, 96 Geo. L.J. 539, 544 (2008).

rule, vb. In AmE, it could not be said that a dissenting judge *rules*, because the dissenter sets forth no binding rule. In BrE, however, it is apparently permissible (though inaccurate) to say that a dissenter *rules* in a certain way—e.g.: "Indeed, Sir Laurence Street in dissent *ruled* in favor of no injunction but an accounting of profits." Letter of Malcolm Turnbull, TLS, 9–15 Dec. 1988, at 1371.

rule; regulation. A *rule* is a principle of guidance that has a close relation to individual conduct and method, or a desire for order and discipline within a group. Typically it implies restriction for the sake of achieving an articulable end, such as conformity to a standard or uniformity of procedure <court rules> <the Rules of Golf>. A *regulation* is typically a specific prescription by authority for the control or management of an agency, organization, system, or industry, especially when issued in some detail by a subordinate authority <FDA regulations> <factory regulations>.

rule, the. When American lawyers in the South and Southwest refer to *the rule*, they invoke an evidentiary and procedural rule by which all witnesses are excluded from the courtroom while another witness is testifying. The purpose of *the rule* is to aid in ascertaining the truth from witnesses by preventing them from hearing what others say on the witness stand. The most frequent idioms containing the phrase are *invoking "the rule"* and *being placed under "the rule"*; legal writers generally use the quotation marks as just shown.

rule absolute. See **decree absolute**.

rule against opinions. See **opinions, rule against**.

Rule against Perpetuities; rule against perpetuities; Rule Against Perpetuities. "In Gray's book [John Chipman Gray, *The Rule against Perpetuities* (1886)] the Rule is capitalized *Rule against Perpetuities*, a style followed by the Blue Book until 1955. In that year, for mysterious reasons—perhaps merely a new font fetish—the Blue Book decreed that the Rule should be capitalized *Rule Against Perpetuities*." Jesse Dukeminier & Stanley M. Johanson, *Family Wealth Transactions* 970 n.1 (1978).

Dukeminier has identified three styles of capitalizing the phrase: the classic style (*Rule against Perpetuities*); the modern style (*rule against perpetuities*); and the *Bluebook* style (*Rule Against Perpetuities*), sanctioned by the *Bluebook* in the ninth edition of 1955. *See* Jesse Dukeminier, *Perpetuities: Contagious Capitalization*, 20 J. Legal Educ. 341 (1968). His research turned up no historical justification for the *Bluebook* style (no longer specifically included in the *Bluebook*), but uncovered long-sanctioned use of both the classic and modern styles (the only ones known in BrE). Dukeminier himself prefers the classic style, perhaps as a nod of respect to Gray. In fact, though, Gray's style merely reflects the predominant 19th-century method of initial capitalization, in which all prepositions (such as *against*), no matter how long, remained lowercase.

Today, though, prepositions of more than four letters are routinely capitalized, so *Rule Against Perpetuities* accords with the prevailing conventions for initial capitals. But why have the initial capitals at all? The lowercase version—*rule against perpetuities*—is now predominant in American legal writing. See CAPITALIZATION (C).

rule against pyramiding inferences. See **pyramiding inferences, rule against.**

rule by law. See **rule of law (C).**

Rule in Shelley's Case; Rule in *Shelley's Case.* British writers tend to italicize the case name; American writers tend not to.

rulemaker. One word.

rulemaking serves best as an adjective <rulemaking authority>, or an abstract noun <rulemaking in administrative law>, but not as a concrete noun <three rulemakings today>. This concrete use—which makes the word a count noun—derives from administrative law, in which it means "the act or an instance of administratively legislating, through promulgated rules." E.g.: "Since that interpretation was issued, the EPA has refused in subsequent *rulemakings* to reconsider it, explaining to disappointed commentators that its earlier decision was conclusive." *Whitman v. American Trucking Ass'n*, 531 U.S. 457, 479 (2001) (per Scalia, J.). The usage smacks of JARGON, but it may well become accepted as standard AmE legal terminology. See PLURALS (B).

rule nisi. See **nisi** & **decree absolute.**

rule of construction. See **rule of law (B).**

rule of four. This phrase denotes, in AmE, the convention that for certiorari to be granted by the U.S. Supreme Court, four Justices must vote in favor of the grant.

rule of law. A. Senses. *Rule of law* = (1) the supremacy of regular as opposed to arbitrary power; (2) the doctrine that every person is subject to the ordinary law of the realm enforced in the ordinary tribunals; (3) the doctrine that general constitutional principles are the result of judicial decisions determining the rights of private individuals in the courts; or (4) any substantive legal principle. *See* A.V. Dicey, *The Law of the Constitution* 110–16 (8th ed. 1915).

Since the 1960s, and especially in popular contexts, sense 1 has taken on more and more concrete connotations. So the phrase often suggests, not the abstract principle of regular power, but the wielders of that power in a given society—the establishment and the police force. E.g.: "Many jurists now complain that there has been a breakdown in respect for 'the *rule of law.*' Their failure to note that the inadequacy of the legal system caused the broad social protest has served only to widen the gulf. The call has gone out for new and stiffer criminal sanctions against civil disobedience." Stephen M. Nagler, "The Language of the Law," in *Language in America* 218, 227–28 (Neil Postman et al. eds., 1969).

B. And *rule of construction.* A *rule of law* is a rule that a court follows to determine the substantive position of the parties; a *rule of construction* is a guide to the court in interpreting a statute or legal instrument. E.g.:

- "The doctrine of ejusdem generis is not a positive *rule of law*, but a *rule of construction* to aid in ascertaining and giving effect to the legislative intent where there is uncertainty." 73 Am. Jur. 2d Statutes § 136 (2001).
- "The court found that this canon was not a *rule of law*, but was only a *rule of construction* used to assist in determining legislative intent." Amir R. Zaidi, *Statutory Interpretation*, 64 Md. L. Rev. 1239, 1250 (2005).
- "A second *rule of construction* states that the nature and purpose of a statute may provide an indication of whether Congress intended a statute to apply beyond the confines of the United States." Charles Doyle, *Extraterritorial Application of American Criminal Law* 7 (2010).

C. And *rule by law.* What a difference a preposition can make. *Rule of law* = (1) a natural-law doctrine that to control the exercise of arbitrary power, such power must be subordinated to impartial and well-defined principles of law; (2) adherence to due process of law as administered by an independent judiciary; or (3) a legal rule. *Rule by law* = government by law, as opposed to lawlessness, even if that law is administered despotically. Actually, though, *rule of law* has historically borne another sense, that of *rule by law*—but the sharing should cease immediately in the interest of linguistic DIFFERENTIATION and legal clearheadedness. E.g.: "The *rule of law*, however, is not merely *rule by law*; rather it demands equal justice for each person under the authority of a constitutional government." John J. Patrick, *Understanding Democracy* 88 (2006).

rule of optional completeness. Under this rule, when a party in an American trial uses deposition testimony, the opposing party may require that more of the passage be read to establish the greater context—e.g.:

- "The part bracketed by us was introduced by appellant under the *rule of optional completeness.*" *Hobson v. State*, 644 S.W.2d 473, 476 n.3 (Tex. Crim. App. 1983).
- "Under the *rule of optional completeness*, hearsay is admissible when it serves to clarify other hearsay evidence elicited by the opposing party." *Wright v. Quarterman*, 470 F.3d 581, 586 (5th Cir. 2006).

rules of law. See CAPITALIZATION (C).

ruling. A *ruling* is the outcome of a court's decision either on some point of law (such as the admissibility of evidence) or on the case as a whole. The word is not synonymous with *opinion*, as here wrongly suggested: "The district court . . . issued a thoughtful 159-page *ruling* [read *opinion*] that discusses in meticulous detail all aspects of the testing as well as each claim in Cooper's petition." *Cooper v. Brown*, 565 F.3d 581, 639 (9th Cir. 2009). See JUDGMENTS, APPELLATE-COURT. Cf. **opinion.**

ruling case = a reported case that determines an issue being litigated. The phrase appears more commonly in BrE than in AmE, in which the phrase *governing caselaw* or *leading case* is often used for this sense. See **leading case.**

run. A. Statutes of Limitation. In AmE, a statute of limitation is said to have *run* when the time limit has passed. In BrE, the usual phraseology is that the period set by the statute of limitation has *expired*—e.g.: "The Supreme Court concluded that the fifteen-day time limit pursuant to Sec. 436 of the Civil Code had *expired*." Helmut Koziol & Barbara C. Steininger, *European Tort Law* 209 (2005). *Run* is also used in BrE, but is considered a casualism. See **laches.**

It is unidiomatic to speak of a statute of limitations *running out*, as opposed to merely *running*—e.g.: "The District 4-E Grievance Committee found [that] the respondent delayed filing suit in a personal injury matter and allowed the statute of limitations to *run out* [read *run*]." *Disciplinary Actions*, 53 Tex. B.J. 1309, 1309 (1990). The period allowed may properly be said to have "run out."

B. *Running with the land.* Covenants are said to *run with the land* when the duty to perform or the right to another's performance is assignable with the land—e.g.:

- "In the case of sales of land the benefit of the vendor's covenants for title '*runs*' with the land purchased." William Geldart, *Introduction to English Law* 123 (D.C.M. Yardley ed., 9th ed. 1984).
- "A lien on real property *runs* with the land and is enforceable against subsequent purchasers." *Permanent Mission of India to the U.N. v. City of N.Y.*, 551 U.S. 193, 198 (2007) (per Thomas, J.).

Cf. **in gross.**

C. Meaning "to apply." This is an idiom properly classed as a LEGALISM—e.g.: "The preliminary injunction *runs* only against the insurers, and they have not contested personal jurisdiction." *Iantosca v. Step Plan Servs., Inc.*, 604 F.3d 24, 31 (1st Cir. 2010).

runnable; runnability. The words are so spelled—as opposed to the incorrect forms *runable and *runability.

RUN-ON SENTENCES do not stop where they should. This is not to say that run-on-sentences are simply overlong, since not all overlong sentences qualify for the approbation. Rather, run-on sentences are ungrammatically joined into one. Many readers will recognize the term from their school days, when teachers would scrawl "run on" in the margins of student papers. The problem usually occurs when the writer is uncertain about how to handle marks of PUNCTUATION or how to handle such adverbs as *however* and *otherwise*, which are often mistakenly treated as conjunctions.

Some grammarians distinguish between a "run-on sentence" (or "fused sentence") and a "comma splice" (or "run-together sentence"). In a run-on sentence, two independent clauses are not joined by a conjunction such as *and*, *but*, *for*, *or*, or *nor* but are incorrectly written with no punctuation between them. In

a comma splice, two such independent clauses have merely a comma between them. A run-on sentence might read, "The decision was unprecedented the court had never heard such a case." As a sentence containing a comma splice, it would read, "The decision was unprecedented, the court had never heard such a case." And correctly, it might read, "The decision was unprecedented; the court had never heard such a case."

The presence or absence of a comma may seem hardly noteworthy, but true run-on sentences symbolize the writer's failure to grasp even the most fundamental rules of writing. They are rare in published legal writing, though they occur distressingly often in the writing of law students.

Comma splices, on the other hand, generally signal a less serious failing because the writer at least understands that some type of stop is necessary. That stop usually needs to be a period or a semicolon instead of a comma. Following are some specimens with suggested remedies:

- "The court has no power to do by indirection what it is prohibited from doing *directly, particularly* is that true in an action for specific performance in which a decree is given as a matter of grace and discretion." *Otis Oil & Gas Corp. v. Maier*, 284 P.2d 653, 657 (Wyo. 1955). A semicolon, not a comma, is needed after *directly*.
- "In its final analysis it fastens liability on the master where his servant is *negligent, otherwise* there is no liability." *Driver v. Smith*, 339 S.W.2d 135, 140 (Tenn. Ct. App. 1960). A semicolon, not a comma, is needed after *negligent*—and a comma is needed after *otherwise*.
- "We do not now decide whether the INS has complied fully with its own *regulations, rather* we decide that it must in the first instance address petitioner's specific factual claims that it failed to do so." *Villegas v. I.N.S.*, 745 F.2d 950, 951 (5th Cir. 1984). A semicolon, not a comma, is needed after *regulations*—and a comma is needed after *rather*.
- "We must reverse and remand given our inability to determine from this record whether the plan is funded by insurance or merely administered by *insurance, nevertheless*, for the sake of completeness and for guidance of the parties upon remand, we discuss the implications of *Werner*, a non-ERISA case." *O'Brien v. Two West Hanover Co.*, 795 A.2d 907, 912 (N.J. Super. Ct. 2002). A semicolon is needed after *insurance*—and a comma is needed after *nevertheless*.

Most usage authorities accept comma splices when (1) the clauses are short and closely related, (2) there is no danger of a MISCUE, and (3) the context is informal. Thus: "Jane likes him, I don't." But even when all three criteria are met, some readers are likely to object.

run the gantlet. See **gantlet.**

run with the land. See **run (B).**

rush to judgment. Lord Erskine, among the greatest advocates ever to practice at the English Bar, was apparently the first to use this phrase, around 1800. He was defending a man accused of trying to assassinate George III: "An attack upon the King is considered to be parricide against the state, and the jury and the witnesses, and even the judges, are the children. It is fit, on that account, that there should be a solemn pause before we *rush to judgment*." Thomas Erskine, "Speech in Defence of James Hadfield," in 4 *Erskine's Speeches* 163, 167 (James L. High ed., 1876).

The term was popularized in 1966 when Mark Lane, a Washington lawyer, published *Rush to Judgment*, a book about the assassination of President John F. Kennedy. William Safire, a linguistic detective, wrote to Mr. Lane to inquire about the phrase, and Lane explained: "When I wrote the book back in '64, I was looking for a title that would have some historic resonance. I came upon the phrase I needed in a speech by Lord Chancellor Thomas Erskine." William Safire, *On Language*, N.Y. Times, 26 Feb. 1995, § 6, at 18.

Today, of course, the phrase is all but ubiquitous whenever an advocate wants to forestall rash judgments, or to keep minds open when public opinion takes an adverse turn.

S

sacrilegious. So spelled. **Sacreligious* is a common misspelling—e.g.:

- "It is a far cry from a situation where a state cannot refuse to license a motion picture on the ground that it is *sacreligious* [read *sacrilegious*], to say that a religious institution is barred from bringing any claim for defamation." *Holy Spirit Ass'n v. Harper & Row, Pubs., Inc.*, 420 N.Y.S.2d 56, 60 (Sup. Ct. 1979).
- "Surely moral merit is at least as elusive as other terms the Court has declared infirm, such as 'gangsters,' 'sacreligious' [read *sacrilegious*],' 'humane,' and 'credible and reliable.'" Deborah L. Rhode, *Moral Character as a Professional Credential*, 94 Yale L.J. 491, 571 (1985).
- "Rudy Guiliani, the former mayor of New York, filed a politically oriented case against the Brooklyn Museum over paintings he thought were *sacreligious* [read *sacrilegious*]." Rebecca French, *Shopping for Religion*, 51 Buff. L. Rev. 127, 153 (Winter 2003).

The correct spelling can be remembered easily if one recalls the noun: *sacrilege*.

sadly. See SENTENCE ADVERBS.

safe; safety. In BrE, these words, when referring to criminal convictions or penalties, denote legal sufficiency. *Safe* = (of a verdict) not liable to be overturned on any ground. *Safety* = a high degree of assurance that a verdict will not be overturned for any reason. E.g.:

- "The judge who tried the PC Blakelock murder case wrote the Home Office four years ago, stating that the verdict against one of the men convicted of the killing was *unsafe*, a defence lawyer claimed last night." David Rose, *Blakelock Judge Told Hurd: Verdict Unsafe*, Observer, 29 Sept. 1991, at 1.
- "The convention organs are apparently disinclined to reach a finding . . . which might cast doubt on the *safety* of the verdict." Stephanos Stavros, *The Guarantees for Accused Persons Under Article 6 of the European Convention on Human Rights* 354 (1993).
- "There were dissents within the Commission against its proposals to . . . limit the ability of appellate courts to overturn convictions on the basis of due-process violations by the police and prosecutor that were not related to the *safety* of the verdict." Kent Roach, *The Role of Innocence Commissions*, 85 Chi.-Kent L. Rev. 89, 93 n.8 (2010).

safe-deposit box. This is the original and correct term, not **safety-deposit box*—e.g.: "He'll just go quietly, back to his day job at Home Depot, doing business with customers who don't know about that silver medal in his *safety-deposit box* [read *safe-deposit box*]." Mike Downey, *Bobsled Pioneer Prepares for a Slower Lifestyle*, Chicago Trib., 13 Feb. 2003, Sports §, at 1. The extra syllable in *safety* probably originated as an auditory error: people heard the phrase and associated the *de-* prefix on *deposit* with the *-ty* suffix on *safety*, and then duplicated the sound. In modern print sources, *safe-deposit box* is three times as common as **safety-deposit box*.

In the full phrase, *safe-deposit* acts as a PHRASAL ADJECTIVE and therefore always requires a hyphen.

safe harbor, a picturesque legal METAPHOR, has a general sense—"a means or area of protection"—as well as a number of specific applications, as in the law of sanctions and in tax law—e.g.: "The unavailability of the *safe harbor* in criminal cases may chill corporate disclosure and may affect what information reasonable investors rely upon when making investment decisions." Wendy Gerwick Couture, *White Collar Crime's Gray Area*, 72 Alb. L. Rev. 1, 2 (2009). Usually, the *safe harbor* is a potential wrongdoer's opportunity to correct a wrong before a penalty comes into effect.

safety. See **safe.**

said. A. Generally. *Said* should be rigorously eschewed as a substitute for *the, that, this,* or any other deictic or "pointing" word. Used for such a word, *said* typifies LEGALESE and is often parodied by nonlawyers. And lawyers occasionally fall into self-parody—e.g.:

> A considerable number of persons were attracted to *said* square by *said* meeting, and *said* bombs and other fireworks which were being exploded there. A portion of the center of the square about 40 to 60 feet was roped off by the police of *said* Chelsea, and *said* bombs or shells were fired off within the space so inclosed, and no spectators were allowed to be within *said* inclosure. The plaintiffs were lawfully in *said* highway at the time of the explosion of *said* mortar, and near *said* ropes, and were in the exercise of due care.
>
> Quoted in *Scanlon v. Wedger*, 31 N.E. 642, 642 (Mass. 1892).

The weed tends to spread profusely in drafted documents such as wills—e.g.:

> If the *said* Grant R. Shelley shall die, and leave surviving him children, it is my desire that, if my wife be then dead, or upon the death of my wife if she should survive *said* son, my trustee shall continue *said* trust for the benefit of *said* children of my son, Grant R. Shelley, and shall make periodic payments for their benefit at intervals of not less than three (3) months apart, and shall hold *said* estate in trust to and until the youngest child of Grant R. Shelley shall attain the age of twenty-one (21) years; thereupon, *said* trust shall terminate, and *said* estate shall be distributed to the children of my son, share and share alike; if any of *said* children die before the youngest attains the age of twenty-one (21) years, *said* distributable estate shall be distributed to the surviving children, share and share alike.
> Quoted in *Shelley v. Shelley*, 354 P.2d 282, 284 (Or. 1960).

This usage had its origins in LOAN TRANSLATION, *said* being the English equivalent of the Latin *dicti*, as in the 17th-century general demurrer: *tam contra pacem dicti nuper Regis* (= against the peace of the said late King).

Among the misinformation recently disseminated about this term is that of Richard Weisberg, who says that *said* "is bizarre, but it is irreplaceable not only to the drafter of wills but to other technical lawyers as well." *When Lawyers Write* 99 (1987). That statement is balderdash. Skilled drafters—no matter how "technical" the subject—have not relied on *said* in more than a century. *Said* never lends greater precision than *the, this, that, these*, or *those*—in many contexts it even introduces imprecision.

B. The said. As used in legal writing, the word *said* is a Middle-English sibling of **aforesaid*, having the sense "above-stated." Originally legal writers would write *the said defendant*—and still do in BrE—just as they would write *the *aforesaid defendant* or *the above-stated defendant*. In AmE, however, *the* was dropped before *said*, which has come to act almost as an article. Hence *the said* seems redundant to American ears, though it was well established at one time. It's more common in BrE cases but occasionally appears in American ones as well—e.g.: " 'Georgaklis and Nieboer . . . intend to set forth their understanding regarding maintenance, upkeep, expenses and profits from the *said* [omit *said*] Property.' " *Mass. Prop. Ins. Underwriting Ass'n v. Georgaklis*, 931 N.E.2d 995, 998 n.8 (Mass. App. Ct. 2010) (quoting a sales agreement).

One writer has stated that "*the said person* is better than *said person*." Elmer A. Driedger, *The Composition of Legislation* 87 (1957). Stylistically, however, both are so horrid that it's better to ask, "Which is less bad?"

C. His said, etc. This collocation is similar to *the said*; both *saids* are quite superfluous here: "He wrongfully, knowingly, intentionally, and maliciously induced *said* [omit *said*] McClure to violate, repudiate, and break *his said* [omit *said*] agreement with the plaintiff." 236 *Reports of Cases Decided in the Court of Appeals of the State of New York* 459 (1924).

D. In Pleadings. *Said* appears at the beginning of legalistically worded pleadings in the SET PHRASE *To the Honorable Judge of Said Court*, the word *said* referring to the name of the court in the caption (usually just above this phrase). Legal stylists generally discard this and similar jargonistic deadwood. Lawyers who want a simpler substitute—who are unwilling to abandon the phrase completely—often write *To the Honorable Court.*

E. As Referring to Preceding Matter. When *said* is used in the way here disapproved, as we must grudgingly accept that it will be, it should refer to something above ("already said"), not to what is about to be said—e.g.: "Any person who does any of the acts hereinafter enumerated thereby submits himself to the jurisdiction of the courts of this State regarding any cause of action arising from any of *said acts* [read *these acts*]: [an enumeration follows]."

F. As a Noun. As suggested above, *said* is merely a pointing word. So it cannot stand on its own as a noun. In this sentence, the writer has misused *said* for *same*: "With regard to the property stolen as a result of the debtor's domestic-relations disputes, the plaintiff failed to prove that the debtor intentionally or deliberately converted *said*." *In re Taylor*, 187 B.R. 736, 739 (Bankr. N.D. Ala. 1995). See **same (A).**

G. Modifying Proper Names. *Said* is especially ludicrous when used to modify a proper name, where no confusion could result from the name alone—e.g.: "The first count of the indictment alleged, in substance, that George Smith was an idiot, and under the care, custody, and control of the respondents . . . that the respondents assaulted *said George* [read *George*]." *Rex. v. William Smith*, [1826] 2 Car. & P. 449.

sailor's will. See **oral will.**

saith; sayeth. The phrase once common in affidavits and still sometimes used—**Further affiant sayeth* (or *saith*) *not*—is superfluous. If it is to be used, the next-to-last word may be spelled either *saith* or *sayeth*. (*Sayeth* is slightly more common in American caselaw.) These are alternative Elizabethan forms. But if we are to write contemporary modern English, and not early modern English, the *-th* forms should disappear altogether.

Why? The *-th* termination for the third-person singular verb for the present tense (*he maketh*) originated in the Midland dialectal form of Middle English; the termination *-s* (*he makes*) originated in northern England and became the predominant form in Shakespeare's day. The *-eth* forms have long been obsolete in every field except religion and law—two fields in which they are obsolescent. See **-ETH.**

When the affiant hath nothing further to say, the affiant generally stoppeth testifying. On the question whether to say *naught* or *not* in this phrase, see **further affiant sayeth naught (A).**

salable; marketable; merchantable; vendible; purchasable. These adjectives all describe the amenability of items to be bought and sold. Both *salable* (not **sellable*) and *marketable* (as well as *merchantable*) stress fitness for the market and the readiness with which potential buyers might be found <a salable building> <marketable securities> <merchantable ice>.

The preferred spellings are *salable* in AmE (*W11* & *W3*) and *saleable* in BrE (*OED* & *COD*). **Sellable*, arguably a more logical form, was formerly used by some writers, but never gained widespread currency.

As between *marketable* and *merchantable*, the first might well be termed a legal ARCHAISM, since it has no nuance not conveyed by the second. E.g.: "The sellers in the Three Rivers Ranch sale agreed to furnish *merchantable* [read *marketable*] title or an owner's title policy." *Jones v. Dickens*, 394 F.2d 233, 234 (10th Cir. 1968). (*Marketable title* = a seller's nondefective title to property.) But *merchantable* appears in many statutes—such as the U.K. Sale of Goods Act—and is therefore unlikely to disappear anytime soon.

Vendible, though the least frequent of these terms, has traditionally been the most versatile, referring not only to commodities but also to people, their talents, and even their honor. So although *vendible* can be used neutrally <vendible wines>, it can also carry with it the strong pejorative sense of venality and corruption <vendible politicians> <vendible women> <vendible votes>. The *-ible* spelling is preferred (and more than five times as common), though **vendable* appears fairly often—e.g.: "O.T. Hodge Chile Parlors only has the right to use 'Hodge's' as a trade name and not as a trademark to identify its *vendable* [read *vendible*] products." *Hodge Chile Co. v. KNA Food Distribs., Inc.*, 575 F.Supp. 210, 211 (E.D. Mo. 1983).

Purchasable describes merely what may be bought, often in reference to an item of such rarity or scarcity that one might think it unobjectionable <you mean that a first edition of Johnson's 1755 *Dictionary* is purchasable today?>. Often, too, *purchasable* applies to items that are obtainable for a price but don't appear to be offered for sale <by the way, all the sculptures you see throughout the hotel are purchasable>. Also, the word can, depending on its referent, imply corruption <purchasable votes> <his loyalty is purchasable>.

salary. See **pay,** n.

sale. See **bailment** & **hard sell.**

sale, contract for; contract of sale. See **contract for sale.**

saleable. See **salable.**

sale and leaseback. See **leaseback.**

salic law; *Salique law. The body of law developed by the Salians (or Salian Franks), after they settled in Gaul under King Pharamond at the beginning of the 5th century, is generally referred to as *Salic law*. Holmes and Holland used this spelling, and so do most other legal writers. E.g.: "A Salian, wherever he might be, in whatever part of France, was judged by the *Salic law*." James Hadley, *Introduction to Roman Law* 28 (1881).

salience; *saliency. The second is a NEEDLESS VARIANT.

*Salique law. See **Salic law.**

salutary; *salutiferous; salubrious. *Salutary* = beneficial; wholesome—e.g.: "Invoking issue preclusion to bar seriatim prosecutions has the *salutary* effect of preventing the Government from circumventing acquittals." *Yeager v. U.S.*, 129 S.Ct. 2360, 2373 (2009) (Scalia, J., dissenting). **Salutory* is a common misspelling. E.g.:

- "The court must be careful to implement this sanction in a way that advances its *salutory* [read *salutary*] purpose while avoiding its potential danger." William W. Kilgarlin & Don Jackson, *Sanctions for Discovery Abuse Under New Rule 215*, 15 St. Mary's L.J. 767, 791 (1984).
- "The rule that jurisdictional facts that are admitted by the parties may establish subject matter jurisdiction over a case is a *salutory* [read *salutary*] one that promotes speedy and inexpensive litigation." *Ferguson v. Neighborhood Hous. Servs. of Cleveland, Inc.*, 780 F.2d 549, 551 (6th Cir. 1986).
- "Whether an award of attorney's fees will have *salutory* [read *salutary*] effect on the area of copyright . . . constitutes a significant consideration in the Court's analysis of BUC's request for attorney's fees." *Luken v. International Yacht Council, Ltd.*, 581 F.Supp.2d 1226, 1239 (S.D. Fla. 2008).

*Salutiferous is a NEEDLESS VARIANT of *salutary*. *Salubrious*, a near-synonym of *salutary*, means "healthful; promoting health or well-being."

SALUTATIONS. See FORMS OF ADDRESS.

*salutiferous. See **salutary.**

salvable. See **savable.**

salvage, n., = (1) the rescue of imperiled property; (2) the property saved or remaining after a fire or other loss; or (3) compensation allowed to a person who, having no duty to do so, helps save a ship or its cargo.

In sense 3 *salvage* is also termed *salvage award*—e.g.: "*Salvage* is often used indifferently to describe the *salvage operation* and the *salvage operation* and the *salvage award*—the latter being the compensation granted for the services rendered." Martin H. Norris, *The Law of Salvage* § 2, at 2 (1958). A *salvor* is the person entitled to the salvage reward.

salvageable. See **savable.**

salvo. See **saving clause (c).**

salvor; salvager; *salvagor. Most dictionaries give preference to *salvager*, but *salvor* has long been the common term in admiralty law. E.g.:

- "The last bottomry bond will ride over all that precedes it; and an abandonment to a *salvor* will supersede every prior claim." *The St. Jago de Cuba*, 22 U.S. (9 Wheat.) 409, 416 (1824) (per Johnson, J.).
- "*Salvors* of human life . . . are entitled to a fair share of the remuneration awarded to the *salvors* of the vessel." 46 U.S.C.A. § 729 (1988).
- "Maritime law . . . is premised on the notion that *salvors* have a right to have their claims heard in a federal forum." *Great Lakes Exploration Group, LLC v. Unidentified Wrecked & Abandoned Sailing Vessel*, 522 F.3d 682, 690 (6th Cir. 2008).

*Salvagor is a NEEDLESS VARIANT of *salvager*.

same. A. As a Pronoun. This usage, commonly exemplified in the phrase *acknowledging same*, is a primary symptom of LEGALESE. H.W. Fowler wrote trenchantly that it "is avoided by all who have any skill in writing" and that those who use it seem bent on giving the worst possible impression of themselves. (*MEU1* 511.) The words *it*, *them*, and the noun itself (that is, *the envelope*, say, and not *same*) are words that come naturally to us all; *same* or *the same* is an unnatural English expression—e.g.:

- "A will may be revoked by burning, tearing, cancelling or obliterating *the same* [read *it*]." Robert Kratovil, *Real Estate Law* 246 (1946).
- "Equity enabled them to hold any kind of property in trust for their own benefit, and to dispose of *the same* [read *it*] at pleasure." Stephen Pfeil, "Law," in 17 *Encyclopedia Americana* 86, 90 (1953).

As these examples illustrate, the phrase is rendered sometimes (and preferably) with the definite article, sometimes without. See **said (F)**.

B. Same . . . as are. *Are* often appears superfluously in statements that two or more things are identical. E.g.:

- "Employees of the government are to be afforded the *same* protection *as are* [omit *are*] employees in the private sector." Harold William Schultz, *Food Law Handbook* 414 (1981).
- "At common law they are in precisely the *same* position *as are* [omit *are*] general partners." Lewis Henry Haney, *Business Organization and Combination* 77 (2009).

See **as . . . as (B)**.

C. Same difference. This phrase is an illogical AmE casualism that is to be avoided not only in writing but in speech as well. "It's all the *same*," "It's the *same* thing," etc., are better.

same time, while at the. See **while at the same time*.

sanative; *sanatory. See **sanitary**.

sanction = (1) to approve; or (2) to penalize. Nonlawyers usually understand *sanction* in sense 1, so lawyers—who use it primarily in sense 2—are liable to be misunderstood. Yet sense 1 also appears in legal writing, as here: "*Thyssen* did not *sanction* relation back of these distinct, albeit related, actions." *Petroleos Mexicanos Refinacion v. M/T King A*, 554 F.3d 99, 109 (3d Cir. 2009) (per Aldisert, J.).

As a noun, *sanction* is burdened by the same AMBIGUITY, meaning either (1) "approval" <governmental sanction to sell the goods>, or (2) "penalty" <the statute provides sanctions for violations of the act>. In phrases such as *give sanction to*, the word means "approval"—while to *issue sanctions against* is a way of showing disapproval.

sanctionable. This word, like *sanction*, carries a double sense of approval and disapproval. Most often, *sanctionable* means "deserving punishment"—e.g.: "Specifically, the court found *sanctionable*: defense counsel's failure to supplement Mignona's deposition testimony." *Perkinson v. Gilbert/Robinson, Inc.*, 821 F.2d 686, 688–89 (D.C. Cir. 1987).

But the word sometimes means "approvable," as here: "It was our visit to the Flower Children . . . that suggested to me the need for an alternative to the polar position—the need for a totally new and socially *sanctionable* drug." Matthew Huxley, *Criteria for a Socially Sanctionable Drug*, 1 Interdisciplinary Sci. Rev. 176, 182 (1976).

sandpapering, in American trial lawyers' JARGON, refers to the preparation of witnesses before trial. The METAPHOR, of course, suggests that counsel can help soften the rough edges of their witnesses—e.g.: "We are not unmindful of the trial court's observations regarding Ms. Haynie's candor, or lack of it, and we suppose that if Diogenes, searching for an honest man, had wandered into the courtroom during the trial of this case, he might not have considered his quest at an end on meeting the plaintiff—although the rough edges on the plaintiff's testimony may have stemmed more from a lack of pre-trial preparation ('sandpapering,' in the trial court's terminology) on the part of her badly overworked counsel than from any inherent defect in the plaintiff's character." *Haynie v. Ross Gear Division of TRW, Inc.*, 799 F.2d 237, 242 (6th Cir. 1986). Cf. **horseshed**.

sanitary; sanative; *sanatory. *Sanitary* = of or relating to health or, more usu., cleanliness. *Sanative* = health-producing; healthful. **Sanatory* is a NEEDLESS VARIANT.

sank. See **sink**.

sans is an archaic literary GALLICISM to be avoided, unless a tongue-in-cheek or archaic effect is intended. *Without* should always be favored over *sans* (as long as one is using the English language)—e.g.:

- "Has Findeisen alleged a deprivation under color of state law of a federally protected property right, *sans* [read *without*] due process?" *Findeisen v. North East Indep. Sch. Dist.*, 749 F.2d 234, 236 (5th Cir. 1984).
- "Neither the record nor International's protestations support a conclusion that the trial judge acted *sans* [read *without*] reason or wisdom." *International Awards, Inc. v. Medina*, 900 S.W.2d 934, 937 (Tex. App.—Amarillo 1995, no pet.).

sans recours. See **without recourse.**

sat, in legal slang, is short for *satisfaction of judgment.* E.g.: "[When a] man finishes paying a judgment, the lawyer involved should send a '*sat*'—a satisfaction of judgment to the county records section." Murray T. Bloom, *The Trouble with Lawyers* 89 (1970) (quoting Robert E. Blackman). See sense 2 of **satisfaction.**

satellite litigation = (1) lawsuits related to a major piece of litigation being conducted in one court, while the others are conducted usu. in other courts and often with different parties; or (2) peripheral skirmishes involved in the prosecution of a lawsuit. The phrase is late-20th-century AmE—e.g.:

- (Sense 1) "The consequences are not limited to this case, but will open legally granted patents to a new source of *satellite litigation* of unforeseen scope." *Symbol Techs. Inc. v. Lemelson Med.*, 277 F.3d 1361, 1369 (Fed. Cir. 2002) (Newman, J., dissenting).
- (Sense 2) "When the deadline ceases to be enforced by the court as written, . . . then *satellite litigation* over issues of waiver and estoppel will not be far behind." E. King Poor, *The Jurisdictional Time Limit for an Appeal*, 102 Nw. U. L. Rev. *Colloquy* 151, 159 (2008).

satire. See **parody.**

satisfaction, as a LEGALISM, has nothing to do with being satisfied in the usual sense. It means (1) "the fulfillment of an obligation or claim, esp. the payment in full of a debt"; or (2) a document showing that an obligation, such as a mortgage or a court's judgment, has been fully paid. See **accord and satisfaction** & **sat.**

savable; salvable; salvageable. *Savable* = capable of being saved. Originally this word was used in theological senses, and it still carries religious connotations. *Salvable*, too, has the theological sense ("admitting of salvation"), as well as the sense (used of ships) "that can be saved or salvaged." *Salvageable*, dated from 1976 in the *OED* but actually much older in AmE, has become common in the sense "that can be salvaged"—e.g.: "His agreement to the foregoing measure of *salvageable* value was not to be construed as an admission of liability." *Wheeler v. Aetna Ins. Co.*, 4 F.Supp. 820, 823 (E.D.N.Y. 1933).

save, as an ARCHAISM equivalent to *except*, is best avoided, although, as the examples following illustrate, it is still common in legal prose:

- "After remand, the Rodgers filed an amended petition, essentially identical to their original petition, *save* [read *except*] in one respect." *Rodgers v. Threlkeld*, 80 S.W.3d 532, 534 (Mo. Ct. App. 2002).
- "The presumption is that a federal court will apply state law in all instances *save* [read *except*] when a countervailing federal interest mandates the application of federal law." *In re Gen. Motors Corp. Dex-Cool Prods. Liability Litig.*, 241 F.R.D. 305, 315 (S.D. Ill. 2007).

- "The notices Durgin received did not reference MCC policy, and instead asserted that all calls, *save* [read *except*] those between attorney and client, would be monitored." *U.S. v. Conley*, 531 F.3d 56, 59 (1st Cir. 2008).

See **except (A).**

save and except is a common but unjustifiable REDUNDANCY. See DOUBLETS, TRIPLETS, AND SYNONYM-STRINGS.

save harmless. See **indemnify (A).**

saving clause; *savings clause; saving-to-suitors clause. A. Generally. *Saving clause* (= a statutory provision exempting from coverage something that would otherwise be included) is the preferred form of this phrase generally, and particularly in admiralty law. *See Territory of Alaska v. American Can Co.*, 246 F.2d 493, 494 (9th Cir. 1957). We are here dealing with statutory construction, not bank accounts, so *saving* is the precise word. *Savings clause is not an uncommon variant, but it is not as good because it (1) suggests financial savings and (2) makes *savings* a nominal rather than a participial adjective when the latter is more specific. E.g.: "NCLB contains a *saving clause*, which provides that '[n]othing in this part shall be construed in a manner inconsistent with any Federal law guaranteeing a civil right.'" *Horne v. Flores*, 129 S.Ct. 2579, 2602 (2009) (per Alito, J.).

The U.S. Constitution grants federal courts jurisdiction over "all Cases of admiralty and maritime Jurisdiction." U.S. Const. art. III, § 2. The statutory grant of this admiralty jurisdiction negated exclusive jurisdiction by "*saving to suitors*, in all cases, the right of a common[-]law remedy where the common law is competent to give it." 28 U.S.C.; § 1333. This language is known as the *saving clause*, or *saving-to-suitors clause*, which allows a plaintiff to bring an action in any forum that will exercise jurisdiction over the case.

Though known especially to American lawyers as a term relating to admiralty jurisdiction, the phrase has long had broader applications—e.g.:

- "We need only suppose for a moment that the supremacy of the State constitutions had been left complete by a *saving clause* in their favor." *The Federalist* No. 44, at 286 (James Madison) (Clinton Rossiter ed., 1961).
- "If all the possible repercussions of the new statute were to be foreseen and provided for, the text necessarily became long, full of enumerations, exceptions, provisions, *saving clauses* and the like." Theodore F.T. Plucknett, *A Concise History of the Common Law* 324 (5th ed. 1956).

B. As a Synonym of *severability clause*. *Saving clause* is sometimes used as a synonym of *severability clause*, whether in a statute or in a contract. But this usage is loose and confusing because *saving clause* generally means something quite different (see (A)) and *severability clause* prevails over *saving clause* in this secondary sense. See **severability clause.**

C. Other Terms. A saving clause is sometimes, especially in older texts, called a *salvo* (common from the 17th to the 19th centuries). For a discussion of one category of saving clauses, see **grandfather clause**.

savings-and-loan association. See **thrift institution**.

sayeth. See **saith**.

sc., the abbreviation for *scilicet* (= that is to say; namely), is a pedantic abbreviation—*namely* or *i.e.* being preferable because they are more widely known. Even *viz.* is better known than *sc.* See **viz.**

scandalous. Court rules in the U.S. and G.B. have long forbidden advocates to put *scandalous matter* in their submissions. *See, e.g.,* Fed. R. Civ. P. 12. The *OED* quotes a phrase from *Vesey's Chancery Cases* (1809)— "The introduction of irrelevant and *scandalous matter* upon affidavits"—defining *scandalous* here as meaning "irrelevant." In yet another sense, the *OED* defines *scandalous* as meaning "defamatory" <scandalous and seditious letters>. And of course, it records the primary meaning: "grossly disgraceful; of the nature of a scandal."

But is the great dictionary correct in saying that *scandalous matter* refers merely to *irrelevant* matter? Some modern legal scholars have scoffed at the suggestion. And they are right: the *OED* definition is incomplete. The phrase *scandalous matter* refers to what is both grossly disgraceful (or defamatory) and *irrelevant*, as an early-20th-century scholar explained: "*Scandal* consists in the allegation of anything [that] is unbecoming the dignity of the court to hear, or is contrary to decency or good manners, or which charges some person with a crime not necessary to be shown in the cause, to which may be added that any unnecessary allegation, bearing cruelly upon the moral character of an individual, is also scandalous. The matter alleged, however, must be not only offensive, but also *irrelevant* to the cause, for however offensive it be, if it be pertinent and material to the cause the party has a right to plead it." Eugene A. Jones, *Manual of Equity Pleading* 50–51 (1916).

scarce; rare. What is *scarce* may be available at some time and not at others <as scarce as out-of-season Vidalia onions>. What is *rare* is always hard to find <a rare 1909-S VDB penny>.

scarlet-letter, adj., = of or relating to a type of punishment, esp. a condition of probation, that results in infamy or public scorn. The phrase alludes to Nathaniel Hawthorne's novella *The Scarlet Letter* (1850), in which Hester Prynne is forced to wear a scarlet *A* on her blouse to proclaim her crime: adultery. In the 1980s, *scarlet-letter punishments* became fashionable in some parts of the U.S.—e.g.:

- "Of particular concern is the growing use of 'scarlet letter' probation conditions which require signs to be posted on the offender's property warning the public by announcing the crime committed." Leonore H. Tavill, Note, *Scarlet Letter Punishment*, 36 Clev. St. L. Rev. 613, 615 (1988).

- "This Note argues that modern *scarlet-letter* probation conditions resembling the historical antecedents of punishment constitute punishment by humiliation." Jon A. Brilliant, Note, *The Modern Day Scarlet Letter*, 1989 Duke L.J. 1357, 1359.

Recorded examples of *scarlet-letter* probation conditions include requiring child molesters to post warning signs on their cars and in their front yards; requiring drunk drivers to proclaim their crimes on T-shirts that they must wear or on bumper stickers; and requiring drunk drivers to place apologies, along with their photographs, in local newspapers.

scatter-gun. See **blunderbuss**.

sceptic. See **skeptic**.

schism (= division; separation) is now usually figurative—e.g.: "Then came the attacks of September 11th and a *schism* at Dar al-Arqam between those who condemned and those who condoned the attacks." *U.S. v. Benkahla*, 530 F.3d 300, 303 (4th Cir. 2008). The word is best pronounced /siz-əm/, not /skiz-əm/. For unimpeachable authority on that pronunciation, see Charles Harrington Elster, *The Big Book of Beastly Mispronunciations* 428–30 (2d ed. 2005).

science. See **legal science**.

scienter /si-en-tər/ (= [1] the fact of an act's having been done knowingly, especially as a ground for damages or criminal punishment; or [2] prior knowledge) is a noun in Anglo-American jurisprudence, although the Latin word *scienter* is an adverb meaning *knowingly*. The term has been common in legal writing since the 19th century.

The term is often stretched beyond its true sense to mean "guilty knowledge," esp. in contexts announcing the standard for intent in fraud contexts. E.g.: "The account executive's *scienter*, defined as intent to defraud or reckless disregard, must be established." *Shad v. Dean Witter Reynolds, Inc.*, 799 F.2d 525, 530 (9th Cir. 1986). Two influential commentators decry this usage, which equates *scienter* with *mens rea*. See Rollin M. Perkins & Ronald N. Boyce, *Criminal Law* 861 (3d ed. 1982).

sci. fa. See **scire facias**.

scilicet. See **sc.**

scintilla (= a spark or minute particle) is often applied to law in the phrase *scintilla of evidence*. Pl. *-las*. The redundant phrase *mere scintilla* has become a legal CLICHÉ.

scire facias, literally "that you cause to know," denotes the judicial writ (which contained these words) founded upon a matter of record requiring the person against whom it is issued to show cause either why the record should not be annulled or vacated, or why a dormant judgment against that person should not be revived. E.g.: "Prior to 1883 the revocation of letters patent involved a procedure commenced in the Court of Chancery in which a writ of *scire facias* would be sought by the challenger." Luigi Palombi, *Gene Cartels* 21 (2009). The phrase is abbreviated *sci. fa.*

scission. See **dépeçage.**

scofflaw (= one who treats the law with contempt) is a 20th-century Americanism. Oddly enough, the word was coined by two entrants in a competition held in 1924 to characterize the "lawless drinker" of liquor illegally made or obtained. *Scofflaw* was chosen from more than 25,000 words, and since that time, of course, it has been extended beyond its original meaning, which lost its pungency with the repeal of Prohibition. Now *scofflaw* refers especially to a person who avoids various laws that are not easily enforced. E.g.:

- "Some *scofflaws* try to avoid detection by hauling make-believe passengers: mannequins, blow-up dolls and dummies." Cecile Sorra, *It Takes Special Training to Tell They Aren't Federal Bureaucrats*, Wall St. J., 19 July 1989, at B1.
- "The meaning of the Constitution should not turn on the antics of tax evaders and *scofflaws*." *Jones v. Flowers*, 547 U.S. 220, 248 (2006) (Thomas, J., dissenting).

sconce. See **penalize.**

score = twenty, though various other numbers are often mistakenly attached to the word. *Four score and seven* = 87.

Scotch law; Scottish law; Scots law. F.T. Wood, an Englishman, writes: "The Scots (or Scotch?) themselves are less particular than the English in the matter of these three words [*Scotch*, *Scottish*, and *Scots*]." *Current English Usage* 207 (1962). He recommends *Scots* for the noun denoting the people; and *Scottish* when referring to characteristics of the country.

Boswell, a Scottish lawyer, used *Scotch law* throughout his *Life of Johnson*, and occasionally *Scottish law* as well. Even modern British writers do not use the terms consistently. E.g.: "It follows that, if the proper law of the arbitration is to be held to be *Scots* law, this conclusion must come about by some inference . . . from the contract. . . . There is absolutely nothing in this contract from which it could be said to be governed by *Scottish* law." *James Miller & Partners Ltd v. Whitworth Street Estates Ltd*, [1970] A.C. 583, 599 (H.L.).

One might defensibly say that the preferred forms are *Scots law*, but *Scottish procedure, Scottish arbitration, Scottish legal forms*. (*Black's Law Dictionary* uses *Scotch law* in references throughout.) *Scotch*, recorded in the *OED* as a "contracted variant of *Scottish*," is best avoided by those in doubt—e.g.:

- "We have, independently of each other, four *Scotch judges* [*Scottish judges* would now be better] and afterwards Sir James Hannen spontaneously arriving at the same conclusion." *Tice Towing Line v. James McWilliams Blue Line*, 51 F.2d 243, 248 (S.D.N.Y. 1931).
- "They followed a *Scottish procedure* by which the husband, in the wife's presence, swore before a sheriff that he was

the child's father, and the child's birth records were then changed to indicate that fact." *Doe v. Doe*, 710 A.2d 1297, 1314 (Conn. 1998).

It is sometimes said that *Scotch* should be used of material objects, as *Scotch tartans, Scotch whisky*, and *Scotch thistle.*

scot-free is a predicative adjective meaning "exempt from injury or punishment." E.g.: "It would be contrary to the decided weight of authority to hold that since plaintiff has a cause of action against the company for breach of contract, Sander should go *scot-free*." *Sorenson v. Chevrolet Motor Co.*, 214 N.W. 754, 756 (Minn. 1927). The phrase derives from the early English "scot" or contribution or payment into a common fund.

It is a mistake to capitalize *scot* as if it referred to someone from Scotland—e.g.: "To allow people to get away with this sort of crime *Scot-free* [read *scot-free*] is a very disturbing trend." James Langton, *The Jury That Saw Two Wrongs as a Right*, Sunday Telegraph, 24 May 1992, at 4 (quoting the Rev. Anthony Higton, rector of Hawkwell in Essex).

scottish; Scots. See **Scotch law.**

scrivener; *scrivenor; scribe. The spelling *scrivener* is preferred over *scrivenor. E.g.:

- "When negotiating and drafting countless contracts in our prior legal careers, we rarely if ever encountered a 'memorandum of understanding' or a 'preliminary agreement' that required nothing more than the wordsmithing of a true *scrivener* to become a 'final contract.' " *Fairbrook Leasing, Inc. v. Mesaba Aviation, Inc.*, 519 F.3d 421, 427 (8th Cir. 2008).
- "While a plan's specific language can aid a court in determining whether that plan qualifies as a top-hat plan, . . . a *scrivener's* choice of plan language cannot be allowed to control the more general interpretive inquiry into what the statute requires." *Alexander v. Brigham & Women's Physicians Org.*, 513 F.3d 37, 45 (1st Cir. 2008).

Scrivener, as illustrated in the two sentences just quoted, and *scribe*, as evidenced in the name of the American lawyers' organization devoted to improved legal writing (*Scribes*), either are frequently taken by lawyers to be terms of praise for the person named, or are unusual lawyers' attempts at self-effacement. Technically, a *scrivener* is merely a copyist or amanuensis, not a legal drafter. In *Bartleby the Scrivener*, Herman Melville described a *scrivener* as "a mere copyist"— "copying law papers being proverbially a dry, husky sort of business."

The same is true of *scribe* in all but historical senses; the *OED* notes that it is additionally "applied to a political pamphleteer or journalist; chiefly with contemptuous notion, a party hack."

Today, *scrivener* is seen most often in the phrase *scrivener's error* ("an error resulting from a minor mistake or inadvertence, esp. in writing or copying

---

something on the record, and not from judicial reasoning or determination." *Black's Law Dictionary* 622 (9th ed. 2009)). E.g.: "The error is simply a *scrivener's error*, however, because the arbitrator correctly implemented the CWA's interpretation in spelling out his remedy." *Verizon Washington, D.C., Inc. v. Communications Workers of Am.*, 571 F.3d 1296, 1300 n.4 (D.C. Cir. 2009).

scrutiny (= close inquiry; investigation) is typically, perhaps invariably, preferable to *scrutinization* (= the act of scrutinizing)—e.g.:

- "[A] *scrutinization* [read *scrutiny*] of Robinson's own testimony reveals that she had not shown any apprehension or fear of Moore during their fight earlier that night." *Robinson v. State*, 875 So.2d 230, 238 (Miss. Ct. App. 2004).
- "[T]he court must offer the same careful *scrutinization* [read *scrutiny*] of the proof in the light most favorable to the party which summary judgment is being sought against." *LaSalle Bank, N.A. v. Shearon*, 850 N.Y.S.2d 871, 877 (Sup. Ct. 2008).
- "The Court's *scrutinization* [read *scrutiny*] of the evidence does not make this Court, or the Seventh Circuit, some sort of an outlaw jurisdiction, as defendants seem to think." *Young v. County of Cook*, 616 F.Supp.2d 856, 860 (N.D. Ill. 2009).

scrutiny, strict. See **strict scrutiny.**

*****sculduggery; *scullduggery.** See **skulduggery.**

scurrility. See **abuse,** n.

Scylla and Charybdis, between. As described by Homer, *Scylla* was a sea monster who had six heads (each with a triple row of teeth) and twelve feet. Though primarily a fish-eater, she was capable of snatching and devouring (in one swoop) six sailors if their ship ventured too near her cave in the Straits of Messina. (In the accounts of later writers, she is depicted as a rocky promontory.) Toward the opposite shore, not far from Scylla's lair, was *Charybdis*, a whirlpool strong enough thrice daily to suck into its vortex whole ships if they came too close.

So *between Scylla and Charybdis* is the literary CLI-CHÉ roughly equivalent to "between a rock and a hard place"—e.g.:

- "A refusal on the part of the federal courts to intervene . . . may place the hapless plaintiff *between the Scylla* of intentionally flouting state law *and the Charybdis* of forgoing what he believes to be constitutionally protected activity to avoid becoming enmeshed in a criminal proceeding." *Steffel v. Thompson*, 415 U.S. 452, 462 (1974) (per Brennan, J.).
- "The alien who is granted voluntary departure but whose circumstances have changed in a manner cognizable by a motion to reopen is between *Scylla and Charybdis*: He or she can leave the United States in accordance with the voluntary departure order; but, pursuant to regulation, the motion to reopen will be deemed withdrawn." *Dada v. Mukasey*, 554 U.S. 1, 18 (2008) (per Kennedy, J.). On the use of *pursuant to in that sentence, see ***pursuant to.**

See LITERARY ALLUSION (A)(4).

seal. A. Origin and Sense. At common law, the seal was an impression made upon wax, a wafer (i.e., gummed paper), or other adhesive substance; attached to a legal document as a formality; and having various types of legal significance, depending on the document. Today, a *seal* is generally an impression stamped or embossed on paper to authenticate a document or attest to a signature, such as a corporate or notary seal. Some jurisdictions—especially U.S. states on the eastern seaboard—require deeds to be sealed. A few even require leases to be under seal. See **L.S., signed, sealed, and delivered** & **wafer.**

B. Contracts Under Seal. Generally, of course, valuable consideration is necessary to make an enforceable contract. But for a *contract under seal*, no consideration is necessary. Traditionally, such a contract carries with it an irrebuttable presumption of consideration: "The Law long ago decided that a *seal*, real or imitation, attached to a promise, amounted to good Consideration for that promise, despite the fact that the man who makes the promise puts the *seal* there." Fred Rodell, *Woe Unto You, Lawyers!* 35 (1939). But statutes in some jurisdictions, such as New York, have made the presumption of consideration rebuttable. In so changing the common law, these jurisdictions have progressed beyond "one of the quaintest freaks of legal conservatism, that the presence or absence of a gummed wafer or engraved mark on a document should, in this rationalistic age, make any difference in its legal effect." Edward Jenks, *The Book of English Law* 291 (P.B. Fairest ed., 6th ed. 1967). See **L.S.**

C. The Idiom *the case is sealed.* This phrase is a figurative extension of the literal contractual sense, the idea being that some occurrence fastens the outcome. E.g.: "The legal errors he made representing himself in the wrongful-death suit probably *sealed* the case against him." *Verdict Against White Supremacist*, A.B.A. J., Jan. 1991, at 22.

sea lawyer. See LAWYERS, DEROGATORY NAMES FOR (B).

seaman; mariner. *Seaman* includes "all persons employed on board ships and vessels, during the voyage, to assist in their navigation and preservation, or to promote the purposes of the voyage." George Wilfred Stumberg, *Harbor Workers and Workmen's Compensation*, 7 Tex. L. Rev. 197, 200 (1929). *Seaman* is common in admiralty contexts, but *mariner* carries the same meaning without the -*man* suffix. (See SEXISM (B).) *Seaman* is so well entrenched, however, that the admiralty bar is unlikely to change it. See **mariner.**

search and seizure. Enshrined in the Fourth Amendment to the U.S. Constitution, the individual's right to be free from unreasonable searches and seizures derives ultimately from Magna Carta. Roscoe Pound and others have connected this important constitutional right with "the clause in Magna Carta that the king would not 'send upon' a free man . . . ." Roscoe

Pound, *The Development of Constitutional Guarantees of Liberty* 49 (1957).

Today, under the exclusionary rule, evidence obtained in violation of the Fourth Amendment right is excluded from any prosecution. Of course, the purposely vague word *unreasonable* has been the source of steady litigation. Today, warrantless searches are generally considered "unreasonable," but there are several exceptions, involving consent, an otherwise lawful arrest, and exigency. See **exclusionary rule, stop-and-frisk rule** & *Terry* **stop.**

When used as a PHRASAL ADJECTIVE, *search and seizure* should be hyphenated: *search-and-seizure rules.*

search-and-seizure order. See *Anton Piller order* under CASE REFERENCES (C).

search warrant. Preferably two words, though some writers have hyphenated the phrase.

seasonable. A. And *seasonal*. *Seasonable* = (1) occurring at the right season; opportune; or (2) (of weather) suitable to the time of year (*OED*). *Seasonal* = (1) pertaining to or characteristic of the seasons of the year, or some one of them; or (2) dependent on the seasons, as certain trades (*OED*). For the noun sense, see **seasonal,** n.

B. And *timely*. In legal contexts, *seasonable* is often used to mean "timely," whereas in lay contexts it ordinarily means "in season." One writer has insisted that "these terms [*seasonable* and *timely*] are not synonymous. That which is *seasonable* is in harmony or keeping with the season or occasion; that which is *timely* is in good time. A thing may be *timely* in appearance that is not *seasonable*." Frank H. Vizetelly, *A Desk-Book of Errors in English* 194 (1907). Yet in American legal writing, the word is regularly used as a synonym of *timely*, whether advisedly or not—e.g.:

- "The bankruptcy court correctly determined that Rafter Seven had all the time it needed to inspect the facially nonconforming goods, and that its rejection was therefore not *seasonable*." *Rafter Seven Ranches LP v. C.H. Brown Co.*, 546 F.3d 1194, 1203 (10th Cir. 2008).
- "Where a buyer's acceptance is as described in UCC § 2-608(1)(b), the majority rule is that he may revoke the acceptance without waiting for a cure, *seasonable* or otherwise, by the seller." *Car Transp. Brokerage Co. v. Blue Bird Body Co.*, 322 Fed. Appx. 891, 895 (11th Cir. 2009).

See **timely.**

seasonal, n., is sometimes used in AmE as an elliptical form of *seasonal worker*. E.g.: "Some year-round employees are consistently coded as temporary *seasonals* while some who received seasonal step-ups are not tracked on the Parks Seasonal Tracking System." *Wright v. Stern*, 450 F.Supp.2d 335, 361 (S.D.N.Y. 2006). See ADJECTIVES (C).

seaworthy. One word—not hyphenated.

secede. See **cede.**

2d; 2nd. The first is preferred in legal citations, the 2nd in all other contexts.

secondary use. See **springing use.**

second bite at the apple—a favorite expression of defense lawyers—is an especially tiresome CLICHÉ. E.g.: "This application was itself Panetti's *second bite at the apple* in the state court on the question of his competency to be executed." *Panetti v. Quarterman*, 551 U.S. 930, 969 n.6 (2007) (per Kennedy, J.). See **one bite at the apple.**

second chair, n.; **second-chair,** vb. In AmE, the *second chair* at trial is a lawyer who helps the lead counsel in court, often by examining some of the witnesses, arguing some of the points of law, and handling parts of the voir dire, opening statement, and summation. For *lead counsel*, see **leader (at the bar).**

Since the late 20th century, the phrase *second-chair* has also come to be used as a verb, preferably hyphenated—e.g.: "I learned this lesson as a novice, *second chairing* [read *second-chairing*] an experienced trial lawyer." Denis McInerney, *Counterclaims as Self-Inflicted Wounds*, Litig., Spring 1992, at 2, 2. See NOUNS AS VERBS.

second degree = the second most serious category of a crime, as in *second-degree murder*. See **degree** & **murder (A).**

second-guess, vb. So hyphenated.

secondhand; *****secondhanded.** The *-ed* suffix is not just unnecessary—it is wrong. E.g.: "Harvey contributed a *secondhanded* [read *secondhand*] boiler and some machinery." *Harvey v. Gartner*, 67 So. 197, 201 (La. 1915).

secondhand evidence. See **hearsay evidence.**

secondly. See **firstly.**

secondment /sə-**kond**-mənt/, primarily a BrE term, means "a person's reassignment from his or her regular employment to some temporary assignment elsewhere." E.g.:

- "Business is conducted . . . through LIA's lawyers, Berwin Leighton, which has had staff on *secondment* at the LIA offices in Tripoli recently." Elena Moya, *Libya Pours Millions into City Investments*, Guardian (London), 25 Aug. 2009, Home §, at 7.
- "Detective Senior Constable Simon Ross, who is on a six-week *secondment* to Sydney from his role with the Port Macquarie child-protection unit, . . . [found] the oldest bandit, 18, holding the night manager hostage." Tim Vollmer & Janet Fife-Yeomans, *Cop's Quick Thinking Saved Hotel Hostage*, Daily Telegraph, 2 Sept. 2009, Local §, at 9.

secretary = a corporate officer who is concerned with the corporation's business management and administration. In corporate law, then, this term denotes an

---

office considerably more elevated than those outside business and law might suspect.

secretaryship; *secretariship. The first spelling is standard.

secrete = (1) to hide; or (2) to exude or ooze through pores or glands; to produce by secretion. **Secrete away* is redundant. Sense 1 is becoming increasingly learned or literary, but it is frequently used in legal writing—e.g.:

- "Redding would not have been the first person to conceal pills in her undergarments. . . . Nor will she be the last after today's decision, which announces the safest place to *secrete* contraband in school." *Safford Unified Sch. Dist. #1 v. Redding,* 129 S.Ct. 2633, 2650 (2009) (Thomas, J., concurring in part & dissenting in part).
- "It is reasonable to conclude that *whomever* [read *whoever*] placed the body of Randall Pinion in the remote area of McDowell County did so to *secrete* the whereabouts of the deceased and avoid detection." *Baum v. Rushton,* 572 F.3d 198, 203 (4th Cir. 2009). For more on *whoever* vs. *whomever,* see **who.**
- "Defendant committed perjury during his trial and then attempted to *secrete* assets in order to frustrate the collection of a fine or restitution." *U.S. v. O'Georgia,* 569 F.3d 281, 303 (6th Cir. 2009).

secret equity. See **equity.**

secretive; secretory. The first is the adjective ("inclined to secrecy; uncommunicative") corresponding to sense 1 of *secrete*; the second is the adjective ("having the function of secreting") corresponding to sense 2 of *secrete. Secretive* is best pronounced /**see**-krə-tiv/ or /si-**kree**-tiv/, and *secretory* /si-**kree**-tə-ree/.

section. In drafting, a *section*—often indicated by the character "§"—is either a subdivision of a document or a subdivision of an article in a document, statutory title, or code. The plural form of the abbreviation is §§.

In contracts, *section* is often used interchangeably with *article* or, more commonly (and unfortunately), *paragraph.* See **paragraph.**

secular, like *lay,* has been extended beyond the religious meaning, namely, "outside the ecclesiastical calling," and now can refer to persons and things outside a profession, most commonly the law. Cf. **temporal.**

securitize = (1) to package (a traditional loan, such as a mortgage) into bondlike securities for resale to investors; or (2) to secure (a debt) with assets. This commercial NEOLOGISM has not yet found its way into most dictionaries, such as the *OED* and *W3.* E.g.:

- (Sense 1) "When card issuers *securitize* credit card debt, they transform the credit card debt into a pool of assets used to pay off bonds. If the pool turns out not to be large enough, the bond investors take the loss. But if there's a surplus, it goes to the card issuer." Adam Levitin, *Two ABI Members Testify Before U.S. Senate Banking, Housing, and Urban Affairs Committee,* 28-2 Am. Bankr. Inst. J. 10, 76 (Mar. 2009).
- (Sense 2) "It is necessary in connection with trusts generally to consider their efficacy relative to security

registration systems that may be in place in the jurisdiction. The trust is often also the preferred legal form for asset *securitization.*" Robert Flannigan, *Business Applications of the Express Trust,* 36 Alberta L. Rev. 630, 634 (1998).

security = (1) an instrument given to secure the performance of an act; (2) collateral used to guarantee repayment of a debt; (3) a surety, or person bound by some type of guaranty [though *surety* is the proper and the more usual term for this sense]; or (4) an instrument (such as a stock, a bond, or an option) indicating one of three things: (a) ownership in a firm, (b) a creditor relationship with a firm or with a national or local government, or (c) some other rights to ownership. Senses 1 and 2 are the traditional legal senses, but sense 4 is the most common modern sense—the investor's sense. Sense 3 ought to be avoided in modern writing.

secus (= not so; otherwise) is an ARCHAISM, a LATINISM, and a LEGALISM—e.g.:

- "If a person devises to trustees, and by express clause gives them the power to appoint agents to manage the land, and they appoint one then solvent and good, though afterwards he proves insolvent, they shall not answer for him; *secus* if he were not solvent when he was nominated." 21 Charles Viner, *General Abridgment of Law and Equity* 525 (1793).
- "In *King v. Hoare,* A.D. 1844, the Court of Exchequer decided that a judgment, without satisfaction, recovered against one of two Joint debtors, is a bar to an action against the other; though *secus* where the debt is joint and several." *Lovejoy v. Murray,* 70 U.S. 1, 4 (1865) (per Miller, J.).
- "Ritual dialogue was unknown to the secular law (*secus* in sacral law, and in public law)." W.W. Buckland, *A Text-Book of Roman Law* 673 (2007).

sedition; treason. *Sedition* = an agreement or communication aimed at stirring up treason or some lesser commotion, or (in BrE) at defaming a member of the royal family or of the government. *Treason* = attempting, through an overt act, to overthrow one's government. The most recent edition of *Black's* reflects the distinction: "The difference between sedition and treason is that the former is committed by preliminary steps, while the latter entails some overt act for carrying out the plan. But if the plan is merely for some small commotion, even accomplishing the plan does not amount to treason." *Black's Law Dictionary* 1479 (9th ed. 2009).

One authority incorrectly states that the distinction between *sedition* and *treason* is that, "though the ultimate object of sedition is a violation of the public peace, or at least such a course of measures as evidently engenders it, yet it does not aim at direct and open violence against the laws or the subversion of the constitution." *Black's Law Dictionary* 1523 (4th ed. 1968). But the distinction does not lie in the objective, even though the objective of sedition may be less serious than what is required for treason; rather, the true distinction is that *sedition* is committed by preliminary steps while *treason* requires some overt act directed toward execution. *See* Rollin M. Perkins & Ronald N. Boyce, *Criminal Law* 508 (3d ed. 1982). See **treason** & **libel**. Cf. **coup d'état**.

seduction; seducement. Although *seducement* is sometimes used for the *seduction*, the two are best kept separate. *Seduction* = the action or an act of seducing (a person, esp. a woman) to err in conduct or belief, esp. of enticing the person to engage in illicit sexual intercourse. It differs from *rape*, in which there is no consent; in *seduction*, the consent is unfairly obtained. English common law had no crime known as *seduction*, but many state statutes in the U.S. make it a misdemeanor (or, formerly, a felony). For the distinction between *rape* and *seduction*, see **rape (B)**.

Seducement = something that seduces or serves as a means of seduction; an insidious temptation (*OED*).

seem. A. As a Weasel Word. The verb *seems* can often destroy the power of a passage, as here: "Synanon makes the astonishing assertion that the alleged wrongdoing—perjured testimony, document destruction, and similar misconduct—constitutes mere discovery abuse for which Synanon has been adequately punished by dismissal of its two lawsuits. Such a characterization *seems* disingenuous." *In re Sealed Case*, 754 F.2d 395, 401 (D.C. Cir. 1985). Given the plaintiff's egregious conduct as catalogued by the judge, *astonishing* is appropriate but the later *seems* is inappropriately weak. See WEASEL WORDS.

B. *Seem (to be)* [+ noun phrase]. In formal writing it is best to include the infinitive *to be*—e.g.:

- "There certainly *seemed* [read *seemed to be*] no enlightening purpose served by giving some slick operator from the K.K.K. a nationwide forum on which to spread his rancid twaddle." James Wolcott, *The Eagles Have Landed*, N.Y. Mag., 1 Nov. 1982, at 72.
- "This definition, however, is a bit vague, and *seems* [read *seems to be*] more of a limitation on implementing a Rocket Docket than an affirmative element of it." Kevin A. Meehan, *Shopping for Expedient, Inexpensive & Predictable Patent Litigation*, 2008 B.C. Intell. Prop. & Tech. F. 102901, ¶ 39.

C. *Would seem.* See **would seem**.

see you in court. This phrase is a CLICHÉ to which litigious people are drawn. E.g.: "To me . . . [the English system of 'loser pays'] discourages frivolous lawsuits and the knee-jerk business reaction of '*see you in court.*'" Mark H. McCormack, *What They Don't Teach You at Harvard Business School* 207 (1984).

segment, vb.; ***segmentalize; *segmentize.*** The first is standard, the others NEEDLESS VARIANTS. See -IZE (A).

segregate for *separate* is often a puffed-up LEGALISM. E.g.: "He then *segregated* [read *separated*] the few jewels that he wished to purchase from the rest of the lot." See **separate**.

segregate out. See **out (A)**.

segregation, de facto; de jure segregation. These phrases denote two types of racial segregation. *De facto segregation* exists in fact but is not required by law. *De jure segregation*, on the other hand, is required by law, as under the long-defunct rule of *Plessy v. Ferguson*, 163 U.S. 537 (1896). (See **separate but equal**.) *De jure segregation* is the more invidious type. See **de facto (A)**.

segregative = having the power or property of separating. In American legal writing, the term is used almost exclusively of racial segregation—e.g.:

- "Confronted with *segregative* assignment of faculty and administrators, *segregative* bus transportation of students and other *segregative* post-*Brown* decisions of the Ector County I.S.D., the district court held that the Ector County School District not only continued to fail to meet its duty to dismantle its dual school system, but actually increased the segregation in its schools." *U.S. v. Crucial*, 722 F.2d 1182, 1184 (5th Cir. 1983) (per Randall, J.).
- "Where, as in this case, a policy of intentional segregation has been proved with respect to a significant portion of the school system, the burden is on the school authorities . . . to prove that their actions as to other segregated schools in the system were not likewise motivated by a *segregative* intent." Brian G. Gilmore, Warth *Redux: The Making of* Warth v. Seldin, 6 Hastings Race & Poverty L.J. 147, 158–59 (2009).

See **separate**.

seignorial; *seignoral; seigneurial. In referring to a feudal lord (a *seignor*) in early England, *seignorial* is the predominant adjective in texts dealing with English legal history. **Seignoral* is a NEEDLESS VARIANT. *Seigneurial* describes a feudal lord in France, or a member of the landed gentry in Canada.

seignory (= [1] feudal lordship; or [2] the relation of a lord to the tenants of a manor) is the usual spelling, **seigniory* being a secondary variant.

seise; seize. The two identically pronounced words are related, but they have undergone DIFFERENTIATION. In the legal sense "to put in possession, invest with the fee simple of," the spelling *seise* is preferred in both AmE and BrE—e.g.: "Each feoffee (recipient of a fief), having received the seisin from his feoffor, would be said to be *seised*, or possessed of an interest in the land." Thomas F. Bergin & Paul G. Haskell, *Preface to Estates in Land and Future Interests* 11 (2d ed. 1984). See **disseise**.

Seize is principally a nontechnical lay word meaning: (1) "to take hold of (a thing or person) forcibly or suddenly or eagerly"; (2) "to take possession of (a thing) by legal right" <to seize contraband>; or (3) "to have a sudden overwhelming effect on" <to be seized by fear> (*OAD*). *Seize* should be confined to these senses. So in the following examples, *seise* would have been the better spelling:

- "In 1814 the New York courts decided that the mortgagor was *seized* [read *seised*] of the freehold." William F. Walsh, *A Treatise on Equity* 124–25 (1930).
- "Under the rule prevailing in Kentucky, tenants in common of land are *seized* [read *seised*] by the moiety and by the whole or, as expressed in the ancient rule, *per my et per tout*." *Saulsberry v. Saulsberry*, 121 F.2d 318, 321 (6th Cir. 1941).
- "When a person dies *seized* [read *seised*] of lands . . . his title shall vest immediately in his heirs." Rev. Code Wash. (ARCW) § 11.04.250.

The spelling *seize* would make sense if the noun were predominantly spelled *seizin*; but it is not. See **seisin.**

Seize is not infrequently used in the lay sense 1 in legal writing, a fact that provides still greater impetus for strict DIFFERENTIATION between the spellings: "Equity *seizes* the property on its way from the donor to the appointee, and applies it to the satisfaction of the obligations of the appointor." *Hill v. Treasurer & Receiver Gen.*, 118 N.E. 891, 891 (Mass. 1918).

seised in law; seised in deed. At common law, when the person with *seisin* dies, the heir is said to be *seised in law*—and the heir is *seised in deed* only upon entering the land. During the interval, the heir has some—though by no means all—of the advantages of seisin. See **seisin.**

seisin /**see**-zən/. **A. Sense.** This feudal word originally meant "possession," then grew into a TERM OF ART in 18th- and 19th-century land law, much of which is now defunct. The term *seisin* has persisted, however, the spoor of a complicated history. Today it generally denotes "possession of a freehold estate in land" and connotes peace and quiet. But the word is impossible to define in a way that adequately evokes its historical importance in English law while serving to guide modern lawyers, who speak of ownership as depending upon title (without any reference to physically entering the land). As the leading English textbook states, "*Seisin* is no longer of importance, for the distinctions [that] gave it its peculiar meaning no longer exist." Robert E. Megarry & H.W.R. Wade, *The Law of Real Property* 47 (5th ed. 1984).

The best advice is to view *seisin* as a historical term and to confine it to historical contexts in which the sense is well defined—e.g.: "Livery of *seisin* . . . meant delivery of possession. It was the operative fact of the feoffment . . . and the feoffment dominated the transfer of land." Percy Bordwell, *Seisin and Disseisin*, 34 Harv. L. Rev. 592, 593 (1921). See **feoffment.**

B. Alternative Spelling. The word is sometimes spelled *seizin*, as in *RH2* (surprisingly) and in 2 B.W. Pope, *Legal Definitions* 1453 (1920). The *-zin* form was once more common than it is today, but it still appears from time to time. E.g.: "If the grantor owns only part of the title, or if the grantor has only a life estate, the covenant of *seizin* [read *seisin*] is violated." Robert Kratovil, *Real Estate Law* 45 (1946).

C. Seisin of Personal Property. To speak of the *seisin* of chattels, or of a *lessee's seisin*, is a solecism. For

centuries, *seisin* has been a term appropriate only to real property.

seisinee (= one to whom seisin is transferred), though omitted from the *OED*, *W3*, and other major dictionaries, has appeared in published legal writings—e.g.: "The Statute was considered to have application only where a *seisinee* held to the use of another person and not himself." L.B. Curzon, *English Legal History* 121 (2d ed. 1979). Seemingly a NONCE WORD—and not a very useful one, at that—it is perhaps best forgotten. See -EE.

seize. See **seise.**

seizin. See **seisin (B).**

select, adj.; **selected.** The first is the adjective meaning "choice; esp. excellent." Here the past-participial form of the verb (*selected*) is used inappropriately for the adjective: "[These students] are all educated young men, and—since the law school's standards are known to be high, and the work is notoriously difficult—it may reasonably be supposed that they are a *selected* [read *select*] group." William L. Prosser, "English as She Is Wrote" (1954), in *Classic Essays on Legal Advocacy* 737, 737 (George Rossman ed., 2010).

selectee. See -EE.

selectman is an Americanism dating from 1635 and meaning "one of a board of officers elected annually to manage various local concerns in a New England township." Today there is a tendency to change the word to *selectperson*, which is not necessarily a happy development. (See SEXISM (B).) The term *selectman* is a difficult one for which to find a nonsexist equivalent formed from the same root; hence one book recommends replacing it with *representative*. See Bobbye D. Sorrels, *The Nonsexist Communicator* 149 (1983). Yet some writers prefer to use *selectman* as if it were gender-neutral—e.g.:

- "*Selectman* Elizabeth Roth cautioned that cutting the budget to the bone could create problems down the road for the community." Derrick Perkins, *Dark Cloud Hangs over First 2010 Budget Review*, Union Leader (Manchester, N.H.), 2 Sept. 2009, at 2.
- "Among the residents interested in expanding the responsibilities of the town administrator is former *Selectman* Linda W. Young." Sandra E. Constantine, *Job Change Eyed in South Hadley*, The Republican (Springfield, Mass.), 3 Sept. 2009, at C2.
- "In 2007, the town settled a lawsuit brought by a former officer who claimed her civil rights were violated because local officials told her she would lose her police job if she ran for *selectman*." Brian Lee, *State Police Investigating Former Chief*, Worcester Tel. & Gaz., 4 Sept. 2009, at B1.

self-admitted, like **self-confessed**, is a REDUNDANCY—e.g.: "Rep. Gerry E. Studds, 53, and Rep. Barney Frank, 50, . . . are *self-admitted* [read *admitted*] homosexuals, but that is not automatically grounds for Congressional expulsion." *Walter Scott's Personality Parade*, Dallas Morning News (Parade Mag.), 22 July 1990, at 2. See **self-confessed.*

self-aggrandizing. See **self-interested.**

*self-complacent is redundant; *complacent* is sufficient.

*self-confessed is a common REDUNDANCY—e.g.:

- "A court that frees a *self-confessed* [read *confessed*] murderer on a technicality would seem to bear responsibility for any harm that criminal may do in the future." Mario Pei, *Words in Sheep's Clothing* 86 (1969).
- "Van Rijn is now a *self-confessed* [read *confessed*] art smuggler who has offered assistance to law enforcement officials." Derek Fincham, *How Adopting the Lex Originis Rule Can Impede the Flow of Illicit Cultural Property*, 32 Colum. J.L. & Arts 111, 128 n.106 (2008).

self-crimination. See **incriminate.**

self-dealing (= financial dealing that is not at arm's length; esp., borrowing from or lending to a company by a controlling individual primarily to that individual's own advantage [*W11*]) is an Americanism that originated in the mid-20th century. E.g.: "The conferred right to exercise all these plenary powers of ownership necessarily modified or displaced the otherwise absolute limitation against *self-dealing.*" *In re Flagg's Estate*, 73 A.2d 411, 415 (Pa. 1950) (per Linn, J.). See **deception.**

self-defender = one who resorts to self-defense. E.g.:

- "This testimony indicates that the victim was the only one in the position of a *self-defender.*" *Bedford v. State*, 222 N.W.2d 658, 661 (Wis. 1974).
- "The negligent *self-defender* is arguably less culpable than the negligent rapist." Arnold H. Loewy, *Culpability, Dangerousness, and Harm*, 66 N.C. L. Rev. 283, 301 (1988).

self-defense = (1) the right to defend oneself with reasonable force against an attack, real or threatened; or (2) the right of a state to defend itself against an attack, real or threatened. E.g.:

- (Sense 1) "Not even *self-defence* [so spelled in BrE] would justify a defender in shooting the aggressor's wife in order to persuade him to desist." Glanville Williams, *Textbook of Criminal Law* 449 (1978).
- (Sense 2) "Is the power of raising armies and equipping fleets necessary? . . . It is involved in the power of *self-defense.*" *The Federalist* No. 41, at 256 (James Madison) (Clinton Rossiter ed., 1961).

self-deprecating; self-depreciating. See **deprecate.**

self-executing = not requiring anything additional to make (a document) binding. E.g.: "Despite his strong statement, Justice Story apparently believed that the Constitution, though mandatory, was not *self-executing.*" Charles Alan Wright, *The Law of Federal Courts* 46 (5th ed. 1994).

self-help. In lay usage, this phrase usually represents something good (the work ethic, providing for oneself without relying on others). But in legal usage, it usually represents something bad (redress of perceived wrongs without recourse to law)—e.g.:

- "*Self-help* is indeed but an unsatisfactory means of redress." Thomas E. Holland, *The Elements of Jurisprudence* 323 (13th ed. 1924).
- "Ideally, reform would come according to reason and justice without *self-help* and disturbing, almost violent, forms of protest." Archibald Cox, *Civil Rights, the Constitution, and the Courts*, 40 N.Y. State B.J. 161, 169 (1968).

Still, in the law of oil and gas, if the rule of capture applies, *self-help* is the only recourse available to prevent losing the rights to resources under one's land.

self-incrimination. See **self-inculpation* & **incriminate.**

*self-inculpation is a NEEDLESS VARIANT of *self-incrimination.*

self-interested; self-aggrandizing. These phrases have distinct uses. *Self-interested* = having a personal, esp. a monetary, interest in a transaction or event, in which one may also play a more neutral role. *Self-aggrandizing* = tending to exaggerate one's own importance or embellish one's own accomplishments. Yet *self-aggrandizing* is sometimes misused for *self-interested*—e.g.: "Plaintiffs claim that, in investing so much of the class's funds in Textron stock during the class period, defendants violated duties of loyalty owed to the class and acted in an unlawfully *self-aggrandizing* [read *self-interested*] manner because defendants knew or had reason to know that Textron faced troubles that were certain to cause (and did in fact cause) a significant decline in the value of its stock." *Lalonde v. Textron, Inc.*, 369 F.3d 1, 3 (1st Cir. 2004).

self-killing; self-murder. See **suicide (A).**

self-proving, not included in any of the major dictionaries, denotes a type of affidavit appended to modern wills. *Self-proving affidavits* are signed by the witnesses to the will, and state that the testator was under no compulsion and had a sound mind when signing the will. E.g.: "A useful device for discouraging a will contest is the '*self-proving*' affidavit, which is the sworn statement of the testator and witnesses about the execution ceremony." Barbara Child, *Drafting Legal Documents* 268 (2d ed. 1992).

self-slaughter. See **suicide (A).**

self-stultification = testifying about one's own bad morals. Hence *rule against self-stultification.* See **stultify.**

self-styled. See *soi disant.*

sell. See **hard sell.**

---

sell, contract to. See **contract for sale.**

***sellable.** See **salable.**

seller. See **vendor.**

Semantics. For solid treatments of general semantics as applied to law, see Glanville Williams, *Language and the Law* (pt. 4), 61 Law Q. Rev. 384–406 (1945); F.A. Philbrick, *Language and the Law* (1949); and Walter Probert, *Law, Language and Communication* (1972).

semble /**sem**-bəl/ (= it seems), a LAW FRENCH term, is used in law reports as a technical expression of uncertainty, usually in introducing either an obiter dictum or the writer's less-than-confident interpretation of how a court's holding might be applied or extended. Today the term appears more often in BrE than in AmE—e.g.:

- "If statutory language makes no sense whatever, *semble* it can be treated as *pro non scripto* [= as not written]; but the Court cannot escape the duty of interpretation merely because the language is difficult or ambiguous." Carleton K. Allen, *Law in the Making* 488 (7th ed. 1964).
- "If he has capacity to contract by the system of law with which the contract is most closely connected, the contract will (*semble*) be valid so far as capacity is concerned." 2 Albert Venn Dicey & J.H.C. Morris, *Dicey & Morris on the Conflict of Laws* 96 (11th ed. 1987).
- "However, *semble* that the operator of a search engine might in principle be liable for publication of a defamatory search result by authorisation, approval or acquiescence after notification of the offending URL." *Metropolitan Int'l Schs. Ltd. v. Designtechnica Corp.*, [2009] E.W.H.C. 1765 (Q.B.), at H10.

semiannual (AmE); **half-yearly** (BrE). See **biennial (A).**

Semicolons. See PUNCTUATION (L).

semiweekly. See **biweekly.**

senatorial courtesy has traditionally had a restricted sense in AmE: the tradition that the president must take care in filling high-level federal posts, such as judgeships, with persons agreeable to the nominees' home-state senators, lest the senators defeat confirmation. E.g.:

- "A nomination approved by them [i.e., by senators from the state in which the office lies] is practically certain of final confirmation by the Senate as a whole. The arrangement is a 'logrolling' one, which has been dignified by the name of 'Senatorial courtesy.'" Herbert W. Horwill, *The Usages of the American Constitution* 128–29 (1925).
- "No possible appointment could more have enraged the conservatives, in and out of the Senate, who had done the Court plan to death; but the silly rule of 'Senatorial courtesy,' whereby members of the club never question very deeply the qualifications of a fellow member named to a new post, made Black's confirmation—just as Roosevelt knew it would—almost automatic." Fred Rodell, *Nine Men* 252 (1955).

The term is unfamiliar enough to general audiences as to justify an explanation when it is used in its traditional sense—e.g.: "Dorsey's refusal to 'sign off' on the nomination drew a firestorm of protests and renewed calls to end 'senatorial courtesy,' the tradition that allows home-county senators to block appointments." *An Inside Look at the Week in New Jersey* (Editorial), Star-Ledger (Newark), 2 Aug. 2009, at 18.

As popularized, however, the term refers to civility among senators. Some writers lament the "decline of *senatorial courtesy*" and cite either the defeat of John Tower as President Bush's nominee for secretary of defense, or the treatment of Anita Hill in Clarence Thomas's confirmation for the U.S. Supreme Court. Such uses are loose at best—e.g.: "Sonia Sotomayor, all concede, will be confirmed. . . . [T]he appointee of a popular Democratic president would ascend to the Supreme Court even if no Republicans were seized by *senatorial courtesy* [read, perhaps, *bipartisanship*] or deference to the Latino vote." Patrick McIlheran, *The Week Judicial Liberalism Gave Up*, Milwaukee J. Sentinel, 17 July 2009, News §, at 11.

send. For general purposes, this word is much preferable to *transmit.* See **transmit.**

send back is occasionally used in place of *remand*, the more formal legal term—e.g.: "The conviction was reversed and the case *sent back* for a new trial." *People v. Allen*, 875 N.E.2d 1221, 1231 (Ill. App. Ct. 2007). See **remand (A).** Cf. **return back.**

senior = a Queen's Counsel. See **Q.C.** & **silk.** Cf. **junior.**

senior circuit judge. See **chief judge.**

senior party. See **junior party.**

sensitize; ***sensitivize.** Although H.W. Fowler championed *sensitivize, the first form is now usual in AmE and BrE.

sensory; ***sensatory; sensorial.** *Sensory* = of sensation or the senses. *Sensatory is a NEEDLESS VARIANT. *Sensorial* = primarily responsive to sensations. For a misuse involving *sensory*, see **sensuous** (last par.).

sensuous; sensual. These words derive from the same root, meaning "appeal to the senses," but the precise meanings have undergone DIFFERENTIATION. *Sensuous* = of or relating to the five senses; arousing any of the five senses. The word properly has no risqué connotations, though it is gravely distorted by hack novelists. Here it is correctly used: "Words thus strung together fall on the ear like music. The appeal is *sensuous* rather than intellectual . . . ." W. Somerset Maugham, "Lucidity, Simplicity, Euphony," in *The Summing Up* 321, 322 (1938).

Sensual = relating to gratification of the senses, esp. sexual; salacious; voluptuous <sensual desires>. This is the word intended by the hack novelists who erroneously believe that *sensuous* carries sexy overtones—e.g.:

- "The spray painted drawings of female genitalia at issue here simply are not erotic or *sensual*." *City of St. George v. Turner*, 860 P.2d 929, 934 (Utah 1993).

- "Since the illustrations were selected by the female, feminist editors, this volume was designed to demonstrate that women and feminists may find *sensual* pleasure . . . in sexually explicit imagery." Nadine Strossen, *A Feminist Critique of "the" Feminist Critique of Pornography*, 79 Va. L. Rev. 1099, 1109 (1993).
- "The grounds for the motion were . . . [that] the facts alleged did not offer sufficient indicia of a 'wicked, lustful, unchaste, licentious or *sensual* design' on Mitchell's part." *State v. Mitchell*, 624 So.2d 859, 859 (Fla. Dist. Ct. App. 1993).
- "In order to satisfy her hot-blooded, passionate partner [the stereotype goes], the Latina must also be *sensual* and sexually responsive." Jenny Rivera, *Domestic Violence Against Latinas by Latino Males*, 14 B.C. Third World L.J. 231, 241 (1994).

Still, some writers are oblivious of these associations. They misuse *sensual* for *sensory*—e.g.:

- "It would be stronger still if these witnesses could explain in detail the nature of the *sensual* [read *sensory*] perceptions on which they based their 'conclusion' that the person they had seen was the defendant and that he was responsible for the events they observed." *Spinelli v. U.S.*, 393 U.S. 410, 429 (1969) (Black, J., dissenting).
- "Its true 'converse' would seem to be 'involuntarily,' i.e., an unconscious bodily movement through convulsion, reflex or other *sensual* [read *sensory* or, perhaps, *sensorial*] phenomenon." *Alford v. State*, 866 S.W.2d 619, 625 (Tex. Crim. App. 1993) (en banc) (Clinton, J., concurring).
- "According to [an expert witness], a 'blackout' is a period of time where an individual is receiving *sensual* [read *sensory*] perceptions, or short-term memory, but these . . . do not get processed into the long-term memory." *U.S. v. Zak*, 65 M.J. 786, 791 (Army Crim. App. 2007).

See **sensory.**

sentence. In most jurisdictions, criminal *sentences* (as opposed to *verdicts*) are imposed by judges and not by juries. E.g.: "The Supreme Court of Alabama agrees that 'the jury is not the sentencing authority in . . . Alabama,' and has described the sentencing judge not as a reviewer of the jury's '*sentence*,' but as *the* sentencer." *Baldwin v. Alabama*, 472 U.S. 372, 384 (1985) (per Blackmun, J.) (citations omitted). The term derives ultimately from Roman law. Cf. **verdict.** For the DIFFERENTIATION of *concurrent*, *consecutive*, and *cumulative sentences*, see **concurrent sentences.**

SENTENCE ADVERBS are adverbs conveying the writer's comment on the statement being made rather than adverbs qualifying a single word in the sentence. A sentence adverb does not resolve itself into the form *in a —— manner*, as most adverbs do. In *Happily, the bill did not go beyond the committee*, the introductory adverb *happily* conveys the writer's opinion on the message being imparted. The following words are among the most frequent sentence adverbs ending in *-ly*:

accordingly	importantly	paradoxically
admittedly	interestingly	regrettably
arguably	ironically	sadly
concededly	legally	strangely
consequently	logically	theoretically
curiously	mercifully	
fortunately	oddly	

Improvising sentence adverbs from traditional adverbs like *hopefully* (= in a hopeful manner) and *thankfully* (= in a thankful manner) is objectionable to many stylists but seems to be on the rise. E.g.:

- "*Explanatorily* [read *By way of explanation*], these consolidated causes were positioned as the ordinary and uncomplicated condemnation case." *O'Neil Corp. v. Perry Gas Transmission, Inc.*, 648 S.W.2d 335, 341 (Tex. App.—Amarillo 1983). See **corollarily.*
- "Taxation is the single greatest impingement by which the government makes its presence felt. *Corollarily* [read, perhaps, *At the same time*], entitlement spending is by far the largest share of government spending, and is also the fastest-growing." Judd Gregg & Charles Blahous, *Mobilizing the Marketplace to Renew American Productivity*, 35 Harv. J. on Legis. 63, 65 (1998).

Avoid newfangled sentence adverbs of this kind. In formal prose, even those like *hopefully* and *thankfully* should be avoided: they're increasingly common, but they have a beleaguered history.

Because sentence adverbs reveal the writer's own thoughts and biases, lawyers often overuse them in argumentation—but danger lurks in words such as *clearly*, *undoubtedly*, and *indisputably*. See **clearly, hopefully, thankfully** & OVERSTATEMENT.

SENTENCE ENDINGS. Karl Llewellyn's understanding of rhythm and emphasis led him to say that a "sentence must be so written that the punch word comes at the end." *A Lecture on Appellate Advocacy*, 29 U. Chi. L. Rev. 627, 628 (1962). He knew, as a rhetorical matter, that the end of a sentence is the position of primary emphasis.

Of course, one must first try to achieve a reasonable average SENTENCE LENGTH, or else there is likely to be no regular position of emphasis. Once the average sentence length hovers around 20 or fewer words, the artistry of stressing final words becomes possible.

But legal writers are often tone-deaf and arrhythmic, hence unemphatic—e.g.:

- "The association's attorney did everything she could under the circumstances to protect the association's interests in this matter." [A possible revision: *The association's attorney did everything she could in this matter to protect the association's interests.*]
- "As the Austin court observed, the gravamen of Plaintiffs' complaint is more properly directed to the legislature if they feel there is a deficiency in the statutory manner in which notice of such legislative proceedings is prescribed

to be given." [A possible revision: *As the Austin court observed, if the Plaintiffs believe that there is a deficiency in the statutory notice provision, then their complaint should be directed to the legislature.*]

- "The application of the court's decision strongly dictates that ESCO cannot be properly sued in Nueces County under Texas Civil Practice and Remedies Code, § 15.037 for foreign corporations." [A possible revision: *Under the Texas venue scheme and caselaw interpreting it, suing ESCO in Nueces County is improper.*]

- "My advice to her would be that it is probably not worth the potential hassles involved in creating a two-tiered pricing system until Tex. Rev. Civ. Stat. Ann. art. 5060-1.12 is repealed or there are cases tried more adequately interpreting it." [A possible revision: *I would advise her that, until article 5060-1.12 is repealed or new cases interpret it better, creating a two-tiered pricing system probably isn't worth the potential hassles.*]

- "It is also the desire of Dr. Goodfellow to amicably resolve any questions or concerns that you may presently have with regard to the contract and your performance of obligations thereunder." [A possible revision: *Dr. Goodfellow wants to resolve any remaining questions amicably.*]

In choosing words that can bear emphasis and ending with them, you can usually rule out ending sentences with the following: (1) dates; (2) citations; and (3) prepositional phrases.

SENTENCE LENGTH. Among the more supportable indictments of legal writing in general is that it reads too slowly. It is plodding. It wastes time.

Among the cures is to reduce the average sentence length in a given piece of writing. Whereas long sentences slow the reader down and create a solemn, portentous impression, short sentences speed the reading and the thought. It is therefore "a counsel of perfection never to write a sentence without asking 'Might it not be better shorter?'" F.L. Lucas, *Style* 103 (1962).

Many things converge in legal writing to create overlong sentences. One is OVERPARTICULARIZA-TION—the wretched habit of trying to say too many things at once, with too much detail and too little sense of relevance. Another is the fear of qualifying a proposition in a separate sentence, as if an entire idea and all its qualifications had to be fitted into a single sentence. A third is the ill-founded fear of being simple and, by implication, simpleminded—of perhaps seeming to be insufficiently sophisticated. Yet a fourth is the nonsense-baggage that so many writers lug around on their backs: the idea that it is poor grammar to begin a sentence with *and* or *but*. See **and (A), but (A)** & SUPERSTITIONS (D).

Of course, many lawyers suffer from these turns of mind. And those who do have much hard work ahead if they wish to pursue a readable or even a clear style. It is not just their sentence length that will suffer. Overlong sentences are merely symptomatic of other problems—chiefly clutter and VERBOSITY.

What should the goal be? Experts in readability commonly say that, in technical writing, you want an average sentence length of 20 words or fewer. Some sentences ought to be 40 or 50 words, and some ought

to be 3 or 4. There needs to be variety, but the average should be 20 or below. The writer who achieves this goal will generally achieve greater speed, clarity, and impact than the writer with longer sentences.

True, E.B. White and others have written long sentences that were perfectly readable. But they were typically writing in a different genre—fiction—and they typically had far greater skill in constructing sentences than most legal writers. Exceptions such as White do not disprove the point that legal writers ought to strive for a shorter average.

Is that goal realistic? Many good writers meet it, even when discussing difficult subjects. Consider how Buckland—with an average sentence length of 13 words—here sums up part of John Austin's philosophy:

> Austin's propositions come to this. There is in every community (but he does not really look beyond our community) a person or body [that] can enact what it will and is under no superior in this matter. That person or body he calls the Sovereign. The general rules [that] the Sovereign lays down are the law. This, at first sight, looks like circular reasoning. Law is law since it is made by the Sovereign. The Sovereign is Sovereign because he makes the law. But this is not circular reasoning; it is not reasoning at all. It is definition. Sovereign and law have much the same relation as centre and circumference. Neither term means anything without the other. In general what Austin says is true for us to-day, though some hold that it might be better to substitute "enforced" for "commanded." Austin is diffuse and repetitive and there is here and there, or seems to be, a certain, not very important, confusion of thought. But, with the limitation that it is not universally true, there is not much to quarrel with in Austin's doctrine. [Total words: 184; avg. words per sentence: 13.]
>
> W.W. Buckland, *Some Reflections on Jurisprudence* 48 (1945).

The style is bold, confident, and quick. More legal writers ought to attempt such a style.

Instead, though, legal readers are too often fed lumpy, indigestible portions of words. Following are some examples, followed by possible revisions:

- "Though a clear case of continuing trespass exists for which the only relief at law, if ejectment should be impracticable, would be successive suits for damages, and therefore equity would intervene normally to prevent a multiplicity of suits, nevertheless equitable relief compelling the removal of the encroachment is denied because of the disproportionate loss to the defendant which would result." William F. Walsh, *A Treatise on Equity* 284 (1930). [Total words: 60; avg. words per sentence: 60. A possible revision: *A clear case of continuing trespass exists for which the only relief at law—if ejectment is impracticable—would be successive suits for damages. Normally, therefore, equity would intervene to prevent a multiplicity of suits. Still, equitable relief compelling the removal of the encroachment is denied because it would result in a disproportionate loss to the defendant.* Total words: 57; avg. words per sentence: 19.]

- "Rules of morality are necessarily unstable and nearly always lacking in precision, changing from age to age, since they reflect mankind's emotional reaction to external conditions, and it should not be expected that the legal decisions and writings which have survived from those periods when a transgression of the current code of ethics was a requisite in criminal guilt can yield any precise definitions and distinctions, especially since the more ancient rule of strict accountability had not then, and indeed has not even now, entirely lost its force." J.W. Cecil Turner, *Kenny's Outlines of Criminal Law* 21 (1952). [Total words: 88; avg. words per sentence: 88. A possible revision: *Rules of morality are necessarily unstable and nearly always lacking in precision. They change from age to age because they reflect humans' emotional reaction to external conditions. And we should not expect to yield any precise definitions and distinctions from legal decisions and writings that have survived from those periods when a transgression of the current code of ethics was a requisite in criminal guilt. For the more ancient rule of strict accountability had not then entirely lost its force. Indeed, it has not even lost it now.* Total words: 88; avg. words per sentence: 18.]

- "In modern codifications, beginning with those of Germany and Switzerland, dating from the turn of the century, to those recent codes and drafts of Czechoslovakia, Ethiopia, Hungary, Italy, the Netherlands, Poland or Portugal, not to speak of France itself, that a structure of the law of obligations which appeared in France's Napoleonic Code and, inspired by the latter, in the Civil Code of Louisiana, has been refashioned along lines of considerably different systematic structure and legislative technique." Max Rheinstein, "Problems and Challenges of Contemporary Civil Law of Obligations," in *Essays on the Civil Law of Obligations* 1, 8–9 (Joseph Dainow ed., 1969). [Total words: 77; avg. words per sentence: 77. A possible revision: *In modern codifications, the structure of the law of obligations—as it originally appeared in the Napoleonic Code and then in the Louisiana Civil Code—has been refashioned. In those codes, the law differs in structure and in legislative technique. The codifications began with Germany and Switzerland at the turn of the century. Among the more recent codes and drafts are those of Czechoslovakia, Ethiopia, Hungary, Italy, the Netherlands, Poland, and Portugal—not to speak of France itself.* Total words: 78; avg. words per sentence: 20.]

- "Though one could logically hold that attempting the impossible is non-criminal even though such attempts are in themselves possible—as, indeed, is held by those who argue that to do the impossible cannot, since it is impossible to do the impossible, be a crime, and that it cannot be a crime to attempt what is not a crime—usually those who have held that attempting the impossible is non-criminal have done so because they held that such an attempt is in itself impossible, while those who have held that attempting the impossible can be a crime have done so because they denied that it is impossible to attempt the impossible." Alan R. White, *Misleading Cases* 13 (1991). [Total words: 112; avg. words per sentence: 112. A possible revision: *One could logically hold that attempting the impossible is noncriminal even though such attempts are in themselves possible. Indeed, some do hold this view. They argue that to do the impossible cannot be a crime, since it is impossible to do the impossible. Further, they say that it cannot be a crime to attempt what is not a crime. But others hold that attempting the impossible is noncriminal for a different reason. They believe that such an attempt is in itself impossible. Still a different group—those who hold that attempting the impossible can be a crime—have done*

so because they denied that it is impossible to attempt the impossible. Total words: 111; avg. words per sentence: 16.]

See ANFRACTUOSITY & PLAIN LANGUAGE (D).

separate. In the legal phrase *to separate the jury*, the verb *separate* means "to segregate." The *OED* suggests that this use of the word is "chiefly in Biblical language" and does not mention the legal use. See BIBLICAL AFFECTATION, **segregate** & **several.**

separate and apart; separate and distinct. Both phrases are common REDUNDANCIES—e.g.:

- "Oil and gas are subject to sale *separate and apart from* [read *separate from* or *apart from*] the surface of the earth." Robert Kratovil, *Real Estate Law* 4 (1946).
- "In all countries where constitutional law is a *separate and distinct* [read *separate*] body of jurisprudence its prescriptions take precedence over all statutory enactments in case of a conflict between the two." James W. Garner, "Law, Constitutional," in 17 *Encyclopedia Americana* 96, 101 (1953).

See DOUBLETS, TRIPLETS, AND SYNONYM-STRINGS.

separate but equal = the now-defunct legal doctrine that blacks could be segregated if granted "equal" opportunities and facilities in education, public transportation, and jobs. Deriving from the infamous decision in *Plessy v. Ferguson*, the term was originally phrased in reverse fashion: *equal but separate. See* 163 U.S. 537, 540 (1896). Notably, if the idea is phrased that way, the idea of separateness receives emphasis, whereas *separate but equal* stresses the (supposed) equality. It is quite conceivable that the phrasing *separate but equal* gained easier acceptance in the popular mind of the late 19th and early 20th centuries. (For the rhetorical rationale for this speculation, see SENTENCE ENDINGS.) The famous civil-rights decisions of the 1950s and 1960s—beginning with *Brown v. Board of Education*, 347 U.S. 483 (1954)—ended the de jure segregation that the separate-but-equal doctrine represented.

As in the previous sentence, when the phrase is used adjectivally, it should be hyphenated: "In cases urging admission of Negroes to a white Texas law school, a white Oklahoma graduate course, and the white section of Southern dining-cars, the main plea was that the entire *separate-but-equal* doctrine be discarded." Fred Rodell, *Nine Men* 323 (1955).

***separate out.** See **out** (A).

separate property = property that a married person owns in his or her own right during marriage. In AmE, the precise meaning of this term varies. In so-called common-law states, this term is contrasted with *marital property*; in community-property states, it is contrasted with *community property.* See **community property.**

separate the jury. See **separate.**

---

separation = (1) an arrangement whereby a married couple stops living together while remaining married, either by mutual consent or by a judicial decree (often called *legal separation* or *judicial separation*); or (2) the status of a husband and wife having begun such an arrangement, or the judgment or contract that brings it about. Because the word *separation* may refer to arrangements involving various degrees of legal formality, on its own it is unclear.

separation of powers. The phrase is usually associated with the U.S. Constitution's demarcation of powers in the executive, legislative, and judicial branches of government. But the idea is much older. John Locke wrote about the separation of legislative and executive powers in his *Two Treatises of Government* (1690). The phrase itself is at least a generation older than the Constitution. In his *Spirit of the Laws* (1748; translated into English in 1750), Montesquieu refined the idea that the virtue of the English constitution was a system of checks and balances among executive, legislature, and judiciary—a *separation of powers*.

When used adjectivally, the phrase needs hyphens: "On all the great *separation-of-powers* questions of our time—executive privilege, legislative vetoes, presidential appointment and impoundment power, and so on—the OLC has provided legal and constitutional guidance for the executive." Barbara H. Craig, *Chadha: The Story of an Epic Constitutional Struggle* 52 (1988). See PHRASAL ADJECTIVES.

sepulcher; sepulchre; sepulture. The preferred spelling of the first term is *sepulcher* in AmE, *sepulchre* in BrE. The word means "burial place; tomb," and is pronounced /**sep**-əl-kər/. *Sepulture*, sometimes a NEEDLESS VARIANT of *sepulcher*, justifies its separate form in the sense "burial." These words are very formal, even literary. They should be used cautiously.

sequential; sequacious. *Sequential* means "forming a sequence or consequence." *Sequacious* means "intellectually servile."

sequential order is often a REDUNDANCY. E.g.: "The Supreme Court's recent decision in *Pearson* overruled that part of *Saucier* [mandating] that courts conduct the two-step qualified-immunity inquiry *in sequential order* [delete the italicized phrase]." *Henry v. Purnell*, 619 F.3d 323, 332 n.6 (4th Cir. 2010).

sequester, n., = (1) in legislative parlance, an across-the-board cut in domestic spending; or (2) a person with whom litigants deposit the property being contested until the case has concluded. Sense 1: "Darman ordered an across-the-board cut in domestic spending—called a *sequester*—of $2.3 million." Stuart Auerbach, *Bill Gives Rostenkowski a Way to Settle Accounts*, Wash. Post, 9 Oct. 1991, at F1.

In sense 2, the word is really a NEEDLESS VARIANT of *sequestrator*—e.g.: "[It] concerned a former husband's suit against a receiver and *sequester* [read *sequestrator*] appointed by a state court to consolidate all the

former husband's property available for fulfilling support obligations." *Firestone v. Cleveland Trust Co.*, 654 F.2d 1212, 1216 (6th Cir. 1981). See **sequestrator.**

sequester, vb.; **sequestrate.** Generally, *sequestrate* means nothing that *sequester*, the more common term, does not also mean. Both terms are old: *sequester* dates from the 14th century, *sequestrate* from the early 16th century. In law, *sequester* = to remove (as property) from the possession of the owner temporarily; to seize and hold the effects of a debtor until the claims of creditors are satisfied (*OED*). The lay meaning of the term, of course, is "to set aside, separate," as *to sequester* (or *separate*) the jury. See **separate.**

Sequestrate is given two slightly different senses by the *OED*, in addition to the overlapping senses: (1) "to divert the income of an estate or benefice, temporarily or permanently, from its owner into other hands"; and (2) (in Scots law) "to place . . . lands belonging to a bankrupt, or [those] of disputed ownership, . . . in the hands of a judicial trustee, for the prevention of waste." These two senses are rare, however, and—except in Scotland—it is best to avoid *sequestrate* as a NEEDLESS VARIANT unless a nuance conveyed by one of these specialized senses is intended.

The sole weakness of this advice is that the agent noun is *sequestrator* and not, ordinarily, *sequesterer*. See **sequestrator.**

Often no such nuance was intended, and *sequester* is the better word—e.g.:

- "The practice of *sequestrating* [read *sequestering*] the property of the defendant to coerce his obedience to the decree was soon developed." Henry Lacey McClintock, *Handbook of Equity* 22 (1936).
- "It is difficult to see why a plaintiff in any action for a personal judgment in tort or contract may not . . . apply to the chancellor for a so-called injunction *sequestrating* [read *sequestering*] his opponent's assets pending recovery and satisfaction of a judgment in such a law action." *De Beers Consol. Mines v. U.S.*, 325 U.S. 212, 222–23 (1945) (per Roberts, J.).

***sequesterer.** See **sequestrator.**

sequestration; attachment; garnishment. In the context of civil remedies, these terms are closely related. *Sequestration* = the removal, by judicial authority, of real or personal property from its possessor, usu. to preserve it until a court has determined who has a right to it. *Attachment* = the prejudgment seizure of property and placement of it under the court's control as security to satisfy a judgment that the plaintiff may recover. (*Attachment* may also refer to the arrest of a person: see **attachment.**) *Garnishment* = a judicial proceeding in which a judgment creditor, or a suitor who may become a judgment creditor, serves notice on a third party who may be indebted to, or on a bailee for, the judgment debtor, that any of the debtor's property held by the person served must be turned over to the judgment creditor.

Garnishment differs from the other two terms in two important ways: it refers to a judicial proceeding—not to a seizure or removal—and the property stays in the third party's hands until judgment is pronounced.

sequestrator; *sequesterer. Though not as logically formed as its alternative, *sequestrator* is the standard term meaning "one who sequesters property"—e.g.: "A substantial amount of assets disappeared from the marital home and, as a result, the court appointed a neutral third-party attorney to act as a *sequestrator*." *Dowling v. Chicago Options Assocs.*, 847 N.E.2d 741, 750 (Ill. App. Ct. 2006). Sometimes, however, *sequestrator* means not the person who seizes, but the party at whose instance the sequestration occurs. Cf. **sequester,** n.

Serbonian bog. See LITERARY ALLUSION (A)(4).

sergeant; serjeant. In medieval times this word (ultimately deriving fr. L. *servient* "serving") came to mean someone performing a specific function in the household or jurisdiction of a king, lord, or deliberative assembly and reporting directly to the top authority under which that person served. From the 14th century until 1875, *serjeants-at-law* were appointed as a superior order of advocates. They wore silk gowns and coifs and (until 1846) had an exclusive right of audience in the Court of Common Pleas. See **silk** & **Order of the Coif.**

Of the more than 50 variant spellings of the term over the centuries, the preferred spelling in AmE today is *sergeant*. In BrE, there is some DIFFERENTIATION between the spellings: *sergeant* is largely military (*sergeant-major*) and *serjeant* largely legal (*serjeant of the coif, serjeant-at-law, serjeant-at-arms*).

*Sargeant is a common misspelling stemming perhaps from the military casualism *sarge*.

SERIAL COMMA. See PUNCTUATION (D).

seriatim = in turn; serially; one after another; in sequence; successively. Though common in references to *seriatim opinions*, this LATINISM in other contexts is generally best replaced with either of its anglicized siblings, *serially* and *in series*, or of one of the phrases used just above in defining the term. E.g.:

- "The State . . . may not bring *seriatim* [read *sequential*] prosecutions for the same offense by alleging separate legal theories." *Whittlesey v. State*, 665 A.2d 223, 255 (Md. 1995).
- "None of these supports the result the Court reaches today. I will apply them *seriatim* [read *in turn*]." *Rothgery v. Gillespie County*, 554 U.S. 191, 226 (2009) (Thomas, J., dissenting).
- "The Appellants advance six arguments on appeal, which we consider *seriatim* [read *in turn*]." *U.S. v. Doe*, 564 F.3d 305, 309 (3d Cir. 2009).

Seriatim is sometimes misspelled *seratim. Because the word is usually an adverb, it's a peculiar error to treat it as the object of a preposition to create a REDUNDANCY such as *in seriatim. Sometimes both errors

crop up together—e.g.: "We will dispose of them *ad seratim* [read *seriatim* or, preferably, *in turn*]." 22 *Bucks County* [Pa.] *Law Reporter* 63 (1972).

For brief account of the decline of seriatim opinions in American courts, see *Garner on Language and Writing* 439–47 (2009).

series may be either singular or plural, although the plural is mandatory when more than one series is intended. Here the verb is a plural noun of multitude: "There *have* been a *series* of efforts made by the central P.L.O. but also splinter groups to move through Jordan into the West Bank." See SYNESIS.

Boswell quoted Samuel Johnson as using the now-obsolete plural *serieses in a legal context: "Entails are good, because it is good to preserve in a country, *serieses* of men, to whom the people are accustomed to look up as their leaders." 2 James Boswell, *Life of Johnson* 428 (1791).

Serious Fraud Office. See **SFO.**

serjeant. See **sergeant.**

serjeanty (or *sergeanty*) is the term for a form of feudal tenure under which a specified personal service was rendered to the king.

The spelling *sergeantry is obsolete. See **sergeant.**

servant. A. And *agent.* See **agent.**

B. And *employee.* See **master (A)** & **employer and employee.**

serve (= to make legal delivery of [a process or a writ] in a legally required manner) as a legal term dates back to the 15th century. In the legal idiom, one who serves process may either *serve* a writ *on* or *upon* another, or *serve* another *with* a writ. See OBJECT-SHUFFLING.

service was once only a noun, but since the late 19th century it has been used as a transitive verb as well. It may mean "to provide service for" <the mechanic serviced the copying machine>; "to pay interest on" <to service a debt>; or generally "to perform services for" <servicing corporate clients>. Ordinarily, the verb *to serve* ought to be used in broad senses; *service*, vb., should be used only where the writer believes that *serve* would not be suitable in idiom or sense.

servicemark. See **trademark (B).**

service of process. See **process.**

servient. See **dominant.**

servitude. A. And *easement. Servitude* is primarily a civil-law term, deriving from L. *servitus* (= subjection), and equivalent to the term *easement* in common law. But even in the common law, *servitude* has a restricted currency in referring to a servient tenement (i.e., land subject to an easement), and meaning "a charge on an estate for the use of another estate belonging to another owner." The DIFFERENTIATION usually observed in common-law countries is that *easement* refers to the personal enjoyment of the burdened property, and *servitude* either to the burden or to the burdened property itself. See **easement.**

International lawyers use *servitude* in an extended sense: "an international agreement giving a territory some permanent status, such as a demilitarized or neutralized status, or creating rights over bodies of water."

B. And *slavery*. "The word *servitude* is of larger meaning than *slavery*, as the latter is popularly understood in this country, and the obvious purpose [of the Thirteenth Amendment] was to forbid all shades and conditions of African slavery." *The Slaughter-House Cases*, 83 U.S. (16 Wall.) 36, 69 (1872). Both terms, in addition to denoting "the condition of being a slave or serf, or of being the property of another person," carry the notion of subjection to excessive labor.

session = (1) the time during which a court or other body meets <court is in session>; or (2) a term of court—that is, a period that constitutes *termtime* <the October session of the Supreme Court>.

By historical extension, *session* came to signify certain courts, the most famous and longest lasting being the Court of Session, the supreme civil court of Scotland, established in 1532 and still in session today. See **cession** & **termtime.**

sessional; *sessionary*. The second is a NEEDLESS VARIANT of the adjective corresponding to the noun *session*.

session laws = the statutes enacted by a legislative body and published in a form identifying them with the term in which the legislative session took place <Session Laws of 1994>. E.g.: "We can scarcely credit, as we know state legislation today, what the *session laws* of an older time disclose." Roscoe Pound, *The Formative Era of American Law* 53 (1938).

set aside. A. In Legal Jargon. This phrase, meaning "to vacate," is sometimes misunderstood by nonlawyers. One lay writer on legal language misinterpreted the phrase as possibly meaning "to lay to the side temporarily, as for review" (as "to take under advisement"). *See* Terri LeClercq, *Jargon 2: Just When You Thought It Was Safe . . . .*, 48 Tex. B.J. 852, 852 (1985) ("So if you are describing the action of a court, you might qualify how the court *set aside* the ruling by adding, for example, that the court *set aside* the ruling for review.").

Such are the linguistic traps that lawyers have needlessly laid for those unfamiliar with legal JARGON, in which this quite ordinary English phrase is given the extraordinary meaning "to annul, to make void." *Migdol v. U.S.*, 298 F.2d 513, 516 (9th Cir. 1961). E.g.: "[*Nullity*] can be used, and most commonly is, to describe a marriage that exists until either party obtains a decree of the court *setting* it *aside*, e.g. on the ground of impotence." Patrick Devlin, *The Enforcement of Morals* 67 (1968). See **overrule.**

B. *Set aside* and *vacate*. See DOUBLETS, TRIPLETS, AND SYNONYM-STRINGS.

setback. To a nonlawyer, of course, this term means "an unexpected interruption of progress." To real-estate lawyers, however, it refers to the amount of space required between a lot line and the building line to ensure that enough light and ventilation reach the ground. In land law, ironically, increased setbacks represent human progress.

setoff, n., = (1) a counterdemand, generally of a liquidated debt growing out of an independent transaction for which a lawsuit might be maintained; or (2) the general right of a debtor to reduce the amount of a debt by any sum that the creditor owes the debtor. It is older than the term *offset* and is considered more correct by purists—e.g.: "Any respondent found liable will be entitled to an equitable *set-off* [read *setoff*] against the settlements appellant has already received." *Chester v. South Carolina Dep't of Pub. Safety*, 698 S.E.2d 559, 560 (S.C. 2010). The *OCL1* includes *set-off*, which is usual in BrE, but not *offset*. See **offset.**

As a verb, the term is written as two words—e.g.: "On the other hand, a *subsequent* agreement between the parties to *set-off* [read *set off*] a claim of the buyer in satisfaction of part of the purchase price may satisfy the statute." Ernest W. Chance, *Principles of Mercantile Law* 236 (Percy W. French ed., 13th ed. 1950).

set over, vb., = to transfer, convey. E.g.: "Ms. Hayden agreed to assign, transfer, and *set over* to Western all her right, title and interest in and to the annuity contract." *Western United Life Assurance Co. v. Hayden*, 64 F.3d 833, 838 (3d Cir. 1995).

SET PHRASES. Fossilized language should not be consciously defossilized—which is to say that one should not try to vary what has been set in stone. So *set in stone* should never become *set in shale*, or whatever other variation one might lamely invent. Nor, to cite another example, should one change *madding crowd* to **maddening crowd*.

Set phrases are sometimes changed out of a sense of cleverness, sometimes out of ignorance. The lawyer who writes, "Time is the essence of this subcontract," simply betrays an ignorance of the idiom *Time is of the essence (of this subcontract)*.

Many expressions are so well entrenched in the English language that the slightest change will make them un-English. For example, we have the phrase *out from under*, ruined by a metamorphosis in this sentence: "[Plaintiff] was injured when the back of the teller stool on which she was sitting fell off and the chair rolled *out from underneath her* [read *out from under her*]." *Syrie v. Knoll Int'l*, 748 F.2d 304, 305 (5th Cir. 1984).

Wilson Follett called set phrases "inviolable" (if not quite inviolate): "the attempt to liven up old clichés by inserting modifiers into the set phrase is a mistake: the distended phrase is neither original, nor unobtrusive, nor brief, and sometimes it has ceased to be immediately clear, as in *They have been reticent to a tactical fault.*" *Modern American Usage* 303 (1966).

In addition to the fault of inserting modifiers into set phrases, three other faults commonly occur. First, it is wrong to wrench a set phrase into ungrammatical contexts, as here: "This was reported to *we the people.*" The phrase *we the people*, of course, derives from the U.S. Constitution; but the sentence calls for the objective *us*.

Second, it is bad style to substitute an alien word for the familiar one in a well-known phrase. For example, changing *in large part* or *in large measure* to *in large degree* simply does not work: "The prejudice to appellant is attributable *in large degree* [read *in large part*] to appellant's own conduct."

Third, it is poor to aim at novelty by reversing the usual order of a phrase: "The cost to individual patients in terms of lost autonomy and control could lower their perceived quality of life and thus their *well-being and health.*" Mark Weitz et al., *In Whose Interest?*, 31 J.L. Med. & Ethics 292, 298 (2003). (The standard phrase is *health and well-being*.) Cf. INELEGANT VARIATION.

settle. Ordinarily, litigants who compromise in order to end the litigation are said to *settle* the lawsuit. By extension in AmE, a judge who pressures the parties to compromise is likewise said to *settle* the lawsuit—e.g.: "Frustrated by a huge backlog of asbestos liability cases, a federal judge and a New York state judge have combined forces to try to *settle* hundreds of the lawsuits." Wade Lambert & Jill Abramson, *Judges Join Forces on Asbestos Litigation*, Wall St. J., 31 Jan. 1990, at B2.

settled. See **well-settled.**

settlement. See **compromise** & **accord and satisfaction.** For the phrase *property settlement*, see **estate planning.**

settlement sheet. See **closing statement.**

settler; settlor. The two forms usually convey different senses. *Settler* = (1) one who settles; or (2) a homesteader. *Settlor* = the creator of a trust; a party to an instrument. *Settlor* has also been used—confusingly—in reference to one who settles a case: "A number of factors should be considered when determining whether a settlement is made in good faith, including (1) 'a rough approximation of plaintiffs' total recovery and the *settlor's* [read *settler's*] proportionate liability' . . . , and (4) 'a recognition that the *settlor* [read *settler*] should pay less in settlement than [it] would if [it] were found liable after a trial.'" *In re Methyl Tertiary Butyl Ether Prods. Liab. Litig.*, 578 F.Supp.2d 519, 525 (S.D.N.Y. 2008).

settlor; trustor; donor; creator. These four terms are used to name the person who establishes a trust. The first is the most common. It should be spelled with the *-or* suffix to differentiate it from the quite different word *settler*. Of these four forms, *trustor* is the least usual and most awkward, although *trustee* is the common name for the holder of the property in trust. See **creator** & **donor.** Cf. **settler.**

set up = to raise (as a defense). Both civil and criminal defendants are traditionally said to *set up* defenses—e.g.:

- "The dishonest contractor [could not] *set up* his original dishonest intent as an excuse for non-performance." Thomas E. Holland, *The Elements of Jurisprudence* 262 (13th ed. 1924).
- "Suppose that D breaks and enters a house, and on a charge of burglary *sets up* the defence of insanity." Glanville Williams, *Criminal Law* 523 (2d ed. 1961).
- "The promisee can *set up* such a promise as a defence to an action but cannot himself sue upon it." P.S. Atiyah, *An Introduction to the Law of Contract* 126 (3d ed. 1981).

severability clause = a contractual or statutory provision—usu. boilerplate—preventing the complete loss of the contract or statute if a court were to hold a single provision invalid. Typically, a *severability clause* states, "If any part of this agreement is for any reason found to be unenforceable, all other parts nevertheless remain enforceable." A variant name for this provision is *saving clause*. See **saving clause (B).**

several for *separate*, an archaic remnant of Middle English, has survived only in legal language. The usage survives primarily in the phrase *joint and several liability*, but thrives in other contexts as well—e.g.:

- "A tenancy in common is property held by two or more persons by *several* and distinct titles." *Windell v. Miller*, 687 N.E.2d 585, 587–88 (Ind. Ct. App. 1997).
- "These mental-health professionals *severally* opined that Murphy suffered from various psychological dysfunctions at the time of the offenses." *U.S. v. Harris*, 61 M.J. 391, 396–97 (Armed Forces Ct. App. 2005).
- "We note that Doe 3 *several* times mentions the copyright doctrine of 'fair use.'" *Arista Records, LLC v. Doe 3*, 604 F.3d 110, 123 (2d Cir. 2010).

See **each (A), common** & **joint and several.**

severally. See **each (A).**

severalty = the condition of being separate or distinct. The legal phrase *in severalty* is used in law in reference to land, and means "held by an individual absolutely, not jointly or in common with another"—e.g.:

- "The whole transaction required the cooperation of all for its success; the division of the shares among them was as much a part of it as any other; they selected each other as owners *in severalty*; and they should be held liable for any defaults of those whom they chose, although their liability is secondary." *Marcus v. Otis*, 168 F.2d 649, 659 (2d Cir. 1948).

- "Suppose that Twose had thought that the common was land belonging to her *in severalty*." Glanville Williams, *Criminal Law* 309 (2d ed. 1961).

severance pay. This AmE phrase, dating from 1940–1945, denotes money (apart from backpay and wages) paid to an employee who is dismissed, often for reasons outside the employer's control. E.g.: "In a more complex form, a termination clause might combine several of these possibilities, and it might add such considerations as acts of third parties, or further conditions, or some kind of '*severance pay*.'" David Crump, *The Five Elements of a Contract*, 43 Tex. B.J. 370, 371 (1980). The BrE equivalent is *redundancy pay*.

sewer; sewerage; sewage. The first two terms denote a wastewater system, although *sewerage* more broadly includes the processing plant and other facilities. *Sewage* is the feculent matter carried in the system.

sex, adj.; **sexual.** Both *sex discrimination* and *sexual discrimination* appear in law reports. *Sex* is perhaps better, since *sexual* has come to refer more to sexual intercourse and things pertaining to it than to questions of maleness or femaleness. See **gender.**

Sexism. Many who at first shrugged off feminists' claims that the English language can be detrimentally sexist have come to acknowledge that many of the contentions are undeniably valid. And with that acknowledgment come certain responsibilities—and difficulties—for the writer concerned with maintaining credibility.

How does one deal with linguistic forms that have traditionally been sexist? The best course today is to eliminate sexist language while not resorting to ugly or awkward linguistic artifices. The purpose, of course, is to avoid distracting any variety of readers, from traditional grammarians to feminists.

A. The Pronoun Problem. English has a number of common-sex general words, such as *person, anyone, everyone,* and *no one,* but it has no common-sex singular personal pronouns. Instead, we have *he, she,* and *it,* the first denoting a male; the second denoting a female; and the third denoting a nonhuman object or being (though occasionally a baby). In general literary and legal usage, the traditional approach has been to use the masculine pronouns *he* and *him* to cover all persons, male and female alike. That this practice has come under increasing attack has caused the single most difficult problem in the realm of sexist language. Other snarls are far more readily solvable.

The inadequacy of the English language in this respect becomes apparent when one reads, for example, the words from an appellate brief excerpted in an opinion addressing medical malpractice in the performance of a hysterectomy: "The objective of the doctrine [of informed consent], the plaintiff asserts, 'is to insure the patient's right to self-determination by requiring that *he* have access to all [the] knowledge necessary for him to give an intelligent and informed consent.'" *Bly v. Rhoads*, 222 S.E.2d 783, 785 (Va. 1976).

Actually, the generic masculine pronoun also sits uneasily in a sentence containing a female to which it is meant to refer—e.g.:

- "When a person, whether male or female, dies without leaving a will, *he* is called an 'intestate.'" Thomas E. Atkinson, *Handbook of the Law of Wills* 4 (2d ed. 1953).
- "That is not to say that the accessory will necessarily be punished as severely as the principal. Yet sometimes *he* may be the guiltier, as Lady Macbeth was. The master mind and guiding spirit of a crime ring will probably receive a heavier sentence than *his* tools." Glanville Williams, *Criminal Law* 404 (2d ed. 1961).
- "Anyone, including a married woman, who has attained the age of twenty-one, has sufficient sense to know what *he* is doing, and is not under the influence of terror or fraud, can make a valid will." Edward Jenks, *The Book of English Law* 299 (P.B. Fairest ed., 6th ed. 1967).
- "If a testator fails to provide by will for *his* surviving spouse [a *she*?] who married the testator after the execution of the will, the omitted spouse shall receive the same share of the estate *he* [i.e., the spouse] would have received if the decedent left no will . . . ." Unif. Probate Code § 2-301(a) (1969).

Even when the context does not make the masculine pronoun somewhat ludicrous, one may feel bludgeoned by its use at every turn—e.g.: "In the acquisition of background information a judge should be left to *his* own devices. If *he* is left to *himself* to find *his* own sources of background information where *he* thinks *he* needs it and if in the acquisition of it *he* behaves in a discreet way, *he* will not be criticized." Patrick Devlin, *The Judge* 52 (1979).

"There are," H.W. Fowler notes, with contributions from Gowers,

> three makeshifts: first, *as anybody can see for himself or herself*; second, *as anybody can see for themselves*; and third, *as anybody can see for himself*. No one who can help it chooses the first; it is correct, and is sometimes necessary, but it is so clumsy as to be ridiculous except when explicitness is urgent, and it usually sounds like a bit of pedantic humour. The second is the popular solution; it sets the literary man's teeth on edge, and he exerts himself to give the same meaning in some entirely different way if he is not prepared to risk the third, which is here recommended. It involves the convention (statutory in the interpretation of documents) that where the matter of sex is not conspicuous or important the masculine form shall be allowed to represent a person instead of a man, or say a man (*homo*) instead of a man (*vir*).
>
> *MEU2* 404 (1965).

At least two other makeshifts are now available. The first is commonly used by American academics: *as anybody can see for herself.* Such phrases are often alternated with those containing masculine pronouns, or, in some writing, appear uniformly. Whether this phraseology will cease to sound strange to most readers only time will tell. This is one possibility, however, of (1) maintaining a grammatical construction; and (2) avoiding the awkwardness of alternatives such as *himself or herself.*

But the method carries two risks. First, unintended connotations may invade the writing. A recent novel was published in two versions, one using generic masculine pronouns and the other using generic feminine pronouns; the effects on readers of the two versions were reported to have been startlingly different in ways far too complex for discussion here. Second, this makeshift is likely to do a disservice to women in the long run, for it would likely be adopted only by a small minority of writers: the rest would continue with the generic masculine pronoun.

A second new makeshift has entered Canadian legislation: *as anybody can see for themself; if a judge decides to recuse themself.* The word **themself* fills the need for a gender-neutral reflexive pronoun, but many readers and writers—especially Americans—bristle at the sight or the sound of it. So for the legal writer, this makeshift carries a considerable risk of distracting readers. See **themself.*

Typographical gimmickry may once have served a political purpose, but it should be avoided as an answer to the problem. It is trendy, ugly, distracting, and usually unpronounceable. E.g.:

- "A district judge who, on reflection, concludes that *s/he* erred may rectify that error when ruling on post-trial motions." *U.S. v. Miller,* 753 F.2d 19, 23 (3d Cir. 1985).
- "*S/he* is required to hold an appropriate qualification specified in the Companies Act and *s/he* must be appointed to hold office." S.B. Marsh & J.B. Bailey, *Terminology of Business and Company Law* 9 (1987).

Variants are **he/she* and **she/he,* and even the gloriously misbegotten double entendre, **s/he/it.* If we must have alternatives, *he or she* is the furthest we should go. See **he or she.**

For the persuasive writer—for whom credibility is all—the writer's point of view does not matter as much as the reader's. So if one is writing for an unknown or a broad readership, the only course that does not risk damaging one's credibility is to write around the problem. For this purpose, every writer ought to have available a repertoire of methods to avoid the generic masculine pronoun. No single method is sufficient. In a given context, one might consider doing any of the following:

- *Delete the pronoun reference altogether.* E.g.: "A judge who was not regarded as impartial could not get disputes submitted *to him* [delete *to him*] for resolution: one party would always refuse." William M. Landes & Richard A. Posner, *Adjudication as a Private Good,* 8 J. Legal Stud. 235, 237 (1979).
- *Repeat the noun instead of using a pronoun, especially when the two are separated by several words.* E.g.: "The easy but timid way out for a trial judge is to leave all cases tried to a jury for jury determination, but in so doing *he* [read *the judge*] fails *his* [read *in the*] duty to take a case from the jury when the evidence would not warrant a verdict by it." *Wilkerson v. McCarthy,* 336 U.S. 53, 65 (1949) (Frankfurter, J., concurring).

- *Change the pronoun to an article, such as* a *or* the. E.g.: "[A] judgment creditor may enforce *his* [read *the*] judgment as if no levy or sale had been made." David Gray Carlson, *Critique of Money Judgment Part One,* 82 St. John's L. Rev. 1291, 1348 (2008).
- *Pluralize, so that* he *becomes* they. E.g.: "A judge [read *Judges*] should not have to worry about whether *his* [read *their*] rulings will offend powerful political figures." Todd Davidson Peterson, *Oh, Behave!,* Legal Affairs 16 (Dec. 2005).
- *Use the relative pronoun* who, *especially when the generic* he *follows an* if. E.g.: "If a prisoner disagrees with the prison's response to his request, *he* may 'resubmit the concern' and it will then be treated as a grievance." *Phipps v. Sheriff of Cook County,* 681 F.Supp.2d 899, 907 (N.D. Ill. 2009). [Read *A prisoner who disagrees with the prison's response may resubmit the concern, and it will then be treated as a grievance.*]

For a sensible discussion of the generic masculine pronoun, see Beverly Ray Burlingame, *Reaction and Distraction: The Pronoun Problem in Legal Persuasion,* 1 Scribes J. Legal Writing 87 (1990). For a fascinating study, see Leslie M. Rose, *The Supreme Court and Gender-Neutral Language,* 17 Duke J. Gender L. & Pol'y 81 (2010).

Though the masculine singular personal pronoun may survive awhile longer as a generic term, it will probably be displaced ultimately by *they,* which is coming to be used alternatively as singular or plural. (See CONCORD (B).) This usage is becoming commonplace—e.g.:

- "*Anyone* who has subscribed to the Literary Review for more than one year may join, as long as *they* are proposed by a writer known to the committee." K. Saunders, *Literati, Glitterati, Choose Your Party,* Sunday Times, 10 Sept. 1989, at F1.
- "It is assumed that, if *someone* is put under enough pressure, *they* will tell the truth, or the truth will emerge despite the teller." Robin T. Lakoff, *Talking Power: The Politics of Language in Our Lives* 90 (1990).
- "How the Elizabethans reacted is, alas, unknown, since *nobody* thought Shakespeare's plays important enough to bother recording *their* impressions." John Carey, *Stages of Hatred,* Sunday Times (Books), 4 Oct. 1992, § 6, at 8.
- "*Anyone* planning a dissertation on Hollywood's fling with yuppie demonology will want to include 'The Temp' in *their* calculations." Janet Maslin, *A Perfect Secretary, Temporarily,* N.Y. Times, 13 Feb. 1993, at 8.

Speakers of AmE resist this development more than speakers of BrE, in which the indeterminate *they* is already more or less standard. That it sets many literate Americans' teeth on edge is an unfortunate setback to what promises to be the ultimate solution to the problem. For a similar etymological progression, see **none.**

B. Words Ending in *-man.* "For the lawyer more than for most men, it is true that he who knows but cannot express what he knows might as well be ignorant." That sentence opens chapter 1 of Henry Weihofen's *Legal Writing Style* (2d ed. 1980)—a sentence that, ironically, is flanked by warnings against sexist

---

An asterisk (✽) precedes words and phrases that are invariably inferior forms.

language (pp. vii, 19–20). If Weihofen were writing today, no doubt he would express himself in neutral language.

Throughout the English-speaking world, writers' awareness of sexism seems to have been heightened most markedly during the 1980s. In September 1984, the Commonwealth Attorney-General's Department in Canberra, Australia, issued a press release entitled "Moves to Modify Language Sex Bias in Legislation." The release states that "the Government accepts that drafting in 'masculine' language may contribute to some extent to the perpetuation of a society in which men and women see women as lesser beings." The press release recommends, "where possible and appropriate, avoidance of the use of words ending in *man*, such as *chairman, serviceman, seaman,* and so on." *See* Note, *The De-Masculinisation of Language in Federal Legislation,* 58 Aus. L.J. 685, 685–86 (1984).

Three years later, the U.S. Supreme Court announced its adoption of changes in the Federal Rules of Civil Procedure to weed out gender-specific references: Rule 4(b) was changed so that *him* and *his* became *the defendant* and *the defendant's. See* 55 U.S.L.W. 1137, 4265–90 (10 Mar. 1987).

The process is at work elsewhere. The *Longshoremen's* and Harbor Workers' Compensation Act, 33 U.S.C. § 901 (1927), was amended by the *Longshore* and Harbor Workers' Compensation Act (1984).

Similarly, American courts have begun to write opinions in more neutral language, sometimes obtrusively neutral—e.g.:

- "Edison argues that the district court should have construed the 'doubtful' language of the escalation clause against the appellee, as the *draftsperson* [read *drafter*]." *RCI Northeast Servs. Div. v. Boston Edison Co.,* 822 F.2d 199, 203 n.3 (1st Cir. 1987).
- "Plaintiff . . . is engaged in the business of franchising independent *businesspersons* [read *businesspeople*] to operate Baskin-Robbins stores throughout the United States." *Dunkin' Donuts Franchised Rests. LLC v. KEV Enters., Inc.,* 634 F.Supp.2d 1324, 1329 (M.D. Fla. 2009).

Some of the extremes to which the trend has been taken seem absurd—e.g.: "This case presents another example of the waste of time, energy, legal and judicial *personpower* and consequent waste of money occasioned by the existence of the Family Court as a separate court of limited jurisdiction." *In re Anthony T.,* 389 N.Y.S.2d 86, 87 (Fam. Ct. 1976).

As a nonsexist alternative, the suffix *-person* leaves much to be desired. For every **anchorperson, *chairperson, *draftsperson, *ombudsperson,* and **tribesperson,* there is a superior substitute: *anchor, chair, drafter, ombuds,* and *tribe member.* Words ending in *-person* are at once wooden and pompous.

The traditional language of the law, of course, abounds in *-man* words: *remainderman, venireman, warehouseman, materialman, foreman, landman, bondsman,* and **juryman.* The last of these is virtually obsolete alongside *juror;* it was in common use, however, through the mid-20th century. Courts have experimented with replacements for *foreman*—e.g.:

"We are unable to conclude that the state trial judge erred in deciding that the *foreperson's* statement that the jury was unable to agree was more than an expression of present inability to agree." *Fay v. McCotter,* 765 F.2d 475, 478 (5th Cir. 1985). Because the *-person* words are so ugly and ineffective, a better nonsexist expression is *presiding juror.*

Venireman is gradually undergoing transmutation, or, more accurately, emasculation—e.g.:

- "During the voir dire, the *venirepersons* [read *veniremembers*] were asked, as a group, a roster of seventeen questions." *Wright v. State,* 983 A.2d 519, 521 (Md. 2009).
- "Once the trial judge refused to allow appellant to define murder for these *venirepersons* [read *veniremembers*], . . . appellant was left without the means to make informed decisions about challenges for cause or the exercise of his peremptory challenges." *State v. Bixby,* 698 S.E.2d 572, 590 (S.C. 2010).

Justice Rehnquist used both *venireman* and *veniremember* in a single opinion. *See Wainwright v. Witt,* 469 U.S. 412, 418–19 (1985). (See INELEGANT VARIATION.) In that opinion, one use of *venireman* was specifically in reference to a woman, a Mrs. Colby. (*See id.*) Justice Rehnquist was right, however, to avoid the *-person* form. *Veniremember* is the better option.

Remainderman, warehouseman, and *longshoreman* are less easily neutralized. Legal writers have experimented with *remainderperson, remainderer, -or,* and *remainor.* None is quite satisfactory. The *-er* suffix does show promise, though: *warehouser* is listed in *W3;* it would certainly take some getting used to, like all linguistic changes. Yet *longshorer* and *remainderer* are more difficult to pronounce distinctly with the *-er.* Perhaps we can satisfy ourselves, however, that, in having reached these words in our analysis of sexist terminology, we have traveled to the furthest reaches of the language.

For other entries bearing on this issue, see **castle doctrine, chairman, drafter, foreman, mechanic's lien, reasonable person** & **venireman.**

C. Feminine Forms in -*ess* and -*trix*. Legal prose is perhaps the last bastion of these feminine forms. We have **prosecutrix, *testatrix, *tutrix, *relatrix, *conciliatrix, *concilatress, *heritrix, *heritress, *inheritrix, *inheritress,* and even such rarely seen oddities as **dictatrix, *dictatress, *victrix, *victress, *aviatress,* and **aviatrix.* Most of these moribund terms ought to be sped along to their graves.

For most legal writers, it is far less bothersome to read of a *woman testator* than it is to read of a *lady booksalesman.* The Latinate agent nouns in *-or* are almost universally perceived as being common-sex terms. We have never, for example, thought it odd that women may be termed *litigators;* we have gotten along fine without **litigatrix.* With the loss of terms in *-ess* and *-trix* we lose a nuance in the language, but the nuance is not worth preserving: the sex of a testator does not matter. See ***lawyeress.**

D. Equivalences. Among the subtler problems of nonsexist usage is to refer to men and women in equivalent terms: not *man and wife*, but *husband and wife*; not *chairmen* and *chairs* (the latter being female), but *chairs* (for all); not *men* and *girls* (a word that diminishes the status of an adult female), but *men* and *women*.

Even *Mr.*, on the one hand, as contrasted with *Miss* or *Mrs.*, on the other, causes problems on this score. Differentiating between one woman and another on the basis of her marital status is invidious, really, if we do not make the same distinction for men. The idea that it matters as an item of personal information whether a woman is married—but that it doesn't matter whether a man is married—is surely an outmoded one. Though many people once considered *Ms.* an abomination, it is today accepted as the standard way of addressing a married or unmarried woman. Unless the writer knows that a woman prefers to use *Mrs.*, the surest course today is to use *Ms.*

E. Statute of Limitations. Those committed to nonsexist usage ought to adopt a statute of limitations that goes something like this: in quoted matter dating from before 1980, passages containing bland sexism—such as the use of the generic *he* or of *chairman*—can be quoted in good conscience because in those days the notions of gender-inclusiveness were entirely different from today's notions. Although it is quite fair to discuss cultural changes over time, it is unfair to criticize our predecessors for not conforming to present-day standards. How could they have done so? Therefore, using "[*sic*]" at every turn to point out old sexist phrases is at best an otiose exercise, at worst a historically irresponsible example of mean-spiritedness. For a choice example of this, see James R. Nafziger, *A Sicness unto Death*, 1 Scribes J. Legal Writing 149 (1990).

sexting. See **texting.**

sexual. See **sex.**

sexual assault. See **rape (c).**

SFO, in England, refers to the Serious Fraud Office—e.g.: "Set up by the Criminal Justice Act of 1987, the *SFO* already has two major investment cases apart from Guinness in the courts . . . plus 63 other cases at different stages." *The Fraud Buster with 66 Cases on His Hands*, Sunday Telegraph, 11 Feb. 1990, at 28.

shadow jury (AmE) = a group of mock jurors who are culled from jury lists and paid to sit through a trial and report to a jury consultant hired by one of the litigants. The *shadow jury*, which is matched as closely as possible to the jury, regularly reports on their reactions to what is taking place in the courtroom and thereby provide counsel with information about the jurors' likely perceptions.

shadow of a doubt, beyond the. This phrase is a CLICHÉ to be avoided. E.g.: "The process by which the Pledge was amended . . . demonstrates *beyond any shadow of a doubt* that the purpose driving the amendment was predominantly, and indeed overwhelmingly, religious in nature." *Newdow v. Rio Linda Union Sch. Dist.*, 597 F.3d 1007, 1057 (9th Cir. 2010).

shady lawyer. See LAWYERS, DEROGATORY NAMES FOR (A).

shall. See WORDS OF AUTHORITY (A).

shall and will. See DOUBLETS, TRIPLETS, AND SYNONYM-STRINGS.

shall mean. See DEFINITIONS (C).

shall not. See WORDS OF AUTHORITY (A), (B).

sham, adj. (= pretended; counterfeit), is frequently used in legal writing in phrases such as *sham corporation*, *sham marriage*, and *sham wedding*. E.g.:

- "It is alleged that a 'bride' would enter into a *sham marriage* with one of the 'aliens' in order to enable the alien, a native of Portugal, to apply for and obtain a non-quota immigrant visa to which he would not otherwise be entitled." *U.S. v. Rodriguez*, 182 F.Supp. 479, 482 (S.D. Cal. 1960).
- "In that case 193 persons who had been individually induced, by means of a fraudulent prospectus, to invest their money in a *sham corporation* were permitted to join in one action for fraud against the promoters." Charles Alan Wright, *The Law of Federal Courts* 503 (5th ed. 1994).
- "Appellants asserted that Pro Net was a *sham corporation* organized to allow Amway to gain greater control over the BSM market." *Nitro Distrib., Inc. v. Alticor, Inc.*, 565 F.3d 417, 422 (8th Cir. 2009).

For more on this word and its near-synonyms, see **imposture.**

sham plea. See **false plea.**

shanghai, vb. (= [1] to drug or otherwise make insensible and then abduct for service on a ship needing crew members; or [2] to influence by fraud or compulsion), makes *shanghaied* and *shanghaiing*. See VOWEL CLUSTERS.

shareholder; shareowner; stockholder. All three terms refer to one who owns shares in a corporation.

shareholder derivative suit. See **derivative action.**

shareowner. See **shareholder.**

shares. See **stock.**

shark. See LAWYERS, DEROGATORY NAMES FOR (A).

shark repellent (= a device by which a company, in either its bylaws or its articles of incorporation, makes it more difficult for an outsider to mount a corporate takeover) is one of several colorful METAPHORS that emerged in corporate law during the 1970s and 1980s. E.g.:

- "Intent on capturing its prey, G-P increased its offer to $63 per share on November 19. . . . An avalanche of intense activity, in and out of court, descended during the next few months. Truncating the tale, it suffices to say that matters did not go well for GNN's directors and their *shark repellents*." *Weinberger v. Great N. Nekoosa Corp.*, 925 F.2d 518, 521 (1st Cir. 1991).
- "Corporate management has developed a bewildering array of defensive devices to fend off unwelcome tender offers. Recognized defensive tactics include *shark-repellent* amendments, lock-up options with a white knight, greenmail, poison pills, golden parachutes for management, and, if all else fails, a management buyout." Carol Goforth, *Proxy Reform as a Means of Increasing Shareholder Participation in Corporate Governance*, 43 Am. U. L. Rev. 379, 423–24 (Winter 1994).
- "No Delaware case has yet cogently distinguished the self-disablement effected by bond indentures, no shop clauses, employment agreements, fair-price *shark repellents*, nonredeemable standard pills, and their ilk from the self-disablement effected by no shops or no hand pills." Daniel C. Davis, Omnicare v. NCS Healthcare: *A Critical Appraisal*, 4 Berkeley Bus. L.J. 177, 199 (Spring 2007).

sharp practice. This phrase originally, in the early 19th century, referred merely to hard bargaining in business. But by the mid-19th century, it came to be associated with lawyers as well as businesspeople, and it took on more strongly negative connotations. Since then, *sharp practice* has referred to unethical practices and trickery—e.g.:

- "What raised the court's ire was the plaintiff's '*sharp practice*' in moving to strike." Monroe Freedman, In the Matter of Manners, Legal Times, 11 Mar. 1991, at 23, 25.
- "Michael Joseph, author of *Lawyers Can Seriously Damage Your Health*, which first exposed *sharp practice* by solicitors five years ago, said only an independent complaints system can salvage solicitors' reputations." John Rowland, *Lawyers Bar Door to Outside Policing*, Sunday Times, 24 Mar. 1991, Features §.
- "The quest for prestige has served as a justification for bad behavior by law schools. . . . [This] suggests to every graduate that *sharp practice* is acceptable so long as one doesn't get caught. One could not imagine worse training for a lawyer." Richard A. Matasar, *Defining Our Responsibilities*, 17 J. Contemp. Legal Issues 67, 114 (2008).
- "His communications with GEICO were misleading and constituted unacceptably *sharp practice*." Douglas R. Richmond, *Lawyers' Professional Responsibilities and Liabilities in Negotiations*, 22 Geo. J. Legal Ethics 249, 273 (2009).

Shays's Rebellion (1786–1787) is so spelled—preferably not **Shays' Rebellion*. See POSSESSIVES (A).

*s/he. See SEXISM (A) & **he or she.**

shear. See **sheer.**

sheaves is the plural both of *sheaf* (= a bundle) and of *sheave* (= a pulley). *Sheaves* is also, as a verb, the

third-person singular of the verb *to sheave* (= to bind into a sheaf).

sheer; shear. *Sheer* describes flimsy material <a sheer veil>, a steep cliff <a sheer dropoff>, or intensity <the sheer gall of that man>. To *shear* is to cut, as fleece from a sheep.

Shelley's Case, the Rule in. See **Rule in Shelley's Case** & CAPITALIZATION (C).

shepardize is a mid-20th-century -IZE NEOLOGISM derived from *Shepard's Citators*. Originally, the word was capitalized as a tradename—e.g.: "If you have before you a recent case in a nisi prius court or in an intermediate court of appeal, do not rest content with *Shepardizing* it." Paxton Blair, *Appellate Briefs and Advocacy*, 18 Fordham L. Rev. 30, 40 (1949). But today, the word is increasingly written without the initial capital, as the tradename threatens to lose its uniqueness and become generic—e.g.:

- "Apparently failing to properly *shepardize* that case, neither plaintiff's nor defendant's counsel *cited to* [read *cited*] this Court a Florida case . . . that specifically rejects *Toussaint*." *Caster v. Hennessey*, 727 F.2d 1075, 1077 (11th Cir. 1984). See **cite (B).**
- "Keen legal minds at the Dickinson School of Law, having time to spare since computers freed them from the drudgery of *shepardizing*, found application of the chess clock first to the teaching, thence to the practice of law." Robert E. Rains, *Of Clocks and Things*, 39 J. Legal Educ. 259, 259 (1989).
- "To be sure, had Lutheran's permanent counsel . . . *shepardized* section 2000e-9, he would have unearthed 29 C.F.R. § 1601.16(b)(1)." *EEOC v. Lutheran Soc. Servs.*, 186 F.3d 959, 964 (D.C. Cir. 1999).
- "Mr. Erausquin claims 2.2 hours to perform 'Legal research re: boilerplate objections, *shepardize* cases from Schneider' — Plaintiffs' counsel do not explain what this entry means, nor its relevance to the case[.]" *Yu Zhang v. GC Servs., LP*, 537 F.Supp.2d 805, 815 (E.D. Va. 2008).

The process of shepardizing cases—once extremely tedious—has been greatly simplified by computer-assisted research. Now, instead of laboriously checking several volumes, one merely punches a button. But the process retains the old name. Some writers seem to have forgotten the origin of the verb— e.g.: "*Shepardize* our cases on *Keycite*." *Blair v. Ing*, 31 P.3d 184, 191 (Haw. 2001) (quoting from an attorney's time sheet). See **Keycite.**

In G.B., the equivalent volumes are termed *Current Law Citations*, or *noter-ups*, and one *notes up* one's cases. See **note up.**

sheriff. In England, a sheriff is the Crown's chief executive officer in a shire or county, responsible (now nominally in most areas) for keeping the peace, overseeing elections, and administering justice generally. In the U.S., the sheriff, an officer elected within each county, has similar responsibilities, but they are real, not nominal. An American sheriff has substantial police powers. In Scotland, the *sheriff principal* and the *sheriffs* are the judges of the main local courts.

sheriffalty; shrievalty. Both terms date from the early 16th century and refer to a sheriff: to the jurisdiction, to the term of office, to the responsibilities in office, or to all three. In English antiquity, the sheriff represented the royal authority in a district (i.e., a shire) and presided at the shire-moot, the judicial assembly of the shire. Today the position of high sheriff of a county (i.e., of a shire, a term no longer used officially, though it continues to have historical and literary meaning) is an honorary one, largely nominal and ceremonial.

W3 and the *OED* suggest that *shrievalty* is the more widely used term and that *sheriffalty* is a NEEDLESS VARIANT, even though *shrieve* is an obsolete variant of *sheriff*. Actually, both are extremely rare, with one citation apiece in federal decisions in the U.S.—and they are both 19th-century citations. If such a noun is needed today, *sheriffalty*—the form used in the Constitution of West Virginia (art. 9, § 3)—is surely more widely comprehensible.

sheriffdom; sheriffwick. See **bailiwick.**

sheriff principal. See **sheriff.**

shew, an obsolete spelling of *show*, occurred in AmE and BrE writing—legal and nonlegal—up to the early 19th century.

shield law = (1) a state law governing a journalist's right to refuse to testify about sources of information or information not used in the journalist's reporting, such as notes and outtakes; or (2) a statute that restricts or prohibits the use, in rape or sexual-assault cases, of evidence about the victim's past sexual conduct (*Black's Law Dictionary* 1502 (9th ed. 2009)). Sense 1 is older—e.g.:

- "The term '*shield law*' is commonly and widely applied to statutes granting newsmen and other media representatives the privilege of declining to reveal confidential sources of information." *In re Farber*, 394 A.2d 330, 335 n.2 (N.J. 1978).
- "When the Enquirer was served with grand jury subpoenas it asserted its *Shield Law* [read *shield-law*] privilege and established a screening process designed to withhold materials identifying confidential sources." *Ventura v. Cincinnati Enquirer*, 396 F.3d 784, 789 (6th Cir. 2005).

In sense 2, the term is often *rape shield law*—e.g.:

- "The [appellate] court specifically held that evidence that Matthews and Russell were living together at the time of trial was not barred by the State's *rape shield law*." *Olden v. Kentucky*, 488 U.S. 227, 230 (1988) (per curiam).
- "His Sixth Amendment confrontation right was indisputably contravened, however, by the state circuit court's application of a per se rule restricting cross-examination of the prosecution's expert under the state *rape shield law*." *Barbe v. McBride*, 521 F.3d 443, 445 (4th Cir. 2008).

shifting use. See **springing use.**

shingle, to hang out (or set up) one's. This AmE casualism, meaning "to begin to practice a profession such as law or medicine, esp. on one's own," originated in the 1840s and has always been closely associated with law. The METAPHOR is not, of course, to be taken literally.

ship-money (= [in English legal history] a tax on ports and localities for providing ships for the king's service) is so hyphenated.

shipowner. One word.

ship's lawyer. See LAWYERS, DEROGATORY NAMES FOR (A).

shire. See **sheriffalty.**

shire court is sometimes hyphenated *shire-court*, but most legal historians write it as two words. E.g.: "The old *shire court* had nothing in common with the modern county court established by an Act of 1846." H.G. Hanbury, *English Courts of Law* 29 (2d ed. 1953).

shock the conscience. This phrase, a CLICHÉ, expresses judicial disapproval of some type of outrageous conduct or outcome. It originated in equity courts in the early 19th century; an 1825 decision by the Ohio Supreme Court quotes Lord Eldon as using the phrase in a legal standard: "In the case of *Coles v. Trecothick*, 9 Ves. 246 [1804], Lord Eldon declared, that unless the inadequacy of price was such as to *shock the conscience*, . . . it was not itself a sufficient ground for refusing a specific performance." *Wills v. Cowper*, 2 Ohio 124, 148 (1825).

Over the years, the phrase has appeared in various ways, not just as a verb phrase. Justice Benjamin Cardozo used it as a noun phrase (*a shock to conscience*): "Still more common are the cases where the evil is less obvious, where there is room for difference of opinion, where some of the judges believe that the existing rules are right, at all events where there is no such *shock to conscience* that precedents will be abandoned." *A Ministry of Justice*, 35 Harv. L. Rev. 113, 119 (1921). The phrase now sometimes appears attributively, as a PHRASAL ADJECTIVE: "A study of the cases indicates that the courts in thus parroting the rule had no occasion to insert the *shock-the-conscience* clause in the particular cases under consideration." *Golden v. Tomiyasu*, 387 P.2d 989, 993 (Nev. 1963).

The MALAPROPISM **shock the conscious* is shockingly common—e.g.:

- "Courts are told to disturb the jury's verdict only when it is 'manifestly unjust,' '*shocks the conscious*' [read '*shocks the conscience*'], or 'clearly demonstrates bias.'" Earl R. Waddell III & Tracy L. Abell, *A New Evidentiary Standard for Criminal Appellate Review*, 3 Tex. Wes. L. Rev. 235, 245–46 (1997).

- "After argument on Johns Hopkins's motion, Judge Schwait stated, 'I find this verdict excessive. I find it grossly excessive. It *shocks my conscious* [read *shocks my conscience*].'" *Mahler v. Johns Hopkins Hosp., Inc.*, 907 A.2d 276, 281 (Md. Ct. App. 2006).
- "*County of Sacramento* recognized that the requisite state of mind for action by an executive official to satisfy the '*shocks the conscious*' [read *shocks-the-conscience*] test will vary according to the circumstances." *Pabon v. Wright*, 459 F.3d 241, 251 (2d Cir. 2006).
- "This concession may have been precipitous with regard to the '*shocks the conscious*' [read *shocks-the-conscience*] element of the test. When a state actor is in a high-pressure situation in which rapid decision-making is required, such as a high-speed car chase, the required mens rea will typically be intent-to-harm." *Ye v. U.S.*, 484 F.3d 634, 639 n.2 (3d Cir. 2007).

*shoe-in. See **shoo-in.**

shoo-in (= a candidate or competitor who is sure to win), a colloquialism, is so spelled—not **shoe-in.*

shopping. See **forum-shopping** & **judge-shopping.**

shotgun. See **blunderbuss.**

shotgun instruction. See **dynamite charge.**

should. Oddly, *should*, like *may*, is sometimes used to create mandatory standards, as in the ABA Code of Judicial Conduct. In that code, in which "the canons . . . establish mandatory standards unless otherwise indicated," six of the seven canons begin, "A Judge *should* . . . ." See **may, ought (B)** & words of authority (A).

*should/could is the type of monstrosity that would-be profound writers, or terminally wishy-washy ones, are fond of. E.g.: "*Should/could* states impose additional requirements that must be met in order to obtain a hearing?" Typographical gimmickry of this sort ought to be avoided; surely the perpetrator does not actually believe he or she conveys otherwise overlooked nuances. See ***and/or (A).**

show > showed > shown. *Showed* is less good than *shown* as the past participle.

show [+ **(to be) (as)**]. The infinitive *to be* is generally preferable to *as* after this verb when the sense is "prove to be"—e.g.: "It is incumbent upon the district court to weigh that claim in light of the facts at hand and in light of any alternatives that may be *shown as* [read *shown to be*] feasible and more promising in their effectiveness." But when the sense is "enter as," "declare as," or the like, *as* is the right choice—e.g.: "Should the real property or other property be under litigation it is still to be *shown as* an asset." Frank Bennett, *Bennett on Bankruptcy* 848 (9th ed. 2006).

show cause (= to give a legally satisfactory reason) is common legal jargon—e.g.:

- "The magistrate judge ordered Allen to *show cause* why his petition should not be dismissed for failure to exhaust state remedies." *Allen v. Zavaras*, 568 F.3d 1197, 1198 (10th Cir. 2009).
- "At the time of the November 8 teleconference, plaintiff's counsel was subject to an order to *show cause* why he should not be sanctioned *pursuant to* [read *under*] Rule 11 in another case before the District Court." *Gollomp v. Spitzer*, 568 F.3d 355, 361 (2d Cir. 2009). For more on the suggested edit, see ***pursuant to.**
- "On Friday, December 14, 1990, then-Secretary of Defense Dick Cheney directed the Secretary of the Navy to *show cause* by January 4, 1991, why the A-12 program should not be terminated." *McDonnell Douglas Corp. v. U.S.*, 567 F.3d 1340, 1344 (Fed. Cir. 2009).

This verb phrase has recently given rise to a corresponding phrasal adjective. The phrase should be hyphenated but not capitalized—e.g.:

- "The magistrate's *show cause order* [read *show-cause order*] informed Allen he could proceed on his exhausted claims." *Allen v. Zavaras*, 568 F.3d 1197, 1199 (10th Cir. 2009).
- "The specificity and detail of the *Show Cause Order* [read *show-cause order*], as clarified by the prehearing brief, provided Volkman with notice with the nature of the DEA's case." *Volkman v. United States DEA*, 567 F.3d 215, 221 (6th Cir. 2009).

Cf. **good cause shown.**

showed. See **show.**

shown. See **show.**

show trial = a trial, usu. in a nondemocratic country, that is staged primarily for propagandistic purposes, with the outcome predetermined. E.g.:

- "In a case described by critics as a '*show trial*,' five democracy campaigners were convicted on Friday, Mr. Maude's last day in Peking, for using loudhailers." Andrew Higgins, *China Gives Maude a Stinging Send-Off*, The Independent, 30 July 1990, at 9.
- "The Stalin period [was] a time of purges, *show trials*, fabricated plots, executions and mass exile." Geneive Abdo, *Spoon Tells Tale of Suffering in Stalinist Camp*, L.A. Times, 5 Aug. 1990, at A3.
- "We must realize that this sort of 'legal' murder was a favorite Nazi trick. *Adolphe Légalité*, as he was at times sarcastically called, was starting out his thousand-years reign by tasting the joys of a *show-trial*." Hans Bernd Gisevius, *To the Bitter End: An Insider's Account of the Plot to Kill Hitler* 27 (1998).
- "In West Siberia, there was a regional *show trial* of 'wreckers' accused of trying to murder the local leader Eikhe—and of trying to assassinate Molotov during his earlier trip there." Simon Sebag Montefiore, *Stalin: The Court of the Red Tsar* 202 (2008).

shrank. See **shrink.**

shrievalty. See **sheriffalty.**

shrink > shrank > shrunk. Some writers mistakenly use *shrunk* as the past-tense form.

shudder; shutter. These words sound the same, but they are otherwise very different. To *shudder* is to tremble or quiver. A *shutter* is the device, such as a screen for a window, that limits the passage of light.

Most literate people know this distinction, but some writers forget.

shun and avoid. See DOUBLETS, TRIPLETS, AND SYNONYM-STRINGS.

shutter. See **shudder.**

shyster = a rascally lawyer; one that is shrewdly dishonest. The word has long been an enigma to English-language etymologists, who have posited a dozen possible derivations. In his 124-page monograph entitled *Origin of the Term "Shyster"* (1982), Gerald L. Cohen conclusively solves the enigma by citing previously overlooked material in a New York City newspaper (1843–1844).

Shyster arose as part of the editor's crusade against legal and political corruption in the city. The correct etymology is that which derives from the vulgar German word *Scheisse* (= excrement); hence *Scheisser* became *shyster*.

Among the mistaken hypotheses are that the word comes from the proper name *Scheuster*, supposedly the name of a corrupt practitioner; from the Gaelic *siostair* (= barrator); from an allusion to Shylock, Shakespeare's villain in *The Merchant of Venice* (ca. 1596); and variously from words in Yiddish, Dutch, and Anglo-Saxon.

Shyster referred originally to an unscrupulous lawyer, and it still carries that association for many— e.g.: "Appellants have other arguments, but displaying them would do little more than illustrate why some members of the public believe that '*shyster*' and 'lawyer' are synonyms. This is a frivolous, doomed, and sanctionable appeal." *Kale v. Obuchowski*, 985 F.2d 360, 363 (7th Cir. 1993) (per Easterbrook, J.).

But its meaning has now widened to include unscrupulous persons in other professions as well. E.g.: "He told the group of cutters that the union officials were a bunch of *shysters*." *N.L.R.B. v. Lettie Lee, Inc.*, 140 F.2d 243, 245 (9th Cir. 1944). So although the phrase *shyster lawyer* would have seemed redundant in the late 19th century, it did not by the mid-20th century: "The *shyster lawyer* assigned by the court wanted to squeeze all the money he could out of the boy's family." Ephraim Tutt, *Yankee Lawyer* 106 (1943). See **pettifogger** & LAWYERS, DEROGATORY NAMES FOR (A).

S.I., in British legal writing, is an abbreviation for *Statutory Instruments*, formerly known as *Statutory Rules and Orders* (or *S.R. & O.*).

sibling (= brother or sister) is sometimes mistakenly thought to mean "child"—e.g.: "I went to see Tate. He opened the door himself, his youngest *sibling* [read *child*] clutching with sticky hands at the legs of his corduroy trousers." Angus Ross, *The Leeds Fiasco* 109 (1975).

sic. **A. Generally.** *Sic* (= thus; so), invariably put in brackets, is used to indicate that a preceding word

or phrase in a quoted passage is reproduced as it appeared in the original document. *Sic* at its best is intended to aid the reader (or a typesetter following copy), who may be confused by whether it was the quoter or the quoted writer who is responsible for the spelling or grammatical anomaly.

This interpolation has been much on the rise: In Westlaw's Allstates-Old database, which includes all state-court opinions from the 19th century up to 1944, the word appeared 1,239 times; from 1945 to 2010, the word appeared 218,110 times. A similarly spectacular rise can be seen in recent federal opinions (from 616 in Allfeds-Old to 150,701 in Allfeds). This increase may result from a number of factors, but one major factor is the benighted use of *sic*, discussed just below.

B. Benighted Uses. Some writers use *sic* meanly— with a false sense of superiority. Its use may frequently reveal more about the quoter than about the author of the quoted material. For example, a recent book review of an English legal text contained a *sic* in its first sentence after the verb *analyse*, which appeared thus on the book's dustjacket. In AmE, of course, the preferred spelling is *analyze*; in BrE, however, the spelling *analyse* is not uncommon and certainly does not deserve a *sic*. In fact, all the quoter (or overzealous editor) demonstrated was ignorance of British usage: "The dust jacket tells us: 'In this book, the author brings to bear empirical evidence and legal theory in a critical comparison of English and American discovery, and *analyses* [sic] and evaluates the differences between the two systems.'" *See* Book Review, 61 Tex. L. Rev. 929, 929 (1983). The same publication also *sic*'d Plucknett's spelling of *skilful* (BrE)—see Thomas Lund, *The Modern Mind of the Medieval Lawyer*, 64 Tex. L. Rev. 1267, 1270 n.14 (1986).

Another irksome use occurs when writers insert *sic* in others' citations, as if to belittle the person quoted for ignorance of correct citation form. For example, a federal appeals court judge had the audacity to *sic* the Supreme Court's citation of one of its own cases: "We strike the balance in favor of institutional security, which we have noted is 'central to all other corrections goals,' *Pell v. Procunier*, 417 U.S., [sic] at 823, 94 S.Ct., [sic] at 2804." *Thorne v. Jones*, 765 F.2d 1270, 1275 (5th Cir. 1985). The better course would be to leave the citations as they are without comment or to give one's own "correct" version in brackets without comment.

C. Ironic Uses. In the following example, the author inserted *sic* after his own word choice, as if to say, "I really do think this is the right word": "In 1951, it was the blessing bestowed on Judge Harold Medina's *prosecution* [sic] of the eleven so-called 'top native Communists,' which blessing meant giving the Smith Act the judicial nod of constitutionality." Fred Rodell, *Nine Men* 302 (1955).

sic transit. A fairly common Latin maxim from Classical literature is *Sic transit gloria mundi*: "So passes away the glory of the world." Some legal writers have adapted the first words of the phrase to denote the lamentable passing of a convention or doctrine—e.g.:

- "Barely a month ago this Court emphatically reaffirmed the exhaustion doctrine. . . . But today . . . *Rose v. Lundy* is not applied. *Sic transit gloria Lundy!* In scarcely a month, the bloom is off the *Rose.*" *Engle v. Isaac*, 456 U.S. 107, 141 (1982) (Brennan, J., dissenting).
- "The goal of the panel majority . . . seems to come as close as possible to making First Amendment free speech an absolute when it comes to indecency or profanity. If this goal is attained, *sic transit* commerce-power and police-power protection of morality." Thomas C. Marks Jr., *The Decline of American Culture*, 37 Stetson L. Rev. 769, 796 (2008).

sic utere. The *sic utere* doctrine embodies the Latin maxim *sic utere tuo, ut alienum non lædas*, which means "use your own property in such a manner as not to injure that of another"—e.g.: "All of these cases are consonant with the *sic utere* principle limiting the rights of proprietors or custodians of things in the use of their land." *Perkins v. F.I.E. Corp.*, 762 F.2d 1250, 1256 (5th Cir. 1985). Justice Holmes called this Latin maxim an "empty general proposition" that leads to "hollow deductions." Oliver Wendell Holmes, "Privilege, Malice, and Intent," in *Collected Legal Papers* 120 (1920). See MAXIMS.

sidebar. A. Sense. Originally, *sidebar* referred to a small fencelike partition, either in the Outer Parliament House in Edinburgh or in Westminster Hall. Each morning in term, attorneys argued motions to the judges *ex parte* from within the sidebar. Today, most American lawyers think of the *sidebar*, in its literal sense, as the side of the judge's bench, where counsel can confer with the judge beyond the jury's earshot. See **at bar** & **bar.**

B. *Sidebar conference.* The phrase *sidebar conference* now usually refers to a discussion among the judge and counsel—usually over an evidentiary objection—outside the jury's hearing. At times, however—especially during voir dire—it has been used in reference to a discussion between the judge and a juror or veniremember. See **bar.**

C. *Sidebar* as an Ellipsis. The word *sidebar* is often used in AmE as a shortening of *sidebar conference.* E.g.: "Appellate specialist John Pollok stuck strictly to arguing questions of procedure and admissibility during *sidebars.*" Gregg Krupa, *Teamwork, Sidebars Tipped Gotti Case*, Manhattan Law., Mar. 1990, at 1.

D. As a Popularized Legal Technicality. By the mid-20th century, journalists had come to use *sidebar* to refer to a short, secondary article within or accompanying a main story in a publication. Also, we speak of *sidebar remarks* or *sidebar comments*, which are comments incidental to the main point. These extended senses almost certainly derived from the connotation that *sidebar* has long carried in legal contexts—i.e., that the discussion is peripheral to the main issues. See POPULARIZED LEGAL TECHNICALITIES.

Siete Partidas. See *Las Partidas.*

sight unseen. From a strictly logical point of view, the phrase makes little sense. In practice, however, it has an accepted and useful meaning: an item is bought *sight unseen* when it has not been inspected before the purchase.

sign; signage. *Signage* (= signs collectively or a system of signs used to identify, warn, or direct) is sometimes used where *sign* or *signs* suffices, or some other word is meant. E.g.:

- "At the time, City Sports displayed no *signage* [read *signs* or *notices*] that identified any of its merchandise as counterfeit." *Diallo v. State*, 928 N.E.2d 250, 251 (Ind. Ct. App. 2010).
- "In station evaluations of North Main Texaco, Texaco noted concerns such as employees not being appropriately dressed, lack of approved landscaping, lack of proper *signage* [read *signs*], unavailability of 'pay at the pump,' and substandard maintenance of the facilities." *Richitelli v. Motiva Enters., LLC*, 697 S.E.2d 667, 669 (S.C. Ct. App. 2010). On the use of *employees* instead of the possessive *employees'* before the gerund *being*, see FUSED PARTICIPLES.

Cf. **assent (A).**

signatary, adj. See **signatory,** adj.

signatary, n.; **signatory;** *****signator.** Fowler and Krapp both recommended in the 1920s that *signatary* be adopted as the preferred noun. See H.W. Fowler, *MEU1* 534; George P. Krapp, *A Comprehensive Guide to Good English* 540 (1927). Today, however, *signatary* is virtually never used; the *COD* and *W11* contain *signatory* only. E.g.:

- "The Court has no jurisdiction to rectify the articles, even if it is proved that they were not in accordance with the intention of the original *signatories.*" J. Charlesworth, *The Principles of Company Law* 25 (4th ed. 1945).
- "If the *signatory* is restating the testimonial statements of the true analysts—whoever they might be—then those analysts, too, must testify in person." *Melendez-Diaz v. Mass.*, 129 S.Ct. 2527, 2546 (2009) (Kennedy, J., dissenting).
- "The implication seems clear that both *signatories* to the Treaty envisioned that members of the Navajo Nation committing crimes would lose certain rights under the treaty." *U.S. v. Fox*, 573 F.3d 1050, 1055 (10th Cir. 2009).

Signatory may be an adjective as well as a noun (Krapp considered it the only adjectival form), often a POSTPOSITIVE ADJECTIVE. When it does follow the noun, *signatory* stays unchanged and the noun takes the plural form—e.g.: "The states of Colorado, Kansas, and Nebraska and the United States are *party signatory* [read *parties signatory*] to the Republican River Compact of 1943." *Garey v. Nebraska Dep't of Natural Res.*, 759 N.W.2d 919, 922 (Neb. 2009). See POSTPOSITIVE ADJECTIVES.

*****Signator*, modeled on Latinate agent nouns, is a NEEDLESS VARIANT of *signatory*, n. E.g.: "AFL-CIO-affiliated unions in good standing are *signators* [read *signatories*] to a standing no-raiding policy." R. Emmett Murray, *The Lexicon of Labor* 147 (2010).

signatory, adj.; **signatural.** *Signatory* = forming one of those (persons or governments) whose signatures are attached to a document (*OED*) <the convention gives the signatory states rights to search one another's fishing vessels>. (See **signatary**.) *Signatural* = of or pertaining to signatures.

signature. See **countersignature.**

signed, sealed, and delivered. This phrase traditionally appears in the attestation clause of a deed, a contract under seal, or a specialty contract. (See **deed** & **specialty**.) The only requirements of such a contract are that it be intended as such and that it be signed, sealed, and delivered. But two of three past participles in the triplet *signed, sealed, and delivered* are now FIC-TIONS. Today, the seal is largely symbolic—a sticky wafer simply being attached to the document instead of a genuine seal. (See **seal (A)**.) Likewise, "delivery" is not literally necessary, as long as the parties clearly intended the deed to be operative. E.g.: "*Specialty Contracts . . .* must be executed with certain formalities. There must be a document, in print or in writing, and it must be *signed, sealed and delivered.*" 1 Ernest W. Chance, *Principles of Mercantile Law* 10 (Percy W. French ed., 13th ed. 1950). See **seal (A), (B)**, POPULAR-IZED LEGAL TECHNICALITIES & DOUBLETS, TRIPLETS, AND SYNONYM-STRINGS.

significance; signification. These should be distinguished. *Significance* = (1) a subtly or indirectly conveyed meaning; suggestiveness; the quality of implying; or (2) the quality of being important or significant.

  Signification = (1) the act of signifying, as by symbols; or (2) the sense intended to be conveyed by a word or other symbol. Writers occasionally misuse *significance* for *signification* (sense 2)—e.g.: "There may be social observances existing before it or without it, but they are not law in any proper *significance* [read *signification* or, better, *sense*] of that term." Carleton K. Allen, *Law in the Making* 2 (7th ed. 1964).

silk; silk gown. These terms are metonymic for "King's or Queen's Counsel." In England, a Queen's Counsel wears a silk gown; hence to obtain, receive, or take *silk* means to become a Queen's Counsel, and *silk* and *silk gown* have come to denote a person who has achieved this rank. E.g.:

- "Yet when North J. was first appointed to the Bench on November 1, 1881, he was assigned to the Queen's Bench Division, although his practice both as a junior and as a *silk* had lain on the Chancery side." R.E. Megarry, *Miscellany-at-Law* 10 (1955).
- "Among the members of the Bar, there is a comparatively small group of senior [barristers], enjoying certain privileges and subject to certain disabilities, known as Queen's Counsel, or (from the fact that they wear silk instead of 'stuff' gowns in court) *silks.*" Edward Jenks, *The Book of English Law* 67 (P.B. Fairest ed., 6th ed. 1967).

See **dispatent** & **take silk.**

silk-stocking lawyer. See LAWYERS, DEROGATORY NAMES FOR (A).

similar and like. See DOUBLETS, TRIPLETS, AND SYNONYM-STRINGS.

SIMILES, very simply, are comparisons constructed with *like* or *as*. They differ from METAPHORS because, with similes, the comparisons are explicit (e.g., "trying this case is like wrestling a grizzly bear"), not implicit (e.g., "this case is a real bear").

  E.B. White's insight is characteristically telling: "The simile is a common device and a useful one, but similes coming in rapid fire, one right on top of another, are more distracting than illuminating. The reader needs time to catch his breath; he can't be expected to compare everything else, and no relief in sight." William Strunk Jr. & E.B. White, *The Elements of Style* 80 (3d ed. 1979). That similes are useful is not to be doubted—e.g.:

- "To waste time and argument in proving that, without [the authority to make necessary and proper laws,] Congress might carry its powers into execution, would be not much less idle than to hold a lighted taper to the sun." *M'Culloch v. Maryland*, 17 U.S. (4 Wheat.) 316, 419 (1819) (per Marshall, C.J.).
- "Like a coral reef, the common law thus becomes a structure of fossils." Robert H. Jackson, *The Struggle for Judicial Supremacy* 295 (1941).
- "The position of a judge has been likened to that of an oyster—anchored in one place, unable to take the initiative, unable to go out after things, restricted to working on and digesting what the fortuitous eddies and currents of litigation may wash his way." Calvert Magruder, *Mr. Justice Brandeis*, 55 Harv. L. Rev. 193, 194 (1941).
- "Just as, perforce, the musical composer delegates some subordinate creative activity to musical performers, so, perforce, the legislature delegates some subordinate (judicial) legislation—i.e., creative activity—to the courts." Jerome Frank, *Courts on Trial* 308 (1949).
- "The [European Community] Treaty is like an incoming tide. It flows into the estuaries and up the rivers. It cannot be held back." *Bulmer Ltd v. Bollinger S.A.*, [1974] 2 All E.R. 1226 (C.A.) (per Lord Denning).
- "As a moth is drawn to the light, so is a litigant drawn to the United States." *Smith Kline & French Labs. v. Bloch*, [1982] 1 W.L.R. 730, 733 (C.A.) (per Lord Denning).
- "The common law came down through the centuries with some of its past sticking to it, like a skin it never quite succeeded in molting." Lawrence M. Friedman, *A History of American Law* 24 (2d ed. 1985).

But as White noted, the enthusiastic users of similes can easily fall into OVERSTATEMENT, and sometimes into foolish-sounding PURPLE PROSE—e.g.:

- "[It] would be like exonerating the Nazis because they were influenced by Hitler's propaganda during World War II." Michele Munn, Note, *The Effects of Free Speech*, 21 Am. J. Crim. L. 433, 478 (1994).
- "Such a strategy would be like the rabbis putting the yetzer hara in a barrel." Adam Candeub, *An Economic Theory of Criminal Excuse*, 50 B.C. L. Rev. 87, 111 (2009).

- "It would be like a Shakespeare scholar rewriting lines of Hamlet instead of quoting the original." David Mongillo, *The Girl Talk Dilemma*, 9 U. Pitt. J. Tech. L. Pol'y 3, 28 (2009).

simony. See **barratry.**

simple. In a phrase such as *fee simple*, the word *simple* denotes that the estate is inheritable by the owner's heirs with no conditions concerning *tail*; in the phrase *simple contract*, the word *simple* means that the contract was not made under seal. See **tail** & **simple contract.**

simple contract = a contract not under seal, whether express or implied, and whether oral or in writing. Oddly enough, the term *parol contract* is synonymous, even when the contract is in writing. Williston preferred the term *informal contract*, believing that the phrase *simple contract* could mislead. See **informal contract.**

simple larceny. See **larceny (B).**

simple negligence. See **negligence (A).**

simplex dictum. See **dictum (B).**

simpliciter (= simply; summarily; taken alone; unconditionally; absolutely) can usually be said more simpliciter—e.g.:

- "I concur heartily in the court's judgment that a grand-jury subpoena *simpliciter* [read *simply* or, depending on the sense, *taken alone*] does not satisfy the more rigorous requirements." *Doe v. DiGenova*, 779 F.2d 74, 92 (D.C. Cir. 1985) (Starr, J., concurring).
- "Both the Georgia statute and the Georgia prosecutor thus completely fail to provide the Court with any support for the conclusion that homosexual sodomy, *simpliciter* [read *by itself*], is considered unacceptable conduct in that State." *Bowers v. Hardwick*, 478 U.S. 186, 220 (1986) (Stevens, J., dissenting).
- "If we think that discrimination *simpliciter is* [read *is absolutely*] wrong, then even reverse discrimination is wrong." Simon Lee, *Law and Morals* 74 (1986).
- "Our view is quite different *than* [read *from*] the Third Circuit's, both as to the allocation of burdens and as to the role given negligence *simpliciter* [read *alone*]." *Espinoza v. Sabol*, 558 F.3d 83, 89 (1st Cir. 2009). For more on the first suggested edit, see **different from.**

The LATINISM adds only obscurity. See FORBIDDEN WORDS (A).

simplistic is a pejorative adjective meaning "over-simple; facile"—e.g.:

- "Petitioners next suggest that an employer in fact must be in violation of the disparate-impact provision before it can use compliance as a defense in a disparate-treatment suit. Again, this is overly *simplistic* and too restrictive of Title VII's purpose." *Ricci v. DeStefano*, 129 S.Ct. 2658, 2674 (2009) (per Thomas, J.). Delete *overly*. And see **overly.**
- "Although specified liability losses must obviously 'arise under' federal law rather than merely be 'related to' it, we believe that formulation is, by itself, too *simplistic* to be determinative here." *In re Harvard Indus.*, 568 F.3d 444, 457 (3d Cir. 2009).

- "The court adopts a *simplistic* universal rule . . . . The effect of this decision on innovation in complex fields of science and technology is unknown to the court, for we have had no advice on the consequences of this change of law." *Abbott Labs. v. Sandoz, Inc.*, 566 F.3d 1282, 1300–01 (Fed. Cir. 2009) (Newman, J., dissenting).

simulacrum. See **imposture.**

simultaneous death. In cases of intestacy, this phrase denotes the death of two or more persons in the same mishap in circumstances making it impossible to determine who was the first to die or the last to survive. It describes a presumption, not necessarily a reality. See *commorientes.*

In the phrase *simultaneous-death statute*, the hyphen is necessary because *simultaneous-death* functions as a PHRASAL ADJECTIVE.

since. See **as (A)** & SUPERSTITIONS (G).

*****since . . . then** mangles the syntax of a causal construction—e.g.: "*Since* plaintiff has not [shown] and cannot show that defendants' slander lawsuit . . . was 'objectively baseless,' *then* plaintiff cannot prevail on his claim against them." *Bryant v. Mississippi Military Dept.*, 569 F.Supp.2d 680, 683 (S.D. Miss. 2008). The problem is remedied by omitting *then*. Some *since . . . then* sentences could be clarified still further by changing *since* to *because*.

sine damno (= without damage) is an unnecessary LATINISM usually found in the phrase *injuria sine damno*—e.g.:

- "The result is, the legal paradox: *Injuria sine damno*. The plaintiff is wronged, but not harmed; it may sue, but may not recover." *Pacific R.R. v. International Coal Mining Co.*, 230 U.S. 184, 247 (1913) (Pitney, J., dissenting).
- "Courts came to recognize that trespassory interferences could be legitimately restrained even when the damage was not necessarily significant physically or monetarily, a possible allusion to normative damages (captured by the injury–damage distinction, or the rule of *injuria sine damno*—'legal injury without actual damage')." Shyamkrishna Balganesh, *Demystifying the Right to Exclude*, 31 Harv. J.L. & Pub. Pol'y 593, 644 (2008).

See *damnum.*

sine die (= without a day being fixed) is used to indicate that no date has been set for resumption. The phrase is OFFICIALESE for "indefinitely." E.g.: "The court adjourned *sine die*." *Appointment of Iredell*, 2 U.S. (2 Dall.) 400, 400 (1790) (term notation). *Sine die* is used exclusively in reference to adjournment taken with no date set for resumption of the proceedings or meeting. See **go hence without day** & **day in court.**

A linguist complains that the phrase is "horribly mispronounced to the point where the first part sounds like the trigonometric function and the second like a synonym for 'perish.'" Mario Pei, *Words in Sheep's Clothing* 83 (1969). But /sɪ-ni dɪ-ee/ has long been established as the usual English-language pronunciation.

sine qua non /**sɪ**-nee kwah **non**/ (L. "without which not") = an indispensable condition or thing. This LATINISM is common in both lay and legal writing and should remain unmolested by plain-English reform—e.g.:

- "Ambiguity of constitutional language and uncertainty about constitution-makers' intent is the very *sine qua non* of judicial review as it has operated in the United States." Robert G. McCloskey, *The American Supreme Court* 117–18 (1960).
- "While knowledge of the right to refuse consent is one factor to be taken into account, the government need not establish such knowledge as the *sine qua non* of an effective consent." *Schneckloth v. Bustamonte*, 412 U.S. 218, 227 (1973) (per Stewart, J.).
- "The *sine qua non* of copyright is originality." *Feist Pub., Inc. v. Rural Tel. Serv. Co.*, 499 U.S. 340, 345 (1991) (per O'Connor, J.).
- "Attracting crowds is not merely an unforeseen byproduct of street performing, it is its *sine qua non*: A street performer who never gathers an audience would give up the pursuit very quickly." *Berger v. City of Seattle*, 569 F.3d 1029, 1073 (9th Cir. 2009).

Cf. **but for.**

sink > sank > sunk. In AmE, some writers misuse the past participle for the simple past—e.g.:

- "The original owner of the vessel had failed to remove it after it *sunk* [read *sank* or *had sunk*]." *Magno v. Corros*, 630 F.2d 224, 227 (4th Cir. 1980).
- "After he sold the house, it *sunk* [read *sank*] into underlying permafrost." *Alaska Pac. Assurance Co. v. Collins*, 794 P.2d 936, 937 (Alaska 1990).

sister, as an adjective <sister state>, is rather quaintly used in a number of expressions, perhaps more commonly today in legal than in lay contexts. Like *she* in reference to states or ships, *sister* may be obsolescent because of whatever latent SEXISM may appear to those who seek to eliminate every vestige of male–female DIFFERENTIATION in the language.

Sister has traditionally been used in a number of contexts—e.g.:

- "We find the rationale of our *sister states* persuasive and hold that when a person enters into a purported marriage contract or relationship at a time when the person already has a living spouse, the crime of bigamy has been committed." *State v. Fitzgerald*, 726 P.2d 1344, 1347 (Kan. 1986).
- "The fact that a number of Illinois's *sister states* have chosen a different rule is not enough to require certification." *Rennert v. Great Dane Ltd. P'ship*, 543 F.3d 914, 918–19 (7th Cir. 2008).

Not only does a state have 49 *sister states* in the U.S., but also the federal judicial circuits, by analogy, have *sister circuits*—e.g.:

- "The issue before us—whether section 3582(a) allows a sentencing court to treat rehabilitation as a reason for lengthening a defendant's prison term—has divided our *sister circuits*." *In re Sealed Case*, 573 F.3d 844, 848 (D.C. Cir. 2009).

- "As our *sister circuits* have recognized, when a pending appeal may preclude the necessity of a retrial, it must be resolved before the statutory clock can start ticking." *U.S. v. Hutchinson*, 573 F.3d 1011, 1028 (10th Cir. 2009).

sistren is the archaic and dialectal equivalent of *brethren*. Karl Llewellyn began his last speech with the jocular remark, "Well, Brethren and *Sistren*, I find myself in a completely impossible position." Karl Llewellyn, *A Lecture on Appellate Advocacy*, 29 U. Chi. L. Rev. 627, 627 (1962). See **brethren.**

sit = (1) of a judge, to occupy a judicial seat; or (2) of a court, to hold judicial proceedings. E.g.:

- (Sense 1) "Yet President Washington had difficulty finding men of national stature willing to *sit* on so inconsequential a court." Robert G. McCloskey, *The American Supreme Court* v (1960).
- (Sense 2) "No court in Britain normally *sits* behind closed doors, so you can walk in boldly and listen to its proceedings." Glanville Williams, *Learning the Law* 17 (11th ed. 1982).

site, n. See **cite (D)** & **situs.**

site, vb., = to locate, place, or provide with a site—e.g.:

- "When the completed septic system was inspected in June 1996, the inspector noted that the house was *sited* too close to the street and that, if septic problems occurred, the property owners would be required 'to install [a] pump to pump to back of lot.'" *Fayne v. Vincent*, 301 S.W.3d 162, 167 (Tenn. 2009).
- "The wells would be *sited* along the Gordon River, near the wastewater treatment plant, and drilled deep below the drinking-water supply." *Around the States: Florida*, Clean Water Rep., 26 June 2009, at 4.

situate, p.pl.; **situated.** The language of the law abounds in needless ARCHAISMS, and *situate* used as a past participle is one of them. Historically, it is one of a great many English participial adjectives formed from Latin perfect passive participles—e.g., *corrupt* (from the Latin *corruptus*, "having been spoiled"), *select*, *compact*, *effeminate*, *legitimate*, and *adequate*. In the Renaissance, many more such participial adjectives existed than do today. Those that have not survived in the Latinate *t*-form (ending in *-t* or *-te*) have been thoroughly anglicized, taking on the English past-participial suffix *-ed*. The verb *to situate* is among these.

Many wills contain phrases such as the following:

- "I give, devise, and bequeath to my son all of the rest, residue, and remainder of my property and estate, real, personal, and mixed, of whatsoever nature and character and wheresoever *situate* [read *situated*] of which I may die seized or possessed or in or to which I may have any right, title, claim, interest, or reversion." *Miller v. Todd*, 447 S.E.2d 9, 10 n.3 (W. Va. 1994) (quoting will).
- "All the rest, residue, and remainder of my estate whether real, personal, or mixed, of every kind and description, whether now owned or hereafter acquired, and

wheresoever *situate* [read *situated*], . . . I hereby give, devise, bequeath, and appoint unto my sister." *Shipley v. Matlack*, 776 A.2d 74, 76 (Md. Ct. Spec. App. 2001) (quoting will).

The usage appears even in judicial opinions, commentary, and statutes—e.g.:

- "The tract of land in question, *situate* [read *situated*] in the Borough of Morris Plains, was purchased by the plaintiff's father in 1924." *Vreeland v. Dawson*, 151 A.2d 62, 63 (N.J. Super. Ct. Ch. Div. 1959).
- "The celebration must take place . . . in a recognized place of worship or Registrar's office *situate* [read *situated*] in the district in which one at least of the parties resides." William Geldart, *Introduction to English Law* 52–53 (D.C.M. Yardley ed., 9th ed. 1984).
- "The county court of the district in which the registered office of the company is *situate* [read *situated*] shall . . . have concurrent jurisdiction with the High Court." Companies Act 1948 § 218(3).

Shakespeare, in *Love's Labour's Lost* (ca. 1588), had one of his comically pompous characters say, "I know where it is *situate.*" Some lawyers continue to use the word similarly, probably unaware of the comic pomposity of the word. It is time they came into the 21st century and wrote *situated.*

One other point about this word merits attention. *Situate* is often superfluous, as in "Flaherty remained in the police vehicle, and defendant was *situated* under a streetlight about 100 feet away." *People v. Newbill*, 873 N.E.2d 408, 410 (Ill. App. Ct. 2007). The word could be dropped from the sentence with no change in meaning, and with enhanced concision.

situated. See **situate**, p.pl.

situate, lying, and being in. See DOUBLETS, TRIPLETS, AND SYNONYM-STRINGS.

situation has, in one of its senses, become a VOGUE WORD, and is often used superfluously, as here: "In offshoring *situations* [omit *situations*], it is usually safe to assume that the Acquired-Rights Directive does not apply." Carole A. Spink & Ute Krudewagen, *From Acquired Rights to Reverse TUPE*, 9 Chi.-Kent J. Int'l & Comp. L. 46, 61–62 (2009).

It is also often used illogically: "He might be significantly affected by the *situation* he seeks to litigate." Fred Shapiro, *The Most-Cited Law-Review Articles* 1291 (1987). One does not litigate a *situation. Dispute, issue,* and *claim* are all more specific examples of what can be litigated. See **litigate.**

situs (= the location or position of [something] for legal purposes) is a legal word not quite equivalent to *site.* E.g.: "Admiralty jurisdiction generally requires both that the injury occur on navigable waters and that the activity bear a sufficient relationship to maritime commerce. These are sometimes described as the locality or *situs* and the nexus or relationship requirements." *Whitcombe v. Stevedoring Servs. of Am.*, 2 F.3d 312, 314 n.2 (9th Cir. 1993).

As a legal term, the word dates from the early 19th century: "Personal contracts have no *situs*; they are to be governed by the law of the place, where they are to be performed." *Maisonnaire v. Keating*, 16 F. Cas. 513, 516 (C.C.D. Mass. 1815) (No. 8,978). Pl. *situs.*

Sometimes *situs* is misleading: "If the will contains a devise of land, the will must be probated *at the situs of the land* [read *in the jurisdiction in which the land is located*] in order to establish title." John Ritchie et al., *Case and Materials on Decedents' Estates and Trusts* 330 (1982). It is not necessary that probate be obtained at the very site where the land is; rather, the will must be probated by a court having territorial jurisdiction over the land. See ***lex situs*** & **locus.**

six of one, half a dozen of the other is one of our most shopworn CLICHÉS.

sizable. So spelled in AmE—but *sizeable* in BrE. See MUTE E.

S.J.D. See. **J.D.**

skeptic; sceptic. The first is the AmE spelling, the second the BrE spelling.

skillful. So spelled in AmE—but *skilful* in BrE. Cf. **willful.**

skulduggery. So spelled—not **skullduggery.* Avoid the variants **sculduggery* and **scullduggery.* The word denotes trickery or unscrupulous behavior.

skyjack; hijack. Today airline *hijackings* are still sometimes termed *skyjackings.* But *hijacking* remains the more common word. See **hijack** & PORTMANTEAU WORDS.

slander. See **libel** & **defamation.**

*slanderize is a NEEDLESS VARIANT of *slander*, vb. E.g.: "Think of advertising: you just don't slam your brand, unless you are Joan Rivers and *self-slanderization* [read *self-slander*] is your brand." Marcelle Langan DiFalco & Jocelyn Greenky Herz, *The Big Sister's Guide to the World of Work* 127 (2004).

slander of title denotes the tort committed by a person who makes false statements, orally or in writing, that cast doubt on another person's ownership of real property. Despite the name, this tort has nothing to do with *slander* in the sense of oral defamation. E.g.:

- "Not dissimilar to the acts just discussed are statements in disparagement of title to property, giving rise to the action for '*slander of title.*'" Thomas E. Holland, *The Elements of Jurisprudence* 189 (13th ed. 1924).
- "A false denial of the plaintiff's title to his property, whereby he was hindered in selling it, was actually called '*slander of title.*'" J.H. Baker, *An Introduction to English Legal History* 521 (3d ed. 1990).

SLAPP is an ACRONYM for "Strategic Lawsuit Against Public Participation," i.e., one brought usu. by a developer, corporate executive, or elected official to stifle those who protest against some type of high-dollar initiative (often involving the environment). The term *SLAPP* is ordinarily used as a noun—e.g.:

- "While *SLAPP* suits 'masquerade as ordinary lawsuits,' the conceptual features that reveal them as *SLAPP*s are that they are generally meritless suits brought by large private interests to deter common citizens from exercising their political or legal rights or to punish them for doing so." *Wilcox v. Superior Ct.*, 33 Cal. Rptr. 2d 446, 450 (Ct. App. 1994).
- "States like California have even adopted Anti-*SLAPP* statutes, which have made an art out of disposing of defamation suits at an early procedural stage." Aaron Perzanowski, Comment, *Relative Access to Corrective Speech*, 94 Calif. L. Rev. 833, 870 (2006).

But it appears also as a verb—e.g.: "Those doing the *SLAPPing* almost always lose; the First Amendment generally protects activists like Betty Blake, whose case is pending." *SLAPPing the Opposition*, Newsweek, 5 Mar. 1990, at 22.

slash. See PUNCTUATION (N).

slavery. See **servitude (B).**

slay. See **kill (A).**

slip-and-fall case = (1) a lawsuit brought by a plaintiff for injuries sustained in slipping and falling, usu. on the defendant's property; or, by extension, (2) any minor case in tort. Sense 2 arose because the *slip-and-fall case* is the archetypal minor tort case—e.g.: "Young, who mostly hears '*slip and fall*' cases, soon will tackle a custody battle between Blount County's Junior and Marry Sue Davis that could set a legal precedent in the USA." *Judge to Decide Embryo Custody*, USA Today, 17 May 1989, at 2A. Because the phrase contains a PHRASAL ADJECTIVE, it should be hyphenated as at the outset of this entry.

slip opinion; advance sheet. In the U.S., reported opinions are published first individually in *slip opinions*, and are then collected in soft-cover *advance sheets*, before appearing in the hardcover reporters.

In some courts, the phrase *slip opinion* formerly referred to a preliminary draft of an opinion not yet ready for publication—e.g.: "On the margin of one '*slip opinion*,' the preliminary draft of an opinion [that] is circulated among the justices, McReynolds wrote, 'This statement makes me sick.'" Donald D. Jackson, *Judges* 336 (1974).

slippery slope. This once-clever METAPHOR—a way of saying that if we take the first step there will be no stopping—has been all but exhausted as a legal CLICHÉ. First used in the mid-1960s, it gained widespread currency in the 1980s. Here are the first examples recorded in federal and state caselaw:

- "If agency power to designate programming 'not in the public interest' is a *slippery slope*, the Commission and the courts started down it too long ago to go back to the top now unless Congress or the Constitution sends them." *Banzhaf v. FCC*, 405 F.2d 1082, 1094 (D.C. Cir. 1968) (per Bazelon, C.J.).
- "It seems more likely that a future court, armed with today's decision, will take one more 'logical' step down the *slippery slope* to absolute liability." *Renslow v. Mennonite Hosp.*, 367 N.E.2d 1250, 1265 (Ill. 1977) (Ryan, J., dissenting).

Legal writers sometimes play cleverly with the metaphor—e.g.:

- "I, for one, however, do not believe that a '*slippery slope*' is necessarily without a constitutional toehold." *Walz v. Tax Comm'n*, 397 U.S. 664, 699–700 (1970) (Harlan, J., dissenting).
- "Judges and lawyers live on the *slippery slope* of analogies; they are not supposed to ski it to the bottom." Robert H. Bork, *The Tempting of America* 169 (1997).

When used attributively, the phrase needs a hyphen: *slippery-slope argument, slippery-slope reasoning*. See PHRASAL ADJECTIVES (A).

SLIPSHOD EXTENSION. Several individual entries in this dictionary refer to this heading. Slipshod extension denotes the mistaken stretching of a word beyond what it is generally accepted as denoting or connoting, the mistake lying in a misunderstanding of the true sense. It occurs most often, explained H.W. Fowler, "when some accident gives currency among the uneducated to words of learned origin, and the more if they are isolated or have few relatives in the vernacular" (*MEU1* 540).

Today one might rightly accuse not only the uneducated, but the educated as well, of the linguistic distortion of *a priori* and *protagonist*, to name but two of any number of possible examples. For examples, see **ad hoc, alias, alibi, a priori, calculus, compound, dilemma, duplicity, enjoinder, factor, hopefully, literally, material, medicine, protagonist, veracity, verbal, viable** & **vitiate.** See also POPULARIZED LEGAL TECHNICALITIES.

slow has long been treated as an immediate adverb, that is, one not requiring the *-ly* suffix. It is ill-informed pedantry to insist that *slow* can be only an adjective. Though *slowly* is the more common adverb, and is certainly correct, *slow* is often just as good in the adverbial sense. Euphony should govern the choice. For example, Coleridge wrote, in "The Complaint of a Forsaken Indian Woman": "I'll follow you across the snow, / You travel heavily and *slow*." The usage is common in legal contexts: "We should go *slow* before amending the Minnesota Constitution and the United States Constitution to allow for preventive detention." *Joelson v. O'Keefe*, 594 N.W.2d 905, 916 (Minn. Ct. App. 1999).

slush fund. Originally, in the early 19th century, this phrase was a nautical term referring to money collected from the sale of fat or grease obtained from meat boiled on board ship; the money was used to buy luxuries for the crew. By the late 19th century, the phrase had come to denote money used to supplement the salaries of government employees, especially through bribes. Today the phrase always carries connotations of moral impropriety, and sometimes of legal impropriety—e.g.:

- "Siemens, the German engineering giant, paid more than $1.4 billion in bribes to government officials in Asia, Africa, Europe, the Middle East, and Latin America, using its *slush funds* to secure public-works contracts around the world." Sara Sun Beale, *A Response to the Critics of Corporate Criminal Liability*, 46 Am. Crim. L. Rev. 1481, 1484 (2009).
- "Investors' funds were principally deposited into the 703 Account, which was little more than a '*slush fund.*' Money was misappropriated from the 703 Account solely to enrich Madoff and his inner circle." *In re Madoff Inv. Secs.*, 424 B.R. 122, 129 (Bankr. S.D.N.Y. 2010).

small-claims court = a local tribunal in which disputes involving small amounts can be adjudicated quickly and cheaply, usu. without legal representation; the model for *small-claims courts* arose in late-17th- and 18th-century England, and they were revived in the late 20th century. *Small-claims* is a PHRASAL ADJECTIVE when it precedes a noun, and therefore requires a hyphen.

smart money (= punitive damages, i.e., an award that smarts) arose in the 18th century and has been more or less steadily used ever since—e.g.:

- "There has been much discussion in the Courts, and among elementary writers upon the subject of vindictive damages, or '*smart money*' as they are sometimes styled." *Malone v. Murphy*, 2 Kan. 250, 261 (1864).
- "The purpose of punitive damages, sometimes denominated as exemplary damages or *smart money*, is two-fold: to punish the wrongdoing of the defendant and to deter others from engaging in similar conduct." *Rogers v. T.J.X. Cos.*, 404 S.E.2d 664, 666 (N.C. 1991).

Two other senses of *smart money* demand attention. The most common sense in general use is money (or some other form of interest) cannily placed as a wager or invested wisely. This sense is common in legal writing as well—e.g.: "A Court-watcher in the early to mid-1990s would have had a solid backdrop for predicting the mode of analysis, if not the result, of a Sixth Amendment jury-trial case. The *smart money* was on the social scientist and not the historian." G. Ben Cohen & Robert J. Smith, *The Death of Death-Qualification*, 59 Case W. Res. L. Rev. 87, 103 (2008).

The oldest sense is a different legal term, denoting compensation for sailors (or, later, other workers) injured on the job—e.g.: "The pensions given for service and wounds, as well as the pecuniary compensation for accidental hurts received in the service, . . . is known as *smart money*." *The Monthly Mag.* (London) 395 (1825). That sense dates back to the 17th century. The term's growth since that time essentially makes it a POPULARIZED LEGAL TECHNICALITY.

smellfungus (= a faultfinder, grumbler) is too valuable a word, especially for lawyers in ad hominem reference to other lawyers, to be as neglected as it is—e.g.: "*Smellfungus* is the least estimable of the three. He it is that hunts like a truffle-dog for old scandals." Frederick Scott Oliver, *The Endless Adventure* 3 (1935).

***snuck** is a nonstandard past tense of *sneak* common in American dialectal and informal English. The past tense to be used in formal writing is *sneaked*—e.g.: "A degree of federalization was, so to say, *sneaked* in the back door." Grant Gilmore, *The Death of Contract* 96 (1974).

Surprisingly, though, **snuck* appears half as often in American caselaw as *sneaked*—e.g.:

- "During the summer of 2005, R.J. *snuck* [read *sneaked*] out of the house several times to see male friends, including T." *Ashland Sch. Dist. v. Parents of Student R.J.*, 588 F.3d 1004, 1006 (9th Cir. 2009).
- "At that point, Fowler *snuck* [read *sneaked*] up behind Officer Horner and Gamble started talking to Officer Horner to distract him." *U.S. v. Fowler*, 603 F.3d 883, 885 (11th Cir. 2010).
- "Rather than either wait or ask for permission to reapply, she *snuck* [read *sneaked*] back into the United States a month later." *Gonzalez-Balderas v. Holder*, 597 F.3d 869, 869 (7th Cir. 2010) (per Posner, J.).

so. A. Omission of. This error is not uncommon. E.g.: "The court of appeals concluded, although it was the first *court to* [read *court so to*] hold, that the 19th-century joinder cases in this court created a federal, common-law, substantive right in a certain class of persons to be joined in the corresponding lawsuits." *Provident Tradesmens Bank & Trust Co. v. Patterson*, 390 U.S. 102, 119 (1968) (per Harlan, J.).

B. For *very*. The casualism of substituting *so* for *very* or *terribly* should be avoided in formal writing. E.g.: "He cannot reason *so well* [read *very well*]."

C. Displaced by *that*. See that (F).

so as [+ infinitive]. This construction is a common and a useful one in legal writing, but it often leads to problems. Most common among these is the unnecessary repetition of *so*—e.g.:

- "So what did we talk about: how could we have been *so* stupid *so as* [read *as*] not to organize politically?" George E. Marcus, *Corporate Futures* 295 (1998).
- "The term 'concerted activities' has not been defined *so broadly so as* [read *so broadly as*] to cover individual action that is merely intended to benefit coworkers." Alex B. Long, "Mutual Aid or Protection and the Right of Association," in *Retaliation and Whistleblowers* 713, 714 (Paul M. Secunda ed., 2008).

In the following sentences, *as* has been suppressed, leaving the syntax incomplete:

- "We do not believe that the acceptance in the case at bar diverged *so radically* from the terms of the offer *to* [read *as to*] warrant this result." *Southern Idaho Pipe & Steel Co. v. Cal-Cut Pipe & Supply*, 567 P.2d 1246, 1253 (Idaho 1977).
- "If the defendant's activities are not *so pervasive to* [read *so pervasive as to*] subject him to general jurisdiction, then

a court may still assert jurisdiction for a cause of action that arises out of the defendant's forum-related activities." *Haisten v. Grass Valley Med. Reimbursement Fund, Ltd.*, 784 F.2d 1392, 1397 (9th Cir. 1986).

Here, the phrase is simply misused for *to* or *in order to*: "On October 17 he capitulated *so as to avoid* [read *to avoid*] unnecessary bloodshed." Andrew Burstein & Nancy Isenberg, *Madison & Jefferson* 87 (2010). The meaning of this sentence calls for the sense "in order to," not "in such a way as to," so that *to* can stand alone.

Not infrequently, and especially in long sentences, *so as to* and *such as to* are improperly mixed, as here: "The necessity that the plaintiffs should join this association is not *so great*, nor is its relation to the rights of the defendants, as compared with the right of the plaintiffs to be free from molestation, *such as to* [read *as to*] bring the acts of the defendants under the shelter of the principles of trade competition." *Plant v. Woods*, 57 N.E. 1011, 1015 (Mass. 1900). **See such (c)** & **sufficiently . . . as to.**

social. A. And *societal*; *societary. These words overlap to some degree, but may be validly distinguished. *Social* = (1) living in companies or organized communities <humans are social animals>; (2) concerned with the mutual relations of (classes of) human beings <the social compact>; or (3) of or in or toward society <social interactions> (*COD*). *Societal* has replaced **societary* (now merely a NEEDLESS VARIANT) in the sense "of, pertaining to, concerned or dealing with, society or social conditions" (*OED*)—e.g.: "Certainly the defendant will accept the *societal* postulate that parents have the obligation to support their children." *Shelley v. Shelley*, 354 P.2d 282, 286 (Or. 1960).

B. And *sociable*. *Sociable* = ready for companionship; quick to unite with others; gregarious. *Social* = relating to persons in society, communities, or commonwealths.

social harm = an invasion of any social interest that the criminal law protects. Every crime involves a social harm committed by some person.

*social-legal. See **sociolegal.**

societal; *societary. See **social (A).**

societas, the Roman-law term for "partnership," sometimes appears in Anglo-American legal texts—e.g.: "When several persons unite for the purpose of carrying on business in common, which is usually done upon the terms that each of them shall be an agent for all the rest, the contract is called partnership, '*societas*,' and takes various shapes, according to the business contemplated." Thomas E. Holland, *The Elements of Jurisprudence* 304 (13th ed. 1924).

society, in torts and family law, often means "consortium; sexual and other intimate companionship." E.g.:

- "Interest in the wife's *society* is frequently called 'consortium,' though the term traditionally included also the services and assistance of the wife." 1 Charles T. McCormick, *Handbook on the Law of Damages* § 92, at 332 (1935).
- "The spouse of an injured crew member who survives his injury may recover her loss of *society* in an action for unseaworthiness." *Madore v. Ingram Tank Ships, Inc.*, 732 F.2d 475, 479 (5th Cir. 1984).
- "His allegation that Judge Townsend's orders deprived him of his wife's *society* and companionship does not in itself create a constitutional claim cognizable in federal court." *Allen v. Allen*, 48 F.3d 259, 261 (7th Cir. 1995).

See **consortium.**

sociolegal; *social-legal. *Sociolegal* = relating to the field of law and society. E.g.: "Historically, *sociolegal* scholars have not been able to assume the perspective of social scientists—to seek to learn how law as a phenomenon affects behavior in society . . .—because our theory has been tied to a concept of law which was developed by and for the use of judges and lawyers." Paul Lermack, *What Does Law Do?*, 12 Legal Stud. F. 401, 401 (1988).

*Social-legal is a NEEDLESS VARIANT—e.g.: "He had, in effect, created a *social-legal* [read *sociolegal*] counterpart of that mathematical curiosity, the Klein bottle, whose spout curves back into its mouth, so that it became a one-sided surface which is closed and has no boundary." Murray T. Bloom, *The Trouble with Lawyers* 252 (1970).

sociological jurisprudence denotes a philosophical approach to law stressing the actual social effects of legal institutions, doctrines, and practices. E.g.:

- "In 1906, . . . [Roscoe Pound] startled the entire bar with an original, highly critical, and constructive analysis of the American legal system. His address shattered the complacency of many leaders of the bar, jurists and professors of law, and started a movement in the United States toward what is called '*sociological jurisprudence*,' which . . . has made enormous headway and has radically affected, sometimes directly and sometimes indirectly, the thinking of American jurists, judges, and lawyers." René A. Wormser, *The Story of the Law* 484–85 (1962).
- "Both *sociological jurisprudence*—which is the opposite of abstraction, formalism, and purism—and legal realism—which rejects scientism and system-building—emphasize the difficulty and the importance of focusing on the judicial process." John H. Merryman, *The Civil Law Tradition* 71 (1969).

Cf. **analytical jurisprudence.**

socius criminis = a partner in crime; an accessory. This LATINISM, which appears primarily in BrE, is invariably unnecessary for *accessory*. E.g.: "The testimony of an accomplice, or *socius criminis*, who is pardoned, must often be resorted to for the discovery and punishment of crimes." Alexander Macomb, *A Treatise on Martial Law and Courts* 113 (2006).

Socius is sometimes used as an elliptical form of *socius criminis*. E.g.: "As a matter of rule, the *socius* was punished by the same punishment as the principal wrongdoer." Adolf Berger, *Encyclopedic Dictionary of Roman Law* 709 (2002). See **accessory.** Cf. **particeps criminis.**

sodomist; *sodomite. The second is an example of BIBLICAL AFFECTATION. These terms have largely fallen into disuse in the wake of the Supreme Court's holding in *Lawrence v. Texas*, 539 U.S. 558 (2003).

sodomize is plagued by the same ambiguities as *sodomy.* Some writers use adverbs to clarify the meaning—e.g.:

- "He forced her to *orally sodomize* him after vaginal sex." Thomas P. Carney, *Practical Investigation of Sex Crimes* 185 (2003).
- "He also attempted to *anally sodomize* the victim several times." *Borders v. State*, 646 S.E.2d 319, 321 (Ga. Ct. App. 2007).

But not everyone would agree on what the following sentence describes: "LePage put the body in the back of the pickup and drove to a remote location, where he *sodomized* the corpse before disposing of it." *LePage v. Idaho*, 851 F.2d 251, 252 (9th Cir. 1988). See **sodomy.**

sodomy. This ambiguous term may refer to (1) anal or oral copulation of any kind between two people (whether of the same or opposite sexes); or (2) bestiality. Sodomy was originally a crime only in canon law. When it became an English common-law crime also, it was defined as (1) bestiality and (2) anal intercourse between men; later, the scope was broadened to cover anal sex between men and women. Wayne C. Bartee & Alice Fleetwood Bartee, *Litigating Morality: American Legal Thought and Its English Roots* 32 (1992). The definition was relatively fixed until the early 20th century. Then it was rapidly expanded by American statutes and caselaw to include many other "deviant" sexual acts, such as fellatio, cunnilingus, and anilingus. *Id.* at 41–42. *See* 8 William Mark McKinney & Burdett Alberto Rich, *Ruling Case Law* 333–35 (1915). Although the Supreme Court's decision in *Lawrence v. Texas* (539 U.S. 558 (2003)) effectively struck down sodomy statutes that criminalized consensual sex acts between people, it may still be treated as a crime in states that recognize sodomy as a common-law crime. But the problem of what consensual behaviors would be criminal and under what circumstances remains unaddressed.

so far as. See **as . . . as (A)** & **insofar as.**

soft law; hard law. In the JARGON of international lawyers, *soft law* contains general principles that are widely accepted as international norms of conduct, as well as declaratory statements of those principles without specific obligations. *Hard law*, by contrast, is binding and requires an active decision on the part of a state to accede to or ratify it. A convention is an example of *hard law*; an international declaration is an example of *soft law*. E.g.: "Much of the original '*soft law*,' or nonbinding principles, has served as the basis for the *hard law* of international conventions and agreements." Allegra Helfenstein, Comment, *U.S. Controls on International Disposal of Hazardous Waste*, 22 Int'l Law. 775, 784 (1988).

soft-pedal. For a fairly common error involving this term, see **peddle.**

so help me God. This formula concludes the oath as traditionally administered to a Christian witness in an Anglo-American court. The person administering the oath traditionally said, "So help *you* God," and the oath-taker would then say *me*. See 2 Alexander M. Burrill, *A Law Dictionary and Glossary* 472 (1860). Presumably, alternative forms have varied for witnesses of other faiths. Some such witnesses, as well as unbelievers, make an *affirmation* rather than taking an oath. See **affirmance.**

soi disant = self-proclaimed. This French affectation is inferior both to the translation just given and to *self-styled.* See GALLICISMS.

solace (= alleviation of sorrow or trouble; relief from distress) should not be used merely as a synonym of *comfort*, without the circumstance of grief or distress being implied. E.g.: "Companies with the greatest market share often have a tendency to 'sit on a lead.' They will take *solace* [read *undue pride*?] in their numbers, become complacent, and lose their competitive edge." Mark H. McCormack, *What They Don't Teach You at Harvard Business School* 205–06 (1984). For a related MALAPROPISM, see **surcease.**

The following misuse is even more puzzling: "No clear legal framework has ever provided for federal jurisdiction over aviation torts. Instead, cases involving aviation torts *find solace* [read *end up* or *are heard*] in federal courts via diversity or admiralty jurisdiction." Albert Lin, Comment, *Jurisdictional Splashdown*, 60 J. Air L. & Com. 409, 411 (1994).

soldier's will. See **oral will.**

sole (= the one and only, single) should not be used with a plural noun, as in *the sole criteria* [read *the only criteria*]. See **feme sole.**

sole and exclusive is a legalistic REDUNDANCY. See DOUBLETS, TRIPLETS, AND SYNONYM-STRINGS.

sole cause. See CAUSATION (E).

solecism. Generally, *solecism* means "a grammatical or syntactic error." Here it is close to the literal sense: "It is no more a *solecism* to say 'immovable personal property' than it is to say 'removable fixtures,' nor more contradicting than in the division of actions to use the term 'in rem,' when, under the particular state of facts, the action is primarily 'in personam.'" *Hook v. Hoffman*, 147 P. 722, 729 (Ariz. 1915).

The word has been extended to figurative senses, however—e.g.:

- "The common law recognized no such *solecism* as a right in the wife to the estate, and a right in someone else to use it as he pleased, and to enjoy all the advantages of its use." 6 *The American and English Encyclopaedia of Law* 323 (David Shephard Garland et al. eds., 1898).
- "The plaintiff asks for protection only during the season, and needs no more, for the designs are all ephemeral. It seeks in this way to persuade us that, if we interfere only a little, the *solecism*, if there be one, may be pardonable." *Cheney Bros. v. Doris Silk Corp.*, 35 F.2d 279, 280 (2d Cir. 1929) (per L. Hand, J.).

solely. The placement of this word sometimes causes trouble. E.g.: "The responding document states a condition *solely advantageous* [read *advantageous solely*] to the party proposing it." *Southern Idaho Pipe & Steel Co. v. Cal-Cut Pipe & Supply, Inc.*, 567 P.2d 1246, 1254 (Idaho 1977). Cf. **only.**

sole practitioner; solo practitioner. In AmE generally, *sole practitioner* is much more common. But there are areas, such as Texas, where *solo* predominates. And in some states, such as New Jersey, both terms appear with almost equal frequency.

sole proprietor; individual proprietor. These synonymous phrases denote an individual who owns a business and is responsible for all its debts.

solicit. A. For *elicit*. This is a MALAPROPISM. E.g.: "The state avoided any questions that might have *solicited* [read *elicited*] that information." *Wimbley v. State*, 208 P.3d 608, 613 (Wyo. 2009).

B. For What a Solicitor Does. Although *solicitor* is the BrE term for a certain kind of lawyer, it is incorrect to say that what such a lawyer does is *solicit*. (This sense of the verb has long been obsolete.) The confusion appears in this passage in a reference book: "In America, lawyers can both *solicit* cases and plead them in court, but in England *solicitors* handle the preliminaries, while *barristers* alone are members of the bar and can take cases to court." Robert Hendrickson, *Business Talk* 34 (1984). The quoted statement is so phrased that some word such as *prepare* would be necessary to fit the context. Apart from chamber practice (conveyancing, wills, probate), a solicitor prepares cases and instructs counsel. See **instruct** & **solicitor.**

C. And *advertise*. See **advertise (B).**

*****solicitate,** a NEEDLESS VARIANT of *solicit*, was coined as a BACK-FORMATION from *solicitation*. But it serves no purpose—e.g.: "An employer in good faith discharged two employees *whom* [read *who*] it believed had made violent threats against the company when the employees tried to *solicitate* [read *solicit*] union memberships." *M.B. Zaninovich, Inc. v. ALRB*, 171 Cal. Rptr. 55, 66 (Ct. App. 1981). For more on *who* vs. *whom* in this sentence, see HYPERCORRECTION (F).

solicitation. In criminal law, this broad term covers any word or actions by which one requests, urges, advises, counsels, tempts, commands, or otherwise entices or incites someone to commit a crime.

solicitor. In G.B., and many of the former Commonwealth countries, this term refers to a member of one of the two branches into which the legal profession is divided, handling usually general legal and business advice, conveyancing, and instruction of and preparation of cases for counsel (barristers). They may do some pleading, particularly in lower courts. See **attorney (A).**

In AmE, the term generally refers to an advertiser or to one who solicits business—and is frequently used disparagingly. E.g.: "A vocational expert . . . opined that the claimant should be able to perform the work of a telephone *soliciter* [read *solicitor*]." *Beavers v. H.E.W.*, 577 F.2d 383, 385 (6th Cir. 1978). Regardless of the sense, the word should be spelled *solicitor*.

solicitor general; solicitor-general. In BrE and AmE alike, this term denotes the second-highest-ranking legal officer in government, but there the similarities end. In G.B., the *solicitor-general* (hyphenated) is a Crown-appointed law officer who advises the cabinet on legal matters and supervises the passage of bills through Parliament. Ironically, the *solicitor-general* in England is invariably a barrister—not a solicitor. In the U.S., the *solicitor general* (unhyphenated) is the chief courtroom lawyer for the executive branch, with chambers at the Supreme Court as well as at the Justice Department. In AmE, the title *solicitor general* is often, after the first mention of the full title, shortened to *solicitor* or (less good) *general*. On the word *general* as a POSTPOSITIVE ADJECTIVE, and the embarrassing gaffe of saying *General Clement* or *General Kagan*, see **general.**

solicitude has two important senses that may render the word ambiguous: (1) "anxiety"; and (2) "protectiveness."

solidary liability. See **joint and several.**

solidus. See PUNCTUATION (N).

solon, journalese for *legislator*, is derived from the name of Solon, an Athenian statesman, merchant, and poet (ca. 640–560 B.C.). In the early 6th century, Solon achieved important political, commercial, and judicial reforms that greatly improved life in the city-state of Athens. He reversed the trend to convert impoverished Athenians into serfs at home or to sell them abroad as slaves. He also standardized Athenian coinage and its system of weights and measures, granted citizenship to immigrant craftsmen, and enhanced the prosperity and independence of Athenian farmers.

In modern times, his name has been used to denote either a "sage" or a "wiseacre" (*OED*). Today, the term "may be inescapable, and thus grudgingly admissible,

---

An asterisk (✳) precedes words and phrases that are invariably inferior forms.

in headlines, where *legislator, senator,* or *representative* will not fit, but in text it is to be avoided." Roy H. Copperud, *Webster's Dictionary of Usage and Style* 368–69 (1964).

When used in reference to legislating judges, *solon* often carries a mocking tone: "At any rate, concluded the nine *solons,* the dodge works; the statute doesn't cover the case; no tax." Fred Rodell, *Woe Unto You, Lawyers!* 46 (1939).

so long as. See **as long as** & **as . . . as (A).**

solo practitioner. See **sole practitioner.**

soluble; solvable. *Soluble* is usually applied to substances in solvents, whereas *solvable* is usually applied to problems. Although *soluble* is often used in reference to problems, this usage is acceptable—though not preferred. Cf. **resolvable.**

solution may take either *to* or *of* as its preposition.

solvabilité, in French civil law, means "solvency," not "solvability" or "solubility."

solvable. See **soluble.**

solvent. See **insolvent.**

some . . . as for *such . . . as* or *some . . . that.* E.g.:
- "The affidavit was admissible because it . . . set forth *some facts as* [read *such facts as* or *some facts that*] would be admissible in evidence at trial." *Peralta v. Martinez,* 564 P.2d 194, 205 (N.M. Ct. App. 1977).
- "It is the rule in Indiana . . . that a false pretense . . . must be of *some fact as* [read *such fact as* or *some fact that*] would tend to deceive a person of ordinary prudence and common intelligence." *State v. Phelps,* 84 P. 24, 26 (Wash. 1906).

somebody; someone. The words are equally good; euphony should govern the choice of term. *Someone* is often better by that standard. Each is a singular noun and hence, for purposes of CONCORD, the antecedent of a singular pronoun. *Some one* as two words is an obsolete spelling, though Justice Benjamin Cardozo used this spelling as recently as 1928.

someplace is informal for *somewhere*; it is out of place in formal prose, although it is acceptable in speech.

some . . . that. See **some . . . as.**

sometime; some time. *Sometime* = at a time in the future; *some time* = quite a while. The difference may be illustrated by contrasting the following two sentences: *It was not until sometime later that he quit* (he quit at an unspecified later date); *It was not until some time later that he quit* (he quit after a while).

Sometime, in a slightly archaic sense, means "former"—e.g.: "Let me also recall my indebtedness to my former tutor, the late Professor F. deZueta; the late Sir John Miles, *sometime* Warden of Merton College." Carleton K. Allen, *Law in the Making* vi (7th ed. 1964). In such phrases as *my sometime friend,* it does

not properly signify "on-again–off-again" or "on occasion." See **erstwhile.**

somewhat should be avoided as a WEASEL WORD—e.g.: "In approaching solution to this problem we must look *somewhat* [omit *somewhat*] beyond the immediate consequences of the decision in this case." *McCurdy v. McCurdy,* 372 S.W.2d 381, 383 (Tex. Civ. App.—Waco 1963). See FLOTSAM PHRASES & FUSTIAN.

Son-of-Sam law denotes a statute that prevents a criminal from profiting from selling the rights to his or her story to a publisher or moviemaker. New York was the first state to enact such a law, in 1977, when the serial murderer David R. Berkowitz (known as "Son of Sam") was offered large sums for his life story.

About 40 American states have enacted such statutes. Generally, these statutes, enacted mostly in the 1980s, authorize prosecutors to seize royalties from convicted criminals. During his prosecution, O.J. Simpson was able to skirt the issue by arranging for his lawyers to profit from book sales, as opposed to Simpson himself. Further, of course, he had only been accused—not convicted—when he wrote his book entitled *I Want to Tell You* (1995).

sophic; sophical. See **sophistical.**

sophist; sophister. *Sophister* is, except in historical contexts denoting a certain rank of student, a NEEDLESS VARIANT of *sophist,* which today has primarily negative connotations in the sense "one who makes use of fallacious arguments; a specious reasoner." Formerly it was a respectable word meaning "one who is distinguished for learning; a wise or learned man" (*OED*).

sophistical; *sophistic; sophic; sophical. *Sophistical* and *sophic* have opposite connotations. *Sophistical* is a pejorative term meaning "quibbling, specious, or captious in reasoning"; **sophistic* is a variant. *Sophic* means "learned; intellectual"; *sophical* is a variant. The disparaging term is more common—e.g.:
- "'Special pleading' in legal discourse . . . used figuratively, implies a one-sided, disingenuous, or *sophistical* argument." Baden Powell, "On the Study of the Evidences of Christianity" (1860), in *Essays and Reviews* 235, 270 (Victor Shea & William Whitia eds., 2000).
- "Therefore, argues petitioner, there was no 'valid' death penalty in effect in Florida as of the date of his actions. But this *sophistic* [read *sophistical*] argument mocks the substance of the Ex Post Facto Clause." *Dobbert v. Florida,* 432 U.S. 282, 297 (1977) (per Rehnquist, J.).

soraismus. See MINGLE-MANGLE.

sore-back lawyer. See LAWYERS, DEROGATORY NAMES FOR (A).

sort of, adv., is a dialectal casualism to be avoided in writing. E.g.: "The prosecutor *sort of* agreed that . . . ." It is also a FUDGE WORD and a WEASEL WORD.

For the problem raised by the phrase **these sort of,* see ***these kind of.**

so . . . so as. See **so . . . as** [+ infinitive].

sought for. The preposition is unnecessary. E.g.: "As the relief *sought* is the appointment of a trustee, and the necessity for such appointment requires the construction of the will as an incident to the relief *sought for* [read merely *sought*], the complainant is properly here." *Hiles v. Garrison*, 62 A. 865, 865 (N.J. Ch. 1906).

sound, vb. This verb has a special legal sense, "to be actionable (in)"—e.g.:

- "It is, of course, to the advantage of any lienor . . . to plead his claim as *sounding* not in contract but in tort." Grant Gilmore & Charles L. Black Jr., *The Law of Admiralty* 753 (2d ed. 1975).
- "Unlike claims *sounding* in malicious prosecution, false arrest, or false imprisonment, the favorable termination of a criminal proceeding is not an essential element of an independent First Amendment claim." *Johnson v. Bax*, 63 F.3d 154, 159 (2d Cir. 1995).

The *OED* refers to the expression *sound in damages* (= to be concerned only with damages)—e.g.: "This covenant did not create a specifically ascertained debt, but only a claim which *sounded* in damages" (quoted in *OED*). Today the sense has been carried beyond "to be concerned only with," to the meaning set forth at the outset of this entry.

sound bite. So spelled—not **sound byte.*

sound block. See **gavel.**

*sound byte. See **sound bite.**

sound mind. See **mind and memory.**

SOUND OF PROSE, THE. We're all occasionally guilty of having a tin ear. The effective writer is self-trained to avoid undue alliteration, unconscious puns, or unseemly images, for these may irritate or distract the reader. The writers of the sentences in the following sections might have benefited from reading their own prose aloud.

A. Undue Alliteration or Rhyme. Justice Benjamin Cardozo, a masterly stylist, wrote in one of his classic opinions: "Nothing in this situation gave notice that the fallen *package* had in it the *potency* of *peril* to *persons* thus removed." *Palsgraf v. Long Island R.R. Co.*, 162 N.E. 99, 99 (N.Y. 1928). This type of wordplay should be undertaken cautiously, for it declares that one's purpose is to be wry or coy.

Intentional but ineffective alliteration is one thing. Thoughtless alliteration is quite another—e.g.:

- "Here all men contribute to the public *welfare* and *bear their fair share* of the public burdens." Andrew Johnson, First Annual Message (1865), in 6 *A Compilation of the Messages and Papers of the Presidents, 1789–1907* 365 (2010).
- "Relating the premiums of individual policies to the individual policy risk makes little *sense since* that risk is largely diversified away in the insurer's portfolio." Philip S. Borba

& David Appel, *Workers Compensation Insurance Pricing* 164 (1988).

- "In *complex* litigation, . . . a special multi-jurisdictional or national rule . . . would take account of the broad national *complexion* of most air disaster claims." James A.R. Nafziger, *Choice of Law in Air Disaster Cases*, 54 La. L. Rev. 1001, 1012 (1994).

See ALLITERATION.

B. Unwieldy or Illogical Imagery.

- "All of them *come to a head at the FDA* and all of those incentives are in the direction of 'approve the drug.'" Joseph Mercole & Kendra Degen Pearsall, *Sweet Deception* 201 (2007). Two idioms collide in the reader's mind: *come to a head* and *head of an organization or department.*
- "That case held that quasi in rem jurisdiction over a defendant could not be exercised unless the defendant had such 'minimum contacts' with the forum state that in personam jurisdiction could be exercised *over him under International Shoe.*" Steve Emanuel & Lazar Emanuel, *Civil Procedure* 56 (23d ed. 2008). Prepositional clash: *over . . . under*; image: *under . . . Shoe.*

C. Unnecessary or Awkward Repetition. "The subsequent acts of the parties may be *looked to to* identify the land conveyed by a deed." 48 Texas Civil Appeals Reports 572 (1910). (Substitute *examined* for *looked to*; or, if this seems to change the meaning, insert *in order* before the second *to*.) See REDUNDANCY (B).

Having words with the same root in close proximity can be especially jarring. Legal writers often use in succession two different forms of the same root, as an agent noun and a verb. E.g.:

- "In *conference*, the *conferees* scaled back the bill." Charles Metz Cameron, *Veto Bargaining* 243 (2000).
- "It was held in *Renals v. Cowlishaw* that there was no annexation where the *covenantor covenanted* with 'the vendor, their heirs, executors, administrators and assigns,' because there was no reference to any land." Gilbert Kodilinye, *Commonwealth Caribbean Property Law* 161 (2005).

In the following sentence, the same root appears in two words that, in context, have remote senses (the verb *impress* and the noun *impression*): "From what has been said we are convinced that appellant's profits in question were not *impressed* with a trust when they first came into existence. The Board *was obviously of the impression* [read *obviously thought*] that the trust first attached when appellant credited them to the beneficiaries on his books of account." *Brainard v. Commissioner*, 91 F.2d 880, 883 (7th Cir. 1937).

D. Arrhythmic Plodding. "Nevertheless, the lengthy process of securing a final state-court judgment that reviews the Board's denial—which envisions state district court trial, intermediate state court appeal, and state supreme court certiorari review—augurs much-belated and possibly ineffective relief to a recent law-school graduate ultimately held to have been improperly denied a certificate of fitness that would have made him eligible to take a bar examination soon after he had completed his legal studies and received his law degree." *Thomas v. Kadish*, 748 F.2d 276, 281 (5th Cir. 1984). This sentence can hardly be meaningfully read aloud on the first or second try. It should be split into smaller clauses in which the emphasis—the author's implied intonation—is clearer.

E. Jarring Contrasts. Be sensitive to unintended syntactic whiplash—e.g.:

- "That such tenancy found its existence in the lease of July 14, 1904, is admittedly true, for plaintiff contends that defendant is holding *over under* it, and defendant contends that he is holding *under* it." *F.H. Stoltze Land Co. v. Westberg*, 206 P. 407, 409 (Mont. 1922). Who has the upper hand? [Read: . . . *for the plaintiff contends that the defendant is a holdover tenant—in violation of the lease—whereas the defendant contends that he is holding in accordance with the lease.*]
- "*There* is *here* no claimed invasion of any substantive constitutional right." *Findeisen v. North East Indep. Sch. Dist.*, 749 F.2d 234, 240 (5th Cir. 1984). [Contextual rewrite: *Findeisen does not claim that the school has invaded any substantive constitutional right.*]

F. Misleading Parts of Speech. In the following sentence, *will* (futurity) sounds like *will* (testament): "Although the courts have been more liberal in admitting extrinsic evidence for the purpose of integrating holographs than they have for the purpose of integrating attested *wills*, it is likely that the proponent *will* have to rely upon evidence appearing in the various pages because sufficient extrinsic evidence may be impossible to obtain." John Ritchie et al., *Case and Materials on Decedents' Estates and Trusts* 256 (1982).

For related subjects, see ANFRACTUOSITY, INITIALESE, MINGLE-MANGLE, MISCUES & SENTENCE LENGTH.

soup, in England, is legal slang equivalent to *dock brief* or to the fee involved in such a brief. See **dock brief.**

sources of law. As Holland pointed out, this phrase is ambiguous. It is commonly used in four senses, i.e., to refer to: (1) the place from which we obtain our knowledge of the law, e.g., whether from the statute-book, the reports, or treatises (literary source); (2) the ultimate authority that backs up the law, i.e., the state (formal source); (3) the causes that have, seemingly automatically, brought into existence rules that have subsequently acquired legal force, such as custom, religion, and scientific discussion (historical or material sources); or (4) the organs through which the state either grants legal recognition to rules previously unauthoritative, or itself creates new law, such as legislation and adjudication (legal source). *See* Thomas E. Holland, *The Elements of Jurisprudence* 55 (13th ed. 1924).

sovereignty; *sovranty. The first spelling is preferred. Brierly rightly calls *sovereignty* a "much abused word." J.L. Brierly, *The Law of Nations* 150 (5th ed. 1955). It has three primary senses: (1) "supreme dominion, authority, or rule"; (2) "the position, rank, or control of a supreme ruler, such as a monarch, or controlling power, such as a democratically formed government";

or (3) "a territory under the rule of a sovereign, or existing as an independent state." To the international lawyer, *sovereignty* "is not a metaphysical concept, nor is it part of the essence of statehood; it is merely a term which designates an aggregate of particular and very extensive claims that states habitually make for themselves in their relations with other states [sense 1]. To the extent that *sovereignty* ha[s] come to imply that there is something inherent in the nature of states that makes it impossible for them to be subjected to law, it is a false doctrine which the facts of international relations do not support." *Id.* at 48–49.

spatial; *spacial. The first spelling is preferred both in AmE and in BrE.

spatter. See **blood spatter.**

spawn litigation is a legal CLICHÉ.

speaking. A. *Speaking Motions* and the Like. Through HYPALLAGE, *speaking* has evolved in legal JARGON as an adjective denoting some type of impermissible or extraordinary communication. A *speaking motion*, for example, is one that requires consideration of facts outside the pleadings; a *speaking objection* is one laced with comments or arguments that reach beyond the legal grounds for the objection; a *speaking demurrer*, in former practice, was one that introduced a new fact or facts not contained in the original petition.

A related term without the connotation of impermissibility is the phrase *speaking order* (= an order that not only commands but also gives reasons for the court's action). E.g.: "The decision in the *Northumberland Case* opened up new possibilities in certiorari when there was a '*speaking order*'—i.e. a record of judgement or decision giving reasons [that] could, if necessary, be assailed for error of law." Carleton K. Allen, *Law in the Making* 573–74 (7th ed. 1964).

B. As a Sentence Adverb. The word *speaking* is among the few "acceptable danglers" or "disguised conjunctions" when used as a sentence adverb. E.g.:

- "*Speaking in general terms*, it is desirable to speed the growth of technical legal meanings." Lon L. Fuller, *Legal Fictions* 23 (1967).
- "*Speaking very generally*, the answer to this question is that contractual obligations are absolute, and that absence of fault is no defence." P.S. Atiyah, *An Introduction to the Law of Contract* 184 (3d ed. 1981).

See DANGLERS (A) & SENTENCE ADVERBS.

special. See **especial** & **write specially.**

special appearance. See *de bene esse.*

special damages. See **general damages** & **damages.**

special guardian. See **guardian** *ad litem.*

special interrogatory. See **special verdict.**

special issue. See **general issue** & **special verdict.**

speciality. See **specialty.**

special limitation; executory limitation; condition subsequent. The ideas denoted by these terms are so intricate that it is difficult if not impossible to explain them without falling into JARGON. Here is an attempt at least to minimize the jargon. A *special limitation* is a restriction on the estate of a grantee who is a first taker, arising either when the grant creates a possibility of reverter or when a third party acquires a defeasing interest after the grant. An *executory limitation* is a restriction on the estate of a grantee who is the first taker, arising when a defeasing interest in a third party is granted simultaneously with the grantee's present interest. A *condition subsequent* is an event that, when it occurs or fails to occur, gives the grantor or the grantor's successors the right to end an existing estate. See **condition (B)** & **condition precedent.**

special litigation committee = a committee of independent corporate directors assigned to investigate the merits of a derivative shareholder action and, if appropriate, to recommend maintaining or dismissing the suit. The phrase dates from the 1970s, when the device it denotes sprang into existence in response to shareholder litigation.

special pleading. See POPULARIZED LEGAL TECHNICALITIES.

special property. See **general property.**

specialty; speciality. The legal term for a contract under seal is spelled *specialty* in both AmE and BrE. In the general lay sense "a special thing," the word is *specialty* in AmE, *speciality* in BrE.

special verdict; special interrogatory; special issue. These synonymous phrases refer to a jury question that requires detailed, specific answers about each factual issue—as opposed to a *general verdict, general interrogatory,* or *general issue,* which asks merely who wins. See **general issue.**

specie; species. *Specie* /**spee**-shee/ means "coined money"; it has no plural, unless one means to refer to different types of coined money. *Species* /**spee**-sheez/ or /-seez/ is both singular and plural and means "a group of similar plants and animals that can breed with each other but not with others." From that sense have grown natural extensions of the meaning of the word. Sometimes *species* is correctly used as an equivalent of *type,* as here: "Loss of services was the gist of this *species* of action." Sir James Dowling & Archer Ryland, 7 *Reports of Cases Argued and Determined in the Court of King's Bench* 134 (1827). The writer of the following sentence was erroneously attempting to make *specie* a singular of *species:* "Penalties are a *specie* [read *species*] of punishment for wrongdoing

and are not looked upon with favor." 14 *Cyclopedia of Federa* 181 (1944). The same blunder appears in the title of an article: Harold S. Bloomenthal, *Shareholder Derivative Actions Under the Securities Laws—Phoenix or Endangered Specie* [read *Species*]?, 26 Ariz. L. Rev. 767 (1984). For more on *species,* see **genus (A).**

In specie (= in kind; specifically; without any kind of substitution) is a LATINISM that is sometimes justified in providing a valuable nuance to legal writing. E.g.:

- "Apparently the Stuarts sought only to compel forced loans of money and impose taxes and levies under claim of prerogative, but not to take property *in specie.*" Roscoe Pound, *The Development of Constitutional Guarantees of Liberty* 108 (1957).
- "[A] claim of the 'proceeds' of certain property is improper, the property still being *in specie.* . . . But it is not improper if the property has been sold by order of court *before* the time for filing schedules has expired." 1 Harold Remington, *A Treatise on the Bankruptcy Law of the United States* 861 (1915).

In specie has given rise to the elliptical adjectival form *specie:* "The executor will permit beneficiaries of any and all trusts hereunder to enjoy the *specie* use or benefit of any household goods, chattels, or other tangible personal property." John Ritchie et al., *Cases and Materials on Decedents' Estates and Trusts* 203 (1982).

-specific. In legal writing, this word is increasingly used as a combining form, as in *fact-specific, city-specific,* and even *newsrack-specific*—e.g.: "The City of Lakewood finds itself between a rock and a hard place: make the rules *newsrack-specific,* and be accused of drawing the noose too tightly around First Amendment protected activities; apply more general rules to newsracks, and be told that your regulators lack standards sufficiently specific to pass constitutional muster." *City of Lakewood v. Plain Dealer Publ'g Co.,* 486 U.S. 750, 795 (1988) (White, J., dissenting).

specific. See **genus (A).**

specific implement. See **specific performance.**

specific intent. See **intention (E)** & **general intent.**

specific legacy. See **legacy.**

specific performance; specific relief; specific implement. In contract cases in which damages would not be an adequate remedy—as where the sale of rare or valuable articles, or of land, is concerned—the court may use its equitable powers to order *specific performance,* i.e., that the contract be performed. E.g.:

- "What is commonly called the *specific performance* of contracts is the doing of what was agreed to be done, but not at the time when it was agreed to be done; i.e., not till after the time when it was agreed to be done is past, and hence not till the contract is broken." C.C. Langdell, *A Brief Survey of Equity Jurisdiction* (pt. 3), 1 Harv. L. Rev. 355, 355–56 (1888).

An asterisk (✳) precedes words and phrases that are invariably inferior forms.

- "In American commentary it has become a truism to say that the once exceptional remedy of *specific performance* is rapidly becoming the order of the day." Grant Gilmore, *The Death of Contract* 83 (1974).

In both AmE and BrE, *specific relief* is a synonym—e.g.: "Chancery intervened by granting *specific relief*, such as the performance of an obligation, or the return of goods which had been lent to defendant." L.B. Curzon, *English Legal History* 108 (2d ed. 1979).

Specific implement is the equivalent phrase in Scots law.

specious. See **spurious.**

spectate. See BACK-FORMATIONS.

specter; spectre. This favorite word of legal writers is preferably spelled *-er* in AmE, *-re* in BrE. Curiously, however, many Americans cling to the British spelling—e.g.:

- "We were not halted by the *spectre* [read *specter*] of an inability to prejudge every future case." *Dillon v. Legg*, 441 P.2d 912, 922 (Cal. 1968).
- "The majority raise a frightening *spectre* [read *specter*] of long delays in processing applications for permits." *San Diego Coast Reg'l Comm'n v. See the Sea, Ltd.*, 513 P.2d 129, 135 (Cal. 1973) (Mosk, J., dissenting).
- "'Properly constituted military authorities' had raised the *spectre* [read *specter*] of a Japanese invasion." Lawrence M. Friedman, *A History of American Law* 526 (3d ed. 2005).

In American writing, the usual spelling of many other words such as *theater* is *-er*. See -ER (C).

spectrum. Pl. *spectra.* See PLURALS (A).

sped. See **speeded.**

speech, in BrE, can refer to a judgment (i.e., a judicial opinion) in the House of Lords. The term derives from the law lords' custom of delivering their pronouncements orally, as parliamentary "speeches." E.g.:

- "It should, however, be said that not all the law lords agreed with Lord Radcliffe, and that in a number of *speeches* (including, indeed, that of Lord Radcliffe himself) there is evidence of support for a third 'theory.'" P.S. Atiyah, *An Introduction to the Law of Contract* 209–10 (3d ed. 1981).
- "Lord Simon of Glaisdale also canvassed the possibility of prospective overruling in a dissenting *speech* in an earlier case." Rupert Cross & J.W. Harris, *Precedent in English Law* 232 (4th ed. 1991).

See **decision.**

speechify (= to deliver a speech) is typically used in a mocking or derogatory way. Cf. **argufy.**

speed, all deliberate. See **with all deliberate speed.**

speeded; sped. The best preterit and past-participial form of the verb *to speed* is *sped*, except in the PHRASAL VERB *to speed up* (= to accelerate) <she speeded up to 80 m.p.h.>.

speedy trial. The Sixth Amendment to the U.S. Constitution declares that "in all criminal prosecutions, the accused shall enjoy the right to a *speedy . . . trial*." In 1974, Congress enacted the Speedy Trial Act (18 U.S.C. § 3161), which set time limits for indicting, arraigning, and prosecuting federal criminal defendants. *Speedy* refers to the point of beginning important events in the prosecution—not the speed with which they are carried out.

speluncean, adj. Many lawyers and law professors have occasion to use this word because of Lon Fuller's classic law-review article, *The Case of the Speluncean Explorers*, 62 Harv. L. Rev. 616 (1949). Some *spelunkers* /spi-**lənk**-ərz/, during one of their *spelunking* /spi-**lənk**-king/ expeditions, are trapped in a cave, and several survive only by killing and eating one of their number. But back to the key word in the title: *speluncean*. It has a soft *-c-*: /spi-**lən**-see-ən/. That's the only recognized pronunciation of the word, which means "of or pertaining to caves." Yet the great majority of law professors who teach the case, and the lawyers and judges who refer to it, mouth it with a hard /k/ sound in the penultimate syllable—a venial error.

spiel (= a set monologue or rehearsed oral presentation) is pronounced /speel/, not in the mock-Yiddish fashion that has become so common (/shpeel/).

spirit, in matters of interpretation, refers to a general purpose: hence, the *spirit of the law* is frequently contrasted with the *letter of the law*. E.g.:

- "As in all interpretations, the '*spirit*' of constitutional texts or the '*spirit*' of constitutions began to be invoked and it became necessary to give a content to abstract constitutional formulas exactly as the civilian has had to give a content for modern purposes to abstract oracular texts of the Roman Books." Roscoe Pound, *The Formative Era of American Law* 97 (1938).
- "It is an almost inevitable feature of legal systems in their adolescence that the *spirit* of the law is overshadowed by the letter of procedure, . . . the demands of precision far outweigh[ing] those of abstract justice." H.G. Hanbury, *English Courts of Law* 34 (2d ed. 1953).

See **letter of the law.**

spiritual; spiritualistic; spirituous; spiritous; spirituel; spirituelle; spirited. *Spiritual* is the broadest of these terms, meaning "of spirit as opposed to matter; of the soul; concerned with sacred or religious things." *Spiritualistic* = of or relating to spiritualism, i.e., the belief that departed spirits communicate with and show themselves to the living, esp. through mediums. *Spirituous* = alcoholic. E.g.: "The indictment charges the unlawful sale of *spirituous* liquors within two miles of Bethel Methodist Church in Macon County." *State v. Downs*, 21 S.E. 689, 689 (N.C. 1895). *Spiritous* is an ARCHAISM in the sense of "highly refined or dematerialized," and is also a NEEDLESS VARIANT of *spirituous*. *Spirituel* (masculine) or *spirituelle* (feminine) means "witty" or "of a highly refined character or nature, esp. in conjunction with liveliness or quickness of mind" (*OED*). *Spirited* means "vivacious" <a spirited performance> or "of a certain nature" <mean-spirited taunts>.

spit > spat > spat. Occasionally *spit* wrongly displaces *spat* as the past-tense or past-participial form—e.g.: "The portraits of downtown life are almost always moving—in spite of the grime and foul language *spit* [read *spat*] through rotten teeth." Soto, *New Poems, Stories on America's "Unwashed"*, Japan Times, 3 June 1990, at 14.

splatter. See **blood spatter.**

split between (or in) the circuits. See **circuit split.**

SPLIT INFINITIVES abound in legal writing, often needlessly—but they are not invariably wrong. The English language gives us "the inestimable advantage of being able to put adverbs where they will be most effective, coloring the verbs to which they apply and becoming practically part of them . . . . If you think a verb cannot be split in two, just call the adverb a part of the verb and the difficulty will be solved." Joseph Lee, *A Defense of the Split Infinitive*, 37 Mass. L.Q. 65, 66 (1952).

H.W. Fowler divided the English-speaking world into five classes: (1) those who neither know nor care what a split infinitive is; (2) those who do not know, but care very much; (3) those who know and condemn; (4) those who know and approve; and (5) those who know and distinguish. (*MEU2* 579.) It is this last class to which, if we have a good ear, we should aspire. See SUPERSTITIONS (B).

An infinitive, of course, is the tenseless form of a verb preceded by *to*, such as *to reverse* or *to modify*. Splitting the infinitive is placing one or more words between *to* and the verb, such as *to summarily reverse* or *to unwisely modify*.

A. Splits to Be Avoided. If a split is easily fixed by putting the adverb at the end of the phrase, and the meaning remains the same, then avoiding the split is the best course:

> Split: "It is not necessary *to here enlarge* upon them."

> Unsplit: "It is not necessary *to enlarge* upon them *here*."

This is an excellent example of the capricious split infinitive, which serves no purpose, unless that purpose is to jar the reader. Similar examples turn up frequently in legal writing—e.g.:

- "*In order for someone to voluntarily take a risk* [read *For someone to take a risk voluntarily*] he must know the dangers involved, and decide to take the risk anyway." James E. Alatis & G. Richard Tucker, *Language in Public Life* 184 (1979).
- "Officers are expected *to almost automatically possess a sophisticated ability* [read: *to possess an almost automatic, sophisticated ability*] to differentiate a bias crime from an ordinary crime—and of course, relatively few do." David A. Nelwert, *Death on the Fourth of July* 204 (2005).
- "This type of unintentional noncompliance may require IRS *to more clearly explain the EITC requirements* [read: *to explain the EITC requirements more clearly*] within related forms and publications." *Tax Compliance* 19 (report to the Senate Finance Committee, 2005).

Wide splits are to be avoided—e.g.: "This Court encourages Plaintiffs' counsel to utilize best efforts *to understandingly, sympathetically, and professionally arrive at* [read *to arrive understandingly, sympathetically, and professionally at*] a mutual agreement as to the individual allotment of fees." *In re Combustion, Inc.*, 968 F.Supp. 1116, 1141 (W.D. La. 1997).

With correlative conjunctions, a split infinitive simply displays carelessness—e.g.: "White was *to either make or obtain* [read *either to make or to obtain*] a loan." Edward Allan Farnsworth & William Franklin Young, *Cases and Materials on Contracts* 237 (1988). The construction invites unparallel syntax—e.g.: "It is not the mandate of the TPRB *to either make or to enforce* [read *either to make or to enforce*] WTO rules." Yan Luo, *Anti-Dumping in the WTO* 24 (2010). See PARALLELISM.

B. Justified Splits. A number of infinitives are best split. Perhaps the most famous is from the 1960s television series *Star Trek*, in which the opening voice-over included this phrase: *to boldly go where no man*—or, in the revival of the 1980s and 1990s, *where no one*—*has gone before*. The phrase sounds inevitable partly because it is so familiar, but also because the adverb most naturally bears the emphasis, not the verb *go*.

And that example is not a rarity. Consider: *She expects to more than double her profits next year*. We cannot merely move the adverbial phrase in that sentence—to "fix" the split, we would have to eliminate the infinitive, as by writing, *She expects her profits to more than double next year*, thereby giving the sentence a different nuance. (The woman seems less responsible for the increase.)

Again, though, knowing when to split an infinitive requires a good ear and a keen eye. Otherwise, the ability to distinguish—the ability Fowler mentioned—is not attainable. *To flatly state*, for example, suggests something different from *to state flatly*. In the sentences that follow, unsplitting the infinitive would either create an awkwardness or change the sense:

- "[The statute] denies to respondent the right *to reasonably manage* or control its own business." *Minneapolis & St. Louis R.R. v. Minnesota*, 193 U.S. 53, 59 (1904) (per McKenna, J.).
- "The great progress of the art, which owed little to financiers and much to operating men, had reduced costs fast enough *to pretty well cover* the manipulations of the holding companies." Robert H. Jackson, *The Struggle for Judicial Supremacy* 142 (1941).
- "Imagine what the Court would have said if Congress had tried *to expressly delegate* the matter to the Court." Charles P. Curtis Jr., *Lions Under the Throne* 242 (1947).
- "A marketing concept does not by confidentiality create a continuing competitive advantage because once it is implemented it is exposed for the world to see and for

competitors *to legally imitate.*" *Richter v. Westab, Inc.*, 189 U.S.P.Q. (BNA) 321, 324 (6th Cir. 1976). Changing placement of the adverb here would change the meaning.

- "The majority improperly places the burden of proof on appellees *to affirmatively establish* the existence of a statutory exemption." *City of Houston v. Jones*, 679 S.W.2d 557, 560 (Tex. App.—Houston [14th Dist] 1984) (Sears, J., dissenting).
- "There is no compelling reason for courts *to myopically focus* only on policy text in isolation and *to affirmatively avoid* appreciating the connotation and context of the policy." 1 Jeffrey W. Stempel, *Stempel on Insurance Contracts* 4-165 (3d ed. 2006).
- "Children in the reinforcement condition . . . were more likely *to falsely claim* that they had taken the toy." G. Daniel Lassiter, *Interrogations, Confessions, and Entrapment* 113 (2006).
- "Failure *to timely file* the appropriate information return . . . can give rise to a $20 per day penalty." Bruce R. Hopkins, *The Law of Tax-Exempt Organizations* 932 (9th ed. 2007).
- "The current EU ETS is not designed *to directly attain* a competitive market equilibrium on the production market." Stefan Weishaar, *Towards Auctioning* 216 (2009).

Distinguishing these examples from those under (A) may not be easy for all readers. Those who find it difficult might advantageously avoid all splits.

C. Awkwardness Caused by Avoiding Splits. Occasionally, though, sticking to the old "rule" about split infinitives leads to gross phrasing. The following sentences illustrate clumsy attempts to avoid splitting the infinitive. In the first and second examples, the adverb may be placed more naturally than it is without splitting the infinitive; in the third example, a split is called for.

- "The Japanese government's failure to prosecute laborrights violations endured by trafficking women allowed employers to continue *unjustly to enrich themselves* [read *to enrich themselves unjustly*] and thus encouraged the further exploitation of the women." Kinsey Dinan, *Owned Justice: Thai Women Trafficked into Debt Bondage in Japan* 57 (2000).
- "There were too few nurses of calibre *effectively to superintend the unit* [read *to superintend the unit effectively*]." Paul Elliott Rock, *Reconstructing a Women's Prison* 297 (1996).
- "The court declined *judicially to interpret* [read *to judicially interpret*] the noun 'child' as used in the statute to include a 'dependent stepchild.'" Stuart M. Speiser, *Recovery for Wrongful Death* 145 (1990).

split sentence = a criminal penalty involving a short jail term—to expose the offender to the unpleasantness of prison—followed by a period of probation. Its use is described and defended in *ABA Standards for Criminal Justice* ch. 18, at 100–07 (2d ed. 1980), though as an unnamed "intermediate sanction" rather than under the name *split sentence*.

splitting the baby has become a legal CLICHÉ to describe an adjudicated compromise imposed on two contending parties—usually with the implication that such a resolution is unsatisfactory. Alluding to the biblical story of Solomon's ruse that revealed which of two contending women was truly the baby's mother, this phrase appears to have come into legal use in AmE first in the mid-1960s: "Without questioning the Solomonic simplicity of this resolution, it is no more permissible than *splitting the baby* would have been conscionable." *Conlon v. McCoy*, 278 N.Y.S.2d 449, 452 (App. Div. 1967).

spoils; spoil; pillage; plunder; booty; prize; loot. These terms all denote property acquired by successful aggressors. *Spoils* originally denoted the movables that a military victor acquired from a defeated enemy after ransacking a ship, stripping a town of its valuables, etc. By extension, *spoils* came to denote land as well as movable property taken over by conquering forces. By further extension in modern usage (not SLIPSHOD EXTENSION), the term applies to any advantage that comes within the power of a victorious competitor, whether that is a range of political appointments made available to a successful candidate or a prestigious trophy awarded to a winning athlete. Although the singular *spoil* is older—and is more likely to bear the earlier, more literal meanings—the plural *spoils* is now more usual in all senses <to the victor go the spoils> <the spoils of war>.

Pillage suggests a messier kind of wartime violence, as by brigands or disorderly marauders on a rampage. (The word is more commonly a verb <they pillaged the city>.) *Plunder* also suggests outright violence, but it included the acts of criminal bandits and highwaymen as well as soldiers.

Booty is essentially synonymous with *plunder*, but with the added connotation that the valuables will be systematically distributed to members of a band—and to the popular mind the word is especially associated with pirates. Yet in international law, *booty* refers specifically to spoils taken on land, while *prize* refers to spoils (including warships) captured on the high seas or within territorial waters.

If a more disparaging expression is needed, *loot* is essentially interchangeable with any of the terms discussed above. It is especially pejorative because it so often denotes the valuables stolen from the dead or the helpless victims of a natural disaster, as from stores and houses during a violent riot.

spoliation; *spoilation. *Spoliation*, a learned word, is, in the hands and mouths of the less-than-learned, often misspelled and mispronounced **spoilation*, as in a 1992 legal seminar on the subject of "*Spoilation* [read *Spoliation*] of Evidence." The difference between the form of the verb and of the noun—though etymologically the words are identical—is understandably the source of confusion. That difference arises from different paths by which the words came into English: in the 14th century, *spoil* was borrowed from Old French (*espoille*), whereas in the 15th century *spoliation* was borrowed from Latin (*spoliātio*).

spotted pony case. See **whitehorse case.**

spousal, adj. The *OED* defines this term as (1) "of, pertaining to, or relating to espousal or marriage; nuptial; matrimonial"; or (2) "(of a hymn, poem, etc.)

celebrating or commemorating an espousal or marriage." *W3* contains like definitions. In modern American law, however, *spousal* means "of, relating to, or by a spouse or spouses." E.g.: "Palimony is a *spousal* support substitute for alimony or *spousal* support for people who are not married." Sandra Choron & Harry Choron, *Planet Wedding* 162 (2010). See **interspousal**.

spousals; espousals. Both are old-fashioned terms, verging on ARCHAISMS. *Spousals* = the agreement to marry, as opposed to the actual exchange of vows. *Espousals* = the making of any spiritual union, esp. one that depends on a vow or pledge. *Espousals* is sometimes used more specifically as a synonym for *spousals*, but the DIFFERENTIATION between the words is something that careful writers—to the extent that they use the words at all—should want to further.

spouse is a word that lawyers use much more often than nonlawyers, who are accustomed to husbands and wives. Certainly in referring to a particular husband or wife, *spouse* is not the best word—e.g.: "We know that the design and text of the Code bears the inimitable imprint of its chief draftsman, Karl N. Llewellyn, and that his *spouse* [read *wife*], Soia Mentschikoff, had a major hand in the entire project." James J. White & Robert S. Summers, *Uniform Commercial Code* § 1, at 5 (3d ed. 1988).

spread, vb. The figurative parliamentary idiom *to spread upon the minutes* has been extended in legal usage to other printed matter, and, as in the first example, even to unprinted matter. E.g.:

- "Such a context is presented here, where the powerfully incriminating extrajudicial statements of a codefendant, who stands accused side-by-side with the defendant, are deliberately *spread before the jury* in a joint trial." *Bruton v. U.S.*, 391 U.S. 123, 135–36 (1968) (per Brennan, J.).
- "In *Weaver v. Ward* it is said that the facts constituting an excuse, and showing that the defendant was free from negligence, should have been *spread upon the record*, in order that the court might judge." Oliver Wendell Holmes, *The Path of the Law and the Common Law* 129 (J. Craig Williams ed., 2009).

springing use; shifting use. A *springing use* is one that arises on the occurrence of a future event, whereas a *shifting use* is one that operates to terminate a preceding use. A *springing use* arises, for example, when property is given to Johnson to the use of Gilbert when Gilbert marries; Gilbert has a springing use that vests in him when he marries. A *shifting use*, by contrast, might arise when property is given to Johnson to the use of Gilbert, but then to Bradley when Foster pays $1,000 to Burke; Bradley has a shifting use that arises when Foster makes the specified payment. In G.B., *secondary use* is a variant of *shifting use*, although all these terms are of historical interest only there. See **use.**

spurious; specious. *Spurious* is used in reference to things, and *specious* to arguments or reasoning.

Spurious = not genuine. *Specious* = having superficial appeal but false. E.g.: "Many *specious* reasons for practices revolting to our ideas of justice may be found in old books." George W. Warvelle, *Essays in Legal Ethics* 129 (2d ed. 1920).

spurious construction; spurious interpretation. See *spurious interpretation* under INTERPRETATION, MODES OF (B).

S.R. & O. See **S.I.**

ss. A. As Mysterious Legal Abbreviation. The sign *ss.* is an abbreviation that often appears on the top of the first page of an affidavit or acknowledgment—e.g.:

> District of Columbia, *ss.*:
>
> John Rand, being duly sworn, deposes and says that he has read the foregoing bill by him subscribed and knows the contents . . . .
> > Eugene A. Jones, *Manual of Equity Pleading and Practice* 39 (1916).

Many possible etymologies have been suggested for this mysterious abbreviation. One is that it signifies *scilicet* (= namely, to wit), which is usually abbreviated *sc.* or *scil.* Another is that *ss.* represents "the two gold letters at the ends of the chain of office or 'collar' worn by the Lord Chief Justice of the King's Bench." Max Radin, *Law Dictionary* 327 (1955). Mellinkoff suggests that the precise etymology is unknown: "Lawyers have been using *ss* for nine hundred years and still are not sure what it means." David Mellinkoff, *The Language of the Law* 296 (1963).

In fact, though, it is a flourish deriving from the Year Books—an equivalent of the paragraph mark: "§." Hence Lord Hardwicke's statement that *ss.* is nothing more than a division mark. See *Jodderrell v. Cowell*, 95 Eng. Rep. 222, 222 (K.B. 1737) ("The word *ss.*, I verily believe, was not originally meant to the county, but only a denotation of each section or paragraph in the record."). An early formbook writer incorporated it into his forms, and ever since it has been mindlessly perpetuated by one generation after another.

American lawyers have puzzled over its meaning and have even wasted time litigating whether it is necessary in affidavits. *See, e.g., Seay v. Shrader*, 95 N.W. 690, 691 (Neb. 1903). There are no judicious uses of this LEGALISM.

B. As an Equivalent of "§§." In BrE, *ss.* frequently means "sections"—e.g.:

- "Forgery Act 1913 ss. 8(2)." Citation in Glanville Williams, *Textbook of Criminal Law* 389 n.4 (1978).
- "Under the *Statute of Frauds*, 1667, ss. 1, 2, it was enacted that leases . . . had to be in writing." L.B. Curzon, *English Legal History* 317 (2d ed. 1979).

stabilize; *stabilify; *stabilitate. The second and third are NEEDLESS VARIANTS.

stadium. Several dictionaries seem to prefer *stadia* as the plural form, but *stadiums* is the more natural and the more usual form, even in formal legal writing of several generations ago.

stagflation. See MORPHOLOGICAL DEFORMITIES.

stakeholder; stockholder. These terms are not to be confused. *Stakeholder*, missed by the *OED* but included in *W2* and *W3*, originally meant "the holder of a stake or wager," a meaning it still carries. But in modern American legal writing it usually denotes one who holds property, the right or possession of which is disputed between two other parties (as in an interpleader action).

Stockholder = (1) a shareholder in a corporation; or (2) one who is a proprietor of stock in the public funds or the funds of a joint-stock company (*OED*). Sense 1 is labeled an Americanism in the *OED*, although the *COD* definition suggests that this sense is now current in BrE. Sense 2 is largely confined to BrE. See **shareholder.**

stale, in law, means "(of a claim, demand, or offer) having lain dormant for too long to be enforceable." The term provides one of the law's more picturesque METAPHORS—e.g.: "It [may be] clear to the offeree that there has been such a long delay in the transmission of the offer as to make it obvious to the offeree that the offer was *stale* when it reached him." G.H. Treitel, *The Law of Contract* 16 (8th ed. 1991).

stanch. See **staunch.**

stand, n., is an AmE shortening of *witness stand*—e.g.: "As to any differences among themselves these clerical proficients might develop on the *stand*, these could hardly be greater than the direct contradictions exchanged between the remunerated medical experts." Herman Melville, *Billy Budd* 38 (1891; repr. N.Y., Signet, 1979). In the common idiom, a witness *takes the stand* after being sworn. See **witness-box.**

stand, vb., = to remain good law. E.g.: "Amanda Acquisition Corp. . . . claimed that the statute was unconstitutional and that if it were allowed to *stand*, the company's offer would be doomed." Laurie P. Cohen, *Court Upholds State Anti-Takeover Law That Makes Raiders Get Board Approval*, Wall St. J., 26 May 1989, at B3.

standard-form contract (= a preprinted contract, often referred to as an *adhesion contract*) is so hyphenated. E.g.: "*Standard-form contracts* are also widely used in transactions between businessmen." P.S. Atiyah, *An Introduction to the Law of Contract* 15 (3d ed. 1981).

For more on *adhesion contract*, see **adherence (A).**

standards of the industry. See **state of the art.**

stand down, in BrE, means "to step down" either literally <she stood down from the witness box> or figuratively <Tory supporters asked Margaret Thatcher to stand down before the 1990 election>.

*standee. See -EE.

standing; locus standi. These synonymous TERMS OF ART mean "a position from which one may validly make a legal claim or seek to enforce a right or duty." The first is primarily AmE, and the second (a LATINISM) is commonly used in BrE. One is said to have *standing* when one's arguments on the merits of a case can be considered by an adjudicator. E.g.:

- "The corporate interests have been largely taken care of by highly qualified lawyers acting in individual cases and by Bar Associations proposing procedural reforms that define, for example, the 'aggrieved' persons who have *standing* to object to agency orders or decisions." William O. Douglas, *Points of Rebellion* 79–80 (1970).
- "They . . . argue that no individual blind vendor or state agency would have *standing* because none has alleged a 'concrete, perceptible harm of a real, nonspeculative nature.'" *Randolph-Sheppard Vendors v. Weinberger*, 795 F.2d 90, 99 (D.C. Cir. 1986).

Joseph Vining's comments on *standing* show that its history is strikingly similar to that of many other legal NEOLOGISMS:

> The word *standing* is rather recent in the basic judicial vocabulary and does not appear to have been commonly used until the middle of [the 20th] century. No authority that I have found introduces the term with proper explanations or apologies and announces that henceforth *standing* should be used to describe who may be heard by a judge. Nor was there any sudden adoption by tacit consent. The word appears here and there, spreading very gradually with no discernible pattern. Judges and lawyers found themselves using the term and did not ask why they did so or where it came from.
>
> Joseph Vining, *Legal Identity* 55 (1978).

One of the earliest uses of the term occurred in 1877: "The mortgage and bonds under and by virtue of which the appellant claims a *standing* in court were executed by the Alabama and Chattanooga Railroad Company as a corporation." *Wallace v. Loomis*, 97 U.S. 146, 154 (1877) (per Bradley, J.). See ***locus standi.***

standpoint. See **viewpoint.**

standstill agreement (= an agreement to preserve the status quo) has become a commonplace phrase in reference to actions by parties involved in a legal dispute. The original *standstill agreement*, according to the *OED*, was concluded in 1931 between German and what would become Allied banking and commercial institutions, allowing Germany to postpone short-term credit repayments because of the country's severe economic plight. Shortly afterwards, the word came to be used in other banking situations—e.g.: "At this juncture the creditor banks in Chicago agreed to enter into what they term a 'standstill' agreement, by the terms of which they would refrain from foreclosing on their collateral and from pressing for payment on their loans." *Lincoln Printing Co. v. Middle W. Utils. Co.*, 6 F.Supp. 663, 667 (N.D. Ill. 1934). Within a couple of decades, however, the phrase had been extended considerably beyond economic and banking contexts—e.g.: "During the course of the September 14 hearing, the parties reached a 'standstill' agreement which had the effect, in part, of amending the prayer for relief." *Ramsburg v. American Inv. Co.*, 231 F.2d 333, 335 (7th Cir. 1956).

Star Chamber. In 16th- and early-17th-century England, the *Star Chamber* was a special equity court charged with keeping the peace by punishing libels, perjury, jury-packing, contempt of court, and conspiracies to pervert justice in any of the king's courts; it acted on private petition. Unacceptable practices such as compulsory self-accusation, unconscionable searches and seizures, and inquisitorial investigations "were among those intolerable abuses of the *Star Chamber*, which [was] brought . . . to an end at the hands of the Long Parliament in 1640." *Jones v. SEC*, 298 U.S. 1, 28 (1936) (per Sutherland, J.).

The origin of the court's name is unclear. Two explanations are current: (1) that the room in which the court sat had a ceiling decorated with gilded stars (*camera stellata, chambre d'estoiles*)—Coke's view (see 4 Inst. 66); or (2) that Jewish merchants' contracts, known as *starra*, were kept in the chamber in which the court conducted its work. Formerly, some writers conjectured that the name derived from O.E. *steoran* "to steer or govern"; or from its punishing of cozenage, known as *crimen stellionatus*.

Today, the phrase *Star Chamber proceeding* usually refers to an unfair judicial proceeding in which the outcome is predetermined.

stare decisis (L. "to stand by things decided") = the doctrine of precedent, under which it is necessary to follow earlier judicial decisions when the same points arise again in litigation. The full phrase is *stare decisis et quieta non movere* (= to stand by things decided and not disturb settled points). See **precedent (A)**.

Though a verb phrase in Latin, the phrase is used as a noun phrase in English—e.g.:

- "The courts are actually returning more and more to a *stare decisis* of principles [that] prevailed during the earlier centuries of the law's history, as distinguished from a narrow *stare decisis* based on mere decisions." William F. Walsh, *A Treatise on Equity* iii (1930).
- "Judicial precedent has some persuasive effect almost everywhere because *stare decisis* (keep to what has been decided previously) is a maxim of practically universal application." Rupert Cross & J.W. Harris, *Precedent in English Law* 3 (4th ed. 1991).

In AmE, the phrase has even come to be used commonly as an adjectival phrase—e.g.: "If adherence to a precedent actually impedes the stable and orderly adjudication of future cases, its *stare decisis effect* [read *precedential effect*] is also diminished." *Citizens United v. Federal Election Comm'n*, 130 S.Ct. 876, 921 (2010) (Roberts, C.J., dissenting). On the question whether to hyphenate such an adjectival use, see PHRASAL ADJECTIVES (B).

The phrase is pronounced /**stahr**-ee/ or /**stair**-ee də-**sī**-sis/. As one might expect, judges are better at

pronouncing the phrase than senators are: "One unresolved issue appeared to be the pronunciation for 'stare decisis.' Clarence Thomas pronounced 'stare' like the word for a clear night—'starry'—while Sen. Orrin Hatch said 'stairay' and Sen. Patrick Leahy, 'star-ay.'" *Legal Lexicon*, A.B.A. J., Aug. 1993, at 44.

start. See **commence**.

state, n., = (in international law) an institutional system of relations that people within a territory establish among themselves to secure order. Brierly warns that *state* "should not be confused with the whole community of persons living on its territory; it is only one among a multitude of other institutions, such as churches and corporations, [that] a community establishes for securing different objects, though obviously it is one of tremendous importance." J.L. Brierly, *The Law of Nations* 118 (5th ed. 1955).

Within a legal system, as in the U.S., *state* may denote an institution of self-government (e.g., Vermont) within a larger entity (the United States), which can also be called a *state*. Many countries such as Canada have other political subdivisions, such as provinces; others, like England, have counties. The name chosen generally reflects the extent of the smaller entity's powers—*states* having more power than *provinces*, and *provinces* more power than *counties*; but there are no invariable rules on this point.

See **nation** & **people (B)**.

state action (= governmental feasance) is a phrase used in international as well as in constitutional law. E.g.: "What the Crown does to foreigners by its agents is *state action* . . . beyond the scope of domestic jurisdiction." *Johnstone v. Pedlar*, [1921] 2 A.C. 262, 290 (per Lord Sumner).

In constitutional law, *state action* often appears in the context of civil rights and denotes some type of illegal governmental intrusion into a person's life. E.g.: "If the State requires a certain electoral procedure, prescribes a general election ballot made up of party nominees so chosen and limits the choice of the electorate in general elections for state offices, practically speaking, to those whose names appear on such a ballot, it endorses, adopts and enforces the discrimination against Negroes . . . . This is *state action* within the meaning of the Fifteenth Amendment." *Smith v. Allwright*, 321 U.S. 649, 664 (1944) (per Reed, J.). In the wake of *Smith*, the U.S. Supreme Court broadened the concept of state action to strike down segregation laws under the Fourteenth and Fifteenth Amendments.

stated. In the phrase *account stated*, the word *stated* means "settled, closed, at an end." E.g.: "Norell Forest Products (Norell) sued H & S Lumber Company (H & S) on an *account stated*." *Norell Forest Prods. v. H & S Lumber Co.*, 417 S.E.2d 96, 98 (S.C. Ct. App. 1992). The phrase is sometimes written *stated account*. See **account stated**.

---

stated otherwise is a pompous version of *in other words*—e.g.: "*Stated otherwise* [read *In other words*], she must demonstrate that it is more likely than not that the defendant acted with scienter." *Tellabs, Inc. v. Makor Issues & Rights, Ltd.*, 551 U.S. 308, 329 (2007) (per Ginsburg, J.). Cf. **to put it another way.**

statehouse (= a state capitol) is an Americanism dating from the 17th century. For the distinction between *capitol* and *capital*, see **capital.**

statement. Though to a nonlawyer the usage is counterintuitive, the word *statement* in law commonly includes expressive nonverbal behavior as well as the spoken word. For example, Rule 801(a) of the Federal Rules of Evidence defines *statement* as either "(1) an oral or written assertion or (2) nonverbal conduct of a person, if it is intended by the person as an assertion."

statement of claim is the modern BrE phrase for the plaintiff's first pleading. Formerly, at common law, it was called either a *statement of claim* or a *declaration*. (See COMMON-LAW PLEADINGS & **declaration.**) In the U.S., it is usually called either a *complaint* or a *petition*, and in Scotland a *summons* or *initial writ*.

statement of facts. See **record** (B) & **report of proceedings.**

state of the art, n.; **state-of-the-art,** adj. These VOGUE WORDS illustrate the interests of a fast-changing society with rapidly produced technological innovations <state-of-the-art products>. For the moment, they are tainted by association with the cant of salespeople.

Notably, *state of the art* is distinguishable from *standards of the industry* because the former refers to that which the most advanced technology allows, as opposed to that which is in common use within an industry. See *Cantu v. John Deere Co.*, 603 P.2d 839, 840 (Wash. Ct. App. 1979) (saying, "We believe the two phrases are not synonymous.").

state's evidence, to turn. See **turn state's evidence.**

states' rights (= those rights and powers not delegated to the federal government by the U.S. Constitution nor prohibited by it for the states to exercise) is so punctuated, unless used as a PHRASAL ADJECTIVE calling for a hyphen <a states'-rights argument>.

The agent noun is *states'-righter*—e.g.: "In recent times the situation has been the precise reverse, so that solid citizens are not *states'-righters* and liberals put greater faith in the federal government, even under conservative auspices." Fred Rodell, *Nine Men* 77 (1955).

*stati. See **status** (B).

stationary; stationery. The first is the adjective ("remaining in one place"), the second the noun ("materials for writing on or with").

statistic (= a single term or datum in a statistical compilation) is a BACK-FORMATION from *statistics* dating

from the late 19th century. Today its correctness is beyond challenge—e.g.:

- "Brady's daughter's testimony was neither inappropriate nor excessive. It provided some description of the victim as a 'unique human being,' rather than a mere *statistic*, without glorifying or enlarging the victim." *St. Clair v. Commonwealth*, 319 S.W.3d 300, 317 (Ky. 2010).
- "The majority recites the *statistic* that 81.9 percent of sentences imposed in the Fourth Circuit in fiscal year 2009 fell within the advisory Guideline range." *U.S. v. Lewis*, 606 F.3d 193, 208 (4th Cir. 2010) (Goodwin, J., concurring in part & dissenting in part).

statu quo, in. See **in statu quo.**

status. A. Legal Sense. *Status* = a summation of or basis for the legal grounds of various capacities or incapacities, for example, one's age, mental state, and the like. "*Status* is . . . belonging to a particular class of persons to all of whom the law assigns particular legal powers, capacities, liabilities or incapacities." 1 David M. Walker, *Principles of Scottish Private Law* 198 (3d ed. 1982). Generally speaking, as *statuses* have been assimilated in Anglo-American law, *status* has dwindled in interest and importance as a legal topic. See D. Neil MacCormick, "General Legal Concepts," in 11 *The Laws of Scotland: Stair Memorial Encyclopedia* ¶ 1070, at 389 (1990).

B. Plural. *Status* forms the plural *statuses* (or, in Latin, *status*), not **stati*: "But this does not militate against the defendants' essential argument that while the jurors come from all socio-economic *stati* [read *statuses*], they represent, on the whole, the higher echelons of the community as opposed to the lower." *U.S. v. Duke*, 263 F.Supp. 828, 833–34 (S.D. Ind. 1967). See HYPERCORRECTION (A).

status quo; status quo ante; *status in quo. *Status quo* means "the state of affairs at present"; hence **current status quo* is a REDUNDANCY. *Status quo ante* (= the state of affairs at a previous time) is a common and useful LATINISM in contexts involving torts or contracts—e.g.:

- "The first and most obvious result of rescinding a contract is that, so far as is possible, the *status quo ante* must be restored." P.S. Atiyah, *An Introduction to the Law of Contract* 299 (3d ed. 1981).
- "A plaintiff's right to be restored to the *status quo ante* has always to be weighed against the duty to do what is reasonable to mitigate the cost to the defendant." Reginald W.M. Dias & B.S. Markesinis, *Tort Law* 428 (1984).

Status quo in the sense "the original condition" (as opposed to "the present condition") is a LEGALISM to be avoided because lawyers as well as nonlawyers are likely to misunderstand the import. **Status in quo* is an archaic variant of *status quo*. See **in statu quo.**

statutable. See **statutory.**

statute, in AmE, refers to a legislative act that the state gives the force of law. E.g.: "American courts interpret the usual wording of the abortion *statutes*, quite remarkably, to prohibit the removal of a dead fetus from the mother." Glanville Williams, *The Sanctity of Life and the Criminal Law* 191 (1957).

In BrE, however, *statute* bears a broader meaning: "It is common in popular and even, to some extent, in legal language to treat '*statute*' and 'Act of Parliament' as equivalent terms. That is quite incorrect. All Acts of Parliament are statutes; but [not] all statutes are . . . Acts of Parliament." Edward Jenks, *The Book of English Law* 40 (P.B. Fairest ed., 6th ed. 1967). How can that be? In G.B., *statutory instruments*—government orders akin to what in the U.S. are called "administrative regulations" and "executive orders"—are considered statutes. See **statutory instrument.**

statute book is two words—unhyphenated.

STATUTE DRAFTING. See **LEGISLATIVE DRAFTING.**

statute law. See **statutory law.**

statute-making is so hyphenated.

statute of frauds. A. Senses. In 1677, Lord Nottingham (1621–1682) drafted the original Statute of Frauds, the best known act prescribing written formalities for some contracts. (In references to that original act, the words should have initial capitals.) It declared that certain contracts would be judicially unenforceable (but not void) if not committed to writing. Most Anglo-American jurisdictions have statutes modeled in some way on the original.

In BrE, the phrase *statute of frauds* also sometimes refers to an act affording relief against debtors who transfer assets to defraud or foil creditors.

B. Within (or without) the statute of frauds. These idioms, though fairly common, confuse even veteran lawyers. *Within the statute of frauds* = violative of the statute of frauds, i.e., within its coverage. E.g.: "Oral promises to a creditor to answer for the debt or default of another are not *within the statute of frauds* where the promisor is already otherwise obligated, irrespective of his promise, to perform such duty." Laurence P. Simpson, *Handbook on the Law of Suretyship* 128 (1950). *Without the statute of frauds* = not violative of the statute.

statute of limitations = a statute that establishes a time limit for suing or for prosecuting a crime. Although the singular phrase is *statute of limitations*, the plural tends to be *statutes of limitation*—that is, the *-s* gets dropped from *limitations*. The singular phrase is often reduced to the elliptical form *limitations*—e.g.:

- "The district court refused to award damages to any of the *Zuniga* plaintiffs, reasoning that all of those individuals' claims were barred by *limitations*." *Salazar-Calderon v. Presidio Valley Farmers Ass'n*, 765 F.2d 1334, 1351 (5th Cir. 1985).
- "RTC argues that *limitations* were tolled because Spring Branch continued to be adversely dominated by the defendant directors during the period of federal and state

regulatory supervision." *Resolution Trust Corp. v. Holmes*, 839 F.Supp. 449, 451 (S.D. Tex. 1993).
- "The court of appeals reversed, finding a fact issue on whether *limitations* were tolled against Flour Bluff when Bass mistakenly named TASB the defendant in her original petition." *State Office of Risk Mgmt. v. Herrera*, 288 S.W.3d 543, 548 (Tex. App.—Amarillo 2009).

See **run (A), repose, laches (C)** & **limitation.** See also **time-bar** & **toll.**

statute of repose. See **repose.**

***statutorial; *statutorally.** See **statutory (A).**

statutorification (= the excessive reliance upon legislation to cure society's ills) is a NEOLOGISM invented by Guido Calabresi, the dean of Yale Law School in the 1980s and 1990s. It is an ugly word for an ugly process—e.g.:

- "The '*statutorification*' of American law is not the only reason for these varied proposals and events." Guido Calabresi, *A Common Law for the Age of Statutes* 1 (1982).
- "Guido Calabresi has written a provocative book about the '*statutorification*' of American law, a neologism intended to be as ugly as the condition it describes." Dan Rosen, *A Common Law for the Ages of Intellectual Property*, 38 U. Miami L. Rev. 769, 770 (1984).

statutorily, not ***statutorally** or ***statutorially**, is the correct adverbial form—e.g.:

- "Appellant contends that the trial court erred in using a gross-work-loss calculation, rather than a net-work-loss calculation, in determining the date on which the *statutorially* [read *statutorily*] mandated accrued work loss of $15,000 was achieved." *Driscoll v. Travelers Ins. Co.*, 542 A.2d 154, 154 (Pa. Super. Ct. 1988).
- "The privilege is held by patients thereby preventing health care providers designated under the *statutorally* [read *statutorily*] and judicially created exception from disclosing certain health care information to third parties." Paul T. Cuzmanes & Christopher P. Orlando, *Automation of Medical Records*, 6 J. Pharm. & L. 19, 31 (1997).

statutory. A. And *statutorial. *Statutory* = (1) of or relating to legislation <statutory construction>; (2) legislatively created <the law of patents is purely statutory>; or (3) conformable to a statute <a statutory course of conduct>.

***Statutorial** is a NEEDLESS VARIANT not recognized in the dictionaries—e.g.:

- "The hardship driving *statutorial* [read *statutory*] procedure, as interpreted in *Munson*, leaves a hole literally wide enough to drive any motorized vehicle through, calling for swift action by the General Assembly." *Burns v. Director of Revenue*, 784 S.W.2d 918, 919 (Mo. Ct. App. 1990). (See **literally.**)
- "Because the definition of 'employee' in § 7511 applied prior to April 1, 1996 to limit the Board's jurisdiction, incorporating this definition into the Ford Act's *statutorial* [read *statutory*] scheme is the only way to ensure Congress's purpose of resurrecting the right to appeal

by the same 'employees' who could have appealed 'as of March 31, 1996.'" *Roche v. Merit Sys. Prot. Bd.*, 596 F.3d 1375, 1382 (Fed. Cir. 2010). On the use of **prior to* in that sentence, see ***prior to.**

The adverb *statutorily* is not infrequently rendered, by mistake, **statutorially* or **statutorally*. See **statutorily.**

B. And *statutable*. *Statutable* = (1) prescribed, authorized, or permitted by statute; (2) conformed to statutory requirements for quality, size, or amount; or (3) (of an offense) legally punishable (*OED*). So *statutable* overlaps to a significant degree with the more usual word, *statutory*. In the 19th-century specimen that follows, *statutable* is used in a context in which *statutory* would inevitably appear today: "But there are express *statuteable* provisions, which directly apply to the present case." *Gelston v. Hoyt*, 16 U.S. 246, 311 (1818) (per Marshall, J.). As in the preceding quotation, the word has occasionally been spelled **statuteable*, but that spelling is inferior. See MUTE E.

statutory charge. Copperud has observed that in lay parlance *statutory rape*, a precise term, has been stretched into phrases such as *statutory charge* and *statutory offense*. *See* Roy H. Copperud, *American Usage and Style* 363 (1980). These phrases are sometimes considered illogical, since criminal offenses or charges are invariably statutorily defined or codified. But in some jurisdictions, such as Scotland, major crimes such as murder and theft are still defined by the common law only. So the phrase *statutory charge* may be quite sound, if it is used to dispel the possibility that one is referring to a common-law crime.

statutory construction. See **interpretation.**

statutory enactment is a REDUNDANCY for *statute*, and the word *enactment* is used loosely in this phrase—e.g.: "The public policy of a state is the law of that state as found in its constitution, its *statutory enactments* [read *statutes*], and its judicial decisions." *Petty v. El Dorado*, 19 P.3d 167, 172 (Kan. 2001). See **enactment.** Cf. **statutory legislation.**

statutory instrument, in BrE, refers to a government order similar to an executive order or agency regulation in the U.S. E.g.: "The most important kind of legislation is the Act of Parliament (otherwise called a statute), though nowadays what is called delegated legislation, like the many government orders generally known as *statutory instruments*, has come to be of great importance as well." Glanville Williams, *Learning the Law* 24 (11th ed. 1982). See **statute.** Cf. **instrument.**

Statutory Instruments. See **S.I.**

statutory law; statute law. Both forms appear in AmE, but the first is the more common. In BrE, *statute law* (preferably unhyphenated except as a PHRASAL ADJECTIVE) is the predominant form.

In some contexts, the phrases are not entirely synonymous. *Statute law* has two meanings: (1) "a law contained in a statute"; or (2) "the system of law and

body of principles laid down in statutes, as distinct from the common law." *Statutory* law shares sense 2 with *statute law* but not sense 1.

statutory legislation is a REDUNDANCY—e.g.:

- "The distinction between the content of constitutional law and that of ordinary *statutory legislation* [read *legislation*] is largely one of degree and in the States of the American Union this distinction is fast disappearing." James W. Garner, "Law, Constitutional," in 17 *Encyclopedia Americana* 96–100 [page so numbered], 101 (1953).
- "In my view, the plain meaning of 'manslaughter' as used in early *statutory legislation* [read *statutes* or *legislation*] did not contemplate the offense of 'involuntary manslaughter.'" *Morris v. U.S.*, 648 A.2d 958, 964 (D.C. 1994) (Mack, J., dissenting).

Cf. **statutory enactment.**

statutory rape (= sexual intercourse with a person below the age of consent, regardless of whether it occurs against his or her will) is an Americanism that originated in the 19th century. Originally, statutory-rape laws applied only to female victims, but today the great majority of American states have sex-neutral legislation dealing with this offense. The term is a popular one, not a statutory one. See **rape.**

Statutory Rules and Orders. Abbr. **S.R. & O.** See **S.I.**

staunch; stanch. *Staunch* is preferable as the adjective ("trustworthy, loyal"), *stanch* as the verb ("to restrain the flow of [usu. blood]").

stay, n. & vb. In law, *stay* means either (1) "postponement"; or (2) "the order suspending a judicial proceeding or the judgment resulting from that proceeding" <stay of the mandate> <the court's stay of execution>.

Although the verb *to stay* is usually intransitive in lay contexts <he stayed awhile>, it is transitive in its legal senses: (1) to postpone, usu. until the court determines a contested issue <to stay the mandate>; or (2) to halt <to stay waste>. E.g.:

- (Sense 1) "That filing automatically *stayed* both the district-court proceedings and the scheduled foreclosure sale." *R.G. Fin. Corp. v. Vergara-Nunez*, 446 F.3d 178, 181 (1st Cir. 2006).
- (Sense 2) "The remainderman has a remedy by injunction to *stay* waste, or for damages for waste already committed." *Roby v. Newton*, 49 S.E. 694, 698 (Ga. 1905).

See **continue.**

stayable (= capable of being legally postponed or halted) is a legal NEOLOGISM not recorded in the *OED*, *W3*, or most other dictionaries. E.g.: "Judgments in actions for injunctions . . . are not *stayable* as of right." 9 James Wm. Moore et al., *Moore's Federal Practice* ¶ 208.04, at 8-11 (1987).

stay law (= a statute that suspends execution or some other legal procedure) is a 19th-century Americanism. E.g.:

- "No advantage to be taken of *stay laws* or injunctions, &c." *Coe v. Pennock*, 5 F. Cas. 1172, 1172 (C.C.N.D. Ohio 1857).

- "I believe it was once held that a *stay-law* passed after a note was given could not affect that debt . . . ; but where the law is passed before the debt is created, a *stay-law* is good in every State." 2 Cong. Rec. 1,226 (5 Feb. 1874) (statement of Sen. Oliver P. Morton).

stay of execution = the suspending of the operation of a court's judgment or order. In lay parlance, the phrase usually appears in reference to a death sentence, but not in legal parlance.

In the following example, Judge Learned Hand employed a variation on the phrase: "The judge sentenced him to not less than five years nor more than ten, *execution to be stayed*, and the defendant to be placed on probation." *Repouille v. U.S.*, 165 F.2d 152, 153 (2d Cir. 1947).

steadfast. So spelled—not **stedfast.*

steal. A. And Its Near-Synonyms: *rob*; *burglarize*; *pilfer*; *purloin*; *filch.* These verbs share the sense "to wrongfully take personal property." To *steal* is to take what belongs to someone else, typically in a furtive way and without the owner's permission or knowledge <the maid stole her employer's diamond pin and, when confronted, claimed to have " 'borrowed' it>. *Steal* has a narrow and a broad sense. It may mean (narrowly) "to obtain by larceny" or (broadly) "to obtain by any one of the three principal forms of theft—embezzlement, false pretenses, or larceny." (See **rob** & **embezzle**.) To *rob* is to feloniously take valuables from another or from a place, as by fraud, trickery, threats, or violence <they robbed the bank> <they were robbed on the street by thugs>. To *burglarize* is to break and enter a building (most traditionally, a house) in order to steal or commit some other felony <their house was burglarized while they were away in St. Thomas>. *Burglarize* is the only term in this entry that does not imply a success in theft, since all that is required is breaking and entering. (See **burglarize**.) To *pilfer* is to steal in small quantities to avoid being discovered <the nurse pilfered medicines>. The word is also used as a EUPHEMISM for *steal. Purloin* is quite similar in suggesting petty thievery through surreptitious means <three rustlers purloined the cattle>. *Filch* heightens the petty underhandedness partly through its slangy informality <the teenager filched bubble gum from the pharmacy>.

B. More on Idiom: *steal, rob,* and *burglarize.* Things are *stolen* <the watch was stolen from her apartment>; persons or places are *robbed* <he was robbed> <rob a bank>; and only places are *burglarized* <the house had been burglarized>. See **burglary.**

steamroll; steamroller, vb. In recent decades the first has *steamrolled* the second as the preferred verb form, being about four times as common in print—e.g.:

- "Investigator Moore's response was the sort of evasive, question-skipping-over, overriding, or 'steamrolling'

condemned in *Almeida*." *Bean v. State*, 752 So.2d 644, 649 (Fla. Ct. App. 2000).
- "During Reconstruction, the Radical Republicans in Congress . . . were willing to conveniently ignore, or *steamroll* through, the role of the President and the Supreme Court in achieving their goals." Terence J. Lau, *Judicial Independence: A Call for Reform*, 9 Nev. L.J. 79, 114 (2008).

*stedfast. See **steadfast.**

stereotypic; stereotypical. The longer form is preferred in figurative senses—e.g.: "Constitutional concerns are heightened, because the individual permit-application decision may rest upon inaccurate and *stereotypic* [read *stereotypical*] fears." *J.W. v. City of Tacoma*, 720 F.2d 1126, 1130–31 (9th Cir. 1983). *Stereotypic* is the better form for the narrow sense "of or produced by stereotypy (the process of printing from stereotype plates)."

sterility; impotence. The first refers to the inability to procreate, the second to the inability to copulate. See **impotence.**

stigma. Pl. *-mas, -mata.* As with many other such words, the English plural (*-mas*) is preferable. See PLURALS (A).

stimulus. Pl. *-li.* Unlike *stigma*, this word does not make a native-English plural. See PLURALS (A).

stipe is English slang for a *stipendiary magistrate* (= a salaried magistrate who is a lawyer appointed by the Lord Chancellor to hear small claims and minor criminal cases such as those heard by [unsalaried] justices of the peace).

stipend. See **pay,** n.

stipital. See **stirpital.**

stipulate = (1) (of an agreement) to specify (something) as an essential part of the contract; (2) (of a party to an agreement) to require or insist upon (something) as an essential condition; or (3) to make express demand *for* something as a condition of an agreement.

This verb belongs to the language of contracts, and is not felicitously transported into contexts involving statutes, where it becomes a substitute for *provide.* E.g.:

- "The original statute *stipulated* [read *provided*] that parents must leave a portion of their wealth to their progeny." Frances Marcus, *Does Napoleonic Law Have Future in Louisiana?*, N.Y. Times, 1 Dec. 1989, at 27.
- "The statute *stipulates* [read *provides*] that no penalty of death can be imposed unless the Commonwealth proves one or both aggravating factors beyond a reasonable doubt." *Prieto v. Commonwealth*, 682 S.E.2d 910, 932 (Va. 2009).

Nor has the verb traditionally meant "(of counsel) to reach an agreement about business before a court,"

---

although this extension of contractual sense is not uncommon in American trial practice. E.g.:

- "The relevant facts *are stipulated.*" *U.S. v. National Bank of Commerce*, 472 U.S. 713, 715 (1985) (per Blackmun, J.).
- "The parties are to provide the court with a *stipulated* plan within ten days from the date of this order." *In re Baby Girl T.*, 715 A.2d 99, 106 (Del. Fam. Ct. 1998).
- "Counsel made no objection to the evidence *stipulated* to by the State and the guardian ad litem." *In re India B.*, 782 N.E.2d 224, 228 (Ill. 2002).

stipulative; stipulatory; *stipulational. The first two are distinct. *Stipulative* = that stipulates or specifies as an essential condition <a stipulative definition>. *Stipulatory* = of or relating to a stipulation <a stipulatory engagement for the debt>.

*Stipulational is a late-20th-century AmE NEOLOGISM—and it is a NEEDLESS VARIANT of *stipulatory*: "The facts which were thus given *stipulational* [read *stipulatory*] establishment were that the injury to plaintiff had occurred at the Roberts Theater." *Chenette v. Trustees of Iowa Coll.*, 431 F.2d 49, 51 (8th Cir. 1970).

stirpes. See **stirps.**

stirpital; stipital. The preferred adjective corresponding to *stirps* (= a branch of a family), used in reference to a per stirpes distribution, is *stirpital*. *Black's Law Dictionary* (4th & 5th eds.) listed only *stipital* as the correct form, but that changed to *stirpital* in the 6th edition (1990). *W3* defines *stipital* as "of or relating to the stipes," *stipes* being a botanical or zoological term meaning "peduncle" or, less commonly, "stirps." But *W3* does not include *stirpital*. And *Words and Phrases* contains *stirpital* but not *stipital*. The *OED* records *stirpital*, noting that it is ill-formed and would be *stirpal* if properly Latinized, and dates it from 1886 with the following quotation: "A division of the proceeds of sale per stirpes is more in accordance than a division per capita with the original *stirpital* division of the income." The *OED* does not contain *stipital*.

Stirpital is by far the prevalent word—e.g.:

- "Counsel for the defendant Nolan, as an alternative claim, suggest the application of the doctrine of *stirpital* survivorship." *State Bank & Trust Co. v. Nolan*, 130 A. 483, 489 (Conn. 1925).
- "Some courts, on the other hand, take a position contrary, or at least in opposition, to the foregoing . . . *stirpital* distribution." 57 Am. Jur. *Wills* § 1292 (1948).
- "This analysis does not result in a consistently *stirpital* distribution of the settled fund as one might have expected." *Re Drummond's Settlement*, [1988] 1 All E.R. 449, 453.

Though it has the approval of some dictionaries, *stipital* is rarely encountered—e.g.: "Considering the circumstances it may be inferred that it would have been impracticable for the testator to have designated his half brothers as *stipital* progenitors." *Theopold v. Sears*, 258 N.E.2d 559, 561 (Mass. 1970).

Hence there can be no doubt that *stirpital* is better than *stipital* as the adjective of *per stirpes*. Most lawyers know the term *per stirpes* and understand *stirpital*

if they hear or read it; *stipital* is another matter. And if a legal term is obscure to lawyers, what hope is there for the nonlawyer?

Then again, in most contexts the phrase *per stirpes* might be used where an adjective is called for <per stirpes distribution>. The phrase **per stirpital*, however, is a needless hybrid—e.g.:

- "Placing the word 'equally' before 'stirpes' created no inconsistency in a *per stirpital* [read *per stirpes*] distribution because it 'signifie[d] that equality of the one-half share [should] be maintained among the children of each group.'" *In re Trust Estate of Dwight*, 909 P.2d 561, 566 (Haw. 1995).
- "First Union's *per stirpital* [read *per stirpes*] distribution of the Nell Legwen trust remainder interest was not error." *Fleming v. First Union Nat'l Bank*, 555 S.E.2d 728, 730 (Ga. 2001).

stirps. Pl. *stirpes.* See **stirpital.**

stochastic. See **aleatory.**

stock; shares. *Stock* = (1) the capital or principal fund raised by a corporation through subscribers' contributions or the sale of shares; (2) the proportional part of this capital credited to an individual shareholder and represented by the number of units he or she owns; or (3) the goods that a merchant has on hand.

Whereas *stock* is a mass noun, *shares* is a count noun closely related to sense 2 of *stock*. *Shares* = the units of capital that represent an ownership interest in a corporation or in its equity.

stockholder. See **shareholder** & **stakeholder.**

stole, took, and carried away. The traditional phrasing of a larceny charge, these words are "clearly an old form derived from the simplest type of stealing, and [were] made the basis of the theory that larceny is a violation of possession." Theodore F.T. Plucknett, *A Concise History of the Common Law* 448 (5th ed. 1956). The phrase *carried away* met the requirement of alleging that an asportation had taken place. See **asportation.**

stone, etched in. This is a SET PHRASE. Variants such as *carved in stone, cast in concrete, cast in cement*, and the illogical *cast in stone* ought to be avoided.

stop; cease; desist; discontinue; quit. These verbs share the sense "to end or terminate some activity or status." *Stop* refers primarily to action or progress that ends suddenly <stop at the red light>. *Cease*, a FORMAL WORD, applies primarily to a state or condition that gradually or foreseeably ends <when ordered to, the accused infringer ceased selling the product>. *Desist* emphasizes self-restraint or forbearance on the part of the actor, sometimes implying the futility of continuing <the attacker desisted when he heard footsteps>. E.g.: "Nor is extortion committed by an employee who threatens to report the illegal conduct of his or her employer unless the employer *desists* from that conduct." *Flatley v. Mauro*, 139 P.3d 2, 24 n.16 (Cal. 2006).

Discontinue suggests leaving off some habitual activity or regular occupation or offering <negotiations were discontinued before the employees went on strike>. *Quit*, originally an Americanism dating from the early 19th century, is typically an informal word associated with jobs <I quit!> and habits <please quit dipping snuff!>.

stop-and-frisk rule = the American constitutional doctrine (announced in *Terry v. Ohio*, 392 U.S. 1 (1968)) that a police officer may, with neither a warrant nor probable cause, stop and search a person for concealed weapons. The PHRASAL ADJECTIVE should be hyphenated whatever the noun may be: *stop-and-frisk law*, *stop-and-frisk doctrine*, etc.

straightforward manslaughter. See **manslaughter (A).**

straitjacket; *straightjacket. **Straightjacket* is a common error for *straitjacket*—e.g.:

- "Therefore no one should be able to put him in a *straightjacket* [read *straitjacket*] as to his method." *Redevelopment Agency v. Mitsui Inv., Inc.*, 522 P.2d 1370, 1373 (Utah 1974).
- "We do not wish to put a *straightjacket* [read *straitjacket*] on the creative development of new forms of alternative dispute resolution." *Annapolis Prof'l Firefighters v. City of Annapolis*, 642 A.2d 889, 895 n.6 (Md. Ct. Spec. App. 1994).

straitlaced (= prudish; rigidly narrow in moral matters) referred originally, in the 16th century, to a tightly laced corset—*strait* meaning "narrow" or "closely fitting." Over time, writers have forgotten the etymology and have confused *strait* with *straight*. Hence the erroneous form **straightlaced*—e.g.:

- "In former days, a bootlegger would much rather trust his fate to a *straightlaced* [read *straitlaced*] prohibitionist minister than to a former saloonkeeper." *Local 36, Int'l Fishermen & Allied Workers v. U.S.*, 177 F.2d 320, 341 (9th Cir. 1949).
- "The standards of 'the Block' (an area in Baltimore in which there are a number of shops [that] deal with pornographic materials) are not the standards to be applied in this case, any more than the standards of the most *straight-laced* [read *straitlaced*] persons." *U.S. v. Womack*, 509 F.2d 368, 380 (D.C. Cir. 1972).
- "The court finds that the plaintiff is '*straight-laced*' [read *straitlaced*] and professional in her work." *Fox v. Ravinia Club, Inc.*, 761 F.Supp. 797, 799 (N.D. Ga. 1991).
- "Frankfort told [the plaintiff] not to tell Howard Moore, the Executive Vice President . . . of Purchasing, as he was very *straight-laced* [read *straitlaced*] and a family man." *T.L v. Toys 'R' Us, Inc.*, 605 A.2d 1125, 1128 (N.J. Super. Ct. App. Div. 1992).

stranger, in law, means (1) "one not a privy or party to an act" <a stranger to the contract>; or (2) "one not standing toward another in some relation implied in the context" <the trustee was dealing with a stranger>.

stratagem. So spelled—but **strategem*, on the analogy of *strategy*, is a common misspelling. Though

etymologically related, the words *stratagem* and *strategy* came into English by different routes, and their spellings diverged merely as a matter of long-standing convention.

strategy; tactics. *Strategy* is the long-range plan for attaining a goal; *tactics* are specific maneuvers to advance those goals in the long run.

stratum. Although the Latin plural *strata* is thoroughly established, some writers ill-advisedly experiment with an anglicized plural—e.g.: "They say nothing concerning depths, levels or *stratums* [read *strata*]." *Rogers v. Westhoma Oil Co.*, 291 F.2d 726, 732 (10th Cir. 1961) (Bratton, J., dissenting). See PLURALS (A).

straw man, literally "a scarecrow made of straw," has come to mean primarily a fictitious person—always conveniently weak or flawed—used as a seeming adversary in an argument. A *straw-man argument* is easily overcome by the advocate who invents it as a foil to his or her own argument. See SEXISM (B).

stray. See **estray** & **waifs and estrays.**

stricken, though common as a past participle in much legal writing, is considered by the better authorities to be inferior to *struck*. It is an ARCHAISM in all but the adjectival sense <a stricken community>. Most modern uses of *stricken* occur as the ill-advised past participle, though—e.g.:

- "Defendant . . . asserted that the deceased was suddenly *stricken* [read *struck*] with apoplexy, that he sank to the floor of the car, and thereafter died from natural causes." *Crumm v. Allstate Life Ins. Co.*, 24 F.Supp.2d 1134, 1137 n.2 (D. Kan. 1998).
- "Hunt maintains that the restitution condition should be *stricken* [read *struck*] from his sentence." *State v. Hunt*, 214 P.3d 1234, 1238 (Mont. 2009).
- "The court sustained the objection and ordered Stephens' answer *stricken* [read *struck*]." *Elsey v. Commissioner of Correction*, 10 A.3d 578, 593 (Conn. Ct. App. 2011).

Stricken is sometimes used as a preterit in the guise of an adjective—e.g.: "Steagall filed a second amended complaint repleading verbatim the fabrication of evidence allegation [that was] *stricken* by the April 28 order." *Serritella v. Markum*, 119 F.3d 506, 507 (7th Cir. 1997). See **strike (A).**

strict construction; strict constructionism. *Strict construction* is now generally a pejorative term to denote the literal, narrow construction of constitutions, statutes, contracts, and the like. Formerly it was used in fairly neutral ways—e.g.:

- "*Strict construction* of a statute is that which refuses to expand the law by implications or equitable considerations, but confines its operation to cases which are clearly within the letter of the statute, as well as within its spirit or reason, not so as to defeat the manifest purpose of the

Legislature, but so as to resolve all reasonable doubts against the applicability of the statute to the particular case." William M. Lile et al., *Brief Making and the Use of Law Books* 343 (3d ed. 1914).

- "And the Constitution alone could not serve to quiet these misgivings, for, as the warring camps soon discovered, it could be cited on either side, depending on whether a '*strict construction*' or a 'loose construction' were adopted." Robert G. McCloskey, *The American Court* 29 (1960).

Strict constructionism denotes the doctrine that courts should interpret statutory and constitutional words strictly according to the letter, without considering their purpose or "spirit" or "tenor," lest the judges begin unpredictably to imbue statutes and constitutions with their own biases. E.g.: "A judge or scholar who embraces a literalist theory (which is also referred to as '*strict constructionism*') relies on an analysis of the words and phrases of the Constitution and an analysis of the overall structure of government as ordained by the concepts of separation of powers and checks and balances in determining what the Constitution sanctions and what it forbids." Barbara H. Craig, *Chadha: The Story of an Epic Constitutional Struggle* 93 (1988).

The phrase has, unfortunately, acquired connotations that may limit its utility in some contexts. As one commentator observes, *strict construction* has—at least since the 1960s—been used to signal "a proclivity to reach constitutional judgments that will please political conservatives." John H. Ely, *Democracy and Distrust* 1 n.* (1980). But more than that, it is commonly used by those on the left as a term of disparagement. Cf. **interpretivism.**

One who adheres to the doctrine of *strict constructionism* is known, not surprisingly, as a *strict constructionist.* E.g.: "It sounds to me like a voice from the past . . . . It is the voice of the *strict constructionist.*" *Nothman v. Barnet Council*, [1978] 1 W.L.R. 220, 228 (per Denning, M.R.). See **original intent** & *strict interpretation* under INTERPRETATION, MODES OF (B).

strictest sense of the word, in the. See WORD-PATRONAGE & *stricto sensu.*

stricti juris; *strictissimi juris.* The first phrase means "strictly according to the law, esp. as opposed to equity." The second, a stronger phrase, means "most strictly according to the law." These LATINISMS, as infrequently used in modern contexts, are not easily simplified—e.g.: "But this privilege or lien . . . is a secret one; it may operate to the prejudice of general creditors and purchasers without notice; it is therefore '*stricti juris*,' and cannot be extended by construction, analogy, or inference." Grant Gilmore & Charles L. Black Jr., *The Law of Admiralty* 633 (2d ed. 1975).

strict interpretation. See **strict construction** & INTERPRETATION, MODES OF (B).

strict liability; absolute liability; liability without fault. Among these broadly synonymous phrases, meaning "liability that does not depend upon actual negligence or intent to harm," *strict liability* is the most common term in both AmE and BrE. The second and third phrases were formerly common, and are still occasionally used.

In some contexts, legal writers distinguish between *strict* and *absolute liability.* L.B. Curzon, for example, differentiates between the *absolute-liability school of thought*, which views intent as being irrelevant in tort—a school represented by Holdsworth—and the *strict-liability school of thought*, which views intent as being minimally relevant in tort—a school represented by Winfield. See L.B. Curzon, *English Legal History* 254 (2d ed. 1979). But Winfield himself seems to have made no such distinction in sense—only in the choice of words: "Liability, then, we suggest, was never absolute . . . . It remains to add that the description of the rule in *Rylands v. Fletcher* as an example of absolute liability in tort is unhappy in view of some half dozen exceptions . . . [that] are admitted as qualifications of it. '*Strict liability*' seems to be a better term." Percy H. Winfield, *The Myth of Absolute Liability*, 42 Law Q. Rev. 37, 46, 51 (1926).

strictly construe. See **strict construction.**

stricto sensu (= in the strict sense) is an unjustifiable LATINISM. E.g.: "The category of defendant is not limited to manufacturers *stricto sensu* [read *in the strict sense*] either." Reginald W.M. Dias & B.S. Markesinis, *Tort Law* 103 (1984). The phrase is often translated into English—a fine practice: "Because its statutory action did not accrue until it was denied just compensation, *in a strict sense* Del Monte Dunes sought not just compensation per se but rather damages for the unconstitutional denial of such compensation." *Monterey v. Del Monte Dunes at Monterey, Ltd.*, 526 U.S. 687, 710 (1999) (per Kennedy, J.).

strict scrutiny = the standard of review that federal courts apply in equal-protection cases involving the constitutionality of governmental classifications that either are based on race or infringe fundamental constitutional rights. To pass muster, a challenged governmental action must be "closely related to a compelling governmental interest." This standard is the toughest of the three levels of scrutiny applied by federal courts—*ordinary scrutiny* and *heightened scrutiny* being the least tough and the intermediate levels. Few statutes survive a constitutional challenge judged by the standard of strict scrutiny.

Though this phrase did not emerge as a legal standard of appellate constitutional review until the mid-20th century, in *Skinner v. Oklahoma*, 316 U.S. 535 (1942), it first appeared much earlier, in *The Federalist Papers*: "And who is there that will either take the trouble or incur the odium of a *strict scrutiny* into the secret springs of the transaction?" *The Federalist* No. 70, at 428 (Alexander Hamilton) (Clinton Rossiter ed., 1961).

strike, vb. **A. Senses.** This word has more than 100 senses, all told. Among the important law-related senses are these: (1) [intransitive] of an employee or employees, to refuse to continue to work (at a workplace) until certain demands have been met <the employees struck for three days before a settlement was reached>; (2) [transitive] of an employee or employees, to engage in a strike against <the steelworkers struck the Indiana Harbor Works>; (3) [transitive] to reject (a veniremember) by a peremptory challenge <the prosecution then struck several blacks, thereby raising a *Batson* issue>; or (4) [transitive] to expunge, as from a record <motion to strike>.

In sense 1, *strike* denotes only the total or partial cessation of work—not the refusal to accept work. Henry Bournes Higgins, *A New Province for Law and Order*, 32 Harv. L. Rev. 189, 192 (1919).

B. *Strike* for *strike down*. When a court invalidates a statute, it is best to write that the court *strikes it down*—e.g.: "The majority *strikes down* the statute because it is not an 'adequate substitute' for habeas review." *Boumediene v. Bush*, 553 U.S. 723, 808 (2008) (Roberts, C.J., dissenting). *Strike* as a lone verb has so many other meanings that making it more precise in this context is desirable—e.g.: "Will the court *strike* [read *strike down*] the statute as unconstitutional under *Kastigar*?" William Wesley Patton, *Rethinking the Privilege Against Self-Incrimination in Child Abuse Dependency Proceedings*, 11 U.C. Davis J. Juv. L. & Pol'y 101, 117–18 (2007).

C. Inflected Forms. *Strike* yields *struck* for both its past tense and its past participle. *Stricken* is archaic as a past participle, and should be reserved only for adjectival uses <a stricken man>; <stricken with polio>. See **stricken.**

strike suit, in colloquial legal parlance, refers to a suit filed not because the courts are likely to think it meritorious but because the defendant seems likely to settle favorably regardless of the weakness of the plaintiff's case. E.g.: "Of course it is error to deny trial when there is a genuine dispute of facts; but it is just as much error—perhaps more in cases of hardship, or where impetus is given to *strike suits*—to deny or postpone judgment where the ultimate legal result is clearly indicated." *Arnstein v. Porter*, 154 F.2d 464, 480 (2d Cir. 1946) (Clark, J., dissenting). Most specifically, *strike suits* are generally shareholder derivative actions begun "with the hope of winning large attorney's fees or private settlements, and with no intention of benefiting the corporation on behalf of which suit is theoretically brought." Note, *Security for Expenses Litigation*, 52 Colum. L. Rev. 267, 267 (1952).

strive > strove > striven. The past tense seems to cause the most trouble—e.g.: "Negotiators *strived* [read *strove*] to get South African power-sharing talks back on track." *World Wide*, Wall St. J., 20 May 1991, at A1.

struck. See **strike (c)** & **stricken.**

stuff gown. See LAWYERS, DEROGATORY NAMES FOR (A).

stultify (now "to make stupid or cause to appear foolish") formerly meant "to attempt to prove one's own mental incapacity." E.g.: "Dr. Johnson seemed much surprized [*sic*] that such a suit was admitted by Scottish law, and observed that in England no man is allowed to *stultify* himself." (Eng.) The term is now used in British legal writing of a witness who, e.g., casts doubt on his own account of a remark alleged to have been overheard by him by admitting that he was too far away to hear it. See Sidney L. Phipson, *The Law of Evidence* 394 (8th ed. 1959). See **self-stultification.**

The word is sometimes misunderstood as being synonymous with the verb *to disgrace* or *dishonor*. Nor is it equivalent to *retard* or *emasculate*—e.g.: "To hold that the Commission had no alternative in this proceeding but to approve the proposed transaction . . . would be to *stultify* the administrative process." *SEC v. Chenery Corp.*, 332 U.S. 194, 202 (1947).

stupefy. So spelled; **stupify* is a fairly common misspelling—e.g.: "If a man, in order to cause a woman to succumb to his wishes, *stupifies* [read *stupefies*] her by drugs . . . , then of course she does not consent." Glanville Williams, *Textbook of Criminal Law* 520 (1978). Cf. **rarefy.**

stupid. See **ignorant.**

style = (1) in AmE and BrE, a case name <the style of the case>; (2) in BrE, the name or title of a person <royal style and titles>; and (3) in Scots law, a model form or precedent of a deed or pleading (*OCL1*).

STYLE. See LEGAL-WRITING STYLE.

STYLE, WORDS OF. See TERMS OF ART.

stylish; stylistic. *Stylish* = in style, in vogue. *Stylistic* = having to do with style (of general application); in the appropriate style (of music).

stymie; **stymy*. This verb, originally a golf term meaning "to obstruct," is best spelled *stymie*—even in the inflected form *stymieing*. (See VOWEL CLUSTERS.) E.g.: "The criminal rules were not designed with the intention of *stymieing* a defendant's ability to mount a complete defense." *SEC v. Nicholas*, 569 F.Supp.2d 1065, 1071 (C.D. Cal. 2008).

suability. Though *suable* appeared in the 17th century, the noun *suability* began as an Americanism (first used, as far as documentation reveals, by Chief Justice John Jay in 1798) and has remained so. Jay's 18th-century assessment remains valid today: "*Suability* and *suable* are words not in common use, but they concisely and correctly convey the idea annexed to them" (quoted in *OED*). E.g.: Mary Q. Kelly, *Workmen's Compensation and Employer Suability*, 5 St. Mary's L.J. 818 (1974). See **suable.**

suable. The adjective *suable* has existed from the early 17th century. At times it means "capable of being sued" <a suable party>, at other times "capable of being sued out [i.e., enforced]" <a suable writ>. E.g.:

- (Sense 1) "The Supreme Court has held that unincorporated labor unions are *suable* in their own names in the Federal courts for violation of the Anti-Trust Act." Charles E. Hughes, *The Supreme Court* 234 (1928).
- (Sense 2) "The principal contracts known to the common law and *suable* in the King's Courts, a century after the Conquest, were suretyship and debt." Oliver Wendell Holmes Jr., *The Common Law* 289 (1881).

See **suability.**

sua sponte /**soo**-ə **spon**-tee/ (= on its own motion; without prompting) is ordinarily used in reference to courts, especially in AmE. Usually, the LATINISM is readily translatable—e.g.: "Lack of subject-matter jurisdiction may be raised at any time by any party or by the court *sua sponte* [read *on its own motion*]." *In re Estate of Hockemeier*, 786 N.W.2d 680, 682 (Neb. 2010).

The phrase is often used illogically—e.g.: "The trial court granted the defendant's motion for a directed verdict, after considering it *sua sponte*, holding that the claims were barred by the statutes of limitation." *Sinotte v. Waterbury*, 995 A.2d 131, 138 (Conn. App. Ct. 2010). If there was a motion by the defendant before the court, then the court could not have considered it *sua sponte*.

The Latin, it must be remembered, means literally "on his or its own motion." So it is probably wrong for the courts to use this phrase in reference to their own actions, as here: "*Sua sponte* we note that the same problem exists in this case as existed in *Reyes*." *State v. White*, 706 P.2d 1331, 1333 (Haw. Ct. App. 1985). The phrase should have been entirely omitted in that sentence. The phrase may acceptably be used with a plural noun—e.g.: "California trial *courts* can also vacate allegations of prior serious or violent felony convictions, either on motion by the prosecution or *sua sponte*." *Ewing v. California*, 538 U.S. 11, 17 (2003) (per O'Connor, J.).

The phrase starts getting especially pretentious in its first-person variations. For the singular, some judges sitting alone (mostly in New York and Pennsylvania) use *mea sponte* instead of *sua sponte*—e.g.:

- "The question whether I should disqualify myself from presiding in Mr. Moskovits' case is not a new one. I raised it *mea sponte* prior to the original trial." *U.S. v. Moskovits*, 866 F.Supp. 178, 179 (E.D. Pa. 1994) (per Pollak, J.). On the preference for *Moskovits's* over *Moskovits'* as a possessive, see POSSESSIVES (A). On the use of **prior to* in that sentence, see ***prior to.**
- "I must determine, *mea sponte*, whether any of these exceptions applies." *Zapata v. I.N.S.*, 93 F.Supp.2d 355, 359 n.4 (S.D.N.Y. 2000) (per Mukasey, J.).

- "I regard myself as competent to answer the question that I raised *mea sponte*." *U.S. v. Capanelli*, 263 F.Supp.2d 677, 679 (S.D.N.Y. 2003) (per Haight, J.).

Because *mea* is singular, it's a mistake to use *mea sponte* with plural pronouns—e.g.: "*We* raised the question of *our* jurisdiction to hear this action *mea sponte* [delete *mea sponte* altogether] and directed the parties to file briefs addressing two issues." *Shrader v. Legg Mason Wood Walker, Inc.*, 880 F.Supp. 366, 367 (E.D. Pa. 1995).

For the plural, *nostra sponte* (= on our own motion) seems to be the order of the day in the Second Circuit and in New York—e.g.:

- "Similarly, we find that courts are not obligated to investigate, *nostra sponte*, a petitioner's exhaustion of particular issues before the BIA." *Zhong v. U.S. Dep't of Just.*, 461 F.3d 101, 119 n.22 (2d Cir. 2006).
- "We note that although the complaint does not allege that the board member defendants intentionally procured the seller's breach, no contention was made on the motion to dismiss or on this appeal that this cause of action is defective for this reason, and we will not dismiss it *nostra sponte* on this ground." *85 Fifth Ave. 4th Floor, LLC v. I.A. Selig, LLC*, 845 N.Y.S.2d 274, 276 (App. Div. 2007).
- "Although Tutty does not challenge the procedural reasonableness of his sentence, we have the power to consider this error *nostra sponte* in the interest of justice." *U.S. v. Tutty*, 612 F.3d 128, 131 (2d Cir. 2010).

I suggest, *mea sponte*—no, we should all urge, *nostra sponte*—that judges stop all this Latinate sputtering or do things either *on their own motion* or *on their own initiative*. Or perhaps they might find a better way *on their own*.

The phrase is occasionally misspelled **sua sponti*—e.g.: "The district judge, *sua sponti* [read *sua sponte*], had the jurors returned to the courtroom to inquire whether a verdict had been reached." *U.S. v. Stollings*, 501 F.2d 954, 955 (4th Cir. 1974). See **ex parte (B).**

sub-. Legal writers are fond of *sub-* words. This fondness often manifests itself in fussy distinctions drawn as analogues to *subcontract* and *subheading* (e.g., *subcategory, subissue, subaspect, subagent, subbuyer*). The only adequate description of such forms is substandard. E.g.:

- "The element has several *subaspects*." Paul M. Grinvalsky, *Idea Expression in Musical Analysis*, 28 Cal. W. L. Rev. 395, 402 (1992).
- "In his habeas petition, Grim raises two issues with several *subissues*." *Grim v. State*, 971 So.2d 85, 102 (Fla. 2007).

Surely there is a better way of saying that there are two issues within a broad issue, or more than one aspect within a broad aspect; words like *issue* and *aspect* are abstract enough without allowing them to become more so with prefixed forms. See ABSTRACTITIS.

The height of the fetish for this prefix consists in *subsub-*, illustrated in the following examples:

- "Nor is it sufficient that Lake City, a *subsubagent*, might ordinarily have relied upon a subagent . . . to collect and forward funds due." *Lake City Stevedores, Inc. v. East West Shipping Agencies, Inc.*, 474 F.2d 1060, 1064 (5th Cir. 1973).

- "In September 1985, Peoples Construction Company . . . ,
a subcontractor, for a construction project in Foster City,
California, hired Matson as a plastering *subsubcontractor* for that project." *Matson Plastering Co. v. Plasterers
& Shophands Local No. 66*, 852 F.2d 1200, 1201 (9th Cir.
1988).
- "The shipowner [may] lawfully intercept freights due
from the *subsubcharterer* to the subcharterer, where there
is privity of contract between the owner and the subcharterer." William Tetley & Robert C. Wilkins, *Maritime Liens
and Claims* 794 (1998).

The device, though inelegant, saves a little space and
lends greater precision to some contexts.

subaspect. See SUB-.

sub-bidder should be so spelled, with the hyphen.

subcontract (= a contract made by a party to another
contract [*main contract* or *head contract*] for carrying
it out, or a part of it) is now in common usage, though
some judges have objected to it—e.g.: "Being of the
opinion that *subcontract* is a malapropism, we prefer
to use the phrase *contracting out* or *contract out*." *International Union v. Webster Elec. Co.*, 299 F.2d 195, 197
n.2 (7th Cir. 1962).

subcontractor is not hyphenated.

subcontractual is the adjective corresponding to *subcontract*. E.g.:

- "Record evidence suggests that Local 829 had no way of
knowing the existence of *subcontractual* arrangements on
particular shows." *United Scenic Artists v. NLRB*, 655 F.2d
1267, 1270 (D.C. Cir. 1981).
- "An exculpatory clause . . . is not an uncommon occurrence in instances in which a prime contractor with the
federal government establishes a *subcontractual* relationship with other companies." *Atlantic States Constr., Inc.
v. Hand, Arendall, Bedsole, Greaves & Johnston*, 892 F.2d
1530, 1538 (11th Cir. 1990).

See **subcontract**.

*subfeudation. See **subinfeudation**.

*subfeudatory. See **subinfeudatory**.

subheading; subhead. Both *subheading* and *subhead*
are used in reference to a textual subdivision under
a heading. *Subheading* is much more common. *Subhead* is used especially in reference to legislation—e.g.:
"This legislation [Hammurabi's Babylonian code of
2350 B.C.] took the form of a code of 282 paragraphs,
regularly arranged under heads and *subheads*, dealing
with the rights of persons, property, the family, contracts, torts and procedure in a very adequate manner."
Stephen Pfeil, "Law," in 17 *Encyclopedia Americana* 86,
87 (1953). See **head**.

subinfeudate; *subinfeud. This term, a BACK-
FORMATION meaning "(of a feudal tenant-in-chief) to
grant a piece of land to a subtenant, who would hold
the land by one of the medieval tenures such as knight

service, serjeanty, frankalmoin, or socage," is ordinarily spelled *subinfeudate*—the shorter form being a
NEEDLESS VARIANT. E.g.:

- "The feudal lord who '*subinfeudates*' to a feudal tenant
should not be equated with the modern landlord who
'lets' to a tenant under a lease." Peter Butt, *Land Law* 38
(2d ed. 1988).
- "William the Conqueror '*leased*' the land to his chief followers, who in turn '*subinfeudated*' the land to others."
Bellikka v. Green, 762 P.2d 997, 1004 n.10 (Or. 1988) (en
banc).
- "Soon after the Norman Conquest tenants in chief who
held by knight service began to *subinfeudate*—i.e., to grant
portions of their lands." Roger A. Cunningham et al., *The
Law of Property* 15 (2d ed. 1993).

Some legal writers use the term figuratively, but few
readers are likely to follow the METAPHOR: "Indeed,
were that not true, the Commission, when dealing at
the outset with a colony of intricately *subinfeudated*
companies would be obliged to stop unraveling them
as soon as it reached any holding company." *Protective
Comm. for Class A Stockholders v. SEC*, 184 F.2d 646,
648 (2d Cir. 1950).

subinfeudation; *subfeudation. The second is a
NEEDLESS VARIANT.

subinfeudatory, dating from the 19th century, can be
either an adjective ("of or relating to subinfeudation") or
a noun ("one who holds land by subinfeudation"). The
noun use is rarer: "In France . . . the *sub-infeudatories* . . .
were expected to support their *immediate* lord in war."
C. Gordon Post, *An Introduction to the Law* 21 (1963).
*Subfeudatory is a NEEDLESS VARIANT.

subissue. See SUB-.

subject, adj., in the sense "that is or are the subject of
examination or consideration" <the subject property>,
is LEGALESE without redeeming value. E.g.:

- "The first [prerequisite] is a prior, unrelated history of
close and trusted dealings of the same general nature or
scope as *the subject transactions* [read *these transactions*
or *the transactions at issue*]." *Harris v. Sentry Title Co.*, 715
F.2d 941, 948 (5th Cir. 1983).
- "The *subject* [delete *subject*] property comprises 17,191
square feet of land zoned 'Waterfront Business.'" *Golemis
v. Kirby*, 632 F.Supp. 159, 160 (D.R.I. 1985).

For a different adjectival use of *subject*, see **subject to
contract**.

subject, n. See **citizen (A)**.

subjectability = the ability of something to be subject
to (a law, etc.). E.g.: "It would appear that the manufacturer and the importer, whose *subjectability to Oklahoma* [read *Oklahoma's*] jurisdiction is not challenged
before this Court, ought not to be judgment-proof."
World-Wide Volkswagen Corp. v. Woodson, 444 U.S.
286, 317–18 (1980) (Blackmun, J., dissenting). The
word is listed in neither *W2* nor *W3*, and is included

in *OED* merely with the notation "in recent dictionaries." The word is arguably useful, though somewhat inaesthetic.

subject matter; subject-matter. As a noun, two words; as a PHRASAL ADJECTIVE, one (hyphenated) in both AmE and BrE <subject-matter jurisdiction>. Only in BrE is the phrase hyphenated as a noun.

subject-matter jurisdiction; jurisdiction of the subject matter. The phrase is rendered both ways in modern legal writing. The longer form used to predominate—e.g.: "*Jurisdiction of the subject matter* is the power lawfully conferred to deal with the general subject involved in the action." *Hunt v. Hunt*, 72 N.Y. 217, 230 (1878). But today, *subject-matter jurisdiction* is more common and usually less cumbersome.

Subject-matter jurisdiction (= the extent to which a court can claim to affect the conduct of persons) is contrasted with *personal jurisdiction* (= a court's power to bring persons into its adjudicative process).

subject matter of the trust. See **corpus.**

subject to. See **notwithstanding.**

subject to change by mutual agreement. This phrase, seen occasionally in contracts, is worthless: everything in the contract is subject to a change of this kind.

subject to contract is a formulaic expression that has the effect of making a preliminary contract for the sale of land and houses nonbinding—until a formal or final contract records the agreement. The phrase is somewhat more common in G.B. than in the U.S., but it is used on both sides of the Atlantic. E.g.:

- "The Court of Appeal held that, as the preliminary agreement was '*subject to a proper contract*,' neither party had ever become bound." 1 Ernest W. Chance, *Principles of Mercantile Law* 30 (Percy W. French ed., 13th ed. 1950).
- "An acceptance '*subject to contract*' or 'subject to title' or any similar term is conditional, and amounts to a counteroffer which may be accepted or rejected by the original offeror as he desires." *Id.* at 38.

subject to the provisions of this Act. This REDUNDANCY appears frequently in common-law LEGISLATIVE DRAFTING. A variation is *subject to any contrary provision in this Act.* As often as not, it signals poorly organized drafting; certainly it makes the interpreter's job no easier. Cf. **notwithstanding anything to the contrary contained herein.**

SUBJECT–VERB AGREEMENT. A. False Attraction to Noun Intervening Between Subject and Verb. The simple rule is that plural subjects take plural verbs, and singular subjects take singular verbs. This subheading denotes a mistake in number usually resulting when a plural noun intervenes between a singular subject and the verb. The writer's eye is thrown off course by the plural noun that appears nearest the verb—e.g.:

- "Indeed the success of these cooperative enterprises *turn* [read *turns*] on this right." William F. Walsh, *A Treatise on Equity* 354 (1930).
- "The *cost* of all prosecutions *are* [read *is*] met out of the fund provided by the locality in which the proceedings take place." Patrick Devlin, *The Criminal Prosecution in England* 14 (1960).
- "*A group of cases have* [read *A group of cases has*, or *Several cases have*] enacted broad cy pres, or reformation, statutes, of which the Vermont statute is an example." Thomas F. Bergin & Paul G. Haskell, *Preface to Estates in Land and Future Interests* 218 (2d ed. 1984).
- "A third *set* of cases where plaintiffs seek only money *are* [read *includes* or *comprises*] suits to collect debts." Douglas Laycock, *The Death of the Irreparable Injury Rule* 17 (1991).
- "*Compliance* with the administrative complaint requirements of Title VII . . . *are* [read *is*] also *applicable* [read *mandatory*?]." Jack B. Moynihan, *After the Civil Rights Act of 1991*, Tex. B.J., May 1992, at 450, 454.
- "Unnecessary *enumeration* of particulars *are* [read *is*] not uncommon." Elmer Doonan, *Drafting* 38 (1995).

This error sometimes occurs when two or more nouns, seeming to create a plural, intervene between the subject and the verb—e.g.:

- "This amazing transformation has not been achieved solely by a concept of 'interference,' for the *provision* of 'works' (water, drainage, houses, transport, power, schools, hospitals and so on) and of 'facilities' (such as education, health services and social security) *do* [read *does*, because the subject is *provision*] not seem to be essentially interferences except to a one-track mind." R.M. Jackson, *The Machinery of Justice in England* 354 (5th ed. 1967).
- "Barefaced *defiance* of morals and law *were* [read *was*, because the subject is *defiance*] illegal." Lawrence M. Friedman, *Crime and Punishment in American History* 131 (1993).

See SYNESIS.

The reverse error, plural to singular, also occurs—e.g.: "Strict *interpretations* of statutory language *has* [read *have*] been used at one time to mitigate the severity of the law and (much more rarely) at another time to increase it." J.W. Cecil Turner, *Kenny's Outlines of Criminal Law* 38 (1952).

B. Reverse False Attraction. This occurs when the writer ignores the true and proximate subject by wrongly searching for a more remote subject earlier in the sentence—e.g.: "The character of punitive damages . . . depends on the function such damages *serves* [read *serve*]." *Northwestern Nat'l Cas. Co. v. McNulty*, 307 F.2d 432, 434 (Fla. Dist. Ct. App. 1962). (The writer apparently thought *function* to be the subject.)

C. False Attraction to Predicate Noun. Occasionally a writer incorrectly looks to the predicate rather than to the subject for the noun that will govern the verb. The "correct" way of phrasing the sentence is often awkward, so the writer is well advised to find another way of stating the idea—e.g.:

- "The second type of case on which I shall spend a little time *are* [read *is*] cases of negligence." H.L.A. Hart, "Intention and Punishment," in *Punishment and Responsibility: Essays in the Philosophy of Law* 113, 132 (1968). [A suggested edit to avoid awkwardness: *The second type of case on which I shall spend a little time is the case involving negligence . . . .*]

- "The appellate judge's immediate audience *are* [read *is*] his colleagues who sat with him when an appeal was argued." Frank M. Coffin, *The Ways of a Judge* 7 (1980).
- "Another *class* of case in which juries are notoriously more willing to acquit than magistrates *are* [read *is*] cases in which everything hinges upon a conflict between the evidence of police witnesses and of the accused." P.S. Atiyah, *Law and Modern Society* 22 (1983). [A suggested edit to avoid awkwardness: *Another class of case in which juries are notoriously more willing to acquit than magistrates is the case in which everything hinges upon a conflict between the evidence of police witnesses and of the accused.*]

D. Compound Subjects Joined Conjunctively.
E.g.:

- "At the same time, the democratic process and the personal participation of the citizen in his government is [read *are*] not all we want." Charles P. Curtis Jr., *Lions Under the Throne* 49 (1947) *The democratic process* and *personal participation* are different things.
- "During the past thirty years, prodigious empirical and theoretical research and commentary *has* [read *have*] provided an economic perspective on the operation of capital markets." Roger J. Dennis, *Materiality and the Efficient Capital Market Model*, 25 Wm. & Mary L. Rev. 373, 373 (1984). *Research* and *commentary* are different things.

Sometimes the two nouns joined by *and* arguably express a single idea and hence should take a singular verb—e.g.: "The confusion and uncertainty *is* compounded by doubt." Jerred G. Blanchard Jr., *Creeping Asset Acquisitions After TEFRA*, 38 Sw. L.J. 1053, 1053 (1985). (*Confusion and uncertainty* here describes a single mental state.)

One must be careful of the compound-noun phrase followed by a singular noun that properly is the singular subject: "First, we must decide whether the claim presented and the relief sought are of the type [that] *admit* [read *admits*, for the subject of the verb is *type*] of judicial resolution." *Powell v. McCormack*, 395 U.S. 486, 516–17 (1969) (per Warren, C.J.).

E. Alternatives.
The last element in a disjunctive series determines the number of the verb—e.g.:

- "It can hardly be otherwise so long as justices or a court *have* [read *has*] to deal with applications, because they must act on insufficient information." R.M. Jackson, *The Machinery of Justice in England* 156 (5th ed. 1967).
- "The Decree undoubtedly contemplates that the government would be able to object where, as here, the process of combatting discrimination depends not merely upon the development of particular lists, but upon *which* of two alternative lists *are* [read *is*] used." *Vulcan Pioneers, Inc. v. New Jersey Dep't of Civil Serv.*, 588 F.Supp. 727, 730 (D.N.J. 1984).
- "Consent to contract may be vitiated if fraud, error, violence or threats *induce* the consent." *McCarty Corp. v. Pullman-Kellogg, Div. of Pullman, Inc.*, 751 F.2d 750, 755 (5th Cir. 1985).
- "Written defamation (libel) was, nevertheless, treated in a special way by the criminal law, where neither publication nor untruth *were* [read *was*] required to be shown." J.H. Baker, *An Introduction to English Legal History* 506–07 (3d ed. 1990). See **neither . . . nor (A)**.
- "[T]he president or the governor *issue* [read *issues*] an executive order . . . ." Bob Dunn, *Contemplating Our Future*, 55 Tex. B.J. 448, 448 (1992).

See **either (B)**.

F. Plural Words Referred to as Words.
These take a singular verb. E.g.:

- "Neither 'per stirpes' nor 'descendants' *were* [read *was*] used in reference to the part of the estate Sue would get had George died intestate." *Harlan v. Citizens Nat'l Bank of Danville*, 251 S.W.2d 284, 287 (Ky. 1952).
- "But 'per stirpes' *were* [read *was*] not used in the phrase granting the power of appointment, *they were only used* [read *it* (i.e., the phrase) *was only used*] in disposing of the property if George died intestate." *Id.*

G. Misleading Connectives.
The phrases *as well as, added to, coupled with*, and *together with* do not affect the grammatical number of the nouns preceding or following them. When such a phrase joins two singular nouns, the singular verb is called for—e.g.:

- "The provision for the payment of interest on the fund held by appellee, *together with* the fact that there was no designation or segregation of any particular fund from which payment was to be made, *are* [read *is*] of interest in determining the intent." *Pierowich v. Metro. Life Ins. Co.*, 275 N.W. 789, 790 (Mich. 1937).
- "Logic, *as well as* equity, *dictate* [read *dictates*] this result." *Affiliated Capital Corp. v. City of Houston*, 793 F.2d 706, 709 (5th Cir. 1986) (en banc).
- "For example, he says, America's declining ability to compete in the global sale of automobiles and other manufactured products, as well as its status as the world's leading debtor nation, *are* [read *is*] partly the result of the declining cognitive abilities of workers and administrators." Malcolm W. Browne, *What Is Intelligence, and Who Has It?*, N.Y. Times, 16 Oct. 1994, § 7, at 3, 41.

See **together with**.

H. Plural Units Denoting Amounts.
In AmE, a plural noun denoting a small unit by which a larger amount is measured generally takes a singular verb—e.g.:

- "Before the leak was detected and the flow of oil shut down, approximately 2,400 barrels of crude oil *were* [read *was*] discharged into the creek." *Student Pub. Interest Research Group of N.J. v. AT&T Bell Labs.*, 617 F.Supp. 1190, 1194 (D.N.J. 1985).
- "Three or four days *are* [read *is*] enough time to inflict heavy damages on enemies." Gerhard Beestermöller & David Little, *Iraq: Threat and Response* 125 (2003).

See COLLECTIVE NOUNS & SYNESIS.

I. The False Singular.
"The situation of the employer and the employee in today's society is equivalent." *Smith v. Atlas Off-Shore Boat Serv., Inc.*, 653 F.2d 1057, 1061 (5th Cir. 1981). [Read *The situation of the employer and that of the employee in today's society are equivalent.*] It is the situations of the employer and the employee, not the persons themselves, that are being compared. See ILLOGIC (A).

J. Inversion. In the sentence that follows, the two *that*-clauses, dual subjects, demand a plural verb, although the writer was misled by the INVERSION into thinking a singular was needed: "*That this court has jurisdiction* to enforce a covenant between the owner of the land and his neighbor purchasing a part of it, *and that the latter shall either use or abstain* from using the land purchased in a particular way, *is* [read *are*] what I never knew to be disputed." *Tulk v. Moxhay*, [1848] 2 Phillips 774.

The error is less understandable in a simpler sentence: "As usual there *seems* [read *seem*] to be a million things happening around the Texas Law Center." Karen Johnson, *What's Happening at the Texas Law Center?*, Tex. B.J., May 1992, at 514. See **there is (B)**.

As in the preceding example, sentences that begin with the expletive *there* invert the order of the subject and the verb, thereby frequently causing confusion in number—even where, as here, the subject being discussed is grammatical number: "The result of this evolution is that there *is* [read *are*] now both a plural *media* and a singular *media*, and each means something different." Robertson Cochrane, *Verbum Sap*, 21 Verbatim 11, 11 (1994).

K. *Thing after thing (is) (are)*. E.g.:

- "Exception after exception *have* [read *has*] whittled away the rule." *Moore v. McAllister*, 141 A.2d 176, 179 (Md. 1958).
- "Assault after assault on the M'Naghten Rules *were* [read *was*] beaten off until 1957." H.L.A. Hart, "Changing Conceptions of Responsibility," in *Punishment and Responsibility: Essays in the Philosophy of Law* 186, 191 (1968).

Cf. **more . . . than (B)**. See CONCORD (A) & **media**.

L. Subject Area Implied. Some writers fall into the habit of implicitly prefacing plural nouns with UNDERSTOOD WORDS such as *the idea of* or *the law of*. To be sure, some of these wordings are, among lawyers, perfectly idiomatic—e.g.: "Torts is my favorite area of the law."

But the habit should not extend beyond the reach of idiomatic comfort—e.g.:

- "Estates and future interests *is* [read *make up*] a complex, highly technical body of material, foreign to most students' experience, and difficult to grasp." Thomas F. Bergin & Paul G. Haskell, *Preface to Estates in Land and Future Interests* v (2d ed. 1984).
- "Lives in being plus 21 years *has* no purpose in the commercial field." *Id.* at 208. [Read *The concept of lives in being plus 21 years has no purpose in the commercial field.*]

M. *One in five; one of every five*. This construction takes a singular: *one in three is not admitted*; *one of every five achieves a perfect score*. E.g.: "The truth is that in the period 1805–10, one in five of reported crimes *were* [read *was*] not prosecuted." Alan Harding, *A Social History of English Law* 276 (1966).

N. *A number of people (is) (are)*. See SYNESIS.

O. *One of those who (is) (are)*. See **one of those ——s who** (*or* **that**).

P. *Each* as Subject. See **each (A)**.

Q. *What* as Subject. See **what**.

subjoin. See **append**, vb.

sub judice (= before the court; awaiting judicial determination), though almost always an unnecessary phrase, rose tenfold in frequency of use between the 1940s and the 1980s in American judicial opinions. Structurally an adverbial of place, the phrase usually functions as a POSTPOSITIVE ADJECTIVE <case *sub judice*>.

The phrase is easily translated. *Case sub judice* readily becomes *case at bar*. Better yet, one might write *this case* or *the present case*—e.g.:

- "In the *case sub judice* [read *present case*] the pleading alleges the withholding of compensation for no legitimate or arguable reason." *Southern Farm Bureau Cas. Ins. Co. v. Holland*, 469 So.2d 55, 57 (Miss. 1984).
- "*The case sub judice* [read *This case*], like the other cases in which we have applied *Sherbert*, plainly falls into the former category." *Employment Div., Dep't of Human Res. v. Smith*, 494 U.S. 872, 900 (1990) (O'Connor, J., concurring).
- "Rule 404(b) is inapplicable *in the case sub judice* [read *in this case*]." *Williams v. State*, 3 So.3d 105, 112 (Miss. 2009).

See **case at bar** & **instant case**. See also LATINISMS.

The phrase is best pronounced either /sub **joo**-di-see/ or /sub **yoo**-di-kay/—and it ought to be two words, not one.

subjugable. So spelled.

subjugate (= [1] to conquer or bring under control; or [2] to subdue) should not be used for *subordinate*—e.g.: "To do so would be to *subjugate* [read *subordinate*] fairness and common sense to technical nicety." *Port v. Heard*, 764 F.2d 423, 428 (5th Cir. 1985).

SUBJUNCTIVES are concededly obsolete for the most part in English. They still survive in such constructions as "If I were," "If he were," etc. Legal writers frequently omit the subjunctive mood of the verb when they should use it, usually when the situation postulated is hypothetical or contrary to fact—e.g.:

- "Drafting is more than a mechanical process of recording the terms of a transaction in writing. If this *was* [read *were*] all that drafting involved, it would not be necessary to look to lawyers to do drafting." Elmer Doonan, *Drafting* 6–7 (1995).
- "Would your answer be different [hypothetical] if one of the creditors *was* [read *were*] the Internal Revenue Service?" *Estate of Sowell v. U.S.*, 198 F.3d 169, 171 n.3 (5th Cir. 1999) (quoting question asked at trial).
- "Suppose, instead, that the 'independent investigation' *was* [read *were* or *had been*] in equipoise on the misconduct issue." *Coe v. Northern Pipe Prods., Inc.*, 589 F.Supp.2d 1055, 1093 (N.D. Iowa 2008).
- "The claims of workmen for loss of wages who were employed in such a factory and cannot continue to work there because of a fire, represent only a small fraction of the claims which would arise if recovery *is* [read *were*, because the *if* is hypothetical] allowed in this class of cases." Eileen Silverstein, *On Recovery in Tort for Pure Economic Loss*, 32 U. Mich. J.L. Reform 403, 415 (1999).

It is ironic, in view of the sentences just quoted, that legal writers still often cling to basically outmoded subjunctives. Krapp labeled the usage *If I be* an "archaic survival" in 1927. *See* George P. Krapp, *A Comprehensive Guide to Good English* 651–52 (1927). But similar archaic examples abound in legal prose—e.g.:

- "If the nonresident *have* [read *has*] no property in the state, there is nothing upon which the tribunals can adjudicate." *Bowling Green Trust Co. v. Barnett*, 149 S.W. 311, 317 (Mo. 1912).
- "If after conviction a prisoner *become* [read *becomes*] insane, he cannot be hanged until his recovery." J.W. Cecil Turner, *Kenny's Outlines of Criminal Law* 75 (1952).
- "The House of Lords does now enjoy—if that *be* [read *is*] the appropriate word—the freedom not to follow its own previous decisions—a freedom only very recently acquired, and not, it would seem, likely by over-use to degenerate into licence." Leslie Scarman, *English Law— The New Dimension* 5 (1974).

When one relates an indirect question asking about past condition, and no hypothetical or contrariety to truth is implied, the simple past should be employed, and not the subjunctive. Confusion on this point is the most common among those who profess to know how to handle subjunctives—e.g.:

- "One inquired if the money *were* [read *was*] 'lost' property, and the other inquired if the money *were* [read *was*] 'mislaid' property." *Schley v. Couch*, 284 S.W.2d 333, 334 (Tex. 1955).
- "The trial court [held] that defendant breached no legal duty owed to the plaintiff, and that, even if a duty *were* [read *was*] breached, it was not a proximate cause of the accident that caused decedent's death." *Ross v. Ching*, 539 N.Y.S.2d 181, 181 (App. Div. 1989).
- "Even if it *were* [read *was*] error, it was harmless error to exclude the testimony." *Merckling v. Curtis*, 911 S.W.2d 759, 773 (Tex. App.—Houston [1st Dist.] 1995).

The three following sentences contain constructions in which—even in the modern idiom—the subjunctive is needed. In the first example, a demand or intention is expressed (this is one of the few exceptions to the obsolescence of subjunctives); the second sentence describes a condition that is contrary to fact:

- "It is not correct to assume that in the absence of a general verdict a jury understands or intends that its response to an interrogatory *is* [read *be*] a final expression of its conclusion on all the ultimate issues of a case." *Sangster v. Van Heck*, 353 N.E.2d 192, 194 (Ill. App. Ct. 1976).
- "Some courts have construed wills acts patterned upon the Statute of Frauds as if the signature rather than the will *was* [read *were*] the thing to be acknowledged by the testator." John Ritchie et al., *Cases and Materials on Decedents' Estates and Trusts* 234 (7th ed. 1982).

But in the following group of sentences, the subjunctive is vestigial and moribund and should therefore be changed to the indicative:

- "In England, fair comment includes the inference of motives if there *be* [read, in modern prose, *is*] foundation for the inference." *Coleman v. MacLennan*, 98 P. 281, 290 (Kan. 1908).
- "In Iowa, and generally elsewhere, the title to a decedent's real estate, whether he *die* [read *dies*] testate or intestate,

including the right of dower, vests in the heir, devisee or spouse instantly upon the death of the decedent." *Coomes v. Finegan*, 7 N.W.2d 729, 732 (Iowa 1943).

- "It is true that a party is sometimes bound to a promise made by him, even though there *were* [read *was*] no consideration at the time of making." *Northern Commercial Co v. United Airmotive*, 101 F.Supp. 169, 170 (D. Alaska Terr. 1951).

Having cited so many examples of misuse, this article might best end with a correct use of the subjunctive in its most common setting: "If the attesting witness swears he did not see the deed executed, I think it is then to be treated *as if there were no* attesting witnesses." *Allston v. Thompson*, [1840] 2 Campbell N.P.R. 636.

On the consistent progression of mood within a sentence, see TENSES (B).

sublease, n.; subtenancy; underlease. The first is the usual term in AmE and BrE. The other two are primarily BrE variants.

Unlike an *assignment* of a lease, in which the lessee's entire interest is transferred to the assignee from the assignor, a *sublease* transfers only the unexpired portion of the lease (often less one day) to the sublessee from the sublessor, who retains a reversion in the lease.

sublease, vb. See **let** & **underlease**.

sublessee; subtenant; undertenant. See **sublease**.

sublessor (AmE & BrE); **underlessor** (BrE). See **sublease**.

sublet. See **lease,** vb.

submersible; submergible. Though *submergible* seems simpler (cf. *persuadable* and **persuasible*), *submersible* is more common in both AmE and BrE. E.g.: "The defendant was performing workover operations on the plaintiff's gas well aboard a *submersible* drilling barge." *Bergeron v. Blake Drilling & Workover Co.*, 599 So.2d 827, 837 (La. Ct. App. 1992).

submissible; *submissable; *submittable. Even though it is labeled "rare" in the *OED*, *submissible* is frequently used in AmE. *See, e.g.,* Charles Alan Wright, *The Law of Federal Courts* 684 (5th ed. 1994) ("there is a *submissible* issue"). **Submissable* and **submittable* are NEEDLESS VARIANTS.

submission is used in several senses: (1) an argument by counsel in court <in his April 10 submission, Cochran argued to Judge Ito that the prosecution was trying to cause a mistrial>; (2) the agreement to abide by a decision or to obey an authority <our submission was limited to the 1992 dispute>; (3) the action of allowing, or agreement to allow, an authority to decide an issue <the voluntary submission of parties to the jurisdiction of courts>; or (4) the referring of a matter to arbitration <submission to arbitration by consent>.

---

*submittable. See **submissible.**

*submittal (= the act of submitting), though not uncommon in American legal writing, is a NEEDLESS VARIANT of *submission*—e.g.:

- "The public may obtain information, [or] make *submittals* [read *submissions*] or requests." Administrative Procedure Act, 5 U.S.C. § 552(a)(1)(a) (1982).
- "The *submittals* [read *submissions*] of the prosecution assert that testimony will be presented by eye witnesses to the listed incidents." *Rolle v. State*, 236 P.3d 259, 267 (Wyo. 2010).

sub modo (= under a qualification; subject to a restriction or condition) is a recherché LATINISM—e.g.: "But whether a creditor or a grantee of the plaintiff in this case would be entitled to the immediate possession of the property, *or would only take the plaintiff's title sub modo* [read *or would take title subject to the restrictions on plaintiff's title*], need not be decided." *Claflin v. Claflin*, 20 N.E. 454, 456 (Mass. 1889).

sub nom. (fr. L. *sub nomine*) = under the name. This abbreviation is commonly used, and justifiably so, in citations to note that a certain case may have involved different parties at an earlier or later procedural stage. E.g.: "Again, in *In re Morgani*, [1942] Ch. 347, the Court of Appeal . . . was doubtless relieved when it was reversed by the House of Lords *sub nom. Perrin v. Morgan*, [1943] A.C. 399." Carleton K. Allen, *Law in the Making* 382 (7th ed. 1964).

suborn; *subornate. *Suborn* = to get another to commit a crime, esp. perjury. E.g.: "To bribe a trustee, as such, is in fact neither more nor less than to *suborn* him to be guilty of a breach or an abuse of trust." Jeremy Bentham, *An Introduction to the Principles of Morals and Legislation* 240 n.3 (1823; repr. 1948).

*Subornate, a BACK-FORMATION from *subornation*, is a NEEDLESS VARIANT of *suborn*. E.g.: "The evidence . . . of the plaintiff's attempt to bribe the witness and *subornate* [read *suborn*] perjury was not being introduced to prove the plaintiff's character in order to show conformity as provided in Rule 404(b)." *Lay v. Mangum*, 360 S.E.2d 481, 483 (N.C. Ct. App. 1987).

subornation of perjury. Although *subornation* may mean in a general sense "the act of inducing or procuring a person to commit an evil action, by bribery, corruption, or the like" (*OED*), in practice today it almost invariably means "the act of procuring a person to commit perjury." Hence *subornation of perjury* is a virtual REDUNDANCY, though an established and therefore a pardonable one.

The verb corresponding to this noun is *suborn* (= to procure [another] to commit perjury), and the agent noun is *suborner*. See **suborn** & **suborner.**

subornee = one who is suborned. See -EE (A).

suborner is the preferred form, not **subornor*. E.g.: "The *suborner* was originally thought of as committing

a separate crime because it was a more serious offense than perjury—although it was not a felony except in very ancient times." Rollin M. Perkins & Ronald N. Boyce, *Criminal Law* 525 (3d ed. 1982). See -ER (A).

subpart. See SUB-.

*subpena. See **subpoena (B).**

subpoena. A. Sense. *W3* lists *subpoena* as an adverb meaning "under penalty" (or "under pain"). This, of course, is its etymological sense. It virtually never appears in modern legal writing with this meaning, and should be considered obsolete in that use.

The modern use is as a noun. Even in medieval English practice, *subpoena* served as a noun denoting the writ that commenced civil proceedings by ordering the defendant to attend under pain of a monetary penalty. Today, its meaning is "a court order commanding the presence of a witness under a penalty of fine for failure."

B. Form and Pronunciation. **Subpena*, the variant spelling recommended by the *Government Printing Office Manual* up until the early 1980s, appears in any number of American federal statutes. *Subpoena* is, however, by far the more common spelling and for that reason alone is to be preferred. Moreover, the better view is reflected in the *Government Printing Office Style Manual* as revised in 1984.

The form with the digraph *æ*—namely, *subpæna*—is pedantic at best in modern writing.

The plural is *subpoenas*, not **subpoenae*: *In re Two Grand Jury Subpoenae* [read *Subpoenas*] *Duces Tecum*, 769 F.2d 52 (2d Cir. 1985). "The *subpoenae* [read *subpoenas*] specifically called for, once again, interview memoranda. On June 6, 1984, the Government filed a motion to quash the *subpoenae* [read *subpoenas*]." *U.S. v. Omni Int'l Corp.*, 634 F.Supp. 1414, 1427 (D. Md. 1986). The form **subpoenae* results from the mistaken view that *subpoena* is a Latin singular noun, whereas it is a Latin phrase used as an English noun. See HYPERCORRECTION (A).

The word is pronounced /sə-**pee**-nə/ as both noun and verb.

C. Types. A *subpoena ad testificandum* /ad tes-ti-fi-**kan**-dəm/ is a subpoena to testify; usually, when *subpoena* is used alone, the word refers to this type. A *subpoena duces tecum* /doo-səs **tee**-kəm/ commands the witness not only to appear but also to bring specified books, papers, or records.

subpoena, vb. The inflected forms of this verb, which dates from the early 17th century, are *subpoenaed* and *subpoenaing*. The miscast forms **subpoened* and **subpoening* are fairly common—as is **subpoenaeing*.

Subpoena'd is an old BrE past-tense form. *See, e.g.,* Sir John Hawles's *Remarks upon Mr. Cornish's Trial*, [1685] 11 How. St. Tr. 455, 460 ("any person may inform in point of fact, though not *subpoena'd*.").

*subpoenable (= capable of being subpoenaed) is an ungainly NEOLOGISM of questionable utility—e.g.:

- "The results could be *subpoenable*." *People v. Pezzette*, 444 N.E.2d 1386, 1387 (Ill. App. Ct. 1983).
- "That is what Bruce insisted he was entitled to from The Ohio State University, which is the formal and *subpoenable* name of his last employer." *Bruce Passes Up Shot at Last Laugh*, Chicago Trib., 29 Nov. 1987, at C1.

subpoenal (= required or done under penalty) is listed in *W2*, but not in the *OED* or in *W3*. Still, it is occasionally useful as an adjective in the sense "required or done in compliance with a subpoena." E.g.: "Additionally, the petitioners contend that their right to produce witnesses on their own behalf will be impinged upon and that their right against self-incrimination will be violated by requiring them to testify under *subpoenal* compulsion." *A v. Curran*, 306 N.Y.S.2d 753, 755–56 (Sup. Ct. 1969).

subrogate = to put (a person) in the place *of*, or substitute (a person) *for*, another in respect of a right or claim; to cause to succeed *to* the rights of another (*OED*). It was once a general English word, more literary than vernacular; today it is mostly confined to legal contexts.

subrogation. A. Senses. *Subrogation* = (1) generally, the substitution of one party for another as a creditor, with the transfer of rights and duties; esp., an equitable assignment that substitutes a surety to the position of the creditor whom the surety has paid; (2) the principle under which an insurer that has paid the loss under an indemnity policy is entitled to take on all the rights and remedies belonging to the insured against a third party with respect to any injuries or breaches covered by the insurance policy; or (3) in civil law, the attribution of legal qualities usu. attached to one kind of property to a different kind of property. Cf. **novation.**

B. *Legal subrogation* **and** *conventional subrogation.* *Legal subrogation* arises by operation of law or by implication in equity to prevent fraud or injustice. *Conventional subrogation* arises by contract.

C. And *reimbursement; contribution; exoneration.* All of these equitable doctrines serve to prevent the unearned enrichment of one party at the expense of another by creating a relation similar to a constructive trust in favor of the party making payment in the creditor's legal rights. See **constructive trust (B).**

subrogative; *subrogatory; *subrogational. Among these less-than-common adjectives, *subrogative* appears most frequently—twice as frequently as **subrogatory* and more than three times as frequently as **subrogational*. It would therefore be convenient to treat the *-tory* and *-tional* forms as NEEDLESS VARIANTS and avoid them.

subrogee; *subrogatee. The usual form is *subrogee* (= a person put in the place or substituted for another in upholding a right or claim)—e.g.: "Subrogation is

a legal fiction [that] results in the substitution of the *subrogee* to the position of the subrogor." John T. Hood Jr., "Subrogation," in *Essays on the Civil Law of Obligations* 174 (Joseph Dainow ed., 1969). **Subrogatee* is an erroneous form—e.g.: "Any recovery by that company against the Hedger Company upon its cross-claim, up to the value of the barge, might be regarded as a recovery by a *subrogatee* [read *subrogee*], substituted for the creditor." *W.E. Hedger Transp. Corp. v. Gallotta*, 145 F.2d 870, 872 (2d Cir. 1944).

Subrogee is pronounced /sab-ra-**jee**/. Cf. **obligee.** See -EE (B).

subrogor (= one who allows another to be substituted for oneself as creditor, with a transfer of rights and duties) is a 20th-century legal NEOLOGISM created to correspond to *subrogee*. It is listed in *W3* but not in the *OED* or in *W2*. As a term corresponding to *subrogee*, *subrogor* is quite acceptable. The word is pronounced /sab-ra-**gohr**/. Cf. **subrogee.**

subscribe. For *subscribe* and its near-synonyms, see **assent,** vb. For the misuse of *ascribe* for *subscribe*, see **ascribe.**

subsequent. See **consequent (B).**

subsequently. A. For *later.* Using the four-syllable word in place of the two-syllable word is rarely, if ever, a good stylistic choice.

B. And *consequently.* Though both words contain the sense "following" or "occurring later," *consequently* has an added causal nuance: "occurring because of." See **consequent (B).**

*subsequent to is a lawyer's pomposity for *after* or *later*, just as **prior to* is for *before*. E.g.:

- "The marijuana obtained *subsequent to* [read *after*] the execution of the search warrant was lawfully obtained." *Commonwealth v. Rogers*, 741 A.2d 813, 820 (Pa. Super. Ct. 1999).
- "There are no material facts, circumstances, or events cited in defendant's certification that occurred *subsequent to* [read *after*] the divorce that form the good-faith reason for the removal." *Shea v. Shea*, 894 A.2d 711, 713 (N.J. Super. Ct. Ch. Div. 2005).
- "*Subsequent to* [read *After*] filing the motion to disqualify, appellant filed a request for production of documents." *Bank of N.Y. v. Miller*, 923 N.E.2d 651, 652 (Ohio Ct. App. 2009).

Used adjectivally (without *to*), *subsequent* is perfectly acceptable in phrases such as *condition subsequent* and *subsequent history* (of a case). See ***prior to** & **consequent (B).**

subserve is an ARCHAISM for *serve*. E.g.:

- "Religion in prison *subserves* [read *serves*] the rehabilitative function by providing an area within which the inmate may reclaim his dignity and reassert his individuality." *Barnett v. Rodgers*, 410 F.2d 995, 1002 (D.C. Cir. 1969).

- "The Supreme Court explained the important and manifold ends *subserved* [read *served*] by the opinion requirement in *Michigan Employment Relations Comm. v. Detroit Symphony Orchestra, Inc.*" *Nunn v. George A. Cantrick Co.*, 317 N.W.2d 331, 334 (Mich. Ct. App. 1982).
- "The view that the slavery-as-punishment clause *subserves* [read *serves*] the prohibition on cruel and unusual punishments does not comport with original-public-meaning originalism." Scott W. Howe, *Slavery as Punishment*, 51 Ariz. L. Rev. 983, 1033 (2009).

subsidence (= the act or process of settling or sinking) is pronounced /səb-**sɪd**-əns/ or /**sɔb**-sɪd-əns/. The word is sometimes misspelled *subsidance*—e.g.: "Appellant asserts the trial court erred in . . . finding that the passage of a truck trailer over a three to five inch *subsidance* [read *subsidence*] in a road is a 'collision' within the meaning of the policy." *Nutchey v. Three R's Trucking Co.*, 674 S.W.2d 928, 929 (Tex. App.—Amarillo 1984).

subsidiarity = (1) the quality of being subsidiary; or (2) the principle that a central authority, such as the European Community, should have a subsidiary function, performing only tasks that cannot be performed effectively at a more immediate or local level. A NEOLOGISM dating from the 1930s, it arose as a paraphrase of a 1931 speech given by Pope Pius XI, in which he used the German word *subsidiarität* (in sense 1). In legal contexts, sense 1 has traditionally been most usual—e.g.: "The requirement of *subsidiarity*, that no other remedy be available at law, is met because no contract exists under which recovery could be had." *Howell v. Rhoades*, 547 So.2d 1087, 1089 (La. Ct. App. 1989).

sub silentio, adj. & adv., is an often unnecessary LATINISM. In many contexts, *silent(ly)*, *tacit(ly)*, *under silence*, or *in silence* provides a good substitute. E.g.:

- "We do not interpret *Grady* as discarding, *sub silentio* [read *silently*], the civil/criminal methodology that the Court has developed." *State v. Lawton*, 482 N.W.2d 142, 148 (Wis. Ct. App. 1992).
- "The unwillingness of the majority in *Romer v. Evans* to address *Bowers v. Hardwick* did not mean that current U.S. Supreme Court jurisprudence had *accepted sub silentio* [read *tacitly accepted*] the identity model of homosexuality." Nancy J. Knauer, *Science, Identity, and the Construction of the Gay Political Narrative*, 12 Law & Sexuality 1, 55 (2003).

subsist. This verb was formerly used regularly in the sense "to exist." This usage is now a legalistic ARCHAISM. E.g.: "Such laws must be invariably obeyed, as long as the creature itself *subsists* [read, today, *lives*], for its existence depends on that obedience." 1 William Blackstone, *Commentaries on the Laws of England* 39 (1769). The more common word *exist* should now be preferred, especially since the usual meaning of *subsist* today is "to survive with a bare minimum of sustenance, to continue to exist; to keep oneself alive."

In the following sentences, *subsist* is used in its archaic sense:

- "In light of the *subsisting* [read *existing*] doubts surrounding that case and Justice Stevens' concurring opinion today, it ought to be evident that the issue is open to reconsideration." *California v. Deep Sea Research, Inc.*, 523 U.S. 491, 510 (1998) (Kennedy, J., concurring).
- "The plaintiff alleged that the 1996 deed did not destroy the joint tenancy *subsisting* [read *existing*] in the plaintiff." *Sathoff v. Sutterer*, 869 N.E.2d 354, 355 (Ill. App. Ct. 2007).

The general lay sense also appears in legal writing, a fact that may lead to AMBIGUITY if the archaic sense is retained: "On the basis of this sole difference the first class is granted and the second class is denied welfare aid upon which may depend the ability of the families to obtain the very means to *subsist*—food, shelter, and other necessities of life." *Shapiro v. Thompson*, 394 U.S. 618, 627 (1969) (per Brennan, J.).

subsistence is occasionally misspelled **subsistance*.

substantial damages. See **nominal damages.**

substantial performance = the equitable doctrine that, if a plaintiff fails to fulfill some of its detailed obligations under a contract, as by not performing quite on time, the plaintiff may nevertheless hold the defendant to his promise despite that failure if the substantial purpose of the contract is accomplished. E.g.:

- "The rule that gives a remedy in cases of *substantial performance* with compensation for defects of trivial or inappreciable importance has been developed by the courts as an instrument of justice." *Jacob & Youngs, Inc. v. Kent*, 129 N.E. 889, 892 (N.Y. 1921).
- "Rules of '*substantial performance*' were developed to protect plaintiffs who had almost, but not quite, completed performance." Grant Gilmore, *The Death of Contract* 74 (1974).

substantiate. See **authenticate.**

substantive, one of the words most commonly mispronounced by lawyers, has three, not four, syllables /**sʌb**-stən-tiv/. The common error in AmE is to insert what is known as an epenthetical -*e*- after the second syllable /**sʌb**-stə-nə-tiv/. Still another blunder is to accent the second syllable /səb-**stan**-tiv/.

substantive law. See **procedural law.**

*substantuate is solecistic for *substantiate*.

substitute; replace. *Substitute* = to put a person or thing in place of another <she will substitute for him>. *Replace* = (1) to put something or someone back in the same place as before; to restore to a former state; (2) to supply an equivalent of; (3) to return; (4) to repay; or (5) to put in a new place.

substituted service, a phrase contrasted with *personal service*, refers to any means of serving legal papers other than by delivering them directly to the person to be served. Examples of substituted service are service by publication in newspapers and service on the attorney instead of the party. The phrase *substituted service* is more common in AmE than its synonym, *constructive service*.

substitutional; *substitutionary; substitutive. In law, *substitutional* is the preferred form, **substitutionary*, a late-19th-century coinage, being a NEEDLESS VARIANT. Even so, **substitutionary* appears almost as frequently as *-al* in the law of wills. It should, like all other such variants, be uprooted. E.g.: "A remote power . . . will actually be exercised only by *substitutionary* [read *substitutional*] deed." *Commissioner v. Singer's Estate*, 161 F.2d 15, 18–19 (2d Cir. 1947). *Substitutive*, a learned word, almost never occurs in legal contexts.

SUBSUB-. See SUB-.

subsumed takes *under* or *in.*

sub suo periculo (= at his, her, or its peril) is a LATINISM with little to commend it. E.g.:

- "If the parent [who is] granted custody undertakes to foist restrictions [that] a court should not impose, he does so *sub suo periculo* [read *at his peril*]." *Asbell v. Asbell*, 430 S.W.2d 436, 439 (Mo. Ct. App. 1968).
- "When Patrolman Ward, relying on the statement of Regina Bailey, that he would not need his gun and unjudiciously holstered it, he did so '*sub suo periculo*' [read *at his peril*]." *Ward v. State*, 366 N.Y.S.2d 800, 808 (Ct. Cl. 1975).

subtenancy is a chiefly BrE variant of *sublease.* See **sublease.**

subtenant. See **sublessee.**

subterfuge is pronounced /**sub**-tər-fyooj/, not /fyoozh/. For more on this word, see **deception.**

subtle; *subtile. The second is an archaic and NEEDLESS VARIANT—e.g.: "Constitutions are not designed for metaphysical or logical *subtilties* [read *subtleties*]." *Boe v. Foss*, 77 N.W.2d 1, 6 (S.D. 1956).

subtraction, a common mathematical word, has a special meaning in law: "the withdrawal or withholding from a person of any right or privilege to which he or she is lawfully entitled." E.g.: "Among rights 'in personam,' family rights, and their analogues, are infringed by '*subtraction*,' adultery, refusal of due aliment, ingratitude on the part of a freedman, or neglect by a vassal of his feudal duties." Thomas E. Holland, *The Elements of Jurisprudence* 334 (13th ed. 1924).

subvention (= a grant of money—esp. a governmental grant—for the support of an object or institution), chiefly a BrE term, has no live verb corresponding to it: *subvene* and *subvent*, each illustrated with a single pre-1800 citation in the *OED*, are obsolete. But the noun is in fairly frequent use—e.g.: "On the Treasury accounts [legal aid] looks like a huge recurrent *subvention* to an indigent relative." Peter Sedley, *Breaking the Law*, London Rev. Books, 18 May 1989, at 3.

succedent. See **successive.**

succeeding for *after* or *following* is unnecessarily stuffy in most contexts—e.g.: "Those revenue rulings address situations in which the credit elect is needed to pay an estimated-tax liability for the year *succeeding* [read *after*] the overpayment year." *FleetBoston Fin. Corp. v. U.S.*, 483 F.3d 1345, 1352 (Fed. Cir. 2007).

succession, in law, has three primary senses: (1) the act or right of legally or officially coming into a predecessor's office, rank, or functions; (2) "the acquiring of an intestate share of an estate"; or (3) loosely, "the acquiring of property by will." E.g.:

- "Congress had plenary authority to abolish the power of testamentary disposition of Indian property and to alter the rules of intestate *succession*." *Hodel v. Irving*, 481 U.S. 704, 710 (1987) (per O'Connor, J.).
- "Jerold further contended that, when Aubrey died in 1978, the property passed by intestate *succession* to Jerold's mother." *Regions Bank v. Dean*, 29 So.3d 201, 204 (Ala. Ct. App. 2009).

(See **descent (B).**) The adjectival form of *succession* in this sense is *successional*. (See **successive.**)

Like *success*, *succession* is pronounced with the first *-c-* as if it were a *-k-*. Otherwise it is easily confused with *secession*. Cf. **accession, accessory** & **succinct.**

successive; successional; succedent. *Successive* = consecutive; following one after another, in uninterrupted succession. *Successional* = proceeding or passing by succession or descent. (See **succession.**) *Succedent to* is a pompous phrase meaning "following; after."

successor in interest. The phrase need not be hyphenated.

successors and assigns. See DOUBLETS, TRIPLETS, AND SYNONYM-STRINGS.

succinct. The first *-c-* is hard in this word. Cf. **succession, accession** & **accessory.**

such. A. As a Demonstrative Adjective. *Such* is properly used as an adjective when reference has previously been made to a category of persons or things: hence *such* = of this kind, not *this*, *these*, or *those*. With this word two points should be kept in mind. First, when used as a demonstrative adjective to modify a singular noun, *such* typifies LEGALESE as much as **aforesaid* and *same*, n. Contrary to what some think, *such* is no more precise than *the*, *that*, or *those*. Second, *such* is a DEICTIC TERM that must refer to a clear antecedent. In the following sentence, *such* is used once vaguely (without an antecedent), once clearly: "DeGraff Associated, Inc. agreed . . . 'to compile data on all conventions which will occur in cities where there are interested Gray Line members and forward *such* reports to *such* members.' " *Gelfand v. Tanner Motor Tours, Ltd.*, 385 F.2d 116, 118–19 (2d Cir. 1967). The first *such* would best have been omitted; no reports have been referred to—only the compilation of data, which is not necessarily the same as a report. The second *such*, less objectionable because the noun following it is plural, would read better as *those*.

H.W. Fowler calls the use of *such* in place of *the* or *that* "the illiterate *such*." E.g.:

- "*Such* cause of action, if any *such* there was, survived her death." *Koehler v. Waukesha Milk Co.*, 208 N.W. 901, 902 (Wis. 1926). A possible revision: *The cause of action, if there was any, survived her death.*
- "Objection to a juror because of his disqualification is waived by a failure to object to *such* [read *that*] juror until after verdict." *Pelfrey v. Commonwealth*, 842 S.W.2d 524, 526 (Ky. 1992).

Cf. **said** & **same.**

Like *said* and *same*, this word is much beloved of those who believe in the MYTH OF PRECISION. It therefore teems in the work of some drafters—e.g.:

Notwithstanding section 502 of this title, there shall not be allowed in *such* partner's case a claim against *such* partner on which both *such* partner and *such* partnership are liable, except to any extent that *such* claim is secured only by property of *such* partner and not by property of *such* partnership. The claim of the trustee under this subsection is entitled to distribution in *such* partner's case under 726(a) of this title the same as any other claim of a kind specified in *such* section.

/11 U.S.C. § 723 (1994)./

In that passage, all but the last *such* could be advantageously replaced by *the*; the last should be *that*. But from the viewpoint of good drafting, the whole section needs rethinking.

B. As a Pronoun. Although the pronoun use of *such* has ancient history on its side—it dates from the 9th century—today it is best regarded as an ARCHAISM except in a few such phrases as *such is life*. In legal contexts, the word is barbarous-sounding—e.g.: "I must dissent from the majority's holding that appellant's detention and ensuing search and seizure were lawful; *such* [read *that holding*] is pure dictum." (Notice that the last clause is nonsensical—*holding* and *dictum* being antithetical.) Indeed, Krapp called *such* a "crude low colloquialism." George P. Krapp, *A Comprehensive Guide to Good English* 568 (1927).

C. Such . . . as to. This generally unobjectionable construction should not be split by more than a few words: "A partisan attempt to influence its processes would be met with *such* widespread outrage *as to* be self-defeating." Andrew Geddis, *For We Are Young & Free*, 3 Election L.J. 385, 389–90 (2004). See **so as** [+ **infinitive**].

D. Such [noun + s] as are. Rephrase to avoid this archaic construction—e.g.: "We would expect Mrs. Hornback . . . to execute *such instruments as are necessary* [read *any instruments needed*] to place the title to any trailers or vehicles . . . in Mr. Hornback's name." *Hornback v. U.S.*, 298 F.Supp. 977, 980 (D. Mo. 1969).

such . . . as. See **some . . . as.**

sue, in the sense "to sue and win," is a common legal idiom in questions posed in law-school exams, as

in, "Can Y sue X?" As fully expressed, this question means, "Can Y sue X *successfully*?" Glanville Williams laments the exam answer that states, "Y can sue X but he will fail": "This displays the writer's common sense but also his lack of knowledge of legal phraseology. It is true that there is virtually no restriction upon the bringing of actions: for instance, I can at this moment sue the Prime Minister for assault—though I shall fail in the action. But when a lawyer asserts that [Y] can sue [X], what he means is that [Y] can sue [X] successfully; if he meant his words to be taken literally, they would not have been worth the uttering." Glanville Williams, *Learning the Law* 131 (11th ed. 1982).

sue facts (= facts that bear on whether to bring suit, esp. whether to institute a shareholder derivative action alleging a state-law cause of action) is an ungainly phrase from corporate-law JARGON. The phrase turns the verb *sue* into an adjective. Scholars have found this phrase more useful than judges, who have not used it—e.g.:

- "I will skip over Borden's intelligent analysis of the current state of the law in Delaware; interesting material on determining value and '*sue facts*'; the line-by-line dissection of SEC Rule 13e-3." James C. Freund, *Lawyer Confronts Peril in Going-Private Transactions*, Legal Times, 24 Jan. 1983, at 13.
- Harvey Gelb, *Rule 10b-5 and* Santa Fe—*Herein of* Sue Facts, *Shame Facts, and Other Matters*, 87 W. Va. L. Rev. 189 (1985).
- "It would be possible, of course, to interpret clause (b) as prohibiting only misrepresentations relating to investment decisions ('investment facts') rather than decisions to bring suit for an injunction or appraisal ('*sue facts*'), as several commentators have suggested." Dennis S. Karjala, *Federalism, Full Disclosure, and the National Market in the Interpretation of Federal Securities Law*, 80 Nw. U. L. Rev. 1473, 1545 (1986).

sue out. *Sue* is best known to lawyers and nonlawyers alike in the sense "to institute legal proceedings against." Historically it has also been used in the PHRASAL VERBS *sue out* and *sue forth*, more commonly the former, in the sense "to make application before a court for the grant of (a writ or other legal process), often with implication of further proceedings being taken upon the writ" (*OED*). E.g.:

- "[The] certificate from the clerk of the Court . . . [must state] the cause . . . and certify[] that such writ of error or appeal had been duly *sued out* and allowed." Sup. Ct. R. 32, 19 U.S. (6 Wheat.) vii (1821).
- "Again the defendant *sued out* a writ of error." R.E. Megarry, *A Second Miscellany-at-Law* 140 (1973).
- "Shortly after filing the second suit, the petitioner *sued out* writ of error in the first case." *Squire v. District Ct. of Arapahoe County*, 393 P.2d 4, 5 (Colo. 1964).
- "If an execution is not *sued out* within 5 years from the date of any judgment . . . the judgment becomes dormant and shall cease to operate as a lien on the estate of the judgment debtor." *Freis v. Harvey*, 563 N.W.2d 363, 366 (Neb. Ct. App. 1997).

The phrase *sue out*, then, is not one of the phrases in which a preposition (here *out*) is merely an unnecessary particle. See **out** (A) & PARTICLES, UNNECESSARY.

suffer (= to permit or acquiesce in) is legal JARGON— an archaic use of an ordinary English word.

sufferance; *suffrance; suffrage; *sufferage. *Sufferance* (= patent tolerance) is the correct spelling, not **suffrance*. *Suffrage* (= the right to vote) is the correct spelling, not **sufferage*. See **suffrage.**

suffice it to say is an inverted command equivalent to "Let it suffice (for me) to say." E.g.: "*Suffice it to say*, the Court finds that substantial evidence supported defendant's decision." *Berges v. Standard Ins. Co.*, 704 F.Supp.2d 1149, 1188 (D. Kan. 2010). The phrase is sometimes mangled into either *suffice to say* or *sufficient to say*—e.g.:

- "*Sufficient to say* [read *Suffice it to say*] that those are not the circumstances of this case." *Estate of Dillingham v. Commissioner*, 903 F.2d 760, 765 n.7 (10th Cir. 1990).
- "*Suffice to say* [read *Suffice it to say*] at this point that district courts have long struggled, in the absence of guidance from a higher authority, to reconcile the conflict between the common law concerns of § 1681h(e) and the sweeping ambit of § 1681t(b)." *Sites v. Nationstar Mortg. LLC*, 646 F.Supp.2d 699, 705 (M.D. Pa. 2009).

Although the phrase has a cut-to-the-chase quality of introducing a summary, it also sometimes amounts to little more than throat-clearing.

sufficiency; *sufficience. The second is a NEEDLESS VARIANT.

sufficient. See **adequate.**

sufficient doubt. See **bona fide** (C).

sufficiently . . . as to for *sufficiently . . . to* results from confusion with *so . . . as to*—e.g.:

- "These anomalies, however, appear *sufficiently* [read *so*] enmeshed in the current tangled web of the jurisprudence on this subject *as to* be beyond attempted amelioration by a panel of this court." *Findeisen v. North East Indep. Sch. Dist.*, 749 F.2d 234, 241 (5th Cir. 1984).
- "The state misperceives the *Henderson* rule, which is applicable in making an initial determination of whether a given instruction is *sufficiently defective as to* [read *so defective as to*] violate due process concepts." *Morrison v. Holland*, 352 S.E.2d 46, 49 (W. Va. 1986).

See **so as** [+ infinitive].

sufficient number of is verbose for *enough*—e.g.: "It is obvious also that if *a sufficient number of* [read *enough*] individuals so weaken themselves, society will thereby be weakened." Patrick Devlin, *The Enforcement of Morals* 111 (1968).

suffrage (= [1] the right given to a member of a body, state, or society to vote in assent to a proposition or in favor of the election of a person; or [2] by extension, the right to vote for or against any controverted question or nomination) typically calls up notions of *women's suffrage* or *universal suffrage*, the most common phrases in which the word appeared in the 20th century.

But the word has historically referred to the right of enfranchised citizens generally, without reference to disenfranchised groups—e.g.: "If we say that five or six hundred citizens are as many as can jointly exercise their right of *suffrage*, must we not deprive the people of the immediate choice of their public servants in every instance where the administration of the government does not require as many of them as will amount to one for that number of citizens?" *The Federalist* No. 57, at 354 (James Madison) (Clinton Rossiter ed., 1961).

*Sufferage is a common misspelling. Cf. **sufferance.**

*suffrance. See **sufferance.**

suggest. See **allude** (C).

*suggestable. See **suggestible.**

suggestibility; compliance. These two terms have become key words in the law relating to false confessions. *Suggestibility* is the readiness with which a person accepts another's suggestion. Generally speaking, people are more suggestible if they are unassertive, diffident, anxious, or unintelligent. Young people, too, are more suggestible than older people. *Compliance* is the extent to which a person will follow another's wishes to avoid confrontation or for some other short-term gain. A compliant person is usually eager to please and wants to avoid clashing with authority. *Compliance* can result from feelings of guilt. *See* Dorothy Wade, *Why Say "I Did It" If You Didn't?*, The Independent, 23 Feb. 1992, at 22.

suggestible; *suggestable. The first spelling is preferred.

suggestio falsi; suppressio veri. *Suggestio falsi* (lit., "suggestion of an untruth") = misrepresentation without direct falsehood. *Suppressio veri* (lit., "suppression of the truth") = the failure to clarify a false impression in another in circumstances in which a duty to clarify exists; a tacit misrepresentation; a silent lie. These LATINISMS may be useful (probably with an accompanying explanation), for there are no comparably short English phrases that convey the same notions. F.W. Maitland cleverly used the phrases in figurative senses: "That is the worst of our mortgage deed—owing to the action of equity, it is one long *suppressio veri* and *suggestio falsi*. It does not in the least explain the rights of the parties; it suggests that they are other than they really are." F.W. Maitland, *Equity* 182 (J. Brunyate ed., 2d ed. 1936). See **lie,** n.

suicide. A. And *self-killing; self-murder; self-slaughter; felo-de-se.* The five terms are generally synonymous, though the phrases *self-murder* and *self-slaughter* are charged with extremely negative connotations. *Suicide* and *self-killing* are broad terms that include every instance in which a person causes his or her own death within the legal rules of causation.

Not always, though, was *suicide* so broad; when first used in the 17th century, it referred only to "the self-killing of a criminal fearing a worse fate: its scope grew steadily, in step with the tendency, profitable to the crown, to declare forfeit the goods of anyone who died by violence." Alan Harding, *A Social History of English Law* 64 (1966).

Suicide used to be included within the definition of *homicide* (= the killing of a human being by a human being), but the modern trend has been to distinguish the one from the other by defining *homicide* as "the killing of a human being by *another* human being."

B. As an Agent Noun. In the early 18th century, *suicide* took on the secondary sense of "one who dies by his or her own hand," and the word has been steadily used with this meaning ever since—e.g.: "Both the elder of Anne's sisters, Jane, and an aunt, Frances, were *suicides*." John Simon, *Connoisseur of Madness, Addict of Suicide*, New Criterion, Dec. 1991, at 58, 59. Earlier synonyms, now less frequently employed, include *self-destroyer, self-killer, self-murderer, self-slayer,* and *felo-de-se.*

C. As a Verb. The verb has been used intransitively <he suicided>, reflexively <he suicided himself>, and transitively <he suicided her>. In the intransitive and reflexive uses, the senses are self-evident; in the transitive use, the sense is "to drive to suicide." In legal writing, the most common use is the intransitive one—e.g.:

- "Three days later he *suicided* by drowning in Sanhican Creek." *Bullis v. Pitman*, 105 A. 589, 590 (N.J. Ch. 1918).
- "Whatever the diagnosis of Nott's case, the inescapable fact remains that he *suicided* within forty-eight hours after his discharge." *Nott v. State*, 75 N.Y.S.2d 737, 740 (Ct. Cl. 1947).
- "On November 14, 1963, his mother, Lorine Asher Toole, *suicided*." *State v. Toole*, 173 So.2d 872, 873 (La. Ct. App. 1965).

suicide victim, a seeming OXYMORON, is a phrase that suggests a dogmatic stand on the issue whether suicide is ever justifiable. The less doctrinaire equivalent, *suicide* (n.), probably better suits most legal contexts. E.g.: "Typically, in his experience, the gun is found on the seat next to *suicide victims* [read *suicides*] or clutched in their hands." *State v. Barrett*, 445 N.W.2d 749, 756 (Iowa 1989) (Lavorato, J., dissenting).

sui juris; sui generis. *Sui juris* /**soo**-ee **jur**-əs/ = (1) of full age and capacity; or (2) having full social and civil rights. Sense 1 is more usual—e.g.:

- "Unless relieved by the provisions of a will or the consent of *sui juris* beneficiaries, the personal representative of an estate is obligated to convert personalty into cash during the administration of the estate." *In re Estate of Austin*, 920 S.W.2d 209, 212 (Tenn. 1996).
- "Respondent argues that because he was old enough to be *sui juris* and the state constitution granted him the right to bear arms, then he could not be charged with a crime for handgun possession." *State v. Bolin*, 662 S.E.2d 38, 39 (S.C. 2008).
- "Courts typically analyze children's 'interests' rather than 'rights' because the latter inhere in a person who is *sui*

juris." Seymour Moskowitz, *Save the Children*, 43 Akron L. Rev. 107, 143 (2010).

Often this LATINISM is easily translated into ordinary English; when that is so, it should be.

Sui generis /**soo**-ee **jen**-ə-rəs/ (= of its own kind; individual; like only to itself) is an acceptable LATINISM because of its familiarity. The phrase is singular only, and should not be used with plural nouns. E.g.:

- "The canine sniff is *sui generis*. We are aware of no other investigative procedure that is so limited both in the manner in which the information is obtained and in the content of the information revealed by the procedure." *U.S. v. Place*, 462 U.S. 696, 707 (1983) (per O'Connor, J.).
- "Analyzing the hybrid nature of [a] primary liability claim with the character of secondary liability, in light of the *sui generis* nature of terrorism, the court crafted a standard of liability for claims of material support to terrorism." *Abecassis v. Wyatt*, 704 F.Supp.2d 623, 657 (S.D. Tex. 2010).
- "This class of cases presents a *sui generis* issue for applying the enterprise regulation principle." Joanna B. Apolinsky & Jeffrey A. Van Detta, *Rethinking Liability for Vaccine Injury*, 19 Cornell J.L. & Pub. Pol'y 537, 612 (2010).

The terms are sometimes confused. In the following sentence, for example, *sui juris* is wrongly used for *sui generis*: "The expression 'uninhabited dwelling' is *sui juris* [read *sui generis*] and should be given some meaning not covered by the term 'dwelling' itself." *Reeves v. State*, 16 So.2d 699, 702 (Ala. 1943).

suit, n.; lawsuit; action; case; cause. All these nouns denote proceedings instituted for the purpose of enforcing a right or otherwise seeking justice. Although they are all in frequent use as synonyms for a court proceeding, their etymological development has lent them shades of meaning that they still faintly bear. *Suit* stresses the sense of campaign—originally a lover's persistent efforts to win love as a suitor but now a complainant's attempt to redress a wrong, enforce a right, or compel application of a rule. *Suit* is historically most closely associated with proceedings in equity <suit in equity>. In the legal sense, *suit* refers to an ongoing dispute at any stage, from the initial filing to the ultimate resolution. *Lawsuit* more clearly implies courtroom proceedings before a judge, as opposed to a dispute before some other type of tribunal.

Action is close to *suit* and *lawsuit* <action on the case>, but historically *action* was closely tied to legal as opposed to equitable proceedings. Because *action* denotes a mode of proceeding in court not just to enforce a private right or to redress or prevent a private wrong, but also to punish a public offense, it is possible to speak of criminal actions. When the jurisdictional distinction between law and equity existed, an *action* ended at judgment, but a *suit* in equity ended after judgment and execution. Today, since virtually all jurisdictions have merged the administration of law and equity, the terms *action* and *suit* are interchangeable. See **suit.**

Case can apply either to the entire proceedings <the case has been pending for 19 months> or to the merits of the action from either side's point of view <the plaintiff has a good case> <the defendant has a good case>.

Cause, a LEGALISM, emphasizes the merits of the action from the plaintiff's point of view, especially with the connotation of seeking justice <the ex-employee's cause for wrongful discharge>. (See **cause (A).**) Although *cause* and *action* are nearly synonymous, the legal idioms in which the phrases are used differ. So an *action* or *suit* is said to be "commenced," but a *cause* is not. Similarly, a *cause* but not an *action* is said to be "tried." The distinction between the words is subtle: broadly, *action* connotes legal procedure and *cause* denotes the merits of the dispute (again, from the plaintiff's vantage).

The first edition of *Black's Law Dictionary* noted the DIFFERENTIATION between *case* and *cause*, although if it does exist at all it is little heeded: "*case* is of a more limited signification, importing a collection of facts, with the conclusion of law thereon," whereas "*cause* imports a judicial proceeding entire, and is nearly synonymous with *lis* in Latin, or *suit* in English." *Black's Law Dictionary* 181 (1st ed. 1891).

One more point about idiom. *Causes* (or *cases*) are *on dockets*; they may be *remanded* (by an appellate court) or *disposed of* (by any court). But they may not be *reversed* or *affirmed*. E.g.: "This is the keystone of the opinion below: If it is in error, the *cause must be reversed* [read *judgment must be reversed*]." *Great Am. Ins. Co. v. Sharpstown State Bank*, 460 S.W.2d 117, 122 (Tex. 1970). See JUDGMENTS, APPELLATE-COURT.

suit, vb. (= to sue), is obsolete in legal English, although the negative form *nonsuit* is still used as a verb. See **action (A)** & **nonsuit.**

suitability, in the sense "liability to suit" <the suitability of the states of the union>, is recorded in none of the major dictionaries. This sense is obfuscatory at best for lawyer-readers as well as for nonlawyers; it should be avoided. See ***nonsuitability.**

suitable; suitability. See ***nonsuitability.**

suit at law is an especially formal way of saying *lawsuit*, the usual term today. Generally, the careful writer would prefer to use one word rather than three if no nuance is lost. But when law is contrasted with equity, as in the following example, using the phrase makes good sense: "Here, the Neuzils filed the *suit at law* [i.e., as opposed to an equitable action]." *Neuzil v. City of Iowa City*, 451 N.W.2d 159, 163 (Iowa 1990). See **suit.**

suit in equity. See **civil action.**

suit money. In some American jurisdictions, this phrase refers to the husband's payment of the wife's attorney's fees in a divorce action.

suitor has virtually opposite meanings in lay and legal language, though a 17th-century writer found common ground: "Amonge sutors in love and in lawe

money is a comoun medler" (*OED* quot. fr. ca. 1660). The lay *suitor* seeks matrimony; the legal *suitor* seeks legal redress.

Suitor is properly used only of a *complainant* or *plaintiff* in a suit, as opposed to a *defendant*. E.g.:

- "[Congress] could have declined to create any such courts, leaving *suitors* to the remedies afforded by state courts, with such appellate review by this Court as Congress might prescribe." *Lockerty v. Phillips*, 319 U.S. 182, 187 (1943) (per Stone, C.J.).
- "Like other *suitors*, the Government is entitled to a fair and impartial trial before a jury of 12 impartial and unbiased jurors." *U.S. v. Chapman*, 158 F.2d 417, 419 (10th Cir. 1946).
- "Burdensome as the security-for-costs requirement may be, *Cohen* made plain [that] *suitors* could not escape the upfront outlay by resorting to the federal court's diversity jurisdiction." *Shady Grove Orthopedic Assocs. v. Allstate Ins. Co.*, 130 S.Ct. 1431, 1462 (2010) (Ginsburg, J., dissenting).

In the context of mergers and acquisitions, *suitor* retains its overtones of wooing: "The Delaware Supreme Court, in a ruling late yesterday afternoon, blocked a takeover of the publishing company by a rival *suitor*, Kohlberg, Davis, Roberts & Company, the leveraged-buyout firm." Jacob I. Fabrikant, *Maxwell Wins on Macmillan*, N.Y. Times, 3 Nov. 1988, at 29.

suit over. See **over (A).**

suit papers. See **court papers.**

sum certain. See POSTPOSITIVE ADJECTIVES.

summarily = by summary legal procedure. E.g.: "When you are prosecuted for dangerous driving you may, if you wish, refuse to have your case dealt with in the police court—i.e. '*summarily*'—and insist on being tried by a jury." Anon., *The Home Counsellor* 112 ([London: Odhams Press] ca. 1940–1945).

summary judgment = a judgment granted on a claim, about which there is no genuine issue of material fact and upon which the movant is entitled to prevail as a matter of law. See Fed. R. Civ. P. 56.

When used as a PHRASAL ADJECTIVE, *summary judgment* needs to be hyphenated: "And still more pressure was coming from Fish, who might well gut the Hunts' entire case by granting the banks' *summary judgment* [read *summary-judgment*] motion." John A. Jenkins, *The Litigators* 294 (1989).

summary offence; indictable offence. In England, crimes are divided into *summary offences*, which are triable in the lower courts (magistrates' courts) without a jury, and *indictable offences*, which are triable in the Crown Court by jury. A few indictable offences, sometimes known as *hybrid offences* or *dual offences*, are triable either on indictment or summarily. *Summary offences* were formerly known as *petty offences*, but the expression fell into disuse because it minimized the seriousness of the crimes it described.

As Glanville Williams notes, the phrase *summary offence* has two liabilities: it exemplifies HYPALLAGE and misleadingly suggests greater substantive differences than it denotes: "The term '*summary offence*' is now established, and is used in legislation; but it is somewhat inappropriate, since what is summary is not the offence itself but the mode of procedure. Even as applied to the mode of procedure 'summary' is an infelicitous adjective, because the procedure of magistrates' courts is supposed in general to be as careful and formal as trial by jury." Glanville Williams, *Textbook of Criminal Law* 10 (1978).

summation (AmE) = (1) the lawyer's closing argument at trial; or (2) formerly, a judge's closing speech to the jury summarizing the evidence (an equivalent of the BrE sense of *summing-up*)—e.g.: (Sense 2) "The court in its *summation* of the evidence to the jury, referred to that fact." *Kelly v. Georgia*, 68 F. 652, 657 (S.D. Ga. 1895).

summer associate. See **clerk.**

summing-up is the British phrase meaning "the judge's summary for the jury of the main points in evidence, together with his guidance on the form of the verdict to be given." E.g.:

- "In instructing the jury the trial judge, even in those jurisdictions where *summing-up* is held proper, is under no obligation to do so, unless he sees fit." 11 William M. McKinney & Thomas J. Michie, *The Encyclopedia of Pleading and Practice* 200 (1898).
- "The Judge's *summing-up* was brief but thorough, and after a short retirement the jury brought in a verdict of guilty." Stanley Jackson, *The Life and Cases of Mr. Justice Humphreys* 175 (n.d. [1951]).

The AmE equivalent is *jury instructions* or *instructions to the jury*.

In AmE, *summing up* refers to the closing arguments of counsel: "The judge instructs the jury orally at the conclusion of the trial after the *summing-up* arguments of counsel to the jury." Charles Alan Wright, *The Law of Federal Courts* 672 (5th ed. 1994).

summon, vb.; **summons,** vb.; **cite; call; convene; convoke.** All these verbs mean "to demand the presence of one or more people—or, by extension, of things." *Summon* implies an authoritative order or command, often with a sense of urgency <the President summoned his cabinet>. *Summons,* a colloquialism when used as a verb, implies that the summoning is carried out with a written order, such as an official citation that is served as legal process <they were summonsed to court>. (See **summons,** vb.) *Call,* often in the phrase *call up* or *call forth,* is a less formal term that may involve a range of actions from yelling to gain attention <call for help> all the way to the more staid naming of one's next courtroom witness <call your witness>. *Cite,* like

summons, implies a written legal notice to appear in court, either as a party or as a witness; in historical BrE, *cite* in this sense is associated mostly with ecclesiastical courts. *Convoke* suggests a calling together of several or many persons to assemble for legislative or deliberative purposes, or perhaps for religious exercises (hence *convocation*). *Convene* less strongly suggests an imperative order in most modern contexts. Instead, it connotes the drawing together of members for a meeting <let's convene now: we're running a little late>. In civil law, to *convene* is to sue <the defendant was convened by the plaintiff>.

summonee (= one who has been summoned) is omitted from the *OED*, *W3*, and most other dictionaries, but it has proved useful in legal writing. E.g.: "The *summonees*' attempt to bring the *summoned* [read *summonsed*] documents within the work product doctrine is similarly meritless." *U.S. v. Davis*, 636 F.2d 1028, 1039 (5th Cir. 1981). See -EE (A) & **summons,** vb.

summons, n., = (1) formerly, a writ directing a sheriff to summon a defendant to appear in court; or (2) a writ or process commencing the plaintiff's action and requiring a defendant to appear and answer.

summons, vb., dates from the 17th century and is still in fairly common use in the sense (1) "to cite to appear before a court or a judge or magistrate"; or (2) "to request (information) by summons." The verb is properly inflected *summonsed* in the past tense, *summonses* in the third-person singular.

The term *summonsed* has some notable detractors, including U.S. District Judge Lynn N. Hughes, who has criticized the verb in private correspondence, and Glanville Williams: "The horrible expression '*summonsed* for an offence' (turning the noun 'summons' into a verb) has now become accepted usage, but 'summoned' remains not only allowable but preferable." Glanville Williams, *Learning the Law* 15 n.28 (11th ed. 1982).

When used in sense 1, as by saying that a *person* is *summonsed*, the verb appears to be a NEEDLESS VARIANT of *summon,* vb.: "I came here because I had been *summonsed* [read *summoned*] by Medina council to pay £342." David Sapsted, *Poll Tax Case Collapses in Confusion*, Times, 2 June 1990, at 1 (quoting David Icke).

In modern legal usage, however, a latent DIFFERENTIATION has emerged: by HYPALLAGE has arisen the idiom that *information* may be *summonsed*, as in sense 2. E.g.:

- "We view the requirement in this Circuit to be that the taxpayer must show that the Government actually possesses the information *summonsed*, such that enforcement of a summons is 'unnecessary.'" *U.S. v. Texas Heart Inst.*, 755 F.2d 469, 476 (5th Cir. 1985).
- "The record does not contain sufficient summary judgment evidence that the IRS or the MTA obtained or possessed the *summonsed* information." *Bull D., S.A. de C.V. v. U.S.*, 487 F.Supp.2d 772, 779 (W.D. Tex. 2007).

summonses is the correct plural form of *summons*, n. E.g.:

- "The District Court granted summary judgment to respondents because the *summonses* and complaints were not mailed nor service acknowledgments made until after the 6-month period." *West v. Conrail*, 481 U.S. 35, 35 (1987) (per Stevens, J.).
- "The clerk indicated that Gonsalves had failed to respond to the *summonses* and that a warrant had been issued for her arrest." *Hager v. Gonsalves*, 942 A.2d 160, 162 (N.J. Super. Ct. 2008).

sumptuous; sumptuary. These words have almost opposite senses. *Sumptuous* = excessively luxurious; made or produced at great cost <a sumptuous hotel suite>. *Sumptuary* = relating to regulating expenditures by individuals on food, clothing, jewelry, and other personal items <luxury-car taxes are really just modern sumptuary laws>.

sundry (= various) is, in AmE, a quaint term with literary associations. The clichéd DOUBLET *various and sundry* ought to be avoided even in the most casual contexts, for it smacks of glibness.

sunk. See **sink.**

sunset law; sunshine law. Though superficially appearing as if they might be antonyms, these picturesque terms for administrative laws have little relation apart from their both arising in AmE during the 1970s.

Sunset law = a statute under which a governmental agency or program automatically terminates at the end of a fixed period unless it is formally renewed. By extension, the transitive verb *sunset* (= to subject to such a statute) likewise came into existence in the late 1970s. E.g.: "The legislature's failure to provide 'phase-out' deregulation resulted in the *sunsetting* of the entire state motor carrier regulatory scheme." *Alterman Transp. Lines, Inc. v. Department of Transp.*, 519 So.2d 1005, 1008 (Fla. Dist. Ct. App. 1987). The past tense and past participle are awkwardly made *sunsetted*—e.g.: "We cannot decide to send this case first to the Collection Agency Board because it was *sunsetted* effective December 31, 1980." *Wiginton v. Pacific Credit Corp.*, 634 P.2d 111, 117 (Haw. Ct. App. 1981).

Sunshine law = a statute requiring a governmental department or agency to open its meetings and its records to public access. E.g.: "*Sunshine laws* are aimed chiefly at keeping administrative decisions above board. The underlying assumption of *sunshine laws* is that it is unwise to permit our administrators to make public policy decisions behind closed doors." Kenneth F. Warren, *Administrative Law in the American Political System* 187 (1982).

superadd (= to add over and above) is rarely used in lay, and infrequently in legal, contexts. It is usually pompous in place of *add*—e.g.: "In many legal systems, therefore, a discretionary or moderating influence has been *superadded* [read *added*] to the rigour of formulated law." Carleton K. Allen, *Law in the Making* 385 (7th ed. 1964). See **append**, vb.

*supercede. See **supersede.**

supererogatory has two almost opposite sets of connotations, some positive and others negative. The core sense is "going beyond what is required." On the one hand, the word may connote "superfluous," and is often used in this way. On the other hand, it may mean "performing more than duty or circumstances require; doing more than is minimally needed."

superfirm = a large, prestigious law firm. E.g.: "Chris Harvey is from the Dallas *superfirm* of Strasburger, Price, Kelton, Martin and Unis, which has the reputation of being perhaps the best insurance defense office in Texas." Joseph C. Goulden, *The Million Dollar Lawyers* 72 (1978). Cf. **superlawyer**.

SUPERFLUITIES of various kinds may be found in most legal writing. This entry contains a few common examples of unnecessary words: "A foreign mining corporation [may] carry on . . . such functional intrastate operations as *those of* [omit *those of*] mining or refining." *Perkins v. Benguet Consol. Mining Co.*, 342 U.S. 437, 445 (1952) (per Burton, J.).

Verbs are often unnecessarily repeated in comparisons—e.g.: "While neither adoption nor grandparental visitation existed at common law, the former has been statutorily recognized for much longer than *has* [omit *has*] the latter." *Hede v. Gilstrap*, 107 P.3d 158, 171 (Wyo. 2005).

Superfluous commas abound in most older judicial opinions—e.g.:

- "The declaration stated, [omit comma] that the plaintiff . . . ." *Harris v. Watson*, [1791] 170 E.R. 94 (K.B.).
- "The witness who proved this, [omit comma] said . . . ." *Butterfield v. Forrester*, [1809] 11 East. 60 (K.B.).

Even today, sentences just like those two are commonplace.

The best contemporary writing is free from such minor refuse; the fewer impediments we put in the way, the more likely readers are to follow. See CUTTING OUT THE CHAFF & VERBOSITY.

superimpose; *superpose. Both forms are used in legal writing, the older form, *superimpose* (1794), being more familiar to most readers. E.g.: "The privacy rule does not prevent this informal discovery from going forward, it merely *superimposes* procedural

---

prerequisites." *Arons v. Jutkowitz*, 880 N.E.2d 831, 842 (N.Y. 2007). **Superpose*, today rightly counted among NEEDLESS VARIANTS, is recorded from 1823.

super-injunction. In U.S. bankruptcy law, an automatic stay has occasionally been called a *super-injunction* because a creditor receives no notice or hearing before a court issues an order restraining the creditor from taking action on a claim. The term is more common in the U.K., where it means a prohibition on all media from identifying the parties in a legal dispute and even from reporting that restrictions have been imposed on the media—e.g.: "English courts are clamping down harder, granting secret *super-injunctions* to avoid giving internet rumour-chasers any crumb of information." *Press Freedom and the Internet: Barbra Streisand Strikes Again*, Economist, 17 Oct. 2009, at 23. The *super-injunction* may be issued against one specific medium, but it binds all media organizations that are notified of the injunction.

superior. See **inferior.**

superlawyer dates from the early 1960s but was not popularized until Joseph C. Goulden published his book *The Superlawyers* in 1971. The word, largely confined to journalism, is typical of the glitzy, hyperbolic labels characteristic of journalese—as the second and third examples illustrate:

- "The French *notaire* is a *superlawyer*, especially trained for his work, a combination of lawyer, court clerk, and petty judge." René A. Wormser, *The Story of the Law* 213 n.† (1962).
- "This man . . . makes probably as much money a year as . . . the fabled Washington *superlawyers* Clark Clifford and Lloyd Cutler." Joseph C. Goulden, *The Million Dollar Lawyers* 76 (1978).
- "The Harvard law professor and *super-lawyer* has crowded his office in Cambridge, Mass., with enough paraphernalia to stock a Dershowitz museum." Steven Taylor, *Dershowitz on the Offensive*, National Jurist, Apr.–May 1992, at 10.

The adjective *super-lawyerlike* may predate the noun: "In all likelihood, the general slant of the new Justice will be just about the opposite of Reed's—except for a similarly *super-lawyerlike* over-attention to detail." Fred Rodell, *Nine Men* 329 (1955). See **lawyerly.**

superlegislature. This tendentious term, dating from the 1920s, describes a court that usurps the power of the legislative branch of government. E.g.:

- "To decide . . . [these matters] is, in my opinion, an exercise of the powers of a *super-legislature*—not the performance of the constitutional function of judicial review." *Jay Burns Baking Co. v. Bryan*, 264 U.S. 504, 534 (1924) (Brandeis, J., dissenting).
- "Our recent decisions make plain that we do not sit as a *super-legislature* to weigh the wisdom of legislation nor to decide whether the policy which it expresses offends the public welfare." *Day-Brite Lighting, Inc. v. Missouri*, 342 U.S. 421, 423 (1952) (per Douglas, J.).
- "Marshall made of the Court a sort of *superlegislature*, back in 1803." Fred Rodell, *Nine Men* 25 (1955).

- "Rights such as these are in principle indistinguishable from those involved here, and to extend the 'compelling interest' rule to all cases in which such rights are affected would go far toward making this Court a '*superlegislature*.'" *Shapiro v. Thompson*, 394 U.S. 618, 661 (1969) (Harlan, J., dissenting).

superpose. See **superimpose.**

supersede. A. Spelling. This word—from the Latin root *-sed* "to sit," not *-ced* "to move"—is the proper spelling. But so many other English words end in *-cede* or *-ceed* that many writers unconsciously distort the spelling of *supersede*. Spelling it correctly is one of the hallmarks of a punctilious writer. The misspelling occurs in some surprising places, as in Arthur A. Leff, *The Leff Dictionary of Law*, 94 Yale L.J. 1855, 1867 (1985), under "Abortion Act," and in nearly 5,000 federal judicial opinions in the U.S. It has even fouled a statute: "Any demand for a product of discovery *supercedes* [read *supersedes*] any inconsistent order." Tex. Bus. & Com. Code Ann. § 15.10(d)(2) (West 1987). And the title of a law-review article: Charles J. Yeager & Lee Hargrave, *The Power of the Attorney General to Supercede* [read *Supersede*] *a District Attorney*, 51 La. L. Rev. 733 (1991) (and passim in text).

B. Special Sense. In law, *supersede* sometimes carries the specialized sense "to invoke or make applicable the right of supersedeas against [an award of damages]," a sense unknown to nonlawyers, for whom the term means "to replace; to supplant." Following are examples of the special legal use:

- "Rather than *supersede* the final judgment, Old Port Cove agreed to a settlement with Stevens in the amount of the judgment and obtained a release." *General Portland Land Dev. Co. v. Stevens*, 395 So.2d 1296, 1298 (Fla. Dist. Ct. App. 1981).
- "A judgment debtor is entitled to *supersede* the judgment while pursuing an appeal; this defers payment until the matter is resolved but does not halt the accumulation of interest on the judgment." *Miga v. Jensen*, 299 S.W.3d 98, 100 (Tex. 2009).

C. Corresponding Noun. *Supersession* is the noun form, meaning either "the act of superseding" or "the state of being superseded." E.g.: "The writ of tolt died a natural death with the *supersession* of both forms of writ of right by the newer action of ejectment." H.G. Hanbury, *English Courts of Law* 46 (2d ed. 1953).

As with the verb, the internal *-s-* is sometimes incorrectly made *-c-*: "The Louisiana Supreme Court declared the statute authorizing *supercession* [read *supersession*] to be unconstitutional." Charles J. Yeager & Lee Hargrave, *The Power of the Attorney General to Supercede* [sic] *a District Attorney*, 51 La. L. Rev. 733, 734 (1991).

**Supersedure* is a NEEDLESS VARIANT in all but beekeeping contexts, but it still occasionally appears: "Despite the apparent *supersedure* [read *supersession*] of the act, however, some decisions continue to treat it as controlling in this area." Edward W. Cleary, *McCormick on Evidence* § 97, at 24 (3d ed. Supp. 1987).

D. For *surpass*. This is a fairly unusual MALA-PROPISM—e.g.: "Arguably, Russia *supersedes* [read *surpasses*] even England in the publication of Shakespeare's works and the staging of his plays." Melor Sturua, *O.J. Through Russian Eyes*, Wall St. J., 21 Sept. 1994, at A14.

supersede and displace. See DOUBLETS, TRIPLETS, AND SYNONYM-STRINGS.

supersedeas, when used elliptically as an attributive noun for *supersedeas bond* or *writ*, forms the plural in -*es*. E.g.: "It also prescribed the conditions upon which such appeals or writs of error should operate as *supersedeases*." *Holland v. Webster*, 29 So. 625, 630 (Fla. 1901) (Mabry, J., dissenting).

superseding cause. See CAUSATION (E).

***supersedure; supersession.** See **supersede** (C).

SUPERSTITIONS. In 1926, H.W. Fowler used the term "superstitions" in reference to what, in the field of writing, are merely "unintelligent applications of an unintelligent dogma" (*MEU1* 586). Experts in usage have long railed against them as arrant nonsense, yet they retain a firm grip—if not a stranglehold—on the average person's mind when it comes to how best to put words on paper. Most of them are perpetuated in the classrooms in which children and adolescents learn to write.

Most of these superstitions are treated elsewhere in this book, in the entry to which the reader is referred at the end of each subentry. For additional perspectives on these points, below are briefly collected the views of respected authorities on style, grammar, and usage.

A. Never End a Sentence with a Preposition. "The origin of the misguided rule is not hard to ascertain. To begin with, there is the meaning of the word 'preposition' itself: stand before. The meaning derives from Latin, and in the Latin language prepositions do usually stand before the words they govern. But Latin is not English. In English prepositions have been used as terminal words in a sentence since the days of Chaucer, and in that position they are completely idiomatic." Theodore M. Bernstein, *Miss Thistlebottom's Hobgoblins: The Careful Writer's Guide to the Taboos, Bugbears, and Outmoded Rules of English Usage* 177 (1971). See PREPOSITIONS (A).

B. Never Split an Infinitive. E.g.:

- "The split infinitive is in full accord with the spirit of modern English and is now widely used by our best writers." George O. Curme, *English Grammar* 148 (1947).
- "However offensive it may be to many persons, the split infinitive makes clear beyond all doubt what the adverb modifies." G.C. Thornton, *Legislative Drafting* 28 (2d ed. 1979).

See SPLIT INFINITIVES.

C. Never Split a Verb Phrase. "When an adverb is to be used with [a compound verb], its normal place is between the auxiliary (or sometimes the first auxiliary if there are two or more) and the rest. Not only is there no objection to so splitting a compound verb, but any other position for the adverb requires special justification: *I have never seen her*, not *I never have seen her*, is the ordinary idiom, though the rejected order becomes the right one if emphasis is to be put on *have* (I may have had chances of seeing her but I never have). But it is plain . . . that a prejudice has grown up against dividing compound verbs . . . . [I]t is entirely unfounded." H.W. Fowler, *A Dictionary of Modern English Usage* 464 (Ernest Gowers ed., 2d ed. 1965). See ADVERBS (A).

D. Never Begin a Sentence with *and* or *but*. "Next to the groundless notion that it is incorrect to end an English sentence with a preposition, perhaps the most wide-spread of many false beliefs about the use of our language is the equally groundless notion that it is incorrect to begin one with 'but' or 'and.' As in the case of the superstition about the prepositional ending, no textbook supports it, but apparently about half of our teachers of English go out of their way to handicap their pupils by inculcating it. One cannot help wondering whether those who teach such a monstrous doctrine ever read any English themselves." Charles Allen Lloyd, *We Who Speak English* 19 (1938). See **and** (A) & **but** (A).

E. Never Write a One-Sentence Paragraph.

- "To interpose a one-sentence paragraph at intervals—at longish intervals—is prudent. Such a device helps the eye and enables the reader (especially if 'the going is heavy') to regain his breath between one impressive or weighty or abstruse paragraph and the next." Eric Partridge, *Usage and Abusage* 224–25 (5th ed. 1957).
- "Basically, there are three situations . . . that can occasion a one-sentence paragraph: (a) when you wish to emphasize a crucial point that might otherwise be buried; (b) when you wish to dramatize a transition from one stage in your argument to the next; and (c) when instinct tells you that your reader is tiring and would appreciate a mental rest-station." John R. Trimble, *Writing with Style* 94 (1975).

F. Never Begin a Sentence with *because*. So novel and absurd is this superstition that seemingly no authority on writing has countered it in print. It appears to result from concern about fragments—e.g.: "Then the group broke for lunch. Because we were hungry." Of course, the second "sentence" is merely a fragment, not a complete sentence. But problems of that kind simply cannot give rise to a general prohibition against starting a sentence with *because*. Good writers do so frequently—e.g.:

- "*Because* of the war the situation in hospitals is, of course, serious." E.B. White, "A Weekend with the Angels," in *The Second Tree from the Corner* 3, 6 (1954).
- "*Because* the relationship between remarks is often vague in this passage, we could not rewrite it with certainty

without knowing the facts." Donald Hall, *Writing Well* 104 (1973).

G. Never Use *since* to Mean *because*. "It is a delusion that *since* may be used only as an adverb in a temporal sense ('We have been here since ten o'clock'). It is also a causal conjunction meaning *for* or *because*: 'Since it is raining, we had better take an umbrella.'" Roy H. Copperud, *American Usage and Style: The Consensus* 349 (1980). See **as (A).**

H. Never Use *between* with More than Two Objects. "When Miss Thistlebottom taught you in grammar school that *between* applies only to two things and *among* to more than two, she was for the most part correct. *Between* essentially does apply to only two, but sometimes the 'two' relationship is present when more than two elements are involved. For example, it would be proper to say that 'The President was trying to start negotiations between Israel, Egypt, Syria and Jordan' if what was contemplated was not a round-table conference but separate talks involving Israel and each of the other three nations." Theodore M. Bernstein, *Dos, Don'ts & Maybes of English Usage* 29 (1977). See **between (A).**

I. Never Use the First-Person Pronouns *I* and *me*. "If you want to write like a professional, just about the first thing you have to do is get used to the first person singular. Just plunge in and write 'I' whenever 'I' seems to be the word that is called for. Never mind the superstitious notion that it's immodest to do so. It just isn't so." Rudolf Flesch, *A New Way to Better English* 49 (1958). See **FIRST PERSON (A).**

J. Never Use Contractions. "Your style will obviously be warmer and truer to your personality if you use contractions like 'I'll' and 'won't' when they fit comfortably into what you're writing. 'I'll be glad to see them if they don't get mad' is less stiff than 'I will be glad to see them if they do not get mad.' There's no rule against such informality—trust your ear and your instincts." William Zinsser, *On Writing Well* 117 (3d ed. 1985). See **CONTRACTIONS.**

K. Never Use *you* in Referring to Your Reader. "Keep a running conversation with your reader. Use the second-person pronoun whenever you can. Translate everything into *you* language. *This applies to citizens over 65 = if you're over 65, this applies to you. It must be remembered that = you must remember. Many people don't realize = perhaps you don't realize.*

"Always write directly to *you*, the person you're trying to reach with your written message. Don't write in mental isolation; reach out to your reader." Rudolf Flesch, *How to Be Brief: An Index to Simple Writing* 114 (1962). See **you.**

supervene (= to come on or occur as something additional or extraneous; to come directly or shortly after something else, either as a consequence of it or in contrast with it) is rarely seen outside the law. E.g.: "Neither the *supervening* death of an optionor nor an attempted revocation by will terminates an irrevocable offer." *In re Estate of Jorstad*, 447 N.W.2d 283, 286 (N.D. 1989).

supervening cause. See CAUSATION (D) & (E).

supervision. See **oversight.**

supervisory; supervisorial. *Supervisory* = of or relating to supervision. *Supervisorial* = of or relating to a supervisor. E.g.: "There shall be in each county a board of supervisors, to consist of three members who shall be qualified electors of their *supervisorial* district." *McCarthy v. State*, 101 P.2d 449, 451 (Ariz. 1940) (quoting a statute).

supplement. See **appendix.**

supplemental pleading; amended pleading. American caselaw is rife with judicial statements that counsel mislabeled an *amended pleading* by calling it a *supplemental pleading*, or vice versa. The important distinction concerns when the events pleaded occurred. A *supplemental pleading* puts into the record matter that is material to an issue that has arisen after the filing of a pleading. An *amended pleading*, by contrast, puts right a matter that might have been pleaded at the time the pleading being amended was filed, but that was erroneously or inadvertently omitted or misstated. *See* Fed. R. Civ. P. 15(a), 15(d).

supplementary; supplemental; suppletory; *suppletive. *Supplementary* is the ordinary word. The other forms have the same meaning, namely, "of the nature of, forming, or serving as a remedy to the deficiencies of something."

One might jump to brand the three other forms NEEDLESS VARIANTS, yet the law has found niches for two of them in special phrases. In the U.S., we refer usually to a *supplemental pleading*, not *supplementary*. In older Anglo-American law, a *suppletory oath* was "an oath (given by a party in his own favor) admitted to supply a deficiency in legal evidence." These variant forms should be confined to these particular uses. See **supplemental pleading.**

*Suppletive is probably best considered a NEEDLESS VARIANT of *supplementary*—e.g.:

- "Here the legal need is for substantive *suppletive* [read *supplementary*] rules, rules which presuppose and supplement the incomplete private transaction with specific 'terms.'" R.E. Speidel et al., *Commercial Law Teaching Materials* 2 (4th ed. 1987).
- "This framework consists mostly of *suppletive* [read *supplementary*] rules of law." A.N. Yiannopoulos, *Of Legal Usufruct, the Surviving Spouse, and Article 890 of the Louisiana Civil Code*, 49 La. L. Rev. 803, 803 (1989).

supplicant; *suppliant. The second is a NEEDLESS VARIANT of the first, an ARCHAISM referring to one who supplicates—i.e., who begs, prays, or humbly petitions or entreats. *Supplicant* has the advantage of more immediately suggesting the corresponding verb. E.g.:

- "The *suppliant* [read *supplicant*] for a stay must make out a clear case of hardship or inequity in being required to go forward." *Landis v. North Am. Co.*, 299 U.S. 248, 255 (1936) (per Cardozo, J.).

- "It is said sometimes that in the case of a true charitable trust, those to be aided must be *suppliants* [read *supplicants*], and must take their benefits gratuitously." George G. Bogert, *The Law of Trusts* 138 (4th ed.1963).

supply an omission. In the modern idiom, we *make up for* or *remedy* or *compensate for* an omission rather than *supplying* it. E.g.:

- "While the application was pending Jardine amended his claims so as to *supply this omission* [read *remedy the error*]." *Schriber-Schroth Co. v. Cleveland Trust Co.*, 311 U.S. 211, 219 (1940) (per Stone, J.).
- "Parol evidence may be admitted to *supply an omission* [read *fill a gap*] in the terms of the contract." *Malo v. Gilman*, 379 N.E.2d 554, 557 (Ind. Ct. App. 1978).

Nothing can *supply* an omission. One can *supply* (= to make up a deficiency in [*OED*]) in an obsolete sense of the word. But today *supply* is so closely connected with the sense "to provide" that it seems almost contradictory to write of *supplying (providing) an omission*.

supposable; suppositious; supposititious; suppositional; *suppositive, *suppository, adj. *Supposable* = capable of being supposed; presumable. The words *suppositious* and *supposititious* sometimes cause confusion. Although some modern dictionaries list these as variants, some DIFFERENTIATION is both possible and desirable. *Suppositious* should be used to mean "hypothetical; theoretical; assumed." *Supposititious* should be confined to its usual sense, "illegitimate; spurious; counterfeit." E.g.: "May there not be feigned legal relations, fictitious legal rights and duties, *supposititious* titles?" Lon L. Fuller, *Legal Fictions* 27 (1967). In legal contexts, *supposititious* when applied to a child means "falsely presented as a genuine heir" (*W11*). E.g.: "Parents who raised a child not biologically theirs 'as son and heir' (a *supposititious* child) might subject themselves to a lawsuit by the true heir." Philip F. Schuster, *Constitutional and Family Law Implications of the* Sleeper *&* Troxel *Cases*, 36 Willamette L. Rev. 549, 559 n.26 (2000). The phrase *supposititious will* = a fake or falsified will.

Suppositional = conjectural, hypothetical. It has much the same sense as *suppositious*, and is perhaps generally the clearer word. *Suppositive (= characterized by supposition; supposed) is a NEEDLESS VARIANT of *supposititious* and *suppositional*. *Suppository, adj., is an obsolete variant of *suppositious* and a rarely seen NEEDLESS VARIANT of *suppositional*.

*supposal; *suppose, n. See **supposition.**

supposing is inferior to *suppose* in introducing a hypothetical—e.g.: "*Supposing* [read *suppose*] that you have found that the article is malicious if—you have found that the article is both defamatory and malicious, you are required to answer the question on

damages." *Curley v. Curtis Publ'g Co.*, 48 F.Supp. 29, 37 (D. Mass. 1942) (quoting instructions to jury).

supposition; *supposal; *suppose, n. In legal contexts, as in most contexts, *supposition* is the ordinary word, and the others are NEEDLESS VARIANTS. *Supposal is sometimes used by logicians.

supposititious; suppositious; suppositional; *suppositive; *suppository. See **supposable.**

suppressible; *suppressable. The first spelling is standard.

suppressio veri. See **suggestio falsi.**

supra. This citational signal is disfavored in modern legal writing, since short-form citations are more convenient for the reader. An archaic variant of *supra* is *ubi supra* (= as above). E.g.: "Factual details are developed in the opinion of the trial court, *ubi, supra*." *Luxenberg v. Mayfair Extension, Inc.*, 382 F.2d 475, 478 n.5 (D.C. Cir. 1967). See **infra** & **ante.**

supraconstitutional (= above the constitution) is a NEOLOGISM that might be apt in some circumstances but is ready-made for hyperbole. Following is the earliest known example: "Calling the court 'a *supraconstitutional* body that has made itself unaccountable to the people of Illinois,' [Professor Louisin] also took a swipe at the court's inability to 'root out corruption among judges.'" Paul Marcotte, *Auditing Dispute*, A.B.A. J., Aug. 1990, at 16, 16.

supralegal (= above the law) is a NEOLOGISM that has enjoyed moderate success in modern legal writing. E.g.: "We might suppose from this phrase that Bodin intended his sovereign to be an irresponsible *supralegal* power, and some of the language in the *Republic* does seem to support that interpretation." J.L. Brierly, *The Law of Nations* 9 (5th ed. 1955).

supranational is a term used of a body of law that is of higher authority and wider application than national law, but yet is not international or worldwide, such as European Community Law. E.g.: "The decisions of the Community derive their binding force from the fact that they are taken by organs endowed with the appropriate power by the Treaties .... To describe this new type of political organism, the word '*supranational*' has been used." Trevor C. Hartley, *The Foundations of European Community Law* 6–7 (1981).

supra protest. The phrase can be translated *under protest*, and ought to be. Spelling the phrase with a diacritical mark (*suprá protest*) is an error, perhaps the result of HYPERCORRECTION—e.g.: "Then any person, not being a party already liable thereon, may, with the consent of the holder, intervene and accept the bill *suprá protest* [read *under protest* or *supra protest*]."

---

1 Ernest W. Chance, *Principles of Mercantile Law* 187 (Percy W. French ed., 13th ed. 1950).

supreme court, in most American jurisdictions, denotes the highest court of appeal. New York, like South Africa, is an exception; *The New York Times* has editorialized about the names of the New York courts and their judges: "The trial court is misnamed the Supreme Court, which is what most people expect to find at the top. A system that uses the term Supreme Court justice for judges of original jurisdiction is a system that resists modernization and invites cynicism." *Doing Justice to the Court,* N.Y. Times, 3 Jan. 1985, at Y18.

Supreme Court of Judicature, an English court, consists of the *High Court of Justice,* the *Court of Appeal,* and the *Crown Court.* The Supreme Court of Judicature Acts of 1873 and 1875 consolidated the following courts into the *Supreme Court of Judicature*: Queen's Bench, Common Pleas, Exchequer, Chancery, Probate, Divorce and Matrimonial Causes, Admiralty, and (from 1883) the London Court of Bankruptcy. The phrase is a misnomer, really, because the House of Lords is superior to all the courts just mentioned.

Supreme Court of the United Kingdom. Composed of 12 Lords Justices and convened for the first time in 2009, the Supreme Court is the United Kingdom's highest appellate court in all civil cases and in criminal cases from England, Wales, and Northern Ireland; in Scotland, the High Court of Justiciary is the final court of resort in criminal matters. It also hears cases of public and constitutional importance. Formerly it was the appellate committee in the House of Lords, but it is now a separate body from Parliament. The Court's decisions are called *judgments* rather than *opinions*.

Supreme Court of the United States. See **United States Supreme Court.**

supreme law of the land. See **law of the land.**

sur appears in various LAW FRENCH phrases. It means merely "on"; the English word should supplant it wherever possible. E.g.: "About 18 months thereafter the plaintiff caused to be issued an attachment *sur judgment* [read *on the judgment*] in which the City of Philadelphia Police Beneficiary Association was summoned as garnishee." *Mamlin v. Tener,* 23 A.2d 90, 91 (Pa. Super. Ct. 1941). For *action sur le case,* see **action on the case.**

surcease = a cessation; a temporary respite. To confuse this word with *solace* (= that which gives comfort when one has experienced disappointment, stress, or grief) is a MALAPROPISM. E.g.:

- "Chanya opted not to offer the challenged testimony in an acceptable manner. Having done so, he may not draw *surcease* [read *solace*] from *Chambers*." *U.S. v. Chanya,* 723 F.2d 374, 376 (5th Cir. 1984).
- "Knighton sought a stay of execution and other habeas *surcease* [read *solace*] in a petition filed in the district court." *Knighton v. Maggio,* 740 F.2d 1344, 1346 (5th Cir. 1984).

See **death.**

surety, n., in law, usually means either (1) "a formal engagement entered into, a pledge, bond, guarantee, or security given for the fulfillment of an undertaking," or (2) "one who undertakes some specific responsibility on behalf of another." Sense 1, illustrated in the following sentence, is slightly less usual: "One nominated as trustee is not required to take an oath that he will faithfully discharge his duties as trustee, or to execute a bond with satisfactory *sureties* conditioned upon the faithful performance of his duties." The archaic lay sense "certainty" is rarely encountered today.

In the broad sense, a *guarantor* is a type of surety (sense [2]). But some authorities distinguish between the two terms, giving *surety* a narrow sense: a *surety* joins in the same promise as the principal and becomes primarily liable, while a *guarantor* makes a separate promise and is only secondarily liable—i.e., liable only if the principal defaults. See **guarantee (c).**

The word *surety* has three syllables /**shoor**-ə-tee/.

suretyship; ***suretiship.** The first spelling is preferred.

***surmisal** is a NEEDLESS VARIANT of *surmise,* n.

surmise and conjecture. See DOUBLETS, TRIPLETS, AND SYNONYM-STRINGS.

surname; Christian name; christian name; forename. The *surname* is the part of a name not given in baptism but acquired originally by accident or by custom and common to all the members of the family. In many cases it was derived from physical characteristics and later transmitted to descendants; in other cases it indicated paternity, e.g.: Davidson. In Gaelic, *MacDonald* indicated the son of Donald. Such names came to be called *surnames* from the sire or father. A person can adopt any surname so long as he or she does not do so with fraudulent intent. In modern practice a woman, upon marrying, frequently adds (but need not) her husband's surname to her own, e.g., Hillary Rodham Clinton. And often, of course, she keeps her own without adding his.

The *Christian name* or *forename* is older; it was the baptismal name and in medieval England was the only name. Surnames were given later to differentiate, e.g., in a charter *Testibus Willelmo Cancellario et Roberto filio Haemonis.* The first word is usually capitalized—though Chief Justice Charles Evans Hughes made it lowercase in *Ohl & Co. v. Smith Iron Works,* 288 U.S. 170, 177 (1933).

The first name of a person not of the Christian faith is better called a *forename.* E.g.: "Because four of the seven defendants share the *surname* Nguyen, these four defendants are here referred to by both their *forename* and *surname*." *U.S. v. Cuong Gia Le,* 310 F.Supp.2d 763, 770 n.3 (E.D. Va. 2004). See **Christian name.**

surpass. See **supersede** (D).

surplus is the tendentiously humorous group term for lawyers—the invention of Eric Partridge. *See Usage and Abusage* 300 (5th ed. 1957). Hence we have a gaggle of geese, a bevy of quail, a flock of sheep, and a surplus of lawyers.

surplus; surplusage. The distinction is slight. *Surplus*, the fundamental term, means "what remains over, what is not required for the purpose at hand, esp. excess of public revenue over expenditure for the financial year" (*COD*). *Surplusage* is a NEEDLESS VARIANT in all senses but the primarily legal one: "an excess or superabundance of words; a word, clause, or statement in an indictment, plea, or legal instrument that is not necessary to its adequacy, or in a statute that is merely redundant and insignificant." Courts often recite the canon of construction that prevents them from reading statutory or contractual language in a way that renders part of it surplusage. *Surplusage*, like *surplus*, is stressed on the first syllable.

surrebutter; *surrebuttal. See **rebuttal**, -ER (B) & COMMON-LAW PLEADINGS.

surrejoinder. See **rejoinder**, -ER (B) & COMMON-LAW PLEADINGS.

surrender, in the language of nonlawyers, is confined to contexts of battles, literal or metaphorical. In the language of the law, it continues in the archaic sense of yielding up something. For example, in the law of leaseholds, it is a TERM OF ART that denotes "the termination of a lease, which occurs when a tenant gives up his or her interest to the landlord, followed by delivery of possession of the premises"—e.g.: "A lease may be terminated by *surrender*, a 'yielding up' to the owner of the reversion or remainder." 1 *American Law of Property* 390 (A.J. Casner ed., 1952).

For more on this word and its near-synonyms, see **relinquish.**

surrenderee (= one to whom property is surrendered) dates from the 17th century and is still occasionally used. E.g.: "The estate surrendered would merge in the estate of the *surrenderee*." Cornelius J. Moynihan, *Introduction to the Law of Real Property* 169 (2d ed. 1988). See -EE (A).

surrogacy; surrogateship. Both may mean "the position of a surrogate." (See **surrogate.**) *Surrogacy*, the more usual form, is the only one used in the sense "the fact or state of being a surrogate (as a surrogate mother)." E.g.:

- "Proponents of *surrogacy* seek to distinguish *surrogacy* from babyselling and adoption." Irma S. Russell, *Within the Best Interests of the Child*, 27 J. Fam. L. 585 (1989).

- "He lied to Ms. Sullivan in order to induce her to enter into the *surrogacy* contract with him." *State ex rel. A.C.M.*, 221 P.3d 185, 192 (Utah 2009).

For the sense "the office of a [judicial] surrogate," it would be helpful to use *surrogateship* rather than *surrogacy* because of the specialized connotations becoming encrusted on the latter. The *Century Dictionary* supports this usage, which also appears in caselaw— e.g.: "Before his *surrogateship*, [Surrogate David B. Ogden was] regarded by his contemporaries as not second to Webster at the federal bar." *In re de Saulles*, 167 N.Y.S. 445, 449 (Sur. Ct. 1917).

surrogate, n., = (1) something that is put in the place of another as a successor or substitute; (2) in some states of the U.S., a judge with probate jurisdiction; or (3) in G.B., the deputy of an ecclesiastical judge, of a bishop or bishop's chancellor, esp. one who grants licences to marry without banns (*OED*). Sense 1, the generic one, is by far the most widespread—e.g.:

- "To many observers, leading the Western World by standing up to the Soviets and their *surrogates* in this manner was the heart of the President's job." Jonathan A. Bush, 80 Va. L. Rev. 1723, 1723 (1994) (reviewing John H. Ely, *War and Responsibility* (1993)).

- "Market share has long served as a *surrogate* for market power." Michael S. Jacobs, *The New Sophistication in Antitrust*, 79 Minn. L. Rev. 1, 13 n.44 (1994).

- "When a patient is incompetent and no *surrogate* is available, practitioners are forced either to use substituted judgment or to act in the best interest of the patient—in short, to adopt the family's viewpoint and bear their ethical burdens." Peter Cherbas, *Paradigms and Our Shrinking Bioethics*, 69 Ind. L.J. 1105, 1111 (1994).

Sense 2 appears mostly in New York and other jurisdictions in the eastern U.S.—e.g.: "While there undoubtedly is merit to that learned *Surrogate's* objection, it does not seem to this court that an objection of surmise is any more meritorious in the area of revocation of wills, than it is to other areas of probate law." *In re Collins' Will*, 458 N.Y.S.2d 987, 993 (Sur. Ct. 1982).

surrogateship. See **surrogacy.**

surveil is a relatively new, and decidedly useful, verb corresponding to the noun *surveillance*. It is, in fact, a BACK-FORMATION from the noun. The participial and past-tense forms are *surveilling* and *surveilled*. E.g.:

- "Bocardo informed his supervisor that they were attempting to *surveil* the car because they knew that the covert vehicle was not appropriate for making a stop." *Rivera v. Garcia*, 927 N.E.2d 1235, 1238 (Ill. App. Ct. 2010).

- "Carmello involved Turner and Rossetti, who helped *surveil* the armored car facility and plan the robbery." *U.S. v. Merlino*, 592 F.3d 22, 25 (1st Cir. 2010).

The *OED* gives the year 1960 as the date of its first recorded use, by an American court at that: "The

---

plaintiff also stresses that the store as a whole, and the customer exits especially, were closely *surveilled*." *Alexandre of London v. Indemnity Ins. Co.*, 182 F.Supp. 748, 750 (D.D.C. 1960).

William Safire spelled the verb **surveille* in his column dated 6 Oct. 1985, but this spelling is inferior. See *Invasion of the Verbs*, N.Y. Times, 6 Oct. 1985, at 6–12 ("Other Lexicographic Irregulars wince at such back-formations as to *surveille* [read *surveil*].").

surveillance, place under, is an established phrase that was necessary before *surveil* was developed as a verb. But the METAPHOR of *placing under surveillance* does not work in all contexts. *Surveillance* can be had of both persons and places, but only persons can be "placed under surveillance," because the metaphor of "placing" will not work for real property (which, as an immovable, cannot conceivably be "placed"). E.g.: "*When Roth's apartment was placed under surveillance* [read *When the officers conducted a surveillance of Roth's apartment*], Noland was observed there prior to Roth's call to the agents arranging to sell them more drugs." *U.S. v. Noland*, 368 Fed. Appx. 951, 952 (11th Cir. 2010). See **surveil.**

survival statute. See **death statute.**

survivance is not a mere NEEDLESS VARIANT of *survival*, although it is increasingly rare. *Survivance* is used solely in G.B. and means "the succession to an estate, office, etc. of a survivor nominated before the death of the existing occupier or holder; the right of such succession in case of survival" (*OED*). E.g.:

- "The court has admitted evidence that the person whose *survivance* is in question is reputed to be dead." 1 John M'Laren, *The Law of Wills and Successions* 67 (1894). (Scot.)
- "This right of *survivance* gave the judge the same hereditary rights and conditional property rights in office as most royal officers acquired through the paulette." Zoë A. Schneider, *The King's Bench* 326 (2008).

surviving widow(er). The gender-neutral equivalent, *surviving spouse* (= a spouse who outlives the other), is preferable in modern contexts. E.g.: "The proprietary interest of the estate of the appointor is one which arises only in default of appointment and in the event of there being no *surviving widow* [read *surviving spouse*]." *Baird v. Baird*, [1990] 2 All E.R. 300, 305 (P.C.). See **widow,** n.

survivorship = (1) the state or condition of being the one person out of two or more who remains alive after the others die; or (2) the right of a surviving party having a joint interest with others in an estate to take the whole. E.g.: "Tenants in common are owners of undivided shares in the land. There is no *survivorship* between them, i.e., when one dies that person's share in the property passes to the decedent's heirs or devisees." A. James Casner & W. Barton Leach, *Cases and Text on Property* 255 (3d ed. 1984).

susceptible (of) (to) (for). The only prepositions with which this verb may properly be construed are *of* and *to*. Usage has differentiated *susceptible of* from *susceptible to*, the latter now being more common in ordinary lay contexts. *Susceptible to* = capable of receiving and being affected by (external impressions, influences, etc., esp. something injurious); sensitive to; liable or open to (attack, injury, etc.). E.g.: "Propounder has failed to show that Mr. Jones was *susceptible to* undue influence at the time he executed the September will." *In re Will of Jones*, 655 S.E.2d 407, 416 (N.C. Ct. App. 2007).

Susceptible of was formerly used in this sense, but is now confined to the senses, common in law, of (1) "capable of undergoing; admitting of (some action or process such as interpretation)"; (2) "capable of taking or admitting (a form, meaning, or other attribute)"; or (3) "capable of receiving into the mind, conceiving, or being inwardly affected by (a thought, feeling, or emotion)." Sense 1 of *susceptible of* is perhaps most common—e.g.:

- "The degree of contribution is not often *susceptible of* exact proof, with mathematical accuracy." *Southeastern Constr. Co. v. Dependent of Dodson*, 153 So.2d 276, 283 (1963).
- "A decree for dissolution of marriage is *susceptible of interpretation* in the same manner as other instruments." *In re Marriage of Russell*, 559 N.W.2d 636, 637 (Iowa App. Ct. 1996).
- "'Written instrument' encompasses every kind of document and other items deemed *susceptible of* 'deceitful' use in a 'forgery' sense." *State v. Radzvilowicz*, 703 A.2d 767, 788 (Conn. App. Ct. 1997).

Sense 2 also frequently appears—e.g.:

- "Where, as here, an ambiguous treaty provision . . . is *susceptible of* two plausible, and reasonable, interpretations, our precedents require us to defer to the Executive's interpretation." *Hamdan v. Rumsfeld*, 548 U.S. 557, 719 (2006) (Thomas, J., dissenting).
- "We must not give a statute a meaning that will nullify its operation if it is *susceptible of* another interpretation." *Sponsel v. Park County*, 126 P.3d 105, 108 (Wyo. 2006).

In the following sentences, *to* wrongly displaces *of* in sense 2:

- "A contract is ambiguous if its language is reasonably susceptible *to* [read *of*] more than one interpretation." *Brookfield Trade Ctr., Inc. v. County of Ramsey*, 584 N.W.2d 390, 394 (Minn. 1998).
- "The first step in this process is to determine whether the term has a 'plain meaning,' i.e., whether it is susceptible *to* [read *of*] only one plausible interpretation." *Malbco Holdings, LLC v. AMCO Ins. Co.*, 629 F.Supp.2d 1185, 1193–94 (D. Or. 2009).

Rarely is *susceptible of* misused for *susceptible to*, but the mistake does occur—e.g.:

- "Appellant argues that that complaint, labeled conversion, does not state a cause of action because the subject matter is money and mere money is not susceptible *of* [read *to*] conversion." *Shahood v. Cavin*, 316 P.2d 700, 701 (Cal. Ct. App. 1957).
- "A selection procedure that is susceptible *of* [read *to*] abuse or is not racially neutral supports the presumption

of discrimination raised by the statistical showing." *Castaneda v. Partida*, 430 U.S. 482, 494 (1977) (per Blackmun, J.).

*Susceptible for is quite wrong—e.g.: "We remanded for factual findings concerning whether the timberland at issue was '*susceptible for* [read *of*] use' to produce interest, dividends, rents, or royalties." *Zemurray Found. v. U.S.*, 755 F.2d 404, 406 (5th Cir. 1985).

Susceptible is sometimes mispronounced, even by educated speakers, /sək-**sep**-tə-bəl/ rather than the correct /sə-**sep**-tə-bəl/.

suspect, adj.**; suspicious.** Generally, the first denotes a fully formulated impression, while the second denotes only an incipient impression. *Suspect* = regarded with suspicion or distrust; suspected <suspect findings>. *Suspicious* = (1) open to, deserving of, or exciting suspicion <a suspicious character>; or (2) full of, inclined to, or feeling suspicion <an unduly suspicious supervisor>.

suspect, n. See **unknown suspect.**

suspendible; *suspendable; *suspensible. The first is the standard term; the second and third are NEEDLESS VARIANTS.

suspension. See **insolvency (A).**

suspension of deportation; withholding of deportation. In American immigration law, these phrases denote distinctive procedures. A *suspension of deportation*, resulting in permanent residency, is granted when a potential deportee proves "extreme hardship"—an admittedly vague concept. A *withholding of deportation*, resulting only in temporary residency in the U.S., is granted when a potential deportee proves that he or she will suffer persecution (not just discrimination) because of race, religion, political opinion, or social position. See **deportee.**

suspensory; suspensive. *Suspensory conditions* are conditions precedent that suspend the operation of a contractual promise until those conditions are met. The phrase **suspensive conditions* is a NEEDLESS VARIANT—except in Scotland, where it is usual.

suspicious. See **suspect,** adj.

sustain is a CHAMELEON-HUED WORD if ever there was one. Idiomatically, we speak of *sustaining damage*, of *sustaining motions*, and of *sustaining a population*. Other variations with slight nuances are possible, and all are permissible because of historical usage. *Sustain* may mean "to undergo, experience, have to submit to (evil, hardship or damage)" (*OED*). E.g.:

- "Ms. Witthoeft later died from the injuries *sustained* in that accident." *Hospodar v. Schick*, 885 A.2d 986, 990 (Pa. Super. Ct. 2005).
- "At the hearing on damages, G.E. presented evidence that it *sustained* damages totaling $263,648.17." *G.E. Capital*

Info. Tech. Solutions, Inc. v. Oklahoma City Pub. Schs., 173 P.3d 114, 116 (Okla. Ct. App. 2007).

Or it may mean "to uphold the validity of." E.g.: "Defendant maintains that neither statute can be *sustained* under Congress's Commerce Clause power." *U.S. v. Myers*, 591 F.Supp.2d 1312, 1316 (S.D. Fla. 2008).

The sense "to nourish or support life in" is one of the general lay senses of the word. Additionally, *sustain* may mean "to keep up or keep going"—e.g.: "Based on the travel of this case, at least two code-enforcement officers, four district-court judges, two superior-court justices, and the full panoply of justices of the Maine Supreme Judicial Court would have had to be involved with at least two lawyers from a private law firm and with a number of municipal officials in effecting a massive and *sustained* conspiracy." *Marcello v. Maine*, 457 F.Supp.2d 55, 65 (D. Me. 2006).

Given these multifarious senses, few uses of the word seem to be objectionable; in the following sentence, however, it appears to have been used as a turgid substitute for *have*: "Neither the defendant nor the man who made the patterns *sustained* [read *had*] any relation by contract with the plaintiff." *Tabor v. Hoffman*, 23 N.E. 12, 13 (N.Y. 1889).

sustainment; *sustentation. What is the noun corresponding to the verb *sustain*, as in "Objection sustained"? Up to 1940, the learned word **sustentation* was more common in legal texts, but since then *sustainment* has appeared nearly twice as often.

Even so, both forms are BURIED VERBS. So one should try to use the verb instead of either of the nouns—e.g.: "The *sustentation* of the motion for sanctions was plain error only if a manifest injustice resulted therefrom." *State v. Williams*, 828 S.W.2d 894, 898 (Mo. Ct. App. 1992). [Read *In sustaining the motion for sanctions, the court committed plain error only if a manifest injustice resulted.*]

SWAPPING HORSES while crossing the stream is H.W. Fowler's term for "changing a word's sense in the middle of a sentence, by vacillating between two constructions either of which might follow a word legitimately enough, by starting off with a subject that fits one verb but must have something tacitly substituted for it to fit another, and by other such performance." (*MEU1* 589.) E.g.: "The subject of this paper, however, is the evidentiary rule and concerns those situations where evidence is sought from the lawyer through compulsion of law." The writer has switched gears mentally from "subject . . . is" to "paper . . . concerns." [Read *The subject of this paper, however, is the evidentiary rule and those situations in which . . .* , or *This paper, however, concerns the evidentiary rule and those situations in which . . . .*]

For related discussions, see JANUS-FACED TERMS & ZEUGMA AND SYLLEPSIS.

An asterisk (*) precedes words and phrases that are invariably inferior forms.

swear; affirm; asseverate; aver. All mean to declare solemnly, especially under oath or on one's word of honor, that what one says is true. To *swear* (especially before a court or court reporter) is to give an earnest pledge—usually with an appeal to a deity and with the right hand raised, and perhaps also with the other hand on a sacred object such as a holy book—that one will speak only the truth and will refrain from withholding the truth. To *affirm* (in the context of testimony) is to make a similar pledge, but without reference to a deity and without any sacred objects because one's personal scruples or conscience forbids an oath.

Most oaths today simply cover both angles by asking the witness to "swear or affirm" (take your choice). Rarely if ever is a witness asked in advance whether he or she objects to swearing. Although California is tending to lean away from swearing to God, one noted Los Angeles litigator, David A. Battaglia, bucks the trend: "I always try to insist on swearing to God," he writes to me, because "(1) I think it is a more serious oath than swearing to the State of California, and (2) I want the jury to know that he swore to God if he lies." Good point. In any event, though, in any jurisdiction the oath or affirmation must be "calculated to awaken the witness' conscience and impress the witness' mind with the duty to do so." Tex. R. Evid. 603. (On the use of *witness'* instead of the better *witness's*, see **witness (B).**)

The final two headwords are less about testimony than about grave pronouncements. To *asseverate* is to insist with serious emphasis or to declare earnestly, with the implication that what one says is the truth. To *aver* is to assert with a little less solemnity, but still in all seriousness, that something is or isn't so.

swear off. See **abjure (A).**

swear out (= to obtain the issue of [a warrant for arrest] by making a charge upon oath) is an American LEGALISM dating from the 19th century. E.g.: "He walked into the trap, *swore out* a criminal warrant, and haled us before Judge Tompkins sitting as a magistrate." Ephraim Tutt, *Yankee Lawyer* 69 (1943). See **out (A)** & PARTICLES, UNNECESSARY.

sweat > sweat > sweat. So declined.

swing vote = an appellate judge's vote that determines an issue on which the other judges are evenly split. The agent noun is *swing voter*—e.g.: "Since President Reagan appointed O'Connor eight years ago, her role in many divisive issues—thanks in part to the arrival of two additional conservatives—has evolved from that of habitual dissenter to that of frequent *swing voter.*" *All Eyes on Justice O'Connor*, Newsweek, 1 May 1989, at 34.

***sworn affidavit** is a common REDUNDANCY.

syllabus. Pl. *-buses*, *-bi*. American judges and college professors are fond, perhaps overfond, of the Latin plural. Though Gowers wrote (wishfully?) that "the plural *-buses* is now more used than *-bi*" (*MEU2* 610), in American judicial opinions *-bi* outstrips *-buses* by more than 50 to 1. See PLURALS (A).

SYLLEPSIS. See ZEUGMA AND SYLLEPSIS.

symposium. Pl. *-siums.* **Symposia* is a pedantry. See PLURALS (A).

synallagmatic contract (= [in civil law] a contract involving mutual obligations; a bilateral contract) dates back to the early 19th century. But in Anglo-American law, the sensible approach is to use the predominant Anglo-American term: *bilateral contract.* E.g.:

- "Every *synallagmatic* [read *bilateral*] contract contains in it the seeds of the problem: in what event will a party be relieved of his undertaking to do that which he has agreed to do but has not yet done?" *Hong Kong Fir Shipping Co. v. Kawasaki Kisen Kaisha*, [1962] 2 Q.B. 26, 65 (per Diplock, L.J.).
- "The judge referred to the well-known distinction discussed in the speeches between *synallagmatic* [read *bilateral*] contracts and unilateral or 'if' contracts, such as options." *Chiltern Court (Baker Street) Residents Ltd v. Wallabrook, Prop. Co.*, [1988] 2 Est. Gaz. L. Rep. 253, 253.

See **bilateral contract.**

sync, short for *synchronism* or *synchrony*, is preferred to *synch.* E.g.: "Professor Imwinkelried cites Montana as a jurisdiction that is out of *sync* with the rest of the country on this issue." *State v. Stout*, 237 P.3d 37, 59 (Mont. 2010).

synchronous; *synchronic; *synchronal. The second and third are NEEDLESS VARIANTS.

SYNESIS. In some contexts meaning, rather than the strict requirements of grammar or syntax, controls in the question of SUBJECT–VERB AGREEMENT. Henry Sweet, the 19th-century English grammarian, used the term "antigrammatical constructions" for these triumphs of logic over grammar. (Expressions in which grammar triumphs over logic are termed "antilogical.") Modern grammarians call the principle underlying these antigrammatical constructions "synesis."

The classic example of an antigrammatical construction is the phrase *a number of* (= several, many). It is routinely followed by a plural verb, even though technically the singular noun *number* is the subject: "A *number* of scholastic ... dogmas *have* grown up which tend to obscure the real function of precedent in our legal reasoning." Carleton K. Allen, *Law in the Making* 268 (7th ed. 1964). (See **number of, a.**) But if the definite article *the* appears rather than the indefinite *a*, the verb is singular—e.g.: "She said that the number of participants was disappointing."

Of course, some writers use the construction *a number of things is*, but the resulting sentence invariably looks priggish—e.g.:

- "The Maccabaean Lecture aroused an interest greater than it deserved. There *is* [read *are*] a *number* of reasons for this." Patrick Devlin, *The Enforcement of Morals* vii (1968).

- "However, there *is* [read *are*] *a number* of exceptions to this rule, whose importance appears to be increasing today." P.S. Atiyah, *An Introduction to the Law of Contract* 260 (3d ed. 1981).
- "*A number* of federal statutes which deal with the allowance of costs *has* [read *have*] been considered." 6 James W. Moore et al., *Moore's Federal Practice* par. 54.77[2], at 54-410 (1988).

Although writers are perfectly justified in writing *a number of people were there*, some avoid the construction merely to prevent raised eyebrows. Instead, they write *many people* or *several people*. This sound practice keeps readers from being distracted.

If *a number of people were* is grammatically safe, however, similar constructions involving collective nouns are somewhat more precarious. The rule consistently announced in 20th-century grammars is as follows: "Collective nouns take sometimes a singular and sometimes a plural verb. When the persons or things denoted are thought of as individuals, the plural should be used. When the collection is regarded as a unit, the singular should be used." George L. Kittredge & Frank E. Farley, *An Advanced English Grammar* 101 (1913). Generally, then, with nouns of multitude, one can justifiably use a plural verb.

Among the common nouns of multitude are *bulk, bunch, flood, handful, host, mass, majority, minority, percentage, proportion, variety*. Each of these is frequently followed by *of* + [plural noun] + [plural verb]—e.g.:

- "In each of these instances, as so often in our history, a *majority* of the Justices *were* behind the political times." Fred Rodell, *Nine Men* 11 (1955).
- "A high *percentage* of cases *are* of a routine nature." Charles E. Wyzanski Jr., "A Trial Judge," in *Whereas—A Judge's Premises* 3, 4 (1965).
- "Thus, in relation to the total number of prosecutions, only a small *proportion are* taken by the Director." R.M. Jackson, *The Machinery of Justice in England* 138 (5th ed. 1967).
- "A large *mass* of rules of evidence *restrict* the questions that might be asked." *Id.* at 142.
- "The great *mass* of these social prohibitions *is* [read *are*] not directly against the making of contracts as such but against the doing of acts." Patrick Devlin, *The Enforcement of Morals* 55 (1968).
- "There *is* [read *are*] also a *host* of new difficulties that are even more salient in contract than they were in torts." Bruce A. Ackerman, *Reconstructing America* 61 (1984).
- "The vast *bulk* of recorded crimes *falls* [read *fall*] into the category of property offences." Andrew Ashworth, *Principles of Criminal Law* 39 (1991).

As shown in the last two examples, these nouns of multitude are not just acceptably treated as plural. One might go so far as to say that *host* and *mass* are preferably treated as plurals when they are followed by *of* and a plural noun.

Very occasionally, an AMBIGUITY arises: "*There is* now *a variety of* antidepressant drugs that can help lift these people out of their black moods." If the sense of *a variety of* is "several," then *are* is the appropriate verb; if the sense of the phrase is "a type of," then *is* is the appropriate verb.

But the nouns *amount, class, group*, and (ironically) *multitude* all typically call for singular verbs—e.g.:

- "Specific relief will be given if practicable where the *amount* of damages *are* [read *is*] so uncertain and speculative, for any reason, that the fixing of the amount . . . by the jury could not be guided by any definite standard." William F. Walsh, *A Treatise on Equity* 309 (1930).
- "Needless to say, there *are* [read *is*] a *multitude* of examples." Charles P. Curtis Jr., *Lions Under the Throne* 220 (1947).
- "The most important *class* of chattels real *are* [read *is*] leasehold estates." William Geldart, *Introduction to English Law* 80 (D.C.M. Yardley ed., 9th ed. 1984). The BE-VERB follows the number of its subject, not of its predicate.
- "A *group* of states *have* [read *has*] enacted broad cy pres, or reformation, statutes, of which the Vermont statute is an example." Thomas F. Bergin & Paul G. Haskell, *Preface to Estates in Land and Future Interests* 218 (2d ed. 1984).
- "But even if a *group* of members *decide* [read *decides*] to challenge such an agreement . . . there is no guarantee that the government will provide time for a debate or the opportunity of a vote." Michael Zander, *The Law-Making Process* 70 (2d ed. 1985). In a BrE text, this usage is defensible; it would be less so in an AmE text. See COLLECTIVE NOUNS.

There may be little or no logical consistency in the two sets of examples just given—justifiable plurals and less justifiable ones—but the problem lies just outside the realm of logic, in the genius of the language. It is no use trying to explain why we say, on the one hand, *that pair of shoes is getting old*, but on the other hand, *the pair were perfectly happy after their honeymoon*.

For more on grammatical agreement generally, see CONCORD & COLLECTIVE NOUNS.

synonymous (in the sense "coextensive") is a LEGALISM not found in general lay writing. E.g.: "Nor do we subscribe to the argument that Merrill's powers of control over partnership property as general partner of a limited partnership . . . are per se *synonymous* with the partnership's." *Moncrief v. U.S.*, 730 F.2d 276, 285 (5th Cir. 1984). The corresponding noun is used in an analogous sense—e.g.: "Given . . . the *synonymy* between the limits of the Louisiana long-arm statute and those of due process, it becomes necessary to consider only whether the exercise of jurisdiction over a nonresident defendant comports with due process." *Bean Dredging Corp. v. Dredge Tech. Corp.*, 744 F.2d 1081, 1083 (5th Cir. 1984).

The word is frequently misspelled **synonomous*, as here: "'Special inquiry officer' is *synonomous* [read *synonymous*] with immigration judge." *Purba v. INS*, 884 F.2d 516, 517 (9th Cir. 1989).

SYNONYMY. The myth is that no two words in the language can have identical meanings, as stated here: "strictly speaking, no two words have the same meaning. There are connotations that attach to language and even two synonyms will suggest slightly different meanings to a reader." Norman Brand & J.O. White, *Legal Writing: The Strategy of Persuasion* 114 (1976). Adherents to this view must contend that *restitutional* and *restitutionary* are merely different forms of the same word—not different words—and must resort to etymology to distinguish *sedulous* from *assiduous*.

This belief may help explain the inclination of lawyers to use DOUBLETS, TRIPLETS, AND SYNONYM-STRINGS. E.g.:

- "Therefore, in the name of the state of Ohio, I command you to receive . . . George Thomas into your custody . . . to be *kept, confined, and imprisoned* for the term of three days." *Thomas v. Village of Ashland*, 12 Ohio St. 124, 126 (1861).
- "Liquidators did and do by these presents, *grant, bargain, sell, assign, convey, transfer, set over, and deliver* unto the following." *Shalett v. Brownell-Kidd Co.*, 153 So.2d 425, 433 (La. Ct. App. 1963).

Instead of using these verbal strings, the writer should determine which of the words can be subsumed under (and therefore omitted because of the presence of) broader terms. In the first sentence quoted above, *imprison* certainly encompasses *confine* and *keep*; in the second, *grant* or *convey* would easily suffice. Lawyers generally seek to cover every contingency, especially in drafting; we should do so, however, discriminatingly rather than in blunderbuss fashion.

synonymy; *synonymity. *Synonymy* is the preferred form. See **synonymous.**

systematic. See **systemic.**

systematic construction; systematic interpretation. See *systematic interpretation* under INTERPRETATION, MODES OF (B).

systematize; *systemize. The second is a NEEDLESS VARIANT of *systematize.*

systemic; systematic. *Systemic* should be *systematic* unless the reference is systems of the body, as in *systemic disorders.* E.g.: "Race, sex, and disability claims are most vulnerable to this *systemic* [read *systematic*] bias." Donna Meredith Matthews, Note, *Employment Law After* Gilmer, 18 Berkeley J. Emp. & Lab. L. 347, 371 (1997).

*systemize. See **systematize.**

T

table, vb., has nearly opposite senses in AmE and BrE. By *tabling* an item, Americans mean postponing discussion for a later time, while Britons mean putting forward for immediate discussion. So Americans might misunderstand a use like the following one: "MPs from both sides of the Commons will tomorrow *table* parliamentary questions demanding to know what official action has been taken to uncover the facts." John Furbisher & Richard Caseby, *"God's Policeman" Keeps Head Down as Bricks Fly*, Sunday Times, 10 June 1990, at 1–4.

taboo; *tabu. The first spelling is standard. For the verb *to taboo* (= to exclude or prohibit by authority or social influence [COD]), the past tense is *tabooed* rather than **taboo'd.* E.g.: "*Tabooed* violence like a rape . . . is one of the most alienating experiences that . . . you can have." Martha Chamallas, Lucky: *The Sequel*, 80 Ind. L.J. 441, 448 (2005).

tabula rasa (= a blank tablet ready for writing; a clean slate) has been an especially common METAPHOR in legal writing. It has grown into a CLICHÉ. The plural is *tabulae rasae.*

tactics. See **strategy.**

tactile; *tactual. The second has become merely a NEEDLESS VARIANT. *Tactile* is the usual word meaning either "of or relating to touch" or "touchable; tangible."

tail, in the legal sense denoting a type of limited freehold estate, is a LAW FRENCH term, deriving ultimately from the Old French verb *taillier* "to cut, shape, hence to fix the precise form of, to limit." Formerly, the anglicized word was spelled *taille,* but today it is spelled *tail* as in *fee tail* and *in tail.* E.g.: "When the testator gave a life estate to John and then gave an estate in freehold to John's heirs (in this case an estate *in tail* rather than in fee simple because of the words 'to the heirs of his body'), the two estates merged in John by operation of law." Emily Kadens, *Justice Blackstone's Common Law Orthodoxy*, 103 Nw. U. L. Rev. 1553, 1599 (2009). Sometimes the word is used also in the phrase *estate tail,* as here: "Conveyances to one and his or her bodily heirs (creating an *estate tail* under the common law as in the instant deeds) carves out of a grantor's fee-simple estate certain lesser estates." *Hess v. Proffer*, 87 S.W.3d 432, 436 (Mo. Ct. App. 2002). See **fee tail (A).**

Tail may be a noun taking POSTPOSITIVE ADJECTIVES (*tail female, tail special*) or may itself be a postpositive adjective (cf. **fee tail**). Some writers hyphenate *tail-female, tail-male,* and even *estate-tail,* but the hyphens are better omitted. See **entail** & **disentail.**

taint. See **attaint.**

take. A. In Its Ordinary Sense. In its everyday uses, *take* "is an ambiguous word, particularly when one is speaking of an adult 'taking' a child somewhere, which could be construed as simply guiding or accompanying the child, or as a forcible taking." *U.S. v. Macklin*, 671 F.2d 60, 65 n.6 (2d Cir. 1982).

B. In the Context of Estates. *Take* (= to receive (property) by will or intestate succession) is peculiar to the legal idiom. E.g.: "In 1971, William married Liv Kennedy, and, in 1974, he signed a form designating her to *take* benefits . . . but naming no contingent beneficiary to *take* if she disclaimed her interest." *Kennedy v. Plan Adm'r for DuPont Savs. & Inv. Plan*, 129 S.Ct. 865, 869 (2009) (per Souter, J.). See **taker.**

C. In the Phrase *stole, took, and carried away.* See **stole, took, and carried away.**

take articles. See **article,** vb.

take by purchase. See **purchase (B).**

take exception. This phrase means "to object" in general lay contexts, but is used in legal writing in the sense "to posit an error on appeal." E.g.: "On appeal, TriHealth *takes exception* only to the district court's conclusion that the undisputed differences are material." *TriHealth, Inc. v. Board of Comm'rs*, 430 F.3d 783, 790 (6th Cir. 2005).

take-it-or-leave-it contract. For this synonym of *adhesion contract*, see **adherence (A).**

taken. Appeals to higher courts are said, in the legal idiom, to be *taken*. E.g.: "An appeal was *taken* from the order of dismissal." *Kircher v. Putnam Funds Trust*, 547 U.S. 633, 644 (2006) (per Souter, J.).

***taken back, to be** is an illiteracy when used for *to be taken aback.*

take-nothing judgment (= a judgment for the defendant providing that the plaintiff recover nothing) should be so hyphenated. See PHRASAL ADJECTIVES.

take notice. This is a common substitute for—and a better phrase than—*know all men by these presents.* E.g.:

- "*Take notice* that the Application for Parole, filed by the Defendant, George Alan Hunt, will be brought on for hearing on the 13th day of March, 1980, at 10:30 o'clock in the Courtrooms of the Courthouse in Jamestown, North Dakota before the Honorable Bert L. Riskedahl, or as soon thereafter as counsel may be heard." *State v. Hunt*, 293 N.W.2d 419, 425 (N.D. 1980).
- "Please *take notice* that as of this date the Magistrate's report and recommendation attached hereto has been filed." *Scott v. Brunsman*, 694 F.Supp.2d 771, 782 (N.D. Ohio 2009).

The phrase is often, alas, written entirely in capitals. See CAPITALIZATION (A) & **know all men by these presents.**

take-or-pay; take or pay. When used as a PHRASAL ADJECTIVE, *take-or-pay* should be hyphenated, as in *take-or-pay obligations*, *take-or-pay clauses*, and

take-or-pay status. Some writers use quotation marks with this phrase instead of hyphens (i.e., *"take or pay" contract*)—a usage to be avoided.

But when *take* and *pay* are used as alternative verbs, the phrase should not be hyphenated: "This right to restrict flow, however, did not operate to diminish Transmission's obligation to *take-or-pay* [read *take or pay*] for 75% of the wells' estimated yearly output." *Garshman v. Universal Res. Holding Inc.*, 824 F.2d 223, 226 (3d Cir. 1987).

takeover, n. One word.

take precedence. See **precedence.**

taker (= one who receives property by will or intestate succession) is common in the law of wills and trusts—e.g.:

- "Words of recommendation, request, entreaty, wish, or expectation addressed to the legatee or devisee will ordinarily make the first *taker* a trustee for the person or persons in whose favor such expressions are used." *Brinn v. Brinn*, 195 S.E. 793, 796 (N.C. 1938).
- "The terms 'heirs,' 'issue,' and 'children' are commonly used in dispositive instruments to designate a class of *takers*." Thomas F. Bergin & Paul G. Haskell, *Preface to Estates in Land and Future Interests* 230 (2d ed. 1984).

See **take (B).**

take silk is a BrE phrase meaning "to become a Queen's Counsel [Q.C.] or King's Counsel [K.C.]" (*OED*). See **silk.**

take the Fifth Amendment, to. See **Fifth Amendment.**

take the stand. See **stand.**

take under advisement. See **advisement.**

taking (= a taking of property by a governmental entity using eminent domain) is midway between JARGON and a TERM OF ART. Lawyers have long argued about just what constitutes a *taking*, but it is hard now to improve on a general statement of more than a century ago: "Anything may be said to amount to a *taking* [that] deprives the owner of the use, occupation, or enjoyment of his property." Alfred R. Haig, *The Law of Eminent Domain in Pennsylvania*, 39 Am. L. Reg. 449, 463 (1891).

tales; talesman; tales-juror. Originally, *tales* /tay-leez/ (L. pl. meaning "such men") referred to persons selected from among those in court to serve on a jury in a case in which the original jury panel has become deficient in number by challenge or other cause. The *OED* notes that the word is "loosely applied in Eng. as a singular (*a tales*) to the supply of men (or even one man) so provided."

In AmE, this "loose" usage (as it is considered in BrE) was formerly common. That is, *tales* once referred to a supply of people available to replace jury

---

panelists. But AmE, unlike BrE, does not use the term *tales* to refer to a *single* person who is available to serve as such a replacement. *Talesman* is used in this latter sense (though rarely) in both AmE and BrE. See SEXISM (B).

The word *tales* also refers in some contexts to the order or act of supplying such juror substitutes, as to *pray, grant, award a tales*. In England up to 1971, this usage was restricted to a summoning of common jurors to serve on a special jury.

In AmE, the term is becoming obsolete, though a few writers use it as a fancy substitute for *veniremember*—e.g.: "In strong terms, he repeatedly admonished the *talesmen* [read *veniremembers*] that they must 'not start out th[e] case with a predisposed state of mind because of something that happened in the past.'" *Neron v. Tierney*, 841 F.2d 1197, 1202 (1st Cir. 1988). See **venireman.**

Talesman has long been the usual form, *talesjuror* being a variant. Both terms are ARCHAISMS, as methods of selecting venires have become more sophisticated.

talisman (= a charm, amulet, or other thing supposed to be capable of working wonders), a favorite word of judges, is not to be confused with *talesman*. (See **talesman.**) E.g.:

- "The law has outgrown its primitive stage of formation when the precise word was the sovereign *talisman*, and every slip was fatal." *Wood v. Lucy, Lady Duff-Gordon*, 118 N.E. 214, 214 (N.Y. 1917) (per Cardozo, J.).
- "Freedom of choice is not a sacred *talisman*; it is only a means to a constitutionally required end—the abolition of the system of segregation and its effects." *Green v. County Sch. Bd.*, 391 U.S. 430, 440 (1968) (per Brennan, J.).
- "But statutory and Guidelines section numbers are not *talismans*, and a pro se prisoner's failure to recite them doesn't obviate the need for a hearing when the record meets the threshold condition." *U.S. v. Byfield*, 391 F.3d 277, 281 (D.C. Cir. 2004).
- "Security is not a *talisman* that the government may invoke to justify any burden on speech (no matter how oppressive)." *Bl(a)ck Tea Soc'y v. City of Boston*, 378 F.3d 8, 13 (1st Cir. 2004).

The corresponding adjective is *talismanic*—e.g.: "As this Court has made plain, jurors' assurances of impartiality simply are not entitled to this sort of *talismanic* significance." *Skilling v. U.S.*, 130 S.Ct. 2896, 2959 (2010) (Sotomayor, J., concurring in part & dissenting in part). The plural form is *talismans*, not *talismen*.

The corresponding adjective is *talismanic*—e.g.:

- "There is nothing *talismanic* about neutral laws of general applicability." *Employment Div., Dep't of Hum. Res. v. Smith*, 494 U.S. 872, 901 (1990) (O'Connor, J., concurring).
- "Such a *talismanic* requirement would clearly place form over substance." *Commonwealth v. Jermyn*, 533 A.2d 74, 87 (Pa. 1987).

talk to; talk with. The first phrasing suggests a conversation in which the remarks strongly preponderate from one side, as between a superior and an inferior.

The second phrasing suggests a conversation between equals, with equal participation.

Taney, Roger Brooke. The last name of the Chief Justice of the United States from 1836 to 1854 is pronounced /**tah**-nee/, not /**tay**-nee/.

tantamount is an adjective only, meaning "equivalent." Using it as a verb is incorrect—e.g.:

- "The legal effect of the judgment in the class action . . . *tantamounts* [read *amounts*], we think, to removing [Humphrey] from the representative class." *Humphrey v. Knox*, 244 S.W.2d 309, 312 (Tex. Civ. App.—Dallas 1951).
- "The 'waiver doctrine' has been held inapplicable where . . . recalling the government witness *tantamounts* [read *amounts*] to continued cross-examination." *State v. Simpson*, 641 P.2d 320, 326 (Haw. 1982).

tape-record, vb. This obsolescent verb is always hyphenated.

tariff. See **tax.**

task, vb. See VOGUE WORDS.

taskforce is increasingly made one word, especially in BrE. That being so, it would be convenient for writers—in BrE and AmE alike—to make it one. E.g.: "On June 11th he even got round to naming the members of the *taskforce* that will deal with it." *What the Centre Holds*, Economist, 19 June 1993, at 25.

taut; taught. *Taut* (= tight) may be literal <a taut guy-line> or figurative <taut emotions>. A common misspelling of *taut* is its homophone *taught*, the past tense and past participle of *teach*.

tautologous; *tautological. The second, though older, has become a NEEDLESS VARIANT of the first. E.g.:

- "The [lower] court's statement that the plaintiff must seek redress for an injury caused by conduct that RICO was designed to deter is unhelpfully *tautological* [read *tautologous*]." *Sedima, S.P.R.L. v. Imrex Co.*, 473 U.S. 479, 494 (1985) (per White, J.).
- "To the extent Blankenhorn believes that same-sex marriage is both a cause and a symptom of deinstitutionalization, his opinion is *tautological* [read *tautologous*]." *Perry v. Schwarzenegger*, 704 F.Supp.2d 921, 949 (N.D. Cal. 2010).

TAUTOLOGY. "What's the first excellence in a lawyer? Tautology. What the second? Tautology. What the third? Tautology." Richard Steele, *The Funeral* 23 (1701). It is worth pointing out, lest the irony escape those who have used this book at all and still are fond of LEGALESE, that the words quoted are derisive, not serious. Yet tautologies continue to proliferate: "Wide public participation in rule-making avoids the problem of *singling out a single defendant* among a group of competitors for initial imposition of a new and inevitably costly legal obligation." *National Petroleum Refiners Ass'n v. F.T.C.*, 482 F.2d 672, 683 (D.C. Cir. 1973). See REDUNDANCY (B).

tax; assessment; levy; excise; impost; customs; duty; tariff; toll. All these terms denote a compulsory payment exacted by some recognized authority, usu. a governmental authority, imposed for purposes of raising revenue. *Tax* is now the most comprehensive term, although originally in English law it referred only to such an exaction for the holding of real property. *See* Francis W. Bird, *Constitutional Aspects of the Federal Tax on the Income of Corporations*, 24 Harv. L. Rev. 31, 32 (1910–1911). Since medieval times, the term has been broadened to encompass virtually all government-imposed contributions calculated on property, income, transactions, and the like, usually proportionally to the item's value.

An *assessment* is typically levied only on property near some local municipal improvement—property that receives some special benefit different from that of the general public. It can also be a tax inspector's calculation of a tax due and a request for payment.

Levy, etymologically, stresses the compulsory aspect of raising and collecting the contributions. The term applies mainly to special taxes, such as emergency taxes.

An *excise* is a tax imposed on the manufacture, marketing, sale, or consumption of certain commodities, such as cigarettes, liquor, and vehicles, or on the conduct of certain trades or occupations. Although *excise* alone denotes such a tax, it is common to encounter *excise tax*—which is at best fully acceptable and at worst a venial REDUNDANCY. See **excise tax.**

Impost, a quiescent term in the language, today most commonly denotes a customs tax on imports. But today the usual word is *customs*, which is invariably plural in form but singular or plural in sense.

Duty is a broad term that traditionally embraces all customs and excise taxes <duty-free goods>, as well as taxes that occur upon particular events <death duties> <stamp duties>.

A *tariff* is a tax imposed on imported or exported goods <ad valorem tariff>, or else a fee that a public utility or telecommunications company may assess for its services <joint tariffs for multiple shippers>.

A *toll* is a tax or dues paid for the privilege of using something such as a public road, a highway, a bridge, etc.

taxable = (1) subject to taxation <taxable income>; or (2) (of legal costs or fees) assessable <taxable expenses>. Sense 2: "Copies made for the court are *taxable* as costs." *Tirapelli v. Advanced Equities, Inc.*, 222 F.Supp.2d 1081, 1086 (N.D. Ill. 2002).

taxation, in the sense "the taxing of costs," is an unusual idiom to many ears, whether law-trained or not—e.g.: "Petitioners argue that since § 1920 lists which expenses a court 'may' tax as costs, that section only authorizes *taxation* of certain items." *Crawford*

Fitting Co. v. J.T. Gibbons, Inc., 482 U.S. 437, 441 (1987) (per Rehnquist, C.J.).

tax avoidance; tax evasion. The difference between these phrases is the difference between what is legal (*avoidance*) and what is not (*evasion*).

taxpayer. See ARTICLES (B) & **payor.**

teachings = holdings and dicta in a judicial opinion. E.g.:
- "The Pennsylvania Supreme Court ruled that there was no *Mills* violation without ever really applying the *teachings* of *Mills*, and by examining the statute, not the potential for confusion by jurors in what they were told to do." *Banks v. Horn*, 271 F.3d 527, 545 (3d Cir. 2001).
- "The government . . . replied to McKee's contention that the *teachings* of *Miranda* had been violated by demonstrating that McKee was never in custody during any of the three questioning sessions." *U.S. v. Williamson*, 339 F.3d 1295, 1306 (11th Cir. 2003).

See **hold** & **dictum.**

tear gas, n.; **teargas,** vb. This term is spelled as two words for the noun, as one for the verb.

technic. See **technique.**

technical; technological. The distinction is sometimes a fine one. *Technical* = of or in a particular science, art, or handicraft; of or in vocational training. *Technological* = pertaining to the science of practical or industrial arts. *Technological* connotes recent experimental methods and development, whereas *technical* has no such connotation.

technique; technic. The second, a variant spelling, is to be avoided.

technological. See **technical.**

teleological construction; teleological interpretation. See *purposive interpretation* under INTERPRETATION, MODES OF (B).

telephonee. See -EE (A).

telephonic is a highfalutin adjectival form of *telephone*, which ordinarily serves as its own adjective. E.g.:
- "The residence was secured, and the officers obtained a *telephonic warrant* [read *telephone warrant*] and subsequently searched the apartment and seized the marijuana and related paraphernalia." *State v. Will*, 885 P.2d 715, 717–18 (Or. Ct. App. 1994).
- "The fax from Dr. Dorn arguably satisfied the contract requirements of *telephonic notification* [read *notice by telephone*]." *Salitros v. Chrysler Corp.*, 306 F.3d 562, 570 (8th Cir. 2002).
- "The UAC held a *telephonic hearing* [read *hearing by telephone*] with both parties and witnesses, and determined that Morales voluntarily left the employment without

good cause." *Morales v. Florida Unemployment Appeals Comm'n*, 43 So.3d 157, 158 (Fla. Dist. Ct. App. 2010).

temper. See **meddle.**

temperature is pronounced /**tem**-pə-rə-chər/, not */**tem**-pə-rə-tyur/, which is precious, or */**tem**-pə-chər/, which is slovenly. A combination of the precious and the slovenly, */**tem**-pə-tyoor/ is humorously affected.

temporal /**tem**-pər-əl/ = (1) of or relating to time; (2) worldly; (3) nonecclesiastical; (4) transitory; (5) pertaining to the temple (part of one's head); or (6) pertaining to bones in the vertebrae. In other words, this is a classic CHAMELEON-HUED WORD. Usually, *temporal* refers to time (sense 1) in legal writing—e.g.: "For these states, the act of signing closely coincided—both as a functional and a *temporal* matter—with their constitutions' transformation into law." Michael Coenen, Note, *The Significance of Signatures*, 119 Yale L.J. 966, 980 (2010). Sense 2 is also common: "The Pleasant Glade Assembly of God is a Pentecostal church; its members believe that the Bible is literally true and that spiritual forces, including demons, can affect *temporal* bodies." William Drabble, Comment, *Righteous Torts*, 62 Baylor L. Rev. 267, 277 (2010).

Temporal was a favorite word of Justice Holmes, who used it in the special legal sense, a variation on sense 3 given above, namely, "civil or common as opposed to criminal or ecclesiastical." E.g.:

- "Actions of tort are brought for *temporal* damage; the law recognizes *temporal* damage as an evil which its object is to prevent or to address." Oliver Wendell Holmes Jr., *Privilege, Malice, and Intent*, 8 Harv. L. Rev. 1, 1 (1894).
- "In numberless instances the law warrants the intentional infliction of *temporal* damage because it regards it as justified." *Vegelahn v. Guntner*, 44 N.E. 1077, 1079 (Mass. 1896) (Field, C.J., dissenting, joined by Holmes, J.).

temporal limit is unidiomatic and stuffy in place of *time limit*, which is well established. E.g.: "These cases do not hold that, if such actus reus evidence is adduced, there is some *temporal limit* [read *time limit*] on the jury's consideration of consciousness-of-guilt evidence to establish mens rea." *U.S. v. Cassese*, 428 F.3d 92, 106 (2d Cir. 2005).

TEMPORAL SEQUENCES. See TENSES (A).

temporary injunction. See **injunction.**

temporary restraining order; preliminary injunction. A *temporary restraining order* (or *T.R.O.*) is an order provisionally granting injunctive relief in an emergency situation, but only for the short time (usually a matter of days at most) until the court can hear evidence and consider longer-term injunctive relief. See **T.R.O.**

A *preliminary injunction* is just such relief. It is an interlocutory injunction issued after notice and a hearing, and it restrains a party until a trial on the merits is concluded. See **interlocutory relief.**

temporize has three important senses: (1) "to act so as to gain time" <defendant temporized by filing dilatory pleas>; (2) "to comply with the requirements of the occasion" <politicians are adept at temporizing>; or (3) "to negotiate or discuss terms of a compromise" <defendant attempted to temporize with plaintiff rather than go to trial>.

tenancy; tenantship; tenantry. The first is, of course, the usual term, meaning (1) "a holding or possession of lands or tenements, by any title of ownership"; (2) "occupancy of lands or tenements under a lease"; (3) "that which is held by a tenant"; or (4) "the period during which a tenant occupies land or a building."

To the extent that *tenantship* overlaps with any of those four meanings, it is a NEEDLESS VARIANT of *tenancy*; yet it does usefully mean "the state of being a tenant," as distinct from ownership. To the extent that *tenantry* overlaps with any of the senses outlined above, it too is a NEEDLESS VARIANT; yet *tenantry* may stand on its own in the sense "the body of tenants" <the tenantry is dissatisfied with the proposed improvements>.

tenancy by the entireties; tenancy by the entirety. The phrase refers to a joint tenancy between the husband and wife; it arises in some jurisdictions when a single instrument conveys realty to the husband and wife but nothing is said in the deed or will about the character of their ownership. Upon the death of either the husband or wife, the survivor automatically takes title to the deceased spouse's share.

The plural form *entireties* is slightly more common in both AmE and BrE, although *Black's* contains its definition under *estate by entirety*, which is also widespread. *Black's Law Dictionary* 627 (9th ed. 2009).

tenancy from month to month; tenancy from year to year. See **periodic tenancy.**

tenancy in common. See **joint tenancy.**

tenancy *per la verge*; tenancy by the verge; tenancy by the rod. These equivalent phrases denote a copyhold. The first is LAW FRENCH, the second a somewhat anglicized version, and the third an anglicized LOAN TRANSLATION of the first phrase. The terms are little used but in historical contexts (the rod having been delivered for purposes of conveying seisin). Each of these phrases ordinarily requires some explanation by the user. See **seisin.**

tenant. A. Senses. *Tenant* = (1) the holder of land under a contract of tenancy; or (2) the defendant in a writ of right (the plaintiff being known as a *demandant*—see **demandant**).

B. And **tenanter*. The word **tenanter* is a NEEDLESS VARIANT.

tenant at sufferance; *tenant by sufferance. The first is the traditional idiomatic phrase. See **sufferance.**

tenant at will. Although Henry S. Maine, among others, used hyphens (*tenant-at-will*), the noun phrase is best spelled without the hyphens. E.g.: "In a law court, O is probably viewed simply as T's *tenant at will*—that is, as a tenant whose estate may be legally terminated at any time by T." Thomas F. Bergin & Paul G. Haskell, *Preface to Estates in Land and Future Interests* 84 (2d ed. 1984). See **at will.**

tenant by sufferance. See **tenant at sufferance.**

tenant by the curtesy initiate. See **curtesy** & **initiate** **tenant by curtesy.**

tenant by the entirety. See **tenancy by the entirety.**

***tenanter.** See **tenant** (B).

tenant-in-chief (= a person who holds land directly under the king) is most commonly so written—with the hyphens—following the similar convention in the phrase *case-in-chief*. See **case-in-chief.**

In the Latin form of *tenant-in-chief*, namely *tenant-in-capite*, the last two words are best italicized. Cf. **in chief.**

tenantry; tenantship. See **tenancy.**

tendentious means "biased (usu. in favor of something); prejudiced." Its meaning is often misapprehended, as in this specimen, in which the writer apparently thought the word means "frivolous": "We believe he had ample reason to know that his appeal lacked merit and that it was *merely tendentious*." *Texas v. Gulf Water Benefaction Co.*, 679 F.2d 85, 87 (5th Cir. 1982). The phrase *merely tendentious* gives away the writer's ignorance of the meaning of the word *tendentious*.

*Tendencious is a variant spelling to be eschewed.

tender, n. See **bid,** n.

tender, vb., is a FORMAL WORD for *make* or *give*.

tendinitis; *tendonitis. *Tendinitis* = inflammation of a tendon. **Tendonitis* is incorrectly arrived at by association with the spelling of the noun *tendon*.

tenement (= [in law] an estate in land) usually denotes in lay contexts "a building or house." In lawbooks, *tenement* is often associated with the word *messuage*. See **messuage** & **lands, tenements, and hereditaments.**

tenendum. See **habendum.**

TENSES. A. Sequence of. The term *sequence of tenses* refers to the relationship of tenses in subordinate clauses to those in principal clauses. Generally, the former follow from the latter.

In careful writing, the tenses agree both logically and grammatically. The basic rules of tense-sequence are easily stated, although the plethora of examples that follow belie their ostensible simplicity in practice.

1. When the principal clause has a verb in the present (*he says*), present perfect (*he has said*), or future (*he will say*), the subordinate clause has a present-tense verb. Grammarians call this the primary sequence.
2. When the principal clause is in past tense (*he said, he was saying*) or past perfect (*he had said*), the subordinate clause has a past-tense verb. Grammarians call this the secondary sequence.

The primary sequence has proved to be a little less troublesome than the secondary sequence. Examples may be readily found, however, in which the primary sequence is mangled: "It *was* [read *is*] as a teacher more than as the guardian of *Richardson on Evidence* that he *will be* long remembered." Leo Glasser, *In Rememberance: Jerome Prince*, 55 Brook. L. Rev. xvii, xviii (1989).

But it is the secondary sequence that most commonly trips up writers, as in the following examples:

- "It will be seen that Duguit set out to find a rational basis for law (though he cannot be said *to succeed* [read *to have succeeded*])." W.W. Buckland, *Some Reflections on Jurisprudence* 11 (1945).
- "This power to imprison a man without trial, not for what he *had* [read *has*] already done, but for what he might hereafter do, was entrusted by Parliament to the executive." Alfred Denning, *Freedom Under the Law* 11 (1949).
- "Even if the majority *did not go* [read *does not go*] so far as to eliminate the need to allege a delinquent act, absent a statutory definition, one so charged would discover whether he or she actually contributed to another's delinquency only when the finder of fact makes that determination in any given case." *State v. Krueger*, 975 P.2d 489, 499 (Utah Ct. App. 1999) (Davis, J., dissenting).

Continuous tenses cause problems when the action described in the subordinate clause is supposed to have preceded the action that is stated in the past tense in the governing clause—e.g.:

- "A jury *being waived* [read *having been waived*], the case was tried." *State to Use of Woodrome v. Freeman*, 158 S.W. 726, 727 (Mo. Ct. App. 1913).
- "Fossils have been collected from the area on several occasions, the largest collection *being* [read *having been*] made by L. Kohl-Larsen in 1938–39." Mary D. Leakey et al., *Fossil Hominids from the Laetolil Beds, Tanzania* 157 (1978).
- "The policy language excluded coverage for accidents *occurring* [read *that occurred*] 'away from premises owned, rented or controlled by the named insured.'" *Ace Am. Ins. Co. v. RC2 Corp.*, 600 F.3d 763, 768 (7th Cir. 2010).

A related problem occurs with (tenseless) infinitives, which, when put after a past-tense verb, are often wrongly made perfect infinitives, as here:

- "When this happened (and without any negligence on the part of the bus driver) there did not remain sufficient time and distance for the bus driver *to have done* [read *to do*] anything to avoid the collision." *Biggers v. Continental Bus Sys., Inc.*, 303 S.W.2d 359, 370 (Tex. 1957) (Griffin, J., dissenting).
- "Although all but Miser had served the number of years required for their pension benefits *to have accrued* [read *to*

accrue], all were still on active duty when their marriages were dissolved." *Cearley v. Cearley*, 544 S.W.2d 661, 664 (Tex. 1976).

- "Appellants argue that the trial judge was required *to have recused himself* [read *to recuse himself*]." *Reilly v. South-eastern Pa. Transp. Auth.*, 479 A.2d 973, 1002 (Pa. 1984).
- "Christie argued in his first postconviction relief motion that it was error for the trial court to ignore the oral plea agreement and for the trial judge not *to have recused* [read *to recuse*] himself." *Christie v. State*, 996 So.2d 81, 83 (Miss. Ct. App. 2008).

Still another bugbear is the incomplete verb phrase by which the writer attempts to give two tenses, but only one tense is actually completed. The result is one type of zeugma—e.g.:

- "This mischaracterization of pension rights *has, and unless overturned, will continue to result* [read *has resulted and, unless overturned, will continue to result*] in ineq-uitable division of community assets." *In re Marriage of Brown*, 544 P.2d 561, 566 (1976).
- "This diversity case is one of a multitude of asbestos cases, presently filed and reasonably anticipated, in which injured plaintiffs or their survivors *have or will seek damages* [read *have sought or will seek damages*] for injuries associated with exposure to asbestos." *Halphen v. Johns-Manville Sales Corp.*, 752 F.2d 124, 125 (5th Cir. 1985).

See ZEUGMA AND SYLLEPSIS.

B. Subjunctives. As Partridge has pointed out, not sequence but mood is involved in the correct use of SUBJUNCTIVES, but the mistakes are common enough and closely enough related to merit treatment here:

- "If the title *were acquired* [read *was acquired*] by purchase, the disseisee's entry was not barred." Kaplan PMBR, *Property* 17 (2009).
- "[P]arties are not required to articulate how they *would have been* prejudiced if they *were not* [read *had not been*] provided with an expert-witness report." David W. Lee, *Handbook of Section 1983 Litigation* 1066 (2009).

See LEGISLATIVE DRAFTING.

C. The Historical Present. Some writers use the present tense to discuss what happened long ago. To many readers this mannerism is an affectation. E.g.: "As regards the real estate of the deceased, it is set-tled by the end of the thirteenth century that he *can make* no will, except where there is a local custom to that effect." William Geldart, *Introduction to English Law* 36 (D.C.M. Yardley ed., 9th ed. 1984). Cf. FIRST PERSON (B).

D. Present Tense for Ongoing Truth. General and ongoing truths require the present tense, regardless of the tense of the principal verb—e.g.: "But even the most aggressive of these federal courts *had* [read *have*] sought to circumscribe this scrutiny by identifying specific, narrow, and precisely defined circumstances in which such scrutiny *was* [read *is*] justified." Richard H. Pildes, *Judging "New Law" in Election Disputes*, 29 Fla. St. U. L. Rev. 691, 730 (2001).

E. Past-Perfect Tense. Many writers stumble on the correct use of this tense, formerly called the "plu-perfect" tense. The past perfect (*had* [+ past parti-ciple]) represents a past action or state as having

been completed before a more recent time in the past—e.g.: "The assurances were made to the family on the only business day between the time that coun-sel *had decided* that a habeas petition would be futile and actual deportation." *Gutierrez v. Ashcroft*, 289 F.Supp.2d 555, 567 (D.N.J. 2003). Because the sec-ond clause takes us still further back in time from the past-tense main clause, it is in the past perfect (*had decided*).

Increasingly—and especially in AmE—writers want to change the past perfect to the simple past. This trend, formerly characteristic only of colloquial speech, should be avoided—e.g.: "One coworker testi-fied at her deposition that she believed a manager was having an affair because she *heard* [read *had heard*] 'rumors' about the purported relationship from 'lots' of people." *Ellis v. UPS*, 523 F.3d 823, 827 (7th Cir. 2008).

F. In Statute Drafting. See LEGISLATIVE DRAFTING.

tentative trust. See **Totten trust.**

tenurial, the adjective corresponding to *tenure*, is almost exclusively a legal term—e.g.:

- "The basic idea of feudal land 'ownership,' then, was that it was *tenurial* in character—more a holding of land on good behavior than ownership as we think of it today." Thomas F. Bergin & Paul G. Haskell, *Preface to Estates in Land and Future Interests* 4 (2d ed. 1984).
- "Oklahoma jurisprudence on the enforcement of cov-enants respecting realty where the original parties were not in a *tenurial* relationship have similarly omitted any discussion of the horizontal aspect of privity." *Beattie v. State*, 41 P.3d 377, 388 n.25 (Okla. 2002).

tergiversation. See **ambiguity.**

term, n. (= a limit in space or duration), has the spe-cial legal senses "an estate or interest in land for a cer-tain period" <term of years> and, as a plural (*terms*), "conditions or stipulations limiting what is proposed to be granted or done" (*OED*). See **fundamental term** & **terms.**

term for years. See **term of years** & **termor.**

terminal. See **terminus.**

termination. See **expiration.**

termination for convenience. This contractual phrase, which appears to have originated in govern-ment contracts in the mid-20th century, is essentially equivalent to "termination for any reason at all—or no reason." *Termination for convenience* is really just a EUPHEMISM sometimes imposed by the contracting party with greater bargaining power, but the plain-spoken *termination for any reason* is actually more frequent in American contracts.

terminological inexactitude. See **lie,** n.

terminus; terminal, n. *Terminus* = the city at the end of a railroad or bus line. Pl. *termini*. *Terminal* = the station of a transportation line.

terminus a quo; terminus ad quem. The first phrase means "departure point"; the second, "destination." Figuratively, the words are used of the beginning and ending points of an argument. Both figuratively and literally, the phrases are pomposities.

term loan; time loan. These phrases are interchangeable, *term loan* being slightly more common.

term of years; term for years; estate for years; lease for years. These synonymous phrases denote an estate whose duration is known—in years, weeks, and days—from the moment of its creation. As between *term of years* and *term for years,* the first is more common in BrE, whereas both forms are used in AmE.

termor = a person who holds lands or tenements for a term of years, or (rarely) for life. E.g.: "[Scope's theory] would entail great hardship, for it would enable any *termor* to commit waste on the last day of his term without any punishment." Thomas Lund, *Activist Judges of the Early Fourteenth Century,* 2008 Utah L. Rev. 471, 494 (2008).

terms has increasingly been used as an elliptical form of *terms of the contract* or *terms of payment.* See **term.**

terms, in. The phrase *in terms* means "expressly; in plain words." Though the *OED* labels the phrase "obsolete," it continues to thrive in legal contexts—e.g.:

- "The act *in terms* applies to all the courts of the United States." Eugene A. Jones, *Manual of Equity Pleading and Practice* 140 (1916).
- "Deere and Fidelity respond that there are no exceptions to [the statute's] safe harbor, which *in terms* applies to 'any' breach committed by someone 'who is otherwise a fiduciary.'" *Hecker v. Deere & Co.,* 556 F.3d 575, 589 (7th Cir. 2009).

terms and conditions. This phrase is among the most common REDUNDANCIES in legal drafting. But someone might ask, is *term* really broad enough to include *condition*—is not a *condition* something that must be satisfied before a contractual *term* applies? The *OED* defines *terms* as "conditions or stipulations limiting what is proposed to be granted or done," and that is its usual sense in law. Hence *terms* is sufficient.

*terms and provisions is a REDUNDANCY.

TERMS OF ART are words having specific, precise meanings in a given specialty. Having its origins in Lord Coke's *vocabula artis,* the phrase *term of art* is common in law because the legal field has developed many technical words whose meanings are locked tight (e.g., *bailment, replevin*)—as well as JARGON, constituting would-be terms of art, whose meanings are often unhinged.

How can one say "unhinged"? Take *per stirpes,* a phrase that many lawyers cite as a quintessential term of art. Yet as a leading expert in the field of wills and

estates has remarked, "*per stirpes* is a textbook example of legalese that seductively suggests certainty but actually can produce ambiguity and litigation." Stanley M. Johanson, *In Defense of Plain Language,* 3 Scribes J. Legal Writing 37, 37 (1992). The phrase creates a problem in this scenario: Mary's will bequeaths property "to my descendants per stirpes." She has two children—John, who has two children, and Bob, who has four. The complication arises when both of Mary's children die before she does. Some courts would say that the shares are divided between John and Bob, others that the shares must be divided at the level of John's and Bob's children. And in many states, the issue has never been decided and would therefore have to be litigated. *Id.* at 38.

Jargon, then, creates more than just aesthetic problems, though some writers lament those most prominently: "the unnecessary or inartistic employment of more or less technical terms in the drafting of legal documents is by no means rare." *Lancaster Malleable Castings Co. v. Dunie,* 73 A.2d 417, 418 (Pa. 1950). Expert drafters, who know that clear, simple drafting is less subject to misinterpretation than legalistic drafting, recommend avoiding jargon precisely because it invites substantive problems.

On the other hand, "Not to use a technical word, even if it is a long one, in its proper place, would be an affectation as noticeable as the overfrequent use of such words where they are not needed." E.L. Piesse, *The Elements of Drafting* 46 (J.K. Aitken ed., 7th ed. 1987). Lawyers need not invent homegrown ways of saying *res ipsa loquitur.*

One secret of good legal writing is to distinguish rigorously between terms of art and mere jargon. It is elementary to know that *and his heirs* and *elegit* have historically been terms of art; yet only the first is a living term of art, the second having become archaic (and therefore useful primarily in historical contexts).

Is *res gestae* a term of art? Or *scire facias* and *fieri facias*? Many such questions are debatable: but the debate is important, for we must attempt to winnow the useful law words from the verbal baggage amid which so many of them are buried. See JARGON & PLAIN LANGUAGE.

termtime (= the time of year during which a court is in session) is the antonym of *vacation.* E.g.: "A judge of a district court may, either in *termtime* or [in] vacation, grant writs of mandamus." Tex. Govt. Code § 24.011 (West 1988). Cf. **vacation.**

British writers tend to use two words (*term time*)—e.g.: "At common law, serjeants had an exclusive right of audience in the Court of Common Pleas during *term time,* while sitting in banc." R.E. Megarry, *A Second Miscellany-at-Law* 23 (1973).

terre-tenant; *tertenant; land-tenant. As between the first two, *terre-tenant* is the standard spelling of this LAW FRENCH term. *Tertenant*, a Middle English anglicized spelling, never gained widespread use. In the *OED*'s only listed sense of *terre-tenant*—"one who has the actual possession of land; the occupant of land"—the word hardly seems justified. But there is another definition, probably purely AmE: "one who has an interest in a judgment debtor's land after the judgment creditor's lien has attached to the land (such as a subsequent purchaser)." *Black's Law Dictionary* 1610 (9th ed. 2009).

No writer should use the phrase *terre-tenant* without both understanding and making clear the precise sense in which it is used, and without a sound reason for doing so. The thoroughly anglicized form, *land-tenant*, which is listed in some of the older law dictionaries, would be an improvement. See **landman (B)**.

territory; dependency; commonwealth. The distinctions in AmE usage are as follows. *Territory* = a part of the United States not included within any state but organized with a separate legislature (*W11*). Guam and the U.S. Virgin Islands are *territories* of the United States; Alaska and Hawaii were formerly *territories*. *Dependency* = a land or territory geographically distinct from the country governing it, but belonging to it and governed by its laws. The Philippines was once a *dependency* of the United States. *Commonwealth* = a political unit having local autonomy but voluntarily united with the United States. Puerto Rico and the Northern Mariana Islands are *commonwealths*. Puerto Rico is sometimes referred to as a *dependency*, but its proper designation is *commonwealth*.

In BrE, *commonwealth* = a loose association of countries that recognize one sovereign as its head <the British Commonwealth>.

Terry stop (= the act of a police officer's stopping a person whose behavior is reasonably considered suspicious and frisking that person for weapons) derives from *Terry v. Ohio*, 392 U.S. 1 (1968)—e.g.:

- "Upholding the legality of the *Terry stop* of a van that led to Jones' arrest, the D.C. Court of Appeals affirmed Jones' conviction." *D.C. Digests*, Legal Times, 4 Dec. 1989, at 37.
- "A *Terry stop* does not give law enforcement officers carte blanche to stop and detain citizens indefinitely or unreasonably." *State v. Jenkins*, 3 A.3d 806, 824 (Conn. 2010).

See CASE REFERENCES (C).

*****tertenant.** See **terre-tenant.**

***tertius gaudens** = a third party who profits when two others dispute. Literally, the term means "a rejoicing third." It is good to have a term for this concept, which is not uncommon in law, but it is unfortunate that the term is so abstruse.

testable = (1) that may be tested or tried; (2) legally qualified to bear witness; (3) legally qualified to make a will; or (4) willable; devisable by will. Only sense 1 can be said to be thriving; the other three are obsolescent if not obsolete.

testacy; intestacy. *Testacy* = the condition of leaving a valid will at death. *Intestacy* is its antonym. See **intestate.**

testament is not, as is sometimes supposed, obsolete outside the phrase *last will and testament*. In legal prose, it is still sometimes contrasted with *devise*, for in the legal idiom *testament* has come generally to signify a will disposing of personal property, whereas *devise* is traditionally the word for a will disposing of land. E.g.: "That real estate passes by the will of the testator, which he owned at the time of its execution, upon the notion that a devise affecting lands is merely a species of conveyance. Hence the distinction between *devises* and *testaments* of personal chattels." *Jones v. Shewmake*, 35 Ga. 151, 153 (Ga. 1866). Cf. **last will and testament** & **bequeath.**

Usually, however, the word is used not for reasons of fastidiousness, but for less good reasons. In the following sentences, for example, it is an archaic pomposity, for which *will* would have been preferable:

- "A valid *testament* [read *will*] includes two essential elements. There must be a sufficient designation of the beneficiary and of the property given to him." *In re Haak's Estate*, 18 A.2d 671, 673 (Pa. 1941).
- "In *In re Bluestein's Will*, both the language of the *testament* [read *will*] and the attendant circumstances were said to support the conclusion that, in context, the testator's 'request' bespoke a direction, imposing an obligation upon the legatee." *Spencer v. Childs*, 134 N.E.2d 60, 62 (N.Y. 1956).
- "The heirs primarily allege that the 1994 *testament* [read *will*] does not contain the requisite testamentary intent, and, for that reason, the document was not a valid *testament* [read *will*]." *In re Succession of White*, 961 So.2d 439, 441 (La. Ct. App. 2007).

See **will.**

In Scots law, the *testament* was formerly that part of a will in which the testator named an executor. Today, however, and elsewhere in the civil-law world, *testament* is used more broadly as a synonym of *will*—e.g.: "The average citizen, relying on the existing legal framework governing intestate successions, will usually make no *testament*." A.N. Yiannopolous, *Of Legal Usufruct, the Surviving Spouse, and Article 890 of the Louisiana Civil Code*, 49 La. L. Rev. 803, 803 (1989).

*****testamental.** See **testimonial (B).**

testamentary. A. Senses. *Testamentary* = (1) of or relating to a will or testament, as a document <testamentary papers>; (2) provided for or appointed by a will <testamentary guardian>; or (3) created by will <testamentary trust>. In sense 1, the word is not ordinarily confined to contexts involving testaments of personal property (as opposed to devises of real property)—e.g.: "*Testamentary* capacity cannot be destroyed by showing a few isolated acts, foibles, idiosyncrasies, moral or mental irregularities, or departures from the normal unless they directly bear upon and have influenced the *testamentary* act." Marsha

Garrison, *The Empire of Illness*, 49 Wm. & Mary L. Rev. 781, 793 (2007).

B. And *testamental. The word is a NEEDLESS VARIANT that occurs mostly in lay writing.

C. For *testimonial*. Since the early 1960s, this error has become surprisingly common in reported American opinions. Usually, *testamentary* appears in tandem with *documentary*—hence the writer is misled by some kind of "false attraction" to the first suffix—e.g.:

- "A thorough review of the documentary and *testamentary* [read *testimonial*] evidence convinces us that the commissioner's findings on this point are amply supported by the record." *Lambert v. U.S.*, 153 Ct. Cl. 501, 510 (1961).
- "Bankrupts then offered documentary and *testamentary* [read *testimonial*] evidence to rebut the Government's proof." *Solari Furs v. U.S.*, 436 F.2d 683, 685 (8th Cir. 1971).
- "The State did not attempt to present any further documentary or *testamentary* [read *testimonial*] evidence relevant to any of the *Daubert/Shafersman* factors." *State v. Casillas*, 782 N.W.2d 882, 898 (Neb. 2010).

In the following sentence, the distinction is made clear: "Lay witnesses, before they may express a *testimonial* opinion as to *testamentary* capacity, must testify first to facts inconsistent with sanity." *In re Estate of Powers*, 134 N.W.2d 148, 161 (Mich. 1965).

testamentary intent; testamentary intention. See **intention (B).**

testate, n. (= a testate person), though corresponding in form to *intestate*, n., is generally a NEEDLESS VARIANT of *testator*. *Testatus* is the civil-law term. See **intestate.**

testate, vb., = (1) to testify; or (2) to make one's will. In sense 1, the word is a NEEDLESS VARIANT of *testify*. In sense 2, the verb is so rare as to sound affected.

testation = the disposal of property by will <power of testation>. E.g.:

- "But tenants soon acquired the right of alienation in their lifetime[s], though not, until much later, that of *testation*." H.G. Hanbury, *English Courts of Law* 57 (2d ed. 1953).
- "Before 1600, the province of Canterbury (excepting Wales and London) came to permit complete freedom of *testation*, whereas the province of York adhered to the old system of parts until 1692." J.H. Baker, *An Introduction to English Legal History* 436 (3d ed. 1990).
- "This case reveals a broader tension between the competing values of freedom of *testation* on one hand and resistance to 'dead hand' control on the other." *In re Estate of Feinberg*, 919 N.E.2d 888, 894 (Ill. 2009).

testator. A. Senses. *Testator* = (1) a person who dies leaving a will; or (2) a person who makes or has made a will. Sense 1 is more usual, perhaps for two reasons: first, we have more occasion to refer to *testators* who have already died; and second, the living feel uncomfortable being called "*testators*."

B. And *devisor*. Because *testament* historically came to be more or less confined to dispositions of personal property, and *devise* to those of real property, it has been thought that *testator* was at one time confined to a person who left personal, as opposed to real, property. *See, e.g.*, Morton S. Freeman, *A Treasury for Word Lovers* 173 (1983). But no such crabbed meaning ever attached to the word; Blackstone wrote, as long ago as 1766, "that all devises of lands and tenements shall not only be in writing, but signed by the *testator*" (quoted in *OED*). See **testate** & **deviser.**

testatorial; testorial; testatory. The *OED* records only *testatory* as the adjective corresponding to *testator*, but this form is extremely rare. As between *testatorial* and *testorial*, the former is the more logical form—e.g.: "An ademption may occur without *testatorial* intention." J.A. Ballentine, *Ballentine's Law Dictionary* 28 (3d ed. 1969).

But the most common form—which has no foundation in the *OED*, *W3*, or *Black's*—is *testorial*. E.g.:

- "It is enough if the circumstances, taken together, leave no doubt as to the *testorial* [read *testamentary*] intention, and in some cases it is said that the implication may be drawn from slight circumstances appearing from the will." 57 Am. Jur. *Wills* § 1192, at 783 (1948).
- "The *testorial* [read *testamentary*] intention will control." *Hixon v. Hixon*, 715 P.2d 1087, 1090 (Okla. 1985).
- "I am no more able to discern here an actual *testorial* [read *testamentary*] intent than was the court in *Johns v. Cobb*." *Riggs Nat'l Bank v. Summerlin*, 445 F.2d 201, 213 (D.C. Cir. 1971).

Often, *testamentary* will be the best option <testamentary intention>. It changes the meaning slightly, from "testator's intention" to "intention as expressed in the will," but ordinarily the latter is a more precise notion.

testatory. See **testatorial.**

testatrix. The word is useless, *testator* quite properly referring to men and women alike. See SEXISM (C).

testatus. See **testate.**

test case = a lawsuit brought to determine an unsettled legal point in some matter of broad application. E.g.:

- "Should *test cases* be brought directly to the highest court and without the lower court procedure?" David Lawrence, *Nine Honest Men* 123 (1936).
- "The appeal is a *test case*, its purpose being to determine whether a juvenile or criminal court has the power to order compensation to be paid to the victim of crime by the local authority in whose care the child who committed the offence was at the time of the offence." *Leeds City Council v. W. Yorkshire Metro. Police*, [1983] 1 A.C. 29, 37 (H.L.).
- "Constitutional lawyers say the large size of the punitive damages assessed against The Inquirer, if upheld on appeal, could become a *test case* for the United States Supreme Court." Michael deC. Hinds, *Philadelphia Paper*

Assessed $34 Million for Libel, N.Y. Times, 4 May 1990, at A1, A11.

- "The bankruptcy court approved procedures permitting Delta to designate objections to selected sets of TIA claims, which would serve as '*test cases*' governing the disposition of similar claims." *In re Delta Air Lines*, 608 F.3d 139, 144 (2d Cir. 2010).

teste is the name, in drafting, of the clause that states the name of a witness and evidences the act of witnessing. E.g.: "The subpoena shall bear *teste* in the name of the city, shall be signed by the mayor or the mayor's designee, and shall be served by any member of the department of police." *Foxy Lady, Inc. v. City of Atlanta*, 347 F.3d 1232, 1235 (11th Cir. 2003). In older instruments *teste* was used in much the same way as some legal writers use *witnesseth* today. See **witnesseth**. Cf. **testimonium clause**.

Like much legal terminology, this word is not in tune with the times. Several American judges have been known to joke that they would much prefer not to attach a *teste* to a document.

testification is an unnecessary word for *testimony* or *testifying*.

*testifier. See **witness (c).**

testify. See **give evidence.**

testimonial, not *testamentary*, is the adjective corresponding to *testimony*. See **testamentary (c).**

testimonium clause, in a sworn legal document, is the attestation clause that traditionally begins with the phrase *In witness whereof*, which commonly concludes legal instruments and pleadings. Among the traditional forms are the following:

- "In witness whereof I have subscribed my name this _____ day of 20___."
- "Witness my signature this _____ day of 20___."
- "In witness whereof we hereto set our hands and seals."

The plural of *testimonium* is either *-iums* or *-ia*, the former being preferable. See **attestation clause** & **in witness whereof.** Cf. **teste.**

testimony is sometimes loosely used as a count noun, but the more natural-sounding usage is to treat it as a mass noun. E.g.:

- "*These testimonies are* [read *This testimony is*] insufficient to raise genuine issues of material fact." *New York Marine & Gen. Ins. Co. v. Lafarge N. Am., Inc.*, 599 F.3d 102, 120 (2d Cir. 2010).
- "According to the *testimonies* [read *testimony*] of Riley, Frisco, and Black, a 'hundred-rock' is the amount of crack that can be purchased with one hundred dollars and is usually approximately 1 gram." *U.S. v. Carl*, 593 F.3d 115, 118 n.2 (1st Cir. 2010).
- "Here, Benson essentially argues that the portions of coconspirators' *testimonies that are* [read *testimony that is*] not considered hearsay cannot be used as the independent, corroborating evidence to determining whether the hearsay statements meet the *Enright* requirements." *U.S. v. Benson*, 591 F.3d 491, 502 (6th Cir. 2010).

See **evidence (A).** Cf. **evidence (c).**

testing-clause. See **attestation clause.**

*testis [L.] = (1) a witness; or (2) a testicle. Modern witnesses are not likely to take kindly to being called *testes.* See **witness.** Cf. **teste.**

testorial. See **testatorial.**

text as an adjective is inferior to *textual*: "We have examined and considered the decisions of the courts of other states construing similar contracts, as well as recognized *text* [read *textual*] authorities in this field." *Holder v. Hartford Fire Ins. Co.*, 257 So.2d 862, 865 (Miss. 1972). See **textual.**

texting; text-messaging; sexting. *Text-messaging*, usually shortened to *texting*, is the act of communicating by sending a written message or photograph using a cellular phone. *Sexting* (sex + texting), a PORTMANTEAU WORD, applies when the writings or photographs are sexually explicit. The term first appeared in the U.K. in 2005: "Following a string of extramarital affairs and several lurid '*sexting*' episodes, Warne has found himself home alone, with Simone Warne taking their three children and flying the conjugal coop." Yvonne Roberts, *The One and Only*, Sunday Telegraph Mag., 31 July 2005, at 22. It may be expanding to include communications over the Internet. In law, the term appears in contexts such as sexual harassment and child pornography—e.g.:

- "'Sexting,' as defined by plaintiffs, is 'the practice of sending or posting sexually suggestive text messages and images, including nude or semi-nude photographs, via cellular telephones or over the Internet.'" *Miller v. Mitchell*, 598 F.3d 139, 143 (3d Cir. 2010).
- "Overzealous prosecutors across the country have charged teen subjects and recipients of *sext-messages* with possession and distribution of child pornography. These prosecutors argue that *sexting* fits the literal definition of child pornography—a depiction of a nude minor." Marsha Levick & Kristina Moon, *Prosecuting Sexting as Child Pornography*, 44 Val. U. L. Rev. 1035, 1035 (2010).
- "He violated MRPC 8.4(d) . . . when he sent his client inappropriate and sexually suggestive electronic text messages (*sexting*) and touched her in a sexually suggestive manner, all while in a courtroom awaiting a trial to commence." *Attorney Grievance Comm'n of Md. v. Marcalus*, 996 A.2d 350, 365 (Md. 2010) (Harrell, J., concurring in part & dissenting in part).

textual; textuary. As an adjective, the second is a NEEDLESS VARIANT.

textual-integrity canon; whole-act rule. These synonymous phrases denote the canon of construction that the entirety of the text must be considered in the interpretation of a provision. *Textual-integrity canon* can apply to any type of authoritative text, while *whole-act rule* applies only to statutes.

textualism. See INTERPRETATION, MODES OF (A).

textuary. See **textual.**

than. A. Verb Not Repeated After (*than is, than has*). Usually it is unnecessary to repeat *be*-verbs and *have*-verbs after *than*. E.g.:

- "Juries—comprised as they are of a fair cross section of the community—*are* more representative institutions *than is the judiciary* [read *than the judiciary*]." *Spaziano v. Florida*, 468 U.S. 447, 486 (1984) (Stevens, J., concurring in part & dissenting in part).
- "The central issue is whether decision makers, who *are* in a better position *than is the judiciary* [read *than the judiciary*] to decide whether the public interest would be served by a proposed remedy, have created a scheme with which the remedy would interfere." *Heaney v. U.S. Veterans Admin.*, 756 F.2d 1215, 1220 (5th Cir. 1985).

B. *Than what.* This collocation usually signals a poor construction. E.g.: "The Michigan Court of Appeals required more *than what* [omit *what*] the Fourth Amendment demands." *Michigan v. Fisher*, 130 S.Ct. 546, 549 (2009) (per curiam).

C. For *then.* This error is so elementary that one might fairly wonder whether it is merely a lapse in proofreading; but it occurs with some frequency— e.g.: "If Defendant is correct, *than* [read *then*] the government filed its complaint in this action several months after the expiration of the applicable limitations period." *U.S. v. Ruegsegger*, 702 F.Supp. 438, 442 (S.D.N.Y. 1988).

D. Case of Pronoun After (*than me* or *than I*). Traditionally, grammarians have considered *than* a conjunction, not a preposition—hence *He is taller than I* [*am*]. That view has had its detractors, including Eric Partridge, who preferred the objective case: *You are a much greater loser than me. See* Eric Partridge, *Usage and Abusage* 332 (1947). But those siding with Partridge have been a small minority.

For formal contexts, I recommend the traditional usage. The prepositional use of *than* is acceptable only in the most relaxed, colloquial contexts. Here it seems ill-advised, even ironic: "So many of our students seem to struggle . . . . (Are we really that much smarter *than them* [read *than they*]?)" John B. Mitchell, *Current Theories on Expert and Novice Thinking*, 39 J. Legal Educ. 275, 275 (1989).

E. *Than whom.* This idiom, common since the latter part of the 16th century, originated perhaps as a LOAN TRANSLATION of the Latin comparative with *quam.* Strictly speaking, *than who* would have been preferable, since *than* is treated as a conjunction, not a preposition (see (D)). But the phrase *than whom*—as in *Holmes was a judge than whom no other could be considered better*—is now established.

thankfully = gratefully; in a manner expressing thanks. The word should not be misused in the way that *hopefully* is misused, namely, in the sense "thank goodness; I am (or we are) thankful that." Following are three examples of the all-too-common fall from stylistic grace:

- "Our country, *thankfully*, has never chosen that path." *Roberts v. U.S.*, 445 U.S. 552, 571 (1980) (Marshall, J., dissenting).

- "As Mustill L.J. has already remarked the many and complicated issues which were debated over many days before Mr. Justice Saville have now, *thankfully*, been considerably refined." *G & H Montage GmbH v. Irvani*, [1990] 1 W.L.R. 667, 687 (C.A.) (per Purchas, L.J.).
- "*Thankfully*, the boy recovered." *Means v. State*, 43 So.3d 438, 442 (Miss. 2010).

See **hopefully** & SENTENCE ADVERBS.

than me; than I. See **than** (D).

than what. See **than** (B).

than whom. See **than** (E).

that. A. Wrongly Suppressed *that* as Relative Pronoun. Although in any number of constructions it is perfectly permissible, and even preferred, to omit *that* by ellipsis (e.g., *The dog you gave me* rather than *The dog that you gave me*), in formal writing *that* is often ill-advisedly omitted where it creates an AMBIGUITY, even if only momentarily. E.g.:

- "In *Eleason* we held the driver, an epileptic, [read *we held that the driver, an epileptic,*] possessed knowledge that he was likely to have a seizure." *Breunig v. American Family Ins. Co.*, 173 N.W.2d 619, 623 (Wis. 1970). (Miscue: *held the driver.*)
- "She *thought Batman was good* [read *thought that Batman was good*] and was trying to help save the world and *her husband* [read *that her husband*] was possessed of the devil." David E. Seidelson, *Reasonable Expectations and Subjective Standards in Negligence Law*, 50 Geo. Wash. L. Rev. 17, 34 (1981). (Miscue: *save the world and her husband.*)
- "The court *held the defendant was sentenced* [read *held that the defendant had been sentenced*] to 366 days with credit for time served only from the last booking date, which amounted to two days, pursuant to the plea agreement." *Young v. State*, 20 So.3d 965, 965 (Fla. Dist. Ct. App. 2009). (Miscue: *held the defendant.*)

See MISCUES (F).

B. Unnecessarily Repeated *that.* One must be careful not to repeat the conjunction after an intervening phrase; either suspend it till just before the verb, or use it early in the sentence and omit it before the verb. E.g.:

- "Appellant . . . argues *that* since Lent, Inc. was the principal in the indemnity agreement, *that* [omit *that*] it cannot also be an indemnitor in the same agreement." *Commercial Union Ins. Co. v. Melikyan*, 430 So.2d 1217, 1223 (La. Ct. App. 1983).
- "Rule 10b-10(a) requires *that* prior to the completion of a transaction *that* [omit *that*] a written statement be sent or given to a customer setting forth prescribed information relating to the transaction." Harold S. Bloomenthal, *Securities Law Handbook* § 19:10 (2009). On the use of *prior to* in that sentence, see ***prior to.**

C. The Biblical *that.* In lieu of *so that* or *in order that*, *that* often smacks of the biblical, as in:

- "A lawyer may never give unsolicited advice to a layman *that* [read *in order that*] he retain a client."

- "We must preserve the work of art *that* [read *so that*] it may continue to convey to the sympathetic spectator the creative ecstasy that went into its making."

See BIBLICAL AFFECTATION.

D. As an Ellipsis for *the fact that*. This construction is often useful; here, however, the phrase is badly used, because the subject and verb are too far removed: "*That* the district court's order authorizing the sale of the Charles House property and judgment confirming the sale and passage of title to Southmark operated as a final judgment on the merits is evident." *Southmark Props. v. Charles House Corp.*, 742 F.2d 862, 870 (5th Cir. 1984). [Read *It is evident that* . . . .] See **fact that, the.**

E. Relative Adverb. E.g.: "Many charities would fail by change of circumstances and [by] the happening of contingencies [that] no human foresight could provide against." *Jackson v. Phillips*, 96 Mass. 539, 580 (1867). (See PREPOSITIONS (E).) Some lightweight authorities do not understand that the construction in the sentence just quoted is perfectly acceptable. One such manual for legal writers recommends, "The case *on which* the lawyer was working never went to trial," instead of, "The case *that* the lawyer *was* working *on* never went to trial," and labels the latter incorrect. See *Texas Law Review Manual on Style* 28–29 (4th ed. 1979). Actually, both constructions are correct—and the construction with *that* is far more natural-sounding.

F. For *so* or *very*. "The wrongdoer was not *that* culpable." Michael Tonry, *Why Punish?* 371 (2010). This usage is informal and colloquial, and though it hardly merits condemnation in speech, it should be avoided in writing: "The wrongdoer is not *so* [or *very*] culpable."

G. *That of*. This phrase is often used unnecessarily. E.g.: "The decision of the en banc panel of the Court of Appeals for the Sixth Circuit, which the Court reverses, brought that Circuit's caselaw into line with *that of* [omit *that of*] its sister Circuits." *Kentucky. Ret. Sys. v. EEOC*, 554 U.S. 135, 151 (2008) (Kennedy, J., dissenting).

H. And *which*. See **that & which** & REMOTE RELATIVES.

I. And *who*. See **who** (C).

J. The Demonstrative *that*. See DEICTIC TERMS.

that & which. A. Generally. Legal writers who fail to distinguish restrictive from nonrestrictive clauses—and especially *that* from *which*—risk their credibility with careful readers. It's therefore worthwhile to learn the difference so well that, when writing, you use the correct form automatically.

Consider the following sentence: "All the cases that were decided before the 1995 legislation support this argument." It illustrates a *restrictive* clause. Such a clause gives essential information about the preceding noun (here, *cases*) so as to distinguish it from similar items (here, cases that were not decided until after the 1995 legislation) with which it might be confused. In

effect, the clause restricts the field of reference to just this one particular case or class of cases—hence the term *restrictive*. Restrictive clauses take no commas (for commas would present the added information as an aside)—e.g.:

- "With the exception of two 1935 cases invalidating statutes as unconstitutional delegations of power, . . . the Court has upheld every challenge to a congressional delegation of power *that* has been presented to it." *U.S. v. Brown*, 364 F.3d 1266, 1271 (11th Cir. 2004).
- "Hardt then filed a motion under 29 U.S.C. § 1132(g)(1), a fee-shifting statute *that* applies in most ERISA lawsuits." *Hardt v. Reliance Standard Life Ins. Co.*, 130 S.Ct. 2149, 2150 (2010) (per Thomas, J.).
- "Cases *that* predate the era of selective incorporation held that the Grand Jury Clause of the Fifth Amendment and the Seventh Amendment's civil jury requirement do not apply to the States." *McDonald v. City of Chicago*, 130 S.Ct. 3020, 3046 n.30 (2010) (per Alito, J.).

Now let's punctuate our sample sentence differently and change the relative pronoun from *that* to *which*: "All the cases, which were decided before the 1995 legislation, support this argument." This version illustrates a *nonrestrictive* clause. Such a clause typically gives supplemental, nondefining information. Here, we already know from the context which cases we are talking about. The sentence informs us that the cases support this argument—oh, and by the way, they were all decided before the 1995 legislation. The incidental detail is introduced by *which* and set off by commas to signal its relative unimportance—e.g.:

- "Not every electoral law burdening associational rights is subject to strict scrutiny, *which* is appropriate only if the burden is severe." *Clingman v. Beaver*, 544 U.S. 581, 592 (2005) (per Thomas, J.).
- "The Court never establishes, however, that these instances of Delaware's assertion of jurisdiction related to wharves of 'extraordinary character,' *which* is the only jurisdiction that the Court's decree confers upon Delaware." *New Jersey v. Delaware*, 552 U.S. 597, 635 (2008) (Scalia, J., dissenting).
- "The Compact, *which* was approved, . . . allows post-Compact development in Colorado." *Kansas v. Colorado*, 129 S.Ct. 1294, 1297 n.1 (2009) (per Alito, J.).

Restrictive clauses are essential to the grammatical and logical completeness of a sentence. Nonrestrictive clauses, by contrast, are so loosely connected with the essential meaning of the sentence that they might be omitted without changing the essential meaning.

Hence, three guidelines. First, if you cannot omit the clause without changing the basic meaning, the clause is restrictive; use *that* without a comma. Second, if you can omit the clause without changing the basic meaning, the clause is nonrestrictive; use *which* after a comma. Third, if you ever find yourself using a *which* that doesn't follow a comma, it probably needs to be a *that*.

For a good general discussion of these two relative pronouns, see Douglas Laycock, *"That" and "Which"*, 2 Scribes J. Legal Writing 37 (1991).

The word *who* is likewise a relative pronoun. With it, we rely entirely on punctuation to denote whether it functions restrictively or nonrestrictively.

Some of the common errors that occur with the two types of relative clauses are discussed in the following sections.

B. Which for that. Using *which* for *that* is perhaps the most common blunder with these words. In none of the sentences that follow could the phrase introduced by *which* be omitted without a nonsensical result or one with a drastically different sense. The word *which* should therefore be *that*—e.g.:

- "Beaver came and made a dam *which* [read *that*] in time created a lovely pond." William O. Douglas, *Points of Rebellion* 83 (1970).
- "Star Chamber did not usually try felonies *which* [read *that*] involved capital punishment." L.B. Curzon, *English Legal History* 181 (2d ed. 1979).
- "For this reason, the [sentence] *which* [read *that*] follows this passage ought to be either much longer or very short." Richard A. Lanham, *Revising Prose* 15 (1979).
- "Liberty is another value *which* [read *that*] seems to lie at the heart of our concern." Simon Lee, *Law and Morals* 77 (1986).
- "Despite all the uncertainty *which* [read *that*] surrounded the 1994 season—and the doubts *which* [read *that*] still linger like a hangover that just won't quit—Paul O'Neill was sure of one thing." Don Burke, *Yank's Ink O'Neill: 4 Years, $19M*, Star-Ledger (Newark, N.J.), 29 Oct. 1994, at 29.
- "Every right *which* [read *that*] accrued prior to passage of a new law, 'if permitted retroactive effect, would take away the right.'" *In re S.C.S.*, 48 S.W.3d 831, 837 (Tex. App.—Houston [14th Dist.] 2001) (Wittig, J., dissenting). On the use of *prior to* in that sentence, see **prior to.**
- "If any police power were necessary to support this doctrine, it would be the arrest power, a power *which* [read *that*] has been granted to the citizens of Tennessee." *U.S. v. Yoon*, 398 F.3d 802, 811 n.5 (6th Cir. 2005).
- "Spokony informed Anderson that he was treating her failure to attend as 'insubordinate default, an act *which* [read *that*] can lead to disciplinary action.'" *Anderson v. New York*, 614 F.Supp.2d 404, 412 (S.D.N.Y. 2009).
- "Act 88 applies to a dispute *which* [read *that*] arises during the public school employers' and employees' negotiations of questions that arise under their collective-bargaining agreement." *Central Dauphin Sch. Dist. v. Central Dauphin Bus Drivers' Ass'n*, 996 A.2d 47, 53 (Pa. Commw. Ct. 2010).
- "We conclude that these words do not carry the significance *which* [read *that*] Bar Counsel asserts." *In re Williams*, 3 A.3d 1179, 1185 (D.C. 2010).

In the last sentence quoted, the first *that* made the writers want to vary the word in the second phrase, but they should not have succumbed to this misplaced desire.

C. Restrictive Clause Wrongly Made Nonrestrictive. This error is fairly common. The relative clauses illogically set off by commas are necessary to the meaning of the sentence; one could not drop those phrases out of the sentences and retain the intended meaning—e.g.: "A state will not exercise judicial *jurisdiction, which* [read *jurisdiction that*] has been obtained by fraud or unlawful force, over a defendant or his property." Restatement (Second) of Conflict of Laws § 82 (1971).

D. Series. Some writers want to substitute *and who* or *and which* in place of *and that* for the last in a series of relative clauses beginning with a *that*-phrase. This tendency may result from a fear that the relative *that* may be confused with the demonstrative *that*; *which* and *who*, by contrast, are consistently relatives. Despite that concern, which is usually overblown, parallel phrasing is better—e.g.: "The trial court's predisposition or predetermination of respondent's guilt was . . . caused in substantial part by the AGC's unlawful [inclusion] . . . of criminal violations *that* had been filed with the Inquiry Panel, *that* were found by the Inquiry Panel . . . to be groundless, *that* were specifically dismissed by the Panel, and *which* [read *that*] were not part of the charges the Review Board authorized the AGC to file." *Attorney Grievance Comm'n of Md. v. Sheridan*, 741 A.2d 1143, 1150 (Md. 1999).

E. Remote Relative Pronouns. See REMOTE RELATIVES.

that is. The conventional wisdom is that, if this phrase is used to begin a sentence, the result is a fragment. But good writers regularly use it in this way, in place of *in other words*—e.g.:

- "A misrepresentation generally has no effect unless it is material. *That is*, it must be one [that] would affect the judgment of a reasonable person in deciding whether, or on what terms, to enter into the contract." G.H. Treitel, *The Law of Contract* 301 (8th ed. 1991).
- "They are punitive rather than remedial. *That is*, they do not attempt to restore any version of the status quo." Douglas Laycock, *The Death of the Irreparable Injury Rule* 199 (1991).

The longer phrase, *that is to say*, is usually wordy in place of *that is*—e.g.: "The statute does not speak with absolute crystalline clarity . . . . *That is to say* [read *That is*], Congress has chosen, wisely or no, to speak to the precise issue at hand through a Committee Report that was expressly adopted by both Houses." *ACLU v. F.C.C.*, 823 F.2d 1554, 1583 (D.C. Cir. 1987) (Starr, J., dissenting in part). Cf. **viz.** & **namely.**

that is to say. See **that is.**

that of. See **that (G).**

that which; those which; those that. When a noun introduced by *that*, as a DEICTIC TERM, is followed by defining matter, that matter is introduced by *which*. E.g.: "The commission merchant must exercise *that* degree of care *which* a prudent person would exercise in the conduct of his or her own affairs." 38 Tex. Jur. 3d § 8 (2010). Sometimes the construction is wrongly made *that . . . that*, as in: "We must distinguish between a belief in the literal truth and falsity of a statement and *that* type of belief in falsity *that* [read *which*] underlies the fraudulent misrepresentation." *In re Roblin's Estate*, 311 P.2d 459, 463 (Or. 1957). When *that* becomes, in plural, *those*, it is permissible for the second member of this construction to be either *which* or *that*. E.g.:

- "The District Court assumed that it was relevant to compare the challenged fees with *those that* [or *those which*] Harris Associates charged its other clients." *Jones v. Harris Assocs., LP*, 130 S.Ct. 1418, 1424 (2010).
- "In determining whether a new communication technology or device is covered under section 2907.31(D), future courts must determine whether that technology is more similar to ones which are personally directed, like an email, or *those that* [or *those which*] are generally accessible, like postings on a public website." *American Booksellers Found. for Free Expression v. Strickland*, 601 F.3d 622, 628 (6th Cir. 2010).

the. See ARTICLES.

theater; theatre. See -ER (C).

the case of. This FLOTSAM PHRASE is almost always best omitted. See **case (A)**.

the fact that. See **fact that, the**.

theft was not the name of a common-law crime. Rather, statutes such as England's Theft Act of 1968 have made *theft* a statutory crime. In ordinary usage, *theft* denotes the act of stealing. In legal usage, in some jurisdictions, it is used as a synonym of *larceny*.

In still others, such as England, *larceny* has been abolished and replaced by *theft*—which sometimes includes embezzlement and false pretenses. The Model Penal Code makes *theft* the name of all such acquisitive offenses. See **burglary (A)**.

their; they're; there. A book like this one ought not to have to explain such distinctions. So it will not. But:

- "Liberals are again trying to explain why they lost their fifth presidential election in 20 years. They've been talking about what *they're* [read *their*] party should be for." *What's a Liberal For?*, Wall St. J., 13 Jan. 1989, at A6.
- "And that's where these radio stations are really missing the boat, because *there* [read *they're*] missing the folks who hold the purse strings to all the disposable income." Brad Tooley, *Canyon Views*, Canyon News, 13 Jan. 1994, at 1, 2.

*theirself. See ***ourself**.

the law abhors a forfeiture. See **equity abhors a forfeiture**.

*themself is a part-plural, part-singular abomination. Sometimes it is intended as a gender-neutral equivalent of *himself or herself*—e.g.: "A person may be placed in involuntary inpatient placement upon a finding that there is a substantial likelihood that the person will inflict serious bodily harm on *themself* [read *himself or herself*] or another person." *L.T. v. Department of Children & Families*, 967 So.2d 456, 457 n.1 (Fla. Dist. Ct. App. 2007).

In the early 1990s, Canadian statute drafters began using **themself* in legislation.

then. A. Adjective. *Then* should not be hyphenated when used alone as an adverb meaning "at that time (but not now)"—e.g.: "Appellee Reed, *then-mayor* [read *then mayor*] of Harrisburg, vetoed the ordinance." *Reed v. Harrisburg City Council*, 995 A.2d 1137, 1138 (Pa.

2010). The full sense here is *who was then mayor*. This forced use of *then* to modify *mayor* shows why then-phrases are often awkward and better avoided.

When then is part of a PHRASAL ADJECTIVE used before the modified term, the phrase should be hyphenated. E.g.:

- "Plaintiffs claim that [defendants] are liable for the violation of Doe's bodily integrity, which occurred at the hands of *then-teacher* Cathy Curtis." *Doe v. Sch. Admin. Dist. No. 19*, 66 F.Supp.2d 57, 65 (D. Me. 1999).
- "One prominent name was commodities trader Marc Rich, who fled the United States in 1983 to avoid prosecution (by *then prosecutor* [read *then-prosecutor*] Rudy Giuliani) for tax evasion and trading with Iran." Charles Duelfer, *Hide and Seek* 229 (2009).

In these examples, however, the writer could have eliminated *then* altogether with no loss of meaning—a desirable result because of the awkward PHRASING that *then* creates.

B. For *than*. This is a distressingly common error, especially in newsprint but sometimes in legal writing also—e.g.:

- "Unfortunately, Bamburg does nothing more *then* [read *than*] state allegations without evidence, specifically medical testimony, to support his claims." *Bamburg v. St. Francis Med. Ctr.*, 30 So.3d 1071, 1075 (La. Ct. App. 2010).
- "Trinity USA filed its complaint on June 25, 2008, and its motion for summary judgment on August 12, 2008, more *then* [read *than*] thirty days later." *Spectrum Oil, LLC v. West*, 34 So.3d 1213, 1223 (Miss. Ct. App. 2010).

For the reverse error, see **than (C)**.

thence; whence; hence. *Thence* = from that place or source; for that reason. *Whence* = from there. *Hence* = (1) from here; or (2) therefore. These are literaryisms as well as LEGALISMS, acceptable perhaps in the more literary style of legal prose, despite carping by those who advocate "consumer English."

thenceforth; *thenceforward. The second is a NEEDLESS VARIANT.

theoretical; *theoretic. The best, most usual form of the adjective is *theoretical*, not **theoretic*. Of a common use of *theoretical*, Walter Wheeler Cook aptly observed: "Theory [that] will not work in practice is not sound theory. 'It is *theoretically* correct but will not work in practice' is a common but erroneous statement. If a theory is '*theoretically* correct' it will work; if it will not work, it is '*theoretically* incorrect.' " Introduction to Wesley N. Hohfeld, *Fundamental Legal Conceptions* 21 (1919). Holmes likewise observed, "I know no reason why theory should disagree with the facts." Oliver W. Holmes, *The Theory of Legal Interpretation*, 12 Harv. L. Rev. 417, 417 (1899).

therapist; *therapeutist. The standard term is *therapist*.

there. See **their** & **there is**.

thereabouts; thereabout. The form *thereabouts* is preferred. See **whereabouts**.

there are. See **there is** & EXPLETIVES.

*thereat (= there; at it). Even at the turn of the 20th century, when the *OED* was being compiled, this word was considered "formal [= pompous] and archaic." Today it is more so. E.g.:

- "In 1999, she was also treated *thereat* [read *there*] by gastroenterologist Dr. Appaswany M. Gowda." *Bright-Jacobs v. Barnhart*, 386 F.Supp.2d 1295, 1347 (N.D. Ga. 2004).
- "The right of way is a right that a vehicle or pedestrian has to legally go on and with preference over another vehicle or pedestrian approaching *thereat* [omit *thereat*] when the circumstances of speed, direction, and proximity are such that an accident could be precipitated unless one of them yields the way to the other." *Colon-Millin v. Sears Roebuck de Puerto Rico, Inc.*, 455 F.3d 30, 44 (1st Cir. 2006).

The word is not a locative. Cf. *whereat. See HERE- AND THERE-WORDS.

thereby cannot rightly be considered a FORBIDDEN WORD, but see HERE- AND THERE- WORDS.

therefore; therefor. The first (stress on first syllable) means "for that reason," "consequently," or "ergo"— this is the word known to nonlawyers; the second (stress on last syllable) means "for that" or "for it." The proper use of *therefore*, which always states a conclusion, needs no illustration.

A. Proper Use of *therefor* Illustrated. In the following sentences, the musty word *therefor* is properly used—even so, though, it generally ought to be replaced for stylistic reasons. E.g.:

- "The plaintiff discharged union cutters and shop foremen without just cause *therefor* [omit *therefor*]." *David Adler & Sons Co. v. Maglio*, 228 N.W. 123, 124 (Wis. 1929).
- "The hearing testimony quickly exposed the flimflam that had been perpetrated upon the Division and the obvious *reasons therefor* [read *reasons for it*]." *Bayview Towing, Inc. v. Stevenson*, 676 A.2d 325, 327 (R.I. 1996).
- "It has become possible for persons to install an unauthorized, or 'pirate,' decoder device or 'descrambler' onto Plaintiff's cable system and to receive all of Plaintiff's scrambled programming, without authorization or *paying therefor* [read *paying for it*]." *MediaOne of Del., Inc. v. E & A Beepers & Cellulars*, 43 F.Supp.2d 1348, 1351 (S.D. Fla. 1998).

See HERE- AND THERE- WORDS.

B. *Therefore* for *therefor*. In the sentences that follow, *therefore* is wrongly used for *therefor*, a surprising lapse:

- "A primary aim of CERCLA is to provide a mechanism for prompt recovery of monies expended for the costs of remedial actions from persons responsible *therefore* [read *therefor*], rather than forcing taxpayers to bear the cost of environmental clean-up." *Olin Corp. v. Consolidated Aluminum Corp.*, 807 F.Supp. 1133, 1137 (S.D.N.Y. 1992).
- "The state law limited the debtor's ability to pay dividends to funds legally available *therefore* [read *therefor*, or, better, *for that purpose*]." John E. Moose et al., *Is It Debt? Or Is It Equity?*, Am. Bankr. Inst. J. 32, 69 (26 Mar. 2007).

C. *Therefor* for *therefore*. This is the slightly more usual error with these homophones. In the first example, the misuse occurs twice in two sentences:

- "The Delaware statute contains no such limiting language and *therefor* [read *therefore*] must, in my opinion, be construed to authorize any reasonable corporate gift of a charitable or educational nature. Significantly, Alexander Dawson, Inc. was incorporated in Delaware in 1958 after 8 Del.C. § 122(9) was cast in its present form, *therefor* [read *therefore*] no constitutional problem arising out of the effect on a stockholder's property rights of the State's reserved power to amend corporate charters is presented." *Theodora Holding Corp. v. Henderson*, 257 A.2d 398, 405 (Del. Ch. 1969).
- "The court found no evidence that the French bank had notice of the sender's mistake and, *therefor* [read *therefore*], ruled it was entitled to the payment." Robert G. Ballen et al., *Commercial Paper, Bank Deposits, and Collections*, 45 Bus. Law. 2341, 2379 (1990).

D. Punctuation Around *therefore*. One must take care in the punctuation of *therefore*. In short sentences it need not, indeed should not, be set off by commas. Punctuating around it in short sentences creates great awkwardness—e.g.:

- "It, *therefore*, becomes necessary to examine what, when, how and why any particular charge, fee, or cost is assessed." *In re Stewart*, 391 B.R. 327, 334 (Bankr. E.D. La. 2008). Whenever a single word like *it* precedes *therefore*, the latter should not be enclosed in commas unless that initial word is to receive stress.
- "We must, *therefore*, dismiss the appeal." *Citizens' Util. Ratepayer Bd. v. State Corp. Comm'n of Kan.*, 202 P.3d 109, 111 (Kan. Ct. App. 2009). The commas destroy the rhythm and emphasize *we*, as opposed to *dismiss*.
- "The appellate court, *therefore*, remanded the case to the trial court." *State v. Wade*, 998 A.2d 1114, 1118 (Conn. 2010). Who else would remand the action? Omit the commas around *therefore*.

E. Run-On Sentences with *therefore*. One should take care not to create run-on sentences in this common way: "These works might be of paramount public *interest, therefore* [read *interest; therefore*] the rights of their compilers are *accordingly* [omit *accordingly*, which is here redundant] in the public interest." Note, *Personal Letters*, 44 Iowa L. Rev. 693, 705 (1958). See RUN-ON SENTENCES.

F. Confused with *therefrom*. See **therefrom**.

therefrom (= from that or it) for *therefor* (= for that or it) is an odd blunder. E.g.: "[The] petitioner has not presented any valid reason for allowing costs in this particular case and, there being no indication that defendant's removal petition was not made in good faith, the court denies petitioner's request *therefrom* [read *therefor* or, better, *for costs*]." *American Oil Co. v. Egan*, 357 F.Supp. 610, 614 (D. Minn. 1973).

Even in contexts in which *therefrom* is technically correct, it is stilted and often vague. An editor will usually improve on it—e.g.: "The indictment also contained a request for forfeiture, in a minimum amount of $22.5 million, of all proceeds and property traceable *therefrom in respect to the criminal activity alleged* [read *from the criminal activity alleged*]." *U.S. v. Green*, 599 F.3d 360, 364 n.1 (4th Cir. 2010).

For an archaic form of *therefrom*, see *****thereout.**

therein. See HERE- AND THERE- WORDS.

there is; there are. A. As Signals of Clutter. These phrases are enemies of a lean writing style. Rarely do they add anything but clutter to a sentence—e.g.:

- "*In a few jurisdictions there are* [read *A few jurisdictions have*] special statutes of limitations prohibiting the initiation of administration proceedings after a designated number of years." Thomas E. Atkinson, *Handbook of the Law of Wills* 569 (2d ed. 1953).
- "*There is nothing in the record to indicate* [read *Nothing in the record indicates*] that the search was conducted in an abusive manner." *Serna v. Goodno*, 567 F.3d 944, 954 (8th Cir. 2009).

The exceptions to this dictum invariably occur when the writer is addressing the existence of something—e.g.: "In tribal times, *there were* the medicine men. In the Middle Ages, *there were* the priests. Today *there are* the lawyers." Fred Rodell, *Woe Unto You, Lawyers!* 1 (1939).

B. Number with. The number of the verb is controlled by whether the subject that follows the inverted verb is singular or plural. Mistakes are common—e.g.:

- "It has been held (although dealing with exclusions from public places where *there are* [read *there is*] discrimination on the basis of race or color) that *preventative* [read *preventive*] relief is available where a public agency operates the public place." *Orloff v. Los Angeles Turf Club*, 180 P.2d 321, 322 (Cal. 1947). See **preventive.**
- "A trial judge has an affirmative duty . . . to ascertain whether *there is* [read *there are*] irrelevant, immaterial, or privileged matters contained within the records or documents." *Peeples v. The Hon. Fourth Sup. J. Dist.*, 701 S.W.2d 635, 637 (Tex. 1985).

See EXPLETIVES & SUBJECT–VERB AGREEMENT (K).

C. Obliquely Phrased Duties in Drafting. In contractual and LEGISLATIVE DRAFTING, the phrase *there is* or, worse yet, *there shall be* displaces a more direct way of phrasing a duty—e.g.: "*There shall be no physical contact between staff and offender during specimen collection* [read *Staff must not touch offender during specimen collection*]." *LeVine v. Roebuck*, 550 F.3d 684, 685 (8th Cir. 2008).

*****thereof.** Avoid this legalistic word by rephrasing the thought—e.g.: "Kentucky . . . adds 'interest income derived *from obligations of sister states and political subdivisions thereof* [read *from obligations of sister states and their political subdivisions*]' back into the taxable net." *Department of Revenue of Ky. v. Davis*, 553 U.S. 328, 333 (2008) (per Souter, J.). See HERE- AND THERE- WORDS.

thereon. See HERE- AND THERE- WORDS & *****thereto (B).**

*****thereout** is an ARCHAISM for *therefrom*—e.g.:

- "The Arbitration Act rendered a written provision in a contract by the parties to such a transaction, to arbitrate

controversies arising *thereout* [read *therefrom*, or, better, *from the contract*], specifically enforceable." *The Anaconda v. American Sugar Ref. Co.*, 322 U.S. 42, 44 (1944) (per Roberts, J.).

- "The character of the lease is to be such as, in effect, to constitute the lessee the municipality's agent for operating the industry without liability on the municipality to others growing *thereout* [read *therefrom*]." *In re American Gen. Aircraft Corp.*, 190 B.R. 275, 280 (Bankr. N.D. Miss. 1995).

See HERE- AND THERE-WORDS.

there shall be. See **there is (C).**

*****thereto. A. Superfluously Used.** E.g.:

- "Five of the children, including appellant, Oscar Durant Kost, were born prior to the execution of the deed of John and Catherine Kost. The others were born *subsequently thereto* [read *later*]." *Kost v. Foster*, 94 N.E.2d 302, 303 (Ill. 1950). On the use of *****prior to* in that sentence, see *****prior to.**
- "Probate of wills, and *litigation related thereto* [read *related litigation*], belonged to the Church courts until 1857." J.H. Baker, *An Introduction to English Legal History* 436 (3d ed. 1990).

See HERE- AND THERE- WORDS & CUTTING OUT THE CHAFF.

B. For *thereon*. E.g.: "It comes as a surprise that the 1972 Code amendments and official comments *thereto* [read *thereon*] refer to the 'requirement' of filing." Peter Winship, *The "True" Consignment Under the Uniform Commercial Code and Related Peccadilloes*, 29 Sw. L.J. 825, 856 (1975). One *comments on*, not *to*, a statute.

theretofore. See **hitherto.**

*****thereunto appertaining.** Like diplomas, contracts often have catchall language referring to "every right and privilege [or appurtenance] *****thereunto appertaining*." Regardless of the context, though, this language is deadwood.

thereupon, adv., = at that instant. This word can usefully pinpoint the time of an action. The word should ordinarily not be used, however, to begin sentences. See HERE- AND THERE- WORDS & **whereupon.**

the said. See **said.**

thesaurus. Pl. *-es* or *-ri*. See PLURALS (A).

these. See DEICTIC TERMS. For the phrase *both these*, see **both (D).**

*****these kind of; *****these type of; *****these sort of.** These are illogical forms that, in a bolder day, would have been termed illiteracies because the demonstrative adjective *these* should modify a plural noun (e.g., *kinds*), not a singular one (e.g., *kind*). Today they merely brand the speaker or writer as being slovenly—e.g.: "The evidence shows that LTV's Board of Directors gave LTV's General Manager the requisite authority to enter into *these type* [read *these types*] of transactions." *LTV Fed. Credit Union v. UMIC Gov't*

Sec., Inc., 523 F.Supp. 819, 825 (N.D. Tex. 1981). Cf. *these kind of.

they're. See **their.**

thief; larcenist; robber; burglar. All these terms denote one who steals, but there are common-law nuances. A *thief*, generally, is one who takes and removes another's property without consent, usually surreptitiously. This is the least technical of the words. Subcategories include embezzling, pilfering, plagiarizing, purloining, and swindling. A *larcenist* is one who by stealing engages in a misdemeanor (often *petty larceny*) or a felony (often *grand larceny*). Definitions vary by jurisdiction: see **larceny.** A *robber* takes the property either from the owner's person or in the owner's presence, often by means of intimidation or violence. A *burglar* breaks and enters a building with the intent to commit a felony, but usually the intent is to commit theft or larceny. See **burglary.**

thieve, vb., may be either transitive (in the sense "to steal [a thing]") or intransitive (in the sense "to act as a thief"). In legal contexts today, the more common use is transitive—e.g.:

- "Defendant . . . told them he would melt down and dispose of any gold they could *thieve.*" *State v. Lewis*, 293 S.E.2d 638, 641 (N.C. Ct. App. 1982).
- "A safe had been *thieved* and asported from the Canton Food Center." *State v. Gardner*, 429 N.W.2d 60, 62 n.* (S.D. 1988) (Henderson, J., concurring).
- "The district court also refused to instruct the jury about bank theft or allow Mr. Bradshaw to argue that he had *thieved* the funds rather than robbed them." *U.S. v. Bradshaw*, 580 F.3d 1129, 1131 (10th Cir. 2009).

thing. Users of this word are often chastised by ill-informed amateurs of usage. Though frequently derided, *thing* can be very useful in contexts in which no more specific or pseudospecific term is needed. Still, the word can easily be overused.

In law—which borrowed the term from philosophy—a *thing* is "the object of a right; i.e., is whatever is treated by the law as the object over which one person exercises a right, and with reference to which another person lies under a duty." Thomas E. Holland, *The Elements of Jurisprudence* 101 (13th ed. 1924). See **res.**

thing in action. See **chose.**

things, in all. See **in all things.**

think. See **feel (A).**

3d; 3rd. In legal writing, and especially in citations, the first of these abbreviations is preferred. See **2d.**

thirdly. See **firstly.**

third party; third-party. The phrase is spelled as two words as a noun <a third party> and is hyphenated as an adjective <a third-party action> and as a

verb <they were third-partied>. The verb phrase is a casualism meaning "to bring into litigation as a third-party defendant." E.g.: "The defendant hospital did not *third party* [read *third-party*] Travenol." *Richard v. Southwest La. Hosp. Ass'n*, 383 So.2d 83, 90 (La. Ct. App. 1980). This usage is informal at best, although it is increasingly common in AmE. For the origin of this phrase, see **party of the first part.** See NOUNS AS VERBS.

third-party plaintiff. Pl. *third-party plaintiffs*. E.g.: "Unlike in *Miller, Pannozzo, Russell,* and *Shampton,* this case involves a situation where an employee–agent in the course of her duties for her employer–principal allegedly interfered with a relationship between two *third parties-plaintiff* [read *third-party plaintiffs*], West and Visteon's suppliers." *West v. Visteon Corp.*, 367 F.Supp.2d 1160, 1163 (N.D. Ohio 2005).

third person should be pluralized *third persons,* never *third people*.

this. See DEICTIC TERMS & ANTECEDENTS, FALSE.

thither = there; to that place. See **whither.**

thitherto. See **hitherto.**

thoroughgoing = thorough, but connotes zeal or ardor. It is not, therefore, merely a NEEDLESS VARIANT. E.g.: "In *Carhart* the Supreme Court, in striking down a Nebraska ban on 'partial birth abortion,' based its holding on longstanding precedent and a *thoroughgoing* analysis of all available medical information." *Richmond Med. Ctr. for Women v. Hicks*, 422 F.3d 160, 162 (4th Cir. 2005).

those. See DEICTIC TERMS.

*those kind of; *those sort of; *those type of. See ***these kind of.**

those which; those that. See **that which.**

though. See **if (C).**

though . . . yet. See **although . . . yet.**

threaten; menace. Both verbs mean "to project to another person potential or even imminent harm, usu. by words, actions, posture, or facial expressions." To *threaten* is to try to influence by creating an expectation of punishment to be carried out against or reprisals to be inflicted on anyone who disobeys or otherwise behaves objectionably. To *menace* is to alarm to some degree with the definite suggestion of hostility, but not with the implication of trying to influence behavior. *Menace* is also the more literary word.

threefold. See **twofold.**

threshold. So spelled; **threshhold* is a common misspelling (*see, e.g., Zweygardt v. Colorado Nat'l Bank,*

---

52 B.R. 229, 231 (Bankr. D. Colo. 1985)). The word is not a compound of the verb *hold*, but rather a modern form of O.E. *thaerscwold* (= doorsill).

thrice is a literary ARCHAISM, and sometimes a useful one, meaning "three times." E.g.:

- "Respondents rely on the statement, *thrice* repeated in the congressional Reports, that '. . . [Federal Tort Claims Act] appeals will continue to be brought to the regional courts of appeals.'" *U.S. v. Hohri*, 482 U.S. 64, 73 (1987) (per Powell, J.).
- "*Thrice* the Court has considered a challenge to a modern method of execution, and *thrice* it has rejected the challenge, each time emphasizing that the Eighth Amendment is aimed at methods of execution purposely designed to inflict pain." *Baze v. Rees*, 553 U.S. 35, 99 (2008) (Thomas, J., concurring).
- "Taylor had contact with a government witness and *thrice* tested positive for marijuana." *U.S. v. Taylor*, 515 F.3d 845, 848 (8th Cir. 2008).

thrift institution is the current JARGON for *savings and loan association*.

thrive > thrived > thrived. So inflected. *Thrived*, not *throve*, is the better past tense—e.g.: "While solicitors *throve* [read *thrived*] in England, however, the avoues declined in France; in 1971, the profession of avoue was abolished except in the appellate courts." John Leubsdorf, *On the History of French Legal Ethics*, 8 U. Chi. L. Sch. Roundtable 341, 345 (2001).

Likewise, *thrived*, not *thriven*, is the better past participle—e.g.: "That the national and international narcotics trade *has thrived* in the face of vigorous criminal-enforcement efforts suggests that no small number of unscrupulous people will make use of the California exemptions." *Gonzales v. Raich*, 545 U.S. 1, 32 (2005) (per Stevens, J.).

throw out, as legal slang, means "to reverse, overturn, or hold unconstitutional." E.g.:

- "A decision *throwing out* a newly written law may hint to the lawmakers how to get the same thing done in a different way [that] the Justices will then approve." Fred Rodell, *Nine Men* 12 (1955).
- "This was the second trial of Speller the court *threw out*; the first was overturned because he had been tried by an all-white jury." Paul R. Clancy, *Just a Country Lawyer: A Biography of Senator Sam Ervin* 150 (1974).
- "The Rhode Island attorney general . . . declined to prosecute for lack of corroborating evidence, and the charges were *thrown out* by a Rhode Island judge." *Hoffman v. Reali*, 973 F.2d 980, 983 (1st Cir. 1992).

*****thru,** an aborted variant spelling of *through*, should be shunned. Oddly, it appears in parts of the Internal Revenue Code.

thus. A. General Senses. *Thus* has four meanings: (1) in this or that manner <one does it thus>; (2) so <thus far>; (3) hence, consequently <thus, the doctrine does not apply>; and (4) as an example <there are several possible courses of action; thus, one might amend the pleadings, nonsuit the defendants, or move

for dismissal>. In senses 3 and 4, *thus*, when it begins a clause, should usually have a comma following.

Here *thus* is given none of these meanings: "The venue facts are *thus*: (1) that defendant is a corporation; (2) that plaintiff has a cause of action against defendant; (3) that some part of the cause of action arose in Ellis County." *Dr. Pepper Co. v. Crow*, 621 S.W.2d 464, 465 (Tex. 1981). The best approach to remedying the problem in that sentence would be to replace *thus* with *as follows*.

B. *****Thusly.** *Thus* itself being an adverb, it needs no *-ly*. Formerly, one might have labeled the use of *thusly* illiterate. Still, though it has appeared in otherwise respectable writing, it remains a grave lapse—e.g.:

- "*Grubbs* is hardly a surprising decision when it is *thusly interpreted* [read *interpreted thus*]." *Paxton v. Weaver*, 553 F.2d 936, 942 (5th Cir. 1977).
- "He illustrated his concern *thusly* [read *thus*]." Barbara H. Craig, *Chadha: The Story of an Epic Constitutional Struggle* 54 (1988).
- "That rationale generates the question presented here, which may be stated *thusly* [read *thus*]." *Lambrecht v. O'Neal*, 3 A.3d 277, 284 (Del. 2010).

Cf. **overly** & *****muchly.** See ADVERBS (D).

ticket-of-leave. See **parole.**

tidings is an ARCHAISM in AmE, although it persists in BrE literary usage. "A sues B on a policy of insurance, and shows that the vessel insured went to sea, and that after a reasonable time no *tidings* of her have been received, but that her loss has been rumoured; the burden of proving that she has not foundered is on B." James Fitzjames Stephen, *A Digest of the Law of Evidence* 104 (4th ed. 1881).

tie makes *tying*. *****Tieing* is incorrect. E.g.: "At one point, Judge Hoffman 'ordered the gagging and hog-*tieing* [read *tying*]' of one of the defendants." Lawrence M. Friedman, *Lexitainment: Legal Process as Theater*, 50 DePaul L. Rev. 539, 543 (2000).

till; until. *Till* is, like *until*, a bona fide preposition and conjunction. Though less formal than *until*, *till* is neither colloquial nor substandard—e.g.:

- "The present English doctrine was not thoroughly received *till* the nineteenth century." Roscoe Pound, *The Development of Constitutional Guarantees of Liberty* 54 (1957).
- "Our system does not interfere *till* harm has been done and has been proved to have been done with the appropriate *mens rea*." H.L.A. Hart, "Punishment and the Elimination of Responsibility," in *Punishment and Responsibility: Essays in the Philosophy of Law* 158, 182 (1968).
- "He didn't file a workers' compensation claim *till* years later." *Gacek v. American Airlines, Inc.*, 614 F.3d 298, 299 (7th Cir. 2010) (per Posner, J.).

The myth to the contrary persists, as some authors and editors mistakenly think that *till* deserves a bracketed *sic*. See, *e.g.*, William Brewer & Francis B. Majorie, *One Year After* Dondi, 17 Pepp. L. Rev. 833, 842 n.68 (1990).

If any form deserves a *sic*, it is **'til*, which is incorrect. E.g.: R. Michael Otto, Comment, *Wait* 'Til [*read* Till] *Your Mothers Get Home*, 1991 Utah L. Rev. 881 (1991).

These two words should be avoided when expressing times and dates because they have been construed as both inclusive and exclusive.

timbre; timber. These are different words in BrE and AmE. *Timbre* /**tim**-bər/ or /**tam**-bər/ is primarily a musical term meaning "tone quality." *Timber* /**tim**-bər/ is the correct form in all other senses.

time-bar means "a bar to a legal claim arising from the lapse of a defined length of time, often contained in a statute of limitations"—e.g.: "The question of whether such estoppel could be raised against the government to defeat a *time-bar* claim was left unanswered." *Tice v. Pennington*, 30 P.3d 1164, 1170 (Okla. Civ. App. 2000). On the use of *question of whether* in this sentence, see **question (as to) whether.**

Hence *time-barred* = barred by the statute of limitations. The phrase is useful, though somewhat inelegant, shorthand—e.g.:

- "Kossick's action would have been *time-barred* under the federal maritime law." Grant Gilmore & Charles L. Black Jr., *The Law of Admiralty* 466 (2d ed. 1975).
- "The Court of International Trade initially dismissed the suit as *time-barred*." Patrick A. Fitch, *International Trade Law Decisions of the Federal Circuit*, 59 Am. U. L. Rev. 1077, 1086 (2010).

time immemorial. Popularly, this term means "a very long time." More technically, it means "a point in time so far back that no living person has knowledge or proof contradicting the right or custom alleged to have existed since then." See **memory of man runneth not to the contrary.**

time is of the essence. When a contractual stipulation relating to the time of performance is "of the essence" of a contract, a party's failure to meet that stipulation automatically justifies the other party's rescinding the contract—no matter how trivial the failure. If, on the other hand, time is not of the essence, then the failure to comply with a stipulation about time will justify rescission only if there is a substantial failure in performance. Gradually, the phrase *time is of the essence* has become so widespread that it is now classifiable as a POPULARIZED LEGAL TECHNICALITY.

time limit. See **temporal limit.**

time loan. See **term loan.**

timely, adj. & adv. Because *timely* may be an adverb as well as an adjective in AmE, phrases such as *in a timely fashion* and *in a timely manner* are wordy and should be shortened. E.g.:

- "As more patent cases are filed and *subsequently disposed of in a timely fashion* [read *timely disposed of*], judges in districts with local patent rules have more opportunities to enhance their judicial expertise in patent law." Xuan-Thao Nguyen, *Dynamic Federalism and Patent Law Reform*, 85 Ind. L.J. 449, 480 (2010).
- "It would be a mistake to assume that this temporal gap prevents the unification of the two systems, *each of which arose in a timely fashion* [read *each of which timely arose*, or better, omit *in a timely fashion*] when needed." Richard A. Epstein, *The Disintegration of Intellectual Property? A Classical Liberal Response to a Premature Obituary*, 62 Stan. L. Rev. 455, 456 (2010).

This adverbial use of *timely* is archaic in BrE. The rare adverbial form *timelily* is to be avoided. See **seasonable (B).**

In British law reports, *timeous* (= coming in due time) and *timeously* (= in a timely manner) are common. Though some Scots lawyers earnestly defend *timeous*, a Scottish glossary calls it "an inelegant and unnecessary word." Andrew D. Gibb, *Students' Glossary of Scottish Legal Terms* 94 (A.G.M. Duncan ed., 2d ed. 1982). The word *timeous* is pronounced /**tı**-məs/, not /**tim**-ee-əs/. The word never occurs in AmE.

time when. See **reason (B).**

time whereof the memory of man runneth not to the contrary. See **time immemorial** & **memory of man runneth not to the contrary.**

tippee = one who receives a tip (i.e., a critical bit of information); one who is illicitly tipped off. E.g.:

- "Absent other culpable actions by a *tippee* that can fairly be said to outweigh these violations by insiders and broker-dealers, we do not believe that the *tippee* properly can be characterized as being of substantially equal culpability as his tippers." *Bateman Eichler, Hill Richards, Inc. v. Berner*, 472 U.S. 299, 314 (1985) (per Brennan, J.).
- "To convict Bhagat of tipping Gill, the government was required to prove that the tipper, Bhagat, provided the *tippee*, Gill, with material, inside information, prior to the *tippee's* purchase of stock." *U.S. v. Bhagat*, 436 F.3d 1140, 1149 (9th Cir. 2006). On the use of *prior to in that sentence, see **prior to.**

The *OED* records the word from 1897 in a rather different sense: "the recipient of a 'tip' or gratuity." See -EE (A).

tipper; tipster. Both refer to a person who gives tips (i.e., critical pieces of information). *Tipster* often refers to one who gives tips to police in criminal investigations, or sells tips relating to speculative or gambling subjects. Here the latter sense applies: "An accurate description of a subject's readily observable location and appearance . . . will help the police correctly identify the person whom the *tipster* means to accuse." *Florida v. J.L.*, 529 U.S. 266, 272 (2000) (per Ginsburg, J.).

Tipper shares the meaning with *tipster* of an informer who tips off police on illegal activities; more commonly in legal AmE, it signifies "one who gives or sells tips to securities and other investors." See **tippee.**

An asterisk (*) precedes words and phrases that are invariably inferior forms.

tipstaff (= a court crier) has two plural forms: *tipstaves* and *tipstaffs*. The first predominates in American law reports. See **crier.**

tipster. See **tipper.**

title = (1) the legal link between a person and some object of property, e.g., ownership, possession, custody <what sort of title does she have?>; (2) legal ownership of property <no known person has title to the property>; (3) the grounds by which a landowner has rights of possession; or (4) the legal evidence of a person's ownership rights, or the means by which the owner comes to have those rights. Lon Fuller once remarked that *title* is an indispensable device of legal thought and expression, but that it has abuses when one speaks not of apportioning ownership rights between two or more persons: "when one's task necessitates breaking through the cover and apportioning the contents among different individuals, the cover [i.e., the word *title*] should be thrown away." Lon L. Fuller, *Legal Fictions* 121–22 (1967).

title deed = a deed providing evidence of a person's legal ownership. In AmE, the term conveys nothing not included in the simple word *deed*. (See **deed (A).**) But in BrE, in which *deed* continues to refer to any sealed instrument, *title deed* is a useful specification—e.g.:

- "In *Adsit*, the full name of each of the four co-owners of the property was declared in their *title deed*, which had been of record for some ten years before the property was sold for taxes." *Lewis v. Succession of Johnson*, 925 So.2d 1172, 1180 (La. 2006).
- "Full ownership of land requires a registered *title deed*, the *escritura*, and anything less implies imperfect ownership." Jean-Louis Van Gelder, *Tales of Deviance and Control*, 44 Law & Soc'y Rev. 239, 256 (2010).
- "The misplaced boundary is not one which merely strayed slightly off course from the ideal boundary called for in the *title deeds* of the two adjacent landowners." *Loutre Land & Timber Co. v. Roberts*, 47 So.3d 478, 490 (La. Ct. App. 2010).

The plural form *title deeds* is sometimes shortened to *titles*.

title member is synonymous in AmE with *name partner*: "While the three *title members* of the firm were merely expert publicity men who devoted themselves to pulling in the business, the rest of the partners were capable, hard-working, high-minded attorneys who cringed at the antics of their masters, but who, for financial reasons, could not afford to sever their connection." Ephraim Tutt, *Yankee Lawyer* 147 (1943).

Titular Tomfoolery, primarily an outgrowth of weekly newspapers and news magazines in the U.S., consists in the creation of false titles for people. Instead of *Abraham Lincoln, the country lawyer*—or, for that matter, *the country lawyer Abraham Lincoln* (the prefixed *the* making a significant difference)— it is today commonplace to read of *country lawyer Abraham Lincoln*, or, worse yet, *Country Lawyer Abraham Lincoln*. *Officer*, granted, is a title to be prefixed to a person's name; *police officer* is not.

This informal verbal contagion originated in a misplaced desire for economy in both words and punctuation, since APPOSITIVES ordinarily require commas (see most of the revisions below).

- "*Lawyer Hamm* carried the case to the state's highest court, the Supreme Court of California." Murray T. Bloom, *The Trouble with Lawyers* 61 (1970). Hamm has already been identified as a lawyer. This example—as one can tell from the fuller context—seems intended as a slight.
- "A few months ago, *second-year law student Jerry Coleman* [read *a second-year law student, Jerry Coleman,*] was unsure of whether to include on his résumé his membership in Columbia University's Gay and Lesbian Law Students' Association." *Job Opportunities Opening Up for Gays*, Nat'l Jurist, Apr./May 1992, at 6.
- "The district attorney also said he would request a new trial for one of the four policemen acquitted in the 1991 beating of *black motorist Rodney King* [read *Rodney King, a black motorist*]." World-Wide, Wall St. J., 14 May 1992, at A1.
- "*Juror Franklin* stated that even though he had formed some opinion regarding the guilt or innocence of petitioner, he could set whatever impression or opinion he had formed aside and render a verdict based solely on the evidence that he would hear at trial." *Hedrick v. Warden of the Sussex I State Prison*, 570 S.E.2d 840, 859 (Va. 2002). In this sentence, if we already know that Franklin is on the jury, omit *juror*; if not, read *Franklin, one of the jurors, stated . . . .* Moreover, the term *juror* may be inappropriate here because, if the statement was made at voir dire, the proper term would be *veniremember*.
- "The trial court violated the *Witherspoon* rule when it granted the State's challenge to *venireman Osborn* [read *the venireman named Osborn*] for cause." *Allridge v. Cockrell*, 92 Fed. Appx. 60, 63 (5th Cir. 2003).
- "Bonnie Smith, *widow* [read *the widow*] of Phillip M. Smith, appeals the finding of the Workers Compensation Board that Phillip's fatal injuries did not arise out of and in the course of his employment." *Smith v. Winfield Livestock Auction, Inc.*, 106 P.3d 94, 96 (Kan. Ct. App. 2005).
- "Mr. Carpenter, the trial prosecutor, tacitly admitted that he was excluding African Americans from the jury when he responded to *Attorney Rogers'* [read *Rogers's, the defense attorney's,*] objection by stating 'how awful.'" *Lark v. Beard*, 495 F.Supp.2d 488, 493 (E.D. Pa. 2007).
- "Small argues [that] trial counsel were ineffective for not objecting to *juror Graham* [read *the juror named Graham*]." *Commonwealth v. Small*, 980 A.2d 549, 573 (Pa. 2009).

Tmesis /tə-**mee**-sis/, the practice of separating parts of a compound word by inserting another word between those parts, occurs much more frequently in legal than in lay writing. A classic colloquial example—some would say dialectal example—is the phrase a *whole 'nother*, which, surprisingly, has actually appeared in legal contexts: "But that, as they say, is *a whole 'nother* story." *In re Toys "R" Us S'holder Litig.*, 877 A.2d 975, 1004 (Del. Ch. 2005). See SET PHRASES.

The traditional form of tmesis in legal prose, however, occurs with formal legal words ending in *-soever*. E.g.:

- "When a man has committed fornication with a woman, her mother *how high soever*, and her daughters, are prohibited to him." Shama Churun Sircar, *The Muhammadan Law* 309 (1973).

- "Toward this end, beginning on September 29, 1732, all 'Houses, Lands, Negroes, and other Hereditaments and real Estates' were to be liable for 'all just Debts, Duties, and Demands, *of what nature or kind soever.*'" Claire Priest, *Creating an American Property Law*, 120 Harv. L. Rev. 385, 423–24 (2006).

The modern tendency, which we should heartily encourage, is to avoid such stuffiness by writing, e.g., *of whatever nature* and *however high*.

to for *until* or *up to* is a casualism—e.g.: "*To* [read *Up to*] September 1964, no Negro pupil had applied for admission to the New Kent school under this statute." *Green v. County Sch. Bd.*, 391 U.S. 430, 433 (1968) (per Brennan, J.). See **toward (A)** & **upon (B)**.

to all intents and purposes. See **for all intents and purposes.**

together appears in a number of REDUNDANCIES, such as *merge together, *connect together, **consolidate together*, *couple together, and *join together. Avoid these phrases.

together with; coupled with; as well as; added to. These expressions do not affect the number of the terms that precede or follow them <Johnson, together with Tucker and Thurman, was [not *were*] at the hearing>. See **coupled with** & SUBJECT–VERB AGREEMENT (H).

to go on circuit. See **circuit, to ride.**

token. See **pledge.**

tolerance; toleration. The first is the quality, the second the act or practice.

toll. In the context of time limits—especially statutes of limitation—*toll* means "to abate" or "to stop the running of (the statutory period)." E.g.:

- "Robinson argues that the 120-day service period should have been *tolled* until the district court screened his *in forma pauperis* complaint and authorized service of process." *Robinson v. Clipse*, 602 F.3d 605, 608 (4th Cir. 2010).
- "A *tolling* rule can affect a statute of limitations in one of three ways—it can suspend the running of the limitations period; it can extend the limitations period; or it can renew or revive the limitations period." Carli McNeill, *Seeing the Forest*, 85 Notre Dame L. Rev. 1231, 1250 (2010).
- "Mentally retarded death-row offenders then had a year to file their federal petitions, with the limitations period *tolled* during the pendency of state post-conviction proceedings." Lee Kovarsky, *Death Ineligibility and Habeas Corpus*, 95 Cornell L. Rev. 329, 369 (2010).

Toll in this special sense has been misunderstood as meaning "to set into motion"—that is, just the opposite of its true sense. *See Langford v. Shamburger*, 417 S.W.2d 438, 445 syls. 7 & 8 (Tex. Civ. App.—Fort Worth 1967). That blunder is an infrequent one.

Tombs lawyer. See LAWYERS, DEROGATORY NAMES FOR (A).

tome refers not to any book, but to one that is imposingly or forbiddingly large.

too. A. Beginning Sentences with. When it means "also," *too* should not begin a sentence, although there is a tendency in facile journalism today to use the word in this position. E.g.: "*Too* [read *Also*], existing laws are read into contracts in order to fix obligations between the parties." As in the preceding edit, *also* may unobjectionably appear at the beginning of a sentence. Also, words such as *moreover, further,* and *furthermore* serve ably in this position.

B. For *very.* This informal use of *too* occurs almost always in negative constructions, e.g., *not too common.* In such contexts, the word *very* is preferable to *too.*

C. *Too* [+ adj.] *a* [+ n.]. This idiom being perfectly acceptable, there is no reason to insist on the artificiality of *a too —— ——*; that is, *too good a job* is better than *a too good job.* E.g.: "Rights under a contract, in so far as they are not of *too personal a nature*, may form the subject of an assignment." William Geldart, *Introduction to English Law* 122 (D.C.M. Yardley ed., 9th ed. 1984).

toothless (= ineffectual; lacking the means of enforcement) is a snarl-word used, in legal discourse, to describe a statute or court decision that the writer or speaker considers too weak. E.g.: "When South Africa adopted its post-apartheid competition law, it needed to counter the *toothless* competition regime preceding it, which had reinforced the white oligarchy." Eleanor M. Fox, *Antitrust and Institutions: Design and Change*, 41 Loy. U. Chi. L.J. 473, 475 (2010).

top court is a legal casualism referring to the court of last resort within a given jurisdiction. E.g.: "The *top court*, in backing their convictions, rejected the defendants' reasoning." Sam H. Verhovek, *New York Court Says Defendants Can't Reject Jurors Based on Race*, N.Y. Times, 30 Mar. 1990, at A1.

to put it another way; put another way. Either is acceptable, although the first is somewhat better from a literary point of view. Here the two idioms are confused: "The essential issue . . . was whether a simple travel book for first and second graders was the proper place to discuss them, *or, put it another way* [read *or, to put it another way*], whether the omission of these concerns affected the educational suitability of the books." *ACLU of Fla. v. Miami-Dade County Sch. Bd.*, 439 F.Supp.2d 1242, 1286 (S.D. Fla. 2006). Cf. **stated otherwise.**

to ride circuit. See **circuit, to ride.**

tornadic (= of or relating to a tornado or tornadoes) is almost always a pomposity—e.g.:

- "The Bossier Center, Inc. (Center) leased premises in its shopping center to Palais Royal (Palais), whose clothing store was heavily damaged by *the tornadic forces* [read *the tornado*]." *Bossier Ctr., Inc. v. Palais Royal, Inc.*, 385 So.2d 886, 887 (La. Ct. App. 1980).
- "Specifically, plaintiff's allegations challeng[ed] the NWS' failure 'to detect, or to recognize, certain radar signatures' allegedly indicating severe *tornadic activity* [read *tornadoes*]." *Bergquist v. U.S.*, 849 F.Supp. 1221, 1230 (N.D. Ill. 1994).

torpid. See **turbid.**

Torrens system. In 1840, Robert Torrens moved from England to South Australia, where he assumed the post of Collector of Customs. While in that post, he developed a new system of conveyancing based on title certificates and enacted in the Real Property Act 1862.

In the U.S., the *Torrens system* is one of four types of evidence of title to real estate (the other three being *abstract and opinion*, *certificate of title*, and *title insurance*). A few counties with large metropolitan areas—e.g., Boston, Chicago, Minneapolis, and New York City—have adopted the *Torrens system*. Under this system, one who wants to establish title first acquires an abstract of title and then applies to a court for issuance of a certificate. This proceeding amounts to a lawsuit against all claimants to the land. Once the certificate is issued, it is conclusive evidence of ownership.

tort = a civil wrong; the breach of a duty that the law imposes on everyone. But those definitions are barely adequate, because "it is perhaps impossible to give an exact definition of 'a tort,' or 'the law of tort' or 'tortious liability,' and, as a corollary, it is certainly impossible to give a definition [that] will satisfy every theorist who has taken any interest in the topic." T.E. Lewis, *Winfield on Tort* 1 (6th ed. 1954). Why? Because there is no common set of traits that every *tort* possesses.

The word derives from LAW FRENCH, meaning literally "wrong; injustice," and ultimately from L. *tortus* (= twisted; crooked). For the adjectival form, see **tortious.**

tortfeasor was once spelled as two words (as late as 1927 in the U.S. Supreme Court), then was hyphenated, and now has been fused into a single word. See **feasor.**

tortious. A. Two Senses. *Tortious* = (1) of or relating to tort <tortious causes of action>; or (2) constituting a tort <tortious acts that are also criminally punishable>. Sense 2 is now more common than sense 1, which is exemplified in this sentence: "The duty of good faith arises out of the contractual relationship between a lender and a borrower, not any separate *tortious* duty owed to the borrower." *Jo-Ann's Launder Ctr., Inc. v. Chase Manhattan Bank, N.A.*, 854 F.Supp. 387, 391 n.4 (D.V.I. 1994). See **delictual.**

B. And *tortuous; torturous.* Justice Benjamin Cardozo's famous opinion in *Palsgraf* demonstrated that a *tortious* act could result from a *tortuous* chain of events with *torturous* consequences. *Tortuous* = full of twists and turns <a tortuous path through the court system>. *Torturous* = of, characterized by, pertaining to torture <torturous abuse>. The word aptly appears in the phrase "the conscienceless or pitiless crime [that] is unnecessarily *torturous* to the victim." *State v. Dixon*, 283 So.2d 1, 9 (Fla. 1973).

Tortuous is sometimes misused for *tortious*—e.g.:

- "Such duty falls into a very different category [from] the general duty to avoid *tortuous* [read *tortious*] conduct." *Walls v. Rees*, 569 A.2d 1161, 1167 (Del. 1990).
- "Petitioners urge that [defendants] . . . engaged in the intentional *tortuous* [read *tortious*] conduct specified below." *Korson v. Independence Mall I, Ltd.*, 595 So.2d 1174, 1177 (La. Ct. App. 1992).

Similarly, *tortuous* is occasionally misused for *torturous*: "Eight-year-old Jenny, a second grader, left for school as usual at 7 a.m. on Dec. 10, 1991. It was still dark as she walked along the sidewalk. So she never saw the tall, thin stranger sneak up from behind and grab her by the back of the neck. She was forced into an alley and then put on the floorboard of the stranger's car and covered with a blanket. This young child was beginning a long, *tortuous* [read *torturous*] ordeal [involving repeated rapes]." Bill Walsh, *A Coordinated Approach to Crimes Against Children*, 55 Tex. B.J. 488, 488 (1992).

tortious interference with contractual relations; procuring (or inducing) breach of contract; interference with a subsisting contract. The first is the American phrase; the latter two are primarily British. Each one means "the tort of intentionally persuading or inducing someone to breach a contract made with a third party."

tortuous; torturous. See **tortious (B).**

tortured construction; tortured interpretation. See *tortured interpretation* under INTERPRETATION, MODES OF (B).

totaled. See DOUBLING OF FINAL CONSONANTS.

totality of the circumstances is a common legal catchphrase, especially in AmE. E.g.: "Under our general Fourth Amendment approach we examine the *totality of the circumstances* to determine whether a search is reasonable within the meaning of the Fourth Amendment." *Samson v. California*, 547 U.S. 843, 848 (2006) (per Thomas, J.).

to the contrary. See **contrary (B).**

to the effect that is often verbose for *that*.

Totten trust; tentative trust. These phrases, which are equivalent, denote "a revocable trust created by one's deposit of money in one's own name as a trustee for another." E.g.: "A so-called '*Totten*' or *tentative trust* is a revocable savings-account trust, in which the named beneficiaries possess a mere expectancy in the trust proceeds prior to the death of the depositor." *Geyer* *v. Kaspar*, 672 N.Y.S.2d 428, 429 (App. Div. 1998). The name *Totten trust*, which is perhaps slightly more common, derives from the case *In re Totten*, 71 N.E. 748 (N.Y. 1904). See CASE REFERENCES (C).

touch and concern. See DOUBLETS, TRIPLETS, AND SYNONYM-STRINGS.

touching (= concerning; about; bearing on) is today virtually peculiar to the legal idiom. E.g.:

- "The Court appears to adopt as its new test a per se rule under which any regulation *touching* on abortion must be invalidated if it poses 'an unacceptable danger of deterring the exercise of that right.'" *Thornburgh v. American Coll. of Obstetricians & Gynecologists*, 476 U.S. 747, 829 (1986) (O'Connor, J., dissenting).
- "Though the full history of dictionaries is fascinating, this Note does not discuss it, instead *touching* on historical concepts only insomuch as they affect the use of dictionaries in legal interpretation today." Phillip A. Rubin, *War of the Words*, 60 Duke L.J. 167, 177 n.59 (2010).

The *OED* labels this use of the word "somewhat archaic"; today it is rightly considered an ARCHAISM.

toward; *towards. The preferred forms are *toward* in AmE, *towards* in BrE.

to wit. The ordinary progression in such common phrases is from two words, to a hyphenated form, to a single word. Though Mellinkoff idiosyncratically spelled this as a single word throughout *The Language of the Law* (1963), and the hyphenated form was once common, today it seems that *to wit* is destined to remain two words, if indeed its destiny is not oblivion. *To wit* is a legal ARCHAISM in the place of which *namely* is almost always an improvement. Cf. **viz.**

toxic. When the context calls for a noun, the adjective *toxic* (= poisonous) should not displace the noun *toxin* (= poison). E.g.: "The assessment determined that docks could lead to . . . increased turbidity, light reduction, ambient light-pattern alteration, noise disturbance, altered wave-energy patterns, increased exotic species, *toxics* [read *toxins*], nutrients, bacterial introductions, and alteration of water quality." *Samson v. City of Bainbridge Island*, 202 P.3d 334, 347 (Wash. Ct. App. 2009).

toxicology; toxology. *Toxicology* = the science of poisons; *toxology* = the branch of knowledge dealing with archery.

track is sometimes misused for *tract* (= a parcel of land) in the phrase *tract of land*—e.g.: "The defendant and two others cut down over two miles of continuous barbed wire fence on three adjacent *tracks* [read *tracts*] of land in one night." *State v. Lubrano*, 550 So.2d 1283, 1286 (La. Ct. App. 1989).

Of course, the two words should be pronounced differently: *tract* /trakt/ and *track* /trak/.

trade. See **business.**

trademark. A. And tradename. The unhyphenated, one-word spellings are preferred. Formerly, in AmE, these terms were distinguished: A *trademark* was an arbitrary, fanciful, or suggestive name of, or symbol for, a product or service that was protectible under trademark laws. A *tradename*, by contrast, was a descriptive, personal, or geographical name or symbol protectible under the law of unfair competition. With the enactment of the Lanham Act in 1946, this distinction became defunct.

Today in AmE, the term *trademark* embraces all the types of names or symbols just mentioned. Its two primary senses are: (1) "a word, phrase, logo, or other graphic symbol used by a manufacturer or seller to distinguish its products from those of others"; or (2) "the body of law dealing with how businesses distinguish their products and services from those of others." In sense 2, the word encompasses such narrower fields as servicemarks, tradenames, unfair competition, and palming off. See (B).

Tradename continues only in the sense "a symbol used to distinguish a company, partnership, or business (as opposed to a product or service)." *See* 1 J. Thomas McCarthy, *Trademarks and Unfair Competition* §§ 4.02–4.05 (3d ed. 1984); 3 Rudolf Callmann, *The Law of Unfair Competition, Trademarks, and Monopolies* § 17.05 (L. Altman ed., 4th ed. 1983).

In sum, *tradenames* identify businesses; *trademarks* identify goods produced by or services provided by businesses.

B. And *servicemark*. *Servicemark* (= a name, phrase, or other device intended to identify the services of a certain supplier) is a species of *trademark*: "*Trademarks* may be used to identify and distinguish 'goods' or 'services.' The term '*servicemark*' is specifically used with respect to services, such as accounting, banking, travel, and tourism services. While the term '*trademark*' may be used in a narrow sense in connection only with goods, it may also be used in a broader sense to encompass services." Frederick M. Abbott, Thomas Cottier & Francis Gurry, *International Intellectual Property in an Integrated World Economy* 259 (2007).

The term is increasingly made one word, though the transition is spotty. Here, one court has it both ways in the same opinion:

- "In 2001, B.L.W. began using 'WINE KING' (the 'First Mark') as a *service mark*." *MNI Mgmt., Inc. v. Wine King, LLC*, 542 F.Supp.2d 389, 399–400 (D.N.J. 2008).
- "Plaintiff applied for a federal *servicemark* on November 19, 2007." *Id.* at 400.

The federal circuits, though, are steadfast in rendering *servicemark* as two words, e.g.:

- "The district court also issued a permanent injunction prohibiting Unisys from using the trademarks or *service marks* 3D VISIBLE ENTERPRISE, 3D-VE, or VISIBLE in the United States in the enterprise modeling or enterprise architecture fields." *Visible Sys. Corp. v. Unisys Corp.*, 551 F.3d 65, 68 (1st Cir. 2008).

- "The question presented herein is whether the *use in commerce* [read *use-in-commerce*] requirement is met when an applicant uses a *service mark* in the preparatory stages of a service's development, but never offers the service to the public. We hold that it is not." *Aycock Eng'g, Inc. v. Airflite, Inc.*, 560 F.3d 1350, 1353 (Fed. Cir. 2009). For more on why hyphenations are needed in the bracketed material, see PHRASAL ADJECTIVES.

- "After a three-week trial, the jury found in favor of . . . St. Luke's on its six other claims, which included *service mark* infringement, cyberpiracy, and unfair competition." *St. Luke's Cataract & Laser Inst. v. Sanderson*, 573 F.3d 1186, 1190 (11th Cir. 2009).

traduce. See **defame.**

traffic, vb., forms the participles *trafficking* and *trafficked*, but the adjective *trafficable* and the noun *trafficator*. For the noun *traffic*, see **business.**

trammel is inflected *trammeled, trammeling* in AmE; and *trammelled, trammelling* in BrE. See DOUBLING OF FINAL CONSONANTS.

trampler. See LAWYERS, DEROGATORY NAMES FOR (A).

transcendent; transcendental. *Transcendent* = surpassing or excelling others of its kind; preeminent. It is loosely used by some writers in the sense "excellent." *Transcendental* = supernatural; mystical; metaphysical; superhuman. The adverbial forms are *transcendently* and *transcendentally*.

transcript; transcription. The first is the written copy, the second the process of producing it. See **record (B).**

transfer, vb., is traditionally accented on the second syllable, hence the past-tense spelling *transferred*, not **transfered*. *Transferor* but *transferral; transferred, transferring*, but *transferable, transferability*. See DOUBLING OF FINAL CONSONANTS.

transfer, n; **transference; *transferral.** Of these three, *transfer* is the all-purpose noun. E.g.: "If a staff person initiates a prisoner's *transfer* for a retaliatory or other improper reason, that individual cannot escape responsibility simply by following IDOC procedure." *Piggie v. Riggle*, 548 F.Supp.2d 652, 657 (N.D. Ind. 2008). *Transfer* commonly appears in the legal phrase *transfer of venue*. **Transferral* (the spelling included in the *OED*) is a NEEDLESS VARIANT of *transfer*. The *W3* entry and the *W11* notation, strangely, appear under **transferal*.

Transference justifies its separate existence primarily in psychological contexts, in the sense "the redirection of feelings or desires." E.g.: "The variance may be prejudicial in a number of ways, but the problem that is of concern here is the possibility of *transference* or 'spillover' of guilt." *U.S. v. Lazarenko*, 564 F.3d 1026, 1044 (9th Cir. 2009).

transferable; *transferrible. The first spelling is preferred.

transference. See **transfer,** n.

transferor. So spelled in legal contexts—e.g.: "A transfer is effected by sending to the transferee a 'proper instrument of transfer' executed by the *transferor*, together with the share certificate relating to the shares comprised in the transfer." J. Charlesworth, *The Principles of Company Law* 89 (4th ed. 1945).

W3 lists *transferor* as a variant spelling of *transferrer*, but notes under the legal definition "usu. *transferor*." For *transferee*, see -EE (A).

*transferral. See **transfer,** n.

transferred intention. See **intention (F).**

*transferrible. See **transferable.**

transfusible; *transfusable. The first spelling is preferred.

transgression. See **breach (A).**

transience; *transiency. The second is a NEEDLESS VARIANT.

transient; transitory; transitive. *Transient* = impermanent; quickly passing. The word is used in the phrase *transient jurisdiction*. *Transitory*, which has virtually the same meaning, is used in the legal phrase *transitory action* (= an action in which the venue might be proper in any county). *Transitive* is a grammatical term denoting a verb that takes a direct object.

transit in rem indicatam. See MAXIMS.

transitory. See **transient.**

transmissible; *transmittable. The first is preferred; the second is a NEEDLESS VARIANT. E.g.: "She also contends that the defendants were aware of the risk that a *transmissible* agent (later identified as HIV) was contaminating factor products." *Erickson v. Baxter Healthcare, Inc.*, 131 F.Supp.2d 995, 998 (N.D. Ill. 2001).

transmission. See **transmittal.**

transmit is a minor pomposity—but a pomposity nevertheless—for *send*. E.g.: "The State Police must then *transmit* [read *send*] this information to the federal government." *Legislation and Regulations*, 33 Mental & Physical Disability L. Rep. 1060, 1061 (2009).

*transmittable. See **transmissible.**

transmittal; *transmittance; transmission. *Transmittal* is more physical than *transmission*, just as *admittance* is more physical than *admission*. (See **admission.**) *Transmittal*, though labeled rare in the *OED*, is common in AmE legal writing, especially in the phrase *transmittal letter* (= a cover letter accompanying documents or other things being conveyed to another). E.g.:

- "In his letter of *transmittal*, the President opined that the agreement was, with certain exceptions, a positive step toward the goal of 'giving the greatest possible protection to the victims of [non-international] conflicts, consistent with legitimate military requirements.'" Michael N. Schmitt, *Military Necessity and Humanity in International Humanitarian Law*, 50 Va. J. Int'l L. 795, 811 (2010) (quoting Ronald Reagan, Letter of Transmittal to the U.S. Senate (29 Jan. 1987)).

- "The event that invokes coverage under a 'claims-made' policy is the *transmittal* of notice of the claim to the insurance carrier." *St. Paul Fire & Marine Ins. v. Estate of Hunt*, 811 P.2d 432, 434 (Colo. Ct. App. 1991).
- "A January 18, 2006 letter of *transmittal* to South Park was filed into evidence." *Lorick v. Direct Gen. Ins. Co.*, 2 So.3d 1209, 1213 (La. Ct. App. 2009).

*Transmittance is a NEEDLESS VARIANT.

transmutation means "to change," not "to transfer," as used by some legal writers (as in the erroneous phrase used in some legal contexts for *transfer*, but conveys *transmutation of possession*).

transnational. So spelled.

transpire. The traditionally correct meaning of this word is "to pass through a surface; come to light; to become known by degrees"—e.g.: "An indictment against a man as accessory before should be good even if it *transpires* [i.e., becomes known] that he is a principal in reality." Glanville Williams, *Criminal Law* 406 (2d ed. 1961). Because this usage grows rarer by the year, it is probably beyond redemption. Lawyers and judges should therefore be aware of the AMBIGUITY created by the coexistence of the popular meaning: "to happen; to occur."

When used in that sense, *transpire* is a mere pomposity displacing an everyday word (*happen*). The word is badly needed in its true sense, as it is used here: "Suppose that a person were to sell a second-hand car and were to state that the brakes were in good working order. If in fact it *transpired* that the brakes did not work at all the seller would find it difficult to convince a judge that he had merely been negligent rather than dishonest." P.S. Atiyah, *An Introduction to the Law of Contract* 228 (3d ed. 1981).

The loose meaning, of course, is rampant—e.g.:

- "A regulatory taking *transpires* [read *occurs*] when some significant restriction is placed upon an owner's use of his property for which 'justice and fairness' require that compensation be given." *Goldblatt v. Hempstead*, 369 U.S. 590, 594 (1962) (per Clark, J.).
- "That plan was foiled, however, when Sed insisted that the deal *transpire* [read *occur* or *happen*] in the same manner as the first deal." *U.S. v. Sed*, 601 F.3d 224, 226 (3d Cir. 2010).

Another loose usage occurs (not *transpires*) when *transpire* is used for *pass* or *elapse*—e.g.:

- "Finally, plaintiff emphasizes that sixteen days *transpired* [read *passed*] between plaintiff's discrimination complaint and plaintiff's forced administrative leave." *Drwal v. Borough of W. View, Pa.*, 617 F.Supp.2d 397, 422 (W.D. Pa. 2009).

- "Assuming the plaintiff complained to the defendant on the last day of November 2008, one month and five days *transpired* [read *passed*] between her complaint and her termination." *Ash v. Sambodromo, LLC*, 676 F.Supp.2d 1360, 1374 (S.D. Fla. 2009).

The *OED* brands this usage "obsolete, rare, and erroneous"; only the last of these adjectives fits.

transportation; *transportal; *transportment. The second and third forms are NEEDLESS VARIANTS.

transship. So spelled—without a hyphen.

trauma, in pathology, means "a wound, or external bodily injury in general," although in popular contexts it has been largely confined to figurative (emotional) senses.

traverse, vb. & n. This word is obsolescent in AmE, but it appears in many not-so-old cases. As a verb, *traverse* means "to deny a factual allegation made in the opposite party's pleading." E.g.:

- "In reply to a claim, a defendant at common law may *traverse* the allegations of the plaintiff, i.e. deny the truth of his assertions." G.W. Paton, *A Textbook of Jurisprudence* 595 (4th ed. 1972).
- "Mr. Brown has never *traversed* the allegations of paternity in the petition for support and other relief." *Department of Revenue v. Brown*, 980 So.2d 590, 591 n.2 (Fla. Dist. Ct. App. 2008).

As a noun, *traverse* means "a denial of a factual allegation made in the opposite party's pleading." E.g.:

- "At common law the respondent . . . was required to plead specially by distinct *traverse* of the allegations of the writ." *Sansom v. Mercer*, 5 S.W. 62, 65 (Tex. 1887).
- "The state . . . filed a *traverse*/demurrer in which it admitted some paragraphs of the motion, but denied others as immaterial, untrue, or disputed." *State v. Taylor*, 16 So.3d 997, 1001 (Fla. Dist. Ct. App. 2009).

A denial of all the facts was, at common law, called a *general traverse*; a denial of one material fact was called a *special traverse*.

tread. See **trodden.**

treason. This word (fr. L. *tradere* "to give up or betray") originally meant treachery to one's lord rather than to the king. At common law, it was *petit treason* for a vassal to kill his lord, a wife her husband, a servant his master, or a clergyman his prelate; it was *high treason* to kill the king.

In the U.S. today, it is *treason* to levy war against the nation or to materially support its enemies. See **sedition.**

treasonable; treasonous. The distinction between these words is small; they are essentially synonyms. *Treasonable* (= involving or characteristic of treason; treacherous) is the preferred adjective for conduct, words, etc.—e.g.: "In 1762, the English government, seeking to censure authors, printers and publishers of seditious and *treasonable* papers, namely the North Briton, issued general arrest warrants authorizing home searches." *O'Rourke v. Norman*, 875 F.2d 1465, 1472 (10th Cir. 1989). *Treasonous* (= characterized by treachery or treason) is also used in reference to things but much more often in reference to people— e.g.: "*Treasonous* citizens, traitors, and local guides who voluntarily served the enemy or who intentionally misled their own army all were to be put to death." Simon Chesterman, *The Spy Who Came in from the Cold War*, 27 Mich. J. Int'l L. 1071, 1079 (2006).

treasure trove (lit., "treasure found"), a remnant of LAW FRENCH, means treasure (usu. gold or silver) "intentionally hidden for safety in the earth or in some secret place, the owner [upon its discovery] being unknown." Ray Andrews Brown, *The Law of Personal Property* 27 (2d ed. 1955).

treaty; accord; concord; protocol; declaration; act; compact, n.; **pact; paction; entente; convention; cartel; concordat; executive agreement.** Contracts between sovereign states are called by various names, none of which has a fixed meaning. *Treaty* is the generic term for an agreement formally signed, ratified, or adhered to by two or more sovereign states <Treaty of Warsaw>. An *accord* is any type of amicable arrangement between peoples or nations <Geneva Accord>. *Concord* is a more formal, slightly archaic equivalent of *accord*. A *protocol* is a treaty amending or supplementing an earlier treaty <Kyoto Protocol>. A *declaration* is ordinarily an agreement that declares or makes law <Declaration of Paris>. An *act* generally results from a formal conference involving high officials. A *compact* is typically an earnest exchange of promises between sovereigns <United Nations Global Compact>. *Pact*, a less formal equivalent, appears most often either in headlines because of its shortness or in certain SET PHRASES such as *suicide pact*. A *paction* is a compact between two nations to be completed by the performance of a single act; the term is rare today. An *entente*, a shortened form of the French *entente cordiale*, is an amicable agreement between nations relating to some policy or course of action, especially involving foreign affairs <Anglo-Russian Entente>. A *convention* is usually a less formal or more specific type of multilateral treaty <Vienna Convention>. A *cartel* is a written agreement between opposing nations (belligerents) during wartime to regulate whatever dealings will take place between them <cartel for the exchange of prisoners of war>. A *concordat* is an agreement between a secular government and a church, especially the Vatican, for regulating church–state affairs <Concordat of 1801>. See **concord (A).**

In the U.S., an *executive agreement* is an agreement between the U.S. and another nation. Unlike a *treaty*, which must have the advice and consent of the Senate, an *executive agreement* is made by the President but not ratified by the Senate. Some writers loosely refer to *executive agreements* as *treaties*.

treaty, vb. (= to make a treaty with), is a NEOLOGISM that is not widespread—and is therefore subject to the objection that many readers will find it jarring. E.g.: "Although the United States *treatied* [read *made treaties*] with tribes for the majority of the tribes' land claims, such negotiations did not always take place." James E. Torgerson, *Indians Against Immigrants—Old Rivals, New Rules*, 14 Am. Indian L. Rev. 57, 78 (1988).

treble; triple. These words are distinguishable though sometimes interchangeable. *Treble* is more usual as the verb, especially in legal contexts: "The trial court determined what additional damages would be subject to *trebling* if the preponderance of the evidence standard were applied to the plaintiffs' claim." *Stuart v. Stuart*, 996 A.2d 259, 263 (Conn. 2010).

As an adjective, *treble* usually means "three times as much or as many" <treble damages>, whereas *triple* means "having three parts" <a triple bookshelf> <triple bypass surgery>.

trek (fr. Dutch *trekken* "to march or travel") is occasionally misspelled **treck*—e.g.:

- "The campers would engage in such activities as water skiing, scuba diving, horseback *trecks* [read *treks*] into the Grand Canyon, mountain climbing, river trips on rubber rafts and fossil hunting." *Ferman v. Estwing Mfg. Co.*, 334 N.E.2d 171, 172 (Ill. App. Ct. 1975).
- "The arrestees were allowed to retain control of [the potential weapons] during the long *treck* [read *trek*] back." *People v. Brisendine*, 531 P.2d 1099, 1102–03 (Cal. 1975) (en banc).

trespass. A. And Near-Synonyms: *encroach*; *infringe*; *impinge*; *invade*. Although these verbs are used quite differently (some are intransitive, some transitive, and some either), they share the sense "to move wrongfully into someone else's rightful territory." *Trespass*, now invariably intransitive, implies an unlawful entrance or unwarranted intrusion—and it is typically followed by *on* (or, less good, *upon*) <you're trespassing on my land>. *Encroach*, now invariably intransitive, suggests a gradual and hardly perceptible movement into another domain <within eight months, the tree was once again encroaching on the neighbor's property>. Further, *encroach* suggests an unnoticed extension of one's possession of land so as to transgress the proper boundary <the Jensens began encroaching on their neighbors' land when they built a wall beyond their property boundaries in 1958>. *Infringe* implies an encroachment that without question violates another's rights. The verb can be either transitive or intransitive <this act infringed [on] my client's rights>. (See **infringe (A).**) *Impinge* implies a more or less violent collision with something else, and therefore a sudden and striking infringement. (See **infringe (B).**) *Invade*, now almost invariably transitive, implies a clear, abrupt penetration into someone else's rightful domain, usually with both hostility and resulting injury <the paparazzi invaded my privacy>.

B. History of the Term. The LAW FRENCH word for transgression or wrongdoing, *trespass* began not as a

TERM OF ART but as a word so broad as to encompass felony, misdemeanor, and disseisin.

In the later common law, the action of *trespass* took on a variety of forms, among which it is useful to distinguish. *Trespass vi et armis* = an action for intentional injuries to the person. *Trespass de bonis asportatis* (or *trespass de bonis*) = an action for the wrongful taking of chattels. *Trespass quare clausum fregit* (or *trespass q.c.f.*) = an action for invasion of possession of realty. *Trespass on the case* = an action for myriad other injuries, from negligence to nuisance to business torts. See **trespass on the case.**

trespasser; *trespassor. The better spelling is *trespasser.*

trespassers will be prosecuted is, in itself, usually a lie. Trespass to land is a tort, not a crime. But trespassers who cause damage, as by damaging crops or breaking windows, can be prosecuted.

trespass on the case is a form of action that, at common law, provided compensation for a wide spectrum of injuries, from personal injuries caused by negligence to business torts and nuisances.

Case is often used as an elliptical form of the phrase *trespass on the case.* E.g.:

- "In England . . . it was very early held that corporations might be liable in actions on the *case* or in trespass, and afterwards in trover." Samuel Williston, *History of the Law of Business Corporations Before 1800*, 2 Harv. L. Rev. 105, 124 (1888).
- "While federal courts only recognize one form of action today, the common law recognized ten: debt, detinue, covenant, special assumpsit, general assumpsit, trespass, trover, replevin, *case*, and ejectment." Sina Kian, *Pleading Sovereign Immunity*, 61 Stan. L. Rev. 1233, 1245 (2009).

See **action on the case.**

*trespassor. See **trespasser.**

trespassorily. See **trespassory.**

trespassory, dating from 1888, is the adjective corresponding to the noun *trespass.* Included in *W2*, it is, oddly, missing from *W3.* Yet it is common—e.g.:

- "Before that time, South Carolina decisions had indicated a *trespassory* entry was necessary to conviction." *Sodergren v. State*, 715 P.2d 170, 175 (Wyo. 1986).
- "An action on the case for nuisance gave him a remedy for *non-trespassory* interference with the use and enjoyment of his land." Roger A. Cunningham et al., *The Law of Property* 9 (2d ed. 1993).
- "The unauthorized use of a vehicle is a '*trespassory*' offense and as such, it poses a serious risk of head-to-head confrontations with owners, police, and bystanders." *U.S. v. DeJesus-Concepcion*, 607 F.3d 303, 306 (2d Cir. 2010).

The adverb is *trespassorily*—e.g.: "A defendant commits a robbery when, with the intent permanently to deprive, he *trespassorily* takes and carries away the personal property of another from the latter's person or presence by the use of force or threatened force." 4 *Wharton's Criminal Law* § 469, at 40 (14th ed. 1981).

-TRESS. See SEXISM (C).

triable = capable of being tried in a court of law; liable to judicial trial (*OED*). This term is used in reference to persons as well as issues and offenses, but primarily in reference to offenses—e.g.:

- "If there has been a demand but the case is not *triable* to a jury as of right, the case will be tried to the court." Charles Alan Wright, *The Law of Federal Courts* 662 (5th ed. 1994).
- "Pavey analogized the issue of exhaustion to subject-matter jurisdiction, observing that not every factual issue that arises during litigation is *triable* to a jury as a matter of right." *Drippe v. Tobelinski*, 604 F.3d 778, 781 (3d Cir. 2010).

trial, vb. The *OED* records four instances of this verb, in the sense "to test (a thing, esp. a new product)," beginning in 1981 <several models are already being trialed>.

In Australia and the U.S., it is sometimes said that a defendant is "trialled" (or "trialed," as the word would be spelled in AmE). An Australian writer comments: "Apparently the *outré* misused word was supposed to mean that he or she had been brought to trial, or had been put to trial. What an unsavoury ill treatment of the English language." Theo Ruoff, *Murky Muddleheadedness or Magic?*, 61 Law Inst. J. 734, 734 (1987). When this unsavory ill treatment occurs in AmE, it comes usually from the mouth of a nonlawyer—e.g.: "I was *trialed* as a habitual offender."

trial, at; upon trial; on the trial. The usual idiom today is *at trial*, not *upon trial* or *on the trial.* E.g.:

- "But if it develops *on the trial* [read *at trial*] that the plaintiff is not entitled to equitable relief in any form, equity will not retain the case to award damages." William F. Walsh, *A Treatise on Equity* 142 (1930).
- "To what extent, if any, equitable relief may ultimately be granted must rest with exigencies as they appear *upon trial* [read *at trial*]." *High v. Trade Union Courier Pub. Corp.*, 69 N.Y.S.2d 526, 529 (Sup. Ct. 1946).
- "While we conclude that resolution of the ownership question requires a trial on the merits, we express no opinion as to how the question should ultimately be resolved *upon trial* [read *at trial*]." *In re Nat'l Century Fin. Enters.*, 377 Fed. Appx. 531, 537 (6th Cir. 2010).

See **at trial.**

trial lawyer, in AmE, has in two ways come to have connotations somewhat different from *litigator.* First, a *trial lawyer* is usually one who actually feels comfortable going into court for trial, whereas a *litigator* is increasingly thought of as a pretrial paper-pusher.

Second, in journalism and even in some legal writing, *trial lawyer* often denotes one who represents primarily plaintiffs, especially in tort actions. E.g.:

- "Aside from the *trial lawyers* themselves, no group has lobbied as hard to expand the scope of liability as the consumer movement." Walter Olson, *A Naderite Backflip on Liability*, Wall St. J., 11 Mar. 1986, at 30.
- "*Trial lawyers*—used here, the term refers to the advocates for victims of what the law calls torts—are a virtually unknown class of the bar." John A. Jenkins, *The Litigators* xii (1989).

The American Trial Lawyers' Association is composed primarily of the plaintiffs' bar, as opposed to defense counsel.

Just as often, however, *trial lawyer* is used in its broader sense, referring to defense counsel as well as plaintiffs' counsel—e.g.:

- "*Trial lawyers* view a disqualification motion as one of the most difficult maneuvers, because they recognize that they must appear before the judge for the rest of their careers." Stephen Labaton, *Bid to Drop Judge Renews Old Fight*, N.Y. Times, 3 Oct. 1988, at 26.
- "It was thought that surprise, dearly cherished by an earlier generation of *trial lawyers*, would be minimized or ended altogether." Charles Alan Wright, *The Law of Federal Courts* 578 (5th ed. 1994).

Cf. **litigator.**

trial to the bench. See **bench trial.**

tribunal has two senses: (1) "a court or other adjudicative body"; or (2) "the seat, bench, or place where judges sit." In its most usual application—sense 1—*tribunal* is broader than *court* and generally refers to a body, other than a court, that exercises judicial functions <industrial tribunal> <social-security tribunal>.

trier of fact; fact-trier. These terms refer to the finder of fact in a judicial proceeding, i.e., the jury or, in a bench trial, the judge. *Trier of fact* is the older phrase, *fact-trier* a form that has recently come into use in AmE and that reduces the awkwardness of *trier of fact* when a possessive is called for <the fact-trier's impartiality>. See POSSESSIVES (G).

triggerman. See **nontriggerman** & SEXISM (B).

trillion, in the U.S. and France, means "a million millions," and traditionally in G.B., "a million million millions." The difference is more than substantial. But today many British writers follow the American usage. Cf. **billion.**

trip (= appeal) is judges' JARGON in AmE—e.g.: "Because Vanorden did not challenge his sentence on Sixth Amendment grounds in his first *trip* through this circuit, this argument is deemed abandoned." *U.S. v. Vanorden*, 414 F.3d 1321, 1323 (11th Cir. 2005).

triple. See **treble.**

TRIPLETS. See DOUBLETS, TRIPLETS, AND SYNONYM-STRINGS.

triumphant; triumphal. Persons are *triumphant* (= celebrating a triumph), and things are *triumphal* (= of, pertaining to, or of the nature of a triumph).

-TRIX. See SEXISM (C).

T.R.O. = temporary restraining order. The letters in this abbreviation are usually capitalized in AmE. Though the periods are often absent, the better practice is to use them, for *T.R.O.* is an initialism, not an acronym. See ACRONYMS AND INITIALISMS & **temporary restraining order.**

trodden is preferred to *trod* as the past participle of *tread*. Ironically, however, *untrod* is preferred to **untrodden* as the adjectival form.

troll, n. = one who acquires intellectual-property rights solely to collect royalties or infringement damages. Additionally, a *patent troll* has no intention of manufacturing the product or developing it any further. And a *copyright troll* has no involvement in the creative aspects of a work. This pejorative term emerged in the early 2000s. The allusion is to the monster in Norse mythology, and more specifically to the fairy-tale creature that dwells under bridges and demands tolls from anyone who wants to cross.

troops. This plural form, which signifies *soldiers* <the troops were deployed along the crest of the ridge>, is usually modified by an adjective to indicate some special training the soldiers have completed or some special assignment <ski troops> <airborne troops> <desert troops>. An adjective may also designate the upper command level at which the soldiers are currently functioning <divisional troops> <corps troops> <army troops> <allied troops>. In the singular, a *troop* refers not to an individual soldier but to an assembled unit of soldiers of whatever special kind, mission, or affiliation <a troop of parachutists secured the airport> <a troop of cavalry passed in review> <a troop of divisional personnel set up the command post>. The plural term *troops* is meaningful when more than one soldier is referred to <get these troops out of the sun>.

These military terms are not to be confused with the term *troupe* <a troupe of actors> <a troupe of circus performers> <a troupe of high-wire acrobats>.

Both *troop* and *troupe* have their origin in the medieval French term *troupeau*, meaning a crowd or herd.

trove = accumulation, hoard. See **treasure trove.**

trover. See **detinue.**

true bill, n. = the grand jury's notation that a criminal charge should go before a petit jury for trial. The phrase is an 18th-century LOAN TRANSLATION of the medieval LATINISM *billa vera*. E.g.:

- "In theory anyone could put an accusation in a bill, lay it before the grand jury with supporting evidence, and invite them to call it a *true bill*." Patrick Devlin, *The Criminal Prosecution in England* 5 (1960).
- "The Wake County Grand Jury returned *true bills* of indictment against defendant for (1) felonious breaking or entering, (2) felonious larceny, [and] (3) felonious possession of stolen goods." *State v. Tanner*, 695 S.E.2d 97, 99 (N.C. 2010).

See **grand jury (A)** & LAW LATIN.

true-bill, vb. = (1) to indict; or (2) to endorse (an indictment) in a way that shows that the grand jury finds the indictment to be sustained by the evidence. E.g., in sense 2: "It is formal notice at the time the indictment was *true-billed*." Clara Tuma, *Court Expands Weapon Notice Requirements*, Tex. Law., 14 May 1990, at 14. (For another example, see the quotation under NOUNS AS VERBS.)

true facts. Although lawyers often use the word *facts* as shorthand for *alleged facts*—and can therefore make out a (weak) case for writing *true facts*—the latter phrase is usually nothing more than a commonplace REDUNDANCY. E.g.:

- "The status of 'insured' is to be determined by the *true facts* [read *facts*], not false, fraudulent, or otherwise incorrect *facts that might be alleged* [read *allegations*]." *Blue Ridge Ins. Co. v. Hanover Ins. Co.*, 748 F.Supp. 470, 473 (N.D. Tex. 1990).
- "Here, the *true facts are* [read *facts are*] that there is no coverage." *Ohio Cas. Ins. Co. v. Cooper Mach. Corp.*, 817 F.Supp. 45, 48 (N.D. Tex. 1993).

See **facts.** Cf. ***actual fact, in.**

trump, n. & vb. In cards, a *trump* is a card of a suit that, for the time being, ranks above the other three, so that any such card can "take" any card of another suit. So one says that this card *trumps* (i.e., overcomes) that one.

During the late 20th century, legal scholars began using this cardplaying metaphor in discussing legal doctrine. Though sometimes deplored as a casualism, the usage is now established—e.g.:

- "It is hard to understand why . . . the same purpose should not also be sufficient to *trump* the per se rule in all other price-fixing cases that arguably permit cartel members to 'provide better services.'" *Business Elecs. Corp. v. Sharp Elecs. Corp.*, 485 U.S. 717, 756 (1988) (Stevens, J., dissenting).
- "No Member of Congress came to the judgment that the District Court cases would *trump Johnson* on the point at issue here." *Blanchard v. Bergeron*, 489 U.S. 87, 98 (1989) (Scalia, J., concurring in part).
- "Los Angeles contends that the charter *trumps* the PUC decision because the use of power within Los Angeles is a municipal affair." *City of Los Angeles v. Tesoro Ref. & Mktg. Co.*, 115 Cal. Rptr. 3d 811, 817 (Ct. App. 2010).

trust. A. Senses. *Trust* = (1) the confidence reposed in a person who looks after property for another's use or benefit; (2) an equitable estate committed to the charge of a fiduciary (trustee) for a beneficiary; (3) the relationship between the holder of the property and the property so held; or (4) a combination that aims at a monopoly <trustbuster>.

In sense 1, *trust* can apply to a variety of fiduciary relationships, including executorship, guardianship, and agency. The transference in meaning between sense 1 and sense 2 resulted from a type of HYPAL-LAGE; so successful was it that sense 2 is now the predominant one.

Sense 4 is an odd extension of meaning, but it is indeed an extension of sense 2: "The monopolistic *trusts* were originally so called because the stock of the combining corporations was transferred to technical trustees to accomplish a centralization of control." George T. Bogert, *Trusts* § 1, at 2 (6th ed. 1987).

B. *In trust* and *on trust*. In sense 1, the word commonly appears in two idioms. In a formal express trust, it is usual to designate the trustee as such and to state that the transfer is *in trust*. The phrase *on trust* is really just a variation of that idiom—e.g.: "A woman left her residuary estate *on trust* for her husband for life, remainder to trustees for her children." Erwin Griswold, *Cases and Materials on Taxation* 241 (6th ed. 1966).

C. *Trust* Without Qualifying Adjective. When *trust* appears without a qualifying adjective, the sense is almost always "express trust." When a *constructive trust* is intended, the entire phrase invariably appears. *See* Restatement of Restitution § 160 cmt. a, at 642 (1937).

D. Other Names for *constructive trust*. Though *constructive trust* is by far the most common phrase today for a trust imposed by a court on equitable grounds, legal writers formerly used in this sense the phrases *trust* de son tort, *implied trust*, *trust* ex delicto, *trust* ex maleficio, and *involuntary trust*.

trust agreement. See **declaration of trust.**

trust deed. See **deed of trust** & **declaration of trust.**

trust *de son tort*. See **constructive trust (A)** & **trust (D).**

trustee, n. **A. And *trusty*.** *Trustee* = a person who, having a nominal title to property, holds it in trust for the benefit of one or more others, the beneficiaries. *Trusty*, n., is an Americanism meaning "a (trusted) convict or prisoner." E.g.: "A *trusty* who had accompanied the officers crawled under the house and retrieved a lady's girdle from inside one of the vents underneath the house, along with several rectal syringes." *In re Wright*, 282 F.Supp. 999, 1005 (W.D. Ark. 1968).

B. And *executor*. In the context of wills, nonlawyers are frequently confused about the difference between an *executor* and a *trustee*. The *executor* collects the decedent's property, pays the debts, and hands over the remaining property to the persons who are entitled to it under the will. A *trustee* becomes necessary only when the property must be held for a time because it cannot, for some reason, be handed over at once to the persons entitled to it.

trustee, vb., dates from the early 19th century, though it looks like a newfangled verbalization of a noun.

The term has three senses: (1) "to place (a person or a person's property) in the hands of a trustee or trustees"; (2) (AmE) "to appoint (a person) trustee, often of a bankrupt's estate in order to restrain the creditor from collecting moneys due"; and (3) (AmE) "to attach (the effects of a debtor) in the hands of a third person." E.g.: "The defendant in this case . . . is a jointly *trusteed* employee health and welfare benefit plan." *Powers v. South Cent. United Food & Commercial Workers Unions*, 719 F.2d 760, 761 (5th Cir. 1983). The quotation illustrates sense 2, which predominates in AmE.

trust estate. See **corpus.**

trust *ex delicto*; trust *ex maleficio*. See **constructive trust (A)** & **trust (D).**

trustor. See **settlor.**

trust property. See **corpus.**

trusty. See **trustee (A).**

truth, the whole truth, and nothing but the truth. This phrase is the quintessential example of ceremonial legal language—e.g.: "A young girl walked to the witness stand. As she raised her hand and swore that the evidence she gave would be *the truth, the whole truth, and nothing but the truth* so help her God, she seemed somehow fragile-looking, but when she sat facing us in the witness chair she became what she was, a thick-bodied girl accustomed to strenuous labor." Harper Lee, *To Kill a Mockingbird* 181 (1960).

truth and veracity is an old but unjustified DOUBLET. To make any sense in modern English, the phrase should be *truthfulness and veracity*. In other words, *truth* in this phrase is shorthand for either *truthfulness* or *truth-telling*, but even most lawyers would be hard-pressed to explain why, since that meaning of *truth* passed into disuse in the 18th century. Today the phrase needs editing:

- "Parties in both civil and criminal actions are frequently assailed by the character witness who testifies that the reputation of one of the parties to the action is bad for *truth and veracity* [read *truthfulness*]." Asher L. Cornelius, *The Cross-Examination of Witnesses* 103 (1929).
- "The trial court excluded Shank's testimony because in its view the evidence had no bearing on Appellant's reputation in the community for *truth and veracity* [read *truthfulness*] and, therefore, it was irrelevant." *Argenbright v. Commonwealth*, 698 S.E.2d 294, 298 (Va. Ct. App. 2010).

try. In G.B., only judges and juries *try* cases; but in the U.S. lawyers, as well as judges and juries, are said to *try* cases. E.g.: "In our adversary system, prosecutors are permitted to *try* their cases with earnestness and vigor." *U.S. v. Johnson*, 587 F.3d 625, 632 (4th Cir. 2009). See **litigate.**

try and is, in AmE, a casualism for *try to*; in BrE, however, it is a standard idiom.

tu quoque (lit., "you also") = a retort in kind; accusing an accuser of a similar offense.

turbid; turpid; torpid. *Turbid* = (of water) muddy, thick; (fig.) disordered. *Turpid* is a rare word meaning "filthy; worthless." *Torpid* = dormant; sluggish; apathetic.

turn state's evidence; turn Queen's (or King's) evidence. The first is AmE, the second BrE. This idiom dates from the early 18th century: an accomplice to a crime is said to *turn evidence* by cooperating with the prosecutors and testifying against other criminal defendants. This behavioral about-face is often accomplished by the prosecution's promising the defendant either a reduction in sentence or a dismissal of certain charges in the indictment. E.g.:

- "Matthews . . . had *turned Queen's evidence* in the hands of a police officer who was not above suspicion." Patrick Devlin, *The Judge* 170–71 (1979).
- "Another legitimate use for pardons was found, as a means of persuading accomplices to '*turn king's evidence*' and testify against their fellows at their trial of indictment." J.H. Baker, *An Introduction to English Legal History* 589 (3d ed. 1990).

See 2 *Jowitt's Dictionary of English Law* 2311 (Daniel Greenberg ed., 3d ed. 2010).

One who *turns state's evidence* is perhaps best referred to as a *cooperating witness* or an *informant*. (See **informant.**) Far more commonly, however, such a person is called a *snitch*, which may also be used as a verb meaning "to report criminal activity, esp. when the reporting person was more or less involved in the activity." Both uses are common in AmE and BrE. *See* Eric Partridge, *A Dictionary of the Underworld* 655 (1949). While *snitch* was once almost exclusively used by criminals and their defense lawyers, it is now also being used increasingly by prosecutors and judges in referring to cooperating witnesses and informants. Once considered *infra dig* slang, the term has recently been upgraded to printable status even in dignified contexts—e.g.:

- "Respondent's amicus insists that jailhouse *snitches* are so inherently unreliable that this Court should craft a broader exclusionary rule for uncorroborated statements obtained by that means." *Kansas v. Ventris*, 129 S.Ct. 1841, 1847 n.* (2009) (per Scalia, J.).
- "Unbeknownst [read *Unbeknown*] to Strode, *snitches* lay on every side. Both Conway and Askew had met with federal agents prior to meeting at Glover's. The agents had outfitted Conway with a recording device, and, as a consequence, the entire conversation at Glover's was recorded." *U.S. v. Strode*, 552 F.3d 630, 632 (7th Cir. 2009). On the use of *unbeknownst* in that sentence, see **unbeknown.** On the use of **prior to*, see ***prior to.**

While *snitch* is occasionally used dispassionately (one can't quite say nonpejoratively), another common synonym—*rat*—has had no such luck.

turpid. See **turbid.**

turpitude. See **moral turpitude.**

*tutrix is a legal ARCHAISM meaning "a female guardian." The word *guardian* itself suffices. See SEXISM (C).

twelve free and lawful men; twelve good and lawful men; twelve men good and true; twelve good and true men. These hoary references to a 12-member jury are LOAN TRANSLATIONS of either of two Latin phrases: *duodecin liberos et legales homines* and *duodecin bonos et legales homines*. Variations on the phrase have appeared in a wide range of literature, though concerns about SEXISM will surely restrict their use to historical contexts, a tendency already evident—e.g.:

- "He uses every trick of oratory and acting to appeal to the crudest emotions of the *twelve good men and true*." Jerome Frank, *Law and the Modern Mind* 197 (1930).
- "In the meantime make *twelve free and lawful men* of the neighbourhood view the land, and record their names." Alan Harding, *A Social History of English Law* 43 (1966) (translating an assize of novel disseisin from the time of Henry II).
- "Massachusetts, among other states, created a system of these courts in 1775—though, true to ideology, issues of fact were to be decided by '*twelve good and lawful men*.'" Lawrence M. Friedman, *A History of American Law* 53 (2d ed. 1985).
- "The *twelve free and lawful men* mentioned in the writ were summoned to 'make recognition' of the facts, and were sometimes called recognitors." J.H. Baker, *An Introduction to English Legal History* 86 (3d ed. 1990).

With all the variations on this expression, it could hardly be termed a SET PHRASE. So it is hardly surprising to see writers varying it still further—e.g.: "In times of public excitement the participation of a *dozen or two 'good men and true'* may merely serve to lend a veneer of due process to expressions of mass hysteria." Lon L. Fuller, *Anatomy of the Law* 39 (1968).

twofold; threefold; fourfold. These and like terms should be spelled as one word.

two-witness rule = the rule that, to support a perjury conviction, two independent witnesses (or one witness together with corroborating evidence) must establish that the perjurer gave false evidence. In the context of treason, the *two-witness rule* appears in the Constitution: "No person shall be convicted of treason unless on the testimony of two witnesses to the same overt act, or on confession in open court." U.S. Const. art. IV, § 2, cl. 2.

tying. See **tie.**

type of is often used unnecessarily and inelegantly. E.g.: "The *types of* [omit *types of*] cases most commonly recommended for centralized adjudication include those involving federal agencies and law." Paul D. Carrington & Paulina Orchard, *The Federal Circuit: A Model for Reform?*, 78 Geo. Wash. L. Rev. 575, 583–84 (2010).

Of is dropped in the following examples, which are typical of the modern American colloquial trend. Again, however, the phrasing with *type* makes the sentence wordy—e.g.:

- "Speedfast is not entitled to the rigid *type protection* [read *protection*] it seeks." *Julius M. Ames Co. v. Bostitch, Inc.*, 235 F.Supp. 856, 857 (S.D.N.Y. 1964).
- "It was reasonably necessary to employ someone in this *type business* [read *business*] to keep the property rented." *Corpus Christi Bank & Trust v. Roberts*, 597 S.W.2d 752, 754 (Tex. 1980).
- "William Spuhl testified that he operated a gun-cleaning/reloading *type business* [omit *type*] on the property." *Gilbert v. Board of County Comm'rs*, 232 P.3d 17, 21 (Wyo. 2010).

For the problem raised by the phrase **these type of*, see ***these kind of.**

tyrannical; tyrannous. Though the senses often seem to merge, the first corresponds to *tyrant*, the second to *tyranny*. In the following examples, a tyrant is being suggested:

- "Nobody has yet been found to say a good word for King John. He was false, cowardly, and *tyrannical*." H.G. Hanbury, *English Courts of Law* 49 (2d ed. 1953).
- "Even the most *tyrannical* despot, who may operate on the basis that his whim is law, soon discovers that his whims will be most effectively enforced if they are translated into 'real' law." P.S. Atiyah, *Law and Modern Society* 65 (1983).
- "I would submit that imposing an additional criminal sanction for an uncharged crime of which the defendant was not convicted is no less *tyrannical*." *State v. Reyna*, 234 P.3d 761, 779 (Kan. 2010).

But *tyrannous* is the appropriate word when referring to tyranny—e.g.: "The representative character of the Commons forms one half of the safeguard against precipitate or *tyrannous* legislation." H.G. Hanbury, *English Courts of Law* 20 (2d ed. 1953).

Sometimes the two forms provoke suspicions of INELEGANT VARIATION—e.g.: "The colonists regarded the acts as *tyrannous* and oppressive . . . . American historians are generally in agreement that the Navigation Acts . . . , together with the ensuing *tyrannical* physical acts of forcible entry . . . [etc.], were the main causes of the American Revolution." *In re Site for Hunts Point Sewage Treatment Works*, 138 N.Y.S.2d 118, 121 (Sup. Ct. 1954). Perhaps, though, those uses are distinguishable, as *tyrannical* is inevitably more concrete than *tyrannous*.

U

uberrima fides; *uberrimæ fidei.* The first, a noun phrase meaning literally "the utmost good faith," describes a class of contracts (such as insurance contracts) in which one party has a preliminary duty to disclose to the other material facts relevant to the subject matter. In American legal writing, the noun form *uberrima fides* (as defined above) is more common <a contract requiring *uberrima fides*>; meanwhile, in British legal writing the genitive *uberrimæ fidei* (= of the utmost good faith) is prevalent <a contract *uberrimæ fidei*>.

When American lawyers use the genitive form, they sometimes mangle the second word, making it *fidae* (or *fides*) instead of *fidei*—e.g.:

- "We have considered the Underwriter's argument that East Coast owed them [*sic*] a duty *of uberrimae fidae* [read either *of ubberima fides* or *uberrimae fidei*], but we find it unpersuasive." *East Coast Tender Servs., Inc. v. Robert T. Winzinger, Inc.*, 759 F.2d 280, 284 n.3 (3d Cir. 1985).
- "Albany relied on the doctrine of utmost good faith or *uberrimae fidae* [read *uberrimae fidei*], seeking to void the policy from its inception based on the owner's representation as to value." Warren J. Marwedel, *Admiralty Jurisdiction and Recreational Craft Personal Injury Issues*, 68 Tul. L. Rev. 423, 469 (1994).

The phrases are pronounced in this way: *uberrima fides* /yoo-bə-**ree**-mə **fi**-deez/ and *uberrimæ fidei* /yoo-bə-**ree**-mi **fi**-day-ee/. See LATINISMS & PRONUNCIATION (C).

ubi remedium, ibi ius. See MAXIMS.

ubi supra. See *ante* & *supra.*

ukase /yoo-kays/, originally a Russian term, historically meant literally "a decree or edict, having the force of law, issued by the Russian emperor or government" (*OED*). By extension it has come to mean "any proclamation or decree, esp. of a final or arbitrary nature." E.g.: "The petitioner failed to comply . . . and that default caused the immigration judge's *ukase* to mutate into a deportation order." *Lattab v. Ashcroft*, 384 F.3d 8, 13 (1st Cir. 2004).

Ulpian; Ulpianus. Though the Roman form of the name is *Ulpianus*, Anglo-American writers usually refer to this 3rd-century Roman treatise-writer as *Ulpian.*

ult. ([*ultimo*] = of last month); **prox.** ([*proximo*] = of next month); **inst.** ([*instant*] = of this month). These abbreviations, primarily from commercialese, are to be avoided in preference for straightforward terms such as *March 12*, or *next month*, or *last month*. See **inst.**

ultima ratio = the final argument; a last resort (often force). E.g.: "It seems to me clear that the *ultima ratio* . . . is force, and that at the bottom of all private relations, however tempered by sympathy and all the social feelings, is a justifiable self-preference." Oliver Wendell Holmes Jr., *The Common Law* 38 (1881).

ultimate; penultimate; antepenultimate. *Ultimate* = last; *penultimate* = next-to-last; *antepenultimate* = third-from-last.

Penultimate is common among educated writers, both lawyers and nonlawyers. E.g.: "Even when concern for human health or welfare motivates a statute, and environmental protection is only *penultimate*, the connection between regulated activities and human well-being can be roundabout or probabilistic." Christopher S. Elmendorf, *State Courts, Citizen Suits, and the Enforcement of Federal Environmental Law by Non-Article III Plaintiffs*, 110 Yale L.J. 1003, 1004 (2001). But some misuse it as a weird HYPERBOLE for *ultimate*—e.g.: "The Second Amendment has nothing whatever to do with personal self-defense. . . . The *penultimate* [read *ultimate*] expression of this wayward view came in March 2007 in the [D.C.] Circuit's majority ruling in *Parker v. District of Columbia*." Robert J. Spitzer, *Why History Matters*, 1 Alb. Gov't L. Rev. 312, 317 (2008).

ultimate destination is not necessarily a REDUNDANCY, as is often assumed. Where a shipment has a series of stops or transfers—i.e., a series of "immediate destinations"—it may be appropriate to use the phrase *final* or *ultimate destination*. One may be on one's way to Bangkok, with a stopover in Tokyo. If on that flight to Tokyo someone asks about one's destination, it would not be inappropriate to characterize Tokyo as the *immediate destination* (i.e., the destination of that particular flight) and Bangkok as the *ultimate destination* (the destination of the entire trip).

Yet the phrase *final destination* or *ultimate destination* should not be used (as it commonly is) in contexts in which such specificity is not called for. Cf. **final outcome** & **end result.**

ultimately = (1) in the end <she ultimately reached her destination>; or (2) at the beginning <the two doctrines are ultimately related>.

ultimatum. Pl. *-ums.* E.g.: "It was only after these *ultimata* [read *ultimatums*] . . . that RFC reasonably concluded to cease making further loan advances." *Meriden Indus. Co. v. U.S.*, 386 F.2d 885, 895 (Ct. Cl. 1967). See PLURALS (A).

ultimo. See **ult.**

ultra (= [1] beyond due limit; extreme; or [2] extremist; fanatical), when used for *beyond*, is erroneous. E.g.: "Exemplary . . . damages are therefore damages *ultra* [read *beyond*] compensation." *S. H. Kress & Co. v. Powell*, 180 So. 757, 764 (Fla. 1938).

ultra vires /əl-trə **vi**-reez/ (= unauthorized; beyond one's power) is classically used as an adverb, as here: "Petitioner maintains that the commission acted *ultra vires* when it applied its new interpretation of its suspension powers to him." See **intra vires.**

Although *ultra vires* is sometimes misused for *illegal*, the terms are not interchangeable: "*Ultra vires* and *illegality* represent totally different ideas. *Ultra vires* contracts are, strictly speaking, only those which are defective solely because they are beyond the power of the corporation . . . . If the contract is *illegal* as in violation of established principles of public policy, it cannot, of course, be enforced." *Maryland Trust Co. v. National Mechanics Bank*, 102 Md. 608, 614 (1906).

But this naturalized LATINISM is now perhaps more frequently used as an adjective—e.g.:

- "If a director parts with the company's money or property for an *ultra vires* purpose, he will be liable to the company for the loss it has sustained." J. Charlesworth, *The Principles of Company Law* 14 (4th ed. 1945).
- "If the contract is beyond the powers of the company, it is *ultra vires*." 2 Ernest W. Chance, *Principles of Mercantile Law* 214 (Percy W. French ed., 10th ed. 1951).

The phrase has even come to be used as a noun—e.g.: "Under the doctrine of *ultra vires*, there is a limit in point of substance on the transactions into which a corporation may enter." William Geldart, *Introduction to English Law* 62 (D.C.M. Yardley ed., 9th ed. 1984).

UN-. See NEGATIVES.

unalienable. See **indefeasible.**

unapt. See **inapt.**

unavailing = of no avail. E.g.: "The companies . . . argue that . . . Title 26 does not apply to their case as a matter of statutory interpretation. We find this ambitious argument *unavailing*." *U.S. v. Clintwood Elkhorn Mining Co.*, 553 U.S. 1, 11 (2008) (per Roberts, C.J.). See **avail.**

unbeknown; unbeknownst. An early-20th-century lexicographer suggested that both forms are humorous, colloquial, and dialectal. George P. Krapp, *A Comprehensive Guide to Good English* 602 (1927). The *COD* likewise suggests that both are colloquial. Eric Partridge and John Simon have written, in conformity with the *OED*, that *unbeknown* is the preferred form in the phrase *unbeknown to*, and that *unbeknownst* is dialectal. These inconsistent pronouncements serve as confusing guides. We can perhaps accept as British orthodoxy the pronouncement of the *COD* that in BrE the forms are colloquial (for *unknown*). In AmE, neither can really be called dialectal or colloquial, for the word is essentially literary. In current AmE usage, *unbeknownst* far outranges *unbeknown* in frequency of use, and it must therefore be considered at least acceptable. But a stylist might justifiably consider *unbeknown* preferable, since the *-st* forms (e.g., *whilst*, *amidst*) uniformly come less naturally to AmE.

Often, though, the ordinary word *unknown* would serve equally well if not better—e.g.:

- "The latter question has arisen where young girls have been invited to submit to acts in order to train their voice or to improve their breathing—*unbeknown* [read *unknown*] to them, the act [that] they were permitting was sexual intercourse." Andrew Ashworth, *Principles of Criminal Law* 306 (1991).
- "One can always hypothesize unusual cases in which even a prototypically violent crime might not present a genuine risk of injury—for example, an attempted murder where the gun, *unbeknownst* [read *unknown*] to the shooter, had no bullets." *James v. U.S.*, 550 U.S. 192, 208 (2007) (per Alito, J.).

unbelief. See **disbelief.**

unborn child. See **fetus.**

*uncapacitate. See **incapacitate.**

*uncategorically is a silly but distressingly common mistake for *categorically* (= unconditionally; without qualification). And it has gotten wide exposure. In 1991, then Judge Clarence Thomas, testifying before the Senate Judiciary Committee, "uncategorically" denied that he discussed pornographic materials with Anita Hill: "Senator, I would like to start by saying unequivocally, *uncategorically*, that I deny each and every single allegation against me today." *The Thomas Nomination*, N.Y. Times, 13 Oct. 1991, at 1–12.

Even by then, though, the illogically formed "nonword" had already made its way into American law reports—e.g.:

- "The statement . . . purports *uncategorically* [read *categorically*] to announce what a finite set of people—political scientists—think about a given subject—Ollman's scholarship." *Ollman v. Evans*, 750 F.2d 970, 1030 n.115 (D.C. Cir. 1984) (en banc) (Robinson, C.J., dissenting in part).
- "The affidavit of Hogan . . . and interrogatories of Butterworth . . . both state *uncategorically* [read *categorically*] that the religious or ethnic background of the sponsors was never considered or discussed." *Rogers v. Fair*, 902 F.2d 140, 143 (1st Cir. 1990).
- "The Sirianni quote, though useful for some purposes, too seems to possess a hierarchical bias in favor of volunteerism through organizations, which this Article *uncategorically* [read *categorically*] rejects." Alice M. Thomas, *Re-envisioning the Charitable Deduction to Legislate Compassion and Civility*, 19 Kan. J.L. & Pub. Pol'y 269, 331 n.452 (2010).

See **categorically.**

unclean hands. See **clean hands.**

uncollectible. So spelled.

unconscionable = (1) (of persons) having no conscience; or (2) (of actions) showing no regard for conscience; not in accordance with what is right or reasonable. Lawyers use the word a great deal, often without fastidiously observing its meaning. For example, some writers and speakers use it hyperbolically in place of *inequitable*, which is a much softer word. See **conscionable.**

unconstitutional. See **nonconstitutional.**

*uncontrovertible should be *incontrovertible*.

uncounseled (= without the benefit or participation of legal counsel) is generally used today in constructions exhibiting HYPALLAGE; that is, the convict, not the conviction, is uncounseled, though we speak of *uncounseled convictions.* E.g.: "In *Scott v. Illinois*, . . . this Court held that an *uncounseled* misdemeanor conviction is constitutionally valid if the offender is not incarcerated." *Moore v. Georgia*, 484 U.S. 904, 904 (1987) (White, J., dissenting).

uncovered is inherently ambiguous; it may mean (1) "not covered," or (2) "having had the cover removed."

unctuous. So spelled—not *unctious.*

*undefeasible. See **indefeasible.**

undeniably. See **clearly, doubtless & obviously.**

under is preferable to **pursuant to* when the noun that follows refers to a rule, statute, contractual provision, or the like. It is better to say *service under Rule 4* than *service pursuant to Rule 4.* E.g.: "*Under* Rule 32(a)(2), the deposition testimony may be used by an adverse party for any purpose at trial." Mark A. Cymrot, *The Forgotten Rule*, Litig., Spring 1992, at 6, 6. In some contexts, though, *under* may be taken to have a spatial relation to the other words, and may therefore lead to MISCUES such as this one: "You cannot play hide the peanut *under* this rule." *Id.* at 8. See ***pursuant to.**

under advisement. See **advisement.**

under appeal. See **appeal** (A).

underhand; underhanded. Although the shorter form is much older, the longer form is now predominant—and is perfectly acceptable—e.g.:

- "The Fund's *underhanded* use of ellipses to hide what the court was talking about, at best, undermines its argument; the Fund is not entitled to the line-item veto." *In re Radcliffe*, 563 F.3d 627, 633 (7th Cir. 2009).
- "*Underhanded* and constitutionally repugnant as these tactics might have been, any one of them, or all of them together, might just as likely have been the consequence of a Commonwealth Attorney's attempt to win a guilty verdict at that trial." *Sanborn v. Parker*, 629 F.3d 554, 581 (6th Cir. 2010).

underinsurance refers not to a particular type of insurance one can purchase, but to the fact of being underinsured. In the following sentence, the word is used attributively: "Failure by Republic-Franklin Insurance Company to have responded within a reasonable time to notification of a settlement offer will void the subrogation clause in the *underinsurance* motorist provision of its policy, the Supreme Court of Ohio said." *Ohio Supreme Court Decision*, Daily Legal News, 17 Aug. 1989, at 1.

under law; in law; by law; at law. These idioms have long been common in Anglo-American legal writing. They are not interchangeable.

Under law ordinarily means "in accordance with the law" or "in our system of law"—e.g.: "The concept of equal justice *under law* requires the State to govern impartially." *Vieth v. Jubelirer*, 541 U.S. 267, 317 (2004) (Stevens, J., dissenting).

In law most often means "in the eyes of the law"—e.g.: "For section 198(6)(b) to be triggered, the nuisance in question must be actionable *in law*." Sarah Hannett, *Significant United Kingdom Environmental Cases*, 19 J. Envtl. L. 267, 272 (2007).

The phrase *by law*, in contrast, usually means "by statute"—e.g.: "Government agencies are charged *by law* with doing particular tasks." *Engquist v. Oregon Dep't of Agric.*, 553 U.S. 591, 598 (2008) (per Roberts, C.J.).

The idiom *at law* usually signals a contrast with equity—that the *law* being referred to is the common law—e.g.: "The primary difference between the requirements for real covenants and those for equitable servitudes is that courts sitting in equity require neither horizontal nor vertical privity, making it easier for a promissor's successor to assert the benefits of a promise in equity than *at law*." Boudewijn Bouchaert, *Property Law and Economics* 148–49 (2010).

underlawyer. See LAWYERS, DEROGATORY NAMES FOR (A).

underlease is a BrE variant of *sublease*, the usual term in both AmE and BrE. See **sublease.**

underlessee (BrE) = *sublessee* (AmE).

underlessor. See **sublessor.**

underlie. So spelled. **Underly* is an infrequent blunder—e.g.:

- "I have said that the morals [that] *underly* [read *underlie*] the law must be derived from the sense of right and wrong [that] resides in the community as a whole." Patrick Devlin, *The Enforcement of Morals* 22 (1968).
- "It is not enough that the same facts *underly* [read *underlie*] the claims." *Gagne v. Fair*, 835 F.2d 6, 7 (1st Cir. 1987).

Writers fall into this error because they more commonly see the adjectival participle *underlying* than the uninflected verb.

underlying, n. In the law of derivatives (see **derivative**), the underlying asset or factor that is the subject of a derivative contract is typically referred to as the *underlying.* This noun use is admittedly odd—as much derivatives terminology is—but it is established. E.g.: "The future price or value of the *underlying* is quantified by the contractual counterparties when they enter into their derivative contract." John-Peter Castagnino, *Derivatives: The Key Principles* 2 (2009).

under-mentioned. See **below-mentioned.**

under my signature. This expression should not be taken too literally. It means "under my authorization," and has nothing necessarily to do with the physical placement of one's signature.

under oath. See **oath** (A).

under seal. See **seal** (B).

undersigned, rarely used outside legal contexts, is a slightly preposterous way of avoiding the FIRST PERSON. Usually it is an attributive noun <the undersigned agrees to forbear from execution>.

A few lawyers, in writing their clients, actually conclude with, "If you have any questions, please do not hesitate to contact the *undersigned*." That approach is hardly an endearing one.

understanding is a vague word sometimes used in drafting as a weaker word than *agreement* or *contract*. If there is an agreement, then use the word *agreement*; if there is none, then *understanding* may suggest unsatisfactorily that there is. Phrases such as *It is the parties' understanding that* or *In accordance with the parties' understanding* are subject to a variety of interpretations—and ought therefore to be avoided.

understood and agreed. Some contracts teem with provisions that begin, *It is further understood and agreed that the Releasor hereby represents and declares that . . . .* For two reasons, the phrase *understood and agreed* ought to be struck everywhere it appears. First, the lead-in to the agreement already covers the point by saying something like, *The parties therefore agree as follows.* So the phrase *understood and agreed* later in a contract is mere surplusage. Second, if only some of the provisions are graced with the phrase, then the implication is that not every term is *understood and agreed*. The phrase could rightly be classed among FORBIDDEN WORDS. Understood? Agreed?

UNDERSTOOD WORDS are common in English and usually are not very troublesome if we are able to mentally supply them. Often they occur at the outset of sentences. *More important* is short for *What is more important*; *as pointed out earlier* is short for *as was pointed out earlier.*

Objects, too, are often elided with the understanding that the reader will know and mentally supply the missing term—e.g.: "Under Michigan law, courts construe an insurer's duty to *defend* more broadly than its duty to *indemnify*." *Cincinnati Ins. Co. v. Zen Design Group, Ltd.,* 329 F.3d 546, 552 (6th Cir. 2003). In that example, both *defend* and *indemnify* have an implied object: *the insured.*

In a compound sentence, parts of a verb phrase can carry over from the first verb phrase to the second, in which they are understood: "Gorbachev has demanded that Lithuania suspend the declaration of independence before the blockade can be lifted and *talks begun*." *Yeltsin Extends Hand to Lithuania,* L.A. Times, 1 June 1990, at P2. (That sentence is considerably more elegant than it would have been if the second verb phrase had appeared in full: *talks can be begun.*)

On verbs supposedly "understood" whose absence detracts from clarity, see BE-VERBS (A). See also JUDGMENTS, APPELLATE-COURT (next-to-last ¶).

under submission = being considered by the court; under advisement. E.g.: "Prompt disposition of the court's business requires a judge to devote adequate time to judicial duties, to be punctual in attending court, and [to be] expeditious in determining matters *under submission*." Sarah Schultz, *Misconduct or Judicial Discretion*, 40 Conn. L. Rev. 549, 579 (2007).

undertake, a word having both popular and legal senses, may mean (1) "to take upon oneself; to try earnestly" <she has undertaken to help the unfortunate child>; (2) "to bind oneself contractually; to promise" <the builder impliedly undertook that the house would be safe>; or (3) "to become surety or security; to make oneself answer or responsible for a person, fact, or the like" <his friends undertook for his appearance in court>.

In historical contexts, *undertake* is common as a native-English-language equivalent of *assumpsit*—e.g.: "This position was turned by the development of *assumpsit*; the defendant will not be liable unless he '*undertook*' to produce a particular result." Theodore F.T. Plucknett, *A Concise History of the Common Law* 469 (5th ed. 1956). See **assumpsit.**

undertaker. In AmE and BrE alike, this word predominantly refers to a person who is more euphemistically described as a *mortician* or *funeral director*. Using *undertaker* to refer colorlessly to somebody who undertakes to do something—more often today termed a *promisor*—is likely to result in a MISCUE, or at least a momentary distraction. E.g.: "We arrive at the classical form of the doctrine, that a valuable consideration is a benefit given or promised to the *undertaker* [read *promisor*], or some loss or liability incurred by the promisee, in return for the promise given by the *undertaker* [read *promisor*]." Edward Jenks, *The Book of English Law* 317 (P.B. Fairest ed., 6th ed. 1967).

undertaking (= a promise, pledge, or engagement) inhabits almost exclusively the domain of legal JARGON. It is perhaps more common today in BrE than in AmE dominions. E.g.: "There is another form of security, termed 'personal security,' which is an *undertaking* (e.g., a bond), unaccompanied by any charge on goods or property, to pay a debt." 2 Ernest W. Chance, *Principles of Mercantile Law* 30 (Percy W. French ed., 10th ed. 1951).

undertenant (BrE) = *sublessee* (AmE & BrE). See **sublease,** n.

under the circumstances. See **circumstances.**

under (the) law. See **under law.**

under the provisions of is verbose for *under*—e.g.:

- "Only when a voluntary acknowledgment of paternity is revoked *under the provisions of* [read *under*] K.S.A. 38-1115(e), does it not create a presumption as a matter of law." *State ex rel. Sec'y of Soc. & Rehab. Servs. v. Kimbrel*, 231 P.3d 576, 581 (Kan. Ct. App. 2010).
- "The Debtors, filed a voluntary joint petition for relief *under the provisions of* [read *under*] Chapter 7 of the United States Bankruptcy Code." *In re Richmond*, 430 B.R. 846, 851 (Bankr. E.D. Ark. 2010).
- "The letter stated that effective June 20, 2007, Thompson was considered to be off work *under the provisions of* [read *under*] California's . . . Family Rights Act and the Federal Family and Medical Leave Act." *Thompson v. City of Monrovia*, 112 Cal. Rptr. 3d 377, 386 (Ct. App. 2010).

underway; under way. Some dictionaries record the term as two words when used adverbially, one word when used as an adjective preceding the noun <underway refueling>. In the phrases *get underway* (= to get into motion) and *be underway* (= to be in progress), the term is increasingly made one word, and it would be convenient to make that transformation, which is already underway, complete in all uses of the word.

Under weigh for *underway* is a MALAPROPISM.

underwrite. The literal sense, of course, is to write one's name at the bottom of a document. By extension, in everyday language, *underwrite* has come to mean "to support or reinforce." In law and business, however, the term has two specific senses: (1) "to assume a risk by insuring it; to insure life or property"; or (2) "to agree to buy unsold shares of a given number of securities to be offered for public sale." For the shorthand form used in the insurance business, see **write.**

underwriter; assurer; insurer; carrier. Each of these terms is commonly used in referring to one that insures a risk. In the context of marine insurance, *assurer* is the most frequently used term; elsewhere, the other three terms predominate.

Underwriter can also correspond to sense 2 of *underwrite*. In that sense, the agent noun refers to a person or entity—usually a bank or syndicate—that agrees to buy unsold shares of a given number of securities to be offered for public sale. See **underwrite.**

undisclosed principal. See **principal (c).**

undisputedly. See *indisputedly.

undocumented alien; undocumented (migratory) worker; illegal alien. The usual and preferable term in AmE is *illegal alien*. The other forms have arisen as needless EUPHEMISMS, and should be avoided as near-GOBBLEDYGOOK. The problem with *undocumented* is that it is intended to mean, by those who use it in this phrase, "not having the requisite documents to enter or stay in a country legally." But the word strongly suggests "unaccounted for" to those unfamiliar with this quasi-legal JARGON, and it may therefore obscure the meaning.

More than one writer has argued in favor of *undocumented alien*. E.g.: "An alien's unauthorized presence in the United States is not a crime under the Immigration and Naturalization Act of 1952 . . . . So many people find the term *undocumented alien* preferable to *illegal alien*, since the former avoids the implication that one's unauthorized presence in the United States is a crime." Elizabeth Hull, *Undocumented Aliens and the Equal Protection Clause*, 48 Brook. L. Rev. 43, 43 n.2 (1981).

But that statement is only equivocally correct: although illegal aliens' presence in the country is no crime, their *entry* into the country is. As Justice Brennan wrote in *Plyler v. Doe*, 457 U.S. 202, 205 (1982): "Unsanctioned entry into the United States is a crime, 8 U.S.C. § 1325." Moreover, it is wrong to equate illegality with criminality, since many illegal acts are not criminal. *Illegal alien* is not an opprobrious epithet: it describes one present in a country in violation of the immigration laws (hence "illegal").

Those who enter the U.K. illegally are termed by statute *illegal entrants*.

*undoubtably** is an obsolete equivalent of *undoubtedly* and *indubitably*. Cf. **supposable.** See **doubtless.**

undoubtedly. See **clearly, doubtless** & **obviously.**

unearned income, to one unskilled in accountancy, may seem like an OXYMORON. The term refers to income derived from investments as opposed to personal labor.

uneconomical; *uneconomic; noneconomic; *noneconomical. The correct words are *uneconomical* (= not cost-effective) and *noneconomic* (= not relating to economics). The most common error is to use *uneconomic* for *uneconomical*—e.g.: "Manifestly *uneconomic* [read *uneconomical*] projects have been pursued . . . . Lavish spending on the new federal capital, Abuja, is at odds with economic [correct] realities." *Aid and Reform in Nigeria*, Fin. Times, 6 Jan. 1992, at 10. See **economic.**

unenbanc, vb. (= to dismiss motion for hearing en banc after it has already been granted), is a NONCE WORD coined by a judge who enjoyed neologizing: "I dissent to the Court's *unenbancing* the case and refusing to reconsider the panel's opinion." *Burleson v. Coastal Recreation, Inc.*, 595 F.2d 332, 332 (5th Cir. 1978) (Brown, C.J., dissenting). The caselaw contains no examples of a positive form, *enbancing*. But cf. **enbancworthy.**

unenbancworthy. See **enbancworthy.**

unenforceable; *nonenforceable. The first is preferable. See NON-.

unenforceable contract. The most important aspect of a valid contract is that it must be enforceable. So, in a sense, *unenforceable contract* denotes an OXYMORON. (For other phrases using *contract* but involving something other than a true contract, see **contract of record** & **void contract.**) Generally speaking, an *unenforceable contract* is invariably one that is not in writing despite a statute's requiring contracts of its type to be in writing (such as a guaranty or a contract for the sale of land).

unequivocal; *unequivocable. The second is erroneous, yet the error is surprisingly common. The dictionaries contain only *unequivocal*, though undaunted lawyers and judges have written **unequivocable*—e.g.:

- "It is well established that the United States may not be sued without its consent and that its consent must be *unequivocably* [read *unequivocally*] manifested in the text of a statute." *Williams v. U.S.*, 242 F.3d 169, 172 (4th Cir. 2001).
- "The plaintiff in *Veliz* did not use a specially designed work platform, but rather stood on the bare forks of the forklift, a practice that Lull had *unequivocably* [read *unequivocally*] warned against." *Sanders v. Lull Int'l Inc.*, 411 F.3d 1266, 1270 n.6 (11th Cir. 2005).

Even great writers err on this point: "Eastern systems (Hinduism and Buddhism) do not pronounce *unequivocably* [read *unequivocally*] and absolutely against suicide." Glanville Williams, *The Sanctity of Life and the Criminal Law* 249 (1957).

unexceptionable; unexceptional. See **exceptionable.**

unfair competition. This is the name of a body of law that protects the first user of a name, brand, or other symbol in the sale of goods or services against a competitor whose use of the symbol confuses (or will likely confuse) consumers into believing that the first user, rather than the competitor, is the source of the goods or services. *See* Paul Goldstein, *Copyright, Patent, Trademark and Related State Doctrines* 88–89 (2d ed. 1981).

Of course, the phrase also denotes an instance of any practice to which that body of law applies <the company had systematically engaged in unfair competition>.

unfair dismissal; wrongful dismissal. In English law, *unfair dismissal* is a breach of the Employment Protection (Consolidation) Act of 1978, which requires employers to conduct a dismissal fairly and reasonably. *Wrongful dismissal*, by contrast, is a cause of action arising at common law, e.g., when the dismissing employer either fails to give proper notice and to compensate the employee during the period of notice, or does not compensate the employee for the unexpired term of the contract.

In most American jurisdictions, the term equivalent to *wrongful dismissal* is *wrongful discharge* (or *wrongful termination*). For an inadvertently humorous use of *wrongful discharge*, see **prophylactic.**

*unfeasible. See **infeasible.**

unfind (= to undo an earlier factual determination) is a NEOLOGISM dating from the 1950s. It is arguably

quite useful, though it has been slow to spread outside Texas—e.g.:

- "A court of civil appeals has no power to 'find facts,' it may only '*unfind* facts' [that] a jury or trial judge has improperly found." *Alvey v. Goforth*, 263 S.W.2d 313, 319 (Tex. Civ. App.—Fort Worth 1953).
- "A Court of Civil Appeals does not find facts; it only '*unfinds*' a vital fact." Robert W. Calvert, *"No Evidence" and "Insufficient Evidence" Points of Error*, 38 Tex. L. Rev. 361, 368 (1960).
- "A court of appeals cannot make original findings of fact, it can only '*unfind*' facts." *Bellefonte Underwriters Ins. Co. v. Brown*, 704 S.W.2d 742, 745 (Tex. 1986).

unforeseen. So spelled. See FOR-.

*unfrequent. See **infrequent.**

unhappily. See **happily.**

unidentified principal. See **principal (C).**

unidentified suspect. See **unknown suspect.**

unified bar. See **bar,** n.

uniformly is the adverb corresponding to the adjective *uniform*. But many writers get it wrong by writing *uniformally*—e.g.:

- "Judges McAuliffe and Eldridge . . . went so far as to urge trial judges to use *uniformally* [read *uniformly*] the pattern instruction on reasonable doubt." *Joyner-Pitts v. State*, 647 A.2d 116, 122 (Md. Ct. Spec. App. 1994).
- "In both state and federal courts nationwide, cocaine possession, manufacturing, and/or sale is *uniformally* [read *uniformly*] treated far more harshly than similar activity involving marijuana." *In re Doherty*, 650 A.2d 522, 523 (Vt. 1994).
- "The terms used in the 1997 and Harborplace lease are terms of art with *uniformally* [read *uniformly*] . . . understood meanings." *MJ Harbor Hotel v. McCormick Rest. Corp.*, 599 F.Supp.2d 612, 623 (N.D. Md. 2009).

unilateral contract. See **bilateral contract.**

uninheritable. See **inheritable.**

unintentional; involuntary. There is an important distinction between these two words, for one may commit a voluntary act that has unintentional consequences. An *involuntary* act is one outside the control of the will, such as a sneeze; an unintentional act is one not aimed at or desired, such as a person's death resulting from a misdirected shot. *Voluntariness* therefore generally refers to the cause, and *intentionality* to the effect. See **intentional** & **involuntary.**

unintentional murder. See **murder (B).**

uninterest(ed). See **disinterest(ed).**

unique. A. Broad Definition in Contracts. In law, *unique* carries the sense "practically unique"; absolute uniqueness is usually too stringent a definition. E.g.: "The *more unique* the skill involved, the more difficult it is for a court to award monetary damages." Glenn M. Wong, *Essentials of Sports Law* 390 (2010).

B. For *unusual.* Strictly speaking, *unique* means "being one of a kind," not "unusual." Hence to write **very unique*, **quite unique*, **how unique*, and the like is slovenly. The *OED* notes that this tendency to hyperbole—to use *unique* when all that is meant is "uncommon, unusual, remarkable"—began in the 19th century. However old it is, the tendency is worth resisting.

But who can demand responsible use of the language from an ad-writer who is loose enough to say, in a national advertisement, that a certain luxury sedan is "so unique, it's capable of thought"? See ADJECTIVES (B).

United Kingdom. See **Great Britain.**

United States. A century ago, in AmE, this proper noun had "ceased to have any suggestion of plurality about it." Harry T. Peck, *What Is Good English?* 16 (1899). That represented a change, though, from just 50 years before, when particularism for states' rights was rampant: much earlier even than 1850, it was usual to say *the United States have,* as Alexander Hamilton did in *The Federalist* No. 15, at 108 (Clinton Rossiter ed., 1961).

Today, however, it is quite unidiomatic to suggest plurality in referring to the U.S. But some BrE writers use the phrase in this way—e.g.: "It has been shown that under the law of *some* of the United States there is a legal advantage." Glanville Williams, *The Sanctity of Life and the Criminal Law* 183–84 (1957).

United States Court of Appeals; United States Circuit Court of Appeals. The second was the title from 1891 until 1948 but was changed in that year by the new § 43 of the Judicial Code.

United States Supreme Court. The more formal name is the *Supreme Court of the United States.* But if *United States* is used adjectivally—as it usually is—the name should be written as it is in the headword to this entry. Some British writers have made the mistake of putting a possessive apostrophe after *States*—e.g.: "One of the landmark cases in the United *States'* [read *States*] Supreme Court was *United States v. American Trucking Association.*" Rupert Cross, *Statutory Interpretation* 132 (1976). See **United States.**

unitization (= the aggregation of two or more oil-producing properties, owned by different persons, to form a single property so that it can be operated as a single entity or unit under an arrangement for sharing costs and revenues) is a 20th-century NEOLOGISM dating from about 1930. See **communitize (A).**

unitize. See **communitize (A).**

unity. Four unities are traditionally required in creating a joint tenancy: of title, of time, of interest, and of possession. Without all four, a joint tenancy does not exist. *Unity of title* requires that all joint tenants acquire their interests under the same instrument. *Unity of title* requires that all joint tenants' interests vest at the same time. *Unity of interest* requires that the joint tenants' interests be identical in nature, extent, and duration. *Unity of possession* requires that each joint tenant be entitled to possession of the whole property (along with other joint tenants).

universal. On the phrase *more universal*, see ADJECTIVES (B).

unjust enrichment; unjust benefit; *unjustified enrichment. *Unjust enrichment* = (1) a benefit obtained from another, not intended as a gift and not legally justifiable, for which the beneficiary must make restitution or recompense; or (2) the body of law governing claims for benefits of this kind. See **impoverishment.**

Unjust enrichment began its career as an AmE term but is now used on both sides of the Atlantic; *unjust benefit* is a primarily BrE variant, which some Britons stoutly prefer: "I can only surmise that while Lord Wright's position on quasi-contract or restitution was accepted, there was an objection to the expression *unjust enrichment*, perhaps because it was professorial or American." *Estok v. Heguy*, [1963] 43 W.W.R. 167, 173 (B.C.). But the leading British treatise uses *unjust enrichment. See* Robert Goff & Gareth Jones, *The Law of Restitution* 13 (3d ed. 1986).

*Unjustified enrichment is a NEEDLESS VARIANT.

*unknown suspect; unidentified suspect. The phrase **unknown suspect* is an OXYMORON; *unidentified suspect,* on the other hand, is not and is therefore preferable. To have a *suspect,* the authorities must have somebody in particular in mind. They may know a great deal about a suspect without having identified him or her—for example, they may have photographs or DNA samples—but to say *unknown* suggests that the authorities know nothing about the person. E.g.:

- "The officer became faced with the prospect of witnessing an *unknown* [read *unidentified*] suspect depart the area without taking any steps to satisfy himself that he could be found again." *Addison v. State*, 765 S.W.2d 566, 573 (Ark. 1989) (Perroni, S.J., concurring).
- "The books and pamphlet were found in the defendant's room in the house where he lived, along with components for making a bomb and clothing similar to that worn by an *unknown* [read *unidentified*] suspect in a previous bombing." *State v. Starkey*, 516 N.W.2d 918, 926 (Minn. 1994).

A similar—but worse—source of confusion appears in the following case name: *Bivens v. Six Unknown Named Agents of Fed. Bureau of Narcotics*, 403 U.S. 388 (1971).

unlaw = (1) a violation of law; (2) lawlessness; or (3) a fine. The term is rare; Frederick Pollock and F.W. Maitland used it in sense 2: "Times of *unlaw* alternate with times of law." 1 *The History of English Law Before the Time of Edward I* 69 (2d ed. 1898).

unlawful = (1) unauthorized by law; (2) criminally punishable; or (3) involving moral turpitude. Sense 1 is most common, but senses 2 and 3 so complicate matters in using this term that they lessen its utility. See **illegal.**

unlawful assembly. See **riot.**

unlawfully. Though commonly included in criminal statutes, this word is best omitted: "If the courts made a habit of treating '*unlawfully*' as pleonastic, whenever a special meaning is not required, the beneficial result might be that this obscure word would be dropped from criminal statutes." Glanville Williams, *Criminal Law* 29 (2d ed. 1961). The primary problem with the word is that it typically prevents the reader from finding out precisely what conduct is prohibited. If the statute prohibits *unlawfully* engaging in some specified act, then it begs the question of precisely when that act is unlawful.

unless and until. In this doublet, of course, the two words are not synonymous—e.g.: "If the signature is obtained by fraud, . . . the innocent party may take steps to repudiate the contract, but *unless and until* he does so, the document will be binding." P.S. Atiyah, *An Introduction to the Law of Contract* 155–56 (3d ed. 1981). Even so, the meaning of *until* swallows that of *unless* in most contexts, so *until* is ordinarily sufficient. Cf. **if and when.** See DOUBLETS, TRIPLETS, AND SYNONYM-STRINGS.

unlike. A. For *despite what*. This is a solecism. E.g.: "*Unlike some believe* [read *Despite what some believe*], you don't really get 'two wines for the price of one,' as the original volume doesn't increase." 8 *Winemaker* 45 (2005).
  B. For *unlike in*. This misuse leads to faulty comparisons. E.g.:

- "The case before us, however, is the converse scenario of *Klessig*; *unlike* Klessig [read *unlike in* Klessig], Imani did not proceed to trial without counsel." *State v. Imani*, 786 N.W.2d 40, 50 (Wis. 2010).
- "It is also unnecessary to revisit the rule from *Beebe* in those circumstances—*unlike the present case* [read *unlike in the present case*]—where lifesaving medical care is denied, because *Sinclair* remains good law." *Harrison v. Tauheed*, 235 P.3d 547, 561 (Kan. Ct. App. 2010).
- "Again, and *unlike the instant case* [read *unlike in the instant case*], Meatland and Braun were not engaged in a common task or seeking to accomplish a common purpose." *Beazer v. New York City Health & Hosps. Corp.*, 906 N.Y.S.2d 218, 219–20 (App. Div. 2010). (Meatland and Braun were not being compared to the instant case, as the syntax suggests.)

See ILLOGIC (A).
Though some usage critics have called the phrase a "gaucherie" and even worse things, *unlike in*—in

which *unlike* takes on an adverbial sense—is now common usage in AmE and BrE alike. It occurs about 2 percent of the time in which the word *unlike* is used. (More than 10,000 instances of *unlike in* were recorded in the Westlaw database in 2010.) E.g.:

- "It seems unlikely that the deregulation of air traffic transport in Sweden next year—*unlike in* the U.S.—will produce genuine competition with more services and lower fares." Robert Taylor, *SAS to Cut Stake in Domestic Airline*, Fin. Times, 11 Sept. 1990, at 27.
- "But *unlike in* the primary, Cropp won't be running with the support of John Ray's well-financed mayoral campaign." René Sanchez, *D.C. Council in the Throes of an Upheaval*, Wash. Post, 13 Sept. 1990, at C7.

unlimitedly, though an ugly word, has become common in the phrase *unlimitedly liable*, perhaps no longer an exaggeration given the proclivities of American juries. See -EDLY.

unliquidated damages are those that h\ave not been previously specified or contractually provided for. These damages become liquidated only after a court or jury assesses them. Tort actions almost always involve unliquidated damages. Cf. **liquidated damages.**

*unmercilessly is a MALAPROPISM on the order of *uncategorically. *Mercilessly*, of course, is the word (or perhaps *unmercifully*)—e.g.:

- "The Fourth Amendment requirements of warrant *and/or* [read *and*] probable cause should be followed *unmercilessly* [read *mercilessly*]." Samuel Bateman, Note, *Indianapolis v. Edmond*, 2 Nev. L.J. 654, 671 (2002). (For more on the other edit here, see ***and/or.**)
- "Having gained a foothold, the British force set up their cannons, dug emplacements, and commenced to pound Louisburg *unmercilessly* [read *mercilessly*]." Derek Hayes, *Historical Atlas of Canada* 96 (2006).
- "[General] Marmaduke felt that too many Union soldiers had managed to escape and had *unmercilessly* [read *mercilessly*] driven his men to run down the fragmented command." Michael J. Forsyth, *The Camden Expedition of 1864* 116 (2007).
- "The late June sun beat *unmercilessly* [read *unmercifully*] upon the heads of the counseling staff." Gary Chattman, *Don't Tell Me Not to Believe: One Teacher's Odyssey* 18 (2009).

See **mercilessly.**

unmeritorious is certainly preferable to *nonmeritorious, which some writers use, but *meritless* is best when it suffices: of course, an *unmeritorious* applicant in a strong field is not quite the same as a *meritless* applicant.

unmoral. See **immoral.**

*unnamed principal. See **principal (C).**

unnatural. "One of the surest ways of running off the rails," writes the estimable Glanville Williams,

is to introduce the words "natural" and "unnatural." . . . [T]he supposed connection between nature and morals . . . is completely mistaken. It is hardly necessary to point out that men do many things that are unnatural (in the sense of being a merely acquired skill or habit). Miscellaneous examples are washing, shaving, driving automobiles, building cathedrals, and giving blood transfusions, to which may be added all the rest of the intricate routine that has prolonged men's lives upon this planet. . . . The term "unnatural" has been applied at different times to vaccination, anæsthetics, male gynæcologists, the emancipation of women, and the use of steam engines.
Glanville Williams, *The Sanctity of Life and the Criminal Law* 59–60 (1957).

In brief, this term frequently reflects both a fear of the unfamiliar and hidebound conformism.

unobjected to is a common idiom in the law of evidence. When the phrase is placed before the noun, it is hyphenated: "No additional factual hearing is needed since this *unobjected to* [read *unobjected-to*] documentary evidence is in the record." *U.S. v. Jumah*, 599 F.3d 799, 811 n.8 (7th Cir. 2010). See PHRASAL ADJECTIVES (A).

unobjectionable. See *nonobjectionable.

unoccupied. See **vacant.**

unorganized. See **disorganized.**

unpaid, adj. One should not write "the unpaid automobile," because one does not pay an automobile—rather, one pays *for* it. (See HYPALLAGE.) Yet *unpaid-for automobile* is unpalatable because it is awkward. *Unpaid debt on the auto* is better; the loss in brevity is outweighed by the gain in clarity and euphony.

*unphased. See **phase.**

unpractical. See **impractical.**

unproportionate; unproportional. See **proportionate.**

unqualified. See **disqualified.**

unqualifiedly. See **qualifiedly.**

unreadable. See **illegible.**

unreason; unreasonableness; *unreasonability. *Unreason* = absence of reason; indisposition or inability to act or think rationally or reasonably (*OED*). *Unreasonableness* = (1) an act not in accordance with reason or good sense; or (2) the fact of going beyond what is reasonable or equitable. **Unreasonability* is a NEEDLESS VARIANT of *unreasonableness.* Cf. **reasonableness.**

unreasonable. See **reasonable** & **arbitrary.**

unreasonableness; *unreasonability. See **unreason.**

unresponsive; *irresponsive. The first is more common, but *nonresponsive* is more common still. See **nonresponsive.**

unrestricted interpretation. See *free interpretation* under INTERPRETATION, MODES OF (B).

*unrevokable. See **irrevocable.**

unsafe. See **safe.**

unsatisfied. See **dissatisfied.**

unseen. See **sight unseen.**

*unsolvable. See **insoluble.**

*unsubstantial. See **insubstantial.**

unsuitable; unsuitableness. See ***nonsuitability.**

untenable; untenantable. The first means "indefensible" (figuratively) as well as "unable to be occupied." The second means "not capable of being occupied or lived in." In speech, many people seem to say *untenantable* when they mean *untenable.*

until. In the phrase *up until,* the *up* is superfluous, though it's common in speech. Use either *until* or *up to.* See **till.**

until such time as is verbose for *until.*

unto, an ARCHAISM for *to,* is common in legal prose and is easily overdone—e.g.:

- "If the Government becomes a lawbreaker, it breeds contempt for law; it invites every man *to become a law unto himself* [read *to make his own law*]; it invites anarchy." *Olmstead v. U.S.*, 277 U.S. 438, 485 (1928) (Brandeis, J., dissenting).
- "It seems *nigh unto* [read *almost*] superfluous to remind that § 1983 . . . provides a federal civil remedy in federal court for violations, under color of state law, of the rights, privileges and immunities secured by the Constitution and laws of the United States." *Findeisen v. North East Indep. Sch. Dist.*, 749 F.2d 234, 236–37 (5th Cir. 1984).
- "[Grantor] does by these presents remise, release, and forever quit claim *unto* [read *to*] the Fuemmelers the following described lots, tracts, or parcels of land." *Wills v. Whitlock*, 139 S.W.3d 643, 649 (Mo. Ct. App. 2004) (quoting a contract).
- "To have and to hold the same *unto* [read *to*] the said Grantee, his heirs and assigns, forever." *Garza v. Prolithic Energy Co., LP*, 195 S.W.3d 137, 140 (Tex. App.—San Antonio 2006) (quoting a lease).

Margaret M. Bryant prematurely pronounced this usage obsolete in 1930, stating: "Ordinarily [in general English contexts] *unto* denotes 'until.' If Mr. Brown says, 'Unto this day, John has not taken a drink,' he means *until* this day. Its obsolete meaning is *to.* Many illustrations of this meaning are found in the Bible, such as 'Give *unto* the Lord,' signifying 'to the Lord.'" Margaret M. Bryant, *English in the Law Courts* 180 (1930).

untrod; *untrodden. See **trodden.**

untrue allegation. See **facts.**

untrue facts. See **facts** & **true facts.**

untruth. See **lie,** n.

untruthful. See **dishonest.**

*****untypical.** See **atypical.**

unusual. See **unique (B).**

unwed. See **wed (A).**

unwieldy, an adjective meaning "difficult to handle," often seems to be mistaken for an adverb in *-ly.* E.g.: "The FERC offered the carrot of blanket transportation certification . . . without the encumbrance of an *unwieldly* [read *unwieldy*] individual certification process." *Consolidated Edison Co. v. FERC,* 823 F.2d 630, 640 (D.C. Cir. 1987).

unwigged. See **wigged.**

unwisdom (= lack or absence of wisdom; ignorance; folly; stupidity) was common through the Middle Ages, fell into disuse in the 17th century, but was revived in the 19th century, much to the delight of common-law judges, who enjoy writing about it. E.g.:

- "Error or *unwisdom* is not equivalent to abuse." *Uniontown Area Sch. Dist. v. Pennsylvania Human Rels. Comm'n,* 313 A.2d 156, 172 (Pa. 1973).
- "I would join the Court's judgment, despite its *unwisdom.*" *John R. Sand & Gravel Co. v. U.S.,* 552 U.S. 130, 142 (2008) (Stevens, J., dissenting).

unwritten law is something of a misnomer. Though the phrase suggests that it relates to laws that are handed down orally from generation to generation, never being committed to paper, in fact it refers to the part of the law that has never been enacted in the form of a statute or ordinance. Of course, this law is "written," in the sense that it appears in thousands of judicial decisions, but it has not been the subject of legislation. See **caselaw** & *jus scriptum.*

upbraid. See **reprove.**

upholden. See **holden.**

upon is a FORMAL WORD that is usually unnecessary in place of *on,* especially when it seems habitual—e.g.: "The relief sought *upon* [read *on*] the second branch is *upon* [read *on*] a footing entirely apart from that prayed *upon* [read *for*] the first." *E. Edelmann & Co. v. Triple-A Specialty Co.,* 88 F.2d 852, 854 (7th Cir. 1937). As a general matter, then, it is better to write *service on a defendant* than to write *service upon a defendant.*

But *upon* is quite justifiable when it introduces a condition or event—e.g.:

- "*Upon* a proper showing, a permanent or temporary injunction, decree, or restraining order shall be granted without bond." *Brown v. Hecht Co.,* 137 F.2d 689, 694 (D.C. Cir. 1943).
- "*Upon* consideration of plaintiffs' motion for depositions regarding destruction of government computer property, plaintiffs' motion is denied." *Alexander v. FBI,* 541 F.Supp.2d 273, 273 (D.D.C. 2008).

The sense "with little or no interval after" is often an important nuance. E.g.: "The circuit court having jurisdiction over the district shall have power to remove directors or any of them for good cause shown *upon* a petition, notice and hearing." *Inter City Fire Prot. Dist. v. DePung,* 283 S.W.3d 277, 278 (Mo. Ct. App. 2009).

Upon is inferior, however, when a shorter, simpler, and more direct word will suffice.

A. For *on.* E.g.:

- "Defendant's abstract record fails to set forth so much of the record as is necessary for a full understanding of all *of* [delete *of*] the questions presented to this court for decision *upon* [read *on*] this appeal." Frederick S. Knight, *The Insurance Law Journal* 876 (1937). (For more on why to delete *of* after *all,* see **all (A).**)
- "The decisions do not place any limitations *upon* [read *on*] the potentially reliable means of reconstituting a plea record." *Commonwealth v. Diaz,* 914 N.E.2d 129, 133 n.6 (Mass. App. Ct. 2009).

See **on.**

B. For *to.* "The nature of the threats was important irrespective of the effect of the threats *upon* [read *on*] the victim." Donna C. Kline, *Dominion & Health* 122 (1987).

C. For *in.* This is a legalistic ARCHAISM—e.g.: "The giving of testimony and the attendance *upon* [read *in*] court . . . in order to testify are public duties *which* [read *that*] every person within the jurisdiction of the Government is bound to perform." *Blair v. U.S.,* 250 U.S. 273, 281 (1919) (per Pitney, J.). (For more on why *that* is the better choice for restrictive clauses, see **that & which.**)

upon a case stated. See **case stated.**

upon behalf of. See **behalf.**

upon the trial. See **at trial.**

upper court. See **higher court.**

upper house. The meaning depends on the country referred to. Rarely is this phrase used in reference to the U.S. Senate. It is the customary term for Great Britain's House of Lords, Germany's Bundesrat, and India's Rajya Sabha, as well as the upper chambers in the parliaments of Barbados, Japan, Nepal, and Poland, to name a few.

upset (= to set aside; overturn) is legal JARGON. E.g.:

- "Any *mala fides* must be proved very clearly in order to *upset* the title." 1 Ernest W. Chance, *Principles of Mercantile Law* 98 (Percy W. French ed., 13th ed. 1950).
- "The Appeal Court declined to *upset* the judgment of the lower court." Nigel Miller, *"Garden Leave" Enforceable Only in Cases of Real Risk to Employers,* Fin. Times, 22 Feb. 1990, at 18.
- "The Airport filed no cross-petition for certiorari seeking to *upset* the judgment." *N.W. Airlines v. County of Kent,* 510 U.S. 355, 364 (1994) (per Ginsburg, J.).
- "The Court concluded that [the prayed-for relief] would *upset* the policy of the Bankruptcy Code." *Archer v. Warner,* 538 U.S. 314, 324 (2003) (Thomas, J., dissenting).

- "The District Court did not abuse its discretion in denying the Plaintiffs' motion for reconsideration, and we therefore will not *upset* that ruling." *Howard Hess Dental Labs v. Dentsply Int'l*, 602 F.3d 237, 252 (3d Cir. 2010) (per Fisher, J.).

up-to-date should be hyphenated as an adjective, unhyphenated as an adverb <once the log is brought up to date, we will have an up-to-date log>.

up to now is a comfortably idiomatic equivalent of *heretofore* and *hitherto*—e.g.: "It is unquestionably true that *up to now Erie* and the cases following it have not succeeded in articulating a workable doctrine governing choice of law in diversity actions." *Hanna v. Plumer*, 380 U.S. 460, 474 (1965) (Harlan, J., concurring).

up until. See **until.**

urge (in law) = (1) to argue in favor of; or (2) to argue. Sense 1—e.g.:

- "Appellant *urges* this court to follow the reasoning found in *State v. Pierce*." *State v. Collins*, 150 S.W.3d 340, 348 (Mo. Ct. App. 2004).
- "The state *urges* affirmance of the District Court." *Buhmann v. State*, 201 P.3d 70, 82 (Mont. 2008). (See **affirmance.**)

When *urge* in sense 2 precedes a clause, it should be followed by *that*—e.g.:

- "Appellant *urges that* the district court erred in granting a new trial." *Jennings v. Jones*, 587 F.3d 430, 436 (1st Cir. 2009).
- "Appellant *urges there is* [read *urges that there is*] a lack of substantial evidence to support the administrative findings and conclusions." *D.C. Fire & Med. Servs. Dep't v. D.C. Office of Employee Appeals*, 986 A.2d 419, 424 (D.C. 2010).

Sometimes, though, sense 2 is followed by a simple phrase: "Since the causes of action, as well as the facts and legal theories necessary to *urge* such causes of action, are very different in the two suits, a judgment on the merits in either one will not bar proceedings in the other."

usable. So spelled; **useable* is incorrect.

usage, in law, usually means "a customary practice." E.g.:

- "Informed by the *usage* of trade, *usage* of the parties, and the course of performance of the parties, the Court concluded that the asbestosis exclusion 'len[t] itself to only one interpretation.'" *AstenJohnson, Inc. v. Columbia Cas. Co.*, 562 F.3d 213, 220 (3d Cir. 2009).
- "Evidence as to such custom and *usage* is to be considered by the court where necessary to understand the context in which the parties have used terms that are specialized." *Law Debenture Trust Co. v. Maverick Tube Corp.*, 595 F.3d 458, 466 (2d Cir. 2010).

See **use.**

Usage also means "an idiom or form of speech," or forms of speech in general. E.g.:

- "Textualists readily employ certain extratextual interpretive aids such as canons of statutory construction and references to the *usage* of given terms throughout the U.S.

Code." Curtis J. Mahoney, *Treaties as Contracts*, 116 Yale L.J. 824, 844–45 (2007).
- "When Senator Strong reintroduced his amendment in the new Congress, he added three words that by *usage* and tradition transformed his proposal into an explanatory amendment." Bradford R. Clark, *The Eleventh Amendment and the Nature of the Union*, 123 Harv. L. Rev. 1817, 1897 (2010).

Here the *use* [not *usage*] of the word is poor: "But *bad language usage* [read *the bad use of language* or *bad usage*] can hurt good law; *good language usage* [read *the good use of language* or *good usage*] can promote respect for good law." Ronald L. Goldfarb, *Recent Books*, 63 Mich. L. Rev. 180, 182 (1964) (reviewing *The Language of the Law*). Where *use* is possible, it should be used.

Usage for *use*, however, is not an uncommon error—e.g.:

- "Unless their impact on land *usage* [read *use*] denies the owner the 'justice and fairness' guaranteed by the constitution, they should be upheld." *Schafer v. City of New Orleans*, 743 F.2d 1086, 1089–90 (5th Cir. 1984).
- "Though States and local governments have broad power to adopt regulations limiting land *usage* [read *use*], those powers are constrained by the Constitution and by other provisions of state law." *Palazzolo v. Rhode Island*, 533 U.S. 606, 638 (2001) (Stevens, J., concurring in part & dissenting in part).

The opposite error—*use* for *usage*—is quite uncommon but does occur: "This *Concise Dictionary* is primarily a manual for people who aspire to write a clear and forceful American in accord with current good *use* [read *usage*]." Robert C. Whitford & James R. Foster, *Concise Dictionary of American Grammar and Usage* v (1955). Given the title of the book, this sentence also illustrates INELEGANT VARIATION.

usance is unjustified in all senses but one: in mercantile law, the term refers to the customary time (varying in different countries) allowed for the payment of a bill of exchange or the like, esp. one drawn in a foreign country.

U.S. Court of Appeals. See **United States Court of Appeals.**

use, n. In phrases such as *Statute of Uses* and *cestui que use*, the word *use* means "benefit" and not "employment," as in everyday language—e.g.: "An *use* is the right in equity to have the profit or benefit of lands or tenements." 2 Edward Hilliard, *Touchstone of Common Assurances* 501 (7th ed. 1821) (note the archaic use of *an*). The etymology is completely separate from the ordinary word *use*, as F.W. Maitland explained: "It seems that at a very early period the French *oes*, *ues*, from the Latin *opus*, was confused in English with the French *us* from the Latin *usus*, and the *use* of our law is traceable directly to the former rather than to the latter." Note, 3 Law Q. Rev. 115, 116 (1887). E.g.: "The will, therefore, creates a *use*, or, in more modern phraseology, a 'dry,' 'passive,' or 'naked' trust, and as such it is executed by force of the statute of uses."

Bellows v. Page, 188 A. 12, 13 (N.H. 1936). See **trust** & **springing use.**

use; utilization. *Use* is the general all-purpose noun and verb, ordinarily to be preferred over *utilize* and *utilization*. *Utilize* is both more abstract and more favorable connotatively than *use*. See **utilize.**

Where the connotative nuance of using something to its best advantage is missing, *utilization* should not appear. Here it is defensible: "The preceding argument focuses on static efficiency, that is, the efficient *utilization* of information that has already been produced." Gregory M. Silverman, *Rise of the Machines*, 79 Wash. L. Rev. 175, 214 (2004). Here it is not defensible: "Plaintiff's prompt *utilization* [read *use*] of the charge embraced in the criminal prosecution as the basis for a civil action was likewise voluntary." *Fusario v. Cavallaro*, 142 A. 391, 392 (Conn. 1928).

*****useable.** See **usable.**

*****used to could** is a semiliterate "double modal" for *used to be able to* or *could formerly*—e.g.: "Juries *used to could not* [read *used to not be able to* or *formerly could not*] consider parole." *Onumonu v. State*, 787 S.W.2d 958, 960 (Tex. Crim. App. 1990) (en banc) (quoting a prosecutor's argument).

user (= continued use, exercise, or enjoyment of a right) almost always creates a MISCUE in the minds of most modern readers, who are likely to read *user* as an agent noun. E.g.:

- "The fullest enjoyment of land ownership demands the restraint of full freedom by forbidding unreasonable *user* interfering unreasonably with like rights of enjoyment of others." William F. Walsh, *A Treatise on Equity* 222 (1930).
- "Apart from express or implied grant, easements may arise by prescription, that is, by continual *user* over a period of at least 20 years." Peter Butt, *Land Law* 319 (2d ed. 1988).

See -ER (B).

usual construction; usual interpretation. See *tortured interpretation* under INTERPRETATION, MODES OF (B).

usual place of abode. See **dwelling-house.**

usucaption; usucapion. Though neither can be said to be common, *usucaption* (= [in civil law] the prescriptive acquisition of ownership) is the more frequent form in American decisions. Academic writers tend to use either *usucapion* or the Latin form *usucapio*.

usufruct [L. *ususfructus*, Fr. *usufruit*], a civil-law term comparable to the common-law *life estate*, means "the lifelong right of possession, use, or enjoyment of another's property, as far as may be had without causing damage or prejudice to the owner." A common-law will might leave A a life estate with the remainder to B; a civilian will would ordinarily leave the property to B subject to a *usufruct* to A for life. E.g.: "In 1961

Samuel Zemurray bequeathed the naked ownership of his one-half interest [in the land] to the plaintiff and bequeathed to his wife Sarah the *usufruct*." *Zemurray Found. v. U.S.*, 755 F.2d 404, 406 (5th Cir. 1985).

Because *usufruct* is a count noun, one refers to *a usufruct*, *the usufruct*, *this usufruct*, and so on. The word is pronounced /**yoo**-zoo-frəkt/. See **life estate.**

usufructuary, n. & adj., = (adj.) of, relating to, or of the nature of a usufruct; (n.) one having the usufruct of property. E.g.: "The *Williams* decision need not have been dispositive had the Tribe provided sufficient evidence to raise a genuine issue of material fact as to the nature of the Tribe's *usufructuary* rights, i.e., hunting, fishing, and gathering rights." *Ottawa Tribe v. Logan*, 577 F.3d 634, 640–41 (6th Cir. 2009). The word is pronounced /yoo-zoo-**frək**-shoo-air-ee/.

usurious /yoo-**zhuur**-ee-əs/ = of, relating to, or constituting excessive interest. E.g.: "The finance company's motion for summary judgment might be defeated if the borrower had a lawyer who could show that the hidden charges, when cumulated, resulted in *usurious* charges." William O. Douglas, *Points of Rebellion* 61 (1970). See **usury.**

usurp. See **arrogate** (A).

usurpation; *usurpature. The second is a NEEDLESS VARIANT.

usury /**yoo**-zə-ree/ is a word whose content has changed considerably over time. Originally, *usury* meant "compensation for the use of money; the lending of money for interest." By the 18th century, however, its meaning had been narrowed considerably to what it is today: "the lending of money at an excessive interest rate." The corresponding adjective is *usurious*.

As for the pronunciation of *usury* and *usurious*, the first syllable of these words is pronounced "you." Because the words begin with a consonant sound, -*y*-, they should be preceded by *a* and not *an* where an indefinite article is called for: "In its counterclaim, North Texas contended that Miller's prayer for interest amounted to *an usurious* [read *a usurious*] charge of interest in violation of [the statute]." *North Texas Fin. Group v. Carl G. Miller Corp.*, 662 S.W.2d 388, 389 (Tex. App.—Dallas 1983). See **a** (A) & **usurious.**

uterine. See **consanguineous.**

utilization. See **use.**

utilize = to apply profitably; put to good use. It is not an exact synonym of *use*. Cf. **use.**

ut infra = as below. See *ante*.

ut supra = as above. See *ante* & *supra*.

utter is a LEGALISM used in reference to written instruments to mean "to put or send (a document) into circulation." Hence, to *utter* a forged instrument is to present it to another with knowledge that it is a forgery. E.g.: "The State charged Ginn with two counts of forgery, two counts of *uttering* a forged document, and two counts of grand theft." *Ginn v. State*, 26 So.3d 706, 707 (Fla. Dist. Ct. App. 2010).

utter bar. See **outer bar.**

ux., an abbreviation of *uxor* (= wife), was once commonly used in the phrase *et ux.* to indicate that a wife is joined with her husband in a legal action. Today the wife is usually accorded the dignity of being named, or at least she should be. If her name does appear, there is certainly no reason for *et ux.*, as some real-estate brokers seem mistakenly to believe. See SEXISM (D).

In writing *ux.*, one should include the period to show that the word is an abbreviation (for *uxor*).

uxorial; uxorious. The first is neutral, the second pejorative. *Uxorial* = of or relating to a wife; *uxorious* = submissive to or excessively fond of one's wife.

V

v.; vs. A. Form of Abbreviation. Both are acceptable abbreviations of *versus*, but they differ in application: in case names, *v.* is the accepted abbreviation, while *vs.* is more common among nonlawyers.

B. Pronunciation. In pronouncing case names, one should be careful to say *versus* or *against* in AmE, not "vee." For some reason, people generally (not just lawyers) tend to say "Roe vee Wade," though few would say "Brown vee Board of Education." Perhaps "Roe vee Wade" became popular because the name consists of three one-syllable words.

In BrE, the abbreviation *v.* is pronounced "and" in the names of civil cases; in other words, British lawyers write one thing but say something else. See **versus**.

C. Whether to Italicize. In American legal writing, it was formerly common to leave the *v.* in a case citation unitalicized <in *Hughes* v. *Rhodes*, the court declared . . . .>. Today, however, the prevailing practice is to italicize the full case name, including *v.* <in *Hughes v. Rhodes*, the court declared . . . .>. British legal writing has followed a similar evolution, though the unitalicized *v.* remains perhaps more common than in the U.S.

vacant; unoccupied. These words are often used in the context of insurance policies on buildings. They are not synonymous: *vacant* means without inanimate objects, while *unoccupied* means without human occupants.

vacate. See JUDGMENTS, APPELLATE-COURT, **overrule** & **set aside.**

vacation, n., in law may mean: (1) the period during which court is not in term; or (2) the act of vacating. Either sense is likely to amount to a MISCUE for the nonlawyer—e.g.:

- (Sense 1) "The court announced that it was taking the cause under advisement and that a decision and decree would be made in *vacation.*" *Sperier v. Ward*, 233 So.2d 823, 825 (Miss. 1970).
- (Sense 2) "Congress made [a] specific provision, by an independent proceeding, for the *vacation* of a warrant wrongfully issued and for return of the property." *Cogen v. U.S.*, 278 U.S. 221, 226 (1929) (per Brandeis, J.).

Justice Lewis F. Powell once complained of the popular misconception that justices enjoy a three- to four-month vacation (sense 1) each year. *See* Powell, *Myths and Misconceptions About the Supreme Court*, 61 A.B.A. J. 1344, 1344 (1975).

vagueness = (1) uncertain breadth of meaning; or (2) loosely, ambiguity. See **ambiguity** & AMBIGUITY. See also **void for vagueness.**

valebat; valebant. See **quantum meruit.**

validate. See **authenticate.**

valuable consideration. See **consideration** (D).

value received. This phrase is customarily inserted in bills of exchange, but it is invariably superfluous, since value is implied.

vara. This word denotes a measure used in some American states that were once under Spanish dominion. In California, the *vara* is equivalent to 33 inches, but in Texas it is 33^1/$_3$ inches.

variable; variant; variational; variative. *Variable* = subject to variation; characterized by variations. *Variant* = differing in form or in details from the one named or considered, differing thus among themselves (*COD*). *Variational* = of, pertaining to, or marked or characterized by variation. *Variative* shares the senses of *variational*, and, being the rarer word, might be considered a NEEDLESS VARIANT; but the courts have found uses for it—e.g.: "This *variative* approach to intrastate branching was nicely illustrated at the time by the structure in New York." *Northeast Bancorp, Inc. v. Federal Res. Sys.*, 472 U.S. 159, 172 (1985) (per Rehnquist, J.).

variance; at variance; variation; variant, n. *Variance* is common in legal writing in two widely divergent senses: (1) a difference or discrepancy between two statements or documents that ought to agree, such as allegations in the pleadings and the proof actually adduced on the record; or (2) a waiver of or exemption from a zoning law.

Sense 1 commonly appears in contexts referring to charging instruments—e.g.: "Wisham asserts that there was a fatal *variance* between what was alleged in the indictment and [the] proof at trial in that the indictment. . . ." *Wisham v. State*, 585 S.E.2d 675, 676 (Ga. Ct. App. 2003).

At variance = (of persons) in a state of discord; (of things) conflicting; in a state of disagreement or difference. E.g.:

- "In *Boxsius v. Goblet Frères*, Lord Esher expressed views quite *at variance* with his utterance in *Pullman v. Hill*." *Flynn v. Western Union Tel. Co.*, 225 N.W. 742, 744 (Wis. 1929).
- "This exact question has not been decided by this court, and the decisions of the courts of other jurisdictions are somewhat *at variance*." *Wilder v. Howard*, 4 S.E.2d 199, 201 (Ga. 1939).
- "Such a result is plainly *at variance* with the policy of the legislation as a whole." *Allen v. U.S.*, 668 F.Supp. 1242, 1254 (W.D. Wis. 1987).

Variation = (1) a departure from a former or normal condition or action or amount, or from a standard or type; or (2) the extent of this departure. The term is standard equipment in discussions of contract law—e.g.:

- "The rule . . . is always applied in cases in which there is a material *variation* between the actual principal contract and what the surety believes it to be." Laurence P. Simpson, *Handbook on the Law of Suretyship* 92 (1950).
- "A *variation* of a contract may amount to a rescission of the old contract followed by the making of a new one relating to the same subject-matter." G.H. Treitel, *The Law of Contract* 96 (8th ed. 1991).

The terms *variance* and *variation* are especially susceptible to INELEGANT VARIATION—e.g.: "The plaintiffs as a matter of law do not have a cause of action for the allegedly arbitrary and discriminatory denial of their request for a zoning *variance* [sense 2]; in any event the denial of a zoning *variation* [read *variance*] is not a deprivation of property." *Shelton v. City of College Station*, 754 F.2d 1251, 1255 (5th Cir. 1985).

Variant = a form or modification differing in some respect from other forms of the same thing (*OED*)—e.g.: "The very paragraph in which the majority announces its conclusion includes two *variants* of 'the rule' of *Apprendi*." *U.S. v. Humphrey*, 287 F.3d 422, 456 (6th Cir. 2002).

variant; variational; variative. See **variable.**

variety. When the phrase *a variety of* means "many," it is quite proper to use the plural form of the verb: "there *are* a *variety* of court-made rules by which particular orders are treated as 'final' and appealable as such." Charles Alan Wright, *The Law of Federal Courts* 740 (5th ed. 1994). See SYNESIS. For the problem raised by the phrase *these variety of*, see *these kind of.

***various different** is a common REDUNDANCY— e.g.: "Pike then recounted that on *various different*

[read *various*] occasions White had, in her presence, 'threatened to kill his wife.'" *White v. State*, 784 S.W.2d 453, 457 (Tex. App.—Tyler 1989). If, as one authority writes, *various different occasions* means "a number of different occasions," then the better wording would be *several different*.

vehement is pronounced /**vee**-ə-mənt/, not /və-**hee**-mənt/.

vehicle. The -*h*- is not pronounced; hence /**vee**-i-kəl/.

vehicular. A. *Vehicular homicide.* *Vehicular* /vee-**hik**-yə-lər/, an adjective dating from about 1900, is not objectionable per se. Several states in the U.S. have *Vehicular Homicide Statutes*, for which there is no ready substitute for *vehicular*. E.g.: "Under Ohio law, both driving while under the influence of intoxicants and negligent *vehicular homicide* are misdemeanors, while reckless *vehicular homicide* is a felony." *Berkemer v. McCarty*, 468 U.S. 420, 430 (1984) (per Marshall, J.). But see (B).

B. *Vehicular accident.* The phrase is pompous LEGALESE and OFFICIALESE for *traffic accident, car accident,* or *motoring accident.*

C. *Vehicular unit.* The phrase is especially absurd for *car*: "The declaration page . . . provided 'separate coverages for uninsured motorist on three *vehicular units.*'" *Nationwide Mut. Ins. Co. v. Garriga*, 636 So.2d 658, 662 (Miss. 1994). If *car* or *automobile* were too specific, then *vehicle* would suffice.

vel non (lit., "or not"), almost always superfluous, is *always* pompous. *W3* defines *vel non* as "whether or not," but that phrase could hardly be plugged into the following sentences:

- "The trademark attribute of descriptiveness *vel non* is determined from the viewpoint of the purchaser." *In re Gyulay*, 820 F.2d 1216, 1217 (Fed. Cir. 1987).
- "In Judge Feikens's opinion . . . he prophetically described the merits, *vel non*, of Static Control's 'meeting of the minds' argument." *Static Control Components, Inc. v. Lexmark Int'l, Inc.*, 615 F.Supp.2d 575, 587 (E.D. Ky. 2009).
- "If the employer meets this burden, the framework falls away and the issue becomes discrimination *vel non*." *Williamson v. American Nat'l Ins. Co.*, 695 F.Supp.2d 431, 447 (S.D. Tex. 2010).

A more accurate definition of the phrase as frequently used in American legal writing is "or the lack of them (or of it)."

Usually the phrase is pretentious surplusage, since it can be either deleted or translated into simpler words—e.g.:

- "The vice in the decree lies in the fact that it enjoins, not specific acts or omissions, but results, evidence of the existence *vel non* [omit] of which must of necessity be determined by the opinion evidence of witnesses." *Seastrunk Rendering Co. v. Hollingsworth*, 177 S.W.2d 1014, 1016–17 (Tex. Civ. App.—Austin 1944).

- "The ultimate issue, that of discrimination *vel non* [omit], is to be treated by district and appellate courts in the same manner as any other issue of fact." *Williams v. Southwestern Bell Tel. Co.*, 718 F.2d 715, 717 (5th Cir. 1983).
- "The argument bears solely on the nature of the violation, not on the existence of a violation *vel non* [omit]." *RSR Corp. v. Brock*, 764 F.2d 355, 362 (5th Cir. 1985).

For the phrase *devisavit vel non*, see **devastavit.**

venal; venial. These words are frequently mistaken. *Venal* has two closely related senses: (1) "purchasable; for sale"; or (2) "highly mercenary; amenable to bribes; corruptible"—e.g.:

- (Sense 1) "Deviating from such standards on the side of generosity and gullibility rather than *venality* does not render one's act in bad faith." *State Sec. Check Cashing, Inc. v. American Gen. Fin. Servs.*, 972 A.2d 882, 891 (Md. 2009).
- (Sense 2) "Respondent's exploitation of his elderly client was more *venal* than that displayed by some attorneys who have been disbarred for knowing misappropriation." *In re Maguire*, 764 A.2d 432, 433 (N.J. 2001).

Venial = slight (used of sins); pardonable; excusable; trivial. E.g.:

- "There will be no assumption of a purpose to visit *venial* faults with oppressive retribution." *Jacob & Youngs, Inc. v. Kent*, 129 N.E. 889, 891 (1921) (per Cardozo, J.).
- "It is a habit . . . of counsel for the defence to make the most of minor uncertainties or discrepancies and to deal with a police officer in cross-examination as if any *venial* sin to which he might admit justified his professional damnation." Patrick Devlin, *The Criminal Prosecution in England* 40 (1960).

vend is now usually commercialese for *sell*, though it has been established since the 17th century.

*vendable. See **salable.**

vendee, an unnecessary LEGALISM for *buyer* or *purchaser*, is most commonly used in real-estate transactions. Some might argue that it is useful in some contexts as a correlative of *vendor*. But using *vendee* and *vendor* invites serious typographical errors, and in any event, simpler words are available—e.g.:

- "A sale contract was then drawn, naming the Millers individually as *vendors* [read *sellers*], and the lessee's sister as *vendee* [read *buyer*]." *Commissioner v. Court Holding Co.*, 324 U.S. 331, 333 (1945) (per Black, J.).
- "The rule of *Flureau v. Thornhill* restricted *vendee's* [read *the buyer's*] damages for seller's breach of a land contract by failure to make good title to what we would call the *vendee's* [read *buyer's*] reliance expenses—searching title and so on." Grant Gilmore, *The Death of Contract* 51–52 (1974).

Cf. ***breachee.** See -EE (A), (C) & **vendor.**

vendible. See **salable.**

vendor. *Seller* is generally a better word, along with the corresponding *buyer* rather than *vendee*. (See **vendee.**) Using the better-known words increases readability and reduces the possibilities of typographical error. Those possibilities sometimes materialize:

drafters have actually had to testify about their mistakenly using *vendor* in place of *vendee*. See *Prahmcoll Props. v. Sanford*, 474 N.W.2d 639, 643 (Minn. Ct. App. 1991).

In specific contexts, however, a DIFFERENTIATION is emerging: in computer contracting, the practice is to use *vendor* rather than *seller* almost exclusively. The term *vendor* is used in two senses: (1) "any member of the entire class of business entities (often the manufacturers or producers) engaged in marketing the particular product that a prospective purchaser may be interested in acquiring"; and (2) "the individual business entity that makes the ultimate sale (including a lease)." In computer contracting, *vending* and *selling* represent two distinct phases of commerce: *vending* emphasizes the process of engaging in marketing or offering a product for sale rather than the sale itself, while *selling* focuses on the final step in the process—the actual sale.

venerable is a CLICHÉ when used inaccurately for *old*—e.g.: "A firmly rooted principle was first established *in the venerable case of* [read, e.g., *more than a century ago in*] *Strawbridge v. Curtiss*." *Field v. Volkswagenwerk AG*, 626 F.2d 293, 296 (3d Cir. 1980). Properly, *venerable* = (of persons) worthy of being venerated, revered, or highly respected and esteemed, on account of character or position; commanding respect by reason of age combined with high personal character and dignity of appearance; (of things) worthy of veneration or deep respect.

vengeful. See **vindictive** (A).

venial. See **venal.**

venire /və-**nɪ**-ree *or* və-**neer**/ was originally an elliptical form of *venire facias* (lit., "that you cause to come"), the name of the writ directing a sheriff to summon a jury to try a case or cases at issue between parties. Today *venire*—never italicized—is used in the sense "a panel of persons selected for jury duty and from which the jurors are to be chosen."

Jury venire is a fairly common REDUNDANCY—e.g.: "The Supreme Court emphasized the limitations *Witherspoon* imposed on the ability of the state to exclude members of a *jury venire* [read *venire*] from service on a petit capital jury." *Bartee v. Quarterman*, 574 F.Supp.2d 624, 663 (W.D. Tex. 2008).

The phrase *venire panel* is likewise a redundancy—e.g.: "Defense counsel then moved to strike the *venire panel* [read *venire*], arguing that the prospective juror poisoned the entire pool." *Orme v. State*, 25 So.3d 536, 545 (Fla. 2009).

venireman; *venireperson; veniremember. Each means "a prospective juror." The best nonsexist form is *veniremember*, not **venireperson*—e.g.:

- "A defense lawyer in a Mississippi capital case contacted thirty-one of the *veniremembers* in connection with a motion for a new trial." *King v. Lynaugh*, 850 F.2d 1055, 1062 (5th Cir. 1988) (Rubin, J., dissenting).

- "A *Batson* prima facie case cannot be established merely by the numbers of black *venirepersons* [read *veniremembers*] stricken by the state." *People v. Peeples*, 616 N.E.2d 294, 363 (Ill. 1993).

Though today common in legal writing, both *venireperson* and *veniremember* are omitted from the standard English-language dictionaries. See SEXISM (B) & **potential juror.**

An additional advantage of *veniremember* over *venireman* is that the latter is a HYBRID. Hence a famous 20th-century linguist referred to "the ugly *venireman*, in use since 1444," noting that "its Latin part goes back to *venire facias.*" Mario Pei, *Words in Sheep's Clothing* 84 (1969). In fact, the *OED* dates *venireman* to 1895, and the hyphenated *venire-man* to 1780. That makes it pretty well established—but its perceived sexism may prove its undoing. See **venire.**

venire panel. See **venire.**

*****venireperson.** See **venireman.**

venter [L. "womb"] (= one or the other of two or more women who are sources of the same man's offspring) is a term nowadays considered objectionable, because it refers to the woman—almost by way of surreal synecdoche—merely as the possessor of a birth canal—e.g.: " 'That, whereas by the law as it now stands, the issue of an ancestor by one *venter* [read *mother*], cannot inherit to the issue of such ancestor by a different *venter* [read *mother*], whereby the real estate of an ancestor in some instances goes out of the family to the great injury of the remaining issue of such ancestor.' " *Ryder v. Myers*, 167 A. 22, 24 (N.J. Ch. 1933) (quoting *Pierson v. De Hart*, 3 N.J.L. 73, 78 (1809)). Cf. **en ventre sa mere.**

venue = (1) originally, the neighborhood from which a jury had to be selected; (2) the county or other territorial unit over which a trial court has jurisdiction; or (3) the proper or a possible place for the trial of a lawsuit. One court has said that the exact etymology of the word is "obscured by a thick doubt," citing these possibilities: it could be derived "from the French as the anglicized spelling of the past participle of *venir*, to come, and thus it means '(those who) come,' or from the modern French substantive, meaning 'a coming,' or . . . from the Latin *vicinitatum*, meaning 'of the neighborhood,' shortened by usage to *visinetum*, and again in law Latin to *visnetum*, whence *visne*, which in early days was used and written interchangeably for *venue.*" *Blair v. U.S.*, 32 F.2d 130, 132 (8th Cir. 1929) (citation omitted). Modern lexicographers have recorded the modern legal sense from 1531 and suggest a different etymology: it derives immediately from the Middle English word *veneu* (= an assault or attack), which in turn derives from the French verb *venir*, the spelling *venue* being the feminine form of the past participle. See **jurisdiction (B).**

venued, adj. An odd usage has cropped up among some American legal writers, who prefer to say that a case *is venued* in a particular locale, rather than that a local court *has venue*. Most readers are likely to consider this newfangled phrasing unidiomatic—e.g.:

- "The FTC concedes that one of the original plaintiffs . . . was properly *venued* in Delaware." *Exxon Corp. v. F.T.C.*, 588 F.2d 895, 898 (3d Cir. 1978). A possible revision: *The FTC concedes that, for one of the original plaintiffs, venue was proper in Delaware.*
- "Where *a case is improperly venued it may* [read *venue is improper, the case may*], on agreement of counsel, be transferred to the county of proper venue." E.B. Gustafson, *Minnesota Tax Appeals* § 2.03, at 13 (1989).

The usage seems to have arisen in Minnesota at the turn of the 20th century: "The appellant made and served a reply *venued* in the county of Ramsey." *Clay County Land Co. v. Alcox*, 92 N.W. 464, 465 (Minn. 1902).

veracity = (1) truthfulness; observance of the truth; or (2) truth; accuracy. Sense 1, denoting a quality that persons have, is the traditionally correct use. Sense 2 began as a SLIPSHOD EXTENSION in the 18th century and still might be so considered. Yet it is not uncommon in modern legal prose—e.g.:

- "Control Data disputes the *veracity* of each point, but the resolution of these factual issues is for another place and another time." *C.E. Servs., Inc. v. Control Data Corp.*, 759 F.2d 1241, 1246 (5th Cir. 1985).
- "Watson's investigator's affidavit regarding the Reno hotel did not call into question the *veracity* of Rivera's affidavit." *U.S. v. Watson*, 919 F.2d 147, 152 (9th Cir. 1990).
- "Shields requested a hearing pursuant to *Franks v. Delaware* in order to test the *veracity* of the search-warrant affidavit." *U.S. v. Shields*, 458 F.3d 269, 275 (3d Cir. 2006).

Veracity is not to be confused with *voracity* (= greediness of consumption, esp. in eating)—e.g.: "Of greater concern than the need to establish the *voracity* [read *veracity*] of one's claim, for many men at least, is the risk facing of criminal prosecution oneself." Lara Stemple, *Male Rape and Human Rights*, 60 Hastings L.J. 605, 631 (2009). See MALAPROPISMS.

*****verbage.** See **verbiage.**

verbal is, unfortunately, "a term often used as meaning oral, parol, or unwritten." 92 C.J.S. at 995 (1955). But careful writers avoid this sloppy usage because strictly speaking, *verbal* means "of or relating to words"— e.g.: "The transposition of the words 'the court' and the addition of the word 'and' at the beginning of the first sentence [of the Rule] are merely *verbal* changes." Fed. R. Civ. P. 60(b) advisory committee's note. The movie producer Samuel Goldwyn's supposedly ironic remark, "A *verbal* contract isn't worth the paper it's written on," was not ironic at all given the proper sense of the word *verbal*, because a written contract *is*

---

verbal. The phrase requires *oral*, which is restricted to what is spoken. For those senses cited in *Corpus Juris Secundum* and quoted at the outset of this entry, *oral* or *unwritten* should be used. See ***verbal contract.**

The error is especially acute when *verbal* is opposed to *written*—e.g.:

- "Any laborer working on shares of crop or for wages in money or other valuable consideration under *a verbal* [read *an oral*] or written contract to labor on farm lands, who shall receive advances . . . and thereafter wilfully . . . fail to perform the reasonable service required of him . . . shall be liable to prosecution for a misdemeanor." *Franklin v. South Carolina*, 218 U.S. 161, 163 (1910) (quoting statutory language).
- "*A verbal* [read *An oral*] submission is not so advantageous as a written submission." 2 Ernest W. Chance, *Principles of Mercantile Law* 291 (Percy W. French ed., 10th ed. 1951).

The misuse of *verbal* for *oral* has a long history and is still common. Yet the distinction is worth fighting for, especially in legal prose. Ironically, though, as one writer observes, lawyers "are among the chief offenders in the *oral-verbal* confusion." Robert C. Cumbow, *The Subverting of the Goeduck*, 14 U. Puget Sound L. Rev. 755, 778 (1991).

Because *verbal* always refers to words, *verbal definition* is redundant, since there can be no definition without words—e.g.: "We do not believe the subjective quality of an ordinary headache falls within the objective *verbal definition* [omit *verbal*] of serious injury as contemplated by the No-Fault Law." *Rivera v. U.S.*, 994 F.Supp. 406, 407 (E.D.N.Y. 1998). Similarly, *verbal* is redundant in such phrases as *verbal promise*, *verbal denial*, *verbal affirmation*, and *verbal criticism*, since these activities usually cannot occur without words.

VERBAL AWARENESS. Lest writers commit unconscious gaffes or create MISCUES—as by referring to a "prophylactic against a wrongful discharge"—they must be aware of all the meanings of a given word. Although one particular meaning may be intended, other potential meanings may confuse or seem odd. Careful writers pay attention to what they say and read, so as not to let a sign such as "Ears Pierced While You Wait" pass unnoticed. Nor do they overlook the humor in the church bulletin that reads, "All women wishing to become Young Mothers should visit the pastor in his office." Likewise, legal writers ought not to refer to "*Roe v. Wade* and its progeny"—though several prominent writers have done just that. Illustrations from law are legion—e.g.:

- "At stake was no mere matter of taste; ammonium nitrate when wet cakes and is difficult to spread on fields as fertilizer." *Dalehite v. U.S.*, 346 U.S. 15, 50 (1953) (per Reed, J.) The proximity of *taste* and *cakes*, which may not at first be recognized as a verb, and the immediate proximity of *ammonium nitrate*, which must be torturous to the palate, do not make for pleasant reading. A suggested revision: *At stake was no mere matter of personal preference; for ammonium nitrate, when wet, cakes and becomes difficult to spread on fields.*
- "The language of the press may carry 'All the news that's fit to print'; the language of the law expresses the fit and

the unfit, the *fleeting* and what *passes* for permanent." David Mellinkoff, *The Language of the Law* 33 (1963). In that sentence, *passes* should not be used alongside *permanent*—especially just after *fleeting*—because, in another sense, what passes is impermanent.
- " 'There is almost complete accord among many text writers that at common law commission of the crime [i.e. sodomy] required penetration *per anum* and that penetration *per os* did not constitute the offense.' This is the logical position." Rollin M. Perkins & Ronald N. Boyce, *Criminal Law* 466 (3d ed. 1982) (quoting a case). Once again, which position is more logical?

A heightening of verbal awareness would save writers from odd contradictions: "At the time *work stoppage started* [read *workers walked off the job*], many other refineries had already closed because of strikes." *Local Union No. 222, Oil Workers Int'l Union v. Gordon*, 92 N.E.2d 739, 742 (Ill. 1950). Cf. ETYMOLOGICAL AWARENESS & MISCUES.

And who knows exactly what kind of consciousness-raising a writer needs who entitles an article *Apprehending the Fetus En Ventre Sa Mere: A Study in Judicial Sleight of Hand?* See 53 Sask. L. Rev. 113 (1989).

*****verbal contract** should be *oral contract* or *unwritten contract*—e.g.: "It is a safeguard against inadvertence and innocent mistake—e.g. in *verbal* [read *an oral*] contract or in the release of a debt." Carleton K. Allen, *Law in the Making* 395 (7th ed. 1964). See **verbal.** Cf. **informal contract** & **simple contract.**

verbal meaning theory. See INTERPRETATION, MODES OF (A).

verbals (BrE) = any remarks that an accused person has made in the presence of the police. *Concise Dictionary of Law* 434 (2d ed. 1990). The term appears to be an elliptical form of *verbal statements*, itself incorrect for *oral statements*. But *verbals* appears to be ensconced in BrE legal JARGON—e.g.: " 'Verbals'—the oral comments made by defendants once arrested, or rather the comments policemen say they made—are often vital pieces of the prosecution's case. So if his client denies having made them—and imaginative policemen are no more unusual than bent lawyers—a barrister has to pitch in to the police witness." *Yes You Did, No I Didn't*, Economist, 29 Mar. 1972, at 27. See **verbal.**

verbatim; ipsissima verba; literatim. These nearsynonyms carry slight nuances. *Verbatim* = word for word. *Literatim* = letter for letter. Sometimes the phrase *verbatim et literatim* is seen. *Ipsissima verba* (lit., "the selfsame words") = the very words used by someone quoted—e.g.: "When such a circumstance prevails, the transcripts are, *ipsissima verba*, 'testimonial' and can be nothing less." *U.S. v. W.R. Grace*, 455 F.Supp.2d 1199, 1201 (D. Mont. 2006). See *in haec verba* & *ipsissima verba*.

verbiage was formerly unerringly pejorative. It referred to prolix language and redundancies. More recently, it has come to signify, especially to American lawyers, "wording, diction," in a neutral sense. Perhaps it is neutral because lawyers have become inured to their prolixities and inelegancies: "Mr. Smithson was preparing the *verbiage* for the agreement." Strictly, the word should maintain the negative connotations it has always had; *verbiage* describes a vice of language. In the sentence just quoted, the writer might have eliminated some clutter by writing, "Mr. Smithson was preparing the agreement." A somewhat different error is illustrated in this specimen: "It is well settled that the exact *verbiage* [read *wording*] of the statute need not be alleged in an indictment when there is no material difference between the language of the statute and the allegations employed." *Colon v. State*, 680 S.W.2d 31, 33 (Tex. App.—Austin 1984).

*Verbage for *verbiage* is a common error spawned perhaps by the analogy of *herbage*—e.g.: "Parker also forgoes equivocation and cuts through the *verbage* [read *verbiage*]." William Rice, *Clawing Their Way to the Top*, Chicago Trib., 16 Oct. 1986, at 14C.

VERBOSITY. Samuel Johnson once said, "It is unjust, sir, to censure lawyers for multiplying words when they argue; it is often necessary for them to multiply words" (quoted in *Boswell's Life of Johnson* (1781)). Perhaps so. But lawyers must at least attempt to distinguish between those occasions when it is necessary and those when it is not. For verbosity is always an enemy of clarity.

As a result, verbosity is virtually never appropriate (much less necessary) in statutes. Yet it is especially common in LEGISLATIVE DRAFTING. The following statute says nothing more than that the industrial commission is to lay down rules to ensure safety in the handling of liquefied petroleum gases:

> The industrial commission shall ascertain, fix, and order such reasonable standards, rules, or regulations for the design, construction, location, installation, operation, repair, and maintenance of equipment for storage, handling, use, and transportation by tank truck or tank trailer, of liquefied petroleum gases for fuel purposes, and for the odorization of said gases used therewith, as shall render such equipment safe.
>
> Wis. Stat. § 101.105(2) (1963).

Certain BURIED VERBS and other verbose phrases recur in statutes—among the most common are these:

Verbose Expression	Kernel Expression
at the time of her death	when she dies (or died)
give consideration	to consider
give recognition	to recognize
have knowledge of	know
have need of	need
make application	to apply
make payment	pay
make provision for	provide for

Judicial writing is also a sanctuary for verbosity. Following are some typical specimens, with recommended ways of eliminating the clutter:

- "The fact that he had other contracts *in process of performance* [read *in effect* or *under way*] would not relieve defendants of damages resulting from their breach of their contract with plaintiff." *Purvis & Bertram v. Shaw*, 164 S.W.2d 416, 419 (Tex. Civ. App.—Fort Worth 1942).
- "A venture to constitute a joint adventure must be for *profit in a financial or commercial sense* [read *financial profit*]." *Edlebeck v. Hooten*, 121 N.W.2d 240, 244 (Wis. 1963).
- "With the benefit of *hindsight and its unerring superb visual acuity*, one might suggest that the trial strategy chosen by Austin's appointed counsel left much to be desired." *Austin v. McCotter*, 764 F.2d 1142, 1144 (5th Cir. 1985). (Omit that desultory amplification of hindsight, the qualities of which people know well enough.)
- "Upon *the filing of a petition* [read *filing the petition*] to terminate parental rights, a summons regarding the proceeding must be issued to the juvenile." *In re J.A.P.*, 659 S.E.2d 14, 17 (N.C. Ct. App. 2008).

Those are merely sentence-level examples of verbosity. When these sentences are aggregated, and the writings in which they appear are aggregated, OBSCURITY proliferates. As Edgar Allan Poe is reputed to have said: "In one case out of a hundred a point is excessively discussed because it is obscure; in the ninety-nine remaining it is obscure because excessively discussed." Edgar Allan Poe, "The Rationale of Verse," in 2 *The Works of the Late Edgar Allan Poe* 215, 216 (1857). See SUPERFLUITIES & FLOTSAM PHRASES. See also BE-VERBS (B), REDUNDANCY, DOUBLETS, TRIPLETS, AND SYNONYM-STRINGS & SYNONYMY.

VERB PHRASES. A. Incomplete. See ZEUGMA AND SYLLEPSIS.

B. Split. See ADVERBS (A).

C. Phrasal Verbs. See PHRASAL VERBS.

verdict. A. Etymology. *Voir dire* is etymologically equivalent to *verdict*, having passed into English through French. *Verdict* came through Anglo-Norman (*verdit*) but was refashioned after the medieval Latin *vere dictum* or *verdictum*, itself based on the French *verdit*. See **voir dire.**

B. Who Hands Down. Juries, not judges, *hand down* verdicts (both civil and criminal). Strictly, verdicts are *returned by* juries, although we have the lay colloquialisms *to pass a verdict on* and *to give a verdict on*. Cf. **sentence.**

C. *Verdict* for *vote*. The jury collectively renders a *verdict*; individual jurors tender *votes*, not *verdicts*—e.g.: "It must be demonstrated that the relationship would influence the juror's *verdict* [read *vote*]." *State v. Allen*, 682 So.2d 713, 725 (La. 1996).

D. *Verdict* for *judgment*. In journalistic references to appellate-court judgments, this error is frequent—e.g.:

- "A judge may swing his *verdict* [read *judgment*] to one party or the other because of a merely technical superiority in the argument of counsel for one side." Edward Stevens Robinson, *Law and the Lawyer* 240 (1935).

An asterisk (✳) precedes words and phrases that are invariably inferior forms.

- "I talked to John Baker a few months after the Supreme Court *verdict* [read *judgment*]." Murray T. Bloom, *The Trouble with Lawyers* 230 (1970) (referring to Wisconsin's highest appellate court).
- "At the time the Court of Appeal handed down its *verdict* [read *judgment*] on the Birmingham public house bombers in January[,] the Lord Chief Justice made it clear that the court would not welcome further referrals of such cases." *Final Decision*, Daily Telegraph, 19 Nov. 1988, at 12.
- "Associate Justice Sandra Day O'Connor jerked forward in her black leather chair, visibly astonished. . . . The *verdict* [read *decision*] is expected next year." Keith C. Epstein, *Ohio Free Speech Case Shocks Supreme Court*, Plain Dealer (Cleveland), 13 Oct. 1994, at 3A.

The mistake occurs also in reference to taking appeals. One appeals from a *judgment*, not a *verdict*—e.g.:

- "A *verdict* [read *judgment*] for defendant was reversed by the Supreme Court and re-trial ordered." Asher L. Cornelius, *The Cross-Examination of Witnesses* 116 (1929).
- "At a press conference, Mr. Lozano, 31, a Miami policeman for five years, said he would appeal the *verdict* [read *judgment*], and 'keep fighting for my job.'" José de Cordoba & Wade Lambert, *Miami Policeman Is Found Guilty in Deaths of Black Biker, Passenger*, Wall St. J., 8 Dec. 1989, at B5.

See JUDGMENTS, APPELLATE-COURT.

veredicto. See **judgment** *non obstante veredicto*.

verification. See **acknowledgment (B)**.

*verificational (= of or relating to a verification) is, in almost every conceivable context, a NEEDLESS VARIANT of *verified*—e.g.:

- "A *verificational* [read *verified*] letter dated January 14, 1977, signed by the plaintiff . . . ." *Good v. Paine Furniture Co.*, 391 A.2d 741, 743 (Conn. Super. Ct. 1978).
- "Any alleged problem raised by the lack of a jurat was cured by Mundinger's having filed his *verificational* [read *verified*] affidavits with jurats." *Lincoln Nat'l Bank v. Mundinger*, 528 N.E.2d 829, 836 (Ind. Ct. App. 1988).

verify = (1) to confirm by swearing <to verify her accounts by affidavit>; (2) to swear to (a statement) <he duly verified his affidavit at the end>; or (3) to check the accuracy of <to verify all the citations>. See **authenticate.**

verily (= in truth) is an affected ARCHAISM in modern contexts. It appears in old-style affidavits.

One usage critic, Margaret Nicholson, says that *I verily believe* means "it is almost incredible, yet facts surprise me into the belief." The phrase has never been used that way in American law, where the phrase is merely pretentious for *I believe*—e.g.: "*I verily believe* that Mr. White communicated these facts to the Richland County Attorneys [*sic*] office." *State v. Copeland*, 448 N.W.2d 611, 615 n.4 (N.D. 1989) (quoting an affidavit).

veritable. See **authentic.**

versus for *opposed to* is quite acceptable—e.g.: "Without delving deeply into the appropriate standards for long- *versus* short-form disclosure, my sense is that the liability structure should be tied to the regulatory judgment about how necessary special disclosure is for investor protection." Donald C. Langevoort, *Deconstructing Section 11*, 63 Law & Contemp. Probs. 45, 68 (Summer 2000). This word need not be italicized as a foreign word. See **v.**

vertical restraints. See **horizontal restraints.**

very. A. As a Weasel Word. This intensifier, which functions as both an adjective and an adverb, surfaces repeatedly in flabby writing. In almost every context in which it appears, its omission would result in at most a negligible loss; in many contexts the idea would be more powerfully expressed without it—e.g.: "We are *very* reluctant to substitute our views on damages for those of the jury." *Gutierrez v. Exxon Corp.*, 764 F.2d 399, 403 (5th Cir. 1985). Here the word *very* weakens the adjective that follows; a simple statement would be more forceful: "We are reluctant to substitute our views . . . ." See **clearly, obviously** & WEASEL WORDS.

B. *Very disappointed*, **etc.** *Very* modifies adjectives (*sorry, sick*, etc.), and not, properly, past participles (*disappointed, uninterested*, etc.). Follett wrote that "finer ears are offended by past participles modified by *very* without the intervention of the quantitative *much*, which respects the verbal sense of an action undergone. Such writers require *very much disappointed*, *very much pleased, very much engrossed, very well satisfied*, etc. Only a few adjectives from verbs—*tired, drunk*, and possibly *depressed*—have shed enough of their verbal quality to stand an immediately preceding *very*." Wilson Follett, *Modern American Usage* 343 (1966). *Very interested* is another acceptable idiom, although *very much interested* seems preferable in formal contexts. When a past participle has become thoroughly established as an adjective (e.g., *drunk*), it takes *very* rather than *very much*.

C. Displaced by *so*. See **so (C).**
D. Displaced by *that*. See **that (F).**
E. Replaced by *too* in Negative Constructions. See **too (B).**

vest, vb., is used in a number of legal and lay idioms, particularly *to vest in* and *to vest with*. The primary senses are these: (1) "to confer ownership of (property) upon a person"; (2) "to invest (a person) with the full title to property"; and (3) "to give (a person) an immediate, fixed right of present or future enjoyment." In all three senses, "the term has reference to the absence of a condition precedent to the future interest becoming possessory, other than the termination of the preceding estate or estates created by the same conveyance." Cornelius J. Moynihan, *Introduction to the Law of Real Property* 121 n.5 (2d ed. 1988).

At common law, in the ceremony known as investiture, the lord handed the vassal some object representing the land: "The vassal was thus *vested with* the fief and the fief was *vested in* him: from these terms developed the modern meanings of *to vest* as, first, to place or secure something in the possession of a person; secondly, to place or establish a person in possession or occupation of some thing; and, thirdly, to pass into possession—the senses, in other words, which are represented in the current idioms *vest in* or *be vested in* and *vest with* or *be vested with*." J.E.S. Simon, *English Idioms from the Law* (pt. 3), 78 Law Q. Rev. 245, 249 (1962). See **invest.**

vested. A. And *contingent*. These terms are ordinarily opposed in reference to future interests. A *vested* interest is an estate that is invariably fixed in a determinate person, who will take upon the termination of a prior estate. A *contingent* interest, by contrast, involves uncertainty: there is some condition precedent to its taking effect in possession other than the mere termination of the preceding estate.

The word *vested* is occasionally, however, used in quite a different sense: in this sense, *vested* "is defined to mean that there is no condition precedent of survival. Or, as it has sometimes been said, the distinction is really whether or not the interest is 'transmissible' on the death of the owner before the time of distribution named in the creating instrument." 1 *American Law of Property* 460–61 (A. James Casner ed., 1952). This is the loose, confusing sense disapproved in the entry entitled **vested interest subject to a contingent remainder.**

B. *Vested interest* as a Popularized Legal Technicality. In the common idiom, any interest is known as a "vested interest." Whether the use is a SLIPSHOD EXTENSION or a useful METAPHOR is usually a matter of degree—e.g.:

- "In the expense and delay the common run of lawyers had, of course, a *vested interest*; simple cheap conveyancing and certainty of titles do not increase the emoluments of attorneys." A.W.B. Simpson, *An Introduction to the History of the Land Law* 253 (1961).
- "The Pacific War is recalled for the public every year with massive media attention on the anniversary of the atomic bombing of Hiroshima, but no group in Japanese society has any *vested interest* in recalling the indignities and hardship of the first decade after surrender." Roger Buckley, *Japan Today* 53 (2d ed. 1990).

In the first sentence quoted, the phrase *vested interest* seems too attenuated from the literal sense; in the second, however, the metaphor seems quite natural and helpful to the passage. See POPULARIZED LEGAL TECHNICALITIES.

vested interest subject to a contingent remainder. This phrase is an ambiguous one referring apparently to a type of contingent remainder that is alienable or transmissible. "The phrase," according to leading commentators in property law, "is awkward and confusing . . . [and] its use is not desirable. If, by the use of the term, it is meant that the remainder in question is

alienable or transmissible, then the remainder should simply be called alienable or transmissible and the reason given for attributing to it those legal characteristics." Lewis M. Simes & Allan F. Smith, *The Law of Future Interests* § 112, at 95 (2d ed. 1956).

vested interest subject to divestment; vested interest liable to be divested. The first is AmE, the second BrE.

vested remainder; contingent remainder. A *vested remainder* is a present estate of freehold in an existing and ascertained person who has the right to immediate possession whenever the preceding estate ends. A *contingent remainder* is not an estate at all; rather, it is a limitation by which an estate will arise when some contingent event occurs and then vest in possession when a preceding estate ends. See **contingent remainder.**

vestigial. So spelled; **vestigal* is a not uncommon misspelling.

via = (1) by way of (a place); passing through <they flew to Amarillo via Dallas>; or (2) by means of; through the agency of <we sent the letter via facsimile transmission>. Sense 2 is considered "certainly acceptable in informal use" by the *Oxford Guide*, though it remains questionable whenever a simple English preposition would suffice. Gowers called it a vulgarism in the revised edition of H.W. Fowler's *Modern English Usage*, and Wilson Follett (*Modern American Usage*) and Theodore Bernstein (*The Careful Writer*) concur.

The following sentences illustrate the objectionable sense, the result of SLIPSHOD EXTENSION:

- "When a party fails to secure a witness's voluntary cooperation by notice or commission procedure, it may seek discovery *via* [read *through*] a letter rogatory." *Pain v. United Techs. Corp.*, 637 F.2d 775, 788 (D.C. Cir. 1980).
- "The FBI agents showed Cherry their badges and gave him his *Miranda* warnings *via* [read *off* or *by reading aloud*] an advice of rights form." *U.S. v. Cherry*, 759 F.2d 1196, 1199 (5th Cir. 1985) (quoting the trial record).
- "The circuit court has jurisdiction over Tamara as the mother of the three children *via* [read *through*] these divorce proceedings." *Quinn v. Mouw-Quinn*, 552 N.W.2d 843, 847 (S.D. 1996).

Here is an acceptable figurative use of sense 1: "At this point there existed two separate suits in federal court, each having arrived *via* removal from state court." *Mohamed v. Exxon Corp.*, 796 S.W.2d 751, 752 (Tex. App.—Houston [14th Dist.] 1990).

viable originally meant "capable of living; fit to live," a sense that still applies in many phrases, such as *a viable fetus*. By acceptable extension it has come to refer figuratively to immaterial things or concepts, as here:

- "We conclude that Powell's claim for back salary remains *viable* even though he has been seated in the 91st Congress and thus find it unnecessary to determine whether

---

the other issues have become moot." *Powell v. McCormack*, 395 U.S. 486, 496 (1969) (per Warren, C.J.).

- "Ancillary jurisdiction presupposes the existence of an action that a federal court can adjudicate and should not be used to breathe life into a lawsuit that is not otherwise viable." 7 Charles Alan Wright & Arthur Miller, *Federal Practice and Procedure: Civil* § 1610, at 99–100 (1972).

The word has lately been the victim of SLIPSHOD EXTENSION, when used in the sense "feasible, practicable" <a viable plan>. This sense is objectionable not alone in being slovenly, but also in its current status as a VOGUE WORD. One writer has noted that "dictionaries now give [as definitions for *viable*] *real*, *workable*, *vivid*, *practicable*, *important*, newer definitions that seem only to confirm the critics' complaints that the word has had the edge hopelessly ground off it." Roy H. Copperud, *American Usage and Style* 405 (1980). So such uses as the following are to be avoided; it is hard even to know what the writer of this sentence meant: "She intended to transport the aliens 'to the nearest *viable* [read *practical*?] Immigration and Naturalization Service office for the purpose of allowing them to file applications for asylum.'" *U.S. v. Merkt*, 764 F.2d 266, 273 (5th Cir. 1985) (quoting a jury instruction).

vicarious liability; vicarious responsibility. Both terms refer to indirect legal responsibility, such as an employer's liability for an employee's acts or a principal's liability for the agent's torts or contracts. *Vicarious liability* is the usual term in both AmE and BrE; *vicarious responsibility* is a primarily BrE variant.

The antonyms to these phrases are *primary liability* and *primary responsibility*. See **responsibility.**

vice versa (= the other way around; just the opposite) should have mirror-image referents, even if only implied—e.g.: "It is unlikely that any of the participants in the debates about constitutional theory are going to have their minds changed by reading a polemic by a person of another sect, any more than Baptist theologians are likely to convert to Catholicism *or vice versa* [read *or Catholic theologians to the Baptist religion*] when presented with a 'refutation' of [their] position." Sanford Levinson, *The Constitution in American Civil Religion*, 1979 Sup. Ct. Rev. 123, 150. (The uncorrected sentence denotes, through *vice versa*, "or Catholicism is likely to convert to Baptist theologians.")

Vice versa does not work here: "A mother may inherit from an illegitimate child whom she has acknowledged and *vice versa*." If we reverse the equation, we get this: "An illegitimate child may inherit from a mother whom she has acknowledged." *Glona v. American Guar. & Liability Ins. Co.*, 391 U.S. 73, 74–75 (1968) (per Douglas, J.). An illegitimate child does not acknowledge her parent.

Nor does *vice versa* work with a verb like *distribute*—e.g.: "The testatrix intended . . . to give [the trustees] a broader and more discretionary power [that] would permit them, to some extent, to distribute as income what would otherwise go as principal and *vice versa*." *American Sec. & Trust Co. v. Frost*, 117 F.2d 283, 287 (D.C. Cir. 1940). The writer did not intend to say, by *vice versa*, that the trustees had the power *to distribute as principal what would otherwise go as income*. The phraseology would work if the verb had been *to treat as*.

vicinity; vicinage. Though *vicinage* (= neighborhood; the relation of neighbors) is the older term in English, dating from the 14th century, it is (in AmE) a legalistic variant of *vicinity*, which dates from 1560. *Vicinity*, however, has far outranged *vicinage* in its usefulness.

The following example shows *vicinage* as a legalistic affectation for *venue*: "Changes of venue or continuances may subject the parties and courts to inconvenience or expense and may even violate the defendant's right to speedy trial in the *vicinage*." *Press-Enterprise Co. v. Superior Ct.*, 691 P.2d 1026, 1032 (Cal. 1984). H.W. Fowler aptly wrote that "*vicinage* is now, compared with *neighborhood*, a FORMAL WORD, and, compared with *vicinity*, a dying one" (*MEU1* 693).

victim allocution. See **allocution** (final ¶).

victimless = (of a legal offense) having or involving no victims. This useful NEOLOGISM dates from the early 1970s, though the idea came earlier. See E.M. Schur, *Crimes Without Victims* (1965).

victor; *victress; *victrix. *Victor* applies to women as well as to men; the other forms are unnecessary. See SEXISM (C).

victory. The phrase *win a victory* is a common but venial REDUNDANCY.

***victress; *victrix.** See **victor.**

victuals, spelled for colloquial uses *vittles*, is pronounced /**vit**-əlz/ with either spelling. It forms *victualer* (= one who provides food and drink for payment), *victualed*, and *victualing* in AmE; these three inflected forms double the *-l-* in BrE. See DOUBLING OF FINAL CONSONANTS.

videlicet. See **viz.**

vi et armis (= by or with force and arms) is a LEGALISM formerly common, but today moribund. It was a necessary part of the allegation, in medieval pleading, that a trespass had been committed with force and therefore was a matter for the King's Court because it involved a breach of the peace. In England, the term survived as a formal requirement of pleading until 1852 (*CDL*). See **trespass** & LOAN TRANSLATIONS.

viewpoint; point of view; standpoint. The first has been stigmatized by a few writers and grammarians who consider it "inferior to *point of view*" (*AHD*). Eric Partridge wrote that the term "has been deprecated by purists; not being a purist, I occasionally use it, although I perceive that it is unnecessary." *Usage and Abusage* 307 (1973). In fact, *viewpoint*, apart from being extremely common, conveniently says in one word what *point of view* says in three. No stigma should attach. E.g.: "So far prosecutions have been considered from the *viewpoint* of the prosecutor." R.M. Jackson, *The Machinery of Justice in England* 145 (5th ed. 1967).

vilify is misspelled **villify* more than 10% of the time in American caselaw, probably through the reference of *villain.*

vindicable is the proper form—not **vindicatable*, which sometimes appears—e.g.: "Only the named plaintiffs have any *vindicatable* [read *vindicable*] rights." *Schultz v. Owens-Illinois, Inc.*, 560 F.2d 849, 855 (7th Cir. 1977).

vindicate = (1) to clear from censure, criticism, suspicion, or doubt, by means of demonstration; or (2) to assert, maintain, make good, by means of action, esp. in one's own interest; to defend against encroachment or interference (*OED*). Sense 1 is the usual lay sense <I've been vindicated>. Sense 2 is the legal sense—e.g.:

- "An arrest is the initial stage of a criminal prosecution. It is intended to *vindicate* society's interest in having its laws obeyed." *Terry v. Ohio*, 392 U.S. 1, 26 (1968) (per Warren, C.J.).
- "A government contractor need not resort to constitutional tort suits against federal officers to *vindicate* his rights when he feels his contract has been unfairly terminated." *Evers v. Astrue*, 536 F.3d 651, 661 (7th Cir. 2008).

See **exculpate.** For more on *vindicate* and its near-synonyms, see **maintain (A).**

vindictive. A. And *vengeful*; **revengeful*. These adjectives all describe someone who is bent on inflicting retribution for some real or imagined wrong. *Vindictive* stresses the intemperate unforgiveness of the agent <she vindictively spray-painted all his suits pink>. *Vengeful* and its NEEDLESS VARIANT **revengeful* stress the serious nature of the retributive act that is contemplated <the vengeful bombs planted by insurgents>.

B. And *vindicatory*; **vindicative*. *Vindicatory* = (1) providing vindication; or (2) punitive; retributive. **Vindicative* is a NEEDLESS VARIANT that, if ever used, would be liable to confusion with *vindictive*, the common word meaning "given to or characterized by revenge or retribution."

vindictive damages. See **punitive damages.**

*violatable is incorrect for *violable*—e.g.: "The courts may then infer the receipt of confidences *violatable* [read *violable*] by the subsequent representation." *Brasseaux v. Girouard*, 214 So.2d 401, 406 (La. Ct. App. 1968).

violate; contravene; abridge; breach; flout. These verbs are common in legal contexts, and in some contexts have virtually the same senses. *Violate* and *flout* commonly take *law* as an object <to flout the law>.

(See **flaunt.**) *Contravene* is also common, but usually refers to something less well defined, such as public policy <the rule contravenes public policy>. *Violate* and *abridge* are often used in reference to constitutional or statutory rights. (See **abridge.**) And *violate* and *breach* are often used of contractual provisions.

violation. See **breach.**

violative. The phrase *to be violative of* is verbose for *to violate*—e.g.: "[A]s this Court has recognized, discrimination may be so unjustifiable as *to be violative of* [read *to violate*] due process." *Bolling v. Sharpe*, 347 U.S. 497, 499 (1954) (per Warren, C.J.). See BE-VERBS (B).

The *OED* records *violative* from 1856 at the earliest, but the word appeared more than half a century before, in *Marbury v. Madison*: "To withhold his commission, therefore, is an act deemed by the court not warranted by law, but *violative* of a vested legal right." 5 U.S. (1 Cranch) 137, 162 (1803) (per Marshall, C.J.).

viperine construction; viperine interpretation; viperous interpretation. See *viperine interpretation* under INTERPRETATION, MODES OF (B).

vires is an unnecessary LATINISM for *power* or *authority*—e.g.: "Right from the beginning he never had *vires* [read *the power*] to deal with the matters other than by reference to the Act." *James Miller & Partners, Ltd. v. Whitworth St. Estates, Ltd.*, [1970] A.C. 583. See **ultra vires** & *intra vires*.

virgule. See PUNCTUATION (N).

virile (lit., "masculine; manly") bears an odd sense in Louisiana civil law, namely, "that can be rightly attributed to or assessed against (a person)." E.g.:

- "If the obligation arises from a contract, the *virile* portions are equal in the absence of agreement to the contrary." *Sampognaro v. Sampognaro*, 952 So.2d 775, 780 (La. Ct. App. 2007).
- "Rowdy is liable for his *virile* share of the partnership debts." *Lang v. Sproull*, 36 So.3d 407, 414 (La. Ct. App. 2010).

virtual; virtually. These are WEASEL WORDS: they weaken what they modify—e.g.: "Rigid trimester analysis . . . [has made] constitutional law in this area a *virtual* Procrustean bed." *Webster v. Reproductive Health Servs.*, 492 U.S. 490, 517 (1989) (per Rehnquist, C.J.).

virtue of, in & by. *By virtue of*, not *in virtue of*, is currently the idiomatic phrase. But *in virtue of* is an ARCHAISM that remains fairly common in legal writing—e.g.:

- "*In virtue of* the State's jurisdiction over the property of the non-resident situated within its limits, [the state courts] can inquire into that non-resident's obligations to its own citizens . . . only to the extent necessary to control the disposition of the property." *Pennoyer v. Neff*, 95 U.S. 714, 723 (1877) (per Field, J.).

- "If CLS sought to exclude a Muslim student *in virtue of* [better: *by virtue of*] the fact that he 'is' Muslim, the dissent suggests, there would be no problem in Hastings forbidding that. But if CLS sought to exclude the same student *in virtue of* the fact that he subscribes to the Muslim faith, Hastings must stand idly by." *Christian Legal Soc. v. Martinez*, 130 S.Ct. 2971, 2996 n.1 (2010) (Stevens, J., concurring).

visa; green card. A *visa* is a government-issued document that allows an alien to seek entry into the U.S. for a certain purpose and for a specified period but does not guarantee admission. Visas may be issued to nonimmigrants, such as students, tourists, and guest workers, or to immigrants. A *green card* is the informal name for a permanent-resident visa or permanent-resident card, which was printed on green paper from 1947 to 1964. It is given to immigrants who are granted permanent-resident status in the U.S.

vis-à-vis is a CHAMELEON-HUED preposition and adverb in place of which it is usually desirable to use a more precise term. The traditional sense is adverbial, "in a position facing each other." The following sentences contain acceptable figurative uses:

- "*Vis-à-vis* their lord they were unfree, though to some extent protected against ill usage, but *vis-à-vis* the rest of the world they were accorded the rights of free men." A.W.B. Simpson, *An Introduction to the History of the Land Law* 148 (1961).
- "This practical possibility is present in all intrafamilial legal relationships, particularly parent *vis-à-vis* child." *Holodook v. Spencer*, 324 N.E.2d 338, 347 (N.Y. 1974).

As a preposition, *vis-à-vis* has been extended to the senses "opposite to; in relation to; as compared with." Usually simpler, more precise prepositions are better. E.g.:

- "CHA would not be able to invoke the rule of strict construction because CHA 'enjoyed substantial bargaining power *vis-à-vis* [read *over*] the carrier.'" *Bank of the West v. Superior Ct.*, 277 Cal. Rptr. 219, 227 (Ct. App. 1991).
- "Any compact negotiation between the Band and the State . . . will inevitably include a State demand for revenue sharing of some sort; to do otherwise would put the Band in a preferred position *vis-à-vis* [read *over*] the other tribes in California." *Rincon Band of Luiseno Mission Indians v. Schwarzenegger*, 602 F.3d 1019, 1070 (9th Cir. 2010).

viscera (= internal organs) is the plural of *viscus*. See PLURALS (A).

visit, n.; visitation. *Visit*, the ordinary word, means "a call on a person or at a place; temporary residence with a person or at a place" (*COD*). *Visitation* denotes a visit by an official, an unduly long visit, or the divine dispensation of punishment or reward. In family law, *visitation* is used in the phrase *visitation rights* (= provisions for spending time with one's children living with another, usu. the divorced spouse)—e.g.: "[The] paternal grandparents sued the children's mother claiming she wrongfully took the children out of France and brought them to Ireland, not allowing them to return to France to see their grandparents who had *visitation rights*." Timothy John Nolen, Note,

Smacking Lesson, 16 Cardozo J.L. & Gender 519, 541 (2010).

visit upon = to inflict punishment for; to avenge—e.g.: "If no adverse consequences can be *visited upon* the convicted person by reason of further testimony, then there is no further incrimination to be feared." *Mitchell v. U.S.*, 526 U.S. 314, 326 (1999) (per Kennedy, J.).

vis major. See **force majeure**.

visualize does not mean "to see," but "to see in the mind's eye." The word is figurative, not literal. Here the word is wrongly used in a literal sense: "Defendant *visualized* [read *saw*] the nerve on the right side and followed the first technique on that side." *Swope v. Printz*, 468 S.W.2d 34, 37 (Mo. 1971).

vitiate = (1) to impair by the addition of (something); (2) to render corrupt in morals; (3) to corrupt or spoil in respect of substance; or (4) to render of no effect; to invalidate either completely or in part; to destroy or impair the legal effect or force of (a deed, etc.) (*OED*). Sense 1 is the most widely used—e.g.:

- "Reference to the so-called antinoise ordinance may well have misled the jury and *vitiated* the initial instruction." *Herbst v. Balogh*, 184 N.Y.S.2d 718, 721 (App. Div. 1959).
- "The defendant argues [that] her consent was invalid because [it] was *vitiated* by the unlawful police entry onto her property and she was intimidated by the three officers." *State v. LaBarre*, 992 A.2d 733, 739–40 (N.H. 2010).

Here *vitiate* is used in the sense "to impair by the subtraction or omission of something," an unexceptionable use:

- "Excising the racial indicia from Exhibit Z would have *vitiated* its relevance in rebutting the claim of discrimination." *Hackett v. Housing Auth. of San Antonio*, 750 F.2d 1308, 1312 (5th Cir. 1985).
- "Judicial intervention may also be permissible or even necessary when the judge detects a patent omission which might *vitiate* a full adjudication of the defendant's guilt or innocence." *In re T.C.*, 999 A.2d 72, 83 (D.C. 2010).

Sense 4 is the legal sense—e.g.:

- "The existence of that remedy does not *vitiate* the finality of the District Court's resolution of the claims in the instant proceeding." *Green Tree Fin. Corp. v. Randolph*, 531 U.S. 79, 86 (2000) (per Rehnquist, C.J.).
- "[The State's] case rests on the argument that defendant's voluntary consent *vitiated* the effect of the police illegality." *State v. Tyler*, 178 P.3d 282, 285 (Or. Ct. App. 2008).
- "An employment relationship may be *vitiated* when there is a material misrepresentation in the employment contract." *Brayboy v. WorkForce*, 681 S.E.2d 567, 569 (S.C. 2009).

It is perhaps a SLIPSHOD EXTENSION to stretch this sense into "to strike down"—e.g.: "The Supreme Court *vitiated* [read *invalidated*] the statute." *Minarcini v. Strongsville City Sch. Dist.*, 384 F.Supp. 698, 706 (N.D. Ohio 1974).

A frequently misunderstood word, *vitiate* does not mean "to weaken or lessen," as used here: "Anger, evoked by all brutal crimes, [can't] be *vitiated* [read *reduced*] by a change in physical surroundings." *U.S.*

v. Harrelson, 754 F.2d 1153, 1162 (5th Cir. 1985). Nor does it mean "to belie": "If defendant's complaint is that the court, sua sponte, should have required the state to elect between the alternative counts, this assertion is *vitiated* [read *belied*] by the use of MAI-CR 3d 304.14, which forbade a finding of guilt on both counts." *State v. Harden*, 748 S.W.2d 701, 703 (Mo. Ct. App. 1988). Nor "to correct": "The court's later instruction . . . cannot be deemed to have *vitiated* [read *cured* or *corrected*] the prejudice caused by the court's earlier apparent indorsement of the improper questioning." *People v. Wood*, 488 N.E.2d 86, 90 (N.Y. 1985). The word is also sometimes misused for *obviate*. See **obviate.**

vitilitigation; *vitiligation. *Vitilitigation* (= [1] contention; wrangling; [2] vexatious litigation) is an odd word with reduplicative sounds, dating in the English language from the mid-17th century. **Vitiligation* is a "ghost-word" that appeared in *Black's Law Dictionary* from the second edition of 1910 through the sixth edition of 1990—a typographical error that was unwittingly perpetuated in the influential book for most of the 20th century. (I removed it after becoming editor in chief of *Black's* in the mid-1990s.) The error seems never to have spread beyond the confines of those editions into legal language more generally.

vitriol. See **abuse,** n.

vittles is not the literary spelling; *victuals* is. See **victuals.**

vituperation. See **abuse,** n.

vituperative; *vituperous. The first is the preferred adjectival form of *vituperation*. The second is a NEEDLESS VARIANT. See **abuse,** n.

viz. is an abbreviation of the Latin word *videlicet* (fr. *videbere* = to see; *licet* = it is permissible). The English-language equivalents are *namely* or *that is to say*, either of which is preferable to this LATINISM. Like its English counterparts, the term signifies that what follows particularizes a general statement, without contradicting what precedes, or that what follows explains certain obscurities that the writer acknowledges to be lurking in what has just been said. E.g.:

- "[If a testator has] devised certain real estate to his widow, 'her heirs, *viz.*, her children and grandchildren and assigns,' the words following the *videlicet* have been held not to be repugnant to, but explanatory and restrictive of, the word 'heirs,' and to operate to limit the widow's estate to an estate for life." 57 Am. Jur. *Wills* § 1156, at 753 (1948).
- "[Justice Stevens] would prefer to take the course we have repeatedly rejected, *viz.*, to repudiate the *Saucier* procedure." *Bunting v. Mellen*, 541 U.S. 1019, 1026 (2004) (Scalia, J., dissenting).

The abbreviation is odd in two ways. First, how does one derive *viz.* from *videlicet*? The final *z* in the abbreviation represents the medieval Latin symbol of contraction for *et* or *-et* (*OED*). Second, how does one pronounce *viz.*? Preferably by saying "namely." As with *i.e.* and *e.g.*, the abbreviation is customarily set off from the rest of the sentence by a pair of commas. (Or, when given as the first word within a parenthetical expression, it is set off by one comma.) See **i.e.** & **e.g.**

vocation. See **avocation.**

vociferous; *vociferant. The second is a NEEDLESS VARIANT.

Vogue Words are those faddish, trendy, seemingly ubiquitous words that have something novel about them. They may be NEOLOGISMS or they may be old words in new uses or senses. Often they quickly become CLICHÉS or standard idioms, and sometimes they pass into obscurity after a period of feverish popularity. For whatever reason, they have such a grip on the popular mind that they come to be used in contexts in which they serve no real purpose other than suggesting group membership. As they become more popular and appear more frequently, says the *Oxford Guide*, "so their real denotative value drains away, a process that closely resembles monetary inflation. . . . One should carefully guard against using them either because they sound more learned and up to date than the more commonplace words in one's vocabulary, or as a short cut in communicating ideas that would be better set out in simple, clear, basic vocabulary" (1983).

The following list is a representative collection:

constructive
cost-effective
cutting edge, on the
definitely
dialogue
downside (risks)
environment
escalate (= to intensify)
eventuate
exposure (= liability)
framework
identify with (as in "I can identify with you")
impact, vb. (except in reference to wisdom teeth)
interface
-IZE words
lifestyle
matrix
meaningful
need-to-know basis, on a
no-lose situation
no-win situation
oriented (e.g., law-oriented)
overly
parameters
relate, vb. (as in "I can relate to that")
scenario

An asterisk (✳) precedes words and phrases that are invariably inferior forms.

state-of-the-art
upside
user-friendly
viable
win–win situation
-WISE words
worst-case scenario

void; voidable. "It is regrettable that the courts have used the term 'voidable' in the sense of both 'voidable' and 'void.'" Lewis A. Jeffrey, *Infants—Contract of Suretyship*, 3 Tex. L. Rev. 328, 329 (1925). The distinction should be evident. *Void* = absolutely null. *Voidable* = capable of being voided or confirmed. The practical effect is that a *void contract* gives no rights at all; a *voidable contract* gives certain rights, though one of the parties (such as a minor) may abruptly put an end to those rights.

Yet confusion seems to abound, as *Corpus Juris Secundum* points out: "There is great looseness and no little confusion in the books in the use of the words *void* and *voidable*, growing, perhaps, in some degree, out of the imperfection of the language, since there are several kinds of defects which are included under the expressions *void* and *voidable*, while there are but two terms to express them all." 92 C.J.S. at 1020–23 (1955).

The phrases *totally void* and *completely void* are REDUNDANCIES. (See ADJECTIVES (B).) *Null and void* is questionable as a DOUBLET, *void* itself being perfectly strong—e.g.: "The natural tendency of the condition contained in the will is to restrain all marriage and for that reason it is *void*." *In re Liberman*, 18 N.E.2d 658, 662 (N.Y. 1939). See **null and void.**

void *ab initio* is an extremely common phrase, and some lawyers try to justify the LATINISM on grounds that it is not easily translated. But quite respectable writers have used *void from the beginning*—e.g.: "The maxim is '*that which is void in the beginning cannot be cured by waiver, acquiescence or lapse of time.*'" Eugene A. Jones, *Manual of Equity Pleading and Practice* 12 n.24 (1916). See *ab initio.*

voidance. See **avoid.**

void and of no effect; *void and of none effect. This DOUBLET is quite redundant. If the phrase must be used, modern idiom requires *void and of no effect.*

void and unenforceable is a common REDUNDANCY.

void contract. As Patrick Atiyah points out, *void contract* is "really a contradiction in terms inasmuch as a contract has already been defined in terms applicable only to a valid contract. However, the term is convenient and is universally used." P.S. Atiyah, *An Introduction to the Law of Contract* 36–37 (3d ed. 1981). Among typical *void contracts* are those in which:

- no consideration was given;
- the acceptance of an offer was not communicated;
- wagering is involved; or
- family relations are prejudiced.

In essence, a *void contract* is no contract at all—it is not necessarily unlawful, but it has no legal effect. For other phrases using *contract* but not truly involving a contract, see **contract of record** & **unenforceable contract.** See also OXYMORONS.

void for vagueness. This phrase was originally confined to the law of deeds and other instruments affecting real or personal property: if the property was not sufficiently identified—or some other critical provision was vaguely worded—the instrument would be declared *void for vagueness.* This usage first appeared in the mid-19th century and has persisted into the 21st—e.g.:

- "Although our early decisions would hold them *void, for vagueness*, our decisions for the last ten and fifteen years, have gone further, and established the law to be liberal enough to sustain mortgages quite as indefinite and vague as the present." *Utley v. Smith*, 24 Conn. 290, 314 (1855).
- "Secondly, . . . said mortgage is *void, for vagueness*, and uncertainty in respect to the debts intended to be secured." *Gill v. Pinney's Adm'r*, 12 Ohio St. 38, 46 (Ohio 1861).
- "We are therefore of the opinion that the description is sufficient to cover and to convey this particular stock of goods, and that the mortgage is not *void for vagueness* or uncertainty." *Davis v. Turner*, 120 F. 605, 612 (4th Cir. 1903).
- "The description [in the deed] is not *void for vagueness* and it may be aided by parol evidence." *Peel v. Calais*, 31 S.E.2d 440, 443 (N.C. 1944).
- "She argues that . . . both the liquor license provision in the contract for deed and the default notice sent to her are *void for vagueness.*" *Turbiville v. Hansen*, 761 P.2d 389, 391 (Mont. 1988).
- "We agree with appellees that this description was sufficient to constitute a key by which the property may be identified, and thus the contract was not *void for vagueness* due to any insufficiency of the description of the property." *Cole v. Shoffner*, 421 S.E.2d 322, 325 (Ga. Ct. App. 1992) (citation omitted).
- "[T]he basis for the defendants' motion [to dismiss] was . . . that the engagement letter signed by the defendants and the plaintiff was *void for vagueness.*" *Winston & Strawn, LLP v. Doley*, 654 F.Supp.2d 17, 21 (D.D.C. 2009).

Not until the early 20th century did the phrase come to bear what is today its most usual sense, in reference to statutes. If legislation establishes a requirement or a punishment without stating precisely what is required or what conduct is punishable, the courts generally hold that it is *void for vagueness* because it violates due process—e.g.:

- "Four reasons are assigned in the motion to quash, against the validity of the statute under the Constitution, [including] that it is *void for vagueness* and uncertainty." *U.S. v. U.S. Brewers' Ass'n*, 239 F. 163, 165 (W.D. Pa. 1916).
- "The designation of the 'usual transfer delivery zone adjacent to' incorporated cities or towns is *void for vagueness.*" *Ex parte Schmolke*, 248 P. 244, 246 (Cal. 1926).
- "The word 'orchard' has always had a well-understood meaning, and the use of such a term in a statute could not possibly render the statute *void for vagueness.*" *Kelleher v. French*, 22 F.2d 341, 344 (W.D. Va. 1927).

- "[The defendant contends that] the statute under which defendant was prosecuted is *void for vagueness*, because it grants unlimited discretion to the state in deciding how many charges to bring for a course of criminal conduct." *State v. Altgilbers*, 786 P.2d 680, 691 (N.M. Ct. App. 1989).

When the expression is used as a PHRASAL ADJECTIVE, it should be hyphenated <void-for-vagueness doctrine>.

*voidity. See **voidness.**

void marriage, like *void contract*, is an OXYMORON: "The expression '*void marriage*' is but a convenient phrase. A void marriage is no marriage. Considered literally the expression is self-destructive and contradictory." *Ross Smith v. Ross Smith*, [1963] A.C. 280, 314 (per Lord Morris of Borth-y-Gest). See **void contract.**

voidness; *voidity. The first is the usual noun. The second, a NEOLOGISM not recorded in most English-language dictionaries, is a NEEDLESS VARIANT—e.g.: "*Voidity* [read *Voidness*] of marriage requir[es] by the trend of the more modern cases an express statutory declaration." Karl Llewellyn, *The Common Law Tradition: Deciding Appeals* 488 (1960).

voir dire, vb., is a lawyer's colloquialism not listed in general English-language dictionaries. E.g.:

- "When I *voir dired* the jury, I asked each prospective juror whether he could set his prejudices aside." John A. Jenkins, *The Litigators* 379 (1989) (quoting Rex Carr).
- "The prosecutor asked the court to reserve ruling until Dr. Ripple could be *voir dired* about her qualifications and background." *Lee v. State*, 996 A.2d 425, 438 (Md. Ct. Spec. App. 2010).

Among the possible substitutes are the verbs *to examine* and *to question (on voir dire)*. See NOUNS AS VERBS.

voir dire; voire dire, n. Meaning literally "to speak the truth," the phrase is a LAW FRENCH equivalent of the Latinate *verdict* (*voir* having been the Norman-French word for the modern French *vrai*). But the two words have come to denote two distinct aspects of jury trials. The preferred spelling is *voir dire*. It is pronounced /vwah **deer**/, or, in the southern U.S., /vohr **dir**/. See **verdict (A)** & PRONUNCIATION (A).

voire dire, n. See **voir dire.**

volenti non fit injuria (lit., "to a willing person a wrong is not done") denotes the tort defense that the plaintiff voluntarily accepted the risk with full knowledge. The LATINISM is gradually falling into disuse in AmE, though it is still used with great frequency in BrE, in which it is sometimes said that the injured person was *volens*.

The Fifth Circuit once wrote what amounts to a usage note on the phrase: "The joint appellants claim that . . . Mobil was not liable to Gantt under the Texas doctrine of assumption of risk (usually referred to by Texas lawyers and courts in its Latin form, '*volenti non fit injuria*,' or '*volenti*' for short)." *Gantt v. Mobil Chem. Co.*, 463 F.2d 691, 699 (5th Cir. 1972). True, the clipped form *volenti* is fairly common, but in Texas judicial opinions, *assumption of the risk* is more than four times as common as the LATINISM in any form. See **assumption of the risk.**

volitional; *volitive. *Volitional* = of or belonging to volition (i.e., an act of willing or resolving); pertaining to the action of willing—e.g.: "Participation in the program requires admission that a person lacks *volitional* control." *In re Detention of Lieberman*, 929 N.E.2d 616, 623 (Ill. App. Ct. 2010). **Volitive* is a NEEDLESS VARIANT.

voluntary. See **unintentional.**

voluntary manslaughter. See **manslaughter (A).**

voluntary waste. See **waste.**

voracious (= having a huge appetite) is sometimes misused for *vigorous*. Perhaps the confusion arose through the CLICHÉ *voracious reader*, in which many seem to have forgotten the METAPHOR of devouring. With reading (which involves mental ingestion), the metaphor works; with other activities in which the idea of consuming is absent, the metaphor flops—e.g.: "From the start, McCurley's team—which included his lawyer wife, Johanna, two associate attorneys, and a paralegal—attacked *voraciously* [read *vigorously*]. Dozens of depositions were taken, tens of thousands of documents assembled. Expert and character witnesses were flown in from around the country. At times McCurley and his crew worked in shifts, sixteen to twenty hours a day." Dana Rubin, *Courting Costs*, Tex. Monthly, May 1992, at 52, 58.

voracity. See MALAPROPISMS.

votary; *votarist. The second is a NEEDLESS VARIANT.

vote; ballot. These words "are sometimes confused, and, while they are sometimes used synonymously, the '*ballot*' is, in fact, under our form of voting, the instrument by which the voter expresses his choice between candidates or in respect to propositions; and his '*vote*' is his choice or election, as expressed by his *ballot*." *Clary v. Hurst*, 138 S.W. 566, 569 (Tex. 1911).

For the distinction between a juror's *vote* and a jury's verdict, see **verdict (c).**

vote damages, in AmE, is the lawyer's shorthand phrase for *vote to award damages*—e.g.: "An insurance functionary—a guy with a big title and a small salary—loves to go back to the office and write a memo telling his boss that he 'did the right thing' and refused [as a juror] to *vote damages*." Joseph Goulden, *The Million Dollar Lawyers* 71 (1978) (quoting Franklin Jones Jr.).

vouch for. See **attest**.

vouchsafe is not equivalent to *grant* or *provide*, as suggested here: "A person is entitled to the actual and continued enjoyment of his civil rights as *vouchsafed* [read *provided*] by the statute and these cannot be permanently thwarted by some other avenue of escape." *Fletcher v. Coney Island, Inc.*, 134 N.E.2d 371, 377 (Ohio 1956). Rather, today it ordinarily denotes "to grant something in a condescending way," or, more neutrally, "to grant something as a special favor." E.g.: "The Court does not *vouchsafe* the lower courts . . . guidelines for formulating specific, definite, wholly unprecedented remedies." *Baker v. Carr*, 369 U.S. 186, 267 (1962) (Frankfurter, J., dissenting).

VOWEL CLUSTERS are not indigenous to the English language, although one finds them in our imported vocabulary, in words such as *giaour* (= one outside the Muslim faith), *maieutic* (= Socratic), *moueing* (= making a pouting face), *onomatopoeia* (= the use of imitative or echoic words, such as *fizz* and *buzz*), *queuing* (AmE) or *queueing* (BrE). In forming NEOLOGISMS, especially by agglutination, one should be wary of clumping vowels together in a way that would strike readers as un-English. Even three consecutive vowels may have this effect, as in *antiaircraft*, which is better hyphenated: *anti-aircraft*. For two more examples— *shanghaied* and *shanghaiing*—see **shanghai**.

vs. See **v.** & **versus**.

W

wafer, in law, is a small red piece of paper that is stuck on a document under seal—in place of a wax seal. Traditionally, the signer of the document, after signing, would touch the wafer with his or her finger. See **seal (A)**.

wage. See **pay**, n.

waifs and estrays. This legal phrase has passed into common parlance in the sense "abandoned or neglected children," which is an extension of the original sense "unclaimed property; wandering animals." (In lay usage, the second element is often *strays*.) Technically, *waifs* came to mean, at common law, things stolen and thrown away by the thief in flight, but not things left behind or hidden; they belonged to the Crown by prerogative right if they had been seized on its behalf (*OCL1*). *Estrays* = valuable tame animals, found wandering and ownerless; at common law, they belonged to the Crown or, by virtue of grant or prescriptive right, to the lord of the manor (*id.*). See **estray**.

waivable, a word supported in the *OED* with but one citation from 1818, is common in modern legal contexts—e.g.:

• "The defects [that] were not *waivable* under either system were: want of jurisdiction over the subject matter, failure to state a cause of action, and lack of an indispensable party." Fleming James, *Civil Practice* § 4.3, at 135 (1965).
• "The distinction between subject-matter jurisdiction and *waivable* defenses is not a mere nicety of legal metaphysics." *U.S. Catholic Conf. v. Abortion Rights Mobilization, Inc.*, 487 U.S. 72, 77 (1988) (per Kennedy, J.).
• "Even assuming all statutory penalties are *waivable*, the fact that a complaint omitting them could be brought as a class action would not at all prove that [the statute] is addressed only to remedies." *Shady Grove Orthopedic Assocs. P.A. v. Allstate Ins. Co.*, 130 S.Ct. 1431, 1439 (2010) (per Scalia, J.).

The noun *waivability* is likewise common, though it appears in none of the general English-language dictionaries. E.g.:

• "Can finding of waiver of unionized employee's state civil rights and privacy law claims be predicated on federal court's mere assumption of *waivability*?" *Labor*, 57 U.S.L.W. 3727, 3727 (2 May 1989).
• "The second [topic] involv[es] the nature and *waivability* of the Workers' Compensation defense." Robert A. Barker, *Collateral Estoppel*, N.Y.L.J., 23 April 1990, at 3.

waive. A. Narrowing of Sense. This word has undergone what linguists call "specialization," its primary sense having gotten narrower with time. Originally, *waive* was just as broad as *abandon*. In general usage today, *waive* means "to relinquish something that one has the right to expect" <to waive the formalities>. And in legal usage, the word ordinarily means "to relinquish a legal right" <the company waived that defense>. For more on this verb and its near-synonyms, see **relinquish**.

B. For *wave*. *Waive* (= to relinquish or abandon voluntarily) is sometimes used as a MALAPROPISM for *wave* (= to move to and fro with the hand)—e.g.: "But a new bidder—the Blockbuster Bowl, sponsored by the video store chain—threw the deal into doubt by *waiving* [read *waving*] a few extra dollars before the noses of our institutions of higher learning." Frederick C. Klein, *Who Cares Who's No. 1?*, Wall St. J., 3 Jan. 1992, at A5. Cf. **waiver (D), (E)**.

waivee. See **waivor**.

waiver. A. Senses. *Waiver* = (1) the voluntary relinquishment or abandonment of a legal right or advantage <waiver of immunity>; or (2) the instrument by which a person relinquishes such a right or advantage <she signed the waiver>.

B. Imprecise Uses. *Waiver* is "an imprecise and generic term" when used, for example, to describe the action of a landlord who decides not to forfeit a lease that a tenant has breached, but the word is "used in many of the leading cases." Peter Butt, *Land Law* 284 (2d ed. 1988). Sometimes the word is used vaguely as a synonym for *laches*, especially when a lien claimant has lost the lien by delay. As leading admiralty scholars put it, when "a lien has attached at the time . . . services were furnished, *waiver*, unless it refers to an express agreement by which the lienor releases his claim against the ship, seems to be merely a word [that] some judges like to use for stylistic effect, by itself or in double harness with its more industrious companion *laches*." Grant Gilmore & Charles L. Black Jr., *The Law of Admiralty* 786 (2d ed. 1975). Finally, *waiver* is sometimes confused with *estoppel*, but the words are quite "incorrectly regarded as synonymous." *Thomas N. Carlton Estate, Inc. v. Keller*, 52 So.2d 131, 132–33 (Fla. 1951). See **estoppel**.

C. And *estoppel*. *Waiver* = the voluntary relinquishment of a known right. *Estoppel* = the legal abatement of somebody's rights and privileges when it would be inequitable to allow that person to assert them. Though the distinction is a fine one (and a frequently muddled one), it is worth carefully observing. In insurance law, for example, "*waiver* arises by the act of one party; *estoppel* by operation of law. *Waiver* depends upon knowledge of the insurer; *estoppel* upon a prejudicial change of position by the insured. While they may coexist, they are not identical . . . . The term *estoppel* is broader than that of *waiver*, and may embrace it within its scope, in certain instances, since an insurer, after waiving certain rights, would be estopped thereafter to assert them. The converse is not true, as an estoppel need not be founded upon a waiver." 16B John A. Appleman & Jean Appleman, *Insurance Law and Practice* § 9081, at 497 (1981).

D. For *waver*. It is a MALAPROPISM to confuse *waiver* with *waver* (= to vacillate)—e.g.:

- "Mayor Koch . . . *waivered* [read *wavered*] between silence and support for months." *Bess Myerson Accused of Stealing $44 in Goods*, N.Y. Times, 28 May 1988, at 9.
- "The Court has never *waivered* [read *wavered*] on this point." *U.S. v. Bates*, 917 F.2d 388, 395 n.10 (9th Cir. 1990).
- "The firm—and Klein and Farr in particular—*waivered* [read *wavered*] over whether to embrace faster growth." Eleanor Kerlow, *Small Is No Longer Beautiful*, Legal Times, 27 May 1991, at 1.

See **waive (B)**.

E. For *waive*. When *waiver* is not misused for *waver*, it is often displacing the more straightforward verb *waive*: "While none have been approved by EPA, the three 'tertiary' ethers are chemically similar to MTBE and would probably be *waivered* [read *waived*] by the EPA." George H. Unzelman, *U.S. Clean Air Act Expands Role for Oxygenates*, Oil & Gas J., 15 Apr. 1991, at 44, 47–48.

waiver by estoppel. This phrase is a useless jumble: "We feel that the term *waiver by estoppel* is confusing and tends to blur the useful distinction between *waiver* and *estoppel*. The *waiver by estoppel* term in our previous cases has always been applied in estoppel situations and should be understood to refer to estoppel and not waiver." *Reed v. Commercial Ins. Co.*, 432 P.2d 691, 693 (Or. 1967). For the distinction between *waiver* and *estoppel*, see **waiver (C)**.

waive the tort. Many lawyers have heard this idiom but are unsure of its origin and meaning. In common-law pleading, a plaintiff often had the choice of framing a cause of action in contract or in tort. One who chose to sue in contract was said to *waive the tort*.

Actually, though, *waiver of tort* is a misnomer because a party "waives" the tort only in the sense of electing to sue in quasi-contract to recover the defendant's unjust benefit instead of suing in tort to recover damages. The remedies, in other words, are in the alternative. And even when the plaintiff elects to sue in quasi-contract, "the tort is not extinguished. Indeed it is said that it is a *sine qua non* of both remedies that [the plaintiff] should establish that a tort has been committed." Lord Goff of Chieveley & Gareth Jones, *The Law of Restitution* 605 (3d ed. 1986).

waivor; waivee. These terms are surely needless, *waivor* being particularly susceptible of confusion with *waiver*. E.g.:

- "A waiver of one misrepresentation does not constitute a waiver of another when the '*waivor*' [read *waiving party*] had no reason to believe the second representation was also false." *Housour v. Prudential Life Ins. Co.*, 136 N.W.2d 689, 691 (Mich. Ct. App. 1965).
- "A valid waiver requires a known legal right, relinquished for consideration, where such legal right is intended for the *waivor's* [read *waiving party's*] sole benefit and does not infringe on the rights of others." *Brannock v. Brannock*, 722 P.2d 636, 637 (N.M. 1986).
- "[T]he ground for the rejection of an asserted post-deadline unilateral *waiver* was not its timing but the determination that the condition in question was not for the exclusive benefit of the purported *waivor* [read *waiving party*]." Donald H. Clark, *Risk Allocation on Failure of Contingent Conditions*, 19 N.Z.U. L. Rev. 206, 229 (2000).

wake; awake; awaken; wake up; woke; waked; waked up; woke up; awakened; awaked; awoke. The past-tense and past-participial forms of *wake* and its various siblings are perhaps the most vexing in the language. Following are the preferred declensions:

> wake > woke > waked (or woken)
>
> awake > awoke > awaked (or awoken)
>
> awaken > awakened > awakened
>
> wake up > woke up > waked up

waller. See LAWYERS, DEROGATORY NAMES FOR (A).

wane; wax. *Wane* = to decrease in strength or importance. E.g.:

- "There is nothing to indicate that Kansas appellate-court approval for this pattern instruction has *waned*." *Foster v. Klaumann*, 216 P.3d 671, 707 (Kan. Ct. App. 2009).
- "The employer's interest in enforcing its unilateral regulations *wanes* when the employer attempts to reach into purely private matters that have no bearing on the employer's legitimate interests." *Stengart v. Loving Care Agency, Inc.*, 973 A.2d 390, 401 (N.J. Super. Ct. App. Div. 2009).

Wax (= [1] to increase in strength or importance, or [2] to become) is used primarily (in sense 2) in clichés such as *to wax poetic, eloquent*, etc., or (in sense 1) as a correlative of *wane* <the doctrine waxed and waned>.

wangle. See **wrangle.**

want, n. (= lack), is an especially formal word, sometimes used in literary contexts but frequently in legal writing <want of prosecution>. E.g.:

- "Such additional pleading burdens could require a showing of *want* of probable cause or malice." June M. Galkoski, Note, *42 U.S.C. § 1983*, 5 St. Thomas L. Rev. 533, 541 (1993).
- "A dismissal for *want* of jurisdiction foreclosed plaintiff's claim." *Southern-Owners Ins. Co. v. Tomac of Fla., Inc.*, 687 F.Supp.2d 665, 668 (S.D. Tex. 2010).

The participial *wanting* (= lacking) also appears often in legal prose—e.g.:

- "If any material link in the chain of title is *wanting*, the whole is defective for *want* of sufficient authority to support it." *Canaj, Inc. v. Baker & Div. Phase III, LLC*, 893 A.2d 1067, 1092 (Md. 2006).
- "Federal jurisdiction is *wanting*, and this action must be remanded to state court." *Evans v. Infirmary Health Servs., Inc.*, 634 F.Supp.2d 1276, 1282 (S.D. Ala. 2009).

wanton; reckless. The word *wanton* usually denotes a greater degree of culpability than *reckless*. A *reckless* person is generally fully aware of the risks and may even be trying and hoping to avoid harm. A *wanton* person may be risking no more harm than the *reckless* person, but he or she is not trying to avoid the harm and is indifferent about whether it results. In criminal law, *wanton* usually connotes malice, but *reckless* does not. See **malice.**

ward has two primary legal senses today: (1) "a territorial division in a city, usu. defined for purposes of city government" <flooding in the fifth ward>; or (2) "a person—usu. a minor—who is under a guardian's charge or protection" <a ward of the state>. Though these meanings are seemingly unrelated, the term *ward* originally meant "guard"—hence sense 1 refers to a place to be guarded and sense 2 to a person to be guarded.

warehousemen. See sexism (b).

warning of caveat (= a notice given to a person who has entered a caveat, warning the person to appear and state what interest he or she has in the matter) is a curious but established redundancy. See **caveat.**

warrant, n., = (1) a writ directing or authorizing someone to do an act—esp. one directing a law enforcer to make an arrest, a search, or a seizure; or (2) a document conferring authority, esp. to pay or receive money. Sense 2 is often used figuratively—e.g.:

- "What *warrant* then had our four new judges for hoping that history would reject these rival claimants and confirm the Supreme Court's constitutional prerogative?" Robert G. McCloskey, *The American Supreme Court* 11 (1960).

- "Faced with a statute that already draws these lines what *warrant* do we have to draw several more on our own?" *U.S. v. Brock*, 501 F.3d 762, 771 (6th Cir. 2007).

warrant, vb. **A. General Usage.** Today, *warrant* most commonly means "to justify." And in modern idiom, one naturally says that objects or actions are *warranted*, but not so naturally that people are *warranted*. Therefore, "Such a conclusion *warrants* federal judges in substituting their views for those of state legislators" reads better this way: *Such a conclusion warrants federal judges' substituting their views for those of state legislators.* To illustrate this point, we might say that acts or beliefs are *warranted* or *unwarranted*, but not that actors or believers are *warranted* or *unwarranted*.

Nevertheless, the *OED* contains examples of *warrant* used with personal objects from the 17th century, and the usage remains common in law, if not elsewhere. E.g.: "Probable cause exists where 'the facts and circumstances [are] sufficient in themselves to *warrant* a man of reasonable caution in the belief that' an offense has been or is being committed." *Brinegar v. U.S.*, 338 U.S. 160, 175–76 (1949) (per Rutledge, J., quoting *Carroll v. U.S.*, 267 U.S. 132, 162 (1925) (per Taft, C.J.)).

B. Legal Senses. In law, *warrant* may mean (1) "to guarantee the security of (realty or personalty, or even a person)" <the company will warrant him from any harm>; (2) "to give warranty of (title); to give warranty of title to (a person)" <the third party had warranted title>; or (3) "to authorize" <Who has warranted this search?>. In senses 1 and 2, the verb *to warrant* is closely connected with the noun *warranty*. Sometimes, however, lawyers use the word *warrant* loosely—especially in contracts—by stating, for example, that a party *warrants* something when no warranty is intended; in modern usage, if a mere promise is intended, as opposed to a warranty, then *warrant* is the wrong word. See **justify.**

warranted (= authorized by a search warrant) is common in American legal writing. *Warranted* has had the sense "furnished with a legal or official warrant" (*OED*) since the mid-18th century. E.g.:

- "Courts have upheld the use of forceful breaking and entering where necessary to effect a *warranted search*, even though the warrant gave no indication that force had been contemplated." *Dalia v. U.S.*, 441 U.S. 238, 257 n.19 (1979) (per Powell, J.).
- "The evidence found during the *warranted search* showed overwhelmingly that Lennick was growing marijuana in his home." *U.S. v. Lennick*, 18 F.3d 814, 818 (9th Cir. 1994).

The antonym of *warranted* in this sense is *warrantless*, not *unwarranted* (= unjustified). See **warrantless.**

warrantee—properly, the person to whom a warranty is given—is sometimes incorrectly used in place of *warranty*. The *OED* cites two examples of this misusage. See -ee & **guarantee (a).**

*****warranter.** See **warrantor.**

warrantless = (1) without a warrant <a warrantless entry of police upon defendant's premises>; or (2) unjustified <completely warrantless accusations>.

warrantor; *warranter. The first spelling is preferred.

warranty. A. General Senses. "The word *warranty* is multivocal throughout the law." Grant Gilmore & Charles L. Black Jr., *The Law of Admiralty* 63 (2d ed. 1975). The word has three primary senses: (1) "[in property law] a covenant by which the grantor in a deed (a) binds himself or herself, as well as any heirs, to secure to the grantee the estate conveyed in the deed, and (b) pledges to compensate the grantee with other land of equivalent value if the grantee is evicted by someone possessing paramount title"; (2) "[in contract law] an express or implied undertaking by the seller of property that it is or will be as represented or promised to be"; and (3) "[in insurance law] a pledge or stipulation by the insured that the facts relating to the person insured, the thing insured, or the risk insured are as stated."

B. And *condition*. In modern usage, a contractual promise may be a *condition*, a *warranty*, or an intermediate term. The breach of a *condition* gives the innocent party the option of treating the entire contract as discharged, while a breach of a *warranty* (or *covenant*) merely entitles the innocent party to claim damages but does not discharge that party's remaining contractual duties. This distinction in terminology arose fairly recently: in older cases, *warranty* is often used to refer to any contractual term. Because the terms *condition* and *warranty* are often loosely used, courts face difficult questions about whether the parties to a contract intended a term to be a *condition* or a *warranty*. See **condition (A).**

C. And *guarantee*. See **guarantee (A).**

D. And *representation*. See **representations and warranties.**

warranty deed. See **grant, bargain, and sell.**

wastage, as Gowers has noted, "is properly used of loss caused by wastefulness, decay, leakage, etc., or, in a staff, by death or resignation. It would be well if it were confined to this meaning instead of being used, as it habitually is, as a long variant of *waste*" (*MEU2* 688).

waste, as a legal TERM OF ART, carries the sense "permanent harm to real property committed by a tenant (for life or for years) to the prejudice of the heir, the reversioner, or the remainderman." E.g.: "It is the tenant's obligation to replace broken windows and to take other steps to preserve the premises from dilapidation. While a tenant may make repairs, he is not permitted to make any material change in the nature and character of the building leased. The making of such a material change is called *waste*." Robert Kratovil, *Real Estate Law* 300 (1946). The usual legal phrase is *to commit waste*. See **devastavit.**

Waste comes in a variety of types (listed here in order of commonness):

- *Commissive waste* (known also as *voluntary waste*) is caused by the affirmative acts of the tenant.

- *Permissive waste* is caused by the failure of the tenant to make necessary repairs that would prevent deterioration and decay. (A life tenant, as opposed to a tenant for years, is not generally liable for permissive waste unless the instrument creating the tenancy imposes a duty to repair.)

- *Equitable waste* is caused by an exempt life tenant (see just above) who flagrantly destroys or damages the property.

- *Ameliorating waste* (BrE) occurs when a tenant improves the land, as by building a high rise on it. "Understandably," as the leading Australian authority puts it, "remaindermen and reversioners rarely complain about *ameliorating waste*." Peter Butt, *Land Law* 115 (2d ed. 1988). In the U.S., *ameliorating waste* is no waste at all.

wastewater. One word.

water rights; riparian rights; littoral rights. All three terms refer to a person's right to use water from a natural water source, but they differ in meaning. *Water rights*, the predominant term in U.S. law, is also the least well defined, as it refers to a limited or unlimited use-of-water right that may or may not be attached to land. In some states, particularly the eastern states, *riparian rights* denotes a landowner's right to use flowing water that is adjacent to the land. *Littoral rights* denotes a landowner's right to use nonflowing water, such as a lake, adjacent to the land. *Riparian* and *littoral rights* are not severable from land ownership.

Riparian is pronounced /ri-**pair**-ee-ən/; *littoral* is pronounced /**lit**-ə-rəl/, which is literally inconvenient as a homophone of a much more common word. But that's the way it's said.

wave. See **waive (B).**

waver. See **waiver (D).**

wax. See **wane.**

way of necessity. See **easement (B).**

ways and means is—by virtue of the Ways and Means Committee in the U.S. House of Representatives and the House of Lords—a DOUBLET of unimpeachable credentials when used in reference to such a committee, which determines how money will be raised for various governmental projects. The phrase appears in some important 18th-century documents—e.g.: "[The States] have no right to question the propriety of the demand; no discretion beyond that of devising the *ways and means* of furnishing the sums demanded." *The Federalist* No. 30, at 189 (Alexander Hamilton) (Clinton Rossiter ed., 1961). Of course, in modern contexts divorced from historical discussions, *ways and means* is an inexcusable REDUNDANCY.

way which, unseparated by a comma, is erroneous for *way in which*. E.g.: "The Pennsylvania Superior Court . . . lists execution of an 'Agreement and

Authorization to Pay a Claim' as one of the *ways which* [read *ways in which*] the state can recover money paid in assistance to a recipient." *In re Holt*, 11 B.R. 797, 799–800 (Bankr. W.D. Pa. 1981). But in sentences that, like that one, contain relative clauses, it is idiomatic to use *that* in place of *in which*—or even to omit the relative pronoun altogether. This usage is colloquial—e.g.: "The Pennsylvania Superior Court lists execution of an agreement as one of the ways that the state can recover . . . ." See **that & which.**

weald. See **wield.**

wear and tear. In the context of leases, the phrase *wear and tear*—a "reduplicative phrase," as linguists call it—includes not only the action of the weather but also the normal use of property. A tenant is not liable to replace a carpet that becomes dingy from normal use during the tenancy—but a spilled bottle of black ink is another matter. The phrase is usually preceded by a synonym, for good measure: *normal wear and tear, reasonable wear and tear,* and *fair wear and tear* are generally synonymous.

we are persuaded that is often just so much verbal baggage in judicial opinions—e.g.: "*We are persuaded that* the principles elucidated in *Mutina* and its progeny are applicable to section 9 hearings." *In re Miller*, 885 N.E.2d 148, 153 (Mass. App. Ct. 2008). The sentence becomes much more forceful if the phrase is deleted: "The principles elucidated in *Mutina* and its progeny are applicable to section 9 hearings." See **persuade** & FLOTSAM PHRASES.

WEASEL WORDS. Theodore Roosevelt said, in a speech in St. Louis, May 31, 1916: "One of our defects as a nation is a tendency to use what have been called weasel words. When a weasel sucks eggs it sucks the meat out of the egg and leaves it an empty shell. If you use a weasel word after another there is nothing left of the other." Some writers have incorrectly assumed that the METAPHOR suggested itself because of the wriggling, evasive character of the weasel. In any event, sensitive writers are aware of how supposed intensives (for example *very*) actually have the effect of weakening a statement. (See **very.**) Many other words merely have the effect of rendering uncertain or toothless the statements in which they appear. Among these are *significantly, substantially, reasonable, meaningful, compelling, undue, clearly, obviously, manifestly, if practicable, with all deliberate speed* (orig. a weasel phrase, now with a history), *all reasonable means,* or *as soon thereafter as may be, rather, somewhat, duly, virtually,* and *quite.* See **clearly.** Cf. FUDGE WORDS.

weblog. See **blog.**

wed. A. Past Tense and Past Participle. *Wedded* is the preferred past-participial form, but *wed* often edges it out—e.g.:

• "Last year, the singer [Dan Fogelberg] *wed* [read *wedded*] his longtime fiancée, Anastasia Savage, who shares

his love of oil painting." Walter Scott, *Personality Parade*, Dallas Morning News (Parade Mag.), 3 Jan. 1993, at 4.
• "In February 1951, we *wed* [read *wedded*] women we had met at college." Walter Goodman, *In Business for Profit; Imagine That!*, N.Y. Times, 16 Oct. 1994, § 7, at 9.

In the negative, the proper adjective is *unwed* <unwed mothers>.

B. Wrongly Referring to the State of Matrimony. The verb *wed* refers to an act, not to a state—to what happens during a wedding, not to what one is afterward: "That purchase occurred during the interval in which we were legally *wed* [read *married*]." Larry Wallberg, *"Marital Property": Divvying Up Those Intangibles*, Wall St. J., 23 Oct. 1990, at A16. *Married*, by contrast, contains just the AMBIGUITY that the writer just quoted fell into; to say, "I was *married* last Saturday," may mean either that the wedding took place then or that a divorce has since occurred.

C. Figurative Uses. *Wed* is often used metaphorically in American legal prose for *adopt* or *endorse*—e.g.: "Though our Supreme Court has not as yet *wedded* this new doctrine, it has certainly at least paid ardent courtship." *Bailey v. Montgomery Ward & Co.*, 431 P.2d 108, 117 (Ariz. Ct. App. 1967).

*welcher. See **welsher.**

well, when forming an adjective with a past participial verb, is hyphenated when placed before the noun (e.g., *a well-known person, a well-written book*), but is not hyphenated when the phrase follows what it modifies (e.g., *a person who is well known, a book that is well written*). See ADJECTIVES (C).

well-being is hyphenated, not spelled as one word.

well-pleaded complaint; artful pleading. Although these terms may seem related, they are used very differently. A *well-pleaded complaint* is an original or initial claim that sufficiently sets forth a claim for relief, by including the grounds for the court's jurisdiction, the basis for the relief claimed, and a demand for judgment, so that a defendant may draft an answer that is truly responsive on the issues to be decided.

Artful pleading, by contrast, is a derogatory term referring to a plaintiff's disguising a federal claim as if it were solely a state claim in order to prevent a defendant from removing the case from state court to federal court.

well-settled, a CLICHÉ, is usually inferior to *settled* in reference to points of law, because, unfortunately, most legal writers use the one for the other undiscriminatingly. See WEASEL WORDS.

welsher; *welcher. The first is the usual spelling; the term means "one who shirks his or her responsibility in a joint undertaking," and most commonly refers to one who does not pay gambling debts.

Many natives of Wales consider the word insulting, though there is no etymological evidence supporting a connection with *Welsh* (= of, relating to, or hailing from Wales). Even so, the popular mind makes this connection, and the careful writer must be heedful.

we the people. See SET PHRASES.

wharf. Pl. *wharves.*

what. Eric Partridge took the view that *what,* as the subject of a clause, takes a singular verb no matter what follows (not *what follow*). *See Usage and Abusage* 362 (5th ed. 1981). The advice leads to such awkward sentences as this one: "*What* some of these lawyers were seeking *was* opinions that would be sympathetic to their ideas." Andrew J. White, *How to Become an Unsuccessful Lawyer* 253 (1970). But good usage allows more variety than this straitjacketing advice: when used as a pronoun, *what* may be either singular or plural. The possibilities are several.

A. Singular *what* in Noun Clause Followed by Singular Predicate. This construction is the easiest: *what* (= the thing that) takes a singular verb—e.g.: "*What* the legal system needs *is* an amicus curiae process to help reviewing courts understand the standard of care in all court-initiated sanctions cases." Nancy B. Rapoport, *Through Gritted Teeth,* 41 St. Mary's L.J. 701, 729 (2010).

B. Singular *what* in Noun Clause Followed by Plural Predicate. In this construction, as in (A), *what* = the thing that—but the main verb is (illogically) attracted to the plural noun that follows it. E.g.: "But *what worries* restaurateurs more *are* customers like Eric Wyka." Molly O'Neill, *Recession and Guilt Pare Dining Trade and Menus,* N.Y. Times, 31 Mar. 1991, at 1. H.W. Fowler would have recommended rewriting that sentence in this way: *What worries restaurateurs more is customers like Eric Wyka.* (*See MEU2* 691–92.) Either sentence would be correct, but O'Neill's original sentence typifies modern usage more than the revision.

C. Plural *what* in Noun Clause Followed by Plural Predicate. In this construction, *what* means "the things that"—e.g.:

- "*What are* in issue *are* propositions, not facts." 3 Charles F. Chamberlayne, *The Modern Law of Evidence* § 1718a, at 2216 (1912).
- "*What* the judge principally wants to hear *are* the relevant cases." Glanville Williams, *Learning the Law* 163 (11th ed. 1982).
- "Ebullience and eccentricity are to be found on every page but *what are* harder to discover *are* the depths of the Hailsham character." John Mortimer, *High Court Jester,* Sunday Times, 8 July 1990, at 8-1.

D. Indeterminate *what* Followed by Plural Predicate. In many contexts, *what* is the object in a noun clause; when that is so, the word is, in actual usage, plural three times as often as it is singular. The *what*s in this category are hard to resolve into a translated phrase, such as "things that" (a phrase that does not quite fit). E.g.:

- "The jury [will] award to the injured party *what are* called his damages." Edward T. Channing, *Judicial Eloquence,* in

Lectures Read to the Seniors in Harvard College 98, 109 (1856).
- "The Supreme Court case next discussed in the text is . . . the basic authority for turning *what are* essentially breach-of-contract claims into torts *pro hac vice.*" Grant Gilmore & Charles L. Black Jr., *The Law of Admiralty* 740 (2d ed. 1975).
- "We need not now trace *what are* the outer boundaries of extortion liability under the Hobbs Act." *Scheidler v. Nat'l Org. for Women, Inc.,* 537 U.S. 393, 402 (2003) (per Rehnquist, C.J.).

whatever; whatsoever. As an intensive meaning "at all," *whatsoever* is an established idiom in AmE <he had no reason whatsoever>, though it is obsolescent in BrE. Still, many American stylists prefer the shorter word, *whatever*—e.g.:

- "We now consider whether plaintiff . . . was entitled to recover any damages *whatever* for the death of his wife." *Missouri-Kansas-Texas R. Co. v. Canada,* 265 P. 1045, 1046 (Okla. 1928).
- "In the present case, there are no circumstances *whatever* suggesting basic unfairness." *Commonwealth ex rel. LaRue v. Rundle,* 207 A.2d 829, 831 (Pa. 1965).
- "Without expressing any view *whatever* on the scope of that authority, it is enough to note that we see little analogy between our Nation's armed services and the Public Company Accounting Oversight Board." *Free Enter. Fund v. Public Co. Acctg. Oversight Bd.,* 130 S.Ct. 3138, 3160 (2010) (per Roberts, C.J.).

For phrases such as *what nature soever,* see TMESIS.

when. See **where** (A).

*when and as. See ***as and when** & **if and when.**

when and if. See **if and when** (B).

whence (= from where; from which; from what source) is an especially FORMAL WORD that some readers consider stilted. Flesch prematurely called it "obsolete," perhaps to reinforce his absolute recommendation to use *from where* instead. *See* Rudolf Flesch, *The ABC of Style: A Guide to Plain English* 294 (1964). But *from where* would hardly work in every context, and *whence* retains some vigor—e.g.: "If his method is to work at all, it must at least work in the sorts of economic cases *whence* it sprang." Laurence H. Tribe, *Constitutional Calculus,* 98 Harv. L. Rev. 592, 615 (1985). True, the writer might have said *cases from which it sprang,* but surely not *cases from where it sprang.*

From whence is technically a REDUNDANCY—because *whence* implies *from*—but the locution has appeared continually in the great writing from the 16th century to the 21st; for example, Shakespeare, Dryden, and Dickens all used the phrase. And *from whence* is less stilted than *whence* alone, which requires a greater literary knowledge for it to be immediately understandable—e.g.: "That limitation makes eminent sense when one considers the necessity *from whence* this kind of military commission grew: The need to dispense swift justice, often in the form of execution, to illegal belligerents captured on the battlefield." *Hamdan v. Rumsfeld*, 548 U.S. 557, 607 (2006) (per Stevens, J.). Some people object to this usage, however well established; no one would object to *from which.* See **from hence** & **thence.**

whenever. In legal drafting, this term is inferior to *if* or *when*—e.g.: "*Whenever* [read *If* or *When*] a deposition is taken at the instance of the government, or *whenever* [read *if* or *when*] a deposition is taken at the instance of a defendant who is unable to bear the expenses of the taking of the deposition, the court may direct." Fed R. Crim. P. 15(b) (as formerly worded—now revised). See **where (A).**

when, not if. See **if and when (B).**

where. A. And *when*. The best word in stating a circumstance to which a statement relates is either *if* or *when*, the word *where* being archaic and legalistic to nonlegal readers. Hence: "*Where* [read *When*] a person examines goods and subsequently makes an offer to buy or hire–purchase them, it may be an implied term of the offer that the goods should remain in substantially the same state in which they were when the offer was made." G.H. Treitel, *The Law of Contract* 43–44 (8th ed. 1991). But see **where, as here.**

One writer actually suggests a nuance between *when* and *where*, but actual usage has never reflected this distinction: "*Where* is used in cases where frequent occurrences of the event are contemplated. *When* is used when a single or rare occurrence of the event is contemplated." G.C. Thornton, *Legislative Drafting* 24–25 (2d ed. 1979). But the commentator's final words are sound: "*If* . . . is very often a better word because it is the word generally used to introduce a condition in ordinary everyday usage." *Id.* at 25.

B. For *in which*. In formal prose, *where* should not be used as a relative pronoun instead of as a locative. E.g.:

- "In making this finding, we identify three different situations *where* [read *in which*] such agreements might not be enforceable." *Saini v. Int'l Game Tech.*, 434 F.Supp.2d 913, 923 (D. Nev. 2006).
- "The 'compliance interest,' seeks to rescue state and local officials from situations *where* [read *in which*] a tension between constitutional law and a federal statute threatens them with having to violate one or the other." Richard Primus, *The Future of Disparate Impact*, 108 Mich. L. Rev. 1341, 1375 (2010).
- "There are many cases *where* [read *in which*] judges have applied the label 'high conflict' on their own." Rachel Birnbaum & Nicholas Bala, *Toward the Differentiation of High-Conflict Families*, 48 Fam. Ct. Rev. 403, 409 (2010).

When a writer wants a relaxed tone, *where* may be more suitable. In the following example, the contraction *I've* might not comfortably fit in the same sentence as *in which*—hence *where* is justifiable: "*I've* deliberately chosen an example *where* [read *in which*] this unspeakable cluster did *not* stand out." Richard A.

Lanham, *Revising Prose* 29 (1979). See **case where** & CASE REFERENCES (B).

C. Wrongly Used in Defining. Those who are unfamiliar with the art of defining terms often use *where* (or *when*) to create maladroit and ambiguous definitions. E.g.:

- "[A] breach is *where* an employee gives away company property, uses company funds as his own, and takes kickbacks." *Staffilino Chevrolet, Inc. v. Balk*, 813 N.E.2d 940, 951 (Ohio Ct. App. 2004). (Better: *A breach occurs when one employee gives away company property, using company funds as his own, and takes kickbacks.*)
- "Disability-related discrimination is defined as *where* the employer treats the disabled person less favorably for a reason which relates to that person's disability." Diana Kloss, *Occupational Health Law* 301 (2010). (Better: *Disability-related discrimination occurs when an employer treats a disabled person less favorably in a way that relates to the person's disability.*)

See **is when.**

D. *Where . . . at*. This phrasing has long typified uneducated English. The problem is not that the sentence ends with a preposition (as it so often will with this phrasing), but that *where* is a "locative" that includes the notion of *at*. Cf. **reason (A).**

whereabouts; *whereabout*. *Whereabouts* is the preferred form. (See **thereabouts.**) This word may take a singular or a plural verb—e.g.: "The *whereabouts* of the note *are* [or *is*] unknown." *Ex parte Calderon*, 309 S.W.3d 64, 68 (Tex. Crim. App. 2010).

whereas. In the sense "given the fact that," *whereas* is the archetypal LEGALISM—it was formerly every lawyer's idea of how to begin a recital in a contract. The more modern drafting style is to use a heading such as *Recitals* or *Background*, followed by short declarative sentences, as opposed to the sometimes unceasing stream of independent clauses linked by semicolons and *whereases*.

One significant feature of these *whereas* clauses is that they usually have no legal effect: they are merely preliminary statements providing introductory background information before the binding promissory language.

Whereas also has a cluster of literary senses, namely, "although; while on the one hand; on the contrary; but by contrast." Whereas the contractual use is legalistic, these literary uses are a part of the general writer's idiom—e.g.: "*Whereas* both his parents have black hair, he has blond."

One usage critic has stated: "*Whereas* sounds stuffy. In spite of the objections of some grammarians, the common word is now *while*." Rudolf Flesch, *The ABC of Style* 294 (1964). Yet *whereas* is better than *while* if the latter ambiguously suggests a time element—e.g.: "I developed the arguments and marshaled authorities, *while* [read *whereas* if the idea of simultaneity is absent] she wrote the brief itself." See **while.**

where, as here. This is a useful phrase—and one in which an editor would generally be ill-advised to change *where* to *when*—e.g.: "The general interpretive principle . . . is of especial force *where, as here*, resort to legislative history is sought to support a result contrary to the statute's express terms." *ACLU v. F.C.C.*, 823 F.2d 1554, 1568 (D.C. Cir. 1987) (emphasis omitted). But see **where (A)**.

*****whereat** is an old-fashioned word dating back to the 13th century. Still, avoid it in modern writing because the locative *where* includes the concept of "at." E.g.: "Stalnaker, represented by counsel, pled 'not guilty' and the matter proceeded to a jury trial *whereat* [read *where*] he was found guilty as charged." *Stalnaker v. Bobby*, 589 F.Supp.2d 905, 923 (N.D. Ohio 2008). (On the misuse of *pled* for *pleaded* in that sentence, see **pleaded**.) Cf. *****thereat**.

where . . . at. See **where (D)**.

whereby can be a useful word, though it is easily overworked. It means "by means of or by the agency of which; from which (as a source of information); according to which, in the matter of which" (*OED*). E.g.:

- "The trust provision . . . permits the invasion of the trust corpus in case of an emergency *whereby* unusual and extraordinary expenses are necessary for the support of the beneficiary's children." *Shelley v. Shelley*, 354 P.2d 282, 288–89 (Or. 1960).
- "This is a suit by plaintiff, a real-estate broker, for damages for breach of contracts *whereby* defendants allegedly agreed for plaintiff to sell certain properties." *Haury & Smith Realty Co. v. Piccadilly Partners I*, 802 S.W.2d 612, 613 (Tenn. Ct. App. 1990).

wherefore = (1) for what? why? <Wherefore all this expense?>; (2) for which (preferably spelled *wherefor*) <he incurred the debt, the liability *wherefor* accrued more than two years ago>; (3) on account of which <the reason *wherefore* the accident occurred>; (4) therefore <wherefore, premises considered, plaintiff prays . . . .>; or (5) the cause or reason <the whys and wherefores of the situation>. In all but sense 2, the word is preferably spelled *wherefore*, but in none of these senses is the word *wherefore* particularly useful in modern writing. There are almost always more straightforward equivalents—e.g.:

- "Defendant's cigarettes contained . . . harmful ingredients, *wherefore* plaintiff suffered the injuries mentioned above." *Pritchard v. Liggett & Myers Tobacco Co.*, 134 F.Supp. 829, 830 (W.D. Pa. 1955). (A suggested revision: *Defendant's cigarettes contained harmful ingredients that caused plaintiff to suffer the injuries mentioned above*.)
- "It was alleged that [the] officers were elected according to a system of by-laws inconsistent with and contrary to the articles of incorporation. *Wherefore* [read *Further*], it was alleged that the defendants were elected unlawfully and were usurping the offices which they held." *Attaway v. Melton*, 88 So.2d 417, 419 (La. Ct. App. 1956).

Cf. HERE- AND THERE- WORDS.

*****whereof** (= of what; of which) is a FORMAL WORD and an ARCHAISM best avoided except in the SET PHRASE *he knows whereof he speaks*.

*****wheresoever** is an unnecessary and archaic LEGAL-ISM for *wherever*. See **whatever**.

whereupon (= upon [the occurrence or occasion of] which; immediately after and as a result of which) may, by convention, begin a sentence, though it technically creates a FRAGMENT. E.g.:

- "Plaintiff demurred to those pleas, and the court of original jurisdiction gave judgment for the defendant. *Whereupon* the plaintiff brought error." *Christmas v. Russell*, 72 U.S. 290, 306 (1866) (per Clifford, J.).
- "Mr. Lavespere was not in the courtroom, and the bailiff's search of the hallways produced no response from him. *Whereupon*, counsel for Mrs. Lavespere moved that Mr. Lavespere's motion and rule be dismissed, which the court granted." *Lavespere v. Lavespere*, 991 So.2d 81, 83 (La. Ct. App. 2008).

But good legal writers just as often use this FORMAL WORD in midsentence—e.g.: "The general, naturally obeying his commander-in-chief instead of Taney, paid no attention to the writ; *whereupon* Taney quixotically ordered the general arrested for contempt of court." Fred Rodell, *Nine Men* 136 (1955). Cf. **but** & **and**.

wherewithal = means, esp. pecuniary means. Hence *financial wherewithal* is redundant—e.g.: "This doomsday scenario could only happen upon the refusal to pay by a defendant with the *financial wherewithal* [read *wherewithal*] to do so." *State v. Drury*, 36 So.3d 1150, 1152 n.4 (La. Ct. App. 2010). A suggested revision to cure the hopelessly unidiomatic phrasing: *This doomsday scenario could happen only if a defendant having the wherewithal to pay refused to do so*.

whether usually directly follows the noun whose dilemma it denotes: *decision whether, issue whether, question whether*. (See **question (as to) whether**.) E.g.:

- "This court has not previously made a *determination as to whether* [read *determination whether*] a modification to the amount of a money judgment constitutes an affirmation or a reversal of the original judgment." *Schiff v. Winchell*, 237 P.3d 99, 101 (Nev. 2010). Better: *This court has not previously determined whether . . . .*
- "The trial court's analysis was based exclusively upon plaintiff's claims and assertions without any independent *determination concerning whether* [read *determination whether*] class-certification prerequisites were met." *Ondrus v. Citizens Ins. Co.*, 781 N.W.2d 798, 799 (Mich. 2010).

Regardless, an adverb, makes *regardless of whether*. See **regardless (C)**.

A. As to whether. This collocation, though rarely defensible (see **question (as to) whether**), is here justified: "Reasonable men might well reach different conclusions *as to whether* [i.e., on the question whether] the servant was within the area of probable deviation, and therefore within his employment, when the accident occurred." *Kohlman v. Hyland*, 210 N.W. 643, 646 (N.D. 1926).

B. *Issue of whether*. Though this phrase is generally better without the *of* (i.e., as *issue whether*), it has certain uses in which *of* is obligatory, usually when *issue* is modified by an adjective. E.g.: "On cross-appeal, Shoemaker raises the threshold *issue of whether* the trial court's denial of the petition to revoke the Joint Trust is an appealable order." *Phillips v. Shoemaker*, 926 N.E.2d 1103, 1105 (Ind. Ct. App. 2010). See **issue (B)**.

C. *Whether or not*. Despite the SUPERSTITION to the contrary, the words *or not* are usually superfluous, since *whether* implies *or not*—e.g.: "This characterization avoids what is at the heart of the policy controversy, which is the question *whether or not* [read *whether*] research requiring embryo destruction is ethical." Rebecca Dresser, *Stem Cell Research as Innovation*, 38 J.L. Med. & Ethics 332, 337 (2010). The only context in which *or not* necessarily appears occurs when *whether or not* means "regardless of whether" <the meeting will go on whether or not it rains>.

D. *And if*. See **if (A)**.

which. A. *Which* [+ noun]. This construction is somewhat outmoded and stilted, though occasionally it is useful to avoid an AMBIGUITY. In these examples it is unnecessary:

- "The resolution was to award the contract to Ivey 'subject to the approval of the Public Housing Administration,' *which agency* [read *which*] subsequently approved the acceptance." *Crenshaw County Hosp. Bd. v. St. Paul Fire & Marine Ins. Co.*, 411 F.2d 213, 215 (5th Cir. 1969).
- "Southern Idaho enclosed a $20,000 check along with its acceptance, *which check* was deposited in Cal-Cut's bank account." *Southern Idaho Pipe & Steel Co. v. Cal-Cut Pipe & Supply, Inc.*, 567 P.2d 1246, 1247 (Idaho 1977). A suggested revision: *Along with its acceptance, Southern Idaho enclosed a $20,000 check, which was deposited.*

The *which* [+ noun] construction is defensible only if *which* is necessarily separated from its antecedent by a phrase—i.e., it overcomes the difficulty presented by the REMOTE RELATIVE. But *which* [+ noun] should never, as in the following sentence, directly follow its antecedent: "The civil service commission must grant him a public *hearing, which hearing* [omit *hearing*] must be held within a period of 15 days from the filing of the charges in writing and the return written answer thereto." 22 *Summary of Pennsylvania Jurisprudence* 586 (2d ed. 1995).

B. The Overeager *which*. One must be certain, before introducing a subordinate clause with *which*, that this word has a clear antecedent. Often writers actually put the *which*-clause *before* the antecedent. E.g.: "There was no showing or offer to show that plaintiff knew of any such custom, and even if we concede, *which plaintiff directly denies*, that the bank had so drawn for plaintiff in a prior year, that would not show his knowledge of any such custom." *Stewart v. Gregory, Carter & Co.*, 84 N.W. 553, 554–55 (N.D.

1900). A suggested revision: ... *even if we concede that the bank had so drawn for the plaintiff previously—a claim the plaintiff denies—that would not show....* See ANTICIPATORY REFERENCE.

C. *And which, or which*, and *but which*. These constructions often signal trouble, for there is only one quite limited context in which any of them can be proper. Each must follow a primary *which*-clause, with which it is parallel, not left floating at the end of a sentence without a shore in sight, as in the following sentence:

> The offer and sale of the certificates of deposit pursuant to the plan shall be conducted in such a manner as to be a separate, distinct offering not integrated with any related offer and sale of similar instruments pursuant to any subsequent pool or plan and the organizers shall not otherwise enter into subsequent transactions within a time period, *or which* otherwise satisfy the factual criteria set forth above, with the result that they might be integrated with offerings made pursuant to the plan.

To edit that sentence, one might break it into two sentences, neither having an overeager *which*:

> The offer and sale of the CDs under the plan must be conducted separately from any related offer and sale of similar instruments. In addition, the organizers may not, within a given period, either (a) engage in later transactions that satisfy the factual criteria set forth above, or (b) integrate the present offerings with later offerings under the same plan.

D. Without a Proper Antecedent. Grammarians have termed this mistake "broad reference": *which* refers to a general idea or an entire statement rather than to a specific antecedent. This fault should be carefully avoided. E.g.:

- "In 1963 the Western Sahara was [made] a non-self-governing territory under . . . the UN Charter, *after which* [read *under which*] Spain came under pressure . . . to decolonize." Susan Akram, *International Law and the Israeli–Palestinian Conflict* 151 (2011).
- "But the Saudi authorities refused to accept the animals, claiming they were diseased, *which* [read *a charge that*] Australia denied." Richard Ellis, *Sheep Trapped on Death Trip*, Sunday Times, 15 Oct. 1989, at A2.

E. Wrongly Elided. E.g.: "This is to advise you that so long as you continue to use the premises for the purposes [insert *for which*] you are now using them, namely, for sawmill purposes and lumber yard, and pay the rentals, your possession will not be disturbed." *F. H. Stoltze Land Co. v. Westberg*, 206 P. 407, 408 (Mont. 1922) (quoting a letter from the land's owner to the former leaseholder).

F. In Rhetorical Disclaimers for *and*. E.g.:

- "If mining is to be taxed (*which* [read *and*] I think it should not be), the least oppressive and least offensive method would be to tax the gold at the mint." Martha Edgerton Plassmann, "Biographical Sketch of Hon. Sidney Edgerton," in 3 *Contributions to the Historical Society of Montana* 331, 334 (1900).
- "Even if the court found one or both of the two challenged provisions to be unenforceable, *which* [read *and*] the court does not, it would still not invalidate the entire

employment agreement." *PrecisionIR Inc. v. Clepper*, 693 F.Supp.2d 286, 296 (S.D.N.Y. 2010).

G. And *that*. See *that & which*.

H. The Remote *which*. See REMOTE RELATIVES.

I. And *who* or *whom*. See *who* (C), (D).

while for *although* or *whereas* is permissible and often all but necessary, despite what purists say about the word's inherent temporality. Though *while* is a more relaxed and conversational term than *although* or *whereas*, it is usually quite at home in formal contexts. E.g.:

- "*While* in form our law is chiefly the work of judges, in great part judges simply put the guinea stamp of the state's authority upon propositions [that] they found worked out for them in advance." Roscoe Pound, *The Formative Era of American Law* 138 (1938).
- "It is settled, too, that orders granting or denying a preliminary injunction are appealable, *while* similar orders involving a temporary restraining order are not." Charles Alan Wright, *The Law of Federal Courts* 708 (4th ed. 1983).

See **whereas**.

The writer who uses *while* in this way should be on guard for AMBIGUITIES. For instance, does it denote time or concession in the following sentences?

- "*While* [read *Although* or *During the time when*?] the police still were on the scene and the victim was seated in one of the police cruisers, the defendant repeatedly telephoned her on her cellular telephone." *State v. Strong*, 999 A.2d 765, 769 (Conn. App. Ct. 2010).
- "*While* [read *Although* or *During the time when*?] the police were dragging Wes away, he threatened to kill everyone when he got out of jail." *People v. Cowan*, 236 P.3d 1074, 1098 (Cal. 2010).

While should not be used merely for *and*—e.g.: "The former husband has an advantage in that he is a lawyer *while* [read *and*] the former wife is not." *Paulson v. Evander*, 633 So.2d 540, 541 (Fla. Dist. Ct. App. 1994). Sometimes this sloppy usage leads to preposterous statements—e.g.: "Mr. Taney made the opening statement *while* Mr. Pigman examined the witnesses." Edward S. Delaplaine, *Chief Justice Roger B. Taney: His Career as a Lawyer*, 52 Am. L. Rev. 535, 565 (1918).

*while at the same time is a common REDUNDANCY—e.g.:

- "Motivate them to keep selling the company *while at the same time* [read *while*] taking credit for their particular accomplishment." Mark H. McCormack, *What They Don't Teach You at Harvard Business School* 194 (1984).
- "We view the evidence as a whole and indulge all reasonable inferences in favor of the jury's verdict *while at the same time* [read *while*] asking whether any rational trier of fact could have found the essential elements of the crime beyond a reasonable doubt." *State v. Johnson*, 229 P.3d 523, 538 (N.M. 2010).

while away; *wile away. The phrase *while away* (= to spend [time] idly) dates from the early 17th century and remains the predominant form. **Wile away*, a synonymous phrase dating from about 1800, began as a corrupt form but is included in modern dictionaries such as *W11* and *AHD* without any cautionary note. Most commonly, of course, *wile* is a noun meaning "a stratagem intended to deceive" or "trickery"; it may also function as a verb in the corresponding sense "to lure or entice." However old the mistaken form **wile away* is—and never mind that Charles Dickens used it—still inferior to *while away*. E.g.:

- "Pizzas were ordered and the boys *wiled* [read *whiled*] away the time by examining defendant's unloaded guns." *Dino v. State*, 405 So.2d 213, 214 (Fla. Dist. Ct. App. 1981).
- "Before Kim Peek saw *Rain Man*, the 1988 award-winning movie loosely based on his life, he stayed home and *wiled* [read *whiled*] away the time working and reading books." Rhonda Smith, *Into the World*, Austin American-Statesman, 28 Apr. 1994, at D1.

whilom. See **erstwhile**.

whilst, though a correct form, is virtually obsolete in AmE and reeks of pretension in a modern American writer. But *whilst* is still common in BrE—e.g.:

- "Defendant, knowing the premises, maliciously intended to injure plaintiff as lessee and manager of the theatre *whilst* the agreement with Wagner was in force." *Lumley v. Gye*, [1853] 118 Eng. Rptr. 749, 751 (Q.B.).
- "L damaged D's car and, *whilst* it was being repaired, D hired a car from A." David Kelly et al., *Business Law* 511 (2005).

Like its sibling *while*, it may be used for *although* or *whereas*, although this is not good modern usage in AmE. E.g.:

- "*Whilst* [read *While*], therefore, their professions are those of lawabiding citizens, their conduct was that of anarchists, recognizing no governing power save unbridled passion." *Warner v. Talbot*, 36 So. 743, 831 (La. 1903).
- "*Whilst* [read *While*] it is true that on some other provision of our law the husband, as master of the community, was the proper party to bring the suit, it is also true that under our community law, the wife had an interest in making the claim." *Holley v. Butler Furniture Co.*, 37 So.2d 476, 479 (La. Ct. App. 1948).

For *amongst*, see **among** (A).

whistleblower (= an informant) is best written as one word, as the Whistleblower Protection Act of 1989 (U.S.).

Whiteacre is the mythical tract of land contrasted with *Blackacre* in hypothetical legal problems. E.g.:

- "Let it be assumed, further, that, in consideration of $100 actually paid by A to B, the latter agrees with A never to enter on X's land, *Whiteacre*." Wesley Newcomb Hohfeld, *Fundamental Legal Conceptions* 76 (1923).

- "Assume that Maria is an investor in real estate, and owns *Whiteacre*, which is unimproved land held for long-term appreciation." James A. Fellows, *Bargain Sales of Property to Tax-Exempt Organizations*, 39 Real Est. L.J. 89, 89 (2010).

See **Blackacre.**

White Book = the two-volume compilation—published in white hardcover editions—of the procedural and administrative rules of the Supreme Court of England and Wales. Cf. **White Paper.**

whitehorse case; horse case; gray mule case; spotted pony case; pony case; goose case. These are terms meaning "a reported case with virtually identical facts, the disposition of which should determine the outcome of the instant case." The terms are now less commonly used in the law schools than formerly; but they are useful terms. E.g.: "The decision mentioned is rather a '*white horse*' case." *Roosth & Genecov Prod. Co. v. White*, 262 S.W.2d 99, 101 (Tex. 1953).

All the quadruped METAPHORS make some sense: they might be said to *run on all fours*. (See **on all fours.**) But *goose case*, common in the southern U.S., especially in Louisiana, is anomalous—e.g.:

- "Counsel for intervenor in his brief before this Court frankly confesses this failure to dig deeply enough into the books to discover the '*goose*' case until after he had felt the sting of adverse judicial opinion." *McGuffin v. Barkett*, 44 So.2d 195, 198 (La. Ct. App. 1950).
- "Although the Supreme Court has not yet been presented with a '*goose*' case, it is difficult to imagine that it would not conclude that the knowing failure to curb student-on-student harassment is actionable." *Rowinsky v. Bryan Indep. Sch. Dist.*, 80 F.3d 1006, 1023 (5th Cir. 1996).
- "The *goose case*, not mentioned by anybody, is *State v. Shaw.* . . . We noted there, and I note here, that the consensual disclosure of contraband is not even a search—it is a plain-view seizure and clearly admissible." *State v. Malone*, 912 So.2d 394, 399 (La. Ct. App. 2005).

Cf. **on all fours.**

White Paper; Green Paper. In British governmental affairs, a *White Paper* announces a firm government policy to be implemented (cf. **White Book**). A *Green Paper* announces a tentative proposal for discussion.

white-powder bar is a derogatory name for defense lawyers who represent cocaine dealers. E.g.: "Neal R. Sonnett, the president of the National Association of Criminal Defense Lawyers, said such behavior was offensive to most trial lawyers, as was the term '*white-powder bar*.' 'There's no such thing as a '*white-powder bar*,' he said. 'It's a very pejorative term.'" Neil A. Lewis, *Drug Lawyers' Quandary: Lure of Money vs. Ethics*, N.Y. Times, 9 Feb. 1990, at A1, B11. See *white-powder lawyer* under LAWYERS, DEROGATORY NAMES FOR (A).

white-powder lawyer. See LAWYERS, DEROGATORY NAMES FOR (A).

white-shoe lawyer. See LAWYERS, DEROGATORY NAMES FOR (A).

whither is an ARCHAISM meaning (1) "to what place or position" <Whither shall we go?>; or (2) "to which" <at Chelsea Square, whither we had gone>. It has virtually no place in modern writing. Cf. **thither.**

who. A. *Who & whom.* Edward Sapir, the philosopher of language, prophesied that "within a couple of hundred years from to-day not even the most learned jurist will be saying 'Whom did you see?' By that time the *whom* will be as delightfully archaic as the Elizabethan *his* for *its*. No logical or historical argument will avail to save this hapless *whom*." Edward Sapir, *Language* 156–57 (1921). A safer bet might have been that no one will be spelling *to-day* with a hyphen. In any event, writers in the late 20th and early 21st centuries ought to understand how the words *who* and *whom* are correctly used.

The distinction to keep in mind is that *who* acts as the subject of a verb, whereas *whom* acts as the object of a verb or preposition. Though not commonly observed in informal speech, the distinction is one to be strictly followed in formal legal prose.

Some lapses are so flagrant that one can hardly fathom how they could have been committed. E.g.: "The three top finishers on the bar exam were Beverly Ray, Michelle Monse, and Kenneth Buck, *all of who* [read *all of whom*] took our bar review course!" Others are more forgivable because the correct use is less obvious:

- "Boyer said she knew the person *who* [read *whom*] she identified as Roy Summers as 'Tiny's' brother." *State v. Iwakiri*, 682 P.2d 571, 593 (Idaho 1984).
- "And he [Judge Stephen G. Breyer, as nominee to the Supreme Court] promised, following the admonition of the late Justice Arthur Goldberg, *who* [read *whom*] he served as a law clerk 30 years ago, to do his best to avoid footnotes." Ruth Marcus, *Judge Breyer Gets Day in Rose Garden*, Wash. Post, 17 May 1994, at A8.
- "At trial, Miller refused to testify unless the district court excluded four young African-American men *whom* [read *who*] she felt posed a threat to her personal safety." *Feazell v. State*, 906 P.2d 727, 728 (Nev. 1995).
- "She acknowledged that the defendant named other people, *whom* [read *who*] he said were setting fires." *U.S. v. Irons*, 646 F.Supp.2d 927, 948 (E.D. Tenn. 2009).

Although *whom* might seem to be the object of *reveal* in the sentence that follows, in fact the relative pronoun is the subject of an implied verb—*failed to reveal who* [*might have wanted to kill Robert Nachtsheim*]. Therefore, *who* is correct: "There are a number of people who might have wanted to kill Robert Nachtsheim in his Minneapolis flower shop early one morning in 1973, but the intervening two decades have failed to reveal *whom* [read *who*]." Kevin Diaz, *$4 Million Award's a Start Toward a Clean Slate*, Star Tribune (Minneapolis), 22 Oct. 1994, at 1A.

Many writers have announced the demise of *whom*, but it persists—especially in AmE. *Who* would be impossible, for example, in this sentence: "If the person on *whom* the duty of electing rests elects to take in conformity with the will or other instrument of donation, he thereby relinquishes his own property, and must release or convey it to the donee upon *whom* the instrument had assumed to confer it." *Sellick v. Sellick*, 173 N.W. 609, 612 (Mich. 1919). And in formal writing, the following instances of *whom* seem natural:

- "It will not much affect the type of case which it is supposed to affect, or restrain the person *whom* it purports to restrain, namely, the litigious troublemaker." *Barry v. American Sec. & Trust Co.*, 135 F.2d 470, 473 (D.C. Cir. 1943).
- "A fundamental principle of our representative democracy is, in Hamilton's words, 'that the people should choose *whom* they please to govern them.'" *Powell v. McCormack*, 395 U.S. 486, 547 (1969) (per Warren, C.J.).
- "Proprietors of private enterprises, such as places of amusement and resort, had no such obligation and were privileged to serve *whomever* they pleased." *Jacobson v. New York Racing Ass'n, Inc.*, 305 N.E.2d 765, 767 (N.Y. 1973).

The correct uses of *who* are sometimes tricky, often because of distracting text between the subject and verb of the clause. But if the pronoun acts as the subject of a clause, it must be *who*, never *whom*—e.g.:

- "An ostensible agent is one *who has* no authority, but *who* the principal has by conduct led third persons to believe *is* clothed with authority." Essel Ray Dillavou, *Principles of Business Law* 104 (2d ed. 1938). *Who* is the subject of *has* in the first clause and of *is* in the badly phrased second clause.
- "If the servant, without authority, entrusts the instrumentality to one *whom* [read *who*], on account of his age, inexperience, or recklessness, he has reason to believe *is* likely to harm others, the master would be liable." Warren Abner Seavey, *Cases on Agency* 118 (1945). *Who* is the subject of *is*.
- "It may, for instance, be negligent on the part of the employer to hire an employee *who* the employer should realize *is* unfit and poses a risk to others." Steven Emanuel, *Torts Caselines* 329 (2007). *Who* is the subject of *is*.

Among the toughest contexts in which to get the pronouns right are those involving linking verbs. We say, for example, *who it is* for the same reason we say *It is I*, but some very good writers have nodded—e.g.:

- "The distinguished political and social philosopher Russell Kirk used the word 'energumen' to describe . . . *whom* [read *who*] it is I agitate against." William F. Buckley, *The Jeweler's Eye* 284 (1969).
- "Trials on indictment are in the name of the Queen . . . ; thus a criminal case is generally called *Reg. v. whomever* [read *whoever*] it is." Glanville Williams, *Learning the Law* 17 (11th ed. 1982).

See HYPERCORRECTION (F).

William Safire takes an interesting approach for those caught between feeling pedantic (by using *whom*) or incorrect (by using *who* for *whom*): "When *whom* is correct, recast the sentence." *On Language*, N.Y. Times, 4 Oct. 1992, § 6, at 12. So *Whom do you trust?* becomes, in a political campaign, *Which candidate do you trust?* See PHRASING & PRONOUNS (B).

B. Placement of. In well-constructed sentences, *who* directly follows the name it refers to, or is interrupted at most by a parenthesis properly set off. Writers who violate this principle risk befuddling their readers—e.g.: "The largest collection [of fossils was] made by L. Kohl-Larson in 1938–1939, who also found a small fragment of hominid maxilla." Walter W. Bishop, *Geological Background to Fossil Man* 157 (1978). [Read *The largest collection of fossils was made in 1938–1939 by L. Kohl-Larson, who also found a small fragment of hominid maxilla.*] See REMOTE RELATIVES.

C. Improper Use in Reference to Nonhuman Entities (*who* for *that* or *which*). *Who* and *that* are the relative pronouns for human beings; *that* and *which* are the relative pronouns for anything other than human beings. But writers sometimes forget this elementary point—e.g.:

- "In this diversity action, we are called upon to decide whether a drawee bank *who* [read *that*] has missed the midnight deadline [is accountable under these circumstances]." *Starcraft Co. v. C.J. Heck Co.*, 748 F.2d 982, 984 (5th Cir. 1984) (per Randall, J.).
- "Many companies, I believe, *who* [read *that*] are busy buying new businesses and bringing in new management teams haven't even tested the outside edge of their profitability." Mark H. McCormack, *What They Don't Teach You at Harvard Business School* 203 (1984).

D. *Which* for *who* or *whom*. This misuse—the opposite of that illustrated in (C)—occurs when writers use *which* in referring to human beings—e.g.:

- "Exhibit No. 9 names the clients *which* [read *whom* or *that*] Kroenecke serviced." *Henshaw v. Kroenecke*, 656 S.W.2d 416, 419 (Tex. 1983).
- "The driver of the first car, *which* [read *who*] was the only occupant, also died at the scene." *2 Killed in 3-Vehicle Crash on Highway 360*, Dallas Morning News, 7 July 2003 at B2. Because the writer used *which* instead of *who*, it seems at first as if the car was its own passenger and died in the accident.

The word *that*, of course, is permissible when referring to humans: *the people that were present* or *the people who were present*. Editors tend, however, to prefer the latter phrasing.

whoever. See **who(so)ever.**

whole. See **in whole.**

whole-act rule. See **textual-integrity canon.**

*wholistic is a mistaken form of *holistic*.

whom. See **who (A).**

whom(so)ever; whomso(ever). See **who(so)ever.**

whoredom = (1) prostitution; or (2) idolatry.

who's; whose. The first is the contraction of *who is*; the second is the possessive form of *who*. The two forms are occasionally confused, usually when *who's* erroneously displaces *whose*—e.g.:

- "At the very least, the burden of proof carried by one who would have rights cancelled should be greater than the burden of one *who's* [read *whose*] only purpose is to prevent a registration from issuing." *Food Specialty Co. v. Catz Am. Co.*, 433 F.2d 817, 819 (C.C.P.A. 1970) (Baldwin, J., dissenting).
- "Mr. Hahn also identified $628.00 as cashed checks, *who's* [read *whose*] purpose was unknown." *U.S. v. Curry*, 681 F.2d 406, 413 n.16 (5th Cir. 1982).
- "Because Rady did not provide evidence that she performed work that was equal, and not merely similar, to that of the male location manager *who's* [read *whose*] pay was increased to $20.80 per hour on May 19, 2009, she cannot use that male as a comparator for purposes of her Equal Pay Act claim." *Prise v. Alderwoods Group, Inc.*, 657 F.Supp.2d 564, 627 n.22 (W.D. Pa. 2009).

whose may usefully refer to nonpersons <an idea whose time has come>. This use of *whose*, formerly decried by some 19th-century grammarians and their predecessors, is often an inescapable way of avoiding clumsiness. *Which*, unfortunately, has no other possessive form, apart from *of which*, an inaesthetic phrase in many contexts—e.g.: "What is commonly termed ownership is in fact tenancy, *the continuance of which* [read *whose continuance*] is contingent upon legally recognized rights of tenure, with corresponding duties." Everett Fraser, *Cases and Readings on Property* 34 (3d ed. 1954).

But *whose* in place of *of which* can lead to such problems as these: "One of those dealers was J & S Government Securities, Inc., *whose* home office was in New York, but *who* also had offices in Houston." (See ANTHROPOMORPHISM.) The sentence could be recast in myriad ways—e.g.: "which had its home office in New York, but offices in Houston as well." (In the corrected sentence, *offices* is a plural noun, not a verb. See **office**.)

who(so)ever; whom(so)ever; *whoso(ever); *whomso(ever). A. Choice of Term. The forms *whoever* and *whomever* are preferred in modern writing. Users of *whosoever* and *whomsoever*, as well as **who(m)so*, are liable to criticism for using LEGALESE, ARCHAISMS, and BIBLICAL AFFECTATION. Often these terms are superfluous, as here: "It expressly limits the liability of the employer and abolishes all rights and remedies of every person *whomsoever* [omit *whomsoever*] against the employer." *Roseberry v. Phillips Petroleum Co.*, 369 P.2d 403, 405 (N.M. 1962).

B. Case. The problem of proper case arises with these words, just as it does with *who* and *whom*. E.g.:

- "Ohio should . . . go after the defendant or *whomever* [read *whoever*] is responsible." *Jenkins v. Ohio Cas. Ins. Co.*, 794 So.2d 228, 235 (Miss. 2001).
- "*Whomever* [read *Whoever*] wrote the Report, of course, would have had access to the major Federalist speeches

and pamphlets defending the Acts." Kurt T. Lash & Alicia Harrison, *Minority Report: John Marshall and the Defense of the Alien and Sedition Acts*, 68 Ohio St. L.J. 435, 504 n.349 (2007).

The *Oxford Guide* contains this rather poor advice: "Use *whoever* for the objective case as well as the subjective, rather than *whomever*, which is rather stilted" (135). Stilted, perhaps, but correct when called for, and really not very stilted in formal prose. See PRONOUNS (B).

C. Possessives. *Whoever's* (colloquial) is incorrect (in formal prose) for *whosever*. E.g.:

- "He denied telling appellant that she was going to jail, although he did admit saying that *whoever's* [read *whosever*] fingerprints were found in that vault could go to jail." *Williams v. State*, 441 So.2d 653, 655 (Fla. Dist. Ct. App. 1983).
- "The detective in charge of the interrogation testified that prior to the interrogation he had had a conversation with the fingerprint expert in which both agreed to almost a hundred per cent certainty that *whoever's* [read *whosever*] finger prints were on one side of the door panel which had been removed, the palm prints matched because they were in perfect configuration." *Commonwealth v. Haynes*, 577 A.2d 564, 572 n.2 (Pa. Super. Ct. 1990). On the use of *prior to in that sentence, see ***prior to.**

Justice Holmes sometimes used *whosesoever*, a correct form made unnecessary by the modern preference of *who(s)ever* over *who(se)soever*.

wide; broad. *Wide*, when used in contexts in which idiomatic English would require *broad*, is a LEGALISM. E.g.:

- "A public body has *wide* discretion in soliciting and accepting bids for public improvements." *Baxter's Asphalt & Concrete, Inc. v. Dep't of Transp.*, 475 So.2d 1284, 1287 (Fla. Dist. Ct. App. 1985).
- "Trial courts are vested with *wide* discretion when making evidentiary rulings." *Von Sternberg v. Caffee*, 692 N.W.2d 549, 554 (S.D. 2005).

Wide is used more commonly in BrE in this sense—e.g.: "The words 'the broadest terms' are too wide." 1 William Oldnall Russell et al., *A Treatise on Crimes and Misdemeanors* 177 (1910).

widely regarded. See **regard (B)**.

widespread was, until the early 20th century, spelled as two words, but now it should always appear as one.

*widespreadedly is a bastard formation. W3 records no adverbial form of the adjective *widespread*, although if there were one it would be *widespreadly*. E.g.: "An adherent to current American doctrine in the negligence field would hardly reject a principle already so *widespreadly* [read *widely*] accepted by judges and other scholars alike." *Hewitt v. Safeway Stores, Inc.*, 404 F.2d 1247, 1254 (D.C. Cir. 1968).

The form *widespreadedly, malformed perhaps on the spurious analogy of *allegedly* and *reportedly*, wrongly assumes the existence of a past-tense form *spreaded. E.g.: "The area of public interest to which [the publications] relate—conditions allegedly capable of *wide-spreadedly* [read *widely*] affecting public health—would seem . . . to be one of such inherent public concern and stake that there could be no possible question as to the applicability of the *New York Times* standard for any defeasance." *United Med. Labs., Inc. v. Columbia Broad. Sys., Inc.*, 404 F.2d 706, 711 (9th Cir. 1968). See -EDLY.

widow, n. The Supreme Court's phrase *surviving widows who administer estates* is a REDUNDANCY. *See Reed v. Reed*, 404 U.S. 71, 75 (1971) (paraphrased). A *widow* who administers her deceased husband's estate must—by the very nature of the situation—have survived him.

widow, vb., may apply to a spouse of either sex. So *widowed man* is unobjectionable, although to many it may seem at first unnatural.

widow; widower. Does this term still apply when one remarries? No.

wield; weald. *Wield* is the verb meaning "to control; handle; hold and use" <he wields his power with good judgment>. Its rare homophone, *weald*, is the noun meaning "a forest" or "an uncultivated upland region."

wigged; unwigged. These attributive nouns denote barristers and solicitors, respectively—e.g.: "The two sides—the *wigged* and the *unwigged*—are kept severely apart: solicitors cannot have lunch in the barristers' Inns of Court, and barristers must never be seen at the solicitors' Law Society." Anthony Sampson, *Anatomy of Britain* 148 (1962).

*****wile away.** See **while away.**

wilful. See **willful.**

will. A. Definition. What is the meaning of *will*? It's not so easy as one might think. Most jurisdictions simply define a *will* as a revocable instrument that gives away property upon the maker's death. But some jurisdictions have much broader definitions—e.g.:

- "A *will* is an oral declaration or written instrument [satisfying formal requirements] to take effect upon death, whereby a person disposes of property or directs how it shall not be disposed of, disposes of his body or any part thereof, exercises a power, appoints a fiduciary or makes any other provision for the administration of his estate, and [that] is revocable during his lifetime." N.Y. Estate Powers & Trusts Law § 1-2.19 (1998).
- "'Will' includes codicil and any testamentary instrument that merely appoints an executor, revokes or revises another *will*, nominates a guardian, or expressly excludes or limits the right of an individual or class to succeed to property of the decedent passing by intestate succession." Unif. Prob. Code § 1-201(55) (2004).

The New York reference to bodies and body parts is said to be "particularly rare." Roger W. Andersen & Ira Mark Bloom, *Fundamentals of Trusts and Estates* (3d ed. 2007). Meanwhile, the Uniform Probate Code

definition is truly circular: a "*will*" includes a "testamentary instrument." Well what, precisely, is that? You might say it's a *will*.

B. And *testament*. A common belief among lawyers is that, at common law, a *will* disposed of real property and a *testament* of personal property. This belief is, strictly speaking, erroneous, although from the 18th century such a distinction in usage (unfounded in the substantive law) began to emerge. The distinction is now obsolete, however, so that in modern legal usage the words are interchangeable, *will* remaining the usual term.

The archaic distinction between the words is said to have grown out of the historical development of property dispositions. Ecclesiastical courts had jurisdiction of cases involving the distribution and use of personal property; appeals from these courts were to Rome, under the Catholic hierarchy, until 1533. The common-law courts of England, meanwhile, decided cases involving the use and disposition of real property. The two court systems developed distinct terms for decedents' estates. As a result of the bifurcated judicial system, the myth goes, the terminology was Anglo-Saxon (*will*) for real-property dispositions, and Latinate (*testament*) for personal-property dispositions, the latter term having derived from Roman law.

But history, especially linguistic history, never comes so neatly packaged. It is not surprising, then, to discover that medieval writers are recorded as having used *will* in reference to personal property and *testament* in reference to land. Even so, the myth concerning these terms may be valid insofar as it explains the tendencies in usage that would later give rise to an idiomatic DIFFERENTIATION. It is at least possible that the DOUBLET *last will and testament* had in its origins a purpose for the inclusion of both real and personal property. (See **last will and testament.**) In any event, *will* now denotes the entire testamentary instrument, a place formerly said to be occupied by *devise*. See also **codicil** & **testament.**

will, vb., has two senses: (1) "must; going to; tending to"; or (2) "to dispose of by will." For a discussion of sense 1, see WORDS OF AUTHORITY (D). In sense 2, *will* is always transitive—e.g.:

- "If an employee had a vested right in compensation, he could *will* it away." *Bry-Block Mercantile Co. v. Carson*, 288 S.W. 726, 728 (Tenn. 1926).
- "If he has only one child he can *will* her two-thirds of his property." *Succession of Lauga*, 624 So.2d 1156, 1178 (La. 1993).
- "I *will* and bequeath all of my property owned by me at my death to my wife." *In re Clark*, 6 So.3d 266, 267 (La. Ct. App. 2009) (quoting testament).

See **devise,** vb.

willable = transferable by will. E.g.: "Kerr, without providing any case law to support her claim, states that 'sperm has not been held to be legally *willable*.'"

Ronald Chester, *Double Trouble*, 44 St. Louis U. L.J. 451, 455 n.21 (2000). The *OED* traces this sense back to only 1880.

willful; wilful. A. Senses. *Willful* = (1) intentional; or (2) malicious; bad-faith. The AMBIGUITY of the term is no recommendation of it.

"*Wilful* is not a term of art," commented Lord Justice Wright, "and is often used as meaning no more than a high degree of carelessness or recklessness. It is not necessarily limited in its use to intentional or deliberate wrong-doing." *Caswell v. Powell Duffryn Assoc. Collieries*, [1940] A.C. 152, 177 (H.L.). The same problem exists in AmE: "The word *wilful* or *wilfully* when used in the definition of a crime, it has been said time and again, means only intentionally or purposely as distinguished from accidentally or negligently and does not require any actual impropriety; while on the other hand it has been stated with equal repetition and insistence that the requirement added by such a word is not satisfied unless there is a bad purpose or evil intent." Rollin M. Perkins & Ronald N. Boyce, *Criminal Law* 875–76 (3d ed. 1982). One influential writer has sensibly suggested that the word should not be used because of its AMBIGUITY. See G.W. Paton, *A Textbook of Jurisprudence* 313 n.2 (4th ed. 1972).

B. Spelling. *Willful* is the preferred spelling in AmE, *wilful* in BrE. *Willfull, a misspelling, occasionally appears.

willfulness; malice aforethought. These terms are sometimes confused in criminal contexts. *Willfulness* is the broader term—e.g.: "An act is done *willfully* if done voluntarily and intentionally, and with the specific intent to do something the law forbids." 1 Edward J. Devitt & Charles Blackmar, *Federal Jury Practice and Instructions* 384 (1977). But see **willful.**

Malice aforethought is used in the context of homicide—e.g.: "*Malice aforethought* means an intent, at the time of a killing, wilfully to take the life of a human being, or an intent wilfully to act in callous or wanton disregard of the consequences to human life; but *malice aforethought* does not necessarily imply any ill will, spite, or hatred toward the individual killed." 2 Edward J. Devitt & Charles Blackmar, *Federal Jury Practice and Instructions* 215 (1977). See **malice** & **malice aforethought.**

willy-nilly (= willingly or unwillingly; by compulsion) is an English equivalent of the LATINISM *nolens volens*. E.g.: "This Court may not *willy-nilly* apply standards—even manageable standards—having no relation to constitutional harms." *Vieth v. Jubelirer*, 541 U.S. 267, 295 (2004) (per Scalia, J.). It is sometimes, as the *OED* remarks, erroneously used for "undecided, shilly-shally" <a willy-nilly disposition>.

win a victory, to. See **victory.**

winner. See **loser.**

-WISE. Phrases arrived at with this combining form are generally to be discouraged. They often displace a more direct wording, and they are invariably graceless and inelegant. E.g.:

- "Just compensation means that the owners must be put in as good a position *money-wise* [read *financially*] as they would have occupied had their property not been taken." *State v. Noble*, 305 P.2d 495, 497 (Utah 1957).
- "Even if acceptable *populationwise* [read *as applied to the population as a whole*], the . . . plan was invidiously discriminatory because a 'political fairness principle' was followed." *Gaffney v. Cummings*, 412 U.S. 735, 752 (1973) (per White, J.).
- "The choice of the corporate form for doing business confers certain *advantages taxwise* [read *tax advantages*]." *Dolese v. U.S.*, 605 F.2d 1146, 1154 (10th Cir. 1979).
- "Every corporate executive in this country knows that it is cheaper *taxwise* [read *for tax purposes*] to raise money through borrowing than through equity financing." Constantine N. Katsoris, *The Level Playing Field*, 17 Fordham Urb. L.J. 419, 480 n.435 (1989).
- "Even speech that, *content-wise* [omit *content-wise*, together with surrounding commas], lies near the core of the First Amendment's protection—archetypical public speech—may be deemed private speech." *Mitchell v. Hillsborough County*, 468 F.3d 1276, 1284 (11th Cir. 2006). On *archetypal* vs. *archetypical, see **archetypal.**

wise (= manner; fashion; way) is an ARCHAISM that still appears infrequently in legal writing—e.g.:

- "The defendant . . . is hereby enjoined from coming around or *in any wise* [read *in any way*] interfering with or molesting the complainant." *Sartin v. Sartin*, 405 So.2d 84, 84 (Miss. 1981).
- "Jou made no cognizable allegation that MIEC's failure to respond to his inquiries regarding waiver *in any wise* [read *in any way*] derogated that protection or security." *Jou v. Medical Ins. Exch. of Cal.*, 70 P.3d 662, 678 (Haw. Ct. App. 2003).

See **nowise.**

wit, to. See **to wit.**

withal is an ARCHAISM for *besides, nevertheless, with*, or *therewith*. E.g.: "Society has labored long and hard—yet *withal* [omit *withal*], perhaps neither long enough nor hard enough—to understand and come to grips with this affliction." *Donahue v. R.I. Dep't of Mental Health, Retardation & Hosps.*, 632 F.Supp. 1456, 1480 (D.R.I. 1986).

with all deliberate speed calls to mind the LATINISM *festina lente* (= make haste slowly). Made famous in *Brown v. Board of Education*, 349 U.S. 294, 301 (1955), the phrase is thought to have originated in English Chancery Courts: "A state cannot be expected to move with the celerity of a private business man; it is enough if it proceeds, in the language of the English Chancery, *with all deliberate speed*." *Virginia v. West Virginia*, 222 U.S. 17, 19–20 (1911) (per Holmes, J.). But the more frequent phrase in equity courts was *with all convenient speed*.

Deliberate speed, on the other hand, has literary as well as equitable origins. The English poets Lord Byron (1788–1824) and Francis Thompson (1859–1907) both used the phrase, as did Goethe (1749–1832), if one forces the translation a little.

The phrase "resembles poetry and resembles equity techniques of discretionary accommodation between principle and expediency, but [it] fits precisely one thing only, namely, the unique function of judicial review in the American system. . . . It means only that the Court, having announced its principle, and having required a measure of initial compliance, resumed its posture of passive receptiveness to the complaints of litigants." Alexander M. Bickel, *The Least Dangerous Branch* 253–54 (1962). However grandiose that may sound, the Court later said that the phrase "has turned out to be only a soft EUPHEMISM for delay." *Alexander v. Holmes County Bd. of Educ.*, 396 U.S. 1218, 1219 (1969) (per Black, J.). See OXYMORONS & WEASEL WORDS.

with force and arms. See *vi et armis.*

withholding of deportation. See **suspension of deportation.**

within, adj. "The legal tone is still too strong for common use in the *within* letter." Wilson Follett, *Modern American Usage* 45 (1966). Indeed, it is perhaps too strong even for use by legal writers, for *enclosed* is far more common and more natural. E.g.:

- "The *within* property shall not be sold or encumbered without the express written consent of the *within* mortgagees, or their assigns." *Sanders v. Hicks*, 317 So.2d 61, 62 63 (Miss. 1975). This use is apparently elliptical for *within-named*; the writer should have omitted the word or phrase completely, for it adds nothing.
- "The Clerk is hereby directed to transmit a copy of the *within* [read *enclosed*] to the parties and the Magistrate Judge." *Burns v. Marley Co. Pension Plan*, 663 F.Supp.2d 135, 146 (E.D.N.Y. 2009).

within, prep. See **no later than.**

within-named. See **within.**

within the statute. See **statute of frauds (B).**

without is a FORMAL WORD when used as an equivalent of *outside.* Usually, *without* is contrasted to *with*; but in law it is frequently an opposite of *within.* Though somewhat archaic, in formal legal prose this usage should be considered unexceptionable. E.g.:

- "Erlichman, by reason of the prior litigation, was cast in the role of the 'wrongdoer' and thus fell *without* the pale of the public-policy protection envisioned by the Safety Responsibility Act." *Farmers Ins. Co. v. Erlichman*, 634 P.2d 582, 584 (Ariz. Ct. App. 1981).
- "When parties settle the issue of outstanding fees, it is *without* our realm to instruct them how to arrive at a mutually acceptable amount." *Pennsylvania Envtl. Def. Found. v. Canon-McMillan Sch. Dist.*, 152 F.3d 228, 238 (3d Cir. 1998).

without day. See **go hence without day,** *sine die* & LOAN TRANSLATIONS.

*without limiting the generality of the foregoing. See **including but not limited to.**

without prejudice (= without loss of any rights) is peculiar to legal JARGON. The phrase describes a legal action—either judicial or among private parties—that in no way harms or cancels the legal rights or privileges of a party. The antonym is *with prejudice.* See **prejudice (A).**

without recourse; *sans recours.* The English phrase *without recourse* is preferred over the GALLICISM *sans recours* for the stipulation that the drawer or indorser of a bill of exchange may add to his signature, repudiating his liability to the holder.

without the statute. See **statute of frauds (B).**

with prejudice. See **without prejudice.**

with regard to. See **regard (A).**

with respect to. See **respect.**

with the object of ——ing is verbose for a simple infinitive, e.g., *with the object of preventing* in place of *to prevent.*

witness, n. **A. Generally.** *Witness* = (1) one who sees or knows something and testifies about it; (2) one who gives evidence under oath or affirmation, either orally or by affidavit or deposition; or (3) one who, to vouch for the genuineness of a signature, affixes his or her name to an instrument that another has signed.

B. And Its Near-Synonyms: *eyewitness; earwitness; observer; onlooker; looker-on; bystander.* These terms all refer to one who can account for what has occurred as a result of sensory perceptions. A *witness* is one who knows firsthand and is therefore competent to testify <call the witness to the stand>. An *eyewitness* has perceived firsthand with the eyes; an *earwitness* has directly perceived with the ears. An *observer* is one who attends closely to details—often one who is trained in systematic observation and who takes down an account of perceptions. An *onlooker* or *looker-on* is casually detached from the action as a happenstance spectator <onlookers told police what they saw>. A *bystander* has even less to do with the spectacle than an *onlooker.* A *bystander* is someone who stands by when something of some significance occurs but has no other connection with it <the photographer, a bystander on the sidelines, was injured when the tight end caught the ball on the sideline and fell into his knees>.

C. Possessive Form of *witness.* The preferable possessive form is *witness's.*

D. And **testifier* or **testis.* **Testifier* is rarely if ever justified in practice; **testis* never is. They are both NEEDLESS VARIANTS. See **testis.*

witness, vb. = to attest or act as a witness <to witness a will>. This LEGALISM is fairly familiar in the lay idiom. See **attest.**

---

witness-box; witness stand. The first is primarily BrE, the second primarily AmE—although there is some overlap on both sides of the Atlantic. Following are modern English and American examples of *witness box*:

- "It often becomes a difficult question for the court to decide *whether or not* [read *whether*] the defendant can go into the *witness-box* and give evidence." Walter S. Shirley, *An Elementary Treatise on Magisterial Law and on the Practice of Magistrates*, 26 (1880). For more on the edit here, see **whether (c)**.

- "The court rearranged the *witness box* so that the jury would be unable to see the shackles." *State v. Calhoun*, 554 So.2d 127, 132 (La. Ct. App. 1989).

Cf. **jurybox.**

A British philologist writes that "in the middle 'fifties, a British judge vehemently rebuked the American defendant's use in 'his' court of the expression *witness-stand* and insisted with some heat on having *witness-box*." Brian Foster, *The Changing English Language* 61–62 (1968). Before the end of the decade, however, *witness stand* had found its way onto BBC airwaves. *Id.* at 62. See **stand.**

witnesseth is commonly used at the outset of contracts and affidavits. E.g.: "[The deed] contains the following relevant language: . . . '*Witnesseth*, That for and in consideration of the sum of Five Hundred ($500.00) dollars, paid by the Grantee to the Grantor, . . . the Grantor does hereby grant and convey . . . an easement.'" *Borek Cranberry Marsh, Inc. v. Jackson County*, 785 N.W.2d 615, 618 (Wis. 2010). Says one writer: *Witnesseth that* is a phrase "admittedly archaic but so firmly entrenched in the draftsman's vocabulary as to allow of few, if any, substitutes." Sidney F. Parham, *The Fundamentals of Legal Writing* 23 (1976). Actually, the whole mess is easily dispensed with; drafters should get right to the point, without *whereas* preceding the recital and without *witnesseth* to introduce the *whereas*-clauses.

The modern use of *witnesseth* is premised on a mistake: that the word is a command in the imperative mood. In fact, though, it is the third-person singular verb in the indicative mood—she *singeth* = she *sings*; he *sayeth* = he *says*; she *witnesseth* = she *witnesses*. The word at the outset of instruments is really just a remnant of a longer phrase, such as *This document witnesseth that* . . . . Hence to make WITNESSETH shout in all capitals from the top of a document makes no literal sense. It seems to have originated in an early formbook writer's mistake. See -ETH & **whereas.**

witness whereof, in. See **in witness whereof.**

woefully is a CLICHÉ, especially when coupled with an adjective like *inadequate* or *insufficient*. E.g.:

- "We find this single, benign reference to an 'estranged relative' to be a *woefully* inadequate factual basis for banishment under *McCreary* factors." *Mackey v. State*, 37 So.3d 1161, 1166 (Miss. 2010).

- "The growing number of exonerations illustrate that the problem of wrongful convictions is real and that current safeguards are *woefully* insufficient." Michele K. Mulhausen, *A Second Chance at Justice*, 81 U. Colo. L. Rev. 309, 337–38 (2010).

woke; woke up; woken. See **wake.**

womankind. See **humankind** & SEXISM (D).

woodshed, vb. See **horseshed.**

Woolf reforms. Before the late 1990s, England had several sets of civil rules of procedure applicable in high courts and county courts. The Lord Chancellor appointed Lord Woolf, Master of the Rolls, to head a committee dedicated to consolidating and rewriting the rules in plain language, both to help laypeople understand them and to make the judicial process faster and less expensive. The overriding objective (summarized at the beginning of the new Civil Rules of Procedure) was to enhance justice, so now judges are granted discretion to interpret and apply the rules in a particular case—rather than adhere strictly to precedent—to satisfy this objective. Paula Loughlin & Stephen M. Gerlis, *Civil Procedure* 1–8 (2004); *see also* 2 *Jowitt's Dictionary of English Law* 2435–36 (Daniel Greenberg ed., 3d ed. 2010).

Some of the primary terminological changes effected by the reforms were these:

Old Term	New Term
Anton Piller order	search order
chancery motion	interim application
contribution proceeding	Part 20 claim
counterclaim	counterclaims/Part 20 claim
defendant	defendant/Part 20 claimant
discovery	disclosure
ex parte	without notice
ex parte motion	application without notice
guardian ad litem	litigator's friend
in camera/ in chambers	in private
inter partes	with notice
inter partes motion	interim application with notice
interrogatories	request for further information
leave of court	permission
Mareva injunction	freezing injunction; freezing order
minor	child
originating summons	Part 8 claim
plaintiff	claimant
pleading	statement of case
request for further and better particulars of a pleading	request for further information
statement of claim/ particulars of claim	particulars of claim

subpoena (n.)	witness statement
subpoena (vb.)	summon
taxation of costs	assessment of costs
third party	Part 20 defendant
third-party claim	Part 20 claim
writ/county court summons	claim form
writ/default summons	claim form

Not all the terminological changes met with enthusiasm: "Legal procedure allows for third-party claims, by which a defendant, a main contractor perhaps, can pass on the employer's claim to a sub-contractor (or third party) if it is the sub-contractor who has really caused the problem. Lord Woolf, believing that most people do not understand third-party proceedings, has lumped them together with counterclaims in Part 20 of his new CPR. From now on they will be known as 'Part 20 Claims'— is the client any the wiser?" Kim Franklin, *Woolf at the Door for Latin Lovers as Legal Jargon Is Abolished*, Architects J., 6 May 1999. Indeed, the references to *Part 8* and *Part 20* seem to replace old JARGON with new, even less-comprehensible jargon. But the new terminology has arrived in BrE.

WOOLLINESS is the quality in expression of being confused and hazy, indefinite and indistinct. Excessive use of cross-references in writing, as in the Internal Revenue Code, is perhaps the apotheosis of *woolliness*—e.g.: "For purposes of paragraph (3), an organization described in paragraph (2) shall be deemed to include an organization described in section 501(c)(4), (5), or (6) which would be described in paragraph (2) if it were an organization described in section 501(c)(3)." I.R.C. § 509(a). See OBSCURITY (A) & PLAIN LANGUAGE (D).

woolsack in G.B. refers to the sack of wool used as the Lord Chancellor's seat when he presides over the House of Lords. E.g.: "Shaftesbury again took the *woolsack*, and they continued debating until the procession entered." Percy H. Fitzgerald, *The Life and Times of William IV* 391 (1884). By extension *woolsack* is sometimes used in the general sense "a seat of justice." Cf. **ermine.**

WORDINESS. See CUTTING OUT THE CHAFF, REDUNDANCY & VERBOSITY.

WORD-PATRONAGE is "the tendency to take out one's words and look at them, to apologize for expressions that either need no apology or should be quietly refrained from" (*MEU1* 733). E.g.: "Only the last qualifies as instrumental use in the narrow sense, yet we expect to derive—*to use an ugly word*—utility from each of these acts." Marcel Wissenberg, *Green Liberalism: The Free and the Green Society* 96 (1998). In his preface to *MEU2*, Gowers indulged mildly in word-patronage when he wrote: "This was indeed an epoch-making book in the strict sense of that over-worked phrase" (p. iii). The tendency is not at all uncommon—e.g.:

- "He came to the conclusion then that the best way of exploiting this invention was to use the mills himself and to what has been described as 'trade grind'—*rather a lengthy split infinitive.*" *Young v. Wilson*, [1955] 72 R.P.C. 351, 353 (Ch.D.) (per Upjohn, J.). See SPLIT INFINITIVES.
- "You have got to so frame yours so that it 'sells the Court,' *to use the term of the marketplace, which I abhor.*" Karl N. Llewellyn, *A Lecture on Appellate Advocacy*, 29 U. Chi. L. Rev. 627, 630 (1962). In that sentence, the *which*-clause is ambiguous: it may refer to either *the marketplace* or (as Llewellyn intended) *the term of the marketplace.* See REMOTE RELATIVES.
- "The language of this description is perhaps not very elegant, for it homologates (*if I may use that horrible word*) the noun 'dealer' with the participles which appear in the parenthesis." *Walter Chadburn and Son Ltd. v. Leeds Corp.*, [1969] 20 P.&C.R. 241, 246 (C.A.).
- "The House of Lords does now enjoy—*if that be the word*—the freedom not to follow its own previous decisions." Leslie Scarman, *English Law—The New Dimension* 5 (1974).
- "*The last sentence is rather clumsy,* but what I mean is this." Glanville Williams, *Learning the Law* 75 (11th ed. 1982).
- "*Although it is a cliché to say so,* it is in every way encyclopedic: every form of every description in connection with any Queen's Bench action is here." Charles Joseph, *Books for Lawyers*, 83 Law Soc. Gazette 3667 (1986) (reviewing *Chitty and Jacob's Queen's Bench Forms*).

A variation of this mannerism occurs when one defends one's choice of words in anticipation of the reader's distaste—e.g.:

- "The Maryland statute *appears to be unique in the proper use* of that much misused word." *Williams v. Patuxent Inst.*, 347 A.2d 179, 187 (Md. 1975).
- "The 'philosophy' of the Act (*if I may be forgiven this neologistic use*) was to allow a legally aided party to civil proceedings only one successful bite at the legal cherry." *Megarity v. Law Soc'y*, [1982] A.C. 81, 103 (per Lord Diplock).
- "The bank may and should be held liable for gratuitously, officiously, and affirmatively—*a surfeit of adverbs never hurt anyone*—telling the government how to place its grasp upon its customer's funds." *Schuster v. Banco de Iberoamerica, S.A.*, 476 So.2d 253, 255 (Fla. Dist. Ct. App. 1985) (Schwartz, J., dissenting).
- "Even a murderer can look forward to a parole after 17 years, in a manner best characterized by that *much-misused word, 'hopefully.'*" *In re Clements*, 440 N.W.2d 133, 137 (Minn. Ct. App. 1989) (Irvine, J., dissenting).

See **if you will.**

word processing, n. Two words. But as a PHRASAL ADJECTIVE, the term is hyphenated <word-processing equipment>.

wordsmithing. In an oddly dismissive way, lawyers frequently refer to someone else's "*wordsmithing.*" They will praise another lawyer (faintly) as being a "*wordsmith.*" They will deflect attention from their

---

inability to frame a workable provision (in a legislative bill, rule, contract, etc.) by suggesting that they will leave the "*wordsmithing*" to others—as if it were a ministerial matter for low-level colleagues at the bar. In fact, though, *wordsmithing* is the lawyer's stock in trade. Every entry in this dictionary is a matter of *wordsmithing*. And mastering the English vocabulary, and then the legal vocabulary, is one of the highest attainments to which a lawyer can aspire. Not always, but often, the lawyer who speaks of *wordsmithing* has little idea what it entails.

WORDS OF ART. See TERMS OF ART.

WORDS OF AUTHORITY. Few reforms would improve legal drafting more than if drafters were to begin paying closer attention to the modal verbs by which they set forth duties, rights, prohibitions, and entitlements. In the current state of common-law drafting, these verbs are a horrific muddle—and, what is even more surprising, few drafters even recognize this fact. The primary problem is *shall*, to which we must immediately turn.

A. Shall. This word runs afoul of several basic principles of good drafting. The first is that a word used repeatedly in a given context is presumed to bear the same meaning throughout. (*Shall* commonly shifts its meaning even in midsentence.) The second principle is strongly allied with the first: when a word takes on too many senses and cannot be confined to one sense in a given document, it becomes useless to the drafter. (Depending on how finely you slice the semantic nuances, *shall* can bear five to eight senses even in a single document. *Black's Law Dictionary* (9th ed. 2009) lists five main senses.) The third principle has been recognized in the literature on legal drafting since the mid-19th century: good drafting generally ought to be in the present tense, not the future. (*Shall* is commonly used as a future-tense modal verb.) In fact, the selfsame quality in *shall*—the fact that it is a CHAMELEON-HUED WORD—causes it to violate each of those principles.

How can *shall* be so slippery, one may ask, when every lawyer knows that it denotes a mandatory action? Well, perhaps every lawyer has heard that it's mandatory, but very few consistently use it in that way. And as a result, courts in virtually every English-speaking jurisdiction have held—by necessity—that *shall* means *may* in some contexts, and vice versa. These holdings have been necessary primarily to give effect to slipshod drafting.

What, then, are the meanings of *shall*? The shadings are sometimes subtle, but the following examples illustrate the more common shades:

- "The court *shall* enter an order directing the county clerk to issue a tax deed." *Strong v. City of Peoria*, 930 N.E.2d 561, 564 (Ill. App. Ct. 2010). The word imposes a duty on the subject of the sentence. This is the most traditional and correct use of the term—the one that most drafters think they're using most of the time.
- "Service *shall* be made, whenever possible, upon the more responsible officers." *Imperial Towers, Inc. v. Dade Home*

Servs., Inc., 199 So.2d 518, 520–21 (Fla. Dist. Ct. App. 1967). The word imposes a duty on an unnamed person, but not on the subject of the sentence (*service*, an abstract thing).
- "Such time *shall* not be further extended except for cause shown." *In re Maurice*, 167 B.R. 114, 123 (Bankr. N.D. Ill. 1994). The word *shall* gives permission (as opposed to a duty), and *shall not* denies permission (i.e., it means "may not"). This problem *shall* being equivalent to *may* frequently appears also in the statutory phrase *No person shall*. Logically the correct construction is *No person may*, because the provision negates permission, not a duty. See (E).
- "The sender *shall* have fully complied with the requirement to send notice when the sender obtains electronic confirmation that the transmission has been received." *In re Nowling*, 279 B.R. 607, 610 (Bankr. S.D. Fla. 2002). The word acts as a future-tense modal verb (the full verb phrase being the future perfect). Many readers of this sentence, however, encounter a MISCUE in reading the sentence, which confusingly suggests that the sender has a duty.
- "The debtor *shall* be brought forthwith before the court that issued the order." 11 U.S.C.A. § 2005 (West 2005). The word seems at first to impose a duty on the debtor but actually imposes it on some unnamed actor.
- "Any objection to the proposed modification *shall* be filed and served on the debtor." *In re Smith*, 388 B.R. 603, 607 (Bankr. E.D. Pa. 2008). The word purports to impose a duty on parties to object to proposed modifications, though the decision to object is discretionary. This amounts to a conditional duty: a party that wants to object must file and serve the objections.
- "The prevailing party *shall* be reimbursed by the other for all reasonable costs." *Monarch Fire Protec. Dist. v. Freedom Consulting & Auditing Servs., Inc.*, 678 F.Supp.2d 927, 940 (E.D. Mo. 2009). The word expresses an entitlement, not a duty.
- "If any person *shall* curse or abuse anyone, or use vulgar, profane, or threatening or indecent language over any telephone in this state, he *shall* be guilty of a misdemeanor." Va. Code Ann. § 18.1-238 (1975). The first *shall* is the "false future"; it should simply be a present-tense verb (*curses or abuses*). The second *shall* is a true future, equivalent to *will*. But it would all be better in present tense. A suggested revision: *Any person who curses or abuses anyone—or uses vulgar, profane, or threatening or indecent language—over any telephone in this state is guilty of a misdemeanor.*

So much for the "Golden Rule" of legal drafting, which Reed Dickerson put this way: "The competent draftsman makes sure that each recurring word or term has been used consistently. He carefully avoids using the same word or term in more than one sense . . . . In brief, he always expresses the same idea in the same way and always expresses different ideas differently." *The Fundamentals of Legal Drafting* § 2.3.1, at 15–16 (2d ed. 1986).

One solution to the problem that *shall* poses is to restrict it to one sense. This solution—called the "American rule" because it is an approach followed by some careful American drafters—is to use *shall* only to mean "has a duty to." Under the American rule, only the first of the eight bulleted items above would be correct. The drafter might well say that a party *shall* send notice, but not that notice *shall* be sent by the party. (If this "has-a-duty-to" sense is the drafter's convention, *must* serves when the subject of the sentence is an inanimate object.) This solution leads to much greater consistency than is generally found in American drafting.

Another solution is the "ABC rule," so called because, in the late 1980s, it was most strongly advocated by certain Australian, British, and Canadian drafters. The ABC rule holds that legal drafters cannot be trusted to use the word *shall* under any circumstances. Under this view, lawyers are not educable on the subject of *shall*, so the only solution is complete abstinence. As a result, the drafter must always choose a more appropriate word: *must, may, will, is entitled to,* or some other expression.

This view has much to be said for it. American lawyers and judges who try to restrict *shall* to the sense "has a duty to" find it difficult to apply the convention consistently. Indeed, few lawyers have the semantic acuity to identify correct and incorrect *shall*s even after a few hours of study. That being so, there can hardly be much hope of the profession's using *shall* consistently.

Small wonder, then, that the ABC rule has fast been gaining ground in the U.S. For example, the federal government's Style Subcommittee—part of the Standing Committee on Rules of Practice and Procedure—a subcommittee that since 1991 has worked on all amendments to the various sets of federal court rules, adopted the approach of disallowing *shall* in late 1992. (This came after a year of using *shall* only to impose a duty on the subject of the verb.) As a result, the rules have become sharper because the drafters are invariably forced into thinking more clearly and specifically about meaning.

There is, of course, a third approach: to allow *shall* its traditional promiscuity while pretending, as we have for centuries, that preserving its chastity is either hopeless or unimportant. Of course, that approach breeds litigation, as attested in more than 120 pages of small-type cases reported in *Words and Phrases,* all interpreting the word *shall*. As long as the mass of the profession remains unsensitized to the problems that *shall* causes, this appears to be the most likely course of inaction.

For more on the use of *must* as opposed to *shall* under the ABC rule, see (C). For further discussion of the general problem, see Dale E. Sutton, *Use of "Shall" in Statutes,* 4 John Marshall L.Q. 204 (1938–39); Robert Eagleson & Michèle Asprey, *Must We Continue with "Shall"?,* 63 Austl. L.J. 75 (1989); Robert Eagleson & Michèle Asprey, *We Must Abandon "Shall",* 63 Austl. L.J. 726 (1989); Jim Main, *"Must" Versus "Shall",* 63 Austl. L.J. 860 (1989); Michèle Asprey, *Plain Language for Lawyers* 149–52 (1991); Joseph Kimble, *The*

Many Misuses of "Shall", 3 Scribes J. Legal Writing 61 (1992); Michèle Asprey, *"Shall" Must Go,* 3 Scribes J. Legal Writing 79 (1992); Bryan A. Garner, *Legal Writing in Plain English* 105–07 (2001). For a contrary (and unpersuasive) point of view, see J.M. Bennett, *In Defence of "Shall",* 63 Austl. L.J. 522 (1989); J.M. Bennett, *Final Observations on the Use of "Shall",* 64 Austl. L.J. 168 (1990); Kenneth A. Adams, *A Manual of Style for Contract Drafting* 31–44 (2d ed. 2008).

A major cause of the litigation over *shall* is the relative strength of the word. That is, what are the consequences when somebody fails to honor a contractual or statutory duty? If it's a contractual duty, does a failure to honor a *shall*-provision always amount to a breach? Does it entitle the other party to rescind? If it's a statutory requirement, does a violation invalidate the proceedings? Or is it merely a directory provision? This unclarity about consequences is a continuing problem in any system that we adopt, however linguistically principled that system might be.

B. Shall not. Under the American rule (see (A)), this phrasing works as long as it means "has a duty not to." So "Thou *shalt not* steal" works, but not "The money *shall not* remain in the court's registry for more than 30 days." In the latter example, the proper choice is either *must not* or *may not*. See (F).

C. Must. Under the American rule (see (A)), this word means "is required to" and is used primarily when an inanimate object appears as subject of the clause. Hence, "Notice *must* be sent within 30 days."

Under the ABC rule (see (A)), *must* denotes all required actions, whether or not the subject of the clause performs the action of the verb—e.g.:

- "The employee *must* send notice within 30 days."
- "Notice *must* be sent within 30 days."

The advantage of *must* over *shall* is that its meaning is fastened down more tightly in any given sentence. Take, for example, a sentence from a widely used commercial lease: "The premises *shall* be used by the tenant for general office purposes and for no other purposes." Once one decides to follow the ABC rule, the dilemma in meaning becomes clear: are we mandating something with that sentence (use of the premises), or are we merely limiting the tenant's freedom to use the premises for other purposes? One might revise the sentence—removing the PASSIVE VOICE—in either of two ways: (1) *The tenant must use the premises for general office purposes;* or (2) *The tenant may use the premises only for general office purposes.* Which meaning is correct? Perhaps somebody should litigate the question so that we might all find out.

In private drafting—contracts as opposed to statutes, rules, and regulations—some drafters consider *must* inappropriately bossy. The word may strike the wrong tone particularly when both parties to a contract are

---

An asterisk (*) precedes words and phrases that are invariably inferior forms.

known quantities, such as two well-known corporations. It seems unlikely that, for example, an American car manufacturer and a Japanese car manufacturer engaging in a joint venture would want the word *must* to set forth their various responsibilities. Indeed, it seems odd to draft one's own contractual responsibilities with *must*: a lawyer for Ford Motor Company is unlikely to write *Ford must . . . Ford must . . . Ford must . . . .* The word *will* is probably the best solution here. See (D).

On the other hand, in a consumer contract or other adhesion contract, *must* is entirely appropriate for the party lacking the bargaining power. In the 1994 revision of its form residential lease—a document signed by a million Texas residents every year—the Texas Apartment Association changed the traditional *shall* to either *must* or *will*. The landlord became *we*, and the tenant became *you*, so that the form reads as follows: *You must . . . You must . . . You must . . . We will . . . We will . . . We will . . . .* Although one might think that the resulting tone would be irksome, none of the typical users on whom the form was tested expressed that thought. Indeed, the distinctive use of *must* for the tenant and *will* for the landlord is very much in keeping with the natural rhetoric of an adhesion contract. And it certainly informs the consumer precisely what his or her obligations are.

Must is a useful device to uncover client misunderstandings about obligations. Hence, some lawyers use it despite the danger of a bossy tone. And because present-tense drafting reduces the incidence of *must*, the *musts* that remain in a given document will—in many contexts—offend no one.

D. Will. This word, like any other, ought to bear a consistent meaning within any drafted document. Two of its possible meanings are discussed in (C): it may express one's own client's obligations in an adhesion contract (as in a residential lease), or it may express both parties' obligations when the relationship is a delicate one (as in a corporate joint venture).

There is still a third possibility: if a future tense really is needed, as to express a future contingency, then *will* is the word. But this circumstance is not common, since the best drafting should generally be in the present, not the future, tense. See LEGISLATIVE DRAFTING.

E. May. This term, very simply, means "has discretion to; is permitted to." It should be the only term used to denote these senses. One would never write *the licensee is free to sell as many units as it desires*, as opposed to *the licensee may sell as many units as it desires*.

Sometimes, *may* should replace *shall*—e.g.: "No person *shall* [read *may*] enter upon immovable property owned by another without express, legal, or implied authorization." La. Rev. Stat. 14:63(B) (2009). That sentence does not negate a duty; it negates permission. This formulation is a pervasive problem. See (A) & LEGISLATIVE DRAFTING.

F. Must not; may not. These two are nearly synonymous. *Must not* = is required not to. *May not* = is not permitted to. For those following the ABC rule (see (A)), the phrase *must not* is usually the more appropriate wording.

Some drafters avoid *may not* because it is sometimes ambiguous—it can mean either "is not permitted to" or (especially in AmE) "might not." For example, an application to a law school states: "This office *may not* consider applications received after April 30." Some readers would take that to mean that the office has discretion whether to consider applications received after April 30, whereas others would infer that some rule or regulation prohibits the office from doing so.

G. Is entitled to. This is the wording for expressing an entitlement. It means "has a right to." E.g.: "Guardians ad litem *shall* [read *are entitled to*] be reimbursed for the mileage expenses incurred in representing their client." N.H. Sup. Ct. Rule 48-A (2008). See (A).

H. Using a Consistent Glossary. A disciplined drafter uses words of authority consistently. This involves, in part, restricting the vocabulary by which one sets forth duties, rights, prohibitions, and entitlements. The drafter who proliferates ways of wording duties, for example, flirts with the danger that somebody interpreting the document—most disastrously, in court—will presume that a difference in wording imports a difference in meaning.

Yet drafted documents are commonly riddled with inconsistencies. It is not uncommon, in American contracts, to find the following variations in paragraph after paragraph:

- "The employee *shall follow . . . .*"
- "The employee *agrees to follow . . . .*"
- "The employee *is to follow . . . .*"
- "The employee *must follow . . . .*"
- "The employee *understands her duty to follow . . . .*"
- "The employee *will follow . . . .*"
- "*It is the responsibility* of the employee *to follow . . . .*"

The better practice is this: after the lead-in (which states, "The parties therefore agree as follows: . . . ."), use only words of authority. An adherent of the American rule would make each of the above items *the employee shall follow*; an adherent of the ABC rule would make each one *the employee must follow*.

The careful drafter might consider adopting either of the following glossaries, preferably the latter:

American Rule

shall	=	has a duty to
must	=	is required to [used for all requirements that are not duties imposed on the subject of the clause]
may not	=	is not permitted to; is disallowed from
must not	=	is required not to; is disallowed from; is not permitted to
may	=	has discretion to; is permitted to
is entitled to	=	has a right to
will	=	(expresses a future contingency)
should	=	(denotes a directory provision)

ABC Rule (Preferred)

must	=	is required to
must not	=	is required not to; is disallowed from; is not permitted to
may	=	has discretion to; is permitted to
may not	=	is not permitted to; is disallowed from
is entitled to	=	has a right to
will	=	[one of the following:]
		a. expresses a future contingency
		b. in an adhesion contract, expresses one's own client's obligations
		c. where the relationship is a delicate one, expresses both parties' obligations
should	=	denotes a directory provision

words of conveyance are the words—usually DOU-BLETS, TRIPLETS, AND SYNONYM-STRINGS—that effect a transfer of ownership in a deed. In a warranty deed, for example, the standard words of conveyance are *convey and warrant* or *grant, bargain, and sell*; in a quitclaim deed, the words are usually *remise, release, and forever quitclaim* or *convey and quitclaim.*

words of purchase; words of limitation. In a grant or conveyance of a freehold estate, *words of purchase* designate the persons who are to receive the grant, and *words of limitation* describe the extent or quality of the estate. E.g.: "In a transfer 'to A and his heirs,' the words 'and his heirs' are now *words of limitation* (words denoting the duration of the estate), not *words of purchase* (words denoting who is getting the estate). The name 'A' is the only *word of purchase*; A is the only person who is getting an estate." Thomas F. Bergin & Paul G. Haskell, *Preface to Estates in Land and Future Interests* 27 (2d ed. 1984).

wordy does not mean "sesquipedalian," as many seem to suppose; it means, rather, "verbose; prolix."

workaholic. See -AHOLIC & MORPHOLOGICAL DEFORMITIES.

work an ademption. See **adeem** & **ademption.**

worker. See **workman.**

worker's comp. See **comp.**

workers' compensation; workmen's compensation. These words contain a plural possessive, hence *workers'* and *workmen's*, not *worker's* and *workman's*. The former phrase is becoming more and more common, doubtless because of a sensitivity to the SEXISM of the other.

workforce; workload. Each is one word.

working man. See **workman.**

workload. See **workforce.**

workman; workingman. Because of the growing awareness of sexism, it is better to use *worker* rather than either of these words. See SEXISM (B).

workplace. One word. Cf. **worksite.**

workproduct is increasingly spelled as one word. The dictionaries still record the term as two words. But in legal contexts the trend, which is wholly salutary, is to hyphenate it or make it one word. E.g.: "To what extent is the Court's equal-protection *workproduct* based on a determinate political-moral principle?" Michael J. Perry, *Modern Equal Protection*, 79 Colum. L. Rev. 1023, 1024 (1979). Cf. **decision-making** & **policymaking.**

worksite. One word. Cf. **jobsite.**

World Court; International Court of Justice in The Hague. The second is the official name, the former the popular name, for the tribunal that adjudicates international disputes between nations. The principal judicial organ of the U.N., it is the successor to the Permanent Court of International Justice, set up in 1920 under the League of Nations.

WORLD COURT PLEADINGS. The pleadings in an action before the World Court are as follows: (1) a *memorial* by the applicant state; (2) a *countermemorial* by the respondent state; (3) a *reply* by the applicant state; and (4) a *rejoinder* by the respondent state. Cf. COMMON-LAW PLEADINGS & EQUITY PLEADINGS.

worse comes to worst. See **worst comes to worst.**

worshiped; worshipped; worshiping; worshipping; worshiper; worshipper. The *-p-* spellings are the preferred forms in AmE; the *-pp-* forms appear in BrE. See DOUBLING OF FINAL CONSONANTS.

worst comes to worst; worse comes to worst. The traditional idiom, evidenced in the *OED* consistently from the 16th century, is *worst comes to (the) worst* (= [if] things turn out as badly as possible). But the more modern and more logical idiom, *worse comes to worst*—with its progression from comparative to superlative—is equally common in legal sources and is the better choice. E.g.:

- "The total cost to the customer if *worse comes to worst* will be at most $100 (and likely much less, after discounting for the time value of money)." Ken Heyer, *Predicting the Competitive Effects of Mergers by Listening to Customers*, 74 Antitrust L.J. 87, 103 (2007).
- "And, if *worse comes to worst*, in the end who really knows what is truth?" Andrew L. Kaufman & David B. Wilkins, *Problems in Professional Responsibility for a Changing Profession* 155 (2009).

SEE ILLOGIC.

worth. When this word is used with amounts, the preceding term denoting the amount should be possessive. E.g.:

- "Findeisen's claim is not for a few *dollars worth* [read *dollars' worth*] of hobby goods [that] were negligently lost; it involves his career." *Findeisen v. North East Indep. Sch. Dist.*, 749 F.2d 234, 239 (5th Cir. 1984).
- "According to Brandon's testimony . . . the Manhattan property underwent thousands of *dollars worth* [read *dollars' worth*] of repairs." *Estate of Stewart v. Commissioner*, 617 F.3d 148, 151 (2d Cir. 2010).

See POSSESSIVES (B).

worthless check. See **check, worthless.**

worthless person. In this legal ARCHAISM, *worthless* means "without worldly goods." But the double sense of the word makes the phrase unworthy in modern writing.

worthwhile. One word.

***wot** (= to know) is an ARCHAISM that H.W. Fowler called a "Wardour Street" term, i.e., an "oddment" calculated to establish (in the eyes of some readers) the writer's claim to be someone of taste and the source of beautiful English. In modern writing, it is a gross affectation—e.g.: "Of the financial status of the other two [lawyers] we *wot* [read *know*] not." *Schine v. Schine*, 309 N.Y.S.2d 51, 52 (App. Div. 1970).

would is often used as a hedge-word, qualifying the absoluteness of the verb following it. For example, a federal court states: "*This court would agree* with the Texas Supreme Court's statement of the measure of damages." If the writer intended to question the applicability of the Texas Supreme Court's statement in certain circumstances, the sentence as written is perhaps right; but it would be better to say *This court agrees* if a direct statement is intended. See SUBJUNCTIVES & **appear.**

would have for *had*. This error is an example of a confused sequence of tenses. E.g.:

- "If the trial judge *would have* [read *had*] allowed impeachment with a limiting instruction . . . , Robinson would be before this court arguing that this alternative solution was error." *U.S. v. Robinson*, 783 F.2d 64, 68 (7th Cir. 1986).
- "Even if the judge *would have* [read *had*] admitted this hearsay evidence, there is no reason to believe that it would have helped the defendant; it might well have hurt him." *Commonwealth v. Mosher*, 920 N.E.2d 285, 287 (Mass. 2010).

would have liked. This phrase should invariably be followed by a present-tense infinitive—hence *would have liked to go, would have liked to read*, not *would have liked to have gone, would have liked to have read*—e.g.:

- "Many Americans *would have liked to put* the administration of justice wholly on a non-technical basis of natural equity." Roscoe Pound, *The Formative Era of American Law* 107 (1938).
- "Kaiser *would have liked to call* some of these witnesses, however, those he spoke with could not afford to come to New York and may have been reluctant to testify at least in part for financial reasons." *Rosario v. Ercole*, 601 F.3d 118, 131 n.4 (2d Cir. 2010).

would seem is usually inferior to *seems* or *seem*. E.g.: "Mr. Kohl *would seem* [read *seems*] to have made another concession." Alan Riding, *European Leaders Give Their Backing to Monetary Plan*, N.Y. Times, 9 Dec. 1989, at 1.

wrack; rack. *Wrack* = to destroy utterly; to wreck. *Rack* = to torture or oppress.

Wrack is also, and primarily, a noun meaning (1) "wreckage"; or (2) "utter destruction." In sense 2, it most commonly appears in the phrase *wrack and ruin*. But *wrack* is sometimes confused with its homophone—e.g.:

- "[The plaintiff stated] . . . that the building was 'virtually a shell,' having been allowed to go to *rack* [read *wrack*] and ruin." *Hilton v. Federated Brokerage Group, Inc.*, 213 N.Y.S.2d 171, 177 (Sup. Ct. 1961).
- "Experience indicates that the state treasury would not fall to *rack* [read *wrack*] and ruin if the shield of immunity were lifted." *Brown v. Wichita State Univ.*, 547 P.2d 1015, 1037 (Kan. 1976) (Fatzer, C.J., concurring in part & dissenting in part).

wrangle; wangle. The two are occasionally confounded. *Wrangle* = to argue noisily or angrily; *wangle* = (1) [transitive] to accomplish or obtain in a clever way; (2) to manage (a thing) despite difficulties; or (3) [intransitive] to use indirect methods to accomplish some end. E.g.: "He has aptly demonstrated his advertising acumen by *wrangling* [read *wangling*] almost half a million dollars in free print media from *New York* Magazine." Letter of David Curry, N.Y. Mag., 23 Jan. 1989, at 9.

wraparound mortgage is current American legal JARGON meaning "a deed of trust whereby a purchaser incorporates into agreed payments to a grantor or third party the grantor's obligation in the initial mortgage." A court defined it as "a junior mortgage [that] secures a promissory note with a face amount equal to the sum of the principal balance of an existing mortgage note plus any additional funds advanced by the second lender." *Mitchell v. Trustees of U.S. Real Est. Inv. Trust*, 375 N.W.2d 424, 428 (Mich. Ct. App. 1985) (with minor differences in wording).

wreak. The better past tense is *wreaked*, not *wrought*. See **reek.**

wreak havoc. See **havoc.**

wreath; wreathe. *Wreath* is the noun, *wreathe* the verb.

***wreckless** for *reckless* is a written MALAPROPISM that appears to denote precisely the opposite of what it is supposed to mean. As literacy in the higher sense has become ever shakier, it has become disturbingly common—e.g.:

- "The answer contains numerous allegations to the effect . . . that the trucks were being used by plaintiff on the highway in a careless and *wreckless* [read *reckless*] manner and greatly depreciating said trucks." *Place v. Parker*, 180 S.W.2d 538, 542 (Mo. Ct. App. 1944).

- "The trial judge also instructed the jury that if it found that the Union had acted with 'actual malice or *wreckless* [read *reckless*] or wanton indifference to the rights of the plaintiff,' it might award punitive damages." *Int'l Bhd. of Boilermakers v. Braswell*, 388 F.2d 193, 199 (5th Cir. 1968) (quoting trial court).
- "In their petition, plaintiffs allege that the sole cause of accident was the combined negligence, gross negligence, wanton, *wreckless* [read *reckless*] conduct and intentional *wrecklessness* [read *recklessness*] . . . of the executive officers and supervisors." *Benjamin v. First Horizon Ins. Co.*, 563 So.2d 1337, 1339 (La. Ct. App. 1990).
- "Prior to 1969, a number of courts had concluded that the military employee is subject to military discipline pursuant to the UCMJ for *wreckless* [read *reckless*] or drunken operation of a vehicle." Michael P. Frederick, *Scope of Employment Under the Federal Tort Claims Act and Attempts to Expand the Limits*, 33 A.F. L. Rev. 69, 81 (1990). On the use of **prior to* in that sentence, see **prior to*. On the use of **pursuant to*, see **pursuant to*.

One court even went so far as to "correct" the lawyers' use of *reckless*—the bracketed *-w-* being in the reported case: "'Cross-defendants' failure to place and maintain plaintiffs' prior Group Health Policy was negligent, careless, and [*w*]*reckless* . . . .'" *Kuperman v. Great Republic Life Ins. Co.*, 241 Cal. Rptr. 187, 188 (Ct. App. 1987) (quoting a pleading).

writ. A. As a Noun. At common law, a *writ* was any formal legal document in letter form, under seal, and in the king's name. Its meaning has evolved differently in AmE and BrE, though the following definition fits both: "a court's written command or order in the name of the sovereign, state, or other competent legal authority, directing or enjoining the addressee to do or refrain from doing some specified act." In AmE, *writ* generally applies to *judicial writs*, which are either extraordinary writs (e.g., mandamus, prohibition) or writs used in appellate procedure (e.g., writ of error, writ of certiorari).

In BrE, by contrast, *writ* is usually synonymous with *original writ* (= one that begins an action), as an abbreviated form of *writ of summons*. E.g.:

- "Claiming that the price of their homes had dropped because of the presence of their new neighbours, Tim and Sue Poeton, with nine other families, issued *writs* claiming that Heron Homes, the development company, had failed to tell them that part of the estate had been earmarked for council housing." Charles Oulton, *When Neighbours Become Good Enemies*, Sunday Times, 5 Nov. 1989, at A13.
- "Lord Denning, 93, former Master of the Rolls, has had a High Court *writ* issued against him over his old school at Whitchurch, Hants." Sunday Telegraph, 24 May 1992, at 2.

As in the first of the two examples just quoted, it is good colloquial BrE to say that the plaintiff issues the *writ*, although in truth the court does the issuing at the plaintiff's request.

B. As a Verb. The *OED* records the verbal sense of *writ* ("to serve [a person] with a writ or summons" <he was writted>), and notes that it is Anglo-Irish.

C. As a Past Participle. As a past participle, *writ* is an ARCHAISM for *written*, except in the CLICHÉ *writ large*. E.g.: "If article 9 were *writ large*, it would set out that a director is not to be removed against his will." (Eng.)

writable. So spelled—not **writeable*. See MUTE E.

write for *underwrite* is common in the insurance business. E.g.: "St. Paul Fire & Marine *writes* about $2,500,000 worth of premiums in the lawyers' malpractice field and has become the largest in the field." Murray T. Bloom, *The Trouble with Lawyers* 57 (1970).

writer is an obsolescent Scottishism in the sense "an attorney or law-agent; an ordinary legal practitioner in country towns; a law-clerk" (*OED*).

writer, the present. See FIRST PERSON (A).

write specially = to concur in a separate opinion. E.g.:

- "Five justices *wrote specially* to express concern regarding a fourth issue unrelated to jury instructions." Michael H. Hoffheimer, *The Future of Constitutionally Required Lesser Included Offenses*, 67 U. Pitt. L. Rev. 585, 623 n.173 (2006).
- "I *write specially* to note that I believe that the particular circumstances of this case demand attention by our legislature." *M.D.C. v. K.D.*, 39 So.3d 1145, 1145 (Ala. Civ. App. 2009) (Bryan, J., concurring).

writ of attachment. See **attachment**.

writ of certiorari. See **certiorari**.

writ of course. See **of course**.

writ of error. The preferred plural is *writs of error*, not **writs of errors* or **writ of errors*.

writ of prohibition. See **prohibition (A)**.

writ of right is a LOAN TRANSLATION of *breve de recto*, at common law "the highest and most solemn form of action." Cornelius J. Moynihan, *Introduction to the Law of Real Property* 100 (2d ed. 1988). Through the litigation initiated with this writ, the mesne lord would decide whether the demandant or the tenant—that is, the plaintiff or the defendant—had older and better seisin in the disputed property. See ***breve*, demandant** & **form of action**.

written. See **verbal**.

written instrument. See **instrument**.

written law. See **unwritten law** & ***jus scriptum***.

wrong, n. The word is not precisely equivalent to *tort*: legal writers who refer to *civil wrongs* usually include not just torts but also breaches of contract and of trust, breaches of statutory duties, and defects in the performance of public duties. See **civil wrong, tort & false.**

wrong; wrongful. The distinction is an important one in law. *Wrong* = (1) out of order; (2) contrary to law or morality; wicked; or (3) other than the right or suitable or the more or most desirable (*COD*). *Wrongful* = characterized by unfairness or injustice; contrary to law; (of a person) not entitled to the position occupied <the wrongful possessor>. Occasionally the words happen to be coextensive—e.g.: "It is a malicious act, which is in law and in fact a *wrong* act, and therefore a *wrongful* act, and therefore an actionable act if injury ensues from it." *Bowen v. Hall*, [1889] 6 Q.B.D. 333. Cf. **wrongous.**

One commentator takes a benighted view: "Does *wrongful* mean something different from *wrong*? *Wrong* alone implies a moral judgment. *Wrongful*, by adding a syllable, only makes the word more pompous and less clear." Robert C. Cumbow, *The Subverting of the Goeduck*, 14 U. Puget Sound L. Rev. 755, 779 (1991).

For the adverbial use of *wrong*, see **wrongly.** For *wrong* vs. *false*, see **false (A).**

wrongdoer = one who violates the law. The term is used of tortfeasors as well as of criminals. E.g.:

- "The goal of the scheme has not necessarily been realized because the *wrongdoer* has the illicit proceeds in hand." *U.S. v. Turner*, 624 F.Supp.2d 206, 224 (E.D.N.Y. 2009).
- "That two *wrongdoers* are compensated differently for their respective roles in a shared criminal activity may in some situations be significant as to their relative status." *U.S. v. Al-Rikabi*, 606 F.3d 11, 16 (1st Cir. 2010).

wrongful. See **wrong.**

wrongful birth; wrongful life. These phrases refer to different causes of action. A *wrongful-birth* action is brought by parents usually against a doctor for failing to advise them prospectively about their risks of having a child with birth defects. A *wrongful-life* action is brought by or on behalf of a child with birth defects, the allegations ordinarily being that, were it not for the doctor–defendant's negligent advice, the child's parents would not have conceived the child, or if they had conceived, would have aborted the fetus to avoid the pain and suffering resulting from the child's congenital defects.

wrongful death. See **death case** & **death statute.**

wrongful discharge (AmE) = *wrongful dismissal* (BrE). E.g.: "The only other damages the plaintiff could claim if he had been *wrongfully dismissed* would have been purely nominal." (Aus.) *Wrongful termination* is sometimes used in the U.S. See **unfair dismissal.**

wrongful interference with goods. See **detinue.**

wrongful life. See **wrongful birth.**

wrongly; wrong. Both forms are proper adverbs; *wrongly*, which is less common, appears before the verb modified <the suspects were wrongly detained>, whereas *wrong* should be used if the adverb follows the noun <he answered the question wrong>.

wrongous, in Scots law, means "wrongful; illegal; unjust." It should be avoided by other than Scottish lawyers.

wroth (= angry) is an ARCHAISM—e.g.: "Petitti, 37, is so *wroth* [read *angry*] over what he sees in the videotape of his nuptial festivities that he has filed suit." Eric Zorn, *Taped Memories Are More Maddening than Magical*, Chicago Trib., 20 Mar. 1990, at 1C.

X

xerox is a registered trademark (Xerox) that is nevertheless used as a noun <he made a xerox of the document>, adjective <a xerox copy>, and verb <to xerox a will>. Sometimes the word is capitalized, but sometimes not—e.g.: "I had to get some letters from readers *xeroxed* last week." Godfrey Smith, Sunday Times, 22 Oct. 1989, at B3. Careful writers use *photocopy* or some other similar word. **Zerox* is a common misspelling.

X-ray; x-ray. Either form is correct. Although the *Associated Press Stylebook* and other publication guides prescribe the capitalized *X*, the lowercase form is quite common. The term is hyphenated in all parts of speech.

Y

y'all; *ya'll. Perhaps the only time when the correct form of this Southernism arises is in transcriptions of testimony. For the record, *y'all* is the logically preferable and far more common form.

ye. See **hear ye** & **oyez.**

year and a day. The lapse of a year has many important effects in Anglo-American law. At common law, escheat was subject to the Crown's right to hold the land for *ann, jour et wast* (= one year, one day, including the right to commit waste). In English law today and in some American states, an act that causes death is not homicide if the death occurs more than a *year and a day* after the act was committed.

Why a year *and a day*—not just a year? Because several centuries ago, English lawyers computed times by including both the first and the last day, so that a year from January 1, 1500, was considered to be December 31, 1500. Hence the day was tacked on to make up a full year. Today, of course, times are generally computed by excluding the first day.

Year Book; Year-Book; year-book; yearbook. Each of these forms except for the last has appeared in legal history books that discuss the unofficial English law reports dating from 1282 to 1537. The predominant form is *Year Book*, although the leading modern legal historian, J.H. Baker, refers to the *year-books. See* J.H. Baker, *An Introduction to English Legal History* 204–07 (3d ed. 1990). If that usage suggests a trend, then *yearbook* cannot be far away, since the manifest destiny of the hyphen is to disappear.

year of our Lord. See A.D.

yellow-dog contract (= an employment contract forbidding membership in a labor union) has become a part of American legal JARGON. The term dates from 1920. E.g.: "The rapidly increasing use of the so-called '*yellow-dog contracts*' has grown into a serious threat to the very existence of labor unions. In view of the inequitable conditions that surround the formation of such agreements and the unfair division of their obligation, to appeal to equity for their enforcement is to disregard the fundamentally ethical foundations of courts of chancery." Felix Frankfurter & Nathan Greene, *Labor Injunctions and Federal Legislation*, 42 Harv. L. Rev. 766, 779 (1929).

Today such contracts are generally illegal, having been outlawed by the Wagner Act of 1935: "A chocolate manufacturing company proposed an unlawful '*yellow-dog contract*' when its president asked a job applicant if she would sign a statement pledging not to join a union or be affiliated in any way with unions." *Today's Summary and Analysis*, Daily Labor Rep., 3 Apr. 1991, at A-A.

yet. See *as yet & **although . . . yet.**

you, the second-person pronoun, is invaluable in drafting consumer contracts that are meant to be generally intelligible. Consider the difference between the following versions of a lease provision:

> Resident shall promptly reimburse owner for loss, damage, or cost of repairs or service caused in the apartment or community by improper use or negligence of resident or resident's guests or occupants.

vs.

> *You* must promptly reimburse us for loss, damage, or cost of repairs or service caused anywhere in the apartment community by your or any guest's or occupant's improper use.

Of course, the drafter must carefully define *you* and *us*, but doing so is usually a straightforward matter. See SUPERSTITIONS (K).

young person. See **child.**

your; you're. *Your* is possessive <take your time> and *you're* is the contraction (= *you are*) <you're welcome>.

your defendant. See **your petitioner.**

your Honor. This is the accepted American way of addressing a judge in person, especially in oral argument. Of British practice, an eminent barrister writes: "Judges prefer to be known as *my lord* or *your Honour* or *your Worship* (the last of these being an anachronistic but revealing indication of the vanity that can afflict adjudicators in minor courts and tribunals)." David Pannick, *Judges* 157 (1987).

your ladyship; your lordship. See **my lord.**

your petitioner; your defendant; your plaintiff; etc. Phrases such as these are quaint ARCHAISMS to be avoided. E.g.:

- "*Your relator* [read *The relator*], George W. Farmer, makes known that he is a resident and citizen of the state of Nebraska." *State v. Grand Island & W.C.R. Co.*, 43 N.W. 419, 419 (Neb. 1889) (quoting a petition).
- "*Your petitioner* [read *The petitioner*] has reliable information and therefore believes that the defendant is intending to leave the jurisdiction." *National Auto. & Cas. Ins. Co. v. Queck*, 405 P.2d 905, 907 (Ariz. Ct. App. 1965) (quoting a petition).

yours. See FORMS OF ADDRESS (H).

Z

zetetic; zetetick. This adjective, meaning "proceeding by inquiry or investigation," is preferably spelled *zetetic* (*OED & W3*), though some law dictionaries anomalously spell it *zetetick*. The Center for Scientific Anomalies at Eastern Michigan University publishes a journal called *The Zetetic Scholar*, devoted to the skeptical analysis of paranormal claims.

ZEUGMA AND SYLLEPSIS. These are two closely related figures of speech. *Zeugma* is the better-known name, whereas *syllepsis* is the more common phenomenon. Our discussion might therefore usefully begin with the latter.

A. Syllepsis. Literally "a taking together, comprehension," *syllepsis* denotes the figure of speech in which a word—usually a verb or preposition—is applied to two other words or phrases in different senses (often literally in one sense and figuratively in the other). Unlike zeugma, *syllepsis* is not a grammatical error. It is usually both purposeful and humorous—e.g.:

- "Noah Swayne of Ohio . . . was a corporation lawyer, as successful as he was callously unethical, who was not to *change his spots* or *his spottiness* throughout his long judicial career." Fred Rodell, *Nine Men* 137 (1955).
- "In January Dan Breen *took* the *oath* and his *seat* in the Dáil." J. Bowyer Bell, *The Secret Army: The IRA* 58 (1997). (*Take* has two objects, *oath* and *seat*, but applies to them in different senses.)

B. Zeugma. Literally "a yoking or bonding," *zeugma* is a grammatical error. It occurs when a single word is applied to two or more words or phrases when it properly applies to only one of them. One species of *zeugma* (the nontransferable auxiliary) plagues legal writing because lawyers so frequently try to express themselves alternatively—e.g.:

- "A grand jury appearance by a defendant *may—as it often has—lead to* [read *may lead, as it often has led, to*] his complete exoneration." *People v. Goldsborough*, 568 N.Y.S.2d 999, 1001 (Sup. Ct. 1991).
- "On a motion to dismiss . . . , the court does not assess the sufficiency of the evidence that a plaintiff *has or will put* forth to support her claim." *Prince v. Madison Square Garden*, 427 F.Supp.2d 372, 378 (S.D.N.Y. 2006). (*Put* is made to be both a past-tense and a future-tense verb.)
- "Wilkes argues that he can be safely incarcerated and that his life *has and will continue to show* [read *has shown and will continue to show*] 'redeeming qualities,' such as helping others." *Wilkes v. State*, 917 N.E.2d 675, 693 (Ind. 2009).

- "At least two bills and two joint resolutions *have or will be submitted* [read *have been, or will be, submitted*] for consideration." J.D. Stetson, *State Sovereignty, Drunken Driving Will Be Targeted*, Gillette News Record, 16 Jan. 2010, at B8.

Cf. JANUS-FACED TERMS.

zonal; zonary. The adjective corresponding to *zone* is *zonal* in all but medical (obstetric) senses.

zonate; *zonated. The term meaning "arranged in zones" is best made *zonate* rather than *zonated.

zygnomic; mesonomic. These terms are the inventions of Albert Kocourek, the legal theorist and creative neologist. A *zygnomic* jural relation involves an act whose evolution directly abridges the freedom of the *servus* (= the legal person who bears a ligation (i.e., the generic term for the servient side of a jural relation—it includes duty, disability, liability, and inability)) in the enjoyment of a legal advantage. A *mesonomic* jural relation does not, legally speaking, directly affect a human being's natural physical freedom—yet it has legal consequences in its evolution. *See* Albert Kocourek, *Jural Relations* 69 (1927). Julius Stone summed up these NEOLOGISMS well: "Kocourek's *mesonomic–zygnomic* distinction is no doubt a valuable one, even if we shrink back at the neologisms." Julius Stone, *Legal System and Lawyers' Reasonings* 148 (1964). And who does not shrink back? It is all pure JARGON and GOBBLEDYGOOK. Still, for that very reason, it provides what some must consider a fitting conclusion to a law dictionary.

SELECT BIBLIOGRAPHY

English-Language Dictionaries (current versions issued periodically)
The American Heritage Dictionary of the English Language.
Merriam-Webster's Collegiate Dictionary.
The New Oxford American Dictionary.
The New Shorter Oxford English Dictionary (2 vols.).
The Oxford English Dictionary (OED).
The Random House Dictionary of the English Language.
Webster's New International Dictionary of the English Language.
Webster's New World Dictionary.

Usage Guides
Bernstein, Theodore M. *The Careful Writer: A Modern Guide to English Usage.* N.Y.: Atheneum, 1965.
Burchfield, R.W. *The New Fowler's Modern English Usage.* 3d ed. Oxford: Oxford Univ. Press, 1996.
Evans, Bergen; and Cornelia Evans. *A Dictionary of Contemporary American Usage.* N.Y.: Random House, 1957.
Follett, Wilson. *Modern American Usage: A Guide.* 2d ed. rev. Erik Wensberg. N.Y.: Hill & Wang, 1966.
Fowler, H.W. *A Dictionary of Modern English Usage.* 2d ed. rev. Ernest Gowers. N.Y. & Oxford: Oxford Univ. Press, 1965.
Garner, Bryan A. *Garner's Modern American Usage.* 3d ed. N.Y. & Oxford: Oxford Univ. Press, 2009.
Garner, Bryan A. "Grammar and Usage," in *The Chicago Manual of Style* (ch. 5). 16th ed. Chicago: Univ. of Chicago Press, 2010.
Partridge, Eric. *Usage and Abusage: A Guide to Good English.* Rev. ed. Janet Whitcut. N.Y. & London: W.W. Norton & Co., 1994.

General Writing Guides
Baker, Sheridan. *The Practical Stylist.* 8th ed. N.Y.: Longman, 1997.
Graves, Robert; and Alan Hodge. *The Reader over Your Shoulder: A Handbook for Writers of English Prose.* 2d ed. N.Y.: Random House, 1979.
Payne, Lucile Vaughan. *The Lively Art of Writing* (1965). Chicago: Follett, 1982.
Strunk, William, Jr.; and E.B. White. *The Elements of Style.* 4th ed. N.Y.: Macmillan, 2000.
Trimble, John R. *Writing with Style.* 3d ed. Upper Saddle River, N.J.: Pearson, 2011.
Zinsser, William. *On Writing Well: An Informal Guide to Writing Nonfiction.* 7th ed. N.Y.: HarperPerennial, 2006.

Style Manuals
The Associated Press Stylebook and Briefing on Media Law. Rev. ed. Norm Goldstein. Cambridge, Mass.: Perseus, 2000.
The Chicago Manual of Style. 16th ed. Chicago: Univ. of Chicago Press, 2010.
Garner, Bryan A. *The Redbook: A Manual on Legal Style.* 2d ed. St. Paul: West, 2006.
Sabin, William A. *The Gregg Reference Manual: A Manual of Style, Grammar, Usage, and Formatting.* Tribute ed. N.Y.: Career Education, 2010.
Walsh, Bill. *The Elephants of Style.* N.Y.: McGraw-Hill, 2004.

English Grammar
Brown, Goold. *The Grammar of English Grammars.* 10th ed. N.Y.: William Wood & Co., 1851.
Curme, George O. *English Syntax.* Boston & N.Y.: D.C. Heath & Co., 1931.
Curme, George O. *Parts of Speech and Accidence.* N.Y.: D.C. Heath & Co., 1935.
Fernald, James C. *English Grammar Simplified.* Rev. ed. Cedric Gale. N.Y.: Barnes & Noble, 1963.
Garner, Bryan A. "Grammar and Usage," in *The Chicago Manual of Style* (ch. 5). 16th ed. Chicago: Univ. of Chicago Press, 2010.
Good, C. Edward. *A Grammar Book for You and I (Oops, Me!).* Sterling, Va.: Capital Books, 2002.
Jespersen, Otto. *Essentials of English Grammar* (1933). Tuscaloosa: Univ. of Alabama Press, 1964.

Technical Terms
Baldick, Chris. *The Concise Oxford Dictionary of Literary Terms.* Oxford & N.Y.: Oxford Univ. Press, 1990.
Cuddon, J.A. *The Penguin Dictionary of Literary Terms and Literary Theory.* 3d ed. London: Penguin, 1992.
Garner, Bryan A. "Glossary of Grammatical, Rhetorical, and Other Language-Related Terms," in *Garner's Modern American Usage.* 3d ed. pp. 877–923. N.Y. & Oxford: Oxford Univ. Press, 2009.
Lanham, Richard A. *A Handlist of Rhetorical Terms: A Guide for Students of English Literature.* 2d ed. Berkeley: Univ. of California Press, 1991.

Etymology
The Barnhart Dictionary of Etymology. Ed. Robert K. Barnhart. Bronx, N.Y.: H.W. Wilson, 1988.

The Oxford Dictionary of English Etymology. Ed. C.T. Onions et al. Oxford: Clarendon Press, 1966.
Webster's Word Histories. Springfield, Mass.: Merriam-Webster, 1989.
Weekley, Ernest. *Etymological Dictionary of Modern English* (1921). 2 vols. N.Y.: Dover, 1967.

Punctuation
Carey, G.V. *Mind the Stop: A Brief Guide to Punctuation with a Note on Proof-Correction.* Rev. ed. Harmondsworth: Penguin, 1971.
Gordon, Karen E. *The New Well-Tempered Sentence: A Punctuation Handbook for the Innocent, the Eager, and the Doomed.* Rev. & exp. ed. N.Y.: Ticknor & Fields, 1993.
Partridge, Eric. *You Have a Point There: A Guide to Punctuation and Its Allies.* London: Hamish Hamilton, 1953.

Pronunciation
Bender, James F. *NBC Handbook of Pronunciation.* 4th ed. rev. Eugene Ehrlich & Raymond Hand Jr. N.Y.: HarperPerennial, 1991.
Elster, Charles Harrington. *The Big Book of Beastly Mispronunciations.* 2d ed. Boston: Houghton Mifflin, 2006.
Lewis, Norman. *Dictionary of Modern Pronunciation.* N.Y.: Harper & Row, 1963.

Law Dictionaries
Black's Law Dictionary. 9th ed. rev. Bryan A. Garner. St. Paul: West, 2009.
A Dictionary of Law. 7th ed. rev. Jonathan Law & Elizabeth A. Martin. Oxford: Oxford Univ. Press, 2009.
Jowitt's Dictionary of English Law. 3d ed. rev. Daniel Greenberg. London: Thomson/Reuters, 2009.
Words and Phrases. 90 vols. & supps. St. Paul: West, 1940–.

Legal Language Generally
Freedman, Adam. *The Party of the First Part: The Curious World of Legalese.* N.Y.: Henry Holt & Co., 2007.
Garner, Bryan A. *Garner on Language and Writing.* Chicago: ABA, 2009.
Language and the Law: Proceedings of a Conference. Ed. Marlyn Robinson. Buffalo, N.Y.: William S. Hein & Co., 2003.
Law and Language. Ed. Frederick Schauer. N.Y.: N.Y. Univ. Press, 1993.
Mellinkoff, David. *The Language of the Law.* Boston: Little, Brown, 1963.

Mertz, Elizabeth. *The Language of Law School: Learning to Think Like a Lawyer*. Oxford: Oxford Univ. Press, 2007.

The Oxford Handbook on Language and Law. Eds. Lawrence Solan & Peter M. Tiersma. N.Y.: Oxford Univ. Press, 2011.

Tiersma, Peter. *Legal Language*. Chicago: Univ. of Chicago Press, 1999.

Tiersma, Peter. *Parchment, Paper, Pixels: Law and the Technologies of Communication*. Chicago: Univ. of Chicago Press, 2010.

Legal Writing Style

Asprey, Michèle M. *Plain Language for Lawyers*. 4th ed. Sydney: Federation Press, 2010.

Charrow, Veda R.; and Myra K. Erhardt. *Clear and Effective Legal Writing*. Boston: Little, Brown, 1986.

Garner, Bryan A. *The Elements of Legal Style*. 2d ed. N.Y.: Oxford Univ. Press, 2002.

Garner, Bryan A. *Legal Writing in Plain English*. Chicago: Univ. of Chicago Press, 2001.

Garner, Bryan A. *The Redbook: A Manual on Legal Style*. 2d ed. St. Paul: West, 2006.

Good, Edward C. *Mightier than the Sword*. Charlottesville, Va.: Blue Jeans Press, 1989.

Kimble, Joseph. *Lifting the Fog of Legalese: Essays on Plain Language*. Durham, N.C.: Carolina Academic Press, 2006.

Painter, Mark. *The Legal Writer*. 2d ed. Cincinnati: Jarndyce & Jarndyce Press, 2003.

Schiess, Wayne. *Better Legal Writing: 15 Topics for Advanced Legal Writers*. Buffalo, N.Y.: William S. Hein & Co., 2005.

Schiess, Wayne. *Writing for the Legal Audience*. Durham, N.C.: Carolina Academic Press, 2003.

Volokh, Eugene. *Academic Legal Writing: Law Review Articles, Student Notes, Seminar Papers, and Getting on Law Review*. 2d ed. N.Y.: Foundation Press, 2005.

Wydick, Richard C. *Plain English for Lawyers*. 5th ed. Durham, N.C.: Carolina Academic Press, 2005.

Plain English

Adler, Mark. *Clarity for Lawyers: The Use of Plain English in Legal Writing*. 2d ed. London: Law Society, 2007.

Eagleson, Robert D. *Writing in Plain English*. Canberra: AGPS Press, 1990.

Flesch, Rudolf. *The Art of Plain Talk*. N.Y.: Harper & Bros., 1946.

Gowers, Ernest. *The Complete Plain Words*. 3d ed. rev. Sidney Greenbaum & Janet Whitcut. Boston: D.R. Godine, 1986.

Gunning, Robert. *The Technique of Clear Writing*. Rev. ed. N.Y.: McGraw-Hill, 1968.

Lauchman, Richard. *Plain Style: Techniques for Simple, Concise, Emphatic Business Writing*. N.Y.: AMACOM, 1993.

Plain Language: Principles and Practice. Ed. Erwin R. Steinberg. Detroit: Wayne State Univ. Press, 1991.

Brief-Writing

Classic Essays on Legal Advocacy (1960). Ed. George Rossman. Clark, N.J.: Lawbook Exchange, 2010.

Garner, Bryan A. *The Winning Brief: 100 Tips on Persuasive Briefing in Trial and Appellate Courts*. 2d ed. N.Y.: Oxford Univ. Press, 2004.

Peck, Girvan. *Writing Persuasive Briefs*. Boston: Little, Brown, 1984.

Scalia, Antonin; and Bryan A. Garner. *Making Your Case: The Art of Persuading Judges*. St. Paul: West, 2008.

Commercial Drafting

Adams, Kenneth A. *A Manual of Style for Contract Drafting*. Chicago: ABA, 2004.

Burnham, Scott. *The Contract Drafting Guidebook*. Charlottesville, Va.: Michie Co., 1992.

Burnham, Scott. *Drafting and Analyzing Contracts*. Newark: LexisNexis, 2003.

Butt, Peter; and Richard Castle. *Modern Legal Drafting: A Guide to Using Clearer Language*. 2d ed. N.Y.: Cambridge Univ. Press, 2006.

Child, Barbara. *Drafting Legal Documents*. 2d ed. St. Paul: West, 1992.

Dickerson, Reed. *The Fundamentals of Legal Drafting*. 2d ed. Boston: Little, Brown, 1986.

Felsenfeld, Carl; and Alan Siegel. *Writing Contracts in Plain English*. St. Paul: West, 1981.

Flesch, Rudolf. *How to Write Plain English: A Book for Lawyers and Consumers*. N.Y.: Harper & Row, 1979.

Garner, Bryan A. *Securities Disclosure in Plain English*. Chicago: CCH, 1999.

Kuney, George W. *The Elements of Contract Drafting*. St. Paul: West, 2003.

Piesse, E.L. *The Elements of Legal Drafting*. 9th ed. rev. J.K. Aitken & Peter J. Butt. Sydney: Law Book, 1996.

Schiess, Wayne. *Preparing Legal Documents Nonlawyers Can Read and Understand*. Chicago: ABA, 2008.

Stark, Tina. *Drafting Contracts*. N.Y.: Aspen Pubs., 2007.

Wincor, Richard. *Contracts in Plain English*. N.Y.: McGraw-Hill, 1976.

Legislative Drafting

Cutts, Martin. *Lucid Law*. High Peak, Derbyshire (U.K.): Plain Language Commission, 2000.

Haggard, Thomas; and George W. Kuney. *Legal Drafting in a Nutshell*. 3d ed. St. Paul: West, 2007.

Rule-Drafting

Garner, Bryan A. *Guidelines for Drafting and Editing Court Rules*. Washington, D.C.: Administrative Office of the U.S. Courts, 1995.

Kimble, Joseph. *Lessons in Drafting from the New Federal Rules of Civil Procedure*. 12 Scribes J. Legal Writing 26 (2008–2009).

Murawski, Thomas. *Writing Readable Regulations*. Durham, N.C.: Carolina Academic Press, 1999.

Redish, Janice. *How to Write Regulations and Other Documents in Clear English*. Washington, D.C.: American Institutes for Research, 1991.

Judicial Opinions

Aldisert, Ruggero J. *Opinion Writing*. 2d ed. Bloomington, Ind.: AuthorHouse, 2009.

Garner, Bryan A. "Opinions, Style of," in *The Oxford Companion to the Supreme Court of the United States*. 2d ed. N.Y.: Oxford Univ. Press, 2005.

George, Joyce J. *Judicial Opinion Writing Handbook*. 3d ed. Buffalo, N.Y.: William S. Hein & Co., 1993.

Jury Instructions

Tiersma, Peter. *Communicating with Juries: How to Write More Understandable Jury Instructions*. Williamsburg, Va.: National Center for State Courts, 2007.

Legal Citations

The Bluebook: A Uniform System of Citation. 19th ed. Cambridge, Mass.: Harvard Law Review, 2010.

Dickerson, Darby A. *The ALWD Citation Manual: A Professional System of Citation*. 4th ed. Frederick, Md.: Aspen, 2010.

ACKNOWLEDGMENTS OF PERMISSION

Grateful acknowledgment is made to the following publishers and journals for their permission to quote from the works listed below.

Little, Brown & Co.
David Mellinkoff, *The Language of the Law* (1963).

New York University Law Review
Walker Gibson, *Literary Minds and Judicial Style,* 36 N.Y.U. L. Rev. 915 (1961).

Oxford University Press
A Dictionary of Law (7th ed. 2009).
H.W. Fowler, *A Dictionary of Modern English Usage* (1926 & 2d ed. 1965).
The Oxford English Dictionary (1933 & 2d ed. 1989).
David M. Walker, *The Oxford Companion to the Law* (1980).
E.S.C. Weiner, *The Oxford Guide to English Usage* (1983).

Pepperdine Law Review
James C. Raymond, *Editing Law Reviews: Practical Suggestions and a Moderately Revolutionary Proposal.* Reprinted from Pepperdine Law Review, Volume 12, Number 2, 1985, Copyright © 1985 by Pepperdine University School of Law.

Texas Tech Law Review
Robert W. Calvert, *Appellate Court Judgments,* 6 Tex. Tech L. Rev. 915 (1975).

Yale Law Journal
Arthur A. Leff, *The Leff Dictionary of Law: A Fragment.* By permission of The Yale Law Journal Company and Fred B. Rothman & Company from The Yale Law Journal, Vol. 94, pp. 1855–2251 (1985).

SELECT INDEX OF WRITERS CITED

INDEX OF PERIODICALS CITED